INDEX OF ECONOMIC ARTICLES
In Journals and Collective Volumes

Index of
Economic Articles

IN JOURNALS AND COLLECTIVE VOLUMES

Volume XXXI · 1989

Part Two—Author Index

Prepared under the auspices of

THE JOURNAL OF ECONOMIC LITERATURE

of the

AMERICAN ECONOMIC ASSOCIATION

JOHN PENCAVEL

Editor

MOSES ABRAMOVITZ
Associate Editor

DRUCILLA EKWURZEL
Associate Editor

ASATOSHI MAESHIRO
Editorial Consultant

MARY KAY AKERMAN
Assistant Editor

NASHVILLE, TENNESSEE
AMERICAN ECONOMIC ASSOCIATION
1992

Copyright © 1992, American Economic Association
Executive Office
2014 Broadway, Suite 305, Nashville, Tennessee 37203

Library of Congress Catalog Card Number: 61–8020
International Standard Book Number: 0–917290–20–8
International Standard Serial Number: 0536–647X
Printed in the United States of America

TABLE OF CONTENTS

INTRODUCTORY DISCUSSION

This volume of the *Index* lists, both by subject category and by author, articles in major economic journals and in collective volumes published during the year 1989. The articles listed include all articles published in English or with English summaries in the journals and books identified in the following sections. Part One includes the Subject Index of Articles in Journals and Collective Volumes, and Part Two consists of an alphabetical Author Index of all the articles indexed in Part One.

Relationship to JEL

This *Index* is prepared largely as an adjunct to the bibliographic activities of the *Journal of Economic Literature (JEL)*. Economies of joint production are pursued throughout the production process. Journals included are those indexed in the *JEL* quarterly; collective volumes are selected from the annotated 1989 books; the classification system is a more detailed version of the 1989 *JEL* system.

Journals Included

The 329 journals listed represent, in general, those journals that we believe will be most helpful to research workers and teachers of economics. These journals are listed below on page x.

Generally, articles, notes, communications, comments, replies, rejoinders, as well as papers and formal discussions in proceedings and review articles have been indexed. There are some exceptions; only articles in English or with English summaries are included—this practice results in a slightly reduced coverage compared with the *JEL* quarterly. Articles lacking author identification are omitted, as are articles without economic content. Identical articles appearing in two different journals in 1989 are listed from both sources. The journal issues included usually fall within a single volume. When a volume of a journal overlaps two calendar years, for example, Fall 1988 to Summer 1989, we include the issues relating to 1989 as best we can determine.

Collective Volumes

The collective volumes consist of the following:
1. *Festschriften*
2. Conference publications with individual papers
3. Collected essays, original, by one or more authors
4. Collected essays, reprinted, by one or more authors
5. Proceedings volumes
6. Books of readings

All original articles in English are indexed with the exception of unsigned articles or articles without economic content. Reprinted articles are included on the basis that a researcher would be interested in knowing about another source of the article. The original publication dates are shown in italics on the citations of reprinted articles. Excerpts are not included. The same article appearing for the first time in different collective volumes in the same year is cited from both publications.

In the article citation, reference to the book in which the article appears is by author or editor of the volume. If the same person or persons wrote or edited more than one book included in the 1989 *Index*, it is indicated by a I or II appearing in both the source given in the article citation and the bibliographic reference in the book listing. If the same person wrote one book and edited another in 1989, the specification of "ed." in the reference indicates which book is being cited.

The collective volumes are listed alphabetically by author or editor beginning on page xvi and include a full bibliographic reference. If there is more than one edition, the publisher cited is the one on the copy the *JEL* received, usually the American publisher.

Arrangement

The *Index* consists of two parts:
1. A Subject Index in which the articles are arranged by subject.
2. An Author Index.

Part One—Subject Index

In Part One, all articles are listed alphabetically by first author under each 4-digit subject category. Joint authors are listed up to three; beyond that, only the first author is listed, followed by *et al.*

There is one exception to the alphabetical author arrangement. In the 0322 category, a subdivision of **History of Thought** entitled **Individuals,** the arrangement is first alphabetical by the individual discussed in the article and then alphabetical by the article's author.

Articles with empirical content or discussing a particular geographic area carry a geographic descriptor (see discussion below).

Classification System

The classification system is an expansion of the 3-digit classification system used in the 1989 *Journal of Economic Literature* to a 4-digit system with slightly over 300 subcategories. The classification system, itself, is shown beginning on page xxxvi (Part One). In most cases, the classification heading is self-explanatory; however, in some cases, notes have been added to clarify the coverage or indicate alternative subject classifications. The basic approach in classification is from the point of view of the researcher rather than the teacher; course content does not necessarily coincide with subfields of our classification system. In all cases where there are two or more 4-digit classifications under a 3-digit category, there is a zero classification; in most instances this is labeled "General." The zero or general category has been used both as an inclusive and a residual category. For example, an article discussing *all* aspects of international trade theory appears in the general category. There are also some articles that do not fall in any of the individual subcategories and these, too, are classified in the general or zero category.

The criterion used in the classifying process is whether persons interested in this topic would wish to have the article drawn to their attention. With the advent of our online ECONOMIC LITERATURE INDEX on Dialog and our compact disc EconLit available from SilverPlatter, the interpretation of "interest" has broadened slightly to include cross-classifications that indicate the subject matter, particularly in such categories as industry studies or occupational designations. Over half of the articles are classified in more than one subcategory. From time to time, we find it desirable to add subject classifications as particular topics become prominent or to change subject headings to make them more descriptive of the contents of the category.

Geographic Descriptors

Geographic descriptors appear in brackets at the end of any article entry in the Subject Index where the article cites data from or refers to a particular country or area. Research workers interested in these countries, thus, are made aware of the empirical content in the article. The descriptors used are countries or broader areas, such as Southeast Asia (S.E. Asia); articles referring to cities or regions within a country are classified under the country. In general, the country name is written out in full with some adaptations and abbreviations, *e.g.*, U.S. is used for United States, U.K. for United Kingdom, and U.S.S.R. for Union of Soviet Socialist Republics. Abbreviations include: W. for West, E. for East, S. for South, N. for North. A shortened name such as W. Germany is used rather than the correct, but longer, Federal Republic of Germany. When broader regions are used as descriptors, the article may or may not refer to the full unit. For example, OECD has been used at times when most, but not all, of the OECD member countries are referred to.

Index volumes prior to 1979 sometimes did not include geographic descriptors on articles listed under subject categories 1210, 1211, 1220, 1221, 1230, 1240, and 1241 involving general or comparative economic country studies. In the 1979 *Index* and later volumes, these articles carry geographic descriptors in order to facilitate identification in the ECONOMIC LITERATURE INDEX and on EconLit. Because the descriptor fields are limited to five, very general descriptors, such as LDCs (developing countries) and MDCs (developed countries), are often used on articles.

The fact that an article carries a geographic descriptor does not necessarily preclude its being primarily theoretical in nature. Any theoretical article drawing on empirical data to demonstrate its findings will carry a geographic descriptor.

Topical Guide to the Classification System

There is an alphabetical listing of standard economic terms and concepts at the end of Part One. References are to the appropriate 4-digit classification numbers, not to page numbers.

Part Two—Author Index

Part two consists of an alphabetical Author Index in which citations appear under each author (up to three) of an article. Wherever possible, the full first name and middle initial or middle name(s) are used. Wherever it could be definitely ascertained, articles by the same person are grouped together with only one listing of the name. Authors' first names and initials are listed differently in various journals and books; for example, an individual may be identified as John L. Smith, J. L. Smith, or John Smith. Thus, despite our best efforts, we were left in doubt in several instances. Joint authors are listed up to three; beyond that, only the first author is listed, followed by *et al.* Under each author, articles are listed alphabetically. Names carrying prefixes are alphabetized according to the first *capitalized* letter, with occasional exceptions following national practices; thus, van Arkadie would appear under A and D'Alabro under D.

LIST OF JOURNALS INDEXED 1989

Accounting Review, Vol. 64.

Acta Oeconomica, Vols. 40–41.

L'Actualité Economique, Vol. 65.

African Economic History, Issue no. 18.

American Economic Review, Vol. 79.

American Economist, Vol. 33.

American Historical Review, Vol. 94.

American Journal of Agricultural Economics, Vol. 71.
　Title changed from **Journal of Farm Economics** in 1968.

American Journal of Economics and Sociology, Vol. 48.

American Real Estate and Urban Economics Association Journal, Vol. 17.

Annales d'Economie et de Statistique, Issue nos. 13–16, 1989.
　Title changed from **Annales de l'INSEE** in 1986.

Annals of Public and Cooperative Economics, Vol. 60.

Annals of Regional Science, Vol. 23.

Antitrust Bulletin, Vol. 34, Issue nos. 1–3.

Applied Economics, Vol. 21.

Asian-Pacific Economic Literature, Vol. 3.

Atlantic Economic Journal, Vol. 17.

Aussenwirtschaft, Vol. 44.

Australian Bulletin of Labour, Vol. 15, Issue nos. 2–5.

Australian Economic History Review, Vol. 29.
　Title changed from **Business Archives and History** in 1967; entitled **Bulletin of the Business Archives Council of Australia** prior to 1962.

Australian Economic Papers, Vol. 28.

Australian Economic Review, Issue nos. 85–88.

Australian Journal of Agricultural Economics, Vol. 33.

Australian Tax Forum, Vol. 6.

Banca Nazionale del Lavoro Quarterly Review, Issue nos. 168–171.

Bangladesh Development Studies, Vol. 17.

Bank of Japan Monetary and Economic Studies, Vol. 7.

British Journal of Industrial Relations, Vol. 27.

British Review of Economic Issues, Vol. 11.

Brookings Papers on Economic Activity, Issue nos. 1–2, 1989; Microeconomics 1989.

Bulletin for International Fiscal Documentation, Vol. 43.

Bulletin of Economic Research, Vol. 41.
　Title changed from **Yorkshire Bulletin of Economic and Social Research** in 1971.

Bulletin of Indonesian Economic Studies, Vol. 25.

Business Economics, Vol. 24.

Business History Review, Vol. 63.
　Title changed from **Bulletin of the Business Historical Society** in 1954.

Cahiers Économiques de Bruxelles, Issue nos. 121–124.

Cambridge Journal of Economics, Vol. 13.

Canadian Journal of Agricultural Economics, Vol. 37.

Canadian Journal of Development Studies, Vol. 10.

Canadian Journal of Economics, Vol. 22.

Canadian Public Policy, Vol. 15.

Carnegie–Rochester Conference Series on Public Policy, Vols. 30–31.
　Vols. 1–17 were listed as supplements to the **Journal of Monetary Economics**.

Cato Journal, Vol. 8, Issue no. 3; Vol. 9, Issue nos. 1–2.

Cepal Review, Issue nos. 37–39.

Challenge, Vol. 32.

Chinese Economic Studies, Vol. 22, Issue nos. 2–4; Vol. 23, Issue no. 1.

Colección Estudios CIEPLAN, Issue nos. 26–27.

Comparative Economic Studies, Vol. 31.
　Title changed from **ACES Bulletin** in 1985.

Contemporary Policy Issues, Vol. 7.

Cuadernos de Economia, Vol. 26, Issue nos. 78–79.

Czechoslovak Economic Digest, Issue nos. 1–7, 1989.

Czechoslovak Economic Papers, Issue nos. 26–27.

Demography, Vol. 26.

Developing Economies, Vol. 27.

Eastern Africa Economic Review, Vol. 5; Special Issue.

Eastern Economic Journal, Vol. 15.

Eastern European Economics, Vol. 27, Issue nos. 3–4; Vol. 28, Issue nos. 1–2.

Econometric Reviews, Vol. 8.

Econometrica, Vol. 57.

Economia (Portuguese Catholic University), Vol. 13.

Economia Internazionale, Vol. 42.

Economia e Lavoro, Vol. 23.

Economia Politica, Vol. 6.

Economia delle Scelte Pubbliche/Journal of Public Finance and Public Choice, Vol. 7.

Economic Analysis and Workers' Management, Vol. 23.

Economic Computation and Economic Cybernetics Studies and Research, Vol. 24.
　Title changed from **Studii şi Cercetări Economicè** in 1974. Changed from issue numbers to volume numbers in 1978.

Economic Development and Cultural Change, Vol. 37, Issue nos. 2–4; Vol. 38, Issue no. 1.

Economic Geography, Vol. 65.

Economic History Review, Vol. 42.

Economic Inquiry, Vol. 27.
　Title changed from **Western Economic Journal** in 1974.

Economic Journal, Vol. 99.

Economic Modelling, Vol. 6.

Economic Notes, Issue nos. 1–3, 1989.

Economic Policy: A European Forum, Issue nos. 8–9, 1989.

Economic Record, Vol. 65.

Economic Review (Keizai Kenkyu), Vol. 40.

Economic and Social Review, Vol. 20, Issue nos. 2–4; Vol. 21, Issue no. 1.

Economic Studies Quarterly, Vol. 40.

Economica, Vol. 56.
　Title changed from **Economica, N.S.** in 1974.

Económica (National University of La Plata), Vol. 35.

Economic Systems Research, Vol. 1.

Economics of Education Review, Vol. 8.

Economics Letters, Vols. 29–31.

Economics and Philosophy, Vol. 5.

Economics and Politics, Vol. 1.

Économie Appliquée, Vol. 42.

Économies et Sociétés, Vol. 23.

De Economist, Vol. 137.

Ekonomiska Samfundets Tidskrift, Vol. 42.

Empirica, Vol. 16.

Empirical Economics, Vol. 14.

Energy Economics, Vol. 11.

Energy Journal, Vol. 10.

Environment and Planning A, Vol. 21.

Estudios Económico, Vol. 4.

European Economic Review, Vol. 33.

European Review of Agricultural Economics, Vol. 16.

Explorations in Economic History, Vol. 26.
　Title changed from **Explorations in Entrepreneurial History** in 1969–70.

Federal Reserve Bank of Atlanta Economic Review, Vol. 74.

Federal Reserve Bank of Dallas Economic Review, January, March, May, July, September, November, 1989.

Federal Reserve Bank of Minneapolis Quarterly Review, Vol. 13.

Federal Reserve Bank of New York Quarterly Review, Vol. 13, Issue no. 4; Vol. 14; Special Issue.

Journal of Conflict Resolution, Vol. 33.

Journal of Consumer Affairs, Vol. 23.

Journal of Consumer Research, Vol. 15, Issue no. 4; Vol. 16, Issue nos. 1–3.

Journal of Cultural Economics, Vol. 13.

Journal of Developing Areas, Vol. 23, Issue nos. 2–4; Vol. 24, Issue no. 1.

Journal of Development Economics, Vols. 30–31.

Journal of Development Studies, Vol. 25, Issue nos. 2–4; Vol. 26, Issue no. 1.

Journal of Econometrics, Vols. 40–41; Vol. 42, Issue nos. 1–2.

Journal of Economic Behavior and Organization, Vols. 11–12.

Journal of Economic Development, Vol. 14.

Journal of Economic Dynamics and Control, Vol. 13.

Journal of Economic Education, Vol. 20.

Journal of Economic History, Vol. 49.

Journal of Economic Issues, Vol. 23.

Journal of Economic Literature, Vol. 27.

Journal of Economic Perspectives, Vol. 3.

Journal of Economic Psychology, Vol. 10.

Journal of Economic and Social Measurement, Vol. 15.

Journal of Economic Studies, Vol. 16.

Journal of Economic Surveys, Vol. 3.

Journal of Economic Theory, Vols. 47–49.

Journal of Economics (Zeitschrift für Nationalökonomie), Vols. 49–50.
 Title changed from Zeitschrift für Nationalökonomie in 1986.

Journal of Economics and Business, Vol. 41.
 Title changed from Economics and Business Bulletin in 1972–73.

Journal of Energy and Development, Vol. 14, Issue no. 2; Vol. 15, Issue no. 1.

Journal of Environmental Economics and Management, Vols. 16–17.

Journal of European Economic History, Vol. 18.

Journal of Finance, Vol. 44.

Journal of Financial Economics, Vols. 23–25.

Journal of Financial and Quantitative Analysis, Vol. 24.

Journal of Financial Research, Vol. 12.

Journal of Financial Services Research, Vols. 2–3.

Journal of Futures Markets, Vol. 9.

Journal of Health Economics, Vol. 8, Issue nos. 1–3.

Journal of Human Resources, Vol. 24.

Journal of Industrial Economics, Vol. 37, Issue nos. 3–4; Vol. 38, Issue nos. 1–2.

Journal of Institutional and Theoretical Economics, Vol. 145.
 Title changed from Zeitschrift für die gesamte Staatswissenschaft in 1986.

Journal of International Economics, Vols. 26–27.

Journal of International Money and Finance, Vol. 8.

Journal of the Japanese and International Economies, Vol. 3.

Journal of King Abdulaziz University: Islamic Economics, Vol. 1.

Journal of Labor Economics, Vol. 7.

Journal of Labor Research, Vol. 10.

Journal of Law and Economics, Vol. 32.

Journal of Law, Economics, and Organization, Vol. 5.

Journal of Legal Studies, Vol. 18.

Journal of Macroeconomics, Vol. 11

Journal of Mathematical Economics, Vol. 18.

Journal of Monetary Economics, Vols. 23–24.

Journal of Money, Credit and Banking, Vol. 21.

Journal of Policy Analysis and Management, Vol. 8.

Journal of Policy Modeling, Vol. 11.

Journal of Political Economy, Vol. 97.

Journal of Population Economics, Vol. 1, Issue no. 4; Vol. 2.

Journal of Portfolio Management, Vol. 15, Issue nos. 2–4; Vol. 16, Issue no. 1.

Policy Sciences, Vol. 22.

Politica Economica, Vol. 5.

Population and Development Review, Vol. 15.

Population Research and Policy Review, Vol. 8.

Population Studies, Vol. 43.

Problems of Economics, Vol. 31, Issue nos. 9–12; Vol. 32, Issue nos. 1–8.

Public Budgeting and Finance, Vol. 9.

Public Choice, Vols. 60–63.

Public Finance, Vol. 44.

Public Finance Quarterly, Vol. 17.

Quarterly Journal of Business and Economics, Vol. 28.
Title changed from Nebraska Journal of Economics and Business in 1983.

Quarterly Journal of Economics, Vol. 104.

Quarterly Review of Economics and Business, Vol. 29.

Rand Journal of Economics, Vol. 20.
Title changed from Bell Journal of Economics in 1984.

Recherches Economiques de Louvain, Vol. 55.

Regional Science Perspectives, Vol. 19.

Regional Science and Urban Economics, Vol. 19.

Regional Studies, Vol. 23.

Resources and Energy, Vol. 11, Issue no. 1.

Review of Black Political Economy, Vol. 17, Issue nos. 3–4; Vol. 18, Issue nos. 1–2.

Review of Economic Conditions in Italy, Issue nos. 1–3, 1989.

Review of Economic Studies, Vol. 56.

Review of Economics and Statistics, Vol. 71.
Title changed from The Review of Economic Statistics in 1948.

Review of Financial Studies, Vol. 2, Issue nos. 1–2.

Review of Income and Wealth, Vol. 35.

Review of Marketing and Agricultural Economics, Vol. 57.

Review of Radical Political Economics, Vol. 21.

Review of Regional Studies, Vol. 19.

Review of Social Economy, Vol. 47.

Revista Española de Economía, Vol. 6.

Revue d'Economie Politique, Vol. 99.

Revue Économique, Vol. 40.

Ricerche Economiche, Vol. 43.

Rivista Internazionale di Scienze Economiche e Commerciali, Vol. 36.

Rivista di Storia Economica, Vol. 6.

Scandinavian Economic History Review, Vol. 37.

Scandinavian Journal of Economics, Vol. 91.
Title changed from Swedish Journal of Economics in 1976; entitled Ekonomisk Tidskrift prior to 1965.

Schweizerische Zeitschrift für Volkswirtschaft und Statistik, Vol. 125.

Science and Society, Vol. 53.

Scottish Journal of Political Economy, Vol. 36.

Singapore Economic Review, Vol. 34.
Title changed from Malayan Economic Review in 1983.

Social Choice and Welfare, Vol. 6.

Social and Economic Studies, Vol. 38.

Social Science Quarterly, Vol. 70.

Social Security Bulletin, Vol. 52.

South African Journal of Economics, Vol. 57.

Southern Economic Journal, Vol. 55, Issue nos. 3–4; Vol. 56, Issue nos. 1–2.

Southern Journal of Agricultural Economics, Vol. 21.

Soviet and Eastern European Foreign Trade, Vol. 25.

Soviet Economy, Vol. 5.

Statistical Journal, Vol. 6.

Studi Economici, Vol. 44, Issue nos. 37, 39.

Survey of Current Business, Vol. 69.

Tijdschrift voor Economie en Management, Vol. 34.
Title changed from Tijdschrift voor Economie in 1975.

Urban Studies, Vol. 26.

Water Resources Research, Vol. 25.

LIST OF COLLECTIVE VOLUMES INDEXED 1989

ABRAMOVITZ, MOSES. *Thinking about growth: And other essays on economic growth and welfare.* Studies in Economic History and Policy: The United States in the Twentieth Century. Cambridge; New York and Melbourne: Cambridge University Press, 1989.

[ADAMS, F. G.] *Economics in theory and practice: An eclectic approach. Essays in honor of F. G. Adams.* Edited by LAWRENCE R. KLEIN AND JAIME MARQUEZ. Advanced Studies in Theoretical and Applied Econometrics, vol. 17. Dordrecht; Boston and London: Kluwer Academic, 1989.

ADELMAN, IRMA AND LANE, SYLVIA, eds. *The balance between industry and agriculture in economic development: Proceedings of the Eighth World Congress of the International Economic Association, Delhi, India. Volume 4. Social effects.* New York: St. Martin's Press in association with the International Economic Association, 1989.

AGASSI, JUDITH BUBER AND HEYCOCK, STEPHEN, eds. *The redesign of working time: Promise or threat?* Berlin: Edition Sigma, 1989.

AHLBRANDT, ROGER S., JR., ed. *Managing in a global competitive environment: Conference proceedings.* Pittsburgh: University of Pittsburgh, Joseph M. Katz Graduate School of Business, 1989.

ALBRECHT, JAMES W., ET AL. *MOSES code.* Stockholm: Industrial Institute for Economic and Social Research; distributed by Almqvist and Wiksell International, 1989.

ALEXANDER, HERBERT E., ed. *Comparative political finance in the 1980s.* With the assistance of JOEL FEDERMAN. Advances in Political Science: An International Series. Cambridge; New York and Melbourne: Cambridge University Press, 1989.

ALLEN, CHRIS, ET AL. *Benin–The Congo–Burkina Faso: Economics, politics and society.* Marxist Regimes Series. New York and London: Pinter; distributed by Columbia University Press, New York, 1989.

ALTMANN, JURGEN AND ROTBLAT, JOSEPH, eds. *Verification of arms reductions: Nuclear, conventional and chemical.* New York; Berlin; London and Tokyo: Springer in cooperation with the Peace Research Institute Frankfurt, 1989.

AMJAD, RASHID, ed. *To the Gulf and back: Studies on the economic impact of Asian labour migration.* Asian Regional Programme on International Labour Migration series. New Delhi: International Labour Organisation, Asian Employment Programme; New York: United Nations Development Programme, 1989.

ANDERSON, JOCK R. AND HAZELL, PETER B. R., eds. *Variability in grain yields: Implications for agricultural research and policy in developing countries.* Baltimore and London: Johns Hopkins University Press for the International Food Policy Research Institute, 1989.

ANDERSSON, AKE E., ET AL., eds. *Advances in spatial theory and dynamics.* Studies in Regional Science and Urban Economics, vol. 20. Amsterdam; Oxford and Tokyo: North-Holland; distributed in the U.S. and Canada by Elsevier Science, New York, 1989.

ANDERSSON, AKE E.; BATTEN, DAVID F. AND KARLSSON, CHARLIE, eds. *Knowledge and industrial organization.* With contributions by A. E. ANDERSSON ET AL. New York; Berlin; London and Tokyo: Springer, 1989.

ARCHETTI, F.; LUCERTINI, M. AND SERAFINI, P., eds. *Operations research models in flexible manufacturing systems.* International Centre for Mechanical Sciences Courses and Lectures series, no. 306. New York and Vienna: Springer, 1989.

ATKINSON, ANTHONY BARNES. *Poverty and social security.* New York; London; Toronto and Sydney: Simon and Schuster International, Harvester Wheatsheaf, 1989.

AUDRETSCH, DAVID B.; SLEUWAEGEN, LEO AND YAMAWAKI, HIDEKI, eds. *The convergence of international and domestic markets.* Contributions to Economic Analysis, no. 180. Amsterdam; New York; Oxford and Tokyo: North-Holland; distributed in the U.S. and Canada by Elsevier Science, New York, 1989.

AVERY, WILLIAM P. AND RAPKIN, DAVID P., eds. *Markets, politics, and change in the global political economy.* International Political Economy Yearbook, vol. 4. Boulder, Colo. and London: Rienner, 1989.

BAEK, KWANG-IL; McLAURIN, RONALD D. AND MOON, CHUNG-IN, eds. *The dilemma of third world defense industries: Supplier control or recipient autonomy?* CIS Monographs, Pacific and World Studies Series, no. 3. Inchon, S. Korea: Center for International Studies, Inha University; Boulder: Westview Press, 1989.

BALASSA, BELA. *Comparative advantage, trade policy and economic development.* New York: New York University Press; distributed by Columbia University Press, 1989.

BALZER, WOLFGANG AND HAMMINGA, BERT, eds. *Philosophy of economics.* Norwell, Mass.; Dordrecht and London: Kluwer Academic, 1989.

BAMBERG, GUNTER AND SPREMANN, KLAUS, eds. *Agency theory, information, and incentives.* Corrected reprint. With contributions by W. BALLWIESER ET AL. New York; Berlin; London and Tokyo: Springer, [1987] 1989.

BARBASH, JACK AND BARBASH, KATE, eds. *Theories and concepts in comparative industrial relations.* Studies in Industrial Relations series. Columbia: University of South Carolina Press, 1989.

BARBER, JOHN; METCALFE, J. STANLEY AND PORTEOUS, MIKE, eds. *Barriers to growth in small firms.* Small Business Series. London and New York: Routledge, 1989.

BARDHAN, PRANAB, ed. *Conversations between economists and anthropologists: Methodological issues in measuring economic change in rural India.* Delhi; Oxford; New York and Toronto: Oxford University Press, 1989. (I)

BARDHAN, PRANAB, ed. *The economic theory of agrarian institutions.* Oxford; New York; Toronto and Melbourne: Oxford University Press, 1989. (II)

BARNETT, WILLIAM A.; GEWEKE, JOHN AND SHELL, KARL, eds. *Economic complexity: Chaos, sunspots, bubbles, and nonlinearity. Proceedings of the Fourth International Symposium in Economic Theory and Econometrics.* International Symposia in Economic Theory and Econometrics series. Cambridge; New York and Melbourne: Cambridge University Press, 1989.

BARRERE, ALAIN, ed. *Money, credit and prices in Keynesian perspective: Proceedings of a conference held at the University of Paris I–Panthéon-Sorbonne.* New York: St. Martin's Press, 1989.

BARRO, ROBERT J., ed. *Modern business cycle theory.* Cambridge, Mass.: Harvard University Press, 1989.

BAUER, SIEGFRIED AND HENRICHSMEYER, WILHELM, eds. *Agricultural sector modelling: Proceedings of the 16th Symposium of the European Association of Agricultural Economists (EAAE), April 14th–15th, 1988, Bonn, FRG.* Kiel: Wissenschaftsverlag Vauk, 1989.

BAWDEN, D. LEE AND SKIDMORE, FELICITY, eds. *Rethinking employment policy.* Washington, D.C.: Urban Institute Press; distributed in the U.S. and Canada by University Press of America, Lanham, Md., 1989.

BAYARD, THOMAS O. AND YOUNG, SOO-GIL, eds. *Economic relations between the United States and Korea: Conflict or cooperation?* Special Report series, no. 8. Washington, D.C.: Institute for International Economics, 1989.

BEACH, CHARLES M. AND GREEN, ALAN G. *Policy forum on the role of immigration in Canada's future.* Policy Forum Series, no. 15. Kingston, Ont.: Queen's University, John Deutsch Institute for the Study of Economic Policy, 1989.

BEAN, FRANK D.; SCHMANDT, JURGEN AND WEINTRAUB, SIDNEY, eds. *Mexican and Central American population and U.S. immigration policy.* Austin: University of Texas at Austin, Center for Mexican American Studies, 1989.

BEAUREGARD, ROBERT A., ed. *Atop the urban hierarchy.* Totowa, N.J.: Rowman and Littlefield, 1989.

BERG, MAXINE, ET AL. *Französische Revolution und Politische Ökonomie: Gehalten anlässlich des Kolloquiums am 27. und 28. Mai 1988 im Studienzentrum Karl-Marx-Haus, Trier (French Revolution and Political Economy: A colloquium organized by the Karl Marx Haus on May 27 and 28, 1988).* Schriften aus dem Karl-Marx-Haus, no. 41. Trier, W. Germany: Friedrich-Ebert-Stiftung, 1989.

BERGSON, ABRAM. *Planning and performance in socialist economies: The USSR and Eastern Europe.*

Winchester, Mass. and London: Unwin Hyman; Sydney and Wellington, New Zealand: Allen and Unwin, 1989.

BERLINER, J. S.; KOSTA, H. G. J. AND HAKOGI, MASUMI, eds. *Economics of the socialist countries.* Fukushima, Japan: Fukushima International Symposium Organizing Committee; distributed by Maruzen, Tokyo, 1989.

BHAGWATI, JAGDISH N. AND WILSON, JOHN DOUGLAS, eds. *Income taxation and international mobility.* Foreword by RICHARD A. MUSGRAVE. Cambridge, Mass. and London: MIT Press, 1989.

BIRD, GRAHAM, ed. *Third world debt: The search for a solution.* Aldershot, U.K.: Elgar; Brookfield, Vt.: Gower, 1989.

BLACK, STANLEY W., ed. *Productivity growth and the competitiveness of the American economy.* Studies in Productivity Analysis series: A Carolina Public Policy Conference Volume. Norwell, Mass.; Dordrecht and London: Kluwer Academic, 1989.

BLANCHARD, OLIVIER JEAN AND FISCHER, STANLEY, eds. *NBER macroeconomics annual: 1989.* Cambridge, Mass. and London: MIT Press, 1989.

BLEJER, MARIO I. AND CHU, KE-YOUNG, eds. *Fiscal policy, stabilization, and growth in developing countries.* Washington, D.C.: International Monetary Fund, 1989.

BLINDER, ALAN S. *Macroeconomics under debate.* Ann Arbor, University of Michigan Press, 1989.

BLOMSTROM, MAGNUS. *Foreign investment and spillovers.* London and New York: Routledge, 1989.

BLYTON, PAUL, ET AL. *Time, work and organization.* London and New York: Routledge, 1989.

BOSWORTH, BARRY P., ET AL. *Critical choices.* Washington, D.C.: Brookings Institution, 1989.

BOTTOMORE, TOM AND BRYM, ROBERT J., eds. *The capitalist class: An international study.* New York: New York University Press, 1989.

BRENNAN, GEOFFREY AND LOMASKY, LOREN E., eds. *Politics and process: New essays in democratic thought.* Cambridge; New York and Melbourne: Cambridge University Press, 1989.

BROCK, PHILIP L.; CONNOLLY, MICHAEL B. AND GONZALEZ-VEGA, CLAUDIO, eds. *Latin American debt and adjustment: External shocks and macroeconomic policies.* New York and London: Greenwood Press, Praeger, 1989.

BROOK, TIMOTHY, ed. *The Asiatic mode of production in China.* Chinese Studies on China. Armonk, N.Y. and London: Sharpe, 1989.

BROWN, IAN, ed. *The economies of Africa and Asia in the inter-war depression.* London and New York: Routledge, 1989.

BRUCE, NEIL, ed. *Tax expenditures and government policy: Proceedings of a conference held at Queen's University, 17–18 November, 1988.* Seventh John Deutsch Roundtable on Economic Policy. Kingston, Ont.: John Deutsch Institute for the Study of Economic Policy, Queen's University, 1989.

BRUNNER, KARL AND MELTZER, ALLAN H. *Monetary economics.* Oxford and New York: Blackwell, 1989.

BRYANT, RALPH C., ET AL., eds. *Macroeconomic policies in an interdependent world.* Washington, D.C.: International Monetary Fund; Washington, D.C.: Brookings Institution; London: Centre for Economic Policy Research, 1989.

BUCHANAN, JAMES M. *Essays on the political economy.* Honolulu: University of Hawaii Press, 1989. (I)

BUCHANAN, JAMES M. *Explorations into constitutional economics.* Compiled and with a preface by ROBERT D. TOLLISON AND VIKTOR J. VANBERG. Texas A&M University Economics Series, no. 9. College Station: Texas A&M University Press, 1989. (II)

BUITER, WILLEM H. *Macroeconomic theory and stabilization policy.* Ann Arbor: University of Michigan Press, 1989.

BULGARIAN ACADEMY OF SCIENCES, INSTITUTE OF ECONOMICS. *Economic thought, 1989.* Year 5. Sofia: Author, 1989.

BULMER-THOMAS, VICTOR, ed. *Britain and Latin America: A changing relationship.* Cambridge; New York and Melbourne: Cambridge University Press in association with the Royal Institute of International Affairs, 1989.

Buse, Rueben C., ed. *The economics of meat demand: Proceedings of the conference on the economics of meat demand, October 20–21, 1986, Charleston, South Carolina.* Madison, Wis.: Author, 1989.

Butler, J. R. G. and Doessel, D. P., eds. *Health economics: Australian readings.* Mosman, N.S.W.: Australian Professional Publications, 1989.

Button, Kenneth and Swann, Dennis, eds. *The age of regulatory reform.* Oxford; New York; Toronto and Melbourne: Oxford University Press, Clarendon Press, 1989.

Byrt, William, ed. *Management education: An international survey.* London and New York: Routledge, 1989.

Calzonetti, Frank J., et al. *Power from the Appalachians: A solution to the Northeast's electricity problems?* Contributions in Economics and Economic History, no. 89. Westport, Conn. and London: Greenwood Press, 1989.

Campbell, Bonnie K., ed. *Political dimensions of the international debt crisis.* International Political Economy Series. New York: St. Martin's Press, 1989.

Campbell, Bonnie K. and Loxley, John, eds. *Structural adjustment in Africa.* International Political Economy Series. New York: St. Martin's Press, 1989.

Canak, William L., ed. *Lost promises: Debt, austerity, and development in Latin America.* Boulder, Colo. and London: Westview Press, 1989.

Candemir, Yucel, ed. *Approaches to regional transport problems: Middle East requirements: Papers and proceedings.* Assistants to the editor: Nurhan Yenturk Coban and N. Lerzan Ozkale. Istanbul: Istanbul Technical University, Transportation and Vehicles Research Center, 1989.

Carriere, Jean; Haworth, Nigel and Roddick, Jacqueline, eds. *The state, industrial relations and the labour movement in Latin America.* Volume 1. New York: St. Martin's Press, 1989.

Cavaciocchi, Simonetta, ed. *Metodi risultati e prospettive della storia economica.* Secc. 13–18. *Atti della "Ventesima Settimana di Studi" 19–23 Aprile 1988.* Istituto Internazionale di Storia Economica "F. Datini" Prato, serie 2: Atti delle "Settimane di Studi" e altri Convegni, no. 20. Florence: Monnier, 1989.

Cerami, Charles A., ed. *A Marshall Plan for the 1990s: An international roundtable on world economic development.* New York and London: Greenwood Press, Praeger, 1989.

Chakravarty, Sukhamoy, ed. *The balance between industry and agriculture in economic development: Proceedings of the Eighth World Congress of the International Economic Association, Delhi, India.* Volume 3. *Manpower and transfers.* New York: St. Martin's Press in association with the International Economic Association, 1989.

Chan, James L. and Patton, James M., eds. *Research in governmental and nonprofit accounting.* Volume 5. A Research Annual. Greenwich, Conn. and London: JAI Press, 1989.

Chapman, John W. and Pennock, J. Roland, eds. *Markets and justice.* Yearbook of the American Society for Political and Legal Philosophy, nomos 31. New York and London: New York University Press, 1989.

Chiancone, Aldo and Messere, Ken, eds. *Changes in revenue structures: Proceedings of the 42nd Congress of the International Institute of Public Finance, Athens, 1986.* Detroit: Wayne State University Press, 1989.

Chiao, Chien and Tapp, Nicholas, eds. *Ethnicity and ethnic groups in China.* With the assistance of Kam-yin Ho. Hong Kong: Chinese University of Hong Kong, New Asia College, 1989.

Chirot, Daniel, ed. *The origins of backwardness in Eastern Europe: Economics and politics from the Middle Ages until the early twentieth century.* Berkeley and Oxford: University of California Press, 1989.

Choudhury, Masudul Alam. *Islamic economic co-operation.* Preface by Ozay Mehmet. Foreword by Syed Ahmad. New York: St. Martin's Press, 1989.

Chubb, John E. and Peterson, Paul E., eds. *Can the government govern?* Washington, D.C.: Brookings Institution, 1989.

Chung, Kae H. and Lee, Hak Chong, eds. *Korean managerial dynamics.* New York and London: Greenwood Press, Praeger, 1989.

CLARK, JOHN MAURICE, ET AL. *Adam Smith, 1776–1926: Lectures to commemorate the sesquicentennial of the publication of* "The Wealth of Nations." Reprints of Economic Classics. Fairfield, N.J.: Kelley, [1928] 1989.

COLANDER, DAVID C. AND COATS, A. W., eds. *The spread of economic ideas.* Cambridge; New York and Melbourne: Cambridge University Press, 1989.

COOPER, RICHARD N., ET AL. *Can nations agree? Issues in international economic cooperation.* Studies in International Economics series. Washington, D.C.: Brookings Institution, 1989.

CORNET, BERNARD AND TULKENS, HENRY, eds. *Contributions to operations research and economics: The twentieth anniversary of CORE.* Cambridge, Mass. and London: MIT Press, 1989.

COUPER, A. D., ed. *Development and social change in the Pacific islands.* Ocean Management and Policy Series. London and New York: Routledge, 1989.

COY, MICHAEL W., ed. *Apprenticeship: From theory to method and back again.* SUNY Series in the Anthropology of Work. Albany: State University of New York Press, 1989.

CRANDALL, ROBERT W. AND FLAMM, KENNETH, eds. *Changing the rules: Technological change, international competition, and regulation in communications.* Washington, D.C.: Brookings Institution, 1989.

CRANE, EDWARD H. AND BOAZ, DAVID. *An American vision: Policies for the '90s.* Washington, D.C.: Cato Institute, 1989.

CREW, MICHAEL A., ed. *Deregulation and diversification of utilities.* Topics in Regulatory Economics and Policy Series. Norwell, Mass.; Dordrecht and Lancaster, U.K.: Kluwer Academic, 1989.

CRUISE O'BRIEN, DONAL B.; DUNN, JOHN AND RATHBONE, RICHARD, eds. *Contemporary West African states.* African Studies Series, no. 65. Cambridge; New York and Melbourne: Cambridge University Press, 1989.

CUMMINGS, L. L. AND STAW, BARRY M., eds. *Research in organizational behavior.* Volume 11. Annual Series of Analytical Essays and Critical Reviews. Greenwich, Conn. and London: JAI Press, 1989.

DAHRENDORF, SIR RALF, ET AL. *Whose Europe? Competing visions for 1992.* Foreword by CENTO VELJANOVSKI. IEA Readings, no. 29. London: Institute of Economic Affairs, 1989.

DAMS, THEODOR AND MATSUGI, TAKASHI, eds. *Adjustment problems in advanced open economies: Japan and Germany.* Schriften zu Regional- und Verkehrsproblemen in Industrie- und Entwicklungsländern, Band 49. Berlin: Duncker and Humblot, 1989.

DAVENPORT-HINES, R. P. T. AND JONES, GEOFFREY, eds. *British business in Asia since 1860.* Cambridge; New York; Toronto and Melbourne: Cambridge University Press, 1989.

DAVIDSON, PAUL AND KREGEL, JAN, eds. *Macroeconomic problems and policies of income distribution: Functional, personal, international.* Aldershot, U.K.: Elgar; Brookfield, Vt.: Gower, 1989.

DAVIES, JULIA, ET AL., eds. *The challenge to Western management development: International alternatives.* New York and London: Routledge, 1989.

DE CECCO, MARCELLO AND GIOVANNINI, ALBERTO, eds. *A European central bank? Perspectives on monetary unification after ten years of the EMS.* Cambridge; New York and Melbourne: Cambridge University Press, 1989.

DEGREGORI, THOMAS R., ed. *Development economics: Theory, practice, and prospects.* Recent Economic Thought Series. Norwell, Mass.; Dordrecht and London: Kluwer Academic, 1989.

DEMSETZ, HAROLD. *The organization of economic activity.* Volume 2. *Efficiency, competition, and policy.* Oxford and New York: Blackwell, 1989.

DIAMOND, PETER AND ROTHSCHILD, MICHAEL, eds. *Uncertainty in economics: Readings and exercises.* Revised edition. Economic Theory, Econometrics, and Mathematical Economics series. San Diego; London; Sydney and Toronto: Harcourt Brace Jovanovich, Academic Press, 1989.

[DIAZ-ALEJANDRO, CARLOS] *Debt, stabilization and development: Essays in memory of Carlos Díaz-Alejandro.* Edited by GUILLERMO CALVO ET AL. Oxford and Cambridge, Mass.: Blackwell; Helsinki: United Nations University, World Institute for Development Economics Research, 1989.

VAN DIJK, JOUKE, ET AL., eds. *Migration and labor market adjustment.* Dordrecht; Norwell, Mass. and London: Kluwer Academic, 1989.

sented at a seminar held in Abu Dhabi, United Arab Emirates, December 5–7, 1988. Washington, D.C.: International Monetary Fund, 1989.

ELSON, DIANE AND PEARSON, RUTH, eds. *Women's employment and multinationals in Europe.* London: Macmillan Press; distributed by International Specialized Book Services, Portland, Oreg., 1989.

ENDERWICK, PETER. *Multinational service firms.* London and New York: Routledge, 1989.

[EVANS, JOHN K.] *The oil market in the 1990s: Challenges for the new era. Essays in honor of John K. Evans.* Edited by ROBERT G. REED III AND FEREIDUN FESHARAKI. Westview Special Studies in International Economics and Business series. Boulder, Colo. and London: Westview Press in cooperation with Pacific Resources and the East–West Center, 1989.

FAIRBURN, JAMES AND KAY, JOHN, eds. *Mergers and merger policy.* Oxford; New York; Toronto and Melbourne: Oxford University Press, 1989.

FAURE, MICHAEL AND VAN DEN BERGH, ROGER, eds. *Essays in law and economics: Corporations, accident prevention and compensation for losses.* Foreword by RICHARD POSNER. Antwerp: MAKLU, 1989.

FEDERAL HOME LOAN BANK OF SAN FRANCISCO. *The future of the thrift industry: Proceedings of the fourteenth annual conference, December 8–9, 1988, San Francisco, California.* San Francisco: Author, 1989.

FEDERAL RESERVE BANK OF KANSAS CITY. *Monetary policy issues in the 1990s: A symposium sponsored by the Federal Reserve Bank of Kansas City, Jackson Hole, Wyoming, August 30–September 1, 1989.* Symposium Series. Kansas City: Author, 1989.

FEENSTRA, ROBERT C., ed. *Trade policies for international competitiveness.* National Bureau of Economic Research Conference Report series. Chicago and London: University of Chicago Press, 1989.

FEIGE, EDGAR L., ed. *The underground economies: Tax evasion and information distortion.* Cambridge; New York and Melbourne: Cambridge University Press, 1989.

FEIWEL, GEORGE R., ed. *The economics of imperfect competition and employment: Joan Robinson and beyond.* New York: New York University Press; distributed by Columbia University Press, 1989. (I)

FEIWEL, GEORGE R., ed. *Joan Robinson and modern economic theory.* New York: New York University Press; distributed by Columbia University Press, 1989. (II)

FELS, GERHARD AND VON FURSTENBERG, GEORGE M., eds. *A supply-side agenda for Germany: Sparks from the United States–Great Britain–European integration.* New York; London; Berlin and Tokyo: Springer, 1989.

FELTON, JOHN RICHARD AND ANDERSON, DALE G., eds. *Regulation and deregulation of the motor carrier industry.* Ames: Iowa State University Press, 1989.

FERRIER, R. W. AND FURSENKO, A., eds. *Oil in the world economy.* London and New York: Routledge, 1989.

FERRIS, GERALD R. AND ROWLAND, KENDRITH M., eds. *Research in personnel and human resources management.* Volume 7. A Research Annual. Greenwich, Conn. and London: JAI Press, 1989.

FIENBERG, STEPHEN E., ed. *The evolving role of statistical assessments as evidence in the courts.* New York; Berlin; London and Tokyo: Springer, 1989.

FINKELSTEIN, JOSEPH, ed. *Windows on a new world: The third industrial revolution.* Contributions in Economics and Economic History series, no. 88. Westport, Conn. and London: Greenwood Press, 1989.

FISCHER, STANLEY AND DE TRAY, DENNIS, eds. *Proceedings of the World Bank Annual Conference on Development Economics 1989.* Washington, D.C.: World Bank, 1989.

[FISCHER, WOLFRAM] *Interactions in the world economy: Perspectives from international economic history.* Edited by CARL-LUDWIG HOLTFRERICH. New York: New York University Press, 1989.

FISHELSON, GIDEON, ed. *Economic cooperation in the Middle East.* Westview Special Studies on the Middle East. Boulder, Colo. and London: Westview Press, 1989.

FITZGERALD, E. V. K. AND VOS, ROB. *Financing economic development: A structural approach to monetary policy.* Aldershot, U.K.; Brookfield, Vt.; Singapore and Sydney: Gower, 1989.

FOGLESONG, RICHARD E. AND WOLFE, JOEL D., eds. *The politics of economic adjustment: Pluralism, corporatism, and privatization.* Contributions in Political Science, no. 237. Westport, Conn. and London: Greenwood Press, 1989.

FOLMER, H. AND VAN IERLAND, E., eds. *Valuation methods and policy making in environmental economics: Selected and integrated papers from the congress "Environmental Policy in a Market Economy," Wageningen, the Netherlands, 8–11 September 1987.* Studies in Environmental Science, no. 36. Amsterdam; Oxford; New York and Tokyo: Elsevier Science, 1989.

FRANCIS, ARTHUR AND GROOTINGS, PETER, eds. *New technologies and work: Capitalist and socialist perspectives.* London and New York: Routledge in cooperation with the European Co-ordination Centre for Research and Documentation in Social Science, 1989.

FRANCIS, ARTHUR AND THARAKAN, P. K. M., eds. *The competitiveness of European industry.* London and New York: Routledge, 1989.

FRANKEL, ANDREW V. AND HECK, CHARLES B., eds. *The Paris plenary, April 1989.* Trialogue series, no. 41. New York: Trilateral Commission, 1989.

FRANZ, ALFRED AND RAINER, NORBERT, eds. *Compilation of input–output data: Proceedings of the 2nd International Meeting on Problems of Compilation of Input–Output Tables, organized by the Austrian Statistical Society, Baden near Vienna, Austria, 13–19 March, 1988.* With contributions by S. BAR-ELIEZER ET AL. Schriftenreihe der Österreichischen Statistischen Gesellschaft, Band 4. Vienna: Wirtschaftsverlag Orac, 1989.

FRANZ, OTMAR, ed. *European currency in the making.* Contributions by ERNST-GUNTHER BRODER, ET AL. Sindelfingen, W. Germany: Libertas, 1989.

FREEMAN, RICHARD B. *Labor markets in action: Essays in empirical economics.* Cambridge and London: Harvard University Press, 1989.

FRENKEL, JACOB A.; DOOLEY, MICHAEL P. AND WICKHAM, PETER, eds. *Analytical issues in debt.* Washington, D.C.: International Monetary Fund, 1989.

FRIED, EDWARD R. AND TREZISE, PHILIP H., eds. *Third world debt: The next phase.* Brookings Dialogues on Public Policy series. Washington, D.C.: Brookings Institution, 1989.

GABRISCH, HUBERT, ed. *Economic reforms in Eastern Europe and the Soviet Union.* Westview Special Studies in International Economics series. Vienna Institute for Comparative Economic Studies Yearbook 1—1988. Boulder, Colo. and London: Westview Press in cooperation with the Vienna Institute for Comparative Economic Studies, 1989.

GALENSON, DAVID W., ed. *Markets in history: Economic studies of the past.* Cambridge; New York and Melbourne: Cambridge University Press, 1989.

GAMBLE, ANDREW, ET AL. *Ideas, interests and consequences.* Foreword by CENTO VELJANOVSKI. IEA Readings, no. 30. London: Institute of Economic Affairs, 1989.

GANGOLLY, JAGDISH, ed. *Advances in accounting.* Supplement 1. MARCOS MASSOUD AND DENNIS B. KNEIER, Associate Editors. A Research Annual. Greenwich, Conn. and London: JAI Press, 1989.

GEARY, DICK, ed. *Labour and socialist movements in Europe before 1914.* Oxford and Munich: Berg; distributed in the U.S. and Canada by St. Martin's Press, New York, 1989.

GEMPER, BODO B., ed. *The market system, structural change and efficient economies: The international trend towards indicative targeting.* Reprint. New Brunswick, N.J. and London: Transaction, 1989.

GIAQUINTA, MARIANO, ed. *Topics in calculus of variations: Lectures given at the 2nd 1987 session of the Centro Internazionale Matematico Estivo (C.I.M.E.) held at Montecatini Terme, Italy, July 20–28, 1987.* Lecture Notes in Mathematics series, vol. 1365. New York; Berlin; London and Tokyo: Springer, 1989.

GIBBS, DAVID, ed. *Government policy and industrial change.* Geography and Environment series. London and New York: Routledge, 1989.

GIBSON, LAY JAMES AND STIMSON, ROBERT J., eds. *Regional structural change: Experience and prospects in two mature economies.* Peace Dale, R.I.: Regional Science Research Institute, 1989.

GIERSCH, HERBERT, ed. *Services in world economic growth: Symposium 1988*. Tubingen, West Germany: Mohr (Siebeck); Boulder, Colo. and London: Westview Press, 1989.

GOLDEN, BRUCE L.; WASIL, EDWARD A. AND HARKER, PATRICK T., eds. *The analytic hierarchy process: Applications and studies*. New York; Berlin; London and Tokyo: Springer, 1989.

GOLDMAN, LAWRENCE, ed. *The blind Victorian: Henry Fawcett and British liberalism*. Cambridge; New York and Melbourne: Cambridge University Press, 1989.

GOLDSCHEIDER, FRANCES K. AND GOLDSCHEIDER, CALVIN, eds. *Ethnicity and the new family economy: Living arrangements and intergenerational financial flows*. Social Inequality Series. Boulder and London: Westview Press, 1989.

GOMULKA, STANISLAW; HA, YONG-CHOOL AND KIM, CAE-ONE, eds. *Economic reforms in the socialist world*. Armonk, N.Y.: Sharpe, 1989.

GOODMAN, DAVID AND REDCLIFT, MICHAEL, eds. *The international farm crisis*. New York: St. Martin's Press, 1989.

GOODMAN, DAVID S. G., ed. *China's regional development*. New York and London: Routledge for the Royal Institute of International Affairs, 1989.

GOODMAN, EDWARD AND BAMFORD, JULIA, eds. *Small firms and industrial districts in Italy*. With PETER SAYNOR. London and New York: Routledge, 1989.

[GORDENKER, LEON] *The United Nations in the world political economy: Essays in honour of Leon Gordenker*. Edited by DAVID P. FORSYTHE. International Political Economy Series. New York: St. Martin's Press, 1989.

GORDON, IAN AND THIRLWALL, A. P., eds. *European factor mobility: Trends and consequences. Proceedings of the Conference of the Confederation of European Economic Associations, University of Kent at Canterbury, 29 June–3 July 1986*. New York and London: St. Martin's Press, 1989.

GOTTDIENER, M. AND KOMNINOS, NICOS, eds. *Capitalist development and crisis theory: Accumulation, regulation and spatial restructuring*. New York: St. Martin's Press, 1989.

GRANTHAM, GEORGE AND LEONARD, CAROL S., eds. *Agrarian organization in the century of industrialization: Europe, Russia, and North America*. Research in Economic History series, supplement 5, pt. A. Greenwich, Conn. and London: JAI Press, 1989.

GRANTHAM, GEORGE AND LEONARD, CAROL S., eds. *Agrarian organization in the century of industrialization: Europe, Russia, and North America*. Research in Economic History series, supplement 5, pt. B. Greenwich, Conn. and London: JAI Press, 1989.

GRAY, H. PETER, ed. *The modern international environment*. Research in International Business and Finance series, vol. 7. Greenwich, Conn. and London: JAI Press, 1989.

GREENAWAY, DAVID, ed. *Current issues in macroeconomics*. Current Issues in Economics series, vol. 2. New York: St. Martin's Press, 1989.

GREENAWAY, DAVID; HYCLAK, THOMAS AND THORNTON, ROBERT J., eds. *Economic aspects of regional trading arrangements*. New York: New York University Press; distributed by Columbia University Press, 1989.

GREENAWAY, DAVID AND PRESLEY, JOHN R., eds. *Pioneers of modern economics in Britain*. Volume 2. New York: St. Martin's Press, 1989.

GROSSMAN, SANFORD J. *The informational role of prices*. Wicksell Lectures. Cambridge, Mass. and London: MIT Press, 1989.

[GRUEN, FRED H.] *Australian economic growth: Essays in honour of Fred H. Gruen*. Edited by BRUCE CHAPMAN. South Melbourne: Macmillan; distributed by International Specialized Book Service, Portland, Oreg., 1989.

GRUNERT, KLAUS G. AND OLANDER, FOLKE, eds. *Understanding economic behaviour*. Theory and Decision Library Series A: Philosophy and Methodology of the Social Sciences, vol. 11. Norwell, Mass.; Dordrecht and London: Kluwer Academic, 1989.

GUARDUCCI, ANNALISA, ed. *Investimenti e civiltà urbana secoli 13–18: Atti della "Nona Settimana di Studi," 22–28 Aprile 1977*. Istituto Internazionale di Storia Economica "F. Datini" Prato, Serie 2: Atti delle "Settimane di Studi" e altri Convegni, no. 9. Florence: Monnier, 1989.

GULLEDGE, THOMAS R., JR. AND LITTERAL, LEWIS A., eds. *Cost analysis applications of economics*

and London: New York University Press; distributed by Columbia University Press, New York, 1989.

HEIDENHEIMER, ARNOLD J.; JOHNSTON, MICHAEL AND LEVINE, VICTOR T., eds. *Political corruption: A handbook*. New Brunswick, N.J. and Oxford: Transaction Books, 1989.

HELD, DAVID AND THOMPSON, JOHN B., eds. *Social theory of modern societies: Anthony Giddens and his critics*. Cambridge; New York and Melbourne: Cambridge University Press, 1989.

HELM, DIETER, ed. *The economic borders of the state*. Oxford; New York; Toronto and Melbourne: Oxford University Press, 1989.

HELM, DIETER; KAY, JOHN AND THOMPSON, DAVID, eds. *The market for energy*. Oxford; New York; Toronto and Melboune: Oxford University Press, 1989.

HELMUTH, JOHN W. AND JOHNSON, STANLEY R., eds. *1988 World Food Conference proceedings*. Volume 1. *Policy addresses*. Foreword by TERRY E. BRANSTAD. Ames: Iowa State University Press for the Center for Agricultural and Rural Development, 1989.

HELMUTH, JOHN W. AND JOHNSON, STANLEY R., eds. *1988 World Food Conference proceedings*. Volume 2: *Issue papers*. Ames: Iowa State University Press for the Center for Agricultural and Rural Development, 1989.

HERMAN, ROBERT D. AND VAN TIL, JON, eds. *Nonprofit boards of directors: Analyses and applications*. New Brunswick, N.J. and Oxford: Transaction Books, 1989.

HEY, JOHN D., ed. *Current issues in microeconomics*. Current Issues in Economics series, vol. 1. New York: St. Martin's Press, 1989.

HIGGINS, BENJAMIN AND ZAGORSKI, KRZYSZTOF, eds. *Australian regional developments: Readings in regional experiences, policies and prospects*. Australian Regional Developments series, no. 10. Canberra: Department of Immigration, Local Government and Ethnic Affairs, Office of Local Government; distributed by Australian Government Publishing Service, 1989.

HILL, HAL, ed. *Unity and diversity: Regional economic development in Indonesia since 1970*. South-East Asian Social Science Monographs. Singapore; Oxford; New York and Melbourne: Oxford University Press, 1989.

HILL, M. ANNE AND KILLINGSWORTH, MARK R., eds. *Comparable worth: Analyses and evidence*. Ithaca, N.Y.: ILR Press, 1989.

HIRSHLEIFER, JACK. *Time, uncertainty and information*. Uncertainty and Expectations in Economics series. Oxford and New York: Blackwell, 1989.

HIRST, PAUL AND ZEITLIN, JONATHAN, eds. *Reversing industrial decline? Industrial structure and policy in Britain and her competitors*. Oxford and Hamburg: Berg; distributed in the U.S. and Canada by St. Martin's Press, New York, 1989.

HODGMAN, DONALD R. AND WOOD, GEOFFREY E., eds. *Macroeconomic policy and economic interdependence*. New York: St. Martin's Press, 1989.

HOLMLUND, BERTIL; LOFGREN, KARL-GUSTAF AND ENGSTROM, LARS. *Trade unions, employment, and unemployment duration*. FIEF Studies in Labour Markets and Economic Policy. Oxford; New York; Toronto and Melbourne: Oxford University Press, Clarendon Press, 1989.

HORWICH, GEORGE AND LYNCH, GERALD J., eds. *Food, policy, and politics: A perspective on agriculture and development*. Westview Special Studies in Agriculture Science and Policy. Boulder, Colo. and London: Westview Press, 1989.

HOWE, CHRISTOPHER AND WALKER, KENNETH R., eds. *The foundations of the Chinese planned economy: A documentary survey, 1953–65*. New York: St. Martin's Press, 1989.

HUANG, WEI-CHIAO, ed. *Organized labor at the crossroads*. Kalamazoo, Mich.: W. E. Upjohn Institute for Employment Research, 1989.

HUDSON, PAT, ed. *Regions and industries: A perspective on the industrial revolution in Britain*. Cambridge; New York and Melbourne: Cambridge University Press, 1989.

HUGHES, GORDON AND VINES, DAVID, eds. *Deregulation and the future of commercial television*. Hume Paper, no. 12. Glasgow: Pergamon, Aberdeen University Press, 1989.

HUSAIN, ISHRAT AND DIWAN, ISHAC, eds. *Dealing with the debt crisis*. A World Bank Symposium. Washington, D.C.: World Bank, 1989.

INTERNATIONAL FISCAL ASSOCIATION, ed. *Administrative and compliance costs of taxation*. Studies

KAUSHIK, SURENDRA K., ed. *International capital markets: New directions*. New York: Simon and Schuster, New York Institute of Finance, 1989.

KIEFER, NICHOLAS M. AND NEUMANN, GEORGE R. *Search models and applied labor economics*. Cambridge; New York and Melbourne: Cambridge University Press, 1989.

KIM, YOON HYUNG AND SMITH, KIRK R., eds. *Electricity in economic development: The experience of Northeast Asia*. Assisted by KENNON BREAZEALE. Contributions in Economics and Economic History series, no. 85. Westport, Conn. and London: Greenwood Press, 1989.

KOLLINTZAS, TRYPHON, ed. *The rational expectations equilibrium inventory model: Theory and applications*. Lecture Notes in Economics and Mathematical Systems series, vol. 322. New York; Berlin; London and Tokyo: Springer, 1989.

KOPCKE, RICHARD W. AND ROSENGREN, ERIC S., eds. *Are the distinctions between debt and equity disappearing? Proceedings of a conference held at Melvin Village, New Hampshire, October 1989*. Conference Series, no. 33. Boston: Federal Reserve Bank of Boston, 1989.

KOTLIKOFF, LAURENCE J. *What determines savings?* Cambridge, Mass. and London: MIT Press, 1989.

KRAMER, CAROL S., ed. *The political economy of U.S. agriculture: Challenges for the 1990s*. National Center for Food and Agricultural Policy Annual Policy Review. Washington, D.C.: Resources for the Future, 1989.

KRAMER, WALTER, ed. *Econometrics of structural change*. Studies in Empirical Economics series. Heidelberg: Physica; New York: Springer, 1989.

KRELLE, WILHELM, ed. *The future of the world economy: Economic growth and structural change*. New York; Berlin; London and Tokyo: Springer, 1989.

KRUEGER, ANNE O.; MICHALOPOULOS, CONSTANTINE AND RUTTAN, VERNON W. *Aid and development*. With KEITH JAY ET AL. Johns Hopkins Studies in Development. Baltimore and London: Johns Hopkins University Press, 1989.

KUZNETS, SIMON. *Economic development, the family, and income distribution: Selected essays*. Studies in Economic History and Policy: The United States in the Twentieth Century. Cambridge; New York and Melbourne: Cambridge University Press, 1989.

KWOKA, JOHN E., JR. AND WHITE, LAWRENCE J., eds. *The antitrust revolution*. Glenview, Ill. and London: Scott, Foresman, 1989.

LABYS, WALTER C.; TAKAYAMA, TAKASHI AND URI, NOEL D., eds. *Quantitative methods for market-oriented economic analysis over space and time*. Aldershot, U.K.; Brookfield, Vt.; Hong Kong and Sydney: Gower, Avebury, 1989.

LANGE, PETER AND REGINI, MARINO, eds. *State, market, and social regulation: New perspectives on Italy*. Cambridge Studies in Modern Political Economies. Cambridge; New York and Melbourne: Cambridge University Press, 1989.

LARNER, ROBERT J. AND MEEHAN, JAMES W., JR., eds. *Economics and antitrust policy*. Westport, Conn. and London: Greenwood Press, Quorum Books, 1989.

LAWLER, EDWARD J. AND MARKOVSKY, BARRY, eds. *Advances in group processes*. Volume 6. A Research Annual. Greenwich, Conn. and London: JAI Press, 1989.

LAWSON, TONY; PALMA, J. GABRIEL AND SENDER, JOHN, eds. *Kaldor's political economy*. London and San Diego: Academic Press, 1989.

LEE, CHENG F., ed. *Advances in financial planning and forecasting*. Volume 3. A Research Annual. Greenwich, Conn. and London: JAI Press, 1989.

LEE, CHENG F. AND HU, SHENG-CHENG, eds. *Taiwan's foreign investment, exports and financial analysis*. Advances in Financial Planning and Forecasting series, supplement no. 1. Greenwich, Conn. and London: JAI Press, 1989.

LEIBENSTEIN, HARVEY. *The collected essays of Harvey Leibenstein*. Volume 1. *Population, development and welfare*. Edited by KENNETH BUTTON. New York: New York University Press; distributed by Columbia University Press, 1989.

LEIBENSTEIN, HARVEY. *The collected essays of Harvey Leibenstein*. Volume 2. *X-efficiency and micro–micro theory*. Edited by KENNETH BUTTON. New York: New York University Press; distributed by Columbia University Press, 1989.

LEONARD, H. JEFFREY, ed. *Environment and the poor: Development strategies for a common agenda.* Overseas Development Council U.S.–Third World Policy Perspectives, no. 11. New Brunswick, N.J. and Oxford: Transaction Books, 1989.

LEVIN, SIMON A.; HALLAM, THOMAS G. AND GROSS, LOUIS J., eds. *Applied mathematical ecology.* Biomathematics series, vol. 18. New York; Berlin and Tokyo: Springer, 1989.

LEWANDOWSKI, ANDRZEJ AND WIERZBICKI, ANDRZEJ PIOTR, eds. *Aspiration based decision support systems: Theory, software and applications.* Lecture Notes in Economics and Mathematical Systems series, vol. 331. Berlin; New York; London and Tokyo: Springer, 1989.

LEWIN, MARION EIN AND SULLIVAN, SEAN, eds. *The care of tomorrow's elderly.* AEI Studies, no. 487. Washington, D.C.: American Enterprise Institute for Public Policy Research, 1989.

LIBECAP, GARY D., ed. *American international competitiveness.* Advances in the Study of Entrepreneurship, Innovation, and Economic Growth series, vol. 3. Greenwich, Conn. and London: JAI Press, 1989.

LINEBERRY, WILLIAM P., ed. *Assessing participatory development: Rhetoric versus reality.* With a foreword by IDRISS JAZAIRY. Boulder, Colo. and London: Westview Press in cooperation with the International Fund for Agricultural Development, 1989.

LINGE, GODFREY J. R. AND VAN DER KNAAP, G. A., eds. *Labour, environment and industrial change.* New York and London: Routledge for the International Geographical Union's Commission on Industrial Change, 1989.

LIPSEY, ROBERT E. AND TICE, HELEN STONE, eds. *The measurement of saving, investment, and wealth.* National Bureau of Economic Research Studies in Income and Wealth, vol. 52. Chicago and London: University of Chicago Press, 1989.

LLEWELLYN, DAVID T., ed. *Reflections on money.* Foreword by LORD EZRA. New York: St. Martin's Press, 1989.

LOCKETT, A. G. AND ISLEI, G., eds. *Improving decision making in organizations: Proceedings of the Eighth International Conference on Multiple Criteria Decision Making held at Manchester Business School, University of Manchester, UK, August 21st–26th, 1988.* Lecture Notes in Economics and Mathematical Systems, vol. 335. New York; Berlin; London and Tokyo: Springer, 1989.

LODEWIJKS, JOHN AND ZERBY, JOHN, eds. *Recent developments in the South Pacific island economies.* Research Report series. Kensington, Australia: University of New South Wales, Centre for Applied Economic Research, East Asian Trade and Development Programme, 1989.

LODGE, JULIET, ed. *The European Community and the challenge of the future.* New York: St. Martin's Press, 1989.

LOISTL, OTTO AND LANDES, THOMAS, ed. *The dynamic pricing of financial assets.* New York; Hamburg; Montreal and Sydney: McGraw-Hill, 1989.

MACAVOY, PAUL W., ET AL. *Privatization and state-owned enterprises: Lessons from the United States, Great Britain and Canada.* Rochester Studies in Economics and Policy Issues series. Norwell, Mass.; Dordrecht and Lancaster, U.K.: Kluwer Academic in cooperation with the University of Rochester, William E. Simon Graduate School of Business Administration, Bradley Policy Research Center, 1989.

MACDONALD, RONALD AND TAYLOR, MARK P., eds. *Exchange rates and open economy macroeconomics.* Oxford and Cambridge, Mass.: Blackwell, 1989.

MACESICH, GEORGE, ed. *Essays on the Yugoslav economic model.* With the assistance of RIKARD LANG AND DRAGOMIR VOJNIC. Westport, Conn. and London: Praeger, 1989.

MACEWAN, ARTHUR AND TABB, WILLIAM K., eds. *Instability and change in the world economy.* New York: Monthly Review Press, 1989.

MADDISON, ANGUS AND PRINCE, GE, eds. *Economic growth in Indonesia, 1820–1940.* Verhandelingen van Het Koninklijk Instituut Voor Taal-, Land- en Volkenkunde, 137. Providence and Dordrecht: Foris, 1989.

MAGNOU-NORTIER, ELISABETH, ET AL. *Historia economica y de las instituciones financieras en Europa. Trabajos en homenaje a Ferran Valls i Taberner.* Estudios interdisciplinares en homenaje a Ferran Valls i Taberner con ocasión del centenario de su nacimiento. Barcelona: Universidad de Málaga, Cátedra de Historia del Derecho y de las Instituciones, 1989.

MAKIN, JOHN H. AND HELLMANN, DONALD C., eds. *Sharing world leadership? A new era for America and Japan.* AEI Studies, no. 488. Washington, D.C.: American Enterprise Institute for Public Policy Research; distributed by National Book Network, Lanham, Md., 1989.

MANSFIELD, ROGER, ed. *Frontiers of management.* London and New York: Routledge, 1989.

DE MARCHI, NEIL AND GILBERT, CHRISTOPHER, eds. *History and methodology of econometrics.* Oxford; New York; Toronto and Melbourne: Oxford University Press, Clarendon Press, 1989.

MARIANO, ROBERTO S.; LIM, K. S. AND LING, K. D., eds. *Advances in statistical analysis and statistical computing.* Volume 2. *Theory and applications.* Greenwich, Conn. and London: JAI Press, 1989.

[MARJOLIN, ROBERT] *International economics and financial markets:* The AMEX Bank Review prize essays. *In memory of Robert Marjolin.* Edited by RICHARD O'BRIEN AND TAPAN DATTA. Oxford; New York; Toronto and Melbourne: Oxford University Press for *The AMEX Bank Review,* 1989.

MARTIN, MICHAEL T. AND KANDAL, TERRY R., eds. *Studies of development and change in the modern world.* New York and Oxford: Oxford University Press, 1989.

MATHIAS, PETER AND POLLARD, SIDNEY, eds. *The Cambridge economic history of Europe.* Volume 8. *The industrial economies: The development of economic and social policies.* Cambridge; New York and Melbourne: Cambridge University Press, 1989.

MATSUO, HIROFUMI, ed. *Understanding Japanese business.* Japan Business Study Program series. Austin: University of Texas, Bureau of Business Research; Houston: Japan External Trade Organization, 1989.

MATZER, JOHN, JR., ed. *Capital projects: New strategies for planning, management, and finance.* Practical Management Series. Washington, D.C.: International City Management Association, 1989.

McKEE, DAVID L., ed. *Hostile takeovers: Issues in public and corporate policy.* New York and London: Greenwood Press, Praeger, 1989.

McLENNAN, KENNETH AND MEYER, JACK A., eds. *Care and cost: Current issues in health policy.* Westview Special Studies in Health Care and Medical Science series. Boulder, Colo. and London: Westview Press, 1989.

McRAE, DONALD AND MUNRO, GORDON, eds. *Canadian oceans policy: National strategies and the new law of the sea.* Canada and International Relations series, no. 2. Vancouver: University of British Columbia Press, 1989.

MEINERS, ROGER E. AND YANDLE, BRUCE, eds. *Regulation and the Reagan era: Politics, bureaucracy and the public interest.* Foreword by ROBERT CRANDALL. Independent Studies in Political Economy. New York and London: Holmes and Meier, 1989.

MESA-LAGO, CARMELO, ed. *Cuban Studies,* Volume 19. Pittsburgh: University of Pittsburgh Press; Pittsburgh: University of Pittsburgh, Center for Latin American Studies, 1989.

MICHAEL, ROBERT T.; HARTMANN, HEIDI I. AND O'FARRELL, BRIGID, eds. *Pay equity: Empirical inquiries.* Washington, D.C.: National Academy Press, 1989.

MILLER, MARCUS; EICHENGREEN, BARRY AND PORTES, RICHARD, eds. *Blueprints for exchange-rate management.* London; San Diego; Sydney and Toronto: Harcourt Brace Jovanovich, Academic Press, 1989.

MILLER, RONALD E.; POLENSKE, KAREN R. AND ROSE, ADAM Z., eds. *Frontiers of input–output analysis.* New York and Oxford: Oxford University Press, 1989.

MINTZ, JACK AND WHALLEY, JOHN, eds. *The economic impacts of tax reform.* Canadian Tax Paper series, no. 84. Toronto: Canadian Tax Foundation, 1989.

MISSOURI VALLEY ECONOMIC ASSOCIATION. *The Journal of Economics.* Volume 15. Cape Girardeau, Mo.: Author, 1989.

MODIGLIANI, FRANCO. *The collected papers of Franco Modigliani.* Volume 4. *Monetary theory and stabilization policies.* Edited by SIMON JOHNSON. Cambridge, Mass. and London: MIT Press, 1989.

MODIGLIANI, FRANCO. *The collected papers of Franco Modigliani.* Volume 5. *Saving, deficits, inflation, and financial theory.* Edited by SIMON JOHNSON. Cambridge, Mass. and London: MIT Press, 1989.

MOHAN, JOHN, ed. *The political geography of contemporary Britain.* London: Macmillan; distributed by Sheridan House, Dobbs Ferry, N.Y., 1989.

MOHRMAN, ALLAN M., JR., ET AL. *Large-scale organizational change.* Jossey-Bass Management Series. San Francisco and London: Jossey-Bass, 1989.

MOMMSEN, WOLFGANG J. *The political and social theory of Max Weber: Collected essays.* Chicago: University of Chicago Press; Cambridge, U.K.: Polity Press, 1989.

MONTI, MARIO, ed. *Fiscal policy, economic adjustment, and financial markets: Papers presented at a seminar sponsored by the International Monetary Fund and Centro di Economia monetaria e finanziaria, Università Bocconi, held in Milan on January 28–30, 1988.* Washington, D.C.: International Monetary Fund; Milan: Centro di Economia monetaria e finanziaria, 1989.

MORRIS-SUZUKI, TESSA AND SEIYAMA, TAKURO, eds. *Japanese capitalism since 1945: Critical perspectives.* An East Gate Book. Armonk, N.Y. and London: Sharpe, 1989.

MOSES, LEON N. AND SAVAGE, IAN, eds. *Transportation safety in an age of deregulation.* New York and Oxford: Oxford University Press, 1989.

[MOUNTJOY, ALAN B.] *The geography of urban–rural interaction in developing countries: Essays for Alan B. Mountjoy.* Edited by ROBERT B. POTTER AND TIM UNWIN. London and New York: Routledge, 1989.

MRAK, MOJMIR, ed. *External debt problem: Current issues and perspectives.* Ljubljana, Yugoslavia: Centre for International Cooperation and Development, 1989.

MULLER, F. AND ZWEZERIJNEN, W. J., eds. *The role of economic policy in society.* The Hague: Universitaire Pers Rotterdam, 1989.

NABLI, MUSTAPHA K. AND NUGENT, JEFFREY B., eds. *The new institutional economics and development: Theory and applications to Tunisia.* Contributions to Economic Analysis, no. 183. Amsterdam; Oxford and Tokyo: North-Holland; distributed in the U.S. and Canada by Elsevier Science, New York, 1989.

NATIONAL ECONOMIC RESEARCH ASSOCIATES. *Telecommunications in a competitive environment: Proceedings of the Third Biennial Telecommunications Conference, Marriott's Camelback Inn, Scottsdale, Arizona, April 12–15, 1989.* White Plains, N.Y.: Author, 1989.

NAU, HENRY R., ed. *Domestic trade politics and the Uruguay Round.* New York: Columbia University Press, 1989.

NAYA, SEIJI, ET AL., eds. *Lessons in development: A comparative study of Asia and Latin America.* Panama and San Francisco: Institute for Contemporary Studies, International Center for Economic Growth, 1989.

NEDD, ALBERT, ed. *International human resources management.* Research in Personnel and Human Resources Management series, supplement 1. Greenwich, Conn. and London: JAI Press, 1989.

NEE, VICTOR AND STARK, DAVID, eds. *Remaking the economic institutions of socialism: China and Eastern Europe.* With MARK SELDON. Stanford, Calif.: Stanford University Press, 1989.

NEGANDHI, ANANT R., ed. *Multinationals and newly industrialized countries: Strategies, environmental imperatives, and practices.* In collaboration with NORIHIKO SUZUKI AND TSAI-MEI LIN. Research in International Business and International Relations series, vol. 3. Greenwich, Conn. and London: JAI Press, 1989.

NELSON, JOAN M., ed. *Fragile coalitions: The politics of economic adjustment.* U.S.–Third World Policy Perseptives series, no. 12. New Brunswick, N.J. and Oxford: Transaction Books, 1989.

NICKELL, STEPHEN J., ET AL. *The nature of unemployment in Britain: Studies of the DHSS cohort.* Oxford; New York; Toronto and Melbourne: Oxford University Press, 1989.

NIEUWENHUYSEN, JOHN, ed. *Towards freer trade between nations.* Committee for Economic Development of Australia Study, P.32. Melbourne; New York; Oxford and Toronto: Oxford University Press, 1989.

NORTH–SOUTH INSTITUTE. *Trade, protectionism and industrial adjustment: Three North American case studies.* Ottawa: Author, 1989.

NOYELLE, THIERRY, ed. *New York's financial markets: The challenges of globalization.* Conservation of Human Resources Studies in the New Economy. Boulder, Colo. and London: Westview Press, 1989.

ODEN, BERTIL AND OTHMAN, HAROUB, eds. *Regional cooperation in southern Africa: A post-apartheid perspective.* Seminar Proceedings, no. 22. Uppsala, Sweden: Scandinavian Institute of African Studies, 1989.

OPITZ, OTTO, ed. *Conceptual and numerical analysis of data: Proceedings of the 13th conference of the Gesellschaft für Klassifikation e. V., University of Augsburg, April 10–12, 1989.* In cooperation with W. GAUL, H. SCHNELLING, AND P. O. DEGENS. New York; Berlin; London and Tokyo: Springer, 1989.

ORAM, P. A., ET AL. *Climate and food security: Papers presented at the International Symposium on Climate Variability and Food Security in Developing Countries, 5–9 February 1987, New Delhi, India.* Manila: International Rice Research Institute in collaboration with the American Association for the Advancement of Science, 1989.

ORDESHOOK, PETER C., ed. *Models of strategic choice in politics.* Ann Arbor: University of Michigan Press, 1989.

ORGANIZATION FOR ECONOMIC CO-OPERATION AND DEVELOPMENT. *Labour market flexibility: Trends in enterprises.* Paris: Author, 1989.

OWEN, A. D., ed. *World environmental and energy issues: Their impact on the Australian economy: Proceedings of a seminar held at the Hilton Hotel, Sydney, Australia, 15 August 1989.* Kensington, Australia: University of New South Wales, Centre for Applied Economic Research, 1989.

PARK, SUNG-JO, ed. *East Asia: International review of economic, political, and social development.* East Asia series, vol. 5. Frankfurt am Main: Campus; Boulder, Colo.: Westview Press, 1989.

PARRY, J. AND BLOCH, M., eds. *Money and the morality of exchange.* Cambridge; New York and Melbourne: Cambridge University Press, 1989.

PEACOCK, ALAN AND WILLGERODT, HANS, eds. *German neo-liberals and the social market economy.* With the assistance of DANIEL JOHNSON. New York: St. Martin's Press, 1989. (I)

PEACOCK, ALAN AND WILLGERODT, HANS, eds. *Germany's social market economy: Origins and evolution.* New York: St. Martin's Press, 1989. (II)

PECHMAN, JOSEPH A., ed. *The role of the economist in government: An international perspective.* New York; London; Toronto and Tokyo. Harvester Wheatsheaf, 1989.

PEDERSEN, JORGEN LINDGAARD, ed. *Technology policy in Denmark.* Copenhagen: New Social Science Monographs, 1989.

PENCAK, WILLIAM AND WRIGHT, CONRAD EDICK, eds. *New York and the rise of American capitalism: Economic development and the social and political history of an American state, 1780–1870.* New York: New York Historical Society, 1989.

PERKINS, EDWIN J., ed. *Essays in economic and business history: Selected papers from the Economic and Business Historical Society, 1988.* Volume 7. With the editorial assistance of BRENDA JOHNSON. Los Angeles: University of Southern California for the Economic and Business Historical Society, 1989.

PERRUCCI, ROBERT AND POTTER, HARRY R., eds. *Networks of power: Organizational actors at the national, corporate, and community levels.* Social Institutions and Social Change series. New York: Aldine de Gruyter, 1989.

PHEBY, JOHN, ed. *New directions in post-Keynesian economics.* New Directions in Modern Economics. Aldershot, U.K.: Elgar; Brookfield, Vt.: Gower, 1989.

PINKERTON, EVELYN, ed. *Co-operative management of local fisheries: New directions for improved management and community development.* Vancouver: University of British Columbia Press, 1989.

PLATT, D. C. M., ed. *Social welfare, 1850–1950: Australia, Argentina and Canada compared.* London: Macmillan; distributed by International Specialized Book Services, Portland, Oreg., 1989.

POLLAK, ROBERT A. *The theory of the cost-of-living index.* New York and Oxford: Oxford University Press, 1989.

Lexington, Mass. and Toronto: Heath, Lexington Books; Washington, D.C.: Ludwig von Mises Institute, 1989.

RUESCHEMEYER, MARILYN AND LEMKE, CHRISTIANE, eds. *The quality of life in the German Democratic Republic: Changes and developments in a state socialist society.* Armonk, N.Y. and London: Sharpe, 1989.

RUESCHHOFF, NORLIN AND SCHAUM, KONRAD, eds. *Christian business values in an intercultural environment.* Volkswirtschaftliche Schriften, Heft 393. Berlin: Duncker and Humblot, 1989.

RUGMAN, ALAN M., ed. *International business in Canada: Strategies for management.* Scarborough, Ont.: Prentice-Hall Canada, 1989.

SABAGH, GEORGES, ed. *The modern economic and social history of the Middle East in its world context.* Giorgio Levi Della Vida conferences, no. 10. Cambridge; New York and Melbourne: Cambridge University Press, 1989.

SACHS, JEFFREY D., ed. *Developing country debt and economic performance.* Volume 1. *The international financial system.* National Bureau of Economic Research Project Report series. Chicago and London: University of Chicago Press, 1989. (I)

SACHS, JEFFREY D., ed. *Developing country debt and the world economy.* National Bureau of Economic Research Project Report series. Chicago and London: University of Chicago Press, 1989. (II)

SACHS, JEFFREY D. AND COLLINS, SUSAN M., eds. *Developing country debt and economic performance.* Volume 3. *Country studies—Indonesia, Korea, Philippines, Turkey.* National Bureau of Economic Research Project Report series. Chicago and London: University of Chicago Press, 1989.

SAIIN, DAVID E., ed. *Seasonal variability in third world agriculture: The consequences for food security.* Baltimore and London: Johns Hopkins University Press for the International Food Policy Research Institute, 1989.

SALAMON, LESTER M., ed. *Beyond privatization: The tools of government action.* Assisted by MICHAEL S. LUND. Washington, D.C.: Urban Institute Press; distributed in the U.S. and Canada by University Press of America, Lanham, Md., 1989.

SAMUELS, WARREN J., ed. *Fundamentals of the economic role of government.* Prepared under the auspices of the Policy Studies Organization. Contributions in Economics and Economic History, no. 98. Westport, Conn. and London: Greenwood Press, 1989. (I)

SAMUELS, WARREN J., ed. *Research in the history of economic thought and methodology.* Volume 6. A Research Annual. Greenwich, Conn. and London: JAI Press, 1989. (II)

[SANDFORD, CEDRIC] *Fiscal policy: Essays in honour of Cedric Sandford.* Edited by DAVID COLLARD. Aldershot, U.K.; Brookfield, Vt.; Hong Kong and Sydney: Gower, Avebury, 1989.

SAPSFORD, DAVID AND TZANNATOS, ZAFIRIS, eds. *Current issues in labour economics.* Current Issues in Economics, vol. 3. New York: St. Martin's Press, 1989.

SATO, RYUZO AND NEGISHI, TAKASHI, eds. *Developments in Japanese economics.* Tokyo; San Diego; London and Toronto: Harcourt Brace Jovanovich, Academic Press, 1989.

SCHAEFFER, ROBERT K., ed. *War in the world-system.* Contributions in Economics and Economic History, no. 93. Studies in the Political Economy of the World-System. Westport, Conn. and London: Greenwood Press, 1989.

SCHEFFLER, RICHARD M. AND ROSSITER, LOUIS F., eds. *Risk-based payments under public programs.* Advances in Health Economics and Health Services Research Series, vol. 10. Greenwich, Conn. and London: JAI Press, 1989.

SCHMAHL, WINFRIED, ed. *Redefining the process of retirement: An international perspective.* With contributions by L. BELLMANN ET AL. London; Paris; Tokyo and Hong Kong: Springer, 1989.

SCHMALENSEE, RICHARD AND WILLIG, ROBERT D., eds. *Handbook of industrial organization.* Volume 1. Handbooks in Economics, no. 10. Amsterdam; Oxford and Tokyo: North-Holland; distributed in the U.S. and Canada by Elsevier Science, New York, 1989.

SCHMALENSEE, RICHARD AND WILLIG, ROBERT D., eds. *Handbook of industrial organization.* Volume 2. Handbooks in Economics, no. 10. Amsterdam; Oxford and Tokyo: North-Holland; distributed in the U.S. and Canada by Elsevier Science, New York, 1989.

SICHEL, WERNER, ed. *The state of economic science: Views of six Nobel Laureates.* Kalamazoo, Mich.: W. E. Upjohn Institute for Employment Research, 1989.

SICULAR, TERRY, ed. *Food price policy in Asia: A comparative study.* Ithaca and London: Cornell University Press, 1989.

SIJBEN, JAC J., ed. *Financing the world economy in the nineties.* Financial and Monetary Policy Studies, vol. 18. Norwell, Mass. and Dordrecht: Kluwer Academic, 1989.

SIMEONE, BRUNO, ed. *Combinatorial optimization: Lectures given at the 3rd session of the Centro Internazionale Matematico Estivo (C.I.M.E.) held at Como, Italy, August 25–September 2, 1986.* Lecture Notes in Mathematics, vol. 1403. Berlin; New York; London and Tokyo: Springer, 1989.

SINGER, ELEANOR AND PRESSER, STANLEY, eds. *Survey research methods: A reader.* Chicago and London: University of Chicago Press, 1989.

SINGER, HANS W. AND SHARMA, SOUMITRA, eds. *Economic development and world debt.* New York: St. Martin's Press, 1989. (I)

SINGER, HANS W. AND SHARMA, SOUMITRA, eds. *Growth and external debt management.* New York: St. Martin's Press, 1989. (II)

SMITH, C. SELBY, ed. *Economics and health: 1989. Proceedings of the Eleventh Australian Conference of Health Economists.* Clayton, Victoria: Public Sector Management Institute, 1989.

SMITH, MICHAEL PETER, ed. *Pacific Rim cities in the world economy.* Comparative Urban and Community Research series, vol. 2. New Brunswick, N.J. and London: Transaction, 1989.

STALLINGS, BARBARA AND KAUFMAN, ROBERT, eds. *Debt and democracy in Latin America.* Boulder, Colo. and London: Westview Press, 1989.

STARR, ROSS M., ed. *General equilibrium models of monetary economies: Studies in the static foundations of monetary theory.* Economic Theory, Econometrics, and Mathematical Economics series. San Diego; London; Sydney and Toronto: Harcourt Brace Jovanovich, Academic Press, 1989.

STEEDMAN, IAN. *From exploitation to altruism.* Aspects of Political Economy series. Boulder, Colo.: Westview Press; Cambridge, U.K.: Polity Press in association with Blackwell, 1989.

STEINBRUNER, JOHN D., ed. *Restructuring American foreign policy.* Washington, D.C.: Brookings Institution, 1989.

STEPHENS, MICHAEL D., ed. *Universities, education and the national economy.* London and New York: Routledge, 1989.

STERN, ROBERT M., ed. *Trade and investment relations among the United States, Canada, and Japan.* Chicago: University of Chicago Press, 1989.

STOECKEL, ANDREW B.; VINCENT, DAVID AND CUTHBERTSON, SANDY, eds. *Macroeconomic consequences of farm support policies.* Duke Press Policy Studies. Canberra: Centre for International Economics; Durham and London: Duke University Press, 1989.

STONE, COURTENAY C., ed. *Financial risk: Theory, evidence and implications. Proceedings of the Eleventh Annual Economic Policy Conference of the Federal Reserve Bank of St. Louis.* Norwell, Mass.; Dordrecht and Lancaster, U.K.: Kluwer Academic, 1989.

[STONE, LAWRENCE] *The first modern society: Essays in English history in honour of Lawrence Stone.* Edited by A. L. BEIER, DAVID CANNADINE, AND JAMES M. ROSENHEIM. Past and Present Publications. Cambridge; New York and Melbourne: Cambridge University Press, 1989.

STROSBERG, MARTIN A.; FEIN, I. ALAN AND CARROLL, JAMES D., eds. *Rationing of medical care for the critically ill.* Brookings Dialogues on Public Policy series. Washington, D.C.: Brookings Institution, 1989.

SUMMERS, LAWRENCE H., ed. *Tax policy and the economy.* Volume 3. Cambridge, Mass. and London: MIT Press for the National Bureau of Economic Research, 1989.

SWEGLE, WAYNE E. AND LIGON, POLLY C., eds. *Aid, trade, and farm policies: A sourcebook on issues and interrelationships. Proceedings of a workshop, January 4–5, 1989, Washington, D.C.* Winrock Development Education Series. Morrilton, Ark.: Winrock International Institute for Agricultural Development; distributed by Winrock Publication Sales, Arlington, Va., 1989.

TARDITI, SECONDO, ET AL., eds. *Agricultural trade liberalization and the European Community.*

Oxford; New York; Toronto and Melbourne: Oxford University Press, Clarendon Press, 1989.

TEICHOVA, ALICE; LÉVY-LEBOYER, MAURICE AND NUSSBAUM, HELGA, eds. *Historical studies in international corporate business.* Cambridge; New York and Melbourne: Cambridge University Press; Paris: Éditions de la Maison des Sciences de l'Homme, 1989.

DI TELLA, GUIDO AND DORNBUSCH, RUDIGER, eds. *The political economy of Argentina, 1946–83.* Pitt Latin American Series. Pittsburgh: University of Pittsburgh Press, 1989.

THARAKAN, P. K. M. AND KOL, JACOB, eds. *Intra-industry trade: Theory, evidence and extensions.* New York: St. Martin's Press, 1989.

THOMAS, CAROLINE AND SARAVANAMUTTU, PAIKIASOTHY, eds. *Conflict and consensus in South/North security.* Ford/Southampton Studies in North/South Security Relations. Cambridge; New York and Melbourne: Cambridge University Press, 1989.

THYNNE, IAN AND ARIFF, MOHAMED, eds. *Privatisation: Singapore's experience in perspective.* Singapore: Longman Singapore, Professional Books, 1989.

TOOL, MARC R. AND SAMUELS, WARREN J., eds. *The economy as a system of power.* Second edition. New Brunswick, N.J. and Oxford: Transaction, [1980] 1989. (I)

TOOL, MARC R. AND SAMUELS, WARREN J., eds. *The methodology of economic thought.* Second edition. New Brunswick, N.J. and Oxford: Transaction, [1980] 1989. (II)

TOOL, MARC R. AND SAMUELS, WARREN J., eds. *State, society and corporate power.* Second edition. New Brunswick, N.J. and Oxford: Transaction Books, [1979] 1989. (III)

TSIANG, S. C. *Finance constraints and the theory of money: Selected papers.* Edited by MEIR KOHN. With contributions by JOHN HICKS, DAVID LAIDLER, AND ALAN STOCKMAN. Economic Theory, Econometrics, and Mathematical Economics series. San Diego; London; Sydney and Toronto: Harcourt Brace Jovanovich, Academic Press, 1989.

TURNER, JOHN A. AND BELLER, DANIEL J., eds. *Trends in pensions.* Washington, D.C.: U.S. Department of Labor, Pension and Welfare Benefits Administration, 1989.

TURVEY, RALPH. *Consumer price indices: An ILO manual.* With contributions by D. J. SELLWOOD ET AL. Geneva: International Labour Office, 1989.

TWEETEN, LUTHER, ed. *Agricultural policy analysis tools for economic development.* Westview Special Studies in Agricultural Science and Policy. Boulder, Colo.: Westview Press; London: Intermediate Technology Publications, 1989.

ULLAH, AMAN, ed. *Semiparametric and nonparametric econometrics.* Studies in Empirical Economics. Heidelberg: Physica; New York: Springer, 1989.

UNITED NATIONS DEPARTMENT OF TECHNICAL CO-OPERATION FOR DEVELOPMENT, DEVELOPMENT ADMINISTRATION DIVISION. *Role and extent of competition in improving the performance of public enterprises: Proceedings of a United Nations Interregional Seminar on Performance Improvement of Public Enterprises, New Delhi, India, 12–19 April 1989.* New York: United Nations, 1989.

VAN NESS, PETER, ed. *Market reforms in socialist societies: Comparing China and Hungary.* With contributions by G. BARANY ET AL. Boulder and London: Rienner, 1989.

VELJANOVSKI, CENTO, ed. *Freedom in broadcasting.* Hobart Paperback series, no. 29. London: Institute of Economic Affairs, 1989. (I)

VELJANOVSKI, CENTO, ed. *Privatisation and competition: A market prospectus.* Hobart Paperback series, no. 28. London: Institute of Economic Affairs, 1989. (II)

VENTURA-DIAS, VIVIANNE, ed. *South–South trade: Trends, issues, and obstacles to its growth.* New York and London: Greenwood Press, Praeger, 1989.

[VERHEYEN, PIET] *Dynamic policy games in economics: Essays in honour of Piet Verheyen.* Edited by FREDERICK VAN DER PLOEG AND AART DE ZEEUW. Contributions to Economic Analysis, no. 181. Amsterdam; New York; Oxford and Tokyo: North-Holland; distributed in the U.S. and Canada by Elsevier Science, New York, 1989.

VOSGERAU, HANS-JURGEN, ed. *New institutional arrangements for the world economy.* Studies in International Economics and Institutions. New York; Berlin; London and Tokyo: Springer, 1989.

WALKER, DONALD A., ed. *Perspectives on the history of economic thought.* Volume 1. *Classical and neoclassical economic thought. Selected papers from the History of Economics Society Con-*

ference, 1987. Aldershot, U.K.: Elgar for the History of Economics Society; Brookfield, Vt.: Gower, 1989.

WARD, PETER M., ed. *Corruption, development and inequality: Soft touch or hard graft?* London and New York: Routledge, 1989.

WATKINS, G. CAMPBELL, ed. *Petro markets: Probing the economics of continental energy.* Contributions by M. A. ADELMAN ET AL. Vancouver: Fraser Institute, 1989.

WEEKS, JOHN F., ed. *Debt disaster? Banks, governments, and multilaterals confront the crisis.* Geonomics Institute for International Economic Advancement Series. New York and London: New York University Press; distributed by Columbia University Press, 1989.

WEHMAN, PAUL AND KREGEL, JOHN, eds. *Supported employment for persons with disabilities: Focus on excellence.* New York: Plenum, Human Sciences Press, 1989.

WEIL, VIVIAN AND SNAPPER, JOHN W., eds. *Owning scientific and technical information: Value and ethical issues.* New Brunswick and London: Rutgers University Press, 1989.

[WEINTRAUB, SIDNEY] *Inflation and income distribution in capitalist crisis: Essays in memory of Sidney Weintraub.* Edited by J. A. KREGEL. New York: New York University Press; distributed by Columbia University Press, 1989.

WEISS, LEONARD W., ed. *Concentration and price.* Cambridge, Mass. and London: MIT Press, 1989.

WHALLEY, JOHN, ed. *Developing countries and the global trading system.* Volume 1. *Thematic studies from a Ford Foundation project.* Studies in International Trade Policy. Ann Arbor: University of Michigan Press, 1989.

WHALLEY, JOHN, ed. *Developing countries and the global trading system.* Volume 2. *Country studies from a Ford Foundation project.* Studies in International Trade Policy. Ann Arbor: University of Michigan Press, 1989.

WHITE, LAWRENCE H. *Competition and currency: Essays on free banking and money.* A Cato Institute Book. New York and London: New York University Press, 1989.

WHITESIDE, ALAN W., ed. *Industrialization and investment incentives in southern Africa.* Pietermaritzburg, South Africa: University of Natal Press; London: Currey; distributed in the U.S. and Canada by Heinemann Educational Books, Portsmouth, N.H., 1989.

[WILLEMS, JAN C.] *Three decades of mathematical system theory: A collection of surveys at the occasion of the 50th birthday of Jan C. Willems.* Edited by H. NIJMEIJER AND J. M. SCHUMACHER. Lecture Notes in Control and Information Sciences, vol. 135. New York; Berlin; London and Tokyo: Springer, 1989.

WILLEMS, JAN C., ed. *From data to model.* New York; Berlin; London and Tokyo: Springer, 1989.

WILLIAMS, OLIVER F.; REILLY, FRANK K. AND HOUCK, JOHN W., eds. *Ethics and the investment industry.* Savage, Md.: Rowman and Littlefield, 1989.

WILLIAMSON, JEFFREY G. AND PANCHAMUKHI, VADIRAJ R., eds. *The balance between industry and agriculture in economic development: Proceedings of the Eighth World Congress of the International Economic Association, Delhi, India.* Volume 2. *Sector proportions.* New York: St. Martin's Press in association with the International Economic Association, 1989.

WISE, DAVID A., ed. *The economics of aging.* National Bureau of Economic Research Project Report series. Chicago and London: University of Chicago Press, 1989.

WISEMAN, JACK. *Cost, choice and political economy.* Aldershot, U.K.: Elgar; Brookfield, Vt.: Gower, 1989.

VON WITZKE, HARALD; RUNGE, C. FORD AND JOB, BRIAN, eds. *Policy coordination in world agriculture.* Kiel: Wissenschaftsverlag Vauk, 1989.

WOHLMUTH, KARL, ed. *Structural adjustment in the world economy and East–West–South economic cooperation.* Bremen: University of Bremen, Institute for World Economics and International Management, 1989.

WOOD, JOHN CUNNINGHAM AND WOODS, RONALD N., eds. *Sir John R. Hicks: Critical assessments.* Volume 1. Critical Assessments of Contemporary Economists series. London and New York: Routledge, 1989.

WOOD, JOHN CUNNINGHAM AND WOODS, RONALD N., eds. *Sir John R. Hicks: Critical assessments.*
Volume 2. Critical Assessments of Contemporary Economists series. London and New York:
Routledge, 1989.

WOOD, JOHN CUNNINGHAM AND WOODS, RONALD N., eds. *Sir John R. Hicks: Critical assessments.*
Volume 3. Critical Assessments of Contemporary Economists series. London and New York:
Routledge, 1989.

WOOD, JOHN CUNNINGHAM AND WOODS, RONALD N., eds. *Sir John R. Hicks: Critical assessments.*
Volume 4. Critical Assessments of Contemporary Economists series. London and New York:
Routledge, 1989.

WORLD BANK AND ISTITUTO ITALO-AFRICANO. *Strengthening local governments in sub-Saharan
Africa: Proceedings of two workshops held in Poretta Terme, Italy, March 5–17, 1989.* EDI
Policy Seminar Report, no. 21. Washington, D.C.: World Bank, 1989.

WORLD HEALTH ORGANIZATION, PAN AMERICAN HEALTH ORGANIZATION. *Health economics: Latin
American perspectives.* Scientific Publication, no. 517. New York: Author, 1989.

WORRELL, DELISLE AND BOURNE, COMPTON, eds. *Economic adjustment policies for small nations:
Theory and experience in the English-speaking Caribbean.* New York and London: Greenwood
Press, Praeger, 1989.

YANNOPOULOS, GEORGE N., ed. *European integration and the Iberian economies.* New York: St.
Martin's Press, 1989.

YANOWITCH, MURRAY, ed. *New directions in Soviet social thought: An anthology.* Armonk, N.Y.
and London: Sharpe, 1989.

ZASLAVSKAIA, TAT'IANA I. *A voice of reform: Essays.* Edited with an introduction by MURRAY YANO-
WITCH. Armonk, N.Y. and London: Sharpe, 1989.

ZERBE, RICHARD O., ed. *Research in law and economics.* Volume 12. Greenwich, Conn. and
London: JAI Press, 1989.

ZERBY, JOHN, ed. *Contemporary economic issues in China.* Research Report series. Kensington,
Australia: University of New South Wales, Centre for Applied Economic Research, East Asian
Trade and Development Programme, 1989.

Author Index of Articles
in Current Periodicals and Collective Volumes

Abbreviated titles for journals are the same as those used in the *Journal of Economic Literature*. Full titles of journals may be found on pages x–xvi.

Books have been identified by author or editor (noted *ed.*). In rare cases where two books by the same author appear, volumes are distinguished by I or II after the name. In some cases there appear two books by the same person, once as author, once as editor. These are distinguished by *ed.* noted for the edited volume. Full titles and bibliographic references for books may be found on pages xvii–xl.

Aaron, Henry J. Politics and the Professors Revisited. *Amer. Econ. Rev.*, May 1989, 79(2), pp. 1–15.

———. Rationing of Medical Care for the Critically Ill: Lessons from the United Kingdom. In *Strosberg, M. A.; Fein, I. A. and Carroll, J. D., eds.*, 1989, pp. 24–31.

———. Tax Increases: Choosing among Four Broad Options. In *Bosworth, B. P., et al.*, 1989, pp. 143–46.

———; **Bosworth, Barry P. and Burtless, Gary.** How Social Security Affects the Deficit. In *Bosworth, B. P., et al.*, 1989, pp. 139–43.

——— **and Burtless, Gary.** Fiscal Policy and the Dynamic Inconsistency of Social Security Forecasts. *Amer. Econ. Rev.*, May 1989, 79(2), pp. 91–96.

Abadía, Antonio. Evolución del tipo efectivo en los impuestos directos. (With English summary.) *Invest. Econ.*, January 1989, 13(1), pp. 45–65.

Abalkin, Leonid. A New Conception of Centralism. In *Jones, A. and Moskoff, W., eds.*, 1989, 1987, pp. 91–98.

———. The Renewal of Socialist Property. *Prob. Econ.*, August 1989, 32(4), pp. 6–16.

———. Restructuring the Economy: The Soviet Point of View. *Prob. Econ.*, December 1989, 32(8), pp. 7–18.

———. Restructuring the Management of the Economy: A Continuation of the Work of the October Revolution. In *Jones, A. and Moskoff, W., eds.*, 1989, pp. 3–20.

Abbasi, Sami M.; Hollman, Kenneth W. and Murrey, Joe H., Jr. Islamic Economics: Foundations and Practices. *Int. J. Soc. Econ.*, 1989, 16(5), pp. 5–17.

Abbott, George C. Britain's Debt Relief Programme. In *Singer, H. W. and Sharma, S., eds. (I)*, 1989, pp. 309–19.

Abbott, Michael G. Labour Market Adjustment: Immigration and Labour Market Adjustment. In *Beach, C. M. and Green, A. G.*, 1989, pp. 27–39.

Abdel-Rahman, A. M. M. A Nonlinear Model of the Sudanese Economy. *Middle East Bus. Econ. Rev.*, July 1989, 1(2), pp. 19–26.

Abdel-Rahman, Ibrahim Helmy and Abu Ali, Mohammed Sultan. Role of the Public and Private Sectors with Special Reference to Privatization: The Case of Egypt. In *El-Naggar, S., ed.*, 1989, pp. 141–81.

Abdou, J. Convexity of Integer Veto and Elimination Procedures. *Soc. Choice Welfare*, January 1989, 6(1), pp. 63–70.

——— **and Mertens, Jean-François.** Correlated Effectivity Functions. *Econ. Letters*, August 1989, 30(2), pp. 97–101.

Abdul Ghani, Othman. Impacts of Global Adjustment on the Asian-Pacific Economy: Comment. In *Shinohara, M. and Lo, F., eds.*, 1989, pp. 277–78.

Abdul Rasool, Faik Ali. The Fiscal Impact of Privatization, with Some Examples from Arab Countries: Comment. In *El-Naggar, S., ed.*, 1989, pp. 113–19.

Abdullah, Dewan A. and Rangazas, Peter. Inflation, Tax Rates, and Investment with Endogenous Financial Behavior. *Southern Econ. J.*, April 1989, 55(4), pp. 870–79.

——— **and Tank, Frederick E.** The Determinants of Fixed Investment over the Business Cycle: Some Time Series Evidence. *J. Macroecon.*, Winter 1989, 11(1), pp. 49–65.

Abdullah, Mohammed. The Effect of Seasonality on Intrahousehold Food Distribution and Nutrition in Bangladesh. In *Sahn, D. E., ed.*, 1989, pp. 57–65.

Abe, Fumio and Katayama, Seiichi. Optimal Investment Policy of the Regulated Firm. *J. Econ. Dynam. Control*, October 1989, 13(4), pp. 533–52.

Abe, Kenzo and Okamura, Makoto. The Welfare Effects of International Tax Harmonization. *Econ. Stud. Quart.*, September 1989, 40(3), pp. 203–11.

Abe, Kiyoshi. A Comparative Study of the Economic Development and Debt Problem of Asian and Latin American NICs. In *Singer, H. W. and Sharma, S., eds. (I)*, 1989, pp. 413–21.

Abed, F. H. and Chowdhury, A. M. R. The Role of NGOs in International Health Development. In *Reich, M. R. and Marui, E., eds.*, 1989, pp. 76–88.

Abeele, P. Vanden; Butaye, I. and Srinivasan, V. The Factor Structure of Multidimensional Response to Marketing Stimuli: A Comparison of Two Approaches. *Marketing Sci.*, Winter 1989, 8(1), pp. 78–88.

Abel, Andrew B. Birth, Death and Taxes. *J. Public Econ.*, June 1989, 39(1), pp. 1–15.

———, **et al.** Assessing Dynamic Efficiency: Theory and Evidence. *Rev. Econ. Stud.*, January 1989, *56*(1), pp. 1–19.

Abell, John D. The Impact of Demand Management Policies on Black vs. White Employment. *Rev. Black Polit. Econ.*, Fall 1989, *18*(2), pp. 43–60.

———— **and Krueger, Thomas M.** Macroeconomic Influences on Beta. *J. Econ. Bus.*, May 1989, *41*(2), pp. 185–93.

Abella, Irving. Panel Discussion on Canadian Immigration Objectives: Levels, Composition, and Directions. In *Beach, C. M. and Green, A. G.*, 1989, pp. 80–83.

Abken, Peter A. An Analysis of Intra-market Spreads in Heating Oil Futures. *J. Futures Markets*, February 1989, *9*(1), pp. 77–86.

————. Interest-Rate Caps, Collars, and Floors. *Fed. Res. Bank Atlanta Econ. Rev.*, Nov.–Dec. 1989, *74*(6), pp. 2–24.

Abler, David G. Vote Trading on Farm Legislation in the U.S. House. *Amer. J. Agr. Econ.*, August 1989, *71*(3), pp. 583–91.

Ablin, Richard. The Shrinking Realm of Laissez-Faire. *Challenge*, March–April 1989, *32*(2), pp. 23–25.

Abosedra, Salah and Baghestani, Hamid. New Evidence on the Causal Relationship between United States Energy Consumption and Gross National Product. *J. Energy Devel.*, Spring 1989, *14*(2), pp. 285–92.

Abou-Ezze, P.; Butterfield, David W. and Kubursi, Atif A. The Economic Case for the Emergence of New Producers of Petrochemicals in the Hydrocarbon-Rich Developing Countries. *Industry Devel.*, June 1989, (27), pp. 31–43.

Abouchar, Alan. Through the (Economics) Glass Darkly. *Challenge*, May–June 1989, *32*(3), pp. 41–47.

Abowd, John M. The Effect of Wage Bargains on the Stock Market Value of the Firm. *Amer. Econ. Rev.*, September 1989, *79*(4), pp. 774–800.

———— **and Card, David.** On the Covariance Structure of Earnings and Hours Changes. *Econometrica*, March 1989, *57*(2), pp. 411–45.

———— **and Tracy, Joseph S.** Market Structure, Strike Activity, and Union Wage Settlements. *Ind. Relat.*, Spring 1989, *28*(2), pp. 227–50.

Abraham-Frois, Gilbert. Krach boursier, crise financière et crise économique. (Stock Exchange Crash, Financial Crisis and Economic Crisis. With English summary.) *Écon. Societes*, March 1989, *23*(3), pp. 129–42.

———— **and Berrebi, Edmond.** Á la recherche de l'étalon invariable des valeurs. (With English summary.) *Revue Écon. Politique*, Jan.–Feb. 1989, *99*(1), pp. 123–40.

Abraham, Haim and Whittaker, John. Is Dynamic Stability of Walrasian Equilibrium Achieved through Falling Target Utilities? *Int. Econ. Rev.*, August 1989, *30*(3), pp. 507–11.

Abraham, Katharine G. and Houseman, Susan N. Job Security and Work Force Adjustment: How Different Are U.S. and Japanese Practices? *J. Japanese Int. Economies*, December 1989, *3*(4), pp. 500–521.

Abraham, Kenneth S. and Jeffries, John C., Jr. Punitive Damages and the Rule of Law: The Role of Defendant's Wealth. *J. Legal Stud.*, June 1989, *18*(2), pp. 415–25.

Abrahamowicz, M. and Ramsay, J. O. Binomial Regression with Monotone Splines: A Psychometric Application. *J. Amer. Statist. Assoc.*, December 1989, *84*(408), pp. 906–15.

Abrahamsen, Yngve and Schips, Bernd. Specification and Stability Tests versus Jackknifing: Some Illustrative Examples. In *Hackl, P., ed.*, 1989, pp. 37–43.

Abrahamsson, Hans. Transport Structures and Dependency Relations in Southern Africa: The Need for a Reorientation of Nordic Aid. In *Odén, B. and Othman, H., eds.*, 1989, pp. 103–26.

Abramovitz, Moses. Catching Up, Forging Ahead, and Falling Behind. In *Abramovitz, M.*, 1989, *1988*, pp. 220–42.

————. Economic Goals and Social Welfare in the Next Generation. In *Abramovitz, M.*, 1989, *1958*, pp. 301–07.

————. Economic Growth in the United States: A Review Article. In *Abramovitz, M.*, 1989, pp. 148–72.

————. Economics of Growth. In *Abramovitz, M.*, 1989, *1952*, pp. 80–124.

————. Growing Up in an Affluent Society. In *Abramovitz, M.*, 1989, *1960*, pp. 308–21.

————. Manpower, Capital, and Technology. In *Abramovitz, M.*, 1989, *1972*, pp. 173–86.

————. The Nature and Significance of Kuznets Cycles. In *Abramovitz, M.*, 1989, *1961*, pp. 245–75.

————. The Passing of the Kuznets Cycle. In *Abramovitz, M.*, 1989, *1968*, pp. 276–97.

————. Rapid Growth Potential and Its Realization: The Experience of Capitalist Economies in the Postwar Period. In *Abramovitz, M.*, 1989, *1979*, pp. 187–219.

————. Resource and Output Trends in the United States since 1870. In *Abramovitz, M.*, 1989, *1956*, pp. 127–47.

————. The Retreat from Economic Advance: Changing Ideas about Economic Progress. In *Abramovitz, M.*, 1989, *1982*, pp. 322–51.

————. Thinking about Growth. In *Abramovitz, M.*, 1989, pp. 3–79.

————. Thinking about Growth: And Other Essays on Economic Growth and Welfare: Preface. In *Abramovitz, M.*, 1989, pp. xi–xviii.

————. Welfare Quandaries and Productivity Concerns. In *Abramovitz, M.*, 1989, *1981*, pp. 352–77.

Abrar, Mohammed B. The Interest Elasticity of Saving and the Functional Form of the Utility Function. *Southern Econ. J.*, January 1989, *55*(3), pp. 594–600.

Abreu, Marcelo de Paiva. Developing Countries and the Uruguay Round of Trade Negotiations. In *Fischer, S. and de Tray, D., eds.*, 1989, pp. 21–46.

———— **and Fritsch, Winston.** Market Access for

Manufactured Exports from Developing Countries: Trends and Prospects. In *Whalley, J., ed., Vol. 1,* 1989, pp. 112–31.

_____ and Fritsch, Winston. Obstacles to Brazilian Export Growth and the Present Multilateral Trade Negotiations. In *Whalley, J., ed., Vol. 2,* 1989, pp. 179–201.

Abromeit, Heidrun. Privatisation: Singapore's Experience in Perspective: An International Perspective I: British Privatisation Policy. In *Thynne, I. and Ariff, M., eds.,* 1989, *1988,* pp. 143–65.

Abu Ali, Mohammed Sultan and Abdel-Rahman, Ibrahim Helmy. Role of the Public and Private Sectors with Special Reference to Privatization: The Case of Egypt. In *El-Naggar, S., ed.,* 1989, pp. 141–81.

Accornero, Aris. Recent Trends and Features in Youth Unemployment. *Labour,* Spring 1989, *3*(1), pp. 127–47.

Acemoglu, Daron and Lambert, Peter J. Equiproportionate Growth of Incomes and Fiscal Drag. *Bull. Econ. Res.,* October 1989, *41*(4), pp. 295–302.

Acevedo F. de P., Rommel. Adjustment Policies in Latin America and the Role of the Public and Private International Financial System. In *Mrak, M., ed.,* 1989, pp. 203–17.

Achary, K. K. A Direct Simplex Type Method for Determining All Efficient Solution Pairs of Time–Cost Transportation Problem. *Econ. Computat. Econ. Cybern. Stud. Res.,* 1989, *24*(2–3), pp. 139–50.

Acharya, H. S.; Rao, N. Ganga Prasada and Rao, G. R. K. Yield Stability of Sorghum and Millet across Climates. In *Oram, P. A., et al.,* 1989, pp. 165–86.

Acharya, Sankarshan and Dreyfus, Jean-Francois. Optimal Bank Reorganization Policies and the Pricing of Federal Deposit Insurance. *J. Finance,* December 1989, *44*(5), pp. 1313–33.

Acheson, Keith. Power Steering the Canadian Automotive Industry: The 1965 Canada–U.S.A. Auto Pact and Political Exchange. *J. Econ. Behav. Organ.,* March 1989, *11*(2), pp. 237–51.

_____ and Maule, Christopher. Trade Policy Responses to New Technology in the Film and Television Industry. *J. World Trade,* April 1989, *23*(2), pp. 35–48.

Acker, Duane. Food Aid Programs, Food Consumption, and Incentives for the Agriculture of Less Developed Countries and the United States. In *Helmuth, J. W. and Johnson, S. R., eds., Vol. 1,* 1989, pp. 161–66.

Acs, Zoltan J. and Audretsch, David B. Births and Firm Size. *Southern Econ. J.,* October 1989, *56*(2), pp. 467–75.

_____ and Audretsch, David B. Patents as a Measure of Innovative Activity. *Kyklos,* 1989, *42*(2), pp. 171–80.

_____ and Audretsch, David B. Patents Innovative Activity. *Eastern Econ. J.,* Oct.–Dec. 1989, *15*(4), pp. 373–76.

_____ and Audretsch, David B. Small-Firm Entry in U.S. Manufacturing. *Economica,* May 1989, *56*(222), pp. 255–65.

_____ and Audretsch, David B. Small Firms in U.S. Manufacturing: A First Report. *Econ. Letters,* December 1989, *31*(4), pp. 399–402.

_____ and Fitzroy, Felix R. Inside the Firm and Organizational Capital: Review Article. *Int. J. Ind. Organ.,* June 1989, *7*(2), pp. 309–14.

Acton, Jan Paul and Vogelsang, Ingo. Price-Cap Regulation: Introduction. *Rand J. Econ.,* Autumn 1989, *20*(3), pp. 369–72.

Aczél, János and Gehrig, W. Determination of All Generalized Hicks-Neutral Production Functions. *Math. Soc. Sci.,* February 1989, *17*(1), pp. 33–45.

_____ and Roberts, Fred S. On the Possible Merging Functions. *Math. Soc. Sci.,* June 1989, *17*(3), pp. 205–43.

Adam, Dietrich. Probleme der belastungsorientierten Auftragsfreigabe. (With English summary.) *Z. Betriebswirtshaft,* April 1989, *59*(4), pp. 443–47.

Adam, Jan. Work-Teams: A New Phenomenon in Income Distribution in Hungary. *Comp. Econ. Stud.,* Spring 1989, *31*(1), pp. 46–66.

Adamec, Ladislav. Report on the Development of the National Economy and the Present Tasks. *Czech. Econ. Digest.,* September 1989, (6), pp. 3–51.

Adamowicz, Wiktor L.; Fletcher, Jerald J. and Graham-Tomasi, Theodore. Functional Form and the Statistical Properties of Welfare Measures. *Amer. J. Agr. Econ.,* May 1989, *71*(2), pp. 414–21.

_____; Graham-Tomasi, Theodore and Fletcher, Jerald J. Inequality Constrained Estimation of Consumer Surplus. *Can. J. Agr. Econ.,* November 1989, *37*(3), pp. 407–20.

Adams, Brock. Deregulation's Negative Effect on Safety. In *Moses, L. N. and Savage, I., eds.,* 1989, pp. 21–27.

Adams, F. Gerard. The Macroeconomic Impacts of Increasing the Minimum Wage. *J. Policy Modeling,* Summer 1989, *11*(2), pp. 179–89.

_____; Faulhaber, Gerald R. and Siwaraksa, Subhak. Measuring Services Output—The Wharton Index of Services Production. *J. Econ. Soc. Meas.,* 1989, *15*(2), pp. 155–66.

_____ and Kroch, Eugene. The Computer in the Teaching of Macroeconomics. *J. Econ. Educ.,* Summer 1989, *20*(3), pp. 269–80.

Adams, James D. and Kenny, Lawrence W. The Retention of State Governors. *Public Choice,* July 1989, *62*(1), pp. 1–13.

Adams, John. The Emptiness of Peasant "Rationality": "Demirationality" as an Alternative. In *Tool, M. R. and Samuels, W. J., eds. (II),* 1989, *1982,* pp. 429–38.

Adams, Michael. New Activities and the Efficient Liability Rules. In *Faure, M. and Van den Bergh, R., eds.,* 1989, pp. 103–06.

Adams, Paul D. and Wyatt, Steve B. On the Pricing of European and American Foreign Currency Options: A Clarification. *J. Int. Money Finance,* June 1989, *8*(2), pp. 305–11.

Adams, Philip D. The Extended Linear Expenditure System with Financial Assets. *Econ. Letters,* December 1989, *31*(2), pp. 179–82.

_____. Recent Developments in the Australian Economy: An Update to 1988–89. *Australian Econ. Rev.*, Spring 1989, (87), pp. 39–44.

_____ and Dixon, Peter B. Forecasts for the Australian Economy in 1989–90 and 1990–91. *Australian Econ. Rev.*, Summer 1989, (88), pp. 5–31.

_____ and Parmenter, B. R. Economic Prospects: 1988–89 to 1994–95. *Australian Econ. Rev.*, Spring 1989, (87), pp. 5–15.

Adams, Richard H., Jr. Worker Remittances and Inequality in Rural Egypt. *Econ. Devel. Cult. Change*, October 1989, 38(1), pp. 45–71.

Adams, Richard M.; Connor, Jeffery D. and Glyer, J. David. Some Further Evidence on the Derived Demand for Irrigation Electricity: A Dual Cost Function Approach. *Water Resources Res.*, July 1989, 25(7), pp. 1461–68.

_____ and Johnson, Neal S. On the Marginal Value of a Fish: Some Evidence from a Steelhead Fishery. *Marine Resource Econ.*, 1989, 6(1), pp. 43–55.

_____, et al. User Fees and Equity Issues in Public Hunting Expenditures: The Case of Ring-Necked Pheasants in Oregon. *Land Econ.*, November 1989, 65(4), pp. 376–85.

Adams, Roy J. North American Industrial Relations: Divergent Trends in Canada and the United States. *Int. Lab. Rev.*, 1989, 128(1), pp. 47–64.

Adams, Walter and Brock, James W. Corporate Power and Economic Sabotage. In *Tool, M. R. and Samuels, W. J., eds. (I)*, 1989, 1986, pp. 383–404.

_____ and Brock, James W. Corporate Size and the Bailout Factor. In *Tool, M. R. and Samuels, W. J., eds. (I)*, 1989, 1987, pp. 405–29.

_____ and Brock, James W. The Evidence and Public Policy. In *McKee, D. L., ed.*, 1989, pp. 143–52.

_____ and Brock, James W. Government and Competitive Free Enterprise. In *Samuels, W. J., ed. (I)*, 1989, pp. 1–7.

_____ and Brock, James W. Merger-Mania: An Empirical Critique. In *McKee, D. L., ed.*, 1989, pp. 33–43.

Adams, William James. Exposure of French Manufacturing to International Competition: 1959–1980. In *Audretsch, D. B.; Sleuwaegen, L. and Yamawaki, H., eds.*, 1989, pp. 85–134.

Adanir, Fikret. Tradition and Rural Change in Southeastern Europe during Ottoman Rule. In *Chirot, D., ed.*, 1989, pp. 131–76.

Adda, William. Privatisation in Ghana. In *Ramanadham, V. V., ed.*, 1989, pp. 303–21.

Addison, John T. The Absence of Job Protection Legislation: A Source of Competitive Advantage for the United States? In *Libecap, G. D., ed.*, 1989, pp. 157–217.

_____. The Controversy over Advance Notice Legislation in the United States. *Brit. J. Ind. Relat.*, July 1989, 27(2), pp. 235–63.

_____. Job Rights and Economic Dislocation. In *Drago, R. and Perlman, R., eds.*, 1989, pp. 130–54.

_____; Burton, John and Torrance, Thomas S. Causation, Social Science and Sir John Hicks. In *Wood, J. C. and Woods, R. N., eds., Vol. 4*, 1989, 1984, pp. 27–37.

_____; Genosko, Joachim and Schnabel, Claus. Gewerkschaften, Produktivität und Rent Seeking. (Union, Productivity, and Rent Seeking. With English summary.) *Jahr. Nationalökon. Statist.*, March 1989, 206(2), pp. 102–16.

_____ and Hirsch, Barry T. Union Effects on Productivity, Profits, and Growth: Has the Long Run Arrived? *J. Lab. Econ.*, January 1989, 7(1), pp. 72–105.

_____ and Portugal, Pedro. The Endogeneity of Union Status and the Application of the Hausman Test. *J. Lab. Res.*, Fall 1989, 10(4), pp. 437–41.

_____ and Portugal, Pedro. Job Displacement, Relative Wage Changes, and Duration of Unemployment. *J. Lab. Econ.*, July 1989, 7(3), pp. 281–302.

_____ and Portugal, Pedro. On the Costs of Worker Displacement: The Case of Dissipated Firm-Specific Training Investments. *Southern Econ. J.*, July 1989, 56(1), pp. 166–82.

Addison, Tony and Demery, Lionel. The Impact of Liberalisation on Growth and Equity. In *Renshaw, G. T., ed.*, 1989, pp. 1–37.

Adegbulugbe, Anthony O.; Dayo, Felix and Gurtler, Thomas. Optimal Structure of the Nigerian Energy Supply Mix. *Energy J.*, April 1989, 10(2), pp. 165–76.

Adelman, Irma; Bourniaux, Jean-Marc and Waelbroeck, Jean. Agricultural Development-Led Industrialisation in a Global Perspective. In *Williamson, J. G. and Panchamukhi, V. R., eds.*, 1989, pp. 320–39.

_____ and Lane, Sylvia. The Balance between Industry and Agriculture in Economic Development: Introduction. In *Adelman, I. and Lane, S., eds.*, 989, pp. xviii–xxi.

_____ and Morris, Cynthia Taft. Nineteenth-century Development Experience and Lessons for Today. *World Devel.*, Special Issue, September 1989, 17(9), pp. 1417–32.

_____; Robinson, Sherman and Kilkenny, Maureen. The Effect of Agricultural Trade Liberalization on the U.S. Economy: Projections to 1991. In *Stoeckel, A. B.; Vincent, D. and Cuthbertson, S., eds.*, 1989, pp. 222–59.

_____ and Sunding, David. Joan Robinson as a Development Economist. In *Feiwel, G. R., ed. (II)*, 1989, pp. 702–22.

_____, et al. Optimal Adjustment to Trade Shocks under Alternative Development Strategies. *J. Policy Modeling*, Winter 1989, 11(4), pp. 451–505.

Adelman, M. A. The Evolution of World Oil Markets. In *Watkins, G. C., ed.*, 1989, pp. 1–16.

_____. Mideast Governments and the Oil Price Prospect. *Energy J.*, April 1989, 10(2), pp. 15–24.

_____ and Shahi, Manoj. Oil Development–Operating Cost Estimates, 1955–85. *Energy Econ.*, January 1989, 11(1), pp. 2–10.

Adelstein, Richard P. "Islands of Conscious Power": Louis D. Brandeis and the Modern

Corporation. *Bus. Hist. Rev.*, Autumn 1989, *63*(3), pp. 614–56.

Adeoye, S. O. and Edozien, John. Privatisation in Nigeria. In *Ramanadham, V. V., ed.*, 1989, pp. 283–302.

Adinugroho, Bambang; Tabor, Steven R. and Altemeier, Klaus. Foodcrop Demand in Indonesia: A Systems Approach. *Bull. Indonesian Econ. Stud.*, August 1989, *25*(2), pp. 31–51.

Adkins, Lee C. and Hill, R. Carter. Risk Characteristics of a Stein-Like Estimator for the Probit Regression Model. *Econ. Letters*, 1989, *30*(1), pp. 19–26.

Adler, Paul S. Technology Strategy: A Guide to the Literatures. In *Rosenbloom, R. S. and Burgelman, R. A., eds.*, 1989, pp. 25–151.

Admati, Anat R. and Pfleiderer, Paul. Divide and Conquer: A Theory of Intraday and Day-of-the-Week Mean Effects. *Rev. Financial Stud.*, 1989, *2*(2), pp. 189–223.

Adnan, M. Anuar and Saleh, M. Zainuddin. Resource Endowment and Allocation in Islamic Countries for Economic Co-operation: Appendix. In *Choudhury, M. A.*, 1989, pp. 155–58.

Adrangi, Bahram; Doroodian, Khosrow and Raffiee, Kambiz. Exchange Rates, Import Costs, and Domestic Wage and Price Levels. *Atlantic Econ. J.*, March 1989, *17*(1), pp. 91.

Adrian, John L., Jr.; Zwingli, Michael E. and Hardy, William E., Jr. Reduced Risk Rotations for Fresh Vegetable Crops: An Analysis for the Sand Mountain and Tennessee Valley Regions of Alabama. *Southern J. Agr. Econ.*, December 1989, *21*(2), pp. 155–65.

Adrian, Manuella and Ferguson, Brian S. The Effects of Community-Based Facilities on the Use of Hospital Beds in the Treatment of Alcohol-Related Problems in Ontario 1971–1985. In *Smith, C. S., ed.*, 1989, pp. 242–61.

Afanas'ev, M. On the Analysis of Bureaucracy under Real Socialism. *Prob. Econ.*, September 1989, *32*(5), pp. 69–79.

Affleck-Graves, John and McDonald, Bill. Nonnormalities and Tests of Asset Pricing Theories. *J. Finance*, September 1989, *44*(4), pp. 889–908.

_____ **and Miller, Robert E.** Regulatory and Procedural Effects on the Underpricing of Initial Public Offerings. *J. Finan. Res.*, Fall 1989, *12*(3), pp. 193–202.

Afriat, Sidney N. Von Neumann's Economic Model. In *Dore, M.; Chakravarty, S. and Goodwin, R., eds.*, 1989, pp. 193–220.

Aftab, Khalid and Rahim, Eric. 'Barriers' to the Growth of Informal Sector Firms: A Case Study. *J. Devel. Stud.*, July 1989, *25*(4), pp. 490–507.

Afxentiou, Panayiotis C. Basic Needs: Some Critical Issues. *Econ. Int.*, Feb.–March 1989, *42*(1–2), pp. 1–21.

_____ **and Serletis, Apostolos.** Long Term Trends in Canadian Economic Development. *Econ. Notes*, 1989, (3), pp. 362–75.

Aganbegyan, A. G. What *Perestroika* Means for Soviet Enterprises. *Int. Lab. Rev.*, 1989, *128*(1), pp. 85–101.

Agarwal, Manmohan. The Role of the External Sector in India's Development Strategy: Implications for MTN. In *Whalley, J., ed., Vol. 2*, 1989, pp. 101–20.

_____. South–South Trade: Building Block or Bargaining Chip? In *Whalley, J., ed., Vol. 1*, 1989, pp. 189–209.

Agarwala, N. The Unequal Exchange Thesis—A Critical Evaluation. *Indian Econ. Rev.*, Jan.–June 1989, *24*(1), pp. 67–81.

Agarwala, Ramgopal; Please, Stanley and Landell-Mills, Pierre. From Crisis to Sustainable Growth in Sub-Saharan Africa. *Finance Devel.*, December 1989, *26*(4), pp. 26–29.

Agassi, Judith Buber. The Design of Working Time and the Status of Women. In *Agassi, J. B. and Heycock, S., eds.*, 1989, pp. 249–55.

_____. The Redesign of Working Time: Promise or Threat? Introduction. In *Agassi, J. B. and Heycock, S., eds.*, 1989, pp. 11–21.

Agatsuma, Nobuhiko; Nakamura, Akihiro and Nakamura, Yoichi. Structure of the Japanese Economy in the Year 2000. *Econ. Systems Res.*, 1989, *1*(1), pp. 69–85.

Agbeyegbe, Terence D. Interest Rates and Metal Price Movements: Further Evidence. *J. Environ. Econ. Manage.*, March 1989, *16*(2), pp. 184–92.

_____. On the Demand for Money in Nigeria. *Atlantic Econ. J.*, March 1989, *17*(1), pp. 88.

Agell, Jonas. Inflation, Taxes, and Asset Prices: A Note on Wealth Effects and Asset Complementarity. *J. Public Econ.*, October 1989, *40*(1), pp. 151–57.

_____ **and Edin, Per-Anders.** Tax Reform and Individual Investor Response: Evidence from Swedish Tax Return Data. *Public Finance*, 1989, *44*(2), pp. 183–203.

Aggarwal, Raj and Durnford, Jon. Market Assessment of International Banking Activity: A Study of U.S. Bank Holding Companies. *Quart. Rev. Econ. Bus.*, Spring 1989, *29*(1), pp. 58–67.

_____; **Rao, Ramesh P. and Hiraki, Takato.** Skewness and Kurtosis in Japanese Equity Returns: Empirical Evidence. *J. Finan. Res.*, Fall 1989, *12*(3), pp. 253–60.

_____ **and Soenen, Luc A.** The ECU Currency Cocktail: Its Performance as a Risk-Reducing Investment. *Rivista Int. Sci. Econ. Com.*, Oct.–Nov. 1989, *36*(10–11), pp. 1019–32.

Aggarwal, Reena and Rivoli, Pietra. Seasonal and Day-of-the-Week Effects in Four Emerging Stock Markets. *Financial Rev.*, November 1989, *24*(4), pp. 541–50.

Aggarwal, Vinod K. Interpreting the History of Mexico's External Debt Crises. In *Eichengreen, B. and Lindert, P. H., eds.*, 1989, pp. 140–88.

Aghion, Philippe and Bolton, Patrick. The Financial Structure of the Firm and the Problem of Control. *Europ. Econ. Rev.*, March 1989, *33*(2/3), pp. 286–93.

Agnelli, Giovanni. The Europe of 1992. *Foreign Aff.*, Fall 1989, *68*(4), pp. 61–70.

_____. Europe 1992: An Industrialist's Point of

View. In *Frankel, A. V. and Heck, C. B., eds.*, 1989, pp. 52–54.

Agosin, Manuel R. Maquiladoras: Mexico's Tiger by the Tail? A Comment. *Challenge*, Nov.–Dec. 1989, 32(6), pp. 60–61.

Agrawal, Nisha. The Macroeconomic Effects of Alternative Employment-Generating Policies. *Australian Bull. Lab.*, December 1989, 15(5), pp. 353–69.

Aguilar, Renato and Zejan, Mario C. Debt Repayment Capacity in Argentina and Uruguay. In *Singer, H. W. and Sharma, S., eds. (I)*, 1989, pp. 383–95.

Aguirre, B. E.; Saenz, Rogelio and Hwang, Sean-Shong. Discrimination and the Assimilation and Ethnic Competition Perspectives. *Soc. Sci. Quart.*, September 1989, 70(3), pp. 594–606.

Aguirre-Baca, Francisco. Latin America. In *Cerami, C. A., ed.*, 1989, pp. 113–27.

Aharoni, A. and Ronen, Joshua. The Choice among Accounting Alternatives and Management Compensation: Effects of Corporate Tax. *Accounting Rev.*, January 1989, 64(1), pp. 69–86.

Ahene, Rexford A. Nobel Laureates in Economic Sciences: A Biographical Dictionary: William Arthur Lewis: 1979. In *Katz, B. S., ed.*, 1989, pp. 173–87.

Ahiakpor, James C. W. Creating the Structures for an Efficient and Dynamic Economy: The Case of Ghana. In *Gemper, B. B., ed.*, 1989, pp. 189–202.

_____. Do Firms Choose Inappropriate Technology in LDCs? *Econ. Devel. Cult. Change*, April 1989, 37(3), pp. 557–71.

_____ and Amirkhalkhali, Saleh. On the Difficulty of Eliminating Deficits with Higher Taxes: Some Canadian Evidence. *Southern Econ. J.*, July 1989, 56(1), pp. 24–31.

Ahking, Francis W. The Dollar/Pound Exchange Rate in the 1920s: An Empirical Investigation. *Southern Econ. J.*, April 1989, 55(4), pp. 924–34.

Ahlbrandt, Roger S., Jr. Management is the Key to Global Competitiveness. In *Ahlbrandt, R. S., Jr., ed.*, 1989, pp. 1–7.

Ahlén, Kristina. Swedish Collective Bargaining under Pressure: Inter-union Rivalry and Incomes Policies. *Brit. J. Ind. Relat.*, November 1989, 27(3), pp. 330–46.

Ahlstrand, Bruce and Purcell, John. Corporate Strategy and the Management of Employee Relations in the Multi-divisional Company. *Brit. J. Ind. Relat.*, November 1989, 27(3), pp. 396–417.

Ahluwalia, Isher Judge and Rangarajan, C. A Study of Linkages between Agriculture and Industry: The Indian Experience. In *Williamson, J. G. and Panchamukhi, V. R., eds.*, 1989, pp. 219–50.

Ahmad, Jaleel. Commodity Price Stabilization and Economic Growth. *J. Econ. Devel.*, June 1989, 14(1), pp. 35–45.

_____. South–South Trade in Manufactures: A Modified Heckscher–Ohlin Model of Bilateral Trade and Some Preliminary Estimates. *Int. Econ. J.*, Spring 1989, 3(1), pp. 35–48.

_____. Trade, Protectionism and Industrial Adjustment: Three North American Case Studies: Case Study 1: The North American Clothing Industry. In *North–South Institute*, 1989, pp. 1–61.

Ahmad, Khan Masood. Euro-Dollar and U.S. Interest Rates: An Empirical Investigation of Causality. *J. Quant. Econ.*, July 1989, 5(2), pp. 349–60.

_____. Lending Decisions and Spreads: The Syndicated Euro-currency Credit Market. *Indian Econ. Rev.*, Jan.–June 1989, 24(1), pp. 83–100.

Ahmad, Muzaffer and Islam, A. F. M. Mafizul. Nominal and Effective Rates of Protection in Bangladesh Textile Economy. *Bangladesh Devel. Stud.*, March–June 1989, 17(1–2), pp. 57–75.

Ahmad, S. Foreign Exchange and Economic Development: The Case of Bangladesh. *Bangladesh Devel. Stud.*, September 1989, 17(3), pp. 1–20.

Ahmad, Syed and Kubursi, Atif A. Imitation, Adaptation and Innovation: A Note on Typology and Consequences. *Industry Devel.*, April 1989, (26), pp. 83–87.

Ahmadi-Esfahani, Fredoun Z. Estimation of Price Elasticities of Export Demand for Canadian and U.S. Wheat: A Nontraditional Approach. *Can. J. Agr. Econ.*, July 1989, 37(2), pp. 173–90.

_____. A Simulation of Economic Effects of Technology Transfer in Cereal Production: A Comment. *Can. J. Agr. Econ.*, November 1989, 37(3), pp. 539–46.

Ahmed, Ehsan; Rosser, J. Barkley, Jr. and Sheehan, Richard G. A Comparison of National and International Aggregate Supply and Demand VAR Models: The United States, Japan and the European Economic Community. *Weltwirtsch. Arch.*, 1989, 125(2), pp. 252–72.

Ahmed, Iftikhar. Advanced Agricultural Biotechnologies: Some Empirical Findings on their Social Impact. *Int. Lab. Rev.*, 1989, 128(5), pp. 553–70.

Ahmed, S.; Hassan, Rashid M. and Fletcher, Lehman B. Unequal Wealth Accumulation and Income Inequality in a Unimodal Agriculture: Sudan's Radad Irrigation Scheme. *J. Devel. Stud.*, October 1989, 26(1), pp. 120–30.

Ahmed, Shaghil. Islamic Banking and Finance: A Review Essay. *J. Monet. Econ.*, July 1989, 24(1), pp. 157–67.

Ahmed, Syed M. The Effects of the Joint Cost of Strikes on Strikes in Canadian Manufacturing Industries—A Test of the Reder–Neumann–Kennan Theory. *Appl. Econ.*, October 1989, 21(10), pp. 1353–67.

Ahmed, Zia U. Effective Costs of Rural Loans in Bangladesh. *World Devel.*, March 1989, 17(3), pp. 357–63.

Ahn, Byung-Joon. Political Economy of Reforms in China. In *Gomulka, S.; Ha, Y.-C. and Kim, C.-O., eds.*, 1989, pp. 11–24.

Ahn, Chang Mo. The Effect of Temporal Risk Aversion on Optimal Consumption, the Equity Premium, and the Equilibrium Interest Rate. *J. Finance*, December 1989, *44*(5), pp. 1411–20.

Ahn, Suck-Kyo. Theoretical and Practical Aspects of the Economic Reform in China. In *Gomulka, S.; Ha, Y.-C. and Kim, C.-O., eds.*, 1989, pp. 25–35.

Ahn, Taesik, et al. DEA and Ratio Efficiency Analyses for Public Institutions of Higher Learning in Texas. In *Chan, J. L. and Patton, J. M., eds.*, 1989, pp. 165–85.

Aho, Seppo. Introducing a Common System of Sabbatical Leave in Various Professions. In *Agassi, J. B. and Heycock, S., eds.*, 1989, pp. 273–82.

Ahonen, Guy. On the Empirical Content of Keynes' *General Theory*. *Ricerche Econ.*, Jan.–June 1989, *43*(1–2), pp. 256–69.

Ahsan, Syed M. Choice of Tax Base under Uncertainty: Consumption or Income? *J. Public Econ.*, October 1989, *40*(1), pp. 99–134.

_____; **Kwan, Andy C. C. and Sahni, Balbir S.** Causality between Government Consumption Expenditure and National Income: OECD Countries. *Public Finance*, 1989, *44*(2), pp. 204–24.

Ahtiala, Pekka. A Note on Fiscal Policy under Flexible Exchange Rates. *Europ. Econ. Rev.*, September 1989, *33*(7), pp. 1481–86.

Aigner, Dennis J. and Ghali, Khalifa. Self-Selection in the Residential Electricity Time-of-Use Pricing Experiments. *J. Appl. Econometrics*, Supplement, December 1989, *4*, pp. S131–44.

Aiken, Linda H. Keeping Medicare Financially Viable. In *Eisdorfer, C.; Kessler, D. A. and Spector, A. N., eds.*, 1989, pp. 88–105.

Airaksinen, Timo and Kanniainen, Vesa. Financial Hierarchy, Risk and Taxes in the Determination of Corporate Debt Policy: Preliminary Results with Finnish Data. *Liiketaloudellinen Aikak.*, 1989, *38*(4), pp. 279–92.

Aiyagari, S. Rao. Can There Be Short-Period Deterministic Cycles When People Are Long Lived? *Quart. J. Econ.*, February 1989, *104*(1), pp. 163–85.

_____. Equilibrium Existence in an Overlapping Generations Model with Altruistic Preferences. *J. Econ. Theory*, February 1989, *47*(1), pp. 130–52.

_____. Gresham's Law in a Lemons Market for Assets. *Can. J. Econ.*, August 1989, *22*(3), pp. 686–97.

_____. How Should Taxes Be Set? *Fed. Res. Bank Minn. Rev.*, Winter 1989, *13*(1), pp. 22–32.

_____; **Eckstein, Zvi and Eichenbaum, Martin.** Inventories and Price Fluctuations under Perfect Competition and Monopoly. In *Kollintzas, T., ed.*, 1989, pp. 34–68.

Aizenman, Joshua. Country Risk and Contingencies. *Int. Econ. J.*, Spring 1989, *3*(1), pp. 81–102.

_____. Country Risk, Incomplete Information and Taxes on International Borrowing. *Econ. J.*, March 1989, *99*(394), pp. 147–61.

_____. Investment, Openness, and Country Risk. In *Frenkel, J. A.; Dooley, M. P. and Wickham, P., eds.*, 1989, pp. 83–101.

_____. Labour Markets and the Choice of Technology in an Open Developing Economy. *J. Devel. Stud.*, January 1989, *25*(2), pp. 210–25.

_____. Market Power and Exchange Rate Adjustment in the Presence of Quotas. *J. Int. Econ.*, November 1989, *27*(3–4), pp. 265–82.

_____. Monopolistic Competition, Relative Prices, and Output Adjustment in the Open Economy. *J. Int. Money Finance*, March 1989, *8*(1), pp. 5–28.

_____ **and Borensztein, Eduardo R.** Debt and Conditionality under Endogenous Terms of Trade Adjustment. In *Frenkel, J. A.; Dooley, M. P. and Wickham, P., eds.*, 1989, pp. 102–29.

Ajinkya, Bipin B. and Jain, Prem C. The Behavior of Daily Stock Market Trading Volume. *J. Acc. Econ.*, November 1989, *11*(4), pp. 331–59.

Ajjan, N. and Rajagopalan, V. An Analysis of Supply Response of the Tea Industry in South India. *Singapore Econ. Rev.*, October 1989, *34*(2), pp. 89–96.

_____ **and Rajagopalan, V.** An Analysis of Supply Response of the Tea Industry in South India. *Singapore Econ. Rev.*, April 1989, *34*(1), pp. 68–74.

Akaah, Ishmael P. and Gyimah-Brempong, Kwabena. Military Participation and Economic Development in LDCs: New Evidence. *J. Econ. Devel.*, June 1989, *14*(1), pp. 115–34.

Akaike, Hirotugu. Application of the Multivariate Autoregressive Model. In *Mariano, R. S.; Lim, K. S. and Ling, K. D., eds.*, 1989, pp. 43–58.

_____. Bayesian Modeling for Time Series Analysis. In *Mariano, R. S.; Lim, K. S. and Ling, K. D., eds.*, 1989, pp. 59–69.

Akbari, Ather H. The Benefits of Immigrants to Canada: Evidence on Tax and Public Services. *Can. Public Policy*, December 1989, *15*(4), pp. 424–35.

Akella, R. Real Time Part Dispatch in Flexible Assembly Test and Manufacturing Systems. In *Archetti, F.; Lucertini, M. and Serafini, P., eds.*, 1989, pp. 1–73.

Akerlof, George A. The Market for "Lemons": Quality Uncertainty and the Market Mechanism. In *Diamond, P. and Rothschild, M., eds.*, 1989, *1970*, pp. 237–49.

_____ **and Katz, Lawrence F.** Workers' Trust Funds and the Logic of Wage Profiles. *Quart. J. Econ.*, August 1989, *104*(3), pp. 525–36.

Akgiray, Vedat. Conditional Heteroscedasticity in Time Series of Stock Returns: Evidence and Forecasts. *J. Bus.*, January 1989, *62*(1), pp. 55–80.

_____; **Booth, G. Geoffrey and Loistl, Otto.** German Stock Market's Resiliency to World-Wide Panics. *Z. Betriebswirtshaft*, September 1989, *59*(9), pp. 968–78.

_____; **Booth, G. Geoffrey and Loistl, Otto.** Statistical Models of German Stock Returns. *J. Econ. (Z. Nationalökon.)*, 1989, *50*(1), pp. 17–33.

_____ and Lamoureux, Christopher G. Estimation of Stable-Law Parameters: A Comparative Study. *J. Bus. Econ. Statist.*, January 1989, 7(1), pp. 85–93.

_____, et al. A Causal Analysis of Black and Official Exchange Rates: The Turkish Case. *Weltwirtsch. Arch.*, 1989, 125(2), pp. 337–45.

Akiba, Hiroya and Waragai, Tomoki. An Analysis of Structural Changes in the Seven Major Exchange Rates. In *Singer, H. W. and Sharma, S., eds. (II)*, 1989, pp. 146–59.

_____ and Waragai, Tomoki. An Arbitrariness-Free Method of Detecting Structural Changes. *Econ. Letters*, 1989, 29(1), pp. 27–30.

Akins, Nancy. New Direction in Sacred Lands Claims: *Lyng v. Northwest Indian Cemetery Protective Association*. *Natural Res. J.*, Spring 1989, 29(2), pp. 593–605.

Akiyama, Yutaka; Torii, Yasuhiko and Shim, Seung-Jin. Effects of Tariff Reductions on Trade in the Asia-Pacific Region. In *Miller, R. E.; Polenske, K. R. and Rose, A. Z., eds.*, 1989, pp. 165–79.

Akrasanee, Narongchai. The Changing Role of ASEAN in the Coming Decades: Post-Manila-Summit Perspectives: Comment. In *Shinohara, M. and Lo, F., eds.*, 1989, pp. 174–75.

_____ and Chirathivat, Suthiphand. Trade Issues among ASEAN, Asian NICs and Japan. In *Shinohara, M. and Lo, F., eds.*, 1989, pp. 400–433.

Akridge, Jay T. Measuring Productive Efficiency in Multiple Product Agribusiness Firms: A Dual Approach. *Amer. J. Agr. Econ.*, February 1989, 71(1), pp. 116–25.

Aktan, Okan H. The Second Enlargement of the European Communities. In *Jacquemin, A. and Sapir, A., eds.*, 1989, 1985, pp. 143–72.

Al-Badri, K. S. and Cain, M. An Inter-sectoral, Inter-regional Dynamic Model for Production and Trade of the GCC Region. *Middle East Bus. Econ. Rev.*, January 1989, 1(1), pp. 3–10.

Al-Chalabi, Fadhil J. OPEC's Energy Policy. *Energy J.*, April 1989, 10(2), pp. 7–13.

Al-Hamad, Abdlatif Y. Privatization and the Regional Public Joint Ventures in the Gulf Cooperation Council Region: Comment. In *El-Naggar, S., ed.*, 1989, pp. 207–09.

Al-Hammad, M. A. Urban Transportation Planning in Arab Cities—An Overview. In *Candemir, Y., ed.*, 1989, pp. 510–18.

Al-Isa, M. S.; Chu, Chausi and Albar, H. O. Traffic Engineering Services and Management in Saudi Arabia. In *Candemir, Y., ed.*, 1989, pp. 495–509.

Al-Mejren, Abbas. Demand Forecast for Petroleum Distillates in the Arab World. *J. Energy Devel.*, Autumn 1989, 15(1), pp. 95–109.

Al-Qudsi, Sulayman S. Returns to Education, Sectoral Pay Differentials and Determinants in Kuwait. *Econ. Educ. Rev.*, 1989, 8(3), pp. 263–76.

Al-Sahlawi, Mohammed A. The Demand for Natural Gas: A Survey of Price and Income Elasticities. *Energy J.*, January 1989, 10(1), pp. 77–90.

_____. The Future Role of OPEC in the World Oil Market. *J. Energy Devel.*, Spring 1989, 14(2), pp. 213–20.

Alaluf, Mateo. Atypical Employment and the Trade Unions in Belgium: The Precariousness of Strategies. In *Rodgers, G. and Rodgers, J., eds.*, 1989, pp. 249–66.

Alam, M. Shahid. Anatomy of Corruption: An Approach to the Political Economy of Underdevelopment. *Amer. J. Econ. Sociology*, October 1989, 48(4), pp. 441–56.

_____. The South Korean 'Miracle': Examining the Mix of Government and Markets. *J. Developing Areas*, January 1989, 23(2), pp. 233–57.

Alameda, José I. and Mann, Arthur J. Energy Price Shocks, Input Price Changes, and Developmental Implications: A Translog Model Applied to Puerto Rico. *J. Devel. Stud.*, April 1989, 25(3), pp. 329–43.

Alamgir, Mohiuddin. Participatory Development: The IFAD Experience. In *Lineberry, W. P., ed.*, 1989, pp. 3–18.

Alaouze, Chris M. and Fitzpatrick, Campbell R. A Mixed Integer Linear Programming Evaluation of Salinity and Waterlogging Control Options in the Murray–Darling Basin of Australia. *Australian J. Agr. Econ.*, December 1989, 33(3), pp. 203–18.

Alauddin, Mohammad and Tisdell, Clem A. Biochemical Technology and Bangladeshi Land Productivity: Diwan and Kallianpur's Analysis Reapplied and Critically Examined. *Appl. Econ.*, June 1989, 21(6), pp. 741–60.

_____ and Tisdell, Clem A. New Crop Varieties: Impact on Diversification and Stability of Yields. *Australian Econ. Pap.*, June 1989, 28(52), pp. 123–40.

_____ and Tisdell, Clem A. Poverty, Resource Distribution and Security: The Impact of New Agricultural Technology in Rural Bangladesh. *J. Devel. Stud.*, July 1989, 25(4), pp. 550–70.

Alba, Francisco. The Mexican Demographic Situation. In *Bean, F. D.; Schmandt, J. and Weintraub, S., eds.*, 1989, pp. 5–32.

Albach, Horst. Dienstleistungsunternehmen in Deutschland. (With English summary.) *Z. Betriebswirtschaft*, April 1989, 59(4), pp. 397–420.

_____. Führungsdistanz und optimale Unternehmensführung. (With English summary.) *Z. Betriebswirtschaft*, November 1989, 59(11), pp. 1219–28.

_____. Innovationsstrategien zur Verbesserung der Wettbewerbsfähigkeit. (With English summary.) *Z. Betriebswirtschaft*, December 1989, 59(12), pp. 1338–52.

Albar, H. O.; Al-Isa, M. S. and Chu, Chausi. Traffic Engineering Services and Management in Saudi Arabia. In *Candemir, Y., ed.*, 1989, pp. 495–509.

Albaum, Gerald S. and Tull, Donald S. Bias in Random Digit Dialed Surveys. In *Singer, E. and Presser, S., eds.*, 1989, 1977, pp. 11–17.

Albeda, W. Labor Relations and Neo-corporatist Decisionmaking. In *Barbash, J. and Barbash, K., eds.*, 1989, pp. 9–21.

Albæk, Karsten and Madsen, Erik Strøjer. Den solidariske lønpolitik og beskæftigelsen af lavtlønnede. (The Employment Effects of the 1977 Increase in the Danish Minimum Wage. With English summary.) *Nationaløkon. Tidsskr.*, 1989, *127*(2), pp. 184–99.

Alberro, José-Luis and Ibarra, David. The Role of the Economist in Government: An International Perspective: Mexico. In *Pechman, J. A., ed.*, 1989, pp. 147–70.

Albers, Sönke. Der Wert einer Absatzreaktionsfunktion für das Erlös-Controlling: Entgegnung. (With English summary.) *Z. Betriebswirtshaft*, November 1989, *59*(11), pp. 1235–42.

_____. Ein System zur IST-SOLL-Abweichungs-Ursachenanalyse von Erlösen. (With English summary.) *Z. Betriebswirtshaft*, June 1989, *59*(6), pp. 637–54.

Albert, Michel. The Role of the Economist in Government: An International Perspective: France. In *Pechman, J. A., ed.*, 1989, pp. 73–88.

Alberts, William W. and Varaiya, Nikhil P. Assessing the Profitability of Growth by Acquisition: A 'Premium Recapture' Approach. *Int. J. Ind. Organ.*, Special Issue, March 1989, *7*(1), pp. 133–49.

Albin, Peter S. Qualitative Effects of Monetary Policy in "Rich" Dynamic Systems. In *Semmler, W., ed.*, 1989, pp. 168–87.

Albon, Robert Peter. Alfred Marshall and the Consumers' Loss from the British Post Office Monopoly. *Hist. Polit. Econ.*, Winter 1989, *21*(4), pp. 679–88.

_____. Some Observations on the Efficiency of British Postal Pricing. *Appl. Econ.*, April 1989, *21*(4), pp. 461–73.

Albrecht, James W.; Holmlund, Bertil and Lang, Harald. Job Search and Youth Unemployment: Analysis of Swedish Data. *Europ. Econ. Rev.*, March 1989, *33*(2/3), pp. 416–25.

_____ and Lindberg, Thomas. The Micro Initialization of MOSES. In *Albrecht, J. W., et al.*, 1989, pp. 67–132.

Albu, Martin and Glover, Michael. The Regulation of Road Freight Transport in Great Britain. In *Moses, L. N. and Savage, I., eds.*, 1989, pp. 289–99.

Alburo, Florian. Trade and Economic Cooperation in the Asian-Pacific Region: Comment. In *Shinohara, M. and Lo, F., eds.*, 1989, pp. 512–14.

d'Alcantara, G. The Emergence of Service Economics. In *Krelle, W., ed.*, 1989, pp. 561–69.

Alchon, Guy. Lillian Gilbreth and the Science of Management, 1900–1920. In *Perkins, E. J., ed.*, 1989, pp. 25–39.

Alcouffe, Alain. The Institutionalization of Political Economy in French Universities: 1819–1896. *Hist. Polit. Econ.*, Summer 1989, *21*(2), pp. 313–44.

Aldag, Ramon J. and Brief, Arthur P. The Economic Functions of Work. In *Ferris, G. R. and Rowland, K. M., eds.*, 1989, pp. 1–23.

Alderman, Harold and Sahn, David E. Understanding the Seasonality of Employment, Wages, and Income. In *Sahn, D. E., ed.*, 1989, pp. 81–106.

Aldershof, Brian and Ruppert, David. Transformations to Symmetry and Homoscedasticity. *J. Amer. Statist. Assoc.*, June 1989, *84*(406), pp. 437–46.

Alderson, Michael J. On Research in Corporate Pension Policy. In *Lee, C. F., ed.*, 1989, pp. 263–79.

_____ and Zivney, Terry L. Optimal Cross-Hedge Portfolios for Hedging Stock Index Options. *J. Futures Markets*, February 1989, *9*(1), pp. 67–75.

Aldrich, John. Autonomy. In *de Marchi, N. and Gilbert, C., eds.*, 1989, pp. 15–34.

_____. Autonomy. *Oxford Econ. Pap.*, January 1989, *41*(1), pp. 15–34.

Aldrich, Mark. The Gender Gap in Earnings during World War II: New Evidence. *Ind. Lab. Relat. Rev.*, April 1989, *42*(3), pp. 415–29.

_____ and Buchele, Robert. Where to Look for Comparable Worth: The Implications of Efficiency Wages. In *Hill, M. A. and Killingsworth, M. R., eds.*, 1989, pp. 11–28.

Aleksashenko, S.; Iasin, E. G. and Mashchits, V. The Thirteenth Five-Year Plan: From Economic Norms to Taxation of Enterprises. *Prob. Econ.*, December 1989, *32*(8), pp. 78–92.

von Alemann, Ulrich. Bureaucratic and Political Corruption Controls: Reassessing the German Record. In *Heidenheimer, A. J.; Johnston, M. and LeVine, V. T., eds.*, 1989, pp. 855–69.

Alesina, Alberto. Alternative Approaches to the Political Business Cycle: Comments. *Brookings Pap. Econ. Act.*, 1989, (2), pp. 50–56.

_____. The Costs and Benefits of a European Currency: Discussion. In *De Cecco, M. and Giovannini, A., eds.*, 1989, pp. 209–12.

_____. Politics and Business Cycles in Industrial Democracies. *Econ. Policy: A Europ. Forum*, April 1989, (8), pp. 55–98.

_____ and Tabellini, Guido. External Debt, Capital Flight and Political Risk. *J. Int. Econ.*, November 1989, *27*(3–4), pp. 199–220.

Alessie, Rob; Kapteyn, Arie and Melenberg, Bertrand. The Effects of Liquidity Constraints on Consumption: Estimation from Household Panel Data. *Europ. Econ. Rev.*, March 1989, *33*(2/3), pp. 547–55.

Alexander, Herbert E. American Presidential Elections since Public Funding, 1976–84. In *Alexander, H. E., ed.*, 1989, pp. 95–123.

_____. Comparative Political Finance in the 1980s: Introduction. In *Alexander, H. E., ed.*, 1989, pp. 1–8.

_____. Money and Politics: Rethinking a Conceptual Framework. In *Alexander, H. E., ed.*, 1989, pp. 9–23.

Alexander, J. Davidson. The Political Economy of Tax-Based Incomes Policy: Wealth Effects of Post Keynesian TIP. *J. Econ. Issues*, March 1989, *23*(1), pp. 135–46.

Alexander, J. N. and Trivedi, P. K. Reemployment Probability and Multiple Unemployment

Spells: A Partial-Likelihood Approach. *J. Bus. Econ. Statist.*, July 1989, *7*(3), pp. 395–401.

Alexander, Joyce M. An Analysis of Conflict in Northern Ireland. **In** *Golden, B. L.; Wasil, E. A. and Harker, P. T.*, eds., 1989, pp. 225–41.

Alexander, Myrna. Privatisation in Africa. **In** *Ramanadham, V. V.*, ed., 1989, pp. 322–51.

Alexander, Paul. Lessons for the Pacific Technology Transfer and Fishing Communities: The Sri Lankan Experience. **In** *Couper, A. D.*, ed., 1989, pp. 63–73.

Alexander, Robert J. A Keynesian Defense of the Reagan Deficit: The Real Issue Is How Big Should Federal Budgets Be and How Should They Be Met. *Amer. J. Econ. Sociology*, January 1989, *48*(1), pp. 47–54.

Alexander, William E. Liberalization of Financial Markets and the Volatility of Exchange Rates: Some Empirical Considerations. **In** *Stern, R. M.*, ed., 1989, pp. 374–78.

Alexeev, Michael. Privileges in a Queue-Rationed CPE with Black Markets: Note. *J. Econ. Theory*, April 1989, *47*(2), pp. 422–30.

Alföldi, István. Information Technology at the Hungarian Central Statistical Office: Experiences and Plans. *Statist. J.*, 1989, *6*(2), pp. 159–66.

Alford, Robert R. and Feige, Edgar L. Information Distortions in Social Systems: The Underground Economy and Other Observer–Subject–Policymaker Feedbacks. **In** *Feige, E. L.*, ed., 1989, pp. 57–79.

Alhadeff, Peter. Social Welfare and the Slump: Argentina in the 1930s. **In** *Platt, D. C. M.*, ed., 1989, pp. 169–78.

Alho, Juha M. Relating Changes in Life Expectancy to Changes in Mortality. *Demography*, November 1989, *26*(4), pp. 705–09.

Ali, Abbas. A Comparative Study of Managerial Beliefs about Work in the Arab States. **In** *Prasad, S. B.*, ed., 1989, pp. 95–112.

Ali, Mubarik and Flinn, John C. Profit Efficiency among Basmati Rice Producers in Pakistan Punjab. *Amer. J. Agr. Econ.*, May 1989, *71*(2), pp. 303–10.

Ali, Mukhtar M. Tests for Autocorrelation and Randomness in Multiple Time Series. *J. Amer. Statist. Assoc.*, June 1989, *84*(406), pp. 533–40.

_____ **and Silver, J. Lew.** Testing Slutsky Symmetry in Systems of Linear Demand Equations. *J. Econometrics*, June 1989, *41*(2), pp. 251–66.

Ali, Syed Mubashir. Determinants of Family Size Preferences in Pakistan. *Pakistan Devel. Rev.*, Autumn 1989, *28*(3), pp. 207–31.

Aliber, Robert Z. Protection and the Structure of the Banking Industry in an International Context. **In** *Giersch, H.*, ed., 1989, pp. 198–218.

_____. U.S. Fiscal Deficits and the Foreign Exchange Value of the U.S. Dollar. **In** *Hodgman, D. R. and Wood, G. E.*, eds., 1989, pp. 141–57.

Alidaee, Bahram. Analyzing Total Cost for a Single Machine and n Jobs, by Use of a Symmetric Matrix Arising from a Quadratic Form of Service Times. *Logist. Transp. Rev.*, December 1989, *25*(4), pp. 367–74.

Allais, Maurice. L'économie des infrastructures de transport et les fondements du calcul économique. (With English summary.) *Revue Écon. Politique*, March–April 1989, *99*(2), pp. 159–97.

_____. My Life Philosophy. *Amer. Economist*, Fall 1989, *33*(2), pp. 3–17.

Allard, Marie; Bronsard, Camille and Richelle, Yves. Temporary Pareto Optimum Theory. *J. Public Econ.*, April 1989, *38*(3), pp. 343–68.

Allemane, Rémy and Portait, Roland. L'évaluation et la gestion d'un portefeuille comprenant des contrats MATIF, BTAN et des options sur BTAN et sur contrats MATIF. (Valuation and Management of a Portfolio Including Interest Rate Futures, Bonds and Options on Bonds and Futures. With English summary.) *Finance*, June 1989, *10*(1), pp. 41–67.

Allen, Beth and Hellwig, Martin. The Approximation of Competitive Equilibria by Bertrand–Edgeworth Equilibria in Large Markets. *J. Math. Econ.*, 1989, *18*(2), pp. 103–27.

Allen, Chris. Benin: Politics, Economics and Society. **In** *Allen, C., et al.*, 1989, pp. 1–144.

Allen, Christopher S. Political Consequences of Change: The Chemical Industry. **In** *Katzenstein, P. J.*, ed., 1989, pp. 157–84.

_____. The Underdevelopment of Keynesianism in the Federal Republic of Germany. **In** *Hall, P. A.*, ed., 1989, pp. 263–89.

_____ **and Riemer, Jeremiah M.** The Industrial Policy Controversy in West Germany: Organized Adjustment and the Emergence of Meso-corporatism. **In** *Foglesong, R. E. and Wolfe, J. D.*, eds., 1989, pp. 45–64.

Allen, D. E. and Mizuno, H. The Determinants of Corporate Capital Structure: Japanese Evidence. *Appl. Econ.*, May 1989, *21*(5), pp. 569–85.

Allen, D. N.; Travers, T. C. and Clements, L. C. Pricing of New Vehicles in the Australian Consumer Price Index: Adjusting for Quality Change. **In** *Turvey, R.*, 1989, pp. 163–65.

Allen, Franklin. The Changing Nature of Debt and Equity: A Financial Perspective. **In** *Kopcke, R. W. and Rosengren, E. S.*, eds., 1989, pp. 12–38.

_____ **and Faulhaber, Gerald R.** Signaling by Underpricing in the IPO Market. *J. Finan. Econ.*, August 1989, *23*(2), pp. 303–23.

Allen, Linda; Peristiani, Stavros and Saunders, Anthony. Bank Size, Collateral, and Net Purchase Behavior in the Federal Funds Market: Empirical Evidence. *J. Bus.*, October 1989, *62*(4), pp. 501–15.

Allen, P. M. and Sanglier, M. Evolutionary Models of Urban Systems: An Application to the Belgian Provinces. *Environ. Planning A*, April 1989, *21*(4), pp. 477–98.

Allen, Ralph C. and Stone, Jack H. The Locational Criteria of Footloose Firms: A Formal

Model. *Rev. Reg. Stud.*, Spring 1989, *19*(2), pp. 13–17.

Allen, Robert C. Enclosure, Farming Methods, and the Growth of Productivity in the South Midlands. In *Grantham, G. and Leonard, C. S., eds.*, Pt. A, 1989, pp. 69–88.

――――. Le due rivoluzioni agrarie inglesi, 1450–1850. (The Two English Agricultural Revolutions, 1450–1850. With English summary.) *Rivista Storia Econ.*, *S.S.*, October 1989, *6*(3), pp. 255–82.

Allen, Robert F. and Hagin, Allan Scott. Scale Related Efficiencies as a (Minor) Source of the Profits–Market Share Relationship. *Rev. Econ. Statist.*, August 1989, *71*(3), pp. 523–26.

Allen, Roy E. Globalisation of the U.S. Financial Markets: The New Structure for Monetary Policy. In *[Marjolin, R.]*, 1989, pp. 267–86.

Allen, Sheila. Flexibility of Work and Working Time: A Gendered Approach. In *Agassi, J. B. and Heycock, S., eds.*, 1989, pp. 238–48.

Allen, Steven G. Why Construction Industry Productivity Is Declining: Reply. *Rev. Econ. Statist.*, August 1989, *71*(3), pp. 547–48.

――――; **McDermed, Ann A. and Clark, Robert L.** Pension Wealth, Age–Wealth Profiles, and the Distribution of Net Worth. In *Lipsey, R. E. and Tice, H. S., eds.*, 1989, pp. 689–731.

Allen, Stuart D. and Connolly, Robert A. Financial Market Effects on Aggregate Money Demand: A Bayesian Analysis. *J. Money, Credit, Banking*, May 1989, *21*(2), pp. 158–75.

Allenby, Greg M. A Unified Approach to Identifying, Estimating and Testing Demand Structures with Aggregate Scanner Data. *Marketing Sci.*, Summer 1989, *8*(3), pp. 265–80.

Allison, Graham. National Security Strategy for the 1990s. In *Hamilton, E. K., ed.*, 1989, pp. 198–241.

Allison, Timothy; Calzonetti, Frank J. and Witt, Tom S. Electricity Supply and Demand. In *Calzonetti, F. J., et al.*, 1989, pp. 19–51.

―――― **and Rose, Adam Z.** On the Plausibility of the Supply-Driven Input–Output Model: Empirical Evidence on Joint Stability. *J. Reg. Sci.*, August 1989, *29*(3), pp. 451–58.

Allon, J. and Pfeffermann, D. Multivariate Exponential Smoothing: Method and Practice. *Int. J. Forecasting*, 1989, *5*(1), pp. 83–98.

Allsopp, Christopher. The Macro-economic Role of the State. In *Helm, D., ed.*, 1989, pp. 180–217.

―――― **and Chrystal, K. Alec.** Exchange Rate Policy in the 1990s. *Oxford Rev. Econ. Policy*, Autumn 1989, *5*(3), pp. 1–23.

―――― **and Rhys, John.** The Macroeconomic Impact of North Sea Oil. In *Helm, D.; Kay, J. and Thompson, D., eds.*, 1989, pp. 377–410.

Alm, James. The Immovable Property Transfer Tax. In *Schroeder, L., ed.*, 1989, pp. 89–114.

――――; **Miller, Barbara Diane and Wozny, James.** The Land Development Tax. In *Schroeder, L., ed.*, 1989, pp. 115–43.

Almansi, Aquiles A. Patterns of External Adjustment in LDC's: Do We Understand Them? *Int. Econ. Rev.*, February 1989, *30*(1), pp. 77–84.

Almon, Clopper. Industrial Impacts of Macroeconomic Policies in the INFORUM Model. In *Miller, R. E.; Polenske, K. R. and Rose, A. Z., eds.*, 1989, pp. 12–21.

Alogoskoufis, George S. The Labour Market in the Open Economy. In *Sapsford, D. and Tzannatos, Z., eds.*, 1989, pp. 208–26.

――――. Monetary, Nominal Income and Exchange Rate Targets in a Small Open Economy. *Europ. Econ. Rev.*, April 1989, *33*(4), pp. 687–705.

――――. Stabilization Policy, Fixed Exchange Rates and Target Zones. In *Miller, M.; Eichengreen, B. and Portes, R., eds.*, 1989, pp. 75–94.

Alonso-Concheiro, Antonio. Technology: Development, International Trade and Cooperation. In *Fishelson, G., ed.*, 1989, pp. 209–36.

Alonzo, Ruperto P. Trends in Poverty and Labour Market Outcomes in the Metro Manila Area. In *Rodgers, G., ed.*, 1989, pp. 173–99.

Alperovich, Gershon. The Distribution of City Size: A Sensitivity Analysis. *J. Urban Econ.*, January 1989, *25*(1), pp. 93–102.

Alpert, W. T.; Greenberg, E. and Pollard, W. A. Statistical Properties of Data Stretching. *J. Appl. Econometrics*, Oct.–Dec. 1989, *4*(4), pp. 383–91.

Alston, Julian M.; Wohlgenant, Michael K. and Mullen, J. D. The Impact of Farm and Processing Research on the Australian Wool Industry. *Australian J. Agr. Econ.*, April 1989, *33*(1), pp. 32–47.

Alston, Lee J. and Ferrie, Joseph P. Social Control and Labor Relations in the American South before the Mechanization of the Cotton Harvest in the 1950s. *J. Inst. Theoretical Econ.*, March 1989, *145*(1), pp. 133–57.

―――― **and Gillespie, William.** Resource Coordination and Transaction Costs: A Framework for Analyzing the Firm/Market Boundary. *J. Econ. Behav. Organ.*, March 1989, *11*(2), pp. 191–212.

Alston, Richard M. and Chi, Wan Fu. Graphing the Model or Modeling the Graph? Not-So-Subtle Problems in Linear *IS–LM* Analysis. *J. Econ. Educ.*, Summer 1989, *20*(3), pp. 261–67.

Alt, Raimund; Ploberger, Werner and Krämer, Walter. A Modification of the CUSUM Test in the Linear Regression Model with Lagged Dependent Variables. In *Kramer, W., ed.*, 1989, pp. 1–11.

――――; **Ploberger, Werner and Krämer, Walter.** A Modification of the CUSUM Test in the Linear Regression Model with Lagged Dependent Variables. *Empirical Econ.*, 1989, *14*(2), pp. 65–75.

Altemeier, Klaus; Adinugroho, Bambang and Tabor, Steven R. Foodcrop Demand in Indonesia: A Systems Approach. *Bull. Indonesian Econ. Stud.*, August 1989, *25*(2), pp. 31–51.

Alter, A. The Disregard of a Legal Entity for Tax Purposes: Israel. In *International Fiscal Association, ed. (II)*, 1989, pp. 325–34.

Alter, George and Riley, James C. Fraility, Sickness, and Death: Models of Morbidity and Mortality in Historical Populations. *Population Stud.*, March 1989, *43*(1), pp. 25–45.

Althaus, Paul G. and Schachter, Joseph. An Equilibrium Model of Gross Migration. *J. Reg. Sci.*, May 1989, *29*(2), pp. 143–59.

Altig, David and Davis, Steve J. Government Debt, Redistributive Fiscal Policies, and the Interaction between Borrowing Constraints and Intergenerational Altruism. *J. Monet. Econ.*, July 1989, *24*(1), pp. 3–29.

Altman, Andrew. Power, Politics, and Economics. In *Samuels, W. J., ed. (I)*, 1989, pp. 9–16.

Altman, Edward I. Measuring Corporate Bond Mortality and Performance. *J. Finance*, September 1989, *44*(4), pp. 909–22.

Altman, Irwin and Sundstrom, Eric. Physical Environments and Work-Group Effectiveness. In *Cummings, L. L. and Staw, B. M., eds.*, 1989, pp. 175–209.

Altman, Stuart H.; Greenberg, Jay N. and Leutz, Walter N. The Social Health Maintenance Organization. In *Eisdorfer, C.; Kessler, D. A. and Spector, A. N., eds.*, 1989, pp. 197–223.

Altman, Yochanan. Second Economy Activities in the USSR: Insights from the Southern Republics. In *Ward, P. M., ed.*, 1989, pp. 58–72.

Altmann, Franz-Lothar. Marx, Socialism and Innovation: Discussion. In *Berliner, J. S.; Kosta, H. G. J. and Hakogi, M., eds.*, 1989, pp. 144–46.

————. Restructuring of the Czechoslovak Economic Mechanism. In *Berliner, J. S.; Kosta, H. G. J. and Hakogi, M., eds.*, 1989, pp. 103–15.

Altmann, Jürgen. Verification Techniques for Heavy Land Vehicles Using Short-Range Sensors. In *Altmann, J. and Rotblat, J., eds.*, 1989, pp. 184–94.

Altuğ, Sumru. Time-to-Build and Aggregate Fluctuations: Some New Evidence. *Int. Econ. Rev.*, November 1989, *30*(4), pp. 889–920.

Alvarez, Antonio; Cox, Thomas A. and Buse, Rueben C. Effect of Demographics on Changes in At-Home Meat Consumption. In *Buse, R. C., ed.*, 1989, pp. 217–42.

Alvarez Garrido, Fernando. Base estadística en España de la contabilidad nacional trimestral. (With English summary.) *Revista Española Econ.*, 1989, *6*(1–2), pp. 59–83.

Alverson, Hoyt. Culture and Economy: Games That "Play People." In *Tool, M. R. and Samuels, W. J., eds. (II)*, 1989, *1986*, pp. 7–25.

Alvey, Jim and Duhs, Alan. Schumacher's Political Economy. *Int. J. Soc. Econ.*, 1989, *16*(6), pp. 67–76.

Alvi, Shafiq A. and Islam, Muhammed N. Wage Settlement Spillovers between the Private and Public Sectors in Canada. *J. Quant. Econ.*, January 1989, *5*(1), pp. 171–86.

Alwin, Duane F. and Krosnick, Jon A. The Measurement of Values in Surveys: A Comparison of Ratings and Rankings. In *Singer, E. and Presser, S., eds.*, 1989, *1985*, pp. 124–41.

Alworth, Julian S. International Aspects of Capital Income Taxation: A Survey of Recent Developments and Possible Reforms. In *Chiancone, A. and Messere, K., eds.*, 1989, pp. 123–42.

Aly, Hassan Y. and Grabowski, Richard. Measuring the Rate and Bias of Technical Innovation in Japanese Agriculture: An Alternative Approach. *Europ. Rev. Agr. Econ.*, 1989, *16*(1), pp. 65–81.

Amadeo, Edward J. and Franco, Gustavo H. B. Entre Keynes e Robertson: *finance*, poupança e investimento. (With English summary.) *Pesquisa Planejamento Econ.*, August 1989, *19*(2), pp. 379–95.

Amann, Erwin and Jäger, Albert. Staatsschuldenarithmetik: Zwei unerfreuliche Beispiele. (Public Debt Arithmetic: Two Unpleasant Examples. With English summary.) *Kredit Kapital*, 1989, *22*(2), pp. 221–34.

Amanor-Boadu, Vincent and Turvey, Calum G. Evaluating Premiums for a Farm Income Insurance Policy. *Can. J. Agr. Econ.*, July 1989, *37*(2), pp. 233–47.

Amariglio, Jack; Callari, Antonio and Cullenberg, Stephen. Analytical Marxism: A Critical Overview. *Rev. Soc. Econ.*, Winter 1989, *47*(4), pp. 415–32.

Ambachtsheer, Keith P. The Persistence of Investment Risk. *J. Portfol. Manage.*, Fall 1989, *16*(1), pp. 69–71.

Ambler, Steve. Does Money Matter in Canada? Evidence from a Vector Error Correction Model. *Rev. Econ. Statist.*, November 1989, *71*(4), pp. 651–58.

————. The International Transmission of Policy Announcement Effects. *J. Int. Money Finance*, June 1989, *8*(2), pp. 219–232.

————. La stationnarité en économétrie et en macroéconomique: Un guide pour les non initiés. (With English summary.) *L'Actual. Econ.*, December 1989, *65*(4), pp. 590–609.

———— **and Phaneuf, Louis.** Accommodation, Price Flexibility and Fluctuations. *Econ. Letters*, September 1989, *30*(3), pp. 185–90.

———— **and Phaneuf, Louis.** The Stablizing Effects of Price Flexibility in Contract-Based Models. *J. Macroecon.*, Spring 1989, *11*(2), pp. 233–46.

Ambrosi, Klaus. Computer-Based and Quantitative Methods in Market Research. In *Opitz, O., ed.*, 1989, pp. 335–55.

Amel, Dean F. and Jacowski, Michael J. Trends in Banking Structure since the Mid-1970s. *Fed. Res. Bull.*, March 1989, *75*(3), pp. 120–33.

———— **and Rhoades, Stephen A.** Empirical Evidence on the Motives for Bank Mergers. *Eastern Econ. J.*, Jan.–March 1989, *15*(1), pp. 17–27.

Amelung, Torsten. The Determinants of Protection in Developing Countries: An Extended Interest-Group Approach. *Kyklos*, 1989, *42*(4), pp. 515–32.

Amemiya, Takeshi and Shimono, Keiko. An Application of Nested Logit Models to the Labor

Supply of the Elderly. *Econ. Stud. Quart.*, March 1989, *40*(1), pp. 14–22.

Amenc, Noël and Huet, Josiane. Innovations financières et comportements stratégiques des entreprises: L'émergence d'und stratégie financière pure. (Financial Innovations and Strategic Behavior in Companies: The Emergence of a Pure Financial Strategy. With English summary.) *Écon. Societes*, January 1989, *23*(1), pp. 7–27.

Amend, Donald F. Alaska's Regional Aquaculture Associations Co-management of Salmon in Southern Southeast Alaska. **In** *Pinkerton, E., ed.*, 1989, pp. 125–34.

Amendola, M. Towards a Dynamic Analysis of the "Traverse." **In** *Wood, J. C. and Woods, R. N., eds., Vol. 4,* 1989, *1984*, pp. 18–26.

Amershi, Amin H. and Hughes, John S. Multiple Signals, Statistical Sufficiency, and Pareto Orderings of Best Agency Contracts. *Rand J. Econ.*, Spring 1989, *20*(1), pp. 102–12.

Ames, Glenn C. W. and Yu, Ming-Fang. An Analysis of Removal of Agricultural Trade Barriers between the United States and Canada with Emphasis on the Southeast. *Can. J. Agr. Econ.*, Part 2, December 1989, *37*(4), pp. 1035–43.

Amezquita C., Manuel de Jesus. Food and Agricultural Policies and Programs in the Caribbean. **In** *Helmuth, J. W. and Johnson, S. R., eds., Vol. 1,* 1989, pp. 84–90.

Amico, Joseph C. Developing and Implementing Tax Treaty Policy: The Tax Sparing Clause: Brazil. *Bull. Int. Fiscal Doc.*, Aug.–Sept. 1989, *43*(8–9), pp. 408–11.

Amihud, Yakov and Mendelson, Haim. The Effects of Beta, Bid–Ask Spread, Residual Risk, and Size on Stock Returns. *J. Finance*, June 1989, *44*(2), pp. 479–86.

_____ **and Mendelson, Haim.** Inventory Behaviour and Market Power: An Empirical Investigation. *Int. J. Ind. Organ.*, June 1989, *7*(2), pp. 269–80.

Amin, Ash. A Model of the Small Firm in Italy. **In** *Goodman, E. and Bamford, J., eds.,* 1989, pp. 111–22.

_____. Specialization without Growth: Small Footwear Firms in Naples. **In** *Goodman, E. and Bamford, J., eds.,* 1989, pp. 239–58.

_____ **and Pywell, C.** Is Technology Policy Enough for Local Economic Revitalization? The Case of Tyne and Wear in the North East of England. *Reg. Stud.*, October 1989, *23*(5), pp. 463–77.

Amirkhalkhali, Saleh and Ahiakpor, James C. W. On the Difficulty of Eliminating Deficits with Higher Taxes: Some Canadian Evidence. *Southern Econ. J.*, July 1989, *56*(1), pp. 24–31.

Amit, Raphael; Livnat, Joshua and Zarowin, Paul. The Mode of Corporate Diversification: Internal Ventures versus Acquisitions. *Managerial Dec. Econ.*, June 1989, *10*(2), pp. 89–100.

Amjad, Rashid. Economic Impact of Migration to the Middle East on the Major Asian Labour

Sending Countries—An Overview. **In** *Amjad, R., ed.,* 1989, pp. 1–27.

Amla, B. L. Postharvest Losses and Food Preservation. **In** *Oram, P. A., et al.,* 1989, pp. 277–88.

Amos, Orley M., Jr. An Inquiry into the Causes of Increasing Regional Income Inequality in the United States. *Rev. Reg. Stud.*, Spring 1989, *19*(2), pp. 1–12.

_____. A Reevaluation of Long Cycle Theories: Development as the Satisfaction of Hierarchial Needs. *Soc. Sci. Quart.*, June 1989, *70*(2), pp. 341–55.

_____ **and Currier, Kevin M.** The Foundations of a Hierarchial Theory of the Long-Wave Phenomenon. *Southern Econ. J.*, July 1989, *56*(1), pp. 142–56.

Amuah, Alex K. and Goddard, Ellen W. The Demand for Canadian Fats and Oils: A Case Study of Advertising Effectiveness. *Amer. J. Agr. Econ.*, August 1989, *71*(3), pp. 741–49.

An, Xi-Ji. The Alternatives and World Impacts of Food Policy in China. **In** *Helmuth, J. W. and Johnson, S. R., eds., Vol. 2,* 1989, pp. 243–54.

_____. Policy Options for Improving the Functioning of the World Food Production and Distribution Systems: Reaction. **In** *Helmuth, J. W. and Johnson, S. R., eds., Vol. 1,* 1989, pp. 231–33.

Anagnost, Ann. Prosperity and Counterprosperity: The Moral Discourse on Wealth in Post-Mao China. **In** *Dirlik, A. and Meisner, M., eds.,* 1989, pp. 210–34.

Anam, Mahmudul. Rural–Urban Wage Differential, Rent Seeking, and a Justification for Free Trade. *J. Urban Econ.*, November 1989, *26*(3), pp. 328–34.

_____. Terms of Trade Shocks and Domestic Prices under Tariffs and Quotas: Note. *Europ. Econ. Rev.*, July 1989, *33*(6), pp. 1279–82.

_____ **and Zandi, Farrokh R.** Immiserising Factor Growth and the Non-equivalence of Quotas and VERs. *Int. Econ. J.*, Autumn 1989, *3*(3), pp. 23–30.

Anand, Punam and McGill, Ann L. The Effect of Vivid Attributes on the Evaluation of Alternatives: The Role of Differential Attention and Cognitive Elaboration. *J. Cons. Res.*, September 1989, *16*(2), pp. 188–96.

Anand, Ritu and van Wijnbergen, Sweder. Inflation and the Financing of Government Expenditure: An Introductory Analysis with an Application to Turkey. *World Bank Econ. Rev.*, January 1989, *3*(1), pp. 17–38.

Anani, Jawad and Khalaf, Rima M. Privatization in Jordan. **In** *El-Naggar, S., ed.,* 1989, pp. 210–25.

Anas, Alex. Statistical Properties of Mathematical Programming Models of Stochastic Network Equilibrium: Erratum. *J. Reg. Sci.*, February 1989, *29*(1), pp. 107–08.

Anbarci, Nejat. The Kalai/Smorodinsky Solution with Time Preferences. *Econ. Letters*, November 1989, *31*(1), pp. 5–7.

Anderlini, Luca. Theoretical Modelling of Banks

and Bank Runs. **In** *Hahn, F., ed.,* 1989, pp. 297–311.

Anders, Gary C. Social and Economic Consequences of Federal Indian Policy: A Case Study of the Alaska Natives. *Econ. Devel. Cult. Change,* January 1989, *37*(2), pp. 285–303.

Andersen, Arthur. Guide to Taxation, Trade and Investment: Brazil. *Bull. Int. Fiscal Doc.,* Aug.–Sept. 1989, *43*(8–9), pp. 355–63.

Andersen, Torben M. Credibility of Policy Announcements: The Output and Inflation Costs of Disinflationary Policies. *Europ. Econ. Rev.,* January 1989, *33*(1), pp. 13–30.

_____. New Classical Macroeconomics: A Sympathetic Account: Comment. *Scand. J. Econ.,* 1989, *91*(2), pp. 253–58.

_____ **and Christensen, Michael.** Relative Wages and Employment Fluctuations. *J. Macroecon.,* Fall 1989, *11*(4), pp. 477–92.

Anderson, Andrew and Rugman, Alan M. Subsidies in the U.S. Steel Industry: A New Conceptual Framework and Literature Review. *J. World Trade,* December 1989, *23*(6), pp. 59–83.

Anderson, B. D. O. and Deistler, Manfred. Linear Dynamic Errors-in-Variables Models: Some Structure Theory. *J. Econometrics,* May 1989, *41*(1), pp. 39–63.

Anderson, Barbara A. and Silver, Brian D. The Changing Shape of Soviet Mortality, 1958–1985: An Evaluation of Old and New Evidence. *Population Stud.,* July 1989, *43*(2), pp. 243–65.

_____ **and Silver, Brian D.** Demographic Sources of the Changing Ethnic Composition of the Soviet Union. *Population Devel. Rev.,* December 1989, *15*(4), pp. 609–56.

_____ **and Silver, Brian D.** Patterns of Cohort Mortality in the Soviet Population. *Population Devel. Rev.,* September 1989, *15*(3), pp. 471–501.

Anderson, Barry. Budget Accounting: Viewpoints. *Public Budg. Finance,* Autumn 1989, *9*(3), pp. 94–101.

Anderson, Carl G.; Wood, Wendell C. and Shafer, Carl E. Frequency and Duration of Profitable Hedging Margins for Texas Cotton Producers, 1980–1986. *J. Futures Markets,* December 1989, *9*(6), pp. 519–28.

Anderson, Clark. Annual Review of Nations: Year 1988: Nigeria. **In** *Haberman, L. and Sacks, P. M., eds.,* 1989, pp. 233–45.

Anderson, Curt L.; Garcia, L. Miguel and Lichty, Richard W. Water Analysis: A Systems Approach Incorporating Linear Programming. *Growth Change,* Winter 1989, *20*(1), pp. 80–89.

Anderson, Dale G. and Falcon, Elmo T. Rural Impacts of Economic Regulation: A Case Study. **In** *Felton, J. R. and Anderson, D. G., eds.,* 1989, *1981*, pp. 121–30.

_____ **and Huttsell, Ray C., Jr.** Trucking Regulation, 1935–1980. **In** *Felton, J. R. and Anderson, D. G., eds.,* 1989, pp. 14–41.

_____ **and Sarwar, Ghulam.** Railroad Rate Deregulation and Uncertainty of Farm-Level

Prices for Corn. *Amer. J. Agr. Econ.,* November 1989, *71*(4), pp. 883–91.

Anderson, David and Throup, David. The Agrarian Economy of Central Province, Kenya, 1918 to 1939. **In** *Brown, I., ed.,* 1989, pp. 8–28.

Anderson, Dennis. Economic Aspects of Afforestation and Soil Conservation Projects. **In** *Schramm, G. and Warford, J. J., eds.,* 1989, pp. 172–84.

_____. Infrastructure Pricing Policies and the Public Revenue in African Countries. *World Devel.,* April 1989, *17*(4), pp. 525–42.

Anderson, Donald. The Single European Market and the Real Economy. *Bus. Econ.,* October 1989, *24*(4), pp. 10–16.

Anderson, Erin and Weitz, Barton. Determinants of Continuity in Conventional Industrial Channel Dyads. *Marketing Sci.,* Fall 1989, *8*(4), pp. 310–23.

Anderson, Gary A. and Roberts, David L. Stability in the Present Value Assessment of Lost Earnings. *J. Risk Ins.,* March 1989, *56*(1), pp. 50–66.

Anderson, Gary M. The Butcher, the Baker, and the Policy-Maker: Adam Smith on Public Choice. *Hist. Polit. Econ.,* Winter 1989, *21*(4), pp. 641–59.

_____; **Ekelund, Robert B., Jr. and Tollison, Robert D.** Nassau Senior as Economic Consultant: The Factory Acts Reconsidered. *Economica,* February 1989, *56*(221), pp. 71–81.

_____; **Levy, David M. and Tollison, Robert D.** The Half-Life of Dead Economists. *Can. J. Econ.,* February 1989, *22*(1), pp. 174–83.

_____; **Shughart, William F., II and Tollison, Robert D.** On the Incentives of Judges to Enforce Legislative Wealth Transfers. *J. Law Econ.,* April 1989, *32*(1), pp. 215–28.

_____; **Shughart, William F., II and Tollison, Robert D.** Political Entry Barriers and Tax Incidence: The Political Economy of Sales and Excise Taxes. *Public Finance,* 1989, *44*(1), pp. 8–18.

Anderson, Gordon J. and Mizon, Grayham E. What Can Statistics Contribute to the Analysis of Economic Structural Change? **In** *Hackl, P., ed.,* 1989, pp. 3–21.

Anderson, James. Nationalisms in a Disunited Kingdom. **In** *Mohan, J., ed.,* 1989, pp. 35–50.

_____ **and Emerson, William.** A Spatial Allocation Model for the New England Fisheries. *Marine Resource Econ.,* 1989, *6*(2), pp. 123–44.

Anderson, James E. Government and the Economy: What Is Fundamental? **In** *Samuels, W. J., ed. (I),* 1989, pp. 17–23.

Anderson, Jock R. Reconsiderations on Risk Deductions in Public Project Appraisal. *Australian J. Agr. Econ.,* August 1989, *33*(2), pp. 136–40.

_____; **Findlay, Carly J. and Wan, G. H.** Are Modern Cultivars More Risky? A Question of Stochastic Efficiency. **In** *Anderson, J. R. and Hazell, P. B. R., eds.,* 1989, pp. 301–08.

_____ **and Hazell, Peter B. R.** Synthesis and

Needs in Agricultural Research and Policy. In *Anderson, J. R. and Hazell, P. B. R., eds.,* 1989, pp. 339–56.

Anderson, John E. and Bunch, Howard C. Agricultural Property Tax Relief: Tax Credits, Tax Rates, and Land Values. *Land Econ.,* February 1989, *65*(1), pp. 13–22.

Anderson, Kathryn H.; Burkhauser, Richard V. and Butler, John S. Work and Health after Retirement: A Competing Risks Model with Semiparametric Unobserved Heterogeneity. *Rev. Econ. Statist.,* February 1989, *71*(1), pp. 46–53.

_____ **and Mitchell, Jean M.** Mental Health and the Labor Force Participation of Older Workers. *Inquiry,* Summer 1989, *26*(2), pp. 262–71.

Anderson, Kym. Korea: A Case of Agricultural Protection. In *Sicular, T., ed.,* 1989, pp. 109–53.

_____ **and Park, Young-il.** China and the International Relocation of World Textile and Clothing Activity. *Weltwirtsch. Arch.,* 1989, *125*(1), pp. 129–48.

_____ **and Tyers, Rodney.** Price Elasticities in International Food Trade: Synthetic Estimates from a Global Model. *J. Policy Modeling,* Fall 1989, *11*(3), pp. 315–44.

Anderson, Lee G. Enforcement Issues in Selecting Fisheries Management Policy. *Marine Resource Econ.,* 1989, *6*(3), pp. 261–77.

_____. Optimal Intra- and Interseasonal Harvesting Strategies When Price Varies with Individual Size. *Marine Resource Econ.,* 1989, *6*(2), pp. 145–62.

Anderson, Margot and Garcia, Philip. Exchange Rate Uncertainty and the Demand for U.S. Soybeans. *Amer. J. Agr. Econ.,* August 1989, *71*(3), pp. 721–29.

Anderson, Max G. Benefit Analysis of Agricultural Research: A Comment. *Can. J. Agr. Econ.,* March 1989, *37*(1), pp. 145–48.

Anderson, Ronald W.; Gilbert, Christopher L. and Powell, Andrew. Securitization and Commodity Contingency in International Lending. *Amer. J. Agr. Econ.,* May 1989, *71*(2), pp. 523–30.

Anderson, Seth C. and Born, Jeffery A. The Selling and Seasoning of Investment Company Offerings. *J. Finan. Services Res.,* June 1989, *2*(2), pp. 115–31.

Anderson, Simon P. Socially Optimal Spatial Pricing. *Reg. Sci. Urban Econ.,* February 1989, *19*(1), pp. 69–86.

_____ **and Devereux, Michael.** Profit-Sharing and Optimal Labour Contracts. *Can. J. Econ.,* May 1989, *22*(2), pp. 425–33.

_____; **Donsimoni, Marie-Paule and Gabszewicz, Jean Jaskold.** Is International Trade Profitable to Oligopolistic Industries? *Int. Econ. Rev.,* November 1989, *30*(4), pp. 725–33.

_____ **and Fischer, Ronald D.** Multi-market Oligopoly with Production before Sales. *J. Ind. Econ.,* December 1989, *38*(2), pp. 167–82.

_____ **and Neven, Damien J.** Market Efficiency with Combinable Products. *Europ. Econ. Rev.,* April 1989, *33*(4), pp. 707–19.

_____; **de Palma, André and Thisse, Jacques-François.** Demand for Differentiated Products, Discrete Choice Models, and the Characteristics Approach. *Rev. Econ. Stud.,* January 1989, *56*(1), pp. 21–35.

_____; **de Palma, André and Thisse, Jacques-François.** Spatial Price Policies Reconsidered. *J. Ind. Econ.,* September 1989, *38*(1), pp. 1–18.

Anderson, T. W. Linear Latent Variable Models and Covariance Structures. *J. Econometrics,* May 1989, *41*(1), pp. 91–119.

Anderson, Terry L. Protecting the Environment. In *Crane, E. H. and Boaz, D.,* 1989, pp. 311–23.

_____ **and Leal, Donald R.** Building Coalitions for Water Marketing. *J. Policy Anal. Manage.,* Summer 1989, *8*(3), pp. 432–45.

Anderson, William P. An Evolutionary Model of Growth in a Two Region Economy. *Ann. Reg. Sci.,* 1989, *23*(2), pp. 105–20.

_____ **and Rigby, David L.** Estimating Capital Stocks and Capital Ages in Canada's Regions: 1961–1981. *Reg. Stud.,* April 1989, *23*(2), pp. 117–26.

Andersson, Åke E.; Batten, David F. and Karlsson, Charlie. From the Industrial Age to the Knowledge Economy. In *Andersson, Å. E.; Batten, D. F. and Karlsson, C., eds.,* 1989, pp. 1–13.

_____; **Batten, David F. and Kobayashi, Kiyoshi.** Knowledge, Nodes and Networks: An Analytical Perspective. In *Andersson, Å. E.; Batten, D. F. and Karlsson, C., eds.,* 1989, pp. 31–46.

_____ **and Kobayashi, Kiyoshi.** Some Theoretical Aspects of Spatial Equilibria with Public Goods. In *Andersson, Å. E., et al., eds.,* 1989, pp. 207–21.

Anderstig, Christer and Karlsson, Charlie. Spatial Diffusion of Information Technology in Sweden. In *Andersson, Å. E.; Batten, D. F. and Karlsson, C., eds.,* 1989, pp. 157–76.

_____ **and Mattsson, Lars-Göran.** Interregional Allocation Models of Infrastructure Investments. *Ann. Reg. Sci.,* 1989, *23*(4), pp. 287–98.

Anderton, Bob; Britton, Andrew and Gregg, Paul. The Home Economy. *Nat. Inst. Econ. Rev.,* November 1989, (130), pp. 7–22.

_____; **Britton, Andrew and Gregg, Paul.** The Home Economy. *Nat. Inst. Econ. Rev.,* August 1989, (129), pp. 6–21.

Anderton, Charles H. Arms Race Modeling: Problems and Prospects. *J. Conflict Resolution,* June 1989, *33*(2), pp. 346–67.

Anderton, Douglas L. Starting, Stopping, and Spacing during the Early Stages of Fertility Transition: Comment. *Demography,* August 1989, *26*(3), pp. 467–70.

Andiappan, P. and Chaison, Gary N. An Analysis of the Barriers to Women Becoming Local Union Officers. *J. Lab. Res.,* Spring 1989, *10*(2), pp. 149–62.

Andison, Nancy Brown. Getting Beyond the Management Illusion. *Can. J. Agr. Econ.*, Part 1, December 1989, 37(4), pp. 743–46.

Andjiga, N. G. and Moulen, J. Necessary and Sufficient Conditions for *l*-Stability of Games in Constitutional Form. *Int. J. Game Theory,* 1989, 18(1), pp. 91–110.

Ando, Albert. Consumption, Income, and Interest Rates: Reinterpreting the Time Series Evidence: Comment. In *Blanchard, O. J. and Fischer, S., eds.,* 1989, pp. 234–44.

Andoh, Samuel Kojo and Gately, Dermot. The U.S. Demand for Cocoa: Explaining the Apparent Insignificance of Income Growth. *Appl. Econ.,* November 1989, 21(11), pp. 1421–32.

Andorka, Rudolf. Economic and Social Development and Demographic Changes in Hungary. In *Chakravarty, S., ed.,* 1989, pp. 24–42.

Andre, Rae. Mixed-National Training Programmes: Some Unintended Consequences. In *Davies, J., et al., eds.,* 1989, pp. 211–23.

Andreae, Clemens-August and Koester, Reinhard B. Values and Policies in the Global Economy: A European–American Institutional Challenge. In *Rueschhoff, N. and Schaum, K., eds.,* 1989, pp. 9–20.

_____ **and Skurski, Roger.** Global Values, Institutions and Policies: A Conceptual Framework. In *Rueschhoff, N. and Schaum, K., eds.,* 1989, pp. 1–3.

Andreasjan, R. World Energy Crisis and the Middle East. In *Ferrier, R. W. and Fursenko, A., eds.,* 1989, pp. 37–49.

Andreff, Wladimir. Testing the Soviet-Type Industrialisation Model in Socialist-Oriented Developing Countries. In *Gomulka, S.; Ha, Y.-C. and Kim, C.-O., eds.,* 1989, pp. 183–99.

Andreoni, James. Giving with Impure Altruism: Applications to Charity and Ricardian Equivalence. *J. Polit. Econ.,* December 1989, 97(6), pp. 1447–58.

Andrew, Michael J. An Overview of Research and Development Incentives: Australia. *Bull. Int. Fiscal Doc.,* November 1989, 43(11), pp. 511–17.

Andrews, Clinton J. Anticipating Air Conditioning's Impact on the World's Electricity Producers. *Energy J.,* July 1989, 10(3), pp. 107–20.

Andrews, Donald W. K. Power in Econometric Applications. *Econometrica,* September 1989, 57(5), pp. 1059–90.

Andrews, Frank M. Construct Validity and Error Components of Survey Measures: A Structural Modeling Approach. In *Singer, E. and Presser, S., eds.,* 1989, 1984, pp. 391–424.

Andrews, Neil and Lewis, Philip. Household Demand in China. *Appl. Econ.,* June 1989, 21(6), pp. 793–807.

Andrews, Stephen H. and Nguyen, Sang V. The Effect of Energy Aggregation on Energy Elasticities: Some Evidence from U.S. Manufacturing Data. *Energy J.,* January 1989, 10(1), pp. 149–56.

_____ **and Nguyen, Sang V.** Stage-of-Fabrication Inventory Behavior in Durable Goods Manu-facturing Industries. *J. Post Keynesian Econ.,* Summer 1989, 11(4), pp. 561–88.

_____ **and Nguyen, Sang V.** Stage-of-Fabrication Inventory Behaviour: A General Target-Adjustment Model. *Appl. Econ.,* February 1989, 21(2), pp. 175–92.

Andrikopoulos, Andreas A.; Brox, James A. and Paraskevopoulos, Christos C. Interfuel and Interfactor Substitution in Ontario Manufacturing, 1962–82. *Appl. Econ.,* December 1989, 21(12), pp. 1667–81.

Androkovich, Robert A. An Attempt at Making the Principal–Agent Paradigm Operational. *Europ. Rev. Agr. Econ.,* 1989, 16(2), pp. 285–300.

_____ **and Stollery, K. R.** Regulation of Stochastic Fisheries: A Comparison of Alternative Methods in the Pacific Halibut Fishery. *Marine Resource Econ.,* 1989, 6(2), pp. 109–22.

Aneja, Yash P.; Chandra, Ramesh and Gunay, Erdal. A Portfolio Approach to Estimating the Average Correlation Coefficient for the Constant Correlation Model. *J. Finance,* December 1989, 44(5), pp. 1435–38.

Ang, B. W. Energy End-Use Structure of an Urban Society: The Case of Singapore. *Energy J.,* January 1989, 10(1), pp. 127–37.

Ang, James S. On Merchant Banking. *J. Finan. Services Res.,* October 1989, 3(1), pp. 33–53.

_____ **and Megginson, William L.** Restricted Voting Shares, Ownership Structure, and the Market Value of Dual-Class Firms. *J. Finan. Res.,* Winter 1989, 12(4), pp. 301–18.

Angel, David P. The Labor Market for Engineers in the U.S. Semiconductor Industry. *Econ. Geogr.,* April 1989, 65(2), pp. 99–112.

Angell, Wayne D. and Kelley, Edward W., Jr. Statement to the U.S. House Subcommittee on Domestic Monetary Policy of the Committee on Banking, Finance and Urban Affairs, August 3, 1989. *Fed. Res. Bull.,* October 1989, 75(10), pp. 677–84.

Angelmar, R.; Prahalad, C. K. and Doz, Yves. Assessing the Scope of Innovations: A Dilemma for Top Management. In *Rosenbloom, R. S. and Burgelman, R. A., eds.,* 1989, pp. 257–81.

Angresano, James. An Evolutionary-Institutional Approach to the Study of Comparative Economies. *J. Econ. Issues,* June 1989, 23(2), pp. 511–17.

Angrist, Joshua D. Using the Draft Lottery to Measure the Effect of Military Service on Civilian Labor Market Outcomes. In *Ehrenberg, R. G., ed.,* 1989, pp. 265–310.

Anheier, Helmut K. Private Voluntary Organizations and Development in West Africa: Comparative Perspectives. In *James, E., ed.,* 1989, pp. 339–57.

Anikin, Andrei V. The Soviet Union Joins the International Economy. *Challenge,* May–June 1989, 32(3), pp. 4–9.

Aninat, Eduardo. The Chilean Economy in the Eighties: Adjustment and Recovery: Comment. In *Edwards, S. and Larrain, F., eds.,* 1989, pp. 234–36.

Anker, Martha and Anker, Richard. Measuring the Female Labour Force in Egypt. *Int. Lab. Rev.*, 1989, *128*(4), pp. 511–20.

Anker, Richard and Anker, Martha. Measuring the Female Labour Force in Egypt. *Int. Lab. Rev.*, 1989, *128*(4), pp. 511–20.

Annerstedt, Jan. Industrial Modernists and 'National Programmers' for High Technology. In *Pedersen, J. L., ed.*, 1989, pp. 125–58.

Ansari, Mohammed I. The Dutch Disease: The Canadian Evidence. *Weltwirtsch. Arch.*, 1989, *125*(4), pp. 804–13.

Antal, László. It Must Not Happen Again (Contributions to the Evaluation of the Anti-reform of the Early 1970s). *Acta Oecon.*, 1989, *40*(1–2), pp. 138–49.

Antel, John; Hosek, James R. and Peterson, Christine E. Military Enlistment and Attrition: An Analysis of Decision Reversal. In *Ehrenberg, R. G., ed.*, 1989, pp. 207–63.

Antle, John M. Nonstructural Risk Attitude Estimation. *Amer. J. Agr. Econ.*, August 1989, *71*(3), pp. 774–84.

_____ **and Capalbo, Susan M.** Incorporating Social Costs in the Returns to Agricultural Research. *Amer. J. Agr. Econ.*, May 1989, *71*(2), pp. 458–63.

Anton, James J. and Yao, Dennis A. Split Awards, Procurement, and Innovation. *Rand J. Econ.*, Winter 1989, *20*(4), pp. 538–52.

Antonelli, Cristiano. A Failure-Inducement Model of Research and Development Expenditure: Italian Evidence from the Early 1980s. *J. Econ. Behav. Organ.*, October 1989, *12*(2), pp. 159–80.

_____; **Petit, Pascal and Tahar, Gabriel.** Technological Diffusion and Investment Behaviour: The Case of the Textile Industry. *Weltwirtsch. Arch.*, 1989, *125*(4), pp. 782–803.

Antonides, Gerrit. An Attempt at Integration of Economic and Psychological Theories of Consumption. *J. Econ. Psych.*, March 1989, *10*(1), pp. 77–99.

Antoniou, A. and Rowley, J. C. R. Canadian Corporate Structure: The Importance of Shadow Groups. *S. Afr. J. Econ.*, December 1989, *57*(4), pp. 380–92.

Anušić, Zoran; Škegro, Borislav and Gapinski, James H. Policy Initiatives for Improving Yugoslav Economic Performance. *Int. Econ. J.*, Winter 1989, *3*(4), pp. 95–107.

Anxo, Dominique and Bigsten, Arne. Working Hours and Productivity in Swedish Manufacturing. *Scand. J. Econ.*, 1989, *91*(3), pp. 613–19.

Anyadike-Danes, Michael and Godley, Wynne. Real Wages and Employment: A Sceptical View of Some Recent Empirical Work. *Manchester Sch. Econ. Soc. Stud.*, June 1989, *57*(2), pp. 172–87.

_____ **and Godley, Wynne.** Real Wages and Employment: Response. *Manchester Sch. Econ. Soc. Stud.*, September 1989, *57*(3), pp. 285.

Aoki, Kunihiko. Marx, Socialism and Innovation. In *Berliner, J. S.; Kosta, H. G. J. and Hakogi, M., eds.*, 1989, pp. 133–44.

Aoki, Masahiko. The Nature of the Japanese Firm as a Nexus of Employment and Financial Contracts: An Overview. *J. Japanese Int. Economies*, December 1989, *3*(4), pp. 345–66.

_____ **and Rosenberg, Nathan.** The Japanese Firm as an Innovating Institution. In *Shiraishi, T. and Tsuru, S., eds.*, 1989, pp. 137–54.

Aoki, Masanao and Havenner, Arthur M. A Method for Approximate Representation of Vector-Valued Time Series and Its Relation to Two Alternatives. *J. Econometrics*, October 1989, *42*(2), pp. 181–99.

Aoki, Torao. Administrative and Compliance Costs of Taxation: Japan. In *International Fiscal Association, ed. (I)*, 1989, pp. 437–60.

Apedaile, Leonard P. and Calkins, Peter H. Development Theory and Chinese Agricultural Development. *Can. J. Agr. Econ.*, Part 2, December 1989, *37*(4), pp. 953–74.

_____ **and Li, Y.** A Simulation of Economic Effects of Technology Transfer in Cereal Production: A Reply. *Can. J. Agr. Econ.*, November 1989, *37*(3), pp. 547–48.

Apostolou, Nicholas; Kee, Robert and Robbins, Walter. Capital Budgeting Practices of U.S. Cities: A Survey. In *Matzer, J., Jr., ed.*, 1989, *1987*, pp. 100–109.

Appadurai, Arjun. Small-Scale Techniques and Large-Scale Objectives. In *Bardhan, P., ed. (I)*, 1989, pp. 250–82.

Appel, Peter A. Administrative Procedure and the Internal Revenue Service: Delimiting the Substantial Understatement Penalty. *Yale Law J.*, May 1989, *98*(7), pp. 1435–56.

Appelbaum, Eileen. The Growth in the U.S. Contingent Labour Force. In *Drago, R. and Perlman, R., eds.*, 1989, pp. 62–82.

Appleyard, Dennis R.; Conway, Patrick J. and Field, Alfred J., Jr. The Effects of Customs Unions on the Pattern and Terms of Trade in a Ricardian Model with a Continuum of Goods. *J. Int. Econ.*, August 1989, *27*(1–2), pp. 147–64.

_____; **Field, Alfred J., Jr. and Conway, Patrick J.** Trade Agreements vs. Unilateral Tariff Reductions: Evidence from Modeling with a Continuum of Goods. *Int. Econ. Rev.*, November 1989, *30*(4), pp. 775–94.

Apps, Patricia. Welfare Options under Less Progressive Tax Rates: An Analysis of Distributional Effects for Working Families. *Australian Econ. Rev.*, Summer 1989, (88), pp. 52–65.

_____ **and Savage, Elizabeth.** Labour Supply, Welfare Rankings and the Measurement of Inequality. *J. Public Econ.*, August 1989, *39*(3), pp. 335–64.

Arabsheibani, Gholamreza. The Wiles Test Revisited. *Econ. Letters*, 1989, *29*(4), pp. 361–64.

Aradhyula, Satheesh V. and Holt, Matthew T. Risk Behavior and Rational Expectations in the U.S. Broiler Market. *Amer. J. Agr. Econ.*, November 1989, *71*(4), pp. 892–902.

Araghi, Farshad A. Land Reform Policies in Iran: Comment. *Amer. J. Agr. Econ.*, November 1989, *71*(4), pp. 1046–49.

Arai, Kazuhiro. A Cross-sectional Analysis of the

Determinants of Enrollment in Higher Education in Japan. *Hitotsubashi J. Econ.*, December 1989, *30*(2), pp. 101–20.

_____. A Theory of Employment Structure. *Hitotsubashi J. Econ.*, June 1989, *30*(1), pp. 49–63.

Arai, Mahmood. Monitoring and Additional Wages in Labour Extraction. *J. Econ. Behav. Organ.*, January 1989, *11*(1), pp. 115–25.

Araiza, William D. Notice-and-Comment Rights for Administrative Decisions Affecting International Trade: Heightened Need, No Response. *Yale Law J.*, December 1989, *99*(3), pp. 669–87.

Araji, A. A. Return to Public Investment in Wheat Research in the Western United States. *Can. J. Agr. Econ.*, November 1989, *37*(3), pp. 467–79.

Araki, Toshihiro. Information Technology and Legal Issues. In *Jussawalla, M.; Okuma, T. and Araki, T.*, eds., 1989, pp. 193–96.

Aranko, Jorma. Bankinspektionens roll på en förändrad finansieringsmarknad. (The Role of the Bank Inspectorate on a Changed Financial Market. With English summary.) *Ekon. Samfundets Tidskr.*, 1989, *42*(3), pp. 179–84.

Aranoff, Gerald. Output-Flexibility and Diverse Technology. *Scot. J. Polit. Econ.*, May 1989, *36*(2), pp. 141–59.

Aranson, Peter H. The Democratic Order and Public Choice. In *Brennan, G. and Lomasky, L. E.*, eds., 1989, pp. 97–148.

Araujo, A. and Monteiro, P. K. Equilibrium without Uniform Conditions. *J. Econ. Theory*, August 1989, *48*(2), pp. 416–27.

de Araújo, João Lizardo and da Motta, Ronaldo Serôa. Decomposição dos efeitos de intensidade energética no setor industrial brasileiro. (With English summary.) *Pesquisa Planejamento Econ.*, April 1989, *19*(1), pp. 113–31.

de Araujo, José Tavares, Jr. Os mercados intersetoriais da ecnomia brasileira nos anos 70. (With English summary.) *Pesquisa Planejamento Econ.*, December 1989, *19*(3), pp. 579–95.

Araujo, Luis and Easton, Geoffrey. The Network Approach: An Articulation. In *Hallén, L. and Johanson, J.*, eds., 1989, pp. 97–119.

_____, et al. Social Approaches to the Competitive Process. In *Francis, A. and Tharakan, P. K. M.*, eds., 1989, pp. 137–64.

Araya, Kensei. Soviet Economic Reform and Technical Progress: Discussion. In *Berliner, J. S.; Kosta, H. G. J. and Hakogi, M.*, eds., 1989, pp. 52–54.

Arbatov, Alexei. Concepts of Conventional Stability and Reductions of Arms in Europe. In *Altmann, J. and Rotblat, J.*, eds., 1989, pp. 126–30.

Arbetman, Marina and Kugler, Jacek. Exploring the "Phoenix Factor" with the Collective Goods Perspective. *J. Conflict Resolution*, March 1989, *33*(1), pp. 84–112.

Arbib, Claudio. A Polynomial Algorithm for Partitioning Line-Graphs. In *Simeone, B.*, ed., 1989, pp. 198–208.

_____; **Lucertini, M. and Nicolò, F.** Optimiza-tion Models for Flexible Manufacturing Systems. In *Archetti, F.; Lucertini, M. and Serafini, P.*, eds., 1989, pp. 75–89.

Arcelli, Mario. Credit Constraints and Investment Finance: Some Evidence from Greece: Comment. In *Monti, M.*, ed., 1989, pp. 183–87.

_____. Monetary and Fiscal Policies in Italy in the Present Phase of Transition towards Europe. *Rev. Econ. Cond. Italy*, May–Aug. 1989, (2), pp. 201–07.

Archetti, F. and Sciomachen, A. Development, Analysis and Simulation of Petri Net Models: An Application to AGV Systems. In *Archetti, F.; Lucertini, M. and Serafini, P.*, eds., 1989, pp. 91–113.

Archibald, G. C. and Eaton, B. Curtis. Two Applications of Characteristics Theory. In *Feiwel, G. R.*, ed. (*I*), 1989, pp. 409–36.

Archibald, Robert B. and Elliott, Catherine S. Subjective Framing and Attitudes towards Risk. *J. Econ. Psych.*, November 1989, *10*(3), pp. 321–28.

_____ **and Elliott, Catherine S.** Trial-and-Error Learning and Economic Models. *Kyklos*, 1989, *42*(1), pp. 39–59.

Archibugi, Daniele and Santarelli, Enrico. Tecnologia e struttura del commercio internazionale: La posizione dell'Italia. (Technology and Trade Structure: The Case of Italy. With English summary.) *Ricerche Econ.*, Oct.–Dec. 1989, *43*(4), pp. 427–55.

Arda, Mehmet. South–South Trade in Agricultural Products. In *Ventura-Dias, V.*, ed., 1989, pp. 110–30.

Ardeni, Pier Giorgio. Does the Law of One Price Really Hold for Commodity Prices? *Amer. J. Agr. Econ.*, August 1989, *71*(3), pp. 661–69.

_____ **and Lubian, Diego.** Co-integration and Trend Reversion in Purchasing Power Parity. *Giorn. Econ.*, March–April 1989, *48*(3–4), pp. 109–28.

_____ **and Lubian, Diego.** Purchasing Power Parity during the 1920s. *Econ. Letters*, October 1989, *30*(4), pp. 357–62.

Arellano, Manuel. An Efficient GLS Estimator of Triangular Models with Covariance Restrictions. *J. Econometrics*, October 1989, *42*(2), pp. 267–73.

_____. A Note on the Anderson–Hsiao Estimator for Panel Data. *Econ. Letters*, December 1989, *31*(4), pp. 337–41.

_____. On the Efficient Estimation of Simultaneous Equations with Covariance Restrictions. *J. Econometrics*, October 1989, *42*(2), pp. 247–65.

Arena, Richard. Keynes après Lucas: Quelques enseignements récents de la macroéconomie monétaire. (Keynes after Lucas: Some Recent Conclusions of Monetary Economics. With English summary.) *Écon. Societes*, April–May 1989, *23*(4–5), pp. 13–42.

_____. A propos du "Détour de valeur." (Comment on "Détour de valeur." With English summary.) *Revue Écon.*, January 1989, *40*(1), pp. 89–109.

Arestis, Philip. On the Post Keynesian Challenge to Neoclassical Economics: A Complete Quantitative Macro-model for the U.K. Economy. *J. Post Keynesian Econ.*, Summer 1989, *11*(4), pp. 611–29.

_____ **and Marshall, Michael Graham.** 'Reaganomics' and Supply-Side Economics: A British View. *J. Econ. Issues*, December 1989, *23*(4), pp. 965–75.

_____ **and Skuse, Frank.** Austerity Policies and the New Right: Recent UK Experience. *Écon. Appl.*, 1989, *42*(1), pp. 171–202.

d'Arge, Ralph C. and Shogren, Jason F. Nonmarket Asset Prices: A Comparison of Three Valuation Approaches. In *Folmer, H. and van Ierland, E., eds.*, 1989, pp. 15–36.

Argimón, Isabel and Molina, Ascensión. El impuesto sobre el matrimonio. (With English summary.) *Invest. Econ.*, January 1989, *13*(1), pp. 67–83.

_____; **Valdés, Teófilo and Raymond, José Luis.** Evolución de la recaudación en el IRPF: Determinación de las causas y estimación de efectos. (With English summary.) *Invest. Econ.*, January 1989, *13*(1), pp. 15–43.

Argy, Victor. Financial Integration, Short Run Exchange Rate Volatility in Portfolio Balance Models. *Australian Econ. Pap.*, June 1989, *28*(52), pp. 29–38.

Argyris, Chris. The Discipline of Management and Academic Defensive Routines. In *Mansfield, R., ed.*, 1989, pp. 8–20.

Ariff, Mohamed. The Changing Role of ASEAN in the Coming Decades: Post-Manila-Summit Perspectives. In *Shinohara, M. and Lo, F., eds.*, 1989, pp. 154–73.

_____. Privatisation: Singapore's Experience in Perspective: A Financial Management Perspective. In *Thynne, I. and Ariff, M., eds.*, 1989, pp. 83–99.

_____. Trade and Economic Cooperation in the Asain-Pacific Region: Comment. In *Shinohara, M. and Lo, F., eds.*, 1989, pp. 463–65.

_____. TRIMs: A North–South Divide or a Non-issue? *World Econ.*, September 1989, *12*(3), pp. 347–60.

_____. The U.S.–ASEAN Free Trade Area Option: Scope and Implications. In *Schott, J. J., ed.*, 1989, pp. 201–16.

Arize, Augustine. An Econometric Investigation of Money Demand Behavior in Four Asian Developing Countries. *Int. Econ. J.*, Winter 1989, *3*(4), pp. 79–93.

van Ark, Bart and Maddison, Angus. International Comparison of Purchasing Power, Real Output and Labour Productivity: A Case Study of Brazilian, Mexican and U.S. Manufacturing, 1975. *Rev. Income Wealth*, March 1989, *35*(1), pp. 31–55.

Armentano, Dominick T. Antitrust and Insurance: Should the McCarran Act Be Repealed? *Cato J.*, Winter 1989, *8*(3), pp. 729–49.

_____. Antitrust Reform: Predatory Practices and the Competitive Process. In *Rothbard, M. N. and Block, W., eds.*, 1989, pp. 61–74.

Armitage, Jane and Schramm, Gunter. Managing the Supply of and Demand for Fuelwood in Africa. In *Schramm, G. and Warford, J. J., eds.*, 1989, pp. 139–71.

Armstrong, Glen W. and Phillips, William E. The Optimal Timing of Land Use Changes from Forestry to Agriculture. *Can. J. Agr. Econ.*, March 1989, *37*(1), pp. 125–34.

Armstrong, Harvey. Community Regional Policy. In *Lodge, J., ed.*, 1989, pp. 167–85.

Armstrong, J. Scott. Combining Forecasts: The End of the Beginning or the Beginning of the End? *Int. J. Forecasting*, 1989, *5*(4), pp. 585–88.

_____. Reflections on Forecasting in the 1980's: Editorial. *Int. J. Forecasting*, 1989, *5*(4), pp. 467–68.

_____ **and Dakin, Stephen.** Predicting Job Performance: A Comparison of Expert Opinion and Research Findings. *Int. J. Forecasting*, 1989, *5*(2), pp. 187–94.

Arnade, Carlos A. and Davison, Cecil W. Testing for Aggregation and Simultaneous Bias in U.S. Soybean Export Equations. *Southern J. Agr. Econ.*, December 1989, *21*(2), pp. 129–37.

_____; **Hallahan, Charles B. and Davison, Cecil W.** Box–Cox Estimation of U.S. Soybean Exports. *J. Agr. Econ. Res.*, Summer 1989, *41*(3), pp. 8–16.

Arnaudo, Aldo A. Expectativas inflacionarias de los ejecutivos de finanzas Argentina. 1983–1985. (Inflationary Expectations of the Financing Executives. Argentina 1983–1985. With English summary.) *Económica (La Plata)*, 1989, *35*(1–2), pp. 3–14.

Arndt, H. W. Mr Hicks's Trade Cycle Theory. In *Wood, J. C. and Woods, R. N., eds., Vol. 1*, 1989, *1951*, pp. 132–45.

Arndt, Sven. The Impact of Microeconomic Policies on European Unemployment. *J. Lab. Res.*, Winter 1989, *10*(1), pp. 45–50.

Arnfred, Niels; Hansen, Annegrethe and Pedersen, Jørgen Lindgaard. Bio-technology and Politics, Danish Experiences. In *Pedersen, J. L., ed.*, 1989, pp. 159–84.

Arnold, Barry C. and Press, S. James. Bayesian Estimation and Prediction for Pareto Data. *J. Amer. Statist. Assoc.*, December 1989, *84*(408), pp. 1079–84.

_____ **and Villaseñor, José A.** Elliptical Lorenz Curves. *J. Econometrics*, February 1989, *40*(2), pp. 327–38.

Arnold, Brian J. The Impact of Tax Reform on International Capital Flows and Investment: Comment. In *Mintz, J. and Whalley, J., eds.*, 1989, pp. 218–22.

Arnold, Michael H. and Austin, Roger B. Plant Breeding and Yield Stability. In *Anderson, J. R. and Hazell, P. B. R., eds.*, 1989, pp. 127–32.

_____ **and Austin, Roger B.** Variability in Wheat Yields in England: Analysis and Future Prospects. In *Anderson, J. R. and Hazell, P. B. R., eds.*, 1989, pp. 101–06.

Arnold, Roger A. and Wyrick, Thomas L. Earmarking as a Deterrent to Rent-Seeking. *Public Choice*, March 1989, *60*(3), pp. 283–91.

Arnon, Arie. The Early Tooke and Ricardo: A Political Alliance and First Signs of Theoretical Disagreements. *Hist. Polit. Econ.*, Spring 1989, *21*(1), pp. 1–14.

Arnott, Richard J. Housing Vacancies, Thin Markets, and Idiosyncratic Tastes. *J. Real Estate Finance Econ.*, February 1989, *2*(1), pp. 5–30.

_____ **and Stiglitz, Joseph E.** Congestion Pricing to Improve Air Travel Safety. In *Moses, L. N. and Savage, I.*, eds., 1989, pp. 167–85.

Arnott, Robert D. The Future for Quantitative Investment Products: Reply. *J. Portfol. Manage.*, Winter 1989, *15*(2), pp. 79.

_____, **et al.** Forecasting Factor Returns: An Intriguing Possibility. *J. Portfol. Manage.*, Fall 1989, *16*(1), pp. 28–35.

Arnould, Eric J. Toward a Broadened Theory of Preference Formation and the Diffusion of Innovations: Cases from Zinder Province, Niger Republic. *J. Cons. Res.*, September 1989, *16*(2), pp. 239–67.

Aronson, Jonathan D. Market Access and Telecommunication Services. In *Robinson, P.; Sauvant, K. P. and Govitrikar, V. P.*, eds., 1989, pp. 239–55.

_____. Trade Negotiations, Telecom Services, and Interdependence. In *Jussawalla, M.; Okuma, T. and Araki, T.*, eds., 1989, pp. 137–49.

Aronson, Lisa. To Weave or Not to Weave: Apprenticeship Rules among the Akwete Igbo of Nigeria and the Baule of the Ivory Coast. In *Coy, M. W.*, ed., 1989, pp. 149–62.

Arora, Harjit and Smyth, David J. A Temporary Equilibrium Model of the Mortgage Market. *J. Macroecon.*, Spring 1989, *11*(2), pp. 261–68.

Arora, Harjit K. and Dua, Pami. Do Expected Budget Deficits Affect Household Expectations of Interest Rates? *J. Macroecon.*, Fall 1989, *11*(4), pp. 551–62.

Arriagada, Ana Maria and Psacharopoulos, George. The Determinants of Early Age Human Capital Formation: Evidence from Brazil. *Econ. Devel. Cult. Change*, July 1989, *37*(4), pp. 683–708.

Arriazu, Ricardo. Fiscal Adjustment, Debt Management, and Conditionality: Comment. In *Monti, M.*, ed., 1989, pp. 138–47.

Arrighi, Giovanni. Custom and Innovation: Long Waves and Stages of Capitalist Development. In *Di Matteo, M.; Goodwin, R. M. and Vercelli, A.*, eds., 1989, pp. 89–113.

_____; **Keyder, Çağlar and Wallerstein, Immanuel.** Southern Europe in the World Economy in the Twentieth Century: Implications for Political and Social Transformations. In *Martin, M. T. and Kandal, T. R.*, eds., 1989, pp. 409–17.

Arrondel, Luc and Masson, André. Déterminants individuels de la composition du patrimoine: France 1980. (Individual Factors of Wealth Composition: France 1980. With English summary.) *Revue Écon.*, May 1989, *40*(3), pp. 441–502.

Arrow, Kenneth J. The State of Economic Science: Views of Six Nobel Laureates: Dr. Kenneth J. Arrow. In *Sichel, W.*, ed., 1989, pp. 11–22.

_____. Uncertainty and the Welfare Economics of Medical Care. In *Diamond, P. and Rothschild, M.*, eds., 1989, *1963*, pp. 347–75.

_____. Von Neumann and the Existence Theorem for General Equilibrium. In *Dore, M.; Chakravarty, S. and Goodwin, R.*, eds., 1989, pp. 15–28.

_____ **and Lind, Robert C.** Uncertainty and the Evaluation of Public Investment Decisions. In *Diamond, P. and Rothschild, M.*, eds., 1989, *1970*, pp. 405–19.

Arshad, Fatimah Mohd. Policy Options for Improving the Functioning of the World Food Production and Distribution Systems: Reaction. In *Helmuth, J. W. and Johnson, S. R.*, eds., Vol. 1, 1989, pp. 235–37.

_____ **and Chong, Eddie Chiew Fook.** Food Trade among Developing Countries. In *Helmuth, J. W. and Johnson, S. R.*, eds., Vol. 2, 1989, pp. 276–302.

Arshad, Mohammad Fayyaz. Regional Patterns of Industrialisation in Pakistan. *Pakistan Econ. Soc. Rev.*, Summer 1989, *27*(1), pp. 17–31.

Arshadi, Nasser. Capital Structure, Agency Problems, and Deposit Insurance in Banking Firms. *Financial Rev.*, February 1989, *24*(1), pp. 31–52.

_____; **Lawrence, Edward C. and Kummer, Donald R.** Incentive Problems in Bank Insider Borrowing. *J. Finan. Services Res.*, October 1989, *3*(1), pp. 17–31.

Arshanapalli, Bala G. and Dalal, Ardeshir J. Effects of Expected Cash and Futures Prices on Hedging and Production: Comments and Extensions. *J. Futures Markets*, August 1989, *9*(4), pp. 337–45.

Artana, Daniel A. Las regulaciones a los hidrocarburos en la Argentina. El costo de los controles de precios. (With English summary.) *Cuadernos Econ.*, August 1989, *26*(78), pp. 263–80.

Arthur, W. Brian. Competing Technologies, Increasing Returns, and Lock-In by Historical Events. *Econ. J.*, March 1989, *99*(394), pp. 116–31.

Artis, Michael J. International Economic Policy Co-ordination: Theory and Practice. *Oxford Rev. Econ. Policy*, Autumn 1989, *5*(3), pp. 83–93.

_____. Wage Inflation. In *Greenaway, D.*, ed., 1989, pp. 91–109.

_____ **and Gazioglu, S.** Modelling Asymmetric Exchange Rate Unions: A Stylized Model of the EMS. *Greek Econ. Rev.*, 1989, *11*(1), pp. 177–202.

_____ **and Taylor, Mark P.** Abolishing Exchange Control: The UK Experience. *Greek Econ. Rev.*, 1989, *11*(1), pp. 19–48.

_____ **and Taylor, Mark P.** The Achievements of the European Monetary System. *Econ. Soc. Rev.*, January 1989, *20*(2), pp. 121–45.

_____ **and Taylor, Mark P.** Some Issues Concerning the Long-Run Credibility of the European Monetary System. In *MacDonald, R. and Taylor, M. P.*, eds., 1989, pp. 295–306.

Artle, Roland. Micro–Macro Interactions and U.S. Industrial Change. In *Andersson, Å. E.; Batten, D. F. and Karlsson, C., eds.*, 1989, pp. 291–96.

Artoni, Roberto. Keynes: politiche fiscali e disavanzi strutturali. (With English summary.) *Politica. Econ.*, December 1989, *5*(3), pp. 345–87.

—— **and Lippi, Marco.** Nota sulla ripresa di un punto di vista keynesiano in macroeconomia. (A Neo-Keynesian Perspective in Macroeconomics. With English summary.) *Politica. Econ.*, August 1989, *5*(2), pp. 221–30.

Artstein, Zvi and Wets, Roger J.-B. Decentralized Allocation of Resources among Many Producers. *J. Math. Econ.*, 1989, *18*(4), pp. 303–24.

Artus, Patrick. De la rigueur salariale ou existe-t-il un salaire réel "optimal"? (On the Existence of an "Optimal" Real Wage. With English summary.) *Ann. Écon. Statist.*, Jan.–March 1989, (13), pp. 77–91.

——. Désintermédiation, déréglementation, efficacité des politiques économiques et stabilité de l'économie. (Desintermediation, Deregulation, Efficiency of Economics Policies and Stability of the Economy. With English summary.) *Écon. Societes*, April–May 1989, *23*(4–5), pp. 71–109.

—— **and Bleuze, Eric.** Les choix de portefeuille des ménages en France. (With English summary.) *Rech. Écon. Louvain*, 1989, *55*(2), pp. 129–53.

Arvan, Lanny. Endogenous Monitoring Intensity, the Period of Contractual Precommitment, and the Slope of the Wage-Earnings Profile. *Econ. Letters*, 1989, *29*(2), pp. 173–77.

——. Optimal Labor Contracts with On-the-Job Search: Are Involuntary Layoffs Used as an Incentive Device to Make Workers Search Harder? *J. Lab. Econ.*, April 1989, *7*(2), pp. 147–69.

Arzac, Enrique R. Income Insurance with Uncertain Output. *Int. Econ. Rev.*, August 1989, *30*(3), pp. 561–69.

Asabere, Paul K.; Hachey, George and Grubaugh, Stephen G. Architecture, Historic Zoning, and the Value of Homes. *J. Real Estate Finance Econ.*, September 1989, *2*(3), pp. 181–95.

Asada, Toichiro. Monetary Stabilization Policy in a Keynes–Goodwin Model of the Growth Cycle. In *Semmler, W., ed.*, 1989, pp. 145–67.

Asami, Yasushi. An Axiomatic Approach to a Measure of Land-Use Mixture. *Environ. Planning A*, April 1989, *21*(4), pp. 509–22.

—— **and Isard, Walter.** Imperfect Information, Uncertainty and Optimal Sampling in Location Theory: An Initial Reexamination of Hotelling, Weber and von Thünen. *J. Reg. Sci.*, November 1989, *29*(4), pp. 507–21.

Asano, Chooichiro; Matsuda, Yoshiro and Matsui, Sachiko. A System for Generating Publication Statistics Based on Bibliographic Information—Bibliometric Analysis for the Development of Economic and Social Thought.

Hitotsubashi J. Econ., December 1989, *30*(2), pp. 121–56.

Asanuma, Banri. Manufacturer–Supplier Relationships in Japan and the Concept of Relation-Specific Skill. *J. Japanese Int. Economies*, March 1989, *3*(1), pp. 1–30.

Asch, Peter and Levy, David T. Speeding, Coordination, and the 55-MPH Limit: Comment. *Amer. Econ. Rev.*, September 1989, *79*(4), pp. 913–15.

Aschauer, David Alan. Does Public Capital Crowd Out Private Capital? *J. Monet. Econ.*, September 1989, *24*(2), pp. 171–88.

——. Is Public Expenditure Productive? *J. Monet. Econ.*, March 1989, *23*(2), pp. 177–200.

Ascher, William. Beyond Accuracy. *Int. J. Forecasting*, 1989, *5*(4), pp. 469–84.

Ash, Ronald A., et al. Job Applicant Training and Work Experience Evaluation in Personnel Selection. In *Ferris, G. R. and Rowland, K. M., eds.*, 1989, pp. 183–226.

Ashcraft, Marie L. F. and Thomas, J. William. Measuring Severity of Illness: A Comparison of Interrater Reliability among Severity Methodologies. *Inquiry*, Winter 1989, *26*(4), pp. 483–92.

Ashcroft, Brian and Love, J. H. Evaluating the Effects of External Takeover on the Performance of Regional Companies: The Case of Scotland, 1965 to 1980. *Environ. Planning A*, February 1989, *21*(2), pp. 197–220.

—— **and McGregor, Peter G.** The Demand for Industrial Development Certificates and the Effect of Regional Policy. *Reg. Stud.*, August 1989, *23*(4), pp. 301–13.

Ashenfelter, Orley. Evidence on U.S. Experiences with Dispute Resolution Systems. In *Huang, W.-C., ed.*, 1989, pp. 139–62.

——. How Auctions Work for Wine and Art. *J. Econ. Perspectives*, Summer 1989, *3*(3), pp. 23–36.

Asher, Mukul G. Privatisation: Singapore's Experience in Perspective: An Economic Perspective. In *Thynne, I. and Ariff, M., eds.*, 1989, pp. 59–82.

——. Tax Reforms in East Asian Developing Countries: Motivations, Directions, and Implications. *Asian-Pacific Econ. Lit.*, March 1989, *3*(1), pp. 39–63.

Ashford, Susan J. Self-Assessments in Organizations: A Literature Review and Integrative Model. In *Cummings, L. L. and Staw, B. M., eds.*, 1989, pp. 133–74.

Ashley, Richard A. and Patterson, Douglas M. Linear versus Nonlinear Macroeconomies: A Statistical Test. *Int. Econ. Rev.*, August 1989, *30*(3), pp. 685–704.

Ashoff, Guido. Die historische Entwicklungssequenz kleiner Industrieländer als Modell für heutige kleine Entwicklungsländer? Ein Beitrag zur Diskussion über Entwicklungsnachteile kleiner Länder. (The Historical Development Pattern of Small Industrialized Countries as a Model for Today's Small Developing Countries? A Contribution to the Debate on Development Disadvantages of Small Countries. With English summary.) *Konjunkturpolitik*, 1989, *35*(4), pp. 213–50.

Ashraf, Javed. Updating Estimates of Union Nonunion Wage Differentials in the United States. *Econ. Letters*, December 1989, *31*(2), pp. 205–09.

Ashton, David. Management Development in a British Multi-national Company. In *Davies, J., et al., eds.*, 1989, pp. 199–210.

Ashton, R. K. A Note on the Role of the Average Cost Curve in the Neoclassical Theory of the Firm. *Managerial Dec. Econ.*, March 1989, *10*(1), pp. 77–79.

_____. Production and Short-run Decision Making in a Neo-classical Context. *Managerial Dec. Econ.*, December 1989, *10*(4), pp. 321–26.

Ashton, Robert H. and Wright, Arnold. Identifying Audit Adjustments with Attention-Directing Procedures. *Accounting Rev.*, October 1989, *64*(4), pp. 710–28.

Ashtor, E. The Factors of Technological and Industrial Progress in the Later Middle Ages. *J. Europ. Econ. Hist.*, Spring 1989, *18*(1), pp. 7–36.

Asimakopulos, Athanasios. Financing Social Security—Who Pays? *J. Post Keynesian Econ.*, Summer 1989, *11*(4), pp. 655–60.

_____. Harrod and Robinson on the Equilibrium Rate of Growth. *Banca Naz. Lavoro Quart. Rev.*, September 1989, (170), pp. 345–58.

_____. Kalecki and Robinson. In *Sebastiani, M., ed.*, 1989, pp. 10–24.

_____. Kalecki and Robinson: An "Outsider's" Influence. *J. Post Keynesian Econ.*, Winter 1988–89, *11*(2), pp. 261–78.

_____. Kalecki and the Determinants of Profits: United States Profits in the Reagan Years. In *Davidson, P. and Kregel, J., eds.*, 1989, pp. 256–69.

_____. The Nature and Role of Equilibrium in Keynes's General Theory. *Australian Econ. Pap.*, June 1989, *28*(52), pp. 16–28.

Aslanbeigui, Nahid. Marshall's and Pigou's Policy Prescriptions on Unemployment, Socialism and Inequality. In *Walker, D. A., ed.*, 1989, pp. 191–204.

_____ **and Summerfield, Gale.** Impact of the Responsibility System on Women in Rural China: An Application of Sen's Theory of Entitlements. *World Devel.*, March 1989, *17*(3), pp. 343–50.

Asp, Erkki. Reduction and Flexibility of Working Time in Finland and Its Consequences. In *Agassi, J. B. and Heycock, S., eds.*, 1989, pp. 263–72.

Asprem, Mads. Stock Prices, Asset Portfolios and Macroeconomic Variables in Ten European Countries. *J. Banking Finance*, September 1989, *13*(4–5), pp. 589–612.

d'Aspremont, Claude. CORE as a Macrocosm of Game-Theoretic Research, 1967–1987: Comments: What Is Bob Aumann Trying to Accomplish? In *Cornet, B. and Tulkens, H., eds.*, 1989, pp. 16–18.

_____; **Dos Santos Ferreira, Rodolphe and Gérard-Varet, Louis-André.** Unemployment in a

Cournot Oligopoly Model with Ford Effects. *Rech. Écon. Louvain*, 1989, *55*(1), pp. 33–60.

_____; **Dos Santos Ferreira, Rodolphe and Gérard-Varet, Louis-André.** Unemployment in an Extended Cournot Oligopoly Model. *Oxford Econ. Pap.*, July 1989, *41*(3), pp. 490–505.

Aspromourgos, Tony. The Logic of Economic Austerity. *Écon. Appl.*, 1989, *42*(1), pp. 23–45.

_____. The Theory of Production and Distribution in Cantillon's *Essai*. *Oxford Econ. Pap.*, April 1989, *41*(2), pp. 356–73.

Asquith, Paul; Healy, Paul and Palepu, Krishna G. Earnings and Stock Splits. *Accounting Rev.*, July 1989, *64*(3), pp. 387–403.

_____; **Mullins, David W., Jr. and Wolff, Eric D.** Original Issue High Yield Bonds: Aging Analyses of Defaults, Exchanges, and Calls. *J. Finance*, September 1989, *44*(4), pp. 923–52.

Asra, Abuzar. Inequality Trends in Indonesia, 1969–1981: A Re-examination. *Bull. Indonesian Econ. Stud.*, August 1989, *25*(2), pp. 100–110.

Assar, Nasir H. and Kymn, Kern O. The Impact of the Declining Saving Rate on the Great Ratios of Economics. *Rivista Int. Sci. Econ. Com.*, January 1989, *36*(1), pp. 29–38.

Asselain, Jean-Charles. Continuités, traumatismes, mutations. (The French Economy in the Revolutionary Storm: Continuity and Change. With English summary.) *Revue Écon.*, November 1989, *40*(6), pp. 1137–88.

Assmann, Georg; Nagel, Detlev and Stollberg, Rudhard. The Introduction of New Technology in Industrial Enterprises of the German Democratic Republic: Two Case Studies. In *Francis, A. and Grootings, P., eds.*, 1989, pp. 61–87.

Assouline, Gérald. Concentration, innovation, pratiques concurrentielles dans l'industrie des phytosanitaires. (Concentration, Innovation, Competition Practices in the Phytosanitary Industry. With English summary.) *Écon. Societes*, July 1989, *23*(7), pp. 107–34.

Assouline, Mireille; Epaulard, Anne and Moncomble, Jean-Eudes. Alignement des régimes de TVA français sur une norme européenne, l'analyse du modèle Hermès-France. (With English summary.) *Revue Écon. Politique*, May–June 1989, *99*(3), pp. 497–516.

Astorga Lira, Enrique and Commander, Simon. Agricultural Commercialisation and the Growth of a Migrant Labour Market in Mexico. *Int. Lab. Rev.*, Special Issue, 1989, *128*(6), pp. 769–89.

Åström, Sven-Erik. Britain's Timber Imports from the Baltic, 1775–1830: Some New Figures and Viewpoints. *Scand. Econ. Hist. Rev.*, 1989, *37*(1), pp. 57–71.

Atack, Jeremy and Bateman, Fred. Land and the Development of Mid–Nineteenth Century American Agriculture in the Northern States. In *Grantham, G. and Leonard, C. S., eds.*, Pt. B, 1989, pp. 279–312.

Ateş, Hüseyin and Kirim, Arman. Technical

Change and Technological Capability in the Turkish Textile Sector. *METU*, 1989, *16*(1–2), pp. 1–30.

Atherton, Terry; Train, Kenneth E. and Ben-Akiva, Moshe. Consumption Patterns and Self-selecting Tariffs. *Rev. Econ. Statist.*, February 1989, *71*(1), pp. 62–73.

Athukorala, Premachandra and Bandara, Jayatilleke S. Growth of Manufactured Exports, Primary Commodity Dependence, and Net Export Earnings: Sri Lanka. *World Devel.*, June 1989, *17*(6), pp. 897–903.

Atkins, F. J. Co-integration, Error Correction and the Fisher Effect. *Appl. Econ.*, December 1989, *21*(12), pp. 1611–20.

_____; **Kerr, William A. and McGivern, D. B.** A Note on Structural Change in Canadian Beef Demand. *Can. J. Agr. Econ.*, November 1989, *37*(3), pp. 513–24.

Atkinson, Anthony B. Analysis of a Partial Basic Income Scheme. In *Atkinson, A. B.*, 1989, pp. 327–35.

_____. The Analysis of Personal Taxation and Social Security. In *Atkinson, A. B.*, 1989, *1983*, pp. 286–308.

_____. The Cost of Social Dividend and Tax Credit Schemes. In *Atkinson, A. B.*, 1989, pp. 309–26.

_____. Family Income Supplement and Two-Parent Families, 1971–1980. In *Atkinson, A. B.*, 1989, pp. 208–24.

_____. How Should We Measure Poverty? Some Conceptual Issues. In *Atkinson, A. B.*, 1989, pp. 7–24.

_____. Inter-generational Continuities in Deprivation. In *Atkinson, A. B.*, 1989, pp. 77–86.

_____. On the Measurement of Poverty. In *Atkinson, A. B.*, 1989, *1987*, pp. 25–39.

_____. Poverty in Britain from the 1930s to the 1980s. In *Atkinson, A. B.*, 1989, pp. 40–61.

_____. Poverty in York: A Re-analysis of Rowntree's 1950 Survey. In *Atkinson, A. B.*, 1989, *1981*, pp. 62–76.

_____. The Poverty Trap in Britain. In *Atkinson, A. B.*, 1989, pp. 181–89.

_____. Poverty, Unemployment and the Future. In *Atkinson, A. B.*, 1989, pp. 87–95.

_____. Social Insurance and Income Maintenance. In *Atkinson, A. B.*, 1989, pp. 104–24.

_____. Social Security, Taxation and the Working Population over the Next Ten Years. In *Atkinson, A. B.*, 1989, *1984*, pp. 256–85.

_____. State Pensions, Taxation and Retirement Income, 1981–2031. In *Atkinson, A. B.*, 1989, *1982*, pp. 231–55.

_____. The Take-Up of Social Security Benefits. In *Atkinson, A. B.*, 1989, pp. 190–207.

_____. TAXMOD. In *Atkinson, A. B.*, 1989, *1988*, pp. 336–59.

_____. Turning the Screw: Benefits for the Unemployed, 1979–1988. In *Atkinson, A. B.*, 1989, pp. 125–57.

_____. Unemployment Benefit, Duration and Incentives in Britain: How Robust Is the Evidence? In *Atkinson, A. B.*, 1989, *1984*, pp. 158–80.

_____; **Gordon, James P. F. and Harrison, Alan.** Trends in the Shares of Top Wealth-Holders in Britain, 1923–1981. *Oxford Bull. Econ. Statist.*, August 1989, *51*(3), pp. 315–32.

_____ **and Micklewright, John.** Turning the Screw: Benefits for the Unemployed 1979–88. In *Dilnot, A. and Walker, I.*, eds., 1989, pp. 17–51.

Atkinson, David. Trade, Aid and Investment since 1950. In *Bulmer-Thomas, V.*, ed., 1989, pp. 103–20.

Atkinson, Lloyd C. International Monetary Reform: A View from the Trenches. *Can. Public Policy*, Supplement, February 1989, *15*, pp. S52–54.

Atkinson, Scott E. and Kerkvliet, Joe. Dual Measures of Monopoly and Monopsony Power: An Application to Regulated Electric Utilities. *Rev. Econ. Statist.*, May 1989, *71*(2), pp. 250–57.

Atmiyanandana, Vinita; Lawler, John J. and Zaidi, Mahmood A. Human Resource Strategies in Southeast Asia: The Case of Thailand. In *Nedd, A.*, ed., 1989, pp. 201–21.

Atoda, Naosumi; Hashimoto, Kyoji and Homma, Masaaki. Welfare Analysis of the 1988 Tax Reform in Japan. *Econ. Stud. Quart.*, December 1989, *40*(4), pp. 336–48.

Atrostic, B. K. Using Panel Data to Assess the Bias in Cross-Sectional Inferences of Life-Cycle Changes in the Level and Composition of Household Wealth: Comment. In *Lipsey, R. E. and Tice, H. S.*, eds., 1989, pp. 640–44.

Attanasio, Orazio P. and Weber, Guglielmo. Intertemporal Substitution, Risk Aversion and the Euler Equation for Consumption. *Econ. J.*, Supplement, 1989, *99*(395), pp. 59–73.

Attaran, Mohsen and Zwick, Martin. An Information Theory Approach to Measuring Industrial Diversification. *J. Econ. Stud.*, 1989, *16*(1), pp. 19–30.

Attwood, Donald W. Does Competition Help Co-operation? *J. Devel. Stud.*, October 1989, *26*(1), pp. 5–27.

Atwood, J. R. and Lister, C. International Antitrust Enforcement in the George Bush Administration: The Enforcement Guidelines and Beyond. *J. World Trade*, April 1989, *23*(2), pp. 97–117.

Atwood, Joseph A.; Segar, James and Hatch, Upton. An Application of Safety-First Probability Limits in a Discrete Stochastic Farm Management Programming Model. *Southern J. Agr. Econ.*, July 1989, *21*(1), pp. 65–72.

Aubert, Gabriel. Collective Agreements and Industrial Peace in Switzerland. *Int. Lab. Rev.*, 1989, *128*(3), pp. 373–88.

Aubin, Jean-Pierre. Quality and Process Improvements in Dynamic Production Processes. In *Andersson, Å. E., et al.*, eds., 1989, pp. 45–52.

Auboin, Marc. Le contrôle de la demande de monnaie (M1), déréglementation et compétition bancaire: Une étude comparative (France, Grande-Bretagne, Etats-Unis). (The Control of the M1 Money Demand, Deregulation and

Competition in the Banking Sector: A Comparative Study [France, the United Kingdom and the United States of America]. With English summary.) *Écon. Appl.*, 1989, *42*(2), pp. 55–85.

Audretsch, David B. The Determinants of Conglomerate Mergers. *Amer. Economist*, Spring 1989, *33*(1), pp. 52–60.

_____. Legalized Cartels in West Germany. *Antitrust Bull.*, Fall 1989, *34*(3), pp. 579–600.

_____ **and Acs, Zoltan J.** Births and Firm Size. *Southern Econ. J.*, October 1989, *56*(2), pp. 467–75.

_____ **and Acs, Zoltan J.** Patents as a Measure of Innovative Activity. *Kyklos*, 1989, *42*(2), pp. 171–80.

_____ **and Acs, Zoltan J.** Patents Innovative Activity. *Eastern Econ. J.*, Oct.–Dec. 1989, *15*(4), pp. 373–76.

_____ **and Acs, Zoltan J.** Small-Firm Entry in U.S. Manufacturing. *Economica*, May 1989, *56*(222), pp. 255–65.

_____ **and Acs, Zoltan J.** Small Firms in U.S. Manufacturing: A First Report. *Econ. Letters*, December 1989, *31*(4), pp. 399–402.

_____; **Sleuwaegen, Leo E. and Yamawaki, Hideki.** The Convergence of International and Domestic Markets: Foreword. In *Audretsch, D. B.; Sleuwaegen, L. and Yamawaki, H., eds.*, 1989, pp. vii–x.

_____; **Sleuwaegen, Leo E. and Yamawaki, Hideki.** The Dynamics of Export Competition. In *Audretsch, D. B.; Sleuwaegen, L. and Yamawaki, H., eds.*, 1989, pp. 211–45.

Auerbach, Alan J. Après Reagan, Le Déluge? A Review Article. *J. Monet. Econ.*, September 1989, *24*(2), pp. 299–311.

_____. Capital Gains Taxation and Tax Reform. *Nat. Tax J.*, September 1989, *42*(3), pp. 391–401.

_____. The Deadweight Loss from 'Non-neutral' Capital Income Taxation. *J. Public Econ.*, October 1989, *40*(1), pp. 1–36.

_____. Tax Policy and Corporate Borrowing. In *Kopcke, R. W. and Rosengren, E. S., eds.*, 1989, pp. 136–62.

_____. Tax Reform and Adjustment Costs: The Impact on Investment and Market Value. *Int. Econ. Rev.*, November 1989, *30*(4), pp. 939–62.

_____. Taxes in Canada, Japan, and the United States: Influences on Trade and Investment Flows, and the Role of Tax-Based Trade Irritants: Comment. In *Stern, R. M., ed.*, 1989, pp. 240–43.

_____ **and Kotlikoff, Laurence J.** An Examination of Empirical Tests of Social Security and Savings. In *Kotlikoff, L. J.*, 1989, *1983*, pp. 479–98.

_____ **and Kotlikoff, Laurence J.** Investment versus Savings Incentives: The Size of the Bang for the Buck and the Potential for Self-Financing Business Tax Cuts. In *Kotlikoff, L. J.*, 1989, *1983*, pp. 264–89.

_____ **and Kotlikoff, Laurence J.** Simulating Alternative Social Security Responses to the Demographic Transition. In *Kotlikoff, L. J.*, 1989, *1985*, pp. 337–57.

_____, **et al.** The Economic Dynamics of Ageing Population: The Case of Four OECD Countries. *OECD Econ. Stud.*, Spring 1989, (12), pp. 97–130.

Augustine, Norman R. and Trimble, Robert F. Procurement Competition at Work: The Manufacturer's Experience. *Yale J. Regul.*, Summer 1989, *6*(2), pp. 333–47.

Augusztinovics, Maria. The Costs of Human Life. *Econ. Systems Res.*, 1989, *1*(1), pp. 5–26.

_____. Primary Incomes and Intersectoral Pricing. *J. Policy Modeling*, Spring 1989, *11*(1), pp. 31–44.

Aukes, Robert G. Double Counting and Windfalls: A Reply. *Can. J. Agr. Econ.*, July 1989, *37*(2), pp. 331–32.

Aulin-Ahmavaara, Pirkko. A Complete Dynamic Input–Output Model Including the Production of Human Capital and Labour. *Econ. Systems Res.*, 1989, *1*(1), pp. 121–29.

Aulin, Arvid. The Condition of Self-steering of Economic Development. *Math. Soc. Sci.*, December 1989, *18*(3), pp. 239–61.

Ault, David E. and Rutman, Gilbert L. Land Scarcity, Economic Efficiency, and African Common Law. In *Zerbe, R. O., ed.*, 1989, pp. 33–54.

Ault, Richard W.; Saba, Richard P. and Caudill, Steven B. Efficient Estimation of the Costs of Rent Controls. *Rev. Econ. Statist.*, February 1989, *71*(1), pp. 154–59.

Aumann, Robert J. CORE as a Macrocosm of Game-Theoretic Research, 1967–1987. In *Cornet, B. and Tulkens, H., eds.*, 1989, pp. 5–16.

_____ **and Sorin, Sylvain.** Cooperation and Bounded Recall. *Games Econ. Behav.*, March 1989, *1*(1), pp. 5–39.

Austen-Smith, David. Sincere Voting in Models of Legislative Elections. *Soc. Choice Welfare*, October 1989, *6*(4), pp. 287–99.

_____ **and Banks, Jeffrey S.** Electoral Accountability and Incumbency. In *Ordeshook, P. C., ed.*, 1989, pp. 121–48.

Austin, Barbara. Managing Marketing in a Commodities Manufacturing Firm: Dominion Textile. In *Hausman, W. J., ed.*, 1989, pp. 168–77.

Austin, Kenneth E. Foreign Exchange Restrictions, Monetary Policy, and Macroeconomic Stability in the Third World. *J. Econ. Devel.*, December 1989, *14*(2), pp. 7–33.

Austin, Roger B. The Climatic Vulnerability of Wheat. In *Oram, P. A., et al.*, 1989, pp. 123–35.

_____ **and Arnold, Michael H.** Plant Breeding and Yield Stability. In *Anderson, J. R. and Hazell, P. B. R., eds.*, 1989, pp. 127–32.

_____ **and Arnold, Michael H.** Variability in Wheat Yields in England: Analysis and Future Prospects. In *Anderson, J. R. and Hazell, P. B. R., eds.*, 1989, pp. 101–06.

Austin, Roy L. Family Environment, Educational Aspiration and Performance in St. Vincent.

Rev. Black Polit. Econ., Winter 1989, *17*(3), pp. 101–22.

Austrom, Douglas R. and Lad, Lawrence J. Issues Management Alliances: New Responses, New Values., and New Logics. **In** *Post, J. E., ed.*, 1989, pp. 233–55.

Ausubel, Lawrence M. and Deneckere, Raymond J. A Direct Mechanism Characterization of Sequential Bargaining with One-Sided Incomplete Information. *J. Econ. Theory*, June 1989, *48*(1), pp. 18–46.

—— **and Deneckere, Raymond J.** Reputation in Bargaining and Durable Goods Monopoly. *Econometrica*, May 1989, *57*(3), pp. 511–31.

Auten, Gerald E.; Burman, Leonard E. and Randolph, William C. Estimation and Interpretation of Capital Gains Realization Behavior: Evidence from Panel Data. *Nat. Tax J.*, September 1989, *42*(3), pp. 353–74.

Auty, Richard M. The Internal Determinants of Eight Oil-Exporting Countries' Resource-Based Industry Performance. *J. Devel. Stud.*, April 1989, *25*(3), pp. 354–72.

Aven, Petr O. The Distribution Mechanism and Social Justice. **In** *Yanowitch, M., ed.*, 1989, *1987*, pp. 187–99.

——. The Distribution Mechanism and Social Justice. **In** *Jones, A. and Moskoff, W., eds.*, 1989, *1988*, pp. 233–48.

—— **and Shironin, V. M.** The Reform of the Economic Mechanism: The Realism of the Projected Transformations. **In** *Jones, A. and Moskoff, W., eds.*, 1989, *1988*, pp. 251–66.

Avenell, Simon; Leeson, Robert and Wood, Gavin. Measuring Exchange Rate Uncertainty: The Case of the Australian Dollar 1969 to 1987. *Australian Econ. Rev.*, Winter 1989, (86), pp. 34–42.

Avenier, Marie-José. "Méthodes de terrain" et recherche en management stratégique. (Field Methods and Research in Strategic Management. With English summary.) *Écon. Societes*, December 1989, *23*(12), pp. 199–218.

Avery, David and Sullivan, Gene D. Southeastern Manufacturing: Recent Changes and Prospects. *Fed. Res. Bank Atlanta Econ. Rev.*, Jan.–Feb. 1989, *74*(1), pp. 2–15.

Avery, Robert B. Long-Term Trends in U.S. Wealth Inequality: Methodological Issues and Results: Comment. **In** *Lipsey, R. E. and Tice, H. S., eds.*, 1989, pp. 839–44.

Avery, William P. and Rapkin, David P. Markets, Politics, and Change in the Global Political Economy. **In** *Avery, W. P. and Rapkin, D. P., eds.*, 1989, pp. 1–16.

Avila, Ricardo Avila and Orellana G., Arturo René. Poverty and Labour Market Access in Guatemala City. **In** *Rodgers, G., ed.*, 1989, pp. 81–96.

Avouyi-Dovi, S.; Boutillier, M. and Topol, R. Du peu de pertinence des anticipations sur le taux d'intérêt à court terme: Retour à la théorie de l'habitat préféré. (Weak Relevance of Short Term Interest Rate Expectations and Return to the Preferred Habitat Theory. With English

summary.) *Écon. Societes*, April–May 1989, *23*(4–5), pp. 43–70.

Avramović, Dragoslav. Debt Problem: What Next? **In** *Mrak, M., ed.*, 1989, pp. 23–48.

Awerbuch, Shimon. Efficient Income Measures and the Partially Regulated Firm. **In** *Crew, M. A., ed.*, 1989, pp. 65–88.

Axelrod, Donald. Jesse Burkhead: An Appreciation. *Public Budg. Finance*, Summer 1989, *9*(2), pp. 3–10.

Axilrod, Stephen H. Central Bank Credibility: An Alternative to Private Money. *Cato J.*, Fall 1989, *9*(2), pp. 363–66.

——. Comments on Co-ordination of Economic Policies. *Can. Public Policy*, Supplement, February 1989, *15*, pp. S39–44.

Ayako, A. B. Contract Farming and Outgrower Schemes in Kenya: Comparative Analysis. *Eastern Afr. Econ. Rev.*, Special Issue, August 1989, pp. 15–19.

——, **et al.** Contract Farming and Outgrower Schemes in Kenya: Case Studies. *Eastern Afr. Econ. Rev.*, Special Issue, August 1989, pp. 4–14.

Ayanian, Robert. Geopolitics and the Dollar. *J. Int. Money Finance*, September 1989, *8*(3), pp. 391–99.

——. Nuclear Consequences of the Welfare State Revisited: Danger in the Data. *Public Choice*, May 1989, *61*(2), pp. 167–69.

——. Perestroika and Arms Control. *Contemp. Policy Issues*, January 1989, *7*(1), pp. 70–74.

Aydin, Shahizer and Lenz, Ilse. Fighting Plant Closure: Women in the Strike at Videocolor. **In** *Elson, D. and Pearson, R., eds.*, 1989, pp. 165–82.

Ayers, Michael and Munkirs, John R. Political and Policy Implications of Centralized Private Sector Planning. **In** *Tool, M. R. and Samuels, W. J., eds. (I)*, 1989, *1983*, pp. 321–36.

Ayling, Simon and Cromie, Stanley. The Motivation, Satisfaction and Company Goals of Business Proprietors. **In** *Mansfield, R., ed.*, 1989, pp. 221–32.

Ayres, Clarence E. Ideological Responsibility. **In** *Tool, M. R. and Samuels, W. J., eds. (II)*, 1989, *1967*, pp. 26–34.

Ayres, Frances L.; Jackson, Betty R. and Hite, Peggy A. The Economic Benefits of Regulation: Evidence from Professional Tax Preparers. *Accounting Rev.*, April 1989, *64*(2), pp. 300–12.

Ayres, Ian and Gertner, Robert. Filling Gaps in Incomplete Contracts: An Economic Theory of Default Rules. *Yale Law J.*, October 1989, *99*(1), pp. 87–130.

Ayres, Robert U. The Barrier-Breakthrough Model of Innovation and the Life Cycle Model of Industrial Evolution as Applied to the U.S. Electrical Industry. **In** *Andersson, Å. E.; Batten, D. F. and Karlsson, C., eds.*, 1989, pp. 115–32.

——. U.S. Competitiveness in Manufacturing. *Managerial Dec. Econ.*, Special Issue, Spring 1989, pp. 3–12.

Ayton, Peter and Wright, George. Judgemental Probability Forecasts for Personal and Impersonal Events. *Int. J. Forecasting*, 1989, 5(1), pp. 117–25.

Azabou, Mongi; Bouzaïane, Lotfi and Nugent, Jeffrey B. Contractual Choice in Tunisian Fishing. In *Nabli, M. K. and Nugent, J. B., eds.*, 1989, pp. 158–77.

———; **Kuran, Timur and Nabli, Mustapha K.** The Wholesale Produce Market of Tunis and Its Porters: A Tale of Market Degeneration. In *Nabli, M. K. and Nugent, J. B., eds.*, 1989, pp. 352–74.

——— **and Nugent, Jeffrey B.** Tax Farming: Anachronism or Optimal Contract? (An Illustration with Respect to Tunisia's Weekly Markets). In *Nabli, M. K. and Nugent, J. B., eds.*, 1989, pp. 178–99.

Azam, Jean-Paul. L'effet Chichilnisky et le cycle des termes de l'échange. (With English summary.) *Revue Écon. Politique*, Sept.–Oct. 1989, 99(5), pp. 720–33.

——— **and Besley, Timothy J.** General Equilibrium with Parallel Markets for Goods and Foreign Exchange: Theory and Application to Ghana. *World Devel.*, December 1989, 17(12), pp. 1921–30.

Azis, Iwan J. Key Issues in Indonesian Regional Development. In *Hill, H., ed.*, 1989, pp. 55–74.

Baade, Robert A. and Nazmi, Nader. Currency Substitution and Money Demand in the United States, West Germany and Japan. *Kredit Kapital*, 1989, 22(3), pp. 363–74.

Baba, Vishwanath V. and Harris, Marion J. Stress and Absence: A Cross-Cultural Perspective. In *Nedd, A., ed.*, 1989, pp. 317–37.

Babb, Emerson M. and Schiek, William A. Impact of Reverse Osmosis on Southeast Milk Markets. *Southern J. Agr. Econ.*, December 1989, 21(2), pp. 63–75.

Babbel, David F. Insuring Banks against Systematic Credit Risk. *J. Futures Markets*, December 1989, 9(6), pp. 487–505.

——— **and Ohtsuka, Eisaku.** Aspects of Optimal Multiperiod Life Insurance. *J. Risk Ins.*, September 1989, 56(3), pp. 460–81.

Babcock, Michael W. and German, H. Wade. Changing Determinants of Truck-Rail Market Shares. *Logist. Transp. Rev.*, September 1989, 25(3), pp. 251–70.

——— **and German, H. Wade.** Public Policy, Motor Carriers and Strategic Planning. In *Missouri Valley Economic Association*, 1989, pp. 16–24.

Babić, Mate. Yugoslav External Debt: A Constraint for Macroeconomic Policy. In *Singer, H. W. and Sharma, S., eds. (I)*, 1989, pp. 219–24.

Babievsky, Kirill and Enikolopov, Nikolai. Chemical Disarmament: Reliable and Efficient Control. In *Rotblat, J. and Goldanskii, V. I., eds.*, 1989, pp. 112–16.

Babula, Ronald A. Contemporaneous Correlation and Modeling Canada's Imports of U.S. Crops. *J. Agr. Econ. Res.*, Winter 1989, 41(1), pp. 33–38.

——— **and Bessler, David A.** Farmgate, Pro-

cessor, and Consumer Price Transmissions in the Wheat Sector. *J. Agr. Econ. Res.*, Summer 1989, 41(3), pp. 23–28.

Babusiaux, Denis. Rentabilité globale, rentabilité des capitaux propres et méthode des intérêts seulement déductibles. (Overall Profitability, Own Capital Profitability and "Shadow Interest" Method. With English summary.) *Écon. Societes*, January 1989, 23(1), pp. 29–54.

Bach, Christopher L. U.S. International Transactions, Fourth Quarter and Year 1988. *Surv. Curr. Bus.*, March 1989, 69(3), pp. 26–57.

———. U.S. International Transactions, Second Quarter 1989. *Surv. Curr. Bus.*, September 1989, 69(9), pp. 28–52.

Bach, Jonathan P. Requiring Due Care in the Process of Patient Deinstitutionalization: Toward a Common Law Approach to Mental Health Care Reform. *Yale Law J.*, April 1989, 98(6), pp. 1153–72.

Bach, Wilfrid. Growing Consensus and Challenges Regarding a Greenhouse Climate. In *Oram, P. A., et al.*, 1989, pp. 289–304.

Bacha, Edmar L. Economic Trends in Latin America. In *Naya, S., et al., eds.*, 1989, pp. 39–51.

———. Um modelo de três hiatos. (With English summary.) *Pesquisa Planejamento Econ.*, August 1989, 19(2), pp. 213–32.

Bacharach, Michael. Expecting and Affecting. *Oxford Econ. Pap.*, April 1989, 41(2), pp. 339–55.

———. The Role of 'Verstehen' in Economic Theory. *Ricerche Econ.*, Jan.–June 1989, 43(1–2), pp. 129–50.

Baches-Gellner, Uschi and Zanders, Eva. Lehre und Forschung als Verbundproduktion. Data-Envelopment-Analysen und organisationsökonomische Interpretationen der Realität in wirtschaftswissenschaftlichen Fachbereichen. (With English summary.) *Z. Betriebswirtshaft*, March 1989, 59(3), pp. 271–90.

Bachman, Jerald G. and O'Malley, Patrick M. When Four Months Equal a Year: Inconsistencies in Student Reports of Drug Use. In *Singer, E. and Presser, S., eds.*, 1989, 1981, pp. 173–85.

Bachman, Sara S., et al. Preferred Provider Organizations: Options for Medicare. *Inquiry*, Spring 1989, 26(1), pp. 24–34.

Bachtler, J. and Davies, P. L. Economic Restructuring and Services Policy. In *Gibbs, D., ed.*, 1989, pp. 154–75.

Backhaus, Jürgen G. Banking Institutions in Historical and Comparative Perspective: Germany, Great Britain and United States in the Nineteenth and Early Twentieth Century: Comment. *J. Inst. Theoretical Econ.*, March 1989, 145(1), pp. 210–14.

———. Efficient Statute Law. In *Faure, M. and Van den Bergh, R., eds.*, 1989, pp. 23–32.

———. Gustav von Schmoller and Social Economics. *Int. J. Soc. Econ.*, 1989, 16(9–10–11), pp. 6–16.

———. Privatization and Nationalization: A Suggested Approach. *Ann. Pub. Coop. Econ.*, 1989, *60*(3), pp. 307–28.

———. Sombart's Modern Capitalism. *Kyklos*, 1989, *42*(4), pp. 599–611.

———. Taxation and Entrepreneurship: An Austrian Approach to Public Finance. *J. Econ. Stud.*, 1989, *16*(2), pp. 5–22.

———. A Transactional Approach to Explaining Historical Contract Structures. *Int. Rev. Law Econ.*, December 1989, *9*(2), pp. 223–26.

———; Holcombe, Randall G. and Zardkoohi, Asghar. Public Investment and the Burden of the Public Debt: Reply. *Southern Econ. J.*, October 1989, *56*(2), pp. 532–34.

Backus, David K. and Gregory, Allan W. Risk Premiums in Asset Prices and Returns: A Comment. *Econometric Rev.*, 1989, *8*(2), pp. 187–95.

———; Gregory, Allan W. and Zin, Stanley E. Risk Premiums in the Term Structure: Evidence from Artificial Economies. *J. Monet. Econ.*, November 1989, *24*(3), pp. 371–99.

——— and Kehoe, Patrick J. On the Denomination of Government Debt: A Critique of the Portfolio Balance Approach. *J. Monet. Econ.*, May 1989, *23*(3), pp. 359–76.

Backwell, K. R. Formal Tender Evaluation. In *Lockett, A. G. and Islei, G., eds.*, 1989, pp. 179–90.

Bacon, Peter W., et al. Long-term Catastrophic Care: A Financial Planning Perspective. *J. Risk Ins.*, March 1989, *56*(1), pp. 146–54.

Bácskai, Tamás. The Reorganization of the Banking System in Hungary. *Eastern Europ. Econ.*, Fall 1989, *28*(1), pp. 79–92.

Badelt, Christoph. Government versus Private Provision of Social Services: The Case of Austria. In *James, E., ed.*, 1989, pp. 162–76.

Baden-Fuller, Charles W. F. Exit from Declining Industries and the Case of Steel Castings. *Econ. J.*, December 1989, *99*(398), pp. 949–61.

Badenhorst, J. A. Reklamepraktyke in Kleinsakeondernemings. (With English summary.) *J. Stud. Econ. Econometrics*, March 1989, *13*(1), pp. 65–75.

Bader, Barry S. Keys to Better Hospital Governance through Better Information. In *Herman, R. D. and Van Til, J., eds.*, 1989, pp. 118–30.

Bader, Kenneth L. U.S. Agriculture's Stake in Aid and Trade. In *Swegle, W. E. and Ligon, P. C., eds.*, 1989, pp. 11–15.

Badrinath, S. G.; Gay, Gerald D. and Kale, Jayant R. Patterns of Institutional Investment, Prudence, and the Managerial "Safety-Net" Hypothesis. *J. Risk Ins.*, December 1989, *56*(4), pp. 605–29.

Baehr, Peter R. The General Assembly: Negotiating the Convention on Torture. In *[Gordenker, L.]*, 1989, pp. 36–53.

Baek, Kwang-il and Moon, Chung-in. Technological Dependence, Supplier Control and Strategies for Recipient Autonomy: The Case of South Korea. In *Baek, K.-I.; McLaurin, R. D. and Moon, C., eds.*, 1989, pp. 153–83.

Baek, Yong-Ho. The Measurement of Change in Consumption. *Int. Econ. J.*, Spring 1989, *3*(1), pp. 49–54.

Baer, Herbert. Expanded Powers after the Crash(es). *Amer. Econ. Rev.*, May 1989, *79*(2), pp. 156–60.

Baer, Werner; Biller, Dan and McDonald, Curtis T. Austerity under Different Political Regimes: The Case of Brazil. In *Handelman, H. and Baer, W., eds.*, 1989, pp. 19–42.

——— and Handelman, Howard. The Economic and Political Costs of Austerity: Introduction. In *Handelman, H. and Baer, W., eds.*, 1989, pp. 1–17.

Baethge, Martin and Oberbeck, Herbert. Computer and Pinstripes: Financial Institutions. In *Katzenstein, P. J., ed.*, 1989, pp. 275–303.

Baffes, John. Factor Demands of Louisiana Rice Producers: An Econometric Investigation: Comment. *Southern J. Agr. Econ.*, December 1989, *21*(2), pp. 221–22.

——— and Vasavada, Utpal. On the Choice of Functional Forms in Agricultural Production Analysis. *Appl. Econ.*, August 1989, *21*(8), pp. 1053–61.

Baffoe-Bonnie, John. Family Labour Supply and Labour Market Segmentation. *Appl. Econ.*, January 1989, *21*(1), pp. 69–83.

Baffoe, Frank. Lesotho: Investment Incentives as an Instrument for Industrialization. In *Whiteside, A. W., ed.*, 1989, pp. 66–83.

Baffuto, Thomas and Major, Thomas. Supported Competitive Employment in New Jersey. In *Wehman, P. and Kregel, J., eds.*, 1989, pp. 207–23.

Bagchi, Prabir K. Carrier Selection: The Analytic Hierarchy Process. *Logist. Transp. Rev.*, March 1989, *25*(1), pp. 63–73.

Bagchi-Sen, Sharmistha and Wheeler, James O. A Spatial and Temporal Model of Foreign Direct Investment in the United States. *Econ. Geogr.*, April 1989, *65*(2), pp. 113–29.

Baggott, Rob. The Politics of the Market. In *Robinson, D.; Maynard, A. and Chester, R., eds.*, 1989, pp. 148–66.

Baghestani, Hamid and Abosedra, Salah. New Evidence on the Causal Relationship between United States Energy Consumption and Gross National Product. *J. Energy Devel.*, Spring 1989, *14*(2), pp. 285–92.

Baginski, Stephen P. Management Forecasts and Release-Specific Directional Information Transfer. *Quart. Rev. Econ. Bus.*, Winter 1989, *29*(4), pp. 49–62.

Bagnoli, Mark and Lipman, Barton L. Provision of Public Goods: Fully Implementing the Core through Private Contributions. *Rev. Econ. Stud.*, October 1989, *56*(4), pp. 583–601.

———; Salant, Stephen W. and Swierzbinski, Joseph E. Durable-Goods Monopoly with Discrete Demand. *J. Polit. Econ.*, December 1989, *97*(6), pp. 1459–78.

Bagó, Eszter and Móra, Mária. The Economic Management and Market Behaviour of the Decentralized Enterprises in Hungarian Industry. *Acta Oecon.*, 1989, *41*(3–4), pp. 341–58.

Bagozzi, Richard P.; Baumgartner, Johann and Yi, Youjae. An Investigation into the Role of Intentions as Mediators of the Attitude–Behavior Relationship. *J. Econ. Psych.*, March 1989, *10*(1), pp. 35–62.

Bagwell, Kyle and Staiger, Robert W. The Role of Export Subsidies When Product Quality is Unknown. *J. Int. Econ.*, August 1989, *27*(1–2), pp. 69–89.

Bagwell, Laurie Simon and Shoven, John B. Cash Distributions to Shareholders. *J. Econ. Perspectives*, Summer 1989, *3*(3), pp. 129–40.

Baharsjah, Sjarifudin; Hadiwigeno, Soetatwo and Hedley, Douglas. Agricultural Policy and Food Self-Sufficiency in Developing Countries. In *Helmuth, J. W. and Johnson, S. R., eds., Vol. 2*, 1989, pp. 121–37.

Bahl, Roy. Intergovernmental Grants. In *Schroeder, L., ed.*, 1989, pp. 51–88.

Bahmani-Oskooee, Mohsen. Devaluation and the J-Curve: Some Evidence for LDCs: Errata. *Rev. Econ. Statist.*, August 1989, *71*(3), pp. 553–54.

_____. Effects of the U.S. Government Budget on Its Current Account: An Empirical Inquiry. *Quart. Rev. Econ. Bus.*, Winter 1989, *29*(4), pp. 76–91.

_____ **and Niroomand, Farhang.** On the Exchange-Rate Elasticity of the Demand for International Reserves: Some Evidence from Industrial Countries: A Reply. *Weltwirtsch. Arch.*, 1989, *125*(2), pp. 394–96.

Bahner, Flemming and Kerndrup, Søren. Assessment of Technology as the Lever of Regional Industrial Planning. In *Pedersen, J. L., ed.*, 1989, pp. 209–35.

Bahr, Michael D.; Dotson, Peter K. and Tolley, H. Dennis. A Statistical Method for Monitoring Social Insurance Claims. *J. Risk Ins.*, December 1989, *56*(4), pp. 670–85.

Baigent, Nick. Some Further Remarks on Preference Proximity. *Quart. J. Econ.*, February 1989, *104*(1), pp. 191–93.

Bailar, Barbara A. Information Needs, Surveys, and Measurement Errors. In *Kasprzyk, D., et al., eds.*, 1989, pp. 1–24.

Bailey, DeeVon and Brorsen, B. Wade. Price Asymmetry in Spatial Fed Cattle Markets. *Western J. Agr. Econ.*, December 1989, *14*(2), pp. 246–52.

_____; **Kumbhakar, Subal C. and Biswas, Basudeb.** A Study of Economic Efficiency of Utah Dairy Farmers: A System Approach. *Rev. Econ. Statist.*, November 1989, *71*(4), pp. 595–604.

_____, **et al.** An Analysis of Technical, Allocative, and Scale Inefficiency: The Case of Ecuadorian Dairy Farms. *Western J. Agr. Econ.*, July 1989, *14*(1), pp. 30–37.

Bailey, Elizabeth E. Enhancing the Performance of the Deregulated Air Transportation System: Comments. *Brookings Pap. Econ. Act., Microeconomics*, 1989, pp. 112–21.

_____ **and Boisvert, Richard N.** A Comparison of Risk Efficiency Criteria in Evaluating Groundnut Performance in Drought-Prone Ar-

eas. *Australian J. Agr. Econ.*, December 1989, *33*(3), pp. 153–69.

_____ **and Kirstein, David M.** Can Truth in Airline Scheduling Alleviate the Congestion and Delay Problem? In *Moses, L. N. and Savage, I., eds.*, 1989, pp. 153–66.

Bailey, Kenneth W. The Impact of the Food Security Act of 1985 on U.S. Wheat Exports. *Southern J. Agr. Econ.*, December 1989, *21*(2), pp. 116–28.

Bailey, Mark D. The Concept of the Margin in the Medieval English Economy. *Econ. Hist. Rev., 2nd Ser.*, February 1989, *42*(1), pp. 1–17.

Bailey, Mark W. and Boyce, Gordon. The Manufacturing and Marketing of Steel in Canada: Dofasco Inc., 1912–1970. In *Hausman, W. J., ed.*, 1989, pp. 228–37.

Bailey, Martin J. and Tavlas, George S. Trade and Investment under Floating Rates: The U.S. Experience. In *Dorn, J. A. and Niskanen, W. A., eds.*, 1989, *1988*, pp. 207–28.

Bailey, Richard. Coal—The Ultimate Privatisation. *Nat. Westminster Bank Quart. Rev.*, August 1989, pp. 2–17.

Bailey, Warren. The Effect of U.S. Money Supply Announcements on Canadian Stock, Bond, and Currency Prices. *Can. J. Econ.*, August 1989, *22*(3), pp. 607–18.

_____. The Market for Japanese Stock Index Futures: Some Preliminary Evidence. *J. Futures Markets*, August 1989, *9*(4), pp. 283–95.

_____ **and Stulz, René M.** The Pricing of Stock Index Options in a General Equilibrium Model. *J. Finan. Quant. Anal.*, March 1989, *24*(1), pp. 1–12.

Baillie, Richard T. Commodity Prices and Aggregate Inflation: Would a Commodity Price Rule Be Worthwhile? *Carnegie–Rochester Conf. Ser. Public Policy*, Autumn 1989, *31*, pp. 185–240.

_____. Econometric Tests of Rationality and Market Efficiency: Reply. *Econometric Rev.*, 1989, *8*(2), pp. 213–16.

_____. Econometric Tests of Rationality and Market Efficiency. *Econometric Rev.*, 1989, *8*(2), pp. 151–86.

_____. Forecast Master: A Review. *J. Appl. Econometrics*, July–Sept. 1989, *4*(3), pp. 305–07.

_____ **and Bollerslev, Tim.** Common Stochastic Trends in a System of Exchange Rates. *J. Finance*, March 1989, *44*(1), pp. 167–81.

_____ **and Bollerslev, Tim.** The Message in Daily Exchange Rates: A Conditional-Variance Tale. *J. Bus. Econ. Statist.*, July 1989, *7*(3), pp. 297–305.

_____ **and DeGennaro, Ramon P.** The Impact of Delivery Terms on Stock Return Volatility. *J. Finan. Services Res.*, October 1989, *3*(1), pp. 55–76.

Baiman, Stanley and Lewis, Barry L. An Experiment Testing the Behavioral Equivalence of Strategically Equivalent Employment Contracts. *J. Acc. Res.*, Spring 1989, *27*(1), pp. 1–20.

Bain, Laurel and Liburd, Eustace E. Financial Intermediation and Economic Growth in the OECS. *Soc. Econ. Stud.*, December 1989, 38(4), pp. 201–18.

Bairam, Erkin I. Learning-by-Doing, Variable Elasticity of Substitution and Economic Growth in Japan, 1878–1939. *J. Devel. Stud.*, April 1989, 25(3), pp. 344–53.

_____. Returns to Scale in Branches of New Zealand Manufacturing Industry: A Cross-Section Production Function Study, 1983/84. *Keio Econ. Stud.*, 1989, 26(1), pp. 43–52.

_____ **and Howells, John M.** Strike Incidence in New Zealand: A New Econometric Approach. *Australian Econ. Pap.*, June 1989, 28(52), pp. 93–102.

Baird, Charles W. James Buchanan and the Austrians: The Common Ground. *Cato J.*, Spring–Summer 1989, 9(1), pp. 201–30.

Bairoch, Paul. European Trade Policy, 1815–1914. In *Mathias, P. and Pollard, S., eds.,* 1989, pp. 1–160.

_____. L'économie française dans le contexte européen à la fin du XVIIIᵉ siècle. (The French Economy in the Europen Context at the End of the Eighteenth Century. With English summary.) *Revue Écon.*, November 1989, 40(6), pp. 939–64.

_____. The Paradoxes of Economic History: Economic Laws and History. *Europ. Econ. Rev.*, March 1989, 33(2/3), pp. 225–49.

_____. Urbanization and the Economy in Preindustrial Societies: The Findings of Two Decades of Research. *J. Europ. Econ. Hist.*, Fall 1989, 18(2), pp. 239–90.

_____. Wages as an Indicator of Gross National Product. In *Scholliers, P., ed.,* 1989, pp. 51–60.

Bajeux, Isabelle. Gestion de portefeuille dans un modèle binomial. (Portfolio Selection in a Binomial Model. With English summary.) *Ann. Écon. Statist.*, Jan.–March 1989, (13), pp. 49–76.

_____ **and Rochet, Jean-Charles.** Opérations d'initiés: une analyse de surplus. (Insider Trading: A Surplus Analysis. With English summary.) *Finance*, June 1989, 10(1), pp. 7–19.

Bajt, A. Socialist Market Economy. *Acta Oecon.*, 1989, 40(3–4), pp. 180–83.

Bajwa, Mohammad S. and Mallela, Parthasaradhi. ML and MINQU Estimation of ARCH Models: Relative Importance of Money Supply and Wage Rate for Explaining U.S. Inflation. *J. Quant. Econ.*, January 1989, 5(1), pp. 155–69.

Baker, Donald I. Antitrust Law and Economics at the Political Frontier. In *Larner, R. J. and Meehan, J. W., Jr., eds.,* 1989, pp. 141–50.

Baker, Gary. Board–Staff Planning and Implementation Processes in Innovative Performance–Benefit Plan. In *Herman, R. D. and Van Til, J., eds.,* 1989, pp. 131–38.

Baker, George P. and Wruck, Karen Hopper. Organizational Changes and Value Creation in Leveraged Buyouts: The Case of the O.M. Scott and Sons Company. *J. Finan. Econ.*, December 1989, 25(2), pp. 163–90.

Baker, H. Kent and Edelman, Richard B. The Dynamics of Neglect and Return: Reply. *J. Portfol. Manage.*, Winter 1989, 15(2), pp. 77.

Baker, Jonathan B. Identifying Cartel Policing under Uncertainty: The U.S. Steel Industry, 1933–1939. *J. Law Econ.*, Part 2, October 1989, 32(2), pp. S47–76.

Baker, Laurie and Thomassin, Paul J. Institutional Change and Its Impact on Farm Management. *Can. J. Agr. Econ.*, Part 1, December 1989, 37(4), pp. 775–94.

Baker, Paul; Blundell, Richard W. and Micklewright, John. Modelling Household Energy Expenditures Using Micro-data. *Econ. J.*, September 1989, 99(397), pp. 720–38.

Baker, R. G. V. and Garner, B. J. On the Space-Time Associations in the Consumer Patronage of Planned Shopping Centres. *Environ. Planning A*, September 1989, 21(9), pp. 1179–94.

Baker, Robert. Beyond Do-Not-Resuscitate Orders. In *Strosberg, M. A.; Fein, I. A. and Carroll, J. D., eds.,* 1989, pp. 52–63.

_____, **et al.** Caring for the Critically Ill: Proposals for Reform. In *Strosberg, M. A.; Fein, I. A. and Carroll, J. D., eds.,* 1989, pp. 87–91.

Baker, Samuel H. and Pratt, James B. Experience as a Barrier to Contestability in Airline Markets. *Rev. Econ. Statist.*, May 1989, 71(2), pp. 352–56.

Baker, Stewart Abercrombie. "Like" Products and Commercial Reality. In *Jackson, J. H. and Vermulst, E. A., eds.,* 1989, pp. 287–94.

Baker, Timothy G. and Turvey, Calum G. Optimal Hedging under Alternative Capital Structures and Risk Aversion. *Can. J. Agr. Econ.*, March 1989, 37(1), pp. 135–43.

Baker, William Gary and Eck, James R. Federal Tort Reform to Solve the Medical Malpractice Insurance Crisis. In *Missouri Valley Economic Association,* 1989, pp. 105–09.

Bakir, Siti Zainab and Humaidi, Mochtar. Lampung: Spontaneous Transmigration. In *Hill, H., ed.,* 1989, pp. 349–62.

Bakos, Gabor. CMEA in the Light of National Mechanisms. In *Berliner, J. S.; Kosta, H. G. J. and Hakogi, M., eds.,* 1989, pp. 15–35.

_____. The Soviet Reform Concept and Its Impact on Economic Reforms in Eastern Europe: Discussion. In *Berliner, J. S.; Kosta, H. G. J. and Hakogi, M., eds.,* 1989, pp. 74–75.

_____. Structure of Capital Financing—A Case Study in Hungary: Discussion. In *Berliner, J. S.; Kosta, H. G. J. and Hakogi, M., eds.,* 1989, pp. 131–32.

_____ **and Hakogi, Masumi.** Economics of the Socialist Countries: Introduction. In *Berliner, J. S.; Kosta, H. G. J. and Hakogi, M., eds.,* 1989, pp. 1–5.

Balaban, Oded. The Positivistic Nature of the Critical Theory. *Sci. Society*, Winter 1989–90, 53(4), pp. 442–58.

Balachandran, Chandra S.; Fisher, Peter F. and Stanley, Michael A. An Expert System Approach to Rural Development: A Prototype

(TIHSO). *J. Developing Areas*, January 1989, 23(2), pp. 259–70.

Balaji, S. and Haridoss, R. Engel Elasticity and Economies of Scale in Household Consumption: A Micro Analysis. *Margin*, Oct. 1989–March 1990, 22(1–2), pp. 103–07.

Baland, Jean-Marie. Social Disarticulation Models: An Analytical Critique and a Re-exposition. *J. Devel. Stud.*, July 1989, 25(4), pp. 521–36.

Balasko, Yves and Cass, David. The Structure of Financial Equilibrium with Exogenous Yields: The Case of Incomplete Markets. *Econometrica*, January 1989, 57(1), pp. 135–62.

Balassa, Bela. The Adding Up Problem. *Banca Naz. Lavoro Quart. Rev.*, March 1989, (168), pp. 47–72.

_____. The Adjustment Experience of Developing Economies after 1973. In *Balassa, B.*, 1989, *1983*, pp. 251–75.

_____. An Empirical Demonstration of Classical Comparative Cost Theory. In *Balassa, B.*, 1989, *1983*, pp. 3–17.

_____. The Changing Pattern of Comparative Advantage in Manufactured Goods. In *Balassa, B.*, 1989, *1979*, pp. 18–30.

_____. Comparative Advantage in Manufactured Goods: A Reappraisal. In *Balassa, B.*, 1989, *1986*, pp. 31–40.

_____. Comparative Advantage, Trade Policy and Economic Development: Introduction—An Autobiographical Essay. In *Balassa, B.*, 1989, pp. xv–xxv.

_____. Economic Incentives and Agricultural Exports in Developing Countries. In *Islam, N.*, *ed.*, 1989, pp. 181–96.

_____. Europe 1992 and Its Possible Implications for Nonmember Countries. In *Schott, J. J.*, *ed.*, 1989, pp. 293–312.

_____. Export Incentives and Export Performance in Developing Countries: A Comparative Analysis. In *Balassa, B.*, 1989, *1978*, pp. 282–313.

_____. Exports and Economic Growth: Further Evidence. In *Balassa, B.*, 1989, *1978*, pp. 314–22.

_____. Exports, Policy Choices and Economic Growth in Developing Countries after the 1973 Oil Shock. In *Balassa, B.*, 1989, *1985*, pp. 323–35.

_____. The Extent and the Cost of Protection in Developed–Developing Country Trade. In *Balassa, B.*, 1989, *1987*, pp. 206–25.

_____. Growth Strategies in Semi-industrial Countries. In *Balassa, B.*, 1989, *1970*, pp. 229–50.

_____. Industrial Protection in the Developed Countries. In *Balassa, B.*, 1989, *1984*, pp. 187–205.

_____. Intra-industry Specialization in a Multi-country and Multi-industry Framework. In *Balassa, B.*, 1989, *1987*, pp. 140–59.

_____. My Life Philosophy. *Amer. Economist*, Spring 1989, 33(1), pp. 16–23.

_____. Next Steps in the Hungarian Economic Reform. *Eastern Europ. Econ.*, Fall 1989,

28(1), pp. 34–52.

_____. Policy Responses to Exogenous Shocks in Developing Countries. In *Balassa, B.*, 1989, *1986*, pp. 276–81.

_____. A Quantitative Appraisal of Adjustment Lending. *Pakistan Devel. Rev.*, Summer 1989, 28(2), pp. 73–94.

_____. 'Revealed' Comparative Advantage Revisited. In *Balassa, B.*, 1989, *1977*, pp. 63–79.

_____. Subsidies and Countervailing Measures: Economic Considerations. *J. World Trade*, April 1989, 23(2), pp. 63–79.

_____. Tariff Protection in Industrial Countries: An Evaluation. In *Balassa, B.*, 1989, *1965*, pp. 160–86.

_____. Tariff Reductions and Trade in Manufactures among the Industrial Countries. In *Balassa, B.*, 1989, *1966*, pp. 131–39.

_____. Temporary Windfalls and Compensation Arrangements. *Weltwirtsch. Arch.*, 1989, 125(1), pp. 97–113.

_____. Trade Creation and Trade Diversion in the European Common Market. In *Balassa, B.*, 1989, *1967*, pp. 109–30.

_____. Trade Liberalization and 'Revealed' Comparative Advantage. In *Balassa, B.*, 1989, *1965*, pp. 41–62.

_____ **and Bauwens, Luc.** The Determinants of Intra-European Trade in Manufactured Goods. In *Jacquemin, A. and Sapir, A., eds.*, 1989, *1988*, pp. 185–201.

_____ **and Noland, Marcus.** The Changing Comparative Advantage of Japan and the United States. In *Balassa, B.*, 1989, pp. 80–106.

_____ **and Noland, Marcus.** The Changing Comparative Advantage of Japan and the United States. *J. Japanese Int. Economies*, June 1989, 3(2), pp. 174–88.

_____, **et al.** The Determinants of Export Supply and Export Demand in Two Developing Countries: Greece and Korea. *Int. Econ. J.*, Spring 1989, 3(1), pp. 1–16.

Balasubramanyam, V. N. ASEAN and Regional Trade Cooperation in Southeast Asia. In *Greenaway, D.; Hyclak, T. and Thornton, R. J., eds.*, 1989, pp. 167–87.

_____. Capital Exports, 1870–1914: Comments. *Econ. Hist. Rev.*, 2nd Ser., May 1989, 42(2), pp. 260–64.

_____. International Trade in Services: The Issues of Market Presence and Right of Establishment. In *Robinson, P.; Sauvant, K. P. and Govitrikar, V. P., eds.*, 1989, pp. 131–53.

Balasundaram, S. K. and Namasivayam, D. Subsidy in the Risk-Preference of Allied Agricultural Projects: A Sensitivity Analysis. *Margin*, April–June 1989, 21(3), pp. 89–103.

Balat, Jean-Charles. International Tax Aspects of Charitable Giving and Philanthropic Organisations: French Aspects. *Bull. Int. Fiscal Doc.*, December 1989, 43(12), pp. 566–69.

Balcerowicz, L. On the "Socialist Market Economy." *Acta Oecon.*, 1989, 40(3–4), pp. 184–89.

Baldacchino, G. and Zammit, E. L. Fifth International Conference on the Economics of Self-management (Vienna, Austria, July 1988):

Workers on the Board—A Sociological Comment on Recent Developments in Workers' Participation in Malta. *Econ. Anal. Workers' Manage.*, 1989, *23*(1), pp. 79–94.

Balderjahn, Ingo. Robustness of Estimation Methods against Small Sample Sizes and Nonnormality in Confirmatory Factor Analysis Models. In *Opitz, O., ed.*, 1989, pp. 3–11.

Balderston, T. War Finance and Inflation in Britain and Germany, 1914–1918. *Econ. Hist. Rev., 2nd Ser.*, May 1989, *42*(2), pp. 222–44.

Balducci, Renato. Coordinamento delle politiche macroeconomiche e stabilità del tasso di cambio. (International Macroeconomic Policy Coordination and Real Exchange Rate Stability. With English summary.) *Giorn. Econ.*, May–June 1989, *48*(5–6), pp. 203–24.

Baldwin, E. Dean; Henderson, Dennis R. and Rhodus, W. Timothy. Pricing Accuracy and Efficiency in a Pilot Electronic Hog Market. *Amer. J. Agr. Econ.*, November 1989, *71*(4), pp. 874–82.

Baldwin, John R. and Gorecki, Paul K. Measuring the Dynamics of Market Structure: Concentration and Mobility Statistics for the Canadian Manufacturing Sector. *Ann. Écon. Statist.*, July–Dec. 1989, (15–16), pp. 315–32.

Baldwin, Richard E. Exporting the Capital Markets: Comparative Advantage and Capital Market Imperfections. In *Audretsch, D. B.; Sleuwaegen, L. and Yamawaki, H., eds.*, 1989, pp. 135–52.

_____. The Growth Effects of 1992. *Econ. Policy: A Europ. Forum*, October 1989, (9), pp. 247–81.

_____ and Flam, Harry. Strategic Trade Policies in the Market for 30–40 Seat Commuter Aircraft. *Weltwirtsch. Arch.*, 1989, *125*(3), pp. 484–500.

_____ and Krugman, Paul R. Persistent Trade Effects of Large Exchange Rate Shocks. *Quart. J. Econ.*, November 1989, *104*(4), pp. 635–54.

Baldwin, Robert E. The Political Economy of Trade Policy. *J. Econ. Perspectives*, Fall 1989, *3*(4), pp. 119–35.

_____. Trade and Investment Patterns and Barriers in the United States, Canada, and Japan: Comment. In *Stern, R. M., ed.*, 1989, pp. 126–33.

_____. The U.S. Basic Industries in the 1980s: Can Fiscal Policies Explain Their Changing Competitive Position? Comment. In *Black, S. W., ed.*, 1989, pp. 71–74.

_____. U.S. Trade Policy: Recent Changes and Future U.S. Interests. *Amer. Econ. Rev.*, May 1989, *79*(2), pp. 128–33.

Balestra, Gabriella and Tsoukias, Alexis. Preparing an Intelligent Interface for the Use of Multicriteria Outranking Methods. In *Lockett, A. G. and Islei, G., eds.*, 1989, pp. 575–84.

Balisacan, Arsenio M. Survey of Philippine Research on the Economics of Agriculture. *Philippine Rev. Econ. Bus.*, June 1989, *26*(1), pp. 14–46.

Balk, Bert M. Changing Consumer Preferences and the Cost-of-Living Index: Theory and Nonparametric Expressions. *J. Econ. (Z. Nationalökon.)*, 1989, *50*(2), pp. 157–69.

Balke, Nathan S. and Gordon, Robert J. The Estimation of Prewar Gross National Product: Methodology and New Evidence. *J. Polit. Econ.*, February 1989, *97*(1), pp. 38–92.

Balkin, David B. Union Influences on Pay Policy: A Survey. *J. Lab. Res.*, Summer 1989, *10*(3), pp. 299–310.

_____ and Gomez-Mejia, Luis R. Effectiveness of Individual and Aggregate Compensation Strategies. *Ind. Relat.*, Fall 1989, *28*(3), pp. 431–45.

Ball, David E. and Mangum, Stephen L. The Transferability of Military-Provided Occupational Training in the Post-Draft Era. *Ind. Lab. Relat. Rev.*, January 1989, *42*(2), pp. 230–45.

Ball, James [Sir]. The United Kingdom Economy: Miracle or Mirage? *Nat. Westminster Bank Quart. Rev.*, February 1989, pp. 43–59.

Ball, Laurence and Romer, David H. Are Prices Too Sticky? *Quart. J. Econ.*, August 1989, *104*(3), pp. 507–24.

_____ and Romer, David H. The Equilibrium and Optimal Timing of Price Changes. *Rev. Econ. Stud.*, April 1989, *56*(2), pp. 179–98.

Ball, M. Misguided Rhetoric on Rent: Reply. *Environ. Planning A*, December 1989, *21*(12), pp. 1667–68.

Ball, Michael O.; Liu, Wei-Guo and Pulleyblank, William R. Two-Terminal Steiner Tree Polyhedra. In *Cornet, B. and Tulkens, H., eds.*, 1989, pp. 251–84.

Ball, Nicole. Disarmament for Development. In *Rotblat, J. and Goldanskii, V. I., eds.*, 1989, pp. 226–34.

Ball, Ray and Finn, Frank J. The Effect of Block Transactions on Share Prices: Australian Evidence. *J. Banking Finance*, July 1989, *13*(3), pp. 397–419.

_____ and Kothari, S. P. Nonstationary Expected Returns: Implications for Tests of Market Efficiency and Serial Correlation in Returns. *J. Finan. Econ.*, November 1989, *25*(1), pp. 51–74.

Ball, V. E.; Somwaru, A. and Vasavada, Utpal. Modeling Dynamic Adjustment Subject to Integrability Conditions. In *Bauer, S. and Henrichsmeyer, W., eds.*, 1989, pp. 279–86.

Ballantyne, Harry C. Social Security Financing in North America. *Soc. Sec. Bull.*, April 1989, *52*(4), pp. 2–13.

Ballwieser, Wolfgang. Auditing in an Agency Setting. In *Bamberg, G. and Spremann, K., eds.*, 1989, pp. 327–46.

Baltagi, Badi H.; Garvin, Susan and Kerman, Stephen. Further Monte Carlo Evidence on Seemingly Unrelated Regressions with Unequal Number of Observations. *Ann. Écon. Statist.*, April–June 1989, (14), pp. 103–15.

_____ and Griffin, James M. Alternative Models of Managerial Behavior: Empirical Tests for the Petroleum Industry. *Rev. Econ. Statist.*, November 1989, *71*(4), pp. 579–85.

Balzer, Wolfgang and Häendler, Ernst W. Ordinary Least Squares as a Method of Measurement. In *Balzer, W. and Hamminga, B., eds.*, 1989, pp. 129–46.

Bamber, E. Michael. The Effect of Perceived Expertise on Auditors' Review Judgments. In *Schwartz, B. N., ed.*, 1989, pp. 153–72.

_____; **Snowball, Doug and Tubbs, Richard M.** Audit Structure and Its Relation to Role Conflict and Role Ambiguity: An Empirical Investigation. *Accounting Rev.*, April 1989, *64*(2), pp. 285–99.

Bamber, Greg and Snape, Ed. Managerial and Professional Employees: Conceptualising Union Strategies and Structures. *Brit. J. Ind. Relat.*, March 1989, *27*(1), pp. 93–110.

_____ **and Snape, Ed.** Managers as Employees: Britain. In *Roomkin, M. J., ed.*, 1989, pp. 17–56.

Bamberg, Günter. Risk Sharing and Subcontracting. In *Bamberg, G. and Spremann, K., eds.*, 1989, pp. 61–79.

Bana e Costa, Carlos A. and Neves, Cesar F. Dinis das. Describing and Formalizing the Evaluation Process of Portuguese Navy Officers. In *Lockett, A. G. and Islei, G., eds.*, 1989, pp. 355–69.

Bandara, Jayatilleke S. and Athukorala, Premachandra. Growth of Manufactured Exports, Primary Commodity Dependence, and Net Export Earnings: Sri Lanka. *World Devel.*, June 1989, *17*(6), pp. 897–903.

_____ **and Hazari, Bharat R.** Basic Needs and Linkages: A Case Study of Sri Lanka. *J. Econ. Devel.*, December 1989, *14*(2), pp. 99–106.

Bandow, Doug. Leaving the Third World Alone. In *Crane, E. H. and Boaz, D.*, 1989, pp. 203–18.

Banerjee, Anindya and Beggs, Alan. Efficiency in Hierarchies: Implementing the First-Best Solution by Sequential Actions. *Rand J. Econ.*, Winter 1989, *20*(4), pp. 637–45.

Banerjee, Avijit and Burton, Jonathan S. Lot Sizing and Work-in-Process Inventories in Single Stage Production Systems. In *Gulledge, T. R., Jr. and Litteral, L. A., eds.*, 1989, pp. 283–97.

Banham, John. Vocational Training in British Business. *Nat. Westminster Bank Quart. Rev.*, February 1989, pp. 4–12.

Banker, Rajiv D. Econometric Estimation and Data Envelopment Analysis. In *Chan, J. L. and Patton, J. M., eds.*, 1989, pp. 231–43.

_____; **Bunch, Beverly S. and Strauss, Robert P.** Factors Influencing School District Financial Reporting Practices. In *Chan, J. L. and Patton, J. M., eds.*, 1989, pp. 27–56.

_____; **Das, Somnath and Datar, Srikant M.** Analysis of Cost Variances for Management Control in Hospitals. In *Chan, J. L. and Patton, J. M., eds.*, 1989, pp. 269–91.

_____ **and Datar, Srikant M.** Sensitivity, Precision, and Linear Aggregation of Signals for Performance Evaluation. *J. Acc. Res.*, Spring 1989, *27*(1), pp. 21–39.

_____ **and Morey, Richard C.** Incorporating Value Judgments in Efficiency Analysis. In *Chan, J. L. and Patton, J. M., eds.*, 1989,

pp. 245–67.

_____, **et al.** An Introduction to Data Envelopment Analysis with Some of Its Models and Their Uses. In *Chan, J. L. and Patton, J. M., eds.*, 1989, pp. 125–63.

Banks, Gary. A Role for ERAs in the GATT Forum? *World Econ.*, June 1989, *12*(2), pp. 219–36.

Banks, Jeffrey S. and Austen-Smith, David. Electoral Accountability and Incumbency. In *Ordeshook, P. C., ed.*, 1989, pp. 121–48.

_____; **Ledyard, John O. and Porter, David P.** Allocating Uncertain and Unresponsive Resources: An Experimental Approach. *Rand J. Econ.*, Spring 1989, *20*(1), pp. 1–25.

Banks, P. David; Wehman, Paul and Kregel, John. Competitive Employment for Persons with Mental Retardation: A Decade Later. In *Wehman, P. and Kregel, J., eds.*, 1989, pp. 97–113.

Banks, Taunya Lovell. AIDS and Government: A Plan of Action? *Mich. Law Rev.*, May 1989, *87*(6), pp. 1321–37.

Bansal, Vipul K.; Pruitt, Stephen W. and Wei, K. C. John. An Empirical Reexamination of the Impact of CBOE Option Initiation on the Volatility and Trading Volume of the Underlying Equaties: 1973–1986. *Financial Rev.*, February 1989, *24*(1), pp. 19–29.

Banta, Susan M. Consumer Expenditures in Different-Size Cities. *Mon. Lab. Rev.*, December 1989, *112*(12), pp. 44–47.

Bao, Ke and Wu, Mingyu. Policy Studies in China. In *Zerby, J., ed.*, 1989, pp. 110–17.

Bar-El, Raphael and Felsenstein, Daniel. Technological Profile and Industrial Structure: Implications for the Development of Sophisticated Industry in Peripheral Areas. *Reg. Stud.*, June 1989, *23*(3), pp. 253–66.

Bar-Eliezer, Simcha. Compilation of Import Matrices. In *Franz, A. and Rainer, N., eds.*, 1989, pp. 21–42.

Bar-Ilan, Avner. Effect of Time Preferences on Indexation. *Econ. Letters*, December 1989, *31*(2), pp. 125–28.

Barany, George. Problems and Perspectives on Market Reforms in Hungary: A Comment on Ránki, Marer, and Kornai. In *Van Ness, P., ed.*, 1989, pp. 107–18.

Barat, Josef. A Brief Review of the Development of Urban Transportation in Brazil. *Int. J. Soc. Econ.*, 1989, *16*(12), pp. 44–57.

Barbash, Jack. Equity as Function: Its Rise and Attrition. In *Barbash, J. and Barbash, K., eds.*, 1989, pp. 114–22.

_____. John R. Commons: Pioneer of Labor Economics. *Mon. Lab. Rev.*, May 1989, *112*(5), pp. 44–49.

_____. Theories and Concepts in Comparative Industrial Relations: Introduction. In *Barbash, J. and Barbash, K., eds.*, 1989, pp. 3–6.

Barber, John; Metcalfe, Stanley and Porteous, Mike. Barriers to Growth: The ACARD Study. In *Barber, J.; Metcalfe, J. S. and Porteous, M., eds.*, 1989, pp. 1–19.

Barber, Richard J. and Wedemeyer, Dan J.

Emerging Technological Possibilities: ISDN and Its Impact on Interdependence, 1986–2016. In *Jussawalla, M.; Okuma, T. and Araki, T., eds.*, 1989, pp. 247–63.

Barber, Richard L. and Brodie, J. Douglas. A Sequential Approach to Derivation of Stand Treatment and Forest-Wide Harvest Prescription or Supply. *Natural Res. Modeling*, Spring 1989, *3*(2), pp. 217–39.

Barber, Stephen. Long-Term Unemployment: The Role of the European Social Fund. In *Dyson, K., ed.*, 1989, pp. 75–83.

Barber, William J. Nobel Laureates in Economic Sciences: A Biographical Dictionary: Robert Merton Solow: 1987. In *Katz, B. S., ed.*, 1989, pp. 277–84.

_____. The Spread of Economic Ideas between Academia and Government: A Two-Way Street. In *Colander, D. C. and Coats, A. W., eds.*, 1989, pp. 119–26.

Barbezat, Daniel. Belgian Domestic Steel Cartels and the Re-rollers, 1933–38. In *Hausman, W. J., ed.*, 1989, pp. 218–27.

_____. Cooperation and Rivalry in the International Steel Cartel, 1926–1933. *J. Econ. Hist.*, June 1989, *49*(2), pp. 435–47.

Barbezat, Debra A. Affirmative Action in Higher Education: Have Two Decades Altered Salary Differentials by Sex and Race? In *Ehrenberg, R. G., ed.*, 1989, pp. 107–56.

_____. The Effect of Collective Bargaining on Salaries in Higher Education. *Ind. Lab. Relat. Rev.*, April 1989, *42*(3), pp. 443–55.

Barbier, Edward B. Cash Crops, Food Crops, and Sustainability: The Case of Indonesia. *World Devel.*, June 1989, *17*(6), pp. 879–95.

Barbolla, Rosa and Corchón, Luis C. An Elementary Proof of the Existence of a Competitive Equilibrium in a Special Case. *Quart. J. Econ.*, May 1989, *104*(2), pp. 385–89.

Barbone, Luca and Poret, Pierre. Structural Conditions and Macroeconomic Responses to Shocks: A Sensitivity Analysis for Four European Countries. *OECD Econ. Stud.*, Spring 1989, (12), pp. 131–58.

Barbosa, Fernando de Holanda. As origens e conseqüências de inflação na América Latina. (With English summary.) *Pesquisa Planejamento Econ.*, December 1989, *19*(3), pp. 505–24.

_____ and McNelis, Paul D. Indexation and Inflationary Inertia: Brazil 1964–1985. *World Bank Econ. Rev.*, September 1989, *3*(3), pp. 339–57.

_____ and Sanchez de la Cal, Manuel. Brazilian Experience with External Debt and Prospects for Growth. In *Singer, H. W. and Sharma, S., eds. (I)*, 1989, pp. 397–412.

Barbuto, João Guilherme Marzagão and Latorraca, Nilton. National Tax System—The 1988 Constitution: Brazil. *Bull. Int. Fiscal Doc.*, Aug.–Sept. 1989, *43*(8–9), pp. 394–98.

Barca, Fabrizio and Caselli, Paola. Competitività internazionale e ristrutturazione della industria italiana negli anni '80. (International Competitiveness and Recovery of the Italian Industry

in the Eighties. With English summary.) *Politica. Econ.*, August 1989, *5*(2), pp. 231–72.

Barclay, Michael J. and Holderness, Clifford G. Private Benefits from Control of Public Corporations. *J. Finan. Econ.*, December 1989, *25*(2), pp. 371–95.

Bardach, Eugene. Social Regulation as a Generic Policy Instrument. In *Salamon, L. M., ed.*, 1989, pp. 197–229.

Bardhan, Pranab. Alternative Approaches to the Theory of Institutions in Economic Development. In *Bardhan, P., ed. (II)*, 1989, pp. 3–17.

_____. Conversations between Economists and Anthropologists: Introduction. In *Bardhan, P., ed. (I)*, 1989, pp. 1–12.

_____. The New Institutional Economics and Development Theory: A Brief Critical Assessment. *World Devel.*, Special Issue, September 1989, *17*(9), pp. 1389–95.

_____. A Note on Interlinked Rural Economic Arrangements. In *Bardhan, P., ed. (II)*, 1989, pp. 237–42.

_____. Poverty and Employment Characteristics of Urban Households in West Bengal, India: An Analysis of the Results of the National Sample Survey, 1977–78. In *Rodgers, G., ed.*, 1989, pp. 201–15.

_____. The Role of Institutions in Development: Comment. In *Fischer, S. and de Tray, D., eds.*, 1989, pp. 181–85.

Bårdsen, Gunnar. Estimation of Long Run Coefficients in Error Correction Models. *Oxford Bull. Econ. Statist.*, August 1989, *51*(3), pp. 345–50.

Barentsen, Wim and Nijkamp, Peter. Modelling Non-linear Processes in Time and Space. In *Andersson, Å. E., et al., eds.*, 1989, pp. 175–92.

Baribeau, Mark B. Leverage Risk in the Nonfinancial Corporate Sector. *Bus. Econ.*, July 1989, *24*(3), pp. 34–39.

Bark, Taeho and de Melo, Jaime. Efficiency and Export Earnings Implications of Two-Tier Quota Allocation Rules. *Int. Econ. J.*, Autumn 1989, *3*(3), pp. 31–42.

Barkai, Haim. The Old Historical School: Roscher on Money and Monetary Issues. *Hist. Polit. Econ.*, Summer 1989, *21*(2), pp. 179–200.

Barkema, Alan and Drabenstott, Mark R. The Farm Recovery Is Complete. *Challenge*, July–Aug. 1989, *32*(4), pp. 57–58.

Barker, David. A Periphery in Genesis and Exodus: Reflections on Rural–Urban Relations in Jamaica. In *[Mountjoy, A. B.]*, 1989, pp. 294–322.

_____. Review Essay. *Soc. Econ. Stud.*, December 1989, *38*(4), pp. 265–74.

Barker, George R. and Chapman, Ralph B. Evaluating Labor Market Contracting and Regulation: A Transaction Costs Perspective with Particular Reference to New Zealand. *J. Inst. Theoretical Econ.*, June 1989, *145*(2), pp. 317–42.

Barker, Randolph; Mount, Timothy D. and Bindlish, Vishva. Can Yield Variability Be Offset by Improved Information? The Case of Rice in India. In *Anderson, J. R. and Hazell, P. B. R., eds.*, 1989, pp. 287–300.

Barla, Philippe and Perelman, Sergio. Technical Efficiency in Airlines under Regulated and Deregulated Environments. *Ann. Pub. Coop. Econ.*, 1989, *60*(1), pp. 103–24.

Barlow, Colin. A Comparison of Factors Influencing Agricultural Development in Malaya and Indonesia, 1870–1940. In *Maddison, A. and Prince, G., eds.*, 1989, pp. 227–58.

_____ **and Thee, Kian Wie.** North Sumatra: Growth with Unbalanced Development. In *Hill, H., ed.*, 1989, pp. 408–36.

Barman, Samir; Tersine, Richard J. and Larson, Paul D. An Economic Inventory/Transport Model with Freight Rate Discounts. *Logist. Transp. Rev.*, December 1989, *25*(4), pp. 291–306.

Barmby, Tim and Doornik, Jurgen. Modelling Trip Frequency as a Poisson Variable. *J. Transp. Econ. Policy*, September 1989, *23*(3), pp. 309–15.

_____ **and Treble, John G.** A Note on Absenteeism. *Brit. J. Ind. Relat.*, March 1989, *27*(1), pp. 155–58.

Barnard, Charles H. and Butcher, Walter R. Landowner Characteristics: A Basis for Locational Decisions in the Urban Fringe. *Amer. J. Agr. Econ.*, August 1989, *71*(3), pp. 679–84.

Barnard, Freddie L. and Dobson, William D. The Prospects for Successfully Restructuring the Farm Credit System. In *Horwich, G. and Lynch, G. J., eds.*, 1989, pp. 238–66.

Barnes, T. J. Rhetoric, Metaphor, and Mathematical Modelling: Commentary. *Environ. Planning A*, October 1989, *21*(10), pp. 1281–84.

Barnett, A. H.; Caudill, Steven B. and Jackson, John D. Job Search Duration and Marginal Tax Rates: An Empirical Inquiry. *Southern Econ. J.*, October 1989, *56*(2), pp. 476–89.

Barnett, William, II. Comment on Professor Timberlake's Squared Rule for the Equilibrium Value for the Marginal Utility of Money. In *Rothbard, M. N. and Block, W., eds.*, 1989, pp. 151–57.

_____. Subjective Cost Revisited. In *Rothbard, M. N. and Block, W., eds.*, 1989, pp. 137–38.

Barnett, William A. and Choi, Seungmook S. A Comparison between the Conventional Econometric Approach to Structural Inference and the Nonparametric Chaotic Attractor Approach. In *Barnett, W. A.; Geweke, J. and Shell, K., eds.*, 1989, pp. 141–212.

_____ **and Choi, Seungmook S.** A Monte Carlo Study of Tests of Blockwise Weak Separability. *J. Bus. Econ. Statist.*, July 1989, *7*(3), pp. 363–77.

Barney, L. Dwayne, Jr. and Reynolds, R. Larry. An Economic Analysis of Transplant Organs. *Atlantic Econ. J.*, September 1989, *17*(3), pp. 12–20.

Barnhart, Scott W. The Effects of Macroeconomic

Announcements on Commodity Prices. *Amer. J. Agr. Econ.*, May 1989, *71*(2), pp. 389–403.

_____ **and Darrat, Ali F.** Federal Deficits and Money Growth in the United States: A Vector Autoregressive Analysis. *J. Banking Finance*, March 1989, *13*(1), pp. 137–49.

_____ **and Hardouvelis, Gikas A.** The Evolution of Federal Reserve Credibility: 1978–1984. *Rev. Econ. Statist.*, August 1989, *71*(3), pp. 385–93.

Barnow, Burt S. Government Training as a Means of Reducing Unemployment. In *Bawden, D. L. and Skidmore, F., eds.*, 1989, pp. 109–35.

Baron, David P. Design of Regulatory Mechanisms and Institutions. In *Schmalensee, R. and Willig, R. D., eds.*, Vol. 2, 1989, pp. 1347–1447.

_____. Service-Induced Campaign Contributions and the Electoral Equilibrium. *Quart. J. Econ.*, February 1989, *104*(1), pp. 45–72.

_____. Service-Induced Campaign Contributions, Incumbent Shirking, and Reelection Opportunities. In *Ordeshook, P. C., ed.*, 1989, pp. 93–120.

_____ **and Ferejohn, John.** The Power to Propose. In *Ordeshook, P. C., ed.*, 1989, pp. 343–66.

Baron, James N. and Newman, Andrew E. Pay the Man: Effects of Demographic Composition on Prescribed Wage Rates in the California Civil Service. In *Michael, R. T.; Hartmann, H. I. and O'Farrell, B., eds.*, 1989, pp. 107–30.

Barone, E. and Cuoco, D. The Italian Market for 'Premium' Contracts: An Application of Option Pricing Theory. *J. Banking Finance*, September 1989, *13*(4–5), pp. 709–45.

Barr, David G. Exchange Rate Dynamics: An Empirical Analysis. In *MacDonald, R. and Taylor, M. P., eds.*, 1989, pp. 109–29.

Barr, G. D. I. and Kantor, B. S. Money and Economic Activity, a Response to the Reserve Bank. *S. Afr. J. Econ.*, September 1989, *57*(3), pp. 292–98.

_____ **and Whittaker, John.** The Price Elasticity of Electricity Demand in South Africa. *Appl. Econ.*, September 1989, *21*(9), pp. 1153–57.

Barre, Raymond. Tour d'Horizon. In *Frankel, A. V. and Heck, C. B., eds.*, 1989, pp. 39–43.

Barrell, R. J. Manufacturing Export Prices for the G7. *Nat. Inst. Econ. Rev.*, May 1989, (128), pp. 90–91.

_____ **and Gurney, Andrew.** The World Economy. *Nat. Inst. Econ. Rev.*, February 1989, (127), pp. 26–45.

_____ **and Gurney, Andrew.** The World Economy. *Nat. Inst. Econ. Rev.*, May 1989, (128), pp. 20–38.

_____ **and Gurney, Andrew.** The World Economy. *Nat. Inst. Econ. Rev.*, November 1989, (130), pp. 23–45.

_____ **and Gurney, Andrew.** The World Economy. *Nat. Inst. Econ. Rev.*, August 1989, (129), pp. 22–41.

Barrère, Alain. Money, Credit and Prices in

Keynesian Perspective: Introduction. In *Barrère, A., ed.*, 1989, pp. xiii–xxv.

Barrére, Christian. Keynesian Assumptions and the Dynamics of Price. In *Barrère, A., ed.*, 1989, pp. 137–61.

Barrett, C. Richard and Pattanaik, Prasanta K. Fuzzy Sets, Preference and Choice: Some Conceptual Issues. *Bull. Econ. Res.*, October 1989, *41*(4), pp. 229–53.

Barrett, Ina. A Critique of In-Service Training in the Public Service. *Soc. Econ. Stud.*, September 1989, *38*(3), pp. 223–38.

Barrett, Nancy J. and Bustillo, Ines. Symposium on the Slowdown in Productivity Growth: Comment. *J. Econ. Perspectives*, Summer 1989, *3*(3), pp. 179–81.

Barrett, Sean D. Measuring Poverty in Ireland: An Assessment of Recent Studies. *Econ. Soc. Rev.*, July 1989, *20*(4), pp. 353–60.

Barro, Robert J. An Efficiency-Wage Theory of the Weather. *J. Polit. Econ.*, August 1989, *97*(4), pp. 999–1001.

_____. Interest-Rate Targeting. *J. Monet. Econ.*, January 1989, *23*(1), pp. 3–30.

_____. Modern Business Cycle Theory: Introduction. In *Barro, R. J., ed.*, 1989, pp. 1–15.

_____. The Neoclassical Approach to Fiscal Policy. In *Barro, R. J., ed.*, 1989, pp. 178–235.

_____. New Classicals and Keynesians, or the Good Guys and the Bad Guys. *Schweiz. Z. Volkswirtsch. Statist.*, September 1989, *125*(3), pp. 263–73.

_____. The Ricardian Approach to Budget Deficits. *J. Econ. Perspectives*, Spring 1989, *3*(2), pp. 37–54.

_____ **and Becker, Gary S.** Fertility Choice in a Model of Economic Growth. *Econometrica*, March 1989, *57*(2), pp. 481–501.

Barron, John M.; Black, Dan A. and Loewenstein, Mark A. Job Matching and On-the-Job Training. *J. Lab. Econ.*, January 1989, *7*(1), pp. 1–19.

de Barros, Ricardo Paes and de Mendonça, Rosane S. Pinto. Família e distribuição de renda: O impacto da participação das esposas no mercado de trabalho. (With English summary.) *Pesquisa Planejamento Econ.*, December 1989, *19*(3), pp. 483–504.

Barrow, Michael and Wagstaff, Adam. Efficiency Measurement in the Public Sector: An Appraisal. *Fisc. Stud.*, February 1989, *10*(1), pp. 72–97.

Barry, Bernard. Management Education in Great Britain. In *Byrt, W., ed.*, 1989, pp. 56–77.

Barry, Christopher B. Initial Public Offering Underpricing: The Issuer's View—A Comment. *J. Finance*, September 1989, *44*(4), pp. 1099–1103.

Barry, Frank G. Payroll Taxes: Capital Grants and Irish Unemployment. *Econ. Soc. Rev.*, October 1989, *21*(1), pp. 107–21.

_____. Taxation and the Choice of Employment Policy. *Econ. Soc. Rev.*, April 1989, *20*(3), pp. 189–99.

Barry, Lynn M. Eighth District Banks: Back in the Black. *Fed. Res. Bank St. Louis Rev.*, May–June 1989, *71*(3), pp. 14–22.

Barry, Nancy. The Noncompetitive Theory of International Trade and Trade Policy: Comment. In *Fischer, S. and de Tray, D., eds.*, 1989, pp. 223–25.

Barry, Norman P. Ideas and Interests: The Problem Reconsidered. In *Gamble, A., et al.*, 1989, pp. 53–74.

_____. Political and Economic Thought of German Neo-liberals. In *Peacock, A. and Willgerodt, H., eds. (1)*, 1989, pp. 105–24.

Barry, Peter J. Publishing in Professional Journals. *J. Agr. Econ. Res.*, Winter 1989, *41*(1), pp. 2–3.

_____ **and Ellinger, Paul N.** Credit Scoring, Loan Pricing, and Farm Business Performance. *Western J. Agr. Econ.*, July 1989, *14*(1), pp. 45–55.

_____; **Schnitkey, Gary D. and Taylor, C. Robert.** Evaluating Farmland Investments Considering Dynamic Stochastic Returns and Farmland Prices. *Western J. Agr. Econ.*, July 1989, *14*(1), pp. 143–56.

Barry, Ursula and Jackson, Pauline. Women's Employment and Multinationals in the Republic of Ireland: The Creation of a New Female Labour Force. In *Elson, D. and Pearson, R., eds.*, 1989, pp. 38–59.

Barsky, Robert B. Why Don't the Prices of Stocks and Bonds Move Together? *Amer. Econ. Rev.*, December 1989, *79*(5), pp. 1132–45.

_____ **and Miron, Jeffrey A.** The Seasonal Cycle and the Business Cycle. *J. Polit. Econ.*, June 1989, *97*(3), pp. 503–34.

Barsoux, Jean-Louis. Management Education in France. In *Byrt, W., ed.*, 1989, pp. 120–50.

Barston, R. P. The International Debt Crisis: Evolving Management Methods. *J. World Trade*, February 1989, *23*(1), pp. 69–82.

_____. The International Debt Crisis: Evolving Management Methods. *J. World Trade*, February 1989, *23*(1), pp. 69–82.

Bartel, Ann P. Where Do the New U.S. Immigrants Live? *J. Lab. Econ.*, October 1989, *7*(4), pp. 371–91.

Bartels, Andrew H. Volcker's Revolution at the Fed. In *Guttmann, R., ed.*, 1989, *1985*, pp. 31–38.

Barten, Anton P. Toward a Levels Version of the Rotterdam and Related Demand Systems. In *Cornet, B. and Tulkens, H., eds.*, 1989, pp. 441–65.

_____ **and Bettendorf, L. J.** Price Formation of Fish: An Application of an Inverse Demand System. *Europ. Econ. Rev.*, October 1989, *33*(8), pp. 1509–25.

_____ **and Dhaene, Geert.** When It All Began: The 1936 Tinbergen Model Revisited. *Econ. Modelling*, April 1989, *6*(2), pp. 203–19.

Barth, James R. and Bradley, Michael D. Evidence on the Real Interest Rate Effects of Money, Debt, and Government Spending. *Quart. Rev. Econ. Bus.*, Spring 1989, *29*(1), pp. 49–57.

_____ **and Bradley, Michael G.** The Ailing S&Ls:

Causes and Cures. *Challenge*, March–April 1989, 32(2), pp. 30–38.

———— **and Bradley, Michael G.** Thrift Deregulation and Federal Deposit Insurance. *J. Finan. Services Res.*, September 1989, 2(3), pp. 231–59.

————, **et al.** The Thrift Industry's Rough Road Ahead. In *Guttmann, R., ed.*, 1989, 1986, pp. 97–102.

Barthelemy, Philippe. The Underground Economy in France. In *Feige, E. L., ed.*, 1989, pp. 281–94.

Bartholdi, J. J., III; Tovey, C. A. and Trick, Michael A. The Computational Difficulty of Manipulating an Election. *Soc. Choice Welfare*, July 1989, 6(3), pp. 227–41.

————; **Tovey, C. A. and Trick, Michael A.** Voting Schemes for Which It Can Be Difficult to Tell Who Won the Election. *Soc. Choice Welfare*, April 1989, 6(2), pp. 157–65.

Bartholomew, Wayne; Joray, Paul and Kochanowski, Paul. The Shift-Share Methodology: Deficiencies and Proposed Remedies. *Reg. Sci. Persp.*, 1989, 19(1), pp. 65–88.

Bartik, Timothy J. Small Business Start-Ups in the United States: Estimates of the Effects of Characteristics of States. *Southern Econ. J.*, April 1989, 55(4), pp. 1004–18.

Bartlett, Bruce. The State and the Market in Sub-Saharan Africa. *World Econ.*, September 1989, 12(3), pp. 293–314.

Bartlett, Will. Optimal Control of the Labour-Managed Firm. *Econ. Anal. Workers' Manage.*, 1989, 23(4), pp. 321–34.

Bartoli, Gloria. Fiscal Expansion and External Current Account Imbalances. In *Blejer, M. I. and Chu, K., eds.*, 1989, pp. 171–207.

Bartolomei, Sonia M. and Sweet, Arnold L. A Note on a Comparison of Exponential Smoothing Methods for Forecasting Seasonal Series. *Int. J. Forecasting*, 1989, 5(1), pp. 111–116.

Barton, David R. and Caves, Richard E. Efficiency, Productivity Growth, and International Trade. In *Audretsch, D. B.; Sleuwaegen, L. and Yamawaki, H., eds.*, 1989, pp. 3–27.

Barton, Stephen E. Property Rights and Human Rights: Efficiency and Democracy as Criteria for Regulatory Reform. In *Tool, M. R. and Samuels, W. J., eds. (III)*, 1989, 1983, pp. 221–36.

Bas, Daniel. On-the-Job Training in Africa. *Int. Lab. Rev.*, 1989, 128(4), pp. 485–96.

Başar, Tamer. Time Consistency and Robustness of Equilibria in Non-cooperative Dynamic Games. In *[Verheyen, P.]*, 1989, pp. 9–54.

Basevi, Giorgio. Economic Policy and Adjustment in Denmark: Comment. In *Monti, M., ed.*, 1989, pp. 106–08.

————. On the International Capital Ownership Pattern at the Turn of the Twenty-First Century: Comment. *Europ. Econ. Rev.*, May 1989, 33(5), pp. 1080–83.

————; **Kind, Paolo and Poli, Giorgio.** International Co-operation of Monetary Policies and Confrontation of Commercial and Financial Policies: An Application to U.S.–EC Relations

and to Problems of the European Monetary System. In *Hodgman, D. R. and Wood, G. E., eds.*, 1989, pp. 217–49.

Bashevkin, Sylvia. Free Trade and Canadian Feminism: The Case of the National Action Committee on the Status of Women. *Can. Public Policy*, December 1989, 15(4), pp. 363–75.

Basile, Liliana. Uncertainty in Economic Theory: An Epistemological Perspective. *Ricerche Econ.*, Jan.–June 1989, 43(1–2), pp. 218–35.

Baskin, Jonathan. Dividend Policy and the Volatility of Common Stocks. *J. Portfol. Manage.*, Spring 1989, 15(3), pp. 19–25.

Baslé, Maurice. Les phases récessives auto-entretenues dans le cycle des affairs: Un survol des analyses récentes et une illustration de la nécessité d'un modèle intégré par le cas de la France. (Self-sustained Recessions in Business Cycles. A Survey of New Analysis and an Example of the Necessity of an Integrated Model in the Case of France. With English summary.) *Écon. Societes*, March 1989, 23(3), pp. 57–74.

Basmann, R. L.; Nieswiadomy, Michael L. and Slottje, Daniel J. On the Empirical Relationship between Several Well-Known Inequality Measures. *J. Econometrics*, September 1989, 42(1), pp. 49–66.

Basu, Alaka Malwade. Is Discrimination in Food Really Necessary for Explaining Sex Differentials in Childhood Mortality? *Population Stud.*, July 1989, 43(2), pp. 193–210.

Basu, Amiya K. and Srinivasan, V. The Metric Quality of Ordered Categorical Data. *Marketing Sci.*, Summer 1989, 8(3), pp. 205–30.

Basu, Kaushik. Causality and Economic Theory. In *Wood, J. C. and Woods, R. N., eds., Vol. 3*, 1989, 1981, pp. 274–85.

————. Rural Credit Markets: The Structure of Interest Rates, Exploitation, and Efficiency. In *Bardhan, P., ed. (II)*, 1989, pp. 147–65.

————. Technological Stagnation, Tenurial Laws, and Adverse Selection. *Amer. Econ. Rev.*, March 1989, 79(1), pp. 251–55.

————. A Theory of Association: Social Status, Prices and Markets. *Oxford Econ. Pap.*, October 1989, 41(4), pp. 653–71.

Basu, Santonu. Deregulation: Small Business Access to the Capital Market—Theoretical Issues with Special Reference to Australian Bank Finance. *Australian Econ. Pap.*, June 1989, 28(52), pp. 141–59.

Baswir, Revrisond and Mubyarto. Central Kalimantan: The Dayak Heartland. In *Hill, H., ed.*, 1989, pp. 502–10.

Batchelor, Roy A. and Dua, Pami. Household versus Economist Forecasts of Inflation: A Reassessment: A Note. *J. Money, Credit, Banking*, May 1989, 21(2), pp. 252–57.

———— **and Jonung, Lars.** Cross-Sectional Evidence on the Rationality of the Mean and Variance of Inflation Expectations. In *Grunert, K. G. and Ölander, F., eds.*, 1989, pp. 93–105.

Bateman, B. W. "Human Logic" and Keynes's Economics: A Comment. *Eastern Econ. J.*, Jan.–March 1989, 15(1), pp. 63–67.

Bateman, D. I. Heroes for Present Purposes?—

A Look at the Changing Idea of Communal Land Ownership in Britain: Presidential Address. *J. Agr. Econ.*, September 1989, *40*(3), pp. 269–89.

Bateman, Fred and Atack, Jeremy. Land and the Development of Mid–Nineteenth Century American Agriculture in the Northern States. In *Grantham, G. and Leonard, C. S., eds., Pt. B*, 1989, pp. 279–312.

Bates, Constance. A Global Study of the Capitalization Process and Employment Levels. In *Negandhi, A. R., ed.*, 1989, pp. 51–75.

Bates, J. M.; McDonald, J. R. S. and Rayner, A. J. Market Power in the Food Industry: A Note. *J. Agr. Econ.*, January 1989, *40*(1), pp. 101–08.

Bates, Timothy. The Changing Nature of Minority Business: A Comparative Analysis of Asian, Nonminority, and Black-Owned Businesses. *Rev. Black Polit. Econ.*, Fall 1989, *18*(2), pp. 25–42.

_____. Small Business Viability in the Urban Ghetto. *J. Reg. Sci.*, November 1989, *29*(4), pp. 625–43.

Bateson, Jeff and Swan, Peter L. Economies of Scale and Utilization: An Analysis of the Multiplant Generation Costs of the Electricity Commission of New South Wales, 1970/71–1984/85. *Econ. Rec.*, December 1989, *65*(191), pp. 329–44.

Batey, Peter W. J. and Weeks, Melvyn J. The Effects of Household Disaggregation in Extended Input–Output Models. In *Miller, R. E.; Polenske, K. R. and Rose, A. Z., eds.*, 1989, pp. 119–33.

Bathke, Allen W., Jr.; Hassell, John M. and Lorek, Kenneth S. New Evidence on the Accuracy of Management Forecasts and Time-Series Forecasts of Annual Earnings. In *Schwartz, B. N., ed.*, 1989, pp. 67–84.

_____; **Lorek, Kenneth S. and Willinger, G. Lee.** Firm-Size and the Predictive Ability of Quarterly Earnings Data. *Accounting Rev.*, January 1989, *64*(1), pp. 49–68.

Batie, Sandra S. and Shugart, Herman H. The Biological Consequences of Climate Changes: An Ecological and Economic Assessment. In *Rosenberg, N. J., et al., eds.*, 1989, pp. 121–31.

Bator, Francis M. GNP Budgeting: Old Theory, New Reality. *Challenge*, Sept.–Oct. 1989, *32*(5), pp. 21–27.

_____. Must We Retrench? *Foreign Aff.*, Spring 1989, *68*(2), pp. 93–123.

Batra, Raveendra N. and Naqvi, Nadeem. Nontraded and Intermediate Goods and the Theory of Protection. *Europ. Econ. Rev.*, April 1989, *33*(4), pp. 721–35.

Batten, Dallas S. and Hafer, R. W. The Impact of the Exchange Rate on U.S. Inflation and GNP Growth: Reply. *Southern Econ. J.*, April 1989, *55*(4), pp. 1052–55.

Batten, David F. and Johansson, Börje. Comparative Structural Change in the Urban Economies of Australia and the United States: Techniques for Assessment and Policy Formulation.

In *Gibson, L. J. and Stimson, R. J., eds.*, 1989, pp. 73–88.

_____ **and Johansson, Börje.** Dynamics of Product Substitution. In *Andersson, Å. E., et al., eds.*, 1989, pp. 23–44.

_____; **Karlsson, Charlie and Andersson, Åke E.** From the Industrial Age to the Knowledge Economy. In *Andersson, Å. E.; Batten, D. F. and Karlsson, C., eds.*, 1989, pp. 1–13.

_____; **Kobayashi, Kiyoshi and Andersson, Åke E.** Knowledge, Nodes and Networks: An Analytical Perspective. In *Andersson, Å. E.; Batten, D. F. and Karlsson, C., eds.*, 1989, pp. 31–46.

_____ **and Nijkamp, Peter.** Progress in Spatial Theory and Dynamics: A Prefatory Review. In *Andersson, Å. E., et al., eds.*, 1989, pp. 1–11.

Batterham, R. L.; Fisher, B. S. and MacAulay, T. G. Solution of Spatial Trading Systems with Concave Cubic Programming. *Australian J. Agr. Econ.*, December 1989, *33*(3), pp. 170–86.

Battese, G. E.; Coelli, T. J. and Colby, T. C. Estimation of Frontier Production Functions and the Efficiencies of Indian Farms Using Panel Data from ICRISAT's Village Level Studies. *J. Quant. Econ.*, July 1989, *5*(2), pp. 327–48.

Batty, M.; Longley, P. and Fotheringham, S. Urban Growth and Form: Scaling, Fractal Geometry, and Diffusion-Limited Aggregation. *Environ. Planning A*, November 1989, *21*(11), pp. 1447–72.

Batygin, G. S. "Virtue" against Interests: Notes on the Reflection of Distributive Relations in Mass Consciousness. In *Yanowitch, M., ed.*, 1989, *1987*, pp. 170–86.

Bauchet, Pierre. Essai sur la nouvelle division internationale du travail: L'exemple de la filière maritime. (Essay on the New International Division of Labor: The Example of the Maritime Related Industries. With English summary.) *Revue Écon.*, September 1989, *40*(5), pp. 817–37.

Baucus, Melissa S. Why Firms Do It and What Happens to Them: A Reexamination of the Theory of Illegal Corporate Behavior. In *Post, J. E., ed.*, 1989, pp. 93–118.

Bauer, Anne and Cahuc, Pierre. Conflits, inefficience du capitalisme et politique économique. (Conflict, Dynamic Inefficiency of Capitalism and Economic Policy. With English summary.) *Revue Écon.*, July 1989, *40*(4), pp. 621–47.

Bauer, Leonard. The Future Role of the Farm Business Management Expert. *Can. J. Agr. Econ.*, Part 1, December 1989, *37*(4), pp. 795–99.

Bauer, P. T. Economic History as Theory—Review. In *Wood, J. C. and Woods, R. N., eds., Vol. 2*, 1989, *1971*, pp. 147–62.

Bauer, Richard J. Marketing of Nonferrous Metals: A Customer Perspective. In *Jackson, L. M. and Richardson, P. R., eds.*, 1989, pp. 1–6.

Bauer, S. Historical Review, Experiences and

Perspectives in Sector Modelling. **In** *Bauer, S. and Henrichsmeyer, W., eds.*, 1989, pp. 3–22.

_____. Some Lessons from the Dynamic Analysis and Prognosis System (DAPS). **In** *Bauer, S. and Henrichsmeyer, W., eds.*, 1989, pp. 325–43.

_____ **and Kasnakoglu, H.** Concept and Application of an Agricultural Sector Model for Policy Analysis in Turkey. **In** *Bauer, S. and Henrichsmeyer, W., eds.*, 1989, pp. 71–84.

Bäuerle, Paul. Zur Problematik der Konstruktion praktikabler Entscheidungsmodelle. (With English summary.) *Z. Betriebswirtshaft*, February 1989, *59*(2), pp. 175–92.

Baum, Christopher F. and Thies, Clifford F. The Term Structure of Interest Rates and the Demand for Money during the Great Depression. *Southern Econ. J.*, October 1989, *56*(2), pp. 490–98.

Baum, Sandra R. Nobel Laureates in Economic Sciences: A Biographical Dictionary: Jan Tinbergen: 1969. **In** *Katz, B. S., ed.*, 1989, pp. 304–17.

_____ **and Schwartz, Saul.** What Strategy for the "Education President"? *Challenge*, Jan.–Feb. 1989, *32*(1), pp. 44–50.

Bauman, W. Scott and Dowen, Richard J. The Dynamics of Neglect and Return: Comment. *J. Portfol. Manage.*, Winter 1989, *15*(2), pp. 76–77.

Bauman, Zygmunt. Hermeneutics and Modern Social Theory. **In** *Held, D. and Thompson, J. B., eds.*, 1989, pp. 33–55.

Baumel, C. Phillip; Lee, Tenpao and Kim, Tae-Kyun. Impact of Deregulation on the Financial Performance of the Class I Railroads: Errata. *Logist. Transp. Rev.*, March 1989, *25*(1), pp. 91–94.

_____; **Schnell, Daniel and Hanson, Steven D.** Impact of Railroad Contracts on Grain Bids to Farmers. *Amer. J. Agr. Econ.*, August 1989, *71*(3), pp. 638–46.

Baumgartner, Johann; Yi, Youjae and Bagozzi, Richard P. An Investigation into the Role of Intentions as Mediators of the Attitude–Behavior Relationship. *J. Econ. Psych.*, March 1989, *10*(1), pp. 35–62.

Baumol, William J. The Income Distribution Frontier and Taxation of Migrants. **In** *Bhagwati, J. N. and Wilson, J. D., eds.*, 1989, *1982*, pp. 159–78.

_____. John R. Hicks', *Contribution to Economics*. **In** *Wood, J. C. and Woods, R. N., eds.*, Vol. 2, 1989, *1972*, pp. 189–212.

_____. Lionel Robbins, 1898–1984. **In** *Greenaway, D. and Presley, J. R., eds.*, 1989, pp. 11–23.

_____. Reflections on Modern Economics: Review. *Cambridge J. Econ.*, June 1989, *13*(2), pp. 353–58.

_____ **and Benhabib, Jess.** Chaos: Significance, Mechanism, and Economic Applications. *J. Econ. Perspectives*, Winter 1989, *3*(1), pp. 77–105.

_____ **and Tobin, James.** The Optimal Cash Bal-

ance Proposition: Maurice Allais' Priority. *J. Econ. Lit.*, September 1989, *27*(3), pp. 1160–62.

_____ **and Wolff, Edward N.** Three Fundamental Productivity Concepts: Principles and Measurement. **In** *Feiwel, G. R., ed. (II)*, 1989, pp. 638–59.

Bausch, Thomas. Sample Techniques Used in Marketing Research. **In** *Opitz, O., ed.*, 1989, pp. 356–66.

Bautista, Carlos C. Numerical Exercises on Devaluation and Debt Repudiation. *Philippine Rev. Econ. Bus.*, December 1989, *26*(2), pp. 302–07.

Bautista, Romeo M. Domestic Terms of Trade and Agricultural Growth in Developing Countries. **In** *Islam, N., ed.*, 1989, pp. 17–38.

Bauwens, Luc and Balassa, Bela. The Determinants of Intra-European Trade in Manufactured Goods. **In** *Jacquemin, A. and Sapir, A., eds.*, 1989, *1988*, pp. 185–201.

Bawden, D. Lee. Rethinking Employment Policy: Introduction. **In** *Bawden, D. L. and Skidmore, F., eds.*, 1989, pp. 1–36.

Baxandall, Phineas. National and Class Consequences of the Federal Debt. *Rev. Radical Polit. Econ.*, Winter 1989, *21*(4), pp. 93–97.

Baxter, Joan and Somerville, Keith. Burkina Faso: Politics, Economics and Society. **In** *Allen, C., et al.*, 1989, pp. 237–86.

Baxter, Marianne. Money and Market Incompleteness in Overlapping Generations Models. *J. Monet. Econ.*, July 1989, *24*(1), pp. 69–91.

_____. Rational Response to Unprecedented Policies: The 1979 Change in Federal Reserve Operating Procedures. *Carnegie–Rochester Conf. Ser. Public Policy*, Autumn 1989, *31*, pp. 247–95.

_____ **and Stockman, Alan C.** Business Cycles and the Exchange-Rate Regime: Some International Evidence. *J. Monet. Econ.*, May 1989, *23*(3), pp. 377–400.

Bayard, Thomas O. Economic Relations between the United States and Korea: Conflict or Cooperation? Introduction and Overview. **In** *Bayard, T. O. and Young, S.-G., eds.*, 1989, pp. 1–6.

Bayarri, M. J. and DeGroot, M. H. Optimal Reporting of Predictions. *J. Amer. Statist. Assoc.*, March 1989, *84*(405), pp. 214–22.

Bayart, Jean-François. Contemporary West African States: Cameroon. **In** *Cruise O'Brien, D. B.; Dunn, J. and Rathbone, R., eds.*, 1989, pp. 31–48.

Bayer, Amanda S. and Porter, Richard D. Monetary Perspective on Underground Economic Activity in the United States. **In** *Feige, E. L., ed.*, 1989, pp. 129–57.

Bayley, David H. The Effects of Corruption in a Developing Nation. **In** *Heidenheimer, A. J.; Johnston, M. and LeVine, V. T., eds.*, 1989, *1966*, pp. 935–52.

Bayri, Tulay Y. and Furtan, W. Hartley. The Impact of New Wheat Technology on Income Distribution: A Green Revolution Case Study,

Turkey, 1960–1983. *Econ. Devel. Cult. Change*, October 1989, *38*(1), pp. 113–27.

Baytas, Ahmet. Financial Innovation, Deregulation, and the Slope of the LM. *Atlantic Econ. J.*, March 1989, *17*(1), pp. 89.

———— **and Marty, Alvin L.** The Interest Elasticity of Money Demand: Further Evidence. *Eastern Econ. J.*, April–June 1989, *15*(2), pp. 107–11.

Bazerman, Max H. and Farber, Henry S. Divergent Expectations as a Cause of Disagreement in Bargaining: Evidence from a Comparison of Arbitration Schemes. *Quart. J. Econ.*, February 1989, *104*(1), pp. 99–120.

Beach, Charles M. Dollars and Dreams: A Reduced Middle Class? Alternative Explanations. *J. Human Res.*, Winter 1989, *24*(1), pp. 162–93.

Beach, E. F. Hicks on Ricardo on Machinery. In *Wood, J. C. and Woods, R. N., eds., Vol. 2, 1989, 1971*, pp. 163–69.

Beamish, Paul. Note on Licensing. In *Rugman, A. M., ed., 1989, 1987*, pp. 395–405.

Bean, Charles R. Capital Shortages and Persistent Unemployment. *Econ. Policy: A Europ. Forum*, April 1989, (8), pp. 11–53.

————. Economic Policy and Adjustment in Denmark: Comment. In *Monti, M., ed., 1989*, pp. 109–11.

———— **and Layard, Richard.** Why Does Unemployment Persist? *Scand. J. Econ.*, 1989, *91*(2), pp. 371–96.

———— **and Symons, James S. V.** Ten Years of Mrs. T. In *Blanchard, O. J. and Fischer, S., eds., 1989*, pp. 13–61.

Bean, Frank D.; Schmandt, Jurgen and Weintraub, Sidney. Mexican and Central American Population and U.S. Immigration Policy: Introduction. In *Bean, F. D.; Schmandt, J. and Weintraub, S., eds., 1989*, pp. 1–4.

————, **et al.** The Spanish-Origin Population in the American Southwest. In *Bean, F. D.; Schmandt, J. and Weintraub, S., eds., 1989*, pp. 65–112.

Bearden, William O. and Lichtenstein, Donald R. Contextual Influences on Perceptions of Merchant-Supplied Reference Prices. *J. Cons. Res.*, June 1989, *16*(1), pp. 55–66.

————; **Netemeyer, Richard G. and Teel, Jesse E.** Measurement of Consumer Susceptibility to Interpersonal Influence. *J. Cons. Res.*, March 1989, *15*(4), pp. 473–81.

Beath, John; Katsoulacos, Yannis and Ulph, David. The Game-Theoretic Analysis of Innovation: A Survey. *Bull. Econ. Res.*, July 1989, *41*(3), pp. 163–84.

————; **Katsoulacos, Yannis and Ulph, David.** Strategic R&D Policy. *Econ. J.*, Supplement, 1989, *99*(395), pp. 74–83.

Beatley, Timothy. The Role of Expectations and Promises in Land Use Decisionmaking. *Policy Sciences*, March 1989, *22*(1), pp. 27–50.

Beatty, Randolph P. Auditor Reputation and the Pricing of Initial Public Offerings. *Accounting Rev.*, October 1989, *64*(4), pp. 693–709.

Beaudreau, Bernard C. Entrepreneurial Ability,

International Trade and Foreign Direct Investment. *Int. Econ. J.*, Autumn 1989, *3*(3), pp. 1–22.

Beaujot, Roderic. Panel Discussion on Canadian Immigration Objectives: Levels, Composition, and Directions. In *Beach, C. M. and Green, A. G., 1989*, pp. 84–87.

Beaulieu, Anne; Patry, Michel and Raynauld, Jacques. L'analyse de la productivité des transporteurs aériens canadiens dans le années soixante-dix: Pour un autre plan de vol. (With English summary.) *L'Actual. Econ.*, June 1989, *65*(2), pp. 183–207.

Beauman, Christopher. Competition and Flotation. In *Veljanovski, C., ed. (II), 1989*, pp. 220–23.

Beaumont, C. D., et al. Advertising Assessment—Myth or Reality? *Environ. Planning A*, May 1989, *21*(5), pp. 629–41.

Beaumont, John R. Towards an Integrated Information System for Retail Management. *Environ. Planning A*, March 1989, *21*(3), pp. 299–309.

———— **and Inglis, K.** Geodemographics in Practice: Developments in Britain and Europe. *Environ. Planning A*, May 1989, *21*(5), pp. 587–604.

Beaumont, P. B. and Harris, R. I. D. The North–South Divide in Britain: The Case of Trade Union Recognition. *Oxford Bull. Econ. Statist.*, November 1989, *51*(4), pp. 413–28.

Beaumont, Paul M. and Rose, Adam Z. Interrelational Income Distribution Multipliers for the U.S. Economy. In *Miller, R. E.; Polenske, K. R. and Rose, A. Z., eds., 1989*, pp. 134–47.

Beauregard, Robert A. Atop the Urban Hierarchy: Preface. In *Beauregard, R. A., ed., 1989*, pp. xiii–xx.

————. Postwar Spatial Transformations. In *Beauregard, R. A., ed., 1989*, pp. 1–44.

————. The Spatial Transformation of Postwar Philadelphia. In *Beauregard, R. A., ed., 1989*, pp. 195–238.

————. Urban Restructuring in Comparative Perspective. In *Beauregard, R. A., ed., 1989*, pp. 239–74.

———— **and Feagin, Joe R.** Houston: Hyperdevelopment in the Sunbelt. In *Beauregard, R. A., ed., 1989*, pp. 153–94.

Beaver, William, et al. Financial Reporting, Supplemental Disclosures, and Bank Share Prices. *J. Acc. Res.*, Autumn 1989, *27*(2), pp. 157–78.

Bebchuk, Lucian Arye. Takeover Bids below the Expected Value of Minority Shares. *J. Finan. Quant. Anal.*, June 1989, *24*(2), pp. 171–84.

Becattini, Giacomo. Henry Fawcett and the Labour Question in Mid-Victorian Britain. In *Goldman, L., ed., 1989*, pp. 120–43.

————. Sectors and/or Districts: Some Remarks on the Conceptual Foundations of Industrial Economics. In *Goodman, E. and Bamford, J., eds., 1989*, pp. 123–35.

Bechri, Mohamed Z. The Political Economy of Interest Rate Determination in Tunisia. In *Nabli, M. K. and Nugent, J. B., eds., 1989*, pp. 375–403.

Beck, John H. and Parai, Amar K. The Incidence of Classified Property Taxes in a Three-Sector Model with an Imperfectly Mobile Population. *J. Urban Econ.*, January 1989, *25*(1), pp. 77–92.

Beck, Paul J. and Jung, Woon-Oh. Taxpayers' Reporting Decisions and Auditing under Information Asymmetry. *Accounting Rev.*, July 1989, *64*(3), pp. 468–87.

_____ **and Maher, Michael W.** Competition, Regulation and Bribery. *Managerial Dec. Econ.*, March 1989, *10*(1), pp. 1–12.

Beck, Peter. British Relations with Latin America: The Antarctic Dimension. In *Bulmer-Thomas, V., ed.*, 1989, pp. 164–85.

Beck, Roger L. and Hussey, Donald. Politics, Property Rights, and Cottage Development. *Can. Public Policy*, March 1989, *15*(1), pp. 25–33.

Becker, Brian E. and Gao, Yang. The Chinese Urban Labor System: Prospects for Reform. *J. Lab. Res.*, Fall 1989, *10*(4), pp. 411–28.

_____ **and Olson, Craig A.** Unionization and Shareholder Interests. *Ind. Lab. Relat. Rev.*, January 1989, *42*(2), pp. 246–62.

Becker, Gary S. On the Economics of the Family: Reply to a Skeptic. *Amer. Econ. Rev.*, June 1989, *79*(3), pp. 514–18.

_____. Political Competition among Interest Groups. In *Shogren, J. F., ed.*, 1989, pp. 13–27.

_____ **and Barro, Robert J.** Fertility Choice in a Model of Economic Growth. *Econometrica*, March 1989, *57*(2), pp. 481–501.

Becker, Joao L. and Sarin, Rakesh K. Decision Analysis Using Lottery-Dependent Utility. *J. Risk Uncertainty*, April 1989, *2*(1), pp. 105–17.

Becker, Mark P. Models for the Analysis of Association in Multivariate Contingency Tables. *J. Amer. Statist. Assoc.*, December 1989, *84*(408), pp. 1014–19.

Becker, Robert A.; Boyd, John H., III and Sung, Bom Yong. Recursive Utility and Optimal Capital Accumulation. I. Existence. *J. Econ. Theory*, February 1989, *47*(1), pp. 76–100.

_____ **and Majumdar, Mukul.** Optimality and Decentralization in Infinite Horizon Economies. In *Feiwel, G. R., ed. (II)*, 1989, pp. 436–504.

Becker, William E. and Waldman, Donald M. A Graphical Interpretation of Probit Coefficients. *J. Econ. Educ.*, Fall 1989, *20*(4), pp. 371–78.

Beckerman, Paul. Austerity, External Debt, and Capital Formation in Peru. In *Handelman, H. and Baer, W., eds.*, 1989, pp. 104–42.

Beckerman, Wilfred. A Difference of Opinion on How Keynesianism Was Spread. *Challenge*, July–Aug. 1989, *32*(4), pp. 54.

_____. How Large a Public Sector? In *Helm, D., ed.*, 1989, pp. 66–91.

Beckford, George L. Plantation Capitalism, Underdevelopment, and Transformation: With Special Reference to the Caribbean. In *Martin,*

M. T. and Kandal, T. R., eds., 1989, pp. 150–65.

Beckman, Barry A. and Hertzberg, Marie P. Business Cycle Indicators: Revised Composite Indexes. *Surv. Curr. Bus.*, January 1989, *69*(1), pp. 23–28.

Beckman, Steve. Producer's Dilemma Experiments. *J. Econ. Behav. Organ.*, January 1989, *11*(1), pp. 27–46.

Beckmann, Martin J. Einkommens- und Preiselastizitäten bei additiver Nutzenfunktion. (Income and Price Elasticities When Utility Functions are Additive. With English summary.) *Jahr. Nationalökon. Statist.*, October 1989, *206*(4–5), pp. 279–84.

_____. Managers as Principals and Agents. In *Bamberg, G. and Spremann, K., eds.*, 1989, pp. 379–88.

_____. A Note on Spatial Price Policy When Demand Is Linear but Non-uniform. *Reg. Sci. Urban Econ.*, February 1989, *19*(1), pp. 103–06.

_____. On the Shape and Size of Market Areas. *Ann. Reg. Sci.*, 1989, *23*(2), pp. 81–91.

_____ **and Papageorgiou, Yorgos Y.** Heterogeneous Tastes and Residential Location. *J. Reg. Sci.*, August 1989, *29*(3), pp. 317–23.

Becquart-Leclercq, Jeanne. Paradoxes of Political Corruption: A French View. In *Heidenheimer, A. J.; Johnston, M. and LeVine, V. T., eds.*, 1989, pp. 191–210.

Becuwe, Stéphane. Les déterminants macro-économiques du commerce intra-branche de la France: Une approche de long terme (1850–1980). (The Macroeconomic Determinants of Intra-industry Trade of France: A Long Term Approach [1850–1980]. With English summary.) *Revue Écon.*, September 1989, *40*(5), pp. 863–86.

Bednarzik, Robert W. and Shiells, Clinton R. Labor Market Changes and Adjustments: How Do the U.S. and Japan Compare? *Mon. Lab. Rev.*, February 1989, *112*(2), pp. 31–42.

Beebower, Gilbert L. The Future for Quantitative Investment Products: Comment. *J. Portfol. Manage.*, Winter 1989, *15*(2), pp. 78.

Beeghley, Leonard and Dwyer, Jeffrey W. Income Transfers and Income Inequality. *Population Res. Policy Rev.*, May 1989, *8*(2), pp. 119–42.

Beenstock, Michael. A Democratic Model of the "Rent-Sought" Benefit Cycle. *Public Choice*, October 1989, *63*(1), pp. 1–14.

_____. The Determinants of the Money Multiplier in the United Kingdom. *J. Money, Credit, Banking*, November 1989, *21*(4), pp. 464–80.

_____ **and Vergottis, Andreas.** An Econometric Model of the World Market for Dry Cargo Freight and Shipping. *Appl. Econ.*, March 1989, *21*(3), pp. 339–56.

_____ **and Vergottis, Andreas.** An Econometric Model of the World Tanker Market. *J. Transp. Econ. Policy*, September 1989, *23*(3), pp. 263–80.

Beesley, J. Alan. The Future of International

Oceans Management. **In** *McRae, D. and Munro, G., eds.,* 1989, pp. 217–37.

Beesley, Mark and Rothwell, Roy. The Importance of Technology Transfer. **In** *Barber, J.; Metcalfe, J. S. and Porteous, M., eds.,* 1989, pp. 87–104.

Beesley, Michael E. Transport Research and Economics. *J. Transp. Econ. Policy,* January 1989, *23*(1), pp. 17–28.

_____ **and Hensher, David A.** Contracts, Competitive Bidding and Market Forces: Recent Experiences in the Supply of Local Bus Services. *Australian Econ. Pap.,* December 1989, *28*(53), pp. 236–45.

_____ **and Littlechild, Stephen C.** The Regulation of Privatized Monopolies in the United Kingdom. *Rand J. Econ.,* Autumn 1989, *20*(3), pp. 454–72.

Beeson, Patricia E. and Eberts, Randall W. Identifying Productivity and Amenity Effects in Interurban Wage Differentials. *Rev. Econ. Statist.,* August 1989, *71*(3), pp. 443–52.

_____ **and Husted, Steven.** Patterns and Determinants of Productive Efficiency in State Manufacturing. *J. Reg. Sci.,* February 1989, *29*(1), pp. 15–28.

Begalli, Diego; Perali, Federico and Berni, Pietro. Importance of Risk in the Acreage Supply Decision of Italian Rice Producers. **In** *Bauer, S. and Henrichsmeyer, W., eds.,* 1989, pp. 43–52.

Begg, David. Domestic and Cross-Border Consequences of U.S. Macroeconomic Policies: Comment. **In** *Bryant, R. C., et al., eds.,* 1989, pp. 119–21.

_____. Floating Exchange Rates in Theory and Practice. *Oxford Rev. Econ. Policy,* Autumn 1989, *5*(3), pp. 24–39.

_____, **et al.** Symmetric and Asymmetric Persistence of Labor Market Shocks. *J. Japanese Int. Economies,* December 1989, *3*(4), pp. 554–77.

Begg, Iain. European Integration and Regional Policy. *Oxford Rev. Econ. Policy,* Summer 1989, *5*(2), pp. 90–104.

_____. The Regional Dimension of the '1992' Proposals. *Reg. Stud.,* August 1989, *23*(4), pp. 368–76.

Beggs, Alan. A Note on Switching Costs and Technology Choice. *J. Ind. Econ.,* June 1989, *37*(4), pp. 437–40.

_____ **and Banerjee, Anindya.** Efficiency in Hierarchies: Implementing the First-Best Solution by Sequential Actions. *Rand J. Econ.,* Winter 1989, *20*(4), pp. 637–45.

Behdad, Sohrab. Property Rights in Contemporary Islamic Economic Thought: A Critical Perspective. *Rev. Soc. Econ.,* Summer 1989, *47*(2), pp. 185–211.

Behrman, Jere R. The Simple Analytics of Contraceptive Social Marketing. *World Devel.,* October 1989, *17*(10), pp. 1499–1521.

_____ **and Deolalikar, Anil B.** Agricultural Wages in India: The Role of Health, Nutrition, and Seasonality. **In** *Sahn, D. E., ed.,* 1989, pp. 107–17.

_____ **and Deolalikar, Anil B.** Is Variety the Spice of Life? Implications for Calorie Intake. *Rev. Econ. Statist.,* November 1989, *71*(4), pp. 666–72.

_____ **and Deolalikar, Anil B.** . . . Of the Fittest? Duration of Survival of Manufacturing Establishments in a Developing Country. *J. Ind. Econ.,* December 1989, *38*(2), pp. 215–26.

_____ **and Deolalikar, Anil B.** Seasonal Demands for Nutrient Intakes and Health Status in Rural South India. **In** *Sahn, D. E., ed.,* 1989, pp. 66–78.

_____; **Lewis, Jeffrey D. and Lofti, Sherif.** The Impact of Commodity Price Instability: Experiments with a General Equilibrium Model for Indonesia. **In** *[Adams, F. G.],* 1989, pp. 59–100.

_____; **Pollack, Robert A. and Taubman, Paul.** Family Resources, Family Size, and Access to Financing for College Education. *J. Polit. Econ.,* April 1989, *97*(2), pp. 398–419.

_____ **and Taubman, Paul.** Is Schooling "Mostly in the Genes"? Nature–Nurture Decomposition Using Data on Relatives. *J. Polit. Econ.,* December 1989, *97*(6), pp. 1425–46.

_____ **and Taubman, Paul.** A Test of the Easterlin Fertility Model Using Income for Two Generations and a Comparison with the Becker Model. *Demography,* February 1989, *26*(1), pp. 117–23.

_____ **and Wolfe, Barbara L.** Does More Schooling Make Women Better Nourished and Healthier? Adult Sibling Random and Fixed Effects Estimates for Nicaragua. *J. Human Res.,* Fall 1989, *24*(4), pp. 644–63.

Beier, A. L. Poverty and Progress in Early Modern England. **In** *[Stone, L.],* 1989, pp. 201–39.

Beiji, Paul R. and Groeneweyen, John P. M. The French Communication Industry Defined and Analyzed through the Social Fabric Matrix, the *Filière* Approach, and Network Analysis. *J. Econ. Issues,* December 1989, *23*(4), pp. 1059–74.

Beilock, Richard; Burkhart, Jeffrey and Welsh, Richard. Risk Permits: An Alterntive Approach to Transportation Safety Regulations. *Logist. Transp. Rev.,* September 1989, *25*(3), pp. 195–207.

Beishuizen, J. Octogenarian John Kenneth Galbraith: Sunday Scientist or Superstar? *De Economist,* 1989, *137*(2), pp. 131–54.

Bej, Emil. Some Aspects of Industrial Planning under Brezhnev–Kossygin Rule. *Jahr. Wirtsch. Osteuropas,* 1989, *13*(1), pp. 176–97.

Beja, Avraham. Finite and Infinite Complexity in Axioms of Rational Choice *or* Sen's Characterization of Preference-Compatibility Cannot Be Improved. *J. Econ. Theory,* December 1989, *49*(2), pp. 339–46.

Bekker, Paul A. Identification in Restricted Factor Models and the Evaluation of Rank Conditions. *J. Econometrics,* May 1989, *41*(1), pp. 5–16.

Bekolo-Ebe, Bruno. Le système des tontines: Liquidité, intermédiation et comportement d'épargne. (With English summary.) *Revue*

Écon. Politique, July–Aug. 1989, *99*(4), pp. 616–38.

Bekx, P. and Tullio, Giuseppe. A Note on the European Monetary System, and the Determination of the DM–Dollar Exchange Rate. *Cah. Écon. Bruxelles*, 3rd Trimester 1989, (123), pp. 329–43.

Beladi, Hamid. Urban Unemployment, Economies of Scale and the Theory of Customs Unions. *Keio Econ. Stud.*, 1989, *26*(2), pp. 5–15.

_____; **Biswas, Basudeb and Tribedy, Gopal.** General Equilibrium Analysis of Negative Value-Added. *J. Econ. Stud.*, 1989, *16*(1), pp. 47–53.

_____ **and Lyon, Kenneth S.** Government Expenditures and the ex ante Crowding-Out Effect: An Examination. *Appl. Econ.*, October 1989, *21*(10), pp. 1411–20.

_____ **and Samanta, Subarna K.** Price Advertising Decision under Uncertainty. *Indian Econ. J.*, Oct.–Dec. 1989, *37*(2), pp. 28–39.

Bélanger, Danny and Bernard, Jean-Thomas. Electricity Exports and Hydro-Québec's 1986–2000 Development Plan. *Energy J.*, January 1989, *10*(1), pp. 139–47.

Bélanger, Jacques. Job Control and Productivity: New Evidence from Canada. *Brit. J. Ind. Relat.*, November 1989, *27*(3), pp. 347–64.

Belden, Susan. Policy Preferences of FOMC Members as Revealed by Dissenting Votes. *J. Money, Credit, Banking*, November 1989, *21*(4), pp. 432–41.

Belenky, Peter W. Spatial Competition with Free Entry, Chamberlinian Tangencies, and Social Efficiency: A Correction. *J. Urban Econ.*, July 1989, *26*(1), pp. 75–83.

Belk, Russell W. Extended Self and Extending Paradigmatic Perspective: Comment. *J. Cons. Res.*, June 1989, *16*(1), pp. 129–32.

_____ **and O'Guinn, Thomas C.** Heaven on Earth: Consumption at Heritage Village, USA. *J. Cons. Res.*, September 1989, *16*(2), pp. 227–38.

_____; **Wallendorf, Melanie and Sherry, John F., Jr.** The Sacred and the Profane in Consumer Behavior: Theodicy on the Odyssey. *J. Cons. Res.*, June 1989, *16*(1), pp. 1–38.

_____; **Zhou, Nan and Tse, David K.** Becoming a Consumer Society: A Longitudinal and Cross-cultural Content Analysis of Print Ads from Hong Kong, the People's Republic of China, and Taiwan. *J. Cons. Res.*, March 1989, *15*(4), pp. 457–72.

Belkin, V. D. Restructuring Creates Favorable Conditions for the Development and Application of EMM. *Matekon*, Spring 1989, *25*(3), pp. 60–62.

Bell, Christopher Ross. Between Anarchy and Leviathan: A Note on the Design of Federal States. *J. Public Econ.*, July 1989, *39*(2), pp. 207–21.

Bell, Clive. The Choice of Tenancy Contract. In *Adelman, I. and Lane, S., eds.*, 1989, pp. 161–78.

_____. A Comparison of Principal–Agent and

Bargaining Solutions: The Case of Tenancy Contracts. In *Bardhan, P., ed. (II)*, 1989, pp. 73–92.

_____ **and Devarajan, Shantayanan.** Project Appraisal and Foreign Exchange Constraints: A Rejoinder. *Econ. J.*, June 1989, *99*(396), pp. 481–82.

_____ **and Srinivasan, T. N.** Interlinked Transactions in Rural Markets: An Empirical Study of Andhra Pradesh, Bihar and Punjab. *Oxford Bull. Econ. Statist.*, February 1989, *51*(1), pp. 73–83.

_____ **and Srinivasan, T. N.** Some Aspects of Linked Product and Credit Market Contracts among Risk-Neutral Agents. In *Bardhan, P., ed. (II)*, 1989, pp. 221–36.

_____ **and Zusman, Pinhas.** The Equilibrium Vector of Pairwise-Bargained Agency Contracts with Diverse Actors and Principals Owning a Fixed Resource. *J. Econ. Behav. Organ.*, January 1989, *11*(1), pp. 91–114.

Bell, Derrick. The Final Report: Harvard's Affirmative Action Allegory. *Mich. Law Rev.*, August 1989, *87*(8), pp. 2382–2410.

Bell, Frederick W. Main Quarry Hypothesis and Salmon Angling. *Marine Resource Econ.*, 1989, *6*(1), pp. 71–82.

Bell, Linda A. Union Concessions in the 1980s. *Fed. Res. Bank New York Quart. Rev.*, Summer 1989, *14*(2), pp. 44–58.

Bell, R. T. Content Protection in the Motor Vehicle Industry in the Presence of Joint Ventures. *S. Afr. J. Econ.*, June 1989, *57*(2), pp. 103–23.

Bell, William R. Sources of Uncertainty in Seasonal Adjustment: Comment. *J. Amer. Statist. Assoc.*, March 1989, *84*(405), pp. 22–24.

Bellacicco, Antonio and Errigo, Antonello. La disoccupazione giovanile nei paesi industrializzati: Un modello interpretativo. (Youth Unemployment in Industrialized Countries. With English summary.) *Econ. Lavoro*, April–June 1989, *23*(2), pp. 39–49.

Bellamy, Donald F. and Irving, Allan. Social Welfare in Developed Market Countries: Canada. In *Dixon, J. and Scheurell, R. P., eds.*, 1989, pp. 47–88.

Bellandi, Marco. The Industrial District in Marshall. In *Goodman, E. and Bamford, J., eds.*, 1989, pp. 136–52.

_____. The Role of Small Firms in the Development of Italian Manufacturing Industry. In *Goodman, E. and Bamford, J., eds.*, 1989, pp. 31–68.

Belle, Françoise. Cadres au féminin: De la revendication d'égalité à la recherche d'identité. (Women in Management: From a Demand for Equality towards a Quest for Identity. With English summary.) *Écon. Societes*, January 1989, *23*(1), pp. 113–37.

Beller, Andrea H. and Graham, John W. The Effect of Child Support Payments on the Labor Supply of Female Family Heads: An Econometric Analysis. *J. Human Res.*, Fall 1989, *24*(4), pp. 664–88.

Beller, Daniel J. Coverage and Vesting Patterns in Private Pension Plans, 1975–1985. In

Turner, J. A. and Beller, D. J., eds., 1989, pp. 39–67.

—— **and Turner, John A.** Trends in Pensions: Introduction and Summary of Major Findings. In *Turner, J. A. and Beller, D. J., eds.*, 1989, pp. 1–14.

Bellet, Adam Z. Employer-Sponsored Life Insurance: A New Look. *Mon. Lab. Rev.*, October 1989, *112*(10), pp. 25–28.

Bellinger, William K. A Utility-Production Model of Union Behavior. *J. Lab. Res.*, Winter 1989, *10*(1), pp. 135–45.

Bellis, Jean-François. The EEC Antidumping System. In *Jackson, J. H. and Vermulst, E. A., eds.*, 1989, pp. 41–97.

——; **Vermulst, Edwin A. and Waer, Paul.** Further Changes in the EEC Anti-dumping Regulation: A Codification of Controversial Methodologies. *J. World Trade*, April 1989, *23*(2), pp. 21–34.

Bellmann, Lutz. Seniority-Based Wage System and Postponed Retirement. In *Schmähl, W., ed.*, 1989, pp. 151–62.

——; **Breitung, Jörg and Wagner, Joachim.** Bias Correction and Bootstrapping of Error Component Models for Panel Data: Theory and Applications. *Empirical Econ.*, 1989, *14*(4), pp. 329–42.

—— **and Wagner, Joachim.** Adjustment Strategies and Employment in Import-Sensitive Manufacturing Industries: An Econometric Study for the Federal Republic of Germany, 1976–1983. In *Wohlmuth, K., ed.*, 1989, pp. 379–401.

—— **and Wagner, Joachim.** The Employment of Female and Foreign Workers in West Germany Manufacturing Industries, 1977–1983. *Econ. Lavoro*, Jan.–March 1989, *23*(1), pp. 131–38.

Belloc, Bernard and Freixas, Xavier. Refinancement, liquidation et rationnement du crédit: Une approche bayésienne. (Extending Credit, Liquidation and Credit Rationing: A Bayesian Approach. With English summary.) *Ann. Écon. Statist.*, July–Dec. 1989, (15–16), pp. 231–66.

Bellofiore, Riccardo. In ricordo di un economista critico. Il percorso intellettuale di Claudio Napoleoni. (In Memory of a Political Economist: Claudio Napoleoni. With English summary.) *Rivista Storia Econ.*, S.S., February 1989, *6*(1), pp. 1–38.

——. A Monetary Labor Theory of Value. *Rev. Radical Polit. Econ.*, 1989, *21*(1–2), pp. 1–25.

Belman, Dale L. and Heywood, John S. Establishment Size, Public Administration and Government Wage Differentials. *Econ. Letters*, 1989, *29*(1), pp. 95–98.

—— **and Heywood, John S.** Government Wage Differentials: A Sample Selection Approach. *Appl. Econ.*, April 1989, *21*(4), pp. 427–38.

—— **and Weiss, Leonard W.** Concentration and Wages: Direct and Indirect Effects. In *Weiss, L. W., ed.*, 1989, pp. 85–111.

Belongia, Michael T. and Chalfant, James A. The Changing Empirical Definition of Money: Some Estimates from a Model of the Demand for Money Substitutes. *J. Polit. Econ.*, April 1989, *97*(2), pp. 387–97.

—— **and Hermann, Werner.** Can a Central Bank Influence Its Currency's Real Value? The Swiss Case. *Fed. Res. Bank St. Louis Rev.*, Jan.–Feb. 1989, *71*(1), pp. 47–55.

—— **and Ott, Mack.** The U.S. Monetary Policy Regime, Interest Differentials, and Dollar Exchange Rate Risk Premia. *J. Int. Money Finance*, March 1989, *8*(1), pp. 137–45.

Belous, Richard S. How Human Resource Systems Adjust to the Shift toward Contingent Workers. *Mon. Lab. Rev.*, March 1989, *112*(3), pp. 7–12.

——. Human Resource Flexibility and Equity: Difficult Questions for Business, Labor, and Government. *J. Lab. Res.*, Winter 1989, *10*(1), pp. 67–72.

Belsky, Jill and Buttel, Frederick H. Biotechnology, Plant Breeding, and Intellectual Property: Social and Ethical Dimensions. In *Weil, V. and Snapper, J. W., eds.*, 1989, pp. 110–32.

Belton, Valerie and Vickers, Stephen P. V·I·S·A—VIM for MCDA. In *Lockett, A. G. and Islei, G., eds.*, 1989, pp. 287–304.

Beltramo, Mark A. Modelling Fuel-Switching between Natural Gas and Fuel Oil in U.S. Manufacturing. *Energy Econ.*, January 1989, *11*(1), pp. 70–78.

Beltratti, Andrea and Grilli, Vittorio U. U.S. Military Expenditure and the Dollar. *Econ. Inquiry*, October 1989, *27*(4), pp. 737–44.

Bemmels, Brian G. and Zaidi, Mahmood A. Industrial Relations: The Minnesota Model. In *Barbash, J. and Barbash, K., eds.*, 1989, pp. 203–10.

Ben-Akiva, Moshe; Atherton, Terry and Train, Kenneth E. Consumption Patterns and Self-selecting Tariffs. *Rev. Econ. Statist.*, February 1989, *71*(1), pp. 62–73.

——; **de Palma, André and Thisse, Jacques-François.** Spatial Competition with Differentiated Products. *Reg. Sci. Urban Econ.*, February 1989, *19*(1), pp. 5–19.

Ben-Horim, Moshe and Callen, Jeffrey L. The Cost of Capital, McCaulay's Duration, and Tobin's q. *J. Finan. Res.*, Summer 1989, *12*(2), pp. 143–56.

Ben-Shahar, Haim. Economic Cooperation in the Middle East: From Dream to Reality. In *Fishelson, G., ed.*, 1989, pp. 1–12.

Ben-Tal, A. and Teboulle, M. A Smoothing Technique for Nondifferentiable Optimization Problems. In *Dolecki, S., ed.*, 1989, pp. 1–11.

Ben-Zion, Uri and Kim, Moshe. The Structure of Technology in a Multioutput Branch Banking Firm. *J. Bus. Econ. Statist.*, October 1989, *7*(4), pp. 489–96.

Bénabou, Roland. Optimal Price Dynamics and Speculation with a Storable Good. *Econometrica*, January 1989, *57*(1), pp. 41–80.

Bénard, Jean. Le calcul économique public: conflit des paradigmes et résistance des organisations et des mentalités. (With English summary.) *Revue Écon. Politique*, March–April 1989, *99*(2), pp. 307–21.

_____. Socialist Incentive Schemes and the Price-Setting Problem. In *Gomulka, S.; Ha, Y.-C. and Kim, C.-O., eds.*, 1989, pp. 214–33.

_____ **and Chiappori, Pierre-André.** Second Best Optimum under Morishima Separability and Exogenous Price Constraints. *Europ. Econ. Rev.*, September 1989, *33*(7), pp. 1313–28.

Benassy, Jean-Pascal. Market Size and Substitutability in Imperfect Competition: A Bertrand–Edgeworth–Chamberlin Model. *Rev. Econ. Stud.*, April 1989, *56*(2), pp. 217–34.

_____ **and Blad, Michael C.** On Learning and Rational Expectations in an Overlapping Generations Model. *J. Econ. Dynam. Control*, July 1989, *13*(3), pp. 379–400.

Benavie, Arthur and Froyen, Richard. Optimal Monetary-Fiscal Stabilizers under an Indexed versus Nonindexed Tax Structure: Reply. *J. Econ. Bus.*, February 1989, *41*(1), pp. 93–94.

Bench, Bryan G. South and Southern Africa: Overview of Socio-political Trends and Short- to Medium-Term Projections. In *Whiteside, A. W., ed.*, 1989, pp. 11–30.

Bendekovic, Jadranko. Investment Project Evaluation. In *Macesich, G., ed.*, 1989, pp. 133–46.

Bender, Bruce. A Simple General Equilibrium Analysis of the Relationship between Real Tax Revenue and the Tax Rate. *Scot. J. Polit. Econ.*, November 1989, *36*(4), pp. 321–33.

_____ **and Fixler, Dennis.** The Median Voter, Voting, and Local Government Employment. *J. Reg. Sci.*, February 1989, *29*(1), pp. 29–46.

Bendick, Marc, Jr. Matching Workers and Job Opportunities: What Role for the Federal–State Employment Service? In *Bawden, D. L. and Skidmore, F., eds.*, 1989, pp. 81–108.

Benedict, Mary Ellen and Montgomery, Edward. The Impact of Bargainer Experience on Teacher Strikes. *Ind. Lab. Relat. Rev.*, April 1989, *42*(3), pp. 380–92.

Benería, Lourdes. Gender and the Global Economy. In *MacEwan, A. and Tabb, W. K., eds.*, 1989, pp. 241–58.

_____. Subcontracting and Employment Dynamics in Mexico City. In *Portes, A.; Castells, M. and Benton, L. A., eds.*, 1989, pp. 173–88.

Bengston, David N. A Price Index for Deflating State Agricultural Experiment Station Research Expenditures. *J. Agr. Econ. Res.*, Fall 1989, *41*(4), pp. 12–20.

Benhabib, Jess and Baumol, William J. Chaos: Significance, Mechanism, and Economic Applications. *J. Econ. Perspectives*, Winter 1989, *3*(1), pp. 77–105.

_____ **and Nishimura, Kazuo.** Stochastic Equilibrium Oscillations. *Int. Econ. Rev.*, February 1989, *30*(1), pp. 85–102.

Benigni, M. Ester. Il concetto di dipendenza nel commercio internazionale: Studio di alcuni indicatori. (The Concept of Dependence in International Trade: An Analysis of a Few Indica-

tors. With English summary.) *Rivista Int. Sci. Econ. Com.*, April–May 1989, *36*(4–5), pp. 413–36.

Benington, John. Poverty, Unemployment, and the European Community: Lessons from Experience. In *Dyson, K., ed.*, 1989, pp. 84–113.

Benjamin, Daniel K. A User's Guide to the Regulatory Bureaucracy. In *Meiners, R. E. and Yandle, B., eds.*, 1989, pp. 253–74.

Benjamin, John D.; Sa-Aadu, J. and Sirmans, C. F. Financing and House Prices. *J. Finan. Res.*, Spring 1989, *12*(1), pp. 83–91.

_____; **Shilling, James D. and Sirmans, C. F.** Flood Insurance, Wealth Redistribution, and Urban Property Values. *J. Urban Econ.*, July 1989, *26*(1), pp. 43–53.

Benjamin, Jules R. Interpreting the U.S. Reaction to the Cuban Revolution, 1959–1960. In *Mesa-Lago, C., ed.*, 1989, pp. 145–65.

Benjamin, Lois and Stewart, James B. The Self-Concept of Black and White Women: The Influences upon Its Formation of Welfare Dependency, Work Effort, Family Networks, and Illnesses. *Amer. J. Econ. Sociology*, April 1989, *48*(2), pp. 165–75.

_____ **and Stewart, James B.** Values, Beliefs, and Welfare Recipiency: Is There a Connection? *Rev. Black Polit. Econ.*, Winter 1989, *17*(3), pp. 43–67.

Benjamin, Nancy C.; Devarajan, Shantayanan and Weiner, Robert J. The 'Dutch' Disease in a Developing Country: Oil Reserves in Cameroon. *J. Devel. Econ.*, January 1989, *30*(1), pp. 71–92.

Benjamin, Roger. Some Public Policy Implications of the Information Revolution. In *Jussawalla, M.; Okuma, T. and Araki, T., eds.*, 1989, pp. 47–53.

Bennett, Adam. The Accelerator's Debt to Simultaneity: A Demonstration on French Data. *Revue Écon.*, January 1989, *40*(1), pp. 81–87.

Bennett, Craig and Cooper, John. The Development of a Program Classification of Health Services for the South Australian Health Commission—Reflections on the First Three Years. In *Butler, J. R. G. and Doessel, D. P., eds.*, 1989, *1984*, pp. 266–77.

Bennett, James T. Mandated Rigidities in U.S. Labor Markets: The Implications for Organized Labor. *J. Lab. Res.*, Winter 1989, *10*(1), pp. 83–89.

Bennett, Karl M. Financing Economic Growth with Special Reference to Jamaica. *Soc. Econ. Stud.*, December 1989, *38*(4), pp. 95–114.

Bennett, M. D.; Greenlick, M. R. and Hornbrook, M. C. Adjusting the AAPCC for Selectivity and Selection Bias under Medicare Risk Contracts. In *Scheffler, R. M. and Rossiter, L. F., eds.*, 1989, pp. 111–49.

Bennett, R. E.; Kamath, Shyam J. and Jensen, K. C. Reprise and Clarification [Money in the Production Function—An Alternative Test Procedure]. *Eastern Econ. J.*, July–Sept. 1989, *15*(3), pp. 241–43.

Bennett, Randall W. and Fizel, John L. The Impact of College Football Telecasts on College

Football Attendance. *Soc. Sci. Quart.*, December 1989, *70*(4), pp. 980–88.

_____ and **Loucks, Christine.** Price (De)Regulation and Quality Rivalry: The Case of Branch Banking Revisited. *Quart. J. Bus. Econ.*, Winter 1989, *28*(1), pp. 68–82.

Bennett, Robert J.; Haining, R. P. and **Griffith, D. A.** Statistical Analysis of Spatial Data in the Presence of Missing Observations: A Methodological Guide and an Application to Urban Census Data. *Environ. Planning A*, November 1989, *21*(11), pp. 1511–23.

_____ and **Krebs, Günter.** Regional Policy Incentives and the Relative Costs of Capital in Assisted Areas in Britain and Germany. *Reg. Stud.*, June 1989, *23*(3), pp. 201–18.

Benson, Bruce L. Further Thoughts on Rent-Seeking, Bureaucratic Output, and the Price of Complements. *Public Choice*, December 1989, *63*(3), pp. 279–81.

_____. The Spontaneous Evolution of Commercial Law. *Southern Econ. J.*, January 1989, *55*(3), pp. 644–61.

_____ and **Cosimano, Thomas F.** Spatial Competition with Free Entry, Chamberlinian Tangencies, and Social Efficiency: A Reevaluation. *J. Urban Econ.*, July 1989, *26*(1), pp. 84–89.

Benston, George J. The Federal "Safety Net" and the Repeal of the Glass–Steagall Act's Separation of Commercial and Investment Banking. *J. Finan. Services Res.*, October 1989, *2*(4), pp. 287–305.

_____. Party Realignments and the Growth of Federal Economic Regulation, 1861–1986: Comments. *J. Finan. Services Res.*, September 1989, *2*(3), pp. 227–29.

Bentley, George G. and **Cross, Sam Y.** Treasury and Federal Reserve Foreign Exchange Operations. *Fed. Res. Bank New York Quart. Rev.*, Autumn 1989, *14*(3), pp. 54–60.

Bentley, Orville G. Technology Development and World Food Production Patterns. In *Helmuth, J. W. and Johnson, S. R., eds., Vol. 1*, 1989, pp. 156–60.

Benton, Gregor. Communist Guerrilla Bases in Southeast China after the Start of the Long March. In *Hartford, K. and Goldstein, S. M., eds.*, 1989, pp. 62–91.

Benton, Lauren A. Homework and Industrial Development: Gender Roles and Restructuring in the Spanish Shoe Industry. *World Devel.*, February 1989, *17*(2), pp. 255–66.

_____. Industrial Subcontracting and the Informal Sector: The Politics of Restructuring in the Madrid Electronics Industry. In *Portes, A.; Castells, M. and Benton, L. A., eds.*, 1989, pp. 228–44.

_____; **Portes, Alejandro** and **Castells, Manuel.** The Policy Implications of Informality: Conclusion. In *Portes, A.; Castells, M. and Benton, L. A., eds.*, 1989, pp. 298–311.

Bentzen, Jan. Betalingsbalancehensyn og skyggevalutakurs i samfundsøkonomiske cost benefit analyser. (On the Use of Shadow Prices in Social Cost Benefit Analysis with Persistent Balance of Payments Problems. With English summary.) *Nationaløkon. Tidsskr.*, 1989, *127*(2), pp. 255–63.

Benveniste, Lawrence M. and **Spindt, Paul A.** How Investment Bankers Determine the Offer Price and Allocation of New Issues. *J. Finan. Econ.*, October 1989, *24*(2), pp. 343–61.

Benzing, Cynthia. An Update on Money in the Production Function. *Eastern Econ. J.*, July–Sept. 1989, *15*(3), pp. 235–39.

Bera, Anil K. and **Robinson, Peter M.** Tests for Serial Dependence and Other Specification Analysis in Models of Markets in Disequilibrium. *J. Bus. Econ. Statist.*, July 1989, *7*(3), pp. 343–52.

Berbel, Julio. Analysis of Protected Cropping: An Application of Multiobjective Programming Techniques to Spanish Horticulture. *Europ. Rev. Agr. Econ.*, 1989, *16*(2), pp. 203–16.

Berend, Iván T. A Debate on the Crisis of the Hungarian Reform in the 1970s. *Acta Oecon.*, 1989, *40*(1–2), pp. 105–38.

_____. In Agreement and At Issue. *Acta Oecon.*, 1989, *40*(1–2), pp. 159–63.

Bereskin, C. Gregory. An Econometric Alternative to URCS (Uniform Railroad Costing System). *Logist. Transp. Rev.*, June 1989, *25*(2), pp. 99–128.

Berezneva, T. D. Convergence of Price Adjustment Processes with Monotonic Demand Functions. *Matekon*, Spring 1989, *25*(3), pp. 31–39.

Berg, Anne Marie. Part-Time Employment: A Response to Economic Crisis? In *Rosenberg, S., ed.*, 1989, pp. 221–31.

Berg, Elliot. The Liberalization of Rice Marketing in Madagascar. *World Devel.*, May 1989, *17*(5), pp. 719–28.

van den Berg, Frank J. M. Patenting Activity and Elements of Market Structure in the Dutch Manufacturing Industry. *De Economist*, 1989, *137*(4), pp. 476–92.

Berg, Gerald C. and **Méndez, José A.** The Effects of Steel Import Restraints on U.S. Steel-Consuming Industries. *J. World Trade*, August 1989, *23*(4), pp. 35–44.

Berg, Gordon. Frances Perkins and the Flowering of Economic and Social Policies. *Mon. Lab. Rev.*, June 1989, *112*(6), pp. 28–32.

Berg, Maxine. Progress and Providence in Early Nineteenth Century Political Economy. In *Berg, M., et al.*, 1989, pp. 150–64.

Berg, Norman A. Land Use: What You Need to Know. In *Dysart, B. C., III and Clawson, M., eds.*, 1989, pp. 135–42.

van der Berg, S. On Interracial Income Distribution in South Africa to the End of the Century. *S. Afr. J. Econ.*, March 1989, *57*(1), pp. 35–51.

Berg, Sanford V. The Production of Compatibility: Technical Standards as Collective Goods. *Kyklos*, 1989, *42*(3), pp. 361–83.

_____. Technical Standards as Public Goods: Demand Incentives for Cooperative Behavior. *Public Finance Quart.*, January 1989, *17*(1), pp. 29–54.

van Bergeijk, Peter A. G. Success and Failure

of Economic Sanctions. *Kyklos*, 1989, *42*(3), pp. 385–404.

_____. The Viability of Commodity Cartels: The Case of Oil. *J. Econ. Educ.*, Fall 1989, *20*(4), pp. 364–70.

Berger, Allen N. and Craine, Roger. Why Random Walk Models of the Term Structure Are Hard to Reject. *J. Bus. Econ. Statist.*, April 1989, *7*(2), pp. 161–67.

_____ **and Hannan, Timothy H.** Deposit Interest Rates and Local Market Concentration. In *Weiss, L. W., ed.*, 1989, pp. 255–65.

_____ **and Hannan, Timothy H.** The Price–Concentration Relationship in Banking. *Rev. Econ. Statist.*, May 1989, *71*(2), pp. 291–99.

Berger, Franklin D. and Long, William T., III. The Texas Industrial Production Index. *Fed. Res. Bank Dallas Econ. Rev.*, November 1989, pp. 21–38.

Berger, Ida E. and Mitchell, Andrew A. The Effect of Advertising on Attitude Accessibility, Attitude Confidence, and the Attitude–Behavior Relationship. *J. Cons. Res.*, December 1989, *16*(3), pp. 269–79.

Berger, Karin; Landes, Thomas and Loistl, Otto. Simulation of Synergetic Stock Price Modelling. In *Loistl, O. and Landes, T., ed.*, 1989, pp. 109–27.

Berger, Lawrence A. Economics and Hermeneutics. *Econ. Philos.*, October 1989, *5*(2), pp. 209–33.

_____; **Kleindorfer, Paul R. and Kunreuther, Howard.** A Dynamic Model of the Transmission of Price Information in Auto Insurance Markets. *J. Risk Ins.*, March 1989, *56*(1), pp. 17–33.

Berger, Marguerite. Giving Women Credit: The Strengths and Limitations of Credit as a Tool for Alleviating Poverty. *World Devel.*, July 1989, *17*(7), pp. 1017–32.

Berger, Mark C. Demographic Cycles, Cohort Size, and Earnings. *Demography*, May 1989, *26*(2), pp. 311–21.

_____; **Black, Dan A. and Scott, Frank A., Jr.** Effects of the Tax Treatment of Fringe Benefits on Labor Market Segmentation. *Ind. Lab. Relat. Rev.*, January 1989, *42*(2), pp. 216–29.

_____ **and Leigh, J. Paul.** Schooling, Self-Selection, and Health. *J. Human Res.*, Summer 1989, *24*(3), pp. 433–55.

Berger, Thomas J. Banks, Governments and International Debt: Where Do We Go from Here? In *Hamouda, O. F.; Rowley, R. and Wolf, B. M., eds.*, 1989, pp. 4–9.

Bergère, Marie-Claire. The Consequences of the Post First World War Depression for the China Treaty-Port Economy 1921–3. In *Brown, I., ed.*, 1989, pp. 221–52.

Bergholm, Fredrik; Hanson, Kenneth A. and Hartler, Christina. Semi-technical Specification of Pricing in MOSES. In *Albrecht, J. W., et al.*, 1989, pp. 221–31.

_____, **et al.** The MOSES APL Program Code. In *Albrecht, J. W., et al.*, 1989, pp. 245–354.

_____. The MOSES Technical Specification

Code. In *Albrecht, J. W., et al.*, 1989, pp. 147–220.

Bergin, James. A Characterization of Sequential Equilibrium Strategies in Infinitely Repeated Incomplete Information Games. *J. Econ. Theory*, February 1989, *47*(1), pp. 51–65.

_____. We Eventually Agree. *Math. Soc. Sci.*, February 1989, *17*(1), pp. 57–66.

_____ **and MacLeod, W. Bentley.** Entry, Sunk Costs and Renegotiation in Duopoly. *Ann. Écon. Statist.*, July–Dec. 1989, (15–16), pp. 173–91.

Bergland, Olvar. The Importance of Functional Form in the Estimation of Welfare: Discussion. *Western J. Agr. Econ.*, July 1989, *14*(1), pp. 175–76.

Berglund, Tom and Gripenberg, Maria. Prissättning av ränteoptioner, en översikt. (Option Pricing: A Review. With English summary.) *Ekon. Samfundets Tidskr.*, 1989, *42*(2), pp. 123–36.

_____; **Liljeblom, Eva and Löflund, Anders.** Estimating Betas on Daily Data for a Small Stock Market. *J. Banking Finance*, March 1989, *13*(1), pp. 41–64.

Bergmann, Barbara R. Does the Market for Women's Labor Need Fixing? *J. Econ. Perspectives*, Winter 1989, *3*(1), pp. 43–60.

Bergson, Abram. Annual Plan Fulfillment in Soviet Industry, 1961–1985. In *Bergson, A.*, 1989, pp. 235–43.

_____. Comparative Productivity: The USSR, Eastern Europe, and the West. In *Bergson, A.*, 1989, pp. 9–31.

_____. Economics of Perestroika: An Inauspicious Beginning. *Challenge*, May–June 1989, *32*(3), pp. 10–15.

_____. Entrepreneurship under Labor Participation: The Yugoslav Case. In *Bergson, A.*, 1989, pp. 177–233.

_____. The Geometry of COMECON Trade. In *Bergson, A.*, 1989, pp. 245–60.

_____. Income Inequality under Soviet Socialism. In *Bergson, A.*, 1989, pp. 55–102.

_____. Inventories: East and West. In *Bergson, A.*, 1989, pp. 33–38.

_____. On Soviet Real Investment Growth. In *Bergson, A.*, 1989, pp. 263–81.

_____. On the Measurement of Soviet Real Defense Outlays. In *Bergson, A.*, 1989, pp. 283–96.

_____. Planning and Performance in Socialist Economies: The USSR and Eastern Europe: Introduction. In *Bergson, A.*, 1989, pp. 1–5.

_____. The Production Function in Soviet Postwar Industrial Growth. In *Bergson, A.*, 1989, pp. 151–61.

_____. Soviet Consumption in Comparative Perspective. In *Bergson, A.*, 1989, pp. 39–54.

_____. The Soviet Slowdown: Can It Be Reversed? In *Bergson, A.*, 1989, pp. 163–74.

_____. Soviet Technological Progress. In *Bergson, A.*, 1989, pp. 105–49.

Bergsten, C. Fred. America in the World Economy: A Strategy for the 1990s. In *Hamilton, E. K., ed.*, 1989, pp. 82–112.

———. The Paris Summit: Lost Opportunities. *Challenge*, Sept.–Oct. 1989, *32*(5), pp. 52–53.

———. The Second Debt Crisis Is Coming. In *Guttmann, R., ed.,* 1989, *1985*, pp. 236–43.

———. U.S. International Macroeconomic Policy. In *Bayard, T. O. and Young, S.-G., eds.,* 1989, pp. 19–33.

Bergstrand, Jeffrey H. The Generalized Gravity Equation, Monopolistic Competition, and the Factor–Proportions Theory in International Trade. *Rev. Econ. Statist.,* February 1989, *71*(1), pp. 143–53.

Bergstrom, John C. and Centner, Terence J. Agricultural Nuisances and Right-to-Farm Laws: Implications of Changing Liability Rules. *Rev. Reg. Stud.,* Winter 1989, *19*(1), pp. 23–30.

——— **and Stoll, John R.** Application of Experimental Economics Concepts and Precepts to CVM Field Survey Procedures. *Western J. Agr. Econ.,* July 1989, *14*(1), pp. 98–109.

———; **Stoll, John R. and Randall, Alan.** Information Effects in Contingent Markets. *Amer. J. Agr. Econ.,* August 1989, *71*(3), pp. 685–91.

Bergstrom, Theodore C. A Fresh Look at the Rotten Kid Theorem—and Other Household Mysteries. *J. Polit. Econ.,* October 1989, *97*(5), pp. 1138–59.

———. Love and Spaghetti, the Opportunity Cost of Virtue. *J. Econ. Perspectives,* Spring 1989, *3*(2), pp. 165–73.

Berkes, Fikret. Co-management and the James Bay Agreement. In *Pinkerton, E., ed.,* 1989, pp. 189–208.

———; **Pinkerton, Evelyn and Rettig, R. Bruce.** The Future of Fisheries Co-management: A Multi-disciplinary Assessment. In *Pinkerton, E., ed.,* 1989, pp. 273–89.

Berkman, Lisa F.; Kapp, Mary C. and Smits, Helen L. The Value of Medical Care: Four Case Studies. In *Eisdorfer, C.; Kessler, D. A. and Spector, A. N., eds.,* 1989, pp. 322–40.

———; **Singer, Burton and Manton, Kenneth G.** Black/White Differences in Health Status and Mortality among the Elderly. *Demography,* November 1989, *26*(4), pp. 661–78.

Berkovec, James. A General Equilibrium Model of Housing Consumption and Investment. *J. Real Estate Finance Econ.,* September 1989, *2*(3), pp. 157–72.

——— **and Fullerton, Don.** The General Equilibrium Effects of Inflation on Housing Consumption and Investment. *Amer. Econ. Rev.,* May 1989, *79*(2), pp. 277–82.

Berkovitch, Elazar; Bradley, Michael and Khanna, Naveen. Tender Offer Auctions, Resistance Strategies, and Social Welfare. *J. Law, Econ., Organ.,* Fall 1989, *5*(2), pp. 395–412.

Berkowitz, Edward D. Allocating Resources for Rehabilitation: A Historical and Ethical Framework. *Soc. Sci. Quart.,* March 1989, *70*(1), pp. 40–52.

——— **and Berkowitz, Monroe.** Incentives for Reducing the Costs of Disability. In *McLennan, K. and Meyer, J. A., eds.,* 1989, pp. 203–26.

Berkowitz, Monroe and Berkowitz, Edward D. Incentives for Reducing the Costs of Disability. In *McLennan, K. and Meyer, J. A., eds.,* 1989, pp. 203–26.

Berlan, Jean-Pierre. Capital Accumulation, Transformation of Agriculture, and the Agricultural Crisis: A Long-Term Perspective. In *MacEwan, A. and Tabb, W. K., eds.,* 1989, pp. 205–24.

Berliner, Diane T. and Pugliaresi, Lucian. Policy Analysis at the Department of State: The Policy Planning Staff. *J. Policy Anal. Manage.,* Summer 1989, *8*(3), pp. 379–94.

Berliner, Joseph S. Soviet Economic Reform and Technical Progress. In *Berliner, J. S.; Kosta, H. G. J. and Hakogi, M., eds.,* 1989, pp. 41–52.

———. The Soviet Far East and the Transbaikal: A New Strategy on the Back of Old Problems: Discussion. In *Berliner, J. S.; Kosta, H. G. J. and Hakogi, M., eds.,* 1989, pp. 99–101.

———. Soviet Female Labor Participation: A Regional Cross-section Analysis. *J. Compar. Econ.,* September 1989, *13*(3), pp. 446–72.

Berman, Katrina V. and Berman, Matthew D. An Empirical Test of the Theory of the Labor-Managed Firm. *J. Compar. Econ.,* June 1989, *13*(2), pp. 281–300.

Berman, Matthew D. and Berman, Katrina V. An Empirical Test of the Theory of the Labor-Managed Firm. *J. Compar. Econ.,* June 1989, *13*(2), pp. 281–300.

Berman, Peter; Sisler, Daniel G. and Habicht, Jean-Pierre. Equity in Public-Sector Primary Health Care: The Role of Service Organization in Indonesia. *Econ. Devel. Cult. Change,* July 1989, *37*(4), pp. 778–803.

Bermúdez, Augusto and Gana, Eduardo. Options for Regional Integration. *CEPAL Rev.,* April 1989, (37), pp. 79–93.

Bernanke, Ben S. Regulation of Debt and Equity: Discussion. In *Kopcke, R. W. and Rosengren, E. S., eds.,* 1989, pp. 207–11.

——— **and Blinder, Alan S.** Credit, Money, and Aggregate Demand. In *Blinder, A. S.,* 1989, *1988*, pp. 93–100.

——— **and Gertler, Mark.** Agency Costs, Net Worth, and Business Fluctuations. *Amer. Econ. Rev.,* March 1989, *79*(1), pp. 14–31.

——— **and Parkinson, Martin.** Unemployment, Inflation, and Wages in the American Depression: Are There Lessons for Europe? *Amer. Econ. Rev.,* May 1989, *79*(2), pp. 210–14.

Bernard, Jean-Thomas. Réglementation des prix de l'électricité à l'exportation par l'one. (With English summary.) *L'Actual. Econ.,* March 1989, *65*(1), pp. 71–85.

———. A Ricardian Theory of Hydroelectric Power Development: Some Canadian Evidence. *Can. J. Econ.,* May 1989, *22*(2), pp. 328–39.

——— **and Bélanger, Danny.** Electricity Exports and Hydro-Québec's 1986–2000 Development Plan. *Energy J.,* January 1989, *10*(1), pp. 139–47.

Bernard, Victor L. and Frost, Carol A. The Role

of Debt Covenants in Assessing the Economic Consequences of Limiting Capitalization of Exploration Costs. *Accounting Rev.*, October 1989, *64*(4), pp. 788–808.

———— **and Stober, Thomas L.** The Nature and Amount of Information in Cash Flows and Accruals. *Accounting Rev.*, October 1989, *64*(4), pp. 624–52.

———— **and Thomas, Jacob K.** Post-Earnings-Announcement Drift: Delayed Price Response or Risk Premium? *J. Acc. Res.*, Supplement, 1989, *27*, pp. 1–36.

Bernardi, Luigi. Income Tax Restructuring through Rate Reduction and Base Broadening: Some Special Problems. In *Chiancone, A. and Messere, K., eds.*, 1989, pp. 73–85.

Bernardo, Daniel J. A Dynamic Model for Determining Optimal Range Improvement Programs. *Western J. Agr. Econ.*, December 1989, *14*(2), pp. 223–34.

Bernardo, John J. Stochastic Preference and Randomized Strategies for Consumer Choice. *J. Behav. Econ.*, Summer 1989, *18*(2), pp. 115–27.

————; **Steuer, Ralph E. and Gardiner, Lorraine R.** Multiple Criteria Trajectory Decision Support Using Polyscreen Workstations: A Production Planning Illustration. In *Lockett, A. G. and Islei, G., eds.*, 1989, pp. 486–97.

Berndt, Ernst R. and Greenberg, Paul E. Canadian Energy Demand after the Oil Shocks. In *Watkins, G. C., ed.*, 1989, pp. 69–103.

————; **Wood, David O. and Harper, Michael J.** Rates of Return and Capital Aggregation Using Alternative Rental Prices. In *Jorgenson, D. W. and Landau, R., eds.*, 1989, pp. 331–72.

Berner, Ole and Thage, Bent. Kvartalsvise nationalregnskaber fra Danmarks Statistik—Og nogle udenlandske erfaringer. (The Sources and Methods of the New Official Quarterly National Accounts for Denmark. With English summary.) *Nationaløkon. Tidsskr.*, 1989, *127*(1), pp. 95–109.

Bernhardt, Dan. Money and Loans. *Rev. Econ. Stud.*, January 1989, *56*(1), pp. 89–100.

———— **and Enders, Alice.** Free Trade Equilibria to Multi-country Quota Games. *J. Int. Econ.*, November 1989, *27*(3–4), pp. 319–33.

Bernheim, B. Douglas. Incentive Effects of the Corporate Alternative Minimum Tax. In *Summers, L. H., ed.*, 1989, pp. 69–95.

————. Intergenerational Altruism, Dynastic Equilibria and Social Welfare. *Rev. Econ. Stud.*, January 1989, *56*(1), pp. 119–28.

————. A Neoclassical Perspective on Budget Deficits. *J. Econ. Perspectives*, Spring 1989, *3*(2), pp. 55–72.

————. The Timing of Retirement: A Comparison of Expectations and Realizations. In *Wise, D. A., ed.*, 1989, pp. 335–55.

———— **and Levin, Lawrence.** Social Security and Personal Saving: An Analysis of Expectations. *Amer. Econ. Rev.*, May 1989, *79*(2), pp. 97–102.

———— **and Ray, Debraj.** Collective Dynamic Consistency in Repeated Games. *Games Econ. Behav.*, December 1989, *1*(4), pp. 295–326.

———— **and Ray, Debraj.** Markov Perfect Equilibria in Altruistic Growth Economies with Production Uncertainty. *J. Econ. Theory*, February 1989, *47*(1), pp. 195–202.

Bernholz, Peter. Currency Competition, Inflation, Gresham's Law and Exchange Rate. *J. Inst. Theoretical Econ.*, September 1989, *145*(3), pp. 465–88.

————. Implications of Alternative International Exchange Rate Arrangements for the Developing Countries: Comments. In *Vosgerau, H.-J., ed.*, 1989, pp. 85–88.

————. Ordo-Liberals and the Control of the Money Supply. In *Peacock, A. and Willgerodt, H., eds. (I)*, 1989, pp. 191–215.

———— **and Jaksch, Hans Jürgen.** An Implausible Theory of Inflation. *Weltwirtsch. Arch.*, 1989, *125*(2), pp. 359–65.

Berni, Pietro; Begalli, Diego and Perali, Federico. Importance of Risk in the Acreage Supply Decision of Italian Rice Producers. In *Bauer, S. and Henrichsmeyer, W., eds.*, 1989, pp. 43–52.

Bernie, J. E. and Hitchens, D. M. W. N. Economic Development in Northern Ireland: Has Pathfinder Lost Its Way? A Reply. *Reg. Stud.*, October 1989, *23*(5), pp. 477–83.

de Bernis, Gérard. L'Europe et l'industrie. (Europe and Industry. With English summary.) *Écon. Appl.*, 1989, *42*(4), pp. 13–29.

Berns, E. E. Value and Time in Menger's *Grundsätze. J. Econ. Stud.*, 1989, *16*(2), pp. 84–108.

Bernstein, Edward M. Perils of the Gold Standard. In *Guttmann, R., ed.*, 1989, *1981*, pp. 300–304.

————. The Search for Exchange Stability: Before and after Bretton Woods. In *Hamouda, O. F.; Rowley, R. and Wolf, B. M., eds.*, 1989, pp. 27–34.

Bernstein, Jeffrey I. An Examination of the Equilibrium Specification and Structure of Production for Canadian Telecommunications. *J. Appl. Econometrics*, July–Sept. 1989, *4*(3), pp. 265–82.

————. The Structure of Canadian Inter-industry R&D Spillovers, and the Rates of Return to R&D. *J. Ind. Econ.*, March 1989, *37*(3), pp. 315–28.

———— **and Nadiri, M. Ishaq.** Research and Development and Intra-industry Spillovers: An Empirical Application of Dynamic Duality. *Rev. Econ. Stud.*, April 1989, *56*(2), pp. 249–67.

Bernstein, Michael A. Northern Labor Finds a Southern Champion: A Note on the Radical Democracy, 1833–1849. In *Pencak, W. and Wright, C. E., eds.*, 1989, pp. 147–67.

Bernstein, Peter L. The Lender's View of Debt and Equity: The Case of Pension Funds: Discussion. In *Kopcke, R. W. and Rosengren, E. S., eds.*, 1989, pp. 125–30.

———— **and Heilbroner, Robert L.** Abolishing the Deficit. *Challenge*, May–June 1989, *32*(3), pp. 54–55.

Bernstein, Richard J. Social Theory as Critique. In *Held, D. and Thompson, J. B., eds.,* 1989, pp. 19–33.

Berque, Augustin. Cultural, Territorial, Urban and Architectural Environment in South Korea. In *Park, S.-J., ed.,* 1989, pp. 105–35.

Berrebi, Edmond and Abraham-Frois, Gilbert. Á la recherche de l'étalon invariable des valeurs. (With English summary.) *Revue Écon. Politique,* Jan.–Feb. 1989, *99*(1), pp. 123–40.

Berrebi, Z. M. and Silber, Jacques G. Deprivation, the Gini Index of Inequality and the Flatness of an Income Distribution. *Math. Soc. Sci.,* December 1989, *18*(3), pp. 229–37.

Berridge, Virginia. History and Addiction Control: The Case of Alcohol. In *Robinson, D.; Maynard, A. and Chester, R., eds.,* 1989, pp. 24–42.

Berrios, Ruben. Soviet–Latin American Economic Relations. *Comp. Econ. Stud.,* Winter 1989, *31*(4), pp. 53–88.

Berry, Albert. Policy-Induced Inflows of Foreign Capital in the Presence of Rigid-Wage Unemployment: Comment. In *[Díaz-Alejandro, C.],* 1989, pp. 389–92.

Berry, Brian J. L. Howard G. Roepke Lecture in Economic Geography: Comparative Geography of the Global Economy: Cultures, Corporations, and the Nation-State. *Econ. Geogr.,* January 1989, *65*(1), pp. 1–18.

Berry, J. and Maclean, F. Managing the Development of a Customer Marketing Data-Base. *Environ. Planning A,* May 1989, *21*(5), pp. 617–23.

Berry, Mike. Industrialisation, De-industrialisation and Uneven Development: The Case of the Pacific Rim. In *Gottdiener, M. and Komninos, N., eds.,* 1989, pp. 174–216.

Berry, Steven. Entry into Deregulated Airline Markets. In *Weiss, L. W., ed.,* 1989, pp. 167–78.

Berry, Tom and Lane, Julia. A Multi-state Analysis of the Targeted Jobs Tax Credit Programme. *Appl. Econ.,* January 1989, *21*(1), pp. 85–94.

Berthoud, Richard. Social Security and the Economics of Housing. In *Dilnot, A. and Walker, I., eds.,* 1989, pp. 88–98.

Berting, Jan and van de Braak, Hans. Technological Changes in Two Dutch Factories: Control, Flexibility and Learning. In *Francis, A. and Grootings, P., eds.,* 1989, pp. 296–325.

Bertocchi, Graziella. Private Saving and Public Debt: A Review Essay. *J. Monet. Econ.,* September 1989, *24*(2), pp. 313–20.

Bertola, Giuseppe. Factor Flexibility, Uncertainty and Exchange Rate Regimes. In *De Cecco, M. and Giovannini, A., eds.,* 1989, pp. 95–119.

Besanko, David and Spulber, Daniel F. Antitrust Enforcement under Asymmetric Information. *Econ. J.,* June 1989, *99*(396), pp. 408–25.

_____ **and Spulber, Daniel F.** Delegated Law Enforcement and Noncooperative Behavior. *J. Law, Econ., Organ.,* Spring 1989, *5*(1), pp. 25–52.

Besen, Stanley M. and Kirby, Sheila Nataraj. Private Copying, Appropriability, and Optimal Copying Royalties. *J. Law Econ.,* Part 1, October 1989, *32*(2), pp. 255–80.

_____ **and Saloner, Garth.** The Economics of Telecommunications Standards. In *Crandall, R. W. and Flamm, K., eds.,* 1989, pp. 177–220.

_____ **and Terasawa, Katsuaki L.** The Prototype Model of Defense Procurement. In *Gulledge, T. R., Jr. and Litteral, L. A., eds.,* 1989, pp. 1–33.

Besharov, Douglas J. and Silver, Jessica Dunsay. Rationing Access to Advanced Medical Techniques. In *McLennan, K. and Meyer, J. A., eds.,* 1989, pp. 41–66.

_____ **and Tramontozzi, Paul N.** Federal Child Care Assistance: A Growing Middle-Class Entitlement. *J. Policy Anal. Manage.,* Spring 1989, *8*(2), pp. 313–18.

Besley, Timothy J. Commodity Taxation and Imperfect Competition: A Note on the Effects of Entry. *J. Public Econ.,* December 1989, *40*(3), pp. 359–67.

_____. A Definition of Luxury and Necessity for Cardinal Utility Functions. *Econ. J.,* September 1989, *99*(397), pp. 844–49.

_____. The Demand for Health Care and Health Insurance. *Oxford Rev. Econ. Policy,* Spring 1989, *5*(1), pp. 21–33.

_____. Ex Ante Evaluation of Health States and the Provision for Ill-Health. *Econ. J.,* March 1989, *99*(394), pp. 132–46.

_____. Publicly Provided Disaster Insurance for Health and the Control of Moral Hazard. *J. Public Econ.,* July 1989, *39*(2), pp. 141–56.

_____ **and Azam, Jean-Paul.** General Equilibrium with Parallel Markets for Goods and Foreign Exchange: Theory and Application to Ghana. *World Devel.,* December 1989, *17*(12), pp. 1921–30.

Bessler, David A. and Babula, Ronald A. Farmgate, Processor, and Consumer Price Transmissions in the Wheat Sector. *J. Agr. Econ. Res.,* Summer 1989, *41*(3), pp. 23–28.

_____ **and Fuller, Stephen.** Effect of Deregulating Motor Carriage of Agricultural Commodities in Texas: An Examination of the Rate Structure for Fresh Vegetables. *Logist. Transp. Rev.,* December 1989, *25*(4), pp. 343–53.

_____ **and Kling, John L.** Calibration-Based Predictive Distributions: An Application of Prequential Analysis to Interest Rates, Money, Prices, and Output. *J. Bus.,* October 1989, *62*(4), pp. 477–99.

_____ **and Kling, John L.** The Forecast and Policy Analysis. *Amer. J. Agr. Econ.,* May 1989, *71*(2), pp. 503–06.

_____ **and McCarl, Bruce A.** Estimating an Upper Bound on the Pratt Risk Aversion Coefficient When the Utility Function Is Unknown. *Australian J. Agr. Econ.,* April 1989, *33*(1), pp. 56–63.

_____ **and Nelson, Robert G.** Subjective Probabilities and Scoring Rules: Experimental Evidence. *Amer. J. Agr. Econ.,* May 1989, *71*(2), pp. 363–69.

Best, Michael H. Sector Strategies and Industrial Policy: The Furniture Industry and the Greater London Enterprise Board. In *Hirst, P. and Zeitlin, J., eds.*, 1989, pp. 191–222.

Best, Paul J. Insurance in Imperial Russia. *J. Europ. Econ. Hist.*, Spring 1989, *18*(1), pp. 139–69.

Besteman, Catherine. Economic Strategies of Farming Households in Penabranca, Portugal. *Econ. Devel. Cult. Change*, October 1989, *38*(1), pp. 129–43.

Bester, Helmut. Incentive-Compatible Long-term Contracts and Job Rationing. *J. Lab. Econ.*, April 1989, *7*(2), pp. 238–55.

_____. Non-cooperative Bargaining and Imperfect Competition: A Survey. *Z. Wirtschaft. Sozialwissen.*, 1989, *109*(2), pp. 265–86.

_____. Noncooperative Bargaining and Spatial Competition. *Econometrica*, January 1989, *57*(1), pp. 97–113.

_____ **and Hellwig, Martin.** Moral Hazard and Equilibrium Credit Rationing: An Overview of the Issues. In *Bamberg, G. and Spremann, K., eds.*, 1989, pp. 135–66.

Betancourt, Roger and Robles, Barbara. Credit, Money and Production: Empirical Evidence. *Rev. Econ. Statist.*, November 1989, *71*(4), pp. 712–17.

Bethel, T. A. and Melfi, C. A. A Probit Model of NLRB Bargaining Order Cases in the Appellate Courts. *J. Lab. Res.*, Summer 1989, *10*(3), pp. 255–70.

Bethell, Leslie. Britain and Latin America in Historical Perspective. In *Bulmer-Thomas, V., ed.*, 1989, pp. 1–24.

Bethke, William M. and Boyd, Susan E. Should Dividend Discount Models Be Yield Tilted? Response. *J. Portfol. Manage.*, Winter 1989, *15*(2), pp. 82–83.

Bethune, John J. The Work Disincentive Effects of Government Income Maintenance Programs: A Reply. *Amer. Economist*, Fall 1989, *33*(2), pp. 70.

Bettelheim, Ch. What Motivates Managers? *Acta Oecon.*, 1989, *40*(3–4), pp. 189–94.

Bettendorf, L. J. and Barten, Anton P. Price Formation of Fish: An Application of an Inverse Demand System. *Europ. Econ. Rev.*, October 1989, *33*(8), pp. 1509–25.

Bettio, Francesca and Villa, Paola. Non-wage Work and Disguised Wage Employment in Italy. In *Rodgers, G. and Rodgers, J., eds.*, 1989, pp. 149–78.

Betts, Julian R. Two Exact, Non-arbitrary and General Methods of Decomposing Temporal Change. *Econ. Letters*, August 1989, *30*(2), pp. 151–56.

Beukema, Leni. The Quality of Work: It's Indispensability for Working-Time Policy. In *Agassi, J. B. and Heycock, S., eds.*, 1989, pp. 283–97.

Beumer, L.; Boeckhout, I. J. and Molle, Willem T. M. The Location of Information Intensive Economic Activities in the European Community. In *Punset, E. and Sweeney, G., eds.*, 1989, pp. 161–72.

Bevan, David L.; Collier, Paul and Gunning, Jan Willem. Black Markets: Illegality, Information, and Rents. *World Devel.*, December 1989, *17*(12), pp. 1955–63.

_____; **Collier, Paul and Gunning, Jan Willem.** Fiscal Response to a Temporary Trade Shock: The Aftermath of the Kenyan Coffee Boom. *World Bank Econ. Rev.*, September 1989, *3*(3), pp. 359–78.

Bevan, Gwyn. Financing UK Hospital and Community Health Services. *Oxford Rev. Econ. Policy*, Spring 1989, *5*(1), pp. 124–35.

_____. Reforming UK Health Care: Internal Markets or Emergent Planning? *Fisc. Stud.*, February 1989, *10*(1), pp. 53–71.

Bewley, Ronald. Weighted Least Squares Estimation from Grouped Observations. *Rev. Econ. Statist.*, February 1989, *71*(1), pp. 187–88.

_____ **and Kearney, Colm.** A Systems Approach to Modelling the EMS Exchange Rate Mechanism. *Econ. Soc. Rev.*, January 1989, *20*(2), pp. 111–20.

Bey, Roger P. and Johnson, Larry J. The Impact of Taxes on Discount Bond Valuation and Risk. *Financial Rev.*, November 1989, *24*(4), pp. 589–97.

de Beyer, J. and Knight, J. B. The Role of Occupation in the Determination of Wages. *Oxford Econ. Pap.*, July 1989, *41*(3), pp. 595–618.

Beyers, William B. Structural Change in Interregional Input–Output Models: Form and Regional Economic Development Implications. In *Miller, R. E.; Polenske, K. R. and Rose, A. Z., eds.*, 1989, pp. 180–92.

Beynon, J. G. Pricism v. Structuralism in Sub-Saharan African Agriculture. *J. Agr. Econ.*, September 1989, *40*(3), pp. 323–35.

Bezdek, Roger H. and Whitman, Ray D. Federal Reimbursement for Mandates on State and Local Governments. *Public Budg. Finance*, Spring 1989, *9*(1), pp. 47–62.

Bezuneh, Mesfin; Deaton, Brady and Norton, George W. Farm Level Impacts of Food-for-Work in a Semi-arid Region of Kenya. *Eastern Afr. Econ. Rev.*, June 1989, *5*(1), pp. 1–8.

Bhaduri, Amit. Employment and Livelihood: The Rural Labour Process and the Formulation of Development Policy. *Int. Lab. Rev.*, Special Issue, 1989, *128*(6), pp. 685–700.

Bhagwati, Jagdish N. Is Free Trade Passé after All? *Weltwirtsch. Arch.*, 1989, *125*(1), pp. 17–44.

_____. Trade Policy and Protectionism: A Conversation with Jagdish Bhagwati. *Eastern Econ. J.*, July–Sept. 1989, *15*(3), pp. 173–76.

_____ **and Hamada, Koichi.** Tax Policy in the Presence of Emigration. In *Bhagwati, J. N. and Wilson, J. D., eds.*, 1989, *1982*, pp. 113–40.

_____ **and Wilson, John Douglas.** Income Taxation in the Presence of International Personal Mobility: An Overview. In *Bhagwati, J. N. and Wilson, J. D., eds.*, 1989, pp. 3–39.

Bhambri, Arvind and Hocevar, Susan Page. Corporate Social Performance: A Model of Assessment Criteria. In *Post, J. E., ed.*, 1989, pp. 1–20.

Bhandari, Arvind, et al. Risk and Return on Newly Listed Stocks: The Post-Listing Experience. *J. Finan. Res.*, Summer 1989, *12*(2), pp. 93–102.

Bhandari, Jagdeep S. Trade Reform under Partial Currency Convertibility: Some Suggestive Results. *Int. Monet. Fund Staff Pap.*, June 1989, *36*(2), pp. 494–513.

————; Horne, Jocelyn P. and Flood, Robert P. Evolution of Exchange Rate Regimes. *Int. Monet. Fund Staff Pap.*, December 1989, *36*(4), pp. 810–35.

Bhar, Robin. Marketing of Nonferrous Metals: The Role of Terminal Markets. In *Jackson, L. M. and Richardson, P. R., eds.*, 1989, pp. 55–57.

Bhargava, Alok. Testing Covariance Restrictions in Systems of Simultaneous Equations with Vector Autoregressive Errors. *Int. Econ. Rev.*, May 1989, *30*(2), pp. 357–72.

Bhaskar, V. Quick Responses in Duopoly Ensure Monopoly Pricing. *Econ. Letters*, 1989, *29*(2), pp. 103–07.

Bhatia, Kul B. Short Run and Long Run in the Theory of Tax Incidence. *Public Finance*, 1989, *44*(3), pp. 343–60.

Bhatia, N. L. and Sarna, A. C. Transport Systems for Metropolitan Cities of India—A Review. In *Candemir, Y., ed.*, 1989, pp. 539–51.

Bhatt, Ela. Toward Empowerment. *World Devel.*, July 1989, *17*(7), pp. 1059–65.

Bhatt, G. K. and Tilak, Jandhyala B. G. Educational Development in Haryana: An Inter-district Analysis. *Margin*, Oct. 1989–March 1990, *22*(1–2), pp. 108–23.

Bhatt, Gita. Europe 1992: The Quest for Economic Integration. *Finance Devel.*, June 1989, *26*(2), pp. 40–42.

Bhatt, Swati. Demand Uncertainty in a Durable Goods Monopoly. *Int. J. Ind. Organ.*, September 1989, *7*(3), pp. 341–55.

Bhatt, V. V. On Competitive Impulses and Public Enterprise Performance. In *UNDTCD*, 1989, pp. 52–61.

Bhattacharya, N. and Chattopadhyay, M. Time Trends in the Level of Living in Rural India: A Critical Study of the Evidence from Large-Scale Surveys. In *Bardhan, P., ed. (I)*, 1989, pp. 32–75.

Bhattacharya, Subir. Efficient Allocation of Resources with CES Production Function: An Exploration. *Indian Econ. J.*, Oct.–Dec. 1989, *37*(2), pp. 83–92.

Bhattacharyay, Biswa N. Money and Income in India—Application of Time Domain Causality Test. *Margin*, Oct. 1989–March 1990, *22*(1–2), pp. 36–51.

Bhattacharyya, Manas. Import-Intensity of Exports: A Case-Study of Indian Economy. *Indian Econ. J.*, Jan.–March 1989, *36*(3), pp. 94–98.

Bhattacharyya, Rabindra N.; Snyder, Donald L. and Biswas, Basudeb. The Optimal Forest Rotation: Some Economic Dimensions. *Indian Econ. J.*, Oct.–Dec. 1989, *37*(2), pp. 69–82.

Bhatty, I. Z. Rise in Consumption Levels in India and Consumerism. *Margin*, April–June 1989, *21*(3), pp. 32–51.

Bhole, L. M. and Sundararajan, S. Functional Form of the Import Demand Function. *Margin*, April–June 1989, *21*(3), pp. 52–65.

Bhullar, N. S. and Dhesi, Autar Singh. A Simplified Approach to District Agriculture Plan Formulation. *Margin*, April–June 1989, *21*(3), pp. 66–88.

Bhushan, Ravi. Collection of Information about Publicly Traded Firms: Theory and Evidence. *J. Acc. Econ.*, July 1989, *11*(2–3), pp. 183–206.

————. Firm Characteristics and Analyst Following. *J. Acc. Econ.*, July 1989, *11*(2–3), pp. 255–74.

Bhuyan, A. R. Beginnings of Cooperation in South Asia. In *Naya, S., et al., eds.*, 1989, pp. 143–55.

Biagi, Marco. Democracy and Trade Union Action: A Comparative Overview. *Labour*, Spring 1989, *3*(1), pp. 171–85.

Bianchi, Marco. Nuovi orientamenti nella teoria del ciclo e della crescita: Un approccio di analisi delle serie storiche nel contesto della nuova macroeconomia classica. (New Trends in the Theory of Cycle and Growth: An Approach Based on the Analysis of Time Series in the New Classical Macroeconomics. With English summary.) *Giorn. Econ.*, March–April 1989, *48*(3–4), pp. 129–46.

Bianchi, Marina. Cambiamento endogeno ed economia come processo: Il caso della teoria neo-austriaca. (Endogenous Change and Economy as a Process: The Case of Neo-Austrian Theory. With English summary.) *Econ. Politica*, April 1989, *6*(1), pp. 9–30.

Bianchi, Patrizio and Gualtieri, Giuseppina. Mergers and Acquisitions in Italy and the Debate on Competition Policy. *Antitrust Bull.*, Fall 1989, *34*(3), pp. 601–24.

Bianchi, Tancredi. The Taxation of the Financial Assets and Liabilities of Credit Firms. *Rev. Econ. Cond. Italy*, Sept.–Dec. 1989, (3), pp. 301–29.

Bianchini, Marco. Some Fundamental Aspects of Italian Eighteenth-Century Economic Thought. In *Walker, D. A., ed.*, 1989, pp. 53–67.

Bianconi, Marcelo. Política monetaria y margen de ganancia variable en una economía pequeña y abierta con inflación: Consideraciones dinámicas y estratígicas. (Monetary Policy and Variable Markup in a Small Open Economy with Inflation Dynamic and Strategic Considerations. With English summary.) *Estud. Econ.*, July–Dec. 1989, *4*(2), pp. 201–35.

———— and Turnovsky, Stephen J. Strategic Wages Policy and the Gains from Cooperation. In *[Verheyen, P.]*, 1989, pp. 191–222.

Bibikov, Michail. Specializzazione e diversificazione dell'economia rurale: Interventi degli esperti. (In English.) In *Cavaciocchi, S., ed.*, 1989, pp. 148–53.

Biçakci, Osman. The Transportation to Iran and

Other East Countries from Trabzon Harbour. In *Candemir, Y., ed.*, 1989, pp. 257–65.

Bićanić, Ivan. Systemic Aspects of the Social Crisis in Yugoslavia. In *Gomulka, S.; Ha, Y.-C. and Kim, C.-O., eds.*, 1989, pp. 139–55.

Bicchieri, Cristina. Progress without Growth? The Case of the "Marginalist Revolution" in Economics. *Ricerche Econ.*, Jan.–June 1989, *43*(1–2), pp. 236–55.

_____. Self-Refuting Theories of Strategic Interaction: A Paradox of Common Knowledge. In *Balzer, W. and Hamminga, B., eds.*, 1989, pp. 69–85.

Bickel, P. J. and Krieger, A. M. Confidence Bands for a Distribution Function Using the Bootstrap. *J. Amer. Statist. Assoc.*, March 1989, *84*(405), pp. 95–100.

Bidard, Christian. Equilibrium with a Qualitative Walras' Law. *J. Econ. Theory*, February 1989, *47*(1), pp. 203–05.

_____ **and Woods, John E.** Taxes, Lands and Non-basics in Joint Production. *Oxford Econ. Pap.*, October 1989, *41*(4), pp. 802–12.

Biddle, Elyce A. and Personick, Martin E. Job Hazards Underscored in Woodworking Study. *Mon. Lab. Rev.*, September 1989, *112*(9), pp. 18–23.

Biddle, Jeff E. and Zarkin, Gary A. Choice among Wage-Hours Packages: An Empirical Investigation of Male Labor Supply. *J. Lab. Econ.*, October 1989, *7*(4), pp. 415–37.

Bidwell, Miles O. and Ware, Harold. Regulatory Scrutiny of Marketing Expenses: Competitive Necessity vs. Regulatory Hang-Ups. In *National Economic Research Associates*, 1989, pp. 117–31.

Bienen, Henry. Change, Stability, and Slogans. In *Martin, M. T. and Kandal, T. R., eds.*, 1989, pp. 96–107.

_____ **and Waterbury, John.** The Political Economy of Privatization in Developing Countries. *World Devel.*, May 1989, *17*(5), pp. 617–32.

Bienkowski, Wojciech. CMEA Countries' Competitiveness in Western Markets. In *Berliner, J. S.; Kosta, H. G. J. and Hakogi, M., eds.*, 1989, pp. 147–63.

_____. CMEA in the Light of National Mechanisms: Discussion. In *Berliner, J. S.; Kosta, H. G. J. and Hakogi, M., eds.*, 1989, pp. 35–37.

_____. New Development of East–West Trade Relations—Focussing on Technology Transfer from Japan: Discussion. In *Berliner, J. S.; Kosta, H. G. J. and Hakogi, M., eds.*, 1989, pp. 190–92.

_____. The Soviet Reform Concept and Its Impact on Economic Reforms in Eastern Europe: Answer. In *Berliner, J. S.; Kosta, H. G. J. and Hakogi, M., eds.*, 1989, pp. 75–78.

Bierens, Herman J. and Hartog, Joop. Estimating a Hedonic Earnings Function with a Nonparametric Method. In *Ullah, A., ed.*, 1989, 1988, pp. 145–72.

Bierwag, G. O., et al. Duration as a Measure of Basis Risk: The Wrong Answer at Low Cost—

Rejoinder. *J. Portfol. Manage.*, Summer 1989, *15*(4), pp. 82–85.

Biewener, Carole. Socialist Politics and Theories of Money and Credit. *Rev. Radical Polit. Econ.*, Fall 1989, *21*(3), pp. 58–63.

Biger, Nahum and Israel, Ronen. A Note on the Pricing of Double Choice Bonds. *J. Banking Finance*, May 1989, *13*(2), pp. 181–90.

Bigsten, Arne and Anxo, Dominique. Working Hours and Productivity in Swedish Manufacturing. *Scand. J. Econ.*, 1989, *91*(3), pp. 613–19.

Biller, Dan; McDonald, Curtis T. and Baer, Werner. Austerity under Different Political Regimes: The Case of Brazil. In *Handelman, H. and Baer, W., eds.*, 1989, pp. 19–42.

Billingsley, Randall S.; Fraser, Donald R. and Thompson, G. Rodney. Shareholder Wealth and Stock Repurchases by Bank Holding Companies. *Quart. J. Bus. Econ.*, Winter 1989, *28*(1), pp. 3–25.

Bilquees, Faiz. Monetary Approach to Balance of Payments: The Evidence on Reserve Flow from Pakistan. *Pakistan Devel. Rev.*, Autumn 1989, *28*(3), pp. 195–206.

Bils, Mark. Pricing in a Customer Market. *Quart. J. Econ.*, November 1989, *104*(4), pp. 699–718.

Bina, Cyrus. Competition, Control and Price Formation in the International Energy Industry. *Energy Econ.*, July 1989, *11*(3), pp. 162–68.

_____. Global Oil and the Transformation of OPEC. *Rev. Radical Polit. Econ.*, Fall 1989, *21*(3), pp. 105–11.

_____ **and Taixeira, John A.** Leveraged Buyouts: Robber Barons of the Eighties. *Challenge*, Sept.–Oct. 1989, *32*(5), pp. 53–57.

Bindlish, Vishva; Barker, Randolph and Mount, Timothy D. Can Yield Variability Be Offset by Improved Information? The Case of Rice in India. In *Anderson, J. R. and Hazell, P. B. R., eds.*, 1989, pp. 287–300.

Bing, Zhao and Wei, Ning. Developments in Foreign Trade Reform. In *Zerby, J., ed.*, 1989, pp. 33–45.

_____ **and Wei, Ning.** Direct Foreign Investment in China. In *Zerby, J., ed.*, 1989, pp. 46–58.

Binger, Brian R. and Hoffman, Elizabeth. Institutional Persistence and Change: The Question of Efficiency. *J. Inst. Theoretical Econ.*, March 1989, *145*(1), pp. 67–84.

Bini Smaghi, Lorenzo. Fiscal Prerequisites for Further Monetary Convergence in the EMS. *Banca Naz. Lavoro Quart. Rev.*, June 1989, (169), pp. 165–89.

_____ **and Micossi, S.** Managing Exchange Markets in the EMS with Free Capital. *Banca Naz. Lavoro Quart. Rev.*, December 1989, (171), pp. 395–430.

_____ **and Vona, Stefano.** The Effects of Economic Convergence and Competitiveness on Trade among the EMS Countries. In *Hodgman, D. R. and Wood, G. E., eds.*, 1989, pp. 272–326.

Binkley, James K. Estimation of Variances in the Grouped Heteroskedasticity Model. *Rev.*

Econ. Statist., November 1989, *71*(4), pp. 659–65.

Binmore, Ken. Social Contract I: Harsani and Rawls. *Econ. J.*, Supplement, 1989, *99*(395), pp. 84–102.

_____; **Shaked, Avner and Sutton, John.** An Outside Option Experiment. *Quart. J. Econ.*, November 1989, *104*(4), pp. 753–70.

Binstock, Robert H. Aging and the Politics of Health-Care Reform. In *Eisdorfer, C.; Kessler, D. A. and Spector, A. N., eds.*, 1989, pp. 422–47.

Binswanger, Hans P. The Policy Response of Agriculture. In *Fischer, S. and de Tray, D., eds.*, 1989, pp. 231–58.

_____ **and Elgin, Miranda.** Quais são as perspectivas para a reforma agrária? (With English summary.) *Pesquisa Planejamento Econ.*, April 1989, *19*(1), pp. 1–18.

_____; **McIntire, John and Udry, Chris.** Production Relations in Semi-arid African Agriculture. In *Bardhan, P., ed. (II)*, 1989, pp. 122–44.

_____ **and Quizon, Jaime B.** What Can Agriculture Do for the Poorest Rural Groups? In *Adelman, I. and Lane, S., eds.*, 1989, pp. 110–35.

Bjørn, Erik; Holmøy, Erling and Olsen, Øystein. Gross and Net Capital, and the Form of the Survival Function: Theory and Some Norwegian Evidence. *Rev. Income Wealth*, June 1989, *35*(2), pp. 133–49.

_____ **and Olsen, Hilde.** Production–Demand Adjustment in Norwegian Manufacturing: A Quarterly Error Correction Model. *Econ. Modelling*, April 1989, *6*(2), pp. 189–202.

Birch, Dan and Rabin, Alan. Aggregate Demand Curves: A Reply. *J. Macroecon.*, Winter 1989, *11*(1), pp. 145–47.

Birch, David L. Change, Innovation, and Job Generation. *J. Lab. Res.*, Winter 1989, *10*(1), pp. 33–38.

Birchenhall, C. R., et al. A Seasonal Model of Consumption. *Econ. J.*, September 1989, *99*(397), pp. 837–43.

Bird, Graham. The Developing Countries and the International Economic Order: A View from the North. In *Thomas, C. and Saravanamuttu, P., eds.*, 1989, pp. 59–74.

_____. Strategic Plans or Muddling Through: The Generics of Third World Debt Policy. In *Bird, G., ed.*, 1989, pp. 189–217.

_____. Third World Debt: The Search for a Solution: Introduction. In *Bird, G., ed.*, 1989, pp. 1–19.

_____. World Debt, Financing, Structural Adjustment and the Official Sector. In *Singer, H. W. and Sharma, S., eds. (I)*, 1989, pp. 245–59.

Bird, Richard M. Tax Expenditures and Public Management and Accounting: Comment. In *Bruce, N., ed.*, 1989, pp. 123–26.

_____. Tax Reform in Canada: Some Continuing Issues and an International Perspective. In *Mintz, J. and Whalley, J., eds.*, 1989, pp. 433–42.

_____. Taxation in Papua New Guinea: Backwards

to the Future? *World Devel.*, August 1989, *17*(8), pp. 1145–57.

_____ **and Miller, Barbara Diane.** The Incidence of Indirect Taxes on Low-Income Households in Jamaica. *Econ. Devel. Cult. Change*, January 1989, *37*(2), pp. 393–409.

Birdsall, Nancy. Economic Analyses of Rapid Population Growth. *World Bank Res. Observer*, January 1989, *4*(1), pp. 23–50.

Birkin, Mark and Clarke, Martin. The Generation of Individual and Household Incomes at the Small Area Level Using Synthesis. *Reg. Stud.*, December 1989, *23*(6), pp. 535–48.

Birman, Beatrice F. and Kennedy, Mary M. The Politics of the National Assessment of Chapter 1. *J. Policy Anal. Manage.*, Fall 1989, *8*(4), pp. 613–32.

Birman, Graciela and Ghobrial, Atef. A Perspective on Airline Competition in Less Developed Countries: An Econometric Approach. In *Candemir, Y., ed.*, 1989, pp. 519–29.

Birnie, J. E. and Hitchens, D. M. W. N. Productivity Levels in Northern Ireland Manufacturing Industry: A Comparison with Great Britain. *Reg. Stud.*, October 1989, *23*(5), pp. 447–54.

Birnie, Pat W. International Legal Issues in the Management and Protection of the Whale: A Review of Four Decades of Experience. *Natural Res. J.*, Fall 1989, *29*(4), pp. 903–34.

Bishara, Halim and Lee, Moon H. Recent Canadian Experience on the Profitability of Insider Trades. *Financial Rev.*, May 1989, *24*(2), pp. 235–49.

Bishop, George F., et al. Pseudo-opinions on Public Affairs. In *Singer, E. and Presser, S., eds.*, 1989, *1980*, pp. 425–36.

Bishop, John A.; Chakraborti, S. and Thistle, Paul D. Asymptotically Distribution-Free Statistical Inference for Generalized Lorenz Curves. *Rev. Econ. Statist.*, November 1989, *71*(4), pp. 725–27.

Bishop, John Hillman. Is the Test Score Decline Responsible for the Productivity Growth Decline? *Amer. Econ. Rev.*, March 1989, *79*(1), pp. 178–97.

_____. Occupational Training in High School: When Does It Pay Off? *Econ. Educ. Rev.*, 1989, *8*(1), pp. 1–15.

_____. Toward More Valid Evaluations of Training Programs Serving the Disadvantaged. *J. Policy Anal. Manage.*, Spring 1989, *8*(2), pp. 209–28.

_____ **and Kang, Suk.** Vocational and Academic Education in High School: Complements or Substitutes? *Econ. Educ. Rev.*, 1989, *8*(2), pp. 133–48.

Bishop, Matthew R. and Kay, J. A. Privatization and the Performance of Public Firms. In *UNDTCD*, 1989, pp. 33–51.

_____ **and Kay, John A.** Privatization in the United Kingdom: Lessons from Experience. *World Devel.*, May 1989, *17*(5), pp. 643–57.

Bishop, Robert L. Imperfect Competition after Fifty Years. In *Feiwel, G. R., ed. (I)*, 1989, pp. 197–211.

———. A Zeuthen–Hicks Theory of Bargaining. In *Wood, J. C. and Woods, R. N., eds.*, Vol. 2, 1989, *1964*, pp. 52–60.

Bisky, Lothar. Media Use in Free Time by the GDR Population. In *Rueschemeyer, M. and Lemke, C., eds.*, 1989, pp. 182–93.

Bisschop, J.; Dorhout, B. and Drud, A. Structural Dependence and Systems of Equations. In *Simeone, B., ed.*, 1989, pp. 209–24.

Biswas, Basudeb; Bailey, DeeVon and Kumbhakar, Subal C. A Study of Economic Efficiency of Utah Dairy Farmers: A System Approach. *Rev. Econ. Statist.*, November 1989, *71*(4), pp. 595–604.

———; **Bhattacharyya, Rabindra N. and Snyder, Donald L.** The Optimal Forest Rotation: Some Economic Dimensions. *Indian Econ. J.*, Oct.–Dec. 1989, *37*(2), pp. 69–82.

———; **Tribedy, Gopal and Beladi, Hamid.** General Equilibrium Analysis of Negative Value-Added. *J. Econ. Stud.*, 1989, *16*(1), pp. 47–53.

Bittlingmayer, George. Shareholder Heterogeneity and the Gains from Merger. In *Faure, M. and Van den Bergh, R., eds.*, 1989, pp. 49–70.

Bivin, David G. Rationales for the Dual Existence of Finished Goods and Raw Materials Inventories. *Southern Econ. J.*, April 1989, *55*(4), pp. 962–73.

Bixby, Ann Kallman. Benefits and Beneficiaries under Public Employee Retirement Systems, Calendar Year 1986. *Soc. Sec. Bull.*, May 1989, *52*(5), pp. 32–36.

———. Overview of Public Social Welfare Expenditures, Fiscal Year 1987. *Soc. Sec. Bull.*, November 1989, *52*(11), pp. 29–31.

Bizer, David S. and Judd, Kenneth L. Taxation and Uncertainty. *Amer. Econ. Rev.*, May 1989, *79*(2), pp. 331–36.

Bjorkegren, Dag. Some Limitations in the Western Model of Executive Training: A Case Study. In *Davies, J., et al., eds.*, 1989, pp. 185–98.

Björklund, Anders. The Duration of Unemployment: Theory and Evidence: Comment. In *Holmlund, B.; Löfgren, K.-G. and Engström, L.*, 1989, pp. 227–29.

———. Potentials and Pitfalls of Panel Data: The Case of Job Mobility. *Europ. Econ. Rev.*, March 1989, *33*(2/3), pp. 537–46.

——— **and Holmlund, Bertil.** Effects of Extended Unemployment Compensation in Sweden. In *Gustafsson, B. A. and Klevmarken, N. A., eds.*, 1989, pp. 165–83.

——— **and Holmlund, Bertil.** Job Mobility and Subsequent Wages in Sweden. In *van Dijk, J., et al., eds.*, 1989, pp. 201–16.

Bjørndal, Trond. Production in a Schooling Fishery: The Case of the North Sea Herring Fishery. *Land Econ.*, February 1989, *65*(1), pp. 49–56.

Bjørstad, Heidi; Hefting, Tom and Stensland, Gunnar. A Model for Exploration Decisions. *Energy Econ.*, July 1989, *11*(3), pp. 189–200.

Bjuggren, Per-Olof. Ownership and Efficiency in Companies Listed on Stockholm Stock Exchange 1985. In *Faure, M. and Van den Bergh, R., eds.*, 1989, pp. 71–79.

Black, Anthony H. Decentralization Incentives and Investment in the South African Periphery. In *Whiteside, A. W., ed.*, 1989, pp. 121–41.

Black, Dan A.; Hayes, Kathy J. and Slottje, Daniel J. Demographic Change and Inequality in the Size Distributions of Labor and Nonlabor Income. *Rev. Income Wealth*, September 1989, *35*(3), pp. 283–96.

——— **and Hoyt, William H.** Bidding for Firms. *Amer. Econ. Rev.*, December 1989, *79*(5), pp. 1249–56.

———; **Loewenstein, Mark A. and Barron, John M.** Job Matching and On-the-Job Training. *J. Lab. Econ.*, January 1989, *7*(1), pp. 1–19.

———; **Scott, Frank A., Jr. and Berger, Mark C.** Effects of the Tax Treatment of Fringe Benefits on Labor Market Segmentation. *Ind. Lab. Relat. Rev.*, January 1989, *42*(2), pp. 216–29.

Black, Fischer. How We Came Up With the Option Formula. *J. Portfol. Manage.*, Winter 1989, *15*(2), pp. 4–8.

Black, Georgina Dopico. The Limits of Expression: Intellectual Freedom in Postrevolutionary Cuba. In *Mesa-Lago, C., ed.*, 1989, pp. 107–42.

Black, Jane M. and Bulkley, I. George. Do Trade Unions Reduce Job Opportunities of Nonmembers? *Econ. J.*, March 1989, *99*(394), pp. 177–86.

——— **and Bulkley, I. George.** Insiders and Outsiders and Efficient Asymmetric Information Contracts. *Econ. Letters*, 1989, *29*(3), pp. 265–69.

——— **and Bulkley, I. George.** A Ratio Criterion for Signing the Effects of an Increase in Uncertainty. *Int. Econ. Rev.*, February 1989, *30*(1), pp. 119–30.

Black, P. A. and Cooper, J. H. Economic Sanctions and Interest Group Analysis: Some Reservations. *S. Afr. J. Econ.*, June 1989, *57*(2), pp. 188–93.

Black, Stanley W. Economic Background and Introduction to the Papers. In *Black, S. W., ed.*, 1989, pp. 1–7.

Blackburn, Keith and Christensen, Michael. Monetary Policy and Policy Credibility: Theories and Evidence. *J. Econ. Lit.*, March 1989, *27*(1), pp. 1–45.

Blackburn, McKinley L. Interpreting the Magnitude of Changes in Measures of Income Inequality. *J. Econometrics*, September 1989, *42*(1), pp. 21–25.

———. Poverty Measurement: An Index Related to a Theil Measure of Inequality. *J. Bus. Econ. Statist.*, October 1989, *7*(4), pp. 475–81.

Blackhurst, Richard. Modern Service Sector Growth: Causes and Effects: Comment. In *Giersch, H., ed.*, 1989, pp. 35–37.

Blackley, Paul R. The Measurement and Determination of State Equilibrium Unemployment Rates. *Southern Econ. J.*, October 1989, *56*(2), pp. 440–56.

Blackman, Courtney N. New Directions for Central Banking in the Caribbean. *Soc. Econ. Stud.*, December 1989, *38*(4), pp. 219–40.

Blackorby, Charles; Lovell, C. A. Knox and Thursby, M. C. Extended Hicks Neutral Technical Change. In *Wood, J. C. and Woods, R. N., eds., Vol. 3*, 1989, *1976*, pp. 153–62.

_____ and Russell, R. Robert. The Morishima Elasticity of Substitution; Symmetry, Constancy, Separability, and Its Relationship to the Hicks and Allen Elasticities. In *Wood, J. C. and Woods, R. N., eds., Vol. 3*, 1989, *1981*, pp. 258–73.

_____ and Russell, R. Robert. Will the Real Elasticity of Substitution Please Stand Up? (A Comparison of the Allen/Uzawa and Morishima Elasticities). *Amer. Econ. Rev.*, September 1989, *79*(4), pp. 882–88.

Blackstone, Erwin A. and Fuhr, Joseph P., Jr. *The Economics of Public Utility Regulation:* Review Article. *Atlantic Econ. J.*, June 1989, *17*(2), pp. 68–73.

Blackwell, Michael and Nocera, Simon. Debt–Equity Swaps. In *Frenkel, J. A.; Dooley, M. P. and Wickham, P., eds.*, 1989, pp. 311–45.

Blad, Michael C. and Benassy, Jean-Pascal. On Learning and Rational Expectations in an Overlapping Generations Model. *J. Econ. Dynam. Control*, July 1989, *13*(3), pp. 379–400.

Bladen Hovell, Robin and Green, Christopher J. Crowding-Out and Pulling-In of Fiscal Policy under Fixed and Flexible Exchange Rates. In *MacDonald, R. and Taylor, M. P., eds.*, 1989, pp. 251–74.

Blades, Derek. Revision of the System of National Accounts: A Note on Objectives and Key Issues. *OECD Econ. Stud.*, Spring 1989, (12), pp. 205–19.

Blain, Nicholas. The Underlying Philosophy of the Industrial Relations Theory Course at the University of Western Australia. In *Barbash, J. and Barbash, K., eds.*, 1989, pp. 211–25.

Blaine, Thomas W.; Mohammad, Golam and Hoehn, John P. Probit Model Procedures to the Estimation of Probabilities: An Empirical Exposition to a Dichotomous Decision Model. *Can. J. Agr. Econ.*, Part 2, December 1989, *37*(4), pp. 1071–79.

Blair, Andrew R. Managing in a Global Competitive Environment: Comments. In *Ahlbrandt, R. S., Jr., ed.*, 1989, pp. 67–68.

Blair, Douglas H.; Golbe, Devra L. and Gerard, James M. Unbundling the Voting Rights and Profit Claims of Common Shares. *J. Polit. Econ.*, April 1989, *97*(2), pp. 420–43.

Blair, John P. and Fichtenbaum, Rudy. Regional Differences in Labor Demand in the United States. *Rev. Reg. Stud.*, Winter 1989, *19*(1), pp. 72–76.

Blair, Peter D. and Wyckoff, Andrew W. The Changing Structure of the U.S. Economy: An Input–Output Analysis. In *Miller, R. E.; Polenske, K. R. and Rose, A. Z., eds.*, 1989, pp. 293–307.

Blair, Roger D.; Kaserman, David L. and Romano, Richard E. A Pedagogical Treatment of Bilateral Monopoly. *Southern Econ. J.*, April 1989, *55*(4), pp. 831–41.

Blais, André; Cousineau, Jean-Michel and McRoberts, Kenneth. The Determinants of Minimum Wage Rates. *Public Choice*, July 1989, *62*(1), pp. 15–24.

Blake, David. The Investments and Returns of Private Sector Pension Funds in the UK 1963–1978. *J. Econ. Soc. Meas.*, 1989, *15*(3–4), pp. 181–224.

_____. Testing Models Generating Time Varying Asset Return Expectations and Risks: The Case of the UK Private Sector Pension Funds. *Econ. Modelling*, April 1989, *6*(2), pp. 220–40.

Blake, John D. Management Education in Canada. In *Byrt, W., ed.*, 1989, pp. 104–19.

Blakemore, Arthur E. and Faith, Roger L. Bargaining Effect and Membership Effect in Public Sector Unions. *Southern Econ. J.*, April 1989, *55*(4), pp. 908–23.

_____ and Hoffman, Dennis L. Seniority Rules and Productivity: An Empirical Test. *Economica*, August 1989, *56*(223), pp. 359–71.

Blakey, G. Robert and O'Hara, Patricia A. Legal Aspects of Insider Trading. In *Williams, O. F.; Reilly, F. K. and Houck, J. W., eds.*, 1989, pp. 101–20.

Blanchard, Olivier Jean. New Classical Macroeconomics: A Sympathetic Account: Comment. *Scand. J. Econ.*, 1989, *91*(2), pp. 259–64.

_____. A Traditional Interpretation of Macroeconomic Fluctuations. *Amer. Econ. Rev.*, December 1989, *79*(5), pp. 1146–64.

_____ and Diamond, Peter A. The Beveridge Curve. *Brookings Pap. Econ. Act.*, 1989, (1), pp. 1–60.

_____ and Quah, Danny. The Dynamic Effects of Aggregate Demand and Supply Disturbances. *Amer. Econ. Rev.*, September 1989, *79*(4), pp. 655–73.

Blanchflower, David G. and Oswald, Andrew J. Housing, Wages and UK Labour Markets: Comments. *Oxford Bull. Econ. Statist.*, March 1989, *51*(2), pp. 137–43.

_____ and Oswald, Andrew J. Housing, Wages and UK Labour Markets: Reply. *Oxford Bull. Econ. Statist.*, March 1989, *51*(2), pp. 159–62.

Blandford, David. Bringing Agriculture into the GATT. *Can. J. Agr. Econ.*, Part 2, December 1989, *37*(4), pp. 813–23.

_____ and Zwart, Anthony C. Market Intervention and International Price Stability. *Amer. J. Agr. Econ.*, May 1989, *71*(2), pp. 379–88.

Blandy, Richard; Sloan, Judith and Wooden, Mark. Reforming the Trade Union Structure in Australia. *Australian Bull. Lab.*, December 1989, *15*(5), pp. 370–83.

Blanes Jiménez, José. Cocaine, Informality, and the Urban Economy in La Paz, Bolivia. In *Portes, A.; Castells, M. and Benton, L. A., eds.*, 1989, pp. 135–49.

Blank, Emily C. Changes in the Stock of On-the-Job Training, Race, and Wage Growth. *Rev. Black Polit. Econ.*, Spring 1989, *17*(4), pp. 45–57.

_____. Mobility and Wage Growth of Male

Household Heads. *Appl. Econ.*, April 1989, *21*(4), pp. 475–85.

Blank, Rebecca M. Analyzing the Length of Welfare Spells. *J. Public Econ.*, August 1989, *39*(3), pp. 245–73.

_____. Disaggregating the Effect of the Business Cycle on the Distribution of Income. *Economica*, May 1989, *56*(222), pp. 141–63.

_____. The Economics of Comparable Worth: Theoretical Considerations: Discussion. In *Hill, M. A. and Killingsworth, M. R., eds.*, 1989, pp. 51–53.

_____. The Effect of Medical Need and Medicaid on AFDC Participation. *J. Human Res.*, Winter 1989, *24*(1), pp. 54–87.

_____. The Role of Part-Time Work in Women's Labor Market Choices over Time. *Amer. Econ. Rev.*, May 1989, *79*(2), pp. 295–99.

Blank, Steven C. Research on Futures Markets: Issues, Approaches, and Empirical Findings. *Western J. Agr. Econ.*, July 1989, *14*(1), pp. 126–39.

Blankart, Charles B. and Knieps, Günter. What Can We Learn from Comparative Institutional Analysis? The Case of Telecommunications. *Kyklos*, 1989, *42*(4), pp. 579–98.

Blankenburg, Erhard; Staudhammer, Rainer and Steinert, Heinz. Political Scandals and Corruption Issues in West Germany. In *Heidenheimer, A. J.; Johnston, M. and LeVine, V. T., eds.*, 1989, pp. 913–32.

Bläsing, Joachim F. D. Promising and Stimulating: Modern Business History in Germany and the Netherlands. *J. Econ. Hist.*, September 1989, *49*(3), pp. 720–24.

Blattberg, Robert C. and Wisniewski, Kenneth J. Price-Induced Patterns of Competition. *Marketing Sci.*, Fall 1989, *8*(4), pp. 291–309.

Blattner, Niklaus and Sheldon, George. Foreign Labour, Growth and Productivity: The Case of Switzerland. In *Gordon, I. and Thirlwall, A. P., eds.*, 1989, pp. 148–65.

Blau, David M. and Robins, Philip K. Fertility, Employment, and Child-Care Costs. *Demography*, May 1989, *26*(2), pp. 287–99.

Blau, Francine D. and Kahn, Lawrence M. A Model of Joint Wage and Hiring Discrimination. In *Ehrenberg, R. G., ed.*, 1989, pp. 157–205.

Blau, J. H. and Brown, D. J. The Structure of Neutral Monotonic Social Functions. *Soc. Choice Welfare*, January 1989, *6*(1), pp. 51–61.

Blau, Zena Smith. The Social Structure, Socialization Processes, and School Competence of Black and White Children. In *Shulman, S. and Darity, W., Jr., eds.*, 1989, pp. 315–34.

Blaug, Mark. Nicholas Kaldor, 1908–86. In *Greenaway, D. and Presley, J. R., eds.*, 1989, pp. 68–95.

Blaut, J. M. Colonialism and the Rise of Capitalism. *Sci. Society*, Fall 1989, *53*(3), pp. 260–96.

Blaylock, James R. An Economic Model of Grocery Shopping Frequency. *Appl. Econ.*, June 1989, *21*(6), pp. 843–52.

_____ **and Blisard, William N.** The Distribution of U.S. Income and Food Expenditures. *J. Cons. Aff.*, Winter 1989, *23*(2), pp. 226–42.

_____; **Smallwood, David M. and Haidacher, Richard C.** A Review of the Research Literature on Meat Demand. In *Buse, R. C., ed.*, 1989, pp. 93–124.

Bleaney, Michael. Can Gorbachev's Reforms Improve Soviet Economic Performance? *World Econ.*, June 1989, *12*(2), pp. 253–61.

_____ **and Greenaway, David.** Recent Developments in Macroeconomics. In *Greenaway, D., ed.*, 1989, pp. 1–21.

Blecha, Betty J. Nobel Laureates in Economic Sciences: A Biographical Dictionary: James Tobin: 1981. In *Katz, B. S., ed.*, 1989, pp. 317–33.

Blecher, Marc. Structural Change and the Political Articulation of Social Interest in Revolutionary and Socialist China. In *Dirlik, A. and Meisner, M., eds.*, 1989, pp. 190–209.

Blecker, Robert A. International Competition, Income Distribution and Economic Growth. *Cambridge J. Econ.*, September 1989, *13*(3), pp. 395–412.

_____. Markup Pricing, Import Competition, and the Decline of the American Steel Industry. *J. Post Keynesian Econ.*, Fall 1989, *12*(1), pp. 70–87.

Bleiberg, Steven. How Little We Know. *J. Portfol. Manage.*, Summer 1989, *15*(4), pp. 26–31.

Blejer, Mario I. The Global Economic Environment and Prospects for Recovery in Latin America: Comment. In *Edwards, S. and Larrain, F., eds.*, 1989, pp. 153–55.

_____. Regional Integration in Latin America: The Experience and the Outlook for Further Cooperation. In *Fishelson, G., ed.*, 1989, pp. 181–208.

_____ **and Cheasty, Adrienne.** Fiscal Policy and Mobilization of Savings for Growth. In *Blejer, M. I. and Chu, K., eds.*, 1989, *1986*, pp. 33–49.

_____ **and Cheasty, Adrienne.** High Inflation, "Heterodox" Stabilization, and Fiscal Policy. In *Blejer, M. I. and Chu, K., eds.*, 1989, *1988*, pp. 72–98.

_____ **and Chu, Ke-young.** Fiscal Policy, Stabilization, and Growth in Developing Countries: Introduction. In *Blejer, M. I. and Chu, K., eds.*, 1989, pp. 3–10.

Blessing, Linda. Governmental Accounting, Auditing and Financial Reporting: One View. *Public Budg. Finance*, Summer 1989, *9*(2), pp. 104–06.

Bletzinger, Matthias and Walz, Uwe. Zum Schattenpreis- und Einkommensbegriff in der ökonomischen Theorie der Fertilität. (Shadow Price and Income Concepts in the Economic Theory of Fertility. With English summary.) *Jahr. Nationalökon. Statist.*, December 1989, *206*(6), pp. 591–98.

Bleuze, Eric and Artus, Patrick. Les choix de portefeuille des ménages en France. (With English summary.) *Rech. Écon. Louvain*, 1989, *55*(2), pp. 129–53.

Blickle, Marina. Information Systems and the Design of Optimal Contracts. In *Bamberg, G. and Spremann, K., eds.*, 1989, pp. 93–103.

Blight, Catherine Montgomery. "What if That Snail Had Been in a Bottle of Milk?" or Product Liability in the UK—The Special Case of Agricultural Products. In *Faure, M. and Van den Bergh, R., eds.*, 1989, pp. 215–32.

Blinder, Alan S. The Challenge of High Unemployment. In *Blinder, A. S.*, 1989, *1988*, pp. 139–59.

_____. The Comparative Statics of a Credit-Rationing Bank. In *Blinder, A. S.*, 1989, pp. 61–72.

_____. Credit Rationing and Effective Supply Failures. In *Blinder, A. S.*, 1989, *1987*, pp. 25–60.

_____. In Honor of Robert M. Solow: Nobel Laureate in 1987. *J. Econ. Perspectives*, Summer 1989, *3*(3), pp. 99–105.

_____. Indexing the Economy through Financial Intermediation. In *Blinder, A. S.*, 1989, *1977*, pp. 160–93.

_____. Institutional Change and the Efficacy of Monetary Policy: Comments. *Brookings Pap. Econ. Act.*, 1989, (1), pp. 111–14.

_____. Keynes after Lucas. In *Blinder, A. S.*, 1989, *1986*, pp. 101–15.

_____. Keynes, Lucas, and Scientific Progress. In *Blinder, A. S.*, 1989, *1987*, pp. 116–27.

_____. A Skeptical Note on the New Econometrics. In *Blinder, A. S.*, 1989, *1986*, pp. 128–38.

_____. The Stylized Facts about Credit Aggregates. In *Blinder, A. S.*, 1989, pp. 73–92.

_____ **and Bernanke, Ben S.** Credit, Money, and Aggregate Demand. In *Blinder, A. S.*, 1989, *1988*, pp. 93–100.

_____ **and Solow, Robert M.** Does Fiscal Policy Matter? In *Blinder, A. S.*, 1989, *1973*, pp. 1–16.

_____ **and Stiglitz, Joseph E.** Money, Credit Constraints, and Economic Activity. In *Blinder, A. S.*, 1989, *1983*, pp. 17–24.

Blinder, Edward H.; Gagnon, Louis and Mensah, Samuel. Hedging Canadian Corporate Debt: A Comparative Study of the Hedging Effectiveness of Canadian and U.S. Bond Futures. *J. Futures Markets*, February 1989, *9*(1), pp. 29–39.

Bline, Dennis M. and Gregson, Terry. The Relationship of Communication Satisfaction to Turnover Intentions and Job Satisfaction for Certified Public Accountants. In *Schwartz, B. N., ed.*, 1989, pp. 203–22.

Blisard, William N. and Blaylock, James R. The Distribution of U.S. Income and Food Expenditures. *J. Cons. Aff.*, Winter 1989, *23*(2), pp. 226–42.

Bliss, Robert R., Jr. and Ronn, Ehud I. Arbitrage-Based Estimation of Nonstationary Shifts in the Term Structure of Interest Rates. *J. Finance*, July 1989, *44*(3), pp. 591–610.

Blissett, Marlan; Wilson, Robert H. and Monts, Ken. Weather Normalization of Electricity Sales to the School Sector: Potential Model

Misspecification. *Energy Econ.*, April 1989, *11*(2), pp. 127–32.

Blitz, Rudolph C. The Religious Reforms of Joseph II (1780–1790) and Their Economic Significance. *J. Europ. Econ. Hist.*, Winter 1989, *18*(3), pp. 583–94.

Bloch, Anthony M. Identification and Estimation of Dynamic Errors-in-Variables Models. *J. Econometrics*, May 1989, *41*(1), pp. 145–58.

Bloch, B. An Extension to the Kinked-Demand Curve Theory of Oligopoly. *S. Afr. J. Econ.*, December 1989, *57*(4), pp. 412–15.

Bloch, Harry and Wirth, Michael O. Concentration and the Price of Local Television Advertising Time. In *Weiss, L. W., ed.*, 1989, pp. 155–58.

Bloch, Howard and High, Jack. On the History of Ordinal Utility Theory: 1900–1932. *Hist. Polit. Econ.*, Summer 1989, *21*(2), pp. 351–65.

Bloch, Maurice. The Symbolism of Money in Imerina. In *Parry, J. and Bloch, M., eds.*, 1989, pp. 165–90.

_____ **and Parry, Jonathan.** Money and the Morality of Exchange: Introduction. In *Parry, J. and Bloch, M., eds.*, 1989, pp. 1–32.

Block, John R. Agricultural Trade—The Hardest Test. In *Cerami, C. A., ed.*, 1989, pp. 203–12.

Block, Stephen R. and Leduc, Robert F. Conjoint Directorship: Clarifying Management Roles between the Board of Directors and the Executive Director. In *Herman, R. D. and Van Til, J., eds.*, 1989, pp. 67–76.

Block, Walter. The Justification for Taxation in the Public Finance Literature: An Unorthodox View. *Econ. Scelte Pubbliche/J. Public Finance Public Choice*, Sept.–Dec. 1989, *7*(3), pp. 141–58.

_____. A Look at *Subjectivism, Intelligibility and Economic Understanding: Essays in Honor of Ludwig M. Lachmann on His Eightieth Birthday*. In *Rothbard, M. N. and Block, W., eds.*, 1989, pp. 215–36.

_____. Privatization in Canada: Ideology, Symbolism or Substance? Comment. In *MacAvoy, P. W., et al.*, 1989, pp. 331–36.

Blocker, T. Jean and Eckberg, Douglas Lee. Environmental Issues as Women's Issues: General Concerns and Local Hazards. *Soc. Sci. Quart.*, September 1989, *70*(3), pp. 586–93.

Blomley, Nicholas K. *Store Choice, Store Location and Market Analysis:* Book Review Essay. *Econ. Geogr.*, April 1989, *65*(2), pp. 153–59.

Blomquist, N. Sören. Comparative Statics for Utility Maximization Models with Nonlinear Budget Constraints. *Int. Econ. Rev.*, May 1989, *30*(2), pp. 275–96.

_____ **and Siven, Claes-Henric.** Nobel Laureates in Economic Sciences: A Biographical Dictionary: Bertil Ohlin: 1977. In *Katz, B. S., ed.*, 1989, pp. 229–40.

Blomqvist, Hans C. A Note on the Predictive Power of a Simple Demand–Supply Model of Unemployment. *Appl. Econ.*, February 1989, *21*(2), pp. 219–23.

_____. The 'Rationality' of Expectations: An Experimental Approach. *J. Econ. Psych.*, June 1989, *10*(2), pp. 275–99.

————. Tillväxt och strukturförändring i den finländska ekonomin. En utvecklingsteoretisk ansats. (Growth and Structural Change in the Finnish Economy. With English summary.) *Ekon. Samfundets Tidskr.*, 1989, *42*(1), pp. 25–45.

———— and Lundahl, Mats. Utvecklingsekonomins utveckling. En översikt. (The Progress of Development Economics. A Survey. With English summary.) *Ekon. Samfundets Tidskr.*, 1989, *42*(3), pp. 185–202.

Blomström, Magnus. A Comparison of the Performance of Foreign and Domestic Firms in Mexico. In *Blomström, M.*, 1989, pp. 11–27.

————. Foreign Investment and Spillover of Efficiency. In *Blomström, M.*, 1989, pp. 35–53.

————. Foreign Investment and Spillovers: Introduction. In *Blomström, M.*, 1989, pp. 1–10.

————. Labour Productivity Differences between Foreign and Mexican Firms. In *Blomström, M.*, 1989, *1988*, pp. 28–34.

————. Multinationals and Market Structure in Mexico. In *Blomström, M.*, 1989, *1986*, pp. 74–89.

————. The Nature of Spillovers. In *Blomström, M.*, 1989, pp. 54–73.

————. Summary and Some Suggestions for Future Research on Spillovers. In *Blomström, M.*, 1989, pp. 90–96.

———— and Lipsey, Robert E. The Export Performance of U.S. and Swedish Multinationals. *Rev. Income Wealth*, September 1989, *35*(3), pp. 245–64.

———— and Lipsey, Robert E. U.S. Multinationals in Latin American Service Industries. *World Devel.*, November 1989, *17*(11), pp. 1769–76.

Bloom, David E. The Poverty of Widows: Future Prospects: Comment. In *Wise, D. A., ed.*, 1989, pp. 223–29.

Bloom, Paul N. and Smith, Darlene Brannigan. Using Content Analysis to Understand the Consumer Movement. *J. Cons. Aff.*, Winter 1989, *23*(2), pp. 301–28.

Bloomfield, Arthur I. Aspects of the Theory of International Trade in France: 1800–1914. *Oxford Econ. Pap.*, July 1989, *41*(3), pp. 619–39.

Blose, Laurence E. and Martin, John D. Federal Government Leasing: Costs, Incentives, and Effects. *Public Budg. Finance*, Summer 1989, *9*(2), pp. 66–75.

Blosser, Lois; Marlowe, Julia and Selnow, Gary. A Content Analysis of Problem-Resolution Appeals in Television Commercials. *J. Cons. Aff.*, Summer 1989, *23*(1), pp. 175–94.

Blum, Alain and Monnier, Alain. Recent Mortality Trends in the U.S.S.R.: New Evidence. *Population Stud.*, July 1989, *43*(2), pp. 211–41.

Blum, Terry C. and Roman, Paul M. Employee Assistance Programs and Human Resources Management. In *Ferris, G. R. and Rowland, K. M., eds.*, 1989, pp. 259–312.

Blum, Ulrich C. H. and Dudley, Leonard. A Spatial Approach to Structural Change: The Making of the French Hexagon. *J. Econ. Hist.*, September 1989, *49*(3), pp. 657–75.

Blum V., Roberto; Rubio F., Luis and Rodriguez D., Cristina. The Making of Mexico's Trade Policy and the Uruguay Round. In *Nau, H. R., ed.*, 1989, pp. 167–90.

Blume, Marshall E.; MacKinlay, A. Craig and Terker, Bruce. Order Imbalances and Stock Price Movements on October 19 and 20, 1987. *J. Finance*, September 1989, *44*(4), pp. 827–48.

Blümle, Gerold and Hauser, Siegfried. Exports of Baden-Württemberg within the Frame of the Federal Republic of Germany Structure—Concentration. In *Dams, T. and Matsugi, T., eds.*, 1989, pp. 191–214.

Blundell, Richard W.; Micklewright, John and Baker, Paul. Modelling Household Energy Expenditures Using Micro-data. *Econ. J.*, September 1989, *99*(397), pp. 720–38.

———— and Smith, Richard J. Estimation in a Class of Simultaneous Equation Limited Dependent Variable Models. *Rev. Econ. Stud.*, January 1989, *56*(1), pp. 37–57.

Blyth, Douglas. Determining Appropriate Technology for Diverse Socioeconomic Conditions: With Particular Reference to the Textile Industry. In *Negandhi, A. R., ed.*, 1989, pp. 305–22.

Blyton, Paul. Time and Labour Relations. In *Blyton, P., et al.*, 1989, pp. 105–31.

————, et al. Time, Work and Organization: Conclusions. In *Blyton, P., et al.*, 1989, pp. 132–37.

————. Time, Work and Organization: Introduction. In *Blyton, P., et al.*, 1989, pp. 1–12.

Boadway, Robin W. Information, Incentives, and General Equilibrium: Comment. In *Cornet, B. and Tulkens, H., eds.*, 1989, pp. 45–50.

————. The Role of Government in a Market Economy. In *Samuels, W. J., ed. (I)*, 1989, pp. 25–31.

———— and Flatters, Frank. Tax Expenditures and Alternatives for Evaluating Government Activities Conducted through the Tax System. In *Bruce, N., ed.*, 1989, pp. 67–104.

———— and McKenzie, Ken. The Treatment of Resource Industries in the 1987 Federal Tax Reform. In *Mintz, J. and Whalley, J., eds.*, 1989, pp. 286–325.

————; Pestieau, Pierre and Wildasin, David E. Non-cooperative Behavior and Efficient Provision of Public Goods. *Public Finance*, 1989, *44*(1), pp. 1–17.

————; Pestieau, Pierre and Wildasin, David E. Tax-Transfer Policies and the Voluntary Provision of Public Goods. *J. Public Econ.*, July 1989, *39*(2), pp. 157–76.

———— and Wildasin, David E. A Median Voter Model of Social Security. *Int. Econ. Rev.*, May 1989, *30*(2), pp. 307–28.

———— and Wildasin, David E. Voting Models of Social Security Determination. In *Gustafsson, B. A. and Klevmarken, N. A., eds.*, 1989, pp. 29–50.

Boardman, Anthony E. and Vining, Aidan R. Ownership and Performance in Competitive Environments: A Comparison of the Performance of Private, Mixed, and State-Owned Enterprises. *J. Law Econ.*, April 1989, *32*(1), pp. 1–33.

Boaz, David. Saving the Inner City. In *Crane, E. H. and Boaz, D.*, 1989, pp. 283–95.

———— **and Crane, Edward H.** An American Vision: Policies for the '90s: Introduction. In *Crane, E. H. and Boaz, D.*, 1989, pp. 1–10.

Boaz, Rachel Floersheim. Social Security Rules and the Early Acceptance of Social Security Benefits. *Soc. Sci. Quart.*, March 1989, *70*(1), pp. 72–87.

Bobko, Philip; Johnson, Nancy Brown and Sambharya, Rakesh B. Deregulation, Business Strategy, and Wages in the Airline Industry. *Ind. Relat.*, Fall 1989, *28*(3), pp. 419–30.

Bobrow, Davis B. Stories Remembered and Forgotten. *J. Conflict Resolution*, June 1989, *33*(2), pp. 187–209.

Bobrowski, Paul M. and Kern, Gary M. A Multiple Vehicle Scheduling Algorithm Employing Subtour Elimination and Operator Theory. *Logist. Transp. Rev.*, March 1989, *25*(1), pp. 75–89.

van Bochove, Cornelis A. and van Sorge, Wim. Constant Wealth National Income: Accounting for War Damage with an Application to the Netherlands, 1940–45. *Rev. Income Wealth*, June 1989, *35*(2), pp. 187–208.

Bock, Hans-Hermann. Probabilistic Aspects in Cluster Analysis. In *Opitz, O., ed.*, 1989, pp. 12–44.

Bockelmann, Horst. The Need for Worldwide Coordination of Economic Policies. In *Sijben, J. J., ed.*, 1989, pp. 39–53.

Böckenholt, Ingo and Gaul, Wolfgang. Generalized Latent Class Analysis: A New Methodology for Market Structure Analysis. In *Opitz, O., ed.*, 1989, pp. 367–76.

Bockstael, Nancy E.; McConnell, Kenneth E. and Strand, Ivar E., Jr. Measuring the Benefits of Improvements in Water Quality: The Chesapeake Bay. *Marine Resource Econ.*, 1989, *6*(1), pp. 1–18.

————; **McConnell, Kenneth E. and Strand, Ivar E., Jr.** A Random Utility Model for Sportfishing: Some Preliminary Results for Florida. *Marine Resource Econ.*, 1989, *6*(3), pp. 245–60.

Bod, Péter Ákos. Deregulation and Institution Building. Lessons from the Reforms of the Hungarian Public Sector. *Jahr. Wirtsch. Osteuropas*, 1989, *13*(1), pp. 110–26.

————. Market Strategy of the Hungarian Enterprise: Sources of Inadequate Response to Environmental Challenges. *Eastern Europ. Econ.*, Winter 1989–90, *28*(2), pp. 153–71.

————. The View from the Opposition: Interview. *Challenge*, Nov.–Dec. 1989, *32*(6), pp. 18–21.

Boda, György. Importbedarf der ungarischen Wirtschaft. Wirtschaftspolitische Schwierigkeiten zu seiner Deckung. (On the Import Intensity of the Hungarian Economy. With En-

glish summary.) *Konjunkturpolitik*, 1989, *35*(3), pp. 160–87.

———— **and Falussy, Béla.** Changes in Total Worktime per Unit of Free Time as a Function of Economic Development. *Statist. J.*, 1989, *6*(1), pp. 51–68.

————; **Koós Balsay, Éva and Molnár, István.** Compilation of Input–Output Tables in Hungary. In *Franz, A. and Rainer, N., eds.*, 1989, pp. 43–67.

Boddie, John W. Federal Financial Management: Another View. *Public Budg. Finance*, Summer 1989, *9*(2), pp. 99–103.

Bode, Eckhardt. Einige kritische Anmerkungen zu empirischen Tests des Ricardianischen Äquivalenztheorems. (Some Critical Remarks upon Empirical Tests of the Ricardian Equivalence Theorem. With English summary.) *Jahr. Nationalökon. Statist.*, March 1989, *206*(2), pp. 128–35.

Bodemann, Y. Michal and Spohn, Willfried. The Capitalist Class: Federal Republic of Germany. In *Bottomore, T. and Brym, R. J., eds.*, 1989, pp. 73–108.

Bodie, Zvi. The Lender's View of Debt and Equity: The Case of Pension Funds. In *Kopcke, R. W. and Rosengren, E. S., eds.*, 1989, pp. 106–24.

Bodström, Lennart. Swedish Science Policy: The Government's New Research Bill. In *Andersson, Å. E.; Batten, D. F. and Karlsson, C., eds.*, 1989, pp. 297–301.

de Bodt, Eric. Systèmes experts et diagnostic financier: Une méthodologie de raisonnement structuré. (Experts Systems and Financial Diagnosis: A Methodology for Structured Reasoning. With English summary.) *Écon. Societes*, December 1989, *23*(12), pp. 59–81.

Bodvarsson, Örn B. Educational Screening with Output Variability and Costly Monitoring. *Atlantic Econ. J.*, March 1989, *17*(1), pp. 16–23.

Boeckhout, I. J.; Molle, Willem T. M. and Beumer, L. The Location of Information Intensive Economic Activities in the European Community. In *Punset, E. and Sweeney, G., eds.*, 1989, pp. 161–72.

Boehm, Ernst A. and Martin, Vance L. An Investigation into the Major Causes of Australia's Recent Inflation and Some Policy Implications. *Econ. Rec.*, March 1989, *65*(188), pp. 1–15.

Boemio, Thomas R. and Edwards, Gerald A., Jr. Asset Securitization: A Supervisory Perspective. *Fed. Res. Bull.*, October 1989, *75*(10), pp. 659–69.

Boeren, Clasina C. M. and Sithole, Vincent Majozi. Contract Farming Schemes in Swaziland: Vuvulane Irrigated Farms and Mphetseni Settlement Scheme. *Eastern Afr. Econ. Rev.*, Special Issue, August 1989, pp. 59–69.

Boeri, Tito. Does Firm Size Matter? *Giorn. Econ.*, Sept.–Oct. 1989, *48*(9–10), pp. 477–95.

Boeschoten, W. C. and Fase, M. M. G. The Way We Pay with Money. *J. Bus. Econ. Statist.*, July 1989, *7*(3), pp. 319–26.

Boettke, Peter J. Evolution and Economics: Austrians as Institutionalists. In *Samuels, W. J., ed. (II)*, 1989, pp. 73–89.

——. Information and the Coase Theorem: Comment. *J. Econ. Perspectives*, Spring 1989, *3*(2), pp. 195–98.

——. A Reply: Austrian Institutionalism. In *Samuels, W. J., ed. (II)*, 1989, pp. 181–202.

Bofinger, Peter. Zum "Bericht zur Wirtschafts- und Währungunion in der Europäischen Gemeinschaft" des "Ausschusses zur Prüfung der Wirtschafts- und Währungsunion": "Delors-Bericht." (Report on Economic and Monetary Union in the European Community. With English summary.) *Kredit Kapital*, 1989, *22*(3), pp. 429–47.

Bogahawatte, C. and Vergani, G. An Interregional Equilibrium Model to Evaluate the Impact of Agricultural Policy Measures or Development Projects on the Agricultural Sector of Developing Countries. Case Study: Sri Lanka. In *Bauer, S. and Henrichsmeyer, W., eds.*, 1989, pp. 85–95.

Bogaschewsky, Ronald. Dynamische Materialdisposition im Beschaffungsbereich. (With English summary.) *Z. Betriebswirtshaft*, August 1989, *59*(8), pp. 855–74.

Bogen, Kenneth T.; Lichtenberg, Erik and Zilberman, David. Regulating Environmental Health Risks under Uncertainty: Groundwater Contamination in California. *J. Environ. Econ. Manage.*, July 1989, *17*(1), pp. 22–34.

Bogetić, Željko. A Model of the Mixed Household in Yugoslavia. *Econ. Anal. Workers' Manage.*, 1989, *23*(2), pp. 99–128.

Boggess, William G.; Moss, Charles B. and Muraro, Ronald P. Distortionary Impacts of the 1982 and 1986 U.S. Tax Codes on Capital Investments: A Case Study of Investment in Orange Groves. *Southern J. Agr. Econ.*, December 1989, *21*(2), pp. 107–15.

Boggio, Luciano and Tirelli, Patrizio. Economic Growth, Exports and International Competitiveness. *Econ. Int.*, Feb.–March 1989, *42*(1–2), pp. 22–46.

Bogunović, Aleksandar. Yugoslav Debt Crisis Management. In *Singer, H. W. and Sharma, S., eds. (II)*, 1989, pp. 271–75.

Bohac, Rodney. Agricultural Structure and the Origins of Migration in Central Russia, 1810–1850. In *Grantham, G. and Leonard, C. S., eds., Pt. B*, 1989, pp. 369–87.

Bohara, Alok K. and McNown, Robert F. Monetary and Inflationary Linkages between India and Nepal: A Vector Autoregression Analysis. *Indian Econ. J.*, July–Sept. 1989, *37*(1), pp. 40–55.

Bohi, Douglas R. Regulatory Failure, Regulatory Reform, and Structural Change in the Electrical Power Industry: Comments. *Brookings Pap. Econ. Act.*, Microeconomics, 1989, pp. 200–203.

Böhm, Franz. Rule of Law in a Market Economy. In *Peacock, A. and Willgerodt, H., eds. (II)*, 1989, *1966*, pp. 46–67.

——; **Eucken, Walter and Grossman-Doerth, Hans.** The Ordo Manifesto of 1936. In *Peacock,*

A. and Willgerodt, H., eds. (II), 1989, *1936*, pp. 15–26.

Böhm, Stephan. Subjectivism and Post-Keynesianism: Towards a Better Understanding. In *Pheby, J., ed.*, 1989, pp. 59–93.

Bohrer, Robert; Yancey, T. A. and Judge, G. G. Sampling Performance of Some Joint One-Sided Preliminary Test Estimators under Squared Error Loss. *Econometrica*, September 1989, *57*(5), pp. 1221–28.

Boidman, Nathan. The Section 482 White Paper: A Canadian Perspective. *Bull. Int. Fiscal Doc.*, November 1989, *43*(11), pp. 483–97.

Boissevain, Jeremy. Patronage in Sicily. In *Heidenheimer, A. J.; Johnston, M. and LeVine, V. T., eds.*, 1989, *1966*, pp. 307–25.

de Boissieu, Christian. Credit Constraints and Investment Finance: Some Evidence from Greece: Comment. In *Monti, M., ed.*, 1989, pp. 188–92.

——. The 'Overdraft Economy', the 'Auto-economy' and the Rate of Interest. In *Barrère, A., ed.*, 1989, pp. 79–104.

Boisvert, Richard N. and Bailey, Elizabeth E. A Comparison of Risk Efficiency Criteria in Evaluating Groundnut Performance in Drought-Prone Areas. *Australian J. Agr. Econ.*, December 1989, *33*(3), pp. 153–69.

Boitani, A. and Christodoulakis, N. A Note on IS–LM and Stock Adjustment Processes. *Metroecon.*, February 1989, *40*(1), pp. 67–85.

Boivin, Jean. Industrial Relations: A Field and a Discipline. In *Barbash, J. and Barbash, K., eds.*, 1989, pp. 91–108.

Bojnec-Fakin, Barbara. Distributivne krive jugoslavenske privrede. (Distributive Curves for the Yugoslav Economy. With English summary.) *Econ. Anal. Workers' Manage.*, 1989, *23*(3), pp. 253–71.

Bokhari, Riyaz. Privatisation in Pakistan. In *Ramanadham, V. V., ed.*, 1989, pp. 145–77.

Bold, Frederick and Hull, Brooks B. Towards an Economic Theory of the Church. *Int. J. Soc. Econ.*, 1989, *16*(7), pp. 5–15.

Boldrin, Michele. Paths of Optimal Accumulation in Two-Sector Models. In *Barnett, W. A.; Geweke, J. and Shell, K., eds.*, 1989, pp. 231–52.

Boldyreva, Tat'iana. Columns of Figures or an Instrument of Social Policy? *Prob. Econ.*, July 1989, *32*(3), pp. 89–102.

Boleat, Mark. British Thrifts Thrive. In *Schwartz, E. and Vasconcellos, G. M., eds.*, 1989, pp. 71–77.

Bolger, E. M. A Set of Axioms for a Value for Partition Function Games. *Int. J. Game Theory*, 1989, *18*(1), pp. 37–44.

Bollard, Alan. Trade and Economic Cooperation in the Asian-Pacific Region: Comment. In *Shinohara, M. and Lo, F., eds.*, 1989, pp. 465–66.

Bolle, Friedel. Levels of Aspiration, Promises, and the Possibility of Revaluation. In *Grunert, K. G. and Ölander, F., eds.*, 1989, pp. 199–211.

Bollerslev, Tim and Baillie, Richard T. Common

Stochastic Trends in a System of Exchange Rates. *J. Finance*, March 1989, *44*(1), pp. 167–81.

_____ **and Baillie, Richard T.** The Message in Daily Exchange Rates: A Conditional-Variance Tale. *J. Bus. Econ. Statist.*, July 1989, *7*(3), pp. 297–305.

Bollini, Andrea C. and Rossi, Nicola. Demographic Variables in Demand Systems and Related Measures of the Cost of Changing Family Size. *Giorn. Econ.*, Sept.–Oct. 1989, *48*(9–10), pp. 449–65.

Bollman, Ray D. Who Receives Farm Government Payments? *Can. J. Agr. Econ.*, November 1989, *37*(3), pp. 351–78.

Bolon, Donald S. and Hunt, David M. A Review of Five Versions of Theory Z: Does Z Have a Future? **In** *Prasad, S. B., ed.*, 1989, pp. 201–20.

Bolster, Paul J.; Lindsey, Lawrence B. and Mitrusi, Andrew W. Tax-Induced Trading: The Effect of the 1986 Tax Reform Act on Stock Market Activity. *J. Finance*, June 1989, *44*(2), pp. 327–44.

_____ **and Srinivasan, Venkat.** An Expert System for Assigning Investment Quality Ratings Using the AHP. **In** *Lockett, A. G. and Islei, G., eds.*, 1989, pp. 563–74.

_____; **Srinivasan, Venkat and Kim, Yong H.** A Framework for Integrating the Leasing Alternative with the Capital Budgeting Decision. **In** *Lee, C. F., ed.*, 1989, pp. 75–93.

Boltho, Andrea. Did Policy Activism Work? *Europ. Econ. Rev.*, December 1989, *33*(9), pp. 1709–26.

_____. European and United States Regional Differentials: A Note. *Oxford Rev. Econ. Policy*, Summer 1989, *5*(2), pp. 105–15.

Bolton, Patrick and Aghion, Philippe. The Financial Structure of the Firm and the Problem of Control. *Europ. Econ. Rev.*, March 1989, *33*(2/3), pp. 286–93.

Bolton, Ruth N. The Relationship between Market Characteristics and Promotional Price Elasticities. *Marketing Sci.*, Spring 1989, *8*(2), pp. 153–69.

Bombach, Gottfried. Jean-Baptiste Say und sein "Gesetz." (Jean-Baptiste Say and His "Law." With English summary.) *Jahr. Nationalökon. Statist.*, October 1989, *206*(4–5), pp. 285–94.

Bomhoff, E. J. The Need for Further Dollar Depreciation: Commentary. **In** *Sijben, J. J., ed.*, 1989, pp. 35–37.

Bon, Ranko. Qualitative Input–Output Analysis. **In** *Miller, R. E.; Polenske, K. R. and Rose, A. Z., eds.*, 1989, pp. 222–31.

Bona, Jerry L. and Santos, Manuel S. On the Structure of the Equilibrium Price Set of Overlapping-Generations Economies. *J. Math. Econ.*, 1989, *18*(3), pp. 209–30.

Bonanno, Giacomo. Sudden and Surprising Changes of Attitude during Negotiations. *Econ. Notes*, 1989, (1), pp. 55–68.

Bonaparte, T. H. George on Free Trade, at Home and Abroad: The American Economist and Social Philosopher Envisioned a World Unhin-

dered in Production and Exchange. *Amer. J. Econ. Sociology*, April 1989, *48*(2), pp. 245–56.

Bond, Eric W. Optimal Policy toward International Factor Movements with a Country-Specific Factor. *Europ. Econ. Rev.*, September 1989, *33*(7), pp. 1329–44.

_____ **and Coulson, N. Edward.** Externalities, Filtering, and Neighborhood Change. *J. Urban Econ.*, September 1989, *26*(2), pp. 231–49.

_____ **and Samuelson, Larry.** Bargaining with Commitment, Choice of Techniques, and Direct Foreign Investment. *J. Int. Econ.*, February 1989, *26*(1/2), pp. 77–97.

_____ **and Samuelson, Larry.** Strategic Behaviour and the Rules for International Taxation of Capital. *Econ. J.*, December 1989, *99*(398), pp. 1099–1111.

Bond, Gary and Pfeffermann, Guy. IFC and Development. *Finance Devel.*, December 1989, *26*(4), pp. 41–43.

Bone, John. A Note on Concavity and Scalar Properties in Production. *Bull. Econ. Res.*, July 1989, *41*(3), pp. 213–17.

Bonev, Valentin B. Customs-Free Zones in the People's Republic of Bulgaria. **In** *Bulgarian Academy of Sciences, Institute of Economics*, 1989, pp. 125–34.

Bonine, John E. A Voice from the Wilderness, Calling Your Name. *Yale J. Regul.*, Summer 1989, *6*(2), pp. 392–402.

Bonnans, J. F. Local Study of Newton Type Algorithms for Constrained Problems. **In** *Dolecki, S., ed.*, 1989, pp. 13–24.

Bonnen, James T. On the Role of Data and Measurement in Agricultural Economics Research. *J. Agr. Econ. Res.*, Fall 1989, *41*(4), pp. 2–5.

_____. Relevancy of the Social Sciences in the Policy Arena: Implications for Agricultural Economics. *Southern J. Agr. Econ.*, July 1989, *21*(1), pp. 41–50.

_____ **and Browne, William P.** Why Is Agricultural Policy So Difficult to Reform? **In** *Krämer, C. S., ed.*, 1989, pp. 7–33.

Bonnier, Karl-Adam and Bruner, Robert F. An Analysis of Stock Price Reaction to Management Change in Distressed Firms. *J. Acc. Econ.*, February 1989, *11*(1), pp. 95–106.

Bonnieux, Francois. Estimating Regional-Level Input Demand for French Agriculture Using a Translog Production Function. *Europ. Rev. Agr. Econ.*, 1989, *16*(2), pp. 229–41.

Bontempo, Hélio Cézar. Política cambial e superávit comercial. (With English summary.) *Pesquisa Planejamento Econ.*, April 1989, *19*(1), pp. 45–64.

Bonus, Holger. Institutional Persistence and Change: The Question of Efficiency: Comment. *J. Inst. Theoretical Econ.*, March 1989, *145*(1), pp. 95–97.

Boo, King Ong. Privatisation: Singapore's Experience in Perspective: A Legal Perspective. **In** *Thynne, I. and Ariff, M., eds.*, 1989, pp. 127–42.

Boomgaard, Peter. Java's Agricultural Production, 1775–1875. **In** *Maddison, A. and Prince, G., eds.*, 1989, pp. 97–131.

Boonekamp, Clemens. Industrial Policies of Industrial Countries. *Finance Devel.*, March 1989, *26*(1), pp. 14–17.

Boonin, Leonard G. The University, Scientific Research, and the Ownership of Knowledge. **In** *Weil, V. and Snapper, J. W., eds.*, 1989, pp. 253–67.

Booth, Alan. Britain in the 1930s: A Managed Economy? A Reply. *Econ. Hist. Rev., 2nd Ser.*, November 1989, *42*(4), pp. 548–56.

Booth, Alison L. The Bargaining Structure of British Establishments. *Brit. J. Ind. Relat.*, July 1989, 27(2), pp. 425–34.

———— **and Chatterji, Monojit.** Redundancy Payments and Firm-Specific Training. *Economica*, November 1989, 56(224), pp. 505–21.

Booth, Anne. Exports and Growth in the Colonial Economy, 1830–1940. **In** *Maddison, A. and Prince, G., eds.*, 1989, pp. 67–96.

————. Indonesian Agricultural Development in Comparative Perspective. *World Devel.*, August 1989, *17*(8), pp. 1235–54.

————. Repelita V and Indonesia's Medium Term Economic Strategy. *Bull. Indonesian Econ. Stud.*, August 1989, *25*(2), pp. 3–30.

———— **and Damanik, Konta.** Central Java and Yogyakarta: Malthus Overcome? **In** *Hill, H., ed.*, 1989, pp. 283–305.

Booth, Douglas E. Hydroelectric Dams and the Decline of Chinook Salmon in the Columbia River Basin. *Marine Resource Econ.*, 1989, *6*(3), pp. 195–211.

Booth, G. Geoffrey and Koveos, Peter E. Purchasing Power Parity: A Reexamination of Prediction Errors. **In** *Lee, C. F., ed.*, 1989, pp. 143–62.

————; **Loistl, Otto and Akgiray, Vedat.** German Stock Market's Resiliency to World-Wide Panics. *Z. Betriebswirtshaft*, September 1989, *59*(9), pp. 968–78.

————; **Loistl, Otto and Akgiray, Vedat.** Statistical Models of German Stock Returns. *J. Econ. (Z. Nationalökon.)*, 1989, *50*(1), pp. 17–33.

Booth, James R. An Analysis of Senior/Subordinated Passthroughs: Implications for Thrifts. **In** *Federal Home Loan Bank of San Francisco*, 1989, pp. 131–50.

Booth, Laurence. Hedging Foreign Exchange Exposure. **In** *Rugman, A. M., ed.*, 1989, pp. 291–309.

Booth, P. and Vaughan, D. R. The Economic Importance of Tourism and the Arts in Merseyside. *J. Cult. Econ.*, December 1989, *13*(2), pp. 21–34.

Booth, Richard A. State Takeover Statutes Revisited. *Mich. Law Rev.*, October 1989, *88*(1), pp. 120–29.

Boothe, Paul M. and Reid, Bradford G. Asset Returns and Government Budgets in a Small Open Economy: Empirical Evidence for Canada. *J. Monet. Econ.*, January 1989, 23(1), pp. 65–77.

Booysen, A. and Fourie, F. C. v. N. Economic Concentration and Macro-economic Instability in South Africa. *J. Stud. Econ. Econometrics*, November 1989, *13*(3), pp. 75–90.

Borchard, G. and Glasmeier, A. Research Policy and Review 31. From Branch Plants to Back Offices: Prospects for Rural Services Growth. *Environ. Planning A*, December 1989, *21*(12), pp. 1565–83.

Bordes, Christian and Driscoll, Michael J. Intégration des marchés des capitaux en Europe: Résultats des tests d'égalité des taux marginaux de substitution intertemporels. (The Integration of Capital Markets in Europe: Testing the Equality between Intertemporal Marginal Rates of Substitution. With English summary.) *Écon. Societes*, April–May 1989, *23*(4–5), pp. 133–64.

————; **Driscoll, Michael J. and Strauss-Kahn, Marc-Olivier.** Price Inertia and Nominal Aggregate Demand in Major European Countries. *Rech. Écon. Louvain*, 1989, *55*(2), pp. 105–28.

Bordes, Georges and Le Breton, Michel. Arrovian Theorems with Private Alternatives Domains and Selfish Individuals. *J. Econ. Theory*, April 1989, *47*(2), pp. 257–81.

Bordignon, Silvano and Gaetan, Carlo. Indicatori multipli dell'occupazione e domanda di lavoro: Alcune analisi empiriche con un modello DYMIMIC. (Multiple Indicators of Employment and Labor Demand: Some Empirical Analyses with a DYMIMIC Model. With English summary.) *Econ. Lavoro*, April–June 1989, *23*(2), pp. 19–38.

———— **and Trivellato, Ugo.** The Optimal Use of Provisional Data in Forecasting with Dynamic Models. *J. Bus. Econ. Statist.*, April 1989, *7*(2), pp. 275–86.

Bordley, Robert F. Generating Market Elasticity Estimates Using Cross-Sectional First-Choice and Second-Choice Data. *J. Bus. Econ. Statist.*, January 1989, *7*(1), pp. 141–46.

————. Relaxing the Loyalty Condition in the Colombo/Morrison Model. *Marketing Sci.*, Winter 1989, *8*(1), pp. 100–103.

Bordo, Michael D. The Contribution of *A Monetary History of the United States, 1867–1960* to Monetary History. **In** *[Schwartz, A. J.]*, 1989, pp. 15–70.

————. Money, History, and International Finance: Essays in Honor of Anna J. Schwartz: Introduction. **In** *[Schwartz, A. J.]*, 1989, pp. 1–11.

———— **and Schwartz, Anna J.** Transmission of Real and Monetary Disturbances under Fixed and Floating Exchange Rates. **In** *Dorn, J. A. and Niskanen, W. A., eds.*, 1989, *1988*, pp. 237–58.

Boreham, Paul; Clegg, Stewart and Dow, Geoff. Political Organisation and Economic Policy. **In** *Duncan, G., ed.*, 1989, pp. 253–76.

Borenstein, Severin. The Economics of Costly Risk Sorting in Competitive Insurance Markets. *Int. Rev. Law Econ.*, June 1989, *9*(1), pp. 25–39.

————. Hubs and High Fares: Dominance and Market Power in the U.S. Airline Industry.

Rand J. Econ., Autumn 1989, *20*(3), pp. 344–65.

_____ **and Cournat, Paul N.** How to Carve a Medical Degree: Human Capital Assets in Divorce Settlements. *Amer. Econ. Rev.*, December 1989, *79*(5), pp. 992–1009.

_____ **and Zimmerman, Martin B.** Losses in Airline Demand and Value Following Accidents. In *Moses, L. N. and Savage, I., eds.*, 1989, pp. 50–55.

Borensztein, Eduardo R. The Effect of External Debt on Investment. *Finance Devel.*, September 1989, *26*(3), pp. 17–19.

_____. Fiscal Policy and Foreign Debt. *J. Int. Econ.*, February 1989, *26*(1/2), pp. 53–75.

_____. How to Cope with a Debt Overhang: Cut Flows Rather Than Stocks: Comment. In *Husain, I. and Diwan, I., eds.*, 1989, pp. 235–37.

_____ **and Aizenman, Joshua.** Debt and Conditionality under Endogenous Terms of Trade Adjustment. In *Frenkel, J. A.; Dooley, M. P. and Wickham, P., eds.*, 1989, pp. 102–29.

_____ **and Ghosh, Atish Rex.** Foreign Borrowing and Export Promotion Policies. *Int. Monet. Fund Staff Pap.*, December 1989, *36*(4), pp. 904–33.

Borg, J. Rody; Borg, Mary O'Malley and Leeth, John D. The Success of Mergers in the 1920s: A Stock Market Appraisal of the Second Merger Wave. *Int. J. Ind. Organ.*, Special Issue, March 1989, *7*(1), pp. 117–31.

Borg, Mary O'Malley. The Income–Fertility Relationship: Effect of the Net Price of a Child. *Demography*, May 1989, *26*(2), pp. 301–10.

_____; **Leeth, John D. and Borg, J. Rody.** The Success of Mergers in the 1920s: A Stock Market Appraisal of the Second Merger Wave. *Int. J. Ind. Organ.*, Special Issue, March 1989, *7*(1), pp. 117–31.

_____; **Mason, Paul M. and Shapiro, Stephen L.** The Case of Effort Variables in Student Performance. *J. Econ. Educ.*, Summer 1989, *20*(3), pp. 308–13.

_____; **Mason, Paul M. and Shapiro, Stephen L.** Gaming Tax Incidence for Three Groups of Las Vegas Gamblers. *Appl. Econ.*, September 1989, *21*(9), pp. 1267–77.

Borgerhoff Mulder, Monique. Marital Status and Reproductive Performance in Kipsigis Women: Re-evaluating the Polygyny–Fertility Hypothesis. *Population Stud.*, July 1989, *43*(2), pp. 285–304.

Borgers, A. W. J.; van der Heijden, R. E. C. M. and Timmermans, H. J. P. A Variety Seeking Model of Spatial Choice-Behaviour. *Environ. Planning A*, August 1989, *21*(8), pp. 1037–48.

Börgers, Tilman. Perfect Equilibrium Histories of Finite and Infinite Horizon Games. *J. Econ. Theory*, February 1989, *47*(1), pp. 218–27.

Borjas, George J. Immigrant and Emigrant Earnings: A Longitudinal Study. *Econ. Inquiry*, January 1989, *27*(1), pp. 21–37.

_____ **and Bronars, Stephen G.** Consumer Discrimination and Self-employment. *J. Polit. Econ.*, June 1989, *97*(3), pp. 581–605.

Borland, Jeff. Trade Unions in Australia. *Australian Econ. Rev.*, Summer 1989, (88), pp. 66–73.

Borland, Melvin V. and Pulsinelli, Robert W. Household Commodity Production and Social Harassment Costs. *Southern Econ. J.*, October 1989, *56*(2), pp. 291–301.

Borlaug, Norman E. Address to the 1988 World Food Conference. In *Helmuth, J. W. and Johnson, S. R., eds., Vol. 1*, 1989, pp. 79–83.

Born, Jeffery A. and Anderson, Seth C. The Selling and Seasoning of Investment Company Offerings. *J. Finan. Services Res.*, June 1989, *2*(2), pp. 115–31.

Borna, Shaheen and Mantripragada, Krishna G. Morality of Public Deficits: A Historical Perspective. *Public Budg. Finance*, Spring 1989, *9*(1), pp. 33–46.

Borner, Silvio. Competitiveness and Internationalization of Industry: The Case of Switzerland. In *Francis, A. and Tharakan, P. K. M., eds.*, 1989, pp. 64–90.

_____. Economic Analysis of Debt–Equity Swaps: Comments. In *Vosgerau, H.-J., ed.*, 1989, pp. 234–37.

Bornstein, Gary and Rapoport, Amnon. Solving Public Good Problems in Competition between Equal and Unequal Size Groups. *J. Conflict Resolution*, September 1989, *33*(3), pp. 460–79.

Borrie, Gordon [Sir]. Merger Policy: Current Policy Concerns. In *Fairburn, J. and Kay, J., eds.*, 1989, pp. 246–63.

Borrie, W. D. The Population. In *Hancock, K., ed.*, 1989, pp. 119–42.

Börsch-Supan, Axel. Household Dissolution and the Choice of Alternative Living Arrangements among Elderly Americans. In *Wise, D. A., ed.*, 1989, pp. 119–46.

Borum, Finn. The IT People: Their Qualifications, Skill Acquirement, and Management. In *Punset, E. and Sweeney, G., eds.*, 1989, pp. 89–105.

Bös, Dieter. Arguments on Privatization. In *Fels, G. and von Furstenberg, G. M., eds.*, 1989, pp. 217–44.

_____ **and von Weizsäcker, Robert K.** Economic Consequences of an Aging Population. *Europ. Econ. Rev.*, March 1989, *33*(2/3), pp. 345–54.

Bos, H. C. On a Socialist Optimum Economic Regime. *Acta Oecon.*, 1989, *40*(3–4), pp. 194–98.

Bos, Ted and Newbold, Paul. On Exponential Smoothing and the Assumption of Deterministic Trend Plus White Noise Data-Generating Models. *Int. J. Forecasting*, 1989, *5*(4), pp. 523–27.

Bosch, Darrell J. and Shabman, Leonard A. The Decline of Private Sector Oyster Culture in Virginia: Causes and Remedial Policies. *Marine Resource Econ.*, 1989, *6*(3), pp. 227–43.

Bosch, Gerhard and Sengenberger, Werner. Employment Policy, the State, and the Unions in the Federal Republic of Germany. In *Rosenberg, S., ed.*, 1989, pp. 87–106.

Bosch, J. C. Alternative Measures of Rates of Return: Some Empirical Evidence. *Managerial Dec. Econ.*, September 1989, *10*(3), pp. 229–39.

Bosch, J. K. Empirical Investigations into the Primary and Secondary Goals of Listed and Unlisted Firms: Part 1. *J. Stud. Econ. Econometrics*, November 1989, *13*(3), pp. 61–73.

Boschen, John F. and Newman, John L. Monetary Effects on the Real Interest Rate in an Open Economy: Evidence from the Argentine Indexed Bond Market. *J. Int. Money Finance*, June 1989, *8*(2), pp. 201–17.

Bose, Amitava. Short Period Equilibrium in a Less Developed Economy. In *Rakshit, M., ed.*, 1989, pp. 26–41.

Bosi, Paolo; Golinelli, Roberto and Stagni, Anna. Le origini del debito pubblico e il costo della stabilizzazione. (With English summary.) *Politica. Econ.*, December 1989, *5*(3), pp. 389–425.

Boskin, Michael J. Fiscal Policy and U.S. International Competitiveness. In *Libecap, G. D., ed.*, 1989, pp. 83–103.

_____. Lessons from the United States Economy in the 1980s and Their Applicability to Europe. In *Fels, G. and von Furstenberg, G. M., eds.*, 1989, pp. 298–38.

_____ **and Kotlikoff, Laurence J.** Public Debt and United States Saving: A New Test of the Neutrality Hypothesis. In *Kotlikoff, L. J.*, 1989, *1985*, pp. 455–78.

_____; **Robinson, Marc S. and Huber, Alan M.** Government Saving, Capital Formation, and Wealth in the United States, 1947–85. In *Lipsey, R. E. and Tice, H. S., eds.*, 1989, pp. 287–353.

_____; **Robinson, Marc S. and Roberts, John M.** New Estimates of Federal Government Tangible Capital and Net Investment. In *Jorgenson, D. W. and Landau, R., eds.*, 1989, pp. 451–83.

Bossard, Andreas. Das konsumgestützte Kapitalmarktmodell: Empirische Ergebnisse für die Schweiz. (The Consumption-Based Capital Asset Pricing Model: Empirical Evidence for Switzerland. With English summary.) *Schweiz. Z. Volkswirtsch. Statist.*, June 1989, *125*(2), pp. 135–56.

Bossert, Walter. The Impossibility of an Intermediate Solution in a One-Dimensional Location Model. *Reg. Sci. Urban Econ.*, February 1989, *19*(1), pp. 113–23.

_____. On the Extension of Preferences over a Set to the Power Set: An Axiomatic Characterization of a Quasi-ordering. *J. Econ. Theory*, October 1989, *49*(1), pp. 84–92.

Bossier, F., et al. HERMES: A Macrosectoral Model for the Belgian Economy. *Econ. Modelling*, October 1989, *6*(4), pp. 374–98.

Bossons, John. Efficiency and Distributional Effects of the Tax Reform Package: Comment. In *Mintz, J. and Whalley, J., eds.*, 1989, pp. 399–402.

Bostaph, Samuel. Jevons's "Antipodean Interlude": The Question of Early Influences. *Hist. Polit. Econ.*, Winter 1989, *21*(4), pp. 601–23.

_____. Jevons's "Antipodean Interlude": The Question of Early Influences: Response. *Hist. Polit. Econ.*, Winter 1989, *21*(4), pp. 631–33.

Bostock, Frances and Jones, Geoffrey. British Business in Iran, 1860s–1970s. In *Davenport-Hines, R. P. T. and Jones, G., eds.*, 1989, pp. 31–67.

Boswell, A. M. and Cluff, M. E. The Changing International Meat Market and the Outlook for the North American Livestock Sector. *Can. J. Agr. Econ.*, Part 2, December 1989, *37*(4), pp. 1199–1214.

Boswell, Terry E. The Utility of World-System Theory for Explaining Social Revolutions: A Comparison of Skocpol and Lenin. In *Martin, M. T. and Kandal, T. R., eds.*, 1989, pp. 77–95.

_____; **Sweat, Mike and Brueggemann, John.** War in the Core of the World-System: Testing the Goldstein Thesis. In *Schaeffer, R. K., ed.*, 1989, pp. 9–26.

Bosworth, Barry P. Institutional Change and the Efficacy of Monetary Policy. *Brookings Pap. Econ. Act.*, 1989, (1), pp. 77–110.

_____. There's No Simple Explanation for the Collapse in Saving. *Challenge*, July–Aug. 1989, *32*(4), pp. 27–32.

_____; **Burtless, Gary and Aaron, Henry J.** How Social Security Affects the Deficit. In *Bosworth, B. P., et al.*, 1989, pp. 139–43.

_____ **and Lawrence, Robert Z.** America in the World Economy. In *Bosworth, B. P., et al.*, 1989, pp. 49–70.

_____ **and Lawrence, Robert Z.** America's Global Role: From Dominance to Interdependence. In *Steinbruner, J. D., ed.*, 1989, pp. 12–47.

Bosworth, Derek L. Barriers to Growth: The Labour Market. In *Barber, J.; Metcalfe, J. S. and Porteous, M., eds.*, 1989, pp. 58–86.

_____ **and Jacobs, Chris.** Management Attitudes, Behaviour, and Abilities as Barriers to Growth. In *Barber, J.; Metcalfe, J. S. and Porteous, M., eds.*, 1989, pp. 20–38.

_____ **and Wilson, R. A.** Infrastructure for Technological Change: Intellectual Property Rights. In *Andersson, Å. E.; Batten, D. F. and Karlsson, C., eds.*, 1989, pp. 197–215.

Botarelli, Simonetta. Redditi da lavoro dipendente ed evasione. (With English summary.) *Studi. Econ.*, 1989, *44*(39), pp. 137–77.

Botha, D. J. J. Economic Historians and the Economy (Review Article). *S. Afr. J. Econ.*, September 1989, *57*(3), pp. 299–310.

Botner, Stanley B. Trends and Developments in Budgeting and Financial Mangement in Large Cities of the United States. *Public Budg. Finance*, Autumn 1989, *9*(3), pp. 37–42.

Bottazzi, Laura. La liberalizzazione dei movimenti di capitali in una economia ad alto debito pubblico. (The Liberalization of Capital Movements in a Large Public Debt Economy. With English summary.) *Rivista Int. Sci. Econ. Com.*, Oct.–Nov. 1989, *36*(10–11), pp. 931–50.

Bottomley, P. and Thirtle, C. The Rate of Return to Public Sector Agricultural R&D in the UK,

1965–80. *Appl. Econ.*, August 1989, *21*(8), pp. 1063–86.

Bottomore, Tom. The Capitalist Class. In *Bottomore, T. and Brym, R. J., eds.*, 1989, pp. 1–18.

_____. Economic Systems, Government, and Group Interests. In *Samuels, W. J., ed. (I)*, 1989, pp. 33–39.

_____. Max Weber and the Capitalist State. In *Duncan, G., ed.*, 1989, pp. 123–32.

Bouaouaja, Mohammed. Privatization in Tunisia: Objectives and Limits. In *El-Naggar, S., ed.*, 1989, pp. 234–46.

Bouchet, Frédéric; Orden, David and Norton, George W. Sources of Growth in French Agriculture. *Amer. J. Agr. Econ.*, May 1989, *71*(2), pp. 280–93.

Bouchet, Michel H. and Hay, Jonathan. The Rise of the Market-Based "Menu" Approach and Its Limitations. In *Husain, I. and Diwan, I., eds.*, 1989, pp. 146–59.

Boudreaux, Donald J. Imperfectly Competitive Firms, Non-price Competition, and Rent Seeking. *J. Inst. Theoretical Econ.*, December 1989, *145*(4), pp. 597–612.

_____ **and Holcombe, Randall G.** The Coasian and Knightian Theories of the Firm. *Managerial Dec. Econ.*, June 1989, *10*(2), pp. 147–54.

_____ **and Holcombe, Randall G.** Government by Contract. *Public Finance Quart.*, July 1989, *17*(3), pp. 264–80.

_____ **and Shughart, William F., II.** The Effects of Monetary Instability on the Extent of Vertical Integration. *Atlantic Econ. J.*, June 1989, *17*(2), pp. 1–10.

Bouët, Antoine. Politique tarifaire: Le cœur et le nucléolus du jeu interne comme fonction de réaction du jeu externe. (On Tariffs: The Core and Nucleolus of the Internal Game as Reaction Functions of External Game. With English summary.) *Revue Écon.*, September 1989, *40*(5), pp. 791–815.

Boughton, James M. Commodity Price Indicators: A Case for Discretion Rather Than Rules: Discussion. In *Miller, M.; Eichengreen, B. and Portes, R., eds.*, 1989, pp. 121–23.

_____. Commodity Prices and Inflation. *Finance Devel.*, June 1989, *26*(2), pp. 27–29.

_____. Policy Assignment Strategies with Somewhat Flexible Exchange Rates. In *Miller, M.; Eichengreen, B. and Portes, R., eds.*, 1989, pp. 125–54.

_____. The Stabilizing Properties of Target Zones: Comment. In *Bryant, R. C., et al., eds.*, 1989, pp. 278–82.

_____**; Haas, Richard D. and Masson, Paul R.** The Role of Exchange Rate Movements in Transmitting International Disturbances. In *Hodgman, D. R. and Wood, G. E., eds.*, 1989, pp. 180–213.

Bouhsina, Z. and Collombel, B. Biotechnologies, bioindustries et IAA. (Biotechnology, Bio-industry and Food Industry. With English summary.) *Écon. Societes*, July 1989, *23*(7), pp. 135–57.

Boulding, Kenneth E. A Bibliographical Autobiography. *Banca Naz. Lavoro Quart. Rev.*, December 1989, (171), pp. 365–93.

_____. The Implications of Macrodistribution for Personal Distribution. In *Davidson, P. and Kregel, J., eds.*, 1989, pp. 6–17.

_____. A Personal Note on Joan Robinson. In *Feiwel, G. R., ed. (II)*, 1989, pp. 853–60.

Bound, John. The Health and Earnings of Rejected Disability Insurance Applicants. *Amer. Econ. Rev.*, June 1989, *79*(3), pp. 482–503.

_____ **and Freeman, Richard B.** Black Economic Progress: Erosion of the Post-1965 Gains in the 1980s? In *Shulman, S. and Darity, W., Jr., eds.*, 1989, pp. 32–49.

Bourbeau, Philip E. Mobile Work Crews: An Approach to Achieve Long-Term Supported Employment. In *Wehman, P. and Kregel, J., eds.*, 1989, pp. 83–94.

Bourdet, Yves. Policy toward Market Power and Restrictive Practices in Sweden. *Antitrust Bull.*, Fall 1989, *34*(3), pp. 533–78.

Bourey, James M. Managing Growth and Infrastructure Development. In *Matzer, J., Jr., ed.*, 1989, pp. 38–47.

Bourgeois, Raymond C. and Crowley, Ronald W. The Rationale and Future Directions of Canada's Oceans Policy: Domestic Aspects. In *McRae, D. and Munro, G., eds.*, 1989, pp. 253–68.

Bourguignon, François. Family Size and Social Utility: Income Distribution Dominance Criteria. *J. Econometrics*, September 1989, *42*(1), pp. 67–80.

Bourke, Philip. Concentration and Other Determinants of Bank Profitability in Europe, North America and Australia. *J. Banking Finance*, March 1989, *13*(1), pp. 65–79.

Bourne, Compton. A Monetary Research Agenda for the Future. In *Worrell, D. and Bourne, C., eds.*, 1989, pp. 157–62.

_____. Some Fundamentals of Monetary Policy in the Caribbean. *Soc. Econ. Stud.*, June 1989, *38*(2), pp. 265–90.

Bourniaux, Jean-Marc; Waelbroeck, Jean and Adelman, Irma. Agricultural Development-Led Industrialisation in a Global Perspective. In *Williamson, J. G. and Panchamukhi, V. R., eds.*, 1989, pp. 320–39.

Boussard, J.-M. On Agricultural Production Functions. In *Bauer, S. and Henrichsmeyer, W., eds.*, 1989, pp. 207–18.

_____. Round Table Discussion: Conclusions and Outlook: Methodological Aspects. In *Bauer, S. and Henrichsmeyer, W., eds.*, 1989, pp. 345.

Boutillier, M.; Topol, R. and Avouyi-Dovi, S. Du peu de pertinence des anticipations sur le taux d'intérêt à court terme: Retour à la théorie de l'habitat préféré. (Weak Relevance of Short Term Interest Rate Expectations and Return to the Preferred Habitat Theory. With English summary.) *Écon. Societes*, April–May 1989, *23*(4–5), pp. 43–70.

Bouvier, Leon F. and Espenshade, Thomas J. The Stable Population Model, Migration, and

Complementarity. *Population Res. Policy Rev.*, May 1989, *8*(2), pp. 165–79.

Bouyssou, Denis. Modelling Inaccurate Determination, Uncertainty, Imprecision Using Multiple Criteria. In *Lockett, A. G. and Islei, G., eds.*, 1989, pp. 78–87.

Bouzaïane, Lotfi; Nugent, Jeffrey B. and Azabou, Mongi. Contractual Choice in Tunisian Fishing. In *Nabli, M. K. and Nugent, J. B., eds.*, 1989, pp. 158–77.

Bovard, James. Draining the Agricultural Policy Swamp. In *Crane, E. H. and Boaz, D.*, 1989, pp. 297–309.

Bovenberg, A. Lans. The Effects of Capital Income Taxation on International Competitiveness and Trade Flows. *Amer. Econ. Rev.*, December 1989, *79*(5), pp. 1045–64.

_____. Tax Policy and National Saving in the United States: A Survey. *Nat. Tax J.*, June 1989, *42*(2), pp. 123–38.

_____ **and Tanzi, Vito.** Economic Interdependence and the International Implications of Supply-Side Policies. In *Fels, G. and von Furstenberg, G. M., eds.*, 1989, pp. 153–79.

Bover, Olympia. Estimating Intertemporal Labour Supply Elasticities Using Structural Models. *Econ. J.*, December 1989, *99*(398), pp. 1026–39.

_____. Intertemporal Consumer Behaviour under Structural Changes in Income: Comment. *Econometric Rev.*, 1989, *8*(1), pp. 89–91.

_____; **Muellbauer, John and Murphy, Anthony.** Housing, Wages and UK Labour Markets. *Oxford Bull. Econ. Statist.*, March 1989, *51*(2), pp. 97–136.

Bowe, M.; Klein, Kurt K. and Klein, S. A. Adverse Selection and Warble Flies in Alberta. *Can. J. Agr. Econ.*, March 1989, *37*(1), pp. 111–23.

Bowen, Brent L. Statement to the U.S. House Subcommittee on Domestic Monetary Policy of the Committee on Banking, Finance and Urban Affairs, August 3, 1989. *Fed. Res. Bull.*, October 1989, *75*(10), pp. 684–88.

Bowen, H. V. Investment and Empire in the Later Eighteenth Century: East India Stockholding, 1756–1791. *Econ. Hist. Rev., 2nd Ser.*, May 1989, *42*(2), pp. 186–206.

Bowen, Harry P. Developing Country Export Competitiveness in Manufactured Goods. In *Audretsch, D. B.; Sleuwaegen, L. and Yamawaki, H., eds.*, 1989, pp. 189–209.

_____. Differentiated Products, Economies of Scale, and Access to the Japanese Market: Comment. In *Feenstra, R. C., ed.*, 1989, pp. 180–83.

Bowen, Ken. Research on Decision-Aiding: How to Be a DSS. In *Lockett, A. G. and Islei, G., eds.*, 1989, pp. 510–16.

Bowen, Robert M.; Johnson, Marilyn F. and Shevlin, Terry. Informational Efficiency and the Information Content of Earnings during the Market Crash of October 1987. *J. Acc. Econ.*, July 1989, *11*(2–3), pp. 225–54.

_____ **and Pfeiffer, Glenn M.** The Year-End LIFO Purchase Decision: The Case of Farmer

Brothers Company. *Accounting Rev.*, January 1989, *64*(1), pp. 152–71.

Bower, Nancy L. Firm Value and the Choice of Offering Method in Initial Public Offerings. *J. Finance*, July 1989, *44*(3), pp. 647–62.

Bowers, John K.; Dobson, Stephen M. and Goddard, John A. The Property Market and Industrial Location. *Scot. J. Polit. Econ.*, February 1989, *36*(1), pp. 1–18.

Bowes, Michael D. and Krutilla, John V. Economics and Public Forestland Management. *Natural Res. J.*, Summer 1989, *29*(3), pp. 737–49.

_____ **and Krutilla, John V.** Socially Optimal Forestry: A Comment. *J. Environ. Econ. Manage.*, November 1989, *17*(3), pp. 309–10.

Bowker, J. M. and Richardson, James W. Impacts of Alternative Farm Policies on Rural Communities. *Southern J. Agr. Econ.*, December 1989, *21*(2), pp. 35–46.

Bowler, M. Kenneth. Preparing Members of Congress to Make Binary Decisions on Complex Policy Issues: The 1986 Tax Reform Bill. *J. Policy Anal. Manage.*, Winter 1989, *8*(1), pp. 35–45.

Bowles, David; Ulbrich, Holley H. and Wallace, Myles S. Default Risk, Interest Differentials and Fiscal Policy: A New Look at Crowding Out. *Eastern Econ. J.*, July–Sept. 1989, *15*(3), pp. 203–12.

Bowles, Paul. Recipient Needs and Donor Interests in the Allocation of EEC Aid to Developing Countries. *Can. J. Devel. Stud.*, 1989, *10*(1), pp. 7–19.

_____ **and MacPhail, Fiona.** Technical Change and Intra-household Welfare: A Case Study of Irrigated Rice Production in South Sulawesi, Indonesia. *J. Devel. Stud.*, October 1989, *26*(1), pp. 58–80.

_____ **and White, Gordon.** Contradictions in China's Financial Reforms: The Relationship between Banks and Enterprises. *Cambridge J. Econ.*, December 1989, *13*(4), pp. 481–95.

Bowles, Roger and Skogh, Göran. Reputation, Monitoring and the Organisation of the Law Firm. In *Faure, M. and Van den Bergh, R., eds.*, 1989, pp. 33–47.

Bowles, Samuel. Social Institutions and Technical Change. In *Di Matteo, M.; Goodwin, R. M. and Vercelli, A., eds.*, 1989, pp. 67–87.

_____; **Gordon, David M. and Weisskopf, Thomas E.** Business Ascendancy and Economic Impasse: A Structural Retrospective on Conservative Economics, 1979–87. *J. Econ. Perspectives*, Winter 1989, *3*(1), pp. 107–34.

Bowlin, William F. An Intertemporal Assessment of the Efficiency of Air Force Accounting and Finance Offices. In *Chan, J. L. and Patton, J. M., eds.*, 1989, pp. 293–310.

Bowman, John H. and Mikesell, John L. Elected versus Appointed Assessors and the Achievement of Assessment Uniformity. *Nat. Tax J.*, June 1989, *42*(2), pp. 181–89.

Bowman, Rhead S. Jevons's Economic Theory in Relation to Social Change and Public Policy.

J. Econ. Issues, December 1989, *23*(4), pp. 1123–47.

Bowsher, Charles A. Federal Financial Management: One View. *Public Budg. Finance*, Summer 1989, *9*(2), pp. 91–98.

Boxley, Robert F. Agricultural and Rural Data Paradigms. *J. Agr. Econ. Res.*, Winter 1989, *41*(1), pp. 21–26.

Boyce, Gordon. The Development of the Cargo Fleet Iron Company, 1900–1914: Entrepreneurship, Costs, and Structural Rigidity in the Northeast Coast Steel Industry. *Bus. Hist. Rev.*, Winter 1989, *63*(4), pp. 839–75.

———— **and Bailey, Mark W.** The Manufacturing and Marketing of Steel in Canada: Dofasco Inc., 1912–1970. In *Hausman, W. J., ed.*, 1989, pp. 228–37.

Boyce, James K. Population Growth and Real Wages of Agricultural Labourers in Bangladesh. *J. Devel. Stud.*, July 1989, *25*(4), pp. 467–89.

Boyd-Barrett, Oliver. Multinational News Agencies. In *Enderwick, P.*, 1989, pp. 107–31.

Boyd, Colin, et al. Fare Evasion and Non-compliance: A Simple Model. *J. Transp. Econ. Policy*, May 1989, *23*(2), pp. 189–97.

Boyd, John H., III; Sung, Bom Yong and Becker, Robert A. Recursive Utility and Optimal Capital Accumulation. I. Existence. *J. Econ. Theory*, February 1989, *47*(1), pp. 76–100.

Boyd, Monica. Immigration and Income Security Policies in Canada: Implications for Elderly Immigrant Women. *Population Res. Policy Rev.*, January 1989, *8*(1), pp. 5–24.

————. Policy Forum on the Role of Immigration in Canada's Future: General Themes. In *Beach, C. M. and Green, A. G.*, 1989, pp. 96–97.

————. Social Adjustment: Immigration, Income Security Programs, and Social Policy Issues. In *Beach, C. M. and Green, A. G.*, 1989, pp. 54–61.

Boyd, Robert L. Population Research: Book Review Article. *Population Res. Policy Rev.*, September 1989, *8*(3), pp. 301–06.

Boyd, Roy and Turnbull, Geoffrey K. Dynamic Adjustment to Land Taxation Policy: Neutrality and Welfare Implications. *J. Environ. Econ. Manage.*, May 1989, *16*(3), pp. 242–52.

———— **and Turnbull, Geoffrey K.** The Effects of Greenspace Tax Laws on Urban Development. *Rev. Reg. Stud.*, Spring 1989, *19*(2), pp. 30–39.

———— **and Uri, Noel D.** The Effects on Agriculture in the United States of an Oil Import Fee. *Appl. Econ.*, December 1989, *21*(12), pp. 1647–66.

———— **and Uri, Noel D.** The Impacts of an Oil Import Fee on U.S. Agriculture. *J. Econ. Devel.*, December 1989, *14*(2), pp. 55–75.

Boyd, Susan E. and Bethke, William M. Should Dividend Discount Models Be Yield Tilted? Response. *J. Portfol. Manage.*, Winter 1989, *15*(2), pp. 82–83.

Boyer, George R. Malthus Was Right after All: Poor Relief and Birth Rates in Southeastern England. *J. Polit. Econ.*, February 1989, *97*(1), pp. 93–114.

———— **and Williamson, Jeffrey G.** A Quantitative Assessment of the Fertility Transition in England, 1851–1911. In *Ransom, R. L., ed.*, 1989, pp. 93–117.

Boyer, Kenneth D. The Safety Effects of Mode Shifting Following Deregulation. In *Moses, L. N. and Savage, I., eds.*, 1989, pp. 258–76.

Boyer, Marcel and Dionne, Georges. An Empirical Analysis of Moral Hazard and Experience Rating. *Rev. Econ. Statist.*, February 1989, *71*(1), pp. 128–34.

———— **and Dionne, Georges.** More on Insurance, Protection, and Risk. *Can. J. Econ.*, February 1989, *22*(1), pp. 202–04.

————; **Dionne, Georges and Kihlstrom, Richard.** Insurance and the Value of Publicly Available Information. In *[Hadar, J.]*, 1989, pp. 137–55.

———— **and Laffont, Jean-Jacques.** Expanding the Informativeness of the Price System with Law. *Can. J. Econ.*, May 1989, *22*(2), pp. 217–27.

———— **and Moreaux, Michel.** Endogenous Rationing in a Differentiated Product Duopoly. *Int. Econ. Rev.*, November 1989, *30*(4), pp. 877–88.

———— **and Moreaux, Michel.** Rationnement endogène et structure de marche. (With English summary.) *L'Actual. Econ.*, March 1989, *65*(1), pp. 119–45.

———— **and Moreaux, Michel.** Uncertainty, Capacity and Flexibility: The Monopoly Case. *Ann. Écon. Statist.*, July–Dec. 1989, (15–16), pp. 291–313.

Boyer, Mark A. Trading Public Goods in the Western Alliance System. *J. Conflict Resolution*, December 1989, *33*(4), pp. 700–727.

Boyer, Robert. Wage Labor Nexus, Technology and Long Run Dynamics: An Interpretation and Preliminary Tests for U.S. In *Di Matteo, M.; Goodwin, R. M. and Vercelli, A., eds.*, 1989, pp. 46–66.

Boyes, William J. and Happel, Stephen K. Auctions as an Allocation Mechanism in Academia: The Case of Faculty Offices. *J. Econ. Perspectives*, Summer 1989, *3*(3), pp. 37–40.

————; **Hoffman, Dennis L. and Low, Stuart A.** An Econometric Analysis of the Bank Credit Scoring Problem. *J. Econometrics*, January 1989, *40*(1), pp. 3–14.

———— **and McDowell, John M.** The Selection of Public Utility Commissioners: A Reexamination of the Importance of Institutional Setting. *Public Choice*, April 1989, *61*(1), pp. 1–13.

Boyle, G. E. and Guyomard, H. Inferring Long-run Supply Elasticities from a Short-run Variable-Revenue Function. *Econ. Soc. Rev.*, October 1989, *21*(1), pp. 127–37.

Boyle, Glenn W. and Young, Leslie. Forward and Futures Prices in a General Equilibrium Monetary Model. *J. Finan. Econ.*, October 1989, *24*(2), pp. 319–41.

Boyle, Kevin J. Building the Vanguard: Walter Reuther and Radical Politics in 1936. *Labor Hist.*, Summer 1989, *30*(3), pp. 433–48.

──────. Commodity Specification and the Framing of Contingent-Valuation Questions. *Land Econ.*, February 1989, *65*(1), pp. 57–63.

Boyle, Maureen. Spending Patterns and Income of Single and Married Parents. *Mon. Lab. Rev.*, March 1989, *112*(3), pp. 37–41.

Boyle, Phelim P. The Quality Option and Timing Option in Futures Contracts. *J. Finance*, March 1989, *44*(1), pp. 101–13.

──────; **Evnine, Jeremy and Gibbs, Stephen.** Numerical Evaluation of Multivariate Contingent Claims. *Rev. Financial Stud.*, 1989, *2*(2), pp. 241–50.

────── **and Turnbull, Stuart M.** Pricing and Hedging Capped Options. *J. Futures Markets*, February 1989, *9*(1), pp. 41–54.

Boynton, G. R. The Senate Agriculture Committee Produces a Homeostat. *Policy Sciences*, March 1989, *22*(1), pp. 51–80.

van de Braak, Hans and Berting, Jan. Technological Changes in Two Dutch Factories: Control, Flexibility and Learning. In *Francis, A. and Grootings, P., eds.*, 1989, pp. 296–325.

van Brabant, Jozef M. Market Socialism: Its Meaning, Feasibility, and Bearing on Economic Reform. *Acta Oecon.*, 1989, *40*(3–4), pp. 198–204.

──────. Regional Integration, Economic Reform, and Convertibility in Eastern Europe. *Jahr. Wirtsch. Osteuropas*, 1989, *13*(1), pp. 44–81.

──────. The Soviet Union and the International Trade Regime: A Reply. *Soviet Econ.*, Oct.–Dec. 1989, *5*(4), pp. 372–77.

Bracken, I. and Martin, D. The Generation of Spatial Population Distributions from Census Centroid Data. *Environ. Planning A*, April 1989, *21*(4), pp. 537–43.

Brada, Josef C. The Soviet Union and the GATT: A Framework for Western Policy. *Soviet Econ.*, Oct.–Dec. 1989, *5*(4), pp. 360–71.

──────. Technological Progress and Factor Utilization in Eastern European Economic Growth. *Economica*, November 1989, *56*(224), pp. 433–48.

──────. What Is Comparative Economics, and What Ought It Be? *Comp. Econ. Stud.*, Fall 1989, *31*(3), pp. 16–23.

────── **and Dobozi, István.** Economic Reform in Hungary: An Overview and Assessment. *Eastern Europ. Econ.*, Fall 1989, *28*(1), pp. 3–13.

────── **and Petrakos, George.** Metropolitan Concentration in Developing Countries. *Kyklos*, 1989, *42*(4), pp. 557–78.

Bradburd, Ralph M. and Ross, David R. Can Small Firms Find and Defend Strategic Niches? A Test of the Porter Hypothesis. *Rev. Econ. Statist.*, May 1989, *71*(2), pp. 258–62.

────── **and Srinagesh, Padmanabhan.** Quality Distortion by a Discriminating Monopolist. *Amer. Econ. Rev.*, March 1989, *79*(1), pp. 96–105.

Bradburn, Norman M. and Miles, Carrie. Vague Quantifiers. In *Singer, E. and Presser, S., eds.*, 1989, *1979*, pp. 155–64.

────── **and Schaeffer, Nora Cate.** Respondent Behavior in Magnitude Estimation. *J. Amer.*

Statist. Assoc., June 1989, *84*(406), pp. 402–13.

──────, **et al.** Question Threat and Response Bias. In *Singer, E. and Presser, S., eds.*, 1989, *1978*, pp. 371–84.

Bradbury, Bruce; Whiteford, Peter and Saunders, Peter. Unemployment Benefit Replacement Rates. *Australian Bull. Lab.*, June 1989, *15*(3), pp. 223–44.

Bradbury, John. Strategies in Local Communities to Cope with Industrial Restructuring. In *Linge, G. J. R. and van der Knaap, G. A., eds.*, 1989, pp. 167–84.

Bradbury, Katharine L.; Case, Karl E. and Dunham, Constance R. Geographic Patterns of Mortgage Lending in Boston, 1982–1987. *New Eng. Econ. Rev.*, Sept.–Oct. 1989, pp. 3–30.

Braden, John B.; Herricks, Edwin E. and Larson, Robert S. Economic Targeting of Nonpoint Pollution Abatement for Fish Habitat Protection. *Water Resources Res.*, December 1989, *25*(12), pp. 2399–405.

──────; **Johnson, Gary V. and Wu, Pei-Ing.** Efficient Control of Cropland Sediment: Storm Event versus Annual Average Loads. *Water Resources Res.*, February 1989, *25*(2), pp. 161–68.

──────; **Roh, Jae-Sun and Nelson, Carl H.** Asset Fixity and Investment Asymmetry in Agriculture. *Amer. J. Agr. Econ.*, November 1989, *71*(4), pp. 970–79.

──────, **et al.** Optimal Spatial Management of Agricultural Pollution. *Amer. J. Agr. Econ.*, May 1989, *71*(2), pp. 404–13.

Bradfield, R. E. Social Cost–Benefit Analysis in Project Evaluation: A Practical Framework for Decision Making. *J. Stud. Econ. Economet-rics*, August 1989, *13*(2), pp. 25–35.

Bradford, Colin I., Jr. Transnational Corporations and Brazilian Auto Sector Exports. In *Ventura-Dias, V., ed.*, 1989, pp. 276–90.

Bradford, David F. An Uncluttered Income Tax: The Next Reform Agenda? In *Fels, G. and von Furstenberg, G. M., eds.*, 1989, pp. 379–98.

──────. Tax Expenditures and the Problem of Accounting for Government. In *Bruce, N., ed.*, 1989, pp. 427–34.

──────. Tax Policy and Corporate Borrowing: Discussion. In *Kopcke, R. W. and Rosengren, E. S., eds.*, 1989, pp. 163–68.

Bradley, Bill. Third World Debt: The Next Phase: Perspectives of Politicians. In *Fried, E. R. and Trezise, P. H., eds.*, 1989, pp. 79–80.

Bradley, Michael; Khanna, Naveen and Berkovitch, Elazar. Tender Offer Auctions, Resistance Strategies, and Social Welfare. *J. Law, Econ., Organ.*, Fall 1989, *5*(2), pp. 395–412.

Bradley, Michael D. and Barth, James R. Evidence on the Real Interest Rate Effects of Money, Debt, and Government Spending. *Quart. Rev. Econ. Bus.*, Spring 1989, *29*(1), pp. 49–57.

────── **and Jansen, Dennis W.** The Optimality of Nominal Income Targeting When Wages Are Indexed to Price. *Southern Econ. J.*, July 1989, *56*(1), pp. 13–23.

—— and **Jansen, Dennis W.** Understanding Nominal GNP Targeting. *Fed. Res. Bank San Francisco Rev.*, Nov.–Dec. 1989, 71(6), pp. 31–40.

—— and **Peden, Edgar A.** Government Size, Productivity, and Economic Growth: The Postwar Experience. *Public Choice*, June 1989, 61(3), pp. 229–45.

Bradley, Michael E. John Stuart Mill's Demand Curves. *Hist. Polit. Econ.*, Spring 1989, 21(1), pp. 43–56.

Bradley, Michael G. and Barth, James R. The Ailing S&Ls: Causes and Cures. *Challenge*, March–April 1989, 32(2), pp. 30–38.

—— and **Barth, James R.** Thrift Deregulation and Federal Deposit Insurance. *J. Finan. Services Res.*, September 1989, 2(3), pp. 231–59.

Bradley, Paul G. Petroleum Supply: Lessons of the 1980s. In *Watkins, G. C., ed.*, 1989, pp. 41–68.

Bradshaw, Benjamin S. and Rosenwaike, Ira. Mortality of the Spanish Surname Population of the Southwest: 1980. *Soc. Sci. Quart.*, September 1989, 70(3), pp. 631–41.

Bradshaw, Jonathan and Huby, Meg. Trends in Dependence on Supplementary Benefit. In *Dilnot, A. and Walker, I., eds.*, 1989, pp. 69–87.

Brady, N. C. Progress in Agricultural Research. In *International Rice Research Institute*, 1989, pp. 25–34.

——. Theory and Practice in World Agriculture. In *DeGregori, T. R., ed.*, 1989, pp. 47–77.

Brady, Nicholas F. Third World Debt: Appendix. In *Dornbusch, R.; Makin, J. H. and Zlowe, D., eds.*, 1989, pp. 115–21.

——. Third World Debt: The Next Phase: A Reexamination of the Debt Strategy. In *Fried, E. R. and Trezise, P. H., eds.*, 1989, pp. 69–76.

Braeutigam, Ronald R. Optimal Policies for Natural Monopolies. In *Schmalensee, R. and Willig, R. D., eds., Vol. 2*, 1989, pp. 1289–1346.

——. The Role of Technological and Market Structure in Regulatory Reform. *J. Finan. Services Res.*, September 1989, 2(3), pp. 189–203.

—— and **Panzar, John C.** Diversification Incentives under "Price-Based" and "Cost-Based" Regulation. *Rand J. Econ.*, Autumn 1989, 20(3), pp. 373–91.

Braga, Francesco S.; Martin, Larry J. and Meilke, Karl D. Cross Hedging the Italian Lira/U.S. Dollar Exchange Rate with Deutsch Mark Futures. *J. Futures Markets*, April 1989, 9(2), pp. 87–99.

Braga, Helson C. and Rossi, José W. A produtividade total dos fatores de produção na indústria brasileira: 1970/83. (With English summary.) *Pesquisa Planejamento Econ.*, August 1989, 19(2), pp. 255–76.

Brahmananda, P. R. The Economics of John Hicks. In *Wood, J. C. and Woods, R. N., eds., Vol. 2*, 1989, 1972, pp. 213–31.

Braid, Ralph M. The Optimal Locations of Multiple Bridges, Connecting Facilities, or Product

Varieties. *J. Reg. Sci.*, February 1989, 29(1), pp. 63–70.

——. Retail Competition along Intersecting Roadways. *Reg. Sci. Urban Econ.*, February 1989, 19(1), pp. 107–12.

——. Uniform versus Peak-Load Pricing of a Bottleneck with Elastic Demand. *J. Urban Econ.*, November 1989, 26(3), pp. 320–27.

Brajer, Victor and Martin, Wade E. Allocating a 'Scarce' Resource, Water in the West: More Market-Like Incentives Can Extend Supply, but Constraints Demand Equitable Policies. *Amer. J. Econ. Sociology*, July 1989, 48(3), pp. 259–71.

——, **et al.** The Strengths and Weaknesses of Water Markets as They Affect Water Scarcity and Sovereignty Interests in the West. *Natural Res. J.*, Spring 1989, 29(2), pp. 489–509.

Bramley, Donald G.; Wunnava, Phanindra V. and Robinson, Michael D. A Note on Union–Non-union Benefit Differentials and Size of Establishment. *Econ. Letters*, 1989, 30(1), pp. 85–88.

Bramley, Glen. Standards for the Distribution of a Subsidized Local Public Service: Indoor Recreation. *Public Finance*, 1989, 44(3), pp. 361–83.

Brand, Horst and Bryant, Kelly. Productivity Trends in Agricultural Chemicals. *Mon. Lab. Rev.*, March 1989, 112(3), pp. 21–28.

Brand, S. S. Demografie, skuld en ekonomiese ontwikkeling. (Demography, Debt and Economic Development. With English summary.) *S. Afr. J. Econ.*, December 1989, 57(4), pp. 317–35.

Brandenburger, Adam and Dekel, Eddie. The Role of Common Knowledge Assumptions in Game Theory. In *Hahn, F., ed.*, 1989, pp. 46–61.

Brander, J. R. G.; Cook, B. A. and Rowcroft, J. E. Deregulated Airline Markets as Open Access Commons. *De Economist*, 1989, 137(4), pp. 466–75.

Brander, James A. and Spencer, Barbara J. Moral Hazard and Limited Liability: Implications for the Theory of the Firm. *Int. Econ. Rev.*, November 1989, 30(4), pp. 833–49.

Brandes, Joseph. International Price Maintenance: Control of Commodity Trade in the 1920s. In *Teichova, A.; Lévy-Leboyer, M. and Nussbaum, H., eds.*, 1989, pp. 57–67.

Brandes, Wilhelm. On the Limitations of Armchair Economics: Some Views of an Armchair Agricultural Economist. *Europ. Rev. Agr. Econ.*, 1989, 16(3), pp. 319–43.

Brandis, Royall. Time Concepts in the History of Economic Thought: The Case of the Stationary State. In *Walker, D. A., ed.*, 1989, pp. 71–81.

Brandsma, Andries S. and Hughes Hallett, Andrew J. The Design of Interdependent Policies with Incomplete Information: A New Argument for Coordinating Economic Policies. *Econ. Modelling*, October 1989, 6(4), pp. 432–46.

Brandt, Jon A., et al. Foreign Trade and Its Impact on the Domestic Livestock Market. In *Buse, R. C., ed.*, 1989, pp. 307–27.

———. The Impact of Domestic Policies and Programs on Producers of Meat and Animal Products. In *Buse, R. C., ed.*, 1989, pp. 328–45.

Brandt, Karl. Entwicklungslinien der deutschen Volkswirtschaftslehre in der ersten Hälfte des zwanzigsten Jahrhunderts. (German Theories of Political Economy in the First Half of the Twentieth Century. With English summary.) *Jahr. Nationalökon. Statist.*, October 1989, *206*(4–5), pp. 295–306.

Brandt, Loren and Sargent, Thomas J. Interpreting New Evidence about China and U.S. Silver Purchases. *J. Monet. Econ.*, January 1989, *23*(1), pp. 31–51.

Brandts, Jordi and Matutes, Carmen. Impacto de la imposición indirecta en los beneficios economicos en un marco de equilibrio general. (With English summary.) *Invest. Econ.*, September 1989, *13*(3), pp. 319–36.

Brännlund, Runar. The Social Loss from Imperfect Competition—The Case of the Swedish Pulpwood Market. *Scand. J. Econ.*, 1989, *91*(4), pp. 689–704.

Brannman, Lance; Klein, J. Douglass and Weiss, Leonard W. The Price Effects of Increased Competition in Auction Markets. In *Weiss, L. W., ed.*, 1989, pp. 67–84.

Brannman, Lance E. and Meitzen, Mark E. Differential Compensation and Worker Turnover. In *Missouri Valley Economic Association*, 1989, pp. 156–61.

Branscomb, Anne W. Legal Rights of Access to Transnational Data. In *Robinson, P.; Sauvant, K. P. and Govitrikar, V. P., eds.*, 1989, pp. 287–304.

Branson, William H. Exchange Rate Pass-Through in the 1980s: The Case of U.S. Imports of Manufacturers: Comments. *Brookings Pap. Econ. Act.*, 1989, (1), pp. 330–33.

———. The Exchange Rate Question in Europe: Comment. In *Bryant, R. C., et al., eds.*, 1989, pp. 305–07.

———. Factor Flexibility, Uncertainity and Exchange Rate Regimes: Discussion. In *De Cecco, M. and Giovannini, A., eds.*, 1989, pp. 119–21.

——— and de Macedo, Jorge Braga. Smuggler's Blues at the Central Bank: Lessons from Sudan. In *[Díaz-Alejandro, C.]*, 1989, pp. 191–207.

Brass, William. Is Britain Facing the Twilight of Parenthood? In *Joshi, H., ed.*, 1989, pp. 12–26.

Bratton, Michael. The Politics of Government–NGO Relations in Africa. *World Devel.*, April 1989, *17*(4), pp. 569–87.

Braun, Bradley M. Energy: Markets and Regulation: Review Article. *Atlantic Econ. J.*, September 1989, *17*(3), pp. 56–60.

Braun, H. J. and Pfeiffer, W. H. Yield Stability in Bread Wheat. In *Anderson, J. R. and Hazell, P. B. R., eds.*, 1989, pp. 157–74.

Braun, Heiko and Brockhoff, Klaus. Optimierung der Sendezeit im Werbefernsehen. (With En-

glish summary.) *Z. Betriebswirtshaft*, June 1989, *59*(6), pp. 609–19.

von Braun, Joachim and Sahn, David E. The Implications of Variability in Food Production for National and Household Food Security. In *Anderson, J. R. and Hazell, P. B. R., eds.*, 1989, pp. 320–38.

——— and Webb, Patrick J. R. The Impact of New Crop Technology on the Agricultural Division of Labor in a West African Setting. *Econ. Devel. Cult. Change*, April 1989, *37*(3), pp. 513–34.

Braun, Ottmar L. and Wicklund, Robert A. Psychological Antecedents of Conspicuous Consumption. *J. Econ. Psych.*, June 1989, *10*(2), pp. 161–87.

Braun, Phillip and Zarnowitz, Victor. New Indexes of Coincident and Leading Economic Indicators: Comment. In *Blanchard, O. J. and Fischer, S., eds.*, 1989, pp. 397–408.

Braunstein, Yale M. Economics of Intellectual Property Rights in the International Arena. In *Jussawalla, M.; Okuma, T. and Araki, T., eds.*, 1989, pp. 183–92.

Braverman, Avishay. The Policy Response of Agriculture: Comment. In *Fischer, S. and de Tray, D., eds.*, 1989, pp. 259–62.

——— and Guasch, J. Luis. Institutional Analysis of Credit Co-operatives. In *Bardhan, P., ed. (II)*, 1989, pp. 340–55.

——— and Guasch, J. Luis. Rural Credit Reforms in LDCs: Issues and Evidence. *J. Econ. Devel.*, June 1989, *14*(1), pp. 7–34.

——— and Stiglitz, Joseph E. Credit Rationing, Tenancy, Productivity, and the Dynamics of Inequality. In *Bardhan, P., ed. (II)*, 1989, pp. 185–202.

Bray, Margaret. Rational Expectations, Information, and Asset Markets. In *Hahn, F., ed.*, 1989, pp. 243–77.

Braz de Oliveira e Silva, Antonio and Ramos, Roberto Luis Olinto. A Commodity Flow Balancing Procedure for the Base Year of the New Brazilian System of National Accounts. In *Franz, A. and Rainer, N., eds.*, 1989, pp. 301–24.

Brazelton, W. Robert. Alvin Harvey Hansen: Economic Growth and a More Perfect Society: The Economist's Role in Defining the Stagnation Thesis and in Popularizing Keynesianism. *Amer. J. Econ. Sociology*, October 1989, *48*(4), pp. 427–40.

Brecher, Richard A. Policy-Induced Inflows of Foreign Capital in the Presence of Rigid-Wage Unemployment. In *[Díaz-Alejandro, C.]*, 1989, pp. 376–88.

——— and Long, Ngo Van. Trade Unions in an Open Economy: A General Equilibrium Analysis. *Econ. Rec.*, September 1989, *65*(190), pp. 234–39.

Breckling, Jens and Stoeckel, Andrew B. Some Economywide Effects of Agricultural Policies in the European Community: A General Equilibrium Study. In *Stoeckel, A. B.; Vincent, D. and Cuthbertson, S., eds.*, 1989, pp. 94–124.

Bredahl, Maury E. and Forsythe, Kenneth W.

Harmonizing Phyto-sanitary and Sanitary Regulations. *World Econ.*, June 1989, *12*(2), pp. 189–206.

Breeden, Douglas T.; Gibbons, Michael R. and Litzenberger, Robert H. Empirical Tests of the Consumption-Oriented CAPM. *J. Finance*, June 1989, *44*(2), pp. 231–62.

Breen, William; Glosten, Lawrence R. and Jagannathan, Ravi. Economic Significance of Predictable Variations in Stock Index Returns. *J. Finance*, December 1989, *44*(5), pp. 1177–89.

Brege, Staffan and Moberg, Claes. Price Policies and Relationship Stability after a Devaluation. In *Hallén, L. and Johanson, J., eds.*, 1989, pp. 37–55.

Breimyer, Harold F. Environmental Issues Could Reshape Farm Programs. *Challenge*, May–June 1989, *32*(3), pp. 59–62.

Breitung, Jörg; Wagner, Joachim and Bellmann, Lutz. Bias Correction and Bootstrapping of Error Component Models for Panel Data: Theory and Applications. *Empirical Econ.*, 1989, *14*(4), pp. 329–42.

Brem, Natalie; Durden, Garey and Gaynor, Patricia. The Effect of Government Employment on Income Inequality Overall and in the South: Evidence from Congressional District Data. *Rev. Reg. Stud.*, Spring 1989, *19*(2), pp. 40–47.

Breman, Jan. Extension of Scale in Fieldwork: From Village to Region in Southern Gujarat. In *Bardhan, P., ed. (I)*, 1989, pp. 127–36.

Brems, Hans. The Founding Fathers of the Swedish School: Wicksell and Cassel. In *Walker, D. A., ed.*, 1989, pp. 145–54.

_____. Gustav Cassel Revisited. *Hist. Polit. Econ.*, Summer 1989, *21*(2), pp. 165–78.

_____. Hours and Employment. *Jahr. Nationalökon. Statist.*, October 1989, *206*(4–5), pp. 307–14.

_____. A Solution of the Keynes–Hicks–Hansen Non-linear Employment Model. In *Wood, J. C. and Woods, R. N., eds., Vol. 1*, 1989, *1956*, pp. 184–93.

Brændgaard, Asger. Nations, National Systems of Production, Politics the Role of Technology Policy. In *Pedersen, J. L., ed.*, 1989, pp. 61–89.

Brennan, Ellen M. and Richardson, Harry W. Asian Megacity Characteristics, Problems, and Policies. *Int. Reg. Sci. Rev.*, 1989, *12*(2), pp. 117–29.

Brennan, Geoffrey and Buchanan, James M. Predictive Power and the Choice among Regimes. In *Buchanan, J. M. (II)*, 1989, pp. 3–23.

_____ and **Buchanan, James M.** Tax Instruments as Constraints on the Disposition of Public Revenues. In *Buchanan, J. M. (II)*, 1989, pp. 264–82.

_____ and **Buchanan, James M.** Voter Choice: Evaluating Political Alternatives. In *Buchanan, J. M. (II)*, 1989, pp. 101–15.

_____ and **Lomasky, Loren E.** Large Numbers, Small Costs: The Uneasy Foundation of Democratic Rule. In *Brennan, G. and Lomasky, L. E., eds.*, 1989, pp. 42–59.

_____ and **Lomasky, Loren E.** Politics and Process: New Essays in Democratic Thought: Introduction. In *Brennan, G. and Lomasky, L. E., eds.*, 1989, pp. 1–10.

Brennan, John P. An Analysis of the Economic Potential of Some Innovations in a Wheat Breeding Programme. *Australian J. Agr. Econ.*, April 1989, *33*(1), pp. 48–55.

_____; **Godyn, Dirk L. and Johnston, Brian G.** An Economic Framework for Evaluating New Wheat Varieties. *Rev. Marketing Agr. Econ.*, April, Aug., Dec. 1989, *57*(1–2–3), pp. 75–92.

Brennan, Michael J. and Schwartz, Eduardo S. Portfolio Insurance and Financial Market Equilibrium. *J. Bus.*, October 1989, *62*(4), pp. 455–72.

_____ and **Solnik, B.** International Risk Sharing and Capital Mobility. *J. Int. Money Finance*, September 1989, *8*(3), pp. 359–73.

Brennan, Timothy J. Exclusive Dealing, Limiting Outside Activity, and Conflict of Interest. *Southern Econ. J.*, October 1989, *56*(2), pp. 323–35.

_____. A Methodological Assessment of Multiple Utility Frameworks. *Econ. Philos.*, October 1989, *5*(2), pp. 189–208.

Brenner, Gabrielle A. and Brenner, Reuven. Les innovations et la loi sur la concurrence. (With English summary.) *L'Actual. Econ.*, March 1989, *65*(1), pp. 146–62.

Brenner, Menachem; Courtadon, Georges and Subrahmanyam, Marti G. Options on Stock Indices and Options on Futures. *J. Banking Finance*, September 1989, *13*(4–5), pp. 773–82.

_____; **Subrahmanyam, Marti G. and Uno, Jun.** The Behavior of Prices in the Nikkei Spot and Futures Market. *J. Finan. Econ.*, August 1989, *23*(2), pp. 363–83.

Brenner, Reuven and Brenner, Gabrielle A. Les innovations et la loi sur la concurrence. (With English summary.) *L'Actual. Econ.*, March 1989, *65*(1), pp. 146–62.

Brenner, Robert. Bourgeois Revolution and Transition to Capitalism. In *[Stone, L.]*, 1989, pp. 271–304.

_____. Economic Backwardness in Eastern Europe in Light of Developments in the West. In *Chirot, D., ed.*, 1989, pp. 15–52.

_____ and **Glick, Mark.** The Regulation Approach to the History of Capitalism. *Écon. Societes*, November 1989, *23*(11), pp. 89–131.

Brenner, Y. S. Distribution Theory with Imperfect Competition. In *Davidson, P. and Kregel, J., eds.*, 1989, pp. 270–79.

Brent, Robert J. The Farmers Home Administration's Social Discount Rate. *Appl. Econ.*, September 1989, *21*(9), pp. 1247–56.

Brenton, Paul A. The Allocation Approach to Trade Modelling: Some Tests of Separability between Imports and Domestic Production and between Different Imported Commodity Groups. *Weltwirtsch. Arch.*, 1989, *125*(2), pp. 230–51.

_____. Modeling Bilateral Trade Flows: An Empirical Analysis Using Disaggregate Commodity Data. *J. Policy Modeling*, Winter 1989, *11*(4), pp. 547–67.

Bresler, Eshel; Dagan, Gideon and Feinerman, Eli. Optimization of Inputs in a Spatially Variable Natural Resource: Unconditional vs. Conditional Analysis. *J. Environ. Econ. Manage.*, September 1989, *17*(2), pp. 140–54.

_____; **Feinerman, Eli and Shani, Y.** Economic Optimisation of Sprinkler Irrigation Considering Uncertainty of Spatial Water Distribution. *Australian J. Agr. Econ.*, August 1989, *33*(2), pp. 88–107.

Breslin, Shaun. Shanxi: China's Powerhouse. In *Goodman, D. S. G., ed.*, 1989, pp. 135–52.

Bresnahan, Timothy F. Empirical Studies of Industries with Market Power. In *Schmalensee, R. and Willig, R. D., eds., Vol. 2*, 1989, pp. 1011–57.

_____ **and Suslow, Valerie Y.** Oligopoly Pricing with Capacity Constraints. *Ann. Écon. Statist.*, July–Dec. 1989, (15–16), pp. 267–89.

_____ **and Suslow, Valerie Y.** Short-run Supply with Capacity Constraints. *J. Law Econ.*, Part 2, October 1989, *32*(2), pp. S11–42.

Bresnock, Anne E.; Graves, Philip E. and White, Nancy. Multiple-Choice Testing: Question and Response Position. *J. Econ. Educ.*, Summer 1989, *20*(3), pp. 239–45.

Bresser Pereira, Luiz Carlos. What's Good for U.S. Banks Is Disaster for Brazil. *Challenge*, Jan.–Feb. 1989, *32*(1), pp. 20–26.

Bresser, Rudi K. F. Kollektive Unternehmensstrategien. (With English summary.) *Z. Betriebswirtshaft*, May 1989, *59*(5), pp. 545–64.

Brester, Gary W. and Marsh, John M. Intertemporal Price Adjustments in the Beef Market: A Reduced Form Analysis of Weekly Data. *Western J. Agr. Econ.*, December 1989, *14*(2), pp. 235–45.

Breton, Albert. The Growth of Competitive Governments. *Can. J. Econ.*, November 1989, *22*(4), pp. 717–50.

Bretschger, Lucas. Eine neokeynesianische Analyse der schweizerischen Exportmärkte. (A Neokeynesian Study of Swiss Export Markets. With English summary.) *Schweiz. Z. Volkswirtsch. Statist.*, March 1989, *125*(1), pp. 67–87.

_____. Regimeabhängige Konjunkturdynamik in einer offenen Volkswirtschaft: Das Beispiel der Schwiez. (Regime-Dependent Dynamics of the Business Cycle in an Open Economy: The Case of Switzerland. With English summary.) *Schweiz. Z. Volkswirtsch. Statist.*, September 1989, *125*(3), pp. 309–26.

Bretschneider, Stuart I., et al. Political and Organizational Influences on the Accuracy of Forecasting State Government Revenues. *Int. J. Forecasting*, 1989, *5*(3), pp. 307–19.

Breusch, Trevor S.; Mizon, Grayham E. and Schmidt, Peter. Efficient Estimation Using Panel Data. *Econometrica*, May 1989, *57*(3), pp. 695–700.

Breuss, Fritz. A Generalization of the Phillips Curve. *Z. Wirtschaft. Sozialwissen.*, 1989, *109*(1), pp. 19–47.

Brewer, Elijah, III. Relationship between Bank Holding Company Risk and Nonbank Activity. *J. Econ. Bus.*, November 1989, *41*(4), pp. 337–53.

_____; **Garcia, Gillian G. and Reichert, Alan K.** A Statistical Analysis of S&L Accounting Profits. In *Lee, C. F., ed.*, 1989, pp. 163–93.

Brewer, H. L. Risk Reduction for Mortgage Portfolios: The Role of Portfolio Theory. In *Lee, C. F., ed.*, 1989, pp. 245–61.

_____ **and Mann, Patrick C.** Regulator Selection and Financial Performance for Public Utilities: Selection Method and the Returns Experienced by Common Equity Owners. *Energy Econ.*, January 1989, *11*(1), pp. 39–45.

Brewin, Christopher and McAllister, Richard. Annual Review of the Activities of the European Communities in 1988. *J. Common Market Stud.*, June 1989, *27*(4), pp. 323–57.

Breyer, Friedrich. On the Intergenerational Pareto Efficiency of Pay-as-You-Go Financed Pension Systems. *J. Inst. Theoretical Econ.*, December 1989, *145*(4), pp. 643–58.

Brezinski, Horst. Structural Impacts of CMEA Integration on Cuba, Mongolia, and Vietnam. In *Wohlmuth, K., ed.*, 1989, pp. 437–79.

Brice, Helene and Wegner, Trevor. A Quantitative Approach to Corporate Social Responsibility Programme Formulation. *Managerial Dec. Econ.*, June 1989, *10*(2), pp. 163–71.

Bricker, Dennis L. and Nyman, John A. Profit Incentives and Technical Efficiency in the Production of Nursing Home Care. *Rev. Econ. Statist.*, November 1989, *71*(4), pp. 586–94.

Bricker, Robert. An Empirical Investigation of the Structure of Accounting Research. *J. Acc. Res.*, Autumn 1989, *27*(2), pp. 246–62.

Brickner, Philip W. and Scharer, Linda K. Alcoholism among the Elderly. In *Eisdorfer, C.; Kessler, D. A. and Spector, A. N., eds.*, 1989, pp. 341–57.

Brief, Arthur P. and Aldag, Ramon J. The Economic Functions of Work. In *Ferris, G. R. and Rowland, K. M., eds.*, 1989, pp. 1–23.

Brien, Kevin M. Marx, Reason, and the Art of Freedom: Review: Reply. *Rev. Radical Polit. Econ.*, 1989, *21*(1–2), pp. 166–68.

_____. The Scientific Marx: Review. *Rev. Radical Polit. Econ.*, 1989, *21*(1–2), pp. 159–63.

Brien, Michael; Cunningham, James and O'Neill, June. Effects of Comparable Worth Policy: Evidence from Washington State. *Amer. Econ. Rev.*, May 1989, *79*(2), pp. 305–09.

Briesemeister, Janee and Horrigan, John. Telecommunications Policy and Economic Development: Conclusion: Perspectives on the New State Role. In *Schmandt, J.; Williams, F. and Wilson, R. H., eds.*, 1989, pp. 267–83.

_____ **and Treuer, Philip.** Telecommunications Policy and Economic Development: The New State Role: Vermont. In *Schmandt, J.; Williams, F. and Wilson, R. H., eds.*, 1989, pp. 185–212.

Briggs, Hugh. The Effects of Concentration and

Cartels on Nineteenth-Century Railroad Freight Rates. In *Weiss, L. W., ed.*, 1989, pp. 194–205.

Briguglio, Lino. The Impact of a Devaluation on the Maltese Trade Balance with Special Reference to the Price and Income Reversal Effects. *Appl. Econ.*, March 1989, *21*(3), pp. 325–37.

_____. Price and Income Reversal Effects Associated with a Devaluation of the Maltese Lira. *Middle East Bus. Econ. Rev.*, July 1989, *1*(2), pp. 11–18.

Brillet, Jean-Louis. Econometric Modelling on Microcomputers: A Review of Major Software Packages. *J. Appl. Econometrics*, Jan.–March 1989, *4*(1), pp. 73–92.

_____. A Long-Term Simulation of the French Economy. In *Krelle, W., ed.*, 1989, pp. 335–51.

Brilmayer, Lea. Rights, Fairness, and Choice of Law. *Yale Law J.*, May 1989, *98*(7), pp. 1277–1319.

Brimmer, Andrew F. Distinguished Lecture on Economics in Government: Central Banking and Systemic Risks in Capital Markets. *J. Econ. Perspectives*, Spring 1989, *3*(2), pp. 3–16.

_____. New Horizons of Macroeconomic Policy: A Conversation. *Eastern Econ. J.*, April–June 1989, *15*(2), pp. 87–90.

Brink, Lars. Agricultural Protection in Finland, Norway and Sweden. *Can. J. Agr. Econ.*, Part 2, December 1989, *37*(4), pp. 1145–54.

Brinkman, George L.; Fox, Glenn C. and Widmer, Lorne. Benefit Analysis of Agricultural Research: A Reply. *Can. J. Agr. Econ.*, March 1989, *37*(1), pp. 149–52.

_____; Haque, A. K. Enamul and Fox, Glenn C. Product Market Distortions and the Returns to Federal Laying-Hen Research in Canada. *Can. J. Agr. Econ.*, March 1989, *37*(1), pp. 29–46.

_____; Zachariah, O. E. R. and Fox, Glenn C. Product Market Distortions and the Returns to Broiler Chicken Research in Canada. *J. Agr. Econ.*, January 1989, *40*(1), pp. 40–51.

Brinkman, Richard L. China: Trade and the Drive to Modernization. In *Gemper, B. B., ed.*, 1989, pp. 124–40.

Brinner, Roger E. and Winsby, Roger. The Evolution of the Business of Business Economics. *Bus. Econ.*, April 1989, *24*(2), pp. 32–34.

Brioschi, Francesco; Buzzacchi, Luigi and Colombo, Massimo G. Risk Capital Financing and the Separation of Ownership and Control in Business Groups. *J. Banking Finance*, September 1989, *13*(4–5), pp. 747–72.

Brisoux, Jacques E. and Laroche, Michel. Incorporating Competition into Consumer Behavior Models: The Case of the Attitude–Intention Relationship. *J. Econ. Psych.*, November 1989, *10*(3), pp. 343–62.

Brissimis, Sophocles N. and Leventakis, John A. The Effectiveness of Devaluation: A General Equilibrium Assessment with Reference to Greece. *J. Policy Modeling*, Summer 1989, *11*(2), pp. 247–71.

Brister, Jozell and Lynn, Monty L. Trends in

Union Organizing Issues and Tactics. *Ind. Relat.*, Winter 1989, *28*(1), pp. 104–13.

Brito, Dagobert L. and Intriligator, Michael D. Arms Races and Arms Control in the Middle East. In *Fishelson, G., ed.*, 1989, pp. 105–22.

_____ and Intriligator, Michael D. A Dynamic Heuristic Game Theory Model of an Arms Race. In *[Verheyen, P.]*, 1989, pp. 73–90.

Brito, M. Paula and Diday, Edwin. Symbolic Cluster Analysis. In *Opitz, O., ed.*, 1989, pp. 45–84.

Brittan, Samuel. The Case for the Consumer Market. In *Veljanovski, C., ed. (I)*, 1989, pp. 25–50.

Britten, Mike. Zimbabwe: Industrial Development in an Environment with No Incentives. In *Whiteside, A. W., ed.*, 1989, pp. 184–203.

Britton, Andrew. The Public Sector in Surplus. *Fisc. Stud.*, May 1989, *10*(2), pp. 13–23.

_____; Gregg, Paul and Anderton, Bob. The Home Economy. *Nat. Inst. Econ. Rev.*, August 1989, (129), pp. 6–21.

_____; Gregg, Paul and Anderton, Bob. The Home Economy. *Nat. Inst. Econ. Rev.*, November 1989, (130), pp. 7–22.

_____; Gregg, Paul and Joyce, Michael. The Home Economy. *Nat. Inst. Econ. Rev.*, February 1989, (127), pp. 7–25.

_____; Gregg, Paul and Joyce, Michael. The Home Economy. *Nat. Inst. Econ. Rev.*, May 1989, (128), pp. 5–19.

Britton, J. N. H. Innovation Policies for Small Firms. *Reg. Stud.*, April 1989, *23*(2), pp. 167–73.

Briys, Eric; Dionne, Georges and Eeckhoudt, Louis. More on Insurance as a Giffen Good. *J. Risk Uncertainty*, December 1989, *2*(4), pp. 415–20.

Broadbent, Jeffrey. "The Technopolis Strategy" vs. Deindustrialization: High-Tech Development Sites in Japan. In *Smith, M. P., ed.*, 1989, pp. 231–53.

Broadberry, Stephen N. Monetary Interdependence and Deflation in Britain and the United States between the Wars. In *Miller, M.; Eichengreen, B. and Portes, R., eds.*, 1989, pp. 47–69.

Broadbridge, Seymour A. Aspects of Economic and Social Policy in Japan, 1868–1945. In *Mathias, P. and Pollard, S., eds.*, 1989, pp. 1106–45.

Broadman, Harry G. and Kalt, Joseph P. How Natural Is Monopoly? The Case of Bypass in Natural Gas Distribution Markets. *Yale J. Regul.*, Summer 1989, *6*(2), pp. 181–208.

Broadus, James M. and Solow, Andrew R. Loss Functions in Estimating Offshore Oil Resources. *Resources & Energy*, March 1989, *11*(1), pp. 81–92.

Broadway, Michael J. and Snyder, Susan D. The Persistence of Urban Deprivation: The Example of Wichita, Kansas, in the 1970s. *Growth Change*, Spring 1989, *20*(2), pp. 50–61.

Brocato, Joe; Kumar, Akhil and Smith, Kenneth L. Individual versus Group Spot Price Forecasting in the International Petroleum Market:

A Case Study. *Managerial Dec. Econ.*, March 1989, *10*(1), pp. 13–24.

_____ and **Smith, Kenneth L.** Velocity and the Variability of Money Growth: Evidence from Granger-Causality Tests: Comment. *J. Money, Credit, Banking*, May 1989, *21*(2), pp. 258–61.

Brocci, Wilmaro. Reform of the Interbank Market. *Rev. Econ. Cond. Italy*, Jan.–April 1989, (1), pp. 61–98.

Brock, Gerald W. Dominant Firm Response to Competitive Challenge: Peripheral Equipment Manufacturers' Suits against IBM. In *Kwoka, J. E., Jr. and White, L. J., eds.*, 1989, pp. 160–82.

Brock, James W. and Adams, Walter. Corporate Power and Economic Sabotage. In *Tool, M. R. and Samuels, W. J., eds. (I)*, 1989, *1986*, pp. 383–404.

_____ and **Adams, Walter.** Corporate Size and the Bailout Factor. In *Tool, M. R. and Samuels, W. J., eds. (I)*, 1989, *1987*, pp. 405–29.

_____ and **Adams, Walter.** The Evidence and Public Policy. In *McKee, D. L., ed.*, 1989, pp. 143–52.

_____ and **Adams, Walter.** Government and Competitive Free Enterprise. In *Samuels, W. J., ed. (I)*, 1989, pp. 1–7.

_____ and **Adams, Walter.** Merger-Mania: An Empirical Critique. In *McKee, D. L., ed.*, 1989, pp. 33–43.

Brock, Philip L. The Chilean Financial Collapse. In *Brock, P. L.; Connolly, M. B. and González-Vega, C., eds.*, 1989, pp. 112–30.

_____. La crisis financiera chilena. (With English summary.) *Cuadernos Econ.*, August 1989, *26*(78), pp. 177–94.

_____. Reserve Requirements and the Inflation Tax. *J. Money, Credit, Banking*, February 1989, *21*(1), pp. 106–21.

_____. The Transmission of Terms-of-Trade Shocks. In *Brock, P. L.; Connolly, M. B. and González-Vega, C., eds.*, 1989, pp. 52–61.

_____ and **Meléndez, Dennis.** Exchange Controls and the Breakdown of Central American Trade in the 1980s. In *Brock, P. L.; Connolly, M. B. and González-Vega, C., eds.*, 1989, pp. 171–86.

Brock, William A.; Rothschild, Michael and Stiglitz, Joseph E. Stochastic Capital Theory. In *Feiwel, G. R., ed. (II)*, 1989, pp. 591–622.

Bröcker, J. How to Eliminate Certain Defects of the Potential Formula. *Environ. Planning A*, June 1989, *21*(6), pp. 817–30.

Brockhoff, Klaus and Braun, Heiko. Optimierung der Sendezeit im Werbefernsehen. (With English summary.) *Z. Betriebswirtshaft*, June 1989, *59*(6), pp. 609–19.

Brockman, Brenda A. Ramie: The Opening and Controlling of a Loophole in the Multifibre Arrangement. In *Gray, H. P., ed.*, 1989, pp. 243–54.

Brockway, George P. Ask Not for Whom the Junk Bond Fails. *Challenge*, May–June 1989, *32*(3), pp. 48–50.

_____. The Future of Business Ethics. In *Wil-liams, O. F.; Reilly, F. K. and Houck, J. W., eds.*, 1989, pp. 175–89.

Bröder, Günther. The Importance of the Ecu for the European Investment Bank. In *Franz, O., ed.*, 1989, pp. 53–56.

Broder, Ivy E. and Langbein, Laura. Wage Differentials among Regulated, Private and Government Sectors: A Case Study. *Eastern Econ. J.*, July–Sept. 1989, *15*(3), pp. 189–201.

Brodie, J. Douglas and Barber, Richard L. A Sequential Approach to Derivation of Stand Treatment and Forest-Wide Harvest Prescription or Supply. *Natural Res. Modeling*, Spring 1989, *3*(2), pp. 217–39.

_____ and **Paredes, Gonzalo L.** Land Value and the Linkage between Stand and Forest Level Analyses. *Land Econ.*, May 1989, *65*(2), pp. 158–66.

Brodsky, Melvin. International Developments in Apprenticeship. *Mon. Lab. Rev.*, July 1989, *112*(7), pp. 40–41.

_____. OECD Social Ministers Focus on Rising Pension, Health Costs. *Mon. Lab. Rev.*, February 1989, *112*(2), pp. 47–48.

Bródy, András. Physical (Phenomenological) Economics? (A Semi-centennial for J. von Neumann and W. Leontief). *Acta Oecon.*, 1989, *41*(3–4), pp. 257–66.

Brody, Andrew. Economics and Thermodynamics. In *Dore, M.; Chakravarty, S. and Goodwin, R., eds.*, 1989, pp. 141–48.

Brody, David. Labor History, Industrial Relations, and the Crisis of American Labor. *Ind. Lab. Relat. Rev.*, October 1989, *43*(1), pp. 7–18.

_____. Time and Work during Early American Industrialism. *Labor Hist.*, Winter 1989, *30*(1), pp. 5–46.

Brody, Elaine M. and Brody, Stanley J. The Informal System of Health Care. In *Eisdorfer, C.; Kessler, D. A. and Spector, A. N., eds.*, 1989, pp. 259–77.

Brody, Stanley J. and Brody, Elaine M. The Informal System of Health Care. In *Eisdorfer, C.; Kessler, D. A. and Spector, A. N., eds.*, 1989, pp. 259–77.

_____ and **Magel, Judith S.** Long-Term Care: The Long and Short of It. In *Eisdorfer, C.; Kessler, D. A. and Spector, A. N., eds.*, 1989, pp. 235–58.

Broehl, Wayne. The Family Business. In *Hausman, W. J., ed.*, 1989, pp. 1–10.

van den Broek, Peter. Retrospectivity and Transitional Relief in Tax Law. *Australian Tax Forum*, 1989, *6*(2), pp. 201–16.

Broemeling, Lyle D. Structural Change and Time Series Analysis. In *Hackl, P., ed.*, 1989, pp. 273–78.

Broer, D. P. and Jansen, W. J. Employment, Schooling and Productivity Growth. *De Economist*, 1989, *137*(4), pp. 425–53.

Broesterhuizen, G. A. A. M. The Unrecorded Economy and the National Income Accounts in the Netherlands: A Sensitivity Analysis. In *Feige, E. L., ed.*, 1989, pp. 159–74.

Brohman, John. Prerevolutionary Nicaraguan Agricultural Development. In *Martin, M. T. and Kandal, T. R., eds.*, 1989, pp. 216–41.

Broman, Elizabeth M. The Bilateral Monopoly Model: Approaching Certainty under the Split-the-Difference Mechanism. *J. Econ. Theory*, June 1989, *48*(1), pp. 134–51.

Bromley, Daniel W. The Culture of Science, Epistemology, and Resource Policy. *Soc. Sci. Quart.*, June 1989, *70*(2), pp. 479–86.

————. Entitlements, Missing Markets, and Environmental Uncertainty. *J. Environ. Econ. Manage.*, September 1989, *17*(2), pp. 181–94.

————. Institutional Change and Economic Efficiency. *J. Econ. Issues*, September 1989, *23*(3), pp. 735–59.

————. Property Relations and Economic Development: The Other Land Reform. *World Devel.*, June 1989, *17*(6), pp. 867–77.

————. Waste Recycled. *Soc. Sci. Quart.*, December 1989, *70*(4), pp. 991–93.

———— **and Chavas, Jean-Paul.** On Risk, Transactions, and Economic Development in the Semiarid Tropics. *Econ. Devel. Cult. Change*, July 1989, *37*(4), pp. 719–36.

Bromwich, Michael and Noke, Christopher. Money, Measurement and Accounting. In *Llewellyn, D. T., ed.*, 1989, pp. 167–90.

Bronars, Stephen G. and Borjas, George J. Consumer Discrimination and Self-employment. *J. Polit. Econ.*, June 1989, *97*(3), pp. 581–605.

———— **and Lott, John R., Jr.** Why Do Workers Join Unions? The Importance of Rent Seeking. *Econ. Inquiry*, April 1989, *27*(2), pp. 305–24.

Bronckers, M. and Quick, R. What Is a Countervailable Subsidy under EEC Trade Law? *J. World Trade*, December 1989, *23*(6), pp. 5–31.

Bronfenbrenner, Martin. Economics of the Socialist Countries: General Comment. In *Berliner, J. S.; Kosta, H. G. J. and Hakogi, M., eds.*, 1989, pp. 193–96.

————. Economy and Culture: The Case of U.S.–Japan Economic Relations: Commentary. In *Hayashi, K., ed.*, 1989, pp. 14–18.

————. International Economics in Embryo. In *Feiwel, G. R., ed. (II)*, 1989, pp. 727–38.

————. A Monetarist on Keynes—Unemployment without the Unemployed. *Keio Econ. Stud.*, 1989, *26*(2), pp. 53–61.

Broniatowski, Michel and Kébabdjian, Gèrard. The Role of Prices in the Establishment of Keynesian Short-Run Equilibrium. In *Barrère, A., ed.*, 1989, pp. 113–36.

Bronisz, Piotr; Krus, Lech and Lopuch, Bozena. MCBARG: A System Supporting Multicriteria Bargaining. In *Lewandowski, A. and Wierzbicki, A. P., eds.*, 1989, pp. 388–90.

————; **Krus, Lech and Wierzbicki, Andrzej P.** Towards Interactive Solutions in a Bargaining Problem. In *Lewandowski, A. and Wierzbicki, A. P., eds.*, 1989, pp. 251–68.

Bronsard, Camille; Richelle, Yves and Allard, Marie. Temporary Pareto Optimum Theory. *J. Public Econ.*, April 1989, *38*(3), pp. 343–68.

Bronstein, Arturo S. The Evolution of Labour

Relations in Uruguay: Achievements and Challenges. *Int. Lab. Rev.*, 1989, *128*(2), pp. 195–212.

Brook, Timothy. The Asiatic Mode of Production in China: Introduction. In *Brook, T., ed.*, 1989, pp. 3–34.

Brooks, C. W. Interpersonal Conflict and Social Tension: Civil Litigation in England, 1640–1830. In *[Stone, L.]*, 1989, pp. 357–99.

Brooks, Daniel G. Competitive Subsidization in Regional Development. *Reg. Sci. Urban Econ.*, December 1989, *19*(4), pp. 589–99.

Brooks, LeRoy D.; Oberhelman, H. Dennis and D'Souza, Rudolph E. A General Stationary Stochastic Regression Model for Estimating and Predicting Beta. *Financial Rev.*, May 1989, *24*(2), pp. 299–317.

Brooks, Michael A. and Heijdra, Ben J. An Exploration of Rent Seeking. *Econ. Rec.*, March 1989, *65*(188), pp. 32–50.

Brooks, Neil. Direct Expenditures versus Tax Expenditures for Economic and Social Policy: Comment. In *Bruce, N., ed.*, 1989, pp. 324–29.

Brooks, Robert. Investment Decision Making with Derivative Securities. *Financial Rev.*, November 1989, *24*(4), pp. 511–27.

————. Investment Decision Making with Index Futures and Index Futures Options. *J. Futures Markets*, April 1989, *9*(2), pp. 143–62.

———— **and Levy, Haim.** An Empirical Analysis of Term Premiums Using Stochastic Dominance. *J. Banking Finance*, May 1989, *13*(2), pp. 245–60.

————; **Levy, Haim and Livingston, Miles.** The Coupon Effect on Term Premiums. *J. Finan. Res.*, Spring 1989, *12*(1), pp. 15–21.

Broome, John. Should Social Preferences Be Consistent? *Econ. Philos.*, April 1989, *5*(1), pp. 7–17.

————. What's the Good of Equality? In *Hey, J. D., ed.*, 1989, pp. 236–62.

Brorsen, B. Wade. Liquidity Costs and Scalping Returns in the Corn Futures Market. *J. Futures Markets*, June 1989, *9*(3), pp. 225–36.

———— **and Bailey, DeeVon.** Price Asymmetry in Spatial Fed Cattle Markets. *Western J. Agr. Econ.*, December 1989, *14*(2), pp. 246–52.

———— **and DeBoer, Larry.** The Demand for and Supply of Military Labor. *Southern Econ. J.*, April 1989, *55*(4), pp. 853–69.

———— **and DeBoer, Larry.** A Note on Congressional Military Pay Setting. *Public Finance Quart.*, January 1989, *17*(1), pp. 96–107.

————; **Farris, Paul L. and Oellermann, Charles M.** Price Discovery for Feeder Cattle. *J. Futures Markets*, April 1989, *9*(2), pp. 113–21.

————; **Irwin, Scott H. and Hall, Joyce A.** The Distribution of Futures Prices: A Test of the Stable Paretian and Mixture of Normals Hypotheses. *J. Finan. Quant. Anal.*, March 1989, *24*(1), pp. 105–16.

———— **and Lukac, Louis P.** The Usefulness of Historical Data in Selecting Parameters for Technical Trading Systems. *J. Futures Markets*, February 1989, *9*(1), pp. 55–65.

_____; **Oellermann, Charles M. and Farris, Paul L.** The Live Cattle Futures Market and Daily Cash Price Movements. *J. Futures Markets*, August 1989, *9*(4), pp. 273–82.

Brose, Hanns-Georg; Schulze-Böing, Matthias and Wohlrab-Sahr, Monika. Discontinuity and Flexibility in Working Time and Work Careers: The Example of Temporary Work. In *Agassi, J. B. and Heycock, S., eds.*, 1989, pp. 99–113.

Brosio, Giorgio and Pola, Giancarlo. A Survey of Various Attempts to Explain the Distribution of Tax Revenues among Levels of Government. In *Chiancone, A. and Messere, K., eds.*, 1989, pp. 403–20.

Broske, Mary S. and Levy, Haim. The Stochastic Dominance Estimation of Default Probability. In *[Hadar, J.]*, 1989, pp. 91–112.

Brotherton, D. I. The Evolution and Implications of Mineral Planning Policy in the National Parks of England and Wales. *Environ. Planning A*, September 1989, *21*(9), pp. 1229–40.

Brouwer, Floor, et al. Sign-Solvability in Economic Models through Plausible Restrictions. *Atlantic Econ. J.*, June 1989, *17*(2), pp. 21–26.

Browder, John O. Development Alternatives for Tropical Rain Forests. In *Leonard, H. J., ed.*, 1989, pp. 111–33.

Browder, Joseph B. Siting Industrial Facilities in the Western United States. In *Dysart, B. C., III and Clawson, M., eds.*, 1989, pp. 99–113.

Brown, Bryan W. and Mariano, Roberto S. Measures of Deterministic Prediction Bias in Nonlinear Models. *Int. Econ. Rev.*, August 1989, *30*(3), pp. 667–84.

_____ **and Mariano, Roberto S.** Stochastic Simulation, Prediction and Validation of Nonlinear Models. In *[Adams, F. G.]*, 1989, pp. 17–36.

_____ **and Walker, Mary Beth.** The Random Utility Hypothesis and Inference in Demand Systems. *Econometrica*, July 1989, *57*(4), pp. 815–29.

Brown, C. K. Regional Cooperation in Post-Apartheid Southern Africa: The Need for a Uniform Information System and Data Base in the SADCC Region. In *Odén, B. and Othman, H., eds.*, 1989, pp. 77–90.

Brown, Charles C. and Medoff, James. The Employer Size–Wage Effect. *J. Polit. Econ.*, October 1989, *97*(5), pp. 1027–59.

Brown, D. J. and Blau, J. H. The Structure of Neutral Monotonic Social Functions. *Soc. Choice Welfare*, January 1989, *6*(1), pp. 51–61.

Brown, David T. Claimholder Incentive Conflicts in Reorganization: The Role of Bankruptcy Law. *Rev. Financial Stud.*, 1989, *2*(1), pp. 109–23.

Brown, Doug. Is Institutional Economics Existential Economics? In *Dugger, W. M., ed.*, 1989, pp. 65–82.

Brown, Drusilla K. A Computational Analysis of Japan's Generalized System of Preferences. *J. Devel. Econ.*, January 1989, *30*(1), pp. 103–28.

_____. Market Structure, the Exchange Rate, and Pricing Behavior by Firms: Some Evidence from Computable General Equilibrium Trade Models. *Weltwirtsch. Arch.*, 1989, *125*(3), pp. 441–63.

_____. Trade and Welfare Effects of the European Schemes of the Generalized System of Preferences. *Econ. Devel. Cult. Change*, July 1989, *37*(4), pp. 757–77.

_____ **and Stern, Robert M.** Computable General Equilibrium Estimates of the Gains from U.S.–Canadian Trade Liberalisation. In *Greenaway, D.; Hyclak, T. and Thornton, R. J., eds.*, 1989, pp. 69–108.

_____ **and Stern, Robert M.** U.S.–Canada Bilateral Tariff Elimination: The Role of Product Differentiation and Market Structure. In *Feenstra, R. C., ed.*, 1989, pp. 217–45.

Brown, Eleanor P. Involuntary Employment in Contracts with Risky Job Search. *Econ. Inquiry*, January 1989, *27*(1), pp. 93–104.

Brown, Graham S. International Tax Aspects of Charitable Giving and Philanthropic Organisations: English Law and Practice. *Bull. Int. Fiscal Doc.*, December 1989, *43*(12), pp. 549–53.

Brown, Gregory; Jacobs, Eva and Shipp, Stephanie. Families of Working Wives Spending More on Services and Nondurables. *Mon. Lab. Rev.*, February 1989, *112*(2), pp. 15–23.

Brown, Harold. Choices for the 1990s: Preserving American Security Interests through the Century's End. In *Hamilton, E. K., ed.*, 1989, pp. 126–65.

Brown, Ian. The Economies of Africa and Asia in the Inter-war Depression: Introduction. In *Brown, I., ed.*, 1989, pp. 1–7.

_____. Some Comments on Industrialisation in the Philippines during the 1930s. In *Brown, I., ed.*, 1989, pp. 203–20.

Brown, James; Haggblade, Steven and Hazell, Peter B. R. Farm–Nonfarm Linkages in Rural Sub-Saharan Africa. *World Devel.*, August 1989, *17*(8), pp. 1173–1201.

Brown, James N. Why Do Wages Increase with Tenure? On-the-Job Training and Life-Cycle Wage Growth Observed within Firms. *Amer. Econ. Rev.*, December 1989, *79*(5), pp. 971–91.

Brown, John C. Public Reform for Private Gain? The Case of Investments in Sanitary Infrastructure: Germany, 1880–1887. *Urban Stud.*, February 1989, *26*(1), pp. 2–12.

Brown, Kaye and Burrows, Colin. Bogged Down in Marginal Analysis: Neuhauser and Lewicki Revisited. In *Smith, C. S., ed.*, 1989, pp. 91–120.

_____; **Ngui, Michael and Burrows, Colin.** Health Insurance Choice: An Econometric Analysis of A.B.S. Health and Health Insurance Surveys. In *Smith, C. S., ed.*, 1989, pp. 172–94.

Brown, Keith C. Reserves and Reserve Production Ratios in Imperfect Markets. *Energy J.*, April 1989, *10*(2), pp. 177–86.

Brown, Kenneth D. Models in History: A Microstudy of Late Nineteenth-Century British Entrepreneurship. *Econ. Hist. Rev., 2nd Ser.*, November 1989, *42*(4), pp. 528–37.

Brown, Lawrence A.; England, Kim V. L. and Goetz, Andrew R. Location, Social Categories, and Individual Labor Market Experiences in Developing Economies: The Venezuelan Case. *Int. Reg. Sci. Rev.*, 1989, *12*(1), pp. 1–28.

────── **and Lawson, Victoria A.** Polarization Reversal, Migration Related Shifts in Human Resource Profiles, and Spatial Growth Policies: A Venezuelan Study. *Int. Reg. Sci. Rev.*, 1989, *12*(2), pp. 165–88.

Brown, Lawrence D.; McLaughlin, Catherine G. and Zellers, Wendy K. Health Care Coalitions: Characteristics, Activities, and Prospects. *Inquiry*, Spring 1989, *26*(1), pp. 72–83.

Brown, Lester R. Global Ecology at the Brink. *Challenge*, March–April 1989, *32*(2), pp. 14–22.

Brown, Malcolm C. Empirical Determinants of Physician Incomes—Evidence from Canadian Data. *Empirical Econ.*, 1989, *14*(4), pp. 273–89.

Brown, Mark G. and Lee, Jonq-Ying. Consumer Demand for Food Diversity. *Southern J. Agr. Econ.*, December 1989, *21*(2), pp. 47–53.

Brown, Murray and Wolfstetter, Elmar. Tripartite Income–Employment Contracts and Coalition Incentive Compatibility. *Rand J. Econ.*, Autumn 1989, *20*(3), pp. 291–307.

Brown, Pamela Clark. A Risk-Averse Buyer's Contract Design. *Europ. Econ. Rev.*, October 1989, *33*(8), pp. 1527–44.

Brown, Philip. Invited Remarks: Ball and Brown [1968]. *J. Acc. Res.*, Supplement, 1989, *27*, pp. 202–17.

Brown, R. A. Comment: The Impact of the Tax Reform Proposals on the Resource Industries. In *Mintz, J. and Whalley, J., eds.*, 1989, pp. 326–35.

Brown, R. G. Social Security and Welfare. In *Hancock, K., ed.*, 1989, pp. 44–69.

Brown, R. Michael and Cochran, John P. What's Wrong Here? *Econ. Inquiry*, July 1989, *27*(3), pp. 541–45.

Brown, Richard. The Rationale and Effects of the IMF Stabilisation Programme in Sudan. In *Campbell, B. K., ed.*, 1989, pp. 51–91.

Brown, Robert D. The Economic Impacts of Tax Reform: Overview. In *Mintz, J. and Whalley, J., eds.*, 1989, pp. 443–50.

Brown, Robert L. and Easton, Stephen A. Weak-Form Efficiency in the Nineteenth Century: A Study of Daily Prices in the London Market for 3 Per Cent Consols, 1821–1860. *Economica*, February 1989, *56*(221), pp. 61–70.

Brown, Seyom. Inherited Geopolitics and Emergent Global Realities. In *Hamilton, E. K., ed.*, 1989, pp. 166–97.

Brown, Stephen J. The Number of Factors in Security Returns. *J. Finance*, December 1989, *44*(5), pp. 1247–62.

Brown, Stephen P. A. and Phillips, Keith R. Oil Demand and Prices in the 1990s. *Fed. Res. Bank Dallas Econ. Rev.*, January 1989, pp. 1–8.

Brown, Stuart S. Export Uncertainty in Centrally Planned Economies and Administered Protection. *J. Compar. Econ.*, December 1989, *13*(4), pp. 553–65.

Brown, William J. Farm Enterprise Size and Diversification in Prairie Agriculture. In *Schmitz, A., ed.*, 1989, pp. 249–302.

Brown, William S. and Hands, D. Wade. Expanding the Neoclassical Vision: Comment. *Rev. Soc. Econ.*, Spring 1989, *47*(1), pp. 84–87.

Browne, Francis X. A New Test of the Buffer Stock Money Hypothesis. *Manchester Sch. Econ. Soc. Stud.*, June 1989, *57*(2), pp. 154–71.

Browne, Lynn E. The Labor Force, Unemployment Rates, and Wage Pressures. *New Eng. Econ. Rev.*, Jan.–Feb. 1989, pp. 21–29.

──────. Shifting Regional Fortunes: The Wheel Turns. *New Eng. Econ. Rev.*, May–June 1989, pp. 27–40.

Browne, M. Neil and Hoag, John H. The Formative Use of Student Evaluations of Teaching: An Empirical Demonstration of the Incompleteness of Global Ratings. In *Missouri Valley Economic Association*, 1989, pp. 32–40.

Browne, Robert S. Africa: Time for a New Development Strategy. In *Martin, M. T. and Kandal, T. R., eds.*, 1989, pp. 399–408.

Browne, William P. and Bonnen, James T. Why Is Agricultural Policy So Difficult to Reform? In *Krämer, C. S., ed.*, 1989, pp. 7–33.

Browning, Edgar K. Elasticities, Tax Rates, and Tax Revenue. *Nat. Tax J.*, March 1989, *42*(1), pp. 45–58.

──────. Inequality and Poverty. *Southern Econ. J.*, April 1989, *55*(4), pp. 819–30.

Browning, Martin J. The Intertemporal Allocation of Expenditure on Non-durables, Services, and Durables. *Can. J. Econ.*, February 1989, *22*(1), pp. 22–36.

──────. A Nonparametric Test of the Life-Cycle Rational Expectations Hypothesis. *Int. Econ. Rev.*, November 1989, *30*(4), pp. 979–92.

Brownstone, David and Small, Kenneth A. Efficient Estimation of Nested Logit Models. *J. Bus. Econ. Statist.*, January 1989, *7*(1), pp. 67–74.

Brox, James A.; Paraskevopoulos, Christos C. and Andrikopoulos, Andreas A. Interfuel and Interfactor Substitution in Ontario Manufacturing, 1962–82. *Appl. Econ.*, December 1989, *21*(12), pp. 1667–81.

Broze, L.; Gourieroux, Christian and Szafarz, A. Speculative Bubbles and Exchange of Information on the Market of a Storable Good. In *Barnett, W. A.; Geweke, J. and Shell, K., eds.*, 1989, pp. 101–18.

Bruce, Judith. Homes Divided. *World Devel.*, July 1989, *17*(7), pp. 979–91.

Bruce, Neil. The Impact of Tax Reform on International Capital Flows and Investment. In *Mintz, J. and Whalley, J., eds.*, 1989, pp. 193–217.

──────. Pathways to Tax Expenditures: A Survey

of Conceptual Issues and Controversies. **In** *Bruce, N., ed.*, 1989, pp. 21–61.

———. Tax Expenditures and Government Policy: An Introduction to the Conference Volume. **In** *Bruce, N., ed.*, 1989, pp. 3–12.

Bruce, Peter G. Political Parties and Labor Legislation in Canada and the U.S. *Ind. Relat.*, Spring 1989, *28*(2), pp. 115–41.

Brudny, Yitzhak M. The Heralds of Opposition to *Perestroyka. Soviet Econ.*, April–June 1989, *5*(2), pp. 162–200.

Brueckner, Jan K. Local Income Redistribution: A Club-Theoretic Analysis. *J. Urban Econ.*, May 1989, *25*(3), pp. 310–24.

——— **and Follain, James R.** ARMs and the Demand for Housing. *Reg. Sci. Urban Econ.*, May 1989, *19*(2), pp. 163–87.

——— **and Lee, Kangoh.** Club Theory with a Peer-Group Effect. *Reg. Sci. Urban Econ.*, August 1989, *19*(3), pp. 399–420.

——— **and O'Brien, Kevin M.** Modeling Government Behavior in Collective Bargaining: A Test for Self-interested Bureaucrats. *Public Choice*, October 1989, *63*(1), pp. 15–41.

Brueggemann, John; Boswell, Terry E. and Sweat, Mike. War in the Core of the World-System: Testing the Goldstein Thesis. **In** *Schaeffer, R. K., ed.*, 1989, pp. 9–26.

Brugger, Bill. Mao, Science, Technology, and Humanity. **In** *Dirlik, A. and Meisner, M., eds.*, 1989, pp. 117–35.

Bruggink, Thomas H. Nobel Laureates in Economic Sciences: A Biographical Dictionary: George J. Stigler: 1982. **In** *Katz, B. S., ed.*, 1989, pp. 284–93.

Bruguière, Michel. Révolution et finances. Réflexions sur un impossible bilan. (The Financial Impact of the French Revolution: An Impossible Balance-Sheet. With English summary.) *Revue Écon.*, November 1989, *40*(6), pp. 985–1000.

Brumbaugh, R. Dan, Jr.; Carron, Andrew S. and Litan, Robert E. Cleaning Up the Depository Institutions Mess. *Brookings Pap. Econ. Act.*, 1989, (1), pp. 243–83.

——— **and Litan, Robert E.** Facing Up to the Crisis in American Banking. **In** *Bosworth, B. P., et al.*, 1989, pp. 122–27.

Brune, Lester H. Guns and Butter: The Pre–Korean War Dispute over Budget Allocations: Nourse's Conservative Keynesianism Loses Favor against Keyserling's Economic Expansion Plan. *Amer. J. Econ. Sociology*, July 1989, *48*(3), pp. 357–71.

Bruneel, Didier. Recent Evolution of Financial Structures and Monetary Policy in France. **In** *Hodgman, D. R. and Wood, G. E., eds.*, 1989, pp. 3–61.

Brunello, Giorgio. The Employment Effects of Shorter Working Hours: An Application to Japanese Data. *Economica*, November 1989, *56*(224), pp. 473–86.

Bruner, Robert F. and Bonnier, Karl-Adam. An Analysis of Stock Price Reaction to Management Change in Distressed Firms. *J. Acc. Econ.*, February 1989, *11*(1), pp. 95–106.

Brunet, Jean-Michel; Souton, Marc and Dumontier, Pascal. Les caractéristiques financières des sociétés françaises acquises par offre publique. (Financial Ratios as Predictors of French Takeovers. With English summary.) *Écon. Societes*, December 1989, *23*(12), pp. 107–28.

Brunhes, Bernard. Labour Flexibility in Enterprises: A Comparison of Firms in Four European Countries. **In** *OECD*, 1989, pp. 11–36.

Bruni, Franco; Penati, Alessandro and Porta, Angelo. Financial Regulation, Implicit Taxes, and Fiscal Adjustment in Italy. **In** *Monti, M., ed.*, 1989, pp. 197–230.

Bruni, Michele. An Integrated Accounting for Firms, Job Positions and Employment. *Labour*, Winter 1989, *3*(3), pp. 73–92.

———. Una contabilità integrata delle imprese, dei posti di lavoro e degli occupati. (An Integrated Accounting for Enterprises, Job Positions and the Employed Population. With English summary.) *Econ. Lavoro*, April–June 1989, *23*(2), pp. 3–17.

Bruning, Edward R. The Economic Implications of the Changing Merger Process. **In** *McKee, D. L., ed.*, 1989, pp. 47–58.

——— **and Kuzma, Ann T.** Airline Accidents and Stock Return Performance. *Logist. Transp. Rev.*, June 1989, *25*(2), pp. 157–68.

——— **and Register, Charles A.** Technical Efficiency within Hospitals: Do Profit Incentives Matter? *Appl. Econ.*, September 1989, *21*(9), pp. 1217–33.

Brunk, Gregory G. The Role of Statistical Heuristics in Public Policy Analysis. *Cato J.*, Spring–Summer 1989, *9*(1), pp. 165–89.

Brunner K., José Joaquín. Los intelectuales y los problemas de la cultura del desarrollo. (With English summary.) *Cuadernos Econ.*, December 1989, *26*(79), pp. 311–19.

Brunner, Karl. Fiscal Policy in Macro Theory: A Survey and Evaluation. **In** *Brunner, K. and Meltzer, A. H.*, 1989, *1986*, pp. 259–338.

———. The Role of Money and Monetary Policy. *Fed. Res. Bank St. Louis Rev.*, Sept.–Oct. 1989, *71*(5), pp. 4–22.

———; **Cukierman, Alex and Meltzer, Allan H.** Money and Economic Activity, Inventories and Business Cycles. **In** *Brunner, K. and Meltzer, A. H.*, 1989, *1983*, pp. 193–229.

——— **and Friedman, Milton.** Anna J. Schwartz: An Appreciation: A Life of Scholarship. **In** *[Schwartz, A. J.]*, 1989, pp. 245–47.

——— **and Meltzer, Allan H.** An Aggregative Theory for a Closed Economy. **In** *Brunner, K. and Meltzer, A. H.*, 1989, *1976*, pp. 159–92.

——— **and Meltzer, Allan H.** A Credit Market Theory of the Money Supply and an Explanation of Two Puzzles in U.S. Monetary Policy. **In** *Brunner, K. and Meltzer, A. H.*, 1989, *1966*, pp. 97–120.

——— **and Meltzer, Allan H.** The Federal Reserves Attachment to the Free Reserve Concept. **In** *Brunner, K. and Meltzer, A. H.*, 1989, pp. 21–96.

——— **and Meltzer, Allan H.** Liquidity Traps

for Money, Bank Credit, and Interest Rates. In *Brunner, K. and Meltzer, A. H.*, 1989, *1968*, pp. 121–58.

———— **and Meltzer, Allan H.** Monetary Economics: Introduction. In *Brunner, K. and Meltzer, A. H.*, 1989, pp. 1–19.

———— **and Meltzer, Allan H.** Mr Hicks and the 'Monetarists.' In *Wood, J. C. and Woods, R. N., eds., Vol. 2*, 1989, *1973*, pp. 232–48.

———— **and Meltzer, Allan H.** The Uses of Money: Money in the Theory of an Exchange Economy. In *Brunner, K. and Meltzer, A. H.*, 1989, *1971*, pp. 230–58.

Bruno, James E. Using MCW–APM Test Scoring to Evaluate Economics Curricula. *J. Econ. Educ.*, Winter 1989, *20*(1), pp. 5–22.

Bruno, Michael. Econometrics and the Design of Economic Reform. *Econometrica*, March 1989, *57*(2), pp. 275–306.

————. Overview [Monetary Policy, Capital Controls and Seigniorage in an Open Economy] [Seigniorage in Europe]. In *De Cecco, M. and Giovannini, A., eds.*, 1989, pp. 88–89.

————. Theoretical Developments in the Light of Macroeconomic Policy and Empirical Research. *Scand. J. Econ.*, 1989, *91*(2), pp. 307–33.

Bruno, Sergio and Sardoni, Claudio. Productivity Competitiveness among Non Cooperating Integrated Economies: A Negative-Sum Game. *Labour*, Spring 1989, *3*(1), pp. 73–94.

Brunstad, R. J. and Vårdal, E. Goal Conflicts in the Norwegian Farming Industry: Allocational Loss through the Pursuit of Non-efficiency Goals. In *Bauer, S. and Henrichsmeyer, W., eds.*, 1989, pp. 97–101.

Brus, Wlodzimierz. Evolution of the Communist Economic System: Scope and Limits. In *Nee, V. and Stark, D., eds.*, 1989, pp. 255–77.

————. From Revisionism to Pragmatism. Sketches towards a Self-Portrait of a 'Reform Economist.' *Acta Oecon.*, 1989, *40*(3–4), pp. 204–10.

———— **and Laski, Kazimierz.** Capital Market and the Problem of Full Employment. *Europ. Econ. Rev.*, March 1989, *33*(2/3), pp. 439–47.

Brusco, Sebastiano. A Policy for Industrial Districts. In *Goodman, E. and Bamford, J., eds.*, 1989, pp. 259–69.

———— **and Villa, Paola.** The State, the Unions, and the Labor Market: The Italian Case, 1969–1985. In *Rosenberg, S., ed.*, 1989, pp. 127–50.

Bryan, William R. and Linke, Charles M. Estimating the Present Value of Future Income Losses: An Historical Simulation 1900–1982: Comment. *J. Risk Ins.*, September 1989, *56*(3), pp. 555–59.

Bryant, John. Interest-Bearing Currency, Legal Restrictions, and the Rate of Return Dominance of Money: A Note. *J. Money, Credit, Banking*, May 1989, *21*(2), pp. 240–45.

————. Money, Banking and Intertemporal Substitution. *J. Banking Finance*, May 1989, *13*(2), pp. 171–79.

Bryant, Kelly and Brand, Horst. Productivity

Trends in Agricultural Chemicals. *Mon. Lab. Rev.*, March 1989, *112*(3), pp. 21–28.

Bryant, Ralph C. Changing Effects of Monetary Policy on Real Economic Activity: Commentary. In *Federal Reserve Bank of Kansas City*, 1989, pp. 113–27.

————; **Helliwell, John F. and Hooper, Peter.** Domestic and Cross-Border Consequences of U.S. Macroeconomic Policies. In *Bryant, R. C., et al., eds.*, 1989, pp. 59–115.

———— **and Hodgkinson, Edith.** Problems of International Cooperation. In *Cooper, R. N., et al.*, 1989, pp. 1–11.

————, **et al.** Macroeconomic Policies in an Interdependent World: Introduction. In *Bryant, R. C., et al., eds.*, 1989, pp. 1–13.

Bryant, Richard and Wilhite, Al. Additional Interpretations of Dummy Variables in Semilogarithmic Equations. *Atlantic Econ. J.*, December 1989, *17*(4), pp. 88.

Brym, Robert J. The Capitalist Class: Canada. In *Bottomore, T. and Brym, R. J., eds.*, 1989, pp. 177–206.

Brzezinski, Zbigniew. The Death of Communism: Interview. *Challenge*, May–June 1989, *32*(3), pp. 16–23.

————. The New U.S. Administration: People, Procedures, Policies. In *Frankel, A. V. and Heck, C. B., eds.*, 1989, pp. 75–78.

Bsaies, Abdeljabbar. Educational Change and the Ulama in the 19th and Early 20th Centuries. In *Nabli, M. K. and Nugent, J. B., eds.*, 1989, pp. 265–88.

Bublitz, Bruce and Ettredge, Michael. The Information in Discretionary Outlays: Advertising, Research, and Development. *Accounting Rev.*, January 1989, *64*(1), pp. 108–24.

Bubnys, Edward L. and Lee, Cheng Few. Linear and Generalized Functional Form Market Models for Electric Utility Firms. *J. Econ. Bus.*, August 1989, *41*(3), pp. 213–23.

————; **Lee, Cheng Few and Wei, K. C. John.** The APT versus the Multi-factor CAPM: Empirical Evidence. *Quart. Rev. Econ. Bus.*, Winter 1989, *29*(4), pp. 6–25.

Bucay, Nisso and Pérez Motta, Eduardo. Trade Negotiation Strategy for Mexico. In *Whalley, J., ed., Vol. 2*, 1989, pp. 230–43.

Buccellato, Claudio and Palazzi, Paolo. Deindustrializzazione e sviluppo: Alcuni confronti internazionali. (Deindustrialization and Development: Some International Comparison. With English summary.) *Econ. Lavoro*, Jan.–March 1989, *23*(1), pp. 53–75.

Buccola, Steven T. Pricing Efficiency in Agricultural Markets: Issues, Methods, and Results. *Western J. Agr. Econ.*, July 1989, *14*(1), pp. 111–21.

Buchanan, James M. The Achievement and Limits of Public Choice in Diagnosing Government Failure and in Offering Bases for Constructive Reform. In *Buchanan, J. M. (II)*, 1989, *1983*, pp. 24–36.

————. The Adam Smith Lecture: On the Structure of an Economy: A Re-emphasis of Some

Classical Foundations. *Bus. Econ.*, January 1989, *24*(1), pp. 6–12.

_____. An Outside Economist's Defense of Pesek and Saving. In *Buchanan, J. M. (II)*, 1989, *1969*, pp. 149–53.

_____. Better than Plowing. In *Buchanan, J. M. (I)*, 1989, *1986*, pp. 67–85.

_____. Breton and Weldon on Public Goods. In *Buchanan, J. M. (II)*, 1989, pp. 208–12.

_____. Can Policy Activism Succeed? In *Buchanan, J. M. (II)*, 1989, pp. 154–64.

_____. The Coase Theorem and the Theory of the State. In *Buchanan, J. M. (II)*, 1989, pp. 385–400.

_____. Coercive Taxation in Constitutional Contract. In *Buchanan, J. M. (II)*, 1989, pp. 309–28.

_____. Constitutional Economics. In *Buchanan, J. M. (II)*, 1989, pp. 57–67.

_____. Contractarian Presuppositions and Democratic Governance. In *Brennan, G. and Lomasky, L. E., eds.*, 1989, pp. 174–82.

_____. The Ethics of Constitutional Order. In *Buchanan, J. M. (I)*, 1989, pp. 25–31.

_____. Free Trade and Producer-Interest Politics. In *Buchanan, J. M. (I)*, 1989, pp. 52–66.

_____. Ideas, Institutions, and Political Economy: A Plea for Disestablishment. In *Buchanan, J. M. (II)*, 1989, pp. 165–75.

_____. The Institutional Structure of Externality. In *Buchanan, J. M. (II)*, 1989, pp. 371–84.

_____. Man and State. In *Buchanan, J. M. (II)*, 1989, pp. 51–56.

_____. Market Failure and Political Failure. In *Buchanan, J. M. (II)*, 1989, pp. 418–29.

_____. Nobelity. *Eastern Econ. J.*, Oct.–Dec. 1989, *15*(4), pp. 339–48.

_____. Notes on Irrelevant Externalities, Enforcement Costs, and the Atrophy of Property Rights. In *Buchanan, J. M. (II)*, 1989, pp. 359–70.

_____. On the Work Ethic. In *Buchanan, J. M. (I)*, 1989, pp. 47–51.

_____. The Political Economy of the Budget Deficit. In *Buchanan, J. M. (I)*, 1989, pp. 1–12.

_____. Predictability: The Criterion of Monetary Constitutions. In *Buchanan, J. M. (II)*, 1989, *1962*, pp. 129–48.

_____. Private Ownership and Common Usage. In *Buchanan, J. M. (II)*, 1989, pp. 344–58.

_____. The Public-Choice Perspective. In *Buchanan, J. M. (I)*, 1989, pp. 13–24.

_____. Public Goods in Theory and Practice. In *Buchanan, J. M. (II)*, 1989, *1967*, pp. 213–17.

_____. Rational Choice Models in the Social Sciences. In *Buchanan, J. M. (II)*, 1989, pp. 37–50.

_____. Reductionist Reflections on the Monetary Constitution. *Cato J.*, Fall 1989, *9*(2), pp. 295–99.

_____. The Relatively Absolute Absolutes. In *Buchanan, J. M. (I)*, 1989, pp. 32–46.

_____. Richard Musgrave, Public Finance, and Public Choice: Review Article. *Public Choice*, June 1989, *61*(3), pp. 289–91.

_____. The State of Economic Science: Views of Six Nobel Laureates: Dr. James M. Buchanan. In *Sichel, W., ed.*, 1989, pp. 79–95.

_____. What If There Is No Majority Motion? In *Buchanan, J. M. (II)*, 1989, pp. 87–100.

_____ and Brennan, Geoffrey. Predictive Power and the Choice among Regimes. In *Buchanan, J. M. (II)*, 1989, pp. 3–23.

_____ and Brennan, Geoffrey. Tax Instruments as Constraints on the Disposition of Public Revenues. In *Buchanan, J. M. (II)*, 1989, pp. 264–82.

_____ and Brennan, Geoffrey. Voter Choice: Evaluating Political Alternatives. In *Buchanan, J. M. (II)*, 1989, pp. 101–15.

_____ and Congleton, Roger D. Proportional and Progressive Income Taxation with Utility-Maximizing Governments. In *Buchanan, J. M. (II)*, 1989, pp. 294–308.

_____ and Faith, Roger L. Entrepreneurship and the Internalization of Externalities. In *Buchanan, J. M. (II)*, 1989, *1981*, pp. 401–17.

_____ and Faith, Roger L. Toward a Theory of Yes–No Voting. In *Buchanan, J. M. (II)*, 1989, pp. 71–86.

_____ and Forte, Francesco. The Evaluation of Public Services. In *Buchanan, J. M. (II)*, 1989, *1961*, pp. 176–93.

_____ and Forte, Francesco. Fiscal Choice through Time: A Case for Indirect Taxation? In *Buchanan, J. M. (II)*, 1989, pp. 228–45.

_____ and Goetz, Charles J. Efficiency Limits of Fiscal Mobility. In *Buchanan, J. M. (II)*, 1989, pp. 246–63.

_____ and Kafoglis, Milton. A Note on Public Goods Supply. In *Buchanan, J. M. (II)*, 1989, *1963*, pp. 194–207.

_____ and Lee, Dwight R. Vote Buying in a Stylized Setting. In *Buchanan, J. M. (II)*, 1989, pp. 116–28.

_____ and Pinto Barbosa, António S. Convexity Constraints in Public Goods Theory. In *Buchanan, J. M. (II)*, 1989, pp. 218–27.

_____ and Vanberg, Viktor. Organization Theory and Fiscal Economics: Society, State, and Public Debt. In *Buchanan, J. M. (II)*, 1989, pp. 329–43.

_____ and Vanberg, Viktor. A Theory of Leadership and Deference in Constitutional Construction. *Public Choice*, April 1989, *61*(1), pp. 15–27.

_____ and Wagner, Richard E. Dialogues Concerning Fiscal Religion. In *Buchanan, J. M. (II)*, 1989, pp. 283–93.

Buchanan, John T. and Daellenbach, Hans G. Desirable Properties of Interactive Multi-objective Programming Methods. In *Lockett, A. G. and Islei, G., eds.*, 1989, pp. 212–23.

Buchele, Robert and Aldrich, Mark. Where to Look for Comparable Worth: The Implications of Efficiency Wages. In *Hill, M. A. and Killingsworth, M. R., eds.*, 1989, pp. 11–28.

Buchholz, John D. Soft Wear for Roads. In *Matzer, J., Jr., ed.*, 1989, *1987*, pp. 211–16.

Buchner-Jeziorska, Anna. Working Time in Poland—Some Regulations and General Tendencies. In *Agassi, J. B. and Heycock, S., eds.,* 1989, pp. 161–66.

Büchtemann, Christoph F. More Jobs through Less Employment Protection? Evidence for West Germany. *Labour,* Winter 1989, *3*(3), pp. 23–56.

———. The Socio-economics of Individual Working Time Reduction: Empirical Evidence for the Federal Republic of Germany. In *Agassi, J. B. and Heycock, S., eds.,* 1989, pp. 178–206.

——— and Quack, Sigrid. "Bridges" or "Traps"? Non-standard Employment in the Federal Republic of Germany. In *Rodgers, G. and Rodgers, J., eds.,* 1989, pp. 109–48.

Buckholtz, P. and Hartwick, John M. Zero Time Preference with Discounting. *Econ. Letters,* 1989, *29*(1), pp. 1–6.

de Buckle, Teresa Salazar; Holaday, William and Castella, Guillermo. Agro-food Industry in Latin America. *Industry Devel.,* June 1989, (27), pp. 1–29.

Buckley, John E. Variations in Holidays, Vacations, and Area Pay Levels. *Mon. Lab. Rev.,* February 1989, *112*(2), pp. 24–30.

Buckley, Peter J. The Institutionalist Perspective òn Recent Theories of Direct Foreign Investment: A Comment. *J. Econ. Issues,* September 1989, *23*(3), pp. 879–85.

———. Predictions of the Economic Theory of the Multinational Enterprise. In *Negandhi, A. R., ed.,* 1989, pp. 79–104.

——— and Prescott, Kate. The Structure of British Industry's Sales in Foreign Markets. *Managerial Dec. Econ.,* September 1989, *10*(3), pp. 189–208.

Bucklin, Randolph E.; Caves, Richard E. and Lo, Andrew W. Games of Survival in the U.S. Newspaper Industry. *Appl. Econ.,* May 1989, *21*(5), pp. 631–49.

Buckner, Georgette C. and Sandelands, Lloyd E. Of Art and Work: Aesthetic Experience and the Psychology of Work Feelings. In *Cummings, L. L. and Staw, B. M., eds.,* 1989, pp. 105–131.

Buckwell, A. Policy Requirements and Dialogue with Modellers. In *Bauer, S. and Henrichsmeyer, W., eds.,* 1989, pp. 351–54.

Budd, Alan. The Peacock Report—Some Unanswered Questions. In *Veljanovski, C., ed. (I),* 1989, pp. 63–75.

Buechler, Hans. Apprenticeship and Transmission of Knowledge in La Paz, Bolivia. In *Coy, M. W., ed.,* 1989, pp. 31–50.

Buechner, M. Northrup. Roundaboutness and Productivity in Böhm-Bawerk. *Southern Econ. J.,* October 1989, *56*(2), pp. 499–510.

Buell, Stephen G. and Guerard, John B., Jr. An Econometric Analysis of Energy Financing. *Energy J.,* April 1989, *10*(2), pp. 47–67.

Bueno de Mesquita, Bruce and Lalman, David. The Road to War Is Strewn with Peaceful Intentions. In *Ordeshook, P. C., ed.,* 1989, pp. 253–66.

Buerger, Robert and Kahn, James R. New York

Value of Chesapeake Striped Bass. *Marine Resource Econ.,* 1989, *6*(1), pp. 19–25.

Buescu, Mircea. Oil in Developing Countries in South America. In *Ferrier, R. W. and Fursenko, A., eds.,* 1989, pp. 28–36.

Buffie, Edward F. Imported Inputs, Real Wage Rigidity and Devaluation in the Small Open Economy. *Europ. Econ. Rev.,* September 1989, *33*(7), pp. 1345–61.

———. Mexico 1958–86: From Stabilizing Development to the Debt Crisis. In *Sachs, J. D., ed. (II),* 1989, pp. 141–68.

———. Smuggler's Blues at the Central Bank: Lessons from Sudan: Comment. In *[Díaz-Alejandro, C.],* 1989, pp. 208–10.

Buganov, Viktor Ivanovich. The Russian Peasant Movement in the Eighteenth and Nineteenth Century. In *Grantham, G. and Leonard, C. S., eds., Pt. B,* 1989, pp. 411–28.

Bugos, Glenn E. Testing the F-4 Phantom II: Engineering Practice in the Development of American Military Aircraft, 1954–1969. In *Hausman, W. J., ed.,* 1989, pp. 13–18.

Buhl, Hans Ulrich. Finanzanalyse des Hersteller–Leasings. (With English summary.) *Z. Betriebswirtschaft,* April 1989, *59*(4), pp. 421–39.

———. Much Ado about Leasing? Entgegnung. (Reply. With English summary.) *Z. Betriebswirtschaft,* October 1989, *59*(10), pp. 1095–97.

Bühler, Wolfgang and Herzog, Walter. Die Duration—Eine geeignete Kennzahl für die Steuerung von Zinsänderungsrisiken in Kreditinstituten? (Teil I). (The Duration-Based Concept—A Meaningful Approach to Managing Banking Institutions' Risk of Interest Changes? [Part I]. With English summary.) *Kredit Kapital,* 1989, *22*(3), pp. 403–28.

——— and Herzog, Walter. Die Duration—eine geeignete Kennzahl für die Steuerung von Zinsänderungsrisiken in Kredinstituten? (Teil II). (The Duration-Based Concept—A Meaningful Approach to Managing Banking Institutions' Risk of Interest Changes? [Part II]. With English summary.) *Kredit Kapital,* 1989, *22*(4), pp. 524–63.

Bui-Lan, A.; Paul, P. B. and Sar, N. L. Forecasting Sawntimber Consumption: The Application of an End-Use Model. *Australian J. Agr. Econ.,* December 1989, *33*(3), pp. 219–32.

Buigues, Pierre and Goybet, Ph. The Community's Industrial Competitiveness and International Trade in Manufactured Products. In *Jacquemin, A. and Sapir, A., eds.,* 1989, pp. 227–47.

——— and Jacquemin, Alexis. Strategies of Firms and Structural Environments in the Large Internal Market. *J. Common Market Stud.,* September 1989, *28*(1), pp. 53–67.

Buijink, Willem and Jegers, Marc. Accounting Rates of Return: Comment. *Amer. Econ. Rev.,* March 1989, *79*(1), pp. 287–89.

Buijtenhuijs, Robert. Chad: The Narrow Escape of an African State, 1965–1987. In *Cruise O'Brien, D. B.; Dunn, J. and Rathbone, R., eds.,* 1989, pp. 49–58.

Buiter, Willem H. After the New Classical Macroeconomics. In *Buiter, W. H.*, 1989, pp. 1–53.

_____. 'Crowding' Out of Private Capital Formation by Government Borrowing in the Presence of Intergenerational Gifts and Bequests. In *Buiter, W. H.*, 1989, *1980*, pp. 255–82.

_____. Death, Birth, Productivity Growth and Debt Neutrality. In *Buiter, W. H.*, 1989, *1988*, pp. 315–31.

_____. Debt Neutrality, Professor Vickrey and Henry George's 'Single Tax.' *Econ. Letters*, 1989, *29*(1), pp. 43–47.

_____. Expectations and Control Theory. In *Buiter, W. H.*, 1989, *1983*, pp. 110–16.

_____. Granger-Causality and Policy Effectiveness. In *Buiter, W. H.*, 1989, *1984*, pp. 168–80.

_____. The Macroeconomics of Dr Pangloss: A Critical Survey of the New Classical Macroeconomics. In *Buiter, W. H.*, 1989, *1980*, pp. 57–76.

_____. Policy Evaluation and Design for Continuous Time Linear Rational Expectations Models: Some Recent Developments. In *Buiter, W. H.*, 1989, *1986*, pp. 228–52.

_____. Predetermined and Non-predetermined Variables in Rational Expectations Models. In *Buiter, W. H.*, 1989, *1982*, pp. 105–09.

_____. Real Effects of Anticipated and Unanticipated Money: Some Problems of Estimation and Hypothesis Testing. In *Buiter, W. H.*, 1989, *1983*, pp. 151–67.

_____. The Right Combination of Demand and Supply Policies: The Case for a Two-Handed Approach. In *Buiter, W. H.*, 1989, *1988*, pp. 117–47.

_____. The Superiority of Contingent Rules over Fixed Rules in Models with Rational Expectations. In *Buiter, W. H.*, 1989, *1981*, pp. 77–104.

_____. The Theory of Optimum Deficits and Debt. In *Buiter, W. H.*, 1989, *1983*, pp. 289–314.

_____. A Viable Gold Standard Requires Flexible Monetary and Fiscal Policy. *Rev. Econ. Stud.*, January 1989, *56*(1), pp. 101–17.

_____. Walras' Law and All That: Budget Constraints and Balance Sheet Constraints in Period Models and Continuous Time Models. In *Buiter, W. H.*, 1989, *1980*, pp. 349–64.

_____ and Carmichael, Jeffrey. Government Debt: Comment. In *Buiter, W. H.*, 1989, *1984*, pp. 283–88.

_____ and Jewitt, Ian. Staggered Wage Setting with Real Wage Relativities: Variations on a Theme of Taylor. In *Buiter, W. H.*, 1989, *1981*, pp. 183–99.

_____; Kletzer, Kenneth M. and Srinivasan, T. N. Some Thoughts on the Brady Plan: Putting a Fourth Leg on the Donkey? *World Devel.*, October 1989, *17*(10), pp. 1661–64.

_____ and Lorie, Henri. Some Unfamiliar Properties of a Familiar Macroeconomic Model. In *Buiter, W. H.*, 1989, *1977*, pp. 335–48.

_____ and Miller, Marcus H. Costs and Benefits of an Anti-inflationary Policy: Questions and Issues. In *Buiter, W. H.*, 1989, *1985*, pp. 200–228.

Bulkley, I. George and Black, Jane M. Do Trade Unions Reduce Job Opportunities of Nonmembers? *Econ. J.*, March 1989, *99*(394), pp. 177–86.

_____ and Black, Jane M. Insiders and Outsiders and Efficient Asymmetric Information Contracts. *Econ. Letters*, 1989, *29*(3), pp. 265–69.

_____ and Black, Jane M. A Ratio Criterion for Signing the Effects of an Increase in Uncertainty. *Int. Econ. Rev.*, February 1989, *30*(1), pp. 119–30.

_____ and Tonks, Ian. Are U.K. Stock Prices Excessively Volatile? Trading Rules and Variance Bounds Tests. *Econ. J.*, December 1989, *99*(398), pp. 1083–98.

Bull, Clive and Tedeschi, Piero. Optimal Probation for New Hires. *J. Inst. Theoretical Econ.*, December 1989, *145*(4), pp. 627–42.

Bullock, Nicholas. Fragments of a Post-War Utopia; Housing in Finsbury 1945–51. *Urban Stud.*, February 1989, *26*(1), pp. 46–58.

Bulmer, Simon and Paterson, William. West Germany's Role in Europe: 'Man-Mountain' or 'Semi-Gulliver'? *J. Common Market Stud.*, December 1989, *28*(2), pp. 95–117.

Bulmer-Thomas, Victor. Britain and Latin America: A Changing Relationship: Preface. In *Bulmer-Thomas, V., ed.*, 1989, pp. ix–xii.

_____. British Relations with Latin America into the 1990s. In *Bulmer-Thomas, V., ed.*, 1989, pp. 205–29.

_____. Can Regional Import Substitution and Export-Led Growth be Combined? In *Irvin, G. and Holland, S., eds.*, 1989, pp. 67–88.

Bulow, Jeremy. Empirical Evidence on Implicit Government Guarantees of Bank Foreign Loan Exposure: Comment. *Carnegie–Rochester Conf. Ser. Public Policy*, Spring 1989, *30*, pp. 163–66.

_____ and Roberts, John M. The Simple Economics of Optimal Auctions. *J. Polit. Econ.*, October 1989, *97*(5), pp. 1060–90.

_____ and Rogoff, Kenneth. A Constant Recontracting Model of Sovereign Debt. *J. Polit. Econ.*, February 1989, *97*(1), pp. 155–78.

_____ and Rogoff, Kenneth. Multilateral Negotiations for Rescheduling Developing Country Debt. In *Frenkel, J. A.; Dooley, M. P. and Wickham, P., eds.*, 1989, pp. 194–207.

_____ and Rogoff, Kenneth. Sovereign Debt: Is to Forgive to Forget? *Amer. Econ. Rev.*, March 1989, *79*(1), pp. 43–50.

Bumpass, Larry and McLanahan, Sara. Unmarried Motherhood: Recent Trends, Composition, and Black–White Differences. *Demography*, May 1989, *26*(2), pp. 279–86.

Bunce, Valerie. The Political Economy of the Soviet Bloc. In *Van Ness, P., ed.*, 1989, pp. 215–61.

Bunch, Beverly S.; Strauss, Robert P. and Banker, Rajiv D. Factors Influencing School District Financial Reporting Practices. In *Chan, J. L. and Patton, J. M., eds.*, 1989, pp. 27–56.

Bunch, Howard C. and Anderson, John E. Agricultural Property Tax Relief: Tax Credits, Tax

Rates, and Land Values. *Land Econ.*, February 1989, *65*(1), pp. 13–22.

Bundt, Thomas P.; Chiesa, Jeffrey Scott and Keating, Barry P. Common Bond Type and Credit Union Behavior. *Rev. Soc. Econ.*, Spring 1989, *47*(1), pp. 27–42.

_____ **and Schweitzer, Robert.** Deregulation, Deposit Markets, and Banks' Costs of Funds. *Financial Rev.*, August 1989, *24*(3), pp. 417–30.

Bundy, William P. The 1950s versus the 1990s. In *Hamilton, E. K., ed.*, 1989, pp. 33–81.

Bunker, John P.; Shoven, John B. and Sundberg, Jeffrey O. The Social Security Cost of Smoking. In *Wise, D. A., ed.*, 1989, pp. 231–50.

Bunn, Derek and Vlahos, Kiriakos. Evaluation of the Long-term Effects on UK Electricity Prices following Privatisation. *Fisc. Stud.*, November 1989, *10*(4), pp. 104–16.

_____ **and Vlahos, Kiriakos.** Evaluation of the Nuclear Constraint in a Privatised Electricity Supply Industry. *Fisc. Stud.*, February 1989, *10*(1), pp. 41–52.

Bunting, David. The Consumption Function "Paradox." *J. Post Keynesian Econ.*, Spring 1989, *11*(3), pp. 347–59.

_____ **and Mizruchi, Mark S.** The Transfer of Control in Large Corporations: 1905–1919. In *Tool, M. R. and Samuels, W. J., eds. (1)*, 1989, 1982, pp. 263–81.

Buongiorno, Joseph and Orr, Blair. Improving Estimates of Employment in Small Geographic Areas. *J. Econ. Soc. Meas.*, 1989, *15*(3–4), pp. 225–35.

Buono, Mark J. The Relationship between the Variability of Inflation and Stock Returns: An Empirical Investigation. *J. Finan. Res.*, Winter 1989, *12*(4), pp. 329–39.

Burbidge, Andrew. Families and the New Tax Provisions. *Australian Tax Forum*, 1989, *6*(3), pp. 347–68.

Burbidge, J. B. and Robb, A. L. Consumption, Income, and Retirement. *Can. J. Econ.*, August 1989, *22*(3), pp. 522–42.

Burchell, Brendan. The Impact on Individuals of Precariousness in the United Kingdom Labour Market. In *Rodgers, G. and Rodgers, J., eds.*, 1989, pp. 225–48.

Burdekin, Richard C. K. International Transmission of U.S. Macroeconomic Policy and the Inflation Record of Western Europe. *J. Int. Money Finance*, September 1989, *8*(3), pp. 401–23.

_____ **and Burkett, Paul G.** Conflict Inflation and the Institutionalisation of Nonactivist Monetary Policy. *Brit. Rev. Econ. Issues*, Spring 1989, *11*(24), pp. 103–20.

_____ **and Burkett, Paul G.** Conflicting Claims as a Source of Inflationary Credit Expansion in the U.S. Economy. *Manchester Sch. Econ. Soc. Stud.*, September 1989, *57*(3), pp. 213–34.

_____ **and Burkett, Paul G.** Distributional Conflict, Monetary Policy, and the Expectations-Augmented Phillips Curve. *Rivista Int. Sci.*

Econ. Com., Oct.–Nov. 1989, *36*(10–11), pp. 951–62.

_____ **and Burkett, Paul G.** Government Budget Deficits, Private Sector Pressure, and Federal Reserve Policy, 1961–1985. *Econ. Notes*, 1989, (2), pp. 229–42.

Burdett, Kenneth and Wright, Randall. Optimal Firm Size, Taxes, and Unemployment. *J. Public Econ.*, August 1989, *39*(3), pp. 275–87.

_____ **and Wright, Randall.** Unemployment Insurance and Short-Time Compensation: The Effects on Layoffs, Hours per Worker, and Wages. *J. Polit. Econ.*, December 1989, *97*(6), pp. 1479–96.

Burešová, Helena. The History and Theory of "Economics." *Czech. Econ. Pap.*, 1989, (27), pp. 95–109.

Burgat, Paul and Jeanrenaud, Claude. L'équilibre budgétaire et l'endettement des collectivités publiques locales. (Budgetary Balance and Local Government Debt. With English summary.) *Schweiz. Z. Volkswirtsch. Statist.*, December 1989, *125*(4), pp. 597–608.

Burgelman, Robert A. and Rosenbloom, Richard S. Technology Strategy: An Evolutionary Process Perspective. In *Rosenbloom, R. S. and Burgelman, R. A., eds.*, 1989, pp. 1–23.

Burger, Anton. Zur Revisionshypothese in entscheidungsorientierten Kostenrechnungen. (With English summary.) *Z. Betriebswirtshaft*, September 1989, *59*(9), pp. 957–67.

Burger, Kees and Smit, Hidde P. Long-term and Short-term Analysis of the Natural Rubber Market. *Weltwirtsch. Arch.*, 1989, *125*(4), pp. 718–47.

Burgess, David F. Lower World Energy Prices: Good News or Bad News? *Can. J. Econ.*, August 1989, *22*(3), pp. 487–502.

_____. The Social Opportunity Cost of Capital in the Presence of Labour Market Distortions. *Can. J. Econ.*, May 1989, *22*(2), pp. 245–62.

Burgess, Richard D. Major Issues and Implications of Tracing Survey Respondents. In *Kasprzyk, D., et al., eds.*, 1989, pp. 52–74.

Burgess, Simon M. Employment and Turnover in UK Manufacturing Industries, 1963–82. *Oxford Bull. Econ. Statist.*, March 1989, *51*(2), pp. 163–92.

_____ **and Dolado, Juan J.** Intertemporal Rules with Variable Speed of Adjustment: An Application to U.K. Manufacturing Employment. *Econ. J.*, June 1989, *99*(396), pp. 347–65.

Burgio, Mario B. The Reorganization of the Common Market's Savings Taxation Regime as Proposed by the European Communities Commission. *Rev. Econ. Cond. Italy*, Sept.–Dec. 1989, (3), pp. 337–61.

Burgstahler, David; Jiambalvo, James and Noreen, Eric. Changes in the Probability of Bankruptcy and Equity Value. *J. Acc. Econ.*, July 1989, *11*(2–3), pp. 207–24.

Burgstaller, André. A Classical Model of Growth, Expectations and General Equilibrium. *Economica*, August 1989, *56*(223), pp. 373–93.

Burke, J. E. Materials and Modern Technology. In *Finkelstein, J., ed.*, 1989, pp. 41–65.

Burke, James E. Europe 1992: An American Perspective. In *Frankel, A. V. and Heck, C. B.*, *eds.*, 1989, pp. 57–59.

Burke, Jonathan L. Arc-Connectedness of the Set of Efficient Allocations in Overlapping-Generations Economies. *J. Econ. Theory*, October 1989, *49*(1), pp. 179–88.

Burke, Peter. Investment and Culture in Three Seventeenth-Century Cities. In *Guarducci, A., ed.*, 1989, pp. 515–30.

Burke, S. P. and Godfrey, L. G. Some Results on the Finite Sample Significance Levels of Instrumental Variable Tests for Non-nested Models. *Econ. Letters*, December 1989, *31*(4), pp. 343–47.

Burkett, John P. and Škegro, Borislav. Capitalism, Socialism, and Productivity: An Econometric Analysis of CES and Translog Functions. *Europ. Econ. Rev.*, July 1989, *33*(6), pp. 1115–33.

Burkett, Paul G. Expectations and Marxian Crisis Theory: Notes on the Work of Paul Sweezy. *Rev. Radical Polit. Econ.*, Fall 1989, *21*(3), pp. 33–39.

_____ **and Burdekin, Richard C. K.** Conflict Inflation and the Institutionalisation of Nonactivist Monetary Policy. *Brit. Rev. Econ. Issues*, Spring 1989, *11*(24), pp. 103–20.

_____ **and Burdekin, Richard C. K.** Conflicting Claims as a Source of Inflationary Credit Expansion in the U.S. Economy. *Manchester Sch. Econ. Soc. Stud.*, September 1989, *57*(3), pp. 213–34.

_____ **and Burdekin, Richard C. K.** Distributional Conflict, Monetary Policy, and the Expectations-Augmented Phillips Curve. *Rivista Int. Sci. Econ. Com.*, Oct.–Nov. 1989, *36*(10–11), pp. 951–62.

_____ **and Burdekin, Richard C. K.** Government Budget Deficits, Private Sector Pressure, and Federal Reserve Policy, 1961–1985. *Econ. Notes*, 1989, (2), pp. 229–42.

_____ **and Wohar, Mark E.** External Shocks and Fiscal Deficits in a Monetary Model of International Reserve Determination: Honduras, 1960–83. *Appl. Econ.*, July 1989, *21*(7), pp. 921–29.

Burkhart, Jeffrey; Welsh, Richard and Beilock, Richard. Risk Permits: An Alterntive Approach to Transportation Safety Regulations. *Logist. Transp. Rev.*, September 1989, *25*(3), pp. 195–207.

Burkhauser, Richard V.; Butler, John S. and Anderson, Kathryn H. Work and Health after Retirement: A Competing Risks Model with Semiparametric Unobserved Heterogeneity. *Rev. Econ. Statist.*, February 1989, *71*(1), pp. 46–53.

_____ **and Duncan, Greg J.** Economic Risks of Gender Roles: Income Loss and Life Events over the Life Course. *Soc. Sci. Quart.*, March 1989, *70*(1), pp. 3–23.

_____ **and Finegan, T. Aldrich.** The Minimum Wage and the Poor: The End of a Relationship. *J. Policy Anal. Manage.*, Winter 1989, *8*(1), pp. 53–71.

_____ **and Quinn, Joseph F.** American Patterns of Work and Retirement. In *Schmähl, W., ed.*, 1989, pp. 91–113.

Burkhead, Jesse. The Changing Economic Role of Government. In *Samuels, W. J., ed. (I)*, 1989, pp. 41–47.

Burlacu, Veronica and Pugna, Irina. Optimizing the Reliability of Coherent Binary Systems in the Designing Stage. *Econ. Computat. Econ. Cybern. Stud. Res.*, 1989, *24*(2–3), pp. 51–60.

Burley, Peter. A von Neumann Representation of Lonergan's Production Model. *Econ. Systems Res.*, 1989, *1*(3), pp. 317–30.

Burman, Leonard E.; Randolph, William C. and Auten, Gerald E. Estimation and Interpretation of Capital Gains Realization Behavior: Evidence from Panel Data. *Nat. Tax J.*, September 1989, *42*(3), pp. 353–74.

Burmeister, E. Synthesizing the Neo-Austrian and Alternative Approaches to Capital Theory: A Survey. In *Wood, J. C. and Woods, R. N., eds., Vol. 3*, 1989, *1974*, pp. 1–62.

Burn, David L. Financial Institutions and Tax Reform: Comment. In *Mintz, J. and Whalley, J., eds.*, 1989, pp. 250–54.

Burnell, Stephen. The Economics of Missing Markets, Information, and Games: Sunspots. In *Hahn, F., ed.*, 1989, pp. 394–409.

Burnett, William B. and Kovacic, William E. Reform of United States Weapons Acquisitions Policy: Competition, Teaming Agreements, and Dual-Sourcing. *Yale J. Regul.*, Summer 1989, *6*(2), pp. 249–317.

Burney, Nadeem A. A Macro-economic Analysis of the Impact of Workers' Remittances on Pakistan's Economy. In *Amjad, R., ed.*, 1989, pp. 197–222.

Burniaux, Jean-Marc. Intersectoral Effects of CAP Trade Liberalization. In *Tarditi, S., et al., eds.*, 1989, pp. 47–69.

_____ ; **van der Mensbrugghe, Dominique and Martin, John P.** How Robust Are WALRAS Results? *OECD Econ. Stud.*, Winter 1989–1990, (13), pp. 173–204.

_____ , **et al.** WALRAS—A Multi-sector, Multicountry Applied General Equilibrium Model for Quantifying the Economy-Wide Effects of Agricultural Policies. *OECD Econ. Stud.*, Winter 1989–1990, (13), pp. 69–102.

Burns, Ailsa; Russell, Graeme and Goodnow, Jacqueline. Australian Families: Pictures and Interpretations. In *Hancock, K., ed.*, 1989, pp. 23–43.

Burns, E. Bradford. Establishing the Patterns of Progress and Poverty in Central America. In *Martin, M. T. and Kandal, T. R., eds.*, 1989, pp. 202–15.

Burns, Lee and Woellner, Robin. International Information Flows—The Tax Implications. *Australian Tax Forum*, 1989, *6*(2), pp. 143–200.

Burns, Malcolm R. New Evidence on Predatory Price Cutting. *Managerial Dec. Econ.*, December 1989, *10*(4), pp. 327–30.

Burra, Neera. Out of Sight, Out of Mind: Working Girls in India. *Int. Lab. Rev.*, 1989, *128*(5), pp. 651–60.

Burrell, Alison. The Demand for Fertiliser in the United Kingdom. *J. Agr. Econ.*, January 1989, 40(1), pp. 1–20.

Burrows, Colin and Brown, Kaye. Bogged Down in Marginal Analysis: Neuhauser and Lewicki Revisited. In *Smith, C. S., ed.*, 1989, pp. 91–120.

_____; **Brown, Kaye and Ngui, Michael.** Health Insurance Choice: An Econometric Analysis of A.B.S. Health and Health Insurance Surveys. In *Smith, C. S., ed.*, 1989, pp. 172–94.

Burrows, Paul. Getting a Stranglehold with the Eminent Domain Clause. *Int. Rev. Law Econ.*, December 1989, 9(2), pp. 129–47.

Burt, Oscar R. Testing for the Length of a Distributed Lag with a Differencing Transformation. *Econ. Letters*, 1989, 29(3), pp. 221–23.

_____ **and Taylor, C. Robert.** Reduction of State Variable Dimension in Stochastic Dynamic Optimization Models Which Use Time-Series Data. *Western J. Agr. Econ.*, December 1989, 14(2), pp. 213–22.

Burtless, Gary. A Dynamic Programming Model of Retirement Behavior: Comment. In *Wise, D. A., ed.*, 1989, pp. 398–403.

_____ **and Aaron, Henry J.** Fiscal Policy and the Dynamic Inconsistency of Social Security Forecasts. *Amer. Econ. Rev.*, May 1989, 79(2), pp. 91–96.

_____; **Aaron, Henry J. and Bosworth, Barry P.** How Social Security Affects the Deficit. In *Bosworth, B. P., et al.*, 1989, pp. 139–43.

Burton, Daniel. International Competition and American Jobs. In *Bawden, D. L. and Skidmore, F., eds.*, 1989, pp. 227–48.

Burton, Ian. Human Dimensions of Global Change: Toward a Research Agenda. In *Rosenberg, N. J., et al., eds.*, 1989, pp. 159–65.

Burton, John; Torrance, Thomas S. and Addison, John T. Causation, Social Science and Sir John Hicks. In *Wood, J. C. and Woods, R. N., eds.*, Vol. 4, 1989, 1984, pp. 27–37.

Burton, John R.; Mayer, Robert N. and Zick, Cathleen D. Consumer Representation and Local Telephone Rates. *J. Cons. Aff.*, Winter 1989, 23(2), pp. 267–84.

Burton, Jonathan S. and Banerjee, Avijit. Lot Sizing and Work-in-Process Inventories in Single Stage Production Systems. In *Gulledge, T. R., Jr. and Litteral, L. A., eds.*, 1989, pp. 283–97.

Busch, Axel. Telecommunications and the Scope of the Market in Services: Comment. In *Giersch, H., ed.*, 1989, pp. 166–72.

Busch, Klaus. Nation-State and European Integration: Structural Problems in the Process of Economic Integration within the European Community. In *Gottdiener, M. and Komninos, N., eds.*, 1989, pp. 123–53.

Buse, A. Efficient Estimation of a Structural Equation with First Order Autocorrelation. *J. Quant. Econ.*, January 1989, 5(1), pp. 59–72.

_____. Hicks, Lutz, Meiselman and the Expectations Theory. In *Wood, J. C. and Woods, R. N., eds., Vol. 2*, 1989, 1970, pp. 106–20.

Buse, Rueben C. What Is America Eating and What Is Happening to Meat Consumption? In *Buse, R. C., ed.*, 1989, pp. 18–56.

_____; **Alvarez, Antonio and Cox, Thomas A.** Effect of Demographics on Changes in At-Home Meat Consumption. In *Buse, R. C., ed.*, 1989, pp. 217–42.

_____ **and Haidacher, Richard C.** The Economics of Meat Demand: Introduction. In *Buse, R. C., ed.*, 1989, pp. 1–5.

Bush, Paul D. The Concept of "Progressive" Institutional Change and Its Implications for Economic Policy Formation. *J. Econ. Issues*, June 1989, 23(2), pp. 455–64.

_____. Institutionalist Methodology and Hermeneutics: A Comment. *J. Econ. Issues*, December 1989, 23(4), pp. 1159–72.

Bushkin, Arthur A. The Use of Communications: A Vehicle for International Cooperation and Development. In *Jussawalla, M.; Okuma, T. and Araki, T., eds.*, 1989, pp. 150–53.

Bushman, Robert; Dickhaut, John and Kanodia, Chandra. Escalation Errors and the Sunk Cost Effect: An Explanation Based on Reputation and Information Asymmetries. *J. Acc. Res.*, Spring 1989, 27(1), pp. 59–77.

Busiahn, Thomas R. The Development of State/ Tribal Co-management of Wisconsin Fisheries. In *Pinkerton, E., ed.*, 1989, pp. 170–85.

Buss, James A.; Peterson, G. Paul and Nantz, Kathryn A. A Comparison of Distributive Justice in OECD Countries. *Rev. Soc. Econ.*, Spring 1989, 47(1), pp. 1–14.

Bussmann, Johannes. Die Bestimmung der Zinsstruktur am deutschen Kapitalmarkt. Eine empirische Untersuchung für den Zeitraum 1978 bis 1986. (Determination of the Interest Rate Regime on the German Capital Market—An Empirical Study for the Period 1978/1986. With English summary.) *Kredit Kapital*, 1989, 22(1), pp. 117–37.

_____. Tests verschiedener Zinsänderungsrisikomasse mit Daten des deutschen Rentenmarktes. (With English summary.) *Z. Betriebswirtshaft*, July 1989, 59(7), pp. 747–65.

Bustillo, Ines and Barrett, Nancy J. Symposium on the Slowdown in Productivity Growth: Comment. *J. Econ. Perspectives*, Summer 1989, 3(3), pp. 179–81.

Butaye, I.; Srinivasan, V. and Abeele, P. Vanden. The Factor Structure of Multidimensional Response to Marketing Stimuli: A Comparison of Two Approaches. *Marketing Sci.*, Winter 1989, 8(1), pp. 78–88.

Butcher, Walter R. and Barnard, Charles H. Landowner Characteristics: A Basis for Locational Decisions in the Urban Fringe. *Amer. J. Agr. Econ.*, August 1989, 71(3), pp. 679–84.

_____ **and Elder, Eric E.** Including the Economic Impact of Cost Paying in Regional Input–Output Analysis. *Western J. Agr. Econ.*, July 1989, 14(1), pp. 78–84.

Butel, Paul. Succès et déclin du commerce colonial français, de la Révolution à la Restauration. (Growth and Decline of French Colonial Trade [1793–1830]. With English summary.) *Revue*

Écon., November 1989, *40*(6), pp. 1079–96.

Butenko, A. P. On the Nature of Property under the Conditions of Real Socialism. In *Yanowitch, M., ed.*, 1989, *1988*, pp. 295–307.

Butler, J. R. G. The Economics of Australian Hospitals: Forum: On the Use of Inter-governmental Grants to Provide Universal Hospital Insurance. In *Smith, C. S., ed.*, 1989, pp. 305–07.

_____. The Effects of Community-Based Facilities on the Use of Hospital Beds in the Treatment of Alcohol-Related Problems in Ontario 1972–1985: Commentary. In *Smith, C. S., ed.*, 1989, pp. 262–64.

_____. Factors Affecting the Demand for Ambulance Services. In *Butler, J. R. G. and Doessel, D. P., eds.*, 1989, *1981*, pp. 238–49.

_____. A Model for Prioritising Therapeutic Devices for Evaluation. In *Smith, C. S., ed.*, 1989, pp. 64–87.

_____. The Queensland Public Hospital System—An Economic Perspective. In *Butler, J. R. G. and Doessel, D. P., eds.*, 1989, *1987*, pp. 303–21.

_____ **and Doessel, D. P.** The Australian Health Industry: Structure and Sources of Funds. In *Butler, J. R. G. and Doessel, D. P., eds.*, 1989, pp. 63–72.

_____ **and Doessel, D. P.** Health Economics: Australian Readings: General Introduction. In *Butler, J. R. G. and Doessel, D. P., eds.*, 1989, pp. xi–xvi.

Butler, John S.; Anderson, Kathryn H. and Burkhauser, Richard V. Work and Health after Retirement: A Competing Risks Model with Semiparametric Unobserved Heterogeneity. *Rev. Econ. Statist.*, February 1989, *71*(1), pp. 46–53.

_____; **Quddus, Munir and Liu, Jin-Tan.** Money, Prices, and Causality: The Chinese Hyperinflation, 1946–49, Reexamined. *J. Macroecon.*, Summer 1989, *11*(3), pp. 447–53.

Butler, Kenneth D. A Comparative Analysis of Cross-Cultural-Interface Management: The United States and Japan: Commentary. In *Hayashi, K., ed.*, 1989, pp. 79–86.

Butler, Michael R. and McNertney, Edward M. The Allocation of Death in the Vietnam War: Comment. *Southern Econ. J.*, April 1989, *55*(4), pp. 1029–33.

Butler, Nicholas. China and GATT. In *[Marjolin, R.]*, 1989, pp. 177–90.

Butler, Richard J.; Heckman, James J. and Payner, Brook S. The Impact of the Economy and the State on the Economic Status of Blacks: A Study of South Carolina. In *Galenson, D. W., ed.*, 1989, pp. 231–346.

_____ **and McDonald, James B.** Using Incomplete Moments to Measure Inequality. *J. Econometrics*, September 1989, *42*(1), pp. 109–19.

Butler, Richard V. and Huston, John H. How Contestable Are Airline Markets? *Atlantic Econ. J.*, June 1989, *17*(2), pp. 27–35.

_____ **and Huston, John H.** Merger Mania and Airline Fares. *Eastern Econ. J.*, Jan.–March 1989, *15*(1), pp. 7–16.

Butler, Stephen A. and Newman, Harry A. Agency Control Mechanism Effectiveness and Decision Making in an Executive's Final Year with a Firm. *J. Inst. Theoretical Econ.*, September 1989, *145*(3), pp. 451–64.

Butlin, N. G. The Palaeoeconomic History of Aboriginal Migration. *Australian Econ. Hist. Rev.*, September 1989, *29*(2), pp. 3–57.

_____ **and Gregory, Robert G.** Trevor Winchester Swan: 1918–1989. *Econ. Rec.*, December 1989, *65*(191), pp. 369–77.

Butt, Abdul Rauf and Khan, Mohammad Nawaz. Who Receives the Benefits of Public Higher Education in Pakistan? *Pakistan Econ. Soc. Rev.*, Summer 1989, *27*(1), pp. 1–15.

Buttel, Frederick H. Resources, Institutions, and Political–Economic Processes: Beyond Allegory and Allegation. *Soc. Sci. Quart.*, June 1989, *70*(2), pp. 468–70.

_____. The U.S. Farm Crisis and the Restructuring of American Agriculture: Domestic and International Dimensions. In *Goodman, D. and Redclift, M., eds.*, 1989, pp. 46–83.

_____ **and Belsky, Jill.** Biotechnology, Plant Breeding, and Intellectual Property: Social and Ethical Dimensions. In *Weil, V. and Snapper, J. W., eds.*, 1989, pp. 110–32.

den Butter, Frank A. G. and van de Gevel, Frans J. J. S. Prediction of the Netherlands' Money Stock. *De Economist*, 1989, *137*(2), pp. 173–201.

Butterfield, David W. and Chami, Saade N. The Implications of Myopic Policy-Making for Macroeconomic Performance. *Int. J. Forecasting*, 1989, *5*(1), pp. 49–58.

_____; **Kubursi, Atif A. and Abou-Ezze, P.** The Economic Case for the Emergence of New Producers of Petrochemicals in the Hydrocarbon-Rich Developing Countries. *Industry Devel.*, June 1989, (27), pp. 31–43.

Butters, Gerard R. Equilibrium Distributions of Sales and Advertising Prices. In *Diamond, P. and Rothschild, M., eds.*, 1989, *1977*, pp. 495–513.

Büttler, Hans-Jürg. An Expository Note on the Valuation of Foreign Exchange Options. *J. Int. Money Finance*, June 1989, *8*(2), pp. 295–304.

Button, Kenneth J. Economic Theories of Regulation and the Regulation of the United Kingdom's Bus Industry. *Antitrust Bull.*, Fall 1989, *34*(3), pp. 489–515.

_____. Liberalising the Canadian Scheduled Aviation Market. *Fisc. Stud.*, November 1989, *10*(4), pp. 19–52.

_____ **and Fleming, Michael.** Regulatory Reform in the UK. In *Button, K. and Swann, D., eds.*, 1989, pp. 79–103.

_____ **and Pearce, David W.** Infrastructure Restoration as a Tool for Stimulating Urban Renewal—The Glasgow Canal. *Urban Stud.*, December 1989, *26*(6), pp. 559–71.

_____ **and Swann, Dennis.** European Community Airlines—Deregulation and Its Problems. *J. Common Market Stud.*, June 1989, *27*(4), pp. 259–82.

_____ **and Swann, Dennis.** Regulatory Reform:

The Way Forward. In *Button, K. and Swann, D., eds.*, 1989, pp. 321–32.

Butz, Earl L. The Family Farm: Shall We Freeze It in Place or Free It to Adjust? In *Horwich, G. and Lynch, G. J., eds.*, 1989, pp. 279–84.

Buvinić, Mayra. Investing in Poor Women: The Psychology of Donor Support. *World Devel.*, July 1989, *17*(7), pp. 1045–57.

Buyst, Erik and Van der Wee, Herman. Europe and the World Economy during the Inter-war Period. In *[Fischer, W.]*, 1989, pp. 239–59.

Buzacott, J. A. Flexible Models of Flexible Manufacturing Systems. In *Archetti, F.; Lucertini, M. and Serafini, P., eds.*, 1989, pp. 115–22.

_____. Modelling Flexible Manufacturing Systems. In *Archetti, F.; Lucertini, M. and Serafini, P., eds.*, 1989, *1984*, pp. 123–34.

Buzdalov, I. Cooperation and Democratic Reforms in the Economy. In *Yanowitch, M., ed.*, 1989, *1987*, pp. 269–79.

Buzgalin, A. and Kolganov, A. How Was the "Administrative System" Created? *Prob. Econ.*, September 1989, *32*(5), pp. 35–52.

_____ and Kolganov, A. Planning without Bureaucratic Administration. In *Yanowitch, M., ed.*, 1989, *1987*, pp. 53–57.

Buzzacchi, Luigi; Colombo, Massimo G. and Brioschi, Francesco. Risk Capital Financing and the Separation of Ownership and Control in Business Groups. *J. Banking Finance*, September 1989, *13*(4–5), pp. 747–72.

Buzzi, Roberto. The Use of the Logical Programming Language PROLOG as a Classification Method. In *Opitz, O., ed.*, 1989, pp. 377–88.

Byatt, Ian. The Record of Tax Reform in Great Britain and Its Contribution to the Supply Side. In *Fels, G. and von Furstenberg, G. M., eds.*, 1989, pp. 355–76.

Bye, Barry V. and Riley, Gerald F. Eliminating the Medicare Waiting Period for Social Security Disabled-Worker Beneficiaries. *Soc. Sec. Bull.*, May 1989, *52*(5), pp. 2–15.

Byerlee, Derek. Bread and Butter Issues in Ecuadorian Food Policy: A Comparative Advantage Approach. *World Devel.*, October 1989, *17*(10), pp. 1585–96.

Byers, C. Randall and Steinhorst, R. Kirk. An Alternative Interpretation of Freedman's Nonresponse Case Study: Reply. *J. Bus. Econ. Statist.*, January 1989, *7*(1), pp. 33.

_____ and Steinhorst, R. Kirk. An Alternative Interpretation of Freedman's Nonresponse Case Study. *J. Bus. Econ. Statist.*, January 1989, *7*(1), pp. 27–28.

Byrd, William A. Plan and Market in the Chinese Economy: A Simple General Equilibrium Model. *J. Compar. Econ.*, June 1989, *13*(2), pp. 177–204.

Byrne, Mark J. and Maloney, Kevin J. An Equilibrium Debt Option Pricing Model in Discrete Time. *J. Banking Finance*, July 1989, *13*(3), pp. 421–42.

Byrnes, Patricia and Valdmanis, Vivian. Variable Cost Frontiers and Efficiency: An Investigation of Labor Costs in Hospitals. In *Gulledge, T.*

R., Jr. and Litteral, L. A., eds., 1989, pp. 160–75.

Byron, R. P. and Takahashi, H. An Analysis of the Effect of Schooling, Experience and Sex on Earnings in the Government and Private Sectors of Urban Java. *Bull. Indonesian Econ. Stud.*, April 1989, *25*(1), pp. 105–17.

Byron, William J. On the Protection and Promotion of the Right to Food: An Ethical Reflection. In *Helmuth, J. W. and Johnson, S. R., eds., Vol. 1*, 1989, pp. 108–22.

Byrt, William. Conclusion: Achievement and the Future. In *Byrt, W., ed.*, 1989, pp. 210–26.

_____. Management Education. In *Byrt, W., ed.*, 1989, pp. 1–17.

_____. Management Education in Australia. In *Byrt, W., ed.*, 1989, pp. 78–103.

Caballero Sanz, Francisco; Ortí Lahoz, Angel and Orts Rios, Vicente. Direct Foreign Investment and International Trade in Spain. In *Yannopoulos, G. N., ed.*, 1989, pp. 227–53.

Caballeros, Rómulo. Central America's External Debt: Past Growth and Projected Burden. In *Irvin, G. and Holland, S., eds.*, 1989, pp. 111–38.

Cabeza, Felix; McMullen, B. Starr and Martin, Michael V. The Impacts of Transportation Deregulation on Wheat Shipments in the Pacific Northwest. *Western J. Agr. Econ.*, December 1989, *14*(2), pp. 253–60.

Cabezas, Mabel and Meller, Patricio. Estimación de las elasticidades ingreso y precio de las importaciones chilenas 1974–1987. (Income and Price Elasticities of Chilean Imports 1974–1987. With English summary.) *Colección Estud. CIEPLAN*, June 1989, (26), pp. 127–70.

Cable, John and Wilson, Nicholas. Profit-Sharing and Productivity: An Analysis of UK Engineering Firms. *Econ. J.*, June 1989, *99*(396), pp. 366–75.

Cabral, Luis M. B. A Simple Proof of the No-Retraction Theorem. *Economia (Portugal)*, October 1989, *13*(3), pp. 389–94.

_____. Política de preços do sector das telecomunicações: Uma análise de equilíbrio geral. (With English summary.) *Economia (Portugal)*, January 1989, *13*(1), pp. 82–113.

Cabrera, E. The Medieval Origins of the Great Landed Estates of the Guadalquivir Valley. *Econ. Hist. Rev.*, 2nd Ser., November 1989, *42*(4), pp. 465–83.

Cáceres, Luis René and Irvin, George. The Reconstruction of the CACM and European Cooperation. In *Irvin, G. and Holland, S., eds.*, 1989, pp. 163–88.

Caffarelli, Luis A. Free Boundary Problems: A Survey. In *Giaquinta, M., ed.*, 1989, pp. 31–61.

Cagan, Phillip. Money-Income Causality—A Critical Review of the Literature since *A Monetary History*. In *[Schwartz, A. J.]*, 1989, pp. 117–51.

Cage, Robert. Spending Differences across Occupational Fields. *Mon. Lab. Rev.*, December 1989, *112*(12), pp. 33–43.

Çağli, Uğur and Durukan, Levent. Sex Role Portrayals in Turkish TV Advertising: Some Preliminary Findings. *METU*, 1989, *16*(1–2), pp. 153–75.

Cahen, Alfred. Africa: Development under Duress. In *Cerami, C. A., ed.*, 1989, pp. 129–51.

Cahill, Carmel and Legg, Wilfrid. Estimation of Agricultural Assistance Using Producer and Consumer Subsidy Equivalents: Theory and Practice. *OECD Econ. Stud.*, Winter 1989–1990, (13), pp. 13–43.

Cahill, Sean; Surry, Yves and McClatchy, Don. Exchange Rates and Multilateral Free Trade in Agriculture. *Can. J. Agr. Econ.*, Part 2, December 1989, *37*(4), pp. 993–1007.

Cahuc, Pierre. Modes de formation des salaires et stagflation: Une analyse en termes de théorie des jeux. (Centralized versus Decentralized Wage Setting: Inflation and Unemployment Implications. With English summary.) *Revue Écon.*, May 1989, *40*(3), pp. 421–40.

_____ and Bauer, Anne. Conflits, inefficience du capitalisme et politique économique. (Conflict, Dynamic Inefficiency of Capitalism and Economic Policy. With English summary.) *Revue Écon.*, July 1989, *40*(4), pp. 621–47.

Caiden, Naomi. Budgeting for Time-Bombs: Recent General Accounting Office Reports on the Crisis of the Nuclear Weapons Complex and the Savings and Loan Industry. *Public Budg. Finance*, Winter 1989, *9*(4), pp. 83–93.

_____. National Economic Commission: Another View. *Public Budg. Finance*, Autumn 1989, *9*(3), pp. 74–75.

Cain, M. and Al-Badri, K. S. An Inter-sectoral, Inter-regional Dynamic Model for Production and Trade of the GCC Region. *Middle East Bus. Econ. Rev.*, January 1989, *1*(1), pp. 3–10.

Cain, Pamela Stone. Empirical Consequences of Comparable Worth: Discussion. In *Hill, M. A. and Killingsworth, M. R., eds.*, 1989, pp. 112–16.

Cain, Stephen Alexis. Strategic Nuclear Forces: Unrealistic Planning. *Public Budg. Finance*, Winter 1989, *9*(4), pp. 94–108.

Caire, Guy. Analyse micro-économique du travail féminin: Apports et apories. (With English summary.) *Revue Écon. Politique*, May–June 1989, *99*(3), pp. 446–65.

_____. Atypical Wage Employment in France. In *Rodgers, G. and Rodgers, J., eds.*, 1989, pp. 75–108.

Cairncross, Alec. Argentina's Nationalism: Myth or Reality?: Comment. In *di Tella, G. and Dornbusch, R., eds.*, 1989, pp. 56–58.

_____. In Praise of Economic History. *Econ. Hist. Rev.*, 2nd Ser., May 1989, *42*(2), pp. 173–85.

_____. The Role of the Economist in Government: An International Perspective: The United Kingdom. In *Pechman, J. A., ed.*, 1989, pp. 25–46.

Cairns, Robert D. Dynamic Rent Seeking. *J. Public Econ.*, August 1989, *39*(3), pp. 315–34.

_____. A Note on MacLeod's Treatment of Contestability. *Can. J. Econ.*, May 1989, *22*(2), pp. 434–37.

Calcoen, Francis; Eeckhoudt, Louis and Sneessens, Henri. L'épargne de précaution: Une analyse géométrique. (Precautionary Saving: A Geometric Analysis. With English summary.) *Revue Écon.*, January 1989, *40*(1), pp. 21–34.

Calder, Kent E. Multinational Firms and Global Information Industry Development. In *Jussawalla, M.; Okuma, T. and Araki, T., eds.*, 1989, pp. 301–04.

Caldwell, Bruce J. Austrians and Institutionalists: The Historical Origins of Their Shared Characteristics. In *Samuels, W. J., ed. (II)*, 1989, pp. 91–100.

_____. The Trend of Methodological Thinking. *Ricerche Econ.*, Jan.–June 1989, *43*(1–2), pp. 8–20.

Caldwell, John C. and Caldwell, Pat. Changing Health Conditions. In *Reich, M. R. and Marui, E., eds.*, 1989, pp. 23–36.

_____; Caldwell, Pat and Quiggin, Pat. The Social Context of AIDS in Sub-Saharan Africa. *Population Devel. Rev.*, June 1989, *15*(2), pp. 185–234.

Caldwell, Pat and Caldwell, John C. Changing Health Conditions. In *Reich, M. R. and Marui, E., eds.*, 1989, pp. 23–36.

_____; Quiggin, Pat and Caldwell, John C. The Social Context of AIDS in Sub-Saharan Africa. *Population Devel. Rev.*, June 1989, *15*(2), pp. 185–234.

Calhoun, Charles. Estimating the Distribution of Desired Family Size and Excess Fertility. *J. Human Res.*, Fall 1989, *24*(4), pp. 709–24.

Calingaert, Michael. What Europe 1992 Means for U.S. Business. *Bus. Econ.*, October 1989, *24*(4), pp. 30–36.

Calkins, Peter H. Toward a Unified Theory of Economic Development. *Can. J. Agr. Econ.*, Part 2, December 1989, *37*(4), pp. 913–31.

_____ and Apedaile, Leonard P. Development Theory and Chinese Agricultural Development. *Can. J. Agr. Econ.*, Part 2, December 1989, *37*(4), pp. 953–74.

Callaghan, John. Fabian Socialism, Democracy and the State. In *Duncan, G., ed.*, 1989, pp. 159–80.

Callaghan, Joseph H.; Mittelstaedt, H. Fred and Yardley, James A. Auditors' Incompatible Economic Incentives. In *Gangolly, J., ed.*, 1989, pp. 57–64.

Callaghy, Thomas M. Toward State Capability and Embedded Liberalism in the Third World: Lessons for Adjustment. In *Nelson, J. M., ed.*, 1989, pp. 115–38.

Callahan, Carolyn M. and Mohr, Rosanne M. The Determinants of Systematic Risk: A Synthesis. *Financial Rev.*, May 1989, *24*(2), pp. 157–81.

Callahan, Colleen M. EC Enlargement and U.S.–EC Trade Frictions. In *Greenaway, D.; Hyclak, T. and Thornton, R. J., eds.*, 1989, pp. 153–66.

Callan, Scott J. and Thomas, Janet M. Constant

and Morgado, Hugo. Labour Market Performance and Urban Poverty in Panama. In *Rodgers, G., ed.*, 1989, pp. 97–116.

Cambria, Rocco, et al. Local Implementation of Supported Employment: Three Programs Making It Work. In *Wehman, P. and Kregel, J., eds.*, 1989, pp. 177–205.

Camdessus, Michel. The Role of the IMF in a Challenging World Economy. *Nationaløkon. Tidsskr.*, 1989, *127*(2), pp. 236–43.

_____. Third World Debt: The Next Phase: Status, Issues, and Prospects: Comment. In *Fried, E. R. and Trezise, P. H., eds.*, 1989, pp. 23–25.

Camerer, Colin F. An Experimental Test of Several Generalized Utility Theories. *J. Risk Uncertainty*, April 1989, *2*(1), pp. 61–104.

_____. Bubbles and Fads in Asset Prices. *J. Econ. Surveys*, 1989, *3*(1), pp. 3–41.

_____. Does the Basketball Market Believe in the 'Hot Hand'? *Amer. Econ. Rev.*, December 1989, *79*(5), pp. 1257–61.

_____ **and Kunreuther, Howard.** Decision Processes for Low Probability Events: Policy Implications. *J. Policy Anal. Manage.*, Fall 1989, *8*(4), pp. 565–92.

_____ **and Kunreuther, Howard.** Experimental Markets for Insurance. *J. Risk Uncertainty*, September 1989, *2*(3), pp. 265–99.

_____; **Loewenstein, George and Weber, Martin.** The Curse of Knowledge in Economic Settings: An Experimental Analysis. *J. Polit. Econ.*, October 1989, *97*(5), pp. 1232–54.

Cameron, Rondo. The Growth of International Banking to 1914. In *[Fischer, W.]*, 1989, pp. 191–219.

Cameron, Samuel. An Empirical Analysis of the Determinants of Cigarette Tax Rates. *Econ. Scelte Pubbliche/J. Public Finance Public Choice*, Jan.–Aug. 1989, *7*(1–2), pp. 45–54.

_____. Determinants of the Prison Population: An Empirical Analysis. *Int. J. Soc. Econ.*, 1989, *16*(8), pp. 17–25.

_____. On the Welfare Economics of Capital Punishment. *Australian Econ. Pap.*, December 1989, *28*(53), pp. 253–66.

_____. Police Cost Function Estimates for England and Wales. *Appl. Econ.*, October 1989, *21*(10), pp. 1279–89.

_____. A Subjectivist Perspective on the Economics of Crime. In *Rothbard, M. N. and Block, W., eds.*, 1989, pp. 31–43.

_____. The Unacceptability of Money as a Gift and Its Status as a Medium of Exchange. *J. Econ. Psych.*, June 1989, *10*(2), pp. 253–55.

_____. Victim Compensation Does Not Increase the Supply of Crime. *J. Econ. Stud.*, 1989, *16*(4), pp. 52–59.

Cameron, Trudy Ann and Huppert, Daniel D. OLS versus ML Estimation of Non-market Resource Values with Payment Card Interval Data. *J. Environ. Econ. Manage.*, November 1989, *17*(3), pp. 230–46.

Camilleri, Arthur; Lester, Michael and Elek, Andrew. Innovation and Technological Change in Australia: Problems and Prospects. In *[Gruen, F. H.]*, 1989, pp. 190–209.

Cammarota, Mark T. The Impact of Unseasonable Weather on Housing Starts. *Amer. Real Estate Urban Econ. Assoc. J.*, Fall 1989, *17*(3), pp. 300–313.

Campan, Eliane and Grimaud, André. Lc syndrome hollandais. (With English summary.) *Revue Écon. Politique*, Nov.–Dec. 1989, *99*(6), pp. 810–34.

Campbell, Adrian; Currie, Wendy and Warner, Malcolm. Innovation, Skills and Training: Micro-electronics and Manpower in the United Kingdom and West Germany. In *Hirst, P. and Zeitlin, J., eds.*, 1989, pp. 133–54.

Campbell, Bonnie K. Indebtedness and Adjustment Lending in the Ivory Coast: Elements for a Structural Critique. In *Campbell, B. K., ed.*, 1989, pp. 129–62.

_____. Political Dimensions of the International Debt Crisis: Introduction. In *Campbell, B. K., ed.*, 1989, pp. 1–14.

_____ **and Loxley, John.** Structural Adjustment in Africa: Introduction. In *Campbell, B. K. and Loxley, J., eds.*, 1989, pp. 1–11.

Campbell, Carl M., III. Sectoral Wage Rigidity in the Canadian and French Economies. *Europ. Econ. Rev.*, December 1989, *33*(9), pp. 1727–49.

Campbell, Charles A. Differential Cyclic Employment Response in a Subregion. *Rev. Reg. Stud.*, Fall 1989, *19*(3), pp. 31–36.

Campbell, Donald E. Arrow's Theorem for Economic Environments and Effective Social Preferences. *Soc. Choice Welfare*, October 1989, *6*(4), pp. 325–29.

_____. Equilibrium and Efficiency with Property Rights and Local Consumption Externalities. *Soc. Choice Welfare*, July 1989, *6*(3), pp. 189–203.

_____. Wilson's Theorem for Economic Environments and Continuous Social Preferences. *Soc. Choice Welfare*, October 1989, *6*(4), pp. 315–23.

Campbell, H. F. Fishery Buy-Back Programmes and Economic Welfare. *Australian J. Agr. Econ.*, April 1989, *33*(1), pp. 20–31.

_____ **and Lindner, R. K.** A Note on Optimal Effort in the Maldivian Tuna Fishery. *Marine Resource Econ.*, 1989, *6*(2), pp. 173–76.

Campbell, J. K. Village Friendship and Patronage. In *Heidenheimer, A. J.; Johnston, M. and LeVine, V. T., eds.*, 1989, pp. 327–37.

Campbell, John L. Corporations, Collective Organization, and the State: Industry Response to the Accident at Three Mile Island. *Soc. Sci. Quart.*, September 1989, *70*(3), pp. 650–66.

Campbell, John Y. Finance Theory and the Term Structure: A Comment. *Carnegie–Rochester Conf. Ser. Public Policy*, Autumn 1989, *31*, pp. 177–84.

_____ **and Deaton, Angus S.** Why Is Consumption So Smooth? *Rev. Econ. Stud.*, July 1989, *56*(3), pp. 357–73.

_____ **and Mankiw, N. Gregory.** Consumption, Income, and Interest Rates: Reinterpreting the Time Series Evidence. In *Blanchard, O. J. and Fischer, S., eds.*, 1989, pp. 185–216.

_____ **and Mankiw, N. Gregory.** International Evidence on the Persistence of Economic Fluctuations. *J. Monet. Econ.*, March 1989, *23*(2), pp. 319–33.

_____ **and Shiller, Robert J.** The Dividend Ratio Model and Small Sample Bias: A Monte Carlo Study. *Econ. Letters*, 1989, *29*(4), pp. 325–31.

Campbell, M. Karen and Donner, Allan. Classification Efficiency of Multinomial Logistic Regression Relative to Ordinal Logistic Regression. *J. Amer. Statist. Assoc.*, June 1989, *84*(406), pp. 587–91.

Campbell, Nigel C. G. Network Analysis of a Global Capital Equipment Industry. In *Hallén, L. and Johanson, J.*, eds., 1989, pp. 75–91.

Campbell, Tim. Environmental Dilemmas and the Urban Poor. In *Leonard, H. J.*, ed., 1989, pp. 165–87.

Campbell, Tim S.; Chan, Yuk-Shee and Marino, Anthony M. Incentive Contracts for Managers Who Discover and Manage Investment Projects. *J. Econ. Behav. Organ.*, December 1989, *12*(3), pp. 353–64.

Campos, Jose Edgardo L. Legislative Institutions, Lobbying, and the Endogenous Choice of Regulatory Instruments: A Political Economy Approach to Instrument Choice. *J. Law, Econ., Organ.*, Fall 1989, *5*(2), pp. 333–53.

Canak, William L. Debt, Austerity, and Latin America in the New International Division of Labor. In *Canak, W. L.*, ed., 1989, pp. 9–27.

_____. Lost Promises: Debt, Austerity, and Development in Latin America: Introduction. In *Canak, W. L.*, ed., 1989, pp. 1–5.

_____ **and Levi, Danilo.** Social Costs of Adjustment in Latin America. In *Weeks, J. F.*, ed., 1989, pp. 143–63.

Canarella, Giorgio and Pollard, Stephen K. Unanticipated Monetary Growth, Output, and the Price Level in Latin America: An Empirical Investigation. *J. Devel. Econ.*, April 1989, *30*(2), pp. 345–58.

Canavan, T. Christopher. Annual Review of Nations: Year 1988: Venezuela. In *Haberman, L. and Sacks, P. M.*, eds., 1989, pp. 377–92.

_____ **and Sacks, Paul M.** Safe Passage through Dire Straits: Managing an Orderly Exit from the Debt Crisis. In *Weeks, J. F.*, ed., 1989, pp. 75–87.

Cancelo de la Torre, José Ramón and Espasa Terrades, Antoni. Modelos univariantes en el análisis económico. (With English summary.) *Revista Española Econ.*, 1989, *6*(1–2), pp. 85–107.

Candela, Guido and Denicolò, Vincenzo. Firms' Location and the Central Business District. *Rivista Int. Sci. Econ. Com.*, August 1989, *36*(8), pp. 703–22.

Candemir, Yücel. Towards Advancing Cooperation in the Region. In *Candemir, Y.*, ed., 1989, pp. 25–38.

Caniglia, Alan and Flaherty, Sean. Unionism and Income Inequality: Comment. *Ind. Lab. Relat. Rev.*, October 1989, *43*(1), pp. 131–37.

Canlar, Mehmet and Man, Chand Maloo. Assessing the Further Impact of College-Level Accounting Study on Student Performance in the MBA-Level Managerial Accounting Course. In *Schwartz, B. N.*, ed., 1989, pp. 129–39.

Canlas, Dante B. and Tan, Edita A. Migrant's Saving Remittance and Labour Supply Behaviour: The Philippines Case. In *Amjad, R.*, ed., 1989, pp. 223–54.

Cannadine, David. The Last Hanoverian Sovereign?: The Victorian Monarchy in Historical Perspective, 1688–1988. In *[Stone, L.]*, 1989, pp. 127–65.

Cannell, Charles F. and Miller, Peter V. A Study of Experimental Techniques for Telephone Interviewing. In *Singer, E. and Presser, S.*, eds., 1989, *1982*, pp. 304–23.

Canner, Glenn B.; Luckett, Charles A. and Durkin, Thomas A. Home Equity Lending. *Fed. Res. Bull.*, May 1989, *75*(5), pp. 333–44.

Canning, David. Bargaining Theory. In *Hahn, F.*, ed., 1989, pp. 163–87.

_____. Optimal Monetary Policy with Missing Markets. *Economica*, November 1989, *56*(224), pp. 449–58.

Cannings, Kathy. An Exit-Voice Model of Managerial Attachment. *J. Econ. Behav. Organ.*, August 1989, *12*(1), pp. 107–29.

Cannon, T. International Marketing. *Environ. Planning A*, May 1989, *21*(5), pp. 643–53.

Cannon, Terry. National Minorities and the Internal Frontier. In *Goodman, D. S. G.*, ed., 1989, pp. 164–79.

_____ **and Kirkby, Richard.** China's Regional Development: Introduction. In *Goodman, D. S. G.*, ed., 1989, pp. 1–19.

Canterbery, E. Ray and McLeod, William. The Doctrine of Inherent Productivity: Keynes, Sraffa, and Kalecki. *J. Post Keynesian Econ.*, Summer 1989, *11*(4), pp. 630–40.

_____ **and McLeod, William.** The Doctrine of Inherent Productivity: Keynes, Sraffa, and Kalecki. *J. Post Keynesian Econ.*, Summer 1989, *11*(4), pp. 630–40.

Canto, Victor A. Debt and Adjustment in the Dominican Republic: The Second Time Around. In *Brock, P. L.; Connolly, M. B. and González-Vega, C.*, eds., 1989, pp. 153–70.

Cantor, David. Substantive Implications of Longitudinal Design Features: The National Crime Survey as a Case Study. In *Kasprzyk, D., et al.*, eds., 1989, pp. 25–51.

Cantor, Richard. Increased Price Flexibility and Output Stability. *J. Macroecon.*, Fall 1989, *11*(4), pp. 563–74.

_____. Interest Rates, Household Cash Flow, and Consumer Expenditures. *Fed. Res. Bank New York Quart. Rev.*, Summer 1989, *14*(2), pp. 59–67.

Cantwell, John. The Changing Form of Multinational Enterprise Expansion in the Twentieth Century. In *Teichova, A.; Lévy-Leboyer, M. and Nussbaum, H.*, eds., 1989, pp. 15–28.

Canzoneri, Matthew B. Adverse Incentives in the Taxation of Foreigners. *J. Int. Econ.*, November 1989, *27*(3–4), pp. 283–97.

_____ **and Henderson, Dale W.** Optimal Choice of Monetary Policy Instruments in a Simple

Two-Country Game. In *[Verheyen, P.]*, 1989, pp. 223–40.

_____ **and Minford, Patrick.** Policy Interdependence: Does Strategic Behaviour Pay? An Empirical Investigation Using the Liverpool World Model. In *Hodgman, D. R. and Wood, G. E., eds.*, 1989, pp. 158–79.

Cao, Chengzhang. The Single-Product Agriculture of Rice and the Reform of Economic Structure of the Dai Nationality. In *Chiao, C. and Tapp, N., eds.*, 1989, pp. 89–102.

Cao, Siyuan. A Proposition on How to Handle Enterprises Long in the Red. *Chinese Econ. Stud.*, Winter 1988–89, *22*(2), pp. 10–15.

Caouris, Y. G.; Kantsos, E. T. and Zagouras, N. G. Production and Cost Functions of Water Low-Temperature Solar Desalination. *Appl. Econ.*, September 1989, *21*(9), pp. 1177–89.

Capalbo, Susan M. and Antle, John M. Incorporating Social Costs in the Returns to Agricultural Research. *Amer. J. Agr. Econ.*, May 1989, *71*(2), pp. 458–63.

Capdevielle, Patricia. International Comparisons of Hourly Compensation Costs. *Mon. Lab. Rev.*, June 1989, *112*(6), pp. 10–12.

Cape, J. N.; Smith, R. I. and Fowler, D. The Statistics of Phytotoxic Air Pollutants. *J. Roy. Statist. Society*, 1989, *152*(2), pp. 183–98.

Capecchi, Vittorio. The Informal Economy and the Development of Flexible Specialization in Emilia–Romagna. In *Portes, A.; Castells, M. and Benton, L. A., eds.*, 1989, pp. 189–215.

Capie, Forrest H.; Pradhan, Mahmood and Wood, Geoffrey E. Prices and Price Controls: Are Price Controls a Policy Instrument? In *Hodgman, D. R. and Wood, G. E., eds.*, 1989, pp. 109–38.

_____ **and Wood, Geoffrey E.** Anna Schwartz's Perspective on British Economic History. In *[Schwartz, A. J.]*, 1989, pp. 79–104.

Caples, S. C.; Herbst, Anthony F. and Kare, D. D. Hedging Effectiveness and Minimum Risk Hedge Ratios in the Presence of Autocorrelation: Foreign Currency Futures. *J. Futures Markets*, June 1989, *9*(3), pp. 185–97.

Capocaccia, Riccardo and Caselli, Graziella. Age, Period, Cohort and Early Mortality: An Analysis of Adult Mortality in Italy. *Population Stud.*, March 1989, *43*(1), pp. 133–53.

Caporaso, James. International Economic Strategies, the State, and Domestic Society: A Comment. In *Van Ness, P., ed.*, 1989, pp. 301–05.

Capozza, Dennis R. and Helsley, Robert W. The Fundamentals of Land Prices and Urban Growth. *J. Urban Econ.*, November 1989, *26*(3), pp. 295–306.

_____ **and Schwann, Gregory M.** The Asset Approach to Pricing Urban Land: Empirical Evidence. *Amer. Real Estate Urban Econ. Assoc. J.*, Summer 1989, *17*(2), pp. 161–74.

_____ **and Van Order, Robert.** Spatial Competition with Consistent Conjectures. *J. Reg. Sci.*, February 1989, *29*(1), pp. 1–13.

Cappelli, Peter and Sherer, Peter D. Spanning the Union/Nonunion Boundary. *Ind. Relat.*, Spring 1989, *28*(2), pp. 206–26.

Capps, Oral, Jr. Added Convenience as a Factor in At-Home Animal Products Demand. In *Buse, R. C., ed.*, 1989, pp. 284–96.

_____. Utilizing Scanner Data to Estimate Retail Demand Functions for Meat Products. *Amer. J. Agr. Econ.*, August 1989, *71*(3), pp. 750–60.

Cappuccio, Nunzio. Analisi di una equazione strutturale: Specificazione, stima e verifica dell'ipotesi di esogeneità. (Analysis of One Structural Equation: Specification, Estimation and Exogeneity Hypothesis Testing. With English summary.) *Giorn. Econ.*, May–June 1989, *48*(5–6), pp. 225–52.

Capron, Henri. The Political Economy of the Fiscal Pressure in Belgium. *Econ. Scelte Pubbliche/J. Public Finance Public Choice*, Jan.–Aug. 1989, *7*(1–2), pp. 89–98.

Capros, Pantelis; Karadeloglou, P. and Mentzas, G. N. Energy Policy Extensions of KLE-Based Macroeconomic Models. *J. Policy Modeling*, Winter 1989, *11*(4), pp. 507–30.

_____, **et al.** A New Modeling Framework for Medium-term Energy-Economy Analysis in Europe. *Energy J.*, October 1989, *10*(4), pp. 1–27.

Caputo, David A. Network Perspectives and Policy Analysis: A Skeptical View. In *Perrucci, R. and Potter, H. R., eds.*, 1989, pp. 111–17.

Caputo, Enzo. Enabling Local Economic Growth. In *World Bank and Istituto Italo-Africano*, 1989, pp. 111–16.

Caputo, Michael R. The Qualitative Content of Renewable Resource Models. *Natural Res. Modeling*, Spring 1989, *3*(2), pp. 241–59.

Caramazza, Francesco. Macroeconomic Co-ordination and the Summit. *Can. Public Policy*, Supplement, February 1989, *15*, pp. S83–86.

Caravale, Giovanni A. On Marx's Interpretation of Ricardo: A Note. *Atlantic Econ. J.*, December 1989, *17*(4), pp. 6–12.

_____. On the Question of Continuity in Classical Economic Thought. In *Walker, D. A., ed.*, 1989, pp. 104–13.

Caravani, Paolo. Evaluating the Efficiency of Local Labor Markets. In *van Dijk, J., et al., eds.*, 1989, pp. 267–78.

Carbaugh, Robert and Wassink, Darwin. Dollar–Yen Exchange Rate Effects on Trade. *Rivista Int. Sci. Econ. Com.*, December 1989, *36*(12), pp. 1075–88.

_____ **and Wassink, Darwin.** Evaluation of U.S.–Canada Free Trade Agreement. In *Missouri Valley Economic Association*, 1989, pp. 135–42.

Card, David and Abowd, John M. On the Covariance Structure of Earnings and Hours Changes. *Econometrica*, March 1989, *57*(2), pp. 411–45.

Cardebring, Peter and Jansson, Jan Owen. A Comparative Study of Road User Taxation in Different Countries. *Int. J. Transport Econ.*, February 1989, *16*(1), pp. 79–89.

_____ **and Jansson, Jan Owen.** Swedish Railway

Policy 1979–88. *J. Transp. Econ. Policy*, September 1989, *23*(3), pp. 329–37.

Cardoso, Eliana A. Financiamiento del díficit y dinámica monetaria en America Latina. (Deficit Finance and Monetary Dynamics in Latin America. With English summary.) *Estud. Econ.*, July–Dec. 1989, *4*(2), pp. 175–200.

_____. Hyperinflation in Latin America. *Challenge*, Jan.–Feb. 1989, *32*(1), pp. 11–19.

_____. Latin America's Debt: Which Way Now? In *Guttmann, R., ed.*, 1989, *1987*, pp. 198–204.

_____. Lessons from the 1890s for the 1980s: Comment. In *[Díaz-Alejandro, C.]*, 1989, pp. 48–53.

_____ **and Dornbusch, Rudiger.** Brazilian Debt: A Requiem for Muddling Through. In *Edwards, S. and Larrain, F., eds.*, 1989, pp. 294–318.

_____ **and Dornbusch, Rudiger.** Brazilian Debt Crises: Past and Present. In *Eichengreen, B. and Lindert, P. H., eds.*, 1989, pp. 106–39.

_____ **and Fishlow, Albert.** The Macroeconomics of the Brazilian External Debt. In *Sachs, J. D., ed. (II)*, 1989, pp. 81–99.

Carey, Kathleen. Tourism Development in LDCs: Hotel Capacity Expansion with Reference to Barbados. *World Devel.*, January 1989, *17*(1), pp. 59–67.

Carey, Robin. The Sherman Act: What Did Congress Intend? *Antitrust Bull.*, Summer 1989, *34*(2), pp. 337–58.

Cargill, Thomas F. CAMEL Ratings and the CD Market. *J. Finan. Services Res.*, December 1989, *3*(4), pp. 347–58.

Carhill, Michael. The Dual-Decision Hypothesis in Light of Recent Developments. *J. Post Keynesian Econ.*, Summer 1989, *11*(4), pp. 547–60.

Carlén, Göran and Sundberg, Lennart. Allocation Mechanisms in Public Provision of Transport and Communication Infrastructure. *Ann. Reg. Sci.*, 1989, *23*(4), pp. 311–27.

Carlin, J. B. and Dempster, A. P. Sensitivity Analysis of Seasonal Adjustments: Empirical Case Studies. *J. Amer. Statist. Assoc.*, March 1989, *84*(405), pp. 6–20.

_____ **and Dempster, A. P.** Sensitivity Analysis of Seasonal Adjustments: Empirical Case Studies: Rejoinder. *J. Amer. Statist. Assoc.*, March 1989, *84*(405), pp. 30–32.

Carlin, Paul S. Why the Incidence of Shirking Varies across Employers. *J. Behav. Econ.*, Summer 1989, *18*(2), pp. 61–73.

Carlin, Wendy and Jacob, Ralf. Austerity Policy in West Germany: Origins and Consequences. *Écon. Appl.*, 1989, *42*(1), pp. 203–38.

_____ **and Soskice, David.** Medium-Run Keynesianism: Hysteresis and Capital Scrapping. In *Davidson, P. and Kregel, J., eds.*, 1989, pp. 241–55.

Carlino, Gerald and Lang, Richard. Interregional Flows of Funds as a Measure of Economic Integration in the United States. *J. Urban Econ.*, July 1989, *26*(1), pp. 20–29.

_____ **and Mills, Edwin S.** Dynamics of County Growth. In *Andersson, Å. E., et al., eds.*, 1989, pp. 195–205.

de Carlos Pablo, Juan and Dornbusch, Rudiger. Debt and Macroeconomic Instability in Argentina. In *Sachs, J. D., ed. (II)*, 1989, pp. 37–56.

Carlson, Barbara Lepidus; Cohen, Steven B. and Johnson, Ayah E. An Analysis of Part-Year Nonresponse in the Household Component of the National Medical Expenditure Survey. *J. Econ. Soc. Meas.*, 1989, *15*(3–4), pp. 281–99.

Carlson, Christopher K., et al. A Contract Termination Processing Model and System for Naval Supply Demand Review (SDR) Actions. In *Gulledge, T. R., Jr. and Litteral, L. A., eds.*, 1989, pp. 34–44.

Carlson, Cynthia and Edwards, Steven F. On Estimating Compensation for Injury to Publicly Owned Marine Resources. *Marine Resource Econ.*, 1989, *6*(1), pp. 27–42.

Carlson, George N. and Patrick, Melanie K. Addressing the Regressivity of a Value-Added Tax. *Nat. Tax J.*, September 1989, *42*(3), pp. 339–51.

Carlson, Gerald A. Externalities and Research Priorities in Agricultural Pest Control. *Amer. J. Agr. Econ.*, May 1989, *71*(2), pp. 453–57.

_____. Pest-Resistant Varieties, Pesticides, and Crop Yield Variability: A Review. In *Anderson, J. R. and Hazell, P. B. R., eds.*, 1989, pp. 242–50.

Carlson, John A. and Dunkelberg, William C. Market Perceptions and Inventory–Price–Employment Plans. *Rev. Econ. Statist.*, May 1989, *71*(2), pp. 318–24.

Carlson, John B. Debt Growth and the Financial System. In *Guttmann, R., ed.*, 1989, *1986*, pp. 103–08.

Carlson, Keith M. Do Price Indexes Tell Us about Inflation? A Review of the Issues. *Fed. Res. Bank San Francisco Rev.*, Nov.–Dec. 1989, *71*(6), pp. 12–30.

_____. Federal Budget Trends and the 1981 Reagan Economic Plan. *Fed. Res. Bank St. Louis Rev.*, Jan.–Feb. 1989, *71*(1), pp. 18–31.

Carlsson, Bo. Flexibility and the Theory of the Firm. *Int. J. Ind. Organ.*, June 1989, *7*(2), pp. 179–203.

Carlton, David L. and Coclanis, Peter A. Capital Mobilization and Southern Industry, 1880–1905: The Case of the Carolina Piedmont. *J. Econ. Hist.*, March 1989, *49*(1), pp. 73–94.

Carlton, Dennis W. The Theory and the Facts of How Markets Clear: Is Industrial Organization Valuable for Understanding Macroeconomics? In *Schmalensee, R. and Willig, R. D., eds., Vol. 1*, 1989, pp. 909–46.

_____ **and Gertner, Robert.** Market Power and Mergers in Durable-Good Industries. *J. Law Econ.*, Part 2, October 1989, *32*(2), pp. S203–26.

Carmichael, Benoit. Anticipated Monetary Policy in a Cash-in-Advance Economy. *Can. J. Econ.*, February 1989, *22*(1), pp. 93–108.

Carmichael, H. Lorne. Self-Enforcing Contracts,

Shirking, and Life Cycle Incentives. *J. Econ. Perspectives*, Fall 1989, *3*(4), pp. 65–83.

Carmichael, Jeffrey. The Debt Crisis: Where Do We Stand after Seven Years? *World Bank Res. Observer*, July 1989, *4*(2), pp. 121–42.

———— **and Buiter, Willem H.** Government Debt: Comment. **In** *Buiter, W. H.*, 1989, *1984*, pp. 283–88.

———— **and Dews, Nigel.** Investment and Australian Economic Growth. **In** *[Gruen, F. H.]*, 1989, pp. 101–32.

Caro, Francis G. Alternatives to Institutionalization: Community Long-Term Care. **In** *Eisdorfer, C.; Kessler, D. A. and Spector, A. N.*, *eds.*, 1989, pp. 50–70.

Caroleo, Floro E. Le cause economiche nei differenziali regionali del tasso di disoccupazione. (The Economic Causes of Regional Differentials for Employment Levels. With English summary.) *Econ. Lavoro*, July–Sept. 1989, *23*(3), pp. 41–53.

Carpenter, Gerald. *Strategy and Structure* Revisited: Jersey Standard's 1960 Reorganization as a Case Study. **In** *Perkins, E. J.*, *ed.*, 1989, pp. 76–90.

Carpenter, Paul R.; Graves, Frank C. and Read, James A., Jr. Estimating the Cost of Switching Rights on Natural Gas Pipelines. *Energy J.*, October 1989, *10*(4), pp. 59–81.

Carpenter, Ted Galen. Beyond U.S. Paternalism: A New Security Strategy for the Pacific Basin. **In** *Crane, E. H. and Boaz, D.*, 1989, pp. 167–81.

Carr, A. Barry. Biotechnology and Agriculture in the Congressional Policy Arena: Commentary. **In** *Krämer, C. S.*, *ed.*, 1989, pp. 201–02.

————. Relevancy of the Social Sciences in the Policy Arena: Implications for Agricultural Economics: Discussion. *Southern J. Agr. Econ.*, July 1989, *21*(1), pp. 51–52.

Carr, Jack L. Government Size and Economic Growth: A New Framework and Some Evidence from Cross-Section and Time-Series Data: Comment. *Amer. Econ. Rev.*, March 1989, *79*(1), pp. 267–71.

————; **Glied, Sherry and Mathewson, Frank.** Unlimited Liability and Free Banking in Scotland: A Note. *J. Econ. Hist.*, December 1989, *49*(4), pp. 974–78.

Carr, Lois Green and Menard, Russell R. Land, Labor, and Economies of Scale in Early Maryland: Some Limits to Growth in the Chesapeake System of Husbandry. *J. Econ. Hist.*, June 1989, *49*(2), pp. 407–18.

Carraro, Carlo. The Tastes of European Central Bankers. **In** *De Cecco, M. and Giovannini, A.*, *eds.*, 1989, pp. 162–89.

———— **and Siniscalco, Domenico.** L'OPEC e il mercato del greggio: Uno schema di oligopolio. (OPEC and the Oil Market: An Oligopoly Model. With English summary.) *Econ. Politica*, April 1989, *6*(1), pp. 31–65.

Carrière, Jean; Haworth, Nigel and Roddick, Jacqueline. Proletarianisation, Industrialisation and Patterns of Action. **In** *Carrière, J.;*

Haworth, N. and Roddick, J., *eds.*, 1989, pp. 1–20.

Carroll, Kathleen A. Industrial Structure and Monopoly Power in the Federal Bureaucracy: An Empirical Analysis. *Econ. Inquiry*, October 1989, *27*(4), pp. 683–703.

Carroll, Raymond J.; Künsch, Hans R. and Stefanski, Leonard A. Conditionally Unbiased Bounded-Influence Estimation in General Regression Models, with Applications to Generalized Linear Models. *J. Amer. Statist. Assoc.*, June 1989, *84*(406), pp. 460–66.

Carroll, Sidney L. Taxing Wealth: An Accessions Tax Proposal for the U.S. *J. Post Keynesian Econ.*, Fall 1989, *12*(1), pp. 49–69.

Carroll, Wayne. Fixed-Percentage Commissions and Moral Hazard in Residential Real Estate Brokerage. *J. Real Estate Finance Econ.*, December 1989, *2*(4), pp. 349–65.

Carron, Andrew S. The Thrift Industry Crisis of the 1980s: What Went Wrong? **In** *Federal Home Loan Bank of San Francisco*, 1989, pp. 23–35.

————; **Litan, Robert E. and Brumbaugh, R. Dan, Jr.** Cleaning Up the Depository Institutions Mess. *Brookings Pap. Econ. Act.*, 1989, (1), pp. 243–83.

Carruthers, David T. Housing Market Models and the Regional Housing System. *Urban Stud.*, April 1989, *26*(2), pp. 214–222.

Carsberg, Bryan. Injecting Competition into Telecommunications. **In** *Veljanovski, C.*, *ed.* *(II)*, 1989, pp. 81–95.

————. Lessons from the British Experience with Price Cap Regulation. **In** *National Economic Research Associates*, 1989, pp. 191–202.

Carson, Edgar. Social Networks in the Labour Market—The Sociology of Job Search. *Australian Bull. Lab.*, September 1989, *15*(4), pp. 287–312.

Cartelier, Jean and De Vroey, Michel. L'approche de la régulation. Un nouveau paradigme? (With English summary.) *Écon. Societes*, November 1989, *23*(11), pp. 63–87.

———— **and Froeschlé, C.** A Model of a Monetary Economy: Principles and Study of Stability. *Metroecon.*, October 1989, *40*(3), pp. 189–209.

Carter, Anne P. Input–Output Recipes in an Information Economy. *Econ. Systems Res.*, 1989, *1*(1), pp. 27–43.

———— **and Petri, Peter A.** Leontief's Contribution to Economics. *J. Policy Modeling*, Spring 1989, *11*(1), pp. 7–30.

Carter, April. Industrial Democracy and the Capitalist State. **In** *Duncan, G.*, *ed.*, 1989, pp. 277–93.

Carter, Ashton B. Telecommunications Policy and U.S. National Security. **In** *Crandall, R. W. and Flamm, K.*, *eds.*, 1989, pp. 221–53.

Carter, Colin A. Arbitrage Opportunities between Thin and Liquid Futures Markets. *J. Futures Markets*, August 1989, *9*(4), pp. 347–53.

————. Trade in Primary Products: Canada, the United States, and Japan: Comment. **In** *Stern, R. M.*, *ed.*, 1989, pp. 170–73.

_____; **Karrenbrock, Jeffrey D. and Wilson, William W.** Freer Trade in the North American Beer and Flour Markets. In *Schmitz, A., ed.*, 1989, pp. 139–86.

_____ **and Pick, Daniel H.** The J-Curve Effect and the U.S. Agricultural Trade Balance. *Amer. J. Agr. Econ.*, August 1989, *71*(3), pp. 712–20.

Carter, Michael J. Financial Innovation and Financial Fragility. *J. Econ. Issues*, September 1989, *23*(3), pp. 779–93.

Carter, Michael R. The Impact of Credit on Peasant Productivity and Differentiation in Nicaragua. *J. Devel. Econ.*, July 1989, *31*(1), pp. 13–36.

_____. A Wisconsin Institutionalist Perspective on Microeconomic Theory of Institutions: The Insufficiency of Pareto Efficiency. In *Tool, M. R. and Samuels, W. J., eds. (II)*, 1989, *1985*, pp. 389–405.

Carter, R. A. L.; Srivastava, Virendra K. and Ullah, Aman. Corrigendum [The Sampling Distribution of Shrinkage Estimators and Their *F*-Ratios in the Regression Model]. *J. Econometrics*, February 1989, *40*(2), pp. 339.

Carter, T. R. and Parry, Martin L. The Effect of Climatic Variations of Food Production. In *Oram, P. A., et al.*, 1989, pp. 429–49.

Carter, Thomas L. Keys to Quality: Management Leadership and Commitment to the Customer. In *Ahlbrandt, R. S., Jr., ed.*, 1989, pp. 37–39.

Carter, Walter H., Jr.; Gennings, Chris and Chinchilli, Vernon M. Response Surface Analysis with Correlated Data: A Nonlinear Model Approach. *J. Amer. Statist. Assoc.*, September 1989, *84*(407), pp. 805–09.

Carter, William H. and Wachter, Michael L. Norm Shifts in Union Wages: Will 1989 Be a Replay of 1969? *Brookings Pap. Econ. Act.*, 1989, (2), pp. 233–64.

Cartwright, I.; Carver, A. and King, M. G. Fisheries Development in Pacific Islands: Some Problems in Paradise. In *Couper, A. D., ed.*, 1989, pp. 47–62.

Cartwright, Joseph V. Regional Science and Public Management. *Rev. Reg. Stud.*, Fall 1989, *19*(3), pp. 1–3.

deCarufel, André and Goh, Swee C. Perceptions of Managerial Effectiveness: An Experimental Study in Sri Lanka and Implications for Leadership Training. In *Nedd, A., ed.*, 1989, pp. 301–15.

Caruso, Guy F. Structural Adjustment in the Oil Industry: Evolutionary Change and an Information Revolution. In *[Evans, J. K.]*, 1989, pp. 1–10.

Carvalho, António Joaquim. Le coût de la perception de l'impôt à charge de l'administration et des contribuables: Portugal. (Administrative and Compliance Costs of Taxation: Portugal. With English summary.) In *International Fiscal Association, ed. (I)*, 1989, pp. 511–28.

de Carvalho, Fernando J. Cardim. Some Short- and Long-Term Barriers to Income Redistribution in a Monetary Production Economy: An Illustration from the Recent Brazilian Experience. In *Davidson, P. and Kregel, J., eds.*, 1989, pp. 195–215.

Carvalho, Joe W. and Holland, David W. Agricultural and Economic Development in Lesotho: Analysis Using a Social Accounting Matrix. *Eastern Afr. Econ. Rev.*, December 1989, *5*(2), pp. 104–20.

Carvalho, Ruy de Quadros and Schmitz, Hubert. Automation and Labour in the Brazilian Car Industry. *J. Devel. Stud.*, October 1989, *26*(1), pp. 81–119.

Carver, A.; King, M. G. and Cartwright, I. Fisheries Development in Pacific Islands: Some Problems in Paradise. In *Couper, A. D., ed.*, 1989, pp. 47–62.

Carwright, William S.; Hu, Teh-wei and Huang, Lien-Fu. Demand for Medigap Insurance by the Elderly: A Micro-simulation Analysis. *Appl. Econ.*, October 1989, *21*(10), pp. 1325–39.

Casanegra de Jantscher, Milka and Tanzi, Vito. The Use of Presumptive Income in Modern Tax Systems. In *Chiancone, A. and Messere, K., eds.*, 1989, pp. 37–51.

Casares, Enrique; Garza, Gilma and Kelly, Rafael. Control adaptable de un modelo no lineal de crecimiento monetario neoclásico. (Adaptive Control of a Nonlinear Neoclassical Monetary Growth Model. With English summary.) *Estud. Econ.*, Jan.–June 1989, *4*(1), pp. 109–26.

Casas, François R. Monopoly as a Basis for Trade. *Can. J. Econ.*, February 1989, *22*(1), pp. 195–201.

_____ **and Choi, Eun Kwan.** Transport Costs and Immiserizing Growth under Variable Returns to Scale. *Int. J. Transport Econ.*, February 1989, *16*(1), pp. 3–18.

Cascio, Wayne F. Gaining and Sustaining Competitive Advantage: Challenges for Human Resource Management. In *Nedd, A., ed.*, 1989, pp. 137–51.

Cascioli, Ettore. Un modello per la classificazione automatica di osservazioni multidimensionali. (A Model for the Automatic Classification of Multidimensional Observations. With English summary.) *Giorn. Econ.*, Jan.–Feb. 1989, *48*(1–2), pp. 55–71.

Case, Bradford and Ebel, Robert D. Using State Consumer Tax Credits for Achieving Equity. *Nat. Tax J.*, September 1989, *42*(3), pp. 323–37.

Case, Karl E. The Asset Approach to Pricing Urban Land: Empirical Evidence: Comments. *Amer. Real Estate Urban Econ. Assoc. J.*, Summer 1989, *17*(2), pp. 175–76.

_____ **and Cook, Leah.** The Distributional Effects of Housing Price Booms: Winners and Losers in Boston, 1980–88. *New Eng. Econ. Rev.*, May–June 1989, pp. 3–12.

_____; **Dunham, Constance R. and Bradbury, Katharine L.** Geographic Patterns of Mortgage Lending in Boston, 1982–1987. *New Eng. Econ. Rev.*, Sept.–Oct. 1989, pp. 3–30.

_____ **and Shiller, Robert J.** The Efficiency of

the Market for Single-Family Homes. *Amer. Econ. Rev.*, March 1989, *79*(1), pp. 125–37.

Casella, Alessandra. Testing for Rational Bubbles with Exogenous or Endogenous Fundamentals: The German Hyperinflation Once More. *J. Monet. Econ.*, July 1989, *24*(1), pp. 109–22.

_____ **and Feinstein, Jonathan S.** Management of a Common Currency. **In** *De Cecco, M. and Giovannini, A., eds.*, 1989, pp. 131–56.

Caselli, Graziella and Capocaccia, Riccardo. Age, Period, Cohort and Early Mortality: An Analysis of Adult Mortality in Italy. *Population Stud.*, March 1989, *43*(1), pp. 133–53.

Caselli, Lorenzo. Trasformazioni dell'impresa e valorizzazione delle risorse umane. (The Transformation of Enterprises and Optimizing Human Resources. With English summary.) *Econ. Lavoro*, Oct.–Dec. 1989, *23*(4), pp. 49–60.

Caselli, Paola and Barca, Fabrizio. Competitività internazionale e ristrutturazione della industria italiana negli anni '80. (International Competitiveness and Recovery of the Italian Industry in the Eighties. With English summary.) *Politica. Econ.*, August 1989, *5*(2), pp. 231–72.

Casetti, E. The Onset and Spread of Modern Economic Growth in Europe: An Empirical Test of a Catastrophe Model. *Environ. Planning A*, November 1989, *21*(11), pp. 1473–89.

Casey, Bernard. Early Retirement: The Problems of "Instrument Substitution" and "Cost Shifting" and Their Implications for Restructuring the Process of Retirement. **In** *Schmähl, W., ed.*, 1989, pp. 133–50.

_____ **and Creigh, Stephen.** "Marginal" Groups in the Labour Force Survey. *Scot. J. Polit. Econ.*, August 1989, *36*(3), pp. 282–300.

_____, **et al.** Temporary Employment in Great Britain and the Federal Republic of Germany: An Overview. *Int. Lab. Rev.*, 1989, *128*(4), pp. 449–66.

Casey, Tom. Technical Information Flow in Ireland. **In** *Punset, E. and Sweeney, G., eds.*, 1989, pp. 146–60.

Cashel-Cordo, Peter and Craig, Steven G. Donors, Development, and Debt: The Role of External Assistance and External Indebtedness. **In** *DeGregori, T. R., ed.*, 1989, pp. 231–83.

Caskey, John P. The IMF and Concerted Lending in Latin American Debt Restructurings: A Formal Analysis. *J. Int. Money Finance*, March 1989, *8*(1), pp. 105–20.

_____ **and Fazzari, Steven.** Debt Commitments and Aggregate Demand: A Critique of the Neoclassical Synthesis and Policy. **In** *Semmler, W., ed.*, 1989, pp. 188–99.

Casler, Stephen D. A Theoretical Context for Shift and Share Analysis. *Reg. Stud.*, February 1989, *23*(1), pp. 43–48.

_____ **and Hannon, Bruce.** Readjustment Potentials in Industrial Energy Efficiency and Structure. *J. Environ. Econ. Manage.*, July 1989, *17*(1), pp. 93–108.

Caspari, Andrea and Martinos, Haris. Local Labour-Market Development and Long-Term

Unemployment in the EC Countries. **In** *Dyson, K., ed.*, 1989, pp. 114–31.

Caspari, Volker. A Marshallian Perspective of Keynes' General Theory. *Metroecon.*, June 1989, *40*(2), pp. 101–18.

Cass, David. Sunspots and Incomplete Financial Markets: The Leading Example. **In** *Feiwel, G. R., ed. (I)*, 1989, pp. 677–93.

_____ **and Balasko, Yves.** The Structure of Financial Equilibrium with Exogenous Yields: The Case of Incomplete Markets. *Econometrica*, January 1989, *57*(1), pp. 135–62.

_____ **and Shell, Karl.** Sunspot Equilibrium in an Overlapping-Generations Economy with an Idealized Contingent-Commodities Market. **In** *Barnett, W. A.; Geweke, J. and Shell, K., eds.*, 1989, pp. 3–20.

Cassidy, Glenn; Epple, Dennis and Romer, Thomas. Redistribution by Local Governments in a Monocentric Urban Area. *Reg. Sci. Urban Econ.*, August 1989, *19*(3), pp. 421–54.

_____; **Kamlet, Mark S. and Nagin, Daniel S.** An Empirical Examination of Bias in Revenue Forecasts by State Governments. *Int. J. Forecasting*, 1989, *5*(3), pp. 321–31.

Cassidy, Judith H.; Friedberg, Alan H. and Strawser, Jerry R. Factors Affecting Materiality Judgments: A Comparison of "Big Eight" Accounting Firms' Materiality Views with the Results of Empirical Research. **In** *Schwartz, B. N., ed.*, 1989, pp. 187–201.

Cassiers, Isabelle. Historical Change in the Institutional Determinants of Wages. **In** *Scholliers, P., ed.*, 1989, pp. 194–200.

Casson, John J. The Contribution of the Economic Forecast to the Business Plan. *Bus. Econ.*, April 1989, *24*(2), pp. 14–19.

Castaneda, Chris and Pratt, Joseph. New Markets, Outmoded Manufacturing: The Transition from Manufactured Gas to Natural Gas by Northeastern Utilities after World War II. **In** *Hausman, W. J., ed.*, 1989, pp. 238–47.

Castañeda, Tarsicio. The Chilean Health System: Organization, Operation, and Financing. **In** *WHO, Pan American Health Organization*, 1989, pp. 3–25.

Castelino, Mark G. Basis Volatility: Implications for Hedging. *J. Finan. Res.*, Summer 1989, *12*(2), pp. 157–72.

Castella, Guillermo; de Buckle, Teresa Salazar and Holaday, William. Agro-food Industry in Latin America. *Industry Devel.*, June 1989, (27), pp. 1–29.

Castellino, Onorato. On the Price of Different Classes of Shares. *Banca Naz. Lavoro Quart. Rev.*, March 1989, (168), pp. 109–23.

Castells, Antoni. Revisión límites del Estado del Bienestar tradicional. (Limits and Revision of the Traditional Welfare State. With English summary.) *Écon. Societes*, February 1989, *23*(2), pp. 69–100.

Castells, Manuel; Benton, Lauren A. and Portes, Alejandro. The Policy Implications of Informality: Conclusion. **In** *Portes, A.; Castells, M. and Benton, L. A., eds.*, 1989, pp. 298–311.

_____ **and Portes, Alejandro.** World Underneath: The Origins, Dynamics, and Effects of the Informal Economy. In *Portes, A.; Castells, M. and Benton, L. A., eds.*, 1989, pp. 11–37.

Casterline, Gary; Dinar, Ariel and Zilberman, David. The Adoption of Modern Irrigation Technologies in the United States. In *Schmitz, A., ed.*, 1989, pp. 222–48.

Casterline, John B.; Cooksey, Elizabeth C. and Ismail, Abdel Fattah E. Household Income and Child Survival in Egypt. *Demography*, February 1989, *26*(1), pp. 15–35.

de Castilho, B. and Navin, F. P. D. A Rule-Based Highway Location System. In *Candemir, Y., ed.*, 1989, pp. 334–48.

Castillo Bonet, Manuel and Tabors, Richard. Load Management. In *Kim, Y. H. and Smith, K. R., eds.*, 1989, pp. 65–105.

Castillo Gimenez, Juana; Reig Martínez, Ernest and Sanchis i Marco, Manuel. Spain's Trade and Development Strategies. In *Yannopoulos, G. N., ed.*, 1989, pp. 40–65.

del Castillo, Graciana. The Role of Transnational Corporations in South–South Trade: Issues and Evidence. In *Ventura-Dias, V., ed.*, 1989, pp. 249–62.

del Castillo Hermosa, Jaime. Cris économique, changements dans l'investissement étranger et intégration de l'économie espagnole au marché mondial. (Economic Crisis, Changes in Foreign Investment and the Integration of the Spanish Economy in the International Market. With English summary.) *Écon. Societes*, February 1989, *23*(2), pp. 5–25.

del Castillo, Pilar. Financing of Spanish Political Parties. In *Alexander, H. E., ed.*, 1989, pp. 172–99.

Castle, Emery N. Economic Theory in Agricultural Economics Research. *J. Agr. Econ. Res.*, Summer 1989, *41*(3), pp. 3–7.

_____. Is Farming a Constant Cost Industry? *Amer. J. Agr. Econ.*, August 1989, *71*(3), pp. 574–82.

Castles, Lance. Jakarta: The Growing Centre. In *Hill, H., ed.*, 1989, pp. 232–53.

Castleton, Anne and Goldscheider, Frances K. Are Mormon Families Different? In *Goldscheider, F. K. and Goldscheider, C., eds.*, 1989, pp. 93–109.

de Castro, Newton. Demanda derivada de energia no transporte de passageiros. (With English summary.) *Pesquisa Planejamento Econ.*, April 1989, *19*(1), pp. 85–111.

Cataquet, Harold. Country Risk Management: How to Juggle with Your Arms in a Straitjacket? In *Singer, H. W. and Sharma, S., eds. (I)*, 1989, pp. 337–54.

ten Cate, Arie and van Nes, Floor. Software for Econometric Research with a Personal Computer. *Int. J. Forecasting*, 1989, *5*(2), pp. 263–78.

Cather, David A. and Howe, Vince. Conflict and Channel Management in Property-Liability Distribution Systems. *J. Risk Ins.*, September 1989, *56*(3), pp. 535–43.

Catinat, Michel. The Large Internal Market under the Microscope: Problems and Challenges.

In *Jacquemin, A. and Sapir, A., eds.*, 1989, pp. 334–56.

Caudill, Steven B.; Ault, Richard W. and Saba, Richard P. Efficient Estimation of the Costs of Rent Controls. *Rev. Econ. Statist.*, February 1989, *71*(1), pp. 154–59.

_____ **and Holcombe, Randall G.** Taxation and the Redistribution of Income. *Atlantic Econ. J.*, September 1989, *17*(3), pp. 39–42.

_____; **Jackson, John D. and Barnett, A. H.** Job Search Duration and Marginal Tax Rates: An Empirical Inquiry. *Southern Econ. J.*, October 1989, *56*(2), pp. 476–89.

Cauvin, Pierre. Illusion, désillusion et mécanismes de défense dans le fonctionnement des organismes de service à but non lucratif. (Illusion, Disillusions and Defence Mechanisms in the Functioning of Non Profit Organisations. With English summary.) *Écon. Societes*, January 1989, *23*(1), pp. 139–61.

Cavagnac, Michel. Information et différenciation du produit sur un marché de duopole. (Information and Product Differentiation in a Duopoly Market. With English summary.) *Ann. Écon. Statist.*, April–June 1989, (14), pp. 39–64.

Cavallo, Domingo and Mundlak, Yair. On the Nature and Implications of Intersectoral Resource Allocations: Argentina 1913–84. In *Adelman, I. and Lane, S., eds.*, 1989, pp. 143–60.

Cave, Martin. An Introduction to Television Economics. In *Hughes, G. and Vines, D., eds.*, 1989, pp. 9–37.

_____. The Conduct of Auctions for Broadcast Franchises. *Fisc. Stud.*, February 1989, *10*(1), pp. 17–31.

_____. Nobel Laureates in Economic Sciences: A Biographical Dictionary: Leonid Kantorovich: 1975. In *Katz, B. S., ed.*, 1989, pp. 109–21.

_____. Regulating a Partly-Deregulated Broadcasting System. In *Hughes, G. and Vines, D., eds.*, 1989, pp. 126–38.

_____ **and Melody, William H.** Models of Broadcast Regulation: The UK and North American Experience. In *Veljanovski, C., ed. (I)*, 1989, pp. 224–43.

Caves, Douglas W.; Herriges, Joseph A. and Kuester, Kathleen A. Load Shifting under Voluntary Residential Time-of-Use Rates. *Energy J.*, October 1989, *10*(4), pp. 83–99.

Caves, Richard E. International Differences in Industrial Organization. In *Schmalensee, R. and Willig, R. D., eds., Vol. 2*, 1989, pp. 1225–50.

_____. Mergers, Takeovers, and Economic Efficiency: Foresight vs. Hindsight. *Int. J. Ind. Organ.*, Special Issue, March 1989, *7*(1), pp. 151–74.

_____ **and Barton, David R.** Efficiency, Productivity Growth, and International Trade. In *Audretsch, D. B.; Sleuwaegen, L. and Yamawaki, H., eds.*, 1989, pp. 3–27.

_____; **Lo, Andrew W. and Bucklin, Randolph E.** Games of Survival in the U.S. Newspaper

Industry. *Appl. Econ.*, May 1989, *21*(5), pp. 631–49.

Caves, Roger W. An Historical Analysis of Federal Housing Policy from the Presidential Perspective: An Intergovernmental Focus. *Urban Stud.*, February 1989, *26*(1), pp. 59–76.

Cawson, Alan. European Consumer Electronics: Corporate Strategies and Public Policy. In *Sharp, M. and Holmes, P., eds.*, 1989, pp. 56–79.

_____. Is There a Corporatist Theory of the State? In *Duncan, G., ed.*, 1989, pp. 233–52.

_____; **Shepherd, Geoffrey and Webber, Douglas.** Governments, Markets, and Regulation in the West European Consumer Electronics Industry. In *Hancher, L. and Moran, M., eds.*, 1989, pp. 109–33.

Cayley, Michael. Recent Trends in Company Taxation. In *Chiancone, A. and Messere, K., eds.*, 1989, pp. 103–12.

van Cayseele, Patrick J. National Policy Responses to Innovative Multinationals: A Club Theoretic Approach with an Application to the Pharmaceutical Industry. In *Audretsch, D. B.; Sleuwaegen, L. and Yamawaki, H., eds.*, 1989, pp. 249–68.

Cebula, Richard J. The Analysis of Geographic Living-Cost Differentials: A Brief Empirical Note. *Land Econ.*, February 1989, *65*(1), pp. 64–67.

_____. A Brief Empirical Note on Federal Budget Deficits and the Yield Curve in the United States. *Public Finance*, 1989, *44*(2), pp. 316–19.

_____. Federal Budget Deficits, International Capital Flows, and the Long-term Nominal Rate of Interest in the United States. *Schweiz. Z. Volkswirtsch. Statist.*, June 1989, *125*(2), pp. 157–64.

_____. More on Budget Deficits and Interest Rates in the United States. *Public Choice*, January 1989, *60*(1), pp. 93–97.

_____ and **Koch, James V.** An Empirical Note on Deficits, Interest Rates, and International Capital Flows. *Quart. Rev. Econ. Bus.*, Autumn 1989, *29*(3), pp. 121–27.

_____ and **Koch, James V.** Welfare Policies and Migration of the Poor in the United States: An Empirical Note. *Public Choice*, May 1989, *61*(2), pp. 171–76.

Ceccarelli, Paolo. The Territorial Aspects of Decentralization. In *World Bank and Istituto Italo-Africano*, 1989, pp. 75–78.

de Cecco, Marcello. The Founding of the Fed and the Destabilization of the Post-1914 U.S. Economy: Discussion. In *De Cecco, M. and Giovannini, A., eds.*, 1989, pp. 328–32.

_____. Keynes and Italian Economics. In *Hall, P. A., ed.*, 1989, pp. 195–229.

_____ and **Giovannini, Alberto.** Does Europe Need Its Own Central Bank? In *De Cecco, M. and Giovannini, A., eds.*, 1989, pp. 1–12.

Cecen, A. Aydin. X-Inefficiency, Productivity and Inflation: An Empirical Investigation. *Atlantic Econ. J.*, March 1989, *17*(1), pp. 43–46.

Ceglowski, Janet. Dollar Depreciation and U.S.

Industry Performance. *J. Int. Money Finance*, June 1989, *8*(2), pp. 233–51.

_____ and **Kasman, Bruce.** External Adjustment and U.S. Macroeconomic Performance. *Fed. Res. Bank New York Quart. Rev.*, Winter–Spring 1989, *13-14*(4–1), pp. 16–32.

Celasun, Merih. Income Distribution and Employment Aspects of Turkey's Post-1980 Adjustment. *METU*, 1989, *16*(3–4), pp. 1–31.

_____ and **Rodrik, Dani.** Debt, Adjustment, and Growth: Turkey. In *Sachs, J. D. and Collins, S. M., eds.*, 1989, pp. 615–808.

_____ and **Rodrik, Dani.** Turkish Experience with Debt: Macroeconomic Policy and Performance. In *Sachs, J. D., ed. (II)*, 1989, pp. 193–211.

Çelik, Fazil and Güçmen, Özer. A Program for Simulating the Conflicting Traffic Flows of Over-Saturated Priority Intersections. In *Candemir, Y., ed.*, 1989, pp. 445–54.

Cella, Gianprimo. Criteria of Regulation in Italian Industrial Relations: A Case of Weak Institutions. In *Lange, P. and Regini, M., eds.*, 1989, pp. 167–85.

Cellerino, Rita. Environmental Expenditure in Italian State and Regional Planning. *Statist. J.*, 1989, *6*(2), pp. 111–25.

Centi, César. Les leçons d'un échec: Molinari et le marché du travail. (The Lessons of a Failure: Molinari and the Labour Market. With English summary.) *Écon. Societes*, October 1989, *23*(10), pp. 31–75.

Centner, Terence J. Invent in America: Pitfalls for Foreigners under U.S. Intellectual Property Rights Legislation. *Can. J. Agr. Econ.*, Part 2, December 1989, *37*(4), pp. 1307–13.

_____ and **Bergstrom, John C.** Agricultural Nuisances and Right-to-Farm Laws: Implications of Changing Liability Rules. *Rev. Reg. Stud.*, Winter 1989, *19*(1), pp. 23–30.

_____ and **White, Fred C.** Protecting Inventors' Intellectual Property Rights in Biotechnology. *Western J. Agr. Econ.*, December 1989, *14*(2), pp. 189–99.

Cerami, Charles A. Both Sides of the Question. In *Cerami, C. A., ed.*, 1989, pp. 21–31.

_____. The Frightening Numbers. In *Cerami, C. A., ed.*, 1989, pp. 5–12.

_____. A Marshall Plan for the 1990s: An International Roundtable on World Economic Development: Introduction. In *Cerami, C. A., ed.*, 1989, pp. 1–3.

_____. A Plan to Create New Markets. In *Cerami, C. A., ed.*, 1989, pp. 13–19.

_____. This Much Is Certain. In *Cerami, C. A., ed.*, 1989, pp. 237–42.

_____. Why Today is Different. In *Cerami, C. A., ed.*, 1989, pp. 33–40.

Cerruti, Giancarlo and Rieser, Vittorio. Professionalità in transizione. (Professionalism in Transition. With English summary.) *Econ. Lavoro*, July–Sept. 1989, *23*(3), pp. 99–117.

Cesar, Herman and de Haan, Jakob. Predicting the Money Multiplier in the Netherlands Once More. *Empirical Econ.*, 1989, *14*(3), pp. 215–27.

Cesco, J. C. and Neme, A. A Nash Type Equilibrium in Games without Transitive Preferences. *Math. Soc. Sci.*, February 1989, *17*(1), pp. 47–56.

Česka, Jaroslav. Comparison of Gross Domestic Product and Net Material Product. In *Krelle, W., ed.*, 1989, pp. 581–96.

Chabotar, Kent John. Measuring the Costs of Magnet Schools. *Econ. Educ. Rev.*, 1989, *8*(2), pp. 169–83.

Chadha, Binky. Is Increased Price Inflexibility Stabilizing? *J. Money, Credit, Banking*, November 1989, *21*(4), pp. 481–97.

Chae, Suchan and Esteban, Joan. The Bounded Core of an Overlapping Generations Economy. *Int. Econ. Rev.*, August 1989, *30*(3), pp. 519–25.

Chaffin, Wilkie W. and Talley, Wayne K. Diffusion Indexes and a Statistical Test for Predicting Turning Points in Business Cycles. *Int. J. Forecasting*, 1989, *5*(1), pp. 29–36.

Chaillou, Paul; Hansen, Pierre and Mahieu, Yvon. Best Network Flow Bounds for the Quadratic Knapsack Problem. In *Simeone, B., ed.*, 1989, pp. 225–35.

Chaison, Gary N. and Andiappan, P. An Analysis of the Barriers to Women Becoming Local Union Officers. *J. Lab. Res.*, Spring 1989, *10*(2), pp. 149–62.

Chakraborti, S.; Thistle, Paul D. and Bishop, John A. Asymptotically Distribution-Free Statistical Inference for Generalized Lorenz Curves. *Rev. Econ. Statist.*, November 1989, *71*(4), pp. 725–27.

Chakraborty, Chandana and Diwan, Romesh. R&D and Components of Technical Change. *Eastern Econ. J.*, Oct.–Dec. 1989, *15*(4), pp. 365–71.

Chakraborty, Debasish and Kulkarni, Kishore G. An Empirical Evidence of Purchasing Power Parity Theory: A Case of Indian Rupee and U.S. Dollar. *Margin*, Oct. 1989–March 1990, *22*(1–2), pp. 52–56.

Chakraborty, Debesh; Das, Tuhin and ten Raa, Thijs. Working Capital in an Input–Output Model. *Econ. Systems Res.*, 1989, *1*(1), pp. 53–68.

Chakravarty, Satya R. The Optimum Size Distribution of Firms. *Math. Soc. Sci.*, August 1989, *18*(1), pp. 99–105.

Chakravarty, Sukhamoy. British Perceptions of Indian Economic Problems: Dr. Vera Anstey and Her Book. *Indian Econ. J.*, Oct.–Dec. 1989, *37*(2), pp. 1–7.

_____. John von Neumann's Model of an Expanding Economy: An Essay in Interpretation. In *Dore, M.; Chakravarty, S. and Goodwin, R., eds.*, 1989, pp. 69–81.

_____. Nicholas Kaldor on Indian Economic Problems. In *Lawson, T.; Palma, J. G. and Sender, J., eds.*, 1989, pp. 237–44.

_____. Nicholas Kaldor on Indian Economic Problems. *Cambridge J. Econ.*, March 1989, *13*(1), pp. 237–44.

_____; Goodwin, Richard M. and Dore, Mohammed H. I. John von Neumann and Modern Economics: Introduction. In *Dore, M.; Chakravarty, S. and Goodwin, R., eds.*, 1989, pp. 1–11.

Chalfant, James A. and Belongia, Michael T. The Changing Empirical Definition of Money: Some Estimates from a Model of the Demand for Money Substitutes. *J. Polit. Econ.*, April 1989, *97*(2), pp. 387–97.

Chalk, Andrew J. Market Forces and Aircraft Safety: Comment. *Econ. Inquiry*, April 1989, *27*(2), pp. 355–56.

Chalklin, C. W. Cultural Activities and Investment in Public Buildings in the Provincial Towns of Georgian England. In *Guarducci, A., ed.*, 1989, pp. 585–608.

Chalmers, James A.; Graves, Philip E. and Greenwood, Michael J. Regional Location Patterns in the United States: Recent Changes and Future Prospects. In *van Dijk, J., et al., eds.*, 1989, pp. 23–45.

Chaloupka, Frank and Saffer, Henry. Breath Testing and Highway Fatality Rates. *Appl. Econ.*, July 1989, *21*(7), pp. 901–12.

_____; Yamada, Tetsuji and Yamada, Tadashi. Nutrition and Infant Health in Japan. *J. Human Res.*, Fall 1989, *24*(4), pp. 725–36.

Chalupa, Svatopluk. The Restructuring of the Economic Mechanism in Agriculture. *Czech. Econ. Digest.*, May 1989, (3), pp. 31–36.

Chalupský, Zdeněk. The Council for Mutual Economic Assistance: The New Tasks. *Czech. Econ. Digest.*, September 1989, (6), pp. 52–64.

Chamberlain, Trevor W. Maturity Effects in Futures Markets: Some Evidence from the City of London. *Scot. J. Polit. Econ.*, February 1989, *36*(1), pp. 90–95.

_____ and Gordon, Myron J. Liquidity, Profitability, and Long-run Survival: Theory and Evidence on Business Investment. *J. Post Keynesian Econ.*, Summer 1989, *11*(4), pp. 589–610.

Chambers, Robert and Leach, Melissa. Trees as Savings and Security for the Rural Poor. *World Devel.*, March 1989, *17*(3), pp. 329–42.

Chambers, Robert G. Concentrated Objective Functions for Nonlinear Taxation Models. *J. Public Econ.*, August 1989, *39*(3), pp. 365–75.

_____. Insurability and Moral Hazard in Agricultural Insurance Markets. *Amer. J. Agr. Econ.*, August 1989, *71*(3), pp. 604–16.

_____. Recent Developments in Production Economics. *Econ. Rec.*, September 1989, *65*(190), pp. 243–64.

_____. Workfare or Welfare? *J. Public Econ.*, October 1989, *40*(1), pp. 79–97.

_____ and Just, Richard E. Estimating Multioutput Technologies. *Amer. J. Agr. Econ.*, November 1989, *71*(4), pp. 980–95.

_____ and Pope, Rulon D. Price Aggregation When Price-Taking Firms' Prices Vary. *Rev. Econ. Stud.*, April 1989, *56*(2), pp. 297–309.

_____ and Vasavada, Utpal. Technical Change and Applications of Dynamic Duality to Agriculture: Reply. *Amer. J. Agr. Econ.*, August 1989, *71*(3), pp. 803–04.

Chambua, Samwel; Hyuha, Theodora and Ma-

ganya, Ernest N. Outgrower Schemes in Tanzania: The Case of Tea and Sugarcane. *Eastern Afr. Econ. Rev.*, Special Issue, August 1989, pp. 70–82.

Chami, Saade N. and Butterfield, David W. The Implications of Myopic Policy-Making for Macroeconomic Performance. *Int. J. Forecasting,* 1989, 5(1), pp. 49–58.

Chamoux, Jean-Pierre. Privacy, Security, and Transborder Data Flow: A European View. In *Jussawalla, M.; Okuma, T. and Araki, T., eds.,* 1989, pp. 177–82.

Champion, Tony. Internal Migration and the Spatial Distribution of Population. In *Joshi, H., ed.,* 1989, pp. 110–32.

Champsaur, Paul. Information, Incentives, and General Equilibrium. In *Cornet, B. and Tulkens, H., eds.,* 1989, pp. 23–44.

_____ and Rochet, Jean-Charles. Multiproduct Duopolists. *Econometrica,* May 1989, 57(3), pp. 533–57.

Chan, Anthony and Chen, Carl R. Interest Rate Sensitivity, Asymmetry, and the Stock Returns of Financial Institutions. *Financial Rev.,* August 1989, 24(3), pp. 457–73.

Chan, Arthur H. The Changing View of Property Rights in Natural Resources Management. *Amer. J. Econ. Sociology,* April 1989, 48(2), pp. 193–201.

_____. To Market or Not to Market: Allocating Water Rights in New Mexico. *Natural Res. J.,* Summer 1989, 29(3), pp. 629–43.

_____. To Market or Not to Market: Allocation of Interstate Waters. *Natural Res. J.,* Spring 1989, 29(2), pp. 529–47.

Chan, K. C. and Stulz, René M. Risk and the Economy: A Finance Perspective. In *Stone, C. C., ed.,* 1989, pp. 79–117.

Chan, K. S. and Tong, Howell. A Survey on the Statistical Analysis of a Univariate Threshold Autoregressive Model. In *Mariano, R. S.; Lim, K. S. and Ling, K. D., eds.,* 1989, pp. 1–42.

Chan, Kenneth S. and Park, Se-Hark. A Cross-Country Input–Output Analysis of Intersectoral Relationships between Manufacturing and Services and Their Employment Implications. *World Devel.,* February 1989, 17(2), pp. 199–212.

_____ and Park, Se-Hark. A Cross-Country Study on the Role of the Service Sector. *J. Econ. Devel.,* December 1989, 14(2), pp. 35–54.

Chan, Yuk-Shee; Marino, Anthony M. and Campbell, Tim S. Incentive Contracts for Managers Who Discover and Manage Investment Projects. *J. Econ. Behav. Organ.,* December 1989, 12(3), pp. 353–64.

Chand, Sheetal K. Toward a Growth-Oriented Model of Financial Programming. *World Devel.,* April 1989, 17(4), pp. 473–90.

Chander, Parkash and Leruth, Luc. The Optimal Product Mix for a Monopolist in the Presence of Congestion Effects: A Model and Some Results. *Int. J. Ind. Organ.,* December 1989, 7(4), pp. 437–49.

Chandra, Ramesh; Gunay, Erdal and Aneja,

Yash P. A Portfolio Approach to Estimating the Average Correlation Coefficient for the Constant Correlation Model. *J. Finance,* December 1989, 44(5), pp. 1435–38.

_____ and Rohrbach, Kermit. The Power of Beaver's U against a Variance Increase in Market Model Residuals. *J. Acc. Res.,* Spring 1989, 27(1), pp. 145–55.

Chandy, P. R. and Hsueh, L. Paul. An Examination of the Yield Spread between Insured and Uninsured Debt. *J. Finan. Res.,* Fall 1989, 12(3), pp. 235–44.

Chaney, Paul K. Moral Hazard and Capital Budgeting. *J. Finan. Res.,* Summer 1989, 12(2), pp. 113–28.

Chang, Chan Sup. Human Resource Management in Korea. In *Chung, K. H. and Lee, H. C., eds.,* 1989, pp. 195–205.

Chang, Cyril F. and Tuckman, Howard P. Teacher Training and Teacher Optimism about the American Economic System. *J. Econ. Educ.,* Fall 1989, 20(4), pp. 335–45.

Chang, Eric C. and Pinegar, J. Michael. Seasonal Fluctuations in Industrial Production and Stock Market Seasonals. *J. Finan. Quant. Anal.,* March 1989, 24(1), pp. 59–74.

Chang, Eui Tae. Barriers to Korea's Manufactured Exports and Negotiating Options. In *Whalley, J., ed., Vol. 2,* 1989, pp. 139–58.

Chang, Hiuze and Yang, Haitian. Contracting, Leasing, and Selling All Unprofitable Enterprises. *Chinese Econ. Stud.,* Winter 1988–89, 22(2), pp. 95–104.

Chang, Hui-Shung and Green, Richard D. The Effects of Advertising on Food Demand Elasticities. *Can. J. Agr. Econ.,* November 1989, 37(3), pp. 481–94.

Chang, Kyung-Sup and Shin, Eui-Hang. Intra- and Intersectoral Processes of Wage Growth: An Examination of Wage Growth Dynamics and Contexts. *Soc. Sci. Quart.,* June 1989, 70(2), pp. 323–40.

Chang, S. J. and Chen, Son-Nan. Stock Price Adjustment to Earnings and Dividend Surprises. *Quart. Rev. Econ. Bus.,* Spring 1989, 29(1), pp. 68–81.

_____ and Chen, Son-Nan. A Study of Call Price Behavior under a Stationary Return Generating Process. *Financial Rev.,* August 1989, 24(3), pp. 335–54.

Chang, T. L.; Yen, Eva C. and Yen, Gili. On the Management of State-Owned Manufacturing Enterprises in Taiwan: An Application of Financial Ratio Analysis. In *Lee, C. F. and Hu, S.-C., eds.,* 1989, pp. 243–62.

Chang, Wen-Ya and Lai, Ching-Chong. The Fleming Proposition with Oligopolistic Pricing. *J. Post Keynesian Econ.,* Spring 1989, 11(3), pp. 460–73.

_____ and Lai, Ching-Chong. Income Taxes, Supply-Side Effects, and Currency Devaluation. *J. Macroecon.,* Spring 1989, 11(2), pp. 281–295.

_____ and Lai, Ching-Chong. Unionized Wages and Employment. *Atlantic Econ. J.,* June 1989, 17(2), pp. 76.

_____; Lai, Ching-Chong and Chu, Yun-Peng. Exchange Rate Dynamics under Dual Exchange Rates: The Case of Neutral Intervention Policy. *Manchester Sch. Econ. Soc. Stud.*, September 1989, *57*(3), pp. 235–47.

Chang, Winston W. and Kim, Jae-Cheol. Competition in Quality-Differentiated Products and Optimal Trade Policy. *Keio Econ. Stud.*, 1989, *26*(1), pp. 1–17.

_____ and Michael, Michael S. Optimal Commercial Policy for an Open Economy with Domestic Distortions. *Econ. Letters*, December 1989, *31*(2), pp. 163–67.

Chang, Yang-Ming and Pillarisetti, Janaki Ram. Debt and the Developing Countries: A Note on Optimal International Borrowing. *J. Devel. Stud.*, July 1989, *25*(4), pp. 576–79.

Chant, John F. Financial Institutions and Tax Reform. In *Mintz, J. and Whalley, J., eds.*, 1989, pp. 223–49.

Chao, Kalvin and Ravallion, Martin. Targeted Policies for Poverty Alleviation under Imperfect Information: Algorithms and Applications. *J. Policy Modeling*, Summer 1989, *11*(2), pp. 213–24.

Chaples, E. A. Public Funding of Elections in Australia. In *Alexander, H. E., ed.*, 1989, pp. 76–94.

Chapman, Bruce. Australian Economic Growth: Introduction. In *[Gruen, F. H.]*, 1989, pp. 1–6.

_____. Australian Economic Growth: Preface. In *[Gruen, F. H.]*, 1989, pp. x–xv.

Chapman, John W. and Pennock, J. Roland. Markets and Justice: NOMOS XXXI: Introduction. In *Chapman, J. W. and Pennock, J. R., eds.*, 1989, pp. 1–10.

Chapman, Ralph B. and Barker, George R. Evaluating Labor Market Contracting and Regulation: A Transaction Costs Perspective with Particular Reference to New Zealand. *J. Inst. Theoretical Econ.*, June 1989, *145*(2), pp. 317–42.

Chapman, Robert E.; Harris, Carl M. and Gass, Saul I. Analyzing the Economic Impacts of a Military Mobilization. In *Gulledge, T. R., Jr. and Litteral, L. A., eds.*, 1989, pp. 353–86.

Chappell, David and Dowd, Kevin. A Simple Model of Macroeconomic Policy. *Econ. Modelling*, October 1989, *6*(4), pp. 447–51.

Chard, J. S. and Mellor, C. J. Intellectual Property Rights and Parallel Imports. *World Econ.*, March 1989, *12*(1), pp. 69–83.

Charemza, Wojcieh W. Computational Controversies in Disequilibrium and Shortage Modelling of Centrally Planned Economies. *J. Econ. Surveys*, 1989, *3*(4), pp. 305–24.

Chari, Varadarajan V. Banking without Deposit Insurance or Bank Panics: Lessons from a Model of the U.S. National Banking System. *Fed. Res. Bank Minn. Rev.*, Summer 1989, *13*(3), pp. 3–19.

_____. Differences of Opinion in Financial Markets: Commentary. In *Stone, C. C., ed.*, 1989, pp. 38–40.

_____ and Jagannathan, Ravi. Adverse Selection

in a Model of Real Estate Lending. *J. Finance*, June 1989, *44*(2), pp. 499–508.

_____; Jones, Larry E. and Manuelli, Rodolfo E. Labor Contracts in a Model of Imperfect Competition. *Amer. Econ. Rev.*, May 1989, *79*(2), pp. 358–63.

_____; Kehoe, Patrick J. and Prescott, Edward C. Time Consistency and Policy. In *Barro, R. J., ed.*, 1989, pp. 265–305.

Charity, Douglas A.; Rasmussen, David W. and Fournier, Gary M. The Impact of Cost of Living Differentials on Migration of Elderly People to Florida. *Rev. Reg. Stud.*, Spring 1989, *19*(2), pp. 48–54.

Charles, Anthony T. Revisions to "In-Season Fishery Management: A Bayesian Model." *Natural Res. Modeling*, Spring 1989, *3*(2), pp. 289–90.

Charles, D. R. and Howells, Jeremy R. Research and Technological Development and Regional Policy: A European Perspective. In *Gibbs, D., ed.*, 1989, pp. 23–54.

Charles, Joni S. James. Information Externalities: Information Dissemination as a Policy Tool to Achieve Efficient Investment Decisions in a Two-Firm Oil Drilling Industry. *Studi. Econ.*, 1989, *44*(39), pp. 29–49.

Charles, Roger. Canada–United States Free Trade Agreement: A Canadian's Personal Perspective. *Nat. Westminster Bank Quart. Rev.*, May 1989, pp. 17–26.

Charlesworth, Neil. The Peasant and the Depression: The Case of the Bombay Presidency, India. In *Brown, I., ed.*, 1989, pp. 59–73.

Charnes, A.; Clarke, R. L. and Cooper, W. W. An Approach to Testing for Organizational Slack via Banker's Game Theoretic DEA Formulations. In *Chan, J. L. and Patton, J. M., eds.*, 1989, pp. 211–29.

_____, et al. Comparisons of DEA and Existing Ratio and Regression Systems for Effecting Efficiency Evaluations of Regulated Electric Cooperatives in Texas. In *Chan, J. L. and Patton, J. M., eds.*, 1989, pp. 187–210.

Charpin, Françoise. Les contraintes de liquidité dans la théorie du cycle de vie. (Liquidity Constraints in the Life Cycle Model. With English summary.) *Ann. Écon. Statist.*, April–June 1989, (14), pp. 65–101.

Chase-Dunn, Christopher and O'Reilly, Kenneth. Core Wars of the Future. In *Schaeffer, R. K., ed.*, 1989, pp. 47–64.

Chase-Lansdale, P. Lindsay; Michael, Robert T. and Desai, Sonalde. Mother or Market? Effects of Maternal Employment on the Intellectual Ability of 4-Year-Old Children. *Demography*, November 1989, *26*(4), pp. 544–61.

Chase, Richard X. The Popperian Legacy in Economics: A Review Article. *J. Econ. Issues*, December 1989, *23*(4), pp. 1149–58.

_____. Unity in the Social Thought of Adolph Lowe: A Review of "Essays in Political Economics: Public Control in a Democratic Society." *Amer. J. Econ. Sociology*, January 1989, *48*(1), pp. 101–11.

Chase-Wilde, Linda and Klein, Kurt K. Growth

and Development of Value-Added Activities. **In** *Schmitz, A., ed.*, 1989, pp. 88–138.

Chasse, John Dennis. John R. Commons and the Democratic State. **In** *Tool, M. R. and Samuels, W. J., eds. (III)*, 1989, *1986*, pp. 131–56.

Chateau, J.-P.D. Liability Management of Financial Intermediaries in a Dynamic and Uncertain Perspective: Corrigendum. *Europ. Econ. Rev.*, September 1989, *33*(7), pp. 1487–88.

Chateauneuf, Alain and Jaffray, Jean-Yves. Some Characterizations of Lower Probabilities and Other Monotone Capacities through the Use of Möbius Inversion. *Math. Soc. Sci.*, June 1989, *17*(3), pp. 263–83.

Chatfield, Robert E.; Moyer, R. Charles and Sisneros, Phillip M. The Accuracy of Long-term Earnings Forecasts for Industrial Firms. *Quart. J. Bus. Econ.*, Summer 1989, *28*(3), pp. 91–104.

———; **Sisneros, Phillip M. and Moyer, R. Charles.** Security Analysts Monitoring Activity: Agency Costs and Information Demands. *J. Finan. Quant. Anal.*, December 1989, *24*(4), pp. 503–12.

Chatterjee, Lata. Women and Technological Development. **In** *Andersson, Å. E., et al., eds.*, 1989, pp. 53–66.

Chatterjee, S. K. Forty Years of International Action for Trade Liberalization. *J. World Trade*, August 1989, *23*(4), pp. 45–64.

Chatterjee, Satyajit and Cooper, Russell. Multiplicity of Equilibria and Fluctuations in Dynamic Imperfectly Competitive Economies. *Amer. Econ. Rev.*, May 1989, *79*(2), pp. 353–57.

Chatterjee, Sris and Scott, James H., Jr. Explaining Differences in Corporate Capital Structure: Theory and New Evidence. *J. Banking Finance*, May 1989, *13*(2), pp. 283–309.

Chatterji, Monojit and Booth, Alison L. Redundancy Payments and Firm-Specific Training. *Economica*, November 1989, *56*(224), pp. 505–21.

——— **and Lahiri, Sajal.** Private Foreign Investment and Welfare in LDCs. **In** *Singer, H. W. and Sharma, S., eds. (II)*, 1989, pp. 220–29.

Chattopadhyay, M. and Bhattacharya, N. Time Trends in the Level of Living in Rural India: A Critical Study of the Evidence from Large-Scale Surveys. **In** *Bardhan, P., ed. (I)*, 1989, pp. 32–75.

Chaudhry, Kiren Aziz. The Price of Wealth: Business and State in Labor Remittance and Oil Economies. *Int. Organ.*, Winter 1989, *43*(1), pp. 101–45.

Chaudhry, M. Ghaffer. The Agrarian Sector in Pakistan's Development Process—Historical Evidence and Implications for Policy and Theory: Comments. *Pakistan Devel. Rev.*, Winter 1989, *28*(4), pp. 526–28.

Chaudhuri, Sarmila and Chaudhuri, Tamal Datta. The Extent of Wage Indexation in Indian Industries. *J. Macroecon.*, Summer 1989, *11*(3), pp. 455–61.

Chaudhuri, Tamal Datta. A Theoretical Analysis

of the Informal Sector. *World Devel.*, March 1989, *17*(3), pp. 351–55.

——— **and Chaudhuri, Sarmila.** The Extent of Wage Indexation in Indian Industries. *J. Macroecon.*, Summer 1989, *11*(3), pp. 455–61.

Chaudhury, Mohammed M. An Approximately Unbiased Estimator for the Theoretical Black-Scholes European Call Valuation. *Bull. Econ. Res.*, April 1989, *41*(2), pp. 137–46.

Chaudry-Shah, Anwar M. A Capitalization Approach to Fiscal Incidence at the Local Level. *Land Econ.*, November 1989, *65*(4), pp. 359–75.

Chavas, Jean-Paul. How Restrictive Is the Prais–Houthakker Model? *Europ. Econ. Rev.*, September 1989, *33*(7), pp. 1363–72.

———. On the Structure of Demand for Meat. **In** *Buse, R. C., ed.*, 1989, pp. 125–35.

——— **and Bromley, Daniel W.** On Risk, Transactions, and Economic Development in the Semiarid Tropics. *Econ. Devel. Cult. Change*, July 1989, *37*(4), pp. 719–36.

———; **Stoll, John R. and Sellar, Christine.** On the Commodity Value of Travel Time in Recreational Activities. *Appl. Econ.*, June 1989, *21*(6), pp. 711–22.

Cheadle, Allen. Explaining Patterns of Profit-Sharing Activity. *Ind. Relat.*, Fall 1989, *28*(3), pp. 387–400.

———; **Scheffler, Richard M. and Haas-Wilson, Deborah.** Demand for Mental Health Services: An Episode of Treatment Approach. *Southern Econ. J.*, July 1989, *56*(1), pp. 219–32.

Cheasty, Adrienne and Blejer, Mario I. Fiscal Policy and Mobilization of Savings for Growth. **In** *Blejer, M. I. and Chu, K., eds.*, 1989, *1986*, pp. 33–49.

——— **and Blejer, Mario I.** High Inflation, "Heterodox" Stabilization, and Fiscal Policy. **In** *Blejer, M. I. and Chu, K., eds.*, 1989, *1988*, pp. 72–98.

Cheater, A. P. and Jackson, J. C. Contract Farming: Sugar, Tea and Cotton in Zimbabwe. *Eastern Afr. Econ. Rev.*, Special Issue, August 1989, pp. 97–107.

Checchi, Daniele. Economic Interdependence and Structural Change. Some Results from Principal Component Analysis. *Econ. Notes*, 1989, (1), pp. 16–36.

———. Economic Interdependence and Structural Change: An Investigation on Business Cycle Transmission. *Int. Rev. Applied Econ.*, January 1989, *3*(1), pp. 57–88.

——— **and Valli, Vittorio.** Investimenti ed occupazione: Un approccio strutturale. (Investment and Employment: A Structural Approach. With English summary.) *Giorn. Econ.*, Jan.–Feb. 1989, *48*(1–2), pp. 3–34.

Checchio, Elizabeth; Shupe, Steven J. and Weatherford, Gary D. Western Water Rights: The Era of Reallocation. *Natural Res. J.*, Spring 1989, *29*(2), pp. 413–34.

Checkland, S. G. British Public Policy, 1776–1939. **In** *Mathias, P. and Pollard, S., eds.*, 1989, pp. 607–40.

Chee, Peng Lim. The Changing Role of Transnational Corporations in the Asian-Pacific Region. In *Shinohara, M. and Lo, F., eds.*, 1989, pp. 351–81.

Chelius, James and Lee, Barbara A. Government Regulation of Labor–Management Corruption: The Casino Industry Experience in New Jersey. *Ind. Lab. Relat. Rev.*, July 1989, *42*(4), pp. 536–48.

Chelliah, Raja J. Changes in Tax Revenue Structure: A Case Study of India. In *Chiancone, A. and Messere, K., eds.*, 1989, pp. 153–65.

Chen, Andrew H. and Ling, David C. Optimal Mortgage Refinancing with Stochastic Interest Rates. *Amer. Real Estate Urban Econ. Assoc. J.*, Fall 1989, *17*(3), pp. 278–99.

Chen, Carl R. Some Evidence on Yield Changes and the Systematic Risk of Bonds. *Quart. J. Bus. Econ.*, Winter 1989, *28*(1), pp. 43–54.

_____ **and Chan, Anthony.** Interest Rate Sensitivity, Asymmetry, and the Stock Returns of Financial Institutions. *Financial Rev.*, August 1989, *24*(3), pp. 457–73.

Chen, Chau-nan and Lai, Ching-Chong. Money, Consumption, and Terms-of-Trade Dynamics: A Note. *Int. Econ. Rev.*, November 1989, *30*(4), pp. 1005–09.

_____; **Tsaur, Tien-wang and Liu, Shun-chieh.** Currency Substitution, Foreign Inflation, and Terms-of-Trade Dynamics. *J. Polit. Econ.*, August 1989, *97*(4), pp. 955–64.

Chen, Chien-Hsun. Monetary Aggregates and Macroeconomic Performance in Mainland China. *J. Compar. Econ.*, June 1989, *13*(2), pp. 314–24.

Chen, Edward K. Y. The Changing Role of the Asian NICs in the Asian-Pacific Region towards the Year 2000. In *Shinohara, M. and Lo, F., eds.*, 1989, pp. 207–31.

_____. Towards the Asian-Pacific Age: Comment. In *Shinohara, M. and Lo, F., eds.*, 1989, pp. 132–34.

_____. Trade Policy in Asia. In *Naya, S., et al., eds.*, 1989, pp. 55–76.

Chen, Guo-quan and Yu, Eden S. H. On Fuzzy Quantity and Fuzzy Isoquant. *Math. Soc. Sci.*, February 1989, *17*(1), pp. 17–31.

Chen, H. K. and Nagurney, Anna. An Algorithm for the Solution of a Quadratic Programming Problem, with Application to Constrained Matrix and Spatial Price Equilibrium Problems. *Environ. Planning A*, January 1989, *21*(1), pp. 99–114.

Chen, Jiasheng. China's Market Reforms in Comparative Perspective. In *Van Ness, P., ed.*, 1989, pp. 123–42.

Chen, K. C.; Hite, Gailen L. and Cheng, David C. Barriers to Entry, Concentration, and Tobin's q Ratio. *Quart. J. Bus. Econ.*, Spring 1989, *28*(2), pp. 32–49.

Chen, Liren. China's Current Population Situation and the Raising of Labour Productivity. In *Howe, C. and Walker, K. R., eds.*, 1989, *1957*, pp. 323–25.

Chen, Marty. A Sectoral Approach to Promoting Women's Work: Lessons from India. *World Devel.*, July 1989, *17*(7), pp. 1007–16.

Chen, Peter and Veeman, Michele. Estimating Market Demand Functions for Meat: An Update of Elasticity Estimates. *Can. J. Agr. Econ.*, Part 2, December 1989, *37*(4), pp. 1061–69.

Chen, Qiwei. Policies for Economic Reform in China. In *Zerby, J., ed.*, 1989, pp. 97–109.

Chen, Shenshen. Clarifying Property Rights Relationships Is a Necessary Premise: A Second Discussion on Establishing a New Order of Market Economy. *Chinese Econ. Stud.*, Fall 1989, *23*(1), pp. 57–63.

_____. On the Question of Ownership and Property Rights: Editor's Introduction. *Chinese Econ. Stud.*, Fall 1989, *23*(1), pp. 3–7.

Chen, Son-Nan and Chang, S. J. Stock Price Adjustment to Earnings and Dividend Surprises. *Quart. Rev. Econ. Bus.*, Spring 1989, *29*(1), pp. 68–81.

_____ **and Chang, S. J.** A Study of Call Price Behavior under a Stationary Return Generating Process. *Financial Rev.*, August 1989, *24*(3), pp. 335–54.

Chen, Thomas P. The Internationalization of the Taiwanese Economy. In *Lee, C. F. and Hu, S.-C., eds.*, 1989, pp. 201–11.

Chen, Wen Ya. Incentives for Management in China: The Economic Responsibility System. In *Davies, J., et al., eds.*, 1989, pp. 97–111.

Chen, Xikang. Input–Output Techniques in China. *Econ. Systems Res.*, 1989, *1*(1), pp. 87–95.

Chen, Yizi; Wang, Xiaoqiang and Gao, Shangquan. Investigation of Reforms in Hungary and Yugoslavia. *Chinese Econ. Stud.*, Spring 1989, *22*(3), pp. 80–88.

Chen, Yun. The Present Situation in Finance and Economics and Certain Measures to Overcome Difficulties. In *Howe, C. and Walker, K. R., eds.*, 1989, *1962*, pp. 115–30.

Cheng, David C.; Chen, K. C. and Hite, Gailen L. Barriers to Entry, Concentration, and Tobin's q Ratio. *Quart. J. Bus. Econ.*, Spring 1989, *28*(2), pp. 32–49.

_____; **Gup, Benton E. and Wall, Larry D.** Financial Determinants of Bank Takeovers: A Note. *J. Money, Credit, Banking*, November 1989, *21*(4), pp. 524–36.

Cheng, Joseph L. C. Toward a Contextual Approach to Cross-National Organization Research: A Macro Perspective. In *Prasad, S. B., ed.*, 1989, pp. 3–18.

Cheng, Leonard K. Intermittent Trade Disruptions and Optimal Production. *Int. Econ. Rev.*, November 1989, *30*(4), pp. 753–74.

Cheng, Louis; Davidson, Wallace N., III and Dutia, Dipa. A Re-examination of the Market Reaction to Failed Mergers. *J. Finance*, September 1989, *44*(4), pp. 1077–83.

Cheng, Soo May. Worker Participation in Private Companies in Singapore: Corporate and Individual Orientations. In *Nedd, A., ed.*, 1989, pp. 97–120.

Cheng, Tun-jen and Haggard, Stephan. The New Bilateralism: The East Asian NICs in American

Foreign Economic Policy. In *Haggard, S. and Moon, C., eds.*, 1989, pp. 305–29.

Cheng, Wei-Yuan. Testing the Food-First Hypothesis: A Cross-National Study of Dependency, Sectoral Growth and Food Intake in Less Developed Countries. *World Devel.*, January 1989, *17*(1), pp. 17–27.

Cheng, Yannian and Xin, Naiquan. The Relationship between Fluctuations in Food Crop Yields and Meteorological Conditions in China. In *Oram, P. A., et al.*, 1989, pp. 85–92.

Cheong, Ken and Foster, Robin. Auctioning the ITV Franchises. In *Hughes, G. and Vines, D., eds.*, 1989, pp. 91–125.

Chern, Wen S. The Energy Sector and Economic Growth. In *James, W. E., ed.*, 1989, pp. 17–28.

Chernick, Howard and Reschovsky, Andrew. Federal Tax Reform and the Taxation of Urban Residents. *Public Finance Quart.*, April 1989, *17*(2), pp. 123–57.

Chernomas, Robert. The Restructuring of the U.S. Health Care System: Comment on Reynolds's "Medical Care and Institutional Change." *J. Econ. Issues*, December 1989, *23*(4), pp. 1172–79.

Chernotsky, Harry I. Trade Adjustment and Foreign Direct Investment: Japan in the United States. In *Haggard, S. and Moon, C., eds.*, 1989, pp. 275–303.

Cherry, Robert. Controversies in the Marxian Analysis of Racial Discrimination: Reply. *Rev. Radical Polit. Econ.*, Winter 1989, *21*(4), pp. 80–82.

_____. Minimum Wage and Pure Discrimination: A Note. *Eastern Econ. J.*, Jan.–March 1989, *15*(1), pp. 55–62.

Chesher, Andrew. Hájek Inequalities, Measures of Leverage and the Size of Heteroskedasticity Robust Wald Tests. *Econometrica*, July 1989, *57*(4), pp. 971–77.

Cheshire, Paul and Sheppard, Stephen. British Planning Policy and Access to Housing: Some Empirical Estimates. *Urban Stud.*, October 1989, *26*(5), pp. 469–85.

Cheshkov, M. Bureaucracy in the Modern World. *Prob. Econ.*, September 1989, *32*(5), pp. 80–88.

Chesney, Marc and Scott, Louis O. Pricing European Currency Options: A Comparison of the Modified Black–Scholes Model and a Random Variance Model. *J. Finan. Quant. Anal.*, September 1989, *24*(3), pp. 267–84.

Chesshire, John. The Energy Demand Impact of Conservation Technology. In *Hawdon, D., ed.*, 1989, pp. 39–53.

Chestnut, Lauraine G.; Violette, Daniel M. and Fisher, Ann. The Value of Reducing Risks of Death: A Note on New Evidence. *J. Policy Anal. Manage.*, Winter 1989, *8*(1), pp. 88–100.

Cheung, C. S. and Gaa, J. C. Controlling Opportunistic Behavior in Corporate Governance: The Role of Disproportionate Voting Shares and Coat-Tail Provisions. *J. Inst. Theoretical Econ.*, September 1989, *145*(3), pp. 438–50.

Cheung, Steven N. S. Privatization vs. Special Interests: The Experience of China's Economic Reforms. *Cato J.*, Winter 1989, *8*(3), pp. 585–96.

_____. Privatization vs. Special Interests: The Experience of China's Economic Reforms. *Hong Kong Econ. Pap.*, 1989, (19), pp. 1–8.

_____. Transaction Costs, Risk Aversion, and the Choice of Contractual Arrangements. In *Diamond, P. and Rothschild, M., eds.*, 1989, *1969*, pp. 379–98.

de la Chevallerie, Oskar. Bevölkerungsstruktur und Altersversorgung. Überlegungen zum Umlage- und Kapitaldeckungsverfahren bei alternativen Geburtenzahlen. (Population Structure and Social Security for the Old: Social Insurance on a Pay-as-You-Go or Fully Funded Basis at Various Birth Rates. With English summary.) *Konjunkturpolitik*, 1989, *35*(5), pp. 276–87.

Chevan, Albert. The Growth of Home Ownership: 1940–1980. *Demography*, May 1989, *26*(2), pp. 249–66.

Chevez, Pablo; Kiehnle, Herman and Sainz O., Manuel. The Disregard of a Legal Entity for Tax Purposes: Mexico. In *International Fiscal Association, ed. (II)*, 1989, pp. 381–89.

Chew, Rosalind and Chew, Soon Beng. Industrial Relations in Singapore. *Singapore Econ. Rev.*, October 1989, *34*(2), pp. 47–63.

Chew, Soo Hong and Epstein, Larry G. The Structure of Preferences and Attitudes towards the Timing of the Resolution of Uncertainty. *Int. Econ. Rev.*, February 1989, *30*(1), pp. 103–17.

_____ and Epstein, Larry G. A Unifying Approach to Axiomatic Non-expected Utility Theories. *J. Econ. Theory*, December 1989, *49*(2), pp. 207–40.

Chew, Soon Beng and Chew, Rosalind. Industrial Relations in Singapore. *Singapore Econ. Rev.*, October 1989, *34*(2), pp. 47–63.

Chewning, Gene; Pany, Kurt and Wheeler, Stephen. Auditor Reporting Decisions Involving Accounting Principle Changes: Some Evidence on Materiality Thresholds. *J. Acc. Res.*, Spring 1989, *27*(1), pp. 78–96.

Cheysson, Claude. Europe's Dilemma. In *Cerami, C. A., ed.*, 1989, pp. 83–91.

Chhibber, Ajay and Thomas, Vinod. Experience with Policy Reforms under Adjustment. *Finance Devel.*, March 1989, *26*(1), pp. 28–31.

Chi, Eric M. and Reinsel, Gregory C. Models for Longitudinal Data with Random Effects and AR(1) Errors. *J. Amer. Statist. Assoc.*, June 1989, *84*(406), pp. 452–59.

Chi, Hua-Shan. Substitution between Production Labor and Other Imputs in Unionized and Nonunionized Manufacturing: Comment. *Rev. Econ. Statist.*, August 1989, *71*(3), pp. 549–52.

Chi, Wan Fu and Alston, Richard M. Graphing the Model or Modeling the Graph? Not-So-Subtle Problems in Linear *IS–LM* Analysis. *J. Econ. Educ.*, Summer 1989, *20*(3), pp. 261–67.

Chiancone, Aldo. Changes in Revenue Structures. In *Chiancone, A. and Messere, K., eds.*, 1989, pp. 1–7.

Chiang, Raymond and Lasser, Dennis J. Tax Timing Options on Futures Contracts and the 1981 Economic Recovery Act. *Financial Rev.*, February 1989, *24*(1), pp. 75–92.

Chiao, Yen-Shong and Gillingham, Allan. The Value of Stabilizing Fertilizer under Carry-Over Conditions. *Amer. J. Agr. Econ.*, May 1989, *71*(2), pp. 352–62.

Chiappori, Pierre-André and Bénard, Jean. Second Best Optimum under Morishima Separability and Exogenous Price Constraints. *Europ. Econ. Rev.*, September 1989, *33*(7), pp. 1313–28.

_____ **and Guesnerie, Roger.** On Stationary Sunspot Equilibria of Order *k*. In *Barnett, W. A.; Geweke, J. and Shell, K., eds.*, 1989, pp. 21–44.

Chiarella, Carl; Kemp, Murray C. and Long, Ngo Van. Innovation and the Transfer of Technology: A Leader–Follower Model. *Econ. Modelling*, October 1989, *6*(4), pp. 452–56.

Chiarini, Bruno. Il mercato del lavoro nei modelli macroeconomici. Una rassegna dell'evidenza econometrica nei modelli italiani. (The Labor Market in Macroeconomic Models. An Outline of the Econometric Evidence of Italian Models. With English summary.) *Econ. Lavoro*, July–Sept. 1989, *23*(3), pp. 3–24.

_____. Models with Rational Expectations: Technical Issues. *Econ. Notes*, 1989, (3), pp. 314–34.

_____. Specifying the Objective Function. *Rivista Int. Sci. Econ. Com.*, July 1989, *36*(7), pp. 623–41.

Chib, Siddhartha; Cooley, Thomas F. and Parke, William R. Predictive Efficiency for Simple Non-linear Models. *J. Econometrics*, January 1989, *40*(1), pp. 33–44.

_____; **Tiwari, R. C. and Jammalamadaka, S. R.** Bayes Prediction Density and Regression Estimation—A Semiparametric Approach. In *Ullah, A., ed.*, 1989, *1988*, pp. 87–100.

Chick, V. A Comment on '*IS–LM:* An Explanation.' In *Wood, J. C. and Woods, R. N., eds.*, Vol. 3, 1989, *1982*, pp. 302–06.

Chicoine, David L. and Deller, Steven C. Economic Diversification and the Rural Economy: Evidence from Consumer Behavior. *Reg. Sci. Persp.*, 1989, *19*(2), pp. 41–55.

_____; **Walzer, N. and Deller, Steven C.** Representative vs. Direct Democracy and Government Spending in a Median Voter Model. *Public Finance*, 1989, *44*(2), pp. 225–36.

Chiesa, Jeffrey Scott; Keating, Barry P. and Bundt, Thomas P. Common Bond Type and Credit Union Behavior. *Rev. Soc. Econ.*, Spring 1989, *47*(1), pp. 27–42.

Chiesi, Antonio M. and Martinelli, Alberto. The Capitalist Class: Italy. In *Bottomore, T. and Brym, R. J., eds.*, 1989, pp. 109–39.

_____ **and Martinelli, Alberto.** The Representation of Business Interests as a Mechanism of Social Regulation. In *Lange, P. and Regini, M., eds.*, 1989, pp. 187–213.

Childs, Nathan W. and Hammig, Michael D. An Empirical Examination of the Link between Monetary Policy and U.S. Agricultural Commodity Exports. *Appl. Econ.*, February 1989, *21*(2), pp. 155–73.

Chilosi, Alberto. Kalecki's Quest for the Microeconomic Foundations of His Macroeconomic Theory. In *Sebastiani, M., ed.*, 1989, pp. 101–20.

Chinchilli, Vernon M.; Carter, Walter H., Jr. and Gennings, Chris. Response Surface Analysis with Correlated Data: A Nonlinear Model Approach. *J. Amer. Statist. Assoc.*, September 1989, *84*(407), pp. 805–09.

_____; **Schwab, Barry H. and Sen, Pranab K.** Inference Based on Ranks for the Multiple-Design Multivariate Linear Model. *J. Amer. Statist. Assoc.*, June 1989, *84*(406), pp. 517–24.

Chinloy, Peter. The Probability of Prepayment. *J. Real Estate Finance Econ.*, December 1989, *2*(4), pp. 267–83.

Chinn, Menzie. A Tale of Two Markets: Capital Market Integration and the Determination of Exchange Rates. In *[Marjolin, R.]*, 1989, pp. 193–212.

Chiplin, Brian; Coyne, John and Wright, Mike. The Market for Corporate Control: The Divestment Option. In *Fairburn, J. and Kay, J., eds.*, 1989, pp. 116–32.

Chipman, John S. The Classical Transfer Problem and the Theory of Foreign Exchanges. In *Feiwel, G. R., ed. (II)*, 1989, pp. 739–73.

_____. A Public Choice Analysis of Strategies for Restoring International Economic Stability: Comments. In *Vosgerau, H.-J., ed.*, 1989, pp. 31–33.

_____. Reminiscences of Joan Robinson. In *Feiwel, G. R., ed. (II)*, 1989, pp. 868–69.

Chirathivat, Suthiphand and Akrasanee, Narongchai. Trade Issues among ASEAN, Asian NICs and Japan. In *Shinohara, M. and Lo, F., eds.*, 1989, pp. 400–433.

Chirco, Alessandra. Analisi statica e analisi dinamica nei modelli di "search equilibrium." (Statics and Dynamics in Equilibrium Search Models. With English summary.) *Econ. Politica*, April 1989, *6*(1), pp. 67–98.

Chirikos, Thomas N. and Nestel, Gilbert. Functional Capacities of Older Men for Extended Work Lives. *Soc. Sec. Bull.*, August 1989, *52*(8), pp. 14–16.

Chirot, Daniel. Causes and Consequences of Backwardness. In *Chirot, D., ed.*, 1989, pp. 1–14.

Chishti, Salim and Hasan, M. Aynul. Relative Prices and Inflation Variability. *Pakistan J. Appl. Econ.*, Summer 1989, *8*(1), pp. 73–84.

Chisman, Forrest. An Effective Employment Policy: The Missing Middle. In *Bawden, D. L. and Skidmore, F., eds.*, 1989, pp. 249–64.

Chiswick, Barry R. Immigrant Earnings Adjustment: An International Comparison. In *Beach, C. M. and Green, A. G.*, 1989, pp. 40–53.

Chiswick, Carmel U. The Impact of Immigration on the Human Capital of Natives. *J. Lab. Econ.*, October 1989, *7*(4), pp. 464–86.

Chittenden, William T.; Evans, Dorla A. and Holcomb, James H. The Relationship between Risk-Return Preference and Knowledge in Experimental Financial Markets. *J. Behav. Econ.*, Spring 1989, *18*(1), pp. 19–40.

Chizhova, L. Regulating the Employment of the Population. *Prob. Econ.*, May 1989, *32*(1), pp. 52–64.

Chmura, Christine and Ihrig, Jane. Changes in Manufacturing Employment in North Carolina Counties, 1980–85. *Fed. Res. Bank Richmond Econ. Rev.*, Sept.–Oct. 1989, *75*(5), pp. 37–46.

Cho, Dong Sung. Diversification Strategy of Korean Firms. In *Chung, K. H. and Lee, H. C., eds.*, 1989, pp. 99–112.

Cho, Soon. U.S. International Macroeconomic Policy: Discussion. In *Bayard, T. O. and Young, S.-G., eds.*, 1989, pp. 34–37.

Cho, Yoon Je. Finance and Development: The Korean Approach. *Oxford Rev. Econ. Policy*, Winter 1989, *5*(4), pp. 88–102.

Choguill, Charles L. Small Towns and Development: A Tale from Two Countries. *Urban Stud.*, April 1989, *26*(2), pp. 267–74.

Choi, Chong-Ki. Structural Adjustment in the World Economy and East–West–South Economic Cooperation: A Study on Regional Cooperation in the Pacific Basin. In *Wohlmuth, K., ed.*, 1989, pp. 515–44.

Choi, Daniel F. S. and Ward, Charles W. R. The Reconciliation of the Smith's and Jarrow and Rudd's Option Sensitivity Formulae: A Teaching Note. *Financial Rev.*, August 1989, *24*(3), pp. 507–10.

Choi, Dosoung; Kamma, Sreenivas and Weintrop, Joseph. The Delaware Courts, Poison Pills, and Shareholder Wealth. *J. Law, Econ., Organ.*, Fall 1989, *5*(2), pp. 375–93.

Choi, Eun Kwan and Casas, François R. Transport Costs and Immiserizing Growth under Variable Returns to Scale. *Int. J. Transport Econ.*, February 1989, *16*(1), pp. 3–18.

_____ **and Johnson, Stanley R.** Stochastic Dominance and Uncertain Price Prospects. *Southern Econ. J.*, January 1989, *55*(3), pp. 699–709.

_____ **and Lapan, Harvey E.** Errata [Tariffs versus Quotas under Uncertainty: Restricting Imports and the Role of Preferences]. *Int. Econ. J.*, Spring 1989, *3*(1), pp. 103.

Choi, J. Y. and Shastri, Kuldeep. Bid–Ask Spreads and Volatility Estimates: The Implications for Option Pricing. *J. Banking Finance*, May 1989, *13*(2), pp. 207–19.

Choi, Jongmoo Jay; Fabozzi, Frank J. and Yaari, Uzi. Optimum Corporate Leverage with Risky Debt: A Demand Approach. *J. Finan. Res.*, Summer 1989, *12*(2), pp. 129–42.

Choi, Seungmook S. and Barnett, William A. A Comparison between the Conventional Econometric Approach to Structural Inference and the Nonparametric Chaotic Attractor Approach. In *Barnett, W. A.; Geweke, J. and Shell, K., eds.*, 1989, pp. 141–212.

_____ **and Barnett, William A.** A Monte Carlo Study of Tests of Blockwise Weak Separability.

J. Bus. Econ. Statist., July 1989, *7*(3), pp. 363–77.

Choi, Yong Yil. Cross-Technology Trade and the Positive Sum Effect. *Int. Econ. J.*, Summer 1989, *3*(2), pp. 57–71.

Choi, Young Back. Political Economy of Han Feitzu. *Hist. Polit. Econ.*, Summer 1989, *21*(2), pp. 367–90.

Choie, Kenneth S. and Novomestky, Frederick. Replication of Long-term with Short-term Options. *J. Portfol. Manage.*, Winter 1989, *15*(2), pp. 17–19.

_____ **and Seff, Eric J.** TIPP: Insurance without Complexity: Comment. *J. Portfol. Manage.*, Fall 1989, *16*(1), pp. 107–08.

Choksi, Armeane; Papageorgiou, Demetris and Michaely, Michael. The Design of Trade Liberalization. *Finance Devel.*, March 1989, *26*(1), pp. 2–5.

Chong, Eddie Chiew Fook and Arshad, Fatimah Mohd. Food Trade among Developing Countries. In *Helmuth, J. W. and Johnson, S. R., eds., Vol. 2*, 1989, pp. 276–302.

Choo, E. U.; Wedley, William C. and Lam, K. F. Linear Goal Programming in Estimation of Classification Probability. In *Lockett, A. G. and Islei, G., eds.*, 1989, pp. 166–78.

Chopra, Navin and Ritter, Jay R. Portfolio Rebalancing and the Turn-of-the-Year Effect. *J. Finance*, March 1989, *44*(1), pp. 149–66.

Choudhry, Muhammad A. and Calzonetti, Frank J. The Power Trade Alternative. In *Calzonetti, F. J., et al.*, 1989, pp. 75–99.

Choudhury, Masudul Alam. Application of Optimal Debt Financing and Managed International Trade Arrangements to Islamic Countries. In *Choudhury, M. A.*, 1989, pp. 248–71.

_____ . Appropriateness of the Basic Needs Approach to Regional Economic Co-operation among Islamic Countries. In *Choudhury, M. A.*, 1989, pp. 230–47.

_____ . The Blending of Religious and Social Orders in Islam. *Int. J. Soc. Econ.*, 1989, *16*(2), pp. 13–45.

_____ . Critique and Alternatives to Contemporary Approaches in International Economic Co-operation. In *Choudhury, M. A.*, 1989, pp. 42–65.

_____ . Decision-Making under Consensus: The Case of Economic Co-operation. In *Choudhury, M. A.*, 1989, pp. 23–41.

_____ . The Humanomic Structure of Islamic Economic Theory. In *Choudhury, M. A.*, 1989, pp. 1–22.

_____ . The Idea of Islamic Economic Co-operation in Contemporary Perspectives. In *Choudhury, M. A.*, 1989, pp. 66–93.

_____ . The Idea of Islamic Economic Cooperation in Contemporary Perspectives. *J. Econ. Devel.*, December 1989, *14*(2), pp. 77–97.

_____ . Inter-Islamic Economic Co-operation and Integration: Institutions, Strategies and Obstacles. In *Choudhury, M. A.*, 1989, pp. 203–29.

_____ . Islamic Economic Co-operation: Conclusion. In *Choudhury, M. A.*, 1989, pp. 411–19.

——. Islamic Economic Co-operation in the South–South Context. In *Choudhury, M. A.*, 1989, pp. 375–410.

——. Islamic Economic Thought in Comparative Perspectives. *Middle East Bus. Econ. Rev.*, July 1989, *1*(2), pp. 43–50.

——. Manpower Exchange and Social Security System for Islamic Economic Co-operation. In *Choudhury, M. A.*, 1989, pp. 316–51.

——. The Potential for Labour Mobility between Islamic Countries as an Example of Islamic Economic Co-operation: The Case of the Arab Gulf Region in the 1980s. In *Choudhury, M. A.*, 1989, pp. 295–315.

——. The Potential Impact of Islamic Economic Co-operation on the World Economy. In *Choudhury, M. A.*, 1989, pp. 352–74.

——. Principles and Instruments of Islamic Economic Co-operation. In *Choudhury, M. A.*, 1989, pp. 94–132.

——. Privatisation of the Islamic Dinar as an Instrument for the Development of an Islamic Capital Market. In *Choudhury, M. A.*, 1989, pp. 272–94.

——. Resource Endowment and Allocation in Islamic Countries for Economic Co-operation. In *Choudhury, M. A.*, 1989, pp. 133–55.

——. Some Critical Issues in Development Financing for the Low- and Middle-Income Countries with a Special Reference to Selected Islamic Countries. In *Choudhury, M. A.*, 1989, pp. 159–202.

Choudhury, Saud A. and Islam, Muhammed N. The Flypaper Effect and the Revenue Impact of Grants-in-Aid. *Econ. Letters*, October 1989, *30*(4), pp. 351–56.

Chouraqui, J. C.; Driscoll, Michael J. and Strauss-Kahn, Marc-Olivier. The Effects of Monetary Policy on the Real Sector: What Do We Know? *Banca Naz. Lavoro Quart. Rev.*, March 1989, (168), pp. 3–46.

Chow, Chee W.; McNamee, Alan H. and Plumlee, R. David. Focusing Audit Aids for Enhanced Audit Efficiency and Effectiveness. In *Gangolly, J., ed.*, 1989, pp. 195–204.

——; **Shields, Michael D. and Whittenburg, Gerald E.** The Quality of Practioners' Judgments Regarding Substantial Authority: An Exploratory Empirical Investigation. In *Jones, S. M., ed.*, 1989, pp. 165–80.

Chow, Garland. Deregulation, Financial Distress, and Safety in the General Freight Trucking Industry. In *Moses, L. N. and Savage, I., eds.*, 1989, pp. 219–40.

Chow, Gregory C. Rational versus Adaptive Expectations in Present Value Models. *Rev. Econ. Statist.*, August 1989, *71*(3), pp. 376–84.

Chow, Peter C. Y. Causality between Export Growth and Industrial Development: Empirical Evidence from the NICs—Reply. *J. Devel. Econ.*, October 1989, *31*(2), pp. 416–17.

——. Monetary Coordination in a Tripartite World: An Empirical Test of the International

Monetary Rule. In *Missouri Valley Economic Association*, 1989, pp. 55–62.

—— **and Kellman, Mitchell.** The Comparative Homogeneity of the East Asian NIC Exports of Similar Manufacturers. *World Devel.*, February 1989, *17*(2), pp. 267–73.

Chowdhury, A. M. R. and Abed, F. H. The Role of NGOs in International Health Development. In *Reich, M. R. and Marui, E., eds.*, 1989, pp. 76–88.

Chowdhury, Abdur R. Financial Innovations and the Interest Elasticity of Money Demand in Canada. *Econ. Letters*, November 1989, *31*(1), pp. 43–48.

——. Monetary and Fiscal Policy as a Stabilization Tool: The Case of Korea and Turkey. *Quart. Rev. Econ. Bus.*, Spring 1989, *29*(1), pp. 33–48.

Chowdhury, Gopa; Green, Christopher J. and Miles, David K. Company Bank Borrowing and Liquid Lending. *Nat. Westminster Bank Quart. Rev.*, November 1989, pp. 42–52.

—— **and Miles, David K.** Modelling Companies' Debt and Dividend Decisions with Company Accounts Data. *Appl. Econ.*, November 1989, *21*(11), pp. 1483–1508.

Chowdhury, Nuimuddin. Bangladesh's Handloom Economy in Transition: A Case of Unequal Growth, Structural Adjustment and Economic Mobility Amid Laissez-Faire Markets: A Synthesis. *Bangladesh Devel. Stud.*, March–June 1989, *17*(1–2), pp. 1–22.

——. Credit Relations and Factor Productivity in Bangladesh's Handloom Industry. *Bangladesh Devel. Stud.*, March–June 1989, *17*(1–2), pp. 77–99.

——. Distributional Costs of Grey Fabrics of Handloom and Powerloom Industries in Bangladesh. *Bangladesh Devel. Stud.*, March–June 1989, *17*(1–2), pp. 189–99.

——. The Handloom Economy of Bangladesh in Transition: Editor's Introduction. *Bangladesh Devel. Stud.*, March–June 1989, *17*(1–2), pp. iii–xii.

—— **and Latif, Muhammad Abdul.** Resource Allocation in Bangladesh Handloom Industry: A Production Function Approach. *Bangladesh Devel. Stud.*, March–June 1989, *17*(1–2), pp. 175–87.

Chowdhury, Osman H. Equity and Efficiency Tradeoff in Bangladesh Tax Policy Reform: A Computable General Equilibrium Model. *Philippine Rev. Econ. Bus.*, December 1989, *26*(2), pp. 262–86.

Chressanthis, George A. Capital Punishment and the Deterrent Effect Revisited: Recent Time-Series Econometric Evidence. *J. Behav. Econ.*, Summer 1989, *18*(2), pp. 81–97.

Christelow, Dorothy B. U.S.–Japan Joint Ventures: Who Gains? *Challenge*, Nov.–Dec. 1989, *32*(6), pp. 29–38.

Christensen, Anders Møller. Kvartalsvise nationalregnskaber i Nationalbanken. (The Methods Used in the Central Bank of Denmark for Compiling Quarterly National Accounts for Den-

mark. With English summary.) *Nationaløkon.*
Tidsskr., 1989, *127*(1), pp. 110–23.

Christensen, Dianne C., et al. Capital in the U.S.
Postal Service. In *Jorgenson, D. W. and Landau, R., eds.*, 1989, pp. 409–50.

**Christensen, Donald G.; Roenfeldt, Rodney L.
and Moore, William T.** Equity Valuation Effects of Forming Master Limited Partnerships.
J. Finan. Econ., September 1989, *24*(1), pp.
107–24.

Christensen, Michael and Andersen, Torben M.
Relative Wages and Employment Fluctuations.
J. Macroecon., Fall 1989, *11*(4), pp. 477–92.

_____ **and Blackburn, Keith.** Monetary Policy
and Policy Credibility: Theories and Evidence.
J. Econ. Lit., March 1989, *27*(1), pp. 1–45.

Christensen, Paul P. Hobbes and the Physiological Origins of Economic Science. *Hist. Polit.
Econ.*, Winter 1989, *21*(4), pp. 689–709.

**Christian, Charles W. and Frischmann, Peter
J.** Attrition in the Statistics of Income Panel
of Individual Returns. *Nat. Tax J.*, December
1989, *42*(4), pp. 495–501.

Christian, John W. Financing Infrastructure
Maintenance through Public Trusts. In *Matzer, J., Jr., ed.*, 1989, 1987, pp. 181–84.

Christian, Patricia B. Nonfamily Households and
Housing among Young Adults. In *Goldscheider, F. K. and Goldscheider, C., eds.*,
1989, pp. 57–73.

Christiano, Lawrence J. Consumption, Income,
and Interest Rates: Reinterpreting the Time
Series Evidence: Comment. In *Blanchard, O.
J. and Fischer, S., eds.*, 1989, pp. 216–33.

_____. *P**: Not the Inflation Forecaster's Holy
Grail. *Fed. Res. Bank Minn. Rev.*, Fall 1989,
13(4), pp. 3–18.

_____. Understanding Japan's Saving Rate: The
Reconstruction Hypothesis. *Fed. Res. Bank
Minn. Rev.*, Spring 1989, *13*(2), pp. 10–25.

_____ **and Eichenbaum, Martin.** Temporal Aggregation and the Stock Adjustment Model of
Inventories. In *Kollintzas, T., ed.*, 1989, pp.
70–108.

Christiansen, Hans. Boligmarkedet i uligevægt:
En empirisk model. (An Empirical Model of
the Danish Housing Market. With English
summary.) *Nationaløkon. Tidsskr.*, 1989,
127(3), pp. 308–20.

Christiansen, Peter Munk. The Danish Policy on
Technology—From Market-Direction to Structural Change. In *Pedersen, J. L., ed.*, 1989,
pp. 31–60.

**Christiansen, Robert E. and Stackhouse, Lee
Ann.** The Privatization of Agricultural Trading
in Malawi. *World Devel.*, May 1989, *17*(5), pp.
729–40.

Christianson, J. B. Capitation of Mental Health
Care in Public Programs. In *Scheffler, R. M.
and Rossiter, L. F., eds.*, 1989, pp. 281–311.

Christie, Cedric R. S. Charitable Donations and
Philanthropic Organisations in Ireland: International. *Bull. Int. Fiscal Doc.*, December
1989, *43*(12), pp. 554–58.

Christie, Virginia and Miller, Paul W. Attitudes

towards Unions and Union Membership. *Econ.
Letters*, September 1989, *30*(3), pp. 263–68.

Christodoulakis, N. and Boitani, A. A Note on
IS–LM and Stock Adjustment Processes. *Metroecon.*, February 1989, *40*(1), pp. 67–85.

Christodoulou, Efthimios. Establishing of a European Monetary Authority. In *Franz, O., ed.*,
1989, pp. 126–30.

Christoff, Peggy Spitzer. U.S.–Taiwan Scientific
and Technological Relations: A Socio-political
Comparison with U.S.–PRC Scientific and
Technological Relations. In *Park, S.-J., ed.*,
1989, pp. 136–60.

Christoffersen, Leif. Environmental Action Plans
in Africa. *Finance Devel.*, December 1989,
26(4), pp. 9.

Christopher, Janice and Farrell, Terrence W.
Macro-monetary Relationships in the Caribbean: An Eclectic Review of the Literature.
In *Worrell, D. and Bourne, C., eds.*, 1989,
pp. 12–27.

Christopherson, Susan and Storper, Michael.
The Effects of Flexible Specialization on Industrial Politics and the Labor Market: The Motion
Picture Industry. *Ind. Lab. Relat. Rev.*, April
1989, *42*(3), pp. 331–47.

**Christy, Francis T., Jr. and Robinson, Michael
A.** The State of Worldwide Fishery Statistics:
A Modest Proposal: Comment. *Marine Resource Econ.*, 1989, *6*(1), pp. 83–84.

Christy, Ralph D. and Connor, John M. Economic Forces Influencing Value-Added Food
Industries: Implications for Southern Agriculture. *Southern J. Agr. Econ.*, July 1989, *21*(1),
pp. 13–22.

Chrystal, K. Alec. In Defence of Monetarism.
In *Llewellyn, D. T., ed.*, 1989, pp. 37–57.

_____. Overshooting Models of the Exchange
Rate. In *Greenaway, D., ed.*, 1989, pp. 214–
30.

_____ **and Allsopp, Christopher.** Exchange Rate
Policy in the 1990s. *Oxford Rev. Econ. Policy*,
Autumn 1989, *5*(3), pp. 1–23.

_____ **and Dowd, Kevin.** Disaggregate Supply:
Evidence for the UK. *Appl. Econ.*, October
1989, *21*(10), pp. 1397–1409.

Chu, Chausi; Albar, H. O. and Al-Isa, M. S.
Traffic Engineering Services and Management
in Saudi Arabia. In *Candemir, Y., ed.*, 1989,
pp. 495–509.

Chu, Ke-young. External Shocks and Fiscal Adjustment in Developing Countries: Recent Experiences. In *Blejer, M. I. and Chu, K., eds.*,
1989, pp. 109–31.

_____ **and Blejer, Mario I.** Fiscal Policy, Stabilization, and Growth in Developing Countries:
Introduction. In *Blejer, M. I. and Chu, K.,
eds.*, 1989, pp. 3–10.

Chu, Wan-wen. Determinants of Marketing
Channel Choice: Extent of Demand, Differential Costs and Entry Threats. *Southern Econ.
J.*, October 1989, *56*(2), pp. 349–62.

Chu, Yun-han. State Structure and Economic Adjustment of the East Asian Newly Industrializing Countries. *Int. Organ.*, Autumn 1989,
43(4), pp. 647–72.

Chu, Yun-Peng; Chang, Wen-Ya and Lai, Ching-Chong. Exchange Rate Dynamics under Dual Exchange Rates: The Case of Neutral Intervention Policy. *Manchester Sch. Econ. Soc. Stud.*, September 1989, 57(3), pp. 235–47.

_____ **and Lin, Chung-cheng.** Interest Rates Interactions between Dual Financial Markets. *J. Econ. Devel.*, December 1989, 14(2), pp. 107–15.

Chubb, John E. U.S. Energy Policy: A Problem of Delegation. In *Chubb, J. E. and Peterson, P. E., eds.*, 1989, pp. 47–99.

_____ **and Peterson, Paul E.** American Political Institutions and the Problem of Governance. In *Chubb, J. E. and Peterson, P. E., eds.*, 1989, pp. 1–43.

Chudnovsky, Daniel. South–South Trade in Capital Goods: The Experiences of Argentina and Brazil. In *Ventura-Dias, V., ed.*, 1989, pp. 216–48.

_____ **and Porta, Fernando.** On Argentine–Brazilian Economic Integration. *CEPAL Rev.*, December 1989, (39), pp. 115–34.

Chun, T. S. and Lahiri, Kajal. Some Tests for Unbiasedness in the Long Run Using Survey Data. *Int. Econ. J.*, Summer 1989, 3(2), pp. 27–42.

Chun, Youngsub. A New Axiomatization of the Shapley Value. *Games Econ. Behav.*, June 1989, 1(2), pp. 119–30.

_____. A Noncooperative Justification for Egalitarian Surplus Sharing. *Math. Soc. Sci.*, June 1989, 17(3), pp. 245–61.

_____ **and Thomson, William.** Bargaining Solutions and Relative Guarantees. *Math. Soc. Sci.*, June 1989, 17(3), pp. 285–95.

Chung, Byung Jae and Von Glinow, Mary Ann. Comparative Human Resource Management Practices in the United States, Japan, Korea, and the People's Republic of China. In *Nedd, A., ed.*, 1989, pp. 153–71.

_____ **and Von Glinow, Mary Ann.** Korean Chaebols and the Changing Business Environment. In *Chung, K. H. and Lee, H. C., eds.*, 1989, pp. 27–38.

Chung, Kae H. An Overview of Korean Management. In *Chung, K. H. and Lee, H. C., eds.*, 1989, pp. 1–8.

_____ **and Lee, Hak Chong.** National Differences in Managerial Practices. In *Chung, K. H. and Lee, H. C., eds.*, 1989, pp. 163–80.

_____ **and Lie, Harry K.** Labor–Management Relations in Korea. In *Chung, K. H. and Lee, H. C., eds.*, 1989, pp. 217–31.

Chung, Kee Ho and Kim, Yong H. Inventory Management under Uncertainty: A Financial Theory for the Transactions Motive. *Managerial Dec. Econ.*, December 1989, 10(4), pp. 291–98.

_____ **and Pyun, Chong Soo.** The Effects of Risk, Inflation and Dividend Yield on Common Stock Returns: The Case of Korea. *Int. Econ. J.*, Winter 1989, 3(4), pp. 69–78.

Chung, S.-H. and Putman, S. H. Effects of Spatial System Design on Spatial Interaction Models: 1. The Spatial System Definition Problem. *En-viron. Planning A*, January 1989, 21(1), pp. 27–46.

Church, Andrew and Hutchinson, Gillian. Wage Determination in Britain: Is There a Local Dimension? *Reg. Stud.*, August 1989, 23(4), pp. 289–300.

_____ **and Hutchinson, Gillian.** Wages, Unions, the Youth Training Scheme and the Young Workers Scheme. *Scot. J. Polit. Econ.*, May 1989, 36(2), pp. 160–82.

Church, Thomas W. and Heumann, Milton. The Underexamined Assumptions of the Invisible Hand: Monetary Incentives as Policy Instruments. *J. Policy Anal. Manage.*, Fall 1989, 8(4), pp. 641–57.

Chwe, Michael Suk-Young. The Discrete Bid First Auction. *Econ. Letters*, December 1989, 31(4), pp. 303–06.

Ciampi, Carlo Azeglio. Informazione, politica economica, sistema finanziario. (Information, Economic Policy and the Financial System. With English summary.) *Giorn. Econ.*, May–June 1989, 48(5–6), pp. 191–201.

Ciaschini, Maurizio. Scale and Structure in Economic Modelling. *Econ. Modelling*, October 1989, 6(4), pp. 355–73.

Ciaurro, Gian Franco. Public Financing of Parties in Italy. In *Alexander, H. E., ed.*, 1989, pp. 153–71.

Cicarelli, James and Cicarelli, Julianne. Nobel Laureates in Economic Sciences: A Biographical Dictionary: Herbert Alexander Simon: 1978. In *Katz, B. S., ed.*, 1989, pp. 264–76.

Cicarelli, Julianne and Cicarelli, James. Nobel Laureates in Economic Sciences: A Biographical Dictionary: Herbert Alexander Simon: 1978. In *Katz, B. S., ed.*, 1989, pp. 264–76.

Cieślik, Jerzy. Relationships and Contractual Arrangements in East–West Trade. In *Hallén, L. and Johanson, J., eds.*, 1989, pp. 25–35.

_____. *Perestroika* and the New Dimensions of East–West Business Relations. *J. World Trade*, April 1989, 23(2), pp. 7–19.

Cigno, Alessandro. Home-Production and the Allocation of Time. In *Sapsford, D. and Tzannatos, Z., eds.*, 1989, pp. 7–32.

_____ **and Ermisch, John F.** A Microeconomic Analysis of the Timing of Births. *Europ. Econ. Rev.*, April 1989, 33(4), pp. 737–60.

Cigola, Margherita and Salinelli, Ernesto. Sui contratti di "Interest Rate Swap" a capitale variabile. (On Roller-Coaster Swaps. With English summary.) *Giorn. Econ.*, Nov.–Dec. 1989, 48(11–12), pp. 593–606.

Ciravegna, Daniele. Le variabili economiche che influenzano il comportamento dell'offerta di lavoro. (The Economic Variables that Influence Labor Supply Behavior. With English summary.) *Econ. Lavoro*, July–Sept. 1989, 23(3), pp. 25–40.

Ciria, Alberto. Canada and Argentina: Researching National Identities. *Can. J. Devel. Stud.*, 1989, 10(2), pp. 303–13.

Cirio, Felix M. and Otero, Manuel. Agricultural Trade in Argentina: Impacts on the Global Economy and Strategies for the GATT Negotiations. In *Whalley, J., ed., Vol. 2*, 1989, pp. 161–78.

Citrin, Daniel. The Recent Behavior of U.S. Trade Prices. *Int. Monet. Fund Staff Pap.*, December 1989, *36*(4), pp. 934–49.

Civelek, M. A. and Rawabdeh, M. A. An Empirical Investigation of the Portfolio Behaviour of the Jordanian Commercial Banks. *Middle East Bus. Econ. Rev.*, July 1989, *1*(2), pp. 27–35.

Cizakca, Murat. Tax-Farming and Resource Allocation in Past Islamic Societies. *J. King Abdulaziz Univ.: Islamic Econ.*, 1989, *1*, pp. 59–81.

Čížkovský, Milan. Czechoslovakia's External Economic Relations. *Czech. Econ. Digest.*, February 1989, (1), pp. 3–20.

Claassen, Emil-Maria. IMS, EMS, and the (N – 1) Problem. *Econ. Soc. Rev.*, January 1989, *20*(2), pp. 91–96.

Claessens, Stijn and Diwan, Ishac. Liquidity, Debt Relief, and Conditionality. In *Husain, I. and Diwan, I., eds.*, 1989, pp. 213–25.

_____ **and Diwan, Ishac.** Market-Based Debt Reduction. In *Husain, I. and Diwan, I., eds.*, 1989, pp. 258–72.

Clague, Christopher. The National Price Level: Theory and Estimation: A Comment. *J. Macroecon.*, Summer 1989, *11*(3), pp. 375–81.

Clain, Suzanne Heller and Leppel, Karen. Fringe Benefits and the Effect of Tax Reform. *Appl. Econ.*, May 1989, *21*(5), pp. 681–95.

Clair, Robert T. and Tucker, Paula K. Interstate Banking and the Federal Reserve: A Historical Perspective. *Fed. Res. Bank Dallas Econ. Rev.*, November 1989, pp. 1–20.

Clapham, Christopher. Contemporary West African States: Liberia. In *Cruise O'Brien, D. B.; Dunn, J. and Rathbone, R., eds.*, 1989, pp. 99–111.

Clarence-Smith, Gervase. The Effects of the Great Depression on Industrialisation in Equatorial and Central Africa. In *Brown, I., ed.*, 1989, pp. 170–202.

Clarete, Ramon L. The Economic Effects of Trade Liberalization on Philippine Agriculture. *Philippine Rev. Econ. Bus.*, December 1989, *26*(2), pp. 208–35.

_____. The Recent Philippine Trade Liberalization: Can the Multilateral Trade System Sustain It? In *Whalley, J., ed., Vol. 2*, 1989, pp. 121–38.

_____ **and Whalley, John.** Trade-Restricting Effects of Exchange Rate Regimes: Implications for Developed–Developing Country Trade Negotiations. In *Whalley, J., ed., Vol. 1*, 1989, pp. 66–88.

Clark, Barry S. and Elliott, John E. Richard Henry Tawney on the Democratic Economy. *Int. J. Soc. Econ.*, 1989, *16*(3), pp. 44–58.

Clark, Cal. External Shocks and Instability in Taiwan: The Dog That Didn't Bark. In *Avery, W. P. and Rapkin, D. P., eds.*, 1989, pp. 173–97.

Clark, Charles M. A. Equilibrium for What? Reflections on Social Order in Economics. *J. Econ. Issues*, June 1989, *23*(2), pp. 597–606.

Clark, Colin W. Bioeconomic Modeling and Resource Management. In *Levin, S. A.; Hallam, T. G. and Gross, L. J., eds.*, 1989, pp. 11–57.

Clark, David E. and Kahn, James R. The Two-Stage Hedonic Wage Approach: A Methodology for the Valuation of Environmental Amenities. *J. Environ. Econ. Manage.*, March 1989, *16*(2), pp. 106–20.

Clark, Don P. Measurement of Trade Concentration under the United States' Caribbean Basin Initiative. *World Devel.*, June 1989, *17*(6), pp. 861–65.

_____. Regulation of International Trade: The United States' Caribbean Basin Economic Recovery Act. *Developing Econ.*, March 1989, *27*(1), pp. 75–82.

_____; **Sawyer, W. Charles and Sprinkle, Richard L.** Determinants of Industry Participation under Offshore Assembly Provisions in the United States Tariff Code. *J. World Trade*, October 1989, *23*(5), pp. 123–30.

Clark, G. L. Remaking the Map of Corporate Capitalism: The Arbitrage Economy of the 1990s: Commentary. *Environ. Planning A*, August 1989, *21*(8), pp. 997–1000.

Clark, Gregory. Economic Growth without Accumulation or Technical Change: Agriculture before Mechanization. In *Feiwel, G. R., ed. (II)*, 1989, pp. 791–817.

_____. Productivity Growth without Technical Change in European Agriculture: Reply. *J. Econ. Hist.*, December 1989, *49*(4), pp. 979–91.

_____. Why Isn't the Whole World Developed? A Reply. *J. Econ. Hist.*, September 1989, *49*(3), pp. 707–14.

Clark, John Maurice. Adam Smith and the Currents of History. In *Clark, J. M., et al.*, 1989, pp. 53–76.

Clark, Leroy D. Insuring Equal Opportunity in Employment through Law. In *Bawden, D. L. and Skidmore, F., eds.*, 1989, pp. 173–203.

Clark, Paul F. Organizing the Organizers: Professional Staff Unionism in the American Labor Movement. *Ind. Lab. Relat. Rev.*, July 1989, *42*(4), pp. 584–99.

Clark, Peter K. Trend Reversion in Real Output and Unemployment. *J. Econometrics*, January 1989, *40*(1), pp. 15–32.

Clark, Richard A. and Sunley, Emil M. Corporate Debt: What Are the Issues and What Are the Choices. *Nat. Tax J.*, September 1989, *42*(3), pp. 273–82.

Clark, Robert L.; Allen, Steven G. and McDermed, Ann A. Pension Wealth, Age–Wealth Profiles, and the Distribution of Net Worth. In *Lipsey, R. E. and Tice, H. S., eds.*, 1989, pp. 689–731.

_____ **and McDermed, Ann A.** Determinants of Retirement by Married Women. *Soc. Sec. Bull.*, January 1989, *52*(1), pp. 33–35.

Clark, Roger A. U.K.–U.S.S.R. and U.S.–

U.S.S.R. Joint Research Programmes in Seismic Verification. **In** *Altmann, J. and Rotblat, J., eds.*, 1989, pp. 99–111.

Clark, Simon. Comparing Iterative Planning Procedures: A Proposed Method and Some Numerical Results. *J. Compar. Econ.*, March 1989, *13*(1), pp. 61–84.

Clark, W. A. V. Residential Segregation in American Cities: Common Ground and Differences in Interpretation. *Population Res. Policy Rev.*, May 1989, *8*(2), pp. 193–97.

_____; **Deurloo, M. C. and Dieleman, F. M.** A Comparative View of Housing Choices in Controlled and Uncontrolled Housing Markets. *Urban Stud.*, October 1989, *26*(5), pp. 457–68.

Clarke, Harry R. and Reed, William J. The Tree-Cutting Problem in a Stochastic Environment: The Case of Age-Dependent Growth. *J. Econ. Dynam. Control*, October 1989, *13*(4), pp. 569–95.

_____ **and Shrestha, Ram M.** Traditional Energy Programs and the Theory of Open Access Forest Resources. *Energy J.*, July 1989, *10*(3), pp. 139–55.

_____ **and Shrestha, Ram M.** Traditional Energy Programs with an Open Access Forest Resource: Policy Implications. *Energy J.*, October 1989, *10*(4), pp. 45–57.

Clarke, Judith A. and Giles, David E. A. Preliminary-Test Estimation of the Scale Parameter in a Mis-specified Regression Model. *Econ. Letters*, September 1989, *30*(3), pp. 201–05.

Clarke, K. J. Technological Change and Strategic Management: Technological Transilience and the British Automotive Components Sector. **In** *Mansfield, R., ed.*, 1989, pp. 109–26.

Clarke, Martin and Birkin, Mark. The Generation of Individual and Household Incomes at the Small Area Level Using Synthesis. *Reg. Stud.*, December 1989, *23*(6), pp. 535–48.

Clarke, R. L.; Cooper, W. W. and Charnes, A. An Approach to Testing for Organizational Slack via Banker's Game Theoretic DEA Formulations. **In** *Chan, J. L. and Patton, J. M., eds.*, 1989, pp. 211–29.

Clarke, R. Oliver. Industrial Relations Theory and Practice: A Note. **In** *Barbash, J. and Barbash, K., eds.*, 1989, pp. 197–202.

Clarke, Richard N. SICs as Delineators of Economic Markets. *J. Bus.*, January 1989, *62*(1), pp. 17–31.

Clarke, Ronald F. Re-defining Resources: Turning the Minimum into the Optimum. **In** *Davies, J., et al., eds.*, 1989, pp. 224–37.

Clarke, Stephen V. O. A Cashless Society Would Cripple the Trade in Illicit Drugs. *Challenge*, March–April 1989, *32*(2), pp. 56–57.

Clarke, Sue and Diamond, Ian. Demographic Patterns among Britain's Ethnic Groups. **In** *Joshi, H., ed.*, 1989, pp. 177–98.

Clarkson, Kenneth W. Privatization and Economic Performance in Britain: A Comment. *Carnegie–Rochester Conf. Ser. Public Policy*, Autumn 1989, *31*, pp. 345–51.

_____. Privatization at the State and Local Level. **In** *MacAvoy, P. W., et al.*, 1989, pp. 143–94.

Clarkson, Leslie A. The Environment and Dynamic of Pre-factory Industry in Northern Ireland. **In** *Hudson, P., ed.*, 1989, pp. 252–70.

_____. The Transformation of Australian Economic and Social History. *Australian Econ. Hist. Rev.*, September 1989, *29*(2), pp. 79–82.

Claude, Dominique. Production and Commercialisation of Rice in Cameroon: The Semry Project. **In** *Campbell, B. K. and Loxley, J., eds.*, 1989, pp. 202–33.

Claudon, Michael P. Foreign Lending at the Brink. **In** *Weeks, J. F., ed.*, 1989, pp. 243–53.

Clauretie, Terrence M. Resolution of Incentive Conflicts in the Mortgage Industry: Comment. *J. Real Estate Finance Econ.*, February 1989, *2*(1), pp. 71–72.

_____. State Foreclosure Laws, Risk Shifting, and the Private Mortgage Insurance Industry. *J. Risk Ins.*, September 1989, *56*(3), pp. 544–54.

Clausen, A. W. Third World Debt: The Next Phase: Perspectives of Commercial Bank Creditors. **In** *Fried, E. R. and Trezise, P. H., eds.*, 1989, pp. 47–49.

Clauson, Annette L. The U.S. Sugar Industry and GATT. *Can. J. Agr. Econ.*, Part 2, December 1989, *37*(4), pp. 1135–43.

Clawson, Marion and Dysart, Benjamin C., III. Public Interest in the Use of Private Lands: An Overview. **In** *Dysart, B. C., III and Clawson, M., eds.*, 1989, pp. 1–8.

Claycombe, Richard J. Wages, Corners and the Wife's Work at Home. *Amer. Economist*, Fall 1989, *33*(2), pp. 64–67.

Claydon, Tim. Union Derecognition in Britain in the 1980s. *Brit. J. Ind. Relat.*, July 1989, *27*(2), pp. 214–24.

Clayton, Elizabeth and Richardson, Thomas. Soviet Control of City Size. *Econ. Devel. Cult. Change*, October 1989, *38*(1), pp. 155–65.

Clayton, Richard R.; Johnson, Timothy P. and Hougland, James G., Jr. Obtaining Reports of Sensitive Behavior: A Comparison of Substance Use Reports from Telephone and Face-to-Face Interviews. *Soc. Sci. Quart.*, March 1989, *70*(1), pp. 174–83.

Clayton, Ronnie; Delozier, John and Ehrhardt, Michael C. A Note on January Returns in the U.S. Government Bond Market: The Term Effect. *J. Finan. Services Res.*, October 1989, *2*(4), pp. 307–18.

Cleeton, David L. Equilibrium Conditions for Efficient Rent Seeking: The Nash–Cournot Solution. *Quart. Rev. Econ. Bus.*, Summer 1989, *29*(2), pp. 6–14.

_____. The Medical Uninsured: A Case of Market Failure? *Public Finance Quart.*, January 1989, *17*(1), pp. 55–83.

Clegg, Stewart; Dow, Geoff and Boreham, Paul. Political Organisation and Economic Policy. **In** *Duncan, G., ed.*, 1989, pp. 253–76.

Cleland, J. and Verma, V. The World Fertility Survey: An Appraisal of Methodology. *J. Amer.*

Statist. Assoc., September 1989, *84*(407), pp. 756–67.

Clem, Andrew G. Milestones in Producer Price Index Methodology and Presentation. *Mon. Lab. Rev.*, August 1989, *112*(8), pp. 41–42.

_____; **Mosimann, Thomas J. and Howell, Craig.** Price Highlights of 1988: Rising Pressures on Consumer Prices. *Mon. Lab. Rev.*, May 1989, *112*(5), pp. 3–10.

Clemen, Robert T. Combining Forecasts: A Review and Annotated Bibliography. *Int. J. Forecasting*, 1989, *5*(4), pp. 559–83.

_____ **and Guerard, John B., Jr.** Econometric GNP Forecasts: Incremental Information Relative to Naive Extrapolation. *Int. J. Forecasting*, 1989, *5*(3), pp. 417–26.

Clément, Alain. Emergence d'un concept: La dépendance alimentaire. (Birth of a Concept: Food Dependance. With English summary.) *Écon. Societes*, June 1989, *23*(6), pp. 201–15.

Clement, Reiner. Regionale und sektorale Auswirkungen des europäischen Binnenmarktes: Eine Analyse am Beispiel der Industrie. (Regional and Structural Implications of the European Internal Market: Prospects for Industry. With English summary.) *Konjunkturpolitik*, 1989, *35*(4), pp. 201–14.

Clement, Robert C. and McCormick, Robert E. Coaching Team Production. *Econ. Inquiry*, April 1989, *27*(2), pp. 287–304.

Clements, Alan W. Money in International Trade. In *Llewellyn, D. T.*, ed., 1989, pp. 139–66.

Clements, L. C. Treatment of Seasonal Fresh Fruit and Vegetables in CPI. In *Turvey, R.*, 1989, pp. 179–81.

_____; **Allen, D. N. and Travers, T. C.** Pricing of New Vehicles in the Australian Consumer Price Index: Adjusting for Quality Change. In *Turvey, R.*, 1989, pp. 163–65.

Clemhout, Simone and Wan, Henry, Jr. On Games of Cake-Eating. In *[Verheyen, P.]*, 1989, pp. 121–55.

Cleminson, F. Ronald. Conventional Arms Reduction in Europe: A Verification Model. In *Altmann, J. and Rotblat, J.*, eds., 1989, pp. 158–66.

Clerico, Giuseppe. Equità, efficienza e diritti di proprietà. (Equity, Efficiency and Property Rights. With English summary.) *Econ. Scelte Pubbliche/J. Public Finance Public Choice*, Sept.–Dec. 1989, *7*(3), pp. 173–90.

Cleveland, Paul A. Domestic Trunk Air Transportation: From Regulatory Control to Deregulation. In *Perkins, E. J.*, ed., 1989, pp. 176–89.

Cleveland, William S. Sensitivity Analysis of Seasonal Adjustments: Empirical Case Studies: Comment. *J. Amer. Statist. Assoc.*, March 1989, *84*(405), pp. 24–27.

Cline, William R. The Baker Plan and Brady Reformulation: An Evaluation. In *Husain, I. and Diwan, I.*, eds., 1989, pp. 176–93.

_____. Brazilian Debt: A Requiem for Muddling Through: Comment. In *Edwards, S. and Larrain, F.*, eds., 1989, pp. 319–23.

_____. The Issue Is Illiquidity, Not Insolvency. In *Guttmann, R.*, ed., 1989, *1984*, pp. 189–
97.

_____. Latin American Debt: Progress, Prospects, and Policy. In *Edwards, S. and Larrain, F.*, eds., 1989, pp. 31–64.

_____. Macroeconomic Influences on Trade Policy. *Amer. Econ. Rev.*, May 1989, *79*(2), pp. 123–27.

Clinton, Roy J. and Troutt, Marvin D. Interactive Optimization: An Optimal Scaling and Step Sizing Approach for the Method of Abstract Forces. In *Lockett, A. G. and Islei, G.*, eds., 1989, pp. 58–67.

Cloete, J. J. Workings of a Managed Floating Exchange Rate System: A Comment. *S. Afr. J. Econ.*, June 1989, *57*(2), pp. 181–87.

Cloutier, A. Pierre and Fortin, Bernard. Converting Exemptions and Deductions into Credits: An Economic Assessment. In *Mintz, J. and Whalley, J.*, eds., 1989, pp. 45–73.

Cloutier, Norman R. and Loviscek, Anthony L. AFDC Benefits and the Inter-urban Variation in Poverty among Female-Headed Households. *Southern Econ. J.*, October 1989, *56*(2), pp. 315–22.

Clower, Robert W. The State of Economics: Hopeless but Not Serious? In *Colander, D. C. and Coats, A. W.*, eds., 1989, pp. 23–41.

Cluff, M. E. and Boswell, A. M. The Changing International Meat Market and the Outlook for the North American Livestock Sector. *Can. J. Agr. Econ.*, Part 2, December 1989, *37*(4), pp. 1199–1214.

Clyde, Steven E. Adapting to the Changing Demand for Water Use through Continued Refinement of the Prior Appropriation Doctrine: An Alternative Approach to Wholesale Reallocation. *Natural Res. J.*, Spring 1989, *29*(2), pp. 435–55.

Cnossen, Sijbren. Broad-Based Consumption Taxes: VAT, RST, or BTT? *Australian Tax Forum*, 1989, *6*(4), pp. 391–422.

_____. The Role of Excises in OECD Member Countries. In *Chiancone, A. and Messere, K.*, eds., 1989, pp. 285–304.

_____. The Value-Added Tax: Key to a Better Tax Mix. *Australian Tax Forum*, 1989, *6*(3), pp. 265–81.

Coate, Douglas and Fowles, Richard. Is There Statistical Evidence for a Blood Lead–Blood Pressure Relationship? *J. Health Econ.*, June 1989, *8*(2), pp. 173–84.

Coate, Malcolm B. The Dynamics of Price–Cost Margins in Concentrated Industries. *Appl. Econ.*, February 1989, *21*(2), pp. 261–72.

_____ **and Fratrik, Mark R.** Dual Distribution as a Vertical Control Device. *J. Behav. Econ.*, Spring 1989, *18*(1), pp. 1–17.

Coate, Stephen. Cash versus Direct Food Relief. *J. Devel. Econ.*, April 1989, *30*(2), pp. 199–224.

Coates, David. The Capitalist Class: Britain. In *Bottomore, T. and Brym, R. J.*, eds., 1989, pp. 19–45.

Coats, A. W. Economic Ideas and Economists in Government: Accomplishments and Frustrations. In *Colander, D. C. and Coats, A. W.*, *eds.*, 1989, pp. 109–18.

_____. Reflections on the Austrian/Institutionalism Symposium. In *Samuels, W. J., ed. (II)*, 1989, pp. 101–06.

_____ and **Colander, David C.** An Introduction to the Spread of Economic Ideas. In *Colander, D. C. and Coats, A. W., eds.*, 1989, pp. 1–19.

Coats, Warren L., Jr. LDC Debt: The Role of the International Monetary Fund. *Contemp. Policy Issues*, April 1989, *7*(2), pp. 41–49.

Cobbs, Elizabeth A. Entrepreneurship as Diplomacy: Nelson Rockefeller and the Development of the Brazilian Capital Market. *Bus. Hist. Rev.*, Spring 1989, *63*(1), pp. 88–121.

Cobham, David. Financial Innovation and the Abandonment of Monetary Targets: The UK Case. In *[Marjolin, R.]*, 1989, pp. 245–65.

_____. Strategies for Monetary Integration Revisited. *J. Common Market Stud.*, March 1989, *27*(3), pp. 203–18.

Cocco, Flavio and Fischer, Andreas M. Are Announcement Effects Time Dependent? *Econ. Letters*, August 1989, *30*(2), pp. 157–59.

Cochran, John P. and Brown, R. Michael. What's Wrong Here? *Econ. Inquiry*, July 1989, *27*(3), pp. 541–45.

Cochran, Steven J.; Froio, Gregory L. and Mansur, Iqbal. The Relationship between the Equity Return Levels of Airline Companies and Unanticipated Events: The Case of the 1979 DC-10 Grounding. *Logist. Transp. Rev.*, December 1989, *25*(4), pp. 355–65.

Cochrane, Hal. The Economics of Dam Failure: Another Look at Catastrophic Losses. *Water Resources Res.*, September 1989, *25*(9), pp. 1931–35.

Cochrane, John H. The Return of the Liquidity Effect: A Study of the Short-run Relation between Money Growth and Interest Rates. *J. Bus. Econ. Statist.*, January 1989, *7*(1), pp. 75–83.

_____. The Sensitivity of Tests of the Intertemporal Allocation of Consumption to Near-Rational Alternatives. *Amer. Econ. Rev.*, June 1989, *79*(3), pp. 319–37.

Cocklin, C.; Harte, M. and Lonergan, S. Patterns of Change in the Use of Energy in the New Zealand Economy. *Environ. Planning A*, September 1989, *21*(9), pp. 1141–56.

Coclanis, Peter A. and Carlton, David L. Capital Mobilization and Southern Industry, 1880–1905: The Case of the Carolina Piedmont. *J. Econ. Hist.*, March 1989, *49*(1), pp. 73–94.

Coddington, A. Hicks's Contribution to Keynesian Economics. In *Wood, J. C. and Woods, R. N., eds., Vol. 3*, 1989, 1979, pp. 187–208.

Coder, John; Rainwater, Lee and Smeeding, Timothy M. Inequality among Children and Elderly in Ten Modern Nations: The United States in an International Context. *Amer. Econ. Rev.*, May 1989, *79*(2), pp. 320–24.

Codognato, Giulio. L'equilibrio "Cournot–Walras": Un riesame critico. ("Cournot–Walras" Equilibrium: A Critical Reappraisal. With English summary.) *Ricerche Econ.*, July–Sept. 1989, *43*(3), pp. 382–97.

Codrington, Harold. Country Size and Taxation in Developing Countries. *J. Devel. Stud.*, July 1989, *25*(4), pp. 508–20.

_____ and **Coppin, Addington.** The Financial Structure and the Allocation of Credit in Barbados, 1977–1987. *Soc. Econ. Stud.*, December 1989, *38*(4), pp. 165–79.

_____ and **Worrell, DeLisle.** Trade and Economic Growth in Small Developing Economies: Research on the Caribbean. In *Worrell, D. and Bourne, C., eds.*, 1989, pp. 28–47.

Cody, Brian J. Imposing Exchange Controls to Dampen Currency Speculation: Political Risk and the French Franc, 1976–1984. *Europ. Econ. Rev.*, December 1989, *33*(9), pp. 1751–68.

Coelli, T. J.; Colby, T. C. and Battese, G. E. Estimation of Frontier Production Functions and the Efficiencies of Indian Farms Using Panel Data from ICRISAT's Village Level Studies. *J. Quant. Econ.*, July 1989, *5*(2), pp. 327–48.

Coenen, Dan T. Untangling the Market-Participant Exemption to the Dormant Commerce Clause. *Mich. Law Rev.*, December 1989, *88*(3), pp. 395–488.

Coes, Donald V. Real Exchange Rates: Definition, Measurement, and Trends in France, West Germany, Italy and the United Kingdom. In *Hodgman, D. R. and Wood, G. E., eds.*, 1989, pp. 250–71.

Coffin, Donald A. The Impact of Historical Districts on Residential Property Values. *Eastern Econ. J.*, July–Sept. 1989, *15*(3), pp. 221–28.

Coffman, W. Ronnie and Hargrove, T. R. Modern Rice Varieties as a Possible Factor in Production Variability. In *Anderson, J. R. and Hazell, P. B. R., eds.*, 1989, pp. 133–46.

Cohen, Alan H. and Goodman, Laurie S. Pay-in-Kind Debentures: An Innovation. *J. Portfol. Manage.*, Winter 1989, *15*(2), pp. 9–16.

Cohen, Alvin. Nobel Laureates in Economic Sciences: A Biographical Dictionary: Gunnar Myrdal: 1974. In *Katz, B. S., ed.*, 1989, pp. 218–28.

Cohen, Avi J. Prices, Capital, and the One-Commodity Model in Neoclassical and Classical Theories. *Hist. Polit. Econ.*, Summer 1989, *21*(2), pp. 231–51.

Cohen, Benjamin J. The Brady Plan: Good News and Bad. In *Mrak, M., ed.*, 1989, pp. 11–21.

_____. Debtors in Wonderland. *Challenge*, Nov.–Dec. 1989, *32*(6), pp. 57–60.

_____. LDC Debt: Is Activism Required? In *Bird, G., ed.*, 1989, pp. 130–68.

_____. LDC Debt: Towards a Genuinely Cooperative Solution. In *Hamouda, O. F.; Rowley, R. and Wolf, B. M., eds.*, 1989, pp. 174–94.

Cohen, Daniel. The Costs and Benefits of a European Currency. In *De Cecco, M. and Giovannini, A., eds.*, 1989, pp. 195–209.

_____. How to Cope with a Debt Overhang: Cut Flows Rather Than Stocks. In *Husain, I. and Diwan, I., eds.*, 1989, pp. 229–35.

_____. Monetary and Fiscal Policy in an Open Economy with or without Policy Coordination. *Europ. Econ. Rev.*, March 1989, *33*(2/3), pp. 303–09.

_____ and Wyplosz, Charles. The European Monetary Union: An Agnostic Evaluation. In *Bryant, R. C., et al., eds.*, 1989, pp. 311–37.

Cohen, Donna and Hastings, Margaret M. Mental Health in the Elderly. In *Eisdorfer, C.; Kessler, D. A. and Spector, A. N., eds.*, 1989, pp. 358–77.

Cohen, Fay G. Treaty Indian Tribes and Washington State: The Evolution of Tribal Involvement in Fisheries Management in the U.S. Pacific Northwest. In *Pinkerton, E., ed.*, 1989, pp. 37–48.

Cohen, Gary. Taxation of Foreign Source Income: Practical Aspects of the Foreign Tax Credit and Imputation Systems. *Australian Tax Forum*, 1989, *6*(1), pp. 115–23.

Cohen, Jacob. The U.S. as the World's No. 1 Foreign Debtor: Causes and Consequences. In *Singer, H. W. and Sharma, S., eds. (I)*, 1989, pp. 355–67.

Cohen, Jeffrey and Kida, Thomas. The Impact of Analytical Review Results, Internal Control Reliability, and Experience on Auditors' Use of Analytical Review. *J. Acc. Res.*, Autumn 1989, *27*(2), pp. 263–76.

Cohen, Joel B. An Over-Extended Self? Comment. *J. Cons. Res.*, June 1989, *16*(1), pp. 125–28.

Cohen, Joel E. The World Fertility Survey: An Appraisal of Methodology: Comment. *J. Amer. Statist. Assoc.*, September 1989, *84*(407), pp. 772–74.

Cohen, Joshua. Contractualism and Property Systems. In *Chapman, J. W. and Pennock, J. R., eds.*, 1989, pp. 72–85.

Cohen, Lloyd R. Deregulation at the U.S. International Trade Commission. In *Meiners, R. E. and Yandle, B., eds.*, 1989, pp. 166–85.

Cohen, Mark A. The Role of Criminal Sanctions in Antitrust Enforcement. *Contemp. Policy Issues*, October 1989, *7*(4), pp. 36–46.

Cohen, Natalie R. Municipal Default Patterns: An Historical Study. *Public Budg. Finance*, Winter 1989, *9*(4), pp. 55–65.

Cohen, Robert B. The Foreign Challenge to U.S. Commercial Banks. In *Noyelle, T., ed.*, 1989, pp. 31–50.

Cohen, S. I. The Agrarian Sector in Pakistan's Development Process—Historical Evidence and Implications for Policy and Theory: Comments. *Pakistan Devel. Rev.*, Winter 1989, *28*(4), pp. 522–25.

_____. The Interface between Population and Development Models, Plans and Policies. *Pakistan Devel. Rev.*, Winter 1989, *28*(4), pp. 385–404.

_____. Multiplier Analyses in Social Accounting and Input–Output Frameworks: Evidence for Several Countries. In *Miller, R. E.; Polenske, K. R. and Rose, A. Z., eds.*, 1989, pp. 79–99.

Cohen, Steven B.; Johnson, Ayah E. and Carlson, Barbara Lepidus. An Analysis of Part-Year Nonresponse in the Household Component of the National Medical Expenditure Survey. *J. Econ. Soc. Meas.*, 1989, *15*(3–4), pp. 281–99.

Cohen, Wesley M. and Levin, Richard C. Empirical Studies of Innovation and Market Structure. In *Schmalensee, R. and Willig, R. D., eds., Vol. 2*, 1989, pp. 1059–1107.

_____ and Levinthal, Daniel A. Innovation and Learning: The Two Faces of R&D. *Econ. J.*, September 1989, *99*(397), pp. 569–96.

Cohn, Elchanan. The Federal Role in Vocational Education: A Case Study of South Carolina. *Econ. Educ. Rev.*, 1989, *8*(1), pp. 107–16.

_____; Kiker, B. F. and de Oliviera, M. Mendes. Tenure, Earnings and Productivity. *Oxford Bull. Econ. Statist.*, February 1989, *51*(1), pp. 1–14.

_____; Rhine, Sherrie L. W. and Santos, Maria C. Institutions of Higher Education as Multiproduct Firms: Economies of Scale and Scope. *Rev. Econ. Statist.*, May 1989, *71*(2), pp. 284–90.

Cohn, Richard A. and Modigliani, Franco. Inflation and Corporate Financial Management. In *Modigliani, F., Vol. 5*, 1989, *1985*, pp. 414–42.

_____ and Modigliani, Franco. Inflation and the Stock Market. In *Modigliani, F., Vol. 5*, 1989, *1982*, pp. 331–49.

_____ and Modigliani, Franco. Inflation, Rational Valuation and the Market. In *Modigliani, F., Vol. 5*, 1989, *1979*, pp. 304–24.

Cohn, Samuel and Eaton, Adrienne E. Historical Limits on Neoclassical Strike Theories: Evidence from French Coal Mining, 1890–1935. *Ind. Lab. Relat. Rev.*, July 1989, *42*(4), pp. 649–62.

Cohon, Jared; Klimberg, Ronald K. and ReVelle, Charles. NMIS: A National Model for Inspection Selection with Limited Resources. In *Lockett, A. G. and Islei, G., eds.*, 1989, pp. 244–53.

Coker, Christopher. Alliances, Bases and Security: A Northern Perspective. In *Thomas, C. and Saravanamuttu, P., eds.*, 1989, pp. 89–103.

Colaert, Anne-Marie. La non-reconnaissance des personnes juridiques en matière fiscale: Belgique. (The Disregard of a Legal Entity for Tax Purposes: Belgium. With English summary.) In *International Fiscal Association, ed. (II)*, 1989, pp. 191–213.

Colander, David C. Money and the Spread of Ideas. In *Colander, D. C. and Coats, A. W., eds.*, 1989, pp. 229–33.

_____. Research on the Economics Profession. *J. Econ. Perspectives*, Fall 1989, *3*(4), pp. 137–48.

_____ and Coats, A. W. An Introduction to the Spread of Economic Ideas. In *Colander, D. C. and Coats, A. W., eds.*, 1989, pp. 1–19.

Colby, Bonnie G. Estimating the Value of Water in Alternative Uses. *Natural Res. J.*, Spring 1989, *29*(2), pp. 511–27.

_____ and Cory, Dennis C. Valuing Amenity Resources under Uncertainty: Does the Existence of Fair Contingent Claims Markets Matter? *J. Environ. Econ. Manage.*, March 1989, *16*(2), pp. 149–55.

Colby, T. C.; Battese, G. E. and Coelli, T. J. Estimation of Frontier Production Functions and the Efficiencies of Indian Farms Using Panel Data from ICRISAT's Village Level Studies. *J. Quant. Econ.*, July 1989, *5*(2), pp. 327–48.

Cole, Harold Linh. General Competitive Analysis in an Economy with Private Information: Comment. *Int. Econ. Rev.*, February 1989, *30*(1), pp. 249–52.

_____. Internationalization of Financial Markets and Balance of Payments Imbalances: A Japanese Perspective: Comment. *Carnegie–Rochester Conf. Ser. Public Policy*, Spring 1989, *30*, pp. 221–29.

Cole, Rebel; Guilkey, David K. and Miles, Mike. The Motivation for Institutional Real Estate Sales and Implications for Asset Class Returns. *Amer. Real Estate Urban Econ. Assoc. J.*, Spring 1989, *17*(1), pp. 70–86.

Cole, Robert E. Economy and Culture: The Case of U.S.–Japan Economic Relations. In *Hayashi, K., ed.*, 1989, pp. 1–13.

_____. Large-Scale Change and the Quality Revolution. In *Mohrman, A. M., Jr., et al.*, 1989, pp. 229–54.

Cole, Rosanne; Dulberger, Ellen R. and Triplett, Jack E. The Postwar Evolution of Computer Prices: Comment. In *Jorgenson, D. W. and Landau, R., eds.*, 1989, pp. 215–19.

Cole, Sam. Expenditure Lags in Impact Analysis. *Reg. Stud.*, April 1989, *23*(2), pp. 105–16.

_____. World Bank Forecasts and Planning in the Third World. *Environ. Planning A*, February 1989, *21*(2), pp. 175–96.

Colella, Adrienne and Wanous, John P. Organizational Entry Research: Current Status and Future Directions. In *Ferris, G. R. and Rowland, K. M., eds.*, 1989, pp. 59–120.

Coleman, Jules. Rationality and the Justification of Democracy. In *Brennan, G. and Lomasky, L. E., eds.*, 1989, pp. 194–220.

Coleman, Thomas S. Unemployment Behavior: Evidence from the CPS Work Experience Survey. *J. Human Res.*, Winter 1989, *24*(1), pp. 1–38.

Coles, Melvyn and Malcomson, James M. Contract Theory and Incentive Compatibility. In *Hey, J. D., ed.*, 1989, pp. 127–51.

Collard, David. The Ascent of High Theory: A View from the Foothills. In *Wood, J. C. and Woods, R. N., eds.*, *Vol. 4*, 1989, *1984*, pp. 45–56.

_____. How Much Investigation? In *[Sandford, C.]*, 1989, pp. 104–15.

Collas-Monsod, Solita. Credit Availability and Economic Growth. In *Helmuth, J. W. and Johnson, S. R., eds.*, *Vol. 1*, 1989, pp. 66–78.

Colledge, Michael J. Coverage and Classification Maintenance Issues in Economic Surveys. In *Kasprzyk, D., et al., eds.*, 1989, pp. 80–107.

Collender, Robert N. Estimation Risk in Farm Planning under Uncertainty. *Amer. J. Agr. Econ.*, November 1989, *71*(4), pp. 996–1002.

_____ **and Zilberman, David.** Land Allocation under Uncertainty for Alternative Specifications of Return Distributions: Reply. *Amer. J. Agr. Econ.*, May 1989, *71*(2), pp. 441–42.

Collier, Irwin L., Jr. The Measurement and Interpretation of Real Consumption and Purchasing Power Parity for a Quantity-Constrained Economy: The Case of East and West Germany. *Economica*, February 1989, *56*(221), pp. 109–20.

_____. The NEW Comparative Economics. *Comp. Econ. Stud.*, Fall 1989, *31*(3), pp. 23–32.

Collier, Kenneth; Ordeshook, Peter C. and Williams, Kenneth. The Rationally Uninformed Electorate: Some Experimental Evidence. *Public Choice*, January 1989, *60*(1), pp. 3–29.

Collier, Paul. Contractual Constraints on Labour Exchange in Rural Kenya. *Int. Lab. Rev.*, Special Issue, 1989, *128*(6), pp. 745–68.

_____; **Gunning, Jan Willem and Bevan, David L.** Black Markets: Illegality, Information, and Rents. *World Devel.*, December 1989, *17*(12), pp. 1955–63.

_____; **Gunning, Jan Willem and Bevan, David L.** Fiscal Response to a Temporary Trade Shock: The Aftermath of the Kenyan Coffee Boom. *World Bank Econ. Rev.*, September 1989, *3*(3), pp. 359–78.

_____ **and Joshi, Vijay.** Exchange Rate Policy in Developing Countries. *Oxford Rev. Econ. Policy*, Autumn 1989, *5*(3), pp. 94–113.

_____ **and Mayer, Colin.** Financial Liberalization, Financial Systems, and Economic Growth: The Assessment. *Oxford Rev. Econ. Policy*, Winter 1989, *5*(4), pp. 1–12.

Collini, Stefan. 'Manly Fellows': Fawcett, Stephen and the Liberal Temper. In *Goldman, L., ed.*, 1989, pp. 41–59.

Collins, A. Store Location Planning: Its Role in Marketing Strategy. *Environ. Planning A*, May 1989, *21*(5), pp. 625–28.

Collins, Daniel W. and Kothari, S. P. An Analysis of Intertemporal and Cross-sectional Determinants of Earnings Response Coefficients. *J. Acc. Econ.*, July 1989, *11*(2–3), pp. 143–81.

Collins, E. J. T. The "Machinery Question" in English Agriculture in the Nineteenth Century. In *Grantham, G. and Leonard, C. S., eds., Pt. A*, 1989, pp. 203–17.

Collins, Kevin. Management Education in Japan. In *Byrt, W., ed.*, 1989, pp. 172–209.

Collins, Michael. The Banking Crisis of 1878. *Econ. Hist. Rev., 2nd Ser.*, November 1989, *42*(4), pp. 504–27.

Collins, Robert A. and Gbur, Edward E. A Small-Sample Comparison of Estimators in the EU-MGF Approach to Decision Making. *Amer. J. Agr. Econ.*, February 1989, *71*(1), pp. 202–10.

Collins, Susan M. Debt, Policy, and Performance: An Introduction. In *Sachs, J. D. and Collins, S. M., eds.*, 1989, pp. 1–16.

_____ **and Park, Won-Am.** External Debt and

Macroeconomic Performance in South Korea. In *Sachs, J. D. and Collins, S. M., eds.*, 1989, pp. 151–369.

_____ and **Park, Won-Am.** External Debt and Macroeconomic Performance in South Korea. In *Sachs, J. D., ed. (II)*, 1989, pp. 121–40.

Collombel, B. and Bouhsina, Z. Biotechnologies, bioindustries et IAA. (Biotechnology, Bio-industry and Food Industry. With English summary.) *Écon. Societes*, July 1989, *23*(7), pp. 135–57.

Colman, David. Economic Issues from the Broads Grazing Marshes Conservation Scheme. *J. Agr. Econ.*, September 1989, *40*(3), pp. 336–44.

Colombier, Michel and Hourcade, Jean-Charles. Développement des réseaux et modulations spatio-temporelles des tarifs: L'équité territoriale revisitée. (Development of Electrical Grids and Spatio-Temporal Modulations of Tariffs: Territorial Equity Revisited. With English summary.) *Revue Écon.*, July 1989, *40*(4), pp. 649–77.

Colombo, Caterina. Dinamica dei prezzi in cambi flessibili: Un modello di concorrenza monopolistica con costi di aggiustamento dei prezzi. (Price Dynamics under Flexible Exchange Rates: Monopolistic Competition and Costs of Price Adjustment. With English summary.) *Ricerche Econ.*, July–Sept. 1989, *43*(3), pp. 304–29.

_____. Rigidità dei prezzi e cambi flessibili: Alcuni risultati empirici. (Flexible Exchange Rates and Sticky Prices: Some Empirical Implication. With English summary.) *Politica. Econ.*, August 1989, *5*(2), pp. 273–300.

Colombo, Massimo G.; Brioschi, Francesco and Buzzacchi, Luigi. Risk Capital Financing and the Separation of Ownership and Control in Business Groups. *J. Banking Finance*, September 1989, *13*(4–5), pp. 747–72.

Colombo, Richard A. and Morrison, Donald G. A Brand Switching Model with Implications for Marketing Strategies. *Marketing Sci.*, Winter 1989, *8*(1), pp. 89–99.

_____ and **Morrison, Donald G.** A Brand Switching Model with Implications for Marketing Strategies: Reply. *Marketing Sci.*, Winter 1989, *8*(1), pp. 106.

Colwell, Peter F. and Scheu, Tim. Optimal Lot Size and Configuration. *J. Urban Econ.*, July 1989, *26*(1), pp. 90–109.

Comanor, William S. and Leibenstein, Harvey. Allocative Efficiency, X-Efficiency and the Measurement of Welfare Losses. In *Leibenstein, H., Vol. 2*, 1989, *1969*, pp. 27–32.

Combs, George F., Jr. The Economics of Strategic Choice: U.S. Uranium Enrichment in the World Market: A Comment. *Energy J.*, January 1989, *10*(1), pp. 175–78.

Comisso, E. Property Rights in Focus. *Acta Oecon.*, 1989, *40*(3–4), pp. 210–16.

Commander, Simon and Astorga Lira, Enrique. Agricultural Commercialisation and the Growth of a Migrant Labour Market in Mexico.

Int. Lab. Rev., Special Issue, 1989, *128*(6), pp. 769–89.

Common, M. S. The Choice of Pollution Control Instruments: Why Is So Little Notice Taken of Economists' Recommendations? *Environ. Planning A*, October 1989, *21*(10), pp. 1297–1314.

Compte, O.; Lesourne, J. and Lévy, B. La formation endogène d'un syndicat sur le marché du travial. (The Endogenous Forming of a Union on a Labour Market. With English summary.) *Écon. Appl.*, 1989, *42*(3), pp. 171–94.

Conable, Barber B. Development and the Environment: A Global Balance. *Finance Devel.*, December 1989, *26*(4), pp. 2–4.

_____. Third World Debt: The Next Phase: Status, Issues, and Prospects: Comment. In *Fried, E. R. and Trezise, P. H., eds.*, 1989, pp. 21–23.

Conant, John L. and Kaserman, David L. Union Merger Incentives and Pecuniary Externalities. *J. Lab. Res.*, Summer 1989, *10*(3), pp. 243–53.

Conant, Melvin A. Long-Range U.S. Oil Security. In *[Evans, J. K.]*, 1989, pp. 11–19.

Conerly, Michael D. and Mansfield, Edward R. An Approximate Test for Comparing Independent Regression Models with Unequal Error Variances. *J. Econometrics*, February 1989, *40*(2), pp. 239–59.

Conforti, Michele. (K_4-e)-Free Perfect Graphs and Star Cutsets. In *Simeone, B., ed.*, 1989, pp. 236–53.

Congdon, Peter. Modelling Migration Flows between Areas: An Analysis for London Using the Census and OPCS Longitudinal Study. *Reg. Stud.*, April 1989, *23*(2), pp. 87–103.

Congdon, Tim. Credit, Broad Money and the Economy. In *Llewellyn, D. T., ed.*, 1989, pp. 59–82.

Congleton, Roger D. Campaign Finances and Political Platforms: The Economics of Political Controversy. *Public Choice*, August 1989, *62*(2), pp. 101–18.

_____. Efficient Status Seeking: Externalities, and the Evolution of Status Games. *J. Econ. Behav. Organ.*, March 1989, *11*(2), pp. 175–90.

_____. Monitoring Rent-Seeking Managers: Advantages of Diffuse Ownership. *Can. J. Econ.*, August 1989, *22*(3), pp. 662–72.

_____ and **Buchanan, James M.** Proportional and Progressive Income Taxation with Utility-Maximizing Governments. In *Buchanan, J. M. (II)*, 1989, pp. 294–308.

de Coning, T. J.; Tromp, D. and Smit, E. van der M. Die Soeke na Suksesfaktore in Klein Ondernemings—'n Pragmatiese Benadering. (With English summary.) *J. Stud. Econ. Econometrics*, March 1989, *13*(1), pp. 1–17.

Conlisk, John. An Aggregate Model of Technical Change. *Quart. J. Econ.*, November 1989, *104*(4), pp. 787–821.

_____. Ranking Mobility Matrices. *Econ. Letters*, 1989, *29*(3), pp. 231–35.

_____. Three Variants on the Allais Example. *Amer. Econ. Rev.*, June 1989, *79*(3), pp. 392–

407.

Conlon, Edward J. and Leatherwood, Marya L.
Sunk Costs and Financial Decision Making: Integration and Implications. In *Lee, C. F., ed.*,
1989, pp. 37–61.

Connelly, Rachel. Occupational Choice under
Uncertainty When Experience Is a Determinant of Earnings. *Econometrica*, September
1989, *57*(5), pp. 1215–19.

Connolly, Michael B. and Taylor, Dean. Adjustment to Interest Rate Shocks in Latin America
and the Caribbean. In *Brock, P. L.; Connolly,
M. B. and González-Vega, C., eds.*, 1989, pp.
80–95.

Connolly, Robert A. An Examination of the Robustness of the Weekend Effect. *J. Finan.
Quant. Anal.*, June 1989, *24*(2), pp. 133–69.

────── **and Allen, Stuart D.** Financial Market
Effects on Aggregate Money Demand: A
Bayesian Analysis. *J. Money, Credit, Banking*,
May 1989, *21*(2), pp. 158–75.

**Connor, Jeffery D.; Glyer, J. David and Adams,
Richard M.** Some Further Evidence on the
Derived Demand for Irrigation Electricity: A
Dual Cost Function Approach. *Water Resources Res.*, July 1989, *25*(7), pp. 1461–68.

Connor, John M. and Christy, Ralph D. Economic Forces Influencing Value-Added Food
Industries: Implications for Southern Agriculture. *Southern J. Agr. Econ.*, July 1989, *21*(1),
pp. 13–22.

Connor, Walter D. Imperial Dilemmas: Soviet
Interests and Economic Reform. In *Nee, V.
and Stark, D., eds.*, 1989, pp. 306–27.

Connors, Peter J. Current Issues Regarding New
Financial Products: United States. *Bull. Int.
Fiscal Doc.*, March 1989, *43*(3), pp. 104–14.

**Conrad, B. Lynne; Thistle, Paul D. and McLeod,
Robert W.** Interest Rates and Bank Portfolio
Adjustments. *J. Banking Finance*, March 1989,
13(1), pp. 151–61.

Conrad, Jennifer. The Price Effect of Option Introduction. *J. Finance*, June 1989, *44*(2), pp.
487–98.

────── **and Kaul, Gautam.** Mean Reversion in
Short-Horizon Expected Returns. *Rev. Financial Stud.*, 1989, *2*(2), pp. 225–40.

Conrad, Jon M. Bioeconomics and the Bowhead
Whale. *J. Polit. Econ.*, August 1989, *97*(4), pp.
974–87.

Conrad, Klaus. Productivity and Cost Gaps in
Manufacturing Industries in U.S., Japan and
Germany. *Europ. Econ. Rev.*, July 1989, *33*(6),
pp. 1135–59.

──────. Tests for Optimizing Behavior and for Patterns of Conjectural Variations. *Kyklos*, 1989,
42(2), pp. 231–55.

────── **and Morrison, Catherine J.** The Impact
of Pollution Abatement Investment on Productivity Change: An Empirical Comparison of
the U.S., Germany, and Canada. *Southern
Econ. J.*, January 1989, *55*(3), pp. 684–98.

Considine, John and Narayan, Jack. Intervention
Analysis to Assess the Impact of Price Changes
on Ridership in a Transit System: A Case

Study. *Logist. Transp. Rev.*, March 1989,
25(1), pp. 53–61.

Considine, Timothy J. Estimating the Demand
for Energy and Natural Resource Inputs:
Trade-Offs in Global Properties. *Appl. Econ.*,
July 1989, *21*(7), pp. 931–45.

──────. Separability, Functional Form and Regulatory Policy in Models of Interfuel Substitution. *Energy Econ.*, April 1989, *11*(2), pp. 82–
94.

Constantinescu, P. and Czedly, I. Optimizing the
Efficiency of Fixed Assets in the Conditions
of Productivity Growth. *Econ. Computat.
Econ. Cybern. Stud. Res.*, 1989, *24*(2–3), pp.
7–16.

Constantino, Luis and Townsend, Gary. Modeling Operating Rate Decisions in the Canadian
Forest Industries. *Western J. Agr. Econ.*, December 1989, *14*(2), pp. 268–80.

Constantinou, S. T. and Diamantides, N. D.
Modeling the Macrodynamics of International
Migration: Determinants of Emigration from
Cyprus, 1946–85. *Environ. Planning A*, July
1989, *21*(7), pp. 927–50.

Conte, Michael A. A Simple Method for Estimating Quarterly Local-Area Personal Income. *J.
Reg. Sci.*, February 1989, *29*(1), pp. 89–105.

Conti, Sergio. Labour Market Models in Their
Spatial Expression. In *Linge, G. J. R. and van
der Knaap, G. A., eds.*, 1989, pp. 20–38.

Contini, Bruno. The Irregular Economy of Italy:
A Survey of Contributions. In *Feige, E. L.,
ed.*, 1989, pp. 237–50.

──────. Organization, Markets and Persistence of
Profits in Italian Industry. *J. Econ. Behav. Organ.*, October 1989, *12*(2), pp. 181–95.

Convain, Anne-Sophie and Mouillart, Michel.
Démographie et construction de logements.
(With English summary.) *Revue Écon. Politique*, July–Aug. 1989, *99*(4), pp. 639–59.

Converse, Jean M. and Schuman, Howard. The
Effects of Black and White Interviewers on
Black Responses. In *Singer, E. and Presser,
S., eds.*, 1989, *1971*, pp. 247–71.

**Conway, Patrick J.; Appleyard, Dennis R. and
Field, Alfred J., Jr.** Trade Agreements vs. Unilateral Tariff Reductions: Evidence from Modeling with a Continuum of Goods. *Int. Econ.
Rev.*, November 1989, *30*(4), pp. 775–94.

──────; **Field, Alfred J., Jr. and Appleyard, Dennis R.** The Effects of Customs Unions on the
Pattern and Terms of Trade in a Ricardian
Model with a Continuum of Goods. *J. Int.
Econ.*, August 1989, *27*(1–2), pp. 147–64.

**Conway, Roger K.; LeBlanc, Michael R. and
Swamy, P. A. V. B.** The Stochastic Coefficients
Approach to Econometric Modeling, Part III:
Estimation, Stability Testing, and Prediction.
J. Agr. Econ. Res., Winter 1989, *41*(1), pp.
4–20.

Cook, Alan [Sir]. Universities, Education and the
National Economy: Case Studies: Science. In
Stephens, M. D., ed., 1989, pp. 117–27.

Cook, Alice H. Public Policies to Help Dual-
Earner Families Meet the Demands of the
Work World. *Ind. Lab. Relat. Rev.*, January
1989, *42*(2), pp. 201–15.

Cook, B. A.; Rowcroft, J. E. and Brander, J. R. G. Deregulated Airline Markets as Open Access Commons. *De Economist*, 1989, *137*(4), pp. 466–75.

Cook, Ellen. How Do the Japanese Compete? *J. Behav. Econ.*, Winter 1989, *18*(4), pp. 251–63.

Cook, Leah and Case, Karl E. The Distributional Effects of Housing Price Booms: Winners and Losers in Boston, 1980–88. *New Eng. Econ. Rev.*, May–June 1989, pp. 3–12.

Cook, Miles R. Macroeconomic Policy Changes and the Forward Exchange Premium. *Amer. Economist*, Spring 1989, *33*(1), pp. 69–79.

Cook, Timothy. Determinants of the Federal Funds Rate: 1979–1982. *Fed. Res. Bank Richmond Econ. Rev.*, Jan.–Feb. 1989, *75*(1), pp. 3–19.

_____ **and Hahn, Thomas.** The Effect of Changes in the Federal Funds Rate Target on Market Interest Rates in the 1970s. *J. Monet. Econ.*, November 1989, *24*(3), pp. 331–51.

Cooke, Stephen C. and Sundquist, W. Burt. Cost Efficiency in U.S. Corn Production. *Amer. J. Agr. Econ.*, November 1989, *71*(4), pp. 1003–10.

Cooke, William N. Improving Productivity and Quality through Collaboration. *Ind. Relat.*, Spring 1989, *28*(2), pp. 299–319.

Cooksey, Elizabeth C.; Ismail, Abdel Fattah E. and Casterline, John B. Household Income and Child Survival in Egypt. *Demography*, February 1989, *26*(1), pp. 15–35.

Cooley, Thomas F. and Hansen, Gary D. The Inflation Tax in a Real Business Cycle Model. *Amer. Econ. Rev.*, September 1989, *79*(4), pp. 733–48.

_____ **; Parke, William R. and Chib, Siddhartha.** Predictive Efficiency for Simple Non-linear Models. *J. Econometrics*, January 1989, *40*(1), pp. 33–44.

_____ **and Smith, Bruce D.** Dynamic Coalition Formation and Equilibrium Policy Selection. *J. Monet. Econ.*, September 1989, *24*(2), pp. 211–33.

Coombs, Cynthia A., et al. Lessons from the Program for Hospitals Initiatives in Long-Term Care. In *Eisdorfer, C.; Kessler, D. A. and Spector, A. N., eds.*, 1989, pp. 184–96.

Cooper, Chester L. Greenhouse Warming: Abatement and Adaptation: Epilogue. In *Rosenberg, N. J., et al., eds.*, 1989, pp. 175–82.

Cooper, David A. and Elias, D. J. Estimated Economic Cost of HIV/AIDS: 1988/89 to 1992/3. In *Smith, C. S., ed.*, 1989, pp. 18–26.

Cooper, Eugene. Apprenticeship as Field Method: Lessons from Hong Kong. In *Coy, M. W., ed.*, 1989, pp. 137–48.

Cooper, J. H. On Income Distribution and Economic Sanctions. *S. Afr. J. Econ.*, March 1989, *57*(1), pp. 14–21.

_____ . On the Policy Implications for South Africa of Zero Foreign Capital Mobility. *J. Stud. Econ. Econometrics*, August 1989, *13*(2), pp. 71–77.

_____ **and Black, P. A.** Economic Sanctions and Interest Group Analysis: Some Reservations. *S. Afr. J. Econ.*, June 1989, *57*(2), pp. 188–93.

Cooper, John and Bennett, Craig. The Development of a Program Classification of Health Services for the South Australian Health Commission—Reflections on the First Three Years. In *Butler, J. R. G. and Doessel, D. P., eds.*, 1989, *1984*, pp. 266–77.

Cooper, Lauren and Honadle, George. Beyond Coordination and Control: An Interorganizational Approach to Structural Adjustment, Service Delivery, and Natural Resource Management. *World Devel.*, October 1989, *17*(10), pp. 1531–41.

Cooper, P. J. M.; Harris, Hazel C. and Goebel, W. Climatic Variability and Food Production in West Asia and North Africa. In *Oram, P. A., et al.*, 1989, pp. 69–83.

Cooper, Richard N. Europe without Borders. *Brookings Pap. Econ. Act.*, 1989, (2), pp. 325–40.

_____ . International Cooperation in Public Health as a Prologue to Macroeconomic Cooperation. In *Cooper, R. N., et al.*, 1989, pp. 178–254.

_____ . Is Private Money Optimal? *Cato J.*, Fall 1989, *9*(2), pp. 393–97.

_____ . Toward an International Commodity Standard? In *Dorn, J. A. and Niskanen, W. A., eds.*, 1989, *1988*, pp. 111–34.

Cooper, Robert and Fox, Stephen. Two Modes of Organization. In *Mansfield, R., ed.*, 1989, pp. 247–61.

Cooper, Russell and Chatterjee, Satyajit. Multiplicity of Equilibria and Fluctuations in Dynamic Imperfectly Competitive Economies. *Amer. Econ. Rev.*, May 1989, *79*(2), pp. 353–57.

_____ **and Riezman, Raymond.** Uncertainty and the Choice of Trade Policy in Oligopolistic Industries. *Rev. Econ. Stud.*, January 1989, *56*(1), pp. 129–40.

_____ , **et al.** Communication in the Battle of the Sexes Game: Some Experimental Results. *Rand J. Econ.*, Winter 1989, *20*(4), pp. 568–87.

Cooper, S. Y. and Oakey, R. P. High Technology Industry, Agglomeration and the Potential for Peripherally Sited Small Firms. *Reg. Stud.*, August 1989, *23*(4), pp. 347–60.

Cooper, Thomas E. Indirect Competition with Spatial Product Differentiation. *J. Ind. Econ.*, March 1989, *37*(3), pp. 241–57.

Cooper, W. W.; Charnes, A. and Clarke, R. L. An Approach to Testing for Organizational Slack via Banker's Game Theoretic DEA Formulations. In *Chan, J. L. and Patton, J. M., eds.*, 1989, pp. 211–29.

Cooperstein, Richard L. Quantifying the Decision to Become a First-Time Home Buyer. *Urban Stud.*, April 1989, *26*(2), pp. 223–33.

Cooter, Robert D. Rawl's Lexical Orderings Are Good Economics. *Econ. Philos.*, April 1989, *5*(1), pp. 47–54.

_____ **and Rubinfeld, Daniel L.** Economic Analysis of Legal Disputes and Their Resolution. *J. Econ. Lit.*, September 1989, *27*(3), pp. 1067–97.

Copeland, Brian R. Efficiency Wages in a Ricardian Model of International Trade. *J. Int. Econ.*, November 1989, *27*(3–4), pp. 221–44.

———. Of Mice and Elephants: The Canada–U.S. Free Trade Agreement. *Contemp. Policy Issues*, July 1989, *7*(3), pp. 42–60.

———. Tariffs and Quotas: Retaliation and Negotiation with Two Instruments of Protection. *J. Int. Econ.*, February 1989, *26*(1/2), pp. 179–88.

———; **Tower, Edward and Webb, Michael A.** On Negotiated Quotas, Tariffs, and Transfers. *Oxford Econ. Pap.*, October 1989, *41*(4), pp. 774–88.

Copeland, Laurence S. Exchange Rates and News: A Vector Autoregression Approach. In *MacDonald, R. and Taylor, M. P., eds.*, 1989, pp. 218–38.

———. Market Efficiency Before and After the Crash. *Fisc. Stud.*, August 1989, *10*(3), pp. 13–33.

Copeland, Ronald M. and Espahbodi, Hassan. Accommodating Multicollinearity in Financial Forecasting and Business Research. In *Lee, C. F., ed.*, 1989, pp. 311–22.

Copes, Parzival. Canadian Fisheries Management Policy: International Dimensions. In *McRae, D. and Munro, G., eds.*, 1989, pp. 3–16.

Copley, Paul A. The Determinants of Local Government Audit Fees: Additional Evidence. In *Chan, J. L. and Patton, J. M., eds.*, 1989, pp. 3–23.

Copp, Terry. The Child Welfare Movement in Montreal to 1920. In *Platt, D. C. M., ed.*, 1989, pp. 45–59.

Coppin, Addington and Codrington, Harold. The Financial Structure and the Allocation of Credit in Barbados, 1977–1987. *Soc. Econ. Stud.*, December 1989, *38*(4), pp. 165–79.

Corak, Miles. Policy in an Era of Free Trade: Some Comments on the de Grandpré Report: Review Article. *Can. Public Policy*, September 1989, *15*(3), pp. 335–38.

Corbae, Dean and Ouliaris, Sam. A Random Walk through the Gibson Paradox. *J. Appl. Econometrics*, July–Sept. 1989, *4*(3), pp. 295–303.

Corbo, Vittorio and McNelis, Paul D. The Pricing of Manufactured Goods during Trade Liberalization: Evidence from Chile, Israel, and Korea. *Rev. Econ. Statist.*, August 1989, *71*(3), pp. 491–99.

——— **and de Melo, Jaime.** External Shocks and Policy Reforms in the Southern Cone: A Reassessment. In *[Díaz-Alejandro, C.]*, 1989, pp. 235–58.

Corbridge, Stuart. Urban–Rural Relations and the Counter-revolution in Development Theory and Policy. In *[Mountjoy, A. B.]*, 1989, pp. 233–56.

Corchón, Luis C. and Barbolla, Rosa. An Elementary Proof of the Existence of a Competi-

tive Equilibrium in a Special Case. *Quart. J. Econ.*, May 1989, *104*(2), pp. 385–89.

Corcoran, Patrick. Commercial Mortgage Measuring Risk and Return. *J. Portfol. Manage.*, Winter 1989, *15*(2), pp. 69–75.

Corcoran, Rosaleen and O'Shea, Eamon. The Placement of Elderly Persons: A Logit Estimation and Cost Analysis. *Econ. Soc. Rev.*, April 1989, *20*(3), pp. 219–41.

Corden, W. Max. An International Debt Facility? In *Frenkel, J. A.; Dooley, M. P. and Wickham, P., eds.*, 1989, pp. 151–71.

———. Australian Macroeconomic Policy Experience. *Econ. Rec.*, June 1989, *65*(189), pp. 152–64.

———. Debt Relief and Adjustment Incentives. In *Frenkel, J. A.; Dooley, M. P. and Wickham, P., eds.*, 1989, pp. 242–57.

———. Economies of Scale and Customs Union Theory. In *Jacquemin, A. and Sapir, A., eds.*, 1989, *1972*, pp. 33–43.

———. Macroeconomic Adjustment in Developing Countries. *World Bank Res. Observer*, January 1989, *4*(1), pp. 51–64.

———. The Relevance for Developing Countries of Recent Developments in Macroeconomic Theory. In *[Díaz-Alejandro, C.]*, 1989, pp. 267–85.

——— **and Dooley, Michael P.** Issues in Debt Strategy: An Overview. In *Frenkel, J. A.; Dooley, M. P. and Wickham, P., eds.*, 1989, pp. 10–37.

Corder, Larry S. and Horvitz, Daniel G. Panel Effects in the National Medical Care Utilization and Expenditure Survey. In *Kasprzyk, D., et al., eds.*, 1989, pp. 304–18.

Cordes, Joseph J.; Goldfarb, Robert S. and Johnson, Richard L. Design and Implementation of Job Loss Compensation Provisions: Lessons from the Airline Deregulation Experience. *Int. J. Transport Econ.*, February 1989, *16*(1), pp. 35–55.

——— **and Sullivan, Martin A.** Resolving the Thrift Industry Crisis: A Public Finance Perspective. *Nat. Tax J.*, September 1989, *42*(3), pp. 233–47.

Coriat, Benjamin. Le débat théorique sur la désindustrialisation: Arguments, enjeux et perspectives. (The Theoretical Debate on De-industrialisation—Review of the Arguments, and Perspectives. With English summary.) *Écon. Appl.*, 1989, *42*(4), pp. 31–66.

Corker, Robert. External Adjustment and the Strong Yen: Recent Japanese Experience. *Int. Monet. Fund Staff Pap.*, June 1989, *36*(2), pp. 464–93.

———; **Evans, Owen and Kenward, Lloyd.** Tax Policy and Business Investment in the United States: Evidence from the 1980s. *Int. Monet. Fund Staff Pap.*, March 1989, *36*(1), pp. 31–62.

Corley, T. A. B. The Nature of Multinationals, 1870–1939. In *Teichova, A.; Lévy-Leboyer, M. and Nussbaum, H., eds.*, 1989, pp. 43–55.

Cornaglia, Anna. Consumo, risparmio, eredità con vita residua incerta. (Consumption, Saving, Bequest with Uncertain Lifespan. With English summary.) *Giorn. Econ.*, Sept.–Oct. 1989, *48*(9–10), pp. 467–75.

Cornelisse, Peter A. Human Capital Accumulation in Post-green Revolution Pakistan: Some Preliminary Results: Comments. *Pakistan Devel. Rev.*, Winter 1989, *28*(4), pp. 434–36.

_____ **and Naqvi, Syed Nawab Haider.** An Appraisal of Wheat Market Policy in Pakistan. *World Devel.*, March 1989, *17*(3), pp. 409–19.

Cornelius, Peter. Macroeconomic Forecasting in Germany: A Comment. *Jahr. Nationalökon. Statist.*, July 1989, *206*(3), pp. 264–66.

Cornelius, Wayne A. Impacts of the 1986 U.S. Immigration Law on Emigration from Rural Mexican Sending Communities. *Population Devel. Rev.*, December 1989, *15*(4), pp. 689–705.

Cornell, Bradford. The Impact of Data Errors on Measurement of the Foreign Exchange Risk Premium. *J. Int. Money Finance*, March 1989, *8*(1), pp. 147–57.

_____ **and Landsman, Wayne R.** Security Price Response to Quarterly Earnings Announcements and Analysts' Forecast Revisions. *Accounting Rev.*, October 1989, *64*(4), pp. 680–92.

Corner, Lorraine. East and West Nusa Tenggara: Isolation and Poverty. In *Hill, H., ed.*, 1989, pp. 178–206.

Cornes, Richard and Milne, Frank. A Simple Analysis of Mutually Disadvantageous Trading Opportunities. *Econ. Stud. Quart.*, June 1989, *40*(2), pp. 122–34.

_____ **and Sandler, Todd.** Public Goods, Growth, and Welfare. *Soc. Choice Welfare*, July 1989, *6*(3), pp. 243–51.

Cornet, Bernard. Existence of Equilibria in Economies with Increasing Returns. In *Cornet, B. and Tulkens, H., eds.*, 1989, pp. 79–97.

Cornforth, Chris and Thomas, Alan. A Model for Democratic Decision-Making: The Case of Worker Co-operatives. *Econ. Anal. Workers' Manage.*, 1989, *23*(1), pp. 1–15.

Cornwall, John. Inflation as a Cause of Economic Stagnation: A Dual Model. In *[Weintraub, S.]*, 1989, pp. 99–122.

_____. The Welfare State in a Programme of Economic Recovery. In *Davidson, P. and Kregel, J., eds.*, 1989, pp. 138–58.

Corradi, Valentina. Una stima non parametrica della funzione di reazione della banca d'Italia. (A Nonparametric Estimation of the Reaction Function of the Bank of Italy. With English summary.) *Rivista Int. Sci. Econ. Com.*, Oct.–Nov. 1989, *36*(10–11), pp. 963–76.

Corrado, Charles J. A Nonparametric Test for Abnormal Security-Price Performance in Event Studies. *J. Finan. Econ.*, August 1989, *23*(2), pp. 385–95.

Correa, Carlos Maria. Informatics in Latin America: Promises and Realities. *J. World Trade*, April 1989, *23*(2), pp. 81–96.

Corrigan, E. Gerald. Economic Policy: Main Challenges, Main Directions. In *Frankel, A. V. and Heck, C. B., eds.*, 1989, pp. 67–70.

_____. Future Priorities in Banking and Finance. *Fed. Res. Bank New York Quart. Rev.*, Winter 1989–90, *14*(4), pp. 1–7.

_____. Legislative Priorities. *Fed. Res. Bank New York Quart. Rev.*, Summer 1989, *14*(2), pp. 1–6.

_____. A Perspective on Recent Financial Disruptions. *Fed. Res. Bank New York Quart. Rev.*, Winter 1989–90, *14*(4), pp. 8–15.

_____. Securing a More Balanced Global Economy. *Fed. Res. Bank New York Quart. Rev.*, Special Issue, 1989, pp. 48–52.

_____. Trends in International Banking in the United States and Japan. *Fed. Res. Bank New York Quart. Rev.*, Autumn 1989, *14*(3), pp. 1–6.

Corsi, Thomas M. and Fanara, Philip, Jr. Effects of New Entrants on Motor Carrier Safety. In *Moses, L. N. and Savage, I., eds.*, 1989, pp. 241–57.

_____; **Jarrell, Judith L. and Grimm, Curtis M.** U.S. Motor Carrier Cost Structure under Deregulation. *Logist. Transp. Rev.*, September 1989, *25*(3), pp. 231–49.

Corstjens, Marcel and Doyle, Peter. Evaluating Alternative Retail Repositioning Strategies. *Marketing Sci.*, Spring 1989, *8*(2), pp. 170–80.

Cortázar, René. Austerity under Authoritarianism: The Neoconservative Revolution in Chile. In *Handelman, H. and Baer, W., eds.*, 1989, pp. 43–63.

Cory, Dennis C. and Colby, Bonnie G. Valuing Amenity Resources under Uncertainty: Does the Existence of Fair Contingent Claims Markets Matter? *J. Environ. Econ. Manage.*, March 1989, *16*(2), pp. 149–55.

Cosh, A. D., et al. Institutional Investment, Mergers and the Market for Corporate Control. *Int. J. Ind. Organ.*, Special Issue, March 1989, *7*(1), pp. 73–100.

Cosimano, Thomas F. and Benson, Bruce L. Spatial Competition with Free Entry, Chamberlinian Tangencies, and Social Efficiency: A Reevaluation. *J. Urban Econ.*, July 1989, *26*(1), pp. 84–89.

_____ **and Van Huyck, John B.** Dynamic Monetary Control and Interest Rate Stabilization. *J. Monet. Econ.*, January 1989, *23*(1), pp. 53–63.

Costa, Alcides Jorge. The Disregard of a Legal Entity for Tax Purposes: Brazil. In *International Fiscal Association, ed. (II)*, 1989, pp. 215–21.

Costa, Antonio M. Taxation of Financial Activities: Round Table. *Rev. Econ. Cond. Italy*, Sept.–Dec. 1989, (3), pp. 365–72.

Costa Campi, Ma. Teresa. Décentrage productif et diffusion industrielle. (Productive Decentralisation and Industrial Diffusion. With English summary.) *Écon. Societes*, February 1989, *23*(2), pp. 27–47.

Costa, Frank; Rosenberg, Robert Allen and Hendon, Willliam S. The General Public and the Art Museum: Case Studies of Visitors to Several Institutions Identify Characteristics of

Their Publics. *Amer. J. Econ. Sociology*, April 1989, *48*(2), pp. 231–43.

Costake, N. and Ticovschi, V. On Some Aspects of Scientific Research, Technological Development and the Application of Technical Advances. *Econ. Computat. Econ. Cybern. Stud. Res.*, 1989, *24*(1), pp. 25–36.

_____ **and Ticovschi, V.** On Some Aspects of Scientific Research, Technological Development and the Application of Technical Advance (III). *Econ. Computat. Econ. Cybern. Stud. Res.*, 1989, *24*(4), pp. 5–19.

_____ **and Ticovschi, V.** On Some Aspects of Scientific Research, Technological Development and the Application of Technical Advance (II). *Econ. Computat. Econ. Cybern. Stud. Res.*, 1989, *24*(2–3), pp. 17–27.

Cot, Annie L. Le gène et l'intérêt: L'anamorphose d'Irving Fisher. (Gene and Interest: On Irving Fisher's Anamorphosis. With English summary.) *Écon. Societes*, June 1989, *23*(6), pp. 89–107.

Cote, Daniel O. Firm Efficiency and Ownership Structure: The Case of U.S. Electric Utilities Using Panel Data. *Ann. Pub. Coop. Econ.*, 1989, *60*(4), pp. 431–50.

Cothren, Richard. Firm-Specific Training in an Incentive-Compatible Contract. *Econ. Letters*, December 1989, *31*(2), pp. 129–32.

Cotner, John S. and Horrell, James F. An Analysis of Index Option Pricing. *J. Futures Markets*, October 1989, *9*(5), pp. 449–59.

Cotta, Alain. The French Economy. In *Frankel, A. V. and Heck, C. B., eds.*, 1989, pp. 24–28.

Cotter, Kevin D. and Jensen, Gail A. Choice of Purchasing Arrangements in Insurance Markets. *J. Risk Uncertainty*, December 1989, *2*(4), pp. 405–14.

Cotter, Patrick S. and Willke, Richard J. Young Physicians and Changes in Medical Practice Characteristics between 1975 and 1987. *Inquiry*, Spring 1989, *26*(1), pp. 84–99.

Cotton, Jeremiah. The Declining Relative Economic Status of Black Families. *Rev. Black Polit. Econ.*, Summer 1989, *18*(1), pp. 75–85.

_____. Opening the Gap: The Decline in Black Economic Indicators in the 1980s. *Soc. Sci. Quart.*, December 1989, *70*(4), pp. 803–19.

Cottrell, Allin. Price Expectations and Equilibrium When the Interest Rate Is Pegged. *Scot. J. Polit. Econ.*, May 1989, *36*(2), pp. 125–40.

Cotula, Franco and Sannucci, Valeria. Nota sulla ricerca storica della Banca d'Italia. (Note on the Historical Research Undertaken by the Bank of Italy. With English summary.) *Rivista Storia Econ.*, S.S., October 1989, *6*(3), pp. 369–75.

Couch, Kenneth A. and Makin, John H. Saving, Pension Contributions, and the Real Interest Rate. *Rev. Econ. Statist.*, August 1989, *71*(3), pp. 401–07.

Coughlan, Anne T. and Sen, Subrata K. Salesforce Compensation: Theory and Managerial Implications. *Marketing Sci.*, Fall 1989, *8*(4), pp. 324–42.

Coughlin, Cletus C. and Mandelbaum, Thomas B. Have Federal Spending and Taxation Contributed to the Divergence of State Per Capita Incomes in the 1980s? *Fed. Res. Bank St. Louis Rev.*, July–Aug. 1989, *71*(4), pp. 29–42.

_____; **Terza, Joseph V. and Khalifah, Noor Aini.** The Determinants of Escape Clause Petitions. *Rev. Econ. Statist.*, May 1989, *71*(2), pp. 341–47.

_____ **and Wood, Geoffrey E.** An Introduction to Non-tariff Barriers to Trade. *Fed. Res. Bank St. Louis Rev.*, Jan.–Feb. 1989, *71*(1), pp. 32–46.

Coughlin, Peter J. Economic Policy Advice and Political Preferences. *Public Choice*, June 1989, *61*(3), pp. 201–16.

_____ **and Howe, Eric C.** Policies over Time and Pareto Optimality. *Soc. Choice Welfare*, October 1989, *6*(4), pp. 259–73.

Coulhon, T. and Mongin, P. Social Choice Theory in the Case of von Neumann–Morgenstern Utilities. *Soc. Choice Welfare*, July 1989, *6*(3), pp. 175–87.

Coulomb, Pierre and Delorme, Hélène. French Agriculture and the Failure of Its European Strategy. In *Goodman, D. and Redclift, M., eds.*, 1989, pp. 84–112.

Coulombe, Serge; Lavoie, Marc and Grenier, Gilles. Discrimination versus English Proficiency in the National Hockey League: A Reply. *Can. Public Policy*, March 1989, *15*(1), pp. 98–101.

Coulon, Christian and Cruise O'Brien, Donal B. Contemporary West African States: Senegal. In *Cruise O'Brien, D. B.; Dunn, J. and Rathbone, R., eds.*, 1989, pp. 145–64.

Coulson, N. Edward. The Empirical Content of the Linearity-as-Repackaging Hypothesis. *J. Urban Econ.*, May 1989, *25*(3), pp. 295–309.

_____ **and Bond, Eric W.** Externalities, Filtering, and Neighborhood Change. *J. Urban Econ.*, September 1989, *26*(2), pp. 231–49.

Counte, Michael A.; Homan, Rick K. and Glandon, Gerald L. Perceived Risk: The Link to Plan Selection and Future Utilization. *J. Risk Ins.*, March 1989, *56*(1), pp. 67–82.

Couper, A. D. Changes in Port and Shipping Technology in the Pacific and Their Social Impact. In *Couper, A. D., ed.*, 1989, pp. 145–52.

_____. Development and Social Change in the Pacific Islands: Introduction. In *Couper, A. D., ed.*, 1989, pp. 1–3.

_____. Fishery Developments and Social Change in the Pacific. In *Couper, A. D., ed.*, 1989, pp. 22–32.

Coupland, Rex E. Universities, Education and the National Economy: Case Studies: Medicine. In *Stephens, M. D., ed.*, 1989, pp. 87–116.

Courakis, Anthony S. Does Constant Relative Risk Aversion Imply Asset Demands That Are Linear in Expected Returns? *Oxford Econ. Pap.*, July 1989, *41*(3), pp. 553–66.

Cournat, Paul N. and Borenstein, Severin. How to Carve a Medical Degree: Human Capital

Assets in Divorce Settlements. *Amer. Econ. Rev.*, December 1989, 79(5), pp. 992–1009.

Courtadon, Georges; Subrahmanyam, Marti G. and Brenner, Menachem. Options on Stock Indices and Options on Futures. *J. Banking Finance*, September 1989, 13(4–5), pp. 773–82.

Courtois, Pierre and Tirard, Jean-Marc. La non-reconnaissance des personnes juridiques en matière fiscale: France. (The Disregard of a Legal Entity for Tax Purposes: France. With English summary.) In *International Fiscal Association, ed. (II)*, 1989, pp. 269–87.

Cousineau, Jean-Michel; McRoberts, Kenneth and Blais, André. The Determinants of Minimum Wage Rates. *Public Choice*, July 1989, 62(1), pp. 15–24.

Covelli, Lucille. Dominant Class Culture and Legitimation: Female Volunteer Directors. In *Herman, R. D. and Van Til, J., eds.*, 1989, pp. 24–35.

Cover, James Peery. International Evidence on Output–Inflation Trade-Offs: Results from a Covariance-Bounds Test. *J. Macroecon.*, Summer 1989, 11(3), pp. 397–408.

_____ **and Hooks, Donald L.** Credit versus Monetary Theories of Macroeconomic Fluctuations. *Atlantic Econ. J.*, June 1989, 17(2), pp. 41–46.

_____ **and Keeler, James P.** Estimating Money Demand in Log-First-Difference Form: Reply. *Southern Econ. J.*, April 1989, 55(4), pp. 1040–43.

Covi, Antonio. L'ordine dei discorsi economici: Napoleoni su Keynes e Sraffa. (Napoleoni on Keynes and Sraffa. With English summary.) *Rivista Int. Sci. Econ. Com.*, April–May 1989, 36(4–5), pp. 339–58.

Cowan, Simon G. B. Trade and Competition Policies for Oligopolies. *Weltwirtsch. Arch.*, 1989, 125(3), pp. 464–83.

Cowell, Frank A. Honesty Is Sometimes the Best Policy. *Europ. Econ. Rev.*, March 1989, 33(2/3), pp. 605–17.

_____. Sampling Variance and Decomposable Inequality Measures. *J. Econometrics*, September 1989, 42(1), pp. 27–41.

Cowen, Janna L. and Felton, John Richard. Operating-Ratio Regulation by the States. In *Felton, J. R. and Anderson, D. G., eds.*, 1989, 1985, pp. 99–112.

Cowen, Tyler. Are All Tastes Constant and Identical? A Critique. *J. Econ. Behav. Organ.*, January 1989, 11(1), pp. 127–35.

_____. Normative Population Theory. *Soc. Choice Welfare*, January 1989, 6(1), pp. 33–43.

_____ **and Kroszner, Randall.** Scottish Banking before 1845: A Model for Laissez-Faire? *J. Money, Credit, Banking*, May 1989, 21(2), pp. 221–31.

Cowling, Keith and Sugden, Roger. Exchange Rate Adjustment and Oligopoly Pricing Behaviour. *Cambridge J. Econ.*, September 1989, 13(3), pp. 373–93.

Cox, Annette. Marketing at Burlington Industries,

1923–1962. In *Hausman, W. J., ed.*, 1989, pp. 160–67.

Cox, Anthony D. and Kellaris, James J. The Effects of Background Music in Advertising: A Reassessment. *J. Cons. Res.*, June 1989, 16(1), pp. 113–18.

Cox, Barry; Stratford, Mike and Islei, Gerd. Ranking, Monitoring and Control of Research Projects in the Pharmaceutical Industry. In *Lockett, A. G. and Islei, G., eds.*, 1989, pp. 191–202.

Cox, Donald and Nye, John Vincent. Male–Female Wage Discrimination in Nineteenth-Century France. *J. Econ. Hist.*, December 1989, 49(4), pp. 903–20.

Cox, Graham; Lowe, Philip and Winter, Michael. The Farm Crisis in Britain. In *Goodman, D. and Redclift, M., eds.*, 1989, pp. 113–34.

Cox, James C. and Epstein, Seth. Preference Reversals without the Independence Axiom. *Amer. Econ. Rev.*, June 1989, 79(3), pp. 408–26.

_____ **and Oaxaca, Ronald L.** Laboratory Experiments with a Finite-Horizon Job-Search Model. *J. Risk Uncertainty*, September 1989, 2(3), pp. 301–29.

Cox, John C. and Huang, Chi-fu. Optimal Consumption and Portfolio Policies When Asset Prices Follow a Diffusion Process. *J. Econ. Theory*, October 1989, 49(1), pp. 33–83.

Cox, Joseph C. and Warf, Barney. Military Prime Contracts and Taxes in the New York Metropolitan Region: A Short-run Analysis. *Reg. Stud.*, June 1989, 23(3), pp. 241–51.

Cox, Steven R. Advertising Restrictions among Professionals: *Bates v. State Bar of Arizona*. In *Kwoka, J. E., Jr. and White, L. J., eds.*, 1989, pp. 134–59.

Cox, Thomas A.; Buse, Rueben C. and Alvarez, Antonio. Effect of Demographics on Changes in At-Home Meat Consumption. In *Buse, R. C., ed.*, 1989, pp. 217–42.

Cox, William Michael and Lown, Cara S. The Capital Gains and Losses on U.S. Government Debt: 1942–1987. *Rev. Econ. Statist.*, February 1989, 71(1), pp. 1–14.

_____ **and Rosenblum, Harvey.** Money and Inflation in a Deregulated Financial Environment: An Overview. *Fed. Res. Bank Dallas Econ. Rev.*, May 1989, pp. 1–19.

Coy, Michael W. Apprenticeship: From Theory to Method and Back Again: Introduction. In *Coy, M. W., ed.*, 1989, pp. xi–xv.

_____. Being What We Pretend to Be: The Usefulness of Apprenticeship as a Field Method. In *Coy, M. W., ed.*, 1989, pp. 115–35.

Coyle, Barry T. A Comment on the Specification of Linear Equations for Consumer Demand, Output Supply and Factor Demand. *Can. J. Agr. Econ.*, July 1989, 37(2), pp. 263–68.

Coyne, Christopher; Fabozzi, Frank J. and Yaari, Uzi. Taxation of Capital Gains with Deferred Realization. *Nat. Tax J.*, December 1989, 42(4), pp. 475–85.

Coyne, John; Wright, Mike and Chiplin, Brian. The Market for Corporate Control: The Divestment Option. In *Fairburn, J. and Kay, J., eds.*, 1989, pp. 116–32.

Coyte, Peter C. and Landon, Stuart. The Impact of Competition on Advertising: The Case of Political Campaign Expenditures. *Can. J. Econ.*, November 1989, *22*(4), pp. 795–818.

Crabbe, Leland. The International Gold Standard and U.S. Monetary Policy from World War I to the New Deal. *Fed. Res. Bull.*, June 1989, *75*(6), pp. 423–40.

Crabbé, Philippe J. and Long, Ngo Van. Optimal Forest Rotation under Monopoly and Competition. *J. Environ. Econ. Manage.*, July 1989, *17*(1), pp. 54–65.

Crabtree, J. R. and Macmillan, D. C. UK Fiscal Changes and New Forestry Planting. *J. Agr. Econ.*, September 1989, *40*(3), pp. 314–22.

Crafts, Nick F. R. Duration of Marriage, Fertility and Women's Employment Opportunities in England and Wales in 1911. *Population Stud.*, July 1989, *43*(2), pp. 325–35.

_____. Long-term Unemployment and the Wage Equation in Britain, 1925–1939. *Economica*, May 1989, *56*(222), pp. 247–54.

_____. The New View of British Growth and Gerschenkron's Hypotheses. *Rivista Storia Econ.*, S.S., February 1989, *6*(1), pp. 39–59.

_____. Real Wages, Inequality and Economic Growth in Britain, 1750–1850: A Review of Recent Research. In *Scholliers, P., ed.*, 1989, pp. 75–95.

_____. Revealed Comparative Advantage in Manufacturing, 1899–1950. *J. Europ. Econ. Hist.*, Spring 1989, *18*(1), pp. 127–37.

_____; **Leybourne, S. J. and Mills, Terence C.** The Climacteric in Late Victorian Britain and France: A Reappraisal of the Evidence. *J. Appl. Econometrics*, April–June 1989, *4*(2), pp. 103–17.

_____; **Leybourne, S. J. and Mills, Terence C.** Trends and Cycles in British Industrial Production, 1700–1913. *J. Roy. Statist. Society*, 1989, *152*(1), pp. 43–60.

Crahan, Margaret E. Catholicism in Cuba. In *Mesa-Lago, C., ed.*, 1989, pp. 3–24.

Craig, Barbara and Pardey, Philip G. Causal Relationships between Public Sector Agricultural Research Expenditures and Output. *Amer. J. Agr. Econ.*, February 1989, *71*(1), pp. 9–19.

Craig, J. G. and Sira, F. N. Dilemmas in Cooperative Development in Third World Countries. *Ann. Pub. Coop. Econ.*, 1989, *60*(2), pp. 229–49.

Craig, Steven G. and Cashel-Cordo, Peter. Donors, Development, and Debt: The Role of External Assistance and External Indebtedness. In *DeGregori, T. R., ed.*, 1989, pp. 231–83.

_____ **and Heikkila, Eric J.** Urban Safety in Vancouver: Allocation and Production of a Congestible Public Good. *Can. J. Econ.*, November 1989, *22*(4), pp. 867–84.

Craigwell, R. C.; Sealy, R. C. and Rock, L. L. Public Deficits and Private Consumption: Empirical Evidence from Small Open Economies. *Appl. Econ.*, May 1989, *21*(5), pp. 697–710.

Crain, Ben W. Comment: Is Managed Money the Root of All Evil? In *Dorn, J. A. and Niskanen, W. A., eds.*, 1989, *1988*, pp. 57–62.

Craine, Roger. Risky Business: The Allocation of Capital. *J. Monet. Econ.*, March 1989, *23*(2), pp. 201–18.

_____ **and Berger, Allen N.** Why Random Walk Models of the Term Structure Are Hard to Reject. *J. Bus. Econ. Statist.*, April 1989, *7*(2), pp. 161–67.

Cram, Fiona and Ng, Sik Hung. Children's Endorsement of Ownership Attributes. *J. Econ. Psych.*, March 1989, *10*(1), pp. 63–75.

von Cramon-Taubadel, Stephan. The Agri-Monetary System and Agricultural Trade Flows within the EC. *Europ. Rev. Agr. Econ.*, 1989, *16*(1), pp. 37–52.

Crampton, Graham and Evans, Alan W. Myth, Reality and Employment in London. *J. Transp. Econ. Policy*, January 1989, *23*(1), pp. 89–108.

Crandall, Robert W. The 'Competitiveness' of the U.S. Economy. In *Libecap, G. D., ed.*, 1989, pp. 13–32.

_____. Regulatory Reform: Are We Ready for the Next Phase? In *Bosworth, B. P., et al.*, 1989, pp. 134–39.

_____. The Role of the U.S. Local Operating Companies. In *Crandall, R. W. and Flamm, K., eds.*, 1989, pp. 114–46.

_____ **and Flamm, Kenneth.** Changing the Rules: Technological Change, International Competition, and Regulation in Communications: Overview. In *Crandall, R. W. and Flamm, K., eds.*, 1989, pp. 1–10.

_____ **and Graham, John D.** The Effect of Fuel Economy Standards on Automobile Safety. *J. Law Econ.*, April 1989, *32*(1), pp. 97–118.

Crane, Barbara B. and Finkle, Jason L. The United States, China, and the United Nations Population Fund: Dynamics of U.S. Policymaking. *Population Devel. Rev.*, March 1989, *15*(1), pp. 23–59.

Crane, Edward H. and Boaz, David. An American Vision: Policies for the '90s: Introduction. In *Crane, E. H. and Boaz, D.*, 1989, pp. 1–10.

Cranor, Carl F. Patenting Body Parts: A Sketch of Some Moral Issues. In *Weil, V. and Snapper, J. W., eds.*, 1989, pp. 200–212.

Craswell, Richard. Performance, Reliance, and One-Sided Information. *J. Legal Stud.*, June 1989, *18*(2), pp. 365–401.

Crawford, Allan and Ferguson, Brian S. Supplier-Induced Demand: A Disequilibrium Test. *Appl. Econ.*, May 1989, *21*(5), pp. 597–609.

Crawford, James. Australian Law after Two Centuries. In *Hancock, K., ed.*, 1989, pp. 192–207.

Crawford, Samuel H. Annual Review of Nations: Year 1988: Italy. In *Haberman, L. and Sacks, P. M., eds.*, 1989, pp. 155–72.

Cray, David. The Use of Symbols in Multicriteria Decision Making. In *Lockett, A. G. and Islei, G., eds.*, 1989, pp. 100–111.

Cray, Randy F. Estimating the Impact of Higher

Electricity Rates on Intersectoral Prices: An Input–Output Approach. *Rev. Reg. Stud.*, Spring 1989, *19*(2), pp. 18–29.

Cready, Cynthia Matthews and Weissert, William G. A Prospective Budgeting Model for Home- and Community-Based Long-Term Care. *Inquiry*, Spring 1989, *26*(1), pp. 116–29.

Creed, Carolyn F.; McCay, Bonnie J. and Gatewood, John B. Labor and the Labor Process in a Limited Entry Fishery. *Marine Resource Econ.*, 1989, *6*(4), pp. 311–30.

Creedy, John. Whewell's "Translation" of J. S. Mill. *Scot. J. Polit. Econ.*, August 1989, *36*(3), pp. 266–81.

_____ **and Disney, Richard.** The Australian Pension Scheme: Some Basic Analytics. *Econ. Rec.*, December 1989, *65*(191), pp. 357–68.

_____ **and Disney, Richard.** Can We Afford to Grow Older? Population Aging and Social Security. *Europ. Econ. Rev.*, March 1989, *33*(2/3), pp. 367–76.

_____ **and Disney, Richard.** The New Pension Scheme in Britain. In *Dilnot, A. and Walker, I., eds.*, 1989, pp. 224–38.

_____ **and Disney, Richard.** Public and Private Partnerships in Social Security: Recent UK Policy. In *Gustafsson, B. A. and Klevmarken, N. A., eds.*, 1989, pp. 211–35.

_____ **and Disney, Richard.** The "Twin-Pillar" Approach to Social Insurance in the UK. *Scot. J. Polit. Econ.*, May 1989, *36*(2), pp. 113–24.

_____ **and McDonald, Ian M.** Trade Unions, Wages and Taxation. *Fisc. Stud.*, August 1989, *10*(3), pp. 50–59.

Creigh, Stephen and Casey, Bernard. "Marginal" Groups in the Labour Force Survey. *Scot. J. Polit. Econ.*, August 1989, *36*(3), pp. 282–300.

Cremer, Helmuth; Marchand, Maurice and Thisse, Jacques-François. The Public Firm as an Instrument for Regulating an Oligopolistic Market. *Oxford Econ. Pap.*, April 1989, *41*(2), pp. 283–301.

Crémer, Jacques and Salehi-Isfahani, Djavad. The Rise and Fall of Oil Prices: A Competitive View. *Ann. Écon. Statist.*, July–Dec. 1989, (15–16), pp. 427–54.

Cressie, Noel. Empirical Bayes Estimation of Undercount in the Decennial Census. *J. Amer. Statist. Assoc.*, December 1989, *84*(408), pp. 1033–44.

Crew, Michael A. Competition, Diversification, and Disintegration in Regulated Industries. In *Crew, M. A., ed.*, 1989, pp. 1–4.

_____ **and Rowley, Charles K.** Feasibility of Deregulation: A Public Choice Analysis. In *Crew, M. A., ed.*, 1989, pp. 5–20.

Cribbett, P. F.; Lye, J. N. and Ullah, Aman. Evaluation of the Two-Stage Least Squares Distribution Function by Imhof's Procedure. *J. Quant. Econ.*, January 1989, *5*(1), pp. 91–96.

Crichton, Noel and de Silva, Charles. Financial Development and Economic Growth: Trinidad and Tobago, 1973–1987. *Soc. Econ. Stud.*, December 1989, *38*(4), pp. 133–64.

Crick, Bernard. Republicanism, Liberalism and Capitalism: A Defence of Parliamentarianism. In *Duncan, G., ed.*, 1989, pp. 63–84.

Criddle, Keith R. and Havenner, Arthur M. Forecasting Halibut Biomass Using System Theoretic Time-Series Methods. *Amer. J. Agr. Econ.*, May 1989, *71*(2), pp. 422–31.

Crihfield, John B. A Structural Empirical Analysis of Metropolitan Labor Demand. *J. Reg. Sci.*, August 1989, *29*(3), pp. 347–71.

Crimmins, Eileen M.; Saito, Yasuhiko and Ingegneri, Dominique. Changes in Life Expectancy and Disability-Free Life Expectancy in the United States. *Population Devel. Rev.*, June 1989, *15*(2), pp. 235–67.

Crisp, M. R. and Marcus, B. M. Administrative and Compliance Costs of Taxation: South Africa. In *International Fiscal Association, ed. (I)*, 1989, pp. 121–37.

Crist, Raymond E. Export Agriculture and the Expansion of Urban Slum Areas. *Amer. J. Econ. Sociology*, April 1989, *48*(2), pp. 143–49.

Crittenden, Brian. Education in Australia: Conformity and Diversity. In *Hancock, K., ed.*, 1989, pp. 70–93.

Crocker, Thomas D. On the Value of the Condition of a Forest Stock: Reply. *Land Econ.*, February 1989, *65*(1), pp. 73–75.

Crockett, Andrew. International Monetary Reform, Coordination and Indicators. In *Hamouda, O. F.; Rowley, R. and Wolf, B. M., eds.*, 1989, pp. 11–26.

_____. The Role of International Institutions in Surveillance and Policy Coordination. In *Bryant, R. C., et al., eds.*, 1989, pp. 343–64.

Croes, Edwin and FitzGerald, E. V. K. The Regional Monetary System and Economic Recovery. In *Irvin, G. and Holland, S., eds.*, 1989, pp. 139–61.

Cromie, Stanley and Ayling, Simon. The Motivation, Satisfaction and Company Goals of Business Proprietors. In *Mansfield, R., ed.*, 1989, pp. 221–32.

Cromley, Robert G. and Hanink, Dean M. A Financial–Economic von Thünen Model. *Environ. Planning A*, July 1989, *21*(7), pp. 951–60.

_____ **and Leinbach, Thomas R.** Modeling Integrated Development Investments in Rural Areas: An Indonesian Illustration. *Int. Reg. Sci. Rev.*, 1989, *12*(2), pp. 229–43.

Crompton, Gerald. 'Squeezing the Pulpless Orange': Labour and Capital on the Railways in the Inter-war Years. In *Harvey, C. and Turner, J., eds.*, 1989, pp. 66–83.

Cromwell, Jerry and Puskin, Dena. Hospital Productivity and Intensity Trends: 1980–87. *Inquiry*, Fall 1989, *26*(3), pp. 366–80.

_____, **et al.** Using Physician Time and Complexity to Identify Mispriced Procedures. *Inquiry*, Spring 1989, *26*(1), pp. 7–23.

Crook, Jonathan. The Demand for Retailer-Financed Instalment Credit: An Econometric Analysis. *Managerial Dec. Econ.*, December 1989, *10*(4), pp. 311–19.

Crookell, Harold. Managing Canadian Subsidiaries in a Free Trade Environment. In *Rugman, A. M., ed.,* 1989, *1987,* pp. 189–99.

Croskery, Patrick. The Intellectual Property Literature: A Structured Approach. In *Weil, V. and Snapper, J. W., eds.,* 1989, pp. 268–81.

Cross, Mark L.; Davidson, Wallace N., III and Thornton, John H. The Impact of Directors and Officers' Liability Suits on Firm Value. *J. Risk Ins.,* March 1989, *56*(1), pp. 128–36.

Cross, Sam Y. The Growth and Changing Character of the Foreign Exchange Market. In *Kaushik, S. K., ed.,* 1989, pp. 83–94.

_____. Treasury and Federal Reserve Foreign Exchange Operations. *Fed. Res. Bull.,* October 1989, *75*(10), pp. 670–74.

_____. Treasury and Federal Reserve Foreign Exchange Operations. *Fed. Res. Bull.,* July 1989, *75*(7), pp. 485–90.

_____. Treasury and Federal Reserve Foreign Exchange Operations, November 1988–January 1989. *Fed. Res. Bank New York Quart. Rev.,* Winter–Spring 1989, *13-14*(4–1), pp. 103–07.

_____. Treasury and Federal Reserve Foreign Exchange Operations: February–April 1989. *Fed. Res. Bank New York Quart. Rev.,* Summer 1989, *14*(2), pp. 68–74.

_____. Treasury and Federal Reserve Foreign Exchange Operations: November 1989–January 1990. *Fed. Res. Bank New York Quart. Rev.,* Winter 1989–90, *14*(4), pp. 69–75.

_____. Treasury and Federal Reserve Foreign Exchange Operations. *Fed. Res. Bull.,* February 1989, *75*(2), pp. 58–62.

_____ and Bentley, George G. Treasury and Federal Reserve Foreign Exchange Operations. *Fed. Res. Bank New York Quart. Rev.,* Autumn 1989, *14*(3), pp. 54–60.

_____ and Weintraub, Cathy. Treasury and Federal Reserve Foreign Exchange Operations: May–June 1989. *Fed. Res. Bank New York Quart. Rev.,* Autumn 1989, *14*(3), pp. 61–66.

Crossa, J.; Pham, H. N. and Waddington, S. R. Yield Stability of CIMMYT Maize Germplasm in International and On-Farm Trials. In *Anderson, J. R. and Hazell, P. B. R., eds.,* 1989, pp. 185–205.

Crossland, Philip D. and Weinel, Ivan. The Scientific Foundations of Technological Progress. *J. Econ. Issues,* September 1989, *23*(3), pp. 795–808.

Crosson, Pierre R. Agricultural Land: The Values at Stake. In *Dysart, B. C., III and Clawson, M., eds.,* 1989, pp. 83–98.

_____. Climate Change: Problems of Limits and Policy Responses. In *Rosenberg, N. J., et al., eds.,* 1989, pp. 69–82.

_____; Easterling, William E., III and Parry, Martin L. Adapting Future Agriculture to Changes in Climate. In *Rosenberg, N. J., et al., eds.,* 1989, pp. 91–104.

Crotty, James. The Limits of Keynesian Macroeconomic Policy in the Age of the Global Marketplace. In *MacEwan, A. and Tabb, W. K., eds.,* 1989, pp. 82–100.

Crough, Greg J. and Wheelwright, Edward L. The Changing Pacific Rim Economy, with Special Reference to Japanese Transnational Corporations: A View from Australia. In *Shiraishi, T. and Tsuru, S., eds.,* 1989, pp. 61–78.

Crous, M. J.; Jooste, C. J. and Nortje, J. D. Selfdoenmodules as Onderrigmedium vir die Kleinsakesektor in die RAS. (With English summary.) *J. Stud. Econ. Econometrics,* March 1989, *13*(1), pp. 89–101.

Croushore, Dean D. The Effect of Government Deficits on Consumption and Interest Rates: A Two Equation Approach. *Quart. J. Bus. Econ.,* Spring 1989, *28*(2), pp. 85–129.

_____. What Neutrality Means in Macroeconomics: Reply. *Eastern Econ. J.,* April–June 1989, *15*(2), pp. 150–52.

Crouzet, François M. Les conséquences des guerres de la Révolution et de l'Empire pour l'économie britannique (1793–1815). (The Impact of the French Wars on the British Economy. With English summary.) *Revue Écon.,* November 1989, *40*(6), pp. 1119–36.

_____. Les conséquences économiques de la Révolution française. Réflexions sur un débat. (The Economic Consequences of the French Revolution: Some Comments. With English summary.) *Revue Écon.,* November 1989, *40*(6), pp. 1189–1204.

_____. Opportunity and Risk in Atlantic Trade during the French Revolution. In *[Fischer, W.],* 1989, pp. 90–150.

Crow, John W. Monetary Policy Issues in the 1990s: Overview: Central Bank Perspectives. In *Federal Reserve Bank of Kansas City,* 1989, pp. 291–97.

Crowe, B. L. and Hailey, D. M. The Economics of Australian Hospitals: Forum: Cost-Effectiveness of Diagnostic Technology: MRI—A Case Study. In *Smith, C. S., ed.,* 1989, pp. 301–04.

Crowley, Ronald W. and Bourgeois, Raymond C. The Rationale and Future Directions of Canada's Oceans Policy: Domestic Aspects. In *McRae, D. and Munro, G., eds.,* 1989, pp. 253–68.

Cruise O'Brien, Donal B. and Coulon, Christian. Contemporary West African States: Senegal. In *Cruise O'Brien, D. B.; Dunn, J. and Rathbone, R., eds.,* 1989, pp. 145–64.

_____ and Rathbone, Richard. Contemporary West African States: Introduction. In *Cruise O'Brien, D. B.; Dunn, J. and Rathbone, R., eds.,* 1989, pp. 1–11.

Crum, Michael R. U.S. Transportation Management Developments since Deregulation. *Int. J. Transport Econ.,* October 1989, *16*(3), pp. 263–95.

Crumbley, D. Larry; Thomas, Christopher R. and Maurice, S. Charles. Vertical Integration, Price Squeezing, and the Percentage Depletion Allowance. *Quart. Rev. Econ. Bus.,* Winter 1989, *29*(4), pp. 26–36.

Crump, Jeffrey R. The Spatial Distribution of Military Spending in the United States 1941–1985. *Growth Change,* Summer 1989, *20*(3), pp. 50–62.

de la Cruz Navarro, María; Martinez Mongay, Carlos and Sanz, Fernando. Selección y explotación de los sistemas de alarma y prevención de quiebra. (With English summary.) *Invest. Ecón.*, September 1989, *13*(3), pp. 465–84.

Csaba, László. Investment and Innovation—The Experience of Three Reforms. *Eastern Europ. Econ.*, Spring 1989, *27*(3), pp. 85–104.

_____. Osteuropa zwischen erneuerungszwang un stagnation. (With English summary.) *Jahr. Wirtsch. Osteuropas*, 1989, *13*(1), pp. 82–109.

Csáki, Csaba. Experiences with Agricultural Policy Models for Centrally Planned Economies. In *Bauer, S. and Henrichsmeyer, W., eds.*, 1989, pp. 193–205.

_____. The Relationship between Industry and Agriculture in the Development of the Hungarian Economy. In *Williamson, J. G. and Panchamukhi, V. R., eds.*, 1989, pp. 264–87.

_____. World Hunger, Malnutrition, and Food Production and Distribution Systems: Reaction. In *Helmuth, J. W. and Johnson, S. R., eds.*, Vol. *1*, 1989, pp. 193–94.

_____ **and Rabár, Ferenc.** Current and Prospective Problems of Hunger and Malnutrition: Beyond the Reach of the Invisible Hand. In *Helmuth, J. W. and Johnson, S. R., eds.*, Vol. 2, 1989, pp. 141–55.

Csath, Magdolna. Management Education for Developing Entrepreneurship in Hungary. In *Davies, J., et al., eds.*, 1989, pp. 137–51.

Csikós-Nagy, B. Personal Comments on the Socialist Market Economy. *Acta Oecon.*, 1989, *40*(3–4), pp. 216–19.

Cuairán, Rogelio; Sanz, Fernando and Sanso, Marcos. Flujos bilaterales de comercio internacional, ecuación de gravedad y teoria Heckscher–Ohlin. (With English summary.) *Invest. Ecón.*, January 1989, *13*(1), pp. 155–66.

Cubukgil, A.; Harltos, Z. J. and Soberman, R. M. Transportation Research Needs of Developing Countries: The Case for a New Centre. In *Candemir, Y., ed.*, 1989, pp. 196–209.

Cuculeanu, Georgeta. Some Considerations on Industrial Robot Optimal Command. *Econ. Computat. Econ. Cybern. Stud. Res.*, 1989, *24*(1), pp. 71–76.

Cuddington, John T. Commodity Export Booms in Developing Countries. *World Bank Res. Observer*, July 1989, *4*(2), pp. 143–65.

_____. The Extent and Causes of the Debt Crisis of the 1980s. In *Husain, I. and Diwan, I., eds.*, 1989, pp. 15–42.

_____ **and Urzúa, Carlos M.** Trends and Cycles in Colombia's Real GDP and Fiscal Deficit. *J. Devel. Econ.*, April 1989, *30*(2), pp. 325–43.

_____ **and Urzúa, Carlos M.** Trends and Cycles in the Net Barter Terms of Trade: A New Approach. *Econ. J.*, June 1989, *99*(396), pp. 426–42.

Cude, Brenda J. Consumer Response to Telecommunications Deregulation: The Equal Access Decision. *J. Cons. Aff.*, Winter 1989, *23*(2), pp. 285–300.

Cude, Wilfred. Graduate Education Is in Trouble. *Challenge*, Sept.–Oct. 1989, *32*(5), pp. 59–63.

Cuff, Robert D. Creating Control Systems: Edwin F. Gay and the Central Bureau of Planning and Statistics, 1917–1919. *Bus. Hist. Rev.*, Autumn 1989, *63*(3), pp. 588–613.

Cugno, Franco. Supervisione e salari di efficienza nell'economia partecipativa di Weitzman. (Supervision and Efficiency Wages in Weitzman's Share Economy. With English summary.) *Rivista Int. Sci. Econ. Com.*, April–May 1989, *36*(4–5), pp. 325–38.

Cukierman, Alex and Meltzer, Allan H. A Political Theory of Government Debt and Deficits in a Neo-Ricardian Framework. *Amer. Econ. Rev.*, September 1989, *79*(4), pp. 713–32.

_____; **Meltzer, Allan H. and Brunner, Karl.** Money and Economic Activity, Inventories and Business Cycles. In *Brunner, K. and Meltzer, A. H.*, 1989, *1983*, pp. 193–229.

Culbertson, J. M. The Term Structure of Interest Rates. In *Wood, J. C. and Woods, R. N., eds.*, Vol. *1*, 1989, *1957*, pp. 194–220.

Culbertson, W. Patton. Beer–Cash Laws: Their Economic Impact and Antitrust Implications. *Antitrust Bull.*, Spring 1989, *34*(1), pp. 209–29.

_____. Empirical Regularities in Black Markets for Currency. *World Devel.*, December 1989, *17*(12), pp. 1907–19.

Cullenberg, Stephen; Amariglio, Jack and Callari, Antonio. Analytical Marxism: A Critical Overview. *Rev. Soc. Econ.*, Winter 1989, *47*(4), pp. 415–32.

Cullison, William E. The Changing Labor Force: Some Provocative Findings. *Fed. Res. Bank Richmond Econ. Rev.*, Sept.–Oct. 1989, *75*(5), pp. 30–36.

_____. The U.S. Productivity Slowdown: What the Experts Say. *Fed. Res. Bank Richmond Econ. Rev.*, July–Aug. 1989, *75*(4), pp. 10–21.

Culyer, A. J. Economics of Health Systems. In *Butler, J. R. G. and Doessel, D. P., eds.*, 1989, pp. 145–66.

_____. The Normative Economics of Health Care Finance and Provision. *Oxford Rev. Econ. Policy*, Spring 1989, *5*(1), pp. 34–58.

Cumby, Robert E. and van Wijnbergen, Sweder. Financial Policy and Speculative Runs with a Crawling Peg: Argentina 1979–1981. *J. Int. Econ.*, August 1989, *27*(1–2), pp. 111–27.

Cummings, L. L. Models of Man in Industrial Relations Research: Discussion. The Essential Nature of Models of Humans in Industrial Relations Research. *Ind. Lab. Relat. Rev.*, October 1989, *43*(1), pp. 93–96.

Cummings, Thomas G.; Mohrman, Allan M., Jr. and Mitroff, Ian I. The Actors in Large-Scale Organizational Change. In *Mohrman, A. M., Jr., et al.*, 1989, pp. 91–99.

Cunningham, James; O'Neill, June and Brien, Michael. Effects of Comparable Worth Policy: Evidence from Washington State. *Amer. Econ. Rev.*, May 1989, *79*(2), pp. 305–09.

Cunningham, Malcolm T. Competitive Strategy

in European Markets. In *Hallén, L. and Johanson, J., eds.*, 1989, pp. 277–305.

Cunningham, Thomas J. The Federal Budget Deficit and the Social Security Surplus. *Fed. Res. Bank Atlanta Econ. Rev.*, March–April 1989, *74*(2), pp. 2–13.

Cunningham, William T. Portuguese Tax Reform: A Closer Look at Corporate Taxation. *Bull. Int. Fiscal Doc.*, March 1989, *43*(3), pp. 123–26.

_____. Withholding Taxes: Portugal. *Bull. Int. Fiscal Doc.*, May 1989, *43*(5), pp. 223–24.

Cuny, Thomas J. The Evolution of Accounting for Receipts in the Federal Budget. *Public Budg. Finance*, Winter 1989, *9*(4), pp. 21–39.

Cuoco, D. and Barone, E. The Italian Market for 'Premium' Contracts: An Application of Option Pricing Theory. *J. Banking Finance*, September 1989, *13*(4–5), pp. 709–45.

Curien, Hubert. Research and Innovation. In *Frankel, A. V. and Heck, C. B., eds.*, 1989, pp. 16–18.

Curien, Nicolas and Gensollen, Michel. L'ouverture des réseaux: Planification ou concurrence dans les télécommunications et d'autres services publics. (The Opening-Up of Networks: Planning or Competition in the Telecommunications Industry and Other Public Utilities. With English summary.) *Ann. Écon. Statist.*, July–Dec. 1989, (15–16), pp. 355–88.

Curran, Christopher and Dwyer, Gerald P., Jr. The Effect of the Double Nickel Speed Limit on Death Rates. In *Faure, M. and Van den Bergh, R., eds.*, 1989, pp. 117–56.

Currie, David A. Implications of Policy Rules for the World Economy: Comment. In *Bryant, R. C., et al., eds.*, 1989, pp. 197–202.

_____. A Macroeconomic View of the 1989 Budget. *Fisc. Stud.*, May 1989, *10*(2), pp. 1–12.

_____; **Gaines, Jessica and Levine, Paul.** The Use of Simple Rules for International Policy Agreements. In *Miller, M.; Eichengreen, B. and Portes, R., eds.*, 1989, pp. 281–319.

_____ **and Hall, Stephen G.** A Stock–Flow Model of the Determination of the UK Effective Exchange Rate. In *MacDonald, R. and Taylor, M. P., eds.*, 1989, pp. 130–41.

_____; **Holtham, Gerald and Hughes Hallett, Andrew J.** The Theory and Practice of International Policy Coordination: Does Coordination Pay? In *Bryant, R. C., et al., eds.*, 1989, pp. 14–46.

_____ **and Wren-Lewis, Simon.** An Appraisal of Alternative Blueprints for International Policy Coordination. *Europ. Econ. Rev.*, December 1989, *33*(9), pp. 1769–85.

_____ **and Wren-Lewis, Simon.** A Comparison of Alternative Regimes for International Macropolicy Coordination. In *Miller, M.; Eichengreen, B. and Portes, R., eds.*, 1989, pp. 181–201.

_____ **and Wren-Lewis, Simon.** Evaluating Blueprints for the Conduct of International Macro Policy. *Amer. Econ. Rev.*, May 1989, *79*(2), pp. 264–69.

Currie, Janet. Who Uses Interest Arbitration? The Case of British Columbia's Teachers, 1947–1981. *Ind. Lab. Relat. Rev.*, April 1989, *42*(3), pp. 363–79.

Currie, Lauchlin. The Role of the Economist in Government: An International Perspective: Colombia. In *Pechman, J. A., ed.*, 1989, pp. 213–27.

Currie, Wendy; Warner, Malcolm and Campbell, Adrian. Innovation, Skills and Training: Micro-electronics and Manpower in the United Kingdom and West Germany. In *Hirst, P. and Zeitlin, J., eds.*, 1989, pp. 133–54.

Currier, Kevin M. An Algorithm for Ramsey Pricing by Multiproduct Public Firms under Incomplete Information. *J. Econ. Dynam. Control*, April 1989, *13*(2), pp. 283–300.

_____ **and Amos, Orley M., Jr.** The Foundations of a Hierarchial Theory of the Long-Wave Phenomenon. *Southern Econ. J.*, July 1989, *56*(1), pp. 142–56.

Curry, David J. and Menasco, Michael B. Utility and Choice: An Empirical Study of Wife/Husband Decision Making. *J. Cons. Res.*, June 1989, *16*(1), pp. 87–97.

Curry, Leslie. Spatial Trade and Factor Markets. *Econ. Geogr.*, October 1989, *65*(4), pp. 271–79.

Curry, Michael R. *A Ground for Common Search:* Book Review Essay. *Econ. Geogr.*, April 1989, *65*(2), pp. 146–52.

Curry, Robert L., Jr. The Basic Needs Strategy, the Congressional Mandate, and U.S. Foreign Aid Policy. *J. Econ. Issues*, December 1989, *23*(4), pp. 1085–96.

_____. Mining Revenues for Development Finance: Some Added Comments. *Amer. J. Econ. Sociology*, July 1989, *48*(3), pp. 323–26.

Curtain, R. F. Representations of Infinite-Dimensional Systems. In *[Willems, J. C.]*, 1989, pp. 101–28.

Curtin, Richard T.; Juster, F. Thomas and Morgan, James N. Survey Estimates of Wealth: An Assessment of Quality. In *Lipsey, R. E. and Tice, H. S., eds.*, 1989, pp. 473–548.

Curzon, Gerard. International Economic Order: Contribution of Ordo-Liberals. In *Peacock, A. and Willgerodt, H., eds. (I)*, 1989, pp. 179–90.

Cushing, Brian J. Use and Misuse of the Allocation Rate in Models of Population Migration. *Ann. Reg. Sci.*, 1989, *23*(1), pp. 51–58.

Cushman, David O. U.S.–Japanese Bilateral Trade and the Yen–Dollar Exchange Rate: Comment. *Southern Econ. J.*, October 1989, *56*(2), pp. 511–23.

Cutcher-Gershenfeld, Joel and Kochan, Thomas A. Innovation or Confrontation: Alternative Directions for American Industrial Relations. In *Huang, W.-C., ed.*, 1989, pp. 27–62.

Cuthbertson, Keith and Taylor, Mark P. Anticipated and Unanticipated Variables in the Demand for M1 in the U.K. *Manchester Sch. Econ. Soc. Stud.*, December 1989, *57*(4), pp. 319–39.

Cuthbertson, Sandy; Stoeckel, Andrew B. and Vincent, David. Macroeconomic Consequences of Farm Support Policies: Overview.

In *Stoeckel, A. B.; Vincent, D. and Cuthbertson, S., eds.*, 1989, pp. 1–63.

Cutler, David M.; Poterba, James M. and Summers, Lawrence H. What Moves Stock Prices? *J. Portfol. Manage.*, Spring 1989, *15*(3), pp. 4–12.

Cutler, Harvey. Aggregate Supply and Demand Disturbances, and the Business Cycle. *J. Macroecon.*, Spring 1989, *11*(2), pp. 247–59.

Cvetković, Ljiljana and Herceg, Dragoslav. On the Extrapolation Method and the U.S.A. Algorithm. *J. Econ. Dynam. Control*, April 1989, *13*(2), pp. 301–11.

Czedly, I. and Constantinescu, P. Optimizing the Efficiency of Fixed Assets in the Conditions of Productivity Growth. *Econ. Computat. Econ. Cybern. Stud. Res.*, 1989, *24*(2–3), pp. 7–16.

Czyzewski, Adam B. and Welfe, Wladyslaw. The Growth of the Polish Economy and Prospects for Structural Change. In *Krelle, W., ed.*, 1989, pp. 419–43.

D'Adda, Carlo. An Economy of Industries and Its Aggregate Representation. *Banca Naz. Lavoro Quart. Rev.*, March 1989, (168), pp. 97–107.

————. Franco Modigliani: il contributo alla macroeconomia e alla teoria della finanza. (With English summary.) *Studi. Econ.*, 1989, *44*(39), pp. 3–28.

D'Alessandro Pereyra, R. and Díaz Paulos, A. M. Administrative and Compliance Costs of Taxation: Uruguay. In *International Fiscal Association, ed. (1)*, 1989, pp. 621–35.

D'Silva, B.; Hallam, Arne and Hassan, Rashid M. Measuring Stochastic Technology for the Multi-product Firm: The Irrigated Farms of Sudan. *Can. J. Agr. Econ.*, November 1989, *37*(3), pp. 495–512.

D'Souza, Rudolph E.; Brooks, LeRoy D. and Oberhelman, H. Dennis. A General Stationary Stochastic Regression Model for Estimating and Predicting Beta. *Financial Rev.*, May 1989, *24*(2), pp. 299–317.

———— **and Puglisi, Donald J.** A Note on Fiscal Agent Pricing of Federal Agency Debt. *J. Banking Finance*, May 1989, *13*(2), pp. 311–20.

van Daal, Jan. On Production in Walras' Theory of General Economic Equilibrium. In *Muller, F. and Zwezerijnen, W. J., eds.*, 1989, pp. 179–96.

———— **and Jolink, Albert.** Leon Walras' Latest Book: *Melanges d'economie politique et sociale. De Economist*, 1989, *137*(3), pp. 351–59.

———— **and Merkies, Arnold H. Q. M.** A Note on the Quadratic Expenditure Model. *Econometrica*, November 1989, *57*(6), pp. 1439–43.

Dąbrowski, Marek. The Economic Effectiveness of the Self-Managed Enterprise—A Review of the Theoretical Literature. *Acta Oecon.*, 1989, *40*(1–2), pp. 39–54.

Dabscheck, Braham. A Survey of Theories of Industrial Relations. In *Barbash, J. and Barbash, K., eds.*, 1989, pp. 155–83.

Dadhwal, V. K. Effect of Temperature on Wheat in India. In *Oram, P. A., et al.*, 1989, pp. 137–44.

Dadkhah, Kamran M. and Mookerjee, Rajen. Money and Corporate Profits in a Developing Country: Theory and Evidence. *J. Banking Finance*, May 1989, *13*(2), pp. 191–205.

Daelemans, Frank. Wages of Servants of the 'Cense-du-Sart' in Ernage (Brabant), 1783–1849. In *Scholliers, P., ed.*, 1989, pp. 48–50.

Daellenbach, Hans G. and Buchanan, John T. Desirable Properties of Interactive Multi-objective Programming Methods. In *Lockett, A. G. and Islei, G., eds.*, 1989, pp. 212–23.

Dagan, Gideon; Feinerman, Eli and Bresler, Eshel. Optimization of Inputs in a Spatially Variable Natural Resource: Unconditional vs. Conditional Analysis. *J. Environ. Econ. Manage.*, September 1989, *17*(2), pp. 140–54.

Dagum, Camilo. Poverty as Perceived by the Leyden Income Evaluation Project. A Survey of Hagenaars' Contribution on the Perception of Poverty. *Econ. Notes*, 1989, (1), pp. 99–111.

Dagum, Estela Bee. The Future of the Forecasting Profession: Editorial. *Int. J. Forecasting*, 1989, *5*(2), pp. 155–57.

Dahl, Carol. Spatially Analysing the Impact of a 'No New Nukes' Policy on European Natural Gas Markets. *Energy Econ.*, October 1989, *11*(4), pp. 262–74.

———— **and Gjelsvik, Eystein.** Simulating Norwegian Troll Gas Prospects in a Competitive Spatial Model. *Resources & Energy*, March 1989, *11*(1), pp. 35–63.

Dahl, Drew and Shrieves, Ronald E. Evidence on the Role of Holding Company Acquisitions in the Management of Bank Capital. *J. Finan. Services Res.*, February 1989, *2*(1), pp. 21–37.

Dahlgaard, Jens J. A Comparative Study of Quality Control Methods and Principles in Japan, South Korea and Denmark. In *Park, S.-J., ed.*, 1989, pp. 71–90.

Dahlgran, Roger A. Is U.S. Meat Demand in Equilibrium? In *Buse, R. C., ed.*, 1989, pp. 187–200.

Dahlman, Carl J. Technological Change in Industry in Developing Countries. *Finance Devel.*, June 1989, *26*(2), pp. 13–15.

Dahmann, Donald C. The Survey of Income and Program Participation as a Source of Migration Data. *J. Econ. Soc. Meas.*, 1989, *15*(1), pp. 57–70.

Dahrendorf, Ralf [Sir]. The Future of Europe? In *Dahrendorf, R., et al.*, 1989, pp. 1–9.

Dailey, Lorna M. Private Pension Statistics in Nine Countries. In *Turner, J. A. and Beller, D. J., eds.*, 1989, pp. 287–339.

———— **and Turner, John A.** U.S. Pensions in World Perspective. In *Turner, J. A. and Beller, D. J., eds.*, 1989, pp. 15–27.

Dakin, Stephen and Armstrong, J. Scott. Predicting Job Performance: A Comparison of Expert Opinion and Research Findings. *Int. J. Forecasting*, 1989, *5*(2), pp. 187–94.

Dalal, Ardeshir J. and Arshanapalli, Bala G. Effects of Expected Cash and Futures Prices on Hedging and Production: Comments and Extensions. *J. Futures Markets*, August 1989, 9(4), pp. 337–45.

Dalal, Siddhartha R.; Fowlkes, Edward B. and Hoadley, Bruce. Risk Analysis of the Space Shuttle: Pre-*Challenger* Prediction of Failure. *J. Amer. Statist. Assoc.*, December 1989, 84(408), pp. 945–57.

Dalamagas, Basil A. A Comparison of the Stabilization Effects of Fiscal and Monetary Policy Instruments in Five European Countries. *Indian Econ. J.*, July–Sept. 1989, 37(1), pp. 15–39.

Dale, Charles; Drisko, Alan F. and Schmitz, Edward J. The Use of the Army College Fund: Implications for Program Cost Effectiveness. In *Gulledge, T. R., Jr. and Litteral, L. A., eds.*, 1989, pp. 407–22.

Dale, Norman. Getting to Co-management: Social Learning in the Redesign of Fisheries Management. In *Pinkerton, E., ed.*, 1989, pp. 49–72.

Dale, Richard. International Financial Regulation: The Separation Issue. In *Button, K. and Swann, D., eds.*, 1989, pp. 217–35.

Dale, Richard S. International Banking Is Out of Control. In *Guttmann, R., ed.*, 1989, *1983*, pp. 266–70.

Daley, Anthony. Industrial Adjustment in the French Steel Industry. In *Foglesong, R. E. and Wolfe, J. D., eds.*, 1989, pp. 107–26.

Daley, Judy R. and Personick, Martin E. Profiles in Safety and Health: Work Hazards of Mobile Homes. *Mon. Lab. Rev.*, July 1989, 112(7), pp. 15–20.

Dalgaard, Esben. An Input–Output Analysis of Danish Trade and Specialization 1966–1983. *J. Econ. Soc. Meas.*, 1989, 15(2), pp. 105–30.

Dalgic, Tevfik and Kaynak, Erdener. From Subcontracting to Multinationality: Internationalization of LDC Construction Companies. In *Negandhi, A. R., ed.*, 1989, pp. 263–82.

Dallago, Bruno. The Non-socialized Sector in Hungary: An Attempt at Estimation of Its Importance. *Jahr. Wirtsch. Osteuropas*, 1989, 13(2), pp. 67–92.

Dalpé, Robert and DeBresson, Christian. Le secteur public comme premier utilisateur d'innovations. (With English summary.) *L'Actual. Econ.*, March 1989, 65(1), pp. 53–70.

Dalto, Guy C. A Structural Approach to Women's Hometime and Experience–Earnings Profiles: Maternity Leave and Public Policy. *Population Res. Policy Rev.*, September 1989, 8(3), pp. 247–66.

Daly, Donald J. Canada's International Competitiveness. In *Rugman, A. M., ed.*, 1989, pp. 37–54.

Daly, Maurice T. The Changing Role of Transnational Corporations in the Asian-Pacific Region: Comment. In *Shinohara, M. and Lo, F., eds.*, 1989, pp. 382–83.

Dalziel, Paul C. Cambridge (U.K.) versus Cambridge (Mass.): A Keynesian Solution of "Pasinetti's Paradox." *J. Post Keynesian Econ.*, Summer 1989, 11(4), pp. 648–53.

Damanik, Konta and Booth, Anne. Central Java

and Yogyakarta: Malthus Overcome? In *Hill, H., ed.*, 1989, pp. 283–305.

van Damme, Eric. Renegotiation-Proof Equilibria in Repeated Prisoners' Dilemma. *J. Econ. Theory*, February 1989, 47(1), pp. 206–17.

_____. Stable Equilibria and Forward Induction. *J. Econ. Theory*, August 1989, 48(2), pp. 476–96.

Damodaran, Aswath and Landsman, Wayne R. A Comparison of Quarterly Earnings per Share Forecasts Using James–Stein and Unconditional Least Squares Parameter Estimators. *Int. J. Forecasting*, 1989, 5(4), pp. 491–500.

_____ **and Landsman, Wayne R.** Using Shrinkage Estimators to Improve upon Time-Series Model Proxies for the Security Market's Expectation of Earnings. *J. Acc. Res.*, Spring 1989, 27(1), pp. 97–115.

Dana, Rose-Anne, et al. Asymptotic Properties of a Leontief Economy. *J. Econ. Dynam. Control*, October 1989, 13(4), pp. 553–68.

_____. Production Prices and General Equilibrium Prices: A Long-run Property of a Leontief Economy. *J. Math. Econ.*, 1989, 18(3), pp. 263–80.

Danaher, Peter J. A Markov Mixture Model for Magazine Exposure. *J. Amer. Statist. Assoc.*, December 1989, 84(408), pp. 922–26.

Daniel, Betty C. One-Sided Uncertainty about Future Fiscal Policy. *J. Money, Credit, Banking*, May 1989, 21(2), pp. 176–89.

Daniel, William D., Jr. and Might, Robert J. Decision Support for War Games. In *Golden, B. L.; Wasil, E. A. and Harker, P. T., eds.*, 1989, pp. 171–81.

Dániel, Zsuzsa. Housing Demand in a Shortage Economy: Results of a Hungarian Survey. *Acta Oecon.*, 1989, 41(1–2), pp. 157–79.

Daniels, Gordon. EC–Japan: Past, Present and Future. In *Lodge, J., ed.*, 1989, pp. 279–84.

Daniels, Peter W.; Thrift, Nigel J. and Leyshon, A. Internationalisation of Professional Producer Services: Accountancy Conglomerates. In *Enderwick, P.*, 1989, pp. 79–106.

Daniels, Rudolph. The Agrarian Land Question in South Africa in Its Historical Context, 1652–1988. *Amer. J. Econ. Sociology*, July 1989, 48(3), pp. 327–38.

Danielson, Anders. Struggle for the Surplus: Jamaica, 1970–84. *METU*, 1989, 16(1–2), pp. 127–52.

Danielson, Leon E. and Palmquist, Raymond B. A Hedonic Study of the Effects of Erosion Control and Drainage on Farmland Values. *Amer. J. Agr. Econ.*, February 1989, 71(1), pp. 55–62.

Danns, George K. and Matthews, Lear K. Perspectives on the Development and Underdevelopment of Communities in Guyana: A Sociohistorical Analysis. In *Martin, M. T. and Kandal, T. R., eds.*, 1989, pp. 166–201.

Danson, M.; Lloyd, G. and Newlands, D. 'Scottish Enterprise': Towards a Model Agency or a Flawed Initiative? *Reg. Stud.*, December 1989, 23(6), pp. 557–63.

Danthine, Jean-Pierre. Growth and Unemployment in Europe: A Review Essay. *J. Monet. Econ.*, November 1989, *24*(3), pp. 479–84.

_____. Modélisation des fluctuations conjoncturelles: Survol de quelques récents développements. (With English summary.) *Rech. Écon. Louvain*, 1989, *55*(3), pp. 213–44.

_____; Donaldson, John B. and Mehra, Rajnish. On Some Computational Aspects of Equilibrium Business Cycle Theory. *J. Econ. Dynam. Control*, July 1989, *13*(3), pp. 449–70.

_____ and Girardin, Michel. Business Cycles in Switzerland: A Comparative Study. *Europ. Econ. Rev.*, January 1989, *33*(1), pp. 31–50.

Dantzig, George B.; McAllister, Patrick H. and Stone, John C. Deriving a Utility Function for the U.S. Economy. *J. Policy Modeling*, Fall 1989, *11*(3), pp. 391–424.

_____; McAllister, Patrick H. and Stone, John C. Integrability of the Multiple-Period Equilibrium Model: Part II. *J. Policy Modeling*, Winter 1989, *11*(4), pp. 569–92.

Danziger, Errol. The Disregard of a Legal Entity for Tax Purposes: South Africa. In *International Fiscal Association*, ed. *(II)*, 1989, pp. 121–37.

Danziger, Leif. Risk Aversion and the Duration of Labor Contracts. In *Ehrenberg, R. G., ed.*, 1989, pp. 311–36.

Danziger, Sheldon and Gottschalk, Peter. Increasing Inequality in the U.S.: What We Know and What We Don't. In *Davidson, P. and Kregel, J., eds.*, 1989, pp. 78–97.

_____ and Gottschalk, Peter. Increasing Inequality in the United States: What We Know and What We Don't. *J. Post Keynesian Econ.*, Winter 1988–89, *11*(2), pp. 174–95.

_____; Gottschalk, Peter and Smolensky, Eugene. How the Rich Have Fared, 1973–87. *Amer. Econ. Rev.*, May 1989, *79*(2), pp. 310–14.

Danzon, Patricia M. Market Incentives and the Costs of Medical Malpractice. In *McLennan, K. and Meyer, J. A., eds.*, 1989, pp. 119–32.

Daouli, J. and Demoussis, M. P. The Impact of Inflation on Prices Received and Paid by Greek Farmers. *J. Agr. Econ.*, May 1989, *40*(2), pp. 232–39.

Dar, Atul A. and Dodds, C. Interest Rates, the Emergency Fund Hypothesis and Saving through Endowment Policies: Some Empirical Evidence for the U.K. *J. Risk Ins.*, September 1989, *56*(3), pp. 415–33.

Daranagama, D. A. U. and Fernando, G. B. A. The Energy–Economy Link in Sri Lanka. In *James, W. E., ed.*, 1989, pp. 183–93.

Darby, Michael R. Comment: Real Exchange Rates and Freedom of International Trade and Capital Flows. In *Dorn, J. A. and Niskanen, W. A., eds.*, 1989, *1988*, pp. 259–61.

_____ and Lothian, James R. The International Transmission of Inflation Afloat. In *[Schwartz, A. J.]*, 1989, pp. 203–36.

_____ and Lott, John R., Jr. Qualitative Information, Reputation, and Monopolistic Competition. *Int. Rev. Law Econ.*, June 1989, *9*(1), pp. 87–103.

_____; Mascaro, Angelo R. and Marlow, Mi-

chael L. The Empirical Reliability of Monetary Aggregates as Indicators: 1983–1987. *Econ. Inquiry*, October 1989, *27*(4), pp. 555–85.

Darity, William A., Jr. Is to Forgive the Debt Divine? In *Weeks, J. F., ed.*, 1989, pp. 233–41.

_____. Profitability of the British Trade in Slaves Once Again: Comment. *Exploration Econ. Hist.*, July 1989, *26*(3), pp. 380–84.

_____. Race, Radicalism, and Reform: Selected Papers, Abram L. Harris: Introduction: The Odyssey of Abram Harris from Howard to Chicago. In *Harris, A. L.*, 1989, pp. 1–34.

_____. The Simple Analytics of Aggregate Demand Price and Aggregate Supply Price Analysis. In *[Weintraub, S.]*, 1989, pp. 9–24.

_____. The Terms of Trade from the Long View. In *Davidson, P. and Kregel, J., eds.*, 1989, pp. 159–73.

_____. What's Left of the Economic Theory of Discrimination? In *Shulman, S. and Darity, W., Jr., eds.*, 1989, pp. 335–74.

_____ and Marrero, Wanda I. A Common Error: Reply. *J. Macroecon.*, Winter 1989, *11*(1), pp. 149–50.

_____ and Shulman, Steven. The Question of Discrimination: Racial Inequality in the U.S. Labor Market: Introduction. In *Shulman, S. and Darity, W., Jr., eds.*, 1989, pp. 1–6.

Darling, O. Leonard. Still Searching for Optimal Capital Structure: Discussion. In *Kopcke, R. W. and Rosengren, E. S., eds.*, 1989, pp. 96–99.

Darmstadter, Joel. Energy and the Global Environment. In *Owen, A. D., ed.*, 1989, pp. 4–12.

_____ and Edmonds, Jae. Human Development and Carbon Dioxide Emissions: The Current Picture and the Long-Term Prospects. In *Rosenberg, N. J., et al., eds.*, 1989, pp. 35–51.

Darnell, Adrian C. "General to Specific" Modelling: A Methodological Perspective. *Brit. Rev. Econ. Issues*, Summer 1989, *11*(25), pp. 53–87.

Daroesman, Ruth and Siahaan, Pulo. West Kalimantan: Uneven Development? In *Hill, H., ed.*, 1989, pp. 528–47.

Darrat, Ali F. Fiscal Deficits and Long-term Interest Rates: Further Evidence from Annual Data. *Southern Econ. J.*, October 1989, *56*(2), pp. 363–74.

_____ and Barnhart, Scott W. Federal Deficits and Money Growth in the United States: A Vector Autoregressive Analysis. *J. Banking Finance*, March 1989, *13*(1), pp. 137–49.

_____ and Glascock, John L. Real Estate Returns, Money and Fiscal Deficits: Is the Real Estate Market Efficient? *J. Real Estate Finance Econ.*, September 1989, *2*(3), pp. 197–208.

_____; LaBarge, Karin P. and LaBarge, Richard A. Is Financial Deepening a Reliable Prescription for Economic Growth? *Amer. Economist*, Fall 1989, *33*(2), pp. 25–33.

_____ and Lopez, F. A. Has Inflation Uncertainty Hampered Economic Growth in Latin America? *Int. Econ. J.*, Summer 1989, *3*(2), pp. 1–15.

Darrough, Masako N. and Stoughton, Neal M. A Bargaining Approach to Profit Sharing in Joint Ventures. *J. Bus.*, April 1989, *62*(2), pp. 237–70.

Darvish, Tikva and Kahana, Nava. The Ratchet Principle: A Multi-period Flexible Incentive Scheme. *Europ. Econ. Rev.*, January 1989, *33*(1), pp. 51–57.

Das, Chandana. Food Policy in a Dual Economy. In *Rakshit, M., ed.*, 1989, pp. 66–93.

Das Gupta, Bejoy. Determinants of Exports from Developing Countries: Exchange Rate Policy and Exports in the 1990s. In *[Marjolin, R.]*, 1989, pp. 117–33.

Das, P. K. Stochastic Models for Rainfall Prediction. In *Oram, P. A., et al.*, 1989, pp. 311–19.

Das, Pulak. Job Search and Internal Migration. *Indian Econ. J.*, Oct.–Dec. 1989, *37*(2), pp. 65–68.

Das, Sandwip Kumar and Pant, Manoj. On Export Diversification and Earning Instability—Theory and Evidence. *Indian Econ. J.*, Jan.–March 1989, *36*(3), pp. 65–71.

Das, Satya P. and Donnenfeld, Shabtai. Oligopolistic Competition and International Trade: Quantity and Quality Restrictions. *J. Int. Econ.*, November 1989, *27*(3–4), pp. 299–318.

Das, Somnath; Datar, Srikant M. and Banker, Rajiv D. Analysis of Cost Variances for Management Control in Hospitals. In *Chan, J. L. and Patton, J. M., eds.*, 1989, pp. 269–91.

Das, Sujit and Lee, Russell. Changes in Business-as-Usual Forecasts in a Petroleum Trade Model. *Energy Econ.*, January 1989, *11*(1), pp. 11–32.

Das, Tuhin; ten Raa, Thijs and Chakraborty, Debesh. Working Capital in an Input–Output Model. *Econ. Systems Res.*, 1989, *1*(1), pp. 53–68.

Dasgupta, Ajit K. and Paul, Satya. Inheritance and Wealth Inequality: The Case of the Punjab. *J. Devel. Econ.*, April 1989, *30*(2), pp. 301–24.

Dasgupta, Dipankar. Procurement Price, Market Price, Employment and Effective Demand. In *Rakshit, M., ed.*, 1989, pp. 42–65.

Dasgupta, Partha. The Economics of Parallel Research. In *Hahn, F., ed.*, 1989, pp. 129–48.

———. Positive Freedom, Markets, and the Welfare State. In *Helm, D., ed.*, 1989, pp. 110–26.

———. Some Theoretical Considerations. *Europ. Econ. Rev.*, March 1989, *33*(2/3), pp. 619–24.

———. Welfare, Positive Freedom and Economic Development. In *Adelman, I. and Lane, S., eds.*, 1989, pp. 18–31.

Dasgupta, Sudipto and Sinha, Anup K. Erratic Dynamics of Dual Economies. In *Rakshit, M., ed.*, 1989, pp. 129–47.

Daskin, Alan J. and Wolken, John D. An Empirical Investigation of the Critical Herfindahl Index in Banking. *J. Econ. Bus.*, May 1989, *41*(2), pp. 95–105.

Dastmalchian, Ali and Ng, Ignace. Determinants of Grievance Outcomes: A Case Study. *Ind.*

Lab. Relat. Rev., April 1989, *42*(3), pp. 393–403.

Data-Chaudhuri, Mrinal and Singh, Nirvikar. Tariffs vs. Quotas with Uncertain Substitutability between Inputs. *J. Quant. Econ.*, July 1989, *5*(2), pp. 251–65.

Datar, Srikant M. and Banker, Rajiv D. Sensitivity, Precision, and Linear Aggregation of Signals for Performance Evaluation. *J. Acc. Res.*, Spring 1989, *27*(1), pp. 21–39.

———; **Banker, Rajiv D. and Das, Somnath.** Analysis of Cost Variances for Management Control in Hospitals. In *Chan, J. L. and Patton, J. M., eds.*, 1989, pp. 269–91.

Datcher-Loury, Linda. Family Background and School Achievement among Low Income Blacks. *J. Human Res.*, Summer 1989, *24*(3), pp. 528–44.

Datta, Ansu. Strategies for Regional Cooperation in Post-Apartheid Southern Africa—the Role of Non-governmental Organizations. In *Odén, B. and Othman, H., eds.*, 1989, pp. 91–102.

Datta, Deepak K. and Yu, Po-Lung. Acquisitions, Mergers and Habitual Domains Analysis. In *Lockett, A. G. and Islei, G., eds.*, 1989, pp. 1–12.

Datta, Ramesh C. and Rao, M. J. Manohar. Rates of Return in the Indian Private Sector. *Econ. Letters*, October 1989, *30*(4), pp. 373–78.

——— **and Rao, M. J. Manohar.** The Screening Hypothesis and the Marginal Productivity Theory. *Econ. Letters*, October 1989, *30*(4), pp. 379–84.

Datta, Rathin. The Disregard of a Legal Entity for Tax Purposes: India. In *International Fiscal Association, ed. (II)*, 1989, pp. 311–23.

Datta, Samar K. and Nugent, Jeffrey B. Transaction Cost Economics and Contractual Choice: Theory and Evidence. In *Nabli, M. K. and Nugent, J. B., eds.*, 1989, pp. 34–79.

Dattatreya, Ravi E. and Fabozzi, Frank J. A Simplified Model for Valuing Debt Options. *J. Portfol. Manage.*, Spring 1989, *15*(3), pp. 64–72.

Daunton, Martin J. Income Flows, the Family Economy and Survival Strategies. In *Scholliers, P., ed.*, 1989, pp. 143–48.

Davar, Ezra. Input–Output and General Equilibrium. *Econ. Systems Res.*, 1989, *1*(3), pp. 331–43.

Dave, Upendra. On Probabilistic Scheduling Period Inventory System with Instantaneous Demand. *Econ. Computat. Econ. Cybern. Stud. Res.*, 1989, *24*(1), pp. 81–87.

Davelaar, Evert Jan and Nijkamp, Peter. Innovative Behaviour of Industrial Firms: Results from a Dutch Empirical Study. In *Andersson, Å. E.; Batten, D. F. and Karlsson, C., eds.*, 1989, pp. 177–86.

——— **and Nijkamp, Peter.** The Role of the Metropolitan Milieu as an Incubation Centre for Technological Innovations: A Dutch Case Study. *Urban Stud.*, October 1989, *26*(5), pp. 517–25.

——— **and Nijkamp, Peter.** Spatial Dispersion

of Technological Innovation: A Case Study for the Netherlands by Means of Partial Least Squares. *J. Reg. Sci.*, August 1989, *29*(3), pp. 325–46.

Davenport-Hines, R. P. T. Vickers and Schneider: A Comparison of New British and French Multinational Strategies 1916–26. In *Teichova, A.; Lévy-Leboyer, M. and Nussbaum, H., eds.*, 1989, pp. 123–34.

_____ **and Jones, Geoffrey.** British Business in Asia since 1860. In *Davenport-Hines, R. P. T. and Jones, G., eds.*, 1989, pp. 1–30.

_____ **and Jones, Geoffrey.** British Business in Asia since 1860: Preface. In *Davenport-Hines, R. P. T. and Jones, G., eds.*, 1989, pp. xv–xvi.

_____ **and Jones, Geoffrey.** British Business in Japan since 1868. In *Davenport-Hines, R. P. T. and Jones, G., eds.*, 1989, pp. 217–44.

Daveri, Francesco. Motivazioni egoistiche e altruistiche dell'aiuto italiano allo sviluppo. Un'analisi empirica. (Selfish and Altruistic Motivations of Italian Aid Flows. An Empirical Analysis. With English summary.) *Rivista Int. Sci. Econ. Com.*, June 1989, *36*(6), pp. 543–72.

Davey, William J. Antidumping Laws in the GATT and the EC. In *Jackson, J. H. and Vermulst, E. A., eds.*, 1989, pp. 295–301.

David, Cristina C. ASEAN Economic Structure and Changes in Agricultural Protection. *Philippine Rev. Econ. Bus.*, June 1989, *26*(1), pp. 47–66.

_____. Philippines: Price Policy in Transition. In *Sicular, T., ed.*, 1989, pp. 154–82.

David, Jean-François and Ghysels, Eric. Y a-t-il des biais systématiques dans les annonces budgétaires canadiennes? (With English summary.) *Can. Public Policy*, September 1989, *15*(3), pp. 313–21.

David, Martin H. Managing Panel Data for Scientific Analysis: The Role of Relational Data Base Management Systems. In *Kasprzyk, D., et al., eds.*, 1989, pp. 226–41.

_____. Year-Apart Estimates of Household Net Worth from the Survey of Income and Program Participation: Comment. In *Lipsey, R. E. and Tice, H. S., eds.*, 1989, pp. 462–71.

Daviddi, Renzo. Soviet Foreign Trade Reform. Short Term Adjustment versus Structural Variations. *Jahr. Wirtsch. Osteuropas*, 1989, *13*(1), pp. 221–53.

_____ **and Espa, Efisio.** The Economics of Rouble Convertibility. New Scenarios for the Soviet Monetary Economy. *Banca Naz. Lavoro Quart. Rev.*, December 1989, (171), pp. 441–67.

Davidova, Sophia. Contemporary Trends in International Trade and Their Relation to the Quality of Satisfying Consumer Needs. In *Bulgarian Academy of Sciences, Institute of Economics*, 1989, pp. 112–24.

Davidson, Basil. Was Colonialism Really Useless? A Review Article. *Scand. Econ. Hist. Rev.*, 1989, *37*(3), pp. 60–64.

Davidson, Duncan M. Reverse Engineering Soft-

ware under Copyright Law: The IBM PC BIOS. In *Weil, V. and Snapper, J. W., eds.*, 1989, pp. 147–68.

Davidson, Lawrence S. and Kang, Heejoon. Changes in Long-term Economic Trends: Before and after the 1930s. *J. Macroecon.*, Winter 1989, *11*(1), pp. 1–23.

Davidson, Marilyn. Restructuring Women's Employment in British Petroleum. In *Elson, D. and Pearson, R., eds.*, 1989, pp. 206–21.

Davidson, Paul. Achieving a Civilized Society. *Challenge*, Sept.–Oct. 1989, *32*(5), pp. 40–46.

_____. Corrected Version of: Patinkin's Interpretation of Keynes and the Keynesian Cross. *Hist. Polit. Econ.*, Winter 1989, *21*(4), pp. 737–41.

_____. A Modest Set of Proposals for Resolving the International Debt Problem. In *Gray, H. P., ed.*, 1989, pp. 29–42.

_____. On the Endogeneity of Money Once More: Reply. *J. Post Keynesian Econ.*, Spring 1989, *11*(3), pp. 488–90.

_____. Only in America: Neither the Homeless nor the Yachtless Are Economic Problems. *J. Post Keynesian Econ.*, Fall 1989, *12*(1), pp. 164–66.

_____. Patinkin's Interpretation of Keynes and the Keynesian Cross. *Hist. Polit. Econ.*, Fall 1989, *21*(3), pp. 549–53.

_____. Policies for Prices and Incomes: An Essay in Honour of Sidney Weintraub. In *Barrère, A., ed.*, 1989, pp. 182–88.

_____ **and Kregel, Jan A.** Macroeconomic Problems and Policies of Income Distribution: Functional, Personal, International: Introduction. In *Davidson, P. and Kregel, J., eds.*, 1989, pp. 1–5.

Davidson, Russell, et al. On the Welfare Effects of Anti-discrimination Regulations in the EC Car Market. *Int. J. Ind. Organ.*, June 1989, *7*(2), pp. 205–30.

Davidson, Scott. Free Movement of Goods, Workers, Services and Capital. In *Lodge, J., ed.*, 1989, pp. 111–28.

Davidson, Wallace N., III and Dutia, Dipa. A Note on the Behavior of Security Returns: A Test of Stock Market Overreaction and Efficiency. *J. Finan. Res.*, Fall 1989, *12*(3), pp. 245–52.

_____; **Dutia, Dipa and Cheng, Louis.** A Reexamination of the Market Reaction to Failed Mergers. *J. Finance*, September 1989, *44*(4), pp. 1077–83.

_____ **and Garrison, Sharon H.** The Stock Market Reaction to Significant Tender Offer Repurchases of Stock: Size and Purpose Perspective. *Financial Rev.*, February 1989, *24*(1), pp. 93–107.

_____; **Thornton, John H. and Cross, Mark L.** The Impact of Directors and Officers' Liability Suits on Firm Value. *J. Risk Ins.*, March 1989, *56*(1), pp. 128–36.

Davidsson, Per. Need for Achievement and Entrepreneurial Activity in Small Firms. In *Grunert, K. G. and Ölander, F., eds.*, 1989, pp. 47–64.

Davies, A. R. Selection of Prepaid or Fee-for-Service Care by Medicaid Families: Examining the Health-Risk Hypothesis. In *Scheffler, R. M. and Rossiter, L. F.*, eds., 1989, pp. 183–98.

Davies, C. S. L. The Enfant Terrible? In *[Stone, L.]*, 1989, pp. 9–13.

Davies, J. E. Impediments to Contestability in Liner Markets. *Logist. Transp. Rev.*, December 1989, *25*(4), pp. 325–42.

_____. A Rejoinder [Competition, Contestability, and the Liner Shipping Industry]. *J. Transp. Econ. Policy*, May 1989, *23*(2), pp. 204–08.

Davies, James B. Incidence of Tax Expenditures in a Lifetime Framework: Theory and an Application to RRSPs. In *Bruce, N.*, ed., 1989, pp. 339–67.

_____ **and Shorrocks, A. F.** Optimal Grouping of Income and Wealth Data. *J. Econometrics*, September 1989, *42*(1), pp. 97–108.

_____; **Whalley, John and Hamilton, Bob.** Capital Income Taxation in a Two-Commodity Life Cycle Model: The Role of Factor Intensity and Asset Capitalization Effects. *J. Public Econ.*, June 1989, *39*(1), pp. 109–26.

Davies, Julia, et al. The Challenge to Western Management Development: International Alternatives: Introduction. In *Davies, J., et al.*, eds., 1989, pp. 1–7.

Davies, P. L. and Bachtler, J. Economic Restructuring and Services Policy. In *Gibbs, D.*, ed., 1989, pp. 154–75.

Davies, R. W. Economic and Social Policy in the USSR, 1917–41. In *Mathias, P. and Pollard, S.*, eds., 1989, pp. 984–1047.

Dávila, Carlos. Grounding Management Education in Local Research: A Latin American Experience. In *Davies, J., et al.*, eds., 1989, pp. 40–56.

Davis, Bruce. Wilderness Conservation in Australia: Eight Governments in Search of a Policy. *Natural Res. J.*, Winter 1989, *29*(1), pp. 103–13.

Davis, Byron L.; Kick, Edward L. and Kiefer, David. The World-System, Militarization, and National Development. In *Schaeffer, R. K.*, ed., 1989, pp. 27–45.

Davis, Don. Tax Increment Financing. *Public Budg. Finance*, Spring 1989, *9*(1), pp. 63–73.

Davis, Evan. The Single Market in Financial Services. In *Dahrendorf, R., et al.*, 1989, pp. 69–88.

Davis, George K. Income and Substitution Effects for Mean-Preserving Spreads. *Int. Econ. Rev.*, February 1989, *30*(1), pp. 131–36.

_____. A Note on Inflation Uncertainty and Monetary Policy. *J. Macroecon.*, Summer 1989, *11*(3), pp. 435–46.

_____. Relative Uncertainty. *Econ. Letters*, 1989, *29*(4), pp. 307–10.

Davis, Herbert J. and Hossain, Sakhawat. Some Thoughts on International Personnel Management as an Emerging Field. In *Nedd, A.*, ed., 1989, pp. 121–36.

Davis, John A. Socialism and the Working Classes in Italy before 1914. In *Geary, D.*, ed., 1989, pp. 182–230.

Davis, John B. Axiomatic General Equilibrium Theory and Referentiality. *J. Post Keynesian Econ.*, Spring 1989, *11*(3), pp. 424–38.

_____. Distribution in Ricardo's Machinery Chapter. *Hist. Polit. Econ.*, Fall 1989, *21*(3), pp. 457–80.

_____. Keynes on Atomism and Organicism. *Econ. J.*, December 1989, *99*(398), pp. 1159–72.

_____. Smith's Invisible Hand and Hegel's Cunning of Reason. *Int. J. Soc. Econ.*, 1989, *16*(6), pp. 50–66.

Davis, Karen. National Health Insurance: A Proposal. *Amer. Econ. Rev.*, May 1989, *79*(2), pp. 349–52.

_____; **Rowland, Diane and Lyons, Barbara.** Catastrophic Coverage under the Medicare Program. In *Eisdorfer, C.; Kessler, D. A. and Spector, A. N.*, eds., 1989, pp. 106–24.

Davis, Kathryn W. and Goldman, Marshall I. Gorbachev's Challenge: Economic Reform in the Age of High Technology. *Aussenwirtschaft*, December 1989, *44*(3–4), pp. 385–98.

Davis, Lance E.; Gallman, Robert E. and Hutchins, Teresa D. Productivity in American Whaling: The New Bedford Fleet in the Nineteenth Century. In *Galenson, D. W.*, ed., 1989, pp. 97–147.

_____ **and Huttenback, Robert A.** Businessmen, the Raj, and the Pattern of Government Expenditures: The British Empire, 1860–1912. In *Galenson, D. W.*, ed., 1989, pp. 190–230.

Davis, Lee N. The Patent System and Industrial Innovation. In *Pedersen, J. L.*, ed., 1989, pp. 91–122.

Davis, Michael. Patents, Natural Rights, and Natural Property. In *Weil, V. and Snapper, J. W.*, eds., 1989, pp. 241–49.

Davis, Michael L. and Porter, Philip K. A Test for Pure or Apparent Ideology in Congressional Voting. *Public Choice*, February 1989, *60*(2), pp. 101–11.

Davis, Peggy C. Law as Microaggression. *Yale Law J.*, June 1989, *98*(8), pp. 1559–77.

Davis, Steve J. and Altig, David. Government Debt, Redistributive Fiscal Policies, and the Interaction between Borrowing Constraints and Intergenerational Altruism. *J. Monet. Econ.*, July 1989, *24*(1), pp. 3–29.

Davis, Wayne J. and Whitford, David T. Tests of Composition Models for Resource Allocation: Good News and Bad News. In *Lee, C. F.*, ed., 1989, pp. 375–93.

Davis, William M. Major Collective Bargaining Settlements in Private Industry in 1988. *Mon. Lab. Rev.*, May 1989, *112*(5), pp. 34–43.

_____ **and Sleemi, Fehmida.** Collective Bargaining in 1989: Negotiators Will Face Diverse Issues. *Mon. Lab. Rev.*, January 1989, *112*(1), pp. 10–24.

Davison, Cecil W. and Arnade, Carlos A. Testing for Aggregation and Simultaneous Bias in U.S. Soybean Export Equations. *Southern J. Agr. Econ.*, December 1989, *21*(2), pp. 129–37.

———; **Arnade, Carlos A. and Hallahan, Charles B.** Box–Cox Estimation of U.S. Soybean Exports. *J. Agr. Econ. Res.*, Summer 1989, *41*(3), pp. 8–16.

Davutyan, Nurhan. Bank Failures as Poisson Variates. *Econ. Letters*, 1989, *29*(4), pp. 333–38.

———. Central Bank Intervention with Sample Selection, Japan 1977–1979. *Econ. Letters*, 1989, *29*(2), pp. 167–71.

———. Explaining Innovations: A Technical Note. *De Economist*, 1989, *137*(4), pp. 493–99.

——— **and Pippenger, John.** Excess Returns and Official Intervention: Canada 1952–1960. *Econ. Inquiry*, July 1989, *27*(3), pp. 489–500.

Davydov, Valerii. Prevention of Nuclear Weapons Proliferation. In *Rotblat, J. and Goldanskii, V. I., eds.*, 1989, pp. 46–51.

Dawkins, Peter and Kenyon, Peter. A Time Series Analysis of Labour Absence in Australia. *Rev. Econ. Statist.*, May 1989, *71*(2), pp. 232–39.

———; **Wooden, Mark and Kriegler, Roy.** Towards Organizational Effectiveness: An Overview with an Australian Perspective. *Australian Bull. Lab.*, March 1989, *15*(2), pp. 115–38.

Dawood, Dayan and Sjafrizal. Aceh: The LNG Boom and Enclave Development. In *Hill, H., ed.*, 1989, pp. 107–23.

Dawson, P. J. and Lingard, J. Measuring Farm Efficiency over Time on Philippine Rice Farms. *J. Agr. Econ.*, May 1989, *40*(2), pp. 168–77.

Day, Colin. Journals, University Presses, and the Spread of Ideas. In *Colander, D. C. and Coats, A. W., eds.*, 1989, pp. 61–72.

Day, Richard H. Comparative Monetary and Fiscal Policy Dynamics. In *Semmler, W., ed.*, 1989, pp. 119–44.

——— **and Walter, Jean-Luc.** Economic Growth in the Very Long Run: On the Multiple-Phase Interaction of Population, Technology, and Social Infrastructure. In *Barnett, W. A.; Geweke, J. and Shell, K., eds.*, 1989, pp. 253–89.

Dayal, Sahab. Collective Bargaining and Contemporary Management–Labor Relations: Analysis and Prospects. In *Prasad, S. B., ed.*, 1989, pp. 45–59.

Dayo, Felix; Gurtler, Thomas and Adegbulugbe, Anthony O. Optimal Structure of the Nigerian Energy Supply Mix. *Energy J.*, April 1989, *10*(2), pp. 165–76.

De Alessi, Louis. The Performance and Management of United States Federal Government Corporations: Comment. In *MacAvoy, P. W., et al.*, 1989, pp. 139–42.

——— **and Staaf, Robert J.** Subjective Value in Contract Law. *J. Inst. Theoretical Econ.*, December 1989, *145*(4), pp. 561–77.

De Boer, A. John. Sustainable Approaches to Hillside Agricultural Development. In *Leonard, H. J., ed.*, 1989, pp. 135–63.

De Boer, P. M. C. and Harkema, R. Some Evidence on the Performance of Size Correction Factors in Testing Consumer Demand Models. *Econ. Letters*, 1989, *29*(4), pp. 311–15.

De Bondt, Werner F. M. and Thaler, Richard H. A Mean-Reverting Walk Down Wall Street. *J. Econ. Perspectives*, Winter 1989, *3*(1), pp. 189–202.

De Borger, Bruno. Estimating the Welfare Implications of In-Kind Government Programs: A General Numerical Approach. *J. Public Econ.*, March 1989, *38*(2), pp. 215–26.

De George, Richard T. Ethics and the Financial Community: An Overview. In *Williams, O. F.; Reilly, F. K. and Houck, J. W., eds.*, 1989, pp. 197–216.

De Grauwe, Paul. Disinflation in the EMS and in the Non-EMS Countries. What Have We Learned? *Empirica*, 1989, *16*(2), pp. 161–76.

De Krey, Gary S. The London Whigs and the Exclusion Crisis Reconsidered. In *[Stone, L.]*, 1989, pp. 457–82.

De Lathouwer, L.; Van den Bosch, K. and Deleeck, H. Regional Differences in the Distribution of Social Security Benefits in Belgium: Facts and Causes. *Cah. Écon. Bruxelles*, 3rd Trimester 1989, (123), pp. 265–310.

De Long, J. Bradford. Senior's Last Hour: Reply. *Hist. Polit. Econ.*, Summer 1989, *21*(2), pp. 309–10.

———, **et al.** The Size and Incidence of the Losses from Noise Trading. *J. Finance*, July 1989, *44*(3), pp. 681–96.

De Villé, Philippe and Menard, Claude. An Insolent Founding Father. *Europ. Econ. Rev.*, March 1989, *33*(2/3), pp. 494–502.

De Vroey, Michel and Cartelier, Jean. L'approche de la régulation. Un nouveau paradigme? (With English summary.) *Écon. Societes*, November 1989, *23*(11), pp. 63–87.

Deacon, Robert T. An Empirical Model of Fishery Dynamics. *J. Environ. Econ. Manage.*, March 1989, *16*(2), pp. 167–83.

——— **and Sonstelie, Jon.** Price Controls and Rent-Seeking Behavior in Developing Countries. *World Devel.*, December 1989, *17*(12), pp. 1945–54.

——— **and Sonstelie, Jon.** The Welfare Costs of Rationing by Waiting. *Econ. Inquiry*, April 1989, *27*(2), pp. 179–96.

Deaconescu, Ecaterina. Methods for Estimating the Volume of the Potentially Recyclable Textiles. *Econ. Computat. Econ. Cybern. Stud. Res.*, 1989, *24*(1), pp. 61–69.

Deadman, Derek and Ghatak, Subrata. Money, Prices and Stabilization Policies in Some Developing Countries. *Appl. Econ.*, July 1989, *21*(7), pp. 853–65.

Deafenbaugh, Linda. Hausa Weaving: Surviving amid the Paradoxes. In *Coy, M. W., ed.*, 1989, pp. 163–79.

Deak, Peter. Restructuring Conventional Forces in Defensive Modes. In *Rotblat, J. and Goldanskii, V. I., eds.*, 1989, pp. 86–92.

Deakin, Edward B. Rational Economic Behavior and Lobbying on Accounting Issues: Evidence from the Oil and Gas Industry. *Accounting Rev.*, January 1989, *64*(1), pp. 137–51.

Dealtry, Michael. External Impacts of the United States' Financial Policies: Comment. In *Hamouda, O. F.; Rowley, R. and Wolf, B. M., eds.*, 1989, pp. 129–30.

_____. The Future of the International Monetary System: Comment. In *Hamouda, O. F.; Rowley, R. and Wolf, B. M., eds.*, 1989, p. 117.

Dean, C. and Lawless, J. F. Tests for Detecting Overdispersion in Poisson Regression Models. *J. Amer. Statist. Assoc.*, June 1989, *84*(406), pp. 467–72.

Dean, James W. Conservative versus Liberal Regulation of International Banking. *J. World Trade*, February 1989, *23*(1), pp. 5–16.

_____. Conservative versus Liberal Regulation of International Banking. *J. World Trade*, February 1989, *23*(1), pp. 5–16.

_____. Does Money Supply Endogeneity Matter? A Reply. *S. Afr. J. Econ.*, June 1989, *57*(2), pp. 203–07.

Deane, Phyllis. Henry Fawcett: The Plain Man's Political Economist. In *Goldman, L., ed.*, 1989, pp. 93–110.

DeAngelo, Harry and DeAngelo, Linda. Proxy Contests and the Governance of Publicly Held Corporations. *J. Finan. Econ.*, June 1989, *23*(1), pp. 29–59.

DeAngelo, Linda and DeAngelo, Harry. Proxy Contests and the Governance of Publicly Held Corporations. *J. Finan. Econ.*, June 1989, *23*(1), pp. 29–59.

Dearden, Philip. Wilderness and Our Common Future. *Natural Res. J.*, Winter 1989, *29*(1), pp. 205–21.

_____; Dumbrell, John and Sewell, W. R. Derrick. Wilderness Decisionmaking and the Role of Environmental Interest Groups: A Comparison of the Franklin Dam, Tasmania and South Moresby, British Columbia Cases. *Natural Res. J.*, Winter 1989, *29*(1), pp. 147–69.

Dearden, S. An Analysis of Labour Turnover in British Railways. *Appl. Econ.*, November 1989, *21*(11), pp. 1465–82.

Deardorff, Alan V. Economic Perspectives on Antidumping Law. In *Jackson, J. H. and Vermulst, E. A., eds.*, 1989, pp. 23–39.

_____. "Market Access" in International Trade: Comment. In *Stern, R. M., ed.*, 1989, pp. 284–88.

_____; Shiells, Clinton R. and Stern, Robert M. Estimates of the Elasticities of Substitution between Imports and Home Goods for the United States: Reply. *Weltwirtsch. Arch.*, 1989, *125*(2), pp. 371–74.

Deas, Malcolm. Further Forward Thoughts on the Falklands. In *Bulmer-Thomas, V., ed.*, 1989, pp. 151–63.

Deaton, Angus S. Looking for Boy–Girl Discrimination in Household Expenditure Data. *World Bank Econ. Rev.*, January 1989, *3*(1), pp. 1–15.

_____. Reflections on Empirical Microeconomics. *Econ. Rec.*, March 1989, *65*(188), pp. 73–76.

_____. Rice Prices and Income Distribution in Thailand: A Non-parametric Analysis. *Econ. J.*, Supplement, 1989, *99*(395), pp. 1–37.

_____. Saving in Developing Countries: Theory and Review. In *Fischer, S. and de Tray, D., eds.*, 1989, pp. 61–96.

_____ and Campbell, John Y. Why Is Consumption So Smooth? *Rev. Econ. Stud.*, July 1989, *56*(3), pp. 357–73.

_____; Ruiz-Castillo, Javier and Thomas, Duncan. The Influence of Household Composition on Household Expenditure Patterns: Theory and Spanish Evidence. *J. Polit. Econ.*, February 1989, *97*(1), pp. 179–200.

Deaton, Brady; Norton, George W. and Bezuneh, Mesfin. Farm Level Impacts of Food-for-Work in a Semi-arid Region of Kenya. *Eastern Afr. Econ. Rev.*, June 1989, *5*(1), pp. 1–8.

Deaves, Richard. North American Money Surprises and Financial Market Reactions: An Empirical Note. *Econ. Letters*, December 1989, *31*(2), pp. 155–58.

Deb, Rajat; Fomby, Thomas B. and Lam, Chun H. Deregulation and the Demand for Money Market Mutual Funds. *J. Macroecon.*, Spring 1989, *11*(2), pp. 297–308.

DeBardeleben, Joan. "The Future Has Already Begun": Environmental Damage and Protection in the GDR. In *Rueschemeyer, M. and Lemke, C., eds.*, 1989, pp. 144–64.

Debertin, David L.; Sjarkowi, Fachurrozi and Pagoulatos, Angelos. Soil Erosion, Intertemporal Profit, and the Soil Conservation Decision. *Southern J. Agr. Econ.*, December 1989, *21*(2), pp. 55–62.

DeBoer, Larry. The Responsiveness of Heavy Vehicle Registrations to Local Tax Differentials. *Atlantic Econ. J.*, December 1989, *17*(4), pp. 89.

_____ and Brorsen, B. Wade. The Demand for and Supply of Military Labor. *Southern Econ. J.*, April 1989, *55*(4), pp. 853–69.

_____ and Brorsen, B. Wade. A Note on Congressional Military Pay Setting. *Public Finance Quart.*, January 1989, *17*(1), pp. 96–107.

_____ and Seeborg, Michael C. The Unemployment Rates of Men and Women: A Transition Probability Analysis. *Ind. Lab. Relat. Rev.*, April 1989, *42*(3), pp. 404–14.

DeBondt, Raymond R.; Dehandschutter, Wim V. and Sleuwaegen, Leo E. The Herfindahl Index and Concentration Ratios Revisited. *Antitrust Bull.*, Fall 1989, *34*(3), pp. 625–40.

Debrah, Siegfried. Impacts of Rising Energy Prices on Saskatchewan Agriculture: A Comment. *Can. J. Agr. Econ.*, July 1989, *37*(2), pp. 319–21.

DeBresson, Christian. Breeding Innovation Clusters: A Source of Dynamic Development. *World Devel.*, January 1989, *17*(1), pp. 1–16.

_____ and Dalpé, Robert. Le secteur public comme premier utilisateur d'innovations. (With English summary.) *L'Actual. Econ.*, March 1989, *65*(1), pp. 53–70.

Debreu, Gerard. Theoretic Models: Mathematical Form and Economic Content. In *Feiwel, G. R., ed. (II), 1989, 1986*, pp. 264–81.

Decker, Paul T. and Hamilton, Bruce W. Taxation of Compensating Wage Variation. *Econ.*

Stud. Quart., September 1989, *40*(3), pp. 239–50.

Decker, Reinhold and Gaul, Wolfgang. Classification and Selection of Consumer Purchase Behaviour Models. In *Opitz, O., ed.*, 1989, pp. 389–98.

Decoster, André and Schokkaert, Erik. Equity and Efficiency of a Reform of Belgian Indirect Taxes. *Rech. Écon. Louvain*, 1989, *55*(2), pp. 155–76.

Dee, Philippa. The Effects of Government Size on Economic Performance: A Quantitative Assessment of a Budget Reduction. *Australian Econ. Rev.*, Autumn 1989, (85), pp. 24–38.

Deeble, J. S. Changes in Private Medical Service Use, 1976 to 1986: Commentary. In *Smith, C. S., ed.*, 1989, pp. 217–18.

——. Health Care under Universal Insurance: The First Three Years of Medicare. In *Butler, J. R. G. and Doessel, D. P., eds.*, 1989, pp. 189–211.

——. Integrating Medicare with Private Health Insurance: The Best of Both Worlds? Commentary. In *Smith, C. S., ed.*, 1989, pp. 239–41.

—— **and Scotton, R. B.** Compulsory Health Insurance for Australia. In *Butler, J. R. G. and Doessel, D. P., eds.*, 1989, *1968*, pp. 128–44.

Deeks, William. The Intellect of Resource Marketing: Or the How and the Why We Do It at Noranda Sales. In *Jackson, L. M. and Richardson, P. R., eds.*, 1989, pp. 66–76.

Deere, Donald R. On the Potential for Private Insurers to Reduce the Inefficiencies of Moral Hazard. *Int. Rev. Law Econ.*, December 1989, *9*(2), pp. 219–22.

Defeo, Victor J.; Lambert, Richard A. and Larcker, David F. The Executive Compensation Effects of Equity-for-Debt Swaps. *Accounting Rev.*, April 1989, *64*(2), pp. 201–27.

Defraigne, Pierre. Macroeconomic Interactions between the North and South: Comment. In *Bryant, R. C., et al., eds.*, 1989, pp. 414–16.

DeGennaro, Ramon P. The Determinants of Wagering Behavior. *Managerial Dec. Econ.*, September 1989, *10*(3), pp. 221–28.

—— **and Baillie, Richard T.** The Impact of Delivery Terms on Stock Return Volatility. *J. Finan. Services Res.*, October 1989, *3*(1), pp. 55–76.

Degens, Paul O. and Tittel, Manfred. Isotonic Regression—For a Monotone Index on a Hierarchy. In *Opitz, O., ed.*, 1989, pp. 212–21.

—— **and Wolf, Karin.** On Properties of Additive Tree Algorithms. In *Opitz, O., ed.*, 1989, pp. 256–65.

DeGregori, Thomas R. The Development Challenge: Theory, Practice, and Prospects. In *DeGregori, T. R., ed.*, 1989, pp. 1–46.

——. Power and Illusion in the Marketplace: Institutions and Technology. In *Tool, M. R. and Samuels, W. J., eds. (I)*, 1989, *1974*, pp. 37–48.

DeGroot, M. H. and Bayarri, M. J. Optimal Reporting of Predictions. *J. Amer. Statist. Assoc.*, March 1989, *84*(405), pp. 214–22.

Dehandschutter, Wim V.; Sleuwaegen, Leo E. and DeBondt, Raymond R. The Herfindahl Index and Concentration Ratios Revisited. *Antitrust Bull.*, Fall 1989, *34*(3), pp. 625–40.

Dehapiot, Tanguy and Manchet, Stéphane. Modèle de volatilité aléatoire et prix des options. (Stochastic Volatility and Option Pricing: A Simplified Approach. With English summary.) *Finance*, December 1989, *10*(2), pp. 7–25.

Deighton, John; Romer, Daniel and McQueen, Josh. Using Drama to Persuade. *J. Cons. Res.*, December 1989, *16*(3), pp. 335–43.

Deimezis, N., et al. DRY: Un modèle macrosectoriel de l'économie belge. (With English summary.) *Cah. Écon. Bruxelles*, 3rd Trimester 1989, (123), pp. 345–81.

——, **et al.** DRY: Un modèle macrosectoriel de l'économie belge (suite). (With English summary.) *Cah. Écon. Bruxelles*, 4th Trimester 1989, (124), pp. 393–413.

Deistler, Manfred. Linear System Identification—A Survey. In *Willems, J. C., ed.*, 1989, pp. 1–25.

——. Symmetric Modeling in System Identification. In *[Willems, J. C.]*, 1989, pp. 129–47.

—— **and Anderson, B. D. O.** Linear Dynamic Errors-in-Variables Models: Some Structure Theory. *J. Econometrics*, May 1989, *41*(1), pp. 39–63.

Deitsch, Clarence R. and Dilts, David A. The Arbitration Literature: Who Contributes? *J. Lab. Res.*, Spring 1989, *10*(2), pp. 207–14.

DeJean, Niels and Olmstead, Dennis J. Belgium–U.S. and France–U.S. Protocols: Highlighting U.S. Tax Treaty Concerns. *Bull. Int. Fiscal Doc.*, January 1989, *43*(1), pp. 3–8.

Dejene, Alemneh. The Training and Visit Agricultural Extension in Rainfed Agriculture: Lessons from Ethiopia. *World Devel.*, October 1989, *17*(10), pp. 1647–59.

Dejon, Bruno; Güldner, Bernhard and Wenzel, Georg. Direct Equilibria of Economies and Their Perfect Homogeneity Limits. In *Andersson, Å. E., et al., eds.*, 1989, pp. 81–105.

Dekel, Eddie. Asset Demands without the Independence Axiom. *Econometrica*, January 1989, *57*(1), pp. 163–69.

—— **and Brandenburger, Adam.** The Role of Common Knowledge Assumptions in Game Theory. In *Hahn, F., ed.*, 1989, pp. 46–61.

Dekle, Robert. An Analysis of Female Labor Supply, Housing Demand and the Saving Rate in Japan: Comment. *Europ. Econ. Rev.*, May 1989, *33*(5), pp. 1023–26.

——. The Relationship between Defense Spending and Economic Performance in Japan. In *Makin, J. H. and Hellmann, D. C., eds.*, 1989, pp. 127–49.

——. A Simulation Model of Saving, Residential Choice, and Bequests of the Japanese Elderly. *Econ. Letters*, 1989, *29*(2), pp. 129–33.

Del Boca, Alessandra and Rota, Paola. Wage Compensation and Employment: Some Empirical Evidence from Microdata. *Giorn. Econ.*, March–April 1989, *48*(3–4), pp. 147–57.

Del Monte, Alfredo and de Luzenberger, Raul.

The Effect of Regional Policy on New Firm Formation in Southern Italy. *Reg. Stud.*, June 1989, *23*(3), pp. 219–30.

Delaney, Charles J. and Smith, Marc T. Impact Fees and the Price of New Housing: An Empirical Study. *Amer. Real Estate Urban Econ. Assoc. J.*, Spring 1989, *17*(1), pp. 41–54.

_____ **and Smith, Marc T.** Pricing Implications of Development Exactions on Existing Housing Stock. *Growth Change*, Fall 1989, *20*(4), pp. 1–12.

Delaney, John Thomas and Sockell, Donna. The Mandatory-Permissive Distinction and Collective Bargaining Outcomes. *Ind. Lab. Relat. Rev.*, July 1989, *42*(4), pp. 566–83.

Delbecque, Bernard. Exchange-Rate Dynamics in a Model with Imperfect Capital Mobility and Asset Substitutability. *Europ. Econ. Rev.*, July 1989, *33*(6), pp. 1161–73.

Delbono, Flavio. Competizioni tecnologiche e struttura di mercato: Risultati teorici e prospettive di ricerca. (Technological Competition and Market Structure: Theoretical Findings and Directions of Research. With English summary.) *Econ. Politica*, April 1989, *6*(1), pp. 151–81.

_____ . Endogenous Market Competition in Technologically Asymmetric Duopolies. *Rivista Int. Sci. Econ. Com.*, August 1989, *36*(8), pp. 723–28.

_____ . Market Leadership with a Sequence of History Dependent Patent Races. *J. Ind. Econ.*, September 1989, *38*(1), pp. 95–101.

_____ . Patterns of Technological Leadership: A Simple Model with Uncertainty. *Metroecon.*, October 1989, *40*(3), pp. 257–77.

_____ **and Denicolò, Vincenzo.** Asymmetric Equilibria in a Dynamic Model of R&D. *Econ. Notes*, 1989, (2), pp. 192–209.

_____ **and de Fraja, Giovanni.** Alternative Strategies of a Public Enterprise in Oligopoly. *Oxford Econ. Pap.*, April 1989, *41*(2), pp. 302–11.

Deleeck, H.; De Lathouwer, L. and Van den Bosch, K. Regional Differences in the Distribution of Social Security Benefits in Belgium: Facts and Causes. *Cah. Écon. Bruxelles*, 3rd Trimester 1989, (123), pp. 265–310.

Delfaud, Pierre. La protectionnisme comme antidote à la vassalisation de l'économie française. (Protectionism as an Antidote to the Vassalization of the French Economy. With English summary.) *Écon. Societes*, August 1989, *23*(8), pp. 59–76.

Delgado, Christopher and Sahn, David E. The Nature and Implications for Market Interventions of Seasonal Food Price Variability. **In** *Sahn, D. E., ed.*, 1989, pp. 179–95.

Dell'Aringa, Carlo and Neri, Fabio. Illegal Immigrants and the Informal Economy in Italy. **In** *Gordon, I. and Thirlwall, A. P., eds.*, 1989, pp. 133–47.

Dell, Sidney. Electronic Highways for World Trade: Services: National Objectives. **In** *Robinson, P.; Sauvant, K. P. and Govitrikar, V. P., eds.*, 1989, pp. 43–70.

_____ . The Future of the International Monetary System. **In** *Hamouda, O. F.; Rowley, R. and Wolf, B. M., eds.*, 1989, pp. 89–116.

Dellas, Harris and Stockman, Alan C. International Portfolio Nondiversification and Exchange Rate Variability. *J. Int. Econ.*, May 1989, *26*(3/4), pp. 271–89.

Deller, Steven C. and Chicoine, David L. Economic Diversification and the Rural Economy: Evidence from Consumer Behavior. *Reg. Sci. Persp.*, 1989, *19*(2), pp. 41–55.

_____ ; **Chicoine, David L. and Walzer, N.** Representative vs. Direct Democracy and Government Spending in a Median Voter Model. *Public Finance*, 1989, *44*(2), pp. 225–36.

Delorme, François and van der Mensbrugghe, Dominique. Assessing the Role of Scale Economies and Imperfect Competition in the Context of Agricultural Trade Liberalisation: A Canadian Case Study. *OECD Econ. Stud.*, Winter 1989–1990, (13), pp. 205–36.

Delorme, Hélène and Coulomb, Pierre. French Agriculture and the Failure of Its European Strategy. **In** *Goodman, D. and Redclift, M., eds.*, 1989, pp. 84–112.

Delorme, Robert. A New View on the Economic Theory of the State: A Case Study of France. **In** *Tool, M. R. and Samuels, W. J., eds. (III)*, 1989, *1984*, pp. 101–30.

Delors, Jacques. Europe 1992. **In** *Frankel, A. V. and Heck, C. B., eds.*, 1989, pp. 48–51.

Delozier, John; Ehrhardt, Michael C. and Clayton, Ronnie. A Note on January Returns in the U.S. Government Bond Market: The Term Effect. *J. Finan. Services Res.*, October 1989, *2*(4), pp. 307–18.

Delp, Peter. Strategies of Development: A Survey: Commentary. **In** *DeGregori, T. R., ed.*, 1989, pp. 179–90.

DeMarco, Edward J. and Mays, Elizabeth. The Demand for Federal Home Loan Bank Advances by Thrift Institutions: Some Recent Evidence. *Amer. Real Estate Urban Econ. Assoc. J.*, Fall 1989, *17*(3), pp. 363–79.

Demaria, Giovanni. Il saggio di interesse in Italia. (The Rate of Interest in Italy. With English summary.) *Rivista Int. Sci. Econ. Com.*, Oct.–Nov. 1989, *36*(10–11), pp. 881–86.

Demas, William G. Alister McIntyre and Caribbean Political Economy. *Soc. Econ. Stud.*, June 1989, *38*(2), pp. 25–35.

DeMasi, Paula and Lorie, Henri. How Resilient Are Military Expenditures? *Int. Monet. Fund Staff Pap.*, March 1989, *36*(1), pp. 130–65.

Dembélé, N. Nango; Staatz, John M. and Dioné, Josué. Cereals Market Liberalization in Mali. *World Devel.*, May 1989, *17*(5), pp. 703–18.

Dementiev, N. P. Turnpike Theorem: The Case When Utility Is Not Additively Separable with Respect to Time. *J. Math. Econ.*, 1989, *18*(4), pp. 385–97.

Demers, Fanny and Demers, Michel. A Privately Revealing Rational Expectations Equilibrium for the Futures Market. *Europ. Econ. Rev.*, April 1989, *33*(4), pp. 663–85.

Demers, Michel and Demers, Fanny. A Privately

Revealing Rational Expectations Equilibrium for the Futures Market. *Europ. Econ. Rev.*, April 1989, *33*(4), pp. 663–85.

Demery, Lionel and Addison, Tony. The Impact of Liberalisation on Growth and Equity. In *Renshaw, G. T., ed.*, 1989, pp. 1–37.

Demetriades, Panikos O. The Relationship between the Level and Variability of Inflation: Theory and Evidence. *J. Appl. Econometrics*, July–Sept. 1989, *4*(3), pp. 239–50.

Demetrius, Lloyd. The Demographic Evolution of Human Populations: The Role of Selection and Environmental Factors. *Demography*, August 1989, *26*(3), pp. 353–72.

Demirdjian, Z. S. Marketing Strategy: A Competitive System Analysis. *Liiketaloudellinen Aikak.*, 1989, *38*(3), pp. 159–70.

Demougin, Dominique M. A Renegotiation-Proof Mechanism for a Principal–Agent Model with Moral Hazard and Adverse Selection. *Rand J. Econ.*, Summer 1989, *20*(2), pp. 256–67.

Demoussis, M. P. and Daouli, J. The Impact of Inflation on Prices Received and Paid by Greek Farmers. *J. Agr. Econ.*, May 1989, *40*(2), pp. 232–39.

Dempsey, Stephen J. Predisclosure Information Search Incentives, Analyst Following, and Earnings Announcement Price Response. *Accounting Rev.*, October 1989, *64*(4), pp. 748–57.

Dempster, A. P. and Carlin, J. B. Sensitivity Analysis of Seasonal Adjustments: Empirical Case Studies: Rejoinder. *J. Amer. Statist. Assoc.*, March 1989, *84*(405), pp. 30–32.

_____ **and Carlin, J. B.** Sensitivity Analysis of Seasonal Adjustments: Empirical Case Studies. *J. Amer. Statist. Assoc.*, March 1989, *84*(405), pp. 6–20.

Dempster, Danny. Implications of the Canada–U.S. Trade Agreement for Horticulture in Canada. *Can. J. Agr. Econ.*, Part 2, December 1989, *37*(4), pp. 1277–82.

Demsetz, Harold. Accounting for Advertising as a Barrier to Entry. In *Demsetz, H.*, 1989, pp. 139–54.

_____. Amenity Potential, Indivisibilities, and Political Competition. In *Demsetz, H.*, 1989, pp. 263–79.

_____. The Amenity Potential of Newspapers and the Reporting of Presidential Campaigns. In *Demsetz, H.*, 1989, pp. 245–62.

_____. The Antitrust Dilemma. In *Demsetz, H.*, 1989, *1974*, pp. 208–16.

_____. Barriers to Entry. In *Demsetz, H.*, 1989, *1982*, pp. 25–39.

_____. Competition in the Public Sector. In *Demsetz, H.*, 1989, *1982*, pp. 280–94.

_____. Economics as a Guide to Antitrust Regulation. In *Demsetz, H.*, 1989, *1976*, pp. 195–207.

_____. The Growth of Government. In *Demsetz, H.*, 1989, *1982*, pp. 295–307.

_____. Inconsistencies of Monopolistic Competition. In *Demsetz, H.*, 1989, *1972*, pp. 67–72.

_____. The Indivisibility Rent Theory of Measured Oligopoly Profit. In *Demsetz, H.*, 1989, pp. 112–38.

_____. Information and Efficiency: Another Viewpoint. In *Demsetz, H.*, 1989, *1969*, pp. 3–24.

_____. Perfect Competition, Regulation, and the Stock Market. In *Demsetz, H.*, 1989, *1969*, pp. 225–42.

_____. Purchasing Monopoly. In *Demsetz, H.*, 1989, *1984*, pp. 155–67.

_____. The Social Variable in Economic Analysis. In *Demsetz, H.*, 1989, pp. 40–46.

_____. The Technostructure, Forty-six Years Later. In *Demsetz, H.*, 1989, *1968*, pp. 168–81.

_____. The Trust behind Antitrust. In *Demsetz, H.*, 1989, pp. 217–24.

_____. Two Systems of Belief about Monopoly. In *Demsetz, H.*, 1989, *1974*, pp. 91–111.

_____. Welfare and Empirical Implications of Monopolistic Competition. In *Demsetz, H.*, 1989, *1964*, pp. 47–66.

_____. Where Is the New Industrial State? In *Demsetz, H.*, 1989, *1974*, pp. 182–92.

_____. Why Regulate Utilities? In *Demsetz, H.*, 1989, *1968*, pp. 75–86.

_____. Why Regulate Utilities? Postscript: Contestability and Competition for the Field. In *Demsetz, H.*, 1989, pp. 86–90.

Demski, Joel S. and Sappington, David E. M. Hierarchical Structure and Responsibility Accounting. *J. Acc. Res.*, Spring 1989, *27*(1), pp. 40–58.

Dendrinos, Dimitrios S. Growth Patterns of the Eight Regions in the People's Republic of China (1980–1985). *Ann. Reg. Sci.*, 1989, *23*(3), pp. 213–22.

Deneckere, Raymond J. and Ausubel, Lawrence M. A Direct Mechanism Characterization of Sequential Bargaining with One-Sided Incomplete Information. *J. Econ. Theory*, June 1989, *48*(1), pp. 18–46.

_____ **and Ausubel, Lawrence M.** Reputation in Bargaining and Durable Goods Monopoly. *Econometrica*, May 1989, *57*(3), pp. 511–31.

Deng, Zihui. On Internal Contradictions within, and Democratic Management of, Agricultural Co-operatives. In *Howe, C. and Walker, K. R., eds.*, 1989, *1956*, pp. 212–36.

_____. Speech Concerning Rural Work and Problems of Agricultural Socialist Reform. In *Howe, C. and Walker, K. R., eds.*, 1989, *1954*, pp. 203–11.

Denicolò, Vincenzo. La teoria dell'attuazione delle regole di scelta collettiva: Una rassegna. (The Theory of Implementation of Collective Choice Rules: A Survey. With English summary.) *Econ. Politica*, December 1989, *6*(3), pp. 427–62.

_____ **and Candela, Guido.** Firms' Location and the Central Business District. *Rivista Int. Sci. Econ. Com.*, August 1989, *36*(8), pp. 703–22.

_____ **and Delbono, Flavio.** Asymmetric Equilibria in a Dynamic Model of R&D. *Econ. Notes*, 1989, (2), pp. 192–209.

Denizet, Jean. Debt, Credit and the Rate of Investment: Concluding Remarks. In *Barrère, A., ed.*, 1989, pp. 105–10.

Dennerlein, John; Power, Anthony and Kruger, Michael W. Deciphering Distribution Effects: Commentary. *Marketing Sci.*, Spring 1989, 8(2), pp. 129–30.

Denning, G. L. and Flinn, John C. Agroeconomic Opportunities in Rice-Based Farming Systems Research. In *International Rice Research Institute*, 1989, pp. 239–54.

Dennis, Kenneth. Ismatically Speaking: Are Austrians Institutionalists? In *Samuels, W. J., ed. (II)*, 1989, pp. 107–14.

————. Provable Theorems and Refutable Hypotheses: The Case of Competitive Theory. In *Tool, M. R. and Samuels, W. J., eds. (II)*, 1989, pp. 152–69.

Dennis, Michael. Individual Burden—Societal Requirement? In *Rueschemeyer, M. and Lemke, C., eds.*, 1989, pp. 95–114.

Dennis, Richard. 'Hard to Let' in Edwardian London. *Urban Stud.*, February 1989, 26(1), pp. 77–89.

Densen, Paul M.; Jones, Ellen W. and Katz, Sidney. Using Field Data to Shape New Policies. In *Eisdorfer, C.; Kessler, D. A. and Spector, A. N., eds.*, 1989, pp. 521–44.

Denslow, Dave and Rush, Mark. Supply Shocks and the Interest Rate. *Econ. Inquiry*, July 1989, 27(3), pp. 501–10.

Dente, Bruno and Regonini, Gloria. Politics and Policies in Italy. In *Lange, P. and Regini, M., eds.*, 1989, pp. 51–79.

Denton, Nancy A. and Massey, Douglas S. Hypersegregation in U.S. Metropolitan Areas: Black and Hispanic Segregation Along Five Dimensions. *Demography*, August 1989, 26(3), pp. 373–91.

Denton, Ross. Overview of the Discussion during the Comparative Antidumping Law Mini-conference, November 6 and 7, 1988. In *Jackson, J. H. and Vermulst, E. A., eds.*, 1989, pp. 467–76.

Deolalikar, Anil B. and Behrman, Jere R. Agricultural Wages in India: The Role of Health, Nutrition, and Seasonality. In *Sahn, D. E., ed.*, 1989, pp. 107–17.

———— **and Behrman, Jere R.** Is Variety the Spice of Life? Implications for Calorie Intake. *Rev. Econ. Statist.*, November 1989, 71(4), pp. 666–72.

———— **and Behrman, Jere R.** . . . Of the Fittest? Duration of Survival of Manufacturing Establishments in a Developing Country. *J. Ind. Econ.*, December 1989, 38(2), pp. 215–26.

———— **and Behrman, Jere R.** Seasonal Demands for Nutrient Intakes and Health Status in Rural South India. In *Sahn, D. E., ed.*, 1989, pp. 66–78.

———— **and Evenson, Robert E.** Technology Production and Technology Purchase in Indian Industry: An Econometric Analysis. *Rev. Econ. Statist.*, November 1989, 71(4), pp. 689–92.

———— **and Röller, Lars-Hendrik.** Patenting by Manufacturing Firms in India: Its Production and Impact. *J. Ind. Econ.*, March 1989, 37(3), pp. 303–14.

———— **and Sundaram, Anant K.** Technology

Choice, Adaptation and Diffusion in Private- and State-Owned Enterprises in India. In *James, J., ed.*, 1989, pp. 73–138.

DePass, Rudolph E. and Friedenberg, Howard L. Per Capita Personal Income: Continued Widening of Regional Differences in 1988. *Surv. Curr. Bus.*, April 1989, 69(4), pp. 35–36.

Deprez, Johan. Income Distribution in Keynes' Aggregate Supply Function with Vintage Fixed Capital. In *Missouri Valley Economic Association*, 1989, pp. 70–79.

Deprins, Dominique and Simar, Léopold. Estimating Technical Inefficiencies with Correction for Environmental Conditions: With an Application to Railway Companies. *Ann. Pub. Coop. Econ.*, 1989, 60(1), pp. 81–102.

———— **and Simar, Léopold.** Estimation de frontières déterministes avec facteurs exogènes d'inefficacité. (Estimating Deterministic Frontier Functions with Exogeneous Factors for the Inefficiency. With English summary.) *Ann. Écon. Statist.*, April–June 1989, (14), pp. 117–50.

Deravi, Keivan; Gregorowicz, Philip and Hegji, Charles E. Deficit Financing Announcements and Asset Prices. *J. Econ. Bus.*, May 1989, 41(2), pp. 171–83.

Dernberger, Robert F. Reforms in China: Implications for U.S. Policy. *Amer. Econ. Rev.*, May 1989, 79(2), pp. 21–25.

Derr, Bruce W. and Wadley, Susan S. Karimpur 1925–1984: Understanding Rural India through Restudies. In *Bardhan, P., ed. (I)*, 1989, pp. 76–126.

Dervis, Kemal. Foreign Trade and Industrial Policy: Historical Perspective and Basic Policy Options. In *Roe, A.; Roy, J. and Sengupta, J.*, 1989, pp. 66–78.

Desai, Ashok V. India in the Uruguay Round. *J. World Trade*, December 1989, 23(6), pp. 33–58.

————. The Politics of India's Trade Policy. In *Nau, H. R., ed.*, 1989, pp. 91–110.

Desai, Meghnad. The Scourge of the Monetarists: Kaldor on Monetarism and on Money. In *Lawson, T.; Palma, J. G. and Sender, J., eds.*, 1989, pp. 171–82.

————. The Scourge of the Monetarists: Kaldor on Monetarism and on Money. *Cambridge J. Econ.*, March 1989, 13(1), pp. 171–82.

Desai, Sonalde; Chase-Lansdale, P. Lindsay and Michael, Robert T. Mother or Market? Effects of Maternal Employment on the Intellectual Ability of 4-Year-Old Children. *Demography*, November 1989, 26(4), pp. 544–61.

Desax, Marcus. Die Nichtanerkennung von juristischen Personen im Steuerrecht: Schwiez. (The Disregard of a Legal Entity for Tax Purposes: Switzerland. With English summary.) In *International Fiscal Association, ed. (II)*, 1989, pp. 501–24.

Desbrières, Philippe. Dividendes et fiscalité, une alternative à l'effet de clientèle: L'hypothèse des transactions à court terme. (Dividends and Taxes, an Alternative to the Clientele Effect:

The Short Term Trading Hypothesis. With English summary.) *Écon. Societes,* January 1989, 23(1), pp. 55–71.

_____. Les stock-options en France: Arbitrages et conditions de réussite. (Stock-Options in France: Arbitrages and Conditions of Success. With English summary.) *Écon. Societes,* December 1989, 23(12), pp. 83–106.

Deserti, L. and Nedda Giraldo, L. FMS: A Classification of Recent Literature. In *Archetti, F.; Lucertini, M. and Serafini, P.,* eds., 1989, pp. 289–92.

Deshpande, Anirudh. Sailors and the Crowd: Popular Protest in Karchi, 1946. *Indian Econ. Soc. Hist. Rev.,* Jan.–March 1989, 26(1), pp. 1–28.

Deshpande, Rohit and Stayman, Douglas M. Situational Ethnicity and Consumer Behavior. *J. Cons. Res.,* December 1989, 16(3), pp. 361–71.

Despotakis, Kostas A. and Fisher, Anthony C. Energy Taxes and Economic Performance: A Regional General Equilibrium Analysis. *Energy Econ.,* April 1989, 11(2), pp. 153–57.

Desprairies, Pierre. Energy Economists in the 21st Century. *Energy J.,* January 1989, 10(1), pp. 21–28.

Destler, I. M. United States Trade Policymaking in the Uruguay Round. In *Nau, H. R.,* ed., 1989, pp. 191–207.

Desvousges, William H. and Smith, V. Kerry. Subjective versus Technical Risk Estimates: Do Risk Communication Policies Increase Consistency? *Econ. Letters,* December 1989, 31(3), pp. 287–91.

Deurloo, M. C.; Dieleman, F. M. and Clark, W. A. V. A Comparative View of Housing Choices in Controlled and Uncontrolled Housing Markets. *Urban Stud.,* October 1989, 26(5), pp. 457–68.

Deutsch, Joseph and Syrquin, Moshe. Economic Development and the Structure of Production. *Econ. Systems Res.,* 1989, 1(4), pp. 447–64.

Devaney, Barbara and Fraker, Thomas. The Dietary Impacts of the School Breakfast Program. *Amer. J. Agr. Econ.,* November 1989, 71(4), pp. 932–48.

_____ and Fraker, Thomas. The Effect of Food Stamps on Food Expenditures: An Assessment of Findings from the Nationwide Food Consumption Survey. *Amer. J. Agr. Econ.,* February 1989, 71(1), pp. 99–104.

Devarajan, Shantayanan and Bell, Clive. Project Appraisal and Foreign Exchange Constraints: A Rejoinder. *Econ. J.,* June 1989, 99(396), pp. 481–82.

_____; Jones, Christine and Roemer, Michael. Markets under Price Controls in Partial and General Equilibrium. *World Devel.,* December 1989, 17(12), pp. 1881–93.

_____ and Offerdal, Erik. Capital Markets and Computable General Equilibrium Models: Comparative Statics without Apology? *J. Policy Modeling,* Summer 1989, 11(2), pp. 191–212.

_____ and Rodrik, Dani. Trade Liberalization in Developing Countries: Do Imperfect Com-

petition and Scale Economies Matter? *Amer. Econ. Rev.,* May 1989, 79(2), pp. 283–87.

_____ and Weiner, Robert J. Dynamic Policy Coordination: Stockpiling for Energy Security. *J. Environ. Econ. Manage.,* January 1989, 16(1), pp. 9–22.

_____; Weiner, Robert J. and Benjamin, Nancy C. The 'Dutch' Disease in a Developing Country: Oil Reserves in Cameroon. *J. Devel. Econ.,* January 1989, 30(1), pp. 71–92.

Devereux, Michael. A Positive Theory of Inflation and Inflation Variance. *Econ. Inquiry,* January 1989, 27(1), pp. 105–16.

_____ and Anderson, Simon P. Profit-Sharing and Optimal Labour Contracts. *Can. J. Econ.,* May 1989, 22(2), pp. 425–33.

_____ and Wilson, Thomas A. International Coordination of Macroeconomic Policies: A Review. *Can. Public Policy,* Supplement, February 1989, 15, pp. S20–34.

Devereux, Michael P. The British Experience of Taxing Oil Extraction. In *Helm, D.; Kay, J. and Thompson, D.,* eds., 1989, pp. 411–27.

_____. Tax Asymmetries, the Cost of Capital and Investment: Some Evidence from United Kingdom Panel Data. *Econ. J.,* Supplement, 1989, 99(395), pp. 103–12.

Devine, James. Paradigms as Ideologies: Liberal vs. Marxian Economics. *Rev. Soc. Econ.,* Fall 1989, 47(3), pp. 293–312.

_____ and Dymski, Gary A. Roemer's Theory of Capitalist Exploitation: The Contradictions of Walrasian Marxism. *Rev. Radical Polit. Econ.,* Fall 1989, 21(3), pp. 13–17.

Devinney, Timothy M. Rationally Determined Irrationality: An Extension of the Thesis of Rationality as Anti-entropic. *J. Econ. Psych.,* November 1989, 10(3), pp. 303–19.

Devlin, Robert. Options for Tackling the External Debt Problem. *CEPAL Rev.,* April 1989, (37), pp. 27–44.

Devoto, Fernando J. The Origins of an Italian Neighbourhood in Buenos Aires in the Mid XIX Century. *J. Europ. Econ. Hist.,* Spring 1989, 18(1), pp. 37–64.

Dewald, William G. and Gavin, William T. The Effect of Disinflationary Policies on Monetary Velocity. *Cato J.,* Spring–Summer 1989, 9(1), pp. 149–64.

_____ and Ulan, Michael. The U.S. Net International Investment Position: Misstated and Misunderstood. In *Dorn, J. A. and Niskanen, W. A.,* eds., 1989, pp. 363–94.

Dewatripont, Mathias. Renegotiation and Information Revelation over Time: The Case of Optimal Labor Contracts. *Quart. J. Econ.,* August 1989, 104(3), pp. 589–619.

Dewees, Peter A. The Woodfuel Crisis Reconsidered: Observations on the Dynamics of Abundance and Scarcity. *World Devel.,* August 1989, 17(8), pp. 1159–72.

Dewhurst, John H. Ll. Australian State Consumption Functions 1951–1984. *Australian Econ. Pap.,* June 1989, 28(52), pp. 112–22.

_____. Below Capacity Working and Potential Output in Scottish Manufacturing Industry.

Scot. J. Polit. Econ., February 1989, *36*(1), pp. 71–89.

Dews, Nigel and Carmichael, Jeffrey. Investment and Australian Economic Growth. In *[Gruen, F. H.]*, 1989, pp. 101–32.

Dex, Shirley and Sloane, Peter. The Economics of Discrimination: How Far Have We Come? In *Drago, R. and Perlman, R.*, eds., 1989, pp. 83–104.

Dey, Harendra Kanti. The Genesis and Spread of Economic Corruption: A Microtheoretic Interpretation. *World Devel.*, April 1989, *17*(4), pp. 503–11.

Deyak, Timothy A. and Dunlevy, James A. Seasonal, Cyclical and Secular Stability of Canadian Aggregate Demand for Merchandise Imports, 1957–1982. *Appl. Econ.*, April 1989, *21*(4), pp. 449–59.

_____; **Sawyer, W. Charles and Sprinkle, Richard L.** An Empirical Examination of the Structural Stability of Disaggregated U.S. Import Demand. *Rev. Econ. Statist.*, May 1989, *71*(2), pp. 337–41.

Dhaene, Geert and Barten, Anton P. When It All Began: The 1936 Tinbergen Model Revisited. *Econ. Modelling*, April 1989, *6*(2), pp. 203–19.

Dhaliwal, Naginder S.; Yanagida, John F. and Sarwar, Ghulam. Uncertainty and the Stability of Money Demand Functions for the U.S. Agricultural Sector. *Can. J. Agr. Econ.*, July 1989, *37*(2), pp. 279–89.

Dhesi, Autar Singh and Bhullar, N. S. A Simplified Approach to District Agriculture Plan Formulation. *Margin*, April–June 1989, *21*(3), pp. 66–88.

_____ **and Singh, Harbhajan.** Education, Labour Market Distortions and Relative Earnings of Different Religion-Caste Categories in India (A Case Study of Delhi.) *Can. J. Devel. Stud.*, 1989, *10*(1), pp. 75–89.

Dhillon, Upinder S. and Wansley, James W. Determinants of Valuation Effects for Security Offerings of Commercial Bank Holding Companies. *J. Finan. Res.*, Fall 1989, *12*(3), pp. 217–33.

Di Matteo, Massimo. Early Discussions on Long Waves. In *Di Matteo, M.; Goodwin, R. M. and Vercelli, A.*, eds., 1989, pp. 403–18.

_____; **Goodwin, Richard M. and Vercelli, Alessandro.** Technological and Social Factors in Long Term Fluctuations: Proceedings of an International Workshop Held in Siena, Italy, December 16–18, 1986: Introduction. In *Di Matteo, M.; Goodwin, R. M. and Vercelli, A.*, eds., 1989, pp. v–ix.

Diakosavvas, Dimitris. On the Causes of Food Insecurity in Less Developed Countries: An Empirical Evaluation. *World Devel.*, February 1989, *17*(2), pp. 223–35.

Diamantaras, Dimitrios and Thomson, William. A Refinement and Extension of the No-Envy Concept. *Econ. Letters*, August 1989, *30*(2), pp. 103–07.

Diamantides, N. D. and Constantinou, S. T. Modeling the Macrodynamics of International

Migration: Determinants of Emigration from Cyprus, 1946–85. *Environ. Planning A*, July 1989, *21*(7), pp. 927–50.

Diamantopoulos, Adamantios and Mathews, Brian. Factors Affecting the Nature and Effectiveness of Subjective Revision in Sales Forecasting: An Empirical Study. *Managerial Dec. Econ.*, March 1989, *10*(1), pp. 51–59.

Diamond, Arthur M., Jr. and Locay, Luis. Investment in Sister's Children as Behavior towards Risk. *Econ. Inquiry*, October 1989, *27*(4), pp. 719–35.

Diamond, Charles A.; Simon, Curtis J. and Warner, John T. Evidence on the Fit of the Log-Linear Income Model versus a General Statistical Specification. *Econ. Letters*, December 1989, *31*(3), pp. 293–98.

Diamond, Douglas W. Reputation Acquisition in Debt Markets. *J. Polit. Econ.*, August 1989, *97*(4), pp. 828–62.

Diamond, Ian. Education and Changing Numbers of Young People. In *Joshi, H.*, ed., 1989, pp. 72–89.

_____ **and Clarke, Sue.** Demographic Patterns among Britain's Ethnic Groups. In *Joshi, H.*, ed., 1989, pp. 177–98.

Diamond, Jack. A Note on the Public Choice Approach to the Growth in Government Expenditure. *Public Finance Quart.*, October 1989, *17*(4), pp. 445–61.

Diamond, Peter A. Aggregate Demand Management in Search Equilibrium. In *Diamond, P. and Rothschild, M.*, eds., 1989, *1982*, pp. 557–70.

_____. Building Blocks of Market Clearing Business Cycle Models: Comment. In *Blanchard, O. J. and Fischer, S.*, eds., 1989, pp. 291–300.

_____. The Role of a Stock Market in a General Equilibrium Model with Technological Uncertainty. In *Diamond, P. and Rothschild, M.*, eds., 1989, *1967*, pp. 211–25.

_____. Wage Determination and Efficiency in Search Equilibrium. In *Diamond, P. and Rothschild, M.*, eds., 1989, *1982*, pp. 543–53.

_____ **and Blanchard, Olivier Jean.** The Beveridge Curve. *Brookings Pap. Econ. Act.*, 1989, (1), pp. 1–60.

_____ **and Fudenberg, Drew.** Rational Expectations Business Cycles in Search Equilibrium. *J. Polit. Econ.*, June 1989, *97*(3), pp. 606–19.

Dias, Antonio José R.; Façanha, Luis Otávio and Rodrigues, Denise A. Financiamentos públicos para projetos de pesquisa e desenvolvimento: Uma experiência de avaliação na Finep. (With English summary.) *Pesquisa Planejamento Econ.*, April 1989, *19*(1), pp. 133–60.

Diatkine, Sylvie. La mesure en unités de salaire réel ou monétaire: Une comparaison entre Smith et Keynes. (Real or Monetary Wage Unit of Measurement: Smith and Keynes. With English summary.) *Écon. Societes*, October 1989, *23*(10), pp. 157–78.

Díaz-Alejandro, Carlos. Peronist Economic Policies, 1946–55: Comments on Two (or More)

Peronisms. **In** *di Tella, G. and Dornbusch, R., eds.*, 1989, pp. 86–88.

Díaz-Briquets, Sergio. The Central American Demographic Situation: Trends and Implications. **In** *Bean, F. D.; Schmandt, J. and Weintraub, S., eds.*, 1989, pp. 33–64.

Díaz Paulos, A. M. and D'Alessandro Pereyra, R. Administrative and Compliance Costs of Taxation: Uruguay. **In** *International Fiscal Association, ed. (I)*, 1989, pp. 621–35.

Dichter, Thomas W. The Enterprise Concept: A Comment on Innovations in Participatory Approaches to Development. **In** *Lineberry, W. P., ed.*, 1989, pp. 131–37.

Dick, H. W. Alternative Technology—Small Commercial Sailing Vessels. A Lost Cause? **In** *Couper, A. D., ed.*, 1989, pp. 168–78.

Dicke, Hugo, et al. Effects of Agricultural Trade Liberalization on West Germany's Economy. **In** *Stoeckel, A. B.; Vincent, D. and Cuthbertson, S., eds.*, 1989, pp. 125–49.

Dickens, William T., et al. Employee Crime and the Monitoring Puzzle. *J. Lab. Econ.*, July 1989, *7*(3), pp. 331–47.

Dickhaut, John; Kanodia, Chandra and Bushman, Robert. Escalation Errors and the Sunk Cost Effect: An Explanation Based on Reputation and Information Asymmetries. *J. Acc. Res.*, Spring 1989, *27*(1), pp. 59–77.

Dickie, Mark and Gerking, Shelby. Benefits of Reduced Morbidity from Air Pollution Control: A Survey. **In** *Folmer, H. and van Ierland, E., eds.*, 1989, pp. 105–22.

_____ **and Gerking, Shelby.** Interregional Wage Differentials in the United States: A Survey. **In** *van Dijk, J., et al., eds.*, 1989, pp. 111–45.

Dickinson, Amy and Peterson, David R. Seasonality in the Option Market. *Financial Rev.*, November 1989, *24*(4), pp. 529–40.

Dickson, Keith; Smith, Helen Lawton and Smith, Stephen R. Interfirm Collaboration and Innovation: Strategic Alliances or Reluctant Partnerships? **In** *Mansfield, R., ed.*, 1989, pp. 140–60.

Dickson, Peter R.; Wilkie, William L. and Urbany, Joel E. Buyer Uncertainty and Information Search. *J. Cons. Res.*, September 1989, *16*(2), pp. 208–15.

Dickson, V. A. and Yu, Weiqiu. Welfare Losses in Canadian Manufacturing under Alternative Oligopoly Regimes. *Int. J. Ind. Organ.*, June 1989, *7*(2), pp. 257–67.

Diday, Edwin and Brito, M. Paula. Symbolic Cluster Analysis. **In** *Opitz, O., ed.*, 1989, pp. 45–84.

Diebold, Francis X. Forecast Combination and Encompassing: Reconciling Two Divergent Literatures. *Int. J. Forecasting*, 1989, *5*(4), pp. 589–92.

_____. Intertemporal Consumer Behaviour under Structural Changes in Income: Comment. *Econometric Rev.*, 1989, *8*(1), pp. 93–99.

_____. State Space Modeling of Time Series: A Review Essay. *J. Econ. Dynam. Control*, October 1989, *13*(4), pp. 597–612.

_____. Structural Time Series Analysis and Modelling Package: A Review. *J. Appl. Econometrics*, April–June 1989, *4*(2), pp. 195–204.

_____ **and Nerlove, Marc.** The Dynamics of Exchange Rate Volatility: A Multivariate Latent Factor Arch Model. *J. Appl. Econometrics*, Jan.–March 1989, *4*(1), pp. 1–21.

_____ **and Pauly, Peter.** Forecasting in Situations of Structural Change: A General Approach. **In** *Hackl, P., ed.*, 1989, pp. 297–318.

_____ **and Rudebusch, Glenn D.** Long Memory and Persistence in Aggregate Output. *J. Monet. Econ.*, September 1989, *24*(2), pp. 189–209.

_____ **and Rudebusch, Glenn D.** Scoring the Leading Indicators. *J. Bus.*, July 1989, *62*(3), pp. 369–91.

Diederich, Werner. The Development of Marx's Economic Theory. **In** *Balzer, W. and Hamminga, B., eds.*, 1989, pp. 147–64.

Diefendorf, Jeffry M. Urban Reconstruction in Europe after World War II. *Urban Stud.*, February 1989, *26*(1), pp. 128–43.

Diekmann, Achim. Automobilproduktion als arbeitsteiliger Prozess. (Technological and Structural Aspects of the Automobile Industry. With English summary.) *Jahr. Nationalökon. Statist.*, October 1989, *206*(4–5), pp. 315–28.

Dieleman, F. M.; Clark, W. A. V. and Deurloo, M. C. A Comparative View of Housing Choices in Controlled and Uncontrolled Housing Markets. *Urban Stud.*, October 1989, *26*(5), pp. 457–68.

Dielman, Terry E. and Pfaffenberger, Roger C. Efficiency of Ordinary Least Squares for Linear Models with Autocorrelation. *J. Amer. Statist. Assoc.*, March 1989, *84*(405), pp. 248.

Dienes, Leslie. *Perestroyka* and the Slavic Regions. *Soviet Econ.*, July–Sept. 1989, *5*(3), pp. 251–75.

Dietrich, J. Richard. Voluntary Disclosure Choice and Earnings Information Transfer: Discussion. *J. Acc. Res.*, Supplement, 1989, *27*, pp. 106–10.

Dietz, James L. Radicals and Institutionalists: Holes, Wholes, and Future Directions. **In** *Dugger, W. M., ed.*, 1989, pp. 51–63.

Dietzenbacher, Erik. The Dynamics of Population Growth, Differential Fertility, and Inequality: Comment. *Amer. Econ. Rev.*, June 1989, *79*(3), pp. 584–87.

_____. The Implications of Technical Change in a Marxian Framework. *J. Econ. (Z. Nationalökon.)*, 1989, *50*(1), pp. 35–46.

_____. On the Relationship between the Supply-Driven and the Demand-Driven Input–Output Model. *Environ. Planning A*, November 1989, *21*(11), pp. 1533–39.

Diewert, W. E.; Turunen-Red, A. H. and Woodland, A. D. Productivity- and Pareto-Improving Changes in Taxes and Tariffs. *Rev. Econ. Stud.*, April 1989, *56*(2), pp. 199–215.

DiFranceisco, Wayne and Gitelman, Zvi. Soviet Political Culture and Modes of Covert Influence. **In** *Heidenheimer, A. J.; Johnston, M.*

and LeVine, V. T., eds., 1989, *1984*, pp. 467–88.

Digby, M. P. Marketing Margins in the Meat Sector, England and Wales 1978–1987. *J. Agr. Econ.*, May 1989, *40*(2), pp. 129–42.

Diggle, Peter J. and Zeger, Scott L. A Non-Gaussian Model for Time Series with Pulses. *J. Amer. Statist. Assoc.*, June 1989, *84*(406), pp. 354–59.

Dignan, Tony, et al. Land and Landlessness among Rural-to-Rural Migrants in Nepal's Terai Region. *Int. Reg. Sci. Rev.*, 1989, *12*(2), pp. 189–209.

van Dijk, Jouke, et al. Equilibrating and Adjustment Tendencies of Interregional Migration: An Introduction. In *van Dijk, J., et al., eds.*, 1989, pp. 3–20.

———. Labor Market Institutions and the Efficiency of Interregional Migration: A Cross-Nation Comparison. In *van Dijk, J., et al., eds.*, 1989, pp. 61–83.

Dijkstra, Theo K. Reduced Form Estimation, Hedging against Possible Misspecification. *Int. Econ. Rev.*, May 1989, *30*(2), pp. 373–90.

Dike, Enwre. Food Imports and Agricultural Decline: Some Evidence from Nigeria. *Eastern Afr. Econ. Rev.*, December 1989, *5*(2), pp. 133–59.

DiLiberto, Maryann Fogarty. The Fixed Exchange Rate Period versus the Flexible Rate Period: An Examination of U.S. International Investment for Structural Change. *Quart. J. Bus. Econ.*, Autumn 1989, *28*(4), pp. 77–99.

Dilla, William N. Information Evaluation in a Competitive Environment: Context and Task Effects. *Accounting Rev.*, July 1989, *64*(3), pp. 404–32.

Dillard, Dudley. The Paradox of Money in the Economics of Joan Robinson. In *Feiwel, G. R., ed. (I)*, 1989, pp. 599–612.

Dilley, Roy M. Secrets and Skills: Apprenticeship among Tukolor Weavers. In *Coy, M. W., ed.*, 1989, pp. 181–98.

Dillinger, William. External Sources of Local Government Finance. In *World Bank and Istituto Italo-Africano*, 1989, pp. 105–10.

——— and **Ljung, P.** Approaches for Strengthening Local Governments. In *World Bank and Istituto Italo-Africano*, 1989, pp. 130–35.

Dillon, Carl R.; Mjelde, James W. and McCarl, Bruce A. Biophysical Simulation in Support of Crop Production Decisions: A Case Study in the Blacklands Region of Texas. *Southern J. Agr. Econ.*, July 1989, *21*(1), pp. 73–86.

Dillon, William R.; Mulani, Narendra and Frederick, Donald G. On the Use of Component Scores in the Presence of Group Structure. *J. Cons. Res.*, June 1989, *16*(1), pp. 106–12.

Dilnot, Andrew. Social Security Policy, Defining the Borders of the State. In *Helm, D., ed.*, 1989, pp. 237–50.

——— and **Disney, Richard.** Pensions Schemes after the 1989 Budget. *Fisc. Stud.*, August 1989, *10*(3), pp. 34–49.

——— and **Helm, Dieter.** Energy Policy, Merit Goods, and Social Security. In *Helm, D.; Kay,*

J. and Thompson, D., eds., 1989, *1987*, pp. 55–73.

——— and **Kell, Michael.** Male Unemployment and Women's Work. In *Dilnot, A. and Walker, I., eds.*, 1989, pp. 153–68.

——— and **Stark, Graham.** The Poverty Trap, Tax Cuts, and the Reform of Social Security. In *Dilnot, A. and Walker, I., eds.*, 1989, pp. 169–78.

——— and **Walker, Ian.** Economic Issues in Social Security: Introduction. In *Dilnot, A. and Walker, I., eds.*, 1989, pp. 1–15.

——— and **Webb, Steven.** Reforming National Insurance Contributions: A Progress Report. *Fisc. Stud.*, May 1989, *10*(2), pp. 38–47.

——— and **Webb, Steven.** The 1988 Social Security Reforms. In *Dilnot, A. and Walker, I., eds.*, 1989, pp. 239–67.

Dilts, David A. and Deitsch, Clarence R. The Arbitration Literature: Who Contributes? *J. Lab. Res.*, Spring 1989, *10*(2), pp. 207–14.

Dimand, Robert W. A Neglected Monetary Standard Alternative: Gold/Commodity Bimetallism: Comment. In *Hamouda, O. F.; Rowley, R. and Wolf, B. M., eds.*, 1989, pp. 212–13.

Dimelis, Sophia P. and Kollintzas, Tryphon. A Linear Rational Expectations Equilibrium Model of the American Petroleum Industry. In *Kollintzas, T., ed.*, 1989, pp. 110–97.

Dimitri, Nicola. Some Results on Ranked Contracts. *Econ. Notes*, 1989, (2), pp. 274–81.

Dimsdale, N. H.; Nickell, Stephen J. and Horsewood, N. Real Wages and Unemployment in Britain during the 1930s. *Econ. J.*, June 1989, *99*(396), pp. 271–92.

Dimson, Elroy. The Discount Rate for a Power Station. *Energy Econ.*, July 1989, *11*(3), pp. 175–80.

Dinan, Terry M. and Miranowski, John A. Estimating the Implicit Price of Energy Efficiency Improvements in the Residential Housing Market: A Hedonic Approach. *J. Urban Econ.*, January 1989, *25*(1), pp. 52–67.

Dinar, Ariel. Provision of and Request for Agricultural Extension Services. *Amer. J. Agr. Econ.*, May 1989, *71*(2), pp. 294–302.

———; **Zilberman, David and Casterline, Gary.** The Adoption of Modern Irrigation Technologies in the United States. In *Schmitz, A., ed.*, 1989, pp. 222–48.

Dinenis, Elias, et al. The London Business School Econometric Model: Some Recent Developments. *Econ. Modelling*, July 1989, *6*(3), pp. 243–351.

Dinenzon, Marcelo and Hopenhayn, Benjamin. Debt and World Money. In *Singer, H. W. and Sharma, S., eds. (I)*, 1989, pp. 181–98.

Dingemans, Dennis and Munn, Andrew. Acquisition-Based Assessment and Property Tax Inequalities after California's 1978 Proposition Thirteen. *Growth Change*, Winter 1989, *20*(1), pp. 55–66.

Dinh, Khoan T. and Herbert, John H. A Note on Bias from Proxy Variables with Systematic Errors. *Econ. Letters*, September 1989, *30*(3), pp. 207–09.

Dini, Lamberto. Economic Policy and European Unemployment. *Aussenwirtschaft*, April 1989, *44*(1), pp. 75–92.

Dinkins, David N. NEA Twentieth Anniversary Luncheon: Keynote Address. *Rev. Black Polit. Econ.*, Summer 1989, *18*(1), pp. 31–36.

Dinopoulos, Elias. Dynamic Duopoly with Output Adjustment Costs in International Markets: Taking the Conjecture out of Conjectual Variations: Comment. In *Feenstra, R. C., ed.*, 1989, pp. 138–39.

_____ **and Kreinin, Mordechai E.** Import Quotas and VERs: A Comparative Analysis in a Three-Country Framework. *J. Int. Econ.*, February 1989, *26*(1/2), pp. 169–78.

Dinwiddy, Caroline and Teal, Francis. Project Appraisal and Foreign Exchange Constraints: A Response. *Econ. J.*, June 1989, *99*(396), pp. 483.

_____ **and Teal, Francis.** Relative Shadow Prices and the Shadow Exchange Rate. *J. Public Econ.*, December 1989, *40*(3), pp. 349–58.

Dioné, Josué; Dembélé, N. Nango and Staatz, John M. Cereals Market Liberalization in Mali. *World Devel.*, May 1989, *17*(5), pp. 703–18.

Dionne, Georges and Boyer, Marcel. An Empirical Analysis of Moral Hazard and Experience Rating. *Rev. Econ. Statist.*, February 1989, *71*(1), pp. 128–34.

_____ **and Boyer, Marcel.** More on Insurance, Protection, and Risk. *Can. J. Econ.*, February 1989, *22*(1), pp. 202–04.

_____ **; Eeckhoudt, Louis and Briys, Eric.** More on Insurance as a Giffen Good. *J. Risk Uncertainty*, December 1989, *2*(4), pp. 415–20.

_____ **; Kihlstrom, Richard and Boyer, Marcel.** Insurance and the Value of Publicly Available Information. In *[Hadar, J.]*, 1989, pp. 137–55.

Dirlik, Arif. Postsocialism? Reflections on "Socialism with Chinese Characteristics." In *Dirlik, A. and Meisner, M., eds.*, 1989, pp. 362–84.

_____. Revolutionary Hegemony and the Language of Revolution: Chinese Socialism between Present and Future. In *Dirlik, A. and Meisner, M., eds.*, 1989, pp. 27–39.

_____ **and Meisner, Maurice.** Politics, Scholarship, and Chinese Socialism. In *Dirlik, A. and Meisner, M., eds.*, 1989, pp. 3–26.

Dirninger, Christian. Schmoller's Approach to Economic Policy, Especially Industrial and Commercial Policy. *Int. J. Soc. Econ.*, 1989, *16*(9–10–11), pp. 117–31.

Dirrigl, Hans and Schaum, Wolfgang. Ausschüttungsplanung nach der Steurerreform 1990. (With English summary.) *Z. Betriebswirtshaft*, March 1989, *59*(3), pp. 291–309.

Disney, Richard and Creedy, John. The Australian Pension Scheme: Some Basic Analytics. *Econ. Rec.*, December 1989, *65*(191), pp. 357–68.

_____ **and Creedy, John.** Can We Afford to Grow Older? Population Aging and Social Security. *Europ. Econ. Rev.*, March 1989, *33*(2/3), pp. 367–76.

_____ **and Creedy, John.** The New Pension Scheme in Britain. In *Dilnot, A. and Walker, I., eds.*, 1989, pp. 224–38.

_____ **and Creedy, John.** Public and Private Partnerships in Social Security: Recent UK Policy. In *Gustafsson, B. A. and Klevmarken, N. A., eds.*, 1989, pp. 211–35.

_____ **and Creedy, John.** The "Twin-Pillar" Approach to Social Insurance in the UK. *Scot. J. Polit. Econ.*, May 1989, *36*(2), pp. 113–24.

_____ **and Dilnot, Andrew.** Pensions Schemes after the 1989 Budget. *Fisc. Stud.*, August 1989, *10*(3), pp. 34–49.

_____ **and Gospel, Howard F.** The Seniority Model of Trade Union Behaviour: A (Partial) Defence. *Brit. J. Ind. Relat.*, July 1989, *27*(2), pp. 179–95.

_____ **and Webb, Steven.** Is There a Market Failure in Occupational Sick Pay? In *Dilnot, A. and Walker, I., eds.*, 1989, pp. 52–68.

Disney, W. Terry; Duffy, Patricia A. and Hardy, William E., Jr. A Markov Chain Analysis of Pork Farm Size Distributions in the South: Reply. *Southern J. Agr. Econ.*, December 1989, *21*(2), pp. 219–20.

Dittmar, Rolf. Development and Problems of Reform in the Chinese Economic System. In *Gemper, B. B., ed.*, 1989, pp. 118–23.

Dittus, Peter. The Budgetary Dimension of the Debt Crisis in Low-Income Sub-Saharan Countries. *J. Inst. Theoretical Econ.*, June 1989, *145*(2), pp. 358–66.

Divisekera, Sarath and Felmingham, B. S. Sri Lankan Economic Performance and Income Distribution in Various Policy Epochs. *Singapore Econ. Rev.*, April 1989, *34*(1), pp. 43–49.

Diwakar, Ashok and Sharma, H. R. Transfer of Technology and Response of Small Farmers. *Margin*, Jan.–March 1989, *21*(2), pp. 45–51.

Diwan, Ishac. Foreign Debt, Crowding Out and Capital Flight. *J. Int. Money Finance*, March 1989, *8*(1), pp. 121–36.

_____ **and Claessens, Stijn.** Liquidity, Debt Relief, and Conditionality. In *Husain, I. and Diwan, I., eds.*, 1989, pp. 213–25.

_____ **and Claessens, Stijn.** Market-Based Debt Reduction. In *Husain, I. and Diwan, I., eds.*, 1989, pp. 258–72.

_____ **and Husain, Ishrat.** Dealing with the Debt Crisis: Introduction. In *Husain, I. and Diwan, I., eds.*, 1989, pp. 1–11.

Diwan, Romesh and Chakraborty, Chandana. R&D and Components of Technical Change. *Eastern Econ. J.*, Oct.–Dec. 1989, *15*(4), pp. 365–71.

_____ **and Qureshi, Muzaffar.** Inter-firm Diffusion of Innovations: Shuttleless Looms in Pakistan. *Indian J. Quant. Econ.*, 1989, *5*(1), pp. 47–62.

Dixit, Avinash K. Entry and Exit Decisions under Uncertainty. *J. Polit. Econ.*, June 1989, *97*(3), pp. 620–38.

_____. Hysteresis, Import Penetration, and Exchange Rate Pass-Through. *Quart. J. Econ.*, May 1989, *104*(2), pp. 205–28.

_____. Intersectoral Capital Reallocation under

Price Uncertainty. *J. Int. Econ.*, May 1989, *26*(3/4), pp. 309–25.

———. Trade and Insurance with Adverse Selection. *Rev. Econ. Stud.*, April 1989, *56*(2), pp. 235–47.

———. Trade and Insurance with Imperfectly Observed Outcomes. *Quart. J. Econ.*, February 1989, *104*(1), pp. 195–203.

Dixit, Praveen M. and Roningen, Vernon O. Quantitative Impacts of Creating an Agricultural Free Trade Area between the United States and Canada. *Can. J. Agr. Econ.*, Part 2, December 1989, *37*(4), pp. 1023–33.

Dixon, Bruce L.; Sonka, Steven T. and Hornbaker, Robert H. Estimating Production Activity Costs for Multioutput Firms with a Random Coefficient Regression Model. *Amer. J. Agr. Econ.*, February 1989, *71*(1), pp. 167–77.

———; **Sonka, Steven T. and Mjelde, James W.** Estimating the Value of Sequential Updating Solutions for Intrayear Crop Management. *Western J. Agr. Econ.*, July 1989, *14*(1), pp. 1–8.

——— and **Ward, Ronald W.** Effectiveness of Fluid Milk Advertising since the Dairy and Tobacco Adjustment Act of 1983. *Amer. J. Agr. Econ.*, August 1989, *71*(3), pp. 730–40.

Dixon, J. E. From Centralism to Devolution: Reforming Local Government in New Zealand. *Reg. Stud.*, June 1989, *23*(3), pp. 267–71.

Dixon, John and Scheurell, Robert P. Social Welfare in Developed Market Countries: Preface. In *Dixon, J. and Scheurell, R. P.*, eds., 1989, pp. vii–xii.

Dixon, John A. Multilevel Resource Analysis and Management: The Case of Watersheds. In *Schramm, G. and Warford, J. J.*, eds., 1989, pp. 185–200.

Dixon, Peter B. and Adams, Philip D. Forecasts for the Australian Economy in 1989–90 and 1990–91. *Australian Econ. Rev.*, Summer 1989, (88), pp. 5–31.

——— and **McDonald, Daina.** The Australian Economy in 1988–89 and 1989–90. *Australian Econ. Rev.*, Autumn 1989, (85), pp. 3–23.

Dixon, Rob. Venture Capitalists and Investment Appraisal. *Nat. Westminster Bank Quart. Rev.*, November 1989, pp. 2–21.

Dixon, Robert. Industrial Structure. In *[Gruen, F. H.]*, 1989, pp. 81–100.

———. The Wage-Share and the Rate of Exchange of Labor Time. In *Feiwel, G. R.*, ed. *(II)*, 1989, pp. 677–83.

——— and **McCombie, J. S. L.** Inter-industry Differences in the Factor-Augmenting Bias of Technological Change. *Australian Econ. Pap.*, June 1989, *28*(52), pp. 103–11.

Djajić, Slobodan. Current-Account Effects of a Temporary Change in Government Expenditure. *Scand. J. Econ.*, 1989, *91*(1), pp. 83–96.

———. Dynamics of the Exchange Rate in Anticipation of Pegging. *J. Int. Money Finance*, December 1989, *8*(4), pp. 559–71.

———. Migrants in a Guest-Worker System: A Utility Maximizing Approach. *J. Devel. Econ.*, October 1989, *31*(2), pp. 327–39.

———. Skills and the Pattern of Migration: The Role of Qualitative and Quantitative Restrictions on International Labor Mobility. *Int. Econ. Rev.*, November 1989, *30*(4), pp. 795–809.

——— and **Kierzkowski, Henryk.** Goods, Services and Trade. *Economica*, February 1989, *56*(221), pp. 83–95.

Djarova, J. and Panov, O. Strategic Planning and Economic Growth in Bulgaria. In *Krelle, W.*, ed., 1989, pp. 407–17.

Djeto, Assane and Pourgerami, Abbas. Inflation–Growth Trade-Off in an Export-Oriented Rural Economy: The Case of Ghana. *Eastern Afr. Econ. Rev.*, June 1989, *5*(1), pp. 32–41.

Dlamini, B. Sibusiso. Extracts from Budget Speech 1989: Swaziland. *Bull. Int. Fiscal Doc.*, June 1989, *43*(6), pp. 291–92.

Dmitriev, V. V. What We Don't Know. *Prob. Econ.*, July 1989, *32*(3), pp. 59–71.

Dnes, Antony W. Rent Seeking, Conflict and Property Rights. *Scot. J. Polit. Econ.*, November 1989, *36*(4), pp. 366–74.

Doak, Ervin John. Income Tax Progressivity and Reform. *Atlantic Econ. J.*, June 1989, *17*(2), pp. 47–52.

Dobos, K. and Ligeti, C. Markov Chain Modelling of Differentiation of Farms. In *Bauer, S. and Henrichsmeyer, W.*, eds., 1989, pp. 157–64.

Dobozi, István. Patterns, Determinants, and Prospects of East–South Economic Relations. In *Schulz, B. H. and Hansen, W. W.*, eds., 1989, pp. 111–36.

——— and **Brada, Josef C.** Economic Reform in Hungary: An Overview and Assessment. *Eastern Europ. Econ.*, Fall 1989, *28*(1), pp. 3–13.

Dobrinsky, Rumen Nikolov. The CMEA Country Models of the Bonn–IIASA Project: Closed CPE Models in an Open Environment. *Acta Oecon.*, 1989, *41*(3–4), pp. 313–40.

———. Comparison of Gross Domestic Product and Net Material Product: Appendix: GDP Estimates for the CMEA Countries in the Bonn–IIASA Project. In *Krelle, W.*, ed., 1989, pp. 597–99.

———. Economic Growth and Structural Change of CMEA Countries. In *Krelle, W.*, ed., 1989, pp. 119–42.

———. The Macroeconomic Models of the European CMEA Countries. In *Krelle, W.*, ed., 1989, pp. 143–171.

——— and **Székely, István.** Growth in and Interdependent World Economy: Linking the National Models through International Trade. In *Krelle, W.*, ed., 1989, pp. 199–232.

Dobrowolski, Grzegorz and Rys, Tomasz. Architecture and Functionality of MIDA. In *Lewandowski, A. and Wierzbicki, A. P.*, eds., 1989, pp. 339–70.

——— and **Zebrowski, Maciej.** Basic Model of an Industrial Structure. In *Lewandowski, A. and Wierzbicki, A. P.*, eds., 1989, pp. 287–93.

——— and **Zebrowski, Maciej.** Hierarchical Multiobjective Approach to a Programming Problem. In *Lewandowski, A. and Wierzbicki, A. P., eds.,* 1989, pp. 310–21.

_____, et al. POSTAN 3 and PLP: Extensions of MINOS for Postoptimal Analysis. In *Lewandowski, A. and Wierzbicki, A. P., eds.,* 1989, pp. 391–99.

Dobson, Stephen M. Jobs in Space: Some Evidence on Spatial Uniformity in the Job Generation Process. *Urban Stud.,* December 1989, 26(6), pp. 611–25.

_____ **and Gerrard, Bill J.** Growth and Profitability in the Leeds Engineering Sector. *Scot. J. Polit. Econ.,* November 1989, 36(4), pp. 334–52.

_____; **Goddard, John A. and Bowers, John K.** The Property Market and Industrial Location. *Scot. J. Polit. Econ.,* February 1989, 36(1), pp. 1–18.

Dobson, William D. and Barnard, Freddie L. The Prospects for Successfully Restructuring the Farm Credit System. In *Horwich, G. and Lynch, G. J., eds.,* 1989, pp. 238–66.

Döckel, J. A. and Pringle, W. A. The South African Angora Goat and Mohair Industry. *S. Afr. J. Econ.,* September 1989, 57(3), pp. 215–30.

Dockès, Pierre and Rosier, Bernard. Un schéma explicatif des rythmes longs: Application à la "crise" contemporaine. (A Schema for Explaining Long Waves: An Application to the Present Crisis. With English summary.) *Écon. Societes,* March 1989, 23(3), pp. 43–55.

Dockner, Engelbert J.; Feichtinger, Gustav and Mehlmann, Alexander. Noncooperative Solutions for a Differential Game Model of Fishery. *J. Econ. Dynam. Control,* January 1989, 13(1), pp. 1–20.

_____ **and Kaitala, Veijo.** On Efficient Equilibrium Solutions in Dynamic Games of Resource Management. *Resources & Energy,* March 1989, 11(1), pp. 23–34.

Dodds, C. and Dar, Atul A. Interest Rates, the Emergency Fund Hypothesis and Saving through Endowment Policies: Some Empirical Evidence for the U.K. *J. Risk Ins.,* September 1989, 56(3), pp. 415–33.

Dodge, D. A. Economic Objectives of Tax Reform. In *Mintz, J. and Whalley, J., eds.,* 1989, pp. 36–44.

Dodson, Joe. Advertising Experiments at the Campbell Soup Company: Commentary. *Marketing Sci.,* Winter 1989, 8(1), pp. 72–73.

Doern, G. Bruce. Tax Expenditure Decisions and the Budgetary Decision Process. In *Bruce, N., ed.,* 1989, pp. 105–22.

_____ **and Prince, Michael J.** The Political Administration of School Closures: Administrators, Trustees and Community Groups. *Can. Public Policy,* December 1989, 15(4), pp. 450–69.

Doessel, D. P. Cost–Benefit Analysis of Water Fluoridation in Townsville, Australia. In *Butler, J. R. G. and Doessel, D. P., eds.,* 1989, 1985, pp. 291–98.

_____. Economic Analysis and End-Stage Renal Disease—An Australian Study. In *Butler, J.*

R. G. and Doessel, D. P., eds., 1989, 1978, pp. 278–90.

_____. Should Government Regulate Technology to Reduce Health Expenditures? Some Australian Results for the Policy Debate. In *Butler, J. R. G. and Doessel, D. P., eds.,* 1989, 1987, pp. 250–61.

_____ **and Butler, J. R. G.** The Australian Health Industry: Structure and Sources of Funds. In *Butler, J. R. G. and Doessel, D. P., eds.,* 1989, pp. 63–72.

_____ **and Butler, J. R. G.** Health Economics: Australian Readings: General Introduction. In *Butler, J. R. G. and Doessel, D. P., eds.,* 1989, pp. xi–xvi.

Doganis, Rigas. Regulatory Changes in International Air Transport. In *Button, K. and Swann, D., eds.,* 1989, pp. 166–88.

Doghri, Lamine; Nabli, Mustapha K. and Nugent, Jeffrey B. The Size Distribution and Ownership Type of Firms in Tunisian Manufacturing. In *Nabli, M. K. and Nugent, J. B., eds.,* 1989, pp. 200–232.

Doherty, Neil A. Risk-Bearing Contracts for Space Enterprises. *J. Risk Ins.,* September 1989, 56(3), pp. 396–414.

Dohner, Robert S. and Intal, Ponciano, Jr. Debt Crisis and Adjustment in the Philippines. In *Sachs, J. D., ed. (II),* 1989, pp. 169–91.

_____ **and Intal, Ponciano, Jr.** The Marcos Legacy: Economic Policy and Foreign Debt in the Philippines. In *Sachs, J. D. and Collins, S. M., eds.,* 1989, pp. 371–614.

Dohse, Knut; Jürgens, Ulrich and Malsch, Thomas. From "Fordism" to "Toyotaism"? The Social Organization of the Labor Process in the Japanese Automobile Industry. In *Park, S.-J., ed.,* 1989, pp. 9–43.

Doi, Noriyuki. Enterprise Groups and Market Performance in Japanese Manufacturing Industries. *Rivista Int. Sci. Econ. Com.,* February 1989, 36(2), pp. 143–53.

_____ **and Shinjo, Koji.** Welfare Loss Calculation for Japanese Industries. *Int. J. Ind. Organ.,* June 1989, 7(2), pp. 243–56.

Dokko, Yoon. Are Changes in Inflation Expectations Capitalized into Stock Prices? A Microfirm Test for the Nominal Contracting Hypothesis. *Rev. Econ. Statist.,* May 1989, 71(2), pp. 309–17.

_____ **and Edelstein, Robert H.** How Well Do Economists Forecast Stock Market Prices? A Study of the Livingston Surveys. *Amer. Econ. Rev.,* September 1989, 79(4), pp. 865–71.

Dökmeci, Vedia F. Multi-plant Location with Respect to Uniform Pricing. *Ann. Reg. Sci.,* 1989, 23(1), pp. 29–39.

_____. Multiplant Location with Respect to Price-Elastic Demand. *Environ. Planning A,* September 1989, 21(9), pp. 1169–78.

Dolado, Juan J. and Burgess, Simon M. Intertemporal Rules with Variable Speed of Adjustment: An Application to U.K. Manufacturing Employment. *Econ. J.,* June 1989, 99(396), pp. 347–65.

_____ **and Maravall, A.** Intertemporal Consumer Behaviour under Structural Changes in Income: Comment. *Econometric Rev.*, 1989, 8(1), pp. 101–09.

Dolan, James G. Choosing Initial Antibiotic Therapy for Acute Pyelonephritis. In *Golden, B. L.; Wasil, E. A. and Harker, P. T., eds.*, 1989, pp. 213–24.

Dollar, David. Employment and Income Effects of Multinational Production by U.S. Computer Firms. *Int. Econ. J.*, Winter 1989, 3(4), pp. 1–17.

Dollery, B. E. Capital, Labour and State: A General Equilibrium Perspective on Liberal and Revisionist Approaches to South African Political Economy. *S. Afr. J. Econ.*, June 1989, 57(2), pp. 124–36.

———. Capital, Labour and State: A Rent-Seeking Framework for South African Political Economy. *J. Stud. Econ. Econometrics*, August 1989, 13(2), pp. 59–70.

———. Financial Sanctions against South Africa. *S. Afr. J. Econ.*, December 1989, 57(4), pp. 393–401.

Dölling, Irene. Culture and Gender. In *Rueschemeyer, M. and Lemke, C., eds.*, 1989, pp. 27–47.

Dolton, P. J.; Makepeace, G. H. and Van Der Klaauw, W. Occupational Choice and Earnings Determination: The Role of Sample Selection and Non-pecuniary Factors. *Oxford Econ. Pap.*, July 1989, 41(3), pp. 573–94.

Domanski, Boleslaw. Attitudes to Industrial Development and Quality of Life in Poland. In *Linge, G. J. R. and van der Knaap, G. A., eds.*, 1989, pp. 50–66.

Domar, Evsey D. An Index-Number Tournament. In *Domar, E. D.*, 1989, *1967*, pp. 107–25.

———. The Blind Men and the Elephant: An Essay on Isms. In *Domar, E. D.*, 1989, pp. 29–46.

———. Capitalism, Socialism, and Serfdom: Foreword. In *Domar, E. D.*, 1989, pp. xi–xix.

———. The Causes of Slavery or Serfdom: A Hypothesis. In *Domar, E. D.*, 1989, *1970*, pp. 225–38.

———. On the Measurement of Comparative Efficiency. In *Domar, E. D.*, 1989, *1971*, pp. 126–40.

———. On the Measurement of Technological Change. In *Domar, E. D.*, 1989, *1961*, pp. 49–72.

———. On the Optimal Compensation of a Socialist Manager. In *Domar, E. D.*, 1989, *1974*, pp. 202–22.

———. On Total Productivity and All That: A Review Article. In *Domar, E. D.*, 1989, *1962*, pp. 73–90.

———. Poor Old Capitalism: A Review Article. In *Domar, E. D.*, 1989, *1974*, pp. 15–28.

———. Reflections on Economic Development. In *Domar, E. D.*, 1989, *1966*, pp. 3–14.

———. The Soviet Collective Farm as a Producer Cooperative. In *Domar, E. D.*, 1989, *1966*, pp. 176–201.

———. Special Features of Industrialization in Planned Economies: A Comparison between the Soviet Union and the United States. In *Domar, E. D.*, 1989, *1965*, pp. 143–75.

———. Were Russian Serfs Overcharged for Their Land by the 1861 Emancipation? The History of One Historical Table. In *Grantham, G. and Leonard, C. S., eds., Pt. B*, 1989, pp. 429–39.

———. Were Russian Serfs Overcharged for Their Land by the 1861 Emancipation? The History of One Historical Table. In *Domar, E. D.*, 1989, pp. 280–88.

——— **and Machina, Mark J.** On the Profitability of Russian Serfdom. In *Domar, E. D.*, 1989, *1984*, pp. 239–79.

———, **et al.** Economic Growth and Productivity in the United States, Canada, United Kingdom, Germany, and Japan in the Post-war Period. In *Domar, E. D.*, 1989, *1964*, pp. 91–106.

Domberger, Simon. A Reconsideration of Franchise Contracts for Natural Monopolies. In *UNDTCD*, 1989, pp. 62–75.

——— **and Sherr, Avrom.** The Impact of Competition on Pricing and Quality of Legal Services. *Int. Rev. Law Econ.*, June 1989, 9(1), pp. 41–56.

Dombois, Rainer. Flexibility by Law? The West German Employment Promotion Act and Temporary Employment. *Cambridge J. Econ.*, June 1989, 13(2), pp. 359–71.

Dome, Takuo. A Theoretical Analysis of Sismondi's Tableau Economique. *Metroecon.*, June 1989, 40(2), pp. 119–34.

Domingo, Jannette O. Employment, Income and Economic Identity in the U.S. Virgin Islands. *Rev. Black Polit. Econ.*, Summer 1989, 18(1), pp. 37–57.

Domínguez, Jorge I. International and National Aspects of the Catholic Church in Cuba. In *Mesa-Lago, C., ed.*, 1989, pp. 43–60.

Domínguez, José M.; Molina, Agustín and Sanchez, José. El impuesto sobre el gasto personal: Algunas cuestiones básicas para el caso español. (With English summary.) *Invest. Ecón.*, May 1989, 13(2), pp. 269–81.

Domínguez Ugá, María Alicia. Economic Analysis of the Vaccination Strategies Adopted in Brazil in 1982. In *WHO, Pan American Health Organization*, 1989, pp. 123–41.

Dominique, C. René. An Alternative to Goodwill in Advertising Competition Models. *Metroecon.*, June 1989, 40(2), pp. 147–58.

Dommel, Paul R. and Rasey, Keith P. Coping with the Loss of General Revenue Sharing in Ohio. *Public Budg. Finance*, Autumn 1989, 9(3), pp. 43–51.

Domowitz, Ian and Calomiris, Charles W. Asset Substitution, Money Demand, and the Inflation Process in Brazil. *J. Money, Credit, Banking*, February 1989, 21(1), pp. 78–89.

Donaldson, A. R. The World Bank on Trade Liberalisation. *S. Afr. J. Econ.*, March 1989, 57(1), pp. 79–87.

Donaldson, C. and Gerard, K. Effects of Payment

and Ownership on Hospital Efficiency. **In** *Smith, C. S., ed.,* 1989, pp. 265–82.

_____ **and Glasziou, P.** Cost Utility Analysis: The Compatibility of Measurement Techniques and the Measurement of Utility through Time: Commentary. **In** *Smith, C. S., ed.,* 1989, pp. 61–63.

Donaldson, John B.; Mehra, Rajnish and Danthine, Jean-Pierre. On Some Computational Aspects of Equilibrium Business Cycle Theory. *J. Econ. Dynam. Control,* July 1989, *13*(3), pp. 449–70.

Donatos, George S. and Mergos, George J. Consumer Behaviour in Greece: An Application of the Almost Ideal Demand System. *Appl. Econ.,* July 1989, *21*(7), pp. 983–93.

_____ **and Mergos, George J.** Demand for Food in Greece: An Almost Ideal Demand System Analysis. *J. Agr. Econ.,* May 1989, *40*(2), pp. 178–84.

_____ **and Mergos, George J.** Energy Demand in Greece: The Impact of the Two Energy Crises. *Energy Econ.,* April 1989, *11*(2), pp. 147–52.

Donescu, Al. The Simplex Algorithm with the Aid of a Gauss–Seidel Method. *Econ. Computat. Econ. Cybern. Stud. Res.,* 1989, *24*(2–3), pp. 127–32.

Dong, Fureng. On the Question of the Forms of Socialist Ownership in China. *Chinese Econ. Stud.,* Fall 1989, *23*(1), pp. 8–23.

Donges, Juergen B. The 1980s Economic Growth Weakness in Europe: Focusing on the Supply Side. *Econ. Rec.,* June 1989, *65*(189), pp. 165–76.

_____; **Klodt, Henning and Schmidt, Klaus-Dieter.** Prospective Structural Changes in the West German Economy. **In** *Krelle, W., ed.,* 1989, pp. 385–98.

_____ **and Schatz, Klaus-Werner.** The Iberian Countries in the EEC—Risks and Chances for Their Manufacturing Industries. **In** *Yannopoulos, G. N., ed.,* 1989, pp. 254–306.

Donkers, H. W. J., et al. Adjusting the CPI for Indirect Taxes. **In** *Turvey, R.,* 1989, pp. 139–45.

Donn, Clifford B. Concession Bargaining in the Ocean-Going Maritime Industry. *Ind. Lab. Relat. Rev.,* January 1989, *42*(2), pp. 189–200.

Donnelly, Tom and Thoms, David. Trade Unions, Management and the Search for Production in the Coventry Motor Car Industry, 1939–75. **In** *Harvey, C. and Turner, J., eds.,* 1989, pp. 98–113.

Donnenfeld, Shabtai and Das, Satya P. Oligopolistic Competition and International Trade: Quantity and Quality Restrictions. *J. Int. Econ.,* November 1989, *27*(3–4), pp. 299–318.

Donner, Allan and Campbell, M. Karen. Classification Efficiency of Multinomial Logistic Regression Relative to Ordinal Logistic Regression. *J. Amer. Statist. Assoc.,* June 1989, *84*(406), pp. 587–91.

Donohue, John J., III. Diverting the Coasean River: Incentive Schemes to Reduce Unemployment Spells: Reply. *Yale Law J.,* Decem-

ber 1989, *99*(3), pp. 635–36.

_____. Diverting the Coasean River: Incentive Schemes to Reduce Unemployment Spells. *Yale Law J.,* December 1989, *99*(3), pp. 549–609.

Donsimoni, Marie-Paule; Gabszewicz, Jean Jaskold and Anderson, Simon P. Is International Trade Profitable to Oligopolistic Industries? *Int. Econ. Rev.,* November 1989, *30*(4), pp. 725–33.

_____ **and Polemarchakis, H. M.** Intertemporal Equilibrium and Disadvantageous Growth. *Europ. Econ. Rev.,* January 1989, *33*(1), pp. 59–65.

Donthu, Naveen and Rust, Roland T. Estimating Geographic Customer Densities Using Kernel Density Estimation. *Marketing Sci.,* Spring 1989, *8*(2), pp. 191–203.

Donzelli, Franco. Individualismo metodologico ed equilibrio economico: Una risposta. (Methodological Individualism and Economic Equilibrium: A Reply. With English summary.) *Econ. Politica,* April 1989, *6*(1), pp. 133–46.

_____ **and Zamagni, Stefano.** Epistemology and Economic Theory: Introduction. *Ricerche Econ.,* Jan.–June 1989, *43*(1–2), pp. 3–7.

Dooley, Michael P. Assessing Buy-Back Benefits: Reply. *Int. Monet. Fund Staff Pap.,* September 1989, *36*(3), pp. 736–37.

_____. Buy-Backs, Debt-Equity Swaps, Asset Exchanges, and Market Prices of External Debt. **In** *Frenkel, J. A.; Dooley, M. P. and Wickham, P., eds.,* 1989, pp. 130–50.

_____. Debt Relief and Leveraged Buy-Outs. *Int. Econ. Rev.,* February 1989, *30*(1), pp. 71–75.

_____. Macroeconomic Interactions between the North and South: Comment. **In** *Bryant, R. C., et al., eds.,* 1989, pp. 413–14.

_____. Market Valuation of External Debt. **In** *Frenkel, J. A.; Dooley, M. P. and Wickham, P., eds.,* 1989, pp. 75–82.

_____. World Payments Imbalances and U.S. Statistics: Comment. **In** *Lipsey, R. E. and Tice, H. S., eds.,* 1989, pp. 429–30.

_____ **and Corden, W. Max.** Issues in Debt Strategy: An Overview. **In** *Frenkel, J. A.; Dooley, M. P. and Wickham, P., eds.,* 1989, pp. 10–37.

_____; **Lizondo, José Saúl and Mathieson, Donald J.** The Currency Composition of Foreign Exchange Reserves. *Int. Monet. Fund Staff Pap.,* June 1989, *36*(2), pp. 385–434.

_____ **and Spinelli, Franco.** The Early Stages of Financial Innovation and Money Demand in France and Italy. *Manchester Sch. Econ. Soc. Stud.,* June 1989, *57*(2), pp. 107–24.

_____ **and Symansky, Steven A.** Comparing Menu Items: Methodological Considerations and Policy Issues. **In** *Frenkel, J. A.; Dooley, M. P. and Wickham, P., eds.,* 1989, pp. 398–411.

_____ **and Watson, C. Maxwell.** Reinvigorating the Debt Strategy. *Finance Devel.,* September 1989, *26*(3), pp. 8–11.

_____; **Wickham, Peter and Frenkel, Jacob A.**

An Introduction to Analytical Issues in Debt. In *Frenkel, J. A.; Dooley, M. P. and Wickham, P., eds.*, 1989, pp. 1–9.

Dooley, Peter C. Ricardo and Keynes on War Finance. *Atlantic Econ. J.*, September 1989, *17*(3), pp. 21–33.

Doolittle, Susan. The Business Economist at Work: The Port of Seattle. *Bus. Econ.*, January 1989, *24*(1), pp. 46–47.

van Doorn, J. The Role of a National Investment Bank in Macroeconomic Policy. In *Muller, F. and Zwezerijnen, W. J., eds.*, 1989, pp. 107–21.

Doornik, Jurgen and Barmby, Tim. Modelling Trip Frequency as a Poisson Variable. *J. Transp. Econ. Policy*, September 1989, *23*(3), pp. 309–15.

van Doorslaer, Eddy; Paci, Pierella and Wagstaff, Adam. Equity in the Finance and Delivery of Health Care: Some Tentative Cross-country Comparisons. *Oxford Rev. Econ. Policy*, Spring 1989, *5*(1), pp. 89–112.

Döpcke, Wolfgang. 'Magomo's Maize': State and Peasants during the Depression in Colonial Zimbabwe. In *Brown, I., ed.*, 1989, pp. 29–58.

Dopfer, Kurt. Causality and Consciousness in Economics: Concepts of Change in Orthodox and Heterodox Economics. In *Tool, M. R. and Samuels, W. J., eds. (II)*, 1989, *1986*, pp. 50–64.

Doppegieter, J. J.; Hamman, W. D. and Lambrechts, I. J. The Importance of Public Utilities in South Africa. *J. Stud. Econ. Econometrics*, August 1989, *13*(2), pp. 37–47.

_____; **Hamman, W. D. and Lambrechts, I. J.** Tariff Policies for Public Utilities: The Accounting Cost Approach. *J. Stud. Econ. Econometrics*, August 1989, *13*(2), pp. 49–57.

Dor, Avi. Can "One Country, Two Governments" Resolve the Israeli–Palestinian Conflict? Some Second Thoughts. *J. Policy Anal. Manage.*, Fall 1989, *8*(4), pp. 668–84.

_____. The Costs of Medicare Patients in Nursing Homes in the United States: A Multiple Output Analysis. *J. Health Econ.*, December 1989, *8*(3), pp. 253–70.

Doran, Charles F. Systemic Disequilibrium, Foreign Policy Role, and the Power Cycle. *J. Conflict Resolution*, September 1989, *33*(3), pp. 371–401.

Dore, Mohammed H. I. Game Theoretic Growth: A Numerical Illustration. In *Dore, M.; Chakravarty, S. and Goodwin, R., eds.*, 1989, pp. 151–61.

_____. The Legacy of John von Neumann. In *Dore, M.; Chakravarty, S. and Goodwin, R., eds.*, 1989, pp. 82–99.

_____. A Return Visit to the International Debt Problem of the LDCs: Comment. In *Hamouda, O. F.; Rowley, R. and Wolf, B. M., eds.*, 1989, pp. 170–72.

_____; **Chakravarty, Sukhamoy and Goodwin, Richard M.** John von Neumann and Modern Economics: Introduction. In *Dore, M.; Chak-*

ravarty, S. and Goodwin, R., eds., 1989, pp. 1–11.

Dore, Ronald. Meritocracy, Employment and Citizenship in Japan and Elsewhere. *Rivista Int. Sci. Econ. Com.*, February 1989, *36*(2), pp. 101–06.

_____. Technology in a World of National Frontiers. *World Devel.*, November 1989, *17*(11), pp. 1665–75.

Dorfman, Jeffrey H. and Heien, Dale M. The Effects of Uncertainty and Adjustment Costs on Investment in the Almond Industry. *Rev. Econ. Statist.*, May 1989, *71*(2), pp. 263–74.

Dorfman, Robert. Thomas Robert Malthus and David Ricardo. *J. Econ. Perspectives*, Summer 1989, *3*(3), pp. 153–64.

Dorhout, B.; Drud, A. and Bisschop, J. Structural Dependence and Systems of Equations. In *Simeone, B., ed.*, 1989, pp. 209–24.

Dorman, Peter. Alienation and Preference Theory. *Rev. Radical Polit. Econ.*, Fall 1989, *21*(3), pp. 1–6.

Dormont, Brigitte. Employment in Disequilibrium: A Disaggregated Approach on a Panel of French Firms. *Rech. Écon. Louvain*, 1989, *55*(1), pp. 61–93.

Dorn, James A. Alternatives to Government Fiat Money: Introduction. *Cato J.*, Fall 1989, *9*(2), pp. 277–94.

_____. The Changing World Economy. In *Dorn, J. A. and Niskanen, W. A., eds.*, 1989, pp. 1–27.

_____. The Depoliticization of Economic Life in China. *Cato J.*, Winter 1989, *8*(3), pp. 597–606.

_____. Economic Reform in China: Introduction. *Cato J.*, Winter 1989, *8*(3), pp. 563–66.

_____. Judicial Choice and Constitutional Order. In *Crane, E. H. and Boaz, D.*, 1989, pp. 327–45.

Dornbusch, Rudiger. Argentina after Martínez de Hoz, 1981–83. In *di Tella, G. and Dornbusch, R., eds.*, 1989, pp. 286–315.

_____. Comment: The McKinnon Standard: How Persuasive? In *Dorn, J. A. and Niskanen, W. A., eds.*, 1989, *1988*, pp. 171–79.

_____. Debt Problems and the World Macroeconomy. In *Sachs, J. D., ed. (I)*, 1989, pp. 331–57.

_____. Debt Problems and the World Macroeconomy. In *Sachs, J. D., ed. (II)*, 1989, pp. 299–311.

_____. The Dollar in the 1990s: Competitiveness and the Challenges of New Economic Blocs. In *Federal Reserve Bank of Kansas City*, 1989, pp. 245–73.

_____. Europe 1992: Macroeconomic Implications. *Brookings Pap. Econ. Act.*, 1989, (2), pp. 341–62.

_____. From Adjustment with Recession to Adjustment with Growth. In *Weeks, J. F., ed.*, 1989, pp. 207–21.

_____. How to Turn Mexico's Debt and Inflation into Growth. *Challenge*, Jan.–Feb. 1989, *32*(1), pp. 4–10.

_____. International Coordination of Fiscal Policies: Current and Future Issues: Comment. In *Monti, M., ed.*, 1989, pp. 38–45.

_____. Ireland's Disinflation: Credibility, Debt and Unemployment: Ireland's Failed Stabilization. *Econ. Policy: A Europ. Forum*, April 1989, (8), pp. 173–209.

_____. Korean International Macroeconomic Policy: Discussion. In *Bayard, T. O. and Young, S.-G., eds.*, 1989, pp. 66–71.

_____. The Latin American Debt Problem: Anatomy and Solutions. In *Stallings, B. and Kaufman, R., eds.*, 1989, pp. 7–22.

_____. The Latin American Dimension. In *Guttmann, R., ed.*, 1989, *1984*, pp. 205–12.

_____. The Need for Further Dollar Depreciation. In *Sijben, J. J., ed.*, 1989, pp. 19–34.

_____. Real Exchange Rates and Macroeconomics: A Selective Survey. *Scand. J. Econ.*, 1989, *91*(2), pp. 401–32.

_____. Reducing Transfers from Debtor Countries. In *Dornbusch, R.; Makin, J. H. and Zlowe, D., eds.*, 1989, pp. 21–42.

_____. Seigniorage in Europe: Discussion. In *De Cecco, M. and Giovannini, A., eds.*, 1989, pp. 79–84.

_____. The U.S. Economy and the Dollar. *Can. Public Policy*, Supplement, February 1989, *15*, pp. S10–19.

_____ **and Cardoso, Eliana A.** Brazilian Debt: A Requiem for Muddling Through. In *Edwards, S. and Larrain, F., eds.*, 1989, pp. 294–318.

_____ **and Cardoso, Eliana A.** Brazilian Debt Crises: Past and Present. In *Eichengreen, B. and Lindert, P. H., eds.*, 1989, pp. 106–39.

_____ **and de Carlos Pablo, Juan.** Debt and Macroeconomic Instability in Argentina. In *Sachs, J. D., ed. (II)*, 1989, pp. 37–56.

_____ **and Makin, John H.** Alternative Solutions to Developing-Country Debt Problems: Introduction. In *Dornbusch, R.; Makin, J. H. and Zlowe, D., eds.*, 1989, pp. 1–6.

_____ **and Reynoso, Alejandro.** Financial Factors in Economic Development. *Amer. Econ. Rev.*, May 1989, *79*(2), pp. 204–09.

_____ **and di Tella, Guido.** The Political Economy of Argentina, 1946–83: Introduction. In *di Tella, G. and Dornbusch, R., eds.*, 1989, pp. 1–15.

Dornelles, Francisco. The Relevance of Double Taxation Treaties for Developing Countries: Brazil. *Bull. Int. Fiscal Doc.*, Aug.–Sept. 1989, *43*(8–9), pp. 383–88.

Doron, Gideon. A Rational Policy Solution to the Israeli–Palestinian Conflict. *J. Policy Anal. Manage.*, Fall 1989, *8*(4), pp. 663–67.

Doroodian, Khosrow; Raffiee, Kambiz and Adrangi, Bahram. Exchange Rates, Import Costs, and Domestic Wage and Price Levels. *Atlantic Econ. J.*, March 1989, *17*(1), pp. 91.

_____ **and Seldon, Barry J.** A Simultaneous Model of Cigarette Advertising: Effects on Demand and Industry Response to Public Policy. *Rev. Econ. Statist.*, November 1989, *71*(4), pp. 673–77.

Dos Santos Ferreira, Rodolphe. Équilibre mar-

shallien et équilibre walrasien. (With English summary.) *Rech. Écon. Louvain*, 1989, *55*(4), pp. 399–424.

_____. La dynamique classique est-elle une alternative à la macro-économie traditionnelle? A propos des modèles de Duménil et Lévy. (Is Classical Dynamics an Alternative to Traditional Macroeconomics? A Comment on Dumenil and Levy Models. With English summary.) *Revue Écon.*, September 1989, *40*(5), pp. 887–98.

_____; **Gérard-Varet, Louis-André and d'Aspremont, Claude.** Unemployment in a Cournot Oligopoly Model with Ford Effects. *Rech. Écon. Louvain*, 1989, *55*(1), pp. 33–60.

_____; **Gérard-Varet, Louis-André and d'Aspremont, Claude.** Unemployment in an Extended Cournot Oligopoly Model. *Oxford Econ. Pap.*, July 1989, *41*(3), pp. 490–505.

Dosi, Giovanni. The Japanese Firm as an Innovating Institution: Comment. In *Shiraishi, T. and Tsuru, S., eds.*, 1989, pp. 155–59.

Dotsey, Michael. An Examination of International Trade Data in the 1980s. *Fed. Res. Bank Richmond Econ. Rev.*, March–April 1989, *75*(2), pp. 21–27.

_____. Monetary Control under Alternative Operating Procedures. *J. Money, Credit, Banking*, August 1989, *21*(3), pp. 273–90.

Dotson, Peter K.; Tolley, H. Dennis and Bahr, Michael D. A Statistical Method for Monitoring Social Insurance Claims. *J. Risk Ins.*, December 1989, *56*(4), pp. 670–85.

Doubleday, Nancy C. Co-management Provisions of the Inuvialuit Final Agreement. In *Pinkerton, E., ed.*, 1989, pp. 209–27.

Dougan, William R. and Munger, Michael C. The Rationality of Ideology. *J. Law Econ.*, April 1989, *32*(1), pp. 119–42.

Douglas, Evan J. The Simple Analytics of the Principal–Agent Incentive Contract. *J. Econ. Educ.*, Winter 1989, *20*(1), pp. 39–51.

Douglas, George W. The Importance of Entry Conditions: Texas Air's Acquisition of Eastern Airlines. In *Kwoka, J. E., Jr. and White, L. J., eds.*, 1989, pp. 99–120.

_____ **and Metrinko, Peter.** Civil Aeronautics Board Sunset: Sunrise at the Department of Transportation? In *Meiners, R. E. and Yandle, B., eds.*, 1989, pp. 186–206.

Douglas, Hernán Cortés. Lessons of the Past: The Role of External Shocks in Chilean Recessions, 1926–1982. In *Brock, P. L.; Connolly, M. B. and González-Vega, C., eds.*, 1989, pp. 40–51.

Douglas, Mike. The Future of Cities on the Pacific Rim. In *Smith, M. P., ed.*, 1989, pp. 9–67.

Douglas, Paul H. Smith's Theory of Value and Distribution. In *Clark, J. M., et al.*, 1989, pp. 77–115.

Douglas, Richard W., Jr. A Three-Asset Determination of the Transactions Demand for Money. *J. Macroecon.*, Winter 1989, *11*(1), pp. 95–108.

Doukas, John. Contagion Effect on Sovereign Interest Rate Spreads. *Econ. Letters*, 1989, *29*(3), pp. 237–41.

Doupnik, Timothy S. and Rolfe, Robert J. The Relevance of Level of Aggregation of Geographic Area Data in the Assessment of Foreign Investment Risk. In *Schwartz, B. N., ed.*, 1989, pp. 51–65.

Douwes Dekker, L. C. G. The Concept of Corporatism from an Industrial Relations Perspective. In *Barbash, J. and Barbash, K., eds.*, 1989, pp. 43–58.

Dow, Alexander C. and Dow, Sheila C. Endogenous Money Creation and Idle Balances. In *Pheby, J., ed.*, 1989, pp. 147–64.

Dow, Geoff; Boreham, Paul and Clegg, Stewart. Political Organisation and Economic Policy. In *Duncan, G., ed.*, 1989, pp. 253–76.

Dow, J. C. R. The Role of the Economist in Government: An International Perspective: The Organization for Economic Cooperation and Development. In *Pechman, J. A., ed.*, 1989, pp. 255–78.

Dow, James. Apprentice Shaman. In *Coy, M. W., ed.*, 1989, pp. 199–209.

Dow, Sheila C. and Dow, Alexander C. Endogenous Money Creation and Idle Balances. In *Pheby, J., ed.*, 1989, pp. 147–64.

Dowall, David E. Bangkok: A Profile of an Efficiently Performing Housing Market. *Urban Stud.*, June 1989, *26*(3), pp. 327–39.

Dowd, Bryan; Feldman, Roger and Finch, Michael. The Role of Health Practices in HMO Selection Bias: A Confirmatory Study. *Inquiry*, Fall 1989, *26*(3), pp. 381–87.

Dowd, Kevin. The Case against a European Central Bank. *World Econ.*, September 1989, *12*(3), pp. 361–72.

_____. Nobel Laureates in Economic Sciences: A Biographical Dictionary: Richard Stone: 1984. In *Katz, B. S., ed.*, 1989, pp. 294–304.

_____ **and Chappell, David.** A Simple Model of Macroeconomic Policy. *Econ. Modelling*, October 1989, *6*(4), pp. 447–51.

_____ **and Chrystal, K. Alec.** Disaggregate Supply: Evidence for the UK. *Appl. Econ.*, October 1989, *21*(10), pp. 1397–1409.

Dowen, Richard J. The Relation of Firm Size, Security Analyst Bias, and Neglect. *Appl. Econ.*, January 1989, *21*(1), pp. 19–23.

_____ **and Bauman, W. Scott.** The Dynamics of Neglect and Return: Comment. *J. Portfol. Manage.*, Winter 1989, *15*(2), pp. 76–77.

Downes, Andrew S. Budgetary Theory and Policy in a Small Developing Country: The Case of Barbados, 1960–1988. *Bull. Int. Fiscal Doc.*, October 1989, *43*(10), pp. 446–57.

Downes, Patrick T. Managing Foreign Exchange Reserves. *Finance Devel.*, December 1989, *26*(4), pp. 20–21.

Downs, Anthony. The Housing Challenge. In *Bosworth, B. P., et al.*, 1989, pp. 117–21.

Dowrick, Steve. Sectoral Change, Catching Up and Slowing Down: OECD Post-war Economic Growth Revisited. *Econ. Letters*, December 1989, *31*(4), pp. 331–35.

_____. Union–Oligopoly Bargaining. *Econ. J.*, December 1989, *99*(398), pp. 1123–42.

_____ **and Nguyen, D. T.** OECD Comparative Economic Growth 1950–85: Catch-Up and Convergence. *Amer. Econ. Rev.*, December 1989, *79*(5), pp. 1010–30.

_____ **and Nguyen, Tom.** Measurement and International Comparison. In *[Gruen, F. H.]*, 1989, pp. 34–59.

Doyle, Allan. Management during the Third Industrial Revolution. In *Finkelstein, J., ed.*, 1989, pp. 193–218.

Doyle, Christopher. Strategy Variables and Theories of Industrial Organization. In *Hahn, F., ed.*, 1989, pp. 149–62.

Doyle, Jack. Biotechnology and Thoroughbred Agriculture: More May Be Less. In *Dysart, B. C., III and Clawson, M., eds.*, 1989, pp. 47–60.

Doyle, Pat. Data Base Strategies for Panel Surveys. In *Kasprzyk, D., et al., eds.*, 1989, pp. 163–89.

Doyle, Peter and Corstjens, Marcel. Evaluating Alternative Retail Repositioning Strategies. *Marketing Sci.*, Spring 1989, *8*(2), pp. 170–80.

Doz, Yves. Competence and Strategy. In *Punset, E. and Sweeney, G., eds.*, 1989, pp. 47–55.

_____; **Angelmar, R. and Prahalad, C. K.** Assessing the Scope of Innovations: A Dilemma for Top Management. In *Rosenbloom, R. S. and Burgelman, R. A., eds.*, 1989, pp. 257–81.

Drabek, Zdenek. CMEA: The Primitive Socialist Integration and Its Prospects. In *Greenaway, D.; Hyclak, T. and Thornton, R. J., eds.*, 1989, pp. 235–54.

Drabenstott, Mark R. and Barkema, Alan. The Farm Recovery Is Complete. *Challenge*, July–Aug. 1989, *32*(4), pp. 57–58.

Draghi, Mario. The Exchange Rate Question in Europe: Comment. In *Bryant, R. C., et al., eds.*, 1989, pp. 307–10.

Drago, Robert. Comparative Productivity and Unemployment. *Econ. Anal. Workers' Manage.*, 1989, *23*(4), pp. 355–60.

_____. The Extent of Wage Discrimination in Australia. *Australian Bull. Lab.*, September 1989, *15*(4), pp. 313–25.

_____ **and Heywood, John S.** Support for Worker Participation. *J. Post Keynesian Econ.*, Summer 1989, *11*(4), pp. 522–30.

_____ **and Heywood, John S.** Tournaments, Piece Rates, and the Shape of the Payoff Function. *J. Polit. Econ.*, August 1989, *97*(4), pp. 992–98.

_____ **and McDonough, Terrence.** Crises of Capitalism and the First Crisis of Marxism: A Theoretical Note on the Bernstein–Kautsky Debate. *Rev. Radical Polit. Econ.*, Fall 1989, *21*(3), pp. 27–32.

_____ **and Perlman, Richard.** Microeconomic Issues in Labour Economics: New Approaches: Introduction. In *Drago, R. and Perlman, R., eds.*, 1989, pp. 1–15.

_____ **and Perlman, Richard.** Supervision and

High Wages as Competing Incentives: A Basis for Labour Segmentation Theory. In *Drago, R. and Perlman, R., eds.*, 1989, pp. 41–61.

Dragun, Andrew K. and Gleeson, Victor. From Water Law to Transferability in New South Wales. *Natural Res. J.*, Summer 1989, *29*(3), pp. 645–61.

Draibe, Sonia Miriam. An Overview of Social Development in Brazil. *CEPAL Rev.*, December 1989, (39), pp. 47–61.

Drake, Paul W. Debt and Democracy in Latin America, 1920s–1980s. In *Stallings, B. and Kaufman, R., eds.*, 1989, pp. 39–58.

Drakopoulos, Stavros A. The Historical Perspective of the Problem of Interpersonal Comparisons of Utility. *J. Econ. Stud.*, 1989, *16*(4), pp. 35–51.

Dranove, David. Medicaid Drug Formulary Restrictions. *J. Law Econ.*, April 1989, *32*(1), pp. 143–62.

Draper, Alan. Labor and the 1966 Elections. *Labor Hist.*, Winter 1989, *30*(1), pp. 78–92.

Dravie, A. Attempting a Patrimony Account for Land in Ivory Coast: Information System and Agricultural Development. *Statist. J.*, 1989, *6*(1), pp. 27–50.

Drazen, Allan. Monetary Policy, Capital Controls and Seigniorage in an Open Economy. In *De Cecco, M. and Giovannini, A., eds.*, 1989, pp. 13–32.

———— **and Eckstein, Zvi.** On the Organization of Rural Markets and the Process of Economic Development: Reply. *Amer. Econ. Rev.*, December 1989, *79*(5), pp. 1299.

Dreisbach, Timothy A. Building Globally through Incremental Commitments. In *Ahlbrandt, R. S., Jr., ed.*, 1989, pp. 22–25.

Drennan, M. P. Information Intensive Industries in Metropolitan Areas of the United States of America. *Environ. Planning A*, December 1989, *21*(12), pp. 1603–18.

Dresher, William H. Marketing of Nonferrous Metals: The Role of Trade Associations. In *Jackson, L. M. and Richardson, P. R., eds.*, 1989, pp. 58–65.

Drewes, Torben. The Economics of Labour Markets: A Review of Current Texts. *Bull. Econ. Res.*, October 1989, *41*(4), pp. 303–15.

Drews, Jürgen. Forschung im Pharmaunternehmen. (With English summary.) *Z. Betriebswirtshaft*, February 1989, *59*(2), pp. 129–40.

Drexl, Andreas. Heuristische Scheduling-Verfahren zur Personaleinsatzplanung bei Unternehmensprüfungen. (With English summary.) *Z. Betriebswirtshaft*, February 1989, *59*(2), pp. 193–212.

Dreyfus, Daniel A. Deregulation of Utilities: The Natural Gas Experience. *Bus. Econ.*, April 1989, *24*(2), pp. 41–47.

Dreyfus, Jean-Francois and Acharya, Sankarshan. Optimal Bank Reorganization Policies and the Pricing of Federal Deposit Insurance. *J. Finance*, December 1989, *44*(5), pp. 1313–33.

Dreyfuss, Rochelle Cooper. General Overview of the Intellectual Property System. In *Weil,*

V. and Snapper, J. W., eds., 1989, pp. 17–40.

Drèze, Jacques H. Axiomatic Theories of Choice, Cardinal Utility and Subjective Probability: A Review. In *Diamond, P. and Rothschild, M., eds.*, 1989, *1974*, pp. 37–57.

————. L'arbitrage entre équité et efficacité en matière d'emploi et de salaires. (With English summary.) *Rech. Écon. Louvain*, 1989, *55*(1), pp. 3–31.

————. Maurice Allais and the French Marginalist School. *Scand. J. Econ.*, 1989, *91*(1), pp. 5–16.

————. The Standard Goods Hypothesis. In *Jacquemin, A. and Sapir, A., eds.*, 1989, pp. 13–32.

———— **and Modigliani, Franco.** The Trade-Off between Real Wages and Employment in an Open Economy (Belgium). In *Modigliani, F., Vol. 4*, 1989, *1981*, pp. 202–42.

Drèze, Jean P. and Mukherjee, Anindita. Labour Contracts in Rural India: Theories and Evidence. In *Chakravarty, S., ed.*, 1989, pp. 233–65.

Driffill, John. Exchange Rate Bands and Realignments in a Stationary Stochastic Setting: Discussion. In *Miller, M.; Eichengreen, B. and Portes, R., eds.*, 1989, pp. 175–77.

————. Macroeconomic Policy Games with Incomplete Information: Some Extensions. In *[Verheyen, P.]*, 1989, pp. 289–322.

Driscoll, Michael J. and Bordes, Christian. Intégration des marchés des capitaux en Europe: Résultats des tests d'égalité des taux marginaux de substitution intertemporels. (The Integration of Capital Markets in Europe: Testing the Equality between Intertemporal Marginal Rates of Substitution. With English summary.) *Écon. Societes*, April–May 1989, *23*(4–5), pp. 133–64.

————; **Strauss-Kahn, Marc-Olivier and Bordes, Christian.** Price Inertia and Nominal Aggregate Demand in Major European Countries. *Rech. Écon. Louvain*, 1989, *55*(2), pp. 105–28.

————; **Strauss-Kahn, Marc-Olivier and Chouraqui, J. C.** The Effects of Monetary Policy on the Real Sector: What Do We Know? *Banca Naz. Lavoro Quart. Rev.*, March 1989, (168), pp. 3–46.

Driskill, Robert A. and McCafferty, Stephen. Dynamic Duopoly with Adjustment Costs: A Differential Game Approach. *J. Econ. Theory*, December 1989, *49*(2), pp. 324–38.

———— **and McCafferty, Stephen.** Dynamic Duopoly with Output Adjustment Costs in International Markets: Taking the Conjecture out of Conjectural Variations. In *Feenstra, R. C., ed.*, 1989, pp. 125–37.

Drisko, Alan F.; Schmitz, Edward J. and Dale, Charles. The Use of the Army College Fund: Implications for Program Cost Effectiveness. In *Gulledge, T. R., Jr. and Litteral, L. A., eds.*, 1989, pp. 407–22.

Driver, B. L.; McLaughlin, William J. and Harris, Charles C. Improving the Contingent Valuation Method: A Psychological Perspective.

J. Environ. Econ. Manage., November 1989, *17*(3), pp. 213–29.

Drobny, A. and Hall, Stephen G. An Investigation of the Long-run Properties of Aggregate Non-durable Consumers' Expenditure in the United Kingdom. *Econ. J.*, June 1989, *99*(396), pp. 454–60.

Drost, F. C., et al. Power Approximations to Multinomial Tests of Fit. *J. Amer. Statist. Assoc.*, March 1989, *84*(405), pp. 130–41.

Drud, A.; Bisschop, J. and Dorhout, B. Structural Dependence and Systems of Equations. In *Simeone, B., ed.*, 1989, pp. 209–24.

Drummond, Di. 'Specifically Designed'? Employers' Labour Strategies and Worker Responses in British Railway Workshops, 1838–1914. In *Harvey, C. and Turner, J., eds.*, 1989, pp. 8–31.

Drummond, Michael F. Output Measurement for Resource Allocation Decisions in Health Care. *Oxford Rev. Econ. Policy*, Spring 1989, *5*(1), pp. 59–74.

Drysdale, Peter. Trade and Economic Cooperation in the Asian-Pacific Region: Comment. In *Shinohara, M. and Lo, F., eds.*, 1989, pp. 466–68.

_____ **and Garnaut, Ross.** A Pacific Free Trade Area? In *Schott, J. J., ed.*, 1989, pp. 217–54.

Du Boff, Richard B. What Military Spending Really Costs. *Challenge*, Sept.–Oct. 1989, *32*(5), pp. 4–10.

_____ **and Herman, Edward S.** The Promotional–Financial Dynamic of Merger Movements: A Historical Perspective. *J. Econ. Issues*, March 1989, *23*(1), pp. 107–33.

Du Toit, Pierre. Bargaining about Bargaining: Inducing the Self-negating Prediction in Deeply Divided Societies—The Case of South Africa. *J. Conflict Resolution*, June 1989, *33*(2), pp. 210–30.

Dua, Pami and Arora, Harjit K. Do Expected Budget Deficits Affect Household Expectations of Interest Rates? *J. Macroecon.*, Fall 1989, *11*(4), pp. 551–62.

_____ **and Batchelor, Roy A.** Household versus Economist Forecasts of Inflation: A Reassessment: A Note. *J. Money, Credit, Banking*, May 1989, *21*(2), pp. 252–57.

_____ **and Smyth, David J.** The Public's Indifference Map between Inflation and Unemployment: Empirical Evidence for the Nixon, Ford, Carter and Reagan Presidencies. *Public Choice*, January 1989, *60*(1), pp. 71–85.

_____**; Smyth, David J. and Washburn, Susan K.** Social Preferences, Inflation, Unemployment, and Political Business Cycles: Econometric Evidence for the Reagan Presidency. *Southern Econ. J.*, October 1989, *56*(2), pp. 336–48.

Duann, Daniel J. Direct Gas Purchases by Local Distribution Companies: Supply Reliability and Cost Implications. *J. Energy Devel.*, Autumn 1989, *15*(1), pp. 61–93.

Dubacher, René and Zimmermann, Heinz. A Simple Measure of Bond Convexity with Appli-

cations. *Jahr. Nationalökon. Statist.*, January 1989, *206*(1), pp. 48–60.

Dubin, Jeffrey A. and Rothwell, Geoffrey S. Risk and Reactor Safety Systems Adoption. *J. Econometrics*, October 1989, *42*(2), pp. 201–18.

_____**; Wilde, Louis L. and Graetz, Michael J.** Administrative and Compliance Costs of Taxation: United States. In *International Fiscal Association, ed. (1)*, 1989, pp. 311–47.

Dubman, Robert W.; Gunter, Lewell F. and Miller, Bill R. Revenue and Cost Uncertainty, Generalized Mean–Variance and the Linear Complementarity Problem: Comment. *Amer. J. Agr. Econ.*, August 1989, *71*(3), pp. 806–09.

Dubofsky, David A. and Fraser, Donald R. The Differential Impact of Two Significant Court Decisions Concerning Banking Consolidation. *J. Banking Finance*, July 1989, *13*(3), pp. 339–54.

_____ **and Fraser, Donald R.** The Texas Probable Future Competition Cases and the Transformation of the Bank Expansion Movement: Evidence from the Equity Market. *Antitrust Bull.*, Summer 1989, *34*(2), pp. 395–410.

Dubovsky, S. V. and Eismont, O. A. Long-Range Modeling of the USSR Economy. In *Krelle, W., ed.*, 1989, pp. 311–24.

Duchin, Faye. An Input–Output Approach to Analyzing the Future Economic Implications of Technological Change. In *Miller, R. E.; Polenske, K. R. and Rose, A. Z., eds.*, 1989, pp. 281–92.

_____. International Trade and the Use of Capital and Labor in the U.S. Economy. *Econ. Systems Res.*, 1989, *1*(3), pp. 345–50.

Duckett, S. J. The Economics of Australian Hospitals: Forum: Is Federalism Dead? The Case of Commonwealth-State Financial Relations in the Hospital Field. In *Smith, C. S., ed.*, 1989, pp. 318–29.

_____. Structural Interests and Australian Health Policy. In *Butler, J. R. G. and Doessel, D. P., eds.*, 1989, *1984*, pp. 73–86.

Dudek, Daniel J. and Tripp, James T. B. Institutional Guidelines for Designing Successful Transferable Rights Programs. *Yale J. Regul.*, Summer 1989, *6*(2), pp. 369–91.

Dudley, Leonard and Blum, Ulrich C. H. A Spatial Approach to Structural Change: The Making of the French Hexagon. *J. Econ. Hist.*, September 1989, *49*(3), pp. 657–75.

_____ **and Lasserre, Pierre.** Information as a Substitute for Inventories. *Europ. Econ. Rev.*, January 1989, *33*(1), pp. 67–88.

Due, Jean M. and White-Jones, Marcia. Differences in Earning, Labour Inputs, Decision-Making and Perception of Development between Farm and Market: A Case Study in Zambia. *Eastern Afr. Econ. Rev.*, December 1989, *5*(2), pp. 91–103.

Due, John F. Erratum [The Tax Structure of Botswana]. *Bull. Int. Fiscal Doc.*, June 1989, *43*(6), pp. 288.

_____. Erratum [The Tax Structure of Botswana].

Bull. Int. Fiscal Doc., April 1989, *43*(4), pp. 180.

———. The Tax Structure of Botswana. *Bull. Int. Fiscal Doc.*, January 1989, *43*(1), pp. 9–16.

Duewer, Lawrence A. and Nelson, Kenneth E. ERS's Measures of Red Meat Consumption. In *Buse, R. C., ed.*, 1989, pp. 57–73.

Duffie, Darrell. Corrigendum [Stochastic Equilibria with Incomplete Financial Markets]. *J. Econ. Theory*, December 1989, *49*(2), pp. 384.

——— **and Sonnenschein, Hugo.** Arrow and General Equilibrium Theory. *J. Econ. Lit.*, June 1989, *27*(2), pp. 565–98.

——— **and Zame, William.** The Consumption-Based Capital Asset Pricing Model. *Econometrica*, November 1989, *57*(6), pp. 1279–97.

Duffy, Patricia A.; Hardy, William E., Jr. and Disney, W. Terry. A Markov Chain Analysis of Pork Farm Size Distributions in the South: Reply. *Southern J. Agr. Econ.*, December 1989, *21*(2), pp. 219–20.

——— **and Molnar, Joseph J.** Attitudes toward Governmental Involvement in Agriculture: Results of a National Survey. *Southern J. Agr. Econ.*, July 1989, *21*(1), pp. 121–30.

———; **Young, George and Mims, Anne M.** Effects of Alternative Acreage Restriction Provisions on Alabama Cotton Farms. *Southern J. Agr. Econ.*, December 1989, *21*(2), pp. 85–94.

Dufour, Jean-Marie. Investment, Taxation, and Econometric Policy Evaluation: Some Evidence on the Lucas Critique. In *Hackl, P., ed.*, 1989, pp. 441–73.

———. Nonlinear Hypotheses, Inequality Restrictions, and Non-nested Hypotheses: Exact Simultaneous Tests in Linear Regressions. *Econometrica*, March 1989, *57*(2), pp. 335–55.

——— **and Roy, R.** Some Robust Exact Results on Sample Autocorrelations and Tests of Randomness: Corrigendum. *J. Econometrics*, June 1989, *41*(2), pp. 279–81.

Dufournaud, Christian, et al. Long-term Contracts for Crude Oil Imports into Costa Rica: A General Equilibrium Analysis. *Energy J.*, January 1989, *10*(1), pp. 119–25.

Dugan, Michael T. and Shriver, Keith A. The Effects of Estimation Period, Industry, and Proxy on the Calculation of the Degree of Operating Leverage. *Financial Rev.*, February 1989, *24*(1), pp. 109–22.

——— **and Shriver, Keith A.** FASB Statement 33 Data Base: Compositional Characteristics, Potential Uses, and Sources of Measurement Error. *J. Econ. Soc. Meas.*, 1989, *15*(1), pp. 27–36.

Dugger, William M. An Institutional Analysis of Corporate Power. In *Tool, M. R. and Samuels, W. J., eds. (I)*, 1989, *1988*, pp. 211–43.

———. Austrians vs. Institutionalists: Who Are the Real Dissenters? In *Samuels, W. J., ed. (II)*, 1989, pp. 115–23.

———. Democratic Economic Planning and Worker Ownership. In *Tool, M. R. and Samuels, W. J., eds. (III)*, 1989, *1987*, pp. 375–87.

———. Emulation: An Institutional Theory of Value Formation. *Rev. Soc. Econ.*, Summer 1989, *47*(2), pp. 134–54.

———. Instituted Process and Enabling Myth: The Two Faces of the Market. *J. Econ. Issues*, June 1989, *23*(2), pp. 607–15.

———. Power: An Institutional Framework of Analysis. In *Tool, M. R. and Samuels, W. J., eds. (I)*, 1989, *1980*, pp. 133–43.

———. Radical Institutionalism: Basic Concepts. In *Dugger, W. M., ed.*, 1989, pp. 1–20.

———. Radical Institutionalism: Conclusion. In *Dugger, W. M., ed.*, 1989, pp. 125–33.

———. Radical Institutionalism: Contemporary Voices: Introduction. In *Dugger, W. M., ed.*, 1989, pp. vii–xii.

———. A Research Agenda for Institutional Economics. In *Dugger, W. M., ed.*, 1989, pp. 105–23.

———. Rhoads's *The Economist's View of the World* and Whynes's *What Is Political Economy:* Review Essay. In *Samuels, W. J., ed. (II)*, 1989, pp. 253–60.

———. The State: Power and Dichotomy. In *Samuels, W. J., ed. (I)*, 1989, pp. 49–57.

Duguay, Pierre and Rabeau, Yves. Les effets macro-économiques de la politique budgétaire: De Keynes à la synthèse néo-classique. (The Macroeconomic Effects of Fiscal Policy: From Keynes to the Neo-classical Synthesis. With English summary.) *Revue Écon.*, July 1989, *40*(4), pp. 597–620.

Duhs, Alan and Alvey, Jim. Schumacher's Political Economy. *Int. J. Soc. Econ.*, 1989, *16*(6), pp. 67–76.

van Duijn, J. J. Near the End of the Downswing—Approaching the Beginning of a New Upswing. In *Muller, F. and Zwezerijnen, W. J., eds.*, 1989, pp. 224–41.

Duke, John and Usher, Lisa. Multifactor Productivity Slips in the Nonrubber Footwear Industry. *Mon. Lab. Rev.*, April 1989, *112*(4), pp. 32–38.

Dukes, William P. and Mukherjee, Tarun K. A Multivariate Analysis of Small Bank Stock Valuation. *Quart. J. Bus. Econ.*, Spring 1989, *28*(2), pp. 3–18.

Dulberger, Ellen R. The Application of a Hedonic Model to a Quality-Adjusted Price Index for Computer Processors. In *Jorgenson, D. W. and Landau, R., eds.*, 1989, pp. 37–75.

———; **Triplett, Jack E. and Cole, Rosanne.** The Postwar Evolution of Computer Prices: Comment. In *Jorgenson, D. W. and Landau, R., eds.*, 1989, pp. 215–19.

Duleep, Harriet Orcutt. Measuring Socioeconomic Mortality Differentials over Time. *Demography*, May 1989, *26*(2), pp. 345–51.

Dulman, Scott P. The Development of Discounted Cash Flow Techniques in U.S. Industry. *Bus. Hist. Rev.*, Autumn 1989, *63*(3), pp. 555–87.

DuMars, Charles T. and Johnson, Norman K. A Survey of the Evolution of Western Water Law in Response to Changing Economic and Public Interest Demands. *Natural Res. J.*, Spring 1989, *29*(2), pp. 347–87.

_____ **and Tarlock, A. Dan.** New Challenges to State Water Allocation Sovereignty: Symposium Introduction. *Natural Res. J.*, Spring 1989, *29*(2), pp. 331–46.

Dumas, Bernard. Two-Person Dynamic Equilibrium in the Capital Market. *Rev. Financial Stud.*, 1989, *2*(2), pp. 157–88.

Dumas, Roland. Europe in a Changing International Environment. In *Frankel, A. V. and Heck, C. B., eds.*, 1989, pp. 44–46.

Dumbrell, John; Sewell, W. R. Derrick and Dearden, Philip. Wilderness Decisionmaking and the Role of Environmental Interest Groups: A Comparison of the Franklin Dam, Tasmania and South Moresby, British Columbia Cases. *Natural Res. J.*, Winter 1989, *29*(1), pp. 147–69.

Duménil, Gérard and Lévy, Dominique. The Competitive Process in a Fixed Capital Environment: A Classical View. *Manchester Sch. Econ. Soc. Stud.*, March 1989, *57*(1), pp. 34–57.

_____ **and Lévy, Dominique.** Labor Values and the Imputation of Labor Contents. *Metroecon.*, June 1989, *40*(2), pp. 159–78.

_____ **and Lévy, Dominique.** Les métamorphoses du cycle industriel. L'exemple des Etats-Unis. (The Foundations of the Business Cycle, the Case of the United States. With English summary.) *Écon. Societes*, March 1989, *23*(3), pp. 75–106.

_____ **and Lévy, Dominique.** The Real and Financial Determinants of Stability: The Law of the Tendency toward Increasing Instability. In *Semmler, W., ed.*, 1989, pp. 87–115.

Dumez, Hervé. A propos de "the thinking organization" quelques réflexions sur la cognition et les sciences de gestion. (About "The Thinking Organization": Remarks about Cognition and Management Sciences. With English summary.) *Écon. Societes*, December 1989, *23*(12), pp. 185–95.

Dumitrescu, Vl.; Somnea, D. and Patrulescu, M. Software Simulation of Bigger Fonts Printing on Dot Matrix Graphical Printers. *Econ. Computat. Econ. Cybern. Stud. Res.*, 1989, *24*(2–3), pp. 103–09.

Dumitru, V. and Luban, Florica. A Generalized Huard–Iri Function for Unconstrained Optimization. *Econ. Computat. Econ. Cybern. Stud. Res.*, 1989, *24*(1), pp. 77–80.

Dumontier, Pascal; Brunet, Jean-Michel and Souton, Marc. Les caractéristiques financières des sociétés françaises acquises par offre publique. (Financial Ratios as Predictors of French Takeovers. With English summary.) *Écon. Societes*, December 1989, *23*(12), pp. 107–28.

Dunaev, E. On Forms of Realization of Socialist Property. *Prob. Econ.*, August 1989, *32*(4), pp. 82–96.

Duncan, Alan and Hassan, John A. The Role of Energy Supplies during Western Europe's Golden Age, 1950–1972. *J. Europ. Econ. Hist.*, Winter 1989, *18*(3), pp. 479–508.

Duncan, Cheryl and Lovell, Michael. The Pen-

sion Subsidy of Educational Inequality. *Econ. Educ. Rev.*, 1989, *8*(4), pp. 313–21.

Duncan, George and Lambert, Diane. The Risk of Disclosure for Microdata. *J. Bus. Econ. Statist.*, April 1989, *7*(2), pp. 207–17.

Duncan, Graeme. A Defence of the Welfare State. In *Duncan, G., ed.*, 1989, pp. 297–315.

_____. Democracy and the Capitalist State: Introduction. In *Duncan, G., ed.*, 1989, pp. 1–12.

_____. Mill, Marx and the State. In *Duncan, G., ed.*, 1989, pp. 105–21.

Duncan, Greg J. and Burkhauser, Richard V. Economic Risks of Gender Roles: Income Loss and Life Events over the Life Course. *Soc. Sci. Quart.*, March 1989, *70*(1), pp. 3–23.

_____ **and Hill, Daniel H.** Assessing the Quality of Household Panel Data: The Case of the Panel Study of Income Dynamics. *J. Bus. Econ. Statist.*, October 1989, *7*(4), pp. 441–52.

_____; **Solenberger, Peter and Servais, Marita.** Data Base Management Approaches to Household Panel Studies. In *Kasprzyk, D., et al., eds.*, 1989, pp. 190–225.

Duncan, Joseph W. Statistics and 1992 in Europe. *Bus. Econ.*, July 1989, *24*(3), pp. 52–53.

_____. The Statistics Corner. *Bus. Econ.*, January 1989, *24*(1), pp. 48–50.

_____. The Statistics Corner: Gatekeepers for Federal Statistics. *Bus. Econ.*, April 1989, *24*(2), pp. 51–52.

Duncan, Simon and Goodwin, Mark. The Crisis of Local Government: Uneven Development and the Thatcher Administrations. In *Mohan, J., ed.*, 1989, pp. 69–86.

Duncan, Steven S. and Ladd, George W. Decomposition of Structural and Exogenous Changes. *Appl. Econ.*, January 1989, *21*(1), pp. 125–37.

Duncan, William A.; LaRue, David and Reckers, Philip M. J. An Empirical Examination of the Influence of Selected Economic and Noneconomic Variables on Decision Making by Tax Professionals. In *Jones, S. M., ed.*, 1989, pp. 91–106.

Dundas-Grant, Valerie. Vocational and Technical Education in France. *Nat. Westminster Bank Quart. Rev.*, February 1989, pp. 30–42.

Dunford, Mick. Technopoles, Politics and Markets: The Development of Electronics in Grenoble and Silicon Glen. In *Sharp, M. and Holmes, P., eds.*, 1989, pp. 80–118.

Dung, Tran Huu. International Investment, Taxes, and Welfare. *Int. Econ. J.*, Spring 1989, *3*(1), pp. 63–79.

_____ **and Kumar, Rishi.** The Transfer Problem under Uncertainty. *Indian Econ. Rev.*, July–Dec. 1989, *24*(2), pp. 197–205.

Dunham, Constance R. New Banks in New England. *New Eng. Econ. Rev.*, Jan.–Feb. 1989, pp. 30–41.

_____; **Bradbury, Katharine L. and Case, Karl E.** Geographic Patterns of Mortgage Lending in Boston, 1982–1987. *New Eng. Econ. Rev.*, Sept.–Oct. 1989, pp. 3–30.

Dunham, Daniel B. Vocational Education in the

Secondary School: The Case for Continuation. *Econ. Educ. Rev.*, 1989, 8(1), pp. 69–74.

Dunham, N. C., et al. Wisconsin: The Impact of an HMO-Based Health Plan for Indigent Adults. In *Scheffler, R. M. and Rossiter, L. F., eds.*, 1989, pp. 201–19.

Dunkelberg, William C. Analyzing Consumer Spending and Debt. *Bus. Econ.*, July 1989, 24(3), pp. 17–22.

———— **and Carlson, John A.** Market Perceptions and Inventory–Price–Employment Plans. *Rev. Econ. Statist.*, May 1989, 71(2), pp. 318–24.

Dunlevy, James A. and Deyak, Timothy. Seasonal, Cyclical and Secular Stability of Canadian Aggregate Demand for Merchandise Imports, 1957–1982. *Appl. Econ.*, April 1989, 21(4), pp. 449–59.

Dunlop, D. M. and Lerohl, M. L. The Impact of Transport Cost Shifts on Production and Welfare in the Prairie Grains Industry. *Can. J. Agr. Econ.*, Part 2, December 1989, 37(4), pp. 1251–63.

Dunn, James A., Jr. The Asian Auto Imbroglio: Patterns of Trade Policy and Business Strategy. In *Haggard, S. and Moon, C., eds.*, 1989, pp. 155–83.

Dunn, John. Contemporary West African States: Conclusion. In *Cruise O'Brien, D. B.; Dunn, J. and Rathbone, R., eds.*, 1989, pp. 181–92.

Dunn, Kenneth B. and Eades, Kenneth M. Voluntary Conversion of Convertible Securities and the Optimal Call Strategy. *J. Finan. Econ.*, August 1989, 23(2), pp. 273–301.

Dunn, R. and Walker, P. District-Level Variations in the Configuration of Service Provision in England: A Graphical Approach to Classification. *Environ. Planning A*, October 1989, 21(10), pp. 1397–1411.

Dunne, Timothy; Roberts, Mark J. and Samuelson, Larry. Firm Entry and Postentry Performance in the U.S. Chemical Industries. *J. Law Econ.*, Part 2, October 1989, 32(2), pp. S233–71.

————; **Roberts, Mark J. and Samuelson, Larry.** The Growth and Failure of U.S. Manufacturing Plants. *Quart. J. Econ.*, November 1989, 104(4), pp. 671–98.

————; **Roberts, Mark J. and Samuelson, Larry.** Plant Turnover and Gross Employment Flows in the U.S. Manufacturing Sector. *J. Lab. Econ.*, January 1989, 7(1), pp. 48–71.

Dunnett, Peter J. S. Canadian Auto Policy Revisited. *Can. Public Policy*, March 1989, 15(1), pp. 102–06.

Dunning, John H. Trade and Foreign-Owned Production in Services: Some Conceptual and Theoretical Issues. In *Giersch, H., ed.*, 1989, pp. 108–50.

Dunphy, Dexter C. and Hackman, B. Katarina. Locus of Control in Human Resource Management: A Comparison of the United States and China. In *Nedd, A., ed.*, 1989, pp. 33–44.

Dunz, Karl. Some Comments on Majority Rule Equilibria in Local Public Good Economies. *J. Econ. Theory*, February 1989, 47(1), pp. 228–34.

Dupont, Frédéric and Reus, Estiva. Le profit macroéconomique monétaire. (Monetary Macroeconomic Profit. With English summary.) *Écon. Appl.*, 1989, 42(2), pp. 87–114.

Dupree, Marguerite. The Community Perspective in Family History: The Potteries during the Nineteenth Century. In *[Stone, L.]*, 1989, pp. 549–73.

Dupuy, Jean-Pierre. Convention et Common knowledge. (Convention and Common Knowledge. With English summary.) *Revue Écon.*, March 1989, 40(2), pp. 361–400.

Durand, J.-J. and Prat, G. Analyse de la relation entre la masse monétaire et la base monétaire en France, 1950–1987. (Analysis of the Relationship between the Money Stock and the Monetary Base in France, 1950–1987. With English summary.) *Écon. Societes*, April–May 1989, 23(4–5), pp. 185–230.

Durden, Garey; Gaynor, Patricia and Brem, Natalie. The Effect of Government Employment on Income Inequality Overall and in the South: Evidence from Congressional District Data. *Rev. Reg. Stud.*, Spring 1989, 19(2), pp. 40–47.

van Duren, Erna and Martin, Larry J. The Role of Economic Analysis in Countervailing Duty Disputes: Cases Involving Agriculture. *Can. Public Policy*, June 1989, 15(2), pp. 162–74.

Durkin, Thomas A.; Canner, Glenn B. and Luckett, Charles A. Home Equity Lending. *Fed. Res. Bull.*, May 1989, 75(5), pp. 333–44.

———— **and Elliehausen, Gregory E.** Theory and Evidence of the Impact of Equal Credit Opportunity: An Agnostic Review of the Literature. *J. Finan. Services Res.*, June 1989, 2(2), pp. 89–114.

Durlauf, Steven N. Output Persistence, Economic Structure, and the Choice of Stabilization Policy. *Brookings Pap. Econ. Act.*, 1989, (2), pp. 69–116.

Durnford, Jon and Aggarwal, Raj. Market Assessment of International Banking Activity: A Study of U.S. Bank Holding Companies. *Quart. Rev. Econ. Bus.*, Spring 1989, 29(1), pp. 58–67.

Duruflé, Gilles. Evaluating Structural Adjustment Policies for Senegal. In *Campbell, B. K., ed.*, 1989, pp. 92–128.

————. Structural Disequilbria and Adjustment Programmes in Madagascar. In *Campbell, B. K. and Loxley, J., eds.*, 1989, pp. 169–201.

————. Structural Disequilibria and Adjustment Policies in the Ivory Coast. In *Campbell, B. K. and Loxley, J., eds.*, 1989, pp. 132–68.

Durukan, Levent and Çağli, Uğur. Sex Role Portrayals in Turkish TV Advertising: Some Preliminary Findings. *METU*, 1989, 16(1–2), pp. 153–75.

Dusansky, Richard. The Demand for Money and Goods in the Theory of Consumer Choice with Money. *Amer. Econ. Rev.*, September 1989, 79(4), pp. 895–901.

————. Diamonds Are a Government's Best Friend: Burden-Free Taxes on Goods Valued for Their Values: Comments. *Amer. Econ. Rev.*, December 1989, 79(5), pp. 1285–88.

———. On the Economics of Institutional Care of the Elderly in the U.S.: The Effects of a Change in Government Reimbursement. *Rev. Econ. Stud.*, January 1989, 56(1), pp. 141–50.

Dutia, Dipa; Cheng, Louis and Davidson, Wallace N., III. A Re-examination of the Market Reaction to Failed Mergers. *J. Finance*, September 1989, 44(4), pp. 1077–83.

——— **and Davidson, Wallace N., III.** A Note on the Behavior of Security Returns: A Test of Stock Market Overreaction and Efficiency. *J. Finan. Res.*, Fall 1989, 12(3), pp. 245–52.

Dutkowsky, Donald H. and Foote, William G. The Dynamic Demand for Bank Discount Window Borrowing with Non-negativity Constraints. *Atlantic Econ. J.*, June 1989, 17(2), pp. 36–41.

——— **and Kao, Chihwa.** An Application of Nonlinear Bounded Influence Estimation to Aggregate Bank Borrowing from the Federal Reserve. *J. Amer. Statist. Assoc.*, September 1989, 84(407), pp. 700–709.

Dutt, Amitava Krishna. Accumulation, Distribution and Inflation in a Marxian/Post-Keynesian Model with a Rentier Class. *Rev. Radical Polit. Econ.*, Fall 1989, 21(3), pp. 18–26.

———. Trade, Debt, and Uneven Development in a North–South Model. *Metroecon.*, October 1989, 40(3), pp. 211–33.

———. Uneven Development in Alternative Models of North–South Trade. *Eastern Econ. J.*, April–June 1989, 15(2), pp. 91–106.

Dutta, Bhaskar and Ray, Debraj. A Concept of Egalitarianism under Participation Constraints. *Econometrica*, May 1989, 57(3), pp. 615–35.

———; **Ray, Debraj and Sengupta, Kunal.** Contracts with Eviction in Infinitely Repeated Principal–Agent Relationships. In *Bardhan, P., ed. (II)*, 1989, pp. 93–121.

———, **et al.** A Consistent Bargaining Set. *J. Econ. Theory*, October 1989, 49(1), pp. 93–112.

Dutta, J. and Polemarchakis, H. M. Credit Constraints and Investment Finance: Some Evidence from Greece. In *Monti, M., ed.*, 1989, pp. 158–82.

Dutta, Prajit K. and Mitra, Tapan. Maximum Theorems for Convex Structures with an Application to the Theory of Optimal Intertemporal Allocation. *J. Math. Econ.*, 1989, 18(1), pp. 77–86.

——— **and Mitra, Tapan.** On Continuity of the Utility Function in Intertemporal Allocation Models: An Example. *Int. Econ. Rev.*, August 1989, 30(3), pp. 527–36.

Dutz, Mark A. Horizontal Mergers in Declining Industries: Theory and Evidence. *Int. J. Ind. Organ.*, Special Issue, March 1989, 7(1), pp. 11–33.

Duvick, Donald N. Possible Genetic Causes of Increased Variability in U.S. Maize Yields. In *Anderson, J. R. and Hazell, P. B. R., eds.*, 1989, pp. 147–56.

Dvořák, Jiří. The Reform of the Economic Mecha-

nism in Czechoslovakia. *Czech. Econ. Pap.*, 1989, (26), pp. 7–17.

Dworak, Stephen and Jussawalla, Meheroo. The Impact of Telematics on Financial Intermediaries and Market Interdependencies. In *Jussawalla, M.; Okuma, T. and Araki, T., eds.*, 1989, pp. 85–101.

Dworkin, Gerald. Commentary: Legal and Ethical Issues. In *Weil, V. and Snapper, J. W., eds.*, 1989, pp. 250–52.

Dworkin, James B. and Fain, James R. Success in Multiple Union Elections: Exclusive Jurisdiction vs. Competition. *J. Lab. Res.*, Winter 1989, 10(1), pp. 91–101.

Dwyer, Gerald P., Jr. and Curran, Christopher. The Effect of the Double Nickel Speed Limit on Death Rates. In *Faure, M. and Van den Bergh, R., eds.*, 1989, pp. 117–56.

——— **and Gilbert, R. Alton.** Bank Runs and Private Remedies. *Fed. Res. Bank St. Louis Rev.*, May–June 1989, 71(3), pp. 43–61.

——— **and Hafer, R. W.** Interest Rates and Economic Announcements. *Fed. Res. Bank St. Louis Rev.*, March–April 1989, 71(2), pp. 34–46.

Dwyer, Hubert J. and Lynn, Richard. Small Capitalization Companies: What Does Financial Analysis Tell Us about Them? *Financial Rev.*, August 1989, 24(3), pp. 397–415.

Dwyer, Jeffrey W. and Beeghley, Leonard. Income Transfers and Income Inequality. *Population Res. Policy Rev.*, May 1989, 8(2), pp. 119–42.

Dyba, Karel. On Socialist Market Economy—From a Czechoslovak Viewpoint. *Acta Oecon.*, 1989, 40(3–4), pp. 219–21.

———. Understanding Czechoslovak Economic Development: 1968–1988. Growth, Adjustment, and Reform. *Jahr. Wirtsch. Osteuropas*, 1989, 13(2), pp. 141–65.

———, **et al.** Question of Growth Strategy. *Czech. Econ. Digest.*, May 1989, (3), pp. 3–15.

Dye, Thomas R. State Factor Scores: Atheoretical and Unreliable. *Soc. Sci. Quart.*, March 1989, 70(1), pp. 193–94.

Dyer, Alan W. Making Semiotic Sense of Money as a Medium of Exchange. *J. Econ. Issues*, June 1989, 23(2), pp. 503–10.

Dyer, Christopher. The Consumer and the Market in the Later Middle Ages. *Econ. Hist. Rev.*, 2nd Ser., August 1989, 42(3), pp. 305–27.

Dyer, Davis and Sicilia, David B. From Commodity to Specialty Chemicals: Cellulose Products and Naval Stores at the Hercules Powder Company, 1919–1939. In *Hausman, W. J., ed.*, 1989, pp. 59–71.

Dyer, Douglas; Kagel, John H. and Levin, Dan. A Comparison of Naive and Experienced Bidders in Common Value Offer Auctions: A Laboratory Analysis. *Econ. J.*, March 1989, 99(394), pp. 108–15.

———; **Kagel, John H. and Levin, Dan.** Resolving Uncertainty about the Number of Bidders in Independent Private-Value Auctions: An Experimental Analysis. *Rand J. Econ.*, Summer 1989, *20*(2), pp. 268–79.

Dyer, James; Vedlitz, Arnold and Worchel, Stephen. Social Distance among Racial and Ethnic Groups in Texas: Some Demographic Correlates. *Soc. Sci. Quart.*, September 1989, *70*(3), pp. 607–16.

Dyhr, Peter and Hemmingsen, Kjeld. The Disregard of a Legal Entity for Tax Purposes: Denmark. In *International Fiscal Association, ed. (II)*, 1989, pp. 249–58.

van Dyk, Esbeth and Schreüder, Willem A. A Multidimensional Scaling Model for Qualitative Pair Wise Comparisons. In *Lockett, A. G. and Islei, G., eds.*, 1989, pp. 68–77.

Dykacz, Janice M. and Hennessey, John C. Postrecovery Experience of Disabled-Worker Beneficiaries. *Soc. Sec. Bull.*, September 1989, *52*(9), pp. 42–66.

_____ **and Hennessey, John C.** Projected Outcomes and Length of Time in the Disability Insurance Program. *Soc. Sec. Bull.*, September 1989, *52*(9), pp. 2–41.

Dykes, Sayre Ellen and Whitehouse, Michael A. The Establishment and Evolution of the Federal Reserve Board: 1913–23. *Fed. Res. Bull.*, April 1989, *75*(4), pp. 227–43.

Dyl, Edward A. Agency, Corporate Control and Accounting Methods—The LIFO–FIFO Choice. *Managerial Dec. Econ.*, June 1989, *10*(2), pp. 141–45.

Dymski, Gary A. Keynesian versus Credit Theories of Money and Banking: A Reply. *J. Post Keynesian Econ.*, Fall 1989, *12*(1), pp. 157–63.

_____ **and Devine, James.** Roemer's Theory of Capitalist Exploitation: The Contradictions of Walrasian Marxism. *Rev. Radical Polit. Econ.*, Fall 1989, *21*(3), pp. 13–17.

_____ **and Elliot, John E.** The Taxonomy of Primary Exploitation. *Rev. Soc. Econ.*, Winter 1989, *47*(4), pp. 338–76.

Dynarski, Mark; Schwab, Robert and Zampelli, Ernest M. Local Characteristics and Public Production: The Case of Education. *J. Urban Econ.*, September 1989, *26*(2), pp. 250–63.

Dysart, Benjamin C., III and Clawson, Marion. Public Interest in the Use of Private Lands: An Overview. In *Dysart, B. C., III and Clawson, M., eds.*, 1989, pp. 1–8.

Dyson, Kenneth. Combating Long-Term Unemployment: Introduction. In *Dyson, K., ed.*, 1989, pp. 1–4.

_____. Combating Long-Term Unemployment: Some Conclusions. In *Dyson, K., ed.*, 1989, pp. 237–47.

_____. Long-Term Unemployment: The Ideological Perspective. In *Dyson, K., ed.*, 1989, pp. 5–27.

Dyson, Tim. The Population History of Berar since 1881 and Its Potential Wider Significance. *Indian Econ. Soc. Hist. Rev.*, April–June 1989, *26*(2), pp. 167–201.

Dziechciarz, Józef. Changing and Random Coefficient Models. A Survey. In *Hackl, P., ed.*, 1989, pp. 217–51.

Dziobek, Claudia. The Transfer Debate, the Role of the International Monetary Fund and the Missing Link between Willingness and Ability to Pay the Foreign Debts. In *Wohlmuth, K., ed.*, 1989, pp. 231–57.

Eades, Kenneth M. and Dunn, Kenneth B. Voluntary Conversion of Convertible Securities and the Optimal Call Strategy. *J. Finan. Econ.*, August 1989, *23*(2), pp. 273–301.

Eagleburger, Lawrence S. The 21st Century: American Foreign Policy Challenges. In *Hamilton, E. K., ed.*, 1989, pp. 242–60.

Eaker, Mark and Grant, Dwight. Complex Hedges: How Well Do They Work? *J. Futures Markets*, February 1989, *9*(1), pp. 15–27.

Earl, Peter E. Bounded Rationality, Psychology and Financial Evolution: Some Behavioural Perspectives on Post-Keynesian Analysis. In *Pheby, J., ed.*, 1989, pp. 165–89.

Earle, Peter. The Female Labour Market in London in the Late Seventeenth and Early Eighteenth Centuries. *Econ. Hist. Rev., 2nd Ser.*, August 1989, *42*(3), pp. 328–53.

Earley, James S. and Evans, Gary R. The Problem Is Bank Liability Management. In *Guttmann, R., ed.*, 1989, 1982, pp. 61–64.

Easingwood, Christopher J. An Analogical Approach to the Long Term Forecasting of Major New Product Sales. *Int. J. Forecasting*, 1989, *5*(1), pp. 69–82.

Easley, David and Kiefer, Nicholas M. Optimal Learning with Endogenous Data. *Int. Econ. Rev.*, November 1989, *30*(4), pp. 963–78.

Eastall, Richard and Kleinman, Mark. A Behavioural Model of the Supply of Re-lets of Council Housing in England. *Urban Stud.*, December 1989, *26*(6), pp. 535–48.

Easterby-Smith, Mark and Tanton, Morgan. Is the Western View Inevitable? A Model of the Development of Management Education. In *Davies, J., et al., eds.*, 1989, pp. 11–22.

Easterling, William E., III; Parry, Martin L. and Crosson, Pierre R. Adapting Future Agriculture to Changes in Climate. In *Rosenberg, N. J., et al., eds.*, 1989, pp. 91–104.

_____ **and Sonka, Steven T.** Economic Adjustments to Climatic Variability. In *Oram, P. A., et al.*, 1989, pp. 389–404.

_____ **and Wilhite, D. A.** Improving Response to Drought. In *Oram, P. A., et al.*, 1989, pp. 321–31.

Easterly, William R. Fiscal Adjustment and Deficit Financing during the Debt Crisis. In *Husain, I. and Diwan, I., eds.*, 1989, pp. 91–113.

Eastlack, Joseph O., Jr. and Rao, Ambar G. Advertising Experiments at the Campbell Soup Company. *Marketing Sci.*, Winter 1989, *8*(1), pp. 57–71.

_____ **and Rao, Ambar G.** Advertising Experiments at the Campbell Soup Company: Reply. *Marketing Sci.*, Winter 1989, *8*(1), pp. 76–77.

Easton, Geoffrey and Araujo, Luis. The Network Approach: An Articulation. In *Hallén, L. and Johanson, J., eds.*, 1989, pp. 97–119.

Easton, Peter D. and Zmijewski, Mark E. Cross-sectional Variation in the Stock Market Response to Accounting Earnings Announcements. *J. Acc. Econ.*, July 1989, *11*(2–3), pp. 117–41.

Easton, Stephen A. and Brown, Robert L. Weak-Form Efficiency in the Nineteenth Century: A Study of Daily Prices in the London Market for 3 Per Cent Consols, 1821–1860. *Economica*, February 1989, *56*(221), pp. 61–70.

Easton, Stephen T. Free Trade, Nationalism, and the Common Man: The Free Trade Agreement between Canada and the United States. *Contemp. Policy Issues*, July 1989, *7*(3), pp. 61–77.

_____ **and Jones, Ronald W.** Perspectives on 'Buy-Outs' and the Ramaswami Effect. *J. Int. Econ.*, November 1989, *27*(3–4), pp. 363–71.

Eaton, Adrienne E. and Cohn, Samuel. Historical Limits on Neoclassical Strike Theories: Evidence from French Coal Mining, 1890–1935. *Ind. Lab. Relat. Rev.*, July 1989, *42*(4), pp. 649–62.

_____ **and Voos, Paula B.** The Ability of Unions to Adapt to Innovative Workplace Arrangements. *Amer. Econ. Rev.*, May 1989, *79*(2), pp. 172–76.

Eaton, B. Curtis and Archibald, G. C. Two Applications of Characteristics Theory. In *Feiwel, G. R., ed. (I)*, 1989, pp. 409–36.

_____ **and Lipsey, Richard G.** Product Differentiation. In *Schmalensee, R. and Willig, R. D., eds., Vol. 1*, 1989, pp. 723–68.

Eaton, Jonathan. Beyond the Debt Crisis: Alternative Forms of Financing Growth: Comment. In *Husain, I. and Diwan, I., eds.*, 1989, pp. 306–308.

_____. Monopoly Wealth and International Debt. *Int. Econ. Rev.*, February 1989, *30*(1), pp. 33–48.

_____ **and Gersovitz, Mark.** Country Risk and the Organization of International Capital Transfer. In *[Díaz-Alejandro, C.]*, 1989, pp. 109–29.

Eaton, Mark. Japanese Industrial Policy. In *Matsuo, H., ed.*, 1989, pp. 36–49.

Ebel, Karl-H. Manning the Unmanned Factory. *Int. Lab. Rev.*, 1989, *128*(5), pp. 535–51.

Ebel, Robert D. and Case, Bradford. Using State Consumer Tax Credits for Achieving Equity. *Nat. Tax J.*, September 1989, *42*(3), pp. 323–37.

Ebeling, Dietrich. Some Remarks on the Relationship between Overall Economic Output and Real Wages in the Pre-industrial Period. In *Scholliers, P., ed.*, 1989, pp. 61–65.

Ebenroth, Carsten-Thomas. Competing Institutional Arrangements and Internationalization. In *Vosgerau, H.-J., ed.*, 1989, pp. 438–78.

Ebert, Robert R. The Price of Pipe Organs: An Eighteenth and Twentieth Century Comparison. *J. Cult. Econ.*, June 1989, *13*(1), pp. 77–88.

Eberts, Randall W. and Beeson, Patricia E. Identifying Productivity and Amenity Effects in Interurban Wage Differentials. *Rev. Econ. Statist.*, August 1989, *71*(3), pp. 443–52.

Ebrahimi, Bahman; Miner, John B. and Wachtel,

Jeffrey M. The Managerial Motivation of Potential Managers in the United States and Other Countries of the World: Implications for National Competitiveness and the Productivity Problem. In *Prasad, S. B., ed.*, 1989, pp. 147–70.

Echeverri-Carroll, Elsie. Japanese Maquilas: Opportunities for Expanding Texas Manufacturing. In *Matsuo, H., ed.*, 1989, pp. 64–74.

Eck, James R. and Baker, William Gary. Federal Tort Reform to Solve the Medical Malpractice Insurance Crisis. In *Missouri Valley Economic Association*, 1989, pp. 105–09.

Eckart, Christel. Learning from History? Notes on Part-Time Work as a Sign of Social Reproductive Needs. In *Agassi, J. B. and Heycock, S., eds.*, 1989, pp. 169–77.

Eckberg, Douglas Lee and Blocker, T. Jean. Environmental Issues as Women's Issues: General Concerns and Local Hazards. *Soc. Sci. Quart.*, September 1989, *70*(3), pp. 586–93.

Eckbo, B. Espen. The Role of Stock Market Studies in Formulating Antitrust Policy toward Horizontal Mergers: Comment. *Quart. J. Bus. Econ.*, Autumn 1989, *28*(4), pp. 22–38.

_____ **and Langohr, Herwig.** Information Disclosure, Method of Payment, and Takeover Premiums: Public and Private Tender Offers in France. *J. Finan. Econ.*, October 1989, *24*(2), pp. 363–403.

Eckel, Catherine C. and Holt, Charles A. Strategic Voting in Agenda-Controlled Committee Experiments. *Amer. Econ. Rev.*, September 1989, *79*(4), pp. 763–73.

_____ **and Vermaelen, Theo.** The Financial Fallout from Chernobyl: Risk Perceptions and Regulatory Response. In *Crew, M. A., ed.*, 1989, pp. 183–201.

Eckert, J. B. and Mullins, D. Income Redistribution and Its Effects on the South African Economy. *J. Stud. Econ. Econometrics*, November 1989, *13*(3), pp. 1–20.

Eckstein, Zvi and Drazen, Allan. On the Organization of Rural Markets and the Process of Economic Development: Reply. *Amer. Econ. Rev.*, December 1989, *79*(5), pp. 1299.

_____; **Eichenbaum, Martin and Aiyagari, S. Rao.** Inventories and Price Fluctuations under Perfect Competition and Monopoly. In *Kollintzas, T., ed.*, 1989, pp. 34–68.

_____ **and Wolpin, Kenneth I.** Dynamic Labour Force Participation of Married Women and Endogenous Work Experience. *Rev. Econ. Stud.*, July 1989, *56*(3), pp. 375–90.

_____ **and Wolpin, Kenneth I.** The Specification and Estimation of Dynamic Stochastic Discrete Choice Models: A Survey. *J. Human Res.*, Fall 1989, *24*(4), pp. 562–98.

Economides, Nicholas. Desirability of Compatibility in the Absence of Network Externalities. *Amer. Econ. Rev.*, December 1989, *79*(5), pp. 1165–81.

_____. Quality Variations and Maximal Variety Differentiation. *Reg. Sci. Urban Econ.*, February 1989, *19*(1), pp. 21–29.

_____. Symmetric Equilibrium Existence and

Optimality in Differentiated Product Markets. *J. Econ. Theory*, February 1989, *47*(1), pp. 178–94.

Eddie, Scott M. Economic Policy and Economic Development in Austria–Hungary, 1867–1913. In *Mathias, P. and Pollard, S., eds.*, 1989, pp. 814–86.

————. The Social Distribution of Landed Wealth in Hungary ca. 1910. In *Grantham, G. and Leonard, C. S., eds., Pt. A*, 1989, pp. 219–49.

Edebalk, Per Gunnar and Wadensjö, Eskil. Contractually Determined Insurance Schemes for Manual Workers. In *Gustafsson, B. A. and Klevmarken, N. A., eds.*, 1989, pp. 195–210.

Edelman, Mark A.; Orazem, Peter F. and Otto, Daniel M. An Analysis of Farmers' Agricultural Policy Preferences. *Amer. J. Agr. Econ.*, November 1989, *71*(4), pp. 837–46.

Edelman, Richard B. and Baker, H. Kent. The Dynamics of Neglect and Return: Reply. *J. Portfol. Manage.*, Winter 1989, *15*(2), pp. 77.

Edelstein, Joel. Market Reforms in Socialist Societies: Comparing China and Hungary: Conclusion. In *Van Ness, P., ed.*, 1989, pp. 306–12.

Edelstein, Robert H. and Dokko, Yoon. How Well Do Economists Forecast Stock Market Prices? A Study of the Livingston Surveys. *Amer. Econ. Rev.*, September 1989, *79*(4), pp. 865–71.

Eden, Benjamin and Landsburg, Steven E. On the Competitive Resolution of Trading Uncertainty. *J. Econ. Theory*, February 1989, *47*(1), pp. 66–75.

Eden, Lorraine. Compulsory Licensing and Canadian Pharmaceutical Policy. In *Rugman, A. M., ed.*, 1989, pp. 245–67.

Edey, Malcolm L. Risk Effects versus Monetary Effects in the Determination of Short-term Interest Rates. *Economica*, August 1989, *56*(223), pp. 311–22.

Edge, Stephen. The United Kingdom Approach to Anti-tax Avoidance Provisions. *Bull. Int. Fiscal Doc.*, February 1989, *43*(2), pp. 82–83.

Edgell, Stephen and Tilman, Rick. The Intellectual Antecedents of Thorstein Veblen: A Reappraisal. *J. Econ. Issues*, December 1989, *23*(4), pp. 1003–26.

Edgington, David W. Foreign Multinationals in Australian Cities and Regions. In *Higgins, B. and Zagorski, K., eds.*, 1989, pp. 234–50.

Edgren, Gus. Structural Adjustment, the Enterprise and the Workers. In *Edgren, G., ed.*, 1989, pp. 1–27.

Edin, Per-Anders. Unemployment Duration and Competing Risks: Evidence from Sweden. *Scand. J. Econ.*, 1989, *91*(4), pp. 639–53.

———— **and Agell, Jonas.** Tax Reform and Individual Investor Response: Evidence from Swedish Tax Return Data. *Public Finance*, 1989, *44*(2), pp. 183–203.

Edmister, Robert O. and Merriken, Harry E. Measuring Interest Rate Sensitivity of Consumer Depositors. *J. Finan. Services Res.*, June 1989, *2*(2), pp. 133–45.

Edmonds, Jae and Darmstadter, Joel. Human Development and Carbon Dioxide Emissions: The Current Picture and the Long-Term Prospects. In *Rosenberg, N. J., et al., eds.*, 1989, pp. 35–51.

Edozien, John and Adeoye, S. O. Privatisation in Nigeria. In *Ramanadham, V. V., ed.*, 1989, pp. 283–302.

Edwards, Alejandra Cox. Labor Market Adjustment with Wage Indexation: The Case of Chile between 1974 and 1980. In *Brock, P. L.; Connolly, M. B. and González-Vega, C., eds.*, 1989, pp. 133–50.

————. Labor Supply Price, Market Wage, and the Social Opportunity Cost of Labor. *Econ. Devel. Cult. Change*, October 1989, *38*(1), pp. 31–43.

————. Understanding Differences in Wages Relative to Income *Per Capita:* The Case of Teachers' Salaries. *Econ. Educ. Rev.*, 1989, *8*(2), pp. 197–203.

Edwards, Christine and Heery, Edmund. Recession in the Public Sector: Industrial Relations in Freightliner 1981–1985. *Brit. J. Ind. Relat.*, March 1989, *27*(1), pp. 57–71.

Edwards, Franklin R. Prologue to Conference on Regulatory Reform of Stock and Futures Markets. In *Edwards, F. R., ed.*, 1989, pp. 1–2.

————. Prologue to Conference on Regulatory Reform of Stock and Futures Markets. *J. Finan. Services Res.*, December 1989, *3*(2–3), pp. 99–100.

Edwards, Geoff. Big Problems Facing Small Societies. *Australian J. Agr. Econ.*, August 1989, *33*(2), pp. 71–87.

Edwards, Gerald A., Jr. and Boemio, Thomas R. Asset Securitization: A Supervisory Perspective. *Fed. Res. Bull.*, October 1989, *75*(10), pp. 659–69.

Edwards, Linda N. The Future of Public Sector Unions: Stagnation or Growth? *Amer. Econ. Rev.*, May 1989, *79*(2), pp. 161–65.

Edwards, P. S. A. The Disregard of a Legal Entity for Tax Purposes: Hong Kong. In *International Fiscal Association, ed. (II)*, 1989, pp. 289–310.

Edwards, Phillip M. and King, Maxwell L. Transformations for an Exact Goodness-of-Fit Test of Structural Change in the Linear Regression Model. In *Kramer, W., ed.*, 1989, pp. 49–57.

———— **and King, Maxwell L.** Transformations for an Exact Goodness-of-Fit Test of Structural Change in the Linear Regression Model. *Empirical Econ.*, 1989, *14*(2), pp. 113–21.

Edwards, Sebastian. Debt Crisis, Trade Liberalization, Structural Adjustment, and Growth: Some Policy Considerations. *Contemp. Policy Issues*, July 1989, *7*(3), pp. 30–41.

————. Economic Liberalization and the Equilibrium Real Exchange Rate in Developing Countries. In *[Díaz-Alejandro, C.]*, 1989, pp. 163–84.

————. Exchange Controls, Devaluations, and Real Exchange Rates: The Latin American Experience. *Econ. Devel. Cult. Change*, April 1989, *37*(3), pp. 457–94.

————. Exchange Rate Misalignment in Developing Countries. *World Bank Res. Observer*, January 1989, *4*(1), pp. 3–21.

_____. Implications of Alternative International Exchange Rate Arrangements for the Developing Countries. In *Vosgerau, H.-J., ed.*, 1989, pp. 34–84.

_____. The International Monetary Fund and the Developing Countries: A Critical Evaluation. *Carnegie–Rochester Conf. Ser. Public Policy*, Autumn 1989, *31*, pp. 7–68.

_____. Policy Reform and the Resolution of the Debt Crisis: Comment. *Carnegie–Rochester Conf. Ser. Public Policy*, Spring 1989, *30*, pp. 115–27.

_____. Structural Adjustment Policies in Highly Indebted Countries. In *Sachs, J. D., ed. (I)*, 1989, pp. 159–207.

_____. Structural Adjustment Policies in Highly Indebted Countries. In *Sachs, J. D., ed. (II)*, 1989, pp. 249–62.

_____. Tariffs, Capital Controls, and Equilibrium Real Exchange Rates. *Can. J. Econ.*, February 1989, *22*(1), pp. 79–92.

_____. Temporary Terms-of-Trade Disturbances, the Real Exchange Rate and the Current Account. *Economica*, August 1989, *56*(223), pp. 343–57.

_____. What Does the International Monetary Fund Really Do? Reply. *Carnegie–Rochester Conf. Ser. Public Policy*, Autumn 1989, *31*, pp. 77–81.

_____ and Larraín, Felipe. Debt, Adjustment, and Recovery in Latin America: An Introduction. In *Edwards, S. and Larrain, F., eds.*, 1989, pp. 1–27.

_____ and Montiel, Peter J. Devaluation Crises and the Macroeconomic Consequences of Postponed Adjustment in Developing Countries. *Int. Monet. Fund Staff Pap.*, December 1989, *36*(4), pp. 875–903.

_____ and Montiel, Peter J. The Price of Postponed Adjustment. *Finance Devel.*, September 1989, *26*(3), pp. 34–37.

_____ and Savastano, Miguel. Latin America's Intra-regional Trade: Evolution and Future Prospects. In *Greenaway, D.; Hyclak, T. and Thornton, R. J., eds.*, 1989, pp. 189–233.

Edwards, Steven F. and Carlson, Cynthia. On Estimating Compensation for Injury to Publicly Owned Marine Resources. *Marine Resource Econ.*, 1989, *6*(1), pp. 27–42.

Edwards, W. F. and Thompson, James F. The Retail Price Effect of the Kentucky and Tennessee Milk Marketing Laws. *Southern J. Agr. Econ.*, December 1989, *21*(2), pp. 211–15.

Edwardson, William. Improvement of the Small-Scale Food Industry in Developing Countries. *Industry Devel.*, June 1989, (27), pp. 67–79.

Eeckhoudt, Louis; Briys, Eric and Dionne, Georges. More on Insurance as a Giffen Good. *J. Risk Uncertainty*, December 1989, *2*(4), pp. 415–20.

_____ and Hansen, Pierre. Minimum Prices and Optimal Production under Multiple Sources of Risk: A Note. *Europ. Rev. Agr. Econ.*, 1989, *16*(3), pp. 411–18.

_____; Sneessens, Henri and Calcoen, Francis. L'épargne de précaution: Une analyse géométrique. (Precautionary Saving: A Geometric Analysis. With English summary.) *Revue Écon.*, January 1989, *40*(1), pp. 21–34.

van den Eeckhout, Patricia. Wage Formation: Some More Problems. In *Scholliers, P., ed.*, 1989, pp. 40–47.

Eele, Graham. The Organization and Management of Statistical Services in Africa: Why Do They Fail? *World Devel.*, March 1989, *17*(3), pp. 431–38.

Eff, E. Anton. History of Thought as Ceremonial Genealogy: The Neglected Influence of Herbert Spencer on Thorstein Veblen. *J. Econ. Issues*, September 1989, *23*(3), pp. 689–716.

Eftekhari, Hossein. Vertical Integration and Power Generation in the United States. In *Missouri Valley Economic Association*, 1989, pp. 25–31.

Efthymoglou, Prodromos G. and Vlachou, Andriana S. Productivity in the Vertically Integrated System of the Greek Electricity Utility, 1970–85. *Energy Econ.*, April 1989, *11*(2), pp. 119–26.

Egan, Daniel L.; Herrmann, Douglas J. and Jones, Derek C. Evidence on Attitudes toward Alternative Sharing Arrangements. *Ind. Relat.*, Fall 1989, *28*(3), pp. 411–18.

_____ and Martin, Philip L. The Makewhole Remedy in California Agriculture. *Ind. Lab. Relat. Rev.*, October 1989, *43*(1), pp. 120–30.

Eggers, Mitchell; Preston, Samuel H. and Himes, Christine. Demographic Conditions Responsible for Population Aging. *Demography*, November 1989, *26*(4), pp. 691–704.

Eggerstedt, Harald and Maennig, Wolfgang. Anpassungsprogramme und wirtschaftliche Projektionen der Weltbank. Eine theoretische und praktische Analyse. (Adjustment Programs and Economic Projections by the World Bank: A Theoretical and Practical Assessment. With English summary.) *Konjunkturpolitik*, 1989, *35*(6), pp. 346–60.

Egorova, Elena N. and Shejhetov, Boris M. Simulated Analysis of the Integration of Science and Industry. *Econ. Systems Res.*, 1989, *1*(4), pp. 481–89.

Ehrat, Felix R. National and International Tax Aspects of Charities and Charitable Contributions: Swiss Report. *Bull. Int. Fiscal Doc.*, December 1989, *43*(12), pp. 570–75.

Ehrbar, Hans. Mathematics and the Labor Theory of Value. *Rev. Radical Polit. Econ.*, Fall 1989, *21*(3), pp. 7–12.

Ehrenberg, Ronald G. Empirical Consequences of Comparable Worth. In *Hill, M. A. and Killingsworth, M. R., eds.*, 1989, pp. 90–106.

_____. Women's Pay in Australia, Great Britain, and the United States: The Role of Laws, Regulations, and Human Capital: Commentary. In *Michael, R. T.; Hartmann, H. I. and O'Farrell, B., eds.*, 1989, pp. 243–46.

_____. Workers' Rights: Rethinking Protective Labor Legislation. In *Bawden, D. L. and Skidmore, F., eds.*, 1989, pp. 137–72.

_____ and Jakubson, George H. Advance Notification of Plant Closing: Does It Matter? *Ind. Relat.*, Winter 1989, 28(1), pp. 60–71.

Ehrenhaft, Peter D. The Application of Antidumping Duties to Imports from "Non-market Economies." In *Jackson, J. H. and Vermulst, E. A., eds.*, 1989, pp. 302–10.

Ehrhardt, Michael C. A New Linear Programming Approach to Bond Portfolio Management: A Comment. *J. Finan. Quant. Anal.*, December 1989, 24(4), pp. 533–37.

_____; Clayton, Ronnie and Delozier, John. A Note on January Returns in the U.S. Government Bond Market: The Term Effect. *J. Finan. Services Res.*, October 1989, 2(4), pp. 307–18.

Ehrlich, Anne and Ehrlich, Paul. The Environmental Dimensions of National Security. In *Rotblat, J. and Goldanskii, V. I., eds.*, 1989, pp. 180–90.

Ehrlich, Paul and Ehrlich, Anne. The Environmental Dimensions of National Security. In *Rotblat, J. and Goldanskii, V. I., eds.*, 1989, pp. 180–90.

Ehui, Simeon K. and Hertel, Thomas W. Deforestation and Agricultural Productivity in the Côte d'Ivoire. *Amer. J. Agr. Econ.*, August 1989, 71(3), pp. 703–11.

Eichberger, Jürgen. A Note on Bankruptcy Rules and Credit Constraints in Temporary Equilibrium. *Econometrica*, May 1989, 57(3), pp. 707–15.

_____ and Harper, Ian R. On Deposit Interest Rate Regulation and Deregulation. *J. Ind. Econ.*, September 1989, 38(1), pp. 19–30.

Eichenbaum, Martin. Some Empirical Evidence on the Production Level and Production Cost Smoothing Models of Inventory Investment. *Amer. Econ. Rev.*, September 1989, 79(4), pp. 853–64.

_____; Aiyagari, S. Rao and Eckstein, Zvi. Inventories and Price Fluctuations under Perfect Competition and Monopoly. In *Kollintzas, T., ed.*, 1989, pp. 34–68.

_____ and Christiano, Lawrence J. Temporal Aggregation and the Stock Adjustment Model of Inventories. In *Kollintzas, T., ed.*, 1989, pp. 70–108.

Eichenberg, Luiz C. and Salm, Cláudio. Integration Trends in the Brazilian Labour Market. *CEPAL Rev.*, December 1989, (39), pp. 63–72.

Eichenberger, Reiner and Frey, Bruno S. Anomalies and Institutions. *J. Inst. Theoretical Econ.*, September 1989, 145(3), pp. 423–37.

_____ and Frey, Bruno S. Choice under Uncertainty: Problems Solved and Unsolved: Comment. *J. Econ. Perspectives*, Summer 1989, 3(3), pp. 181–83.

_____ and Frey, Bruno S. Zur Bedeutung entscheidungstheoretischer Anomalien für die Ökonomik. (How Important Are Choice Anomalies for Economics? With English summary.) *Jahr. Nationalökon. Statist.*, March 1989, 206(2), pp. 81–101.

Eichengreen, Barry. The Founding of the Fed and the Destablization of the Post-1914 U.S.

Economy: Discussion. In *De Cecco, M. and Giovannini, A., eds.*, 1989, pp. 333–36.

_____. Hegemonic Stability Theories of the International Monetary System. In *Cooper, R. N., et al.*, 1989, pp. 255–98.

_____. House Calls of the Money Doctor: The Kemmerer Missions to Latin America, 1917–1931. In *[Díaz-Alejandro, C.]*, 1989, pp. 57–77.

_____. How Do Fixed-Exchange-Rate Regimes Work? Evidence from the Gold Standard, Bretton Woods and the EMS: Discussion. In *Miller, M.; Eichengreen, B. and Portes, R., eds.*, 1989, pp. 43–46.

_____. The Political Economy of the Smoot–Hawley Tariff. In *Ransom, R. L., ed.*, 1989, pp. 1–43.

_____. Resolving Debt Crises: An Historical Perspective. In *Edwards, S. and Larrain, F., eds.*, 1989, pp. 68–96.

_____. The U.S. Capital Market and Foreign Lending, 1920–1955. In *Sachs, J. D., ed. (II)*, 1989, pp. 237–48.

_____. The U.S. Capital Market and Foreign Lending, 1920–1955. In *Sachs, J. D., ed. (I)*, 1989, pp. 107–55.

_____ and Goulder, Lawrence H. Savings Promotion, Investment Promotion, and International Competitiveness. In *Feenstra, R. C., ed.*, 1989, pp. 5–44.

_____ and Goulder, Lawrence H. The U.S. Basic Industries in the 1980s: Can Fiscal Policies Explain Their Changing Competitive Position? In *Black, S. W., ed.*, 1989, pp. 9–70.

_____ and Lindert, Peter H. The International Debt Crisis in Historical Perspective: Overview. In *Eichengreen, B. and Lindert, P. H., eds.*, 1989, pp. 1–11.

_____ and Portes, Richard. After the Deluge: Default, Negotiation, and Readjustment during the Interwar Years. In *Eichengreen, B. and Lindert, P. H., eds.*, 1989, pp. 12–47.

_____ and Portes, Richard. Dealing with Debt: The 1930s and the 1980s. In *Husain, I. and Diwan, I., eds.*, 1989, pp. 69–86.

_____; Portes, Richard and Miller, Marcus H. Blueprints for Exchange-Rate Management: Introduction. In *Miller, M.; Eichengreen, B. and Portes, R., eds.*, 1989, pp. 1–10.

Eichenseher, John W. and Shields, David. Corporate Capital Structure and Auditor 'Fit.' In *Gangolly, J., ed.*, 1989, pp. 39–56.

Eichner, Alfred S. The Further Theoretical Development of the Weintraub Aggregate Price Equation. In *[Weintraub, S.]*, 1989, pp. 83–98.

Eidsvik, Harold K. The Status of Wilderness: An International Overview. *Natural Res. J.*, Winter 1989, 29(1), pp. 57–82.

van Eijk, C. J. Concerted Action: A Remedy against Persistent Unemployment? In *Muller, F. and Zwezerijnen, W. J., eds.*, 1989, pp. 62–71.

Einy, Ezra. On Preference Relations Which Satisfy Weak Independence Property. *J. Math. Econ.*, 1989, 18(3), pp. 291–300.

—— and **Lehrer, Ehud.** Regular Simple Games. *Int. J. Game Theory*, 1989, *18*(2), pp. 195–207.

—— and **Neyman, Abraham.** Large Symmetric Games Are Characterized by Completeness of the Desirability Relation. *J. Econ. Theory*, August 1989, *48*(2), pp. 369–85.

Eisdorfer, Carl; Kessler, David A. and Spector, Abby N. Caring for the Elderly: Introduction. In *Eisdorfer, C.; Kessler, D. A. and Spector, A. N., eds.,* 1989, pp. xix–xxi.

Eiselt, Horst A. and Laporte, Gilbert. The Maximum Capture Problem in a Weighted Network. *J. Reg. Sci.*, August 1989, *29*(3), pp. 433–39.

Eisenstadt, Abraham S. Political Corruption in American History. In *Heidenheimer, A. J.; Johnston, M. and LeVine, V. T., eds.,* 1989, *1978*, pp. 537–56.

Eismont, O. A. and Dubovsky, S. V. Long-Range Modeling of the USSR Economy. In *Krelle, W., ed.,* 1989, pp. 311–24.

Eisner, Robert. Budget Deficits: Rhetoric and Reality. *J. Econ. Perspectives*, Spring 1989, *3*(2), pp. 73–93.

——. Debt and Deficit and Other Illusions. In *Feiwel, G. R., ed. (1),* 1989, pp. 709–20.

——. Divergences of Measurement and Theory and Some Implications for Economic Policy. *Amer. Econ. Rev.*, March 1989, *79*(1), pp. 1–13.

——. Employer Approaches to Reducing Unemployment. In *Bawden, D. L. and Skidmore, F., eds.,* 1989, pp. 59–80.

——. Government Saving, Capital Formation, and Wealth in the United States, 1947–85: Comment. In *Lipsey, R. E. and Tice, H. S., eds.,* 1989, pp. 353–56.

——. Les déficits budgétaires: De la rhétorique à la réalité. (Budget Deficits: Rhetoric and Reality. With English summary.) *Écon. Appl.*, 1989, *42*(1), pp. 135–59.

——. On Keynesian Underemployment, Prices, and Wealth Effects of Government Debt. In *Barrère, A., ed.,* 1989, pp. 162–69.

—— and **Pieper, Paul J.** Inflation-Adjusted Government Budget Deficits and Real Economic Activity: Rejoinder. *Ann. Écon. Statist.*, Jan.–March 1989, (13), pp. 139–47.

Ekanayake, S. A. B. and Jayasuriya, Sisira K. Change, Adjustment and the Role of Specific Experience: Evidence from Sri Lankan Rice Farming. *Australian J. Agr. Econ.*, August 1989, *33*(2), pp. 123–35.

Ekelund, Robert B., Jr. and Hébert, Robert F. Consumer Surplus: The First Hundred Years. In *Wood, J. C. and Woods, R. N., eds., Vol. 4,* 1989, *1985*, pp. 198–230.

——; **Hébert, Robert F. and Tollison, Robert D.** An Economic Model of the Medieval Church: Usury as a Form of Rent Seeking. *J. Law, Econ., Organ.*, Fall 1989, *5*(2), pp. 307–31.

—— and **Shieh, Yeung-Nan.** Jevons on Utility, Exchange, and Demand Theory: A Reassessment. *Manchester Sch. Econ. Soc. Stud.*, March 1989, *57*(1), pp. 17–33.

—— and **Thommesen, Sven.** Disequilibrium Theory and Thornton's Assault on the Laws of Supply and Demand. *Hist. Polit. Econ.*, Winter 1989, *21*(4), pp. 567–92.

——; **Tollison, Robert D. and Anderson, Gary M.** Nassau Senior as Economic Consultant: The Factory Acts Reconsidered. *Economica*, February 1989, *56*(221), pp. 71–81.

Ekstrom, Carl D. Budgetary Practices in Smaller Units of Government. *Public Budg. Finance*, Summer 1989, *9*(2), pp. 76–82.

El-Amir, M. R. Rice Processing and Handling Technologies. In *International Rice Research Institute,* 1989, pp. 329–32.

El-Beblawi, Hazem. Privatization: Opportunities for Financial Market Development: Comment. In *El-Naggar, S., ed.,* 1989, pp. 137–40.

El-Bushra, El-Sayed. The Urban Crisis and Rural–Urban Migration in Sudan. In *[Mountjoy, A. B.],* 1989, pp. 109–40.

El-Gabaly, M. M. The Role of Early-Maturing Rice Varieties in the Cropping Systems of Egypt. In *International Rice Research Institute,* 1989, pp. 35–39.

El-Gaghdadi, Mahdi and Suliman, M. Osman. Global Approaches to Commodity Price Stabilization. *J. World Trade*, August 1989, *23*(4), pp. 25–34.

El-Naggar, Said. Privatization and Structural Adjustment: The Basic Issues. In *El-Naggar, S., ed.,* 1989, pp. 1–17.

El Reedy, Tarek and Harajli, Ali. Transport Strategy for Greater Amman: A Look into the Future. In *Candemir, Y., ed.,* 1989, pp. 433–44.

El-Sahrigi, A. F. and Ishihara, S. Mechanization of Rice Production in Egypt. In *International Rice Research Institute,* 1989, pp. 167–73.

El Serafy, Salah and Lutz, Ernst. Environmental and Natural Resource Accounting. In *Schramm, G. and Warford, J. J., eds.,* 1989, pp. 23–38.

El Shazly, Mona R. The Oil-Price Effect on the Dollar/Pound Rate of Exchange. *Int. Econ. J.*, Autumn 1989, *3*(3), pp. 73–83.

Elbaum, Bernard. Why Apprenticeship Persisted in Britain but Not in the United States. *J. Econ. Hist.*, June 1989, *49*(2), pp. 337–49.

Elder, Eric E. and Butcher, Walter R. Including the Economic Impact of Cost Paying in Regional Input–Output Analysis. *Western J. Agr. Econ.*, July 1989, *14*(1), pp. 78–84.

Elder, Harold W. Trials and Settlements in the Criminal Courts: An Empirical Analysis of Dispositions and Sentencing. *J. Legal Stud.*, January 1989, *18*(1), pp. 191–208.

—— and **Misiolek, Walter S.** Exclusionary Manipulation of Markets for Pollution Rights. *J. Environ. Econ. Manage.*, March 1989, *16*(2), pp. 156–66.

Eldor, Rafael; Pines, David and Schwartz, Abba. Determinants of an Individual's Demand for Hedging Instruments. *J. Futures Markets*, April 1989, *9*(2), pp. 135–41.

Elek, Andrew; Camilleri, Arthur and Lester, Michael. Innovation and Technological Change in Australia: Problems and Prospects. **In** *[Gruen, F. H.]*, 1989, pp. 190–209.

Elfring, Tom. New Evidence on the Expansion of Service Employment in Advanced Economies. *Rev. Income Wealth*, December 1989, 35(4), pp. 409–40.

Elg, Ulf; Johansson, Ulf and Wikström, Solveig R. From the Consumption of Necessities to Experience-Seeking Consumption. **In** *Grunert, K. G. and Ölander, F.*, eds., 1989, pp. 287–308.

Elgin, Miranda and Binswanger, Hans P. Quais são as perspectivas para a reforma agrária? (With English summary.) *Pesquisa Planejamento Econ.*, April 1989, 19(1), pp. 1–18.

Elias, D. J. and Cooper, David A. Estimated Economic Cost of HIV/AIDS: 1988/89 to 1992/3. **In** *Smith, C. S.*, ed., 1989, pp. 18–26.

Eliashberg, Jehoshua; Robertson, Thomas S. and Gatignon, Hubert. Modeling Multinational Diffusion Patterns: An Efficient Methodology. *Marketing Sci.*, Summer 1989, 8(3), pp. 231–47.

Eliasson, Gunnar. Modeling the Experimentally Organized Economy—Overview of the MO-SES Model. **In** *Albrecht, J. W., et al.*, 1989, pp. 7–65.

Elish, Herbert. Employee Ownership Works for All Parties. **In** *Ahlbrandt, R. S., Jr.*, ed., 1989, pp. 58–60.

Ellickson, Robert C. The Case for Coase and against "Coaseanism." *Yale Law J.*, December 1989, 99(3), pp. 611–30.

———. A Hypothesis of Wealth-Maximizing Norms: Evidence from the Whaling Industry. *J. Law, Econ., Organ.*, Spring 1989, 5(1), pp. 83–97.

Elliehausen, Gregory E. and Durkin, Thomas A. Theory and Evidence of the Impact of Equal Credit Opportunity: An Agnostic Review of the Literature. *J. Finan. Services Res.*, June 1989, 2(2), pp. 89–114.

Ellinger, Paul N. and Barry, Peter J. Credit Scoring, Loan Pricing, and Farm Business Performance. *Western J. Agr. Econ.*, July 1989, 14(1), pp. 45–55.

Elliot, John E. and Dymski, Gary A. The Taxonomy of Primary Exploitation. *Rev. Soc. Econ.*, Winter 1989, 47(4), pp. 338–76.

Elliott, Barbara J. and Rossmiller, George E. Agriculture in the GATT: A Perspective from the United States. *Can. J. Agr. Econ.*, Part 2, December 1989, 37(4), pp. 853–61.

Elliott, Catherine S. and Archibald, Robert B. Subjective Framing and Attitudes towards Risk. *J. Econ. Psych.*, November 1989, 10(3), pp. 321–28.

——— **and Archibald, Robert B.** Trial-and-Error Learning and Economic Models. *Kyklos*, 1989, 42(1), pp. 39–59.

Elliott, David and Marshall, Michael. Sector Strategy in the West Midlands. **In** *Hirst, P. and Zeitlin, J.*, eds., 1989, pp. 223–47.

Elliott, John E. Gorbachev's Perestroika. *Contemp. Policy Issues*, January 1989, 7(1), pp. 35–52.

———. The Three Facts of John Locke: Fundamental Ambiguities in Government's Economic Functions. **In** *Samuels, W. J.*, ed. (I), 1989, pp. 59–67.

——— **and Clark, Barry S.** Richard Henry Tawney on the Democratic Economy. *Int. J. Soc. Econ.*, 1989, 16(3), pp. 44–58.

Elliott, Robert F. and Murphy, Philip D. Evasion of Incomes Policy: A Model of Non-compliance. *Econ. J.*, December 1989, 99(398), pp. 1054–64.

Ellis, Christopher J. An Equilibrium Politico–Economic Model. *Econ. Inquiry*, July 1989, 27(3), pp. 521–28.

Ellis, M. Ocean Energy Developments: Prospects for Pacific Island Nations. **In** *Couper, A. D.*, ed., 1989, pp. 127–44.

Ellis, M. E. and Ma, Christopher K. Selecting Industries as Inflation Hedges. *J. Portfol. Manage.*, Summer 1989, 15(4), pp. 45–48.

Ellis, Randall P. Employee Choice of Health Insurance. *Rev. Econ. Statist.*, May 1989, 71(2), pp. 215–23.

———; **McGuire, Thomas G. and Freiman, Marc P.** Provider Response to Medicare's PPS: Reductions in Length of Stay for Psychiatric Patients Treated in Scatter Beds. *Inquiry*, Summer 1989, 26(2), pp. 192–201.

Ellison, Julian. Race, Radicalism, and Reform: Selected Papers: Review Essay. *Rev. Black Polit. Econ.*, Fall 1989, 18(2), pp. 97–103.

Ellsworth, Lynn and Shapiro, Kenneth. Seasonality in Burkina Faso Grain Marketing: Farmer Strategies and Government Policy. **In** *Sahn, D. E.*, ed., 1989, pp. 196–205.

Elmendorf, Douglas W. and Feldstein, Martin. Budget Deficits, Tax Incentives, and Inflation: A Surprising Lesson from the 1983–1984 Recovery. **In** *Summers, L. H.*, ed., 1989, pp. 1–23.

Elshabani, Abdelgader and White, Graham S. Regional Transportation Planning Issues in the Context of Comprehensive Development Plans. **In** *Candemir, Y.*, ed., 1989, pp. 161–83.

Elsner, Wolfram. Adam Smith's Model of the Origins and Emergence of Institutions: The Modern Findings of the Classical Approach. *J. Econ. Issues*, March 1989, 23(1), pp. 189–213.

Elson, Diane. Bound by One Thread: The Restructuring of UK Clothing and Textile Multinationals. **In** *MacEwan, A. and Tabb, W. K.*, eds., 1989, pp. 187–204.

———. The Cutting Edge: Multinationals in the EEC Textiles and Clothing Industry. **In** *Elson, D. and Pearson, R.*, eds., 1989, pp. 80–110.

——— **and Pearson, Ruth.** Nimble Fingers and Foreign Investments: Introduction. **In** *Elson, D. and Pearson, R.*, eds., 1989, pp. 1–11.

Elster, Jon. Social Norms and Economic Theory. *J. Econ. Perspectives*, Fall 1989, 3(4), pp. 99–117.

Elterich, G. J. and Gempesaw, C. M., II. The Importance of International Students in the Academic Market for Agricultural Economists.

Amer. J. Agr. Econ., May 1989, 71(2), pp. 275–79.

Eltis, David. Trade between Western Africa and the Atlantic World before 1870: Estimates of Trends in Value, Composition and Direction. In *Ransom, R. L., ed.*, 1989, pp. 197–239.

Eltis, Walter. Argentina's Economy under a Labour-Based Government, 1973–76: Comment. In *di Tella, G. and Dornbusch, R., eds.*, 1989, pp. 247–53.

———. Ten Years of Mrs. T.: Comment. In *Blanchard, O. J. and Fischer, S., eds.*, 1989, pp. 67–71.

Elton, Edwin J.; Gruber, Martin J. and Rentzler, Joel. New Public Offerings, Information, and Investor Rationality: The Case of Publicly Offered Commodity Funds. *J. Bus.*, January 1989, 62(1), pp. 1–15.

Elvers, Eva. Quality Presentation in Environment Statistics—Some Swedish Examples. *Statist. J.*, 1989, 6(3), pp. 269–82.

Ely, David P. and Robinson, Kenneth J. The Stock Market and Inflation: A Synthesis of the Theory and Evidence. *Fed. Res. Bank Dallas Econ. Rev.*, March 1989, pp. 17–29.

Elzinga, Kenneth G. Collusive Predation: *Matsushita v. Zenith.* In *Kwoka, J. E., Jr. and White, L. J., eds.*, 1989, pp. 241–62.

———. Unmasking Monopoly: Four Types of Economic Evidence. In *Larner, R. J. and Meehan, J. W., Jr., eds.*, 1989, pp. 11–38.

Emami, Ali; Martin, Michael V. and Lev, Larry. United States Agricultural Trade: Where Are the Gains? Comment. *Western J. Agr. Econ.*, December 1989, 14(2), pp. 310–12.

Embardo, Robert J. "Summer Lightning," 1907: The Wobblies in Bridgeport. *Labor Hist.*, Fall 1989, 30(4), pp. 518–35.

Embry, Olice H. First Businesses of Columbus—Georgia's First Planned City. In *Perkins, E. J., ed.*, 1989, pp. 237–46.

Emel'ianov, A. The Economic Mechanism and the Socialist Market for the Means of Production. *Prob. Econ.*, February 1989, 31(10), pp. 95–107.

Emerson, Michael. The Emergence of the New European Economy of 1992. *Bus. Econ.*, October 1989, 24(4), pp. 5–9.

Emerson, Robert D. Migratory Labor and Agriculture. *Amer. J. Agr. Econ.*, August 1989, 71(3), pp. 617–29.

Emerson, William and Anderson, James. A Spatial Allocation Model for the New England Fisheries. *Marine Resource Econ.*, 1989, 6(2), pp. 123–44.

Emmott, William. The Limits to Japanese Power. In *[Marjolin, R.]*, 1989, pp. 5–18.

Emons, Winand. On the Limitation of Warranty Duration. *J. Ind. Econ.*, March 1989, 37(3), pp. 287–301.

———. The Theory of Warranty Contracts. *J. Econ. Surveys*, 1989, 3(1), pp. 43–57.

Encaoua, David. Différenciation des produits et structures de marché: Un tour d'horizon. (Production Differentiation and Market Structure:

A Survey. With English summary.) *Ann. Écon. Statist.*, July–Dec. 1989, (15–16), pp. 51–83.

———. Market Dynamics and Industrial Structure: Forward. *Ann. Écon. Statist.*, July–Dec. 1989, (15–16), pp. 21–38.

——— and **Santini, Jean-Jacques.** Les privatisations en France: Éléments d'analyse et bilan. (With English summary.) *L'Actual. Econ.*, March 1989, 65(1), pp. 21–52.

Encarnation, Dennis. American–Japanese Cross Investment: A Second Front of Economic Rivalry. In *Haggard, S. and Moon, C., eds.*, 1989, pp. 209–50.

Enders, Alice and Bernhardt, Dan. Free Trade Equilibria to Multi-country Quota Games. *J. Int. Econ.*, November 1989, 27(3–4), pp. 319–33.

Enders, Walter. Unit Roots and the Real Exchange Rate before World War I: The Case of Britain and the USA. *J. Int. Money Finance*, March 1989, 8(1), pp. 59–73.

——— and **Gauger, Jean A.** Money Neutrality at Aggregate and Sectoral Levels. *Southern Econ. J.*, January 1989, 55(3), pp. 771–78.

Enderwick, Peter. Multinational Contracting. In *Enderwick, P.*, 1989, pp. 132–51.

———. Multinational Service Firms: Conclusions. In *Enderwick, P.*, 1989, pp. 245–55.

———. Policy Issues in International Trade and Investment in Services. In *Enderwick, P.*, 1989, pp. 215–44.

———. Some Economics of Service-Sector Multinational Enterprises. In *Enderwick, P.*, 1989, pp. 3–34.

Endres, Alfred. Liability and Information. *J. Inst. Theoretical Econ.*, June 1989, 145(2), pp. 249–74.

Enelow, James M. and Hinich, Melvin J. A General Probabilistic Spatial Theory of Elections. *Public Choice*, May 1989, 61(2), pp. 101–13.

Engel, Charles. The Trade Balance and Real Exchange Rate under Currency Substitution. *J. Int. Money Finance*, March 1989, 8(1), pp. 47–58.

——— and **Kletzer, Kenneth M.** Saving and Investment in an Open Economy with Nontraded Goods. *Int. Econ. Rev.*, November 1989, 30(4), pp. 735–52.

——— and **Rodrigues, Anthony P.** Tests of International CAPM with Time-Varying Covariances. *J. Appl. Econometrics*, April–June 1989, 4(2), pp. 119–38.

Engels, Friedrich. Conditions et perspectives d'une guerre de la Sainte-Alliance contre une France révolutionnaire en 1852. (Conditions and Perspectives of the War of the Holy Alliance against Revolutionary France in 1852. With English summary.) *Écon. Societes*, September 1989, 23(9), pp. 75–95.

Engels, Wolfram. Tax Reform Here and There. In *Fels, G. and von Furstenberg, G. M., eds.*, 1989, pp. 341–52.

Engineer, Merwan. Bank Runs and the Suspension of Deposit Convertibility. *J. Monet. Econ.*, November 1989, 24(3), pp. 443–54.

———. Taxes, Public Goods, and the Ruling

Class: An Exploration of the Territory between Brennan and Buchanan's Leviathan and Conventional Public Finance. *Public Finance*, 1989, *44*(1), pp. 19–30.

England, Catherine. A Market Approach to the Savings and Loan Crisis. In *Crane, E. H. and Boaz, D.*, 1989, pp. 105–28.

England, George W. and Quintanilla, S. Antonio Ruiz. Major Work Meaning Patterns in the National Labor Forces of Germany, Japan and the United States. In *Prasad, S. B., ed.*, 1989, pp. 77–94.

England, Kim V. L.; Goetz, Andrew R. and Brown, Lawrence A. Location, Social Categories, and Individual Labor Market Experiences in Developing Economies: The Venezuelan Case. *Int. Reg. Sci. Rev.*, 1989, *12*(1), pp. 1–28.

Englander, A. Steven and Steindel, Charles. Evaluating Recent Trends in Capital Formation. *Fed. Res. Bank New York Quart. Rev.*, Autumn 1989, *14*(3), pp. 7–19.

_____ **and Stone, Gary.** Inflation Expectations Surveys as Predictors of Inflation and Behavior in Financial and Labor Markets. *Fed. Res. Bank New York Quart. Rev.*, Autumn 1989, *14*(3), pp. 20–32.

Englander, Ernest J.; Marcus, Alfred A. and Kaufman, Allen M. Structure and Implementation in Issues Management: Transaction Costs and Agency Theory. In *Post, J. E., ed.*, 1989, pp. 257–71.

Engle, R. F.; Granger, C. W. J. and Hallman, Jeffrey J. Merging Short- and Long-run Forecasts: An Application of Seasonal Cointegration to Monthly Electricity Sales Forecasting. *J. Econometrics*, January 1989, *40*(1), pp. 45–62.

English, William B.; Miron, Jeffrey A. and Wilcox, David W. Seasonal Fluctuations and the Life Cycle–Permanent Income Model of Consumption: A Correction. *J. Polit. Econ.*, August 1989, *97*(4), pp. 988–91.

Englund, Peter. Monetary Policy and Bank Regulations in an Economy with Financial Innovations. *Economica*, November 1989, *56*(224), pp. 459–72.

_____; **Hörngren, Lars and Viotti, Staffan.** Discount Window Borrowing and Money Market Interest Rates. *Scand. J. Econ.*, 1989, *91*(3), pp. 517–33.

Engström, Lars and Löfren, Karl-Gustaf. The Duration of Unemployment: Theory and Evidence. In *Holmlund, B.; Löfgren, K.-G. and Engström, L.*, 1989, pp. 133–220.

Enikolopov, Nikolai and Babievsky, Kirill. Chemical Disarmament: Reliable and Efficient Control. In *Rotblat, J. and Goldanskii, V. I., eds.*, 1989, pp. 112–16.

Enis, Charles R. and Hunt, Herbert G., III. Economic Analysis of Broad-Based Income and Consumption Taxes. In *Jones, S. M., ed.*, 1989, pp. 223–45.

Enke, Harald. Tertiarisierung und internationale Arbeitsteilung. Überlegungen und Materialien zur Bedeutung von Tertiarisierungsbefunden in der offenen Volkswirtschaft. (Increasing

Share of Tertiary Activities and International Division of Labour. With English summary.) *Jahr. Nationalökon. Statist.*, October 1989, *206*(4–5), pp. 329–46.

Ennew, C. T. and White, B. The Implications of Quotas and Supply Control Policy in the British Potato Market. *Europ. Rev. Agr. Econ.*, 1989, *16*(2), pp. 243–56.

_____, **et al.** Simulation and Optimisation in Agricultural Policy Analysis: The Case of the British Potato Market. In *Bauer, S. and Henrichsmeyer, W., eds.*, 1989, pp. 175–81.

Enos, J. L. Transfer of Technology. *Asian-Pacific Econ. Lit.*, March 1989, *3*(1), pp. 3–37.

Enria, Andrea. Sraffa e Keynes: Note su moneta, valore e incertezza. (Sraffa and Keynes: Notes on Money, Value and Uncertainty. With English summary.) *Econ. Politica*, August 1989, *6*(2), pp. 215–33.

Enrich, Enric and Girbau, Ramón. International Tax Aspects of Philanthropic and Other Nonprofit Organisations: Spain. *Bull. Int. Fiscal Doc.*, December 1989, *43*(12), pp. 576–78.

Enriquez de Salamanca, Rafael. Política de financiación óptima en la Seguridad Social. (With English summary.) *Invest. Ecón.*, September 1989, *13*(3), pp. 485–516.

Entwisle, Barbara. Measuring Components of Family Planning Program Effort. *Demography*, February 1989, *26*(1), pp. 53–76.

_____. Measuring Components of Family Planning Program Effort: Reply. *Demography*, February 1989, *26*(1), pp. 81–84.

Epaulard, Anne; Moncomble, Jean-Eudes and Assouline, Mireille. Alignement des régimes de TVA français sur une norme européenne, l'analyse du modèle Hermès-France. (With English summary.) *Revue Écon. Politique*, May–June 1989, *99*(3), pp. 497–516.

Epperson, J. E. and Lei, L. F. A Regional Analysis of Vegetable Production with Changing Demand for Row Crops Using Quadratic Programming. *Southern J. Agr. Econ.*, July 1989, *21*(1), pp. 87–96.

Epple, Dennis and Romer, Thomas. On the Flexibility of Municipal Boundaries. *J. Urban Econ.*, November 1989, *26*(3), pp. 307–19.

_____; **Romer, Thomas and Cassidy, Glenn.** Redistribution by Local Governments in a Monocentric Urban Area. *Reg. Sci. Urban Econ.*, August 1989, *19*(3), pp. 421–54.

Epplin, Francis M. and Stoecker, Arthur L. Mathematical Programming. In *Tweeten, L., ed.*, 1989, pp. 212–37.

Epstein, Edward C. Austerity and Trade Unions in Latin America. In *Canak, W. L., ed.*, 1989, pp. 169–89.

_____. What Difference Does Regime Type Make? Economic Austerity Programs in Argentina. In *Handelman, H. and Baer, W., eds.*, 1989, pp. 64–80.

Epstein, Gerald A. Financial Instability and the Structure of the International Monetary System. In *MacEwan, A. and Tabb, W. K., eds.*, 1989, pp. 101–20.

_____ **and Schor, Juliet B.** The Divorce of the

Banca d'Italia and the Italian Treasury: A Case Study of Central Bank Independence. In *Lange, P. and Regini, M., eds.*, 1989, pp. 147–64.

Epstein, José D. Old Wine in New Bottles: Policy-Based Lending in the 1980s. In *Weeks, J. F., ed.*, 1989, pp. 131–40.

Epstein, Larry G. and Chew, Soo Hong. The Structure of Preferences and Attitudes towards the Timing of the Resolution of Uncertainty. *Int. Econ. Rev.*, February 1989, *30*(1), pp. 103–17.

———— **and Chew, Soo Hong.** A Unifying Approach to Axiomatic Non-expected Utility Theories. *J. Econ. Theory*, December 1989, *49*(2), pp. 207–40.

———— **and Zin, Stanley E.** Substitution, Risk Aversion, and the Temporal Behavior of Consumption and Asset Returns: A Theoretical Framework. *Econometrica*, July 1989, *57*(4), pp. 937–69.

Epstein, Richard A. Beyond Foreseeability: Consequential Damages in the Law of Contract. *J. Legal Stud.*, January 1989, *18*(1), pp. 105–38.

Epstein, Roy J. The Fall of OLS in Structural Estimation. *Oxford Econ. Pap.*, January 1989, *41*(1), pp. 94–107.

————. The Fall of OLS in Structural Estimation. In *de Marchi, N. and Gilbert, C., eds.*, 1989, pp. 94–107.

Epstein, Seth and Cox, James C. Preference Reversals without the Independence Axiom. *Amer. Econ. Rev.*, June 1989, *79*(3), pp. 408–26.

Erasmus, G. J. The Informal Sector in Selected Settlement Areas in South Africa. *J. Stud. Econ. Econometrics*, March 1989, *13*(1), pp. 55–64.

Erb, Richard D. The Role of Central Banks. *Finance Devel.*, December 1989, *26*(4), pp. 11–13.

Erbas, S. Nuri. The Limits on Bond Financing of Government Deficits under Optimal Fiscal Policy. *J. Macroecon.*, Fall 1989, *11*(4), pp. 589–98.

Erber, Georg. Structural Change in World Trade: Analyses and Forecasts of the FIND Model. In *Krelle, W., ed.*, 1989, pp. 499–513.

Erdös, Tibor. Monetary Regulation and Its Perplexities in Hungary. *Acta Oecon.*, 1989, *40*(1–2), pp. 1–15.

————. Wanted: A Well Founded Economic Policy—Problems of External and Internal Equilibrium, Economic Growth and Inflation. *Acta Oecon.*, 1989, *41*(3–4), pp. 359–76.

Erekson, O. Homer; Moser, James W. and Schwartz, Steven. Evenhandedness in Arbitration: The Case of Major League Baseball. *Eastern Econ. J.*, April–June 1989, *15*(2), pp. 117–27.

Ergin, Esin. Reconciling the East and West: Management and Management Education in Turkey. In *Davies, J., et al., eds.*, 1989, pp. 125–36.

Ericksen, Eugene P.; Kadane, Joseph B. and Tu-

key, John W. Adjusting the 1980 Census of Population and Housing. *J. Amer. Statist. Assoc.*, December 1989, *84*(408), pp. 927–44.

Erickson, Charlotte J. Emigration from the British Isles to the U.S.A. in 1841: Part I. Emigration from the British Isles. *Population Stud.*, November 1989, *43*(3), pp. 346–67.

Erickson, Nancy S. Muller v. Oregon Reconsidered: The Origins of a Sex-Based Doctrine of Liberty of Contract. *Labor Hist.*, Spring 1989, *30*(2), pp. 228–50.

Erickson, Rodney A. Export Performance and State Industrial Growth. *Econ. Geogr.*, October 1989, *65*(4), pp. 280–92.

Erickson, Timothy. Proper Posteriors from Improper Priors for an Unidentified Errors-in-Variables Model. *Econometrica*, November 1989, *57*(6), pp. 1299–1316.

Eriksson, Ljusk Ola and Sallnäs, Ola. Management Variation and Price Expectations in an Intertemporal Forest Sector Model. *Natural Res. Modeling*, Summer 1989, *3*(3), pp. 385–98.

Eriksson, Tor. Employment Length in the Private Sector. *Liiketaloudellinen Aikak.*, 1989, *38*(3), pp. 171–83.

————. International Migration and Regional Differentials in Unemployment and Wages: Some Empirical Evidence from Finland. In *Gordon, I. and Thirlwall, A. P., eds.*, 1989, pp. 59–73.

Erkes, H. T. and Witzke, H. P. Base Model (Version B): Feed Component. In *Bauer, S. and Henrichsmeyer, W., eds.*, 1989, pp. 399–405.

Ermini, Luigi. Excessive Sensitivity of Consumption and Postponed Revision of the Optimum Plans. *J. Macroecon.*, Summer 1989, *11*(3), pp. 409–22.

————. Some New Evidence on the Timing of Consumption Decisions and on Their Generating Process. *Rev. Econ. Statist.*, November 1989, *71*(4), pp. 643–50.

Ermisch, John F. Divorce: Economic Antecedents and Aftermath. In *Joshi, H., ed.*, 1989, pp. 42–55.

———— **and Cigno, Alessandro.** A Microeconomic Analysis of the Timing of Births. *Europ. Econ. Rev.*, April 1989, *33*(4), pp. 737–60.

———— **and Wright, Robert E.** Welfare Benefits and the Duration of Single Parenthood. *Nat. Inst. Econ. Rev.*, November 1989, (130), pp. 85–90.

Ernsberger, C. Nicole and Munnell, Alicia H. Public Pension Surpluses and National Saving: Foreign Experience. *New Eng. Econ. Rev.*, Mar.–Apr. 1989, pp. 16–38.

Ernst, Daniel. The Yellow-Dog Contract and Liberal Reform, 1917–1932. *Labor Hist.*, Spring 1989, *30*(2), pp. 251–74.

Ernst, Lawrence R. Weighting Issues for Longitudinal Household and Family Estimates. In *Kasprzyk, D., et al., eds.*, 1989, pp. 139–59.

Ernst, Maurice. How Not to Create Jobs: Lessons from the West European Experience. *J. Lab. Res.*, Winter 1989, *10*(1), pp. 39–43.

Ernst, William and Grasewicz, Paul J. Impact

Fees: When, Where, and How? In *Matzer, J., Jr., ed.*, 1989, *1988*, pp. 170–75.

van Erp, F. A. M., et al. A Monetary Model of the Dutch Economy: A Quarterly Submodel of Freia–Kompas. *Econ. Modelling*, January 1989, *6*(1), pp. 56–93.

Erreygers, Guido. On Indirect Taxation and Weakly Basic Commodities. *J. Econ. (Z. Nationalökon.)*, 1989, *50*(2), pp. 139–56.

Errico, Darrell and Reed, William J. A New Look at Whole-Forest Modeling. *Natural Res. Modeling*, Summer 1989, *3*(3), pp. 399–427.

Errigo, Antonello and Bellacicco, Antonio. La disoccupazione giovanile nei paesi industrializzati: Un modello interpretativo. (Youth Unemployment in Industrialized Countries. With English summary.) *Econ. Lavoro*, April–June 1989, *23*(2), pp. 39–49.

Errington, A. Estimating Enterprise Input–Output Coefficients from Regional Farm Data. *J. Agr. Econ.*, January 1989, *40*(1), pp. 52–56.

Erritt, M. J. The Organisation and Management of Statistical Programmes in the United Kingdom. *Statist. J.*, 1989, *6*(1), pp. 17–26.

Errunza, Vihang R. and Losq, Etienne. Capital Flow Controls, International Asset Pricing, and Investors' Welfare: A Multi-country Framework. *J. Finance*, September 1989, *44*(4), pp. 1025–37.

_____ **and Moreau, Arthur F.** Debt-for-Equity Swaps under a Rational Expectations Equilibrium. *J. Finance*, July 1989, *44*(3), pp. 663–80.

Ershov, E. B. It Is Necessary and Possible to Produce a Working Document for Unifying the Efforts and Results of Our Research Direction. *Matekon*, Spring 1989, *25*(3), pp. 71–74.

Ersoy, Arif. Liberal Economic Strategy for Debt Crisis Management: The Case of Turkey. In *Singer, H. W. and Sharma, S., eds. (II)*, 1989, pp. 256–70.

Ervin, R. Terry and Segarra, Eduardo. Agricultural Economists and Multidisciplinary Research: Comment. *Amer. J. Agr. Econ.*, May 1989, *71*(2), pp. 437–38.

Escudé, Carlos Andrés. Health in Buenos Aires in the Second Half of the Nineteenth Century. In *Platt, D. C. M., ed.*, 1989, pp. 60–70.

Escudier, Jean-Louis. Le mouvement long de l'économie: Terminologie et options théoriques. (The Long-term Movement of the Economy: Terminology and Theorical Options. With English summary.) *Revue Écon.*, September 1989, *40*(5), pp. 839–62.

Esen, Oğuz. Heterodoks Istikrar Programlari: Teori ve Uygulama. (Hetrodox Stabilization Programs: Theory and Policy. With English summary.) *METU*, 1989, *16*(3–4), pp. 33–64.

Esfahani, Hadi S. and Mojtahed, Ahmad. Agricultural Policy and Performance in Iran: The Post-revolutionary Experience. *World Devel.*, June 1989, *17*(6), pp. 839–60.

_____ **and Salehi-Isfahani, Djavad.** Effort Observability and Worker Productivity: Towards an Explanation of Economic Dualism. *Econ. J.*, September 1989, *99*(397), pp. 818–36.

Eshag, Eprime. Some Suggestions for Improving the Operation of IMF Stabilisation Programmes. *Int. Lab. Rev.*, 1989, *128*(3), pp. 297–320.

Espa, Efisio and Daviddi, Renzo. The Economics of Rouble Convertibility. New Scenarios for the Soviet Monetary Economy. *Banca Naz. Lavoro Quart. Rev.*, December 1989, (171), pp. 441–67.

Espahbodi, Hassan and Copeland, Ronald M. Accommodating Multicollinearity in Financial Forecasting and Business Research. In *Lee, C. F., ed.*, 1989, pp. 311–22.

Esparon, N. M. and Sturgess, Neil H. The Measurement of Technical Efficiency Using Frontier Production Functions of Rice Farms in West Java. *Bull. Indonesian Econ. Stud.*, December 1989, *25*(3), pp. 99–119.

Esparza, Adrian. Defense Impact Analysis within a Social Accounting Framework. *Growth Change*, Summer 1989, *20*(3), pp. 63–79.

_____ **and Krmenec, Andrew.** Manufacturing and the Externalization of Services: A Theoretical Model. *Reg. Sci. Persp.*, 1989, *19*(2), pp. 29–40.

Espasa Terrades, Antoni and Cancelo de la Torre, José Ramón. Modelos univariantes en el análisis económico. (With English summary.) *Revista Española Econ.*, 1989, *6*(1–2), pp. 85–107.

Espenshade, Thomas J. Growing Imbalances between Labor Supply and Labor Demand in the Caribbean Basin. In *Bean, F. D.; Schmandt, J. and Weintraub, S., eds.*, 1989, pp. 113–60.

_____ **and Bouvier, Leon F.** The Stable Population Model, Migration, and Complementarity. *Population Res. Policy Rev.*, May 1989, *8*(2), pp. 165–79.

Esser, Josef and Fach, Wolfgang. Crisis Management "Made in Germany": The Steel Industry. In *Katzenstein, P. J., ed.*, 1989, pp. 221–48.

d'Estaing, Valéry Giscard; Nakasone, Yasuhiro and Kissinger, Henry A. East–West Relations. *Foreign Aff.*, Summer 1989, *68*(3), pp. 1–21.

Esteban, Joan and Chae, Suchan. The Bounded Core of an Overlapping Generations Economy. *Int. Econ. Rev.*, August 1989, *30*(3), pp. 519–25.

Estes, Carroll L. and Lee, Philip R. Toward National Health Insurance. In *Eisdorfer, C.; Kessler, D. A. and Spector, A. N., eds.*, 1989, pp. 137–51.

Estrada, Javier and Fugleberg, Ole. Price Elasticities of Natural Gas Demand in France and West Germany. *Energy J.*, July 1989, *10*(3), pp. 77–90.

Estrin, Saul and Wadhwani, Sushil. Profit-Sharing. In *Sapsford, D. and Tzannatos, Z., eds.*, 1989, pp. 227–58.

Eswaran, Mukesh and Kotwal, Ashok. Credit and Agrarian Class Structure. In *Bardhan, P., ed. (II)*, 1989, pp. 166–84.

_____ **and Kotwal, Ashok.** Credit as Insurance in Agrarian Economies. *J. Devel. Econ.*, July 1989, *31*(1), pp. 37–53.

—— **and Kotwal, Ashok.** Why Are Capitalists the Bosses? *Econ. J.*, March 1989, *99*(394), pp. 162–76.

Etemad, Hamid. Production Management and Structure. In *Rugman, A. M., ed.*, 1989, pp. 347–64.

Etherington, Dan M. and Forster, Keith. The Complex Case of the Chinese Tea Industry. *Food Res. Inst. Stud.*, 1989, *21*(3), pp. 265–308.

Etherington, K. Administrative and Compliance Costs of Taxation: United Kingdom. In *International Fiscal Association, ed. (I)*, 1989, pp. 541–61.

Ethier, Wilfred and Horn, Henrik. A New Look at Economic Integration. In *Jacquemin, A. and Sapir, A., eds.*, 1989, *1984*, pp. 71–93.

Etner, François. Partisans et adversaires de l'économie mathématique en France. (How Mathematical Economics Was Received in France in the XIXth Century. With English summary.) *Revue Écon.*, May 1989, *40*(3), pp. 541–48.

Ettredge, Michael and Bublitz, Bruce. The Information in Discretionary Outlays: Advertising, Research, and Development. *Accounting Rev.*, January 1989, *64*(1), pp. 108–24.

Etxezarreta, Miren and Viladomiu, Lourdes. The Restructuring of Spanish Agriculture, and Spain's Accession to the EEC. In *Goodman, D. and Redclift, M., eds.*, 1989, pp. 156–82.

Etzioni, Amitai. School Reform: A Serious Challenge for Business. *Challenge*, May–June 1989, *32*(3), pp. 51–54.

Etzioni-Halevy, Eva. Exchanging Material Benefits for Political Support: A Comparative Analysis. In *Heidenheimer, A. J.; Johnston, M. and LeVine, V. T., eds.*, 1989, pp. 287–304.

Eubanks, L. and Wyckoff, J. Voluntary Contributions to State Nongame Wildlife Programs. *J. Environ. Econ. Manage.*, January 1989, *16*(1), pp. 38–44.

Eucken, Walter. What Kind of Economic and Social System? In *Peacock, A. and Willgerodt, H., eds. (II)*, 1989, *1948*, pp. 27–45.

——; **Grossman-Doerth, Hans and Böhm, Franz.** The Ordo Manifesto of 1936. In *Peacock, A. and Willgerodt, H., eds. (II)*, 1989, *1936*, pp. 15–26.

Eugene, Darrick and McCarty, David. Telecommunications Policy and Economic Development: The New State Role: Florida. In *Schmandt, J.; Williams, F. and Wilson, R. H., eds.*, 1989, pp. 41–61.

Eun, Cheol S. and Shim, Sangdal. International Transmission of Stock Market Movements. *J. Finan. Quant. Anal.*, June 1989, *24*(2), pp. 241–56.

Eusepi, Giuseppe. Buchanan's Critique of the Neoclassical Model and the Rediscovery of the Italian Tradition in Public Finance. *Rivista Int. Sci. Econ. Com.*, September 1989, *36*(9), pp. 801–22.

——. Public Debt Burden: An Institutional Approach. *Econ. Int.*, Aug.–Nov. 1989, *42*(3–4), pp. 175–90.

Euzéby, Alain and Vessillier, Elisabeth. Analyse d'un prélèvement sur les salaires: Les cotisations sociales. (With English summary.) In *Chiancone, A. and Messere, K., eds.*, 1989, pp. 323–37.

Euzéby, Chantal. Non-contributory Old-Age Pensions: A Possible Solution in the OECD Countries. *Int. Lab. Rev.*, 1989, *128*(1), pp. 11–28.

Evanoff, Douglas D. Bank Deposit Rate Deregulation and Customer Service Levels. *J. Cons. Aff.*, Summer 1989, *23*(1), pp. 161–74.

Evans, Alan W. Housing Costs and the Retail Price Index. *Nat. Westminster Bank Quart. Rev.*, August 1989, pp. 39–55.

—— **and Crampton, Graham.** Myth, Reality and Employment in London. *J. Transp. Econ. Policy*, January 1989, *23*(1), pp. 89–108.

Evans, David B. Bogged Down in Marginal Analysis: Neuhauser and Lewicki Revisited: Commentary. In *Smith, C. S., ed.*, 1989, pp. 121–22.

—— **and Hasibuan, Nurimansjah.** South Sumatra: Dualism and Export Orientation. In *Hill, H., ed.*, 1989, pp. 454–72.

Evans, David S. and Jovanovic, Boyan. An Estimated Model of Entrepreneurial Choice under Liquidity Constraints. *J. Polit. Econ.*, August 1989, *97*(4), pp. 808–27.

—— **and Leighton, Linda S.** Some Empirical Aspects of Entrepreneurship. *Amer. Econ. Rev.*, June 1989, *79*(3), pp. 519–35.

—— **and Leighton, Linda S.** Why Do Smaller Firms Pay Less? *J. Human Res.*, Spring 1989, *24*(2), pp. 299–318.

Evans, Dorla A.; Holcomb, James H. and Chittenden, William T. The Relationship between Risk-Return Preference and Knowledge in Experimental Financial Markets. *J. Behav. Econ.*, Spring 1989, *18*(1), pp. 19–40.

Evans, Gary R. and Earley, James S. The Problem Is Bank Liability Management. In *Guttmann, R., ed.*, 1989, *1982*, pp. 61–64.

Evans, George W. The Conduct of Monetary Policy and the Natural Rate of Unemployment: A Note. *J. Money, Credit, Banking*, November 1989, *21*(4), pp. 498–507.

——. The Fragility of Sunspots and Bubbles. *J. Monet. Econ.*, March 1989, *23*(2), pp. 297–317.

——. A Measure of the U.S. Output Gap. *Econ. Letters*, 1989, *29*(4), pp. 285–89.

——. Output and Unemployment Dynamics in the United States: 1950–1985. *J. Appl. Econometrics*, July–Sept. 1989, *4*(3), pp. 213–37.

Evans, Hugh Emrys. National Development and Rural–Urban Policy: Past Experience and New Directions in Kenya. *Urban Stud.*, April 1989, *26*(2), pp. 253–66.

Evans, Lewis and Wells, Graeme. Time Series Estimates of Tariff Incidence. *Appl. Econ.*, September 1989, *21*(9), pp. 1191–1202.

Evans, M.; Mondor, R. and Flaten, D. Expert Systems and Farm Management. *Can. J. Agr. Econ.*, Part 1, December 1989, *37*(4), pp. 639–66.

Evans, Michael. John Stuart Mill and Karl Marx:

Some Problems and Perspectives. *Hist. Polit. Econ.*, Summer 1989, *21*(2), pp. 273–98.

Evans, Neil. Two Paths to Economic Development: Wales and the North-east of England. In *Hudson, P., ed.*, 1989, pp. 201–27.

Evans, Owen; Kenward, Lloyd and Corker, Robert. Tax Policy and Business Investment in the United States: Evidence from the 1980s. *Int. Monet. Fund Staff Pap.*, March 1989, *36*(1), pp. 31–62.

Evans, Paul. A Test of Steady-State Government-Debt Neutrality. *Econ. Inquiry*, January 1989, *27*(1), pp. 39–55.

Evans, Peter B. Declining Hegemony and Assertive Industrialization: U.S.–Brazil Conflicts in the Computer Industry. *Int. Organ.*, Spring 1989, *43*(2), pp. 207–38.

_____ **and Tigre, Paulo Bastos.** Going Beyond Clones in Brazil and Korea: A Comparative Analysis of NIC Strategies in the Computer Industry. *World Devel.*, November 1989, *17*(11), pp. 1751–68.

Evans, Ray. Property Rights, Markets and Competition in Electricity Supply. In *Veljanovski, C., ed. (II)*, 1989, pp. 135–43.

Evans, Robert. Sequential Bargaining with Correlated Values. *Rev. Econ. Stud.*, October 1989, *56*(4), pp. 499–510.

_____ **and Maskin, Eric.** Efficient Renegotiation—Proof Equilibria Repeated Games. *Games Econ. Behav.*, December 1989, *1*(4), pp. 361–69.

Evans, Sara M. and Nelson, Barbara J. The Impact of Pay Equity on Public Employees: State of Minnesota Employees' Attitudes toward Wage Policy Innovation. In *Michael, R. T.; Hartmann, H. I. and O'Farrell, B., eds.*, 1989, pp. 200–221.

Evansohn, John. The Effects of Mechanisms of Managerial Control of Unionization. *Ind. Relat.*, Winter 1989, *28*(1), pp. 91–103.

Evenhouse, Eirik and Long, Millard. Restructuring Distressed Financial Systems. *Finance Devel.*, September 1989, *26*(3), pp. 4–7.

Evensky, Jerry M. The Evolution of Adam Smith's Views on Political Economy. *Hist. Polit. Econ.*, Spring 1989, *21*(1), pp. 123–45.

_____. Expanding the Scope of Neoclassical Vision: Reply. *Rev. Soc. Econ.*, Spring 1989, *47*(1), pp. 88–90.

_____ **and Spuches, Charles M.** The Syracuse University Experience: Lessons in Multiteacher Course Design. *J. Econ. Educ.*, Spring 1989, *20*(2), pp. 181–98.

Evenson, Robert E. Spillover Benefits of Agricultural Research: Evidence from U.S. Experience. *Amer. J. Agr. Econ.*, May 1989, *71*(2), pp. 447–52.

_____ **and Deolalikar, Anil B.** Technology Production and Technology Purchase in Indian Industry: An Econometric Analysis. *Rev. Econ. Statist.*, November 1989, *71*(4), pp. 689–92.

_____ **and Huffman, Wallace E.** Supply and Demand Functions for Multiproduct U.S. Cash Grain Farms: Biases Caused by Research and Other Policies. *Amer. J. Agr. Econ.*, August 1989, *71*(3), pp. 761–73.

Evers, Gerard H. M. Simultaneous Models for Migration and Commuting: Macro and Micro Economic Approaches. In *van Dijk, J., et al., eds.*, 1989, pp. 177–97.

Evers, Hans-Dieter. Urban Poverty and Labour Supply Strategies in Jakarta. In *Rodgers, G., ed.*, 1989, pp. 145–72.

Evers, Martin A. and Swaney, James A. The Social Cost Concepts of K. William Kapp and Karl Polanyi. *J. Econ. Issues*, March 1989, *23*(1), pp. 7–33.

Evnine, Jeremy; Gibbs, Stephen and Boyle, Phelim P. Numerical Evaluation of Multivariate Contingent Claims. *Rev. Financial Stud.*, 1989, *2*(2), pp. 241–50.

Evren, Gungor and Gercek, Haluk. A Preliminary Evaluation of the Container Transportation on the Turkish Railway Network. In *Candemir, Y., ed.*, 1989, pp. 285–99.

Ewbank, Douglas C. Estimating Birth Stopping and Spacing Behavior. *Demography*, August 1989, *26*(3), pp. 473–83.

Ewert, Ralf. The Financial Theory of Agency as a Tool for an Analysis of Problems in External Accounting. In *Bamberg, G. and Spremann, K., eds.*, 1989, pp. 281–309.

Eymard-Duvernay, François. Conventions de qualité et formes de coordination. (Definitions of Quality and Forms of Organisation. With English summary.) *Revue Écon.*, March 1989, *40*(2), pp. 329–59.

Eyre, Stephen C. Financial Markets and Foreign Investment in the United States. In *Kaushik, S. K., ed.*, 1989, pp. 141–44.

Eyssell, Thomas H. Partial Acquisitions and Firm Performance. *J. Econ. Bus.*, February 1989, *41*(1), pp. 69–88.

_____; **Fraser, Donald R. and Rangan, Nanda K.** Debt–Equity Swaps, Regulation K, and Bank Stock Returns. *J. Banking Finance*, December 1989, *13*(6), pp. 853–68.

Eyzaguirre, Nicolás. Saving and Investment under External and Fiscal Constraints. *CEPAL Rev.*, August 1989, (38), pp. 31–47.

Ezaki, Mitsuo. Macro-impacts of Oil Price Changes: A CGE Analysis of the Japanese Economy. (In Japanese. With English summary.) *Econ. Stud. Quart.*, June 1989, *40*(2), pp. 135–51.

_____. Oil Price Declines and Structural Adjustment Policies in Indonesia: A Static CGE Analysis for 1980 and 1985. *Philippine Rev. Econ. Bus.*, December 1989, *26*(2), pp. 173–207.

Ezejelue, A. C. 1989 Budgetary Changes to Tax Laws: Nigeria. *Bull. Int. Fiscal Doc.*, November 1989, *43*(11), pp. 522–27.

Ezz, Esmat. Preventing Proliferation of Nuclear Weapons: Hopes and Realities. In *Rotblat, J. and Goldanskii, V. I., eds.*, 1989, pp. 36–45.

Fabella, Raul V. Monopoly Deregulation in the Presence of Tullock Activities. *Public Choice*, September 1989, *62*(3), pp. 287–93.

_____. Separability and Risk in the Static Household Production Model. *Southern Econ. J.*, April 1989, 55(4), pp. 954–61.

———. Uncertain Monopoly Rent and the Social Cost of Rent Seeking. *Econ. Letters,* 1989, 29(3), pp. 199–203.

Faber, Mike. Beware of Debtspeak. In *Bird, G., ed.*, 1989, pp. 218–35.

———. If Sisyphus Stops Pushing the Mountain of Third World Debt? In *Singer, H. W. and Sharma, S., eds. (I)*, 1989, pp. 39–49.

Faber, Ronald J. and O'Guinn, Thomas C. Compulsive Buying: A Phenomenological Exploration. *J. Cons. Res.*, September 1989, 16(2), pp. 147–57.

Fabian, Cs., et al. Information System for the Management of Steel Smelting Process in Electric Furnaces. *Econ. Computat. Econ. Cybern. Stud. Res.*, 1989, 24(2–3), pp. 41–50.

Fabozzi, Frank J. and Dattatreya, Ravi E. A Simplified Model for Valuing Debt Options. *J. Portfol. Manage.*, Spring 1989, 15(3), pp. 64–72.

———; **Yaari, Uzi and Choi, Jongmoo Jay.** Optimum Corporate Leverage with Risky Debt: A Demand Approach. *J. Finan. Res.*, Summer 1989, 12(2), pp. 129–42.

———; **Yaari, Uzi and Coyne, Christopher.** Taxation of Capital Gains with Deferred Realization. *Nat. Tax J.*, December 1989, 42(4), pp. 475–85.

Façanha, Luis Otávio; Rodrigues, Denise A. and Dias, Antonio José R. Financiamentos públicos para projetos de pesquisa e desenvolvimento: Uma experiência de avaliação na Finep. (With English summary.) *Pesquisa Planejamento Econ.*, April 1989, 19(1), pp. 133–60.

Fach, Wolfgang and Esser, Josef. Crisis Management "Made in Germany": The Steel Industry. In *Katzenstein, P. J., ed.*, 1989, pp. 221–48.

Fachini, Stefano. A Montecarlo Experiment on the Power of Variable Addition Tests for Parameter Stability. *Giorn. Econ.*, Sept.–Oct. 1989, 48(9–10), pp. 497–506.

Fackler, James S. and McMillin, W. Douglas. Federal Debt and Macroeconomic Activity. *Southern Econ. J.*, April 1989, 55(4), pp. 994–1003.

Fackler, Paul L. A Note on Alternative Market and Governmental Risk Transference Mechanisms. *Southern J. Agr. Econ.*, December 1989, 21(2), pp. 203–09.

——— **and Orden, David.** Identifying Monetary Impacts on Agricultural Prices in VAR Models. *Amer. J. Agr. Econ.*, May 1989, 71(2), pp. 495–502.

Fadaei-Tehrani, Reza. The Costs of Crime: Unemployment and Poverty. *Int. J. Soc. Econ.*, 1989, 16(12), pp. 34–43.

Fadil, Farah G. Money, Income and Sterilization: Tests for Causality in the Oil Economy of Kuwait. *Appl. Econ.*, October 1989, 21(10), pp. 1305–24.

Fafchamps, Marcel; de Janvry, Alain and Sadoulet, Elisabeth. Agrarian Structure, Technological Innovations, and the State. In *Bardhan, P., ed. (II)*, 1989, pp. 356–82.

Fahey, Charles J. The Ethical Underpinnings of Public Policy. In *Eisdorfer, C.; Kessler, D. A. and Spector, A. N., eds.*, 1989, pp. 413–21.

Fahrion, Roland. Fifth Generation Technology—Basic Principles and Economic Implications. In *Dams, T. and Matsugi, T., eds.*, 1989, pp. 91–105.

Fahrmeir, Ludwig. Analysis of Nonnormal Longitudinal Data with Generalized Linear Models. In *Opitz, O., ed.*, 1989, pp. 85–104.

Faig, Miquel. Seasonal Fluctuations and the Demand for Money. *Quart. J. Econ.*, November 1989, 104(4), pp. 847–61.

Fain, James R. and Dworkin, James B. Success in Multiple Union Elections: Exclusive Jurisdiction vs. Competition. *J. Lab. Res.*, Winter 1989, 10(1), pp. 91–101.

Faini, Riccardo and Rossi, Nicola. La macroeconometria ed il comportamento degli agenti privati: Il caso del modello econometrico della Banca d'Italia. (With English summary.) *Politica. Econ.*, April 1989, 5(1), pp. 69–89.

Fainstein, Norman I.; Fainstein, Susan S. and Schwartz, Alex. Economic Shifts and Land Use in the Global City: New York, 1940–1987. In *Beauregard, R. A., ed.*, 1989, pp. 45–85.

Fainstein, Susan S.; Schwartz, Alex and Fainstein, Norman I. Economic Shifts and Land Use in the Global City: New York, 1940–1987. In *Beauregard, R. A., ed.*, 1989, pp. 45–85.

Fair, Ray C. The Production-Smoothing Model Is Alive and Well. *J. Monet. Econ.*, November 1989, 24(3), pp. 353–70.

——— **and Shiller, Robert J.** The Informational Context of Ex Ante Forecasts. *Rev. Econ. Statist.*, May 1989, 71(2), pp. 325–31.

Fairbank, Alan. Expanding Insurance Coverage to Alternative Types of Psychotherapists: Demand and Substitution Effects of Direct Reimbursement to Social Workers. *Inquiry*, Summer 1989, 26(2), pp. 170–81.

Fairbrother, Peter. State Workers: Class Position and Collective Action. In *Duncan, G., ed.*, 1989, pp. 187–213.

Fairburn, James A. The Evolution of Merger Policy in Britain. In *Fairburn, J. and Kay, J., eds.*, 1989, pp. 193–230.

——— **and Geroski, Paul A.** The Empirical Analysis of Market Structure and Performance. In *Fairburn, J. and Kay, J., eds.*, 1989, pp. 175–92.

——— **and Kay, John A.** Mergers and Merger Policy: Introduction. In *Fairburn, J. and Kay, J., eds.*, 1989, pp. 1–29.

Fairris, David. Compensating Wage Differentials in the Union and Nonunion Sectors. *Ind. Relat.*, Fall 1989, 28(3), pp. 356–72.

Faith, Roger L. and Blakemore, Arthur E. Bargaining Effect and Membership Effect in Public Sector Unions. *Southern Econ. J.*, April 1989, 55(4), pp. 908–23.

——— **and Buchanan, James M.** Entrepreneurship and the Internalization of Externalities. In *Buchanan, J. M. (II)*, 1989, *1981*, pp. 401–17.

_____ and Buchanan, James M. Toward a Theory of Yes–No Voting. In *Buchanan, J. M. (II)*, 1989, pp. 71–86.

Falcon, Elmo T. and Anderson, Dale G. Rural Impacts of Economic Regulation: A Case Study. In *Felton, J. R. and Anderson, D. G., eds.*, 1989, *1981*, pp. 121–30.

Faletto, Enzo. The Specificity of the Latin American State. *CEPAL Rev.*, August 1989, (38), pp. 69–87.

Falk, Barry and Orazem, Peter F. Measuring Market Responses to Error-Ridden Government Announcements. *Quart. Rev. Econ. Bus.*, Summer 1989, 29(2), pp. 41–55.

_____ and Orazem, Peter F. The Role of Systematic Fed Errors in Explaining the Money Supply Announcements Puzzle: A Note. *J. Money, Credit, Banking*, August 1989, 21(3), pp. 401–06.

Falk, Jonathan S. Investment in Equipment Modernization: The Question of Prudence. In *National Economic Research Associates*, 1989, pp. 103–15.

Falk, Karl L. Explaining the American Dream: Telling Chinese Academics What 'Liberty and Justice For All' Means Taxes Even an Eager Audience. *Amer. J. Econ. Sociology*, October 1989, 48(4), pp. 385–92.

Falk, Richard. Perspective on the United Nations. In *[Gordenker, L.]*, 1989, pp. 199–211.

Falkus, Malcolm. Early British Business in Thailand. In *Davenport-Hines, R. P. T. and Jones, G., eds.*, 1989, pp. 117–56.

Fallis, George. Political Economy of Tax Expenditures: Comment. In *Bruce, N., ed.*, 1989, pp. 415–18.

_____ and Smith, Lawrence B. Tax Reform and Residential Real Estate. In *Mintz, J. and Whalley, J., eds.*, 1989, pp. 336–65.

Falls, Gregory A. and Zangeneh, Hamid. The Interest Rate Volatility and the Demand for Money: The Empirical Evidence. *Quart. J. Bus. Econ.*, Winter 1989, 28(1), pp. 26–42.

Falmagne, Jean-Claude and Fishburn, Peter C. Binary Choice Probabilities and Rankings. *Econ. Letters*, December 1989, 31(2), pp. 113–17.

Falola, Toyin. Cassava Starch for Export in Nigeria during the Second World War. *African Econ. Hist.*, 1989, (18), pp. 73–98.

Falussy, Béla and Boda, György. Changes in Total Worktime per Unit of Free Time as a Function of Economic Development. *Statist. J.*, 1989, 6(1), pp. 51–68.

Falvey, Rodney E. Trade, Quality Reputations and Commercial Policy. *Int. Econ. Rev.*, August 1989, 30(3), pp. 607–22.

_____ and Tyers, Rodney. Border Price Changes and Domestic Welfare in the Presence of Subsidised Exports. *Oxford Econ. Pap.*, April 1989, 41(2), pp. 434–51.

Fama, Eugene F. and French, Kenneth R. Business Conditions and Expected Returns on Stocks and Bonds. *J. Finan. Econ.*, November 1989, 25(1), pp. 23–49.

Famulari, Melissa and Manser, Marilyn E. Employer-Provided Benefits: Employer Cost versus Employee Value. *Mon. Lab. Rev.*, December 1989, 112(12), pp. 24–32.

Fan, Chuen-mei and Fan, Liang-Shing. The Demand for International Reserves of Asian Countries and the Irrational Case of Taiwan. In *Lee, C. F. and Hu, S.-C., eds.*, 1989, pp. 191–200.

Fan, Liang-Shing and Fan, Chuen-mei. The Demand for International Reserves of Asian Countries and the Irrational Case of Taiwan. In *Lee, C. F. and Hu, S.-C., eds.*, 1989, pp. 191–200.

Fanara, Philip, Jr. and Corsi, Thomas M. Effects of New Entrants on Motor Carrier Safety. In *Moses, L. N. and Savage, I., eds.*, 1989, pp. 241–57.

Fand, David I. Classical Mercantilism, Neomercantilism and Contemporary Rent Seeking. *Econ. Scelte Pubbliche/J. Public Finance Public Choice*, Jan.–Aug. 1989, 7(1–2), pp. 1–16.

_____. From a Random-Walk Monetary Standard to a Monetary Constitution. *Cato J.*, Fall 1989, 9(2), pp. 323–37.

Fandel, Günter and François, Peter. Just-in-Time-Produktion und -Beschaffung Funktionsweise, Einsatzvoraussetzungen und Grenzen. (With English summary.) *Z. Betriebswirtshaft*, May 1989, 59(5), pp. 531–44.

_____ and Reese, Joachim. "Just-in-Time"-Logistik am Beispiel eines Zulieferbetriebs in der Automobilindustrie. (With English summary.) *Z. Betriebswirtshaft*, January 1989, 59(1), pp. 55–69.

Fanti, M. P.; Turchiano, B. and Maione, B. Large Scale Markov Chain Modelling of Transfer Lines. In *Archetti, F.; Lucertini, M. and Serafini, P., eds.*, 1989, pp. 193–211.

Farber, Henry S. Trends in Worker Demand for Union Representation. *Amer. Econ. Rev.*, May 1989, 79(2), pp. 166–71.

_____ and Bazerman, Max H. Divergent Expectations as a Cause of Disagreement in Bargaining: Evidence from a Comparison of Arbitration Schemes. *Quart. J. Econ.*, February 1989, 104(1), pp. 99–120.

Farber, Kit D. and Rutledge, Gary L. Pollution Abatement and Control Expenditures, 1984–87. *Surv. Curr. Bus.*, June 1989, 69(6), pp. 19–26.

Farber, Stephen C. The Dependence of Parametric Efficiency Tests on Measures of the Price of Capital and Capital Stock for Electric Utilities. *J. Ind. Econ.*, December 1989, 38(2), pp. 199–213.

_____ and Newman, Robert J. Regional Wage Differentials and the Spatial Convergence of Worker Characteristic Prices. *Rev. Econ. Statist.*, May 1989, 71(2), pp. 224–31.

Färe, Rolf; Grosskopf, Shawna and Kokkelenberg, Edward C. Measuring Plant Capacity, Utilization and Technical Change: A Nonparametric Approach. *Int. Econ. Rev.*, August 1989, 30(3), pp. 655–66.

_____; Grosskopf, Shawna and Pasurka, Carl. The Effect of Environmental Regulations on the Efficiency of Electric Utilities: 1969 versus

1975. *Appl. Econ.*, February 1989, *21*(2), pp. 225–35.

———; **Grosskopf, Shawna and Weber, William L.** Measuring School District Performance. *Public Finance Quart.*, October 1989, *17*(4), pp. 409–28.

———; **Herr, W. and Njinkeu, Dominique.** Returns to Scale and Efficiency in Production: A Distance Function Approach to Southern Illinois Hog Farms. In *Gulledge, T. R., Jr. and Litteral, L. A., eds.*, 1989, pp. 145–59.

———; **Logan, James and Lovell, C. A. Knox.** Some Economics of Content Protection. *J. Econ. (Z. Nationalökon.)*, 1989, *50*(2), pp. 171–80.

——— **and Mitchell, Thomas M.** A Family Tree of Linearly Homogeneous Production Functions. *Scand. J. Econ.*, 1989, *91*(4), pp. 749–57.

——— **and Njinkeu, Dominique.** Computing Returns to Scale under Alternative Models. *Econ. Letters*, 1989, *30*(1), pp. 55–59.

———, **et al.** Multilateral Productivity Comparisons When Some Outputs Are Undesirable: A Nonparametric Approach. *Rev. Econ. Statist.*, February 1989, *71*(1), pp. 90–98.

Farebrother, R. W. Systems of Axioms for the Estimators of the Parameters in the Standard Linear Model. *Oxford Bull. Econ. Statist.*, February 1989, *51*(1), pp. 91–94.

Fargeix, André and Perloff, Jeffrey M. The Effect of Tariffs in Markets with Vertical Restraints. *J. Int. Econ.*, February 1989, *26*(1/2), pp. 99–117.

Fargues, Philippe and Khlat, Myriam. Child Mortality in Beirut: Six Indirect Estimates Based on Data Collected at the Time of a Birth. *Population Stud.*, November 1989, *43*(3), pp. 497–513.

Farhadian-Lorie, Ziba and Katz, Menachem. Fiscal Dimensions of Trade Policy. In *Blejer, M. I. and Chu, K., eds.*, 1989, pp. 276–306.

Farkas, George and Hotchkiss, Lawrence. Incentives and Disincentives for Subject Matter Difficulty and Student Effort: Course Grade Determinants across the Stratification System. *Econ. Educ. Rev.*, 1989, *8*(2), pp. 121–32.

———; **Hotchkiss, Lawrence and Stromsdorfer, Ernest W.** Vocational Training, Supply Constraints, and Individual Economic Outcomes. *Econ. Educ. Rev.*, 1989, *8*(1), pp. 17–30.

——— **and Olsen, Randall J.** Endogenous Covariates in Duration Models and the Effect of Adolescent Childbirth on Schooling. *J. Human Res.*, Winter 1989, *24*(1), pp. 39–53.

Farley, Dean E. Measuring Casemix Specialization and the Concentration of Diagnoses in Hospitals Using Information Theory. *J. Health Econ.*, June 1989, *8*(2), pp. 185–207.

Farmer, Richard N. Selling Them to Death. In *Negandhi, A. R., ed.*, 1989, pp. 171–85.

——— **and Forney, Charles P.** Long-Term Sales Success in the U.S. Auto Market. In *Negandhi, A. R., ed.*, 1989, pp. 251–59.

Farness, Donald H. Detecting the Economic Base: New Challenges. *Int. Reg. Sci. Rev.*, 1989, *12*(3), pp. 319–28.

Farnsworth, Lee W. 'Clan Politics' and Japan's Changing Policy-making Structure. *World Econ.*, June 1989, *12*(2), pp. 163–74.

Farrell, Carlyle A. J. and Tyrchniewicz, Edward W. Trade Preferences for Developing Countries: An Analysis of Canada's Trade with the Caribbean Basin. *Can. J. Agr. Econ.*, Part 2, December 1989, *37*(4), pp. 1231–40.

Farrell, John P. Financial 'Crisis' in the CPEs or "Vsyo Normalno"? *Comp. Econ. Stud.*, Winter 1989, *31*(4), pp. 1–9.

Farrell, Joseph and Gibbons, Robert. Cheap Talk Can Matter in Bargaining. *J. Econ. Theory*, June 1989, *48*(1), pp. 221–37.

——— **and Gibbons, Robert.** Cheap Talk with Two Audiences. *Amer. Econ. Rev.*, December 1989, *79*(5), pp. 1214–23.

——— **and Lander, Eric.** Competition between and within Teams: The Lifeboat Principle. *Econ. Letters*, 1989, *29*(3), pp. 205–08.

——— **and Maskin, Eric.** Renegotiation in Repeated Games. *Games Econ. Behav.*, December 1989, *1*(4), pp. 327–60.

——— **and Maskin, Eric.** Renegotiation-Proof Equilibrium: Reply. *J. Econ. Theory*, December 1989, *49*(2), pp. 376–78.

——— **and Shapiro, Carl.** Optimal Contracts with Lock-In. *Amer. Econ. Rev.*, March 1989, *79*(1), pp. 51–68.

Farrell, Terrence W. Monetary Policy in Trinidad and Tobago, 1974–1985. In *Worrell, D. and Bourne, C., eds.*, 1989, pp. 147–56.

——— **and Christopher, Janice.** Macro-monetary Relationships in the Caribbean: An Eclectic Review of the Literature. In *Worrell, D. and Bourne, C., eds.*, 1989, pp. 12–27.

Farris, Paul L.; Brorsen, B. Wade and Oellermann, Charles M. The Live Cattle Futures Market and Daily Cash Price Movements. *J. Futures Markets*, August 1989, *9*(4), pp. 273–82.

———; **Oellermann, Charles M. and Brorsen, B. Wade.** Price Discovery for Feeder Cattle. *J. Futures Markets*, April 1989, *9*(2), pp. 113–21.

Farris, Paul W.; Olver, James and de Kluyver, Cornelis. The Relationship between Distribution and Market Share: Reply. *Marketing Sci.*, Spring 1989, *8*(2), pp. 131–32.

———; **Olver, James and de Kluyver, Cornelis.** The Relationship between Distribution and Market Share. *Marketing Sci.*, Spring 1989, *8*(2), pp. 107–28.

Farrow, Scott and Krautkraemer, Jeffrey A. Extraction at the Intensive Margin: Metal Supply and Grade Selection in Response to Anticipated and Unanticipated Price Changes. *Resources & Energy*, March 1989, *11*(1), pp. 1–21.

Fase, M. M. G. and Boeschoten, W. C. The Way We Pay with Money. *J. Bus. Econ. Statist.*, July 1989, *7*(3), pp. 319–26.

Fast, Janet; Vosburgh, Richard E. and Frisbee, William R. The Effects of Consumer Education on Consumer Search. *J. Cons. Aff.*, Summer 1989, *23*(1), pp. 65–90.

Fatti, L. Paul. Water Research Planning in South Africa. In *Golden, B. L.; Wasil, E. A. and Harker, P. T., eds.*, 1989, pp. 122–37.

Faulhaber, Gerald R. Telecommunications and the Scope of the Market in Services. In *Giersch, H., ed.*, 1989, pp. 156–65.

_____ **and Allen, Franklin.** Signaling by Underpricing in the IPO Market. *J. Finan. Econ.*, August 1989, 23(2), pp. 303–23.

_____; **Siwaraksa, Subhak and Adams, F. Gerard.** Measuring Services Output—The Wharton Index of Services Production. *J. Econ. Soc. Meas.*, 1989, 15(2), pp. 155–66.

_____ **and Yao, Dennis A.** "Fly-By-Night" Firms and the Market for Product Reviews. *J. Ind. Econ.*, September 1989, 38(1), pp. 65–77.

Faulwetter, Helmut. The Socialist Countries' Conception of the New International Economic Order. In *Schulz, B. H. and Hansen, W. W., eds.*, 1989, pp. 77–89.

Faure, Michael and Van den Bergh, Roger. Essays in Law and Economics: Corporations, Accident Prevention and Compensation for Losses: Introduction. In *Faure, M. and Van den Bergh, R., eds.*, 1989, pp. 15–20.

Fauré, Yves A. Côte d'Ivoire: Analysing the Crisis. In *Cruise O'Brien, D. B.; Dunn, J. and Rathbone, R., eds.*, 1989, pp. 59–73.

Faust, Jon. Supernovas in Monetary Theory: Does the Ultimate Sunspot Rule Out Money? *Amer. Econ. Rev.*, September 1989, 79(4), pp. 872–81.

Fausten, Dietrich K. A Note on External Adjustment. *Kredit Kapital*, 1989, 22(3), pp. 344–62.

Favereau, Olivier. Marchés internes, marchés externes. (Internal and External Markets. With English summary.) *Revue Écon.*, March 1989, 40(2), pp. 273–328.

_____. Vers un calcul économique organisationnel? (With English summary.) *Revue Écon. Politique*, March–April 1989, 99(2), pp. 322–54.

Favorskaia, A. A Proof in Favor of Democracy. In *Yanowitch, M., ed.*, 1989, 1988, pp. 78–81.

Faxén, Karl-Olof and Lundgren, Håkan. Managers as Employees: Sweden. In *Roomkin, M. J., ed.*, 1989, pp. 176–201.

Fay, Charles H. Where to Look for Comparable Worth: The Implications of Efficiency Wages: Discussion. In *Hill, M. A. and Killingsworth, M. R., eds.*, 1989, pp. 31–35.

Fay, Jeanie. How California's Cities Are Using Mello–Roos. In *Matzer, J., Jr., ed.*, 1989, 1987, pp. 176–80.

Fay, Robert E. Estimating Nonignorable Nonresponse in Longitudinal Surveys through Causal Modeling. In *Kasprzyk, D., et al., eds.*, 1989, pp. 375–99.

Fazio, Antonio. Problems of European Monetary and Financial Integration. *Rev. Econ. Cond. Italy*, May–Aug. 1989, (2), pp. 191–200.

Fazio, Russell H.; Powell, Martha C. and Williams, Carol J. The Role of Attitude Accessibility in the Attitude-to-Behavior Process. *J. Cons. Res.*, December 1989, 16(3), pp. 280–89.

Fazzari, Steven and Caskey, John. Debt Commitments and Aggregate Demand: A Critique of the Neoclassical Synthesis and Policy. In *Semmler, W., ed.*, 1989, pp. 188–99.

Feagin, Joe R. and Beauregard, Robert A. Houston: Hyperdevelopment in the Sunbelt. In *Beauregard, R. A., ed.*, 1989, pp. 153–94.

Fearne, Andrew P. The CAP in 1995—A Qualitative Approach to Policy Forecasting. *Europ. Rev. Agr. Econ.*, 1989, 16(1), pp. 113–27.

_____. A 'Satisficing' Model of CAP Decision-Making. *J. Agr. Econ.*, January 1989, 40(1), pp. 71–81.

Feather, Peter M. and Kaylen, Michael S. Conditional Qualitative Forecasting. *Amer. J. Agr. Econ.*, February 1989, 71(1), pp. 195–201.

Featherstone, Kevin. The Mediterranean Challenge: Cohesion and External Preferences. In *Lodge, J., ed.*, 1989, pp. 186–201.

Fecher, Fabienne and Perelman, Sergio. Productivité, progrès technique et efficacité: Une étude comparative de 14 secteurs industriels belges. (Total Factor Productivity, Technical Progress and Efficiency: A Comparative Study of 14 Belgian Industrial Sectors. With English summary.) *Ann. Écon. Statist.*, Jan.–March 1989, (13), pp. 93–118.

Feder, Gershon L. and Onchan, Tongroj. Land Ownership Security and Farm Investment: Reply. *Amer. J. Agr. Econ.*, February 1989, 71(1), pp. 215–16.

_____, **et al.** Agricultural Credit and Farm Performance in China. *J. Compar. Econ.*, December 1989, 13(4), pp. 508–26.

Feder, Judith; Hadley, Jack and Zukerman, Stephen. Profits and Fiscal Pressure in the Prospective Payment System: Their Impacts on Hospitals. *Inquiry*, Fall 1989, 26(3), pp. 354–65.

_____ **and Scanlon, William J.** Paying for Long-Term Care. In *Eisdorfer, C.; Kessler, D. A. and Spector, A. N., eds.*, 1989, pp. 125–36.

_____ **and Scanlon, William J.** Problems and Prospects in Financing Long-Term Care. In *McLennan, K. and Meyer, J. A., eds.*, 1989, pp. 67–85.

Fedor, Max. Accelerating the Product Development Process and Reducing Risk. In *Ahlbrandt, R. S., Jr., ed.*, 1989, pp. 41–44.

Fedorov, Valeri V. Latent Variables in Regression Analysis. In *Hackl, P., ed.*, 1989, pp. 265–72.

Fedrizzi, Mario and Kacprzyk, Janusz. A 'Human-Consistent' Degree of Consensus Based on Fuzzy Logic with Linguistic Quantifiers. *Math. Soc. Sci.*, December 1989, 18(3), pp. 275–90.

Feehan, James P. Pareto-Efficiency with Three Varieties of Public Input. *Public Finance*, 1989, 44(2), pp. 237–48.

Feenberg, Daniel R. and Skinner, Jonathan. Sources of IRA Saving. In *Summers, L. H., ed.*, 1989, pp. 25–46.

_____, **et al.** Testing the Rationality of State Revenue Forecasts. *Rev. Econ. Statist.*, May 1989, 71(2), pp. 300–308.

Feeney, Griffith, et al. Recent Fertility Dynamics

in China: Results from the 1987 One Percent Population Survey. *Population Devel. Rev.*, June 1989, *15*(2), pp. 297–322.

Feenstra, Robert C. Symmetric Pass-Through of Tariffs and Exchange Rates under Imperfect Competition: An Empirical Test. *J. Int. Econ.*, August 1989, *27*(1–2), pp. 25–45.

————. Trade Policies for International Competitiveness: Introduction. In *Feenstra, R. C., ed.*, 1989, pp. 1–4.

————; **Ware, Roger and Lewis, Tracy R.** Eliminating Price Supports: A Political Economy Perspective. *J. Public Econ.*, November 1989, *40*(2), pp. 159–85.

Feeny, David. The Decline of Property Rights in Man in Thailand, 1800–1913. *J. Econ. Hist.*, June 1989, *49*(2), pp. 285–96.

Fehr, Ernst. A Theory of Short- and Long-run Equilibrium Unemployment. *J. Econ. (Z. Nationalökon.)*, 1989, *50*(3), pp. 201–22.

————. Vollbeschäftigung durch Gewinnbeteiligung? Kritische Anmerkungen zum Weitzman-Plan. (Full Employment through Profit-Sharing? A Critical Assessment of Weitzmans' Proposal. With English summary.) *Jahr. Nationalökon. Statist.*, July 1989, *206*(3), pp. 225–42.

Feibel, Charles Edward. The Efficiency and Effectiveness of Road Based Urban Public Transport Modes: A Case Study of Istanbul. In *Candemir, Y., ed.*, 1989, pp. 69–82.

Feichtinger, Gustav; Mehlmann, Alexander and Dockner, Engelbert J. Noncooperative Solutions for a Differential Game Model of Fishery. *J. Econ. Dynam. Control*, January 1989, *13*(1), pp. 1–20.

———— and **Sorger, Gerhard.** Intertemporal Sharecropping: A Differential Game Approach. In *Bamberg, G. and Spremann, K., eds.*, 1989, pp. 415–38.

Feige, Edgar L. The Meaning and Measurement of the Underground Economy. In *Feige, E. L., ed.*, 1989, pp. 13–56.

————. The Underground Economies: Tax Evasion and Information Distortion: Introduction. In *Feige, E. L., ed.*, 1989, pp. 1–9.

———— and **Alford, Robert R.** Information Distortions in Social Systems: The Underground Economy and Other Observer–Subject–Policymaker Feedbacks. In *Feige, E. L., ed.*, 1989, pp. 57–79.

———— and **McGee, Robert T.** Policy Illusion, Macroeconomic Instability, and the Unrecorded Economy. In *Feige, E. L., ed.*, 1989, pp. 81–109.

Feigenbaum, Harvey B. Democracy at the Margins: The International System and Policy Change in France. In *Foglesong, R. E. and Wolfe, J. D., eds.*, 1989, pp. 87–106.

Feinberg, Richard E. The Rise of the Market-Based "Menu" Approach and Its Limitations: Comment. In *Husain, I. and Diwan, I., eds.*, 1989, pp. 160–62.

———— and **Gwin, Catherine.** Pulling Together: Reforming the Fund. In *Gwin, C. and Feinberg, R. E., eds.*, 1989, pp. 3–29.

———— and **Hanson, Gordon H.** LDC Debt Will Restructure U.S. Banking. *Challenge*, March–April 1989, *32*(2), pp. 44–49.

Feinberg, Robert M. The Effects of Foreign Exchange Movements on U.S. Domestic Prices. *Rev. Econ. Statist.*, August 1989, *71*(3), pp. 505–11.

————. Exchange Rates and "Unfair Trade." *Rev. Econ. Statist.*, November 1989, *71*(4), pp. 704–07.

————. Imports as a Threat to Cartel Stability. *Int. J. Ind. Organ.*, June 1989, *7*(2), pp. 281–88.

———— and **Hirsch, Barry T.** Industry Rent Seeking and the Filing of 'Unfair Trade' Complaints. *Int. J. Ind. Organ.*, September 1989, *7*(3), pp. 325–40.

Feinerman, Eli; Bresler, Eshel and Dagan, Gideon. Optimization of Inputs in a Spatially Variable Natural Resource: Unconditional vs. Conditional Analysis. *J. Environ. Econ. Manage.*, September 1989, *17*(2), pp. 140–54.

————; **Shani, Y. and Bresler, Eshel.** Economic Optimisation of Sprinkler Irrigation Considering Uncertainty of Spatial Water Distribution. *Australian J. Agr. Econ.*, August 1989, *33*(2), pp. 88–107.

Feinman, Joshua and Poole, William. Federal Reserve Policymaking: An Overview and Analysis of the Policy Process: Comment. *Carnegie–Rochester Conf. Ser. Public Policy*, Spring 1989, *30*, pp. 63–74.

Feinstein, Charles H. Wages and the Paradox of the 1880s: Comment. *Exploration Econ. Hist.*, April 1989, *26*(2), pp. 237–47.

Feinstein, Jerald L. Introduction to Expert Systems. *J. Policy Anal. Manage.*, Spring 1989, *8*(2), pp. 182–87.

Feinstein, Jonathan S. The Safety Regulation of U.S. Nuclear Power Plants: Violations, Inspections, and Abnormal Occurrences. *J. Polit. Econ.*, February 1989, *97*(1), pp. 115–54.

———— and **Casella, Alessandra.** Management of a Common Currency. In *De Cecco, M. and Giovannini, A., eds.*, 1989, pp. 131–56.

———— and **McFadden, Daniel.** The Dynamics of Housing Demand by the Elderly: Wealth, Cash Flow, and Demographic Effects. In *Wise, D. A., ed.*, 1989, pp. 55–86.

Feinstein, Steven P. Forecasting Stock-Market Volatility Using Options on Index Futures. *Fed. Res. Bank Atlanta Econ. Rev.*, May–June 1989, *74*(3), pp. 12–30.

Feiveson, Harold. A Strategy to Stop the Spread of Fissile Material. In *Rotblat, J. and Goldanskii, V. I., eds.*, 1989, pp. 61–69.

Feiwel, George R. Joan Robinson inside and outside the Stream. In *Feiwel, G. R., ed. (II)*, 1989, pp. 1–120.

————. Kalecki and Keynes Revisited. *Keio Econ. Stud.*, 1989, *26*(2), pp. 25–52.

————. The Legacies of Kalecki and Keynes. In *Sebastiani, M., ed.*, 1989, pp. 45–80.

————. The Paradox of Joan Robinson. *Rivista Int. Sci. Econ. Com.*, June 1989, *36*(6), pp. 481–96.

——. Towards an Integration of Imperfect Competition and Macrodynamics: Kalecki, Keynes, Joan Robinson. In *Feiwel, G. R., ed. (I)*, 1989, pp. 3–145.

Feketekuty, Geza. International Network Competition in Telecommunications. In *Robinson, P.; Sauvant, K. P. and Govitrikar, V. P., eds.*, 1989, pp. 257–85.

Feld, Scott L.; Owen, Guillermo and Grofman, Bernard. Proving a Distribution-Free Generalization of the Condorcet Jury Theorem. *Math. Soc. Sci.*, February 1989, *17*(1), pp. 1–16.

Feldbrugge, F. J. M. The Soviet Second Economy in a Political and Legal Perspective. In *Feige, E. L., ed.*, 1989, pp. 297–338.

Felder, Stefan. Sind Externalitäten in jedem Fall zu internalisieren? Eine Anmerkung zu "Konkurrenz und Umweltschutz." (Should Externalities Always Be Internalized? With English summary.) *Schweiz. Z. Volkswirtsch. Statist.*, June 1989, *125*(2), pp. 189–94.

Feldman, Allan M. Bilateral Trading Processes, Pairwise Optimality, and Pareto Optimality. In *Starr, R. M., ed.*, 1989, *1973*, pp. 85–95.

Feldman, David. The Term Structure of Interest Rates in a Partially Observable Economy. *J. Finance*, July 1989, *44*(3), pp. 789–812.

Feldman, David H. The Trade-off between GNP and Unemployment in a Dual Economy. *Southern Econ. J.*, July 1989, *56*(1), pp. 46–55.

Feldman, Gerald D. Foreign Penetration of German Enterprises after the First World War: The Problem of Überfremdung. In *Teichova, A.; Lévy-Leboyer, M. and Nussbaum, H., eds.*, 1989, pp. 87–110.

Feldman, Marshall M. A. and Kraushaar, Robert. Industrial Restructuring and the Limits of Industry Data: Examples from Western New York. *Reg. Stud.*, February 1989, *23*(1), pp. 49–62.

Feldman, Robert Alan. Implementing Structural Reforms in Industrial Countries. *Finance Devel.*, September 1989, *26*(3), pp. 24–26.

Feldman, Roger; Finch, Michael and Dowd, Bryan. The Role of Health Practices in HMO Selection Bias: A Confirmatory Study. *Inquiry*, Fall 1989, *26*(3), pp. 381–87.

——, **et al.** The Demand for Employment-Based Health Insurance Plans. *J. Human Res.*, Winter 1989, *24*(1), pp. 115–42.

Feldsieper, Manfred. Monetary Policy Concepts of the German Bundesbank and the German Council of Economic Advisers. *Hong Kong Econ. Pap.*, 1989, (19), pp. 13–20.

Feldstein, Martin. The Case against Trying to Stabilize the Dollar. *Amer. Econ. Rev.*, May 1989, *79*(2), pp. 36–40.

——. How the CEA Advises Presidents. *Challenge*, Nov.–Dec. 1989, *32*(6), pp. 51–55.

——. Tax Policy for the 1990s: Personal Saving, Business Investment, and Corporate Debt. *Amer. Econ. Rev.*, May 1989, *79*(2), pp. 108–12.

—— **and Elmendorf, Douglas W.** Budget Defi-

cits, Tax Incentives, and Inflation: A Surprising Lesson from the 1983–1984 Recovery. In *Summers, L. H., ed.*, 1989, pp. 1–23.

Felix, David. Financial Globalisation and the LDC Debt Crisis. In *Singer, H. W. and Sharma, S., eds. (I)*, 1989, pp. 151–65.

——. Import Substitution and Late Industrialization: Latin America and Asia Compared. *World Devel.*, Special Issue, September 1989, *17*(9), pp. 1455–69.

—— **and Sanchez, Juana.** Pooling Foreign Assets and Liabilities of Latin American Debtors to Solve Their Debt Crisis: Estimates of Capital Flight and Alternative Pooling Mechanisms. In *Gray, H. P., ed.*, 1989, pp. 43–61.

Fell, John P. C. Growth, Migration and Causality: A Comment on Tests for Macroeconomic Feedback from Large-Scale Migration Based on the Irish Experience, 1948–87. *Econ. Soc. Rev.*, April 1989, *20*(3), pp. 267–73.

——. In Search of a Causal Relationship between Industrial Output and Employment in Ireland. *Econ. Soc. Rev.*, October 1989, *21*(1), pp. 51–67.

Fellingham, John C. and Young, Richard A. Special Allocations, Investment Decisions, and Transactions Costs in Partnerships. *J. Acc. Res.*, Autumn 1989, *27*(2), pp. 179–200.

Felmingham, B. S. and Divisekera, Sarath. Sri Lankan Economic Performance and Income Distribution in Various Policy Epochs. *Singapore Econ. Rev.*, April 1989, *34*(1), pp. 43–49.

Fels, Gerhard. West Germany's Current Troubles and Challenges. In *Fels, G. and von Furstenberg, G. M., eds.*, 1989, pp. 18–20.

—— **and von Furstenberg, George M.** A Supply-Side Agenda for Germany: Introducing the Agenda. In *Fels, G. and von Furstenberg, G. M., eds.*, 1989, pp. 1–16.

Felsenstein, Daniel and Bar-El, Raphael. Technological Profile and Industrial Structure: Implications for the Development of Sophisticated Industry in Peripheral Areas. *Reg. Stud.*, June 1989, *23*(3), pp. 253–66.

Feltenstein, Andrew. Agricultural Policies and the U.S. Federal Budget and U.S. Trade Deficit. In *Stoeckel, A. B.; Vincent, D. and Cuthbertson, S., eds.*, 1989, pp. 200–221.

Felton, John Richard. Background of the Motor Carrier Act of 1935. In *Felton, J. R. and Anderson, D. G., eds.*, 1989, pp. 3–13.

——. Inherent Structure, Behavior, and Performance. In *Felton, J. R. and Anderson, D. G., eds.*, 1989, *1978*, pp. 42–52.

——. Motor Carrier Act of 1980: An Assessment. In *Felton, J. R. and Anderson, D. G., eds.*, 1989, pp. 143–62.

——. Rate Inflexibility and the Backhaul Problem. In *Felton, J. R. and Anderson, D. G., eds.*, 1989, *1981*, pp. 66–81.

——. Regulatory Rigidity and Seasonal Variations in Demand. In *Felton, J. R. and Anderson, D. G., eds.*, 1989, *1981*, pp. 82–98.

——. Rural Impacts of Economic Regulation: Internal Subsidization. In *Felton, J. R. and*

Anderson, D. G., eds., 1989, *1980*, pp. 113–20.

——. Social Costs of Regulation. In *Felton, J. R. and Anderson, D. G., eds.*, 1989, *1978*, pp. 53–65.

—— and Cowen, Janna L. Operating-Ratio Regulation by the States. In *Felton, J. R. and Anderson, D. G., eds.*, 1989, *1985*, pp. 99–112.

—— and Huttsell, Ray C., Jr. Entry Regulation: The Nebraska Experience. In *Felton, J. R. and Anderson, D. G., eds.*, 1989, pp. 131–42.

Felton, Marianne Victorius. Major Influences on the Demand for Opera Tickets. *J. Cult. Econ.*, June 1989, *13*(1), pp. 53–64.

Fender, John and Yip, Chong K. Tariffs and Employment: An Intertemporal Approach. *Econ. J.*, September 1989, *99*(397), pp. 806–17.

Fenn, Paul; Mayhew, Ken and McGuire, Alistair. The Assessment: The Economics of Health Care. *Oxford Rev. Econ. Policy*, Spring 1989, *5*(1), pp. 1–20.

Ferber, Marianne A. and Sander, William. Of Women, Men, and Divorce: Not by Economics Alone. *Rev. Soc. Econ.*, Spring 1989, *47*(1), pp. 15–26.

Ferber, P. Demand Component. In *Bauer, S. and Henrichsmeyer, W., eds.*, 1989, pp. 391–93.

—— and Wolfgarten, H. Market Component. In *Bauer, S. and Henrichsmeyer, W., eds.*, 1989, pp. 395–98.

Ferdinand, Peter. The Economic and Financial Dimension. In *Goodman, D. S. G., ed.*, 1989, pp. 38–56.

——. Shandong: An Atypical Costal Province? In *Goodman, D. S. G., ed.*, 1989, pp. 153–63.

Ferejohn, John and Baron, David P. The Power to Propose. In *Ordeshook, P. C., ed.*, 1989, pp. 343–66.

Ferguson, Brian S. and Adrian, Manuella. The Effects of Community-Based Facilities on the Use of Hospital Beds in the Treatment of Alcohol-Related Problems in Ontario 1972–1985. In *Smith, C. S., ed.*, 1989, pp. 242–61.

—— and Crawford, Allan. Supplier-Induced Demand: A Disequilibrium Test. *Appl. Econ.*, May 1989, *21*(5), pp. 597–609.

Ferguson, Ed. Value Theory and Colonial Capitalism: The Case of Zanzibar, 1897–1945. *African Econ. Hist.*, 1989, (18), pp. 25–56.

Ferguson, James M. Newspaper Advertizing Rates. In *Weiss, L. W., ed.*, 1989, pp. 149–54.

Ferleger, Lou and Mandle, Jay R. The Saving Shortfall. *Challenge*, March–April 1989, *32*(2), pp. 57–59.

Fernandes, C. and Harvey, Andrew C. Time Series Models for Count or Qualitative Observations: Reply. *J. Bus. Econ. Statist.*, October 1989, *7*(4), pp. 422.

—— and Harvey, Andrew C. Time Series Models for Count or Qualitative Observations. *J.*

Bus. Econ. Statist., October 1989, *7*(4), pp. 407–17.

Fernandez-Arena, Jose Antonio. Mexican Operative and Administrative Culture. In *Rueschhoff, N. and Schaum, K., eds.*, 1989, pp. 88–105.

Fernández Guerrero, Ismael; Gonzalez, Agustin and Suárez Burguet, Celestino. Spanish External Trade and EEC Preferences. In *Yannopoulos, G. N., ed.*, 1989, pp. 144–68.

Fernández-Kelly, M. Patricia. International Development and Industrial Restructuring: The Case of Garment and Electronics Industries in Southern California. In *MacEwan, A. and Tabb, W. K., eds.*, 1989, pp. 147–65.

—— and García, Anna M. Informalization at the Core: Hispanic Women, Homework, and the Advanced Capitalist State. In *Portes, A.; Castells, M. and Benton, L. A., eds.*, 1989, pp. 247–64.

Fernandez, Raquel. Can Interindustry Wage Differentials Justify Strategic Trade Policy? Comment. In *Feenstra, R. C., ed.*, 1989, pp. 120–24.

Fernández, Roque B. Institucionalidad económica y estabilidad política. (With English summary.) *Cuadernos Econ.*, August 1989, *26*(78), pp. 169–76.

—— and Mantel, Rolf R. Fiscal Lags and the Problem of Stabilization: Argentina's Austral Plan. In *Brock, P. L.; Connolly, M. B. and González-Vega, C., eds.*, 1989, pp. 65–79.

Fernando, Adrian and Maxwell, Simon. Cash Crops in Developing Countries: The Issues, the Facts, the Policies. *World Devel.*, November 1989, *17*(11), pp. 1677–1708.

Fernando, G. B. A. and Daranagama, D. A. U. The Energy–Economy Link in Sri Lanka. In *James, W. E., ed.*, 1989, pp. 183–93.

Fernando, Lloyd S. The South Asian Economy and Asian-Pacific Region: Comment. In *Shinohara, M. and Lo, F., eds.*, 1989, pp. 245–46.

Ferns, H. S. Argentina and Canada, 1880–1930: Problems and Solutions in Immigrant Communities. In *Platt, D. C. M., ed.*, 1989, pp. 151–68.

Ferrara, Peter J. Social Security: A New Compact between the Generations. In *Crane, E. H. and Boaz, D.*, 1989, pp. 221–37.

Ferrari, M. and Zweifel, P. Multiple Versorgungsrisiken und optimale Reservekapazitäten in der schweizerischen Energieversorgung. (Multiple Risks in Energy Supply and Optimal Reserve Capacities—The Case of Switzerland. With English summary.) *Schweiz. Z. Volkswirtsch. Statist.*, March 1989, *125*(1), pp. 1–17.

Ferreira, Eurico J. and Sirmans, G. Stacy. Selling Price, Financing Premiums, and Days on the Market. *J. Real Estate Finance Econ.*, September 1989, *2*(3), pp. 209–22.

Ferrera, Maurizio. Politics, Institutional Features, and the Government of Industry. In *Lange, P. and Regini, M., eds.*, 1989, pp. 111–27.

——. Social Welfare in Developed Market

Countries: Italy. In *Dixon, J. and Scheurell, R. P., eds.*, 1989, pp. 122–46.

Ferretti, Mario. Un modello walrasiano d'equilibrio di lugno periodo. (A Walrasian Model of Long-run Equilibrium. With English summary.) *Giorn. Econ.*, Sept.–Oct. 1989, *48*(9–10), pp. 415–47.

Ferri, Giovanni. An Endogenous Infrastructural Investment Cycle. In *Di Matteo, M.; Goodwin, R. M. and Vercelli, A., eds.*, 1989, pp. 36–45.

Ferri, Michael G.; Moore, Scott B. and Schirm, David C. The Listing, Size, and Value of Equity Warrants. *Financial Rev.*, February 1989, *24*(1), pp. 135–46.

_____; **Schirm, David C. and Sheehan, Richard G.** Financial Market Responses to Treasury Debt Announcements: A Note. *J. Money, Credit, Banking*, August 1989, *21*(3), pp. 394–400.

Ferrie, Joseph P. and Alston, Lee J. Social Control and Labor Relations in the American South before the Mechanization of the Cotton Harvest in the 1950s. *J. Inst. Theoretical Econ.*, March 1989, *145*(1), pp. 133–57.

Ferris, John W. and Klarquist, Virginia L. Productivity in the Carburetors, Pistons, and Valves Industry. *Mon. Lab. Rev.*, February 1989, *112*(2), pp. 43–46.

Fershtman, Chaim. Fixed Rules and Decision Rules: Time Consistency and Subgame Perfection. *Econ. Letters*, September 1989, *30*(3), pp. 191–94.

_____. Self-Enforceable Agreements in an N-Player Dynamic Game. In *[Verheyen, P.]*, 1989, pp. 55–72.

_____ **and Pirchi, Anat.** Perceived Wealth and Government Bonds: A Diagrammatic Exposition. *Amer. Economist*, Spring 1989, *33*(1), pp. 83–86.

Ferson, Wayne E. Changes in Expected Security Returns, Risk, and the Level of Interest Rates. *J. Finance*, December 1989, *44*(5), pp. 1191–1217.

Fesharaki, Fereidun. The International Petroleum Market: Changing Structure and the Future Outlook. In *James, W. E., ed.*, 1989, pp. 3–16.

_____ **and Isaak, David T.** Oil Refining: Planning Long-Term Strategies in a Short-Term Market. In *[Evans, J. K.]*, 1989, pp. 20–34.

Fess, Philip E. and Ziegler, Richard E. Perceptions of Bankers and Analysts of the CPA's Responsibilities for Audited Financial Statements. In *Gangolly, J., ed.*, 1989, pp. 65–88.

Fetter, Steve; Prilutskii, Oleg F. and Rodionov, Stanislav N. Passive Detection of Nuclear Warheads. In *Altmann, J. and Rotblat, J., eds.*, 1989, pp. 48–59.

Fewell, Carla-Marie and Mooney, Linda A. Crime in One Long-Lived Comic Strip: An Evaluation of Chester Gould's 'Dick Tracy.' *Amer. J. Econ. Sociology*, January 1989, *48*(1), pp. 89–100.

de Feydeau, Henri and Kulbokas, François. Le coût de la perception de l'impôt à charge de l'administration et des contribuables: France. (Administrative and Compliance Costs of Taxation: France. With English summary.) In *International Fiscal Association, ed. (I)*, 1989, pp. 361–85.

Ffrench-Davis, Ricardo. Economic Integration in Latin America. In *Naya, S., et al., eds.*, 1989, pp. 157–80.

_____. El conflicto entre la deuda y el crecimiento en Chile: Tendencias y perspectivas. (The Conflict between Debt and Growth in Chile: Trends and Perspectives. With English summary.) *Colección Estud. CIEPLAN*, June 1989, (26), pp. 61–89.

_____. Lessons from the 1890s for the 1980s: Comment. In *[Díaz-Alejandro, C.]*, 1989, pp. 54–56.

Fichtenbaum, Rudy. The Productivity Slowdown and the Underground Economy. *Quart. J. Bus. Econ.*, Summer 1989, *28*(3), pp. 78–90.

_____ **and Blair, John P.** Regional Differences in Labor Demand in the United States. *Rev. Reg. Stud.*, Winter 1989, *19*(1), pp. 72–76.

Fiebiger, H. On the Methodology of Time Budget Surveys in the GDR. *Statist. J.*, 1989, *6*(3), pp. 207–12.

Fiedler, Klaus and Pethig, Rüdiger. Effluent Charges on Municipal Wastewater Treatment Facilities: In Search of Their Theoretical Rationale. *J. Econ. (Z. Nationalökon.)*, 1989, *49*(1), pp. 71–94.

Fiegenbaum, Avi and Primeaux, Walter J., Jr. An Empirical Examination of Strategic Groups in Three Manufacturing Industries. In *Lee, C. F., ed.*, 1989, pp. 281–310.

Field, Alfred J., Jr.; Appleyard, Dennis R. and Conway, Patrick J. The Effects of Customs Unions on the Pattern and Terms of Trade in a Ricardian Model with a Continuum of Goods. *J. Int. Econ.*, August 1989, *27*(1–2), pp. 147–64.

_____; **Conway, Patrick J. and Appleyard, Dennis R.** Trade Agreements vs. Unilateral Tariff Reductions: Evidence from Modeling with a Continuum of Goods. *Int. Econ. Rev.*, November 1989, *30*(4), pp. 775–94.

Field, Barry C. The Evolution of Property Rights. *Kyklos*, 1989, *42*(3), pp. 319–45.

Field, Daniel. The Polarization of Peasant Households in Prerevolutionary Russia: Zemstvo Censuses and Problems of Measurement. In *Grantham, G. and Leonard, C. S., eds., Pt. B*, 1989, pp. 477–505.

Fields, Gary S. Changes in Poverty and Inequality in Developing Countries. *World Bank Res. Observer*, July 1989, *4*(2), pp. 167–85.

_____. On-the-Job Search in a Labor Market Model: Ex Ante Choices and Ex Post Outcomes. *J. Devel. Econ.*, January 1989, *30*(1), pp. 159–78.

_____ **and Wan, Henry, Jr.** Wage-Setting Institutions and Economic Growth. *World Devel.*, Special Issue, September 1989, *17*(9), pp. 1471–83.

Fields, Joseph A. and Murphy, Neil B. An Analysis of Efficiency in the Delivery of Financial

Services: The Case of Life Insurance Agencies. *J. Finan. Services Res.*, October 1989, *2*(4), pp. 343–56.

Fields, M. Andrew. Should Dividend Discount Models Be Yield Tilted? Comment. *J. Portfol. Manage.*, Winter 1989, *15*(2), pp. 80–82.

_____; **Hall, Thomas E. and Fields, T. Windsor.** On Allocating the Variance of Output Growth to Trend and Cycle Components. *Econ. Letters*, October 1989, *30*(4), pp. 323–26.

Fields, T. Windsor; Fields, M. Andrew and Hall, Thomas E. On Allocating the Variance of Output Growth to Trend and Cycle Components. *Econ. Letters*, October 1989, *30*(4), pp. 323–26.

Fieleke, Norman S. Europe in 1992. *New Eng. Econ. Rev.*, May–June 1989, pp. 13–26.

_____. International Payments Imbalances in the 1980s: An Overview. *New Eng. Econ. Rev.*, Mar.–Apr. 1989, pp. 3–14.

_____. The Terms on Which Nations Trade. *New Eng. Econ. Rev.*, Nov.–Dec. 1989, pp. 3–12.

Fienberg, Stephen E. The Evolving Role of Statistical Assessments as Evidence in the Courts: Case Studies. In *Fienberg, S. E., ed.*, 1989, pp. 17–83.

_____. The Evolving Role of Statistical Assessments as Evidence in the Courts: Introduction. In *Fienberg, S. E., ed.*, 1989, pp. 1–16.

_____. Modeling Considerations: Discussion from a Modeling Perspective. In *Kasprzyk, D., et al., eds.*, 1989, pp. 566–74.

_____. Review of the Use of Statistics in Selected Areas of Litigation. In *Fienberg, S. E., ed.*, 1989, pp. 85–137.

_____. Some Partial Solutions to the Problems Arising from Expert Statistical Testimony. In *Fienberg, S. E., ed.*, 1989, pp. 155–89.

_____. Statistics, Law, and Expert Testimony. In *Fienberg, S. E., ed.*, 1989, pp. 139–54.

Figlewski, Stephen. Options Arbitrage in Imperfect Markets. *J. Finance*, December 1989, *44*(5), pp. 1289–1311.

Fik, Timothy J. and Mulligan, Gordon F. Asymmetrical Price Conjectural Variation in Spatial Competition Models. *Econ. Geogr.*, January 1989, *65*(1), pp. 19–32.

_____ and **Mulligan, Gordon F.** Price Variation in Spatial Markets: The Case of Perfectly Inelastic Demand. *Ann. Reg. Sci.*, 1989, *23*(3), pp. 187–201.

Filardo, Peter. Annual Bibliography on American Labor History: 1988. *Labor Hist.*, Fall 1989, *30*(4), pp. 585–94.

Filc, Wolfgang. The Ecu with a View towards Stabilising Exchange Rates and Furthering the Economic Integration of Europe. In *Franz, O., ed.*, 1989, pp. 38–48.

Filer, Randall K. Occupational Segregation, Compensating Differentials, and Comparable Worth. In *Michael, R. T.; Hartmann, H. I. and O'Farrell, B., eds.*, 1989, pp. 153–70.

Filios, Vassilios P. Monitoring Social Change through Accounting: The Case of Greece. *Rivista Int. Sci. Econ. Com.*, June 1989, *36*(6), pp. 513–24.

Filippi, Francesco. "Keynes dopo Lucas." Una nota. ("Keynes dopo Lucas." A Note. With English summary.) *Econ. Politica*, August 1989, *6*(2), pp. 255–63.

Filippini, L. and Rovetta, A. Economic Aspects in Factory Automation in Relation to System Flexibility. In *Archetti, F.; Lucertini, M. and Serafini, P., eds.*, 1989, pp. 135–51.

Filippini, Mariano and Olcese, Maria Angélica. Transitional Economic Policies, 1971–73. In *di Tella, G. and Dornbusch, R., eds.*, 1989, pp. 189–205.

Fina, Lluis; Meixide, Alberto and Toharia, Luis. Reregulating the Labor Market amid an Economic and Political Crisis: Spain, 1975–1986. In *Rosenberg, S., ed.*, 1989, pp. 107–25.

Finch, C. David. The Use of IMF Credit: Conditional Finance for Industrial Countries: Comment. In *Gwin, C. and Feinberg, R. E., eds.*, 1989, pp. 93–99.

Finch, Michael; Dowd, Bryan and Feldman, Roger. The Role of Health Practices in HMO Selection Bias: A Confirmatory Study. *Inquiry*, Fall 1989, *26*(3), pp. 381–87.

_____; **Lurie, N. and Moscovice, I.** Minnesota: Plan Choice by the Mentally Ill in Medicaid Prepaid Health Plans. In *Scheffler, R. M. and Rossiter, L. F., eds.*, 1989, pp. 265–78.

Fincher, R. Multicultural matters: Commentary. *Environ. Planning A*, November 1989, *21*(11), pp. 1423–26.

Findlay, Carly J.; Wan, G. H. and Anderson, Jock R. Are Modern Cultivars More Risky? A Question of Stochastic Efficiency. In *Anderson, J. R. and Hazell, P. B. R., eds.*, 1989, pp. 301–08.

Findlay, Patricia. Fighting Plant Closure—Women in the Plessey Occupation. In *Elson, D. and Pearson, R., eds.*, 1989, pp. 183–205.

Findlay, Ronald. National and Global Perspectives on Economic Development—The Two Models of Arthur Lewis: W. Arthur Lewis Lecture. *Rev. Black Polit. Econ.*, Summer 1989, *18*(1), pp. 17–29.

_____. North–South Models and the Evolution of Global Interdependence. In *[Díaz-Alejandro, C.]*, 1989, pp. 397–414.

Findley, Carter Vaughn. Knowledge and Education in the Modern Middle East: A Comparative View. In *Sabagh, G., ed.*, 1989, pp. 130–54.

Fine, Charles H. and Li, Lode. Equilibrium Exit in Stochastically Declining Industries. *Games Econ. Behav.*, March 1989, *1*(1), pp. 40–59.

Fine, Michelle; Sudman, Seymour and Rothbart, George S. On Finding and Interviewing the Needles in the Haystack: The Use of Multiplicity Sampling. In *Singer, E. and Presser, S., eds.*, 1989, *1982*, pp. 18–31.

Finegan, T. Aldrich and Burkhauser, Richard V. The Minimum Wage and the Poor: The End of a Relationship. *J. Policy Anal. Manage.*, Winter 1989, *8*(1), pp. 53–71.

Finer, Samuel E. Patronage and the Public Service in Britain and America. In *Heidenheimer,*

A. J.; Johnston, M. and LeVine, V. T., eds., 1989, *1952*, pp. 101–28.

Fingard, Judith. Evangelical Social Work in Canada: Salvationists and Sailors' Friends, 1890–1920. In *Platt, D. C. M., ed.*, 1989, pp. 25–44.

Finger, J. Michael. North–South Trade in Services: Some Empirical Evidence: Comment. In *Giersch, H., ed.*, 1989, pp. 272–73.

———. Protectionist Rules and Internationalist Discretion in the Making of National Trade Policy. In *Vosgerau, H.-J., ed.*, 1989, pp. 310–23.

Fink, Justin. Community Agency Boards of Directors: Viability and Vestigiality, Substance and Symbol. In *Herman, R. D. and Van Til, J., eds.*, 1989, pp. 89–117.

Finkelstein, Joseph. Windows on a New World: Introduction. In *Finkelstein, J., ed.*, 1989, pp. xv–xxi.

——— and Newman, David. The Third Industrial Revolution. In *Finkelstein, J., ed.*, 1989, pp. 219–32.

Finkelstein, Lawrence S. The Struggle to Control UNESCO. In *[Gordenker, L.]*, 1989, pp. 144–64.

Finkle, Jason L. and Crane, Barbara B. The United States, China, and the United Nations Population Fund: Dynamics of U.S. Policymaking. *Population Devel. Rev.*, March 1989, *15*(1), pp. 23–59.

Finn, Chester E., Jr. An Executive Branch Perspective: Comment. *J. Policy Anal. Manage.*, Fall 1989, *8*(4), pp. 633–38.

Finn, Frank J. and Ball, Ray. The Effect of Block Transactions on Share Prices: Australian Evidence. *J. Banking Finance*, July 1989, *13*(3), pp. 397–419.

Finn, Mary. An Econometric Analysis of the Intertemporal General-Equilibrium Approach to Exchange Rate and Current Account Determination. *J. Int. Money Finance*, December 1989, *8*(4), pp. 467–86.

Finnerty, John D. Measuring the Duration of a Floating-Rate Bond. *J. Portfol. Manage.*, Summer 1989, *15*(4), pp. 67–72.

Finsinger, Jörg and von der Schulenburg, J.-Matthias Graf. Der Sonntagsverkauf. (The Effects of Sunday Trading. With English summary.) *Z. Wirtschaft. Sozialwissen.*, 1989, *109*(1), pp. 119–28.

——— and Simon, Jürgen. An Economic Assessment of the EC Product Liability Directive and the Product Liability Law of the Federal Republic of Germany. In *Faure, M. and Van den Bergh, R., eds.*, 1989, pp. 185–214.

Finsterbusch, Kurt and Van Wicklin, Warren A., III. Beneficiary Participation in Development Projects: Empirical Tests of Popular Theories. *Econ. Devel. Cult. Change*, April 1989, *37*(3), pp. 573–93.

Finucane, Thomas J. Black–Scholes Approximations of Call Option Prices with Stochastic Volatilities: A Note. *J. Finan. Quant. Anal.*, December 1989, *24*(4), pp. 527–32.

———. A Simple Linear Weighting Scheme for

Black–Scholes Implied Volatilities: Note. *J. Banking Finance*, May 1989, *13*(2), pp. 321–26.

Fiocca, Renato and Snehota, Ivan. High Technology and Management of the Market Differential. In *Hallén, L. and Johanson, J., eds.*, 1989, pp. 199–209.

Fiore, Lyle C.; Zuber, Richard A. and Johnson, R. Stafford. The Investment Performance of Common Stocks in Relation to Their Price–Earnings Ratios: An Update of the Basu Study. *Financial Rev.*, August 1989, *24*(3), pp. 499–505.

Fiorentini, Gianluca. Externalities and Property Rights: Some Policy Implications. *Econ. Notes*, 1989, (3), pp. 343–61.

Firchau, Volker. Information Systems for Principal–Agent Problems. In *Bamberg, G. and Spremann, K., eds.*, 1989, pp. 81–92.

Firer, C. and Knight, E. T. The Performance of South African Unit Trusts 1977–1986. *S. Afr. J. Econ.*, March 1989, *57*(1), pp. 52–68.

Firman, James P. Health-Care Cooperatives. In *Eisdorfer, C.; Kessler, D. A. and Spector, A. N., eds.*, 1989, pp. 278–87.

Fischbeck, G. Variability in Winter Wheat and Spring Barley Yields in Bavaria. In *Anderson, J. R. and Hazell, P. B. R., eds.*, 1989, pp. 118–24.

Fischel, Daniel R. The Economics of Lender Liability. *Yale Law J.*, October 1989, *99*(1), pp. 131–54.

Fischel, William A. Did *Serrano* Cause Proposition 13? *Nat. Tax J.*, December 1989, *42*(4), pp. 465–73.

——— and Shapiro, Perry. A Constitutional Choice Model of Compensation for Takings. *Int. Rev. Law Econ.*, December 1989, *9*(2), pp. 115–28.

Fischer, Andreas M. Interpreting the Term Structure of Interest Rates Using Weekly Money Announcements. *Schweiz. Z. Volkswirtsch. Statist.*, March 1989, *125*(1), pp. 43–53.

———. Policy Regime Changes and Monetary Expectations: Testing for Super Exogeneity. *J. Monet. Econ.*, November 1989, *24*(3), pp. 423–36.

———. Unit Roots and Survey Data. *Oxford Bull. Econ. Statist.*, November 1989, *51*(4), pp. 451–63.

——— and Cocco, Flavio. Are Announcement Effects Time Dependent? *Econ. Letters*, August 1989, *30*(2), pp. 157–59.

Fischer, Charles C. Bell, Merton and Mills as Veblen Critics: A Comment. *Amer. J. Econ. Sociology*, July 1989, *48*(3), pp. 321–22.

Fischer, David A. V. The IAEA's Controls on Fissile Material: Limits and Successes. In *Altmann, J. and Rotblat, J., eds.*, 1989, pp. 68–79.

Fischer, David W. Returns to Society from Offshore Hard Mineral Resource Development: Special Interests Are Seeking to Monopolize Public Land under the Sea by Doing Away with the 1953 Act. *Amer. J. Econ. Sociology,* January 1989, *48*(1), pp. 31–46.

Fischer, Dietrich. Economic Cooperation as a Means of Improving East–West Relations. **In** *Feiwel, G. R., ed. (I),* 1989, pp. 741–48.

Fischer, Edwin O.; Heinkel, Robert and Zechner, Josef. Dynamic Capital Structure Choice: Theory and Tests. *J. Finance,* March 1989, *44*(1), pp. 19–40.

———; **Heinkel, Robert and Zechner, Josef.** Dynamic Recapitalization Policies and the Role of Call Premia and Issue Discounts. *J. Finan. Quant. Anal.,* December 1989, *24*(4), pp. 427–46.

Fischer, Georges and Thierstein, Alain. Internationale Wettbewerbsfähigkeit und regionale Entwicklung. (International Competitiveness and Regional Development. With English summary.) *Aussenwirtschaft,* June 1989, *44*(2), pp. 197–222.

Fischer, Günther; Parikh, Kirit S. and Frohberg, Klaus K. International Effects of CAP Trade Liberalization. **In** *Tarditi, S., et al., eds.,* 1989, pp. 27–46.

Fischer, Jeffrey H. Anomalies: The Ultimatum Game; Comment. *J. Econ. Perspectives,* Summer 1989, *3*(3), pp. 184.

Fischer, Lutz. Die Kosten der Steuererhebung für Verwaltung und Steuerpflichtige: Deutschland. (Administrative and Compliance Costs of Taxation: West Germany. With English summary.) **In** *International Fiscal Association, ed. (I), 1989,* pp. 139–76.

Fischer, Manfred M. Innovation, Diffusion and Regions. **In** *Andersson, Å. E.; Batten, D. F. and Karlsson, C., eds.,* 1989, pp. 47–61.

Fischer, Ronald D. Dynamic Duopoly with Output Adjustment Costs in International Markets: Taking the Conjecture out of Conjectual Variations: Comment. **In** *Feenstra, R. C., ed.,* 1989, pp. 141–43.

——— **and Anderson, Simon P.** Multi-market Oligopoly with Production before Sales. *J. Ind. Econ.,* December 1989, *38*(2), pp. 167–82.

Fischer, Stanley. The Effect of the Stock Market on Investment: A Comparative Study: Comment. *Europ. Econ. Rev.,* May 1989, *33*(5), pp. 956–59.

———. Factor Mobility and the International Monetary System. *Bank Japan Monet. Econ. Stud.,* August 1989, *7*(2), pp. 15–23.

———. The Key Question is the Bargaining. **In** *Dornbusch, R.; Makin, J. H. and Zlowe, D., eds.,* 1989, pp. 75–78.

———. Resolving the International Debt Crisis. **In** *Sachs, J. D., ed. (I),* 1989, pp. 359–85.

———. Resolving the International Debt Crisis. **In** *Sachs, J. D., ed. (II),* 1989, pp. 313–23.

———. Simulating the Effects of Some Simple Coordinated versus Uncoordinated Policy Rules: Comment. **In** *Bryant, R. C., et al., eds.,* 1989, pp. 245–47.

——— **and Modigliani, Franco.** Towards an Understanding of the Real Effects and Costs of Inflation. **In** *Modigliani, F., Vol. 5,* 1989, *1978,* pp. 280–303.

——— **and Summers, Lawrence H.** Should Governments Learn to Live with Inflation? *Amer. Econ. Rev.,* May 1989, *79*(2), pp. 382–87.

——— **and de Tray, Dennis.** Proceedings of the World Bank Annual Conference on Development Economics 1989: Introduction. **In** *Fischer, S. and de Tray, D., eds.,* 1989, pp. 1–9.

Fischer, Thomas R. Die Bereitschaft der Banken zur Übernahme von Kreditrisiken. (The Banks' Willingness to Assume Credit Risks. With English summary.) *Kredit Kapital,* 1989, *22*(2), pp. 267–95.

Fischer, Vivienne C. States Rescue Localities with Creative Financing. **In** *Matzer, J., Jr., ed.,* 1989, *1988,* pp. 156–61.

Fish, Mary and Gibbons, Jean D. A Comparison of the Publications of Female and Male Economists. *J. Econ. Educ.,* Winter 1989, *20*(1), pp. 93–105.

Fishback, Price V. Can Competition among Employers Reduce Governmental Discrimination? Coal Companies and Segregated Schools in West Virginia in the Early 1900s. *J. Law Econ.,* Part 1, October 1989, *32*(2), pp. 311–28.

———. Debt Peonage in Postbellum Georgia. *Exploration Econ. Hist.,* April 1989, *26*(2), pp. 219–36.

——— **and La Croix, Sumner J.** Firm-Specific Evidence on Racial Wage Differentials and Workforce Segregation in Hawaii's Sugar Industry. *Exploration Econ. Hist.,* October 1989, *26*(4), pp. 403–23.

——— **and Lauszus, Dieter.** The Quality of Services in Company Towns: Sanitation in Coal Towns during the 1920s. *J. Econ. Hist.,* March 1989, *49*(1), pp. 125–44.

——— **and Terza, Joseph V.** Are Estimates of Sex Discrimination by Employers Robust? The Use of Never-Marrieds. *Econ. Inquiry,* April 1989, *27*(2), pp. 271–85.

Fishburn, Peter C. Non-transitive Measurable Utility for Decision under Uncertainty. *J. Math. Econ.,* 1989, *18*(2), pp. 187–207.

———. Retrospective on the Utility Theory of von Neumann and Morgenstern. *J. Risk Uncertainty,* June 1989, *2*(2), pp. 127–57.

———. Stochastic Dominance in Nonlinear Utility Theory. **In** *[Hadar, J.],* 1989, pp. 3–20.

——— **and Falmagne, Jean-Claude.** Binary Choice Probabilities and Rankings. *Econ. Letters,* December 1989, *31*(2), pp. 113–17.

Fishelson, Gideon. Imperfect Competition under Uncertainty. *J. Econ. Bus.,* August 1989, *41*(3), pp. 253–63.

———. Key Findings of the Middle East Economic Cooperation Projects. **In** *Fishelson, G., ed.,* 1989, pp. 347–65.

Fisher, Ann; Chestnut, Lauraine G. and Violette, Daniel M. The Value of Reducing Risks of Death: A Note on New Evidence. *J. Policy Anal. Manage.,* Winter 1989, *8*(1), pp. 88–100.

Fisher, Anthony C. and Despotakis, Kostas A. Energy Taxes and Economic Performance: A Regional General Equilibrium Analysis. *Energy Econ.,* April 1989, *11*(2), pp. 153–57.

Fisher, Arthur. Investment in the United States: A Summary of the Technical and Miscellaneous Revenue Act of 1988 and the Sec. 482 White Paper. *Bull. Int. Fiscal Doc.*, April 1989, *43*(4), pp. 173–76.

Fisher, B. S.; MacAulay, T. G. and Batterham, R. L. Solution of Spatial Trading Systems with Concave Cubic Programming. *Australian J. Agr. Econ.*, December 1989, *33*(3), pp. 170–86.

Fisher, Cynthia D.; Shaw, James B. and Ismail, Abdul Jalil Bin. A Cognitive Categorization Approach to Managerial Performance Appraisal: Analysis of the Singapore Manager. In *Nedd, A., ed.*, 1989, pp. 339–57.

Fisher, Douglas. The Price Revolution: A Monetary Interpretation. *J. Econ. Hist.*, December 1989, *49*(4), pp. 883–902.

_____ **and Serletis, Apostolos.** Velocity and the Growth of Money in the United States, 1970–1985. *J. Macroecon.*, Summer 1989, *11*(3), pp. 323–32.

_____ **and Thurman, Walter N.** Sweden's Financial Sophistication in the Nineteenth Century: An Appraisal. *J. Econ. Hist.*, September 1989, *49*(3), pp. 621–34.

Fisher, Eric. Exchange Rate Pass-Through and the Relative Concentration of German and Japanese Manufacturing Industries. *Econ. Letters*, November 1989, *31*(1), pp. 81–85.

_____. A Model of Exchange Rate Pass-Through. *J. Int. Econ.*, February 1989, *26*(1/2), pp. 119–37.

Fisher, Franklin M. Games Economists Play: A Noncooperative View. *Rand J. Econ.*, Spring 1989, *20*(1), pp. 113–24.

_____. It Takes *t** to Tango: Trading Coalitions with Fixed Prices. *Rev. Econ. Stud.*, July 1989, *56*(3), pp. 391–403.

Fisher, Jeffrey D. and Lentz, George H. Tax Reform and Organizational Forms for Holding Investment Real Estate: Corporation vs. Partnership. *Amer. Real Estate Urban Econ. Assoc. J.*, Fall 1989, *17*(3), pp. 314–37.

Fisher, M. R. Professor Hicks and the Keynesians. In *Wood, J. C. and Woods, R. N., eds.*, Vol. 3, 1989, *1976*, pp. 127–37.

Fisher, P. G., et al. Comparative Properties of Models of the UK Economy. *Nat. Inst. Econ. Rev.*, August 1989, (129), pp. 69–87.

Fisher, Peter F.; Stanley, Michael A. and Balachandran, Chandra S. An Expert System Approach to Rural Development: A Prototype (TIHSO). *J. Developing Areas*, January 1989, *23*(2), pp. 259–70.

Fisher, Robert. Urban Policy in Houston, Texas. *Urban Stud.*, February 1989, *26*(1), pp. 144–54.

Fisher, Ronald C.; Goddeeris, John H. and Young, James C. Participation in Tax Amnesties: The Individual Income Tax. *Nat. Tax J.*, March 1989, *42*(1), pp. 15–27.

Fisher, Zara and Goldscheider, Frances K. Household Structure and Living Alone in Israel. In *Goldscheider, F. K. and Goldscheider, C., eds.*, 1989, pp. 148–61.

Fishkin, James S. In Quest of the Social Contract. In *Brennan, G. and Lomasky, L. E., eds.*, 1989, pp. 183–93.

Fishlow, Albert. Conditionality and Willingness to Pay: Some Parallels from the 1890s. In *Eichengreen, B. and Lindert, P. H., eds.*, 1989, pp. 86–105.

_____. The Extent and Causes of the Debt Crisis of the 1980s: Comment. In *Husain, I. and Diwan, I., eds.*, 1989, pp. 42–44.

_____. Hard Times: Latin America in the 1930s and 1980s. In *[Fischer, W.]*, 1989, pp. 314–37.

_____. Lessons from the 1890s for the 1980s. In *[Díaz-Alejandro, C.]*, 1989, pp. 19–47.

_____ **and Cardoso, Eliana A.** The Macroeconomics of the Brazilian External Debt. In *Sachs, J. D., ed. (II)*, 1989, pp. 81–99.

Fishman, G. S. Statistical Considerations in the Simulation of Flexible Manufacturing Systems. In *Archetti, F.; Lucertini, M. and Serafini, P., eds.*, 1989, pp. 153–83.

Fishman, Michael J. Preemptive Bidding and the Role of the Medium of Exchange in Acquisitions. *J. Finance*, March 1989, *44*(1), pp. 41–57.

_____ **and Hagerty, Kathleen M.** Disclosure Decisions by Firms and the Competition for Price Efficiency. *J. Finance*, July 1989, *44*(3), pp. 633–46.

Fishwick, Francis. Definition of Monopoly Power in the Antitrust Policies of the United Kingdom and the European Community. *Antitrust Bull.*, Fall 1989, *34*(3), pp. 451–88.

Fitzgerald, Bruce and Monson, Terry. Preferential Credit and Insurance as Means to Promote Exports. *World Bank Res. Observer*, January 1989, *4*(1), pp. 89–114.

FitzGerald, E. V. K. The Analytics of Stabilization Policy in the Small Semi-industrialized Economy. In *Fitzgerald, E. V. K. and Vos, R.*, 1989, pp. 83–114.

_____. Problems in Financing a Revolution: Accumulation, Defence and Income Distribution in Nicaragua 1979–86. In *Fitzgerald, E. V. K. and Vos, R.*, 1989, pp. 262–98.

_____ **and Croes, Edwin.** The Regional Monetary System and Economic Recovery. In *Irvin, G. and Holland, S., eds.*, 1989, pp. 139–61.

_____ **and Vos, Rob.** Financing Economic Development: A Structural Approach to Monetary Policy: Introduction. In *Fitzgerald, E. V. K. and Vos, R.*, 1989, pp. 1–15.

_____ **and Vos, Rob.** The Foundations of Development Finance: Economic Structure, Accumulation Balances and Income Distribution. In *Fitzgerald, E. V. K. and Vos, R.*, 1989, pp. 17–54.

Fitzgerald, John and Callan, Tim. Price Determination in Ireland: Effects of Changes in Exchange Rates and Exchange Rate Regimes. *Econ. Soc. Rev.*, January 1989, *20*(2), pp. 165–88.

Fitzgerald, John M. The Taste for Bequests and Well-Being of Widows: A Model of Life Insurance Demand by Married Couples. *Rev. Econ. Statist.*, May 1989, *71*(2), pp. 206–14.

Fitzgerald, Robert. Employers' Labour Strategies, Industrial Welfare, and the Response to New Unionism at Bryant and May, 1888–1930. In *Harvey, C. and Turner, J., eds.,* 1989, pp. 48–65.

_____. Rowntree and Market Strategy, 1897–1939. In *Hausman, W. J., ed.,* 1989, pp. 45–58.

Fitzgerald, Terry J. and Miller, Preston J. A Simple Way to Estimate Current-Quarter GNP. *Fed. Res. Bank Minn. Rev.,* Fall 1989, *13*(4), pp. 27–31.

FitzGerald, Vince and Urban, Peter. Causes and Consequences of Changes in the Terms of Trade and the Balance of Payments. In *[Gruen, F. H.],* 1989, pp. 240–61.

Fitzpatrick, Campbell R. and Alaouze, Chris M. A Mixed Integer Linear Programming Evaluation of Salinity and Waterlogging Control Options in the Murray–Darling Basin of Australia. *Australian J. Agr. Econ.,* December 1989, *33*(3), pp. 203–18.

Fitzroy, Felix R. and Acs, Zoltan J. Inside the Firm and Organizational Capital: Review Article. *Int. J. Ind. Organ.,* June 1989, *7*(2), pp. 309–14.

_____ **and Kraft, Kornelius.** Profitability and Profit Sharing: Reply. *J. Ind. Econ.,* September 1989, *38*(1), pp. 115–17.

Fitzsimmons, Edward L. Textbooks, Taxes, and Objectivity in Economics Instruction. *J. Econ. Educ.,* Summer 1989, *20*(3), pp. 247–52.

Fixler, Dennis and Bender, Bruce. The Median Voter, Voting, and Local Government Employment. *J. Reg. Sci.,* February 1989, *29*(1), pp. 29–46.

Fizel, John L. and Bennett, Randall W. The Impact of College Football Telecasts on College Football Attendance. *Soc. Sci. Quart.,* December 1989, *70*(4), pp. 980–88.

Flacco, Paul R. and Zeager, Lester A. The Competitive Firm with Uncertainty in the Rate of Labor Turnover. *Southern Econ. J.,* October 1989, *56*(2), pp. 457–66.

Flaherty, Sean and Caniglia, Alan. Unionism and Income Inequality: Comment. *Ind. Lab. Relat. Rev.,* October 1989, *43*(1), pp. 131–37.

Flaig, Gebhard and Steiner, Viktor. Stability and Dynamic Properties of Labour Demand in West German Manufacturing. *Oxford Bull. Econ. Statist.,* November 1989, *51*(4), pp. 395–412.

Flaim, Paul O. How Many New Jobs since 1982? Data from Two Surveys Differ. *Mon. Lab. Rev.,* August 1989, *112*(8), pp. 10–15.

Flakierski, Henryk. Economic Reform and Income Distribution in Yugoslavia. *Comp. Econ. Stud.,* Spring 1989, *31*(1), pp. 67–102.

_____. The Economic System and Income Distribution in Yugoslavia. *Eastern Europ. Econ.,* Summer 1989, *27*(4), pp. 1–104.

Flam, Harry and Baldwin, Richard E. Strategic Trade Policies in the Market for 30–40 Seat Commuter Aircraft. *Weltwirtsch. Arch.,* 1989, *125*(3), pp. 484–500.

Flamm, Kenneth. Technological Advance and Costs: Computers versus Communications. In *Crandall, R. W. and Flamm, K., eds.,* 1989, pp. 13–61.

_____ **and Crandall, Robert W.** Changing the Rules: Technological Change, International Competition, and Regulation in Communications: Overview. In *Crandall, R. W. and Flamm, K., eds.,* 1989, pp. 1–10.

_____ **and McNaugher, Thomas L.** Rationalizing Technology Investments. In *Steinbruner, J. D., ed.,* 1989, pp. 119–57.

Flanagan, Robert J. Compliance and Enforcement Decisions under the National Labor Relations Act. *J. Lab. Econ.,* July 1989, *7*(3), pp. 257–80.

Flanigan, George B., et al. Experience from Early Tort Reforms: Comparative Negligence Since 1974. *J. Risk Ins.,* September 1989, *56*(3), pp. 525–34.

Flannery, Mark J. Capital Regulation and Insured Banks' Choice of Individual Loan Default Risks. *J. Monet. Econ.,* September 1989, *24*(2), pp. 235–58.

Flassbeck, Heiner. Von der Klassik zur Moderne—Ein Essay über den Erkenntnisfortschritt von 200 Jahren Macroökonomie. (From Classical to Modern Macroeconomics—An Essay on Scientific Progress in the Last 200 Years. With English summary.) *Konjunkturpolitik,* 1989, *35*(1–2), pp. 1–21.

Flaten, D.; Evans, M. and Mondor, R. Expert Systems and Farm Management. *Can. J. Agr. Econ.,* Part 1, December 1989, *37*(4), pp. 639–66.

Flath, David. Vertical Integration by Means of Shareholding Interlocks. *Int. J. Ind. Organ.,* September 1989, *7*(3), pp. 369–80.

_____ **and Nariu, Tatsuhiko.** Returns Policy in the Japanese Marketing System. *J. Japanese Int. Economies,* March 1989, *3*(1), pp. 49–63.

Flatters, Frank and Boadway, Robin W. Tax Expenditures and Alternatives for Evaluating Government Activities Conducted through the Tax System. In *Bruce, N., ed.,* 1989, pp. 67–104.

Fleischer, Ernest M. Alternative Strategies for Success: Panel Presentation. In *Federal Home Loan Bank of San Francisco,* 1989, pp. 107–08.

Fleisher, Arthur A., III; Shughart, William F., II and Tollison, Robert D. Ownership Structure in Professional Sports. In *Zerbe, R. O., ed.,* 1989, pp. 71–75.

Fleisher, Belton M. and Kopecky, Kenneth J. The Loanable-Funds Approach to Teaching Macroeconomics: Reply. *J. Econ. Educ.,* Summer 1989, *20*(3), pp. 259–60.

Fleisher, Beverly. The Economic Risks of Deliberately Released Genetically Engineered Microorganisms. *Amer. J. Agr. Econ.,* May 1989, *71*(2), pp. 480–84.

Fleming, Euan M. and Piggott, Roley R. Assessment of Policy Options for Agricultural Export Stabilization in the South Pacific. *J. Developing Areas,* January 1989, *23*(2), pp. 271–89.

Fleming, Michael and Button, Kenneth J. Regulatory Reform in the UK. In *Button, K. and Swann, D.*, eds., 1989, pp. 79–103.

Flemming, John S. Examples Set by Great Britain and the United States. In *Fels, G. and von Furstenberg, G. M.*, eds., 1989, pp. 181–84.

———. The Tastes of European Central Bankers: Discussion. In *De Cecco, M. and Giovannini, A.*, eds., 1989, pp. 189–91.

———. Theoretical Developments in the Light of Macroeconomic Policy and Empirical Research: Comment. *Scand. J. Econ.*, 1989, 91(2), pp. 335–37.

Fletcher, Jerald J.; Adamowicz, Wiktor L. and Graham-Tomasi, Theodore. Inequality Constrained Estimation of Consumer Surplus. *Can. J. Agr. Econ.*, November 1989, 37(3), pp. 407–20.

———; **Graham-Tomasi, Theodore and Adamowicz, Wiktor L.** Functional Form and the Statistical Properties of Welfare Measures. *Amer. J. Agr. Econ.*, May 1989, 71(2), pp. 414–21.

Fletcher, Lehman B.; Ahmed, S. and Hassan, Rashid M. Unequal Wealth Accumulation and Income Inequality in a Unimodal Agriculture: Sudan's Radad Irrigation Scheme. *J. Devel. Stud.*, October 1989, 26(1), pp. 120–30.

Fletcher, Richard D. Undervaluation, Adjustment, and Growth. In *Weeks, J. F.*, ed., 1989, pp. 125–30.

Fletcher, Stanley M.; Houston, Jack E. and Jeong, Kihong. Varietal Sales and Quality Differentiation: The Case of Certified Soybean Seed in the Southeastern U.S. *Southern J. Agr. Econ.*, July 1989, 21(1), pp. 113–20.

Fleury, Alfonso Carlos Correa. The Technological Behaviour of State-Owned Enterprises in Brazil. In *James, J.*, ed., 1989, pp. 194–229.

Flinn, John C. and Ali, Mubarik. Profit Efficiency among Basmati Rice Producers in Pakistan Punjab. *Amer. J. Agr. Econ.*, May 1989, 71(2), pp. 303–10.

——— and **Denning, G. L.** Agroeconomic Opportunities in Rice-Based Farming Systems Research. In *International Rice Research Institute*, 1989, pp. 239–54.

——— and **Garrity, Dennis P.** Yield Stability and Modern Rice Technology. In *Anderson, J. R. and Hazell, P. B. R.*, eds., 1989, pp. 251–64.

Flood, Robert P. Commodity Prices and Aggregate Inflation: Would a Commodity Price Rule Be Worthwhile? A Comment. *Carnegie–Rochester Conf. Ser. Public Policy*, Autumn 1989, 31, pp. 241–46.

———; **Bhandari, Jagdeep S. and Horne, Jocelyn P.** Evolution of Exchange Rate Regimes. *Int. Monet. Fund Staff Pap.*, December 1989, 36(4), pp. 810–35.

——— and **Isard, Peter.** Monetary Policy Strategies. *Int. Monet. Fund Staff Pap.*, September 1989, 36(3), pp. 612–32.

Florens, Jean-Pierre and Mouchart, Michel. Bayesian Specification Tests. In *Cornet, B. and Tulkens, H.*, eds., 1989, pp. 467–90.

Flores, Benito E. The Utilization of the Wilcoxon Test to Compare Forecasting Methods: A Note. *Int. J. Forecasting*, 1989, 5(4), pp. 529–35.

Flores de Frutos, Rafael. Análisis de las relaciones entre el PIB español, el PNB de Estados Unidos y el PNB del conjunto de países industrializados. (With English summary.) *Invest. Econ.*, May 1989, 13(2), pp. 301–16.

Floto, Edgardo. The Centre–Periphery System and Unequal Exchange. *CEPAL Rev.*, December 1989, (39), pp. 135–54.

Fløttum, Erling Joar. Norwegian Practices on Integrated Input–Output Compilation in the National Accounts: General Features and Special Issues. In *Franz, A. and Rainer, N.*, eds., 1989, pp. 169–89.

Flowerdew, R. and Goldstein, W. Geodemographics in Practice: Developments in North America. *Environ. Planning A*, May 1989, 21(5), pp. 605–16.

Flowers, Edward B. Taiwan's Potential for Foreign Direct Investment in the United States. In *Lee, C. F. and Hu, S.-C.*, eds., 1989, pp. 91–118.

Flowers, Marilyn R. Public Investment and the Burden of the Public Debt: Comment. *Southern Econ. J.*, October 1989, 56(2), pp. 529–31.

Flynn, Andrew and Lowe, Philip. Environmental Politics and Policy in the 1980s. In *Mohan, J.*, ed., 1989, pp. 255–79.

Flynn, John J. Fundamentals of the Economic Role of Government: The Chicken and the Egg. In *Samuels, W. J.*, ed. (I), 1989, pp. 69–78.

Flynn, Joseph E. and Mayo, John W. Firm Entry and Exit: Causality Tests and Economic-Base Linkages. *J. Reg. Sci.*, November 1989, 29(4), pp. 645–62.

Foddy, Margaret. Information Control as a Bargaining Tactic in Social Exchange. In *Lawler, E. J. and Markovsky, B.*, eds., 1989, pp. 139–78.

Fodella, Gianni. Internazionalizzazione economica e scenari anni 90: Si può parlare di un'area del pacifico? (Economic Internationalization and Prospects for the 1990's: Is There a Pacific Area? With English summary.) *Rivista Int. Sci. Econ. Com.*, February 1989, 36(2), pp. 97–100.

———. Orgware: The Key of Japanese Success. *Rivista Int. Sci. Econ. Com.*, December 1989, 36(12), pp. 1057–62.

Foders, Federico. The Fisheries Regime in the Member Countries of the EC: Legal and Economic Aspects. *Econ. Scelte Pubbliche/J. Public Finance Public Choice*, Jan.–Aug. 1989, 7(1–2), pp. 67–79.

Fodor, Jorge. Argentina's Nationalism: Myth or Reality? In *di Tella, G. and Dornbusch, R.*, eds., 1989, pp. 31–55.

Fogarty, John. Social Experiments in Regions of Recent Settlement: Australia, Argentina and Canada. In *Platt, D. C. M.*, ed., 1989, pp. 179–99.

Fogel, Robert William. Afterword: Some Notes on the Scientific Methods of Simon Kuznets. In *Kuznets, S.*, 1989, pp. 413–38.

Foglesong, Richard E. The Politics of Industrial Policy in the United States. In *Foglesong, R. E. and Wolfe, J. D., eds.*, 1989, pp. 27–43.

_____ **and Wolfe, Joel D.** The Politics of Economic Adjustment: Pluralism, Corporatism, and Privatization: Introduction. In *Foglesong, R. E. and Wolfe, J. D., eds.*, 1989, pp. 1–8.

Fohlin, Caroline; Robinson, Sherman and Schluter, Gerald. Terms of Trade and Factor Commitments in Agriculture. *J. Agr. Econ. Res.*, Fall 1989, *41*(4), pp. 6–11.

Foighel, Isi. Taxation of Income from Capital: The Danish Experience. In *Chiancone, A. and Messere, K., eds.*, 1989, pp. 113–22.

Földi, Tamás. An Actual Reverse Motion? *Acta Oecon.*, 1989, *40*(3–4), pp. 222–24.

_____. Discussion on Socialist Market Economy: Answers to an Inquiry. *Acta Oecon.*, 1989, *40*(3–4), pp. 179.

Foley, Duncan K. Economic Equilibrium with Costly Marketing. In *Starr, R. M., ed.*, 1989, *1970*, pp. 184–99.

_____. Endogenous Financial-Production Cycles in a Macroeconomic Model. In *Barnett, W. A.; Geweke, J. and Shell, K., eds.*, 1989, pp. 89–99.

_____. Joan Robinson: An Informal Memoir. In *Feiwel, G. R., ed. (II)*, 1989, pp. 874–76.

Foley, Thomas P. Congress and the Administration. In *Frankel, A. V. and Heck, C. B., eds.*, 1989, pp. 71–74.

Folkerts-Landau, David. The Internationalization of Financial Markets and the Regulatory Response. In *Vosgerau, H.-J., ed.*, 1989, pp. 175–209.

_____. Management of Interest Rate Risk by LDCs. *Finance Devel.*, June 1989, *26*(2), pp. 20–23.

_____. Marked-to-Market Interest Rate Swaps: A Solution to the Interest Rate Risk Management Problem of Indebted Developing Countries. In *Frenkel, J. A.; Dooley, M. P. and Wickham, P., eds.*, 1989, pp. 372–97.

_____ **and Rodriguez, Carlos Alfredo.** Mexican Debt Exchange: Lessons and Issues. In *Frenkel, J. A.; Dooley, M. P. and Wickham, P., eds.*, 1989, pp. 359–71.

Follain, James R. Inferring an Investment Return Series for Real Estate from Observations on Sales: Comments. *Amer. Real Estate Urban Econ. Assoc. J.*, Summer 1989, *17*(2), pp. 231–34.

_____ **and Brueckner, Jan K.** ARMs and the Demand for Housing. *Reg. Sci. Urban Econ.*, May 1989, *19*(2), pp. 163–87.

_____ **and Mills, Edwin S.** Interactions between Finance and Urban Development. *Amer. Real Estate Urban Econ. Assoc. J.*, Summer 1989, *17*(2), pp. 137–41.

Folland, Sherman and Stano, Miron. Sources of Small Area Variations in the Use of Medical Care. *J. Health Econ.*, March 1989, *8*(1), pp. 85–107.

Follmann, Dean A. and Kostiuk, Peter F. Learning Curves, Personal Characteristics, and Job Performance. *J. Lab. Econ.*, April 1989, *7*(2), pp. 129–46.

_____ **and Lambert, Diane.** Generalizing Logistic Regression by Nonparametric Mixing. *J. Amer. Statist. Assoc.*, March 1989, *84*(405), pp. 295–300.

Folmer, C., et al. Modelling Alternative Common Agricultural Policies: Some Simulation Outcomes from the European Community Agricultural Model, ECAM. In *Bauer, S. and Henrichsmeyer, W., eds.*, 1989, pp. 287–305.

Folmer, Hendrik and Hutten, Theo. Some Reflections on Innovation Stimulating Policy. In *Andersson, Å. E.; Batten, D. F. and Karlsson, C., eds.*, 1989, pp. 271–78.

_____ **and van Ierland, Ekko.** Valuation Methods and Policy Making in Environmental Economics: Relevance and Scope. In *Folmer, H. and van Ierland, E., eds.*, 1989, pp. 1–11.

Folsom, Ralph; LaVange, Lisa and Williams, Rick L. A Probability Sampling Perspective on Panel Data Analysis. In *Kasprzyk, D., et al., eds.*, 1989, pp. 108–38.

Folsom, Roger Nils; Mehay, Stephen L. and Gonzalez, Rodolfo A. Bureaucracy, Publicness and Local Government Expenditures Revisited: Comment. *Public Choice*, July 1989, *62*(1), pp. 71–77.

Fomby, Thomas B. and Hirschberg, Joseph G. Texas in Transition: Dependence on Oil and the National Economy. *Fed. Res. Bank Dallas Econ. Rev.*, January 1989, pp. 11–28.

_____; **Lam, Chun H. and Deb, Rajat.** Deregulation and the Demand for Money Market Mutual Funds. *J. Macroecon.*, Spring 1989, *11*(2), pp. 297–308.

Fonfara, Krzysztof. Relationships in the Complex Construction Venture Market. In *Hallén, L. and Johanson, J., eds.*, 1989, pp. 235–47.

Fonseca, Lois and Tayman, Jeff. Postcensal Estimates of Household Income Distributions. *Demography*, February 1989, *26*(1), pp. 149–59.

da Fonseca, Roberto Giannetti and Kennedy, J. Ray. Brazilian Trade Policy and the Uruguay Round. In *Nau, H. R., ed.*, 1989, pp. 29–49.

Fontaine, Juan A. The Chilean Economy in the Eighties: Adjustment and Recovery. In *Edwards, S. and Larrain, F., eds.*, 1989, pp. 208–33.

Fontela, Emilio. Industrial Structures and Economic Growth: An Input–Output Perspective. *Econ. Systems Res.*, 1989, *1*(1), pp. 45–52.

Fontvieille, Louis. The Movement of Capital's Composition: Long Term Fluctuations and Trend. In *Di Matteo, M.; Goodwin, R. M. and Vercelli, A., eds.*, 1989, pp. 177–205.

Fooks, John H. Total Quality Management. In *Ahlbrandt, R. S., Jr., ed.*, 1989, pp. 30–33.

Foot, David K. Panel Discussion on Canadian Immigration Objectives: Levels, Composition, and Directions. In *Beach, C. M. and Green, A. G.*, 1989, pp. 88–91.

_____. Public Expenditures, Population Aging and Economic Dependency in Canada, 1921–2021. *Population Res. Policy Rev.*, January 1989, *8*(1), pp. 97–117.

_____ **and Milne, William J.** Multiregional Estimation of Gross Internal Migration Flows. *Int. Reg. Sci. Rev.*, 1989, *12*(1), pp. 29–43.

———— **and Stager, David A. A.** Intertemporal Market Effect on Gender Earnings Differentials: Lawyers in Canada, 1970–80. *Appl. Econ.*, August 1989, *21*(8), pp. 1011–28.

———— **and Stager, David A. A.** Lawyers' Earnings under Market Growth and Differentiation, 1970–80. *Can. J. Econ.*, February 1989, *22*(1), pp. 150–63.

Foote, William G. The Rationality and Efficiency of Stock Price Relative to Money Announcement Information. *Financial Rev.*, May 1989, *24*(2), pp. 281–98.

———— **and Dutkowsky, Donald H.** The Dynamic Demand for Bank Discount Window Borrowing with Non-negativity Constraints. *Atlantic Econ. J.*, June 1989, *17*(2), pp. 36–41.

Forbes, Kevin F. and Zampelli, Ernest M. Is Leviathan a Mythical Beast? *Amer. Econ. Rev.*, June 1989, *79*(3), pp. 568–77.

Forbes, Shawn M. and Mayne, Lucille S. The Asymmetric Prime: An Empirical Note. *Econ. Letters*, December 1989, *31*(4), pp. 371–74.

———— **and Mayne, Lucille S.** A Friction Model of the Prime. *J. Banking Finance*, March 1989, *13*(1), pp. 127–35.

Forcina, Antonio and Galeotti, Gianluigi. Political Loyalties and the Economy: The U.S. Case. *Rev. Econ. Statist.*, August 1989, *71*(3), pp. 512–17.

Ford, A. G. International Financial Policy and the Gold Standard, 1870–1914. In *Mathias, P. and Pollard, S., eds.*, 1989, pp. 197–249.

Ford, Deborah Ann. The Effect of Historic District Designation on Single-Family Home Prices. *Amer. Real Estate Urban Econ. Assoc. J.*, Fall 1989, *17*(3), pp. 353–62.

Ford, J. L. G. L. S. Shackle, 1903– In *Greenaway, D. and Presley, J. R., eds.*, 1989, pp. 24–67.

Ford, Kathleen, et al. Birth-Interval Dynamics in Rural Bangladesh and Maternal Weight. *Demography*, August 1989, *26*(3), pp. 425–37.

Foreman-Peck, James. Foreign Investment and Imperial Exploitation: Balance of Payments Reconstruction for Nineteenth-Century Britain and India. *Econ. Hist. Rev., 2nd Ser.*, August 1989, *42*(3), pp. 354–74.

Forget, Evelyn L. J. S. Mill and J. E. Cairnes on Natural Value: The Role of Expectations in Late-Classical Thought. *Hist. Polit. Econ.*, Spring 1989, *21*(1), pp. 103–21.

Formánek, Karel. The Wage Policy in the Conditions of the Restructuring of the Economic Mechanism. *Czech. Econ. Digest.*, May 1989, (3), pp. 51–59.

Formby, John P. and Millner, Edward L. Output and Welfare Effects of Optimal Price Discrimination in Markets Segmented at the Initiative of the Seller. *Europ. Econ. Rev.*, July 1989, *33*(6), pp. 1175–81.

————; **Seaks, Terry G. and Smith, W. James.** On the Measurement and Trend of Inequality: A Reconsideration. *Amer. Econ. Rev.*, March 1989, *79*(1), pp. 256–64.

Fornari, Fabio. The Contribution of the Ecu to Exchange-Rate Stability: A Further Comment. *Banca Naz. Lavoro Quart. Rev.*, December 1989, (171), pp. 469–76.

Forney, Charles P. and Farmer, Richard N. Long-Term Sales Success in the U.S. Auto Market. In *Negandhi, A. R., ed.*, 1989, pp. 251–59.

Forsgren, Mats. Foreign Acquisitions: Internalization or Network Interdependency? In *Hallén, L. and Johanson, J., eds.*, 1989, pp. 141–59.

Forssell, Osmo. The Input–Output Framework for Analysing Transmission of Technical Progress between Industries. *Econ. Systems Res.*, 1989, *1*(4), pp. 429–45.

Forster, Bruce A. Optimal Health Investment Strategies. *Bull. Econ. Res.*, January 1989, *41*(1), pp. 45–57.

————. Unskilled Labor Migration and Capital Mobility: A Diagrammatic Exposition. *J. Econ. Educ.*, Fall 1989, *20*(4), pp. 355–62.

Forster, Keith and Etherington, Dan M. The Complex Case of the Chinese Tea Industry. *Food Res. Inst. Stud.*, 1989, *21*(3), pp. 265–308.

Forsund, Hildegunn M. Social Welfare in Developed Market Countries: Norway. In *Dixon, J. and Scheurell, R. P., eds.*, 1989, pp. 228–63.

Forsyth, Peter and Kay, John A. The Economic Implications of North Sea Oil Revenues. In *Helm, D.; Kay, J. and Thompson, D., eds.*, 1989, *1980*, pp. 349–76.

Forsythe, David P. The Political Economy of UN Refugee Programmes. In *[Gordenker, L.]*, 1989, pp. 131–43.

————. The United Nations in the World Economy: Introduction. In *[Gordenker, L.]*, 1989, pp. 1–10.

Forsythe, Kenneth W. and Bredahl, Maury E. Harmonizing Phyto-sanitary and Sanitary Regulations. *World Econ.*, June 1989, *12*(2), pp. 189–206.

Forsythe, Robert; Isaac, R. Mark and Palfrey, Thomas R. Theories and Tests of "Blind Bidding" in Sealed-Bid Auctions. *Rand J. Econ.*, Summer 1989, *20*(2), pp. 214–38.

Forte, Francesco and Buchanan, James M. The Evaluation of Public Services. In *Buchanan, J. M. (II)*, 1989, *1961*, pp. 176–93.

———— **and Buchanan, James M.** Fiscal Choice through Time: A Case for Indirect Taxation? In *Buchanan, J. M. (II)*, 1989, pp. 228–45.

Fortin, Bernard. Incidence of Tax Expenditures in a Lifetime Framework: Theory and an Application to RRSPs: Comment. In *Bruce, N., ed.*, 1989, pp. 368–71.

————. Une réduction de la semaine légale de travail augmente-t-elle la demande de travailleurs? (Does a Reduction of the Legal Work Week Increase the Demand for Labour? With English summary.) *L'Actual. Econ.*, September 1989, *65*(3), pp. 423–43.

———— **and Cloutier, A. Pierre.** Converting Exemptions and Deductions into Credits: An

Economic Assessment. **In** *Mintz, J. and Whalley, J., eds.*, 1989, pp. 45–73.

Fortin, Guy and Tingley, Daniel H. The Disregard of a Legal Entity for Tax Purposes: Canada. **In** *International Fiscal Association, ed. (II)*, 1989, pp. 223–37.

Fortin, Pierre. How 'Natural' is Canada's High Unemployment Rate? *Europ. Econ. Rev.*, January 1989, *33*(1), pp. 89–110.

_____. L'impact du choc démographique sur le niveau de vie à long terme. (With English summary.) *L'Actual. Econ.*, September 1989, *65*(3), pp. 364–95.

_____. Tax Reform and the Macroeconomy: Jobs, Inflation, and Growth. **In** *Mintz, J. and Whalley, J., eds.*, 1989, pp. 403–29.

_____ and Vaillancourt, François. Panel Discussion on Canadian Immigration Objectives: Levels, Composition, and Directions. **In** *Beach, C. M. and Green, A. G.*, 1989, pp. 92–93.

Fortin, Richard D.; Grube, R. Corwin and Joy, O. Maurice. Seasonality in NASDAQ Dealer Spreads. *J. Finan. Quant. Anal.*, September 1989, *24*(3), pp. 395–407.

Fortuna, Juan Carlos and Prates, Suzana. Informal Sector versus Informalized Labor Relations in Uruguay. **In** *Portes, A.; Castells, M. and Benton, L. A., eds.*, 1989, pp. 78–94.

Fortune, Peter. An Assessment of Financial Market Volatility: Bills, Bonds, and Stocks. *New Eng. Econ. Rev.*, Nov.–Dec. 1989, pp. 13–28.

Fossett, Mark A. and Kiecolt, K. Jill. The Relative Size of Minority Populations and White Racial Attitudes. *Soc. Sci. Quart.*, December 1989, *70*(4), pp. 820–35.

Foster, F. Douglas. Syndicate Size, Spreads, and Market Power during the Introduction of Shelf Registration. *J. Finance*, March 1989, *44*(1), pp. 195–204.

Foster, J. Fagg. The Relation between the Theory of Value and Economic Analysis. **In** *Tool, M. R. and Samuels, W. J., eds. (II)*, 1989, *1981*, pp. 353–59.

Foster, Jerry R. and Thompson, Alicia. Motor Carrier Salespeople: Can They Adapt? *Logist. Transp. Rev.*, December 1989, *25*(4), pp. 307–24.

Foster, John. The Macroeconomics of Keynes: An Evolutionary Perspective. **In** *Pheby, J., ed.*, 1989, pp. 124–46.

Foster, John Bellamy. The Age of Restructuring. **In** *MacEwan, A. and Tabb, W. K., eds.*, 1989, pp. 281–97.

_____. The Uncoupling of the World Order: A Survey of Global Crisis Theories. **In** *Gottdiener, M. and Komninos, N., eds.*, 1989, pp. 99–122.

Foster, Richard W. Identifying Experimental Program Effects with Confounding Price Changes and Selection Bias. *J. Human Res.*, Spring 1989, *24*(2), pp. 253–79.

Foster, Robin and Cheong, Ken. Auctioning the ITV Franchises. **In** *Hughes, G. and Vines, D., eds.*, 1989, pp. 91–125.

Foster, William and Just, Richard E. Measuring Welfare Effects of Product Contamination with Consumer Uncertainty. *J. Environ. Econ. Manage.*, November 1989, *17*(3), pp. 266–83.

Foster, William E. and Rausser, Gordon C. A Coherent Policy for U.S. Agriculture. **In** *Horwich, G. and Lynch, G. J., eds.*, 1989, pp. 191–237.

_____ and Rausser, Gordon C. Impacts of Economic Reform for Agricultural and Food Policy: Reaction. **In** *Helmuth, J. W. and Johnson, S. R., eds., Vol. 1*, 1989, pp. 95–99.

Fosu, Joseph. Subsistence Farming and Labor Market Participation of Non-commercial Farmers in Zambia: A Framework for Analysis. **In** *Missouri Valley Economic Association*, 1989, pp. 116–22.

Fotheringham, S.; Batty, M. and Longley, P. Urban Growth and Form: Scaling, Fractal Geometry, and Diffusion-Limited Aggregation. *Environ. Planning A*, November 1989, *21*(11), pp. 1447–72.

Fougère, Denis. Recherche d'emploi en présence de contrats de travail de courte durée: modélisation et estimation sur données individuelles. (Job-Search and Short-term Labor Contracts: Modelling and Estimation Using Individual Data. With English summary.) *Ann. Écon. Statist.*, April–June 1989, (14), pp. 225–57.

Fountain, John. Radio Spectrum Management: An Economic Critique of the Trustee Model. **In** *Veljanovski, C., ed. (I)*, 1989, pp. 129–64.

Fourie, F. C. v. N. The Nature of Firms and Markets: Do Transactions Approaches Help? *S. Afr. J. Econ.*, June 1989, *57*(2), pp. 142–60.

_____. Unemployment in Conventional Macroeconomic Theory: A Suggestion. *S. Afr. J. Econ.*, March 1989, *57*(1), pp. 69–78.

_____ and Booysen, A. Economic Concentration and Macro-economic Instability in South Africa. *J. Stud. Econ. Econometrics*, November 1989, *13*(3), pp. 75–90.

_____ and Smit, M. R. Trends in Economic Concentration in South Africa. *S. Afr. J. Econ.*, September 1989, *57*(3), pp. 241–56.

Fournier, Gary M.; Charity, Douglas A. and Rasmussen, David W. The Impact of Cost of Living Differentials on Migration of Elderly People to Florida. *Rev. Reg. Stud.*, Spring 1989, *19*(2), pp. 48–54.

_____ and Zuehlke, Thomas W. Litigation and Settlement: An Empirical Approach. *Rev. Econ. Statist.*, May 1989, *71*(2), pp. 189–95.

Fowler, D.; Cape, J. N. and Smith, R. I. The Statistics of Phytotoxic Air Pollutants. *J. Roy. Statist. Society*, 1989, *152*(2), pp. 183–98.

Fowler, David J.; Rorke, C. Harvey and Jog, Vijay M. A Bias-Correcting Procedure for Beta Estimation in the Presence of Thin Trading. *J. Finan. Res.*, Spring 1989, *12*(1), pp. 23–32.

Fowler, Kenneth. Investment in Urban Defence: The Frontier Regions of France and England during the Fourteenth Century. **In** *Guarducci, A., ed.*, 1989, pp. 149–82.

Fowler, Robert J. The Impacts of International Regulation of Greenhouse Gas Emissions. **In** *Owen, A. D., ed.*, 1989, pp. 38–50.

Fowles, Richard and Coate, Douglas. Is There Statistical Evidence for a Blood Lead–Blood Pressure Relationship? *J. Health Econ.*, June 1989, *8*(2), pp. 173–84.

—— and Loeb, Peter D. Speeding, Coordination, and the 55-MPH Limit: Comment. *Amer. Econ. Rev.*, September 1989, *79*(4), pp. 916–21.

Fowlkes, Edward B.; Hoadley, Bruce and Dalal, Siddhartha R. Risk Analysis of the Space Shuttle: Pre-*Challenger* Prediction of Failure. *J. Amer. Statist. Assoc.*, December 1989, *84*(408), pp. 945–57.

Fox, Glenn C.; Brinkman, George L. and Haque, A. K. Enamul. Product Market Distortions and the Returns to Federal Laying-Hen Research in Canada. *Can. J. Agr. Econ.*, March 1989, *37*(1), pp. 29–46.

——; Brinkman, George L. and Zachariah, O. E. R. Product Market Distortions and the Returns to Broiler Chicken Research in Canada. *J. Agr. Econ.*, January 1989, *40*(1), pp. 40–51.

——; McKenney, D. W. and van Vuuren, Willem. An Economic Comparison of Alternative Tree Improvement Strategies: A Simulation Approach. *Can. J. Agr. Econ.*, July 1989, *37*(2), pp. 211–32.

——; Moschini, Giancarlo and Oxley, James. An Analysis of the Structural and Welfare Effects of Bovine Somatotropin on the Ontario Dairy Industry. *Can. J. Agr. Econ.*, November 1989, *37*(3), pp. 393–406.

—— and van Vuuren, Willem. Estimating the Costs of Soil Erosion: A Comment. *Can. J. Agr. Econ.*, November 1989, *37*(3), pp. 549–53.

——; Widmer, Lorne and Brinkman, George L. Benefit Analysis of Agricultural Research: A Reply. *Can. J. Agr. Econ.*, March 1989, *37*(1), pp. 149–52.

Fox, Karl A. Agricultural Economists in the Econometric Revolution: Institutional Background, Literature and Leading Figures. *Oxford Econ. Pap.*, January 1989, *41*(1), pp. 53–70.

——. Agricultural Economists in the Econometric Revolution: Institutional Background, Literature and Leading Figures. In *de Marchi, N. and Gilbert, C., eds.*, 1989, pp. 53–70.

Fox, Stephen and Cooper, Robert. Two Modes of Organization. In *Mansfield, R., ed.*, 1989, pp. 247–61.

Fox, William F.; Herzog, Henry W., Jr. and Schlottmann, Alan M. Metropolitan Fiscal Structure and Migration. *J. Reg. Sci.*, November 1989, *29*(4), pp. 523–36.

Fraas, Arthur G. and Munley, Vincent G. Economic Objectives within a Bureaucratic Decision Process: Setting Pollution Control Requirements under the Clean Water Act. *J. Environ. Econ. Manage.*, July 1989, *17*(1), pp. 35–53.

Frackowiak, Waldemar. Mutual Relations among Firms, Local Labor Markets and Consumers in an Economy of Shortages: The Case of Po-

land. *Rev. Reg. Stud.*, Spring 1989, *19*(2), pp. 59–64.

Fraenkel, A. S. and Harary, F. Geodetic Contraction Games on Graphs. *Int. J. Game Theory*, 1989, *18*(3), pp. 327–38.

Fraga-Iribarne, Manuel. The Economics of Liberty and How More Nations Can Join the First World. In *Cerami, C. A., ed.*, 1989, pp. 103–12.

Frain, Lewis F. The Monthly OASDI One-Percent Sample File. *Soc. Sec. Bull.*, June 1989, *52*(6), pp. 8–15.

de Fraja, Giovanni and Delbono, Flavio. Alternative Strategies of a Public Enterprise in Oligopoly. *Oxford Econ. Pap.*, April 1989, *41*(2), pp. 302–11.

Fraker, Thomas and Devaney, Barbara. The Dietary Impacts of the School Breakfast Program. *Amer. J. Agr. Econ.*, November 1989, *71*(4), pp. 932–48.

—— and Devaney, Barbara. The Effect of Food Stamps on Food Expenditures: An Assessment of Findings from the Nationwide Food Consumption Survey. *Amer. J. Agr. Econ.*, February 1989, *71*(1), pp. 99–104.

Fraley, C. and Vial, Jean-Philippe. Numerical Study of Projective Methods for Linear Programming. In *Dolecki, S., ed.*, 1989, pp. 25–38.

Framingham, Charles F. Principles of Planning and Management: The Family. *Can. J. Agr. Econ.*, Part 1, December 1989, *37*(4), pp. 755–60.

France, Judith; Summary, Rebecca M. and Vasegh-Daneshvary, Nasser. The Impact of Economic Education Courses on the Knowledge and Retention of Knowledge of Secondary and Primary School Teachers. *J. Econ. Educ.*, Fall 1989, *20*(4), pp. 346–54.

Francis, Arthur. The Competitiveness of European Industry: Introduction. In *Francis, A. and Tharakan, P. K. M., eds.*, 1989, pp. 1–4.

——. The Concept of Competitiveness. In *Francis, A. and Tharakan, P. K. M., eds.*, 1989, pp. 5–20.

——. Technological Change in Four British Factories: Some Lessons from the Introduction of CNC Machine Tools. In *Francis, A. and Grootings, P., eds.*, 1989, pp. 227–61.

Francis, Carlene Y. Monetary and Credit Policies in the Bahamas since 1974. In *Worrell, D. and Bourne, C., eds.*, 1989, pp. 79–88.

Franco, Carlos. Participation and Concentration in Social Policies. *CEPAL Rev.*, April 1989, (37), pp. 123–30.

Franco, Gustavo H. B. Inércia e coordenação: Pactos, congelamentos e seus problemas. (With English summary.) *Pesquisa Planejamento Econ.*, April 1989, *19*(1), pp. 65–84.

—— and Amadeo, Edward J. Entre Keynes e Robertson: *finance, poupança e investimento*. (With English summary.) *Pesquisa Planejamento Econ.*, August 1989, *19*(2), pp. 379–95.

Francois, Joseph F. Estimating Homeownership Costs: Owners' Estimates of Implicit Rents and the Relative Importance of Rental Equivalence

Problems of the EEC Single Market. With English summary.) *Konjunkturpolitik*, 1989, 35(6), pp. 311–28.

Franzosi, Roberto. One Hundred Years of Strike Statistics: Methodological and Theoretical Issues in Quantitative Strike Research. *Ind. Lab. Relat. Rev.*, April 1989, 42(3), pp. 348–62.

Fraser, Clive and Hollander, Abraham. Advance Delivery Contracts, Revenue Pools and Price Discrimination. *J. Econ. Behav. Organ.*, March 1989, 11(2), pp. 285–91.

Fraser, Donald R. and Dubofsky, David A. The Differential Impact of Two Significant Court Decisions Concerning Banking Consolidation. *J. Banking Finance*, July 1989, 13(3), pp. 339–54.

_____ **and Dubofsky, David A.** The Texas Probable Future Competition Cases and the Transformation of the Bank Expansion Movement: Evidence from the Equity Market. *Antitrust Bull.*, Summer 1989, 34(2), pp. 395–410.

_____ **and Kannan, Srinivasan.** The Risk Implications of Forecast Errors of Bank Earnings, 1976–1986. *J. Finan. Res.*, Fall 1989, 12(3), pp. 261–68.

_____ **; Rangan, Nanda K. and Eyssell, Thomas H.** Debt–Equity Swaps, Regulation K, and Bank Stock Returns. *J. Banking Finance*, December 1989, 13(6), pp. 853–68.

_____ **; Thompson, G. Rodney and Billingsley, Randall S.** Shareholder Wealth and Stock Repurchases by Bank Holding Companies. *Quart. J. Bus. Econ.*, Winter 1989, 28(1), pp. 3–25.

Fraser, Douglas G. and Lee, Edward G. The Rationale and Future Directions of Canada's Oceans Policy: International Dimensions. **In** *McRae, D. and Munro, G., eds.*, 1989, pp. 238–52.

Fraser, Peter. Australian Tax Haven Measures. *Australian Tax Forum*, 1989, 6(1), pp. 99–113.

Fraser, R. W. Uncertainty and the Positive Theory of the Public Enterprise. *Bull. Econ. Res.*, April 1989, 41(2), pp. 147–55.

Frater, Philip and Rice, Phillip. The Demand for Petrol with Explicit New Car Fuel Efficiency Effects: A UK Study 1977–86. *Energy Econ.*, April 1989, 11(2), pp. 95–104.

Fratianni, Michele. The European Monetary System: How Well Has It Worked? **In** *Dorn, J. A. and Niskanen, W. A., eds.*, 1989, 1988, pp. 263–87.

Fratrik, Mark R. and Coate, Malcolm B. Dual Distribution as a Vertical Control Device. *J. Behav. Econ.*, Spring 1989, 18(1), pp. 1–17.

Fraumeni, Barbara M. The Economics of Technical Progress: A Comment. *Eastern Econ. J.*, Oct.–Dec. 1989, 15(4), pp. 337.

_____ **and Jorgenson, Dale W.** The Accumulation of Human and Nonhuman Capital, 1948–84. **In** *Lipsey, R. E. and Tice, H. S., eds.*, 1989, pp. 227–82.

Frazao, Elizabeth and Sumner, Daniel A. Wage Rates in a Poor Rural Area with Emphasis on the Impact of Farm and Nonfarm Experience. *Econ. Devel. Cult. Change*, July 1989, 37(4),

pp. 709–18.

Frederick, Donald G.; Dillon, William R. and Mulani, Narendra. On the Use of Component Scores in the Presence of Group Structure. *J. Cons. Res.*, June 1989, 16(1), pp. 106–12.

Frederick, Kenneth D. and Gleick, Peter H. Water Resources and Climate Change. **In** *Rosenberg, N. J., et al., eds.*, 1989, pp. 133–43.

Freebairn, John W. The Role and Consequences of Labour Market Arrangements. **In** *[Gruen, F. H.]*, 1989, pp. 162–89.

_____. Some Effects of Reducing Excess in Infrastructure Charges on the Export Coal Industry. *Econ. Rec.*, December 1989, 65(191), pp. 345–56.

Freedman, Charles. Monetary Policy in the 1990s: Lessons and Challenges. **In** *Federal Reserve Bank of Kansas City*, 1989, pp. 1–45.

Freedman, D. A. An Alternative Interpretation of Freedman's Nonresponse Case Study: Comment. *J. Bus. Econ. Statist.*, January 1989, 7(1), pp. 31–32.

Freeman, Christopher. Technical Change and Depression in the 1930s and 1980s. **In** *Di Matteo, M.; Goodwin, R. M. and Vercelli, A., eds.*, 1989, pp. 419–42.

_____. Technical Change and Productivity. *Finance Devel.*, September 1989, 26(3), pp. 46–48.

Freeman, Iris C. and Vladeck, Bruce C. The Nursing Home Conundrum. **In** *Eisdorfer, C.; Kessler, D. A. and Spector, A. N., eds.*, 1989, pp. 224–34.

Freeman, Milton M. R. The Alaska Eskimo Whaling Commission: Successful Co-management under Extreme Conditions. **In** *Pinkerton, E., ed.*, 1989, pp. 137–53.

Freeman, Richard B. Black Economic Progress since 1964. **In** *Freeman, R. B.*, 1989, 1978, pp. 105–20.

_____. The Changing Status of Unionism around the World: Some Emerging Patterns. **In** *Huang, W.-C., ed.*, 1989, pp. 111–37.

_____. Contraction and Expansion: The Divergence of Private Sector and Public Sector Unionism in the United States. **In** *Freeman, R. B.*, 1989, 1988, pp. 221–48.

_____. Does the New Generation of Labor Economists Know More than the Older Generation? **In** *Freeman, R. B.*, 1989, 1988, pp. 317–42.

_____. The Effect of Demographic Factors on Age–Earnings Profiles. **In** *Freeman, R. B.*, 1989, 1979, pp. 74–102.

_____. Effects of Unions on the Economy. **In** *Freeman, R. B.*, 1989, 1986, pp. 197–217.

_____. Evaluating the European View That the United States Has No Unemployment Problem. **In** *Freeman, R. B.*, 1989, 1988, pp. 270–79.

_____. The Exit–Voice Tradeoff in the Labor Market: Unionism, Job Tenure, Quits and Separations. **In** *Freeman, R. B.*, 1989, 1980, pp. 169–96.

_____. Expectations and Marginal Decision-Making. **In** *Freeman, R. B.*, 1989, 1971, pp. 51–73.

———. Functioning of the College Graduates' Job Market. In *Freeman, R. B.*, 1989, *1976*, pp. 21–50.

———. Individual Mobility and Union Voice in the Labor Market. In *Freeman, R. B.*, 1989, *1976*, pp. 159–68.

———. Job Satisfaction as an Economic Variable. In *Freeman, R. B.*, 1989, *1978*, pp. 283–91.

———. Labor Markets in Action: Essays in Empirical Economics: Introduction. In *Freeman, R. B.*, 1989, pp. ix–xii.

———. Longitudinal Analyses of the Effects of Trade Unions. In *Freeman, R. B.*, 1989, *1984*, pp. 292–316.

———. Supply and Salary Adjustments to the Changing Market for Physicists. In *Freeman, R. B.*, 1989, *1975*, pp. 3–20.

——— and Bound, John. Black Economic Progress: Erosion of the Post-1965 Gains in the 1980s? In *Shulman, S. and Darity, W., Jr., eds.*, 1989, pp. 32–49.

——— and Hall, Brian. Permanent Homelessness in America? In *Freeman, R. B.*, 1989, *1987*, pp. 134–56.

——— and Holzer, Harry J. Young Blacks and Jobs. In *Freeman, R. B.*, 1989, *1985*, pp. 121–33.

———; Lauer, Harrison and Ichniowski, Casey. Collective Bargaining Laws, Threat Effects, and the Determination of Police Compensation. *J. Lab. Econ.*, April 1989, 7(2), pp. 191–209.

——— and Rebick, Marcus E. Crumbling Pillar? Declining Union Density in Japan. *J. Japanese Int. Economies*, December 1989, 3(4), pp. 578–605.

——— and Weitzman, Martin L. Bonuses and Employment in Japan. In *Freeman, R. B.*, 1989, *1987*, pp. 249–69.

Freeman, Robert N. and Tse, Senyo. The Multiperiod Information Content of Accounting Earnings: Confirmations and Contradictions of Previous Earnings Reports. *J. Acc. Res.*, Supplement, 1989, 27, pp. 49–79.

Freeman, Scott J. Fiat Money as a Medium of Exchange. *Int. Econ. Rev.*, February 1989, 30(1), pp. 137–51.

——— and Murphy, Robert G. Inside Money and the Open Economy. *J. Int. Econ.*, February 1989, 26(1/2), pp. 29–51.

Freese, Jan. Computers and Law. In *Jussawalla, M.; Okuma, T. and Araki, T., eds.*, 1989, pp. 172–76.

Freidkes, Nahum and Gavish, Moshe. Administrative and Compliance Costs of Taxation: Israel. In *International Fiscal Association, ed. (I)*, 1989, pp. 403–24.

Freiman, Marc P. Reimbursement Decisions for Hospital Services: The Case of Psychiatric Units under Medicare. *Inquiry*, Fall 1989, 26(3), pp. 399–405.

———; Ellis, Randall P. and McGuire, Thomas G. Provider Response to Medicare's PPS: Reductions in Length of Stay for Psychiatric Patients Treated in Scatter Beds. *Inquiry*, Summer 1989, 26(2), pp. 192–201.

Freixas, Xavier and Belloc, Bernard. Refinancement, liquidation et rationnement du crédit: Une approche bayésienne. (Extending Credit, Liquidation and Credit Rationing: A Bayesian Approach. With English summary.) *Ann. Écon. Statist.*, July–Dec. 1989, (15–16), pp. 231–66.

Fremdling, Rainer. British Coal on Continental Markets, 1850–1913. In *[Fischer, W.]*, 1989, pp. 168–90.

Fremling, Gertrud M. and Lott, John R., Jr. Deadweight Losses and the Saving Response to a Deficit. *Econ. Inquiry*, January 1989, 27(1), pp. 117–29.

——— and Lott, John R., Jr. Time Dependent Information Costs, Price Controls, and Successive Government Intervention. *J. Law, Econ., Organ.*, Fall 1989, 5(2), pp. 293–306.

French, Kenneth R. and Fama, Eugene F. Business Conditions and Expected Returns on Stocks and Bonds. *J. Finan. Econ.*, November 1989, 25(1), pp. 23–49.

French, Michael. Manufacturing and Marketing: Vertical Integration in the U.S. Tire Manufacturing Industry, 1890–1980s. In *Hausman, W. J., ed.*, 1989, pp. 178–87.

French, Simon and Insua, David Rios. Partial Information and Sensitivity Analysis in Multiobjective Decision Making. In *Lockett, A. G. and Islei, G., eds.*, 1989, pp. 424–33.

Frendreis, John P. Migration as a Source of Changing Party Strength. *Soc. Sci. Quart.*, March 1989, 70(1), pp. 211–20.

Freni, Giuseppe. Equilibri multipli ed instabilitá dello stato stazionario in un semplice modello dinamico ricardiano. (Multiple Equilibria and Instability of the Stationary State in a Simple Ricardian Dynamical Model. With English summary.) *Econ. Politica*, December 1989, 6(3), pp. 363–79.

Frenk, Julio. Financing as an Instrument of Public Policy: Commentary. In *WHO, Pan American Health Organization*, 1989, pp. 167–73.

Frenkel, Jacob A.; Dooley, Michael P. and Wickham, Peter. An Introduction to Analytical Issues in Debt. In *Frenkel, J. A.; Dooley, M. P. and Wickham, P., eds.*, 1989, pp. 1–9.

——— and Goldstein, Morris. The International Monetary System: Developments and Prospects. In *Dorn, J. A. and Niskanen, W. A., eds.*, 1989, *1988*, pp. 89–110.

———; Goldstein, Morris and Masson, Paul R. International Dimensions of Monetary Policy: Coordination versus Autonomy. In *Federal Reserve Bank of Kansas City*, 1989, pp. 183–232.

———; Goldstein, Morris and Masson, Paul R. Simulating the Effects of Some Simple Coordinated versus Uncoordinated Policy Rules. In *Bryant, R. C., et al., eds.*, 1989, pp. 203–39.

——— and Razin, Assaf. Exchange-Rate Management Viewed as Tax Policies. *Europ. Econ. Rev.*, April 1989, 33(4), pp. 761–81.

——— and Razin, Assaf. International Effects of Tax Reforms. *Econ. J.*, Supplement, 1989, 99(395), pp. 38–58.

Frenkel, Stephen J. and Shaw, Marguerite. No

Tears for the Second Tier: Productivity Bargaining in the Australian Metal Industry. *Australian Bull. Lab.*, March 1989, *15*(2), pp. 90–114.

Freshwater, David. Canadian Agricultural Finance in the 1980s and 1990s. *Can. J. Agr. Econ.*, March 1989, *37*(1), pp. 1–27.

_____. The Political Economy of Farm Credit Reform: The Agricultural Credit Act of 1987. In *Krämer, C. S.*, ed., 1989, pp. 105–39.

Freund, D. A., et al. Interim Findings from the Medicaid Competition Demonstrations. In *Scheffler, R. M. and Rossiter, L. F.*, eds., 1989, pp. 153–81.

Frey, Bruno S. How Large (or Small) Should the Underground Economy Be? In *Feige, E. L.*, ed., 1989, pp. 111–26.

_____ and Eichenberger, Reiner. Anomalies and Institutions. *J. Inst. Theoretical Econ.*, September 1989, *145*(3), pp. 423–37.

_____ and Eichenberger, Reiner. Choice under Uncertainty: Problems Solved and Unsolved: Comment. *J. Econ. Perspectives*, Summer 1989, *3*(3), pp. 181–83.

_____ and Eichenberger, Reiner. Zur Bedeutung entscheidungstheoretischer Anomalien für die Ökonomik. (How Important Are Choice Anomalies for Economics? With English summary.) *Jahr. Nationalökon. Statist.*, March 1989, *206*(2), pp. 81–101.

_____ and Heggli, Beat. An Ipsative Theory of Business Behaviour. *J. Econ. Psych.*, March 1989, *10*(1), pp. 1–20.

_____ and Pommerehne, Werner W. Art Investment: An Empirical Inquiry. *Southern Econ. J.*, October 1989, *56*(2), pp. 396–409.

Frey, Donald E. A Structural Approach to the Economic Base Multiplier. *Land Econ.*, November 1989, *65*(4), pp. 352–58.

Friar, Shirley A. and Wardlow, Penelope S. Local Government Procurement of CPA Audit Services: The Role of the States. *Public Budg. Finance*, Spring 1989, *9*(1), pp. 92–106.

Fricke, Friedrich. Asymmetric Information between Investors and Managers under the New German Accounting Legislation. In *Bamberg, G. and Spremann, K.*, eds., 1989, pp. 311–26.

Fridlizius, Gunnar. The Deformation of Cohorts: Nineteenth Century Mortality Decline in a Generational Perspective. *Scand. Econ. Hist. Rev.*, 1989, *37*(3), pp. 3–17.

Fried, Edward R. and Trezise, Philip H. Third World Debt: The Next Phase: Overview. In *Fried, E. R. and Trezise, P. H.*, eds., 1989, pp. 3–16.

_____ and Trezise, Philip H. Third World Debt: The Next Phase: Preface. In *Fried, E. R. and Trezise, P. H.*, eds., 1989, pp. vii–viii.

Friedberg, Alan H.; Strawser, Jerry R. and Cassidy, Judith H. Factors Affecting Materiality Judgments: A Comparison of "Big Eight" Accounting Firms' Materiality Views with the Results of Empirical Research. In *Schwartz, B. N.*, ed., 1989, pp. 187–201.

Frieden, Jeffry A. Oil and the Evolution of U.S.

Policy towards the Developing Areas, 1900–1950: An Essay in Interpretation. In *Ferrier, R. W. and Fursenko, A.*, eds., 1989, pp. 53–73.

_____. Winners and Losers in the Latin America Debt Crisis: The Political Implications. In *Stallings, B. and Kaufman, R.*, eds., 1989, pp. 23–37.

Friedenberg, Howard L. and DePass, Rudolph E. Per Capita Personal Income: Continued Widening of Regional Differences in 1988. *Surv. Curr. Bus.*, April 1989, *69*(4), pp. 35–36.

Friedländer, Michael. Changes in the Banking System in the CMEA Area. In *Gabrisch, H.*, ed., 1989, pp. 193–200.

_____. More Austerity and More Reform Announced in Hungary. In *Gabrisch, H.*, ed., 1989, pp. 125–31.

Friedman, Benjamin M. Changing Effects of Monetary Policy on Real Economic Activity. In *Federal Reserve Bank of Kansas City*, 1989, pp. 55–111.

_____. Cleaning Up the Depository Institutions Mess: Comments. *Brookings Pap. Econ. Act.*, 1989, (1), pp. 284–90.

_____. Does Monetary Policy Matter? A New Test in the Spirit of Friedman and Schwartz: Comment. In *Blanchard, O. J. and Fischer, S.*, eds., 1989, pp. 177–82.

_____. The Lender's View of Debt and Equity: The Case of Pension Funds: Discussion. In *Kopcke, R. W. and Rosengren, E. S.*, eds., 1989, pp. 131–35.

_____ and Laibson, David I. Economic Implications of Extraordinary Movements in Stock Prices. *Brookings Pap. Econ. Act.*, 1989, (2), pp. 137–72.

Friedman, Daniel. Producers' Markets: A Model of Oligopoly with Sales Costs. *J. Econ. Behav. Organ.*, May 1989, *11*(3), pp. 381–98.

_____. The S-Shaped Value Function as a Constrained Optimum. *Amer. Econ. Rev.*, December 1989, *79*(5), pp. 1243–48.

Friedman, David D. An Economic Analysis of Alternative Damage Rules for Breach of Contract. *J. Law Econ.*, Part 1, October 1989, *32*(2), pp. 281–310.

Friedman, Edward. Theorizing the Democratization of China's Leninist State. In *Dirlik, A. and Meisner, M.*, eds., 1989, pp. 171–89.

Friedman, Irving S. The World Economy and the International Financial System. In *Kaushik, S. K.*, ed., 1989, pp. 3–16.

Friedman, Joseph; Hakim, Simon and Spiegel, Uriel. The Difference between Short and Long Run Effects of Police Outlays on Crime: Policing Deters Criminals Initially, but Later They May 'Learn by Doing.' *Amer. J. Econ. Sociology*, April 1989, *48*(2), pp. 177–91.

_____; Hakim, Simon and Weinblatt, J. Casino Gambling as a "Growth Pole" Strategy and Its Effect on Crime. *J. Reg. Sci.*, November 1989, *29*(4), pp. 615–23.

Friedman, Lawrence M. Law, Lawyers, and Popular Culture. *Yale Law J.*, June 1989, *98*(8), pp. 1579–1606.

Friedman, Milton. Anna J. Schwartz: An Appreciation: A Life of Scholarship: Collaboration in Economics. In *[Schwartz, A. J.]*, 1989, pp. 247–50.

_____. The Case for Overhauling the Federal Reserve. In *Guttmann, R., ed.*, 1989, *1985*, pp. 39–47.

_____. Using the Market for Social Development. *Cato J.*, Winter 1989, *8*(3), pp. 567–79.

_____ **and Brunner, Karl.** Anna J. Schwartz: An Appreciation: A Life of Scholarship. In *[Schwartz, A. J.]*, 1989, pp. 245–47.

Friedmann, Daniel. The Efficient Breach Fallacy. *J. Legal Stud.*, January 1989, *18*(1), pp. 1–24.

Friedrich, Carl J. Corruption Concepts in Historical Perspective. In *Heidenheimer, A. J.; Johnston, M. and LeVine, V. T., eds.*, 1989, pp. 15–24.

Friedricks, William B. A Metropolitan Entrepreneur Par Excellence: Henry E. Huntington and the Growth of Southern California, 1898-1927. *Bus. Hist. Rev.*, Summer 1989, *63*(2), pp. 329–55.

Friesen, R. A. Corporate Tax Reform and Its Economic Impact: An Evaluation of the Phase 1 Proposals: Comment. In *Mintz, J. and Whalley, J., eds.*, 1989, pp. 125–29.

Friesz, T. L. On the Use of Network-Equilibrium Models in Urban and Regional Analyses: The Emergence of Dynamic Concepts of Equilibrium: Commentary. *Environ. Planning A*, April 1989, *21*(4), pp. 425–28.

Frieze, Irene Hanson and Olson, Josephine E. Job Interruptions and Part-Time Work: Their Effect on MBAs' Income. *Ind. Relat.*, Fall 1989, *28*(3), pp. 373–86.

Friezer, Mark and Green, Don. Taxation of the Income of Non-resident Trusts: The Consultative Document Proposals. *Australian Tax Forum*, 1989, *6*(1), pp. 41–63.

Frisbee, William R.; Fast, Janet and Vosburgh, Richard E. The Effects of Consumer Education on Consumer Search. *J. Cons. Aff.*, Summer 1989, *23*(1), pp. 65–90.

Frisch, Daniel J. The BALRM Approach to Transfer Pricing. *Nat. Tax J.*, September 1989, *42*(3), pp. 261–71.

Frischmann, Peter J. and Christian, Charles W. Attrition in the Statistics of Income Panel of Individual Returns. *Nat. Tax J.*, December 1989, *42*(4), pp. 495–501.

Frischtak, Claudio. Competition as a Tool of LDC Industrial Policy. *Finance Devel.*, September 1989, *26*(3), pp. 27–29.

Fristrup, Peter and Kleiding, Hans. A Note on Asymptotical Strategy-Proofness. *Econ. Letters*, December 1989, *31*(4), pp. 307–12.

Fritsch, Winston. The New Minilateralism and Developing Countries. In *Schott, J. J., ed.*, 1989, pp. 337–52.

_____ **and Abreu, Marcelo de Paiva.** Market Access for Manufactured Exports from Developing Countries: Trends and Prospects. In *Whalley, J., ed., Vol. 1*, 1989, pp. 112–31.

_____ **and Abreu, Marcelo de Paiva.** Obstacles to Brazilian Export Growth and the Present Multilateral Trade Negotiations. In *Whalley, J., ed., Vol. 2*, 1989, pp. 179–201.

Fritz, Judy M. and Fritz, Richard G. Linguistic Structure and Economic Method. In *Tool, M. R. and Samuels, W. J., eds. (II)*, 1989, *1985*, pp. 316–42.

Fritz, Richard G. Strategic Planning with a System Dynamics Model for Regional Tourism Site Development. *Rev. Reg. Stud.*, Winter 1989, *19*(1), pp. 57–71.

_____ **and Fritz, Judy M.** Linguistic Structure and Economic Method. In *Tool, M. R. and Samuels, W. J., eds. (II)*, 1989, *1985*, pp. 316–42.

Froeb, Luke. Evaluating Mergers in Durable Goods Industries. *Antitrust Bull.*, Spring 1989, *34*(1), pp. 99–119.

Froeschlé, C. and Cartelier, Jean. A Model of a Monetary Economy: Principles and Study of Stability. *Metroecon.*, October 1989, *40*(3), pp. 189–209.

Frohberg, Klaus K.; Fischer, Günther and Parikh, Kirit S. International Effects of CAP Trade Liberalization. In *Tarditi, S., et al., eds.*, 1989, pp. 27–46.

_____ **and Pierani, Pierpaolo.** Impact of CAP Trade Liberalization on Agricultural Supply. In *Tarditi, S., et al., eds.*, 1989, pp. 123–41.

_____; **Womack, Abner W. and Meyers, William H.** Food and Agricultural Policies and Programs of Major Countries and Regions: Reaction. In *Helmuth, J. W. and Johnson, S. R., eds., Vol. 1*, 1989, pp. 39–41.

_____, **et al.** Benefits and Costs of Policy Reform in World Food Production and Distribution Systems. In *Helmuth, J. W. and Johnson, S. R., eds., Vol. 2*, 1989, pp. 59–73.

Fröhlich, Hans-Peter. International Competitiveness: Alternative Macroeconomic Strategies and Changing Perceptions in Recent Years. In *Francis, A. and Tharakan, P. K. M., eds.*, 1989, pp. 21–40.

_____. Supply-Side Policies in Germany: Economics versus Politics. In *Fels, G. and von Furstenberg, G. M., eds.*, 1989, pp. 21–44.

Frohlich, Samuel M. Adjusting to Change in the Global Marketplace. In *Ahlbrandt, R. S., Jr., ed.*, 1989, pp. 26–28.

Froio, Gregory L.; Mansur, Iqbal and Cochran, Steven J. The Relationship between the Equity Return Levels of Airline Companies and Unanticipated Events: The Case of the 1979 DC-10 Grounding. *Logist. Transp. Rev.*, December 1989, *25*(4), pp. 355–65.

Froment, E. Les innovations en matière de cartes face aux fonctions de transaction, de paiement et d'intermédiation. (Card Innovations, Intermediation and the Medium-of-Exchange Function of Money. With English summary.) *Écon. Societes*, April–May 1989, *23*(4–5), pp. 165–83.

Froot, Kenneth A. Buybacks, Exit Bonds, and the Optimality of Debt and Liquidity Relief. *Int. Econ. Rev.*, February 1989, *30*(1), pp. 49–70.

_____. Can Interindustry Wage Differentials Justify Strategic Trade Policy? Comment. In *Feenstra, R. C., ed.*, 1989, pp. 117–20.

_____. Consistent Covariance Matrix Estimation with Cross-Sectional Dependence and Heteroskedasticity in Financial Data. *J. Finan. Quant. Anal.*, September 1989, *24*(3), pp. 333–55.

_____. Do the Secondary Markets Believe in Life after Debt? Comment. In *Husain, I. and Diwan, I., eds.*, 1989, pp. 293.

_____. New Hope for the Expectations Hypothesis of the Term Structure of Interest Rates. *J. Finance*, June 1989, *44*(2), pp. 283–305.

_____ and Frankel, Jeffrey A. Forward Discount Bias: Is It an Exchange Risk Premium? *Quart. J. Econ.*, February 1989, *104*(1), pp. 139–61.

_____ and Ito, Takatoshi. On the Consistency of Short-run and Long-run Exchange Rate Expectations. *J. Int. Money Finance*, December 1989, *8*(4), pp. 487–510.

_____ and Klemperer, Paul D. Exchange Rate Pass-Through When Market Share Matters. *Amer. Econ. Rev.*, September 1989, *79*(4), pp. 637–54.

_____; Scharfstein, David S. and Stein, Jeremy C. LDC Debt: Forgiveness, Indexation, and Investment Incentives. *J. Finance*, December 1989, *44*(5), pp. 1335–50.

Frost, Carol A. and Bernard, Victor L. The Role of Debt Covenants in Assessing the Economic Consequences of Limiting Capitalization of Exploration Costs. *Accounting Rev.*, October 1989, *64*(4), pp. 788–808.

Frost, Peter J. The Role of Organizational Power and Politics in Human Resource Management. In *Nedd, A., ed.*, 1989, pp. 1–21.

Froyen, Richard and Benavie, Arthur. Optimal Monetary-Fiscal Stabilizers under an Indexed versus Nonindexed Tax Structure: Reply. *J. Econ. Bus.*, February 1989, *41*(1), pp. 93–94.

Fruhling, Hugo. Nonprofit Organizations as Opposition to Authoritarian Rule: The Case of Human Rights Organizations in Chile. In *James, E., ed.*, 1989, pp. 358–76.

Fry, Clifford L. Hicks's 'The Two Triads. Lecture 1' and the Transactions Demand for Money. In *Wood, J. C. and Woods, R. N., eds., Vol. 3*, 1989, *1975*, pp. 107–13.

_____ and Lee, Insup. OSHA Sanctions and the Value of the Firm. *Financial Rev.*, November 1989, *24*(4), pp. 599–610.

Fry, Maxwell J. Financial Development: Theories and Recent Experience. *Oxford Rev. Econ. Policy*, Winter 1989, *5*(4), pp. 13–28.

_____. Foreign Debt Instability: An Analysis of National Saving and Domestic Investment Responses to Foreign Debt Accumulation in 28 Developing Countries. *J. Int. Money Finance*, September 1989, *8*(3), pp. 315–44.

Fry, Vanessa and Pashardes, Panos. Constructing the True Cost of Living Index from the Engel Curves of the Piglog Model. *J. Appl. Econometrics*, Jan.–March 1989, *4*(1), pp. 41–56.

_____ and Stark, Graham. The Take-Up of Supplementary Benefit: Gaps in the 'Safety Net'? In *Dilnot, A. and Walker, I., eds.*, 1989, pp. 179–91.

Frye, Alton and Stevenson, Adlai E. Trading with the Communists. *Foreign Aff.*, Spring 1989, *68*(2), pp. 53–71.

Fuchs, Victor R. Women's Quest for Economic Equality. *J. Econ. Perspectives*, Winter 1989, *3*(1), pp. 25–41.

Fuchs-Seliger, Susanne. Money-Metric Utility Functions in the Theory of Revealed Preference. *Math. Soc. Sci.*, December 1989, *18*(3), pp. 199–210.

Fudenberg, Drew and Diamond, Peter A. Rational Expectations Business Cycles in Search Equilibrium. *J. Polit. Econ.*, June 1989, *97*(3), pp. 606–19.

_____ and Levine, David K. Reputation and Equilibrium Selection in Games with a Patient Player. *Econometrica*, July 1989, *57*(4), pp. 759–78.

_____ and Tirole, Jean. Noncooperative Game Theory for Industrial Organization: An Introduction and Overview. In *Schmalensee, R. and Willig, R. D., eds., Vol. 1*, 1989, pp. 259–327.

Fuentes, Juan Alberto. Central American Economic Integration: Renewed Prospects in the Midst of Crisis. In *Irvin, G. and Holland, S., eds.*, 1989, pp. 89–109.

_____. Negotiating Trade Preferences in Central America. In *Whalley, J., ed., Vol. 2*, 1989, pp. 202–29.

Fugleberg, Ole and Estrada, Javier. Price Elasticities of Natural Gas Demand in France and West Germany. *Energy J.*, July 1989, *10*(3), pp. 77–90.

Fuhr, Joseph P., Jr. and Blackstone, Erwin A. The Economics of Public Utility Regulation: Review Article. *Atlantic Econ. J.*, June 1989, *17*(2), pp. 68–73.

Fuhrmann, Wilfried. Aussenwirtschaftliche Persistenzen und Wechselkurselastizitäten. (Persistent Trade Effects and the Exchange-Rate Elasticity. With English summary.) *Z. Wirtschaft. Sozialwissen.*, 1989, *109*(4), pp. 585–602.

Fujii, Yataro. Changing Boundaries of State Activity: From Nationalisation to Privatisation: Comment. In *Shiraishi, T. and Tsuru, S., eds.*, 1989, pp. 210–12.

Fujimagari, David. The Sources of Change in Canadian Industry Output. *Econ. Systems Res.*, 1989, *1*(2), pp. 187–201.

Fujimoto, Takao. Cournot Oligopoly Model with Multi-product Firms. *Econ. Stud. Quart.*, December 1989, *40*(4), pp. 364–68.

_____. Generalized Gross Substitute Systems with D-Stability: A Reformulation. *Econ. Stud. Quart.*, December 1989, *40*(4), pp. 369–73.

Fujimura, Toshiro. Economic Reform and Rural Economy in China. In *Berliner, J. S.; Kosta, H. G. J. and Hakogi, M., eds.*, 1989, pp. 197–203.

Fujita, Kuniko and Hill, Richard Child. Global Production and Regional "Hollowing Out" in Japan. In *Smith, M. P., ed.*, 1989, pp. 200–230.

Fujita, Masahiro. Internationalization of Japanese Commercial Banking and the Yen: The Recent Experience of City Banks. In *Sato, R. and Negishi, T., eds.*, 1989, pp. 217–51.

Fujita, Masahisa and Kashiwadani, Masuo. Testing the Efficiency of Urban Spatial Growth: A Case Study of Tokyo. *J. Urban Econ.*, March 1989, *25*(2), pp. 156–92.

_____ **and Ogawa, H.** Nonmonocentric Urban Configurations in a Two-Dimensional Space. *Environ. Planning A*, March 1989, *21*(3), pp. 363–74.

Fujita, Natsuki. Input–Output Analysis of Agricultural Production Quotas: A Case Study of the Hokkaido Region. *Ann. Reg. Sci.*, 1989, *23*(1), pp. 41–50.

_____ **and James, William E.** Export Promotion and the "Heavy Industrialization" of Korea, 1973–83. *Developing Econ.*, September 1989, *27*(3), pp. 236–50.

Fukamachi, Ikuya. Structural Change of International Capital Market Flows in a Historical Perspective. In *Singer, H. W. and Sharma, S., eds. (I)*, 1989, pp. 199–218.

Fukami, Hiroaki. The Japanese Economy and Oil Importation. In *Ferrier, R. W. and Fursenko, A., eds.*, 1989, pp. 116–28.

Fukao, Mitsuhiro. Exchange Rate Fluctuations, Balance of Payments Imbalances and Internationalization of Financial Markets. *Bank Japan Monet. Econ. Stud.*, August 1989, *7*(2), pp. 25–71.

_____. Some Comparative Macroeconomics of the United States, Japan, and Canada: Comment. In *Stern, R. M., ed.*, 1989, pp. 86–89.

_____ **and Okina, Kunio.** Internationalization of Financial Markets and Balance of Payments Imbalances: A Japanese Perspective. *Carnegie–Rochester Conf. Ser. Public Policy*, Spring 1989, *30*, pp. 167–220.

Fukiharu, Toshitaka. On Cournot–Nash Non-cooperative Games. *Kobe Univ. Econ.*, 1989, (35), pp. 33–67.

Fukuda, Shin-ichi. Monetary and Fiscal Policies under Two Alternative Types of Rules. *J. Econ. Dynam. Control*, July 1989, *13*(3), pp. 401–20.

Fukui, Haruhiro and Weatherford, M. Stephen. Domestic Adjustment to International Shocks in Japan and the United States. *Int. Organ.*, Autumn 1989, *43*(4), pp. 585–623.

Fukushige, Mototsugu. A New Approach to the Economic Inequality Based upon the Permanent Income Hypothesis. *Econ. Letters*, 1989, *29*(2), pp. 183–87.

Fukushima, Takashi. The Structure of Indirect Taxation and Economic Welfare: A Note. *Econ. Stud. Quart.*, December 1989, *40*(4), pp. 349–54.

_____ **and Hatta, Tatsuo.** Why Not Tax Uniformly Rather Than Optimally? *Econ. Stud. Quart.*, September 1989, *40*(3), pp. 220–38.

_____ **and Kim, Namdoo.** Welfare Improving Tariff Changes: A Case of Many Goods and Countries. *J. Int. Econ.*, May 1989, *26*(3/4), pp. 383–88.

Fuller, Chris J. Misconceiving the Grain Heap: A Critique of the Concept of the Indian Jajmani System. In *Parry, J. and Bloch, M., eds.*, 1989, pp. 33–63.

Fuller, J. David and Gerchak, Yigal. Risk Aversion and Plant Size: Theory and Application to Tar-Sands Oil Plants. *Can. J. Econ.*, February 1989, *22*(1), pp. 164–73.

Fuller, Stephen and Bessler, David A. Effect of Deregulating Motor Carriage of Agricultural Commodities in Texas: An Examination of the Rate Structure for Fresh Vegetables. *Logist. Transp. Rev.*, December 1989, *25*(4), pp. 343–53.

Fuller, Wayne A. Estimation of Cross-Sectional and Change Parameters: Discussion. In *Kasprzyk, D., et al., eds.*, 1989, pp. 480–85.

Fullerton, Don and Berkovec, James. The General Equilibrium Effects of Inflation on Housing Consumption and Investment. *Amer. Econ. Rev.*, May 1989, *79*(2), pp. 277–82.

_____ **and Henderson, Yolanda Kodrzycki.** A Disaggregate Equilibrium Model of the Tax Distortions among Assets, Sectors, and Industries. *Int. Econ. Rev.*, May 1989, *30*(2), pp. 391–413.

_____ **and Henderson, Yolanda Kodrzycki.** The Marginal Excess Burden of Different Capital Tax Instruments. *Rev. Econ. Statist.*, August 1989, *71*(3), pp. 435–42.

_____ **and Mackie, James B.** Economic Efficiency in Recent Tax Reform History: Policy Reversals or Consistent Improvements. *Nat. Tax J.*, March 1989, *42*(1), pp. 1–13.

Fullerton, Howard N., Jr. New Labor Force Projections, Spanning 1988 to 2000. *Mon. Lab. Rev.*, November 1989, *112*(11), pp. 3–12.

Fullerton, Thomas M., Jr. A Composite Approach to Forecasting State Government Revenues: Case Study of the Idaho Sales Tax. *Int. J. Forecasting*, 1989, *5*(3), pp. 373–80.

Fulponi, L. The Almost Ideal Demand System: An Application to Food and Meat Groups for France. *J. Agr. Econ.*, January 1989, *40*(1), pp. 82–92.

Fulton, Murray E. The Impact of Export Markets on Rural Communities. *Can. J. Agr. Econ.*, Part 2, December 1989, *37*(4), pp. 1113–34.

_____ **and Just, Richard E.** Antitrust, Exploration, and Social Optimality in Nonrenewable Resource Markets. *J. Environ. Econ. Manage.*, July 1989, *17*(1), pp. 1–21.

_____ **and Karp, Larry S.** Estimating the Objectives of a Public Firm in a Natural Resource Industry. *J. Environ. Econ. Manage.*, May 1989, *16*(3), pp. 268–87.

_____; **Rosaasen, Ken A. and Furtan, W. Hartley.** Agricultural Subsidies in Canada: Explicit and Implicit. In *Schmitz, A., ed.*, 1989, pp. 329–62.

Fung, K. C. Profit-Sharing and European Unemployment. *Europ. Econ. Rev.*, December 1989, *33*(9), pp. 1787–98.

_____. Tariffs, Quotas, and International Oligopoly. *Oxford Econ. Pap.*, October 1989, *41*(4), pp. 749–57.

_____. Unemployment, Profit-Sharing and Japan's Economic Success. *Europ. Econ. Rev.*, April 1989, *33*(4), pp. 783–96.

Funke, Helmut. Incentive Compatible Mechanisms for the Allocation of Public Goods. **In** *Bamberg, G. and Spremann, K., eds.*, 1989, pp. 105–16.

Funke, Michael. Asset Prices and Real Investment in West Germany: Evidence from Vector Autoregressive Models. *Empirical Econ.*, 1989, *14*(4), pp. 307–28.

_____. On the U.S. Trade Imbalances. *Konjunkturpolitik*, 1989, *35*(1–2), pp. 77–98.

_____; **Wadewitz, Sabine and Willenbockel, Dirk.** Tobin's Q and Sectoral Investment in West Germany and Great Britain: A Pooled Cross-Section and Time-Series Study. *Z. Wirtschaft. Sozialwissen.*, 1989, *109*(3), pp. 399–420.

Furlong, Frederick T. Commodity Prices as a Guide for Monetary Policy. *Fed. Res. Bank San Francisco Econ. Rev.*, Winter 1989, (1), pp. 21–38.

_____. International Dimensions of U.S. Economic Policy in the 1980s. *Fed. Res. Bank San Francisco Econ. Rev.*, Spring 1989, (2), pp. 3–16.

_____ **and Keeley, Michael C.** Capital Regulation and Bank Risk-Taking: A Note. *J. Banking Finance*, December 1989, *13*(6), pp. 883–91.

Furno, Marilena. Robust Methods in Econometrics: A Review Essay. *Econ. Notes*, 1989, (1), pp. 76–98.

von Furstenberg, George M. Helpful Insights from Supply-Side Economics. **In** *Fels, G. and von Furstenberg, G. M., eds.*, 1989, pp. 101–05.

_____. Measuring Household Saving: Recent Experience from the Flow-of-Funds Perspective: Comment. **In** *Lipsey, R. E. and Tice, H. S., eds.*, 1989, pp. 145–52.

_____ **and Fels, Gerhard.** A Supply-Side Agenda for Germany: Introducing the Agenda. **In** *Fels, G. and von Furstenberg, G. M., eds.*, 1989, pp. 1–16.

_____ **and Jeon, Bang Nam.** International Stock Price Movements: Links and Messages. *Brookings Pap. Econ. Act.*, 1989, (1), pp. 125–67.

Furtan, W. Hartley and Bayri, Tulay Y. The Impact of New Wheat Technology on Income Distribution: A Green Revolution Case Study, Turkey, 1960–1983. *Econ. Devel. Cult. Change*, October 1989, *38*(1), pp. 113–27.

_____; **Fulton, Murray E. and Rosaasen, Ken A.** Agricultural Subsidies in Canada: Explicit and Implicit. **In** *Schmitz, A., ed.*, 1989, pp. 329–62.

Furth, Dave. A General Theory of Equilibrium Selection in Games: A Review Article. *J. Inst. Theoretical Econ.*, December 1989, *145*(4), pp. 730–38.

Furubotn, Eirik G. Distributional Issues in Contracting for Property Rights: Comment. *J. Inst. Theoretical Econ.*, March 1989, *145*(1), pp. 25–31.

_____. Group Behavior and Economic Growth: Some Questions. *Soc. Sci. Quart.*, September 1989, *70*(3), pp. 659–62.

_____. Organizational Economics and the Analysis of Codetermination: Reply. *Ann. Pub. Coop. Econ.*, 1989, *60*(4), pp. 463–74.

_____. Property Rights in Information and the Multinational Firm: The Case of Technical Learning in a Multiplant System. **In** *Vosgerau, H.-J., ed.*, 1989, pp. 368–400.

_____ **and Richter, Rudolf.** The New Institutional Approach to Economic History. *J. Inst. Theoretical Econ.*, March 1989, *145*(1), pp. 1–15.

Furukawa, Shunichi; Lo, Fu-chen and Song, Byung-Nak. Patterns of Development and Interdependence among the East and Southeast Asian Economies. **In** *Shinohara, M. and Lo, F., eds.*, 1989, pp. 108–27.

Fusfeld, Daniel R. Keynes and the Keynesian Cross: Reply. *Hist. Polit. Econ.*, Fall 1989, *21*(3), pp. 545–47.

_____. The Rise of the Corporate State in America. **In** *Tool, M. R. and Samuels, W. J., eds. (I)*, 1989, *1972*, pp. 171–92.

_____. Toward a Revision of the Economic Theory of Individual Behavior. *J. Econ. Issues*, June 1989, *23*(2), pp. 357–66.

Futagami, Koichi. A Game Theoretical Approach to Reconstruction of Public Finance. *J. Public Econ.*, October 1989, *40*(1), pp. 135–50.

Fux, Beat. Überlagerte kulturelle Faktoren: Ein Sättigungsmodell zur Erklärung des schweizerischen Geburtenrückgangs. (Overlied Cultural Factors: Saturation of Tensions as an Explication of Fertility Decline in Switzerland. With English summary.) *Schweiz. Z. Volkswirtsch. Statist.*, June 1989, *125*(2), pp. 165–88.

Fyfe, Nicholas R. Policing the Recession. **In** *Mohan, J., ed.*, 1989, pp. 238–54.

Gaa, J. C. and Cheung, C. S. Controlling Opportunistic Behavior in Corporate Governance: The Role of Disproportionate Voting Shares and Coat-Tail Provisions. *J. Inst. Theoretical Econ.*, September 1989, *145*(3), pp. 438–50.

van der Gaag, Jacques; Stelcner, Morton and Vijverberg, Wim. Wage Differentials and Moonlighting by Civil Servants: Evidence from Côte d'Ivoire and Peru. *World Bank Econ. Rev.*, January 1989, *3*(1), pp. 67–95.

_____ **and Vijverberg, Wim.** Wage Determinants in Côte d'Ivoire: Experience, Credentials, and Human Capital. *Econ. Devel. Cult. Change*, January 1989, *37*(2), pp. 371–81.

_____; **Vijverberg, Wim and Stelcner, Morton.** A Switching Regression Model of Public–Private Sector Wage Differentials in Peru: 1985–86. *J. Human Res.*, Summer 1989, *24*(3), pp. 545–59.

Gabel, Jon R. and Jensen, Gail A. The Price of State Mandated Benefits. *Inquiry*, Winter 1989, *26*(4), pp. 419–31.

Gábor, Istvan R. Second Economy and Socialism: The Hungarian Experience. **In** *Feige, E. L., ed.*, 1989, pp. 339–60.

_____. Second Economy in State Socialism: Past Experience and Future Prospects: The Case of Hungary. *Europ. Econ. Rev.*, March 1989, 33(2/3), pp. 597–604.

_____ and Kövári, Gy. Can the Promises of the Hungarian "Wage Reform" Come True? (Social Mechanism of Wage Determination and the Competency of Wage Theories). *Acta Oecon.*, 1989, 40(3–4), pp. 307–18.

Gabriel, Jürg Martin. Das amerikanische Exportkontroll-System. (The American Export Control Regime. With English summary.) *Aussenwirtschaft*, April 1989, 44(1), pp. 59–74.

Gabriel, Paul E. and Schmitz, Susanne. The Effect of Occupational Segregation on the Relative Earnings of Black Males. *Econ. Letters*, 1989, 30(1), pp. 77–83.

Gabriel, Stuart A. and Rosenthal, Stuart S. Household Location and Race: Estimates of a Multinomial Logit Model. *Rev. Econ. Statist.*, May 1989, 71(2), pp. 240–49.

_____; Rothberg, James P. and Nothaft, Frank E. On the Determinants of Yield Spreads between Mortgage Pass-Through and Treasury Securities. *J. Real Estate Finance Econ.*, December 1989, 2(4), pp. 301–15.

Gabrisch, Hubert. Economic Reforms in Eastern Europe and the Soviet Union: Introduction. In *Gabrisch, H., ed.*, 1989, pp. 1–6.

_____. The "Second Stage of the Economic Reform" in Poland. In *Gabrisch, H., ed.*, 1989, pp. 175–90.

_____ and Stankovsky, Jan. Special Forms of East–West Trade. *Soviet E. Europ. Foreign Trade*, Spring 1989, 25(1), pp. 1–132.

_____ and Stankovsky, Jan. Special Forms of East–West Trade. *Soviet E. Europ. Foreign Trade*, Summer 1989, 25(2), pp. 1–117.

Gabszewicz, Jean Jaskold. Cournot 150 Years After: Introductory Remarks. *Europ. Econ. Rev.*, March 1989, 33(2/3), pp. 491–93.

_____; Anderson, Simon P. and Donsimoni, Marie-Paule. Is International Trade Profitable to Oligopolistic Industries? *Int. Econ. Rev.*, November 1989, 30(4), pp. 725–33.

_____ and Thisse, Jacques-François. Competitive Discriminatory Pricing. In *Feiwel, G. R., ed. (I)*, 1989, pp. 387–406.

Gács, János. Changes in the Structure of Industrial Production and Foreign Trade in the Period of Restrictions, 1978–1986. *Eastern Europ. Econ.*, Winter 1989–90, 28(2), pp. 126–52.

_____. Changes in the Structure of Production and Foreign Trade of the Hungarian Industry in the Period of Restrictions (1978–1986). *Acta Oecon.*, 1989, 40(1–2), pp. 79–103.

Gadbois, Millie A. and Jolly, Curtis M. Foreign Aid as a Promotional Strategy. *Rev. Black Polit. Econ.*, Summer 1989, 18(1), pp. 59–74.

Gadgil, Sulachana. Monsoon Variability and Its Relationship to Agricultural Strategies. In *Oram, P. A., et al.*, 1989, pp. 249–56.

Gadiel, David L. Estimated Economic Cost of HIV/AIDS: 1988/89 to 1992/3: Commentary. In *Smith, C. S., ed.*, 1989, pp. 27–30.

Gadó, Ottó and Suranyi, György. Desirable Changes in the Hungarian Tax Structure. In *Chiancone, A. and Messere, K., eds.*, 1989, pp. 167–81.

Gaetan, Carlo and Bordignon, Silvano. Indicatori multipli dell'occupazione e domanda di lavoro: Alcune analisi empiriche con un modello DYMIMIC. (Multiple Indicators of Employment and Labor Demand: Some Empirical Analyses with a DYMIMIC Model. With English summary.) *Econ. Lavoro*, April–June 1989, 23(2), pp. 19–38.

Gafar, John S. Employment and Output Functions for Trinidad and Tobago Manufacturing Industries. *Singapore Econ. Rev.*, October 1989, 34(2), pp. 78–88.

Gafni, Amiram and Yuan, Yufei. Students Performance vs. Hospital Performance in the Labor Market for Medical Interns and Residents: Do Hospitals Perform Better Due to Asymmetry in Information Available to Them Relative to Students? *J. Health Econ.*, December 1989, 8(3), pp. 353–60.

Gafny, Arnon. The Middle East Development Fund. In *Fishelson, G., ed.*, 1989, pp. 167–79.

Gagnon, Jean-Marie and Suret, Jean-Marc. The Canadian Tax Reform and Dividends: A Reexamination. *Finance*, December 1989, 10(2), pp. 27–49.

Gagnon, Joseph E. Adjustment Costs and International Trade Dynamics. *J. Int. Econ.*, May 1989, 26(3/4), pp. 327–44.

Gagnon, Louis; Mensah, Samuel and Blinder, Edward H. Hedging Canadian Corporate Debt: A Comparative Study of the Hedging Effectiveness of Canadian and U.S. Bond Futures. *J. Futures Markets*, February 1989, 9(1), pp. 29–39.

Gahlen, Bernhard. Zum wirtschaftlichen Wachstum in der Bundesrepublik Deutschland in den 80er Jahren. (On Economic Growth in West Germany in the 1980s. With English summary.) *Jahr. Nationalökon. Statist.*, October 1989, 206(4–5), pp. 347–56.

Gahvari, Firouz. Licensing and Nontransferable Rents: Comment. *Amer. Econ. Rev.*, September 1989, 79(4), pp. 906–09.

_____. The Nature of Government Expenditures and the Shape of the Laffer Curve. *J. Public Econ.*, November 1989, 40(2), pp. 251–60.

Gaidis, William C.; Reingen, Peter H. and Kelley, Craig A. The Use of Vivid Stimuli to Enhance Comprehension of the Content of Product Warning Messages. *J. Cons. Aff.*, Winter 1989, 23(2), pp. 243–66.

Gaiha, Raghav. Poverty, Agricultural Production and Prices in Rural India—A Reformulation. *Cambridge J. Econ.*, June 1989, 13(2), pp. 333–52.

Gaile, Gary L. and Grant, Richard. Trade, Power, and Location: The Spatial Dynamics of the Relationship between Exchange and Political–Economic Strength. *Econ. Geogr.*, October 1989, 65(4), pp. 329–37.

Gaimmarino, Ronald M. The Resolution of Financial Distress. *Rev. Financial Stud.*, 1989, 2(1), pp. 25–47.

Gaines, Jessica; Levine, Paul and Currie, David A. The Use of Simple Rules for International Policy Agreements. In *Miller, M.; Eichengreen, B. and Portes, R., eds.*, 1989, pp. 281–319.

Gajda, Jan B. Structural Change in Foreign Trade of the CMEA Countries. In *Krelle, W., ed.*, 1989, pp. 259–76.

Gakenheimer, Ralph. Approaches to Regional Transport Problems: Middle East Requirements: Presentation of the Reporter General. In *Candemir, Y., ed.*, 1989, pp. 10–16.

——. Comparison and Choice in Urban Transportation. In *Candemir, Y., ed.*, 1989, pp. 212–29.

Gal-Or, Esther. Warranties as a Signal of Quality. *Can. J. Econ.*, February 1989, *22*(1), pp. 50–61.

Galai, Dan. Equilibrium Warrant Pricing Models and Accounting for Executive Stock Options: A Note. *J. Acc. Res.*, Autumn 1989, *27*(2), pp. 313–15.

Galasi, Péter and Kertesi, Gábor. Rat Race and Equilibria in Markets with Side Payments under Socialism. *Acta Oecon.*, 1989, *41*(3–4), pp. 267–91.

—— **and Sziráczki, György.** State Regulation, Enterprise Behavior, and the Labor Market in Hungary, 1968–1983. In *Rosenberg, S., ed.*, 1989, pp. 151–70.

Galaskiewicz, Joseph. Interorganizational Networks Mobilizing Action at the Metropolitan Level. In *Perrucci, R. and Potter, H. R., eds.*, 1989, pp. 81–96.

Galbraith, James K. The Exchange of Favors in the Market for Commitments. In *Colander, D. C. and Coats, A. W., eds.*, 1989, pp. 127–40.

——. On the Goals of Economic Policy. In *Feiwel, G. R., ed. (I)*, 1989, pp. 721–37.

Galbraith, Jay R. From Recovery to Development through Large-Scale Changes. In *Mohrman, A. M., Jr., et al.*, 1989, pp. 62–87.

Galbraith, John Kenneth. Ideology and Economic Reality. *Challenge*, Nov.–Dec. 1989, *32*(6), pp. 4–9.

——. A Look Back: Affirmation and Error. *J. Econ. Issues*, June 1989, *23*(2), pp. 413–16.

Galderisi, Peter and Goetze, David. Explaining Collective Action with Rational Models. *Public Choice*, July 1989, *62*(1), pp. 25–39.

Gale, Douglas and Hellwig, Martin. Repudiation and Renegotiation: The Case of Sovereign Debt. *Int. Econ. Rev.*, February 1989, *30*(1), pp. 3–31.

Gale, Ian L. and Stiglitz, Joseph E. The Informational Content of Initial Public Offerings. *J. Finance*, June 1989, *44*(2), pp. 469–77.

Gale, James R.; Shen, Patrick and Lu, Wen-he. Cross Section Evidence on the Demand for Money by the Household Sector. In *Missouri Valley Economic Association*, 1989, pp. 63–69.

Galenson, David W. Labor Market Behavior in Colonial America: Servitude, Slavery, and Free Labor. In *Galenson, D. W., ed.*, 1989, pp. 52–96.

—— **and Pope, Clayne L.** Economic and Geographic Mobility on the Farming Frontier: Evidence from Appanoose County, Iowa, 1850–1870. *J. Econ. Hist.*, September 1989, *49*(3), pp. 635–55.

Galenson, Walter and Leibenstein, Harvey. Investment Criteria, Productivity, and Economic Development. In *Leibenstein, H., Vol. 1*, 1989, *1955*, pp. 173–200.

Galeotti, Gianluigi and Forcina, Antonio. Political Loyalties and the Economy: The U.S. Case. *Rev. Econ. Statist.*, August 1989, *71*(3), pp. 512–17.

Galeotti, M. and Gori, F. Uniqueness of Periodic Orbitis in Lienard-Type Business-Cycle Models. *Metroecon.*, June 1989, *40*(2), pp. 135–46.

Galetovic P., Alexander and Lagos M., Luis Felipe. Los planes Austral y Cruzado: Por qué no detuvieron la inflación? (With English summary.) *Cuadernos Econ.*, August 1989, *26*(78), pp. 217–42.

Gallagher, Daniel P., Jr. Managing in a Global Competitive Environment: Comments. In *Ahlbrandt, R. S., Jr., ed.*, 1989, pp. 69–70.

Gallagher, Raymond B. American Television: Fact and Fantasy. In *Veljanovski, C., ed. (I)*, 1989, pp. 178–207.

Gallagher, Sally and Whiteside, Alan. Mozambique: Incentives and Industrialization in a Centrally Planned State. In *Whiteside, A. W., ed.*, 1989, pp. 103–20.

Gallant, Ronald and Tauchen, George. Seminonparametric Estimation of Conditionally Constrained Heterogeneous Processes: Asset Pricing Applications. *Econometrica*, September 1989, *57*(5), pp. 1091–1120.

Gallarotti, Giulio M. Legitimacy as a Capital Asset of the State. *Public Choice*, October 1989, *63*(1), pp. 43–61.

Gallastegui, Immaculada; Tusell, Fernando and Zubiri, Ignacio. Cálculo del efecto de alteraciones fiscales en una economía abierta: El caso del I.V.A. en el País Vasco. (With English summary.) *Invest. Ecón.*, May 1989, *13*(2), pp. 283–300.

Gallaway, Lowell and Vedder, Richard. The Tullock–Bastiat Hypothesis and Rawlsian Distribution Strategies. *Public Choice*, May 1989, *61*(2), pp. 177–81.

Gallegati, Mauro and Perri, Stefano. Un modello ricardiano di crescita e distribuzione: Un approccio integrato. (A Ricardian Model of Distribution and Growth: An Integrated Approach. With English summary.) *Econ. Politica*, December 1989, *6*(3), pp. 381–402.

Galli, Giampaolo; Terlizzese, Daniele and Visco, Ignazio. Un modello trimestrale per la previsione e la politica economica: Le proprietà di breve e di lungo periodo del modello della Banca d'Italia. (With English summary.) *Politica. Econ.*, April 1989, *5*(1), pp. 3–51.

Gallini, Nancy and Karp, Larry S. Sales and Consumer Lock-In. *Economica*, August 1989, *56*(223), pp. 279–94.

Gallman, Robert E.; Hutchins, Teresa D. and Davis, Lance E. Productivity in American Whaling: The New Bedford Fleet in the Nineteenth Century. In *Galenson, D. W., ed.*, 1989, pp. 97–147.

Gallo, Frank and Levitan, Sar A. Can Employee Associations Negotiate New Growth? *Mon. Lab. Rev.*, July 1989, *112*(7), pp. 5–14.

_____ **and Levitan, Sar A.** Collective Bargaining and Private Sector Professionals. *Mon. Lab. Rev.*, September 1989, *112*(9), pp. 24–33.

_____ **and Levitan, Sar A.** The Shortsighted Focus on Labor Shortages. *Challenge*, Sept.–Oct. 1989, *32*(5), pp. 28–32.

Galor, Oded and Ryder, Harl E. Existence, Uniqueness, and Stability of Equilibrium in an Overlapping-Generations Model with Productive Capital. *J. Econ. Theory*, December 1989, *49*(2), pp. 360–75.

Galster, George. Residential Segregation in American Cities: A Further Response. *Population Res. Policy Rev.*, May 1989, *8*(2), pp. 181–92.

Gambale, Sergio. Tax Structure and Export Performance. The Italian Case. *Rev. Econ. Cond. Italy*, May–Aug. 1989, (2), pp. 219–34.

Gamble, Andrew. Ideas and Interests in British Economic Policy. In *Gamble, A., et al.*, 1989, pp. 1–21.

_____. Thatcherism and the New Politics. In *Mohan, J., ed.*, 1989, pp. 1–17.

Gamble, Ralph C., Jr. Excise Taxes and the Price Elasticity of Demand. *J. Econ. Educ.*, Fall 1989, *20*(4), pp. 379–89.

Gammill, James F., Jr. and Perold, André F. The Changing Character of Stock Market Liquidity. *J. Portfol. Manage.*, Spring 1989, *15*(3), pp. 13–18.

Gamst, Frederick C. The Railroad Apprentice and the 'Rules': Historic Roots and Contemporary Practices. In *Coy, M. W., ed.*, 1989, pp. 65–86.

Gan, Chin Lee and Lee, David Kuo Chuen. An Economic Analysis of Fertility, Market Participation and Marriage Behaviour in Recent Japan. *Appl. Econ.*, January 1989, *21*(1), pp. 59–68.

_____ **and Lee, David Kuo Chuen.** Corrigendum [An Economic Analysis of Fertility, Market Participation and Marriage Behaviour in Recent Japan]. *Appl. Econ.*, June 1989, *21*(6), pp. 740.

Gan, See Khem. A Comparative Analysis of Human Resource Management in Foreign and Local Banks in Singapore. In *Nedd, A., ed.*, 1989, pp. 223–34.

Gana, Eduardo and Bermúdez, Augusto. Options for Regional Integration. *CEPAL Rev.*, April 1989, (37), pp. 79–93.

Gandar, John M.; Zuber, Richard A. and Russo, Benjamin. Market Rationality Tests Based on Cross-Equation Restrictions. *J. Monet. Econ.*, November 1989, *24*(3), pp. 455–70.

Gandhi, Devinder K.; Rashid, Muhammad and Riener, Kenneth D. Intertemporal Resolution of Uncertainty and Portfolio Behavior. *Financial Rev.*, August 1989, *24*(3), pp. 491–97.

Gangolli, A. and Plambeck, T. A Note on Periodicity in Some Octal Games. *Int. J. Game Theory*, 1989, *18*(3), pp. 311–20.

Gant, David R. and Lashgari, Malek K. Social Investing: The Sullivan Principles. *Rev. Soc. Econ.*, Spring 1989, *47*(1), pp. 74–83.

Ganugi, Piero. Financial deepening, risparmio forzato e accumulazione in Italia, 1881–1936. (Financial Deepening, Forced Saving and Capital Formation in Italy, 1881–1936. With English summary.) *Rivista Storia Econ.*, S.S., October 1989, *6*(3), pp. 321–57.

Ganzia, S. and Kopach, N. Leasing as a Form of Realization of Public Property. *Prob. Econ.*, November 1989, *32*(7), pp. 79–91.

Gao, Liangzhi; Juan, Fang and Li, Bingbai. Climatic Variation and Food Production in Jiangsu, China. In *Oram, P. A., et al.*, 1989, pp. 557–62.

Gao, Shangquan; Chen, Yizi and Wang, Xiaoqiang. Investigation of Reforms in Hungary and Yugoslavia. *Chinese Econ. Stud.*, Spring 1989, *22*(3), pp. 80–88.

Gao, Yang and Becker, Brian E. The Chinese Urban Labor System: Prospects for Reform. *J. Lab. Res.*, Fall 1989, *10*(4), pp. 411–28.

Gapinski, James H.; Anušić, Zoran and Škegro, Borislav. Policy Initiatives for Improving Yugoslav Economic Performance. *Int. Econ. J.*, Winter 1989, *3*(4), pp. 95–107.

_____; **Škegro, Borislav and Zuehlke, Thomas W.** A Model of Yugoslav Economic Performance. *J. Compar. Econ.*, March 1989, *13*(1), pp. 15–46.

Garand, James C. Measuring Government Size in the American States: Implications for Testing Models of Government Growth. *Soc. Sci. Quart.*, June 1989, *70*(2), pp. 487–96.

Garbacz, Christopher. Gasoline, Diesel and Motorfuel Demand in Taiwan. *Energy J.*, April 1989, *10*(2), pp. 153–63.

_____. Smoke Detector Effectiveness and the Value of Saving a Life. *Econ. Letters*, December 1989, *31*(3), pp. 281–86.

_____. Traffic Fatalities in Taiwan. *J. Transp. Econ. Policy*, September 1989, *23*(3), pp. 317–27.

Garber, Alan M. Long-Term Care, Wealth, and Health of the Disabled Elderly Living in the Community. In *Wise, D. A., ed.*, 1989, pp. 255–77.

Garber, Peter M. Tulipmania. *J. Polit. Econ.*, June 1989, *97*(3), pp. 535–60.

_____. Who Put the Mania in Tulipmania? *J. Portfol. Manage.*, Fall 1989, *16*(1), pp. 53–60.

_____ **and Grilli, Vittorio U.** Bank Runs in Open Economies and the International Transmission of Panics. *J. Int. Econ.*, August 1989, *27*(1–2), pp. 165–75.

Garber, Steven. The Reserve-Labor Hypothesis, Short-run Pricing Theories, and the Employment–Output Relationship. *J. Econometrics*, October 1989, *42*(2), pp. 219–45.

Garcia Alvarez-Coque, José Maréa and Rivera

Vilas, Luis Miguel. El modelo multiatributo de utilidad esperada con relaciones de sustitución constantes. (With English summary.) *Invest. Ecón.*, September 1989, *13*(3), pp. 453–63.

García, Álvero; Infante, Ricardo and Tokman, Víctor E. Paying Off the Social Debt in Latin America. *Int. Lab. Rev.*, 1989, *128*(4), pp. 467–83.

García, Anna M. and Fernández-Kelly, M. Patricia. Informalization at the Core: Hispanic Women, Homework, and the Advanced Capitalist State. In *Portes, A.; Castells, M. and Benton, L. A., eds.*, 1989, pp. 247–64.

Garcia, Danny B., III and Watad, Mahmoud. Telecommunications Policy and Economic Development: The New State Role: California. In *Schmandt, J.; Williams, F. and Wilson, R. H., eds.*, 1989, pp. 17–39.

García de la Sienra, Adolfo. Open Problems in the Foundations of Price Formation Dynamics. In *Balzer, W. and Hamminga, B., eds.*, 1989, pp. 87–99.

Garcia, Gillian G. The Lender of Last Resort in the Wake of the Crash. *Amer. Econ. Rev.*, May 1989, *79*(2), pp. 151–55.

_____. The Thrift Industry Crisis of the 1980s: What Went Wrong? A Panel Presentation. In *Federal Home Loan Bank of San Francisco*, 1989, pp. 37–43.

_____; **Reichert, Alan K. and Brewer, Elijah, III.** A Statistical Analysis of S&L Accounting Profits. In *Lee, C. F., ed.*, 1989, pp. 163–93.

García-Huidobro, Guillermo; Morgado, Hugo and Camazón, Daniel. Labour Market Performance and Urban Poverty in Panama. In *Rodgers, G., ed.*, 1989, pp. 97–116.

Garcia, Jaime. Incentive and Welfare Effects of Reforming the British Benefit System: A Simulation Study for the Wives of the Unemployed. In *Nickell, S. J., et al.*, 1989, pp. 164–98.

_____ **and Stern, Jon.** Real Earnings, Gains, and Losses from Unemployment. In *Nickell, S. J., et al.*, 1989, pp. 78–107.

Garcia, L. Miguel; Lichty, Richard W. and Anderson, Curt L. Water Analysis: A Systems Approach Incorporating Linear Programming. *Growth Change*, Winter 1989, *20*(1), pp. 80–89.

Garcia-Milà, Teresa. Some Empirical Evidence on Government Purchase Multipliers. *Econ. Letters*, December 1989, *31*(4), pp. 375–80.

Garcia, Philip and Anderson, Margot. Exchange Rate Uncertainty and the Demand for U.S. Soybeans. *Amer. J. Agr. Econ.*, August 1989, *71*(3), pp. 721–29.

Gardiner, John A. and Lyman, Theodore R. The Logic of Corruption Control. In *Heidenheimer, A. J.; Johnston, M. and LeVine, V. T., eds.*, 1989, pp. 827–40.

Gardiner, Lorraine R.; Bernardo, John J. and Steuer, Ralph E. Multiple Criteria Trajectory Decision Support Using Polyscreen Workstations: A Production Planning Illustration. In *Lockett, A. G. and Islei, G., eds.*, 1989, pp. 486–97.

_____; **Stam, Antonie and Joachimsthaler, Erich A.** Multicriteria Issues in Marketing: A Sales Resource Allocation Example and Potential Areas of Future Research. In *Lockett, A. G. and Islei, G., eds.*, 1989, pp. 224–33.

Gardner, B. Delworth; Huffaker, Ray G. and Wilen, James E. Multiple Use Benefits on Public Rangelands: An Incentive-Based Fee System. *Amer. J. Agr. Econ.*, August 1989, *71*(3), pp. 670–78.

Gardner, Bruce L. Rollover Hedging and Missing Long-term Futures Markets. *Amer. J. Agr. Econ.*, May 1989, *71*(2), pp. 311–18.

Gardner, Grant W. and Kimbrough, Kent P. The Behavior of U.S. Tariff Rates. *Amer. Econ. Rev.*, March 1989, *79*(1), pp. 211–18.

_____ **and Kimbrough, Kent P.** Tariffs, Interest Rates, and the Trade Balance in the World Economy. *J. Int. Econ.*, August 1989, *27*(1–2), pp. 91–110.

Gardner, J. C.; Huefner, R. J. and Lotfi, V. An Interactive Multi-criteria Model for Audit Workload Planning. In *Lockett, A. G. and Islei, G., eds.*, 1989, pp. 234–43.

Garegnani, Pierangelo. On Sraffa's Contribution to Economic Theory. In *Feiwel, G. R., ed. (II)*, 1989, pp. 368–74.

_____. Some Notes on Capital, Expectations and the Analysis of Changes. In *Feiwel, G. R., ed. (II)*, 1989, pp. 344–67.

Garella, Paolo G. Adverse Selection and the Middleman. *Economica*, August 1989, *56*(223), pp. 395–400.

_____ **and Martínez-Giralt, Xavier.** Price Competition in Markets for Dichotomous Substitutes. *Int. J. Ind. Organ.*, September 1989, *7*(3), pp. 357–67.

Garen, John E. Job-Match Quality as an Error Component and the Wage–Tenure Profile: A Comparison and Test of Alternative Estimators. *J. Bus. Econ. Statist.*, April 1989, *7*(2), pp. 245–52.

Garenne, Michel and van de Walle, Etienne. Polygyny and Fertility among the Sereer of Senegal. *Population Stud.*, July 1989, *43*(2), pp. 267–83.

Garfinkel, Irwin and Oellerich, Donald. Noncustodial Fathers' Ability to Pay Child Support. *Demography*, May 1989, *26*(2), pp. 219–33.

Garfinkel, Michelle R. The Causes and Consequences of Leveraged Buyouts. *Fed. Res. Bank St. Louis Rev.*, Sept.–Oct. 1989, *71*(5), pp. 23–34.

_____. The FOMC in 1988: Uncertainty's Effects on Monetary Policy. *Fed. Res. Bank St. Louis Rev.*, March–April 1989, *71*(2), pp. 16–33.

_____. Global Macroeconomics: Policy Conflict and Cooperation: A Review Essay. *J. Monet. Econ.*, March 1989, *23*(2), pp. 345–52.

_____. What Is an "Acceptable" Rate of Inflation?—A Review of the Issues. *Fed. Res. Bank St. Louis Rev.*, July–Aug. 1989, *71*(4), pp. 3–15.

_____ **and Thornton, Daniel L.** The Link between M1 and the Monetary Base in the 1980s.

Fed. Res. Bank St. Louis Rev., Sept.–Oct. 1989, 71(5), pp. 35–52.

Garganas, Nicholas C. Financial Regulation, Implicit Taxes, and Fiscal Adjustment in Italy: Comment. In Monti, M., ed., 1989, pp. 231–34.

Garlick, Steve and Taylor, Michael. Commonwealth Government Involvement in Regional Development in the 1980s: A Local Approach. In Higgins, B. and Zagorski, K., eds., 1989, pp. 79–103.

Gärling, Tommy; Lindberg, Erik and Montgomery, Henry. Beliefs about Attainment of Life Satisfaction as Determinants of Preferences for Everyday Activities. In Grunert, K. G. and Ölander, F., eds., 1989, pp. 33–46.

Garman, David M. and Richards, Daniel J. Policy Rules, Inflationary Bias, and Cyclical Stability. J. Money, Credit, Banking, November 1989, 21(4), pp. 409–21.

Garnaut, Ross and Drysdale, Peter. A Pacific Free Trade Area? In Schott, J. J., ed., 1989, pp. 217–54.

Garner, B. J. and Baker, R. G. V. On the Space-Time Associations in the Consumer Patronage of Planned Shopping Centres. Environ. Planning A, September 1989, 21(9), pp. 1179–94.

Garner, C. Alan. Commodity Prices: Policy Target or Information Variable? A Note. J. Money, Credit, Banking, November 1989, 21(4), pp. 508–14.

Garner, Thesia I.; Zieschang, Kimberley D. and Miller, Richard D. Using the Consumer Expenditure Survey Data: Past, Present, and Future Research. J. Econ. Soc. Meas., 1989, 15(3–4), pp. 237–79.

Garnick, Daniel H. Growth in Metropolitan and Nonmetropolitan Areas: An Update. Surv. Curr. Bus., April 1989, 69(4), pp. 37–38.

Garofalo, Gasper A. and Malhotra, Devinder M. Intertemporal and Interspatial Productivity Differentials in U.S. Manufacturing. Ann. Reg. Sci., 1989, 23(2), pp. 121–36.

Garofoli, Gioacchino. Industrial Districts: Structure and Transformation. Econ. Notes, 1989, (1), pp. 37–54.

Garretsen, Harry and Lensink, Robert. International Policy Coordination and European Wage Rigidity. De Economist, 1989, 137(1), pp. 76–90.

Garrison, Roger W. The Austrian Theory of the Business Cycle in the Light of Modern Macroeconomics. In Rothbard, M. N. and Block, W., eds., 1989, pp. 3–29.

Garrison, Sharon H. and Davidson, Wallace N., III. The Stock Market Reaction to Significant Tender Offer Repurchases of Stock: Size and Purpose Perspective. Financial Rev., February 1989, 24(1), pp. 93–107.

Garrity, Dennis P. and Flinn, John C. Yield Stability and Modern Rice Technology. In Anderson, J. R. and Hazell, P. B. R., eds., 1989, pp. 251–64.

Garten, Jeffrey E. Japan and Germany: American Concerns. Foreign Aff., Winter 1989–90, 68(5), pp. 84–101.

_____. Regulating the Global Stock Market. In Kaushik, S. K., ed., 1989, pp. 181–94.

Garud, Raghu and Van de Ven, Andrew H. A Framework for Understanding the Emergence of New Industries. In Rosenbloom, R. S. and Burgelman, R. A., eds., 1989, pp. 195–225.

Garvin, Susan; Kerman, Stephen and Baltagi, Badi H. Further Monte Carlo Evidence on Seemingly Unrelated Regressions with Unequal Number of Observations. Ann. Écon. Statist., April–June 1989, (14), pp. 103–15.

Garwin, Richard. Deep Cuts in Strategic Nuclear Weapons: Possible? Desirable? In Rotblat, J. and Goldanskii, V. I., eds., 1989, pp. 2–13.

Garwood, Griffith L. Statement to the U.S. Senate Subcommittee on Consumer and Regulatory Affairs, Committee on Banking, Housing, and Urban Affairs, July 31, 1989. Fed. Res. Bull., September 1989, 75(9), pp. 619–24.

Gary-Bobo, Robert J. Cournot, a Great Forerunner of Mathematical Economics. Europ. Econ. Rev., March 1989, 33(2/3), pp. 515–22.

_____. Cournot–Walras and Locally Consistent Equilibria. J. Econ. Theory, October 1989, 49(1), pp. 10–32.

de la Garza, E. Long-Term U.S. Food and Agricultural Policies: A Legislative Perspective. In Helmuth, J. W. and Johnson, S. R., eds., Vol. 1, 1989, pp. 25–29.

Garza, Gilma; Kelly, Rafael and Casares, Enrique. Control adaptable de un modelo no lineal de crecimiento monetario neoclásico. (Adaptive Control of a Nonlinear Neoclassical Monetary Growth Model. With English summary.) Estud. Econ., Jan.–June 1989, 4(1), pp. 109–26.

Gascoigne, John. Church and State Allied: The Failure of Parliamentary Reform of the Universities, 1688–1800. In [Stone, L.], 1989, pp. 401–29.

Gasiorek, Michael; Smith, Alasdair and Venables, Anthony J. Tariffs, Subsidies and Retaliation. Europ. Econ. Rev., March 1989, 33(2/3), pp. 480–89.

Gasperini, E. Intégration européenne et accroissement des disparités régionales. La politique régionale de la communauté économique européenne en question. (European Integration and Extension of Regional Disparities. EEC Regional Politics in Question. With English summary.) Écon. Societes, February 1989, 23(2), pp. 129–59.

Gass, Saul I.; Chapman, Robert E. and Harris, Carl M. Analyzing the Economic Impacts of a Military Mobilization. In Gulledge, T. R., Jr. and Litteral, L. A., eds., 1989, pp. 353–86.

Gassmann, H. P. Telecommunications Market Structure Changes: Expectations and Experiences. In Jussawalla, M.; Okuma, T. and Araki, T., eds., 1989, pp. 236–43.

Gastwirth, Joseph L. and Nayak, Tapan K. The Use of Diversity Analysis to Assess the Relative Influence of Factors Affecting the Income Distribution. J. Bus. Econ. Statist., October 1989, 7(4), pp. 453–60.

_____; Nayak, Tapan K. and Wang, Jane-Ling. Statistical Properties of Measures of Between-Group Income Differentials. *J. Econometrics*, September 1989, *42*(1), pp. 5–19.

Gately, Dermot and Andoh, Samuel Kojo. The U.S. Demand for Cocoa: Explaining the Apparent Insignificance of Income Growth. *Appl. Econ.*, November 1989, *21*(11), pp. 1421–32.

Gatev, Kiril. An Approach in Measuring and Analysing Regional Specialization and Concentration. In *Bulgarian Academy of Sciences, Institute of Economics*, 1989, pp. 153–63.

Gatewood, John B.; Creed, Carolyn F. and McCay, Bonnie J. Labor and the Labor Process in a Limited Entry Fishery. *Marine Resource Econ.*, 1989, *6*(4), pp. 311–30.

Gathon, Henry-Jean. Etude comparative des performances des societes de chemins de fer. (Comparative Study of the Performance of Railway Companies. With English summary.) *Ann. Pub. Coop. Econ.*, 1989, *60*(1), pp. 61–80.

_____. Indicators of Partial Productivity and Technical Efficiency in the European Urban Transit Sector. *Ann. Pub. Coop. Econ.*, 1989, *60*(1), pp. 43–59.

Gatignon, Hubert; Eliashberg, Jehoshua and Robertson, Thomas S. Modeling Multinational Diffusion Patterns: An Efficient Methodology. *Marketing Sci.*, Summer 1989, *8*(3), pp. 231–47.

Gatsios, Konstantine. Imperfect Competition and International Trade. In *Hahn, F., ed.*, 1989, pp. 188–207.

_____ and Seabright, Paul. Regulation in the European Community. *Oxford Rev. Econ. Policy*, Summer 1989, *5*(2), pp. 37–60.

Gaudet, Gérard and Howitt, Peter. A Note on Uncertainty and the Hotelling Rule. *J. Environ. Econ. Manage.*, January 1989, *16*(1), pp. 80–86.

Gaudry, Marc and Laferriére, Richard. The Box–Cox Transformation: Power Invariance and a New Interpretation. *Econ. Letters*, 1989, *30*(1), pp. 27–29.

Gauger, Jean A. The Generated Regressor Correction: Impacts upon Inferences in Hypothesis Testing. *J. Macroecon.*, Summer 1989, *11*(3), pp. 383–95.

_____ and Enders, Walter. Money Neutrality at Aggregate and Sectoral Levels. *Southern Econ. J.*, January 1989, 55(3), pp. 771–78.

Gaul, Wolfgang and Böckenholt, Ingo. Generalized Latent Class Analysis: A New Methodology for Market Structure Analysis. In *Opitz, O., ed.*, 1989, pp. 367–76.

_____ and Decker, Reinhold. Classification and Selection of Consumer Purchase Behaviour Models. In *Opitz, O., ed.*, 1989, pp. 389–98.

Gaus, Gerald F. A Contractual Justification of Redistributive Capitalism. In *Chapman, J. W. and Pennock, J. R., eds.*, 1989, pp. 89–121.

Gauvin, Annie. L'invention de l'emploi . . . masculin? (Was Employment Invention Only Male Employment Invention? With English summary.) *Écon. Societes*, October 1989, *23*(10), pp. 77–106.

_____ and Michon, François. Work-Sharing Public Policy in France, 1981–1986. In *Rosenberg, S., ed.*, 1989, pp. 207–20.

Gavin, Michael. The Stock Market and Exchange Rate Dynamics. *J. Int. Money Finance*, June 1989, *8*(2), pp. 181–200.

Gavin, William T. and Dewald, William G. The Effect of Disinflationary Policies on Monetary Velocity. *Cato J.*, Spring–Summer 1989, *9*(1), pp. 149–64.

Gavish, Moshe and Freidkes, Nahum. Administrative and Compliance Costs of Taxation: Israel. In *International Fiscal Association, ed. (I)*, 1989, pp. 403–24.

Gay, Gerald D.; Kale, Jayant R. and Badrinath, S. G. Patterns of Institutional Investment, Prudence, and the Managerial "Safety-Net" Hypothesis. *J. Risk Ins.*, December 1989, *56*(4), pp. 605–29.

_____; Kale, Jayant R. and Noe, Thomas H. Share Repurchase through Transferable Put Rights: Theory and Case Study. *J. Finan. Econ.*, November 1989, *25*(1), pp. 141–60.

_____; Kolb, Robert W. and Yung, Kenneth. Trader Rationality in the Exercise of Futures Options. *J. Finan. Econ.*, August 1989, *23*(2), pp. 339–61.

_____, et al. Noisy Juries and the Choice of Trial Mode in a Sequential Signalling Game: Theory and Evidence. *Rand J. Econ.*, Summer 1989, *20*(2), pp. 196–213.

Gay, Robert S. and Wascher, William L. Persistence Effects in Labor Force Participation. *Eastern Econ. J.*, July–Sept. 1989, *15*(3), pp. 177–87.

Gaynor, Martin. Competition within the Firm: Theory Plus Some Evidence from Medical Group Practice. *Rand J. Econ.*, Spring 1989, *20*(1), pp. 59–76.

_____. The Presence of Moral Hazard in Budget Breaking. *Public Choice*, June 1989, *61*(3), pp. 261–67.

_____ and Kleindorfer, Paul R. Misperceptions, Equilibrium, and Incentives in Groups and Organizations. In *Bamberg, G. and Spremann, K., eds.*, 1989, pp. 389–414.

Gaynor, Patricia; Brem, Natalie and Durden, Garey. The Effect of Government Employment on Income Inequality Overall and in the South: Evidence from Congressional District Data. *Rev. Reg. Stud.*, Spring 1989, *19*(2), pp. 40–47.

Gazeley, Ian. The Cost of Living for Urban Workers in Late Victorian and Edwardian Britain. *Econ. Hist. Rev., 2nd Ser.*, May 1989, *42*(2), pp. 207–21.

Gazier, Bernard. L'Envers du plein emploi. Eléments d'analyse épistémologique des normes d'employabilité. (The Other Side of Employment. Elements of an Epistemological Analysis of Employability Norms. With English summary.) *Écon. Societes*, October 1989, *23*(10), pp. 135–56.

Gazioglu, S. and Artis, Michael J. Modelling Asymmetric Exchange Rate Unions: A Stylized Model of the EMS. *Greek Econ. Rev.*, 1989, *11*(1), pp. 177–202.

Gbur, Edward E. A Comparison of Alternative Estimators for Revised Monthly Import Statistics. *J. Bus. Econ. Statist.*, January 1989, *7*(1), pp. 21–25.

_____ **and Collins, Robert A.** A Small-Sample Comparison of Estimators in the EU-MGF Approach to Decision Making. *Amer. J. Agr. Econ.*, February 1989, *71*(1), pp. 202–10.

Ge, Minghao; Sun, Li-Teh and Zhang, Shi-Ying. Prospects of Chinese Wage Reform: A Synergy of Market and Planning Systems. *Int. J. Soc. Econ.*, 1989, *16*(8), pp. 26–34.

Geanakoplos, John and Mas-Colell, Andreu. Real Indeterminacy with Financial Assets. *J. Econ. Theory*, February 1989, *47*(1), pp. 22–38.

_____; **Pearce, David G. and Stacchetti, Ennio.** Psychological Games and Sequential Rationality. *Games Econ. Behav.*, March 1989, *1*(1), pp. 60–79.

Gear, Tony and Read, Martin. On-Line Group Decision Support. In *Lockett, A. G. and Islei, G., eds.*, 1989, pp. 124–33.

Geare, A. J. New Directions in New Zealand Labour Legislation: The Labour Relations Act 1987. *Int. Lab. Rev.*, 1989, *128*(2), pp. 213–28.

Geary, Dick. Labour and Socialist Movements in Europe before 1914: Introduction. In *Geary, D., ed.*, 1989, pp. 1–10.

_____. Socialism and the German Labour Movement before 1914. In *Geary, D., ed.*, 1989, pp. 101–36.

Geary, F. and Johnson, W. Unemployment, Participation Rates and Unemployment Legislation between the Wars. *Appl. Econ.*, October 1989, *21*(10), pp. 1341–52.

Geary, Patrick T. Irish Migration: The Search for the Efficiency and Equity Basis of a European Regional Policy: A Comment. *Econ. Soc. Rev.*, October 1989, *21*(1), pp. 85–86.

_____. The Measurement and Alleviation of Poverty: A Review of Some Issues. *Econ. Soc. Rev.*, July 1989, *20*(4), pp. 293–307.

_____ **and Ó Gráda, Cormac.** Post-war Migration between Ireland and the United Kingdom: Models and Estimates. In *Gordon, I. and Thirlwall, A. P., eds.*, 1989, pp. 53–58.

Gebauer, Rolf H. Towards a New Socioeconomic Classification Scheme for Farm Households Using a Cluster Analysis Technique. In *Opitz, O., ed.*, 1989, pp. 399–406.

Gebauer, Wolfgang. Towards a European Monetary Constitution—Basic Issues and Practical Steps. In *Franz, O., ed.*, 1989, pp. 118–25.

Geddes, Earl. Transportation and Management. *Can. J. Agr. Econ.*, Part 1, December 1989, *37*(4), pp. 761–63.

Gedizlioğlu, Ergun. Traffic Flow on Bosphorus Bridge and Approaches. In *Candemir, Y., ed.*, 1989, pp. 455–63.

Gehrig, Gerhard. Ein Energienachfragemodell für den Sudan. (An Energy Demand Model for Sudan. With English summary.) *Jahr. Na-*

tionalökon. *Statist.*, October 1989, *206*(4–5), pp. 357–68.

Gehrig, W. and Aczél, János. Determination of All Generalized Hicks-Neutral Production Functions. *Math. Soc. Sci.*, February 1989, *17*(1), pp. 33–45.

Gehrlein, William V. The Probability of Intransitivity of Pairwise Comparisons in Individual Preference. *Math. Soc. Sci.*, February 1989, *17*(1), pp. 67–75.

Geiger, Helmut. Ecu and EMS. In *Franz, O., ed.*, 1989, pp. 21–25.

Geiger, Linwood T. Expropriation and External Capital Flows. *Econ. Devel. Cult. Change*, April 1989, *37*(3), pp. 535–56.

Geiger, Marshall A. and Hunt, Herbert G., III. Capital Gain Taxation: A Critical Analysis of Historical and Current Issues. In *Jones, S. M., ed.*, 1989, pp. 21–39.

_____ **and Kirch, David.** What Does "Total Return" Really Mean? A Comment. *J. Portfol. Manage.*, Summer 1989, *15*(4), pp. 80–81.

Geithman, Frederick and Marion, Bruce W. Live Cattle Prices and Packer–Buyer Concentration. In *Weiss, L. W., ed.*, 1989, pp. 213–18.

Gelles, Gregory M. and Mitchell, Douglas W. An Approximation Theorem for the Polynomial Inverse Lag. *Econ. Letters*, August 1989, *30*(2), pp. 129–32.

_____; **Speaker, Paul J. and Mitchell, Douglas W.** Geometric Combination Lags as Flexible Infinite Distributed Lag Estimators. *J. Econ. Dynam. Control*, April 1989, *13*(2), pp. 171–85.

Gellings, Clark W. and Harper, Jerome P. End-Use R&D: Technology Development Strategy for an Integrated Market. *Energy J.*, July 1989, *10*(3), pp. 19–33.

Geltner, David. Bias in Appraisal-Based Returns. *Amer. Real Estate Urban Econ. Assoc. J.*, Fall 1989, *17*(3), pp. 338–52.

_____. Estimating Real Estate's Systematic Risk from Aggregate Level Appraisal-Based Returns. *Amer. Real Estate Urban Econ. Assoc. J.*, Winter 1989, *17*(4), pp. 463–81.

_____. On the Use of the Financial Option Price Model to Value and Explain Vacant Urban Land. *Amer. Real Estate Urban Econ. Assoc. J.*, Summer 1989, *17*(2), pp. 142–58.

van Gemert, H. G., et al. Theo van de Klundert: A Frontier Economist. *De Economist*, 1989, *137*(3), pp. 257–78.

Gemmell, Norman. The Economics of Authors' Royalty Contracts: Some Analytics. *J. Econ. Stud.*, 1989, *16*(4), pp. 23–34.

_____. Is There a Conflict between Authors and Publishers over Royalty Terms? *Econ. Letters*, 1989, *29*(1), pp. 7–11.

_____. Optimal International Borrowing—How Should It Be Defined? A Reply. *J. Devel. Stud.*, July 1989, *25*(4), pp. 580–82.

Gemper, Bodo B. Redefining the Government's Role in Contemporary National Economies: Essentials of State Participation in Market Economies. In *Gemper, B. B., ed.*, 1989, pp. 11–20.

Gempesaw, C. M., II and Elterich, G. J. The Importance of International Students in the Academic Market for Agricultural Economists. *Amer. J. Agr. Econ.*, May 1989, *71*(2), pp. 275–79.

Genberg, Hans. Exchange Rate Management and Macroeconomic Policy: A National Perspective. *Scand. J. Econ.*, 1989, *91*(2), pp. 439–69.

———— **and Swoboda, Alexander K.** Policy and Current Account Determination under Floating Exchange Rates. *Int. Monet. Fund Staff Pap.*, March 1989, *36*(1), pp. 1–30.

Geng, Shuhai and Li, Hua. Reform and Social Mentality of Workers. *Chinese Econ. Stud.*, Summer 1989, *22*(4), pp. 8–17.

Gennings, Chris; Chinchilli, Vernon M. and Carter, Walter H., Jr. Response Surface Analysis with Correlated Data: A Nonlinear Model Approach. *J. Amer. Statist. Assoc.*, September 1989, *84*(407), pp. 805–09.

Genosko, Joachim; Schnabel, Claus and Addison, John T. Gewerkschaften, Produktivität und Rent Seeking. (Union, Productivity, and Rent Seeking. With English summary.) *Jahr. Nationalökon. Statist.*, March 1989, *206*(2), pp. 102–16.

Genovese, Frank C. This Journal's Reason for Being. *Amer. J. Econ. Sociology*, July 1989, *48*(3), pp. 257–58.

Genser, Bernd. Competitive Performance, Regulation and Trade in Banking Services: Comments. In *Vosgerau, H.-J., ed.*, 1989, pp. 251–53.

Gensior, Sabine and Schöler, Bärbel. Women's Employment and Multinationals in the Federal Republic of Germany: The Job-Export Question. In *Elson, D. and Pearson, R., eds.*, 1989, pp. 60–79.

Gensollen, Michel and Curien, Nicolas. L'ouverture des réseaux: Planification ou concurrence dans les télécommunications et d'autres services publics. (The Opening-Up of Networks: Planning or Competition in the Telecommunications Industry and Other Public Utilities. With English summary.) *Ann. Écon. Statist.*, July–Dec. 1989, (15–16), pp. 355–88.

Gentry, William M. Do State Revenue Forecasters Utilize Available Information? *Nat. Tax J.*, December 1989, *42*(4), pp. 429–39.

Georgakopoulos, Theodore A. Harmonisation of Commodity Taxes: The Restricted Origin Principle—Comment. *J. Public Econ.*, June 1989, *39*(1), pp. 137–39.

George, David. Social Evolution and the Role of Knowledge. *Rev. Soc. Econ.*, Spring 1989, *47*(1), pp. 55–73.

George, Kenneth. Do We Need a Merger Policy? In *Fairburn, J. and Kay, J., eds.*, 1989, pp. 281–300.

George, M. V. and Perreault, J. Methodological Issues in the Projection of Households and Families in Canada. *Statist. J.*, 1989, *6*(4), pp. 325–36.

Georgianna, Daniel and Hogan, William. U.S. Fish Processing Capacity and Imports of Whole Groundfish from Canada. *Marine Resource Econ.*, 1989, *6*(3), pp. 213–25.

Georgiev, Iliya. Qualitatively New Organizational and Economic Conditions for Economic Activities. In *Bulgarian Academy of Sciences, Institute of Economics*, 1989, pp. 47–57.

Georgiou, George C. Changing Pattern of U.S.–Latin American Trade. *Atlantic Econ. J.*, September 1989, *17*(3), pp. 84.

Gerard, James M.; Blair, Douglas H. and Golbe, Devra L. Unbundling the Voting Rights and Profit Claims of Common Shares. *J. Polit. Econ.*, April 1989, *97*(2), pp. 420–43.

Gerard, K. and Donaldson, C. Effects of Payment and Ownership on Hospital Efficiency. In *Smith, C. S., ed.*, 1989, pp. 265–82.

Gérard-Varet, Louis-André. Pouvoirs de marché et informations privées en équilibre général: La théorie peut-elle avoir un pouvoir prédictif? (With English summary.) *Rech. Écon. Louvain*, 1989, *55*(4), pp. 313–38.

————; **d'Aspremont, Claude and Dos Santos Ferreira, Rodolphe.** Unemployment in a Cournot Oligopoly Model with Ford Effects. *Rech. Écon. Louvain*, 1989, *55*(1), pp. 33–60.

————; **d'Aspremont, Claude and Dos Santos Ferreira, Rodolphe.** Unemployment in an Extended Cournot Oligopoly Model. *Oxford Econ. Pap.*, July 1989, *41*(3), pp. 490–505.

Gerardin, Bernard. Financing of Great Transport Infrastructure Projects Contributions of New Financing Techniques. In *Candemir, Y., ed.*, 1989, pp. 243–56.

Gerasimovich, V. N. and Ovsienko, V. V. A Reform of the Mechanism of International Economic Relations: Basic Concepts and Problems. *Matekon*, Winter 1989–90, *26*(2), pp. 27–37.

Gerber, Jim and Singh, Harinder. On-the-Job Leisure–Income Tradeoffs: A Test of Rational Behavior. *Econ. Letters*, 1989, *29*(1), pp. 91–94.

Gercek, Haluk and Evren, Gungor. A Preliminary Evaluation of the Container Transportation on the Turkish Railway Network. In *Candemir, Y., ed.*, 1989, pp. 285–99.

Gerchak, Yigal and Fuller, J. David. Risk Aversion and Plant Size: Theory and Application to Tar-Sands Oil Plants. *Can. J. Econ.*, February 1989, *22*(1), pp. 164–73.

Gercheva, Dafina and Naidenov, Naiden. Economic Aspects of the Environmental Policy of the People's Republic of Bulgaria. In *Bulgarian Academy of Sciences, Institute of Economics*, 1989, pp. 107–11.

Gerchunoff, Pablo. Peronist Economic Policies, 1946–55. In *di Tella, G. and Dornbusch, R., eds.*, 1989, pp. 59–85.

————. The 'Revolución Libertadora', 1955–58: A Note. In *di Tella, G. and Dornbusch, R., eds.*, 1989, pp. 103–07.

Gereffi, Gary and Wyman, Donald. Determinants of Development Strategies in Latin America and East Asia. In *Haggard, S. and Moon, C., eds.*, 1989, pp. 23–52.

Gerhaeusser, Klaus. Output–Inflation Trade-Offs

in Industrial and Developing Countries: A Corrective Note. *J. Macroecon.*, Summer 1989, *11*(3), pp. 463–65.

Gerhart, Barry A. and Milkovich, George T. Salaries, Salary Growth, and Promotions of Men and Women in a Large, Private Firm. In *Michael, R. T.; Hartmann, H. I. and O'Farrell, B., eds.*, 1989, pp. 23–43.

Gerking, Shelby and Dickie, Mark. Benefits of Reduced Morbidity from Air Pollution Control: A Survey. In *Folmer, H. and van Ierland, E., eds.*, 1989, pp. 105–22.

_____ and Dickie, Mark. Interregional Wage Differentials in the United States: A Survey. In *van Dijk, J., et al., eds.*, 1989, pp. 111–45.

_____; Weiss, Peter and Maier, Gunther. The Economics of Traffic Accidents on Austrian Roads: Risk Lovers or Policy Deficit? *Empirica*, 1989, *16*(2), pp. 177–92.

Gerlach, Stefan. Information, Persistence, and Real Business Cycles. *J. Econ. Dynam. Control*, April 1989, *13*(2), pp. 187–99.

_____. Intertemporal Speculation, Devaluation, and the 'J-Curve.' *J. Int. Econ.*, November 1989, *27*(3–4), pp. 335–45.

Gerli, Massimo. Equilbrio esterno e movimenti di capitale in Italia. (With English summary.) *Studi. Econ.*, 1989, *44*(39), pp. 51–77.

Gerlowski, Daniel A. and Thies, Clifford F. Deposit Insurance: A History of Failure. *Cato J.*, Winter 1989, *8*(3), pp. 677–93.

Germain, Marc. Externalités, taxation et traitement de la pollution dans le cadre d'un duopole de Cournot. (With English summary.) *Rech. Écon. Louvain*, 1989, *55*(3), pp. 273–92.

German, H. Wade and Babcock, Michael W. Changing Determinants of Truck-Rail Market Shares. *Logist. Transp. Rev.*, September 1989, *25*(3), pp. 251–70.

_____ and Babcock, Michael W. Public Policy, Motor Carriers and Strategic Planning. In *Missouri Valley Economic Association*, 1989, pp. 16–24.

Geroski, Paul A. The Effect of Entry on Profit Margins in the Short and Long Run. *Ann. Écon. Statist.*, July–Dec. 1989, (15–16), pp. 333–53.

_____. Entry, Innovation and Productivity Growth. *Rev. Econ. Statist.*, November 1989, *71*(4), pp. 572–78.

_____. European Industrial Policy and Industrial Policy in Europe. *Oxford Rev. Econ. Policy*, Summer 1989, *5*(2), pp. 20–36.

_____. The Interaction between Domestic and Foreign Based Entrants. In *Audretsch, D. B.; Sleuwaegen, L. and Yamawaki, H., eds.*, 1989, pp. 59–83.

_____ and Fairburn, James A. The Empirical Analysis of Market Structure and Performance. In *Fairburn, J. and Kay, J., eds.*, 1989, pp. 175–92.

_____ and Jacquemin, Alexis. Industrial Change, Barriers to Mobility, and European Industrial Policy. In *Jacquemin, A. and Sapir, A., eds.*, 1989, *1985*, pp. 298–333.

_____; Thompson, David and Toker, Saadet. Vertical Separation and Price Discrimination: Cellular Phones in the UK. *Fisc. Stud.*, November 1989, *10*(4), pp. 83–103.

Gerpott, Torsten J. Ökonomische Spurenelemente in der Personalwirtschaftslehre: Ansätze zur Bestimmung ökonomischer Erfolgswirkungen von Personalauswahlverfahren. (With English summary.) *Z. Betriebswirtshaft*, August 1989, *59*(8), pp. 888–912.

Gerrard, Bill J. and Dobson, Stephen M. Growth and Profitability in the Leeds Engineering Sector. *Scot. J. Polit. Econ.*, November 1989, *36*(4), pp. 334–52.

Gerschenkron, A. Mercator Gloriosus. In *Wood, J. C. and Woods, R. N., eds., Vol. 2*, 1989, *1971*, pp. 174–88.

Gerson, Judith M. The Wage Effects of Occupational Sex Composition: A Review and New Findings: Discussion. In *Hill, M. A. and Killingsworth, M. R., eds.*, 1989, pp. 80–82.

Gersovitz, Mark. Transportation, State Marketing, and the Taxation of the Agricultural Hinterland. *J. Polit. Econ.*, October 1989, *97*(5), pp. 1113–37.

_____ and Eaton, Jonathan. Country Risk and the Organization of International Capital Transfer. In *[Díaz-Alejandro, C.]*, 1989, pp. 109–29.

Gertler, Mark. Restrictions on Financial Intermediaries and Implications for Aggregate Fluctuations: Canada and the United States 1870–1913: Comment. In *Blanchard, O. J. and Fischer, S., eds.*, 1989, pp. 340–45.

_____ and Bernanke, Ben S. Agency Costs, Net Worth, and Business Fluctuations. *Amer. Econ. Rev.*, March 1989, *79*(1), pp. 14–31.

Gertler, Paul J. Subsidies, Quality, and the Regulation of Nursing Homes. *J. Public Econ.*, February 1989, *38*(1), pp. 33–52.

_____ and Frank, Richard G. The Effect of Medicaid Policy on Mental Health and Poverty. *Inquiry*, Summer 1989, *26*(2), pp. 283–90.

_____; Locay, Luis and Sanderson, Warren. Are User Fees Regressive? The Welfare Implications of Charging for Medical Care in Peru. In *WHO, Pan American Health Organization*, 1989, pp. 86–106.

Gertner, Robert and Ayres, Ian. Filling Gaps in Incomplete Contracts: An Economic Theory of Default Rules. *Yale Law J.*, October 1989, *99*(1), pp. 87–130.

_____ and Carlton, Dennis W. Market Power and Mergers in Durable-Good Industries. *J. Law Econ.*, Part 2, October 1989, *32*(2), pp. S203–26.

Gestrin, B. V. Macroeconomic Adjustment Policy Issues: Comment. In *Hamouda, O. F.; Rowley, R. and Wolf, B. M., eds.*, 1989, pp. 157–59.

Getis, A. A Spatial Causal Model of Economic Interdependency among Neighboring Communities. *Environ. Planning A*, January 1989, *21*(1), pp. 115–20.

Getzel, Elizabeth Evans; Kregel, John and Veldheer, Linda C. Projecting the Service Needs of Transition-Aged Young Adults Exiting Pub-

lic School Programs: A Statewide Analysis. **In**
Wehman, P. and Kregel, J., eds., 1989, pp.
243–56.

Gevel, Ad and Mayes, David G. 1992: Removing
the Barriers. *Nat. Inst. Econ. Rev.*, August
1989, (129), pp. 42–51.

**van de Gevel, Frans J. J. S. and den Butter,
Frank A. G.** Prediction of the Netherlands'
Money Stock. *De Economist*, 1989, *137*(2), pp.
173–201.

Gewalli, Lars Erik. Statistical Data Bank Services
in Denmark. *Statist. J.*, 1989, *6*(1), pp. 99–
104.

Geweke, John. Bayesian Inference in Econometric Models Using Monte Carlo Integration.
Econometrica, November 1989, *57*(6), pp.
1317–39.

_____. Exact Predictive Densities for Linear
Models with ARCH Disturbances. *J. Econometrics*, January 1989, *40*(1), pp. 63–86.

_____. Modeling with Normal Polynomial Ex-
pansions. **In** *Barnett, W. A.; Geweke, J. and
Shell, K., eds.*, 1989, pp. 337–59.

_____. Sensitivity Analysis of Seasonal Adjust-
ments: Empirical Case Studies: Comment. *J.
Amer. Statist. Assoc.*, March 1989, *84*(405), pp.
28–30.

Geyer, Hermanus S. Industrial Development
Policy in South Africa—The Past, Present and
Future. *World Devel.*, March 1989, *17*(3), pp.
379–96.

Ghali, Khalifa and Aigner, Dennis J. Self-Selec-
tion in the Residential Electricity Time-of-Use
Pricing Experiments. *J. Appl. Econometrics*,
Supplement, December 1989, *4*, pp. S131–44.

Ghani, Ejaz. Alternative Approaches to Devaluation. **In** *Renshaw, G. T., ed.*, 1989, pp. 39–
70.

Ghatak, Subrata and Deadman, Derek. Money,
Prices and Stabilization Policies in Some Developing Countries. *Appl. Econ.*, July 1989,
21(7), pp. 853–65.

Ghaus, Aisha. The Incidence of Public Expenditure in Karachi. *Pakistan J. Appl. Econ.*, Summer 1989, *8*(1), pp. 85–109.

_____. Municipal, Finances—A Case Study of
Karachi. *Pakistan Econ. Soc. Rev.*, Winter
1989, *27*(2), pp. 77–108.

_____; **Malik, Salman and Pasha, Hafiz A.** The
Economic Cost of Power Outages in the Industrial Sector of Pakistan. *Energy Econ.*, October
1989, *11*(4), pp. 301–18.

Ghazal, G. A. A Short Term Macroeconomic
Model of Egypt (1950–1982). *Middle East Bus.
Econ. Rev.*, January 1989, *1*(1), pp. 20–31.

Ghiat, Boufeldja and Willey, Phillip C. T. The
Impact of Local Culture and Attitudes on Orga-
nizational Effectiveness in Algeria. **In** *Davies,
J., et al., eds.*, 1989, pp. 66–74.

Ghisellini, Fabrizio. A Short-run Model for the
Lira/U.S. Dollar Exchange Rate. *Econ. Notes*,
1989, (1), pp. 112–34.

Ghobrial, Atef. Competition between U.S. and
Foreign Air Carriers: An Econometric Approach. *Int. J. Transport Econ.*, February
1989, *16*(1), pp. 19–33.

_____ **and Birman, Graciela.** A Perspective on
Airline Competition in Less Developed Coun-
tries: An Econometric Approach. **In** *Candemir,
Y., ed.*, 1989, pp. 519–29.

Ghorban, N. National Oil Companies with Reference to the Middle East 1900–73. **In** *Ferrier,
R. W. and Fursenko, A., eds.*, 1989, pp. 17–
27.

Ghosal, Vivek. Market Structures, Price–Cost
Margins, and Unionism: An Empirical Note.
Econ. Letters, 1989, *29*(2), pp. 179–82.

Ghose, A. K. Rural Poverty and Relative Prices
in India. *Cambridge J. Econ.*, June 1989, *13*(2),
pp. 307–31.

**Ghosh, Arabinda; Kolodny, Richard and Lau-
rence, Martin.** In Search of Excellence...for
Whom? *J. Portfol. Manage.*, Spring 1989,
15(3), pp. 56–60.

Ghosh, Atish Rex and Borensztein, Eduardo R.
Foreign Borrowing and Export Promotion Policies. *Int. Monet. Fund Staff Pap.*, December
1989, *36*(4), pp. 904–33.

Ghosh, C. and Woolridge, J. R. Stock-Market
Reaction to Growth-Induced Dividend Cuts:
Are Investors Myopic? *Managerial Dec. Econ.*,
March 1989, *10*(1), pp. 25–35.

Ghosh, Damayanti. Maximum Likelihood Estimation of the Dynamic Shock-Error Model.
J. Econometrics, May 1989, *41*(1), pp. 121–43.

_____. A Monte Carlo Study of the Maximum
Likelihood Estimator of a Dynamic Shock-Error Model. *J. Quant. Econ.*, January 1989, *5*(1),
pp. 97–126.

Ghosh, Malay and Sen, Pranab K. Median Unbiasedness and Pitman Closeness. *J. Amer.
Statist. Assoc.*, December 1989, *84*(408), pp.
1089–91.

Ghosh, S.; Lall, Sanjaya and Ray, S. The Determinants and Promotion of South–South Trade
in Manufactured Products. **In** *Ventura-Dias,
V., ed.*, 1989, pp. 131–64.

Ghosh, Sukesh K. Currency Substitution and Demand for Money in Canada: Further Evidence.
J. Macroecon., Winter 1989, *11*(1), pp. 81–93.

Ghuman, B. S. A Planning Model for Punjab in
Consistency Framework. *Indian Econ. Rev.*,
Jan.–June 1989, *24*(1), pp. 101–23.

Ghysels, Eric and David, Jean-François. Y a-t-il
des biais systématiques dans les annonces budgétaires canadiennes? (With English summary.) *Can. Public Policy*, September 1989,
15(3), pp. 313–21.

Giacomino, Don E. and Mielke, David E. Learning Styles of Public Accountants: Measurement
and Applicability to Practice Management. **In**
Schwartz, B. N., ed., 1989, pp. 241–56.

**Giammarino, Ronald; Schwartz, Eduardo S. and
Zechner, Josef.** Market Valuation of Bank As-
sets and Deposit Insurance in Canada. *Can.
J. Econ.*, February 1989, *22*(1), pp. 109–27.

Giannaros, D. and Kolluri, Bharat R. The Impact
of Budget Deficits on Real Interest Rates: An
International Empirical Investigation. *Int.
Econ. J.*, Summer 1989, *3*(2), pp. 17–25.

Giannias, Dimitrios A. Consumer Benefit from

Air Quality Improvements. *Appl. Econ.*, August 1989, *21*(8), pp. 1099–1108.

Giannopoulos, G. A. Cooperation in the Transport Field: The European Experience. In *Candemir, Y., ed.*, 1989, pp. 39–52.

Giap, The Siauw. Socio-economic Role of the Chinese in Indonesia, 1820–1940. In *Maddison, A. and Prince, G., eds.*, 1989, pp. 159–83.

Giarratani, Frank and Houston, David B. Structural Change and Economic Policy in a Declining Metropolitan Region: Implications of the Pittsburgh Experience. *Urban Stud.*, December 1989, *26*(6), pp. 549–58.

Giavazzi, Francesco. The European Monetary System: Lessons from Europe and Perspectives in Europe. *Econ. Soc. Rev.*, January 1989, *20*(2), pp. 73–90.

_____. The Exchange Rate Question in Europe. In *Bryant, R. C., et al., eds.*, 1989, pp. 283–304.

_____ and Giovannini, Alberto. Monetary Policy Interactions under Managed Exchange Rates. *Economica*, May 1989, *56*(222), pp. 199–213.

_____ and Spaventa, Luigi. Italy: The Real Effects of Inflation and Disinflation. *Econ. Policy: A Europ. Forum*, April 1989, (8), pp. 133–71.

Gibbons, Jean D. and Fish, Mary. A Comparison of the Publications of Female and Male Economists. *J. Econ. Educ.*, Winter 1989, *20*(1), pp. 93–105.

Gibbons, Kenneth M. Toward an Attitudinal Definition of Corruption. In *Heidenheimer, A. J.; Johnston, M. and LeVine, V. T., eds.*, 1989, pp. 165–71.

_____. Variations in Attitudes toward Corruption in Canada. In *Heidenheimer, A. J.; Johnston, M. and LeVine, V. T., eds.*, 1989, pp. 763–80.

Gibbons, Michael and Metcalfe, J. S. Technology, Variety and Organization: A Systematic Perspective on the Competitive Process. In *Rosenbloom, R. S. and Burgelman, R. A., eds.*, 1989, pp. 153–93.

Gibbons, Michael R. On the Volatility of Bond Prices. *Carnegie–Rochester Conf. Ser. Public Policy*, Autumn 1989, *31*, pp. 139–75.

_____; Litzenberger, Robert H. and Breeden, Douglas T. Empirical Tests of the Consumption-Oriented CAPM. *J. Finance*, June 1989, *44*(2), pp. 231–62.

_____; Ross, Stephen A. and Shanken, Jay. A Test of the Efficiency of a Given Portfolio. *Econometrica*, September 1989, *57*(5), pp. 1121–52.

Gibbons, Robert and Farrell, Joseph. Cheap Talk Can Matter in Bargaining. *J. Econ. Theory*, June 1989, *48*(1), pp. 221–37.

_____ and Farrell, Joseph. Cheap Talk with Two Audiences. *Amer. Econ. Rev.*, December 1989, *79*(5), pp. 1214–23.

Gibbs, David C. Government Policy and Industrial Change: An Overview. In *Gibbs, D., ed.*, 1989, pp. 1–20.

Gibbs, Stephen; Boyle, Phelim P. and Evnine, Jeremy. Numerical Evaluation of Multivariate

Contingent Claims. *Rev. Financial Stud.*, 1989, *2*(2), pp. 241–50.

Gibert, Patrick. L'analyse de politique. (With English summary.) *Revue Écon. Politique*, March–April 1989, *99*(2), pp. 355–92.

Gibson, Heather D. and Thirlwall, A. P. An International Comparison of the Causes of Changes in the Debt Service Ratio 1980–1985. *Banca Naz. Lavoro Quart. Rev.*, March 1989, (168), pp. 73–95.

_____ and Thirlwall, A. P. Errata Corrige [An International Comparison of the Causes of Changes in the Debt Service Ratio 1980–1985]. *Banca Naz. Lavoro Quart. Rev.*, June 1989, (169), pp. 245.

Gibson, L. J. and Stimson, R. J. The United States and Australia: Observations and Speculations about Two Mature Economies. In *Gibson, L. J. and Stimson, R. J., eds.*, 1989, pp. 1–6.

Gibson, Thomas H. Limitations on the Foreign Tax Credit: United States. *Bull. Int. Fiscal Doc.*, October 1989, *43*(10), pp. 423–45.

Gicquiau, Hervé. Portrait of the Sixty-eight Soviet Enterprises with Access to the International Market. *Soviet E. Europ. Foreign Trade*, Fall 1989, *25*(3), pp. 9–67.

Giddens, Anthony. A Reply to My Critics. In *Held, D. and Thompson, J. B., eds.*, 1989, pp. 249–301.

Gideonse, Sarah K. and Meyers, William R. Why the Family Support Act Will Fail. *Challenge*, Sept.–Oct. 1989, *32*(5), pp. 33–39.

Giersch, Herbert. An Employment Policy without Inflation. In *Peacock, A. and Willgerodt, H., eds. (II)*, 1989, *1972*, pp. 208–18.

Gies, David L. and McAdam, Terry W. Managing Expectations: What Effective Board Members Ought to Expect from Nonprofit Organizations. In *Herman, R. D. and Van Til, J., eds.*, 1989, pp. 77–88.

Giffin, Phillip E.; Hutchinson, E. Bruce and Kushner, Joseph W. The Conventional Wisdom about Cross-Haul. *Eastern Econ. J.*, Jan.–March 1989, *15*(1), pp. 29–34.

Gifford, Roger M. Exploiting the Fertilizer Effect of Increasing Atmospheric Carbon Dioxide. In *Oram, P. A., et al.*, 1989, pp. 477–87.

Giglio, Joseph M. Infrastructure in Trouble. In *Matzer, J., Jr., ed.*, 1989, *1988*, pp. 13–18.

de Gijsel, Peter. On the Role of General Equilibrium Theory in Walras's Theory of a Just Society. In *Walker, D. A., ed.*, 1989, pp. 133–44.

Gil-Diaz, Francisco. Mexico's Debt Burden. In *Edwards, S. and Larrain, F., eds.*, 1989, pp. 270–91.

Gilad, B.; Kaish, S. and Ronen, Joshua. Information, Search, and Entrepreneurship: A Pilot Study. *J. Behav. Econ.*, Fall 1989, *18*(3), pp. 217–35.

Gilbert, Christopher L. Economic Theory and Econometric Models. *Econ. Soc. Rev.*, October 1989, *21*(1), pp. 1–25.

_____. The Impact of Exchange Rates and Developing Country Debt on Commodity Prices. *Econ. J.*, September 1989, *99*(397), pp. 773–84.

_____. LSE and the British Approach to Time Series Econometrics. In *de Marchi, N. and Gilbert, C., eds.*, 1989, pp. 108–28.

_____. LSE and the British Approach to Time Series Econometrics. *Oxford Econ. Pap.*, January 1989, *41*(1), pp. 108–28.

_____ and de Marchi, Neil. History and Methodology of Econometrics: Introduction. *Oxford Econ. Pap.*, January 1989, *41*(1), pp. 1–11.

_____ and de Marchi, Neil. History and Methodology of Econometrics: Introduction. In *de Marchi, N. and Gilbert, C., eds.*, 1989, pp. 1–11.

_____; Powell, Andrew and Anderson, Ronald W. Securitization and Commodity Contingency in International Lending. *Amer. J. Agr. Econ.*, May 1989, *71*(2), pp. 523–30.

Gilbert, R. Alton. Payments System Risk: What Is It and What Will Happen if We Try to Reduce It? *Fed. Res. Bank St. Louis Rev.*, Jan.–Feb. 1989, *71*(1), pp. 3–17.

_____ and Dwyer, Gerald P., Jr. Bank Runs and Private Remedies. *Fed. Res. Bank St. Louis Rev.*, May–June 1989, *71*(3), pp. 43–61.

_____ and Kochin, Levis A. Local Economic Effects of Bank Failures. *J. Finan. Services Res.*, December 1989, *3*(4), pp. 333–45.

Gilbert, Richard J. Mobility Barriers and the Value of Incumbency. In *Schmalensee, R. and Willig, R. D., eds., Vol. 1*, 1989, pp. 475–535.

_____. The Role of Potential Competition in Industrial Organization. *J. Econ. Perspectives*, Summer 1989, *3*(3), pp. 107–27.

Gilboa, Itzhak. Expectation and Variation in Multi-period Decisions. *Econometrica*, September 1989, *57*(5), pp. 1153–69.

_____ and Samet, Dov. Bounded versus Unbounded Rationality: The Tyranny of the Weak. *Games Econ. Behav.*, September 1989, *1*(3), pp. 213–21.

_____ and Schmeidler, David. Maxmin Expected Utility with Non-unique Prior. *J. Math. Econ.*, 1989, *18*(2), pp. 141–53.

_____ and Zemel, Eitan. Nash and Correlated Equilibria: Some Complexity Considerations. *Games Econ. Behav.*, March 1989, *1*(1), pp. 80–93.

Gilder, George. Let a Billion Flowers Bloom. *Cato J.*, Winter 1989, *8*(3), pp. 669–75.

_____. Liberty is Destiny. In *Crane, E. H. and Boaz, D.*, 1989, pp. 347–55.

Gilderbloom, John I. Socioeconomic Influences on Rentals for U.S. Urban Housing: Assumptions of Open Access to a Perfectly Competitive 'Free Market' Are Confronted with the Facts. *Amer. J. Econ. Sociology*, July 1989, *48*(3), pp. 273–92.

Giles, Anthony. Industrial Relations Theory, the State, and Politics. In *Barbash, J. and Barbash, K., eds.*, 1989, pp. 123–54.

Giles, David E. A. Coefficient Sign Changes When Restricting Regression Models under Instrumental Variables Estimation. *Oxford Bull. Econ. Statist.*, November 1989, *51*(4), pp. 465–67.

_____ and Clarke, Judith A. Preliminary-Test Estimation of the Scale Parameter in a Misspecified Regression Model. *Econ. Letters*, September 1989, *30*(3), pp. 201–05.

_____ and McCann, Ewen. Divisia Monetary Aggregates and the Real User Cost of Money. *J. Quant. Econ.*, January 1989, *5*(1), pp. 127–41.

Giliberto, S. Michael and Houston, Arthur L., Jr. Relocation Opportunities and Mortgage Default. *Amer. Real Estate Urban Econ. Assoc. J.*, Spring 1989, *17*(1), pp. 55–69.

_____ and Thibodeau, Thomas G. Modeling Conventional Residential Mortgage Refinancings. *J. Real Estate Finance Econ.*, December 1989, *2*(4), pp. 285–99.

_____ and Varaiya, Nikhil P. The Winner's Curse and Bidder Competition in Acquisitions: Evidence from Failed Bank Auctions. *J. Finance*, March 1989, *44*(1), pp. 59–75.

Gilje, Paul A. Culture of Conflict: The Impact of Commercialization on New York Workingmen, 1787–1829. In *Pencak, W. and Wright, C. E., eds.*, 1989, pp. 249–70.

Gill, Andrew M. The Role of Discrimination in Determining Occupational Structure. *Ind. Lab. Relat. Rev.*, July 1989, *42*(4), pp. 610–23.

_____ and Long, Stewart. Is There an Immigration Status Wage Differential between Legal and Undocumented Workers? Evidence from the Los Angeles Garment Industry. *Soc. Sci. Quart.*, March 1989, *70*(1), pp. 164–73.

Gill, David. Privatization: Opportunities for Financial Market Development. In *El-Naggar, S., ed.*, 1989, pp. 120–36.

Gill, Harley Leroy and Roberts, David C. New Car Warranty Repair: Theory and Evidence. *Southern Econ. J.*, January 1989, *55*(3), pp. 662–78.

Gilleard, Christopher J. The Achieving Society Revisited: A Further Analysis of the Relation between National Economic Growth and Need Achievement. *J. Econ. Psych.*, March 1989, *10*(1), pp. 21–34.

Gillen, David W.; Oum, Tae Hoon and Tretheway, Michael W. Privatization of Air Canada: Why It Is Necessary in a Deregulated Environment. *Can. Public Policy*, September 1989, *15*(3), pp. 285–99.

Gilles, Christian. Charges as Equilibrium Prices and Asset Bubbles. *J. Math. Econ.*, 1989, *18*(2), pp. 155–67.

Gillespie, A. E.; Thwaites, A. T. and Williams, H. Industrial Dynamics and Policy Debate in the Information Technology Production Industries. In *Gibbs, D., ed.*, 1989, pp. 55–69.

Gillespie, William and Alston, Lee J. Resource Coordination and Transaction Costs: A Framework for Analyzing the Firm/Market Boundary. *J. Econ. Behav. Organ.*, March 1989, *11*(2), pp. 191–212.

Gilliam, Franklin D., Jr. and Whitby, Kenny J. Race, Class, and Attitudes toward Social Welfare Spending: An Ethclass Interpretation. *Soc. Sci. Quart.*, March 1989, *70*(1), pp. 88–100.

Gilligan, Thomas W. and Krehbiel, Keith. Collective Choice without Procedural Commitment. In *Ordeshook, P. C., ed.*, 1989, pp. 295–314.

———; **Marshall, William J. and Weingast, Barry R.** Regulation and the Theory of Legislative Choice: The Interstate Commerce Act of 1887. *J. Law Econ.*, April 1989, *32*(1), pp. 35–61.

Gillingham, Allan and Chiao, Yen-Shong. The Value of Stabilizing Fertilizer under Carry-Over Conditions. *Amer. J. Agr. Econ.*, May 1989, *71*(2), pp. 352–62.

Gilmer, Robert William. Energy Labels and Economic Search: An Example from the Residential Real Estate Market. *Energy Econ.*, July 1989, *11*(3), pp. 213–18.

———; **Keil, Stanley R. and Mack, Richard S.** The Service Sector in a Hierarchy of Rural Places: Potential for Export Activity. *Land Econ.*, August 1989, *65*(3), pp. 217–27.

——— **and Pulsipher, Allan G.** Structural Change in Southern Manufacturing: Expansion in the Tennessee Valley. *Growth Change*, Spring 1989, *20*(2), pp. 62–70.

Gilroy, Bernard Michael. Intra-firm Trade. *J. Econ. Surveys*, 1989, *3*(4), pp. 325–43.

Gilson, Stuart C. Management Turnover and Financial Distress. *J. Finan. Econ.*, December 1989, *25*(2), pp. 241–62.

Ginglinger, Edith and Levasseur, Michel. Déductibilité des dividendes versés aux actions nouvelles, décisions de financement et valeur le la firme. (Tax Deductible Dividends, Financing Decisions and the Value of the Firm. With English summary.) *Écon. Societes*, January 1989, *23*(1), pp. 73–84.

van Ginneken, Wouter and van der Hoeven, Rolph. Industrialisation, Employment and Earnings (1950–87): An International Survey. *Int. Lab. Rev.*, 1989, *128*(5), pp. 571–99.

Ginsberg, Roy H. US–EC Relations. In *Lodge, J., ed.*, 1989, pp. 256–78.

Ginsburgh, Victor and Kiekens, Jean-Pierre. A Note on the Computation of the Shadow Wage Rate in an Autarkic Agricultural Environment. *Europ. Rev. Agr. Econ.*, 1989, *16*(1), pp. 137–44.

——— **and Vanhamme, Geneviève.** Price Differences in the EC Car Market: Some Further Results. *Ann. Écon. Statist.*, July–Dec. 1989, (15–16), pp. 137–49.

Gintis, Herbert. Financial Markets and the Democratic Enterprise. In *Drago, R. and Perlman, R., eds.*, 1989, pp. 155–76.

———. Financial Markets and the Political Structure of the Enterprise. *J. Econ. Behav. Organ.*, May 1989, *11*(3), pp. 311–22.

Ginzberg, Eli. How to Think about Health Care for the Elderly. In *Eisdorfer, C.; Kessler, D. A. and Spector, A. N., eds.*, 1989, pp. 451–66.

Giordano, James N. A Trucker's Dilemma: Managerial Behavior under an Operating-Ratio Standard. *Managerial Dec. Econ.*, September 1989, *10*(3), pp. 241–51.

Giordano, Robert M. Foreign Financing of the Federal Budget Deficit: Myths and Realities. In *Kaushik, S. K., ed.*, 1989, pp. 113–25.

Giordano, Rosanna and Veall, Michael R. A Note on Log–Log Regressions with Dummy Variables: Why Units Matter. *Oxford Bull. Econ. Statist.*, February 1989, *51*(1), pp. 95–96.

Giorgi, Giovanni Maria and Pallini, Andrea. Upper Bounds on Gini Index: A Measure for Geometric Comparison. *Econ. Notes*, 1989, (2), pp. 282–86.

Giovannetti, Giorgia. Aggregate Imports and Expenditure Components in Italy: An Econometric Analysis. *Appl. Econ.*, July 1989, *21*(7), pp. 957–71.

Giovannini, Alberto. Capital Taxation: National Tax Systems versus the European Capital Market. *Econ. Policy: A Europ. Forum*, October 1989, (9), pp. 345–86.

———. The European Monetary Union: An Agnostic Evaluation: Comment. In *Bryant, R. C., et al., eds.*, 1989, pp. 340–42.

———. Export Prices and Exchange Rates: An Industry Approach: Comment. In *Feenstra, R. C., ed.*, 1989, pp. 206–10.

———. How Do Fixed-Exchange-Rate Regimes Work? Evidence from the Gold Standard, Bretton Woods and the EMS. In *Miller, M.; Eichengreen, B. and Portes, R., eds.*, 1989, pp. 13–41.

———. Symposium on Europe 1992: Comments. *Brookings Pap. Econ. Act.*, 1989, (2), pp. 363–68.

———. The Tastes of European Central Bankers: Discussion. In *De Cecco, M. and Giovannini, A., eds.*, 1989, pp. 191–94.

———. Uncertainty and Liquidity. *J. Monet. Econ.*, March 1989, *23*(2), pp. 239–58.

——— **and de Cecco, Marcello.** Does Europe Need Its Own Central Bank? In *De Cecco, M. and Giovannini, A., eds.*, 1989, pp. 1–12.

——— **and Giavazzi, Francesco.** Monetary Policy Interactions under Managed Exchange Rates. *Economica*, May 1989, *56*(222), pp. 199–213.

——— **and Jorion, Philippe.** The Time Variation of Risk and Return in the Foreign Exchange and Stock Markets. *J. Finance*, June 1989, *44*(2), pp. 307–25.

——— **and Rotemberg, Julio J.** Exchange-Rate Dynamics with Sticky Prices: The Deutsche Mark, 1974–1982. *J. Bus. Econ. Statist.*, April 1989, *7*(2), pp. 169–78.

Giraldo, Germán and Mann, Arthur J. Latin American External Debt Growth: A Current Account Explanatory Model, 1973–1984. *J. Developing Areas*, October 1989, *24*(1), pp. 47–57.

Girardin, Michel and Danthine, Jean-Pierre. Business Cycles in Switzerland: A Comparative Study. *Europ. Econ. Rev.*, January 1989, *33*(1), pp. 31–50.

Girbau, Ramón and Enrich, Enric. International Tax Aspects of Philanthropic and Other Nonprofit Organisations: Spain. *Bull. Int. Fiscal Doc.*, December 1989, *43*(12), pp. 576–78.

Giroux, Gary. Monopoly Power and Monitoring:

A Test Using the Gonzalez and Mehay Model. *Public Choice*, October 1989, *63*(1), pp. 73–78.

Girvan, Norman P. Technological Change and the Caribbean: Formulating Strategic Responses. *Soc. Econ. Stud.*, June 1989, *38*(2), pp. 111–35.

Gisser, Micha. Price Leadership and Welfare Losses in U.S. Manufacturing: Reply. *Amer. Econ. Rev.*, June 1989, *79*(3), pp. 610–13.

_____ **and Sass, Tim R.** Agency Cost, Firm Size, and Exclusive Dealing. *J. Law Econ.*, Part 1, October 1989, *32*(2), pp. 381–400.

Gitelman, Zvi and DiFranceisco, Wayne. Soviet Political Culture and Modes of Covert Influence. In *Heidenheimer, A. J.; Johnston, M. and LeVine, V. T., eds.*, 1989, *1984*, pp. 467–88.

Giuliano, G. Research Policy and Review 27. New Directions for Understanding Transportation and Land Use. *Environ. Planning A*, February 1989, *21*(2), pp. 145–59.

Givon, Moshe. Taste Tests: Changing the Rules to Improve the Game. *Marketing Sci.*, Summer 1989, *8*(3), pp. 281–90.

Gjelsvik, Eystein and Dahl, Carol. Simulating Norwegian Troll Gas Prospects in a Competitive Spatial Model. *Resources & Energy*, March 1989, *11*(1), pp. 35–63.

Glachant, Jean-Michel. Maurice Allais et la fondation d'une seconde école française de tarification rationnelle des entreprises publiques. (Maurice Allais and the Founding of the Second French School of Rational Pricing in Public Enterprises. With English summary.) *Écon. Societes*, June 1989, *23*(6), pp. 109–40.

Glade, William. Privatization in Rent-Seeking Societies. *World Devel.*, May 1989, *17*(5), pp. 673–82.

Gladwin, Christina H. and McMillan, Della. Is a Turnaround in Africa Possible without Helping African Women to Farm? *Econ. Devel. Cult. Change*, January 1989, *37*(2), pp. 345–69.

Glaessner, Gert-Joachim. Technological Transformation and Educational Policy. In *Rueschemeyer, M. and Lemke, C., eds.*, 1989, pp. 77–94.

Glahe, Fred and Vorhies, Frank. Liberty and Development in Africa. *S. Afr. J. Econ.*, September 1989, *57*(3), pp. 279–91.

_____ **and Vorhies, Frank.** Religion, Liberty and Economic Development: An Empirical Investigation. *Public Choice*, September 1989, *62*(3), pp. 201–15.

Glance, S. and Goddard, Ellen W. Demand for Fats and Oils in Canada, United States and Japan. *Can. J. Agr. Econ.*, November 1989, *37*(3), pp. 421–43.

Glandon, Gerald L.; Counte, Michael A. and Homan, Rick K. Perceived Risk: The Link to Plan Selection and Future Utilization. *J. Risk Ins.*, March 1989, *56*(1), pp. 67–82.

Glanz, Milton P. and Kerns, Wilmer L. Private Social Welfare Expenditures, 1972–87. *Soc. Sec. Bull.*, November 1989, *52*(11), pp. 18–26.

Glascock, John L. and Darrat, Ali F. Real Estate Returns, Money and Fiscal Deficits: Is the Real Estate Market Efficient? *J. Real Estate Finance Econ.*, September 1989, *2*(3), pp. 197–208.

_____ **and Karafiath, Imre.** Intra-industry Effects of a Regulatory Shift: Capital Market Evidence from Penn Square. *Financial Rev.*, February 1989, *24*(1), pp. 123–34.

Glasmeier, A. and Borchard, G. Research Policy and Review 31. From Branch Plants to Back Offices: Prospects for Rural Services Growth. *Environ. Planning A*, December 1989, *21*(12), pp. 1565–83.

Glasner, David. On Some Classical Monetary Controversies. *Hist. Polit. Econ.*, Summer 1989, *21*(2), pp. 201–29.

Glass, J. C. and McKillop, D. G. A Multi-product Multi-input Cost Function Analysis of Northern Ireland Agriculture, 1955–85. *J. Agr. Econ.*, January 1989, *40*(1), pp. 57–70.

Glassman, Marc B.; Singer, Eleanor and Frankel, Martin R. The Effect of Interviewer Characteristics and Expectations on Response. In *Singer, E. and Presser, S., eds.*, 1989, *1983*, pp. 272–87.

Glasziou, P. and Donaldson, C. Cost Utility Analysis: The Compatibility of Measurement Techniques and the Measurement of Utility through Time: Commentary. In *Smith, C. S., ed.*, 1989, pp. 61–63.

Glauber, Joseph; Helmberger, Peter and Miranda, Mario. Four Approaches to Commodity Market Stabilization: A Comparative Analysis. *Amer. J. Agr. Econ.*, May 1989, *71*(2), pp. 326–37.

Glaude, Michel and Gombert, Monique. Household Income by Socio-occupational Category. *Statist. J.*, 1989, *6*(2), pp. 127–45.

Glazer, Amihai. Politics and the Choice of Durability. *Amer. Econ. Rev.*, December 1989, *79*(5), pp. 1207–13.

_____. The Social Discount Rate under Majority Voting. *Public Finance*, 1989, *44*(3), pp. 384–93.

_____ **and Grofman, Bernard.** Why Representatives Are Ideologists though Voters Are Not. *Public Choice*, April 1989, *61*(1), pp. 29–39.

Glazer, Jacob and Ma, Ching-To Albert. Efficient Allocation of a "Prize"—King Solomon's Dilemma. *Games Econ. Behav.*, September 1989, *1*(3), pp. 222–33.

Glazer, Rashi; Steckel, Joel H. and Winer, Russell S. The Formation of Key Marketing Variable Expectations and Their Impact on Firm Performance: Some Experimental Evidence. *Marketing Sci.*, Winter 1989, *8*(1), pp. 18–34.

Gleason, Alan H. The Level of Living in Japan and the United States: A Long-term International Comparison. *Econ. Devel. Cult. Change*, January 1989, *37*(2), pp. 261–84.

Gleason, J. E. and Kauffman, Harold E. Climatic Vulnerability of Major Food Crops: Soybeans. In *Oram, P. A., et al.*, 1989, pp. 155–64.

Gleeson, Victor and Dragun, Andrew K. From Water Law to Transferability in New South

Wales. *Natural Res. J.*, Summer 1989, *29*(3), pp. 645–61.

Gleicher, David. Labor Specialization and the Transformation Problem. *Rev. Radical Polit. Econ.*, 1989, *21*(1–2), pp. 75–95.

————. Wage Rate Differentials in Capitalist Economies. *Sci. Society*, Spring 1989, *53*(1), pp. 29–46.

Gleick, Peter H. Global Climatic Change, Water Resources, and Food Security. In *Oram, P. A., et al.*, 1989, pp. 415–27.

————. Global Environmental Issues and International Politics. In *Rotblat, J. and Goldanskii, V. I., eds.*, 1989, pp. 204–17.

———— **and Frederick, Kenneth D.** Water Resources and Climate Change. In *Rosenberg, N. J., et al., eds.*, 1989, pp. 133–43.

Glenday, Graham. Personal Savings and Portfolio Composition: Changing Tax Incentives. In *Mintz, J. and Whalley, J., eds.*, 1989, pp. 142–82.

————. Tax Expenditure Budget from Inside the Government: Comment. In *Bruce, N., ed.*, 1989, pp. 273–77.

Glennon, Dennis. Estimating the Income, Price, and Interest Elasticities of Housing Demand. *J. Urban Econ.*, March 1989, *25*(2), pp. 219–29.

————. A Note on the Long-run Effects of Bond Financed Government Expenditures. *Public Finance*, 1989, *44*(3), pp. 394–405.

————; **McCabe, James and Lane, Julia.** Measures of Local Business Climate: Alternative Approaches. *Reg. Sci. Persp.*, 1989, *19*(1), pp. 89–106.

Gleske, Leonhard. Monetary Policy Issues in the 1990s: Overview: Central Bank Perspectives. In *Federal Reserve Bank of Kansas City*, 1989, pp. 299–307.

Glete, Jan. Long-term Firm Growth and Ownership Organization: A Study of Business Histories. *J. Econ. Behav. Organ.*, December 1989, *12*(3), pp. 329–51.

Glezen, G. William and Wilson, Arlette C. The Effect of the Length of Prediction Interval on Prediction Error of Regression Models Used in Analytical Review. In *Schwartz, B. N., ed.*, 1989, pp. 173–86.

Glick, Mark and Brenner, Robert. The Regulation Approach to the History of Capitalism. *Écon. Societes*, November 1989, *23*(11), pp. 89–131.

Glick, Reuven and Hutchison, Michael M. Exchange Rates and Monetary Policy. *Fed. Res. Bank San Francisco Econ. Rev.*, Spring 1989, (2), pp. 17–29.

Glickman, Norman J. International Trade, Investment, and American Cities and Regions. In *[Adams, F. G.]*, 1989, pp. 227–47.

Glied, Sherry; Mathewson, Frank and Carr, Jack L. Unlimited Liability and Free Banking in Scotland: A Note. *J. Econ. Hist.*, December 1989, *49*(4), pp. 974–78.

Gligorov, Kiro. The Economic System of Yugoslavia. In *Macesich, G., ed.*, 1989, pp. 1–11.

Globerman, Steven. Regulation of Multinationals

in Canada. In *Rugman, A. M., ed.*, 1989, pp. 162–77.

Glombowski, Jörg and Krüger, Michael. Changes of Labour Productivity Growth in a Model of Cyclical Growth. *Écon. Societes*, March 1989, *23*(3), pp. 201–17.

Glosten, Lawrence R. Insider Trading, Liquidity, and the Role of the Monopolist Specialist. *J. Bus.*, April 1989, *62*(2), pp. 211–35.

————; **Jagannathan, Ravi and Breen, William.** Economic Significance of Predictable Variations in Stock Index Returns. *J. Finance*, December 1989, *44*(5), pp. 1177–89.

Glover, David J. Special Issue on Contract Farming and Smallholder Outgrower Schemes in Eastern and Southern Africa: Preface. *Eastern Afr. Econ. Rev.*, Special Issue, August 1989, pp. 1–3.

————. Special Issue on Contract Farming and Smallholder Outgrower Schemes in Eastern and Southern Africa: Conclusions. *Eastern Afr. Econ. Rev.*, Special Issue, August 1989, pp. 108–16.

Glover, Keith. A Tutorial on Hankel-Norm Approximation. In *Willems, J. C., ed.*, 1989, pp. 26–48.

Glover, Michael and Albu, Martin. The Regulation of Road Freight Transport in Great Britain. In *Moses, L. N. and Savage, I., eds.*, 1989, pp. 289–99.

Glyer, J. David; Adams, Richard M. and Connor, Jeffery D. Some Further Evidence on the Derived Demand for Irrigation Electricity: A Dual Cost Function Approach. *Water Resources Res.*, July 1989, *25*(7), pp. 1461–68.

Glytsos, Nicholas P. and Katseli, Louka T. Theoretical and Empirical Determinants of International Labour Mobility: A Greek–German Perspective. In *Gordon, I. and Thirlwall, A. P., eds.*, 1989, pp. 95–115.

Godard, Xavier. Experience of International Cooperation in Transport Research in Developing Countries. What Lessons? In *Candemir, Y., ed.*, 1989, pp. 187–95.

Goddard, Ellen W. and Amuah, Alex K. The Demand for Canadian Fats and Oils: A Case Study of Advertising Effectiveness. *Amer. J. Agr. Econ.*, August 1989, *71*(3), pp. 741–49.

———— **and Glance, S.** Demand for Fats and Oils in Canada, United States and Japan. *Can. J. Agr. Econ.*, November 1989, *37*(3), pp. 421–43.

Goddard, F. O. Harrod-Neutral Economic Growth with Hicks-Biased Technological Progress. In *Wood, J. C. and Woods, R. N., eds., Vol. 2*, 1989, *1970*, pp. 92–105.

Goddard, John A.; Bowers, John K. and Dobson, Stephen M. The Property Market and Industrial Location. *Scot. J. Polit. Econ.*, February 1989, *36*(1), pp. 1–18.

Goddeeris, John H. Modeling Interest-Group Campaign Contributions. *Public Finance Quart.*, April 1989, *17*(2), pp. 158–84.

————; **Young, James C. and Fisher, Ronald C.** Participation in Tax Amnesties: The Individual

Income Tax. *Nat. Tax J.*, March 1989, *42*(1), pp. 15–27.

Goddu, André. "Eurosclerosis" and the Political Integration of Western Europe—A Historical Perspective. In *Rueschhoff, N. and Schaum, K., eds.*, 1989, pp. 21–39.

Godfrey, Christine. Price Regulation. In *Robinson, D.; Maynard, A. and Chester, R., eds.*, 1989, pp. 110–30.

Godfrey, James T. and Wardlow, Penelope S. Pers Reports and Users' Information Needs. In *Chan, J. L. and Patton, J. M., eds.*, 1989, pp. 71–97.

———; **Wurst, John and Neter, John.** Efficiency of Sieve Sampling in Auditing. *J. Bus. Econ. Statist.*, April 1989, *7*(2), pp. 199–205.

Godfrey, L. G. and Burke, S. P. Some Results on the Finite Sample Significance Levels of Instrumental Variable Tests for Non-nested Models. *Econ. Letters*, December 1989, *31*(4), pp. 343–47.

Godley, Wynne and Anyadike-Danes, Michael. Real Wages and Employment: A Sceptical View of Some Recent Empirical Work. *Manchester Sch. Econ. Soc. Stud.*, June 1989, *57*(2), pp. 172–87.

——— **and Anyadike-Danes, Michael.** Real Wages and Employment: Response. *Manchester Sch. Econ. Soc. Stud.*, September 1989, *57*(3), pp. 285.

——— **and Zezza, Gennaro.** Foreign Debt, Foreign Trade and Living Conditions, with Special Reference to Denmark. *Nationaløkon. Tidsskr.*, 1989, *127*(2), pp. 229–35.

Godwin, Michael. Compliance with Excise Taxes and VAT: Differences in Administrative Expectations. In *[Sandford, C.]*, 1989, pp. 46–54.

Godwin, Stephen R. and Peterson, George E. Developing a Comprehensive Condition Assessment System. In *Matzer, J., Jr., ed.*, 1989, *1984*, pp. 65–73.

Godyn, Dirk L.; Johnston, Brian G. and Brennan, John P. An Economic Framework for Evaluating New Wheat Varieties. *Rev. Marketing Agr. Econ.*, April, Aug., Dec. 1989, *57*(1–2–3), pp. 75–92.

Goebel, W.; Cooper, P. J. M. and Harris, Hazel C. Climatic Variability and Food Production in West Asia and North Africa. In *Oram, P. A., et al.*, 1989, pp. 69–83.

Goecke, O.; Korte, Bernhard and Lovász, L. Examples and Algorithmic Properties of Greedoids. In *Simeone, B., ed.*, 1989, pp. 113–61.

Goeckel, Robert F. Church and Society in the GDR. In *Rueschemeyer, M. and Lemke, C., eds.*, 1989, pp. 210–27.

Goel, Rajeev K. and Rich, Daniel P. On the Economic Incentives for Taking Bribes. *Public Choice*, June 1989, *61*(3), pp. 269–75.

Goel, Ratan Lal. International Trade, Protectionism and Third World Debt. In *Singer, H. W. and Sharma, S., eds. (I)*, 1989, pp. 79–85.

Goetz, Andrew R.; Brown, Lawrence A. and England, Kim V. L. Location, Social Categories, and Individual Labor Market Experiences in Developing Economies: The Venezuelan

Case. *Int. Reg. Sci. Rev.*, 1989, *12*(1), pp. 1–28.

Goetz, Charles J. and Buchanan, James M. Efficiency Limits of Fiscal Mobility. In *Buchanan, J. M. (II)*, 1989, pp. 246–63.

Goetze, Bernd A. Verification of Confidence and Security Building Measures: Evolution and Future Prospects. In *Altmann, J. and Rotblat, J., eds.*, 1989, pp. 140–50.

Goetze, David and Galderisi, Peter. Explaining Collective Action with Rational Models. *Public Choice*, July 1989, *62*(1), pp. 25–39.

Goff, Brian L. and Tollison, Robert D. The Allocation of Death in the Vietnam War: Reply. *Southern Econ. J.*, April 1989, *55*(4), pp. 1034–35.

Goh, Siew, et al. A Generalized Stochastic Dominance Program for the IBM PC. *Southern J. Agr. Econ.*, December 1989, *21*(2), pp. 175–82.

Goh, Swee C. and deCarufel, André. Perceptions of Managerial Effectiveness: An Experimental Study in Sri Lanka and Implications for Leadership Training. In *Nedd, A., ed.*, 1989, pp. 301–15.

Gohmann, Stephan F. and Spector, Lee C. Test Scrambling and Student Performance. *J. Econ. Educ.*, Summer 1989, *20*(3), pp. 235–38.

Goisis, Gianandrea. Budget Deficit and Interest Rates. *Rivista Int. Sci. Econ. Com.*, Oct.–Nov. 1989, *36*(10–11), pp. 887–903.

———. Disavanzi pubblici e tassi di interesse: Conferme e nuove prospettive. (Public Deficits and Interest Rates: Some Confirmations and New Hypotheses. With English summary.) *Giorn. Econ.*, Nov.–Dec. 1989, *48*(11–12), pp. 521–40.

Gokhberg, Mikhail. Soviet–American Collaboration on Seismic Monitoring. In *Rotblat, J. and Goldanskii, V. I., eds.*, 1989, pp. 22–24.

Golan, Amos. On the Natural Fluctuation of the Economy. *Math. Soc. Sci.*, April 1989, *17*(2), pp. 161–75.

Golan, Lorette; Shechter, Mordechai and Kim, Moshe. Valuing a Public Good: Direct and Indirect Valuation Approaches to the Measurement of the Benefits from Pollution Abatement. In *Folmer, H. and van Ierland, E., eds.*, 1989, pp. 123–37.

Golbe, Devra L.; Gerard, James M. and Blair, Douglas H. Unbundling the Voting Rights and Profit Claims of Common Shares. *J. Polit. Econ.*, April 1989, *97*(2), pp. 420–43.

Gold, Bela. Forces Tending to Reduce Concentration Levels in U.S. Industries. *Managerial Dec. Econ.*, June 1989, *10*(2), pp. 115–19.

Goldar, Bishwanath. Determinants of India's Export Performance in Engineering Products, 1960–79. *Developing Econ.*, March 1989, *27*(1), pp. 3–18.

Goldberg, Lawrence G., et al. Relative Revenue Distribution in the Securities Industry. *Quart. Rev. Econ. Bus.*, Autumn 1989, *29*(3), pp. 86–94.

Goldberg, Michael A.; Helsley, Robert W. and Levi, Maurice D. The Location of International Financial Activity: An Interregional Analysis. *Reg. Stud.*, February 1989, *23*(1), pp. 1–7.

Goldberg, Michael J. The Teamsters' Board of Monitors: An Experiment in Union Reform Litigation. *Labor Hist.*, Fall 1989, *30*(4), pp. 563–84.

Goldberger, Arthur S. Economic and Mechanical Models of Intergenerational Transmission. *Amer. Econ. Rev.*, June 1989, *79*(3), pp. 504–13.

Golden, Bruce L. and Wang, Qiwen. An Alternate Measure of Consistency. In *Golden, B. L.; Wasil, E. A. and Harker, P. T., eds.*, 1989, pp. 68–81.

———; **Wasil, Edward A. and Harker, Patrick T.** The Analytic Hierarchy Process: Applications and Studies: Introduction. In *Golden, B. L.; Wasil, E. A. and Harker, P. T., eds.*, 1989, pp. 1–2.

———; **Wasil, Edward A. and Levy, Doug E.** Applications of the Analytic Hierarchy Process: A Categorized, Annotated Bibliography. In *Golden, B. L.; Wasil, E. A. and Harker, P. T., eds.*, 1989, pp. 37–58.

Goldenberg, David H. Memory and Equilibrium Futures Prices. *J. Futures Markets*, June 1989, *9*(3), pp. 199–213.

Goldfarb, Robert S.; Johnson, Richard L. and Cordes, Joseph J. Design and Implementation of Job Loss Compensation Provisions: Lessons from the Airline Deregulation Experience. *Int. J. Transport Econ.*, February 1989, *16*(1), pp. 35–55.

Goldhaber, Gerald M. and deTurck, Mark A. Effectiveness of Product Warning Labels: Effects of Consumers' Information Processing Objectives. *J. Cons. Aff.*, Summer 1989, *23*(1), pp. 111–26.

Goldin, Claudia. Life-Cycle Labor-Force Participation of Married Women: Historical Evidence and Implications. *J. Lab. Econ.*, January 1989, *7*(1), pp. 20–47.

———. The Wage Effects of Occupational Sex Composition: A Review and New Findings: Discussion. In *Hill, M. A. and Killingsworth, M. R., eds.*, 1989, pp. 83–89.

——— **and Margo, Robert A.** The Poor at Birth: Birth Weights and Infant Mortality at Philadelphia's Almshouse Hospital, 1848–1873. *Exploration Econ. Hist.*, July 1989, *26*(3), pp. 360–79.

——— **and Parsons, Donald O.** Parental Altruism and Self-Interest: Child Labor among Late Nineteenth-Century American Families. *Econ. Inquiry*, October 1989, *27*(4), pp. 637–59.

Goldman, Alan H. Ethical Issues in Proprietary Restrictions on Research Results. In *Weil, V. and Snapper, J. W., eds.*, 1989, pp. 69–82.

Goldman, Fred; Joyce, Theodore J. and Grossman, Michael. An Assessment of the Benefits of Air Pollution Control: The Case of Infant Health. *J. Urban Econ.*, January 1989, *25*(1), pp. 32–51.

Goldman, Howard H. and Taube, Carl A. State Strategies to Restructure Psychiatric Hospitals:

A Selective Review. *Inquiry*, Summer 1989, *26*(2), pp. 146–56.

Goldman, Lawrence. 'An Advanced Liberal': Henry Fawcett, 1833–1884: Introduction. In *Goldman, L., ed.*, 1989, pp. 1–38.

———. The Blind Victorian Henry Fawcett and British Liberalism: Preface. In *Goldman, L., ed.*, 1989, pp. xi–xiv.

———. Henry Fawcett and the Social Science Association: Liberal Politics, Political Economy and the Working Class in Mid-Victorian Britain. In *Goldman, L., ed.*, 1989, pp. 147–79.

Goldman, Marshall I. and Davis, Kathryn W. Gorbachev's Challenge: Economic Reform in the Age of High Technology. *Aussenwirtschaft*, December 1989, *44*(3–4), pp. 385–98.

Goldman, Noreen; Westoff, Charles F. and Moreno, Lorenzo. The Demographic Impact of Changes in Contraceptive Practice in Third World Populations. *Population Devel. Rev.*, March 1989, *15*(1), pp. 91–106.

Goldman, Steven M. and Starr, Ross M. Pairwise, *t*-Wise, and Pareto Optimalities. In *Starr, R. M., ed.*, 1989, *1982*, pp. 99–112.

Goldscheider, Calvin and Goldscheider, Frances K. Ethnicity and the New Family Economy. In *Goldscheider, F. K. and Goldscheider, C., eds.*, 1989, pp. 185–97.

——— **and Goldscheider, Frances K.** The New Family Economy: Residential and Economic Relationships among the Generations. In *Goldscheider, F. K. and Goldscheider, C., eds.*, 1989, pp. 1–16.

——— **and Jones, Mali B.** Living Arrangements among the Older Population. In *Goldscheider, F. K. and Goldscheider, C., eds.*, 1989, pp. 75–91.

Goldscheider, Frances K. Children Leaving Home and the Household Economy. In *Goldscheider, F. K. and Goldscheider, C., eds.*, 1989, pp. 111–25.

——— **and Castleton, Anne.** Are Mormon Families Different? In *Goldscheider, F. K. and Goldscheider, C., eds.*, 1989, pp. 93–109.

——— **and Fisher, Zara.** Household Structure and Living Alone in Israel. In *Goldscheider, F. K. and Goldscheider, C., eds.*, 1989, pp. 148–61.

——— **and Goldscheider, Calvin.** Ethnicity and the New Family Economy. In *Goldscheider, F. K. and Goldscheider, C., eds.*, 1989, pp. 185–97.

——— **and Goldscheider, Calvin.** The New Family Economy: Residential and Economic Relationships among the Generations. In *Goldscheider, F. K. and Goldscheider, C., eds.*, 1989, pp. 1–16.

Goldsmith, Art. Dental Hygienists' Wages: The Role of Human Capital and Institutional Factors. *Quart. Rev. Econ. Bus.*, Summer 1989, *29*(2), pp. 56–67.

Goldsmith, Arthur A. and Lele, Uma J. The Development of National Agricultural Research Capacity: India's Experience with the Rockefeller Foundation and Its Significance for Africa. *Econ. Devel. Cult. Change*, January 1989, 37(2), pp. 305–43.

Goldsmith, William W. Poverty, Isolation and Urban Politics. *Rev. Radical Polit. Econ.*, Fall 1989, 21(3), pp. 91–98.

Goldstein, Harvey A. and Luger, Michael I. Federal Labor Protections and the Privatization of Public Transit. *J. Policy Anal. Manage.*, Spring 1989, 8(2), pp. 229–50.

Goldstein, Henry N. and Haynes, Stephen E. Monetary Policy Activism under Managed-Floating Exchange Rates: A Cross-country Comparison. *Contemp. Policy Issues*, April 1989, 7(2), pp. 27–40.

Goldstein, Judith. The Impact of Ideas on Trade Policy: The Origins of U.S. Agricultural and Manufacturing Policies. *Int. Organ.*, Winter 1989, 43(1), pp. 31–71.

Goldstein, Morris. The International Monetary Fund and the Developing Countries: A Critical Evaluation: A Comment. *Carnegie–Rochester Conf. Ser. Public Policy*, Autumn 1989, 31, pp. 69–75.

_____ **and Frenkel, Jacob A.** The International Monetary System: Developments and Prospects. In *Dorn, J. A. and Niskanen, W. A.*, *eds.*, 1989, 1988, pp. 89–110.

_____; **Masson, Paul R. and Frenkel, Jacob A.** International Dimensions of Monetary Policy: Coordination versus Autonomy. In *Federal Reserve Bank of Kansas City*, 1989, pp. 183–232.

_____; **Masson, Paul R. and Frenkel, Jacob A.** Simulating the Effects of Some Simple Coordinated versus Uncoordinated Policy Rules. In *Bryant, R. C., et al., eds.*, 1989, pp. 203–39.

Goldstein, Nance. Gender and "Post-Industrial" Work in the Microelectronics Industry in Scotland. *Rev. Radical Polit. Econ.*, Fall 1989, 21(3), pp. 64–69.

_____. Silicon Glen: Women and Semiconductor Multinationals. In *Elson, D. and Pearson, R., eds.*, 1989, pp. 111–28.

Goldstein, Richard, et al. Survival Analysis Software on MS/PC-DOS Computers. *J. Appl. Econometrics*, Oct.–Dec. 1989, 4(4), pp. 393–414.

Goldstein, Steven M. and Hartford, Kathleen. Perspectives on the Chinese Communist Revolution: Introduction. In *Hartford, K. and Goldstein, S. M., eds.*, 1989, pp. 3–33.

Goldstein, W. and Flowerdew, R. Geodemographics in Practice: Developments in North America. *Environ. Planning A*, May 1989, 21(5), pp. 605–16.

Goldthwaite, Richard. Processi di urbanizzazione: Interventi degli esperti. (In English.) In *Cavaciocchi, S., ed.*, 1989, pp. 244–47.

Gole, Barbara S. Accounting for Our Infrastructure. In *Matzer, J., Jr., ed.*, 1989, 1988, pp. 61–64.

Golembe, Carter H. Long-term Trends in Bank Regulation. *J. Finan. Services Res.*, September 1989, 2(3), pp. 171–83.

Golinelli, Roberto; Stagni, Anna and Bosi, Paolo. Le origini del debito pubblico e il costo della stabilizzazione. (With English summary.) *Po-litica. Econ.*, December 1989, 5(3), pp. 389–425.

Gollehon, Noel R. and Ogg, Clayton W. Western Irrigation Response to Pumping Costs: A Water Demand Analysis Using Climatic Regions. *Water Resources Res.*, May 1989, 25(5), pp. 767–73.

Gollier, Christian. Flexibilité et discrimination des salaires: Un réexamen à la lumière de la théorie économique du risque. (With English summary.) *Rech. Écon. Louvain*, 1989, 55(3), pp. 245–55.

Gollop, Frank M. Regulatory Failure, Regulatory Reform, and Structural Change in the Electrical Power Industry: Comments. *Brookings Pap. Econ. Act.*, Microeconomics, 1989, pp. 203–07.

Golob, Thomas F. The Causal Influences of Income and Car Ownership on Trip Generation by Mode. *J. Transp. Econ. Policy*, May 1989, 23(2), pp. 141–62.

Golub, Stephen S. Foreign-currency Government Debt, Asset Markets, and the Balance of Payments. *J. Int. Money Finance*, June 1989, 8(2), pp. 285–94.

Golubev, G. The World Climate Impact Studies Programme. In *Oram, P. A., et al.*, 1989, pp. 333–39.

Gombert, Monique and Glaude, Michel. Household Income by Socio-occupational Category. *Statist. J.*, 1989, 6(2), pp. 127–45.

Gomes-Casseres, Benjamin. Ownership Structures of Foreign Subsidiaries: Theory and Evidence. *J. Econ. Behav. Organ.*, January 1989, 11(1), pp. 1–25.

Gomes, Lawrence J. and Islam, Muhammad M. Market Power and Cost of Capital under Uncertainty. *Quart. J. Bus. Econ.*, Autumn 1989, 28(4), pp. 61–76.

Gomez-Mejia, Luis R. and Balkin, David B. Effectiveness of Individual and Aggregate Compensation Strategies. *Ind. Relat.*, Fall 1989, 28(3), pp. 431–45.

Gomez, Rosario. Un modelo de equilibrio general de imposición lineal óptima. (With English summary.) *Invest. Econ.*, September 1989, 13(3), pp. 387–406.

Gomulka, Stanislaw. Gorbachev's Economic Reforms in the Context of the Soviet Political System. In *Gomulka, S.; Ha, Y.-C. and Kim, C.-O., eds.*, 1989, pp. 59–78.

_____. 'Technological Revolution' as an Innovation Superwave in the World Technological Frontier Area. In *Di Matteo, M.; Goodwin, R. M. and Vercelli, A., eds.*, 1989, pp. 16–35.

Gonce, R. A. Comment on the Comparing of the Austrian and Institutionalist Schools of Economic Thought. In *Samuels, W. J., ed. (II)*, 1989, pp. 125–32.

Gondwe, Derrick K. and Griffith, Winston H. Trade Creation and Trade Diversion: A Case Study of MDCs in CARIFTA, 1968–1974. *Soc. Econ. Stud.*, September 1989, 38(3), pp. 149–75.

Gondzio, Jacek and Ruszczynski, Andrzej. A Sensitivity Method for Solving Multistage Stochastic Linear Programming Problems. **In** *Lewandowski, A. and Wierzbicki, A. P., eds.*, 1989, pp. 68–79.

Gönül, Füsun F. Comparison of Hazard Functions with Duration Dependence and Stayer–Mover Structure with an Application to Divorce. *Econ. Letters*, 1989, *30*(1), pp. 31–36.

———. Dynamic Labor Force Participation Decisions of Males in the Presence of Layoffs and Uncertain Job Offers. *J. Human Res.*, Spring 1989, *24*(2), pp. 195–220.

Gonzales, Juan J.; Franz, Lori S. and Reeves, Gary R. The Effect of Decision Maker Characteristics on Group Decision Making. **In** *Lockett, A. G. and Islei, G., eds.*, 1989, pp. 134–42.

Gonzalez, Agustin; Suárez Burguet, Celestino and Fernández Guerrero, Ismael. Spanish External Trade and EEC Preferences. **In** *Yannopoulos, G. N., ed.*, 1989, pp. 144–68.

González Echevarría, Roberto. Cuban Criticism and Literature: A Reply to Smith. **In** *Mesa-Lago, C., ed.*, 1989, pp. 101–06.

Gonzalez, Rodolfo A.; Folsom, Roger Nils and Mehay, Stephen L. Bureaucracy, Publicness and Local Government Expenditures Revisited: Comment. *Public Choice*, July 1989, *62*(1), pp. 71–77.

González-Vega, Claudio. Debt, Stabilization, and Liberalization in Costa Rica: Political Economy Responses to a Fiscal Crisis. **In** *Brock, P. L.; Connolly, M. B. and González-Vega, C., eds.*, 1989, pp. 197–209.

Gonzalez, Yvette. The Best Equitable Defense Is a Good Offense. *Natural Res. J.*, Summer 1989, *29*(3), pp. 849–59.

Gonzi, Marco. The New Palgrave on Causality: A Critical Appraisal. *Int. J. Transport Econ.*, February 1989, *16*(1), pp. 91–96.

Good, Charles M. AIDS and Ethnomedicine in Africa: International Cooperation for Disease Control. **In** *Reich, M. R. and Marui, E., eds.*, 1989, pp. 264–94.

Goode, Frank M. Rural Industrial Location versus Rural Industrial Growth. *Ann. Reg. Sci.*, 1989, *23*(1), pp. 59–68.

Goode, Richard. Forward-Shifting of the Corporate Tax in the Presence of Competing Imports: A Reply. *Public Finance*, 1989, *44*(2), pp. 327–28.

——— **and Kamarck, Andrew M.** The Role of the Economist in Government: An International Perspective: The International Monetary Fund and the World Bank. **In** *Pechman, J. A., ed.*, 1989, pp. 231–54.

Goodhart, Charles A. E. The Conduct of Monetary Policy. *Econ. J.*, June 1989, *99*(396), pp. 293–346.

———. The Development of Monetary Theory. **In** *Llewellyn, D. T., ed.*, 1989, pp. 25–36.

———. The Establishment of a Central Bank: Italy in the 19th Century: Discussion. **In** *De Cecco, M. and Giovannini, A., eds.*, 1989, pp. 280–85.

———. Has Moore Become Too Horizontal? *J.*

Post Keynesian Econ., Fall 1989, *12*(1), pp. 29–34.

———. Purchasing Power Parity as a Monetary Standard: Comment. **In** *Hamouda, O. F.; Rowley, R. and Wolf, B. M., eds.*, 1989, pp. 65–67.

———. A Return Visit to the International Debt Problem of the LDCs: Comment. **In** *Hamouda, O. F.; Rowley, R. and Wolf, B. M., eds.*, 1989, pp. 173.

Goodman, Allen C. Estimation of Offset and Income Effects on the Demand for Mental Health Treatment. *Inquiry*, Summer 1989, *26*(2), pp. 235–48.

———. Identifying Willingness-to-Pay for Heterogeneous Goods with Factorial Survey Methods. *J. Environ. Econ. Manage.*, January 1989, *16*(1), pp. 58–79.

Goodman, David and Redclift, Michael. The International Farm Crisis: Introduction. **In** *Goodman, D. and Redclift, M., eds.*, 1989, pp. 1–22.

Goodman, David S. G. Political Perspectives. **In** *Goodman, D. S. G., ed.*, 1989, pp. 20–37.

Goodman, Edward. The Political Economy of the Small Firm in Italy: Introduction. **In** *Goodman, E. and Bamford, J., eds.*, 1989, pp. 1–30.

Goodman, John. Industrial Relations and Restructuring in Manufacturing: Three Case Studies in the United Kingdom. *Int. Lab. Rev.*, 1989, *128*(5), pp. 601–20.

Goodman, Laurie S. and Cohen, Alan H. Pay-in-Kind Debentures: An Innovation. *J. Portfol. Manage.*, Winter 1989, *15*(2), pp. 9–16.

Goodman, Margaret. Preserving Privilege in Yucatan. **In** *Heidenheimer, A. J.; Johnston, M. and LeVine, V. T., eds.*, 1989, *1974*, pp. 639–58.

Goodnow, Jacqueline; Burns, Ailsa and Russell, Graeme. Australian Families: Pictures and Interpretations. **In** *Hancock, K., ed.*, 1989, pp. 23–43.

Goodspeed, Timothy J. A Re-examination of the Use of Ability to Pay Taxes by Local Governments. *J. Public Econ.*, April 1989, *38*(3), pp. 319–42.

Goodstein, Eban. Landownership, Development, and Poverty in Southern Appalachia. *J. Developing Areas*, July 1989, *23*(4), pp. 519–33.

Goodwin, Cathy and Verhage, Bronislaw J. Role Perceptions of Services: A Cross-cultural Comparison with Behavioral Implications. *J. Econ. Psych.*, 1989, *10*(4), pp. 543–58.

Goodwin, Craufurd D. Doing Good and Spreading the Gospel (Economic) **In** *Colander, D. C. and Coats, A. W., eds.*, 1989, pp. 157–73.

Goodwin, Mark and Duncan, Simon. The Crisis of Local Government: Uneven Development and the Thatcher Administrations. **In** *Mohan, J., ed.*, 1989, pp. 69–86.

Goodwin, Richard M. Joan Robinson—Passionate Seeker after Truth. **In** *Feiwel, G. R., ed. (II)*, 1989, pp. 916–17.

———. Kalecki's Economic Dynamics: A Personal View. **In** *Sebastiani, M., ed.*, 1989, pp. 249–51.

_____. Swinging along the Autostrada: Cyclical Fluctuations along the von Neumann Ray. In *Dore, M.; Chakravarty, S. and Goodwin, R., eds.*, 1989, pp. 125–40.

_____. Towards a Theory of Long Waves. In *Di Matteo, M.; Goodwin, R. M. and Vercelli, A., eds.*, 1989, pp. 1–15.

_____; **Dore, Mohammed H. I. and Chakravarty, Sukhamoy.** John von Neumann and Modern Economics: Introduction. In *Dore, M.; Chakravarty, S. and Goodwin, R., eds.*, 1989, pp. 1–11.

_____; **Vercelli, Alessandro and Di Matteo, Massimo.** Technological and Social Factors in Long Term Fluctuations: Proceedings of an International Workshop Held in Siena, Italy, December 16–18, 1986: Introduction. In *Di Matteo, M.; Goodwin, R. M. and Vercelli, A., eds.*, 1989, pp. v–ix.

Goody, Esther N. Learning, Apprenticeship and the Division of Labor. In *Coy, M. W., ed.*, 1989, pp. 233–56.

de Gooijer, Jan G. Testing Non-linearities in World Stock Market Prices. *Econ. Letters*, November 1989, *31*(1), pp. 31–35.

Gopalakrishnan, Chennat. Transnational Corporations and Ocean Technology Transfer: New Economic Zones Are Being Developed by Public/Private Partnerships but Deep Sea Miners Balk on Royalties. *Amer. J. Econ. Sociology*, July 1989, *48*(3), pp. 373–83.

_____; **Khaleghi, Gholam H. and Shrestha, Rajendra B.** Energy–Non-energy Input Substitution in U.S. Agriculture: Some Findings. *Appl. Econ.*, May 1989, *21*(5), pp. 673–79.

Gordon, Andrew. Non-OPEC Crude Production. In *Hawdon, D., ed.*, 1989, pp. 54–60.

Gordon, Barry and Ohrenstein, Roman A. Quantitative Dimensions of Human Capital Analysis in the Talmudic Tradition. *Int. J. Soc. Econ.*, 1989, *16*(6), pp. 5–13.

Gordon, Daniel V. A Revenue-Function Approach to the Measurement of Output-Substitution Possibilities in Agriculture. *J. Bus. Econ. Statist.*, October 1989, *7*(4), pp. 483–87.

Gordon, David A.; Gordon, Myron J. and Gould, Lawrence I. Choice among Methods of Estimating Share Yield. *J. Portfol. Manage.*, Spring 1989, *15*(3), pp. 50–55.

Gordon, David B. and Levine, Ross. The 'Problem' of Capital Flight—A Cautionary Note. *World Econ.*, June 1989, *12*(2), pp. 237–52.

Gordon, David M. What Makes Epochs? A Comparative Analysis of Technological and Social Explanations of Long Economic Swings. In *Di Matteo, M.; Goodwin, R. M. and Vercelli, A., eds.*, 1989, pp. 267–304.

_____; **Weisskopf, Thomas E. and Bowles, Samuel.** Business Ascendancy and Economic Impasse: A Structural Retrospective on Conservative Economics, 1979–87. *J. Econ. Perspectives*, Winter 1989, *3*(1), pp. 107–34.

Gordon, Ian. The Role of International Migration in the Changing European Labour Market. In *Gordon, I. and Thirlwall, A. P., eds.*, 1989, pp. 13–29.

_____ **and Thirlwall, A. P.** European Factor Mobility: Introduction. In *Gordon, I. and Thirlwall, A. P., eds.*, 1989, pp. 1–12.

Gordon, James P. F. Individual Morality and Reputation Costs as Deterrents to Tax Evasion. *Europ. Econ. Rev.*, April 1989, *33*(4), pp. 797–805.

_____. A Many Good, Many Person, Corlett–Hague Tax Rule. *Econ. Letters*, 1989, *29*(2), pp. 157–61.

_____. Tax Reform via Commodity Grouping. *J. Public Econ.*, June 1989, *39*(1), pp. 67–81.

_____; **Harrison, Alan and Atkinson, Anthony B.** Trends in the Shares of Top Wealth-Holders in Britain, 1923–1981. *Oxford Bull. Econ. Statist.*, August 1989, *51*(3), pp. 315–32.

Gordon, Kenneth. Comments on the Papers by Falk, Bidwell and Ware. In *National Economic Research Associates*, 1989, pp. 133–38.

_____. Hicks and Hollander on Ricardo: A Mathematical Note. In *Wood, J. C. and Woods, R. N., eds., Vol. 4*, 1989, *1983*, pp. 1–5.

Gordon, Kenneth R. and Palmer, Michael. A Comparison of the Financial Institutions' View and the Market's View of Country Creditworthiness. *J. Finan. Services Res.*, June 1989, *2*(2), pp. 73–87.

Gordon, Moira and O'Connor, Kevin. Operation of Regional Labour Markets in Australia. In *Higgins, B. and Zagorski, K., eds.*, 1989, pp. 196–217.

Gordon, Myron J. and Chamberlain, Trevor W. Liquidity, Profitability, and Long-run Survival: Theory and Evidence on Business Investment. *J. Post Keynesian Econ.*, Summer 1989, *11*(4), pp. 589–610.

_____; **Gould, Lawrence I. and Gordon, David A.** Choice among Methods of Estimating Share Yield. *J. Portfol. Manage.*, Spring 1989, *15*(3), pp. 50–55.

Gordon, Peter; Kumar, Ajay and Richardson, Harry W. Congestion, Changing Metropolitan Structure, and City Size in the United States. *Int. Reg. Sci. Rev.*, 1989, *12*(1), pp. 45–56.

_____; **Kumar, Ajay and Richardson, Harry W.** Gender Differences in Metropolitan Travel Behavior. *Reg. Stud.*, December 1989, *23*(6), pp. 499–510.

_____; **Kumar, Ajay and Richardson, Harry W.** The Influence of Metropolitan Spatial Structure on Commuting Time. *J. Urban Econ.*, September 1989, *26*(2), pp. 138–51.

_____; **Kumar, Ajay and Richardson, Harry W.** The Spatial Mismatch Hypothesis: Some New Evidence. *Urban Stud.*, June 1989, *26*(3), pp. 315–26.

_____ **and Moore, J. E., II.** Endogenizing the Rise and Fall of Urban Subcenters via Discrete Programming Models. *Environ. Planning A*, September 1989, *21*(9), pp. 1195–1203.

Gordon, Robert. The Disregard of a Legal Entity for Tax Purposes: Australia. In *International Fiscal Association, ed. (II)*, 1989, pp. 169–84.

Gordon, Robert J. Assessing the Federal Reserve's Measures of Capacity and Utilization: Comments. *Brookings Pap. Econ. Act.*, 1989, (1), pp. 226–35.

_____. Fresh Water, Salt Water, and Other Macroeconomic Elixirs. *Econ. Rec.*, June 1989, 65(189), pp. 177–84.

_____. Hysteresis in History: Was There Ever a Phillips Curve? *Amer. Econ. Rev.*, May 1989, 79(2), pp. 220–25.

_____. Political and Economic Determinants of Budget Deficits in the Industrial Democracies: Comment. *Europ. Econ. Rev.*, May 1989, 33(5), pp. 934–38.

_____. The Postwar Evolution of Computer Prices. In *Jorgenson, D. W. and Landau, R.*, eds., 1989, pp. 77–125.

_____. Price and Technological Change in a Capital Good: A Survey of Research on Computers: Comment and Rejoinder. In *Jorgenson, D. W. and Landau, R.*, eds., 1989, pp. 221–24.

_____ and Balke, Nathan S. The Estimation of Prewar Gross National Product: Methodology and New Evidence. *J. Polit. Econ.*, February 1989, 97(1), pp. 38–92.

Gordon, Roger H. and Varian, Hal R. Taxation of Asset Income in the Presence of a World Securities Market. *J. Int. Econ.*, May 1989, 26(3/4), pp. 205–26.

_____ and Wilson, John Douglas. Measuring the Efficiency Cost of Taxing Risky Capital Income. *Amer. Econ. Rev.*, June 1989, 79(3), pp. 427–39.

Gordon, Wendell. Comparing Austrian and Institutional Economics. In *Samuels, W. J., ed. (II)*, 1989, pp. 133–41.

_____. The Debate over Monetarism: Monetary Policy and Economic Development: Commentary. In *DeGregori, T. R.*, ed., 1989, pp. 223–29.

_____. Donors, Development, and Debt: The Role of External Assistance and External Indebtedness: Commentary. In *DeGregori, T. R.*, ed., 1989, pp. 285–89.

Gorecki, Henryk and Skulimowski, Andrzej M. J. Safety Principle in Multiobjective Decision Support in the Decision Space Defined by Availability of Resources. In *Lewandowski, A. and Wierzbicki, A. P.*, eds., 1989, pp. 145–57.

Gorecki, Paul K. and Baldwin, John R. Measuring the Dynamics of Market Structure: Concentration and Mobility Statistics for the Canadian Manufacturing Sector. *Ann. Écon. Statist.*, July–Dec. 1989, (15–16), pp. 315–32.

Goreux, Louis M. The Fund and the Low-Income Countries. In *Gwin, C. and Feinberg, R. E.*, eds., 1989, pp. 141–64.

Gori, F. and Galeotti, M. Uniqueness of Periodic Orbitis in Lienard-Type Business-Cycle Models. *Metroecon.*, June 1989, 40(2), pp. 135–46.

Goriushkin, Leonid Mikhailovich. The General and the Specific in Siberian Agrarian Development in the Second Half of the Nineteenth and Beginning of the Twentieth Century. In *Grantham, G. and Leonard, C. S.*, eds., Pt. B, 1989, pp. 441–54.

Gorodetskii, D. The Braking Mechanism and Its Socioeconomic Foundations. *Prob. Econ.*, September 1989, 32(5), pp. 53–59.

Gorski, Marian. The Scale of Disequilibrium on the Consumer Market and Sources of Price Inflation in Poland. Empirical Evidence for the 1980s. *Jahr. Wirtsch. Osteuropas*, 1989, 13(2), pp. 93–113.

de Gorter, Harry and Meilke, Karl D. Efficiency of Alternative Policies for the EC's Common Agricultural Policy. *Amer. J. Agr. Econ.*, August 1989, 71(3), pp. 592–603.

Gorton, Gary. The Role of Technological and Market Structure in Regulatory Reform: Comments. *J. Finan. Services Res.*, September 1989, 2(3), pp. 205–11.

Gorton, Slade. Not One Debt Problem but Hundreds. In *Dornbusch, R.; Makin, J. H. and Zlowe, D.*, eds., 1989, pp. 87–89.

Gosling, S. M. Asymmetric Pricing as a Source of Bias in Price Level Movements. *Australian Econ. Pap.*, December 1989, 28(53), pp. 267–79.

Gospel, Howard F. Product Markets, Labour Markets, and Industrial Relations: The Case of Flour Milling. In *Harvey, C. and Turner, J.*, eds., 1989, pp. 84–97.

_____ and Disney, Richard. The Seniority Model of Trade Union Behaviour: A (Partial) Defence. *Brit. J. Ind. Relat.*, July 1989, 27(2), pp. 179–95.

Goss, John. Breastfeeding in the Philippines: Empirical Study of Its Effects on Child Development: Commentary. In *Smith, C. S.*, ed., 1989, pp. 16–17.

Gossop, Michael. Many Problems in Many Forms. In *Robinson, D.; Maynard, A. and Chester, R.*, eds., 1989, pp. 43–62.

Goto, Akira and Suzuki, Kazuyuki. R&D Capital, Rate of Return on R&D Investment and Spillover of R&D in Japanese Manufacturing Industries. *Rev. Econ. Statist.*, November 1989, 71(4), pp. 555–64.

Goto, Fumihiro. Input–Output Tables in Japan and Construction of International Input–Output Tables. In *Franz, A. and Rainer, N.*, eds., 1989, pp. 69–85.

Goto, Junichi. The Multifibre Arrangement and Its Effects on Developing Countries. *World Bank Res. Observer*, July 1989, 4(2), pp. 203–27.

Gott, Edwin H., Jr. Productivity, Quality and Work Force Participation. In *Ahlbrandt, R. S., Jr.*, ed., 1989, pp. 34–36.

Gottdiener, M. Crisis Theory and Socio-spatial Restructuring: The U.S. Case. In *Gottdiener, M. and Komninos, N.*, eds., 1989, pp. 365–90.

_____ and Komninos, Nicos. Capitalist Development and Crisis Theory: Accumulation, Regulation and Spatial Restructuring: Introduction. In *Gottdiener, M. and Komninos, N.*, eds., 1989, pp. 1–17.

Gottfries, Nils; Persson, Torsten and Palmer, Edward E. Regulation, Financial Buffer Stocks, and Short-run Adjustment: An Econometric

Case-Study of Sweden, 1970–82. *Europ. Econ. Rev.*, October 1989, *33*(8), pp. 1545–65.

Gottinger, Hans W. Assessment of Social Value for a Nuclear-Fueled Electric Economy with Application to the European Community. *Z. Wirtschaft. Sozialwissen.*, 1989, *109*(1), pp. 93–117.

_____. Stochastics of Innovation Processes. *J. Econ. (Z. Nationalökon.)*, 1989, *49*(2), pp. 123–38.

Gottlieb, Daniel. On the Determinants of a Country's Creditworthiness: The Case of Israel, 1971 to 1983. *J. Econ. Devel.*, June 1989, *14*(1), pp. 65–91.

Gottschalk, Peter and Danziger, Sheldon. Increasing Inequality in the U.S.: What We Know and What We Don't. In *Davidson, P. and Kregel, J., eds.*, 1989, pp. 78–97.

_____ **and Danziger, Sheldon.** Increasing Inequality in the United States: What We Know and What We Don't. *J. Post Keynesian Econ.*, Winter 1988–89, *11*(2), pp. 174–95.

_____; **Smolensky, Eugene and Danziger, Sheldon.** How the Rich Have Fared, 1973–87. *Amer. Econ. Rev.*, May 1989, *79*(2), pp. 310–14.

_____; **Wolfe, Barbara L. and Haveman, Robert H.** Health Care Financing in the U.S., U.K. and Netherlands: Distributional Consequences. In *Chiancone, A. and Messere, K., eds.*, 1989, pp. 351–73.

Gottstein, Klaus. Obstacles to Confidence-Building: How Can They Be Overcome? In *Rotblat, J. and Goldanskii, V. I., eds.*, 1989, pp. 143–46.

Goudreau, Robert E. and Whitehead, David D. Commercial Bank Profitability: Improved in 1988. *Fed. Res. Bank Atlanta Econ. Rev.*, July–Aug. 1989, *74*(4), pp. 34–47.

Gould, Brian W. and Saupe, William E. Off-Farm Labor Market Entry and Exit. *Amer. J. Agr. Econ.*, November 1989, *71*(4), pp. 960–69.

_____; **Saupe, William E. and Klemme, Richard M.** Conservation Tillage: The Role of Farm and Operator Characteristics and the Perception of Soil Erosion. *Land Econ.*, May 1989, *65*(2), pp. 167–82.

Gould, George A. Transfer of Water Rights. *Natural Res. J.*, Spring 1989, *29*(2), pp. 457–77.

Gould, Lawrence I.; Gordon, David A. and Gordon, Myron J. Choice among Methods of Estimating Share Yield. *J. Portfol. Manage.*, Spring 1989, *15*(3), pp. 50–55.

Gould, Michael S. and Zobrist, Frederick A. An Overview of Water Resources Planning in West Africa. *World Devel.*, November 1989, *17*(11), pp. 1717–22.

Goulder, Lawrence H. Tax Policy, Housing Prices, and Housing Investment. *Reg. Sci. Urban Econ.*, May 1989, *19*(2), pp. 281–304.

_____ **and Eichengreen, Barry.** Savings Promotion, Investment Promotion, and International Competitiveness. In *Feenstra, R. C., ed.*, 1989, pp. 5–44.

_____ **and Eichengreen, Barry.** The U.S. Basic Industries in the 1980s: Can Fiscal Policies Explain Their Changing Competitive Position? In *Black, S. W., ed.*, 1989, pp. 9–70.

_____ **and Summers, Lawrence H.** Tax Policy, Asset Prices, and Growth: A General Equilibrium Analysis. *J. Public Econ.*, April 1989, *38*(3), pp. 265–96.

Goulet, Denis. Participation in Development: New Avenues. *World Devel.*, February 1989, *17*(2), pp. 165–78.

Gourevitch, Peter A. Keynesian Politics: The Political Sources of Economic Policy Choices. In *Hall, P. A., ed.*, 1989, pp. 87–106.

Gourieroux, Christian; Monfort, Alan and Renault, Eric. Testing for Common Roots. *Econometrica*, January 1989, *57*(1), pp. 171–85.

_____; **Szafarz, A. and Broze, L.** Speculative Bubbles and Exchange of Information on the Market of a Storable Good. In *Barnett, W. A.; Geweke, J. and Shell, K., eds.*, 1989, pp. 101–18.

Gourvish, T. R. The Genesis of State-Owned Enterprises in the United Kingdom—Transport, Coal and Electricity. In *Magnou-Nortier, E., et al.*, 1989, pp. 3607–23.

Govind, Har. Application of the Law to the Computer Industry: India. *Bull. Int. Fiscal Doc.*, April 1989, *43*(4), pp. 166–72.

Gowa, Joanne. Bipolarity and the Postwar International Economic Order. In *Katzenstein, P. J., ed.*, 1989, pp. 33–50.

Goybet, Ph. and Buigues, Pierre. The Community's Industrial Competitiveness and International Trade in Manufactured Products. In *Jacquemin, A. and Sapir, A., eds.*, 1989, pp. 227–47.

Goza, Franklin W. and Hakkert, Ralph. The Demographic Consequences of Austerity in Latin America. In *Canak, W. L., ed.*, 1989, pp. 69–97.

Gozzi, Giancarlo. La teoria della crescita: Dalla modellistica aggregata ai modelli multisettoriali di crescita disproporzionale. (Growth Theory: From Aggregate Models to Multisector Analysis of Non Steady-State Growth. With English summary.) *Econ. Politica*, August 1989, *6*(2), pp. 281–342.

Graaff, J. de V. Kaldor on Welfare. In *Lawson, T.; Palma, J. G. and Sender, J., eds.*, 1989, pp. 19–23.

_____. Kaldor on Welfare. *Cambridge J. Econ.*, March 1989, *13*(1), pp. 19–23.

Graafland, J. J. Can Hysteresis Explain Different Labour Market Operations between Europe and the United States? *Appl. Econ.*, January 1989, *21*(1), pp. 95–111.

Grabowski, Henry G. An Analysis of U.S. International Competitiveness in Pharmaceuticals. *Managerial Dec. Econ.*, Special Issue, Spring 1989, pp. 27–33.

Grabowski, Richard. Development as Displacement: A Critique and Alternative. *J. Developing Areas*, July 1989, *23*(4), pp. 505–18.

_____ **and Aly, Hassan Y.** Measuring the Rate and Bias of Technical Innovation in Japanese Agriculture: An Alternative Approach. *Europ. Rev. Agr. Econ.*, 1989, *16*(1), pp. 65–81.

_____ **and Pasurka, Carl.** The Relative Efficiency of Slave Agriculture: An Application of a Stochastic Production Frontier. *Appl. Econ.*, May 1989, *21*(5), pp. 587–95.

_____ **and Pasurka, Carl.** The Relative Technical Efficiency of Slave and Non-slave Farms in Southern Agriculture. *Eastern Econ. J.*, July–Sept. 1989, *15*(3), pp. 245–58.

_____ **and Shields, Michael P.** Lewis and Ricardo: A Reinterpretation. *World Devel.*, February 1989, *17*(2), pp. 193–97.

Gracia-Diez, Mercedes. Compositional Changes of the Labor Force and the Increase of the Unemployment Rate: An Estimate for the United States. *J. Bus. Econ. Statist.*, April 1989, *7*(2), pp. 237–43.

Graczynski, Manfred. Observations of Military Exercises and On-Site Inspections. In *Altmann, J. and Rotblat, J., eds.*, 1989, pp. 151–56.

Grad, Susan. Income and Assets of Social Security Beneficiaries by Type of Benefit. *Soc. Sec. Bull.*, January 1989, *52*(1), pp. 2–10.

Graddy, Elizabeth and Nichol, Michael B. Public Members on Occupational Licensing Boards: Effects on Legislative Regulatory Reforms. *Southern Econ. J.*, January 1989, *55*(3), pp. 610–25.

Gradison, Willis D., Jr. Rationing of Medical Care for the Critically Ill: Federal Policy and Intensive Care. In *Strosberg, M. A.; Fein, I. A. and Carroll, J. D., eds.*, 1989, pp. 37–40.

Gradus, Raymond H. J. M. A Differential Game between Government and Firms: A Non-cooperative Approach. *J. Econ. (Z. Nationalökon.)*, 1989, *50*(3), pp. 237–56.

Grady, Gerald J. and Schreiber, Richard K. Expert System Applications in the IRS. *J. Policy Anal. Manage.*, Spring 1989, *8*(2), pp. 193–99.

Grady, William R.; Hayward, Mark D. and Hardy, Melissa A. Labor Force Withdrawal Patterns among Older Men in the United States. *Soc. Sci. Quart.*, June 1989, *70*(2), pp. 425–48.

Graen, George and Wakabayashi, Mitsuru. Human Resource Development of Japanese Managers: Leadership and Career Investment. In *Nedd, A., ed.*, 1989, pp. 235–56.

Graetz, Michael J.; Dubin, Jeffrey A. and Wilde, Louis L. Administrative and Compliance Costs of Taxation: United States. In *International Fiscal Association, ed. (I)*, 1989, pp. 311–47.

Graf, William D. The Theory of the Non-capitalist Road. In *Schulz, B. H. and Hansen, W. W., eds.*, 1989, pp. 27–52.

Grafstein, R. Getting the Whole to Play Its Part: A Review. *Soc. Choice Welfare*, January 1989, *6*(1), pp. 77–83.

de Graft-Johnson, Kweku T. The World Fertility Survey: An Appraisal of Methodology: Comment. *J. Amer. Statist. Assoc.*, September 1989, *84*(407), pp. 769–70.

Grafton, Quentin and Seguino, Stephanie. The Haitian Coffee Market: A Case Study of Different Approaches to Social Science Research. *Can. J. Devel. Stud.*, 1989, *10*(1), pp. 91–102.

Graham, Cosmo. Regulating the Company. In *Hancher, L. and Moran, M., eds.*, 1989, pp. 199–223.

Graham, John D. Communicating about Chemical Hazards. *J. Policy Anal. Manage.*, Spring 1989, *8*(2), pp. 307–13.

_____ **and Crandall, Robert W.** The Effect of Fuel Economy Standards on Automobile Safety. *J. Law Econ.*, April 1989, *32*(1), pp. 97–118.

Graham, John W. International Differences in Saving Rates and the Life Cycle Hypothesis: Reply and Further Evidence. *Europ. Econ. Rev.*, September 1989, *33*(7), pp. 1499–1507.

_____ **and Beller, Andrea H.** The Effect of Child Support Payments on the Labor Supply of Female Family Heads: An Econometric Analysis. *J. Human Res.*, Fall 1989, *24*(4), pp. 664–88.

Graham, Robert. British Policy towards Latin America. In *Bulmer-Thomas, V., ed.*, 1989, pp. 52–67.

Graham-Tomasi, Theodore; Adamowicz, Wiktor L. and Fletcher, Jerald J. Functional Form and the Statistical Properties of Welfare Measures. *Amer. J. Agr. Econ.*, May 1989, *71*(2), pp. 414–21.

_____; **Fletcher, Jerald J. and Adamowicz, Wiktor L.** Inequality Constrained Estimation of Consumer Surplus. *Can. J. Agr. Econ.*, November 1989, *37*(3), pp. 407–20.

Gram, Harvey. Ideology and Time: Criticisms of General Equilibrium. In *Feiwel, G. R., ed. (II)*, 1989, pp. 285–302.

_____. Memories of Joan Robinson. In *Feiwel, G. R., ed. (II)*, 1989, pp. 877–80.

Gramley, Lyle E. Monetary Policy in the 1990s: Lessons and Challenges: Commentary. In *Federal Reserve Bank of Kansas City*, 1989, pp. 47–53.

Gramlich, Edward M. Budget Deficits and National Saving: Are Politicians Exogenous? *J. Econ. Perspectives*, Spring 1989, *3*(2), pp. 23–35.

_____. Economists' View of the Welfare System. *Amer. Econ. Rev.*, May 1989, *79*(2), pp. 191–96.

_____; **Kasten, Richard and Sammartino, Frank.** Deficit Reduction and Income Redistribution. *Amer. Econ. Rev.*, May 1989, *79*(2), pp. 315–19.

Gramm, Warren S. Analytic and Political Elements in Exegesis of Marx's Social Economics. *Atlantic Econ. J.*, December 1989, *17*(4), pp. 39–46.

_____. Oligarchic Capitalism: Arguable Reality, Thinkable Future? In *Tool, M. R. and Samuels, W. J., eds. (III)*, 1989, 1980, pp. 353–74.

_____. The Selective Interpretation of Adam Smith. In *Tool, M. R. and Samuels, W. J., eds. (II)*, 1989, 1980, pp. 277–300.

_____; **Hoaas, David J. and Johnson, L. E.** Marx's Law of Profit: The Current State of the Controversy. *Atlantic Econ. J.*, December 1989, *17*(4), pp. 55–62.

Grammatikos, Theoharry. Dividend Stripping, Risk Exposure, and the Effect of the 1984 Tax

Reform Act on the Ex-dividend Day Behavior. *J. Bus.*, April 1989, *62*(2), pp. 157–73.

Grampp, William D. The Justice of the Market. *Écon. Societes*, June 1989, *23*(6), pp. 141–50.

_____. Rent-Seeking in Arts Policy. *Public Choice*, February 1989, *60*(2), pp. 113–21.

Granaglia, Elena. Public Intervention and Health Policy: An Analysis of Tendencies in Progress. In *Lange, P. and Regini, M., eds.*, 1989, pp. 235–48.

Granberg, Alexandr G. The Restructuring of the Soviet Economy and Prospects for Siberia's Development. *Int. Reg. Sci. Rev.*, 1989, *12*(3), pp. 291–304.

Grandmont, Jean-Michel. Keynesian Issues and Economic Theory. *Scand. J. Econ.*, 1989, *91*(2), pp. 265–93.

_____. Local Bifurcations and Stationary Sunspots. In *Barnett, W. A.; Geweke, J. and Shell, K., eds.*, 1989, pp. 45–60.

_____. On the Short-Run Equilibrium in a Monetary Economy. In *Starr, R. M., ed.*, 1989, *1974*, pp. 309–23.

_____. Report on Maurice Allais' Scientific Work. *Scand. J. Econ.*, 1989, *91*(1), pp. 17–28.

Grandy, Christopher. Can Government Be Trusted to Keep Its Part of a Social Contract?: New Jersey and the Railroads, 1825–1888. *J. Law, Econ., Organ.*, Fall 1989, *5*(2), pp. 249–69.

_____. The Economics of Multiple Governments: New Jersey Corporate Chartermongering 1875–1929. In *Hausman, W. J., ed.*, 1989, pp. 19–21.

_____. New Jersey Corporate Chartermongering, 1875–1929. *J. Econ. Hist.*, September 1989, *49*(3), pp. 677–92.

Grangeas, Geneviève. Cyclical Behaviour of the Cost of Labour and Long Waves. In *Di Matteo, M.; Goodwin, R. M. and Vercelli, A., eds.*, 1989, pp. 225–41.

_____ **and Lecaillon, Jacques.** Cycles courts et cycles longs de la répartition (France, 1820–1985). (Short and Long Cycles of Income Distribution [France, 1820–1985]. With English summary.) *Écon. Societes*, March 1989, *23*(3), pp. 106–27.

Granger, C. W. J.; Hallman, Jeffrey J. and Engle, R. F. Merging Short- and Long-run Forecasts: An Application of Seasonal Cointegration to Monthly Electricity Sales Forecasting. *J. Econometrics*, January 1989, *40*(1), pp. 45–62.

_____ **and Lee, T. H.** Investigation of Production, Sales and Inventory Relationships Using Multicointegration and Non-symmetric Error Correction Models. *J. Appl. Econometrics*, Supplement, December 1989, *4*, pp. S145–59.

_____; **White, Halbert and Kamstra, Mark.** Interval Forecasting: An Analysis Based upon ARCH-Quantile Estimators. *J. Econometrics*, January 1989, *40*(1), pp. 87–96.

Grannemann, T. W. Should Risk-Based Payments Be Used for Long-Term Care? In *Scheffler, R. M. and Rossiter, L. F., eds.*, 1989, pp. 335–49.

Gransow, Volker. Colleague Frankenstein and the Pale Light of Progress. In *Rueschemeyer, M. and Lemke, C., eds.*, 1989, pp. 194–209.

Grant, Charles. Policies for Employment Creation. In *Gemper, B. B., ed.*, 1989, pp. 47–62.

Grant, Dwight and Eaker, Mark. Complex Hedges: How Well Do They Work? *J. Futures Markets*, February 1989, *9*(1), pp. 15–27.

Grant, James C. Global Trade in Services: A Corporate Perspective on Telecommunication and Data Services. In *Robinson, P.; Sauvant, K. P. and Govitrikar, V. P., eds.*, 1989, pp. 101–20.

Grant, James P. and Jolly, Richard. The New Economics of Child Health and Survival. In *Adelman, I. and Lane, S., eds.*, 1989, pp. 32–44.

Grant, John. Foreign Exchange Markets: A View from the Trenches. *Can. Public Policy*, Supplement, February 1989, *15*, pp. S63–66.

Grant, K. Gary. The Impact of Quotas on the Optimal Adjustment of Milk Production at the Farm Level: A Comment. *Europ. Rev. Agr. Econ.*, 1989, *16*(4), pp. 515–22.

Grant, Marcus. Controlling Alcohol Abuse. In *Robinson, D.; Maynard, A. and Chester, R., eds.*, 1989, pp. 63–83.

Grant, Richard and Gaile, Gary L. Trade, Power, and Location: The Spatial Dynamics of the Relationship between Exchange and Political–Economic Strength. *Econ. Geogr.*, October 1989, *65*(4), pp. 329–37.

Grant, Warren R.; Ito, Shoichi and Peterson, E. Wesley F. Rice in Asia: Is It Becoming an Inferior Good? *Amer. J. Agr. Econ.*, February 1989, *71*(1), pp. 32–42.

Grantham, George. Agrarian Organization in the Century of Industrialization: Europe, Russia and North America. In *Grantham, G. and Leonard, C. S., eds., Pt. A*, 1989, pp. 1–24.

_____. Agricultural Supply during the Industrial Revolution: French Evidence and European Implications. *J. Econ. Hist.*, March 1989, *49*(1), pp. 43–72.

_____. Capital and Agrarian Structure in Early Nineteenth-Century France. In *Grantham, G. and Leonard, C. S., eds., Pt. A*, 1989, pp. 137–59.

_____. Jean Meuvret and the Subsistence Problem in Early Modern France. *J. Econ. Hist.*, March 1989, *49*(1), pp. 184–200.

Granwell, Alan W. and Kaufman, Nancy H. Working with Passive Foreign Investment Companies: How to Minimize the Hurt: United States. *Bull. Int. Fiscal Doc.*, July 1989, *43*(7), pp. 303–11.

Grasewicz, Paul J. and Ernst, William. Impact Fees: When, Where, and How? In *Matzer, J., Jr., ed.*, 1989, *1988*, pp. 170–75.

Grasshoff, Ulrike; Mahmood, Talat and Schwalbach, Joachim. The Dynamics of Corporate Profits. *Europ. Econ. Rev.*, October 1989, *33*(8), pp. 1625–39.

Grassi, Anneliese and Makin, John H. Sharing World Leadership? A New Era for America and Japan: Introduction. **In** *Makin, J. H. and Hellmann, D. C., eds.*, 1989, pp. xix–xxiii.

Gravelle, Jane G. Differential Taxation of Capital Income: Another Look at the 1986 Tax Reform Act. *Nat. Tax J.*, December 1989, *42*(4), pp. 441–63.

———— **and Kotlikoff, Laurence J.** The Incidence and Efficiency Costs of Corporate Taxation When Corporate and Noncorporate Firms Produce the Same Good. *J. Polit. Econ.*, August 1989, *97*(4), pp. 749–80.

———— **and Taylor, Jack.** Financing Long-term Care for the Elderly. *Nat. Tax J.*, September 1989, *42*(3), pp. 219–32.

Graves, Bennie. Informal Aspects of Apprenticeship in Selected American Occupations. **In** *Coy, M. W., ed.*, 1989, pp. 51–64.

Graves, Frank C.; Read, James A., Jr. and Carpenter, Paul R. Estimating the Cost of Switching Rights on Natural Gas Pipelines. *Energy J.*, October 1989, *10*(4), pp. 59–81.

Graves, Philip E.; Greenwood, Michael J. and Chalmers, James A. Regional Location Patterns in the United States: Recent Changes and Future Prospects. **In** *van Dijk, J., et al., eds.*, 1989, pp. 23–45.

———— **and Knapp, Thomas A.** On the Role of Amenities in Models of Migration and Regional Development. *J. Reg. Sci.*, February 1989, *29*(1), pp. 71–87.

————**; Lee, Dwight R. and Sexton, Robert L.** Statutes versus Enforcement: The Case of the Optimal Speed Limit. *Amer. Econ. Rev.*, September 1989, *79*(4), pp. 932–36.

————**; White, Nancy and Bresnock, Anne E.** Multiple-Choice Testing: Question and Response Position. *J. Econ. Educ.*, Summer 1989, *20*(3), pp. 239–45.

Graw, Stephen. Company Share Buy-Backs—The Sequel. *Australian Tax Forum*, 1989, *6*(4), pp. 495–507.

————. Company Share Buy-Backs: The Taxation Problems. *Australian Tax Forum*, 1989, *6*(3), pp. 369–90.

Gray, A. M. and McGuire, Alistair. Factor Input in NHS Hospitals. *Appl. Econ.*, March 1989, *21*(3), pp. 397–411.

Gray, Alan. Measuring Preference for In-marriage: A Response. *Population Stud.*, March 1989, *43*(1), pp. 163–66.

Gray, Clive. On Measuring the Shadow Price of Uncommitted Fiscal Resources in Africa. *World Devel.*, February 1989, *17*(2), pp. 213–21.

Gray, Colin. From Unemployment to Self-Employment: A Manageable Change? *Econ. Lavoro*, July–Sept. 1989, *23*(3), pp. 119–39.

Gray, David J. Social Science and Social Policy: A Comment. *Amer. J. Econ. Sociology*, July 1989, *48*(3), pp. 307–09.

Gray, Edwin J. What Went Wrong? **In** *Schwartz, E. and Vasconcellos, G. M., eds.*, 1989, pp. 53–61.

Gray, H. Peter. The Multi-Fibre Arrangement and the Least Developed Countries. *Industry Devel.*, April 1989, (26), pp. 89–96.

————. A Question of Departed Tranquility? **In** *Gray, H. P., ed.*, 1989, pp. 3–14.

————. Research in International Business and Finance: Introduction. **In** *Gray, H. P., ed.*, 1989, pp. ix–xii.

————. Services and Comparative Advantage Theory. **In** *Giersch, H., ed.*, 1989, pp. 85–103.

————. Social Science: Quasi-science? *Eastern Econ. J.*, Oct.–Dec. 1989, *15*(4), pp. 273–86.

———— **and Gray, Jean M.** International Payments in a Flow-of-Funds Format. *J. Post Keynesian Econ.*, Winter 1988–89, *11*(2), pp. 241–60.

Gray, Jean M. and Gray, H. Peter. International Payments in a Flow-of-Funds Format. *J. Post Keynesian Econ.*, Winter 1988–89, *11*(2), pp. 241–60.

Gray, John. Contractarian Method, Private Property, and the Market Economy. **In** *Chapman, J. W. and Pennock, J. R., eds.*, 1989, pp. 13–58.

————. Hayek on the Market Economy and the Limits of State Action. **In** *Helm, D., ed.*, 1989, pp. 127–43.

Gray, Tara and Olson, Kent W. A Cost–Benefit Analysis of the Sentencing Decision for Burglars. *Soc. Sci. Quart.*, September 1989, *70*(3), pp. 708–22.

Gray, Thomas A. Let Small Business Do What It Does Best—Create Jobs. *J. Lab. Res.*, Winter 1989, *10*(1), pp. 73–81.

Gray, William S. The Anatomy of a Stock Market Forecast. *J. Portfol. Manage.*, Fall 1989, *16*(1), pp. 36–44.

Grayson, Leslie E. and Morris, Robert K. The Implications for Future Contingency Planning of the 1979 Gasoline Shortage. **In** *[Adams, F. G.]*, 1989, pp. 207–25.

Graziani, Augusto. Credit Constraints and Investment Finance: Some Evidence from Greece: Comment. **In** *Monti, M., ed.*, 1989, pp. 193–96.

————. Money and Finance in Joan Robinson's Works. **In** *Feiwel, G. R., ed. (I)*, 1989, pp. 613–30.

————. Schumpeter and Italian Economic Thought in the Inter-war Period. *Studi. Econ.*, 1989, *44*(37), pp. 41–83.

Graziano, Loretta. If You're So Smart, Why Aren't You Tall? A Cross-Cultural Perspective on the Nature of Entrepreneurship. *J. Behav. Econ.*, Fall 1989, *18*(3), pp. 205–15.

Graziosi, Andrea. Keynes in Russia nel 1925. (With English summary.) *Studi. Econ.*, 1989, *44*(37), pp. 125–43.

Greasley, David. British Wages and Income, 1856–1913: A Revision. *Exploration Econ. Hist.*, April 1989, *26*(2), pp. 248–59.

Grebenik, E. Demography, Democracy, and Demonology. *Population Devel. Rev.*, March 1989, *15*(1), pp. 1–22.

Green, A. E. and Owen, D. W. The Changing Geography of Occupations in Engineering in Britain, 1978–1987. *Reg. Stud.*, February 1989, *23*(1), pp. 27–42.

———— **and Owen, D. W.** Labour Market Accounts for Travel-to-Work Areas, 1981–1984. *Reg. Stud.*, February 1989, 23(1), pp. 69–72.

Green, Alan. Policy Forum on the Role of Immigration in Canada's Future: Introductory Remarks. **In** *Beach, C. M. and Green, A. G.*, 1989, pp. 1–2.

Green, Bill and Richardson, Miles. The Fisheries Co-management Initiative in Haida Gwaii. **In** *Pinkerton, E., ed.*, 1989, pp. 249–61.

Green, Christopher. The London Metal Exchange. **In** *Jackson, L. M. and Richardson, P. R., eds.*, 1989, pp. 46–54.

Green, Christopher J. Model Comparison When the Endogenous Variable Is Uncertain: An Application of Non-nested Testing Procedures. *Econ. Letters*, December 1989, 31(4), pp. 349–54.

_____ **and Bladen Hovell, Robin.** Crowding-Out and Pulling-In of Fiscal Policy under Fixed and Flexible Exchange Rates. **In** *MacDonald, R. and Taylor, M. P., eds.*, 1989, pp. 251–74.

_____ **and Kiernan, Eric.** Multicollinearity and Measurement Error in Econometric Financial Modelling. *Manchester Sch. Econ. Soc. Stud.*, December 1989, 57(4), pp. 357–69.

_____; **Miles, David K. and Chowdhury, Gopa.** Company Bank Borrowing and Liquid Lending. *Nat. Westminster Bank Quart. Rev.*, November 1989, pp. 42–52.

Green, Don and Friezer, Mark. Taxation of the Income of Non-resident Trusts: The Consultative Document Proposals. *Australian Tax Forum*, 1989, 6(1), pp. 41–63.

Green, H. A. J. When Are Goods More Goods? **In** *Wood, J. C. and Woods, R. N., eds., Vol. 2*, 1989, 1958, pp. 28.

Green, Jerry R. and Jullien, Bruno. Ordinal Independence in Nonlinear Utility Theory: Erratum. *J. Risk Uncertainty*, April 1989, 2(1), pp. 119.

Green, Milford B. and McNaughton, Rod B. Interurban Variation in Venture Capital Investment Characteristics. *Urban Stud.*, April 1989, 26(2), pp. 199–213.

_____ **and McNaughton, Rod B.** Spatial Patterns of Canadian Venture Capital Investment. *Reg. Stud.*, February 1989, 23(1), pp. 9–18.

Green, Raúl H. Les déterminants de la restructuration des grands groupes agro-alimentaires au niveau mondial. (The Determinants of Structural Change of the World's Biggest Industrial Groups in Food Industry. With English summary.) *Écon. Societes*, July 1989, 23(7), pp. 27–52.

Green, Richard D. and Chang, Hui-Shung. The Effects of Advertising on Food Demand Elasticities. *Can. J. Agr. Econ.*, November 1989, 37(3), pp. 481–94.

Green, Rodney D. and Heidarian, Jamshid. The Impact of Oil-Export Dependency on a Developing Country. *Energy Econ.*, October 1989, 11(4), pp. 247–61.

Greenaway, David. Commercial Policy and Policy Conflict: An Evaluation of the Incidence of Protection in a Non-industrialized Economy. *Manchester Sch. Econ. Soc. Stud.*, June 1989, 57(2), pp. 125–41.

_____. James Meade, 1907– **In** *Greenaway, D. and Presley, J. R., eds.*, 1989, pp. 120–43.

_____. The Non-equivalence of Equivalent Restrictions: A Further Example. *J. Econ. Stud.*, 1989, 16(1), pp. 61–64.

_____. Regional Trading Arrangements and Intra-Industry Trade: Evidence and Policy Issues. **In** *Greenaway, D.; Hyclak, T. and Thornton, R. J., eds.*, 1989, pp. 31–42.

_____. Tariff and Non-tariff Protection in Britain: Managing Freer Trade. **In** *Nieuwenhuysen, J., ed.*, 1989, pp. 100–114.

_____ **and Bleaney, Michael.** Recent Developments in Macroeconomics. **In** *Greenaway, D., ed.*, 1989, pp. 1–21.

_____ **and Milner, Chris.** Effective Protection Analysis and Optimal Trade Policy with Intra-industry Specialisation and Imperfect Competition. **In** *Tharakan, P. K. M. and Kol, J., eds.*, 1989, pp. 145–62.

_____ **and Milner, Chris.** Nominal and Effective Tariffs in a Small Industrializing Economy: The Case of Mauritius. *Appl. Econ.*, August 1989, 21(8), pp. 995–1009.

Greenbaum, Stuart I. The Thrift Industry Crisis of the 1980s: What Went Wrong? A Panel Presentation. **In** *Federal Home Loan Bank of San Francisco*, 1989, pp. 45–47.

_____; **Kanatas, George and Venezia, Itzhak.** Equilibrium Loan Pricing under the Bank–Client Relationship. *J. Banking Finance*, May 1989, 13(2), pp. 221–35.

_____ **and Thakor, Anjan V.** Bank Reserve Requirements as an Impediment to Signaling. *Econ. Inquiry*, January 1989, 27(1), pp. 75–91.

Greenberg, E.; Pollard, W. A. and Alpert, W. T. Statistical Properties of Data Stretching. *J. Appl. Econometrics*, Oct.–Dec. 1989, 4(4), pp. 383–91.

Greenberg, Irwin. Strategies for Reliability Incentive Contracting. **In** *Gulledge, T. R., Jr. and Litteral, L. A., eds.*, 1989, pp. 62–71.

Greenberg, Jay N.; Leutz, Walter N. and Altman, Stuart H. The Social Health Maintenance Organization. **In** *Eisdorfer, C.; Kessler, D. A. and Spector, A. N., eds.*, 1989, pp. 197–223.

_____ **and Meiners, Mark R.** Improving the Role of Private Markets in Financing Long-Term Care Services. **In** *McLennan, K. and Meyer, J. A., eds.*, 1989, pp. 87–115.

Greenberg, Joseph. An Application of the Theory of Social Situations to Repeated Games. *J. Econ. Theory*, December 1989, 49(2), pp. 278–93.

_____. Deriving Strong and Coalition-Proof Nash Equilibria from an Abstract System. *J. Econ. Theory*, October 1989, 49(1), pp. 195–202.

Greenberg, Paul E. and Berndt, Ernst R. Canadian Energy Demand after the Oil Shocks. **In** *Watkins, G. C., ed.*, 1989, pp. 69–103.

Greene, J. Edward. Developing Centres of Excellence through North/South Linkages in Higher Education. *Soc. Econ. Stud.*, June 1989, 38(2), pp. 37–67.

Greene, Jerome D. A Brand Switching Model with Implications for Marketing Strategies: Commentary. *Marketing Sci.*, Winter 1989, 8(1), pp. 104–05.

Greene, Joshua. The African Debt Problem. In *[Marjolin, R.]*, 1989, pp. 103–15.

———. The Debt Problem of Sub-Saharan Africa. *Finance Devel.*, June 1989, 26(2), pp. 9–12.

———. The External Debt Problem of Sub-Saharan Africa. *Int. Monet. Fund Staff Pap.*, December 1989, 36(4), pp. 836–74.

———. External Debt Problem of Sub-Saharan Africa. In *Frenkel, J. A.; Dooley, M. P. and Wickham, P.*, eds., 1989, pp. 38–74.

Greene, Kenneth R. The Social Context and Hispanics' Evaluations of Municipal Services. *Soc. Sci. Quart.*, March 1989, 70(1), pp. 204–10.

Greenfield, Robert L. and Yeager, Leland B. Can Monetary Disequilibrium Be Eliminated? *Cato J.*, Fall 1989, 9(2), pp. 405–21.

Greenhouse, Carol J. Just in Time: Temporality and the Cultural Legitimation of Law. *Yale Law J.*, June 1989, 98(8), pp. 1631–51.

Greenhut, M. L. and Lane, W. J. A Theory of Oligopolistic Competition. *Manchester Sch. Econ. Soc. Stud.*, September 1989, 57(3), pp. 248–61.

Greenlick, M. R.; Hornbrook, M. C. and Bennett, M. D. Adjusting the AAPCC for Selectivity and Selection Bias under Medicare Risk Contracts. In *Scheffler, R. M. and Rossiter, L. F.*, eds., 1989, pp. 111–49.

Greenspan, Alan. Deficits Do Matter: Comment. *Challenge*, Jan.–Feb. 1989, 32(1), pp. 51–54.

———. The Great Malaise. In *Guttmann, R.*, ed., 1989, 1980, pp. 117–20.

———. Monetary Policy Issues in the 1990s: Overview: Central Bank Perspectives. In *Federal Reserve Bank of Kansas City*, 1989, pp. 309–13.

———. Statement to the Deficit Commission: Statement to the National Economic Commission, November 16, 1988. *Fed. Res. Bull.*, January 1989, 75(1), pp. 15–18.

———. Statement to the U.S. House Committee on Ways and Means, February 2, 1989. *Fed. Res. Bull.*, April 1989, 75(4), pp. 267–72.

———. Statement to the U.S. House Federal Reserve System before the Committee on Banking, Finance and Urban Affairs, January 24, 1989. *Fed. Res. Bull.*, March 1989, 75(3), pp. 139–42.

———. Statement to the U.S. House Subcommittee on Domestic Monetary Policy of the Committee on Banking, Finance and Urban Affairs, October 25, 1989. *Fed. Res. Bull.*, December 1989, 75(12), pp. 795–803.

———. Statement to the U.S. Senate Committee on Banking, Housing, and Foreign Affairs, February 23, 1989. *Fed. Res. Bull.*, April 1989, 75(4), pp. 278–82.

———. Statement to the U.S. Senate Committee on Banking, Housing, and Urban Affairs, February 21, 1989. *Fed. Res. Bull.*, April 1989, 75(4), pp. 272–77.

———. Statement to the U.S. Senate Committee on Banking, Housing, and Urban Affairs, August 1, 1989. *Fed. Res. Bull.*, September 1989, 75(9), pp. 614–19.

———. Statement to the U.S. Senate Committee on Finance, January 26, 1989. *Fed. Res. Bull.*, March 1989, 75(3), pp. 142–46.

———. Statement to the U.S. Senate Committee on the Budget, February 28, 1989. *Fed. Res. Bull.*, April 1989, 75(4), pp. 282–86.

———. Statement to the U.S. Senate Subcommittee on Securities of the Committee on Banking, Housing, and Urban Affairs, June 14, 1989. *Fed. Res. Bull.*, August 1989, 75(8), pp. 557–63.

———. Statement to the U.S. Subcommittee on Financial Institutions Supervision, Regulation and Insurance of the Committee on Banking, Finance and Urban Affairs of March 22, 1989. *Fed. Res. Bull.*, May 1989, 75(5), pp. 347–50.

Greenwald, Bruce C. and Stiglitz, Joseph E. Toward a Theory of Rigidities. *Amer. Econ. Rev.*, May 1989, 79(2), pp. 364–69.

Greenwald, Joseph A. A Free Trade Agreement between Mexico and the United States? Comments. In *Schott, J. J.*, ed., 1989, pp. 268–70.

Greenwood, Jeremy and Williamson, Stephen D. International Financial Intermediation and Aggregate Fluctuations under Alternative Exchange Rate Regimes. *J. Monet. Econ.*, May 1989, 23(3), pp. 401–31.

Greenwood, John G. Forum on the Negative Interest Rate Scheme. *Hong Kong Econ. Pap.*, 1989, (19), pp. 67–70.

Greenwood, Justin; Williams, Alan M. and Shaw, Gareth. From Tourist to Tourism Entrepreneur, From Consumption to Production: Evidence from Cornwall, England. *Environ. Planning A*, December 1989, 21(12), pp. 1639–53.

Greenwood, Michael J.; Chalmers, James A. and Graves, Philip E. Regional Location Patterns in the United States: Recent Changes and Future Prospects. In *van Dijk, J., et al.*, eds., 1989, pp. 23–45.

———— and Hunt, Gary L. Jobs versus Amenities in the Analysis of Metropolitan Migration. *J. Urban Econ.*, January 1989, 25(1), pp. 1–16.

Greenwood, Ronald G. and Wrege, Charles. Origins of Midvale Steel (1866–1880): Birthplace of Scientific Management. In *Perkins, E. J.*, ed., 1989, pp. 206–19.

Greer, Harold. Baptists in Western Cuba: From the Wars of Independence to Revolution. In *Mesa-Lago, C.*, ed., 1989, pp. 61–77.

Gregg, Paul; Anderton, Bob and Britton, Andrew. The Home Economy. *Nat. Inst. Econ. Rev.*, August 1989, (129), pp. 6–21.

———; Anderton, Bob and Britton, Andrew. The Home Economy. *Nat. Inst. Econ. Rev.*, November 1989, (130), pp. 7–22.

———; Joyce, Michael and Britton, Andrew. The Home Economy. *Nat. Inst. Econ. Rev.*, February 1989, (127), pp. 7–25.

———; Joyce, Michael and Britton, Andrew. The Home Economy. *Nat. Inst. Econ. Rev.*, May 1989, (128), pp. 5–19.

Gregorowicz, Philip and Hegji, Charles E. Short-term Movement in Exchange Rates and Information on the Money Stock. *Quart. J. Bus. Econ.*, Spring 1989, *28*(2), pp. 19–31.

_____; Hegji, Charles E. and Deravi, Keivan. Deficit Financing Announcements and Asset Prices. *J. Econ. Bus.*, May 1989, *41*(2), pp. 171–83.

Gregory, Allan W. A Nonparametric Test for Autoregressive Conditional Heteroscedasticity: A Markov-Chain Approach. *J. Bus. Econ. Statist.*, January 1989, *7*(1), pp. 107–15.

_____ and Backus, David K. Risk Premiums in Asset Prices and Returns: A Comment. *Econometric Rev.*, 1989, *8*(2), pp. 187–95.

_____ and Sampson, Michael J. Markov Chain Tests of the Unbiasedness Hypothesis in the Forward Foreign Exchange Market. *J. Quant. Econ.*, January 1989, *5*(1), pp. 143–54.

_____; Zin, Stanley E. and Backus, David K. Risk Premiums in the Term Structure: Evidence from Artificial Economies. *J. Monet. Econ.*, November 1989, *24*(3), pp. 371–99.

Gregory, Ann. Political Risk Management. In *Rugman, A. M., ed.*, 1989, pp. 310–29.

Gregory, Derek. Presences and Absences: Time–Space Relations and Structuration Theory. In *Held, D. and Thompson, J. B., eds.*, 1989, pp. 185–214.

Gregory, Paul R. The Role of the State in Promoting Economic Development: A Case Study of Russia. *Rivista Storia Econ.*, *S.S.*, June 1989, *6*(2), pp. 165–81.

_____. The Soviet Bureaucracy and Perestroika. *Comp. Econ. Stud.*, Spring 1989, *31*(1), pp. 1–45.

Gregory, Robert G. and Butlin, N. G. Trevor Winchester Swan: 1918–1989. *Econ. Rec.*, December 1989, *65*(191), pp. 369–77.

_____, et al. Women's Pay in Australia, Great Britain, and the United States: The Role of Laws, Regulations, and Human Capital. In *Michael, R. T.; Hartmann, H. I. and O'Farrell, B., eds.*, 1989, pp. 222–42.

Gregson, Nicky. On the (Ir)Relevance of Structuration Theory to Empirical Research. In *Held, D. and Thompson, J. B., eds.*, 1989, pp. 235–48.

_____. Tawney Revisited: Custom and the Emergence of Capitalist Class Relations in Northeast Cumbria: 1600–1830. *Econ. Hist. Rev.*, *2nd Ser.*, February 1989, *42*(1), pp. 18–42.

Gregson, Terry and Bline, Dennis M. The Relationship of Communication Satisfaction to Turnover Intentions and Job Satisfaction for Certified Public Accountants. In *Schwartz, B. N., ed.*, 1989, pp. 203–22.

Greif, Avner. Reputation and Coalitions in Medieval Trade: Evidence on the Maghribi Traders. *J. Econ. Hist.*, December 1989, *49*(4), pp. 857–82.

Gremillion, Joseph. The Church as Transnational Source and Carrier of Values Affecting Economic and Business Institutions and Policies. In *Rueschhoff, N. and Schaum, K., eds.*, 1989, pp. 173–81.

Grenier, Gilles; Coulombe, Serge and Lavoie, Marc. Discrimination versus English Proficiency in the National Hockey League: A Reply. *Can. Public Policy*, March 1989, *15*(1), pp. 98–101.

Grennes, Thomas. The Multifiber Arrangement and the Management of International Textile Trade. *Cato J.*, Spring–Summer 1989, *9*(1), pp. 107–31.

Gresik, Thomas A. and Satterthwaite, Mark A. The Rate at Which a Simple Market Converges to Efficiency as the Number of Traders Increases: An Asymptotic Result for Optimal Trading Mechanisms. *J. Econ. Theory*, June 1989, *48*(1), pp. 304–32.

Grewlich, Klaus W. Cooperative Communications Policies: Europe's Contribution to the International Information Economy. In *Jussawalla, M.; Okuma, T. and Araki, T., eds.*, 1989, pp. 60–68.

Grier, Kevin B. Campaign Spending and Senate Elections, 1978–84. *Public Choice*, December 1989, *63*(3), pp. 201–19.

_____ and Tullock, Gordon. An Empirical Analysis of Cross-National Economic Growth, 1951–80. *J. Monet. Econ.*, September 1989, *24*(2), pp. 259–76.

Griesinger, Harriet and Kahn, Shulamit. Female Mobility and the Returns to Seniority: Should EEO Policy Be Concerned with Promotion? *Amer. Econ. Rev.*, May 1989, *79*(2), pp. 300–304.

Grieson, Ronald E. and White, James R. The Existence and Capitalization of Neighborhood Externalities: A Reassessment. *J. Urban Econ.*, January 1989, *25*(1), pp. 68–76.

Grieves, Robin; Khaksari, Shahriar and Kamath, Ravindra. A New Approach to Determining Optimum Portfolio Mix. *J. Portfol. Manage.*, Spring 1989, *15*(3), pp. 43–49.

Griffin, James M. Previous Cartel Experience: Any Lessons for OPEC? In *[Adams, F. G.]*, 1989, pp. 179–206.

_____ and Baltagi, Badi H. Alternative Models of Managerial Behavior: Empirical Tests for the Petroleum Industry. *Rev. Econ. Statist.*, November 1989, *71*(4), pp. 579–85.

Griffith, D. A.; Bennett, Robert J. and Haining, R. P. Statistical Analysis of Spatial Data in the Presence of Missing Observations: A Methodological Guide and an Application to Urban Census Data. *Environ. Planning A*, November 1989, *21*(11), pp. 1511–23.

Griffith-Jones, Stephany. The Bargaining Position of Debtor Nations. In *Bird, G., ed.*, 1989, pp. 41–69.

_____. Cross-Conditionality or the Spread of Obligatory Adjustment. In *Singer, H. W. and Sharma, S., eds. (II)*, 1989, pp. 59–79.

_____. Financial Relations between Britain and Latin America. In *Bulmer-Thomas, V., ed.*, 1989, pp. 121–35.

_____. The International Debt Problem: Prospects and Solutions. In *Singer, H. W. and Sharma, S., eds. (I)*, 1989, pp. 3–21.

_____. Nicholas Kaldor's Contribution to the

Analysis of International Monetary Reform. *Cambridge J. Econ.*, March 1989, *13*(1), pp. 223–35.

_____. Nicholas Kaldor's Contribution to the Analysis of International Monetary Reform. In *Lawson, T.; Palma, J. G. and Sender, J., eds.*, 1989, pp. 223–35.

_____. Whose Crisis Is the Debt Crisis? A View from the South. In *Thomas, C. and Saravanamuttu, P., eds.*, 1989, pp. 107–22.

Griffith, Robin. Antidumping Duties on Parts in the EEC. In *Jackson, J. H. and Vermulst, E. A., eds.*, 1989, pp. 311–25.

Griffith, Winston H. and Gondwe, Derrick K. Trade Creation and Trade Diversion: A Case Study of MDCs in CARIFTA, 1968–1974. *Soc. Econ. Stud.*, September 1989, *38*(3), pp. 149–75.

Griffiths, Pat. Using Information Systems and Technology to Gain Competitive Advantage. In *Punset, E. and Sweeney, G., eds.*, 1989, pp. 78–88.

Griffiths, W. E. and Surekha, K. Additive and Multiplicative Heteroscedasticity: A Bayesian Analysis with an Application to an Expenditure Model. *J. Quant. Econ.*, January 1989, *5*(1), pp. 43–58.

Griliches, Zvi. Patents: Recent Trends and Puzzles. *Brookings Pap. Econ. Act.*, Microeconomics, 1989, pp. 291–319.

_____ and Lichtenberg, Frank R. Errors of Measurement in Output Deflators. *J. Bus. Econ. Statist.*, January 1989, *7*(1), pp. 1–9.

Grillenzoni, Carlo. Alternative Modelings of Multiple Time Series. *Ricerche Econ.*, July–Sept. 1989, *43*(3), pp. 330–56.

Grilli, Vittorio U. Europe 1992: Issues and Prospects for the Financial Markets. *Econ. Policy: A Europ. Forum*, October 1989, (9), pp. 387–421.

_____. Exchange Rates and Seigniorage. *Europ. Econ. Rev.*, March 1989, *33*(2/3), pp. 580–87.

_____. Financial Markets and 1992. *Brookings Pap. Econ. Act.*, 1989, (2), pp. 301–24.

_____. Seigniorage in Europe. In *De Cecco, M. and Giovannini, A., eds.*, 1989, pp. 53–79.

_____ and Beltratti, Andrea. U.S. Military Expenditure and the Dollar. *Econ. Inquiry*, October 1989, *27*(4), pp. 737–44.

_____ and Garber, Peter M. Bank Runs in Open Economies and the International Transmission of Panics. *J. Int. Econ.*, August 1989, *27*(1–2), pp. 165–75.

Grimaldi, Antonio. The Sociopolitical Heritage of Rural Latin America and Its Influence on Managerial Performance. In *Negandhi, A. R., ed.*, 1989, pp. 187–202.

Grimaud, André. Agglomeration Economies and Building Height. *J. Urban Econ.*, January 1989, *25*(1), pp. 17–31.

_____. Nonoptimal Ranking of Households in Urban Space: An Example. *Environ. Planning A*, February 1989, *21*(2), pp. 257–63.

_____ and Campan, Eliane. Le syndrome hollandais. (With English summary.) *Revue Écon.*

Politique, Nov.–Dec. 1989, *99*(6), pp. 810–34.

_____ and Laffont, Jean-Jacques. Existence of a Spatial Equilibrium. *J. Urban Econ.*, March 1989, *25*(2), pp. 213–18.

Grimes, Paul W. and Niss, James F. Concentrated Study Time and Improved Learning Efficiency: An Experiment Using *Economics U$A*. *J. Econ. Educ.*, Spring 1989, *20*(2), pp. 133–38.

_____, et al. The Effectiveness of *Economics U$A* on Learning and Attitudes. *J. Econ. Educ.*, Spring 1989, *20*(2), pp. 139–52.

Grimm, Curtis M.; Corsi, Thomas M. and Jarrell, Judith L. U.S. Motor Carrier Cost Structure under Deregulation. *Logist. Transp. Rev.*, September 1989, *25*(3), pp. 231–49.

Grimstone, Gerry. Privatisation: Macroeconomics and Modalities. In *Ramanadham, V. V., ed.*, 1989, pp. 103–17.

Grinblatt, Mark and Hwang, Chuan Yang. Signalling and the Pricing of New Issues. *J. Finance*, June 1989, *44*(2), pp. 393–420.

_____ and Titman, Sheridan D. Mutual Fund Performance: An Analysis of Quarterly Portfolio Holdings. *J. Bus.*, July 1989, *62*(3), pp. 393–416.

Grindle, Merilee S. The Response to Austerity: Political and Economic Strategies of Mexico's Rural Poor. In *Canak, W. L., ed.*, 1989, pp. 190–215.

_____ and Thomas, John W. Policy Makers, Policy Choices, and Policy Outcomes: The Political Economy of Reform in Developing Countries. *Policy Sciences*, November 1989, *22*(3–4), pp. 213–48.

Grinold, Richard C. The Fundamental Law of Active Management. *J. Portfol. Manage.*, Spring 1989, *15*(3), pp. 30–37.

_____; Rudd, Andrew and Stefek, Dan. Gobal Factors: Fact or Fiction? *J. Portfol. Manage.*, Fall 1989, *16*(1), pp. 79–88.

Grinols, Earl L. Procedural Protectionism: The American Trade Bill and New Interventionist Mode. *Weltwirtsch. Arch.*, 1989, *125*(3), pp. 501–21.

de Grip, Andres. The Economics of Overeducation: Comment. *Econ. Educ. Rev.*, 1989, *8*(2), pp. 205–07.

Gripaios, Peter, et al. High Technology Industry in a Peripheral Area: The Case of Plymouth. *Reg. Stud.*, April 1989, *23*(2), pp. 151–57.

Gripenberg, Maria and Berglund, Tom. Prissättning av ränteoptioner, en översikt. (Option Pricing: A Review. With English summary.) *Ekon. Samfundets Tidskr.*, 1989, *42*(2), pp. 123–36.

Grissa, Abdessatar. An Interest Group Analysis of Tunisia's State Enterprises. In *Nabli, M. K. and Nugent, J. B., eds.*, 1989, pp. 404–27.

Grobar, Lisa M. and Porter, Richard C. Benoit Revisited: Defense Spending and Economic Growth in LDCs. *J. Conflict Resolution*, June 1989, *33*(2), pp. 318–45.

_____ and Stern, Robert M. A Data Set on International Trade in Armaments for the Major Western Industrialized and Developing Countries for 1980: Sources and Methodological Issues. *Weltwirtsch. Arch.*, 1989, *125*(4), pp. 748–62.

Grodal, B. and Hildenbrand, Werner. The Weak Axiom of Revealed Preference in a Productive Economy. *Rev. Econ. Stud.*, October 1989, *56*(4), pp. 635–39.

Groenewegen, Peter D. The Australian Indirect Taxation Regime: Targeting the Defects. *Australian Tax Forum*, 1989, *6*(3), pp. 283–302.

———. New Light on the Origins of Modern Economics. *Econ. Rec.*, June 1989, *65*(189), pp. 136–49.

Groeneweyen, John P. M. and Beiji, Paul R. The French Communication Industry Defined and Analyzed through the Social Fabric Matrix, the *Filière* Approach, and Network Analysis. *J. Econ. Issues*, December 1989, *23*(4), pp. 1059–74.

Groenewold, Nicolaas. The Adjustment of the Real Interest Rate to Inflation. *Appl. Econ.*, July 1989, *21*(7), pp. 947–56.

Groff, David H. The "Revolt" of Assikasso of 1898: An Episode in the Colonial Restructuring of an African Regional Economy. *African Econ. Hist.*, 1989, (18), pp. 1–24.

Groff, James E. and Wingender, John R. On Stochastic Dominance Analysis of Day-of-the-Week Return Patterns. *J. Finan. Res.*, Spring 1989, *12*(1), pp. 51–55.

——— **and Wright, Charlotte J.** The Market for Corporate Control and Its Implications for Accounting Policy Choice. In *Schwartz, B. N., ed.*, 1989, pp. 3–21.

Grofman, Bernard; Feld, Scott L. and Owen, Guillermo. Proving a Distribution-Free Generalization of the Condorcet Jury Theorem. *Math. Soc. Sci.*, February 1989, *17*(1), pp. 1–16.

——— **and Glazer, Amihai.** Why Representatives Are Ideologists though Voters Are Not. *Public Choice*, April 1989, *61*(1), pp. 29–39.

Groll, Shalom and Orzech, Ze'ev B. From Marx to the Okishio Theorem: A Genealogy. *Hist. Polit. Econ.*, Summer 1989, *21*(2), pp. 253–72.

——— **and Orzech, Ze'ev B.** Stages in the Development of a Marxian Concept: The Composition of Capital. *Hist. Polit. Econ.*, Spring 1989, *21*(1), pp. 57–76.

Gromkovskii, V.; Starodubrovskaia, I. and Tolstikov, S. Bureaucratism in the Socialist Economy: Its Essence and Forms, and Means of Overcoming It. *Prob. Econ.*, September 1989, *32*(5), pp. 13–34.

Gronbeck, Bruce E. The Rhetoric of Political Corruption. In *Heidenheimer, A. J.; Johnston, M. and LeVine, V. T., eds.*, 1989, *1978*, pp. 173–89.

de Groot, Hans and Pommer, Evert. The Stability of Stated Preferences for Public Goods: Evidence from Recent Budget Games. *Public Choice*, February 1989, *60*(2), pp. 123–32.

de Groote, Jacques. Firmer Foundations for Lasting Prosperity. In *Cerami, C. A., ed.*, 1989, pp. 223–36.

Grootings, Peter. Conditions and Consequences of the Introduction of New Technology at Work. In *Francis, A. and Grootings, P., eds.*, 1989, pp. 1–34.

Gros, Daniel. On the Volatility of Exchange Rates: Tests of Monetary and Portfolio Balance Models of Exchange Rate Determination. *Weltwirtsch. Arch.*, 1989, *125*(2), pp. 273–95.

———. Paradigms for the Monetary Union of Europe. *J. Common Market Stud.*, March 1989, *27*(3), pp. 219–30.

Gross, Dominique M. Structural Shifts and Unemployment in Switzerland. *Schweiz. Z. Volkswirtsch. Statist.*, June 1989, *125*(2), pp. 113–33.

Gross, Paul F. Breastfeeding in the Philippines: Empirical Study of Its Effects on Child Development. In *Smith, C. S., ed.*, 1989, pp. 1–15.

Gross, William H. Selling the Noise. *J. Portfol. Manage.*, Spring 1989, *15*(3), pp. 61–63.

Grossberg, Adam J. Labor Supply under Real Wage Uncertainty: A New Look at the Intertemporal Substitution Hypothesis. *Southern Econ. J.*, April 1989, *55*(4), pp. 974–86.

Grosser, Ilse. Economic Reforms in Bulgaria. In *Gabrisch, H., ed.*, 1989, pp. 99–109.

Grosskopf, Shawna; Kokkelenberg, Edward C. and Färe, Rolf. Measuring Plant Capacity, Utilization and Technical Change: A Nonparametric Approach. *Int. Econ. Rev.*, August 1989, *30*(3), pp. 655–66.

———; **Pasurka, Carl and Färe, Rolf.** The Effect of Environmental Regulations on the Efficiency of Electric Utilities: 1969 versus 1975. *Appl. Econ.*, February 1989, *21*(2), pp. 225–35.

———; **Weber, William L. and Färe, Rolf.** Measuring School District Performance. *Public Finance Quart.*, October 1989, *17*(4), pp. 409–28.

Grossman-Doerth, Hans; Böhm, Franz and Eucken, Walter. The Ordo Manifesto of 1936. In *Peacock, A. and Willgerodt, H., eds. (II)*, 1989, *1936*, pp. 15–26.

Grossman, Gene M. and Helpman, Elhanan. Product Development and International Trade. *J. Polit. Econ.*, December 1989, *97*(6), pp. 1261–83.

——— **and Levinsohn, James A.** Import Competition and the Stock Market Return to Capital. *Amer. Econ. Rev.*, December 1989, *79*(5), pp. 1065–87.

Grossman, Gregory. Informal Personal Incomes and Outlays of the Soviet Urban Population. In *Portes, A.; Castells, M. and Benton, L. A., eds.*, 1989, pp. 150–70.

———. The Second Economy: Boon or Bane for the Reform of the First Economy? In *Gomulka, S.; Ha, Y.-C. and Kim, C.-O., eds.*, 1989, pp. 79–96.

Grossman, Herschel I. Forecasting Monetary Policy: A Comment. *Carnegie–Rochester Conf. Ser. Public Policy*, Autumn 1989, *31*, pp. 297–301.

——— **and Haraf, William S.** Shunto, Rational Expectations, and Output Growth in Japan. *Empirical Econ.*, 1989, *14*(3), pp. 193–213.

Grossman, Jean Baldwin. The Work Disincentive Effect of Extended Unemployment Compensation: Recent Evidence. *Rev. Econ. Statist.*, February 1989, *71*(1), pp. 159–64.

_____ **and Roberts, Judith.** Welfare Savings from Employment and Training Programs for Welfare Recipients. *Rev. Econ. Statist.*, August 1989, *71*(3), pp. 532–37.

Grossman, Michael; Goldman, Fred and Joyce, Theodore J. An Assessment of the Benefits of Air Pollution Control: The Case of Infant Health. *J. Urban Econ.*, January 1989, *25*(1), pp. 32–51.

Grossman, Philip J. Federalism and the Size of Government. *Southern Econ. J.*, January 1989, *55*(3), pp. 580–93.

_____. Fiscal Decentralization and Government Size: An Extension. *Public Choice*, July 1989, *62*(1), pp. 63–69.

_____. Intergovernmental Grants and Grantor Government Own-Purpose Expenditures. *Nat. Tax J.*, December 1989, *42*(4), pp. 487–94.

_____ **and Kenyon, Peter.** Artists' Subsidy of the Arts: Comment. *Australian Econ. Pap.*, December 1989, *28*(53), pp. 280–87.

Grossman, Sanford J. The Allocational Role of Takeover Bids in Situations of Asymmetric Information. **In** *Grossman, S. J.*, 1989, pp. 143–65.

_____. An Analysis of the Implications for Stock and Futures Price Volatility of Program Trading and Dynamic Hedging Strategies. **In** *Grossman, S. J.*, 1989, pp. 117–42.

_____. An Introduction to the Theory of Rational Expectations under Asymmetric Information. **In** *Grossman, S. J.*, 1989, pp. 11–39.

_____. The Existence of Futures Markets, Noisy Rational Expectations, and Informational Externalities. **In** *Grossman, S. J.*, 1989, pp. 62–90.

_____. Further Results on the Informational Efficiency of Competitive Stock Markets. **In** *Grossman, S. J.*, 1989, pp. 40–61.

_____. The Informational Role of Prices: Introduction. **In** *Grossman, S. J.*, 1989, pp. 1–10.

_____. The Informational Role of Warranties and Private Disclosure about Product Quality. **In** *Grossman, S. J.*, 1989, pp. 166–89.

_____. On the Impossibility of Informationally Efficient Markets. **In** *Grossman, S. J.*, 1989, pp. 91–116.

_____. Rational Expectations and the Informational Role of Prices. **In** *Barro, R. J.*, *ed.*, 1989, pp. 128–52.

_____. Unemployment with Observable Aggregate Shocks. **In** *Grossman, S. J.*, 1989, pp. 190–212.

_____ **and Vila, Jean-Luc.** Portfolio Insurance in Complete Markets: A Note. *J. Bus.*, October 1989, *62*(4), pp. 473–76.

Grove, Hugh and Murray, Dennis. Participation in Software Selection: Effects on Students' Motivation and Performance. **In** *Schwartz, B. N.*, *ed.*, 1989, pp. 141–49.

Groves, Miles; Lee, Frederic S. and Milberg, William. The Power of Ideas and the Impact of One Man, Alfred Eichner 1937–1988. *J. Post Keynesian Econ.*, Spring 1989, *11*(3), pp. 491–96.

Groves, Robert M. Actors and Questions in Telephone and Personal Interview Surveys. **In** *Singer, E. and Presser, S., eds.*, 1989, *1979*, pp. 208–23.

_____; **Lepkowski, James M. and Traugott, Michael W.** Using Dual Frame Designs to Reduce Nonresponse in Telephone Surveys. **In** *Singer, E. and Presser, S., eds.*, 1989, *1987*, pp. 79–96.

_____ **and Magilavy, Lou J.** Measuring and Explaining Interviewer Effects in Centralized Telephone Surveys. **In** *Singer, E. and Presser, S., eds.*, 1989, *1986*, pp. 288–303.

_____ **and Miller, Peter V.** Matching Survey Responses to Official Records: An Exploration of Validity in Victimization Reporting. **In** *Singer, E. and Presser, S., eds.*, 1989, *1985*, pp. 356–70.

Grown, Caren A. and Sebstad, Jennefer. Introduction: Toward a Wider Perspective on Women's Employment. *World Devel.*, July 1989, *17*(7), pp. 937–52.

Grubaugh, Stephen G.; Asabere, Paul K. and Hachey, George. Architecture, Historic Zoning, and the Value of Homes. *J. Real Estate Finance Econ.*, September 1989, *2*(3), pp. 181–95.

_____; **Stollar, Andrew J. and Thompson, G. Rodney.** Socialist Structural Gaps: A Simultaneous Inference Analysis. *Rev. Econ. Statist.*, November 1989, *71*(4), pp. 693–98.

_____ **and Sumner, Scott.** Commodity Prices, Money Surprises, and Fed Credibility: A Comment. *J. Money, Credit, Banking*, August 1989, *21*(3), pp. 407–08.

Grubb, W. Norton. Dropouts, Spells of Time, and Credits in Postsecondary Education: Evidence from Longitudinal Surveys. *Econ. Educ. Rev.*, 1989, *8*(1), pp. 49–67.

_____ **and Wilson, Robert H.** Sources of Increasing Inequality in Wages and Salaries, 1960–80. *Mon. Lab. Rev.*, April 1989, *112*(4), pp. 3–13.

Grube, R. Corwin; Joy, O. Maurice and Fortin, Richard D. Seasonality in NASDAQ Dealer Spreads. *J. Finan. Quant. Anal.*, September 1989, *24*(3), pp. 395–407.

Grubel, Herbert G. Does the World Need a GATT for Services? **In** *Vosgerau, H.-J., ed.*, 1989, pp. 257–75.

_____. Issues in Free Trade in Services between Canada and the United States. **In** *Greenaway, D.; Hyclak, T. and Thornton, R. J., eds.*, 1989, pp. 109–24.

_____. Multinational Banking. **In** *Enderwick, P.*, 1989, pp. 61–78.

_____; **Hammes, David L. and Rosa, Jean-Jacques.** The National Accounts, Household Service Consumption and Its Monetization. *Kyklos*, 1989, *42*(1), pp. 3–15.

_____ **and Walker, Michael A.** Services and the Changing Economic Structure. **In** *Giersch, H., ed.*, 1989, pp. 1–34.

Gruben, William C. and Phillips, Keith R. Diversifying Texas: Recent History and Prospects. *Fed. Res. Bank Dallas Econ. Rev.*, July 1989, pp. 1–12.

Gruber, Andreas. Signalling and Market Behavior. In *Bamberg, G. and Spremann, K.*, eds., 1989, pp. 205–27.

Gruber, Martin J.; Rentzler, Joel and Elton, Edwin J. New Public Offerings, Information, and Investor Rationality: The Case of Publicly Offered Commodity Funds. *J. Bus.*, January 1989, 62(1), pp. 1–15.

Gruber, Utta. Zustandsunabhängige Löhne und heterogene Arbeit. (State-Invariant Wages and Heterogeneous Labour. With English summary.) *Jahr. Nationalökon. Statist.*, October 1989, 206(4–5), pp. 369–82.

Gruchy, Allan G. Institutionalism in the New Palgrave Dictionary of Economics. *J. Econ. Issues*, September 1989, 23(3), pp. 857–63.

_____. Neoinstitutionalism and the Economics of Dissent. In *Tool, M. R. and Samuels, W. J.*, eds. *(II)*, 1989, 1969, pp. 35–49.

Gruen, Fred. Australian Economic Growth: Some Concluding Thoughts. In *[Gruen, F. H.]*, 1989, pp. 262–64.

Gruenberg, L.; Tompkins, C. and Porell, F. The Health Status and Utilization Patterns of the Elderly: Implications for Setting Medicare Payments to HMOs. In *Scheffler, R. M. and Rossiter, L. F.*, eds., 1989, pp. 41–73.

Gruenspecht, Howard K. and Lave, Lester B. The Economics of Health, Safety, and Environmental Regulation. In *Schmalensee, R. and Willig, R. D.*, eds., Vol. 2, 1989, pp. 1507–50.

Grumet, Barbara R. Legal Perspectives on the Allocation of Intensive Care Services. In *Strosberg, M. A.; Fein, I. A. and Carroll, J. D.*, eds., 1989, pp. 76–79.

Grunert, Klaus G. Another Attitude towards Multi-attribute Attitude Theories. In *Grunert, K. G. and Ölander, F.*, eds., 1989, pp. 213–30.

_____. Attributes, Attribute Values and Their Characteristics: A Unifying Approach and an Example Involving a Complex Household Investment. *J. Econ. Psych.*, June 1989, 10(2), pp. 229–51.

_____ and Ölander, Folke. Understanding Economic Behaviour: Introduction. In *Grunert, K. G. and Ölander, F.*, eds., 1989, pp. 1–5.

Grunert, Susanne C. Personality Traits as Elements in a Model of Eating Behaviour. In *Grunert, K. G. and Ölander, F.*, eds., 1989, pp. 309–32.

Grushin, B. A. The Possibility and Prospects of Freedom: Ten Polemical Questions and Answers. In *Yanowitch, M.*, ed., 1989, 1988, pp. 82–100.

Grüske, Karl-Dieter. Additional Costs of Taxation: Administration and Compliance Costs—Some Empirical Evidence. In *Chiancone, A. and Messere, K.*, eds., 1989, pp. 243–64.

Gruver, Gene W. On the Plausibility of the Supply-Driven Input–Output Model: A Theoretical Basis for Input-Coefficient Change. *J. Reg. Sci.*, August 1989, 29(3), pp. 441–50.

Guadagni, Alieto Aldo. Economic Policy during Illia's Period in Office, 1963–66. In *di Tella, G. and Dornbusch, R.*, eds., 1989, pp. 147–61.

Gual, Jordi. Discriminación de precios y diferenciación de productos en el mercado europeo del autómovil. Un análisis descriptivo. (With English summary.) *Invest. Econ.*, January 1989, 13(1), pp. 115–35.

Gualtieri, Giuseppina and Bianchi, Patrizio. Mergers and Acquisitions in Italy and the Debate on Competition Policy. *Antitrust Bull.*, Fall 1989, 34(3), pp. 601–24.

Guan, Jian. Tourism, Cultural Survival and Host Ethnic Participation. In *Chiao, C. and Tapp, N.*, eds., 1989, pp. 75–78.

Guasch, J. Luis and Braverman, Avishay. Institutional Analysis of Credit Co-operatives. In *Bardhan, P.*, ed. *(II)*, 1989, pp. 340–55.

_____ and Braverman, Avishay. Rural Credit Reforms in LDCs: Issues and Evidence. *J. Econ. Devel.*, June 1989, 14(1), pp. 7–34.

Gubitz, Andrea. Seigniorage—Hindernis auf dem Weg zur Europäischen Währungsunion? (Seigniorage—A Barrier on the Way to the European Monetary Union. With English summary.) *Konjunkturpolitik*, 1989, 35(5), pp. 288–96.

Güçmen, Özer and Çelik, Fazil. A Program for Simulating the Conflicting Traffic Flows of Over-Saturated Priority Intersections. In *Candemir, Y.*, ed., 1989, pp. 445–54.

Guerard, John B., Jr. Mergers, Stock Prices, and Industrial Production: Further Evidence. *Econ. Letters*, August 1989, 30(2), pp. 161–64.

_____ and Buell, Stephen G. An Econometric Analysis of Energy Financing. *Energy J.*, April 1989, 10(2), pp. 47–67.

_____ and Clemen, Robert T. Econometric GNP Forecasts: Incremental Information Relative to Naive Extrapolation. *Int. J. Forecasting*, 1989, 5(3), pp. 417–26.

Guerin-Calvert, Margaret E. Vertical Integration as a Threat to Competition: Airline Computer Reservations Systems. In *Kwoka, J. E., Jr. and White, L. J.*, eds., 1989, pp. 338–70.

Guerin, Joseph R. The Just Wage and the Two-Earner Family. *Int. J. Soc. Econ.*, 1989, 16(3), pp. 5–8.

Guerra-Borges, Alfredo. Industrial Development in Central America, 1960–1980: Issues of Debate. In *Irvin, G. and Holland, S.*, eds., 1989, pp. 45–66.

Guesnerie, Roger. First-Best Allocation of Resources with Nonconvexities in Production. In *Cornet, B. and Tulkens, H.*, eds., 1989, pp. 99–143.

_____. Modern Economic Theory and the Multiplicity Issue. *Econ. Rec.*, March 1989, 65(188), pp. 77–81.

_____ and Chiappori, Pierre-André. On Stationary Sunspot Equilibria of Order k. In *Barnett,*

W. A.; *Geweke, J. and Shell, K., eds.*, 1989, pp. 21–44.

_____; **Picard, Pierre and Rey, Patrick.** Adverse Selection and Moral Hazard with Risk Neutral Agents. *Europ. Econ. Rev.*, April 1989, *33*(4), pp. 807–23.

Gueugnon, Jean-François. Un exemple d'application de la stratégie d'immunisation pure à la gestion d'un portefeuille d'obligations à taux fixe. (An Application of the Immunization Strategy to Bond Portfolio Management. With English summary.) *Écon. Societes*, December 1989, *23*(12), pp. 129–58.

Guha, Ashok. Consumption, Efficiency and Surplus Labour. *J. Devel. Econ.*, July 1989, *31*(1), pp. 1–12.

Guha, Sumit. The Handloom Industry of Central India: 1825–1950. *Indian Econ. Soc. Hist. Rev.*, July–Sept. 1989, *26*(3), pp. 297–318.

Gui, Benedetto. Una semplice modellizzazione degli effetti macroeconomici dei sussidi marginali all'occupazione. (The Macroeconomic Effects of Marginal Employment Subsidies: A Simple Model. With English summary.) *Rivista Int. Sci. Econ. Com.*, August 1989, *36*(8), pp. 767–80.

Guibert, Bernard. Le capital symoblique. Généalogie sartrienne d'un concept marxien. (Symbolic Capital: The Sartrian Genesis of a Marxian Notion. With English summary.) *Écon. Societes*, June 1989, *23*(6), pp. 151–83.

Guidotti, Pablo E. Exchange Rate Determination, Interest Rates, and an Integrative Approach to the Demand for Money. *J. Int. Money Finance*, March 1989, *8*(1), pp. 29–45.

Guilkey, David K.; Haines, Pamela S. and Popkin, Barry M. Food Consumption Changes of Adult Women between 1977 and 1985. *Amer. J. Agr. Econ.*, November 1989, *71*(4), pp. 949–59.

_____; **Miles, Mike and Cole, Rebel.** The Motivation for Institutional Real Estate Sales and Implications for Asset Class Returns. *Amer. Real Estate Urban Econ. Assoc. J.*, Spring 1989, *17*(1), pp. 70–86.

_____ **and Schmidt, Peter.** Extended Tabulations for Dickey–Fuller Tests. *Econ. Letters*, December 1989, *31*(4), pp. 355–57.

_____, **et al.** Prenatal Care and Pregnancy Outcome in Cebu, Philippines. *J. Devel. Econ.*, April 1989, *30*(2), pp. 241–72.

Guillaume, Y.; Meulders, Danièle and Plasman, Robert. Simulation des impacts de l'achèvement du marché intérieur. Le cas de la Belgique. (With English summary.) *Cah. Écon. Bruxelles*, 4th Trimester 1989, (124), pp. 449–73.

Guillaumont, Patrick and Guillaumont, Sylviane. The Implications of European Monetary Union for African Countries. *J. Common Market Stud.*, December 1989, *28*(2), pp. 139–53.

Guillaumont, Sylviane and Guillaumont, Patrick. The Implications of European Monetary Union for African Countries. *J. Common Market Stud.*, December 1989, *28*(2), pp. 139–53.

Guimarães, Eduardo Augusto. A indústria auto-

mobiléstica brasileira na década de 80. (With English summary.) *Pesquisa Planejamento Econ.*, August 1989, *19*(2), pp. 347–77.

Guimarães, Roberto P. The Ecopolitics of Development in Brazil. *CEPAL Rev.*, August 1989, (38), pp. 89–103.

Guindo, Ousmane. The Role of Adaptive Research in Increasing Agricultural Productivity: The Experience from Haiti. *Can. J. Agr. Econ.*, Part 2, December 1989, *37*(4), pp. 887–97.

Guiomard, Cathal and Hurley, Margaret. Determinants of Money Demand in Ireland 1971 to 1988: Rounding-Up the Usual Suspects. *Econ. Soc. Rev.*, October 1989, *21*(1), pp. 139–49.

Guitián, Manuel. Fiscal Adjustment, Debt Management, and Conditionality. In *Monti, M., ed.*, 1989, pp. 112–37.

Gul, Faruk. Bargaining Foundations of Shapley Value. *Econometrica*, January 1989, *57*(1), pp. 81–95.

Gülalp, Haldun. The Stages and Long-Cycles of Capitalist Development. *Rev. Radical Polit. Econ.*, Winter 1989, *21*(4), pp. 83–92.

Gulati, Umesh C. Dynamics of Economic Restructuring in Small NIC. *Indian Econ. J.*, Oct.–Dec. 1989, *37*(2), pp. 40–56.

Guldmann, Jean-Michel. Capacity Cost Allocation in the Provision of Urban Public Services: The Case of Gas Distribution. *Growth Change*, Spring 1989, *20*(2), pp. 1–18.

Güldner, Bernhard; Wenzel, Georg and Dejon, Bruno. Direct Equilibria of Economies and Their Perfect Homogeneity Limits. In *Andersson, Å. E., et al., eds.*, 1989, pp. 81–105.

Gulhati, Ravi. Trade Policy Reforms in Sub-Saharan Africa. In *Singer, H. W. and Sharma, S., eds. (II)*, 1989, pp. 246–55.

Gulland, J. A. The State of Worldwide Fishery Statistics: A Modest Proposal: Comments. *Marine Resource Econ.*, 1989, *6*(1), pp. 85–86.

Gullason, Edward T. The Consumption Value of Schooling: An Empirical Estimate of One Aspect. *J. Human Res.*, Spring 1989, *24*(2), pp. 287–98.

_____. New Evidence Supporting the Screening Hypothesis. *Atlantic Econ. J.*, June 1989, *17*(2), pp. 80.

Gulley, O. David and Scott, Frank A., Jr. Lottery Effects on Pari-mutual Tax Revenues. *Nat. Tax J.*, March 1989, *42*(1), pp. 89–93.

Gultekin, Mustafa N.; Gultekin, N. Bulent and Penati, Alessandro. Capital Controls and International Capital Market Segmentation: The Evidence from the Japanese and American Stock Markets. *J. Finance*, September 1989, *44*(4), pp. 849–69.

Gultekin, N. Bulent; Penati, Alessandro and Gultekin, Mustafa N. Capital Controls and International Capital Market Segmentation: The Evidence from the Japanese and American Stock Markets. *J. Finance*, September 1989, *44*(4), pp. 849–69.

_____ **and Rogalski, Richard J.** Duration as a Measure of Basis Risk: The Wrong Answer at

Low Cost—Answer to Rejoinder. *J. Portfol. Manage.*, Summer 1989, *15*(4), pp. 86–87.

_____ **and Rogalski, Richard J.** Duration: Response to Critics: Comment. *J. Portfol. Manage.*, Spring 1989, *15*(3), pp. 83–87.

Gump, James. Ecological Change and Pre-Shakan State Formation. *African Econ. Hist.*, 1989, (18), pp. 57–71.

Gunasekera, H. Don B. H. Intraindustry Specialization in Production and Trade in Newly Industrializing Countries: A Conceptual Framework and Some Empirical Evidence from East Asia. *World Devel.*, August 1989, *17*(8), pp. 1279–87.

_____. The Relationship between the Variation in Protection within Manufacturing Industries and Intra-industry trade in Korea: A Preliminary Analysis. *Developing Econ.*, March 1989, *27*(1), pp. 83–93.

_____; **Parsons, David and Kirby, Michael G.** Liberalizing Agricultural Trade: Some Perspectives for Developing Countries. In *Whalley, J., ed., Vol. 1*, 1989, pp. 238–57.

Gunay, Erdal; Aneja, Yash P. and Chandra, Ramesh. A Portfolio Approach to Estimating the Average Correlation Coefficient for the Constant Correlation Model. *J. Finance*, December 1989, *44*(5), pp. 1435–38.

Gunderson, Gerald. Privatization and the 19th-Century Turnpike. *Cato J.*, Spring–Summer 1989, *9*(1), pp. 191–200.

Gunderson, Morley. Male–Female Wage Differentials and Policy Responses. *J. Econ. Lit.*, March 1989, *27*(1), pp. 46–72.

_____; **Kervin, John and Reid, Frank.** The Effect of Labour Relations Legislation on Strike Incidence. *Can. J. Econ.*, November 1989, *22*(4), pp. 779–94.

Gunjal, Kisan and Kebede, Yohannes. Economic Evaluation of a Postdrought Recovery Agricultural Project in Ethiopia. *Can. J. Agr. Econ.*, Part 2, December 1989, *37*(4), pp. 899–907.

Günlük-Şenesen, G. and Şenesen, M. U. An Analysis of the Turkish Transportation Sector in the Context of a Two-Group Industry Model. In *Candemir, Y., ed.*, 1989, pp. 145–60.

Gunn, L. Ray. The Crisis of Distributive Politics: The Debate over State Debts and Development Policy in New York, 1837–1842. In *Pencak, W. and Wright, C. E., eds.*, 1989, pp. 168–201.

Gunning, J. Patrick. Mises on the Evenly Rotating Economy. In *Rothbard, M. N. and Block, W., eds.*, 1989, pp. 123–35.

_____. Professor Caldwell on Ludwig von Mises' Methodology. In *Rothbard, M. N. and Block, W., eds.*, 1989, pp. 163–76.

Gunning, Jan Willem; Bevan, David L. and Collier, Paul. Black Markets: Illegality, Information, and Rents. *World Devel.*, December 1989, *17*(12), pp. 1955–63.

_____; **Bevan, David L. and Collier, Paul.** Fiscal Response to a Temporary Trade Shock: The Aftermath of the Kenyan Coffee Boom. *World Bank Econ. Rev.*, September 1989, *3*(3), pp. 359–78.

Gunst, Péter. Agrarian Systems of Central and Eastern Europe. In *Chirot, D., ed.*, 1989, pp. 53–91.

Gunter, Frank R. Customs Union Theory: Retrospect and Prospect. In *Greenaway, D.; Hyclak, T. and Thornton, R. J., eds.*, 1989, pp. 1–30.

Gunter, Lewell F. and McNamara, Kevin T. Off-Farm Earnings: The Impact of Economic Structure. *Rev. Reg. Stud.*, Fall 1989, *19*(3), pp. 37–45.

_____; **Miller, Bill R. and Dubman, Robert W.** Revenue and Cost Uncertainty, Generalized Mean–Variance and the Linear Complementarity Problem: Comment. *Amer. J. Agr. Econ.*, August 1989, *71*(3), pp. 806–09.

Gunther, William D. Foreign Direct Investment in the United States: Implications for Corporate Control. In *McKee, D. L., ed.*, 1989, pp. 103–15.

Guo, Chong Dao. The Developing World and the Multifiber Arrangement. In *Whalley, J., ed., Vol. 2*, 1989, pp. 83–100.

Guo, Jinhua. The Educational and Technical Qualities of the Contemporary Worker. *Chinese Econ. Stud.*, Summer 1989, *22*(4), pp. 18–31.

_____; **He, Bing and Hao, Chengyi.** Conditions of Workers' Material and Mental Lives and Trends in Their Development. *Chinese Econ. Stud.*, Summer 1989, *22*(4), pp. 32–38.

_____ **and Wu, Shouhui.** Workers' Evaluation of and Hopes for Trade Unions. *Chinese Econ. Stud.*, Summer 1989, *22*(4), pp. 55–68.

Gup, Benton E.; Wall, Larry D. and Cheng, David C. Financial Determinants of Bank Takeovers: A Note. *J. Money, Credit, Banking*, November 1989, *21*(4), pp. 524–36.

_____ **and Walter, John R.** Top Performing Small Banks: Making Money the Old-Fashioned Way. *Fed. Res. Bank Richmond Econ. Rev.*, Nov.–Dec. 1989, *75*(6), pp. 23–35.

Gupta, Arjun K.; Saleh, A. K. Md. Ehsanes and Sen, Pranab K. Improved Estimation in a Contingency Table: Independence Structure. *J. Amer. Statist. Assoc.*, June 1989, *84*(406), pp. 525–32.

Gupta, Atul and Misra, Lalatendu. Public Information and Pre-announcement Trading in Takeover Stocks. *J. Econ. Bus.*, August 1989, *41*(3), pp. 225–33.

Gupta, G. S. Growth Variations across Developing Countries: How Much and Why? *Indian Econ. J.*, Jan.–March 1989, *36*(3), pp. 49–64.

Gupta, Kanhaya L. Budget Deficits and Interest Rates in the United States. *Public Choice*, January 1989, *60*(1), pp. 87–92.

_____ **and Moazzami, B.** Demand for Money in Asia. *Econ. Modelling*, October 1989, *6*(4), pp. 467–73.

Gupta, Manash Ranjan. Credit and Share-Cropping: Comments. *J. Devel. Econ.*, October 1989, *31*(2), pp. 403–11.

_____. Nutrition, Dependants and the Mode of Wage Payment. *Oxford Econ. Pap.*, October 1989, *41*(4), pp. 737–48.

Gupta, N. S. Cultural Dynamics and Management

Development. In *Davies, J., et al., eds.*, 1989, pp. 57–65.

Gupta, Prakash C. International Cooperation in Dealing with Health Problems Caused by Tobacco. In *Reich, M. R. and Marui, E., eds.*, 1989, pp. 209–33.

Gupta, Sanjeev; Lipschitz, Leslie and Mayer, Thomas. The Common Agricultural Policy of the EC. *Finance Devel.*, June 1989, *26*(2), pp. 37–39.

Guria, Jagadish C. An Assessment of the Effects of Road Freight Transport Regulations in Developing Countries. *Int. J. Transport Econ.*, October 1989, *16*(3), pp. 237–62.

Gurney, Andrew. Obtaining Estimates for the Standard Errors of Long-run Parameters. *Nat. Inst. Econ. Rev.*, May 1989, (128), pp. 89–90.

_____ **and Barrell, R. J.** The World Economy. *Nat. Inst. Econ. Rev.*, November 1989, (130), pp. 23–45.

_____ **and Barrell, R. J.** The World Economy. *Nat. Inst. Econ. Rev.*, February 1989, (127), pp. 26–45.

_____ **and Barrell, R. J.** The World Economy. *Nat. Inst. Econ. Rev.*, August 1989, (129), pp. 22–41.

_____ **and Barrell, R. J.** The World Economy. *Nat. Inst. Econ. Rev.*, May 1989, (128), pp. 20–38.

Gurrieri, Adolfo. Features and Phases of the "Swedish Model": Comments. *CEPAL Rev.*, December 1989, (39), pp. 27–29.

Gurry, Francis. Electronic Highways for World Trade: Issues in Telecommunication and Data Services: Institutional Aspects. In *Robinson, P.; Sauvant, K. P. and Govitrikar, V. P., eds.*, 1989, pp. 197–219.

Gurtler, Thomas; Adegbulugbe, Anthony O. and Dayo, Felix. Optimal Structure of the Nigerian Energy Supply Mix. *Energy J.*, April 1989, *10*(2), pp. 165–76.

Gussin, Arnold E. S. Windows on a New World: Biotechnology. In *Finkelstein, J., ed.*, 1989, pp. 109–30.

Gustafson, Cole R. Stochastic Dynamic Modeling: An Aid to Agricultural Lender Decision Making. *Western J. Agr. Econ.*, July 1989, *14*(1), pp. 157–65.

Gustafson, Elizabeth and Hadley, Lawrence. Labor Supply and Money Illusion: A Dynamic Simultaneous Equations Model. *Quart. Rev. Econ. Bus.*, Winter 1989, *29*(4), pp. 63–75.

Gustafsson, Björn and Klevmarken, N. Anders. The Political Economy of Social Security: Editor's Introduction and Summary. In *Gustafsson, B. A. and Klevmarken, N. A., eds.*, 1989, pp. 1–9.

Gustavo Secchi, Angel and Matheu, Luis María. Administrative and Compliance Costs of Taxation: Argentina. In *International Fiscal Association, ed.* (*I*), 1989, pp. 177–91.

Gustman, Alan L. and Steinmeier, Thomas L. An Analysis of Pension Benefit Formulas, Pension Wealth, and Incentives from Pensions. In *Ehrenberg, R. G., ed.*, 1989, pp. 53–106.

Guth, Michael A. S. Intrinsic Uncertainty and Common-Knowledge Priors in Financial Economics. *J. Finan. Res.*, Winter 1989, *12*(4), pp. 269–83.

_____ **and Philippatos, George C.** A Reexamination of Arbitrage Pricing Theory (APT) under Common Knowledge Beliefs. *Rivista Int. Sci. Econ. Com.*, August 1989, *36*(8), pp. 729–46.

Gutman, Patrick. The Export of "Complete Plants" with Buy-Back Agreements: A Substitute for Direct Investment in East–South Relations? In *Schulz, B. H. and Hansen, W. W., eds.*, 1989, pp. 153–80.

Guttman, Joel M. and Schnytzer, Adi. Strategic Work Interactions and the Kibbutz–Kolkhoz Paradox. *Econ. J.*, September 1989, *99*(397), pp. 686–99.

Guttmann, Robert. Changing of the Guard at the Fed. In *Guttmann, R., ed.*, 1989, *1987*, pp. 156–61.

_____. Financial Restructuring and Innovation. In *Guttmann, R., ed.*, 1989, pp. 134–38.

_____. The Great Recession as a Historic Turning Point. In *Guttmann, R., ed.*, 1989, pp. 109–11.

_____. The International Monetary System. In *Guttmann, R., ed.*, 1989, pp. 15–22.

_____. The Long-Term Consequences of Excessive Indebtedness. In *Guttmann, R., ed.*, 1989, pp. 65–68.

_____. Managing Credit Money. In *Guttmann, R., ed.*, 1989, pp. 3–8.

_____. The Post-War Monetary Regime. In *Guttmann, R., ed.*, 1989, pp. 307–17.

_____. Regulating Financial Institutions. In *Guttmann, R., ed.*, 1989, pp. 9–14.

_____. The Saving Shortfall Reconsidered. *Challenge*, Sept.–Oct. 1989, *32*(5), pp. 47–51.

_____. The Socio-economic Foundations of Financial Accounting. *Brit. Rev. Econ. Issues*, Spring 1989, *11*(24), pp. 75–102.

_____. Stable Exchange Rates and a Proper Form of World Money. In *Guttmann, R., ed.*, 1989, pp. 252–56.

_____. The Structure and Policy Options of the Federal Reserve. In *Guttmann, R., ed.*, 1989, pp. 25–30.

_____. Temporary Illiquidity versus Long-Term Insolvency. In *Guttmann, R., ed.*, 1989, pp. 175–79.

_____. The Transition to a New Monetary Regime. In *Guttmann, R., ed.*, 1989, pp. 318–27.

_____. The United States as a Debtor Nation. In *Guttmann, R., ed.*, 1989, pp. 219–22.

Guyer, Jane. From Seasonal Income to Daily Diet in a Partially Commercialized Rural Economy (Southern Cameroon). In *Sahn, D. E., ed.*, 1989, pp. 137–50.

Guyomard, H. and Boyle, G. E. Inferring Long-run Supply Elasticities from a Short-run Variable-Revenue Function. *Econ. Soc. Rev.*, October 1989, *21*(1), pp. 127–37.

_____ **and Vermersch, D.** Economy and Technology of the French Cereal Sector: A Dual Approach. In *Bauer, S. and Henrichsmeyer, W., eds.*, 1989, pp. 260–77.

Guzanova, A.; Liberman, L. and Shokhin, A. Prices through the Eyes of the Population. *Prob. Econ.*, June 1989, *32*(2), pp. 6–13.

Guzda, Henry P. United Auto Workers 29th Constitutional Convention. *Mon. Lab. Rev.*, October 1989, *112*(10), pp. 34–36.

Gwartney, James D. and Holcombe, Randall G. Political Parties and the Legislative Principal–Agent Relationship. *J. Inst. Theoretical Econ.*, December 1989, *145*(4), pp. 669–75.

Gwiazda, Adam. International Economic Interdependence and the Prospects for East–West–South Cooperation. In *Wohlmuth, K., ed.*, 1989, pp. 103–21.

_____. Poland's Foreign Trade Performance and Policy Changes. *Jahr. Wirtsch. Osteuropas*, 1989, *13*(1), pp. 127–52.

Gwilliam, Ken M. Setting the Market Free: Deregulation of the Bus Industry. *J. Transp. Econ. Policy*, January 1989, *23*(1), pp. 29–43.

Gwin, Catherine and Feinberg, Richard E. Pulling Together: Reforming the Fund. In *Gwin, C. and Feinberg, R. E., eds.*, 1989, pp. 3–29.

Gwinn, Lawrence. The Transmission of U.S. Income Disturbances to Canada under Fixed Exchange Rates. *Appl. Econ.*, July 1989, *21*(7), pp. 867–79.

Gyimah-Brempong, Kwabena. Demand for Factors of Production in Municipal Police Departments. *J. Urban Econ.*, March 1989, *25*(2), pp. 247–59.

_____. Functional Substitution among Crimes: Some Evidence. *Eastern Econ. J.*, April–June 1989, *15*(2), pp. 129–40.

_____. Is the Tradeoff between Defense Spending and Social Welfare an Illusion?—Some Evidence from Tropical Africa. *Eastern Afr. Econ. Rev.*, December 1989, *5*(2), pp. 74–90.

_____. Production of Public Safety: Are Socioeconomic Characteristics of Local Communities Important Factors? *J. Appl. Econometrics*, Jan.–March 1989, *4*(1), pp. 57–71.

_____ and Akaah, Ishmael P. Military Participation and Economic Development in LDCs: New Evidence. *J. Econ. Devel.*, June 1989, *14*(1), pp. 115–34.

Gyimesi, Sandor. Incomes, Public Constructions and Investments in the Hungarian Towns in the 18th Century. In *Guarducci, A., ed.*, 1989, pp. 97–112.

Gyourko, Joseph and Han, Jaehye Kim. Housing Wealth, Housing Finance, and Tenure in Korea. *Reg. Sci. Urban Econ.*, May 1989, *19*(2), pp. 211–34.

_____ and Linneman, Peter D. Equity and Efficiency Aspects of Rent Control: An Empirical Study of New York City. *J. Urban Econ.*, July 1989, *26*(1), pp. 54–74.

_____ and Tracy, Joseph S. The Importance of Local Fiscal Conditions in Analyzing Local Labor Markets. *J. Polit. Econ.*, October 1989, *97*(5), pp. 1208–31.

_____ and Tracy, Joseph S. Local Public Sector Rent-Seeking and Its Impact on Local Land Values. *Reg. Sci. Urban Econ.*, August 1989, *19*(3), pp. 493–516.

_____ and Tracy, Joseph S. On the Political Economy of Land Value Capitalization and Local Public Sector Rent Seeking in a Tiebout Model. *J. Urban Econ.*, September 1989, *26*(2), pp. 152–73.

Ha, Yong-Chool. The Soviet Communist Party and Economic Reform: A Case Study. In *Gomulka, S.; Ha, Y.-C. and Kim, C.-O., eds.*, 1989, pp. 108–20.

Ha, Young-Won and Hoch, Stephen J. Ambiguity, Processing Strategy, and Advertising–Evidence Interactions. *J. Cons. Res.*, December 1989, *16*(3), pp. 354–60.

Haag, Günter. Spatial Interaction Models and Their Micro-foundation. In *Andersson, Å. E., et al., eds.*, 1989, pp. 165–74.

de Haan, Jakob and Cesar, Herman. Predicting the Money Multiplier in the Netherlands Once More. *Empirical Econ.*, 1989, *14*(3), pp. 215–27.

_____ and Zelhorst, Dick. Stabilization of the Economy: Some More International Evidence. *Banca Naz. Lavoro Quart. Rev.*, December 1989, (171), pp. 431–40.

Haanes-Olsen, Leif. Worldwide Trends and Developments in Social Security, 1985–87. *Soc. Sec. Bull.*, February 1989, *52*(2), pp. 14–26.

Haaparanta, Pertti J. The Intertemporal Effects of International Transfers. *J. Int. Econ.*, May 1989, *26*(3/4), pp. 371–82.

Haas, Jack. The Process of Apprenticeship: Ritual Ordeal and the Adoption of a Cloak of Competence. In *Coy, M. W., ed.*, 1989, pp. 87–105.

Haas, Peter M. Do Regimes Matter? Epistemic Communities and Mediterranean Pollution Control. *Int. Organ.*, Summer 1989, *43*(3), pp. 377–403.

Haas, Richard D.; Masson, Paul R. and Boughton, James M. The Role of Exchange Rate Movements in Transmitting International Disturbances. In *Hodgman, D. R. and Wood, G. E., eds.*, 1989, pp. 180–213.

Haas-Wilson, Deborah. Employment Choices and Earnings of Social Workers: Comparing Private Practice and Salaried Employment. *Inquiry*, Summer 1989, *26*(2), pp. 182–90.

_____. Strategic Regulatory Entry Deterrence: An Empirical Test in the Ophthalmic Market. *J. Health Econ.*, December 1989, *8*(3), pp. 339–52.

_____; Cheadle, Allen and Scheffler, Richard M. Demand for Mental Health Services: An Episode of Treatment Approach. *Southern Econ. J.*, July 1989, *56*(1), pp. 219–32.

Haber, Susan and McCall, Nelda. Use of Nonphysician Providers in the Medicare Program: Assessment of the Direct Reimbursement of Clinical Social Workers Demonstration Project. *Inquiry*, Summer 1989, *26*(2), pp. 158–69.

Haberler, Gottfried. Should Floating Continue? In *Dorn, J. A. and Niskanen, W. A., eds.*, 1989, pp. 293–301.

Habermeier, Karl F. Competing Technologies,

the Learning Curve, and Rational Expectations. *Europ. Econ. Rev.*, September 1989, *33*(7), pp. 1293–1311.

Habib, Ahsanul and Stahl, Charles W. The Impact of Overseas Workers' Remittances on Indigenous Industries: Evidence from Bangladesh. *Developing Econ.*, September 1989, *27*(3), pp. 269–85.

Habibagahi, Hamid and Quirk, James. Hicksian Stability and Walras' Law. In *Wood, J. C. and Woods, R. N., eds., Vol. 2, 1989, 1973*, pp. 249–61.

Habibi, Nader. Cultural Conflict and Economic Development in Traditional Societies: Note. *J. Compar. Econ.*, March 1989, *13*(1), pp. 134–37.

Habicht, Jean-Pierre; Berman, Peter and Sisler, Daniel G. Equity in Public-Sector Primary Health Care: The Role of Service Organization in Indonesia. *Econ. Devel. Cult. Change*, July 1989, *37*(4), pp. 778–803.

Hachette, Dominique. The Chilean Economy in the Eighties: Adjustment and Recovery: Comment. In *Edwards, S. and Larrain, F., eds.,* 1989, pp. 237–40.

Hachey, George; Grubaugh, Stephen G. and Asabere, Paul K. Architecture, Historic Zoning, and the Value of Homes. *J. Real Estate Finance Econ.*, September 1989, *2*(3), pp. 181–95.

ten Hacken, Peter; Kapteyn, Arie and Woittiez, Isolde. Unemployment Benefits and the Labor Market, A Micro/Macro Approach. In *Gustafsson, B. A. and Klevmarken, N. A., eds.,* 1989, pp. 143–64.

Hackett, D. W. and Kabir, M. Is Atlantic Canada Becoming More Dependent on Federal Transfers? *Can. Public Policy*, March 1989, *15*(1), pp. 43–48.

Hackett, Rick D. and Jain, Harish C. Measuring Effectiveness of Employment Equity Programs in Canada: Public Policy and a Survey. *Can. Public Policy*, June 1989, *15*(2), pp. 189–204.

Hackl, Peter and Katzenbeisser, Walter. Tests against Nonconstancy in Linear Models Based on Counting Statistics. In *Hackl, P., ed.,* 1989, pp. 53–70.

_____ **and Westlund, Anders H.** Statistical Analysis of "Structural Change": An Annotated Bibliography. *Empirical Econ.*, 1989, *14*(2), pp. 167–92.

_____ **and Westlund, Anders H.** Statistical Analysis of "Structural Change": An Annotated Bibliography. In *Kramer, W., ed.,* 1989, pp. 103–28.

Hackman, B. Katarina and Dunphy, Dexter C. Locus of Control in Human Resource Management: A Comparison of the United States and China. In *Nedd, A., ed.,* 1989, pp. 33–44.

Hackman, Steven T. and Passy, Ury. A Consistent, Reflexive Duality Framework of Production: An Application of Quasi-Concave Conjugacy Theory. *J. Econ. (Z. Nationalökon.),* 1989, *49*(2), pp. 183–198.

Hackmann, Johannes. Einkommensteuerliche Investitionswirkungen bei unterschiedlichen Fassungen des steuerlichen Einkommensbe-griffs. (Tax Effects on Investment Decisions with Different Definitions of Taxable Income. With English summary.) *Z. Wirtschaft. Sozialwissen.,* 1989, *109*(1), pp. 49–74.

Hadaway, Beverly L. and Hadaway, Samuel C. Do Institutional Constraints Hobble Performance? *J. Portfol. Manage.*, Winter 1989, *15*(2), pp. 33–37.

Hadaway, Samuel C. and Hadaway, Beverly L. Do Institutional Constraints Hobble Performance? *J. Portfol. Manage.*, Winter 1989, *15*(2), pp. 33–37.

Haddad, L. The Role of the State in the Light of Ibn Khaldun's Economics. *Middle East Bus. Econ. Rev.*, January 1989, *1*(1), pp. 54–62.

Hadden, Susan G. The Future of Expert Systems in Government. *J. Policy Anal. Manage.*, Spring 1989, *8*(2), pp. 203–08.

Hadden, W. James, Jr. Expert Systems for Environmental Permits. *J. Policy Anal. Manage.*, Spring 1989, *8*(2), pp. 187–93.

Haden, Kimberly L. and Johnson, Larry A. Factors Which Contribute to the Financial Performance of Selected Tennessee Dairies. *Southern J. Agr. Econ.*, July 1989, *21*(1), pp. 105–12.

Hadiwigeno, Soetatwo; Hedley, Douglas and Baharsjah, Sjarifudin. Agricultural Policy and Food Self-Sufficiency in Developing Countries. In *Helmuth, J. W. and Johnson, S. R., eds., Vol. 2,* 1989, pp. 121–37.

Hadley, Eleanor M. The Diffusion of Keynesian Ideas in Japan. In *Hall, P. A., ed.,* 1989, pp. 291–309.

Hadley, Jack and Swartz, Katherine. The Impacts on Hospital Costs between 1980 and 1984 of Hospital Rate Regulation, Competition, and Changes in Health Insurance Coverage. *Inquiry*, Spring 1989, *26*(1), pp. 35–47.

_____; **Zukerman, Stephen and Feder, Judith.** Profits and Fiscal Pressure in the Prospective Payment System: Their Impacts on Hospitals. *Inquiry*, Fall 1989, *26*(3), pp. 354–65.

Hadley, Lawrence and Gustafson, Elizabeth. Labor Supply and Money Illusion: A Dynamic Simultaneous Equations Model. *Quart. Rev. Econ. Bus.*, Winter 1989, *29*(4), pp. 63–75.

Häendler, Ernst W. and Balzer, Wolfgang. Ordinary Least Squares as a Method of Measurement. In *Balzer, W. and Hamminga, B., eds.,* 1989, pp. 129–46.

Haeusler, Juergen and Hirsch, Joachim. Political Regulation: The Crisis of Fordism and the Transformation of the Party System in West Germany. In *Gottdiener, M. and Komninos, N., eds.,* 1989, pp. 300–327.

Hafer, R. W. Does Dollar Depreciation Cause Inflation? *Fed. Res. Bank St. Louis Rev.*, July–Aug. 1989, *71*(4), pp. 16–28.

_____ **and Batten, Dallas S.** The Impact of the Exchange Rate on U.S. Inflation and GNP Growth: Reply. *Southern Econ. J.*, April 1989, *55*(4), pp. 1052–55.

_____ **and Dwyer, Gerald P., Jr.** Interest Rates and Economic Announcements. *Fed. Res.*

Bank St. Louis Rev., March–April 1989, *71*(2), pp. 34–46.

_____ and **Hein, Scott E.** Comparing Futures and Survey Forecasts of Near-Term Treasury Bill Rates. *Fed. Res. Bank St. Louis Rev.*, May–June 1989, *71*(3), pp. 33–42.

_____ and **Sheehan, Richard G.** The Sensitivity of VAR Forecasts to Alternative Lag Structures. *Int. J. Forecasting*, 1989, *5*(3), pp. 399–408.

Hagan, Joe D. Domestic Political Regime Changes and Third World Voting Realignments in the United Nations, 1946–84. *Int. Organ.*, Summer 1989, *43*(3), pp. 505–41.

Hagemann, Robert P. and Nicoletti, Giuseppe. Population Ageing: Economic Effects and Some Policy Implications for Financing Public Pensions. *OECD Econ. Stud.*, Spring 1989, (12), pp. 51–96.

Hagen, Daniel A. and Vincent, James W. On the Pricing of Independently-Generated Electricity. *Southern Econ. J.*, April 1989, *55*(4), pp. 935–53.

von Hagen, Jürgen. Monetary Targeting with Exchange Rate Constraints: The Bundesbank in the 1980s. *Fed. Res. Bank St. Louis Rev.*, Sept.–Oct. 1989, *71*(5), pp. 53–69.

_____. Relative Commodity Prices and Cointegration. *J. Bus. Econ. Statist.*, October 1989, *7*(4), pp. 497–503.

Hagen, William W. Seventeenth-Century Crisis in Brandenburg: The Thirty Years' War, the Destabilization of Serfdom, and the Rise of Absolutism. *Amer. Historical Rev.*, April 1989, *94*(2), pp. 302–35.

Hagenaars, Aldi and Renes, Gusta. The Perceived Distribution of Job Characteristics. *Europ. Econ. Rev.*, April 1989, *33*(4), pp. 845–62.

Hagerty, Kathleen M. and Fishman, Michael J. Disclosure Decisions by Firms and the Competition for Price Efficiency. *J. Finance*, July 1989, *44*(3), pp. 633–46.

Haggard, Stephan. The International Politics of Industrial Change: Introduction. **In** *Haggard, S. and Moon, C., eds.*, 1989, pp. 1–21.

_____ and **Cheng, Tun-jen.** The New Bilateralism: The East Asian NICs in American Foreign Economic Policy. **In** *Haggard, S. and Moon, C., eds.*, 1989, pp. 305–29.

_____ and **Kaufman, Robert R.** Economic Adjustment in New Democracies. **In** *Nelson, J. M., ed.*, 1989, pp. 57–77.

_____ and **Kaufman, Robert R.** The Politics of Stabilization and Structural Adjustment. **In** *Sachs, J. D., ed. (II)*, 1989, pp. 263–74.

_____ and **Kaufman, Robert R.** The Politics of Stabilization and Structural Adjustment. **In** *Sachs, J. D., ed. (I)*, 1989, pp. 209–54.

Haggblade, Steven; Hazell, Peter B. R. and Brown, James. Farm–Nonfarm Linkages in Rural Sub-Saharan Africa. *World Devel.*, August 1989, *17*(8), pp. 1173–1201.

Hagin, Allan Scott and Allen, Robert F. Scale Related Efficiencies as a (Minor) Source of the Profits–Market Share Relationship. *Rev. Econ.*

Statist., August 1989, *71*(3), pp. 523–26.

Hahn, Albert. Brazil: The 'Alcohol Plan' Reviewed. **In** *[Marjolin, R.]*, 1989, pp. 151–59.

Hahn, Chan K. Korean Manufacturing Strategy. **In** *Chung, K. H. and Lee, H. C., eds.*, 1989, pp. 131–44.

_____ and **Kim, Jay S.** The Korean Chaebol as an Organizational Form. **In** *Chung, K. H. and Lee, H. C., eds.*, 1989, pp. 51–64.

Hahn, Dietger. Integrierte und flexible Unternehmensführung durch computergestütztes Controlling. (With English summary.) *Z. Betriebswirtshaft*, November 1989, *59*(11), pp. 1135–58.

Hahn, Frank H. The Economics of Missing Markets, Information, and Games: Introduction. **In** *Hahn, F., ed.*, 1989, pp. 1–4.

_____. Equilibrium with Transaction Costs. **In** *Starr, R. M., ed.*, 1989, *1971*, pp. 203–25.

_____. Information Dynamics and Equilibrium. **In** *Hahn, F., ed.*, 1989, pp. 106–26.

_____. Kaldor on Growth. **In** *Lawson, T.; Palma, J. G. and Sender, J., eds.*, 1989, pp. 47–57.

_____. Kaldor on Growth. *Cambridge J. Econ.*, March 1989, *13*(1), pp. 47–57.

_____. On Some Problems of Proving the Existence of an Equilibrium in a Monetary Economy. **In** *Starr, R. M., ed.*, 1989, *1966*, pp. 298–306.

_____. Reflections on the Invisible Hand. **In** *Johnson, C., ed.*, 1989, pp. 86–105.

Hahn, Robert W. Economic Prescriptions for Environmental Problems: Not Exactly What the Doctor Ordered. **In** *Shogren, J. F., ed.*, 1989, pp. 131–89.

_____. Economic Prescriptions for Environmental Problems: How the Patient Followed the Doctor's Orders. *J. Econ. Perspectives*, Spring 1989, *3*(2), pp. 95–114.

_____. A New Approach to the Design of Regulation in the Presence of Multiple Objectives. *J. Environ. Econ. Manage.*, September 1989, *17*(2), pp. 195–211.

_____ and **Hester, Gordon L.** Where Did All the Markets Go? An Analysis of EPA's Emissions Trading Program. *Yale J. Regul.*, Winter 1989, *6*(1), pp. 109–53.

Hahn, Thomas and Cook, Timothy. The Effect of Changes in the Federal Funds Rate Target on Market Interest Rates in the 1970s. *J. Monet. Econ.*, November 1989, *24*(3), pp. 331–51.

Haidacher, Richard C. The Demand for Meat: Symposium Objectives. **In** *Buse, R. C., ed.*, 1989, pp. 9–17.

_____; **Blaylock, James R. and Smallwood, David M.** A Review of the Research Literature on Meat Demand. **In** *Buse, R. C., ed.*, 1989, pp. 93–124.

_____ and **Buse, Rueben C.** The Economics of Meat Demand: Introduction. **In** *Buse, R. C., ed.*, 1989, pp. 1–5.

_____ and **Huang, Kuo S.** An Assessment of Price and Income Effects on Changes in Meat Consumption. **In** *Buse, R. C., ed.*, 1989, pp. 139–56.

Haider, Donald. Grants as a Tool of Public Policy. In *Salamon, L. M., ed.*, 1989, pp. 93–124.

Haig, Bryan. International Comparisons of Australian GDP in the 19th Century. *Rev. Income Wealth*, June 1989, *35*(2), pp. 151–62.

Haila, A. Misguided Rhetoric on Rent: A Comment. *Environ. Planning A*, November 1989, *21*(11), pp. 1525–32.

Hailey, D. M. A Model for Prioritising Therapeutic Devices for Evaluation: Commentary. In *Smith, C. S., ed.*, 1989, pp. 88–90.

———— **and Crowe, B. L.** The Economics of Australian Hospitals: Forum: Cost-Effectiveness of Diagnostic Technology: MRI—A Case Study. In *Smith, C. S., ed.*, 1989, pp. 301–04.

Haines, Andrew. The Role of Health Care in Alleviating Underdevelopment. In *Rotblat, J. and Goldanskii, V. I., eds.*, 1989, pp. 248–52.

Haines, Michael R. American Fertility in Transition: New Estimates of Birth Rates in the United States, 1900–1910. *Demography*, February 1989, *26*(1), pp. 137–48.

————. Social Class Differentials during Fertility Decline: England and Wales Revisited. *Population Stud.*, July 1989, *43*(2), pp. 305–23.

Haines, Pamela S.; Popkin, Barry M. and Guilkey, David K. Food Consumption Changes of Adult Women between 1977 and 1985. *Amer. J. Agr. Econ.*, November 1989, *71*(4), pp. 949–59.

Haining, R. P.; Griffith, D. A. and Bennett, Robert J. Statistical Analysis of Spatial Data in the Presence of Missing Observations: A Methodological Guide and an Application to Urban Census Data. *Environ. Planning A*, November 1989, *21*(11), pp. 1511–23.

Hájek, Mojmír and Toms, Miroslav. Theoretical Questions of Forecasting the Intensification Process and Its Growth Rate Alternatives. *Czech. Econ. Pap.*, 1989, (26), pp. 51–71.

Hajivassiliou, Vassilis A. Do the Secondary Markets Believe in Life after Debt? In *Husain, I. and Diwan, I., eds.*, 1989, pp. 276–92.

Hakanoğlu, Erol; Kopprasch, Robert and Roman, Emmanuel. Constant Proportion Portfolio Insurance for Fixed-Income Investment. *J. Portfol. Manage.*, Summer 1989, *15*(4), pp. 58–66.

Hakchung, Choo. The Asian Newly Industrializing Economies (NIEs): Are "Economic Miracles" Equally Miraculous? *Singapore Econ. Rev.*, April 1989, *34*(1), pp. 2–12.

Hakim, Peter and Stedman, Louellen. Political Change and Economic Policy in Latin America and the Caribbean in 1988. In *Weeks, J. F., ed.*, 1989, pp. 165–74.

Hakim, Simon; Spiegel, Uriel and Friedman, Joseph. The Difference between Short and Long Run Effects of Police Outlays on Crime: Policing Deters Criminals Initially, but Later They May 'Learn by Doing.' *Amer. J. Econ. Sociology*, April 1989, *48*(2), pp. 177–91.

————; **Weinblatt, J. and Friedman, Joseph.** Casino Gambling as a "Growth Pole" Strategy and Its Effect on Crime. *J. Reg. Sci.*, November 1989, *29*(4), pp. 615–23.

Hakkert, Ralph and Goza, Franklin W. The Demographic Consequences of Austerity in Latin America. In *Canak, W. L., ed.*, 1989, pp. 69–97.

Hakkio, Craig S. and Rush, Mark. Market Efficiency and Cointegration: An Application to the Sterling and Deutschemark Exchange Markets. *J. Int. Money Finance*, March 1989, *8*(1), pp. 75–88.

Hakogi, Masumi. New Development of East–West Trade Relations—Focussing on Technology Transfer from Japan. In *Berliner, J. S.; Kosta, H. G. J. and Hakogi, M., eds.*, 1989, pp. 177–90.

———— **and Bakos, Gabor.** Economics of the Socialist Countries: Introduction. In *Berliner, J. S.; Kosta, H. G. J. and Hakogi, M., eds.*, 1989, pp. 1–5.

Hale, C. and Vanags, A. Spot and Period Rates in the Dry Bulk Market: Some Tests for the Period 1980–1986. *J. Transp. Econ. Policy*, September 1989, *23*(3), pp. 281–91.

Halevi, J. Lowe, Dobb and Hicks. In *Wood, J. C. and Woods, R. N., eds., Vol. 4*, 1989, *1984*, pp. 6–17.

Haley, John O. The Context and Content of Regulatory Change in Japan. In *Button, K. and Swann, D., eds.*, 1989, pp. 124–38.

————. Mission to Manage: The U.S. Forest Service as a "Japanese" Bureaucracy. In *Hayashi, K., ed.*, 1989, pp. 196–225.

Halfmann, Jost. Social Change and Political Mobilization in West Germany. In *Katzenstein, P. J., ed.*, 1989, pp. 51–86.

Hall, A. D. and McAleer, Michael. A Monte Carlo Study of Some Tests of Model Adequacy in Time Series Analysis. *J. Bus. Econ. Statist.*, January 1989, *7*(1), pp. 95–106.

Hall, Alastair. On the Calculation of the Information Matrix Test in the Normal Linear Regression Model. *Econ. Letters*, 1989, *29*(1), pp. 31–35.

Hall, Brian and Freeman, Richard B. Permanent Homelessness in America? In *Freeman, R. B.*, 1989, *1987*, pp. 134–56.

Hall, Christopher D. A Dutch Auction Information Exchange. *J. Law Econ.*, April 1989, *32*(1), pp. 195–213.

Hall, Darwin C., et al. Organic Food and Sustainable Agriculture. *Contemp. Policy Issues*, October 1989, *7*(4), pp. 47–72.

Hall, Graham. Lack of Finance as a Constraint on the Expansion of Innovatory Small Firms. In *Barber, J.; Metcalfe, J. S. and Porteous, M., eds.*, 1989, pp. 39–57.

Hall, Jane. Cost Benefit Analysis of Non-drug Treatment of Hypertension: Commentary. In *Smith, C. S., ed.*, 1989, pp. 144–46.

————; **Salkeld, G. and Richardson, J.** Cost Utility Analysis: The Compatibility of Measurement Techniques and the Measurement of Utility through Time. In *Smith, C. S., ed.*, 1989, pp. 31–60.

Hall, John B. Liberal Reformism and Declining Capital Formation in Hungary: The Developing Capitalist Sector Is Its Only Frontier but This Threatens the Party Dictatorship. *Amer. J. Econ. Sociology*, October 1989, *48*(4), pp. 473–88.

Hall, Joyce A.; Brorsen, B. Wade and Irwin, Scott H. The Distribution of Futures Prices: A Test of the Stable Paretian and Mixture of Normals Hypotheses. *J. Finan. Quant. Anal.*, March 1989, *24*(1), pp. 105–16.

Hall, Maximilian J. G. The BIS Capital Adequacy "Rules": A Critique. *Banca Naz. Lavoro Quart. Rev.*, June 1989, (169), pp. 207–27.

Hall, Peter A. The Political Power of Economic Ideas: Keynesianism across Nations: Conclusion: The Politics of Keynesian Ideas. In *Hall, P. A., ed.*, 1989, pp. 361–91.

_____. The Political Power of Economic Ideas: Keynesianism across Nations: Introduction. In *Hall, P. A., ed.*, 1989, pp. 3–26.

Hall, Peter H. and Treadgold, Malcolm L. Aggregate Demand Curves: A Response. *J. Macroecon.*, Winter 1989, *11*(1), pp. 141–43.

Hall, Robert E. The Beveridge Curve: Comments. *Brookings Pap. Econ. Act.*, 1989, (1), pp. 61–64.

_____. Industry Rents: Evidence and Implications: Comments. *Brookings Pap. Econ. Act.*, Microeconomics, 1989, pp. 276–80.

_____. Modern Business Cycle Theory: Consumption. In *Barro, R. J., ed.*, 1989, pp. 153–77.

Hall, Stephen G. Maximum Likelihood Estimation of Cointegration Vectors: An Example of the Johansen Procedure. *Oxford Bull. Econ. Statist.*, March 1989, *51*(2), pp. 213–18.

_____ and Currie, David A. A Stock–Flow Model of the Determination of the UK Effective Exchange Rate. In *MacDonald, R. and Taylor, M. P., eds.*, 1989, pp. 130–41.

_____ and Drobny, A. An Investigation of the Long-run Properties of Aggregate Non-durable Consumers' Expenditure in the United Kingdom. *Econ. J.*, June 1989, *99*(396), pp. 454–60.

_____; Miles, David K. and Taylor, Mark P. Modelling Asset Prices with Time-Varying Betas. *Manchester Sch. Econ. Soc. Stud.*, December 1989, *57*(4), pp. 340–56.

_____, et al. The UK Labour Market; Expectations and Disequilibrium. *Appl. Econ.*, November 1989, *21*(11), pp. 1509–23.

Hall, Thomas D. Is Historical Sociology of Peripheral Regions Peripheral? In *Martin, M. T. and Kandal, T. R., eds.*, 1989, pp. 349–72.

Hall, Thomas E.; Fields, T. Windsor and Fields, M. Andrew. On Allocating the Variance of Output Growth to Trend and Cycle Components. *Econ. Letters*, October 1989, *30*(4), pp. 323–26.

Hall, V. B.; Truong, T. P. and Nguyen, V. A. Responses to World Oil and Coal Shocks, in a Short-run Fuel Substitution Tax Model. *Australian Econ. Rev.*, Spring 1989, (87), pp. 25–38.

Hallahan, Charles B.; Davison, Cecil W. and Arnade, Carlos A. Box–Cox Estimation of U.S.

Soybean Exports. *J. Agr. Econ. Res.*, Summer 1989, *41*(3), pp. 8–16.

Hallam, Arne; Hassan, Rashid M. and D'Silva, B. Measuring Stochastic Technology for the Multi-product Firm: The Irrigated Farms of Sudan. *Can. J. Agr. Econ.*, November 1989, *37*(3), pp. 495–512.

Hallén, Lars and Johanson, Jan. International Business Relationships and Industrial Networks: Introduction. In *Hallén, L. and Johanson, J., eds.*, 1989, pp. xiii–xxiii.

_____; Mohamed, Nazeem Seyed and Johanson, Jan. Relationships and Exchange in International Business. In *Hallén, L. and Johanson, J., eds.*, 1989, pp. 7–23.

Haller, Andreas and Stoll, Hans R. Market Structure and Transaction Costs: Implied Spreads in the German Stock Market. *J. Banking Finance*, September 1989, *13*(4–5), pp. 697–708.

Haller, Gert. The Impact of Fiscal Policy on the Balance of Payments: Recent Experience in the United States: Comment. In *Monti, M., ed.*, 1989, pp. 72–76.

Halliday, J. E. Attitudes towards Farm Diversification: Results from a Survey of Devon Farms. *J. Agr. Econ.*, January 1989, *40*(1), pp. 93–100.

Hallman, Jeffrey J.; Engle, R. F. and Granger, C. W. J. Merging Short- and Long-run Forecasts: An Application of Seasonal Cointegration to Monthly Electricity Sales Forecasting. *J. Econometrics*, January 1989, *40*(1), pp. 45–62.

_____; Porter, Richard D. and Small, David H. M2 per Unit of Potential GNP as an Anchor for the Price Level. *Fed. Res. Bull.*, April 1989, *75*(4), pp. 263–64.

Hallwood, C. Paul. Foreign Ownership and Industrial Organization in the Scottish Offshore Oil-Supply Industry. *J. Energy Devel.*, Spring 1989, *14*(2), pp. 221–36.

Halme, Merja and Korhonen, Pekka. Nondominated Tradeoffs and Termination in Interactive Multiple Objective Linear Programming. In *Lockett, A. G. and Islei, G., eds.*, 1989, pp. 410–23.

Halperin, Graeme I. Taxing the Mind: Is Know-How an Asset for Capital Gains Tax Purposes? *Australian Tax Forum*, 1989, *6*(2), pp. 217–63.

Halpern, László. Effects of Devaluation in a Macroeconometric Model for Hungary. *Acta Oecon.*, 1989, *41*(3–4), pp. 293–311.

_____ and Molnár, György. Macro Features of the Hungarian Economy since 1970. *Econ. Systems Res.*, 1989, *1*(1), pp. 111–20.

Halstead, Jim. SOVPLAN: An In-class Simulation of Central Planning. *Econ. Inquiry*, April 1989, *27*(2), pp. 357–61.

Haltiwanger, John C. and Maccini, Louis J. Inventories, Orders, Temporary and Permanent Layoffs: An Econometric Analysis. *Carnegie–Rochester Conf. Ser. Public Policy*, Spring 1989, *30*, pp. 301–66.

_____ and Waldman, Michael. Limited Rationality and Strategic Complements: The Implications for Macroeconomics. *Quart. J. Econ.*, August 1989, *104*(3), pp. 463–83.

_____ **and Waldman, Michael.** Rational Expectations in the Aggregate. *Econ. Inquiry*, October 1989, *27*(4), pp. 619–36.

Halverson, Philip; Hamilton, Joel R. and Whittlesey, Norman K. Interruptible Water Markets in the Pacific Northwest. *Amer. J. Agr. Econ.*, February 1989, *71*(1), pp. 63–75.

Hamada, Koichi. Correcting Global Imbalances: A Simulation Approach: Comment. In *Stern, R. M., ed.*, 1989, pp. 427–30.

_____. The Effect of the Stock Market on Investment: A Comparative Study: Comment. *Europ. Econ. Rev.*, May 1989, *33*(5), pp. 959–61.

_____ **and Bhagwati, Jagdish N.** Tax Policy in the Presence of Emigration. In *Bhagwati, J. N. and Wilson, J. D., eds.*, 1989, *1982*, pp. 113–40.

_____ **and Iwata, Kazumasa.** On the International Capital Ownership Pattern at the Turn of the Twenty-First Century. *Europ. Econ. Rev.*, May 1989, *33*(5), pp. 1055–79.

Hamalainen, Raimo P. and Ruusunen, Jukka. Project Selection by an Integrated Decision Aid. In *Golden, B. L.; Wasil, E. A. and Harker, P. T., eds.*, 1989, pp. 101–21.

Hamao, Yasushi. Japanese Stocks, Bonds, Bills, and Inflation, 1973–87. *J. Portfol. Manage.*, Winter 1989, *15*(2), pp. 20–26.

Hamburger, Philip A. The Constitution's Accommodation of Social Change. *Mich. Law Rev.*, November 1989, *88*(2), pp. 239–327.

Hamdar, Bassam and Turay, Abdul M. The New International Debt Strategy for Indebted Nations: A Problem of Liquidity. *Econ. Int.*, Aug.–Nov. 1989, *42*(3–4), pp. 219–33.

Hamermesh, Daniel S. Labor Demand and the Structure of Adjustment Costs. *Amer. Econ. Rev.*, September 1989, *79*(4), pp. 674–89.

_____. What Do We Know about Worker Displacement in the U.S.? *Ind. Relat.*, Winter 1989, *28*(1), pp. 51–59.

_____. Why Do Individual-Effects Models Perform So Poorly? The Case of Academic Salaries. *Southern Econ. J.*, July 1989, *56*(1), pp. 39–45.

Hamid, Naved and Nabi, Ijaz. Private Finance Companies in LDCs: Lessons from an Experiment. *World Devel.*, August 1989, *17*(8), pp. 1289–97.

Hamilton, Bob; Davies, James B. and Whalley, John. Capital Income Taxation in a Two-Commodity Life Cycle Model: The Role of Factor Intensity and Asset Capitalization Effects. *J. Public Econ.*, June 1989, *39*(1), pp. 109–26.

_____ **and Whalley, John.** Efficiency and Distributional Effects of the Tax Reform Package. In *Mintz, J. and Whalley, J., eds.*, 1989, pp. 373–98.

_____ **and Whalley, John.** Geographically Discriminatory Trade Arrangements. In *Jacquemin, A. and Sapir, A., eds.*, 1989, *1985*, pp. 213–26.

_____ **and Whalley, John.** Reforming Indirect

Taxes in Canada: Some General Equilibrium Estimates. *Can. J. Econ.*, August 1989, *22*(3), pp. 561–75.

Hamilton, Bruce W. Market Failure in the Land of Lösch. *J. Urban Econ.*, March 1989, *25*(2), pp. 143–55.

_____. Wasteful Commuting Again. *J. Polit. Econ.*, December 1989, *97*(6), pp. 1497–1504.

_____ **and Decker, Paul T.** Taxation of Compensating Wage Variation. *Econ. Stud. Quart.*, September 1989, *40*(3), pp. 239–50.

Hamilton, Carl B. The Political Economy of Transient "New" Protectionism. *Weltwirtsch. Arch.*, 1989, *125*(3), pp. 522–46.

Hamilton, Clive. Fixed Capital in Linkage-Based Planning Models. *Appl. Econ.*, September 1989, *21*(9), pp. 1203–16.

_____. The Irrelevance of Economic Liberalization in the Third World. *World Devel.*, October 1989, *17*(10), pp. 1523–30.

Hamilton, Colleen and Whalley, John. Coalitions in the Uruguay Round. *Weltwirtsch. Arch.*, 1989, *125*(3), pp. 547–62.

_____ **and Whalley, John.** Developing Countries and the Global Trading System: Introduction. In *Whalley, J., ed., Vol. 1*, 1989, pp. 3–25.

Hamilton, David. The Myth Is Not the Reality: Income Maintenance and Welfare. In *Tool, M. R. and Samuels, W. J., eds. (II)*, 1989, *1984*, pp. 439–54.

_____. On Staying for the Canoe Building, or Why Ideology Is Not Enough. *J. Econ. Issues*, June 1989, *23*(2), pp. 535–43.

_____. Thorstein Veblen as the First Professor of Marketing Science. *J. Econ. Issues*, December 1989, *23*(4), pp. 1097–1104.

Hamilton, Edward K. America's Global Interests: A New Agenda: Introduction and Overview. In *Hamilton, E. K., ed.*, 1989, pp. 3–32.

Hamilton, Gary G. and Orru, Marco. Organizational Structure of East Asian Companies. In *Chung, K. H. and Lee, H. C., eds.*, 1989, pp. 39–47.

Hamilton, James D. The Long-run Behavior of the Velocity of Circulation: A Review Essay. *J. Monet. Econ.*, March 1989, *23*(2), pp. 335–44.

_____. A New Approach to the Economic Analysis of Nonstationary Time Series and the Business Cycle. *Econometrica*, March 1989, *57*(2), pp. 357–84.

Hamilton, Joel R.; Whittlesey, Norman K. and Halverson, Philip. Interruptible Water Markets in the Pacific Northwest. *Amer. J. Agr. Econ.*, February 1989, *71*(1), pp. 63–75.

Hamilton, Jonathan H.; Sheshinski, Eytan and Slutsky, Steven M. Production Externalities and Long-run Equilibria: Bargaining and Pigovian Taxation. *Econ. Inquiry*, July 1989, *27*(3), pp. 453–71.

_____; **Thisse, Jacques-François and Weskamp, Anita.** Spatial Discrimination: Bertrand vs. Cournot in a Model of Location Choice. *Reg. Sci. Urban Econ.*, February 1989, *19*(1), pp. 87–102.

Hamilton, Lee H. Can We Break the Budget

Deadlock? *Challenge*, July–Aug. 1989, *32*(4), pp. 14–21.

Hamilton, Marybeth. "The Life of a Citizen in the Hands of a Woman": Sexual Assault in New York City, 1790–1820. **In** *Pencak, W. and Wright, C. E., eds.*, 1989, pp. 228–48.

Hamilton, R. T. Unemployment and Business Formation Rates: Reconciling Time-Series and Cross-section Evidence. *Environ. Planning A*, February 1989, *21*(2), pp. 249–55.

_____ **and Shergill, G. S.** Diversification Patterns in New Zealand Listed Companies. *New Zealand Econ. Pap.*, 1989, *23*, pp. 3–11.

Hamissa, M. R. and Mahrous, F. N. Fertilizer Use Efficiency in Rice. **In** *International Rice Research Institute*, 1989, pp. 129–39.

Hamlen, Susan S. and Hamlen, William A., Jr. Decentralized Pricing in Natural Monopolies. **In** *Crew, M. A., ed.*, 1989, pp. 89–105.

Hamlen, William A., Jr. and Hamlen, Susan S. Decentralized Pricing in Natural Monopolies. **In** *Crew, M. A., ed.*, 1989, pp. 89–105.

_____ **and Southwick, Lawrence, Jr.** Quality in the MBA Program: Inputs, Outputs or Value Added? *J. Econ. Soc. Meas.*, 1989, *15*(1), pp. 1–26.

Hamlin, Alan P. Rights, Indirect Utilitarianism, and Contractarianism. *Econ. Philos.*, October 1989, *5*(2), pp. 167–87.

Hamm, Walter. The Welfare State at Its Limit. **In** *Peacock, A. and Willgerodt, H., eds. (II)*, 1989, *1981*, pp. 171–94.

Hamman, W. D.; Lambrechts, I. J. and Doppegieter, J. J. The Importance of Public Utilities in South Africa. *J. Stud. Econ. Econometrics*, August 1989, *13*(2), pp. 37–47.

_____; **Lambrechts, I. J. and Doppegieter, J. J.** Tariff Policies for Public Utilities: The Accounting Cost Approach. *J. Stud. Econ. Econometrics*, August 1989, *13*(2), pp. 49–57.

Hammer, Jerry A. On Biases Reported in Studies of the Black–Scholes Option Pricing Model. *J. Econ. Bus.*, May 1989, *41*(2), pp. 153–69.

Hammer, Peter L. and Kalantari, B. A Bound on the Roof-Duality Gap. **In** *Simeone, B., ed.*, 1989, pp. 254–57.

_____ **and Simeone, Bruno.** Quadratic Functions of Binary Variables. **In** *Simeone, B., ed.*, 1989, pp. 1–56.

Hammerstein, Peter. Biological Games. *Europ. Econ. Rev.*, March 1989, *33*(2/3), pp. 635–44.

Hammes, David L.; Rosa, Jean-Jacques and Grubel, Herbert G. The National Accounts, Household Service Consumption and Its Monetization. *Kyklos*, 1989, *42*(1), pp. 3–15.

Hammig, Michael D. and Childs, Nathan W. An Empirical Examination of the Link between Monetary Policy and U.S. Agricultural Commodity Exports. *Appl. Econ.*, February 1989, *21*(2), pp. 155–73.

Hamminga, Bert. Sneed versus Nowak: An Illustration in Economics. **In** *Balzer, W. and Hamminga, B., eds.*, 1989, pp. 247–65.

Hammitt, James K. Adding an Economic Dimension to Risk Assessment: Discussion. *Amer. J. Agr. Econ.*, May 1989, *71*(2), pp. 487–88.

Hammond, Elizabeth; Helm, Dieter and Thompson, David. Competition in Electricity Supply: Has the Energy Act Failed? **In** *Helm, D.; Kay, J. and Thompson, D., eds.*, 1989, *1986*, pp. 157–77.

Hammond, Peter J. Consistent Plans, Consequentialism, and Expected Utility. *Econometrica*, November 1989, *57*(6), pp. 1445–49.

_____. Information, Incentives, and General Equilibrium: Comment. **In** *Cornet, B. and Tulkens, H., eds.*, 1989, pp. 50–58.

_____. Some Assumptions of Contemporary Neoclassical Economic Theology. **In** *Feiwel, G. R., ed. (II)*, 1989, pp. 186–257.

_____; **Kaneko, Mamoru and Wooders, Myrna Holtz.** Continuum Economies with Finite Coalitions: Core, Equilibria, and Widespread Externalities. *J. Econ. Theory*, October 1989, *49*(1), pp. 113–34.

Hammond, Thomas H. and Thomas, Paul A. The Impossibility of a Neutral Hierarchy. *J. Law, Econ., Organ.*, Spring 1989, *5*(1), pp. 155–84.

Hamnett, Chris. The Political Geography of Housing in Contemporary Britain. **In** *Mohan, J., ed.*, 1989, pp. 208–23.

_____. Sociotenurial Polarisation in London and the South East: A Reply. *Environ. Planning A*, April 1989, *21*(4), pp. 545–48.

Hamori, Shigeyuki. Information Costs, Learning Process and the Effectiveness of Monetary Policy. *Scand. J. Econ.*, 1989, *91*(3), pp. 535–46.

Hamouda, Omar F. The Evolution of Hicks' Theory of Money. **In** *Wood, J. C. and Woods, R. N., eds., Vol. 4*, 1989, *1985*, pp. 159–77.

_____ **and Harcourt, Geoff C.** Post-Keynesianism: From Criticism to Coherence? **In** *Pheby, J., ed.*, 1989, *1988*, pp. 1–34.

_____ **and Rowley, Robin.** Disturbance in the World Economy. **In** *Hamouda, O. F.; Rowley, R. and Wolf, B. M., eds.*, 1989, pp. 1–3.

Han, Aaron K. Asymptotic Efficiency Calculations of the Partial Likelihood Estimator. *J. Econometrics*, June 1989, *41*(2), pp. 237–50.

_____ **and Park, Daekeun.** Testing for Structural Change in Panel Data: Application to a Study of U.S. Foreign Trade in Manufacturing Goods. *Rev. Econ. Statist.*, February 1989, *71*(1), pp. 135–42.

Han, Jaehye Kim and Gyourko, Joseph. Housing Wealth, Housing Finance, and Tenure in Korea. *Reg. Sci. Urban Econ.*, May 1989, *19*(2), pp. 211–34.

Han, Jerry C. Y.; Wild, John J. and Ramesh, K. Managers' Earnings Forecasts and Intra-industry Information Transfers. *J. Acc. Econ.*, February 1989, *11*(1), pp. 3–33.

Han, Qing. Achievements Are the Main Feature of Construction Work in the Textile Industry in Recent Years. **In** *Howe, C. and Walker, K. R., eds.*, 1989, *1957*, pp. 158–64.

Hanappi, Gerhard. The Stages of Industrial Capitalism. **In** *Di Matteo, M.; Goodwin, R. M. and Vercelli, A., eds.*, 1989, pp. 353–83.

Hanaut, Anne. Le commerce de "perfectionnement" de la France, une forme de segmentation internationale des processus productifs.

(With English summary.) *Revue Écon. Politique*, Jan.–Feb. 1989, *99*(1), pp. 78–95.

———. Les échanges internationaux entre la France et l'Espagne sous le régime du perfectionnement passif. Communication aux journées Franco–Espagnoles, Bilbao du 27 au 29 mai 1987. ("Outward Processing" Trade between France and Spain. With English summary.) *Écon. Societes*, February 1989, *23*(2), pp. 49–68.

Hanchar, John J.; Kim, C. S. and Moore, Michael R. A Dynamic Model of Adaptation to Resource Depletion: Theory and an Application to Groundwater Mining. *J. Environ. Econ. Manage.*, July 1989, *17*(1), pp. 66–82.

Hancher, Leigh. Regulating Drug Prices: The West German and British Experience. In *Hancher, L. and Moran, M., eds.*, 1989, pp. 79–108.

———. Regulating Pharmaceutical Prices and Corporate R&D Strategies in Britain and in France. In *Sharp, M. and Holmes, P., eds.*, 1989, pp. 160–85.

——— **and Moran, Michael.** Capitalism, Culture, and Economic Regulation: Introduction. In *Hancher, L. and Moran, M., eds.*, 1989, pp. 1–7.

——— **and Moran, Michael.** Organizing Regulatory Space. In *Hancher, L. and Moran, M., eds.*, 1989, pp. 271–99.

Hancock, D. G. Fiscal Policy, Monetary Policy and the Efficiency of the Stock Market. *Econ. Letters*, November 1989, *31*(1), pp. 65–69.

Hancock, Keith and Rawson, Don. Industrial Relations: Stability and Turmoil. In *Hancock, K., ed.*, 1989, pp. 166–91.

Hand, John R. M. Did Firms Undertake Debt–Equity Swaps for an Accounting Paper Profit or True Financial Gain? *Accounting Rev.*, October 1989, *64*(4), pp. 587–623.

Handa, Jagdish and Ma, Barry K. Four Tests for the Random Walk Hypothesis: Power versus Robustness. *Econ. Letters*, 1989, *29*(2), pp. 141–45.

Handa, Puneet; Kothari, S. P. and Wasley, Charles E. The Relation between the Return Interval and Betas: Implications for the Size Effect. *J. Finan. Econ.*, June 1989, *23*(1), pp. 79–100.

Handelman, Howard and Baer, Werner. The Economic and Political Costs of Austerity: Introduction. In *Handelman, H. and Baer, W., eds.*, 1989, pp. 1–17.

Hands, D. Wade and Brown, William S. Expanding the Neoclassical Vision: Comment. *Rev. Soc. Econ.*, Spring 1989, *47*(1), pp. 84–87.

Hanemann, W. Michael. Information and the Concept of Option Value. *J. Environ. Econ. Manage.*, January 1989, *16*(1), pp. 23–37.

———. Welfare Evaluations in Contingent Valuation Experiments with Discrete Response Data: Reply. *Amer. J. Agr. Econ.*, November 1989, *71*(4), pp. 1057–61.

——— **and LaFrance, Jeffrey T.** The Dual Structure of Incomplete Demand Systems. *Amer. J. Agr. Econ.*, May 1989, *71*(2), pp. 262–74.

Hanf, C.-Henning. Research Organization and Cooperation in the Field of Agricultural Sector Modelling. In *Bauer, S. and Henrichsmeyer, W., eds.*, 1989, pp. 355–58.

——— **and Noell, C.** Farm Based Modelling Concepts: Experiences with Farm Sample Models in Sector Analysis. In *Bauer, S. and Henrichsmeyer, W., eds.*, 1989, pp. 103–11.

Hanink, Dean M. Trade Theories, Scale, and Structure: Introduction. *Econ. Geogr.*, October 1989, *65*(4), pp. 267–70.

——— **and Cromley, Robert G.** A Financial–Economic von Thünen Model. *Environ. Planning A*, July 1989, *21*(7), pp. 951–60.

Hanke, Helmut. Leisure Time in the GDR. In *Rueschemeyer, M. and Lemke, C., eds.*, 1989, pp. 167–81.

Hanke, John. Forecasting in Business Schools: A Follow-Up Survey. *Int. J. Forecasting*, 1989, *5*(2), pp. 259–62.

Hanke, Steve H. Privatization at the State and Local Level: Comment. In *MacAvoy, P. W., et al.*, 1989, pp. 195–202.

Hanley, N. D. Valuing Non-market Goods Using Contingent Valuation. *J. Econ. Surveys*, 1989, *3*(3), pp. 235–52.

———. Valuing Rural Recreation Benefits: An Empirical Comparison of Two Approaches. *J. Agr. Econ.*, September 1989, *40*(3), pp. 361–74.

Hannan, Timothy H. and Berger, Allen N. Deposit Interest Rates and Local Market Concentration. In *Weiss, L. W., ed.*, 1989, pp. 255–65.

——— **and Berger, Allen N.** The Price–Concentration Relationship in Banking. *Rev. Econ. Statist.*, May 1989, *71*(2), pp. 291–99.

——— **and Wolken, John D.** Returns to Bidders and Targets in the Acquisition Process: Evidence from the Banking Industry. *J. Finan. Services Res.*, October 1989, *3*(1), pp. 5–16.

Hannes, Jules and Scholliers, Peter. Some Conclusions and Suggestions for Further Research. In *Scholliers, P., ed.*, 1989, pp. 229–35.

Hannon, Bruce and Casler, Stephen D. Readjustment Potentials in Industrial Energy Efficiency and Structure. *J. Environ. Econ. Manage.*, July 1989, *17*(1), pp. 93–108.

Hansen, Ann. Inventories, Inflation, and Price Expectations. *J. Post Keynesian Econ.*, Spring 1989, *11*(3), pp. 439–59.

Hansen, Annegrethe; Pedersen, Jørgen Lindgaard and Arnfred, Niels. Bio-technology and Politics, Danish Experiences. In *Pedersen, J. L., ed.*, 1989, pp. 159–84.

Hansen, Bent. Capital and Lopsided Development in Egypt under British Occupation. In *Sabagh, G., ed.*, 1989, pp. 66–88.

Hansen, Gary D. and Cooley, Thomas F. The Inflation Tax in a Real Business Cycle Model. *Amer. Econ. Rev.*, September 1989, *79*(4), pp. 733–48.

Hansen, Gerd and Sienknecht, Hans-Peter. A Comparison of Demand Systems—A Case Study for West Germany. *Empirical Econ.*, 1989, *14*(1), pp. 43–61.

Hansen, N. Environmental Impacts of Human Settlement System Growth in the U.S. Southwest. In *Gibson, L. J. and Stimson, R. J., eds.*, 1989, pp. 135–43.

Hansen, Pierre and Eeckhoudt, Louis. Minimum Prices and Optimal Production under Multiple Sources of Risk: A Note. *Europ. Rev. Agr. Econ.*, 1989, *16*(3), pp. 411–18.

_____; **Mahieu, Yvon and Chaillou, Paul.** Best Network Flow Bounds for the Quadratic Knapsack Problem. In *Simeone, B., ed.*, 1989, pp. 225–35.

Hansen, Ronald W. Stimulating Product Innovation and Reforming the Health Care Reimbursement System. In *McLennan, K. and Meyer, J. A., eds.*, 1989, pp. 147–64.

Hansen, William W. East–South Relations: An Introduction. In *Schulz, B. H. and Hansen, W. W., eds.*, 1989, pp. 1–7.

Hansohm, Dirk. IMF/World Bank Policies in Sudan and Its Critics. In *Wohlmuth, K., ed.*, 1989, pp. 259–80.

_____ **and Wohlmuth, Karl.** Sudan's East–South and South–South Economic Cooperation. In *Wohlmuth, K., ed.*, 1989, pp. 481–513.

Hanson, Gordon H. and Feinberg, Richard E. LDC Debt Will Restructure U.S. Banking. *Challenge*, March–April 1989, *32*(2), pp. 44–49.

Hanson, John R., II. Education, Economic Development, and Technology Transfer: A Colonial Test. *J. Econ. Hist.*, December 1989, *49*(4), pp. 939–57.

Hanson, Kathleen M. and Woodhouse, Thomas J. The Treatment of Finance-Related Commodities in a Consumers' Price Index. In *Turvey, R.*, 1989, pp. 155–61.

Hanson, Kenneth A. Firm Entry in MOSES: A User Manual. In *Albrecht, J. W., et al.*, 1989, pp. 233–44.

_____. Flow Presentation of MOSES Initialization and Simulation. In *Albrecht, J. W., et al.*, 1989, pp. 133–45.

_____; **Hartler, Christina and Bergholm, Fredrik.** Semi-technical Specification of Pricing in MOSES. In *Albrecht, J. W., et al.*, 1989, pp. 221–31.

Hanson, Kirk O. Ethics and Takeovers: A Debate (2) A Cautionary Assessment of Wall Street Ethics. In *Williams, O. F.; Reilly, F. K. and Houck, J. W., eds.*, 1989, pp. 77–83.

Hanson, Steven D.; Baumel, C. Phillip and Schnell, Daniel. Impact of Railroad Contracts on Grain Bids to Farmers. *Amer. J. Agr. Econ.*, August 1989, *71*(3), pp. 638–46.

Hansson, Ingemar. The Underground Economy in Sweden. In *Feige, E. L., ed.*, 1989, pp. 219–36.

_____ **and Stuart, Charles.** The Marginal Cost of Public Funds: Methods and Prospects. In *Chiancone, A. and Messere, K., eds.*, 1989, pp. 231–41.

_____ **and Stuart, Charles.** Social Security as Trade among Living Generations. *Amer. Econ. Rev.*, December 1989, *79*(5), pp. 1182–95.

_____ **and Stuart, Charles.** Why Is Investment

Subsidized? *Int. Econ. Rev.*, August 1989, *30*(3), pp. 549–59.

Hansson, Pär and Lundberg, Lars. Comparative Costs and Elasticities of Substitution as Determinants of Inter- and Intra-industry Trade. In *Tharakan, P. K. M. and Kol, J., eds.*, 1989, pp. 31–50.

Hanus, H. and Schoop, P. Influence of Nitrogen Fertilizer and Fungicide on Yield and Yield Variability in Wheat and Barley. In *Anderson, J. R. and Hazell, P. B. R., eds.*, 1989, pp. 265–84.

Hanusch, Horst and Weiss, Karl-Heinz. Tax Reform in a Recovering Economy: From Income Taxes to Indirect Taxation. In *Chiancone, A. and Messere, K., eds.*, 1989, pp. 197–213.

Hanushek, Eric A. Expenditures, Efficiency, and Equity in Education: The Federal Government's Role. *Amer. Econ. Rev.*, May 1989, *79*(2), pp. 46–51.

Hao, Chengyi; Guo, Jinhua and He, Bing. Conditions of Workers' Material and Mental Lives and Trends in Their Development. *Chinese Econ. Stud.*, Summer 1989, *22*(4), pp. 32–38.

Happel, Stephen K. and Boyes, William J. Auctions as an Allocation Mechanism in Academia: The Case of Faculty Offices. *J. Econ. Perspectives*, Summer 1989, *3*(3), pp. 37–40.

Haque, A. K. Enamul; Fox, Glenn C. and Brinkman, George L. Product Market Distortions and the Returns to Federal Laying-Hen Research in Canada. *Can. J. Agr. Econ.*, March 1989, *37*(1), pp. 29–46.

Haque, Mainul. Demand for Money in the United Kingdom: An Empirical Measurement. *Indian Econ. J.*, July–Sept. 1989, *37*(1), pp. 74–81.

Haque, Mohammed Ohidul. Estimation of Engel Elasticities from Concentration Curves. *J. Econ. Devel.*, June 1989, *14*(1), pp. 93–114.

_____. Functional Forms for Engel Curves. *Indian J. Quant. Econ.*, 1989, *5*(1), pp. 13–34.

Haque, Nadeem U. and Montiel, Peter J. Consumption in Developing Countries: Tests for Liquidity Constraints and Finite Horizons. *Rev. Econ. Statist.*, August 1989, *71*(3), pp. 408–15.

Haraf, William S. and Grossman, Herschel I. Shunto, Rational Expectations, and Output Growth in Japan. *Empirical Econ.*, 1989, *14*(3), pp. 193–213.

Harajli, Ali and El Reedy, Tarek. Transport Strategy for Greater Amman: A Look into the Future. In *Candemir, Y., ed.*, 1989, pp. 433–44.

Harary, F. and Fraenkel, A. S. Geodetic Contraction Games on Graphs. *Int. J. Game Theory*, 1989, *18*(3), pp. 327–38.

Harberger, Arnold C. Applications of Real Exchange Rate Analysis. *Contemp. Policy Issues*, April 1989, *7*(2), pp. 1–26.

Harbury, Colin. Privatization: British Style. *J. Behav. Econ.*, Winter 1989, *18*(4), pp. 265–88.

Harcourt, Geoff C. and Hamouda, Omar F. Post-Keynesianism: From Criticism to Coherence? In *Pheby, J., ed.*, 1989, *1988*, pp. 1–34.

Hardie, Ian W. and Larson, Douglas M. Seller Behavior in Stumpage Markets with Imperfect

Information. *Land Econ.*, August 1989, *65*(3), pp. 239–53.

Harding, Harry and Hewett, Ed A. Dealing with Reforms in China and the Soviet Union. In *Bosworth, B. P., et al.*, 1989, pp. 166–70.

_____ **and Hewett, Ed A.** Socialist Reforms and the World Economy. In *Steinbruner, J. D., ed.*, 1989, pp. 158–84.

_____ **and Lincoln, Edward J.** The East Asian Laboratory. In *Steinbruner, J. D., ed.*, 1989, pp. 185–220.

Hardjodimedjo, Martono and Meyer, Paul A. Maluku: The Modernization of the Spice Islands. In *Hill, H., ed.*, 1989, pp. 548–65.

Hardjono, Joan and Hill, Hal. West Java: Population Pressure and Regional Diversity. In *Hill, H., ed.*, 1989, pp. 254–82.

Härdle, Wolfgang and Stoker, Thomas M. Investigating Smooth Multiple Regression by the Method of Average Derivatives. *J. Amer. Statist. Assoc.*, December 1989, *84*(408), pp. 986–95.

Hardouvelis, Gikas A. Stock Market Margin Requirements and Volatility: Commentary. *J. Finan. Services Res.*, December 1989, *3*(2–3), pp. 139–51.

_____ . Stock Market Margin Requirements and Volatility: Commentary. In *Edwards, F. R., ed.*, 1989, pp. 41–53.

_____ **and Barnhart, Scott W.** The Evolution of Federal Reserve Credibility: 1978–1984. *Rev. Econ. Statist.*, August 1989, *71*(3), pp. 385–93.

_____ **and Peristiani, Stavros.** Do Margin Requirements Matter? Evidence from U.S. and Japanese Stock Markets. *Fed. Res. Bank New York Quart. Rev.*, Winter 1989–90, *14*(4), pp. 16–35.

Hardwick, Philip. Economies of Scale in Building Societies. *Appl. Econ.*, October 1989, *21*(10), pp. 1291–1304.

Hardy, Melissa A.; Grady, William R. and Hayward, Mark D. Labor Force Withdrawal Patterns among Older Men in the United States. *Soc. Sci. Quart.*, June 1989, *70*(2), pp. 425–48.

Hardy, William E., Jr.; Adrian, John L., Jr. and Zwingli, Michael E. Reduced Risk Rotations for Fresh Vegetable Crops: An Analysis for the Sand Mountain and Tennessee Valley Regions of Alabama. *Southern J. Agr. Econ.*, December 1989, *21*(2), pp. 155–65.

_____ ; **Disney, W. Terry and Duffy, Patricia A.** A Markov Chain Analysis of Pork Farm Size Distributions in the South: Reply. *Southern J. Agr. Econ.*, December 1989, *21*(2), pp. 219–20.

Hare, Paul G. Economic Development in Eastern Europe: A Review Article. *Oxford Econ. Pap.*, October 1989, *41*(4), pp. 672–97.

_____ **and Yushi, Mao.** Chinese Experience in the Introduction of a Market Mechanism into a Planned Economy: The Role of Pricing. *J. Econ. Surveys*, 1989, *3*(2), pp. 137–58.

Harford, Jon D. Efficient Scale of the Pollution-

Abating Firm: Comment. *Land Econ.*, November 1989, *65*(4), pp. 413–16.

Hargrove, T. R. and Coffman, W. Ronnie. Modern Rice Varieties as a Possible Factor in Production Variability. In *Anderson, J. R. and Hazell, P. B. R., eds.*, 1989, pp. 133–46.

Hargroves, Jeannette S. The Basic Skills Crisis: One Bank Looks at Its Training Investment. *New Eng. Econ. Rev.*, Sept.–Oct. 1989, pp. 58–68.

Haridoss, R. and Balaji, S. Engel Elasticity and Economies of Scale in Household Consumption: A Micro Analysis. *Margin*, Oct. 1989–March 1990, *22*(1–2), pp. 103–07.

Haring, John. The U.S. "Experience" with Price Caps. In *National Economic Research Associates*, 1989, pp. 203–12.

Harkema, R. and De Boer, P. M. C. Some Evidence on the Performance of Size Correction Factors in Testing Consumer Demand Models. *Econ. Letters*, 1989, *29*(4), pp. 311–15.

Harker, Patrick T. The Art and Science of Decision Making: The Analytic Hierarchy Process. In *Golden, B. L.; Wasil, E. A. and Harker, P. T., eds.*, 1989, pp. 3–36.

_____ ; **Golden, Bruce L. and Wasil, Edward A.** The Analytic Hierarchy Process: Applications and Studies: Introduction. In *Golden, B. L.; Wasil, E. A. and Harker, P. T., eds.*, 1989, pp. 1–2.

Harkness, Jon. The Economic Cost of AIDS in Canada. *Can. Public Policy*, December 1989, *15*(4), pp. 405–12.

Harl, Neil E. Break-Out Session II—Conference Consensus: Recommendations: International Debt Restructuring and Financing of Economic Development. In *Helmuth, J. W. and Johnson, S. R., eds., Vol. 1*, 1989, pp. 198–200.

_____ . The Political Economy of Farm Credit Reform: The Agricultural Credit Act of 1987: Commentary. In *Krämer, C. S., ed.*, 1989, pp. 140–43.

_____ . 1988 World Food Conference: Proceedings: A Policy Agenda for World Agriculture. In *Helmuth, J. W. and Johnson, S. R., eds., Vol. 1*, 1989, pp. 252–61.

Harless, David W. More Laboratory Evidence on the Disparity between Willingness to Pay and Compensation Demanded. *J. Econ. Behav. Organ.*, May 1989, *11*(3), pp. 359–79.

Harley, C. Knick. Coal Exports and British Shipping, 1850–1913. *Exploration Econ. Hist.*, July 1989, *26*(3), pp. 311–38.

Harley, M. Overview of the OECD Ministerial Trade Mandate Model. In *Bauer, S. and Henrichsmeyer, W., eds.*, 1989, pp. 171–74.

Harley, Nancy and Poddar, Satya N. Problems in Moving from a Flawed to a Neutral and Broad-Based Consumption Tax: The Canadian Experience. *Australian Tax Forum*, 1989, *6*(3), pp. 303–26.

Harlow, W. V. and Rao, Ramesh K. S. Asset Pricing in a Generalized Mean-Lower Partial Moment Framework: Theory and Evidence.

J. Finan. Quant. Anal., September 1989, *24*(3), pp. 285–311.

Harltos, Z. J.; Soberman, R. M. and Cubukgil, A. Transportation Research Needs of Developing Countries: The Case for a New Centre. In *Candemir, Y., ed.*, 1989, pp. 196–209.

Harmatz, H. R. and Wharton, J. D. An Exploratory Investigation of How Cultural Attitudes Relate to Life Insurance Holdings: A Cross-Cultural Comparison. *J. Econ. Psych.*, June 1989, *10*(2), pp. 217–27.

Harmon, Bruce R.; Ward, Lisa M. and Palmer, Paul R. Schedule Estimating Relationships for Tactical Aircraft. In *Gulledge, T. R., Jr. and Litteral, L. A., eds.*, 1989, pp. 259–80.

Harmon, Oskar Ragnar. A New View of the Incidence of the Property Tax: The Case of New Jersey. *Public Finance Quart.*, July 1989, *17*(3), pp. 323–48.

———. **and Lambrinos, James.** An Empirical Evaluation of Two Methods for Estimating Economic Damages. *J. Risk Ins.*, December 1989, *56*(4), pp. 733–39.

Harmstone, Richard C. Note on the "Moral" Aspect of Soviet Capital Retirement Statistics. *Comp. Econ. Stud.*, Winter 1989, *31*(4), pp. 89–94.

Harnett, Ian and Patterson, Kerry D. An Analysis of Changes in the Structural and Simulation Properties of the Bank of England Quarterly Model of the UK Economy. *Econ. Modelling*, January 1989, *6*(1), pp. 20–55.

Harper, Carolyn R. and Zilberman, David. Pest Externalities from Agricultural Inputs. *Amer. J. Agr. Econ.*, August 1989, *71*(3), pp. 692–702.

Harper, Ian R. and Eichberger, Jürgen. On Deposit Interest Rate Regulation and Deregulation. *J. Ind. Econ.*, September 1989, *38*(1), pp. 19–30.

——— **and Lim, G. C.** Is Monetary Policy Too Tight? *Australian Econ. Rev.*, Winter 1989, (86), pp. 15–28.

Harper, Jerome P. and Gellings, Clark W. End-Use R&D: Technology Development Strategy for an Integrated Market. *Energy J.*, July 1989, *10*(3), pp. 19–33.

Harper, Joellen M. and Younger, Benet. Telecommunications Policy and Economic Development: The New State Role: Nebraska. In *Schmandt, J.; Williams, F. and Wilson, R. H., eds.*, 1989, pp. 83–110.

Harper, Michael J.; Berndt, Ernst R. and Wood, David O. Rates of Return and Capital Aggregation Using Alternative Rental Prices. In *Jorgenson, D. W. and Landau, R., eds.*, 1989, pp. 331–72.

Harrigan, Frank and McGregor, Peter G. Neoclassical and Keynesian Perspectives on the Regional Macro-economy: A Computable General Equilibrium Approach. *J. Reg. Sci.*, November 1989, *29*(4), pp. 555–73.

Harrington, Charlene A. The Structured Approaches. In *Eisdorfer, C.; Kessler, D. A. and Spector, A. N., eds.*, 1989, pp. 31–49.

Harrington, David E. An Intertemporal Model of Housing Demand: Implications for the Price Elasticity. *J. Urban Econ.*, March 1989, *25*(2), pp. 230–46.

——— **and Krynski, Kathy J.** State Pricing of Vanity License Plates. *Nat. Tax J.*, March 1989, *42*(1), pp. 95–99.

Harrington, James W., Jr. Implications of the Canada–United States Free Trade Agreement for Regional Provision of Producer Services. *Econ. Geogr.*, October 1989, *65*(4), pp. 314–28.

——— **and Lombard, J. R.** Producer-Service Firms in a Declining Manufacturing Region. *Environ. Planning A*, January 1989, *21*(1), pp. 65–79.

Harrington, Joseph E., Jr. The Advantageous Nature of Risk Aversion in a Three-Player Bargaining Game Where Acceptance of a Proposal Requires a Simple Majority. *Econ. Letters*, September 1989, *30*(3), pp. 195–200.

———. Collusion among Asymmetric Firms: The Case of Different Discount Factors. *Int. J. Ind. Organ.*, June 1989, *7*(2), pp. 289–307.

———. Collusion and Predation under (Almost) Free Entry. *Int. J. Ind. Organ.*, September 1989, *7*(3), pp. 381–401.

———. If *Homo Economicus* Could Choose His Own Utility Function, Would He Want One with a Conscience?: Comment. *Amer. Econ. Rev.*, June 1989, *79*(3), pp. 588–93.

———. A Re-evaluation of Perfect Competition as the Solution to the Bertrand Price Game. *Math. Soc. Sci.*, June 1989, *17*(3), pp. 315–28.

Harrington, Scott E. and VanDerhei, Jack L. Pension Asset Reversions. In *Turner, J. A. and Beller, D. J., eds.*, 1989, pp. 187–210.

Harrington, Winston; Krupnick, Alan J. and Spofford, Walter O., Jr. The Economic Losses of a Waterborne Disease Outbreak. *J. Urban Econ.*, January 1989, *25*(1), pp. 116–37.

Harris, Abram L. Black Communists in Dixie. In *Harris, A. L.*, 1989, *1925*, pp. 140–48.

———. Defining the Negro Problem. In *Harris, A. L.*, 1989, *1925*, pp. 60–63.

———. Economic Evolution: Dialectical and Darwinian. In *Harris, A. L.*, 1989, *1934*, pp. 362–401.

———. Economic Foundations of American Race Division. In *Harris, A. L.*, 1989, *1927*, pp. 167–81.

———. The Economics of the Founding Fathers. In *Harris, A. L.*, 1989, *1937*, pp. 216–29.

———. Education and the Economic Status of Negroes in the United States. In *Harris, A. L.*, 1989, *1964*, pp. 100–123.

———. J. S. Mill on Monopoly and Socialism: A Note. In *Harris, A. L.*, 1989, *1959*, pp. 461–71.

———. John Stuart Mill: Servant of the East India Company. In *Harris, A. L.*, 1989, *1964*, pp. 487–507.

———. The Marxian Right to the Whole Product. In *Harris, A. L.*, 1989, *1935*, pp. 236–75.

———. Mill on Freedom and Voluntary Association. In *Harris, A. L.*, 1989, *1960*, pp. 472–86.

———. Monopoly, Business Cycles, and Imperialism. In *Harris, A. L.*, 1989, pp. 414–23.

———. The Negro and Economic Radicalism. In *Harris, A. L.*, 1989, *1925*, pp. 130–39.

———. The Negro and the New Economic Life. In *Harris, A. L.*, 1989, *1929*, pp. 182–92.

———. The Negro in the Coal Mining Industry. In *Harris, A. L.*, 1989, *1926*, pp. 149–57.

———. Negro Labor's Quarrel with White Workingmen. In *Harris, A. L.*, 1989, *1926*, pp. 158–66.

———. Negro Migration to the North. In *Harris, A. L.*, 1989, *1924*, pp. 53–59.

———. The Negro Population in Minneapolis: A Study of Race Relations. In *Harris, A. L.*, 1989, pp. 64–99.

———. The Negro Problem as Viewed by Negro Leaders. In *Harris, A. L.*, 1989, *1923*, pp. 43–52.

———. The Negro Worker: A Problem of Progressive Labor Action. In *Harris, A. L.*, 1989, *1930*, pp. 193–99.

———. Our Second Bourgeois Revolution. In *Harris, A. L.*, 1989, *1938*, pp. 213–15.

———. Pure Capitalism and the Disappearance of the Middle Class. In *Harris, A. L.*, 1989, *1939*, pp. 276–301.

———. Reconstruction and the Negro. In *Harris, A. L.*, 1989, *1935*, pp. 209–12.

———. Review of Bernard Rosenberg's *The Values of Veblen: A Critical Appraisal*. In *Harris, A. L.*, 1989, *1959*, pp. 424–27.

———. Sombart and German (National) Socialism. In *Harris, A. L.*, 1989, *1942*, pp. 428–53.

———. Types of Institutionalism. In *Harris, A. L.*, 1989, *1932*, pp. 337–61.

———. Utopian Elements in Marx's Thought. In *Harris, A. L.*, 1989, *1950*, pp. 302–29.

———. Veblen and the Social Phenomenon of Capitalism. In *Harris, A. L.*, 1989, *1951*, pp. 402–13.

Harris, Barry C. and Simons, Joseph J. Focusing Market Definition: How Much Substitution Is Necessary? In *Zerbe, R. O.*, ed., 1989, pp. 207–26.

Harris, Carl M.; Gass, Saul I. and Chapman, Robert E. Analyzing the Economic Impacts of a Military Mobilization. In *Gulledge, T. R., Jr. and Litteral, L. A.*, eds., 1989, pp. 353–86.

Harris, Charles C.; Driver, B. L. and McLaughlin, William J. Improving the Contingent Valuation Method: A Psychological Perspective. *J. Environ. Econ. Manage.*, November 1989, *17*(3), pp. 213–29.

Harris, Charles P. Local Government and Regional Planning. In *Higgins, B. and Zagorski, K.*, eds., 1989, pp. 104–22.

Harris, Charles W. Federal and Local Interests in the Nation's Capital: Congress and District of Columbia Appropriations. *Public Budg. Finance*, Winter 1989, *9*(4), pp. 66–82.

Harris, Christopher J.; Heady, Christopher J. and Mitra, Pradeep K. Investment and Shadow Pricing in a Growing Economy with Tax Restrictions. *J. Public Econ.*, August 1989,

39(3), pp. 289–313.

Harris, D. J. Military Radicalism and African State Consolidation: A Review Article. *Can. J. Devel. Stud.*, 1989, *10*(1), pp. 135–39.

Harris, Elmer. Monetary Policy in Guyana, 1974–1985. In *Worrell, D. and Bourne, C.*, eds., 1989, pp. 115–24.

Harris, Emma. J. & P. Coats Ltd in Poland. In *Teichova, A.; Lévy-Leboyer, M. and Nussbaum, H.*, eds., 1989, pp. 135–42.

Harris, Frederick H. deB. Institutional Persistence and Change: The Question of Efficiency: Comment. *J. Inst. Theoretical Econ.*, March 1989, *145*(1), pp. 85–94.

Harris, Harold M. The SAEA: After Twenty Years: Discussion. *Southern J. Agr. Econ.*, July 1989, *21*(1), pp. 61–64.

Harris, Hazel C.; Goebel, W. and Cooper, P. J. M. Climatic Variability and Food Production in West Asia and North Africa. In *Oram, P. A., et al.*, 1989, pp. 69–83.

——— and Jones, Michael J. Climatic Variability and Agronomic Management in Mediterranean Barley–Livestock Farming Systems. In *Oram, P. A., et al.*, 1989, pp. 563–72.

Harris, Ian W. Administrative and Compliance Costs of Taxation: Hong Kong. In *International Fiscal Association, ed. (I)*, 1989, pp. 387–402.

———. Budget 1989/1990: Predictable and Boring: Hong Kong. *Bull. Int. Fiscal Doc.*, June 1989, *43*(6), pp. 270–73.

Harris, Jack C. The Effect of Real Rates of Interest on Housing Prices. *J. Real Estate Finance Econ.*, February 1989, *2*(1), pp. 47–60.

Harris, Jeffrey S. What Employers Can Do about Medical Care Costs: Managing Health and Productivity. In *McLennan, K. and Meyer, J. A.*, eds., 1989, pp. 167–202.

Harris, Lawrence. A Day-End Transaction Price Anomaly. *J. Finan. Quant. Anal.*, March 1989, *24*(1), pp. 29–45.

———. The October 1987 S&P 500 Stock-Futures Basis. *J. Finance*, March 1989, *44*(1), pp. 77–99.

———. Professor Hicks and the Foundations of Monetary Economics. In *Wood, J. C. and Woods, R. N.*, eds., Vol. 2, 1989, *1969*, pp. 80–91.

———. S&P 500 Cash Stock Price Volatilities. *J. Finance*, December 1989, *44*(5), pp. 1155–75.

Harris, Lorelei. Women's Response to Multinationals in County Mayo. In *Elson, D. and Pearson, R.*, eds., 1989, pp. 144–64.

Harris, Malcolm C., Sr. and Wynne, Kevin J. Explaining the Decline of Nuclear Power in the United States: Evidence from Plant Cancellation Decisions. *J. Energy Devel.*, Spring 1989, *14*(2), pp. 251–67.

Harris, Marion J. and Baba, Vishwanath V. Stress and Absence: A Cross-Cultural Perspective. In *Nedd, A.*, ed., 1989, pp. 317–37.

Harris, Milton and Raviv, Artur. The Design of Securities. *J. Finan. Econ.*, October 1989, *24*(2), pp. 255–87.

Harris, Nigel. The Pacific Rim: Review Article. *J. Devel. Stud.*, April 1989, *25*(3), pp. 408–16.

Harris, Olivia. The Earth and the State: The Sources and Meanings of Money in Northern Potosí, Bolivia. In *Parry, J. and Bloch, M., eds.*, 1989, pp. 232–68.

Harris, Peter. Socialist Graft: The Soviet Union and the People's Republic of China. In *Heidenheimer, A. J.; Johnston, M. and LeVine, V. T., eds.*, 1989, *1986*, pp. 513–33.

Harris, R. I. D. and Beaumont, P. B. The North–South Divide in Britain: The Case of Trade Union Recognition. *Oxford Bull. Econ. Statist.*, November 1989, *51*(4), pp. 413–28.

Harris, Richard G. "Market Access" in International Trade. In *Stern, R. M., ed.*, 1989, pp. 263–84.

_____. The New Protectionism Revisited. *Can. J. Econ.*, November 1989, *22*(4), pp. 751–78.

Harris, Robert S. and Franks, Julian R. Shareholder Wealth Effects of Corporate Takeovers: The U.K. Experience 1955–1985. *J. Finan. Econ.*, August 1989, *23*(2), pp. 225–49.

_____ **and Franks, Julian R.** Shareholder Wealth Effects of UK Takeovers: Implications for Merger Policy. In *Fairburn, J. and Kay, J., eds.*, 1989, pp. 148–74.

Harrison, Alan; Atkinson, Anthony B. and Gordon, James P. F. Trends in the Shares of Top Wealth-Holders in Britain, 1923–1981. *Oxford Bull. Econ. Statist.*, August 1989, *51*(3), pp. 315–32.

_____ **and Stewart, Mark.** Cyclical Fluctuations in Strike Durations. *Amer. Econ. Rev.*, September 1989, *79*(4), pp. 827–41.

Harrison, Anne. Environmental Issues and the SNA. *Rev. Income Wealth*, December 1989, *35*(4), pp. 377–88.

Harrison, B. and Kluver, J. Reassessing the 'Massachusetts Miracle': Reindustrialization and Balanced Growth, or Convergence to 'Manhattanization'? *Environ. Planning A*, June 1989, *21*(6), pp. 771–801.

Harrison, George L. Some Essentials of Monetary Stability. *Fed. Res. Bank New York Quart. Rev.*, Special Issue, 1989, pp. 15–20.

Harrison, Glenn W. Theory and Misbehavior of First-Price Auctions. *Amer. Econ. Rev.*, September 1989, *79*(4), pp. 749–62.

_____ **and Hirshleifer, Jack.** An Experimental Evaluation of Weakest Link/Best Shot Models of Public Goods. *J. Polit. Econ.*, February 1989, *97*(1), pp. 201–25.

_____**; Rutherford, Thomas F. and Wooton, Ian.** The Economic Impact of the European Community. *Amer. Econ. Rev.*, May 1989, *79*(2), pp. 288–94.

_____**; Rutström, E. E. and Wigle, Randall M.** Costs of Agricultural Trade Wars. In *Stoeckel, A. B.; Vincent, D. and Cuthbertson, S., eds.*, 1989, pp. 330–67.

Harrison, Larry. The Information Component. In *Robinson, D.; Maynard, A. and Chester, R., eds.*, 1989, pp. 183–202.

Harrison, R. T. The Politics of Industrial Decline and Restructuring in the Northern Ireland Shipbuilding Industry. In *Gibbs, D., ed.*, 1989, pp. 117–53.

Harrison, William B. and Wood, D. Robley, Jr. The Development of a Bank Classification Scheme through Discriminant Analysis. *Atlantic Econ. J.*, March 1989, *17*(1), pp. 35–42.

_____ **and Yoo, Jang H.** Altruism in the "Market" for Giving and Receiving: A Case of Higher Education. *Econ. Educ. Rev.*, 1989, *8*(4), pp. 367–76.

Harriss, Barbara. Commercialisation, Distribution and Consumption: Rural–Urban Grain and Resource Transfers in Peasant Society. In *[Mountjoy, A. B.]*, 1989, pp. 204–32.

Harriss, C. Lowell. Guidance from and Economics Classic: The Centennial of Henry George's 'Protection or Free Trade.' *Amer. J. Econ. Sociology*, July 1989, *48*(3), pp. 351–56.

_____. True Fundamentals of the Economic Role of Government. In *Samuels, W. J., ed. (I)*, 1989, pp. 79–85.

Harriss, John. Knowing about Rural Economic Change: Problems Arising from a Comparison of the Results of 'Macro' and 'Micro' Research in Tamil Nadu. In *Bardhan, P., ed. (I)*, 1989, pp. 137–73.

_____. Vulnerable Workers in the Indian Urban Labour Market. In *Rodgers, G., ed.*, 1989, pp. 217–57.

Hárs, Ágnes. Hopeless Prospects—Unemployment in Hungary: Review Article. *Acta Oecon.*, 1989, *41*(1–2), pp. 193–236.

Harsanyi, John C. An Equilibrium-Point Interpretation of the von Neumann–Morgenstern Solution and a Proposed Alternative Definition. In *Dore, M.; Chakravarty, S. and Goodwin, R., eds.*, 1989, pp. 162–90.

_____. Approaches to the Bargaining Problem before and after the Theory of Games: A Critical Discussion of Zeuthen's, Hicks', and Nash's Theories. In *Wood, J. C. and Woods, R. N., eds., Vol. 1*, 1989, *1956*, pp. 169–83.

Hart, Albert Gailord. A Neglected Monetary Standard Alternative: Gold/Commodity Bimetallism. In *Hamouda, O. F.; Rowley, R. and Wolf, B. M., eds.*, 1989, pp. 197–209.

Hart, Douglas B. and Munger, Michael C. Declining Electoral Competitiveness in the House of Representatives: The Differential Impact of Improved Transportation Technology. *Public Choice*, June 1989, *61*(3), pp. 217–28.

Hart, Gillian. Changing Mechanisms of Persistence: Reconfigurations of Petty Production in a Malaysian Rice Region. *Int. Lab. Rev.*, Special Issue, 1989, *128*(6), pp. 815–31.

_____. The Growth Linkages Controversy: Some Lessons from the Muda Case. *J. Devel. Stud.*, July 1989, *25*(4), pp. 571–75.

Hart, Jeffrey A. High Technology and the UN. In *[Gordenker, L.]*, 1989, pp. 112–27.

_____. The Origins of the U.S.–Japan Semiconductor Dispute. In *Haggard, S. and Moon, C., eds.*, 1989, pp. 129–53.

Hart, Michael. Dumping and Free Trade Areas.

In *Jackson, J. H. and Vermulst, E. A., eds.*, 1989, pp. 326–42.

Hart, Oliver D. Bargaining and Strikes. *Quart. J. Econ.*, February 1989, *104*(1), pp. 25–43.

————. The Changing Nature of Debt and Equity: A Financial Perspective: Discussion. In *Kopcke, R. W. and Rosengren, E. S., eds.*, 1989, pp. 39–43.

Hart, Robert A. The Employment and Hours Effects of a Marginal Employment Subsidy. *Scot. J. Polit. Econ.*, November 1989, *36*(4), pp. 385–95.

Hart, Sergiu and Mas-Colell, Andreu. Potential, Value, and Consistency. *Econometrica*, May 1989, *57*(3), pp. 589–614.

Harte, M.; Lonergan, S. and Cocklin, C. Patterns of Change in the Use of Energy in the New Zealand Economy. *Environ. Planning A*, September 1989, *21*(9), pp. 1141–56.

Hartford, Kathleen. Repression and Communist Success: The Case of Jin-Cha-Ji, 1938–1943. In *Hartford, K. and Goldstein, S. M., eds.*, 1989, pp. 92–127.

———— and **Goldstein, Steven M.** Perspectives on the Chinese Communist Revolution: Introduction. In *Hartford, K. and Goldstein, S. M., eds.*, 1989, pp. 3–33.

Hartigan, James C.; Kamma, Sreenivas and Perry, Philip R. The Injury Determination Category and the Value of Relief from Dumping. *Rev. Econ. Statist.*, February 1989, *71*(1), pp. 183–86.

Hartler, Christina; Bergholm, Fredrik and Hanson, Kenneth A. Semi-technical Specification of Pricing in MOSES. In *Albrecht, J. W., et al.*, 1989, pp. 221–31.

Hartley, Keith. Industry, Employment and Control Policy. In *Robinson, D.; Maynard, A. and Chester, R., eds.*, 1989, pp. 167–82.

———— and **Hutton, John.** Large Purchasers. In *Barber, J.; Metcalfe, J. S. and Porteous, M., eds.*, 1989, pp. 105–27.

Hartley, Michael J. and Swanson, Eric V. Maximum Likelihood Estimation of the Truncated and Censored Normal Regression Models. In *Mariano, R. S.; Lim, K. S. and Ling, K. D., eds.*, 1989, pp. 159–204.

———— and **Swanson, Eric V.** Retention of Basic Skills among Dropouts from Egyptian Primary Schools. In *Mariano, R. S.; Lim, K. S. and Ling, K. D., eds.*, 1989, pp. 205–45.

Hartley, Peter R. and Kyle, Albert S. Equilibrium Investment in an Industry with Moderate Investment Economies of Scale. *Econ. J.*, June 1989, *99*(396), pp. 392–407.

Hartman, Bart P. and Sami, Heibatollah. The Impact of the Accounting Treatment of Leasing Contracts on Use Decision Making: A Field Experiment. In *Schwartz, B. N., ed.*, 1989, pp. 23–35.

Hartman, Raymond S. An Empirical Model of Product Design and Pricing Strategy. *Int. J. Ind. Organ.*, December 1989, *7*(4), pp. 419–36.

————. Hedonic Methods for Evaluating Product Design and Pricing Strategies. *J. Econ. Bus.*, August 1989, *41*(3), pp. 197–212.

Hartmann, Heidi I. and Michael, Robert T. Pay Equity: Assessing the Issues. In *Michael, R. T.; Hartmann, H. I. and O'Farrell, B., eds.*, 1989, pp. 1–19.

Hartmann-Wendels, Thomas. Dividend Policy under Asymmetric Information. In *Bamberg, G. and Spremann, K., eds.*, 1989, pp. 229–53.

————. Principal-Agent–Theorie und asymmetrische Informationsverteilung. (With English summary.) *Z. Betriebswirtshaft*, July 1989, *59*(7), pp. 714–34.

Hartog, J. A.; Hinloopen, E. and Nijkamp, Peter. A Sensitivity Analysis of Multicriteria Choice-Methods An Application on the Basis of the Optimal Site Selection for a Nuclear Power Plant. *Energy Econ.*, October 1989, *11*(4), pp. 293–300.

Hartog, Joop. Distribution Policies in the Netherlands. In *Muller, F. and Zwezerijnen, W. J., eds.*, 1989, pp. 17–46.

————. Survey Non-response in Relation to Ability and Family Background: Structure and Effects on Estimated Earnings Functions. *Appl. Econ.*, March 1989, *21*(3), pp. 387–95.

———— and **Bierens, Herman J.** Estimating a Hedonic Earnings Function with a Nonparametric Method. In *Ullah, A., ed.*, 1989, *1988*, pp. 145–72.

————; **Pfann, Gerard A. and Ridder, Geert.** (Non-)graduation and the Earnings Function: An Inquiry on Self-Selection. *Europ. Econ. Rev.*, September 1989, *33*(7), pp. 1373–95.

———— and **Vriend, Nick.** Post-war International Labour Mobility: The Netherlands. In *Gordon, I. and Thirlwall, A. P., eds.*, 1989, pp. 74–94.

Hartwell, R. M. The Political Economy of Policy Formation: The Case of England. In *Gamble, A., et al.*, 1989, pp. 99–122.

Hartwick, John M. On the Development of the Theory of Land Rent. *Land Econ.*, November 1989, *65*(4), pp. 410–12.

———— and **Buckholtz, P.** Zero Time Preference with Discounting. *Econ. Letters*, 1989, *29*(1), pp. 1–6.

———— and **Spencer, Michael.** An Oil-Exporting Region versus an Industrialized Region. In *Andersson, Å. E., et al., eds.*, 1989, pp. 67–79.

———— and **Yeung, David.** Production Cost Uncertainty and Industry Equilibrium for Nonrenewable Resource Extraction. *Natural Res. Modeling*, Fall 1989, *3*(4), pp. 577–88.

Harvey, Andrew C. and Fernandes, C. Time Series Models for Count or Qualitative Observations: Reply. *J. Bus. Econ. Statist.*, October 1989, *7*(4), pp. 422.

———— and **Fernandes, C.** Time Series Models for Count or Qualitative Observations. *J. Bus. Econ. Statist.*, October 1989, *7*(4), pp. 407–17.

———— and **Phillips, Garry D. A.** Testing for Structural Change in Simultaneous Equation Models. In *Hackl, P., ed.*, 1989, pp. 25–36.

Harvey, Campbell R. Time-Varying Conditional Covariances in Tests of Asset Pricing Models. *J. Finan. Econ.*, October 1989, *24*(2), pp. 289–317.

Harvey, Charles and Press, Jon. Overseas Investment and the Professional Advance of British Metal Mining Engineers, 1851–1914. *Econ. Hist. Rev.*, *2nd Ser.*, February 1989, *42*(1), pp. 64–86.

Harvey, David. Alternatives to Present Price Policies for the CAP. *Europ. Rev. Agr. Econ.*, 1989, *16*(1), pp. 83–111.

Harvey, R., et al. Changes in Private Medical Service Use, 1976 to 1986. In *Smith, C. S., ed.*, 1989, pp. 196–216.

Harvie, Charles. Oil Production, Wages, and Macroeconomic Adjustment. *J. Energy Devel.*, Autumn 1989, *15*(1), pp. 25–49.

Harvie, Christopher. Fawcett as Professional Politician. In *Goldman, L., ed.*, 1989, pp. 180–88.

Hasan, M. Aynul and Chishti, Salim. Relative Prices and Inflation Variability. *Pakistan J. Appl. Econ.*, Summer 1989, *8*(1), pp. 73–84.

_____ **and Nishat, Mohammed.** Determinants of Multinational Investments in Pakistan: An Exploratory Analysis. *Pakistan Econ. Soc. Rev.*, Summer 1989, *27*(1), pp. 49–60.

Hasan, Zubair. Towards an Islamic Macro Model of Distribution: A Comparative Approach: Comments. *J. King Abdulaziz Univ.: Islamic Econ.*, 1989, *1*, pp. 121–27.

Hasche-Preusse, Christine. Europäischer Finanzraum—Perspektiven für die Kapitalmärkte, die Finanzindustrien und die Währungspolitik. (Financing in Europe—Capital Market, Financial Industry and Monetary Policy Perspectives. With English summary.) *Kredit Kapital*, 1989, *22*(1), pp. 138–60.

Hase, Tatsuo and Odagiri, Hiroyuki. Are Mergers and Acquisitions Going to Be Popular in Japan Too? An Empirical Study. *Int. J. Ind. Organ.*, Special Issue, March 1989, *7*(1), pp. 49–72.

Hasegawa, Hikaru. Bayesian Estimator of the Linear Regression Model with an Interval Constraint on Coefficients. *Econ. Letters*, November 1989, *31*(1), pp. 9–12.

Haseltine, John B. The View of the Banking Community. In *Dornbusch, R.; Makin, J. H. and Zlowe, D., eds.*, 1989, pp. 83–86.

Haseyama, Takahiko; Honobe, Susumu and O'uchi, Minoru. New Issues of Economic Cooperation. In *Shinohara, M. and Lo, F., eds.*, 1989, pp. 469–502.

Hashemi, Ibrahim S. J. Al and Najjar, George K. Strategic Choices in Management Education: The Bahrain Experience. In *Davies, J., et al., eds.*, 1989, pp. 29–39.

Hashimoto, Hideo and Takayama, Takashi. A Comparative Study of Linear Complementarity Programming Models and Linear Programming Models in Multi-region Investment Analysis: Aluminium and Bauxite. In *Labys, W. C.; Takayama, T. and Uri, N. D., eds.*, 1989, pp. 129–63.

Hashimoto, Kyoji; Homma, Masaaki and Atoda, Naosumi. Welfare Analysis of the 1988 Tax Reform in Japan. *Econ. Stud. Quart.*, December 1989, *40*(4), pp. 336–48.

Hashimoto, Masanori and Raisian, John. Investments in Employer–Employee Attachments by Japanese and U.S. Workers in Firms of Varying Size. *J. Japanese Int. Economies*, March 1989, *3*(1), pp. 31–48.

Hashimoto, Noriko. Small Sample Properties of Modified Prais–Winston Estimators in Hypothesis Testing in a Linear Model with AR(1) Errors. *Econ. Letters*, 1989, *29*(2), pp. 147–52.

Hasibuan, Nurimansjah and Evans, David B. South Sumatra: Dualism and Export Orientation. In *Hill, H., ed.*, 1989, pp. 454–72.

Haslag, Joseph H. and Hein, Scott E. Federal Reserve System Reserve Requirements, 1959–1988: A Note. *J. Money, Credit, Banking*, November 1989, *21*(4), pp. 515–23.

_____ **and Hein, Scott E.** Reserve Requirements, the Monetary Base, and Economic Activity. *Fed. Res. Bank Dallas Econ. Rev.*, March 1989, pp. 1–15.

Hassan, John A. International Responses to the Energy Crises of 1986. *Brit. Rev. Econ. Issues*, Summer 1989, *11*(25), pp. 1–26.

_____ **and Duncan, Alan.** The Role of Energy Supplies during Western Europe's Golden Age, 1950–1972. *J. Europ. Econ. Hist.*, Winter 1989, *18*(3), pp. 479–508.

Hassan, Mahmud; Sloan, Frank A. and Wedig, Gerard J. Hospital Investment Decisions and the Cost of Capital. *J. Bus.*, October 1989, *62*(4), pp. 517–37.

Hassan, Rashid M.; D'Silva, B. and Hallam, Arne. Measuring Stochastic Technology for the Multi-product Firm: The Irrigated Farms of Sudan. *Can. J. Agr. Econ.*, November 1989, *37*(3), pp. 495–512.

_____ **; Fletcher, Lehman B. and Ahmed, S.** Unequal Wealth Accumulation and Income Inequality in a Unimodal Agriculture: Sudan's Radad Irrigation Scheme. *J. Devel. Stud.*, October 1989, *26*(1), pp. 120–30.

Hassard, John. Time and Industrial Sociology. In *Blyton, P., et al.*, 1989, pp. 13–34.

_____. Time and Organization. In *Blyton, P., et al.*, 1989, pp. 79–104.

Hasseldine, D. John. An Analysis of the New Residence Requirements: New Zealand. *Bull. Int. Fiscal Doc.*, April 1989, *43*(4), pp. 153–56.

_____. Dividend Imputation: The New Zealand Model. *Bull. Int. Fiscal Doc.*, May 1989, *43*(5), pp. 203–13.

_____. Increasing Voluntary Compliance: The Case of Tax Amnesties. *Australian Tax Forum*, 1989, *6*(4), pp. 509–23.

_____. 1989 Budget: Calm amidst an Upheaval: New Zealand. *Bull. Int. Fiscal Doc.*, October 1989, *43*(10), pp. 467–68.

Hassell, John M.; Lorek, Kenneth S. and Bathke, Allen W., Jr. New Evidence on the Accuracy of Management Forecasts and Time-Series Forecasts of Annual Earnings. In *Schwartz, B. N., ed.*, 1989, pp. 67–84.

Hastak, Manoj and Olson, Jerry C. Assessing the Role of Brand-Related Cognitive Responses as Mediators of Communication Effects on Cognitive Structure. *J. Cons. Res.*, March 1989, 15(4), pp. 444–56.

Hastie, Trevor and Stuetzle, Werner. Principal Curves. *J. Amer. Statist. Assoc.*, June 1989, 84(406), pp. 502–16.

Hastings, Margaret M. and Cohen, Donna. Mental Health in the Elderly. In *Eisdorfer, C.; Kessler, D. A. and Spector, A. N.*, eds., 1989, pp. 358–77.

Hasymi, Ali and Potter, Lesley. South Kalimantan: The Banjarese Heartland. In *Hill, H.*, ed., 1989, pp. 473–99.

Hatch, Upton; Atwood, Joseph A. and Segar, James. An Application of Safety-First Probability Limits in a Discrete Stochastic Farm Management Programming Model. *Southern J. Agr. Econ.*, July 1989, 21(1), pp. 65–72.

Hathaway, Dale E. Modifying U.S. Farm Policy: Helping Others while Helping Ourselves. In *Swegle, W. E. and Ligon, P. C.*, eds., 1989, pp. 41–49.

Hatta, Tatsuo and Fukushima, Takashi. Why Not Tax Uniformly Rather Than Optimally? *Econ. Stud. Quart.*, September 1989, 40(3), pp. 220–38.

Hattori, Tamio. Japanese Zaibatsu and Korean Chaebol. In *Chung, K. H. and Lee, H. C.*, eds., 1989, pp. 79–95.

Hattwick, Richard E., et al. On the Alleged Decline in Business Ethics. *J. Behav. Econ.*, Summer 1989, 18(2), pp. 129–43.

Hatzipanayotou, Panos. Commercial Policies in a Model of an Open Economy with Restricted Supply of Domestic Goods. *Greek Econ. Rev.*, 1989, 11(2), pp. 291–304.

_____ and Michael, Michael S. Capital Flows, Tariffs, and the Host Country's Welfare. *Econ. Int.*, Aug.–Nov. 1989, 42(3–4), pp. 191–97.

Haubrich, Joseph G. Financial Intermediation: Delegated Monitoring and Long-term Relationships. *J. Banking Finance*, March 1989, 13(1), pp. 9–20.

Hauer, Ezra. The Reign of Ignorance in Road Safety: A Case for Separating Evaluation from Implementation. In *Moses, L. N. and Savage, I.*, eds., 1989, pp. 56–69.

Haugen, Robert A. Pension Management in the Context of Corporate Risk Management. *J. Portfol. Manage.*, Fall 1989, 16(1), pp. 72–78.

Haugen, Steven E. Employment Gains Slow in the First Half of 1989. *Mon. Lab. Rev.*, August 1989, 112(8), pp. 3–9.

Haughton, Graham. Community and Industrial Restructuring: Responses to the Recession and Its Aftermath in the Illawarra Region of Australia. *Environ. Planning A*, February 1989, 21(2), pp. 233–47.

_____ and Peck, Jamie A. Local Labour Market Analysis, Skill Shortages and the Skills Audit Approach. *Reg. Stud.*, June 1989, 23(3), pp. 271–76.

Haughton, Jonathan. Should OPEC Use Dollars in Pricing Oil? *J. Energy Devel.*, Spring 1989, 14(2), pp. 193–211.

Hauke, Wolfgang; Opitz, Otto and Pauly, Ralf. Explorative Data Analysis and Macroeconomics. In *Opitz, O.*, ed., 1989, pp. 416–31.

Haupt, Reinhard and Knobloch, Thomas. Kostentheoretische Anpassungsprozesse bei zeitvariablen Faktoreinsätzen. (With English summary.) *Z. Betriebswirtshaft*, May 1989, 59(5), pp. 504–24.

Haurie, Alain. Duopole et percées technologiques: Un modèle de jeu différentiel déterministe par morceaux. (With English summary.) *L'Actual. Econ.*, March 1989, 65(1), pp. 105–18.

Haurin, Donald R. Women's Labor Market Reactions to Family Disruptions. *Rev. Econ. Statist.*, February 1989, 71(1), pp. 54–61.

_____ and Lee, Kyubang. A Structural Model of the Demand for Owner-Occupied Housing. *J. Urban Econ.*, November 1989, 26(3), pp. 348–60.

Haury, Susanne and Meier, Alfred. Kollektive Bewältigung von Unsicherheit nach dem Börsencrash vom 19. Oktober 1987. (Collective Measures of Uncertainty Management after the Stock Market Crash of 1987. With English summary.) *Aussenwirtschaft*, June 1989, 44(2), pp. 253–72.

Haus, Joseph W. and Schroeder, John. Lasers: Now the Age of Light. In *Finkelstein, J.*, ed., 1989, pp. 67–107.

Hause, John C. Indemnity, Settlement, and Litigation, or I'll Be Suing You. *J. Legal Stud.*, January 1989, 18(1), pp. 157–79.

_____. Short-run Supply with Capacity Constraints: Comment. *J. Law Econ.*, Part 2, October 1989, 32(2), pp. S43–46.

Hauser, Heinz. Property Rights in Information and the Multinational Firm: The Case of Technical Learning in a Multiplant System: Comments. In *Vosgerau, H.-J.*, ed., 1989, pp. 401–08.

Hauser, Siegfried and Blümle, Gerold. Exports of Baden-Württemberg within the Frame of the Federal Republic of Germany Structure—Concentration. In *Dams, T. and Matsugi, T.*, eds., 1989, pp. 191–214.

Häusermann, Hartmut and Krämer-Badoni, Thomas. The Change of Regional Inequality in the Federal Republic of Germany. In *Gottdiener, M. and Komninos, N.*, eds., 1989, pp. 331–47.

Hausman, Daniel M. Arbitrage Arguments. In *Balzer, W. and Hamminga, B.*, eds., 1989, pp. 5–22.

_____. Decision Theory and the Deductive Method. *Ricerche Econ.*, Jan.–June 1989, 43(1–2), pp. 199–217.

_____. Economic Methodology in a Nutshell. *J. Econ. Perspectives*, Spring 1989, 3(2), pp. 115–27.

_____. On Justifying the Ways of Mammon to Man. In *Feiwel, G. R.*, ed. (II), 1989, pp. 821–32.

Hausman, Jerry A. and Tardiff, Timothy J. Competition in Telecommunications for Large Users in New York. In *National Economic Research Associates*, 1989, pp. 1–19.

Haveman, Robert H. Economics and Public Policy: On the Relevance of Conventional Economic Advice. *Quart. Rev. Econ. Bus.*, Autumn 1989, *29*(3), pp. 6–20.

———; **Gottschalk, Peter and Wolfe, Barbara L.** Health Care Financing in the U.S., U.K. and Netherlands: Distributional Consequences. In *Chiancone, A. and Messere, K., eds.*, 1989, pp. 351–73.

Havenga, J. J. D. Determinants in the Start-Up and Growth of Small and Medium-Sized Firms. *J. Stud. Econ. Econometrics*, March 1989, *13*(1), pp. 19–31.

Havenner, Arthur M. and Aoki, Masanao. A Method for Approximate Representation of Vector-Valued Time Series and Its Relation to Two Alternatives. *J. Econometrics*, October 1989, *42*(2), pp. 181–99.

——— **and Criddle, Keith R.** Forecasting Halibut Biomass Using System Theoretic Time-Series Methods. *Amer. J. Agr. Econ.*, May 1989, *71*(2), pp. 422–31.

Havet, José L. Points of View and Comments: Introduction. *Can. J. Devel. Stud.*, 1989, *10*(2), pp. 289–91.

Havlik, Peter. Foreign Trade System and Joint Ventures in the CMEA Region. In *Gabrisch, H., ed.*, 1989, pp. 201–12.

———. Gorbachev's Reform Course Confirmed. In *Gabrisch, H., ed.*, 1989, pp. 87–98.

Havrilesky, Thomas. A Compassionate Solution to Distributional Conflict. *Challenge*, March–April 1989, *32*(2), pp. 55–56.

———. Monetary Activism as Addiction. *Challenge*, May–June 1989, *32*(3), pp. 55–57.

Hawdon, David. Changing Oil Price Expectations. In *Hawdon, D., ed.*, 1989, pp. 115–27.

———. Oil Prices in the 1990s: Introduction. In *Hawdon, D., ed.*, 1989, pp. xi–xviii.

———. Transport Costs and Capacity Adjustment in the Tanker Market. In *Hawdon, D., ed.*, 1989, pp. 80–104.

Hawk, Barry E. Airline Deregulation after Ten Years: The Need for Vigorous Antitrust Enforcement and Intergovernmental Agreements. *Antitrust Bull.*, Summer 1989, *34*(2), pp. 267–305.

Hawkins, Michael. Ambiguity and Contradiction in 'the Rise of Professionalism': The English Clergy, 1570–1730. In *[Stone, L.]*, 1989, pp. 241–69.

Haworth, Nigel. The State, Industrial Relations and the Labour Movement in Latin America: Volume 1: Peru. In *Carrière, J.; Haworth, N. and Roddick, J., eds.*, 1989, pp. 21–66.

———; **Roddick, Jacqueline and Carrière, Jean.** Proletarianisation, Industrialisation and Patterns of Action. In *Carrière, J.; Haworth, N. and Roddick, J., eds.*, 1989, pp. 1–20.

Hax, Herbert. The New Institutional Economics and the Process of Economic Development: Comment. *J. Inst. Theoretical Econ.*, March 1989, *145*(1), pp. 63–66.

Hay, Donald A. and Louri, Helen. Firms as Portfolios: A Mean–Variance Analysis of Unquoted UK Companies. *J. Ind. Econ.*, December 1989, *38*(2), pp. 141–65.

Hay, George A. Merger Policy in the U.S. In *Fairburn, J. and Kay, J., eds.*, 1989, pp. 231–45.

———. Practices That Facilitate Cooperation: The *Ethyl* Case. In *Kwoka, J. E., Jr. and White, L. J., eds.*, 1989, pp. 183–207.

Hay, Jonathan and Bouchet, Michel H. The Rise of the Market-Based "Menu" Approach and Its Limitations. In *Husain, I. and Diwan, I., eds.*, 1989, pp. 146–59.

Hayami, Yujiro. Agricultural Policies in Disarray: The Players. In *von Witzke, H.; Runge, C. F. and Job, B., eds.*, 1989, pp. 56–88.

——— **and Kawagoe, Toshihiko.** Farm Mechanization, Scale Economies and Polarization: The Japanese Experience. *J. Devel. Econ.*, October 1989, *31*(2), pp. 221–39.

——— **and Kawagoe, Toshihiko.** Farmers and Middlemen in a Transmigration Area in Indonesia. *Bull. Indonesian Econ. Stud.*, December 1989, *25*(3), pp. 73–97.

——— **and Morooka, Yoshinori.** Contract Choice and Enforcement in an Agrarian Community: Agricultural Tenancy in Upland Java. *J. Devel. Stud.*, October 1989, *26*(1), pp. 28–42.

Hayashi, Fumio. Is Japan's Saving Rate High? *Fed. Res. Bank Minn. Rev.*, Spring 1989, *13*(2), pp. 3–9.

———. Saving in Developing Countries: Theory and Review: Comment. In *Fischer, S. and de Tray, D., eds.*, 1989, pp. 97–99.

Hayashi, Kichiro. Assumptions on Decisions, Decisions on Assumptions—Some Future Perspectives. In *Hayashi, K., ed.*, 1989, pp. 313–39.

———. A Comparative Analysis of Cross-Cultural-Interface Management: The United States and Japan. In *Hayashi, K., ed.*, 1989, pp. 22–74.

———. The U.S.–Japanese Economic Relationship: Can It Be Improved? Preface. In *Hayashi, K., ed.*, 1989, pp. vii–xiv.

Hayashibara, Masayuki and Jones, Ronald W. Should a Factor-Market Distortion Be Widened? *Econ. Letters*, December 1989, *31*(2), pp. 159–62.

Hayden, F. Gregory. Institutionalism For What: To Understand Inevitable Progress or for Policy Relevance? *J. Econ. Issues*, June 1989, *23*(2), pp. 633–45.

———. Public Pension Power for Socioeconomic Investments. *J. Econ. Issues*, December 1989, *23*(4), pp. 1027–45.

———. Social Fabric Matrix: From Perspective to Analytical Tool. In *Tool, M. R. and Samuels, W. J., eds. (II)*, 1989, *1982*, pp. 565–90.

Haydu, Jeffrey. Trade Agreement vs. Open Shop: Employers' Choices before WWI. *Ind. Relat.*, Spring 1989, *28*(2), pp. 159–73.

von Hayek, Friedrich August. The Pretence of Knowledge. *Amer. Econ. Rev.*, December 1989, *79*(6), pp. 3–7.

Hayes, Alfred E. The International Monetary System—Retrospect and Prospect. *Fed. Res. Bank New York Quart. Rev.*, Special Issue, 1989, pp. 29–34.

Hayes, Dermot J. Incorporating Credit in Demand Analysis. *J. Cons. Aff.*, Summer 1989, 23(1), pp. 1–20.

Hayes, Kathy J. A Specification Test for Choosing the "Right" Public-Good Price. *J. Bus. Econ. Statist.*, April 1989, 7(2), pp. 267–73.

_____ and **Slottje, Daniel J.** The Efficacy of State and Local Governments' Redistributional Policies. *Public Finance Quart.*, July 1989, 17(3), pp. 304–22.

_____; **Slottje, Daniel J. and Black, Dan A.** Demographic Change and Inequality in the Size Distributions of Labor and Nonlabor Income. *Rev. Income Wealth*, September 1989, 35(3), pp. 283–96.

Hayes, Radar. Determining the Consumer Information Content of Newspapers: A Proposed Analytical Framework and Illustrative Application. *J. Cons. Aff.*, Summer 1989, 23(1), pp. 127–44.

Hayes-Renshaw, Fiona; Lequesne, Christian and Mayor Lopez, Pedro. The Permanent Representations of the Member States to the European Communities. *J. Common Market Stud.*, December 1989, 28(2), pp. 119–37.

Hayes, Robert E., Jr. The Business Economist at Work: K mart Corporation. *Bus. Econ.*, April 1989, 24(2), pp. 48–50.

Hayford, Marc. Liquidity Constraints and the Ricardian Equivalence Theorem: A Note. *J. Money, Credit, Banking*, August 1989, 21(3), pp. 380–87.

Hayghe, Howard V. Children in 2-Worker Families and Real Family Income. *Mon. Lab. Rev.*, December 1989, 112(12), pp. 48–52.

Hayn, Carla. Tax Attributes as Determinants of Shareholder Gains in Corporate Acquisitions. *J. Finan. Econ.*, June 1989, 23(1), pp. 121–53.

Haynes, Cleviston and Holder, Carlos. Monetary and Fiscal Policy in Barbados, 1970–1985. In *Worrell, D. and Bourne, C., eds.*, 1989, pp. 89–104.

Haynes, Kingsley E. and Krmenec, Andrew. A Sensitivity Assessment of Uncertainty in Infrastructure Expansion. *Ann. Reg. Sci.*, 1989, 23(4), pp. 299–309.

Haynes, Stephen E. and Goldstein, Henry N. Monetary Policy Activism under Managed-Floating Exchange Rates: A Cross-country Comparison. *Contemp. Policy Issues*, April 1989, 7(2), pp. 27–40.

_____; **Hutchison, Michael M. and Mikesell, Raymond F.** U.S.–Japanese Bilateral Trade and the Yen–Dollar Exchange Rate: Reply. *Southern Econ. J.*, October 1989, 56(2), pp. 524–28.

_____ and **Stone, Joe A.** An Integrated Test for Electoral Cycles in the U.S. Economy. *Rev. Econ. Statist.*, August 1989, 71(3), pp. 426–34.

Hayter, R. and Ofori-Amoah, B. Labour Turnover Characteristics at the Eurocan Pulp and Paper Mill, Kitimat: A Log-Linear Analysis. *Environ. Planning A*, November 1989, 21(11), pp. 1491–1510.

Hayton, K. The Future of Local Economic Development. *Reg. Stud.*, December 1989, 23(6), pp. 549–57.

Hayton, Robert D. and Utton, Albert E. Transboundary Groundwaters: The Bellagio Draft Treaty. *Natural Res. J.*, Summer 1989, 29(3), pp. 663–722.

Hayward, Fred M. Sierra Leone: State Consolidation, Fragmentation and Decay. In *Cruise O'Brien, D. B.; Dunn, J. and Rathbone, R., eds.*, 1989, pp. 165–80.

Hayward, Mark D.; Hardy, Melissa A. and Grady, William R. Labor Force Withdrawal Patterns among Older Men in the United States. *Soc. Sci. Quart.*, June 1989, 70(2), pp. 425–48.

_____, **et al.** Occupational Influences on Retirement, Disability, and Death. *Demography*, August 1989, 26(3), pp. 393–409.

Hazari, Bharat R. and Bandara, Jayatilleke S. Basic Needs and Linkages: A Case Study of Sri Lanka. *J. Econ. Devel.*, December 1989, 14(2), pp. 99–106.

_____; **Muir, S. and Sgro, Pasquale M.** Rationing Black Markets and Welfare of the Poor. *Indian Econ. J.*, April–June 1989, 36(4), pp. 39–47.

Hazelkorn, Ellen. Why Is There No Socialism in Ireland? Theoretical Problems of Irish Marxism. *Sci. Society*, Summer 1989, 53(2), pp. 136–64.

Hazell, Peter B. R. Changing Patterns of Variability in World Cereal Production. In *Anderson, J. R. and Hazell, P. B. R., eds.*, 1989, pp. 13–34.

_____ and **Anderson, Jock R.** Synthesis and Needs in Agricultural Research and Policy. In *Anderson, J. R. and Hazell, P. B. R., eds.*, 1989, pp. 339–56.

_____; **Brown, James and Haggblade, Steven.** Farm–Nonfarm Linkages in Rural Sub-Saharan Africa. *World Devel.*, August 1989, 17(8), pp. 1173–1201.

Hazledine, Tim. Industrial Organisation Foundations of Trade Policy Modelling. *Australian J. Agr. Econ.*, April 1989, 33(1), pp. 1–19.

_____ and **Wigington, Ian.** Canadian Auto Policy Revisited: Reply. *Can. Public Policy*, March 1989, 15(1), pp. 107–08.

_____, **et al.** Trade, Protectionism and Industrial Adjustment: Three North American Case Studies: Case Study 2: North American and European Community Policies: Effect on Southeast Asian Vegetable Oil Exports. In *North–South Institute*, 1989, pp. 65–104.

Hazlett, Thomas W. Cabling America: Economic Forces in a Political World. In *Veljanovski, C., ed. (I)*, 1989, pp. 208–23.

Hazzard, William R. Prevention and Early Intervention. In *Eisdorfer, C.; Kessler, D. A. and Spector, A. N., eds.*, 1989, pp. 378–99.

He, Bing; Hao, Chengyi and Guo, Jinhua. Conditions of Workers' Material and Mental Lives and Trends in Their Development. *Chinese Econ. Stud.*, Summer 1989, *22*(4), pp. 32–38.

He, Weiling. The Impact and Influence of the New View of Science on China's Reform. *Cato J.*, Winter 1989, *8*(3), pp. 637–40.

Head, Ivan L. South–North Dangers. *Foreign Aff.*, Summer 1989, *68*(3), pp. 71–86.

Heady, Christopher J.; Mitra, Pradeep K. and Harris, Christopher J. Investment and Shadow Pricing in a Growing Economy with Tax Restrictions. *J. Public Econ.*, August 1989, *39*(3), pp. 289–313.

Heald, David. The Valuation of Power Stations by the Modern Equivalent Asset Method. *Fisc. Stud.*, May 1989, *10*(2), pp. 86–108.

Healey, Derek and Lütkenhorst, Wilfried. Export Processing Zones: The Case of the Republic of Korea. *Industry Devel.*, April 1989, (26), pp. 1–56.

Healy, Paul; Palepu, Krishna G. and Asquith, Paul. Earnings and Stock Splits. *Accounting Rev.*, July 1989, *64*(3), pp. 387–403.

Heaney, James P. and Ng, Elliot K. Efficient Total Enumeration of Water Resources Alternatives. *Water Resources Res.*, April 1989, *25*(4), pp. 583–90.

Heath, John. Privatisation: Modalities and Strategy. In *Ramanadham, V. V., ed.*, 1989, pp. 118–24.

Heath, Julia A. An Econometric Model of the Role of Gender in Economic Education. *Amer. Econ. Rev.*, May 1989, *79*(2), pp. 226–30.

Heather, Randall W. Annual Review of Nations: Year 1988: Federal Republic of Germany (West Germany). In *Haberman, L. and Sacks, P. M., eds.*, 1989, pp. 75–95.

_____. Annual Review of Nations: Year 1988: France. In *Haberman, L. and Sacks, P. M., eds.*, 1989, pp. 97–116.

Hébert, Robert F. and Ekelund, Robert B., Jr. Consumer Surplus: The First Hundred Years. In *Wood, J. C. and Woods, R. N., eds.*, Vol. 4, 1989, *1985*, pp. 198–230.

_____; **Tollison, Robert D. and Ekelund, Robert B., Jr.** An Economic Model of the Medieval Church: Usury as a Form of Rent Seeking. *J. Law, Econ., Organ.*, Fall 1989, *5*(2), pp. 307–31.

Heckman, James J. The Impact of Government on the Economic Status of Black Americans. In *Shulman, S. and Darity, W., Jr., eds.*, 1989, pp. 50–80.

_____ and **Hotz, V. Joseph.** Choosing among Alternative Nonexperimental Methods for Estimating the Impact of Social Programs: The Case of Manpower Training. *J. Amer. Statist. Assoc.*, December 1989, *84*(408), pp. 862–74.

_____ and **Hotz, V. Joseph.** Choosing among Alternative Nonexperimental Methods for Estimating the Impact of Social Programs: The Case of Manpower Training: Rejoinder. *J. Amer. Statist. Assoc.*, December 1989, *84*(408), pp. 878–80.

_____ and **Payner, Brook S.** Determining the Impact of Federal Antidiscrimination Policy on the Economic Status of Blacks: A Study of South Carolina. *Amer. Econ. Rev.*, March 1989, *79*(1), pp. 138–77.

_____; **Payner, Brook S. and Butler, Richard J.** The Impact of the Economy and the State on the Economic Status of Blacks: A Study of South Carolina. In *Galenson, D. W., ed.*, 1989, pp. 231–346.

_____ and **Robb, Richard.** The Value of Longitudinal Data for Solving the Problem of Selection Bias in Evaluating the Impact of Treatments on Outcomes. In *Kasprzyk, D., et al., eds.*, 1989, pp. 512–38.

_____ and **Walker, James R.** Forecasting Aggregate Period-Specific Birth Rates: The Time Series Properties of a Microdynamic Neoclassical Model of Fertility. *J. Amer. Statist. Assoc.*, December 1989, *84*(408), pp. 958–65.

Hedge, David M.; Menzel, Donald C. and Krause, Mark A. The Intergovernmental Milieu and Street-Level Implementation. *Soc. Sci. Quart.*, June 1989, *70*(2), pp. 285–99.

Hedley, Douglas. Break-Out Session II—Conference Consensus: Recommendations: Harmonizing Macroeconomic, Financial, Food Consumption, and Agricultural Policies. In *Helmuth, J. W. and Johnson, S. R., eds.*, Vol. 1, 1989, pp. 200–201.

_____; **Baharsjah, Sjarifudin and Hadiwigeno, Soetatwo.** Agricultural Policy and Food Self-Sufficiency in Developing Countries. In *Helmuth, J. W. and Johnson, S. R., eds.*, Vol. 2, 1989, pp. 121–37.

Heen, Knut. Impact Analysis of Multispecies Marine Resource Management. *Marine Resource Econ.*, 1989, *6*(4), pp. 331–48.

Heertje, Arnold. Nicolaas Gerard Pierson. In *Walker, D. A., ed.*, 1989, pp. 167–90.

Heery, Edmund and Edwards, Christine. Recession in the Public Sector: Industrial Relations in Freightliner 1981–1985. *Brit. J. Ind. Relat.*, March 1989, *27*(1), pp. 57–71.

_____ and **Kelly, John.** Full-time Officers and Trade Union Recruitment. *Brit. J. Ind. Relat.*, July 1989, *27*(2), pp. 196–213.

Heffern, Gordon E. Ethical Considerations in Takeovers. In *McKee, D. L., ed.*, 1989, pp. 79–84.

Hefting, Tom; Stensland, Gunnar and Bjørstad, Heidi. A Model for Exploration Decisions. *Energy Econ.*, July 1989, *11*(3), pp. 189–200.

Hegazi, Abdul Aziz. Role of the Public and Private Sectors with Special Reference to Privatization: The Case of Egypt: Comment. In *El-Naggar, S., ed.*, 1989, pp. 182–88.

Hegde, Shantaram P. On the Value of the Implicit Delivery Options. *J. Futures Markets*, October 1989, *9*(5), pp. 421–37.

_____ and **Miller, Robert E.** Market-Making in Initial Public Offerings of Common Stocks: An Empirical Analysis. *J. Finan. Quant. Anal.*, March 1989, *24*(1), pp. 75–90.

Hegedüs, András. Merely a Beauty-Spot. *Acta Oecon.*, 1989, *40*(3–4), pp. 225–27.

_____. Theses on the Crisis of Ethics and the

Economic Crisis. *Acta Oecon.*, 1989, *40*(1–2), pp. 55–63.

Heggie, Ian G. Reforming Transport Policy. *Finance Devel.*, March 1989, *26*(1), pp. 42–44.

Heggli, Beat and Frey, Bruno S. An Ipsative Theory of Business Behaviour. *J. Econ. Psych.*, March 1989, *10*(1), pp. 1–20.

Hegji, Charles E. FOMC Targets, Base Drift and Inflationary Expectations. *Eastern Econ. J.*, Jan.–March 1989, *15*(1), pp. 45–54.

_____; **Deravi, Keivan and Gregorowicz, Philip.** Deficit Financing Announcements and Asset Prices. *J. Econ. Bus.*, May 1989, *41*(2), pp. 171–83.

_____ **and Gregorowicz, Philip.** Short-term Movement in Exchange Rates and Information on the Money Stock. *Quart. J. Bus. Econ.*, Spring 1989, *28*(2), pp. 19–31.

Heidarian, Jamshid and Green, Rodney D. The Impact of Oil-Export Dependency on a Developing Country. *Energy Econ.*, October 1989, *11*(4), pp. 247–61.

Heidenheimer, Arnold J. Perspectives on the Perception of Corruption. In *Heidenheimer, A. J.; Johnston, M. and LeVine, V. T., eds.*, 1989, pp. 149–63.

_____. Problems of Comparing American Political Corruption. In *Heidenheimer, A. J.; Johnston, M. and LeVine, V. T., eds.*, 1989, *1978*, pp. 573–85.

_____; **Johnston, Michael and LeVine, Victor T.** Political Corruption: A Handbook: Terms, Concepts, and Definitions: An Introduction. In *Heidenheimer, A. J.; Johnston, M. and LeVine, V. T., eds.*, 1989, pp. 3–14.

Heien, Dale M. and Dorfman, Jeffrey H. The Effects of Uncertainty and Adjustment Costs on Investment in the Almond Industry. *Rev. Econ. Statist.*, May 1989, *71*(2), pp. 263–74.

_____ **and Pompelli, Greg.** The Demand for Alcoholic Beverages: Economic and Demographic Effects. *Southern Econ. J.*, January 1989, *55*(3), pp. 759–70.

Heij, C. and Willems, J. C. A Deterministic Approach to Approximate Modelling. In *Willems, J. C., ed.*, 1989, pp. 49–134.

van der Heijden, R. E. C. M.; Timmermans, H. J. P. and Borgers, A. W. J. A Variety Seeking Model of Spatial Choice-Behaviour. *Environ. Planning A*, August 1989, *21*(8), pp. 1037–48.

Heijdra, Ben J. and Brooks, Michael A. An Exploration of Rent Seeking. *Econ. Rec.*, March 1989, *65*(188), pp. 32–50.

Heikkila, Eric J. and Craig, Steven G. Urban Safety in Vancouver: Allocation and Production of a Congestible Public Good. *Can. J. Econ.*, November 1989, *22*(4), pp. 867–84.

_____, **et al.** What Happened to the CBD-Distance Gradient? Land Values in a Policentric City. *Environ. Planning A*, February 1989, *21*(2), pp. 221–32.

Heilbroner, Robert L. Examining Stein's Proposals. *Challenge*, July–Aug. 1989, *32*(4), pp. 10–13.

_____. On the Possibility of a Political Economics.

In *Tool, M. R. and Samuels, W. J., eds. (II)*, 1989, *1970*, pp. 519–40.

_____. Rereading *The Affluent Society*. *J. Econ. Issues*, June 1989, *23*(2), pp. 367–77.

_____ **and Bernstein, Peter L.** Abolishing the Deficit. *Challenge*, May–June 1989, *32*(3), pp. 54–55.

Heimert, A. Michael. On Controlling the Maintenance of Durable Goods When Contractual Enforcement Is Costly. *Econ. Letters*, 1989, *29*(2), pp. 109–13.

Heimler, Alberto. Productive Restructuring, Costs, and Profit Margins in the Industrial Countries. *J. Policy Modeling*, Fall 1989, *11*(3), pp. 345–59.

Heimlich, Ralph E. Productivity of Highly Erodible Cropland. *J. Agr. Econ. Res.*, Summer 1989, *41*(3), pp. 17–22.

Hein, Scott E. and Hafer, R. W. Comparing Futures and Survey Forecasts of Near-Term Treasury Bill Rates. *Fed. Res. Bank St. Louis Rev.*, May–June 1989, *71*(3), pp. 33–42.

_____ **and Haslag, Joseph H.** Federal Reserve System Reserve Requirements, 1959–1988: A Note. *J. Money, Credit, Banking*, November 1989, *21*(4), pp. 515–23.

_____ **and Haslag, Joseph H.** Reserve Requirements, the Monetary Base, and Economic Activity. *Fed. Res. Bank Dallas Econ. Rev.*, March 1989, pp. 1–15.

_____ **and MacDonald, S. Scott.** Futures Rates and Forward Rates as Predictors of Near-Term Treasury Bill Rates. *J. Futures Markets*, June 1989, *9*(3), pp. 249–62.

Heiner, Ronald A. Imperfect Choice and Self-stabilizing Rules. *Econ. Philos.*, April 1989, *5*(1), pp. 19–32.

_____. The Origin of Predictable Dynamic Behavior. *J. Econ. Behav. Organ.*, October 1989, *12*(2), pp. 233–57.

Heinkel, Robert; Zechner, Josef and Fischer, Edwin O. Dynamic Capital Structure Choice: Theory and Tests. *J. Finance*, March 1989, *44*(1), pp. 19–40.

_____; **Zechner, Josef and Fischer, Edwin O.** Dynamic Recapitalization Policies and the Role of Call Premia and Issue Discounts. *J. Finan. Quant. Anal.*, December 1989, *24*(4), pp. 427–46.

Heinrichs, Wolfgang and Steinitz, Klaus. Problems of an Industrial Economy with Intensive Agricultural Production: The German Democratic Republic. In *Williamson, J. G. and Panchamukhi, V. R., eds.*, 1989, pp. 288–301.

Heinsohn, Gunnar and Steiger, Otto. The Veil of Barter: The Solution to 'The Task of Obtaining Representations of an Economy in Which Money Is Essential.' In *[Weintraub, S.]*, 1989, pp. 175–201.

Heizmann, Bernhard. Analyse ökonomisch bzw. ökologisch motivierter Substitutionen—Eine Untersuchung des zeitlichen Verlaufes und der Bestimmungsfaktoren. (With English summary.) *Z. Betriebswirtshaft*, February 1989, *59*(2), pp. 155–74.

Hekstra, Gjerrit P. Sea-Level Rise: Regional

Consequences and Responses. In *Rosenberg, N. J., et al., eds.*, 1989, pp. 53–67.

Held, David. Citizenship and Autonomy. In *Held, D. and Thompson, J. B., eds.*, 1989, pp. 162–84.

_____ **and Thompson, John B.** Social Theory of Modern Societies: Anthony Giddens and His Critics: Introduction. In *Held, D. and Thompson, J. B., eds.*, 1989, pp. 1–18.

Helfat, Constance E. Investment Choices in the Petroleum Industry. *J. Econ. Behav. Organ.*, March 1989, *11*(2), pp. 253–83.

_____. Investment in Offshore Oil by Diversified Petroleum Companies. *J. Ind. Econ.*, September 1989, *38*(1), pp. 79–93.

Helfgott, Roy B. On the Demise of the Long Run. *J. Econ. Perspectives*, Fall 1989, *3*(4), pp. 149–52.

Helleiner, Gerald K. Conventional Foolishness and Overall Ignorance: Current Approaches to Global Transformation and Development. *Can. J. Devel. Stud.*, 1989, *10*(1), pp. 107–20.

_____. International Policy Issues Posed by Sub-Saharan African Debt. *World Econ.*, September 1989, *12*(3), pp. 315–24.

_____. New Trade Theory and the Less Developed Countries: Comment. In *[Díaz-Alejandro, C.]*, 1989, pp. 366–70.

_____. The Sub-Saharan African Debt Problem: Issues for International Policy. In *Mrak, M., ed.*, 1989, pp. 173–88.

Heller, H. Robert. Improving America's Competitiveness. *Fed. Res. Bank Richmond Econ. Rev.*, March–April 1989, *75*(2), pp. 17–20.

_____. Money and the International Monetary System. *Fed. Res. Bank St. Louis Rev.*, March–April 1989, *71*(2), pp. 65–71.

_____. Statement to the U.S. House Subcommittee on General Oversight and Investigations of the Committee on Banking, Finance and Urban Affairs, May 17, 1989. *Fed. Res. Bull.*, July 1989, *75*(7), pp. 495–98.

Heller, Peter S. and Schiller, Christian. The Fiscal Impact of Privatization, with Some Examples from Arab Countries. In *El-Naggar, S., ed.*, 1989, pp. 85–112.

_____ **and Schiller, Christian.** The Fiscal Impact of Privatization, with Some Examples from Arab Countries. *World Devel.*, May 1989, *17*(5), pp. 757–67.

Heller, Walter P. and Starr, Ross M. Equilibrium with Non-convex Transactions Costs: Monetary and Non-monetary Economies. In *Starr, R. M., ed.*, 1989, *1976*, pp. 267–87.

Heller, Walter W. Can There Be Another Crash? In *Guttmann, R., ed.*, 1989, *1980*, pp. 112–16.

Helliwell, John F. From Now till Then: Globalization and Economic Co-operation. *Can. Public Policy*, Supplement, February 1989, *15*, pp. S71–77.

_____. Reducing International Imbalances: Evidence from Multicountry Models. *Amer. Econ. Rev.*, May 1989, *79*(2), pp. 258–63.

_____. Some Comparative Macroeconomics of the United States, Japan, and Canada. In *Stern, R. M., ed.*, 1989, pp. 35–80.

_____; **Hooper, Peter and Bryant, Ralph C.** Domestic and Cross-Border Consequences of U.S. Macroeconomic Policies. In *Bryant, R. C., et al., eds.*, 1989, pp. 59–115.

Hellmann, Donald C. The Imperatives for Reciprocity and Symmetry in U.S.–Japanese Economic and Defense Relations. In *Makin, J. H. and Hellmann, D. C., eds.*, 1989, pp. 237–66.

Hellsten, Martin. Socially Optimal Forestry: Reply. *J. Environ. Econ. Manage.*, November 1989, *17*(3), pp. 311–12.

Hellwig, Klaus. Dezentrale Produktions- und Absatzplanung. (With English summary.) *Z. Betriebswirtshaft*, May 1989, *59*(5), pp. 525–30.

_____. A Model of Economic Growth. *Jahr. Nationalökon. Statist.*, July 1989, *206*(3), pp. 252–56.

Hellwig, Martin. Asymmetric Information, Financial Markets, and Financial Institutions: Where Are We Currently Going? *Europ. Econ. Rev.*, March 1989, *33*(2/3), pp. 277–85.

_____ **and Allen, Beth.** The Approximation of Competitive Equilibria by Bertrand–Edgeworth Equilibria in Large Markets. *J. Math. Econ.*, 1989, *18*(2), pp. 103–27.

_____ **and Bester, Helmut.** Moral Hazard and Equilibrium Credit Rationing: An Overview of the Issues. In *Bamberg, G. and Spremann, K., eds.*, 1989, pp. 135–66.

_____ **and Gale, Douglas.** Repudiation and Renegotiation: The Case of Sovereign Debt. *Int. Econ. Rev.*, February 1989, *30*(1), pp. 3–31.

Helm, Dieter. The Economic Borders of the State. In *Helm, D., ed.*, 1989, pp. 9–45.

_____. The Economic Borders of the State: Introduction. In *Helm, D., ed.*, 1989, pp. 1–7.

_____. Mergers, Take-Overs, and the Enforcement of Profit Maximization. In *Fairburn, J. and Kay, J., eds.*, 1989, pp. 133–47.

_____. Predictions and Causes: A Comparison of Friedman and Hicks on Method. In *Wood, J. C. and Woods, R. N., eds., Vol. 4*, 1989, *1984*, pp. 122–38.

_____ **and Dilnot, Andrew.** Energy Policy, Merit Goods, and Social Security. In *Helm, D.; Kay, J. and Thompson, D., eds.*, 1989, *1987*, pp. 55–73.

_____; **Kay, John A. and Thompson, David.** The Market for Energy: Introduction: Energy Policy and the Role of the State in the Market for Energy. In *Helm, D.; Kay, J. and Thompson, D., eds.*, 1989, pp. 1–20.

_____ **and McGowan, Francis.** Electricity Supply in Europe: Lessons for the UK. In *Helm, D.; Kay, J. and Thompson, D., eds.*, 1989, pp. 237–60.

_____ **and Smith, Stephen R.** The Assessment: Economic Integration and the Role of the European Community. *Oxford Rev. Econ. Policy*, Summer 1989, *5*(2), pp. 1–19.

_____ **and Smith, Stephen R.** The Decentralized State: The Economic Borders of Local Government. In *Helm, D., ed.*, 1989, pp. 275–96.

_____; **Thompson, David and Hammond, Elizabeth.** Competition in Electricity Supply: Has the Energy Act Failed? In *Helm, D.; Kay, J.*

and Thompson, D., eds., 1989, 1986, pp. 157–77.

Helman, Amir; Kroll, Yoram and Lampert, Ada. The Kibbutz and Private Property. In *Grunert, K. G. and Ölander, F., eds.*, 1989, pp. 65–74.

Helmberger, Peter; Miranda, Mario and Glauber, Joseph. Four Approaches to Commodity Market Stabilization: A Comparative Analysis. *Amer. J. Agr. Econ.*, May 1989, 71(2), pp. 326–37.

Helmi-Oskoui, Behrouz. A Model of Joint Production of Oil and Gas from Pumping Wells. *J. Energy Devel.*, Autumn 1989, 15(1), pp. 9–24.

Helmstädter, Ernst. Die M-Form des Wachstumszyklus. (The M-Shape of the Growth Cycle. With English summary.) *Jahr. Nationalökon. Statist.*, October 1989, 206(4–5), pp. 383–94.

Helmuth, John W. Background and Perspectives on the 1988 World Food Conference. In *Helmuth, J. W. and Johnson, S. R., eds., Vol. 1*, 1989, pp. 3–14.

Helper, Susan and Mirowski, Philip. Maquiladoras: Mexico's Tiger by the Tail? *Challenge*, May–June 1989, 32(3), pp. 24–30.

Helpman, Elhanan. The Noncompetitive Theory of International Trade and Trade Policy. In *Fischer, S. and de Tray, D., eds.*, 1989, pp. 193–216.

_____. The Simple Analytics of Debt–Equity Swaps. *Amer. Econ. Rev.*, June 1989, 79(3), pp. 440–51.

_____. Voluntary Debt Reduction: Incentives and Welfare. In *Frenkel, J. A.; Dooley, M. P. and Wickham, P., eds.*, 1989, pp. 279–310.

_____. Voluntary Debt Reduction: Incentives and Welfare. *Int. Monet. Fund Staff Pap.*, September 1989, 36(3), pp. 580–611.

_____ **and Grossman, Gene M.** Product Development and International Trade. *J. Polit. Econ.*, December 1989, 97(6), pp. 1261–83.

Helsley, Robert W. and Capozza, Dennis R. The Fundamentals of Land Prices and Urban Growth. *J. Urban Econ.*, November 1989, 26(3), pp. 295–306.

_____; **Levi, Maurice D. and Goldberg, Michael A.** The Location of International Financial Activity: An Interregional Analysis. *Reg. Stud.*, February 1989, 23(1), pp. 1–7.

van Helten, Jean-Jacques and Jones, Geoffrey. British Business in Malaysia and Singapore since the 1870s. In *Davenport-Hines, R. P. T. and Jones, G., eds.*, 1989, pp. 157–88.

Helwege, Ann. Is There Any Hope for Nicaragua? *Challenge*, Nov.–Dec. 1989, 32(6), pp. 22–28.

Hemenway, David. A Failing Grade for Auto Inspections—And Motorists Like It That Way. *J. Policy Anal. Manage.*, Spring 1989, 8(2), pp. 321–25.

Hemmer, Hans-R. and Mannel, C. On the Economic Analysis of the Urban Informal Sector. *World Devel.*, October 1989, 17(10), pp. 1543–52.

Hemmingsen, Kjeld and Dyhr, Peter. The Disregard of a Legal Entity for Tax Purposes: Denmark. In *International Fiscal Association, ed.*

(II), 1989, pp. 249–58.

Hénaff, Patrick. A Newton's Algorithm for Solving Multicountry Econometric Models. *J. Econ. Dynam. Control*, January 1989, 13(1), pp. 41–54.

Hendershott, Patric H. The Future of Thrifts as Home Mortgage Portfolio Lenders. In *Federal Home Loan Bank of San Francisco*, 1989, pp. 153–63.

_____. Social Returns to Housing and Other Fixed Capital: Comments. *Amer. Real Estate Urban Econ. Assoc. J.*, Summer 1989, 17(2), pp. 212–17.

_____. The Tax Reform Act of 1986 and Economic Growth. In *Black, S. W., ed.*, 1989, pp. 121–50.

_____ **and Peek, Joe.** Aggregate U.S. Private Saving: Conceptual Measures and Empirical Tests. In *Lipsey, R. E. and Tice, H. S., eds.*, 1989, pp. 185–223.

_____ **and Peek, Joe.** Household Saving in the United States: Measurement and Behavior. *J. Bus. Econ. Statist.*, January 1989, 7(1), pp. 11–19.

_____ **and Shilling, James D.** The Impact of the Agencies on Conventional Fixed-Rate Mortgage Yields. *J. Real Estate Finance Econ.*, June 1989, 2(2), pp. 101–15.

_____ **and Shilling, James D.** Reforming Conforming Loan Limits: The Impact on Thrift Earnings and Taxpayer Outlays. *J. Finan. Services Res.*, December 1989, 3(4), pp. 311–31.

_____ **and Smith, Marc T.** Transfer Programs and Aggregate Household Formations. *Population Res. Policy Rev.*, September 1989, 8(3), pp. 227–45.

_____ **and Van Order, Robert.** Integration of Mortgage and Capital Markets and the Accumulation of Residential Capital. *Reg. Sci. Urban Econ.*, May 1989, 19(2), pp. 189–210.

Henderson, Dale W. Liberalization of Financial Markets and the Volatility of Exchange Rates: A Theoretical Analysis. In *Stern, R. M., ed.*, 1989, pp. 365–73.

_____ **and Canzoneri, Matthew B.** Optimal Choice of Monetary Policy Instruments in a Simple Two-Country Game. In *[Verheyen, P.]*, 1989, pp. 223–40.

Henderson, David. A New Age of Reform? *Fisc. Stud.*, August 1989, 10(3), pp. 72–90.

_____. Perestroika in the West: Progress, Limits and Implications. In *Nieuwenhuysen, J., ed.*, 1989, pp. 32–43.

_____; **McGregor, Peter G. and McNicoll, Iain H.** Measuring the Effects of Changing Structure on Employment Generation Potential. *Int. Reg. Sci. Rev.*, 1989, 12(1), pp. 57–65.

Henderson, David R. Are We All Supply-Siders Now? *Contemp. Policy Issues*, October 1989, 7(4), pp. 116–28.

_____. The Perverse Effects of a Variable Oil Import Fee. *Energy J.*, October 1989, 10(4), pp. 159–70.

_____. The Supply-Side Tax Revenue Effects of the Child Care Tax Credit. *J. Policy Anal. Manage.*, Fall 1989, 8(4), pp. 673–75.

———. VIF Mortis Est: Rejoinder. *Energy J.*, October 1989, *10*(4), pp. 173–74.

Henderson, Dennis R.; Rhodus, W. Timothy and Baldwin, E. Dean. Pricing Accuracy and Efficiency in a Pilot Electronic Hog Market. *Amer. J. Agr. Econ.*, November 1989, *71*(4), pp. 874–82.

Henderson, Glenn V., Jr. and McIntosh, Willard. Efficiency of the Office Properties Market. *J. Real Estate Finance Econ.*, February 1989, *2*(1), pp. 61–70.

Henderson, J. Vernon and Ioannides, Yannis M. Dynamic Aspects of Consumer Decisions in Housing Markets. *J. Urban Econ.*, September 1989, *26*(2), pp. 212–30.

——— **and Miceli, Thomas J.** Reputation in Land Development Markets. *J. Urban Econ.*, November 1989, *26*(3), pp. 386–408.

Henderson, James P. Jones's *Conflict and Control in the World Economy: Contemporary Economic Realism and Neo-Mercantilism:* Review Essay. In *Samuels, W. J., ed. (II)*, 1989, pp. 247–51.

———. "The Relation of Ethics to Economics": J. S. MacKenzie's Challenge to Neoclassical Economics. *Rev. Soc. Econ.*, Fall 1989, *47*(3), pp. 239–65.

———. Whewell's Solution to the Reciprocal Demand Riddle in Mill's "Great Chapter." *Hist. Polit. Econ.*, Winter 1989, *21*(4), pp. 661–77.

Henderson, Jeffrey. The Political Economy of Technological Transformation in Hong Kong. In *Smith, M. P., ed.*, 1989, pp. 102–55.

Henderson, Richard C. Taxes, Market Structure and International Price Discrimination. *J. World Trade*, December 1989, *23*(6), pp. 147–66.

Henderson, Yolanda Kodrzycki. Capital Gains Rates and Revenues. *New Eng. Econ. Rev.*, Jan.–Feb. 1989, pp. 3–20.

———. The Emergence of the Venture Capital Industry. *New Eng. Econ. Rev.*, July–Aug. 1989, pp. 64–79.

——— **and Fullerton, Don.** A Disaggregate Equilibrium Model of the Tax Distortions among Assets, Sectors, and Industries. *Int. Econ. Rev.*, May 1989, *30*(2), pp. 391–413.

——— **and Fullerton, Don.** The Marginal Excess Burden of Different Capital Tax Instruments. *Rev. Econ. Statist.*, August 1989, *71*(3), pp. 435–42.

Hendon, Willliam S.; Costa, Frank and Rosenberg, Robert Allen. The General Public and the Art Museum: Case Studies of Visitors to Several Institutions Identify Characteristics of Their Publics. *Amer. J. Econ. Sociology*, April 1989, *48*(2), pp. 231–43.

Hendricks, Ann M. Hospital Wage Gradients within U.S. Urban Areas. *J. Health Econ.*, June 1989, *8*(2), pp. 233–46.

Hendricks, Kenneth and Kovenock, Dan. Asymmetric Information, Information Externalities, and Efficiency: The Case of Oil Exploration. *Rand J. Econ.*, Summer 1989, *20*(2), pp. 164–82.

——— **and Porter, Robert H.** Collusion in Auc-

tions. *Ann. Écon. Statist.*, July–Dec. 1989, (15–16), pp. 217–30.

———; **Porter, Robert H. and Spady, Richard H.** Random Reservation Prices and Bidding Behavior in OCS Drainage Auctions. *J. Law Econ.*, Part 2, October 1989, *32*(2), pp. S83–106.

Hendrickx, Laurie; Timmermans, Daniëlle and Vlek, Charles. An Experimental Study of the Effectiveness of Computer-Programmed Decision Support. In *Lockett, A. G. and Islei, G., eds.*, 1989, pp. 13–23.

Hendrikse, George and Peters, Hans. A Note on Partial Vertical Integration. *Econ. Letters*, September 1989, *30*(3), pp. 249–52.

Hendry, Chris; Pettigrew, Andrew M. and Sparrow, Paul. Linking Strategic Change, Competitive Performance and Human Resource Management: Results of a UK Empirical Study. In *Mansfield, R., ed.*, 1989, pp. 195–220.

Hendry, David F. Intertemporal Consumer Behaviour under Structural Changes in Income: Comment. *Econometric Rev.*, 1989, *8*(1), pp. 111–21.

——— **and Morgan, Mary S.** A Re-analysis of Confluence Analysis. *Oxford Econ. Pap.*, January 1989, *41*(1), pp. 35–52.

——— **and Morgan, Mary S.** A Re-analysis of Confluence Analysis. In *de Marchi, N. and Gilbert, C., eds.*, 1989, pp. 35–52.

——— **and Richard, Jean-François.** Recent Developments in the Theory of Encompassing. In *Cornet, B. and Tulkens, H., eds.*, 1989, pp. 393–440.

Hendry, John. Technology, Marketing, and Culture: The Politics of New Product Development. In *Mansfield, R., ed.*, 1989, pp. 96–108.

Heneman, Herbert G., III and Sandver, Marcus H. Union Characteristics and Organizing Success. *J. Lab. Res.*, Fall 1989, *10*(4), pp. 377–89.

Heng, Toh Mun and Low, Linda. Health Care Economics in Singapore: Trends and Issues. In *Smith, C. S., ed.*, 1989, pp. 147–68.

Henin, Pierre-Yves. Sur la non-stationnarité des séries macroéconomiques: Tendances, cycles et persistance. (With English summary.) *Revue Écon. Politique*, Sept.–Oct. 1989, *99*(5), pp. 661–91.

———. Une macroéconomie sans monnaie pour les années 90? Revue critique des travaux théoriques et empiriques sur les cycles réels. (With English summary.) *Revue Écon. Politique*, July–Aug. 1989, *99*(4), pp. 531–96.

Henley, Andrew. Aggregate Profitability and Income Distribution in the UK Corporate Sector, 1963–1985. *Int. Rev. Applied Econ.*, June 1989, *3*(2), pp. 170–90.

———, **et al.** Location Choice and Labour Market Perceptions: A Discrete Choice Study. *Reg. Stud.*, October 1989, *23*(5), pp. 431–45.

Henley, John S. African Employment Relationships and the Future of Trade Unions. *Brit. J. Ind. Relat.*, November 1989, *27*(3), pp. 295–309.

Henn, Rudolf and Nakhaeizadeh, Gholamreza.

Neuere Entwicklungen in der Geldnachfrage. Einige theoretische und empirische Ergebnisse im Überblick. (Recent Developments in the Demand for Money: A Survey of Some Theoretical and Empirical Studies. With English summary.) *Jahr. Nationalökon. Statist.*, October 1989, *206*(4–5), pp. 395–406.

Hennart, Jean-François. The Transaction-Cost Rationale for Countertrade. *J. Law, Econ., Organ.*, Spring 1989, *5*(1), pp. 127–53.

Henneberry, David and Henneberry, Shida. International Trade Policies. In *Tweeten, L., ed.*, 1989, pp. 322–54.

Henneberry, Shida and Henneberry, David. International Trade Policies. In *Tweeten, L., ed.*, 1989, pp. 322–54.

_____; **Tweeten, Luther and Pyles, David.** Supply and Elasticity Estimation. In *Tweeten, L., ed.*, 1989, pp. 73–95.

Henner, Henri-François. La dette et l'ajustement. (With English summary.) *Revue Écon. Politique*, May–June 1989, *99*(3), pp. 482–96.

Hennessey, John C. and Dykacz, Janice M. Postrecovery Experience of Disabled-Worker Beneficiaries. *Soc. Sec. Bull.*, September 1989, *52*(9), pp. 42–66.

_____ **and Dykacz, Janice M.** Projected Outcomes and Length of Time in the Disability Insurance Program. *Soc. Sec. Bull.*, September 1989, *52*(9), pp. 2–41.

Henning, C. Randall and Putnam, Robert D. The Bonn Summit of 1978: A Case Study in Coordination. In *Cooper, R. N., et al.*, 1989, pp. 12–140.

Henning, John C. and Martin, Larry J. An Economic Evaluation of Expanded Canadian 3-M Wheat Exports. *Can. J. Agr. Econ.*, November 1989, *37*(3), pp. 445–65.

Hénocq, Christophe and Kempf, Hubert. Quasirational Expectations. *Econ. Letters*, August 1989, *30*(2), pp. 93–96.

Henrey, Robert. International Tax Aspects of Foreign Currency Transactions: United States. *Bull. Int. Fiscal Doc.*, July 1989, *43*(7), pp. 312–20, 326.

Henrichsmeyer, W. Agricultural Sector Modelling: Introduction and Overview. In *Bauer, S. and Henrichsmeyer, W., eds.*, 1989, pp. 379–83.

_____. Sectoral Production and Income Model for EC-Agriculture (SPEL): SPEL-System: Concept and Overview. In *Bauer, S. and Henrichsmeyer, W., eds.*, 1989, pp. 359–63.

Henripin, Jacques. Panel Discussion on Canadian Immigration Objectives: Levels, Composition, and Directions. In *Beach, C. M. and Green, A. G.*, 1989, pp. 94–95.

Henriques, Maria Helena; Strauss, John and Thomas, Duncan. Mortalidade infantil, estado nutricional e características do domicílio: A evidência brasileira. (With English summary.) *Pesquisa Planejamento Econ.*, December 1989, *19*(3), pp. 427–82.

Henry, C. Michael. Farmer Response to New Technology: An Econometric Appraisal of the Case of Guyana. *Soc. Econ. Stud.*, September 1989, *38*(3), pp. 93–118.

Henry, E. W. An Experiment in Deflating Input–Output Transactions and in Estimating Terms-of-Trade Effects. In *Franz, A. and Rainer, N., eds.*, 1989, pp. 325–42.

Henry, George B. Wall Street Economists: Are They Worth Their Salt? *Bus. Econ.*, October 1989, *24*(4), pp. 44–48.

Henry, Ralph M. Inequality in Plural Societies: An Exploration. *Soc. Econ. Stud.*, June 1989, *38*(2), pp. 69–110.

Hensel, K. Paul. Problems of Worker Democracies. In *Peacock, A. and Willgerodt, H., eds. (II)*, 1989, *1966*, pp. 124–39.

Hensher, David A. and Beesley, Michael E. Contracts, Competitive Bidding and Market Forces: Recent Experiences in the Supply of Local Bus Services. *Australian Econ. Pap.*, December 1989, *28*(53), pp. 236–45.

_____, **et al.** An Empirical Model of Household Automobile Holdings. *Appl. Econ.*, January 1989, *21*(1), pp. 35–57.

Hentschel, Jesko. The Changing Composition of Imports of Highly Indebted Countries. *Econ. Int.*, Feb.–March 1989, *42*(1–2), pp. 79–89.

Hentschel, Volker. German Economic and Social Policy, 1815–1939. In *Mathias, P. and Pollard, S., eds.*, 1989, pp. 752–813.

_____. Institutions and Agriculture in Old-Régime France: Comment. *J. Inst. Theoretical Econ.*, March 1989, *145*(1), pp. 185–88.

Hepworth, Mark E. Geographical Advantage in the Information Economy. In *Punset, E. and Sweeney, G., eds.*, 1989, pp. 26–35.

Herbert, John H. Noisy Data and Uncertain Coefficients: A Comment. *Energy J.*, January 1989, *10*(1), pp. 167–69.

_____ **and Dinh, Khoan T.** A Note on Bias from Proxy Variables with Systematic Errors. *Econ. Letters*, September 1989, *30*(3), pp. 207–09.

_____ **and Kreil, Erik.** Specifying and Evaluating Aggregate Monthly Natural-Gas Demand by Households. *Appl. Econ.*, October 1989, *21*(10), pp. 1369–81.

Herbst, Anthony F.; Kare, D. D. and Caples, S. C. Hedging Effectiveness and Minimum Risk Hedge Ratios in the Presence of Autocorrelation: Foreign Currency Futures. *J. Futures Markets*, June 1989, *9*(3), pp. 185–97.

_____; **Maberly, Edwin D. and Spahr, Ronald W.** An Analysis of Daily Patterns in Stock Returns across Indices: Spot versus Futures. *Quart. J. Bus. Econ.*, Winter 1989, *28*(1), pp. 55–67.

Herceg, Dragoslav and Cvetković, Ljiljana. On the Extrapolation Method and the U.S.A. Algorithm. *J. Econ. Dynam. Control*, April 1989, *13*(2), pp. 301–11.

Herden, Gerhard. Cluster Methods for Qualitative Data. In *Opitz, O., ed.*, 1989, pp. 105–15.

_____. On the Existence of Utility Functions. *Math. Soc. Sci.*, June 1989, *17*(3), pp. 297–313.

_____. On the Existence of Utility Functions II.

Math. Soc. Sci., October 1989, *18*(2), pp. 107–17.

_____. Some Lifting Theorems for Continuous Utility Functions. *Math. Soc. Sci.*, October 1989, *18*(2), pp. 119–34.

Herdt, Robert W. The Impact of Technology and Policy on Seasonal Household Food Security in Asia. In *Sahn, D. E., ed.*, 1989, pp. 235–45.

_____. Rice in Egyptian and Global Agriculture. In *International Rice Research Institute*, 1989, pp. 41–54.

Herek, Gregory M.; Janis, Irving L. and Huth, Paul. Quality of U.S. Decision Making during the Cuban Missile Crisis: Major Errors in Welch's Reassasment. *J. Conflict Resolution*, September 1989, *33*(3), pp. 446–59.

Heri, Erwin W. Expansion der Finanzmärkte: Ursachen, Konsequenzen, Perspektiven. (The Expansion of Financial Markets: Reasons, Consequences, Outlook. With English summary.) *Kyklos*, 1989, *42*(1), pp. 17–37.

Hering, Wolfgang. International Tax Aspects of Philanthropic and Other Non-profit Organisations: German Report. *Bull. Int. Fiscal Doc.*, December 1989, *43*(12), pp. 558–65.

Herlitz, Lars. On the Prehistory of the Trinity: Functional Class Division from Mercantilism to Classicism. *Scand. Econ. Hist. Rev.*, 1989, *37*(2), pp. 5–25.

Herman, Arthur S. Productivity Continued to Rise in Many Industries during 1987. *Mon. Lab. Rev.*, March 1989, *112*(3), pp. 13–20.

Herman, Edward S. and Du Boff, Richard B. The Promotional–Financial Dynamic of Merger Movements: A Historical Perspective. *J. Econ. Issues*, March 1989, *23*(1), pp. 107–33.

Herman, Fernand. European Monetary Policy— A Belgian View. In *Franz, O., ed.*, 1989, pp. 61–65.

Herman, Robert Dean. Board Functions and Board–Staff Relations in Nonprofit Organizations: An Introduction. In *Herman, R. D. and Van Til, J., eds.*, 1989, pp. 1–7.

_____. Concluding Thoughts on Closing the Board Gap. In *Herman, R. D. and Van Til, J., eds.*, 1989, pp. 193–99.

_____ and Tulipana, F. Peter. Board–Staff Relations and Perceived Effectiveness in Nonprofit Organizations. In *Herman, R. D. and Van Til, J., eds.*, 1989, pp. 48–59.

Hermann, Werner and Belongia, Michael T. Can a Central Bank Influence Its Currency's Real Value? The Swiss Case. *Fed. Res. Bank St. Louis Rev.*, Jan.–Feb. 1989, *71*(1), pp. 47–55.

_____ and Santoni, G. J. The Cost of Restricting Corporate Takeovers: A Lesson from Switzerland. *Fed. Res. Bank San Francisco Rev.*, Nov.–Dec. 1989, *71*(6), pp. 3–11.

Hernández Berenguel, Luis. The Disregard of a Legal Entity for Tax Purposes: Peru. In *International Fiscal Association, ed. (II)*, 1989, pp. 439–46.

Hernandez, Donald J. Measuring Components of Family Planning Program Effort: Comment. *Demography*, February 1989, *26*(1), pp. 77–80.

Hernández Iglesias, Feliciano. Argentina after Martínez de Hoz, 1981–83: Comment. In *di Tella, G. and Dornbusch, R., eds.*, 1989, pp. 316–19.

Hernandez, Luis Lazaro. Nonfamily Living Arrangements among Black and Hispanic Americans. In *Goldscheider, F. K. and Goldscheider, C., eds.*, 1989, pp. 17–37.

Herr, Edwin L. The Implementation of the Carl D. Perkins Vocational Education Act in a Large Industrial State: Pennsylvania. *Econ. Educ. Rev.*, 1989, *8*(1), pp. 83–92.

Herr, Ellen M. U.S. Business Enterprises Acquired or Established by Foreign Direct Investors in 1988. *Surv. Curr. Bus.*, May 1989, *69*(5), pp. 22–30.

Herr, Paul M. Priming Price: Prior Knowledge and Context Effects. *J. Cons. Res.*, June 1989, *16*(1), pp. 67–75.

Herr, W.; Njinkeu, Dominique and Färe, Rolf. Returns to Scale and Efficiency in Production: A Distance Function Approach to Southern Illinois Hog Farms. In *Gulledge, T. R., Jr. and Litteral, L. A., eds.*, 1989, pp. 145–59.

Herrero, Maria José. The Nash Program: Nonconvex Bargaining Problems. *J. Econ. Theory*, December 1989, *49*(2), pp. 266–77.

Herrick, Bruce. A New Paradigm for the Study of Economic Development. In *Nabli, M. K. and Nugent, J. B., eds.*, 1989, pp. 429–37.

Herricks, Edwin E.; Larson, Robert S. and Braden, John B. Economic Targeting of Nonpoint Pollution Abatement for Fish Habitat Protection. *Water Resources Res.*, December 1989, *25*(12), pp. 2399–405.

Herrigel, Gary B. Industrial Order and the Politics of Industrial Change: Mechanical Engineering. In *Katzenstein, P. J., ed.*, 1989, pp. 185–220.

Herriges, Joseph A.; Kuester, Kathleen A. and Caves, Douglas W. Load Shifting under Voluntary Residential Time-of-Use Rates. *Energy J.*, October 1989, *10*(4), pp. 83–99.

Herring, Richard J. The Economics of Workout Lending. *J. Money, Credit, Banking*, February 1989, *21*(1), pp. 1–15.

Herriott, Scott R. Competition and Cooperation in Deregulated Bulk Power Markets. In *Crew, M. A., ed.*, 1989, pp. 143–63.

Herrmann, Douglas J.; Jones, Derek C. and Egan, Daniel L. Evidence on Attitudes toward Alternative Sharing Arrangements. *Ind. Relat.*, Fall 1989, *28*(3), pp. 411–18.

Herrmann, R. Agricultural Price Protection, Import Dependence and Economic Development: The Case of Wheat. *J. Agr. Econ.*, May 1989, *40*(2), pp. 152–67.

_____. Modelling National Interests in International Agricultural Policy. In *Bauer, S. and Henrichsmeyer, W., eds.*, 1989, pp. 183–92.

Herrou-Aragón, Alberto. Dinero y ciclo económico en la economía argentina. (With English summary.) *Cuadernos Econ.*, August 1989, *26*(78), pp. 243–62.

Hersch, Joni. Another Look at Compensating Differentials. *J. Behav. Econ.*, Spring 1989, *18*(1), pp. 41–50.

Hersch, Philip L. and McDougall, Gerald S. Do People Put Their Money Where Their Votes Are? The Case of Lottery Tickets. *Southern Econ. J.*, July 1989, *56*(1), pp. 32–38.

_____ **and Netter, Jeffry M.** State Prohibition of Alcohol: An Application of Diffusion Analysis to Regulation. In *Zerbe, R. O., ed.*, 1989, pp. 55–70.

Hertel, Thomas W. Negotiating Reductions in Agricultural Support: Implications of Technology and Factor Mobility. *Amer. J. Agr. Econ.*, August 1989, *71*(3), pp. 559–73.

_____. PSEs and the Mix of Measures to Support Farm Incomes. *World Econ.*, March 1989, *12*(1), pp. 17–27.

_____ **and Ehui, Simeon K.** Deforestation and Agricultural Productivity in the Côte d'Ivoire. *Amer. J. Agr. Econ.*, August 1989, *71*(3), pp. 703–11.

_____; **Preckel, Paul V. and Huang, Wen-Yuan.** The CARD Linear Programming Model of U.S. Agriculture. *J. Agr. Econ. Res.*, Spring 1989, *41*(2), pp. 20–23.

_____; **Thompson, Robert L. and Tsigas, Marinos E.** Economywide Effects of Unilateral Trade and Policy Liberalization in U.S. Agriculture. In *Stoeckel, A. B.; Vincent, D. and Cuthbertson, S., eds.*, 1989, pp. 260–92.

_____ **and Tsigas, Marinos E.** Testing Dynamic Models of the Farm Firm. *Western J. Agr. Econ.*, July 1989, *14*(1), pp. 20–29.

Herting, Jerald R.; Pullum, Thomas W. and Tedrow, Lucky M. Measuring Change and Continuity in Parity Distributions. *Demography*, August 1989, *26*(3), pp. 485–98.

Hertzberg, Marie P. and Beckman, Barry A. Business Cycle Indicators: Revised Composite Indexes. *Surv. Curr. Bus.*, January 1989, *69*(1), pp. 23–28.

Hervouet, Gérard and Mace, Gordon. Canada's Third Option: A Complete Failure? *Can. Public Policy*, December 1989, *15*(4), pp. 387–404.

van Herwijnen, M. and Janssen, R. Definite: A Support System for Decisions on a Finite Set of Alternatives. In *Lockett, A. G. and Islei, G., eds.*, 1989, pp. 534–43.

Herz, Barbara. Bringing Women into the Economic Mainstream. *Finance Devel.*, December 1989, *26*(4), pp. 22–25.

_____. Women in Development: Kenya's Experience. *Finance Devel.*, June 1989, *26*(2), pp. 43–45.

Herz, Diane E. and Rones, Philip L. Institutional Barriers to Employment of Older Workers. *Mon. Lab. Rev.*, April 1989, *112*(4), pp. 14–21.

Herzog, Henry W., Jr.; Schlottmann, Alan M. and Fox, William F. Metropolitan Fiscal Structure and Migration. *J. Reg. Sci.*, November 1989, *29*(4), pp. 523–36.

_____ **and Schlottmann, Alan M.** Environmental Regulation and the Valuation of Life: Interindustry Mobility and the Market Price of Safety.

In *Folmer, H. and van Ierland, E., eds.*, 1989, pp. 139–57.

_____ **and Schlottmann, Alan M.** High-Technology Location and Worker Mobility in the U.S. In *Andersson, Å. E.; Batten, D. F. and Karlsson, C., eds.*, 1989, pp. 219–32.

Herzog, Walter and Bühler, Wolfgang. Die Duration—Eine geeignete Kennzahl für die Steuerung von Zinsänderungsrisiken in Kreditinstituten? (Teil I). (The Duration-Based Concept—A Meaningful Approach to Managing Banking Institutions' Risk of Interest Changes? [Part I]. With English summary.) *Kredit Kapital*, 1989, *22*(3), pp. 403–28.

_____ **and Bühler, Wolfgang.** Die Duration—eine geeignete Kennzahl für die Steuerung von Zinsänderungsrisiken in Kredinstituten? (Teil II). (The Duration-Based Concept—A Meaningful Approach to Managing Banking Institutions' Risk of Interest Changes? [Part II]. With English summary.) *Kredit Kapital*, 1989, *22*(4), pp. 524–63.

Herzstein, Robert. Dumping and Trade Liberalization: A Two-Tiered Approach to Reducing Antidumping Disciplines between Open Trading Partners. In *Jackson, J. H. and Vermulst, E. A., eds.*, 1989, pp. 343–48.

Hess, Peter N. The Military Burden, Economic Growth, and the Human Suffering Index: Evidence from the LDCs. *Cambridge J. Econ.*, December 1989, *13*(4), pp. 497–515.

Hess, Stephen. Making It Happen: Thoughts for a New President on Process, People, and the Press. In *Bosworth, B. P., et al.*, 1989, pp. 95–116.

Hesse, Helmut. Does the World Need a GATT for Services? Comments. In *Vosgerau, H.-J., ed.*, 1989, pp. 276–83.

Hester, Donald D. and Sdogati, Fabio. European Financial Integration: Some Lessons from Italy. *Banca Naz. Lavoro Quart. Rev.*, September 1989, (170), pp. 313–44.

Hester, Gordon L. and Hahn, Robert W. Where Did All the Markets Go? An Analysis of EPA's Emissions Trading Program. *Yale J. Regul.*, Winter 1989, *6*(1), pp. 109–53.

Hetler, Carol B. The Impact of Circular Migration on a Village Economy. *Bull. Indonesian Econ. Stud.*, April 1989, *25*(1), pp. 53–75.

Hetrick, Nancy E. Recent Developments in the El Paso/New Mexico Interstate Groundwater Controversy—The Constitutionality of New Mexico's New Municipality Water Planning Statute. *Natural Res. J.*, Winter 1989, *29*(1), pp. 223–49.

Hettich, Walter and Winer, Stanley L. Tax Expenditures and the Democratic Process. In *Bruce, N., ed.*, 1989, pp. 379–405.

Hetzel, Robert L. M2 and Monetary Policy. *Fed. Res. Bank Richmond Econ. Rev.*, Sept.–Oct. 1989, *75*(5), pp. 14–29.

_____ **and Mehra, Yash P.** The Behavior of Money Demand in the 1980s. *J. Money, Credit, Banking*, November 1989, *21*(4), pp. 455–63.

Heuer, G. A. Reduction of Silverman-Like Games

to Games on Bounded Sets. *Int. J. Game Theory*, 1989, *18*(1), pp. 31–36.

Heumann, Milton and Church, Thomas W. The Underexamined Assumptions of the Invisible Hand: Monetary Incentives as Policy Instruments. *J. Policy Anal. Manage.*, Fall 1989, *8*(4), pp. 641–57.

Heuson, Andrea Jane. Institutional Disparities in the Pricing of Adjustable Rate Mortgage Loans. *J. Real Estate Finance Econ.*, February 1989, *2*(1), pp. 31–45.

————. Offering Rates on Fixed- and Adjustable-Rate Mortgage Loans. *Financial Rev.*, February 1989, *24*(1), pp. 147–56.

Hewett, Ed A. Economic Reform in the USSR, Eastern Europe, and China: The Politics of Economics. *Amer. Econ. Rev.*, May 1989, *79*(2), pp. 16–20.

————. *Perestroyka* and the Congress of People's Deputies. *Soviet Econ.*, Jan.–March 1989, *5*(1), pp. 47–69.

———— **and Harding, Harry.** Dealing with Reforms in China and the Soviet Union. In *Bosworth, B. P., et al.*, 1989, pp. 166–70.

———— **and Harding, Harry.** Socialist Reforms and the World Economy. In *Steinbruner, J. D., ed.*, 1989, pp. 158–84.

Hewings, Geoffrey J. D. and Sonis, Michael. Error and Sensitivity Input–Output Analysis: A New Approach. In *Miller, R. E.; Polenske, K. R. and Rose, A. Z., eds.*, 1989, pp. 232–44.

————; **Sonis, Michael and Jackson, Randall W.** Decomposition Approaches to the Identification of Change in Regional Economies. *Econ. Geogr.*, July 1989, *65*(3), pp. 216–31.

————, **et al.** Key Sectors and Structural Change in the Brazilian Economy: A Comparison of Alternative Approaches and Their Policy Implications. *J. Policy Modeling*, Spring 1989, *11*(1), pp. 67–90.

Hewitt, Adrian. ACP and the Developing World. In *Lodge, J., ed.*, 1989, pp. 285–300.

Hey, John D. Current Issues in Microeconomics: Introduction: Recent Developments in Microeconomics. In *Hey, J. D., ed.*, 1989, pp. 1–11.

————. Reply [Theory versus Empiricism in Academic Economics: Update and Comparison]. *J. Econ. Perspectives*, Fall 1989, *3*(4), pp. 209–10.

Heycock, Stephen. New Technology on the Coal Industry and Its Effects upon the Redesign of Working Time. In *Agassi, J. B. and Heycock, S., eds.*, 1989, pp. 84–95.

Heyndels, B. and Vuchelen, Jef. De efficiëntie van de belastinginning. (With English summary.) *Cah. Écon. Bruxelles*, 2nd Trimester 1989, (122), pp. 221–34.

Heyne, Paul. Do Trade Deficits Matter? In *Dorn, J. A. and Niskanen, W. A., eds.*, 1989, *1983*, pp. 351–62.

Heyssel, Robert M. and Steinberg, Earl P. Medical Research and Teaching in a Market-Driven Health Care System. In *McLennan, K. and Meyer, J. A., eds.*, 1989, pp. 133–45.

Heywood, John S. Discrimination in the Provision of Fringe Benefits. *Econ. Letters*, November 1989, *31*(1), pp. 95–98.

————. Do Union Members Receive Compensating Differentials? The Case of Employment Security. *J. Lab. Res.*, Summer 1989, *10*(3), pp. 271–83.

————. The Effect of Unions and Imports on Monopoly Power: A Comment. *J. Post Keynesian Econ.*, Winter 1988–89, *11*(2), pp. 313–17.

————. Wage Discrimination by Race and Gender in the Public and Private Sectors. *Econ. Letters*, 1989, *29*(1), pp. 99–102.

———— **and Belman, Dale L.** Establishment Size, Public Administration and Government Wage Differentials. *Econ. Letters*, 1989, *29*(1), pp. 95–98.

———— **and Belman, Dale L.** Government Wage Differentials: A Sample Selection Approach. *Appl. Econ.*, April 1989, *21*(4), pp. 427–38.

———— **and Drago, Robert.** Support for Worker Participation. *J. Post Keynesian Econ.*, Summer 1989, *11*(4), pp. 522–30.

———— **and Drago, Robert.** Tournaments, Piece Rates, and the Shape of the Payoff Function. *J. Polit. Econ.*, August 1989, *97*(4), pp. 992–98.

Heywood, Paul. The Labour Movement in Spain before 1914. In *Geary, D., ed.*, 1989, pp. 231–65.

Heyzer, Noeleen. Asian Women Wage-Earners: Their Situation and Possibilities for Donor Intervention. *World Devel.*, July 1989, *17*(7), pp. 1109–23.

Hibbs, John. Privatisation and Competition in Road Passenger Transport. In *Veljanovski, C., ed. (II)*, 1989, pp. 161–77.

Hickerson, Steven R. Legal Counsel, Power, and Institutional Hegemony. In *Tool, M. R. and Samuels, W. J., eds. (III)*, 1989, *1982*, pp. 157–76.

Hickman, Bert G. U.S. Economic Growth in Retrospect and Prospect. In *Krelle, W., ed.*, 1989, pp. 279–300.

————; **Huntington, Hillard G. and Sweeney, James L.** On Economic Policy Responses to Disruptions: Reply. *Energy J.*, October 1989, *10*(4), pp. 189–98.

Hickok, Susan. Japanese Trade Balance Adjustment to Yen Appreciation. *Fed. Res. Bank New York Quart. Rev.*, Autumn 1989, *14*(3), pp. 33–47.

———— **and Orr, James A.** Shifting Patterns of U.S. Trade with Selected Developing Asian Economies. *Fed. Res. Bank New York Quart. Rev.*, Winter 1989–90, *14*(4), pp. 36–47.

Hicks, George. The Four Little Dragons: An Enthusiast's Reading Guide. *Asian-Pacific Econ. Lit.*, September 1989, *3*(2), pp. 35–49.

Hicks, John R. The Assumption of Constant Returns to Scale. *Cambridge J. Econ.*, March 1989, *13*(1), pp. 9–17.

————. The Assumption of Constant Returns to Scale. In *Lawson, T.; Palma, J. G. and Sender, J., eds.*, 1989, pp. 9–17.

————. Complementarity and Interrelations of Shifts in Demand: A Comment. In *Wood, J.*

C. and Woods, R. N., eds., Vol. 1, 1989, *1940*, pp. 42–44.

_____. Hicks on Ricardo on Machinery: A Reply. In *Wood, J. C. and Woods, R. N., eds., Vol. 2, 1989, 1971,* pp. 170–73.

_____. LF and LP. In *Tsiang, S. C.,* 1989, pp. 351–58.

_____. A Note on a Point in *Value and Capital: A Reply.* In *Wood, J. C. and Woods, R. N., eds., Vol. 1,* 1989, pp. 164–68.

_____. On Coddington's Interpretation: A Reply. In *Wood, J. C. and Woods, R. N., eds., Vol. 3, 1989, 1979,* pp. 209–16.

_____. A Suggestion for Simplifying the Theory of Money. In *Starr, R. M., ed.,* 1989, *1935,* pp. 8–23.

_____ and Lange, Oscar. The Interrelations of Shifts in Demand: Replies. In *Wood, J. C. and Woods, R. N., eds., Vol. 1, 1989, 1944,* pp. 97–105.

Hicks, Norman L. Expenditure Reductions in High-Debt Countries. *Finance Devel.,* March 1989, *26*(1), pp. 35–37.

Hiebert, L. Dean. Cost Flexibility and Price Dispersion. *J. Ind. Econ.,* September 1989, *38*(1), pp. 103–09.

Hiemenz, Ulrich and Langhammer, Rolf J. Liberalisation and the Successful Integration of Developing Countries into the World Economy. In *Renshaw, G. T., ed.,* 1989, pp. 105–39.

Hietala, Pekka T. Asset Pricing in Partially Segmented Markets: Evidence from the Finnish Market. *J. Finance,* July 1989, *44*(3), pp. 697–718.

Higgins, Benjamin. Australian Regional Development in International Perspective. In *Higgins, B. and Zagorski, K., eds.,* 1989, pp. 3–16.

_____. Implications for Policy: Conclusions. In *Higgins, B. and Zagorski, K., eds.,* 1989, pp. 251–60.

Higgins, Christopher I. Colin Clark: An Interview. *Econ. Rec.,* September 1989, *65*(190), pp. 296–310.

Higgins, Richard S.; Shughart, William F., II and Tollison, Robert D. Price Leadership with Incomplete Information. *J. Econ. Behav. Organ.,* May 1989, *11*(3), pp. 423–29.

Higgs, Peter J. The Taxation of Australian Agriculture through Assistance to Australian Manufacturing. In *Stoeckel, A. B.; Vincent, D. and Cuthbertson, S., eds.,* 1989, pp. 293–329.

Higgs, Robert. Black Progress and the Persistence of Racial Economic Inequalities, 1865–1940. In *Shulman, S. and Darity, W., Jr., eds.,* 1989, pp. 9–31.

_____. Do Legislators' Votes Reflect Constituency Preference? A Simple Way to Evaluate the Senate. *Public Choice,* November 1989, *63*(2), pp. 175–81.

_____. Organization, Ideology and the Free Rider Problem: Comment. *J. Inst. Theoretical Econ.,* March 1989, *145*(1), pp. 232–37.

High, Jack and Bloch, Howard. On the History of Ordinal Utility Theory: 1900–1932. *Hist. Polit. Econ.,* Summer 1989, *21*(2), pp. 351–65.

Highsmith, Robert J. The Advanced Placement Program. *J. Econ. Educ.,* Winter 1989, *20*(1), pp. 115–20.

_____. Professional Developments and Opportunities. *J. Econ. Educ.,* Winter 1989, *20*(1), pp. 121–24.

_____. Professional Developments and Opportunities. *J. Econ. Educ.,* Fall 1989, *20*(4), pp. 416–20.

Higman, B. W. The Internal Economy of Jamaican Pens, 1760–1890. *Soc. Econ. Stud.,* March 1989, *38*(1), pp. 61–86.

Higuchi, Yoshio. Japan's Changing Wage Structure: The Impact of Internal Factors and International Competition. *J. Japanese Int. Economies,* December 1989, *3*(4), pp. 480–99.

Hildenbrand, Werner. CORE and Equilibria of a Large Economy. In *Cornet, B. and Tulkens, H., eds.,* 1989, pp. 59–77.

_____. Facts and Ideas in Microeconomic Theory. *Europ. Econ. Rev.,* March 1989, *33*(2/3), pp. 251–76.

_____. The Weak Axiom of Revealed Preference for Market Demand Is Strong. *Econometrica,* July 1989, *57*(4), pp. 979–85.

_____ and Grodal, B. The Weak Axiom of Revealed Preference in a Productive Economy. *Rev. Econ. Stud.,* October 1989, *56*(4), pp. 635–39.

_____ and Jerison, Michael. The Demand Theory of the Weak Axioms of Revealed Preference. *Econ. Letters,* 1989, *29*(3), pp. 209–13.

Hildred, William M. and Pinto, James V. Estimates of Passive Tax Expenditures, 1984. *J. Econ. Issues,* March 1989, *23*(1), pp. 93–106.

Hildreth, Andrew. The Ambiguity of Verdoorn's Law: A Case Study of the British Regions. *J. Post Keynesian Econ.,* Winter 1988–89, *11*(2), pp. 279–94.

Hildreth, R. J. Break-Out Session II—Conference Consensus: Recommendations: Coordinating Food and Agricultural Policies among Countries. In *Helmuth, J. W. and Johnson, S. R., eds., Vol. 1,* 1989, pp. 197–98.

_____. A Critique of the World Agricultural Economics Research Establishment. *J. Agr. Econ. Res.,* Spring 1989, *41*(2), pp. 2–4.

Hilke, John C. and Nelson, Philip B. Strategic Behavior and Attempted Monopolization: The *Coffee (General Foods)* Case. In *Kwoka, J. E., Jr. and White, L. J., eds.,* 1989, pp. 208–40.

Hilke, Wolfgang. Development of External Accounting in the FRG According to the 4th and 7th EC Directives—The New German Accounting and Reporting Law. In *Dams, T. and Matsugi, T., eds.,* 1989, pp. 119–47.

Hill, Bruce M. An Alternative Interpretation of Freedman's Nonresponse Case Study: Comment. *J. Bus. Econ. Statist.,* January 1989, *7*(1), pp. 29–30.

Hill, Daniel H. and Duncan, Greg J. Assessing the Quality of Household Panel Data: The Case of the Panel Study of Income Dynamics. *J. Bus. Econ. Statist.,* October 1989, *7*(4), pp. 441–52.

Hill, Elizabeth T. Postsecondary Technical Education, Performance and Employee Development: A Survey of Employers. *Econ. Educ. Rev.*, 1989, *8*(4), pp. 323–33.

Hill, Hal and Hardjono, Joan. West Java: Population Pressure and Regional Diversity. In *Hill, H., ed.*, 1989, pp. 254–82.

_____ **and Weidemann, Anna.** Regional Development in Indonesia: Patterns and Issues. In *Hill, H., ed.*, 1989, pp. 3–54.

Hill, Herbert. Black Labor and Affirmative Action: An Historical Perspective. In *Shulman, S. and Darity, W., Jr., eds.*, 1989, pp. 190–267.

Hill, John K. Demographics and the Trade Balance. *Fed. Res. Bank Dallas Econ. Rev.*, September 1989, pp. 1–11.

_____ **and Robinson, Kenneth J.** Money, Wages, and Factor Scarcity as Predictors of Inflation. *Fed. Res. Bank Dallas Econ. Rev.*, May 1989, pp. 21–29.

Hill, John W. and Ingram, Robert W. Selection of GAAP or RAP in the Savings and Loan Industry. *Accounting Rev.*, October 1989, *64*(4), pp. 667–79.

Hill, Kenneth and Pebley, Anne R. Child Mortality in the Developing World. *Population Devel. Rev.*, December 1989, *15*(4), pp. 657–87.

Hill, Lewis E. Cultural Determinism or Emergent Evolution: An Analysis of the Controversy between Clarence Ayres and David Miller. *J. Econ. Issues*, June 1989, *23*(2), pp. 465–71.

Hill, M. Anne. Female Labor Supply in Japan: Implications of the Informal Sector for Labor Force Participation and Hours of Work. *J. Human Res.*, Winter 1989, *24*(1), pp. 143–61.

_____ **and Killingsworth, Mark R.** Comparable Worth: Analyses and Evidence: Introduction. In *Hill, M. A. and Killingsworth, M. R., eds.*, 1989, pp. 1–10.

Hill, Malcolm R. Soviet and Eastern European Service Multinationals. In *Enderwick, P.*, 1989, pp. 155–99.

Hill, R. Carter and Adkins, Lee C. Risk Characteristics of a Stein-Like Estimator for the Probit Regression Model. *Econ. Letters*, 1989, *30*(1), pp. 19–26.

Hill, Richard Child. Divisions of Labor in Global Manufacturing: The Case of the Automobile Industry. In *MacEwan, A. and Tabb, W. K., eds.*, 1989, pp. 166–86.

_____ **and Fujita, Kuniko.** Global Production and Regional "Hollowing Out" in Japan. In *Smith, M. P., ed.*, 1989, pp. 200–230.

Hill, Robert B. Economic Forces, Structural Discrimination and Black Family Instability. *Rev. Black Polit. Econ.*, Winter 1989, *17*(3), pp. 5–23.

Hill, Stephen. Time at Work: An Economic Analysis. In *Blyton, P., et al.*, 1989, pp. 57–78.

Hilliard, Jimmy E. and Jordan, Susan D. Hedging Interest Rate Risk with Futures Portfolios under Full-Rank Assumptions. *J. Finan. Quant. Anal.*, June 1989, *24*(2), pp. 217–40.

_____ **and Murphy, J. Austin.** An Investigation into the Equilibrium Structure of the Com-

modity Futures Market Anomaly. *Financial Rev.*, February 1989, *24*(1), pp. 1–18.

Hillier, Brian. Time Inconsistency and the Theory of Second Best. *Scot. J. Polit. Econ.*, August 1989, *36*(3), pp. 253–65.

Hillier, John; Kearney, Colm and MacDonald, Ronald. The Efficiency of the Market for Bank Accepted Bills. *Econ. Rec.*, September 1989, *65*(190), pp. 225–33.

Hilling, David. Alan B. Mountjoy: An Appreciation. In *[Mountjoy, A. B.]*, 1989, pp. 1–10.

Hillman, Arye L. Policy Motives and International Trade Restrictions. In *Vosgerau, H.-J., ed.*, 1989, pp. 284–302.

_____. Resolving the Puzzle of Welfare-Reducing Trade Diversion: A Prisoners' Dilemma Interpretation. *Oxford Econ. Pap.*, April 1989, *41*(2), pp. 452–55.

Hillman, Jimmye S. Agricultural Constituencies and Agricultural Institutions in the United States: Implications and Obstacles for a Needed Reform. *Europ. Rev. Agr. Econ.*, 1989, *16*(3), pp. 359–74.

Hillmer, Steven C. and Trabelsi, Abdelwahed. A Benchmarking Approach to Forecast Combination. *J. Bus. Econ. Statist.*, July 1989, 7(3), pp. 353–62.

Hills, John. Counting the Family Silver: The Public Sector's Balance Sheet 1957 to 1987. *Fisc. Stud.*, May 1989, *10*(2), pp. 66–85.

_____. The Voluntary Sector in Housing: The Role of British Housing Associations. In *James, E., ed.*, 1989, pp. 245–66.

Hills, Peter J. Alternative Approaches to the Costing and Valuation of Traffic Accidents. In *Candemir, Y., ed.*, 1989, pp. 83–112.

Hilsenrath, Peter. The Development of Synthetic Fuels in South Africa. *J. Energy Devel.*, Spring 1989, *14*(2), pp. 269–83.

Hilton, Boyd. Manliness, Masculinity and the Mid-Victorian Temperament. In *Goldman, L., ed.*, 1989, pp. 60–70.

Hilton, R. Spence. Capacity Constraints and the Prospects for External Adjustment and Economic Growth: 1989–90. *Fed. Res. Bank New York Quart. Rev.*, Winter–Spring 1989, *13-14*(4–1), pp. 52–68.

Hilton, Ronald W. and Turner, Martha J. Use of Accounting Product-Costing Systems in Making Production Decisions. *J. Acc. Res.*, Autumn 1989, *27*(2), pp. 297–312.

Himarios, Daniel. Do Devaluations Improve the Trade Balance? The Evidence Revisited. *Econ. Inquiry*, January 1989, *27*(1), pp. 143–68.

_____. The Impact of the Exchange Rate on U.S. Inflation and GNP Growth: Comment. *Southern Econ. J.*, April 1989, *55*(4), pp. 1044–51.

Himes, Christine; Eggers, Mitchell and Preston, Samuel H. Demographic Conditions Responsible for Population Aging. *Demography*, November 1989, *26*(4), pp. 691–704.

Hinck, Harriet. Nobel Laureates in Economic Sciences: A Biographical Dictionary: Simon Kuznets: 1971. In *Katz, B. S., ed.*, 1989, pp. 143–59.

Hinde, P. R. Andrew. The Marriage Market in

the Nineteenth Century English Countryside. *J. Europ. Econ. Hist.*, Fall 1989, *18*(2), pp. 383–92.

Hindley, Brian. Integrated World Markets in Services: Problems and Prospects. In *Giersch, H., ed.*, 1989, pp. 222–44.

_____. Liberalization of Service Transactions. In *Fishelson, G., ed.*, 1989, pp. 253–68.

Hindy, Monier I. Saleh. The Use of Markowitz's Model as a Project Selection Technique: A Case Study. *Middle East Bus. Econ. Rev.*, January 1989, *1*(1), pp. 48–53.

Hine, Robert C. Customs Union Enlargement and Adjustment: Spain's Accession to the European Community. *J. Common Market Stud.*, September 1989, *28*(1), pp. 1–27.

_____. Spain's Entry to the European Community: Some Aspects of the Political Economy of Adjustment. In *Greenaway, D.; Hyclak, T. and Thornton, R. J., eds.*, 1989, pp. 125–51.

_____; **Ingersent, K. A. and Rayner, A. J.** Agriculture in the Uruguay Round: From the Punta del Este Declaration to the Geneva Accord. *J. Agr. Econ.*, September 1989, *40*(3), pp. 385–97.

Hinich, Melvin J. and Enelow, James M. A General Probabilistic Spatial Theory of Elections. *Public Choice*, May 1989, *61*(2), pp. 101–13.

_____ **and Munger, Michael C.** Political Investment, Voter Perceptions, and Candidate Strategy: An Equilibrium Spatial Analysis. In *Ordeshook, P. C., ed.*, 1989, pp. 49–67.

_____ **and Patterson, Douglas M.** Evidence of Nonlinearity in the Trade-by-Trade Stock Market Return Generating Process. In *Barnett, W. A.; Geweke, J. and Shell, K., eds.*, 1989, pp. 383–409.

Hinkle, Maureen Kuwano and Reichelderfer, Katherine H. The Evolution of Pesticide Policy: Environmental Interests and Agriculture. In *Krämer, C. S., ed.*, 1989, pp. 147–73.

Hinkovska, Margarita. Trends in Increasing the Economic Role of Customs Tariffs in the Conditions of Economic Self-Management. In *Bulgarian Academy of Sciences, Institute of Economics*, 1989, pp. 145–52.

Hinloopen, E.; Nijkamp, Peter and Hartog, J. A. A Sensitivity Analysis of Multicriteria Choice-Methods An Application on the Basis of the Optimal Site Selection for a Nuclear Power Plant. *Energy Econ.*, October 1989, *11*(4), pp. 293–300.

Hipple, F. Steb. The Changing Role of Multinational Corporations in U.S. International Trade. In *Gray, H. P., ed.*, 1989, pp. 65–80.

Hippler Bello, Judith. Access to Business Confidential Information in Antidumping Proceedings. In *Jackson, J. H. and Vermulst, E. A., eds.*, 1989, pp. 349–53.

Hiraki, Takato; Aggarwal, Raj and Rao, Ramesh P. Skewness and Kurtosis in Japanese Equity Returns: Empirical Evidence. *J. Finan. Res.*, Fall 1989, *12*(3), pp. 253–60.

Hirashima, Shigemochi and Kuchiki, Akifumi. Primary Commodity Issues in Development.

In *Shinohara, M. and Lo, F., eds.*, 1989, pp. 258–73.

Hirata, Akira and Nohara, Takashi. Changing Patterns in International Division of Labour in Asia and the Pacific. In *Shinohara, M. and Lo, F., eds.*, 1989, pp. 434–62.

Hirata, Helena. Production Relocation: An Electronics Multinational in France and Brazil. In *Elson, D. and Pearson, R., eds.*, 1989, pp. 129–43.

Hirlinger, Michael W. and Morgan, David R. Socioeconomic Dimensions of the American States: An Update. *Soc. Sci. Quart.*, March 1989, *70*(1), pp. 184–92.

_____ **and Morgan, David R.** State Factor Scores: Perhaps Not So Bad. *Soc. Sci. Quart.*, March 1989, *70*(1), pp. 195–96.

Hirsch, Barry T. and Addison, John T. Union Effects on Productivity, Profits, and Growth: Has the Long Run Arrived? *J. Lab. Econ.*, January 1989, *7*(1), pp. 72–105.

_____ **and Feinberg, Robert M.** Industry Rent Seeking and the Filing of 'Unfair Trade' Complaints. *Int. J. Ind. Organ.*, September 1989, *7*(3), pp. 325–40.

Hirsch, Jean-Pierre. Revolutionary France, Cradle of Free Enterprise. *Amer. Historical Rev.*, December 1989, *94*(5), pp. 1281–89.

Hirsch, Joachim and Haeusler, Juergen. Political Regulation: The Crisis of Fordism and the Transformation of the Party System in West Germany. In *Gottdiener, M. and Komninos, N., eds.*, 1989, pp. 300–327.

Hirsch, Seev. International Transactions Involving Interactions: A Conceptual Framework Combining Goods and Services. In *Giersch, H., ed.*, 1989, pp. 63–84.

_____. Services and Service Intensity in International Trade. *Weltwirtsch. Arch.*, 1989, *125*(1), pp. 45–60.

_____. Trade Regimes in the Middle East. In *Fishelson, G., ed.*, 1989, pp. 269–82.

Hirsch, Werner Z. Economists' Role in Government at Risk. In *Samuels, W. J., ed. (I)*, 1989, pp. 87–96.

_____. Radical Revenue Restructuring under Federalism and Its Side Effects. In *Chiancone, A. and Messere, K., eds.*, 1989, pp. 421–30.

Hirschberg, Joseph G. Economic Experiment Data: A Primer on the Use of Time of Day Electricity Pricing Data. *J. Econ. Soc. Meas.*, 1989, *15*(2), pp. 131–53.

_____ **and Fomby, Thomas B.** Texas in Transition: Dependence on Oil and the National Economy. *Fed. Res. Bank Dallas Econ. Rev.*, January 1989, pp. 11–28.

_____; **Molina, David J. and Slottje, Daniel J.** Errata [A Selection Criterion for Choosing between Functional Forms of Income Distribution]. *Econometric Rev.*, 1989, *8*(2), pp. 227.

_____ **and Slottje, Daniel J.** Remembrance of Things Past the Distribution of Earnings across Occupations and the Kappa Criterion. *J. Econometrics*, September 1989, *42*(1), pp. 121–30.

Hirschey, Mark and Zaima, Janis K. Insider

Trading, Ownership Structure, and the Market Assessment of Corporate Sell-Offs. *J. Finance*, September 1989, *44*(4), pp. 971–80.

von Hirschhausen, Christian R. and Pourgerami, Abbas. Aggregate Demand for Energy and Dynamics of Energy Demand Elasticities in Non-Oil-Developing Countries. *J. Energy Devel.*, Spring 1989, *14*(2), pp. 237–52.

Hirschman, Albert O. Having Opinions—One of the Elements of Well-Being? *Amer. Econ. Rev.*, May 1989, *79*(2), pp. 75–79.

_____. How Keynes Was Spread from America: Errata. *Challenge*, Jan.–Feb. 1989, *32*(1), pp. 53.

_____. How the Keynesian Revolution Was Exported from the United States, and Other Comments. In *Hall, P. A., ed.*, 1989, pp. 347–59.

_____. Unbalanced Development, 1958–62: Comment. In *di Tella, G. and Dornbusch, R., eds.*, 1989, pp. 126–28.

Hirschowitz, R. The Other Path: The Invisible Revolution in the Third World. *S. Afr. J. Econ.*, December 1989, *57*(4), pp. 402–11.

Hirshleifer, David. Determinants of Hedging and Risk Premia in Commodity Futures Markets. *J. Finan. Quant. Anal.*, September 1989, *24*(3), pp. 313–31.

_____. Futures Trading, Storage, and the Division of Risk: A Multiperiod Analysis. *Econ. J.*, September 1989, *99*(397), pp. 700–719.

_____ **and Rasmusen, Eric.** Cooperation in a Repeated Prisoners' Dilemma with Ostracism. *J. Econ. Behav. Organ.*, August 1989, *12*(1), pp. 87–106.

Hirshleifer, Jack. The Bayesian Approach to Statistical Decision: An Exposition. In *Hirshleifer, J.*, 1989, *1961*, pp. 125–51.

_____. Conflict and Rent-Seeking Success Functions: Ratio vs. Difference Models of Relative Success. *Public Choice*, November 1989, *63*(2), pp. 101–12.

_____. Investment Decision under Uncertainty: Applications of the State-Preference Approach. In *Hirshleifer, J.*, 1989, *1966*, pp. 98–121.

_____. Investment Decision under Uncertainty: Choice-Theoretic Approaches. In *Hirshleifer, J.*, 1989, *1965*, pp. 69–97.

_____. Liquidity, Uncertainty, and the Accumulation of Information. In *Hirshleifer, J.*, 1989, *1972*, pp. 209–19.

_____. A Note on the Bohm-Bawerk/Wicksell Theory of Interest. In *Hirshleifer, J.*, 1989, *1967*, pp. 38–51.

_____. On the Theory of Optimal Investment Decision. In *Hirshleifer, J.*, 1989, *1958*, pp. 5–37.

_____. The Private and Social Value of Information and the Reward to Inventive Activity. In *Diamond, P. and Rothschild, M., eds.*, 1989, *1971*, pp. 573–86.

_____. The Private and Social Value of Information and the Reward to Inventive Activity. In *Hirshleifer, J.*, 1989, *1971*, pp. 220–38.

_____. Speculation and Equilibrium: Information, Risk, and Markets. In *Hirshleifer, J.*, 1989, *1975*, pp. 239–61.

_____. "Sustained Yield" versus Capital Theory. In *Hirshleifer, J.*, 1989, pp. 52–68.

_____. The Theory of Speculation under Alternative Regimes of Markets. In *Hirshleifer, J.*, 1989, *1977*, pp. 262–91.

_____. Two Models of Speculation and Information. In *Hirshleifer, J.*, 1989, pp. 292–300.

_____ **and Harrison, Glenn W.** An Experimental Evaluation of Weakest Link/Best Shot Models of Public Goods. *J. Polit. Econ.*, February 1989, *97*(1), pp. 201–25.

_____ **and Riley, John G.** The Analytics of Uncertainty and Information: An Expository Survey. In *Hirshleifer, J.*, 1989, *1979*, pp. 152–206.

Hirshman, A. O. Avoir des opinions: L'un des éléments du bien-être? (Having Opinions: One of the Elements of Well Being. With English summary.) *Écon. Societes*, June 1989, *23*(6), pp. 3–10.

Hirst, Eric and Trumble, David. Effects of the Hood River Conservation Project on Electricity Use and Savings in Single-Family Homes. *Appl. Econ.*, August 1989, *21*(8), pp. 1029–42.

Hirst, Paul. The Politics of Industrial Policy. In *Hirst, P. and Zeitlin, J., eds.*, 1989, pp. 269–87.

Hitchens, D. M. W. N. and Bernie, J. E. Economic Development in Northern Ireland: Has Pathfinder Lost Its Way? A Reply. *Reg. Stud.*, October 1989, *23*(5), pp. 477–83.

_____ **and Birnie, J. E.** Productivity Levels in Northern Ireland Manufacturing Industry: A Comparison with Great Britain. *Reg. Stud.*, October 1989, *23*(5), pp. 447–54.

_____ **and O'Farrell, P. N.** The Competitiveness and Performance of Small Manufacturing Firms: An Analysis of Matched Pairs in Scotland and England. *Environ. Planning A*, September 1989, *21*(9), pp. 1241–63.

_____ **and O'Farrell, P. N.** The Relative Competitiveness of Small Manufacturing Companies in South Wales and Northern Ireland: Analysis and Policy. In *Gibbs, D., ed.*, 1989, pp. 176–205.

Hite, Gailen L.; Cheng, David C. and Chen, K. C. Barriers to Entry, Concentration, and Tobin's q Ratio. *Quart. J. Bus. Econ.*, Spring 1989, *28*(2), pp. 32–49.

_____ **and Vetsuypens, Michael R.** Management Buyouts of Divisions and Shareholder Wealth. *J. Finance*, September 1989, *44*(4), pp. 953–70.

Hite, Peggy A. A Positive Approach to Taxpayer Compliance. *Public Finance*, 1989, *44*(2), pp. 249–67.

_____; **Ayres, Frances L. and Jackson, Betty R.** The Economic Benefits of Regulation: Evidence from Professional Tax Preparers. *Accounting Rev.*, April 1989, *64*(2), pp. 300–12.

Ho, Lok-Sang. Optimal Cities. *Urban Stud.*, October 1989, *26*(5), pp. 510–16.

Ho, Y. K. Forum on the Negative Interest Rate Scheme. *Hong Kong Econ. Pap.*, 1989, (19), pp. 71–73.

Hoaas, David J.; Johnson, L. E. and Gramm,

Warren S. Marx's Law of Profit: The Current State of the Controversy. *Atlantic Econ. J.*, December 1989, *17*(4), pp. 55–62.

Hoadley, Bruce; Dalal, Siddhartha R. and Fowlkes, Edward B. Risk Analysis of the Space Shuttle: Pre-*Challenger* Prediction of Failure. *J. Amer. Statist. Assoc.*, December 1989, *84*(408), pp. 945–57.

Hoag, Dana L. Budget Planner: User-Oriented Whole-Farm Budgeting Software. *Southern J. Agr. Econ.*, July 1989, *21*(1), pp. 163–69.

Hoag, John H. and Browne, M. Neil. The Formative Use of Student Evaluations of Teaching: An Empirical Demonstration of the Incompleteness of Global Ratings. **In** *Missouri Valley Economic Association*, 1989, pp. 32–40.

Hobbs, Phil. The UK Worker Co-operative Movement in 1988: Review. *Ann. Pub. Coop. Econ.*, 1989, *60*(4), pp. 475–83.

Hobcraft, John. People and Services: Central Assessment of Local Needs. **In** *Joshi, H., ed.*, 1989, pp. 133–56.

_____ **and Joshi, Heather.** Population Matters. **In** *Joshi, H., ed.*, 1989, pp. 1–11.

Hobday, Mike. The European Semiconductor Industry: Resurgence and Rationalization. *J. Common Market Stud.*, December 1989, *28*(2), pp. 155–86.

Hocevar, Susan Page and Bhambri, Arvind. Corporate Social Performance: A Model of Assessment Criteria. **In** *Post, J. E., ed.*, 1989, pp. 1–20.

Hoch, R. Commodity Production with or without Attribute. *Acta Oecon.*, 1989, *40*(3–4), pp. 227–32.

Hoch, Stephen J. and Ha, Young-Won. Ambiguity, Processing Strategy, and Advertising–Evidence Interactions. *J. Cons. Res.*, December 1989, *16*(3), pp. 354–60.

Hoch, Steven L. Bridewealth, Dowry, and Socioeconomic Differentiation in Rural Russia. **In** *Grantham, G. and Leonard, C. S., eds., Pt. B*, 1989, pp. 389–410.

Hochman, Eithan; Levy, Amnon and Justman, Moshe. The Implications of Financial Cooperation in Israel's Semi-cooperative Villages. *J. Devel. Econ.*, January 1989, *30*(1), pp. 25–46.

Hodge, I. D. Compensation for Nature Conservation. *Environ. Planning A*, August 1989, *21*(8), pp. 1027–36.

Hodges-Aeberhard, Jane. The Right to Organise in Article 2 of Convention No. 87: What is Meant by Workers "Without Distinction Whatsoever"? *Int. Lab. Rev.*, 1989, *128*(2), pp. 177–94.

Hodgkinson, Edith and Bryant, Ralph C. Problems of International Cooperation. **In** *Cooper, R. N., et al.*, 1989, pp. 1–11.

Hodgman, Donald R. and Resek, Robert W. Italian Monetary and Foreign Exchange Policy. **In** *Hodgman, D. R. and Wood, G. E., eds.*, 1989, pp. 62–86.

_____ **and Wood, Geoffrey E.** Macroeconomic Policy and Economic Interdependence: Introduction. **In** *Hodgman, D. R. and Wood, G. E., eds.*, 1989, pp. vii–xvi.

Hodgson, Geoff. Institutional Rigidities and Economic Growth. *Cambridge J. Econ.*, March 1989, *13*(1), pp. 79–101.

_____. Institutional Rigidities and Economic Growth. **In** *Lawson, T.; Palma, J. G. and Sender, J., eds.*, 1989, pp. 79–101.

_____. Marxism without Tears: A Review of John E. Roemer's "Free to Lose." *Rev. Soc. Econ.*, Winter 1989, *47*(4), pp. 433–36.

_____. Post-Keynesianism and Institutionalism: The Missing Link. **In** *Pheby, J., ed.*, 1989, pp. 94–123.

_____. The Rationalist Conception of Action. **In** *Tool, M. R. and Samuels, W. J., eds. (II)*, 1989, *1985*, pp. 65–91.

_____ **and Jones, Derek C.** Codetermination: A Partial Review of Theory and Evidence. *Ann. Pub. Coop. Econ.*, 1989, *60*(3), pp. 329–40.

Hodgson, Ray J. Low Cost Responses. **In** *Robinson, D.; Maynard, A. and Chester, R., eds.*, 1989, pp. 101–09.

Hodrick, Robert J. Risk, Uncertainty, and Exchange Rates. *J. Monet. Econ.*, May 1989, *23*(3), pp. 433–59.

_____. U.S. International Capital Flows: Perspectives from Rational Maximizing Models. *Carnegie–Rochester Conf. Ser. Public Policy*, Spring 1989, *30*, pp. 231–88.

Hoehn, John P.; Blaine, Thomas W. and Mohammad, Golam. Probit Model Procedures to the Estimation of Probabilities: An Empirical Exposition to a Dichotomous Decision Model. *Can. J. Agr. Econ.*, Part 2, December 1989, *37*(4), pp. 1071–79.

_____ **and Randall, Alan.** Benefit Estimation for Complex Policies. **In** *Folmer, H. and van Ierland, E., eds.*, 1989, pp. 219–29.

_____ **and Randall, Alan.** Too Many Proposals Pass the Benefit Cost Test. *Amer. Econ. Rev.*, June 1989, *79*(3), pp. 544–51.

van der Hoek, M. Peter. On the Size of the Multiplier. *Atlantic Econ. J.*, June 1989, *17*(2), pp. 75.

_____. Pay Differentials between the Private and the Public Sector in the Netherlands. *Public Finance Quart.*, January 1989, *17*(1), pp. 84–95.

Hoekman, Bernard M. Agriculture and the Uruguay Round. *J. World Trade*, February 1989, *23*(1), pp. 83–96.

_____. Agriculture and the Uruguay Round. *J. World Trade*, February 1989, *23*(1), pp. 83–96.

_____. Determining the Need for Issue Linkages in Multilateral Trade Negotiations. *Int. Organ.*, Autumn 1989, *43*(4), pp. 693–714.

_____ **and Leidy, Michael P.** Dumping, Antidumping and Emergency Protection. *J. World Trade*, October 1989, *23*(5), pp. 27–44.

Hoel, Michael. Efficiency Wages and Local versus Central Wage Bargaining. *Econ. Letters*, August 1989, *30*(2), pp. 175–79.

_____ **and Calmfors, Lars.** Work Sharing, Employment and Shiftwork. *Oxford Econ. Pap.*, October 1989, *41*(4), pp. 758–73.

Hoem, Britta and Hoem, Jan M. The Impact of

Women's Employment on Second and Third Births in Modern Sweden. *Population Stud.*, March 1989, *43*(1), pp. 47–67.

Hoem, Jan M. The Issue of Weights in Panel Surveys of Individual Behavior. In *Kasprzyk, D., et al., eds.*, 1989, pp. 539–65.

———— **and Hoem, Britta.** The Impact of Women's Employment on Second and Third Births in Modern Sweden. *Population Stud.*, March 1989, *43*(1), pp. 47–67.

Hoen, H. W.; Lanjouw, G. J. and van Leeuwen, E. H. Eastern Europe's Participation in the International Financial System. *Jahr. Wirtsch. Osteuropas*, 1989, *13*(2), pp. 41–65.

———— **and Wagener, H.-J.** Hungary's Exports to the OECD: A Constant Market Shares Analysis. *Acta Oecon.*, 1989, *40*(1–2), pp. 65–77.

Hoenack, Stephen. Group Behavior and Economic Growth. *Soc. Sci. Quart.*, September 1989, *70*(3), pp. 744–58.

————. Group Behavior and Economic Growth: A Reply. *Soc. Sci. Quart.*, September 1989, *70*(3), pp. 763–64.

van der Hoeven, Rolph. External Shocks, Adjustment, and Income Distribution. In *Weeks, J. F., ed.*, 1989, pp. 21–40.

———— **and van Ginneken, Wouter.** Industrialisation, Employment and Earnings (1950–87): An International Survey. *Int. Lab. Rev.*, 1989, *128*(5), pp. 571–99.

van der Hoeven, W. H. M. and Thurik, A. R. Manufacturing Margins: Differences between Small and Large Firms. *Econ. Letters*, 1989, *29*(4), pp. 353–59.

———— **and Thurik, A. R.** Profit Margins and Concentration. *Atlantic Econ. J.*, June 1989, *17*(2), pp. 79.

Hof, John G. and Rideout, Douglas B. Limitations of the With and Without Principle in Benefit–Cost Analysis. *Public Finance Quart.*, April 1989, *17*(2), pp. 216–26.

Hoffer, George E. and Millner, Edward L. Has Pricing Behaviour in the U.S. Automobile Industry Become More Competitive? *Appl. Econ.*, March 1989, *21*(3), pp. 295–304.

Hofflander, Alfred E.; Venezian, Emilio C. and Nye, Blaine F. The Distribution of Claims for Professional Malpractice: Some Statistical and Public Policy Aspects. *J. Risk Ins.*, December 1989, *56*(4), pp. 686–701.

Hoffman, Arnold J. Funding Levels of Private Defined Benefit Pension Plans by Industry: The Relationship between Output, Employment and Funding. In *Turner, J. A. and Beller, D. J., eds.*, 1989, pp. 137–52.

————. Pension Funds and the Economy, 1950–87. In *Turner, J. A. and Beller, D. J., eds.*, 1989, pp. 95–117.

Hoffman, Dennis L. and Blakemore, Arthur E. Seniority Rules and Productivity: An Empirical Test. *Economica*, August 1989, *56*(223), pp. 359–71.

————; **Low, Stuart A. and Boyes, William J.** An Econometric Analysis of the Bank Credit Scoring Problem. *J. Econometrics*, January 1989, *40*(1), pp. 3–14.

———— **and Pagan, Adrian R.** Post-Sample Prediction Tests for Generalized Method of Moments Estimators. *Oxford Bull. Econ. Statist.*, August 1989, *51*(3), pp. 333–43.

Hoffman, Elizabeth and Binger, Brian R. Institutional Persistence and Change: The Question of Efficiency. *J. Inst. Theoretical Econ.*, March 1989, *145*(1), pp. 67–84.

Hoffman Friedrichand Rebstock, Wolfgang. Unternehmungsethik. Eine Herausforderung an die Unternehmung. (With English summary.) *Z. Betriebswirtshaft*, June 1989, *59*(6), pp. 667–87.

Hoffman, Lorey Arthur and Macnaughton, Alan. Life Insurance and Tax Reform. In *Mintz, J. and Whalley, J., eds.*, 1989, pp. 255–85.

Hoffman, Philip T. Institutions and Agriculture in Old-Régime France. *J. Inst. Theoretical Econ.*, March 1989, *145*(1), pp. 166–81.

Hoffman, Sharon. Impacts of Deregulation on the Australian Petroleum Industry. In *James, W. E., ed.*, 1989, pp. 97–109.

Hoffmann, Lutz. In Praise of Development Economics: Comments. *Pakistan Devel. Rev.*, Winter 1989, *28*(4), pp. 382–84.

————. South Asia and European Integration—Lessons from the Past and Future Prospects. *Pakistan Devel. Rev.*, Winter 1989, *28*(4), pp. 465–501.

Hoffmann, Stanley. The European Community and 1992. *Foreign Aff.*, Fall 1989, *68*(4), pp. 27–47.

Hoffmeyer, Erik. Delors-rapporten. (An Evaluation of the Delors Committee's Report on an Economic and Monetary Union in Europe. With English summary.) *Nationaløkon. Tidsskr.*, 1989, *127*(2), pp. 160–64.

Hofler, Richard A. and Murphy, Kevin J. Using a Composed Error Model to Estimate the Frictional and Excess-Supply Components of Unemployment. *J. Reg. Sci.*, May 1989, *29*(2), pp. 213–28.

Hogan, William V. and Georgianna, Daniel. U.S. Fish Processing Capacity and Imports of Whole Groundfish from Canada. *Marine Resource Econ.*, 1989, *6*(3), pp. 213–25.

Hogan, William W. A Dynamic Putty–Semi-putty Model of Aggregate Energy Demand. *Energy Econ.*, January 1989, *11*(1), pp. 53–69.

Hogarth, Robin M. On Combining Diagnostic 'Forecasts': Thoughts and Some Evidence. *Int. J. Forecasting*, 1989, *5*(4), pp. 593–97.

———— **and Kunreuther, Howard.** Risk, Ambiguity, and Insurance. *J. Risk Uncertainty*, April 1989, *2*(1), pp. 5–35.

Hogg, Robert V. How to Hope with Statistics. *J. Amer. Statist. Assoc.*, March 1989, *84*(405), pp. 1–5.

Hogler, Raymond L. Labor History and Critical Labor Law: An Interdisciplinary Approach to Workers' Control. *Labor Hist.*, Spring 1989, *30*(2), pp. 165–92.

Hohenberg, Paul M. *Technology and Economic Policy:* Review Article. *Atlantic Econ. J.*, March 1989, *17*(1), pp. 47–50.

Høie, Henning and Vestøl, Jon Åge. Sustainable

Agriculture: Assessments of Agricultural Pollution in the SIMJAR Model. *Statist. J.*, 1989, 6(3), pp. 255–67.

Hojman, David E. Fundamental Equilibrium Exchange Rates under Contractionary Devaluation: A Peruvian Model. *J. Econ. Stud.*, 1989, 16(3), pp. 5–26.

_____. Neoliberal Economic Policies and Infant and Child Mortality: Simulation Analysis of a Chilean Paradox. *World Devel.*, January 1989, 17(1), pp. 933–108.

Hoke, Donald. British and American Horology: A Reply. *J. Econ. Hist.*, September 1989, 49(3), pp. 715–19.

_____. Product Design and Cost Considerations: Clock, Watch, and Typewriter Manufacturing in the 19th Century. In *Hausman, W. J., ed.*, 1989, pp. 119–28.

Holaday, William; Castella, Guillermo and de Buckle, Teresa Salazar. Agro-food Industry in Latin America. *Industry Devel.*, June 1989, (27), pp. 1–29.

Holbik, Karel. Japan's Internal Economic Inefficiencies and Its Trade Balance. *Rivista Int. Sci. Econ. Com.*, February 1989, 36(2), pp. 165–76.

Holbrook, Morris B. and Schindler, Robert M. Some Exploratory Findings on the Development of Musical Tastes. *J. Cons. Res.*, June 1989, 16(1), pp. 119–24.

Holcomb, James H.; Chittenden, William T. and Evans, Dorla A. The Relationship between Risk-Return Preference and Knowledge in Experimental Financial Markets. *J. Behav. Econ.*, Spring 1989, 18(1), pp. 19–40.

Holcombe, Randall G. The Median Voter Model in Public Choice Theory. *Public Choice*, May 1989, 61(2), pp. 115–25.

_____. Non-optimal Unanimous Agreement under Majority Rule: Reply. *Public Choice*, July 1989, 62(1), pp. 89–92.

_____. A Note on Seniority and Political Competition. *Public Choice*, June 1989, 61(3), pp. 285–88.

_____ and Boudreaux, Donald J. The Coasian and Knightian Theories of the Firm. *Managerial Dec. Econ.*, June 1989, 10(2), pp. 147–54.

_____ and Boudreaux, Donald J. Government by Contract. *Public Finance Quart.*, July 1989, 17(3), pp. 264–80.

_____ and Caudill, Steven B. Taxation and the Redistribution of Income. *Atlantic Econ. J.*, September 1989, 17(3), pp. 39–42.

_____ and Gwartney, James D. Political Parties and the Legislative Principal–Agent Relationship. *J. Inst. Theoretical Econ.*, December 1989, 145(4), pp. 669–75.

_____; Zardkoohi, Asghar and Backhaus, Jürgen G. Public Investment and the Burden of the Public Debt: Reply. *Southern Econ. J.*, October 1989, 56(2), pp. 532–34.

Holden, Darryl R.; Nairn, Alasdair G. M. and Swales, J. K. Shift-Share Analysis of Regional Growth and Policy: A Critique. *Oxford Bull.*

Econ. Statist., February 1989, 51(1), pp. 15–34.

Holden, David J. Wardrop's Third Principle: Urban Traffic Congestion and Traffic Policy. *J. Transp. Econ. Policy*, September 1989, 23(3), pp. 239–62.

Holden, K. Macroeconomic Forecasting. In *Greenaway, D., ed.*, 1989, pp. 163–81.

Holden, Merle. A Comparative Analysis of Structural Imbalance in the Face of a Debt Crisis. *S. Afr. J. Econ.*, March 1989, 57(1), pp. 22–34.

_____. Unemployment in a Sector Specific Trade Model in the Presence of Economic Sanctions. *S. Afr. J. Econ.*, June 1989, 57(2), pp. 137–41.

Holden, Steinar. Wage Drift and Bargaining: Evidence from Norway. *Economica*, November 1989, 56(224), pp. 419–32.

Holder, Carlos and Haynes, Cleviston. Monetary and Fiscal Policy in Barbados, 1970–1985. In *Worrell, D. and Bourne, C., eds.*, 1989, pp. 89–104.

_____ and Prescod, Ronald. The Distribution of Personal Income in Barbados. *Soc. Econ. Stud.*, March 1989, 38(1), pp. 87–113.

Holderness, Clifford G. The Assignment of Rights, Entry Effects, and the Allocation of Resources. *J. Legal Stud.*, January 1989, 18(1), pp. 181–89.

_____ and Barclay, Michael J. Private Benefits from Control of Public Corporations. *J. Finan. Econ.*, December 1989, 25(2), pp. 371–95.

Holdren, John. Interaction between Nuclear and Conventional Arms-Control Measures (Report on a Pugwash Workshop, June 1988). In *Rotblat, J. and Goldanskii, V. I., eds.*, 1989, pp. 93–96.

Holland, David W. and Carvalho, Joe W. Agricultural and Economic Development in Lesotho: Analysis Using a Social Accounting Matrix. *Eastern Afr. Econ. Rev.*, December 1989, 5(2), pp. 104–20.

Holland, Forrest D. and Sharples, Jerry A. World Wheat Trade: Implications for U.S. Exports. In *Labys, W. C.; Takayama, T. and Uri, N. D., eds.*, 1989, pp. 299–329.

Holland, Paul W. Choosing among Alternative Nonexperimental Methods for Estimating the Impact of Social Programs: The Case of Manpower Training: It's Very Clear: Comment. *J. Amer. Statist. Assoc.*, December 1989, 84(408), pp. 875–77.

Holland, Stuart and Irvin, George. Central American Integration: A Suitable Case for Treatment. In *Irvin, G. and Holland, S., eds.*, 1989, pp. 1–21.

Hollander, Abraham. La politique de concurrence et les mesures spéciales d'importation dans un marché nord-américain en voie d'intégration. (With English summary.) *L'Actual. Econ.*, March 1989, 65(1), pp. 163–74.

_____ and Fraser, Clive. Advance Delivery Contracts, Revenue Pools and Price Discrimination. *J. Econ. Behav. Organ.*, March 1989, 11(2), pp. 285–91.

Hollander, Jacob H. The Dawn of a Science. In *Clark, J. M., et al.*, 1989, pp. 1–21.

———. The Founder of a School. In *Clark, J. M., et al.*, 1989, pp. 22–52.

Hollander, Samuel. Diminishing Returns and Malthus's First Essay on Population: Theory and Application. *Écon. Societes*, June 1989, 23(6), pp. 11–39.

———. Physics and the "Marginalist Revolution": Comment. *Cambridge J. Econ.*, September 1989, 13(3), pp. 459–70.

Holler, Manfred J. Why the Latin American Countries Do Not Form a Debtors' Cartel. *Kyklos*, 1989, 42(1), pp. 89–102.

Hollingshead, Craig A. and Russon, Manuel G. Aircraft Size as a Quality of Service Variable in a Short-Haul Market. *Int. J. Transport Econ.*, October 1989, 16(3), pp. 297–311.

——— and Russon, Manuel G. Convenience and Circuity in a Short-Haul Model of Air Passenger Demand. *Rev. Reg. Stud.*, Winter 1989, 19(1), pp. 50–56.

Hollingsworth, Ellen Jane and Hollingsworth, J. Rogers. Public Organizations: The Behavior of Hospitals in England and Wales. In *James, E., ed.*, 1989, pp. 110–36.

Hollingsworth, J. Rogers and Hollingsworth, Ellen Jane. Public Organizations: The Behavior of Hospitals in England and Wales. In *James, E., ed.*, 1989, pp. 110–36.

Hollman, Kenneth W.; Murrey, Joe H., Jr. and Abbasi, Sami M. Islamic Economics: Foundations and Practices. *Int. J. Soc. Econ.*, 1989, 16(5), pp. 5–17.

Holloway, Garth J. Distribution of Research Gains in Multistage Production Systems: Further Results. *Amer. J. Agr. Econ.*, May 1989, 71(2), pp. 338–43.

Holloway, Thomas M. An Updated Look at Okun's Law. *Soc. Sci. Quart.*, June 1989, 70(2), pp. 497–504.

———. Measuring the Cyclical Sensitivity of Federal Receipts and Expenditures: Simplified Estimation Procedures. *Int. J. Forecasting*, 1989, 5(3), pp. 347–60.

———. Present NIPA Saving Measures: Their Characteristics and Limitations. In *Lipsey, R. E. and Tice, H. S., eds.*, 1989, pp. 21–93.

Holly, Brian P. Corporate Takeovers and Regional Economic Development: An Ohio Perspective. In *McKee, D. L., ed.*, 1989, pp. 59–68.

Holly, Sean and Smith, Peter. Interrelated Factor Demands for Manufacturing: A Dynamic Translog Cost Function Approach. *Europ. Econ. Rev.*, January 1989, 33(1), pp. 111–26.

Holma, Eero. Finsk försäkring internationaliseras. (The Internationalization of Finnish Insurance. With English summary.) *Ekon. Samfundets Tidskr.*, 1989, 42(3), pp. 165–67.

Holmberg, K. and Jörnsten, K. Exact Methods for Gravity Trip-Distribution Models. *Environ. Planning A*, January 1989, 21(1), pp. 81–97.

Holmes, J. H. Private Disinvestment and Public Investment in Australia's Pastoral Zone: Policy Issues. In *Gibson, L. J. and Stimson, R. J., eds.*, 1989, pp. 145–61.

Holmes, James M. and Hutton, Patricia A. 'Optimal' Model Selection When the True Relationship Is Weak and Occurs with a Delay. *Econ. Letters*, October 1989, 30(4), pp. 333–39.

Holmes, John. New Production Technologies, Labour and the North American Auto Industry. In *Linge, G. J. R. and van der Knaap, G. A., eds.*, 1989, pp. 87–106.

Holmes, Peter and Sharp, Margaret. Conclusions: Farewell to the National Champion. In *Sharp, M. and Holmes, P., eds.*, 1989, pp. 212–39.

——— and Sharp, Margaret. The State: Captor or Captive? In *Sharp, M. and Holmes, P., eds.*, 1989, pp. 1–18.

Holmes, Thomas J. The Effects of Third-Degree Price Discrimination in Oligopoly. *Amer. Econ. Rev.*, March 1989, 79(1), pp. 244–50.

Holmlund, Bertil. Wages and Employment in Unionized Economies: Theory and Evidence. In *Holmlund, B.; Löfgren, K.-G. and Engström, L.*, 1989, pp. 5–104.

——— and Björklund, Anders. Effects of Extended Unemployment Compensation in Sweden. In *Gustafsson, B. A. and Klevmarken, N. A., eds.*, 1989, pp. 165–83.

——— and Björklund, Anders. Job Mobility and Subsequent Wages in Sweden. In *van Dijk, J., et al., eds.*, 1989, pp. 201–16.

———; Lang, Harald and Albrecht, James W. Job Search and Youth Unemployment: Analysis of Swedish Data. *Europ. Econ. Rev.*, March 1989, 33(2/3), pp. 416–25.

——— and Lundborg, Per. Unemployment Insurance Schemes for Reducing the Natural Rate of Unemployment. *J. Public Econ.*, February 1989, 38(1), pp. 1–15.

Holmøy, Erling; Olsen, Øystein and Bjørn, Erik. Gross and Net Capital, and the Form of the Survival Function: Theory and Some Norwegian Evidence. *Rev. Income Wealth*, June 1989, 35(2), pp. 133–49.

Holmstrom, Bengt R. Agency Costs and Innovation. *J. Econ. Behav. Organ.*, December 1989, 12(3), pp. 305–27.

———. Moral Hazard and Observability. In *Diamond, P. and Rothschild, M., eds.*, 1989, 1979, pp. 327–44.

——— and Tirole, Jean. The Theory of the Firm. In *Schmalensee, R. and Willig, R. D., eds.*, Vol. 1, 1989, pp. 61–133.

Holstein-Beck, Maria. Flexibilisation of Working Time in Poland: Former Practice and Future Perspectives. In *Agassi, J. B. and Heycock, S., eds.*, 1989, pp. 41–47.

Holt, Charles A. The Exercise of Market Power in Laboratory Experiments. *J. Law Econ.*, Part 2, October 1989, 32(2), pp. S107–30.

——— and Eckel, Catherine C. Strategic Voting in Agenda-Controlled Committee Experiments. *Amer. Econ. Rev.*, September 1989, 79(4), pp. 763–73.

——— and Scheffman, David T. Strategic Business Behavior and Antitrust. In *Larner, R. J. and Meehan, J. W., Jr., eds.*, 1989, pp. 39–82.

Holt, D. Panel Conditioning: Discussion. In *Kasprzyk, D., et al., eds.*, 1989, pp. 340–47.

Holt, John. Managing Change in Extension. *Amer. J. Agr. Econ.*, November 1989, 71(4), pp. 869–73.

Holt, Matthew T. Bounded Price Variation Models with Rational Expectations and Price Risk. *Econ. Letters*, December 1989, 31(4), pp. 313–17.

_____ **and Aradhyula, Satheesh V.** Risk Behavior and Rational Expectations in the U.S. Broiler Market. *Amer. J. Agr. Econ.*, November 1989, 71(4), pp. 892–902.

_____ **and Johnson, Stanley R.** Bounded Price Variation and Rational Expectations in an Endogenous Switching Model of the U.S. Corn Market. *Rev. Econ. Statist.*, November 1989, 71(4), pp. 605–13.

_____ **and Skold, Karl D.** Dynamic Elasticities and Flexibilities in a Quarterly Model of the U.S. Pork Sector. *Appl. Econ.*, December 1989, 21(12), pp. 1683–1700.

Holt, Wythe. The New American Labor Law History. *Labor Hist.*, Spring 1989, 30(2), pp. 275–93.

Holtbrügge, Dirk. Joint Ventures in der UdSSR: Privatkapitalistische Inseln oder intersystemare Unternehmungskooperation. (Joint Ventures in the USSR. With English summary.) *Aussenwirtschaft*, December 1989, 44(3–4), pp. 399–424.

Holtfrerich, Carl-Ludwig. The Evolution of World Trade, 1720 to the Present: Introduction. In *[Fischer, W.]*, 1989, pp. 1–30.

_____. The Monetary Unification Process in 19th-Century Germany: Relevance and Lessons for Europe Today. In *De Cecco, M. and Giovannini, A., eds.*, 1989, pp. 216–41.

_____. Social Control and Labor Relations in the American South before the Mechanization of the Cotton Harvest in the 1950s: Comment. *J. Inst. Theoretical Econ.*, March 1989, 145(1), pp. 162–65.

Holtham, Gerald. Foreign Exchange Markets and Target Zones. *Oxford Rev. Econ. Policy*, Autumn 1989, 5(3), pp. 73–82.

_____. German Macroeconomic Policy and the 1978 Bonn Economic Summit. In *Cooper, R. N., et al.*, 1989, pp. 141–77.

_____; **Hughes Hallett, Andrew J. and Currie, David A.** The Theory and Practice of International Policy Coordination: Does Coordination Pay? In *Bryant, R. C., et al., eds.*, 1989, pp. 14–46.

_____; **Hutson, Gary and Hughes Hallett, Andrew J.** Exchange-Rate Targeting as Surrogate International Cooperation. In *Miller, M.; Eichengreen, B. and Portes, R., eds.*, 1989, pp. 239–78.

Holtz-Eakin, Douglas; Newey, Whitney K. and Rosen, Harvey S. The Revenues–Expenditures Nexus: Evidence from Local Government Data. *Int. Econ. Rev.*, May 1989, 30(2), pp. 415–29.

_____ **and Rosen, Harvey S.** The 'Rationality' of Municipal Capital Spending: Evidence from New Jersey. *Reg. Sci. Urban Econ.*, August 1989, 19(3), pp. 517–36.

Holub, Hans Werner. Theory versus Empiricism in Academic Economics: Update and Comparison: Comments. *J. Econ. Perspectives*, Fall 1989, 3(4), pp. 207–09.

_____ **and Tappeiner, Gottfried.** An Extension of Input–Output Employment Models. *Econ. Systems Res.*, 1989, 1(3), pp. 297–309.

_____ **and Tappeiner, Gottfried.** Structural Consequences of Different Models of Transformation in the SNA. In *Franz, A. and Rainer, N., eds.*, 1989, pp. 389–410.

Holzer, Harry J. and Freeman, Richard B. Young Blacks and Jobs. In *Freeman, R. B.*, 1989, 1985, pp. 121–33.

Holzman, Franklyn D. Reforms in the USSR: Implications for U.S. Policy. *Amer. Econ. Rev.*, May 1989, 79(2), pp. 26–30.

Holzmüller, Hartmut H. and Kasper, Helmut. Psychostrukturelle Merkmale von Exportmanagern, Organisationskultur und Exporterfolg. Eine kausalanalytische Untersuchung. (With English summary.) *Z. Betriebswirtshaft*, December 1989, 59(12), pp. 1297–1323.

Homan, Rick K.; Glandon, Gerald L. and Counte, Michael A. Perceived Risk: The Link to Plan Selection and Future Utilization. *J. Risk Ins.*, March 1989, 56(1), pp. 67–82.

Homano, Tadashi. On the Non-existence of a Marginal Cost Pricing Equilibrium and the Ioffe Normal Cone. *J. Econ. (Z. Nationalökon.)*, 1989, 50(1), pp. 47–53.

Homburg, Stefan. Some Notes on Overshooting. *Z. Wirtschaft. Sozialwissen.*, 1989, 109(3), pp. 443–47.

Home, Niilo. Kyläkaupan kuolema ja eloonjääminen. (Death and Survival of Rural Stores. With English summary.) *Liiketaloudellinen Aikak.*, 1989, 38(3), pp. 255–62.

Homma, Masaaki; Atoda, Naosumi and Hashimoto, Kyoji. Welfare Analysis of the 1988 Tax Reform in Japan. *Econ. Stud. Quart.*, December 1989, 40(4), pp. 336–48.

Hommes, Cars H. and Nusse, Helena E. Does an Unstable Keynesian Unemployment Equilibrium in a Non-Walrasian Dynamic Macroeconomic Model Imply Chaos? *Scand. J. Econ.*, 1989, 91(1), pp. 161–67.

Honadle, George and Cooper, Lauren. Beyond Coordination and Control: An Interorganizational Approach to Structural Adjustment, Service Delivery, and Natural Resource Management. *World Devel.*, October 1989, 17(10), pp. 1531–41.

Honda, Tetsushi; Nambu, Tsuruhiko and Suzuki, Kazuyuki. Deregulation in Japan. In *Crandall, R. W. and Flamm, K., eds.*, 1989, pp. 147–73.

Hong, Chansik and Zellner, Arnold. Forecasting International Growth Rates Using Bayesian Shrinkage and Other Procedures. *J. Econometrics*, January 1989, 40(1), pp. 183–202.

Hong, Fenglin and Shao, Daosheng. Workers' Assessment of Party Spirit and Interpersonal

Relations. *Chinese Econ. Stud.*, Summer 1989, 22(4), pp. 44–54.

Hong, Lee Fook. New Tax Incentives: Singapore. *Bull. Int. Fiscal Doc.*, March 1989, 43(3), pp. 131–34.

_____. 1989 Budget: Pro-business or Pro-family? Singapore. *Bull. Int. Fiscal Doc.*, June 1989, 43(6), pp. 283–85.

Hong, Sung-Tai and Wyer, Robert S., Jr. Effects of Country-of-Origin and Product-Attribute Information on Product Evaluation: An Information Processing Perspective. *J. Cons. Res.*, September 1989, 16(2), pp. 175–87.

Hong, Wontack. Factor Intensities of Korea's Domestic Demand, Production and Trade: 1960–85. *Int. Econ. J.*, Summer 1989, 3(2), pp. 97–113.

Hong, Y. and Pagan, Adrian R. Some Simulation Studies of Nonparametric Estimators. In *Ullah, A., ed.*, 1989, 1988, pp. 129–44.

Honig, Marjorie. Where to Look for Comparable Worth: The Implications of Efficiency Wages: Discussion. In *Hill, M. A. and Killingsworth, M. R., eds.*, 1989, pp. 29–30.

_____ and Reimers, Cordelia W. Is It Worth Eliminating the Retirement Test? *Amer. Econ. Rev.*, May 1989, 79(2), pp. 103–07.

_____ and Reimers, Cordelia W. The Retirement Process in the United States: Mobility among Full-Time Work, Partial Retirement, and Full Retirement. In *Schmähl, W., ed.*, 1989, pp. 115–31.

Honkapohja, Seppo. Keynesian Issues and Economic Theory: Comment. *Scand. J. Econ.*, 1989, 91(2), pp. 295–99.

_____. Whither Macroeconomics? Editor's Introduction. *Scand. J. Econ.*, 1989, 91(2), pp. 209–21.

Honko, Jaakko. Internationale Konkurrenzfähigkeit und wissenschaftliche Forschung. (With English summary.) *Z. Betriebswirtschaft*, March 1989, 59(3), pp. 265–70.

Honma, Masayoshi. Trade in Primary Products: Canada, the United States, and Japan: Comment. In *Stern, R. M., ed.*, 1989, pp. 168–70.

Honobe, Susumu; O'uchi, Minoru and Haseyama, Takahiko. New Issues of Economic Cooperation. In *Shinohara, M. and Lo, F., eds.*, 1989, pp. 469–502.

Honohan, Patrick and McNelis, Paul D. Is the EMS a DM Zone?—Evidence from the Realignments. *Econ. Soc. Rev.*, January 1989, 20(2), pp. 97–110.

Hont, Istvan. The Political Economy of the "Unnatural and Retrograde" Order: Adam Smith and Natural Liberty. In *Berg, M., et al.*, 1989, pp. 122–49.

Hooijmans, Frans C. and van der Knoop, Han S. A Multivariate Intervention Model for the Dutch Mint Circulation: Estimation and Monte Carlo Simulation. *J. Bus. Econ. Statist.*, April 1989, 7(2), pp. 179–89.

Hook, Alison and Walton, David. Commodity Price Indicators: A Case for Discretion Rather

Than Rules. In *Miller, M.; Eichengreen, B. and Portes, R., eds.*, 1989, pp. 99–119.

Hooks, Donald L. and Cover, James Peery. Credit versus Monetary Theories of Macroeconomic Fluctuations. *Atlantic Econ. J.*, June 1989, 17(2), pp. 41–46.

Hoole, Francis W. and Huang, Chi. The Global Conflict Process. *J. Conflict Resolution*, March 1989, 33(1), pp. 142–63.

Hooper, P. and Wood, C. The Effects of the Relaxation of Planning Controls in Enterprise Zones on Industrial Pollution. *Environ. Planning A*, September 1989, 21(9), pp. 1157–67.

Hooper, Peter. U.S. Net Foreign Saving Has Also Plunged. *Challenge*, July–Aug. 1989, 32(4), pp. 33–38.

_____; Bryant, Ralph C. and Helliwell, John F. Domestic and Cross-Border Consequences of U.S. Macroeconomic Policies. In *Bryant, R. C., et al., eds.*, 1989, pp. 59–115.

_____ and Larin, Kathryn A. International Comparisons of Labor Costs in Manufacturing. *Rev. Income Wealth*, December 1989, 35(4), pp. 335–55.

_____ and Mann, Catherine L. Exchange Rate Pass-Through in the 1980s: The Case of U.S. Imports of Manufacturers. *Brookings Pap. Econ. Act.*, 1989, (1), pp. 297–329.

_____ and Meade, Ellen E. U.S. International Transactions in 1988. *Fed. Res. Bull.*, May 1989, 75(5), pp. 321–32.

Hope, Dave. Building an Enterprise Livestock Data Base for Extension and Research Use. *Can. J. Agr. Econ.*, Part 1, December 1989, 37(4), pp. 591–95.

Hope, Kempe Ronald. Private Direct Investment and Development Policy in the Caribbean: Nationalism and Nationalization Scared Away Foreign Investors but Reagan Initiative's Luring Them. *Amer. J. Econ. Sociology*, January 1989, 48(1), pp. 69–78.

Hopenhayn, Benjamin and Dinenzon, Marcelo. Debt and World Money. In *Singer, H. W. and Sharma, S., eds. (I)*, 1989, pp. 181–98.

Hopkins, R. W. Privatisation: Singapore's Experience in Perspective: An Accounting Perspective. In *Thynne, I. and Ariff, M., eds.*, 1989, pp. 101–25.

Hoppe, Hans-Hermann. In Defense of Extreme Rationalism: Thoughts on Donald McCloskey's *The Rhetoric of Economics*. In *Rothbard, M. N. and Block, W., eds.*, 1989, pp. 179–214.

Hopwood, William; McKeown, James and Mutchler, Jane. A Test of the Incremental Explanatory Power of Opinions Qualified for Consistency and Uncertainty. *Accounting Rev.*, January 1989, 64(1), pp. 28–48.

_____ and Schaefer, Thomas. Firm-Specific Responsiveness to Input Price Changes and the Incremental Information in Current Cost Income. *Accounting Rev.*, April 1989, 64(2), pp. 313–28.

Horen, J. and Wu, S. Y. Vertical Transactions under Uncertainty. In *[Hadar, J.]*, 1989, pp. 157–86.

Hori, Hajime. Rules of Thumb in Expectations

Formation and Stability of Growth Dynamics. In *Sato, R. and Negishi, T., eds.*, 1989, pp. 3–29.

_____ **and Kanaya, Sadao.** Utility Functionals with Nonpaternalistic Intergenerational Altruism. *J. Econ. Theory*, December 1989, *49*(2), pp. 241–65.

_____ **and Tsukui, Jinkichi.** Rolling Plans and the Turnpike in a Dynamic Input–Output System: A Simulation Study. *J. Policy Modeling*, Spring 1989, *11*(1), pp. 91–109.

Horioka, Charles Yuji. Why Is Japan's Private Saving Rate So High? In *Sato, R. and Negishi, T., eds.*, 1989, pp. 145–78.

Horiuchi, Toshihiro. Development Process of Robot Industries in Japan. *Rivista Int. Sci. Econ. Com.*, December 1989, *36*(12), pp. 1089–1108.

Horlick, Gary N. The United States Antidumping System. In *Jackson, J. H. and Vermulst, E. A., eds.*, 1989, pp. 99–166.

_____ **and Oliver, Geoffrey D.** Antidumping and Countervailing Duty Law Provisions of the Omnibus Trade and Competitiveness Act of 1988. *J. World Trade*, June 1989, *23*(3), pp. 5–49.

Hormats, Robert D. Redefining Europe and the Atlantic Link. *Foreign Aff.*, Fall 1989, *68*(4), pp. 71–91.

Horn, B. E. Some Aspects of International Concern in Regional Road Transport. In *Candemir, Y., ed.*, 1989, pp. 53–61.

Horn, Henrik and Ethier, Wilfred. A New Look at Economic Integration. In *Jacquemin, A. and Sapir, A., eds.*, 1989, *1984*, pp. 71–93.

Horn, Murray and Zeckhauser, Richard J. The Control and Performance of State-Owned Enterprises. In *MacAvoy, P. W., et al.*, 1989, pp. 7–57.

Horn, Robin; Jimenez, Emmanuel and Kugler, Bernardo. National In-Service Training Systems in Latin America: An Economic Evaluation of Colombia's SENA. *Econ. Devel. Cult. Change*, April 1989, *37*(3), pp. 595–610.

Hornbaker, Robert H.; Dixon, Bruce L. and Sonka, Steven T. Estimating Production Activity Costs for Multioutput Firms with a Random Coefficient Regression Model. *Amer. J. Agr. Econ.*, February 1989, *71*(1), pp. 167–77.

Hornbrook, M. C.; Bennett, M. D. and Greenlick, M. R. Adjusting the AAPCC for Selectivity and Selection Bias under Medicare Risk Contracts. In *Scheffler, R. M. and Rossiter, L. F., eds.*, 1989, pp. 111–49.

Horne, Jocelyn P.; Flood, Robert P. and Bhandari, Jagdeep S. Evolution of Exchange Rate Regimes. *Int. Monet. Fund Staff Pap.*, December 1989, *36*(4), pp. 810–35.

_____ **and Martin, Vance L.** Exchange Rate Indicators and Optimal Currency Baskets: A Macroeconomic Analysis with Application to Developing Countries. *Appl. Econ.*, September 1989, *21*(9), pp. 1137–52.

_____ **and Martin, Vance L.** Weighted Monetary Aggregates: An Empirical Study Using Australian Monetary Data, 1969–1987. *Australian*

Econ. Pap., December 1989, *28*(53), pp. 181–200.

Horner, Jim. The Role of Technology: An Institutionalist Debate. *J. Econ. Issues*, June 1989, *23*(2), pp. 579–86.

Hörngren, Lars; Viotti, Staffan and Englund, Peter. Discount Window Borrowing and Money Market Interest Rates. *Scand. J. Econ.*, 1989, *91*(3), pp. 517–33.

_____ **and Vredin, Anders.** Exchange Risk Premia in a Currency Basket System. *Weltwirtsch. Arch.*, 1989, *125*(2), pp. 310–25.

Hornsby, H. H. and Williams, C. G. Vocationalism in U.S. and U.K. High Schools. *Econ. Educ. Rev.*, 1989, *8*(1), pp. 37–47.

Hornung-Draus, Renate. Das Vermögen der privaten Haushalte in der Bundesrepublik Deutschland: Bestand, Entwicklung und Verteilung. (The Wealth of Private Households in the Federal Republic of Germany. With English summary.) *Jahr. Nationalökon. Statist.*, January 1989, *206*(1), pp. 18–47.

Horowitz, Harold, et al. Public Support for Art: Viewpoints Presented at the Ottawa Meetings. *J. Cult. Econ.*, December 1989, *13*(2), pp. 1–19.

Horowitz, Ira. The Short-run Policies of the Labor-Managed Uncertain-Export-Price Taker. *Econ. Anal. Workers' Manage.*, 1989, *23*(2), pp. 155–65.

Horowitz, Irving Louis. The Public Costs of Private Blessings. In *Samuels, W. J., ed. (I)*, 1989, pp. 97–104.

Horowitz, Joel L. The Asymptotic Efficiency of Semiparametric Estimators for Censored Linear Regression Models. In *Ullah, A., ed.*, 1989, *1988*, pp. 1–18.

_____ **and Neumann, George R.** Computational and Statistical Efficiency of Semiparametric GLS Estimators. *Econometric Rev.*, 1989, *8*(2), pp. 223–25.

_____ **and Neumann, George R.** Specification Testing in Censored Regression Models: Parametric and Semiparametric Methods. *J. Appl. Econometrics*, Supplement, December 1989, *4*, pp. S61–86.

Horowitz, Stanley A.; Stahl, Joseph W. and Levine, Daniel B. The Effect of Technology on the Supportability and Cost of Avionics Equipment. In *Gulledge, T. R., Jr. and Litteral, L. A., eds.*, 1989, pp. 214–25.

Horrell, James F. and Cotner, John S. An Analysis of Index Option Pricing. *J. Futures Markets*, October 1989, *9*(5), pp. 449–59.

Horrigan, John and Briesemeister, Janee. Telecommunications Policy and Economic Development: Conclusion: Perspectives on the New State Role. In *Schmandt, J.; Williams, F. and Wilson, R. H., eds.*, 1989, pp. 267–83.

_____ **and Rudloff, Darren.** Telecommunications Policy and Economic Development: The New State Role: Illinois. In *Schmandt, J.; Williams, F. and Wilson, R. H., eds.*, 1989, pp. 63–82.

Horsewood, N.; Dimsdale, N. H. and Nickell, Stephen J. Real Wages and Unemployment in Britain during the 1930s. *Econ. J.*, June 1989, *99*(396), pp. 271–92.

Horstbøll, Henrik. Cosmology and Economics: Discontinuity and Continuity in Economic Conceptions on the Market for Popular Prints in Denmark during the Seventeenth and Eighteenth Centuries. *Scand. Econ. Hist. Rev.*, 1989, *37*(2), pp. 26–50.

Horstmann, Ignatius J. and Markusen, James R. Firm-Specific Assets and the Gains from Direct Foreign Investment. *Economica*, February 1989, *56*(221), pp. 41–48.

Horton, Susan and McLaren, John. Supply Constraints in the Tanzanian Economy: Simulation Results from a Macroeconometric Model. *J. Policy Modeling*, Summer 1989, *11*(2), pp. 297–313.

Horvat, Branko. Contemporary Socialist Systems and the Trends in Systemic Reforms Worldwide. In *Gomulka, S.; Ha, Y.-C. and Kim, C.-O., eds.*, 1989, pp. 234–42.

_____. The Pure Labour Theory of Prices and Interest: Basic Principles. *Europ. Econ. Rev.*, July 1989, *33*(6), pp. 1183–1203.

_____. What Is a Socialist Market Economy? *Acta Oecon.*, 1989, *40*(3–4), pp. 233–35.

Horvitz, Daniel G. and Corder, Larry S. Panel Effects in the National Medical Care Utilization and Expenditure Survey. In *Kasprzyk, D., et al., eds.*, 1989, pp. 304–18.

Horvitz, Paul M. The FSLIC Crisis and the Southwest Plan. *Amer. Econ. Rev.*, May 1989, *79*(2), pp. 146–50.

Horwich, George. The Catholic Bishops' Pastoral Draft Statement on American Agriculture: Response. In *Horwich, G. and Lynch, G. J., eds.*, 1989, pp. 274–78.

Horwitz, Abraham. Economics and Health: Beyond Financing: Commentary. In *WHO, Pan American Health Organization*, 1989, pp. 158–66.

Hosek, James R.; Peterson, Christine E. and Antel, John. Military Enlistment and Attrition: An Analysis of Decision Reversal. In *Ehrenberg, R. G., ed.*, 1989, pp. 207–63.

Hosier, Richard H. The Economics of Smallholder Agroforestry: Two Case Studies. *World Devel.*, November 1989, *17*(11), pp. 1827–39.

Hosios, Arthur J. and Peters, Michael. Repeated Insurance Contracts with Adverse Selection and Limited Commitment. *Quart. J. Econ.*, May 1989, *104*(2), pp. 229–53.

Hoskins, W. Lee. NABE Presidential Address: Property Rights in a Global Economy. *Bus. Econ.*, January 1989, *24*(1), pp. 13–19.

Hoskisson, Robert E., et al. Balancing Corporate Strategy and Executive Compensation: Agency Theory and Corporate Governance. In *Ferris, G. R. and Rowland, K. M., eds.*, 1989, pp. 25–57.

Hoskyns, John [Sir]. 1992 and the Brussels Machine. In *Dahrendorf, R., et al.*, 1989, pp. 11–21.

Hosoda, Eiji. Competitive Equilibrium and the Wage–Profit Frontier. *Manchester Sch. Econ.*

Soc. Stud., September 1989, *57*(3), pp. 262–79.

Hossain, Md. Akhtar. A Monetary Model of Inflation for Bangladesh, 1974–1985. *Pakistan Devel. Rev.*, Summer 1989, *28*(2), pp. 133–55.

Hossain, Najmul and Jamal, A. M. M. The Earnings of Industrial Labour in an LDC: The Evidence from Bangladesh. *Bangladesh Devel. Stud.*, December 1989, *17*(4), pp. 71–81.

Hossain, Sakhawat and Davis, Herbert J. Some Thoughts on International Personnel Management as an Emerging Field. In *Nedd, A., ed.*, 1989, pp. 121–36.

Hossain, Shaikh I. Effect of Public Programs on Family Size, Child Education and Health. *J. Devel. Econ.*, January 1989, *30*(1), pp. 145–58.

Hotchkiss, Lawrence and Farkas, George. Incentives and Disincentives for Subject Matter Difficulty and Student Effort: Course Grade Determinants across the Stratification System. *Econ. Educ. Rev.*, 1989, *8*(2), pp. 121–32.

_____; **Stromsdorfer, Ernest W. and Farkas, George.** Vocational Training, Supply Constraints, and Individual Economic Outcomes. *Econ. Educ. Rev.*, 1989, *8*(1), pp. 17–30.

Hotz-Hart, Beat. Innovating Behaviour of Swiss Industry—Findings and Policy Conclusions. In *Andersson, Å. E.; Batten, D. F. and Karlsson, C., eds.*, 1989, pp. 187–96.

Hotz, V. Joseph and Heckman, James J. Choosing among Alternative Nonexperimental Methods for Estimating the Impact of Social Programs: The Case of Manpower Training. *J. Amer. Statist. Assoc.*, December 1989, *84*(408), pp. 862–74.

_____ and **Heckman, James J.** Choosing among Alternative Nonexperimental Methods for Estimating the Impact of Social Programs: The Case of Manpower Training: Rejoinder. *J. Amer. Statist. Assoc.*, December 1989, *84*(408), pp. 878–80.

Houben, Vincent J. H. Economic Policy in the Principalities of Central Java in the Nineteenth Century. In *Maddison, A. and Prince, G., eds.*, 1989, pp. 185–202.

Houck, James P. If Economists Priced Their Own Books: One Author's View. *Quart. Rev. Econ. Bus.*, Autumn 1989, *29*(3), pp. 111–20.

Houff, James N. and Wiatrowski, William J. Analyzing Short-term Disability Benefits. *Mon. Lab. Rev.*, June 1989, *112*(6), pp. 3–9.

Hough, George C., Jr. and Land, Kenneth C. New Methods for Tables of School Life, with Applications to U.S. Data from Recent School Years. *J. Amer. Statist. Assoc.*, March 1989, *84*(405), pp. 63–75.

Hough, Jerry F. The Politics of Successful Economic Reform. *Soviet Econ.*, Jan.–March 1989, *5*(1), pp. 3–46.

Hougland, James G., Jr.; Clayton, Richard R. and Johnson, Timothy P. Obtaining Reports of Sensitive Behavior: A Comparison of Substance Use Reports from Telephone and Face-to-Face Interviews. *Soc. Sci. Quart.*, March 1989, *70*(1), pp. 174–83.

Houpt, James V. and Martinson, Michael G.

Transfer Risk in U.S. Banks. *Fed. Res. Bull.*, April 1989, 75(4), pp. 255–58.

Hourcade, Jean-Charles and Colombier, Michel. Développement des réseaux et modulations spatio-temporelles des tarifs: L'équité territoriale revisitée. (Development of Electrical Grids and Spatio-Temporal Modulations of Tariffs: Territorial Equity Revisited. With English summary.) *Revue Écon.*, July 1989, 40(4), pp. 649–77.

Houseman, Susan N. and Abraham, Katharine G. Job Security and Work Force Adjustment: How Different Are U.S. and Japanese Practices? *J. Japanese Int. Economies*, December 1989, 3(4), pp. 500–521.

Houston, Arthur L., Jr. and Giliberto, S. Michael. Relocation Opportunities and Mortgage Default. *Amer. Real Estate Urban Econ. Assoc. J.*, Spring 1989, 17(1), pp. 55–69.

Houston, David B. Roemer on Exploitation and Class: Review Article. *Rev. Radical Polit. Econ.*, 1989, 21(1–2), pp. 175–87.

———— **and Giarratani, Frank.** Structural Change and Economic Policy in a Declining Metropolitan Region: Implications of the Pittsburgh Experience. *Urban Stud.*, December 1989, 26(6), pp. 549–58.

Houston, Jack E.; Jeong, Kihong and Fletcher, Stanley M. Varietal Sales and Quality Differentiation: The Case of Certified Soybean Seed in the Southeastern U.S. *Southern J. Agr. Econ.*, July 1989, 21(1), pp. 113–20.

————, **et al.** Factors Affecting Local Prices of Shrimp Landings. *Marine Resource Econ.*, 1989, 6(2), pp. 163–72.

van Houwelingen, Jeannet H. and van Raaij, W. Fred. The Effect of Goal-Setting and Daily Electronic Feedback on In-home Energy Use. *J. Cons. Res.*, June 1989, 16(1), pp. 98–105.

Hovenkamp, Herbert. Antitrust's Protected Classes. *Mich. Law Rev.*, October 1989, 88(1), pp. 1–48.

Howard, David H. Implications of the U.S. Current Account Deficit. *J. Econ. Perspectives*, Fall 1989, 3(4), pp. 153–65.

Howard, Jeffrey H. and Kaserman, David L. Proof of Damages in Construction Industry Bid-Rigging Cases. *Antitrust Bull.*, Summer 1989, 34(2), pp. 359–93.

Howard, Lee Milton. The Evolution of Bilateral and Multilateral Cooperation for Health in Developing Countries. **In** *Reich, M. R. and Marui, E., eds.*, 1989, pp. 332–57.

Howard, M. C. and King, J. E. The Rational Choice Marxism of John Roemer: A Critique. *Rev. Soc. Econ.*, Winter 1989, 47(4), pp. 392–414.

Howard, Marcia A. State Tax and Expenditure Limitations: There Is No Story. *Public Budg. Finance*, Summer 1989, 9(2), pp. 83–90.

Howard, Maurice. Transport and Communications. **In** *Goodman, D. S. G., ed.*, 1989, pp. 77–93.

Howard, Michael. Public Sector Financing in Jamaica, Barbados, and Trinidad and Tobago

1974–1984. *Soc. Econ. Stud.*, September 1989, 38(3), pp. 119–48.

Howard, Wayne H. What Our Students Should Know: Perspectives from Business and Academia. *Can. J. Agr. Econ.*, July 1989, 37(2), pp. 303–17.

———— **and McEwan, Kenneth A.** Human Resource Management: A Review with Applications to Agriculture. *Can. J. Agr. Econ.*, Part 1, December 1989, 37(4), pp. 733–42.

———— **and Shumway, C. Richard.** Technical Change and Applications of Dynamic Duality to Agriculture: Reply. *Amer. J. Agr. Econ.*, August 1989, 71(3), pp. 805.

Howarth, Richard B. Energy Use in U.S. Manufacturing: The Impacts of the Energy Shocks on Sectoral Output, Industry Structure, and Energy Intensity. *J. Energy Devel.*, Spring 1989, 14(2), pp. 175–91.

Howe, Eric C. and Coughlin, Peter J. Policies over Time and Pareto Optimality. *Soc. Choice Welfare*, October 1989, 6(4), pp. 259–73.

———— **and Stabler, Jack C.** Canada Divided: The Optimal Division of an Economy into Regions. *J. Reg. Sci.*, May 1989, 29(2), pp. 191–211.

Howe, Vince and Cather, David A. Conflict and Channel Management in Property-Liability Distribution Systems. *J. Risk Ins.*, September 1989, 56(3), pp. 535–43.

Howe, Wayne J. and Parks, William, II. Labor Market Completes Sixth Year of Expansion in 1988. *Mon. Lab. Rev.*, February 1989, 112(2), pp. 3–14.

Howell, Craig; Clem, Andrew G. and Mosimann, Thomas J. Price Highlights of 1988: Rising Pressures on Consumer Prices. *Mon. Lab. Rev.*, May 1989, 112(5), pp. 3–10.

Howell, David R. Production Technology and the Interindustry Wage Structure. *Ind. Relat.*, Winter 1989, 28(1), pp. 32–50.

———— **and Wolff, Edward N.** Labor Quality and Productivity Growth in the United States: An Input–Output Growth-Accounting Framework. **In** *Miller, R. E.; Polenske, K. R. and Rose, A. Z., eds.*, 1989, pp. 148–62.

Howell, Roger, Jr. Resistance to Change: The Political Elites of Provincial Towns during the English Revolution. **In** *[Stone, L.]*, 1989, pp. 433–55.

Howells, Jeremy R. Research and Development, Corporate Organisation and Industrial Location: Prospects for Regional Development. **In** *Andersson, Å. E.; Batten, D. F. and Karlsson, C., eds.*, 1989, pp. 81–99.

———— **and Charles, D. R.** Research and Technological Development and Regional Policy: A European Perspective. **In** *Gibbs, D., ed.*, 1989, pp. 23–54.

Howells, John M. and Bairam, Erkin I. Strike Incidence in New Zealand: A New Econometric Approach. *Australian Econ. Pap.*, June 1989, 28(52), pp. 93–102.

Howenstine, Ned G. U.S. Affiliates of Foreign Companies: 1987 Benchmark Survey Results. *Surv. Curr. Bus.*, July 1989, 69(7), pp. 116–39.

Howitt, Peter and Gaudet, Gérard. A Note on Uncertainty and the Hotelling Rule. *J. Environ. Econ. Manage.*, January 1989, *16*(1), pp. 80–86.

⸺ **and Sinn, Hans-Werner.** Gradual Reforms of Capital Income Taxation. *Amer. Econ. Rev.*, March 1989, *79*(1), pp. 106–24.

Howson, Susan. Cheap Money versus Cheaper Money: A Reply. *Econ. Hist. Rev., 2nd Ser.*, August 1989, *42*(3), pp. 401–05.

Hoy, Michael. The Value of Screening Mechanisms under Alternative Insurance Possibilities. *J. Public Econ.*, July 1989, *39*(2), pp. 177–206.

Hoyer, Wayne D. and Jacoby, Jacob. The Comprehension/Miscomprehension of Print Communication: Selected Findings. *J. Cons. Res.*, March 1989, *15*(4), pp. 434–43.

Hoyt, Robert E. Use of Financial Futures by Life Insurers. *J. Risk Ins.*, December 1989, *56*(4), pp. 740–48.

Hoyt, William H. and Black, Dan A. Bidding for Firms. *Amer. Econ. Rev.*, December 1989, *79*(5), pp. 1249–56.

⸺ **and Smolensky, Eugene.** The Distributed Effects of Revenue Structures. In *Chiancone, A. and Messere, K.*, eds., 1989, pp. 215–30.

⸺ **and Toma, Eugenia Froedge.** State Mandates and Interest Group Lobbying. *J. Public Econ.*, March 1989, *38*(2), pp. 199–213.

Hrezo, Margaret S. and Hrezo, William E. Judicial Regulation of the Environment under Posner's Economic Model of the Law. In *Tool, M. R. and Samuels, W. J.*, eds. (III), 1989, 1984, pp. 199–219.

Hrezo, William E. and Hrezo, Margaret S. Judicial Regulation of the Environment under Posner's Economic Model of the Law. In *Tool, M. R. and Samuels, W. J.*, eds. (III), 1989, 1984, pp. 199–219.

Hrnčíř, Miroslav. From Traditional to Reformed Planned Economy: The Case of Czechoslovakia. *Czech. Econ. Pap.*, 1989, (27), pp. 25–45.

⸺**; Seják, Josef and Klusoň, Václav.** The Directions of Development of Intensive Type Economic Mechanism. *Czech. Econ. Pap.*, 1989, (26), pp. 31–49.

Hrnčířová, M. and Rusmich, Ladislav. Disputes around Economic Prognoses. *Czech. Econ. Digest.*, August 1989, (5), pp. 3–19.

Hsiao, Cheng. Consistent Estimation for Some Nonlinear Errors-in-Variables Models. *J. Econometrics*, May 1989, *41*(1), pp. 159–85.

⸺ **and Mountain, Dean C.** A Combined Structural and Flexible Functional Approach for Modeling Energy Substitution. *J. Amer. Statist. Assoc.*, March 1989, *84*(405), pp. 76–87.

⸺ **and Mountain, Dean C.** Some Remarks on the Identification and Estimation of Translog Models. In *Mariano, R. S.; Lim, K. S. and Ling, K. D.*, eds., 1989, pp. 123–57.

⸺**, et al.** Modeling Ontario Regional Electricity System Demand Using a Mixed Fixed and Random Coefficients Approach. *Reg. Sci.*

Urban Econ., December 1989, *19*(4), pp. 565–87.

Hsiao, Frank S. T. and Hsiao, Mei-chu W. Japanese Experience of Industrialization and Economic Performance of Korea and Taiwan: Tests of Similarity. In *Lee, C. F. and Hu, S.-C.*, eds., 1989, pp. 157–90.

Hsiao, Mei-chu W. and Hsiao, Frank S. T. Japanese Experience of Industrialization and Economic Performance of Korea and Taiwan: Tests of Similarity. In *Lee, C. F. and Hu, S.-C.*, eds., 1989, pp. 157–90.

Hsieh, Chang-tseh and Stephens, Mark A. A Simultaneous-Equations Model for Examining Taiwan–U.S. Trade Relations. In *Lee, C. F. and Hu, S.-C.*, eds., 1989, pp. 139–55.

Hsieh, David A. Modeling Heteroscedasticity in Daily Foreign-Exchange Rates. *J. Bus. Econ. Statist.*, July 1989, *7*(3), pp. 307–17.

⸺. Testing for Nonlinear Dependence in Daily Foreign Exchange Rates. *J. Bus.*, July 1989, *62*(3), pp. 339–68.

Hsing, Yu. Money Is Relevant: A Study of 20 OECD Countries. *Atlantic Econ. J.*, September 1989, *17*(3), pp. 86.

⸺. On the Relationship between Inflation and Unemployment: New Evidence from Six Industrialized Nations. *J. Post Keynesian Econ.*, Fall 1989, *12*(1), pp. 98–108.

⸺. On the Variable Money Demand Elasticity: The Case of Taiwan. *Int. Econ. J.*, Autumn 1989, *3*(3), pp. 43–52.

⸺. Testing for the Flexible Employment Elasticity Hypothesis: Application of an Expanded Box–Cox Model to U.S. Manufacturing. *Quart. Rev. Econ. Bus.*, Summer 1989, *29*(2), pp. 96–107.

⸺. Testing for the Functional Form of Labor-Demand Equations: The Textile Industry. *J. Econ. Bus.*, November 1989, *41*(4), pp. 355–64.

Hsiung, Bingyuang and Putterman, Louis. Pre- and Post-reform Income Distribution in a Chinese Commune: The Case of Dahe Township in Hebei Province. *J. Compar. Econ.*, September 1989, *13*(3), pp. 406–45.

Hsu, Chen-Min. Trade, Inventories, and Forward Exchange under Exchange Rate and Demand Uncertainty. *J. Econ. (Z. Nationalökon.)*, 1989, *50*(2), pp. 113–27.

Hsu, George J. Y. Energy Multipliers for Economic Analysis: An Input–Output Approach. *Energy Econ.*, January 1989, *11*(1), pp. 33–38.

Hsu, John S. J.; Tsui, Kam-Wah and Leonard, Tom. Bayesian Marginal Inference. *J. Amer. Statist. Assoc.*, December 1989, *84*(408), pp. 1051–58.

Hsueh, L. Paul and Chandy, P. R. An Examination of the Yield Spread between Insured and Uninsured Debt. *J. Finan. Res.*, Fall 1989, *12*(3), pp. 235–44.

Hu, Sheng Cheng. Uncertain Lifetime, the Annuity Market, and Estate Taxation. *J. Public Econ.*, November 1989, *40*(2), pp. 217–35.

⸺ **and Lee, Cheng Few.** Advances in Financial Planning and Forecasting: Introduction. In

Lee, C. F. and Hu, S.-C., eds., 1989, pp. 1–7.

Hu, Teh-wei; Huang, Lien-Fu and Carwright, William S. Demand for Medigap Insurance by the Elderly: A Micro-simulation Analysis. *Appl. Econ.,* October 1989, *21*(10), pp. 1325–39.

———— **and Jerrell, Jeanette M.** Cost-Effectiveness of Intensive Clinical and Case Management Compared with an Existing System of Care. *Inquiry,* Summer 1989, *26*(2), pp. 224–34.

Hu, Zhongda. The Asiatic Mode of Production and the Theory of Five Modes of Production. In *Brook, T., ed.,* 1989, pp. 164–75.

Hua, Chang-i. Linking a Housing Vacancy Chain Model and a Behavioral Choice Model for Improved Housing Policy Evaluation. *Ann. Reg. Sci.,* 1989, *23*(3), pp. 203–11.

Hua, Sheng. Privatisation in China. In *Ramanadham, V. V., ed.,* 1989, pp. 250–67.

————, **et al.** On a Path toward Price Reform with a Characteristic Peculiar to China. *Chinese Econ. Stud.,* Spring 1989, *22*(3), pp. 34–49.

————. Restructuring the Microeconomic Base. *Chinese Econ. Stud.,* Winter 1988–89, *22*(2), pp. 47–66.

Huan, Guocang. China's Open-Door Policy: Development, Problems, and Prospects. In *Cerami, C. A., ed.,* 1989, pp. 153–68.

————. China's Open Door Policy, 1978–1988. In *Van Ness, P., ed.,* 1989, pp. 281–300.

Huang, Chi and Hoole, Francis W. The Global Conflict Process. *J. Conflict Resolution,* March 1989, *33*(1), pp. 142–63.

Huang, Chi-fu and Cox, John C. Optimal Consumption and Portfolio Policies When Asset Prices Follow a Diffusion Process. *J. Econ. Theory,* October 1989, *49*(1), pp. 33–83.

Huang, Junting and Lu, Shiguang. The Role of China's Import Trade during the First Five-Year Plan. In *Howe, C. and Walker, K. R., eds.,* 1989, *1957,* pp. 52–62.

Huang, Kuo S. A Forecasting Model for Food and Other Expenditures. *Appl. Econ.,* September 1989, *21*(9), pp. 1235–46.

———— **and Haidacher, Richard C.** An Assessment of Price and Income Effects on Changes in Meat Consumption. In *Buse, R. C., ed.,* 1989, pp. 139–56.

Huang, Lien-Fu; Carwright, William S. and Hu, Teh-wei. Demand for Medigap Insurance by the Elderly: A Micro-simulation Analysis. *Appl. Econ.,* October 1989, *21*(10), pp. 1325–39.

Huang, Peter H. Upper Semi-continuity of the Separating Equilibrium Correspondence. *J. Econ. Theory,* April 1989, *47*(2), pp. 406–12.

Huang, Roger D. An Analysis of Intertemporal Pricing for Forward Foreign Exchange Contracts. *J. Finance,* March 1989, *44*(1), pp. 183–94.

Huang, Shu-De; Zhang, Dazhi and Yu, Po-Lung. Decision Rationality and Habitual Domain

Analysis. In *Lockett, A. G. and Islei, G., eds.,* 1989, pp. 24–33.

Huang, Wei-Chiao. Organized Labor at the Crossroads: Introduction. In *Huang, W.-C., ed.,* 1989, pp. 1–11.

Huang, Wen-Yuan; Hertel, Thomas W. and Preckel, Paul V. The CARD Linear Programming Model of U.S. Agriculture. *J. Agr. Econ. Res.,* Spring 1989, *41*(2), pp. 20–23.

Huang, Youguang and Yang, Xiaokai. Why Should China Implement the Policy of Converting Enterprises to Management by the People in One Single Leap "Across the River"? A Discussion of the Reform of the Ownership System. *Chinese Econ. Stud.,* Fall 1989, *23*(1), pp. 64–81.

Hubbard, R. Glenn and Calomiris, Charles W. Price Flexibility, Credit Availability, and Economic Fluctuations: Evidence from the United States, 1894–1909. *Quart. J. Econ.,* August 1989, *104*(3), pp. 429–52.

———— **and Weiner, Robert J.** Contracting and Price Adjustment in Commodity Markets: Evidence from Copper and Oil. *Rev. Econ. Statist.,* February 1989, *71*(1), pp. 80–89.

Huber, Alan M.; Boskin, Michael J. and Robinson, Marc S. Government Saving, Capital Formation, and Wealth in the United States, 1947–85. In *Lipsey, R. E. and Tice, H. S., eds.,* 1989, pp. 287–353.

Huberman, Gur and Kandel, Shmuel. Firms' Fiscal Years, Size and Industry. *Econ. Letters,* 1989, *29*(1), pp. 69–75.

Hübler, Olaf. Individual Overtime Functions with Double Correction for Selectivity Bias. *Econ. Letters,* 1989, *29*(1), pp. 87–90.

————. Optimal Number of Job Changes. *Z. Wirtschaft. Sozialwissen.,* 1989, *109*(1), pp. 75–92.

Huby, Meg and Bradshaw, Jonathan. Trends in Dependence on Supplementary Benefit. In *Dilnot, A. and Walker, I., eds.,* 1989, pp. 69–87.

Huckins, Larry E. Capital Labor Substitution in Municipal Government. *Public Finance Quart.,* October 1989, *17*(4), pp. 357–74.

Hudec, Robert E. The Structure of South–South Trade Preferences in the 1988 GSTP Agreement: Learning to Say MFMFN. In *Whalley, J., ed., Vol. 1,* 1989, pp. 210–37.

Hudson, John. The Birth and Death of Firms. *Quart. Rev. Econ. Bus.,* Summer 1989, *29*(2), pp. 68–86.

————. The Economics of the National Trust: A Demand Curve for a History Club. *Scot. J. Polit. Econ.,* February 1989, *36*(1), pp. 19–35.

————. Nobel Laureates in Economic Sciences: A Biographical Dictionary: James Meade: 1977. In *Katz, B. S., ed.,* 1989, pp. 187–203.

————. Perceptions of Inflation. In *Grunert, K. G. and Ölander, F., eds.,* 1989, pp. 77–91.

———— **and Lark, Richard.** A Polychotomous Probit Measure and Analysis of Inflationary Expectations. *J. Macroecon.,* Spring 1989, *11*(2), pp. 269–80.

Hudson, Michael A.; Ward, Clement E. and

Kahl, Kandice H. Cash Settlement Issues for Live Cattle Futures Contracts. *J. Futures Markets,* June 1989, *9*(3), pp. 237–48.

Hudson, Pat. Capital and Credit in the West Riding Wool Textile Industry c. 1750–1850. **In** *Hudson, P., ed.,* 1989, pp. 69–99.

_____. The Regional Perspective. **In** *Hudson, P., ed.,* 1989, pp. 5–38.

Hudson, Ray. Rewriting History and Reshaping Geography: The Nationalised Industries and the Political Economy of Thatcherism. **In** *Mohan, J., ed.,* 1989, pp. 113–29.

Huefner, R. J.; Lotfi, V. and Gardner, J. C. An Interactive Multi-criteria Model for Audit Workload Planning. **In** *Lockett, A. G. and Islei, G., eds.,* 1989, pp. 234–43.

Huet, Josiane and Amenc, Noël. Innovations financières et comportements stratégiques des entreprises: L'émergence d'und stratégie financière pure. (Financial Innovations and Strategic Behavior in Companies: The Emergence of a Pure Financial Strategy. With English summary.) *Écon. Societes,* January 1989, *23*(1), pp. 7–27.

Hufbauer, Gary Clyde. Protectionist Rules and Internationalist Discretion in the Making of National Trade Policy: Comments. **In** *Vosgerau, H.-J., ed.,* 1989, pp. 324–29.

_____. The State, the Individual, and the Taxation of Economic Migration. **In** *Bhagwati, J. N. and Wilson, J. D., eds.,* 1989, pp. 83–94.

Huff, David L. and Lutz, James M. Urban Spheres of Influence in Ghana. *J. Developing Areas,* January 1989, *23*(2), pp. 201–20.

Huff, H. Bruce and Moreddu, Catherine. The Ministerial Trade Mandate Model. *OECD Econ. Stud.,* Winter 1989–1990, (13), pp. 45–67.

Huff, W. G. Bookkeeping Barter, Money, Credit, and Singapore's International Rice Trade, 1870–1939. *Exploration Econ. Hist.,* April 1989, *26*(2), pp. 161–89.

Huffaker, Ray G. and Wilen, James E. Dynamics of Optimal Stocking in Plant/Herbivore Systems. *Natural Res. Modeling,* Fall 1989, *3*(4), pp. 553–75.

_____; **Wilen, James E. and Gardner, B. Delworth.** Multiple Use Benefits on Public Rangelands: An Incentive-Based Fee System. *Amer. J. Agr. Econ.,* August 1989, *71*(3), pp. 670–78.

Huffman, Stephen P. The Impact of the Degrees of Operating and Financial Leverage on the Systematic Risk of Common Stocks: Another Look. *Quart. J. Bus. Econ.,* Winter 1989, *28*(1), pp. 83–100.

Huffman, Wallace E. and Evenson, Robert E. Supply and Demand Functions for Multiproduct U.S. Cash Grain Farms: Biases Caused by Research and Other Policies. *Amer. J. Agr. Econ.,* August 1989, *71*(3), pp. 761–73.

_____ **and Lange, Mark D.** Off-Farm Work Decisions of Husbands and Wives: Joint Decision Making. *Rev. Econ. Statist.,* August 1989, *71*(3), pp. 471–80.

_____ **and McNulty, Mark S.** The Sample Spectrum of Time Series with Trading Day Variation. *Econ. Letters,* December 1989, *31*(4), pp. 367–70.

Hufton, Olwen. Bread, Tax and Politics at the End of the Old Regime. **In** *Berg, M., et al.,* 1989, pp. 11–25.

Hughes, Alan. The Impact of Merger: A Survey of Empirical Evidence for the UK. **In** *Fairburn, J. and Kay, J., eds.,* 1989, pp. 30–98.

_____. Small Firms' Merger Activity and Competition Policy. **In** *Barber, J.; Metcalfe, J. S. and Porteous, M., eds.,* 1989, pp. 128–72.

Hughes, Donald A. The Relationship between Distribution and Market Share: Commentary. *Marketing Sci.,* Spring 1989, *8*(2), pp. 128–29.

Hughes, Gordon. The Switch from Domestic Rates to the Community Charge in Scotland. *Fisc. Stud.,* August 1989, *10*(3), pp. 1–12.

_____ **and McCormick, Barry.** Does Migration Reduce Differentials in Regional Unemployment Rates? **In** *van Dijk, J., et al., eds.,* 1989, pp. 85–108.

_____ **and Vines, David.** Regulation and Strategic Behaviour in Commercial Television. **In** *Hughes, G. and Vines, D., eds.,* 1989, pp. 38–90.

Hughes Hallett, Andrew J. Econometrics and the Theory of Economic Policy: The Tinbergen–Theil Contributions 40 Years On. *Oxford Econ. Pap.,* January 1989, *41*(1), pp. 189–214.

_____. Econometrics and the Theory of Economic Policy: The Tinbergen–Theil Contributions 40 Years On. **In** *de Marchi, N. and Gilbert, C., eds.,* 1989, pp. 189–214.

_____. Macroeconomic Interdependence and the Coordination of Economic Policy. **In** *Greenaway, D., ed.,* 1989, pp. 182–213.

_____. What Are the Risks in Co-ordinating Economic Policies Internationally? **In** *MacDonald, R. and Taylor, M. P., eds.,* 1989, pp. 307–41.

_____ **and Brandsma, Andries S.** The Design of Interdependent Policies with Incomplete Information: A New Argument for Coordinating Economic Policies. *Econ. Modelling,* October 1989, *6*(4), pp. 432–46.

_____; **Currie, David A. and Holtham, Gerald.** The Theory and Practice of International Policy Coordination: Does Coordination Pay? **In** *Bryant, R. C., et al., eds.,* 1989, pp. 14–46.

_____; **Holtham, Gerald and Hutson, Gary.** Exchange-Rate Targetting as Surrogate International Cooperation. **In** *Miller, M.; Eichengreen, B. and Portes, R., eds.,* 1989, pp. 239–78.

Hughes, Helen. Toward Clarity and Common Sense. **In** *Naya, S., et al., eds.,* 1989, pp. 259–78.

Hughes, James W. The Effect of Medical Malpractice Reform Laws on Claim Disposition. *Int. Rev. Law Econ.,* June 1989, *9*(1), pp. 57–78.

_____ **and Snyder, Edward A.** Evaluating Medical Malpractice Reforms. *Contemp. Policy Issues,* April 1989, *7*(2), pp. 83–98.

_____ **and Snyder, Edward A.** Policy Analysis

of Medical Malpractice Reforms: What Can We Learn from Claims Data? *J. Bus. Econ. Statist.*, October 1989, 7(4), pp. 423–31.

Hughes, John S. and Amershi, Amin H. Multiple Signals, Statistical Sufficiency, and Pareto Orderings of Best Agency Contracts. *Rand J. Econ.*, Spring 1989, 20(1), pp. 102–12.

Hughes, Jonathan. Variations on a Theme: Longterm Growth of Government. *J. Finan. Services Res.*, September 1989, 2(3), pp. 153–65.

Hughes, Kirsty S. The Changing Dynamics of International Technological Competition. In *Audretsch, D. B.; Sleuwaegen, L. and Yamawaki, H., eds.*, 1989, pp. 269–93.

Hughes, Mark Alan. Concentrated Deviance and the "Underclass" Hypothesis. *J. Policy Anal. Manage.*, Spring 1989, 8(2), pp. 274–81.

———. Misspeaking Truth to Power: A Geographical Perspective on the "Underclass" Fallacy. *Econ. Geogr.*, July 1989, 65(3), pp. 187–207.

Hughey, A. M. Uncertainty and the Joint Extraction of Helium and Natural Gas. *Resources & Energy*, March 1989, 11(1), pp. 65–79.

Hugo, G. J. Regional Implications of Recent Demographic Changes in Australia. In *Gibson, L. J. and Stimson, R. J., eds.*, 1989, pp. 7–31.

Huhne, Christopher. Some Lessons of the Debt Crisis: Never Again? In *[Marjolin, R.]*, 1989, pp. 85–101.

Huigen, René; Van de Stadt, Huib and Zeelenberg, Kees. Socio-Economic Accounts for the Netherlands. *Rev. Income Wealth*, September 1989, 35(3), pp. 317–34.

Huiskamp, Rien J. Large Corporations, Industry Bargaining Structures and National Industrial Relations: A Comparative and Organizational Approach. In *Barbash, J. and Barbash, K., eds.*, 1989, pp. 22–42.

Huizinga, Harry. The Commercial Bank Claims on Developing Countries: How Have Banks Been Affected? In *Husain, I. and Diwan, I., eds.*, 1989, pp. 129–43.

Hujer, Reinhard and Schneider, Hilmar. The Analysis of Labor Market Mobility Using Panel Data. *Europ. Econ. Rev.*, March 1989, 33(2/3), pp. 530–36.

Hula, David G. Intangible Capital, Market Share and Corporate Strategy. *Appl. Econ.*, November 1989, 21(11), pp. 1535–47.

———. Macroeconomic Policy and the Pricing Behavior of Imperfectly Competitive Firms. *Managerial Dec. Econ.*, June 1989, 10(2), pp. 121–25.

Hulbert, Mark. The Debtor Economy. In *Guttmann, R., ed.*, 1989, 1980, pp. 81–86.

Hull, Brooks B. and Bold, Frederick. Towards an Economic Theory of the Church. *Int. J. Soc. Econ.*, 1989, 16(7), pp. 5–15.

Hull, John. Assessing Credit Risk in a Financial Institution's Off-Balance Sheet Commitments. *J. Finan. Quant. Anal.*, December 1989, 24(4), pp. 489–501.

Hulten, Charles R.; Robertson, James W. and Wykoff, Frank C. Energy, Obsolescence, and

the Productivity Slowdown. In *Jorgenson, D. W. and Landau, R., eds.*, 1989, pp. 225–58.

Hultén, Staffan. Theories of Industrial Change and Markets as Networks. In *Hallén, L. and Johanson, J., eds.*, 1989, pp. 181–91.

Hultman, Charles W. and McGee, L. Randolph. Factors Affecting the Foreign Banking Presence in the U.S. *J. Banking Finance*, July 1989, 13(3), pp. 383–96.

Humaidi, Mochtar and Bakir, Siti Zainab. Lampung: Spontaneous Transmigration. In *Hill, H., ed.*, 1989, pp. 349–62.

Humphrey, David B. Market Responses to Pricing Fedwire Daylight Overdrafts. *Fed. Res. Bank Richmond Econ. Rev.*, May–June 1989, 75(3), pp. 23–34.

Humphrey, Thomas M. Lender of Last Resort: The Concept in History. *Fed. Res. Bank Richmond Econ. Rev.*, March–April 1989, 75(2), pp. 8–16.

———. Precursors of the P-Star Model. *Fed. Res. Bank Richmond Econ. Rev.*, July–Aug. 1989, 75(4), pp. 3–9.

———. Unsettled Issues in the Case for Free Banking. *Cato J.*, Fall 1989, 9(2), pp. 461–65.

Humphreys, Charles and Jaeger, William. Africa's Adjustment and Growth. *Finance Devel.*, June 1989, 26(2), pp. 6–8.

——— **and Underwood, John.** The External Debt Difficulties of Low-Income Africa. In *Husain, I. and Diwan, I., eds.*, 1989, pp. 45–65.

Hundley, Greg. Things Unions Do, Job Attributes, and Union Membership. *Ind. Relat.*, Fall 1989, 28(3), pp. 335–55.

Hung, Juann; Pigott, Charles and Rodrigues, Anthony P. Financial Implications of the U.S. External Deficit. *Fed. Res. Bank New York Quart. Rev.*, Winter–Spring 1989, 13-14(4–1), pp. 33–51.

Hunsley, Terrance. Converting Exemptions and Deductions into Credits: An Economic Assessment: Comment: Tax Reform and Income Redistribution. In *Mintz, J. and Whalley, J., eds.*, 1989, pp. 74–78.

Hunt, David M. and Bolon, Donald S. A Review of Five Versions of Theory Z: Does Z Have a Future? In *Prasad, S. B., ed.*, 1989, pp. 201–20.

Hunt, E. K. The Meaning and Significance of the Transformation Problem: Two Contrasting Approaches. *Atlantic Econ. J.*, December 1989, 17(4), pp. 47–54.

Hunt, Gary L. and Greenwood, Michael J. Jobs versus Amenities in the Analysis of Metropolitan Migration. *J. Urban Econ.*, January 1989, 25(1), pp. 1–16.

Hunt, Herbert G., III and Enis, Charles R. Economic Analysis of Broad-Based Income and Consumption Taxes. In *Jones, S. M., ed.*, 1989, pp. 223–45.

——— **and Geiger, Marshall A.** Capital Gain Taxation: A Critical Analysis of Historical and Current Issues. In *Jones, S. M., ed.*, 1989, pp. 21–39.

Hunt, Lester and Manning, Neil. Energy Price- and Income-Elasticities of Demand: Some Estimates for the UK Using the Cointegration Procedure. *Scot. J. Polit. Econ.*, May 1989, *36*(2), pp. 183–93.

Hunt, Margaret. Time-Management, Writing, and Accounting in the Eighteenth-Century English Trading Family: A Bourgeois Enlightenment. In *Hausman, W. J., ed.*, 1989, pp. 150–59.

Hunt, Raymond G.; Lee, Wonsick and Meindl, James R. Individualism–Collectivism and Work Values: Data from the United States, China, Taiwan, Korea, and Hong Kong. In *Nedd, A., ed.*, 1989, pp. 59–77.

Hunter, Gregory S. The Manhattan Company: Managing a Multi-unit Corporation in New York, 1799–1842. In *Pencak, W. and Wright, C. E., eds.*, 1989, pp. 124–46.

Hunter, William Curt and Timme, Stephen G. Does Multiproduct Production in Large Banks Reduce Costs? *Fed. Res. Bank Atlanta Econ. Rev.*, May–June 1989, *74*(3), pp. 2–11.

_____ and **Wall, Larry D.** Bank Merger Motivations: A Review of the Evidence and an Examination of Key Target Bank Characteristics. *Fed. Res. Bank Atlanta Econ. Rev.*, Sept.–Oct. 1989, *74*(5), pp. 2–19.

Hunter, William J. and Nelson, Michael A. Interest Group Demand for Taxation. *Public Choice*, July 1989, *62*(1), pp. 41–61.

Huntington, Hillard G.; Sweeney, James L. and Hickman, Bert G. On Economic Policy Responses to Disruptions: Reply. *Energy J.*, October 1989, *10*(4), pp. 189–98.

Huntington, Samuel P. Modernization and Corruption. In *Heidenheimer, A. J.; Johnston, M. and LeVine, V. T., eds.*, 1989, *1968*, pp. 377–88.

Huppert, Daniel D. Measuring the Value of Fish to Anglers: Application to Central California Anadromous Species. *Marine Resource Econ.*, 1989, *6*(2), pp. 89–107.

_____ and **Cameron, Trudy Ann.** OLS versus ML Estimation of Non-market Resource Values with Payment Card Interval Data. *J. Environ. Econ. Manage.*, November 1989, *17*(3), pp. 230–46.

Hurd, Michael D. The Annuity Value of Social Security. In *Gustafsson, B. A. and Klevmarken, N. A., eds.*, 1989, pp. 67–82.

_____. The Joint Retirement Decision of Husbands and Wives. *Soc. Sec. Bull.*, January 1989, *52*(1), pp. 29–32.

_____. Mortality Risk and Bequests. *Econometrica*, July 1989, *57*(4), pp. 779–813.

_____. The Poverty of Widows: Future Prospects. In *Wise, D. A., ed.*, 1989, pp. 201–22.

_____ and **Mundaca, B. Gabriela.** The Importance of Gifts and Inheritances among the Affluent. In *Lipsey, R. E. and Tice, H. S., eds.*, 1989, pp. 737–58.

_____ and **Wise, David A.** The Wealth and Poverty of Widows: Assets before and after the Husband's Death. In *Wise, D. A., ed.*, 1989, pp. 177–99.

Hurd, Richard W. and Rouse, William. Progressive Union Organizing: The SEIU Justice for Janitors Campaign. *Rev. Radical Polit. Econ.*, Fall 1989, *21*(3), pp. 70–75.

Hurdle, Gloria J., et al. Concentration, Potential Entry, and Performance in the Airline Industry. *J. Ind. Econ.*, December 1989, *38*(2), pp. 119–39.

Hurdle, Sylvia and Pope, Gregory C. Physician Productivity: Trends and Determinants. *Inquiry*, Spring 1989, *26*(1), pp. 100–115.

Hurley, Margaret and Guiomard, Cathal. Determinants of Money Demand in Ireland 1971 to 1988: Rounding-Up the Usual Suspects. *Econ. Soc. Rev.*, October 1989, *21*(1), pp. 139–49.

Hursh, Steven R., et al. The Quantitative Analysis of Economic Behavior with Laboratory Animals. In *Grunert, K. G. and Ölander, F., eds.*, 1989, pp. 393–407.

Hurst, Christopher. Markets for Natural Gas in Developing Countries. *Energy J.*, July 1989, *10*(3), pp. 91–105.

Hurwich, Judith J. Lineage and Kin in the Sixteenth-Century Aristocracy: Some Comparative Evidence on England and Germany. In *[Stone, L.]*, 1989, pp. 33–64.

Hurwicz, Leonid. Effects of Entry on Profits under Monopolistic Competition. In *Feiwel, G. R., ed. (I)*, 1989, pp. 305–64.

_____. Mechanisms and Institutions. In *Shiraishi, T. and Tsuru, S., eds.*, 1989, pp. 87–104.

Husain, Ishrat. Recent Experience with the Debt Strategy. *Finance Devel.*, September 1989, *26*(3), pp. 12–15.

_____ and **Diwan, Ishac.** Dealing with the Debt Crisis: Introduction. In *Husain, I. and Diwan, I., eds.*, 1989, pp. 1–11.

_____ and **Mitra, Saumya.** Future Financing Needs of the Highly Indebted Countries. In *Husain, I. and Diwan, I., eds.*, 1989, pp. 199–209.

Husain, S. Shahid. Reviving Growth in Latin America. *Finance Devel.*, June 1989, *26*(2), pp. 2–5.

Husby, Ralph D. and Leuthold, Jane H. Horizontal Equity and Taxpayer Characteristics: Who Is Advantaged and Disadvantaged by the Federal Income Tax? *Eastern Econ. J.*, Jan.–March 1989, *15*(1), pp. 35–44.

Hušková, Marie and Sen, Pranab K. Nonparametric Tests for Shift and Change in Regression at an Unknown Time Point. In *Hackl, P., ed.*, 1989, pp. 71–85.

Hussain, Syed Tanveer. Economic Development with and without Land Reform in Bangladesh. *Bangladesh Devel. Stud.*, September 1989, *17*(3), pp. 119–47.

Hussey, Donald and Beck, Roger L. Politics, Property Rights, and Cottage Development. *Can. Public Policy*, March 1989, *15*(1), pp. 25–33.

Husted, Steven and Beeson, Patricia E. Patterns and Determinants of Productive Efficiency in State Manufacturing. *J. Reg. Sci.*, February 1989, *29*(1), pp. 15–28.

Husted, Thomas A. Nonmonotonic Demand for Income Redistribution Benefits: The Case of

AFDC. *Southern Econ. J.*, January 1989, *55*(3), pp. 710–27.

Huston, John H. and Butler, Richard V. How Contestable Are Airline Markets? *Atlantic Econ. J.*, June 1989, *17*(2), pp. 27–35.

———— **and Butler, Richard V.** Merger Mania and Airline Fares. *Eastern Econ. J.*, Jan.–March 1989, *15*(1), pp. 7–16.

Huszar, Paul C. Economics of Reducing Off-Site Costs of Wind Erosion. *Land Econ.*, November 1989, *65*(4), pp. 333–40.

Hutchens, Robert M. Seniority, Wages and Productivity: A Turbulent Decade. *J. Econ. Perspectives*, Fall 1989, *3*(4), pp. 49–64.

————; **Jakubson, George H. and Schwartz, Saul.** AFDC and the Formation of Subfamilies. *J. Human Res.*, Fall 1989, *24*(4), pp. 599–628.

Hutchful, Eboe. From 'Revolution' to Monetarism: The Economics and Politics of the Adjustment Programme in Ghana. **In** *Campbell, B. K. and Loxley, J.*, eds., 1989, pp. 92–131.

Hutchins, Teresa D.; Davis, Lance E. and Gallman, Robert E. Productivity in American Whaling: The New Bedford Fleet in the Nineteenth Century. **In** *Galenson, D. W.*, ed., 1989, pp. 97–147.

Hutchinson, E. Bruce; Kushner, Joseph W. and Giffin, Phillip E. The Conventional Wisdom about Cross-Haul. *Eastern Econ. J.*, Jan.–March 1989, *15*(1), pp. 29–34.

———— **and Murray, Michael P.** A Three Factor Cost Function for Multifamily Housing: A Study in Philanthropy. *Urban Stud.*, April 1989, *26*(2), pp. 234–39.

Hutchinson, Gillian and Church, Andrew. Wage Determination in Britain: Is There a Local Dimension? *Reg. Stud.*, August 1989, *23*(4), pp. 289–300.

———— **and Church, Andrew.** Wages, Unions, the Youth Training Scheme and the Young Workers Scheme. *Scot. J. Polit. Econ.*, May 1989, *36*(2), pp. 160–82.

Hutchison, Michael M. and Glick, Reuven. Exchange Rates and Monetary Policy. *Fed. Res. Bank San Francisco Econ. Rev.*, Spring 1989, (2), pp. 17–29.

———— **and Keeley, Michael C.** Estimating the Fisher Effect and the Stochastic Money Growth Process. *Econ. Inquiry*, April 1989, *27*(2), pp. 219–39.

————; **Mikesell, Raymond F. and Haynes, Stephen E.** U.S.–Japanese Bilateral Trade and the Yen–Dollar Exchange Rate: Reply. *Southern Econ. J.*, October 1989, *56*(2), pp. 524–28.

Hutchison, Terence W. The New Institutional Economics and the Process of Economic Development: Comment. *J. Inst. Theoretical Econ.*, March 1989, *145*(1), pp. 59–62.

Huters, Ted. Between Praxis and Essence: The Search for Cultural Expression in the Chinese Revolution. **In** *Dirlik, A. and Meisner, M.*, eds., 1989, pp. 316–37.

Huth, Paul; Herek, Gregory M. and Janis, Irving L. Quality of U.S. Decision Making during the Cuban Missile Crisis: Major Errors in Welch's Reassassment. *J. Conflict Resolution*, September 1989, *33*(3), pp. 446–59.

Huth, William L. and MacDonald, Don N. The Impact of Antitrust Litigation on Shareholder Return. *J. Ind. Econ.*, June 1989, *37*(4), pp. 411–26.

———— **and MacDonald, Don N.** Individual Valuation, Market Valuation, and the Preference Reversal Phenomenon. *J. Behav. Econ.*, Summer 1989, *18*(2), pp. 99–114.

Hutson, Gary; Hughes Hallett, Andrew J. and Holtham, Gerald. Exchange-Rate Targetting as Surrogate International Cooperation. **In** *Miller, M.; Eichengreen, B. and Portes, R.*, eds., 1989, pp. 239–78.

Hutt, W. H. Trade Unions: The Private Use of Coercive Power. **In** *Rothbard, M. N. and Block, W.*, eds., 1989, pp. 108–20.

Hutten, Theo and Folmer, Hendrik. Some Reflections on Innovation Stimulating Policy. **In** *Andersson, Å. E.; Batten, D. F. and Karlsson, C.*, eds., 1989, pp. 271–78.

Huttenback, Robert A. and Davis, Lance E. Businessmen, the Raj, and the Pattern of Government Expenditures: The British Empire, 1860–1912. **In** *Galenson, D. W.*, ed., 1989, pp. 190–230.

Huttin, Christine. The Effects of State Aid on Employment and Investment in the French Textile and Clothing Industry. *Int. J. Ind. Organ.*, December 1989, *7*(4), pp. 489–501.

————. Les effets d'une aide publique sur les décisions d'emploi et d'investissement des entreprises. Une analyse économétrique sur l'industrie française du textile-habillement. (The Effects of a State Aid on Employment and Investment Decisions of Firms: An Econometric Analysis on the French Textile and Clothing Industry. With English summary.) *Revue Écon.*, May 1989, *40*(3), pp. 503–40.

Hutton, John and Hartley, Keith. Large Purchasers. **In** *Barber, J.; Metcalfe, J. S. and Porteous, M.*, eds., 1989, pp. 105–27.

Hutton, Patricia A. and Holmes, James M. 'Optimal' Model Selection When the True Relationship Is Weak and Occurs with a Delay. *Econ. Letters*, October 1989, *30*(4), pp. 333–39.

Huttsell, Ray C., Jr. and Anderson, Dale G. Trucking Regulation, 1935–1980. **In** *Felton, J. R. and Anderson, D. G.*, eds., 1989, pp. 14–41.

———— **and Felton, John Richard.** Entry Regulation: The Nebraska Experience. **In** *Felton, J. R. and Anderson, D. G.*, eds., 1989, pp. 131–42.

Huussen, G. M. Mises and the Praxeological Point of View. *J. Econ. Stud.*, 1989, *16*(2), pp. 121–33.

Huzayyin, Ali S. The Need for Low Cost Transport Improvements in the Developing Countries Metropolis: A New Framework for Implementation. **In** *Candemir, Y.*, ed., 1989, pp. 407–17.

Hveem, Helge. If Not Global, Then (Inter-)Regional: The Mini-NIEO Alternative. **In** *Odén, B. and Othman, H.*, eds., 1989, pp. 181–97.

Hvidding, James M. The Livingston Price Expectations Data: Forecast Horizon and Rationality Tests. *Quart. J. Bus. Econ.*, Summer 1989, 28(3), pp. 105–21.

Hviid, Morten. Risk-Averse Duopolists and Voluntary Information Transmission. *J. Ind. Econ.*, September 1989, 38(1), pp. 49–64.

Hwa, Erh-Cheng. The Contribution of Agriculture to Economic Growth: Some Empirical Evidence. In *Williamson, J. G. and Panchamukhi, V. R., eds.*, 1989, pp. 106–26.

Hwang, Chuan Yang and Grinblatt, Mark. Signalling and the Pricing of New Issues. *J. Finance*, June 1989, 44(2), pp. 393–420.

Hwang, Hong and Mai, Chao-cheng. Export Subsidies and Oligopolistic Rivalry between Labor-Managed and Capitalist Economies. *J. Compar. Econ.*, September 1989, 13(3), pp. 473–80.

_____ **and Mai, Chao-cheng.** On the Optimum Location of Vertically Related Firms with Simultaneous Entry. *J. Reg. Sci.*, February 1989, 29(1), pp. 47–61.

_____ **and Mai, Chao-cheng.** Tariffs versus Ratio Quotas under Duopoly. *J. Int. Econ.*, August 1989, 27(1–2), pp. 177–83.

Hwang, Sean-Shong; Aguirre, B. E. and Saenz, Rogelio. Discrimination and the Assimilation and Ethnic Competition Perspectives. *Soc. Sci. Quart.*, September 1989, 70(3), pp. 594–606.

Hy, M.; Lassaut, B. and Nicolas, F. Concurrence entre les formes industrielles et artisanales de production–distribution des biens alimentaires: Exemples de la boulangerie et de la boucherie. (Competition between Industrial and Artisanal Firms in Food Products Marketing: The Case of Butchers' and Bakers' Trade. With English summary.) *Écon. Societes*, July 1989, 23(7), pp. 197–216.

Hyclak, Thomas J. Economic Aspects of Regional Trading Arrangements: Introduction. In *Greenaway, D.; Hyclak, T. and Thornton, R. J., eds.*, 1989, pp. xiii–xviii.

_____ **and Johnes, Geraint.** Real Wage Rigidity in Regional Labor Markets in the U.K., the U.S., and West Germany. *J. Reg. Sci.*, August 1989, 29(3), pp. 423–32.

_____ **and Johnes, Geraint.** Wage Inflation and Unemployment in Europe: The Regional Dimension. *Reg. Stud.*, February 1989, 23(1), pp. 19–26.

Hyde, William F. Marginal Costs of Managing Endangered Species: The Case of the Red-Cockaded Woodpecker. *J. Agr. Econ. Res.*, Spring 1989, 41(2), pp. 12–19.

Hylleberg, Svend and Mizon, Grayham E. Cointegration and Error Correction Mechanisms. *Econ. J.*, Supplement, 1989, 99(395), pp. 113–25.

_____ **and Mizon, Grayham E.** A Note on the Distribution of the Least Squares Estimator of a Random Walk with Drift. *Econ. Letters*, 1989, 29(3), pp. 225–30.

Hyman, Howard. Privatisation: The Facts. In *Veljanovski, C., ed. (II)*, 1989, pp. 191–219.

Hyman, Leonard S. and West, Heidimarie. Diversification, Deregulation, and Competition: Cost of Capital Implications for Electric Utilities. In *Crew, M. A., ed.*, 1989, pp. 165–81.

Hymes, I. M. The Revolution in Manufacturing. In *Finkelstein, J., ed.*, 1989, pp. 173–91.

Hyuha, Theodora; Maganya, Ernest N. and Chambua, Samwel. Outgrower Schemes in Tanzania: The Case of Tea and Sugarcane. *Eastern Afr. Econ. Rev.*, Special Issue, August 1989, pp. 70–82.

Hyun, Oh-Seok. The Impact of Overseas Migration on National Development: The Case of the Republic of Korea. In *Amjad, R., ed.*, 1989, pp. 143–66.

Iadov, V. The Social Personality Type. In *Yanowitch, M., ed.*, 1989, 1988, pp. 256–66.

Iannaccone, Laurence R. Bandwagons and the Threat of Chaos: Interpersonal Effects Revisited. *J. Econ. Behav. Organ.*, May 1989, 11(3), pp. 431–42.

Ianovchik, V. A. It Is Necessary to Educate EMM Users Patiently. *Matekon*, Spring 1989, 25(3), pp. 77–79.

Iasin, E. G. Administrative System or Economic Mechanism. *Matekon*, Spring 1989, 25(3), pp. 40–56.

_____. Positions on Restructuring and the Price of Competence: A Survey of Economic Publicistics. *Prob. Econ.*, March 1989, 31(11), pp. 68–91.

_____; **Mashchits, V. and Aleksashenko, S.** The Thirteenth Five-Year Plan: From Economic Norms to Taxation of Enterprises. *Prob. Econ.*, December 1989, 32(8), pp. 78–92.

Ibarra, David and Alberro, José-Luis. The Role of the Economist in Government: An International Perspective: Mexico. In *Pechman, J. A., ed.*, 1989, pp. 147–70.

Ibrahim, Barbara. Policies Affecting Women's Employment in the Formal Sector: Strategies for Change. *World Devel.*, July 1989, 17(7), pp. 1097–1107.

Ichino, Andrea. Incentivazione della produttività o suddivisione del rischio? Ipotesi sui motivi della recente diffusione di contratti con incrementi salariali collegati agli andamenti aziendali. (With English summary.) *Politica. Econ.*, December 1989, 5(3), pp. 463–91.

Ichioka, Osamu and Tachibanaki, Toshiaki. General Equilibrium Evaluations of Tariffs, Nontariff Barriers and Subsidies for Agriculture in Japan. *Econ. Stud. Quart.*, December 1989, 40(4), pp. 317–35.

Ichniowski, Casey; Freeman, Richard B. and Lauer, Harrison. Collective Bargaining Laws, Threat Effects, and the Determination of Police Compensation. *J. Lab. Econ.*, April 1989, 7(2), pp. 191–209.

_____ **and Preston, Anne E.** The Persistence of Organized Crime in New York City Construction: An Economic Perspective. *Ind. Lab. Relat. Rev.*, July 1989, 42(4), pp. 549–65.

Ide, Toyonari and Takayama, Akira. On Homothetic Functions. *Scand. J. Econ.*, 1989, 91(3), pp. 621–23.

———— **and Takayama, Akira.** Returns to Scale under Non-homotheticity and Homotheticity and the Shape of Average Cost. *J. Inst. Theoretical Econ.*, June 1989, *145*(2), pp. 367–88.

Idrissi, H.; Lefebvre, O. and Michelot, C. Applications and Numerical Convergence of the Partial Inverse Method. In *Dolecki, S., ed.*, 1989, pp. 39–54.

Idson, Todd L. Establishment Size Differentials in Internal Mobility. *Rev. Econ. Statist.*, November 1989, *71*(4), pp. 721–24.

van Ierland, Ekko and Folmer, Hendrik. Valuation Methods and Policy Making in Environmental Economics: Relevance and Scope. In *Folmer, H. and van Ierland, E., eds.*, 1989, pp. 1–11.

Ietto-Gillies, Grazia. Some Indicators of Multinational Domination of National Economies: Analysis for the UK and Other Developed Countries. *Int. Rev. Applied Econ.*, January 1989, *3*(1), pp. 25–45.

Ifeka, Caroline. Women in Fisheries. Why Women Count: Prospects for Self-Reliant Fisheries Development in the South Pacific Compared to the Indian Ocean. In *Couper, A. D., ed.*, 1989, pp. 89–114.

Iglesias, Enrique V. Third World Debt: The Next Phase: Status, Issues, and Prospects: Comment. In *Fried, E. R. and Trezise, P. H., eds.*, 1989, pp. 25–28.

Ignat'ev, S. M. The Banking System: Paths of Reform. *Prob. Econ.*, May 1989, *32*(1), pp. 89–104.

Ihlanfeldt, Keith R. and Sjoquist, David L. The Impact of Job Decentralization on the Economic Welfare of Central City Blacks. *J. Urban Econ.*, July 1989, *26*(1), pp. 110–30.

Ihori, Toshihiro. On the Degree of Debt Neutrality: Some Evidence for the Japanese Economy. *Econ. Stud. Quart.*, March 1989, *40*(1), pp. 66–74.

————. Tax Reforms in a Debt Financed Economy: The Role of Expectations. *Econ. Stud. Quart.*, September 1989, *40*(3), pp. 251–63.

Ihrig, Jane and Chmura, Christine. Changes in Manufacturing Employment in North Carolina Counties, 1980–85. *Fed. Res. Bank Richmond Econ. Rev.*, Sept.–Oct. 1989, *75*(5), pp. 37–46.

Ikäheimo, Seppo. Filosofisia mietteitä laskentatoimen tutkimuksen kehityksestä ja jaottelusta. (Philosophical Thoughts of the Development and Classification of Accounting Research. With English summary.) *Liiketaloudellinen Aikak.*, 1989, *38*(1), pp. 47–62.

Ikeda, M. Decentralized Control of Large Scale Systems. In *[Willems, J. C.]*, 1989, pp. 219–42.

Ikegami, Jun. Changing Boundaries of State Activity: From Nationalisation to Privatisation: Comment. In *Shiraishi, T. and Tsuru, S., eds.*, 1989, pp. 207–09.

Ikiara, Gerrishon K. Kenya's Participation in Regional and Global Trade Arrangements. In *Whalley, J., ed., Vol. 2*, 1989, pp. 19–39.

Ilha, Adayr da Silva and de Lima, João Eustá-

quio. Impacto da educação na pequena produção agrícola em Minas Gerais. (With English summary.) *Pesquisa Planejamento Econ.*, April 1989, *19*(1), pp. 183–202.

Ilmakunnas, Pekka. Survey Expectations vs. Rational Expectations in the Estimation of a Dynamic Model: Demand for Labour in Finnish Manufacturing. *Oxford Bull. Econ. Statist.*, August 1989, *51*(3), pp. 297–314.

———— **and Törmä, Hannu.** Structural Change in Factor Substitution in Finnish Manufacturing. *Scand. J. Econ.*, 1989, *91*(4), pp. 705–21.

Im, Bae-Geun; Kaserman, David L. and Melese, François. Endogenous Regulation and the Firm's Regulatory Expenditures. *Appl. Econ.*, March 1989, *21*(3), pp. 375–85.

Imada, Pearl; Naya, Seiji and Roy, Suby. Lessons in Development: A Comparative Study of Asia and Latin America: Introduction. In *Naya, S., et al., eds.*, 1989, pp. 3–12.

Imaoka, Hideki. Japanese Corporate Employment and Personnel Systems and Their Transfer to Japanese Affiliates in Asia. *Developing Econ.*, December 1989, *27*(4), pp. 407–26.

Imbert, Claude. French Idiosyncrasy on the Wane? In *Frankel, A. V. and Heck, C. B., eds.*, 1989, pp. 6–10.

Imershein, Allen W. and Rond, Philip C., III. Elite Fragmentation in Health Care: Proprietary and Nonproprietary Hospitals in Florida. *Soc. Sci. Quart.*, March 1989, *70*(1), pp. 53–71.

Imhof, F. W. Administrative and Compliance Costs of Taxation: Netherlands. In *International Fiscal Association, ed. (I)*, 1989, pp. 483–510.

van Imhoff, Evert. Optimal Investment in Human Capital under Conditions of Nonstable Population. *J. Human Res.*, Summer 1989, *24*(3), pp. 414–32.

———— **and Ritzen, Jozef M. M.** Comparing Employment Opportunities of Graduates and Dropouts of Full-Time Education and an In-Service Training Program. *Econ. Educ. Rev.*, 1989, *8*(2), pp. 159–67.

Imrie, R. F. Industrial Restructuring, Labour, and Locality: The Case of the British Pottery Industry. *Environ. Planning A*, January 1989, *21*(1), pp. 3–26.

Imrohoruğlu, Ayşe. Cost of Business Cycles with Indivisibilities and Liquidity Constraints. *J. Polit. Econ.*, December 1989, *97*(6), pp. 1364–83.

Inaba, Fred S. and Wallace, Nancy E. Spatial Price Competition and the Demand for Freight Transportation. *Rev. Econ. Statist.*, November 1989, *71*(4), pp. 614–25.

Inakazu, T. and Koizumi, A. A Multipurpose Optimization Model for Area-Wide Sewerage Systems. *Environ. Planning A*, August 1989, *21*(8), pp. 1015–26.

Indelli, P. The Latent Choice. When It Is Worth Postponing the Decision. *Metroecon.*, February 1989, *40*(1), pp. 17–42.

Infante, Ricardo; Tokman, Víctor E. and García, Álvero. Paying Off the Social Debt in Latin

America. *Int. Lab. Rev.*, 1989, *128*(4), pp. 467–83.

Ingegneri, Dominique; Crimmins, Eileen M. and Saito, Yasuhiko. Changes in Life Expectancy and Disability-Free Life Expectancy in the United States. *Population Devel. Rev.*, June 1989, *15*(2), pp. 235–67.

Ingene, Charles A. and Yu, Eden S. H. Optimal Intervention Policies for a Region Facing Pollution-Induced Uncertainty. *Ann. Reg. Sci.*, 1989, *23*(1), pp. 3–18.

Ingersent, K. A.; Rayner, A. J. and Hine, Robert C. Agriculture in the Uruguay Round: From the Punta del Este Declaration to the Geneva Accord. *J. Agr. Econ.*, September 1989, *40*(3), pp. 385–97.

Ingham, Hilary. Disaggregated Labour Demand: Some Empirical Evidence. *Scot. J. Polit. Econ.*, November 1989, *36*(4), pp. 353–65.

Ingham, Mike. Education and Youth Unemployment: A Reappraisal. *J. Econ. Stud.*, 1989, *16*(3), pp. 27–39.

Ingles, Jerry L. Economics for the Birds. *J. Econ. Issues*, June 1989, *23*(2), pp. 435–42.

Inglis, K. and Beaumont, John R. Geodemographics in Practice: Developments in Britain and Europe. *Environ. Planning A*, May 1989, *21*(5), pp. 587–604.

Ingram, Robert W. and Hill, John W. Selection of GAAP or RAP in the Savings and Loan Industry. *Accounting Rev.*, October 1989, *64*(4), pp. 667–79.

_____; **Raman, K. K. and Wilson, Earl R.** The Information in Governmental Annual Reports: A Contemporaneous Price Reaction Approach. *Accounting Rev.*, April 1989, *64*(2), pp. 250–68.

Ingrao, Bruna. From Walras's General Equilibrium to Hick's Temporary Equilibrium. *Rech. Écon. Louvain*, 1989, *55*(4), pp. 365–98.

_____. The Hidden Epistemology of Rational Expectations and the Paradoxes of Rationality. *Ricerche Econ.*, Jan.–June 1989, *43*(1–2), pp. 100–28.

Inkster, Ian. "Partly Solid and Partly Sophistical": Adam Smith as an Historian of Economic Thought. *Quart. Rev. Econ. Bus.*, Winter 1989, *29*(4), pp. 92–96.

Inman, Robert P. The Local Decision to Tax: Evidence from Large U.S. Cities. *Reg. Sci. Urban Econ.*, August 1989, *19*(3), pp. 455–91.

_____. New Research in Local Public Finance: Introduction. *Reg. Sci. Urban Econ.*, August 1989, *19*(3), pp. 347–52.

Innes, Jon T. and Thornton, Robert J. Interpreting Semilogarithmic Regression Coefficients in Labor Research. *J. Lab. Res.*, Fall 1989, *10*(4), pp. 443–47.

Innes, Robert D. and Rausser, Gordon C. Incomplete Markets and Government Agricultural Policy. *Amer. J. Agr. Econ.*, November 1989, *71*(4), pp. 915–31.

Inoue, Tadashi. Sufficient Conditions for the Existence of the World Production Possibility Frontier: Notes. *Econ. Stud. Quart.*, December 1989, *40*(4), pp. 355–63.

Insua, David Rios and French, Simon. Partial Information and Sensitivity Analysis in Multiobjective Decision Making. In *Lockett, A. G. and Islei, G.*, eds., 1989, pp. 424–33.

Intal, Ponciano, Jr. and Dohner, Robert S. Debt Crisis and Adjustment in the Philippines. In *Sachs, J. D.*, ed. (II), 1989, pp. 169–91.

_____ **and Dohner, Robert S.** The Marcos Legacy: Economic Policy and Foreign Debt in the Philippines. In *Sachs, J. D. and Collins, S. M.*, eds., 1989, pp. 371–614.

Intriligator, Michael D. and Brito, Dagobert L. Arms Races and Arms Control in the Middle East. In *Fishelson, G.*, ed., 1989, pp. 105–22.

_____ **and Brito, Dagobert L.** A Dynamic Heuristic Game Theory Model of an Arms Race. In *[Verheyen, P.]*, 1989, pp. 73–90.

Ioannides, Yannis M. Diffusion of Technological Change and Economic Growth. In *Andersson, Å. E.; Batten, D. F. and Karlsson, C.*, eds., 1989, pp. 101–11.

_____. The Dynamics of Housing Demand by the Elderly: Wealth, Cash Flow, and Demographic Effects: Comment. In *Wise, D. A.*, ed., 1989, pp. 87–91.

_____. Housing, Other Real Estate, and Wealth Portfolios: An Empirical Investigation Based on the 1983 Survey of Consumer Finances. *Reg. Sci. Urban Econ.*, May 1989, *19*(2), pp. 259–80.

_____ **and Henderson, J. Vernon.** Dynamic Aspects of Consumer Decisions in Housing Markets. *J. Urban Econ.*, September 1989, *26*(2), pp. 212–30.

_____; **Pissarides, Christopher A. and Meghir, Costas.** Female Participation and Male Unemployment Duration in Greece: Evidence from the Labour Force Survey. *Europ. Econ. Rev.*, March 1989, *33*(2/3), pp. 395–406.

Ioffe, A. On Some Recent Developments in the Theory of Second Order Optimality Conditions. In *Dolecki, S.*, ed., 1989, pp. 55–68.

Ippolito, Richard A. Efficiency with Costly Information: A Study of Mutual Fund Performance, 1965–1984. *Quart. J. Econ.*, February 1989, *104*(1), pp. 1–23.

Iqbal, S. Humera. Farm Size and Productivity Relationship: Effect of Over-Aggregation in Farm Size Grouping. *Pakistan Econ. Soc. Rev.*, Summer 1989, *27*(1), pp. 61–76.

Ireland, Jonathan and Wren-Lewis, Simon. Terminal Dates and the Dynamic Properties of National Institute Model 11. *Nat. Inst. Econ. Rev.*, May 1989, (128), pp. 91–93.

Ireland, Norman J. and Law, Peter J. Dynamic Allocation in a Labor-Managed Firm: Comment. *J. Compar. Econ.*, June 1989, *13*(2), pp. 335–37.

Ireland, Thomas R. How Shirking Can Help Productivity: A Critiqe of Carlin and the "Shirking as Harm" Theory. *J. Behav. Econ.*, Summer 1989, *18*(2), pp. 75–79.

Irfan, M. Reducing Poverty in Developing Countries—Some Basic Principles for Policy Design: Comments. *Pakistan Devel. Rev.*, Winter 1989, *28*(4), pp. 461–63.

Irie, Itaro and Suzuki, Norihiko. The Cooperative Development of Research Projects on MNCs between Taiwan and Japan: Past, Present, and Future. In *Negandhi, A. R., ed.*, 1989, pp. 231–37.

Irish, Charles R. Gifts without Borders: U.S. Tax Treatment of International Charitable Contributions. *Bull. Int. Fiscal Doc.*, December 1989, 43(12), pp. 544–48.

Iriso-Napal, Pedro Luis and Reher, David Sven. Marital Fertility and Its Determinants in Rural and in Urban Spain, 1887–1930. *Population Stud.*, November 1989, 43(3), pp. 405–27.

Ironmonger, D. S. and Van Hoa, Tran. Equivalence Scales: A Household Production Approach. *Econ. Letters*, December 1989, 31(4), pp. 407–10.

Irvin, George and Cáceres, Luis René. The Reconstruction of the CACM and European Cooperation. In *Irvin, G. and Holland, S., eds.*, 1989, pp. 163–88.

_____ and Holland, Stuart. Central American Integration: A Suitable Case for Treatment. In *Irvin, G. and Holland, S., eds.*, 1989, pp. 1–21.

Irvine, F. Owen; Jianakoplos, Nancy Ammon and Menchik, Paul L. Using Panel Data to Assess the Bias in Cross-Sectional Inferences of Life-Cycle Changes in the Level and Composition of Household Wealth. In *Lipsey, R. E. and Tice, H. S., eds.*, 1989, pp. 553–640.

Irving, Allan and Bellamy, Donald F. Social Welfare in Developed Market Countries: Canada. In *Dixon, J. and Scheurell, R. P., eds.*, 1989, pp. 47–88.

Irwin, Douglas A. Trade Deficit Announcements, Intervention, and the Dollar. *Econ. Letters*, December 1989, 31(3), pp. 257–62.

Irwin, Scott H.; Hall, Joyce A. and Brorsen, B. Wade. The Distribution of Futures Prices: A Test of the Stable Paretian and Mixture of Normals Hypotheses. *J. Finan. Quant. Anal.*, March 1989, 24(1), pp. 105–16.

Isaac, Alan G. Exchange Rate Volatility and Currency Substitution. *J. Int. Money Finance*, June 1989, 8(2), pp. 277–84.

_____. Wealth Effects and the Current Account with Endogenous Terms of Trade. *J. Macroecon.*, Fall 1989, 11(4), pp. 609–12.

Isaac, J. E. The Second Tier and Labour Market Flexibility. *Australian Econ. Rev.*, Autumn 1989, (85), pp. 51–58.

Isaac, R. Mark; Palfrey, Thomas R. and Forsythe, Robert. Theories and Tests of "Blind Bidding" in Sealed-Bid Auctions. *Rand J. Econ.*, Summer 1989, 20(2), pp. 214–38.

_____; Schmidtz, David and Walker, James M. The Assurance Problem in a Laboratory Market. *Public Choice*, September 1989, 62(3), pp. 217–36.

Isaac, William M. The Deposit Insurance System: Focusing the Debate: Panel Presentation. In *Federal Home Loan Bank of San Francisco*, 1989, pp. 209–12.

Isaak, David T. and Fesharaki, Fereidun. Oil Refining: Planning Long-Term Strategies in a

Short-Term Market. In *[Evans, J. K.]*, 1989, pp. 20–34.

Isachsen, Arne Jon and Strøm, Steinar. The Hidden Economy in Norway with Special Emphasis on the Hidden Labor Market. In *Feige, E. L., ed.*, 1989, pp. 251–65.

Isaic-Maniu, Al. and Vodă, V. G. Estimation of the Average Life of Products by the Aid of Minimum Length Confidence Intervals. *Econ. Computat. Econ. Cybern. Stud. Res.*, 1989, 24(1), pp. 53–59.

Isaksen, Jan. Industrial Development in Post-Apartheid Southern Africa: Some Issues for Further Research in a SADRA/Nordic Context. In *Odén, B. and Othman, H., eds.*, 1989, pp. 199–218.

Isard, Peter and Flood, Robert P. Monetary Policy Strategies. *Int. Monet. Fund Staff Pap.*, September 1989, 36(3), pp. 612–32.

Isard, Walter and Asami, Yasushi. Imperfect Information, Uncertainty and Optimal Sampling in Location Theory: An Initial Reexamination of Hotelling, Weber and von Thünen. *J. Reg. Sci.*, November 1989, 29(4), pp. 507–21.

Isenberg, D. L. The Financially Fragile Firm: Is There a Case for It in the 1920s? *Brit. Rev. Econ. Issues*, Summer 1989, 11(25), pp. 27–51.

IsHak, Samir T. and Moore, Robert W. The Influence of Culture on Recruitment and Training: Hofstede's Cultural Consequences as Applied to the Asian Pacific and Korea. In *Nedd, A., ed.*, 1989, pp. 277–300.

Ishi, Hiromitsu. Individual Income Tax Erosion and Tax Equity in Japan. In *Chiancone, A. and Messere, K., eds.*, 1989, pp. 87–101.

_____. Taxes in Canada, Japan, and the United States: Influences on Trade and Investment Flows, and the Role of Tax-Based Trade Irritants: Comment Comment. In *Stern, R. M., ed.*, 1989, pp. 243–46.

Ishihara, S. and El-Sahrigi, A. F. Mechanization of Rice Production in Egypt. In *International Rice Research Institute*, 1989, pp. 167–73.

Ishii, Yasunori. Measures of Risk Aversion and Comparative Statics of Industry Equilibrium: Correction. *Amer. Econ. Rev.*, March 1989, 79(1), pp. 285–86.

Ishikawa, Akihiro. Technology Development and Workers' Attitudes in East Europe—An International Comparative Study. In *Berliner, J. S.; Kosta, H. G. J. and Hakogi, M., eds.*, 1989, pp. 165–74.

Ishikawa, Shigeru. Industrialisation in Primary Export Economies: Introduction. In *Islam, N., ed.*, 1989, pp. 271–78.

Ishiyama, Yoshihide. Industrial Policies of Japan and the United States—Their Mechanisms and International Implications. In *Hayashi, K., ed.*, 1989, pp. 231–64.

Islam, A. F. M. Mafizul and Ahmad, Muzaffer. Nominal and Effective Rates of Protection in Bangladesh Textile Economy. *Bangladesh Devel. Stud.*, March–June 1989, 17(1–2), pp. 57–75.

Islam, Iyanatul. Industrial Restructuring and Industrial Relations in ASEAN—A Firm-Level Chronicle. In *Edgren, G., ed.*, 1989, pp. 81–151.

———— **and Khan, Habibullah.** Trends in International Inequality: A Basic Needs Approach. *J. Econ. Devel.*, December 1989, *14*(2), pp. 143–52.

Islam, Mohammed N. Tiebout Hypothesis and Migration-Impact of Local Fiscal Policies. *Public Finance*, 1989, *44*(3), pp. 406–18.

Islam, Muhammad M. and Gomes, Lawrence J. Market Power and Cost of Capital under Uncertainty. *Quart. J. Bus. Econ.*, Autumn 1989, *28*(4), pp. 61–76.

Islam, Muhammad Q. and Shahin, Wassim N. Economic Methodology Applied to Political Hostage-Taking in Light of the Iran-Contra Affair. *Southern Econ. J.*, April 1989, *55*(4), pp. 1019–24.

Islam, Muhammed N. and Alvi, Shafiq A. Wage Settlement Spillovers between the Private and Public Sectors in Canada. *J. Quant. Econ.*, January 1989, *5*(1), pp. 171–86.

———— **and Choudhury, Saud A.** The Flypaper Effect and the Revenue Impact of Grants-in-Aid. *Econ. Letters*, October 1989, *30*(4), pp. 351–56.

Islam, Nurul. The Balance between Industry and Agriculture in Economic Development: Introduction. In *Islam, N., ed.*, 1989, pp. xxi–xl.

————. Relative Price Changes in Agriculture and Industry: Introduction. In *Islam, N., ed.*, 1989, pp. 3–15.

————. Undernutrition and Poverty: Magnitude, Pattern, and Measures for Alleviation. In *Helmuth, J. W. and Johnson, S. R., eds., Vol. 2*, 1989, pp. 156–77.

————. World Hunger, Malnutrition, and Food Production and Distribution Systems: Reaction. In *Helmuth, J. W. and Johnson, S. R., eds., Vol. 1*, 1989, pp. 182–86.

———— **and Subramanian, A.** Agricultural Exports of Developing Countries: Estimates of Income and Price Elasticities of Demand and Supply. *J. Agr. Econ.*, May 1989, *40*(2), pp. 221–31.

Islam, Shafiqul. Going Beyond the Brady Plan. *Challenge*, July–Aug. 1989, *32*(4), pp. 39–46.

Islei, Gerd; Cox, Barry and Stratford, Mike. Ranking, Monitoring and Control of Research Projects in the Pharmaceutical Industry. In *Lockett, A. G. and Islei, G., eds.*, 1989, pp. 191–202.

Ismail, Abdel Fattah E.; Casterline, John B. and Cooksey, Elizabeth C. Household Income and Child Survival in Egypt. *Demography*, February 1989, *26*(1), pp. 15–35.

Ismail, Abdul Jalil Bin; Fisher, Cynthia D. and Shaw, James B. A Cognitive Categorization Approach to Managerial Performance Appraisal: Analysis of the Singapore Manager. In *Nedd, A., ed.*, 1989, pp. 339–57.

Ismail, Badr E. and Kim, Moon K. On the Association of Cash Flow Variables with Market Risk: Further Evidence. *Accounting Rev.*, January 1989, *64*(1), pp. 125–36.

Israel, Ronen and Biger, Nahum. A Note on the Pricing of Double Choice Bonds. *J. Banking Finance*, May 1989, *13*(2), pp. 181–90.

————; **Ofer, Aharon R. and Siegel, Daniel R.** The Information Content of Equity-for-Debt Swaps: An Investigation of Analyst Forecasts of Firm Cash Flows. *J. Finan. Econ.*, December 1989, *25*(2), pp. 349–70.

Issawi, Charles. The Middle East in the World Context: A Historical View. In *Sabagh, G., ed.*, 1989, pp. 3–28.

Issing, Otmar. Outlook and Issues for Germany. In *Fels, G. and von Furstenberg, G. M., eds.*, 1989, pp. 401–04.

———— **and Masuch, Klaus.** Zur Frage der normativen Interpretation von Leistungsbilanzsalden. (Questions Relating to the Normative Interpretation of Current Balance Data. With English summary.) *Kredit Kapital*, 1989, *22*(1), pp. 1–17.

Itagaki, Takao. The Multinational Enterprise under the Threats of Restriction on Profit Repatriation and Exchange Control. *J. Devel. Econ.*, October 1989, *31*(2), pp. 369–77.

————. Optimal Tariff and Profit Taxes for the Multinational Enterprise. *Manchester Sch. Econ. Soc. Stud.*, March 1989, *57*(1), pp. 58–74.

————. Optimal Tariffs and Quotas under Uncertain International Transfer. In *[Hadar, J.]*, 1989, pp. 187–99.

Italianer, Alexander. Implicações econômicas da integração do mercado interno da Comunidade Européia: Uma revisão. (With English summary.) *Pesquisa Planejamento Econ.*, December 1989, *19*(3), pp. 525–52.

Itami, Hiroyuki. Mobilising Invisible Assets: The Key for Successful Corporate Strategy. In *Punset, E. and Sweeney, G., eds.*, 1989, pp. 36–46.

Ito, Minoru. Microelectronics and the Changing Structure of Workplaces in Japan. In *Park, S.-J., ed.*, 1989, pp. 44–70.

Ito, Shoichi; Peterson, E. Wesley F. and Grant, Warren R. Rice in Asia: Is It Becoming an Inferior Good? *Amer. J. Agr. Econ.*, February 1989, *71*(1), pp. 32–42.

Ito, Takatoshi and Froot, Kenneth A. On the Consistency of Short-run and Long-run Exchange Rate Expectations. *J. Int. Money Finance*, December 1989, *8*(4), pp. 487–510.

———— **and Kang, Kyoungsik.** Bonuses, Overtime, and Employment: Korea vs Japan. *J. Japanese Int. Economies*, December 1989, *3*(4), pp. 424–50.

———— **and Quah, Danny.** Hypothesis Testing with Restricted Spectral Density Matrices, with an Application to Uncovered Interest Parity. *Int. Econ. Rev.*, February 1989, *30*(1), pp. 203–15.

Itoga, Shigeru and Yokoyama, Hisashi. A Test of the Dual-Industrial Growth Hypothesis: The Case of the Philippines and Thailand. *Developing Econ.*, December 1989, *27*(4), pp. 381–88.

Itoh, Motoshige. "Market Access" in International Trade: Comment. In *Stern, R. M., ed.*, 1989, pp. 288–92.

Iversen, Ingrid. Future Financing for Developing Countries. **In** *Bird, G., ed.*, 1989, pp. 169–88.

Iversen, L. H. and Polich, C. L. The Provision of Long-Term Care in Risk-Based HMOs. **In** *Scheffler, R. M. and Rossiter, L. F., eds.*, 1989, pp. 351–60.

Iwamoto, Yasushi. Budget Deficits and Capital Formation: On the Effects of the Inflation Tax. (In Japanese. With English summary.) *Econ. Stud. Quart.*, June 1989, *40*(2), pp. 152–65.

Iwata, Kazumasa. Differences in Income Elasticities and Trends in Real Exchange Rates: Comment. *Europ. Econ. Rev.*, May 1989, *33*(5), pp. 1047–49.

_____ **and Hamada, Koichi.** On the International Capital Ownership Pattern at the Turn of the Twenty-First Century. *Europ. Econ. Rev.*, May 1989, *33*(5), pp. 1055–79.

Iwata, Masayuki. CMEA in the Light of National Mechanisms: Discussion. **In** *Berliner, J. S.; Kosta, H. G. J. and Hakogi, M., eds.*, 1989, pp. 37–39.

_____. Institutional Change for the Future: Socialist Experience and New Horizons: Comment. **In** *Shiraishi, T. and Tsuru, S., eds.*, 1989, pp. 126–31.

Iyengar, N. S. Recent Studies on Poverty in India: A Survey. *J. Quant. Econ.*, July 1989, *5*(2), pp. 223–37.

Iyer, Easwar S.; Smith, Daniel C. and Park, C. Whan. The Effects of Situational Factors on In-Store Grocery Shopping Behavior: The Role of Store Environment and Time Available for Shopping. *J. Cons. Res.*, March 1989, *15*(4), pp. 422–33.

Izák, Vratislav. Planning and Intensive Development. *Czech. Econ. Digest.*, August 1989, (5), pp. 20–36.

Ize, Alain and Ortiz, Guillermo. Fiscal Rigidities, Public Debt, and Capital Flight. **In** *Blejer, M. I. and Chu, K., eds.*, 1989, *1987*, pp. 50–71.

Jaang, Daehong; Kim, Kyung-Soo and Kim, Woo Tack. On the Effectiveness of Capital Gains Tax as a Stabilizer of Real Estate Prices. *Int. Econ. J.*, Winter 1989, *3*(4), pp. 37–44.

Jabara, Cathy L. Effects of Agricultural Protection on Food Manufacturing: The U.S. Sugar Program. *Europ. Rev. Agr. Econ.*, 1989, *16*(3), pp. 375–90.

Jackman, R.; Layard, Richard and Pissarides, Christopher A. On Vacancies. *Oxford Bull. Econ. Statist.*, November 1989, *51*(4), pp. 377–94.

Jackson, Betty R.; Hite, Peggy A. and Ayres, Frances L. The Economic Benefits of Regulation: Evidence from Professional Tax Preparers. *Accounting Rev.*, April 1989, *64*(2), pp. 300–12.

_____ **and Jaouen, Pauline R.** Influencing Taxpayer Compliance through Sanction Threat or Appeals to Conscience. **In** *Jones, S. M., ed.*, 1989, pp. 131–47.

Jackson, Charles L. LEC Gateways: Provision of Audio, Video and Text Services in the U.S.

In *National Economic Research Associates*, 1989, pp. 139–53.

Jackson, J. C. and Cheater, A. P. Contract Farming: Sugar, Tea and Cotton in Zimbabwe. *Eastern Afr. Econ. Rev.*, Special Issue, August 1989, pp. 97–107.

Jackson, James M. A Comment on the Wilderness Debate: A Rancher's View. *Natural Res. J.*, Summer 1989, *29*(3), pp. 843–48.

Jackson, John D.; Barnett, A. H. and Caudill, Steven B. Job Search Duration and Marginal Tax Rates: An Empirical Inquiry. *Southern Econ. J.*, October 1989, *56*(2), pp. 476–89.

_____ **and Lindley, James T.** Measuring the Extent of Wage Discrimination: A Statistical Test and a Caveat. *Appl. Econ.*, April 1989, *21*(4), pp. 515–40.

Jackson, John H. Dumping in International Trade: Its Meaning and Context. **In** *Jackson, J. H. and Vermulst, E. A., eds.*, 1989, pp. 1–22.

Jackson, Marvin R. The Changing Soviet Foreign Trade System: Introduction. *Soviet E. Europ. Foreign Trade*, Fall 1989, *25*(3), pp. 3–8.

Jackson, Moira. Marketing of Nonferrous Metals: Digest of Discussions. **In** *Jackson, L. M. and Richardson, P. R., eds.*, 1989, pp. 99–113.

Jackson, P. M. The Boundaries of the Public Domain. **In** *Samuels, W. J., ed. (I)*, 1989, pp. 105–16.

Jackson, Pauline and Barry, Ursula. Women's Employment and Multinationals in the Republic of Ireland: The Creation of a New Female Labour Force. **In** *Elson, D. and Pearson, R., eds.*, 1989, pp. 38–59.

Jackson, Randall W. Conjoining Interindustry Linkages and Ownership Data: An Empirical Application. *Growth Change*, Winter 1989, *20*(1), pp. 34–54.

_____; **Hewings, Geoffrey J. D. and Sonis, Michael.** Decomposition Approaches to the Identification of Change in Regional Economies. *Econ. Geogr.*, July 1989, *65*(3), pp. 216–31.

_____ **and West, Guy R.** Perspectives on Probabilistic Input–Output Analysis. **In** *Miller, R. E.; Polenske, K. R. and Rose, A. Z., eds.*, 1989, pp. 209–21.

Jackson, Richard P. From Profit-Sailing to Wage-Sailing: Mediterranean Owner-Captains and Their Crews during the Medieval Commercial Revolution. *J. Europ. Econ. Hist.*, Winter 1989, *18*(3), pp. 605–28.

Jacob, Klaus. Aspects of the Verification of Conventional Arms Control Measures in Europe. **In** *Altmann, J. and Rotblat, J., eds.*, 1989, pp. 167–71.

Jacob, Ralf and Carlin, Wendy. Austerity Policy in West Germany: Origins and Consequences. *Écon. Appl.*, 1989, *42*(1), pp. 203–38.

Jacobs, Bruce I. and Levy, Kenneth N. The Complexity of the Stock Market. *J. Portfol. Manage.*, Fall 1989, *16*(1), pp. 19–27.

Jacobs, Chris and Bosworth, Derek L. Management Attitudes, Behaviour, and Abilities as Barriers to Growth. **In** *Barber, J.; Metcalfe, J. S. and Porteous, M., eds.*, 1989, pp. 20–38.

Jacobs, Curtis A. and Silberstein, Adriana R. Symptoms of Repeated Interview Effects in the Consumer Expenditure Interview Survey. In *Kasprzyk, D., et al., eds.*, 1989, pp. 289–303.

Jacobs, Eva; Shipp, Stephanie and Brown, Gregory. Families of Working Wives Spending More on Services and Nondurables. *Mon. Lab. Rev.*, February 1989, *112*(2), pp. 15–23.

Jacobs, Francis G. Observations on the Antidumping Law and Practice of the European Community, and Some Possible Reforms. In *Jackson, J. H. and Vermulst, E. A., eds.*, 1989, pp. 354–59.

Jacobs, James B. and Thacher, Thomas D., II. Attacking Corruption in Union–Management Relations: A Symposium. *Ind. Lab. Relat. Rev.*, July 1989, *42*(4), pp. 501–07.

Jacobs, James J. and Taylor, David T. The Increasing Role of States in Water Management: The Wyoming Experience. *Western J. Agr. Econ.*, December 1989, *14*(2), pp. 261–67.

Jacobs, Klaus and Schmähl, Winfried. The Process of Retirement in Germany: Trends, Public Discussion and Options for Its Redefinition. In *Schmähl, W., ed.*, 1989, pp. 13–38.

Jacobsen, Hanns-Dieter. The Impact of Economic Sanctions. In *Wohlmuth, K., ed.*, 1989, pp. 187–208.

Jacobsen, Joyce P. The Economics of Comparable Worth: Theoretical Considerations. In *Hill, M. A. and Killingsworth, M. R., eds.*, 1989, pp. 36–50.

Jacobson, Charles. Same Game, Different Players: Problems in Urban Public Utility Regulation, 1850–1987. *Urban Stud.*, February 1989, *26*(1), pp. 13–31.

Jacobson, David. Theorizing Irish Industrialization: The Case of the Motor Industry. *Sci. Society*, Summer 1989, *53*(2), pp. 165–91.

Jacobson, Harold K. The United Nations in Crisis. In *[Gordenker, L.]*, 1989, pp. 212–27.

Jacobson, Stephen L. The Effects of Pay Incentives on Teacher Absenteeism. *J. Human Res.*, Spring 1989, *24*(2), pp. 280–86.

Jacoby, Jacob and Hoyer, Wayne D. The Comprehension/Miscomprehension of Print Communication: Selected Findings. *J. Cons. Res.*, March 1989, *15*(4), pp. 434–43.

Jacoby, Sanford M. Reckoning with Company Unions: The Case of Thompson Products, 1934–1964. *Ind. Lab. Relat. Rev.*, October 1989, *43*(1), pp. 19–40.

Jaconis, Stefania. Moneta e credito nella riforma economica sovietica. (With English summary.) *Politica. Econ.*, December 1989, *5*(3), pp. 493–527.

Jacowski, Michael J. and Amel, Dean F. Trends in Banking Structure since the Mid-1970s. *Fed. Res. Bull.*, March 1989, *75*(3), pp. 120–33.

Jacquemin, Alexis. The European Internal Market Challenge and the Role of Microeconomic Analysis. *Ann. Écon. Statist.*, July–Dec. 1989, (15–16), pp. 39–50.

_____. International and Multinational Strategic Behaviour. *Kyklos*, 1989, *42*(4), pp. 495–513.

_____. Les enjeux de la nouvelle économie industrielle. (With English summary.) *L'Actual. Econ.*, March 1989, *65*(1), pp. 8–20.

_____. Strategic Behavior and the Role of Government. In *Samuels, W. J., ed. (I)*, 1989, pp. 117–22.

_____ and Buigues, Pierre. Strategies of Firms and Structural Environments in the Large Internal Market. *J. Common Market Stud.*, September 1989, *28*(1), pp. 53–67.

_____ and Geroski, Paul A. Industrial Change, Barriers to Mobility, and European Industrial Policy. In *Jacquemin, A. and Sapir, A., eds.*, 1989, *1985*, pp. 298–333.

_____ and Sapir, André. The European Internal Market: Introduction: 1992: A Single but Imperfect Market. In *Jacquemin, A. and Sapir, A., eds.*, 1989, pp. 1–9.

_____ and Sapir, André. International Trade and Integration of the European Community: An Econometric Analysis. In *Jacquemin, A. and Sapir, A., eds.*, 1989, *1988*, pp. 202–12.

_____ and Slade, Margaret E. Cartels, Collusion, and Horizontal Merger. In *Schmalensee, R. and Willig, R. D., eds., Vol. 1*, 1989, pp. 415–73.

Jaeger, Alfred M. Organization Development Methods in Practice: A Five-Country Examination. In *Prasad, S. B., ed.*, 1989, pp. 113–30.

Jaeger, K. Economic Policy Effectiveness in Hicksian Analysis: A Note. In *Wood, J. C. and Woods, R. N., eds., Vol. 3*, 1989, *1981*, pp. 291–93.

Jaeger, William and Humphreys, Charles. Africa's Adjustment and Growth. *Finance Devel.*, June 1989, *26*(2), pp. 6–8.

Jaffe, Adam B. Real Effects of Academic Research. *Amer. Econ. Rev.*, December 1989, *79*(5), pp. 957–70.

Jaffe, Jeffrey F.; Keim, Donald B. and Westerfield, Randolph. Earnings Yields, Market Values, and Stock Returns. *J. Finance*, March 1989, *44*(1), pp. 135–48.

_____ and Westerfield, Randolph. Is There a Monthly Effect in Stock Market Returns? Evidence from Foreign Countries. *J. Banking Finance*, May 1989, *13*(2), pp. 237–44.

_____; Westerfield, Randolph and Ma, Christopher K. A Twist on the Monday Effect in Stock Prices: Evidence from the U.S. and Foreign Stock Markets. *J. Banking Finance*, September 1989, *13*(4–5), pp. 641–50.

Jaffee, David. Gender Inequality in Workplace Autonomy and Authority. *Soc. Sci. Quart.*, June 1989, *70*(2), pp. 375–90.

Jaffee, Dwight M. Symposium on Federal Deposit Insurance for S&L Institutions. *J. Econ. Perspectives*, Fall 1989, *3*(4), pp. 3–9.

Jaffray, Jean-Yves and Chateauneuf, Alain. Some Characterizations of Lower Probabilities and Other Monotone Capacities through the Use of Möbius Inversion. *Math. Soc. Sci.*, June 1989, *17*(3), pp. 263–83.

Jagannathan, Ravi; Breen, William and Glosten, Lawrence R. Economic Significance of Predictable Variations in Stock Index Returns. *J.*

Finance, December 1989, *44*(5), pp. 1177–89.

_____ and **Chari, Varadarajan V.** Adverse Selection in a Model of Real Estate Lending. *J. Finance*, June 1989, *44*(2), pp. 499–508.

_____ and **Palfrey, Thomas R.** Effects of Insider Trading Disclosures on Speculative Activity and Future Prices. *Econ. Inquiry*, July 1989, 27(3), pp. 411–30.

Jäger, Albert and Amann, Erwin. Staatsschuldenarithmetik: Zwei unerfreuliche Beispiele. (Public Debt Arithmetic: Two Unpleasant Examples. With English summary.) *Kredit Kapital*, 1989, 22(2), pp. 221–34.

Jager, Henk and de Jong, Eelke. The Contribution of the Ecu to Exchange-Rate Stability: A Further Reply. *Banca Naz. Lavoro Quart. Rev.*, December 1989, (171), pp. 477–81.

Jain, Anil Kumar. Tax Reform in India. *Indian Econ. J.*, April–June 1989, 36(4), pp. 57–70.

Jain, Devaki. Letting the Worm Turn: A Comment on Innovative Poverty Alleviation. In *Lineberry, W. P., ed.*, 1989, pp. 71–83.

Jain, Harish C. and Hackett, Rick D. Measuring Effectiveness of Employment Equity Programs in Canada: Public Policy and a Survey. *Can. Public Policy*, June 1989, 15(2), pp. 189–204.

Jain, Hem C. and Punnett, Betty Jane. Management Styles: Some Similarities and Differences between Japanese and Canadian Managers in Canada. In *Prasad, S. B., ed.*, 1989, pp. 183–97.

Jain, L. R.; Sundaram, K. and Tendulkar, Suresh D. Level of Living and Incidence of Poverty in Rural India—A Cross-Sectional Analysis. *J. Quant. Econ.*, January 1989, 5(1), pp. 187–209.

_____ and **Tendulkar, Suresh D.** On a Relationship between the Real and the Nominal Relative Disparities in the Consumption of Cereals in Rural India. *J. Devel. Econ.*, October 1989, 31(2), pp. 271–95.

Jain, Prem C. and Ajinkya, Bipin B. The Behavior of Daily Stock Market Trading Volume. *J. Acc. Econ.*, November 1989, 11(4), pp. 331–59.

Jain, Raj K. The Seasonal Adjustment Procedures for the Consumer Price Indexes: Some Empirical Results. *J. Bus. Econ. Statist.*, October 1989, 7(4), pp. 461–69.

Jakš, Jaroslav. CMEA–E.E.C. Relations in the Light of the Nascent Single Market of the European Communities. *Czech. Econ. Digest.*, August 1989, (5), pp. 42–56.

Jaksch, Hans Jürgen and Bernholz, Peter. An Implausible Theory of Inflation. *Weltwirtsch. Arch.*, 1989, 125(2), pp. 359–65.

Jakubson, George H. and Ehrenberg, Ronald G. Advance Notification of Plant Closing: Does It Matter? *Ind. Relat.*, Winter 1989, 28(1), pp. 60–71.

_____; **Schwartz, Saul and Hutchens, Robert M.** AFDC and the Formation of Subfamilies. *J. Human Res.*, Fall 1989, 24(4), pp. 599–628.

Jalilvand, Abolhassan and Kryzanowski, Lawrence. Incorporating Contemporaneous Residual Relationships for Security Prices. *Econ. Letters*, December 1989, 31(3), pp. 245–49.

Jamal, A. M. M. and Hossain, Najmul. The Earnings of Industrial Labour in an LDC: The Evidence from Bangladesh. *Bangladesh Devel. Stud.*, December 1989, 17(4), pp. 71–81.

Jamal, Vali. The Demise of the Labor Aristocracy in Africa: Structural Adjustment in Tanzania. In *Weeks, J. F., ed.*, 1989, pp. 175–91.

James, Alan. The Security Council: Paying for Peacekeeping. In *[Gordenker, L.]*, 1989, pp. 13–35.

James, Christopher. Empirical Evidence on Implicit Government Guarantees of Bank Foreign Loan Exposure. *Carnegie–Rochester Conf. Ser. Public Policy*, Spring 1989, 30, pp. 129–61.

James, Dilmus D. Importation and Local Generation of Technology by the Third World: An Institutionalist Perspective. In *DeGregori, T. R., ed.*, 1989, pp. 291–370.

James, Estelle. The Nonprofit Sector in Developing Countries: The Case of Sri Lanka. In *James, E., ed.*, 1989, pp. 289–318.

_____. The Nonprofit Sector in International Perspective: Studies in Comparative Culture and Policy: Introduction. In *James, E., ed.*, 1989, pp. 3–27.

_____. The Private Nonprofit Provision of Education: A Theoretical Model and Application to Japan. In *James, E., ed.*, 1989, pp. 61–83.

_____. The Private Provision of Public Services: A Comparison of Sweden and Holland. In *James, E., ed.*, 1989, pp. 31–60.

_____, **et al.** College Quality and Future Earnings: Where Should You Send Your Child to College? *Amer. Econ. Rev.*, May 1989, 79(2), pp. 247–52.

James, Harold. What Is Keynesian about Deficit Financing? The Case of Interwar Germany. In *Hall, P. A., ed.*, 1989, pp. 231–62.

James, Jeffrey. Bureaucratic, Engineering and Economic Men: Decision-Making for Technology in the United Republic of Tanzania's State-Owned Enterprises. In *James, J., ed.*, 1989, pp. 42–72.

_____. Public Enterprise, Technology and Employment in Developing Countries. In *James, J., ed.*, 1989, pp. 21–41.

_____. The Technological Behaviour of Public Enterprises in Developing Countries: Introduction. In *James, J., ed.*, 1989, pp. 1–20.

James, John A. The Stability of the 19th-Century Phillips Curve Relationship. *Exploration Econ. Hist.*, April 1989, 26(2), pp. 117–34.

James, Scott C. and Lake, David A. The Second Face of Hegemony: Britain's Repeal of the Corn Laws and the American Walker Tariff of 1846. *Int. Organ.*, Winter 1989, 43(1), pp. 1–29.

James, William E. Changes in the Balance of Payments and Capital Flows: Implications for Asia. In *James, W. E., ed.*, 1989, pp. 47–60.

_____ and **Fujita, Natsuki.** Export Promotion and the "Heavy Industrialization" of Korea, 1973–83. *Developing Econ.*, September 1989, 27(3), pp. 236–50.

_____ and **Manopimoke, Wirote.** Property Rights, and Petroleum Exploration and Development in the Asian Developing Countries. In *James, W. E., ed.*, 1989, pp. 61–74.

Jameson, Kenneth P. Austerity Programs under Conditions of Political Instability and Economic Depression: The Case of Bolivia. In *Handelman, H. and Baer, W., eds.*, 1989, pp. 81–103.

_____; **Weaver, James H. and Wilber, Charles K.** Strategies of Development: A Survey. In *DeGregori, T. R., ed.*, 1989, pp. 137–77.

Jammalamadaka, S. R.; Chib, Siddhartha and Tiwari, R. C. Bayes Prediction Density and Regression Estimation—A Semiparametric Approach. In *Ullah, A., ed., 1989, 1988*, pp. 87–100.

Jamshidian, Farshid. An Exact Bond Option Formula. *J. Finance*, March 1989, *44*(1), pp. 205–09.

Janáček, Kamil. Forecast of the Czechoslovak Economy to 2010—Methodology and Principal Results. *Czech. Econ. Pap.*, 1989, (26), pp. 19–30.

Janáčková, Stanislava. Productivity Growth and Intensification of Capitalist Production in the Eighties—Some Open Questions. *Czech. Econ. Pap.*, 1989, (26), pp. 99–108.

Janhunen, Olli. Knowledge-Based Statistical Systems—An Overview. *Statist. J.*, 1989, *6*(4), pp. 315–23.

Janis, Irving L.; Huth, Paul and Herek, Gregory M. Quality of U.S. Decision Making during the Cuban Missile Crisis: Major Errors in Welch's Reassassment. *J. Conflict Resolution*, September 1989, *33*(3), pp. 446–59.

Janisch, Hudson N. The North American Telecommunications Industry. In *Button, K. and Swann, D., eds.*, 1989, pp. 300–320.

Jankowski, P. Mixed-Data Multicriteria Evaluation for Regional Planning: A Systematic Approach to the Decisionmaking Process. *Environ. Planning A*, March 1989, *21*(3), pp. 349–62.

Jankowski, W. B. Competition, Contestability, and the Liner Shipping Industry. *J. Transp. Econ. Policy*, May 1989, *23*(2), pp. 199–203.

_____. The Development of Liner Shipping Conferences: A Game Theoretical Explanation. *Int. J. Transport Econ.*, October 1989, *16*(3), pp. 313–28.

Janover, Louis. "Liberté, Egalité, Proprieéte et Bentham." ("Liberty, Equality, Property and Bentham." With English summary.) *Écon. Societes*, September 1989, *23*(9), pp. 97–120.

Janowitz, M. F. and Schweizer, B. Ordinal and Percentile Clustering. *Math. Soc. Sci.*, October 1989, *18*(2), pp. 135–86.

Jansen, Dennis W. Does Inflation Uncertainty Affect Output Growth? Further Evidence. *Fed. Res. Bank St. Louis Rev.*, July–Aug. 1989, *71*(4), pp. 43–54.

_____ **and Bradley, Michael D.** The Optimality of Nominal Income Targeting When Wages Are Indexed to Price. *Southern Econ. J.*, July 1989, *56*(1), pp. 13–23.

_____ **and Bradley, Michael D.** Understanding Nominal GNP Targeting. *Fed. Res. Bank San*

Francisco Rev., Nov.–Dec. 1989, *71*(6), pp. 31–40.

Jansen, Karel. Monetary Policy and Financial Development. In *Fitzgerald, E. V. K. and Vos, R.*, 1989, pp. 55–82.

_____. Stability and Stabilization in Thailand. In *Fitzgerald, E. V. K. and Vos, R.*, 1989, pp. 154–86.

Jansen, W. J. and Broer, D. P. Employment, Schooling and Productivity Growth. *De Economist*, 1989, *137*(4), pp. 425–53.

Janssen, Maarten C. W. Individualistic Foundation for General Equilibrium Theory: A Review of Some Game Theoretic Approaches. *Rech. Écon. Louvain*, 1989, *55*(4), pp. 425–46.

_____. Structuralist Reconstructions of Classical and Keynesian Macroeconomics. In *Balzer, W. and Hamminga, B., eds.*, 1989, pp. 165–81.

_____ **and Kuipers, Theo A. F.** Stratification of General Equilibrium Theory: A Synthesis of Reconstructions. In *Balzer, W. and Hamminga, B., eds.*, 1989, pp. 183–205.

Janssen, R. and van Herwijnen, M. Definite: A Support System for Decisions on a Finite Set of Alternatives. In *Lockett, A. G. and Islei, G., eds.*, 1989, pp. 534–43.

Janssens de Bisthoven, Olivier and Loute, Etienne. Solving Arborescent Linear Programs with Nested Decomposition. In *Cornet, B. and Tulkens, H., eds.*, 1989, pp. 285–314.

Janssens, M. J. B. T. and Moors, J. J. A. Exact Distributions of Bayesian Cox–Snell Bounds in Auditing. *J. Acc. Res.*, Spring 1989, *27*(1), pp. 135–44.

Jansson, Hans. Marketing to Projects in Southeast Asia. In *Hallén, L. and Johanson, J., eds.*, 1989, pp. 259–76.

Jansson, Jan Owen. Car Demand Modelling and Forecasting: A New Approach. *J. Transp. Econ. Policy*, May 1989, *23*(2), pp. 125–40.

_____ **and Cardebring, Peter.** A Comparative Study of Road User Taxation in Different Countries. *Int. J. Transport Econ.*, February 1989, *16*(1), pp. 79–89.

_____ **and Cardebring, Peter.** Swedish Railway Policy 1979–88. *J. Transp. Econ. Policy*, September 1989, *23*(3), pp. 329–37.

de Janvry, Alain. The Economics of Investment in Rural Development: Private and Social Accounting Experiences from Latin America. In *Lineberry, W. P., ed.*, 1989, pp. 49–69.

_____. Farm Structure, Productivity, and Poverty. In *Horwich, G. and Lynch, G. J., eds.*, 1989, pp. 132–72.

_____ **and Sadoulet, Elisabeth.** Growth and Equity in Agriculture-Led Growth. In *Adelman, I. and Lane, S., eds.*, 1989, pp. 81–96.

_____ **and Sadoulet, Elisabeth.** Investment Strategies to Combat Rural Poverty: A Proposal for Latin America. *World Devel.*, August 1989, *17*(8), pp. 1203–21.

_____ **and Sadoulet, Elisabeth.** A Study in Resistance to Institutional Change: The Lost Game of Latin American Land Reform. *World Devel.*, Special Issue, September 1989, *17*(9), pp. 1397–1407.

_____; Sadoulet, Elisabeth and Fafchamps, Marcel. Agrarian Structure, Technological Innovations, and the State. In *Bardhan, P., ed. (II),* 1989, pp. 356–82.

_____; Sadoulet, Elisabeth and Wilcox, Linda. Rural Labour in Latin America. *Int. Lab. Rev.,* Special Issue, 1989, *128*(6), pp. 701–29.

Jao, Y. C. Money Supply Exogeneity and Endogeneity: A Review of the Monetarist–Post-Keynesian Debate. *Greek Econ. Rev.,* 1989, *11*(2), pp. 203–34.

_____. A Supply-Side Budget: Hong Kong. *Bull. Int. Fiscal Doc.,* June 1989, *43*(6), pp. 274–76.

Jaouen, Pauline R. and Jackson, Betty R. Influencing Taxpayer Compliance through Sanction Threat or Appeals to Conscience. In *Jones, S. M., ed.,* 1989, pp. 131–47.

Jappelli, Tullio and Modigliani, Franco. The Determinants of Interest Rates in the Italian Economy. In *Modigliani, F., Vol. 5,* 1989, *1988,* pp. 228–53.

_____ and Modigliani, Franco. Fiscal Policy and Saving in Italy since 1860. In *Modigliani, F., Vol. 5,* 1989, *1987,* pp. 182–227.

_____ and Pagano, Marco. Consumption and Capital Market Imperfections: An International Comparison. *Amer. Econ. Rev.,* December 1989, *79*(5), pp. 1088–1105.

_____; Pagano, Marco and Modigliani, Franco. The Impact of Fiscal Policy and Inflation on National Saving: A Reply. *Banca Naz. Lavoro Quart. Rev.,* June 1989, (169), pp. 239–44.

Jara-Díaz, Sergio R. and Ortúzar, Juan de Dois. Introducing the Expenditure Rate in the Estimation of Mode Choice Models. *J. Transp. Econ. Policy,* September 1989, *23*(3), pp. 293–308.

Járai, Zsigmond. Development Trends of the Security Market in Hungary: Review Article. *Acta Oecon.,* 1989, *40*(3–4), pp. 353–65.

_____. Goals and Conditions in Setting Up a Stock Market in Hungary, 1988. *Europ. Econ. Rev.,* March 1989, *33*(2/3), pp. 448–55.

Jaramillo, Mauricio and Pinstrup-Andersen, Per. The Impact of Drought and Technological Change in Rice Production on Intrayear Fluctuations in Food Consumption: The Case of North Arcot, India. In *Sahn, D. E., ed.,* 1989, pp. 264–84.

Jaro, Matthew A. Advances in Record-Linkage Methodology as Applied to Matching the 1985 Census of Tampa, Florida. *J. Amer. Statist. Assoc.,* June 1989, *84*(406), pp. 414–20.

Jarre, F. On the Method of Analytic Centers for Solving Smooth Convex Programs. In *Dolecki, S., ed.,* 1989, pp. 69–85.

Jarrell, Gregg A. The Insider Trading Scandal: Understanding the Problem. In *Williams, O. F.; Reilly, F. K. and Houck, J. W., eds.,* 1989, pp. 85–100.

_____ and Poulsen, Annette B. Stock Trading before the Announcement of Tender Offers: Insider Trading or Market Anticipation? *J. Law, Econ., Organ.,* Fall 1989, *5*(2), pp. 225–48.

Jarrell, Judith L.; Grimm, Curtis M. and Corsi, Thomas M. U.S. Motor Carrier Cost Structure under Deregulation. *Logist. Transp. Rev.,* September 1989, *25*(3), pp. 231–49.

Jarrell, Stephen B. and Stanley, T. D. Meta-Regression Analysis: A Quantitative Method of Literature Surveys. *J. Econ. Surveys,* 1989, *3*(2), pp. 161–70.

Jarrow, Robert A. and O'Hara, Maureen. Primes and Scores: An Essay on Market Imperfections. *J. Finance,* December 1989, *44*(5), pp. 1263–87.

_____ and Wiggins, James B. Option Pricing and Implicit Volatilities. *J. Econ. Surveys,* 1989, *3*(1), pp. 59–81.

Jarsulic, Marc. Endogenous Credit and Endogenous Business Cycles. *J. Post Keynesian Econ.,* Fall 1989, *12*(1), pp. 35–48.

Jarvie, Wendy K. Changes in Internal Migration in Australia: Population- or Employment-Led? In *Gibson, L. J. and Stimson, R. J., eds.,* 1989, pp. 47–60.

_____. Migration and Regional Development. In *Higgins, B. and Zagorski, K., eds.,* 1989, pp. 218–33.

Jarvis, Valerie and Prais, S. J. Two Nations of Shopkeepers: Training for Retailing in France and Britain. *Nat. Inst. Econ. Rev.,* May 1989, (128), pp. 58–74.

_____; Wagner, Karin and Prais, S. J. Productivity and Vocational Skills in Services in Britain and Germany: Hotels. *Nat. Inst. Econ. Rev.,* November 1989, (130), pp. 52–74.

Jašić, Zoran. Management of the Third-World Debt. In *Singer, H. W. and Sharma, S., eds. (II),* 1989, pp. 30–45.

_____. Qualitative Factors of Development and the Implementation of the Long-Term Program of Economic Stabilization. In *Macesich, G., ed.,* 1989, pp. 157–67.

Jasinski, Boguslav. Debt Globalisation for Its Management. In *Singer, H. W. and Sharma, S., eds. (II),* 1989, pp. 22–29.

Jaspersen, Fred Z. Macroeconomic Adjustment Policy Issues. In *Hamouda, O. F.; Rowley, R. and Wolf, B. M., eds.,* 1989, pp. 149–56.

Jasso, Guillermina and Rosenzweig, Mark R. Language Skill Acquisition, Labor Markets and Locational Choice: The Foreign-Born in the United States, 1900 and 1980. In *van Dijk, J., et al., eds.,* 1989, pp. 217–39.

Jatobá, Jorge. Urban Poverty, Labour Markets and Regional Differentiation in Brazil. In *Rodgers, G., ed.,* 1989, pp. 35–63.

Jay, Keith E. and Michalopoulos, Constantine. Donor Policies, Donor Interests, and Aid Effectiveness. In *Krueger, A. O.; Michalopoulos, C. and Ruttan, V. W.,* 1989, pp. 68–88.

_____ and Michalopoulos, Constantine. Interaction between Donors and Recipients. In *Krueger, A. O.; Michalopoulos, C. and Ruttan, V. W.,* 1989, pp. 89–108.

Jayasuriya, Sisira K. and Ekanayake, S. A. B. Change, Adjustment and the Role of Specific Experience: Evidence from Sri Lankan Rice

Farming. *Australian J. Agr. Econ.*, August 1989, *33*(2), pp. 123–35.

_____ and Nehen, I. Ketut. Bali: Economic Growth and Tourism. In *Hill, H., ed.*, 1989, pp. 330–48.

Jayatissa, R. A. and Rodrigo, Chandra. Maximising Benefits from Labour Migration: Sri Lanka. In *Amjad, R., ed.*, 1989, pp. 255–302.

Jayawardena, A. S. Privatisation in Sri Lanka. In *Ramanadham, V. V., ed.*, 1989, pp. 199–215.

Jayet, Hubert. State Space Heterogeneity and Space Determination for Markov Models of Mobility. In *van Dijk, J., et al., eds.*, 1989, pp. 279–97.

Jayet, P.-A. Model for Aggregation and Control of Crops Supply. In *Bauer, S. and Henrichsmeyer, W., eds.*, 1989, pp. 219–31.

Jazairy, Idriss. Assessing Participatory Development: Rhetoric versus Reality: Foreword. In *Lineberry, W. P., ed.*, 1989, pp. ix–xii.

Jeanfils, Ph. Impact sur le marché des changes des variations du dollar et de l'intervention de la Banque Centrale. (With English summary.) *Cah. Écon. Bruxelles*, 2nd Trimester 1989, (122), pp. 175–219.

_____; Kestens, P. and Thys-Clément, F. 1992 en perspective 2000: Les performances de la Belgique suite à l'ouverture européenne des frontières. (With English summary.) *Cah. Écon. Bruxelles*, 4th Trimester 1989, (124), pp. 475–91.

_____; Thiry, Bernard and Frank, M. La réforme de 1988 relative à l'impôt sur le revenu et aux droits d'accises. (With English summary.) *Cah. Écon. Bruxelles*, 1st Trimester 1989, (121), pp. 69–115.

Jeannot, Thomas M. Moral Leadership and Practical Wisdom. *Int. J. Soc. Econ.*, 1989, *16*(6), pp. 14–38.

Jeanrenaud, Claude and Burgat, Paul. L'équilibre budgétaire et l'endettement des collectivités publiques locales. (Budgetary Balance and Local Government Debt. With English summary.) *Schweiz. Z. Volkswirtsch. Statist.*, December 1989, *125*(4), pp. 597–608.

Jech, T. A Quantitative Theory of Preferences: Some Results on Transition Functions. *Soc. Choice Welfare*, October 1989, *6*(4), pp. 301–14.

Jee, Beomha. A Comparative Analysis of Alternative Pure Premium Models in the Automobile Risk Classification System. *J. Risk Ins.*, September 1989, *56*(3), pp. 434–59.

Jeffcoat, Colin. Choice under Uncertainty. *J. Econ. Surveys*, 1989, *3*(1), pp. 97–105.

Jefferson, Anne L. Financing Public Education: The Canadian Way. *Econ. Educ. Rev.*, 1989, *8*(3), pp. 247–53.

Jefferson, Gary H. Potential Sources of Productivity Growth within Chinese Industry. *World Devel.*, January 1989, *17*(1), pp. 45–57.

Jeffries, John C., Jr. Compensation for Constitutional Torts: Reflections on the Significance of Fault. *Mich. Law Rev.*, October 1989, *88*(1), pp. 82–103.

_____ and Abraham, Kenneth S. Punitive Damages and the Rule of Law: The Role of Defendant's Wealth. *J. Legal Stud.*, June 1989, *18*(2), pp. 415–25.

Jeffries, Richard. Ghana: The Political Economy of Personal Rule. In *Cruise O'Brien, D. B.; Dunn, J. and Rathbone, R., eds.*, 1989, pp. 75–98.

Jegers, Marc. On the Detection of Strategic Groups and the Relation between Their Occurrence and Industry Profitability. *Rivista Int. Sci. Econ. Com.*, June 1989, *36*(6), pp. 497–511.

_____. The Risk–Return Relation at the Firm and Industry Level: An Empirical Analysis Using Belgian Accounting Data. *Appl. Econ.*, July 1989, *21*(7), pp. 913–20.

_____ and Buijink, Willem. Accounting Rates of Return: Comment. *Amer. Econ. Rev.*, March 1989, *79*(1), pp. 287–89.

Jehle, Geoffrey A. A Note on Some Theorems in the Theory of International Trade. *Eastern Econ. J.*, April–June 1989, *15*(2), pp. 141–45.

Jelassi, M. Tawfik and Ozernoy, Vladimir M. A Framework for Building an Expert System for MCDM Models Selection. In *Lockett, A. G. and Islei, G., eds.*, 1989, pp. 553–62.

Jelen, Ted G. Weaker Vessels and Helpmeets: Gender Role Stereotypes and Attitudes toward Female Ordination. *Soc. Sci. Quart.*, September 1989, *70*(3), pp. 579–85.

Jemrić, Igor. Stabilna optimalizacija konveksnih modela matematickog programiranja. Pregled oblasti. I dio: Lokalna analiza stabilnosti. (Stable Optimization of Convex Models of Mathematical Programming—A Review of the Field. Part One: Local Analysis of Stability. With English summary.) *Econ. Anal. Workers' Manage.*, 1989, *23*(4), pp. 361–412.

Jencks, Christopher and Mayer, Susan E. Poverty and the Distribution of Material Hardship. *J. Human Res.*, Winter 1989, *24*(1), pp. 88–114.

Jeniček, V. Economic and Social Development of Czechoslovak Agriculture. In *Adelman, I. and Lane, S., eds.*, 1989, pp. 185–96.

Jenkins, Glenn P. Comment: Tax Reform and the Savings Incentive. In *Mintz, J. and Whalley, J., eds.*, 1989, pp. 183–85.

_____; Sawchuk, Gary D. and Webster, Gloria. Trade, Protectionism and Industrial Adjustment: Three North American Case Studies: Case Study 3: The Consumer Electronics Industry in North America. In *North–South Institute*, 1989, pp. 105–46.

Jenkins, Keith A. The Jersey Exempt Company. *Bull. Int. Fiscal Doc.*, July 1989, *43*(7), pp. 334–39.

Jenkins, Rhys. Transnational Corporations, Competition and Monopoly. *Rev. Radical Polit. Econ.*, Winter 1989, *21*(4), pp. 12–32.

Jenkins, Stephen P. and Millar, Jane. Income Risk and Income Maintenance: Implications for Incentives to Work. In *Dilnot, A. and Walker, I., eds.*, 1989, pp. 137–52.

_____ and O'Higgins, Michael. Inequality Measurement Using 'Norm Incomes': Were Garvy and Paglin onto Something after All? *Rev. Income Wealth*, September 1989, *35*(3), pp. 265–82.

Jenkis, Helmut W. Gorbachev's Economic Reforms: A Structural or a Technical Alteration? In *Gemper, B. B., ed.*, 1989, pp. 141–68.

Jennings, John F. A Congressional Perspective: Comment. *J. Policy Anal. Manage.*, Fall 1989, *8*(4), pp. 639–40.

Jennings, Ken and McLaughlin, Frank. Wage and Performance Discrimination: The Situation Facing Hispanics and Blacks in Major League Baseball. *J. Behav. Econ.*, Winter 1989, *18*(4), pp. 237–50.

Jennings, Larkin and Sawhney, Harmeet S. Telecommunications Policy and Economic Development: The New State Role: New York. In *Schmandt, J.; Williams, F. and Wilson, R. H., eds.*, 1989, pp. 111–50.

Jennings, William P. and Phillips, G. Michael. Risk as a Discount Rate Determinant in Wrongful Death and Injury Cases. *J. Risk Ins.*, March 1989, *56*(1), pp. 122–27.

Jensen, Gail A. and Cotter, Kevin D. Choice of Purchasing Arrangements in Insurance Markets. *J. Risk Uncertainty*, December 1989, *2*(4), pp. 405–14.

———— **and Gabel, Jon R.** The Price of State Mandated Benefits. *Inquiry*, Winter 1989, *26*(4), pp. 419–31.

Jensen, Hans E. The Civilized Economics of Geoffrey C. Harcourt—A Review Article. *J. Post Keynesian Econ.*, Winter 1988–89, *11*(2), pp. 305–12.

————. Marx and Keynes: Alternative Views on Capitalism? *Atlantic Econ. J.*, December 1989, *17*(4), pp. 29–38.

Jensen, K. C.; Bennett, R. E. and Kamath, Shyam J. Reprise and Clarification [Money in the Production Function—An Alternative Test Procedure]. *Eastern Econ. J.*, July–Sept. 1989, *15*(3), pp. 241–43.

Jensen, Rodney C. and Powell, Roy A. Regional Economic Structure: An Input–Output Approach. In *Higgins, B. and Zagorski, K., eds.*, 1989, pp. 173–95.

———— **and West, Guy R.** On Objectivity in Economic Research: A Response. *Environ. Planning A*, March 1989, *21*(3), pp. 405–07.

Jensen, Svend-Erik Hougaard. International Transmission af økonomisk politik. (International Transmission of Macroeconomic Policies. With English summary.) *Nationaløkon. Tidsskr.*, 1989, *127*(3), pp. 356–70.

Jeon, Bang Nam and von Furstenberg, George M. International Stock Price Movements: Links and Messages. *Brookings Pap. Econ. Act.*, 1989, (1), pp. 125–67.

Jeong, Kihong; Fletcher, Stanley M. and Houston, Jack E. Varietal Sales and Quality Differentiation: The Case of Certified Soybean Seed in the Southeastern U.S. *Southern J. Agr. Econ.*, July 1989, *21*(1), pp. 113–20.

Jepma, C. J. Extensions of the Constant-Market-Shares Analysis with an Application to Long-Term Export Data of Developing Countries. In *Williamson, J. G. and Panchamukhi, V. R., eds.*, 1989, pp. 129–43.

Jerison, Michael and Hildenbrand, Werner. The Demand Theory of the Weak Axioms of Revealed Preference. *Econ. Letters*, 1989, *29*(3), pp. 209–13.

Jerrell, Jeanette M. and Hu, Teh-wei. Cost-Effectiveness of Intensive Clinical and Case Management Compared with an Existing System of Care. *Inquiry*, Summer 1989, *26*(2), pp. 224–34.

Jespersen, Jesper and Velupillai, Kumaraswamy. Et farvel til o "klassiske" økonomer. (The Contributions to Economic Theory of John Hicks [1904–89] and Richard Kahn [1905–89]. With English summary.) *Nationaløkon. Tidsskr.*, 1989, *127*(2), pp. 264–68.

Jessop, Bob. Capitalism, Nation-States and Surveillance. In *Held, D. and Thompson, J. B., eds.*, 1989, pp. 103–28.

————. Conservative Regimes and the Transition to Post-Fordism: The Cases of Great Britain and West Germany. In *Gottdiener, M. and Komninos, N., eds.*, 1989, pp. 261–99.

————. Régulation Theories in Retrospect and Prospect. *Écon. Societes*, November 1989, *23*(11), pp. 7–62.

Jewitt, Ian. An Information Inequality for Agency Problems. *Econ. Letters*, 1989, *29*(4), pp. 295–98.

———— **and Buiter, Willem H.** Staggered Wage Setting with Real Wage Relativities: Variations on a Theme of Taylor. In *Buiter, W. H.*, 1989, *1981*, pp. 183–99.

Ježek, Tomáš. The Role of the Economic Centre. *Czech. Econ. Digest.*, April 1989, (2), pp. 3–12.

———— **and Turek, Otakar.** Structural Changes and the Economic Mechanism. *Czech. Econ. Digest.*, November 1989, (7), pp. 53–79.

Jha, Prem Shankar. Energy—The Challenges and Opportunities before the Developing Countries. *Energy J.*, January 1989, *10*(1), pp. 29–34.

Jhunjhunwala, B. Kaldor–Hicks–Scitovszky Criteria: A Postmortem. In *Wood, J. C. and Woods, R. N., eds.*, Vol. 2, 1989, *1974*, pp. 273–77.

Ji, Xiaoming and Wang, Xiaoqiang. Thoughts on Not Establishing a Stockholding System for Enterprises. *Chinese Econ. Stud.*, Fall 1989, *23*(1), pp. 33–42.

———— **and Wang, Xiaoqiang.** Thoughts on the Model of Nonstock Enterprises. *Chinese Econ. Stud.*, Winter 1988–89, *22*(2), pp. 38–46.

Jiambalvo, James; Noreen, Eric and Burgstahler, David. Changes in the Probability of Bankruptcy and Equity Value. *J. Acc. Econ.*, July 1989, *11*(2–3), pp. 207–24.

Jianakoplos, Nancy Ammon; Menchik, Paul L. and Irvine, F. Owen. Using Panel Data to Assess the Bias in Cross-Sectional Inferences of Life-Cycle Changes in the Level and Composition of Household Wealth. In *Lipsey, R. E. and Tice, H. S., eds.*, 1989, pp. 553–640.

Jiang, Xiaorong and Zhang, Wenxian. The Economic Law of Population Distribution and Migration. *Int. J. Soc. Econ.*, 1989, *16*(1), pp. 5–12.

_____ **and Zhang, Wenxian.** The Transformation of the Agricultural Population and the Urbanisation Process in China. *Int. J. Soc. Econ.*, 1989, *16*(1), pp. 40–51.

Jiggins, Janice. How Poor Women Earn Income in Sub-Saharan Africa and What Works against Them. *World Devel.*, July 1989, *17*(7), pp. 953–63.

Jimenez, Emmanuel. Social Sector Pricing Policy Revisited: A Survey of Some Recent Controversies. In *Fischer, S. and de Tray, D., eds.*, 1989, pp. 109–38.

_____; **Kugler, Bernardo and Horn, Robin.** National In-Service Training Systems in Latin America: An Economic Evaluation of Colombia's SENA. *Econ. Devel. Cult. Change*, April 1989, *37*(3), pp. 595–610.

Jimenez, Felix and Nell, Edward J. The Political Economy of the External Debt and Growth: The Case of Peru. In *Semmler, W., ed.*, 1989, pp. 228–51.

Jin, Lizuo and Wu, Jiaxiang. Establishing a Stockholding System for Enterprises: One Line of Thought for Further Promotion of the Reform. *Chinese Econ. Stud.*, Fall 1989, *23*(1), pp. 24–32.

_____ **and Wu, Jiaxiang.** Sharing Enterprises: An Approach to Further Reform. *Chinese Econ. Stud.*, Winter 1988–89, *22*(2), pp. 24–37.

Jirásek, Jaroslav. Flexible Machining Systems in the Czechoslovak Engineering Industry. In *Francis, A. and Grootings, P., eds.*, 1989, pp. 35–60.

Joachimsthaler, Erich A.; Gardiner, Lorraine R. and Stam, Antonie. Multicriteria Issues in Marketing: A Sales Resource Allocation Example and Potential Areas of Future Research. In *Lockett, A. G. and Islei, G., eds.*, 1989, pp. 224–33.

Job, Brian; von Witzke, Harald and Runge, C. Ford. Policy Coordination in World Agriculture: Introduction. In *von Witzke, H.; Runge, C. F. and Job, B., eds.*, 1989, pp. 1–5.

Jobson, J. D. and Korkie, Bob. A Performance Interpretation of Multivariate Tests of Asset Set Intersection, Spanning, and Mean–Variance Efficiency. *J. Finan. Quant. Anal.*, June 1989, *24*(2), pp. 185–204.

Jodha, N. S. Agronomic Adjustments to Climatic Variation. In *Oram, P. A., et al.*, 1989, pp. 405–13.

_____. Potential Strategies for Adapting to Greenhouse Warming: Perspectives from the Developing World. In *Rosenberg, N. J., et al., eds.*, 1989, pp. 147–58.

_____. Social Science Research on Rural Change: Some Gaps. In *Bardhan, P., ed. (I)*, 1989, pp. 174–99.

Joe, Tom. Policies for People: A Proposal for Redirection of Long-Term Care for the Elderly.

In *Eisdorfer, C.; Kessler, D. A. and Spector, A. N., eds.*, 1989, pp. 507–20.

Joerding, Wayne and Sheffrin, Steven M. Consumption Spending and Output Fluctuations: A Multi-country Study. *Appl. Econ.*, July 1989, *21*(7), pp. 891–99.

Joffé, George. Political Violence and the International System: A View from the South. In *Thomas, C. and Saravanamuttu, P., eds.*, 1989, pp. 159–74.

Jog, Vijay M.; Fowler, David J. and Rorke, C. Harvey. A Bias-Correcting Procedure for Beta Estimation in the Presence of Thin Trading. *J. Finan. Res.*, Spring 1989, *12*(1), pp. 23–32.

_____ **and Mintz, Jack M.** Business Tax Expenditure Accounts: Their Purpose and Measurement. In *Bruce, N., ed.*, 1989, pp. 181–225.

_____ **and Mintz, Jack M.** Corporate Tax Reform and Its Economic Impact: An Evaluation of the Phase 1 Proposals. In *Mintz, J. and Whalley, J., eds.*, 1989, pp. 83–124.

Joglekar, Gitanjali and Zimbalist, Andrew. Dollar GDP per Capita in Cuba: Estimates and Observations on the Use of the Physical Indicators Method. *J. Compar. Econ.*, March 1989, *13*(1), pp. 85–114.

Johanningsmeier, Edward P. William Z. Foster and the Syndicalist League of North America. *Labor Hist.*, Summer 1989, *30*(3), pp. 329–53.

Johanson, Jan and Hallén, Lars. International Business Relationships and Industrial Networks: Introduction. In *Hallén, L. and Johanson, J., eds.*, 1989, pp. xiii–xxiii.

_____; **Hallén, Lars and Mohamed, Nazeem Seyed.** Relationships and Exchange in International Business. In *Hallén, L. and Johanson, J., eds.*, 1989, pp. 7–23.

Johansson, Börje and Batten, David F. Comparative Structural Change in the Urban Economies of Australia and the United States: Techniques for Assessment and Policy Formulation. In *Gibson, L. J. and Stimson, R. J., eds.*, 1989, pp. 73–88.

_____ **and Batten, David F.** Dynamics of Product Substitution. In *Andersson, Å. E., et al., eds.*, 1989, pp. 23–44.

Johansson, Per-Olov. Valuing Public Goods in a Risky World: An Experiment. In *Folmer, H. and van Ierland, E., eds.*, 1989, pp. 37–48.

_____; **Kriström, Bengt and Mäler, Karl Göran.** Welfare Evaluations in Contingent Valuation Experiments with Discrete Response Data: Comment. *Amer. J. Agr. Econ.*, November 1989, *71*(4), pp. 1054–56.

_____ **and Löfgren, Karl-Gustaf.** Disequilibrium Cost–Benefit Rules: An Exposition and Extension. In *Folmer, H. and van Ierland, E., eds.*, 1989, pp. 161–86.

_____; **Löfgren, Karl-Gustaf and Mäler, Karl-Göran.** Recreational Values, Pareto Optimality and Timber Supply. In *Folmer, H. and van Ierland, E., eds.*, 1989, pp. 49–68.

Johansson, Sten and Lindgren, Anders. The Use of Micro-computers at a Statistical Agency: A

Report on Statistics Sweden. *Statist. J.*, 1989, 6(3), pp. 191–205.

Johansson, Ulf; Wikström, Solveig R. and Elg, Ulf. From the Consumption of Necessities to Experience-Seeking Consumption. In *Grunert, K. G. and Ölander, F., eds.*, 1989, pp. 287–308.

Johnes, Geraint. Regional Phillips Curves under Consistent Expectations. *Reg. Sci. Persp.*, 1989, 19(2), pp. 21–28.

_____ **and Hyclak, Thomas J.** Real Wage Rigidity in Regional Labor Markets in the U.K., the U.S., and West Germany. *J. Reg. Sci.*, August 1989, 29(3), pp. 423–32.

_____ **and Hyclak, Thomas J.** Wage Inflation and Unemployment in Europe: The Regional Dimension. *Reg. Stud.*, February 1989, 23(1), pp. 19–26.

Johnes, Jill and Taylor, Jim. The First Destination of New Graduates: Comparisons between Universities. *Appl. Econ.*, March 1989, 21(3), pp. 357–73.

Johns, Lucy. Selective Contracting in California: An Update. *Inquiry*, Fall 1989, 26(3), pp. 345–53.

Johns, Michael and Portes, Alejandro. The Polarization of Class and Space in the Contemporary Latin American City. In *Canak, W. L., ed.*, 1989, pp. 111–37.

Johnsen, Eugene and Mintz, Beth. Organizational versus Class Components of Director Networks. In *Perrucci, R. and Potter, H. R., eds.*, 1989, pp. 57–80.

Johnsen, Paul and Joynt, Patrick. Themes in the History of Industrial Relations in Norway. In *Barbash, J. and Barbash, K., eds.*, 1989, pp. 59–75.

Johnson, Allan N., et al. Differences in Inpatient Resource Use by Type of Health Plan. *Inquiry*, Fall 1989, 26(3), pp. 388–98.

Johnson, Ayah E.; Carlson, Barbara Lepidus and Cohen, Steven B. An Analysis of Part-Year Nonresponse in the Household Component of the National Medical Expenditure Survey. *J. Econ. Soc. Meas.*, 1989, 15(3–4), pp. 281–99.

Johnson, Bruce. The OMB Budget Examiner and the Congressional Budget Process. *Public Budg. Finance*, Spring 1989, 9(1), pp. 5–14.

Johnson, Christopher. The Market on Trail: Introduction. In *Johnson, C., ed.*, 1989, pp. 1–14.

Johnson, D. Gale. The Current Setting of U.S. Agriculture. In *Horwich, G. and Lynch, G. J., eds.*, 1989, pp. 173–90.

Johnson, Dale M. and Levins, Richard A. A Software Package for Teaching Farm Planning. *Southern J. Agr. Econ.*, July 1989, 21(1), pp. 157–62.

Johnson, Dana J. The Risk Behavior of Equity of Firms Approaching Bankruptcy. *J. Finan. Res.*, Spring 1989, 12(1), pp. 33–50.

Johnson, Daniel. Exiles and Half-Exiles: Wilhelm Röpke, Alexander Rüstow and Walter Eucken. In *Peacock, A. and Willgerodt, H., eds. (I)*, 1989, pp. 40–68.

Johnson, Dennis A. Price and the Multiple Product Firm. In *Missouri Valley Economic Association*, 1989, pp. 169–74.

Johnson, Donn M.; McKean, John R. and Walsh, Richard G. Issues in Nonmarket Valuation and Policy Application: A Retrospective Glance. *Western J. Agr. Econ.*, July 1989, 14(1), pp. 178–88.

Johnson, Ellis L. On Binary Group Problems Having the Fulkerson Property. In *Simeone, B., ed.*, 1989, pp. 57–112.

Johnson, Eric J. and Meyer, Robert J. Information Overload and the Nonrobustness of Linear Models: A Comment. *J. Cons. Res.*, March 1989, 15(4), pp. 498–503.

Johnson, F. Reed. Disclosure, Consent, and Environmental Risk Regulation. In *Shogren, J. F., ed.*, 1989, pp. 191–208.

Johnson, Frederick I. Market Definition under the Merger Guidelines: Critical Demand Elasticities. In *Zerbe, R. O., ed.*, 1989, pp. 235–46.

_____. Price Supports under Uncertainty: The U.S. Oats Market. *Amer. Economist*, Spring 1989, 33(1), pp. 36–44.

_____. Two Approaches to Market Definition under the Merger Guidelines. In *Zerbe, R. O., ed.*, 1989, pp. 227–34.

Johnson, Gary V.; Wu, Pei-Ing and Braden, John B. Efficient Control of Cropland Sediment: Storm Event versus Annual Average Loads. *Water Resources Res.*, February 1989, 25(2), pp. 161–68.

Johnson, George E. Do We Know Enough about the Unemployment Problem to Know What, If Anything, Will Help? In *Bawden, D. L. and Skidmore, F., eds.*, 1989, pp. 37–57.

_____. Organized Labor's Political Agenda: An Economist's Evaluation. In *Huang, W.-C., ed.*, 1989, pp. 63–89.

Johnson, H. G. Demand Theory Further Revised or Goods Are Goods. In *Wood, J. C. and Woods, R. N., eds., Vol. 2, 1989, 1958*, pp. 26–27.

Johnson, James H., Jr. and Zeigler, Donald J. Nuclear Protective Action Advisories: A Policy Analysis and Evaluation. *Growth Change*, Fall 1989, 20(4), pp. 51–65.

Johnson, James M.; Pari, Robert A. and Rosenthal, Leonard. The Impact of In-substance Defeasance on Bondholder and Shareholder Wealth. *J. Finance*, September 1989, 44(4), pp. 1049–57.

Johnson, L. E.; Gramm, Warren S. and Hoaas, David J. Marx's Law of Profit: The Current State of the Controversy. *Atlantic Econ. J.*, December 1989, 17(4), pp. 55–62.

Johnson, Larry A. and Haden, Kimberly L. Factors Which Contribute to the Financial Performance of Selected Tennessee Dairies. *Southern J. Agr. Econ.*, July 1989, 21(1), pp. 105–12.

Johnson, Larry J. and Bey, Roger P. The Impact of Taxes on Discount Bond Valuation and Risk. *Financial Rev.*, November 1989, 24(4), pp. 589–97.

Johnson, Leanor Boulin. The Employed Black: The Dynamics of Work–Family Tension. *Rev. Black Polit. Econ.*, Winter 1989, *17*(3), pp. 69–85.

Johnson, Lyman and Millon, David. Misreading the Williams Act. *Mich. Law Rev.*, June 1989, *87*(7), pp. 1862–1923.

_____ **and Millon, David.** Missing the Point about State Takeover Statutes. *Mich. Law Rev.*, February 1989, *87*(4), pp. 846–57.

Johnson, M. Bruce. Privatization in Britain: Comment. In *MacAvoy, P. W., et al.*, 1989, pp. 259–62.

Johnson, Manuel H. Current Perspectives on Monetary Policy. In *Dorn, J. A. and Niskanen, W. A., eds.*, 1989, *1988*, pp. 31–38.

_____. Statement to the U.S. House Committee on Banking, Finance and Urban Affairs, January 5, 1989. *Fed. Res. Bull.*, March 1989, *75*(3), pp. 136–39.

_____. Statement to the U.S. House Subcommittee on Financial Institutions Supervision, Regulation and Insurance of the Committee on Banking, Finance and Urban Affairs, September 19, 1989. *Fed. Res. Bull.*, November 1989, *75*(11), pp. 738–44.

_____. Statement to the U.S. House Subcommittee on Financial Institutions Supervision, Regulation and Insurance of the Committee on Banking, Finance and Urban Affairs, September 26, 1989. *Fed. Res. Bull.*, November 1989, *75*(11), pp. 744–50.

_____. Statement to the U.S. Senate Committee on Banking, Housing, and Urban Affairs, October 25, 1989. *Fed. Res. Bull.*, December 1989, *75*(12), pp. 803–11.

Johnson, Marilyn F.; Shevlin, Terry and Bowen, Robert M. Informational Efficiency and the Information Content of Earnings during the Market Crash of October 1987. *J. Acc. Econ.*, July 1989, *11*(2–3), pp. 225–54.

Johnson, Mark A. Capital Accumulation and Wage Rates: The Development of the California Labor Market in the Nineteenth Century. *Rev. Radical Polit. Econ.*, Fall 1989, *21*(3), pp. 76–81.

Johnson, Merrill L. Industrial Transition and the Location of High-Technology Branch Plants in the Nonmetropolitan Southeast. *Econ. Geogr.*, January 1989, *65*(1), pp. 33–47.

Johnson, Michael D. The Differential Processing of Product Category and Noncomparable Choice Alternatives. *J. Cons. Res.*, December 1989, *16*(3), pp. 300–309.

_____ **and Plott, Charles R.** The Effect of Two Trading Institutions on Price Expectations and the Stability of Supply-Response Lag Markets. *J. Econ. Psych.*, June 1989, *10*(2), pp. 189–216.

Johnson, Michael S. Assessor Behavior in the Presence of Regulatory Constraints. *Southern Econ. J.*, April 1989, *55*(4), pp. 880–95.

Johnson, Nancy Brown; Sambharya, Rakesh B. and Bobko, Philip. Deregulation, Business Strategy, and Wages in the Airline Industry. *Ind. Relat.*, Fall 1989, *28*(3), pp. 419–30.

Johnson, Neal S. and Adams, Richard M. On the Marginal Value of a Fish: Some Evidence from a Steelhead Fishery. *Marine Resource Econ.*, 1989, *6*(1), pp. 43–55.

Johnson, Norman K. and DuMars, Charles T. A Survey of the Evolution of Western Water Law in Response to Changing Economic and Public Interest Demands. *Natural Res. J.*, Spring 1989, *29*(2), pp. 347–87.

Johnson, Norris Brock. Japanese Temple Gardens and the Apprentice Training of Priests. In *Coy, M. W., ed.*, 1989, pp. 211–32.

Johnson, Paul and Lambert, Peter J. Measuring the Responsiveness of Income Tax Revenue to Income Growth: A Review and Some UK Values. *Fisc. Stud.*, November 1989, *10*(4), pp. 1–18.

_____ **and Stark, Graham.** Ten Years of Mrs Thatcher: The Distributional Consequences. *Fisc. Stud.*, May 1989, *10*(2), pp. 29–37.

_____ **and Webb, Steven.** Counting People with Low Incomes: The Impact of Recent Changes in Official Statistics. *Fisc. Stud.*, November 1989, *10*(4), pp. 66–82.

Johnson, Peter S. Employment Change in the Small Establishment Sector in UK Manufacturing. *Appl. Econ.*, February 1989, *21*(2), pp. 251–60.

Johnson, Peter T. The Consistency of a Revolutionary Movement: Peru's Sendero Luminoso and Its Texts, 1965–1986. In *Martin, M. T. and Kandal, T. R., eds.*, 1989, pp. 267–96.

Johnson, R. Stafford; Fiore, Lyle C. and Zuber, Richard A. The Investment Performance of Common Stocks in Relation to Their Price–Earnings Ratios: An Update of the Basu Study. *Financial Rev.*, August 1989, *24*(3), pp. 499–505.

Johnson, R. W. M.; Schroder, W. R. and Taylor, N. W. Deregulation and the New Zealand Agricultural Sector: A Review. *Rev. Marketing Agr. Econ.*, April, Aug., Dec. 1989, *57*(1–2–3), pp. 47–74.

Johnson, Ralph R. Fundamental Market-Oriented Agricultural Reform: Is It Desirable? Is It Achievable? In *Helmuth, J. W. and Johnson, S. R., eds., Vol. 1*, 1989, pp. 207–19.

Johnson, Richard L.; Cordes, Joseph J. and Goldfarb, Robert S. Design and Implementation of Job Loss Compensation Provisions: Lessons from the Airline Deregulation Experience. *Int. J. Transport Econ.*, February 1989, *16*(1), pp. 35–55.

Johnson, Ronald N. and Libecap, Gary D. Agency Growth, Salaries and the Protected Bureaucrat. *Econ. Inquiry*, July 1989, *27*(3), pp. 431–51.

_____ **and Libecap, Gary D.** Bureaucratic Rules, Supervisor Behavior, and the Effect on Salaries in the Federal Government. *J. Law, Econ., Organ.*, Spring 1989, *5*(1), pp. 53–82.

_____ **and Watts, Myles J.** Contractual Stipulations, Resource Use, and Interest Groups: Implications from Federal Grazing Contracts. *J. Environ. Econ. Manage.*, January 1989, *16*(1), pp. 87–96.

Johnson, Ruth C.; Kaserman, David L. and Trimble, John L. Equilibration in a Negotiated Market: Evidence from Housing. *J. Urban Econ.*, July 1989, *26*(1), pp. 30–42.

Johnson, Stanley R. Discussion: Structural Change in Meat Demand: The End of the "Chicken Little" Era. In *Buse, R. C., ed.*, 1989, pp. 201–13.

_____ **and Choi, Eun Kwan.** Stochastic Dominance and Uncertain Price Prospects. *Southern Econ. J.*, January 1989, *55*(3), pp. 699–709.

_____ **and Holt, Matthew T.** Bounded Price Variation and Rational Expectations in an Endogenous Switching Model of the U.S. Corn Market. *Rev. Econ. Statist.*, November 1989, *71*(4), pp. 605–13.

_____, **et al.** 1988 World Food Conference: Proceedings: Summary and Recommendations. In *Helmuth, J. W. and Johnson, S. R., eds., Vol. 1*, 1989, pp. 243–51.

Johnson, Thomas G. and Kraybill, David S. Value-Added Activities as a Rural Development Strategy. *Southern J. Agr. Econ.*, July 1989, *21*(1), pp. 27–36.

Johnson, Timothy P.; Hougland, James G., Jr. and Clayton, Richard R. Obtaining Reports of Sensitive Behavior: A Comparison of Substance Use Reports from Telephone and Face-to-Face Interviews. *Soc. Sci. Quart.*, March 1989, *70*(1), pp. 174–83.

Johnson, W. and Geary, F. Unemployment, Participation Rates and Unemployment Legislation between the Wars. *Appl. Econ.*, October 1989, *21*(10), pp. 1341–52.

Johnston, Brian G.; Brennan, John P. and Godyn, Dirk L. An Economic Framework for Evaluating New Wheat Varieties. *Rev. Marketing Agr. Econ.*, April, Aug., Dec. 1989, *57*(1–2–3), pp. 75–92.

Johnston, Bruce F. The Political Economy of Agricultural Development in the Soviet Union and China. *Food Res. Inst. Stud.*, 1989, *21*(2), pp. 97–137.

_____. The Political Economy of Agricultural Development in Kenya and Tanzania. *Food Res. Inst. Stud.*, 1989, *21*(3), pp. 205–64.

Johnston, Elizabeth Tashjian and McConnell, John J. Requiem for a Market: An Analysis of the Rise and Fall of a Financial Futures Contract. *Rev. Financial Stud.*, 1989, *2*(1), pp. 1–23.

Johnston, Michael. Corruption, Inequality, and Change. In *Ward, P. M., ed.*, 1989, pp. 13–37.

_____. The Political Consequences of Corruption: A Reassessment. In *Heidenheimer, A. J.; Johnston, M. and LeVine, V. T., eds.*, 1989, *1986*, pp. 985–1006.

_____. Right and Wrong in American Politics: Popular Conceptions of Corruption. In *Heidenheimer, A. J.; Johnston, M. and LeVine, V. T., eds.*, 1989, *1986*, pp. 743–61.

_____; **LeVine, Victor T. and Heidenheimer, Arnold J.** Political Corruption: A Handbook: Terms, Concepts, and Definitions: An Intro-

duction. In *Heidenheimer, A. J.; Johnston, M. and LeVine, V. T., eds.*, 1989, pp. 3–14.

Johnston, Neil, et al. The Role of Fiscal Policy in Postwar Australian Economic Growth. In *[Gruen, F. H.]*, 1989, pp. 133–61.

Johnston, R. J. Extending the Research Agenda. *Econ. Geogr.*, October 1989, *65*(4), pp. 338–47.

_____ **and Pattie, C. J.** The Changing Electoral Geography of Great Britain. In *Mohan, J., ed.*, 1989, pp. 51–68.

Johnstone, Derrick. The European Commission and Long-Term Unemployment. In *Dyson, K., ed.*, 1989, pp. 51–74.

Joignaux, Guy and Scrawell, Helga. Enjeux et stratégies autour de la filière bio-éthanol. (Aims and Strategies in the Production of Bio-ethanol. With English summary.) *Écon. Societes*, July 1989, *23*(7), pp. 159–78.

Jolink, Albert and van Daal, Jan. Leon Walras' Latest Book: *Melanges d'economie politique et sociale*. *De Economist*, 1989, *137*(3), pp. 351–59.

Jolly, Alison. The Madagascar Challenge: Human Needs and Fragile Ecosystems. In *Leonard, H. J., ed.*, 1989, pp. 188–215.

Jolly, Curtis M. and Gadbois, Millie A. Foreign Aid as a Promotional Strategy. *Rev. Black Polit. Econ.*, Summer 1989, *18*(1), pp. 59–74.

Jolly, Richard and Grant, James P. The New Economics of Child Health and Survival. In *Adelman, I. and Lane, S., eds.*, 1989, pp. 32–44.

Joly, Pierre-Benoit. Stratégies d'entreprises et rupture technologique dans l'industrie des semences. (From Technological Breakthrough to Firm Strategies: The Case of Seed Industry. With English summary.) *Écon. Societes*, July 1989, *23*(7), pp. 91–106.

Jones, Andrew M. A Double-Hurdle Model of Cigarette Consumption. *J. Appl. Econometrics*, Jan.–March 1989, *4*(1), pp. 23–39.

_____. A Systems Approach to the Demand for Alcohol and Tobacco. *Bull. Econ. Res.*, April 1989, *41*(2), pp. 85–105.

_____. The UK Demand for Cigarettes 1954–1986, a Double-Hurdle Approach. *J. Health Econ.*, March 1989, *8*(1), pp. 133–41.

Jones, Anthony and Moskoff, William. Perestroika and the Economy: New Thinking in Soviet Economics: Introduction. In *Jones, A. and Moskoff, W., eds.*, 1989, pp. vii–xxi.

Jones, Bryn. Flexible Automation and Factory Politics: The United Kingdom in Comparative Perspective. In *Hirst, P. and Zeitlin, J., eds.*, 1989, pp. 95–121.

Jones, Carol Adaire. Standard Setting with Incomplete Enforcement Reviewed. *J. Policy Anal. Manage.*, Winter 1989, *8*(1), pp. 72–87.

Jones, Charles P. and Wilson, Jack W. The Analysis of the January Effect in Stocks and Interest Rates under Varying Monetary Regimes. *J. Finan. Res.*, Winter 1989, *12*(4), pp. 341–54.

Jones, Christine and Roemer, Michael. Modeling and Measuring Parallel Markets in Developing Countries: Editors' Introduction. *World*

Devel., December 1989, *17*(12), pp. 1861–70.

———; **Roemer, Michael and Devarajan, Shantayanan.** Markets under Price Controls in Partial and General Equilibrium. *World Devel.*, December 1989, *17*(12), pp. 1881–93.

Jones, Clive Vaughan. Errata: The Law of Demand and Commodities Sold at a Rate Schedule. *Amer. Economist*, Spring 1989, *33*(1), pp. 4.

———. The Policy Relevance of Process Descriptions of Technical Innovation. *J. Econ. Issues*, December 1989, *23*(4), pp. 1105–22.

Jones, D. R. After Redundancy—Labour Market Adjustment and Hysteresis Effects: Evidence from the Steel Industry. *Oxford Bull. Econ. Statist.*, August 1989, *51*(3), pp. 259–75.

Jones, David R. Europeanizing American Employment Issues. *J. Lab. Res.*, Winter 1989, *10*(1), pp. 1–4.

Jones, Derek C.; Egan, Daniel L. and Herrmann, Douglas J. Evidence on Attitudes toward Alternative Sharing Arrangements. *Ind. Relat.*, Fall 1989, *28*(3), pp. 411–18.

——— **and Hodgson, Geoff.** Codetermination: A Partial Review of Theory and Evidence. *Ann. Pub. Coop. Econ.*, 1989, *60*(3), pp. 329–40.

——— **and Pliskin, Jeffrey.** British Evidence on the Employment Effects of Profit Sharing. *Ind. Relat.*, Spring 1989, *28*(2), pp. 276–98.

Jones, Donald W. Urbanization and Energy Use in Economic Development. *Energy J.*, October 1989, *10*(4), pp. 29–44.

Jones, Ellen W.; Katz, Sidney and Densen, Paul M. Using Field Data to Shape New Policies. In *Eisdorfer, C.; Kessler, D. A. and Spector, A. N., eds.*, 1989, pp. 521–44.

Jones, Eugene and Mutuura, Josephine. The Supply Responsiveness of Small Kenyan Cotton Farmers. *J. Developing Areas*, July 1989, *23*(4), pp. 535–44.

Jones, Gavin W. Sub-national Population Policy: The Case of North Sulawesi. *Bull. Indonesian Econ. Stud.*, April 1989, *25*(1), pp. 77–104.

——— **and Sondakh, Lucky.** North Sulawesi: Unexploited Potential. In *Hill, H., ed.*, 1989, pp. 364–85.

Jones, Geoffrey and Bostock, Frances. British Business in Iran, 1860s–1970s. In *Davenport-Hines, R. P. T. and Jones, G., eds.*, 1989, pp. 31–67.

——— **and Davenport-Hines, R. P. T.** British Business in Asia since 1860. In *Davenport-Hines, R. P. T. and Jones, G., eds.*, 1989, pp. 1–30.

——— **and Davenport-Hines, R. P. T.** British Business in Asia since 1860: Preface. In *Davenport-Hines, R. P. T. and Jones, G., eds.*, 1989, pp. xv–xvi.

——— **and Davenport-Hines, R. P. T.** British Business in Japan since 1868. In *Davenport-Hines, R. P. T. and Jones, G., eds.*, 1989, pp. 217–44.

——— **and van Helten, Jean-Jacques.** British Business in Malaysia and Singapore since the 1870s. In *Davenport-Hines, R. P. T. and Jones, G., eds.*, 1989, pp. 157–88.

Jones-Hendrickson, S. B. Financial Structure and Economic Development in the Organisation of Eastern Caribbean States. *Soc. Econ. Stud.*, December 1989, *38*(4), pp. 71–93.

Jones, Ian. Risk Analysis and Optional Investment in the Electricity Supply Industry. In *Helm, D.; Kay, J. and Thompson, D., eds.*, 1989, pp. 214–36.

Jones, James R. The Budget Outlook and Federal Tax Policy. *Nat. Tax J.*, September 1989, *42*(3), pp. 215–18.

Jones, Jonathan D. A Comparison of Lag-Length Selection Techniques in Tests of Granger Causality between Money Growth and Inflation: Evidence for the U.S., 1959–86. *Appl. Econ.*, June 1989, *21*(6), pp. 809–22.

Jones, Kent. Voluntary Export Restraint: Political Economy, History and the Role of the GATT. *J. World Trade*, June 1989, *23*(3), pp. 125–40.

Jones, Lamar B. Schumpeter versus Darwin: In re Malthus. *Southern Econ. J.*, October 1989, *56*(2), pp. 410–22.

Jones, Larry E.; Manuelli, Rodolfo E. and Chari, Varadarajan V. Labor Contracts in a Model of Imperfect Competition. *Amer. Econ. Rev.*, May 1989, *79*(2), pp. 358–63.

Jones, Lawrence D. Current Wealth and Tenure Choice. *Amer. Real Estate Urban Econ. Assoc. J.*, Spring 1989, *17*(1), pp. 17–40.

Jones, M. C. Discretized and Interpolated Kernel Density Estimates. *J. Amer. Statist. Assoc.*, September 1989, *84*(407), pp. 733–41.

Jones, M. R. The Potential of Decision Analysis As a Means of Integrating the Environment into Energy Policy Decisionmaking. *Environ. Planning A*, October 1989, *21*(10), pp. 1315–27.

Jones, Mali B. and Goldscheider, Calvin. Living Arrangements among the Older Population. In *Goldscheider, F. K. and Goldscheider, C., eds.*, 1989, pp. 75–91.

Jones, Michael. Realistic Options and Relevant Extensions. In *Hamouda, O. F.; Rowley, R. and Wolf, B. M., eds.*, 1989, pp. 85–88.

Jones, Michael J. and Harris, Hazel C. Climatic Variability and Agronomic Management in Mediterranean Barley–Livestock Farming Systems. In *Oram, P. A., et al.*, 1989, pp. 563–72.

Jones, Randall S. Political Economy of Japan's Agricultural Policies. *World Econ.*, March 1989, *12*(1), pp. 29–38.

Jones, Rich and Whalley, John. A Canadian Regional General Equilibrium Model and Some Applications. *J. Urban Econ.*, May 1989, *25*(3), pp. 368–404.

Jones, Robert C. Group Rotation from the Bottom Up. *J. Portfol. Manage.*, Summer 1989, *15*(4), pp. 32–38.

Jones, Ronald W. Co-movements in Relative Commodity Prices and International Capital Flows: A Simple Model. *Econ. Inquiry*, January 1989, *27*(1), pp. 131–41.

———. New Trade Theory and the Less Developed Countries: Comment. In *[Díaz-Alejandro, C.]*, 1989, pp. 371–75.

———— **and Easton, Stephen T.** Perspectives on 'Buy-Outs' and the Ramaswami Effect. *J. Int. Econ.*, November 1989, 27(3–4), pp. 363–71.

———— **and Hayashibara, Masayuki.** Should a Factor-Market Distortion Be Widened? *Econ. Letters*, December 1989, 31(2), pp. 159–62.

———— **and Spencer, Barbara J.** Raw Materials, Processing Activities, and Protectionism. *Can. J. Econ.*, August 1989, 22(3), pp. 469–86.

———— **and Takemori, Shumpei.** Foreign Monopoly and Optimal Tariffs for the Small Open Economy. *Europ. Econ. Rev.*, December 1989, 33(9), pp. 1691–1707.

Jones, Stephen R. G. Have Your Lawyer Call My Lawyer: Bilateral Delegation in Bargaining Situations. *J. Econ. Behav. Organ.*, March 1989, 11(2), pp. 159–74.

————. Job Research Methods, Intensity and Effects. *Oxford Bull. Econ. Statist.*, August 1989, 51(3), pp. 277–96.

————. Reservation Wages and the Cost of Unemployment. *Economica*, May 1989, 56(222), pp. 225–46.

————. The Role of Negotiators in Union–Firm Bargaining. *Can. J. Econ.*, August 1989, 22(3), pp. 630–42.

———— **and McKenna, C. J.** The Effect of Outsiders on Union Contracts. *Europ. Econ. Rev.*, October 1989, 33(8), pp. 1567–73.

Jones, Wayne. Canadian Farm Income Outlook. *Can. J. Agr. Econ.*, Part 2, December 1989, 37(4), pp. 1221–30.

de Jong, A. H. M. Scope for Growth: An Evaluation. In *Muller, F. and Zwezerijnen, W. J., eds.*, 1989, pp. 163–78.

de Jong, E.; Van Kooten, G. C. and Weisensel, Ward P. Estimating the Costs of Soil Erosion: A Reply. *Can. J. Agr. Econ.*, November 1989, 37(3), pp. 555–62.

————; **Van Kooten, G. C. and Weisensel, Ward P.** Estimating the Costs of Soil Erosion in Saskatchewan. *Can. J. Agr. Econ.*, March 1989, 37(1), pp. 63–75.

de Jong, Eelke and Jager, Henk. The Contribution of the Ecu to Exchange-Rate Stability: A Further Reply. *Banca Naz. Lavoro Quart. Rev.*, December 1989, (171), pp. 477–81.

de Jong, Piet. Smoothing and Interpolation with the State-Space Model. *J. Amer. Statist. Assoc.*, December 1989, 84(408), pp. 1085–88.

de Jong, S. Global Company and World Financial Markets: Commentary. In *Sijben, J. J., ed.*, 1989, pp. 75–78.

Jonishi, Arthur. High Technology Industrial Cooperation between the U.S. and Japan. In *Matsuo, H., ed.*, 1989, pp. 58–63.

Jonker, P.; Streng, M. and Twilt, F. Gradient Newton Flows for Complex Polynomials. In *Dolecki, S., ed.*, 1989, pp. 177–90.

Jonung, Lars. Knut Wicksell on Unemployment. *Hist. Polit. Econ.*, Spring 1989, 21(1), pp. 27–42.

———— **and Batchelor, Roy A.** Cross-Sectional Evidence on the Rationality of the Mean and Vari-

ance of Inflation Expectations. In *Grunert, K. G. and Ölander, F., eds.*, 1989, pp. 93–105.

Jonzon, Björn and Wise, Lois Recascino. Getting Young People to Work: An Evaluation of Swedish Youth Employment Policy. *Int. Lab. Rev.*, 1989, 128(3), pp. 337–56.

Jooste, C. J.; Nortje, J. D. and Crous, M. J. Selfdoenmodules as Onderrigmedium vir die Kleinsakesektor in die RAS. (With English summary.) *J. Stud. Econ. Econometrics*, March 1989, 13(1), pp. 89–101.

Joray, Paul; Kochanowski, Paul and Bartholomew, Wayne. The Shift-Share Methodology: Deficiencies and Proposed Remedies. *Reg. Sci. Persp.*, 1989, 19(1), pp. 65–88.

Jorberg, Lennart and Kranz, Olle. Economic and Social Policy in Sweden, 1850–1939. In *Mathias, P. and Pollard, S., eds.*, 1989, pp. 1048–1105.

Jordan, Danny. Negotiating Salmon Management on the Klamath River. In *Pinkerton, E., ed.*, 1989, pp. 73–81.

Jordan, J. S. The Economics of Accounting Information Systems. *Amer. Econ. Rev.*, May 1989, 79(2), pp. 140–45.

Jordan, Jerry L. The Future of Price Stability in a Fiat Money World. *Cato J.*, Fall 1989, 9(2), pp. 471–86.

Jordan, John M.; Meador, Mark and Walters, Stephen J. K. Academic Research Productivity, Department Size and Organization: Further Results. *Econ. Educ. Rev.*, 1989, 8(4), pp. 345–52.

Jordan, Susan D. and Hilliard, Jimmy E. Hedging Interest Rate Risk with Futures Portfolios under Full-Rank Assumptions. *J. Finan. Quant. Anal.*, June 1989, 24(2), pp. 217–40.

Jorde, L. B.; Pitkänen, K. J. and Mielke, J. H. Smallpox and Its Eradication in Finland: Implications for Disease Control. *Population Stud.*, March 1989, 43(1), pp. 95–111.

Jorgensen, Erika and Sachs, Jeffrey D. Default and Renegotiation of Latin American Foreign Bonds in the Interwar Period. In *Eichengreen, B. and Lindert, P. H., eds.*, 1989, pp. 48–85.

Jørgensen, Steffen; Kort, Peter M. and van Schijndel, Geert-Jan C. Th. Optimal Investment, Financing, and Dividends: A Stackelberg Differential Game. *J. Econ. Dynam. Control*, July 1989, 13(3), pp. 339–77.

Jorgenson, Dale W. Capital as a Factor of Production. In *Jorgenson, D. W. and Landau, R., eds.*, 1989, pp. 1–35.

———— **and Fraumeni, Barbara M.** The Accumulation of Human and Nonhuman Capital, 1948–84. In *Lipsey, R. E. and Tice, H. S., eds.*, 1989, pp. 227–82.

Jorion, Philippe. Asset Allocation with Hedged and Unhedged Foreign Stocks and Bonds. *J. Portfol. Manage.*, Summer 1989, 15(4), pp. 49–54.

———— **and Giovannini, Alberto.** The Time Variation of Risk and Return in the Foreign Exchange and Stock Markets. *J. Finance*, June 1989, 44(2), pp. 307–25.

———— **and Stoughton, Neal M.** An Empirical Investigation of the Early Exercise Premium of Foreign Currency Options. *J. Futures Markets*, October 1989, 9(5), pp. 365–75.

Jorner, U. and Nilsson, Sam. Income and Profitability Analysis Based on Farm Models. In *Bauer, S. and Henrichsmeyer, W., eds.*, 1989, pp. 125–39.

Jörnsten, K. and Holmberg, K. Exact Methods for Gravity Trip-Distribution Models. *Environ. Planning A*, January 1989, 21(1), pp. 81–97.

Joseph, A. E.; Smit, B. and McIlravey, G. P. Consumer Preferences for Rural Residences: A Conjoint Analysis in Ontario, Canada. *Environ. Planning A*, January 1989, 21(1), pp. 47–63.

Joshi, Heather. The Changing Form of Women's Economic Dependency. In *Joshi, H., ed.*, 1989, pp. 157–76.

_____ **and Hobcraft, John.** Population Matters. In *Joshi, H., ed.*, 1989, pp. 1–11.

Joshi, Vijay and Collier, Paul. Exchange Rate Policy in Developing Countries. *Oxford Rev. Econ. Policy*, Autumn 1989, 5(3), pp. 94–113.

_____ **and Little, I. M. D.** Indian Macroeconomic Policies. In *[Díaz-Alejandro, C.]*, 1989, pp. 286–308.

Joshi, Yamini and Singh, Sudama. Structural Changes in the Economy of Uttar Pradesh during Seventies: An Input–Output Study. *Indian Econ. J.*, Oct.–Dec. 1989, 37(2), pp. 19–27.

Joskow, Paul L. Regulatory Failure, Regulatory Reform, and Structural Change in the Electrical Power Industry. *Brookings Pap. Econ. Act.*, Microeconomics, 1989, pp. 125–99.

_____ **and Rose, Nancy L.** The Effects of Economic Regulation. In *Schmalensee, R. and Willig, R. D., eds., Vol. 2*, 1989, pp. 1449–1506.

Jossa, Bruno. Class Struggle and Income Distribution in Kaleckian Theory. In *Sebastiani, M., ed.*, 1989, pp. 142–59.

Jouahri, Abdellatif. Privatization in Tunisia: Objectives and Limits: Comment. In *El-Naggar, S., ed.*, 1989, pp. 247–58.

Jouini, Elyes. A Remark on Clarke's Normal Cone and the Marginal Cost Pricing Rule. *J. Math. Econ.*, 1989, 18(1), pp. 95–101.

Joulfaian, David and Marlow, Michael L. The Determinants of Off-Budget Activity of State and Local Governments. *Public Choice*, November 1989, 63(2), pp. 113–23.

Jovane, F. Flexible Automation: A Need for Industry—A Challenge for Research. In *Archetti, F.; Lucertini, M. and Serafini, P., eds.*, 1989, pp. 185–92.

Jovanis, Paul P. A System Perspective on the Effects of Economic Deregulation on Motor Carrier Safety. In *Moses, L. N. and Savage, I., eds.*, 1989, pp. 277–86.

Jovanovic, Boyan. Observable Implications of Models with Multiple Equilibria. *Econometrica*, November 1989, 57(6), pp. 1431–37.

_____ **and Evans, David S.** An Estimated Model of Entrepreneurial Choice under Liquidity Constraints. *J. Polit. Econ.*, August 1989, 97(4), pp. 808–27.

_____ **and Lach, Saul.** Entry, Exit, and Diffusion

with Learning by Doing. *Amer. Econ. Rev.*, September 1989, 79(4), pp. 690–99.

_____ **and Rob, Rafael.** The Growth and Diffusion of Knowledge. *Rev. Econ. Stud.*, October 1989, 56(4), pp. 569–82.

Jovanović, Miroslav N. Industrial Policy and International Trade (Shaping Comparative Advantage). *Econ. Anal. Workers' Manage.*, 1989, 23(1), pp. 55–77.

Jovel, J. Roberto. Natural Disasters and Their Economic and Social Impact. *CEPAL Rev.*, August 1989, (38), pp. 133–45.

Jovičić, Milena. Zavisnost trgovinskog bilansa od stope rasta društvenog proizvoda Jugoslavije. (The Dependence of the Balance of Trade on the Growth Rate of Yugoslavia's Social Product. With English summary.) *Econ. Anal. Workers' Manage.*, 1989, 23(2), pp. 139–53.

Joy, O. Maurice; Fortin, Richard D. and Grube, R. Corwin. Seasonality in NASDAQ Dealer Spreads. *J. Finan. Quant. Anal.*, September 1989, 24(3), pp. 395–407.

Joy, Stewart. Railway Costs and Planning. *J. Transp. Econ. Policy*, January 1989, 23(1), pp. 45–54.

Joyce, Jon M. Effect of Firm Organizational Structure on Incentives to Engage in Price Fixing. *Contemp. Policy Issues*, October 1989, 7(4), pp. 19–35.

Joyce, Joseph P. An Investigation of Government Preference Functions: The Case of Canada, 1970–1981. *J. Macroecon.*, Spring 1989, 11(2), pp. 217–32.

Joyce, Michael; Britton, Andrew and Gregg, Paul. The Home Economy. *Nat. Inst. Econ. Rev.*, February 1989, (127), pp. 7–25.

_____ **; Britton, Andrew and Gregg, Paul.** The Home Economy. *Nat. Inst. Econ. Rev.*, May 1989, (128), pp. 5–19.

Joyce, Theodore J.; Grossman, Michael and Goldman, Fred. An Assessment of the Benefits of Air Pollution Control: The Case of Infant Health. *J. Urban Econ.*, January 1989, 25(1), pp. 32–51.

Joyce, Walter. Soviet Economic Reform and Technical Progress: Discussion. In *Berliner, J. S.; Kosta, H. G. J. and Hakogi, M., eds.*, 1989, pp. 54–55.

_____. The Soviet Far East and the Transbaikal: A New Strategy on the Back of Old Problems. In *Berliner, J. S.; Kosta, H. G. J. and Hakogi, M., eds.*, 1989, pp. 89–99.

Joynt, Patrick. International Strategy: A Study of Norwegian Companies. In *Prasad, S. B., ed.*, 1989, pp. 131–46.

_____ **and Johnsen, Paul.** Themes in the History of Industrial Relations in Norway. In *Barbash, J. and Barbash, K., eds.*, 1989, pp. 59–75.

Józefiak, Cezary. The Polish Reform: A Tentative Evaluation. In *Gabrisch, H., ed.*, 1989, pp. 133–73.

Juan, Fang; Li, Bingbai and Gao, Liangzhi. Climatic Variation and Food Production in Jiangsu, China. In *Oram, P. A., et al.*, 1989, pp. 557–62.

Judd, John P. and Trehan, Bharat. Unemployment-Rate Dynamics: Aggregate-Demand and -Supply Interactions. *Fed. Res. Bank San Francisco Econ. Rev.*, Fall 1989, (4), pp. 20–37.

Judd, Kenneth L. Patent Renewal Data: Comments. *Brookings Pap. Econ. Act.*, Microeconomics, 1989, pp. 402–04.

———— **and Bizer, David S.** Taxation and Uncertainty. *Amer. Econ. Rev.*, May 1989, 79(2), pp. 331–36.

Judge, G. G.; Bohrer, Robert and Yancey, T. A. Sampling Performance of Some Joint One-Sided Preliminary Test Estimators under Squared Error Loss. *Econometrica*, September 1989, 57(5), pp. 1221–28.

Judge, Ken and Smith, Jillian. Purchase of Service in England. In *James, E., ed.*, 1989, pp. 139–61.

Judita, Samuel. Stochastic Dynamic Systems with Controlled Transition Probabilities. *Econ. Computat. Econ. Cybern. Stud. Res.*, 1989, 24(4), pp. 21–39.

Juhász, P. Reform of Cooperative Ownership, and Land. *Acta Oecon.*, 1989, 41(3–4), pp. 421–33.

Juhrs, Patricia D. and Smith, Marcia Datlow. Community-Based Employment for Persons with Autism. In *Wehman, P. and Kregel, J., eds.*, 1989, pp. 163–75.

Jullien, Bruno and Green, Jerry R. Ordinal Independence in Nonlinear Utility Theory: Erratum. *J. Risk Uncertainty*, April 1989, 2(1), pp. 119.

Jump, Bernard. Governmental Accounting, Auditing and Finanacial Reporting: Another View. *Public Budg. Finance*, Summer 1989, 9(2), pp. 107.

Jun, Byoung Heon. Non-cooperative Bargaining and Union Formation. *Rev. Econ. Stud.*, January 1989, 56(1), pp. 59–76.

Junankar, P. N. The Response of Peasant Farmers to Price Incentives: The Use and Misuse of Profit Functions. *J. Devel. Stud.*, January 1989, 25(2), pp. 169–82.

Jung, Joon Pyo. Condorcet Consistent Binary Agendas under Incomplete Information. In *Ordeshook, P. C., ed.*, 1989, pp. 315–41.

Jung, Ku Hyun. Business–Government Relations in Korea. In *Chung, K. H. and Lee, H. C., eds.*, 1989, pp. 11–26.

Jung, Michael and Spremann, Klaus. Transaktionsrisiken. (With English summary.) *Z. Betriebswirtshaft*, January 1989, 59(1), pp. 94–112.

Jung, Woon-Oh and Beck, Paul J. Taxpayers' Reporting Decisions and Auditing under Information Asymmetry. *Accounting Rev.*, July 1989, 64(3), pp. 468–87.

Junne, Gerd. Competitiveness and the Impact of Change: Applications of "High Technologies." In *Katzenstein, P. J., ed.*, 1989, pp. 249–74.

Juoro, Umar. The Determinants of Agglomeration Economies in Indonesia and the Philippines. *Philippine Rev. Econ. Bus.*, June 1989, 26(1), pp. 141–71.

Juretic, Mark; Stolp, Chandler and Warner, David C. Patterns of Inpatient Mental Health, Mental Retardation, and Substance Abuse Service Utilization in California. *Soc. Sci. Quart.*, September 1989, 70(3), pp. 687–707.

Jürgens, Ulrich; Malsch, Thomas and Dohse, Knut. From "Fordism" to "Toyotaism"? The Social Organization of the Labor Process in the Japanese Automobile Industry. In *Park, S.-J., ed.*, 1989, pp. 9–43.

Jurin, Smiljan. Market and Current Key Problems in Socioeconomic Development. In *Macesich, G., ed.*, 1989, pp. 56–70.

Jurković, Lidija. Inflation and Relative Price Variability in Yugoslavia. *Econ. Letters*, 1989, 29(2), pp. 135–39.

Jurkovic, Pero. The Policy of Financing Social Needs in Recent Years. In *Macesich, G., ed.*, 1989, pp. 207–36.

Jussawalla, Meheroo. Overview of Thoughts Expressed on Information Technology and Economic Interdependence. In *Jussawalla, M.; Okuma, T. and Araki, T., eds.*, 1989, pp. 3–8.

———— **and Dworak, Stephen.** The Impact of Telematics on Financial Intermediaries and Market Interdependencies. In *Jussawalla, M.; Okuma, T. and Araki, T., eds.*, 1989, pp. 85–101.

———— **and Snow, Marcellus.** Deregulatory Trends in OECD Countries. In *Jussawalla, M.; Okuma, T. and Araki, T., eds.*, 1989, pp. 21–39.

Just, Richard E. and Chambers, Robert G. Estimating Multioutput Technologies. *Amer. J. Agr. Econ.*, November 1989, 71(4), pp. 980–95.

———— **and Foster, William.** Measuring Welfare Effects of Product Contamination with Consumer Uncertainty. *J. Environ. Econ. Manage.*, November 1989, 17(3), pp. 266–83.

———— **and Fulton, Murray.** Antitrust, Exploration, and Social Optimality in Nonrenewable Resource Markets. *J. Environ. Econ. Manage.*, July 1989, 17(1), pp. 1–21.

———— **and Schmitz, Andrew.** The Effect of U.S. Farm Programs on Diversification. In *Schmitz, A., ed.*, 1989, pp. 303–28.

Juster, F. Thomas; Morgan, James N. and Curtin, Richard T. Survey Estimates of Wealth: An Assessment of Quality. In *Lipsey, R. E. and Tice, H. S., eds.*, 1989, pp. 473–548.

Justice, S. Craig. The Increasing Importance of Financial Capital in the U.S. Economy: A Reply. *J. Econ. Issues*, March 1989, 23(1), pp. 249–50.

Justman, Moshe; Hochman, Eithan and Levy, Amnon. The Implications of Financial Cooperation in Israel's Semi-cooperative Villages. *J. Devel. Econ.*, January 1989, 30(1), pp. 25–46.

Jüttner, D. Johannes. Fundamentals, Bubbles, Trading Strategies: Are They the Causes of Black Monday? *Kredit Kapital*, 1989, 22(4), pp. 470–86.

Kaas, Klaus Peter and Uhlmann, Bernd. Pharma-Marketing. Möglichkeiten und Grenzen nach der Strukturreform des Gesundheitswesens. (With English summary.) *Z. Betriebswirtshaft*, June 1989, *59*(6), pp. 620–36.

Kabir, M. and Hackett, D. W. Is Atlantic Canada Becoming More Dependent on Federal Transfers? *Can. Public Policy*, March 1989, *15*(1), pp. 43–48.

Kaboudan, Mahmoud A. and Marzouk, M. S. A Retrospective Evaluation of Environmental Protection Projects in Kuwait. *J. Developing Areas*, July 1989, *23*(4), pp. 567–82.

Kabra, Kamal Nayan. Growth of the Service Sector and Inflationary Pressures. *Indian Econ. J.*, Oct.–Dec. 1989, *37*(2), pp. 8–18.

Kacprzyk, Janusz and Fedrizzi, Mario. A 'Human-Consistent' Degree of Consensus Based on Fuzzy Logic with Linguistic Quantifiers. *Math. Soc. Sci.*, December 1989, *18*(3), pp. 275–90.

Kadane, Joseph B.; Tierney, Luke and Kass, Robert E. Fully Exponential Laplace Approximations to Expectations and Variances of Nonpositive Functions. *J. Amer. Statist. Assoc.*, September 1989, *84*(407), pp. 710–16.

_____; **Tukey, John W. and Ericksen, Eugene P.** Adjusting the 1980 Census of Population and Housing. *J. Amer. Statist. Assoc.*, December 1989, *84*(408), pp. 927–44.

Kadapakkam, Palani-Rajan and Kon, Stanley J. The Value of Shelf Registration for New Debt Issues. *J. Bus.*, April 1989, *62*(2), pp. 271–92.

Kádár, Béla. Further Development of the Relationship between the Foreign-Economic Decision Making System and the Political Sphere. *Acta Oecon.*, 1989, *41*(1–2), pp. 79–100.

_____. Market Economy—Hungarian Way. *Acta Oecon.*, 1989, *40*(3–4), pp. 235–38.

Kadhim, Mihssen. Saint-Simonism and Its Relevancy to Third World Development. *Rivista Int. Sci. Econ. Com.*, January 1989, *36*(1), pp. 9–27.

Kaelble, Hartmut. Was Prometheus most Unbound in Europe? The Labour Force in Europe during the late XIXth and XXth Centuries. *J. Europ. Econ. Hist.*, Spring 1989, *18*(1), pp. 65–104.

Kaempfer, William H. Immiserising Growth with Globally Optimal Policies. *J. Econ. Stud.*, 1989, *16*(1), pp. 54–60.

_____. Protection of a Domestic Finishing Industry. *J. Econ. Devel.*, December 1989, *14*(2), pp. 117–26.

_____ **and Lowenberg, Anton D.** Sanctioning South Africa: The Politics behind the Policies. *Cato J.*, Winter 1989, *8*(3), pp. 713–27.

_____ **and Lowenberg, Anton D.** The Theory of International Economic Sanctions—A Public Choice Approach: Reply. *Amer. Econ. Rev.*, December 1989, *79*(5), pp. 1304–06.

_____; **McClure, J. Harold, Jr. and Willett, Thomas D.** Incremental Protection and Efficient Political Choice between Tariffs and Quotas. *Can. J. Econ.*, May 1989, *22*(2), pp. 228–36.

_____ **and Willett, Thomas D.** Combining Rent-Seeking and Public Choice Theory in the Anal-

ysis of Tariffs versus Quotas. *Public Choice*, October 1989, *63*(1), pp. 79–86.

Kafoglis, Milton and Buchanan, James M. A Note on Public Goods Supply. In *Buchanan, J. M. (II)*, 1989, *1963*, pp. 194–207.

Kaganovich, I. A. A Progressive Direction in Soviet Economic Science. *Matekon*, Spring 1989, *25*(3), pp. 75–77.

Kagel, John H.; Levin, Dan and Dyer, Douglas. A Comparison of Naive and Experienced Bidders in Common Value Offer Auctions: A Laboratory Analysis. *Econ. J.*, March 1989, *99*(394), pp. 108–15.

_____; **Levin, Dan and Dyer, Douglas.** Resolving Uncertainty about the Number of Bidders in Independent Private-Value Auctions: An Experimental Analysis. *Rand J. Econ.*, Summer 1989, *20*(2), pp. 268–79.

_____, **et al.** First-Price Common Value Auctions: Bidder Behavior and the "Winner's Curse." *Econ. Inquiry*, April 1989, *27*(2), pp. 241–58.

Kagono, Tadao. The Effect of Innovations in Information Technology on Corporate and Industrial Organisation in Japan: Comment. In *Shiraishi, T. and Tsuru, S., eds.*, 1989, pp. 184–87.

Kahan, Arcadius. Data for the Study of Russian History. In *Kahan, A.*, 1989, *1972*, pp. 199–228.

_____. Determinants of the Incidence of Literacy in Rural Nineteenth-Century Russia. In *Kahan, A.*, 1989, *1965*, pp. 186–90.

_____. Forms of Social Protest by the Agrarian Population in Russia. In *Kahan, A.*, 1989, pp. 157–67.

_____. Government Policies and the Industrialization of Russia. In *Kahan, A.*, 1989, *1967*, pp. 91–107.

_____. "Hereditary Workers" Hypothesis and the Development of a Factory Labor Force in Eighteenth- and Nineteenth-Century Russia. In *Kahan, A.*, 1989, *1965*, pp. 179–85.

_____. Notes on Serfdom in Western and Eastern Europe. In *Kahan, A.*, 1989, *1973*, pp. 145–56.

_____. The Russian Economy, 1860–1913. In *Kahan, A.*, 1989, pp. 1–90.

_____. Russian Scholars and Statesmen on Education as an Investment. In *Kahan, A.*, 1989, *1965*, pp. 191–98.

_____. Social Structure, Public Policy, and the Development of Education. In *Kahan, A.*, 1989, *1965*, pp. 168–78.

_____. The Tsar "Hunger" in the Land of the Tsars. In *Kahan, A.*, 1989, pp. 108–44.

Kahan, Marcel. Causation and Incentives to Take Care under the Negligence Rule. *J. Legal Stud.*, June 1989, *18*(2), pp. 427–47.

Kahan, Michael. Annual Review of Nations: Year 1988: South Korea. In *Haberman, L. and Sacks, P. M., eds.*, 1989, pp. 301–13.

_____. Annual Review of Nations: Year 1988: Spain. In *Haberman, L. and Sacks, P. M., eds.*, 1989, pp. 315–34.

Kahana, Nava. The Duality Approach in the Case

of Labour-Managed Firms. *Oxford Econ. Pap.*, July 1989, *41*(3), pp. 567–72.

───── and **Darvish, Tikva.** The Ratchet Principle: A Multi-period Flexible Incentive Scheme. *Europ. Econ. Rev.*, January 1989, *33*(1), pp. 51–57.

───── and **Nitzan, Shmuel.** More on Alternative Objectives of Labor-Managed Firms. *J. Compar. Econ.*, December 1989, *13*(4), pp. 527–38.

Kahl, Kandice H.; Hudson, Michael A. and **Ward, Clement E.** Cash Settlement Issues for Live Cattle Futures Contracts. *J. Futures Markets*, June 1989, *9*(3), pp. 237–48.

───── and **Miller, Stephen E.** Performance of Estimated Hedging Ratios under Yield Uncertainty. *J. Futures Markets*, August 1989, *9*(4), pp. 307–19.

Kahler, Miles. International Financial Institutions and the Politics of Adjustment. **In** *Nelson, J. M., ed.*, 1989, pp. 139–59.

───── and **Odell, John.** Developing Country Coalition-Building and International Trade Negotiations. **In** *Whalley, J., ed., Vol. 1*, 1989, pp. 149–67.

Kahley, William J. Interregional Migration: Boon or Bane for the South? *Fed. Res. Bank Atlanta Econ. Rev.*, Jan.–Feb. 1989, *74*(1), pp. 18–34.

─────. U.S. and Foreign Direct Investment Patterns. *Fed. Res. Bank Atlanta Econ. Rev.*, Nov.–Dec. 1989, *74*(6), pp. 42–57.

Kahn, Alfred E. Telecommunications in a Competitive Environment: Closing Remarks. **In** *National Economic Research Associates*, 1989, pp. 227–33.

Kahn, James R. and **Buerger, Robert.** New York Value of Chesapeake Striped Bass. *Marine Resource Econ.*, 1989, *6*(1), pp. 19–25.

───── and **Clark, David E.** The Two-Stage Hedonic Wage Approach: A Methodology for the Valuation of Environmental Amenities. *J. Environ. Econ. Manage.*, March 1989, *16*(2), pp. 106–20.

Kahn, Lawrence M. and **Blau, Francine D.** A Model of Joint Wage and Hiring Discrimination. **In** *Ehrenberg, R. G., ed.*, 1989, pp. 157–205.

Kahn, Shulamit and **Griesinger, Harriet.** Female Mobility and the Returns to Seniority: Should EEO Policy Be Concerned with Promotion? *Amer. Econ. Rev.*, May 1989, *79*(2), pp. 300–304.

Kahneman, Daniel and **Tversky, Amos.** Judgment under Uncertainty: Heuristics and Biases. **In** *Diamond, P. and Rothschild, M., eds.*, 1989, *1974*, pp. 19–34.

Kain, John F. The Economics of Architecture and Urban Design: Some Preliminary Findings: Comments. *Amer. Real Estate Urban Econ. Assoc. J.*, Summer 1989, *17*(2), pp. 261–65.

Kaiser, Helmut and **Spahn, P. Bernd.** On the Efficiency and Distributive Justice of Consumption Taxes: A Study on VAT in West Germany. *J. Econ. (Z. Nationalökon.)*, 1989, *49*(2), pp. 199–218.

Kaiser, Manfred. Long-Term Unemployment and

Locally-Based Initiatives: West German Experience. **In** *Dyson, K., ed.*, 1989, pp. 152–79.

Kaish, S.; Ronen, Joshua and **Gilad, B.** Information, Search, and Entrepreneurship: A Pilot Study. *J. Behav. Econ.*, Fall 1989, *18*(3), pp. 217–35.

Kaitala, Veijo and **Dockner, Engelbert J.** On Efficient Equilibrium Solutions in Dynamic Games of Resource Management. *Resources & Energy*, March 1989, *11*(1), pp. 23–34.

Kaizuka, Keimei. A Comparative Study on Financial Development. **In** *Sato, R. and Negishi, T., eds.*, 1989, pp. 197–216.

Kakwani, Nanak. On Measuring Undernutrition. *Oxford Econ. Pap.*, July 1989, *41*(3), pp. 528–52.

Kalantari, B. and **Hammer, Peter L.** A Bound on the Roof-Duality Gap. **In** *Simeone, B., ed.*, 1989, pp. 254–57.

Kaldor, Nicholas. Alternative Theories of Distribution. **In** *Kaldor, N.*, 1989, *1956*, pp. 201–28.

─────. Capital Accumulation and Economic Growth. **In** *Kaldor, N.*, 1989, *1958*, pp. 229–81.

─────. Capitalism and Industrial Development: Some Lessons from Britain's Experience. **In** *Kaldor, N.*, 1989, *1977*, pp. 351–69.

─────. The Case for Regional Policies. **In** *Kaldor, N.*, 1989, *1970*, pp. 311–26.

─────. Causes of the Slow Rate of Economic Growth in the United Kingdom. **In** *Kaldor, N.*, 1989, *1966*, pp. 282–310.

─────. Conflicts in National Economic Objectives. **In** *Kaldor, N.*, 1989, *1971*, pp. 495–515.

─────. The Determinateness of Static Equilibrium. **In** *Kaldor, N.*, 1989, *1934*, pp. 27–47.

─────. The Equilibrium of the Firm. **In** *Kaldor, N.*, 1989, *1934*, pp. 48–64.

─────. Equilibrium Theory and Growth Theory. **In** *Kaldor, N.*, 1989, *1977*, pp. 411–33.

─────. How Monetarism Failed. **In** *Guttmann, R., ed.*, 1989, *1985*, pp. 48–57.

─────. Inflation and Recession in the World Economy. **In** *Kaldor, N.*, 1989, *1976*, pp. 516–32.

─────. The Irrelevance of Equilibrium Economics. **In** *Kaldor, N.*, 1989, *1972*, pp. 373–98.

─────. John von Neumann and Modern Economics: Foreword. **In** *Dore, M.; Chakravarty, S. and Goodwin, R., eds.*, 1989, pp. vii–xi.

─────. Keynesian Economics after Fifty Years. **In** *Kaldor, N.*, 1989, *1983*, pp. 164–98.

─────. Limits on Growth. **In** *Wood, J. C. and Woods, R. N., eds., Vol. 4*, 1989, *1986*, pp. 253–64.

─────. Market Imperfection and Excess Capacity. **In** *Kaldor, N.*, 1989, *1935*, pp. 65–83.

─────. A Model of the Trade Cycle. **In** *Kaldor, N.*, 1989, *1940*, pp. 148–63.

─────. Monetary Policy, Economic Stability and Growth. **In** *Kaldor, N.*, 1989, pp. 448–73.

─────. Mr Hicks on the Trade Cycle. **In** *Wood, J. C. and Woods, R. N., eds., Vol. 1*, 1989, *1951*, pp. 146–58.

─────. A New Look at the Expenditure Tax. **In** *Kaldor, N.*, 1989, pp. 437–47.

_____. The New Monetarism. In *Kaldor, N.,* 1989, *1970,* pp. 474–94.

_____. Personal Recollections on Michal Kalecki. In *Sebastiani, M., ed.,* 1989, pp. 3–9.

_____. Prof. Pigou on Money Wages in Relation to Unemployment. In *Kaldor, N.,* 1989, *1937,* pp. 91–100.

_____. The Role of Commodity Prices in Economic Recovery. In *Kaldor, N.,* 1989, *1983,* pp. 533–49.

_____. The Role of Increasing Returns, Technical Progress and Cumulative Causation in the Theory of International Trade and Economic Growth. In *Kaldor, N.,* 1989, *1981,* pp. 327–50.

_____. Speculation and Economic Stability. In *Kaldor, N.,* 1989, pp. 101–47.

_____. Welfare Propositions in Economics. In *Kaldor, N.,* 1989, *1939,* pp. 84–87.

_____. What Is Wrong with Economic Theory. In *Kaldor, N.,* 1989, *1975,* pp. 399–410.

Kale, Jayant R.; Badrinath, S. G. and Gay, Gerald D. Patterns of Institutional Investment, Prudence, and the Managerial "Safety-Net" Hypothesis. *J. Risk Ins.,* December 1989, *56*(4), pp. 605–29.

_____; **Noe, Thomas H. and Gay, Gerald D.** Share Repurchase through Transferable Put Rights: Theory and Case Study. *J. Finan. Econ.,* November 1989, *25*(1), pp. 141–60.

Kalirajan, K. P. On Measuring the Contribution of Human Capital to Agricultural Production. *Indian Econ. Rev.,* July–Dec. 1989, *24*(2), pp. 247–61.

_____. A Test for Heteroscedasticity and Nonnormality of Regression Residuals. *Econ. Letters,* August 1989, *30*(2), pp. 133–36.

_____ **and Shand, R. T.** A Generalized Measure of Technical Efficiency. *Appl. Econ.,* January 1989, *21*(1), pp. 25–34.

_____ **and Tse, Y. K.** Technical Efficiency Measures for the Malaysian Food Manufacturing Industry. *Developing Econ.,* June 1989, *27*(2), pp. 174–84.

Kallaste, Tiit. An Approach to Forecast the Level of Air Pollution. *Statist. J.,* 1989, *6*(4), pp. 349–57.

Kally, Elisha. The Potential for Cooperation in Water Projects in the Middle East at Peace. In *Fishelson, G., ed.,* 1989, pp. 303–25.

Kalt, Joseph P. Exhaustible Resource Price Policy, International Trade, and Intertemporal Welfare. *J. Environ. Econ. Manage.,* September 1989, *17*(2), pp. 109–26.

_____ **and Broadman, Harry G.** How Natural Is Monopoly? The Case of Bypass in Natural Gas Distribution Markets. *Yale J. Regul.,* Summer 1989, *6*(2), pp. 181–208.

Kalton, Graham. Modeling Considerations: Discussion from a Survey Sampling Perspective. In *Kasprzyk, D., et al., eds.,* 1989, pp. 575–85.

_____; **Kasprzyk, Daniel and McMillen, David B.** Nonsampling Errors in Panel Surveys. In *Kasprzyk, D., et al., eds.,* 1989, pp. 249–70.

_____; **Ludwig, Jacob and Schuman, Howard.** Context and Contiguity in Survey Questionnaires. In *Singer, E. and Presser, S., eds.,* 1989, *1983,* pp. 151–54.

Kalua, B. and Nankumba, J. S. Contract Farming in Malawi: Smallholder Sugar and Tea Authorities. *Eastern Afr. Econ. Rev.,* Special Issue, August 1989, pp. 42–58.

Kamal, Salih; Nakamura, Yoichi and Lo, Fuchen. Structural Interdependency and the Outlook for the Asian-Pacific Economy towards the Year 2000. In *Shinohara, M. and Lo, F., eds.,* 1989, pp. 80–107.

Kamal, Yousaf. Energy and the Economy in Pakistan. In *James, W. E., ed.,* 1989, pp. 177–82.

Kamarck, Andrew M. and Goode, Richard. The Role of the Economist in Government: An International Perspective: The International Monetary Fund and the World Bank. In *Pechman, J. A., ed.,* 1989, pp. 231–54.

Kamasaki, Charles. Farm Workers, Agriculture, and the Politics of Immigration Reform: The Immigration Reform and Control Act of 1986: Commentary. In *Krämer, C. S., ed.,* 1989, pp. 258–60.

Kamath, Ravindra; Grieves, Robin and Khaksari, Shahriar. A New Approach to Determining Optimum Portfolio Mix. *J. Portfol. Manage.,* Spring 1989, *15*(3), pp. 43–49.

Kamath, Shyam J. Concealed Takings: Capture and Rent-Seeking in the Indian Sugar Industry. *Public Choice,* August 1989, *62*(2), pp. 119–38.

_____; **Jensen, K. C. and Bennett, R. E.** Reprise and Clarification [Money in the Production Function—An Alternative Test Procedure]. *Eastern Econ. J.,* July–Sept. 1989, *15*(3), pp. 241–43.

Kamecke, U. Non-cooperative Matching Games. *Int. J. Game Theory,* 1989, *18*(4), pp. 423–31.

Kamien, Morton I.; Li, Lode and Samet, Dov. Bertrand Competition with Subcontracting. *Rand J. Econ.,* Winter 1989, *20*(4), pp. 553–67.

Kaminsky, Graciela. Economic Policy without Political Context: Guido, 1962–63: Comment. In *di Tella, G. and Dornbusch, R., eds.,* 1989, pp. 142–45.

Kamlet, Mark S.; Nagin, Daniel S. and Cassidy, Glenn. An Empirical Examination of Bias in Revenue Forecasts by State Governments. *Int. J. Forecasting,* 1989, *5*(3), pp. 321–31.

Kamma, Sreenivas; Perry, Philip R. and Hartigan, James C. The Injury Determination Category and the Value of Relief from Dumping. *Rev. Econ. Statist.,* February 1989, *71*(1), pp. 183–86.

_____; **Weintrop, Joseph and Choi, Dosoung.** The Delaware Courts, Poison Pills, and Shareholder Wealth. *J. Law, Econ., Organ.,* Fall 1989, *5*(2), pp. 375–93.

Kamstra, Mark; Granger, C. W. J. and White, Halbert. Interval Forecasting: An Analysis Based upon ARCH-Quantile Estimators. *J. Econometrics,* January 1989, *40*(1), pp. 87–96.

Kanaan, Taher H. Privatization in Jordan: Comment. In *El-Naggar, S., ed.,* 1989, pp. 226–32.

Kanafani, Adib and Keeler, Theodore E. New Entrants and Safety. In *Moses, L. N. and Savage, I., eds.*, 1989, pp. 115–28.

Kanatas, George. Commercial Paper, Bank Reserve Requirements and the Informational Role of Loan Commitments: Reply. *J. Banking Finance*, May 1989, *13*(2), pp. 279–81.

_____; **Venezia, Itzhak and Greenbaum, Stuart I.** Equilibrium Loan Pricing under the Bank–Client Relationship. *J. Banking Finance*, May 1989, *13*(2), pp. 221–35.

Kanawaty, George, et al. Adjustment at the Micro Level. *Int. Lab. Rev.*, 1989, *128*(3), pp. 269–96.

Kanaya, Sadao and Hori, Hajime. Utility Functionals with Nonpaternalistic Intergenerational Altruism. *J. Econ. Theory*, December 1989, *49*(2), pp. 241–65.

Kanbur, Ravi and Keen, Michael. Poverty, Incentives, and Linear Income Taxation. In *Dilnot, A. and Walker, I., eds.*, 1989, pp. 99–115.

Kandal, Terry R. Marx and Engels on International Relations, Revolution, and Counterrevolution. In *Martin, M. T. and Kandal, T. R., eds.*, 1989, pp. 25–76.

_____ **and Martin, Michael T.** Studies of Development and Change in the Modern World: Introduction. In *Martin, M. T. and Kandal, T. R., eds.*, 1989, pp. 3–21.

Kandel, Shmuel and Huberman, Gur. Firms' Fiscal Years, Size and Industry. *Econ. Letters*, 1989, *29*(1), pp. 69–75.

_____ **and Stambaugh, Robert F.** A Mean–Variance Framework for Tests of Asset Pricing Models. *Rev. Financial Stud.*, 1989, *2*(2), pp. 125–56.

Kane, Edward J. The Bush Plan Is No Cure for the S&L Insurance Malady. *Challenge*, Nov.–Dec. 1989, *32*(6), pp. 39–43.

_____. Changing Incentives Facing Financial-Services Regulators. *J. Finan. Services Res.*, September 1989, *2*(3), pp. 265–74.

_____. The High Cost of Incompletely Funding the FSLIC Shortage of Explicit Capital. *J. Econ. Perspectives*, Fall 1989, *3*(4), pp. 31–47.

_____. International Competition in the Market for Financial Regulatory Services. In *Singer, H. W. and Sharma, S., eds. (II)*, 1989, pp. 230–34.

_____. The Looting of FSLIC: What Went Wrong? Panel Presentation. In *Federal Home Loan Bank of San Francisco*, 1989, pp. 49–59.

Kane, Robert L. and Kane, Rosalie A. Vacating the Premises: A Reevaluation of First Principles. In *Eisdorfer, C.; Kessler, D. A. and Spector, A. N., eds.*, 1989, pp. 490–506.

Kane, Rosalie A. and Kane, Robert L. Vacating the Premises: A Reevaluation of First Principles. In *Eisdorfer, C.; Kessler, D. A. and Spector, A. N., eds.*, 1989, pp. 490–506.

Kaneda, Hiromitsu. Rural Resource Mobility and Intersectoral Balance in Early Modern Growth. In *Williamson, J. G. and Panchamukhi, V. R., eds.*, 1989, pp. 367–89.

Kaneko, Hiroshi and Miyatake, Toshio. The Disregard of a Legal Entity for Tax Purposes: Japan. In *International Fiscal Association, ed. (II)*, 1989, pp. 355–62.

Kaneko, Mamoru and Wooders, Myrna Holtz. The Core of a Continuum Economy with Widespread Externalities and Finite Coalitions: From Finite to Continuum Economies. *J. Econ. Theory*, October 1989, *49*(1), pp. 135–68.

_____; **Wooders, Myrna Holtz and Hammond, Peter J.** Continuum Economies with Finite Coalitions: Core, Equilibria, and Widespread Externalities. *J. Econ. Theory*, October 1989, *49*(1), pp. 113–34.

Kanemitsu, Hideo and Ohnishi, Hiroshi. An Input–Output Analysis of Technological Changes in the Japanese Economy: 1970–1980. In *Miller, R. E.; Polenske, K. R. and Rose, A. Z., eds.*, 1989, pp. 308–23.

Kanemoto, Yoshitsugu and MacLeod, W. Bentley. Optimal Labor Contracts with Non-contractible Human Capital. *J. Japanese Int. Economies*, December 1989, *3*(4), pp. 385–402.

Kang, Heejoon. The Optimal Lag Selection and Transfer Function Analysis in Granger Causality Tests. *J. Econ. Dynam. Control*, April 1989, *13*(2), pp. 151–69.

_____ **and Davidson, Lawrence S.** Changes in Long-term Economic Trends: Before and after the 1930s. *J. Macroecon.*, Winter 1989, *11*(1), pp. 1–23.

Kang, Kyoungsik and Ito, Takatoshi. Bonuses, Overtime, and Employment: Korea vs Japan. *J. Japanese Int. Economies*, December 1989, *3*(4), pp. 424–50.

Kang, Myung-Kyu. Industrial Management and Reforms in North Korea. In *Gomulka, S.; Ha, Y.-C. and Kim, C.-O., eds.*, 1989, pp. 200–211.

Kang, Suk and Bishop, John Hillman. Vocational and Academic Education in High School: Complements or Substitutes? *Econ. Educ. Rev.*, 1989, *8*(2), pp. 133–48.

Kang, Suki and Schreiner, Dean F. Analysis of Public Subsidy to Rural Community Water Systems. *Reg. Sci. Persp.*, 1989, *19*(1), pp. 40–64.

Kang, Zhuo. Chairman Mao Comes to Xushui. In *Howe, C. and Walker, K. R., eds.*, 1989, *1958*, pp. 247–50.

Kanjanapan, Wilawan. The Asian-American Traditional Household. In *Goldscheider, F. K. and Goldscheider, C., eds.*, 1989, pp. 39–55.

Kannai, Yakar. A Characterization of Monotone Individual Demand Functions. *J. Math. Econ.*, 1989, *18*(1), pp. 87–94.

Kannan, Srinivasan and Fraser, Donald R. The Risk Implications of Forecast Errors of Bank Earnings, 1976–1986. *J. Finan. Res.*, Fall 1989, *12*(3), pp. 261–68.

Kannappan, Subbiah. Urban Labor Markets in Developing Countries. *Finance Devel.*, June 1989, *26*(2), pp. 46–48.

Kanniainen, Vesa and Airaksinen, Timo. Financial Hierarchy, Risk and Taxes in the Determination of Corporate Debt Policy: Preliminary Results with Finnish Data. *Liiketaloudellinen Aikak.*, 1989, 38(4), pp. 279–92.

Kanodia, Chandra; Bushman, Robert and Dickhaut, John. Escalation Errors and the Sunk Cost Effect: An Explanation Based on Reputation and Information Asymmetries. *J. Acc. Res.*, Spring 1989, 27(1), pp. 59–77.

Kanovsky, Eliyahu. The Economic Aspects of Peace in the Middle East: Oil and the Arms Race. In *Fishelson, G., ed.*, 1989, pp. 31–54.

Kant, Chander. Perverse Intra-firm Trade. *Southern Econ. J.*, July 1989, 56(1), pp. 233–35.

Kantor, B. S. Estimating the Value of Unrecorded Economic Activity in South Africa. *J. Stud. Econ. Econometrics*, March 1989, 13(1), pp. 33–53.

—— **and Barr, G. D. I.** Money and Economic Activity, a Response to the Reserve Bank. *S. Afr. J. Econ.*, September 1989, 57(3), pp. 292–98.

Kantorovich, Leonid V. Mathematics in Economics: Achievements, Difficulties, Perspectives. *Amer. Econ. Rev.*, December 1989, 79(6), pp. 18–22.

Kantsos, E. T.; Zagouras, N. G. and Caouris, Y. G. Production and Cost Functions of Water Low-Temperature Solar Desalination. *Appl. Econ.*, September 1989, 21(9), pp. 1177–89.

Kao, Chihwa and Dutkowsky, Donald H. An Application of Nonlinear Bounded Influence Estimation to Aggregate Bank Borrowing from the Federal Reserve. *J. Amer. Statist. Assoc.*, September 1989, 84(407), pp. 700–709.

Kapes, Jerome T. Implementation of the Carl D. Perkins Vocational Education Act in Texas. *Econ. Educ. Rev.*, 1989, 8(1), pp. 95–105.

Kaplan, Donald M. Alternative Strategies for Success. In *Federal Home Loan Bank of San Francisco*, 1989, pp. 81–105.

Kaplan, Gilbert and Kuhbach, Susan Haggerty. Recent U.S. Developments in Cost of Production Analysis. In *Jackson, J. H. and Vermulst, E. A., eds.*, 1989, pp. 360–65.

Kaplan, Richard L. Perspectives on International Tax Compliance and Enforcement: Transfer Pricing in the United States. *Australian Tax Forum*, 1989, 6(4), pp. 423–54.

Kaplan, Steven N. Campeau's Acquisitions of Federated: Value Destroyed or Value Added. *J. Finan. Econ.*, December 1989, 25(2), pp. 191–212.

——. The Effects of Management Buyouts on Operating Performance and Value. *J. Finan. Econ.*, October 1989, 24(2), pp. 217–54.

——. Management Buyouts: Evidence on Taxes as a Source of Value. *J. Finance*, July 1989, 44(3), pp. 611–32.

Kaplinsky, Raphael. Industrial and Intellectual Property Rights in the Uruguay Round and Beyond. *J. Devel. Stud.*, April 1989, 25(3), pp. 373–400.

Kaplow, Louis. Horizontal Equity: Measures in Search of a Principle. *Nat. Tax J.*, June 1989, 42(2), pp. 139–54.

Kapp, Mary C.; Smits, Helen L. and Berkman, Lisa F. The Value of Medical Care: Four Case Studies. In *Eisdorfer, C.; Kessler, D. A. and Spector, A. N., eds.*, 1989, pp. 322–40.

Kappel, Robert. Global Trends in International Shipping: Over-Capacities, Liberalization and National State Interference. In *Wohlmuth, K., ed.*, 1989, pp. 319–55.

Kapstein, Ethan B. From Guns to Butter in the USSR. *Challenge*, Sept.–Oct. 1989, 32(5), pp. 11–15.

——. Resolving the Regulator's Dilemma: International Coordination of Banking Regulations. *Int. Organ.*, Spring 1989, 43(2), pp. 323–47.

Kapteyn, Arie; Melenberg, Bertrand and Alessie, Rob. The Effects of Liquidity Constraints on Consumption: Estimation from Household Panel Data. *Europ. Econ. Rev.*, March 1989, 33(2/3), pp. 547–55.

—— **and Wansbeek, Tom.** Estimation of the Error-Components Model with Incomplete Panels. *J. Econometrics*, July 1989, 41(3), pp. 341–61.

——; **Woittiez, Isolde and ten Hacken, Peter.** Unemployment Benefits and the Labor Market, A Micro/Macro Approach. In *Gustafsson, B. A. and Klevmarken, N. A., eds.*, 1989, pp. 143–64.

Kapur, Basant K. Inflation and Financial Deepening: Comment. *J. Devel. Econ.*, October 1989, 31(2), pp. 379–96.

——. The J-Curve and Short-run Exchange-Rate Dynamics. *Int. Econ. J.*, Autumn 1989, 3(3), pp. 85–104.

Karacaoglu, Girol and Kohn, Meir. Aggregation and the Microfoundations of the Monetary Approach to the Balance of Payments. *Can. J. Econ.*, May 1989, 22(2), pp. 290–309.

—— **and Ursprung, Heinrich W.** Exchange-Rate Dynamics under Gradual Portfolio and Commodity-Price Adjustment. *Europ. Econ. Rev.*, July 1989, 33(6), pp. 1205–26.

Karadeloglou, P.; Mentzas, G. N. and Capros, Pantelis. Energy Policy Extensions of KLE-Based Macroeconomic Models. *J. Policy Modeling*, Winter 1989, 11(4), pp. 507–30.

Karafiath, Imre and Glascock, John L. Intra-industry Effects of a Regulatory Shift: Capital Market Evidence from Penn Square. *Financial Rev.*, February 1989, 24(1), pp. 123–34.

Karakitsos, E. Monetary Policy Exchange Rate Dynamics and the Labour Market. *Oxford Econ. Pap.*, April 1989, 41(2), pp. 408–33.

Karamouzis, Nicholas and Lombra, Raymond E. Federal Reserve Policymaking: An Overview and Analysis of the Policy Process. *Carnegie–Rochester Conf. Ser. Public Policy*, Spring 1989, 30, pp. 7–62.

Karanja, R. W. Privatisation in Kenya. In *Ramanadham, V. V., ed.*, 1989, pp. 268–82.

Karataş, Cevat. Economic Evaluation of Istanbul Metro System and Bosphorus Railroad Tube Tunnel Crossing. In *Candemir, Y., ed.*, 1989, pp. 370–96.

_____. 3. Boğaz Köprüsü ile Boğaz Karayolu Tüp Tünel Projesinin Ekonomik Değerlendirmesi. (Third Bosphorus Bridge versus Bosphorus Road Tube Tunnel: An Economic Appraisal. With English summary.) *METU*, 1989, *16*(1–2), pp. 177–225.

Kare, D. D.; Caples, S. C. and Herbst, Anthony F. Hedging Effectiveness and Minimum Risk Hedge Ratios in the Presence of Autocorrelation: Foreign Currency Futures. *J. Futures Markets*, June 1989, *9*(3), pp. 185–97.

Kareem P., Abdul. The Second-Stage of Import Substitution: Case of India. *Indian Econ. J.*, Jan.–March 1989, *36*(3), pp. 88–93.

Karels, Gordon V. Market Forces and Aircraft Safety: An Extension. *Econ. Inquiry*, April 1989, *27*(2), pp. 345–54.

Karfakis, Costas and Moschos, Demetrios. Testing for Long Run Purchasing Power Parity: A Time Series Analysis for the Greek Drachma. *Econ. Letters*, September 1989, *30*(3), pp. 245–48.

Karier, Thomas. New Evidence on the Effect of Unions and Imports on Monopoly Profits: A Rejoinder. *J. Post Keynesian Econ.*, Winter 1988–89, *11*(2), pp. 318–23.

Karkosh, Kedrick; Osborne, Clark and McGrann, James M. Agricultural Financial Analysis Expert Systems: Software Description. *Can. J. Agr. Econ.*, Part 1, December 1989, *37*(4), pp. 695–708.

Karlinsky, Stewart S.; Milliron, Valerie C. and Watkins, Paul R. Policy Judgments of Taxpayers: An Analysis of Criteria Employed. In *Jones, S. M., ed.*, 1989, pp. 201–21.

Karlsson, Charlie; Andersson, Åke E. and Batten, David F. From the Industrial Age to the Knowledge Economy. In *Andersson, Å. E.; Batten, D. F. and Karlsson, C., eds.*, 1989, pp. 1–13.

_____ **and Anderstig, Christer.** Spatial Diffusion of Information Technology in Sweden. In *Andersson, Å. E.; Batten, D. F. and Karlsson, C., eds.*, 1989, pp. 157–76.

Karlsson, Christer. Hindering and Supporting Factors in the Start-Up of New, Small, Technology Based Firms. In *Francis, A. and Tharakan, P. K. M., eds.*, 1989, pp. 91–109.

Karlsson, Per-Arne. Housekeeping Ideology and Equilibrium Policy in Eighteenth-Century Sweden: Socio-economic Theory and Practice prior to the Market Society. *Scand. Econ. Hist. Rev.*, 1989, *37*(2), pp. 51–77.

Karni, Edi. Generalized Expected Utility Analysis of Multivariate Risk Aversion. *Int. Econ. Rev.*, May 1989, *30*(2), pp. 297–305.

_____ **and Safra, Zvi.** Dynamic Consistency, Revelations in Auctions and the Structure of Preferences. *Rev. Econ. Stud.*, July 1989, *56*(3), pp. 421–33.

_____ **and Zilcha, Itzhak.** Aggregate and Distributional Effects of Fair Social Security. *J. Public Econ.*, October 1989, *40*(1), pp. 37–56.

Karotkin, D. and Paroush, Jacob. Robustness of Optimal Majority Rules over Teams with

Changing Size. *Soc. Choice Welfare*, April 1989, *6*(2), pp. 127–38.

Karp, Larry S. and Fulton, Murray E. Estimating the Objectives of a Public Firm in a Natural Resource Industry. *J. Environ. Econ. Manage.*, May 1989, *16*(3), pp. 268–87.

_____ **and Gallini, Nancy.** Sales and Consumer Lock-In. *Economica*, August 1989, *56*(223), pp. 279–94.

_____ **and Perloff, Jeffrey M.** Dynamic Oligopoly in the Rice Export Market. *Rev. Econ. Statist.*, August 1989, *71*(3), pp. 462–70.

_____ **and Perloff, Jeffrey M.** Estimating Market Structure and Tax Incidence: The Japanese Television Market. *J. Ind. Econ.*, March 1989, *37*(3), pp. 225–39.

Karpak, Birsen. Multiple Criteria Decision Support Systems on Microcomputers: An Application in Production Planning. In *Lockett, A. G. and Islei, G., eds.*, 1989, pp. 254–63.

Karpoff, Jonathan M. Characteristics of Limited Entry Fisheries and the Option Component of Entry Licenses. *Land Econ.*, November 1989, *65*(4), pp. 386–93.

_____ **and Malatesta, Paul H.** The Wealth Effects of Second-Generation State Takeover Legislation. *J. Finan. Econ.*, December 1989, *25*(2), pp. 291–322.

_____ **and Rice, Edward M.** Organizational Form, Share Transferability, and Firm Performance: Evidence from the ANCSA Corporations. *J. Finan. Econ.*, September 1989, *24*(1), pp. 69–105.

Karrenbrock, Jeffrey D. The 1988 Drought: Its Impact on District Agriculture. *Fed. Res. Bank St. Louis Rev.*, May–June 1989, *71*(3), pp. 3–13.

_____; **Wilson, William W. and Carter, Colin A.** Freer Trade in the North American Beer and Flour Markets. In *Schmitz, A., ed.*, 1989, pp. 139–86.

Karsten, Siegfried G. Gorbachev's *Perestroika*—Beginning of a Soviet Socialist Social Market Economy? *Int. J. Soc. Econ.*, 1989, *16*(6), pp. 39–49.

Karunaratne, Neil Dias. A Rapid Informatization Strategy for Australia—An Impact Analysis. *Econ. Systems Res.*, 1989, *1*(4), pp. 465–79.

Karwan, Mark H.; Zionts, Stanley and Ramesh, R. Performance Characteristics of Three Interactive Solution Strategies for Bicriteria Integer Programming. In *Lockett, A. G. and Islei, G., eds.*, 1989, pp. 472–85.

Kasa, Kenneth. Solution and Estimation of a Bivariate Interdependent Adjustment Cost Model. *Econ. Letters*, December 1989, *31*(3), pp. 225–30.

Kasanen, Eero; Östermark, Ralf and Zeleny, Milan. Gestalt System of Holistic Graphics: New Management Support View of MCDM. In *Lockett, A. G. and Islei, G., eds.*, 1989, pp. 143–56.

Kasanen, Pirkko and Lakshmanan, T. R. Residential Heating Choices of Finnish Households. *Econ. Geogr.*, April 1989, *65*(2), pp. 130–45.

Kaser, Michael. Soviet Restructuring in Relation to the Chinese Reform. In *Gomulka, S.; Ha, Y.-C. and Kim, C.-O., eds.,* 1989, pp. 97–107.

Kaserman, David L. and Conant, John L. Union Merger Incentives and Pecuniary Externalities. *J. Lab. Res.,* Summer 1989, *10*(3), pp. 243–53.

———— **and Howard, Jeffrey H.** Proof of Damages in Construction Industry Bid-Rigging Cases. *Antitrust Bull.,* Summer 1989, *34*(2), pp. 359–93.

————; **Melese, François and Im, Bae-Geun.** Endogenous Regulation and the Firm's Regulatory Expenditures. *Appl. Econ.,* March 1989, *21*(3), pp. 375–85.

————; **Romano, Richard E. and Blair, Roger D.** A Pedagogical Treatment of Bilateral Monopoly. *Southern Econ. J.,* April 1989, *55*(4), pp. 831–41.

————; **Trimble, John L. and Johnson, Ruth C.** Equilibration in a Negotiated Market: Evidence from Housing. *J. Urban Econ.,* July 1989, *26*(1), pp. 30–42.

Kashiwadani, Masuo and Fujita, Masahisa. Testing the Efficiency of Urban Spatial Growth: A Case Study of Tokyo. *J. Urban Econ.,* March 1989, *25*(2), pp. 156–92.

Kashiwagi, Yusuke. European Currency—A Japanese View. In *Franz, O., ed.,* 1989, pp. 89–93.

————. Third World Debt: The Next Phase: Perspectives of Commercial Bank Creditors. In *Fried, E. R. and Trezise, P. H., eds.,* 1989, pp. 50–54.

Kashyap, S. P. and Tiwari, R. S. Size Distribution of Firms in Diamond Processing Industry in India: An Exploratory Analysis. *Indian J. Quant. Econ.,* 1989, *5*(1), pp. 63–83.

Kasliwal, Pari. Is India Overborrowed? In *Singer, H. W. and Sharma, S., eds. (I),* 1989, pp. 423–35.

Kasman, Bruce. Monetary Policy and U.S. External Balances. *Fed. Res. Bank New York Quart. Rev.,* Winter 1989–90, *14*(4), pp. 62–68.

———— **and Ceglowski, Janet.** External Adjustment and U.S. Macroeconomic Performance. *Fed. Res. Bank New York Quart. Rev.,* Winter–Spring 1989, *13-14*(4–1), pp. 16–32.

Kasnakoglu, H. Data Requirements and Evaluation. In *Bauer, S. and Henrichsmeyer, W., eds.,* 1989, pp. 347–48.

———— **and Bauer, S.** Concept and Application of an Agricultural Sector Model for Policy Analysis in Turkey. In *Bauer, S. and Henrichsmeyer, W., eds.,* 1989, pp. 71–84.

Kasoff, Mark J.; Solocha, Andrew and Soskin, Mark D. Canadian Investment in Northern New York: Impact of Exchange Rates on Foreign Direct Investment. *Growth Change,* Winter 1989, *20*(1), pp. 1–16.

Kasper, Helmut and Holzmüller, Hartmut H. Psychostrukturelle Merkmale von Exportmanagern, Organisationskultur und Exporterfolg. Eine kausalanalytische Untersuchung. (With English summary.) *Z. Betriebswirtshaft,* December 1989, *59*(12), pp. 1297–1323.

Kasprzyk, Daniel; McMillen, David B. and Kalton, Graham. Nonsampling Errors in Panel Surveys. In *Kasprzyk, D., et al., eds.,* 1989, pp. 249–70.

Kass, Robert E.; Kadane, Joseph B. and Tierney, Luke. Fully Exponential Laplace Approximations to Expectations and Variances of Nonpositive Functions. *J. Amer. Statist. Assoc.,* September 1989, *84*(407), pp. 710–16.

Kassalow, Everett M. Employee Representation on U.S., German Boards. *Mon. Lab. Rev.,* September 1989, *112*(9), pp. 39–42.

Kassem, M. S. and Timmins, S. A. A Descriptive of the Need in Family Businesses to Juggle Family Values and Business Decision Making: The Saudi Arabian Case. *Middle East Bus. Econ. Rev.,* July 1989, *1*(2), pp. 37–42.

Kasten, Richard; Sammartino, Frank and Gramlich, Edward M. Deficit Reduction and Income Redistribution. *Amer. Econ. Rev.,* May 1989, *79*(2), pp. 315–19.

Katayama, Seiichi and Abe, Fumio. Optimal Investment Policy of the Regulated Firm. *J. Econ. Dynam. Control,* October 1989, *13*(4), pp. 533–52.

Kato, Hiroo and Matsui, Yukio. Tax Reform in Japan. *Bull. Int. Fiscal Doc.,* November 1989, *43*(11), pp. 498–505.

Kato, Takao. Specific and General Training in the Theory of Labor Turnover. *Econ. Letters,* September 1989, *30*(3), pp. 259–62.

Katosh, John P. and Traugott, Michael W. The Consequences of Validated and Self-Reported Voting Measures. In *Singer, E. and Presser, S., eds.,* 1989, *1981,* pp. 327–43.

Katouzian, Homa. Oil and Economic Development in the Middle East. In *Sabagh, G., ed.,* 1989, pp. 44–65.

————. The Political Economy of Iran since the Revolution: A Macro-historical Analysis. *Comp. Econ. Stud.,* Fall 1989, *31*(3), pp. 55–66.

Katrak, Homi. Imported Technologies and R&D in a Newly Industrialising Country: The Experience of Indian Enterprises. *J. Devel. Econ.,* July 1989, *31*(1), pp. 123–39.

Kats, Amoz. Spatial Oligopoly and Price Discrimination with Downward Sloping Demand. *Reg. Sci. Urban Econ.,* February 1989, *19*(1), pp. 55–68.

Katseli, Louka T. Economic Liberalization and the Equilibrium Real Exchange Rate in Developing Countries: Comment. In *[Díaz-Alejandro, C.],* 1989, pp. 185–87.

———— **and Glytsos, Nicholas P.** Theoretical and Empirical Determinants of International Labour Mobility: A Greek–German Perspective. In *Gordon, I. and Thirlwall, A. P., eds.,* 1989, pp. 95–115.

Katsoulacos, Yannis. On the Welfare Effects of Trade and Innovation in Vertically Differentiated Products. *J. Econ. (Z. Nationalökon.),* 1989, *49*(2), pp. 165–82.

————; **Ulph, David and Beath, John.** The Game-Theoretic Analysis of Innovation: A Survey. *Bull. Econ. Res.,* July 1989, *41*(3), pp. 163–84.

_____; **Ulph, David and Beath, John.** Strategic R&D Policy. *Econ. J.*, Supplement, 1989, *99*(395), pp. 74–83.

Katz, Bernard S. Nobel Laureates in Economic Sciences: A Biographical Dictionary: Introduction. In *Katz, B. S., ed.*, 1989, pp. ix–xii.

Katz, Eliakim and Rosenberg, Jacob. Rent-Seeking for Budgetary Allocation: Preliminary Results for 20 Countries. *Public Choice*, February 1989, *60*(2), pp. 133–44.

_____ **and Stark, Oded.** International Labour Migration under Alternative Informational Regimes: A Diagrammatic Analysis. *Europ. Econ. Rev.*, January 1989, *33*(1), pp. 127–42.

Katz, Jeffrey A. The Evolving Role of IDA. *Finance Devel.*, June 1989, *26*(2), pp. 16–19.

Katz, Katarina and Sterner, Thomas. Värdering av renare luft. En empirisk miljöekonomisk studie. (Payment for Cleaner Air. An Empirical Study of Environmental Behaviour. With English summary.) *Ekon. Samfundets Tidskr.*, 1989, *42*(4), pp. 243–56.

Katz, Lawrence F. Norm Shifts in Union Wages: Will 1989 Be a Replay of 1969? Comments. *Brookings Pap. Econ. Act.*, 1989, (2), pp. 265–70.

_____ **and Akerlof, George A.** Workers' Trust Funds and the Logic of Wage Profiles. *Quart. J. Econ.*, August 1989, *104*(3), pp. 525–36.

_____ **and Revenga, Ana L.** Changes in the Structure of Wages: The United States vs Japan. *J. Japanese Int. Economies*, December 1989, *3*(4), pp. 522–53.

_____ **and Summers, Lawrence H.** Can Interindustry Wage Differentials Justify Strategic Trade Policy? In *Feenstra, R. C., ed.*, 1989, pp. 85–116.

_____ **and Summers, Lawrence H.** Industry Rents: Evidence and Implications. *Brookings Pap. Econ. Act.*, Microeconomics, 1989, pp. 209–75.

Katz, Menachem. Mexico: Anatomy of a Debt Crisis. In *Singer, H. W. and Sharma, S., eds. (I)*, 1989, pp. 369–82.

_____ **and Farhadian-Lorie, Ziba.** Fiscal Dimensions of Trade Policy. In *Blejer, M. I. and Chu, K., eds.*, 1989, pp. 276–306.

Katz, Michael L. Vertical Contractual Relations. In *Schmalensee, R. and Willig, R. D., eds.*, Vol. 1, 1989, pp. 655–721.

Katz, Samuel I. Balance of Payments Adjustment, 1945 to 1986: The IMF Experience. *Atlantic Econ. J.*, December 1989, *17*(4), pp. 71–82.

Katz, Sidney; Densen, Paul M. and Jones, Ellen W. Using Field Data to Shape New Policies. In *Eisdorfer, C.; Kessler, D. A. and Spector, A. N., eds.*, 1989, pp. 521–44.

Katz, Y. Public Participation in the Danish Planning System—A Cybernetics Approach. *Environ. Planning A*, July 1989, *21*(7), pp. 975–82.

Katzenbeisser, Walter and Hackl, Peter. Tests against Nonconstancy in Linear Models Based on Counting Statistics. In *Hackl, P., ed.*, 1989, pp. 53–70.

Katzenstein, Peter J. Industry in a Changing West Germany. In *Katzenstein, P. J., ed.*, 1989, pp. 3–29.

_____. Stability and Change in the Emerging Third Republic. In *Katzenstein, P. J., ed.*, 1989, pp. 307–53.

Katzman, Rubén. The Heterogeneity of Poverty. The Case of Montevideo. *CEPAL Rev.*, April 1989, (37), pp. 131–42.

Katzmann, Robert A. The President and the Federal Courts. In *Bosworth, B. P., et al.*, 1989, pp. 131–33.

Katzner, Donald W. Attitudes, Rationality and Consumer Demand. In *[Weintraub, S.]*, 1989, pp. 133–53.

_____. The "Comparative Statics" of the Shackle–Vickers Approach to Decision-Making in Ignorance. In *[Hadar, J.]*, 1989, pp. 21–43.

Kaucky, Gerhard and Niedereichholz, Joachim. Informationstechnologie und Organisationsänderung. Dargestellt am Beispiel von Investitionsentscheidungen im Grossrechnerbereich. (With English summary.) *Z. Betriebswirtshaft*, June 1989, *59*(6), pp. 655–66.

Kaufer, Erich. Market-Clearing by Corruption: The Political Economy of China's Recent Economic Reforms: Comment. *J. Inst. Theoretical Econ.*, March 1989, *145*(1), pp. 127–29.

Kauffman, Harold E. and Gleason, J. E. Climatic Vulnerability of Major Food Crops: Soybeans. In *Oram, P. A., et al.*, 1989, pp. 155–64.

Kauffman, Jacques and Kauffman, Jean. La non-reconnaissance des personnes juridiques en matière fiscale: Luxembourg. (The Disregard of a Legal Entity for Tax Purposes: Luxemburg. With English summary.) In *International Fiscal Association, ed. (II)*, 1989, pp. 363–79.

Kauffman, Jean and Kauffman, Jacques. La non-reconnaissance des personnes juridiques en matière fiscale: Luxembourg. (The Disregard of a Legal Entity for Tax Purposes: Luxemburg. With English summary.) In *International Fiscal Association, ed. (II)*, 1989, pp. 363–79.

Kauffmann, P. and Rousseau, J. M. La théorie des choix de portefeuille: reformulation par une approche en termes de caractéristiques aléatoires. (Portfolio Theory Revisited: The Analysis of Random Characteristics. With English summary.) *Écon. Societes*, April–May 1989, *23*(4–5), pp. 249–64.

Kaufman, Allen M.; Englander, Ernest J. and Marcus, Alfred A. Structure and Implementation in Issues Management: Transaction Costs and Agency Theory. In *Post, J. E., ed.*, 1989, pp. 257–71.

Kaufman, Bruce E. Labor's Inequality of Bargaining Power: Changes over Time and Implications for Public Policy. *J. Lab. Res.*, Summer 1989, *10*(3), pp. 285–98.

_____. Models of Man in Industrial Relations Research: Reply. *Ind. Lab. Relat. Rev.*, October 1989, *43*(1), pp. 96–102.

_____. Models of Man in Industrial Relations Research. *Ind. Lab. Relat. Rev.*, October 1989, *43*(1), pp. 72–88.

Kaufman, George G. Framework for the Future:

Resurrecting and Legitimizing the Thrift Industry. In *Federal Home Loan Bank of San Francisco*, 1989, pp. 191–207.

――――. Management versus Economic Conditions as Contributors to the Recent Increase in Bank Failures: Commentary. In *Stone, C. C., ed.*, 1989, pp. 149–54.

――――. Thrift Deregulation and Federal Deposit Insurance: Comments. *J. Finan. Services Res.*, September 1989, 2(3), pp. 261–64.

Kaufman, Henry. Danger: Too Much Turbulence. In *Guttmann, R., ed.*, 1989, *1982*, pp. 87–96.

――――. Financial Institutions in Ferment. In *Guttmann, R., ed.*, 1989, *1983*, pp. 146–51.

――――. The Risks in the World Economic Order. In *Guttmann, R., ed.*, 1989, *1987*, pp. 244–51.

――――. Third World Debt: The Next Phase: Concluding Impressions. In *Fried, E. R. and Trezise, P. H., eds.*, 1989, pp. 99–101.

Kaufman, Joan, et al. Family Planning Policy and Practice in China: A Study of Four Rural Counties. *Population Devel. Rev.*, December 1989, 15(4), pp. 707–29.

Kaufman, Nancy H. and Granwell, Alan W. Working with Passive Foreign Investment Companies: How to Minimize the Hurt: United States. *Bull. Int. Fiscal Doc.*, July 1989, 43(7), pp. 303–11.

Kaufman, Robert R. Economic Orthodoxy and Political Change in Mexico: The Stabilization and Adjustment Policies of the de la Madrid Administration. In *Stallings, B. and Kaufman, R., eds.*, 1989, pp. 109–26.

――――. The Politics of Economic Adjustment Policy in Argentina, Brazil, and Mexico: Experiences in the 1980s and Challenges for the Future. *Policy Sciences*, November 1989, 22(3–4), pp. 395–413.

――――. and Haggard, Stephan. Economic Adjustment in New Democracies. In *Nelson, J. M., ed.*, 1989, pp. 57–77.

――――. and Haggard, Stephan. The Politics of Stabilization and Structural Adjustment. In *Sachs, J. D., ed. (I)*, 1989, pp. 209–54.

――――. and Haggard, Stephan. The Politics of Stabilization and Structural Adjustment. In *Sachs, J. D., ed. (II)*, 1989, pp. 263–74.

――――. and Stallings, Barbara. Debt and Democracy in the 1980s: The Latin American Experience. In *Stallings, B. and Kaufman, R., eds.*, 1989, pp. 201–23.

Kaufman, Roger T. The Effects of Statutory Minimum Rates of Pay on Employment in Great Britain. *Econ. J.*, December 1989, 99(398), pp. 1040–53.

Kaufmann, Heinz. On Testing for and against Inequality Restrictions. In *Opitz, O., ed.*, 1989, pp. 116–22.

Kaufmann, Johan. The Economic and Social Council and the New International Economic Order. In *[Gordenker, L.]*, 1989, pp. 54–66.

Kaufmann, Patrick J. and Leibenstein, Harvey. International Business Format Franchising and Retail Entrepreneurship: A Possible Source of Retail Know-How for Developing Countries. In *Leibenstein, H., Vol. 1*, 1989, pp. 259–73.

Kaufmann, William W. A Defense Agenda for Fiscal Years 1990–1994. In *Steinbruner, J. D., ed.*, 1989, pp. 48–93.

――――. Restructuring Defense. In *Bosworth, B. P., et al.*, 1989, pp. 151–60.

Kaul, Gautam and Conrad, Jennifer. Mean Reversion in Short-Horizon Expected Returns. *Rev. Financial Stud.*, 1989, 2(2), pp. 225–40.

Kaulmann, Thomas. Managerialism versus the Property Rights Theory of the Firm. In *Bamberg, G. and Spremann, K., eds.*, 1989, pp. 439–59.

――――. and Picot, Arnold. Comparative Performance of Government-Owned and Privately-Owned Industrial Corporations—Empirical Results from Six Countries. *J. Inst. Theoretical Econ.*, June 1989, 145(2), pp. 298–316.

Kaushik, Surendra K. International Capital Markets: New Directions: Introduction. In *Kaushik, S. K., ed.*, 1989, pp. xxiii–xxxii.

Kaw, Marita. Predicting Soviet Military Intervention. *J. Conflict Resolution*, September 1989, 33(3), pp. 402–29.

Kawabe, Nobuo. The Development of Distribution Systems in Japan before World War II. In *Hausman, W. J., ed.*, 1989, pp. 33–44.

――――. Japanese Business in the United States before the Second World War: The Case of Mitsui and Mitsubishi. In *Teichova, A.; Lévy-Leboyer, M. and Nussbaum, H., eds.*, 1989, pp. 177–89.

Kawagoe, Toshihiko and Hayami, Yujiro. Farm Mechanization, Scale Economies and Polarization: The Japanese Experience. *J. Devel. Econ.*, October 1989, 31(2), pp. 221–39.

――――. and Hayami, Yujiro. Farmers and Middlemen in a Transmigration Area in Indonesia. *Bull. Indonesian Econ. Stud.*, December 1989, 25(3), pp. 73–97.

Kawaguchi, T. and Kennedy, John. On Decision-Making for Maximum Profit Per Unit of Time from Batch Production. *J. Agr. Econ.*, May 1989, 40(2), pp. 209–20.

Kawaller, Ira G. Applications for Options on Currency Futures. In *Kaushik, S. K., ed.*, 1989, pp. 127–37.

――――. and Koch, Timothy W. Yield Opportunities and Hedge Ratio Considerations with Fixed Income Cash-and-Carry Trades. *J. Futures Markets*, December 1989, 9(6), pp. 539–45.

Kawamura, Mikio. A Comparative Analysis of Cross-Cultural-Interface Management: The United States and Japan: Commentary. In *Hayashi, K., ed.*, 1989, pp. 75–78.

Kay, John A. Changing Boundaries of State Activity: From Nationalisation to Privatisation. In *Shiraishi, T. and Tsuru, S., eds.*, 1989, pp. 193–206.

――――. The Economic Functions of the Tax System. In *Helm, D., ed.*, 1989, pp. 218–36.

――――. and Bishop, Matthew R. Privatization and the Performance of Public Firms. In *UNDTCD*, 1989, pp. 33–51.

_____ and **Bishop, Matthew R.** Privatization in the United Kingdom: Lessons from Experience. *World Devel.*, May 1989, *17*(5), pp. 643–57.

_____ and **Fairburn, James A.** Mergers and Merger Policy: Introduction. In *Fairburn, J. and Kay, J., eds.*, 1989, pp. 1–29.

_____ and **Forsyth, Peter.** The Economic Implications of North Sea Oil Revenues. In *Helm, D.; Kay, J. and Thompson, D., eds.*, 1989, *1980*, pp. 349–76.

_____; **Manning, Alan and Szymanski, Stefan.** The Economic Benefits of the Channel Tunnel. *Econ. Policy: A Europ. Forum*, April 1989, (8), pp. 211–34.

_____ and **Posner, M. V.** Routes to Economic Integration: 1992 in the European Community. *Nat. Inst. Econ. Rev.*, August 1989, (129), pp. 55–68.

_____; **Thompson, David and Helm, Dieter.** The Market for Energy: Introduction: Energy Policy and the Role of the State in the Market for Energy. In *Helm, D.; Kay, J. and Thompson, D., eds.*, 1989, pp. 1–20.

Kay, Neil. Post-Keynesian Economics and New Approaches to Industrial Economics. In *Pheby, J., ed.*, 1989, pp. 190–208.

Kayaalp, Orhan. Early Italian Contributions to the Theory of Public Finance: Pantaleoni, De Viti de Marco, and Mazzola. In *Walker, D. A., ed.*, 1989, pp. 155–66.

_____. Early Italian Contributions to the Theory of Public Finance: Pantaleoni, De Viti de Marco, and Mazzola. In *Walker, D. A., ed.*, 1989, pp. 155–66.

_____. The Jacobs Hypothesis of the Urban Origins of Agricultural Activity: Twenty Years Later. *J. Europ. Econ. Hist.*, Winter 1989, *18*(3), pp. 683–91.

_____. Reconciling Economic Postulates: Does "Adaptive" Egoism Satisfice? *J. Behav. Econ.*, Winter 1989, *18*(4), pp. 289–306.

Kaylen, Michael S. and Feather, Peter M. Conditional Qualitative Forecasting. *Amer. J. Agr. Econ.*, February 1989, *71*(1), pp. 195–201.

Kaynak, Erdener and Dalgic, Tevfik. From Subcontracting to Multinationality: Internationalization of LDC Construction Companies. In *Negandhi, A. R., ed.*, 1989, pp. 263–82.

Kazakevich, D. M. Improving Consumer Prices. In *Jones, A. and Moskoff, W., eds.*, 1989, *1986*, pp. 145–56.

Kazi, Shahnaz. Domestic Impact of Overseas Migration: Pakistan. In *Amjad, R., ed.*, 1989, pp. 167–96.

_____ and **Sathar, Zeba A.** Female Employment and Fertility: Further Investigation of an Ambivalent Association. *Pakistan Devel. Rev.*, Autumn 1989, *28*(3), pp. 175–93.

Kazi, Umarfaruk A. An Exploratory Stochastic Framework to Analyse the Relationship between Macro Oil Price Shocks and Economic Development. *Energy Econ.*, July 1989, *11*(3), pp. 228–38.

Kazmierczak, Tamra Kirkpatrick and Taylor, Daniel B. VEGMARC II(c): A Computerized Record Keeping System for Vegetable Marketing Cooperatives. *Southern J. Agr. Econ.*, July 1989, *21*(1), pp. 149–55.

Ke, Changji. Ancient Chinese Society and the Asiatic Mode of Production. In *Brook, T., ed.*, 1989, pp. 47–64.

Kealey, Gregory S. The Canadian State's Attempt to Manage Class Conflict, 1900–1948. In *Platt, D. C. M., ed.*, 1989, pp. 125–47.

Keane, Michael J. Function and Competition among Urban Centers. *J. Reg. Sci.*, May 1989, *29*(2), pp. 265–76.

_____. The Significance of Spatial Dependencies in Small Area Income Determination Models. *Reg. Stud.*, October 1989, *23*(5), pp. 455–62.

Keane, Michael P. and Runkle, David E. Are Economic Forecasts Rational? *Fed. Res. Bank Minn. Rev.*, Spring 1989, *13*(2), pp. 26–33.

Kearney, Colm and Bewley, Ronald. A Systems Approach to Modelling the EMS Exchange Rate Mechanism. *Econ. Soc. Rev.*, January 1989, *20*(2), pp. 111–20.

_____; **MacDonald, Ronald and Hillier, John.** The Efficiency of the Market for Bank Accepted Bills. *Econ. Rec.*, September 1989, *65*(190), pp. 225–33.

Kearney, John F. Co-management or Co-optation? The Ambiguities of Lobster Fishery Management in Southwest Nova Scotia. In *Pinkerton, E., ed.*, 1989, pp. 85–102.

Keating, Barry P. Statistical Software for Economists: Macintosh. *Bus. Econ.*, July 1989, *24*(3), pp. 54–57.

_____; **Bundt, Thomas P. and Chiesa, Jeffrey Scott.** Common Bond Type and Credit Union Behavior. *Rev. Soc. Econ.*, Spring 1989, *47*(1), pp. 27–42.

Kébabdjian, Gèrard and Broniatowski, Michel. The Role of Prices in the Establishment of Keynesian Short-Run Equilibrium. In *Barrère, A., ed.*, 1989, pp. 113–36.

Kebede, Yohannes and Gunjal, Kisan. Economic Evaluation of a Postdrought Recovery Agricultural Project in Ethiopia. *Can. J. Agr. Econ.*, Part 2, December 1989, *37*(4), pp. 899–907.

Kee, James Edwin. The President's FY 1990 Budget: The Last Act in a Decade of Change. *Public Budg. Finance*, Summer 1989, *9*(2), pp. 11–29.

_____ and **Shannon, John.** The Rise of Competitive Federalism. *Public Budg. Finance*, Winter 1989, *9*(4), pp. 5–20.

Kee, Robert; Robbins, Walter and Apostolou, Nicholas. Capital Budgeting Practices of U.S. Cities: A Survey. In *Matzer, J., Jr., ed.*, 1989, *1987*, pp. 100–109.

Keeler, James P. and Cover, James Peery. Estimating Money Demand in Log-First-Difference Form: Reply. *Southern Econ. J.*, April 1989, *55*(4), pp. 1040–43.

Keeler, Theodore E. Deregulation and Scale Economies in the U.S. Trucking Industry: An Econometric Extension of the Survivor Principle. *J. Law Econ.*, Part 1, October 1989, *32*(2), pp. 229–53.

_____ and **Kanafani, Adib.** New Entrants and

Safety. In *Moses, L. N. and Savage, I., eds.*, 1989, pp. 115–28.

Keeley, Michael C. The Stock Price Effects of Bank Holding Company Securities Issuance. *Fed. Res. Bank San Francisco Econ. Rev.*, Winter 1989, (1), pp. 3–19.

_____ **and Furlong, Frederick T.** Capital Regulation and Bank Risk-Taking: A Note. *J. Banking Finance*, December 1989, *13*(6), pp. 883–91.

_____ **and Hutchison, Michael M.** Estimating the Fisher Effect and the Stochastic Money Growth Process. *Econ. Inquiry*, April 1989, *27*(2), pp. 219–39.

Keely, Charles B. Population and Immigration Policy: State and Federal Roles. In *Bean, F. D.; Schmandt, J. and Weintraub, S., eds.*, 1989, pp. 161–78.

Keen, Howard. The Yield Curve as a Predictor of Business Cycle Turning Points. *Bus. Econ.*, October 1989, *24*(4), pp. 37–43.

Keen, Michael. Multilateral Tax and Tariff Reform. *Econ. Stud. Quart.*, September 1989, *40*(3), pp. 195–202.

_____. Pareto-Improving Indirect Tax Harmonisation. *Europ. Econ. Rev.*, January 1989, *33*(1), pp. 1–12.

_____ **and Kanbur, Ravi.** Poverty, Incentives, and Linear Income Taxation. In *Dilnot, A. and Walker, I., eds.*, 1989, pp. 99–115.

Keeran, Roger. The International Workers Order and the Origins of the CIO. *Labor Hist.*, Summer 1989, *30*(3), pp. 385–408.

Kehoe, Patrick J. Policy Cooperation among Benevolent Governments May Be Undesirable. *Rev. Econ. Stud.*, April 1989, *56*(2), pp. 289–96.

_____ **and Backus, David K.** On the Denomination of Government Debt: A Critique of the Portfolio Balance Approach. *J. Monet. Econ.*, May 1989, *23*(3), pp. 359–76.

_____; **Prescott, Edward C. and Chari, Varadarajan V.** Time Consistency and Policy. In *Barro, R. J., ed.*, 1989, pp. 265–305.

Kehoe, Timothy J. Intertemporal General Equilibrium Models. In *Hahn, F., ed.*, 1989, pp. 463–93.

_____; **Levine, David K. and Romer, Paul M.** Steady States and Determinacy of Equilibria in Economies with Infinitely Lived Agents. In *Feiwel, G. R., ed. (II)*, 1989, pp. 521–44.

_____, **et al.** Determinacy of Equilibrium in Large-scale Economies. *J. Math. Econ.*, 1989, *18*(3), pp. 231–62.

_____. Un análisis de equilibrio general de la reforma fiscal de 1986 en España. (With English summary.) *Invest. Econ.*, September 1989, *13*(3), pp. 337–85.

Keil, Stanley R.; Mack, Richard S. and Gilmer, Robert William. The Service Sector in a Hierarchy of Rural Places: Potential for Export Activity. *Land Econ.*, August 1989, *65*(3), pp. 217–27.

Keim, Donald B. Trading Patterns, Bid–Ask Spreads, and Estimated Security Returns: The Case of Common Stocks at Calendar Turning Points. *J. Finan. Econ.*, November 1989, *25*(1), pp. 75–97.

_____; **Westerfield, Randolph and Jaffe, Jeffrey F.** Earnings Yields, Market Values, and Stock Returns. *J. Finance*, March 1989, *44*(1), pp. 135–48.

Keith, John E. The Importance of Functional Form in the Estimation of Welfare: Discussion. *Western J. Agr. Econ.*, July 1989, *14*(1), pp. 177.

_____, **et al.** Energy and Agriculture in Utah: Responses to Water Shortages. *Western J. Agr. Econ.*, July 1989, *14*(1), pp. 85–97.

Keithley, Jane. Social Welfare in Developed Market Countries: United Kingdom. In *Dixon, J. and Scheurell, R. P., eds.*, 1989, pp. 309–44.

Keizer, W. Recent Reinterpretations of the Socialist Calculation Debate. *J. Econ. Stud.*, 1989, *16*(2), pp. 63–83.

Kæjr, Henrik. Kommunernes rolle i erhvervspolitikken. (The Role of Local Government in Industrial Policy. With English summary.) *Nationaløkon. Tidsskr.*, 1989, *127*(3), pp. 339–45.

Kelch, David and Leuck, Dale. Political and Economic Factors Influencing Agricultural Policy Reform in the European Community and the United States. *Can. J. Agr. Econ.*, Part 2, December 1989, *37*(4), pp. 1181–91.

Keleher, Robert E. Comment: Price Level Changes and the Adjustment Process under Fixed Rates. In *Dorn, J. A. and Niskanen, W. A., eds.*, 1989, *1988*, pp. 181–88.

Kelkar, Ujwala R. and Sastry, D. V. S. On Decomposition of Total Inequality by Factor Components. *Margin*, Oct. 1989–March 1990, *22*(1–2), pp. 98–102.

Kell, Michael and Dilnot, Andrew. Male Unemployment and Women's Work. In *Dilnot, A. and Walker, I., eds.*, 1989, pp. 153–68.

Kellaris, James J. and Cox, Anthony D. The Effects of Background Music in Advertising: A Reassessment. *J. Cons. Res.*, June 1989, *16*(1), pp. 113–18.

Keller, André. Econometrics of Technical Change: Techniques and Problems. In *Hackl, P., ed.*, 1989, pp. 367–406.

Keller, Kevin Lane and Staelin, Richard. Assessing Biases in Measuring Decision Effectiveness and Information Overload. *J. Cons. Res.*, March 1989, *15*(4), pp. 504–08.

Keller, Wouter J. and Metz, K. J. The Impact of New Dataprocessing Techniques at the Netherlands Central Bureau of Statistics. *Statist. J.*, 1989, *6*(3), pp. 213–22.

Kellerman, A. Agricultural Location Theory 1: Basic Models. *Environ. Planning A*, October 1989, *21*(10), pp. 1381–96.

_____. Agricultural Location Theory, 2: Relaxation of Assumptions and Applications. *Environ. Planning A*, November 1989, *21*(11), pp. 1427–46.

Kelley, Allen C. The "International Human Suffering Index": Reconsideration of the Evidence. *Population Devel. Rev.*, December 1989, *15*(4), pp. 731–37.

Kelley, Craig A.; Gaidis, William C. and Rein-

gen, Peter H. The Use of Vivid Stimuli to Enhance Comprehension of the Content of Product Warning Messages. *J. Cons. Aff.*, Winter 1989, *23*(2), pp. 243–66.

Kelley, Edward W., Jr. and Angell, Wayne D. Statement to the U.S. House Subcommittee on Domestic Monetary Policy of the Committee on Banking, Finance and Urban Affairs, August 3, 1989. *Fed. Res. Bull.*, October 1989, *75*(10), pp. 677–84.

Kelley, Maryellen R. Unionization and Job Design under Programmable Automation. *Ind. Relat.*, Spring 1989, *28*(2), pp. 174–87.

Kelley, Robin D. G. A New War in Dixie: Communists and the Unemployed in Birmingham, Alabama, 1930–1933. *Labor Hist.*, Summer 1989, *30*(3), pp. 367–84.

Kelley, William B. The Role of the Economist in Government: An International Perspective: The General Agreement on Tariffs and Trade. In *Pechman, J. A., ed.*, 1989, pp. 301–17.

Kellman, Mitchell and Chow, Peter C. Y. The Comparative Homogeneity of the East Asian NIC Exports of Similar Manufacturers. *World Devel.*, February 1989, *17*(2), pp. 267–73.

Kellough, Howard J. The Canadian Approach to Combat Tax Avoidance: The Early Aftermath. *Bull. Int. Fiscal Doc.*, February 1989, *43*(2), pp. 77–81.

Kellow, Aynsley. The Dispute over the Franklin River and South West Wilderness Area in Tasmania, Australia. *Natural Res. J.*, Winter 1989, *29*(1), pp. 129–46.

Kelly, Austin and Krumm, Ronald. Effects of Homeownership on Household Savings. *J. Urban Econ.*, November 1989, *26*(3), pp. 281–94.

Kelly, Jerry S. Conjectures and Unsolved Problems: 6. The Ostrogorski Paradox. *Soc. Choice Welfare*, January 1989, *6*(1), pp. 71–76.

_____. Dictionaries. *Soc. Choice Welfare*, July 1989, *6*(3), pp. 253–58.

_____. Interjacency. *Soc. Choice Welfare*, October 1989, *6*(4), pp. 331–35.

_____. A New Informational Base for Social Choice. *Math. Soc. Sci.*, April 1989, *17*(2), pp. 177–88.

Kelly, John and Heery, Edmund. Full-time Officers and Trade Union Recruitment. *Brit. J. Ind. Relat.*, July 1989, *27*(2), pp. 196–213.

_____ and Richardson, Ray. Annual Review Article 1988. *Brit. J. Ind. Relat.*, March 1989, *27*(1), pp. 133–54.

Kelly, Kenneth. Can Imports Injure a Domestic Industry When They Decline? In *Zerbe, R. O., ed.*, 1989, pp. 119–29.

Kelly, Kirk P. A Knowledge-Based Theory of the Audit Planning Process. In *Gangolly, J., ed.*, 1989, pp. 119–40.

Kelly, Patrick D. Recent Changes in the Patent Law That Affect Inventorship and Ownership. In *Weil, V. and Snapper, J. W., eds.*, 1989, pp. 61–68.

Kelly, Rafael; Casares, Enrique and Garza, Gilma. Control adaptable de un modelo no lineal de crecimiento monetario neoclásico.

(Adaptive Control of a Nonlinear Neoclassical Monetary Growth Model. With English summary.) *Estud. Econ.*, Jan.–June 1989, *4*(1), pp. 109–26.

Kelly, William A., Jr. and Miles, James A. Capital Structure Theory and the Fisher Effect. *Financial Rev.*, February 1989, *24*(1), pp. 53–73.

Kelman, Sander and Rice, Dorothy P. Measuring Comorbidity and Overlap in the Hospitalization Cost for Alcohol and Drug Abuse and Mental Illness. *Inquiry*, Summer 1989, *26*(2), pp. 249–60.

Kelsey, David. An Introduction to Nonlinear Dynamics and Its Application to Economics. In *Hahn, F., ed.*, 1989, pp. 410–34.

Kelton, Christina M. L. and Weiss, Leonard W. Change in Concentration, Change in Cost, Change in Demand, and Change in Price. In *Weiss, L. W., ed.*, 1989, pp. 41–66.

Kemal, A. R. South Asia and Economic Integration—Lessons from the Past and Future Prospects: Comments. *Pakistan Devel. Rev.*, Winter 1989, *28*(4), pp. 505–07.

Kemp, Jack F. Adjusting Our Economies to Accept New Suppliers. In *Cerami, C. A., ed.*, 1989, pp. 195–202.

Kemp, Kathleen A. Party Realignments and the Growth of Federal Economic Regulation, 1861–1986. *J. Finan. Services Res.*, September 1989, *2*(3), pp. 213–25.

Kemp, Murray C. and Long, Ngo Van. Union Power in the Long Run Reconsidered: Comment. *Scand. J. Econ.*, 1989, *91*(4), pp. 747–48.

_____; Long, Ngo Van and Chiarella, Carl. Innovation and the Transfer of Technology: A Leader–Follower Model. *Econ. Modelling*, October 1989, *6*(4), pp. 452–56.

_____ and Shimomura, Koji. A Neglected Corner: Labor Unions and the Pattern of International Trade. In *Feiwel, G. R., ed. (II)*, 1989, pp. 774–90.

Kemp, T. Economic and Social Policy in France. In *Mathias, P. and Pollard, S., eds.*, 1989, pp. 691–751.

Kempf, Hubert. Inflation and Wage Indexation with Multiperiod Contracts: A Comment. *Europ. Econ. Rev.*, September 1989, *33*(7), pp. 1397–1404.

_____ and Hénocq, Christophe. Quasi-rational Expectations. *Econ. Letters*, August 1989, *30*(2), pp. 93–96.

Kendall, Sarah B. Repeated Lending and Business Fluctuations: A Note. *Econ. Letters*, 1989, *29*(1), pp. 37–41.

Kendrick, John W. International Differences in Productivity Advance. *Managerial Dec. Econ.*, Special Issue, Spring 1989, pp. 13–18.

_____. Policy Implications of the Slowdown in U.S. Productivity Growth. In *Black, S. W., ed.*, 1989, pp. 75–109.

Kenen, Peter B. The Use of IMF Credit. In *Gwin, C. and Feinberg, R. E., eds.*, 1989, pp. 69–91.

Kennan, John. Simultaneous Equations Bias in Disaggregated Econometric Models. *Rev.*

Econ. Stud., January 1989, 56(1), pp. 151–56.

_____ and Wilson, Robert B. Strategic Bargaining Models and Interpretation of Strike Data. *J. Appl. Econometrics*, Supplement, December 1989, 4, pp. S87–130.

Kennedy, Bruce Richard. Mobility and Instability in Canadian Earnings. *Can. J. Econ.*, May 1989, 22(2), pp. 383–94.

_____. Refinancing the CCP: The Cost of Acquiescence. *Can. Public Policy*, March 1989, 15(1), pp. 34–42.

Kennedy, C. and Thirlwall, A. P. Extended Hicks Neutral Technical Change—A Comment. In *Wood, J. C. and Woods, R. N., eds., Vol. 3,* 1989, 1977, pp. 178–79.

Kennedy, David. Lessons from Bradford's Experience: The Integrated Approach. In *Dyson, K., ed.,* 1989, pp. 218–26.

Kennedy, J. Ray and da Fonseca, Roberto Giannetti. Brazilian Trade Policy and the Uruguay Round. In *Nau, H. R., ed.,* 1989, pp. 29–49.

Kennedy, John and Kawaguchi, T. On Decision-Making for Maximum Profit Per Unit of Time from Batch Production. *J. Agr. Econ.*, May 1989, 40(2), pp. 209–20.

_____ and Vanzetti, David. Optimal Retaliation in International Commodity Markets. *Rev. Marketing Agr. Econ.*, April, Aug., Dec. 1989, 57(1–2–3), pp. 93–117.

Kennedy, Mary M. and Birman, Beatrice F. The Politics of the National Assessment of Chapter 1. *J. Policy Anal. Manage.*, Fall 1989, 8(4), pp. 613–32.

Kennedy, Peter. Non-nested Hypothesis Tests: A Diagrammatic Exposition. *Australian Econ. Pap.*, June 1989, 28(52), pp. 160–65.

Kennedy, Randall. Martin Luther King's Constitution: A Legal History of the Montgomery Bus Boycott. *Yale Law J.*, April 1989, 98(6), pp. 999–1067.

Kennedy, William P. Market-Clearing by Corruption: The Political Economy of China's Recent Economic Reforms: Comment. *J. Inst. Theoretical Econ.*, March 1989, 145(1), pp. 130–32.

Kennett, David. Annual Review of Nations: Year 1988: United Kingdom. In *Haberman, L. and Sacks, P. M., eds.,* 1989, pp. 353–75.

Kenny, Lawrence W. and Adams, James D. The Retention of State Governors. *Public Choice*, July 1989, 62(1), pp. 1–13.

Kent, Calvin A. The Treatment of Entrepreneurship in Principles of Economics Textbooks. *J. Econ. Educ.*, Spring 1989, 20(2), pp. 153–64.

Kent, Richard J. On the Variability of the Replacement Investment Capital Stock Ratio: Some Evidence from Money. *Appl. Econ.*, August 1989, 21(8), pp. 1129–35.

Kent, Tom. Immigration Issues: A Personal Perspective. In *Beach, C. M. and Green, A. G.,* 1989, pp. 9–11.

Kenward, Lloyd; Corker, Robert and Evans, Owen. Tax Policy and Business Investment in the United States: Evidence from the 1980s. *Int. Monet. Fund Staff Pap.*, March 1989, 36(1), pp. 31–62.

Kenyon, Peter and Dawkins, Peter. A Time Series Analysis of Labour Absence in Australia. *Rev. Econ. Statist.*, May 1989, 71(2), pp. 232–39.

_____ and Grossman, Philip J. Artists' Subsidy of the Arts: Comment. *Australian Econ. Pap.*, December 1989, 28(53), pp. 280–87.

Kenzer, Robert C. The Black Businessman in the Postwar South: North Carolina, 1865–1880. *Bus. Hist. Rev.*, Spring 1989, 63(1), pp. 61–87.

Kephart, George and Palloni, Alberto. The Effects of Breastfeeding and Contraception on the Natural Rate of Increase: Are There Compensating Effects? *Population Stud.*, November 1989, 43(3), pp. 455–78.

Keppler, Erhard. Environmental Problems: A Determining Factor of Future Politics. In *Rotblat, J. and Goldanskii, V. I., eds.,* 1989, pp. 191–203.

Keran, Michael W. The Supply-Side Miracle. *J. Portfol. Manage.*, Summer 1989, 15(4), pp. 73–77.

Keren, Michael and Levhari, David. Decentralization, Aggregation, Control Loss and Costs in a Hierarchical Model of the Firm. *J. Econ. Behav. Organ.*, March 1989, 11(2), pp. 213–36.

Kærgård, Niels. Autonomy, Switching Regimes, and Super Exogeneity. *Europ. Econ. Rev.*, December 1989, 33(9), pp. 1799–1804.

_____. Økonomisk historie—Mellem kildekritik og højere algebra. (Is Economic History Methodologically Different from Other Parts of Economics? With English summary.) *Nationaløkon. Tidsskr.*, 1989, 127(3), pp. 381–92.

Kerkvliet, Joe and Atkinson, Scott E. Dual Measures of Monopoly and Monopsony Power: An Application to Regulated Electric Utilities. *Rev. Econ. Statist.*, May 1989, 71(2), pp. 250–57.

Kerman, Stephen; Baltagi, Badi H. and Garvin, Susan. Further Monte Carlo Evidence on Seemingly Unrelated Regressions with Unequal Number of Observations. *Ann. Écon. Statist.*, April–June 1989, (14), pp. 103–15.

Kermit, Mark L. California: A Model for Continuing Education of Transportation Professionals in a Developing Region. In *Candemir, Y., ed.,* 1989, pp. 230–38.

Kern, Gary M. and Bobrowski, Paul M. A Multiple Vehicle Scheduling Algorithm Employing Subtour Elimination and Operator Theory. *Logist. Transp. Rev.*, March 1989, 25(1), pp. 75–89.

Kern, Horst and Schumann, Michael. New Concepts of Production in West German Plants. In *Katzenstein, P. J., ed.,* 1989, pp. 87–110.

Kern, Louis. Nobel Laureates in Economic Sciences: A Biographical Dictionary: Friedrich August von Hayek: 1974. In *Katz, B. S., ed.,* 1989, pp. 80–93.

Kern, William S. Comment [Austrian and Institutional Economics: Some Common Elements] [Evolution and Economics: Austrians as Institutionalists]. In *Samuels, W. J., ed. (II)*, 1989, pp. 143–49.

Kerndrup, Søren and Bahner, Flemming. Assessment of Technology as the Lever of Regional Industrial Planning. In *Pedersen, J. L., ed.*, 1989, pp. 209–35.

Kernell, Samuel. The Evolution of the White House Staff. In *Chubb, J. E. and Peterson, P. E., eds.*, 1989, pp. 185–237.

Kerns, Wilmer L. and Glanz, Milton P. Private Social Welfare Expenditures, 1972–87. *Soc. Sec. Bull.*, November 1989, *52*(11), pp. 18–26.

Kerr, William A. Diversification of Prairie Agriculture. In *Schmitz, A., ed.*, 1989, pp. 37–87.

———; **McGivern, D. B. and Atkins, F. J.** A Note on Structural Change in Canadian Beef Demand. *Can. J. Agr. Econ.*, November 1989, *37*(3), pp. 513–24.

Kerstein, Robert and Swanstrom, Todd. Job and Housing Displacement: A Review of Competing Policy Perspectives. In *Smith, M. P., ed.*, 1989, pp. 254–96.

Kersten, G. E. and Mallory, G. R. And/Or Graphs, Scenarios and Multiple Criteria: Prototyping in Decision Support. In *Lockett, A. G. and Islei, G., eds.*, 1989, pp. 544–52.

Kertesi, Gábor and Galasi, Péter. Rat Race and Equilibria in Markets with Side Payments under Socialism. *Acta Oecon.*, 1989, *41*(3–4), pp. 267–91.

Kervin, John; Reid, Frank and Gunderson, Morley. The Effect of Labour Relations Legislation on Strike Incidence. *Can. J. Econ.*, November 1989, *22*(4), pp. 779–94.

Keshari, Pradeep Kumar and Saggar, Mridul. A Firm Level Study of the Determinants of Export Performance in Machinery and Transport Equipment Industry of India. *Indian Econ. J.*, Jan.–March 1989, *36*(3), pp. 36–48.

Kesselman, Jonathan R. Direct Expenditures versus Tax Expenditures for Economic and Social Policy. In *Bruce, N., ed.*, 1989, pp. 283–323.

———. Income Tax Evasion: An Intersectoral Analysis. *J. Public Econ.*, March 1989, *38*(2), pp. 137–82.

Kessler, David A.; Spector, Abby N. and Eisdorfer, Carl. Caring for the Elderly: Introduction. In *Eisdorfer, C.; Kessler, D. A. and Spector, A. N., eds.*, 1989, pp. xix–xxi.

Kessler, Denis. The Importance of Gifts and Inheritances among the Affluent: Comment. In *Lipsey, R. E. and Tice, H. S., eds.*, 1989, pp. 758–63.

——— **and Masson, André.** Bequest and Wealth Accumulation: Are Some Pieces of the Puzzle Missing? *J. Econ. Perspectives*, Summer 1989, *3*(3), pp. 141–52.

Kesteloot, Roger. Introduction of Computerised Numerical Control and the Rationalisation of Production: The Belgian Case. In *Francis, A. and Grootings, P., eds.*, 1989, pp. 165–86.

———. Typology of Machine-Tool Technologies: Appendix. In *Francis, A. and Grootings, P., eds.*, 1989, pp. 326–30.

Kestens, P.; Thys-Clément, F. and Jeanfils, Ph. 1992 en perspective 2000: Les performances de la Belgique suite à l'ouverture européenne des frontières. (With English summary.) *Cah. Écon. Bruxelles*, 4th Trimester 1989, (124), pp. 475–91.

Ketkar, Kusum W. and Ketkar, Suhas L. Determinants of Capital Flight from Argentina, Brazil, and Mexico. *Contemp. Policy Issues*, July 1989, *7*(3), pp. 11–29.

Ketkar, Suhas L. and Ketkar, Kusum W. Determinants of Capital Flight from Argentina, Brazil, and Mexico. *Contemp. Policy Issues*, July 1989, *7*(3), pp. 11–29.

Kettani, Ossama and Oral, Muhittin. A Mathematical Programming Model for Market Share Prediction. *Int. J. Forecasting*, 1989, *5*(1), pp. 59–68.

Keuschnigg, Christian. Tax Incentives for Investment: A Dynamic General Equilibrium Perspective. *Empirica*, 1989, *16*(1), pp. 31–51.

Key, Sydney J. Mutual Recognition: Integration of the Financial Sector in the European Community. *Fed. Res. Bull.*, September 1989, *75*(9), pp. 593–609.

Key, V. O., Jr. Techniques of Political Graft. In *Heidenheimer, A. J.; Johnston, M. and LeVine, V. T., eds.*, 1989, pp. 39–49.

Keyder, Çağlar. Social Structure and the Labour Market in Turkish Agriculture. *Int. Lab. Rev.*, Special Issue, 1989, *128*(6), pp. 731–44.

———; **Wallerstein, Immanuel and Arrighi, Giovanni.** Southern Europe in the World Economy in the Twentieth Century: Implications for Political and Social Transformations. In *Martin, M. T. and Kandal, T. R., eds.*, 1989, pp. 409–17.

Keyder, Nur. Velocity and Monetary Targeting in Turkey. *METU*, 1989, *16*(1–2), pp. 31–66.

Keyfitz, Nathan. Putting Trained Labour Power to Work: The Dilemma of Education and Employment. *Bull. Indonesian Econ. Stud.*, December 1989, *25*(3), pp. 35–55.

Keyzer, M. A. Data-Base Management in Relation to Economic Modelling. In *Bauer, S. and Henrichsmeyer, W., eds.*, 1989, pp. 349–50.

———. Some Views on Agricultural Sector Modelling. In *Bauer, S. and Henrichsmeyer, W., eds.*, 1989, pp. 23–30.

Khachaturov, Tigran. Intensification of Land Utilisation. In *Adelman, I. and Lane, S., eds.*, 1989, pp. 216–29.

Khadka, Rup Bahadur. A Survey of the Tax System: Nepal. *Bull. Int. Fiscal Doc.*, March 1989, *43*(3), pp. 135–40.

Khaksari, Shahriar; Kamath, Ravindra and Grieves, Robin. A New Approach to Determining Optimum Portfolio Mix. *J. Portfol. Manage.*, Spring 1989, *15*(3), pp. 43–49.

Khalaf, Rima M. Privatisation in Jordan. In *Ramanadham, V. V., ed.*, 1989, pp. 236–49.

——— **and Anani, Jawad.** Privatization in Jordan. In *El-Naggar, S., ed.*, 1989, pp. 210–25.

Khalaf, Samir. On Loyalties and Social Change. In *Sabagh, G., ed.*, 1989, pp. 89–111.

Khaleghi, Gholam H.; Shrestha, Rajendra B. and Gopalakrishnan, Chennat. Energy–Non-energy Input Substitution in U.S. Agriculture:

Some Findings. *Appl. Econ.*, May 1989, *21*(5), pp. 673–79.

Khalifah, Noor Aini; Coughlin, Cletus C. and Terza, Joseph V. The Determinants of Escape Clause Petitions. *Rev. Econ. Statist.*, May 1989, *71*(2), pp. 341–47.

Khalil, Mohamad A. and Mansour, Ali. Post-war Iraqi Economic Recovery and Development. *J. Energy Devel.*, Autumn 1989, *15*(1), pp. 51–59.

Khambata, Dara and Khambata, Farida. Emerging Capital Markets: A Case Study of Equity Markets in India. *J. Developing Areas*, April 1989, *23*(3), pp. 425–37.

Khambata, Farida and Khambata, Dara. Emerging Capital Markets: A Case Study of Equity Markets in India. *J. Developing Areas*, April 1989, *23*(3), pp. 425–37.

Khan, Ashfaque H. South Asia and Economic Integration—Lessons from the Past and Future Prospects: Comments. *Pakistan Devel. Rev.*, Winter 1989, *28*(4), pp. 502–04.

_____. The Two-Level CES Production Function for the Manufacturing Sector of Pakistan. *Pakistan Devel. Rev.*, Spring 1989, *28*(1), pp. 1–12.

_____ **and Raza, Bilquees.** The Demand for Money in Pakistan: Quarterly Results 1972–1987. *Pakistan Econ. Soc. Rev.*, Summer 1989, *27*(1), pp. 33–48.

Khan, Ghulam Ishaq. Sixth Annual General Meeting of the Pakistan Society of Development Economists, Islamabad, January 8–10, 1990: Inaugural Address. *Pakistan Devel. Rev.*, Winter 1989, *28*(4), pp. 279–87.

Khan, Habibullah and Islam, Iyanatul. Trends in International Inequality: A Basic Needs Approach. *J. Econ. Devel.*, December 1989, *14*(2), pp. 143–52.

Khan, Haider A. and Thorbecke, Erik. Macroeconomic Effects of Technology Choice: Multiplier and Structural Path Analysis within a SAM Framework. *J. Policy Modeling*, Spring 1989, *11*(1), pp. 131–56.

Khan, M. Ali. In Praise of Development Economics. *Pakistan Devel. Rev.*, Winter 1989, *28*(4), pp. 337–78.

_____. Lessons to Be Learned from the European Unemployment of the 80s: Comments. *Pakistan Devel. Rev.*, Winter 1989, *28*(4), pp. 331–33.

_____ **and Peck, N. T.** On the Interiors of Production Sets in Infinite Dimensional Spaces. *J. Math. Econ.*, 1989, *18*(1), pp. 29–39.

Khan, Mohammad Nawaz and Butt, Abdul Rauf. Who Receives the Benefits of Public Higher Education in Pakistan? *Pakistan Econ. Soc. Rev.*, Summer 1989, *27*(1), pp. 1–15.

Khan, Mohsin S. Future Financing Needs of the Highly Indebted Countries: Comment. In *Husain, I. and Diwan, I., eds.*, 1989, pp. 209–10.

_____. How Integrated are World Capital Markets? Some New Tests: Comment. In *[Díaz-Alejandro, C.]*, 1989, pp. 156–59.

_____ **and Mirakhor, Abbas.** The Financial System and Monetary Policy in an Islamic Economy. *J. King Abdulaziz Univ.: Islamic Econ.*, 1989, *1*, pp. 39–58.

_____ **and Montiel, Peter J.** Growth-Oriented Adjustment Programs: A Conceptual Framework. *Int. Monet. Fund Staff Pap.*, June 1989, *36*(2), pp. 279–306.

Khan, Rauf R. The Social and Human Costs of Japanese Management. In *Park, S.-J., ed.*, 1989, pp. 91–104.

Khan, Shahrukh Rafi. Profitability of Islamic PLS Banks Competing with Interest Banks: Problems and Prospects: Comments. *J. King Abdulaziz Univ.: Islamic Econ.*, 1989, *1*, pp. 119–20.

Khan, Showkat Hayat and Miller, Barbara Diane. Voluntarism. In *Schroeder, L., ed.*, 1989, pp. 175–90.

_____ **and Murshed, Hasan.** The Holdings Tax. In *Schroeder, L., ed.*, 1989, pp. 145–59.

Khan, Waqar Masood. Towards an Interest-Free Islamic Economic System. *J. King Abdulaziz Univ.: Islamic Econ.*, 1989, *1*, pp. 3–38.

Khang, Chulsoon. Bhandari's Aggregated Dynamics in an Open Economy: A Reassessment. *Manchester Sch. Econ. Soc. Stud.*, December 1989, *57*(4), pp. 387–91.

Khanna-Chopra, Renu and Sinha, S. K. Impact of Climate Variation on Production of Pulses. In *Oram, P. A., et al.*, 1989, pp. 219–36.

Khanna, Kailash C. Budget 1989/90: Fiscal Juggling? India. *Bull. Int. Fiscal Doc.*, June 1989, *43*(6), pp. 277–79.

Khanna, Naveen; Berkovitch, Elazar and Bradley, Michael. Tender Offer Auctions, Resistance Strategies, and Social Welfare. *J. Law, Econ., Organ.*, Fall 1989, *5*(2), pp. 395–412.

Kharas, Homi. Do the Secondary Markets Believe in Life after Debt? Comment. In *Husain, I. and Diwan, I., eds.*, 1989, pp. 292–93.

_____ **and Pinto, Brian.** Exchange Rate Rules, Black Market Premia and Fiscal Deficits: The Bolivian Hyperinflation. *Rev. Econ. Stud.*, July 1989, *56*(3), pp. 435–47.

Khatkhate, Deena R. Assessing the Level of Interest Rates in Less Developed Countries. In *Worrell, D. and Bourne, C., eds.*, 1989, pp. 65–78.

Khatrawi, Mohammed F. Privatization and the Regional Public Joint Ventures in the Gulf Cooperation Council Region. In *El-Naggar, S., ed.*, 1989, pp. 189–206.

Khazzoom, J. Daniel. Energy Savings from More Efficient Appliances: A Rejoinder. *Energy J.*, January 1989, *10*(1), pp. 157–66.

Khenkin, G. M. and Polterovich, V. M. An Evolutionary Model with Interaction between Development and Adoption of New Technologies. *Matekon*, Fall 1989, *26*(1), pp. 3–19.

Kher, Lov; Sioshansi, F. P. and Sorooshian, Soroosh. Noisy Data and Uncertain Coefficients: A Reply. *Energy J.*, January 1989, *10*(1), pp. 171–74.

Khilji, Nasir M. and Pariser, David B. Monopsony and Federal Coal Leasing—A Bargaining

Approach. *Energy Econ.*, July 1989, *11*(3), pp. 169–74.

Khilnani, Arvind and Tse, Edison T. S. A Note on the Radius of Convergence of the U.S.A. Algorithm. *J. Econ. Dynam. Control*, April 1989, *13*(2), pp. 313–16.

Khlat, Myriam and Fargues, Philippe. Child Mortality in Beirut: Six Indirect Estimates Based on Data Collected at the Time of a Birth. *Population Stud.*, November 1989, *43*(3), pp. 497–513.

Kho, Timothy and Quah, Euston. Economic Aspects of Legal Issues Involving Women in Singapore: Matrimonial Property Division and Rape. *Singapore Econ. Rev.*, April 1989, *34*(1), pp. 30–42.

Khosla, Anil and Teranishi, Juro. Exchange Rate Pass-through in Export Prices—An International Comparison. *Hitotsubashi J. Econ.*, June 1989, *30*(1), pp. 31–48.

Khoury, Nabil T. and Martel, Jean-Marc. A Supply of Storage Theory with Asymmetric Information. *J. Futures Markets*, December 1989, *9*(6), pp. 573–81.

Khrouz, F.; Vlasselaer, M. and Lemaitre, N. Secteur de l'Audit: Analyse structurelle et identification des avantages concurrentiels. (With English summary.) *Cah. Écon. Bruxelles*, 3rd Trimester 1989, (123), pp. 311–27.

Kibola, Hamisi S. Pre-shipment Inspection and the GATT. *J. World Trade*, April 1989, *23*(2), pp. 49–61.

Kick, Edward L.; Kiefer, David and Davis, Byron L. The World-System, Militarization, and National Development. In *Schaeffer, R. K., ed.*, 1989, pp. 27–45.

Kida, Thomas and Cohen, Jeffrey. The Impact of Analytical Review Results, Internal Control Reliability, and Experience on Auditors' Use of Analytical Review. *J. Acc. Res.*, Autumn 1989, *27*(2), pp. 263–76.

Kidane, Asmerom. Demographic Consequences of the 1984–1985 Ethiopian Famine. *Demography*, August 1989, *26*(3), pp. 515–22.

Kidwell, David S.; Marr, M. Wayne and Ogden, Joseph P. The Effect of a Sinking Fund on the Reoffering Yields of New Public Utility Bonds. *J. Finan. Res.*, Spring 1989, *12*(1), pp. 1–13.

Kiecolt, K. Jill and Fossett, Mark A. The Relative Size of Minority Populations and White Racial Attitudes. *Soc. Sci. Quart.*, December 1989, *70*(4), pp. 820–35.

Kiefer, David; Davis, Byron L. and Kick, Edward L. The World-System, Militarization, and National Development. In *Schaeffer, R. K., ed.*, 1989, pp. 27–45.

Kiefer, Nicholas M. A Value Function Arising in the Economics of Information. *J. Econ. Dynam. Control*, April 1989, *13*(2), pp. 201–23.

_____ **and Easley, David.** Optimal Learning with Endogenous Data. *Int. Econ. Rev.*, November 1989, *30*(4), pp. 963–78.

_____ **and Neumann, George R.** An Empirical Job-Search Model, with a Test of the Constant Reservation-Wage Hypothesis. In *Kiefer, N.*

M. and Neumann, G. R., 1989, *1979*, pp. 42–62.

_____ **and Neumann, George R.** Choice or Chance? A Structural Interpretation of Individual Labor Market Histories. In *Kiefer, N. M. and Neumann, G. R.*, 1989, *1984*, pp. 109–38.

_____ **and Neumann, George R.** Earnings, Unemployment, and the Allocation of Time over Time. In *Kiefer, N. M. and Neumann, G. R.*, 1989, *1984*, pp. 83–108.

_____ **and Neumann, George R.** Employment Risk and Labor Market Diversification. In *Kiefer, N. M. and Neumann, G. R.*, 1989, pp. 229–35.

_____ **and Neumann, George R.** Estimation of Wage Offer Distributions and Reservation Wages. In *Kiefer, N. M. and Neumann, G. R.*, 1989, *1979*, pp. 23–41.

_____ **and Neumann, George R.** How Long Is a Spell of Unemployment? Illusions and Biases in the Use of CPS Data. In *Kiefer, N. M. and Neumann, G. R.*, 1989, *1985*, pp. 203–26.

_____ **and Neumann, George R.** Individual Effects in a Nonlinear Model: Explicit Treatment of Heterogeneity in the Empirical Job-Search Model. In *Kiefer, N. M. and Neumann, G. R.*, 1989, *1981*, pp. 63–79.

_____ **and Neumann, George R.** Interfirm Mobility and Earnings. In *Kiefer, N. M. and Neumann, G. R.*, 1989, pp. 247–83.

_____ **and Neumann, George R.** Layoffs and Duration Dependence in a Model of Turnover. In *Kiefer, N. M. and Neumann, G. R.*, 1989, *1985*, pp. 139–59.

_____ **and Neumann, George R.** Methods for Analyzing Employment Contracts and Other Agreements. In *Kiefer, N. M. and Neumann, G. R.*, 1989, *1984*, pp. 284–92.

_____ **and Neumann, George R.** A Proposition and an Example in the Theory of Job Search with Hours Constraints. In *Kiefer, N. M. and Neumann, G. R.*, 1989, *1987*, pp. 236–46.

_____ **and Neumann, George R.** Search Models and Applied Labor Economics: Introduction. In *Kiefer, N. M. and Neumann, G. R.*, 1989, pp. 1–19.

_____ **and Neumann, George R.** Structural and Reduced Form Approaches to Analyzing Unemployment Durations. In *Kiefer, N. M. and Neumann, G. R.*, 1989, *1981*, pp. 163–78.

_____ **and Neumann, George R.** Wages and the Structure of Unemployment Rates. In *Kiefer, N. M. and Neumann, G. R.*, 1989, *1982*, pp. 179–202.

_____ **and Nyarko, Yaw.** Optimal Control of an Unknown Linear Process with Learning. *Int. Econ. Rev.*, August 1989, *30*(3), pp. 571–86.

Kiehnle, Herman; Sainz O., Manuel and Chevez, Pablo. The Disregard of a Legal Entity for Tax Purposes: Mexico. In *International Fiscal Association, ed. (II)*, 1989, pp. 381–89.

Kiekens, Jean-Pierre and Ginsburgh, Victor. A Note on the Computation of the Shadow Wage Rate in an Autarkic Agricultural Environment. *Europ. Rev. Agr. Econ.*, 1989, *16*(1), pp. 137–44.

Kiernan, Eric and Green, Christopher J. Multi-collinearity and Measurement Error in Econometric Financial Modelling. *Manchester Sch. Econ. Soc. Stud.*, December 1989, 57(4), pp. 357–69.

_____ and Madan, Dilip B. Stochastic Stability in Macro Models. *Economica*, February 1989, 56(221), pp. 97–108.

Kiernan, Kathleen E. The Family: Formation and Fission. In *Joshi, H., ed.*, 1989, pp. 27–41.

Kierzkowski, Henryk. Intra-industry Trade in Transportation Services. In *Tharakan, P. K. M. and Kol, J., eds.*, 1989, pp. 92–120.

_____ and Djajic, Slobodan. Goods, Services and Trade. *Economica*, February 1989, 56(221), pp. 83–95.

Kiewiet, D. Roderick and McCubbins, Mathew D. Parties, Committees, and Policymaking in the U.S. Congress: A Comment on the Role of Transaction Costs as Determinants of the Governance Structure of Political Institutions. *J. Inst. Theoretical Econ.*, December 1989, 145(4), pp. 676–85.

Kiguel, Miguel A. Budget Deficits, Stability, and the Monetary Dynamics of Hyperinflation. *J. Money, Credit, Banking*, May 1989, 21(2), pp. 148–57.

Kigyóssy-Schmidt, Eva. Non-market Services in Input–Output Analysis. *Econ. Systems Res.*, 1989, 1(1), pp. 131–45.

Kihlstrom, Richard; Boyer, Marcel and Dionne, Georges. Insurance and the Value of Publicly Available Information. In *[Hadar, J.]*, 1989, pp. 137–55.

Kihwan, Kim and Soo, Chung Hwa. Korea's Domestic Trade Politics and the Uruguay Round. In *Nau, H. R., ed.*, 1989, pp. 135–65.

Kiker, B. F.; de Oliviera, M. Mendes and Cohn, Elchanan. Tenure, Earnings and Productivity. *Oxford Bull. Econ. Statist.*, February 1989, 51(1), pp. 1–14.

Kikeri, Sunita and Nellis, John. The Privatization of Public Enterprises. In *El-Naggar, S., ed.*, 1989, pp. 50–80.

_____ and Nellis, John. Public Enterprise Reform: Privatization and the World Bank. *World Devel.*, May 1989, 17(5), pp. 659–72.

Kilby, Peter and Liedholm, Carl. The Role of Nonfarm Activities in the Rural Economy. In *Williamson, J. G. and Panchamukhi, V. R., eds.*, 1989, pp. 340–66.

Kilduff, Anthony P. Real Wages and Employment: New Evidence. *Can. J. Econ.*, August 1989, 22(3), pp. 619–29.

Kiljunen, Kimmo. Toward a Theory of the International Division of Industrial Labor. *World Devel.*, January 1989, 17(1), pp. 109–38.

Kilkenny, Maureen; Adelman, Irma and Robinson, Sherman. The Effect of Agricultural Trade Liberalization on the U.S. Economy: Projections to 1991. In *Stoeckel, A. B.; Vincent, D. and Cuthbertson, S., eds.*, 1989, pp. 222–59.

Killick, Tony. Issues Arising from the Spread of Obligatory Adjustment. In *Bird, G., ed.*, 1989, pp. 78–117.

Killingsworth, Mark R. and Hill, M. Anne. Comparable Worth: Analyses and Evidence: Introduction. In *Hill, M. A. and Killingsworth, M. R., eds.*, 1989, pp. 1–10.

Kilmann, Ralph H. A Completely Integrated Program for Organizational Change. In *Mohrman, A. M., Jr., et al.*, 1989, pp. 200–228.

Kim, C. S. Gains from Trade Liberalization in the World Wheat Market. *Can. J. Agr. Econ.*, Part 2, December 1989, 37(4), pp. 1009–22.

_____; Moore, Michael R. and Hanchar, John J. A Dynamic Model of Adaptation to Resource Depletion: Theory and an Application to Groundwater Mining. *J. Environ. Econ. Manage.*, July 1989, 17(1), pp. 66–82.

Kim, Cae-One. Economic Reforms in the Socialist World: Introduction. In *Gomulka, S.; Ha, Y.-C. and Kim, C.-O., eds.*, 1989, pp. 1–8.

Kim, Chang-Jin and Nelson, Charles R. The Time-Varying-Parameter Model for Modeling Changing Conditional Variance: The Case of the Lucas Hypothesis. *J. Bus. Econ. Statist.*, October 1989, 7(4), pp. 433–40.

Kim, Chankon. Working Wives' Time-Saving Tendencies: Durable Ownership, Convenience Food Consumption, and Meal Purchases. *J. Econ. Psych.*, November 1989, 10(3), pp. 391–409.

Kim, Chong W. and Kim, Dong Ki. Korean Value Systems and Managerial Practices. In *Chung, K. H. and Lee, H. C., eds.*, 1989, pp. 207–16.

Kim, Dong Ki and Kim, Chong W. Korean Value Systems and Managerial Practices. In *Chung, K. H. and Lee, H. C., eds.*, 1989, pp. 207–16.

Kim, Gew-rae and Markowitz, Harry M. Investment Rules, Margin, and Market Volatility. *J. Portfol. Manage.*, Fall 1989, 16(1), pp. 45–52.

Kim, Jae-Cheol. Advertising, Quality and Signaling. *Metroecon.*, February 1989, 40(1), pp. 43–56.

_____. Trade in Used Goods and Durability Choice. *Int. Econ. J.*, Autumn 1989, 3(3), pp. 53–63.

_____ and Chang, Winston W. Competition in Quality-Differentiated Products and Optimal Trade Policy. *Keio Econ. Stud.*, 1989, 26(1), pp. 1–17.

_____ and Yoo, Byung-Kook. Partial Compliance with the Minimum Wage Law. *Bull. Econ. Res.*, July 1989, 41(3), pp. 197–206.

Kim, Jay S. and Hahn, Chan K. The Korean Chaebol as an Organizational Form. In *Chung, K. H. and Lee, H. C., eds.*, 1989, pp. 51–64.

Kim, Jun Young. Long Run Equilibrium, Income Distribution among Heterogeneous Classes and Taxation in a Two Sector Growing Economy. *Econ. Rev. (Keizai Kenkyu)*, October 1989, 40(4), pp. 357–65.

Kim, K. H. and Roush, Fred W. Kelly's Conjecture. *Math. Soc. Sci.*, April 1989, 17(2), pp. 189–94.

Kim, Kisoo. Trade Restricting Policies under Uncertainty and a Differentiated Duopoly. *Int. Econ. J.*, Winter 1989, 3(4), pp. 45–59.

Kim, Kwan S. and Vorasopontaviporn, P. International Trade, Employment, and Income: The Case of Thailand. *Developing Econ.*, March 1989, 27(1), pp. 60–74.

Kim, Kwang Chung and Kim, Shin. Kinship Group and Patrimonial Executives in a Developing Nation: A Case Study of Korea. *J. Developing Areas*, October 1989, 24(1), pp. 27–45.

Kim, Kyoo-Hong. Optimal Linear Income Taxation, Redistribution and Labour Supply. *Econ. Modelling*, April 1989, 6(2), pp. 174–81.

Kim, Kyung-Soo. International Market Linkages and Optimal Monetary Policy. *Europ. Econ. Rev.*, September 1989, 33(7), pp. 1405–26.

_____; **Kim, Woo Tack and Jaang, Daehong.** On the Effectiveness of Capital Gains Tax as a Stabilizer of Real Estate Prices. *Int. Econ. J.*, Winter 1989, 3(4), pp. 37–44.

Kim, Linsu. Technological Transformation of Korean Firms. In *Chung, K. H. and Lee, H. C., eds.*, 1989, pp. 113–29.

Kim, Mahn-Je and Ro, Sung-Tae. Korean International Macroeconomic Policy. In *Bayard, T. O. and Young, S.-G., eds.*, 1989, pp. 43–65.

Kim, Moon K. and Ismail, Badr E. On the Association of Cash Flow Variables with Market Risk: Further Evidence. *Accounting Rev.*, January 1989, 64(1), pp. 125–36.

_____ **and Wu, Chunchi.** Performance of Mutual Funds in the Pre- versus Post-Mayday Periods. *Quart. J. Bus. Econ.*, Spring 1989, 28(2), pp. 61–84.

Kim, Moshe and Ben-Zion, Uri. The Structure of Technology in a Multioutput Branch Banking Firm. *J. Bus. Econ. Statist.*, October 1989, 7(4), pp. 489–96.

_____; **Golan, Lorette and Shechter, Mordechai.** Valuing a Public Good: Direct and Indirect Valuation Approaches to the Measurement of the Benefits from Pollution Abatement. In *Folmer, H. and van Ierland, E., eds.*, 1989, pp. 123–37.

Kim, Namdoo and Fukushima, Takashi. Welfare Improving Tariff Changes: A Case of Many Goods and Countries. *J. Int. Econ.*, May 1989, 26(3/4), pp. 383–88.

Kim, Shin and Kim, Kwang Chung. Kinship Group and Patrimonial Executives in a Developing Nation: A Case Study of Korea. *J. Developing Areas*, October 1989, 24(1), pp. 27–45.

Kim, Sun-Young and Lombra, Raymond E. Why the Empirical Relationship between Deficits and Interest Rates Appears So Fragile. *J. Econ. Bus.*, August 1989, 41(3), pp. 241–51.

Kim, Sung-Hoon. Korean Trade Policy: Implications for Korea–U.S. Cooperation: Discussion. In *Bayard, T. O. and Young, S.-G., eds.*, 1989, pp. 165–68.

Kim, Sunwoong. Labor Specialization and the Extent of the Market. *J. Polit. Econ.*, June 1989, 97(3), pp. 692–705.

Kim, Tae-Kyun; Baumel, C. Phillip and Lee, Tenpao. Impact of Deregulation on the Financial Performance of the Class I Railroads: Errata. *Logist. Transp. Rev.*, March 1989, 25(1), pp. 91–94.

Kim, Taewon. Bidding in Real Estate: A Game Theoretic Approach. *J. Real Estate Finance Econ.*, December 1989, 2(4), pp. 239–51.

Kim, Tschangcho John and Rho, Jeong Hyun. Solving a Three-Dimensional Urban Activity Model of Land Use Intensity and Transport Congestion. *J. Reg. Sci.*, November 1989, 29(4), pp. 595–613.

Kim, Woo Tack; Jaang, Daehong and Kim, Kyung-Soo. On the Effectiveness of Capital Gains Tax as a Stabilizer of Real Estate Prices. *Int. Econ. J.*, Winter 1989, 3(4), pp. 37–44.

Kim, Woo Taik. Administrative and Compliance Costs of Taxation: Republic of Korea. In *International Fiscal Association, ed. (I)*, 1989, pp. 529–40.

Kim, Yong H.; Bolster, Paul J. and Srinivasan, Venkat. A Framework for Integrating the Leasing Alternative with the Capital Budgeting Decision. In *Lee, C. F., ed.*, 1989, pp. 75–93.

_____ **and Chung, Kee Ho.** Inventory Management under Uncertainty: A Financial Theory for the Transactions Motive. *Managerial Dec. Econ.*, December 1989, 10(4), pp. 291–98.

Kim, Yoon Hyung. Financial Management and Corporate Organization. In *Kim, Y. H. and Smith, K. R., eds.*, 1989, pp. 187–224.

_____ **and Pan, Pu-Sen.** Patterns and Important Issues in Supply. In *Kim, Y. H. and Smith, K. R., eds.*, 1989, pp. 107–43.

_____ **and Smith, Kirk R.** Electric Power in Development: Lessons from Northeast Asia. In *Kim, Y. H. and Smith, K. R., eds.*, 1989, pp. 225–49.

_____ **and Smith, Kirk R.** Electricity in Northeast Asia: The Principal Historical Trends. In *Kim, Y. H. and Smith, K. R., eds.*, 1989, pp. 1–19.

_____; **Yu, Oliver S. and Nakamura, Mitsugu.** Structure, Parameters, and Prediction of Demand. In *Kim, Y. H. and Smith, K. R., eds.*, 1989, pp. 21–64.

Kim, Yoonbai. Is Greater Exchange Rate Flexibility Stabilizing? Some Evidence from U.S. Data. *Econ. Letters*, 1989, 29(1), pp. 57–62.

Kim, Youngsoo. The Role of Consensus and Disagreement in Portfolio Adjustment: A Trading Volume Approach. *Econ. Letters*, 1989, 30(1), pp. 71–76.

Kimball, Miles S. The Effect of Demand Uncertainty on a Precommitted Monopoly Price. *Econ. Letters*, 1989, 30(1), pp. 1–5.

_____ **and Mankiw, N. Gregory.** Precautionary Saving and the Timing of Taxes. *J. Polit. Econ.*, August 1989, 97(4), pp. 863–79.

Kimbrough, Kent P. Optimal Taxation in a Monetary Economy with Financial Intermediaries. *J. Macroecon.*, Fall 1989, 11(4), pp. 493–511.

_____ **and Gardner, Grant W.** The Behavior of U.S. Tariff Rates. *Amer. Econ. Rev.*, March 1989, 79(1), pp. 211–18.

_____ **and Gardner, Grant W.** Tariffs, Interest Rates, and the Trade Balance in the World Economy. *J. Int. Econ.*, August 1989, 27(1–2), pp. 91–110.

Kimenyi, Mwangi S. Immigration and Black–

White Unemployment Rates in the United States. *Konjunkturpolitik*, 1989, *35*(5), pp. 297–309.

——. Interest Groups, Transfer Seeking and Democratization: Competition for the Benefits of Governmental Power May Explain African Political Instability. *Amer. J. Econ. Sociology*, July 1989, *48*(3), pp. 339–49.

—— **and Shughart, William F., II.** Political Successions and the Growth of Government. *Public Choice*, August 1989, *62*(2), pp. 173–79.

Kimura, Mitsuhiko. Public Finance in Korea under Japanese Rule: Deficit in the Colonial Account and Colonial Taxation. *Exploration Econ. Hist.*, July 1989, *26*(3), pp. 285–310.

Kimura, Toru. Energy Trade in Asia and the Pacific. In *James, W. E., ed.*, 1989, pp. 29–45.

Kincaid, John. Fiscal Capacity and Tax Effort of the American States: Trends and Issues. *Public Budg. Finance*, Autumn 1989, *9*(3), pp. 4–26.

Kind, Paolo; Poli, Giorgio and Basevi, Giorgio. International Co-operation of Monetary Policies and Confrontation of Commercial and Financial Policies: An Application to U.S.–EC Relations and to Problems of the European Monetary System. In *Hodgman, D. R. and Wood, G. E., eds.*, 1989, pp. 217–49.

Kindleberger, Charles P. Commercial Policy between the Wars. In *Mathias, P. and Pollard, S., eds.*, 1989, pp. 161–96.

——. The Dollar Yesterday, Today, and Tomorrow. In *Guttmann, R., ed.*, 1989, *1985*, pp. 282–89.

——. From Graduate Student to Professional Peer: An Appreciation of Carlos F. Díaz-Alejandro. In *[Díaz-Alejandro, C.]*, 1989, pp. 4–15.

——. How Ideas Spread among Economists: Examples from International Economics. In *Colander, D. C. and Coats, A. W., eds.*, 1989, pp. 43–59.

——. Reflections on the Papers and the Debate on Multinational Enterprise: International Finance, Markets and Governments in the Twentieth Century: Summary. In *Teichova, A.; Lévy-Leboyer, M. and Nussbaum, H., eds.*, 1989, pp. 229–39.

——. Responsibility in Economic Life. In *Johnson, C., ed.*, 1989, pp. 75–85.

——. The United States and the World Economy in the Twentieth Century. In *[Fischer, W.]*, 1989, pp. 287–313.

King, B. Frank; Tschinkel, Sheila L. and Whitehead, David D. Interstate Banking Developments in the 1980s. *Fed. Res. Bank Atlanta Econ. Rev.*, May–June 1989, *74*(3), pp. 32–51.

King, Desmond. Economic Crisis and Welfare State Recommodification: A Comparative Analysis of the United States and Britain. In *Gottdiener, M. and Komninos, N., eds.*, 1989, pp. 237–60.

King, J. E. and Howard, M. C. The Rational Choice Marxism of John Roemer: A Critique. *Rev. Soc. Econ.*, Winter 1989, *47*(4), pp. 392–414.

King, John P. Socioeconomic Development and Corrupt Campaign Practices in England. In *Heidenheimer, A. J.; Johnston, M. and LeVine, V. T., eds.*, 1989, pp. 233–49.

King, Lambert N. The Need for a Geriatrics Specialty: Reality in the United States. In *Eisdorfer, C.; Kessler, D. A. and Spector, A. N., eds.*, 1989, pp. 307–21.

King, M. G.; Cartwright, I. and Carver, A. Fisheries Development in Pacific Islands: Some Problems in Paradise. In *Couper, A. D., ed.*, 1989, pp. 47–62.

King, Maxwell L. Testing for Fourth-Order Autocorrelation in Regression Disturbances When First-Order Autocorrelation Is Present. *J. Econometrics*, July 1989, *41*(3), pp. 285–301.

—— **and Edwards, Phillip M.** Transformations for an Exact Goodness-of-Fit Test of Structural Change in the Linear Regression Model. *Empirical Econ.*, 1989, *14*(2), pp. 113–21.

—— **and Edwards, Phillip M.** Transformations for an Exact Goodness-of-Fit Test of Structural Change in the Linear Regression Model. In *Kramer, W., ed.*, 1989, pp. 49–57.

King, Mervyn. Economic Growth and the Life-Cycle of Firms. *Europ. Econ. Rev.*, March 1989, *33*(2/3), pp. 325–34.

——. Take-Over Activity in the United Kingdom. In *Fairburn, J. and Kay, J., eds.*, 1989, pp. 99–115.

King, R. J. Capital Switching and the Role of Ground Rent: 2. Switching between Circuits and Switching between Submarkets. *Environ. Planning A*, June 1989, *21*(6), pp. 711–38.

——. Capital Switching and the Role of Ground Rent: 3. Switching between Circuits, Switching between Submarkets, and Social Change. *Environ. Planning A*, July 1989, *21*(7), pp. 853–80.

——. Capital Switching and the Role of Ground Rent: Theoretical Problems. *Environ. Planning A*, April 1989, *21*(4), pp. 445–62.

King, Robin A. and Robinson, Michael D. Assessing Structural Adjustment Programs: A Summary of Country Experience. In *Weeks, J. F., ed.*, 1989, pp. 103–23.

Kingkade, W. Ward. Content, Organization, and Methodology in Recent Soviet Population Censuses. *Population Devel. Rev.*, March 1989, *15*(1), pp. 123–38.

Kingma, Bruce Robert. An Accurate Measurement of the Crowd-Out Effect, Income Effect, and Price Effect for Charitable Contributions. *J. Polit. Econ.*, October 1989, *97*(5), pp. 1197–1207.

Kingma, Hildy L. and Rose, Leslie S. Seasonal Migration of Retired Persons: Estimating Its Extent and Its Implications for the State of Florida. *J. Econ. Soc. Meas.*, 1989, *15*(1), pp. 91–104.

Kingston, Geoffrey. Theoretical Foundations of Constant-Proportion Portfolio Insurance. *Econ. Letters*, 1989, *29*(4), pp. 345–47.

Kingston, Jeff. Annual Review of Nations: Year 1988: Indonesia. In *Haberman, L. and Sacks, P. M., eds.*, 1989, pp. 135–54.

_____. Annual Review of Nations: Year 1988: Malaysia. In *Haberman, L. and Sacks, P. M., eds.*, 1989, pp. 195–211.

Kingston, O. L. Consumer Preferences for Loin and Topside Steaks from Beef Carcasses of Different Classification Criteria. *Rev. Marketing Agr. Econ.*, April, Aug., Dec. 1989, 57(1–2–3), pp. 118–28.

Kingston, Paul William and Nock, Steven L. The Division of Leisure and Work. *Soc. Sci. Quart.*, March 1989, 70(1), pp. 24–39.

Kinney, William R., Jr. and McDaniel, Linda S. Characteristics of Firms Correcting Previously Reported Quarterly Earnings. *J. Acc. Econ.*, February 1989, 11(1), pp. 71–93.

Kinnunen, Juha. The Income Smoothing Effects of Depreciations and Untaxed Reserves in Listed Finnish Firms. *Liiketaloudellinen Aikak.*, 1989, 38(4), pp. 293–305.

Kintis, Andreas A. and Panas, Epaminondas E. The Capital–Energy Controversy: Further Results. *Energy Econ.*, July 1989, 11(3), pp. 201–12.

Kirby, Maurice W. Institutional Rigidities and Britain's Industrial Decline. *Bus. Hist. Rev.*, Winter 1989, 63(4), pp. 930–37.

Kirby, Michael D. Informatics and Democratic Society: Beyond the Tokyo Summit. In *Jussawalla, M.; Okuma, T. and Araki, T., eds.*, 1989, pp. 157–71.

Kirby, Michael G.; Gunasekera, H. Don B. H. and Parsons, David. Liberalizing Agricultural Trade: Some Perspectives for Developing Countries. In *Whalley, J., ed., Vol. 1*, 1989, pp. 238–57.

Kirby, Robert G. Whose Company Is It, Anyway? *J. Portfol. Manage.*, Fall 1989, 16(1), pp. 13–18.

Kirby, Sheila Nataraj and Besen, Stanley M. Private Copying, Appropriability, and Optimal Copying Royalties. *J. Law Econ.*, Part 1, October 1989, 32(2), pp. 255–80.

Kirch, David and Geiger, Marshall A. What Does "Total Return" Really Mean? A Comment. *J. Portfol. Manage.*, Summer 1989, 15(4), pp. 80–81.

Kirchgässner, Gebhard. On the Political Economy of Economic Policy. *Econ. Scelte Pubbliche/J. Public Finance Public Choice*, Jan.–Aug. 1989, 7(1–2), pp. 111–23.

Kirchner, Christian. New Institutional Arrangements in International Economic Law: The Working of Codes of Conduct. In *Vosgerau, H.-J., ed.*, 1989, pp. 409–35.

Kirim, Arman and Ateş, Hüseyin. Technical Change and Technological Capability in the Turkish Textile Sector. *METU*, 1989, 16(1–2), pp. 1–30.

Kirk, John M. Toward an Understanding of the Church–State Rapprochement in Revolutionary Cuba. In *Mesa-Lago, C., ed.*, 1989, pp. 25–42.

Kirkby, Diane. The Australian Experiment of Compulsory Arbitration. In *Platt, D. C. M., ed.*, 1989, pp. 107–24.

Kirkby, Richard and Cannon, Terry. China's Regional Development: Introduction. In *Goodman, D. S. G., ed.*, 1989, pp. 1–19.

Kirkman, Kimberly E. Graduation in the Generalized System of Preferences: The Projected Impact on Remaining Beneficiaries in the United States Scheme. *World Devel.*, October 1989, 17(10), pp. 1597–1600.

Kirkman-Liff, Bradford L. Cost Containment and Physician Payment Methods in the Netherlands. *Inquiry*, Winter 1989, 26(4), pp. 468–82.

Kirkpatrick, Colin. Some Background Observations on Privatisation. In *Ramanadham, V. V., ed.*, 1989, pp. 94–102.

Kirman, Alan. The Intrinsic Limits of Modern Economic Theory: The Emperor Has No Clothes. *Econ. J.*, Supplement, 1989, 99(395), pp. 126–39.

Kirmani, Amna and Wright, Peter. Money Talks: Perceived Advertising Expense and Expected Product Quality. *J. Cons. Res.*, December 1989, 16(3), pp. 344–53.

Kirmani, Naheed. The Uruguay Round: Revitalizing the Global Trading System. *Finance Devel.*, March 1989, 26(1), pp. 6–8.

Kirstein, David M. and Bailey, Elizabeth E. Can Truth in Airline Scheduling Alleviate the Congestion and Delay Problem? In *Moses, L. N. and Savage, I., eds.*, 1989, pp. 153–66.

Kirton, Claremont D. Development Planning in the Grenada Revolution: Applying AFROSIBER. *Soc. Econ. Stud.*, September 1989, 38(3), pp. 1–52.

Kirwan, R. M. Finance for Urban Public Infrastructure. *Urban Stud.*, June 1989, 26(3), pp. 285–300.

Kirzner, Israel M. The Use of Labels in Doctrinal History: Comment on Baird. *Cato J.*, Spring–Summer 1989, 9(1), pp. 231–35.

Kiselev, V. I. Contemporary Trends in Pricing of Industrial and Farm Products in the USSR and Their Impact on Effectiveness of Production. In *Islam, N., ed.*, 1989, pp. 73–85.

Kiser, Edgar. A Principal–Agent Analysis of the Initiation of War in Absolutist States. In *Schaeffer, R. K., ed.*, 1989, pp. 65–82.

Kishida, Tamiki. Entrepreneurship: Management Ideology and Corporate Strategy. In *Dams, T. and Matsugi, T., eds.*, 1989, pp. 21–42.

Kishimoto, Naoki. Pricing Contingent Claims under Interest Rate and Asset Price Risk. *J. Finance*, July 1989, 44(3), pp. 571–89.

Kiss, Judit. Competition or Cooperation? Agricultural Trade of the Socialist and the Developing Countries. In *Wohlmuth, K., ed.*, 1989, pp. 147–84.

Kissinger, Henry A.; d'Estaing, Valéry Giscard and Nakasone, Yasuhiro. East–West Relations. *Foreign Aff.*, Summer 1989, 68(3), pp. 1–21.

Kistner, Klaus-Peter and Switalski, Marion. Hierarchische Produktionsplanung. (With English summary.) *Z. Betriebswirtshaft*, May 1989, 59(5), pp. 477–503.

Kitabatake, Yoshifusa. Backward Incidence of Pollution Damage Compensation Policy. *J. En-*

viron. Econ. Manage., September 1989, *17*(2), pp. 171–80.

———. Optimal Exploitation and Enhancement of Environmental Resources. *J. Environ. Econ. Manage.*, May 1989, *16*(3), pp. 224–41.

Kitchen, John and Rausser, Gordon C. Interest Rates and Commodity Prices. *J. Agr. Econ. Res.*, Spring 1989, *41*(2), pp. 5–11.

Kitron, Uriel. Integrated Disease Management of Tropical Infectious Diseases. In *Reich, M. R. and Marui, E., eds.*, 1989, pp. 234–63.

Kitson, Michael and Solomou, Solomos. The Macroeconomics of Protectionism: The Case of Britain in the 1930s. In *Lawson, T.; Palma, J. G. and Sender, J., eds.*, 1989, pp. 155–69.

——— **and Solomou, Solomos.** The Macroeconomics of Protectionism: The Case of Britain in the 1930s. *Cambridge J. Econ.*, March 1989, *13*(1), pp. 155–69.

Kittelsen, Sverre A. C. Economic Performance of Flexible Functional Forms: Correction and Comment. *Europ. Econ. Rev.*, April 1989, *33*(4), pp. 825–38.

Kiva, A. The Socialist Orientation: Theoretical Pontential of the Concept and Its Reality in Practice. *Prob. Econ.*, June 1989, *32*(2), pp. 66–88.

Kiwiel, Krzysztof C. and Stachurski, Andrzej. Issues of Effectiveness Arising in the Design of a System of Nondifferentiable Optimization Algorithms. In *Lewandowski, A. and Wierzbicki, A. P., eds.*, 1989, pp. 180–92.

Kiyotaki, Nobuhiro and Wright, Randall. On Money as a Medium of Exchange. *J. Polit. Econ.*, August 1989, *97*(4), pp. 927–54.

Klamer, Arjo. An Accountant among Economists: Conservations with Sir John R. Hicks. *J. Econ. Perspectives*, Fall 1989, *3*(4), pp. 167–80.

———. A Conversation with Amartya Sen. *J. Econ. Perspectives*, Winter 1989, *3*(1), pp. 135–50.

Klarquist, Virginia L. and Ferris, John W. Productivity in the Carburetors, Pistons, and Valves Industry. *Mon. Lab. Rev.*, February 1989, *112*(2), pp. 43–46.

Klaus, Václav. The Imperatives of Long-term Prognoses and the Dominant Characteristics of the Economy at Present. *Czech. Econ. Digest.*, November 1989, (7), pp. 31–52.

——— **and Tříska, Dušan.** The Economic Centre: The Restructuring and Equilibrium. *Czech. Econ. Digest.*, February 1989, (1), pp. 34–56.

van Klaveren, Jacob. The Concept of Corruption. In *Heidenheimer, A. J.; Johnston, M. and LeVine, V. T., eds.*, 1989, *1957*, pp. 25–28.

———. Corruption as a Historical Phenomenon. In *Heidenheimer, A. J.; Johnston, M. and LeVine, V. T., eds.*, 1989, pp. 73–86.

———. Corruption: The Special Case of the United States. In *Heidenheimer, A. J.; Johnston, M. and LeVine, V. T., eds.*, 1989, *1959*, pp. 557–66.

Kleckley, James W. and Olson, Kent W. Severance Tax Stability. *Nat. Tax J.*, March 1989, *42*(1), pp. 69–78,.

Kleckner, Dean. Trade and Aid Policies: How U.S. Farmers See It. In *Swegle, W. E. and Ligon, P. C., eds.*, 1989, pp. 17–22.

Kleen, P. The Safeguard Issue in the Uruguay Round–A Comprehensive Approach. *J. World Trade*, October 1989, *23*(5), pp. 73–92.

Kleffe, Jürgen. Updating Parameters of Linear Change Point Models. In *Hackl, P., ed.*, 1989, pp. 319–26.

Klehr, Harvey and Tompson, William. Self-determination in the Black Belt: Origins of a Communist Policy. *Labor Hist.*, Summer 1989, *30*(3), pp. 354–66.

Kleiding, Hans and Fristrup, Peter. A Note on Asymptotical Strategy-Proofness. *Econ. Letters*, December 1989, *31*(4), pp. 307–12.

Kleiman, Ephraim. Open Borders and Labor Mobility: Israel, the West Bank, and Gaza. In *Fishelson, G., ed.*, 1989, pp. 55–78.

Kleiman, Robert T. and Murphy, J. Austin. The Inflation-Hedging Characteristics of Equity REITs: An Empirical Study. *Quart. Rev. Econ. Bus.*, Autumn 1989, *29*(3), pp. 95–101.

Klein, Bohuslav. Joint Ventures in Czechoslovakia: New Law on Joint Ventures Passed. *Czech. Econ. Digest.*, June 1989, (4), pp. 3–12.

Klein, Bruce W. and Rones, Philip L. A Profile of the Working Poor. *Mon. Lab. Rev.*, October 1989, *112*(10), pp. 3–13.

Klein, Deborah P. and Norwood, Janet L. Developing Statistics to Meet Society's Needs. *Mon. Lab. Rev.*, October 1989, *112*(10), pp. 14–19.

Klein, Ira. Population Growth and Mortality, Part I: The Climacteric of Death. *Indian Econ. Soc. Hist. Rev.*, Oct.–Dec. 1989, *26*(4), pp. 387–403.

Klein, J. Douglass. Cooperation and the per se Debate: Evidence from the United Kingdom. *Antitrust Bull.*, Fall 1989, *34*(3), pp. 517–32.

———; **Weiss, Leonard W. and Brannman, Lance.** The Price Effects of Increased Competition in Auction Markets. In *Weiss, L. W., ed.*, 1989, pp. 67–84.

Klein, Jean. The Links between Nuclear and Conventional Forces. In *Rotblat, J. and Goldanskii, V. I., eds.*, 1989, pp. 72–78.

Klein, Kurt K. and Chase-Wilde, Linda. Growth and Development of Value-Added Activities. In *Schmitz, A., ed.*, 1989, pp. 88–138.

———; **Klein, S. A. and Bowe, M.** Adverse Selection and Warble Flies in Alberta. *Can. J. Agr. Econ.*, March 1989, *37*(1), pp. 111–23.

Klein, Lawrence R. Developments and Prospects in Macroeconometric Modeling. *Eastern Econ. J.*, Oct.–Dec. 1989, *15*(4), pp. 287–304.

———. Econometric Aspects of Input–Output Analysis. In *Miller, R. E.; Polenske, K. R. and Rose, A. Z., eds.*, 1989, pp. 3–11.

———. The Economic Principles of Joan Robinson. In *Feiwel, G. R., ed. (II)*, 1989, pp. 258–63.

———. Global Adjustment and the Future of Asian-Pacific Economies. In *Shinohara, M. and Lo, F., eds.*, 1989, pp. 15–27.

———. The Restructuring of the American Economy. In *[Weintraub, S.]*, 1989, pp. 25–45.

———. The State of Economic Science: Views of Six Nobel Laureates: Dr. Lawrence R. Klein. In *Sichel, W., ed.*, 1989, pp. 41–58.

——— and Sojo, E. Combinations of High and Low Frequency Data in Macroeconometric Models. In *[Adams, F. G.]*, 1989, pp. 3–16.

Klein, Linda S. and Peterson, David R. Earnings Forecast Revisions Associated with Stock Split Announcements. *J. Finan. Res.*, Winter 1989, 12(4), pp. 319–28.

Klein, Martin. Arbitrage and Interest Rates on Currency Baskets. *Weltwirtsch. Arch.*, 1989, 125(2), pp. 296–310.

Klein, Noreen M. and Yadav, Manjit S. Context Effects on Effort and Accuracy in Choice: An Enquiry into Adaptive Decision Making. *J. Cons. Res.*, March 1989, 15(4), pp. 411–21.

Klein, Peter W. The China Seas and the World Economy between the Sixteenth and Nineteenth Centuries: The Changing Structures of Trade. In *[Fischer, W.]*, 1989, pp. 61–89.

———. Storia quantitativa e storia economica: Relazione introduttiva. (In English.) In *Cavaciocchi, S., ed.*, 1989, pp. 289–316.

Klein, Philip A. Confronting Power in Economics: A Pragmatic Evaluation. In *Tool, M. R. and Samuels, W. J., eds. (I)*, 1989, *1980*, pp. 63–88.

———. Economics: Allocation or Valuation? In *Tool, M. R. and Samuels, W. J., eds. (I)*, 1989, *1974*, pp. 9–35.

———. Institutionalism Confronts the 1990s. *J. Econ. Issues*, June 1989, 23(2), pp. 545–53.

———. Institutionalist Reflections on the Role of the Public Sector. In *Tool, M. R. and Samuels, W. J., eds. (II)*, 1989, *1984*, pp. 541–64.

Klein, Rudolf. Money, Information and Policy. In *[Sandford, C.]*, 1989, pp. 116–36.

Klein, S. A.; Bowe, M. and Klein, Kurt K. Adverse Selection and Warble Flies in Alberta. *Can. J. Agr. Econ.*, March 1989, 37(1), pp. 111–23.

Klein, Thomas. Sozialhilfeniveau und untere Lohneinkommen. (Social Assistance Level and Low Earnings. With English summary.) *Ifo-Studien*, 1989, 35(1), pp. 53–76.

Kleinberg, Jill. Cultural Clash between Managers: America's Japanese Firms. In *Prasad, S. B., ed.*, 1989, pp. 221–43.

Kleindorfer, Paul R. and Gaynor, Martin. Misperceptions, Equilibrium, and Incentives in Groups and Organizations. In *Bamberg, G. and Spremann, K., eds.*, 1989, pp. 389–414.

———; Kunreuther, Howard and Berger, Lawrence A. A Dynamic Model of the Transmission of Price Information in Auto Insurance Markets. *J. Risk Ins.*, March 1989, 56(1), pp. 17–33.

Kleinholz, Rainer. Ein Anreizsystem mit Signalisierung der Markteinschätzung. (With English summary.) *Z. Betriebswirtshaft*, July 1989, 59(7), pp. 735–41.

Kleinman, Mark and Eastall, Richard. A Behavioural Model of the Supply of Re-lets of Council Housing in England. *Urban Stud.*, December 1989, 26(6), pp. 535–48.

Klemkosky, Robert C. and Resnick, Bruce G. An Analysis of Variance Test for Linearity of the Two-Parameter Asset Pricing Model. *J. Econ. Bus.*, November 1989, 41(4), pp. 265–82.

de Klemm, Cyril. Migratory Species in International Law. *Natural Res. J.*, Fall 1989, 29(4), pp. 935–78.

Klemme, Richard M.; Gould, Brian W. and Saupe, William E. Conservation Tillage: The Role of Farm and Operator Characteristics and the Perception of Soil Erosion. *Land Econ.*, May 1989, 65(2), pp. 167–82.

Klemperer, Paul D. Price Wars Caused by Switching Costs. *Rev. Econ. Stud.*, July 1989, 56(3), pp. 405–20.

——— and Froot, Kenneth A. Exchange Rate Pass-Through When Market Share Matters. *Amer. Econ. Rev.*, September 1989, 79(4), pp. 637–54.

——— and Meyer, Margaret A. Supply Function Equilibria in Oligopoly under Uncertainty. *Econometrica*, November 1989, 57(6), pp. 1243–77.

Klemperer, W. David. An Income Tax Wedge between Buyers' and Sellers' Values of Forests: Erratum. *Land Econ.*, November 1989, 65(4), pp. iii.

———. An Income Tax Wedge between Buyers' and Sellers' Values of Forests. *Land Econ.*, May 1989, 65(2), pp. 146–57.

Klep, Paul. Specializzazione e diversificazione dell'economia rurale: Interventi degli esperti. (In English.) In *Cavaciocchi, S., ed.*, 1989, pp. 165–69.

Klepper, Steven and Nagin, Daniel S. The Anatomy of Tax Evasion. *J. Law, Econ., Organ.*, Spring 1989, 5(1), pp. 1–24.

——— and Nagin, Daniel S. The Role of Tax Preparers in Tax Compliance. *Policy Sciences*, May 1989, 22(2), pp. 167–94.

Kletke, Darrel. Enterprise Budgets. In *Tweeten, L., ed.*, 1989, pp. 189–211.

Kletzer, Kenneth M. Sovereign Debt Renegotiation under Asymmetric Information. In *Frenkel, J. A.; Dooley, M. P. and Wickham, P., eds.*, 1989, pp. 208–41.

——— and Engel, Charles. Saving and Investment in an Open Economy with Non-traded Goods. *Int. Econ. Rev.*, November 1989, 30(4), pp. 735–52.

———; Srinivasan, T. N. and Buiter, Willem H. Some Thoughts on the Brady Plan: Putting a Fourth Leg on the Donkey? *World Devel.*, October 1989, 17(10), pp. 1661–64.

Kletzer, Lori Gladstein. Returns to Seniority after Permanent Job Loss. *Amer. Econ. Rev.*, June 1989, 79(3), pp. 536–43.

Klevmarken, N. Anders. Panel Studies: What Can We Learn from Them? Introduction. *Eu-*

rop. Econ. Rev., March 1989, *33*(2/3), pp. 523–29.

_____ and Gustafsson, Björn. The Political Economy of Social Security: Editor's Introduction and Summary. In *Gustafsson, B. A. and Klevmarken, N. A., eds.*, 1989, pp. 1–9.

Klíma, Arnošt. Domestic Industry, Manufactory and Early Industrialization in Bohemia. *J. Europ. Econ. Hist.*, Winter 1989, *18*(3), pp. 509–27.

Klimberg, Ronald K.; ReVelle, Charles and Cohon, Jared. NMIS: A National Model for Inspection Selection with Limited Resources. In *Lockett, A. G. and Islei, G., eds.*, 1989, pp. 244–53.

Klimenko, L. and Menshikov, S. Long Waves in Economic Structure. In *Di Matteo, M.; Goodwin, R. M. and Vercelli, A., eds.*, 1989, pp. 145–66.

_____ and Menshikov, S. Structural Change and the Long Wave. In *Krelle, W., ed.*, 1989, pp. 543–60.

Kling, Catherine L. The Importance of Functional Form in the Estimation of Welfare. *Western J. Agr. Econ.*, July 1989, *14*(1), pp. 168–74.

_____. A Note on the Welfare Effects of Omitting Substitute Prices and Qualities from Travel Cost Models. *Land Econ.*, August 1989, *65*(3), pp. 290–96.

Kling, John L. and Bessler, David A. Calibration-Based Predictive Distributions: An Application of Prequential Analysis to Interest Rates, Money, Prices, and Output. *J. Bus.*, October 1989, *62*(4), pp. 477–99.

_____ and Bessler, David A. The Forecast and Policy Analysis. *Amer. J. Agr. Econ.*, May 1989, *71*(2), pp. 503–06.

Kling, Robert W. General Equilibrium Effects of Regulation. *Amer. Economist*, Fall 1989, *33*(2), pp. 53–59.

Klitgaard, Robert. Incentive Myopia. *World Devel.*, April 1989, *17*(4), pp. 447–59.

Klock, Mark and Silberman, Jonathan. The Behavior of Respondents in Contingent Valuation: Evidence on Starting Bids. *J. Behav. Econ.*, Spring 1989, *18*(1), pp. 51–60.

Klodt, Henning. Most-Favored-Nation Principle and Negotiating Strategies. In *Robinson, P.; Sauvant, K. P. and Govitrikar, V. P., eds.*, 1989, pp. 181–95.

_____. Services and Comparative Advantage Theory: Comment. In *Giersch, H., ed.*, 1989, pp. 104–07.

_____; Schmidt, Klaus-Dieter and Donges, Juergen B. Prospective Structural Changes in the West German Economy. In *Krelle, W., ed.*, 1989, pp. 385–98.

Kloppenburg, Jack. Biotechnology, Plant Breeding, and Intellectual Property: Social and Ethical Dimensions: Appendix: Agrigenetics and Agricultural Genetics. In *Weil, V. and Snapper, J. W., eds.*, 1989, pp. 132–39.

Kloten, Norbert. Perspektiven der europäischen Währungsintegration. (The Outlook for European Monetary Integration. With English sum-

mary.) *Jahr. Nationalökon. Statist.*, October 1989, *206*(4–5), pp. 407–20.

_____. The Role of the Economist in Government: An International Perspective: West Germany. In *Pechman, J. A., ed.*, 1989, pp. 47–72.

_____. Role of the Public Sector in the Social Market Economy. In *Peacock, A. and Willgerodt, H., eds. (I)*, 1989, pp. 69–104.

Klovland, Jan Tore. A Chronology of Cycles in Real Economic Activity for Norway, 1867–1914. *Scand. Econ. Hist. Rev.*, 1989, *37*(3), pp. 18–38.

Kluender, Richard A. and Pickett, John C. Public Policy Implications for the Supply of Pine Sawlogs. *Natural Res. J.*, Summer 1989, *29*(3), pp. 723–35.

Kluger, Brian D. Implications of Quality Standard Regulation for Multiproduct Monopoly Pricing. *Managerial Dec. Econ.*, March 1989, *10*(1), pp. 61–67.

_____ and Shields, David. Auditor Changes, Information Quality and Bankruptcy Prediction. *Managerial Dec. Econ.*, December 1989, *10*(4), pp. 275–82.

Klump, Rainer. Der Dollar als internationale Schlüsselwährung: Ursachen und Perspektiven. (The Dollar as an International Key Currency: Reasons and Perspectives. With English summary.) *Kredit Kapital*, 1989, *22*(3), pp. 375–402.

van de Klundert, Theo. Wage Differentials and Employment in a Two-Sector Model with a Dual Labour Market. *Metroecon.*, October 1989, *40*(3), pp. 235–56.

_____ and van der Ploeg, Frederick. Fiscal Policy and Finite Lives in Interdependent Economies with Real and Nominal Wage Rigidity. *Oxford Econ. Pap.*, July 1989, *41*(3), pp. 459–89.

_____ and van der Ploeg, Frederick. Wage Rigidity and Capital Mobility in an Optimizing Model of a Small Open Economy. *De Economist*, 1989, *137*(1), pp. 47–75.

Klusoň, Václav. The General and Specific Rules of Economic Control. *Czech. Econ. Pap.*, 1989, (27), pp. 47–64.

_____; Hrnčíř, Miroslav and Seják, Josef. The Directions of Development of Intensive Type Economic Mechanism. *Czech. Econ. Pap.*, 1989, (26), pp. 31–49.

Kluver, J. and Harrison, B. Reassessing the 'Massachusetts Miracle': Reindustrialization and Balanced Growth, or Convergence to 'Manhattanization'? *Environ. Planning A*, June 1989, *21*(6), pp. 771–801.

de Kluyver, Cornelis; Farris, Paul W. and Olver, James. The Relationship between Distribution and Market Share: Reply. *Marketing Sci.*, Spring 1989, *8*(2), pp. 131–32.

_____; Farris, Paul W. and Olver, James. The Relationship between Distribution and Market Share. *Marketing Sci.*, Spring 1989, *8*(2), pp. 107–28.

Kmenta, Jan. Towards a Positive Economic Theory of Institutional Change: Comment. *J. Inst.*

Theoretical Econ., March 1989, *145*(1), pp. 113–15.

van der Knaap, G. A. and van der Laan, L. Spatial Implications of Unionisation, Employment and Labour Activism. In *Linge, G. J. R. and van der Knaap, G. A., eds.*, 1989, pp. 144–66.

_____ **and Linge, G. J. R.** Labour, Environment and Industrial Change. In *Linge, G. J. R. and van der Knaap, G. A., eds.*, 1989, pp. 1–19.

Knaap, Gerrit J. Doctors and Their Workshops: A Spatial Perspective. *Reg. Sci. Urban Econ.*, February 1989, *19*(1), pp. 143–57.

_____. The Political Economy of Growth Management in Oregon: A Historical Review. *Rev. Reg. Stud.*, Winter 1989, *19*(1), pp. 43–49.

Knapp, Keith C. and Paris, Quirino. Estimation of von Liebig Response Functions. *Amer. J. Agr. Econ.*, February 1989, *71*(1), pp. 178–86.

Knapp, Martin. Intersectoral Differences in Cost Effectiveness: Residential Child Care in England and Wales. In *James, E., ed.*, 1989, pp. 193–216.

Knapp, Thomas A. and Graves, Philip E. On the Role of Amenities in Models of Migration and Regional Development. *J. Reg. Sci.*, February 1989, *29*(1), pp. 71–87.

Knaus, William A. Criteria for Admission to Intensive Care Units. In *Strosberg, M. A.; Fein, I. A. and Carroll, J. D., eds.*, 1989, pp. 44–51.

Kneebone, Ronald D. Does Fiscal Policy Matter in a Federal Economy? *J. Macroecon.*, Fall 1989, *11*(4), pp. 599–607.

_____. On Macro-economic Instability under a Monetarist Policy Rule in a Federal Economy. *Can. J. Econ.*, August 1989, *22*(3), pp. 673–85.

Kneschaurek, Francesco. Untersuchungen zur internationalen Konkurrenzfähigkeit der Schweiz: Ein Vergleich. (Comparative Analysis on the International Competitive Position of the Swiss Economy. With English summary.) *Aussenwirtschaft*, June 1989, *44*(2), pp. 179–96.

Knetsch, Jack L. The Endowment Effect and Evidence of Nonreversible Indifference Curves. *Amer. Econ. Rev.*, December 1989, *79*(5), pp. 1277–84.

Knetter, Michael M. Price Discrimination by U.S. and German Exporters. *Amer. Econ. Rev.*, March 1989, *79*(1), pp. 198–210.

Knieps, Günter. Telecommunications Policy—Assessing Recent Experience in the U.S., Japan and Europe and Its Implications for the Completion of the Internal Common Market. In *Giersch, H., ed.*, 1989, pp. 173–89.

_____ **and Blankart, Charles B.** What Can We Learn from Comparative Institutional Analysis? The Case of Telecommunications. *Kyklos*, 1989, *42*(4), pp. 579–98.

Kniesner, Thomas J. and Leeth, John D. Can We Make OSHA and Workers' Compensation Insurance Interact More Effectively in Promoting Workplace Safety? In *Ehrenberg, R. G., ed.*, 1989, pp. 1–51.

_____ **and Leeth, John D.** Separating the Reporting Effects from the Injury Rate Effects of Workers' Compensation Insurance: A Hedonic Simulation. *Ind. Lab. Relat. Rev.*, January 1989, *42*(2), pp. 280–93.

Knight, E. T. and Firer, C. The Performance of South African Unit Trusts 1977–1986. *S. Afr. J. Econ.*, March 1989, *57*(1), pp. 52–68.

Knight, J. B. and de Beyer, J. The Role of Occupation in the Determination of Wages. *Oxford Econ. Pap.*, July 1989, *41*(3), pp. 595–618.

Knight, K. G. Labour Productivity and Strike Activity in British Manufacturing Industries: Some Quantitative Evidence. *Brit. J. Ind. Relat.*, November 1989, *27*(3), pp. 365–74.

Knight, Thomas O., et al. An Analysis of Lenders' Influence on Agricultural Producers' Risk Management Decisions. *Southern J. Agr. Econ.*, December 1989, *21*(2), pp. 21–33.

Knirsch, P. The Socialist Market Economy— Myth or Reality? *Acta Oecon.*, 1989, *40*(3–4), pp. 239–42.

Knobloch, Thomas and Haupt, Reinhard. Kostentheoretische Anpassungsprozesse bei zeitvariablen Faktoreinsätzen. (With English summary.) *Z. Betriebswirtshaft*, May 1989, *59*(5), pp. 504–24.

Knodel, John and McDonald, Peter. The Impact of Changes in Birth Spacing on Age at Last Birth: Response. *Demography*, August 1989, *26*(3), pp. 471–72.

Knoeber, Charles R. A Real Game of Chicken: Contracts, Tournaments, and the Production of Broilers. *J. Law, Econ., Organ.*, Fall 1989, *5*(2), pp. 271–92.

Knoke, David and Laumann, Edward O. Policy Networks of the Organizational State: Collective Action in the National Energy and Health Domains. In *Perrucci, R. and Potter, H. R., eds.*, 1989, pp. 17–55.

Knoll, Michael S. Legal and Economic Framework for the Analysis of Injury by the U.S. International Trade Commission. *J. World Trade*, June 1989, *23*(3), pp. 95–107.

van der Knoop, Han S. and Hooijmans, Frans C. A Multivariate Intervention Model for the Dutch Mint Circulation: Estimation and Monte Carlo Simulation. *J. Bus. Econ. Statist.*, April 1989, *7*(2), pp. 179–89.

Knox, A. D. On a Theory of the Trade Cycle. In *Wood, J. C. and Woods, R. N., eds., Vol. 1*, 1989, *1950*, pp. 123–31.

Knudsen, Dan. Estimation af industrieksportens priselasticitet. (An Estimation of the Price Elasticity for Danish Industrial Export. With English summary.) *Nationaløkon. Tidsskr.*, 1989, *127*(2), pp. 213–28.

Knudson, Mary K. and Larson, Bruce A. A Framework for Examining Technical Change. *J. Agr. Econ. Res.*, Fall 1989, *41*(4), pp. 21–28.

Kobayashi, Kiyoshi and Andersson, Åke E. Some Theoretical Aspects of Spatial Equilibria with Public Goods. In *Andersson, Å. E., et al., eds.*, 1989, pp. 207–21.

_____; **Andersson, Åke E. and Batten, David**

F. Knowledge, Nodes and Networks: An Analytical Perspective. In *Andersson, Å. E.; Batten, D. F. and Karlsson, C., eds.,* 1989, pp. 31–46.

_____; Zhang, Wei-Bin and Yoshikawa, Kazuhiro. Taste Change and Conservation Laws in the Housing Market. In *Andersson, Å. E., et al., eds.,* 1989, pp. 291–307.

Kobayashi, Yotaro. The Challenges Facing Japan in the Heisei Era. In *Frankel, A. V. and Heck, C. B., eds.,* 1989, pp. 62–66.

Koch, Bruce S. and Reed, Sarah A. Resource Allocation Decisions by Charitable Organizations: An Experiment. In *Chan, J. L. and Patton, J. M., eds.,* 1989, pp. 99–122.

Koch, Helmut. Zur Theorie des optimalen Produktprogramms bei Ungewissheit. (With English summary.) *Z. Betriebswirtshaft,* December 1989, 59(12), pp. 1267–84.

Koch, James V. and Cebula, Richard J. An Empirical Note on Deficits, Interest Rates, and International Capital Flows. *Quart. Rev. Econ. Bus.,* Autumn 1989, 29(3), pp. 121–27.

_____ and Cebula, Richard J. Welfare Policies and Migration of the Poor in the United States: An Empirical Note. *Public Choice,* May 1989, 61(2), pp. 171–76.

Koch, Karl-Josef. Mean Demand When Consumers Satisfy the Weak Axiom of Revealed Preference. *J. Math. Econ.,* 1989, 18(4), pp. 347–56.

Koch, Timothy W. and Kawaller, Ira G. Yield Opportunities and Hedge Ratio Considerations with Fixed Income Cash-and-Carry Trades. *J. Futures Markets,* December 1989, 9(6), pp. 539–45.

Kochan, Thomas A. and Cutcher-Gershenfeld, Joel. Innovation or Confrontation: Alternative Directions for American Industrial Relations. In *Huang, W.-C., ed.,* 1989, pp. 27–62.

Kochanowicz, Jacek. The Polish Economy and the Evolution of Dependency. In *Chirot, D., ed.,* 1989, pp. 92–130.

Kochanowski, Paul; Bartholomew, Wayne and Joray, Paul. The Shift-Share Methodology: Deficiencies and Proposed Remedies. *Reg. Sci. Persp.,* 1989, 19(1), pp. 65–88.

Kochin, Levis A. and Gilbert, R. Alton. Local Economic Effects of Bank Failures. *J. Finan. Services Res.,* December 1989, 3(4), pp. 333–45.

Kochman, Ladd M. Trigger Prices for Margin Calls. *Atlantic Econ. J.,* June 1989, 17(2), pp. 78.

Kocklauner, Gerhard. Econometric Problems in Cross-sectional Stochastic Input–Output Analysis. *Econ. Systems Res.,* 1989, 1(3), pp. 311–16.

Koditschek, Theodore. The Dynamics of Class Formation in Nineteenth-Century Bradford. In *[Stone, L.],* 1989, pp. 511–48.

Koedijk, Kees and Schotman, Peter. Dominant Real Exchange Rate Movements. *J. Int. Money Finance,* December 1989, 8(4), pp. 517–31.

Koekkoek, Ad. Tropical Products, Developing

Countries and the Uruguay Round. *J. World Trade,* December 1989, 23(6), pp. 127–36.

Koeller, C. T. A 'Keynesian' Construct in Hicksian IS–LM Analysis: A Comment. In *Wood, J. C. and Woods, R. N., eds., Vol. 3,* 1989, 1977, pp. 173–77.

Koen, Vincent. L'anglomanie des économistes français. (The Anglomania of French Economists. With English summary.) *Écon. Societes,* August 1989, 23(8), pp. 103–15.

Koenig, Evan F. Investment and the Nominal Interest Rate: The Variable Velocity Case. *Econ. Inquiry,* April 1989, 27(2), pp. 325–44.

_____. Recent Trade and Exchange Rate Movements: Possible Explanations. *Fed. Res. Bank Dallas Econ. Rev.,* September 1989, pp. 13–28.

Koenigsberger, H. G. Republics and Courts in Italian and European Culture in the 16th and 17th Centuries. In *Guarducci, A., ed.,* 1989, pp. 483–513.

Koester, Reinhard B. and Andreae, Clemens-August. Values and Policies in the Global Economy: A European–American Institutional Challenge. In *Rueschhoff, N. and Schaum, K., eds.,* 1989, pp. 9–20.

_____ and Kormendi, Roger C. Taxation, Aggregate Activity and Economic Growth: Cross-Country Evidence on Some Supply-Side Hypotheses. *Econ. Inquiry,* July 1989, 27(3), pp. 367–86.

Koester, U. Financial Implications of the EC Set-Aside Programme. *J. Agr. Econ.,* May 1989, 40(2), pp. 240–48.

Kogut, Bruce. The Stability of Joint Ventures: Reciprocity and Competitive Rivalry. *J. Ind. Econ.,* December 1989, 38(2), pp. 183–98.

Koh, Francis and Walter, Terry. A Direct Test of Rock's Model of the Pricing of Unseasoned Issues. *J. Finan. Econ.,* August 1989, 23(2), pp. 251–72.

Kohler, André and Krolak-Schwerdt, Sabine. Relations between Models for Three-Way Factor Analysis and Multidimensional Scaling. In *Opitz, O., ed.,* 1989, pp. 147–58.

Kohlhase, Janet E. and Ohta, Hiroshi. General Equilibrium of Spatial Product and Labor Markets. *J. Reg. Sci.,* November 1989, 29(4), pp. 537–53.

Kohli, Atul. Politics of Economic Liberalization in India. *World Devel.,* March 1989, 17(3), pp. 305–28.

Kohli, Inderjit and Singh, Nirvikar. Exports and Growth: Critical Minimum Effort and Diminishing Returns. *J. Devel. Econ.,* April 1989, 30(2), pp. 391–400.

Kohli, Kedar N. Economic Trends in Asia. In *Naya, S., et al., eds.,* 1989, pp. 13–38.

Kohli, U. Consistent Estimation When the Left-Hand Variable is Exogenous over Part of the Sample Period. *J. Appl. Econometrics,* July–Sept. 1989, 4(3), pp. 283–93.

Kohn, Donald L. Monetary Policy in an Era of Change. *Fed. Res. Bull.,* February 1989, 75(2), pp. 53–57.

_____. Policy Targets and Operating Procedures

in the 1990s. **In** *Federal Reserve Bank of Kansas City*, 1989, pp. 129–41.

Kohn, Meir and Karacaoglu, Girol. Aggregation and the Microfoundations of the Monetary Approach to the Balance of Payments. *Can. J. Econ.*, May 1989, *22*(2), pp. 290–309.

Kohn, Robert E. Efficient Scale of the Pollution-Abating Firm: Reply. *Land Econ.*, November 1989, *65*(4), pp. 417–19.

_____. Variable Outputs along a Production Possibility Frontier with Inputs Constant by Choice. *Rivista Int. Sci. Econ. Com.*, September 1989, *36*(9), pp. 837–46.

Kohsaka, H. An Analysis of Competitive Oscillations between Japanese Twin Cities. *Environ. Planning A*, June 1989, *21*(6), pp. 803–16.

Koistinen, Pertti. Transforming Industrial Work in Finland. **In** *Francis, A. and Grootings, P., eds.*, 1989, pp. 262–95.

Koizumi, A. and Inakazu, T. A Multipurpose Optimization Model for Area-Wide Sewerage Systems. *Environ. Planning A*, August 1989, *21*(8), pp. 1015–26.

Koizumi, Tetsunori. Management of Innovation and Change in Japanese Organizations. **In** *Prasad, S. B., ed.*, 1989, pp. 245–54.

Kojima, Hiroshi. Intergenerational Household Extension in Japan. **In** *Goldscheider, F. K. and Goldscheider, C., eds.*, 1989, pp. 163–84.

Kojima, Kiyoshi. Japanese and American Direct Investment in Asia. **In** *Negandhi, A. R., ed.*, 1989, pp. 125–51.

_____. The Multiple Key Currency Gold-Exchange Standard: A Proposal. *Hitotsubashi J. Econ.*, June 1989, *30*(1), pp. 1–13.

_____. Theory of Internalisation by Multinational Corporations. *Hitotsubashi J. Econ.*, December 1989, *30*(2), pp. 65–85.

Kojima, Makoto. Industrialisation, Income Distribution, and Labour Migration: The Case of India. **In** *Chakravarty, S., ed.*, 1989, pp. 207–32.

Kokkelenberg, Edward C.; Färe, Rolf and Grosskopf, Shawna. Measuring Plant Capacity, Utilization and Technical Change: A Nonparametric Approach. *Int. Econ. Rev.*, August 1989, *30*(3), pp. 655–66.

Kokoski, Mary F. Experimental Cost-of-Living Indexes: A Summary of Current Research. *Mon. Lab. Rev.*, July 1989, *112*(7), pp. 34–39.

Kol, Jacob and Mennes, L. B. M. Corrections for Trade Imbalance: A Survey. *Weltwirtsch. Arch.*, 1989, *125*(4), pp. 703–17.

_____ **and Rayment, Paul.** Allyn Young Specialisation and Intermediate Goods in Intra-industry Trade. **In** *Tharakan, P. K. M. and Kol, J., eds.*, 1989, pp. 51–68.

_____ **and Tharakan, P. K. M.** Intra-industry Trade, Traditional Trade Theory and Its Extensions. **In** *Tharakan, P. K. M. and Kol, J., eds.*, 1989, pp. 1–14.

Kolari, James; McInish, Thomas H. and Saniga, Erwin M. A Note on the Distribution Types of Financial Ratios in the Commercial Banking Industry. *J. Banking Finance*, July 1989, *13*(3), pp. 463–71.

Kolb, Robert W. and Rodriguez, Ricardo J. The Regression Tendencies of Betas: A Reappraisal. *Financial Rev.*, May 1989, *24*(2), pp. 319–34.

_____; **Yung, Kenneth and Gay, Gerald D.** Trader Rationality in the Exercise of Futures Options. *J. Finan. Econ.*, August 1989, *23*(2), pp. 339–61.

Kolbe, Jim. The Need for Debt Concessions and Forgiveness. **In** *Dornbusch, R.; Makin, J. H. and Zlowe, D., eds.*, 1989, pp. 79–81.

Kolganov, A. and Buzgalin, A. How Was the "Administrative System" Created? *Prob. Econ.*, September 1989, *32*(5), pp. 35–52.

_____ **and Buzgalin, A.** Planning without Bureaucratic Administration. **In** *Yanowitch, M., ed.*, 1989, *1987*, pp. 53–57.

Koller, Roland H., II and Weiss, Leonard W. Price Levels and Seller Concentration: The Case of Portland Cement. **In** *Weiss, L. W., ed.*, 1989, pp. 17–40.

Kollewe, Wolfgang. Evaluation of a Survey with Methods of Formal Concept Analysis. **In** *Opitz, O., ed.*, 1989, pp. 123–34.

Kollintzas, Tryphon. The Linear Rational Expectations Equilibrium Inventory Model: An Introduction. **In** *Kollintzas, T., ed.*, 1989, pp. 1–32.

_____ **and Dimelis, Sophia P.** A Linear Rational Expectations Equilibrium Model of the American Petroleum Industry. **In** *Kollintzas, T., ed.*, 1989, pp. 110–97.

Kolluri, Bharat R. and Giannaros, D. The Impact of Budget Deficits on Real Interest Rates: An International Empirical Investigation. *Int. Econ. J.*, Summer 1989, *3*(2), pp. 17–25.

_____; **Panik, Michael J. and Sullivan, Jack J.** Wagner's Law of Public Expenditure Revisited. **In** *Missouri Valley Economic Association*, 1989, pp. 98–104.

Kołodko, Grzegorz W. Economic Reform in Socialism and Inflation: Determinants and Interrelations. *Eastern Europ. Econ.*, Spring 1989, *27*(3), pp. 36–50.

_____. Social and Political Aspects of Inflation. *Eastern Europ. Econ.*, Spring 1989, *27*(3), pp. 51–60.

Kolodny, Richard; Laurence, Martin and Ghosh, Arabinda. In Search of Excellence...for Whom? *J. Portfol. Manage.*, Spring 1989, *15*(3), pp. 56–60.

Kolpin, V. Core Implementation via Dynamic Game Forms. *Soc. Choice Welfare*, July 1989, *6*(3), pp. 205–25.

Kolstad, Charles D. Computing Dynamic Spatial Oligopolistic Equilibrium in an Exhaustible Resource Market: The Case of Coal. **In** *Labys, W. C.; Takayama, T. and Uri, N. D., eds.*, 1989, pp. 87–103.

Koltunov, Viktor. Experience with INF Treaty Verification and Prospects for the Future. **In** *Altmann, J. and Rotblat, J., eds.*, 1989, pp. 27–36.

Komárek, Valtr. Prognostic Self-reflection of the Czechoslovak Society. *Czech. Econ. Digest.*, November 1989, (7), pp. 4–30.

Komiya, Ryutaro. Macroeconomic Development

of China: "Overheating" in 1984–1987 and Problems for Reform. *J. Japanese Int. Economies*, March 1989, *3*(1), pp. 64–121.

Komlos, John. Thinking about the Industrial Revolution. *J. Europ. Econ. Hist.*, Spring 1989, *18*(1), pp. 191–206.

Komninos, Nicos. From National to Local: The Janus Face of Crisis. In *Gottdiener, M. and Komninos, N., eds.*, 1989, pp. 348–64.

_____ **and Gottdiener, M.** Capitalist Development and Crisis Theory: Accumulation, Regulation and Spatial Restructuring: Introduction. In *Gottdiener, M. and Komninos, N., eds.*, 1989, pp. 1–17.

Kompas, Tom and Spotton, Brenda. A Note on Rational Speculative Bubbles. *Econ. Letters*, October 1989, *30*(4), pp. 327–31.

Kon, I. S. The Psychology of Social Inertia. In *Yanowitch, M., ed.*, 1989, *1988*, pp. 241–55.

_____. The Relay Race of Generations: Notes on the Upbringing of Youth. In *Yanowitch, M., ed.*, 1989, *1987*, pp. 226–40.

Kon, Stanley J. and Kadapakkam, Palani-Rajan. The Value of Shelf Registration for New Debt Issues. *J. Bus.*, April 1989, *62*(2), pp. 271–92.

_____ **and Thatcher, John G.** The Effect of Bankruptcy Laws on the Valuation of Risky Consumer Debt. *Financial Rev.*, August 1989, *24*(3), pp. 371–95.

Konate, M. and Traore, Kalilou. Operational Agroclimatic Assistance to Agriculture in Sub-Saharan Africa: A Case Study. In *Oram, P. A., et al.*, 1989, pp. 193–202.

Kondonassis, A. J. The European Economic Community and the Single European Act. In *Missouri Valley Economic Association*, 1989, pp. 129–34.

König, Andreas and Momm, Willi. Community Integration for Disabled People: A New Approach to Their Vocational Training and Employment. *Int. Lab. Rev.*, 1989, *128*(4), pp. 497–509.

König, Heinz and Pohlmeier, Winfried. Worksharing and Factor Prices: A Comparison of Three Flexible Functional Forms for Nonlinear Cost Schemes. *J. Inst. Theoretical Econ.*, June 1989, *145*(2), pp. 343–57.

_____ **and Seitz, Helmut.** Zur Transmission von Nachfrage- und Kostenschocks auf Lagerhaltung, Preise und Produktion. (The Transmission of Demand and Cost Shocks on Inventories, Prices and Production. With English summary.) *Jahr. Nationalökon. Statist.*, October 1989, *206*(4–5), pp. 421–33.

König, Klaus and Siedentopf, Heinrich. Privatisation: Singapore's Experience in Perspective: An International Perspective II: Privatisation and Institutional Modernisation in Asia and Europe. In *Thynne, I. and Ariff, M., eds.*, 1989, pp. 167–86.

de Koning, Jaap. Labour Hoarding in Dutch Manufacturing Industry. *De Economist*, 1989, *137*(2), pp. 155–72.

Konishi, Hideo. The Welfare Effects of Shifting from an Indirect Tax to a Direct Tax. *Econ.*

Stud. Quart., September 1989, *40*(3), pp. 212–20.

Konrad, Anton. Reale Wechselkurse, Leistungsbilanz und Wachstum. (Real Exchange Rates, Balance on Current Account, and Growth. With English summary.) *Kredit Kapital*, 1989, *22*(3), pp. 329–43.

Kontrus, Karl; Ploberger, Werner and Krämer, Walter. A New Test for Structural Stability in the Linear Regression Model. *J. Econometrics*, February 1989, *40*(2), pp. 307–18.

Koo, Bon-Ho. Technological Innovation in the Asian-Pacific Region: Facts and Economic Interpretations: Comment. In *Shinohara, M. and Lo, F., eds.*, 1989, pp. 346–48.

Koo, Helen D. Determinants of Divorce. *Soc. Sec. Bull.*, August 1989, *52*(8), pp. 17–19.

Kooiman, Peter. Estimating Average Excess Supply on Goods and Labor Markets from a Cross Section of Business Survey Reports. In *Cornet, B. and Tulkens, H., eds.*, 1989, pp. 491–519.

Koole, Ruud. The "Modesty" of Dutch Party Finance. In *Alexander, H. E., ed.*, 1989, pp. 200–219.

Koopmans, Carl C.; van Opstal, Rocus and Theeuwes, Jules J. M. Human Capital and Job Levels: Explaining the Age–Income Funnel. *Europ. Econ. Rev.*, December 1989, *33*(9), pp. 1839–49.

Koopmanschap, Marc and Teulings, Coen. An Econometric Model of Crowding Out of Lower Education Levels. *Europ. Econ. Rev.*, October 1989, *33*(8), pp. 1653–64.

Koós Balsay, Éva; Molnár, István and Boda, György. Compilation of Input–Output Tables in Hungary. In *Franz, A. and Rainer, N., eds.*, 1989, pp. 43–67.

Koot, Ronald S. and Walker, David A. Economic Stability and the Federal Deficit. *Rivista Int. Sci. Econ. Com.*, Oct.–Nov. 1989, *36*(10–11), pp. 905–16.

Kop, Yaakov. Fiscal Restraint and Social Expenditure: Israel's Experience in the 1980s. *Int. Monet. Fund Staff Pap.*, March 1989, *36*(1), pp. 262–70.

Kopach, N. and Ganzia, S. Leasing as a Form of Realization of Public Property. *Prob. Econ.*, November 1989, *32*(7), pp. 79–91.

Kopcke, Richard W. No Gain, No Pain: Some Consequences of Taxing Capital Gains. *New Eng. Econ. Rev.*, Mar.–Apr. 1989, pp. 39–55.

_____. The Roles of Debt and Equity in Financing Corporate Investments. *New Eng. Econ. Rev.*, July–Aug. 1989, pp. 25–48.

_____ **and Rosengren, Eric S.** Are the Distinctions between Debt and Equity Disappearing? An Overview. In *Kopcke, R. W. and Rosengren, E. S., eds.*, 1989, pp. 1–11.

_____ **and Rosengren, Eric S.** Regulation of Debt and Equity. In *Kopcke, R. W. and Rosengren, E. S., eds.*, 1989, pp. 173–206.

Kopecky, Kenneth J. and Fleisher, Belton M. The Loanable-Funds Approach to Teaching Macroeconomics: Reply. *J. Econ. Educ.*, Summer 1989, *20*(3), pp. 259–60.

Kopp, Raymond J. and Smith, V. Kerry. Benefit

Estimation Goes to Court: The Case of Natural Resource Damage Assessments. *J. Policy Anal. Manage.*, Fall 1989, *8*(4), pp. 593–612.

Kopprasch, Robert; Roman, Emmanuel and Hakanoğlu, Erol. Constant Proportion Portfolio Insurance for Fixed-Income Investment. *J. Portfol. Manage.*, Summer 1989, *15*(4), pp. 58–66.

Kopytowski, Jerzy and Zebrowski, Maciej. MIDA: Experience in Theory, Software and Application of DSS in the Chemical Industry. In *Lewandowski, A. and Wierzbicki, A. P., eds.*, 1989, pp. 271–86.

Koray, Faik. Money and Functional Distribution of Income. *J. Money, Credit, Banking*, February 1989, *21*(1), pp. 33–48.

_____ **and Lastrapes, William D.** Real Exchange Rate Volatility and U.S. Bilateral Trade: A VAR Approach. *Rev. Econ. Statist.*, November 1989, *71*(4), pp. 708–12.

_____ **and McMillin, W. Douglas.** An Empirical Analysis of the Macroeconomic Effects of Government Debt: Evidence from Canada. *Appl. Econ.*, January 1989, *21*(1), pp. 113–24.

Koren, Stephan. Ausgewählte Steuerreformen im Vergleich. (On the Recent Tax Reforms in Five Industrial Countries. With English summary.) *Konjunkturpolitik*, 1989, *35*(5), pp. 251–75.

Korhonen, Pekka and Halme, Merja. Nondominated Tradeoffs and Termination in Interactive Multiple Objective Linear Programming. In *Lockett, A. G. and Islei, G., eds.*, 1989, pp. 410–23.

_____ **and Wallenius, Jyrki.** A Careful Look at Efficiency in Multiple Objective Linear Programming. In *Lockett, A. G. and Islei, G., eds.*, 1989, pp. 334–44.

Koriagina, T. I. Shadow Services and Legal Services. *Prob. Econ.*, November 1989, *32*(7), pp. 43–48.

Korkie, Bob. Corrections for Trading Frictions in Multivariate Returns. *J. Finance*, December 1989, *44*(5), pp. 1421–34.

_____ **and Jobson, J. D.** A Performance Interpretation of Multivariate Tests of Asset Set Intersection, Spanning, and Mean–Variance Efficiency. *J. Finan. Quant. Anal.*, June 1989, *24*(2), pp. 185–204.

Korkman, Sixten. Bytesbalansen och stabiliseringspolitiken. (The Balance of Current Payments and Stabilization Policy. With English summary.) *Ekon. Samfundets Tidskr.*, 1989, *42*(4), pp. 229–36.

Kormendi, Roger C. and Koester, Reinhard B. Taxation, Aggregate Activity and Economic Growth: Cross-Country Evidence on Some Supply-Side Hypotheses. *Econ. Inquiry*, July 1989, *27*(3), pp. 367–86.

Korn, Francis and de la Torre, Lidia. Housing in Buenos Aires 1887–1914. In *Platt, D. C. M., ed.*, 1989, pp. 87–104.

Kornai, János. The Hungarian Reform Process: Visions, Hopes, and Reality. In *Nee, V. and Stark, D., eds.*, 1989, pp. 32–94.

_____. Some Lessons from the Hungarian Experience for Chinese Reformers. In *Van Ness, P., ed.*, 1989, pp. 75–106.

Kornhauser, Lewis A. and Revesz, Richard L. Sharing Damages among Multiple Tortfeasors. *Yale Law J.*, March 1989, *98*(5), pp. 831–84.

_____; **Rubinstein, Ariel and Wilson, Charles.** Reputation and Patience in the 'War of Attrition.' *Economica*, February 1989, *56*(221), pp. 15–24.

Korostelev, V. A. The Rebirth of Small-Scale Commodity Production. In *Jones, A. and Moskoff, W., eds.*, 1989, pp. 45–59.

Koroteeva, V.; Perepelkin, L. and Shkaratan, O. From Bureaucratic Centralism to Economic Integration of Sovereign Republics. *Prob. Econ.*, July 1989, *32*(3), pp. 36–56.

Kort, Peter M.; van Schijndel, Geert-Jan C. Th. and Jørgensen, Steffen. Optimal Investment, Financing, and Dividends: A Stackelberg Differential Game. *J. Econ. Dynam. Control*, July 1989, *13*(3), pp. 339–77.

Korte, Bernhard; Lovász, L. and Goecke, O. Examples and Algorithmic Properties of Greedoids. In *Simeone, B., ed.*, 1989, pp. 113–61.

Korteweg, P. The Need for Worldwide Coordination of Economic Policies: Commentary. In *Sijben, J. J., ed.*, 1989, pp. 54–58.

Korth, Christopher M. and Schroath, Frederick W. Managerial Barriers to the Internationalization of U.S. Property and Liability Insurers: Theory and Perspectives. *J. Risk Ins.*, December 1989, *56*(4), pp. 630–48.

Kortus, Bronislaw. Industrial Change in Poland and the Working and Living Environment. In *Linge, G. J. R. and van der Knaap, G. A., eds.*, 1989, pp. 39–49.

Korves, Ross C. The Evolution of Pesticide Policy: Environmental Interests and Agriculture: Commentary. In *Krämer, C. S., ed.*, 1989, pp. 174–77.

Korzick, Amy M. and Sarwar, Sehba. Telecommunications Policy and Economic Development: The New State Role: Virginia. In *Schmandt, J.; Williams, F. and Wilson, R. H., eds.*, 1989, pp. 213–39.

Koshal, Manjulika and Koshal, Rajindar K. Economies of Scale of State Road Transport Industry in India. *Int. J. Transport Econ.*, June 1989, *16*(2), pp. 165–73.

Koshal, Rajindar K. and Koshal, Manjulika. Economies of Scale of State Road Transport Industry in India. *Int. J. Transport Econ.*, June 1989, *16*(2), pp. 165–73.

Koskela, Erkki and Virén, Matti. International Differences in Saving Rates and the Life Cycle Hypothesis: A Comment. *Europ. Econ. Rev.*, September 1989, *33*(7), pp. 1489–98.

Koslowski, Peter. Grundlinien der Wirtschaftsethik. (Economic Ethics. With English summary.) *Z. Wirtschaft. Sozialwissen.*, 1989, *109*(3), pp. 345–83.

Kossoudji, Sherrie A. Immigrant Worker Assimilation: Is It a Labor Market Phenomenon? *J. Human Res.*, Summer 1989, *24*(3), pp. 494–527.

_____. Pride and Prejudice: Culture's Role in

Markets. In *Shulman, S. and Darity, W., Jr.*, eds., 1989, pp. 293–314.

Kosta, Jiří. Can Socialist Economic Systems Be Reformed? In *Gabrisch, H., ed.*, 1989, pp. 9–22.

_____. The Soviet Reform Concept and Its Impact on Economic Reforms in Eastern Europe. In *Berliner, J. S.; Kosta, H. G. J. and Hakogi, M., eds.*, 1989, pp. 57–73.

Kostakov, Vladimir G. Employment: Scarcity or Surplus? In *Jones, A. and Moskoff, W., eds.*, 1989, *1987*, pp. 159–75.

Kostecki, Michel M. Electronics Trade Policies in the 1980s. *J. World Trade*, February 1989, 23(1), pp. 17–35.

_____. Electronics Trade Policies in the 1980s. *J. World Trade*, February 1989, 23(1), pp. 17–35.

Kosters, Marvin H. Can Rethinking Some Fundamentals Make Old Age More Productive and Satisfying? In *Lewin, M. E. and Sullivan, S., eds.*, 1989, pp. 69–80.

_____. The Changing Quality of American Jobs? *J. Lab. Res.*, Winter 1989, 10(1), pp. 23–31.

Kösters, Wim. Transmission und Koordination nationaler Wirtschaftspolitiken bei weltwirtschaftlicher Verflechtung. (Transmission and Coordination of National Economic Policies in the Face of Global Economic Integration. With English summary.) *Kredit Kapital*, 1989, 22(1), pp. 18–42.

Kostin, L. Restructuring the System of Payment of Labor. In *Jones, A. and Moskoff, W., eds.*, 1989, *1988*, pp. 176–94.

Kostiuk, Peter F. and Follmann, Dean A. Learning Curves, Personal Characteristics, and Job Performance. *J. Lab. Econ.*, April 1989, 7(2), pp. 129–46.

Kostowska-Watanabe, Elzbieta. Technology Development and Workers' Attitudes in East Europe—An International Comparative Study: Discussion. In *Berliner, J. S.; Kosta, H. G. J. and Hakogi, M., eds.*, 1989, pp. 175–76.

Kostreva, M. M. Nonconvexity in Noncooperative Game Theory. *Int. J. Game Theory*, 1989, 18(3), pp. 247–59.

Kostrzewa, Wojciech. Polens neue Währungsordnung: Vom Devisenschwarzmarkt zur beschränkten Währungskonvertibilität. (Poland's Way from Foreign Exchange Control to Currency Convertibility. With English summary.) *Aussenwirtschaft*, December 1989, 44(3–4), pp. 453–79.

Kosuge, Toshio. Electronic Highways for World Trade: Telecommunications. In *Robinson, P.; Sauvant, K. P. and Govitrikar, V. P., eds.*, 1989, pp. 223–37.

Kothari, S. P. and Ball, Ray. Nonstationary Expected Returns: Implications for Tests of Market Efficiency and Serial Correlation in Returns. *J. Finan. Econ.*, November 1989, 25(1), pp. 51–74.

_____ and Collins, Daniel W. An Analysis of Intertemporal and Cross-sectional Determinants of Earnings Response Coefficients. *J. Acc. Econ.*, July 1989, 11(2–3), pp. 143–81.

_____ and Wasley, Charles E. Measuring Security Price Performance in Size-Clustered Samples. *Accounting Rev.*, April 1989, 64(2), pp. 228–49.

_____; Wasley, Charles E. and Handa, Puneet. The Relation between the Return Interval and Betas: Implications for the Size Effect. *J. Finan. Econ.*, June 1989, 23(1), pp. 79–100.

Kotlikoff, Laurence J. Deficit Delusion. In *Kotlikoff, L. J.*, 1989, *1986*, pp. 290–303.

_____. Economic Impact of Deficit Financing. In *Kotlikoff, L. J.*, 1989, *1984*, pp. 234–63.

_____. Estimating the Wealth Elasticity of Bequests from a Sample of Potential Decedents. In *Kotlikoff, L. J.*, 1989, pp. 404–28.

_____. Health Expenditures and Precautionary Savings. In *Kotlikoff, L. J.*, 1989, pp. 141–62.

_____. Intergenerational Transfers and Savings. In *Kotlikoff, L. J.*, 1989, pp. 68–85.

_____. Is Debt Neutral in the Life Cycle Model? In *Kotlikoff, L. J.*, 1989, pp. 304–10.

_____. On the Contribution of Economics to the Evaluation and Formation of Social Insurance Policy. *Amer. Econ. Rev.*, May 1989, 79(2), pp. 184–90.

_____. Social Security and Equilibrium Capital Intensity. In *Kotlikoff, L. J.*, 1989, *1979*, pp. 316–36.

_____. Some Economic Implications of Life-Span Extension. In *Kotlikoff, L. J.*, 1989, *1981*, pp. 358–74.

_____. Taxation and Savings: A Neoclassical Perspective. In *Kotlikoff, L. J.*, 1989, *1984*, pp. 167–233.

_____. Testing the Theory of Social Security and Life Cycle Accumulation. In *Kotlikoff, L. J.*, 1989, *1979*, pp. 380–403.

_____. What Determines Savings? Introduction. In *Kotlikoff, L. J.*, 1989, pp. 1–35.

_____ and Auerbach, Alan J. An Examination of Empirical Tests of Social Security and Savings. In *Kotlikoff, L. J.*, 1989, *1983*, pp. 479–98.

_____ and Auerbach, Alan J. Investment versus Savings Incentives: The Size of the Bang for the Buck and the Potential for Self-Financing Business Tax Cuts. In *Kotlikoff, L. J.*, 1989, *1983*, pp. 264–89.

_____ and Auerbach, Alan J. Simulating Alternative Social Security Responses to the Demographic Transition. In *Kotlikoff, L. J.*, 1989, *1985*, pp. 337–57.

_____ and Boskin, Michael J. Public Debt and United States Saving: A New Test of the Neutrality Hypothesis. In *Kotlikoff, L. J.*, 1989, *1985*, pp. 455–78.

_____ and Gravelle, Jane G. The Incidence and Efficiency Costs of Corporate Taxation When Corporate and Noncorporate Firms Produce the Same Good. *J. Polit. Econ.*, August 1989, 97(4), pp. 749–80.

_____ and Morris, John N. How Much Care Do the Aged Receive from Their Children? A Bimodal Picture of Contact and Assistance. In *Wise, D. A., ed.*, 1989, pp. 151–75.

_____; Shoven, John B. and Spivak, Avia. Annuity Insurance, Savings, and Inequality. In *Kotlikoff, L. J.*, 1989, pp. 109–40.

——— **and Spivak, Avia.** The Family as an Incomplete Annuities Market. In *Kotlikoff, L. J.*, 1989, *1981*, pp. 88–108.

———; **Spivak, Avia and Summers, Lawrence H.** The Adequacy of Savings. In *Kotlikoff, L. J.*, 1989, *1982*, pp. 429–54.

——— **and Summers, Lawrence H.** The Role of Intergenerational Transfers in Aggregate Capital Accumulation. In *Kotlikoff, L. J.*, 1989, *1981*, pp. 43–67.

——— **and Wise, David A.** Employee Retirement and a Firm's Pension Plan. In *Wise, D. A., ed.*, 1989, pp. 279–330.

Kotobalavu, Jioji and Matos, Cruz A. Ocean Minerals—Prospects for Pacific Island Nations. In *Couper, A. D., ed.*, 1989, pp. 115–26.

Kotouč, Václav. The Collective Concept of International Socialist Division of Labour for the Years 1991–2005. *Czech. Econ. Digest.*, April 1989, (2), pp. 44–66.

Kotwal, Ashok and Eswaran, Mukesh. Credit and Agrarian Class Structure. In *Bardhan, P., ed. (II)*, 1989, pp. 166–84.

——— **and Eswaran, Mukesh.** Credit as Insurance in Agrarian Economies. *J. Devel. Econ.*, July 1989, *31*(1), pp. 37–53.

——— **and Eswaran, Mukesh.** Why Are Capitalists the Bosses? *Econ. J.*, March 1989, *99*(394), pp. 162–76.

Koulen, Mark. Some Problems of Interpretation and Implementation of the GATT Antidumping Code. In *Jackson, J. H. and Vermulst, E. A., eds.*, 1989, pp. 366–73.

Koumanakos, Peter. The Capital Stock Survey Project. *Surv. Curr. Bus.*, May 1989, *69*(5), pp. 31–35.

Kouri, Pentti J. K. Trade, Capital Flows and Dynamics of the Real Exchange Rate. In *[Díaz-Alejandro, C.]*, 1989, pp. 324–43.

Koustas, Zisimos. Some Model-Based Tests of Expectational Rationality. *Atlantic Econ. J.*, June 1989, *17*(2), pp. 53–64.

Kouzelis, A. K. and Pavlopoulos, P. G. Cost Behaviour in the Banking Industry: Evidence from a Greek Commercial Bank. *Appl. Econ.*, March 1989, *21*(3), pp. 285–93.

Kovacic, William E. Federal Antitrust Enforcement in the Reagan Administration: Two Cheers for the Disappearance of the Large Firm Defendant in Nonmerger Cases. In *Zerbe, R. O., ed.*, 1989, pp. 173–206.

——— **and Burnett, William B.** Reform of United States Weapons Acquisitions Policy: Competition, Teaming Agreements, and Dual-Sourcing. *Yale J. Regul.*, Summer 1989, *6*(2), pp. 249–317.

Koval'chenko, I. D. The Peasant Economy in Central Russia in the Late Nineteenth and Early Twentieth Century. In *Grantham, G. and Leonard, C. S., eds.*, Pt. B, 1989, pp. 455–75.

Koval, Vitalina and Nochevnik, Michael. Technological Innovations and Work in the Soviet Union. In *Francis, A. and Grootings, P., eds.*, 1989, pp. 120–39.

Kovalainen, Anne. The Concept of Entrepreneur in Business Economics. *Liiketaloudellinen Aikak.*, 1989, *38*(2), pp. 82–93.

Kövári, Gy. and Gábor, Istvan R. Can the Promises of the Hungarian "Wage Reform" Come True? (Social Mechanism of Wage Determination and the Competency of Wage Theories). *Acta Oecon.*, 1989, *40*(3–4), pp. 307–18.

Kovatchev, Assen. Balancing and Optimization of the Structural Development of the Economy. In *Bulgarian Academy of Sciences, Institute of Economics*, 1989, pp. 66–74.

Kovenock, Dan and Hendricks, Kenneth. Asymmetric Information, Information Externalities, and Efficiency: The Case of Oil Exploration. *Rand J. Econ.*, Summer 1989, *20*(2), pp. 164–82.

——— **and Widdows, Kealoha.** The Sequencing of Union Contract Negotiations. *Managerial Dec. Econ.*, December 1989, *10*(4), pp. 283–89.

Koveos, Peter E. and Booth, G. Geoffrey. Purchasing Power Parity: A Reexamination of Prediction Errors. In *Lee, C. F., ed.*, 1989, pp. 143–62.

Köves, András. Opening to the World Economy and Renewing Hungarian Relations with the CMEA. *Acta Oecon.*, 1989, *41*(1–2), pp. 1–25.

Kowalczyk, Carsten. Trade Negotiations and World Welfare. *Amer. Econ. Rev.*, June 1989, *79*(3), pp. 552–59.

Kowalewski, David. Global Debt Crises in Structural-Cyclical Perspective: 1791–1984. In *Avery, W. P. and Rapkin, D. P., eds.*, 1989, pp. 57–84.

Kowalik, Tadeusz. On Crucial Reform of Real Socialism. In *Gabrisch, H., ed.*, 1989, pp. 23–86.

Kowalski, George. Oil Demand in the 1990s. In *Hawdon, D., ed.*, 1989, pp. 1–19.

Koziara, Edward C.; Yan, Chiou-Shuang and Stone, Susan. Employer Strike Insurance. In *Perkins, E. J., ed.*, 1989, pp. 220–29.

Kozlov, Iu. G. and Osipenko, O. V. What Is It That Casts a Shadow? *Prob. Econ.*, November 1989, *32*(7), pp. 29–42.

Kozlowski, Paul J. Forecasting with Leading Indicators: Regional Economic Sense or Nonsense? *Reg. Sci. Persp.*, 1989, *19*(1), pp. 3–24.

Kozma, F. The Market Mechanism in the Socialist System. *Acta Oecon.*, 1989, *40*(3–4), pp. 243–48.

Kraft, Kornelius. Arbeitszeitverkürzung, Beschäftigung und tatsächliche Arbeitszeit. Ergebnisse einer empirischen Untersuchung. (Reduction in Standard Working Time, Employment and Actual Working Hours. Results of an Empirical Study. With English summary.) *Jahr. Nationalökon. Statist.*, July 1989, *206*(3), pp. 243–51.

———. Determinanten des Überstundeneinsatzes. (Determinants of Overtime Working. With English summary.) *Z. Wirtschaft. Sozialwissen.*, 1989, *109*(3), pp. 431–42.

_____. Expectations and the Adjustment of Hours and Employment. *Appl. Econ.*, April 1989, *21*(4), pp. 487–95.

_____. Market Structure, Firm Characteristics and Innovative Activity. *J. Ind. Econ.*, March 1989, *37*(3), pp. 329–36.

_____ and **FitzRoy, Felix R.** Profitability and Profit Sharing: Reply. *J. Ind. Econ.*, September 1989, *38*(1), pp. 115–17.

Krahn, Harvey and Lowe, Graham S. Computer Skills and Use among High School and University Graduates. *Can. Public Policy*, June 1989, *15*(2), pp. 175–88.

_____ **and Lowe, Graham S.** Recent Trends in Public Support for Unions in Canada. *J. Lab. Res.*, Fall 1989, *10*(4), pp. 391–410.

Krahnen, Jan P. and Meran, Georg. Why Leasing? An Introduction to Comparative Contractual Analysis. In *Bamberg, G. and Spremann, K., eds.*, 1989, pp. 255–80.

Kram, Kathy E.; Yeager, Peter C. and Reed, Gary E. Decisions and Dilemmas: The Ethical Dimension in the Corporate Context. In *Post, J. E., ed.*, 1989, pp. 21–54.

Krämer-Badoni, Thomas and Häusermann, Hartmut. The Change of Regional Inequality in the Federal Republic of Germany. In *Gottdiener, M. and Komninos, N., eds.*, 1989, pp. 331–47.

Kramer, Carol S. Food Safety and International Trade: The U.S.–EC Meat and Hormone Controversies. In *Krämer, C. S., ed.*, 1989, pp. 203–33.

_____, **et al.** Choices and Challenges for the 1990s. In *Krämer, C. S., ed.*, 1989, pp. 267–81.

Kramer, John M. Political Corruption in the U.S.S.R. In *Heidenheimer, A. J.; Johnston, M. and LeVine, V. T., eds.*, 1989, *1977*, pp. 449–65.

Kramer, Ralph M. The Use of Government Funds by Voluntary Social Service Agencies in Four Welfare States. In *James, E., ed.*, 1989, pp. 217–44.

Kramer, Randall A.; Price, J. Michael and McDowell, Howard. An Analysis of U.S. Farm Income Policies: Historical, Market-Determined, and Sector-Wide Stabilization. *Southern J. Agr. Econ.*, December 1989, *21*(2), pp. 1–11.

Krämer, Walter. On the Robustness of the *F*-Test to Autocorrelation among Disturbances. *Econ. Letters*, 1989, *30*(1), pp. 37–40.

_____. The Robustness of the Chow Test to Autocorrelation among Disturbances. In *Hackl, P., ed.*, 1989, pp. 45–52.

_____; **Alt, Raimund and Ploberger, Werner.** A Modification of the CUSUM Test in the Linear Regression Model with Lagged Dependent Variables. *Empirical Econ.*, 1989, *14*(2), pp. 65–75.

_____; **Alt, Raimund and Ploberger, Werner.** A Modification of the CUSUM Test in the Linear Regression Model with Lagged Dependent Variables. In *Kramer, W., ed.*, 1989, pp. 1–11.

_____; **Kontrus, Karl and Ploberger, Werner.** A New Test for Structural Stability in the Linear Regression Model. *J. Econometrics*, February 1989, *40*(2), pp. 307–18.

Kranz, Olle and Jorberg, Lennart. Economic and Social Policy in Sweden, 1850–1939. In *Mathias, P. and Pollard, S., eds.*, 1989, pp. 1048–1105.

Krasa, Stefan. Existence of Competitive Equilibria for Option Markets. *J. Econ. Theory*, April 1989, *47*(2), pp. 413–21.

Krashinsky, Michael. Do Hockey Teams Discriminate against French Canadians?: Comment [Discrimination and Performance Differentials in the National Hockey League]. *Can. Public Policy*, March 1989, *15*(1), pp. 94–97.

Krasner, Stephen D. Trade Conflicts and the Common Defense: The United States and Japan. In *Haggard, S. and Moon, C., eds.*, 1989, pp. 251–74.

Kraus, Alan and Smith, Maxwell. Market Created Risk. *J. Finance*, July 1989, *44*(3), pp. 557–69.

Kraus, Marvin. The Welfare Gains from Pricing Road Congestion Using Automatic Vehicle Identification and On-Vehicle Meters. *J. Urban Econ.*, May 1989, *25*(3), pp. 261–81.

Kraus, Richard C. The Lament of Astrophysicist Fang Lizhi: China's Intellectuals in a Global Context. In *Dirlik, A. and Meisner, M., eds.*, 1989, pp. 294–315.

Krause, Mark A.; Hedge, David M. and Menzel, Donald C. The Intergovernmental Milieu and Street-Level Implementation. *Soc. Sci. Quart.*, June 1989, *70*(2), pp. 285–99.

Kraushaar, Robert and Feldman, Marshall M. A. Industrial Restructuring and the Limits of Industry Data: Examples from Western New York. *Reg. Stud.*, February 1989, *23*(1), pp. 49–62.

Krauss, Melvyn. The European Model Is Not for Us. *J. Lab. Res.*, Winter 1989, *10*(1), pp. 61–65.

_____. The (Negative) Role of Food Aid and Technical Assistance. In *Horwich, G. and Lynch, G. J., eds.*, 1989, pp. 120–29.

Krauth, Joachim. A New Modification of the Rand Index for Comparing Partitions. In *Opitz, O., ed.*, 1989, pp. 135–46.

Krautkraemer, Jeffrey A. Price Expectations, Ore Quality Selection, and the Supply of a Nonrenewable Resource. *J. Environ. Econ. Manage.*, May 1989, *16*(3), pp. 253–67.

_____ **and Farrow, Scott.** Extraction at the Intensive Margin: Metal Supply and Grade Selection in Response to Anticipated and Unanticipated Price Changes. *Resources & Energy*, March 1989, *11*(1), pp. 1–21.

Kraybill, David S. and Johnson, Thomas G. Value-Added Activities as a Rural Development Strategy. *Southern J. Agr. Econ.*, July 1989, *21*(1), pp. 27–36.

Krebs, Günter and Bennett, Robert J. Regional Policy Incentives and the Relative Costs of Capital in Assisted Areas in Britain and Germany. *Reg. Stud.*, June 1989, *23*(3), pp. 201–18.

Kregel, Jan A. Editor's Introduction: In Memory of a Jevonian Seditionist. In *[Weintraub, S.]*, 1989, pp. 1–7.

_____. Keynes, Income Distribution and Incomes Policy. In *Davidson, P. and Kregel, J.*, eds., 1989, pp. 42–55.

_____. Microfoundations and Hicksian Monetary Theory. In *Wood, J. C. and Woods, R. N.*, eds., Vol. 3, 1989, 1982, pp. 314–37.

_____. Money Wages in the Keynesian and Monetarist Explanations of the Transmission Mechanism Linking Money and Prices. In *[Weintraub, S.]*, 1989, pp. 69–81.

_____. Savings, Investment and Finance in Kalecki's Theory. In *Sebastiani, M., ed.*, 1989, pp. 193–205.

_____ **and Davidson, Paul.** Macroeconomic Problems and Policies of Income Distribution: Functional, Personal, International: Introduction. In *Davidson, P. and Kregel, J., eds.*, 1989, pp. 1–5.

Kregel, John. An Analysis of Services Provided by Employment Specialists in the Individual Placement Model of Supported Employment. In *Wehman, P. and Kregel, J., eds.*, 1989, pp. 115–35.

_____; **Banks, P. David and Wehman, Paul.** Competitive Employment for Persons with Mental Retardation: A Decade Later. In *Wehman, P. and Kregel, J., eds.*, 1989, pp. 97–113.

_____; **Veldheer, Linda C. and Getzel, Elizabeth Evans.** Projecting the Service Needs of Transition-Aged Young Adults Exiting Public School Programs: A Statewide Analysis. In *Wehman, P. and Kregel, J., eds.*, 1989, pp. 243–56.

_____ **and Wehman, Paul.** An Analysis of the Employment Outcomes of Young Adults with Mental Retardation. In *Wehman, P. and Kregel, J., eds.*, 1989, pp. 257–67.

_____, **et al.** Community Integration of Young Adults with Mental Retardation: Transition from School to Adulthood. In *Wehman, P. and Kregel, J., eds.*, 1989, pp. 227–41.

Kreglewski, Tomasz. Nonlinear Optimization Techniques in Decision Support Systems. In *Lewandowski, A. and Wierzbicki, A. P., eds.*, 1989, pp. 158–71.

_____, **et al.** IAC–DIDAS–N: A Dynamic Interactive Decision Analysis and Support System for Multicriteria Analysis of Nonlinear Models. In *Lewandowski, A. and Wierzbicki, A. P., eds.*, 1989, pp. 378–81.

Krehbiel, Keith and Gilligan, Thomas W. Collective Choice without Procedural Commitment. In *Ordeshook, P. C., ed.*, 1989, pp. 295–314.

Krehbiel, Timothy L. and McCarthy, Patrick S. An Analysis of the Determinants of Portfolio Selection. *Quart. Rev. Econ. Bus.*, Autumn 1989, 29(3), pp. 43–56.

Kreil, Erik and Herbert, John H. Specifying and Evaluating Aggregate Monthly Natural-Gas Demand by Households. *Appl. Econ.*, October 1989, 21(10), pp. 1369–81.

Kreinin, Mordechai E. An Analytical Survey of Formal and Informal Barriers to International Trade and Investment in the United States, Canada, and Japan: Comment. In *Stern, R. M., ed.*, 1989, pp. 359–61.

_____ **and Dinopoulos, Elias.** Import Quotas and VERs: A Comparative Analysis in a Three-Country Framework. *J. Int. Econ.*, February 1989, 26(1/2), pp. 169–78.

Kreis, Eliahu S. The Inflationary Process in Israel, Fiscal Policy, and the Economic Stabilization Plan of July 1985. In *Blejer, M. I. and Chu, K., eds.*, 1989, pp. 346–83.

Krelle, Wilhelm. Auszeichnung des status quo: Gleichgewichtsbereiche im Dyopol. (Distinction of the Status Quo: Equilibrium Ranges in Duopoly. With English summary.) *Jahr. Nationalökon. Statist.*, October 1989, 206(4–5), pp. 434–45.

_____. Die räumliche wirtschaftsentwicklung im weltmasstab: Ost–West und Nord–Süd-Vergleiche. (With English summary.) *Jahr. Wirtsch. Osteuropas*, 1989, 13(1), pp. 7–43.

_____. Growth, Decay and Structural Change. In *Krelle, W., ed.*, 1989, pp. 3–37.

_____. Main Results of the Bonn–IIASA Research Project. In *Krelle, W., ed.*, 1989, pp. 39–82.

_____ **and Sarrazin, Hermann.** Growth of the West German Economy: Forecast by the Bonn Model 11. In *Krelle, W., ed.*, 1989, pp. 399–405.

_____ **and Welsch, Heinz.** Determination of Exchange Rates and Capital Flows for OECD Countries. In *Gordon, I. and Thirlwall, A. P., eds.*, 1989, pp. 233–50.

Kremeniuk, Terry. Standardization: A Road to Better Information. *Can. J. Agr. Econ.*, Part 1, December 1989, 37(4), pp. 723–26.

Kremers, Jeroen J. M. U.S. Federal Indebtedness and the Conduct of Fiscal Policy. *J. Monet. Econ.*, March 1989, 23(2), pp. 219–38.

Kreps, David M. Out-of-Equilibrium Beliefs and Out-of-Equilibrium Behaviour. In *Hahn, F., ed.*, 1989, pp. 7–45.

Kress, Shirley E. Niskanen Effects in the California Community Colleges. *Public Choice*, May 1989, 61(2), pp. 127–40.

Kretzmer, Peter E. The Cross-Industry Effects of Unanticipated Money in an Equilibrium Business Cycle Model. *J. Monet. Econ.*, March 1989, 23(2), pp. 275–96.

Kreutzer, David W. and Lee, Dwight R. Up-Cheating: Explaining OPEC's Apparent Stability in the 1970s. *J. Energy Devel.*, Autumn 1989, 15(1), pp. 1–7.

Kreuzer, Karl. Domestic Bank Regulation in a World of International Banking: Comments. In *Vosgerau, H.-J., ed.*, 1989, pp. 150–74.

Krever, Rick. New International Tax Regime: Australia. *Bull. Int. Fiscal Doc.*, July 1989, 43(7), pp. 327–33.

Krieger, A. M. and Bickel, P. J. Confidence Bands for a Distribution Function Using the Bootstrap. *J. Amer. Statist. Assoc.*, March 1989, 84(405), pp. 95–100.

Kriegler, Roy; Dawkins, Peter and Wooden, Mark. Towards Organizational Effectiveness: An Overview with an Australian Perspective. *Australian Bull. Lab.*, March 1989, *15*(2), pp. 115–38.

Kriesky, Jill. Acknowledging Labor's Record of Success. *Challenge*, March–April 1989, *32*(2), pp. 50–53.

Kriesler, Peter. Methodological Implications of Kalecki's Microfoundations. In *Sebastiani, M.*, *ed.*, 1989, pp. 121–41.

Krinsky, I. and Rotenberg, W. Signalling and the Valuation of Unseasoned New Issues Revisited. *J. Finan. Quant. Anal.*, June 1989, *24*(2), pp. 257–66.

_____ and Rotenberg, W. The Transition to Competitive Pricing on the Toronto Stock Exchange. *Can. Public Policy*, June 1989, *15*(2), pp. 135–44.

Krishna, Kala. Trade Restrictions as Facilitating Practices. *J. Int. Econ.*, May 1989, *26*(3/4), pp. 251–70.

Krishnaiah, J. and Krishnamoorthy, S. Regional Supply Response Functions for Food Grain in Andhra Pradesh. *Margin*, July–Sept. 1989, *21*(4), pp. 43–52.

Krishnamoorthy, S. and Krishnaiah, J. Regional Supply Response Functions for Food Grain in Andhra Pradesh. *Margin*, July–Sept. 1989, *21*(4), pp. 43–52.

Krishnamurthi, Lakshman; Narayan, Jack and Raj, S. P. Intervention Analysis Using Control Series and Exogenous Variables in a Transfer Function Model: A Case Study. *Int. J. Forecasting*, 1989, *5*(1), pp. 21–27.

Krishnamurty, K.; Pandit, V. N. and Sastry, D. U. India: Medium Term Economic Outlook, 1988–90. In *Reddy, J. M., et al., eds. (II)*, 1989, pp. 1–22.

_____; Pandit, V. N. and Sharma, P. D. Parameters of Growth in a Developing Mixed Economy: The Indian Experience. *J. Quant. Econ.*, July 1989, *5*(2), pp. 295–325.

Krissoff, Barry; Sullivan, John and Wainio, John. Opening Agricultural Markets: Implications for Developing Countries. *Can. J. Agr. Econ.*, Part 2, December 1989, *37*(4), pp. 1265–75.

Kristanto, Kustiah; Makaliwe, Willem H. and Saleh, Abdul Karim. South-east Sulawesi: Isolation and Dispersed Settlement. In *Hill, H.*, *ed.*, 1989, pp. 566–83.

_____; Parenta, Tajuddin and Sturgess, Neil H. South Sulawesi: New Directions in Agriculture? In *Hill, H., ed.*, 1989, pp. 386–407.

Kristensen, Niels Buus. Industrial Growth in Denmark, 1872–1913—In Relation to the Debate on an Industrial Break-through. *Scand. Econ. Hist. Rev.*, 1989, *37*(1), pp. 3–22.

Kristensen, P. S. The Slope of the Union's Resistance Curve in Collective Bargaining—A Solution to the Hicks–Shackle Controversy. In *Wood, J. C. and Woods, R. N., eds., Vol. 3*, 1989, *1980*, pp. 222–25.

Kriström, Bengt; Mäler, Karl Göran and Johansson, Per-Olov. Welfare Evaluations in Contingent Valuation Experiments with Discrete Response Data: Comment. *Amer. J. Agr. Econ.*, November 1989, *71*(4), pp. 1054–56.

Kritzman, Mark. Serial Dependence in Currency Returns: Investment Implications. *J. Portfol. Manage.*, Fall 1989, *16*(1), pp. 96–102.

Krmenec, Andrew and Esparza, Adrian. Manufacturing and the Externalization of Services: A Theoretical Model. *Reg. Sci. Persp.*, 1989, *19*(2), pp. 29–40.

_____ and Haynes, Kingsley E. A Sensitivity Assessment of Uncertainty in Infrastructure Expansion. *Ann. Reg. Sci.*, 1989, *23*(4), pp. 299–309.

Kroch, Eugene and Adams, F. Gerard. The Computer in the Teaching of Macroeconomics. *J. Econ. Educ.*, Summer 1989, *20*(3), pp. 269–80.

Krohn, Gregory A. Corporate Mergers and Investment. *J. Macroecon.*, Winter 1989, *11*(1), pp. 109–20.

Krol, Robert. The Information in the Term Structure of Eurodollar Interest Rates. *Econ. Letters*, December 1989, *31*(3), pp. 251–56.

Krolak-Schwerdt, Sabine and Kohler, André. Relations between Models for Three-Way Factor Analysis and Multidimensional Scaling. In *Opitz, O., ed.*, 1989, pp. 147–58.

Kroll, Heidi. Property Rights and the Soviet Enterprise: Evidence from the Law of Contract. *J. Compar. Econ.*, March 1989, *13*(1), pp. 115–33.

_____. Reform and Damages for Breach of Contract in the Soviet Economy. *Soviet Econ.*, July–Sept. 1989, *5*(3), pp. 276–97.

Kroll, Yoram; Lampert, Ada and Helman, Amir. The Kibbutz and Private Property. In *Grunert, K. G. and Ölander, F., eds.*, 1989, pp. 65–74.

_____ and Levy, Haim. Investment, Capital Structure and Cost of Capital: Revisited. In *[Hadar, J.]*, 1989, pp. 201–24.

Krömer, Wolfgang and Wohltmann, Hans-Werner. On the Notion of Time-Consistency: Comment. *Europ. Econ. Rev.*, July 1989, *33*(6), pp. 1283–88.

Krommenacker, Raymond J. The Impact of Information Technology on Trade Interdependence. In *Jussawalla, M.; Okuma, T. and Araki, T., eds.*, 1989, pp. 124–36.

Kromphardt, Jürgen. Konjunkturtheorie heute: Ein Überblick. (With English summary.) *Z. Wirtschaft. Sozialwissen.*, 1989, *109*(2), pp. 173–231.

Krosnick, Jon A. and Alwin, Duane F. The Measurement of Values in Surveys: A Comparison of Ratings and Rankings. In *Singer, E. and Presser, S., eds.*, 1989, *1985*, pp. 124–41.

Kroszner, Randall and Cowen, Tyler. Scottish Banking before 1845: A Model for Laissez-Faire? *J. Money, Credit, Banking*, May 1989, *21*(2), pp. 221–31.

Krueger, Anne O. A Free Trade Agreement with Australia? Comments. In *Schott, J. J., ed.*, 1989, pp. 197–99.

_____. Korean Trade Policy: Implications for Korea–U.S. Cooperation: Discussion. In *Bayard*,

T. O. and Young, S.-G., eds., 1989, pp. 159–65.

───────. Policy-Induced Inflows of Foreign Capital in the Presence of Rigid-Wage Unemployment: Comment. In *[Díaz-Alejandro, C.]*, 1989, pp. 393–96.

───────. Resolving the Debt Crisis and Restoring Developing Countries' Creditworthiness. *Carnegie–Rochester Conf. Ser. Public Policy*, Spring 1989, *30*, pp. 75–113.

─────── and **Michalopoulos, Constantine.** Recipient Policies, National Development, and Aid Effectiveness. In *Krueger, A. O.; Michalopoulos, C. and Ruttan, V. W.*, 1989, pp. 55–67.

───────; **Michalopoulos, Constantine and Ruttan, Vernon W.** Aid and Development: Introduction. In *Krueger, A. O.; Michalopoulos, C. and Ruttan, V. W.*, 1989, pp. 1–10.

───────; **Michalopoulos, Constantine and Ruttan, Vernon W.** Some Lessons from Development Assistance. In *Krueger, A. O.; Michalopoulos, C. and Ruttan, V. W.*, 1989 , pp. 305–23.

─────── and **Ruttan, Vernon W.** Assistance to Korea. In *Krueger, A. O.; Michalopoulos, C. and Ruttan, V. W.*, 1989, pp. 226–49.

─────── and **Ruttan, Vernon W.** Assistance to Turkey. In *Krueger, A. O.; Michalopoulos, C. and Ruttan, V. W.*, 1989, pp. 250–68.

─────── and **Ruttan, Vernon W.** Development Thought and Development Assistance. In *Krueger, A. O.; Michalopoulos, C. and Ruttan, V. W.*, 1989, pp. 13–31.

─────── and **Ruttan, Vernon W.** Toward a Theory of Development Assistance. In *Krueger, A. O.; Michalopoulos, C. and Ruttan, V. W.*, 1989, pp. 32–52.

─────── and **Urrutia, Miguel.** Remarks on Country Studies. In *Sachs, J. D.*, ed. *(II)*, 1989, pp. 212–22.

Krueger, Russell C. U.S. International Transactions, First Quarter 1989. *Surv. Curr. Bus.*, June 1989, *69*(6), pp. 50–92.

Krueger, Thomas M. and Abell, John D. Macroeconomic Influences on Beta. *J. Econ. Bus.*, May 1989, *41*(2), pp. 185–93.

Krüger, Dietrich. Optimale Ausnutzung des internationalen Steuergefälles durch deutsche Konzerne. (With English summary.) *Z. Betriebswirtshaft*, March 1989, *59*(3), pp. 310–20.

Krüger, Michael and Glombowski, Jörg. Changes of Labour Productivity Growth in a Model of Cyclical Growth. *Écon. Societes*, March 1989, *23*(3), pp. 201–17.

Kruger, Michael W.; Dennerlein, John and Power, Anthony. Deciphering Distribution Effects: Commentary. *Marketing Sci.*, Spring 1989, *8*(2), pp. 129–30.

Kruglak, Gregory. Tripartitism and the ILO. In *[Gordenker, L.]*, 1989, pp. 179–96.

Krugman, Paul R. The Case for Stabilizing Exchange Rates. *Oxford Rev. Econ. Policy*, Autumn 1989, *5*(3), pp. 61–72.

───────. Differences in Income Elasticities and Trends in Real Exchange Rates. *Europ. Econ. Rev.*, May 1989, *33*(5), pp. 1031–46.

───────. Economic Integration in Europe: Some Conceptual Issues. In *Jacquemin, A. and Sapir, A.*, eds., 1989, *1987*, pp. 357–80.

───────. Industrial Organization and International Trade. In *Schmalensee, R. and Willig, R. D.*, eds., Vol. 2, 1989, pp. 1179–1223.

───────. The J-Curve, the Fire Sale, and the Hard Landing. *Amer. Econ. Rev.*, May 1989, *79*(2), pp. 31–35.

───────. Market-Based Approaches to Debt Reduction. In *Dornbusch, R.; Makin, J. H. and Zlowe, D.*, eds., 1989, pp. 43–63.

───────. Market-Based Debt-Reduction Schemes. In *Frenkel, J. A.; Dooley, M. P. and Wickham, P.*, eds., 1989, pp. 258–78.

───────. New Trade Theory and the Less Developed Countries. In *[Díaz-Alejandro, C.]*, 1989, pp. 347–65.

───────. On the International Capital Ownership Pattern at the Turn of the Twenty-First Century: Comment. *Europ. Econ. Rev.*, May 1989, *33*(5), pp. 1083–85.

───────. Private Capital Flows to Problem Debtors. In *Sachs, J. D.*, ed. *(II)*, 1989, pp. 285–98.

───────. Private Capital Flows to Problem Debtors. In *Sachs, J. D.*, ed. *(I)*, 1989, pp. 299–330.

─────── and **Baldwin, Richard E.** Persistent Trade Effects of Large Exchange Rate Shocks. *Quart. J. Econ.*, November 1989, *104*(4), pp. 635–54.

Krugmann, Hartmut. Review of Issues and Research Relating to Improved Cookstoves. *Can. J. Devel. Stud.*, 1989, *10*(1), pp. 121–33.

Krumm, Ronald and Kelly, Austin. Effects of Homeownership on Household Savings. *J. Urban Econ.*, November 1989, *26*(3), pp. 281–94.

Krupnick, Alan J.; Spofford, Walter O., Jr. and Harrington, Winston. The Economic Losses of a Waterborne Disease Outbreak. *J. Urban Econ.*, January 1989, *25*(1), pp. 116–37.

Krupp, Hans-Jürgen. Social Change and the Development of the Financial Situation of the Social Security System in the Federal Republic of Germany. In *Gustafsson, B. A. and Klevmarken, N. A.*, eds., 1989, pp. 11–27.

Krus, Lech; Lopuch, Bozena and Bronisz, Piotr. MCBARG: A System Supporting Multicriteria Bargaining. In *Lewandowski, A. and Wierzbicki, A. P.*, eds., 1989, pp. 388–90.

───────; **Wierzbicki, Andrzej P. and Bronisz, Piotr.** Towards Interactive Solutions in a Bargaining Problem. In *Lewandowski, A. and Wierzbicki, A. P.*, eds., 1989, pp. 251–68.

Kruschwitz, Lutz. Much Ado about Leasing: Anmerkungen. (Comment. With English summary.) *Z. Betriebswirtshaft*, October 1989, *59*(10), pp. 1090–94.

Kruse, Agneta and Söderström, Lars. Early Retirement in Sweden. In *Schmähl, W.*, ed., 1989, pp. 39–61.

Kruth, Harold E. and Morkre, Morris E. Determining Whether Dumped or Subsidized Imports Injure Domestic Industries: International Trade Commission Approach. *Contemp. Policy Issues*, July 1989, *7*(3), pp. 78–95.

Krutilla, John V. and Bowes, Michael D. Economics and Public Forestland Management. *Natural Res. J.*, Summer 1989, *29*(3), pp. 737–49.

_____ **and Bowes, Michael D.** Socially Optimal Forestry: A Comment. *J. Environ. Econ. Manage.*, November 1989, *17*(3), pp. 309–10.

Krutilla, Kerry. Tariff Burdens and Optimal Tariffs under Alternative Transport Cost and Market Structures. *Econ. Letters*, December 1989, *31*(4), pp. 381–86.

Krynski, Kathy J. and Harrington, David E. State Pricing of Vanity License Plates. *Nat. Tax J.*, March 1989, *42*(1), pp. 95–99.

Kryzanowski, Lawrence and Jalilvand, Abolhassan. Incorporating Contemporaneous Residual Relationships for Security Prices. *Econ. Letters*, December 1989, *31*(3), pp. 245–49.

Kubíček, Ladislav. Scientific–Technological Progress in the Restructuring Process. *Czech. Econ. Digest.*, April 1989, (2), pp. 13–18.

Kubík, Stanislav. Science and Technology in the New Economic Mechanism. *Czech. Econ. Digest.*, August 1989, (5), pp. 37–41.

Kubin, Ingrid. Stability in Classical Competition: An Alternative to Nikaido's Approach. *J. Econ. (Z. Nationalökon.)*, 1989, *50*(3), pp. 223–35.

Kubo, Yuji. A Model of Dual-Industrial Development in a Semi-industrial Country. *Developing Econ.*, December 1989, *27*(4), pp. 331–49.

Kubursi, Atif A.; Abou-Ezze, P. and Butterfield, David W. The Economic Case for the Emergence of New Producers of Petrochemicals in the Hydrocarbon-Rich Developing Countries. *Industry Devel.*, June 1989, (27), pp. 31–43.

_____ **and Ahmad, Syed.** Imitation, Adaptation and Innovation: A Note on Typology and Consequences. *Industry Devel.*, April 1989, (26), pp. 83–87.

Kucharski, Mieczysław. The State Budget and Financial Equilibrium. *Eastern Europ. Econ.*, Spring 1989, *27*(3), pp. 24–35.

Kuchiki, Akifumi and Hirashima, Shigemochi. Primary Commodity Issues in Development. In *Shinohara, M. and Lo, F., eds.*, 1989, pp. 258–73.

Kudlow, Lawrence A. Why Dollars Are Scarce. *Challenge*, July–Aug. 1989, *32*(4), pp. 59–60.

Kudoh, Kazuhisa. International Capital Movements, Domestic Assets, and the Current Account. *J. Japanese Int. Economies*, June 1989, *3*(2), pp. 189–208.

Kuenne, Robert E. Conflict Management in Mature Rivalry. *J. Conflict Resolution*, September 1989, *33*(3), pp. 554–66.

_____. The Dynamics of Oligopolistic Location: Present Status and Future Research Directions. In *Andersson, Å. E., et al., eds.*, 1989, pp. 15–21.

_____. On Hicks's Concept of Perfect Stability in Multiple Exchange. In *Wood, J. C. and Woods, R. N., eds., Vol. 2*, 1989, *1959*, pp. 36–42.

_____. Price–Quality Competition in Oligopolistic Interdependence. In *Feiwel, G. R., ed. (I)*, 1989, pp. 437–61.

_____. Rivalrous Consonance: A Theory of Ma-

ture Oligopolistic Behavior in a General Equilibrium Framework. In *Andersson, Å. E., et al., eds.*, 1989, pp. 107–18.

_____. Uncertainty, Spatial Proximity, and the Stability of Oligopoly Pricing. *Environ. Planning A*, August 1989, *21*(8), pp. 1001–13.

Kuester, Kathleen A.; Caves, Douglas W. and Herriges, Joseph A. Load Shifting under Voluntary Residential Time-of-Use Rates. *Energy J.*, October 1989, *10*(4), pp. 83–99.

Kuflik, Arthur. Moral Foundations of Intellectual Property Rights. In *Weil, V. and Snapper, J. W., eds.*, 1989, pp. 219–40.

Kugler, Bernardo; Horn, Robin and Jimenez, Emmanuel. National In-Service Training Systems in Latin America: An Economic Evaluation of Colombia's SENA. *Econ. Devel. Cult. Change*, April 1989, *37*(3), pp. 595–610.

_____ **and Psacharopoulos, George.** Earnings and Education in Argentina: An Analysis of the 1985 Buenos Aires Household Survey. *Econ. Educ. Rev.*, 1989, *8*(4), pp. 353–65.

Kugler, Jacek and Arbetman, Marina. Exploring the "Phoenix Factor" with the Collective Goods Perspective. *J. Conflict Resolution*, March 1989, *33*(1), pp. 84–112.

Kugler, Peter. Cointegration and the Dynamic Relationship between Consumer and Wholesale Prices: An Empirical Investigation. *Rivista Int. Sci. Econ. Com.*, September 1989, *36*(9), pp. 847–55.

_____; **Müller, Urs and Sheldon, George.** Nonneutral Technical Change, Capital, White-Collar and Blue-Collar Labor: Some Empirical Results. *Econ. Letters*, November 1989, *31*(1), pp. 91–94.

Kuhbach, Susan Haggerty and Kaplan, Gilbert. Recent U.S. Developments in Cost of Production Analysis. In *Jackson, J. H. and Vermulst, E. A., eds.*, 1989, pp. 360–65.

Kuhn, Peter and Robert, Jacques. Seniority and Distribution in a Two-Worker Trade Union. *Quart. J. Econ.*, August 1989, *104*(3), pp. 485–505.

Kuhn, Tillo E. Social Market Systems: International Perspectives. In *Gemper, B. B., ed.*, 1989, pp. 21–33.

Kühnberger, Manfred. Der Erfolg in der Lebensversicherung: Entstehung, Darstellung und Beurteilung. (With English summary.) *Z. Betriebswirtshaft*, March 1989, *59*(3), pp. 321–29.

Kühne, Winrich. Nkomati and Soviet Policy on Africa in the Eighties: The End of Ideological Expansion? In *Schulz, B. H. and Hansen, W. W., eds.*, 1989, pp. 181–96.

Kuhnen, Frithjof. The Agrarian Sector in Pakistan's Development Process—Historical Evidence and Implications for Policy and Theory. *Pakistan Devel. Rev.*, Winter 1989, *28*(4), pp. 509–21.

Kuipers, Theo A. F. and Janssen, Maarten C. W. Stratification of General Equilibrium Theory: A Synthesis of Reconstructions. In *Balzer, W. and Hamminga, B., eds.*, 1989, pp. 183–205.

Kulagin, G. A. Product Mix, Price, Profit. In *Jones, A. and Moskoff, W., eds.*, 1989, *1986*, pp. 127–44.

Kulbokas, François and de Feydeau, Henri. Le coût de la perception de l'impôt à charge de l'administration et des contribuables: France. (Administrative and Compliance Costs of Taxation: France. With English summary.) In *International Fiscal Association, ed. (I)*, 1989, pp. 361–85.

Kulikov, V. V. The Structure and Forms of Socialist Property. In *Jones, A. and Moskoff, W., eds.*, 1989, *1988*, pp. 217–32.

Kulkarni, Kishore G. and Chakraborty, Debasish. An Empirical Evidence of Purchasing Power Parity Theory: A Case of Indian Rupee and U.S. Dollar. *Margin*, Oct. 1989–March 1990, *22*(1–2), pp. 52–56.

Kulphanich, Bunchird. Thailand's Energy Sector. In *James, W. E., ed.*, 1989, pp. 147–54.

Kulpinska, Jolanta and Skalmierski, Slawomir. The Taming of New Technology. A Polish Case Study on the Introduction of a Flexible Manufacturing System. In *Francis, A. and Grootings, P., eds.*, 1989, pp. 140–64.

Kulshreshtha, Surendra N. Irrigation and Prairie Agricultural Development. In *Schmitz, A., ed.*, 1989, pp. 187–221.

_____ **and Tewari, Devi D.** Impacts of Rising Energy Prices on Saskatchewan Agriculture: A Reply. *Can. J. Agr. Econ.*, July 1989, *37*(2), pp. 323–25.

Kumar, Ajay; Richardson, Harry W. and Gordon, Peter. Congestion, Changing Metropolitan Structure, and City Size in the United States. *Int. Reg. Sci. Rev.*, 1989, *12*(1), pp. 45–56.

_____ **; Richardson, Harry W. and Gordon, Peter.** Gender Differences in Metropolitan Travel Behavior. *Reg. Stud.*, December 1989, *23*(6), pp. 499–510.

_____ **; Richardson, Harry W. and Gordon, Peter.** The Influence of Metropolitan Spatial Structure on Commuting Time. *J. Urban Econ.*, September 1989, *26*(2), pp. 138–51.

_____ **; Richardson, Harry W. and Gordon, Peter.** The Spatial Mismatch Hypothesis: Some New Evidence. *Urban Stud.*, June 1989, *26*(3), pp. 315–26.

Kumar, Akhil; Smith, Kenneth L. and Brocato, Joe. Individual versus Group Spot Price Forecasting in the International Petroleum Market: A Case Study. *Managerial Dec. Econ.*, March 1989, *10*(1), pp. 13–24.

Kumar, B. Nino and Steinmann, Horst. Small and Medium-Sized Multinationals and Development: Suitability of International Strategy of German Small and Medium-Sized Firms in Newly Industrializing Countries. In *Negandhi, A. R., ed.*, 1989, pp. 105–24.

Kumar, Gopalakrishna. Gender, Differential Mortality and Development: The Experience of Kerala. *Cambridge J. Econ.*, December 1989, *13*(4), pp. 517–39.

Kumar, Manmohan S. The Stabilizing Role of the Compensatory Financing Facility. *Int. Monet. Fund Staff Pap.*, December 1989, *36*(4), pp. 771–809.

Kumar, Mohan S.; Pesaran, M. Hashem and Pierse, Richard G. Econometric Analysis of Aggregation in the Context of Linear Prediction Models. *Econometrica*, July 1989, *57*(4), pp. 861–88.

Kumar, Narinder and Singhal, K. C. India's Export Instability. *Indian Econ. J.*, Jan.–March 1989, *36*(3), pp. 72–79.

Kumar, Nita. Labour, Capital, and the Congress: Delhi Cloth Mills, 1928–38. *Indian Econ. Soc. Hist. Rev.*, Jan.–March 1989, *26*(1), pp. 29–59.

Kumar, R. Nanda and Rao, P. Purnachandra. Savings in Household Sector as a Source of Finance. In *Reddy, J. M., et al., eds. (I)*, 1989, pp. 138–45.

Kumar, Ramesh C. and Tayyab, Ahsan. Money, Working Capital and Production in a Developing Economy: A Disequilibrium Econometric Model of Production for India, 1950–1980. *Empirical Econ.*, 1989, *14*(3), pp. 229–39.

Kumar, Rishi and Dung, Tran Huu. The Transfer Problem under Uncertainty. *Indian Econ. Rev.*, July–Dec. 1989, *24*(2), pp. 197–205.

Kumar, Umesh. Trade Liberalization and Payments Arrangements under the PTA Treaty: An Experiment in Collective Self-Reliance. *J. World Trade*, October 1989, *23*(5), pp. 93–121.

Kumar, Vikram and Morley, Samuel A. Labor Intensity and Employment Creation in a Constrained Economy. *J. Devel. Econ.*, April 1989, *30*(2), pp. 287–300.

Kumbhakar, Subal C. Economic Performance of U.S. Class 1 Railroads: A Stochastic Frontier Approach. *Appl. Econ.*, November 1989, *21*(11), pp. 1433–46.

_____. Estimation of Technical Efficiency Using Flexible Functional Form and Panel Data. *J. Bus. Econ. Statist.*, April 1989, *7*(2), pp. 253–58.

_____. Modelling Technical and Allocative Inefficiency in a Translog Production Function. *Econ. Letters*, December 1989, *31*(2), pp. 119–23.

_____ **; Biswas, Basudeb and Bailey, DeeVon.** A Study of Economic Efficiency of Utah Dairy Farmers: A System Approach. *Rev. Econ. Statist.*, November 1989, *71*(4), pp. 595–604.

_____ **and Summa, Timo.** Technical Efficiency of Finnish Brewing Plants: A Production Frontier Approach. *Scand. J. Econ.*, 1989, *91*(1), pp. 147–60.

Kumcu, M. Ercan. The Savings Behavior of Migrant Workers: Turkish Workers in W. Germany. *J. Devel. Econ.*, April 1989, *30*(2), pp. 273–86.

Kummer, Donald R.; Arshadi, Nasser and Lawrence, Edward C. Incentive Problems in Bank Insider Borrowing. *J. Finan. Services Res.*, October 1989, *3*(1), pp. 17–31.

Kunda, Gideon and Van Maanen, John. "Real Feelings": Emotional Expression and Organizational Culture. In *Cummings, L. L. and Staw, B. M., eds.*, 1989, pp. 43–103.

Kunev, Metodi. On the Identification of Services as Products and on the Economic Estimation of Their Full Volume. In *Bulgarian Academy of Sciences, Institute of Economics,* 1989, pp. 192–97.

Kunreuther, Howard; Berger, Lawrence A. and Kleindorfer, Paul R. A Dynamic Model of the Transmission of Price Information in Auto Insurance Markets. *J. Risk Ins.,* March 1989, *56*(1), pp. 17–33.

_____ **and Camerer, Colin F.** Decision Processes for Low Probability Events: Policy Implications. *J. Policy Anal. Manage.,* Fall 1989, *8*(4), pp. 565–92.

_____ **and Camerer, Colin F.** Experimental Markets for Insurance. *J. Risk Uncertainty,* September 1989, *2*(3), pp. 265–99.

_____ **and Hogarth, Robin M.** Risk, Ambiguity, and Insurance. *J. Risk Uncertainty,* April 1989, *2*(1), pp. 5–35.

Künsch, Hans R.; Stefanski, Leonard A. and Carroll, Raymond J. Conditionally Unbiased Bounded-Influence Estimation in General Regression Models, with Applications to Generalized Linear Models. *J. Amer. Statist. Assoc.,* June 1989, *84*(406), pp. 460–66.

Kunst, Robert M. and Marin, Dalia. On Exports and Productivity: A Causal Analysis. *Rev. Econ. Statist.,* November 1989, *71*(4), pp. 699–703.

Kuo, Lynn. Composite Estimation of Totals for Livestock Surveys. *J. Amer. Statist. Assoc.,* June 1989, *84*(406), pp. 421–29.

Kupiec, Paul H. Initial Margin Requirements and Stock Returns Volatility: Another Look. *J. Finan. Services Res.,* December 1989, *3*(2–3), pp. 287–301.

_____. Initial Margin Requirements and Stock Returns Volatility: Another Look. In *Edwards, F. R., ed.,* 1989, pp. 189–203.

Kuprianov, Anatoli and Mengle, David L. The Future of Deposit Insurance: An Analysis of the Alternatives. *Fed. Res. Bank Richmond Econ. Rev.,* May–June 1989, *75*(3), pp. 3–15.

Kurabayashi, Yoshimasa. Reconciliation of the Input–Output Tables with SNA and Its Implications in Technology Assumptions. In *Franz, A. and Rainer, N., eds.,* 1989, pp. 431–46.

_____ **and Matsuura, Hiroshi.** Progress of Japanese National Accounts in an International Perspective of the SNA Review. In *Sato, R. and Negishi, T., eds.,* 1989, pp. 99–123.

Kuraku, Seinosuke. Management of a Japanese Establishment in the Federal Republic of Germany—A Report on Experiences with Problems and Solution Approaches. In *Dams, T. and Matsugi, T., eds.,* 1989, pp. 65–75.

Kuran, Timur. The Craft Guilds of Tunis and Their Amins: A Study in Institutional Atrophy. In *Nabli, M. K. and Nugent, J. B., eds.,* 1989, pp. 236–64.

_____. Sparks and Prairie Fires: A Theory of Unanticipated Political Revolution. *Public Choice,* April 1989, *61*(1), pp. 41–74.

_____; **Nabli, Mustapha K. and Azabou, Mongi.** The Wholesale Produce Market of Tunis and Its Porters: A Tale of Market Degeneration. In *Nabli, M. K. and Nugent, J. B., eds.,* 1989, pp. 352–74.

Kurashvili, B. P. Restructuring and the Enterprise. In *Jones, A. and Moskoff, W., eds.,* 1989, pp. 21–44.

Kuroda, Haruhiko. Domestic and Cross-Border Consequences of U.S. Macroeconomic Policies: Comment. In *Bryant, R. C., et al., eds.,* 1989, pp. 116–19.

Kuroda, Makoto. Strengthening Japan–U.S. Cooperation and the Concept of Japan–U.S. Free Trade Arrangements. In *Schott, J. J., ed.,* 1989, pp. 121–30.

Kuroda, Tatsuaki. Location of Public Facilities with Spillover Effects: Variable Location and Parametric Scale. *J. Reg. Sci.,* November 1989, *29*(4), pp. 575–94.

Kuroda, Yoshimi. Impacts of Economies of Scale and Technological Change on Agricultural Productivity in Japan. *J. Japanese Int. Economies,* June 1989, *3*(2), pp. 145–73.

Kurre, James A. and Weller, Barry R. Forecasting the Local Economy, Using Time-Series and Shift-Share Techniques. *Environ. Planning A,* June 1989, *21*(6), pp. 753–70.

_____ **and Weller, Barry R.** Regional Cyclical Instability: An Empirical Examination of Wage, Hours and Employment Adjustments, and an Application of the Portfolio Variance Technique. *Reg. Stud.,* August 1989, *23*(4), pp. 315–29.

Kurth, Michael M. and Reid, Joseph D., Jr. Public Employees in Political Firms: Part B. Civil Service and Militancy. *Public Choice,* January 1989, *60*(1), pp. 41–54.

Kurtzweg, Laurie. The Role of the Service Sector in Soviet GNP and Productivity Estimates: Comment. *J. Compar. Econ.,* December 1989, *13*(4), pp. 566–73.

Kurz, Mordecai. Competition, Non-linear Pricing and Rationing in Credit Markets. In *Feiwel, G. R., ed. (I),* 1989, pp. 508–34.

_____. Equilibrium in a Finite Sequence of Markets with Transaction Cost. In *Starr, R. M., ed.,* 1989, *1974,* pp. 245–64.

Kurz-Scherf, Ingrid. Elements of an Emancipatory Working Time Policy: Ten Theses on Making Normal Working Time More Dynamic and Freeing It from Patriarchy. In *Agassi, J. B. and Heycock, S., eds.,* 1989, pp. 256–60.

Kurzhanski, A. B. Identification—A Theory of Guaranteed Estimates. In *Willems, J. C., ed.,* 1989, pp. 135–214.

Kushner, Joseph, et al. Profit Rates, Risk, and Size in Canadian Banks and Trust Companies. *Antitrust Bull.,* Fall 1989, *34*(3), pp. 683–93.

Kushner, Joseph W.; Giffin, Phillip E. and Hutchinson, E. Bruce. The Conventional Wisdom about Cross-Haul. *Eastern Econ. J.,* Jan.–March 1989, *15*(1), pp. 29–34.

Kushnirsky, Fyodor I. and Stull, William J. Productive and Unproductive Labour: Smith, Marx, and the Soviets. In *Walker, D. A., ed.,* 1989, pp. 82–103.

Kutscher, Ronald E. Projections Summary and

Emerging Issues. *Mon. Lab. Rev.*, November 1989, *112*(11), pp. 66–74.

_____. Structural Change in the USA, Past and Prospective: Its Implication for Skill and Educational Requirements. *Econ. Systems Res.*, 1989, *1*(3), pp. 351–91.

_____ and Sorrentino, Constance E. Employment and Unemployment Patterns in the U.S. and Europe, 1973–1987. *J. Lab. Res.*, Winter 1989, *10*(1), pp. 5–22.

Kuwahara, Tetsuya. The Japanese Cotton Spinners' Direct Investments into China before the Second World War. In *Teichova, A.; Lévy-Leboyer, M. and Nussbaum, H., eds.*, 1989, pp. 151–62.

Kuwayama, Mikio. The Technological Potential of the Primary Export Sector. *CEPAL Rev.*, December 1989, (39), pp. 93–114.

Kuyper, Pieter Jan. Judicial Protection and Judicial Review in the EEC. In *Jackson, J. H. and Vermulst, E. A., eds.*, 1989, pp. 374–83.

Kuzma, Ann T. and Bruning, Edward R. Airline Accidents and Stock Return Performance. *Logist. Transp. Rev.*, June 1989, *25*(2), pp. 157–68.

Kuznets, Simon. Children and Adults in the Income Distribution. In *Kuznets, S.*, 1989, *1982*, pp. 370–412.

_____. Demographic Aspects of the Size Distribution of Income: An Exploratory Essay. In *Kuznets, S.*, 1989, *1976*, pp. 131–239.

_____. Distributions of Households by Size: Differences and Trends. In *Kuznets, S.*, 1989, *1982*, pp. 320–69.

_____. Driving Forces of Economic Growth: What Can We Learn from History? In *Kuznets, S.*, 1989, *1980*, pp. 7–29.

_____. Modern Economic Growth and the Less Developed Countries (LDCs). In *Kuznets, S.*, 1989, *1982*, pp. 68–77.

_____. A Note on Production Structure and Aggregate Growth. In *Kuznets, S.*, 1989, *1981*, pp. 30–46.

_____. Notes on Demographic Change. In *Kuznets, S.*, 1989, pp. 78–86.

_____. The Pattern of Shift of Labor Froce from Agriculture, 1950–70. In *Kuznets, S.*, 1989, *1982*, pp. 47–67.

_____. Recent Population Trends in Less Developed Countries and Implications for Internal Income Inequality. In *Kuznets, S.*, 1989, *1980*, pp. 87–130.

_____. Size and Age Structure of Family Households: Exploratory Comparisons. In *Kuznets, S.*, 1989, *1978*, pp. 240–77.

_____. Size of Households and Income Disparities. In *Kuznets, S.*, 1989, *1981*, pp. 278–319.

Kuznetsova, T. Cooperatives: The Tactic Determines the Practice. *Prob. Econ.*, December 1989, *32*(8), pp. 35–42.

Kwan, Andy C. C.; Sahni, Balbir S. and Ahsan, Syed M. Causality between Government Consumption Expenditure and National Income: OECD Countries. *Public Finance*, 1989, *44*(2), pp. 204–24.

Kwasa, S. O. The Debt Problem of Eastern and Southern Africa. In *Singer, H. W. and Sharma, S., eds. (I)*, 1989, pp. 437–43.

Kwast, Myron L. The Impact of Underwriting and Dealing on Bank Returns and Risks. *J. Banking Finance*, March 1989, *13*(1), pp. 101–25.

Kwok, E. C. and Scott, Allen J. Inter-firm Subcontracting and Locational Agglomeration: A Case Study of the Printed Circuits Industry in Southern California. *Reg. Stud.*, October 1989, *23*(5), pp. 405–16.

Kwoka, John E., Jr. International Joint Venture: General Motors and Toyota. In *Kwoka, J. E., Jr. and White, L. J., eds.*, 1989, pp. 46–79.

_____. The Private Profitability of Horizontal Mergers with Non-Cournot and Maverick Behavior. *Int. J. Ind. Organ.*, September 1989, *7*(3), pp. 403–11.

_____ and White, Lawrence J. The Antitrust Revolution: Introduction. In *Kwoka, J. E., Jr. and White, L. J., eds.*, 1989, pp. 1–5.

_____ and White, Lawrence J. The Economic and Legal Context of Horizontal Practices. In *Kwoka, J. E., Jr. and White, L. J., eds.*, 1989, pp. 122–33.

_____ and White, Lawrence J. The Economic and Legal Context of Horizontal Structure. In *Kwoka, J. E., Jr. and White, L. J., eds.*, 1989, pp. 8–18.

_____ and White, Lawrence J. The Economic and Legal Context of Vertical Arrangements. In *Kwoka, J. E., Jr. and White, L. J., eds.*, 1989, pp. 264–72.

Kwon, Ik-Whan and Safranski, Scott R. Religiocultural Values in Management: Isolating Specific Relationships. In *Rueschhoff, N. and Schaum, K., eds.*, 1989, pp. 143–56.

_____ and Safranski, Scott R. Religion and Management: Exploring Specific Relationships. In *Prasad, S. B., ed.*, 1989, pp. 171–82.

Kwon, O. Yul. An Analysis of China's Taxation of Foreign Direct Investment. *Developing Econ.*, September 1989, *27*(3), pp. 251–68.

Kydland, Finn E. Monetary Policy in Models with Capital. In *[Verheyen, P.]*, 1989, pp. 267–88.

Kyer, Ben L. A Test of the Baumol Model of Unbalanced Growth. *Atlantic Econ. J.*, September 1989, *17*(3), pp. 83.

_____; Uri, Noel D. and Mixon, J. Wilson, Jr. An Analysis of the Automatic Stabilizers Associated with Taxes and Transfer Payments. *Int. Rev. Applied Econ.*, January 1989, *3*(1), pp. 46–56.

_____; Uri, Noel D. and Mixon, J. Wilson, Jr. Automatic Stabilizers Reconsidered. *Public Finance*, 1989, *44*(3), pp. 476–91.

Kyle, Albert S. Informed Speculation with Imperfect Competition. *Rev. Econ. Stud.*, July 1989, *56*(3), pp. 317–55.

_____ and Hartley, Peter R. Equilibrium Investment in an Industry with Moderate Investment Economies of Scale. *Econ. J.*, June 1989, *99*(396), pp. 392–407.

Kyloh, Robert H. Flexibility and Structural Adjustment through Consensus: Some Lessons from Australia. *Int. Lab. Rev.*, 1989, *128*(1), pp. 103–23.

Kymn, Kern O. From Unemployment to Golden Age Capital Accumulation in a Two-Sector Growth Model. *Math. Soc. Sci.*, April 1989, *17*(2), pp. 195–200.

_____ **and Assar, Nasir H.** The Impact of the Declining Saving Rate on the Great Ratios of Economics. *Rivista Int. Sci. Econ. Com.*, January 1989, *36*(1), pp. 29–38.

Kysilka, Pavel. Early Efforts at an Economic Reform. *Czech. Econ. Digest.*, June 1989, (4), pp. 13–45.

La Croix, Sumner J. Homogeneous Middleman Groups: What Determines the Homogeneity? *J. Law, Econ., Organ.*, Spring 1989, *5*(1), pp. 211–22.

_____ **and Fishback, Price V.** Firm-Specific Evidence on Racial Wage Differentials and Workforce Segregation in Hawaii's Sugar Industry. *Exploration Econ. Hist.*, October 1989, *26*(4), pp. 403–23.

_____ **and Rose, Louis A.** A Simulation Study of the Interactive Effects of Taxes and Inflation on the Relative Price of Land. *Land Econ.*, May 1989, *65*(2), pp. 100–117.

_____ **and Rose, Louis A.** Urban Land Price: The Extraordinary Case of Honolulu Hawaii. *Urban Stud.*, June 1989, *26*(3), pp. 301–14.

de La Grandville, Olivier. Erratum [In Quest of the Slutsky Diamond]. *Amer. Econ. Rev.*, December 1989, *79*(5), pp. 1307.

_____. In Quest of the Slutsky Diamond. *Amer. Econ. Rev.*, June 1989, *79*(3), pp. 468–81.

La Manna, Manfredi; MacLeod, Ross and de Meza, David. The Case for Permissive Patents. *Europ. Econ. Rev.*, September 1989, *33*(7), pp. 1427–43.

La Rosa, Rosario. Non perfetta mobilita' dei capitali nel modello di macroeconomia aperta a cambi flessibili. (With English summary.) *Studi. Econ.*, 1989, *44*(39), pp. 79–112.

La Via, Vincenzo and Tabellini, Guido. Money, Deficit and Public Debt in the United States. *Rev. Econ. Statist.*, February 1989, *71*(1), pp. 15–25.

van der Laan, L. and van der Knaap, G. A. Spatial Implications of Unionisation, Employment and Labour Activism. In *Linge, G. J. R. and van der Knaap, G. A., eds.*, 1989, pp. 144–66.

van Laanen, Jan T. M. Per Capita Income Growth in Indonesia, 1850–1940. In *Maddison, A. and Prince, G., eds.*, 1989, pp. 43–66.

Labadie, Pamela. Stochastic Inflation and the Equity Premium. *J. Monet. Econ.*, September 1989, *24*(2), pp. 277–98.

Laband, David N. and Lentz, Bernard F. Why So Many Children of Doctors Become Doctors: Nepotism vs. Human Capital Transfers. *J. Human Res.*, Summer 1989, *24*(3), pp. 396–413.

LaBarge, Karin P.; LaBarge, Richard A. and Darrat, Ali F. Is Financial Deepening a Reliable Prescription for Economic Growth? *Amer. Economist*, Fall 1989, *33*(2), pp. 25–33.

LaBarge, Richard A.; Darrat, Ali F. and LaBarge, Karin P. Is Financial Deepening a Reli-

able Prescription for Economic Growth? *Amer. Economist*, Fall 1989, *33*(2), pp. 25–33.

Labys, Walter C. An Integrated Exhaustible Resource Model of Copper Market Dynamics. In *[Adams, F. G.], 1989*, pp. 37–55.

_____. Spatial and Temporal Price and Allocation Models of Mineral and Energy Markets. In *Labys, W. C.; Takayama, T. and Uri, N. D., eds., 1989*, pp. 17–47.

_____ **and Yang, Chin-Wei.** A Sensitivity Analysis of the Linear Complementarity Programming Model: Appalachian Steam Coal and Natural Gas. In *Labys, W. C.; Takayama, T. and Uri, N. D., eds., 1989*, pp. 69–86.

LaCava, Gerald; Parhizgari, Ali M. and Prakash, Arun J. A General Proof of Merton's Analytic Derivation of the Efficient Portfolio Frontier. *Quart. J. Bus. Econ.*, Summer 1989, *28*(3), pp. 67–77.

Lacey, Eric F. Some Comparative and Contrasting Features of OECD Countries' Competition Laws. *Econ. Scelte Pubbliche/J. Public Finance Public Choice*, Jan.–Aug. 1989, *7*(1–2), pp. 81–87.

Lach, Saul and Jovanovic, Boyan. Entry, Exit, and Diffusion with Learning by Doing. *Amer. Econ. Rev.*, September 1989, *79*(4), pp. 690–99.

_____ **and Schankerman, Mark.** Dynamics of R&D and Investment in the Scientific Sector. *J. Polit. Econ.*, August 1989, *97*(4), pp. 880–904.

Lachance, Gabrielle. Le Développement: Un essai d'opérationnalisation du concept. (With English summary.) *Can. J. Devel. Stud.*, 1989, *10*(2), pp. 195–209.

Lachinov, Iu. N. Economic Functions of the Family. *Prob. Econ.*, April 1989, *31*(12), pp. 50–61.

Lachmann, L. M. Sir John Hicks as a Neo-Austrian. In *Wood, J. C. and Woods, R. N., eds., Vol. 2, 1989, 1973*, pp. 262–72.

_____. Sir John Hicks on Capital and Growth (Review Article). In *Wood, J. C. and Woods, R. N., eds., Vol. 2, 1989, 1966*, pp. 61–71.

Lacker, Jeffrey M. Financial Intermediation, Optimality, and Efficiency. *Can. J. Econ.*, May 1989, *22*(2), pp. 364–82.

_____ **and Weinberg, John A.** Optimal Contracts under Costly State Falsification. *J. Polit. Econ.*, December 1989, *97*(6), pp. 1345–63.

Lad, Lawrence J. and Austrom, Douglas R. Issues Management Alliances: New Responses, New Values., and New Logics. In *Post, J. E., ed., 1989*, pp. 233–55.

Ladd, George W. and Duncan, Steven S. Decomposition of Structural and Exogenous Changes. *Appl. Econ.*, January 1989, *21*(1), pp. 125–37.

Ladd, Helen F. and Yinger, John. The Determinants of State Assistance to Central Cities. *Nat. Tax J.*, December 1989, *42*(4), pp. 413–28.

Laferriére, Richard and Gaudry, Marc. The Box–Cox Transformation: Power Invariance and a New Interpretation. *Econ. Letters*, 1989, *30*(1), pp. 27–29.

Laffer, Arthur B. America in the World Economy: A Strategy for the 1990s: Commentary. In *Hamilton, E. K., ed.*, 1989, pp. 122–25.

Laffond, G. La révélation de la qualité par les prix sur un marché en auto-organisation. (Quality Revelation through Prices on a Self-organized Market. With English summary.) *Écon. Appl.*, 1989, 42(3), pp. 129–53.

Laffont, Jean-Jacques. A Brief Overview of the Economics of Incomplete Markets. *Econ. Rec.*, March 1989, 65(188), pp. 54–65.

_____ **and Boyer, Marcel.** Expanding the Informativeness of the Price System with Law. *Can. J. Econ.*, May 1989, 22(2), pp. 217–27.

_____ **and Grimaud, André.** Existence of a Spatial Equilibrium. *J. Urban Econ.*, March 1989, 25(2), pp. 213–18.

_____ **and Maskin, Eric.** Rational Expectations with Imperfect Competition: A Bertrand–Edgeworth Example. *Econ. Letters*, October 1989, 30(4), pp. 269–74.

LaFrance, Jeffrey T. and Hanemann, W. Michael. The Dual Structure of Incomplete Demand Systems. *Amer. J. Agr. Econ.*, May 1989, 71(2), pp. 262–74.

Lagos M., Luis Felipe and Galetovic P., Alexander. Los planes Austral y Cruzado: Por qué no detuvieron la inflación? (With English summary.) *Cuadernos Econ.*, August 1989, 26(78), pp. 217–42.

Lahiri, Ashok K. Dynamics of Asian Savings: The Role of Growth and Age Structure. *Int. Monet. Fund Staff Pap.*, March 1989, 36(1), pp. 228–61.

Lahiri, Kajal and Chun, T. S. Some Tests for Unbiasedness in the Long Run Using Survey Data. *Int. Econ. J.*, Summer 1989, 3(2), pp. 27–42.

_____; **Lankford, R. Hamilton and Numrich, Richard P.** The Estimation and Interpretation of Urban Density Gradients. *J. Bus. Econ. Statist.*, April 1989, 7(2), pp. 227–35.

Lahiri, Sajal. Incidence of Sharecropping in the Presence of Urban Unemployment: A Two Sector Analysis. *J. Quant. Econ.*, January 1989, 5(1), pp. 1–14.

_____. Structural Break, Indivisibilities and Input–Output Analysis. *Econ. Systems Res.*, 1989, 1(2), pp. 155–65.

_____ **and Chatterji, Monojit.** Private Foreign Investment and Welfare in LDCs. In *Singer, H. W. and Sharma, S., eds. (II)*, 1989, pp. 220–29.

_____ **and Ono, Yoshiyasu.** Terms of Trade and Welfare: A General Analysis. *Econ. Rec.*, March 1989, 65(188), pp. 27–31.

Lahiri, Somdeb. The Max–Min Solution for Variable Threat Games. *Econ. Letters*, 1989, 29(3), pp. 215–20.

_____. A New Proof of the Maximum Principle in Optimal Control Theory. *J. Quant. Econ.*, January 1989, 5(1), pp. 37–42.

Lahr, Michael L.; Stevens, Benjamin H. and Treyz, George I. On the Comparative Accuracy of RPC Estimating Techniques. In *Miller, R. E.; Polenske, K. R. and Rose, A. Z., eds.*, 1989, pp. 245–57.

Lahti, Ari and Pylkkönen, Pertti. News and Stock Prices. *Liiketaloudellinen Aikak.*, 1989, 38(3), pp. 184–93.

Lai, Cheng-chung. Adam Smith and Yen Fu: Western Economics in Chinese Perspective. *J. Europ. Econ. Hist.*, Fall 1989, 18(2), pp. 371–82.

_____. Development Strategies and Growth with Equality: Re-evaluation of Taiwan's Experience: 1950's–1970's. *Rivista Int. Sci. Econ. Com.*, February 1989, 36(2), pp. 177–91.

_____. Market Structure and Inter-industry Wage Differences: The Case of Taiwan. *Econ. Letters*, December 1989, 31(2), pp. 199–204.

_____. The Structure and Characteristics of the Chinese Co-operative System: 1928–49. *Int. J. Soc. Econ.*, 1989, 16(2), pp. 59–66.

Lai, Ching-Chong and Chang, Wen-Ya. The Fleming Proposition with Oligopolistic Pricing. *J. Post Keynesian Econ.*, Spring 1989, 11(3), pp. 460–73.

_____ **and Chang, Wen-Ya.** Income Taxes, Supply-Side Effects, and Currency Devaluation. *J. Macroecon.*, Spring 1989, 11(2), pp. 281–295.

_____ **and Chang, Wen-Ya.** Unionized Wages and Employment. *Atlantic Econ. J.*, June 1989, 17(2), pp. 76.

_____ **and Chen, Chau-nan.** Money, Consumption, and Terms-of-Trade Dynamics: A Note. *Int. Econ. Rev.*, November 1989, 30(4), pp. 1005–09.

_____; **Chu, Yun-Peng and Chang, Wen-Ya.** Exchange Rate Dynamics under Dual Exchange Rates: The Case of Neutral Intervention Policy. *Manchester Sch. Econ. Soc. Stud.*, September 1989, 57(3), pp. 235–47.

Lai, Tsong-Yue. An Equilibrium Model of Asset Pricing with Progressive Personal Taxes. *J. Finan. Quant. Anal.*, March 1989, 24(1), pp. 117–27.

Laibson, David I. and Friedman, Benjamin M. Economic Implications of Extraordinary Movements in Stock Prices. *Brookings Pap. Econ. Act.*, 1989, (2), pp. 137–72.

Laidler, David. Anna Schwartz's Perspective on British Economic History: Comment. In *[Schwartz, A. J.]*, 1989, pp. 104–14.

_____. The Context of S. C. Tsiang's Monetary Economics. In *Tsiang, S. C.*, 1989, pp. 359–75.

_____. Dow and Saville's *Critique of Monetary Policy*—A Review Essay. *J. Econ. Lit.*, September 1989, 27(3), pp. 1147–59.

Lainé, J. Processus d'échanges bilatéraux et auto-organisation du marché. (Bilateral Exchange Processes and Market Self-organization. With English summary.) *Écon. Appl.*, 1989, 42(3), pp. 41–61.

Lains, Alfian. West Sumatra: The Road to *Parasamya Purnakarya Nugraha*. In *Hill, H., ed.*, 1989, pp. 437–53.

Laird, Samuel and Yeats, Alexander J. Nontariff Barriers of Developed Countries, 1966–86. *Finance Devel.*, March 1989, 26(1), pp. 12–13.

Laitinen, Erkki K. Efficiency, Productivity and

Profitability Ratios in a Public Enterprise. *Liiketaloudellinen Aikak.*, 1989, *38*(3), pp. 194–224.

_____. Failure Processes in Firms of Different Size and Age. *Liiketaloudellinen Aikak.*, 1989, *38*(4), pp. 306–31.

_____. Framework for an Effective Decision Support System: Part II. *Liiketaloudellinen Aikak.*, 1989, *38*(1), pp. 3–20.

Laitner, John. Dynamic Determinacy and the Existence of Sunspot Equilibria. *J. Econ. Theory*, February 1989, *47*(1), pp. 39–50.

Lake, David A. and James, Scott C. The Second Face of Hegemony: Britain's Repeal of the Corn Laws and the American Walker Tariff of 1846. *Int. Organ.*, Winter 1989, *43*(1), pp. 1–29.

Laki, M. What Is the Solution? *Acta Oecon.*, 1989, *40*(3–4), pp. 248–51.

Lakonishok, Josef and Smidt, Seymour. Past Price Changes and Current Trading Volume. *J. Portfol. Manage.*, Summer 1989, *15*(4), pp. 18–24.

Lakshmanan, T. R. Infrastructure and Economic Transformation. In *Andersson, Å. E., et al.,* eds., 1989, pp. 241–61.

_____. Technological and Institutional Innovations in the Service Sector. In *Andersson, Å. E.; Batten, D. F. and Karlsson, C.,* eds., 1989, pp. 63–79.

_____ **and Kasanen, Pirkko.** Residential Heating Choices of Finnish Households. *Econ. Geogr.*, April 1989, *65*(2), pp. 130–45.

Laky, T. Vanished Myths—Wavering Intentions (Small Enterprises Revisited). *Acta Oecon.*, 1989, *40*(3–4), pp. 285–306.

Lal, Deepak. After the Debt Crisis: Modes of Development for the Longer Run in Latin America. In *Edwards, S. and Larrain, F.,* eds., 1989, pp. 100–120.

_____. The Political Economy of Industrialisation in Primary Product Exporting Economies: Some Cautionary Tales. In *Islam, N., ed.,* 1989, pp. 279–314.

_____. A Simple Framework for Analysing Various Real Aspects of Stabilisation and Structural Adjustment Policies. *J. Devel. Stud.*, April 1989, *25*(3), pp. 291–313.

Lal, Kishori. Canadian System of National Accounts—An Integrated Framework. In *Franz, A. and Rainer, N.,* eds., 1989, pp. 191–214.

Lal, Rajiv and Matutes, Carmen. Price Competition in Multimarket Duopolies. *Rand J. Econ.*, Winter 1989, *20*(4), pp. 516–37.

Lal, Rattan. Soil Degradation in Relation to Climate. In *Oram, P. A., et al.,* 1989, pp. 257–68.

Laleye, O. M. and Olowu, Dele. Decentralization in Africa. In *World Bank and Istituto Italo-Africano,* 1989, pp. 78–85.

_____ **and Olowu, Dele.** Managing Local Governments in Africa. In *World Bank and Istituto Italo-Africano,* 1989, pp. 117–23.

Laliwala, Jafarhusein I. Islamic Economics: Some Issues in Definition and Methodology: Com-

ments. *J. King Abdulaziz Univ.: Islamic Econ.*, 1989, *1*, pp. 129–31.

Lall, K. B. The South Asian Economy and Asian-Pacific Region. In *Shinohara, M. and Lo, F.,* eds., 1989, pp. 234–44.

Lall, Rajiv. Indian Overseas Investment and Exports of Technology and Manufactures: An Overview. In *Ventura-Dias, V., ed.,* 1989, pp. 291–308.

Lall, Sanjaya and Perasso, Giancarlo. Determinants of the Debt Problem in Eastern and Southern Africa: A Statistical Analysis. *Rivista Int. Sci. Econ. Com.*, Oct.–Nov. 1989, *36*(10–11), pp. 985–92.

_____; **Ray, S. and Ghosh, S.** The Determinants and Promotion of South–South Trade in Manufactured Products. In *Ventura-Dias, V., ed.,* 1989, pp. 131–64.

Lallement, Michel. Dialectique et Sens pratique. (Dialectic and Practical Logic. With English summary.) *Écon. Societes*, October 1989, *23*(10), pp. 179–205.

Lalli, Marco and Thomas, Christina. Public Opinion and Decision Making in the Community. Evaluation of Residents' Attitudes towards Town Planning Measures. *Urban Stud.*, August 1989, *26*(4), pp. 435–47.

Lalman, David and Bueno de Mesquita, Bruce. The Road to War Is Strewn with Peaceful Intentions. In *Ordeshook, P. C., ed.,* 1989, pp. 253–66.

Lam, Chun H.; Deb, Rajat and Fomby, Thomas B. Deregulation and the Demand for Money Market Mutual Funds. *J. Macroecon.*, Spring 1989, *11*(2), pp. 297–308.

Lam, K. F.; Choo, E. U. and Wedley, William C. Linear Goal Programming in Estimation of Classification Probability. In *Lockett, A. G. and Islei, G., eds.,* 1989, pp. 166–78.

Lam, Pok-sang. Irreversibility and Consumer Durables Expenditures. *J. Monet. Econ.*, January 1989, *23*(1), pp. 135–50.

Lamas, Enrique J. and McNeil, John M. Year-Apart Estimates of Household Net Worth from the Survey of Income and Program Participation. In *Lipsey, R. E. and Tice, H. S., eds.,* 1989, pp. 431–62.

Lambert, David K. Calf Retention and Production Decisions over Time. *Western J. Agr. Econ.*, July 1989, *14*(1), pp. 9–19.

Lambert, Diane and Duncan, George. The Risk of Disclosure for Microdata. *J. Bus. Econ. Statist.*, April 1989, *7*(2), pp. 207–17.

_____ **and Follmann, Dean A.** Generalizing Logistic Regression by Nonparametric Mixing. *J. Amer. Statist. Assoc.*, March 1989, *84*(405), pp. 295–300.

Lambert, Peter J. and Acemoglu, Daron. Equiproportionate Growth of Incomes and Fiscal Drag. *Bull. Econ. Res.*, October 1989, *41*(4), pp. 295–302.

_____ **and Johnson, Paul.** Measuring the Responsiveness of Income Tax Revenue to Income Growth: A Review and Some UK Values. *Fisc. Stud.*, November 1989, *10*(4), pp. 1–18.

Lambert, Richard A.; Lanen, William N. and

Larcker, David F. Executive Stock Option Plans and Corporate Dividend Policy. *J. Finan. Quant. Anal.*, December 1989, *24*(4), pp. 409–25.

_____ **and Larcker, David F.** Estimating the Marginal Cost of Operating a Service Department When Reciprocal Services Exist. *Accounting Rev.*, July 1989, *64*(3), pp. 449–67.

_____; **Larcker, David F. and Defeo, Victor J.** The Executive Compensation Effects of Equity-for-Debt Swaps. *Accounting Rev.*, April 1989, *64*(2), pp. 201–27.

Lamberton, Donald M. The Regional Information Economy: Its Measurement and Significance. In *Punset, E. and Sweeney, G., eds.*, 1989, pp. 16–25.

Lamborghini, Bruno. The Impact of Information and Information Technology on the Structure of the Firm. In *Punset, E. and Sweeney, G., eds.*, 1989, pp. 56–66.

Lambrechts, I. J.; Doppegieter, J. J. and Hamman, W. D. The Importance of Public Utilities in South Africa. *J. Stud. Econ. Econometrics*, August 1989, *13*(2), pp. 37–47.

_____; **Doppegieter, J. J. and Hamman, W. D.** Tariff Policies for Public Utilities: The Accounting Cost Approach. *J. Stud. Econ. Econometrics*, August 1989, *13*(2), pp. 49–57.

Lambrinos, James and Harmon, Oskar Ragnar. An Empirical Evaluation of Two Methods for Estimating Economic Damages. *J. Risk Ins.*, December 1989, *56*(4), pp. 733–39.

Lambsdorff, Otto Graf. European Currency—A German View. In *Franz, O., ed.*, 1989, pp. 66–75.

Lamdany, Ruben. The Market-Based Menu Approach in Action: The 1988 Brazilian Financing Package. In *Husain, I. and Diwan, I., eds.*, 1989, pp. 163–74.

_____. Voluntary Debt Reduction Operations: Bolivia, Mexico, and Beyond. *Contemp. Policy Issues*, April 1989, *7*(2), pp. 66–82.

Lamm, Donald S. Economics and the Common Reader. In *Colander, D. C. and Coats, A. W., eds.*, 1989, pp. 95–105.

Lamm-Tennant, Joan. Asset/Liability Management for the Life Insurer: Situation Analysis and Strategy Formulation. *J. Risk Ins.*, September 1989, *56*(3), pp. 501–17.

Lamoureux, Christopher G. and Akgiray, Vedat. Estimation of Stable-Law Parameters: A Comparative Study. *J. Bus. Econ. Statist.*, January 1989, *7*(1), pp. 85–93.

_____; **and Frankfurter, George M.** Estimation and Selection Bias in Mean–Variance Portfolio Selection. *J. Finan. Res.*, Summer 1989, *12*(2), pp. 173–81.

_____ **and Frankfurter, George M.** The Relevance of the Distributional Form of Common Stock Returns to the Construction of Optimal Portfolios: Reply. *J. Finan. Quant. Anal.*, March 1989, *24*(1), pp. 131.

_____ **and Sanger, Gary C.** Firm Size and Turn-of-the-Year Effects in the OTC/NASDAQ Market. *J. Finance*, December 1989, *44*(5), pp. 1219–45.

_____ **and Wansley, James W.** The Pricing of When-Issued Securities. *Financial Rev.*, May 1989, *24*(2), pp. 183–98.

Lampe, John R. Imperial Borderlands or Capitalist Periphery? Redefining Balkan Backwardness, 1520–1914. In *Chirot, D., ed.*, 1989, pp. 177–209.

Lampert, Ada; Helman, Amir and Kroll, Yoram. The Kibbutz and Private Property. In *Grunert, K. G. and Ölander, F., eds.*, 1989, pp. 65–74.

Lampert, Heinz. "Denken in Ordnungen" als ungelöste Aufgabe. (On the Interrelations of the Economic and the Social Order. With English summary.) *Jahr. Nationalökon. Statist.*, October 1989, *206*(4–5), pp. 446–56.

Lan, David. Resistance to the Present by the Past: Mediums and Money in Zimbabwe. In *Parry, J. and Bloch, M., eds.*, 1989, pp. 191–208.

Lancaster, K. Revising Demand Theory. In *Wood, J. C. and Woods, R. N., eds., Vol. 2,* 1989, *1957*, pp. 18–25.

Lancry, Pierre-Jean. Le secteur 2 de la médecine libérale un élément de marché? (With English summary.) *Revue Écon. Politique*, Nov.–Dec. 1989, *99*(6), pp. 854–70.

Land, Kenneth C. and Hough, George C., Jr. New Methods for Tables of School Life, with Applications to U.S. Data from Recent School Years. *J. Amer. Statist. Assoc.*, March 1989, *84*(405), pp. 63–75.

Landale, Nancy S. Agricultural Opportunity and Marriage: The United States at the Turn of the Century. *Demography*, May 1989, *26*(2), pp. 203–18.

Landau, Ralph. Technology and Capital Formation. In *Jorgenson, D. W. and Landau, R., eds.*, 1989, pp. 485–505.

Lande, Laurie B. Child Care Options of Employed Women. *Mon. Lab. Rev.*, December 1989, *112*(12), pp. 52.

Landell-Mills, Joslin M. The Demand for International Reserves and Their Opportunity Cost. *Int. Monet. Fund Staff Pap.*, September 1989, *36*(3), pp. 708–32.

_____. The Financial Costs of Holding Reserves. *Finance Devel.*, December 1989, *26*(4), pp. 17–19.

Landell-Mills, Pierre; Agarwala, Ramgopal and Please, Stanley. From Crisis to Sustainable Growth in Sub-Saharan Africa. *Finance Devel.*, December 1989, *26*(4), pp. 26–29.

Lander, Eric and Farrell, Joseph. Competition between and within Teams: The Lifeboat Principle. *Econ. Letters*, 1989, *29*(3), pp. 205–08.

Landes, David S. Some Thoughts on Economic Hegemony: Europe in the Nineteenth-Century World Economy. In *[Fischer, W.]*, 1989, pp. 153–67.

Landes, Thomas and Loistl, Otto. The Dynamic Pricing of Financial Assets: Introduction: The Market Performance at the Microlevel. In *Loistl, O. and Landes, T., ed.*, 1989, pp. 1–12.

_____; **Loistl, Otto and Berger, Karin.** Simulation of Synergetic Stock Price Modelling. In

Loistl, O. and Landes, T., ed., 1989, pp. 109–27.

_____; **Loistl, Otto and Reiss, Winfried.** The Determinants of the Fundamental Value Part of a Share Price. In *Loistl, O. and Landes, T., ed.*, 1989, pp. 129–63.

_____; **Loistl, Otto and Reiss, Winfried.** The Market Microstructure and the Dynamic Pricing of Financial Assets. In *Loistl, O. and Landes, T., ed.*, 1989, pp. 53–108.

Landes, William M. and Posner, Richard A. An Economic Analysis of Copyright Law. *J. Legal Stud.*, June 1989, *18*(2), pp. 325–63.

Landesmann, Michael and Snell, Andrew. The Consequences of Mrs. Thatcher for U.K. Manufacturing Exports. *Econ. J.*, March 1989, *99*(394), pp. 1–27.

_____ **and Snell, Andrew.** Implications of a Modernization Strategy for the United Kingdom. In *Krelle, W., ed.*, 1989, pp. 353–84.

Landgraff, Richard L. The Cross Functional Team Approach to Product Development. In *Ahlbrandt, R. S., Jr., ed.*, 1989, pp. 45–48.

Lando, Henrik. Om imperfekte kapitalmarkeder og konjunkturbevægelser. (The Role of Imperfect Capital Markets in the Business Cycle. With English summary.) *Nationaløkon. Tidsskr.*, 1989, *127*(3), pp. 371–80.

Landon, Stuart and Coyte, Peter C. The Impact of Competition on Advertising: The Case of Political Campaign Expenditures. *Can. J. Econ.*, November 1989, *22*(4), pp. 795–818.

Landsburg, Steven E. and Eden, Benjamin. On the Competitive Resolution of Trading Uncertainty. *J. Econ. Theory*, February 1989, *47*(1), pp. 66–75.

Landsman, Wayne R. The Multiperiod Information Content of Accounting Earnings: Confirmation and Contradictions of Previous Earnings Reports: Discussion. *J. Acc. Res.*, Supplement, 1989, *27*, pp. 80–84.

_____ **and Cornell, Bradford.** Security Price Response to Quarterly Earnings Announcements and Analysts' Forecast Revisions. *Accounting Rev.*, October 1989, *64*(4), pp. 680–92.

_____ **and Damodaran, Aswath.** A Comparison of Quarterly Earnings per Share Forecasts Using James–Stein and Unconditional Least Squares Parameter Estimators. *Int. J. Forecasting*, 1989, *5*(4), pp. 491–500.

_____ **and Damodaran, Aswath.** Using Shrinkage Estimators to Improve upon Time-Series Model Proxies for the Security Market's Expectation of Earnings. *J. Acc. Res.*, Spring 1989, *27*(1), pp. 97–115.

Lane, Jonathan S. and Vandell, Kerry D. The Economics of Architecture and Urban Design: Some Preliminary Findings. *Amer. Real Estate Urban Econ. Assoc. J.*, Summer 1989, *17*(2), pp. 235–60.

Lane, Julia and Berry, Tom. A Multi-state Analysis of the Targeted Jobs Tax Credit Programme. *Appl. Econ.*, January 1989, *21*(1), pp. 85–94.

_____; **Glennon, Dennis and McCabe, James.** Measures of Local Business Climate: Alterna-

tive Approaches. *Reg. Sci. Persp.*, 1989, *19*(1), pp. 89–106.

Lane, Robert E. Market Choice and Human Choice. In *Chapman, J. W. and Pennock, J. R., eds.*, 1989, pp. 226–49.

Lane, Sylvia and Adelman, Irma. The Balance between Industry and Agriculture in Economic Development: Introduction. In *Adelman, I. and Lane, S., eds.*, 989, pp. xviii–xxi.

Lane, Timothy D. Foreign Exchange Market Intervention in Interdependent Economies: A Case for Capricious Policy. *J. Macroecon.*, Fall 1989, *11*(4), pp. 513–31.

Lane, W. J. and Greenhut, M. L. A Theory of Oligopolistic Competition. *Manchester Sch. Econ. Soc. Stud.*, September 1989, *57*(3), pp. 248–61.

Lane, William R.; Looney, Stephen W. and Wansley, James W. An Examination of Misclassifications with Bank Failure Prediction Models. *J. Econ. Bus.*, November 1989, *41*(4), pp. 327–36.

Lanen, William N.; Larcker, David F. and Lambert, Richard A. Executive Stock Option Plans and Corporate Dividend Policy. *J. Finan. Quant. Anal.*, December 1989, *24*(4), pp. 409–25.

Lang, Harald. Herman Wold on Optimal Properties of Exponentially Weighed Forecasts. *J. Econ. Behav. Organ.*, May 1989, *11*(3), pp. 443–46.

_____; **Albrecht, James W. and Holmlund, Bertil.** Job Search and Youth Unemployment: Analysis of Swedish Data. *Europ. Econ. Rev.*, March 1989, *33*(2/3), pp. 416–25.

Lang, Kevin. Why Was There Mandatory Retirement? *J. Public Econ.*, June 1989, *39*(1), pp. 127–36.

Lang, Larry H. P. and Litzenberger, Robert H. Dividend Announcements: Cash Flow Signalling vs. Free Cash Flow Hypothesis? *J. Finan. Econ.*, September 1989, *24*(1), pp. 181–91.

_____; **Stulz, René M. and Walkling, Ralph A.** Managerial Performance, Tobin's Q, and the Gains from Successful Tender Offers. *J. Finan. Econ.*, September 1989, *24*(1), pp. 137–54.

Láng, László. The East–South Economic Interplay in the Eighties: Challenges and Chances. In *Wohlmuth, K., ed.*, 1989, pp. 123–46.

Lang, Richard and Carlino, Gerald. Interregional Flows of Funds as a Measure of Economic Integration in the United States. *J. Urban Econ.*, July 1989, *26*(1), pp. 20–29.

Lang, Rikard; Marendic, Bozo and Vojnic, Dragomir. The Socioeconomic Model of Socialist Self-Management. In *Macesich, G., ed.*, 1989, pp. 12–55.

Lang, William W. and Nakamura, Leonard I. Information Losses in a Dynamic Model of Credit. *J. Finance*, July 1989, *44*(3), pp. 730–46.

Langbein, Laura and Broder, Ivy E. Wage Differentials among Regulated, Private and Government Sectors: A Case Study. *Eastern Econ. J.*, July–Sept. 1989, *15*(3), pp. 189–201.

Langdon, Steve J. Prospects for Co-management

of Marine Mammals in Alaska. **In** *Pinkerton, E., ed.*, 1989, pp. 154–69.

Lange, Dirk. Economic Development and Agricultural Export Pattern: An Empirical Cross-Country Analysis. *Europ. Rev. Agr. Econ.*, 1989, *16*(2), pp. 187–202.

Lange, Kenneth L.; Little, Roderick J. A. and Taylor, Jeremy M. G. Robust Statistical Modeling Using the *t* Distribution. *J. Amer. Statist. Assoc.*, December 1989, *84*(408), pp. 881–96.

Lange, Mark D. and Huffman, Wallace E. Off-Farm Work Decisions of Husbands and Wives: Joint Decision Making. *Rev. Econ. Statist.*, August 1989, *71*(3), pp. 471–80.

———; **Zacharias, Thomas P. and Ojemakinde, Abiodun.** Modelling the Firm-Level Multiproduct Cost Structure of Agricultural Production. **In** *Gulledge, T. R., Jr. and Litteral, L. A., eds.*, 1989, pp. 117–29.

Lange, Oscar. Complementarity and Interrelations of Shifts in Demand. **In** *Wood, J. C. and Woods, R. N., eds., Vol. 1*, 1989, *1940*, pp. 35–41.

——— **and Hicks, John R.** The Interrelations of Shifts in Demand: Replies. **In** *Wood, J. C. and Woods, R. N., eds., Vol. 1*, 1989, *1944*, pp. 97–105.

Lange, Peter and Regini, Marino. Interests and Institutions—Forms of Social Regulation and Public Policy-Making. **In** *Lange, P. and Regini, M., eds.*, 1989, pp. 1–25.

——— **and Regini, Marino.** The Italian Case between Continuity and Change. **In** *Lange, P. and Regini, M., eds.*, 1989, pp. 249–72.

Langenfeld, James. Identifying Cartel Policing under Uncertainty: The U.S. Steel Industry, 1933–1939: Comment. *J. Law Econ.*, Part 2, October 1989, *32*(2), pp. S77–82.

——— **and Scheffman, David T.** Innovation and U.S. Competition Policy. *Antitrust Bull.*, Spring 1989, *34*(1), pp. 1–63.

——— **and Walton, Thomas F.** Regulatory Reform under Reagan—The Right Way and the Wrong Way. **In** *Meiners, R. E. and Yandle, B., eds.*, 1989, pp. 41–70.

Langetieg, Terence C. and Leibowitz, Martin L. Shortfall Risk and the Asset Allocation Decision: A Simulation Analysis of Stock and Bond Risk Profiles. *J. Portfol. Manage.*, Fall 1989, *16*(1), pp. 61–68.

Langfeldt, Enno. The Underground Economy in the Federal Republic of Germany: A Preliminary Assessment. **In** *Feige, E. L., ed.*, 1989, pp. 197–217.

Langhammer, Rolf J. Services and International Division of Labour. **In** *Giersch, H., ed.*, 1989, pp. 248–71.

——— **and Hiemenz, Ulrich.** Liberalisation and the Successful Integration of Developing Countries into the World Economy. **In** *Renshaw, G. T., ed.*, 1989, pp. 105–39.

Langlois, Catherine. Markup Pricing versus Marginalism: A Controversy Revisited. *J. Post Keynesian Econ.*, Fall 1989, *12*(1), pp. 127–51.

———. A Model of Target Inventory and Markup

with Empirical Testing Using Automobile Industry Data. *J. Econ. Behav. Organ.*, January 1989, *11*(1), pp. 47–74.

Langlois, Jean-Pierre P. Modeling Deterrence and International Crises. *J. Conflict Resolution*, March 1989, *33*(1), pp. 67–83.

Langlois, Richard N. and Robertson, Paul L. Explaining Vertical Integration: Lessons from the American Automobile Industry. *J. Econ. Hist.*, June 1989, *49*(2), pp. 361–75.

Langohr, Herwig and Eckbo, B. Espen. Information Disclosure, Method of Payment, and Takeover Premiums: Public and Private Tender Offers in France. *J. Finan. Econ.*, October 1989, *24*(2), pp. 363–403.

Langrehr, Frederick W. and Langrehr, Virginia B. Measuring the Ability to Repay: The Residual Income Ratio. *J. Cons. Aff.*, Winter 1989, *23*(2), pp. 393–406.

Langrehr, Virginia B. and Langrehr, Frederick W. Measuring the Ability to Repay: The Residual Income Ratio. *J. Cons. Aff.*, Winter 1989, *23*(2), pp. 393–406.

Langsen, Arnold L. and Lowenthal, Franklin. The Omega Matrix. *Managerial Dec. Econ.*, June 1989, *10*(2), pp. 155–58.

Langworthy, Mark and Thompson, Gary D. Profit Function Approximations and Duality Applications to Agriculture. *Amer. J. Agr. Econ.*, August 1989, *71*(3), pp. 791–98.

Lanjouw, G. J.; van Leeuwen, E. H. and Hoen, H. W. Eastern Europe's Participation in the International Financial System. *Jahr. Wirtsch. Osteuropas*, 1989, *13*(2), pp. 41–65.

Lankford, R. Hamilton; Numrich, Richard P. and Lahiri, Kajal. The Estimation and Interpretation of Urban Density Gradients. *J. Bus. Econ. Statist.*, April 1989, *7*(2), pp. 227–35.

Lansbury, Russell D. and Quince, Annabelle. Managers as Employees: Australia. **In** *Roomkin, M. J., ed.*, 1989, pp. 97–130.

Lanthier, Pierre. Multinationals and the French Electrical Industry, 1889–1940. **In** *Teichova, A.; Lévy-Leboyer, M. and Nussbaum, H., eds.*, 1989, pp. 143–50.

Lantieri, Charles and Riviére, Pascal. Peut-on estimer la demande d'actifs á partir d'un modèle de portefeuille? (An Estimation of the Demand for Money Derived from a Portfolio Model. With English summary.) *Revue Écon.*, January 1989, *40*(1), pp. 55–79.

Lantto, Kari. Is Abuse a Problem in Social Insurance? **In** *Gustafsson, B. A. and Klevmarken, N. A., eds.*, 1989, pp. 185–94.

Lanvin, Bruno. Participation of Developing Countries in a Telecommunication and Data Services Agreement: Some Elements for Consideration. **In** *Robinson, P.; Sauvant, K. P. and Govitrikar, V. P., eds.*, 1989, pp. 71–99.

Lanza, Alessandro. Considerazioni su un metodo per lo studio dei linkages in un contesto input-output. (An Approach to the Analysis of Linkages in an Input–Output Context. With English summary.) *Rivista Int. Sci. Econ. Com.*, March 1989, *36*(3), pp. 221–31.

Lanzetta de Pardo, Mónica and Murillo Castaño,

Gabriel. The Articulation of Formal and Informal Sectors in the Economy of Bogotá, Colombia. In *Portes, A.; Castells, M. and Benton, L. A., eds.*, 1989, pp. 95–110.

Lanzinger, Klaus. Europe, Our Old Home: An American Cultural Experience. In *Rueschhoff, N. and Schaum, K., eds.*, 1989, pp. 40–56.

Lapan, Harvey E. and Choi, Eun Kwan. Errata [Tariffs versus Quotas under Uncertainty: Restricting Imports and the Role of Preferences]. *Int. Econ. J.*, Spring 1989, *3*(1), pp. 103.

Lapidus, Gail W. Gorbachev and the "National Question": Restructuring the Soviet Federation. *Soviet Econ.*, July–Sept. 1989, *5*(3), pp. 201–50.

Laporte, Gilbert and Eiselt, Horst A. The Maximum Capture Problem in a Weighted Network. *J. Reg. Sci.*, August 1989, *29*(3), pp. 433–39.

Laqueur, Thomas W. Crowds, Carnival and the State in English Executions, 1604–1868. In *[Stone, L.]*, 1989, pp. 305–55.

Laraki, Karim. Ending Food Subsidies: Nutritional, Welfare, and Budgetary Effects. *World Bank Econ. Rev.*, September 1989, *3*(3), pp. 395–408.

Larcker, David F. Accounting Measurement, Price–Earnings Ratios, and the Information Content of Security Prices: Discussion. *J. Acc. Res.*, Supplement, 1989, *27*, pp. 145–52.

————; **Defeo, Victor J. and Lambert, Richard A.** The Executive Compensation Effects of Equity-for-Debt Swaps. *Accounting Rev.*, April 1989, *64*(2), pp. 201–27.

———— **and Lambert, Richard A.** Estimating the Marginal Cost of Operating a Service Department When Reciprocal Services Exist. *Accounting Rev.*, July 1989, *64*(3), pp. 449–67.

————; **Lambert, Richard A. and Lanen, William N.** Executive Stock Option Plans and Corporate Dividend Policy. *J. Finan. Quant. Anal.*, December 1989, *24*(4), pp. 409–25.

Lardy, Nicholas R. Dilemmas in the Pattern of Resource Allocation in China, 1978–1985. In *Nee, V. and Stark, D., eds.*, 1989, pp. 278–305.

Lareau, Thomas J. and Rae, Douglas A. Valuing WTP for Diesel Odor Reductions: An Application of Contingent Ranking Technique. *Southern Econ. J.*, January 1989, *55*(3), pp. 728–42.

Larichev, O. I., et al. Expert Knowledge Acquisition System. In *Lockett, A. G. and Islei, G., eds.*, 1989, pp. 517–21.

Larin, Kathryn A. and Hooper, Peter. International Comparisons of Labor Costs in Manufacturing. *Rev. Income Wealth*, December 1989, *35*(4), pp. 335–55.

Larjavaara, Tuomas. Export Credits, Credit Subsidies and External Debt Crisis. *Liiketaloudellinen Aikak.*, 1989, *38*(1), pp. 21–30.

Lark, Richard and Hudson, John. A Polychotomous Probit Measure and Analysis of Inflationary Expectations. *J. Macroecon.*, Spring 1989, *11*(2), pp. 269–80.

Larkey, Patrick D. and Smith, Richard A. Bias in the Formulation of Local Government Budget Problems. *Policy Sciences*, May 1989, *22*(2), pp. 123–66.

Larner, Robert J. Vertical Price Restraints: Per se or Rule of Reason? In *Larner, R. J. and Meehan, J. W., Jr., eds.*, 1989, pp. 123–40.

———— **and Meehan, James W., Jr.** Economics and Antitrust Policy: Introduction. In *Larner, R. J. and Meehan, J. W., Jr., eds.*, 1989, pp. 1–9.

———— **and Meehan, James W., Jr.** Postscript: In Memory of H. Michael Mann. In *Larner, R. J. and Meehan, J. W., Jr., eds.*, 1989, pp. 209–14.

———— **and Meehan, James W., Jr.** The Structural School, Its Critics, and Its Progeny: An Assessment. In *Larner, R. J. and Meehan, J. W., Jr., eds.*, 1989, pp. 179–208.

Laroche, Michel and Brisoux, Jacques E. Incorporating Competition into Consumer Behavior Models: The Case of the Attitude–Intention Relationship. *J. Econ. Psych.*, November 1989, *10*(3), pp. 343–62.

Laroque, Guy. Comparative Estimates of a Macroeconomic Disequilibrium Model: France, Germany, the U.K. and the U.S.A. *Europ. Econ. Rev.*, May 1989, *33*(5), pp. 963–89.

————. On Inventories and the Business Cycle. In *Feiwel, G. R., ed. (I)*, 1989, pp. 649–76.

————. On the Inventory Cycle and the Instability of the Competitive Mechanism. *Econometrica*, July 1989, *57*(4), pp. 911–35.

———— **and Salanie, Bernard.** Estimation of Multi-market Fix-Price Models: An Application of Pseudo Maximum Likelihood Methods. *Econometrica*, July 1989, *57*(4), pp. 831–60.

Laroque, Pierre. Towards a New Employment Policy. *Int. Lab. Rev.*, 1989, *128*(1), pp. 1–10.

Larraín, Felipe and Edwards, Sebastian. Debt, Adjustment, and Recovery in Latin America: An Introduction. In *Edwards, S. and Larrain, F., eds.*, 1989, pp. 1–27.

Larsen, Flemming and Wattleworth, Michael. Structural Policies in Industrial Countries. *Finance Devel.*, September 1989, *26*(3), pp. 20–23.

Larsen, James E. and Park, Won J. Non-uniform Percentage Brokerage Commissions and Real Estate Market Performance. *Amer. Real Estate Urban Econ. Assoc. J.*, Winter 1989, *17*(4), pp. 422–38.

Larsen, Ulla and Menken, Jane. Measuring Sterility from Incomplete Birth Histories. *Demography*, May 1989, *26*(2), pp. 185–201.

Larson, Bruce A. Dynamic Factor Demands Using Intertemporal Duality. *J. Agr. Econ. Res.*, Winter 1989, *41*(1), pp. 27–32.

————. Technical Change and Applications of Dynamic Duality to Agriculture: Comment. *Amer. J. Agr. Econ.*, August 1989, *71*(3), pp. 799–802.

———— **and Knudson, Mary K.** A Framework for Examining Technical Change. *J. Agr. Econ. Res.*, Fall 1989, *41*(4), pp. 21–28.

Larson, Bruce D. A Reappraisal of Canard's *The-*

ory of Price Determination. In *Walker, D. A., ed.*, 1989, pp. 38–52.

Larson, Donald K. Transitions of Poverty amidst Employment Growth: Two Nonmetro Case Studies. *Growth Change,* Spring 1989, *20*(2), pp. 19–34.

Larson, Douglas M. and Hardie, Ian W. Seller Behavior in Stumpage Markets with Imperfect Information. *Land Econ.,* August 1989, *65*(3), pp. 239–53.

Larson, Paul D.; Barman, Samir and Tersine, Richard J. An Economic Inventory/Transport Model with Freight Rate Discounts. *Logist. Transp. Rev.,* December 1989, *25*(4), pp. 291–306.

Larson, Robert S.; Braden, John B. and Herricks, Edwin E. Economic Targeting of Nonpoint Pollution Abatement for Fish Habitat Protection. *Water Resources Res.,* December 1989, *25*(12), pp. 2399–405.

Larsson, Gudmund. A Ten-Year Review of Science Policy in Sweden. In *Andersson, Å. E.; Batten, D. F. and Karlsson, C., eds.*, 1989, pp. 303–07.

Larue, Bruno. Optimal Tariff and Trade in Raw and Finished Goods. *Can. J. Agr. Econ.,* Part 2, December 1989, *37*(4), pp. 1081–90.

LaRue, David and Reckers, Philip M. J. An Empirical Examination of the Influence of Selected Factors on Professional Tax Preparers' Decision Processes. In *Schwartz, B. N., ed.*, 1989, pp. 37–50.

_____; **Reckers, Philip M. J. and Duncan, William A.** An Empirical Examination of the Influence of Selected Economic and Noneconomic Variables on Decision Making by Tax Professionals. In *Jones, S. M., ed.*, 1989, pp. 91–106.

Lashgari, Malek K. Information from Daily Closing Prices on the Tokyo Stock Exchange. *Keio Econ. Stud.,* 1989, *26*(2), pp. 17–23.

_____ **and Gant, David R.** Social Investing: The Sullivan Principles. *Rev. Soc. Econ.,* Spring 1989, *47*(1), pp. 74–83.

Laskar, Daniel. Conservative Central Bankers in a Two-Country World. *Europ. Econ. Rev.,* October 1989, *33*(8), pp. 1575–95.

Laski, Kazimierz and Brus, Wlodzimierz. Capital Market and the Problem of Full Employment. *Europ. Econ. Rev.,* March 1989, *33*(2/3), pp. 439–47.

Laslett, John H. M. State Policy towards Labour and Labour Organizations, 1830–1939: Anglo-American Union Movements. In *Mathias, P. and Pollard, S., eds.*, 1989, pp. 495–549.

Laslier, J. F. Développement des entreprises et évolution de la concurrence. (Development of Firms and Evolution of Competition. With English summary.) *Écon. Appl.,* 1989, *42*(3), pp. 155–70.

_____. Diffusion d'informations et évaluations séquentielles. (Diffusion of Information and Sequential Evaluations. With English summary.) *Écon. Appl.,* 1989, *42*(3), pp. 83–128.

_____ **and Lesourne, J.** Rendements croissants et dynamique d'un marché. (Market Dynamics

and Increasing Returns. With English summary.) *Écon. Appl.,* 1989, *42*(3), pp. 63–81.

Lass, Daniel A. and Weaver, Robert D. Corner Solutions in Duality Models: A Cross-Section Analysis of Dairy Production Decisions. *Amer. J. Agr. Econ.,* November 1989, *71*(4), pp. 1025–40.

Lassarre, Dominique and Roland-Lévy, Christine. Understanding Children's Economic Socialization. In *Grunert, K. G. and Ölander, F., eds.*, 1989, pp. 347–68.

Lassaut, B.; Nicolas, F. and Hy, M. Concurrence entre les formes industrielles et artisanales de production–distribution des biens alimentaires: Exemples de la boulangerie et de la boucherie. (Competition between Industrial and Artisanal Firms in Food Products Marketing: The Case of Butchers' and Bakers' Trade. With English summary.) *Écon. Societes,* July 1989, *23*(7), pp. 197–216.

Lasser, Dennis J. and Chiang, Raymond. Tax Timing Options on Futures Contracts and the 1981 Economic Recovery Act. *Financial Rev.,* February 1989, *24*(1), pp. 75–92.

Lasserre, Pierre and Dudley, Leonard. Information as a Substitute for Inventories. *Europ. Econ. Rev.,* January 1989, *33*(1), pp. 67–88.

Lassnigg, Lorenz. The "New Values" and Consumer Behaviour—Some Empirical Findings from Austria. In *Grunert, K. G. and Ölander, F., eds.*, 1989, pp. 333–45.

Lastrapes, William D. Exchange Rate Volatility and U.S. Monetary Policy: An ARCH Application. *J. Money, Credit, Banking,* February 1989, *21*(1), pp. 66–77.

_____ **and Koray, Faik.** Real Exchange Rate Volatility and U.S. Bilateral Trade: A VAR Approach. *Rev. Econ. Statist.,* November 1989, *71*(4), pp. 708–12.

Latham, Gary A. and Napier, Nancy K. Chinese Human Resource Management Practices in Hong Kong and Singapore: An Exploratory Study. In *Nedd, A., ed.*, 1989, pp. 173–99.

Latham, Mark. The Arbitrage Pricing Theory and Supershares. *J. Finance,* June 1989, *44*(2), pp. 263–81.

Latif, Muhammad Abdul. Towards an Estimation of Cloth Supply in Bangladesh: 1955/56–1986/87. *Bangladesh Devel. Stud.,* March–June 1989, *17*(1–2), pp. 23–56.

_____ **and Chowdhury, Nuimuddin.** Resource Allocation in Bangladesh Handloom Industry: A Production Function Approach. *Bangladesh Devel. Stud.,* March–June 1989, *17*(1–2), pp. 175–87.

Latorraca, Nilton and Barbuto, João Guilherme Marzagão. National Tax System—The 1988 Constitution: Brazil. *Bull. Int. Fiscal Doc.,* Aug.–Sept. 1989, *43*(8–9), pp. 394–98.

Latsis, Otto. The Threat to Restructuring. *Prob. Econ.,* March 1989, *31*(11), pp. 48–57.

_____. Why Are You Pushing? [Where Are the *Pirogi* Meatier?]. In *Jones, A. and Moskoff, W., eds.*, 1989, 1988, pp. 111–15.

Lau, Hon-Shiang and Wingender, John R. The Analytics of the Intervaling Effect on Skewness and Kurtosis of Stock Returns. *Financial Rev.*, May 1989, *24*(2), pp. 215–33.

Lau, Lawrence J. and Yotopoulos, Pan A. The Meta-production Function Approach to Technological Change in World Agriculture. *J. Devel. Econ.*, October 1989, *31*(2), pp. 241–69.

Lau, Man-Lui and Shea, Koon-Lam. A Choice Theoretic Model of the Kaldorian Growth: The Most Rapid Approach Path Analysis. *Hong Kong Econ. Pap.*, 1989, (19), pp. 43–47.

Lauer, Harrison; Ichniowski, Casey and Freeman, Richard B. Collective Bargaining Laws, Threat Effects, and the Determination of Police Compensation. *J. Lab. Econ.*, April 1989, 7(2), pp. 191–209.

Läufer, Nikolaus K. A. The Internationalization of Financial Markets and the Regulatory Response: Comments. **In** *Vosgerau, H.-J., ed.*, 1989, pp. 210–12.

_____. Makroökonomik einer neuen Geldangebotshypothese für die BRD. (Macroeconomic Aspects of a New Money Supply Hypothesis for the Federal Republic of Germany. With English summary.) *Kredit Kapital*, 1989, *22*(1), pp. 66–91.

Laughlan, Janet. Technological Change and Economic Theory: Review Article. *Scot. J. Polit. Econ.*, August 1989, *36*(3), pp. 311–14.

Laumann, Edward O. and Knoke, David. Policy Networks of the Organizational State: Collective Action in the National Energy and Health Domains. **In** *Perrucci, R. and Potter, H. R., eds.*, 1989, pp. 17–55.

Laumas, Gurcharan S. Anticipated Federal Budget Deficits, Monetary Policy and the Rate of Interest. *Southern Econ. J.*, October 1989, *56*(2), pp. 375–82.

Laumas, Prem S. An International Comparison of the Savings Function. *Indian Econ. J.*, July–Sept. 1989, *37*(1), pp. 91–96.

_____ **and Williams, Martin.** The Demand for Working Capital: A Reply. *Appl. Econ.*, January 1989, *21*(1), pp. 139–40.

Laurence, Martin; Ghosh, Arabinda and Kolodny, Richard. In Search of Excellence...for Whom? *J. Portfol. Manage.*, Spring 1989, *15*(3), pp. 56–60.

Lauria, Alma. New Rules in Labour Organization: The "Bunsha" System. *Rivista Int. Sci. Econ. Com.*, February 1989, *36*(2), pp. 155–63.

_____. The Position of Women in Japanese Economy and Society. *Rivista Int. Sci. Econ. Com.*, December 1989, *36*(12), pp. 1141–49.

Lauszus, Dieter and Fishback, Price V. The Quality of Services in Company Towns: Sanitation in Coal Towns during the 1920s. *J. Econ. Hist.*, March 1989, *49*(1), pp. 125–44.

Lauterbach, Beni. Consumption Volatility, Production Volatility, Spot-Rate Volatility, and the Returns on Treasury Bills and Bonds. *J. Finan. Econ.*, September 1989, *24*(1), pp. 155–79.

_____ **and Monroe, Margaret.** Evidence on the Effect of Information and Noise Trading on Intraday Gold Futures Returns. *J. Futures Markets*, August 1989, *9*(4), pp. 297–305.

Laux-Meiselbach, Wolfgang. A Note on Import Substitution versus Export Promotion as Strategies for Development. *Kyklos*, 1989, *42*(2), pp. 219–29.

LaVange, Lisa; Williams, Rick L. and Folsom, Ralph. A Probability Sampling Perspective on Panel Data Analysis. **In** *Kasprzyk, D., et al., eds.*, 1989, pp. 108–38.

Lave, Charles. Speeding, Coordination, and the 55-MPH Limit: Reply. *Amer. Econ. Rev.*, September 1989, *79*(4), pp. 926–31.

Lave, Judith R. and Frank, Richard G. A Comparison of Hospital Responses to Reimbursement Policies for Medicaid Psychiatric Patients. *Rand J. Econ.*, Winter 1989, *20*(4), pp. 588–600.

Lave, Lester B. Lead as a Public Health Problem: Is It Overestimated? *J. Health Econ.*, June 1989, *8*(2), pp. 247–50.

_____ **and Gruenspecht, Howard K.** The Economics of Health, Safety, and Environmental Regulation. **In** *Schmalensee, R. and Willig, R. D., eds., Vol. 2*, 1989, pp. 1507–50.

Lavergne, David R.; Vandeveer, Lonnie R. and Paxton, Kenneth W. Irrigation and Potential Diversification Benefits in Humid Climates. *Southern J. Agr. Econ.*, December 1989, *21*(2), pp. 167–74.

Lavers, R. J. Prescription Charges, the Demand for Prescriptions and Morbidity. *Appl. Econ.*, August 1989, *21*(8), pp. 1043–52.

Lavigne, A. Banque centrale, banques de second rang et crédibilité de la politique monétaire. Une analyse stratégique de la nouvelle régulation par les taux d'intérêt en France. (The Central Bank, Commercial Banks and the Credibility of Monetary Policy. With English summary.) *Écon. Societes*, April–May 1989, *23*(4–5), pp. 111–32.

Lavigne, Marie. A Note on Market Socialism. *Acta Oecon.*, 1989, *40*(3–4), pp. 251–53.

Lavoie, Don. Economic Chaos or Spontaneous Order? Implications for Political Economy of the New View of Science. *Cato J.*, Winter 1989, *8*(3), pp. 613–35.

Lavoie, Marc; Grenier, Gilles and Coulombe, Serge. Discrimination versus English Proficiency in the National Hockey League: A Reply. *Can. Public Policy*, March 1989, *15*(1), pp. 98–101.

_____ **and Seccareccia, Mario.** Les idées révolutionnaires de Keynes en politique économique et le déclin du capitalisme rentier. (The Keynesian Revolution in the Theory of Economic Policy and the Twilight of Rentiers Capitalism. With English summary.) *Écon. Appl.*, 1989, *42*(1), pp. 47–70.

Law, C. K. Forum on the Negative Interest Rate Scheme. *Hong Kong Econ. Pap.*, 1989, (19), pp. 75–78.

Law, Peter J. and Ireland, Norman J. Dynamic Allocation in a Labor-Managed Firm: Comment. *J. Compar. Econ.*, June 1989, *13*(2), pp. 335–37.

LaWare, John P. Statement to the U.S. Senate Subcommittee on Consumer and Regulatory Affairs of the Committee on Banking, Housing, and Urban Affairs, October 24, 1989. *Fed. Res. Bull.*, December 1989, 75(12), pp. 790–95.

Lawarrée, Jacques. Collusion et audit d'entreprises publiques. (Collusion and Audit of Public Enterprises. With English summary.) *Ann. Pub. Coop. Econ.*, 1989, 60(2), pp. 217–27.

Lawler, Edward E., III. Strategic Choices for Changing Organizations. In *Mohrman, A. M., Jr., et al.*, 1989, pp. 255–71.

Lawler, Eugene L. Combinatorial Structures and Combinatorial Optimization. In *Simeone, B., ed.*, 1989, pp. 162–97.

Lawler, James J. and Parle, William M. Expansion of the Public Trust Doctrine in Environmental Law: An Examination of Judicial Policy Making by State Courts. *Soc. Sci. Quart.*, March 1989, 70(1), pp. 134–48.

Lawler, John J.; Zaidi, Mahmood A. and Atmiyanandana, Vinita. Human Resource Strategies in Southeast Asia: The Case of Thailand. In *Nedd, A., ed.*, 1989, pp. 201–21.

Lawler, P. Exchange Rate Effects of an Oil Discovery in a Three-Country Model. *Brit. Rev. Econ. Issues*, Summer 1989, 11(25), pp. 89–113.

Lawless, J. F. and Dean, C. Tests for Detecting Overdispersion in Poisson Regression Models. *J. Amer. Statist. Assoc.*, June 1989, 84(406), pp. 467–72.

Lawniczak, Brandon David. Substantiating "Competitive Disadvantage" Claims: A Broad Reading of *Truitt. Mich. Law Rev.*, June 1989, 87(7), pp. 2026–55.

Lawrence, Colin. Banking Costs, Generalized Functional Forms, and Estimation of Economies of Scale and Scope. *J. Money, Credit, Banking*, August 1989, 21(3), pp. 368–79.

Lawrence, Denis. An Aggregator Model of Canadian Export Supply and Import Demand Responsiveness. *Can. J. Econ.*, August 1989, 22(3), pp. 503–21.

Lawrence, Edward C.; Kummer, Donald R. and Arshadi, Nasser. Incentive Problems in Bank Insider Borrowing. *J. Finan. Services Res.*, October 1989, 3(1), pp. 17–31.

Lawrence, Geoffrey. The Rural Crisis Downunder: Australia's Declining Fortunes in the Global Farm Economy. In *Goodman, D. and Redclift, M., eds.*, 1989, pp. 234–74.

Lawrence, Helen H. Trends in Private Pension Plans. In *Turner, J. A. and Beller, D. J., eds.*, 1989, pp. 69–93.

Lawrence, Mark, et al. Seasonal Pattern of Activity and Its Nutritional Consequence in Gambia. In *Sahn, D. E., ed.*, 1989, pp. 47–56.

Lawrence, Paul R. Why Organizations Change. In *Mohrman, A. M., Jr., et al.*, 1989, pp. 48–61.

Lawrence, Peter. Management Education in West Germany. In *Byrt, W., ed.*, 1989, pp. 151–71.

Lawrence, Philip K. The State and Legitimation: The Work of Jürgen Habermas. In *Duncan, G., ed.*, 1989, pp. 133–58.

Lawrence, Robert Z. A Depressed View of Policies for Depressed Industries. In *Stern, R. M., ed.*, 1989, pp. 174–208.

———. Protection: Is There a Better Way? *Amer. Econ. Rev.*, May 1989, 79(2), pp. 118–22.

———. Strengthening Japan–U.S. Cooperation and the Concept of Japan–U.S. Free Trade Arrangements: Comments. In *Schott, J. J., ed.*, 1989, pp. 131–35.

———. Symposium on Europe 1992: Comments. *Brookings Pap. Econ. Act.*, 1989, (2), pp. 368–73.

——— **and Bosworth, Barry P.** America in the World Economy. In *Bosworth, B. P., et al.*, 1989, pp. 49–70.

——— **and Bosworth, Barry P.** America's Global Role: From Dominance to Interdependence. In *Steinbruner, J. D., ed.*, 1989, pp. 12–47.

——— **and Schultze, Charles L.** Barriers to European Growth: Overview. In *Jacquemin, A. and Sapir, A., eds.*, 1989, pp. 251–97.

———; **Schultze, Charles L. and Litan, Robert E.** Improving American Living Standards. In *Bosworth, B. P., et al.*, 1989, pp. 29–48.

Lawson, Colin W. Undergraduate Economics Education in English and Welsh Universities. *J. Econ. Educ.*, Fall 1989, 20(4), pp. 391–404.

Lawson, Nigel. Energy Policy. In *Helm, D.; Kay, J. and Thompson, D., eds.*, 1989, pp. 23–29.

———. The State of the Market. In *Johnson, C., ed.*, 1989, pp. 26–36.

Lawson, T. L. and Pendleton, John W. Climatic Variability and Sustainability of Crop Yields in the Humid Tropics. In *Oram, P. A., et al.*, 1989, pp. 57–68.

Lawson, Tony. Abstraction, Tendencies and Stylised Facts: A Realist Approach to Economic Analysis. *Cambridge J. Econ.*, March 1989, 13(1), pp. 59–78.

———. Abstraction, Tendencies and Stylised Facts: A Realist Approach to Economic Analysis. In *Lawson, T.; Palma, J. G. and Sender, J., eds.*, 1989, pp. 59–78.

———. Realism and Instrumentalism in the Development of Econometrics. In *de Marchi, N. and Gilbert, C., eds.*, 1989, pp. 236–58.

———. Realism and Instrumentalism in the Development of Econometrics. *Oxford Econ. Pap.*, January 1989, 41(1), pp. 236–58.

———; **Palma, J. Gabriel and Sender, John.** Kaldor's Contribution to Economics: An Introduction. *Cambridge J. Econ.*, March 1989, 13(1), pp. 1–8.

Lawson, Victoria A. and Brown, Lawrence A. Polarization Reversal, Migration Related Shifts in Human Resource Profiles, and Spatial Growth Policies: A Venezuelan Study. *Int. Reg. Sci. Rev.*, 1989, 12(2), pp. 165–88.

Layard, Richard. The Duration of Unemployment: Theory and Evidence: Comment. In *Holmlund, B.; Löfgren, K.-G. and Engström, L.*, 1989, pp. 221–26.

——— **and Bean, Charles R.** Why Does Unemployment Persist? *Scand. J. Econ.*, 1989, 91(2), pp. 371–96.

——— **and Nickell, Stephen J.** The Thatcher Miracle? *Amer. Econ. Rev.*, May 1989, 79(2), pp. 215–19.

_____; Pissarides, Christopher A. and Jackman, R. On Vacancies. *Oxford Bull. Econ. Statist.*, November 1989, *51*(4), pp. 377–94.

Layne, Christopher. NATO and the Next Administration. In *Crane, E. H. and Boaz, D.*, 1989, pp. 147–66.

Layton, Allan P. and Moore, Geoffrey H. Leading Indicators for the Service Sector. *J. Bus. Econ. Statist.*, July 1989, *7*(3), pp. 379–86.

Lazar, Fred. Airline Deregulation: A Footnote on the Missing Entrants. *Australian Econ. Pap.*, December 1989, *28*(53), pp. 246–52.

_____. Antidumping Rules Following the Canada–United States Free Trade Agreement. *J. World Trade*, October 1989, *23*(5), pp. 45–71.

Lazear, Edward P. Pay Equality and Industrial Politics. *J. Polit. Econ.*, June 1989, *97*(3), pp. 561–80.

_____. The Timing of Retirement: A Comparison of Expectations and Realizations: Comment. In *Wise, D. A., ed.*, 1989, pp. 356–58.

Le Bas, Christian. La stratégie d'automatisation de la PME: Réflexions à partir d'études de cas. (The Automation Strategy and the Small and Medium Firm: The Implications of Some Experiences. With English summary.) *Écon. Societes*, January 1989, *23*(1), pp. 165–85.

Le Breton, Michel. A Note on Balancedness and Nonemptiness of the Core in Voting Games. *Int. J. Game Theory*, 1989, *18*(1), pp. 111–17.

_____ and Bordes, Georges. Arrovian Theorems with Private Alternatives Domains and Selfish Individuals. *J. Econ. Theory*, April 1989, *47*(2), pp. 257–81.

Le Franc, Elsie. Socio-economic Determinants of Health Status. *Soc. Econ. Stud.*, June 1989, *38*(2), pp. 291–305.

Le Masne, Pierre. La structure des échanges extérieurs dans une approche entrées-sorties: La France et ses voisins européens. (With English summary.) *Revue Écon. Politique*, Nov.–Dec. 1989, *99*(6), pp. 835–53.

Le Nay, Jean and Mathis, Jean. The Impact of Drought on the National Accounts for Livestock in Sahelian Countries. *Rev. Income Wealth*, June 1989, *35*(2), pp. 209–24.

Le Pera, Sergio and Lessa, Pedro. The Disregard of a Legal Entity for Tax Purposes: Argentina. In *International Fiscal Association, ed. (II)*, 1989, pp. 157–68.

Le Roux, Yves. Threshold Price, Expected Price and Aggregation of Micro markets. In *Bauer, S. and Henrichsmeyer, W., eds.*, 1989, pp. 233–51.

Lea, Michael J. and Zorn, Peter M. Mortgage Borrower Repayment Behavior: A Microeconomic Analysis with Canadian Adjustable Rate Mortgage Data. *Amer. Real Estate Urban Econ. Assoc. J.*, Spring 1989, *17*(1), pp. 118–36.

Leach, Jim. Third World Debt: The Next Phase: Perspectives of Politicians. In *Fried, E. R. and Trezise, P. H., eds.*, 1989, pp. 84–88.

Leach, John. Liquidity-Constrained Employment Contracts. *J. Econ. Dynam. Control*, April 1989, *13*(2), pp. 255–69.

Leach, Melissa and Chambers, Robert. Trees as Savings and Security for the Rural Poor. *World Devel.*, March 1989, *17*(3), pp. 329–42.

Leal, Donald R. and Anderson, Terry L. Building Coalitions for Water Marketing. *J. Policy Anal. Manage.*, Summer 1989, *8*(3), pp. 432–45.

Leamer, Edward E. Planning, Criticism, and Revision. *J. Appl. Econometrics*, Supplement, December 1989, *4*, pp. S5–27.

Leary, Ed. Expert Systems at the Social Security Administration. *J. Policy Anal. Manage.*, Spring 1989, *8*(2), pp. 201–03.

Leary, Neil A. and Thornton, Judith. Are Socialist Industries Inoculated against Innovation? A Case Study of Technological Change in Steelmaking. *Comp. Econ. Stud.*, Summer 1989, *31*(2), pp. 42–65.

Leathers, Charles G. Scotland's New Poll Taxes as Hayekian Policy. *Scot. J. Polit. Econ.*, May 1989, *36*(2), pp. 194–201.

_____. Thorstein Veblen's Theories of Governmental Failure: The Critic of Capitalism and Democracy Neglected Some Useful Insights, Hindsight Shows. *Amer. J. Econ. Sociology*, July 1989, *48*(3), pp. 293–306.

Leatherwood, Marya L. and Conlon, Edward J. Sunk Costs and Financial Decision Making: Integration and Implications. In *Lee, C. F., ed.*, 1989, pp. 37–61.

Lebailly, Philippe. Filières agro-industrielles et développement: Le cas de la viande bovine dans les pays sahéliens. (With English summary.) *Can. J. Devel. Stud.*, 1989, *10*(1), pp. 61–73.

LeBaron, Blake and Scheinkman, José A. Nonlinear Dynamics and GNP Data. In *Barnett, W. A.; Geweke, J. and Shell, K., eds.*, 1989, pp. 213–27.

_____ and Scheinkman, José A. Nonlinear Dynamics and Stock Returns. *J. Bus.*, July 1989, *62*(3), pp. 311–37.

LeBlanc, Michael R.; Swamy, P. A. V. B. and Conway, Roger K. The Stochastic Coefficients Approach to Econometric Modeling, Part III: Estimation, Stability Testing, and Prediction. *J. Agr. Econ. Res.*, Winter 1989, *41*(1), pp. 4–20.

Leboutte, René. Passing through a Minefield: International Comparisons of 19th-Century Wages. In *Scholliers, P., ed.*, 1989, pp. 140–42.

Lebreton, Sophie. Crises et mutations spatiales: Un cadre pour l'analyse de l'expérience française de décentralisation. (Crisis and Spatial Changes: A Framework for Decentralization Process. The French Experience. With English summary.) *Écon. Societes*, February 1989, *23*(2), pp. 161–88.

Lecaillon, Jacques and Grangeas, Geneviève. Cycles courts et cycles longs de la répartition (France, 1820–1985). (Short and Long Cycles of Income Distribution [France, 1820–1985]. With English summary.) *Écon. Societes*, March 1989, *23*(3), pp. 106–27.

Leclercq, Vincent. Aims and Constraints of the Brazilian Agro-industrial Strategy: The Case of

Soya. In *Goodman, D. and Redclift, M., eds.*, 1989, pp. 275–91.

Lecocq, Alfred. Disposal of Fissile Material from Nuclear Weapons. In *Altmann, J. and Rotblat, J., eds.*, 1989, pp. 60–67.

Lecraw, Donald J. Management of Countertrade. In *Rugman, A. M., ed.*, 1989, pp. 68–85.

_____. Third World Multinationals in the Service Industries. In *Enderwick, P.*, 1989, pp. 200–212.

Leddin, Anthony. Efficiency in the Forward Exchange Market: An Application of Co-integration: A Comment. *Econ. Soc. Rev.*, April 1989, *20*(3), pp. 281–85.

Ledent, J. and Liaw, K-L. Provincial Out-Migration Patterns of Canadian Elderly: Characterization and Explanation. *Environ. Planning A*, August 1989, *21*(8), pp. 1093–1111.

Ledford, Gerald E., Jr.; Mohrman, Allan M., Jr. and Mohrman, Susan Albers. What We Have Learned about Large-Scale Organizational Change: Conclusion. In *Mohrman, A. M., Jr., et al.*, 1989, pp. 292–302.

_____; **Mohrman, Susan Albers and Mohrman, Allan M., Jr.** Interventions That Change Organizations. In *Mohrman, A. M., Jr., et al.*, 1989, pp. 145–53.

_____, **Jr., et al.** The Phenomenon of Large-Scale Organizational Change. In *Mohrman, A. M., Jr., et al.*, 1989, pp. 1–31.

Ledić, Michèle. The Energy Sector. In *Goodman, D. S. G., ed.*, 1989, pp. 94–111.

Ledolter, Johannes. Adaptive Estimation and Structural Change in Regression and Time Series Models. In *Hackl, P., ed.*, 1989, pp. 191–208.

_____. The Effect of Additive Outliers on the Forecasts from ARIMA Models. *Int. J. Forecasting*, 1989, *5*(2), pp. 231–40.

Leduc, Robert F. and Block, Stephen R. Conjoint Directorship: Clarifying Management Roles between the Board of Directors and the Executive Director. In *Herman, R. D. and Van Til, J., eds.*, 1989, pp. 67–76.

Ledyard, John O. Information Aggregation in Two-Candidate Elections. In *Ordeshook, P. C., ed.*, 1989, pp. 7–30.

_____; **Porter, David P. and Banks, Jeffrey S.** Allocating Uncertain and Unresponsive Resources: An Experimental Approach. *Rand J. Econ.*, Spring 1989, *20*(1), pp. 1–25.

Lee, Barbara A. The Economics of Comparable Worth: Theoretical Consideration: Discussion. In *Hill, M. A. and Killingsworth, M. R., eds.*, 1989, pp. 54–56.

_____ **and Chelius, James.** Government Regulation of Labor–Management Corruption: The Casino Industry Experience in New Jersey. *Ind. Lab. Relat. Rev.*, July 1989, *42*(4), pp. 536–48.

Lee, Barrett A. Stability and Change in an Urban Homeless Population. *Demography*, May 1989, *26*(2), pp. 323–34.

Lee, Bong-Soo. A Nonlinear Expectations Model of the Term Structure of Interest Rates with Time-Varying Risk Premia. *J. Money, Credit, Banking*, August 1989, *21*(3), pp. 348–67.

_____. Solving, Estimating, and Testing a Nonlinear Stochastic Equilibrium Model, with an Example of the Asset Returns and Inflation Relationship. *J. Econ. Dynam. Control*, October 1989, *13*(4), pp. 499–531.

Lee, Bradford A. The Miscarriage of Necessity and Invention: Proto-Keynesianism and Democratic States in the 1930s. In *Hall, P. A., ed.*, 1989, pp. 129–70.

Lee, Catherine and Robinson, Bill. Can Household Surveys Help Explain the Fall in the Savings Ratio? *Fisc. Stud.*, August 1989, *10*(3), pp. 60–71.

Lee, Cheng Few and Bubnys, Edward L. Linear and Generalized Functional Form Market Models for Electric Utility Firms. *J. Econ. Bus.*, August 1989, *41*(3), pp. 213–23.

_____ **and Hu, Sheng-Cheng.** Advances in Financial Planning and Forecasting: Introduction. In *Lee, C. F. and Hu, S.-C., eds.*, 1989, pp. 1–7.

_____ **and Lynge, Morgan J., Jr.** Financial Ratio Comparison of Savings and Loan Associations and Commercial Banks. In *Lee, C. F., ed.*, 1989, pp. 195–229.

_____; **Wei, K. C. John and Bubnys, Edward L.** The APT versus the Multi-factor CAPM: Empirical Evidence. *Quart. Rev. Econ. Bus.*, Winter 1989, *29*(4), pp. 6–25.

_____ **and Wu, Chunchi.** Using Zellner's Errors-in-Variables Model to Reexamine MM's Valuation Model for the Electric Utility Industry. In *Lee, C. F., ed.*, 1989, pp. 63–73.

Lee, Chi-Wen Jevons and Petruzzi, Christopher R. Inventory Accounting Switch and Uncertainty. *J. Acc. Res.*, Autumn 1989, *27*(2), pp. 277–96.

Lee, Christine and Lodewijks, John. Recent Economic Developments in the Papua New Guinea Economy. In *Lodewijks, J. and Zerby, J., eds.*, 1989, pp. 30–49.

_____; **Lodewijks, John and Mahony, Greg.** Recent Developments in the Fijian Economy. In *Lodewijks, J. and Zerby, J., eds.*, 1989, pp. 50–66.

Lee, Chul Song and Lim, Hee Taek. The Disregard of a Legal Entity for Tax Purposes: Republic of Korea. In *International Fiscal Association, ed. (II)*, 1989, pp. 463–71.

Lee, Chung H. and Ramstetter, Eric D. Trade in Services and Returns on Foreign Direct Investment. *Weltwirtsch. Arch.*, 1989, *125*(2), pp. 375–85.

Lee, David Kuo Chuen and Gan, Chin Lee. An Economic Analysis of Fertility, Market Participation and Marriage Behaviour in Recent Japan. *Appl. Econ.*, January 1989, *21*(1), pp. 59–68.

_____ **and Gan, Chin Lee.** Corrigendum [An Economic Analysis of Fertility, Market Participation and Marriage Behaviour in Recent Japan]. *Appl. Econ.*, June 1989, *21*(6), pp. 740.

Lee, Dwight R. Ideology and the Economic Role

of Government. In *Samuels, W. J., ed. (I)*, 1989, pp. 123–30.

_____. The Impossibility of a Desirable Minimal State. *Public Choice*, June 1989, *61*(3), pp. 277–84.

_____. Less Than Unanimous Agreement on the Reason for Unanimous Agreement: Comment. *Public Choice*, July 1989, *62*(1), pp. 83–87.

_____. Special Interest Inefficiency: A Case for or against Government Spending Limits? *Soc. Sci. Quart.*, September 1989, *70*(3), pp. 765–71.

_____ and Buchanan, James M. Vote Buying in a Stylized Setting. In *Buchanan, J. M. (II)*, 1989, pp. 116–28.

_____ and Kreutzer, David W. Up-Cheating: Explaining OPEC's Apparent Stability in the 1970s. *J. Energy Devel.*, Autumn 1989, *15*(1), pp. 1–7.

_____ and McKenzie, Richard B. The International Political Economy of Declinging Tax Rates. *Nat. Tax J.*, March 1989, *42*(1), pp. 79–83.

_____ and Sandler, Todd. On the Optimal Retaliation against Terrorists: The Paid-Rider Option. *Public Choice*, May 1989, *61*(2), pp. 141–52.

_____; Sexton, Robert L. and Graves, Philip E. Statutes versus Enforcement: The Case of the Optimal Speed Limit. *Amer. Econ. Rev.*, September 1989, *79*(4), pp. 932–36.

Lee, Edward G. and Fraser, Douglas G. The Rationale and Future Directions of Canada's Oceans Policy: International Dimensions. In *McRae, D. and Munro, G., eds.*, 1989, pp. 238–52.

Lee, Eric Youngkoo. The Persistent U.S. External Imbalance: Its Causes and Policy Message. *Amer. Economist*, Spring 1989, *33*(1), pp. 28–35.

Lee, Feng-Yao. Exports and Taiwan's Economic Growth. In *Lee, C. F. and Hu, S.-C., eds.*, 1989, pp. 119–37.

Lee, Frederic S. D. H. MacGregor and the Firm: A Neglected Chapter in the History of the Post Keynesian Theory of the Firm. *Brit. Rev. Econ. Issues*, Spring 1989, *11*(24), pp. 21–47.

_____; Milberg, William and Groves, Miles. The Power of Ideas and the Impact of One Man, Alfred Eichner 1937–1988. *J. Post Keynesian Econ.*, Spring 1989, *11*(3), pp. 491–96.

Lee, Hak Chong. Managerial Characteristics of Korean Firms. In *Chung, K. H. and Lee, H. C., eds.*, 1989, pp. 147–62.

_____ and Chung, Kae H. National Differences in Managerial Practices. In *Chung, K. H. and Lee, H. C., eds.*, 1989, pp. 163–80.

Lee, Hee-Yeon. Growth Determinants in the Core–Periphery of Korea. *Int. Reg. Sci. Rev.*, 1989, *12*(2), pp. 147–63.

Lee, Insup and Fry, Clifford L. OSHA Sanctions and the Value of the Firm. *Financial Rev.*, November 1989, *24*(4), pp. 599–610.

_____ and Schweitzer, Robert. Shareholder Wealth Effects of Interstate Banking: The Case of Delaware's Financial Center Development

Act. *J. Finan. Services Res.*, June 1989, *2*(2), pp. 65–72.

Lee, Jonq-Ying. Effect of Sociodemographics on At-Home Red Meat Consumption in the United States. In *Buse, R. C., ed.*, 1989, pp. 243–55.

_____ and Brown, Mark G. Consumer Demand for Food Diversity. *Southern J. Agr. Econ.*, December 1989, *21*(2), pp. 47–53.

Lee, Kangoh and Brueckner, Jan K. Club Theory with a Peer-Group Effect. *Reg. Sci. Urban Econ.*, August 1989, *19*(3), pp. 399–420.

Lee, Kye Sik. Migration, Income and Fertility in Malaysia: A Simultaneous Equations Model with Limited Dependent Variables. *Appl. Econ.*, December 1989, *21*(12), pp. 1589–1610.

Lee, Kyu Sik. Location of Jobs in Developing Cities. *Finance Devel.*, December 1989, *26*(4), pp. 44–46.

Lee, Kyubang and Haurin, Donald R. A Structural Model of the Demand for Owner-Occupied Housing. *J. Urban Econ.*, November 1989, *26*(3), pp. 348–60.

Lee, Kyung W. and Rejda, George E. State Unemployment Compensation Programs: Immediate Reforms Needed. *J. Risk Ins.*, December 1989, *56*(4), pp. 649–69.

Lee, Moon H. and Bishara, Halim. Recent Canadian Experience on the Profitability of Insider Trades. *Financial Rev.*, May 1989, *24*(2), pp. 235–49.

Lee, Myung-Soo and Mittal, Banwari. A Causal Model of Consumer Involvement. *J. Econ. Psych.*, November 1989, *10*(3), pp. 363–89.

Lee, Philip R. and Estes, Carroll L. Toward National Health Insurance. In *Eisdorfer, C.; Kessler, D. A. and Spector, A. N., eds.*, 1989, pp. 137–51.

Lee, Robert H. Insurance and Medical List Prices. *J. Human Res.*, Fall 1989, *24*(4), pp. 689–708.

Lee, Ronald D. and Wachter, Kenneth W. U.S. Births and Limit Cycle Models. *Demography*, February 1989, *26*(1), pp. 99–115.

Lee, Russell and Das, Sujit. Changes in Business-as-Usual Forecasts in a Petroleum Trade Model. *Energy Econ.*, January 1989, *11*(1), pp. 11–32.

Lee, Sang M. Management Styles of Korean Chaebols. In *Chung, K. H. and Lee, H. C., eds.*, 1989, pp. 181–92.

Lee, T. H. and Granger, C. W. J. Investigation of Production, Sales and Inventory Relationships Using Multicointegration and Non-symmetric Error Correction Models. *J. Appl. Econometrics*, Supplement, December 1989, *4*, pp. S145–59.

Lee, Tenpao; Kim, Tae-Kyun and Baumel, C. Phillip. Impact of Deregulation on the Financial Performance of the Class I Railroads: Errata. *Logist. Transp. Rev.*, March 1989, *25*(1), pp. 91–94.

Lee, Wonsick; Meindl, James R. and Hunt, Raymond G. Individualism–Collectivism and Work Values: Data from the United States,

China, Taiwan, Korea, and Hong Kong. In *Nedd, A., ed.*, 1989, pp. 59–77.

Lee, Y. An Allometric Analysis of the U.S. Urban System: 1960–80. *Environ. Planning A*, April 1989, *21*(4), pp. 463–76.

Lee, Young Sun. A Study of the Determinants of Intra-industry Trade among the Pacific Basin Countries. *Weltwirtsch. Arch.*, 1989, *125*(2), pp. 346–58.

Leeds, Michael A. Government Debt, Immigration, and Durable Public Goods. *Public Finance Quart.*, April 1989, *17*(2), pp. 227–35.

Leeds, Roger S. Malaysia: Genesis of Privatization Transaction. *World Devel.*, May 1989, *17*(5), pp. 741–56.

van de Leemput, Cécile; Mubikangiey, Luc and Salengros, Pierre. Psychological and Sociological Perspectives on Precarious Employment in Belgium. In *Rodgers, G. and Rodgers, J., eds.*, 1989, pp. 197–223.

Leen, A. R. Böhm-Bawerk's Goods Characteristics Reactivated for Modern Austrians. *J. Econ. Stud.*, 1989, *16*(2), pp. 109–20.

Leeson, Robert; Wood, Gavin and Avenell, Simon. Measuring Exchange Rate Uncertainty: The Case of the Australian Dollar 1969 to 1987. *Australian Econ. Rev.*, Winter 1989, (86), pp. 34–42.

Leeth, John D.; Borg, J. Rody and Borg, Mary O'Malley. The Success of Mergers in the 1920s: A Stock Market Appraisal of the Second Merger Wave. *Int. J. Ind. Organ.*, Special Issue, March 1989, *7*(1), pp. 117–31.

———— **and Kniesner, Thomas J.** Can We Make OSHA and Workers' Compensation Insurance Interact More Effectively in Promoting Workplace Safety? In *Ehrenberg, R. G., ed.*, 1989, pp. 1–51.

———— **and Kniesner, Thomas J.** Separating the Reporting Effects from the Injury Rate Effects of Workers' Compensation Insurance: A Hedonic Simulation. *Ind. Lab. Relat. Rev.*, January 1989, *42*(2), pp. 280–93.

———— **and Scott, Jonathan A.** The Incidence of Secured Debt: Evidence from the Small Business Community. *J. Finan. Quant. Anal.*, September 1989, *24*(3), pp. 379–94.

de Leeuw, Frank. Aggregate U.S. Private Saving: Conceptual Measures and Empirical Tests: Comment. In *Lipsey, R. E. and Tice, H. S., eds.*, 1989, pp. 223–26.

————. Leading Indicators and the "Prime Mover" View. *Surv. Curr. Bus.*, August 1989, *69*(8), pp. 23–29.

de Leeuw, Jan; van Montfort, Kees and Mooijaart, Ab. Estimation of Regression Coefficients with the Help of Characteristic Functions. *J. Econometrics*, June 1989, *41*(2), pp. 267–78.

van Leeuwen, E. H.; Hoen, H. W. and Lanjouw, G. J. Eastern Europe's Participation in the International Financial System. *Jahr. Wirtsch. Osteuropas*, 1989, *13*(2), pp. 41–65.

Lefebvre, O.; Michelot, C. and Idrissi, H. Applications and Numerical Convergence of the Partial Inverse Method. In *Dolecki, S., ed.*, 1989, pp. 39–54.

Leff, Nathaniel H. Economic Development through Bureaucratic Corruption. In *Heidenheimer, A. J.; Johnston, M. and LeVine, V. T., eds.*, 1989, *1964*, pp. 389–403.

————. Flow-of-Funds and National Income and Product Account Savings Estimates in Latin America: Comment. In *Lipsey, R. E. and Tice, H. S., eds.*, 1989, pp. 180–83.

———— **and Sato, Kazuo.** Modelling the Demand for Foreign Savings in Developing Countries: Testing a Hypothesis with Latin American Data. *J. Devel. Stud.*, July 1989, *25*(4), pp. 537–49.

Lefoll, J. and Calvet, A. L. Risk and Return on Canadian Capital Markets: Seasonality and Size Effect. *Finance*, June 1989, *10*(1), pp. 21–39.

Lefrançois, Pierre. Allowing for Asymmetry in Forecast Errors: Results from a Monte-Carlo Study. *Int. J. Forecasting*, 1989, *5*(1), pp. 99–110.

————. Confidence Intervals for Non-stationary Forecast Errors: Some Empirical Results for the Series in the M-Competition. *Int. J. Forecasting*, 1989, *5*(4), pp. 553–57.

Legg, Wilfrid and Cahill, Carmel. Estimation of Agricultural Assistance Using Producer and Consumer Subsidy Equivalents: Theory and Practice. *OECD Econ. Stud.*, Winter 1989–1990, (13), pp. 13–43.

Leggett, Jeremy. A Comprehensive Test-Ban Verification Regime: Implications of Cooperative Measures in INF and START. In *Rotblat, J. and Goldanskii, V. I., eds.*, 1989, pp. 14–21.

————. Recent Developments and Outlook for the Verification of a Nuclear Test Ban. In *Altmann, J. and Rotblat, J., eds.*, 1989, pp. 86–98.

Lehmann, Bruce N. Volatility, Price Resolution, and the Effectiveness of Price Limits: Commentary. *J. Finan. Services Res.*, December 1989, *3*(2–3), pp. 205–09.

————. Volatility, Price Resolution, and the Effectiveness of Price Limits: Commentary. In *Edwards, F. R., ed.*, 1989, pp. 107–11.

Lehn, Kenneth and Poulsen, Annette B. Free Cash Flow and Stockholder Gains in Going Private Transactions. *J. Finance*, July 1989, *44*(3), pp. 771–87.

Lehrer, Ehud. Lower Equilibrium Payoffs in Two-Player Repeated Games with Non-observable Actions. *Int. J. Game Theory*, 1989, *18*(1), pp. 57–89.

———— **and Einy, Ezra.** Regular Simple Games. *Int. J. Game Theory*, 1989, *18*(2), pp. 195–207.

Lehrman, Lewis E. Back to Gold: Giving Up the "Order of the Jungle." In *Guttmann, R., ed.*, 1989, *1986*, pp. 290–99.

Lei, L. F. and Epperson, J. E. A Regional Analysis of Vegetable Production with Changing Demand for Row Crops Using Quadratic Programming. *Southern J. Agr. Econ.*, July 1989, *21*(1), pp. 87–96.

Leibenstein, Harvey. Allocative Efficiency vs. "X-Efficiency." In *Leibenstein, H., Vol. 2*, 1989, *1966*, pp. 3–26.

_____. An Interpretation of the Economic Theory of Fertility: Promising Path or Blind Alley? In *Leibenstein, H., Vol. 1*, 1989, *1974*, pp. 34–56.

_____. Aspects of the X-Efficiency Theory of the Firm. In *Leibenstein, H., Vol. 2*, 1989, *1975*, pp. 33–59.

_____. Bandwagon, Snob, and Veblen Effects in the Theory of Consumers' Demand. In *Leibenstein, H., Vol. 2*, 1989, *1950*, pp. 93–117.

_____. A Branch of Economics Is Missing: Micro–Micro Theory. In *Leibenstein, H., Vol. 2*, 1989, *1979*, pp. 67–92.

_____. Comment on Inert Areas and the Definition of X-Efficiency. In *Leibenstein, H., Vol. 2*, 1989, *1974*, pp. 340–42.

_____. Comment on the Nature of X-Efficiency. In *Leibenstein, H., Vol. 2*, 1989, *1972*, pp. 370–74.

_____. Competition and X-Efficiency: Reply. In *Leibenstein, H., Vol. 2*, 1989, *1973*, pp. 327–39.

_____. Economic Decision Theory and Human Fertility Behavior: A Speculative Essay. In *Leibenstein, H., Vol. 1*, 1989, *1981*, pp. 57–76.

_____. The Economic Theory of Fertility Decline. In *Leibenstein, H., Vol. 1*, 1989, *1975*, pp. 3–33.

_____. Efficiency Wages, X-Efficiency, and Urban Unemployment. In *Leibenstein, H., Vol. 2*, 1989, *1974*, pp. 280–97.

_____. Entrepreneurship and Development. In *Leibenstein, H., Vol. 1*, 1989, *1968*, pp. 247–58.

_____. Entrepreneurship, Entrepreneurial Training, and X-Efficiency Theory. In *Leibenstein, H., Vol. 2*, 1989, *1987*, pp. 243–57.

_____. The Impact of Population Growth on Economic Welfare—Nontraditional Elements. In *Leibenstein, H., Vol. 1*, 1989, *1971*, pp. 79–102.

_____. The Impact of Population Growth on the American Economy. In *Leibenstein, H., Vol. 1*, 1989, *1972*, pp. 118–30.

_____. Incremental Capital–Output Ratios and Growth Rates in the Short Run. In *Leibenstein, H., Vol. 1*, 1989, *1966*, pp. 277–84.

_____. The Inflation Process: A Micro-behavioral Analysis. In *Leibenstein, H., Vol. 2*, 1989, *1981*, pp. 274–79.

_____. The Japanese Management System: An X-Efficiency–Game Theory Analysis. In *Leibenstein, H., Vol. 2*, 1989, *1984*, pp. 161–87.

_____. The Kibbutz: Motivations, Hierarchy and Efficiency. In *Leibenstein, H., Vol. 1*, 1989, pp. 231–43.

_____. Long-Run Welfare Criteria. In *Leibenstein, H., Vol. 1*, 1989, *1965*, pp. 348–60.

_____. Notes on Welfare Economics and the Theory of Democracy. In *Leibenstein, H., Vol. 1*, 1989, *1962*, pp. 327–47.

_____. On Relaxing the Maximization Postulate. In *Leibenstein, H., Vol. 2*, 1989, *1985*, pp. 142–57.

_____. On the Basic Proposition of X-Efficiency Theory. In *Leibenstein, H., Vol. 2*, 1989, *1978*, pp. 60–64.

_____. On the Economics of Conventions and Institutions: An Exploratory Essay. In *Leibenstein, H., Vol. 2*, 1989, *1984*, pp. 261–73.

_____. Organizational Economics and Institutions as Missing Elements in Economic Development Analysis. *World Devel.*, Special Issue, September 1989, *17*(9), pp. 1361–73.

_____. Organizational or Frictional Equilibria, X-Efficiency, and the Rate of Innovation. In *Leibenstein, H., Vol. 2*, 1989, *1969*, pp. 118–41.

_____. Population Growth and the Take-Off Hypothesis. In *Leibenstein, H., Vol. 1*, 1989, *1963*, pp. 103–17.

_____. The Prisoners' Dilemma in the Invisible Hand: An Analysis of Intrafirm Productivity. In *Leibenstein, H., Vol. 2*, 1989, *1982*, pp. 188–93.

_____. Property Rights and X-Efficiency: Comment. In *Leibenstein, H., Vol. 2*, 1989, *1983*, pp. 352–63.

_____. The Proportionality Controversy and the Theory of Production. In *Leibenstein, H., Vol. 1*, 1989, *1955*, pp. 317–23.

_____. Some Notes on Economic Development Planning and the Rate of Interest under Multiple Sovereignties. In *Leibenstein, H., Vol. 1*, 1989, *1970*, pp. 214–30.

_____. Technical Progress, the Production Function, and Development. In *Leibenstein, H., Vol. 1*, 1989, *1963*, pp. 285–300.

_____. Technical Progress, the Production Function and Dualism. In *Leibenstein, H., Vol. 1*, 1989, *1960*, pp. 301–16.

_____. The Theory of Underemployment in Backward Economies. In *Leibenstein, H., Vol. 1*, 1989, *1957*, pp. 201–13.

_____. What Can We Expect from a Theory of Development? In *Leibenstein, H., Vol. 1*, 1989, *1966*, pp. 133–54.

_____. Why Do We Disagree on Investment Policies for Development? In *Leibenstein, H., Vol. 1*, 1989, *1958*, pp. 155–72.

_____. X-Efficiency, Intrafirm Behavior, and Growth. In *Leibenstein, H., Vol. 2*, 1989, *1980*, pp. 194–211.

_____. X-Efficiency, Technical Efficiency, and Incomplete Information Use: A Comment. In *Leibenstein, H., Vol. 2*, 1989, *1977*, pp. 364–69.

_____. X-Efficiency Theory, Conventional Entrepreneurship, and Excess Capacity Creation in LDCs. In *Leibenstein, H., Vol. 2*, 1989, *1977*, pp. 231–42.

_____. X-Efficiency Theory, Productivity and Growth. In *Leibenstein, H., Vol. 2*, 1989, *1981*, pp. 298–323.

_____. X-Inefficiency Xists—Reply to an Xorcist. In *Leibenstein, H., Vol. 2*, 1989, *1978*, pp. 343–51.

_____ **and Comanor, William S.** Allocative Efficiency, X-Efficiency and the Measurement of Welfare Losses. In *Leibenstein, H., Vol. 2*, 1989, *1969*, pp. 27–32.

_____ **and Galenson, Walter.** Investment Criteria, Productivity, and Economic Development.

In *Leibenstein, H., Vol. 1*, 1989, *1955*, pp. 173–200.

_____ and **Kaufmann, Patrick J.** International Business Format Franchising and Retail Entrepreneurship: A Possible Source of Retail Know-How for Developing Countries. In *Leibenstein, H., Vol. 1*, 1989, pp. 259–73.

_____ and **Weiermair, Klaus.** X-Efficiency, Managerial Discretion, and the Nature of Employment-Relations: A Game-Theoretical Approach. In *Leibenstein, H., Vol. 2*, 1989, *1988*, pp. 212–27.

Leibowitz, Martin L. and **Langetieg, Terence C.** Shortfall Risk and the Asset Allocation Decision: A Simulation Analysis of Stock and Bond Risk Profiles. *J. Portfol. Manage.*, Fall 1989, *16*(1), pp. 61–68.

Leiderman, Leonardo. Economic Adjustment and Exchange Rates in LDC's: A Review Essay. *J. Monet. Econ.*, July 1989, *24*(1), pp. 147–55.

Leidy, Michael P. The Theory of International Economic Sanctions—A Public Choice Approach: Comment. *Amer. Econ. Rev.*, December 1989, *79*(5), pp. 1300–1303.

_____ and **Hoekman, Bernard M.** Dumping, Antidumping and Emergency Protection. *J. World Trade*, October 1989, *23*(5), pp. 27–44.

Leigh, J. Paul. Compensating Wages for Job-Related Death: The Opposing Arguments. *J. Econ. Issues*, September 1989, *23*(3), pp. 823–42.

_____ and **Berger, Mark C.** Schooling, Self-Selection, and Health. *J. Human Res.*, Summer 1989, *24*(3), pp. 433–55.

Leigh-Pemberton, Robin. Europe 1992: Some Monetary Policy Issues. In *Federal Reserve Bank of Kansas City*, 1989, pp. 175–82.

Leigh, Wilhelmina A. Federal Government Policies and the "Housing Quotient" of Black American Families. *Rev. Black Polit. Econ.*, Winter 1989, *17*(3), pp. 25–42.

Leighton, Linda S. and **Evans, David S.** Some Empirical Aspects of Entrepreneurship. *Amer. Econ. Rev.*, June 1989, *79*(3), pp. 519–35.

_____ and **Evans, David S.** Why Do Smaller Firms Pay Less? *J. Human Res.*, Spring 1989, *24*(2), pp. 299–318.

Leigland, James. Selling Bonds Worldwide. In *Matzer, J., Jr., ed.*, 1989, *1988*, pp. 148–55.

Leijonhufvud, A. Hicks on Time and Money. In *Wood, J. C. and Woods, R. N., eds., Vol. 4*, 1989, *1984*, pp. 70–90.

_____. Review of *Economic Perspectives: Further Essays on Money and Growth* by Sir John Hicks. In *Wood, J. C. and Woods, R. N., eds., Vol. 3*, 1989, *1979*, pp. 183–86.

Leinbach, Thomas R. and **Cromley, Robert G.** Modeling Integrated Development Investments in Rural Areas: An Indonesian Illustration. *Int. Reg. Sci. Rev.*, 1989, *12*(2), pp. 229–43.

Leiner, Frederick C. American Service of Process upon Foreign Corporations: The Schlunk Case and Beyond. *J. World Trade*, February 1989, *23*(1), pp. 37–46.

_____. American Service of Process upon Foreign Corporations: The Schlunk Case and Beyond. *J. World Trade*, February 1989, *23*(1), pp. 37–46.

Leininger, Wolfgang. Escalation and Cooperation in Conflict Situations: The Dollar Auction Revisited. *J. Conflict Resolution*, June 1989, *33*(2), pp. 231–54.

_____; **Linhart, Peter B.** and **Radner, Roy.** Equilibria of the Sealed-Bid Mechanism for Bargaining with Incomplete Information. *J. Econ. Theory*, June 1989, *48*(1), pp. 63–106.

Leipert, Christian. National Income and Economic Growth: The Conceptual Side of Defensive Expenditures. *J. Econ. Issues*, September 1989, *23*(3), pp. 843–56.

_____ and **Simonis, Udo Ernst.** Environmental Protection Expenditures: The German Example. *Rivista Int. Sci. Econ. Com.*, March 1989, *36*(3), pp. 255–70.

Leipziger, Danny M. and **Petri, Peter A.** Korean Incentive Policies towards Industry and Agriculture. In *Williamson, J. G. and Panchamukhi, V. R., eds.*, 1989, pp. 167–89.

Leiser, Burton M. Ethics and Equity in the Securities Market. In *Williams, O. F.; Reilly, F. K. and Houck, J. W., eds.*, 1989, pp. 149–74.

Leistikow, Dean. Announcements and Futures Price Variability. *J. Futures Markets*, December 1989, *9*(6), pp. 477–86.

Leite, António P. N. Precommitment and Allocative Efficiency in Long Term Projects. *Economia (Portugal)*, January 1989, *13*(1), pp. 1–16.

_____. Rent Extraction and Efficiency in Long Term Procurement. *Economia (Portugal)*, May 1989, *13*(2), pp. 215–31.

Leitzel, Jim. Damage Measures and Incomplete Contracts. *Rand J. Econ.*, Spring 1989, *20*(1), pp. 92–101.

_____. The New Institutional Economics and a Model of Contract. *J. Econ. Behav. Organ.*, January 1989, *11*(1), pp. 75–89.

Leland, Hayne E. Saving and Uncertainty: The Precautionary Demand for Saving. In *Diamond, P. and Rothschild, M., eds.*, 1989, *1968*, pp. 129–37.

Lele, Uma J. Managing Agricultural Development in Africa. *Finance Devel.*, March 1989, *26*(1), pp. 45–48.

_____. Sources of Growth in East African Agriculture. *World Bank Econ. Rev.*, January 1989, *3*(1), pp. 119–44.

_____ and **Goldsmith, Arthur A.** The Development of National Agricultural Research Capacity: India's Experience with the Rockefeller Foundation and Its Significance for Africa. *Econ. Devel. Cult. Change*, January 1989, *37*(2), pp. 305–43.

Lemaire, B. and **Lemaire-Misonne, C.** An Optimization Problem with a Piecewise Linear Objective and Conditional Threshold Constraints. Solution by Partitioning. In *Dolecki, S., ed.*, 1989, pp. 87–98.

Lemaire-Misonne, C. and **Lemaire, B.** An Optimization Problem with a Piecewise Linear

Objective and Conditional Threshold Constraints. Solution by Partitioning. In *Dolecki, S., ed.*, 1989, pp. 87–98.

Lemaitre, N.; Khrouz, F. and Vlasselaer, M. Secteur de l'Audit: Analyse structurelle et identification des avantages concurrentiels. (With English summary.) *Cah. Écon. Bruxelles*, 3rd Trimester 1989, (123), pp. 311–27.

Leman, Christopher K. The Forgotten Fundamental: Successes and Excesses of Direct Government. In *Salamon, L. M., ed.*, 1989, pp. 51–92.

Lemelin, André. Les déterminants des dépenses de fonctionnement de l'enseignement collégial public au Québec. (With English summary.) *L'Actual. Econ.*, June 1989, 65(2), pp. 208–30.

Lemieux, Catharine M. and Wohlgenant, Michael K. Ex Ante Evaluation of the Economic Impact of Agricultural Biotechnology: The Case of Porcine Somatotropin. *Amer. J. Agr. Econ.*, November 1989, 71(4), pp. 903–14.

Lemin, A. J. Patenting Microorganisms: Threats to Openness. In *Weil, V. and Snapper, J. W., eds.*, 1989, pp. 193–99.

Lemke, Christiane. Political Socialization and the "Micromilieu." In *Rueschemeyer, M. and Lemke, C., eds.*, 1989, pp. 59–73.

——— **and Rueschemeyer, Marilyn.** The Quality of Life in the German Democratic Republic: Conclusion. In *Rueschemeyer, M. and Lemke, C., eds.*, 1989, pp. 228–35.

Lemoine, Jacques. Ethnicity, Culture and Development among Some Minorities of the People's Republic of China. In *Chiao, C. and Tapp, N., eds.*, 1989, pp. 1–9.

Lemov, Penelope. The Municipal Bond Market after Tax Reform. In *Matzer, J., Jr., ed.*, 1989, 1988, pp. 135–47.

Lenel, Hans Otto. Does Germany Still Have a Social Market Economy? In *Peacock, A. and Willgerodt, H., eds. (II)*, 1989, 1971, pp. 261–72.

———. Evolution of the Social Market Economy. In *Peacock, A. and Willgerodt, H., eds. (I)*, 1989, pp. 16–39.

Lengyel, L. Market Economy without Any Attributes. *Acta Oecon.*, 1989, 40(3–4), pp. 253–56.

Lensink, Robert and Garretsen, Harry. International Policy Coordination and European Wage Rigidity. *De Economist*, 1989, 137(1), pp. 76–90.

Lentz, Bernard F. and Laband, David N. Why So Many Children of Doctors Become Doctors: Nepotism vs. Human Capital Transfers. *J. Human Res.*, Summer 1989, 24(3), pp. 396–413.

Lentz, George H. and Fisher, Jeffrey D. Tax Reform and Organizational Forms for Holding Investment Real Estate: Corporation vs. Partnership. *Amer. Real Estate Urban Econ. Assoc. J.*, Fall 1989, 17(3), pp. 314–37.

Lenz, Allen. Slimming the U.S. Trade and Current Account Deficits: How It Will—and Won't—Occur. In *[Marjolin, R.]*, 1989, pp. 21–41.

Lenz, Hansrudi. Urteilsbegründung bei betriebs-

wirtschaftlichen Prüfungen. Indirekte Prüfungen als statistische Begründung rationaler Erwartungen. (With English summary.) *Z. Betriebswirtschaft*, December 1989, 59(12), pp. 1353–66.

Lenz, Ilse and Aydin, Shahizer. Fighting Plant Closure: Women in the Strike at Videocolor. In *Elson, D. and Pearson, R., eds.*, 1989, pp. 165–82.

Leo, Elaine Stahl. Working Part-Time in Male Professions: Social-Psychological Costs and Benefits Reported by Thirty American Women with Families. In *Agassi, J. B. and Heycock, S., eds.*, 1989, pp. 207–26.

Leon, Hyginus. Econometric Modelling: A Methodological Interlude. *Soc. Econ. Stud.*, June 1989, 38(2), pp. 185–213.

Leonard, Carol S. Agrarian Organization in the Century of Industrialization: Europe, Russia, and North America: Postscript. In *Grantham, G. and Leonard, C. S., eds., Pt. B*, 1989, pp. 507–14.

———. The Distribution of Land and Agricultural Output in Non-blackearth Russia on the Eve of Emancipation (Maloga Uezd). In *Grantham, G. and Leonard, C. S., eds., Pt. B*, 1989, pp. 353–68.

Leonard, Daniel. Market Behavior of Rational Addicts. *J. Econ. Psych.*, March 1989, 10(1), pp. 117–44.

Leonard, H. Jeffrey. Environment and the Poor: Development Strategies for a Common Agenda. In *Leonard, H. J., ed.*, 1989, pp. 3–45.

Leonard, Jonathan S. Wage Structure and Dynamics in the Electronics Industry. *Ind. Relat.*, Spring 1989, 28(2), pp. 251–75.

———. Women and Affirmative Action. *J. Econ. Perspectives*, Winter 1989, 3(1), pp. 61–75.

Leonard, Tom; Hsu, John S. J. and Tsui, Kam-Wah. Bayesian Marginal Inference. *J. Amer. Statist. Assoc.*, December 1989, 84(408), pp. 1051–58.

Leone, Robert A. Curriculum and Case Notes. *J. Policy Anal. Manage.*, Fall 1989, 8(4), pp. 704–11.

Leong, Avon K. Liability Rules when Injurers as Well as Victims Suffer Losses. *Int. Rev. Law Econ.*, June 1989, 9(1), pp. 105–111.

Leong, Siew Meng. A Citation Analysis of the *Journal of Consumer Research*. *J. Cons. Res.*, March 1989, 15(4), pp. 492–97.

Leont'eva, E. Social Conflict. *Prob. Econ.*, December 1989, 32(8), pp. 19–34.

Leontief, Wassily. Input–Output Data Base for Analysis of Technological Change. *Econ. Systems Res.*, 1989, 1(3), pp. 287–95.

Lepage, Henri. Countering the Climate of Growing Protectionism: The Need for Free Trade. In *Nieuwenhuysen, J., ed.*, 1989, pp. 13–31.

Lepkowski, James M. Treatment of Wave Nonresponse in Panel Surveys. In *Kasprzyk, D., et al., eds.*, 1989, pp. 348–74.

———; **Traugott, Michael W. and Groves, Robert M.** Using Dual Frame Designs to Reduce Nonresponse in Telephone Surveys. In *Singer,*

E. and Presser, S., eds., 1989, *1987*, pp. 79–96.

Leppel, Karen. Determinants of the Value of the Mother's Time: Evidence from a Developing Country. *Amer. Economist*, Spring 1989, *33*(1), pp. 61–68.

_____ **and Clain, Suzanne Heller.** Fringe Benefits and the Effect of Tax Reform. *Appl. Econ.*, May 1989, *21*(5), pp. 681–95.

Lequesne, Christian; Mayor Lopez, Pedro and Hayes-Renshaw, Fiona. The Permanent Representations of the Member States to the European Communities. *J. Common Market Stud.*, December 1989, *28*(2), pp. 119–37.

Lerman, Donald L. and Lerman, Robert I. Income Sources and Income Inequality: Measurements from Three U.S. Income Surveys. *J. Econ. Soc. Meas.*, 1989, *15*(2), pp. 167–79.

Lerman, Robert I. Employment Opportunities of Young Men and Family Formation. *Amer. Econ. Rev.*, May 1989, *79*(2), pp. 62–66.

_____ **and Lerman, Donald L.** Income Sources and Income Inequality: Measurements from Three U.S. Income Surveys. *J. Econ. Soc. Meas.*, 1989, *15*(2), pp. 167–79.

_____ **and Yitzhaki, Shlomo.** Improving the Accuracy of Estimates of Gini Coefficients. *J. Econometrics*, September 1989, *42*(1), pp. 43–47.

Lerner, A. P. Professor Hicks' Dynamics. **In** *Wood, J. C. and Woods, R. N., eds., Vol. 1,* 1989, *1940*, pp. 28–34.

Lerner, A. Ya. Empirical Data-Based Procedure for Optimal Decision Making. *Math. Soc. Sci.*, December 1989, *18*(3), pp. 291–95.

Lerner, Miri. Paternalism and Entrepreneurship: The Emergence of State-Made Entrepreneurs. *J. Behav. Econ.*, Fall 1989, *18*(3), pp. 149–66.

Lerohl, M. L. and Dunlop, D. M. The Impact of Transport Cost Shifts on Production and Welfare in the Prairie Grains Industry. *Can. J. Agr. Econ.*, Part 2, December 1989, *37*(4), pp. 1251–63.

LeRoy, Stephen F. Efficient Capital Markets and Martingales. *J. Econ. Lit.*, December 1989, *27*(4), pp. 1583–1621.

Leruth, Luc and Chander, Parkash. The Optimal Product Mix for a Monopolist in the Presence of Congestion Effects: A Model and Some Results. *Int. J. Ind. Organ.*, December 1989, *7*(4), pp. 437–49.

_____ **and de Palma, André.** Congestion and Game in Capacity: A Duopoly Analysis in the Presence of Network Externalities. *Ann. Écon. Statist.*, July–Dec. 1989, (15–16), pp. 389–407.

Lesage, Alain. Liaisons inter-industrielles et compétitivité régionale: Éléments d'analyse. (Inter-sectoral Linkages and Regional Competitiveness: Methodological Hints. With English summary.) *Écon. Appl.*, 1989, *42*(4), pp. 67–86.

Lesage, James P. Incorporating Regional Wage Relations in Local Forecasting Models with a Bayesian Prior. *Int. J. Forecasting*, 1989, *5*(1), pp. 37–47.

_____ **and Reed, J. David.** The Dynamic Relationship between Export, Local, and Total Area

Employment. *Reg. Sci. Urban Econ.*, December 1989, *19*(4), pp. 615–36.

_____ **and Reed, J. David.** Interregional Wage Transmission in an Urban Hierarchy: Tests Using Vector Autoregressive Models. *Int. Reg. Sci. Rev.*, 1989, *12*(3), pp. 305–18.

Lesourne, J. L'entreprise en lutte sur deux fronts. (The Two Fighting Fronts of the Firm. With English summary.) *Écon. Appl.*, 1989, *42*(3), pp. 195–202.

_____. L'état des recherches sur l'ordre et le désordre en micro-économie. (A Survey of Research on Order and Disorder in Micro-economics. With English summary.) *Écon. Appl.*, 1989, *42*(3), pp. 11–39.

_____. A propos d'un apologue militaire: Le rôle des personnalités dans un processus historique. (About a Military Story: The Part Played by Personalities in a Historical Process. With English summary.) *Écon. Appl.*, 1989, *42*(3), pp. 203–17.

_____ **and Laslier, J. F.** Rendements croissants et dynamique d'un marché. (Market Dynamics and Increasing Returns. With English summary.) *Écon. Appl.*, 1989, *42*(3), pp. 63–81.

_____; **Lévy, B. and Compte, O.** La formation endogène d'un syndicat sur le marché du travial. (The Endogenous Forming of a Union on a Labour Market. With English summary.) *Écon. Appl.*, 1989, *42*(3), pp. 171–94.

Lessa, Pedro and Le Pera, Sergio. The Disregard of a Legal Entity for Tax Purposes: Argentina. **In** *International Fiscal Association, ed. (II),* 1989, pp. 157–68.

Lessard, Donald R. Beyond the Debt Crisis: Alternative Forms of Financing Growth. **In** *Husain, I. and Diwan, I., eds.,* 1989, pp. 294–306.

_____. Country Risk and the Structure of International Financial Intermediation. **In** *Stone, C. C., ed.,* 1989, pp. 197–227.

_____. Financial Risk Management Needs of Developing Countries: Discussion. *Amer. J. Agr. Econ.*, May 1989, *71*(2), pp. 534–35.

_____ **and Modigliani, Franco.** Inflation and the Housing Market: Problems and Potential Solutions. **In** *Modigliani, F., Vol. 5,* 1989, *1975,* pp. 257–73.

Lesser, Jonathan A. The Economics of Preference Power. **In** *Zerbe, R. O., ed.,* 1989, pp. 131–51.

Lessig, Lawrence. Plastics: Unger and Ackerman on Transformation. *Yale Law J.*, April 1989, *98*(6), pp. 1173–92.

Lester, Michael; Elek, Andrew and Camilleri, Arthur. Innovation and Technological Change in Australia: Problems and Prospects. **In** *[Gruen, F. H.],* 1989, pp. 190–209.

Lesuis, P. J. J. Potentials of Sector Models. **In** *Muller, F. and Zwezerijnen, W. J., eds.,* 1989, pp. 197–223.

Lettman, Amy. Disabling Injuries in Longshore Operations. *Mon. Lab. Rev.*, October 1989, *112*(10), pp. 37–38.

Letwin, Shirley Robin. The Morality of Democracy and the Rule of Law. In *Brennan, G. and Lomasky, L. E., eds.*, 1989, pp. 221–34.

Letwin, William. American Economic Policy, 1865–1939. In *Mathias, P. and Pollard, S., eds.*, 1989, pp. 641–90.

Leube, Kurt R. Social Policy: Hayek and Schmoller Compared. *Int. J. Soc. Econ.*, 1989, *16*(9–10–11), pp. 106–16.

Leuck, Dale and Kelch, David. Political and Economic Factors Influencing Agricultural Policy Reform in the European Community and the United States. *Can. J. Agr. Econ.*, Part 2, December 1989, *37*(4), pp. 1181–91.

Leuthold, Jane H. and Husby, Ralph D. Horizontal Equity and Taxpayer Characteristics: Who Is Advantaged and Disadvantaged by the Federal Income Tax? *Eastern Econ. J.*, Jan.–March 1989, *15*(1), pp. 35–44.

Leuthold, Raymond M., et al. An Examination of the Necessary and Sufficient Conditions for Market Efficiency: The Case of Hogs. *Appl. Econ.*, February 1989, *21*(2), pp. 193–204.

Leutz, Walter N.; Altman, Stuart H. and Greenberg, Jay N. The Social Health Maintenance Organization. In *Eisdorfer, C.; Kessler, D. A. and Spector, A. N., eds.*, 1989, pp. 197–223.

Lev, Baruch. On the Usefulness of Earnings and Earnings Research: Lessons and Directions from Two Decades of Empirical Research. *J. Acc. Res.*, Supplement, 1989, *27*, pp. 153–92.

Lev, Larry; Emami, Ali and Martin, Michael V. United States Agricultural Trade: Where Are the Gains? Comment. *Western J. Agr. Econ.*, December 1989, *14*(2), pp. 310–12.

Levasseur, Michel and Ginglinger, Edith. Déductibilité des dividendes versés aux actions nouvelles, décisions de financement et valeur le la firme. (Tax Deductible Dividends, Financing Decisions and the Value of the Firm. With English summary.) *Écon. Societes*, January 1989, *23*(1), pp. 73–84.

Levcik, Friedrich. Economic Reforms in Czechoslovakia. In *Gabrisch, H., ed.*, 1989, pp. 111–23.

———. Innovation and Structural Adjustment in East and West. In *Berliner, J. S.; Kosta, H. G. J. and Hakogi, M., eds.*, 1989, pp. 7–13.

Leven, Charles L. Cycles, Convergence and Interregional Adjustment. In *van Dijk, J., et al., eds.*, 1989, pp. 47–58.

Leventakis, John A. and Brissimis, Sophocles N. The Effectiveness of Devaluation: A General Equilibrium Assessment with Reference to Greece. *J. Policy Modeling*, Summer 1989, *11*(2), pp. 247–71.

Lever, Harold. The Dollar and the World Economy: The Case for Concerted Management. In *Johnson, C., ed.*, 1989, pp. 139–50.

Lever, W. F. International Comparative Aspects of Government Intervention in Local Economic Policy. In *Gibbs, D., ed.*, 1989, pp. 209–31.

Levesque, Benoît. Les cooperatives au Quebec. Un secteur stratégique, à la recherche d'un projet pour l'an 2000. (The Cooperatives in Quebec, a Strategic Sector on the Trail of a Plan for the Year 2000. With English summary.) *Ann. Pub. Coop. Econ.*, 1989, *60*(2), pp. 181–215.

Levhari, David and Keren, Michael. Decentralization, Aggregation, Control Loss and Costs in a Hierarchical Model of the Firm. *J. Econ. Behav. Organ.*, March 1989, *11*(2), pp. 213–36.

Levi, Danilo and Canak, William L. Social Costs of Adjustment in Latin America. In *Weeks, J. F., ed.*, 1989, pp. 143–63.

Levi, Isaac. The Paradoxes of Allais and Ellsberg: Reply. *Econ. Philos.*, April 1989, *5*(1), pp. 79–90.

Levi, Maurice D.; Goldberg, Michael A. and Helsley, Robert W. The Location of International Financial Activity: An Interregional Analysis. *Reg. Stud.*, February 1989, *23*(1), pp. 1–7.

Levi, Steven C. Labor History and Alaska. *Labor Hist.*, Fall 1989, *30*(4), pp. 595–607.

Levich, Richard M. Is the Foreign Exchange Market Efficient? *Oxford Rev. Econ. Policy*, Autumn 1989, *5*(3), pp. 40–60.

——— **and Walter, Ingo.** The Regulation of Global Financial Markets. In *Noyelle, T., ed.*, 1989, pp. 51–89.

Levin, Dan; Dyer, Douglas and Kagel, John H. A Comparison of Naive and Experienced Bidders in Common Value Offer Auctions: A Laboratory Analysis. *Econ. J.*, March 1989, *99*(394), pp. 108–15.

——— **; Dyer, Douglas and Kagel, John H.** Resolving Uncertainty about the Number of Bidders in Independent Private-Value Auctions: An Experimental Analysis. *Rand J. Econ.*, Summer 1989, *20*(2), pp. 268–79.

Levin, Harvey J. Regulating the Global Commons: A Case Study. In *Zerbe, R. O., ed.*, 1989, pp. 247–66.

Levin, Henry M. Economics of Investment in Educationally Disadvantaged Students. *Amer. Econ. Rev.*, May 1989, *79*(2), pp. 52–56.

——— **and Tsang, Mun C.** The Economics of Overeducation: Reply. *Econ. Educ. Rev.*, 1989, *8*(2), pp. 209.

Levin, Jay H. On the Dynamic Effects of Monetary and Fiscal Policy under Floating Exchange Rates: Simulations with an Asset Market Model. *Weltwirtsch. Arch.*, 1989, *125*(4), pp. 665–80.

Levin, Lawrence and Bernheim, B. Douglas. Social Security and Personal Saving: An Analysis of Expectations. *Amer. Econ. Rev.*, May 1989, *79*(2), pp. 97–102.

Levin, M. Youth and Labor: Reflections of Sociologists and a Journalist. In *Yanowitch, M., ed.*, 1989, *1983*, pp. 203–17.

Levin, Richard C. and Cohen, Wesley M. Empirical Studies of Innovation and Market Structure. In *Schmalensee, R. and Willig, R. D., eds., Vol. 2*, 1989, pp. 1059–1107.

Levin, Stanford L. Measuring Competition for IntraLATA Services. In *National Economic Research Associates*, 1989, pp. 51–61.

Levine, Daniel B.; Horowitz, Stanley A. and

Levy, Brian. Foreign Aid in the Making of Economic Policy in Sri Lanka, 1977–1983. *Policy Sciences,* November 1989, *22*(3–4), pp. 437–61.

_____. Public Enterprises and the Transfer of Technology in the Ammonia Industry. In *James, J., ed.,* 1989, pp. 170–93.

Levy, Daniel. Evaluating Private Institutions: The Case of Latin American Higher Education. In *James, E., ed.,* 1989, pp. 84–109.

Levy, David M. Equilibrium Employment of Inputs by a Rent-Seeking Firm. *Public Choice,* February 1989, *60*(2), pp. 177–84.

_____. The Statistical Basis of Athenian–American Constitutional Theory. *J. Legal Stud.,* January 1989, *18*(1), pp. 79–103.

_____ **and Terleckyj, Nestor E.** Problems Identifying Returns to R&D in an Industry. *Managerial Dec. Econ.,* Special Issue, Spring 1989, pp. 43–49.

_____; **Tollison, Robert D. and Anderson, Gary M.** The Half-Life of Dead Economists. *Can. J. Econ.,* February 1989, *22*(1), pp. 174–83.

Levy, David T. Firm Entry and Postentry Performance in the U.S. Chemical Industries: Comment. *J. Law Econ.,* Part 2, October 1989, *32*(2), pp. S273–75.

_____. Predation, Firm-Specific Assets and Diversification. *J. Ind. Econ.,* December 1989, *38*(2), pp. 227–33.

_____ **and Asch, Peter.** Speeding, Coordination, and the 55-MPH Limit: Comment. *Amer. Econ. Rev.,* September 1989, *79*(4), pp. 913–15.

_____ **and Reiffen, David.** Vertical Integration in a Spatial Setting: Implications of the Successive Monopoly Distortion. *Econ. Letters,* 1989, *29*(1), pp. 77–81.

Lévy, Dominique and Duménil, Gérard. The Competitive Process in a Fixed Capital Environment: A Classical View. *Manchester Sch. Econ. Soc. Stud.,* March 1989, *57*(1), pp. 34–57.

_____ **and Duménil, Gérard.** Labor Values and the Imputation of Labor Contents. *Metroecon.,* June 1989, *40*(2), pp. 159–78.

_____ **and Duménil, Gérard.** Les métamorphoses du cycle industriel. L'exemple des Etats-Unis. (The Foundations of the Business Cycle, the Case of the United States. With English summary.) *Écon. Societes,* March 1989, *23*(3), pp. 75–106.

_____ **and Duménil, Gérard.** The Real and Financial Determinants of Stability: The Law of the Tendency toward Increasing Instability. In *Semmler, W., ed.,* 1989, pp. 87–115.

Levy, Doug E.; Golden, Bruce L. and Wasil, Edward A. Applications of the Analytic Hierarchy Process: A Categorized, Annotated Bibliography. In *Golden, B. L.; Wasil, E. A. and Harker, P. T., eds.,* 1989, pp. 37–58.

_____ **and Lewis, Robert.** Predicting a National Acid Rain Policy. In *Golden, B. L.; Wasil, E. A. and Harker, P. T., eds.,* 1989, pp. 155–70.

Levy, Edmond and Nobay, A. Robert. On the Bivariate Analysis of Speculative Efficiency in Forward Markets. In *MacDonald, R. and Taylor, M. P., eds.,* 1989, pp. 197–217.

Levy, Frank. Recent Trends in U.S. Earnings and Family Incomes. In *Blanchard, O. J. and Fischer, S., eds.,* 1989, pp. 73–113.

Levy, Haim. Two-Moment Decision Models and Expected Utility Maximization: Comment. *Amer. Econ. Rev.,* June 1989, *79*(3), pp. 597–600.

_____ **and Brooks, Robert.** An Empirical Analysis of Term Premiums Using Stochastic Dominance. *J. Banking Finance,* May 1989, *13*(2), pp. 245–60.

_____ **and Broske, Mary S.** The Stochastic Dominance Estimation of Default Probability. In *[Hadar, J.],* 1989, pp. 91–112.

_____ **and Kroll, Yoram.** Investment, Capital Structure and Cost of Capital: Revisited. In *[Hadar, J.],* 1989, pp. 201–24.

_____; **Livingston, Miles and Brooks, Robert.** The Coupon Effect on Term Premiums. *J. Finan. Res.,* Spring 1989, *12*(1), pp. 15–21.

_____ **and Simon, Julian L.** A Generalization That Makes Useful the Dorfman–Steiner Theorem with Respect to Advertising. *Managerial Dec. Econ.,* March 1989, *10*(1), pp. 85–87.

_____ **and Yoder, James A.** Applying the Black–Scholes Model after Large Market Shocks. *J. Portfol. Manage.,* Fall 1989, *16*(1), pp. 103–06.

Levy, Kenneth N. and Jacobs, Bruce I. The Complexity of the Stock Market. *J. Portfol. Manage.,* Fall 1989, *16*(1), pp. 19–27.

Levy, Peter B. The Waterfront Commission of the Port of New York: A History and Appraisal. *Ind. Lab. Relat. Rev.,* July 1989, *42*(4), pp. 508–23.

Levy, Santiago. Export Subsidies and the Balance of Trade. *J. Devel. Econ.,* July 1989, *31*(1), pp. 99–121.

Levy, Victor and Newman, John L. Wage Rigidity: Micro and Macro Evidence on Labor Market Adjustment in the Modern Sector. *World Bank Econ. Rev.,* January 1989, *3*(1), pp. 97–117.

Lewandowski, Andrzej and Wierzbicki, Andrzej P. Decision Support Systems Using Reference Point Optimization. In *Lewandowski, A. and Wierzbicki, A. P., eds.,* 1989, pp. 3–20.

_____, **et al.** Decision Support Systems of DIDAS Family (Dynamic Interactive Decision Analysis and Support). In *Lewandowski, A. and Wierzbicki, A. P., eds.,* 1989, pp. 21–47.

Lewbel, Arthur. A Demand System Rank Theorem. *Econometrica,* May 1989, *57*(3), pp. 701–05.

_____. Exact Aggregation and a Representative Consumer. *Quart. J. Econ.,* August 1989, *104*(3), pp. 621–33.

_____. A Globally Concave, Symmetric, Flexible Cost Function. *Econ. Letters,* December 1989, *31*(3), pp. 211–14.

_____. Household Equivalence Scales and Welfare Comparisons. *J. Public Econ.,* August 1989, *39*(3), pp. 377–91.

_____. Identification and Estimation of Equivalence Scales under Weak Separability. *Rev. Econ. Stud.*, April 1989, *56*(2), pp. 311–16.

_____. Nesting the AIDS and Translog Demand System. *Int. Econ. Rev.*, May 1989, *30*(2), pp. 349–56.

_____. A Path-Independent Divisia-Like Index for PIGLOG Preferences. *Economica*, February 1989, *56*(221), pp. 121–23.

Lewellen, Wilbur; Loderer, Claudio F. and Rosenfeld, Ahron. Mergers, Executive Risk Reduction, and Stockholder Wealth. *J. Finan. Quant. Anal.*, December 1989, *24*(4), pp. 459–72.

Lewin, David. Models of Man in Industrial Relations Research: Discussion. Why Psychology Is Not the Sine Qua Non. *Ind. Lab. Relat. Rev.*, October 1989, *43*(1), pp. 89–92.

Lewin, Marion Ein and Sullivan, Sean. The Care of Tomorrow's Elderly: Introduction. In *Lewin, M. E. and Sullivan, S., eds.*, 1989, pp. 1–10.

_____ **and Wallack, Stanley.** Strategies for Financing Long-Term Care. In *Lewin, M. E. and Sullivan, S., eds.*, 1989, pp. 161–76.

Lewis, Alan. Fiscal Psychology. In *[Sandford, C.]*, 1989, pp. 1–27.

Lewis, Barry L. and Baiman, Stanley. An Experiment Testing the Behavioral Equivalence of Strategically Equivalent Employment Contracts. *J. Acc. Res.*, Spring 1989, *27*(1), pp. 1–20.

Lewis, Darrell R., et al. A Note on the Use of Earning Functions and Human Capital Theory in Assessing Special Education. *Econ. Educ. Rev.*, 1989, *8*(3), pp. 285–90.

Lewis, Frank D. Dependents and the Demand for Life Insurance. *Amer. Econ. Rev.*, June 1989, *79*(3), pp. 452–67.

Lewis, Jeffrey D.; Lofti, Sherif and Behrman, Jere R. The Impact of Commodity Price Instability: Experiments with a General Equilibrium Model for Indonesia. In *[Adams, F. G.]*, 1989, pp. 59–100.

Lewis, Karen K. Can Learning Affect Exchange-Rate Behavior? The Case of the Dollar in the Early 1980's. *J. Monet. Econ.*, January 1989, *23*(1), pp. 79–100.

_____. Changing Beliefs and Systematic Rational Forecast Errors with Evidence from Foreign Exchange. *Amer. Econ. Rev.*, September 1989, *79*(4), pp. 621–36.

_____. On Occasional Monetary Policy Coordinations that Fix the Exchange Rate. *J. Int. Econ.*, February 1989, *26*(1/2), pp. 139–55.

Lewis, Morgan V. Co-ordination of Public Vocational Education with the Job Training Partnership Act. *Econ. Educ. Rev.*, 1989, *8*(1), pp. 75–81.

Lewis, Pam and Thomas, Howard. The Linkage between Strategy, Strategic Groups and Performance in the UK Retail Grocery Industry. In *Mansfield, R., ed.*, 1989, pp. 163–79.

Lewis, Philip and Andrews, Neil. Household Demand in China. *Appl. Econ.*, June 1989, *21*(6), pp. 793–807.

Lewis, Robert and Levy, Doug E. Predicting a National Acid Rain Policy. In *Golden, B. L.; Wasil, E. A. and Harker, P. T., eds.*, 1989, pp. 155–70.

Lewis, Tracy R.; Feenstra, Robert C. and Ware, Roger. Eliminating Price Supports: A Political Economy Perspective. *J. Public Econ.*, November 1989, *40*(2), pp. 159–85.

_____ **and Nickerson, David.** Self-insurance against Natural Disasters. *J. Environ. Econ. Manage.*, May 1989, *16*(3), pp. 209–23.

_____ **and Sappington, David E. M.** Countervailing Incentives in Agency Problems. *J. Econ. Theory*, December 1989, *49*(2), pp. 294–313.

_____ **and Sappington, David E. M.** Inflexible Rules in Incentive Problems. *Amer. Econ. Rev.*, March 1989, *79*(1), pp. 69–84.

_____ **and Sappington, David E. M.** Regulatory Options and Price-Cap Regulation. *Rand J. Econ.*, Autumn 1989, *20*(3), pp. 405–16.

Ley, Robert D. Neoconservative Economics in the Southern Cone of Latin America, 1973–83: Review Article. *Atlantic Econ. J.*, September 1989, *17*(3), pp. 49–55.

Leybourne, S. J. and McCabe, Brendan P. M. Testing for Coefficient Constancy in Random Walk Models with Particular Reference to the Initial Value Problem. In *Kramer, W., ed.*, 1989, pp. 41–48.

_____ **and McCabe, Brendan P. M.** Testing for Coefficient Constancy in Random Walk Models with Particular Reference to the Initial Value Problem. *Empirical Econ.*, 1989, *14*(2), pp. 105–12.

_____; **Mills, Terence C. and Crafts, Nick F. R.** The Climacteric in Late Victorian Britain and France: A Reappraisal of the Evidence. *J. Appl. Econometrics*, April–June 1989, *4*(2), pp. 103–17.

_____; **Mills, Terence C. and Crafts, Nick F. R.** Trends and Cycles in British Industrial Production, 1700–1913. *J. Roy. Statist. Society*, 1989, *152*(1), pp. 43–60.

Leys, Colin. What Is the Problem about Corruption? In *Heidenheimer, A. J.; Johnston, M. and LeVine, V. T., eds.*, 1989, *1965*, pp. 51–66.

Leysen, Y. Two Theories on the Cost of Capital. *Tijdschrift Econ. Manage.*, June 1989, *34*(3), pp. 305–15.

Leyshon, A.; Daniels, Peter W. and Thrift, Nigel J. Internationalisation of Professional Producer Services: Accountancy Conglomerates. In *Enderwick, P.*, 1989, pp. 79–106.

Li, Bingbai; Gao, Liangzhi and Juan, Fang. Climatic Variation and Food Production in Jiangsu, China. In *Oram, P. A., et al.*, 1989, pp. 557–62.

Li, Boxi and Li, Peiyu. Current Analysis and Prospects for China's Economy. In *Zerby, J., ed.*, 1989, pp. 72–96.

Li, Choh-Ming. A Note of Professor Hicks' *Value and Capital*. In *Wood, J. C. and Woods, R. N., eds., Vol. 1*, 1989, *1941*, pp. 92–94.

Li, Elton and Stoecker, Arthur L. Using Microcomputers for Policy Analysis. In *Tweeten, L., ed.*, 1989, pp. 46–55.

Li, Fuchun. For the Sake of Socialist Construction Strengthen Planning Work throughout the Country. In *Howe, C. and Walker, K. R., eds.,* 1989, *1956,* pp. 29–40.

Li, Hua. The Democratic Management of Enterprises and Workers' Awareness of Democracy. *Chinese Econ. Stud.,* Summer 1989, *22*(4), pp. 69–80.

_____ **and Geng, Shuhai.** Reform and Social Mentality of Workers. *Chinese Econ. Stud.,* Summer 1989, *22*(4), pp. 8–17.

Li, Jingwen. Steadfastly Reduce Non-productive Urban Population. In *Howe, C. and Walker, K. R., eds.,* 1989, *1957,* pp. 351–57.

Li, Jingxiong. Climatic Vulnerability of Maize in China. In *Oram, P. A., et al.,* 1989, pp. 145–54.

Li, Lode and Fine, Charles H. Equilibrium Exit in Stochastically Declining Industries. *Games Econ. Behav.,* March 1989, *1*(1), pp. 40–59.

_____; **Samet, Dov and Kamien, Morton I.** Bertrand Competition with Subcontracting. *Rand J. Econ.,* Winter 1989, *20*(4), pp. 553–67.

Li, Peiyu and Li, Boxi. Current Analysis and Prospects for China's Economy. In *Zerby, J., ed.,* 1989, pp. 72–96.

Li, Pu. Do Not Permit Rightists to Make Use of the Population Problem in Order to Promote Political Conspiracies. In *Howe, C. and Walker, K. R., eds.,* 1989, *1957,* pp. 326–34.

Li, Rose Maria. Migration to China's Northern Frontier, 1953–82. *Population Devel. Rev.,* September 1989, *15*(3), pp. 503–38.

Li, Shaomin. China's Population Policy: A Model of a Constant Stream of Births. *Population Res. Policy Rev.,* September 1989, *8*(3), pp. 279–300.

Li, Xu and Wu, Yu. Prerequisite Conditions to Enforcement of the Bankruptcy Law. *Chinese Econ. Stud.,* Winter 1988–89, *22*(2), pp. 16–23.

Li, Y. and Apedaile, Leonard P. A Simulation of Economic Effects of Technology Transfer in Cereal Production: A Reply. *Can. J. Agr. Econ.,* November 1989, *37*(3), pp. 547–48.

Li, Yih-yuan. Four Hundred Years of Ethnic Relations in Taiwan. In *Chiao, C. and Tapp, N., eds.,* 1989, pp. 103–15.

Li, Yining. Conceiving Ownership Reform in China. *Chinese Econ. Stud.,* Winter 1988–89, *22*(2), pp. 72–81.

Li, Yunhe. How to Improve the Management of Agricultural Producers' Co-operatives. The 'Special Management System' and 'Contracting Output Down to the Household' Are Good Methods of Solving the Main Contradictions in the Co-operatives. In *Howe, C. and Walker, K. R., eds.,* 1989, *1957,* pp. 237–46.

Li, Yunqi, et al. The Individualization of Ownership of State-Owned Property: The Trends and Choices in China's Economic Reform (A Letter of Proposals to China's Leaders). *Chinese Econ. Stud.,* Fall 1989, *23*(1), pp. 82–88.

Liang, Kung-Yee and Zeger, Scott L. A Class of Logistic Regression Models for Multivariate Binary Time Series. *J. Amer. Statist. Assoc.,* June 1989, *84*(406), pp. 447–51.

Liang, Nellie. Bank Profits, Risk, and Local Market Concentration. *J. Econ. Bus.,* November 1989, *41*(4), pp. 297–305.

Liang, Zai and Massey, Douglas S. The Long-term Consequences of a Temporary Worker Program: The U.S. Bracero Experience. *Population Res. Policy Rev.,* September 1989, *8*(3), pp. 199–226.

Liao, Jili. Discussing the 'Double-Track System.' In *Howe, C. and Walker, K. R., eds.,* 1989, *1958,* pp. 69–77.

Liao, Shustung. Science and Technology-Related Research Publications from Taiwan: An Overall Comparison with China and Other Countries. In *Lee, C. F. and Hu, S.-C., eds.,* 1989, pp. 263–76.

Liao, Tim Futing. A Flexible Approach for the Decomposition of Rate Differences. *Demography,* November 1989, *26*(4), pp. 717–26.

Liapis, Peter S. Causality of EC Wheat Export Subsidies and U.S. Wheat Export Prices. *Can. J. Agr. Econ.,* Part 2, December 1989, *37*(4), pp. 1155–64.

Liaw, K-L. and Ledent, J. Provincial Out-Migration Patterns of Canadian Elderly: Characterization and Explanation. *Environ. Planning A,* August 1989, *21*(8), pp. 1093–1111.

Liaw, K. Thomas. A Microeconomic Approach to Tariff Reform in the Taiwanese Automobile Market. In *Lee, C. F. and Hu, S.-C., eds.,* 1989, pp. 213–41.

Libby, Lawrence W. Break-Out Session I—Issues for Hunger, Malnutrition, Agriculture, and Food Policy: Recommendations: Farmers and Farm Groups. In *Helmuth, J. W. and Johnson, S. R., eds., Vol. 1,* 1989, pp. 126–28.

Libecap, Gary D. Distributional Issues in Contracting for Property Rights. *J. Inst. Theoretical Econ.,* March 1989, *145*(1), pp. 6–24.

_____. The Political Economy of Crude Oil Cartelization in the United States, 1933–1972. *J. Econ. Hist.,* December 1989, *49*(4), pp. 833–55.

_____ **and Johnson, Ronald N.** Agency Growth, Salaries and the Protected Bureaucrat. *Econ. Inquiry,* July 1989, *27*(3), pp. 431–51.

_____ **and Johnson, Ronald N.** Bureaucratic Rules, Supervisor Behavior, and the Effect on Salaries in the Federal Government. *J. Law, Econ., Organ.,* Spring 1989, *5*(1), pp. 53–82.

Liberatore, Matthew J. A Decision Support Approach for R&D Project Selection. In *Golden, B. L.; Wasil, E. A. and Harker, P. T., eds.,* 1989, pp. 82–100.

Liberman, Iakov G. The Strategy of Accumulation. *Prob. Econ.,* April 1989, *31*(12), pp. 84–91.

Liberman, L.; Shokhin, A. and Guzanova, A. Prices through the Eyes of the Population. *Prob. Econ.,* June 1989, *32*(2), pp. 6–13.

Liburd, Eustace E. and Bain, Laurel. Financial Intermediation and Economic Growth in the OECS. *Soc. Econ. Stud.,* December 1989, *38*(4), pp. 201–18.

_____ and Tempro, Elizabeth M. An Assessment of Monetary and Credit Policies in the OECS Region, 1975–1985. In *Worrell, D. and Bourne, C., eds.*, 1989, pp. 132–46.

Lichtblau, John H. World Oil and U.S. Imports: Is the Past Prologue? In *[Evans, J. K.]*, 1989, pp. 74–82.

Lichtenberg, A. J. and Ujihara, A. Application of Nonlinear Mapping Theory to Commodity Price Fluctuations. *J. Econ. Dynam. Control*, April 1989, *13*(2), pp. 225–46.

Lichtenberg, Erik. Land Quality, Irrigation Development, and Cropping Patterns in the Northern High Plains. *Amer. J. Agr. Econ.*, February 1989, *71*(1), pp. 187–94.

_____ and Zilberman, David. The Econometrics of Damage Contol: Reply. *Amer. J. Agr. Econ.*, May 1989, *71*(2), pp. 445–46.

_____; Zilberman, David and Bogen, Kenneth T. Regulating Environmental Health Risks under Uncertainty: Groundwater Contamination in California. *J. Environ. Econ. Manage.*, July 1989, *17*(1), pp. 22–34.

Lichtenberg, Frank R. Contributions to Federal Election Campaigns by Government Contractors. *J. Ind. Econ.*, September 1989, *38*(1), pp. 31–48.

_____. How Elastic Is the Government's Demand for Weapons. *J. Public Econ.*, October 1989, *40*(1), pp. 57–78.

_____. IR&D Project Data and Theories of R&D Investment. *J. Econ. Dynam. Control*, April 1989, *13*(2), pp. 271–82.

_____ and Griliches, Zvi. Errors of Measurement in Output Deflators. *J. Bus. Econ. Statist.*, January 1989, *7*(1), pp. 1–9.

Lichtenstein, Donald R. and Bearden, William O. Contextual Influences on Perceptions of Merchant-Supplied Reference Prices. *J. Cons. Res.*, June 1989, *16*(1), pp. 55–66.

Lichtenstein, Peter M. Theories of Value and Price in Contemporary Chinese Marxism. *Atlantic Econ. J.*, December 1989, *17*(4), pp. 63–70.

Lichty, Richard W.; Anderson, Curt L. and Garcia, L. Miguel. Water Analysis: A Systems Approach Incorporating Linear Programming. *Growth Change*, Winter 1989, *20*(1), pp. 80–89.

Lie, Harry K. and Chung, Kae H. Labor–Management Relations in Korea. In *Chung, K. H. and Lee, H. C., eds.*, 1989, pp. 217–31.

Liebenthal, Robert and Nicholas, Peter. World Bank-Supported Adjustment Programs. In *Weeks, J. F., ed.*, 1989, pp. 91–102.

Liebeskind, Julia and Rumelt, Richard P. Markets for Experience Goods with Performance Uncertainty. *Rand J. Econ.*, Winter 1989, *20*(4), pp. 601–21.

Liedholm, Carl and Kilby, Peter. The Role of Nonfarm Activities in the Rural Economy. In *Williamson, J. G. and Panchamukhi, V. R., eds.*, 1989, pp. 340–66.

Liedtka, Jeanne. Managerial Values and Corporate Decision-Making: An Empirical Analysis

of Value Congruence in Two Organizations. In *Post, J. E., ed.*, 1989, pp. 55–91.

van Liemt, Gijsbert. Minimum Labour Standards and International Trade: Would a Social Clause Work? *Int. Lab. Rev.*, 1989, *128*(4), pp. 433–48.

Lien, Da-Hsiang Donald. Cash Settlement Provisions on Futures Contracts. *J. Futures Markets*, June 1989, *9*(3), pp. 263–70.

_____. Optical Settlement Specification on Futures Contracts. *J. Futures Markets*, August 1989, *9*(4), pp. 355–58.

_____. Optimal Hedging and Spreading on Wheat Futures Markets. *J. Futures Markets*, April 1989, *9*(2), pp. 163–70.

_____. Sampled Data as a Basis of Cash Settlement Price. *J. Futures Markets*, December 1989, *9*(6), pp. 583–88.

Lienert, Ian. Quantifying Agricultural Policies in the WALRAS Model. *OECD Econ. Stud.*, Winter 1989–1990, (13), pp. 103–30.

Lievesley, Denise and Waterton, Jennifer. Evidence of Conditioning Effects in the British Social Attitudes Panel. In *Kasprzyk, D., et al., eds.*, 1989, pp. 319–39.

Ligeti, C. and Dobos, K. Markov Chain Modelling of Differentiation of Farms. In *Bauer, S. and Henrichsmeyer, W., eds.*, 1989, pp. 157–64.

Ligon, Polly C. and Swegle, Wayne E. Aid, Trade, and Farm Policies: A Sourcebook on Issues and Interrelationships: Introduction. In *Swegle, W. E. and Ligon, P. C., eds.*, 1989, pp. xi–xv.

Liljeblom, Eva. An Analysis of Earnings per Share Forecasts for Stocks Listed on the Stockholm Stock Exchange. *Scand. J. Econ.*, 1989, *91*(3), pp. 565–81.

_____. Företagets finansiella beslut som signaler. (The Signalling of a Company's Financial Decision. With English summary.) *Ekon. Samfundets Tidskr.*, 1989, *42*(2), pp. 73–85.

_____; Löflund, Anders and Berglund, Tom. Estimating Betas on Daily Data for a Small Stock Market. *J. Banking Finance*, March 1989, *13*(1), pp. 41–64.

Lillard, Lee A. Sample Dynamics: Some Behavioral Issues. In *Kasprzyk, D., et al., eds.*, 1989, pp. 497–511.

Lillydahl, Jane H. and Singell, Larry D. Some Alternative Definitions of Youth Unemployment: A Means for Improved Understanding and Policy Formulation. *Amer. J. Econ. Sociology*, October 1989, *48*(4), pp. 457–71.

Lim, Camilo Jose, Jr. Energy and the Economy in the Philippines. In *James, W. E., ed.*, 1989, pp. 155–66.

Lim, Chin. Morality and Economics. *Int. J. Soc. Econ.*, 1989, *16*(2), pp. 3–12.

_____ and Ong, Nai Pew. A Dynamic Model of Advertising and Market Shares. *Can. J. Econ.*, November 1989, *22*(4), pp. 819–33.

Lim, G. C. and Harper, Ian R. Is Monetary Policy Too Tight? *Australian Econ. Rev.*, Winter 1989, (86), pp. 15–28.

Lim, Hee Taek and Lee, Chul Song. The Disregard of a Legal Entity for Tax Purposes: Republic of Korea. In *International Fiscal Association, ed. (II)*, 1989, pp. 463–71.

Lim, Kian-Guan. Dividend Policy and Tax Structure. *Econ. Letters*, December 1989, *31*(3), pp. 269–72.

_____. A New Test of the Three-Moment Capital Asset Pricing Model. *J. Finan. Quant. Anal.*, June 1989, *24*(2), pp. 205–16.

Lim, Raymond S. K. Keynes and the Store of Wealth Function of Money: A Note. *Indian Econ. J.*, July–Sept. 1989, *37*(1), pp. 87–90.

Lim, Suk-Pil and Narayanan, M. P. On the Call Provision in Corporate Zero-Coupon Bonds. *J. Finan. Quant. Anal.*, March 1989, *24*(1), pp. 91–103.

Lim, Youngil. Comparing Brazil and Korea. In *Naya, S., et al., eds.*, 1989, pp. 93–117.

de Lima, João Eustáquio and Ilha, Adayr da Silva. Impacto da educação na pequena produção agrícola em Minas Gerais. (With English summary.) *Pesquisa Planejamento Econ.*, April 1989, *19*(1), pp. 183–202.

Lin, An-loh. Estimation of Multiplicative Measurement-Error Models and Some Simulation Results. *Econ. Letters*, November 1989, *31*(1), pp. 13–20.

Lin, Chung-cheng and Chu, Yun-Peng. Interest Rates Interactions between Dual Financial Markets. *J. Econ. Devel.*, December 1989, *14*(2), pp. 107–15.

Lin, Cyril Zhiren. Open-Ended Economic Reform in China. In *Nee, V. and Stark, D., eds.*, 1989, pp. 95–136.

Lin, D. Y. and Wei, L. J. The Robust Inference for the Cox Proportional Hazards Model. *J. Amer. Statist. Assoc.*, December 1989, *84*(408), pp. 1074–78.

Lin, Justin Yifu. An Economic Theory of Institutional Change: Induced and Imposed Change. *Cato J.*, Spring–Summer 1989, *9*(1), pp. 1–33.

Lin, Steven A. Y. and Otsuka, Allen S. Determinants of U.S. Direct Manufacturing Investments in East Asia. In *Missouri Valley Economic Association*, 1989, pp. 123–28.

Lin, Tsai-Mei. Multinational Corporations in the 1990s and Beyond: With Special Reference to the Economic Development of the Republic of China. In *Negandhi, A. R., ed.*, 1989, pp. 203–14.

Lin, Winston T. Modeling and Forecasting Hospital Patient Movements: Univariate and Multiple Time Series Approaches. *Int. J. Forecasting*, 1989, *5*(2), pp. 195–208.

Lincoln, Edward J. and Harding, Harry. The East Asian Laboratory. In *Steinbruner, J. D., ed.*, 1989, pp. 185–220.

Lincoln, James R. Productivity, Motivation, and Work Attitudes in the United States and Japan. In *Libecap, G. D., ed.*, 1989, pp. 119–55.

Lind, Robert C. and Arrow, Kenneth J. Uncertainty and the Evaluation of Public Investment Decisions. In *Diamond, P. and Rothschild, M., eds.*, 1989, *1970*, pp. 405–19.

Lindahl, Frederick W. Dynamic Analysis of Inventory Accounting Choice. *J. Acc. Res.*, Autumn 1989, *27*(2), pp. 201–26.

Lindahl, Mary. Mesuring Hedging Effectiveness with R^2: A Note. *J. Futures Markets*, October 1989, *9*(5), pp. 469–75.

Lindauer, David L. Parallel, Fragmented, or Black? Defining Market Structure in Developing Economies. *World Devel.*, December 1989, *17*(12), pp. 1871–80.

Lindbeck, Assar. Remaining Puzzles and Neglected Issues in Macroeconomics. *Scand. J. Econ.*, 1989, *91*(2), pp. 495–516.

_____ **and Snower, Dennis J.** Macroeconomic Policy and Insider Power. *Amer. Econ. Rev.*, May 1989, *79*(2), pp. 370–76.

Lindberg, Erik; Montgomery, Henry and Gärling, Tommy. Beliefs about Attainment of Life Satisfaction as Determinants of Preferences for Everyday Activities. In *Grunert, K. G. and Ölander, F., eds.*, 1989, pp. 33–46.

Lindberg, Thomas and Albrecht, James W. The Micro Initialization of MOSES. In *Albrecht, J. W., et al.*, 1989, pp. 67–132.

Lindblad, J. Thomas. The Petroleum Industry in Indonesia before the Second World War. *Bull. Indonesian Econ. Stud.*, August 1989, *25*(2), pp. 53–77.

Lindenberg, Marc. Making Economic Adjustment Work: The Politics of Policy Implementation. *Policy Sciences*, November 1989, *22*(3–4), pp. 359–94.

Linder, Willy. Grundpositionen der Reformpolitik Besondere Aspekte des Aussenhandels. (Fundamentals of Reforms. With English summary.) *Aussenwirtschaft*, December 1989, *44*(3–4), pp. 307–43.

Lindert, Peter H. Response to Debt Crisis: What Is Different about the 1980s? In *Eichengreen, B. and Lindert, P. H., eds.*, 1989, pp. 227–75.

_____ **and Eichengreen, Barry.** The International Debt Crisis in Historical Perspective: Overview. In *Eichengreen, B. and Lindert, P. H., eds.*, 1989, pp. 1–11.

_____ **and Morton, Peter J.** How Sovereign Debt Has Worked. In *Sachs, J. D., ed. (I)*, 1989, pp. 39–106.

_____ **and Morton, Peter J.** How Sovereign Debt Has Worked. In *Sachs, J. D., ed. (II)*, 1989, pp. 225–35.

Lindgren, Anders and Johansson, Sten. The Use of Micro-computers at a Statistical Agency: A Report on Statistics Sweden. *Statist. J.*, 1989, *6*(3), pp. 191–205.

Lindley, James T. and Jackson, John D. Measuring the Extent of Wage Discrimination: A Statistical Test and a Caveat. *Appl. Econ.*, April 1989, *21*(4), pp. 515–40.

_____ **and Moser, James T.** A Simple Formula for Duration: An Extension. *Financial Rev.*, November 1989, *24*(4), pp. 611–15.

_____; **Rudolph, Patricia M. and Selby, Edward B., Jr.** Credit Card Possession and Use: Changes over Time. *J. Econ. Bus.*, May 1989, *41*(2), pp. 127–42.

Lindner, R. K. and Campbell, H. F. A Note on

Optimal Effort in the Maldivian Tuna Fishery. *Marine Resource Econ.*, 1989, *6*(2), pp. 173–76.

Lindsay, Holly. The Indonesian Log Export Ban: An Estimation of Foregone Export Earnings. *Bull. Indonesian Econ. Stud.*, August 1989, *25*(2), pp. 111–23.

Lindsey, Charles W. Commodities, Technology, and Trade: Transnational Corporations and Philippine Economic Development. *Philippine Rev. Econ. Bus.*, June 1989, *26*(1), pp. 67–108.

_____. Free to Lose: An Introduction to Marxist Economic Philosophy: Review Article. *Rev. Radical Polit. Econ.*, 1989, *21*(1–2), pp. 188–89.

Lindsey, Lawrence B.; Mitrusi, Andrew W. and Bolster, Paul J. Tax-Induced Trading: The Effect of the 1986 Tax Reform Act on Stock Market Activity. *J. Finance*, June 1989, *44*(2), pp. 327–44.

Lindsey, Robin. Import Disruptions, Exhaustible Resources, and Intertemporal Security of Supply. *Can. J. Econ.*, May 1989, *22*(2), pp. 340–63.

Lindström, Caj-Gunnar. Leadership in Knowledge Organisations with Special Reference to Universities. *Liiketaloudellinen Aikak.*, 1989, *38*(4), pp. 332–42.

Lindström, Eva Sundkvist and Wijkman, Per Magnus. Pacific Basin Integration: A Step towards Freer Trade. In *Nieuwenhuysen, J., ed.*, 1989, pp. 144–62.

Lines, Marji. Environmental Noise and Nonlinear Models: A Simple Macroeconomic Example. *Econ. Notes*, 1989, (3), pp. 376–94.

Ling, David C. and Chen, Andrew H. Optimal Mortgage Refinancing with Stochastic Interest Rates. *Amer. Real Estate Urban Econ. Assoc. J.*, Fall 1989, *17*(3), pp. 278–99.

Lingard, J. and Dawson, P. J. Measuring Farm Efficiency over Time on Philippine Rice Farms. *J. Agr. Econ.*, May 1989, *40*(2), pp. 168–77.

Linge, G. J. R. and van der Knaap, G. A. Labour, Environment and Industrial Change. In *Linge, G. J. R. and van der Knaap, G. A., eds.*, 1989, pp. 1–19.

Lingle, C. On the Real Costs of Military Conscription. *S. Afr. J. Econ.*, September 1989, *57*(3), pp. 270–78.

Linhart, Peter B. and Radner, Roy. Minimax-Regret Strategies for Bargaining over Several Variables. *J. Econ. Theory*, June 1989, *48*(1), pp. 152–78.

_____; **Radner, Roy and Leininger, Wolfgang.** Equilibria of the Sealed-Bid Mechanism for Bargaining with Incomplete Information. *J. Econ. Theory*, June 1989, *48*(1), pp. 63–106.

_____; **Radner, Roy and Satterthwaite, Mark A.** Symposium on Noncooperative Bargaining: Introduction. *J. Econ. Theory*, June 1989, *48*(1), pp. 1–17.

Linke, Charles M. and Bryan, William R. Estimating the Present Value of Future Income Losses: An Historical Simulation 1900–1982:

Comment. *J. Risk Ins.*, September 1989, *56*(3), pp. 555–59.

Linnamo, Jussi. Kasinoekonomin och värdepappersmarknadens problem. (The Casino Economy and Problems on the Securities Market. With English summary.) *Ekon. Samfundets Tidskr.*, 1989, *42*(4), pp. 239–42.

Linneman, Peter D. and Gyourko, Joseph. Equity and Efficiency Aspects of Rent Control: An Empirical Study of New York City. *J. Urban Econ.*, July 1989, *26*(1), pp. 54–74.

_____ **and Wachter, Susan.** The Impacts of Borrowing Constraints on Homeownership. *Amer. Real Estate Urban Econ. Assoc. J.*, Winter 1989, *17*(4), pp. 389–402.

Lins, David A. Future Directions in Farm Management. *Can. J. Agr. Econ.*, Part 1, December 1989, *37*(4), pp. 765–74.

Lion, Robert. On Decentralization. In *Frankel, A. V. and Heck, C. B., eds.*, 1989, pp. 34–38.

Lipartito, Kenneth. System Building at the Margin: The Problem of Public Choice in the Telephone Industry. *J. Econ. Hist.*, June 1989, *49*(2), pp. 323–36.

Lipietz, Alain. Three Crises: The Metamorphoses of Capitalism and the Labour Movement. In *Gottdiener, M. and Komninos, N., eds.*, 1989, pp. 59–95.

Lipman, Barton L. and Bagnoli, Mark. Provision of Public Goods: Fully Implementing the Core through Private Contributions. *Rev. Econ. Stud.*, October 1989, *56*(4), pp. 583–601.

Lippi, Marco and Artoni, Roberto. Nota sulla ripresa di un punto di vista keynesiano in macroeconomia. (A Neo-Keynesian Perspective in Macroeconomics. With English summary.) *Politica. Econ.*, August 1989, *5*(2), pp. 221–30.

Lippman, Steven A. and Mamer, John W. A Simple Search Model with Procyclical Quits. *J. Econ. Dynam. Control*, April 1989, *13*(2), pp. 247–53.

Lippmann, Walter. A Theory about Corruption. In *Heidenheimer, A. J.; Johnston, M. and Le-Vine, V. T., eds.*, 1989, *1930*, pp. 567–71.

Lipschitz, Leslie; Mayer, Thomas and Gupta, Sanjeev. The Common Agricultural Policy of the EC. *Finance Devel.*, June 1989, *26*(2), pp. 37–39.

Lipsey, Richard G. Agendas for the 1988 and Future Summits. *Can. Public Policy*, Supplement, February 1989, *15*, pp. S87–91.

_____. Unsettled Issues in the Great Free Trade Debate. *Can. J. Econ.*, February 1989, *22*(1), pp. 1–21.

_____ **and Eaton, B. Curtis.** Product Differentiation. In *Schmalensee, R. and Willig, R. D., eds., Vol. 1*, 1989, pp. 723–68.

_____ **and Smith, Murray G.** The Canada–U.S. Free Trade Agreement: Special Case or Wave of the Future? In *Schott, J. J., ed.*, 1989, pp. 317–35.

_____ **and York, Robert.** The Canada–U.S. Free Trade Agreement. In *Rugman, A. M., ed.*, 1989, pp. 123–43.

Lipsey, Robert E. and Blomström, Magnus. The

Export Performance of U.S. and Swedish Multinationals. *Rev. Income Wealth*, September 1989, *35*(3), pp. 245–64.

_____ **and Blomström, Magnus.** U.S. Multinationals in Latin American Service Industries. *World Devel.*, November 1989, *17*(11), pp. 1769–76.

_____ **and Tice, Helen Stone.** The Measurement of Saving, Investment, and Wealth: Introduction. In *Lipsey, R. E. and Tice, H. S., eds.*, 1989, pp. 1–19.

Lipson, Charles. International Debt and National Security: Comparing Victorian Britain and Postwar America. In *Eichengreen, B. and Lindert, P. H., eds.*, 1989, pp. 189–226.

Lipton, Douglas W. and Strand, Ivar E., Jr. The Effect of Common Property on the Optimal Structure of the Fishing Industry. *J. Environ. Econ. Manage.*, January 1989, *16*(1), pp. 45–51.

Lipton, M. The Challenge of Sanctions. *S. Afr. J. Econ.*, December 1989, *57*(4), pp. 336–61.

Lipton, Michael. Agriculture, Rural People, the State and the Surplus in Some Asian Countries: Thoughts on Some Implications of Three Recent Approaches in Social Science. *World Devel.*, October 1989, *17*(10), pp. 1553–71.

_____ **and Longhurst, Richard.** The Role of Agricultural Research and Secondary Food Crops in Reducing Seasonal Food Insecurity. In *Sahn, D. E., ed.*, 1989, pp. 285–97.

Lipumba, Nguyuru H. I. Domestic Supply Constraints versus Market Access: International Trade and Economic Development in Tanzania. In *Whalley, J., ed., Vol. 2*, 1989, pp. 58–80.

Lisichkin, G. A Mixed Economy. *Acta Oecon.*, 1989, *40*(3–4), pp. 256–59.

Lisov, V. A. Factors Differentiating the Material Well-Being of the Rural Population. *Prob. Econ.*, December 1989, *32*(8), pp. 43–57.

_____ **and Shaposhnikov, A. N.** Methods and Results of Constructing a Typology of Families Based on Level of Material Well-Being: Example of the Rural Population. *Prob. Econ.*, May 1989, *32*(1), pp. 33–51.

Lissakers, Karin. Background to the Debt Crisis: Structural Adjustment in the Financial Markets. In *Weeks, J. F., ed.*, 1989, pp. 67–73.

Lissner, Will. Reform of the Federal Reserve? *Amer. J. Econ. Sociology*, April 1989, *48*(2), pp. 192.

_____. Saving a Vital Natural Resource. *Amer. J. Econ. Sociology*, April 1989, *48*(2), pp. 243–44.

Lister, C. and Atwood, J. R. International Antitrust Enforcement in the George Bush Administration: The Enforcement Guidelines and Beyond. *J. World Trade*, April 1989, *23*(2), pp. 97–117.

Lister, Ruth. The Politics of Social Security: An Assessment of the Fowler Review. In *Dilnot, A. and Walker, I., eds.*, 1989, pp. 200–23.

Litan, Robert E. Changing Incentives Facing Financial-Services Regulators: Comments. *J. Fi-*

nan. Services Res., September 1989, *2*(3), pp. 275–79.

_____. Which Way for Congress? In *Guttmann, R., ed.*, 1989, *1987*, pp. 162–69.

_____ **and Brumbaugh, R. Dan, Jr.** Facing Up to the Crisis in American Banking. In *Bosworth, B. P., et al.*, 1989, pp. 122–27.

_____; **Brumbaugh, R. Dan, Jr. and Carron, Andrew S.** Cleaning Up the Depository Institutions Mess. *Brookings Pap. Econ. Act.*, 1989, (1), pp. 243–83.

_____; **Lawrence, Robert Z. and Schultze, Charles L.** Improving American Living Standards. In *Bosworth, B. P., et al.*, 1989, pp. 29–48.

Little, Daniel. *Marx, Reason, and the Art of Freedom:* Review. *Rev. Radical Polit. Econ.*, 1989, *21*(1–2), pp. 163–64.

_____. *The Scientific Marx:* Review: Reply. *Rev. Radical Polit. Econ.*, 1989, *21*(1–2), pp. 165–66.

Little, I. M. D. and Joshi, Vijay. Indian Macroeconomic Policies. In *[Díaz-Alejandro, C.]*, 1989, pp. 286–308.

Little, Jane Sneddon. The Dollar, Structural Change and the New England Miracle. *New Eng. Econ. Rev.*, Sept.–Oct. 1989, pp. 47–57.

_____. Exchange Rates and Structural Change in U.S. Manufacturing Employment. *New Eng. Econ. Rev.*, Mar.–Apr. 1989, pp. 56–70.

Little, Roderick J. A. and Su, Hong-Lin. Item Nonresponse in Panel Surveys. In *Kasprzyk, D., et al., eds.*, 1989, pp. 400–425.

_____; **Taylor, Jeremy M. G. and Lange, Kenneth L.** Robust Statistical Modeling Using the *t* Distribution. *J. Amer. Statist. Assoc.*, December 1989, *84*(408), pp. 881–96.

Littleboy, Bruce and Mehta, Ghanshyam. Patinkin on Keynes's Theory of Effective Demand: A Rejoinder. *Hist. Polit. Econ.*, Winter 1989, *21*(4), pp. 711–21.

Littlechild, Stephen C. Myths and Merger Policy. In *Fairburn, J. and Kay, J., eds.*, 1989, pp. 301–21.

_____. Ten Steps to Denationalisation. In *Veljanovski, C., ed. (II)*, 1989, *1981*, pp. 15–25.

_____ **and Beesley, Michael E.** The Regulation of Privatized Monopolies in the United Kingdom. *Rand J. Econ.*, Autumn 1989, *20*(3), pp. 454–72.

_____ **and Wiseman, Jack.** Crusoe's Kingdom: Cost, Choice and Political Economy. In *Wiseman, J.*, 1989, pp. 234–64.

_____ **and Wiseman, Jack.** The Political Economy of Restriction of Choice. In *Wiseman, J.*, 1989, *1986*, pp. 186–98.

Littman, Mark S. Poverty in the 1980's: Are the Poor Getting Poorer? *Mon. Lab. Rev.*, June 1989, *112*(6), pp. 13–18.

_____. Reasons for Not Working: Poor and Nonpoor Householders. *Mon. Lab. Rev.*, August 1989, *112*(8), pp. 16–21.

Littmann, E.-L. Agricultural Policies in the USSR: Problems, Trends and Prospects. *J. Agr. Econ.*, September 1989, *40*(3), pp. 290–301.

Litvak, Isaiah A. Canadian Multinationals and Foreign Policy. In *Rugman, A. M., ed.*, 1989, pp. 230–44.

Litz, Diane and Moore, Linda. Multifactor Productivity Advances in the Tires and Inner Tubes Industry. *Mon. Lab. Rev.*, June 1989, *112*(6), pp. 19–27.

Litzenberger, Robert H.; Breeden, Douglas T. and Gibbons, Michael R. Empirical Tests of the Consumption-Oriented CAPM. *J. Finance*, June 1989, *44*(2), pp. 231–62.

——— **and Lang, Larry H. P.** Dividend Announcements: Cash Flow Signalling vs. Free Cash Flow Hypothesis? *J. Finan. Econ.*, September 1989, *24*(1), pp. 181–91.

Liu, Alan P. L. The Politics of Corruption in the People's Republic of China. In *Heidenheimer, A. J.; Johnston, M. and LeVine, V. T., eds.*, 1989, *1983*, pp. 489–511.

Liu, Ben-C.; Yen, Eva C. and Yen, Gili. Cultural and Family Effects on Fertility Decisions in Taiwan, R.O.C.: Traditional Values and Family Structure Are as Relevant as Income Measures. *Amer. J. Econ. Sociology*, October 1989, *48*(4), pp. 415–26.

Liu, Jin-Tan; Butler, John S. and Quddus, Munir. Money, Prices, and Causality: The Chinese Hyperinflation, 1946–49, Reexamined. *J. Macroecon.*, Summer 1989, *11*(3), pp. 447–53.

Liu, Karen and Wainio, John. Sources of Instability in the World Soybean Market. *Can. J. Agr. Econ.*, Part 2, December 1989, *37*(4), pp. 1315–23.

Liu, Pu; Smith, Stanley D. and Syed, Azmat A. The Exploitation of Inside Information at the *Wall Street Journal:* A Test of Strong Form Efficiency. *Financial Rev.*, November 1989, *24*(4), pp. 567–79.

Liu, Shun-chieh; Chen, Chau-nan and Tsaur, Tien-wang. Currency Substitution, Foreign Inflation, and Terms-of-Trade Dynamics. *J. Polit. Econ.*, August 1989, *97*(4), pp. 955–64.

Liu, Tai-Ying. The Prospects for Economic Cooperation in the Pacific Basin. In *Negandhi, A. R., ed.*, 1989, pp. 239–49.

Liu, Wei-Guo; Pulleyblank, William R. and Ball, Michael O. Two-Terminal Steiner Tree Polyhedra. In *Cornet, B. and Tulkens, H., eds.*, 1989, pp. 251–84.

Liu, Yih-Wu. China's Foreign Trade Statistics. In *Missouri Valley Economic Association*, 1989, pp. 143–49.

Liu, Yunhui and Wang, Rongjiu. Appraising the Adjustment of Autumn Grain Prices. In *Howe, C. and Walker, K. R., eds.*, 1989, *1959*, pp. 265–67.

Livernois, John R. Marginal Effective Tax Rates for Capital in the Canadian Mining Industry: An Extension. *Can. J. Econ.*, February 1989, *22*(1), pp. 184–94.

——— **and Ryan, David L.** Testing for Non-jointness in Oil and Gas Exploration: A Variable Profit Function Approach. *Int. Econ. Rev.*, May 1989, *30*(2), pp. 479–504.

Livesay, Harold C. Entrepreneurial Dominance in Businesses Large and Small, Past and Pres-

ent. *Bus. Hist. Rev.*, Spring 1989, *63*(1), pp. 1–21.

Livingston, Lori A. and Richards, Steven. U.S. Import and Export Prices Continued to Register Sizable Gains in 1988. *Mon. Lab. Rev.*, May 1989, *112*(5), pp. 11–33.

Livingston, Marie Leigh. Transboundary Environmental Degradation: Market Failure, Power, and Instrumental Justice. *J. Econ. Issues*, March 1989, *23*(1), pp. 79–91.

Livingston, Miles; Brooks, Robert and Levy, Haim. The Coupon Effect on Term Premiums. *J. Finan. Res.*, Spring 1989, *12*(1), pp. 15–21.

Livingstone, Ian. Unemployed Youth: Alternative Approaches to an African Crisis. *Int. Lab. Rev.*, 1989, *128*(3), pp. 389–407.

Livnat, Joshua and Callen, Jeffrey L. Responsibility Accounting and Asymmetry of Information. *Managerial Dec. Econ.*, March 1989, *10*(1), pp. 81–84.

——— **and Melnik, Arie.** Interim Audit Scope, Client Size and Client Familiarity: An Empirical Analysis. *Managerial Dec. Econ.*, March 1989, *10*(1), pp. 69–75.

———; **Zarowin, Paul and Amit, Raphael.** The Mode of Corporate Diversification: Internal Ventures versus Acquisitions. *Managerial Dec. Econ.*, June 1989, *10*(2), pp. 89–100.

Lizondo, José Saúl. Transitional Economic Policies, 1971–73: Comment. In *di Tella, G. and Dornbusch, R., eds.*, 1989, pp. 206–12.

———; **Mathieson, Donald J. and Dooley, Michael P.** The Currency Composition of Foreign Exchange Reserves. *Int. Monet. Fund Staff Pap.*, June 1989, *36*(2), pp. 385–434.

——— **and Montiel, Peter J.** Contractionary Devaluation in Developing Countries: An Analytical Overview. *Int. Monet. Fund Staff Pap.*, March 1989, *36*(1), pp. 182–227.

Ljung, P. and Dillinger, William. Approaches for Strengthening Local Governments. In *World Bank and Istituto Italo-Africano*, 1989, pp. 130–35.

Llewellyn, David T. The Changing Structure of Regulation in the British Financial System. In *Button, K. and Swann, D., eds.*, 1989, pp. 189–216.

———. Reflections on Money: Introduction. In *Llewellyn, D. T., ed.*, 1989, pp. 1–23.

———. Structural Change in the British Financial System. In *Llewellyn, D. T., ed.*, 1989, pp. 109–37.

Llona, Juan Braun. Localización espacial y política económica. (With English summary.) *Cuadernos Econ.*, December 1989, *26*(79), pp. 335–51.

Llorens Urrutia, Juan Luis. Development of the Information Sector in the Basque Country. In *Punset, E. and Sweeney, G., eds.*, 1989, pp. 173–83.

Lloyd-Ellis, H.; McKenzie, G. W. and Thomas, Stephen H. Using Country Balance Sheet Data to Predict Debt Rescheduling. *Econ. Letters*, December 1989, *31*(2), pp. 173–77.

Lloyd, G.; Newlands, D. and Danson, M. 'Scottish Enterprise': Towards a Model Agency or a Flawed Initiative? *Reg. Stud.*, December 1989, 23(6), pp. 557–63.

Lloyd, P. J. A Family of Agronomic Production Functions with Economies of Scope. *Australian J. Agr. Econ.*, August 1989, 33(2), pp. 108–22.

_____. Reflections on Intra-industry Trade Theory and Factor Proportions. In *Tharakan, P. K. M. and Kol, J., eds.*, 1989, pp. 15–30.

Lloyd, Peter E. Fragmenting Markets and the Dynamic Restructuring of Production: Issues for Spatial Policy. *Environ. Planning A*, April 1989, 21(4), pp. 429–44.

_____ and Peck, Jamie A. Conceptualising Processes of Skill Change: A Local Labour Market Approach. In *Linge, G. J. R. and van der Knaap, G. A., eds.*, 1989, pp. 107–27.

Lo, Andrew W.; Bucklin, Randolph E. and Caves, Richard E. Games of Survival in the U.S. Newspaper Industry. *Appl. Econ.*, May 1989, 21(5), pp. 631–49.

_____ and MacKinlay, A. Craig. The Size and Power of the Variance Ratio Test in Finite Samples. *J. Econometrics*, February 1989, 40(2), pp. 203–38.

Lo, Fu-chen; Kamal, Salih and Nakamura, Yoichi. Structural Interdependency and the Outlook for the Asian-Pacific Economy towards the Year 2000. In *Shinohara, M. and Lo, F., eds.*, 1989, pp. 80–107.

_____ and Shinohara, Miyohei. Global Adjustment and the Future of Asian-Pacific Economy: Introduction: An Overview of Issues. In *Shinohara, M. and Lo, F., eds.*, 1989, pp. ix–xxi.

_____; Song, Byung-Nak and Furukawa, Shunichi. Patterns of Development and Interdependence among the East and Southeast Asian Economies. In *Shinohara, M. and Lo, F., eds.*, 1989, pp. 108–27.

Loasby, Brian J. Herbert Simon's Human Rationality. In *Samuels, W. J., ed. (II)*, 1989, pp. 1–17.

Lobel, Jules. Emergency Power and the Decline of Liberalism. *Yale Law J.*, May 1989, 98(7), pp. 1385–1433.

Löber, Heinz H. Die Kosten der Steuererhebung für Verwaltung und Steuerpflichtige: Österreich. (Administrative and Compliance Costs of Taxation: Austria. With English summary.) In *International Fiscal Association, ed. (I)*, 1989, pp. 193–222.

Lobez, Frédéric. Rationnement du crédit et contrats implicites: Théorie et tests économétriques. (Credit Rationing and Implicit Contracts: Theory and Tests. With English summary.) *Finance*, December 1989, 10(2), pp. 59–76.

Lobo, Gerald J. and Mahmoud, Amal A. W. Relationship between Differential Amounts of Prior Information and Security Return Variability. *J. Acc. Res.*, Spring 1989, 27(1), pp. 116–34.

_____ and Song, In-Man. The Incremental Information in SFAS No. 33 Income Disclosures over Historical Cost Income and Its Cash and Accrual Components. *Accounting Rev.*, April 1989, 64(2), pp. 329–43.

Locander, William B.; Pollio, Howard R. and Thompson, Craig J. Putting Consumer Experience Back into Consumer Research: The Philosophy and Method of Existential-Phenomenology. *J. Cons. Res.*, September 1989, 16(2), pp. 133–46.

Locay, Luis. From Hunting and Gathering to Agriculture. *Econ. Devel. Cult. Change*, July 1989, 37(4), pp. 737–56.

_____ and Diamond, Arthur M., Jr. Investment in Sister's Children as Behavior towards Risk. *Econ. Inquiry*, October 1989, 27(4), pp. 719–35.

_____; Sanderson, Warren and Gertler, Paul. Are User Fees Regressive? The Welfare Implications of Charging for Medical Care in Peru. In *WHO, Pan American Health Organization*, 1989, pp. 86–106.

Lockeretz, William. Secondary Effects on Midwestern Agriculture of Metropolitan Development and Decreases in Farmland. *Land Econ.*, August 1989, 65(3), pp. 205–16.

Lockett, Martin. Foreign Trade. In *Goodman, D. S. G., ed.*, 1989, pp. 57–76.

Lockwood, Ben and Manning, Alan. Dynamic Wage–Employment Bargaining with Employment Adjustment Costs. *Econ. J.*, December 1989, 99(398), pp. 1143–58.

_____ and Thomas, Jonathan P. Asymptotic Efficiency in Principal–Agent Models with Hidden Information. *Econ. Letters*, October 1989, 30(4), pp. 297–301.

Loderer, Claudio F.; Rosenfeld, Ahron and Lewellen, Wilbur. Mergers, Executive Risk Reduction, and Stockholder Wealth. *J. Finan. Quant. Anal.*, December 1989, 24(4), pp. 459–72.

_____ and Sheehan, Dennis P. Corporate Bankruptcy and Managers' Self-Serving Behavior. *J. Finance*, September 1989, 44(4), pp. 1059–75.

Lodewijks, John. Dow's *Macroeconomic Thought: A Methodological Approach:* Review Essay. In *Samuels, W. J., ed. (II)*, 1989, pp. 261–68.

_____ and Lee, Christine. Recent Economic Developments in the Papua New Guinea Economy. In *Lodewijks, J. and Zerby, J., eds.*, 1989, pp. 30–49.

_____; Mahony, Greg and Lee, Christine. Recent Developments in the Fijian Economy. In *Lodewijks, J. and Zerby, J., eds.*, 1989, pp. 50–66.

_____, et al. Current and Emerging Policy Issues in the South Pacific. In *Lodewijks, J. and Zerby, J., eds.*, 1989, pp. 22–29.

Lodge, Juliet. EC Policymaking: Institutional Considerations. In *Lodge, J., ed.*, 1989, pp. 26–57.

_____. Environment: Towards a Clean Blue-Green EC? In *Lodge, J., ed.*, 1989, pp. 319–26.

_____. The European Parliament—From 'Assembly' to Co-legislature: Changing the Institutional Dynamics. In *Lodge, J., ed.*, 1989, pp. 58–79.

_____. European Political Cooperation: Towards the 1990s. In *Lodge, J., ed.*, 1989, pp. 223–40.

_____. Introduction: Internal Perspectives. **In** *Lodge, J., ed.,* 1989, pp. 83–93.

_____. Social Europe: Fostering a People's Europe? **In** *Lodge, J., ed.,* 1989, pp. 303–18.

Loeb, Peter D. and Fowles, Richard. Speeding, Coordination, and the 55-MPH Limit: Comment. *Amer. Econ. Rev.,* September 1989, *79*(4), pp. 916–21.

_____ **and Levine, Philip.** Asymmetric Behavior of the Prime Rate of Interest. *Amer. Economist,* Fall 1989, *33*(2), pp. 34–38.

Loef, Hans-E. The Case for Rules in the Conduct of Monetary Policy: A Critique on a Paper by B. T. McCallum. *Weltwirtsch. Arch.,* 1989, *125*(1), pp. 168–78.

Loehnis, Anthony D. European Currency and European Central Bank—A British View. **In** *Franz, O., ed.,* 1989, pp. 76–88.

Loehr, Raymond C. Multi-media Aspects of Waste Management. **In** *Dysart, B. C., III and Clawson, M., eds.,* 1989, pp. 9–26.

Loehr, William and Van Ness, Peter. The Cost of Self-Reliance: The Case of China. **In** *Van Ness, P., ed.,* 1989, pp. 262–80.

Loesch, Dieter. The Difficulties in Reforming Soviet Type Economies: Red China's New Economic Policies in the Light of Eastern European Reform Experiences. **In** *Gemper, B. B., ed.,* 1989, pp. 107–17.

Loewenstein, George and Thaler, Richard H. Intertemporal Choice. *J. Econ. Perspectives,* Fall 1989, *3*(4), pp. 181–93.

_____; **Weber, Martin and Camerer, Colin F.** The Curse of Knowledge in Economic Settings: An Experimental Analysis. *J. Polit. Econ.,* October 1989, *97*(5), pp. 1232–54.

Loewenstein, Mark A.; Barron, John M. and Black, Dan A. Job Matching and On-the-Job Training. *J. Lab. Econ.,* January 1989, *7*(1), pp. 1–19.

Löfgren, Karl-Gustaf. Buying and Selling Behavior in Stochastic Environments with Backstop Markets. *J. Econ. (Z. Nationalökon.),* 1989, *50*(2), pp. 87–112.

_____ **and Johansson, Per-Olov.** Disequilibrium Cost–Benefit Rules: An Exposition and Extension. **In** *Folmer, H. and van Ierland, E., eds.,* 1989, pp. 161–86.

_____; **Mäler, Karl-Göran and Johansson, Per-Olov.** Recreational Values, Pareto Optimality and Timber Supply. **In** *Folmer, H. and van Ierland, E., eds.,* 1989, pp. 49–68.

Löflund, Anders. Kopplingen mellan aktiekurser och makroekonomi. (The Connection between Stock Prices and Macroeconomics. With English summary.) *Ekon. Samfundets Tidskr.,* 1989, *42*(2), pp. 87–94.

_____; **Berglund, Tom and Liljeblom, Eva.** Estimating Betas on Daily Data for a Small Stock Market. *J. Banking Finance,* March 1989, *13*(1), pp. 41–64.

Löfren, Karl-Gustaf and Engström, Lars. The Duration of Unemployment: Theory and Evidence. **In** *Holmlund, B.; Löfgren, K.-G. and Engström, L.,* 1989, pp. 133–220.

Lofti, Sherif; Behrman, Jere R. and Lewis, Jeffrey D. The Impact of Commodity Price Instability: Experiments with a General Equilibrium Model for Indonesia. **In** *[Adams, F. G.],* 1989, pp. 59–100.

Logan, Bob and Shieh, Yeung-Nan. Location and Corporate Decisions in a Truly Profit Maximizing Model. *Reg. Sci. Urban Econ.,* February 1989, *19*(1), pp. 125–31.

Logan, J. and Trengove, C. D. Extract from "Forum on Health Insurance in Australia: Financing Health Care—Which Way from Here?" **In** *Butler, J. R. G. and Doessel, D. P., eds.,* 1989, *1988,* pp. 185–88.

Logan, James; Lovell, C. A. Knox and Färe, Rolf. Some Economics of Content Protection. *J. Econ. (Z. Nationalökon.),* 1989, *50*(2), pp. 171–80.

Logan, John W. and Lutter, Randall W. Guaranteed Lowest Prices: Do They Facilitate Collusion? *Econ. Letters,* December 1989, *31*(2), pp. 189–92.

_____; **Masson, Robert T. and Reynolds, Robert J.** Efficient Regulation with Little Information: Reality in the Limit? *Int. Econ. Rev.,* November 1989, *30*(4), pp. 851–61.

Logan, Robert R. and O'Brien, J. Patrick. Fiscal Illusion, Budget Maximizers, and Dynamic Equilibrium. *Public Choice,* December 1989, *63*(3), pp. 221–35.

Logue, Dennis E. and Maloney, Kevin J. Neglected Complexities in Structured Bond Portfolios. *J. Portfol. Manage.,* Winter 1989, *15*(2), pp. 59–68.

Lohmann, Karl and Rühmann, Peter. Marktverzinsung und Erhaltungskonzeptionen bei abnutzbaren Anlagegegenständen. (With English summary.) *Z. Betriebswirtshaft,* December 1989, *59*(12), pp. 1324–37.

Loistl, Otto; Akgiray, Vedat and Booth, G. Geoffrey. German Stock Market's Resiliency to World-Wide Panics. *Z. Betriebswirtshaft,* September 1989, *59*(9), pp. 968–78.

_____; **Akgiray, Vedat and Booth, G. Geoffrey.** Statistical Models of German Stock Returns. *J. Econ. (Z. Nationalökon.),* 1989, *50*(1), pp. 17–33.

_____; **Berger, Karin and Landes, Thomas.** Simulation of Synergetic Stock Price Modelling. **In** *Loistl, O. and Landes, T., ed.,* 1989, pp. 109–27.

_____ **and Landes, Thomas.** The Dynamic Pricing of Financial Assets: Introduction: The Market Performance at the Microlevel. **In** *Loistl, O. and Landes, T., ed.,* 1989, pp. 1–12.

_____ **and Reiss, Winfried.** Pricebuilding Mechanisms and Their Modelling in the Literature. **In** *Loistl, O. and Landes, T., ed.,* 1989, pp. 13–51.

_____; **Reiss, Winfried and Landes, Thomas.** The Determinants of the Fundamental Value Part of a Share Price. **In** *Loistl, O. and Landes, T., ed.,* 1989, pp. 129–63.

_____; **Reiss, Winfried and Landes, Thomas.** The Market Microstructure and the Dynamic

Pricing of Financial Assets. In *Loistl, O. and Landes, T., ed.*, 1989, pp. 53–108.

Loke, Wing Hong. The Effects of Framing and Incomplete Information on Judgments. *J. Econ. Psych.*, November 1989, *10*(3), pp. 329–41.

Lomasky, Loren E. and Brennan, Geoffrey. Large Numbers, Small Costs: The Uneasy Foundation of Democratic Rule. In *Brennan, G. and Lomasky, L. E., eds.*, 1989, pp. 42–59.

_____ and Brennan, Geoffrey. Politics and Process: New Essays in Democratic Thought: Introduction. In *Brennan, G. and Lomasky, L. E., eds.*, 1989, pp. 1–10.

Lomax, David F. Vocational Training. *Nat. Westminster Bank Quart. Rev.*, February 1989, pp. 2–3.

_____ and Wilkinson, Philip [Sir]. Lessons for Banking from the 1980s and the Recent Past. *Nat. Westminster Bank Quart. Rev.*, May 1989, pp. 2–16.

de Lombaerde, P. and Verbeke, Alain. Assessing International Seaport Competition: A Tool for Strategic Decision Making. *Int. J. Transport Econ.*, June 1989, *16*(2), pp. 175–92.

Lombard, J. R. and Harrington, James W., Jr. Producer-Service Firms in a Declining Manufacturing Region. *Environ. Planning A*, January 1989, *21*(1), pp. 65–79.

Lombardini, Siro. Market and Institutions. In *Shiraishi, T. and Tsuru, S., eds.*, 1989, pp. 27–49.

Lombra, Raymond E. and Karamouzis, Nicholas. Federal Reserve Policymaking: An Overview and Analysis of the Policy Process. *Carnegie–Rochester Conf. Ser. Public Policy*, Spring 1989, *30*, pp. 7–62.

_____ and Kim, Sun-Young. Why the Empirical Relationship between Deficits and Interest Rates Appears So Fragile. *J. Econ. Bus.*, August 1989, *41*(3), pp. 241–51.

Lommerud, Kjell Erik. Educational Subsidies When Relative Income Matters. *Oxford Econ. Pap.*, July 1989, *41*(3), pp. 640–52.

_____. Marital Division of Labor with Risk of Divorce: The Role of "Voice" Enforcement of Contracts. *J. Lab. Econ.*, January 1989, *7*(1), pp. 113–27.

Lonergan, S.; Cocklin, C. and Harte, M. Patterns of Change in the Use of Energy in the New Zealand Economy. *Environ. Planning A*, September 1989, *21*(9), pp. 1141–56.

Loney, Glenn E. Statement to the U.S. House Subcommittee on Policy Research and Insurance of the Committee on Banking, Finance and Urban Affairs, May 31, 1989. *Fed. Res. Bull.*, July 1989, *75*(7), pp. 498–501.

Long, Frank. Manufacturing Exports in the Caribbean and the New International Division of Labour. *Soc. Econ. Stud.*, March 1989, *38*(1), pp. 115–31.

Long, James E. The Effect of the 1986 Tax Act on Personal Interest Deductions. *Public Finance Quart.*, July 1989, *17*(3), pp. 243–63.

Long, Millard and Evenhouse, Eirik. Restructur-

ing Distressed Financial Systems. *Finance Devel.*, September 1989, *26*(3), pp. 4–7.

Long, Ngo Van. On the Organization of Rural Markets and the Process of Economic Development: Comment. *Amer. Econ. Rev.*, December 1989, *79*(5), pp. 1297–98.

_____ and Brecher, Richard A. Trade Unions in an Open Economy: A General Equilibrium Analysis. *Econ. Rec.*, September 1989, *65*(190), pp. 234–39.

_____; Chiarella, Carl and Kemp, Murray C. Innovation and the Transfer of Technology: A Leader–Follower Model. *Econ. Modelling*, October 1989, *6*(4), pp. 452–56.

_____ and Crabbé, Philippe J. Optimal Forest Rotation under Monopoly and Competition. *J. Environ. Econ. Manage.*, July 1989, *17*(1), pp. 54–65.

_____ and Kemp, Murray C. Union Power in the Long Run Reconsidered: Comment. *Scand. J. Econ.*, 1989, *91*(4), pp. 747–48.

_____ and Siebert, Horst. Optimal Foreign Borrowing: The Impact of the Planning Horizon on the Half and Full Debt Cycle. *J. Econ. (Z. Nationalökon.)*, 1989, *49*(3), pp. 279–97.

Long, Stewart and Gill, Andrew M. Is There an Immigration Status Wage Differential between Legal and Undocumented Workers? Evidence from the Los Angeles Garment Industry. *Soc. Sci. Quart.*, March 1989, *70*(1), pp. 164–73.

Long, William T., III and Berger, Franklin D. The Texas Industrial Production Index. *Fed. Res. Bank Dallas Econ. Rev.*, November 1989, pp. 21–38.

Longhurst, Richard and Lipton, Michael. The Role of Agricultural Research and Secondary Food Crops in Reducing Seasonal Food Insecurity. In *Sahn, D. E., ed.*, 1989, pp. 285–97.

Longley, P.; Fotheringham, S. and Batty, M. Urban Growth and Form: Scaling, Fractal Geometry, and Diffusion-Limited Aggregation. *Environ. Planning A*, November 1989, *21*(11), pp. 1447–72.

Longo, C. A. Fiscal Issues and the 1988 Constitution: Brazil. *Bull. Int. Fiscal Doc.*, Aug.–Sept. 1989, *43*(8–9), pp. 389–93.

Longo, Peter J. and Miewald, Robert D. Institutions in Water Policy: The Case of Nebraska. *Natural Res. J.*, Summer 1989, *29*(3), pp. 751–62.

Longstaff, Francis A. A Nonlinear General Equilibrium Model of the Term Structure of Interest Rates. *J. Finan. Econ.*, August 1989, *23*(2), pp. 195–224.

_____. Temporal Aggregation and the Continuous-Time Capital Asset Pricing Model. *J. Finance*, September 1989, *44*(4), pp. 871–87.

Longworth, David. The Profitability of Forward Currency Speculation by Central Banks. *Europ. Econ. Rev.*, April 1989, *33*(4), pp. 839–43.

Lonsdale, R. E. The Nonmetropolitan Western United States and Its Changing Employment Structure. In *Gibson, L. J. and Stimson, R. J., eds.*, 1989, pp. 109–24.

Loo, Thomas and Tower, Edward. Agricultural Protectionism and the Less Developed Countries: The Relationship between Agricultural Prices, Debt Servicing Capacities, and the Need for Development Aid. **In** *Stoeckel, A. B.; Vincent, D. and Cuthbertson, S., eds.*, 1989, pp. 64–93.

Loomes, Graham. Experimental Economics. **In** *Hey, J. D., ed.*, 1989, pp. 152–78.

———; Starmer, Chris and Sugden, Robert. Preference Reversal: Information-Processing Effect or Rational Non-transitive Choice? *Econ. J.*, Supplement, 1989, 99(395), pp. 140–51.

Loomis, John B. Test–Retest Reliability of the Contingent Valuation Method: A Comparison of General Population and Visitor Responses. *Amer. J. Agr. Econ.*, February 1989, 71(1), pp. 76–84.

Looney, J. Jefferson. Cultural Life in the Provinces: Leeds and York, 1720–1820. **In** *[Stone, L.]*, 1989, pp. 483–510.

Looney, Robert E. The Economic Impact of Rent Seeking and Military Expenditures: A Comparison of Third World Military and Civilian Regimes. *Amer. J. Econ. Sociology*, January 1989, 48(1), pp. 11–29.

———. The Impact of Arms Imports and Economic Environments on Third World Debt. **In** *Avery, W. P. and Rapkin, D. P., eds.*, 1989, pp. 85–104.

———. Impact of Arms Production on Income Distribution and Growth in the Third World. *Econ. Devel. Cult. Change*, October 1989, 38(1), pp. 145–53.

———. The Influence of Arms Imports on Third World Debt. *J. Developing Areas*, January 1989, 23(2), pp. 221–31.

———. Macroeconomic Consequences of the Size of Third World Nations: With Special Reference to the Caribbean. *World Devel.*, January 1989, 17(1), pp. 69–83.

———. Profiles of Small, Lesser Developed Economies. *Can. J. Devel. Stud.*, 1989, 10(1), pp. 21–37.

———. The Role of Infrastructure in Saudi Arabia's Development: The Relative Importance of Linkage vs. Spread Effects. *Int. J. Transport Econ.*, February 1989, 16(1), pp. 57–78.

Looney, Stephen W.; Wansley, James W. and Lane, William R. An Examination of Misclassifications with Bank Failure Prediction Models. *J. Econ. Bus.*, November 1989, 41(4), pp. 327–36.

Lopes, Jose da Silva. Policies of Economic Adjustment to Correct External Imbalances. **In** *Roe, A.; Roy, J. and Sengupta, J.*, 1989, pp. 21–33.

Lopez-Claros, Augusto. Growth-Oriented Adjustment: Spain in the 1980s. *Finance Devel.*, March 1989, 26(1), pp. 38–41.

Lopez Diaz, Ligia. The Disregard of a Legal Entity for Tax Purposes: Colombia. **In** *International Fiscal Association, ed. (II)*, 1989, pp. 239–47.

Lopez, F. A. and Darrat, Ali F. Has Inflation

Uncertainty Hampered Economic Growth in Latin America? *Int. Econ. J.*, Summer 1989, 3(2), pp. 1–15.

Lopez-Garcia, Miguel-Angel. Public Debt, Voluntary Intergenerational Transfers and Overlapping Generations. *Econ. Letters*, 1989, 29(2), pp. 115–20.

López M., Cecilia and Pollack, Molly. The Incorporation of Women in Development Policies. *CEPAL Rev.*, December 1989, (39), pp. 37–46.

Lopez, Rigoberto A. Political Economy of U.S. Sugar Policies. *Amer. J. Agr. Econ.*, February 1989, 71(1), pp. 20–31.

Lopuch, Bozena; Bronisz, Piotr and Krus, Lech. MCBARG: A System Supporting Multicriteria Bargaining. **In** *Lewandowski, A. and Wierzbicki, A. P., eds.*, 1989, pp. 388–90.

Lorange, Peter. Cooperative Ventures in Multinational Settings. **In** *Hallén, L. and Johanson, J., eds.*, 1989, pp. 211–33.

Loranger, Jean-Guy. A Reexamination of the Marxian Circuit of Capital: A New Look at Inflation. *Rev. Radical Polit. Econ.*, 1989, 21(1–2), pp. 97–112.

Lord, Montague J. International Commodity Trade and Latin American Exports: An Empirical Investigation. **In** *Brock, P. L.; Connolly, M. B. and González-Vega, C., eds.*, 1989, pp. 227–41.

———. Primary Commodities as an Engine for Export Growth of Latin America. **In** *Islam, N., ed.*, 1989, pp. 129–45.

———. Production Differentiation in International Commodity Trade. *Oxford Bull. Econ. Statist.*, February 1989, 51(1), pp. 35–53.

Lord, William. The Transition from Payroll to Consumption Receipts with Endogenous Human Capital. *J. Public Econ.*, February 1989, 38(1), pp. 53–73.

Lorek, Kenneth S.; Bathke, Allen W., Jr. and Hassell, John M. New Evidence on the Accuracy of Management Forecasts and Time-Series Forecasts of Annual Earnings. **In** *Schwartz, B. N., ed.*, 1989, pp. 67–84.

———; Willinger, G. Lee and Bathke, Allen W., Jr. Firm-Size and the Predictive Ability of Quarterly Earnings Data. *Accounting Rev.*, January 1989, 64(1), pp. 49–68.

Lorenz, Detlef. Newly Industrialising Countries in the World Economy: NICs, SICs, NECs, EPZs or TEs? **In** *[Fischer, W.]*, 1989, pp. 338–66.

———. Trade in Manufactures, Newly Industrializing Economies (NIEs), and Regional Development in the World Economy—A European View. *Developing Econ.*, September 1989, 27(3), pp. 221–35.

Lorenz, Edward H. The Search for Flexibility: Subcontracting Networks in British and French Engineering. **In** *Hirst, P. and Zeitlin, J., eds.*, 1989, pp. 122–32.

Lorenz, Wilhelm and Wagner, Joachim. Einkommensfunktionsschätzungen mit Längsschnittdaten für vollzeiterwerbstätige deutsche Männer. (Estimates of Earnings Functions for Full-Time Working German Men Using Longitudinal Data. With English summary.) *Konjunkturpolitik*, 1989, *35*(1–2), pp. 99–109.

Lorenzen, Gunter. Input–Output Multipliers When Data Are Incomplete or Unreliable. *Environ. Planning A*, August 1989, *21*(8), pp. 1075–92.

_____ **and Maas, Christoph.** Zur Input–Output Analyse mit Intervalldaten. (On Input–Output Analysis with Interval Data. With English summary.) *Jahr. Nationalökon. Statist.*, July 1989, *206*(3), pp. 257–63.

Loridan, P. and Morgan, J. ∈-Regularized Two-Level Optimization Problems: Approximation and Existence Results. In *Dolecki, S., ed.,* 1989, pp. 99–113.

Lorie, Henri and Buiter, Willem H. Some Unfamiliar Properties of a Familiar Macroeconomic Model. In *Buiter, W. H.,* 1989, *1977*, pp. 335–48.

_____ **and DeMasi, Paula.** How Resilient Are Military Expenditures? *Int. Monet. Fund Staff Pap.*, March 1989, *36*(1), pp. 130–65.

Lörinc, Hajna Istvanffy. Conditionality and Adjustment. In *Singer, H. W. and Sharma, S., eds. (II),* 1989, pp. 115–26.

Losq, Etienne and Errunza, Vihang R. Capital Flow Controls, International Asset Pricing, and Investors' Welfare: A Multi-country Framework. *J. Finance*, September 1989, *44*(4), pp. 1025–37.

Lotfi, V.; Gardner, J. C. and Huefner, R. J. An Interactive Multi-criteria Model for Audit Workload Planning. In *Lockett, A. G. and Islei, G., eds.,* 1989, pp. 234–43.

Lothian, James R. and Darby, Michael R. The International Transmission of Inflation Afloat. In *[Schwartz, A. J.],* 1989, pp. 203–36.

Lott, John R., Jr. Explaining Challengers' Campaign Expenditures: The Importance of Sunk Nontransferable Brand Name. *Public Finance Quart.*, January 1989, *17*(1), pp. 108–18.

_____. Licensing and Nontransferable Rents: Reply. *Amer. Econ. Rev.*, September 1989, *79*(4), pp. 910–12.

_____. Racial Employment and Earnings Differentials: The Impact of the Reagan Administration—Comment. *Rev. Black Polit. Econ.*, Spring 1989, *17*(4), pp. 83–84.

_____ **and Bronars, Stephen G.** Why Do Workers Join Unions? The Importance of Rent Seeking. *Econ. Inquiry*, April 1989, *27*(2), pp. 305–24.

_____ **and Darby, Michael R.** Qualitative Information, Reputation, and Monopolistic Competition. *Int. Rev. Law Econ.*, June 1989, *9*(1), pp. 87–103.

_____ **and Fremling, Gertrud M.** Deadweight Losses and the Saving Response to a Deficit. *Econ. Inquiry*, January 1989, *27*(1), pp. 117–29.

_____ **and Fremling, Gertrud M.** Time Dependent Information Costs, Price Controls, and Successive Government Intervention. *J. Law, Econ., Organ.*, Fall 1989, *5*(2), pp. 293–306.

_____ **and Reed, W. Robert.** Shirking and Sort-

ing in a Political Market with Finite-Lived Politicians. *Public Choice*, April 1989, *61*(1), pp. 75–96.

_____ **and Reynolds, Morgan O.** Production Costs and Deregulation. *Public Choice*, May 1989, *61*(2), pp. 183–86.

_____ **and Roberts, Russell D.** Why Comply: One-Sided Enforcement of Price Controls and Victimless Crime Laws. *J. Legal Stud.*, June 1989, *18*(2), pp. 403–14.

Lou, Jiwei and Zhou, Xiaochuan. On the Direction of Reform in the Price System. *Chinese Econ. Stud.*, Spring 1989, *22*(3), pp. 14–23.

Loube, Robert. The Return of the Electric Utility Holding Company and the Future of the Electric Supply Industry. *J. Econ. Issues*, June 1989, *23*(2), pp. 625–32.

Loucks, Christine and Bennett, Randall W. Price (De)Regulation and Quality Rivalry: The Case of Branch Banking Revisited. *Quart. J. Bus. Econ.*, Winter 1989, *28*(1), pp. 68–82.

Loungani, Prakash and Rogerson, Richard. Cyclical Fluctuations and Sectoral Reallocation: Evidence from the PSID. *J. Monet. Econ.*, March 1989, *23*(2), pp. 259–73.

Louri, Helen. Regional Policy and Investment Behaviour: The Case of Greece, 1971–1982. *Reg. Stud.*, June 1989, *23*(3), pp. 231–39.

_____ **and Hay, Donald A.** Firms as Portfolios: A Mean–Variance Analysis of Unquoted UK Companies. *J. Ind. Econ.*, December 1989, *38*(2), pp. 141–65.

Loury, Glenn C. Why Should We Care about Group Inequality? In *Shulman, S. and Darity, W., Jr., eds.,* 1989, pp. 268–90.

Louscher, David J. and Schwarz, Anne Naylor. Patterns of Third World Military Technology Acquisition. In *Baek, K.-I.; McLaurin, R. D. and Moon, C., eds.,* 1989, pp. 33–56.

Loute, Etienne. Twenty Years of Mathematical Programming: Comment. In *Cornet, B. and Tulkens, H., eds.,* 1989, pp. 228–32.

_____ **and Janssens de Bisthoven, Olivier.** Solving Arborescent Linear Programs with Nested Decomposition. In *Cornet, B. and Tulkens, H., eds.,* 1989, pp. 285–314.

Loutfi, Martha F. Development Issues and State Policies in Sub-Saharan Africa. *Int. Lab. Rev.*, 1989, *128*(2), pp. 137–54.

Loutsov, Ivan. The Role of the Cooperative in the Further Development of Socialism. In *Bulgarian Academy of Sciences, Institute of Economics,* 1989, pp. 89–99.

Louviere, J. J., et al. Determinants of Migration of the Elderly in the United States: A Model of Individual-Level Migration Decision Making. In *Gibson, L. J. and Stimson, R. J., eds.,* 1989, pp. 61–71.

Lovász, L.; Goecke, O. and Korte, Bernhard. Examples and Algorithmic Properties of Greedoids. In *Simeone, B., ed.,* 1989, pp. 113–61.

Love, Douglas O. and Torrence, William D. The Value of Advance Notice of Worker Displacement. *Southern Econ. J.*, January 1989, *55*(3), pp. 626–43.

Love, James H. Export Instability and Recurrent and Development Expenditure in a Sample of Developing Countries. *J. Developing Areas*, October 1989, *24*(1), pp. 19–26.

_____. Export Instability, Imports and Investment in Developing Countries. *J. Devel. Stud.*, January 1989, *25*(2), pp. 183–91.

_____. External Takeover and Regional Economic Development: A Survey and Critique. *Reg. Stud.*, October 1989, *23*(5), pp. 417–29.

_____ and **Ashcroft, Brian.** Evaluating the Effects of External Takeover on the Performance of Regional Companies: The Case of Scotland, 1965 to 1980. *Environ. Planning A*, February 1989, *21*(2), pp. 197–220.

Love, Joseph. Modeling Internal Colonialism: History and Prospect. *World Devel.*, June 1989, *17*(6), pp. 905–22.

Lovell, C. A. Knox. Policy Implications of the Slowdown in U.S. Productivity Growth: Comment. **In** *Black, S. W., ed.*, 1989, pp. 111–19.

_____; **Färe, Rolf and Logan, James.** Some Economics of Content Protection. *J. Econ. (Z. Nationalökon.)*, 1989, *50*(2), pp. 171–80.

_____; **Thursby, M. C. and Blackorby, Charles.** Extended Hicks Neutral Technical Change. **In** *Wood, J. C. and Woods, R. N., eds.*, *Vol. 3*, 1989, *1976*, pp. 153–62.

Lovell, Michael and Duncan, Cheryl. The Pension Subsidy of Educational Inequality. *Econ. Educ. Rev.*, 1989, *8*(4), pp. 313–21.

Lovins, Amory B. and Lovins, L. Hunter. Drill Rigs and Battleships Are the Answer! (But What Was the Question?): Oil Efficiency, Economic Rationality, and Security. **In** *[Evans, J. K.]*, 1989, pp. 83–138.

Lovins, L. Hunter and Lovins, Amory B. Drill Rigs and Battleships Are the Answer! (But What Was the Question?): Oil Efficiency, Economic Rationality, and Security. **In** *[Evans, J. K.]*, 1989, pp. 83–138.

Loviscek, Anthony L. and Cloutier, Norman R. AFDC Benefits and the Inter-urban Variation in Poverty among Female-Headed Households. *Southern Econ. J.*, October 1989, *56*(2), pp. 315–22.

Lovrich, Nicholas P.; Warner, Rebecca L. and Steel, Brent S. Conditions Associated with the Advent of Representative Bureaucracy: The Case of Women in Policing. *Soc. Sci. Quart.*, September 1989, *70*(3), pp. 562–78.

Low, Linda and Heng, Toh Mun. Health Care Economics in Singapore: Trends and Issues. **In** *Smith, C. S., ed.*, 1989, pp. 147–68.

Low, Stuart A.; Boyes, William J. and Hoffman, Dennis L. An Econometric Analysis of the Bank Credit Scoring Problem. *J. Econometrics*, January 1989, *40*(1), pp. 3–14.

Low, William; McIntosh, James and Schiantarelli, Fabio. A Qualitative Response Analysis of UK Firms' Employment and Output Decisions. *J. Appl. Econometrics*, July–Sept. 1989, *4*(3), pp. 251–64.

Lowder, Stella. The Distributional Consequences of Nepotism, and Patron–Clientelism: The Case of Cuenca, Ecuador. **In** *Ward, P. M., ed.*, 1989, pp. 123–42.

Lowe, Graham S. and Krahn, Harvey. Computer Skills and Use among High School and University Graduates. *Can. Public Policy*, June 1989, *15*(2), pp. 175–88.

_____ and **Krahn, Harvey.** Recent Trends in Public Support for Unions in Canada. *J. Lab. Res.*, Fall 1989, *10*(4), pp. 391–410.

Lowe, Ian. World Environmental and Energy Issues: Australian Policy Issues. **In** *Owen, A. D., ed.*, 1989, pp. 62–70.

Lowe, J. F. and Silver, Mick S. An Appraisal of the Performance of Manufacturing Industry in Wales. *J. Econ. Stud.*, 1989, *16*(1), pp. 31–46.

Lowe, John C. and Viterito, Arthur. Differential Spatial Attraction of Private Colleges and Universities in the United States. *Econ. Geogr.*, July 1989, *65*(3), pp. 208–15.

Lowe, M. S. Never Mind the Planning. . .Feel the Initiative: Local Government Policy and Worker Co-operatives. **In** *Gibbs, D., ed.*, 1989, pp. 286–308.

Lowe, Philip and Flynn, Andrew. Environmental Politics and Policy in the 1980s. **In** *Mohan, J., ed.*, 1989, pp. 255–79.

_____; **Winter, Michael and Cox, Graham.** The Farm Crisis in Britain. **In** *Goodman, D. and Redclift, M., eds.*, 1989, pp. 113–34.

Lowenberg, Anton D. An Economic Theory of Apartheid. *Econ. Inquiry*, January 1989, *27*(1), pp. 57–74.

_____ and **Kaempfer, William H.** Sanctioning South Africa: The Politics behind the Policies. *Cato J.*, Winter 1989, *8*(3), pp. 713–27.

_____ and **Kaempfer, William H.** The Theory of International Economic Sanctions—A Public Choice Approach: Reply. *Amer. Econ. Rev.*, December 1989, *79*(5), pp. 1304–06.

Lowenstein, Daniel H. Legal Efforts to Define Political Bribery. **In** *Heidenheimer, A. J.; Johnston, M. and LeVine, V. T., eds.*, 1989, *1985*, pp. 29–38.

Lowenthal, Franklin and Langsen, Arnold L. The Omega Matrix. *Managerial Dec. Econ.*, June 1989, *10*(2), pp. 155–58.

Lower, Milton D. The Industrial Economy and International Price Shocks. **In** *Tool, M. R. and Samuels, W. J., eds. (III)*, 1989, *1986*, pp. 461–76.

Lown, Cara S. Interest Rate Spreads, Commodity Prices, and the Dollar: A New Strategy for Monetary Policy? *Fed. Res. Bank Dallas Econ. Rev.*, July 1989, pp. 13–26.

_____ and **Cox, William Michael.** The Capital Gains and Losses on U.S. Government Debt: 1942–1987. *Rev. Econ. Statist.*, February 1989, *71*(1), pp. 1–14.

Lowry, Mark Newton. Competitive Speculative Storage and the Cost of Refinery Product Supply. *Energy J.*, April 1989, *10*(2), pp. 187–93.

Lowry, S. Todd. Bargain and Contract Theory in Law and Economics. **In** *Tool, M. R. and Samuels, W. J., eds. (III)*, 1989, *1976*, pp. 41–62.

Löwy, Michael. Weber against Marx? The Polemic with Historical Materialism in the *Protestant Ethic. Sci. Society,* Spring 1989, *53*(1), pp. 71–83.

Loxley, John. The Devaluation Debate in Tanzania. In *Campbell, B. K. and Loxley, J., eds.,* 1989, pp. 1–36.

_____. The IMF, the World Bank and Reconstruction in Uganda. In *Campbell, B. K. and Loxley, J., eds.,* 1989, pp. 67–91.

_____ and Campbell, Bonnie K. Structural Adjustment in Africa: Introduction. In *Campbell, B. K. and Loxley, J.; eds.,* 1989, pp. 1–11.

Loyns, R. M. A. and Timko, M. Market Information Needs for Prairie Farmers. *Can. J. Agr. Econ.,* Part 1, December 1989, *37*(4), pp. 609–27.

Lu, Shiguang and Huang, Junting. The Role of China's Import Trade during the First Five-Year Plan. In *Howe, C. and Walker, K. R., eds.,* 1989, *1957,* pp. 52–62.

Lu, Wen-he; Gale, James R. and Shen, Patrick. Cross Section Evidence on the Demand for Money by the Household Sector. In *Missouri Valley Economic Association,* 1989, pp. 63–69.

Luban, David. Difference Made Legal: The Court and Dr. King. *Mich. Law Rev.,* August 1989, *87*(8), pp. 2152–2224.

Luban, Florica and Dumitru, V. A Generalized Huard–Iri Function for Unconstrained Optimization. *Econ. Computat. Econ. Cybern. Stud. Res.,* 1989, *24*(1), pp. 77–80.

Lubeck, Paul. Petroleum and Proletarianization: The Life History of a Muslim Nigerian Worker. *African Econ. Hist.,* 1989, (18), pp. 99–112.

Luben, Maydia. Review of Monetary and Credit Policies in Belize, 1976–1986. In *Worrell, D. and Bourne, C., eds.,* 1989, pp. 105–14.

Lubian, Diego and Ardeni, Pier Giorgio. Co-integration and Trend Reversion in Purchasing Power Parity. *Giorn. Econ.,* March–April 1989, *48*(3–4), pp. 109–28.

_____ and Ardeni, Pier Giorgio. Purchasing Power Parity during the 1920s. *Econ. Letters,* October 1989, *30*(4), pp. 357–62.

Lucángeli, Jorge. Technological Behaviour of Argentine Public Enterprises: The Case of Yacimientos Petrolíferos Fiscales. In *James, J., ed.,* 1989, pp. 139–69.

Lucas, R. F. The Bank of Canada and Zero Inflation: A New Cross of Gold? *Can. Public Policy,* March 1989, *15*(1), pp. 84–93.

Lucas, Robert C. A Look at Wilderness Use and Users in Transition. *Natural Res. J.,* Winter 1989, *29*(1), pp. 41–55.

Lucas, Robert E. B. Liberalization of Indian Trade and Industrial Licensing: A Disaggregated Econometric Model with Simulations. *J. Devel. Econ.,* July 1989, *31*(1), pp. 141–75.

_____, Jr. and Prescott, Edward C. Equilibrium Search and Unemployment. In *Diamond, P. and Rothschild, M., eds.,* 1989, *1974,* pp. 517–38.

Lucassen, Jan. The Standard of Living Debate and Social History: A Comment. In *Scholliers, P., ed.,* 1989, pp. 101–06.

de Lucena, Diogo. On the Representation of Information Structures: A Clarification. *Economia (Portugal),* January 1989, *13*(1), pp. 114–18.

Lucertini, M.; Nicolò, F. and Arbib, Claudio. Optimization Models for Flexible Manufacturing Systems. In *Archetti, F.; Lucertini, M. and Serafini, P., eds.,* 1989, pp. 75–89.

Lucey, Brian M. Efficiency in the Forward Exchange Market: An Application of Co-integration: Reply. *Econ. Soc. Rev.,* April 1989, *20*(3), pp. 286–87.

_____. The Real Wage Gap and Its Development over Time: The Irish Experience 1960–87: A Comment. *Econ. Soc. Rev.,* October 1989, *21*(1), pp. 103–05.

_____. Tests for the Macroeconomic Effects of Large-Scale Migration Based on the Irish Experience, 1948–87: A Comment. *Econ. Soc. Rev.,* April 1989, *20*(3), pp. 274–77.

Lucifora, Claudio. Differenziali retributivi per settori e professioni nella provincia di Milano. (Wage Differentials by Sector and Profession in the Milan Area. With English summary.) *Econ. Lavoro,* July–Sept. 1989, *23*(3), pp. 55–70.

Luckett, Charles A.; Durkin, Thomas A. and Canner, Glenn B. Home Equity Lending. *Fed. Res. Bull.,* May 1989, *75*(5), pp. 333–44.

Lucore, Robert E. American Exceptionalism and the Economic Role of the Public Sector: Canada and the U.S. Compared. *Int. J. Soc. Econ.,* 1989, *16*(3), pp. 34–43.

Lüdiger, Martin. Wechselkursovershooting contra effiziente Devisenmärkte. (Exchange Rate Overshooting versus Efficient Foreign Exchange Markets. With English summary.) *Kredit Kapital,* 1989, *22*(2), pp. 173–96.

Ludwig, Jacob; Schuman, Howard and Kalton, Graham. Context and Contiguity in Survey Questionnaires. In *Singer, E. and Presser, S., eds.,* 1989, *1983,* pp. 151–54.

Ludwig, Udo. Input–Output Table Extended to Skilled Labour Input. In *Franz, A. and Rainer, N., eds.,* 1989, pp. 87–110.

Lueck, Dean. The Economic Nature of Wildlife Law. *J. Legal Stud.,* June 1989, *18*(2), pp. 291–324.

Luger, Michael I. and Goldstein, Harvey A. Federal Labor Protections and the Privatization of Public Transit. *J. Policy Anal. Manage.,* Spring 1989, *8*(2), pp. 229–50.

Luis, Luis R. The Rise of the Market-Based "Menu" Approach and Its Limitations: Comment. In *Husain, I. and Diwan, I., eds.,* 1989, pp. 159–60.

Lukac, Louis P. and Brorsen, B. Wade. The Usefulness of Historical Data in Selecting Parameters for Technical Trading Systems. *J. Futures Markets,* February 1989, *9*(1), pp. 55–65.

Lukács, Béla. Once More about Economic Entropy. *Acta Oecon.,* 1989, *41*(1–2), pp. 181–92.

Lukashin, Yuri P. An Adaptive Method of Regression Analysis. In *Hackl, P., ed.,* 1989, pp. 209–16.

Lukasiewicz, John and Silvestri, George. Projections of Occupational Employment, 1988–2000. *Mon. Lab. Rev.*, November 1989, *112*(11), pp. 42–65.

Lukka, Kari. Budjettiharhan luominen organisaatiossa. (Budgetary Biasing in Organizations. With English summary.) *Liiketaloudellinen Aikak.*, 1989, *38*(1), pp. 63–66.

_____. Laskentatoimen käsitteiden ontologia— Esimerkkinä voiton käsitteen analysointi. (An Ontological Analysis of Accounting Concepts. Example: In What Sense Does Accounting Profit Exist? With English summary.) *Liiketaloudellinen Aikak.*, 1989, *38*(2), pp. 94–116.

Lulek, Andrzej F. and Paga, Leslaw A. The Spheres of Inequality in a Centrally Planned Economy: The Case of Poland. *Int. J. Soc. Econ.*, 1989, *16*(1), pp. 27–39.

Lummer, Scott L. and McConnell, John J. Further Evidence on the Bank Lending Process and the Capital-Market Response to Bank Loan Agreements. *J. Finan. Econ.*, November 1989, *25*(1), pp. 99–122.

Lund, Anker Brink. Involving Stakeholders in Technology Assessment: A Case Study of Community Health Informatics. In *Pedersen, J. L.*, ed., 1989, pp. 187–207.

Lund, Michael S. Between Welfare and the Market: Loan Guarantees as a Policy Tool. In *Salamon, L. M.*, ed., 1989, pp. 125–66.

_____ **and Salamon, Lester M.** The Tools Approach: Basic Analytics. In *Salamon, L. M.*, ed., 1989, pp. 23–49.

Lundahl, Mats. Apartheid: *Cui Bono? World Devel.*, June 1989, *17*(6), pp. 825–37.

_____ **and Blomqvist, Hans C.** Utvecklingsekonomins utveckling. En översikt. (The Progress of Development Economics. A Survey. With English summary.) *Ekon. Samfundets Tidskr.*, 1989, *42*(3), pp. 185–202.

_____ **and Vedovato, Claudio.** The State and Economic Development in Haiti and the Dominican Republic. *Scand. Econ. Hist. Rev.*, 1989, *37*(3), pp. 39–59.

Lundberg, Erik. Ricordo della Scuola di Stoccolma. (With English summary.) *Studi. Econ.*, 1989, *44*(37), pp. 3–16.

Lundberg, Lars and Hansson, Pär. Comparative Costs and Elasticities of Substitution as Determinants of Inter- and Intra-industry Trade. In *Tharakan, P. K. M. and Kol, J.*, eds., 1989, pp. 31–50.

Lundberg, Shelly J. Equality and Efficiency: Antidiscrimination Policies in the Labor Market. *Contemp. Policy Issues*, January 1989, *7*(1), pp. 75–94.

Lundborg, Per and Holmlund, Bertil. Unemployment Insurance Schemes for Reducing the Natural Rate of Unemployment. *J. Public Econ.*, February 1989, *38*(1), pp. 1–15.

Lundgren, Håkan and Faxén, Karl-Olof. Managers as Employees: Sweden. In *Roomkin, M. J.*, ed., 1989, pp. 176–201.

Lundvall, Bengt-Åke. Long Waves and the Uneven Development of Capitalism. In *Di Mat-*

teo, M.; Goodwin, R. M. and Vercelli, A., eds., 1989, pp. 332–52.

Lunghini, Giorgio. Il dottorato di ricerca: Ph.D. o borse di studio? (Italian Ph.D. Prgrammes: "Dottore di Ricerca" or "Borsista?" With English summary.) *Econ. Politica*, April 1989, *6*(1), pp. 3–7.

_____; **Rampa, Giorgio and Vaggi, Gianni.** The Age of Waste: Some Ideas on Full Employment. *Écon. Appl.*, 1989, *42*(1), pp. 115–33.

Lunn, John. R&D, Concentration and Advertising: A Simultaneous Equations Model. *Managerial Dec. Econ.*, June 1989, *10*(2), pp. 101–05.

Lunt, Peter K. The Perceived Causal Structure of Unemployment. In *Grunert, K. G. and Ölander, F.*, eds., 1989, pp. 107–20.

Luo, Xiaopeng. The Hierarchical Structure and the System of Ownership in China's Rural Enterprises. *Chinese Econ. Stud.*, Fall 1989, *23*(1), pp. 89–99.

Luo, Zhengfeng. Reflections on the System of Assets Management Responsibility. *Chinese Econ. Stud.*, Winter 1988–89, *22*(2), pp. 67–71.

Lupi, Claudio. Direct Tests of the Rational Expectations Hypothesis: A Study of Italian Entrepreneurs' Inflationary Expectations (1980–1988). *Econ. Notes*, 1989, (3), pp. 395–412.

Lurie, N.; Moscovice, I. and Finch, Michael. Minnesota: Plan Choice by the Mentally Ill in Medicaid Prepaid Health Plans. In *Scheffler, R. M. and Rossiter, L. F.*, eds., 1989, pp. 265–78.

Lusht, Kenneth M. and Saunders, Edward M. Direct Tests of the Divergence of Opinion Hypothesis in the Market for Racetrack Betting. *J. Finan. Res.*, Winter 1989, *12*(4), pp. 285–91.

Lütkenhorst, Wilfried. Industrial Development and Industrial Policy in the Republic of Korea, with Special Emphasis on Engineering Industries. *Industry Devel.*, January 1989, (25), pp. 1–22.

_____ **and Healey, Derek.** Export Processing Zones: The Case of the Republic of Korea. *Industry Devel.*, April 1989, (26), pp. 1–56.

Lütkepohl, Helmut. Prediction Tests for Structural Stability of Multiple Time Series. *J. Bus. Econ. Statist.*, January 1989, *7*(1), pp. 129–35.

_____. The Stability Assumption in Tests of Causality between Money and Income. *Empirical Econ.*, 1989, *14*(2), pp. 139–50.

_____. The Stability Assumption in Tests of Causality between Money and Income. In *Kramer, W.*, ed., 1989, pp. 75–86.

Lutter, Randall W. and Logan, John W. Guaranteed Lowest Prices: Do They Facilitate Collusion? *Econ. Letters*, December 1989, *31*(2), pp. 189–92.

Lutz, Ernst and El Serafy, Salah. Environmental and Natural Resource Accounting. In *Schramm, G. and Warford, J. J.*, eds., 1989, pp. 23–38.

Lutz, Friedrich A. The Functioning of the Gold

Standard. In *Peacock, A. and Willgerodt, H.*, eds. (II), 1989, *1935*, pp. 219–41.

_____. Observations on the Problem of Monopolies. In *Peacock, A. and Willgerodt, H.*, eds. (II), 1989, *1956*, pp. 152–70.

Lutz, James M. and Huff, David L. Urban Spheres of Influence in Ghana. *J. Developing Areas*, January 1989, *23*(2), pp. 201–20.

Lutz, Mark and Wonnacott, Paul. Is There a Case for Free Trade Areas? In *Schott, J. J.*, ed., 1989, pp. 59–84.

Lutz, Martin J. Gemeinschaftspatent und Gemeinschaftsmarke. (Community Patent and Community Trademark. With English summary.) *Aussenwirtschaft*, April 1989, *44*(1), pp. 93–108.

Lutz, Nancy A. Warranties as Signals under Consumer Moral Hazard. *Rand J. Econ.*, Summer 1989, *20*(2), pp. 239–55.

Lützel, Heinrich. Household Production and National Accounts. *Statist. J.*, 1989, *6*(4), pp. 337–48.

Luyten, Paul. Multilateralism versus Preferential Bilateralism: A European View. In *Schott, J. J.*, ed., 1989, pp. 271–79.

Luzadis, Rebecca A. and Mitchell, Olivia S. Pension Responses to Changes in Social Security. *Soc. Sec. Bull.*, August 1989, *52*(8), pp. 12–13.

de Luzenberger, Raul. Soluzioni di aspettative razionali e processi collettivi di scelta. (With English summary.) *Econ. Int.*, Feb.–March 1989, *42*(1–2), pp. 47–78.

_____ **and Del Monte, Alfredo.** The Effect of Regional Policy on New Firm Formation in Southern Italy. *Reg. Stud.*, June 1989, *23*(3), pp. 219–30.

Lye, J. N.; Ullah, Aman and Cribbett, P. F. Evaluation of the Two-Stage Least Squares Distribution Function by Imhof's Procedure. *J. Quant. Econ.*, January 1989, *5*(1), pp. 91–96.

Lyman, Theodore R. and Gardiner, John A. The Logic of Corruption Control. In *Heidenheimer, A. J.; Johnston, M. and LeVine, V. T.*, eds., 1989, pp. 827–40.

Lynas, M. G. and de Waal, D. P. Use of External Support Sources in the Planning Processes of Small Firms in Natal, South Africa. *J. Stud. Econ. Econometrics*, March 1989, *13*(1), pp. 77–88.

Lynch, Gerald J. Subsidies and Support. In *Horwich, G. and Lynch, G. J.*, eds., 1989, pp. 285–90.

_____ **and Watts, Michael.** The Principles Courses Revisited. *Amer. Econ. Rev.*, May 1989, *79*(2), pp. 236–41.

Lynch, J. E. The Implications of Electronic Point-of-Sale Technology on the Marketing/Operations Interface in UK Retailing. In *Mansfield, R.*, ed., 1989, pp. 127–39.

Lynch, Lisa M. The Youth Labor Market in the Eighties: Determinants of Re-employment Probabilities for Young Men and Women. *Rev. Econ. Statist.*, February 1989, *71*(1), pp. 37–45.

_____ **and Osterman, Paul.** Technological Inno-

vation and Employment in Telecommunications. *Ind. Relat.*, Spring 1989, *28*(2), pp. 188–206.

Lynch, Robert G. Centralization and Decentralization Redefined. *J. Compar. Econ.*, March 1989, *13*(1), pp. 1–14.

Lynch, Robin. Compilation of the Input–Output Tables for the United Kingdom 1984. In *Franz, A. and Rainer, N.*, eds., 1989, pp. 343–54.

Lynd, Staughton. Resisting Plant Shutdowns: Essay Review. *Labor Hist.*, Spring 1989, *30*(2), pp. 294–300.

Lyndon, Mary L. Information Economics and Chemical Toxicity: Designing Laws to Produce and Use Data. *Mich. Law Rev.*, June 1989, *87*(7), pp. 1795–1861.

Lynge, Morgan J., Jr. and Lee, Cheng Few. Financial Ratio Comparison of Savings and Loan Associations and Commercial Banks. In *Lee, C. F.*, ed., 1989, pp. 195–229.

Lynk, Edward L. The Demand for Energy by U.K. Manufacturing Industry. *Manchester Sch. Econ. Soc. Stud.*, March 1989, *57*(1), pp. 1–16.

Lynn, Laurence E., Jr. Policy Analysis in the Bureaucracy: How New? How Effective? *J. Policy Anal. Manage.*, Summer 1989, *8*(3), pp. 373–77.

Lynn, Michael. Scarcity Effects on Desirability: Mediated by Assumed Expensiveness? *J. Econ. Psych.*, June 1989, *10*(2), pp. 257–74.

Lynn, Monty L. and Brister, Jozell. Trends in Union Organizing Issues and Tactics. *Ind. Relat.*, Winter 1989, *28*(1), pp. 104–13.

Lynn, Richard and Dwyer, Hubert J. Small Capitalization Companies: What Does Financial Analysis Tell Us about Them? *Financial Rev.*, August 1989, *24*(3), pp. 397–415.

Lynn, Robert and McCarthy, Francis Desmond. Padrões de crescimento dos países em desenvolvimento na década de 80. (With English summary.) *Pesquisa Planejamento Econ.*, August 1989, *19*(2), pp. 309–45.

Lynne, Gary D. Scarcity Rents for Water: A Valuation and Pricing Model: Comment. *Land Econ.*, November 1989, *65*(4), pp. 420–24.

Lyon, Andrew B. The Effect of Changes in the Percentage Depletion Allowance on Oil Firm Stock Prices. *Energy J.*, October 1989, *10*(4), pp. 101–16.

_____. The Effect of the Investment Tax Credit on the Value of the Firm. *J. Public Econ.*, March 1989, *38*(2), pp. 227–47.

Lyon, Charles C. and Thompson, Gary D. Marketing Order Impacts on Farm–Retail Price Spreads: The Suspension of Prorates on California–Arizona Navel Oranges. *Amer. J. Agr. Econ.*, August 1989, *71*(3), pp. 647–60.

Lyon, Kenneth S. and Beladi, Hamid. Government Expenditures and the ex ante Crowding-Out Effect: An Examination. *Appl. Econ.*, October 1989, *21*(10), pp. 1411–20.

Lyon, Randolph M. Transferable Discharge Permit Systems and Environmental Management in Developing Countries. *World Devel.*, August 1989, *17*(8), pp. 1299–1312.

Lyons, Barbara; Davis, Karen and Rowland, Diane. Catastrophic Coverage under the Medicare Program. In *Eisdorfer, C.; Kessler, D. A. and Spector, A. N., eds.*, 1989, pp. 106–24.

Lyons, Bruce. An Empirical Investigation of UK Manufacturing's Trade with the World and the E.E.C.: 1968 and 1980. In *Audretsch, D. B.; Sleuwaegen, L. and Yamawaki, H., eds.*, 1989, pp. 155–87.

_____ **and Varoufakis, Yanis.** Game Theory, Oligopoly and Bargaining. In *Hey, J. D., ed.*, 1989, pp. 79–126.

Lyons, John S. Family Response to Economic Decline: Handloom Weavers in Early Nineteenth-Century Lancashire. In *Ransom, R. L., ed.*, 1989, pp. 45–91.

Lyons, Susan M. C. An Outline of the 1989 Budget Proposals: Mayalsia. *Bull. Int. Fiscal Doc.*, January 1989, *43*(1), pp. 25–28.

Lyson, Thomas A. Industrial Change and the Sexual Division of Labor in New York and Georgia: 1910–1930. *Soc. Sci. Quart.*, June 1989, *70*(2), pp. 356–74.

Lyster, Simon. The Convention on the Conservation of Migratory Species of Wild Animals (The "Bonn Convention"). *Natural Res. J.*, Fall 1989, *29*(4), pp. 979–1000.

Ma, Barry K. and Handa, Jagdish. Four Tests for the Random Walk Hypothesis: Power versus Robustness. *Econ. Letters*, 1989, *29*(2), pp. 141–45.

Ma, Ching-To Albert and Glazer, Jacob. Efficient Allocation of a "Prize"—King Solomon's Dilemma. *Games Econ. Behav.*, September 1989, *1*(3), pp. 222–33.

Ma, Christopher K. and Ellis, M. E. Selecting Industries as Inflation Hedges. *J. Portfol. Manage.*, Summer 1989, *15*(4), pp. 45–48.

_____ **; Jaffe, Jeffrey F. and Westerfield, Randolph.** A Twist on the Monday Effect in Stock Prices: Evidence from the U.S. and Foreign Stock Markets. *J. Banking Finance*, September 1989, *13*(4–5), pp. 641–50.

_____ **; Rao, Ramesh P. and Peterson, Richard L.** The Resiliency of the High-Yield Bond Market: The LTV Default. *J. Finance*, September 1989, *44*(4), pp. 1085–97.

_____ **; Rao, Ramesh P. and Sears, R. Stephen.** Limit Moves and Price Resolution: The Case of the Treasury Bond Futures Market. *J. Futures Markets*, August 1989, *9*(4), pp. 321–35.

_____ **; Rao, Ramesh P. and Sears, R. Stephen.** Volatility, Price Resolution, and the Effectiveness of Price Limits. *J. Finan. Services Res.*, December 1989, *3*(2–3), pp. 165–99.

_____ **; Rao, Ramesh P. and Sears, R. Stephen.** Volatility, Price Resolution, and the Effectiveness of Price Limits. In *Edwards, F. R., ed.*, 1989, pp. 67–101.

_____ **; Wong, G. Wenchi and Maberly, Edwin D.** The Daily Effect in the Gold Market: A Reply. *J. Futures Markets*, April 1989, *9*(2), pp. 175–77.

Ma, Cindy W. Forecasting Efficiency of Energy Futures Prices. *J. Futures Markets*, October 1989, *9*(5), pp. 393–419.

Ma, Xin. The Theory of Marx's "Four Modes of Production." In *Brook, T., ed.*, 1989, pp. 176–83.

Ma, Yinchu. A New Theory of Population. In *Howe, C. and Walker, K. R., eds.*, 1989, 1957, pp. 300–322.

Maani, Sholeh A. The Unemployment Benefit, Unemployment Duration and Wage Requirements of Job Seekers in New Zealand. *New Zealand Econ. Pap.*, 1989, *23*, pp. 12–28.

Maas, Christoph and Lorenzen, Gunter. Zur Input–Output Analyse mit Intervalldaten. (On Input–Output Analysis with Interval Data. With English summary.) *Jahr. Nationalökon. Statist.*, July 1989, *206*(3), pp. 257–63.

Maasdorp, Gavin. Industrialization and Investment Incentives in Southern Africa: Overview: Regional Prospects and Rapid Technological Change. In *Whiteside, A. W., ed.*, 1989, pp. 204–17.

Maasoumi, Esfandiar. Continuously Distributed Attributes and Measures of Multivariate Inequality. *J. Econometrics*, September 1989, *42*(1), pp. 131–44.

_____ **and Pippenger, John.** Transaction Costs and the Interest Parity Theorem: Comment. *J. Polit. Econ.*, February 1989, *97*(1), pp. 236–43.

Maatman, Gerald L. A Proposal for Change: Affordable Automobile Insurance. *J. Risk Ins.*, September 1989, *56*(3), pp. 518–24.

Maberly, Edwin D. The Relationship between Stock Indices and Stock Index Futures from 3:00–3:15: A Note. *J. Futures Markets*, June 1989, *9*(3), pp. 271–72.

_____ **; Ma, Christopher K. and Wong, G. Wenchi.** The Daily Effect in the Gold Market: A Reply. *J. Futures Markets*, April 1989, *9*(2), pp. 175–77.

_____ **; Spahr, Ronald W. and Herbst, Anthony F.** An Analysis of Daily Patterns in Stock Returns across Indices: Spot versus Futures. *Quart. J. Bus. Econ.*, Winter 1989, *28*(1), pp. 55–67.

Macari, John A. Taking Control of Your Municipality's Operating Assets. In *Matzer, J., Jr., ed.*, 1989, 1986, pp. 55–60.

Macaulay, Stewart. Popular Legal Culture: An Introduction. *Yale Law J.*, June 1989, *98*(8), pp. 1545–58.

MacAulay, T. G.; Batterham, R. L. and Fisher, B. S. Solution of Spatial Trading Systems with Concave Cubic Programming. *Australian J. Agr. Econ.*, December 1989, *33*(3), pp. 170–86.

Macauley, Molly K. and Toman, Michael A. No Free Launch: Efficient Space Transportation Pricing. *Land Econ.*, May 1989, *65*(2), pp. 91–99.

_____ **, et al.** Fuelwood Use in Urban Areas: A Case Study of Raipur, India. *Energy J.*, July 1989, *10*(3), pp. 157–80.

MacAvoy, Paul W. and McIsaac, George S. The Performance and Management of United States

Federal Government Corporations. In *Mac-Avoy, P. W., et al.*, 1989, pp. 77–135.

_____; Spulber, Daniel F. and Stangle, Bruce E. Is Competitive Entry Free? Bypass and Partial Deregulation in Natural Gas Markets. *Yale J. Regul.*, Summer 1989, 6(2), pp. 209–47.

MacBean, Alasdair I. Agricultural Exports of Developing Countries: Market Conditions and National Policies. In *Islam, N., ed.*, 1989, pp. 101–27.

MacCharles, Donald C. Canada in a Global Economy. In *Rugman, A. M., ed.*, 1989, pp. 12–36.

Maccini, Louis J. and Haltiwanger, John C. Inventories, Orders, Temporary and Permanent Layoffs: An Econometric Analysis. *Carnegie-Rochester Conf. Ser. Public Policy*, Spring 1989, 30, pp. 301–66.

Maccoby, Michael. Social Character and Organizational Change. In *Mohrman, A. M., Jr., et al.*, 1989, pp. 120–41.

MacCormac, Earl R. Forecasting Loads and Designing Rates for Electric Utilities. In *Golden, B. L.; Wasil, E. A. and Harker, P. T., eds.*, 1989, pp. 138–54.

MacDonald, Don N. and Huth, William L. The Impact of Antitrust Litigation on Shareholder Return. *J. Ind. Econ.*, June 1989, 37(4), pp. 411–26.

_____ and Huth, William L. Individual Valuation, Market Valuation, and the Preference Reversal Phenomenon. *J. Behav. Econ.*, Summer 1989, 18(2), pp. 99–114.

_____ and Wall, Jerry L. An Experimental Study of the Allais Paradox over Losses: Some Preliminary Evidence. *Quart. J. Bus. Econ.*, Autumn 1989, 28(4), pp. 43–60.

Macdonald, Garry and Turner, David S. A Ready Reckoner Package for Macroeconomics Teaching. *Oxford Bull. Econ. Statist.*, March 1989, 51(2), pp. 193–211.

MacDonald, Jack. The *Mochiai* Effect: Japanese Corporate Cross-Holdings. *J. Portfol. Manage.*, Fall 1989, 16(1), pp. 90–94.

MacDonald, James M. Concentration and Railroad Pricing. In *Weiss, L. W., ed.*, 1989, pp. 205–12.

_____. Railroad Deregulation, Innovation, and Competition: Effects of the Staggers Act on Grain Transportation. *J. Law Econ.*, April 1989, 32(1), pp. 63–95.

MacDonald, Ronald; Hillier, John and Kearney, Colm. The Efficiency of the Market for Bank Accepted Bills. *Econ. Rec.*, September 1989, 65(190), pp. 225–33.

_____ and Murphy, Philip D. Testing for the Long Run Relationship between Nominal Interest Rates and Inflation Using Cointegration Techniques. *Appl. Econ.*, April 1989, 21(4), pp. 439–47.

_____ and Speight, Alan E. H. Consumption, Saving and Rational Expectations: Some Further Evidence for the U.K. *Econ. J.*, March 1989, 99(394), pp. 83–91.

_____ and Speight, Alan E. H. Does the Public Sector Obey the Rational Expectations–Permanent Income Hypothesis? A Multi-country Study of the Time Series Properties of Government Expenditures. *Appl. Econ.*, September 1989, 21(9), pp. 1257–66.

_____ and Speight, Alan E. H. Government Expenditure under Rational Expectations: Some Estimates for the U.K., Canada, Germany, and the U.S. *Public Finance*, 1989, 44(3), pp. 419–36.

_____ and Taylor, Mark P. Economic Analysis of Foreign Exchange Markets: An Expository Survey. In *MacDonald, R. and Taylor, M. P., eds.*, 1989, pp. 3–107.

_____ and Taylor, Mark P. Foreign Exchange Market Efficiency and Cointegration: Some Evidence from the Recent Float. *Econ. Letters*, 1989, 29(1), pp. 63–68.

_____ and Taylor, Mark P. Interest Rate Parity: Some New Evidence. *Bull. Econ. Res.*, October 1989, 41(4), pp. 255–74.

_____ and Taylor, Mark P. International Parity Conditions. *Greek Econ. Rev.*, 1989, 11(2), pp. 257–90.

_____ and Taylor, Mark P. Rational Expectations, Risk and Efficiency in the London Metal Exchange: An Empirical Analysis. *Appl. Econ.*, February 1989, 21(2), pp. 143–53.

_____ and Torrance, Thomas S. Some Survey-Based Tests of Uncovered Interest Parity. In *MacDonald, R. and Taylor, M. P., eds.*, 1989, pp. 239–48.

MacDonald, S. Scott and Hein, Scott E. Futures Rates and Forward Rates as Predictors of Near-Term Treasury Bill Rates. *J. Futures Markets*, June 1989, 9(3), pp. 249–62.

MacDonnell, Lawrence. Federal Interests in Western Water Resources: Conflict and Accommodation. *Natural Res. J.*, Spring 1989, 29(2), pp. 389–411.

Mace, Gordon and Hervouet, Gérard. Canada's Third Option: A Complete Failure? *Can. Public Policy*, December 1989, 15(4), pp. 387–404.

de Macedo, Jorge Braga. Financial Regulation, Implicit Taxes, and Fiscal Adjustment in Italy: Comment. In *Monti, M., ed.*, 1989, pp. 235–43.

_____ and Branson, William H. Smuggler's Blues at the Central Bank: Lessons from Sudan. In *[Díaz-Alejandro, C.]*, 1989, pp. 191–207.

_____ and Sebastiao, Manuel. Public Debt and Implicit Taxes: The Portuguese Experience. *Europ. Econ. Rev.*, March 1989, 33(2/3), pp. 573–79.

Macesich, George. Essays on the Yugoslav Economic Model: Introduction. In *Macesich, G., ed.*, 1989, pp. vii–xi.

_____. Fiscal Policy, Deficits and Crowding-Out. In *Singer, H. W. and Sharma, S., eds. (II)*, 1989, pp. 97–114.

_____. International Financial System and World Debt: The Issue of Cooperation. In *Singer, H. W. and Sharma, S., eds. (I)*, 1989, pp. 135–50.

MacEwan, Arthur and Tabb, William K. Instability and Change in the World Economy. In *Mac-*

Ewan, A. and Tabb, W. K., eds., 1989, pp. 23–43.

_____ and Tabb, William K. Instability and Change in the World Economy: Introduction. In MacEwan, A. and Tabb, W. K., eds., 1989, pp. 7–20.

Macfarlane, Ian J. Policy Targets and Operating Procedures: The Australian Case. In Federal Reserve Bank of Kansas City, 1989, pp. 143–59.

MacGregor, Ian [Sir]. The Political Economy of Privatization in Britain: A Narrative. In MacAvoy, P. W., et al., 1989, pp. 263–72.

Machan, Tibor R. The Fantasy of Glasnost. Int. J. Soc. Econ., 1989, 16(2), pp. 46–53.

_____. Individual versus Subjective Values. Int. J. Soc. Econ., 1989, 16(8), pp. 49–59.

Machard, Luc. Le statut des organisations chez Hayek. (The Organizations in Hayek's Thought. With English summary.) Écon. Societes, October 1989, 23(10), pp. 207–26.

Machina, Mark J. Choice under Uncertainty: Problems Solved and Unsolved. In Hey, J. D., ed., 1989, pp. 12–46.

_____. Comparative Statics and Non-expected Utility Preferences. J. Econ. Theory, April 1989, 47(2), pp. 393–405.

_____. Decision-Making in the Presence of Risk. In Hahn, F., ed., 1989, 1987, pp. 278–94.

_____. Dynamic Consistency and Non-expected Utility Models of Choice under Uncertainty. J. Econ. Lit., December 1989, 27(4), pp. 1622–68.

_____ and Domar, Evsey D. On the Profitability of Russian Serfdom. In Domar, E. D., 1989, 1984, pp. 239–79.

Machlup, F. Professor Hicks' Statics. In Wood, J. C. and Woods, R. N., eds., Vol. 1, 1989, 1940, pp. 12–27.

_____. Professor Hicks' Revision of Demand Theory. In Wood, J. C. and Woods, R. N., eds., Vol. 2, 1989, 1957, pp. 1–17.

Machowski, Heinrich. Rückwirkungen der sowjetischen Reformpolitik auf die Zusammenarbeit im "Rat für Gegenseitige Wirtschaftschilfe" (RGW). (The Soviet Proposed Reforms for the COMECON. With English summary.) Aussenwirtschaft, December 1989, 44(3–4), pp. 367–84.

Maciejewicz, Jan and Monkiewicz, Jan. Services in the Socialist Countries of Eastern Europe. Jahr. Wirtsch. Osteuropas, 1989, 13(2), pp. 167–93.

Macintosh, Donald and Whitson, David. Rational Planning vs. Regional Interests: The Professionalization of Canadian Amateur Sport. Can. Public Policy, December 1989, 15(4), pp. 436–49.

Mack, Eric. Dominos and the Fear of Commodification. In Chapman, J. W. and Pennock, J. R., eds., 1989, pp. 198–225.

Mack, Richard S.; Gilmer, Robert William and Keil, Stanley R. The Service Sector in a Hierarchy of Rural Places: Potential for Export Activity. Land Econ., August 1989, 65(3), pp. 217–27.

Macke, Robert and Southgate, Douglas. The Downstream Benefits of Soil Conservation in Third World Hydroelectric Watersheds. Land Econ., February 1989, 65(1), pp. 38–48.

Mackenzie, G. A. Are All Summary Indicators of the Stance of Fiscal Policy Misleading? Int. Monet. Fund Staff Pap., December 1989, 36(4), pp. 743–70.

Mackey, Michael C. Commodity Price Fluctuations: Price Dependent Delays and Nonlinearities as Explanatory Factors. J. Econ. Theory, August 1989, 48(2), pp. 497–509.

Mackie, J. A. C. and Sjahrir. Survey of Recent Developments. Bull. Indonesian Econ. Stud., December 1989, 25(3), pp. 3–34.

_____ and Zain, Djumilah. East Java: Balanced Growth and Diversification. In Hill, H., ed., 1989, pp. 306–29.

Mackie, James B. and Fullerton, Don. Economic Efficiency in Recent Tax Reform History: Policy Reversals or Consistent Improvements. Nat. Tax J., March 1989, 42(1), pp. 1–13.

MacKinlay, A. Craig and Lo, Andrew W. The Size and Power of the Variance Ratio Test in Finite Samples. J. Econometrics, February 1989, 40(2), pp. 203–38.

_____; Terker, Bruce and Blume, Marshall E. Order Imbalances and Stock Price Movements on October 19 and 20, 1987. J. Finance, September 1989, 44(4), pp. 827–48.

MacKinnon, James G. Heteroskedasticity-Robust Tests for Structural Change. Empirical Econ., 1989, 14(2), pp. 77–92.

_____. Heteroskedasticity-Robust Tests for Structural Change. In Kramer, W., ed., 1989, pp. 13–28.

MacKinnon, Mary. Years of Schooling: The Australian Experience in Comparative Perspective. Australian Econ. Hist. Rev., September 1989, 29(2), pp. 58–78.

MacLaury, Bruce K. Third World Debt: The Next Phase: Concluding Impressions. In Fried, E. R. and Trezise, P. H., eds., 1989, pp. 109–10.

Maclean, F. and Berry, J. Managing the Development of a Customer Marketing Data-Base. Environ. Planning A, May 1989, 21(5), pp. 617–23.

MacLeod, J. R. Strategies and Possibilities for Indian Leadership in Co-management Initiatives in British Columbia. In Pinkerton, E., ed., 1989, pp. 262–72.

MacLeod, Ross; de Meza, David and La Manna, Manfredi. The Case for Permissive Patents. Europ. Econ. Rev., September 1989, 33(7), pp. 1427–43.

MacLeod, W. Bentley. Entry, Sunk Costs, and Market Structure: Reply. Can. J. Econ., May 1989, 22(2), pp. 438–41.

_____ and Bergin, James. Entry, Sunk Costs and Renegotiation in Duopoly. Ann. Écon. Statist., July–Dec. 1989, (15–16), pp. 173–91.

_____ and Kanemoto, Yoshitsugu. Optimal Labor Contracts with Non-contractible Human Capital. J. Japanese Int. Economies, December 1989, 3(4), pp. 385–402.

_____ and Malcomson, James M. Implicit Contracts, Incentive Compatibility, and Involuntary Unemployment. *Econometrica*, March 1989, *57*(2), pp. 447–80.

MacLeod, William C. and Rogowsky, Robert A. Consumer Protection at the FTC during the Reagan Administration. In *Meiners, R. E. and Yandle, B., eds.*, 1989, pp. 71–88.

Macmillan, D. C. and Crabtree, J. R. UK Fiscal Changes and New Forestry Planting. *J. Agr. Econ.*, September 1989, *40*(3), pp. 314–22.

Macnaughton, Alan and Hoffman, Lorey Arthur. Life Insurance and Tax Reform. In *Mintz, J. and Whalley, J., eds.*, 1989, pp. 255–85.

Macneil, Ian R. Power, Contract, and the Economic Model. In *Tool, M. R. and Samuels, W. J., eds. (III)*, 1989, *1980*, pp. 63–77.

MacPhail, Fiona and Bowles, Paul. Technical Change and Intra-household Welfare: A Case Study of Irrigated Rice Production in South Sulawesi, Indonesia. *J. Devel. Stud.*, October 1989, *26*(1), pp. 58–80.

MacPhee, Craig R. and Rosenbaum, David I. The Asymmetric Effects of Reversible Tariff Changes under the United States GSP. *Southern Econ. J.*, July 1989, *56*(1), pp. 105–25.

_____ and Rosenbaum, David I. Has the European Community GSP Increased LDC Exports? *Appl. Econ.*, June 1989, *21*(6), pp. 823–41.

Macpherson, C. B. Do We Need a Theory of the State? In *Duncan, G., ed.*, 1989, pp. 15–32.

MacPherson, David A. and Stewart, James B. The Labor Force Participation and Earnings Profiles of Married Female Immigrants. *Quart. Rev. Econ. Bus.*, Autumn 1989, *29*(3), pp. 57–72.

_____ and Stewart, James B. The Labor Supply and School Attendance of Black Women in Extended and Nonextended Households. *Amer. Econ. Rev.*, May 1989, *79*(2), pp. 71–74.

Macrae, Norman. Workplace Flexibility: Past, Present, and Future. *J. Lab. Res.*, Winter 1989, *10*(1), pp. 51–55.

Macrory, Patrick F. J. Cost of Production as the Sole Measure of Dumping. In *Jackson, J. H. and Vermulst, E. A., eds.*, 1989, pp. 384–88.

Macrory, R. B. and Sheate, W. R. Agriculture and the EC Environmental Assessment Directive: Lessons for Community Policy-Making. *J. Common Market Stud.*, September 1989, *28*(1), pp. 68–81.

Madan, Dilip B. and Kiernan, Eric. Stochastic Stability in Macro Models. *Economica*, February 1989, *56*(221), pp. 97–108.

_____; Milne, Frank and Shefrin, Hersh. The Multinomial Option Pricing Model and Its Brownian and Poisson Limits. *Rev. Financial Stud.*, 1989, *2*(2), pp. 251–65.

_____ and Prucha, Ingmar R. A Note on the Estimation of Nonsymmetric Dynamic Factor Demand Models. *J. Econometrics*, October 1989, *42*(2), pp. 275–83.

Madan, Vibhas. Efficiency Wages and Interlinked Markets. *J. Quant. Econ.*, January 1989, *5*(1), pp. 15–28.

Madavo, C. Strengthening Local Governments in Sub-Saharan Africa: Opening Remarks. In *World Bank and Istituto Italo-Africano*, 1989, pp. 65–69.

Madden, David. Indirect Tax Reform in Ireland. *Econ. Soc. Rev.*, October 1989, *21*(1), pp. 27–47.

Madden, Janice Fanning. Empirical Consequences of Comparable Worth: Discussion. In *Hill, M. A. and Killingsworth, M. R., eds.*, 1989, pp. 107–11.

Madden, Paul. General Equilibrium and Disequilibrium and the Microeconomic Foundations of Macroeconomics. In *Hey, J. D., ed.*, 1989, pp. 179–208.

Maddison, Angus. Crescita e slowdown nelle economie capitalistiche avanzate: Tecniche di valutazione quantitativa. (Growth and Slowdown in Advanced Capitalist Economies: Techniques of Quantitative Assessment. With English summary.) *Econ. Lavoro*, Jan.–March 1989, *23*(1), pp. 3–51.

_____. Dutch Income In and From Indonesia, 1700–1938. In *Maddison, A. and Prince, G., eds.*, 1989, pp. 15–41.

_____. World Economic Performance since 1870. In *[Fischer, W.]*, 1989, pp. 223–38.

_____ and van Ark, Bart. International Comparison of Purchasing Power, Real Output and Labour Productivity: A Case Study of Brazilian, Mexican and U.S. Manufacturing, 1975. *Rev. Income Wealth*, March 1989, *35*(1), pp. 31–55.

Maddox, George L. and Manton, Kenneth G. Hospitals: The DRG System. In *Eisdorfer, C.; Kessler, D. A. and Spector, A. N., eds.*, 1989, pp. 71–87.

Madison, James H. Manufacturing Pharmaceuticals: Eli Lilly and Company, 1876–1948. In *Hausman, W. J., ed.*, 1989, pp. 72–78.

Madsen, Erik Kloppenborg. Beyond the Expected Utility Proposition in Rational Decision Making. In *Grunert, K. G. and Ölander, F., eds.*, 1989, pp. 183–97.

Madsen, Erik Strøjer and Albæk, Karsten. Den solidariske lønpolitik og beskæftigelsen af lavtlønnede. (The Employment Effects of the 1977 Increase in the Danish Minimum Wage. With English summary.) *Nationaløkon. Tidsskr.*, 1989, *127*(2), pp. 184–99.

Madura, Jeff. Influence of Foreign Markets on Multinational Stocks: Implications for Investors. *Rivista Int. Sci. Econ. Com.*, Oct.–Nov. 1989, *36*(10–11), pp. 1009–18.

_____ and McDaniel, William R. Market Reaction to Increased Loan Loss Reserves at Money-Center Banks. *J. Finan. Services Res.*, December 1989, *3*(4), pp. 359–69.

Maennig, Wolfgang and Eggerstedt, Harald. Anpassungsprogramme und wirtschaftliche Projektionen der Weltbank. Eine theoretische und praktische Analyse. (Adjustment Programs and Economic Projections by the World Bank: A Theoretical and Practical Assessment. With

English summary.) *Konjunkturpolitik*, 1989, 35(6), pp. 346–60.

Maes, Ivo. IS-LM: The Hicksian Journey. *De Economist*, 1989, 137(1), pp. 91–104.

Maeshiro, Asatoshi and Wichers, C. Robert. Estimating Money Demand in Log-First-Difference Form: Comment. *Southern Econ. J.*, April 1989, 55(4), pp. 1036–39.

―――― **and Wichers, C. Robert.** On the Relationship between the Estimates of Level Models and Difference Models. *Amer. J. Agr. Econ.*, May 1989, 71(2), pp. 432–36.

Maganya, Ernest N.; Chambua, Samwel and Hyuha, Theodora. Outgrower Schemes in Tanzania: The Case of Tea and Sugarcane. *Eastern Afr. Econ. Rev.*, Special Issue, August 1989, pp. 70–82.

Magdoff, Harry. A New State of Capitalism Ahead? In *MacEwan, A. and Tabb, W. K., eds.*, 1989, pp. 349–61.

―――― **and Sweezy, Paul.** The Financial Explosion. In *Guttmann, R., ed.*, 1989, 1985, pp. 129–33.

Magee, Lonnie. An Edgeworth Test Size Correction for the Linear Model with AR(1) Errors. *Econometrica*, May 1989, 57(3), pp. 661–74.

Magee, Stephen P. and Noe, Thomas H. Economic Policy Failure with Endogenous Voting. *Hong Kong Econ. Pap.*, 1989, (19), pp. 9–12.

Magel, Judith S. and Brody, Stanley J. Long-Term Care: The Long and Short of It. In *Eisdorfer, C.; Kessler, D. A. and Spector, A. N., eds.*, 1989, pp. 235–58.

Maggiora, Ferruccio. Una analisi della proposta messicana di "securitisation": Aspetti positivi e negativi. (The Mexico's Proposal of Securitisation: Positive and Negative Aspects. With English summary.) *Rivista Int. Sci. Econ. Com.*, Oct.–Nov. 1989, 36(10–11), pp. 993–1007.

Magilavy, Lou J. and Groves, Robert M. Measuring and Explaining Interviewer Effects in Centralized Telephone Surveys. In *Singer, E. and Presser, S., eds.*, 1989, 1986, pp. 288–303.

Magill, Robert S. Social Welfare in Developed Market Countries: United States of America. In *Dixon, J. and Scheurell, R. P., eds.*, 1989, pp. 345–86.

Magnanti, Thomas L. Twenty Years of Mathematical Programming. In *Cornet, B. and Tulkens, H., eds.*, 1989, pp. 163–227.

Magnus, Jan R. and Pesaran, Bahram. The Exact Multi-period Mean-Square Forecast Error for the First-Order Autoregressive Model with an Intercept. *J. Econometrics*, October 1989, 42(2), pp. 157–79.

Magnus, Peter A. The Canadian Antidumping System. In *Jackson, J. H. and Vermulst, E. A., eds.*, 1989, pp. 167–222.

Magnusson, Lars. Corruption and Civic Order—Natural Law and Economic Discourse in Sweden during the Age of Freedom. *Scand. Econ. Hist. Rev.*, 1989, 37(2), pp. 78–105.

Magnusson, Monica. Employee Designed Working Hours Scheduling—Some Swedish Exam-

ples. In *Agassi, J. B. and Heycock, S., eds.*, 1989, pp. 298–309.

Magraw, Roger. Socialist, Syndicalism and French Labour before 1914. In *Geary, D., ed.*, 1989, pp. 48–100.

Mahar, Dennis J. Deforestation in Brazil's Amazon Region: Magnitude, Rate, and Causes. In *Schramm, G. and Warford, J. J., eds.*, 1989, pp. 87–116.

Maharatna, Arup. Change in Concentration and Growth in Indian Industries 1964–80. *Indian Econ. J.*, Oct.–Dec. 1989, 37(2), pp. 93–102.

Mahdavi, Saeid. The Effects of External Trade, Foreign Resources, and Domestic Policies on Domestic Savings in Some Developing Countries: A Regression Analysis. *De Economist*, 1989, 137(2), pp. 217–31.

Mahdavy, Khashayar and Silver, Mick S. The Measurement of a Nation's Terms of Trade Effect and Real National Disposable Income within a National Accounting Framework. *J. Roy. Statist. Society*, 1989, 152(1), pp. 87–107.

Mahé, Louis P. and Moreddu, Catherine. Analysis of CAP Trade Policy Changes. In *Tarditi, S., et al., eds.*, 1989, pp. 81–98.

―――― **and Munk, Knud J.** The EC Grain Price Policy at the Core of the CAP. In *Bauer, S. and Henrichsmeyer, W., eds.*, 1989, pp. 307–24.

Maher, Chris. Information, Intermediaries and Sales Strategy in an Urban Housing Market: The Implications of Real Estate Auctions in Melbourne. *Urban Stud.*, October 1989, 26(5), pp. 495–509.

Maher, Michael W. and Beck, Paul J. Competition, Regulation and Bribery. *Managerial Dec. Econ.*, March 1989, 10(1), pp. 1–12.

Maher, Patrick. Levi on the Allais and Ellsberg Paradoxes. *Econ. Philos.*, April 1989, 5(1), pp. 69–78.

Mahieu, Yvon; Chaillou, Paul and Hansen, Pierre. Best Network Flow Bounds for the Quadratic Knapsack Problem. In *Simeone, B., ed.*, 1989, pp. 225–35.

Mahloudji, F. Hicks and the Keynesian Revolution. In *Wood, J. C. and Woods, R. N., eds.*, Vol. 4, 1989, 1985, pp. 178–97.

Mahmood, Talat; Schwalbach, Joachim and Grasshoff, Ulrike. The Dynamics of Corporate Profits. *Europ. Econ. Rev.*, October 1989, 33(8), pp. 1625–39.

Mahmood, Zafar. The Interface between Population and Development Models, Plans and Policies: Comments. *Pakistan Devel. Rev.*, Winter 1989, 28(4), pp. 405–07.

Mahmoud, Amal A. W. and Lobo, Gerald J. Relationship between Differential Amounts of Prior Information and Security Return Variability. *J. Acc. Res.*, Spring 1989, 27(1), pp. 116–34.

Mahmoud, Essam. Combining Forecasts: Some Managerial Issues. *Int. J. Forecasting*, 1989, 5(4), pp. 599–600.

Mahmud, Wahiduddin. The Impact of Overseas Labour Migration on the Bangladesh Economy: A Macro-economic Perspective. In *Amjad, R., ed.*, 1989, pp. 55–94.

Mahony, Greg; Lee, Christine and Lodewijks, John. Recent Developments in the Fijian Economy. In *Lodewijks, J. and Zerby, J., eds.,* 1989, pp. 50–66.

Mahrous, F. N. and Hamissa, M. R. Fertilizer Use Efficiency in Rice. In *International Rice Research Institute,* 1989, pp. 129–39.

Mahseredjian, Sophie and Montmarquette, Claude. Could Teacher Grading Practices Account for Unexplained Variation in School Achievements? *Econ. Educ. Rev.,* 1989, 8(4), pp. 335–43.

_____ **and Montmarquette, Claude.** Does School Matter for Educational Achievement? A Two-Way Nested-Error Components Analysis. *J. Appl. Econometrics,* April–June 1989, 4(2), pp. 181–93.

Mai, Chao-cheng. Technological Uncertainty and International Market Share Rivalry. *Rivista Int. Sci. Econ. Com.,* March 1989, 36(3), pp. 271–81.

_____ **and Hwang, Hong.** Export Subsidies and Oligopolistic Rivalry between Labor-Managed and Capitalist Economies. *J. Compar. Econ.,* September 1989, 13(3), pp. 473–80.

_____ **and Hwang, Hong.** On the Optimum Location of Vertically Related Firms with Simultaneous Entry. *J. Reg. Sci.,* February 1989, 29(1), pp. 47–61.

_____ **and Hwang, Hong.** Tariffs versus Ratio Quotas under Duopoly. *J. Int. Econ.,* August 1989, 27(1–2), pp. 177–83.

Maier, Gerhard. Creation of the Ecu and Inflation. In *Franz, O., ed.,* 1989, pp. 26–31.

Maier, Gunther; Gerking, Shelby and Weiss, Peter. The Economics of Traffic Accidents on Austrian Roads: Risk Lovers or Policy Deficit? *Empirica,* 1989, 16(2), pp. 177–92.

Mailath, George J. Simultaneous Signaling in an Oligopoly Model. *Quart. J. Econ.,* May 1989, 104(2), pp. 417–27.

Mainwaring, Lynn. Erratum [Global Accumulation with a Dual Southern Economy]. *J. Post Keynesian Econ.,* Summer 1989, 11(4), pp. 661–62.

_____. Global Accumulation with a Dual Southern Economy. *J. Post Keynesian Econ.,* Spring 1989, 11(3), pp. 399–423.

_____. World Income Shares and the Terms of Trade: A North–South Growth Cycle. *Bull. Econ. Res.,* July 1989, 41(3), pp. 185–96.

Maione, B.; Fanti, M. P. and Turchiano, B. Large Scale Markov Chain Modelling of Transfer Lines. In *Archetti, F.; Lucertini, M. and Serafini, P., eds.,* 1989, pp. 193–211.

Mair, Douglas and Miller, Anne G. Urban Unemployment; A Causal Modelling Approach. *Urban Stud.,* August 1989, 26(4), pp. 379–96.

Maire, P. Cost Calculation Based on RICA Data. In *Bauer, S. and Henrichsmeyer, W., eds.,* 1989, pp. 141–46.

Mairesse, Jacques. An Analysis of Female Labor Supply, Housing Demand and the Saving Rate in Japan: Comment. *Europ. Econ. Rev.,* May 1989, 33(5), pp. 1027–30.

Mais, Eric L.; Moore, William T. and Rogers, Ronald C. A Re-examination of Shareholder Wealth Effects of Calls of Convertible Preferred Stock. *J. Finance,* December 1989, 44(5), pp. 1401–10.

Majchrzak, Janusz. DISCRET: An Interactive Decision Support System for Discrete Alternatives Multicriteria Problems. In *Lewandowski, A. and Wierzbicki, A. P., eds.,* 1989, pp. 382–84.

_____. A Methodological Guide to the Decision Support System DISCRET for Discrete Alternatives Problems. In *Lewandowski, A. and Wierzbicki, A. P., eds.,* 1989, pp. 193–212.

Majd, M. G. Land Reform Policies in Iran: Reply. *Amer. J. Agr. Econ.,* November 1989, 71(4), pp. 1050–53.

_____. The Oil Boom and Agricultural Development: A Reconsideration of Agricultural Policy in Iran. *J. Energy Devel.,* Autumn 1989, 15(1), pp. 125–40.

Majd, Saman and Pindyck, Robert S. The Learning Curve and Optimal Production under Uncertainty. *Rand J. Econ.,* Autumn 1989, 20(3), pp. 331–43.

Majocchi, Alberto. Monetary and Financial Integration: Problems and Perspectives. In *Tarditi, S., et al., eds.,* 1989, pp. 244–56.

Major, Thomas and Baffuto, Thomas. Supported Competitive Employment in New Jersey. In *Wehman, P. and Kregel, J., eds.,* 1989, pp. 207–23.

Majumdar, Mukul and Becker, Robert A. Optimality and Decentralization in Infinite Horizon Economies. In *Feiwel, G. R., ed. (II),* 1989, pp. 436–504.

_____; **Mitra, Tapan and Nyarko, Yaw.** Dynamic Optimization under Uncertainty: Nonconvex Feasible Set. In *Feiwel, G. R., ed. (II),* 1989, pp. 545–90.

Makaliwe-Watupongoh, J. A. A.; Makaliwe, Willem H. and Schreuel, Evert-J. Central Sulawesi: Facing Communication and Erosion Problems. In *Hill, H., ed.,* 1989, pp. 511–27.

Makaliwe, Willem H.; Saleh, Abdul Karim and Kristanto, Kustiah. South-east Sulawesi: Isolation and Dispersed Settlement. In *Hill, H., ed.,* 1989, pp. 566–83.

_____; **Schreuel, Evert-J. and Makaliwe-Watupongoh, J. A. A.** Central Sulawesi: Facing Communication and Erosion Problems. In *Hill, H., ed.,* 1989, pp. 511–27.

Makarov, V. L., et al. Equilibrium, Rationing, and Stability: A Summary of the Proceedings of the Second Novosibirsk School of Mathematical Economics. *Matekon,* Summer 1989, 25(4), pp. 4–95.

Makdisi, Samir A. The Privatization of Public Enterprises: Comment. In *El-Naggar, S., ed.,* 1989, pp. 81–84.

Makepeace, G. H.; Van Der Klaauw, W. and Dolton, P. J. Occupational Choice and Earnings Determination: The Role of Sample Selection and Non-pecuniary Factors. *Oxford Econ. Pap.,* July 1989, 41(3), pp. 573–94.

Makgetla, Neva Seidman and Seidman, Robert B. The Applicability of Law and Economics to Policymaking in the Third World. *J. Econ. Issues*, March 1989, *23*(1), pp. 35–78.

_____ **and Seidman, Robert B.** On the Appropriate Arenas for Government Intervention in the Third World. In *Samuels, W. J., ed. (I)*, 1989, pp. 131–46.

Makhija, Anil K. and Spiro, Michael H. Determinants of Earned Rates of Return on Equity of U.S. Electric Utilities, 1976–1984. *Econ. Letters*, October 1989, *30*(4), pp. 367–71.

Mäki, Uskali. On the Problem of Realism in Economics. *Ricerche Econ.*, Jan.–June 1989, *43*(1–2), pp. 176–98.

Makin, A. J. Is the Current Account Deficit Sustainable? *Australian Econ. Rev.*, Winter 1989, (86), pp. 29–33.

Makin, John H. American Economic and Military Leadership in the Postwar Period. In *Makin, J. H. and Hellmann, D. C., eds.*, 1989, pp. 3–40.

_____. Developing-Country Debt Problems after Seven Years. In *Dornbusch, R.; Makin, J. H. and Zlowe, D., eds.*, 1989, pp. 9–20.

_____. Economic Growth and the Health Care Budget. In *Lewin, M. E. and Sullivan, S., eds.*, 1989, pp. 53–67.

_____. The Impact of Fiscal Policy on the Balance of Payments: Recent Experience in the United States. In *Monti, M., ed.*, 1989, pp. 54–71.

_____ **and Couch, Kenneth A.** Saving, Pension Contributions, and the Real Interest Rate. *Rev. Econ. Statist.*, August 1989, *71*(3), pp. 401–07.

_____ **and Dornbusch, Rudiger.** Alternative Solutions to Developing-Country Debt Problems: Introduction. In *Dornbusch, R.; Makin, J. H. and Zlowe, D., eds.*, 1989, pp. 1–6.

_____ **and Grassi, Anneliese.** Sharing World Leadership? A New Era for America and Japan: Introduction. In *Makin, J. H. and Hellmann, D. C., eds.*, 1989, pp. xix–xxiii.

Makinen, Gail E. and Woodward, G. Thomas. A Monetary Interpretation of the Poincaré Stabilization of 1926. *Southern Econ. J.*, July 1989, *56*(1), pp. 191–211.

_____ **and Woodward, G. Thomas.** The Taiwanese Hyperinflation and Stabilization of 1945–1952. *J. Money, Credit, Banking*, February 1989, *21*(1), pp. 90–105.

Makowski, Louis. Keynes's Liquidity Preference Theory: A Suggested Reinterpretation. In *Hahn, F., ed.*, 1989, pp. 468–75.

Makowski, Marek and Sosnowski, Janusz S. HYBRID: A Mathematical Programming Package. In *Lewandowski, A. and Wierzbicki, A. P., eds.*, 1989, pp. 376–77.

_____ **and Sosnowski, Janusz S.** Mathematical Programming Package HYBRID. In *Lewandowski, A. and Wierzbicki, A. P., eds.*, 1989, pp. 106–44.

Makridakis, Spyros. Why Combining Works? *Int. J. Forecasting*, 1989, *5*(4), pp. 601–03.

Maksimovic, Vojislav; Sick, Gordon A. and Zechner, Josef. Forward Markets, Stock Markets, and the Theory of the Firm: Comment. *J. Finance*, June 1989, *44*(2), pp. 525–28.

Mal'ginova, E. G. and Saenko, O. P. Property and Family Well-Being. *Prob. Econ.*, July 1989, *32*(3), pp. 72–80.

Malaguerra, Carlo. Le programme de l'Office fédéral de la statistique pour les années 1990. (Supply and Demand for Longitudinal Data in Switzerland. With English summary.) *Schweiz. Z. Volkswirtsch. Statist.*, September 1989, *125*(3), pp. 367–90.

Malan, Pedro S. Country Risk and the Organization of International Capital Transfer: Comment. In *[Díaz-Alejandro, C.]*, 1989, pp. 130–33.

Malatesta, Paul H. and Karpoff, Jonathan M. The Wealth Effects of Second-Generation State Takeover Legislation. *J. Finan. Econ.*, December 1989, *25*(2), pp. 291–322.

Malcomson, James M. and Coles, Melvyn. Contract Theory and Incentive Compatibility. In *Hey, J. D., ed.*, 1989, pp. 127–51.

_____ **and MacLeod, W. Bentley.** Implicit Contracts, Incentive Compatibility, and Involuntary Unemployment. *Econometrica*, March 1989, *57*(2), pp. 447–80.

Malczewski, Jacek and Ogryczak, Wlodzimierz. On Health Care Districts Planning by Multiobjective Analysis with the MPSX/370 Package. In *Lockett, A. G. and Islei, G., eds.*, 1989, pp. 314–24.

Maldonado, C. The Underdogs of the Urban Economy Join Forces: Results of an ILO Programme in Mali, Rwanda and Togo. *Int. Lab. Rev.*, 1989, *128*(1), pp. 65–84.

Malecki, Edward J. What about People in High Technology? Some Research and Policy Considerations. *Growth Change*, Winter 1989, *20*(1), pp. 67–79.

Mäler, Karl-Göran. The Acid Rain Game. In *Folmer, H. and van Ierland, E., eds.*, 1989, pp. 231–52.

_____; **Johansson, Per-Olov and Kriström, Bengt.** Welfare Evaluations in Contingent Valuation Experiments with Discrete Response Data: Comment. *Amer. J. Agr. Econ.*, November 1989, *71*(4), pp. 1054–56.

_____; **Johansson, Per-Olov and Löfgren, Karl-Gustaf.** Recreational Values, Pareto Optimality and Timber Supply. In *Folmer, H. and van Ierland, E., eds.*, 1989, pp. 49–68.

Malgrange, Pierre. The Structure of Dynamic Macroeconometric Models. In *Cornet, B. and Tulkens, H., eds.*, 1989, pp. 521–50.

Malhotra, Devinder M. and Garofalo, Gasper A. Intertemporal and Interspatial Productivity Differentials in U.S. Manufacturing. *Ann. Reg. Sci.*, 1989, *23*(2), pp. 121–36.

Maligaya, Arlyn R. and White, Fred C. Agricultural Output Supply and Input Demand Relationships with Endogenous Land Rents. *Southern J. Agr. Econ.*, December 1989, *21*(2), pp. 13–20.

Malik, Muhammad Hussain and Najam-us-Saqib. Tax Incidence by Income Classes in Pakistan. *Pakistan Devel. Rev.*, Spring 1989, *28*(1), pp. 13–25.

Malik, Salman; Pasha, Hafiz A. and Ghaus, Ai-

sha. The Economic Cost of Power Outages in the Industrial Sector of Pakistan. *Energy Econ.*, October 1989, *11*(4), pp. 301–18.

Malik, Sohail J.; Mushtaq, Mohammad and Nazli, Hina. An Analysis of Production Relations in the Large-Scale Textile Manufacturing Sector of Pakistan. *Pakistan Devel. Rev.*, Spring 1989, *28*(1), pp. 27–42.

Maling, C. Hicks' Neo-Austrian Capital Theory. In *Wood, J. C. and Woods, R. N., eds., Vol. 3, 1980*, pp. 240–57.

Malinvaud, Edmond. Human Capital Accumulation in Post-green Revolution Pakistan: Some Preliminary Results: Comments. *Pakistan Devel. Rev.*, Winter 1989, *28*(4), pp. 432–33.

_____. Lessons to Be Learned from the European Unemployment of the 80s. *Pakistan Devel. Rev.*, Winter 1989, *28*(4), pp. 311–28.

_____. Observation in Macroeconomic Theory Building. *Europ. Econ. Rev.*, March 1989, *33*(2/3), pp. 205–23.

_____. Profitability and Factor Demands under Uncertainty. *De Economist*, 1989, *137*(1), pp. 2–15.

_____. Reflecting on the Theory of Capital and Growth. In *Wood, J. C. and Woods, R. N., eds., Vol. 4, 1989, 1986*, pp. 265–82.

Malitz, Ileen B. A Re-examination of the Wealth Expropriation Hypothesis: The Case of Captive Finance Subsidiaries. *J. Finance*, September 1989, *44*(4), pp. 1039–47.

Mallela, Parthasaradhi. On Identification with Covariance Restrictions: A Correction and an Extension. *Int. Econ. Rev.*, November 1989, *30*(4), pp. 993–97.

_____ **and Bajwa, Mohammad S.** ML and MINQU Estimation of ARCH Models: Relative Importance of Money Supply and Wage Rate for Explaining U.S. Inflation. *J. Quant. Econ.*, January 1989, *5*(1), pp. 155–69.

_____ **and Nahata, Babu.** Effects of Horizontal Merger on Price, Profits, and Market Power in a Dominant-Firm Oligopoly. *Int. Econ. J.*, Spring 1989, *3*(1), pp. 55–62.

Malliaris, A. G. Approaches to the Cash Management Problem. In *Lee, C. F., ed., 1989*, pp. 231–43.

Mallory, G. R. and Kersten, G. E. And/Or Graphs, Scenarios and Multiple Criteria: Prototyping in Decision Support. In *Lockett, A. G. and Islei, G., eds., 1989*, pp. 544–52.

Malmer, Håkan and Norrman, Bo. Administrative and Compliance Costs of Taxation: Sweden. In *International Fiscal Association, ed. (I), 1989*, pp. 563–93.

Maloney, Kevin J. and Byrne, Mark J. An Equilibrium Debt Option Pricing Model in Discrete Time. *J. Banking Finance*, July 1989, *13*(3), pp. 421–42.

_____ **and Logue, Dennis E.** Neglected Complexities in Structured Bond Portfolios. *J. Portfol. Manage.*, Winter 1989, *15*(2), pp. 59–68.

_____ **and Rogalski, Richard J.** Call-Option Pricing and the Turn of the Year. *J. Bus.*, October 1989, *62*(4), pp. 539–52.

Maloney, Michael T. and Mitchell, Mark L. Cri-

sis in the Cockpit? The Role of Market Forces in Promoting Air Travel Safety. *J. Law Econ.*, Part 1, October 1989, *32*(2), pp. 329–55.

Malsch, Thomas; Dohse, Knut and Jürgens, Ulrich. From "Fordism" to "Toyotaism"? The Social Organization of the Labor Process in the Japanese Automobile Industry. In *Park, S.-J., ed., 1989*, pp. 9–43.

Malueg, David A. Emission Credit Trading and the Incentive to Adopt New Pollution Abatement Technology. *J. Environ. Econ. Manage.*, January 1989, *16*(1), pp. 52–57.

_____ **and Solow, John L.** A Note on Welfare in the Durable-Goods Monopoly. *Economica*, November 1989, *56*(224), pp. 523–27.

Mamer, John W. and Lippman, Steven A. A Simple Search Model with Procyclical Quits. *J. Econ. Dynam. Control*, April 1989, *13*(2), pp. 247–53.

Man, Chand Maloo and Canlar, Mehmet. Assessing the Further Impact of College-Level Accounting Study on Student Performance in the MBA-Level Managerial Accounting Course. In *Schwartz, B. N., ed., 1989*, pp. 129–39.

Manchester, Joyce M. The Baby Boom, Housing and Loanable Funds. *Can. J. Econ.*, February 1989, *22*(1), pp. 128–49.

_____. How Money Affects Real Output. *J. Money, Credit, Banking*, February 1989, *21*(1), pp. 16–32.

_____ **and Poterba, James M.** Second Mortgages and Household Saving. *Reg. Sci. Urban Econ.*, May 1989, *19*(2), pp. 325–46.

Manchet, Stéphane and Dehapiot, Tanguy. Modèle de volatilité aléatoire et prix des options. (Stochastic Volatility and Option Pricing: A Simplified Approach. With English summary.) *Finance*, December 1989, *10*(2), pp. 7–25.

Mandel, Ernest. Historical and Institutional Determinants of Long-Term Variation of Real Wages. In *Scholliers, P., ed., 1989*, pp. 183–93.

_____. The Infernal Logic of the Debt Crisis. In *Gottdiener, M. and Komninos, N., eds., 1989*, pp. 217–33.

_____. Theories of Crisis: An Explanation of the 1974–82 Cycle. In *Gottdiener, M. and Komninos, N., eds., 1989*, pp. 30–58.

Mandelbaum, Thomas B. The Eighth District Business Economy in 1988: Still Expanding, but More Slowly. *Fed. Res. Bank St. Louis Rev.*, May–June 1989, *71*(3), pp. 23–32.

_____ **and Coughlin, Cletus C.** Have Federal Spending and Taxation Contributed to the Divergence of State Per Capita Incomes in the 1980s? *Fed. Res. Bank St. Louis Rev.*, July–Aug. 1989, *71*(4), pp. 29–42.

Mandle, Jay R. and Ferleger, Lou. The Saving Shortfall. *Challenge*, March–April 1989, *32*(2), pp. 57–59.

Mandy, David M. Forecasting Unemployment Insurance Trust Funds: The Case of Tennessee. *Int. J. Forecasting*, 1989, *5*(3), pp. 381–91.

Manegold, D. EC Agricultural Policy in 1988–89: An Early End to Reform? *Rev. Marketing*

Agr. Econ., April, Aug., Dec. 1989, 57(1–2–3), pp. 11–46.

Manfredini Gasparetoo, Marialuisa. Integrazione economica europea: Il 31.12.1992. (European Economic Integration: December 31, 1992. With English summary.) *Rivista Int. Sci. Econ. Com.*, Oct.–Nov. 1989, 36(10–11), pp. 917–30.

Mangum, Stephen L. and Ball, David E. The Transferability of Military-Provided Occupational Training in the Post-Draft Era. *Ind. Lab. Relat. Rev.*, January 1989, 42(2), pp. 230–45.

Manheim, L. M., et al. New York: Design and Implementation of a Voluntary Medicaid Case-Management Demonstration. In *Scheffler, R. M. and Rossiter, L. F., eds.*, 1989, pp. 241–64.

Maniruzzamanand Schroeder, Larry. Local Government Structure. In *Schroeder, L., ed.*, 1989, pp. 23–50.

Mankiw, N. Gregory. International Stock Price Movements: Links and Messages: Comments. *Brookings Pap. Econ. Act.*, 1989, (1), pp. 168–71.

_____. Real Business Cycles: A New Keynesian Perspective. *J. Econ. Perspectives*, Summer 1989, 3(3), pp. 79–90.

_____ **and Campbell, John Y.** Consumption, Income, and Interest Rates: Reinterpreting the Time Series Evidence. In *Blanchard, O. J. and Fischer, S., eds.*, 1989, pp. 185–216.

_____ **and Campbell, John Y.** International Evidence on the Persistence of Economic Fluctuations. *J. Monet. Econ.*, March 1989, 23(2), pp. 319–33.

_____ **and Kimball, Miles S.** Precautionary Saving and the Timing of Taxes. *J. Polit. Econ.*, August 1989, 97(4), pp. 863–79.

_____ **and Weil, David N.** The Baby Boom, the Baby Bust, and the Housing Market. *Reg. Sci. Urban Econ.*, May 1989, 19(2), pp. 235–58.

Mann, Arthur J. and Alameda, José I. Energy Price Shocks, Input Price Changes, and Developmental Implications: A Translog Model Applied to Puerto Rico. *J. Devel. Stud.*, April 1989, 25(3), pp. 329–43.

_____ **and Giraldo, Germán.** Latin American External Debt Growth: A Current Account Explanatory Model, 1973–1984. *J. Developing Areas*, October 1989, 24(1), pp. 47–57.

Mann, Catherine L. The Effects of Exchange Rate Trends and Volatility on Export Prices: Industry Examples from Japan, Germany, and the United States. *Weltwirtsch. Arch.*, 1989, 125(3), pp. 588–618.

_____ **and Hooper, Peter.** Exchange Rate Pass-Through in the 1980s: The Case of U.S. Imports of Manufacturers. *Brookings Pap. Econ. Act.*, 1989, (1), pp. 297–329.

Mann, Patrick C. and Brewer, H. L. Regulator Selection and Financial Performance for Public Utilities: Selection Method and the Returns Experienced by Common Equity Owners. *Energy Econ.*, January 1989, 11(1), pp. 39–45.

Mann, Prem S. Green Revolution Revisited: The Adoption of High Yielding Variety Wheat

Seeds in India. *J. Devel. Stud.*, October 1989, 26(1), pp. 131–44.

Mann, Steven V. The Dividend Puzzle: A Progress Report. *Quart. J. Bus. Econ.*, Summer 1989, 28(3), pp. 3–35.

Mann, Thomas E. and Schultze, Charles L. Getting Rid of the Budget Deficit: Why We Should and How We Can. In *Bosworth, B. P., et al.*, 1989, pp. 1–28.

Mannan, M. A. Family, Society, Economy and Fertility in Bangladesh. *Bangladesh Devel. Stud.*, September 1989, 17(3), pp. 67–99.

Mannel, C. and Hemmer, Hans-R. On the Economic Analysis of the Urban Informal Sector. *World Devel.*, October 1989, 17(10), pp. 1543–52.

Manning, Alan. An Asymmetric Information Approach to the Comparative Analysis of Participatory and Capitalist Firms. *Oxford Econ. Pap.*, April 1989, 41(2), pp. 312–26.

_____. Implicit-Contract Theory. In *Sapsford, D. and Tzannatos, Z., eds.*, 1989, pp. 63–85.

_____ **and Lockwood, Ben.** Dynamic Wage–Employment Bargaining with Employment Adjustment Costs. *Econ. J.*, December 1989, 99(398), pp. 1143–58.

_____; **Szymanski, Stefan and Kay, John A.** The Economic Benefits of the Channel Tunnel. *Econ. Policy: A Europ. Forum*, April 1989, (8), pp. 211–34.

Manning, Chris and Rumbiak, Michael. Irian Jaya: Economic Change, Migrants, and Indigenous Welfare. In *Hill, H., ed.*, 1989, pp. 76–106.

Manning, Christopher A. Explaining Intercity Home Price Differences. *J. Real Estate Finance Econ.*, June 1989, 2(2), pp. 131–49.

Manning, D. N. The Effect of Political Uncertainty on the Stock Market: The Case of British Telecom. *Appl. Econ.*, July 1989, 21(7), pp. 881–89.

Manning, Neil and Hunt, Lester. Energy Price- and Income-Elasticities of Demand: Some Estimates for the UK Using the Cointegration Procedure. *Scot. J. Polit. Econ.*, May 1989, 36(2), pp. 183–93.

Manning, Peter A. Dealing with Hunger: Corporate Involvement and Food Assistance Policy. In *Post, J. E., ed.*, 1989, pp. 207–32.

Manning, Richard. Search While Consuming. *Econ. Stud. Quart.*, June 1989, 40(2), pp. 97–108.

_____ **and Shea, Koon-Lam.** Perfect Discrimination and the Long-run National Advantage. *J. Econ. (Z. Nationalökon.)*, 1989, 49(3), pp. 299–313.

_____ **and Shea, Koon-Lam.** Perfectly Discriminatory Policy towards International Capital Movements in a Dynamic World. *Int. Econ. Rev.*, May 1989, 30(2), pp. 329–48.

Manning, Robert E. The Nature of America: Visions and Revisions of Wilderness. *Natural Res. J.*, Winter 1989, 29(1), pp. 25–40.

Manopimoke, Wirote and James, William E. Property Rights, and Petroleum Exploration and Development in the Asian Developing

Countries. In *James, W. E., ed.*, 1989, pp. 61–74.

Manove, Michael. The Harm from Insider Trading and Informed Speculation. *Quart. J. Econ.*, November 1989, *104*(4), pp. 823–45.

Manrai, Ajay K. and Sinha, Prabhakant. Elimination-by-Cutoffs. *Marketing Sci.*, Spring 1989, *8*(2), pp. 133–52.

Manser, Marilyn E. and Famulari, Melissa. Employer-Provided Benefits: Employer Cost versus Employee Value. *Mon. Lab. Rev.*, December 1989, *112*(12), pp. 24–32.

Mansfield, Edward R. and Conerly, Michael D. An Approximate Test for Comparing Independent Regression Models with Unequal Error Variances. *J. Econometrics*, February 1989, *40*(2), pp. 239–59.

Mansfield, Edwin. Innovation, R and D, and Firm Growth in Robotics: Japan and the United States. In *Andersson, Å. E.; Batten, D. F. and Karlsson, C., eds.*, 1989, pp. 143–55.

_____. Patent Renewal Data: Comments. *Brookings Pap. Econ. Act.*, Microeconomics, 1989, pp. 405–09.

_____. Technological Change in Robotics: Japan and the United States. *Managerial Dec. Econ.*, Special Issue, Spring 1989, pp. 19–25.

Mansfield, Malcolm. L'organisation du marché du travail et le rôle des bureaux de placement dans "Unemployment. A Problem of Industry" (1909) de William Beveridge. (Labour Market Organization and Employment Agencies Functions in William Beveridge's "Unemployment: A Problem of Industry" [1909]. With English summary.) *Écon. Societes*, October 1989, *23*(10), pp. 5–30.

Mansfield, Mike. The U.S. and Japan: Sharing Our Destinies. *Foreign Aff.*, Spring 1989, *68*(2), pp. 3–15.

Mansfield, Roger. Management Research and the Development of Management Practice. In *Mansfield, R., ed.*, 1989, pp. 3–7.

Manski, Charles F. Anatomy of the Selection Problem. *J. Human Res.*, Summer 1989, *24*(3), pp. 343–60.

_____. Schooling as Experimentation: A Reappraisal of the Postsecondary Dropout Phenomenon. *Econ. Educ. Rev.*, 1989, *8*(4), pp. 305–12.

_____ and Thompson, T. Scott. Estimation of Best Predictors of Binary Response. *J. Econometrics*, January 1989, *40*(1), pp. 97–123.

Mansour, Ali and Khalil, Mohamad A. Post-war Iraqi Economic Recovery and Development. *J. Energy Devel.*, Autumn 1989, *15*(1), pp. 51–59.

Mansur, Ahsan H. Effects of a Budget Deficit on the Current Account Balance: The Case of the Philippines. In *Blejer, M. I. and Chu, K., eds.*, 1989, pp. 309–45.

_____ and Robinson, David J. Transmission of Effects of the Fiscal Deficit in Industrial Countries to the Fiscal Deficit of Developing Countries. In *Blejer, M. I. and Chu, K., eds.*, 1989, pp. 132–68.

Mansur, Iqbal; Cochran, Steven J. and Froio,

Gregory L. The Relationship between the Equity Return Levels of Airline Companies and Unanticipated Events: The Case of the 1979 DC-10 Grounding. *Logist. Transp. Rev.*, December 1989, *25*(4), pp. 355–65.

Mantel, Rolf R. and Fernández, Roque B. Fiscal Lags and the Problem of Stabilization: Argentina's Austral Plan. In *Brock, P. L.; Connolly, M. B. and González-Vega, C., eds.*, 1989, pp. 65–79.

Manton, Kenneth G.; Berkman, Lisa F. and Singer, Burton. Black/White Differences in Health Status and Mortality among the Elderly. *Demography*, November 1989, *26*(4), pp. 661–78.

_____ and Maddox, George L. Hospitals: The DRG System. In *Eisdorfer, C.; Kessler, D. A. and Spector, A. N., eds.*, 1989, pp. 71–87.

Mantripragada, Krishna G. and Borna, Shaheen. Morality of Public Deficits: A Historical Perspective. *Public Budg. Finance*, Spring 1989, *9*(1), pp. 33–46.

Manuelli, Rodolfo E.; Chari, Varadarajan V. and Jones, Larry E. Labor Contracts in a Model of Imperfect Competition. *Amer. Econ. Rev.*, May 1989, *79*(2), pp. 358–63.

Manzoni, Jean-François and Merchant, Kenneth A. The Achievability of Budget Targets in Profit Centers: A Field Study. *Accounting Rev.*, July 1989, *64*(3), pp. 539–58.

Mao, Ching-Sheng. Estimating Intertemporal Elasticity of Substitution: The Case of Log-Linear Restrictions. *Fed. Res. Bank Richmond Econ. Rev.*, Nov.–Dec. 1989, *75*(6), pp. 3–14.

Mao, Zedong. Speech at the Conference of Provincial and Municipal Committee Secretaries. In *Howe, C. and Walker, K. R., eds.*, 1989, *1959*, pp. 78–87.

_____. Talk on the Third Five-Year Plan. In *Howe, C. and Walker, K. R., eds.*, 1989, *1964*, pp. 131–34.

Marais, M. Laurentius. Post-Earnings-Announcement Drift: Delayed Price Response or Risk Premium? Discussion. *J. Acc. Res.*, Supplement, 1989, *27*, pp. 37–48.

_____; Schipper, Katherine and Smith, Abbie. Wealth Effects of Going Private for Senior Securities. *J. Finan. Econ.*, June 1989, *23*(1), pp. 155–91.

Maravall, Agustín. La extracción de señales y el análisis de coyuntura. (With English summary.) *Revista Española Econ.*, 1989, *6*(1–2), pp. 109–30.

_____. On the Dynamic Structure of a Seasonal Component. *J. Econ. Dynam. Control*, January 1989, *13*(1), pp. 81–91.

_____ and Dolado, Juan J. Intertemporal Consumer Behaviour under Structural Changes in Income: Comment. *Econometric Rev.*, 1989, *8*(1), pp. 101–09.

Marceau, Jane. The Capitalist Class: France. In *Bottomore, T. and Brym, R. J., eds.*, 1989, pp. 46–72.

Marcel, Mario. Privatización y finanzas públicas: El caso de Chile, 1985–88. (Privatization and Public Finance: The Chilean Case, 1985–1988.

With English summary.) *Colección Estud. CIEPLAN,* June 1989, (26), pp. 5–60.

_____ **and Palma, J. Gabriel.** Kaldor on the 'Discreet Charm' of the Chilean Bourgeoisie. *Cambridge J. Econ.,* March 1989, *13*(1), pp. 245–72.

_____ **and Palma, J. Gabriel.** Kaldor on the 'Discreet Charm' of the Chilean Bourgeoisie. In *Lawson, T.; Palma, J. G. and Sender, J.,* eds., 1989, pp. 245–72.

Marcet, Albert and Sargent, Thomas J. Convergence of Least-Squares Learning in Environments with Hidden State Variables and Private Information. *J. Polit. Econ.,* December 1989, *97*(6), pp. 1306–22.

_____ **and Sargent, Thomas J.** Convergence of Least Squares Learning Mechanisms in Self-referential Linear Stochastic Models. *J. Econ. Theory,* August 1989, *48*(2), pp. 337–68.

_____ **and Sargent, Thomas J.** Least-Squares Learning and the Dynamics of Hyperflation. In *Barnett, W. A.; Geweke, J. and Shell, K.,* eds., 1989, pp. 119–37.

Marchak, M. Patricia. The Ideology of Free Trade: A Response. *Can. Public Policy,* June 1989, *15*(2), pp. 220–25.

Marchand, Maurice; Pestieau, Pierre and Wibaut, Serge. Optimal Commodity Taxation and Tax Reform under Unemployment. *Scand. J. Econ.,* 1989, *91*(3), pp. 547–63.

_____ ; **Thisse, Jacques-François and Cremer, Helmuth.** The Public Firm as an Instrument for Regulating an Oligopolistic Market. *Oxford Econ. Pap.,* April 1989, *41*(2), pp. 283–301.

Marchand, Roland. The Inward Thrust of Institutional Advertising: General Electric and General Motors in the 1920s. In *Hausman, W. J.,* ed., 1989, pp. 188–96.

Marchant, Garry. Analogical Reasoning and Hypothesis Generation in Auditing. *Accounting Rev.,* July 1989, *64*(3), pp. 500–513.

_____ , **et al.** A Cognitive Model of Tax Problem Solving. In *Jones, S. M.,* ed., 1989, pp. 1–20.

Marchese, Serafino and Nadal de Simone, Franciso. Monotonicity of Indices of "Revealed" Comparative Advantage: Empirical Evidence on Hillman's Condition. *Weltwirtsch. Arch.,* 1989, *125*(1), pp. 158–67.

Marchetti, Aldo. Orario, Flessibilità, formazione: Per una ricomposizione del dibattito sul tempo di lavoro. (On Working Hours, Flexibility and Training: A Realignment of the Debate on Working Time. With English summary.) *Econ. Lavoro,* Jan.–March 1989, *23*(1), pp. 115–29.

Marchi, Ezio. Interchangeability of Equilibrium Points in Extensive Games with Complete Information. *Econ. Letters,* October 1989, *30*(4), pp. 303–06.

de Marchi, Neil and Gilbert, Christopher L. History and Methodology of Econometrics: Introduction. *Oxford Econ. Pap.,* January 1989, *41*(1), pp. 1–11.

_____ **and Gilbert, Christopher L.** History and Methodology of Econometrics: Introduction. In *de Marchi, N. and Gilbert, C.,* eds., 1989, pp. 1–11.

Marcil, Benoît and To, Minh-Chau. La transaction programmée et la volatilité. (With English summary.) *L'Actual. Econ.,* June 1989, *65*(2), pp. 248–62.

Marcus, Alfred A.; Kaufman, Allen M. and Englander, Ernest J. Structure and Implementation in Issues Management: Transaction Costs and Agency Theory. In *Post, J. E.,* ed., 1989, pp. 257–71.

Marcus, B. M. and Crisp, M. R. Administrative and Compliance Costs of Taxation: South Africa. In *International Fiscal Association,* ed. *(I),* 1989, pp. 121–37.

Marcus, Richard D. Freshmen Retention Rates at U.S. Private Colleges: Results from Aggregate Data. *J. Econ. Soc. Meas.,* 1989, *15*(1), pp. 37–55.

_____ **and Zivney, Terry L.** The Day the United States Defaulted on Treasury Bills. *Financial Rev.,* August 1989, *24*(3), pp. 475–89.

Marendic, Bozo; Vojnic, Dragomir and Lang, Rikard. The Socioeconomic Model of Socialist Self-Management. In *Macesich, G.,* ed., 1989, pp. 12–55.

Marer, Paul. East Europe's Debt Situation in Global Perspective: Utopian versus Realistic Solutions. In *Singer, H. W. and Sharma, S.,* eds. *(II),* 1989, pp. 237–45.

_____ . A Five-Point Definition. *Acta Oecon.,* 1989, *40*(3–4), pp. 259.

_____ . Market Mechanism Reforms in Hungary. In *Van Ness, P.,* ed., 1989, pp. 52–74.

Margheim, Loren; Pany, Kurt and Pourciau, Susan. Controlling Audit Staff Underreporting of Time and Premature Signoffs: Some Preliminary Findings. In *Gangolly, J.,* ed., 1989, pp. 181–94.

Margo, Robert A. The Effect of Migration on Black Incomes: Evidence from the 1940 Census. *Econ. Letters,* December 1989, *31*(4), pp. 403–06.

_____ **and Goldin, Claudia.** The Poor at Birth: Birth Weights and Infant Mortality at Philadelphia's Almshouse Hospital, 1848–1873. *Exploration Econ. Hist.,* July 1989, *26*(3), pp. 360–79.

Margolis, Stephen E. Monopolistic Competition and Multiproduct Brand Names. *J. Bus.,* April 1989, *62*(2), pp. 199–209.

Marguerat, Philippe. The Involvement of French Banks in the Oil Industry between the Wars: Paribas and Its Romanian Investments. In *Ferrier, R. W. and Fursenko, A.,* eds., 1989, pp. 107–15.

Mariano, Roberto S. and Brown, Bryan W. Measures of Deterministic Prediction Bias in Nonlinear Models. *Int. Econ. Rev.,* August 1989, *30*(3), pp. 667–84.

_____ **and Brown, Bryan W.** Stochastic Simulation, Prediction and Validation of Nonlinear Models. In *[Adams, F. G.],* 1989, pp. 17–36.

Marimon, Ramon. Stochastic Turnpike Property and Stationary Equilibrium. *J. Econ. Theory,* April 1989, *47*(2), pp. 282–306.

Marin, Dalia. Assessing Structural Change: The

Case of Austria. *Int. Rev. Applied Econ.*, January 1989, *3*(1), pp. 89–106.

———. Trade and Scale Economies: A Causality Test for the U.S., Japan, Germany and the U.K. In *Audretsch, D. B.; Sleuwaegen, L. and Yamawaki, H.*, eds., 1989, pp. 29–56.

——— and Kunst, Robert M. On Exports and Productivity: A Causal Analysis. *Rev. Econ. Statist.*, November 1989, *71*(4), pp. 699–703.

Marin, José. Dos propiedades del impuesto lineal. (With English summary.) *Invest. Ecón.*, January 1989, *13*(1), pp. 3–14.

Marini, Giancarlo. Interest Rate Rules in an Equilibrium Model: A Note. *Manchester Sch. Econ. Soc. Stud.*, March 1989, *57*(1), pp. 75–78.

Marino, Anthony M.; Campbell, Tim S. and Chan, Yuk-Shee. Incentive Contracts for Managers Who Discover and Manage Investment Projects. *J. Econ. Behav. Organ.*, December 1989, *12*(3), pp. 353–64.

Marion, Bruce W. The Concentration–Price Relationship in Food Retailing. In *Weiss, L. W.*, ed., 1989, pp. 185–93.

——— and Geithman, Frederick. Live Cattle Prices and Packer–Buyer Concentration. In *Weiss, L. W.*, ed., 1989, pp. 213–18.

Mariotti, Marco. Being Identical, Behaving Differently: A Theorem on Technological Diffusion. *Econ. Letters*, October 1989, *30*(4), pp. 275–78.

———. Uniformità e varietà nell'attività innovativa: Un modello di oligopolio schumpeteriano. (Uniformity and Variety in Innovation: A Model of Schumpeterian Oligopoly. With English summary.) *Rivista Int. Sci. Econ. Com.*, June 1989, *36*(6), pp. 525–42.

Maris, Brian A. and White, Harry L. Valuing and Hedging Fixed Rate Mortgage Commitments. *J. Real Estate Finance Econ.*, September 1989, *2*(3), pp. 223–32.

Mark, Janette and Weston, Ann. The Havana Charter Experience: Lessons for Developing Countries. In *Whalley, J.*, ed., Vol. 1, 1989, pp. 45–65.

Markandya, Anil and Pearce, David W. Marginal Opportunity Cost as a Planning Concept in Natural Resource Management. In *Schramm, G. and Warford, J. J.*, eds., 1989, pp. 39–55.

Markey, James P. and Parks, William, II. Occupational Change: Pursuing a Different Kind of Work. *Mon. Lab. Rev.*, September 1989, *112*(9), pp. 3–12.

Markowitz, Harry M. and Kim, Gew-rae. Investment Rules, Margin, and Market Volatility. *J. Portfol. Manage.*, Fall 1989, *16*(1), pp. 45–52.

Markowski, Aleksander. Minimac: A Small Integrated Model of the Financial and Real Sectors of the Swedish Economy. *Econ. Modelling*, October 1989, *6*(4), pp. 399–431.

Marks, Denton; Sadanand, Asha and Sadanand, Venkatraman. Probationary Contracts in Agencies with Bilateral Asymmetric Information. *Can. J. Econ.*, August 1989, *22*(3), pp. 643–61.

Marks, Suzanne and Yetley, Mervin. Food Aid

Policy and Food Demand Patterns: Changing Food Demand Patterns Reveal Potential for Trade. In *Helmuth, J. W. and Johnson, S. R.*, eds., Vol. 1, 1989, pp. 136–45.

Markusen, Ann. The Economic, Industrial, and Regional Consequences of Defense-Led Innovation. In *Andersson, Å. E.; Batten, D. F. and Karlsson, C.*, eds., 1989, pp. 251–69.

Markusen, James R. An Analytical Survey of Formal and Informal Barriers to International Trade and Investment in the United States, Canada, and Japan: Comment. In *Stern, R. M.*, ed., 1989, pp. 353–59.

———. Service Trade by the Multinational Enterprise. In *Enderwick, P.*, 1989, pp. 35–57.

———. Trade in Producer Services and in Other Specialized Intermediate Inputs. *Amer. Econ. Rev.*, March 1989, *79*(1), pp. 85–95.

——— and Horstmann, Ignatius J. Firm-Specific Assets and the Gains from Direct Foreign Investment. *Economica*, February 1989, *56*(221), pp. 41–48.

——— and Wigle, Randall M. Nash Equilibrium Tariffs for the United States and Canada: The Roles of Country Size, Scale Economies, and Capital Mobility. *J. Polit. Econ.*, April 1989, *97*(2), pp. 368–86.

Markwald, Ricardo A.; Moreira, Ajax R. Bello and Pereira, Pedro L. Valls. Previsão da produção industrial: Indicadores antecedentes e modelos de série temporal. (With English summary.) *Pesquisa Planejamento Econ.*, August 1989, *19*(2), pp. 233–54.

Marley, Marcia and Wolff, Edward N. Long-Term Trends in U.S. Wealth Inequality: Methodological Issues and Results. In *Lipsey, R. E. and Tice, H. S.*, eds., 1989, pp. 765–839.

Marlow, Michael L.; Darby, Michael R. and Mascaro, Angelo R. The Empirical Reliability of Monetary Aggregates as Indicators: 1983–1987. *Econ. Inquiry*, October 1989, *27*(4), pp. 555–85.

——— and Joulfaian, David. The Determinants of Off-Budget Activity of State and Local Governments. *Public Choice*, November 1989, *63*(2), pp. 113–23.

Marlowe, Julia; Selnow, Gary and Blosser, Lois. A Content Analysis of Problem-Resolution Appeals in Television Commercials. *J. Cons. Aff.*, Summer 1989, *23*(1), pp. 175–94.

Marovitz, Andrew S. Casting a Meaningful Ballot: Applying One-Person, One-Vote to Judicial Elections Involving Racial Discrimination. *Yale Law J.*, April 1989, *98*(6), pp. 1193–1213.

Marques, Maria Silvia Bastos and Werlang, Sérgio Ribeiro da Costa. Moratória interna, dívida pública e juros reais. (With English summary.) *Pesquisa Planejamento Econ.*, April 1989, *19*(1), pp. 19–43.

Marquez, Jaime. Income and Price Elasticities of Foreign Trade Flows: Econometric Estimation and Analysis of the U.S. Trade Deficit. In *[Adams, F. G.]*, 1989, pp. 129–76.

Marquis, Milton H. Interest Rate Volatility in a Partial Equilibrium Model of Household

Money Demand. *J. Macroecon.*, Winter 1989, *11*(1), pp. 67–80.

――― **and Witte, Willard E.** Cash Management and the Demand for Money by Firms. *J. Macroecon.*, Summer 1989, *11*(3), pp. 333–50.

Marr, M. Wayne; Ogden, Joseph P. and Kidwell, David S. The Effect of a Sinking Fund on the Reoffering Yields of New Public Utility Bonds. *J. Finan. Res.*, Spring 1989, *12*(1), pp. 1–13.

Marr, William L. Farm Size of Tenant and Owner-Occupied Farms in York County, Ontario, 1871: A Case Study. In *Grantham, G. and Leonard, C. S., eds., Pt. B*, 1989, pp. 331–45.

Marrero, Wanda I. and Darity, William A., Jr. A Common Error: Reply. *J. Macroecon.*, Winter 1989, *11*(1), pp. 149–50.

Marrese, Michael. The Separability of Hungarian Foreign Trade with Respect to the Soviet Union, the Rest of the CMEA, and the West. *Comp. Econ. Stud.*, Summer 1989, *31*(2), pp. 1–41.

Marret, M. A. Le problème de la mesure de l'évolution des primes d'assurance de dommages et de son introduction dans l'indice des prix à la consommation français. (The Measurement of Liability Insurance Premium Trends and Their Inclusion in the French Consumer Price Index. With English summary.) In *Turvey, R.*, 1989, pp. 131–37.

Marrinan, Jane. Exchange Rate Determination: Sorting Out Theory and Evidence. *New Eng. Econ. Rev.*, Nov.–Dec. 1989, pp. 39–51.

Marris, Stephen. Why the Dollar Won't Come Down. In *Guttmann, R., ed.*, 1989, *1984*, pp. 229–35.

Marron, J. S. Automatic Smoothing Parameter Selection: A Survey. In *Ullah, A., ed.*, 1989, *1988*, pp. 65–86.

Mars, Perry. Competing Theories and Third World Political Practice. In *Martin, M. T. and Kandal, T. R., eds.*, 1989, pp. 373–98.

Marsden, David and Ryan, Paul. Statistical Tests for the Universality of Youth Employment Mechanisms in Segmented Labour Markets. *Int. Rev. Applied Econ.*, June 1989, *3*(2), pp. 148–69.

Marsden, T. K.; Munton, R. J. and Whatmore, S. J. Part-Time Farming and Its Implications for the Rural Landscape: A Preliminary Analysis. *Environ. Planning A*, April 1989, *21*(4), pp. 523–36.

Marsenic, Dragutin. Accumulation and Investment in the Yugoslav Economy: The Developmental and Systemic Aspects. In *Macesich, G., ed.*, 1989, pp. 82–100.

Marsh, John M. and Brester, Gary W. Intertemporal Price Adjustments in the Beef Market: A Reduced Form Analysis of Weekly Data. *Western J. Agr. Econ.*, December 1989, *14*(2), pp. 235–45.

Marsh, John S. The Common Agricultural Policy. In *Lodge, J., ed.*, 1989, pp. 148–66.

Marshall, Adriana. The Fall of Labor's Share in Income and Consumption: A New "Growth

Model" for Argentina? In *Canak, W. L., ed.*, 1989, pp. 47–65.

――― . The Sequel of Unemployment: The Changing Role of Part-Time and Temporary Work in Western Europe. In *Rodgers, G. and Rodgers, J., eds.*, 1989, pp. 17–48.

Marshall, Eileen and Robinson, Colin. Liberalizing the British Coal Industry. In *Helm, D.; Kay, J. and Thompson, D., eds.*, 1989, *1986*, pp. 289–312.

Marshall, J. N. Corporate Reorganization and the Geography of Services: Evidence from the Motor Vehicle Aftermarket in the West Midlands Region of the UK. *Reg. Stud.*, April 1989, *23*(2), pp. 139–50.

Marshall, James N. Nobel Laureates in Economic Sciences: A Biographical Dictionary: Wassily W. Leontief: 1973. In *Katz, B. S., ed.*, 1989, pp. 160–73.

Marshall, John D. Stages of Industrialisation in Cumbria. In *Hudson, P., ed.*, 1989, pp. 132–55.

Marshall, John M. Welfare Analysis under Uncertainty. *J. Risk Uncertainty*, December 1989, *2*(4), pp. 385–403.

Marshall, Michael and Elliott, David. Sector Strategy in the West Midlands. In *Hirst, P. and Zeitlin, J., eds.*, 1989, pp. 223–47.

Marshall, Michael Graham and Arestis, Philip. 'Reaganomics' and Supply-Side Economics: A British View. *J. Econ. Issues*, December 1989, *23*(4), pp. 965–75.

Marshall R., Jorge. Colombia and the Latin American Debt Crisis: Comment. In *Edwards, S. and Larrain, F., eds.*, 1989, pp. 267–69.

――― **and Morandé, Felipe G.** Una interpretación keynesiana-inercialista de la inflación brasileña en los años ochenta. (With English summary.) *Cuadernos Econ.*, December 1989, *26*(79), pp. 353–66.

Marshall, Ray. The Implications of Internationalization for Labor Market Institutions and Industrial Relations Systems. In *Bawden, D. L. and Skidmore, F., eds.*, 1989, pp. 205–25.

Marshall S., Jorge. Resolving Debt Crises: An Historical Perspective: Comment. In *Edwards, S. and Larrain, F., eds.*, 1989, pp. 97–99.

Marshall, William J.; Weingast, Barry R. and Gilligan, Thomas W. Regulation and the Theory of Legislative Choice: The Interstate Commerce Act of 1887. *J. Law Econ.*, April 1989, *32*(1), pp. 35–61.

Marston, Richard C. Real and Nominal Exchange Rate Variability. *Empirica*, 1989, *16*(2), pp. 147–60.

――― . A Reevaluation of Exchange Rate Policy. *Can. Public Policy*, Supplement, February 1989, *15*, pp. S45–51.

Martel, Jean-Marc and Khoury, Nabil T. A Supply of Storage Theory with Asymmetric Information. *J. Futures Markets*, December 1989, *9*(6), pp. 573–81.

Martellaro, Joseph A. South Korea and Taiwan: A Comparative Analysis of the Generation and Distribution of Income. *Rivista Int. Sci. Econ. Com.*, December 1989, *36*(12), pp. 1123–40.

――― . Water Resource Development in China:

A Case Study. *Rivista Int. Sci. Econ. Com.*, April–May 1989, *36*(4–5), pp. 459–76.

Martellato, Dino and Van der Borg, Jan. Dinamica occupazionale nei sistemi urbani italiani. (Employment Dynamics in Italian Urban Systems. With English summary.) *Econ. Lavoro*, Oct.–Dec. 1989, *23*(4), pp. 31–47.

Martens, André. L'ajustement structurel en vitesse de croisière au Sahel? (With English summary.) *Can. J. Devel. Stud.*, 1989, *10*(1), pp. 39–60.

Martijn, Jan K. Real Exchange Rate Changes as a Cause of Protectionism. *De Economist*, 1989, *137*(3), pp. 328–50.

Martikainen, Teppo and Perttunen, Jukka. On the Proportionality Assumption of Financial Ratios. *Liiketaloudellinen Aikak.*, 1989, *38*(4), pp. 343–59.

Martin, Charles L. and Smart, Denise T. Consumer Correspondence: An Exploratory Investigation of Consistency between Business Policy and Practice. *J. Cons. Aff.*, Winter 1989, *23*(2), pp. 364–82.

Martin, Christine A. and Witt, Stephen F. Forecasting Tourism Demand: A Comparison of the Accuracy of Several Quantitative Methods. *Int. J. Forecasting*, 1989, *5*(1), pp. 7–19.

Martin, D. and Bracken, I. The Generation of Spatial Population Distributions from Census Centroid Data. *Environ. Planning A*, April 1989, *21*(4), pp. 537–43.

Martin, David Dale. The Uses and Abuses of Economic Theory in the Social Control of Business. In *Tool, M. R. and Samuels, W. J., eds. (II)*, 1989, *1974*, pp. 360–74.

Martin, Gerald. Britain's Cultural Relations with Latin America. In *Bulmer-Thomas, V., ed.*, 1989, pp. 27–51.

Martin, Ian. Incentives for Foreign Participation in Botswana's Manufacturing Sector. In *Whiteside, A. W., ed.*, 1989, pp. 45–65.

Martin, John D. and Blose, Laurence E. Federal Government Leasing: Costs, Incentives, and Effects. *Public Budg. Finance*, Summer 1989, *9*(2), pp. 66–75.

Martin, John P.; Burniaux, Jean-Marc and van der Mensbrugghe, Dominique. How Robust Are WALRAS Results? *OECD Econ. Stud.*, Winter 1989–1990, (13), pp. 173–204.

_____, **et al.** Economy-Wide Effects of Agricultural Policies in OECD Countries: Simulation Results with WALRAS. *OECD Econ. Stud.*, Winter 1989–1990, (13), pp. 131–72.

Martin, Larry J. and van Duren, Erna. The Role of Economic Analysis in Countervailing Duty Disputes: Cases Involving Agriculture. *Can. Public Policy*, June 1989, *15*(2), pp. 162–74.

_____ **and Henning, John C.** An Economic Evaluation of Expanded Canadian 3-M Wheat Exports. *Can. J. Agr. Econ.*, November 1989, *37*(3), pp. 445–65.

_____; **Meilke, Karl D. and Braga, Francesco S.** Cross Hedging the Italian Lira/U.S. Dollar Exchange Rate with Deutsch Mark Futures. *J. Futures Markets*, April 1989, *9*(2), pp. 87–99.

Martin, Laurence W. Universities, Education and the National Economy: Case Studies: Arts and Social Sciences. In *Stephens, M. D., ed.*, 1989, pp. 43–50.

Martin, Linda G. Living Arrangements of the Elderly in Fiji, Korea, Malaysia, and the Philippines. *Demography*, November 1989, *26*(4), pp. 627–43.

Martin, Michael T. The Current Economic Crisis and the Caribbean/Central American Periphery: U.S. International Economic Policy during the Republican Administration of 1981 to 1984. In *Martin, M. T. and Kandal, T. R., eds.*, 1989, pp. 111–49.

_____ **and Kandal, Terry R.** Studies of Development and Change in the Modern World: Introduction. In *Martin, M. T. and Kandal, T. R., eds.*, 1989, pp. 3–21.

Martin, Michael V.; Cabeza, Felix and McMullen, B. Starr. The Impacts of Transportation Deregulation on Wheat Shipments in the Pacific Northwest. *Western J. Agr. Econ.*, December 1989, *14*(2), pp. 253–60.

_____; **Lev, Larry and Emami, Ali.** United States Agricultural Trade: Where Are the Gains? Comment. *Western J. Agr. Econ.*, December 1989, *14*(2), pp. 310–12.

Martin, Patricia Yancey and Whiddon, Beverly. Organizational Democracy and Work Quality in a State Welfare Agency. *Soc. Sci. Quart.*, September 1989, *70*(3), pp. 667–86.

Martin, Philip L. and Egan, Daniel L. The Makewhole Remedy in California Agriculture. *Ind. Lab. Relat. Rev.*, October 1989, *43*(1), pp. 120–30.

Martin, Ron. Deindustrialisation and State Intervention: Keynesianism, Thatcherism and the Regions. In *Mohan, J., ed.*, 1989, pp. 87–112.

_____. The Growth and Geographical Anatomy of Venture Capitalism in the United Kingdom. *Reg. Stud.*, October 1989, *23*(5), pp. 389–403.

Martin, S. M. The Long Depression: West African Export Producers and the World Economy, 1914–45. In *Brown, I., ed.*, 1989, pp. 74–94.

Martin, Stephen. Sunk Costs, Financial Markets, and Contestability. *Europ. Econ. Rev.*, July 1989, *33*(6), pp. 1089–1113.

Martin, Steve. New Jobs in the Inner City: The Employment Impacts of Projects Assisted under the Urban Development Grant Programme. *Urban Stud.*, December 1989, *26*(6), pp. 627–38.

Martin, Thomas L. Protection or Free Trade: An Analysis of the Ideas of Henry George on International Commerce and Wages. *Amer. J. Econ. Sociology*, October 1989, *48*(4), pp. 489–501.

Martin, Vance L. and Boehm, Ernst A. An Investigation into the Major Causes of Australia's Recent Inflation and Some Policy Implications. *Econ. Rec.*, March 1989, *65*(188), pp. 1–15.

_____ **and Horne, Jocelyn P.** Exchange Rate Indicators and Optimal Currency Baskets: A Macroeconomic Analysis with Application to Developing Countries. *Appl. Econ.*, September 1989, *21*(9), pp. 1137–52.

_____ and Horne, Jocelyn P. Weighted Monetary Aggregates: An Empirical Study Using Australian Monetary Data, 1969–1987. *Australian Econ. Pap.*, December 1989, *28*(53), pp. 181–200.

Martin, W. J. Implications of Changes in the Composition of Australian Exports for Export Sector Instability. *Australian Econ. Rev.*, Autumn 1989, (85), pp. 39–50.

Martin, Wade E. and Brajer, Victor. Allocating a 'Scarce' Resource, Water in the West: More Market-Like Incentives Can Extend Supply, but Constraints Demand Equitable Policies. *Amer. J. Econ. Sociology*, July 1989, *48*(3), pp. 259–71.

Martinelli, Alberto and Chiesi, Antonio M. The Capitalist Class: Italy. In *Bottomore, T. and Brym, R. J., eds.*, 1989, pp. 109–39.

_____ and Chiesi, Antonio M. The Representation of Business Interests as a Mechanism of Social Regulation. In *Lange, P. and Regini, M., eds.*, 1989, pp. 187–213.

Martinelli, Flavia. Struttura industriale e servizi alla produzione nel mezzogiorno. Un'interpretazione degli squilibri regionali nell'offerta di servizi alle imprese in Italia. (With English summary.) *Politica. Econ.*, April 1989, *5*(1), pp. 129–87.

Martinello, Felice. Wage and Employment Determination in a Unionized Industry: The IWA and the British Columbia Wood Products Industry. *J. Lab. Econ.*, July 1989, *7*(3), pp. 303–30.

Martínez-Giralt, Xavier. On Brand Proliferation with Vertical Differentiation. *Econ. Letters*, October 1989, *30*(4), pp. 279–86.

_____ and Garella, Paolo G. Price Competition in Markets for Dichotomous Substitutes. *Int. J. Ind. Organ.*, September 1989, *7*(3), pp. 357–67.

Martínez López, Antonio and Melis Maynar, Francisco. La demanda y la oferta de estadísticas coyunturales. (With English summary.) *Revista Española Econ.*, 1989, *6*(1–2), pp. 7–57.

Martinez Mongay, Carlos; Sanz, Fernando and de la Cruz Navarro, María. Selección y explotación de los sistemas de alarma y prevención de quiebra. (With English summary.) *Invest. Econ.*, September 1989, *13*(3), pp. 465–84.

Martino, Antonio. Budget Deficits and Constitutional Constraints. *Cato J.*, Winter 1989, *8*(3), pp. 695–711.

Martino, Renato R. Food: An Imperative to Share. In *Helmuth, J. W. and Johnson, S. R., eds., Vol. 1*, 1989, pp. 103–07.

Martinos, Haris and Caspari, Andrea. Local Labour-Market Development and Long-Term Unemployment in the EC Countries. In *Dyson, K., ed.*, 1989, pp. 114–31.

Martins, Ana Paula. Preferências intertemporais de consumo e investimento em capital humano. (With English summary.) *Economia (Portugal)*, May 1989, *13*(2), pp. 179–214.

_____. Worker's Characteristics and Production Theory. *Economia (Portugal)*, January 1989, *13*(1), pp. 17–55.

Martinson, Michael G. and Houpt, James V. Transfer Risk in U.S. Banks. *Fed. Res. Bull.*, April 1989, *75*(4), pp. 255–58.

Marttila, John. American Public Opinion: Evolving Definitions of National Security. In *Hamilton, E. K., ed.*, 1989, pp. 261–315.

Marty, Alvin L. and Baytas, Ahmet. The Interest Elasticity of Money Demand: Further Evidence. *Eastern Econ. J.*, April–June 1989, *15*(2), pp. 107–11.

Marui, Eiji. Japan's Experience with Public Health Reform in the Early Occupation Days. In *Reich, M. R. and Marui, E., eds.*, 1989, pp. 145–72.

_____ and Reich, Michael R. International Cooperation for Health: Problems, Prospects, and Priorities: Overview and Introduction. In *Reich, M. R. and Marui, E., eds.*, 1989, pp. 1–20.

Maruyama, Nobuo. China's Economic Policy towards Asian-Pacific Economies: Comment. In *Shinohara, M. and Lo, F., eds.*, 1989, pp. 205–06.

Marvel, Howard P. Concentration and Price in Gasoline Retailing. In *Weiss, L. W., ed.*, 1989, pp. 179–85.

Marx, Karl. La Constitution de la République Française adoptée le 4 Novembre 1848. (The Constitution of the French Republic Adopted 4 November 1848. With English summary.) *Écon. Societes*, September 1989, *23*(9), pp. 61–73.

_____. La Sainte Famille (chapitre VI-Extraits). (The Holy Family [Chapter VI]. With English summary.) *Écon. Societes*, September 1989, *23*(9), pp. 161–87.

Marx, Thomas G. The Role of Business Economics in Strategic Business Planning. *Bus. Econ.*, April 1989, *24*(2), pp. 20–26.

Marzouk, M. S. and Kaboudan, Mahmoud A. A Retrospective Evaluation of Environmental Protection Projects in Kuwait. *J. Developing Areas*, July 1989, *23*(4), pp. 567–82.

Mas-Colell, Andreu. An Equivalence Theorem for a Bargaining Set. *J. Math. Econ.*, 1989, *18*(2), pp. 129–39.

_____. Capital Theory Paradoxes: Anything Goes. In *Feiwel, G. R., ed. (II)*, 1989, pp. 505–20.

_____. Recent Developments in the Theory of Incomplete Markets. *Econ. Rec.*, March 1989, *65*(188), pp. 82–84.

_____ and Geanakoplos, John. Real Indeterminacy with Financial Assets. *J. Econ. Theory*, February 1989, *47*(1), pp. 22–38.

_____ and Hart, Sergiu. Potential, Value, and Consistency. *Econometrica*, May 1989, *57*(3), pp. 589–614.

_____ and Silvestre, Joaquim. Cost Share Equilibria: A Lindahlian Approach. *J. Econ. Theory*, April 1989, *47*(2), pp. 239–56.

Mascaro, Angelo R.; Marlow, Michael L. and Darby, Michael R. The Empirical Reliability of Monetary Aggregates as Indicators: 1983–1987. *Econ. Inquiry*, October 1989, *27*(4), pp. 555–85.

Maschler, M. and Owen, Guillermo. The Consistent Shapley Value for Hyperplane Games. *Int. J. Game Theory*, 1989, *18*(4), pp. 389–407.

Mascotte, John P. The Importance of Board Effectivness in Not-for-Profit Organizations. In *Herman, R. D. and Van Til, J., eds.*, 1989, pp. 152–59.

Masera, Rainer S. Monetary and Financial Markets in Europe: Regulation and Market Forces. *Rev. Econ. Cond. Italy*, Jan.–April 1989, (1), pp. 13–42.

_____. The Prospects for a European Central Bank: Panel Discussion. In *De Cecco, M. and Giovannini, A., eds.*, 1989, pp. 337–43.

Mashchits, V.; Aleksashenko, S. and Iasin, E. G. The Thirteenth Five-Year Plan: From Economic Norms to Taxation of Enterprises. *Prob. Econ.*, December 1989, *32*(8), pp. 78–92.

Masi, Anthony C. Deindustrialization, Economic Performance, and Industrial Policy: British and American Theories Applied to Italy. In *Foglesong, R. E. and Wolfe, J. D., eds.*, 1989, pp. 127–52.

Masi, Paola. L'influenza del debito pubblico sulla costituzione dei sistemi finanziari: Il caso italiano 1860–93. (The Public Debt and the Development of the Financial System: Italy, 1860–93. With English summary.) *Rivista Storia Econ.*, S.S., February 1989, *6*(1), pp. 60–86.

Maskin, Eric and Evans, Robert. Efficient Renegotiation—Proof Equilibria Repeated Games. *Games Econ. Behav.*, December 1989, *1*(4), pp. 361–69.

_____ and Farrell, Joseph. Renegotiation in Repeated Games. *Games Econ. Behav.*, December 1989, *1*(4), pp. 327–60.

_____ and Farrell, Joseph. Renegotiation-Proof Equilibrium: Reply. *J. Econ. Theory*, December 1989, *49*(2), pp. 376–78.

_____ and Laffont, Jean-Jacques. Rational Expectations with Imperfect Competition: A Bertrand–Edgeworth Example. *Econ. Letters*, October 1989, *30*(4), pp. 269–74.

_____ and Riley, John G. Optimal Multi-unit Auctions. In *Hahn, F., ed.*, 1989, pp. 312–35.

Maskus, Keith E. The Determinants of Foreign Direct Investment in the United States, 1979–85: Comment. In *Feenstra, R. C., ed.*, 1989, pp. 77–80.

_____. Large Costs and Small Benefits of the American Sugar Programme. *World Econ.*, March 1989, *12*(1), pp. 85–104.

Mason, Charles F. Exploration Information and AEC Regulation of the Domestic Uranium Industry. *J. Econ. Dynam. Control*, July 1989, *13*(3), pp. 421–48.

Mason, Colin M. Explaining Recent Trends in New Firm Formation in the UK: Some Evidence from South Hampshire. *Reg. Stud.*, August 1989, *23*(4), pp. 331–46.

Mason, Mark. United States Direct Investment in Japan: Studies in Government Policy and Corporate Strategy. In *Hausman, W. J., ed.*, 1989, pp. 22–25.

Mason, Paul M.; Shapiro, Stephen L. and Borg, Mary O'Malley. The Case of Effort Variables in Student Performance. *J. Econ. Educ.*, Summer 1989, *20*(3), pp. 308–13.

_____; Shapiro, Stephen L. and Borg, Mary O'Malley. Gaming Tax Incidence for Three Groups of Las Vegas Gamblers. *Appl. Econ.*, September 1989, *21*(9), pp. 1267–77.

Mass, William. Developing and Utilizing Technological Leadership: Industrial Research, Vertical Integration, and Business Strategy at the Draper Company, 1816–1930. In *Hausman, W. J., ed.*, 1989, pp. 129–39.

_____. Mechanical and Organizational Innovation: The Drapers and the Automatic Loom. *Bus. Hist. Rev.*, Winter 1989, *63*(4), pp. 876–929.

Massad, Carlos. External Shocks and Policy Reforms in the Southern Cone: A Reassessment: Comment. In *[Díaz-Alejandro, C.]*, 1989, pp. 259–62.

_____. A New Integration Strategy. *CEPAL Rev.*, April 1989, (37), pp. 95–103.

Massey, Doreen and Painter, Joe. The Changing Geography of Trade Unions. In *Mohan, J., ed.*, 1989, pp. 130–50.

Massey, Douglas S. and Denton, Nancy A. Hypersegregation in U.S. Metropolitan Areas: Black and Hispanic Segregation Along Five Dimensions. *Demography*, August 1989, *26*(3), pp. 373–91.

_____ and Liang, Zai. The Long-term Consequences of a Temporary Worker Program: The U.S. Bracero Experience. *Population Res. Policy Rev.*, September 1989, *8*(3), pp. 199–226.

Massiah, Joycelin. Women's Lives and Livelihoods: A View from the Commonwealth Caribbean. *World Devel.*, July 1989, *17*(7), pp. 965–77.

Masso, Jordi and Rosenthal, Robert W. More on the 'Anti-Folk Theorem.' *J. Math. Econ.*, 1989, *18*(3), pp. 281–90.

Masson, André and Arrondel, Luc. Déterminants individuels de la composition du patrimoine: France 1980. (Individual Factors of Wealth Composition: France 1980. With English summary.) *Revue Écon.*, May 1989, *40*(3), pp. 441–502.

_____ and Kessler, Denis. Bequest and Wealth Accumulation: Are Some Pieces of the Puzzle Missing? *J. Econ. Perspectives*, Summer 1989, *3*(3), pp. 141–52.

Masson, Paul R.; Boughton, James M. and Haas, Richard D. The Role of Exchange Rate Movements in Transmitting International Disturbances. In *Hodgman, D. R. and Wood, G. E., eds.*, 1989, pp. 180–213.

_____; Frenkel, Jacob A. and Goldstein, Morris. International Dimensions of Monetary Policy: Coordination versus Autonomy. In *Federal Reserve Bank of Kansas City*, 1989, pp. 183–232.

_____; Frenkel, Jacob A. and Goldstein, Morris. Simulating the Effects of Some Simple Coordinated versus Uncoordinated Policy Rules. In *Bryant, R. C., et al., eds.*, 1989, pp. 203–39.

Masson, Robert T.; Reynolds, Robert J. and Logan, John W. Efficient Regulation with Little

Information: Reality in the Limit? *Int. Econ. Rev.*, November 1989, *30*(4), pp. 851–61.

Massone, Pedro. Net Worth Tax: Mexico. *Bull. Int. Fiscal Doc.*, October 1989, *43*(10), pp. 465–66.

Masten, Scott E.; Meehan, James W., Jr. and Snyder, Edward A. Vertical Integration in the U.S. Auto Industry: A Note on the Influence of Transaction Specific Assets. *J. Econ. Behav. Organ.*, October 1989, *12*(2), pp. 265–73.

Masuch, Klaus and Issing, Otmar. Zur Frage der normativen Interpretation von Leistungsbilanzsalden. (Questions Relating to the Normative Interpretation of Current Balance Data. With English summary.) *Kredit Kapital*, 1989, *22*(1), pp. 1–17.

Masunaga, Rei. Macroeconomic Co-ordination and the Summit: International Monetary Reform. *Can. Public Policy*, Supplement, February 1989, *15*, pp. S55–57.

Mata, Eugénia; Valério, Nuno and Nunes, Ana Bela. Portuguese Economic Growth, 1833–1985. *J. Europ. Econ. Hist.*, Fall 1989, *18*(2), pp. 291–330.

Mata-Greenwood, Adriana. Women in Economic Activity: Lessons from Two Surveys in Costa Rica and Kerala. *Statist. J.*, 1989, *6*(4), pp. 293–304.

Mataloni, Raymond J., Jr. Capital Expenditures by Majority-Owned Foreign Affiliates of U.S. Companies, 1990. *Surv. Curr. Bus.*, September 1989, *69*(9), pp. 21–27.

Matějka, Jaromír. The Next Phase of the Restructuring of the Czechoslovak Economy. *Czech. Econ. Digest.*, June 1989, (4), pp. 46–51.

Mates, Neven. Recent Tendencies in the Regulation of Income Distribution in Enterprises. In *Macesich, G., ed.*, 1989, pp. 147–56.

Matesco, Virene and Pinheiro, Armando Castelar. Relação capital/produto incremental: Estimativas para o período 1948/87. (With English summary.) *Pesquisa Planejamento Econ.*, December 1989, *19*(3), pp. 597–612.

Mathar, Rudolf. Algorithms in Multidimensional Scaling. In *Opitz, O., ed.*, 1989, pp. 159–77.

Matheu, Luis María and Gustavo Secchi, Angel. Administrative and Compliance Costs of Taxation: Argentina. In *International Fiscal Association, ed. (I)*, 1989, pp. 177–91.

Mathews, Brian and Diamantopoulos, Adamantios. Factors Affecting the Nature and Effectiveness of Subjective Revision in Sales Forecasting: An Empirical Study. *Managerial Dec. Econ.*, March 1989, *10*(1), pp. 51–59.

Mathews, Jessica Tuchman. Redefining Security. *Foreign Aff.*, Spring 1989, *68*(2), pp. 162–77.

Mathews, Russell. Fiscal Response to Regional Disparities. In *Higgins, B. and Zagorski, K., eds.*, 1989, pp. 123–47.

————. Tax Effectiveness and Taxpayer Compliance: Neglected Canons of Taxation Policy. In *[Sandford, C.]*, 1989, pp. 86–103.

Mathews, William Carl. Conflict and Consensus in the German Political Economy during the Inflation, 1918–1923: Design or Default? In *Perkins, E. J., ed.*, 1989, pp. 101–23.

Mathewson, Frank; Carr, Jack L. and Glied, Sherry. Unlimited Liability and Free Banking in Scotland: A Note. *J. Econ. Hist.*, December 1989, *49*(4), pp. 974–78.

———— **and Winter, Ralph.** The Economic Effects of Automobile Dealer Regulation. *Ann. Écon. Statist.*, July–Dec. 1989, (15–16), pp. 409–26.

Mathiasen, David G. National Economic Commission: Viewpoints. *Public Budg. Finance*, Autumn 1989, *9*(3), pp. 52–63.

Mathieson, Donald J. Exchange Rate Arrangements and Monetary Policy. *Finance Devel.*, March 1989, *26*(1), pp. 21–24.

————; **Dooley, Michael P. and Lizondo, José Saúl.** The Currency Composition of Foreign Exchange Reserves. *Int. Monet. Fund Staff Pap.*, June 1989, *36*(2), pp. 385–434.

Mathios, Alan D. Education, Variation in Earnings, and Nonmonetary Compensation. *J. Human Res.*, Summer 1989, *24*(3), pp. 456–68.

———— **and Plummer, Mark.** The Regulation of Advertising by the Federal Trade Commission: Capital Market Effects. In *Zerbe, R. O., ed.*, 1989, pp. 77–93.

———— **and Rogers, Robert P.** The Impact of Alternative Forms of State Regulation of AT&T on Direct-Dial, Long-Distance Telephone Rates. *Rand J. Econ.*, Autumn 1989, *20*(3), pp. 437–53.

Mathis, Agostino. Information Systems for Networks of Small and Medium-Sized Enterprises: ENEA's Experience. In *Punset, E. and Sweeney, G., eds.*, 1989, pp. 131–45.

Mathis, Edward J. and Zech, Charles E. The Median Voter Model Fails an Empirical Test: The Procedure, Useful in the Absence of a Better One, Is Not Valid for Multidimensional Issues. *Amer. J. Econ. Sociology*, January 1989, *48*(1), pp. 79–87.

Mathis, Jean and Le Nay, Jean. The Impact of Drought on the National Accounts for Livestock in Sahelian Countries. *Rev. Income Wealth*, June 1989, *35*(2), pp. 209–24.

Mathur, A. N. The Effects of Legal and Contractual Regulations on Employment in Indian Industry. In *Edgren, G., ed.*, 1989, pp. 153–202.

Mathur, Gautam. Trotting Platinum Ages. In *Feiwel, G. R., ed. (II)*, 1989, pp. 413–35.

Mathur, Vijay K. Location Theory of the Firm, Clarification, Revisions, and Additions. *J. Urban Econ.*, September 1989, *26*(2), pp. 189–96.

Matlon, Peter and Reardon, Thomas. Seasonal Food Insecurity and Vulnerability in Drought-Affected Regions of Burkina Faso. In *Sahn, D. E., ed.*, 1989, pp. 118–36.

Matos, Cruz A. and Kotobalavu, Jioji. Ocean Minerals—Prospects for Pacific Island Nations. In *Couper, A. D., ed.*, 1989, pp. 115–26.

Matos, Manuel A. C. C. and Miranda, Vladimiro. A Holistic Approach in Multicriteria Decision Aid. In *Lockett, A. G. and Islei, G., eds.*, 1989, pp. 34–45.

Matoussi, Mohamed S. and Nugent, Jeffrey B. The Switch to Sharecropping in Medjez-el-bab. In *Nabli, M. K. and Nugent, J. B., eds.*, 1989, pp. 140–57.

Matson, Cathy. Public Vices, Private Benefit: William Duer and His Circle, 1776–1792. In *Pencak, W. and Wright, C. E., eds.*, 1989, pp. 72–123.

Matsubara, Nozomu. Conflict and Limits of Power. *J. Conflict Resolution,* March 1989, 33(1), pp. 113–41.

Matsuda, Mari J. Public Response to Racist Speech: Considering the Victim's Story. *Mich. Law Rev.,* August 1989, 87(8), pp. 2320–81.

Matsuda, Yoshiro; Matsui, Sachiko and Asano, Chooichiro. A System for Generating Publication Statistics Based on Bibliographic Information—Bibliometric Analysis for the Development of Economic and Social Thought. *Hitotsubashi J. Econ.,* December 1989, 30(2), pp. 121–56.

_____; **Mizoguchi, Toshiyuki and Wang, Hui-Ling.** A Comparison of Real Consumption Level between Japan and People's Republic of China—The First Approach of Application of ICP Method to Chinese Data. *Hitotsubashi J. Econ.,* June 1989, 30(1), pp. 15–29.

Matsugi, Takashi. The Foreign Trade Structure of Japan. In *Dams, T. and Matsugi, T., eds.*, 1989, pp. 149–71.

Matsui, Akihiko. Consumer-Benefited Cartels under Strategic Capital Investment Competition. *Int. J. Ind. Organ.,* December 1989, 7(4), pp. 451–70.

_____. Information Leakage Forces Cooperation. *Games Econ. Behav.,* March 1989, 1(1), pp. 94–115.

Matsui, Sachiko; Asano, Chooichiro and Matsuda, Yoshiro. A System for Generating Publication Statistics Based on Bibliographic Information—Bibliometric Analysis for the Development of Economic and Social Thought. *Hitotsubashi J. Econ.,* December 1989, 30(2), pp. 121–56.

Matsui, Yukio and Kato, Hiroo. Tax Reform in Japan. *Bull. Int. Fiscal Doc.,* November 1989, 43(11), pp. 498–505.

Matsumoto, Yasumi. Social Choice without Completeness. *Econ. Stud. Quart.,* December 1989, 40(4), pp. 289–95.

Matsuo, Hirofumi. Japanese Manufacturing Management. In *Matsuo, H., ed.*, 1989, pp. 32–35.

Matsuo, Toshihide. On Incentive Compatible, Individual Rational, and Ex Post Efficient Mechanisms for Bilateral Trading. *J. Econ. Theory,* October 1989, 49(1), pp. 189–94.

Matsushima, Hitoshi. Efficiency in Repeated Games with Imperfect Monitoring. *J. Econ. Theory,* August 1989, 48(2), pp. 428–42.

Matsushita, Masahiro and Sato, Ryuzo. Estimations of Self-Dual Demand Functions: An International Comparison. In *Sato, R. and Negishi, T., eds.*, 1989, pp. 253–73.

Matsushita, Mitsuo. Comments on Antidumping Law Enforcement in Japan. In *Jackson, J. H. and Vermulst, E. A., eds.*, 1989, pp. 389–95.

Matsuura, Hiroshi and Kurabayashi, Yoshimasa.

Progress of Japanese National Accounts in an International Perspective of the SNA Review. In *Sato, R. and Negishi, T., eds.*, 1989, pp. 99–123.

Matsuyama, Kiminori. Erratum [Chernoff's Dual Axiom, Revealed Preference and Weak Rational Choice Functions]. *J. Econ. Theory,* December 1989, 49(2), pp. 383.

Matte E., Ricardo and Rojas R., Patricio. Evolución reciente del mercado monetario y una estimación de la demanda por dinero en Chile. (With English summary.) *Cuadernos Econ.,* August 1989, 26(78), pp. 195–216.

Matthews, Derek. The British Experience of Profit-Sharing. *Econ. Hist. Rev., 2nd Ser.,* November 1989, 42(4), pp. 439–64.

Matthews, K. G. P. Could Lloyd George Have Done It? The Pledge Re-examined. *Oxford Econ. Pap.,* April 1989, 41(2), pp. 374–407.

_____. Was Sterling Overvalued in 1925? A Reply and Further Evidence. *Econ. Hist. Rev., 2nd Ser.,* February 1989, 42(1), pp. 90–96.

Matthews, Lear K. and Danns, George K. Perspectives on the Development and Underdevelopment of Communities in Guyana: A Sociohistorical Analysis. In *Martin, M. T. and Kandal, T. R., eds.*, 1989, pp. 166–201.

Matthews, Steven A. Veto Threats: Rhetoric in a Bargaining Game. *Quart. J. Econ.,* May 1989, 104(2), pp. 347–69.

_____ **and Postlewaite, Andrew.** Pre-play Communication in Two-Person Sealed-Bid Double Auctions. *J. Econ. Theory,* June 1989, 48(1), pp. 238–63.

Mattila, J. Peter and Orazem, Peter F. Comparable Worth and the Structure of Earnings: The Iowa Case. In *Michael, R. T.; Hartmann, H. I. and O'Farrell, B., eds.*, 1989, pp. 179–99.

Mattingly, Doreen J. and Scott, Allen J. The Aircraft and Parts Industry in Southern California: Continuity and Change from the Inter-war years to the 1990s. *Econ. Geogr.,* January 1989, 65(1), pp. 48–71.

Mattsson, Lars-Göran and Anderstig, Christer. Interregional Allocation Models of Infrastructure Investments. *Ann. Reg. Sci.,* 1989, 23(4), pp. 287–98.

Mattsson, Lars-Gunnar. Development of Firms in Networks: Positions and Investments. In *Hallén, L. and Johanson, J., eds.*, 1989, pp. 121–39.

Matutes, Carmen. Some Considerations about 1992. *Atlantic Econ. J.,* September 1989, 17(3), pp. 1–11.

_____ **and Brandts, Jordi.** Impacto de la imposición indirecta en los beneficios economicos en un marco de equilibrio general. (With English summary.) *Invest. Econ.,* September 1989, 13(3), pp. 319–36.

_____ **and Lal, Rajiv.** Price Competition in Multimarket Duopolies. *Rand J. Econ.,* Winter 1989, 20(4), pp. 516–37.

_____ **and Regibeau, Pierre.** Standardization across Markets and Entry. *J. Ind. Econ.,* June 1989, 37(4), pp. 359–71.

Matykowski, Roman and Stryjakiewicz, Tadeusz.

The Changing Organisation of Labour and Its Impacts on Daily Activities. In *Linge, G. J. R. and van der Knaap, G. A., eds.*, 1989, pp. 128–43.

Matzer, John, Jr. Infrastructure: The State of the Art. In *Matzer, J., Jr., ed.*, 1989, pp. 3–12.

———. Rating Forms for Capital Improvements. In *Matzer, J., Jr., ed.*, 1989, pp. 121–31.

———. Selecting Financing Options. In *Matzer, J., Jr., ed.*, 1989, pp. 191–97.

———. Tools for Condition Assessment. In *Matzer, J., Jr., ed.*, 1989, pp. 74–80.

———. Tools for Planning and Programming. In *Matzer, J., Jr., ed.*, 1989, pp. 48–52.

Mauch, Gerhard and Werner, Josua. Friedrich List und die Lehre von den produktiven Kräften. (Friedrich List and the Theory of Productive Forces. With English summary.) *Jahr. Nationalökon. Statist.*, December 1989, 206(6), pp. 533–45.

Maud, Humphrey. First Steps to Increased Trade. In *Cerami, C. A., ed.*, 1989, pp. 41–52.

Maule, Christopher and Acheson, Keith. Trade Policy Responses to New Technology in the Film and Television Industry. *J. World Trade*, April 1989, 23(2), pp. 35–48.

Maunder, W. John. Climatic Variability and Agricultural Production in Temperate Regions: Six Case Studies. In *Oram, P. A., et al.*, 1989, pp. 45–55.

Maurice, S. Charles; Crumbley, D. Larry and Thomas, Christopher R. Vertical Integration, Price Squeezing, and the Percentage Depletion Allowance. *Quart. Rev. Econ. Bus.*, Winter 1989, 29(4), pp. 26–36.

Mauskopf, Josephine. Adding an Economic Dimension to Risk Assessment: Discussion. *Amer. J. Agr. Econ.*, May 1989, 71(2), pp. 485–86.

Max, Emmanuel. Leprosy Control in India: International Cooperation. In *Reich, M. R. and Marui, E., eds.*, 1989, pp. 295–314.

Maxfield, Sylvia. National Business, Debt-Led Growth and Political Transition in Latin America. In *Stallings, B. and Kaufman, R., eds.*, 1989, pp. 75–90.

Maxwell, Nan L. Demographic and Economic Determinants of United States Income Inequality. *Soc. Sci. Quart.*, June 1989, 70(2), pp. 245–64.

———. Labor Market Effects from Involuntary Job Losses in Layoffs, Plant Closings: The Role of Human Capital in Facilitating Reemployment and Reduced Wage Losses. *Amer. J. Econ. Sociology*, April 1989, 48(2), pp. 129–41.

Maxwell, Simon and Fernando, Adrian. Cash Crops in Developing Countries: The Issues, the Facts, the Policies. *World Devel.*, November 1989, 17(11), pp. 1677–1708.

Mayer, Colin. Public Ownership: Concepts and Applications. In *Helm, D., ed.*, 1989, pp. 251–74.

——— **and Collier, Paul.** Financial Liberalization, Financial Systems, and Economic

Growth: The Assessment. *Oxford Rev. Econ. Policy*, Winter 1989, 5(4), pp. 1–12.

Mayer, Jean. International Labour Standards and Technical Co-operation: The Case of Special Public Works Programmes. *Int. Lab. Rev.*, 1989, 128(2), pp. 155–75.

Mayer, Robert N.; Zick, Cathleen D. and Burton, John R. Consumer Representation and Local Telephone Rates. *J. Cons. Aff.*, Winter 1989, 23(2), pp. 267–84.

Mayer, Susan E. and Jencks, Christopher. Poverty and the Distribution of Material Hardship. *J. Human Res.*, Winter 1989, 24(1), pp. 88–114.

Mayer, Thomas. Economic Structure, the Exchange Rate, and Adjustment in the Federal Republic of Germany: A General Equilibrium Approach. *Int. Monet. Fund Staff Pap.*, June 1989, 36(2), pp. 435–63.

———; **Gupta, Sanjeev and Lipschitz, Leslie.** The Common Agricultural Policy of the EC. *Finance Devel.*, June 1989, 26(2), pp. 37–39.

Mayer, Thomas F. In Defense of Analytical Marxism. *Sci. Society*, Winter 1989–90, 53(4), pp. 416–41.

Mayer, Walter J. Estimating Disequilibrium Models with Limited A Priori Price-Adjustment Information. *J. Econometrics*, July 1989, 41(3), pp. 303–20.

Mayer-Wittman, Karl M. Economic Analysis and Corporate Strategic Planning. *Bus. Econ.*, April 1989, 24(2), pp. 27–31.

Mayers, Judith O. Glossary of Pension and Related Terms. In *Turner, J. A. and Beller, D. J., eds.*, 1989, pp. 470–81.

Mayes, David G. The Effects of Economic Integration on Trade. In *Jacquemin, A. and Sapir, A., eds.*, 1989, 1978, pp. 97–121.

——— **and Gevel, Ad.** 1992: Removing the Barriers. *Nat. Inst. Econ. Rev.*, August 1989, (129), pp. 42–51.

Mayhew, Anne. Dangers in Using the Idea of Property Rights: Modern Property Rights Theory and the Neo-classical Trap. In *Tool, M. R. and Samuels, W. J., eds. (III)*, 1989, 1985, pp. 247–54.

———. Polanyi's Double Movement and Veblen on the Army of the Commonweal. *J. Econ. Issues*, June 1989, 23(2), pp. 555–62.

Mayhew, Ken; McGuire, Alistair and Fenn, Paul. The Assessment: The Economics of Health Care. *Oxford Rev. Econ. Policy*, Spring 1989, 5(1), pp. 1–20.

——— **and Turnbull, Peter.** Models of Union Behaviour: A Critique of Recent Literature. In *Drago, R. and Perlman, R., eds.*, 1989, pp. 105–29.

Maynard, Alan. The Costs of Addiction and the Costs of Control. In *Robinson, D.; Maynard, A. and Chester, R., eds.*, 1989, pp. 84–100.

Maynard, David E. Gambling with Public Funds: State Investment Pools Revisited. *J. Policy Anal. Manage.*, Winter 1989, 8(1), pp. 101–03.

Maynard, Geoffrey. Argentina: Macroeconomic

Policy, 1966–73. In *di Tella, G. and Dornbusch, R., eds.*, 1989, pp. 166–74.

———. The Budget. *Fisc. Stud.*, May 1989, *10*(2), pp. 24–28.

Mayne, Lucille S. and Forbes, Shawn M. The Asymmetric Prime: An Empirical Note. *Econ. Letters*, December 1989, *31*(4), pp. 371–74.

——— **and Forbes, Shawn M.** A Friction Model of the Prime. *J. Banking Finance*, March 1989, *13*(1), pp. 127–35.

Mayo, John W. and Flynn, Joseph E. Firm Entry and Exit: Causality Tests and Economic-Base Linkages. *J. Reg. Sci.*, November 1989, *29*(4), pp. 645–62.

——— **and McFarland, Deborah A.** Regulation, Market Structure, and Hospital Costs. *Southern Econ. J.*, January 1989, *55*(3), pp. 559–69.

Mayo, Wayne. Pricing for Capacity Utilisation with Public Enterprises. *Australian Econ. Rev.*, Spring 1989, (87), pp. 16–24.

Mayor Lopez, Pedro; Hayes-Renshaw, Fiona and Lequesne, Christian. The Permanent Representations of the Member States to the European Communities. *J. Common Market Stud.*, December 1989, *28*(2), pp. 119–37.

Mayrzedt, Hans. Alternativen zu herkömmlichen Bestrebungen einer Reform der Weltwirtschaftsordnung. (Alternatives for a Reform of the World Economic Order. With English summary.) *Aussenwirtschaft*, June 1989, *44*(2), pp. 223–36.

Mays, Elizabeth. A Profit-Maximizing Model of Federal Home Loan Bank Behavior. *J. Real Estate Finance Econ.*, December 1989, *2*(4), pp. 331–47.

——— **and DeMarco, Edward J.** The Demand for Federal Home Loan Bank Advances by Thrift Institutions: Some Recent Evidence. *Amer. Real Estate Urban Econ. Assoc. J.*, Fall 1989, *17*(3), pp. 363–79.

Mazeya, Y. E. and Vitaliano, Donald F. Public Debt and the Size Distribution of Income. In *Davidson, P. and Kregel, J., eds.*, 1989, pp. 56–77.

Mazier, Jacques. Crise, ajustement structurel et régulation. (Crisis, Structural Adjustment and Regulation. With English summary.) *Écon. Societes*, March 1989, *23*(3), pp. 179–200.

Mazur, Mark J. Optimal Linear Taxation with Stochastic Incomes. *Public Finance*, 1989, *44*(1), pp. 31–50.

Mbaku, John M. Does Fiscal Expansion Contribute to Political Instability in Africa? Some Empirical Evidence. *Econ. Scelte Pubbliche/J. Public Finance Public Choice*, Sept.–Dec. 1989, *7*(3), pp. 159–71.

———. Export Growth and Economic Performance in Developing Countries: Further Evidence from Africa. *J. Econ. Devel.*, December 1989, *14*(2), pp. 127–42.

——— **and Paul, Chris.** Political Instability in Africa: A Rent-Seeking Approach. *Public Choice*, October 1989, *63*(1), pp. 63–72.

Mbilima, Deonatus. Regional Organizations in Southern Africa. In *Whiteside, A. W., ed.*, 1989, pp. 31–44.

McAdam, Terry W. and Gies, David L. Managing Expectations: What Effective Board Members Ought to Expect from Nonprofit Organizations. In *Herman, R. D. and Van Til, J., eds.*, 1989, pp. 77–88.

McAfee, R. Preston and McMillan, John. Government Procurement and International Trade. *J. Int. Econ.*, May 1989, *26*(3/4), pp. 291–308.

———; **McMillan, John and Reny, Philip J.** Extracting the Surplus in the Common-Value Auction. *Econometrica*, November 1989, *57*(6), pp. 1451–59.

———; **McMillan, John and Whinston, Michael D.** Multiproduct Monopoly, Commodity Bundling, and Correlation of Values. *Quart. J. Econ.*, May 1989, *104*(2), pp. 371–83.

McAleer, Michael and Hall, A. D. A Monte Carlo Study of Some Tests of Model Adequacy in Time Series Analysis. *J. Bus. Econ. Statist.*, January 1989, *7*(1), pp. 95–106.

——— **and Veall, Michael R.** How Fragile Are Fragile Inferences? A Re-evaluation of the Deterrent Effect of Capital Punishment. *Rev. Econ. Statist.*, February 1989, *71*(1), pp. 99–106.

McAllister, J. Colonial America, 1607–1776. *Econ. Hist. Rev., 2nd Ser.*, May 1989, *42*(2), pp. 245–59.

McAllister, Patrick H.; Stone, John C. and Dantzig, George B. Deriving a Utility Function for the U.S. Economy. *J. Policy Modeling*, Fall 1989, *11*(3), pp. 391–424.

———; **Stone, John C. and Dantzig, George B.** Integrability of the Multiple-Period Equilibrium Model: Part II. *J. Policy Modeling*, Winter 1989, *11*(4), pp. 569–92.

McAllister, Richard and Brewin, Christopher. Annual Review of the Activities of the European Communities in 1988. *J. Common Market Stud.*, June 1989, *27*(4), pp. 323–57.

McCaa, Robert. Isolation or Assimilation? A Log Linear Interpretation of Australian Marriages, 1947–60, 1975, and 1986. *Population Stud.*, March 1989, *43*(1), pp. 155–62.

McCabe, Brendan P. M. Misspecification Tests in Econometrics Based on Ranks. *J. Econometrics*, February 1989, *40*(2), pp. 261–78.

——— **and Leybourne, S. J.** Testing for Coefficient Constancy in Random Walk Models with Particular Reference to the Initial Value Problem. *Empirical Econ.*, 1989, *14*(2), pp. 105–12.

——— **and Leybourne, S. J.** Testing for Coefficient Constancy in Random Walk Models with Particular Reference to the Initial Value Problem. In *Kramer, W., ed.*, 1989, pp. 41–48.

——— **and Phillips, Garry D. A.** A Sequential Approach to Testing for Structural Change in Econometric Models. In *Kramer, W., ed.*, 1989, pp. 87–101.

——— **and Phillips, Garry D. A.** A Sequential Approach to Testing for Structural Change in Econometric Models. *Empirical Econ.*, 1989, *14*(2), pp. 151–65.

McCabe, George M. and Solberg, Donald P. Hedging in the Treasury Bill Futures Market

When the Hedged Instrument and the Deliverable Instrument Are Not Matched. *J. Futures Markets*, December 1989, *9*(6), pp. 529–37.

McCabe, James; Lane, Julia and Glennon, Dennis. Measures of Local Business Climate: Alternative Approaches. *Reg. Sci. Persp.*, 1989, *19*(1), pp. 89–106.

McCabe, Kevin A. Fiat Money as a Store of Value in an Experimental Market. *J. Econ. Behav. Organ.*, October 1989, *12*(2), pp. 215–31.

McCafferty, Stephen and Driskill, Robert A. Dynamic Duopoly with Adjustment Costs: A Differential Game Approach. *J. Econ. Theory*, December 1989, *49*(2), pp. 324–38.

_____ **and Driskill, Robert A.** Dynamic Duopoly with Output Adjustment Costs in International Markets: Taking the Conjecture out of Conjectual Variations. In *Feenstra, R. C., ed.*, 1989, pp. 125–37.

McCain, Roger A. Artists' Resale Dividends: Some Economic–Theoretic Considerations. *J. Cult. Econ.*, June 1989, *13*(1), pp. 35–51.

_____ **and Sullivan, Edward J.** RATS: An Econometric Package for Microcomputers. *J. Econ. Surveys*, 1989, *3*(3), pp. 253–60.

McCall, Nelda. Arizona: The Arizona Health Care Cost Containment System: Implementation by Plan Structure. In *Scheffler, R. M. and Rossiter, L. F., eds.*, 1989, pp. 221–40.

_____ **and Haber, Susan.** Use of Nonphysician Providers in the Medicare Program: Assessment of the Direct Reimbursement of Clinical Social Workers Demonstration Project. *Inquiry*, Summer 1989, *26*(2), pp. 158–69.

McCalla, Alex F. Developing Country Productivity and Trade: Complementary or Competitive? In *Helmuth, J. W. and Johnson, S. R., eds., Vol. 2*, 1989, pp. 255–75.

_____. Improving Policy Coordination in Agriculture. In *von Witzke, H.; Runge, C. F. and Job, B., eds.*, 1989, pp. 212–45.

_____. Policy Options for Improving the Functioning of the World Food Production and Distribution Systems: Reaction. In *Helmuth, J. W. and Johnson, S. R., eds., Vol. 1*, 1989, pp. 233–35.

McCallum, Bennett T. Inflation Prevention by a Monetary Rule. *Cato J.*, Fall 1989, *9*(2), pp. 339–44.

_____. New Classical Macroeconomics: A Sympathetic Account. *Scand. J. Econ.*, 1989, *91*(2), pp. 223–52.

_____. Real Business Cycle Models. In *Barro, R. J., ed.*, 1989, pp. 16–50.

_____. Reply [The Case for Rules in the Conduct of Monetary Policy: A Concrete Example]. *Weltwirtsch. Arch.*, 1989, *125*(1), pp. 179–82.

McCallum, John. Social Welfare in Developed Market Countries: Australia. In *Dixon, J. and Scheurell, R. P., eds.*, 1989, pp. 1–46.

McCann, Dennis P. "Accursed Internationalism" of Finance: Coping with the Resource of Catholic Social Teaching. In *Williams, O. F.; Reilly, F. K. and Houck, J. W., eds.*, 1989, pp. 127–47.

McCann, Ewen and Giles, David E. A. Divisia Monetary Aggregates and the Real User Cost of Money. *J. Quant. Econ.*, January 1989, *5*(1), pp. 127–41.

McCardle, Kevin F. and Winkler, Robert L. All Roads Lead to Risk Preference: A Turnpike Theorem for Conditionally Independent Returns. *J. Finan. Quant. Anal.*, March 1989, *24*(1), pp. 13–28.

McCarl, Bruce A. and Bessler, David A. Estimating an Upper Bound on the Pratt Risk Aversion Coefficient When the Utility Function Is Unknown. *Australian J. Agr. Econ.*, April 1989, *33*(1), pp. 56–63.

_____; **Dillon, Carl R. and Mjelde, James W.** Biophysical Simulation in Support of Crop Production Decisions: A Case Study in the Blacklands Region of Texas. *Southern J. Agr. Econ.*, July 1989, *21*(1), pp. 73–86.

_____ **and Önal, Hayri.** Aggregation of Heterogeneous Firms in Mathematical Programming Models. *Europ. Rev. Agr. Econ.*, 1989, *16*(4), pp. 499–513.

_____ **and Önal, Hayri.** Linear Approximation Using MOTAD and Separable Programming: Should It Be Done? *Amer. J. Agr. Econ.*, February 1989, *71*(1), pp. 158–66.

_____, **et al.** Linking Farm and Sector Models in Spatial Equilibrium Analysis: An Application to Ozone Standards as They Affect Corn Belt Agriculture. In *Labys, W. C.; Takayama, T. and Uri, N. D., eds.*, 1989, pp. 279–98.

McCarthy, David D. and Turner, John A. Pension Rates of Return in Large and Small Plans. In *Turner, J. A. and Beller, D. J., eds.*, 1989, pp. 235–86.

McCarthy, Francis Desmond and Lynn, Robert. Padrões de crescimento dos países em desenvolvimento na década de 80. (With English summary.) *Pesquisa Planejamento Econ.*, August 1989, *19*(2), pp. 309–45.

McCarthy, Mary R. and McCarthy, Thomas G. Irish Migration: The Search for the Efficiency and Equity Basis of a European Regional Policy. *Econ. Soc. Rev.*, October 1989, *21*(1), pp. 71–84.

McCarthy, Patrick S. Accident Involvement and Highway Safety. *Logist. Transp. Rev.*, June 1989, *25*(2), pp. 129–38.

_____ **and Krehbiel, Timothy L.** An Analysis of the Determinants of Portfolio Selection. *Quart. Rev. Econ. Bus.*, Autumn 1989, *29*(3), pp. 43–56.

McCarthy, Thomas G. and McCarthy, Mary R. Irish Migration: The Search for the Efficiency and Equity Basis of a European Regional Policy. *Econ. Soc. Rev.*, October 1989, *21*(1), pp. 71–84.

McCarthy, William F. Evaluation of Computer Assisted Telephone Interviewing as a Survey Methodology by Means of Cost Models and Mathematical Programming. In *Gulledge, T. R., Jr. and Litteral, L. A., eds.*, 1989, pp. 327–37.

McCarty, David. Telecommunications Policy and Economic Development: The New State Role:

Texas. In *Schmandt, J.; Williams, F. and Wilson, R. H., eds.*, 1989, pp. 151–84.

_____ and **Eugene, Darrick.** Telecommunications Policy and Economic Development: The New State Role: Florida. In *Schmandt, J.; Williams, F. and Wilson, R. H., eds.*, 1989, pp. 41–61.

McCauley, Robert N. and Zimmer, Steven A. Explaining International Differences in the Cost of Capital. *Fed. Res. Bank New York Quart. Rev.*, Summer 1989, *14*(2), pp. 7–28.

McCay, Bonnie J. Co-management of a Clam Revitalization Project: The New Jersey "Spawner Sanctuary" Program. In *Pinkerton, E., ed.*, 1989, pp. 103–24.

_____; **Gatewood, John B. and Creed, Carolyn F.** Labor and the Labor Process in a Limited Entry Fishery. *Marine Resource Econ.*, 1989, *6*(4), pp. 311–30.

McChesney, Fred S. Regulation, Taxes, and Political Extortion. In *Meiners, R. E. and Yandle, B., eds.*, 1989, pp. 223–41.

McClatchy, Don; Cahill, Sean and Surry, Yves. Exchange Rates and Multilateral Free Trade in Agriculture. *Can. J. Agr. Econ.*, Part 2, December 1989, *37*(4), pp. 993–1007.

McCleary, William A. Policy Implementation under Adjustment Lending. *Finance Devel.*, March 1989, *26*(1), pp. 32–34.

McClelland, John W.; Wetzstein, Michael E. and Noles, Richard K. Optimal Replacement Policies for Rejuvenated Assets. *Amer. J. Agr. Econ.*, February 1989, *71*(1), pp. 147–57.

McClelland, Robert. Voluntary Donations and Public Expenditures in a Federalist System: Comment and Extension. *Amer. Econ. Rev.*, December 1989, *79*(5), pp. 1291–96.

McClintock, Brent. Direct Foreign Investment: Reply. *J. Econ. Issues*, September 1989, *23*(3), pp. 885–89.

McCloskey, Donald N. Formalism in Economics, Rhetorically Speaking. *Ricerche Econ.*, Jan.–June 1989, *43*(1–2), pp. 57–75.

_____. The Open Fields of England: Rent, Risk, and the Rate of Interest, 1300–1815. In *Galenson, D. W., ed.*, 1989, pp. 5–51.

_____. The Very Idea of Epistemology: Comment. *Econ. Philos.*, April 1989, *5*(1), pp. 1–6.

_____. Why I Am No Longer a Positivist. *Rev. Soc. Econ.*, Fall 1989, *47*(3), pp. 225–38.

McCloud, Darell E. Assessing Climatic Variability from Long-Term Crop Yield Trends. In *Oram, P. A., et al.*, 1989, pp. 203–17.

McClure, J. Harold, Jr.; Willett, Thomas D. and Kaempfer, William H. Incremental Protection and Efficient Political Choice between Tariffs and Quotas. *Can. J. Econ.*, May 1989, *22*(2), pp. 228–36.

McColl, Greg D. Changing Patterns of World Energy Use. In *Owen, A. D., ed.*, 1989, pp. 13–24.

McCombie, J. S. L. Economic Growth, the Harrod Foreign Trade Multiplier and the Hicks Super-Multiplier. In *Wood, J. C. and Woods,*

R. N., eds., Vol. 4, 1989, *1985*, pp. 139–58.

_____. 'Thirlwall's Law' and Balance of Payments Constrained Growth—A Comment on the Debate. *Appl. Econ.*, May 1989, *21*(5), pp. 611–29.

_____ and **Dixon, Robert.** Inter-industry Differences in the Factor-Augmenting Bias of Technological Change. *Australian Econ. Pap.*, June 1989, *28*(52), pp. 103–11.

McConnell, John J. and Johnston, Elizabeth Tashjian. Requiem for a Market: An Analysis of the Rise and Fall of a Financial Futures Contract. *Rev. Financial Stud.*, 1989, *2*(1), pp. 1–23.

_____ and **Lummer, Scott L.** Further Evidence on the Bank Lending Process and the Capital-Market Response to Bank Loan Agreements. *J. Finan. Econ.*, November 1989, *25*(1), pp. 99–122.

McConnell, Kenneth E. and Strand, Ivar E. Benefits from Commercial Fisheries When Demand and Supply Depend on Water Quality. *J. Environ. Econ. Manage.*, November 1989, *17*(3), pp. 284–92.

_____; **Strand, Ivar E., Jr. and Bockstael, Nancy E.** Measuring the Benefits of Improvements in Water Quality: The Chesapeake Bay. *Marine Resource Econ.*, 1989, *6*(1), pp. 1–18.

_____; **Strand, Ivar E., Jr. and Bockstael, Nancy E.** A Random Utility Model for Sportfishing: Some Preliminary Results for Florida. *Marine Resource Econ.*, 1989, *6*(3), pp. 245–60.

McConnell, Sheena. Strikes, Wages, and Private Information. *Amer. Econ. Rev.*, September 1989, *79*(4), pp. 801–15.

McCormick, Barry. Housing, Wages and UK Labour Markets: Comments. *Oxford Bull. Econ. Statist.*, March 1989, *51*(2), pp. 144–50.

_____ and **Hughes, Gordon.** Does Migration Reduce Differentials in Regional Unemployment Rates? In *van Dijk, J., et al., eds.*, 1989, pp. 85–108.

McCormick, James M. and Mitchell, Neil J. Human Rights and Foreign Assistance: An Update. *Soc. Sci. Quart.*, December 1989, *70*(4), pp. 969–79.

McCormick, Ken. An Essay on the Assumption of Rational Behavior in Economics. *Rev. Soc. Econ.*, Fall 1989, *47*(3), pp. 313–21.

_____. Veblen on the Nature of Capital. *Rivista Int. Sci. Econ. Com.*, July 1989, *36*(7), pp. 609–22.

_____ and **Raiklin, Ernest.** The Conditional View of the Neoclassical and Marxist Approaches to the Concept of Productive Labour. *Int. J. Soc. Econ.*, 1989, *16*(1), pp. 13–26.

McCormick, Robert E. A Review of the Economics of Regulation: The Political Process. In *Meiners, R. E. and Yandle, B., eds.*, 1989, pp. 16–37.

_____ and **Clement, Robert C.** Coaching Team Production. *Econ. Inquiry*, April 1989, *27*(2), pp. 287–304.

McCorriston, Steve and Sheldon, Ian M. Measuring Patterns of Intra-industry Specialisation within the EC. *Scot. J. Polit. Econ.*, February

1989, *36*(1), pp. 96–102.

_____ and **Sheldon, Ian M.** Trade and Welfare Effects of EC Accession on the UK Agricultural Supply Industries. *J. Agr. Econ.*, September 1989, *40*(3), pp. 302–13.

_____ and **Sheldon, Ian M.** The Welfare Implications of Nitrogen Limitation Policies. *J. Agr. Econ.*, May 1989, *40*(2), pp. 143–51.

McCoy, James P. Bauxite Processing in Jamaica and Guyana: An Estimate of Income and Foreign Exchange Impacts. *World Devel.*, February 1989, *17*(2), pp. 275–92.

McCoy, Jennifer L. Venezuela: Austerity and the Working Class in a Democratic Regime. In *Handelman, H. and Baer, W., eds.*, 1989, pp. 195–223.

McCoy, John L. and Weems, Kerry. Disabled-Worker Beneficiaries and Disabled SSI Recipients: A Profile of Demographic and Program Characteristics. *Soc. Sec. Bull.*, May 1989, *52*(5), pp. 16–28.

McCracken, Grant. Who Is the Celebrity Endorser? Cultural Foundations of the Endorsement Process. *J. Cons. Res.*, December 1989, *16*(3), pp. 310–21.

McCracken, M. C. Tax Reform and the Macroeconomy: Jobs, Inflation, and Growth: Comment. In *Mintz, J. and Whalley, J., eds.*, 1989, pp. 430–32.

McCracken, Vicki A. The Importance of Demographic Variables on the Probability of Consuming Meat Away from Home. In *Buse, R. C., ed.*, 1989, pp. 256–83.

McCraw, Thomas K. and Reinhardt, Forest. Losing to Win: U.S. Steel's Pricing, Investment Decisions, and Market Share, 1901–1938. *J. Econ. Hist.*, September 1989, *49*(3), pp. 593–619.

McCubbins, Mathew D. and Kiewiet, D. Roderick. Parties, Committees, and Policymaking in the U.S. Congress: A Comment on the Role of Transaction Costs as Determinants of the Governance Structure of Political Institutions. *J. Inst. Theoretical Econ.*, December 1989, *145*(4), pp. 676–85.

McCulloch, Robert E. Local Model Influence. *J. Amer. Statist. Assoc.*, June 1989, *84*(406), pp. 473–78.

McDaniel, Linda S. and Kinney, William R., Jr. Characteristics of Firms Correcting Previously Reported Quarterly Earnings. *J. Acc. Econ.*, February 1989, *11*(1), pp. 71–93.

McDaniel, Paul R. Tax Expenditure Budget from Inside the Government: Comment. In *Bruce, N., ed.*, 1989, pp. 269–72.

_____. Tax Expenditures as Tools of Government Action. In *Salamon, L. M., ed.*, 1989, pp. 167–96.

McDaniel, William R. and Madura, Jeff. Market Reaction to Increased Loan Loss Reserves at Money-Center Banks. *J. Finan. Services Res.*, December 1989, *3*(4), pp. 359–69.

McDermed, Ann A. and Clark, Robert L. Determinants of Retirement by Married Women. *Soc. Sec. Bull.*, January 1989, *52*(1), pp. 33–35.

_____; **Clark, Robert L. and Allen, Steven G.** Pension Wealth, Age–Wealth Profiles, and the Distribution of Net Worth. In *Lipsey, R. E. and Tice, H. S., eds.*, 1989, pp. 689–731.

McDermott, John H. Foreign-Exchange Rationing and Employment in Industrializing Countries. *J. Int. Econ.*, November 1989, *27*(3–4), pp. 245–64.

McDevitt, Catherine L. The Role of the Nominal Tax System in the Common Stock Returns/Expected Inflation Relationship. *J. Monet. Econ.*, July 1989, *24*(1), pp. 93–107.

McDonald, Bill and Affleck-Graves, John. Nonnormalities and Tests of Asset Pricing Theories. *J. Finance*, September 1989, *44*(4), pp. 889–908.

_____ and **Miller, Robert E.** Additional Evidence on the Nature of Size-Related Anomalies. *J. Econ. Bus.*, February 1989, *41*(1), pp. 61–68.

McDonald, Curtis T.; Baer, Werner and Biller, Dan. Austerity under Different Political Regimes: The Case of Brazil. In *Handelman, H. and Baer, W., eds.*, 1989, pp. 19–42.

McDonald, Daina. The Government Accounts and the Deficit. *Australian Econ. Rev.*, Winter 1989, (86), pp. 43–52.

_____ and **Dixon, Peter B.** The Australian Economy in 1988–89 and 1989–90. *Australian Econ. Rev.*, Autumn 1989, (85), pp. 3–23.

McDonald, Frank. The Single European Market: Review Article. *J. Econ. Stud.*, 1989, *16*(4), pp. 60–70.

_____ and **Zis, George.** The European Monetary System: Towards 1992 and Beyond. *J. Common Market Stud.*, March 1989, *27*(3), pp. 183–202.

McDonald, Ian M. The Wage Demands of a Selfish, Plant-Specific Trade Union. *Oxford Econ. Pap.*, July 1989, *41*(3), pp. 506–27.

_____ and **Creedy, John.** Trade Unions, Wages and Taxation. *Fisc. Stud.*, August 1989, *10*(3), pp. 50–59.

McDonald, J. R. S.; Rayner, A. J. and Bates, J. M. Market Power in the Food Industry: A Note. *J. Agr. Econ.*, January 1989, *40*(1), pp. 101–08.

McDonald, James B. Partially Adaptive Estimation of ARMA Time Series Models. *Int. J. Forecasting*, 1989, *5*(2), pp. 217–30.

_____ and **Butler, Richard J.** Using Incomplete Moments to Measure Inequality. *J. Econometrics*, September 1989, *42*(1), pp. 109–19.

McDonald, John F. Econometric Studies of Urban Population Density: A Survey. *J. Urban Econ.*, November 1989, *26*(3), pp. 361–85.

_____. On the Estimation of Localization Economies. *Econ. Letters*, 1989, *29*(3), pp. 275–77.

_____ and **McMillen, Daniel P.** Selectivity Bias in Urban Land Value Functions. *Land Econ.*, November 1989, *65*(4), pp. 341–51.

McDonald, Peter and Knodel, John. The Impact of Changes in Birth Spacing on Age at Last Birth: Response. *Demography*, August 1989, *26*(3), pp. 471–72.

McDonnell, Paul. Trade and Shipping Needs for

Island Economies. In *Couper, A. D., ed.,* 1989, pp. 153–59.

McDonough, Carol C. and Sihag, Balbir S. Shift-Share Analysis: The International Dimension. *Growth Change,* Summer 1989, *20*(3), pp. 80–88.

McDonough, Terrence and Drago, Robert. Crises of Capitalism and the First Crisis of Marxism: A Theoretical Note on the Bernstein–Kautsky Debate. *Rev. Radical Polit. Econ.,* Fall 1989, *21*(3), pp. 27–32.

McDorman, Ted L. Canadian Offshore Oil and Gas: Jurisdiction and Management Issues in the 1980s and Beyond. In *McRae, D. and Munro, G., eds.,* 1989, pp. 39–68.

McDougall, Gerald S. and Hersch, Philip L. Do People Put Their Money Where Their Votes Are? The Case of Lottery Tickets. *Southern Econ. J.,* July 1989, *56*(1), pp. 32–38.

McDowell, Howard; Kramer, Randall A. and Price, J. Michael. An Analysis of U.S. Farm Income Policies: Historical, Market-Determined, and Sector-Wide Stabilization. *Southern J. Agr. Econ.,* December 1989, *21*(2), pp. 1–11.

McDowell, John M. and Boyes, William J. The Selection of Public Utility Commissioners: A Reexamination of the Importance of Institutional Setting. *Public Choice,* April 1989, *61*(1), pp. 1–13.

McDowell, Linda. Women in Thatcher's Britain. In *Mohan, J., ed.,* 1989, pp. 172–86.

McDowell, Moore. Agency, Allocation and Distribution—Evidence on the Motivation of Central to Local Transfers. *Econ. Soc. Rev.,* April 1989, *20*(3), pp. 201–17.

McEwan, Kenneth A. and Howard, Wayne H. Human Resource Management: A Review with Applications to Agriculture. *Can. J. Agr. Econ.,* Part 1, December 1989, *37*(4), pp. 733–42.

McEwen, Ruth Ann. A Comparative Analysis of Error Metrics Applied to Analysts' Forecasts of Earnings. In *Schwartz, B. N., ed.,* 1989, pp. 113–26.

McEwin, R. Ian. No-Fault and Road Accidents: Some Australasian Evidence. *Int. Rev. Law Econ.,* June 1989, *9*(1), pp. 13–24.

McFadden, Daniel. A Method of Simulated Moments for Estimation of Discrete Response Models without Numerical Integration. *Econometrica,* September 1989, *57*(5), pp. 995–1026.

_____. Testing for Stochastic Dominance. In *[Hadar, J.],* 1989, pp. 113–34.

_____ and Feinstein, Jonathan S. The Dynamics of Housing Demand by the Elderly: Wealth, Cash Flow, and Demographic Effects. In *Wise, D. A., ed.,* 1989, pp. 55–86.

McFarland, Deborah A. and Mayo, John W. Regulation, Market Structure, and Hospital Costs. *Southern Econ. J.,* January 1989, *55*(3), pp. 559–69.

McGarity, Thomas O. and Shapiro, Sidney A. Reorienting OSHA: Regulatory Alternatives and Legislative Reform. *Yale J. Regul.,* Winter 1989, *6*(1), pp. 1–63.

McGartland, Albert M.; Oates, Wallace E. and Portney, Paul R. The *Net* Benefits of Incentive-Based Regulation: A Case Study of Environmental Standard Setting. *Amer. Econ. Rev.,* December 1989, *79*(5), pp. 1233–42.

McGee, John. Barriers to Growth: The Effects of Market Structure. In *Barber, J.; Metcalfe, J. S. and Porteous, M., eds.,* 1989, pp. 173–95.

McGee, L. Randolph and Hultman, Charles W. Factors Affecting the Foreign Banking Presence in the U.S. *J. Banking Finance,* July 1989, *13*(3), pp. 383–96.

McGee, M. Kevin. Alternative Transitions to a Consumption Tax. *Nat. Tax J.,* June 1989, *42*(2), pp. 155–66.

_____. The Lifetime Marginal Tax Rate. *Public Finance,* 1989, *44*(1), pp. 51–61.

McGee, Robert T. and Feige, Edgar L. Policy Illusion, Macroeconomic Instability, and the Unrecorded Economy. In *Feige, E. L., ed.,* 1989, pp. 81–109.

McGee, Terry G., et al. Industrial Development, Ethnic Cleavages, and Employment Patterns: Penang State, Malaysia. In *Portes, A.; Castells, M. and Benton, L. A., eds.,* 1989, pp. 265–78.

McGill, Ann L. and Anand, Punam. The Effect of Vivid Attributes on the Evaluation of Alternatives: The Role of Differential Attention and Cognitive Elaboration. *J. Cons. Res.,* September 1989, *16*(2), pp. 188–96.

McGillivray, Mark. The Allocation of Aid among Developing Countries: A Multi-donor Analysis Using a Per Capita Aid Index. *World Devel.,* April 1989, *17*(4), pp. 561–68.

McGivern, D. B.; Atkins, F. J. and Kerr, William A. A Note on Structural Change in Canadian Beef Demand. *Can. J. Agr. Econ.,* November 1989, *37*(3), pp. 513–24.

McGowan, Francis and Helm, Dieter. Electricity Supply in Europe: Lessons for the UK. In *Helm, D.; Kay, J. and Thompson, D., eds.,* 1989, pp. 237–60.

_____ and Seabright, Paul. Deregulating European Airlines. *Econ. Policy: A Europ. Forum,* October 1989, (9), pp. 283–344.

McGowan, Richard. Public Policy Measures and Cigarette Sales: An ARIMA Intervention Analysis. In *Post, J. E., ed.,* 1989, pp. 151–79.

McGrann, James M.; Karkosh, Kedrick and Osborne, Clark. Agricultural Financial Analysis Expert Systems: Software Description. *Can. J. Agr. Econ.,* Part 1, December 1989, *37*(4), pp. 695–708.

McGrath, John and Whiteside, Alan. Industry, Investment Incentives and the Foreign Exchange Crisis: Zambia—A Case Study. In *Whiteside, A. W., ed.,* 1989, pp. 167–83.

McGreevey, William Paul. The High Costs of Health Care in Brazil. In *WHO, Pan American Health Organization,* 1989, pp. 51–72.

McGregor, Patrick P. L. Demographic Pressure and the Irish Famine: Malthus after Mokyr. *Land Econ.,* August 1989, *65*(3), pp. 228–38.

McGregor, Peter G. and Ashcroft, Brian. The

Demand for Industrial Development Certificates and the Effect of Regional Policy. *Reg. Stud.*, August 1989, *23*(4), pp. 301–13.

_____ and Harrigan, Frank. Neoclassical and Keynesian Perspectives on the Regional Macro-economy: A Computable General Equilibrium Approach. *J. Reg. Sci.*, November 1989, *29*(4), pp. 555–73.

_____; McNicoll, Iain H. and Henderson, David. Measuring the Effects of Changing Structure on Employment Generation Potential. *Int. Reg. Sci. Rev.*, 1989, *12*(1), pp. 57–65.

McGuire, Alistair; Fenn, Paul and Mayhew, Ken. The Assessment: The Economics of Health Care. *Oxford Rev. Econ. Policy*, Spring 1989, *5*(1), pp. 1–20.

_____ and Gray, A. M. Factor Input in NHS Hospitals. *Appl. Econ.*, March 1989, *21*(3), pp. 397–411.

McGuire, Martin C. Factor Migration, Trade, and Welfare under Threat of Commercial Disruption. In *Fishelson, G., ed.*, 1989, pp. 141–60.

McGuire, Robert A. and Ohsfeldt, Robert L. Self-interest, Agency Theory, and Political Voting Behavior: The Ratification of the United States Constitution. *Amer. Econ. Rev.*, March 1989, *79*(1), pp. 219–34.

McGuire, Thomas G. Combining Demand- and Supply-Side Cost Sharing: The Case of Inpatient Mental Health Care. *Inquiry*, Summer 1989, *26*(2), pp. 292–303.

_____; Freiman, Marc P. and Ellis, Randall P. Provider Response to Medicare's PPS: Reductions in Length of Stay for Psychiatric Patients Treated in Scatter Beds. *Inquiry*, Summer 1989, *26*(2), pp. 192–201.

McHugh, Richard and Stevens, David W. Combined Training: Evidence of Economic Impact. *Econ. Educ. Rev.*, 1989, *8*(1), pp. 31–35.

McIlravey, G. P.; Joseph, A. E. and Smit, B. Consumer Preferences for Rural Residences: A Conjoint Analysis in Ontario, Canada. *Environ. Planning A*, January 1989, *21*(1), pp. 47–63.

McIlroy, Robert. Mission to Manage: The U.S. Forest Service as a "Japanese" Bureaucracy: Commentary. In *Hayashi, K., ed.*, 1989, pp. 226–30.

McInish, Thomas H.; Saniga, Erwin M. and Kolari, James. A Note on the Distribution Types of Financial Ratios in the Commercial Banking Industry. *J. Banking Finance*, July 1989, *13*(3), pp. 463–71.

McInnis, Marvin. The Size Structure of Farming, Canada West, 1861. In *Grantham, G. and Leonard, C. S., eds., Pt. B*, 1989, pp. 313–29.

McIntire, John; Udry, Chris and Binswanger, Hans P. Production Relations in Semi-arid African Agriculture. In *Bardhan, P., ed. (II)*, 1989, pp. 122–44.

McIntosh, Christopher S. and Shideed, Kamil H. The Effect of Government Programs on Acreage Response over Time: The Case of Corn Production in Iowa. *Western J. Agr. Econ.*, July 1989, *14*(1), pp. 38–44.

McIntosh, James; Schiantarelli, Fabio and Low, William. A Qualitative Response Analysis of UK Firms' Employment and Output Decisions. *J. Appl. Econometrics*, July–Sept. 1989, *4*(3), pp. 251–64.

McIntosh, Willard and Henderson, Glenn V., Jr. Efficiency of the Office Properties Market. *J. Real Estate Finance Econ.*, February 1989, *2*(1), pp. 61–70.

McIntyre, Richard. Economic Rhetoric and Industrial Decline. *J. Econ. Issues*, June 1989, *23*(2), pp. 483–91.

McIntyre, Robert J. Economic Change in Eastern Europe: Other Paths to Socialist Construction. *Sci. Society*, Spring 1989, *53*(1), pp. 5–28.

McIsaac, George S. and MacAvoy, Paul W. The Performance and Management of United States Federal Government Corporations. In *MacAvoy, P. W., et al.*, 1989, pp. 77–135.

McKay, Hugh. Introducing an Operations Management System. In *Matzer, J., Jr., ed.*, 1989, *1988*, pp. 115–20.

McKay, Lindsay. The Disregard of a Legal Entity for Tax Purposes: New Zealand. In *International Fiscal Association, ed. (II)*, 1989, pp. 407–14.

McKay, Niccie L. Quality Choice in Medicaid Markets: The Case of Nursing Homes. *Quart. Rev. Econ. Bus.*, Summer 1989, *29*(2), pp. 27–40.

McKean, John R.; Walsh, Richard G. and Johnson, Donn M. Issues in Nonmarket Valuation and Policy Application: A Retrospective Glance. *Western J. Agr. Econ.*, July 1989, *14*(1), pp. 178–88.

McKee, Arnold F. "Option for the Poor" as a Socio-economic Principle. *Int. J. Soc. Econ.*, 1989, *16*(5), pp. 46–55.

_____. What Is Just Profit? *Rev. Soc. Econ.*, Summer 1989, *47*(2), pp. 173–84.

McKee, David L. Hostile Takeovers: Issues in Public and Corporate Policy: Some Final Policy Reflections. In *McKee, D. L., ed.*, 1989, pp. 153–56.

_____. Schumpeter and the Political Economy of International Change. *Int. J. Soc. Econ.*, 1989, *16*(12), pp. 26–33.

_____ and Tisdell, Clem A. Urbanization and the Development Problem in Small Island Nations. *METU*, 1989, *16*(1–2), pp. 85–98.

McKee, Katharine. Microlevel Strategies for Supporting Livelihoods, Employment, and Income Generation of Poor Women in the Third World: The Challenge of Significance. *World Devel.*, July 1989, *17*(7), pp. 993–1006.

McKee, Michael. Intra-experimental Income Effects and Risk Aversion. *Econ. Letters*, August 1989, *30*(2), pp. 109–15.

McKelvey, R. D. Game Forms for Nash Implementation of General Social Choice Correspondences. *Soc. Choice Welfare*, April 1989, *6*(2), pp. 139–56.

McKenna, C. J. The Theory of Search in Labour Markets. In *Sapsford, D. and Tzannatos, Z., eds.*, 1989, pp. 33–62.

_____ and Jones, Stephen R. G. The Effect of

Outsiders on Union Contracts. *Europ. Econ. Rev.*, October 1989, *33*(8), pp. 1567–73.

_____ and **McNabb, Robert.** Male–Female Earnings: Further Evidence for Australia. *Appl. Econ.*, November 1989, *21*(11), pp. 1525–33.

McKenna, Jack F. Management Education in the United States. In *Byrt, W., ed.*, 1989, pp. 18–55.

McKenney, D. W.; van Vuuren, Willem and Fox, Glenn C. An Economic Comparison of Alternative Tree Improvement Strategies: A Simulation Approach. *Can. J. Agr. Econ.*, July 1989, *37*(2), pp. 211–32.

McKenzie, G. W.; Thomas, Stephen H. and Lloyd-Ellis, H. Using Country Balance Sheet Data to Predict Debt Rescheduling. *Econ. Letters*, December 1989, *31*(2), pp. 173–77.

McKenzie, Ken and Boadway, Robin W. The Treatment of Resource Industries in the 1987 Federal Tax Reform. In *Mintz, J. and Whalley, J., eds.*, 1989, pp. 286–325.

McKenzie, Richard B. Labor Policy in a Competitive World Economy. In *Libecap, G. D., ed.*, 1989, pp. 45–71.

_____ and **Lee, Dwight R.** The International Political Economy of Declining Tax Rates. *Nat. Tax J.*, March 1989, *42*(1), pp. 79–83.

McKeown, James; Mutchler, Jane and Hopwood, William. A Test of the Incremental Explanatory Power of Opinions Qualified for Consistency and Uncertainty. *Accounting Rev.*, January 1989, *64*(1), pp. 28–48.

McKibbin, Warwick J. Time-Consistent Policy: A Survey of the Issues. *Australian Econ. Pap.*, December 1989, *28*(53), pp. 167–80.

_____; **Roubini, Nouriel and Sachs, Jeffrey D.** Correcting Global Imbalances: A Simulation Approach. In *Stern, R. M., ed.*, 1989, pp. 379–424.

_____ and **Sachs, Jeffrey D.** Implications of Policy Rules for the World Economy. In *Bryant, R. C., et al., eds.*, 1989, pp. 151–94.

McKie, James W. U.S. Regulatory Policy. In *Button, K. and Swann, D., eds.*, 1989, pp. 27–48.

McKillop, D. G. The Return–Risk Structure of Lowland Agriculture in Northern Ireland. *Europ. Rev. Agr. Econ.*, 1989, *16*(2), pp. 217–28.

_____ and **Glass, J. C.** A Multi-product Multi-input Cost Function Analysis of Northern Ireland Agriculture, 1955–85. *J. Agr. Econ.*, January 1989, *40*(1), pp. 57–70.

McKinlay, Alan and Zeitlin, Jonathan. The Meanings of Managerial Prerogative: Industrial Relations and the Organisation of Work in British Engineering, 1880–1939. In *Harvey, C. and Turner, J., eds.*, 1989, pp. 32–47.

McKinney, Joseph and Rowley, Keith A. Voluntary Restraint Arrangements on Steel Imports: Policy Development and Sectoral Effects. *J. World Trade*, June 1989, *23*(3), pp. 69–81.

McKinney, Scott. Change in Metropolitan Area Residential Integration, 1970–80. *Population Res. Policy Rev.*, May 1989, *8*(2), pp. 143–64.

_____ and **Schnare, Ann B.** Trends in Residential Segregation by Race: 1960–1980. *J. Urban Econ.*, November 1989, *26*(3), pp. 269–80.

McKinnon, Ronald I. An International Gold Standard without Gold. In *Dorn, J. A. and Niskanen, W. A., eds.*, 1989, *1988*, pp. 147–69.

_____. The Fall of the Dollar and High U.S. Interest Rates: Two Interpretations. In *Kaushik, S. K., ed.*, 1989, pp. 95–112.

_____. Financial Liberalization and Economic Development: A Reassessment of Interest-Rate Policies in Asia and Latin America. *Oxford Rev. Econ. Policy*, Winter 1989, *5*(4), pp. 29–54.

_____. Financial Liberalization and Economic Development: A Reassessment of Interest-Rate Policies in Asia and Latin America. *Greek Econ. Rev.*, 1989, *11*(1), pp. 137–76.

_____. Macroeconomic Instability and Moral Hazard in Banking in a Liberalizing Economy. In *Brock, P. L.; Connolly, M. B. and González-Vega, C., eds.*, 1989, pp. 99–111.

_____. Some Comparative Macroeconomics of the United States, Japan, and Canada: Comment. In *Stern, R. M., ed.*, 1989, pp. 80–86.

_____ and **Ohno, Kenichi.** Purchasing Power Parity as a Monetary Standard. In *Hamouda, O. F.; Rowley, R. and Wolf, B. M., eds.*, 1989, pp. 42–64.

McLanahan, Sara and Bumpass, Larry. Unmarried Motherhood: Recent Trends, Composition, and Black–White Differences. *Demography*, May 1989, *26*(2), pp. 279–86.

McLaren, John and Horton, Susan. Supply Constraints in the Tanzanian Economy: Simulation Results from a Macroeconometric Model. *J. Policy Modeling*, Summer 1989, *11*(2), pp. 297–313.

McLaren, K. R. and UpCher, M. R. Specification, Identification and Estimation of a Continuous-Time Portfolio Model of Asset Demands. *J. Quant. Econ.*, July 1989, *5*(2), pp. 275–94.

McLauchlan, Gregory. World War, the Advent of Nuclear Weapons, and Global Expansion of the National Security State. In *Schaeffer, R. K., ed.*, 1989, pp. 83–97.

McLaughlin, Catherine G.; Zellers, Wendy K. and Brown, Lawrence D. Health Care Coalitions: Characteristics, Activities, and Prospects. *Inquiry*, Spring 1989, *26*(1), pp. 72–83.

McLaughlin, Frank and Jennings, Ken. Wage and Performance Discrimination: The Situation Facing Hispanics and Blacks in Major League Baseball. *J. Behav. Econ.*, Winter 1989, *18*(4), pp. 237–50.

McLaughlin, Mary M. and Wolfson, Martin H. Recent Developments in the Profitability and Lending Practices of Commercial Banks. *Fed. Res. Bull.*, July 1989, *75*(7), pp. 461–84.

McLaughlin, William J.; Harris, Charles C. and Driver, B. L. Improving the Contingent Valuation Method: A Psychological Perspective. *J. Environ. Econ. Manage.*, November 1989, *17*(3), pp. 213–29.

McLaurin, Ronald D. Supplier Restraints: The

European Exporters. In *Baek, K.-I.; McLaurin, R. D. and Moon, C., eds.,* 1989, pp. 113–35.

———. Technology Acquisition: A Case Study of the Supply Side. In *Baek, K.-I.; McLaurin, R. D. and Moon, C., eds.,* 1989, pp. 57–100.

——— **and Smaldone, Joseph P.** Supplier Controls in U.S. Arms Transfer Policy. In *Baek, K.-I.; McLaurin, R. D. and Moon, C., eds.,* 1989, pp. 101–12.

McLean, Ian. Growth in a Small Open Economy: An Historical View. In *[Gruen, F. H.],* 1989, pp. 7–33.

McLean-Meyinsse, Patricia E. and Okunade, Albert Ade. Factor Demands of Louisiana Rice Producers: An Econometric Investigation: Reply. *Southern J. Agr. Econ.,* December 1989, *21*(2), pp. 223–24.

McLean, Richard P. and Levy, Anat. Weighted Coalition Structure Values. *Games Econ. Behav.,* September 1989, *1*(3), pp. 234–49.

——— **and Postlewaite, Andrew.** Excess Functions and Nucleolus Allocations of Pure Exchange Economies. *Games Econ. Behav.,* June 1989, *1*(2), pp. 131–43.

——— **and Riordan, Michael H.** Industry Structure with Sequential Technology Choice. *J. Econ. Theory,* February 1989, *47*(1), pp. 1–21.

McLellan, James W. Hazardous Substances and the Right to Know in Canada. *Int. Lab. Rev.,* 1989, *128*(5), pp. 639–50.

McLennan, Andrew. Consistent Conditional Systems in Noncooperative Game Theory. *Int. J. Game Theory,* 1989, *18*(2), pp. 141–74.

———. Fixed Points of Contractible Valued Correspondences. *Int. J. Game Theory,* 1989, *18*(2), pp. 175–84.

———. The Space of Conditional Systems is a Ball. *Int. J. Game Theory,* 1989, *18*(2), pp. 125–39.

McLennan, Kenneth and Meyer, Jack A. Adopting Market Incentives in Public-Sector Policies. In *McLennan, K. and Meyer, J. A., eds.,* 1989, pp. 13–38.

——— **and Meyer, Jack A.** Containing Health Care Cost Escalation and Improving Access to Services: The Search for a Solution. In *McLennan, K. and Meyer, J. A., eds.,* 1989, pp. 1–11.

McLeod, Robert W.; Conrad, B. Lynne and Thistle, Paul D. Interest Rates and Bank Portfolio Adjustments. *J. Banking Finance,* March 1989, *13*(1), pp. 151–61.

McLeod, William and Canterbery, E. Ray. The Doctrine of Inherent Productivity: Keynes, Sraffa, and Kalecki. *J. Post Keynesian Econ.,* Summer 1989, *11*(4), pp. 630–40.

——— **and Canterbery, E. Ray.** The Doctrine of Inherent Productivity: Keynes, Sraffa, and Kalecki. *J. Post Keynesian Econ.,* Summer 1989, *11*(4), pp. 630–40.

McMahon, Gary. Computable General Equilibrium Modeling: A Survey with Reference to India. *Indian Econ. J.,* July–Sept. 1989, *37*(1), pp. 1–14.

———. The Income Distribution Effects of the Kenyan Coffee Marketing System. *J. Devel. Econ.,* October 1989, *31*(2), pp. 297–326.

McMichael, Susan Manges. Mahon Revisited: *Keystone Bituminous Coal Ass'n v. DeBenedictis,* 480 U.S. 470 (1987): Note. *Natural Res. J.,* Fall 1989, *29*(4), pp. 1057–77.

McMillan, Della and Gladwin, Christina H. Is a Turnaround in Africa Possible without Helping African Women to Farm? *Econ. Devel. Cult. Change,* January 1989, *37*(2), pp. 345–69.

McMillan, John. A Game-Theoretic View of International Trade Negotiations: Implications for the Developing Countries. In *Whalley, J., ed., Vol. 1,* 1989, pp. 26–44.

——— **and McAfee, R. Preston.** Government Procurement and International Trade. *J. Int. Econ.,* May 1989, *26*(3/4), pp. 291–308.

———; **Reny, Philip J. and McAfee, R. Preston.** Extracting the Surplus in the Common-Value Auction. *Econometrica,* November 1989, *57*(6), pp. 1451–59.

———; **Whalley, John and Zhu, Lijing.** The Impact of China's Economic Reforms on Agricultural Productivity Growth. *J. Polit. Econ.,* August 1989, *97*(4), pp. 781–807.

———; **Whinston, Michael D. and McAfee, R. Preston.** Multiproduct Monopoly, Commodity Bundling, and Correlation of Values. *Quart. J. Econ.,* May 1989, *104*(2), pp. 371–83.

McMillan, Melville L. On Measuring Congestion of Local Public Goods. *J. Urban Econ.,* September 1989, *26*(2), pp. 131–37.

McMillen, Daniel P. An Empirical Model of Urban Fringe Land Use. *Land Econ.,* May 1989, *65*(2), pp. 138–45.

——— **and McDonald, John F.** Selectivity Bias in Urban Land Value Functions. *Land Econ.,* November 1989, *65*(4), pp. 341–51.

McMillen, David B.; Kalton, Graham and Kasprzyk, Daniel. Nonsampling Errors in Panel Surveys. In *Kasprzyk, D., et al., eds.,* 1989, pp. 249–70.

McMillin, W. Douglas and Fackler, James S. Federal Debt and Macroeconomic Activity. *Southern Econ. J.,* April 1989, *55*(4), pp. 994–1003.

——— **and Koray, Faik.** An Empirical Analysis of the Macroeconomic Effects of Government Debt: Evidence from Canada. *Appl. Econ.,* January 1989, *21*(1), pp. 113–24.

McMullen, B. Starr; Martin, Michael V. and Cabeza, Felix. The Impacts of Transportation Deregulation on Wheat Shipments in the Pacific Northwest. *Western J. Agr. Econ.,* December 1989, *14*(2), pp. 253–60.

McNabb, Robert. Compensating Wage Differentials: Some Evidence for Britain. *Oxford Econ. Pap.,* April 1989, *41*(2), pp. 327–38.

——— **and McKenna, C. J.** Male–Female Earnings: Further Evidence for Australia. *Appl. Econ.,* November 1989, *21*(11), pp. 1525–33.

——— **and Richardson, Sue.** Earnings, Education and Experience: Is Australia Different?

Australian Econ. Pap., June 1989, *28*(52), pp. 57–75.

_____ and Ryan, Paul. Segmented Labour Markets. In *Sapsford, D. and Tzannatos, Z., eds.*, 1989, pp. 151–76.

McNamara, James Bray and Yang, Chin-Wei. Two Quadratic Programming Acquisition Models with Reciprocal Services. In *Gulledge, T. R., Jr. and Litteral, L. A., eds.*, 1989, pp. 338–49.

McNamara, Kevin T. and Gunter, Lewell F. Off-Farm Earnings: The Impact of Economic Structure. *Rev. Reg. Stud.*, Fall 1989, *19*(3), pp. 37–45.

McNamee, Alan H.; Plumlee, R. David and Chow, Chee W. Focusing Audit Aids for Enhanced Audit Efficiency and Effectiveness. In *Gangolly, J., ed.*, 1989, pp. 195–204.

McNaugher, Thomas L. and Flamm, Kenneth. Rationalizing Technology Investments. In *Steinbruner, J. D., ed.*, 1989, pp. 119–57.

McNaughton, Rod B. and Green, Milford B. Interurban Variation in Venture Capital Investment Characteristics. *Urban Stud.*, April 1989, *26*(2), pp. 199–213.

_____ and Green, Milford B. Spatial Patterns of Canadian Venture Capital Investment. *Reg. Stud.*, February 1989, *23*(1), pp. 9–18.

McNees, Stephen K. Forecasts and Actuals: The Trade-Off between Timeliness and Accuracy. *Int. J. Forecasting*, 1989, *5*(3), pp. 409–16.

_____. How Well Do Financial Markets Predict the Inflation Rate? *New Eng. Econ. Rev.*, Sept.–Oct. 1989, pp. 31–46.

_____. Why Do Forecasts Differ? *New Eng. Econ. Rev.*, Jan.–Feb. 1989, pp. 42–54.

McNeil, John M. and Lamas, Enrique J. Year-Apart Estimates of Household Net Worth from the Survey of Income and Program Participation. In *Lipsey, R. E. and Tice, H. S., eds.*, 1989, pp. 431–62.

McNeill, Thomas J. and Tronstad, Russell. Asymmetric Price Risk: An Econometric Analysis of Aggregate Sow Farrowings, 1973–86. *Amer. J. Agr. Econ.*, August 1989, *71*(3), pp. 630–37.

McNelis, Paul D. and Barbosa, Fernando de Holanda. Indexation and Inflationary Inertia: Brazil 1964–1985. *World Bank Econ. Rev.*, September 1989, *3*(3), pp. 339–57.

_____ and Corbo, Vittorio. The Pricing of Manufactured Goods during Trade Liberalization: Evidence from Chile, Israel, and Korea. *Rev. Econ. Statist.*, August 1989, *71*(3), pp. 491–99.

_____ and Honohan, Patrick. Is the EMS a DM Zone?—Evidence from the Realignments. *Econ. Soc. Rev.*, January 1989, *20*(2), pp. 97–110.

McNertney, Edward M. and Butler, Michael R. The Allocation of Death in the Vietnam War: Comment. *Southern Econ. J.*, April 1989, *55*(4), pp. 1029–33.

McNichols, Maureen. Evidence of Informational Asymmetries from Management Earnings Forecasts and Stock Returns. *Accounting Rev.*, January 1989, *64*(1), pp. 1–27.

McNicoll, Iain H.; Henderson, David and McGregor, Peter G. Measuring the Effects of Changing Structure on Employment Generation Potential. *Int. Reg. Sci. Rev.*, 1989, *12*(1), pp. 57–65.

McNiel, Douglas W. and Yu, Shirley S. Blue Laws: Impact on Regional Retail Activity. *Population Res. Policy Rev.*, September 1989, *8*(3), pp. 267–78.

McNiven, Malcolm A. Advertising Experiments at the Campbell Soup Company: Commentary. *Marketing Sci.*, Winter 1989, *8*(1), pp. 74–75.

McNown, Robert F. and Bohara, Alok K. Monetary and Inflationary Linkages between India and Nepal: A Vector Autoregression Analysis. *Indian Econ. J.*, July–Sept. 1989, *37*(1), pp. 40–55.

_____ and Rogers, Andrei. Forecasting Mortality: A Parameterized Time Series Approach. *Demography*, November 1989, *26*(4), pp. 645–60.

_____ and Wallace, Myles S. Co-integration Tests for Long Run Equilibrium in the Monetary Exchange Rate Model. *Econ. Letters*, December 1989, *31*(3), pp. 263–67.

_____ and Wallace, Myles S. National Price Levels, Purchasing Power Parity, and Cointegration: A Test of Four High Inflation Economies. *J. Int. Money Finance*, December 1989, *8*(4), pp. 533–45.

McNulty, Mark S. and Huffman, Wallace E. The Sample Spectrum of Time Series with Trading Day Variation. *Econ. Letters*, December 1989, *31*(4), pp. 367–70.

McPhee, Peter. The French Revolution, Peasants, and Capitalism. *Amer. Historical Rev.*, December 1989, *94*(5), pp. 1265–80.

McPherson, Glen. The Scientists' View of Statistics—A Neglected Area. *J. Roy. Statist. Society*, 1989, *152*(2), pp. 221–40.

McPherson, M. Peter. The Case for Economic Policy Reform in Developing Countries. In *Helmuth, J. W. and Johnson, S. R., eds., Vol. 1*, 1989, pp. 45–55.

McPherson, Michael S.; Schapiro, Morton Owen and Winston, Gordon C. Recent Trends in U.S. Higher Education Costs and Prices: The Role of Government Funding. *Amer. Econ. Rev.*, May 1989, *79*(2), pp. 253–57.

McQuade, Lawrence C. The Challenge to Business Leadership. In *Cerami, C. A., ed.*, 1989, pp. 183–93.

McQueen, Josh; Deighton, John and Romer, Daniel. Using Drama to Persuade. *J. Cons. Res.*, December 1989, *16*(3), pp. 335–43.

McQuillan, Peter. Comment: Tax Reform—Some Unfinished Business with Respect to the Cost of Capital and Return on Investment. In *Mintz, J. and Whalley, J., eds.*, 1989, pp. 185–92.

McRae, Donald M. Canada and the Delimitation of Maritime Boundaries. In *McRae, D. and Munro, G., eds.*, 1989, pp. 145–64.

McRoberts, Kenneth; Blais, André and Cousineau, Jean-Michel. The Determinants of Minimum Wage Rates. *Public Choice*, July 1989, 62(1), pp. 15–24.

McShan, Scott and Windle, Robert. The Implications of Hub-and-Spoke Routing for Airline Costs and Competitiveness. *Logist. Transp. Rev.*, September 1989, 25(3), pp. 209–30.

McSweeney, Brendan. The Roles of Accounting in Organizational Maintenance and Change: Insights from a Case-Study. In *Mansfield, R., ed.*, 1989, pp. 233–46.

McSweeny, William T. and Shortle, James S. Stochastic Technology and Prices: Comment. *Amer. J. Agr. Econ.*, August 1989, 71(3), pp. 813–16.

McTaggart, Douglas and Salant, David. Time Consistency and Subgame Perfect Equilibria in a Monetary Policy Game. *J. Macroecon.*, Fall 1989, 11(4), pp. 575–88.

McWhinney, Will. Meta-Praxis: A Framework for Making Complex Changes. In *Mohrman, A. M., Jr., et al.*, 1989, pp. 154–99.

Meacci, Ferdinando. Different Divisions of Capital in Smith, Ricardo, and Marx. *Atlantic Econ. J.*, December 1989, 17(4), pp. 13–21.

————. Irving Fisher and the Classics on the Notion of Capital: Upheaval and Continuity in Economic Thought. *Hist. Polit. Econ.*, Fall 1989, 21(3), pp. 409–24.

————. The Principle of Increasing Risk versus the Marginal Efficiency of Capital. In *Sebastiani, M., ed.*, 1989, pp. 231–45.

Meade, Ellen E. and Hooper, Peter. U.S. International Transactions in 1988. *Fed. Res. Bull.*, May 1989, 75(5), pp. 321–32.

Meador, Mark; Walters, Stephen J. K. and Jordan, John M. Academic Research Productivity, Department Size and Organization: Further Results. *Econ. Educ. Rev.*, 1989, 8(4), pp. 345–52.

Meagher, G. A. and Parmenter, B. R. Forecasting the Demand for Engineers in Australia, 1986–87 to 1991–92. *Australian Bull. Lab.*, June 1989, 15(3), pp. 185–99.

Means, Gardiner C. The Problems and Prospects of Collective Capitalism. In *Tool, M. R. and Samuels, W. J., eds. (I)*, 1989, 1969, pp. 157–70.

Mechanic, David. Assumptions in Economic Modeling of the Mental Health Services System. *Inquiry*, Summer 1989, 26(2), pp. 304–06.

Medema, Steven G. Discourse and the Institutional Approach to Law and Economics: Factors that Separate the Institutional Approach to Law and Economics from Alternative Approaches. *J. Econ. Issues*, June 1989, 23(2), pp. 417–25.

Médici, André Cézar. The Financing of Health Policies in Brazil. In *WHO, Pan American Health Organization*, 1989, pp. 26–50.

Medley, Joseph E. Imperialism and Uneven Development: U.S. Policy in Taiwan and Nicaragua. *Rev. Radical Polit. Econ.*, Fall 1989, 21(3), pp. 112–17.

Medoff, James and Brown, Charles C. The Em-

ployer Size–Wage Effect. *J. Polit. Econ.*, October 1989, 97(5), pp. 1027–59.

Medoff, Marshall H. Constituencies, Ideology, and the Demand for Abortion Legislation. *Public Choice*, February 1989, 60(2), pp. 185–91.

————. The Rankings of Economists. *J. Econ. Educ.*, Fall 1989, 20(4), pp. 405–15.

————. The Relative Quality of Black Economists. *Rev. Black Polit. Econ.*, Fall 1989, 18(2), pp. 81–86.

Meehan, James W., Jr. and Larner, Robert J. Economics and Antitrust Policy: Introduction. In *Larner, R. J. and Meehan, J. W., Jr., eds.*, 1989, pp. 1–9.

———— **and Larner, Robert J.** Postscript: In Memory of H. Michael Mann. In *Larner, R. J. and Meehan, J. W., Jr., eds.*, 1989, pp. 209–14.

———— **and Larner, Robert J.** The Structural School, Its Critics, and Its Progeny: An Assessment. In *Larner, R. J. and Meehan, J. W., Jr., eds.*, 1989, pp. 179–208.

————; **Snyder, Edward A. and Masten, Scott E.** Vertical Integration in the U.S. Auto Industry: A Note on the Influence of Transaction Specific Assets. *J. Econ. Behav. Organ.*, October 1989, 12(2), pp. 265–73.

Meen, Geoffrey P. The Ending of Mortgage Rationing and Its Effects on the Housing Market: A Simulation Study. *Urban Stud.*, April 1989, 26(2), pp. 240–52.

van der Meer, Kees. A Comparison of Factors Influencing Economic Development in Thailand and Indonesia, 1820–1940. In *Maddison, A. and Prince, G., eds.*, 1989, pp. 259–93.

van der Meer, Tjemme and Merkies, Arnold H. Q. M. Scope of the Three-Component Model. *Reg. Sci. Urban Econ.*, December 1989, 19(4), pp. 601–14.

van Meerhaeghe, Marcel. Taxation and the European Community. *Econ. Scelte Pubbliche/J. Public Finance Public Choice*, Jan.–Aug. 1989, 7(1–2), pp. 17–28.

Meerschwam, David M. International Capital Imbalances: The Demise of Local Financial Boundaries. In *[Marjolin, R.]*, 1989, pp. 289–307.

Meese, Richard. Empirical Assessment of Foreign Currency Risk Premiums. In *Stone, C. C., ed.*, 1989, pp. 157–80.

Megbolugbe, Isaac F. A Hedonic Index Model: The Housing Market of Jos, Nigeria. *Urban Stud.*, October 1989, 26(5), pp. 486–94.

Megdal, Sharon B. On Regulation, Deregulation, and Economics. *Energy J.*, July 1989, 10(3), pp. 181–95.

Megginson, William L. and Ang, James S. Restricted Voting Shares, Ownership Structure, and the Market Value of Dual-Class Firms. *J. Finan. Res.*, Winter 1989, 12(4), pp. 301–18.

Meghir, Costas; Ioannides, Yannis M. and Pissarides, Christopher A. Female Participation and Male Unemployment Duration in Greece: Evidence from the Labour Force Survey. *Europ. Econ. Rev.*, March 1989, 33(2/3), pp. 395–406.

Megiddo, Nimrod. On Computable Beliefs of Rational Machines. *Games Econ. Behav.*, June 1989, *1*(2), pp. 144–69.

Mehay, Stephen L.; Gonzalez, Rodolfo A. and Folsom, Roger Nils. Bureaucracy, Publicness and Local Government Expenditures Revisited: Comment. *Public Choice*, July 1989, *62*(1), pp. 71–77.

Mehlmann, Alexander; Dockner, Engelbert J. and Feichtinger, Gustav. Noncooperative Solutions for a Differential Game Model of Fishery. *J. Econ. Dynam. Control*, January 1989, *13*(1), pp. 1–20.

Mehmet, Ozay. Islamic Economic Co-operation: Preface. In *Choudhury, M. A.*, 1989, pp. xxiii–xxv.

Mehra, Rajnish; Danthine, Jean-Pierre and Donaldson, John B. On Some Computational Aspects of Equilibrium Business Cycle Theory. *J. Econ. Dynam. Control*, July 1989, *13*(3), pp. 449–70.

Mehra, Rekha. Farm Workers, Agriculture, and the Politics of Immigration Reform: The Immigration Reform and Control Act of 1986. In *Krämer, C. S., ed.*, 1989, pp. 239–57.

Mehra, Yash P. Some Further Results on the Source of Shift in M1 Demand in the 1980s. *Fed. Res. Bank Richmond Econ. Rev.*, Sept.–Oct. 1989, *75*(5), pp. 3–13.

_____. Velocity and the Variability of Money Growth: Evidence from Granger-Causality Tests: Comment. *J. Money, Credit, Banking*, May 1989, *21*(2), pp. 262–66.

_____ **and Hetzel, Robert L.** The Behavior of Money Demand in the 1980s. *J. Money, Credit, Banking*, November 1989, *21*(4), pp. 455–63.

Mehran, Farhad. Longitudinal Analysis of Employment and Unemployment Based on Matched Rotation Samples. *Labour*, Spring 1989, *3*(1), pp. 3–20.

Mehta, Ghanshyam and Littleboy, Bruce. Patinkin on Keynes's Theory of Effective Demand: A Rejoinder. *Hist. Polit. Econ.*, Winter 1989, *21*(4), pp. 711–21.

Mehta, Rajesh; Panchamukhi, Vadiraj R. and Nambiar, R. G. Structural Change and Economic Growth in Developing Countries. In *Williamson, J. G. and Panchamukhi, V. R., eds.*, 1989, pp. 54–84.

Meier, Alfred and Haury, Susanne. Kollektive Bewältigung von Unsicherheit nach dem Börsencrash vom 19. Oktober 1987. (Collective Measures of Uncertainty Management after the Stock Market Crash of 1987. With English summary.) *Aussenwirtschaft*, June 1989, *44*(2), pp. 253–72.

Meier, Gerald M. Misconceptions about External Debt. In *Singer, H. W. and Sharma, S., eds. (I)*, 1989, pp. 27–32.

_____. The Old and New Export Pessimism: A Critical Survey. In *Islam, N., ed.*, 1989, pp. 197–217.

_____. Theoretical Issues Concerning the History of International Trade and Economic Development. In *[Fischer, W.]*, 1989, pp. 33–58.

Meigs, A. James. Dollars and Deficits: Substitut-

ing False for Real Problems. In *Dorn, J. A. and Niskanen, W. A., eds.*, 1989, *1988*, pp. 329–49.

Meilke, Karl D.; Braga, Francesco S. and Martin, Larry J. Cross Hedging the Italian Lira/ U.S. Dollar Exchange Rate with Deutsch Mark Futures. *J. Futures Markets*, April 1989, *9*(2), pp. 87–99.

_____ **and de Gorter, Harry.** Efficiency of Alternative Policies for the EC's Common Agricultural Policy. *Amer. J. Agr. Econ.*, August 1989, *71*(3), pp. 592–603.

_____ **and Moschini, Giancarlo.** Modeling the Pattern of Structural Change in U.S. Meat Demand. *Amer. J. Agr. Econ.*, May 1989, *71*(2), pp. 253–61.

_____ **and Warley, T. K.** Agriculture in the Uruguay Round: A Canadian Perspective. *Can. J. Agr. Econ.*, Part 2, December 1989, *37*(4), pp. 825–52.

Meindl, James R.; Hunt, Raymond G. and Lee, Wonsick. Individualism–Collectivism and Work Values: Data from the United States, China, Taiwan, Korea, and Hong Kong. In *Nedd, A., ed.*, 1989, pp. 59–77.

Meiners, Mark R. and Greenberg, Jay N. Improving the Role of Private Markets in Financing Long-Term Care Services. In *McLennan, K. and Meyer, J. A., eds.*, 1989, pp. 87–115.

Meiners, Roger E. and Yandle, Bruce. Regulatory Lessons from the Reagan Era: Introduction. In *Meiners, R. E. and Yandle, B., eds.*, 1989, pp. 3–15.

Meinhold, Richard J. and Singpurwalla, Nozer D. Robustification of Kalman Filter Models. *J. Amer. Statist. Assoc.*, June 1989, *84*(406), pp. 479–86.

Meisenheimer, Joseph R., II. Employer Provisions for Parental Leave. *Mon. Lab. Rev.*, October 1989, *112*(10), pp. 20–24.

_____ **and Wiatrowski, William J.** Flexible Benefits Plans: Employees Who Have a Choice. *Mon. Lab. Rev.*, December 1989, *112*(12), pp. 17–23.

Meisner, Maurice. The Deradicalization of Chinese Socialism. In *Dirlik, A. and Meisner, M., eds.*, 1989, pp. 341–61.

_____. Marx, Mao, and Deng on the Division of Labor in History. In *Dirlik, A. and Meisner, M., eds.*, 1989, pp. 79–116.

_____ **and Dirlik, Arif.** Politics, Scholarship, and Chinese Socialism. In *Dirlik, A. and Meisner, M., eds.*, 1989, pp. 3–26.

Meital, Yoram. The Economic Relations between Israel and Egypt: Tourism, 1979–1984. In *Fishelson, G., ed.*, 1989, pp. 283–301.

Meitzen, Mark E. and Brannman, Lance E. Differential Compensation and Worker Turnover. In *Missouri Valley Economic Association*, 1989, pp. 156–61.

Meixide, Alberto; Toharia, Luis and Fina, Lluis. Reregulating the Labor Market amid an Economic and Political Crisis: Spain, 1975–1986. In *Rosenberg, S., ed.*, 1989, pp. 107–25.

Mejcher, Helmut. Banking and the German Oil

Industry, 1890–1939. **In** *Ferrier, R. W. and Fursenko, A., eds.,* 1989, pp. 94–106.

Melby, Russell. Break-Out Session I—Issues for Hunger, Malnutrition, Agriculture, and Food Policy: Recommendations: Government and Private Development Assistance Organizations. **In** *Helmuth, J. W. and Johnson, S. R., eds., Vol. 1,* 1989, pp. 130–31.

————. Break-Out Session II—Conference Consensus: Recommendations: Improving Food Distribution Systems, Dietary Status, and Relieving Hunger Problems. **In** *Helmuth, J. W. and Johnson, S. R., eds., Vol. 1,* 1989, pp. 201–03.

Melekhin, V. N. and Melekhina, K. V. On the Instability of Difference Equations Solutions in Production Capacity Planning. *Matekon,* Winter 1989–90, *26*(2), pp. 3–16.

Melekhina, K. V. and Melekhin, V. N. On the Instability of Difference Equations Solutions in Production Capacity Planning. *Matekon,* Winter 1989–90, *26*(2), pp. 3–16.

Melenberg, Bertrand; Alessie, Rob and Kapteyn, Arie. The Effects of Liquidity Constraints on Consumption: Estimation from Household Panel Data. *Europ. Econ. Rev.,* March 1989, *33*(2/3), pp. 547–55.

Meléndez, Dennis and Brock, Philip L. Exchange Controls and the Breakdown of Central American Trade in the 1980s. **In** *Brock, P. L.; Connolly, M. B. and González-Vega, C., eds.,* 1989, pp. 171–86.

Melese, François; Im, Bae-Geun and Kaserman, David L. Endogenous Regulation and the Firm's Regulatory Expenditures. *Appl. Econ.,* March 1989, *21*(3), pp. 375–85.

Melfi, C. A. and Bethel, T. A. A Probit Model of NLRB Bargaining Order Cases in the Appellate Courts. *J. Lab. Res.,* Summer 1989, *10*(3), pp. 255–70.

Melin, Leif. The Field-of-Force Metaphor. **In** *Hallén, L. and Johanson, J., eds.,* 1989, pp. 161–79.

Melis Maynar, Francisco. Sobre la hipótesis de componentes y la extracción de la señal de coyuntura sin previa desestacionalización. (With English summary.) *Revista Española Econ.,* 1989, *6*(1–2), pp. 131–63.

———— **and Martínez López, Antonio.** La demanda y la oferta de estadísticas coyunturales. (With English summary.) *Revista Española Econ.,* 1989, *6*(1–2), pp. 7–57.

Meller, Patricio. Criticisms and Suggestions on the Cross-conditionality of the IMF and the World Bank. *CEPAL Rev.,* April 1989, (37), pp. 65–78.

————. Latin American Debt: Progress, Prospects, and Policy: Comment. **In** *Edwards, S. and Larrain, F., eds.,* 1989, pp. 65–67.

———— **and Cabezas, Mabel.** Estimación de las elasticidades ingreso y precio de las importaciones chilenas 1974–1987. (Income and Price Elasticities of Chilean Imports 1974–1987. With English summary.) *Colección Estud. CIEPLAN,* June 1989, (26), pp. 127–70.

Mellor, C. J. and Chard, J. S. Intellectual Prop-

erty Rights and Parallel Imports. *World Econ.,* March 1989, *12*(1), pp. 69–83.

Mellor, John W. Alleviating Hunger while Building Markets. **In** *Swegle, W. E. and Ligon, P. C., eds.,* 1989, pp. 51–56.

————. Rural Employment Linkages through Agricultural Growth: Concepts, Issues, and Questions. **In** *Williamson, J. G. and Panchamukhi, V. R., eds.,* 1989, pp. 305–19.

————. World Food Situation in Historical Perspective. **In** *Horwich, G. and Lynch, G. J., eds.,* 1989, pp. 50–64.

Melman, Seymour. The Impact of Economics on Technology. **In** *Tool, M. R. and Samuels, W. J., eds. (I),* 1989, *1975,* pp. 49–62.

————. Some Avoided Topics in Economics. *J. Econ. Issues,* June 1989, *23*(2), pp. 563–68.

Melnik, Arie and Livnat, Joshua. Interim Audit Scope, Client Size and Client Familiarity: An Empirical Analysis. *Managerial Dec. Econ.,* March 1989, *10*(1), pp. 69–75.

Melnyk, Andrew. On Ideas and Interests. **In** *Gamble, A., et al.,* 1989, pp. 123–30.

de Melo, Jaime and Bark, Taeho. Efficiency and Export Earnings Implications of Two-Tier Quota Allocation Rules. *Int. Econ. J.,* Autumn 1989, *3*(3), pp. 31–42.

———— **and Corbo, Vittorio.** External Shocks and Policy Reforms in the Southern Cone: A Reassessment. **In** *[Díaz-Alejandro, C.],* 1989, pp. 235–58.

———— **and Robinson, Sherman.** Product Differentiation and the Treatment of Foreign Trade in Computable General Equilibrium Models of Small Economies. *J. Int. Econ.,* August 1989, *27*(1–2), pp. 47–67.

————; **Stanton, Julie and Tarr, David.** Revenue-Raising Taxes: General Equilibrium Evaluation of Alternative Taxation in U.S. Petroleum Industries. *J. Policy Modeling,* Fall 1989, *11*(3), pp. 425–49.

Melody, William H. Efficiency and Social Policy in Telecommunication: Lessons from the U.S. Experience. *J. Econ. Issues,* September 1989, *23*(3), pp. 657–88.

————. The Information Society: Implications for Economic Institutions and Market Theory. **In** *Tool, M. R. and Samuels, W. J., eds. (III),* 1989, *1985,* pp. 477–93.

————. The Marginal Utility of Marginal Analysis in Public Policy Formation. **In** *Tool, M. R. and Samuels, W. J., eds. (II),* 1989, *1974,* pp. 375–88.

———— **and Cave, Martin.** Models of Broadcast Regulation: The UK and North American Experience. **In** *Veljanovski, C., ed. (I),* 1989, pp. 224–43.

Melolidakis, C. On Stochastic Games with Lack of Information on One Side. *Int. J. Game Theory,* 1989, *18*(1), pp. 1–29.

Meltz, Noah M. Industrial Relations: Balancing Efficiency and Equity. **In** *Barbash, J. and Barbash, K., eds.,* 1989, pp. 109–13.

————. Interstate vs. Interprovincial Differences in Union Density. *Ind. Relat.,* Spring 1989, *28*(2), pp. 142–58.

Meltzer, Allan H. Capital Flight and Reflight. In *Dornbusch, R.; Makin, J. H. and Zlowe, D., eds.,* 1989, pp. 71–73.

_____. Efficiency and Stability in World Finance. *Bank Japan Monet. Econ. Stud.,* August 1989, 7(2), pp. 1–14.

_____. Eliminating Monetary Disturbances. *Cato J.,* Fall 1989, 9(2), pp. 423–28.

_____. On Monetary Stability and Monetary Reform. In *Dorn, J. A. and Niskanen, W. A., eds.,* 1989, pp. 63–85.

_____. Some Lessons of Monetary Management. *Kredit Kapital,* 1989, 22(1), pp. 43–65.

_____. Tobin on Macroeconomic Policy: A Review Essay. *J. Monet. Econ.,* January 1989, 23(1), pp. 159–73.

_____. Variability of Prices, Output and Money under Fixed and Fluctuating Exchange Rates: An Empirical Study of Monetary Regimes in Japan and the United States. In *Brunner, K. and Meltzer, A. H.,* 1989, *1986,* pp. 339–78.

_____ **and Brunner, Karl.** An Aggregative Theory for a Closed Economy. In *Brunner, K. and Meltzer, A. H.,* 1989, *1976,* pp. 159–92.

_____ **and Brunner, Karl.** A Credit Market Theory of the Money Supply and an Explanation of Two Puzzles in U.S. Monetary Policy. In *Brunner, K. and Meltzer, A. H.,* 1989, *1966,* pp. 97–120.

_____ **and Brunner, Karl.** The Federal Reserves Attachment to the Free Reserve Concept. In *Brunner, K. and Meltzer, A. H.,* 1989, pp. 21–96.

_____ **and Brunner, Karl.** Liquidity Traps for Money, Bank Credit, and Interest Rates. In *Brunner, K. and Meltzer, A. H.,* 1989, *1968,* pp. 121–58.

_____ **and Brunner, Karl.** Monetary Economics: Introduction. In *Brunner, K. and Meltzer, A. H.,* 1989, pp. 1–19.

_____ **and Brunner, Karl.** Mr Hicks and the 'Monetarists.' In *Wood, J. C. and Woods, R. N., eds., Vol. 2,* 1989, *1973,* pp. 232–48.

_____ **and Brunner, Karl.** The Uses of Money: Money in the Theory of an Exchange Economy. In *Brunner, K. and Meltzer, A. H.,* 1989, *1971,* pp. 230–58.

_____; **Brunner, Karl and Cukierman, Alex.** Money and Economic Activity, Inventories and Business Cycles. In *Brunner, K. and Meltzer, A. H.,* 1989, *1983,* pp. 193–229.

_____ **and Cukierman, Alex.** A Political Theory of Government Debt and Deficits in a Neo-Ricardian Framework. *Amer. Econ. Rev.,* September 1989, 79(4), pp. 713–32.

_____ **and Robinson, Saranna.** Stability under the Gold Standard in Practice. In *[Schwartz, A. J.],* 1989, pp. 163–95.

Melumad, Nahum D. and Mookherjee, Dilip. Delegation as Commitment: The Case of Income Tax Audits. *Rand J. Econ.,* Summer 1989, 20(2), pp. 139–63.

_____ **and Reichelstein, Stefan.** Value of Communication in Agencies. *J. Econ. Theory,* April 1989, 47(2), pp. 334–68.

Melvin, James R. Trade in Producer Services: A Heckscher–Ohlin Approach. *J. Polit. Econ.,* October 1989, 97(5), pp. 1180–96.

Melvin, Michael and de la Parra, Gonzalo Afcha. Dollar Currency in Latin America: A Bolivian Application. *Econ. Letters,* December 1989, 31(4), pp. 393–97.

_____; **Schlagenhauf, Don and Talu, Ayhan.** The U.S. Budget Deficit and the Foreign Exchange Value of the Dollar. *Rev. Econ. Statist.,* August 1989, 71(3), pp. 500–505.

_____ **and Zhou, Su.** Do Centrally Planned Exchange Rates Behave Differently from Capitalist Rates? *J. Compar. Econ.,* June 1989, 13(2), pp. 325–34.

Mena Keymer, Hugo. Consideraciones generales en torno a la medición del crecimiento económico en las cuentas nacionales de Chile. (With English summary.) *Cuadernos Econ.,* December 1989, 26(79), pp. 385–415.

Menard, Claude. Les organisations en économie de marché. (With English summary.) *Revue Écon. Politique,* Nov.–Dec. 1989, 99(6), pp. 771–96.

_____ **and De Villé, Philippe.** An Insolent Founding Father. *Europ. Econ. Rev.,* March 1989, 33(2/3), pp. 494–502.

Menard, Russell R. and Carr, Lois Green. Land, Labor, and Economies of Scale in Early Maryland: Some Limits to Growth in the Chesapeake System of Husbandry. *J. Econ. Hist.,* June 1989, 49(2), pp. 407–18.

Menasco, Michael B. and Curry, David J. Utility and Choice: An Empirical Study of Wife/Husband Decision Making. *J. Cons. Res.,* June 1989, 16(1), pp. 87–97.

Menchik, Paul L.; Irvine, F. Owen and Jianakoplos, Nancy Ammon. Using Panel Data to Assess the Bias in Cross-Sectional Inferences of Life-Cycle Changes in the Level and Composition of Household Wealth. In *Lipsey, R. E. and Tice, H. S., eds.,* 1989, pp. 553–640.

Mendell, Marguerite. Market Reforms and Market Failures: Karl Polanyi and the Paradox of Convergence. *J. Econ. Issues,* June 1989, 23(2), pp. 473–81.

Mendelsohn, Robert and Peterson, George. Welfare Measurement with Expenditure-Constrained Demand Models. *Rev. Econ. Statist.,* February 1989, 71(1), pp. 164–67.

_____ **and Swierzbinski, Joseph E.** Exploration and Exhaustible Resources: The Microfoundations of Aggregate Models. *Int. Econ. Rev.,* February 1989, 30(1), pp. 175–86.

_____ **and Swierzbinski, Joseph E.** Information and Exhaustible Resources: A Bayesian Analysis. *J. Environ. Econ. Manage.,* May 1989, 16(3), pp. 193–208.

Mendelson, Haim and Amihud, Yakov. The Effects of Beta, Bid–Ask Spread, Residual Risk, and Size on Stock Returns. *J. Finance,* June 1989, 44(2), pp. 479–86.

_____ **and Amihud, Yakov.** Inventory Behaviour and Market Power: An Empirical Investigation. *Int. J. Ind. Organ.,* June 1989, 7(2), pp. 269–80.

Mendes, A. J. Marques and Thirlwall, A. P. The

Balance of Payments Constraint and Growth in Portugal: 1951–1984. In *Yannopoulos, G. N., ed.*, 1989, pp. 21–39.

Méndez, José A. and Berg, Gerald C. The Effects of Steel Import Restraints on U.S. Steel-Consuming Industries. *J. World Trade*, August 1989, *23*(4), pp. 35–44.

_____ **and Rousslang, Donald J.** Does the Central American Common Market Benefit Its Members? *Econ. Inquiry*, July 1989, *27*(3), pp. 473–87.

_____ **and Rousslang, Donald J.** Liberalizing U.S. Trade with the Eastern Bloc: What Are the Consequences? *J. Compar. Econ.*, December 1989, *13*(4), pp. 491–507.

Mendilow, Jonathan. Party Financing in Israel: Experience and Experimentation, 1968–85. In *Alexander, H. E., ed.*, 1989, pp. 124–52.

de Mendonça, Rosane S. Pinto and de Barros, Ricardo Paes. Família e distribuição de renda: O impacto da participação das esposas no mercado de trabalho. (With English summary.) *Pesquisa Planejamento Econ.*, December 1989, *19*(3), pp. 483–504.

Meng, Ronald. Collective Bargaining, Firm Size and Pensions in Canada. *Econ. Letters*, November 1989, *31*(1), pp. 99–103.

_____. Compensating Differences in the Canadian Labour Market. *Can. J. Econ.*, May 1989, *22*(2), pp. 413–24.

Mengle, David L. Banking under Changing Rules: The Fifth District since 1970. *Fed. Res. Bank Richmond Econ. Rev.*, March–April 1989, *75*(2), pp. 3–7.

_____ **and Kuprianov, Anatoli.** The Future of Deposit Insurance: An Analysis of the Alternatives. *Fed. Res. Bank Richmond Econ. Rev.*, May–June 1989, *75*(3), pp. 3–15.

Menken, Jane and Larsen, Ulla. Measuring Sterility from Incomplete Birth Histories. *Demography*, May 1989, *26*(2), pp. 185–201.

Menkhaus, Dale J. and Whipple, Glen D. Supply Response in the U.S. Sheep Industry. *Amer. J. Agr. Econ.*, February 1989, *71*(1), pp. 126–35.

Mennemeyer, Stephen T. Competitive Bidding for Medicare Outpatient Laboratory Tests. In *Scheffler, R. M. and Rossiter, L. F., eds.*, 1989, pp. 313–33.

_____ **and Olinger, Lois.** Selective Contracting in California: Its Effect on Hospital Finances. *Inquiry*, Winter 1989, *26*(4), pp. 442–57.

Mennes, L. B. M. and Kol, Jacob. Corrections for Trade Imbalance: A Survey. *Weltwirtsch. Arch.*, 1989, *125*(4), pp. 703–17.

Menon, Vijay. Telecommunications and Development: The Case of India. In *Jussawalla, M.; Okuma, T. and Araki, T., eds.*, 1989, pp. 281–88.

Mensah, Samuel; Blinder, Edward H. and Gagnon, Louis. Hedging Canadian Corporate Debt: A Comparative Study of the Hedging Effectiveness of Canadian and U.S. Bond Futures. *J. Futures Markets*, February 1989, *9*(1), pp. 29–39.

van der Mensbrugghe, Dominique and Delorme,

François. Assessing the Role of Scale Economies and Imperfect Competition in the Context of Agricultural Trade Liberalisation: A Canadian Case Study. *OECD Econ. Stud.*, Winter 1989–1990, (13), pp. 205–36.

_____; **Martin, John P. and Burniaux, Jean-Marc.** How Robust Are WALRAS Results? *OECD Econ. Stud.*, Winter 1989–1990, (13), pp. 173–204.

Menshikov, S. and Klimenko, L. Long Waves in Economic Structure. In *Di Matteo, M.; Goodwin, R. M. and Vercelli, A., eds.*, 1989, pp. 145–66.

_____ **and Klimenko, L.** Structural Change and the Long Wave. In *Krelle, W., ed.*, 1989, pp. 543–60.

Mentzas, G. N.; Capros, Pantelis and Karadeloglou, P. Energy Policy Extensions of KLE-Based Macroeconomic Models. *J. Policy Modeling*, Winter 1989, *11*(4), pp. 507–30.

Menz, Fredric C. and Mullen, John K. Valuing the Effect of Acidification Damages in the Adirondack Fishery: Reply. *Amer. J. Agr. Econ.*, February 1989, *71*(1), pp. 221–22.

Menzel, Donald C.; Krause, Mark A. and Hedge, David M. The Intergovernmental Milieu and Street-Level Implementation. *Soc. Sci. Quart.*, June 1989, *70*(2), pp. 285–99.

Meran, Georg and Krahnen, Jan P. Why Leasing? An Introduction to Comparative Contractual Analysis. In *Bamberg, G. and Spremann, K., eds.*, 1989, pp. 255–80.

Merchant, Kenneth A. and Manzoni, Jean-François. The Achievability of Budget Targets in Profit Centers: A Field Study. *Accounting Rev.*, July 1989, *64*(3), pp. 539–58.

Mereste, U. The Theory of Property and Improvement of the Economic Mechanism. In *Yanowitch, M., ed.*, 1989, *1987*, pp. 280–94.

Mergos, George J. Feed Use of Grain: On Trends and Determinants. *Europ. Rev. Agr. Econ.*, 1989, *16*(1), pp. 1–17.

_____ **and Donatos, George S.** Consumer Behaviour in Greece: An Application of the Almost Ideal Demand System. *Appl. Econ.*, July 1989, *21*(7), pp. 983–93.

_____ **and Donatos, George S.** Demand for Food in Greece: An Almost Ideal Demand System Analysis. *J. Agr. Econ.*, May 1989, *40*(2), pp. 178–84.

_____ **and Donatos, George S.** Energy Demand in Greece: The Impact of the Two Energy Crises. *Energy Econ.*, April 1989, *11*(2), pp. 147–52.

Meric, Gulser and Meric, Ilhan. Potential Gains from International Portfolio Diversification and Inter-temporal Stability and Seasonality in International Stock Market Relationships. *J. Banking Finance*, September 1989, *13*(4–5), pp. 627–40.

Meric, Ilhan and Meric, Gulser. Potential Gains from International Portfolio Diversification and Inter-temporal Stability and Seasonality in International Stock Market Relationships. *J. Banking Finance*, September 1989, *13*(4–5), pp. 627–40.

Merkies, Arnold H. Q. M. and van Daal, Jan. A Note on the Quadratic Expenditure Model. *Econometrica*, November 1989, *57*(6), pp. 1439–43.

_____ **and van der Meer, Tjemme.** Scope of the Three-Component Model. *Reg. Sci. Urban Econ.*, December 1989, *19*(4), pp. 601–14.

Merrett, D. T. Australian Banking Practice and the Crisis of 1893. *Australian Econ. Hist. Rev.*, March 1989, *29*(1), pp. 60–85.

Merrick, John J., Jr. Early Unwindings and Roll-overs of Stock Index Futures Arbitrage Programs: Analysis and Implications for Predicting Expiration Day Effects. *J. Futures Markets*, April 1989, *9*(2), pp. 101–11.

Merriken, Harry E. and Edmister, Robert O. Measuring Interest Rate Sensitivity of Consumer Depositors. *J. Finan. Services Res.*, June 1989, *2*(2), pp. 133–45.

Merrill, Jeffrey C. and Somers, Stephen A. Long-Term Care: The Great Debate on the Wrong Issue. *Inquiry*, Fall 1989, *26*(3), pp. 317–20.

Mertens, Jean-François. CORE as a Macrocosm of Game-Theoretic Research, 1967–1987: Comments. In *Cornet, B. and Tulkens, H., eds.*, 1989, pp. 18–22.

_____ **and Abdou, J.** Correlated Effectivity Functions. *Econ. Letters*, August 1989, *30*(2), pp. 97–101.

Mertes, Eugene R. Entering Global Markets. In *Ahlbrandt, R. S., Jr., ed.*, 1989, pp. 18–21.

Merton, Robert C. The Changing Nature of Debt and Equity: A Financial Perspective: Discussion. In *Kopcke, R. W. and Rosengren, E. S., eds.*, 1989, pp. 44–48.

Merville, Larry J. and Pieptea, Dan R. Stock-Price Volatility, Mean-Reverting Diffusion, and Noise. *J. Finan. Econ.*, September 1989, *24*(1), pp. 193–214.

Mesghenna, Yemane. Italian Colonialism in Eritrea, 1882–1941: Review Article. *Scand. Econ. Hist. Rev.*, 1989, *37*(3), pp. 65–72.

Messer, Ellen. Seasonality in Food Systems: An Anthropological Perspective on Household Food Security. In *Sahn, D. E., ed.*, 1989, pp. 151–75.

Messere, Ken C. and Nørregard, John. Consumption Taxes in OECD Countries over the Last Two Decades: International. *Bull. Int. Fiscal Doc.*, June 1989, *43*(6), pp. 255–68.

_____ **and Owens, Jeffrey P.** Long-Term Revenue Trends and Current Tax Reform Issues in OECD Countries. In *Chiancone, A. and Messere, K., eds.*, 1989, pp. 21–35.

Messerlin, Patrick A. The EC Antidumping Regulations: A First Economic Appraisal, 1980–85. *Weltwirtsch. Arch.*, 1989, *125*(3), pp. 563–87.

Mestelman, Stuart. Taxes, Subsidies, Standards, and Social Choices. *Public Finance*, 1989, *44*(2), pp. 268–84.

Mester, Loretta J. Testing for Expense Preference Behavior: Mutual versus Stock Savings and Loans. *Rand J. Econ.*, Winter 1989, *20*(4), pp. 483–98.

_____. Viability in Multiproduct Industries.

Econ. Letters, December 1989, *31*(3), pp. 273–76.

Metcalf, David. Water Notes Dry Up: The Impact of the Donovan Reform Proposals and Thatcherism at Work on Labour Productivity in British Manufacturing Industry. *Brit. J. Ind. Relat.*, March 1989, *27*(1), pp. 1–31.

Metcalfe, J. S. and Gibbons, Michael. Technology, Variety and Organization: A Systematic Perspective on the Competitive Process. In *Rosenbloom, R. S. and Burgelman, R. A., eds.*, 1989, pp. 153–93.

_____ **and Steedman, Ian.** 'On Foreign Trade.' In *Steedman, I.*, 1989, *1973*, pp. 40–50.

Metcalfe, Stanley; Porteous, Mike and Barber, John. Barriers to Growth: The ACARD Study. In *Barber, J.; Metcalfe, J. S. and Porteous, M., eds.*, 1989, pp. 1–19.

Metrinko, Peter and Douglas, George W. Civil Aeronautics Board Sunset: Sunrise at the Department of Transportation? In *Meiners, R. E. and Yandle, B., eds.*, 1989, pp. 186–206.

Metwally, Mokhtar M. The Role of the Rate of Interest in Contemporary Islamic Societies. *Middle East Bus. Econ. Rev.*, January 1989, *1*(1), pp. 32–47.

Metz, K. J. and Keller, Wouter J. The Impact of New Dataprocessing Techniques at the Netherlands Central Bureau of Statistics. *Statist. J.*, 1989, *6*(3), pp. 213–22.

Metzger, John T. and Weiss, Marc A. Planning for Chicago: The Changing Politics of Metropolitan Growth and Neighborhood Development. In *Beauregard, R. A., ed.*, 1989, pp. 123–51.

Metzler, Helen M. D.; Shafer, Michael S. and Rice, Martha Larus. Integration in the Workplace: Perceptions and Experiences of Employees without Disabilities. In *Wehman, P. and Kregel, J., eds.*, 1989, pp. 137–59.

Metzler, L. A. Stability of Multiple Markets: The Hicks Conditions. In *Wood, J. C. and Woods, R. N., eds.*, *Vol. 1*, 1989, *1945*, pp. 108–22.

Meulders, Danièle; Plasman, Robert and Guillaume, Y. Simulation des impacts de l'achèvement du marché intérieur. Le cas de la Belgique. (With English summary.) *Cah. Écon. Bruxelles*, 4th Trimester 1989, (124), pp. 449–73.

_____ **and Tytgat, Bernard.** The Emergence of Atypical Employment in the European Community. In *Rodgers, G. and Rodgers, J., eds.*, 1989, pp. 179–96.

Meurer, Michael J. The Settlement of Patent Litigation. *Rand J. Econ.*, Spring 1989, *20*(1), pp. 77–91.

Mey, Hansjurg. The Impact of Information Technology on International Financial Flows. In *Jussawalla, M.; Okuma, T. and Araki, T., eds.*, 1989, pp. 102–08.

Meyanathan, Sahathavan. Energy Plans and Strategies: Malaysia. In *James, W. E., ed.*, 1989, pp. 135–45.

Meyer, Bernd. A Multisectoral Econometric Model with Markets for Commodities and Financial Assets. *Econ. Systems Res.*, 1989, *1*(2), pp. 167–86.

———. A Neoclassical Input–Output Model Based on "Make"- and "Use"-Tables. *Empirical Econ.*, 1989, *14*(1), pp. 1–19.

Meyer, Carrie A. Agrarian Reform in the Dominican Republic: An Associative Solution to the Collective/Individual Dilemma. *World Devel.*, August 1989, *17*(8), pp. 1255–67.

Meyer, David R. Midwestern Industrialization and the American Manufacturing Belt in the Nineteenth Century. *J. Econ. Hist.*, December 1989, *49*(4), pp. 921–37.

Meyer, Dirk. Der Bestandsschutz im Arbeitsverhältnis als ökonomisches Gut. Ansätze zu einer effizienten Regelung. (The Protection of the Working Relationship in Labor Contracts as an Economic Good. Dispositions of Efficient Arrangements. With English summary.) *Jahr. Nationalökon. Statist.*, July 1989, *206*(3), pp. 208–24.

———. Rent Seeking durch Rationalisierungsschutz oder die Wohlfahrtsverluste einer Kostensenkungssteuer. (Rent Seeking through Regulations Protecting Human Capital from Devaluation Due to Technological Innovation. With English summary.) *Konjunkturpolitik*, 1989, *35*(3), pp. 188–200.

Meyer, Fritz W. Development Aid in a Free Market System. In *Peacock, A. and Willgerodt, H., eds. (II)*, 1989, *1960*, pp. 242–60.

Meyer, Jack. Stochastic Dominance and Transformations of Random Variables. In *[Hadar, J.]*, 1989, pp. 45–57.

———. Two-Moment Decision Models and Expected Utility Maximization: Reply. *Amer. Econ. Rev.*, June 1989, *79*(3), pp. 603.

——— **and Ormiston, Michael B.** Deterministic Transformations of Random Variables and the Comparative Statics of Risk. *J. Risk Uncertainty*, June 1989, *2*(2), pp. 179–88.

Meyer, Jack A. Matching Policies for Retirement Years with Changing Demographic and Economic Conditions. In *Lewin, M. E. and Sullivan, S., eds.*, 1989, pp. 123–36.

———. Reforming Medicare and Medicaid. In *Lewin, M. E. and Sullivan, S., eds.*, 1989, pp. 103–21.

——— **and McLennan, Kenneth.** Adopting Market Incentives in Public-Sector Policies. In *McLennan, K. and Meyer, J. A., eds.*, 1989, pp. 13–38.

——— **and McLennan, Kenneth.** Containing Health Care Cost Escalation and Improving Access to Services: The Search for a Solution. In *McLennan, K. and Meyer, J. A., eds.*, 1989, pp. 1–11.

Meyer-Krahmer, Frieder and Wessels, Hans. Intersektorale Verflechtung von Technologiegebern und Technologienehmern—Eine empirische Analyse für die Bundesrepublik Deutschland. (Intersectoral Technology Flow: Network between Producer and User—An Empirical Analysis for the Federal Republic of Germany. With English summary.) *Jahr.*

Nationalökon. Statist., December 1989, *206*(6), pp. 563–82.

Meyer, Margaret A. and Klemperer, Paul D. Supply Function Equilibria in Oligopoly under Uncertainty. *Econometrica*, November 1989, *57*(6), pp. 1243–77.

Meyer, Paul A. and Hardjodimedjo, Martono. Maluku: The Modernization of the Spice Islands. In *Hill, H., ed.*, 1989, pp. 548–65.

Meyer, Renate. Extensions of Correspondence Analysis for the Statistical Exploration of Multidimensional Contingency Tables. In *Opitz, O., ed.*, 1989, pp. 178–86.

Meyer, Robert A. Regulation in Multifirm Markets. *Quart. Rev. Econ. Bus.*, Spring 1989, *29*(1), pp. 5–20.

Meyer, Robert J. and Johnson, Eric J. Information Overload and the Nonrobustness of Linear Models: A Comment. *J. Cons. Res.*, March 1989, *15*(4), pp. 498–503.

Meyers-Levy, Joan. The Influence of a Brand Name's Association Set Size and Word Frequency on Brand Memory. *J. Cons. Res.*, September 1989, *16*(2), pp. 197–207.

——— **and Tybout, Alice M.** Schema Congruity as a Basis for Product Evaluation. *J. Cons. Res.*, June 1989, *16*(1), pp. 39–54.

Meyers, William H.; Frohberg, Klaus K. and Womack, Abner W. Food and Agricultural Policies and Programs of Major Countries and Regions: Reaction. In *Helmuth, J. W. and Johnson, S. R., eds., Vol. 1*, 1989, pp. 39–41.

Meyers, William R. and Gideonse, Sarah K. Why the Family Support Act Will Fail. *Challenge*, Sept.–Oct. 1989, *32*(5), pp. 33–39.

de Meza, David. Not Even Strategic Trade Theory Justifies Export Subsidies. *Oxford Econ. Pap.*, October 1989, *41*(4), pp. 720–36.

———; **La Manna, Manfredi and MacLeod, Ross.** The Case for Permissive Patents. *Europ. Econ. Rev.*, September 1989, *33*(7), pp. 1427–43.

——— **and Natale, Piergiovanna.** Efficient Job Creation in LDCs Requires a Tax on Employment. *Econ. J.*, December 1989, *99*(398), pp. 1112–22.

——— **and Webb, David C.** The Role of Interest Rate Taxes in Credit Markets with Divisible Projects and Asymmetric Information. *J. Public Econ.*, June 1989, *39*(1), pp. 33–44.

Miceli, Thomas J. Housing Rental Contracts and Adverse Selection with an Application to the Rent–Own Decision. *Amer. Real Estate Urban Econ. Assoc. J.*, Winter 1989, *17*(4), pp. 403–21.

———. The Optimal Duration of Real Estate Listing Contracts. *Amer. Real Estate Urban Econ. Assoc. J.*, Fall 1989, *17*(3), pp. 267–77.

——— **and Henderson, J. Vernon.** Reputation in Land Development Markets. *J. Urban Econ.*, November 1989, *26*(3), pp. 386–408.

Michael, Michael S. and Chang, Winston W. Optimal Commercial Policy for an Open Economy with Domestic Distortions. *Econ. Letters*, December 1989, *31*(2), pp. 163–67.

——— **and Hatzipanayotou, Panos.** Capital

Flows, Tariffs, and the Host Country's Welfare. *Econ. Int.*, Aug.–Nov. 1989, *42*(3–4), pp. 191–97.

Michael, Robert T.; Desai, Sonalde and Chase-Lansdale, P. Lindsay. Mother or Market? Effects of Maternal Employment on the Intellectual Ability of 4-Year-Old Children. *Demography*, November 1989, *26*(4), pp. 544–61.

_____ **and Hartmann, Heidi I.** Pay Equity: Assessing the Issues. In *Michael, R. T.; Hartmann, H. I. and O'Farrell, B., eds.*, 1989, pp. 1–19.

Michaelis, Jochen. Staatsverschuldung als Quelle der Nicht-Neutralität. Ein Beitrag zum Ricardianischen Äquivalenztheorem. (Government Debt as a Reason for Lacking Neutrality. A Contribution to the Ricardian Equivalence Theorem. With English summary.) *Kredit Kapital*, 1989, *22*(4), pp. 453–69.

Michaels, Robert J. Conjectural Variations and the Nature of Equilibrium in Rent-Seeking Models. *Public Choice*, January 1989, *60*(1), pp. 31–39.

_____. Reorganizing Electricity Supply in New Zealand: Lessons for the United States. *Contemp. Policy Issues*, October 1989, *7*(4), pp. 73–90.

Michaely, Michael; Choksi, Armeane and Papageorgiou, Demetris. The Design of Trade Liberalization. *Finance Devel.*, March 1989, *26*(1), pp. 2–5.

Michalak, Stanley J. UNCTAD as an Agent of Change. In *[Gordenker, L.]*, 1989, pp. 69–85.

Michalopoulos, Constantine. Assistance for Infrastructure Development. In *Krueger, A. O.; Michalopoulos, C. and Ruttan, V. W.*, 1989, pp. 125–39.

_____ **and Jay, Keith E.** Donor Policies, Donor Interests, and Aid Effectiveness. In *Krueger, A. O.; Michalopoulos, C. and Ruttan, V. W.*, 1989, pp. 68–88.

_____ **and Jay, Keith E.** Interaction between Donors and Recipients. In *Krueger, A. O.; Michalopoulos, C. and Ruttan, V. W.*, 1989, pp. 89–108.

_____ **and Krueger, Anne O.** Recipient Policies, National Development, and Aid Effectiveness. In *Krueger, A. O.; Michalopoulos, C. and Ruttan, V. W.*, 1989, pp. 55–67.

_____; **Ruttan, Vernon W. and Krueger, Anne O.** Aid and Development: Introduction. In *Krueger, A. O.; Michalopoulos, C. and Ruttan, V. W.*, 1989, pp. 1–10.

_____; **Ruttan, Vernon W. and Krueger, Anne O.** Some Lessons from Development Assistance. In *Krueger, A. O.; Michalopoulos, C. and Ruttan, V. W.*, 1989 , pp. 305–23.

_____ **and Sukhatme, Vasant A.** The Impact of Development Assistance: A Review of the Quantitative Evidence. In *Krueger, A. O.; Michalopoulos, C. and Ruttan, V. W.*, 1989, pp. 111–24.

Michalowski, W. and Szapiro, T. A Safe Choice Procedure in Interactive Programming. In *Lockett, A. G. and Islei, G., eds.*, 1989, pp. 454–61.

Michalski, Wolfgang. Advanced Information Technologies: Challenges and Opportunities. In *Jussawalla, M.; Okuma, T. and Araki, T., eds.*, 1989, pp. 9–18.

Michelot, C.; Idrissi, H. and Lefebvre, O. Applications and Numerical Convergence of the Partial Inverse Method. In *Dolecki, S., ed.*, 1989, pp. 39–54.

Michener, H. Andrew; Salzer, Mark S. and Richardson, Greg D. Extensions of Value Solutions in Constant-Sum Non-sidepayment Games. *J. Conflict Resolution*, September 1989, *33*(3), pp. 530–53.

Michener, Ronald W. Rules, Commitment, and the Search for Stable Money: A Review Essay. *J. Monet. Econ.*, January 1989, *23*(1), pp. 151–58.

Michon, François and Gauvin, Annie. Work-Sharing Public Policy in France, 1981–1986. In *Rosenberg, S., ed.*, 1989, pp. 207–20.

Mickler, Otfried. The Introduction and Use of CNC in the Federal Republic of Germany. In *Francis, A. and Grootings, P., eds.*, 1989, pp. 187–226.

Micklewright, John. Choice at Sixteen. *Economica*, February 1989, *56*(221), pp. 25–39.

_____ **and Atkinson, Anthony B.** Turning the Screw: Benefits for the Unemployed 1979–88. In *Dilnot, A. and Walker, I., eds.*, 1989, pp. 17–51.

_____; **Baker, Paul and Blundell, Richard W.** Modelling Household Energy Expenditures Using Micro-data. *Econ. J.*, September 1989, *99*(397), pp. 720–38.

_____; **Pearson, Mark and Smith, Stephen R.** Has Britain an Early School-Leaving Problem? *Fisc. Stud.*, February 1989, *10*(1), pp. 1–16.

Mickwitz, Gösta. Miljöskatter och subventioner. (Environmental Taxes and Subsidies. With English summary.) *Ekon. Samfundets Tidskr.*, 1989, *42*(3), pp. 149–51.

Micossi, S. and Bini Smaghi, Lorenzo. Managing Exchange Markets in the EMS with Free Capital. *Banca Naz. Lavoro Quart. Rev.*, December 1989, (171), pp. 395–430.

_____ **and Rossi, S.** Restrictions on International Capital Flows: The Case of Italy. In *Gordon, I. and Thirlwall, A. P., eds.*, 1989, pp. 195–214.

Middleton, Alan. The Changing Structure of Petty Production in Ecuador. *World Devel.*, January 1989, *17*(1), pp. 139–55.

Middleton, Melissa. The Characteristics and Influence of Intraboard Networks: A Case Study of a Nonprofit Board of Directors. In *Herman, R. D. and Van Til, J., eds.*, 1989, pp. 160–92.

Middleton, Peter [Sir]. Economic Policy Formulation in the Treasury in the Post-war Period. *Nat. Inst. Econ. Rev.*, February 1989, (127), pp. 46–51.

Middleton, Roger. Britain in the 1930s: A Managed Economy? A Comment. *Econ. Hist. Rev.*, 2nd Ser., November 1989, *42*(4), pp. 544–47.

Mielke, David E. and Giacomino, Don E. Learning Styles of Public Accountants: Measurement and Applicability to Practice Management. In *Schwartz, B. N., ed.*, 1989, pp. 241–56.

Mielke, J. H.; Jorde, L. B. and Pitkänen, K. J. Smallpox and Its Eradication in Finland: Implications for Disease Control. *Population Stud.*, March 1989, *43*(1), pp. 95–111.

Miernyk, William and Rose, Adam Z. Input–Output Analysis: The First Fifty Years. *Econ. Systems Res.*, 1989, *1*(2), pp. 229–71.

Mies, J. P. W. The Disregard of a Legal Entity for Tax Purposes: Netherlands. In *International Fiscal Association, ed. (II)*, 1989, pp. 415–38.

Mieszkowski, Peter and Zodrow, George R. Taxation and the Tiebout Model: The Differential Effects of Head Taxes, Taxes on Land Rents, and Property Taxes. *J. Econ. Lit.*, September 1989, *27*(3), pp. 1098–1146.

Miewald, Robert D. and Longo, Peter J. Institutions in Water Policy: The Case of Nebraska. *Natural Res. J.*, Summer 1989, *29*(3), pp. 751–62.

Might, Robert J. and Daniel, William D., Jr. Decision Support for War Games. In *Golden, B. L.; Wasil, E. A. and Harker, P. T., eds.*, 1989, pp. 171–81.

Mihăiţă, N. V. The Flexible Structures of the Systems of Relations in Marketing. *Econ. Computat. Econ. Cybern. Stud. Res.*, 1989, *24*(2–3), pp. 29–40.

Mihaljek, Dubravko. Wealth Effects of Inflation and Devaluations in Yugoslavia: Who Gains and Who Loses? *Econ. Anal. Workers' Manage.*, 1989, *23*(3), pp. 207–52.

Mihályi, Péter. East European Consumer Goods Imports from the West, 1962–1986. *Acta Oecon.*, 1989, *41*(1–2), pp. 53–78.

Mikesell, John L. A Note on the Changing Incidence of State Lottery Finance. *Soc. Sci. Quart.*, June 1989, *70*(2), pp. 513–21.

_____ **and Bowman, John H.** Elected versus Appointed Assessors and the Achievement of Assessment Uniformity. *Nat. Tax J.*, June 1989, *42*(2), pp. 181–89.

Mikesell, Raymond F.; Haynes, Stephen E. and Hutchison, Michael M. U.S.–Japanese Bilateral Trade and the Yen–Dollar Exchange Rate: Reply. *Southern Econ. J.*, October 1989, *56*(2), pp. 524–28.

Mikhail, William M. Modelling Labour and Capital Movements between Egypt and Other Arab Countries. *Middle East Bus. Econ. Rev.*, January 1989, *1*(1), pp. 11–19.

Mikheev, I. and Solodkov, M. A Stage-by-Stage Transition to Wholesale Trade in the Means of Production. *Prob. Econ.*, January 1989, *31*(9), pp. 98–112.

Mikić, Mia. External Debt Management. In *Singer, H. W. and Sharma, S., eds. (II)*, 1989, pp. 12–21.

Mikkelson, Wayne H. and Partch, M. Megan. Managers' Voting Rights and Corporate Control. *J. Finan. Econ.*, December 1989, *25*(2), pp. 263–90.

Mikul'skii, K. The Differentiation of Labor Incomes under Socialism: Essence, Functions,

Criteria, and Parameters. *Prob. Econ.*, April 1989, *31*(12), pp. 62–83.

Milana, Carlo. External Constraint and the Labour Oriented Supply-Side Policies in Italy. *Labour*, Winter 1989, *3*(3), pp. 109–28.

Milani, Hamid. Devaluation and the Balance of Trade: A Synthesis of Monetary and Elasticity Approaches. *Int. Econ. J.*, Autumn 1989, *3*(3), pp. 65–72.

Milano, Serge. Jalons pour une histoire du revenu minimum garanti (XIXème–XXème siècle). (Blazing the Trail of an History of Guaranteed Income: From XIXth to XXth Century. With English summary.) *Écon. Societes*, October 1989, *23*(10), pp. 107–34.

Milberg, William; Groves, Miles and Lee, Frederic S. The Power of Ideas and the Impact of One Man, Alfred Eichner 1937–1988. *J. Post Keynesian Econ.*, Spring 1989, *11*(3), pp. 491–96.

Milbourne, Ross D. and Smith, Gregor W. How Informative Are Preliminary Announcements of the Money Stock in Canada? *Can. J. Econ.*, August 1989, *22*(3), pp. 595–606.

Milde, Hellmuth. Managerial Contracting with Public and Private Information. In *Bamberg, G. and Spremann, K., eds.*, 1989, pp. 39–59.

Miles, Carrie and Bradburn, Norman M. Vague Quantifiers. In *Singer, E. and Presser, S., eds.*, 1989, *1979*, pp. 155–64.

Miles, David K. and Chowdhury, Gopa. Modelling Companies' Debt and Dividend Decisions with Company Accounts Data. *Appl. Econ.*, November 1989, *21*(11), pp. 1483–1508.

_____ **; Chowdhury, Gopa and Green, Christopher J.** Company Bank Borrowing and Liquid Lending. *Nat. Westminster Bank Quart. Rev.*, November 1989, pp. 42–52.

_____ **; Taylor, Mark P. and Hall, Stephen G.** Modelling Asset Prices with Time-Varying Betas. *Manchester Sch. Econ. Soc. Stud.*, December 1989, *57*(4), pp. 340–56.

Miles, Ian. Social Implications of Information Technology. In *Jussawalla, M.; Okuma, T. and Araki, T., eds.*, 1989, pp. 222–35.

Miles, James A. and Kelly, William A., Jr. Capital Structure Theory and the Fisher Effect. *Financial Rev.*, February 1989, *24*(1), pp. 53–73.

Miles, Mike; Cole, Rebel and Guilkey, David K. The Motivation for Institutional Real Estate Sales and Implications for Asset Class Returns. *Amer. Real Estate Urban Econ. Assoc. J.*, Spring 1989, *17*(1), pp. 70–86.

Milgrom, Paul. An Essay on Price Discrimination. In *Feiwel, G. R., ed. (I)*, 1989, pp. 365–86.

_____. Auctions and Bidding: A Primer. *J. Econ. Perspectives*, Summer 1989, *3*(3), pp. 3–22.

Miliband, Ralph. Marx and the State. In *Duncan, G., ed.*, 1989, pp. 85–103.

Milios, John. The Problem of Capitalist Development: Theoretical Considerations in View of the Industrial Countries and the New Industrial Countries. In *Gottdiener, M. and Komninos, N., eds.*, 1989, pp. 154–73.

Milkovich, George T. and Gerhart, Barry A. Salaries, Salary Growth, and Promotions of Men and Women in a Large, Private Firm. In *Michael, R. T.; Hartmann, H. I. and O'Farrell, B., eds.*, 1989, pp. 23–43.

Millar, Annie. Selecting Capital Investment Projects for Local Government. In *Matzer, J., Jr., ed.*, 1989, *1988*, pp. 81–99.

Millar, Jane and Jenkins, Stephen P. Income Risk and Income Maintenance: Implications for Incentives to Work. In *Dilnot, A. and Walker, I., eds.*, 1989, pp. 137–52.

Miller, Angela Browne and Scheffler, Richard M. Demand Analysis of Mental Health Service Use among Ethnic Subpopulations. *Inquiry*, Summer 1989, *26*(2), pp. 202–15.

Miller, Anne G. and Mair, Douglas. Urban Unemployment; A Causal Modelling Approach. *Urban Stud.*, August 1989, *26*(4), pp. 379–96.

Miller, Arthur Selwyn. Legal Foundations of the Corporate State. In *Tool, M. R. and Samuels, W. J., eds. (III)*, 1989, *1972*, pp. 79–99.

Miller, Barbara Diane and Bird, Richard M. The Incidence of Indirect Taxes on Low-Income Households in Jamaica. *Econ. Devel. Cult. Change*, January 1989, *37*(2), pp. 393–409.

_____ **and Khan, Showkat Hayat.** Voluntarism. In *Schroeder, L., ed.*, 1989, pp. 175–90.

_____; **Wozny, James and Alm, James.** The Land Development Tax. In *Schroeder, L., ed.*, 1989, pp. 115–43.

Miller, Bill R.; Dubman, Robert W. and Gunter, Lewell F. Revenue and Cost Uncertainty, Generalized Mean–Variance and the Linear Complementarity Problem: Comment. *Amer. J. Agr. Econ.*, August 1989, *71*(3), pp. 806–09.

Miller, Bruce M. Hellfire Missile Competition Case Study. In *Gulledge, T. R., Jr. and Litteral, L. A., eds.*, 1989, pp. 45–61.

Miller, David B. Monumental Building as an Indicator of Economic Trends in Northern Rus' in the Late Kievan and Mongol Periods, 1138–1462. *Amer. Historical Rev.*, April 1989, *94*(2), pp. 360–90.

Miller, Edward M. The Definition of Capital for Solow's Growth Accounting Formula. *Southern Econ. J.*, July 1989, *56*(1), pp. 157–65.

_____. Design of Financial Systems for Economic Stability. *Amer. Economist*, Fall 1989, *33*(2), pp. 39–52.

_____. Explaining Intra-day and Overnight Price Behavior. *J. Portfol. Manage.*, Summer 1989, *15*(4), pp. 10–16.

_____. Keynes' Monetary Theory and Bank Reserves in Britain. *Atlantic Econ. J.*, March 1989, *17*(1), pp. 24–34.

_____. The Unique "Rent Defined" Capital Input Assumption in Investment Theory. *Southern Econ. J.*, April 1989, *55*(4), pp. 987–93.

Miller, Edythe S. Comment [Austrian and Institutional Economics: Some Common Elements] [Evolution and Economics: Austrians as Institutionalists]. In *Samuels, W. J., ed. (II)*, 1989, pp. 151–58.

_____. Economics For What? Economic Folklore and Social Realities. *J. Econ. Issues*, June 1989, *23*(2), pp. 339–56.

Miller, Gary J. Confiscation, Credible Commitment and Progressive Reform in the United States. *J. Inst. Theoretical Econ.*, December 1989, *145*(4), pp. 686–92.

Miller, H. J. and O'Kelly, M. E. A Synthesis of Some Market Area Delimitation Models. *Growth Change*, Summer 1989, *20*(3), pp. 14–33.

Miller, Harris N. Farm Workers, Agriculture, and the Politics of Immigration Reform: The Immigration Reform and Control Act of 1986: Commentary. In *Krämer, C. S., ed.*, 1989, pp. 261–63.

Miller, J. D. B. Australia in the World. In *Hancock, K., ed.*, 1989, pp. 228–43.

Miller, James C., III. Reflections on Fiscal Policy in the 1980s. In *Federal Home Loan Bank of San Francisco*, 1989, pp. 5–17.

Miller, James P. The Product Cycle and High Technology Industry in Nonmetropolitan Areas, 1976–1980. *Rev. Reg. Stud.*, Winter 1989, *19*(1), pp. 1–12.

Miller, Jane E. Is the Relationship between Birth Intervals and Perinatal Mortality Spurious? Evidence from Hungary and Sweden. *Population Stud.*, November 1989, *43*(3), pp. 479–95.

Miller, John A. Social Wage or Social Profit? The Net Social Wage and the Welfare State. *Rev. Radical Polit. Econ.*, Fall 1989, *21*(3), pp. 82–90.

Miller, Marcus H. Plans to Solve the Problem of the Twin U.S. Deficits. *Can. Public Policy*, Supplement, February 1989, *15*, pp. S58–62.

_____ **and Buiter, Willem H.** Costs and Benefits of an Anti-inflationary Policy: Questions and Issues. In *Buiter, W. H.*, 1989, *1985*, pp. 200–228.

_____; **Eichengreen, Barry and Portes, Richard.** Blueprints for Exchange-Rate Management: Introduction. In *Miller, M.; Eichengreen, B. and Portes, R., eds.*, 1989, pp. 1–10.

_____ **and Weller, Paul.** Exchange Rate Bands and Realignments in a Stationary Stochastic Setting. In *Miller, M.; Eichengreen, B. and Portes, R., eds.*, 1989, pp. 161–73.

_____; **Weller, Paul and Williamson, John.** The Stabilizing Properties of Target Zones. In *Bryant, R. C., et al., eds.*, 1989, pp. 248–71.

_____ **and Williamson, John.** The International Monetary System: An Analysis of Alternative Regimes. In *Hamouda, O. F.; Rowley, R. and Wolf, B. M., eds.*, 1989, pp. 68–84.

Miller, Merton H. Volatility, Price Resolution, and the Effectiveness of Price Limits: Commentary. In *Edwards, F. R., ed.*, 1989, pp. 103–05.

_____. Volatility, Price Resolution, and the Effectiveness of Price Limits: Commentary. *J. Finan. Services Res.*, December 1989, *3*(2–3), pp. 201–03.

Miller, Morris. The World Bank and the International Monetary Fund: Roles in and beyond the Debt Crisis. In *Singer, H. W. and Sharma, S., eds. (I)*, 1989, pp. 109–28.

Miller, Paul W. Low-Wage Youth Employment:

A Permanent or Transitory State? *Econ. Rec.*, June 1989, *65*(189), pp. 126–35.

———. The Structure of Aboriginal and Non-aboriginal Youth Unemployment. *Australian Econ. Pap.*, June 1989, *28*(52), pp. 39–56.

——— and Christie, Virginia. Attitudes towards Unions and Union Membership. *Econ. Letters*, September 1989, *30*(3), pp. 263–68.

Miller, Peter V. and Cannell, Charles F. A Study of Experimental Techniques for Telephone Interviewing. In *Singer, E. and Presser, S., eds.*, 1989, *1982*, pp. 304–23.

——— and Groves, Robert M. Matching Survey Responses to Official Records: An Exploration of Validity in Victimization Reporting. In *Singer, E. and Presser, S., eds.*, 1989, *1985*, pp. 356–70.

Miller, Preston J. Gramm–Rudman–Hollings' Hold on Budget Policy: Losing Its Grip? *Fed. Res. Bank Minn. Rev.*, Winter 1989, *13*(1), pp. 11–21.

——— and Fitzgerald, Terry J. A Simple Way to Estimate Current-Quarter GNP. *Fed. Res. Bank Minn. Rev.*, Fall 1989, *13*(4), pp. 27–31.

——— and Runkle, David E. The U.S. Economy in 1989 and 1990: Walking a Fine Line. *Fed. Res. Bank Minn. Rev.*, Winter 1989, *13*(1), pp. 3–10.

Miller, Reuben. Supplier Autonomy A L'outrance: Retransfer of Military Arms and Technology to Terrorist Groups. In *Baek, K.-I.; McLaurin, R. D. and Moon, C., eds.*, 1989, pp. 201–30.

Miller, Richard D.; Garner, Thesia I. and Zieschang, Kimberley D. Using the Consumer Expenditure Survey Data: Past, Present, and Future Research. *J. Econ. Soc. Meas.*, 1989, *15*(3–4), pp. 237–79.

Miller, Robert E. and Affleck-Graves, John. Regulatory and Procedural Effects on the Underpricing of Initial Public Offerings. *J. Finan. Res.*, Fall 1989, *12*(3), pp. 193–202.

——— and Hegde, Shantaram P. Market-Making in Initial Public Offerings of Common Stocks: An Empirical Analysis. *J. Finan. Quant. Anal.*, March 1989, *24*(1), pp. 75–90.

——— and McDonald, Bill. Additional Evidence on the Nature of Size-Related Anomalies. *J. Econ. Bus.*, February 1989, *41*(1), pp. 61–68.

Miller, Ronald E. Stability of Supply Coefficients and Consistency of Supply-Driven and Demand-Driven Input–Output Models: A Comment. *Environ. Planning A*, August 1989, *21*(8), pp. 1113–20.

Miller, Stephen E. and Kahl, Kandice H. Performance of Estimated Hedging Ratios under Yield Uncertainty. *J. Futures Markets*, August 1989, *9*(4), pp. 307–19.

Miller, Stephen M. Money Demand Instability: Has It Ended? *Econ. Letters*, October 1989, *30*(4), pp. 345–49.

——— and Russek, Frank S. Are the Twin Deficits Really Related? *Contemp. Policy Issues*, October 1989, *7*(4), pp. 91–115.

——— and Valliant, Richard. A Class of Multiplicative Estimators of Laspeyres Price Indexes.

J. Bus. Econ. Statist., July 1989, *7*(3), pp. 382–94.

Miller, Susie. The Outlook for Dairy Products. *Can. J. Agr. Econ.*, Part 2, December 1989, *37*(4), pp. 1215–20.

Miller, Ted R., et al. Global Climate Change: A Challenge to Urban Infrastructure Planners. *Rev. Reg. Stud.*, Fall 1989, *19*(3), pp. 4–13.

Miller, Tracy and Tolley, George. Technology Adoption and Agricultural Price Policy. *Amer. J. Agr. Econ.*, November 1989, *71*(4), pp. 847–57.

Milliman, Scott R. and Prince, Raymond. Firm Incentives to Promote Technological Change in Pollution Control. *J. Environ. Econ. Manage.*, November 1989, *17*(3), pp. 247–65.

——— and Town, Robert. Competition in Deregulated Air Fares. In *Weiss, L. W., ed.*, 1989, pp. 163–67.

Milliron, Valerie C.; Watkins, Paul R. and Karlinsky, Stewart S. Policy Judgments of Taxpayers: An Analysis of Criteria Employed. In *Jones, S. M., ed.*, 1989, pp. 201–21.

Millner, Edward L. and Formby, John P. Output and Welfare Effects of Optimal Price Discrimination in Markets Segmented at the Initiative of the Seller. *Europ. Econ. Rev.*, July 1989, *33*(6), pp. 1175–81.

——— and Hoffer, George E. Has Pricing Behaviour in the U.S. Automobile Industry Become More Competitive? *Appl. Econ.*, March 1989, *21*(3), pp. 295–304.

——— and Pratt, Michael D. An Experimental Investigation of Efficient Rent-Seeking. *Public Choice*, August 1989, *62*(2), pp. 139–51.

Millon-Cornett, Marcia H. and Tehranian, Hassan. Stock Market Reactions to the Depository Institutions Deregulation and Monetary Control Act of 1980. *J. Banking Finance*, March 1989, *13*(1), pp. 81–100.

——— and Travlos, Nickolaos G. Information Effects Associated with Debt-for-Equity and Equity-for-Debt Exchange Offers. *J. Finance*, June 1989, *44*(2), pp. 451–68.

——— and Vetsuypens, Michael R. Voting Rights and Shareholder Wealth: The Issuance of Limited Voting Common Stock. *Managerial Dec. Econ.*, September 1989, *10*(3), pp. 175–88.

Millon, David and Johnson, Lyman. Misreading the Williams Act. *Mich. Law Rev.*, June 1989, *87*(7), pp. 1862–1923.

——— and Johnson, Lyman. Missing the Point about State Takeover Statutes. *Mich. Law Rev.*, February 1989, *87*(4), pp. 846–57.

Mills, David E. Is Zoning a Negative-Sum Game? *Land Econ.*, February 1989, *65*(1), pp. 1–12.

Mills, Edwin S. Social Returns to Housing and Other Fixed Capital. *Amer. Real Estate Urban Econ. Assoc. J.*, Summer 1989, *17*(2), pp. 197–211.

——— and Carlino, Gerald. Dynamics of County Growth. In *Andersson, Å. E., et al., eds.*, 1989, pp. 195–205.

——— and Follain, James R. Interactions between Finance and Urban Development.

Amer. Real Estate Urban Econ. Assoc. J., Summer 1989, *17*(2), pp. 137–41.

Mills, G. E. Privatisation in Jamaica, Trinidad and Tobago. In *Ramanadham, V. V., ed.*, 1989, pp. 378–401.

Mills, Gordon. The Reform of Australian Aviation. *J. Transp. Econ. Policy*, May 1989, *23*(2), pp. 209–18.

Mills, Terence C. Four Paradoxes in U.K. GDP. *Econ. Letters*, October 1989, *30*(4), pp. 287–90.

_____; **Crafts, Nick F. R. and Leybourne, S. J.** The Climacteric in Late Victorian Britain and France: A Reappraisal of the Evidence. *J. Appl. Econometrics*, April–June 1989, *4*(2), pp. 103–17.

_____; **Crafts, Nick F. R. and Leybourne, S. J.** Trends and Cycles in British Industrial Production, 1700–1913. *J. Roy. Statist. Society*, 1989, *152*(1), pp. 43–60.

_____ **and Taylor, Mark P.** Random Walk Components in Output and Exchange Rates: Some Robust Tests on UK Data. *Bull. Econ. Res.*, April 1989, *41*(2), pp. 123–35.

Millstone, Erik. The Regulatory Environment: Science and Politics in the Control of a Technology. In *Sharp, M. and Holmes, P., eds.*, 1989, pp. 186–211.

Milne, Frank and Cornes, Richard. A Simple Analysis of Mutually Disadvantageous Trading Opportunities. *Econ. Stud. Quart.*, June 1989, *40*(2), pp. 122–34.

_____; **Shefrin, Hersh and Madan, Dilip B.** The Multinomial Option Pricing Model and Its Brownian and Poisson Limits. *Rev. Financial Stud.*, 1989, *2*(2), pp. 251–65.

Milne, William J. and Foot, David K. Multiregional Estimation of Gross Internal Migration Flows. *Int. Reg. Sci. Rev.*, 1989, *12*(1), pp. 29–43.

Milner, Chris. Harry G. Johnson, 1923–77. In *Greenaway, D. and Presley, J. R., eds.*, 1989, pp. 170–210.

_____. True Protection in "Capital-Rich" and "Capital-Poor" Developing Countries: Some Policy Implications. *J. Econ. Stud.*, 1989, *16*(4), pp. 5–22.

_____ **and Greenaway, David.** Effective Protection Analysis and Optimal Trade Policy with Intra-industry Specialisation and Imperfect Competition. In *Tharakan, P. K. M. and Kol, J., eds.*, 1989, pp. 145–62.

_____ **and Greenaway, David.** Nominal and Effective Tariffs in a Small Industrializing Economy: The Case of Mauritius. *Appl. Econ.*, August 1989, *21*(8), pp. 995–1009.

Milner, Helen V. and Yoffie, David B. Between Free Trade and Protectionism: Strategic Trade Policy and a Theory of Corporate Trade Demands. *Int. Organ.*, Spring 1989, *43*(2), pp. 239–72.

Milon, J. Walter. Contingent Valuation Experiments for Strategic Behavior. *J. Environ. Econ. Manage.*, November 1989, *17*(3), pp. 293–308.

Milot, Jean-Paul; Teillet, Pierre and Vanoli, André. How to Treat Non-produced Assets and Exceptional Events in the National Accounts? Considerations on the Variations in Wealth Accounting. *Rev. Income Wealth*, June 1989, *35*(2), pp. 163–86.

Milstein, Mikhail. Nuclear Forces and Their Relation to Conventional Armaments. In *Rotblat, J. and Goldanskii, V. I., eds.*, 1989, pp. 79–85.

Milward, Alan S. Motives for Currency Convertibility: The Pound and the Deutschmark, 1950–5. In *[Fischer, W.]*, 1989, pp. 260–84.

Mims, Anne M.; Duffy, Patricia A. and Young, George. Effects of Alternative Acreage Restriction Provisions on Alabama Cotton Farms. *Southern J. Agr. Econ.*, December 1989, *21*(2), pp. 85–94.

Minali, Alberto. La derivazione assiomatica delle misure di povertà: Un esame critico della letteratura degli ultimi vent'anni. (The Axiomatic Derivation of Poverty Measures: A Critical Analysis of the Literature over the Past Twenty Years. With English summary.) *Giorn. Econ.*, May–June 1989, *48*(5–6), pp. 253–74.

Minarik, Joseph J. How Tax Reform Came About. In *Colander, D. C. and Coats, A. W., eds.*, 1989, pp. 141–54.

Minato, Tetsuo. A Comparison of Japanese and American Interfirm Production Systems. In *Hayashi, K., ed.*, 1989, pp. 87–122.

Mincer, Jacob. Models of Man in Industrial Relations Research: Discussion. *Ind. Lab. Relat. Rev.*, October 1989, *43*(1), pp. 92–93.

Miner, Jerry. The Reagan Deficit. *Public Budg. Finance*, Spring 1989, *9*(1), pp. 15–32.

Miner, John B.; Wachtel, Jeffrey M. and Ebrahimi, Bahman. The Managerial Motivation of Potential Managers in the United States and Other Countries of the World: Implications for National Competitiveness and the Productivity Problem. In *Prasad, S. B., ed.*, 1989, pp. 147–70.

Miner, William M. Implications of GATT for World Agriculture. In *Helmuth, J. W. and Johnson, S. R., eds., Vol. 2*, 1989, pp. 313–24.

_____. Policy Options for Improving the Functioning of the World Food Production and Distribution Systems: Reaction. In *Helmuth, J. W. and Johnson, S. R., eds., Vol. 1*, 1989, pp. 237–39.

Minford, Patrick. Do Floating Exchange Rates Insulate? In *MacDonald, R. and Taylor, M. P., eds.*, 1989, pp. 275–94.

_____. Europe and the Supply Side. In *Fels, G. and von Furstenberg, G. M., eds.*, 1989, pp. 47–71.

_____. Exchange-Rate Regimes and Policy Coordination. In *Miller, M.; Eichengreen, B. and Portes, R., eds.*, 1989, pp. 207–35.

_____. Housing, Wages and UK Labour Markets: Comments. *Oxford Bull. Econ. Statist.*, March 1989, *51*(2), pp. 150–53.

_____. Implications of Policy Rules for the World Economy: Comment. In *Bryant, R. C., et al., eds.*, 1989, pp. 195–97.

_____. International Coordination of Fiscal Policies: Current and Future Issues: Comment. In *Monti, M., ed.*, 1989, pp. 46–49.

———. Ulysses and the Sirens: A Political Model of Credibility in an Open Economy. *Greek Econ. Rev.*, 1989, *11*(1), pp. 1–18.

——— and Canzoneri, Matthew B. Policy Interdependence: Does Strategic Behaviour Pay? An Empirical Investigation Using the Liverpool World Model. In *Hodgman, D. R. and Wood, G. E., eds.*, 1989, pp. 158–79.

——— and Walters, Alan. Modelling the Role of Government Deficits in Developing Countries. *Econ. Modelling*, April 1989, *6*(2), pp. 106–73.

Mingay, Gordon. Agricultural Productivity and Agricultural Society in Eighteenth-Century England. In *Grantham, G. and Leonard, C. S., eds., Pt. A*, 1989, pp. 31–47.

Mini, Peter V. An Early Statement of the Multiplier. *Economia (Portugal)*, May 1989, *13*(2), pp. 255–57.

Ministry of Public Enterprises. Privatisation in Malaysia. In *Ramanadham, V. V., ed.*, 1989, pp. 216–35.

Minkler, Alanson P. Property Rights, Efficiency and Labor-Managed Firms. *Ann. Pub. Coop. Econ.*, 1989, *60*(3), pp. 341–57.

Mino, Kazuo. Implications of Endogenous Money Supply Rules in Dynamic Models with Perfect Foresight. *J. Macroecon.*, Spring 1989, *11*(2), pp. 181–97.

———. Income Taxation and Endogenous Growth. *Econ. Letters*, December 1989, *31*(4), pp. 325–29.

Minsky, Hyman P. Can "It" Happen Again? A Reprise. In *Guttmann, R., ed.*, 1989, *1982*, pp. 121–28.

———. Economic Implications of Extraordinary Movements in Stock Prices: Comments. *Brookings Pap. Econ. Act.*, 1989, (2), pp. 173–82.

———. Financial Crises and the Evolution of Capitalism: The Crash of '87—What Does It Mean? In *Gottdiener, M. and Komninos, N., eds.*, 1989, pp. 391–403.

———. Financial Structures: Indebtedness and Credit. In *Barrère, A., ed.*, 1989, pp. 49–70.

———. The Macroeconomic Safety Net: Does It Need to Be Improved? In *Gray, H. P., ed.*, 1989, pp. 17–27.

———. Money and the Lender of Last Resort. In *Guttmann, R., ed.*, 1989, *1985*, pp. 74–80.

Mintz, Alex and Steinberg, Gerald. Coping with Supplier Control: The Israeli Experience. In *Baek, K.-I.; McLaurin, R. D. and Moon, C., eds.*, 1989, pp. 137–51.

Mintz, Beth. The Capitalist Class: United States of America. In *Bottomore, T. and Brym, R. J., eds.*, 1989, pp. 207–36.

——— and Johnsen, Eugene. Organizational versus Class Components of Director Networks. In *Perrucci, R. and Potter, H. R., eds.*, 1989, pp. 57–80.

Mintz, Jack M. and Jog, Vijay M. Business Tax Expenditure Accounts: Their Purpose and Measurement. In *Bruce, N., ed.*, 1989, pp. 181–225.

——— and Jog, Vijay M. Corporate Tax Reform and Its Economic Impact: An Evaluation of the Phase 1 Proposals. In *Mintz, J. and Whalley, J., eds.*, 1989, pp. 83–124.

Mirakhor, Abbas and Khan, Mohsin S. The Financial System and Monetary Policy in an Islamic Economy. *J. King Abdulaziz Univ.: Islamic Econ.*, 1989, *1*, pp. 39–58.

Miranda Gutiérrez, Guido. Health as an Economic Value in a Time of Crisis: Commentary. In *WHO, Pan American Health Organization*, 1989, pp. 188–91.

Miranda, Mario; Glauber, Joseph and Helmberger, Peter. Four Approaches to Commodity Market Stabilization: A Comparative Analysis. *Amer. J. Agr. Econ.*, May 1989, *71*(2), pp. 326–37.

Miranda, Vladimiro and Matos, Manuel A. C. C. A Holistic Approach in Multicriteria Decision Aid. In *Lockett, A. G. and Islei, G., eds.*, 1989, pp. 34–45.

Miranowski, John A. and Dinan, Terry M. Estimating the Implicit Price of Energy Efficiency Improvements in the Residential Housing Market: A Hedonic Approach. *J. Urban Econ.*, January 1989, *25*(1), pp. 52–67.

Miranti, Paul J., Jr. The Mind's Eye of Reform: The ICC's Bureau of Statistics and Accounts and a Vision of Regulation, 1887–1940. *Bus. Hist. Rev.*, Autumn 1989, *63*(3), pp. 469–509.

Mirman, Leonard J. and Samuelson, Larry. Information and Equilibrium with Inside Traders. *Econ. J.*, Supplement, 1989, *99*(395), pp. 152–67.

Miron, J. R. Household Formation, Affordability, and Housing Policy. *Population Res. Policy Rev.*, January 1989, *8*(1), pp. 55–77.

Miron, Jeffrey A. The Founding of the Fed and the Destabilization of the Post-1914 U.S. Economy. In *De Cecco, M. and Giovannini, A., eds.*, 1989, pp. 290–328.

——— and Barsky, Robert B. The Seasonal Cycle and the Business Cycle. *J. Polit. Econ.*, June 1989, *97*(3), pp. 503–34.

———; Wilcox, David W. and English, William B. Seasonal Fluctuations and the Life Cycle–Permanent Income Model of Consumption: A Correction. *J. Polit. Econ.*, August 1989, *97*(4), pp. 988–91.

——— and Zeldes, Stephen P. Production, Sales, and the Change in Inventories: An Identity That Doesn't Add Up. *J. Monet. Econ.*, July 1989, *24*(1), pp. 31–51.

——— and Zeldes, Stephen P. Seasonality, Cost Shocks, and the Production Smoothing Model of Inventories. In *Kollintzas, T., ed.*, 1989, pp. 199–244.

Mirowski, Philip. The Measurement without Theory Controversy: Defeating Rival Research Programs by Accusing Them of Naive Empiricism. *Écon. Societes*, June 1989, *23*(6), pp. 65–87.

———. The Probabilistic Counter-Revolution, or How Stochastic Concepts Came to Neoclassical Economic Theory. *Oxford Econ. Pap.*, January 1989, *41*(1), pp. 217–35.

_____. The Probabilistic Counter-revolution, or How Stochastic Concepts Came to Neoclassical Economic Theory. In *de Marchi, N. and Gilbert, C., eds.*, 1989, pp. 217–235.

_____. The Rise and Fall of the Concept of Equilibrium in Economic Analysis. *Rech. Écon. Louvain*, 1989, 55(4), pp. 447–68.

_____. 'Substantive Identity' of Classical and Neoclassical Economics: Reply. *Cambridge J. Econ.*, September 1989, 13(3), pp. 471–77.

_____. 'Tis a Pity Econometrics Isn't an Empirical Endeavor: Mandelbrot, Chaos, and the Noah and Joseph Effects. *Ricerche Econ.*, Jan.–June 1989, 43(1–2), pp. 76–99.

_____ and Helper, Susan. Maquiladoras: Mexico's Tiger by the Tail? *Challenge*, May–June 1989, 32(3), pp. 24–30.

Mirrlees, James A. Migration and Optimal Income Taxes. In *Bhagwati, J. N. and Wilson, J. D., eds.*, 1989, 1982, pp. 179–200.

Mirus, Rolf and Smith, Roger S. Canada's Underground Economy. In *Feige, E. L., ed.*, 1989, pp. 267–80.

_____ and Yeung, Bernard. Exchange Rate Behaviour: Theory and Managerial Implications. In *Rugman, A. M., ed.*, 1989, pp. 270–90.

Mishel, Lawrence R. The Late Great Debate on Deindustrialization. *Challenge*, Jan.–Feb. 1989, 32(1), pp. 35–43.

Mishkin, Frederic S. Econometric Tests of Rationality and Market Efficiency: A Comment. *Econometric Rev.*, 1989, 8(2), pp. 197–200.

Mishra, R. K. Performance of Public Enterprises in Seventh Five-Year Plan. In *Reddy, J. M., et al., eds. (II)*, 1989, pp. 101–11.

Misiolek, Walter S. and Elder, Harold W. Exclusionary Manipulation of Markets for Pollution Rights. *J. Environ. Econ. Manage.*, March 1989, 16(2), pp. 156–66.

Misra, Lalatendu and Gupta, Atul. Public Information and Pre-announcement Trading in Takeover Stocks. *J. Econ. Bus.*, August 1989, 41(3), pp. 225–33.

Misra, R. K. and Reddy, G. Pakki. Surplus Generation by Public Enterprises for the Financing of Seventh Plan: A Case of State Level Public Enterprises of Andhra Pradesh. In *Reddy, J. M., et al., eds. (I)*, 1989, pp. 125–37.

Missler-Behr, Magdalena and Opitz, Otto. Identification of Multiple Criteria Decision Making. In *Opitz, O., ed.*, 1989, pp. 407–15.

Mistri, Maurizio. Sull'esistenza di un equilibrio temporaneo concorrenziale del consumatore in mercato aperto. (The Existence of a Consumer's Competitive Temporary General Equilibrium in an Open Market. (With English summary.) *Rivista Int. Sci. Econ. Com.*, September 1989, 36(9), pp. 823–35.

Mitchell, Andrew A. and Berger, Ida E. The Effect of Advertising on Attitude Accessibility, Attitude Confidence, and the Attitude–Behavior Relationship. *J. Cons. Res.*, December 1989, 16(3), pp. 269–79.

Mitchell, Claire J. A. The Arts and Employment: The Impact of Three Canadian Theatre Compa-

nies. *J. Cult. Econ.*, December 1989, 13(2), pp. 69–79.

_____ and Wall, Geoffrey. The Arts and Employment: A Case Study of the Stratford Festival. *Growth Change*, Fall 1989, 20(4), pp. 31–40.

Mitchell, Daniel J. Stemming the Flow of Red Ink: How to Stop the Federal Spending Crisis. In *Crane, E. H. and Boaz, D.*, 1989, pp. 13–29.

Mitchell, Daniel J. B. Wage Pressures and Labor Shortages: The 1960s and 1980s. *Brookings Pap. Econ. Act.*, 1989, (2), pp. 191–231.

Mitchell, Douglas W. The Marriage Tax Penalty and Subsidy under Tax Reform. *Eastern Econ. J.*, April–June 1989, 15(2), pp. 113–16.

_____ and Gelles, Gregory M. An Approximation Theorem for the Polynomial Inverse Lag. *Econ. Letters*, August 1989, 30(2), pp. 129–32.

_____; Gelles, Gregory M. and Speaker, Paul J. Geometric Combination Lags as Flexible Infinite Distributed Lag Estimators. *J. Econ. Dynam. Control*, April 1989, 13(2), pp. 171–85.

Mitchell, Janet. Credit Rationing, Budget Constraints, and Salaries in Yugoslav Firms. *J. Compar. Econ.*, June 1989, 13(2), pp. 254–80.

Mitchell, Janet B. and Rosenbach, Margo L. Feasibility of Case-Based Payment for Inpatient Radiology, Anesthesia, and Pathology Services. *Inquiry*, Winter 1989, 26(4), pp. 457–67.

Mitchell, Jean M. and Anderson, Kathryn H. Mental Health and the Labor Force Participation of Older Workers. *Inquiry*, Summer 1989, 26(2), pp. 262–71.

Mitchell, John E. and Todd, Michael J. On the Relationship between the Search Directions in the Affine and Projective Variants of Karmarkar's Linear Programming Algorithm. In *Cornet, B. and Tulkens, H., eds.*, 1989, pp. 237–50.

Mitchell, Julian. The Myth and the Man. In *[Stone, L.]*, 1989, pp. 3–7.

Mitchell, Karlyn. Interest Rate Risk at Commercial Banks: An Empirical Investigation. *Financial Rev.*, August 1989, 24(3), pp. 431–55.

Mitchell, Kenneth H. and Wasil, Edward A. AHP in Practice: Applications and Observations from a Management Consulting Perspective. In *Golden, B. L.; Wasil, E. A. and Harker, P. T., eds.*, 1989, pp. 192–212.

Mitchell, Mark L. The Impact of External Parties on Brand-Name Capital: The 1982 Tylenol Poisonings and Subsequent Cases. *Econ. Inquiry*, October 1989, 27(4), pp. 601–18.

_____ and Maloney, Michael T. Crisis in the Cockpit? The Role of Market Forces in Promoting Air Travel Safety. *J. Law Econ.*, Part 1, October 1989, 32(2), pp. 329–55.

_____ and Mulherin, J. Harold. Pensions and Mergers. In *Turner, J. A. and Beller, D. J., eds.*, 1989, pp. 211–34.

_____ and Netter, Jeffry M. Triggering the 1987 Stock Market Crash: Antitakeover Provisions in the Proposed House Ways and Means Tax

Bill? *J. Finan. Econ.*, September 1989, *24*(1), pp. 37–68.

Mitchell, Neil J. and McCormick, James M. Human Rights and Foreign Assistance: An Update. *Soc. Sci. Quart.*, December 1989, *70*(4), pp. 969–79.

Mitchell, Olivia S. and Luzadis, Rebecca A. Pension Responses to Changes in Social Security. *Soc. Sec. Bull.*, August 1989, *52*(8), pp. 12–13.

Mitchell, Thomas M. and Färe, Rolf. A Family Tree of Linearly Homogeneous Production Functions. *Scand. J. Econ.*, 1989, *91*(4), pp. 749–57.

_____ **and Sato, Ryuzo.** The Economics of Technical Progress. *Eastern Econ. J.*, Oct.–Dec. 1989, *15*(4), pp. 309–36.

Mitchell, William C. Chicago Political Economy: A Public Choice Perspective. *Public Choice,* December 1989, *63*(3), pp. 283–92.

_____. More on Military 'Tactics.' *J. Econ. Behav. Organ.*, March 1989, *11*(2), pp. 293–96.

_____. The Calculus of Consent: Enduring Contributions to Public Choice and Political Science. *Public Choice,* March 1989, *60*(3), pp. 201–10.

Mitra, Pradeep K.; Harris, Christopher J. and Heady, Christopher J. Investment and Shadow Pricing in a Growing Economy with Tax Restrictions. *J. Public Econ.*, August 1989, *39*(3), pp. 289–313.

Mitra, Saumya and Husain, Ishrat. Future Financing Needs of the Highly Indebted Countries. In *Husain, I. and Diwan, I., eds.*, 1989, pp. 199–209.

Mitra, Tapan and Dutta, Prajit K. Maximum Theorems for Convex Structures with an Application to the Theory of Optimal Intertemporal Allocation. *J. Math. Econ.*, 1989, *18*(1), pp. 77–86.

_____ **and Dutta, Prajit K.** On Continuity of the Utility Function in Intertemporal Allocation Models: An Example. *Int. Econ. Rev.*, August 1989, *30*(3), pp. 527–36.

_____; **Nyarko, Yaw and Majumdar, Mukul.** Dynamic Optimization under Uncertainty: Nonconvex Feasible Set. In *Feiwel, G. R., ed. (II)*, 1989, pp. 545–90.

Mitroff, Ian I.; Cummings, Thomas G. and Mohrman, Allan M., Jr. The Actors in Large-Scale Organizational Change. In *Mohrman, A. M., Jr., et al.*, 1989, pp. 91–99.

Mitrusi, Andrew W.; Bolster, Paul J. and Lindsey, Lawrence B. Tax-Induced Trading: The Effect of the 1986 Tax Reform Act on Stock Market Activity. *J. Finance,* June 1989, *44*(2), pp. 327–44.

Mitsugi, Mamoru. Technological Development in Japan: Information Processing R&D. In *Matsuo, H., ed.*, 1989, pp. 4–24.

Mitsui, Toshihide and Watanabe, Shinichi. Monetary Growth in a Turnpike Environment. *J. Monet. Econ.*, July 1989, *24*(1), pp. 123–37.

Mittal, Banwari and Lee, Myung-Soo. A Causal Model of Consumer Involvement. *J. Econ. Psych.*, November 1989, *10*(3), pp. 363–89.

Mittelstaedt, H. Fred. An Empirical Analysis of the Factors Underlying the Decision to Remove Excess Assets from Overfunded Pension Plans. *J. Acc. Econ.*, November 1989, *11*(4), pp. 399–418.

_____; **Yardley, James A. and Callaghan, Joseph H.** Auditors' Incompatible Economic Incentives. In *Gangolly, J., ed.*, 1989, pp. 57–64.

Mixon, J. Wilson, Jr.; Kyer, Ben L. and Uri, Noel D. An Analysis of the Automatic Stabilizers Associated with Taxes and Transfer Payments. *Int. Rev. Applied Econ.*, January 1989, *3*(1), pp. 46–56.

_____; **Kyer, Ben L. and Uri, Noel D.** Automatic Stabilizers Reconsidered. *Public Finance,* 1989, *44*(3), pp. 476–91.

Miyagiwa, Kaz. Human Capital and Economic Growth in a Minimum-Wage Economy. *Int. Econ. Rev.*, February 1989, *30*(1), pp. 187–202.

Miyatake, Toshio and Kaneko, Hiroshi. The Disregard of a Legal Entity for Tax Purposes: Japan. In *International Fiscal Association, ed. (II)*, 1989, pp. 355–62.

Mizoguchi, Toshiyuki; Wang, Hui-Ling and Matsuda, Yoshiro. A Comparison of Real Consumption Level between Japan and People's Republic of China—The First Approach of Application of ICP Method to Chinese Data. *Hitotsubashi J. Econ.*, June 1989, *30*(1), pp. 15–29.

Mizon, Grayham E. The Role of Econometric Modelling in Economic Analysis. *Revista Española Econ.*, 1989, *6*(1–2), pp. 165–91.

_____ **and Anderson, Gordon J.** What Can Statistics Contribute to the Analysis of Economic Structural Change? In *Hackl, P., ed.*, 1989, pp. 3–21.

_____ **and Hylleberg, Svend.** Cointegration and Error Correction Mechanisms. *Econ. J.*, Supplement, 1989, *99*(395), pp. 113–25.

_____ **and Hylleberg, Svend.** A Note on the Distribution of the Least Squares Estimator of a Random Walk with Drift. *Econ. Letters,* 1989, *29*(3), pp. 225–30.

_____; **Schmidt, Peter and Breusch, Trevor S.** Efficient Estimation Using Panel Data. *Econometrica,* May 1989, *57*(3), pp. 695–700.

Mizruchi, Mark S. and Bunting, David. The Transfer of Control in Large Corporations: 1905–1919. In *Tool, M. R. and Samuels, W. J., eds. (I)*, 1989, *1982*, pp. 263–81.

Mizuno, H. and Allen, D. E. The Determinants of Corporate Capital Structure: Japanese Evidence. *Appl. Econ.*, May 1989, *21*(5), pp. 569–85.

Mizuno, Masaichi. The Economic Consequences of Government Deficit—The Japanese Case. In *Dams, T. and Matsugi, T., eds.*, 1989, pp. 247–74.

Mjelde, James W.; Dixon, Bruce L. and Sonka, Steven T. Estimating the Value of Sequential Updating Solutions for Intrayear Crop Management. *Western J. Agr. Econ.*, July 1989, *14*(1), pp. 1–8.

_____; **McCarl, Bruce A. and Dillon, Carl R.** Biophysical Simulation in Support of Crop Production Decisions: A Case Study in the Black-lands Region of Texas. *Southern J. Agr. Econ.*, July 1989, *21*(1), pp. 73–86.

_____ and Paggi, Mechel S. An Empirical Analysis of Interregional Price Linkages. *J. Reg. Sci.*, May 1989, *29*(2), pp. 171–89.

Mládek, Jan. Selected Problems of Modelling Consumption in a CPE: The Case of Czechoslovakia 1955–1986. *Jahr. Wirtsch. Osteuropas*, 1989, *13*(2), pp. 195–205.

Mladenka, Kenneth R. Barriers to Hispanic Employment Success in 1,200 Cities. *Soc. Sci. Quart.*, June 1989, *70*(2), pp. 391–407.

Moazzami, B. and Gupta, Kanhaya L. Demand for Money in Asia. *Econ. Modelling*, October 1989, *6*(4), pp. 467–73.

Moberg, Claes and Brege, Staffan. Price Policies and Relationship Stability after a Devaluation. In *Hallén, L. and Johanson, J., eds.*, 1989, pp. 37–55.

Mocan, Naci H. On the Mutual Causalities between Age at Marriage and Divorce. *Atlantic Econ. J.*, March 1989, *17*(1), pp. 94.

Mochizuki, Kiichi. Preconsideration of Policy Model of the Soviet Economy. In *Berliner, J. S.; Kosta, H. G. J. and Hakogi, M., eds.*, 1989, pp. 79–84.

Mock, Theodore J. and Washington, Mary T. Risk Concepts and Risk Assessment in Auditing. In *Gangolly, J., ed.*, 1989, pp. 105–17.

Mockers, J.-P. La conjoncture de crise, les effets pervers des politiques de rigueur et la remise en cause des idées reçues sur certains mécanismes macro-économiques. (The Crisis Conjuncture and the Perverse Effects of the "Stabilization" Policies. With English summary.) *Écon. Societes*, March 1989, *23*(3), pp. 143–78.

Modesto, Leonor. Testing the Rationality of Expectations Using Aggregate Data. *Economia (Portugal)*, October 1989, *13*(3), pp. 303–34.

Modiano, Eduardo Marco. A Short-Run Model of a Semi-industrialised Economy. In *Chakravarty, S., ed.*, 1989, pp. 63–93.

Modica, Salvatore. Business Cycles in Equilibrium: An Example. In *Hahn, F., ed.*, 1989, pp. 452–67.

Modigliani, Andre and Modigliani, Franco. The Growth of the Federal Deficit and the Role of Public Attitudes. In *Modigliani, F., Vol. 5*, 1989, *1987*, pp. 160–81.

Modigliani, Franco. Argentine Economic Policy, 1976–81: Comment. In *di Tella, G. and Dornbusch, R., eds.*, 1989, pp. 276–85.

_____. Comment [Where Have All the Flowers Gone? Economic Growth in the 1960s]. In *Modigliani, F., Vol. 4*, 1989, *1982*, pp. 243–52.

_____. Debt, Dividend Policy, Taxes, Inflation, and Market Valuation: Erratum. In *Modigliani, F., Vol. 5*, 1989, pp. 412–13.

_____. Debt, Dividend Policy, Taxes, Inflation and Market Valuation. In *Modigliani, F., Vol. 5*, 1989, *1982*, pp. 393–411.

_____. The Economics of Public Deficits. In *Modigliani, F., Vol. 5*, 1989, *1987*, pp. 104–46.

_____. Financial Markets. In *Modigliani, F., Vol. 5*, 1989, pp. 325–30.

_____. Government Deficits, Inflation, and Future Generations. In *Modigliani, F., Vol. 5*, 1989, *1983*, pp. 87–103.

_____. The Inflation-Proof Mortgage: The Mortgage for the Young. In *Modigliani, F., Vol. 5*, 1989, pp. 350–68.

_____. Life Cycle, Individual Thrift and the Wealth of Nations. In *Modigliani, F., Vol. 5*, 1989, *1986*, pp. 35–57.

_____. MM—Past, Present, Future. In *Modigliani, F., Vol. 5*, 1989, *1988*, pp. 443–58.

_____. The Monetarist Controversy Revisited. In *Modigliani, F., Vol. 4*, 1989, *1988*, pp. 136–51.

_____. Reagan's Economic Policies: A Critique. In *Modigliani, F., Vol. 4*, 1989, *1988*, pp. 326–55.

_____. The Role of Intergenerational Transfers and Life Cycle Saving in the Accumulation of Wealth. In *Modigliani, F., Vol. 5*, 1989, *1988*, pp. 58–83.

_____. Some Currently Suggested Explanations and Cures for Inflation: A Comment. In *Modigliani, F., Vol. 5*, 1989, *1976*, pp. 274–79.

_____. World Economic Outlook and Its Implications for Italy. In *Modigliani, F., Vol. 4*, 1989, *1988*, pp. 356–62.

_____ and Cohn, Richard A. Inflation and Corporate Financial Management. In *Modigliani, F., Vol. 5*, 1989, *1985*, pp. 414–42.

_____ and Cohn, Richard A. Inflation and the Stock Market. In *Modigliani, F., Vol. 5*, 1989, *1982*, pp. 331–49.

_____ and Cohn, Richard A. Inflation, Rational Valuation and the Market. In *Modigliani, F., Vol. 5*, 1989, *1979*, pp. 304–24.

_____ and Drèze, Jacques H. The Trade-Off between Real Wages and Employment in an Open Economy (Belgium). In *Modigliani, F., Vol. 4*, 1989, *1981*, pp. 202–42.

_____ and Fischer, Stanley. Towards an Understanding of the Real Effects and Costs of Inflation. In *Modigliani, F., Vol. 5*, 1989, *1978*, pp. 280–303.

_____ and Jappelli, Tullio. The Determinants of Interest Rates in the Italian Economy. In *Modigliani, F., Vol. 5*, 1989, *1988*, pp. 228–53.

_____ and Jappelli, Tullio. Fiscal Policy and Saving in Italy since 1860. In *Modigliani, F., Vol. 5*, 1989, *1987*, pp. 182–227.

_____; Jappelli, Tullio and Pagano, Marco. The Impact of Fiscal Policy and Inflation on National Saving: A Reply. *Banca Naz. Lavoro Quart. Rev.*, June 1989, (169), pp. 239–44.

_____ and Lessard, Donald R. Inflation and the Housing Market: Problems and Potential Solutions. In *Modigliani, F., Vol. 5*, 1989, *1975*, pp. 257–73.

_____ and Modigliani, Andre. The Growth of the Federal Deficit and the Role of Public Attitudes. In *Modigliani, F., Vol. 5*, 1989, *1987*, pp. 160–81.

_____; Padoa Schioppa, Fiorella and Rossi, Nicola. Aggregate Unemployment in Italy, 1960–1983. In *Modigliani, F., Vol. 4, 1989, 1986,* pp. 253–87.

_____ **and Papademos, Lucas.** Inflation, Financial and Fiscal Structure, and the Monetary Mechanism. In *Modigliani, F., Vol. 4, 1989, 1983,* pp. 48–95.

_____ **and Papademos, Lucas.** Money, Credit and the Monetary Mechanism. In *Modigliani, F., Vol. 4, 1989, 1987,* pp. 96–135.

_____ **and Papademos, Lucas.** Optimal Demand Policies against Stagflation. In *Modigliani, F., Vol. 4, 1989, 1978,* pp. 155–201.

_____ **and Papademos, Lucas.** The Structure of Financial Markets and the Monetary Mechanism. In *Modigliani, F., Vol. 4, 1989, 1980,* pp. 3–47.

_____ **and Shiller, Robert J.** Coupon and Tax Effects on New and Seasoned Bond Yields and the Measurement of the Cost of Debt Capital. In *Modigliani, F., Vol. 5, 1989, 1979,* pp. 371–92.

_____ **and Sterling, Arlie.** Determinants of Private Saving with Special Reference to the Role of Social Security—Cross-Country Tests. In *Modigliani, F., Vol. 5, 1989, 1983,* pp. 3–34.

_____ **and Sterling, Arlie.** Government Debt, Government Spending and Private Sector Behavior: Comment. In *Modigliani, F., Vol. 5, 1989, 1986,* pp. 147–59.

_____, **et al.** Reducing Unemployment in Europe: The Role of Capital Formation. In *Modigliani, F., Vol. 4, 1989, 1986,* pp. 288–325.

Mody, Ashoka. Information Industries in the Newly Industrializing Countries. In *Crandall, R. W. and Flamm, K., eds.,* 1989, pp. 298–327.

Moe, Terry M. The Politics of Bureaucratic Structure. In *Chubb, J. E. and Peterson, P. E., eds.,* 1989, pp. 267–329.

Moeckel, Cindy L. and Plumlee, R. David. Auditors' Confidence in Recognition of Audit Evidence. *Accounting Rev.,* October 1989, *64*(4), pp. 653–66.

Moen, Jon R. Poverty in the South. *Fed. Res. Bank Atlanta Econ. Rev.,* Jan.–Feb. 1989, *74*(1), pp. 36–46.

Moene, Karl Ove. A Note on Mechanization and Wage Bargaining. *Econ. Letters,* 1989, *29*(4), pp. 379–81.

van **Moeseke, Paul.** Modèle et revenu éthonomiques. (With English summary.) *Kyklos,* 1989, *42*(3), pp. 347–59.

Moesel, Douglas; Schatzer, Raymond Joe and Tilley, Daniel S. Consumer Expenditures at Direct Produce Markets. *Southern J. Agr. Econ.,* July 1989, *21*(1), pp. 131–38.

Moffett, Michael H. The *J*-Curve Revisited: An Empirical Examination for the United States. *J. Int. Money Finance,* September 1989, *8*(3), pp. 425–44.

Moffitt, Michael. Shocks, Deadlocks, and Scorched Earth: Reaganomics and the Decline of U.S. Hegemony. In *Martin, M. T. and Kandal, T. R., eds.,* 1989, pp. 418–51.

Moffitt, Robert. Choosing among Alternative Nonexperimental Methods for Estimating the Impact of Social Programs: The Case of Manpower Training: Comment. *J. Amer. Statist. Assoc.,* December 1989, *84*(408), pp. 877–78.

_____. Estimating the Value of an In-Kind Transfer: The Case of Food Stamps. *Econometrica,* March 1989, *57*(2), pp. 385–409.

_____ **and Rangarajan, Anuradha.** The Effect of Transfer Programmes on Work Effort and Human Capital Formation: Evidence from the U.S. In *Dilnot, A. and Walker, I., eds.,* 1989, pp. 116–36.

Moggridge, D. E. The Gold Standard and National Financial Policies, 1919–39. In *Mathias, P. and Pollard, S., eds.,* 1989, pp. 250–314.

Moghaddam, M. Real Business Cycles—An Inquiry. In *Missouri Valley Economic Association,* 1989, pp. 92–97.

Moghaddam S., M. B. Allocation of Growth of Demand for Energy between Its Sources. *Indian J. Quant. Econ.,* 1989, *5*(1), pp. 35–45.

Mogridge, Martin J. H. The Prediction of Car Ownership and Use Revisited: The Beginning of the End? *J. Transp. Econ. Policy,* January 1989, *23*(1), pp. 55–74.

Mohamed, Nazeem Seyed; Johanson, Jan and Hallén, Lars. Relationships and Exchange in International Business. In *Hallén, L. and Johanson, J., eds.,* 1989, pp. 7–23.

Mohammad, Golam; Hoehn, John P. and Blaine, Thomas W. Probit Model Procedures to the Estimation of Probabilities: An Empirical Exposition to a Dichotomous Decision Model. *Can. J. Agr. Econ.,* Part 2, December 1989, *37*(4), pp. 1071–79.

Mohammed, Azizali F. Liberalization and Privatization: An Overview: Comment. In *El-Naggar, S., ed.,* 1989, pp. 42–44.

Mohan, John. Commercialisation and Centralisation: Towards a New Geography of Health Care. In *Mohan, J., ed.,* 1989, pp. 224–37.

Mohapatra, P. K. J. and Vizayakumar, K. An Approach to Environmental Impact Assessment by Using Cross Impact Simulation. *Environ. Planning A,* June 1989, *21*(6), pp. 831–37.

Mohr, Rosanne M. and Callahan, Carolyn M. The Determinants of Systematic Risk: A Synthesis. *Financial Rev.,* May 1989, *24*(2), pp. 157–81.

Mohrman, Allan M., Jr.; Ledford, Gerald E., Jr. and Mohrman, Susan Albers. Interventions That Change Organizations. In *Mohrman, A. M., Jr., et al.,* 1989, pp. 145–53.

_____; **Mitroff, Ian I. and Cummings, Thomas G.** The Actors in Large-Scale Organizational Change. In *Mohrman, A. M., Jr., et al.,* 1989, pp. 91–99.

_____ **and Mohrman, Susan Albers.** Changing the Organization through Time: A New Paradigm. In *Mohrman, A. M., Jr., et al.,* 1989, pp. 273–91.

_____ **and Mohrman, Susan Albers.** The Environment as an Agent of Change. In *Mohrman, A. M., Jr., et al.,* 1989, pp. 35–47.

———; **Mohrman, Susan Albers and Ledford, Gerald E., Jr.** What We Have Learned about Large-Scale Organizational Change: Conclusion. In *Mohrman, A. M., Jr., et al.*, 1989, pp. 292–302.

Mohrman, Susan Albers; Ledford, Gerald E., Jr. and Mohrman, Allan M., Jr. What We Have Learned about Large-Scale Organizational Change: Conclusion. In *Mohrman, A. M., Jr., et al.*, 1989, pp. 292–302.

——— **and Mohrman, Allan M., Jr.** Changing the Organization through Time: A New Paradigm. In *Mohrman, A. M., Jr., et al.*, 1989, pp. 273–91.

——— **and Mohrman, Allan M., Jr.** The Environment as an Agent of Change. In *Mohrman, A. M., Jr., et al.*, 1989, pp. 35–47.

———; **Mohrman, Allan M., Jr. and Ledford, Gerald E., Jr.** Interventions That Change Organizations. In *Mohrman, A. M., Jr., et al.*, 1989, pp. 145–53.

Mohtadi, Hamid. Migration and Job Search in a Dualistic Economy: A Todaro–Stigler Synthesis. *Econ. Letters*, 1989, *29*(4), pp. 373–78.

Mojtahed, Ahmad and Esfahani, Hadi S. Agricultural Policy and Performance in Iran: The Postrevolutionary Experience. *World Devel.*, June 1989, *17*(6), pp. 839–60.

Mok, Albert L. Sociology of Work and Redesign of Working Time. In *Agassi, J. B. and Heycock, S., eds.*, 1989, pp. 23–26.

Mokhtari, Manouchehr and Rassekh, Farhad. The Tendency towards Factor Price Equalization among OECD Countries. *Rev. Econ. Statist.*, November 1989, *71*(4), pp. 636–42.

Mol, A. P. J. and Opschoor, J. B. Developments in Economic Valuation of Environmental Resources in Centrally Planned Economies. *Environ. Planning A*, September 1989, *21*(9), pp. 1205–28.

Molana, Hassan H. Wealth Allocation, Capital Gains and Private Expenditure in the UK. *Scot. J. Polit. Econ.*, August 1989, *36*(3), pp. 209–37.

——— **and Vines, David.** North–South Growth and the Terms of Trade: A Model on Kaldorian Lines. *Econ. J.*, June 1989, *99*(396), pp. 443–53.

Moldovanu, B. A Note on a Theorem of Aumann and Dreze [Cooperative Games with Coalition Structures]. *Int. J. Game Theory*, 1989, *18*(4), pp. 471–76.

Molho, Ian. A Disaggregate Model of Flows onto Invalidity Benefit. *Appl. Econ.*, February 1989, *21*(2), pp. 237–50.

——— **and Waterson, Michael.** Modelling Supermarket Store Locations. *Scot. J. Polit. Econ.*, November 1989, *36*(4), pp. 375–84.

Molho, Lazoros E. European Financial Integration and Revenue from Seigniorage: The Case of Italy. *Giorn. Econ.*, Nov.–Dec. 1989, *48*(11–12), pp. 541–68.

Molina, Agustín; Sanchez, José and Dominguez, José M. El impuesto sobre el gasto personal: Algunas cuestiones básicas para el caso español.

(With English summary.) *Invest. Ecón.*, May 1989, *13*(2), pp. 269–81.

Molina, Ascensión and Argimón, Isabel. El impuesto sobre el matrimonio. (With English summary.) *Invest. Ecón.*, January 1989, *13*(1), pp. 67–83.

Molina, David J. and Nieswiadomy, Michael L. Comparing Residential Water Demand Estimates under Decreasing and Increasing Block Rates Using Household Data. *Land Econ.*, August 1989, *65*(3), pp. 280–89.

———; **Slottje, Daniel J. and Hirschberg, Joseph G.** Errata [A Selection Criterion for Choosing between Functional Forms of Income Distribution]. *Econometric Rev.*, 1989, *8*(2), pp. 227.

Molinas, César and Prados de la Escosura, Leandro. Was Spain Different? Spanish Historical Backwardness Revisited. *Exploration Econ. Hist.*, October 1989, *26*(4), pp. 385–402.

Moll, Peter G. The Rationality of Farm Size Growth: An Example from 'White' South Africa. *Europ. Rev. Agr. Econ.*, 1989, *16*(3), pp. 345–57.

Molle, Willem T. M.; Beumer, L. and Boeckhout, I. J. The Location of Information Intensive Economic Activities in the European Community. In *Punset, E. and Sweeney, G., eds.*, 1989, pp. 161–72.

——— **and van Mourik, Aad.** A Static Explanatory Model of International Labour Migration to and in Western Europe. In *Gordon, I. and Thirlwall, A. P., eds.*, 1989, pp. 30–52.

Möller, Carola. Flexibilisation: The Impoverishment of Employees, and the Reduction of Work Place Solidarity. In *Agassi, J. B. and Heycock, S., eds.*, 1989, pp. 114–28.

Møller, Michael and Nielsen, Niels Chr. Ejerskab, ledelse og incitamentsstrukturer. (The Interaction between Ownership, Management and Incentives. With English summary.) *Nationaløkon. Tidsskr.*, 1989, *127*(1), pp. 45–58.

Molnár, György and Halpern, László. Macro Features of the Hungarian Economy since 1970. *Econ. Systems Res.*, 1989, *1*(1), pp. 111–20.

Molnár, István; Boda, György and Koós Balsay, Éva. Compilation of Input–Output Tables in Hungary. In *Franz, A. and Rainer, N., eds.*, 1989, pp. 43–67.

Molnar, Joseph J. and Duffy, Patricia A. Attitudes toward Governmental Involvement in Agriculture: Results of a National Survey. *Southern J. Agr. Econ.*, July 1989, *21*(1), pp. 121–30.

Molyneux, Philip. 1992 and Its Impact on Local and Regional Banking Markets. *Reg. Stud.*, December 1989, *23*(6), pp. 523–33.

Momm, Willi and König, Andreas. Community Integration for Disabled People: A New Approach to Their Vocational Training and Employment. *Int. Lab. Rev.*, 1989, *128*(4), pp. 497–509.

Mommsen, Wolfgang J. The Antinomical Structure of Max Weber's Political Thought. In *Mommsen, W. J.*, 1989, 1983, pp. 24–43.

———. Capitalism and Socialism: Weber's Dialogue with Marx. In *Mommsen, W. J.*, 1989, *1985*, pp. 53–73.

_____. Ideal Type and Pure Type: Two Variants of Max Weber's Ideal-Typical Method. In *Mommsen, W. J.*, 1989, pp. 121–32.

_____. Joining the Underdogs? Weber's Critique of the Social Democrats in Wilhelmine Germany. In *Mommsen, W. J.*, 1989, pp. 74–86.

_____. Max Weber in Modern Social Thought. In *Mommsen, W. J.*, 1989, pp. 169–96.

_____. Max Weber on Bureaucracy and Bureaucratization: Threat to Liberty and Instrument of Creative Action. In *Mommsen, W. J.*, 1989, pp. 109–20.

_____. Max Weber's Theory of Legitimacy Today. In *Mommsen, W. J.*, 1989, pp. 44–49.

_____. Politics and Scholarship: The Two Icons in Max Weber's Life. In *Mommsen, W. J.*, 1989, pp. 3–23.

_____. Rationalization and Myth in Weber's Thought. In *Mommsen, W. J.*, 1989, *1983*, pp. 133–44.

_____. Roberto Michels and Max Weber: Moral Conviction versus the Politics of Responsibility. In *Mommsen, W. J.*, 1989, *1987*, pp. 87–105.

_____. The Two Dimensions of Social Change in Max Weber's Sociological Theory. In *Mommsen, W. J.*, 1989, pp. 145–65.

Momtaz, A. Research and Management Strategies for Increased Rice Production in Egypt. In *International Rice Research Institute*, 1989, pp. 55–69.

_____ **and Siddiq, E. A.** Extending Rice Cultivation to New Areas in Egypt. In *International Rice Research Institute*, 1989, pp. 275–90.

Monadjemi, Mehdi S. Fiscal Deficits and Interest Rates: A Multi-country Analysis. *Australian Econ. Pap.*, December 1989, *28*(53), pp. 209–18.

Moncomble, Jean-Eudes; Assouline, Mireille and Epaulard, Anne. Alignement des régimes de TVA français sur une norme européenne, l'analyse du modèle Hermès-France. (With English summary.) *Revue Écon. Politique*, May–June 1989, *99*(3), pp. 497–516.

Moncur, James E. T. and Pollock, Richard L. Scarcity Rents for Water: A Valuation and Pricing Model: Reply. *Land Econ.*, November 1989, *65*(4), pp. 425–28.

Mondal, Abdul Hye. Distribution of Yarn in the Handloom Sector of Bangladesh: A Further Study. *Bangladesh Devel. Stud.*, March–June 1989, *17*(1–2), pp. 101–29.

_____. The Pricing of Cotton Yarn in the Handloom Sector of Bangladesh. *Bangladesh Devel. Stud.*, March–June 1989, *17*(1–2), pp. 131–55.

Monderer, Dov. Weighted Majority Games Have Many μ-Values. *Int. J. Game Theory*, 1989, *18*(3), pp. 321–25.

_____ **and Samet, Dov.** Approximating Common Knowledge with Common Beliefs. *Games Econ. Behav.*, June 1989, *1*(2), pp. 170–90.

Mondor, R.; Flaten, D. and Evans, M. Expert Systems and Farm Management. *Can. J. Agr. Econ.*, Part 1, December 1989, *37*(4), pp. 639–66.

Moneta, Carlos Juan. Latin American Economic Relations with the United States and Japan. In *Naya, S., et al., eds.*, 1989, pp. 197–212.

Money, Arthur; Naude, Peter and Wegner, Trevor. A Comparison of Multi-attribute Utility Generation Methods. In *Lockett, A. G. and Islei, G., eds.*, 1989, pp. 46–57.

Monfort, Alan; Renault, Eric and Gourieroux, Christian. Testing for Common Roots. *Econometrica*, January 1989, *57*(1), pp. 171–85.

Mongin, P. and Coulhon, T. Social Choice Theory in the Case of von Neumann–Morgenstern Utilities. *Soc. Choice Welfare*, July 1989, *6*(3), pp. 175–87.

Mongiovi, Gary. The Role of Demand in the Classical Theory of Price. In *Walker, D. A., ed.*, 1989, pp. 114–30.

Mongkolsmai, Dow and Rosegrant, Mark W. The Effect of Irrigation on Seasonal Rice Prices, Farm Income, and Labor Demand in Thailand. In *Sahn, D. E., ed.*, 1989, pp. 246–63.

Monkiewicz, Grazyna and Monkiewicz, Jan. East–South Capital Cooperation: An Unexploited Possibility? In *Schulz, B. H. and Hansen, W. W., eds.*, 1989, pp. 137–51.

Monkiewicz, Jan. Western Direct Investment in the CMEA: An Instrument for Intensified Technology Inflow and Structural Adjustment? In *Wohlmuth, K., ed.*, 1989, pp. 403–36.

_____ **and Maciejewicz, Jan.** Services in the Socialist Countries of Eastern Europe. *Jahr. Wirtsch. Osteuropas*, 1989, *13*(2), pp. 167–93.

_____ **and Monkiewicz, Grazyna.** East–South Capital Cooperation: An Unexploited Possibility? In *Schulz, B. H. and Hansen, W. W., eds.*, 1989, pp. 137–51.

Monnier, Alain and Blum, Alain. Recent Mortality Trends in the U.S.S.R.: New Evidence. *Population Stud.*, July 1989, *43*(2), pp. 211–41.

Monroe, Margaret and Lauterbach, Beni. Evidence on the Effect of Information and Noise Trading on Intraday Gold Futures Returns. *J. Futures Markets*, August 1989, *9*(4), pp. 297–305.

Monson, Terry and Fitzgerald, Bruce. Preferential Credit and Insurance as Means to Promote Exports. *World Bank Res. Observer*, January 1989, *4*(1), pp. 89–114.

Montanari, Armando. Barcelona and Glasgow: The Similarities and Differences in the History of Two Port Cities. *J. Europ. Econ. Hist.*, Spring 1989, *18*(1), pp. 171–89.

de Montbrial, Thierry. France's Foreign Policy. In *Frankel, A. V. and Heck, C. B., eds.*, 1989, pp. 11–15.

Monteiro, P. K. and Araujo, A. Equilibrium without Uniform Conditions. *J. Econ. Theory*, August 1989, *48*(2), pp. 416–27.

van Montfort, Kees; Mooijaart, Ab and de Leeuw, Jan. Estimation of Regression Coefficients with the Help of Characteristic Functions. *J. Econometrics*, June 1989, *41*(2), pp. 267–78.

Montgomery, B. Ruth. The Influence of Attitudes and Normative Pressures on Voting Decisions in a Union Certification Election. *Ind. Lab. Relat. Rev.*, January 1989, *42*(2), pp. 263–79.

Montgomery, Edward. Employment and Unemployment Effects of Unions. *J. Lab. Econ.*, April 1989, *7*(2), pp. 170–90.

_____ **and Benedict, Mary Ellen.** The Impact of Bargainer Experience on Teacher Strikes. *Ind. Lab. Relat. Rev.*, April 1989, *42*(3), pp. 380–92.

Montgomery, Henry; Gärling, Tommy and Lindberg, Erik. Beliefs about Attainment of Life Satisfaction as Determinants of Preferences for Everyday Activities. **In** *Grunert, K. G. and Ölander, F., eds.*, 1989, pp. 33–46.

Montgomery, James F. Alternative Strategies for Success: Panel Presentation. **In** *Federal Home Loan Bank of San Francisco*, 1989, pp. 111–12.

Montgomery, Mark R. and Sulak, Donna B. Female First Marriage in East and Southeast Asia: A Kiefer–Neumann Model. *J. Devel. Econ.*, April 1989, *30*(2), pp. 225–40.

Monti, Mario. Fiscal Policy, Economic Adjustment, and Financial Markets: Concluding Remarks. **In** *Monti, M., ed.*, 1989, pp. 269–74.

Montias, John Michael. National Values and Economic Reforms in Socialist Economies. *World Devel.*, Special Issue, September 1989, *17*(9), pp. 1433–42.

Monticelli, Carlo. The Effects of Inflation on the Demand for Assets: A Dual Approach. *Rivista Int. Sci. Econ. Com.*, August 1989, *36*(8), pp. 747–66.

Montiel, Peter J. Empirical Analysis of High-Inflation Episodes in Argentina, Brazil, and Israel. *Int. Monet. Fund Staff Pap.*, September 1989, *36*(3), pp. 527–49.

_____ **and Edwards, Sebastian.** Devaluation Crises and the Macroeconomic Consequences of Postponed Adjustment in Developing Countries. *Int. Monet. Fund Staff Pap.*, December 1989, *36*(4), pp. 875–903.

_____ **and Edwards, Sebastian.** The Price of Postponed Adjustment. *Finance Devel.*, September 1989, *26*(3), pp. 34–37.

_____ **and Haque, Nadeem U.** Consumption in Developing Countries: Tests for Liquidity Constraints and Finite Horizons. *Rev. Econ. Statist.*, August 1989, *71*(3), pp. 408–15.

_____ **and Khan, Mohsin S.** Growth-Oriented Adjustment Programs: A Conceptual Framework. *Int. Monet. Fund Staff Pap.*, June 1989, *36*(2), pp. 279–306.

_____ **and Lizondo, José Saúl.** Contractionary Devaluation in Developing Countries: An Analytical Overview. *Int. Monet. Fund Staff Pap.*, March 1989, *36*(1), pp. 182–227.

Montmarquette, Claude. Political Economy of Tax Expenditures: Comment. **In** *Bruce, N., ed.*, 1989, pp. 419–22.

_____ **and Mahseredjian, Sophie.** Could Teacher Grading Practices Account for Unexplained Variation in School Achievements? *Econ. Educ. Rev.*, 1989, *8*(4), pp. 335–43.

_____ **and Mahseredjian, Sophie.** Does School Matter for Educational Achievement? A Two-Way Nested-Error Components Analysis. *J. Appl. Econometrics*, April–June 1989, *4*(2), pp. 181–93.

Monts, Ken; Blissett, Marlan and Wilson, Robert H. Weather Normalization of Electricity Sales to the School Sector: Potential Model Misspecification. *Energy Econ.*, April 1989, *11*(2), pp. 127–32.

Montuschi, Luisa. Sindicatos y negociaciones salariales. El caso argentino. (Trade Unions and Wage Bargaining. The Argentine Case. With English summary.) *Económica (La Plata)*, 1989, *35*(1–2), pp. 15–35.

Moodie, Graeme C. On Political Scandals and Corruption. **In** *Heidenheimer, A. J.; Johnston, M. and LeVine, V. T., eds.*, 1989, *1980*, pp. 873–86.

Mooijaart, Ab; de Leeuw, Jan and van Montfort, Kees. Estimation of Regression Coefficients with the Help of Characteristic Functions. *J. Econometrics*, June 1989, *41*(2), pp. 267–78.

Mookerjee, Rajen and Dadkhah, Kamran M. Money and Corporate Profits in a Developing Country: Theory and Evidence. *J. Banking Finance*, May 1989, *13*(2), pp. 191–205.

Mookherjee, Dilip and Melumad, Nahum D. Delegation as Commitment: The Case of Income Tax Audits. *Rand J. Econ.*, Summer 1989, *20*(2), pp. 139–63.

_____ **and Png, Ivan.** Optimal Auditing, Insurance, and Redistribution. *Quart. J. Econ.*, May 1989, *104*(2), pp. 399–415.

Moomaw, Ronald L. and Williams, Martin. Capital and Labour Efficiencies: A Regional Analysis. *Urban Stud.*, December 1989, *26*(6), pp. 573–85.

Moon, Choon-Geol. A Monte Carlo Comparison of Semiparametric Tobit Estimators. *J. Appl. Econometrics*, Oct.–Dec. 1989, *4*(4), pp. 361–82.

Moon, Chung-in. A Dissenting View on the Pacific Future: Conclusion. **In** *Haggard, S. and Moon, C., eds.*, 1989, pp. 359–74.

_____. Trade Friction and Industrial Adjustment: The Textiles and Apparel in the Pacific Basin. **In** *Haggard, S. and Moon, C., eds.*, 1989, pp. 185–207.

_____ **and Baek, Kwang-il.** Technological Dependence, Supplier Control and Strategies for Recipient Autonomy: The Case of South Korea. **In** *Baek, K.-I.; McLaurin, R. D. and Moon, C., eds.*, 1989, pp. 153–83.

Moon, Marilyn. The Wealth of the Aged and Nonaged, 1984: Comment. **In** *Lipsey, R. E. and Tice, H. S., eds.*, 1989, pp. 684–87.

_____ **and Smeeding, Timothy M.** Can the Elderly Afford Long-Term Care? **In** *Lewin, M. E. and Sullivan, S., eds.*, 1989, pp. 137–60.

Mooney, Linda A. and Fewell, Carla-Marie. Crime in One Long-Lived Comic Strip: An Evaluation of Chester Gould's 'Dick Tracy.' *Amer. J. Econ. Sociology*, January 1989, *48*(1), pp. 89–100.

Moore, Basil J. Does Money Supply Endogeneity Matter? A Comment. *S. Afr. J. Econ.*, June 1989, *57*(2), pp. 194–200.

_____. The Effects of Monetary Policy on Income Distribution. In *Davidson, P. and Kregel, J.*, eds., 1989, pp. 18–41.

_____. Inflation and Financial Deepening: A Reply. *J. Devel. Econ.*, October 1989, *31*(2), pp. 397–401.

_____. Is the Money Stock Really a Control Variable? In *Guttmann, R.*, ed., 1989, *1981*, pp. 58–61.

_____. On the Endogeneity of Money Once More: Comment. *J. Post Keynesian Econ.*, Spring 1989, *11*(3), pp. 479–87.

_____. A Simple Model of Bank Intermediation. *J. Post Keynesian Econ.*, Fall 1989, *12*(1), pp. 10–28.

Moore, C. and Nagurney, Anna. A General Equilibrium Model of Interregional Monetary Flows. *Environ. Planning A*, March 1989, *21*(3), pp. 397–404.

Moore, Des. Erratum [Industrial Relations and the Failure of the Accord: What Should Be Done]. *Australian Bull. Lab.*, September 1989, *15*(4), pp. 343.

_____. Industrial Relations and the Failure of the Accord: What Should Be Done. *Australian Bull. Lab.*, June 1989, *15*(3), pp. 153–84.

Moore, Eric G. Population Issues in Canadian Public Policy: Editorial Introduction. *Population Res. Policy Rev.*, January 1989, *8*(1), pp. 1–14.

_____; **Ray, Brian and Rosenberg, Mark W.** Redistribution of Immigrant Groups in Canada. In *Beach, C. M. and Green, A. G.*, 1989, pp. 62–79.

Moore, Geoffrey H. and Layton, Allan P. Leading Indicators for the Service Sector. *J. Bus. Econ. Statist.*, July 1989, *7*(3), pp. 379–86.

Moore, J. E., II and Gordon, Peter. Endogenizing the Rise and Fall of Urban Subcenters via Discrete Programming Models. *Environ. Planning A*, September 1989, *21*(9), pp. 1195–1203.

Moore, Joan. Is There a Hispanic Underclass? *Soc. Sci. Quart.*, June 1989, *70*(2), pp. 265–84.

Moore, Linda and Litz, Diane. Multifactor Productivity Advances in the Tires and Inner Tubes Industry. *Mon. Lab. Rev.*, June 1989, *112*(6), pp. 19–27.

Moore, M. Roger and Webb, Nick C. Residence in the United Kingdom and the Scope of U.K. Taxation for Individuals—A Consultative Document. *Bull. Int. Fiscal Doc.*, March 1989, *43*(3), pp. 119–21.

Moore, Marian Chapman and Moore, Michael J. Adaptive Learning, Adaptive Utility, and Rational Behavior in a Repeated Prisoner's Dilemma. *J. Risk Uncertainty*, December 1989, *2*(4), pp. 367–83.

Moore, Michael J. Deflationary Consequences of a Hard Currency Peg. *Greek Econ. Rev.*, 1989, *11*(1), pp. 119–36.

_____. Dual Exchange Rates, Capital Controls, and Sticky Prices. *J. Int. Money Finance*, December 1989, *8*(4), pp. 547–58.

_____. Inventories in the Open Economy Macro Model: A Disequilibrium Analysis. *Rev. Econ.*

Stud., January 1989, *56*(1), pp. 157–62.

_____ **and Moore, Marian Chapman.** Adaptive Learning, Adaptive Utility, and Rational Behavior in a Repeated Prisoner's Dilemma. *J. Risk Uncertainty*, December 1989, *2*(4), pp. 367–83.

_____ **and Viscusi, W. Kip.** Promoting Safety through Workers' Compensation: The Efficacy and Net Wage Costs of Injury Insurance. *Rand J. Econ.*, Winter 1989, *20*(4), pp. 499–515.

_____ **and Viscusi, W. Kip.** Rates of Time Preference and Valuations of the Duration of Life. *J. Public Econ.*, April 1989, *38*(3), pp. 297–317.

Moore, Michael R. Native American Water Rights: Efficiency and Fairness. *Natural Res. J.*, Summer 1989, *29*(3), pp. 763–91.

_____; **Hanchar, John J. and Kim, C. S.** A Dynamic Model of Adaptation to Resource Depletion: Theory and an Application to Groundwater Mining. *J. Environ. Econ. Manage.*, July 1989, *17*(1), pp. 66–82.

Moore, Mick. The Fruits and Fallacies of Neoliberalism: The Case of Irrigation Policy. *World Devel.*, November 1989, *17*(11), pp. 1733–50.

_____. What and Where Is Political Economy? Review Article. *J. Devel. Stud.*, July 1989, *25*(4), pp. 583–89.

Moore, Robert W. and IsHak, Samir T. The Influence of Culture on Recruitment and Training: Hofstede's Cultural Consequences as Applied to the Asian Pacific and Korea. In *Nedd, A.*, ed., 1989, pp. 277–300.

Moore, Scott B.; Schirm, David C. and Ferri, Michael G. The Listing, Size, and Value of Equity Warrants. *Financial Rev.*, February 1989, *24*(1), pp. 135–46.

Moore, Thomas Gale. The Myth of Deregulation's Negative Effect on Safety. In *Moses, L. N. and Savage, I.*, eds., 1989, pp. 8–20.

Moore, William J.; Newman, Robert J. and Scott, Loren C. Welfare Expenditures and the Decline of Unions. *Rev. Econ. Statist.*, August 1989, *71*(3), pp. 538–42.

Moore, William T.; Christensen, Donald G. and Roenfeldt, Rodney L. Equity Valuation Effects of Forming Master Limited Partnerships. *J. Finan. Econ.*, September 1989, *24*(1), pp. 107–24.

_____; **Rogers, Ronald C. and Mais, Eric L.** A Re-examination of Shareholder Wealth Effects of Calls of Convertible Preferred Stock. *J. Finance*, December 1989, *44*(5), pp. 1401–10.

_____ **and Schmit, Joan T.** The Risk Retention Act of 1986: Effects on Insurance Firm Shareholders' Wealth. *J. Risk Ins.*, March 1989, *56*(1), pp. 137–45.

Moors, J. J. A. and Janssens, M. J. B. T. Exact Distributions of Bayesian Cox–Snell Bounds in Auditing. *J. Acc. Res.*, Spring 1989, *27*(1), pp. 135–44.

Moorthy, Vivek. Unemployment in Canada and the United States: The Role of Unemployment Insurance Benefits. *Fed. Res. Bank New York*

Quart. Rev., Winter 1989–90, *14*(4), pp. 48–61.

Móra, Mária and Bagó, Eszter. The Economic Management and Market Behaviour of the Decentralized Enterprises in Hungarian Industry. *Acta Oecon.*, 1989, *41*(3–4), pp. 341–58.

Mora y Araujo, Manuel. Political and Economic Crises in Argentina: Comment. In *di Tella, G. and Dornbusch, R.*, eds., 1989, pp. 25–30.

Morales, Juan Antonio and Sachs, Jeffrey D. Bolivia's Economic Crisis. In *Sachs, J. D.*, ed. *(II)*, 1989, pp. 57–79.

Morales, Luis Guillermo. New Tax Measures: Colombia. *Bull. Int. Fiscal Doc.*, April 1989, *43*(4), pp. 81–82.

———. The Taxation of Income from Business and Capital: An Overview of Objectives and Alternatives: Colombia. *Bull. Int. Fiscal Doc.*, May 1989, *43*(5), pp. 225–32.

Morales, Rebecca; Wolff, Goetz and Soja, Edward. Urban Restructuring: An Analysis of Social and Spatial Change in Los Angeles. In *Beauregard, R. A.*, ed., 1989, pp. 87–122.

Moran, Cristian. Economic Stabilization and Structural Transformation: Lessons from the Chilean Experience, 1973–87. *World Devel.*, April 1989, *17*(4), pp. 491–502.

Moran, Larry R. Motor Vehicles, Model Year 1989. *Surv. Curr. Bus.*, November 1989, *69*(11), pp. 21–24.

Moran, Michael. Investor Protection and the Culture of Capitalism. In *Hancher, L. and Moran, M.*, eds., 1989, pp. 49–75.

——— and Hancher, Leigh. Capitalism, Culture, and Economic Regulation: Introduction. In *Hancher, L. and Moran, M.*, eds., 1989, pp. 1–7.

——— and Hancher, Leigh. Organizing Regulatory Space. In *Hancher, L. and Moran, M.*, eds., 1989, pp. 271–99.

Morandé, Felipe G. Controlling Inflation: The Problem of Nonindexed Debt: Comment. In *Edwards, S. and Larrain, F.*, eds., 1989, pp. 176–78.

——— and Marshall R., Jorge. Una interpretación keynesiana-inercialista de la inflación brasileña en los años ochenta. (With English summary.) *Cuadernos Econ.*, December 1989, *26*(79), pp. 353–66.

Moravcsik, Andrew M. Disciplining Trade Finance: The OECD Export Credit Arrangement. *Int. Organ.*, Winter 1989, *43*(1), pp. 173–205.

Morcaldo, Giancarlo. Financial Regulation, Implicit Taxes, and Fiscal Adjustment in Italy: Comment. In *Monti, M.*, ed., 1989, pp. 244–46.

Morck, Randall; Schwartz, Eduardo S. and Stangeland, David. The Valuation of Forestry Resources under Stochastic Prices and Inventories. *J. Finan. Quant. Anal.*, December 1989, *24*(4), pp. 473–87.

———; Shleifer, Andrei and Vishny, Robert W. Alternative Mechanisms for Corporate Control. *Amer. Econ. Rev.*, September 1989, 79(4), pp. 842–52.

Moreau, Arthur F. and Errunza, Vihang R. Debt-for-Equity Swaps under a Rational Expectations Equilibrium. *J. Finance*, July 1989, *44*(3), pp. 663–80.

Moreaux, Michel and Boyer, Marcel. Endogenous Rationing in a Differentiated Product Duopoly. *Int. Econ. Rev.*, November 1989, *30*(4), pp. 877–88.

——— and Boyer, Marcel. Rationnement endogène et structure de marche. (With English summary.) *L'Actual. Econ.*, March 1989, *65*(1), pp. 119–45.

——— and Boyer, Marcel. Uncertainty, Capacity and Flexibility: The Monopoly Case. *Ann. Écon. Statist.*, July–Dec. 1989, (15–16), pp. 291–313.

Moreddu, Catherine and Huff, H. Bruce. The Ministerial Trade Mandate Model. *OECD Econ. Stud.*, Winter 1989–1990, (13), pp. 45–67.

——— and Mahé, Louis P. Analysis of CAP Trade Policy Changes. In *Tarditi, S., et al.*, eds., 1989, pp. 81–98.

Moreira, Ajax R. Bello; Pereira, Pedro L. Valls and Markwald, Ricardo A. Previsão da produção industrial: Indicadores antecedentes e modelos de série temporal. (With English summary.) *Pesquisa Planejamento Econ.*, August 1989, *19*(2), pp. 233–54.

Morell, David L. Effective Toxics Management: A Multi-media Perspective. In *Dysart, B. C., III and Clawson, M.*, eds., 1989, pp. 27–46.

Moreno, Lorenzo; Goldman, Noreen and Westoff, Charles F. The Demographic Impact of Changes in Contraceptive Practice in Third World Populations. *Population Devel. Rev.*, March 1989, *15*(1), pp. 91–106.

Moreno, Ramon. Exchange Rates and Monetary Policy in Singapore and Hong Kong. *Hong Kong Econ. Pap.*, 1989, (19), pp. 21–42.

———. Exchange Rates and Trade Adjustment in Taiwan and Korea. *Fed. Res. Bank San Francisco Econ. Rev.*, Spring 1989, (2), pp. 30–48.

Morera, Esteve. Gramsci's Realism. *Sci. Society*, Winter 1989–90, *53*(4), pp. 459–69.

Moretto, Michele. Durabilità ottima del capitale, flusso di investimenti e incertezza. (The Optimal Durability of Capital, Investment and Demand Uncertainty. With English summary.) *Ricerche Econ.*, Oct.–Dec. 1989, *43*(4), pp. 456–78.

———. L'impresa l'accumulazione e il controllo esterno del tasso di rendimento: Un riesame dell'effetto Averch–Johnson. (Capital Accumulation in the Regulated Firm: Re-examination of the Averch–Johnson Effect. With English summary.) *Rivista Int. Sci. Econ. Com.*, January 1989, *36*(1), pp. 75–95.

Morey, Richard C. Costing Out Quality Changes: An Econometric Frontier Analysis of U.S. Navy Enlistments. In *Gulledge, T. R., Jr. and Litteral, L. A.*, eds., 1989, pp. 176–93.

——— and Banker, Rajiv D. Incorporating Value Judgments in Efficiency Analysis. In *Chan, J. L. and Patton, J. M.*, eds., 1989, pp. 245–67.

Morgado, Hugo; Camazón, Daniel and García-Huidobro, Guillermo. Labour Market Performance and Urban Poverty in Panama. In *Rodgers, G., ed.,* 1989, pp. 97–116.

Morgan, David R. and Hirlinger, Michael W. Socioeconomic Dimensions of the American States: An Update. *Soc. Sci. Quart.,* March 1989, *70*(1), pp. 184–92.

———— **and Hirlinger, Michael W.** State Factor Scores: Perhaps Not So Bad. *Soc. Sci. Quart.,* March 1989, *70*(1), pp. 195–96.

Morgan, Donald P. Monetary Policy Issues in the 1990s: Introduction. In *Federal Reserve Bank of Kansas City,* 1989, pp. xv–xxvii.

Morgan, George Emir and Smith, Stephen D. Some Notes on Risk Management via Forward Contracting. *Southern Econ. J.,* July 1989, *56*(1), pp. 240–52.

Morgan, J. and Loridan, P. ε-Regularized Two-Level Optimization Problems: Approximation and Existence Results. In *Dolecki, S., ed.,* 1989, pp. 99–113.

Morgan, James N.; Curtin, Richard T. and Juster, F. Thomas. Survey Estimates of Wealth: An Assessment of Quality. In *Lipsey, R. E. and Tice, H. S., eds.,* 1989, pp. 473–548.

Morgan, Kevin. Telecom Strategies in Britain and France: The Scope and Limits of Neo-liberalism and Dirigisme. In *Sharp, M. and Holmes, P., eds.,* 1989, pp. 19–55.

Morgan, Mary S. and Hendry, David F. A Re-analysis of Confluence Analysis. *Oxford Econ. Pap.,* January 1989, *41*(1), pp. 35–52.

———— **and Hendry, David F.** A Re-analysis of Confluence Analysis. In *de Marchi, N. and Gilbert, C., eds.,* 1989, pp. 35–52.

Morgan, W. B. The Role of Energy in Urban–Rural Interchange in Tropical Africa. In *[Mountjoy, A. B.],* 1989, pp. 33–67.

Morgan, William E.; Mutti, John and Patridge, Mark. A Regional Equilibrium Model of the United States: Tax Effects on Factor Movements and Regional Production. *Rev. Econ. Statist.,* November 1989, *71*(4), pp. 626–35.

————**; Partridge, Mark and Mutti, John.** The Incidence of Regional Taxes in a General Equilibrium Framework. *J. Public Econ.,* June 1989, *39*(1), pp. 83–107.

Morgenstern, O. Professor Hicks on Value and Capital. In *Wood, J. C. and Woods, R. N., eds., Vol. 1,* 1989, *1941,* pp. 69–91.

Mori, Nobuhiro and Tsutsui, Yoshiro. Bank Market Structure and Performance: Evidence from Japan. *Econ. Stud. Quart.,* December 1989, *40*(4), pp. 296–316.

Mori, Pier Angelo. Salari ed assegnazione alle mansioni nei mercati interni del lavoro con informazione asimmetrica. (Wages and Job Matching in Internal Labour Markets under Asymmetric Information. With English summary.) *Econ. Politica,* April 1989, *6*(1), pp. 99–122.

Mori, Shunsuke and Sawa, Takamitsu. Revaluation of Durable Capital Stock in Japanese Manufacturing and Its Application for the Measurement of Potential Growth Rate during the

OPEC Decade. In *Sato, R. and Negishi, T., eds.,* 1989, pp. 125–44.

Moriarty, B. M. and Moriarty, L. R. Capital Restructuring, Government Policy and the Decentralization of U.S. Manufacturing. In *Gibbs, D., ed.,* 1989, pp. 73–94.

———— **and Moriarty, L. R.** Industrial Restructuring and the Spatial Reorganization of American Manufacturing Employment. In *Gibson, L. J. and Stimson, R. J., eds.,* 1989, pp. 89–107.

Moriarty, L. R. and Moriarty, B. M. Capital Restructuring, Government Policy and the Decentralization of U.S. Manufacturing. In *Gibbs, D., ed.,* 1989, pp. 73–94.

———— **and Moriarty, B. M.** Industrial Restructuring and the Spatial Reorganization of American Manufacturing Employment. In *Gibson, L. J. and Stimson, R. J., eds.,* 1989, pp. 89–107.

Morici, Peter. The Canadian–U.S. Free Trade Agreement: Origins, Contents and Prospects. In *Greenaway, D.; Hyclak, T. and Thornton, R. J., eds.,* 1989, pp. 43–68.

Moriguchi, Chikashi. Driving Forces of Economic Structural Change: The Case of Japan in the Last Decade. In *Krelle, W., ed.,* 1989, pp. 325–34.

————. Economic Structural Adjustments and Macroeconomic Balance of Japan. *Rivista Int. Sci. Econ. Com.,* February 1989, *36*(2), pp. 107–33.

Morimune, Kimio. Test in a Structural Equation. *Econometrica,* November 1989, *57*(6), pp. 1341–60.

Morioka, Koji. The Capitalist Class: Japan. In *Bottomore, T. and Brym, R. J., eds.,* 1989, pp. 140–76.

Moris, Jon R. Indigenous versus Introduced Solutions to Food Stress in Africa. In *Sahn, D. E., ed.,* 1989, pp. 209–34.

Morishima, Michio. A Note on a Point in *Value and Capital.* In *Wood, J. C. and Woods, R. N., eds., Vol. 1,* 1989, *1953,* pp. 159–64.

————. On the Three Hicksian Laws of Comparative Statics. In *Wood, J. C. and Woods, R. N., eds., Vol. 2,* 1989, *1960,* pp. 43–51.

Morishima, Motohiro and Sherer, Peter D. Roads and Roadblocks to Dual Commitment: Similar and Dissimilar Antecedents of Union and Company Commitment. *J. Lab. Res.,* Summer 1989, *10*(3), pp. 311–30.

Morisset, Jacques. The Impact of Foreign Capital Inflows on Domestic Savings Reexamined: The Case of Argentina. *World Devel.,* November 1989, *17*(11), pp. 1709–15.

————. L'affectation du financement externe dans un pays en voie de développement: Un modèle de portefeuille. (With English summary.) *Revue Écon. Politique,* July–Aug. 1989, *99*(4), pp. 597–615.

Morissey, Oliver. Are Non-domestic Rates a Suitable Local Business Tax? In *[Sandford, C.],* 1989, pp. 28–45.

Morita, Tsuneo. Restructuring of the Czechoslovak Economic Mechanism: Discussion. In *Ber-*

liner, J. S.; Kosta, H. G. J. and Hakogi, M., eds., 1989, pp. 115–16.

――――. Structure of Capital Financing—A Case Study in Hungary. In *Berliner, J. S.; Kosta, H. G. J. and Hakogi, M., eds.*, 1989, pp. 117–30.

Mork, Knut Anton. Oil and Macroeconomy When Prices Go Up and Down: An Extension of Hamilton's Results. *J. Polit. Econ.*, June 1989, 97(3), pp. 740–44.

―――― **and Smith, V. Kerry.** Testing the Life-Cycle Hypothesis with a Norwegian Household Panel. *J. Bus. Econ. Statist.*, July 1989, 7(3), pp. 287–96.

Morkre, Morris E. and Kruth, Harold E. Determining Whether Dumped or Subsidized Imports Injure Domestic Industries: International Trade Commission Approach. *Contemp. Policy Issues*, July 1989, 7(3), pp. 78–95.

Morley, Alfred C. Nuturing Professional Standards in the Investment Industry. In *Williams, O. F.; Reilly, F. K. and Houck, J. W., eds.*, 1989, pp. 41–45.

Morley, Morris H. and Petras, James F. The Imperial State in the Rise and Fall of U.S. Imperialism. In *MacEwan, A. and Tabb, W. K., eds.*, 1989, pp. 44–63.

Morley, Samuel A. and Kumar, Vikram. Labor Intensity and Employment Creation in a Constrained Economy. *J. Devel. Econ.*, April 1989, 30(2), pp. 287–300.

Moroney, John R. Output and Energy: An International Analysis. *Energy J.*, July 1989, 10(3), pp. 1–18.

Morooka, Yoshinori and Hayami, Yujiro. Contract Choice and Enforcement in an Agrarian Community: Agricultural Tenancy in Upland Java. *J. Devel. Stud.*, October 1989, 26(1), pp. 28–42.

Morrell, Mike. The Struggle to Integrate Traditional Indian Systems and State Management in the Salmon Fisheries of the Skeena River, British Columbia. In *Pinkerton, E., ed.*, 1989, pp. 231–48.

Morris, Cynthia Taft and Adelman, Irma. Nineteenth-century Development Experience and Lessons for Today. *World Devel.*, Special Issue, September 1989, 17(9), pp. 1417–32.

Morris, John N. and Kotlikoff, Laurence J. How Much Care Do the Aged Receive from Their Children? A Bimodal Picture of Contact and Assistance. In *Wise, D. A., ed.*, 1989, pp. 151–75.

Morris, John S. Rationing of Medical Care for the Critically Ill: Ethics and Scarcity. In *Strosberg, M. A.; Fein, I. A. and Carroll, J. D., eds.*, 1989, pp. 11–16.

Morris, Larry A. Marketing of Nonferrous Metals: Future Market Development Needs. In *Jackson, L. M. and Richardson, P. R., eds.*, 1989, pp. 77–86.

Morris, Michael L. and Newman, Mark D. Official and Parallel Cereals Markets in Senegal: Empirical Evidence. *World Devel.*, December 1989, 17(12), pp. 1895–1906.

Morris, Robert K. and Grayson, Leslie E. The

Implications for Future Contingency Planning of the 1979 Gasoline Shortage. In *[Adams, F. G.]*, 1989, pp. 207–25.

Morris-Suzuki, Tessa. Japanese Economic Growth, Images and Ideologies. In *Morris-Suzuki, T. and Seiyama, T., eds.*, 1989, pp. 3–27.

Morrisette, Peter M. The Evolution of Policy Responses to Stratospheric Ozone Depletion. *Natural Res. J.*, Summer 1989, 29(3), pp. 793–820.

Morrison, Bruce. Facing the Realities of the Debt Crisis. In *Weeks, J. F., ed.*, 1989, pp. 195–206.

Morrison, Catherine J. Export Prices and Exchange Rates: An Industry Approach: Comment. In *Feenstra, R. C., ed.*, 1989, pp. 210–15.

―――― **and Conrad, Klaus.** The Impact of Pollution Abatement Investment on Productivity Change: An Empirical Comparison of the U.S., Germany, and Canada. *Southern Econ. J.*, January 1989, 55(3), pp. 684–98.

Morrison, Damon C. and Sjovold, Arve R. Rocket Propulsion Cost Modeling. In *Gulledge, T. R., Jr. and Litteral, L. A., eds.*, 1989, pp. 226–58.

Morrison, Donald G. and Colombo, Richard A. A Brand Switching Model with Implications for Marketing Strategies. *Marketing Sci.*, Winter 1989, 8(1), pp. 89–99.

―――― **and Colombo, Richard A.** A Brand Switching Model with Implications for Marketing Strategies: Reply. *Marketing Sci.*, Winter 1989, 8(1), pp. 106.

Morrison, Steven A. U.S. Domestic Aviation. In *Button, K. and Swann, D., eds.*, 1989, pp. 141–65.

―――― **and Winston, Clifford.** Enhancing the Performance of the Deregulated Air Transportation System. *Brookings Pap. Econ. Act.*, Microeconomics, 1989, pp. 61–112.

Morrisson, Christian and Thorbecke, Erik. Institutions, Policies and Agricultural Performance: A Comparative Analysis. *World Devel.*, Special Issue, September 1989, 17(9), pp. 1485–98.

Morrow, Glenn R. Adam Smith: Moralist and Philosopher. In *Clark, J. M., et al.*, 1989, pp. 156–79.

Morrow, James D. Bargaining in Repeated Crises: A Limited Information Model. In *Ordeshook, P. C., ed.*, 1989, pp. 207–28.

――――. A Twist of Truth: A Reexamination of the Effects of Arms Races on the Occurrence of War. *J. Conflict Resolution*, September 1989, 33(3), pp. 500–529.

Morsa, Denis. Is It Justified to Use Real Wages as a Standard of Living Index? In *Scholliers, P., ed.*, 1989, pp. 96–100.

Morss, Mark F. The Incidence of Welfare Losses Due to Appliance Efficiency Standards. *Energy J.*, January 1989, 10(1), pp. 111–18.

―――― **and Small, J. L.** Deriving Electricity Demand Elasticities from a Simulation Model. *Energy J.*, July 1989, 10(3), pp. 51–76.

―――― **and Small, J. L.** The Effect of Wood and

Coal Stoves on Household Use of Electricity. *Land Econ.*, February 1989, 65(1), pp. 29–37.

Mortensen, Dale T. The Persistence and Indeterminacy of Unemployment in Search Equilibrium. *Scand. J. Econ.*, 1989, 91(2), pp. 347–70.

Mortimore, Michael. The Conduct of Latin America's Creditor Banks. *CEPAL Rev.*, April 1989, (37), pp. 7–26.

Morton, Peter J. and Lindert, Peter H. How Sovereign Debt Has Worked. In *Sachs, J. D., ed. (II)*, 1989, pp. 225–35.

—— **and Lindert, Peter H.** How Sovereign Debt Has Worked. In *Sachs, J. D., ed. (I)*, 1989, pp. 39–106.

Möschel, Wernhard. Competition Policy from an Ordo Point of View. In *Peacock, A. and Willgerodt, H., eds. (I)*, 1989, pp. 142–59.

Moschini, Giancarlo. Modeling the Supply Response of Supply-Managed Industries: A Review of Issues. *Can. J. Agr. Econ.*, November 1989, 37(3), pp. 379–92.

——. Normal Inputs and Joint Production with Allocatable Fixed Factors. *Amer. J. Agr. Econ.*, November 1989, 71(4), pp. 1021–24.

—— **and Meilke, Karl D.** Modeling the Pattern of Structural Change in U.S. Meat Demand. *Amer. J. Agr. Econ.*, May 1989, 71(2), pp. 253–61.

——; **Oxley, James and Fox, Glenn C.** An Analysis of the Structural and Welfare Effects of Bovine Somatotropin on the Ontario Dairy Industry. *Can. J. Agr. Econ.*, November 1989, 37(3), pp. 393–406.

——; **Prescott, David M. and Stengos, Thanasis.** Nonparametric Kernel Estimation Applied to Forecasting: An Evaluation Based on the Bootstrap. In *Ullah, A., ed.*, 1989, *1988*, pp. 19–32.

Moschos, Demetrios. Export Expansion, Growth and the Level of Economic Development: An Empirical Analysis. *J. Devel. Econ.*, January 1989, 30(1), pp. 93–102.

—— **and Karfakis, Costas.** Testing for Long Run Purchasing Power Parity: A Time Series Analysis for the Greek Drachma. *Econ. Letters*, September 1989, 30(3), pp. 245–48.

Moscovice, I.; Finch, Michael and Lurie, N. Minnesota: Plan Choice by the Mentally Ill in Medicaid Prepaid Health Plans. In *Scheffler, R. M. and Rossiter, L. F., eds.*, 1989, pp. 265–78.

Moser, Caroline O. N. Gender Planning in the Third World: Meeting Practical and Strategic Gender Needs. *World Devel.*, November 1989, 17(11), pp. 1799–1825.

Moser, Donald V. The Effects of Output Interference, Availability, and Accounting Information on Investors' Predictive Judgments. *Accounting Rev.*, July 1989, 64(3), pp. 433–48.

Moser, James T. and Lindley, James T. A Simple Formula for Duration: An Extension. *Financial Rev.*, November 1989, 24(4), pp. 611–15.

Moser, James W.; Schwartz, Steven and Erekson, O. Homer. Evenhandedness in Arbitration: The Case of Major League Baseball. *East-*

ern Econ. J., April–June 1989, 15(2), pp. 117–27.

Moser, Peter. Toward an Open World Order: A Constitutional Economics Approach. *Cato J.*, Spring–Summer 1989, 9(1), pp. 133–47.

Moses, Leon N. and Savage, Ian. The Effect of Airline Pilot Characteristics on Perceptions of Job Safety Risks. *J. Risk Uncertainty*, December 1989, 2(4), pp. 335–51.

—— **and Savage, Ian.** Summary of Other Aviation Issues. In *Moses, L. N. and Savage, I., eds.*, 1989, pp. 206–15.

—— **and Savage, Ian.** Transportation Safety in an Age of Deregulation: Summary and Policy Implications. In *Moses, L. N. and Savage, I., eds.*, 1989, pp. 308–31.

—— **and Savage, Ian.** Transportation Safety in an Age of Deregulation: Introduction. In *Moses, L. N. and Savage, I., eds.*, 1989, pp. 3–7.

Mosimann, Thomas J.; Howell, Craig and Clem, Andrew G. Price Highlights of 1988: Rising Pressures on Consumer Prices. *Mon. Lab. Rev.*, May 1989, 112(5), pp. 3–10.

Moskoff, William and Jones, Anthony. Perestroika and the Economy: New Thinking in Soviet Economics: Introduction. In *Jones, A. and Moskoff, W., eds.*, 1989, pp. vii–xxi.

Moskowitz, Karl. Ownership and Management of Korean Firms. In *Chung, K. H. and Lee, H. C., eds.*, 1989, pp. 65–77.

Mosley, Paul. The Design of Economic Recovery Programmes in Less Developed Countries. In *[Sandford, C.]*, 1989, pp. 150–70.

Moss, Charles B.; Muraro, Ronald P. and Boggess, William G. Distortionary Impacts of the 1982 and 1986 U.S. Tax Codes on Capital Investments: A Case Study of Investment in Orange Groves. *Southern J. Agr. Econ.*, December 1989, 21(2), pp. 107–15.

——; **Shonkwiler, J. S. and Reynolds, John E.** Government Payments to Farmers and Real Agricultural Asset Values in the 1980s. *Southern J. Agr. Econ.*, December 1989, 21(2), pp. 139–53.

Mott, Tracy. A Post Keynesian Perspective on a "Cashless Competitive Payments System." *J. Post Keynesian Econ.*, Spring 1989, 11(3), pp. 360–69.

da Motta, Ronaldo Serôa and de Araújo, João Lizardo. Decomposição dos efeitos de intensidade energética no setor industrial brasileiro. (With English summary.) *Pesquisa Planejamento Econ.*, April 1989, 19(1), pp. 113–31.

Mouallif, K. Variational Convergence and Perturbed Proximal Method for Saddle Point Problems. In *Dolecki, S., ed.*, 1989, pp. 115–40.

Mouchart, Michel. Twenty Years After: Econometrics, 1966–1986: Comments. In *Cornet, B. and Tulkens, H., eds.*, 1989, pp. 383–87.

—— **and Florens, Jean-Pierre.** Bayesian Specification Tests. In *Cornet, B. and Tulkens, H., eds.*, 1989, pp. 467–90.

Mougeot, Michel and Naegelen, Florence. Surplus collectif, enchère optimale et discrimination. (Discrimination in Public Procurement Policy. With English summary.) *Revue Écon.*, September 1989, *40*(5), pp. 765–90.

Mouhoud, E. M. Les stratégies de relocalisation des firmes multinationales. (With English summary.) *Revue Écon. Politique*, Jan.–Feb. 1989, *99*(1), pp. 96–122.

Mouillart, Michel and Convain, Anne-Sophie. Démographie et construction de logements. (With English summary.) *Revue Écon. Politique*, July–Aug. 1989, *99*(4), pp. 639–59.

Moulen, J. and Andjiga, N. G. Necessary and Sufficient Conditions for *l*-Stability of Games in Constitutional Form. *Int. J. Game Theory*, 1989, *18*(1), pp. 91–110.

Moulin, Hervé. Monotonic Surplus Sharing: Characterization Results. *Games Econ. Behav.*, September 1989, *1*(3), pp. 250–74.

_____ **and Roemer, John E.** Public Ownership of the External World and Private Ownership of Self. *J. Polit. Econ.*, April 1989, *97*(2), pp. 347–67.

Moulton, Brent R. and Randolph, William C. Alternative Tests of the Error Components Model. *Econometrica*, May 1989, *57*(3), pp. 685–93.

Mounsey, H. M. and Rhind, D. W. The Chorley Committee and "Handling Geographic Information." *Environ. Planning A*, May 1989, *21*(5), pp. 571–85.

Mount, Timothy D. Policy Analysis with Time-Series Econometric Models: Discussion. *Amer. J. Agr. Econ.*, May 1989, *71*(2), pp. 507–08.

_____ **; Bindlish, Vishva and Barker, Randolph.** Can Yield Variability Be Offset by Improved Information? The Case of Rice in India. In *Anderson, J. R. and Hazell, P. B. R., eds.*, 1989, pp. 287–300.

Mountain, Dean C. A Quadratic Quasi Cobb–Douglas Extension of the Multi-input CES Formulation. *Europ. Econ. Rev.*, January 1989, *33*(1), pp. 143–58.

_____ **and Hsiao, Cheng.** A Combined Structural and Flexible Functional Approach for Modeling Energy Substitution. *J. Amer. Statist. Assoc.*, March 1989, *84*(405), pp. 76–87.

_____ **and Hsiao, Cheng.** Some Remarks on the Identification and Estimation of Translog Models. In *Mariano, R. S.; Lim, K. S. and Ling, K. D., eds.*, 1989, pp. 123–57.

_____ **; Stipdonk, Bill P. and Warren, Cathy J.** Technological Innovation and a Changing Energy Mix—A Parametric and Flexible Approach to Modeling Ontario Manufacturing. *Energy J.*, October 1989, *10*(4), pp. 139–58.

van Mourik, Aad and Molle, Willem T. M. A Static Explanatory Model of International Labour Migration to and in Western Europe. In *Gordon, I. and Thirlwall, A. P., eds.*, 1989, pp. 30–52.

_____ **; Poot, Jacques and Siegers, Jacques J.** Trends in Occupational Segregation of Women and Men in New Zealand: Some New Evidence. *New Zealand Econ. Pap.*, 1989, *23*, pp. 29–50.

Moutos, Thomas. Real Wage Rigidity, Capital Im-

mobility and Stabilisation Policies. *Econ. Notes*, 1989, (3), pp. 335–42.

_____ **and Vines, David.** The Simple Macroeconomics of North–South Interaction. *Amer. Econ. Rev.*, May 1989, *79*(2), pp. 270–76.

Movshovich, S. M. Price Adjustment in the Presence of Queues. *Matekon*, Spring 1989, *25*(3), pp. 19–30.

Moxon, Richard W. Multinational Consortia in Manufacturing. In *Negandhi, A. R., ed.*, 1989, pp. 11–28.

Moyer, R. Charles; Chatfield, Robert E. and Sisneros, Phillip M. Security Analysts Monitoring Activity: Agency Costs and Information Demands. *J. Finan. Quant. Anal.*, December 1989, *24*(4), pp. 503–12.

_____ **; Sisneros, Phillip M. and Chatfield, Robert E.** The Accuracy of Long-term Earnings Forecasts for Industrial Firms. *Quart. J. Bus. Econ.*, Summer 1989, *28*(3), pp. 91–104.

_____ **and Spudeck, Raymond E.** A Note on the Stock Market's Reaction to the Accident at Three Mile Island. *J. Econ. Bus.*, August 1989, *41*(3), pp. 235–40.

Moyes, Patrick. Equiproportionate Growth of Incomes and After-Tax Inequality. *Bull. Econ. Res.*, October 1989, *41*(4), pp. 287–94.

_____. Some Classes of Functions That Preserve the Inequality and Welfare Orderings of Income Distributions. *J. Econ. Theory*, December 1989, *49*(2), pp. 347–59.

Moyo, July Gabarari. The Demand for Urban Services in Africa. In *World Bank and Istituto Italo-Africano*, 1989, pp. 87–92.

Mrak, Mojmir. External Debt Problem: Current Issues and Perspectives: Introduction. In *Mrak, M., ed.*, 1989, pp. 7–10.

_____. Restoring Resource Flow to Developing Countries. In *Mrak, M., ed.*, 1989, pp. 121–43.

Mshomba, Richard E. Price Elasticity of Supply of Tanzania's Major Export Crops. *Eastern Afr. Econ. Rev.*, June 1989, *5*(1), pp. 9–23.

Mubikangiey, Luc; Salengros, Pierre and van de Leemput, Cécile. Psychological and Sociological Perspectives on Precarious Employment in Belgium. In *Rodgers, G. and Rodgers, J., eds.*, 1989, pp. 197–223.

Mubyartoand Baswir, Revrisond. Central Kalimantan: The Dayak Heartland. In *Hill, H., ed.*, 1989, pp. 502–10.

Mückenberger, Ulrich. Non-standard Forms of Employment in the Federal Republic of Germany: The Role and Effectiveness of the State. In *Rodgers, G. and Rodgers, J., eds.*, 1989, pp. 267–285.

Muehlebach, F. Combination of an Animal Breeding Simulation Model with a Sector Model. In *Bauer, S. and Henrichsmeyer, W., eds.*, 1989, pp. 147–56.

Muellbauer, John; Murphy, Anthony and Bover, Olympia. Housing, Wages and UK Labour Markets. *Oxford Bull. Econ. Statist.*, March 1989, *51*(2), pp. 97–136.

Mueller, Dennis C. Democracy: The Public

Choice Approach. In *Brennan, G. and Lomasky, L. E., eds.*, 1989, pp. 78–96.

———. Mergers: Causes, Effects and Policies. *Int. J. Ind. Organ.*, Special Issue, March 1989, 7(1), pp. 1–10.

———. Probabilistic Majority Rule. *Kyklos*, 1989, 42(2), pp. 151–70.

Mueller, Michael J. Natural Resource Economics under Uncertainty: Effect of Futures Markets. *Natural Res. Modeling*, Spring 1989, 3(2), pp. 261–88.

Mueller, Rolf A. E. and Sumner, Daniel A. Are Harvest Forecasts News? USDA Announcements and Futures Market Reactions. *Amer. J. Agr. Econ.*, February 1989, 71(1), pp. 1–8.

Mueller, Willard F. Antitrust in a Planned Economy: Anachronism or an Essential Complement? In *Tool, M. R. and Samuels, W. J., eds. (III)*, 1989, 1975, pp. 285–305.

——— **and Wills, Robert L.** Brand Pricing and Advertising. *Southern Econ. J.*, October 1989, 56(2), pp. 383–95.

Mueser, Peter R. Measuring the Impact of Locational Characteristics on Migration: Interpreting Cross-Sectional Analyses. *Demography*, August 1989, 26(3), pp. 499–513.

———. The Spatial Structure of Migration: An Analysis of Flows between States in the U.S.A. over Three Decades. *Reg. Stud.*, June 1989, 23(3), pp. 185–200.

Mühlbacher, Hans and Vyslozil, Wilfried. Making Corporate Strategies Work: The Role of Values, Norms, and Attitudes. In *Rueschhoff, N. and Schaum, K., eds.*, 1989, pp. 123–42.

Mühlen, Ernest. Economic and Currency Integration as Exemplified by the Swiss and U.S. Federal Republics. In *Franz, O., ed.*, 1989, pp. 49–52.

Muhlrad, N. Integrated Programmes for Transport Safety: The Need for Coordination, International Cooperation, and Professional Training. In *Candemir, Y., ed.*, 1989, pp. 113–25.

Muhondwa, Eustace P. Y. The Role and Impact of Foreign Aid in Tanzania's Health Development. In *Reich, M. R. and Marui, E., eds.*, 1989, pp. 173–206.

Muir, Dana M. Changing the Rules of the Game: Pension Plan Terminations and Early Retirement Benefits. *Mich. Law Rev.*, April 1989, 87(5), pp. 1034–72.

Muir, S.; Sgro, Pasquale M. and Hazari, Bharat R. Rationing Black Markets and Welfare of the Poor. *Indian Econ. J.*, April–June 1989, 36(4), pp. 39–47.

Mujahid-Mukhtar, Eshya and Zahid, Shahid N. Impact of Agricultural Research and Extension on Crop Productivity in Pakistan: A Comment. *World Devel.*, April 1989, 17(4), pp. 589–90.

Mukherjee, Anindita and Drèze, Jean P. Labour Contracts in Rural India: Theories and Evidence. In *Chakravarty, S., ed.*, 1989, pp. 233–65.

Mukherjee, Tarun K. and Dukes, William P. A Multivariate Analysis of Small Bank Stock Valuation. *Quart. J. Bus. Econ.*, Spring 1989, 28(2), pp. 3–18.

Mukherji, Anjan. Quasi-concave Optimisation: Sufficient Conditions for a Maximum. *Econ. Letters*, October 1989, 30(4), pp. 341–43.

———; **Patnaik, Prabhat and Sanyal, Amal.** Stocks, Credit and the Commodity Market: A Preliminary Exercise. In *Rakshit, M., ed.*, 1989, pp. 111–28.

Mukhopadhyay, Arun K. Profitability and Profit Sharing: A Comment. *J. Ind. Econ.*, September 1989, 38(1), pp. 111–14.

Mulani, Narendra; Frederick, Donald G. and Dillon, William R. On the Use of Component Scores in the Presence of Group Structure. *J. Cons. Res.*, June 1989, 16(1), pp. 106–12.

Muldoon, Jacqueline M. and Stoddart, Greg L. Publicly Financed Competition in Health Care Delivery: A Canadian Simulation Model. *J. Health Econ.*, December 1989, 8(3), pp. 313–38.

Mulford, David C. Debt Reduction, Debt-Service Reduction, and New Money. In *Dornbusch, R.; Makin, J. H. and Zlowe, D., eds.*, 1989, pp. 97–103.

Mulherin, J. Harold and Mitchell, Mark L. Pensions and Mergers. In *Turner, J. A. and Beller, D. J., eds.*, 1989, pp. 211–34.

——— **and Muller, Walter J., III.** Resolution of Incentive Conflicts in the Mortgage Industry: A Reply. *J. Real Estate Finance Econ.*, February 1989, 2(1), pp. 73–74.

Muliere, Pietro and Scarsini, Marco. Multivariate Decisions with Unknown Price Vector. *Econ. Letters*, 1989, 29(1), pp. 13–19.

——— **and Scarsini, Marco.** A Note on Stochastic Dominance and Inequality Measures. *J. Econ. Theory*, December 1989, 49(2), pp. 314–23.

Mullahy, John and Sindelar, Jody. Life-Cycle Effects of Alcoholism on Education, Earnings, and Occupation. *Inquiry*, Summer 1989, 26(2), pp. 272–82.

Mullen, J. D.; Alston, Julian M. and Wohlgenant, Michael K. The Impact of Farm and Processing Research on the Australian Wool Industry. *Australian J. Agr. Econ.*, April 1989, 33(1), pp. 32–47.

Mullen, John K. and Menz, Fredric C. Valuing the Effect of Acidification Damages in the Adirondack Fishery: Reply. *Amer. J. Agr. Econ.*, February 1989, 71(1), pp. 221–22.

Müller, Albrecht A. C. Towards Conventional Stability in Europe. In *Rotblat, J. and Goldanskii, V. I., eds.*, 1989, pp. 118–35.

Müller-Armack, Alfred. The Meaning of the Social Market Economy. In *Peacock, A. and Willgerodt, H., eds. (II)*, 1989, 1956, pp. 82–86.

Muller, C. Wolfgang. Social Welfare in Developed Market Countries: Germany, West. In *Dixon, J. and Scheurell, R. P., eds.*, 1989, pp. 89–121.

Muller, Frederik. Capital Costs for Vintage Models. In *Muller, F. and Zwezerijnen, W. J., eds.*, 1989, pp. 82–99.

Müller, Harald. Transforming the East–West Conflict: The Crucial Role of Verification. In *Altmann, J. and Rotblat, J., eds.*, 1989, pp. 2–15.

Müller, Jürgen. Integrated World Markets in Services: Problems and Prospects: Comment. In *Giersch, H., ed.*, 1989, pp. 245–47.

_____ **and Owen, Nicholas.** The Effect of Trade on Plant Size. In *Jacquemin, A. and Sapir, A., eds.*, 1989, *1985*, pp. 173–84.

Muller, L. Scott. Health Insurance Coverage among Recently Entitled Disability Insurance Beneficiaries: Findings from the New Beneficiary Survey. *Soc. Sec. Bull.*, November 1989, *52*(11), pp. 2–17.

Müller, N. Valid Modelling of Institutions That Are Challenged by Rapid Environmental Change—The Case of a Waterworks Coping with Nitrate Compounds in Drinking Water. *Environ. Planning A*, August 1989, *21*(8), pp. 1049–74.

Müller, Paul. Numerical Classification of Biased Estimators. In *Opitz, O., ed.*, 1989, pp. 187–200.

Müller, Ronald. Global Corporations and National Stabilization Policy: The Need for Social Planning. In *Tool, M. R. and Samuels, W. J., eds. (III)*, 1989, *1975*, pp. 437–59.

Müller, Sigrid M. On Complete Securities Markets and the Martingale Property of Securities Prices. *Econ. Letters*, November 1989, *31*(1), pp. 37–41.

_____. Perfect Option Hedging and the Hedge Ratio. *Econ. Letters*, 1989, *29*(3), pp. 243–48.

_____. Perfect Option Hedging and the Hedge Ratio. *Econ. Letters*, November 1989, *31*(1), pp. 71–75.

Müller, Urs. Die Passivseite der Bankbilanz ein Portfolio-Ansatz. (The Liability Side of the Banks Balance Sheet. A Portfolio Approach. With English summary.) *Schweiz. Z. Volkswirtsch. Statist.*, March 1989, *125*(1), pp. 55–66.

_____; **Sheldon, George and Kugler, Peter.** Non-neutral Technical Change, Capital, White-Collar and Blue-Collar Labor: Some Empirical Results. *Econ. Letters*, November 1989, *31*(1), pp. 91–94.

Müller, W. and Rohr-Zänker, R. The Fiscal Crisis and the Local State: Examination of the Structuralist Concept. *Environ. Planning A*, December 1989, *21*(12), pp. 1619–38.

Muller, Walter J., III and Mulherin, J. Harold. Resolution of Incentive Conflicts in the Mortgage Industry: A Reply. *J. Real Estate Finance Econ.*, February 1989, *2*(1), pp. 73–74.

Mulligan, Gordon F. and Fik, Timothy J. Asymmetrical Price Conjectural Variation in Spatial Competition Models. *Econ. Geogr.*, January 1989, *65*(1), pp. 19–32.

_____ **and Fik, Timothy J.** Price Variation in Spatial Markets: The Case of Perfectly Inelastic Demand. *Ann. Reg. Sci.*, 1989, *23*(3), pp. 187–201.

Mullins, D. and Eckert, J. B. Income Redistribution and Its Effects on the South African Economy. *J. Stud. Econ. Econometrics*, November 1989, *13*(3), pp. 1–20.

Mullins, David W., Jr.; Wolff, Eric D. and Asquith, Paul. Original Issue High Yield Bonds: Aging Analyses of Defaults, Exchanges, and Calls. *J. Finance*, September 1989, *44*(4), pp. 923–52.

Mullins, Mark. Meltdown Monday of Meltdown Money?: Causes of the Stock Market Crash. In *[Marjolin, R.]*, 1989, pp. 43–64.

_____ **and Wadhwani, Sushil.** The Effect of the Stock Market on Investment: A Comparative Study. *Europ. Econ. Rev.*, May 1989, *33*(5), pp. 939–56.

Mumey, Glen. Double Counting and Windfalls: A Comment. *Can. J. Agr. Econ.*, July 1989, *37*(2), pp. 327–29.

Mundaca, B. Gabriela and Hurd, Michael D. The Importance of Gifts and Inheritances among the Affluent. In *Lipsey, R. E. and Tice, H. S., eds.*, 1989, pp. 737–58.

Mundell, Robert A. Latin American Debt and the Transfer Problem: Introduction. In *Brock, P. L.; Connolly, M. B. and González-Vega, C., eds.*, 1989, pp. 1–17.

Mundlak, Yair and Cavallo, Domingo. On the Nature and Implications of Intersectoral Resource Allocations: Argentina 1913–84. In *Adelman, I. and Lane, S., eds.*, 1989, pp. 143–60.

Munera, Hector A. Prediction of Preference Reversals by the Linearized Moments Model. In *Grunert, K. G. and Ölander, F., eds.*, 1989, pp. 247–66.

Munger, Michael C. A Simple Test of the Thesis That Committee Jurisdictions Shape Corporate PAC Contributions. *Public Choice*, August 1989, *62*(2), pp. 181–86.

_____ **and Dougan, William R.** The Rationality of Ideology. *J. Law Econ.*, April 1989, *32*(1), pp. 119–42.

_____ **and Hart, Douglas B.** Declining Electoral Competitiveness in the House of Representatives: The Differential Impact of Improved Transportation Technology. *Public Choice*, June 1989, *61*(3), pp. 217–28.

_____ **and Hinich, Melvin J.** Political Investment, Voter Perceptions, and Candidate Strategy: An Equilibrium Spatial Analysis. In *Ordeshook, P. C., ed.*, 1989, pp. 49–67.

Munier, Bertrand. Calcul économique et révision de la théorie de la décision en avenir risque. (With English summary.) *Revue Écon. Politique*, March–April 1989, *99*(2), pp. 276–306.

Munk, Knud J. Effects of Decreasing Common Agricultural Prices. In *Tarditi, S., et al., eds.*, 1989, pp. 142–56.

_____. Price Support to the EC Agricultural Sector: An Optimal Policy? *Oxford Rev. Econ. Policy*, Summer 1989, *5*(2), pp. 76–89.

_____ **and Mahé, Louis P.** The EC Grain Price Policy at the Core of the CAP. In *Bauer, S. and Henrichsmeyer, W., eds.*, 1989, pp. 307–24.

Munkirs, John R. Centralized Private Sector Planning: An Institutionalist's Perspective on the Contemporary U.S. Economy. In *Tool, M. R. and Samuels, W. J., eds. (I)*, 1989, *1983*, pp. 283–319.

_____. Economic Power: A Micro–Macro Nexus. *J. Econ. Issues*, June 1989, *23*(2), pp. 617–23.

_____ and Ayers, Michael. Political and Policy Implications of Centralized Private Sector Planning. In *Tool, M. R. and Samuels, W. J., eds. (I), 1989, 1983,* pp. 321–36.

_____ and Sturgeon, James I. Oligopolistic Cooperation: Conceptual and Empirical Evidence of Market Structure Evolution. In *Tool, M. R. and Samuels, W. J., eds. (I), 1989, 1985,* pp. 337–59.

Munley, Vincent G. and Fraas, Arthur G. Economic Objectives within a Bureaucratic Decision Process: Setting Pollution Control Requirements under the Clean Water Act. *J. Environ. Econ. Manage.,* July 1989, *17*(1), pp. 35–53.

Munn, Andrew and Dingemans, Dennis. Acquisition-Based Assessment and Property Tax Inequalities after California's 1978 Proposition Thirteen. *Growth Change,* Winter 1989, *20*(1), pp. 55–66.

Munnell, Alicia H. It's Time to Tax Employee Benefits. *New Eng. Econ. Rev.,* July–Aug. 1989, pp. 49–63.

_____ and Ernsberger, C. Nicole. Public Pension Surpluses and National Saving: Foreign Experience. *New Eng. Econ. Rev.,* Mar.–Apr. 1989, pp. 16–38.

Munro, Alistair. In-Kind Transfers, Cash Grants and the Supply of Labour. *Europ. Econ. Rev.,* October 1989, *33*(8), pp. 1597–1604.

Munro, Gordon R. and Stokes, Robert L. The Canada–United States Pacific Salmon Treaty. In *McRae, D. and Munro, G., eds.,* 1989, pp. 17–35.

Munton, R. J.; Whatmore, S. J. and Marsden, T. K. Part-Time Farming and Its Implications for the Rural Landscape: A Preliminary Analysis. *Environ. Planning A,* April 1989, *21*(4), pp. 523–36.

Mupawose, Robbie M. Policy Issues to Address the Problem of Hunger and Nutrition. In *Helmuth, J. W. and Johnson, S. R., eds., Vol. 1,* 1989, pp. 167–81.

Murad, Howard. U.S. International Transactions, Third Quarter 1989. *Surv. Curr. Bus.,* December 1989, *69*(12), pp. 22–46.

Murakami, Atsushi. Japan and the United States: Roles in Asian Development. In *Naya, S., et al., eds.,* 1989, pp. 183–96.

Murakami, Naoki and Otsuka, Keijiro. Incentives and Enforcement under Contract: The Taxicab in Kyoto. *J. Japanese Int. Economies,* September 1989, *3*(3), pp. 231–49.

Muraro, Ronald P.; Boggess, William G. and Moss, Charles B. Distortionary Impacts of the 1982 and 1986 U.S. Tax Codes on Capital Investments: A Case Study of Investment in Orange Groves. *Southern J. Agr. Econ.,* December 1989, *21*(2), pp. 107–15.

Murgatroyd, Linda. Only Half the Story: Some Blinkering Effects of 'Malestream' Sociology. In *Held, D. and Thompson, J. B., eds.,* 1989, pp. 147–61.

Murillo Castaño, Gabriel and Lanzetta de Pardo, Mónica. The Articulation of Formal and Informal Sectors in the Economy of Bogotá, Colombia. In *Portes, A.; Castells, M. and Benton, L. A., eds.,* 1989, pp. 95–110.

Murnane, Richard J. and Olsen, Randall J. The Effects of Salaries and Opportunity Costs on Duration in Teaching: Evidence from Michigan. *Rev. Econ. Statist.,* May 1989, *71*(2), pp. 347–52.

_____ and Olsen, Randall J. Will There Be Enough Teachers? *Amer. Econ. Rev.,* May 1989, *79*(2), pp. 242–46.

Murphy, Anthony; Bover, Olympia and Muellbauer, John. Housing, Wages and UK Labour Markets. *Oxford Bull. Econ. Statist.,* March 1989, *51*(2), pp. 97–136.

Murphy, Austin and Nathan, Kevin S. An Analysis of Merger Financing. *Financial Rev.,* November 1989, *24*(4), pp. 551–66.

Murphy, Brendan. Factor Price Changes and Imported Intermediate Goods. *Int. Econ. J.,* Winter 1989, *3*(4), pp. 19–36.

Murphy, C. W. The Budget Strategy and Foreign Debt. *Australian Econ. Rev.,* Summer 1989, (88), pp. 32–51.

Murphy, Eithne. Comparative Advantage in Dairying: An Intercountry Analysis within the European Community. *Europ. Rev. Agr. Econ.,* 1989, *16*(1), pp. 19–36.

Murphy, J. Austin. A Discounted Cash-flow Model of Convertibles Subject to Multiple Calls in a World of Refunding Costs and Stochastic Interest Rates. *Southern Econ. J.,* July 1989, *56*(1), pp. 87–104.

_____ and Hilliard, Jimmy E. An Investigation into the Equilibrium Structure of the Commodity Futures Market Anomaly. *Financial Rev.,* February 1989, *24*(1), pp. 1–18.

_____ and Kleiman, Robert T. The Inflation-Hedging Characteristics of Equity REITs: An Empirical Study. *Quart. Rev. Econ. Bus.,* Autumn 1989, *29*(3), pp. 95–101.

Murphy, Kevin J. The Control and Performance of State-Owned Enterprises: Comment. In *MacAvoy, P. W., et al.,* 1989, pp. 59–68.

_____ and Hofler, Richard A. Using a Composed Error Model to Estimate the Frictional and Excess-Supply Components of Unemployment. *J. Reg. Sci.,* May 1989, *29*(2), pp. 213–28.

Murphy, Kevin M.; Shleifer, Andrei and Vishny, Robert W. Building Blocks of Market Clearing Business Cycle Models. In *Blanchard, O. J. and Fischer, S., eds.,* 1989, pp. 247–87.

_____; Shleifer, Andrei and Vishny, Robert W. Income Distribution, Market Size, and Industrialization. *Quart. J. Econ.,* August 1989, *104*(3), pp. 537–64.

_____; Shleifer, Andrei and Vishny, Robert W. Industrialization and the Big Push. *J. Polit. Econ.,* October 1989, *97*(5), pp. 1003–26.

Murphy, Mary K. Nobel Laureates in Economic Sciences: A Biographical Dictionary: Maurice Allais: 1988. In *Katz, B. S., ed.,* 1989, pp. 1–9.

Murphy, Michael J. Housing the People: From Shortage to Surplus? In *Joshi, H., ed.,* 1989, pp. 90–109.

Murphy, Neil B. and Fields, Joseph A. An Analysis of Efficiency in the Delivery of Financial Services: The Case of Life Insurance Agencies. *J. Finan. Services Res.*, October 1989, *2*(4), pp. 343–56.

Murphy, Philip D. and Elliott, Robert F. Evasion of Incomes Policy: A Model of Non-compliance. *Econ. J.*, December 1989, *99*(398), pp. 1054–64.

_____ and MacDonald, Ronald. Testing for the Long Run Relationship between Nominal Interest Rates and Inflation Using Cointegration Techniques. *Appl. Econ.*, April 1989, *21*(4), pp. 439–47.

Murphy, Robert G. Import Pricing and the Trade Balance in a Popular Model of Exchange Rate Determination. *J. Int. Money Finance*, September 1989, *8*(3), pp. 345–57.

_____. Stock Prices, Real Exchange Rates, and Optimal Capital Accumulation. *Int. Monet. Fund Staff Pap.*, March 1989, *36*(1), pp. 102–29.

_____ and Freeman, Scott J. Inside Money and the Open Economy. *J. Int. Econ.*, February 1989, *26*(1/2), pp. 29–51.

Murray, Dennis and Grove, Hugh. Participation in Software Selection: Effects on Students' Motivation and Performance. In *Schwartz, B. N., ed.*, 1989, pp. 141–49.

_____ and Regel, Roy W. Staff Performance Evaluation by Auditors: The Effect of Training on Accuracy and Consensus. In *Schwartz, B. N., ed.*, 1989, pp. 223–39.

Murray, Michael P. Hicks, Marshall, and Points Off the Demand Curve. In *Wood, J. C. and Woods, R. N., eds., Vol. 3*, 1989, *1976*, pp. 147–52.

_____ and Hutchinson, E. B. A Three Factor Cost Function for Multifamily Housing: A Study in Philanthropy. *Urban Stud.*, April 1989, *26*(2), pp. 234–39.

Murray, Tracy and Rousslang, Donald J. A Method for Estimating Injury Caused by Unfair Trade Practices. *Int. Rev. Law Econ.*, December 1989, *9*(2), pp. 149–64.

Murrey, Joe H., Jr.; Abbasi, Sami M. and Hollman, Kenneth W. Islamic Economics: Foundations and Practices. *Int. J. Soc. Econ.*, 1989, *16*(5), pp. 5–17.

Murrin, John M. The Eminence Rouge? In *[Stone, L.]*, 1989, pp. 21–30.

Murshed, Hasan and Khan, Showkat Hayat. The Holdings Tax. In *Schroeder, L., ed.*, 1989, pp. 145–59.

Murshed, S. Mansoob and Sen, Somnath. Inflation and Macroeconomic Adjustments in a North–South Model. *Greek Econ. Rev.*, 1989, *11*(1), pp. 95–118.

Murthy, K. S. Krishna. Balance from Current Revenue—A Retrospect. In *Reddy, J. M., et al., eds. (I)*, 1989, pp. 67–71.

Murthy, N. R. Vasudeva. The Effects of Taxes and Rates of Return on Foreign Direct Investment in the United States: Some Econometric Comments. *Nat. Tax J.*, June 1989, *42*(2), pp. 205–07.

Murty, M. N. and Ray, Ranjan. A Computational Procedure for Calculating Optimal Commodity Taxes with Illustrative Evidence from Indian Budget Data. *Scand. J. Econ.*, 1989, *91*(4), pp. 655–70.

Muscarella, Chris J. and Vetsuypens, Michael R. A Simple Test of Baron's Model of IPO Underpricing. *J. Finan. Econ.*, September 1989, *24*(1), pp. 125–35.

_____ and Vetsuypens, Michael R. The Underpricing of "Second" Initial Public Offerings. *J. Finan. Res.*, Fall 1989, *12*(3), pp. 183–92.

Muscatelli, Anton and Papi, Luca. Un modello con aspettative razionali per la domanda di moneta: Un giudizio critico. (With English summary.) *Econ. Int.*, Feb.–March 1989, *42*(1–2), pp. 90–108.

_____ and Vines, David. Macroeconomic Interactions between the North and South. In *Bryant, R. C., et al., eds.*, 1989, pp. 381–412.

Muscatelli, Vito Antonio. A Comparison of the 'Rational Expectations' and 'General-to-Specific' Approaches to Modelling the Demand for M1. *Oxford Bull. Econ. Statist.*, November 1989, *51*(4), pp. 353–75.

_____; Stevenson, Andrew and Vines, David. Uncovered Interest Parity, Exchange Rate Risk and Exchange Rate Dynamics. In *MacDonald, R. and Taylor, M. P., eds.*, 1989, pp. 159–77.

Musella, Marco. Moneta e politica monetaria nella teoria di Kaldor. (Money and Monetary Policy in Kaldor's Theory. With English summary.) *Econ. Scelte Pubbliche/J. Public Finance Public Choice*, Jan.–Aug. 1989, *7*(1–2), pp. 99–109.

Musgrave, Frank W.; Vaughan, Michael B. and Thomas, Wade L. The Evolving Health Care System: Economic Integration through Reciprocity. *J. Econ. Issues*, June 1989, *23*(2), pp. 493–502.

Musgrave, Richard A. Income Taxation and International Mobility: Foreword. In *Bhagwati, J. N. and Wilson, J. D., eds.*, 1989, pp. xi–xvii.

_____. The Three Branches Revisited. *Atlantic Econ. J.*, March 1989, *17*(1), pp. 1–7.

Musgrove, Philip. Is Polio Eradication in the Americas Economically Justified? In *WHO, Pan American Health Organization*, 1989, pp. 107–22.

Mushkat, Jerome. Fernando Wood and the Commercial Growth of New York City. In *Pencak, W. and Wright, C. E., eds.*, 1989, pp. 202–27.

Mushkat, Miron. Environmental Turbulence and the Economic Prospects of Hong Kong: A Need for Caution. In *Park, S.-J., ed.*, 1989, pp. 161–78.

Mushtaq, Mohammad; Nazli, Hina and Malik, Sohail J. An Analysis of Production Relations in the Large-Scale Textile Manufacturing Sector of Pakistan. *Pakistan Devel. Rev.*, Spring 1989, *28*(1), pp. 27–42.

Musolf, Lloyd D. The Government-Corporation Tool: Permutations and Possibilities. In *Salamon, L. M., ed.*, 1989, pp. 231–52.

Mussa, Michael. The Stabilizing Properties of Target Zones: Comment. **In** *Bryant, R. C., et al., eds.*, 1989, pp. 272–77.

Mussner, Werner and Rueschhoff, Norlin G. Institutional Infrastructures as an Element of Intercultural Value Analysis. **In** *Rueschhoff, N. and Schaum, K., eds.*, 1989, pp. 106–22.

Musu, Ignazio. Economia e ambiente. (Economics and Environment. With English summary.) *Econ. Politica*, December 1989, *6*(3), pp. 359–62.

Muszynski, Leon and Wolfe, David A. New Technology and Training: Lessons from Abroad. *Can. Public Policy*, September 1989, *15*(3), pp. 245–64.

Mutchler, Jane; Hopwood, William and McKeown, James. A Test of the Incremental Explanatory Power of Opinions Qualified for Consistency and Uncertainty. *Accounting Rev.*, January 1989, *64*(1), pp. 28–48.

Muth, John F. A Stochastic Theory of the Generalized Cobb–Douglas Production Function. **In** *Gulledge, T. R., Jr. and Litteral, L. A., eds.*, 1989, pp. 75–95.

Mutlu, Servet. Population and Agglomeration Trends in the Turkish Settlement System: An Empirical Analysis and Some of Its Implications. *METU*, 1989, *16*(1–2), pp. 99–125.

————. Urban Concentration and Primacy Revisited: An Analysis and Some Policy Conclusions. *Econ. Devel. Cult. Change*, April 1989, *37*(3), pp. 611–39.

Muto, Shigeo. Limit Properties of Power Indices in a Class of Representative Systems. *Int. J. Game Theory*, 1989, *18*(4), pp. 361–88.

————; **Potters, Jos and Tijs, Stef.** Information Market Games. *Int. J. Game Theory*, 1989, *18*(2), pp. 209–26.

Mutran, Elizabeth and Reitzes, Donald C. Labor Force Participation and Health: A Cohort Comparison of Older Male Workers. *Soc. Sci. Quart.*, June 1989, *70*(2), pp. 449–67.

Mutti, John; Morgan, William E. and Partridge, Mark. The Incidence of Regional Taxes in a General Equilibrium Framework. *J. Public Econ.*, June 1989, *39*(1), pp. 83–107.

————; **Patridge, Mark and Morgan, William E.** A Regional Equilibrium Model of the United States: Tax Effects on Factor Movements and Regional Production. *Rev. Econ. Statist.*, November 1989, *71*(4), pp. 626–35.

Mutuura, Josephine and Jones, Eugene. The Supply Responsiveness of Small Kenyan Cotton Farmers. *J. Developing Areas*, July 1989, *23*(4), pp. 535–44.

Muysken, Joan. Classification of Unemployment: Analytical and Policy Relevance. *De Economist*, 1989, *137*(4), pp. 397–424.

Mwabu, Germano M. Nonmonetary Factors in the Household Choice of Medical Facilities. *Econ. Devel. Cult. Change*, January 1989, *37*(2), pp. 383–92.

————. Referral Systems and Health Care Seeking Behavior of Patients: An Economic Analysis. *World Devel.*, January 1989, *17*(1), pp. 85–92.

Mwase, Ngila. Railway Tariffs in Southern Africa: A Case Study of the Tanzania–Zambia Railway Tariff. *Int. J. Transport Econ.*, June 1989, *16*(2), pp. 193–207.

Myers, Lester H. Economic Forces Influencing Value-Added Food Industries: Implications for Southern Agriculture: Discussion. *Southern J. Agr. Econ.*, July 1989, *21*(1), pp. 23–26.

————. What Do We Know and What Does It Mean? **In** *Buse, R. C., ed.*, 1989, pp. 369–75.

Myers, Norman. The Environmental Basis of Sustainable Development. **In** *Schramm, G. and Warford, J. J., eds.*, 1989, pp. 57–68.

Myers, Ramon H. The World Depression and the Chinese Economy 1930–6. **In** *Brown, I., ed.*, 1989, pp. 253–78.

Myers, Robert J. Econometric Testing for Risk Averse Behaviour in Agriculture. *Appl. Econ.*, April 1989, *21*(4), pp. 541–52.

———— **and Thompson, Stanley R.** Generalized Optimal Hedge Ratio Estimation. *Amer. J. Agr. Econ.*, November 1989, *71*(4), pp. 858–68.

———— **and Thompson, Stanley R.** Optimal Portfolios of External Debt in Developing Countries: The Potential Role of Commodity-Linked Bonds. *Amer. J. Agr. Econ.*, May 1989, *71*(2), pp. 517–22.

Myers, Samuel L., Jr. How Voluntary Is Black Unemployment and Black Labor Force Withdrawal? **In** *Shulman, S. and Darity, W., Jr., eds.*, 1989, pp. 81–108.

————. Political Economy, Race, and Morals: NEA Presidential Address. *Rev. Black Polit. Econ.*, Summer 1989, *18*(1), pp. 5–15.

Myers, Stewart C. Still Searching for Optimal Capital Structure. **In** *Kopcke, R. W. and Rosengren, E. S., eds.*, 1989, pp. 80–95.

Myers, William E. Urban Working Children: A Comparison of Four Surveys from South America. *Int. Lab. Rev.*, 1989, *128*(3), pp. 321–35.

Myerson, Roger B. Credible Negotiation Statements and Coherent Plans. *J. Econ. Theory*, June 1989, *48*(1), pp. 264–303.

Myhrman, Johan. The New Institutional Economics and the Process of Economic Development. *J. Inst. Theoretical Econ.*, March 1989, *145*(1), pp. 38–58.

Myles, Gareth D. Imperfect Competition and the Taxation of Intermediate Goods. *Public Finance*, 1989, *44*(1), pp. 62–74.

————. Ramsey Tax Rules for Economies with Imperfect Competition. *J. Public Econ.*, February 1989, *38*(1), pp. 95–115.

Myoung, Kwang-Sik. Evaluation of Rice Market Intervention and Its Rationale in Korea. *J. Econ. Devel.*, June 1989, *14*(1), pp. 175–99.

Myrdal, Gunnar. Corruption as a Hindrance to Modernization in South Asia. **In** *Heidenheimer, A. J.; Johnston, M. and LeVine, V. T., eds.*, 1989, 1968, pp. 405–21.

————. Corruption: Its Causes and Effects. **In** *Heidenheimer, A. J.; Johnston, M. and LeVine, V. T., eds.*, 1989, pp. 953–61.

————. The Equality Issue in World Development. *Amer. Econ. Rev.*, December 1989, 79(6), pp. 8–17.

N'guessan, Tchétché. Un système de contrôle du comportement bureaucratique de la Banque centrale. (With English summary.) *Revue Écon. Politique*, Sept.–Oct. 1989, 99(5), pp. 734–43.

Nabi, Ijaz. Investment in Segmented Capital Markets. *Quart. J. Econ.*, August 1989, 104(3), pp. 453–62.

_____ **and Hamid, Naved.** Private Finance Companies in LDCs: Lessons from an Experiment. *World Devel.*, August 1989, 17(8), pp. 1289–97.

Nabli, Mustapha K.; Azabou, Mongi and Kuran, Timur. The Wholesale Produce Market of Tunis and Its Porters: A Tale of Market Degeneration. In *Nabli, M. K. and Nugent, J. B., eds.*, 1989, pp. 352–74.

_____ **and Nugent, Jeffrey B.** Collective Action, Institutions and Development. In *Nabli, M. K. and Nugent, J. B., eds.*, 1989, pp. 80–137.

_____ **and Nugent, Jeffrey B.** The New Institutional Economics and Development: Concluding Remarks. In *Nabli, M. K. and Nugent, J. B., eds.*, 1989, pp. 438–48.

_____ **and Nugent, Jeffrey B.** The New Institutional Economics and Economic Development: An Introduction. In *Nabli, M. K. and Nugent, J. B., eds.*, 1989, pp. 3–33.

_____ **and Nugent, Jeffrey B.** The New Institutional Economics and Its Applicability to Development. *World Devel.*, Special Issue, September 1989, 17(9), pp. 1333–47.

_____**; Nugent, Jeffrey B. and Doghri, Lamine.** The Size Distribution and Ownership Type of Firms in Tunisian Manufacturing. In *Nabli, M. K. and Nugent, J. B., eds.*, 1989, pp. 200–232.

Nachane, D. M. and Ray, D. The Money-Multiplier: A Re-examination of the Indian Evidence. *Indian Econ. J.*, July–Sept. 1989, 37(1), pp. 56–73.

Nachtigal, Vladimír. The Concept of National Income and Productive Labour. *Czech. Econ. Pap.*, 1989, (26), pp. 73–97.

Nadal de Simone, Franciso and Marchese, Serafino. Monotonicity of Indices of "Revealed" Comparative Advantage: Empirical Evidence on Hillman's Condition. *Weltwirtsch. Arch.*, 1989, 125(1), pp. 158–67.

Nadel, Henry. Crisi e trasformazioni della natura dell'impiego. L'esperienza francese. (Crisis and Transformations in the Nature of Employment: The French Experience. With English summary.) *Econ. Lavoro*, Oct.–Dec. 1989, 23(4), pp. 3–21.

Nadel, Stanley. From the Barricades of Paris to the Sidewalks of New York: German Artisans and the European Roots of American Labor Radicalism. *Labor Hist.*, Winter 1989, 30(1), pp. 47–75.

Nadiri, M. Ishaq and Bernstein, Jeffrey I. Research and Development and Intra-industry Spillovers: An Empirical Application of Dynamic Duality. *Rev. Econ. Stud.*, April 1989, 56(2), pp. 249–67.

Nadler, David A. and Tushman, Michael L. Leadership for Organizational Change. In *Mohrman, A. M., Jr., et al.*, 1989, pp. 100–119.

Nadler, Mark A. The Loanable-Funds Approach to Teaching Macroeconomics: Comment. *J. Econ. Educ.*, Summer 1989, 20(3), pp. 253–58.

_____. Nobel Laureates in Economic Sciences: A Biographical Dictionary: Theodore Schultz: 1979. In *Katz, B. S., ed.*, 1989, pp. 253–64.

Nadler, Paul S. The State of the Industry. In *Federal Home Loan Bank of San Francisco*, 1989, pp. 71–78.

Naegelen, Florence. Le théorème d'équivalence-revenu, une approche en termes de stratégies optimales. (With English summary.) *Revue Écon. Politique*, May–June 1989, 99(3), pp. 466–81.

_____ **and Mougeot, Michel.** Surplus collectif, enchère optimale et discrimination. (Discrimination in Public Procurement Policy. With English summary.) *Revue Écon.*, September 1989, 40(5), pp. 765–90.

Nagahisa, Ryo-ichi. Rational Performance and Gibbard's Pareto-Consistent Libertarian Claim. *Econ. Letters*, November 1989, 31(1), pp. 1–4.

Nagaraja, G. N. and Venkataram, J. V. Institutional Short-Term Loan Facilities for Farmers: A Taluk-Level Study in Karnataka. *Margin*, Oct. 1989–March 1990, 22(1–2), pp. 92–97.

Nagarajan, P. and Spears, Annie. Comment on Causality Testing of the Wagner's Law. *Atlantic Econ. J.*, March 1989, 17(1), pp. 90.

_____ **and Spears, Annie.** "No Causality" between Government Expenditure and Economic Growth: A Comment. *Public Finance*, 1989, 44(1), pp. 134–38.

Nagel, Detlev; Stollberg, Rudhard and Assmann, Georg. The Introduction of New Technology in Industrial Enterprises of the German Democratic Republic: Two Case Studies. In *Francis, A. and Grootings, P., eds.*, 1989, pp. 61–87.

Nagin, Daniel S.; Cassidy, Glenn and Kamlet, Mark S. An Empirical Examination of Bias in Revenue Forecasts by State Governments. *Int. J. Forecasting*, 1989, 5(3), pp. 321–31.

_____ **and Klepper, Steven.** The Anatomy of Tax Evasion. *J. Law, Econ., Organ.*, Spring 1989, 5(1), pp. 1–24.

_____ **and Klepper, Steven.** The Role of Tax Preparers in Tax Compliance. *Policy Sciences*, May 1989, 22(2), pp. 167–94.

Nagurney, Anna. A General Dynamic Spatial Price Equilibrium Model with Gains and Losses. In *Andersson, Å. E., et al., eds.*, 1989, pp. 223–40.

_____. Migration Equilibrium and Variational Inequalities. *Econ. Letters*, November 1989, 31(1), pp. 109–12.

_____ **and Chen, H. K.** An Algorithm for the Solution of a Quadratic Programming Problem, with Application to Constrained Matrix and Spatial Price Equilibrium Problems. *Environ. Planning A*, January 1989, 21(1), pp. 99–114.

_____ and Moore, C. A General Equilibrium Model of Interregional Monetary Flows. *Environ. Planning A*, March 1989, *21*(3), pp. 397–404.

Nagy, András. Monopoly and Liberalization of Foreign Exchange Control. *Acta Oecon.*, 1989, *41*(3–4), pp. 377–401.

Nagy, Katalin. New Technology and Work in Hungary: Technological Innovation without Organisational Adaptation. In *Francis, A. and Grootings, P., eds.*, 1989, pp. 88–119.

Nagy, Sándor. The International Debt Trap: External and Internal Redistribution of Incomes. In *Davidson, P. and Kregel, J., eds.*, 1989, pp. 174–78.

Nagy, T. What Makes a Market Economy Socialist? *Acta Oecon.*, 1989, *40*(3–4), pp. 259–64.

Nahata, Babu and Mallela, Parthasaradhi. Effects of Horizontal Merger on Price, Profits, and Market Power in a Dominant-Firm Oligopoly. *Int. Econ. J.*, Spring 1989, *3*(1), pp. 55–62.

_____ and Olson, Dennis O. On the Definition of Barriers to Entry. *Southern Econ. J.*, July 1989, *56*(1), pp. 236–39.

Nahmias, Antoinette M. and Peck, Anne E. Hedging Your Advice: Do Portfolio Models Explain Hedging? *Food Res. Inst. Stud.*, 1989, *21*(2), pp. 193–204.

Naidenov, Naiden and Gercheva, Dafina. Economic Aspects of the Environmental Policy of the People's Republic of Bulgaria. In *Bulgarian Academy of Sciences, Institute of Economics*, 1989, pp. 107–11.

Naimuddin, M. A Note on the Energy Sector in the Seventh Plan. In *Reddy, J. M., et al., eds. (II)*, 1989, pp. 122–29.

Nainar, S. M. Khalid. Bootstrapping for Consistent Standard Errors for Translog Price Elasticities Some Evidence from Industrial Electricity Demand. *Energy Econ.*, October 1989, *11*(4), pp. 319–22.

Naini, Abbas and Worsick, Janice. The Impact of Energy Prices on Alberta's Economic Outlook. *Energy Econ.*, January 1989, *11*(1), pp. 46–52.

Nair, P. R. Gopinathan. Incidence, Impact and Implications of Migration to the Middle East from Kerala (India). In *Amjad, R., ed.*, 1989, pp. 343–64.

Nairn, Alasdair G. M.; Swales, J. K. and Holden, Darryl R. Shift-Share Analysis of Regional Growth and Policy: A Critique. *Oxford Bull. Econ. Statist.*, February 1989, *51*(1), pp. 15–34.

Naish, Howard F. Labor Market Externalities and the Downward Inflexibility of Nominal Wages. *J. Post Keynesian Econ.*, Fall 1989, *12*(1), pp. 109–26.

Najam-us-Saqiband Malik, Muhammad Hussain. Tax Incidence by Income Classes in Pakistan. *Pakistan Devel. Rev.*, Spring 1989, *28*(1), pp. 13–25.

Najjar, George K. and Hashemi, Ibrahim S. J. Al. Strategic Choices in Management Education: The Bahrain Experience. In *Davies, J., et al., eds.*, 1989, pp. 29–39.

Nakagane, Katsuji. Intersectoral Resource Flows in China Revisited: Who Provided Industrialization Funds? *Developing Econ.*, June 1989, *27*(2), pp. 146–73.

Nakagawa, Masao. The Japanese Banking System. In *Matsuo, H., ed.*, 1989, pp. 50–57.

Nakagome, Masaki. Urban Unemployment and the Spatial Structure of Labor Markets: An Examination of the "Todaro Paradox" in a Spatial Context. *J. Reg. Sci.*, May 1989, *29*(2), pp. 161–70.

Nakajima, Hiroshi. Priorities and Opportunities for International Cooperation: Experiences in the WHO Western Pacific Region. In *Reich, M. R. and Marui, E., eds.*, 1989, pp. 317–31.

Nakamura, Akihiro; Nakamura, Yoichi and Agatsuma, Nobuhiko. Structure of the Japanese Economy in the Year 2000. *Econ. Systems Res.*, 1989, *1*(1), pp. 69–85.

Nakamura, Alice and Nakamura, Masao. Effects of Excess Supply on the Wage Rates of Young Women. In *Michael, R. T.; Hartmann, H. I. and O'Farrell, B., eds.*, 1989, pp. 70–90.

_____ and Nakamura, Masao. Inventory Management Behavior of American and Japanese Firms. *J. Japanese Int. Economies*, September 1989, *3*(3), pp. 270–91.

_____ and Nakamura, Masao. New Measures of Nonwage Compensation Components: Are They Needed? *Surv. Curr. Bus.*, March 1989, *69*(3), pp. 58–61.

Nakamura, Leonard I. and Lang, William W. Information Losses in a Dynamic Model of Credit. *J. Finance*, July 1989, *44*(3), pp. 730–46.

Nakamura, Masao. Asymmetry in the Dividend Behavior of U.S. and Japanese Firms. *Managerial Dec. Econ.*, December 1989, *10*(4), pp. 261–74.

_____ and Nakamura, Alice. Effects of Excess Supply on the Wage Rates of Young Women. In *Michael, R. T.; Hartmann, H. I. and O'Farrell, B., eds.*, 1989, pp. 70–90.

_____ and Nakamura, Alice. Inventory Management Behavior of American and Japanese Firms. *J. Japanese Int. Economies*, September 1989, *3*(3), pp. 270–91.

_____ and Nakamura, Alice. New Measures of Nonwage Compensation Components: Are They Needed? *Surv. Curr. Bus.*, March 1989, *69*(3), pp. 58–61.

Nakamura, Mitsugu; Kim, Yoon Hyung and Yu, Oliver S. Structure, Parameters, and Prediction of Demand. In *Kim, Y. H. and Smith, K. R., eds.*, 1989, pp. 21–64.

Nakamura, Shinichiro. Multilateral TFP Index and Multilateral Similarity of Technology. *Keio Econ. Stud.*, 1989, *26*(1), pp. 31–41.

_____. Productivity and Factor Prices as Sources of Differences in Production Costs between Germany, Japan and the U.S. *Econ. Stud. Quart.*, March 1989, *40*(1), pp. 75–89.

Nakamura, Yasushi. Preconsideration of Policy

Model of the Soviet Economy: Discussion: Discrepancy between Consumption Plan and Income Plan? In *Berliner, J. S.; Kosta, H. G. J. and Hakogi, M., eds.*, 1989, pp. 84–87.

Nakamura, Yoichi; Agatsuma, Nobuhiko and Nakamura, Akihiro. Structure of the Japanese Economy in the Year 2000. *Econ. Systems Res.*, 1989, *1*(1), pp. 69–85.

_____; **Lo, Fu-chen and Kamal, Salih.** Structural Interdependency and the Outlook for the Asian-Pacific Economy towards the Year 2000. In *Shinohara, M. and Lo, F., eds.*, 1989, pp. 80–107.

Nakao, Takehiko. The Foreign Tax Credit System: Recent Amendments: Japan. *Bull. Int. Fiscal Doc.*, November 1989, *43*(11), pp. 506–10,.

Nakao, Takeo. Cost-Reducing R and D in Oligopoly. *J. Econ. Behav. Organ.*, August 1989, *12*(1), pp. 131–48.

_____. Export Subsidy and Antitrust Policies in Oligopoly with and without Threat of Entry. *J. Econ. (Z. Nationalökon.)*, 1989, *50*(3), pp. 269–95.

Nakasone, Yasuhiro; Kissinger, Henry A. and d'Estaing, Valéry Giscard. East–West Relations. *Foreign Aff.*, Summer 1989, *68*(3), pp. 1–21.

Nakata, Yutaka. The Japanese Economy and Internationalization: The Changing Japanese Economy. In *Matsuo, H., ed.*, 1989, pp. 1–3.

Nakatani, Takeshi. Monopoly and the Metamorphoses of Business Cycles. *Kobe Univ. Econ.*, 1989, (35), pp. 15–31.

Nakayama, Hirotaka. An Interactive Support System for Bond Trading. In *Lockett, A. G. and Islei, G., eds.*, 1989, pp. 325–33.

Nakazato, Minoru and Ramseyer, J. Mark. The Rational Litigant: Settlement Amounts and Verdict Rates in Japan. *J. Legal Stud.*, June 1989, *18*(2), pp. 263–90.

Nakazawa, Toshiaki and Weiss, Leonard W. The Legal Cartels of Japan. *Antitrust Bull.*, Fall 1989, *34*(3), pp. 641–53.

Nakhaeizadeh, Gholamreza and Henn, Rudolf. Neuere Entwicklungen in der Geldnachfrage. Einige theoretische und empirische Ergebnisse im Überblick. (Recent Developments in the Demand for Money: A Survey of Some Theoretical and Empirical Studies. With English summary.) *Jahr. Nationalökon. Statist.*, October 1989, *206*(4–5), pp. 395–406.

Nakosteen, Robert A. and Zimmer, Michael A. Minimum Wages and Labor Market Prospects of Women. *Southern Econ. J.*, October 1989, *56*(2), pp. 302–14.

Nalebuff, Barry. The Arbitrage Mirage, Wait Watchers, and More. *J. Econ. Perspectives*, Summer 1989, *3*(3), pp. 165–74.

_____. The Other Person's Envelope Is Always Greener. *J. Econ. Perspectives*, Winter 1989, *3*(1), pp. 171–81.

Namasivayam, D. and Balasundaram, S. K. Subsidy in the Risk-Preference of Allied Agricultural Projects: A Sensitivity Analysis. *Margin*, April–June 1989, *21*(3), pp. 89–103.

Nambiar, R. G.; Mehta, Rajesh and Panchamukhi, Vadiraj R. Structural Change and Economic Growth in Developing Countries. In *Williamson, J. G. and Panchamukhi, V. R., eds.*, 1989, pp. 54–84.

Nambu, Tsuruhiko; Suzuki, Kazuyuki and Honda, Tetsushi. Deregulation in Japan. In *Crandall, R. W. and Flamm, K., eds.*, 1989, pp. 147–73.

Namkoong, G. and Rodriguez, J. Optimum Growth and Reproduction Schedules for Forest Trees. *Natural Res. Modeling*, Fall 1989, *3*(4), pp. 539–51.

Nana-Sinkam, S. C. The Fate of Smallholders and Other Rural Poor in Africa during the Structural Adjustment Transition. In *Lineberry, W. P., ed.*, 1989, pp. 19–48.

Nance, John J. Economic Deregulation's Unintended But Inevitable Impact on Airline Safety. In *Moses, L. N. and Savage, I., eds.*, 1989, pp. 186–205.

Nangaku, Masaaki. Japanese Economic Cooperation to Support the Industrialization of Asian Nations. In *Shinohara, M. and Lo, F., eds.*, 1989, pp. 503–12.

Naniopoulos, A. and Vougias, S. Evaluation of the Port of Volos for the Transport of Goods between Europe and Middle East. In *Candemir, Y., ed.*, 1989, pp. 355–69.

Nankumba, J. S. and Kalua, B. Contract Farming in Malawi: Smallholder Sugar and Tea Authorities. *Eastern Afr. Econ. Rev.*, Special Issue, August 1989, pp. 42–58.

Nantz, Kathryn A. Nobel Laureates in Economic Sciences: A Biographical Dictionary: Tjalling C. Koopmans: 1975. In *Katz, B. S., ed.*, 1989, pp. 136–43.

_____; **Buss, James A. and Peterson, G. Paul.** A Comparison of Distributive Justice in OECD Countries. *Rev. Soc. Econ.*, Spring 1989, *47*(1), pp. 1–14.

Napier, Nancy K. and Latham, Gary A. Chinese Human Resource Management Practices in Hong Kong and Singapore: An Exploratory Study. In *Nedd, A., ed.*, 1989, pp. 173–99.

Naples, Michele I. A Radical Economic Revision of the Transformation Problem. *Rev. Radical Polit. Econ.*, 1989, *21*(1–2), pp. 137–58.

Naqvi, Nadeem and Batra, Raveendra N. Nontraded and Intermediate Goods and the Theory of Protection. *Europ. Econ. Rev.*, April 1989, *33*(4), pp. 721–35.

Naqvi, Syed Nawab Haider. Must Development Economists Watch *Hamlet* without the Prince? *Pakistan Devel. Rev.*, Winter 1989, *28*(4), pp. 291–308.

_____ **and Cornelisse, Peter A.** An Appraisal of Wheat Market Policy in Pakistan. *World Devel.*, March 1989, *17*(3), pp. 409–19.

Narasimhan, Chakravarthi. Incorporating Consumer Price Expectations in Diffusion Models. *Marketing Sci.*, Fall 1989, *8*(4), pp. 343–57.

Naray, Peter. The End of the Foreign Trade Monopoly: The Case of Hungary. *J. World Trade*, December 1989, *23*(6), pp. 85–97.

Narayan, Jack and Considine, John. Intervention

Analysis to Assess the Impact of Price Changes on Ridership in a Transit System: A Case Study. *Logist. Transp. Rev.*, March 1989, 25(1), pp. 53–61.

_____; **Raj, S. P. and Krishnamurthi, Lakshman.** Intervention Analysis Using Control Series and Exogenous Variables in a Transfer Function Model: A Case Study. *Int. J. Forecasting*, 1989, 5(1), pp. 21–27.

Narayana, A. V. L. and Panagariya, Arvind. Excise Tax Evasion: Reply. *Public Finance*, 1989, 44(3), pp. 510–12.

Narayanan, A. and Whiteside, M. M. Reverse Regression, Collinearity, and Employment Discrimination. *J. Bus. Econ. Statist.*, July 1989, 7(3), pp. 403–06.

Narayanan, M. P. and Lim, Suk-Pil. On the Call Provision in Corporate Zero-Coupon Bonds. *J. Finan. Quant. Anal.*, March 1989, 24(1), pp. 91–103.

Narayanan, Shankar, et al. Evaluating the Potential Farm-Level Implications of Multilateral Agricultural Free Trade on Selected Farm Sectors in Canada. *Can. J. Agr. Econ.*, Part 2, December 1989, 37(4), pp. 975–91.

Narayanan, Suresh. Forward-Shifting of the Corporate Tax in the Presence of Competing Imports: A Note. *Public Finance*, 1989, 44(2), pp. 320–26.

Nardone, Thomas and Polivka, Anne E. On the Definition of "Contingent Work." *Mon. Lab. Rev.*, December 1989, 112(12), pp. 9–16.

Nardozzi, Giangiacomo. Sulla dinamica strutturale dei sistemi economici: Colloquio con Luigi Pasinetti. (On the Structural Change of Economic Systems: An Interview with Luigi Pasinetti. With English summary.) *Rivista Storia Econ.*, S.S., October 1989, 6(3), pp. 359–67.

Narduzzi, Susan A. and Theil, Henri. The Statistical Structure of Real-Income Changes. *Econ. Letters*, 1989, 29(3), pp. 271–73.

Narendranathan, Wiji and Nickell, Stephen J. Modelling the Process of Job Search. In *Nickell, S. J., et al.*, 1989, 1985, pp. 47–77.

_____; **Nickell, Stephen J. and Stern, Jon.** The Nature of Unemployment in Britain: Studies of the DHSS Cohort: Introduction. In *Nickell, S. J., et al.*, 1989, pp. 1–10.

_____; **Nickell, Stephen J. and Stern, Jon.** Unemployment Benefits Revisited. In *Nickell, S. J., et al.*, 1989, 1985, pp. 11–46.

Nariu, Tatsuhiko and Flath, David. Returns Policy in the Japanese Marketing System. *J. Japanese Int. Economies*, March 1989, 3(1), pp. 49–63.

Narula, Subhash C. and Weistroffer, H. Roland. Algorithms for Multi-objective Nonlinear Programming Problems: An Overview. In *Lockett, A. G. and Islei, G., eds.*, 1989, pp. 434–43.

Narveson, Jan. The Justice of the Market: Comments on Gray and Radin. In *Chapman, J. W. and Pennock, J. R., eds.*, 1989, pp. 250–76.

Naseem, S. M. Impacts of Global Adjustment on the Asian-Pacific Economy: Comment. In *Shinohara, M. and Lo, F., eds.*, 1989, pp. 274–77.

Nash, Michael. Women and the Pennsylvania Railroad: The World War II Years. *Labor Hist.*, Fall 1989, 30(4), pp. 608–21.

Nasseh, Alireza. The UK's Demand for Money and the Choice of the Appropriate Scale Variable and Interest Rate: An Application of Nonnested Tests. *Appl. Econ.*, July 1989, 21(7), pp. 973–82.

Nassmacher, Karl-Heinz. Structure and Impact of Public Subsidies to Political Parties in Europe: The Examples of Austria, Italy, Sweden and West Germany. In *Alexander, H. E., ed.*, 1989, pp. 236–67.

Nasution, Anwar and Woo, Wing Thye. The Conduct of Economic Policies in Indonesia and Its Impact on External Debt. In *Sachs, J. D., ed. (II)*, 1989, pp. 101–20.

_____ **and Woo, Wing Thye.** Indonesian Economic Policies and Their Relation to External Debt Management. In *Sachs, J. D. and Collins, S. M., eds.*, 1989, pp. 17–149.

Natale, Piergiovanna. Non tutti i dazi vengono per nuocere. (Every Tariff Has a Silver Lining. With English summary.) *Econ. Politica*, August 1989, 6(2), pp. 275–80.

_____ **and de Meza, David.** Efficient Job Creation in LDCs Requires a Tax on Employment. *Econ. J.*, December 1989, 99(398), pp. 1112–22.

Nath, N. C. B. Food Security and Food Stocks: Some Managerial Issues. In *Oram, P. A., et al.*, 1989, pp. 573–77.

Nathan, Alli and Neave, Edwin H. Competition and Contestability in Canada's Financial System: Empirical Results. *Can. J. Econ.*, August 1989, 22(3), pp. 576–94.

Nathan, Kevin S. and Murphy, Austin. An Analysis of Merger Financing. *Financial Rev.*, November 1989, 24(4), pp. 551–66.

_____ **and O'Keefe, Terrence.** The Rise in Takeover Premiums: An Exploratory Study. *J. Finan. Econ.*, June 1989, 23(1), pp. 101–19.

Natividad, Fidelina B. The Concept and Estimation of Direct, Indirect and "Total" Currency Substitution in Money Demand. *Philippine Rev. Econ. Bus.*, December 1989, 26(2), pp. 287–301.

Nato, Takatsugu. Conglutination and Managerial Dominance versus Diversification of Life Values. *Int. J. Soc. Econ.*, 1989, 16(3), pp. 59–67.

Nau, Henry R. Domestic Trade Politics and the Uruguay Round: Preface. In *Nau, H. R., ed.*, 1989, pp. xiii–xvii.

_____. Domestic Trade Politics and the Uruguay Round: An Overview. In *Nau, H. R., ed.*, 1989, pp. 1–27.

Naude, Peter and Scholtz, Edwin. A Hybrid Model of Strategic Planning. In *Lockett, A. G. and Islei, G., eds.*, 1989, pp. 305–13.

_____; **Wegner, Trevor and Money, Arthur.** A Comparison of Multi-attribute Utility Generation Methods. In *Lockett, A. G. and Islei, G., eds.*, 1989, pp. 46–57.

Naughton, Michael C. Regulatory Preferences

and Two-Part Tariffs: The Case of Electricity. *Southern Econ. J.*, January 1989, *55*(3), pp. 743–58.

Naumova, N. F. and Rogovin, V. Z. The Task of Justice. In *Yanowitch, M., ed.*, 1989, *1987*, pp. 155–69.

Navarro, Peter. Creating and Destroying Comparative Advantage: The Role of Regulation in International Trade. *J. Compar. Econ.*, June 1989, *13*(2), pp. 205–26.

———. The U.S. Regulatory Environment and International Trade: Lessons from the Electricity Sector. *J. Policy Anal. Manage.*, Summer 1989, *8*(3), pp. 466–81.

Navarro, Vicente. A National Health Program Is Necessary. *Challenge*, May–June 1989, *32*(3), pp. 36–40.

Navid, Daniel. The International Law of Migratory Species: The Ramsar Convention. *Natural Res. J.*, Fall 1989, *29*(4), pp. 1001–16.

Navin, F. P. D. and de Castilho, B. A Rule-Based Highway Location System. In *Candemir, Y., ed.*, 1989, pp. 334–48.

Navrud, Ståle. Estimating Social Benefits of Environmental Improvements from Reduced Acid Depositions: A Contigent Valuation Survey. In *Folmer, H. and van Ierland, E., eds.*, 1989, pp. 69–102.

Nawata, Kazumitsu. Semiparametric Estimation and Efficiency Bounds of Binary Choice Models When the Models Contain One Continuous Variable. *Econ. Letters*, November 1989, *31*(1), pp. 21–26.

Nawrocki, David and Staples, Katharine. A Customized LPM Risk Measure for Portfolio Analysis. *Appl. Econ.*, February 1989, *21*(2), pp. 205–18.

Naya, Seiji; Roy, Suby and Imada, Pearl. Lessons in Development: A Comparative Study of Asia and Latin America: Introduction. In *Naya, S., et al., eds.*, 1989, pp. 3–12.

Nayak, Tapan K. and Gastwirth, Joseph L. The Use of Diversity Analysis to Assess the Relative Influence of Factors Affecting the Income Distribution. *J. Bus. Econ. Statist.*, October 1989, *7*(4), pp. 453–60.

———; **Wang, Jane-Ling and Gastwirth, Joseph L.** Statistical Properties of Measures of Between-Group Income Differentials. *J. Econometrics*, September 1989, *42*(1), pp. 5–19.

Nayfeld, Alejandro and Velasco, Andres. Annual Review of Nations: Year 1988: Argentina. In *Haberman, L. and Sacks, P. M., eds.*, 1989, pp. 1–18.

Naylor, Robin. Strikes, Free Riders, and Social Customs. *Quart. J. Econ.*, November 1989, *104*(4), pp. 771–85.

Nayyar, Deepak. International Labour Migration from India: A Macro-economic Analysis. In *Amjad, R., ed.*, 1989, pp. 95–142.

Nazarenko, Victor. The Impact of Changes in Policies in Centrally Planned Economies on World Food Trade and Consumption. In *Helmuth, J. W. and Johnson, S. R., eds., Vol. 2*, 1989, pp. 45–58.

Nazli, Hina; Malik, Sohail J. and Mushtaq, Mo-

hammad. An Analysis of Production Relations in the Large-Scale Textile Manufacturing Sector of Pakistan. *Pakistan Devel. Rev.*, Spring 1989, *28*(1), pp. 27–42.

Nazmi, Nader. Economic Growth and Under-development in Iran: 1951–1978. *Comp. Econ. Stud.*, Fall 1989, *31*(3), pp. 33–54.

——— **and Baade, Robert A.** Currency Substitution and Money Demand in the United States, West Germany and Japan. *Kredit Kapital*, 1989, *22*(3), pp. 363–74.

Ndulu, Benno J. Social Sector Pricing Policy Revisited: A Survey of Some Recent Controversies: Comment. In *Fischer, S. and de Tray, D., eds.*, 1989, pp. 139–42.

Neale, Walter C. The Evolution of Colonial Institutions: An Argument Illustrated from the Economic History of British Central Africa. In *Tool, M. R. and Samuels, W. J., eds. (III)*, 1989, *1984*, pp. 425–35.

———. Language and Economics. In *Tool, M. R. and Samuels, W. J., eds. (II)*, 1989, *1982*, pp. 301–15.

———. Property in Land as Cultural Imperialism: Or, Why Ethnocentric Ideas Won't Work in India and Africa. In *Tool, M. R. and Samuels, W. J., eds. (III)*, 1989, *1985*, pp. 255–62.

Neary, J. Peter. Immigration and Real Wages. *Econ. Letters*, August 1989, *30*(2), pp. 171–74.

———. Subsidios a las exportaciones y bienestar nacional. (Export Subsidies and National Welfare. With English summary.) *Estud. Econ.*, July–Dec. 1989, *4*(2), pp. 135–56.

Neave, Edwin H. Canada's Approach to Financial Regulation. *Can. Public Policy*, March 1989, *15*(1), pp. 1–11.

——— **and Nathan, Alli.** Competition and Contestability in Canada's Financial System: Empirical Results. *Can. J. Econ.*, August 1989, *22*(3), pp. 576–94.

Neck, R. Emil Sax's Contribution to Public Economics. *J. Econ. Stud.*, 1989, *16*(2), pp. 23–46.

Necker, Tyll. Telecommunications Policy—Assessing Recent Experience in the U.S., Japan and Europe and Its Implications for the Completion of the Internal Common Market: Comment. In *Giersch, H., ed.*, 1989, pp. 190–97.

Nedda Giraldo, L. and Deserti, L. FMS: A Classification of Recent Literature. In *Archetti, F.; Lucertini, M. and Serafini, P., eds.*, 1989, pp. 289–92.

Nee, Victor. Peasant Entrepreneurship and the Politics of Regulation in China. In *Nee, V. and Stark, D., eds.*, 1989, pp. 169–207.

——— **and Stark, David.** Toward an Institutional Analysis of State Socialism. In *Nee, V. and Stark, D., eds.*, 1989, pp. 1–31.

Neeson, J. M. Parliamentary Enclosure and the Disappearance of the English Peasantry, Revisited. In *Grantham, G. and Leonard, C. S., eds., Pt. A*, 1989, pp. 89–120.

Negandhi, Anant R. Management Strategies and Policies of American, German, and Japanese

Multinational Corporations. **In** *Negandhi, A. R., ed.*, 1989, pp. 29–49.

_____; **Serapio, Manuel G., Jr. and Shin, Mansoo.** Multinationals and Newly Industrialized Countries: Strategies, Environmental Imperatives, and Practices: Introduction: Multinationals in the Twenty-first Century. **In** *Negandhi, A. R., ed.*, 1989, pp. 1–8.

Negishi, Takashi. Competition and the Number of Participants: Lessons of Edgeworth's Theorem. **In** *Feiwel, G. R., ed. (I)*, 1989, pp. 212–24.

_____. Expenditure Patterns and International Trade in Quesnay's Tableau Economique. **In** *Sato, R. and Negishi, T., eds.*, 1989, pp. 85–97.

_____. On Equilibrium and Disequilibrium: A Reply. *Hist. Polit. Econ.*, Winter 1989, *21*(4), pp. 593–600.

Negri, Donald H. The Common Property Aquifer as a Differential Game. *Water Resources Res.*, January 1989, *25*(1), pp. 9–15.

Nehen, I. Ketut and Jayasuriya, Sisira K. Bali: Economic Growth and Tourism. **In** *Hill, H., ed.*, 1989, pp. 330–48.

Neill, Jon R. A Welfare-Theoretic Evaluation of Unemployment Insurance. *Public Finance Quart.*, October 1989, *17*(4), pp. 429–44.

Nelissen, Jan H. M. The Distribution of Lifetime Earnings. *Econ. Letters*, 1989, *29*(2), pp. 189–93.

Nell, Edward J. Accumulation and Capital Theory. **In** *Feiwel, G. R., ed. (II)*, 1989, pp. 377–412.

_____. Joan Robinson: A Memoir. **In** *Feiwel, G. R., ed. (II)*, 1989, pp. 892–94.

_____. Notes on Finance, Risk and Investment Spending. **In** *Barrère, A., ed.*, 1989, pp. 16–47.

_____. On Long-Run Equilibrium in Class Society. **In** *Feiwel, G. R., ed. (II)*, 1989, pp. 323–43.

_____. The Rate of Profit in Kalecki's Theory. **In** *Sebastiani, M., ed.*, 1989, pp. 160–63.

_____ **and Jimenez, Felix.** The Political Economy of the External Debt and Growth: The Case of Peru. **In** *Semmler, W., ed.*, 1989, pp. 228–51.

Nellis, John. The Role of Institutions in Development: Comment. **In** *Fischer, S. and de Tray, D., eds.*, 1989, pp. 177–79.

_____ **and Kikeri, Sunita.** The Privatization of Public Enterprises. **In** *El-Naggar, S., ed.*, 1989, pp. 50–80.

_____ **and Kikeri, Sunita.** Public Enterprise Reform: Privatization and the World Bank. *World Devel.*, May 1989, *17*(5), pp. 659–72.

Nelson, Alan. Average Explanations. **In** *Balzer, W. and Hamminga, B., eds.*, 1989, pp. 23–42.

Nelson, Alex. Efficiency Gains and Adjustment Costs of Reforming the U.S. Rice Program. *Food Res. Inst. Stud.*, 1989, *21*(2), pp. 139–64.

Nelson, Barbara J. and Evans, Sara M. The Impact of Pay Equity on Public Employees: State of Minnesota Employees' Attitudes toward Wage Policy Innovation. **In** *Michael, R. T.; Hartmann, H. I. and O'Farrell, B., eds.*, 1989, pp. 200–221.

Nelson, Carl H.; Braden, John B. and Roh, Jae-Sun. Asset Fixity and Investment Asymmetry in Agriculture. *Amer. J. Agr. Econ.*, November 1989, *71*(4), pp. 970–79.

_____ **and Preckel, Paul V.** The Conditional Beta Distribution as a Stochastic Production Function. *Amer. J. Agr. Econ.*, May 1989, *71*(2), pp. 370–78.

_____ **and Preckel, Paul V.** Erratum [The Conditional Beta Distribution as a Stochastic Production Function]. *Amer. J. Agr. Econ.*, November 1989, *71*(4), pp. 1045.

Nelson, Charles R. Implicit Estimates of the Natural and Cyclical Components of Japan's Real GNP. *Bank Japan Monet. Econ. Stud.*, August 1989, *7*(2), pp. 73–91.

_____ **and Kim, Chang-Jin.** The Time-Varying-Parameter Model for Modeling Changing Conditional Variance: The Case of the Lucas Hypothesis. *J. Bus. Econ. Statist.*, October 1989, *7*(4), pp. 433–40.

_____; **Peck, Stephen C. and Uhler, Robert G.** The NERC Fan in Retrospect and Lessons for the Future. *Energy J.*, April 1989, *10*(2), pp. 91–107.

_____; **Turner, Christopher M. and Startz, Richard.** A Markov Model of Heteroskedasticity, Risk, and Learning in the Stock Market. *J. Finan. Econ.*, November 1989, *25*(1), pp. 3–22.

Nelson, Daniel. Managers and Nonunion Workers in the Rubber Industry: Union Avoidance Strategies in the 1930s. *Ind. Lab. Relat. Rev.*, October 1989, *43*(1), pp. 41–52.

Nelson, Daniel B. Price Volatility, International Market Links, and Their Implications for Regulatory Policies: Commentary. *J. Finan. Services Res.*, December 1989, *3*(2–3), pp. 247–54.

_____. Price Volatility, International Market Links, and Their Implications for Regulatory Policies: Commentary. **In** *Edwards, F. R., ed.*, 1989, pp. 149–56.

Nelson, Douglas. On the High Track to Protection: The U.S. Automobile Industry, 1979–1981. **In** *Haggard, S. and Moon, C., eds.*, 1989, pp. 97–128.

Nelson, Gerald C. Rent Seeking in North–South Agricultural Trade. *Europ. Rev. Agr. Econ.*, 1989, *16*(1), pp. 53–64.

Nelson, J. Gordon. Wilderness in Canada: Past, Present, Future. *Natural Res. J.*, Winter 1989, *29*(1), pp. 83–102.

Nelson, Joan M. Crisis Management, Economic Reform and Costa Rican Democracy. **In** *Stallings, B. and Kaufman, R., eds.*, 1989, pp. 143–61.

_____. The Fund and the Low-Income Countries: The IMF and the Impact of Adjustment on the Poor: Comment. **In** *Gwin, C. and Feinberg, R. E., eds.*, 1989, pp. 165–68.

_____. The Politics of Long-Haul Economic Reform. In *Nelson, J. M., ed.*, 1989, pp. 3–26.

_____. The Politics of Pro-poor Adjustment. In *Nelson, J. M., ed.*, 1989, pp. 95–113.

Nelson, Jon P. and Roberts, Mark J. Ramsey Numbers and the Role of Competing Interest Groups in Electric Utility Regulation. *Quart. Rev. Econ. Bus.*, Autumn 1989, *29*(3), pp. 21–42.

Nelson, Julie A. Individual Consumption within the Household: A Study of Expenditures on Clothing. *J. Cons. Aff.*, Summer 1989, *23*(1), pp. 21–44.

Nelson, Kenneth E. and Duewer, Lawrence A. ERS's Measures of Red Meat Consumption. In *Buse, R. C., ed.*, 1989, pp. 57–73.

Nelson, Michael A. Taxation of Natural Resources and State Economic Growth. *Growth Change*, Fall 1989, *20*(4), pp. 13–30.

_____ **and Hunter, William J.** Interest Group Demand for Taxation. *Public Choice*, July 1989, *62*(1), pp. 41–61.

_____ **and Wyzan, Michael L.** Public Policy, Local Labor Demand, and Migration in Sweden, 1979–84. *J. Reg. Sci.*, May 1989, *29*(2), pp. 247–64.

Nelson, Philip B. and Hilke, John C. Strategic Behavior and Attempted Monopolization: The *Coffee (General Foods)* Case. In *Kwoka, J. E., Jr. and White, L. J., eds.*, 1989, pp. 208–40.

Nelson, Randy A. The Effects of Regulation on Capacity Utilization: Evidence from the Electric Power Industry. *Quart. Rev. Econ. Bus.*, Winter 1989, *29*(4), pp. 37–48.

_____. On the Measurement of Capacity Utilization. *J. Ind. Econ.*, March 1989, *37*(3), pp. 273–86.

Nelson, Richard R. Industry Growth Accounts and Production Functions When Techniques Are Idiosyncratic. *J. Econ. Behav. Organ.*, May 1989, *11*(3), pp. 323–41.

_____. State Labor Legislation Enacted in 1988. *Mon. Lab. Rev.*, January 1989, *112*(1), pp. 40–59.

Nelson, Richard W. Management versus Economic Conditions as Contributors to the Recent Increase in Bank Failures. In *Stone, C. C., ed.*, 1989, pp. 125–48.

Nelson, Robert G. and Bessler, David A. Subjective Probabilities and Scoring Rules: Experimental Evidence. *Amer. J. Agr. Econ.*, May 1989, *71*(2), pp. 363–69.

Nelson, Robert H. The Office of Policy Analysis in the Department of the Interior. *J. Policy Anal. Manage.*, Summer 1989, *8*(3), pp. 395–410.

_____. Privatization of Federal Lands: What Did Not Happen? In *Meiners, R. E. and Yandle, B., eds.*, 1989, pp. 132–65.

_____. The Role of the Economist in Government: An International Perspective: Introduction and Summary. In *Pechman, J. A., ed.*, 1989, pp. 1–22.

Nelson, William. Evaluating the Institutions of Liberal Democracy. In *Brennan, G. and Lomasky, L. E., eds.*, 1989, pp. 60–77.

Nelson, William J., Jr. Workers' Compensation: Coverage, Benefits, and Costs, 1986. *Soc. Sec. Bull.*, March 1989, *52*(3), pp. 34–41.

Neme, A. and Cesco, J. C. A Nash Type Equilibrium in Games without Transitive Preferences. *Math. Soc. Sci.*, February 1989, *17*(1), pp. 47–56.

Nentjes, Andries. Macroeconomic Cost–Benefit Analysis of Environmental Programmes. In *Folmer, H. and van Ierland, E., eds.*, 1989, pp. 187–216.

Neri, Fabio and Dell'Aringa, Carlo. Illegal Immigrants and the Informal Economy in Italy. In *Gordon, I. and Thirlwall, A. P., eds.*, 1989, pp. 133–47.

_____ **and Podrecca, Elena.** Dalla curva di beveridge ad una matrice per qualifiche. (From the Beveridge Curve to a Job Category Matrix. With English summary.) *Econ. Lavoro*, July–Sept. 1989, *23*(3), pp. 87–98.

Nerlove, Marc. The Use of Modern Inputs in the Agricultural Sectors of Developing Countries: The Case of Brazil. In *Chakravarty, S., ed.*, 1989, pp. 299–322.

_____ **and Diebold, Francis X.** The Dynamics of Exchange Rate Volatility: A Multivariate Latent Factor Arch Model. *J. Appl. Econometrics*, Jan.–March 1989, *4*(1), pp. 1–21.

van Nes, Floor and ten Cate, Arie. Software for Econometric Research with a Personal Computer. *Int. J. Forecasting*, 1989, *5*(2), pp. 263–78.

Ness, Gayl D. The Impact of International Population Assistance. In *Krueger, A. O.; Michalopoulos, C. and Ruttan, V. W.*, 1989, pp. 185–200.

Nestel, Gilbert and Chirikos, Thomas N. Functional Capacities of Older Men for Extended Work Lives. *Soc. Sec. Bull.*, August 1989, *52*(8), pp. 14–16.

Netemeyer, Richard G.; Teel, Jesse E. and Bearden, William O. Measurement of Consumer Susceptibility to Interpersonal Influence. *J. Cons. Res.*, March 1989, *15*(4), pp. 473–81.

Neter, John; Godfrey, James T. and Wurst, John. Efficiency of Sieve Sampling in Auditing. *J. Bus. Econ. Statist.*, April 1989, *7*(2), pp. 199–205.

Neto, Francisco P. Bueno. Administrative and Compliance Costs of Taxation: Brazil. In *International Fiscal Association, ed. (I)*, 1989, pp. 251–65.

Netter, Jeffry M. and Hersch, Philip L. State Prohibition of Alcohol: An Application of Diffusion Analysis to Regulation. In *Zerbe, R. O., ed.*, 1989, pp. 55–70.

_____ **and Mitchell, Mark L.** Triggering the 1987 Stock Market Crash: Antitakeover Provisions in the Proposed House Ways and Means Tax Bill? *J. Finan. Econ.*, September 1989, *24*(1), pp. 37–68.

Neubig, Thomas S. The Current Role of the Tax Expenditure Budget in U.S. Policymaking. In *Bruce, N., ed.*, 1989, pp. 239–58.

Neudorfer, Peter and Pichelmann, Karl. Measuring Shock Persistence in Austrian Unemployment: A Note. *Empirica*, 1989, *16*(2), pp. 193–208.

Neufeld, Edward P. Co-ordination of Economic Policies: A View from the Trenches. *Can. Public Policy*, Supplement, February 1989, *15*, pp. S35–38.

Neumann, George R. and Horowitz, Joel L. Computational and Statistical Efficiency of Semiparametric GLS Estimators. *Econometric Rev.*, 1989, *8*(2), pp. 223–25.

_____ **and Horowitz, Joel L.** Specification Testing in Censored Regression Models: Parametric and Semiparametric Methods. *J. Appl. Econometrics*, Supplement, December 1989, *4*, pp. S61–86.

_____ **and Kiefer, Nicholas M.** An Empirical Job-Search Model, with a Test of the Constant Reservation-Wage Hypothesis. **In** *Kiefer, N. M. and Neumann, G. R.*, 1989, *1979*, pp. 42–62.

_____ **and Kiefer, Nicholas M.** Choice or Chance? A Structural Interpretation of Individual Labor Market Histories. **In** *Kiefer, N. M. and Neumann, G. R.*, 1989, *1984*, pp. 109–38.

_____ **and Kiefer, Nicholas M.** Earnings, Unemployment, and the Allocation of Time over Time. **In** *Kiefer, N. M. and Neumann, G. R.*, 1989, *1984*, pp. 83–108.

_____ **and Kiefer, Nicholas M.** Employment Risk and Labor Market Diversification. **In** *Kiefer, N. M. and Neumann, G. R.*, 1989, pp. 229–35.

_____ **and Kiefer, Nicholas M.** Estimation of Wage Offer Distributions and Reservation Wages. **In** *Kiefer, N. M. and Neumann, G. R.*, 1989, *1979*, pp. 23–41.

_____ **and Kiefer, Nicholas M.** How Long Is a Spell of Unemployment? Illusions and Biases in the Use of CPS Data. **In** *Kiefer, N. M. and Neumann, G. R.*, 1989, *1985*, pp. 203–26.

_____ **and Kiefer, Nicholas M.** Individual Effects in a Nonlinear Model: Explicit Treatment of Heterogeneity in the Empirical Job-Search Model. **In** *Kiefer, N. M. and Neumann, G. R.*, 1989, *1981*, pp. 63–79.

_____ **and Kiefer, Nicholas M.** Interfirm Mobility and Earnings. **In** *Kiefer, N. M. and Neumann, G. R.*, 1989, pp. 247–83.

_____ **and Kiefer, Nicholas M.** Layoffs and Duration Dependence in a Model of Turnover. **In** *Kiefer, N. M. and Neumann, G. R.*, 1989, *1985*, pp. 139–59.

_____ **and Kiefer, Nicholas M.** Methods for Analyzing Employment Contracts and Other Agreements. **In** *Kiefer, N. M. and Neumann, G. R.*, 1989, *1984*, pp. 284–92.

_____ **and Kiefer, Nicholas M.** A Proposition and an Example in the Theory of Job Search with Hours Constraints. **In** *Kiefer, N. M. and Neumann, G. R.*, 1989, *1987*, pp. 236–46.

_____ **and Kiefer, Nicholas M.** Search Models and Applied Labor Economics: Introduction. **In** *Kiefer, N. M. and Neumann, G. R.*, 1989, pp. 1–19.

_____ **and Kiefer, Nicholas M.** Structural and Reduced Form Approaches to Analyzing Unemployment Durations. **In** *Kiefer, N. M. and Neumann, G. R.*, 1989, *1981*, pp. 163–78.

_____ **and Kiefer, Nicholas M.** Wages and the Structure of Unemployment Rates. **In** *Kiefer, N. M. and Neumann, G. R.*, 1989, *1982*, pp. 179–202.

Neumann, L. Market Relations in Intra-enterprise Wage Bargaining? *Acta Oecon.*, 1989, *40*(3–4), pp. 319–38.

Neumann, Manfred. Changes in Revenue Structures from the Point of View of Political Economy. **In** *Chiancone, A. and Messere, K., eds.*, 1989, pp. 143–51.

_____. Market Size, Monopoly Power and Innovations under Uncertainty. **In** *Audretsch, D. B.; Sleuwaegen, L. and Yamawaki, H., eds.*, 1989, pp. 295–314.

Neumann, Manfred J. M. Policy Analysis with a Multicountry Model: Comment. **In** *Bryant, R. C., et al., eds.*, 1989, pp. 142–46.

_____, **et al.** The Appropriate Level of Regulation in Europe: Local, National or Community-Wide? A Roundtable Discussion. *Econ. Policy: A Europ. Forum*, October 1989, (9), pp. 467–81.

Neumann, Uwe and Schellhaass, Horst-Manfred. Missbrauchsaufsicht im Lebensmitteleinzelhandel. (With English summary.) *Z. Betriebswirtshaft*, May 1989, *59*(5), pp. 566–78.

Neun, Stephen P. and Santerre, Rexford E. Managerial Control and Executive Compensation in the 1930s: A Reexamination. *Quart. J. Bus. Econ.*, Autumn 1989, *28*(4), pp. 100–118.

Neutze, Max. Urban Development. **In** *Higgins, B. and Zagorski, K., eds.*, 1989, pp. 45–64.

Neven, Damien J. Strategic Entry Deterrence: Recent Developments in the Economics of Industry. *J. Econ. Surveys*, 1989, *3*(3), pp. 213–33.

_____ **and Anderson, Simon P.** Market Efficiency with Combinable Products. *Europ. Econ. Rev.*, April 1989, *33*(4), pp. 707–19.

_____ **and Thisse, Jacques-François.** Choix des produits: Concurrence en qualité et en variété. (Products Selection: Competition in Quality and Variety. With English summary.) *Ann. Écon. Statist.*, July–Dec. 1989, (15–16), pp. 85–112.

Neves, Cesar F. Dinis das and Bana e Costa, Carlos A. Describing and Formalizing the Evaluation Process of Portuguese Navy Officers. **In** *Lockett, A. G. and Islei, G., eds.*, 1989, pp. 355–69.

Nevile, J. W. An Economy in Distress? **In** *Hancock, K., ed.*, 1989, pp. 143–65.

Newbery, David M. Agricultural Institutions for Insurance and Stabilization. **In** *Bardhan, P., ed. (II)*, 1989, pp. 267–96.

_____. Cost Recovery from Optimally Designed Roads. *Economica*, May 1989, *56*(222), pp. 165–85.

_____. Energy Policy Issues after Privatization. **In** *Helm, D.; Kay, J. and Thompson, D., eds.*, 1989, pp. 30–54.

———. Missing Markets: Consequences and Remedies. In *Hahn, F., ed.*, 1989, pp. 211–42.

———. The Theory of Food Price Stabilisation. *Econ. J.*, December 1989, *99*(398), pp. 1065–82.

——— **and Wright, Brian D.** Financial Instruments for Consumption Smoothing by Commodity-Dependent Exporters. *Amer. J. Agr. Econ.*, May 1989, *71*(2), pp. 511–16.

Newbold, Paul and Bos, Ted. On Exponential Smoothing and the Assumption of Deterministic Trend Plus White Noise Data-Generating Models. *Int. J. Forecasting*, 1989, *5*(4), pp. 523–27.

Newburger, Harriet B. Discrimination by a Profit-Maximizing Real Estate Broker in Response to White Prejudice. *J. Urban Econ.*, July 1989, *26*(1), pp. 1–19.

Newcombe, Kenneth J. An Economic Justification for Rural Afforestation: The Case of Ethiopia. In *Schramm, G. and Warford, J. J., eds.*, 1989, pp. 117–38.

Newell, Andrew and Symons, James S. V. Stylised Facts and the Labour Demand Curve. *Labour*, Winter 1989, *3*(3), pp. 3–21.

Newey, Whitney K. Introduction à la théorie des bornes d'efficacité semi-paramétriques. (An Introduction to Semiparametric Efficiency Bounds. With English summary.) *Ann. Écon. Statist.*, Jan.–March 1989, (13), pp. 1–47.

———; **Rosen, Harvey S. and Holtz-Eakin, Douglas.** The Revenues–Expenditures Nexus: Evidence from Local Government Data. *Int. Econ. Rev.*, May 1989, *30*(2), pp. 415–29.

Newfarmer, Richard S. Directions of Trade and Transnational Corporations in Brazil: An Empirical Analysis. In *Ventura-Dias, V., ed.*, 1989, pp. 263–75.

Newlands, D.; Danson, M. and Lloyd, G. 'Scottish Enterprise': Towards a Model Agency or a Flawed Initiative? *Reg. Stud.*, December 1989, *23*(6), pp. 557–63.

Newlon, Daniel H. The Role of the NSF in the Spread of Economic Ideas. In *Colander, D. C. and Coats, A. W., eds.*, 1989, pp. 195–228.

Newman, Andrew E. and Baron, James N. Pay the Man: Effects of Demographic Composition on Prescribed Wage Rates in the California Civil Service. In *Michael, R. T.; Hartmann, H. I. and O'Farrell, B., eds.*, 1989, pp. 107–30.

Newman, Barbara A. and Thomson, Randall J. Economic Growth and Social Development: A Longitudinal Analysis of Causal Priority. *World Devel.*, April 1989, *17*(4), pp. 461–71.

Newman, David and Finkelstein, Joseph. The Third Industrial Revolution. In *Finkelstein, J., ed.*, 1989, pp. 219–32.

Newman, Geoffrey. Towards a Theory of 'Rational' Distortions. *Rivista Int. Sci. Econ. Com.*, April–May 1989, *36*(4–5), pp. 289–323.

Newman, Harry A. Selection of Short-term Accounting-Based Bonus Plans. *Accounting Rev.*, October 1989, *64*(4), pp. 758–72.

——— **and Butler, Stephen A.** Agency Control Mechanism Effectiveness and Decision Making

in an Executive's Final Year with a Firm. *J. Inst. Theoretical Econ.*, September 1989, *145*(3), pp. 451–64.

Newman, Jay. Frontiers in Biophysics: Today's Science for Tomorrow's Technology. In *Finkelstein, J., ed.*, 1989, pp. 131–52.

Newman, Jeffry and Prinzinger, Joseph. Is Hospice a Cost Effective Alternative to Medicaid Conventional Care? *Atlantic Econ. J.*, March 1989, *17*(1), pp. 95.

Newman, John L. and Boschen, John F. Monetary Effects on the Real Interest Rate in an Open Economy: Evidence from the Argentine Indexed Bond Market. *J. Int. Money Finance*, June 1989, *8*(2), pp. 201–17.

——— **and Levy, Victor.** Wage Rigidity: Micro and Macro Evidence on Labor Market Adjustment in the Modern Sector. *World Bank Econ. Rev.*, January 1989, *3*(1), pp. 97–117.

Newman, Mark D. and Morris, Michael L. Official and Parallel Cereals Markets in Senegal: Empirical Evidence. *World Devel.*, December 1989, *17*(12), pp. 1895–1906.

Newman, Robert J. and Farber, Stephen C. Regional Wage Differentials and the Spatial Convergence of Worker Characteristic Prices. *Rev. Econ. Statist.*, May 1989, *71*(2), pp. 224–31.

———; **Scott, Loren C. and Moore, William J.** Welfare Expenditures and the Decline of Unions. *Rev. Econ. Statist.*, August 1989, *71*(3), pp. 538–42.

Newmark, Craig M. Administrative Control, Buyer Concentration, and Price–Cost Margins. *Rev. Econ. Statist.*, February 1989, *71*(1), pp. 74–79.

Newton, Keith. Introducing New Technologies in Canada: Some Human-Resource Implications. In *Punset, E. and Sweeney, G., eds.*, 1989, pp. 106–18.

Newville, Ed. Pueblo Indian Water Rights: Overview and Update on the AAMODT Litigation. *Natural Res. J.*, Winter 1989, *29*(1), pp. 251–78.

Neyman, Abraham. Uniqueness of the Shapley Value. *Games Econ. Behav.*, March 1989, *1*(1), pp. 116–18.

——— **and Einy, Ezra.** Large Symmetric Games Are Characterized by Completeness of the Desirability Relation. *J. Econ. Theory*, August 1989, *48*(2), pp. 369–85.

Ng, Elliot K. and Heaney, James P. Efficient Total Enumeration of Water Resources Alternatives. *Water Resources Res.*, April 1989, *25*(4), pp. 583–90.

Ng, Ignace and Dastmalchian, Ali. Determinants of Grievance Outcomes: A Case Study. *Ind. Lab. Relat. Rev.*, April 1989, *42*(3), pp. 393–403.

Ng, Kenneth and Virts, Nancy. The Value of Freedom. *J. Econ. Hist.*, December 1989, *49*(4), pp. 958–65.

Ng, Lawrence. A DRASTIC Approach to Controlling Groundwater Pollution. *Yale Law J.*, February 1989, *98*(4), pp. 773–91.

Ng, Sik Hung and Cram, Fiona. Children's Endorsement of Ownership Attributes. *J. Econ. Psych.*, March 1989, *10*(1), pp. 63–75.

Ng, Yew-Kwang. Diamonds Are a Government's Best Friend: Burden-Free Taxes on Goods Valued for Their Values: Reply. *Amer. Econ. Rev.*, December 1989, *79*(5), pp. 1289–90.

_____. Economic Efficiency versus Egalitarian Rights: A Response. *Kyklos*, 1989, *42*(2), pp. 261–63.

_____. Hurka's Gamble and Methuselah's Paradox: A Response to Cowen on Normative Population Theory. *Soc. Choice Welfare*, January 1989, *6*(1), pp. 45–49.

_____. Individual Irrationality and Social Welfare. *Soc. Choice Welfare*, April 1989, *6*(2), pp. 87–101.

_____. What Should We Do about Future Generations? Impossibility of Parfit's Theory X. *Econ. Philos.*, October 1989, *5*(2), pp. 235–53.

Ngui, Michael; Burrows, Colin and Brown, Kaye. Health Insurance Choice: An Econometric Analysis of A.B.S. Health and Health Insurance Surveys. In *Smith, C. S., ed.*, 1989, pp. 172–94.

Nguyen, D. T. The Demand for LDC Exports of Manufactures: Estimates from Hong Kong: A Comment. *Econ. J.*, June 1989, *99*(396), pp. 461–66.

_____. Partial Price Stabilisation and National Export Earnings Instability. *J. Econ. Stud.*, 1989, *16*(3), pp. 57–69.

_____ **and Dowrick, Steve.** OECD Comparative Economic Growth 1950–85: Catch-Up and Convergence. *Amer. Econ. Rev.*, December 1989, *79*(5), pp. 1010–30.

Nguyen, Hung. Agricultural Planning Policy and Variability in Syrian Cereal Production. In *Anderson, J. R. and Hazell, P. B. R., eds.*, 1989, pp. 78–96.

Nguyen, Sang and Pallottino, Stefano. Hyperpaths and Shortest Hyperpaths. In *Simeone, B., ed.*, 1989, pp. 258–71.

Nguyen, Sang V. and Andrews, Stephen H. The Effect of Energy Aggregation on Energy Elasticities: Some Evidence from U.S. Manufacturing Data. *Energy J.*, January 1989, *10*(1), pp. 149–56.

_____ **and Andrews, Stephen H.** Stage-of-Fabrication Inventory Behavior in Durable Goods Manufacturing Industries. *J. Post Keynesian Econ.*, Summer 1989, *11*(4), pp. 561–88.

_____ **and Andrews, Stephen H.** Stage-of-Fabrication Inventory Behaviour: A General Target-Adjustment Model. *Appl. Econ.*, February 1989, *21*(2), pp. 175–92.

Nguyen, Tom and Dowrick, Steve. Measurement and International Comparison. In *[Gruen, F. H.]*, 1989, pp. 34–59.

Nguyen, Trien T. The Parallel Market of Illegal Aliens: A Computational Approach. *World Devel.*, December 1989, *17*(12), pp. 1965–78.

_____ **and Whalley, John.** General Equilibrium Analysis of Black and White Markets: A Computational Approach. *J. Public Econ.*, December 1989, *40*(3), pp. 331–47.

Nguyen, V. A.; Hall, V. B. and Truong, T. P.

Responses to World Oil and Coal Shocks, in a Short-run Fuel Substitution Tax Model. *Australian Econ. Rev.*, Spring 1989, (87), pp. 25–38.

Ngwasiri, C. N. The Effect of Legislation on Foreign Investment: The Case of Cameroon. *J. World Trade*, June 1989, *23*(3), pp. 109–23.

Nichol, Michael B. and Graddy, Elizabeth. Public Members on Occupational Licensing Boards: Effects on Legislative Regulatory Reforms. *Southern Econ. J.*, January 1989, *55*(3), pp. 610–25.

Nicholas, Peter and Liebenthal, Robert. World Bank-Supported Adjustment Programs. In *Weeks, J. F., ed.*, 1989, pp. 91–102.

Nickel, Hildegard M. Sex-Role Socialization in Relationships as a Function of the Division of Labor. In *Rueschemeyer, M. and Lemke, C., eds.*, 1989, pp. 48–58.

Nickell, Stephen J. Real Wages and Employment: A Comment. *Manchester Sch. Econ. Soc. Stud.*, September 1989, *57*(3), pp. 280–84.

_____; **Horsewood, N. and Dimsdale, N. H.** Real Wages and Unemployment in Britain during the 1930s. *Econ. J.*, June 1989, *99*(396), pp. 271–92.

_____ **and Layard, Richard.** The Thatcher Miracle? *Amer. Econ. Rev.*, May 1989, *79*(2), pp. 215–19.

_____ **and Narendranathan, Wiji.** Modelling the Process of Job Search. In *Nickell, S. J., et al.*, 1989, *1985*, pp. 47–77.

_____; **Stern, Jon and Narendranathan, Wiji.** The Nature of Unemployment in Britain: Studies of the DHSS Cohort: Introduction. In *Nickell, S. J., et al.*, 1989, pp. 1–10.

_____; **Stern, Jon and Narendranathan, Wiji.** Unemployment Benefits Revisited. In *Nickell, S. J., et al.*, 1989, *1985*, pp. 11–46.

Nickerson, David and Lewis, Tracy R. Self-insurance against Natural Disasters. *J. Environ. Econ. Manage.*, May 1989, *16*(3), pp. 209–23.

Nickson, Andrew. The State, Industrial Relations and the Labour Movement in Latin America: Volume 1: Paraguay. In *Carrière, J.; Haworth, N. and Roddick, J., eds.*, 1989, pp. 67–98.

Nicol, Christopher J. Estimating a Third-Order Translog Using Canadian Cross-Sectional Micro-data. *Can. J. Econ.*, August 1989, *22*(3), pp. 543–60.

_____. Testing a Theory of Exact Aggregation. *J. Bus. Econ. Statist.*, April 1989, *7*(2), pp. 259–65.

Nicolaides, Phedon. Economic Aspects of Services: Implications for a GATT Agreement. *J. World Trade*, February 1989, *23*(1), pp. 125–36.

_____. Economic Aspects of Services: Implications for a GATT Agreement. *J. World Trade*, February 1989, *23*(1), pp. 125–36.

_____. Globalisation of Services and Developing Countries. In *[Marjolin, R.]*, 1989, pp. 161–75.

_____. The Problem of Regulation in Traded Services: The Implications for Reciprocal Liberalization. *Aussenwirtschaft*, April 1989, *44*(1), pp. 29–57.

————. The Usefulness of a Broad Perspective on Services: Comment on D. Nayyar's Article: "Some Reflections on the Uruguay Round and Trade in Services." *J. World Trade*, August 1989, *23*(4), pp. 65–67.

Nicolaissen, Rolf H. Administrative and Compliance Costs of Taxation: Norway. In *International Fiscal Association, ed. (I)*, 1989, pp. 461–82.

Nicolaou-Smokoviti, Litsa. Reorganising Working Time and Social Change: The Case of Greece. In *Agassi, J. B. and Heycock, S., eds.*, 1989, pp. 139–44.

Nicolas, F.; Hy, M. and Lassaut, B. Concurrence entre les formes industrielles et artisanales de production–distribution des biens alimentaires: Exemples de la boulangerie et de la boucherie. (Competition between Industrial and Artisanal Firms in Food Products Marketing: The Case of Butchers' and Bakers' Trade. With English summary.) *Écon. Societes*, July 1989, *23*(7), pp. 197–216.

Nicolau, Ed., et al. Designing Relations for a General Non-linear System of Order Three. *Econ. Computat. Econ. Cybern. Stud. Res.*, 1989, *24*(2–3), pp. 75–84.

Nicolescu, O. Designing Computerized Management Games. *Econ. Computat. Econ. Cybern. Stud. Res.*, 1989, *24*(2–3), pp. 133–37.

Nicoletti, Giuseppe and Hagemann, Robert P. Population Ageing: Economic Effects and Some Policy Implications for Financing Public Pensions. *OECD Econ. Stud.*, Spring 1989, (12), pp. 51–96.

Nicolich, Lillian and Pollack, Gerald A. The Business Economist at Work: Overseas Shipholding Group. *Bus. Econ.*, July 1989, *24*(3), pp. 48–51.

Nicolò, F.; Arbib, Claudio and Lucertini, M. Optimization Models for Flexible Manufacturing Systems. In *Archetti, F.; Lucertini, M. and Serafini, P., eds.*, 1989, pp. 75–89.

Niedereichholz, Joachim and Kaucky, Gerhard. Informationstechnologie und Organisationsänderung. Dargestellt am Beispiel von Investitionsentscheidungen im Grossrechnerbereich. (With English summary.) *Z. Betriebswirtshaft*, June 1989, *59*(6), pp. 655–66.

Niehans, Jürg. Thünen-Vorlesung: Klassik als nationalökonomischer Mythus. (The Mythology of Classical Economics. With English summary.) *Z. Wirtschaft. Sozialwissen.*, 1989, *109*(1), pp. 1–17.

Niehaus, Gregory R. Government Pension Policy and the Cost of Labor and Capital. *J. Finan. Services Res.*, February 1989, *2*(1), pp. 5–20.

————. Ownership Structure and Inventory Method Choice. *Accounting Rev.*, April 1989, *64*(2), pp. 269–84.

van Niekerk, Nico and Roddick, Jacqueline. The State, Industrial Relations and the Labour Movement in Latin America: Volume 1: Bolivia. In *Carrière, J.; Haworth, N. and Roddick, J., eds.*, 1989, pp. 128–77.

Nielsen, A. Hjortshøj and Rasmussen, Svend. The Impact of Quotas on the Optimal Adjust-

ment of Milk Production at the Farm Level: Reply. *Europ. Rev. Agr. Econ.*, 1989, *16*(4), pp. 523–24.

Nielsen, Lars Tyge. Asset Market Equilibrium with Short-Selling. *Rev. Econ. Stud.*, July 1989, *56*(3), pp. 467–73.

————. Valutarisiko, valutagæld og rentespænd. (Exchange Rate Risk and Interest Rate Differential in a Portfolio Model. With English summary.) *Nationaløkon. Tidsskr.*, 1989, *127*(3), pp. 346–55.

Nielsen, Niels Chr. and Møller, Michael. Ejerskab, ledelse og incitamentsstrukturer. (The Interaction between Ownership, Management and Incentives. With English summary.) *Nationaløkon. Tidsskr.*, 1989, *127*(1), pp. 45–58.

Nielsen, Søren Bo. Effects of Macroeconomic Transmission of Tariffs. In *Singer, H. W. and Sharma, S., eds. (II)*, 1989, pp. 211–19.

————. The Puzzle of Welfare-Reducing Trade Diversion: A Supplementary Note. *Oxford Econ. Pap.*, April 1989, *41*(2), pp. 456–57.

Niemi, Albert W., Jr. How Discrimination against Female Workers Is Hidden in U.S. Industry Statistics: Sex Differences in Wages in the Cotton Textile and Boot and Shoe Industries between the World Wars. *Amer. J. Econ. Sociology*, October 1989, *48*(4), pp. 401–14.

Nieswiadomy, Michael L. and Molina, David J. Comparing Residential Water Demand Estimates under Decreasing and Increasing Block Rates Using Household Data. *Land Econ.*, August 1989, *65*(3), pp. 280–89.

————; **Slottje, Daniel J. and Basmann, R. L.** On the Empirical Relationship between Several Well-Known Inequality Measures. *J. Econometrics*, September 1989, *42*(1), pp. 49–66.

Nieuwenhuysen, John. Towards Freer Trade between Nations: Introduction: Major Themes and Proposals for Action. In *Nieuwenhuysen, J., ed.*, 1989, pp. 1–12.

————. Towards Freer Trade for Australia. In *Nieuwenhuysen, J., ed.*, 1989, pp. 115–43.

van Nieuwkerk, M. Model Building and Model Use. In *Muller, F. and Zwezerijnen, W. J., eds.*, 1989, pp. 122–32.

Nieuwoudt, W. L. and Vink, N. The Effects of Increased Earnings from Traditional Agriculture in Southern Africa. *S. Afr. J. Econ.*, September 1989, *57*(3), pp. 257–69.

Niggle, Christopher J. The Correct Conception of Capital: A Reply [The Increasing Importance of Financial Capital in the U.S. Economy]. *J. Econ. Issues*, March 1989, *23*(1), pp. 247–49.

————. The Cyclical Behavior of Corporate Financial Ratios and Minsky's Financial Instability Hypothesis. In *Semmler, W., ed.*, 1989, pp. 203–20.

————. Monetary Policy and Changes in Income Distribution. *J. Econ. Issues*, September 1989, *23*(3), pp. 809–22.

Nijkamp, Peter and Barentsen, Wim. Modelling Non-linear Processes in Time and Space. In *Andersson, Å. E., et al., eds.*, 1989, pp. 175–92.

_____ **and Batten, David F.** Progress in Spatial Theory and Dynamics: A Prefatory Review. In *Andersson, Å. E., et al., eds.*, 1989, pp. 1–11.

_____ **and Davelaar, Evert Jan.** Innovative Behaviour of Industrial Firms: Results from a Dutch Empirical Study. In *Andersson, Å. E.; Batten, D. F. and Karlsson, C., eds.*, 1989, pp. 177–86.

_____ **and Davelaar, Evert Jan.** The Role of the Metropolitan Milieu as an Incubation Centre for Technological Innovations: A Dutch Case Study. *Urban Stud.*, October 1989, *26*(5), pp. 517–25.

_____ **and Davelaar, Evert Jan.** Spatial Dispersion of Technological Innovation: A Case Study for the Netherlands by Means of Partial Least Squares. *J. Reg. Sci.*, August 1989, *29*(3), pp. 325–46.

_____**; Hartog, J. A. and Hinloopen, E.** A Sensitivity Analysis of Multicriteria Choice-Methods An Application on the Basis of the Optimal Site Selection for a Nuclear Power Plant. *Energy Econ.*, October 1989, *11*(4), pp. 293–300.

_____ **and van Pelt, Michiel.** Spatial Impact Analysis in Developing Countries: Method and Application. *Int. Reg. Sci. Rev.*, 1989, *12*(2), pp. 211–28.

_____ **and Reggiani, Aura.** Spatial Interaction and Input–Output Models: A Dynamic Stochastic Multiobjective Framework. In *Miller, R. E.; Polenske, K. R. and Rose, A. Z., eds.*, 1989, pp. 193–205.

_____ **and Rietveld, Piet.** Multiple-Objective Optimization in a Macroeconomic Context. In *Muller, F. and Zwezerijnen, W. J., eds.*, 1989, pp. 133–49.

_____ **and Rouwendal, Jan.** Endogenous Production of R and D and Stable Economic Development. *De Economist*, 1989, *137*(2), pp. 202–16.

Nijmeijer, Hendrik. On Dynamic Decoupling and Dynamic Path Controllability in Economic Systems. *J. Econ. Dynam. Control*, January 1989, *13*(1), pp. 21–39.

_____. On the Theory of Nonlinear Control Systems. In *[Willems, J. C.]*, 1989, pp. 339–57.

Nikic, Gorazd. Structural Adjustment and Exchange Rate Policy in Yugoslavia. In *Singer, H. W. and Sharma, S., eds. (I)*, 1989, pp. 297–307.

Nikiforov, L. V. The Development of the Agro-industrial Complex in the USSR. In *Williamson, J. G. and Panchamukhi, V. R., eds.*, 1989, pp. 253–63.

_____ **and Rutgaizer, V.** Leasing Relations in the Economic System of Socialism. *Prob. Econ.*, November 1989, *32*(7), pp. 49–62.

Nilsson, Sam. The Effect of Science and Technology in Regional and Global Development. In *Fishelson, G., ed.*, 1989, pp. 237–51.

_____ **and Jorner, U.** Income and Profitability Analysis Based on Farm Models. In *Bauer, S. and Henrichsmeyer, W., eds.*, 1989, pp. 125–39.

Nilsson, Stefan. High Speed Train Technology

on Existing Tracks. In *Candemir, Y., ed.*, 1989, pp. 530–38.

Nimni, Ephraim. Marx, Engels and the National Question. *Sci. Society*, Fall 1989, *53*(3), pp. 297–326.

Niou, Emerson M. S. and Ordeshook, Peter C. Stability in International Systems and the Costs of War. In *Ordeshook, P. C., ed.*, 1989, pp. 229–51.

Nirenberg, L. Variational Methods in Nonlinear Problems. In *Giaquinta, M., ed.*, 1989, pp. 100–119.

Niroomand, Farhang and Bahmani-Oskooee, Mohsen. On the Exchange-Rate Elasticity of the Demand for International Reserves: Some Evidence from Industrial Countries: A Reply. *Weltwirtsch. Arch.*, 1989, *125*(2), pp. 394–96.

_____ **and Sawyer, W. Charles.** The Extent of Scale Economies in U.S. Foreign Trade. *J. World Trade*, December 1989, *23*(6), pp. 137–46.

Nishat, Mohammed and Hasan, M. Aynul. Determinants of Multinational Investments in Pakistan: An Exploratory Analysis. *Pakistan Econ. Soc. Rev.*, Summer 1989, *27*(1), pp. 49–60.

Nishi, Takashi. Multiplier Process and Price Fluctuations. *Keio Econ. Stud.*, 1989, *26*(1), pp. 53–60.

Nishimizu, Mieko and Page, John M., Jr. Productivity Change and Growth in Industry and Agriculture: An International Comparison. In *Williamson, J. G. and Panchamukhi, V. R., eds.*, 1989, pp. 390–413.

Nishimura, Kazuo and Benhabib, Jess. Stochastic Equilibrium Oscillations. *Int. Econ. Rev.*, February 1989, *30*(1), pp. 85–102.

Nishimura, Kiyohiko G. Customer Markets and Price Sensitivity. *Economica*, May 1989, *56*(222), pp. 187–98.

_____. Indexation and Monopolistic Competition in Labor Markets. *Europ. Econ. Rev.*, October 1989, *33*(8), pp. 1605–23.

Nishioka, Hideki. An Efficiency Evaluation of the Japanese Tax System—The Marginal Welfare Cost in a Dynamic Equilibrium Model. *Econ. Stud. Quart.*, September 1989, *40*(3), pp. 264–75.

Niskanen, William A. Economic Deregulation in the United States: Lessons for America, Lessons for China. *Cato J.*, Winter 1989, *8*(3), pp. 657–68.

_____. New Institutional Arrangements in International Economic Law: The Working of Codes of Conduct: Comments. In *Vosgerau, H.-J., ed.*, 1989, pp. 436–37.

_____. The Performance and Management of United States Federal Government Corporations: Comment. In *MacAvoy, P. W., et al.*, 1989, pp. 137–38.

_____. A Reply to George Stigler: Evaluating Government Policy. *Bus. Econ.*, January 1989, *24*(1), pp. 20–22.

_____. Rethinking the Case for Central Banking. *Cato J.*, Fall 1989, *9*(2), pp. 467–69.

_____. The Uneasy Relation between the Budget

and Trade Deficits. In *Dorn, J. A. and Niskanen, W. A., eds.*, 1989, *1988*, pp. 305–16.

_____. U.S. Trade Policy: Problems and Prospects. In *Crane, E. H. and Boaz, D.*, 1989, pp. 55–71.

Niss, James F. and Grimes, Paul W. Concentrated Study Time and Improved Learning Efficiency: An Experiment Using *Economics U$A. J. Econ. Educ.*, Spring 1989, *20*(2), pp. 133–38.

Nissan, Edward. An Alternative Index for Quality of Life in Urban Areas. *Rev. Reg. Stud.*, Winter 1989, *19*(1), pp. 77–80.

_____. A Measurement of Economic Growth for Selected Caribbean Nations. *Rev. Black Polit. Econ.*, Fall 1989, *18*(2), pp. 61–79.

_____. Regional Earning Patterns: Note. *Rev. Reg. Stud.*, Spring 1989, *19*(2), pp. 55–58.

Nissen, Bruce. Enterprise Zones as an Economic Development Tool: The Indiana Experience. *Reg. Sci. Persp.*, 1989, *19*(2), pp. 3–20.

Nitzan, Shmuel. More on the Preservation of Preference Proximity and Anonymous Social Choice. *Quart. J. Econ.*, February 1989, *104*(1), pp. 187–90.

_____ and **Kahana, Nava.** More on Alternative Objectives of Labor-Managed Firms. *J. Compar. Econ.*, December 1989, *13*(4), pp. 527–38.

Nixon, Clair J. and VanTassell, Larry W. A Further Look at the Effect of Federal Tax Laws on Optimal Machinery Replacement. *Southern J. Agr. Econ.*, December 1989, *21*(2), pp. 77–84.

Nixson, Frederick. The Less Developed Countries and the Global Economy: Review Article. *J. Devel. Stud.*, October 1989, *26*(1), pp. 145–56.

Njinkeu, Dominique and Färe, Rolf. Computing Returns to Scale under Alternative Models. *Econ. Letters*, 1989, *30*(1), pp. 55–59.

_____; **Färe, Rolf and Herr, W.** Returns to Scale and Efficiency in Production: A Distance Function Approach to Southern Illinois Hog Farms. In *Gulledge, T. R., Jr. and Litteral, L. A., eds.*, 1989, pp. 145–59.

Noam, Eli M. International Telecommunications in Transition. In *Crandall, R. W. and Flamm, K., eds.*, 1989, pp. 257–97.

Nobay, A. Robert and Levy, Edmond. On the Bivariate Analysis of Speculative Efficiency in Forward Markets. In *MacDonald, R. and Taylor, M. P., eds.*, 1989, pp. 197–217.

Noble, Gregory W. The Japanese Industrial Policy Debate. In *Haggard, S. and Moon, C., eds.*, 1989, pp. 53–95.

Noble, James S. and Tanchoco, J. M. A. Cost Modeling for Design Justification. In *Gulledge, T. R., Jr. and Litteral, L. A., eds.*, 1989, pp. 197–213.

da Nóbrega, Mailson F. Tax Policy in Brazil. *Bull. Int. Fiscal Doc.*, Aug.–Sept. 1989, *43*(8–9), pp. 364–70.

Nocera, Simon and Blackwell, Michael. Debt–Equity Swaps. In *Frenkel, J. A.; Dooley, M. P. and Wickham, P., eds.*, 1989, pp. 311–45.

Nochevnik, Michael and Koval, Vitalina. Technological Innovations and Work in the Soviet Union. In *Francis, A. and Grootings, P., eds.*, 1989, pp. 120–39.

Nock, Steven L. and Kingston, Paul William. The Division of Leisure and Work. *Soc. Sci. Quart.*, March 1989, *70*(1), pp. 24–39.

Noe, Thomas H.; Gay, Gerald D. and Kale, Jayant R. Share Repurchase through Transferable Put Rights: Theory and Case Study. *J. Finan. Econ.*, November 1989, *25*(1), pp. 141–60.

_____ and **Magee, Stephen P.** Economic Policy Failure with Endogenous Voting. *Hong Kong Econ. Pap.*, 1989, (19), pp. 9–12.

Noell, C. and Hanf, C. -Henning. Farm Based Modelling Concepts: Experiences with Farm Sample Models in Sector Analysis. In *Bauer, S. and Henrichsmeyer, W., eds.*, 1989, pp. 103–11.

Noell, Edd S. Sir Edward Coke and Adam Smith on Occupational Regulation: Economic Efficiency, Justice, and the Public Good. In *Walker, D. A., ed.*, 1989, pp. 19–37.

Noguchi, Yukio. Land Problem as an Unintended Industrial Policy: Its Mechanism and Limit. *Hitotsubashi J. Econ.*, December 1989, *30*(2), pp. 87–99.

Nogués, Julio. The Role of Debt and the Macroeconomy in the Uruguay Round: The Case of Latin America. In *Gray, H. P., ed.*, 1989, pp. 227–41.

Nohara, Takashi and Hirata, Akira. Changing Patterns in International Division of Labour in Asia and the Pacific. In *Shinohara, M. and Lo, F., eds.*, 1989, pp. 434–62.

Noke, Christopher and Bromwich, Michael. Money, Measurement and Accounting. In *Llewellyn, D. T., ed.*, 1989, pp. 167–90.

Nolan, Brian. An Evaluation of the New Official Low Income Statistics. *Fisc. Stud.*, November 1989, *10*(4), pp. 53–65.

_____. Macroeconomic Conditions and the Size Distribution of Income: Evidence from the UK. In *Davidson, P. and Kregel, J., eds.*, 1989, pp. 115–37.

_____. Macroeconomic Conditions and the Size Distribution of Income: Evidence from the United Kingdom. *J. Post Keynesian Econ.*, Winter 1988–89, *11*(2), pp. 196–221.

_____ and **Callan, Tim.** Evaluating Social Welfare Expenditures: How Well Does the System Perform in Reducing Poverty? *Econ. Soc. Rev.*, July 1989, *20*(4), pp. 329–52.

_____ and **Callan, Tim.** Measuring Trends in Poverty over Time: Some Robust Results for Ireland 1980–87. *Econ. Soc. Rev.*, July 1989, *20*(4), pp. 309–28.

Noland, Marcus. Japanese Trade Elasticities and the *J*-Curve. *Rev. Econ. Statist.*, February 1989, *71*(1), pp. 175–79.

_____ and **Balassa, Bela.** The Changing Comparative Advantage of Japan and the United States. In *Balassa, B.*, 1989, pp. 80–106.

_____ and **Balassa, Bela.** The Changing Comparative Advantage of Japan and the United States.

J. Japanese Int. Economies, June 1989, *3*(2), pp. 174–88.

Noles, Richard K.; McClelland, John W. and **Wetzstein, Michael E.** Optimal Replacement Policies for Rejuvenated Assets. *Amer. J. Agr. Econ.*, February 1989, *71*(1), pp. 147–57.

Noll, Roger G. Economic Perspectives on the Politics of Regulation. In *Schmalensee, R. and Willig, R. D., eds., Vol. 2*, 1989, pp. 1253–87.

———. The Economic Theory of Regulation after a Decade of Deregulation: Comments. *Brookings Pap. Econ. Act.*, Microeconomics, 1989, pp. 48–58.

——— and **Owen, Bruce M.** The Anticompetitive Uses of Regulation: *United States v. AT&T.* In *Kwoka, J. E., Jr. and White, L. J., eds.*, 1989, pp. 290–337.

Nord, Stephen. The Relationships among Labor-Force Participation, Service-Sector Employment, and Underemployment. *J. Reg. Sci.*, August 1989, *29*(3), pp. 407–21.

———; **Phelps, John J.** and **Sheets, Robert G.** Service Industries and Structural Underemployment in Urban Areas in the United States. *Rivista Int. Sci. Econ. Com.*, September 1989, *36*(9), pp. 785–800.

Nordblom, T. L. Rice-Based Crop–Livestock Systems in Egypt. In *International Rice Research Institute*, 1989, pp. 265–67.

Nordhaus, William D. Alternative Approaches to the Political Business Cycle. *Brookings Pap. Econ. Act.*, 1989, (2), pp. 1–49.

———. Patents: Recent Trends and Puzzles: Comments. *Brookings Pap. Econ. Act.*, Microeconomics, 1989, pp. 320–25.

———. Ten Years of Mrs. T.: Comment. In *Blanchard, O. J. and Fischer, S., eds.*, 1989, pp. 61–67.

———. What's Wrong with a Declining National Saving Rate? *Challenge*, July–Aug. 1989, *32*(4), pp. 22–26.

Noreen, Eric; Burgstahler, David and **Jiambalvo, James.** Changes in the Probability of Bankruptcy and Equity Value. *J. Acc. Econ.*, July 1989, *11*(2–3), pp. 207–24.

Norese, Maria Franca and **Ostanello, Anna.** Identification and Development of Alternatives: Introduction to the Recognition of Process Typologies. In *Lockett, A. G. and Islei, G., eds.*, 1989, pp. 112–23.

Norman, George. Monopolistic Competition: Some Extensions from Spatial Competition. *Reg. Sci. Urban Econ.*, February 1989, *19*(1), pp. 31–53.

Norman, Victor D. EFTA and the Internal European Market. *Econ. Policy: A Europ. Forum*, October 1989, (9), pp. 423–65.

———. Trade Policy under Imperfect Competition: Theoretical Ambiguities—Empirical Regularities? *Europ. Econ. Rev.*, March 1989, *33*(2/3), pp. 473–79.

Normandin, Charles P. The Changing Nature of Debt and Equity: A Legal Perspective. In *Kopcke, R. W. and Rosengren, E. S., eds.*, 1989, pp. 49–66.

Nørregard, John and **Messere, Ken C.** Consumption Taxes in OECD Countries over the Last Two Decades: International. *Bull. Int. Fiscal Doc.*, June 1989, *43*(6), pp. 255–68.

Norrman, Bo and **Malmer, Håkan.** Administrative and Compliance Costs of Taxation: Sweden. In *International Fiscal Association, ed. (I)*, 1989, pp. 563–93.

North, Douglass C. Institutional Change and Economic History: Final Remarks. *J. Inst. Theoretical Econ.*, March 1989, *145*(1), pp. 238–45.

———. Institutions and Economic Growth: An Historical Introduction. *World Devel.*, Special Issue, September 1989, *17*(9), pp. 1319–32.

———. A Transaction Cost Approach to the Historical Development of Polities and Economies. *J. Inst. Theoretical Econ.*, December 1989, *145*(4), pp. 661–68.

——— and **Weingast, Barry R.** Constitutions and Commitment: The Evolution of Institutions Governing Public Choice in Seventeenth-Century England. *J. Econ. Hist.*, December 1989, *49*(4), pp. 803–32.

Northrup, Herbert R. Construction Double-breasted Operations and Pre-hire Agreements: Assessing the Issues. *J. Lab. Res.*, Spring 1989, *10*(2), pp. 215–38.

———. From Union Hegemony to Union Disintegration: Collective Bargaining in Cement and Related Industries. *J. Lab. Res.*, Fall 1989, *10*(4), pp. 337–76.

———. The Twelve-Hour Shift in the Petroleum and Chemical Industries Revisited: An Assessment by Human Resource Mangement Executives. *Ind. Lab. Relat. Rev.*, July 1989, *42*(4), pp. 640–48.

Nortje, J. D.; Crous, M. J. and **Jooste, C. J.** Selfdoenmodules as Onderrigmedium vir die Kleinsakesektor in die RAS. (With English summary.) *J. Stud. Econ. Econometrics*, March 1989, *13*(1), pp. 89–101.

Norton, Edgar. Determinants of Capital Structure: A Survey. In *Lee, C. F., ed.*, 1989, pp. 323–50.

Norton, George W.; Bezuneh, Mesfin and **Deaton, Brady.** Farm Level Impacts of Food-for-Work in a Semi-arid Region of Kenya. *Eastern Afr. Econ. Rev.*, June 1989, *5*(1), pp. 1–8.

———; **Bouchet, Frédéric** and **Orden, David.** Sources of Growth in French Agriculture. *Amer. J. Agr. Econ.*, May 1989, *71*(2), pp. 280–93.

Norton, John A. and **Wilson, Lynn O.** Optimal Entry Timing for a Product Line Extension. *Marketing Sci.*, Winter 1989, *8*(1), pp. 1–17.

Norton, R. D. Restructuring the Fortune 500: The View from Ohio. In *McKee, D. L., ed.*, 1989, pp. 69–78.

Norton, Seth W. Franchising, Labor Productivity, and the New Institutional Economics. *J. Inst. Theoretical Econ.*, December 1989, *145*(4), pp. 578–96.

Norwood, Janet L. and **Klein, Deborah P.** Developing Statistics to Meet Society's Needs. *Mon. Lab. Rev.*, October 1989, *112*(10), pp. 14–19.

Nossal, Kim Richard. International Sanctions as International Punishment. *Int. Organ.*, Spring 1989, *43*(2), pp. 301–22.

Nothaft, Frank E.; Gabriel, Stuart A. and **Rothberg, James P.** On the Determinants of Yield Spreads between Mortgage Pass-Through and Treasury Securities. *J. Real Estate Finance Econ.*, December 1989, *2*(4), pp. 301–15.

Nouyrit, Henri. The Ecu as the Key to the Future of the Common Agricultural Policy. In *Franz, O., ed.*, 1989, pp. 57–58.

Novak, Michael. The Elderly "R" Us. In *Lewin, M. E. and Sullivan, S., eds.*, 1989, pp. 177–84.

Nove, Alec. The Limits of Full Economic Accountability. *Prob. Econ.*, July 1989, *32*(3), pp. 25–35.

_____. Market Socialism. *Acta Oecon.*, 1989, *40*(3–4), pp. 264–67.

Novikov, V. Leasing as the Development of Relations of Socialist Property. *Prob. Econ.*, November 1989, *32*(7), pp. 63–78.

Novomestky, Frederick and **Choie, Kenneth S.** Replication of Long-term with Short-term Options. *J. Portfol. Manage.*, Winter 1989, *15*(2), pp. 17–19.

Novos, Ian E. Social Security Wealth Accumulation: Further Microeconomic Evidence. *Rev. Econ. Statist.*, February 1989, *71*(1), pp. 167–71.

Nowak, Eugen. Erratum [Identification of Simultaneous Equation Models with Measurement Errors Based on Time Series Structure]. *J. Econometrics*, October 1989, *42*(2), pp. 285.

_____. Identification of Simultaneous Equation Models with Measurement Errors Based on Time Series Structure. *J. Econometrics*, February 1989, *40*(2), pp. 319–25.

Nowak, Leszek. On the (Idealizational) Structure of Economic Theories. In *Balzer, W. and Hamminga, B., eds.*, 1989, pp. 225–46.

Nowotny, Kenneth R. The Greenhouse Effect and Energy Policy in the United States. *J. Econ. Issues*, December 1989, *23*(4), pp. 1075–84.

Nowzad, Bahram. The Debt Problem and the IMF's Perspective. In *Bird, G., ed.*, 1989, pp. 118–29.

Noyelle, Thierry. New York's Competitiveness. In *Noyelle, T., ed.*, 1989, pp. 91–114.

_____. New York's Financial Markets: The Challenges of Globalization: Overview: Issues for the 1990s. In *Noyelle, T., ed.*, 1989, pp. 1–6.

Nozaki, Seigo. Third World Debt: The Next Phase: Concluding Impressions. In *Fried, E. R. and Trezise, P. H., eds.*, 1989, pp. 103–06.

Nsouli, Saleh M. Structural Adjustment in Sub-Saharan Africa. *Finance Devel.*, September 1989, *26*(3), pp. 30–33.

Nti, Kofi O. More Potential Entrants May Lead to Less Competition. *J. Econ. (Z. Nationalökon.)*, 1989, *49*(1), pp. 47–70.

Nugent, Jeffrey B. Collective Action in Tunisia's Producer Organizations: Some Variations on the Olsonian Theme. In *Nabli, M. K. and Nugent, J. B., eds.*, 1989, pp. 289–322.

_____ **and Azabou, Mongi.** Tax Farming: Anachronism or Optimal Contract? (An Illustration with Respect to Tunisia's Weekly Markets). In *Nabli, M. K. and Nugent, J. B., eds.*, 1989, pp. 178–99.

_____; **Azabou, Mongi** and **Bouzaïane, Lotfi.** Contractual Choice in Tunisian Fishing. In *Nabli, M. K. and Nugent, J. B., eds.*, 1989, pp. 158–77.

_____ **and Datta, Samar K.** Transaction Cost Economics and Contractual Choice: Theory and Evidence. In *Nabli, M. K. and Nugent, J. B., eds.*, 1989, pp. 34–79.

_____; **Doghri, Lamine** and **Nabli, Mustapha K.** The Size Distribution and Ownership Type of Firms in Tunisian Manufacturing. In *Nabli, M. K. and Nugent, J. B., eds.*, 1989, pp. 200–232.

_____ **and Matoussi, Mohamed S.** The Switch to Sharecropping in Medjez-el-bab. In *Nabli, M. K. and Nugent, J. B., eds.*, 1989, pp. 140–57.

_____ **and Nabli, Mustapha K.** Collective Action, Institutions and Development. In *Nabli, M. K. and Nugent, J. B., eds.*, 1989, pp. 80–137.

_____ **and Nabli, Mustapha K.** The New Institutional Economics and Development: Concluding Remarks. In *Nabli, M. K. and Nugent, J. B., eds.*, 1989, pp. 438–48.

_____ **and Nabli, Mustapha K.** The New Institutional Economics and Economic Development: An Introduction. In *Nabli, M. K. and Nugent, J. B., eds.*, 1989, pp. 3–33.

_____ **and Nabli, Mustapha K.** The New Institutional Economics and Its Applicability to Development. *World Devel.*, Special Issue, September 1989, *17*(9), pp. 1333–47.

_____ **and Sanchez, Nicolas.** The Efficiency of the Mesta: A Parable. *Exploration Econ. Hist.*, July 1989, *26*(3), pp. 261–84.

Numrich, Richard P.; Lahiri, Kajal and **Lankford, R. Hamilton.** The Estimation and Interpretation of Urban Density Gradients. *J. Bus. Econ. Statist.*, April 1989, *7*(2), pp. 227–35.

Nunes, Ana Bela; Mata, Eugénia and **Valério, Nuno.** Portuguese Economic Growth, 1833–1985. *J. Europ. Econ. Hist.*, Fall 1989, *18*(2), pp. 291–330.

Nunnally, Bennie H., Jr. and **Plath, D. Anthony.** Leasing versus Borrowing: Evaluating Alternative Forms of Consumer Credit. *J. Cons. Aff.*, Winter 1989, *23*(2), pp. 383–92.

Nunnenkamp, Peter. Capital Drain, Debt Relief, and Creditworthiness of Developing Countries. In *Mrak, M., ed.*, 1989, pp. 95–120.

_____ **and Picht, Hartmut.** Willful Default by Developing Countries in the 1980s: A Cross-Country Analysis of Major Determinants. *Weltwirtsch. Arch.*, 1989, *125*(4), pp. 681–702.

Nurse, Charles. The State, Industrial Relations and the Labour Movement in Latin America: Volume 1: Ecuador. In *Carrière, J.; Haworth, N. and Roddick, J., eds.*, 1989, pp. 99–127.

Nusinovic, Mustafa and **Teodorovic, Ivan.** Investment Decisionmaking. In *Macesich, G., ed.*, 1989, pp. 101–32.

Nusse, Helena E. and Hommes, Cars H. Does an Unstable Keynesian Unemployment Equilibrium in a Non-Walrasian Dynamic Macroeconomic Model Imply Chaos? *Scand. J. Econ.*, 1989, *91*(1), pp. 161–67.

Nuti, Domenico Mario. Michal Kalecki's Contributions to the Theory and Practice of Socialist Planning. In *Sebastiani, M., ed.,* 1989, pp. 317–58.

_____. Remonetisation and Capital Markets in the Reform of Centrally Planned Economies. *Europ. Econ. Rev.*, March 1989, *33*(2/3), pp. 427–38.

Nwanna, Gladson I. Food Prices, Agriculture Labor Supply, and Mechanization. *Atlantic Econ. J.*, March 1989, *17*(1), pp. 93.

Nyarko, Yaw and Kiefer, Nicholas M. Optimal Control of an Unknown Linear Process with Learning. *Int. Econ. Rev.*, August 1989, *30*(3), pp. 571–86.

_____; **Majumdar, Mukul and Mitra, Tapan.** Dynamic Optimization under Uncertainty: Non-convex Feasible Set. In *Feiwel, G. R., ed. (II),* 1989, pp. 545–90.

Nyblom, Jukka. Testing for the Constancy of Parameters over Time. *J. Amer. Statist. Assoc.*, March 1989, *84*(405), pp. 223–30.

Nye, Blaine F.; Hofflander, Alfred E. and Venezian, Emilio C. The Distribution of Claims for Professional Malpractice: Some Statistical and Public Policy Aspects. *J. Risk Ins.*, December 1989, *56*(4), pp. 686–701.

Nye, John Vincent and Cox, Donald. Male–Female Wage Discrimination in Nineteenth-Century France. *J. Econ. Hist.*, December 1989, *49*(4), pp. 903–20.

Nye, Joseph S., Jr. Arms Control after the Cold War. *Foreign Aff.*, Winter 1989–90, *68*(5), pp. 42–64.

_____. Corruption and Political Development: A Cost–Benefit Analysis. In *Heidenheimer, A. J.; Johnston, M. and LeVine, V. T., eds.,* 1989, *1967,* pp. 963–83.

Nygård, Fredrik and Sandström, Arne. Income Inequality Measures Based on Sample Surveys. *J. Econometrics*, September 1989, *42*(1), pp. 81–95.

Nyirongo, Griffin K. and Shula, Emmanuel W. C. Contract Farming and Smallholder Outgrower Schemes in Zambia. *Eastern Afr. Econ. Rev.*, Special Issue, August 1989, pp. 83–96.

Nyman, John A. The Private Demand for Nursing Home Care. *J. Health Econ.*, June 1989, *8*(2), pp. 209–31.

_____ **and Bricker, Dennis L.** Profit Incentives and Technical Efficiency in the Production of Nursing Home Care. *Rev. Econ. Statist.*, November 1989, *71*(4), pp. 586–94.

Nymoen, Ragnar. Modelling Wages in the Small Open Economy: An Error-Correction Model of Norwegian Manufacturing Wages. *Oxford Bull. Econ. Statist.*, August 1989, *51*(3), pp. 239–58.

_____. Wages and the Length of the Working Day. An Empirical Test Based on Norwegian Quarterly Manufacturing Data. *Scand. J. Econ.*, 1989, *91*(3), pp. 599–612.

Nyong, Michael O. The Effect of Quality of Management on the Profitability of Commercial Banks: A Comparative Analysis Based on Nigerian Banking Experience. *Developing Econ.*, September 1989, *27*(3), pp. 286–303.

Nyoni, M. B. Balancing Supply and Disposition Tables and the Derivation of Input–Output Tables—Zimbabwe's Experience. In *Franz, A. and Rainer, N., eds.,* 1989, pp. 355–73.

O'Brien, Anthony Patrick. A Behavioral Explanation for Nominal Wage Rigidity during the Great Depression. *Quart. J. Econ.*, November 1989, *104*(4), pp. 719–35.

_____. How to Succeed in Business: Lessons from the Struggle between Ford and General Motors during the 1920s and 1930s. In *Hausman, W. J., ed.,* 1989, pp. 79–87.

_____. The ICC, Freight Rates, and the Great Depression. *Exploration Econ. Hist.*, January 1989, *26*(1), pp. 73–98.

O'Brien, Bernie. The Effect of Patient Charges on the Utilisation of Prescription Medicines. *J. Health Econ.*, March 1989, *8*(1), pp. 109–32.

O'Brien, D. P. Robbins as a Political *Economist*: A Reply. *Econ. J.*, June 1989, *99*(396), pp. 479–80.

O'Brien, J. Patrick and Logan, Robert R. Fiscal Illusion, Budget Maximizers, and Dynamic Equilibrium. *Public Choice*, December 1989, *63*(3), pp. 221–35.

_____ **and Shieh, Yeung-Nan.** Transportation Rates, Production and Location in the Moses–Weber Triangle: A Note. *Reg. Sci. Urban Econ.*, February 1989, *19*(1), pp. 133–42.

O'Brien, James L. and Read, William A. The Involved Hospital. In *Eisdorfer, C.; Kessler, D. A. and Spector, A. N., eds.,* 1989, pp. 157–83.

O'Brien, John C. Gustav von Schmoller: Social Economist. *Int. J. Soc. Econ.*, 1989, *16*(9–10–11), pp. 16–46.

O'Brien, Joseph E. The Crisis in the Thrift Industry—A Canadian Perspective. In *Schwartz, E. and Vasconcellos, G. M., eds.,* 1989, pp. 79–101.

O'Brien, Kevin M. and Brueckner, Jan K. Modeling Government Behavior in Collective Bargaining: A Test for Self-interested Bureaucrats. *Public Choice*, October 1989, *63*(1), pp. 15–41.

O'Brien, Paul. Recent Developments in Economic Statistics at the Federal Reserve: Part 2. *Bus. Econ.*, July 1989, *24*(3), pp. 40–47.

O'Brien, Peter. Recent Developments in the Machine-Tool Industry: The Prospects for Foreign Direct Investment with Particular Reference to Asian Developing Countries. *Industry Devel.*, January 1989, (25), pp. 23–91.

O'Brien, Robert B., Jr. Easing the Plight of the Thrifts or Savings and Loans at the Crossroads. In *Schwartz, E. and Vasconcellos, G. M., eds.,* 1989, pp. 63–69.

O'Brien, Thomas F. "Rich beyond the Dreams

of Avarice": The Guggenheims in Chile. *Bus. Hist. Rev.*, Spring 1989, *63*(1), pp. 122–59.

O'Bryan, Anne. The Small-Business Supported-Employment Option for Persons with Severe Handicaps. In *Wehman, P. and Kregel, J., eds.*, 1989, pp. 69–82.

O'Connell, Lenahan. Ownerbuilt Housing and Resources: Implications for Self-help Policies. *Urban Stud.*, December 1989, *26*(6), pp. 607–09.

O'Connell, Stephen A. The External Debt Difficulties of Low-Income Africa: Comment. In *Husain, I. and Diwan, I., eds.*, 1989, pp. 66–68.

_____ **and Taylor, Lance.** A Minsky Crisis. In *Semmler, W., ed.*, 1989, pp. 3–17.

O'Connor, James. An Introduction to a Theory of Crisis Theories. In *Gottdiener, M. and Komninos, N., eds.*, 1989, pp. 21–29.

O'Connor, Kevin and Gordon, Moira. Operation of Regional Labour Markets in Australia. In *Higgins, B. and Zagorski, K., eds.*, 1989, pp. 196–217.

O'Connor, Marcus. Models of Human Behaviour and Confidence in Judgement: A Review. *Int. J. Forecasting*, 1989, *5*(2), pp. 159–69.

O'Conor, Karen and Wong, William. Measuring the Precision of the Employment Cost Index. *Mon. Lab. Rev.*, March 1989, *112*(3), pp. 29–36.

O'Donnell, Margaret G. A Historical Note on the Use of Fiction to Teach Principles of Economics. *J. Econ. Educ.*, Summer 1989, *20*(3), pp. 314–20.

O'Driscoll, Gerald P., Jr. A Tribute to F. A. Hayek. *Cato J.*, Fall 1989, *9*(2), pp. 345–52.

O'Farrell, P. N. and Hitchens, D. M. W. N. The Competitiveness and Performance of Small Manufacturing Firms: An Analysis of Matched Pairs in Scotland and England. *Environ. Planning A*, September 1989, *21*(9), pp. 1241–63.

_____ **and Hitchens, D. M. W. N.** The Relative Competitiveness of Small Manufacturing Companies in South Wales and Northern Ireland: Analysis and Policy. In *Gibbs, D., ed.*, 1989, pp. 176–205.

_____ **and Pickles, A. R.** Entrepreneurial Behaviour within Male Work Histories: A Sector-Specific Analysis. *Environ. Planning A*, March 1989, *21*(3), pp. 311–31.

Ó Gráda, Cormac and Geary, Patrick T. Postwar Migration between Ireland and the United Kingdom: Models and Estimates. In *Gordon, I. and Thirlwall, A. P., eds.*, 1989, pp. 53–58.

O'Guinn, Thomas C. and Belk, Russell W. Heaven on Earth: Consumption at Heritage Village, USA. *J. Cons. Res.*, September 1989, *16*(2), pp. 227–38.

_____ **and Faber, Ronald J.** Compulsive Buying: A Phenomenological Exploration. *J. Cons. Res.*, September 1989, *16*(2), pp. 147–57.

O'Hagan, John. Indirect Tax Reform in Ireland: A Comment. *Econ. Soc. Rev.*, October 1989,

21(1), pp. 48–50.

O'Hara, Maureen. Technology and Hedging Behavior: A Proof of Hicks' Conjecture. In *Wood, J. C. and Woods, R. N., eds., Vol. 4*, 1989, pp. 246–52.

_____ **and Jarrow, Robert A.** Primes and Scores: An Essay on Market Imperfections. *J. Finance*, December 1989, *44*(5), pp. 1263–87.

O'Hara, Patricia A. and Blakey, G. Robert. Legal Aspects of Insider Trading. In *Williams, O. F.; Reilly, F. K. and Houck, J. W., eds.*, 1989, pp. 101–20.

O'Hare, Michael. A Typology of Governmental Action. *J. Policy Anal. Manage.*, Fall 1989, *8*(4), pp. 670–72.

O'Higgins, Michael. Assessing the Underground Economy in the United Kingdom. In *Feige, E. L., ed.*, 1989, pp. 175–95.

_____. Dilemmas of the NHS. In *[Sandford, C.]*, 1989, pp. 137–49.

_____ **and Jenkins, Stephen P.** Inequality Measurement Using 'Norm Incomes': Were Garvy and Paglin onto Something after All? *Rev. Income Wealth*, September 1989, *35*(3), pp. 265–82.

_____; **Schmaus, Guenther and Stephenson, Geoffrey.** Income Distribution and Redistribution: A Microdata Analysis for Seven Countries. *Rev. Income Wealth*, June 1989, *35*(2), pp. 107–31.

Ó Huallacháin, Breandán. Agglomeration of Services in American Metropolitan Areas. *Growth Change*, Summer 1989, *20*(3), pp. 34–49.

O'Keefe, Terrence and Nathan, Kevin S. The Rise in Takeover Premiums: An Exploratory Study. *J. Finan. Econ.*, June 1989, *23*(1), pp. 101–19.

O'Kelly, M. E. Equilibrium in a Two-Crop Model with a Low-Cost Transportation Route. *Environ. Planning A*, March 1989, *21*(3), pp. 385–96.

_____ **and Miller, H. J.** A Synthesis of Some Market Area Delimitation Models. *Growth Change*, Summer 1989, *20*(3), pp. 14–33.

O'Malley, Patrick M. and Bachman, Jerald G. When Four Months Equal a Year: Inconsistencies in Student Reports of Drug Use. In *Singer, E. and Presser, S., eds.*, 1989, *1981*, pp. 173–85.

O'Muircheartaigh, Colm. Sources of Nonsampling Error: Discussion. In *Kasprzyk, D., et al., eds.*, 1989, pp. 271–88.

O'Neill, G. J. and Parr, J. B. Aspects of the Lognormal Function in the Analysis of Regional Population Distribution. *Environ. Planning A*, July 1989, *21*(7), pp. 961–73.

O'Neill, June; Brien, Michael and Cunningham, James. Effects of Comparable Worth Policy: Evidence from Washington State. *Amer. Econ. Rev.*, May 1989, *79*(2), pp. 305–09.

O'Reilly, Anthony J. F. Foreign Markets: Friend or Foe? In *Ahlbrandt, R. S., Jr., ed.*, 1989, pp. 8–11.

O'Reilly, Kenneth and Chase-Dunn, Christopher. Core Wars of the Future. In *Schaeffer,*

R. K., ed., 1989, pp. 47–64.

O'Riordan, Jon. Derrick Sewell and the Wilderness Advisory Committee in British Columbia. *Natural Res. J.*, Winter 1989, *29*(1), pp. 115–27.

O'Rourke, Edward W. The Catholic Bishops' Pastoral Draft Statement on American Agriculture. In *Horwich, G. and Lynch, G. J., eds.*, 1989, pp. 267–73.

O'Rourke, Kevin. Tariffs and the Current Account with Short-run Capital Specificity. *Econ. Letters*, 1989, *30*(1), pp. 67–70.

O'Shea, Eamon and Corcoran, Rosaleen. The Placement of Elderly Persons: A Logit Estimation and Cost Analysis. *Econ. Soc. Rev.*, April 1989, *20*(3), pp. 219–41.

O'Shea, Timothy J. C. Annual Review of Nations: Year 1988: Japan. In *Haberman, L. and Sacks, P. M., eds.*, 1989, pp. 173–94.

O'Sullivan, Patrick J. Empirical Testing in Economics and the Theory of Truth. *Ricerche Econ.*, Jan.–June 1989, *43*(1–2), pp. 151–75.

O'uchi, Minoru; Haseyama, Takahiko and Honobe, Susumu. New Issues of Economic Cooperation. In *Shinohara, M. and Lo, F., eds.*, 1989, pp. 469–502.

Oakey, R. P. and Cooper, S. Y. High Technology Industry, Agglomeration and the Potential for Peripherally Sited Small Firms. *Reg. Stud.*, August 1989, *23*(4), pp. 347–60.

Oates, Wallace E. Searching for Leviathan: Reply. *Amer. Econ. Rev.*, June 1989, *79*(3), pp. 578–83.

_____; **Portney, Paul R. and McGartland, Albert M.** The *Net* Benefits of Incentive-Based Regulation: A Case Study of Environmental Standard Setting. *Amer. Econ. Rev.*, December 1989, *79*(5), pp. 1233–42.

Oaxaca, Ronald L. and Cox, James C. Laboratory Experiments with a Finite-Horizon Job-Search Model. *J. Risk Uncertainty*, September 1989, *2*(3), pp. 301–29.

Obasi, G. O. P. Climate and Food Crop Production. In *Oram, P. A., et al.*, 1989, pp. 503–14.

Oberbeck, Herbert and Baethge, Martin. Computer and Pinstripes: Financial Institutions. In *Katzenstein, P. J., ed.*, 1989, pp. 275–303.

Oberhauser, Alois. Internationale Kapitalbewegungen, Änderungen der Leistungsbilanzsalden und Einkommensverteilung. (International Capital Movements, Changes of Current Accounts and the Distribution of Income. With English summary.) *Jahr. Nationalökon. Statist.*, October 1989, *206*(4–5), pp. 457–67.

_____ **and Scherf, Wolfgang.** Interactions between the External Economy and the Fiscal and Monetary Policy of the Federal Republic of Germany, in View of Stabilization Policy. In *Dams, T. and Matsugi, T., eds.*, 1989, pp. 275–97.

Oberhelman, H. Dennis; D'Souza, Rudolph E. and Brooks, LeRoy D. A General Stationary Stochastic Regression Model for Estimating and Predicting Beta. *Financial Rev.*, May 1989, *24*(2), pp. 299–317.

Oberhofer, Tom. The Changing Cultural Discount Rate. *Rev. Soc. Econ.*, Spring 1989, *47*(1), pp. 43–54.

_____. The Cultural Discount Rate, Social Contracts, and Intergenerational Tension. *Soc. Sci. Quart.*, December 1989, *70*(4), pp. 858–69.

_____. Two Hundred Years of Economics: Culture and Values in Tension. *Rivista Int. Sci. Econ. Com.*, January 1989, *36*(1), pp. 1–8.

Obst, Norman P. Monetary Price Rules for Alternative Steady-State Regimes. *Metroecon.*, October 1989, *40*(3), pp. 179–88.

Obstfeld, Maurice. Comment: Reforming the Exchange Rate System. In *Dorn, J. A. and Niskanen, W. A., eds.*, 1989, *1988*, pp. 229–35.

_____. Empirical Assessment of Foreign Currency Risk Premiums: Commentary. In *Stone, C. C., ed.*, 1989, pp. 181–96.

_____. Fiscal Deficits and Relative Prices in a Growing World Economy. *J. Monet. Econ.*, May 1989, *23*(3), pp. 461–84.

_____. How Integrated Are World Capital Markets? Some New Tests. In *[Díaz-Alejandro, C.]*, 1989, pp. 134–55.

_____. U.S. International Capital Flows: Perspectives from Rational Maximizing Models: Comment. *Carnegie–Rochester Conf. Ser. Public Policy*, Spring 1989, *30*, pp. 289–300.

Obzina, Jaromír. Czechoslovakia's Participation in the 40-Year Cooperation of the CMEA Member Countries. *Czech. Econ. Digest.*, February 1989, (1), pp. 85–98.

Ocampo, José Antonio. Colombia and the Latin American Debt Crisis. In *Edwards, S. and Larrain, F., eds.*, 1989, pp. 241–66.

_____. North–South Models and the Evolution of Global Interdependence: Comment. In *[Díaz-Alejandro, C.]*, 1989, pp. 415–20.

Ochoa, Eduardo M. Values, Prices, and Wage–Profit Curves in the U.S. Economy. *Cambridge J. Econ.*, September 1989, *13*(3), pp. 413–29.

Ochs, Jack and Roth, Alvin E. An Experimental Study of Sequential Bargaining. *Amer. Econ. Rev.*, June 1989, *79*(3), pp. 355–84.

Odagiri, Hiroyuki and Hase, Tatsuo. Are Mergers and Acquisitions Going to Be Popular in Japan Too? An Empirical Study. *Int. J. Ind. Organ.*, Special Issue, March 1989, *7*(1), pp. 49–72.

Odaka, Konosuke. A Comparison of U.S.–Japanese Firms' Parts-Supply Systems: What Besides Nationality Matters? Commentary. In *Hayashi, K., ed.*, 1989, pp. 155–57.

Odama, Joseph S. Balancing Food Production Requirements and Policies for Economic Growth. In *Helmuth, J. W. and Johnson, S. R., eds., Vol. 2*, 1989, pp. 178–90.

_____. World Hunger, Malnutrition, and Food Production and Distribution Systems: Reaction. In *Helmuth, J. W. and Johnson, S. R., eds., Vol. 1*, 1989, pp. 186–88.

Odden, Allan. The Educational Excellence Movement: Politics and Impact: An Essay Review. *Econ. Educ. Rev.*, 1989, 8(4), pp. 377–81.

Odedokun, M. O. The Effects of Systematic and Surprise Fiscal Policy Actions in a Developing Economy: Evidence from Nigeria. *Eastern Afr. Econ. Rev.*, December 1989, 5(2), pp. 122–32.

Odell, John and Kahler, Miles. Developing Country Coalition-Building and International Trade Negotiations. In *Whalley, J., ed., Vol. 1*, 1989, pp. 149–67.

Odell, Kerry A. The Integration of Regional and Interregional Capital Markets: Evidence from the Pacific Coast, 1883–1913. *J. Econ. Hist.*, June 1989, 49(2), pp. 297–310.

Odewahn, Charles and Scott, Clyde. An Analysis of Multi-union Elections Involving Incumbent Unions. *J. Lab. Res.*, Spring 1989, 10(2), pp. 197–205.

Oellerich, Donald and Garfinkel, Irwin. Noncustodial Fathers' Ability to Pay Child Support. *Demography*, May 1989, 26(2), pp. 219–33.

Oellermann, Charles M.; Brorsen, B. Wade and Farris, Paul L. Price Discovery for Feeder Cattle. *J. Futures Markets*, April 1989, 9(2), pp. 113–21.

_____; **Farris, Paul L. and Brorsen, B. Wade.** The Live Cattle Futures Market and Daily Cash Price Movements. *J. Futures Markets*, August 1989, 9(4), pp. 273–82.

Oettli, Werner. Note on Pareto Optimality and Duality for Certain Nonlinear Systems. In *Dolecki, S., ed.*, 1989, pp. 141–45.

Ofer, Aharon R.; Siegel, Daniel R. and Israel, Ronen. The Information Content of Equity-for-Debt Swaps: An Investigation of Analyst Forecasts of Firm Cash Flows. *J. Finan. Econ.*, December 1989, 25(2), pp. 349–70.

Ofer, Gur. Budget Deficit, Market Disequilibrium and Soviet Economic Reforms. *Soviet Econ.*, April–June 1989, 5(2), pp. 107–61.

Offer, Avner. Economic Interpretation of War: The German Submarine Campaign, 1915–18. *Australian Econ. Hist. Rev.*, March 1989, 29(1), pp. 21–41.

Offerdal, Erik and Devarajan, Shantayanan. Capital Markets and Computable General Equilibrium Models: Comparative Statics without Apology? *J. Policy Modeling*, Summer 1989, 11(2), pp. 191–212.

Officer, Lawrence H. The National Price Level: Theory and Estimation. *J. Macroecon.*, Summer 1989, 11(3), pp. 351–373.

_____. The Remarkable Efficiency of the Dollar–Sterling Gold Standard, 1890–1906. *J. Econ. Hist.*, March 1989, 49(1), pp. 1–41.

Ofori-Amoah, B. and Hayter, R. Labour Turnover Characteristics at the Eurocan Pulp and Paper Mill, Kitimat: A Log-Linear Analysis. *Environ. Planning A*, November 1989, 21(11), pp. 1491–1510.

Ogawa, H. and Fujita, Masahisa. Nonmonocentric Urban Configurations in a Two-Dimensional Space. *Environ. Planning A*, March 1989, 21(3), pp. 363–74.

Ogden, Joseph P.; Kidwell, David S. and Marr,

M. Wayne. The Effect of a Sinking Fund on the Reoffering Yields of New Public Utility Bonds. *J. Finan. Res.*, Spring 1989, 12(1), pp. 1–13.

Ogden, William, Jr.; Rangan, Nanda K. and Stanley, Thomas. Risk Reduction in S&L Mortgage Loan Portfolios through Geographic Diversification. *J. Finan. Services Res.*, February 1989, 2(1), pp. 39–48.

Ogg, Clayton W. and Gollehon, Noel R. Western Irrigation Response to Pumping Costs: A Water Demand Analysis Using Climatic Regions. *Water Resources Res.*, May 1989, 25(5), pp. 767–73.

Ogryczak, Wlodzimierz and Malczewski, Jacek. On Health Care Districts Planning by Multiobjective Analysis with the MPSX/370 Package. In *Lockett, A. G. and Islei, G., eds.*, 1989, pp. 314–24.

_____; **Studzinski, Krzysztof and Zorychta, Krystian.** DINAS: Dynamic Interactive Network Analysis System. In *Lewandowski, A. and Wierzbicki, A. P., eds.*, 1989, pp. 385–87.

_____; **Studzinski, Krzysztof and Zorychta, Krystian.** Dynamic Interactive Network Analysis System. In *Lockett, A. G. and Islei, G., eds.*, 1989, pp. 444–53.

_____; **Studzinski, Krzysztof and Zorychta, Krystian.** A Generalized Reference Point Approach to Multiobjective Transshipment Problem with Facility Location. In *Lewandowski, A. and Wierzbicki, A. P., eds.*, 1989, pp. 213–29.

_____; **Studzinski, Krzysztof and Zorychta, Krystian.** Solving Multiobjective Distribution–Location Problems with the DINAS System. In *Lewandowski, A. and Wierzbicki, A. P., eds.*, 1989, pp. 230–50.

_____ **and Szymanowski, W.** The Analysis of Liquid Milk Supply to Urban Agglomeration by Bicriterion Linear Transportation Model with the MPSX/370 Package. In *Lockett, A. G. and Islei, G., eds.*, 1989, pp. 203–11.

Ogura, Kazuo. Information Technologies and International Relations: Foreword. In *Jussawalla, M.; Okuma, T. and Araki, T., eds.*, 1989, pp. ix–xiii.

Oh, Seonghwan. A Theory of a Generally Acceptable Medium of Exchange and Barter. *J. Monet. Econ.*, January 1989, 23(1), pp. 101–19.

Ohashi, Isao. On the Determinants of Bonuses and Basic Wages in Large Japanese Firms. *J. Japanese Int. Economies*, December 1989, 3(4), pp. 451–79.

Ohkawa, Masayuki and Tanaka, Kazuyoshi. A Note on Tariffs and Employment under Flexible Exchange Rates. *Scand. J. Econ.*, 1989, 91(4), pp. 741–46.

Ohlin, Göran. House Calls of the Money Doctor: The Kemmerer Missions to Latin America, 1917–1931: Comment. In *[Díaz-Alejandro, C.]*, 1989, pp. 78–79.

Ohlson, James A. Ungarbled Earnings and Dividends: An Analysis and Extension of the Beaver, Lambert, and Morse Valuation Model. *J. Acc. Econ.*, July 1989, 11(2–3), pp. 109–15.

Ohnishi, Hiroshi and Kanemitsu, Hideo. An Input–Output Analysis of Technological Changes in the Japanese Economy: 1970–1980. In *Miller, R. E.; Polenske, K. R. and Rose, A. Z., eds.*, 1989, pp. 308–23.

Ohno, Kenichi. Export Pricing Behavior of Manufacturing: A U.S.–Japan Comparison. *Int. Monet. Fund Staff Pap.*, September 1989, 36(3), pp. 550–79.

_____. Testing Purchasing Power Parity and the Dornbusch Overshooting Model with Vector Autoregression. *J. Japanese Int. Economies*, June 1989, 3(2), pp. 209–26.

_____ **and McKinnon, Ronald I.** Purchasing Power Parity as a Monetary Standard. In *Hamouda, O. F.; Rowley, R. and Wolf, B. M., eds.*, 1989, pp. 42–64.

Ohno, Koichi. A Note on the Dual-Industrial Growth and Learning Effects. *Developing Econ.*, December 1989, 27(4), pp. 350–58.

Ohrenstein, Roman A. Game Theory in the Talmud: An Economic Perspective. *Int. J. Soc. Econ.*, 1989, 16(7), pp. 57–67.

_____ **and Gordon, Barry.** Quantitative Dimensions of Human Capital Analysis in the Talmudic Tradition. *Int. J. Soc. Econ.*, 1989, 16(6), pp. 5–13.

Ohsfeldt, Robert L. and McGuire, Robert A. Self-interest, Agency Theory, and Political Voting Behavior: The Ratification of the United States Constitution. *Amer. Econ. Rev.*, March 1989, 79(1), pp. 219–34.

Ohta, Hiroshi and Kohlhase, Janet E. General Equilibrium of Spatial Product and Labor Markets. *J. Reg. Sci.*, November 1989, 29(4), pp. 537–53.

Ohtake, Fumio and Yoshikawa, Hiroshi. An Analysis of Female Labor Supply, Housing Demand and the Saving Rate in Japan. *Europ. Econ. Rev.*, May 1989, 33(5), pp. 997–1023.

Ohtani, Kazuhiro and Toyoda, Toshihisa. A Switching Regression Model with Different Change-Points for Individual Coefficients and Its Application to the Energy Demand Equations for Japan. *Empirical Econ.*, 1989, 14(2), pp. 93–103.

_____ **and Toyoda, Toshihisa.** A Switching Regression Model with Different Change-Points for Individual Coefficients and Its Application to the Energy Demand Equations for Japan. In *Kramer, W., ed.*, 1989, pp. 29–39.

_____ **and Toyoda, Toshihisa.** Testing Equality between Sets of Coefficients in Two Linear Regressions When Error Terms Are Autocorrelated. *Econ. Stud. Quart.*, March 1989, 40(1), pp. 35–47.

Ohtsuka, Eisaku and Babbel, David F. Aspects of Optimal Multiperiod Life Insurance. *J. Risk Ins.*, September 1989, 56(3), pp. 460–81.

Ohyama, Michihiro. Balance of Payments Adjustment under Price Rigidity. In *Sato, R. and Negishi, T., eds.*, 1989, pp. 31–42.

_____. Bargaining with Differential Skills. *Keio Econ. Stud.*, 1989, 26(2), pp. 1–4.

_____. Factor Endowments and the Pattern of Commodity and Factor Trade. *Keio Econ. Stud.*, 1989, 26(1), pp. 19–29.

_____. On the Stability Properties of the Long-run Stationary Equilibrium in Macro-dynamic Models under Perfect Foresight and Static Expectations. *Econ. Letters*, December 1989, 31(4), pp. 299–301.

_____. Structure and Growth of an Open Dual Economy: Examining Industrial Policy. *Developing Econ.*, December 1989, 27(4), pp. 312–30.

Ojemakinde, Abiodun; Lange, Mark D. and Zacharias, Thomas P. Modelling the Firm-Level Multiproduct Cost Structure of Agricultural Production. In *Gulledge, T. R., Jr. and Litteral, L. A., eds.*, 1989, pp. 117–29.

Okamura, Makoto and Abe, Kenzo. The Welfare Effects of International Tax Harmonization. *Econ. Stud. Quart.*, September 1989, 40(3), pp. 203–11.

Okina, Kunio and Fukao, Mitsuhiro. Internationalization of Financial Markets and Balance of Payments Imbalances: A Japanese Perspective. *Carnegie–Rochester Conf. Ser. Public Policy*, Spring 1989, 30, pp. 167–220.

Okishio, Nobuo. On the Theories of Determination of the Real Wage Rate. *Kobe Univ. Econ.*, 1989, (35), pp. 1–13.

Okita, Saburo. The Current Economic Situation and Future Problems in the Asia-Pacific Region. In *Stern, R. M., ed.*, 1989, pp. 247–59.

_____. The Future of the Asian-Pacific Region and the Role of Japan. In *Shinohara, M. and Lo, F., eds.*, 1989, pp. 42–53.

_____. Japan's Growing Role for Development Financing. In *Reich, M. R. and Marui, E., eds.*, 1989, pp. 358–71.

_____. The Role of the Economist in Government: An International Perspective: Japan. In *Pechman, J. A., ed.*, 1989, pp. 173–91.

Okonkwo, I. C. The Erosion of Agricultural Exports in an Oil Economy: The Case of Nigeria. *J. Agr. Econ.*, September 1989, 40(3), pp. 375–84.

Okpala, Amon O. Child Care and Female Employment in Urban Nigeria. *Rev. Black Polit. Econ.*, Winter 1989, 17(3), pp. 87–99.

_____. Female Employment and Family Size among Urban Nigerian Women. *J. Developing Areas*, April 1989, 23(3), pp. 439–56.

Okuguchi, Koji. The Bertrand and Cournot Equilibria for International Duopoly with Multimarkets. *Int. Econ. J.*, Winter 1989, 3(4), pp. 61–68.

_____ **and Szidarovszky, Ferenc.** An Adaptive Model of Oligopoly with Multi-product Firms. *Econ. Stud. Quart.*, March 1989, 40(1), pp. 48–52.

_____ **and Szidarovszky, Ferenc.** A Non-differentiable Input–Output Model. *Math. Soc. Sci.*, October 1989, 18(2), pp. 187–90.

Okumura, Hiroshi. Features of the Japanese Stock Market. *Rivista Int. Sci. Econ. Com.*, December 1989, 36(12), pp. 1063–73.

Okumura, Ryuhei. Patterns of the Balance of Payments in the Optimal Growth Model. In *Dams, T. and Matsugi, T., eds.*, 1989, pp. 173–90.

Okunade, Albert Ade. A Comment on the Determinants of Saving in Ethiopia and the Role of Demographic Variables. *Eastern Afr. Econ. Rev.*, June 1989, 5(1), pp. 24–31.

_____ **and McLean-Meyinsse, Patricia E.** Factor Demands of Louisiana Rice Producers: An Econometric Investigation: Reply. *Southern J. Agr. Econ.*, December 1989, 21(2), pp. 223–24.

Okuno-Fujiwara, Masahiro. A Depressed View of Policies for Depressed Industries: Comment. In *Stern, R. M., ed.*, 1989, pp. 209–13.

_____. On Labor Incentives and Work Norm in Japanese Firms. *J. Japanese Int. Economies*, December 1989, 3(4), pp. 367–84.

Ölander, Folke and Grunert, Klaus G. Understanding Economic Behaviour: Introduction. In *Grunert, K. G. and Ölander, F., eds.*, 1989, pp. 1–5.

Olcese, Maria Angélica and Filippini, Mariano. Transitional Economic Policies, 1971–73. In *di Tella, G. and Dornbusch, R., eds.*, 1989, pp. 189–205.

Olea, Miguel A. The Latin American Debt Crisis: The Debtor's View. In *Bird, G., ed.*, 1989, pp. 70–77.

Olechowski, Andrzej. Developing Countries and the Uruguay Round of Trade Negotiations: Comment. In *Fischer, S. and de Tray, D., eds.*, 1989, pp. 47–48.

Oleinik, Iu. A. Mathematical Economic Methods: An Integral Part of Soviet Economic Science. *Matekon*, Spring 1989, 25(3), pp. 65–68.

Olekalns, Nilss. Substitution between Private and Public Consumption in Australia. *Econ. Rec.*, March 1989, 65(188), pp. 16–26.

Olgun, Hasan. Some Aspects and Consequences of the Agricultural Price Interventions in Turkey. *Europ. Rev. Agr. Econ.*, 1989, 16(3), pp. 391–410.

Oliner, Stephen D. The Formation of Private Business Capital: Trends, Recent Developments, and Measurement Issues. *Fed. Res. Bull.*, December 1989, 75(12), pp. 771–83.

Olinger, Lois and Mennemeyer, Stephen T. Selective Contracting in California: Its Effect on Hospital Finances. *Inquiry*, Winter 1989, 26(4), pp. 442–57.

Oliver, Daniel. Federal Trade Commission and Domestic Transparency. *World Econ.*, September 1989, 12(3), pp. 339–46.

Oliver, Geoffrey D. and Horlick, Gary N. Antidumping and Countervailing Duty Law Provisions of the Omnibus Trade and Competitiveness Act of 1988. *J. World Trade*, June 1989, 23(3), pp. 5–49.

Oliver, Mark. Radio Deregulation in the UK. In *Veljanovski, C., ed. (I),* 1989, pp. 165–77.

Oliver, Melvin L. and Shapiro, Thomas M. Race and Wealth. *Rev. Black Polit. Econ.*, Spring 1989, 17(4), pp. 5–25.

Oliver, Nick and Wilkinson, Barry. Japanese Manufacturing Techniques and Personnel and

Industrial Relations Practice in Britain: Evidence and Implications. *Brit. J. Ind. Relat.*, March 1989, 27(1), pp. 73–91.

Oliver, Richard L. and Swan, John E. Equity and Disconfirmation Perceptions as Influences on Merchant and Product Satisfaction. *J. Cons. Res.*, December 1989, 16(3), pp. 372–83.

de Oliviera, M. Mendes; Cohn, Elchanan and Kiker, B. F. Tenure, Earnings and Productivity. *Oxford Bull. Econ. Statist.*, February 1989, 51(1), pp. 1–14.

Olmer, Lionel H. Can the United States Still Lead? In *Cerami, C. A., ed.*, 1989, pp. 74–82.

Olmstead, Alan L. and Rhode, Paul. The U.S. Energy Crisis of 1920 and the Search for New Oil Supplies. In *Ferrier, R. W. and Fursenko, A., eds.*, 1989, pp. 83–93.

Olmstead, Dennis J. and DeJean, Niels. Belgium–U.S. and France–U.S. Protocols: Highlighting U.S. Tax Treaty Concerns. *Bull. Int. Fiscal Doc.*, January 1989, 43(1), pp. 3–8.

Olney, Martha L. Consumer Durables in the Interwar Years: New Estimates, New Patterns. In *Ransom, R. L., ed.*, 1989, pp. 119–50.

_____. Credit as a Production-Smoothing Device: The Case of Automobiles, 1913–1938. *J. Econ. Hist.*, June 1989, 49(2), pp. 377–91.

Olowu, Dele and Laleye, O. M. Decentralization in Africa. In *World Bank and Istituto Italo-Africano*, 1989, pp. 78–85.

_____ **and Laleye, O. M.** Managing Local Governments in Africa. In *World Bank and Istituto Italo-Africano*, 1989, pp. 117–23.

Olsen, Hilde and Biørn, Erik. Production–Demand Adjustment in Norwegian Manufacturing: A Quarterly Error Correction Model. *Econ. Modelling*, April 1989, 6(2), pp. 189–202.

Olsen, Katherine; Smith, Amy L. and Wunnava, Phanindra V. An Empirical Study of the Life-Cycle Hypothesis with Respect to Alumni Donations. *Amer. Economist*, Fall 1989, 33(2), pp. 60–63.

Olsen, Ole Jess. Deregulation and Reorganisation: The Case of the Danish Telecommunications. *Ann. Pub. Coop. Econ.*, 1989, 60(2), pp. 251–58.

Olsen, Øystein; Biørn, Erik and Holmøy, Erling. Gross and Net Capital, and the Form of the Survival Function: Theory and Some Norwegian Evidence. *Rev. Income Wealth*, June 1989, 35(2), pp. 133–49.

Olsen, Randall J. and Farkas, George. Endogenous Covariates in Duration Models and the Effect of Adolescent Childbirth on Schooling. *J. Human Res.*, Winter 1989, 24(1), pp. 39–53.

_____ **and Murnane, Richard J.** The Effects of Salaries and Opportunity Costs on Duration in Teaching: Evidence from Michigan. *Rev. Econ. Statist.*, May 1989, 71(2), pp. 347–52.

_____ **and Murnane, Richard J.** Will There Be Enough Teachers? *Amer. Econ. Rev.*, May 1989, 79(2), pp. 242–46.

Olsen, Trond E. Capital Investments and Resource Extraction from Non-identical Deposits.

J. Environ. Econ. Manage., September 1989, 17(2), pp. 127–39.

_____ **and Stensland, Gunnar.** Optimal Sequencing of Resource Pools under Uncertainty. *J. Environ. Econ. Manage.*, July 1989, 17(1), pp. 83–92.

Olson, Craig A. and Becker, Brian E. Unionization and Shareholder Interests. *Ind. Lab. Relat. Rev.*, January 1989, 42(2), pp. 246–62.

Olson, Dennis O. and Nahata, Babu. On the Definition of Barriers to Entry. *Southern Econ. J.*, July 1989, 56(1), pp. 236–39.

_____ **and Shieh, Yeung-Nan.** Estimating Functional Forms in Cost-Prices. *Europ. Econ. Rev.*, September 1989, 33(7), pp. 1445–61.

Olson, Jerry C. and Hastak, Manoj. Assessing the Role of Brand-Related Cognitive Responses as Mediators of Communication Effects on Cognitive Structure. *J. Cons. Res.*, March 1989, 15(4), pp. 444–56.

Olson, Josephine E. and Frieze, Irene Hanson. Job Interruptions and Part-Time Work: Their Effect on MBAs' Income. *Ind. Relat.*, Fall 1989, 28(3), pp. 373–86.

Olson, Kent W. and Gray, Tara. A Cost–Benefit Analysis of the Sentencing Decision for Burglars. *Soc. Sci. Quart.*, September 1989, 70(3), pp. 708–22.

_____ **and Kleckley, James W.** Severance Tax Stability. *Nat. Tax J.*, March 1989, 42(1), pp. 69–78,.

Olson, Lars J. Stochastic Growth with Irreversible Investment. *J. Econ. Theory*, February 1989, 47(1), pp. 101–29.

Olson, Mancur. How Ideas Affect Societies: Is Britain the Wave of the Future? **In** *Gamble, A., et al.*, 1989, pp. 23–51.

_____. A Microeconomic Approach to Macroeconomic Policy. *Amer. Econ. Rev.*, May 1989, 79(2), pp. 377–81.

Olsson, Sven E. Social Welfare in Developed Market Countries: Sweden. **In** *Dixon, J. and Scheurell, R. P., eds.*, 1989, pp. 264–308.

Olver, James; de Kluyver, Cornelis and Farris, Paul W. The Relationship between Distribution and Market Share: Reply. *Marketing Sci.*, Spring 1989, 8(2), pp. 131–32.

_____; **de Kluyver, Cornelis and Farris, Paul W.** The Relationship between Distribution and Market Share. *Marketing Sci.*, Spring 1989, 8(2), pp. 107–28.

Omberg, Edward. The Expected Utility of the Doubling Strategy. *J. Finance*, June 1989, 44(2), pp. 515–24.

Omolehinwa, Eddy and Roe, Emery M. Boom and Bust Budgeting: Repetitive Budgetary Processes in Nigeria, Kenya and Ghana. *Public Budg. Finance*, Summer 1989, 9(2), pp. 43–65.

Onado, Marco. Conditions for Efficiency on the Government Securities Secondary Market: Initial Research Results. *Rev. Econ. Cond. Italy*, May–Aug. 1989, (2), pp. 209–18.

Önal, Hayri and McCarl, Bruce A. Aggregation of Heterogeneous Firms in Mathematical Programming Models. *Europ. Rev. Agr. Econ.*, 1989, 16(4), pp. 499–513.

_____ **and McCarl, Bruce A.** Linear Approximation Using MOTAD and Separable Programming: Should It Be Done? *Amer. J. Agr. Econ.*, February 1989, 71(1), pp. 158–66.

Onchan, Tongroj and Feder, Gershon L. Land Ownership Security and Farm Investment: Reply. *Amer. J. Agr. Econ.*, February 1989, 71(1), pp. 215–16.

Ong, Nai Pew and Lim, Chin. A Dynamic Model of Advertising and Market Shares. *Can. J. Econ.*, November 1989, 22(4), pp. 819–33.

Onida, Fabrizio. Credito agevolato e assicurazione alle esportazioni: Uno strumento obsoleto o ancora valido di politica industriale in economia aperta? (With English summary.) *Politica. Econ.*, April 1989, 5(1), pp. 91–128.

Oniki, Hajime. Computer-Aided Learning for Development. **In** *Jussawalla, M.; Okuma, T. and Araki, T., eds.*, 1989, pp. 293–95.

Onishi, Akira. Prospects for the World Economy and Asian-Pacific Region. **In** *Shinohara, M. and Lo, F., eds.*, 1989, pp. 135–53.

_____. Towards the Asian-Pacific Age: Comment. **In** *Shinohara, M. and Lo, F., eds.*, 1989, pp. 128–32.

Ono, Yoshiyasu and Lahiri, Sajal. Terms of Trade and Welfare: A General Analysis. *Econ. Rec.*, March 1989, 65(188), pp. 27–31.

Onofri, Paolo. Il ruolo delle politiche macroeconomiche nello sviluppo europeo dal dopoguerra ad oggi. (With English summary.) *Politica. Econ.*, December 1989, 5(3), pp. 427–62.

_____. Teoria economica e politiche nel modello Banca d'Italia. (With English summary.) *Politica. Econ.*, April 1989, 5(1), pp. 53–67.

Onyebuchi, Edward I. Alternate Energy Strategies for the Developing World's Domestic Use: A Case Study of Nigerian Households' Fuel Use Patterns and Preferences. *Energy J.*, July 1989, 10(3), pp. 121–38.

Oort, C. The Impact of the Quality of Debts for the Vulnerability of the International Banking System. **In** *Sijben, J. J., ed.*, 1989, pp. 79–96.

Oostendorp, Remco H. and van Praag, Bernard M. S. On the Stability of the Social Security System. **In** *Gustafsson, B. A. and Klevmarken, N. A., eds.*, 1989, pp. 97–111.

Oosterhaven, Jan. The Supply-Driven Input–Output Model: A New Interpretation but Still Implausible. *J. Reg. Sci.*, August 1989, 29(3), pp. 459–65.

_____ **and Stoffelsma, Ronald J.** Social Security Benefits and Interregional Income Inequalities: The Case of the Netherlands. *Ann. Reg. Sci.*, 1989, 23(3), pp. 223–40.

Opitz, Otto and Missler-Behr, Magdalena. Identification of Multiple Criteria Decision Making. **In** *Opitz, O., ed.*, 1989, pp. 407–15.

_____; **Pauly, Ralf and Hauke, Wolfgang.** Explorative Data Analysis and Macroeconomics. **In** *Opitz, O., ed.*, 1989, pp. 416–31.

_____ **and Wiedemann, Raimund.** An Agglomerative Algorithm of Overlapping Clustering. In *Opitz, O., ed.*, 1989, pp. 201–11.

Opocher, Arrigo. Note su equilibri non walrasiani e bilancia commerciale nella piccola economia. (Notes on Non-Walrasian Equilibria and the Balance of Trade in the Small Country. With English summary.) *Rivista Int. Sci. Econ. Com.*, July 1989, *36*(7), pp. 661–81.

Opp, Karl-Dieter. The Economics of Crime and the Sociology of Deviant Behaviour: A Theoretical Confrontation of Basic Propositions. *Kyklos*, 1989, *42*(3), pp. 405–30.

van Oppendoor, S. An Overview of the World's Social Science–Modelling Industry: Applying the XM_{as} Principle: Commentary. *Environ. Planning A*, December 1989, *21*(12), pp. 1561–64.

Oppenheimer, Peter M. External Impacts of the United States' Financial Policies. In *Hamouda, O. F.; Rowley, R. and Wolf, B. M., eds.*, 1989, pp. 118–26.

——. Financial Markets and Economic Well-Being: A Tribute to Fred Hirsch. In *Johnson, C., ed.*, 1989, pp. 17–25.

—— and **Reddaway, Brian.** The U.S. Economy: Performance and Prospects. *Nat. Inst. Econ. Rev.*, February 1989, (127), pp. 52–63.

Opper, Barbara. Improving the Bank's Loan Currency Pool. *Finance Devel.*, June 1989, *26*(2), pp. 24–25.

Opschoor, J. B. and Mol, A. P. J. Developments in Economic Valuation of Environmental Resources in Centrally Planned Economies. *Environ. Planning A*, September 1989, *21*(9), pp. 1205–28.

van Opstal, Rocus; Theeuwes, Jules J. M. and Koopmans, Carl C. Human Capital and Job Levels: Explaining the Age–Income Funnel. *Europ. Econ. Rev.*, December 1989, *33*(9), pp. 1839–49.

Oral, Muhittin and Kettani, Ossama. A Mathematical Programming Model for Market Share Prediction. *Int. J. Forecasting*, 1989, *5*(1), pp. 59–68.

Oram, Peter A. Sensitivity of Agricultural Production to Climatic Change, an Update. In *Oram, P. A., et al.*, 1989, pp. 25–44.

——. Views on "The New Global Context for Agricultural Research: Implications for Policy." In *Oram, P. A., et al.*, 1989, pp. 13–23.

Oran, Ahmad and Rashid, Salim. Fiscal Policy in Early Islam. *Public Finance*, 1989, *44*(1), pp. 75–101.

Orazem, Peter F. and Falk, Barry. Measuring Market Responses to Error-Ridden Government Announcements. *Quart. Rev. Econ. Bus.*, Summer 1989, *29*(2), pp. 41–55.

—— and **Falk, Barry.** The Role of Systematic Fed Errors in Explaining the Money Supply Announcements Puzzle: A Note. *J. Money, Credit, Banking*, August 1989, *21*(3), pp. 401–06.

—— and **Mattila, J. Peter.** Comparable Worth and the Structure of Earnings: The Iowa Case. In *Michael, R. T.; Hartmann, H. I. and O'Farrell, B., eds.*, 1989, pp. 179–99.

——; **Otto, Daniel M. and Edelman, Mark A.** An Analysis of Farmers' Agricultural Policy Preferences. *Amer. J. Agr. Econ.*, November 1989, *71*(4), pp. 837–46.

Ord, J. Keith and Texter, Pamela A. Forecasting Using Automatic Identification Procedures: A Comparative Analysis. *Int. J. Forecasting*, 1989, *5*(2), pp. 209–15.

—— and **Young, Peg.** Model Selection and Estimation for Technological Growth Curves. *Int. J. Forecasting*, 1989, *5*(4), pp. 501–13.

Orden, David and Fackler, Paul L. Identifying Monetary Impacts on Agricultural Prices in VAR Models. *Amer. J. Agr. Econ.*, May 1989, *71*(2), pp. 495–502.

——; **Norton, George W. and Bouchet, Frédéric.** Sources of Growth in French Agriculture. *Amer. J. Agr. Econ.*, May 1989, *71*(2), pp. 280–93.

Ordeshook, Peter C. and Niou, Emerson M. S. Stability in International Systems and the Costs of War. In *Ordeshook, P. C., ed.*, 1989, pp. 229–51.

——; **Williams, Kenneth and Collier, Kenneth.** The Rationally Uninformed Electorate: Some Experimental Evidence. *Public Choice*, January 1989, *60*(1), pp. 3–29.

Ordóñez Plaja, Antonio. Invitation to a Debate on Financing and Health: Commentary. In *WHO, Pan American Health Organization*, 1989, pp. 182–87.

Ordover, Janusz A. and Saloner, Garth. Predation, Monopolization, and Antitrust. In *Schmalensee, R. and Willig, R. D., eds., Vol. 1*, 1989, pp. 537–96.

Orellana G., Arturo René and Avila, Ricardo Avila. Poverty and Labour Market Access in Guatemala City. In *Rodgers, G., ed.*, 1989, pp. 81–96.

d'Orey, Vasco and Turnovsky, Stephen J. The Choice of Monetary Instrument in Two Interdependent Economies under Uncertainty. *J. Monet. Econ.*, January 1989, *23*(1), pp. 121–33.

Oria, Maria E.; Tuss, Joseph P. and Riordan, Timothy H. Dayton's Capital Allocation Process. In *Matzer, J., Jr., ed.*, 1989, *1987*, pp. 21–37.

Orléan, André. Pour une approche cognitive des conventions économiques. (Toward a Cognitive Approach to Economic Conventions. With English summary.) *Revue Écon.*, March 1989, *40*(2), pp. 241–72.

Orlov, B. P. Illusions and Reality of Economic Information. *Prob. Econ.*, May 1989, *32*(1), pp. 15–32.

Orme, Christopher D. Evaluating the Performance of Maximum Likelihood Corrections in the Face of Local Misspecification. *Bull. Econ. Res.*, January 1989, *41*(1), pp. 29–44.

——. On the Uniqueness of the Maximum Likelihood Estimator in Truncated Regression Models. *Econometric Rev.*, 1989, *8*(2), pp. 217–22.

Ormiston, Michael B. and Meyer, Jack. Deterministic Transformations of Random Variables and the Comparative Statics of Risk. *J. Risk Uncertainty*, June 1989, 2(2), pp. 179–88.

Ornstein, Stanley I. Exclusive Dealing and Antitrust. *Antitrust Bull.*, Spring 1989, 34(1), pp. 65–98.

Oropesa, R. S. The Social and Political Foundations of Effective Neighborhood Improvement Associations. *Soc. Sci. Quart.*, September 1989, 70(3), pp. 723–43.

Orr, Blair and Buongiorno, Joseph. Improving Estimates of Employment in Small Geographic Areas. *J. Econ. Soc. Meas.*, 1989, 15(3–4), pp. 225–35.

Orr, James A. The Average Workweek of Capital in Manufacturing, 1952–1984. *J. Amer. Statist. Assoc.*, March 1989, 84(405), pp. 88–94.

———. The Performance of the U.S. Capital Goods Industry: Implications for Trade Adjustment. *Fed. Res. Bank New York Quart. Rev.*, Winter–Spring 1989, 13-14(4–1), pp. 69–82.

——— **and Hickok, Susan.** Shifting Patterns of U.S. Trade with Selected Developing Asian Economies. *Fed. Res. Bank New York Quart. Rev.*, Winter 1989–90, 14(4), pp. 36–47.

Orru, Marco and Hamilton, Gary G. Organizational Structure of East Asian Companies. **In** *Chung, K. H. and Lee, H. C.*, eds., 1989, pp. 39–47.

Ortí Lahoz, Angel; Orts Rios, Vicente and Caballero Sanz, Francisco. Direct Foreign Investment and International Trade in Spain. **In** *Yannopoulos, G. N.*, ed., 1989, pp. 227–53.

Ortiz de Zevallos M., Felipe. Privatisation in Peru. **In** *Ramanadham, V. V.*, ed., 1989, pp. 358–77.

Ortiz Ferrara, G., et al. Wheat: A Complementary Crop for Traditional Rice-Growing Countries of Asia. **In** *International Rice Research Institute*, 1989, pp. 255–63.

Ortiz, Guillermo. The IMF and the Debt Strategy. **In** *Gwin, C. and Feinberg, R. E.*, eds., 1989, pp. 123–39.

——— **and Ize, Alain.** Fiscal Rigidities, Public Debt, and Capital Flight. **In** *Blejer, M. I. and Chu, K.*, eds., 1989, 1987, pp. 50–71.

Ortner, K. M. A Multi-market Model for Policy Impact Assessment. **In** *Bauer, S. and Henrichsmeyer, W.*, eds., 1989, pp. 165–69.

Orts Rios, Vicente; Caballero Sanz, Francisco and Ortí Lahoz, Angel. Direct Foreign Investment and International Trade in Spain. **In** *Yannopoulos, G. N.*, ed., 1989, pp. 227–53.

Ortúzar, Juan de Dois and Jara-Díaz, Sergio R. Introducing the Expenditure Rate in the Estimation of Mode Choice Models. *J. Transp. Econ. Policy*, September 1989, 23(3), pp. 293–308.

Orzech, Ze'ev B. and Groll, Shalom. From Marx to the Okishio Theorem: A Genealogy. *Hist. Polit. Econ.*, Summer 1989, 21(2), pp. 253–72.

——— **and Groll, Shalom.** Stages in the Development of a Marxian Concept: The Composition of Capital. *Hist. Polit. Econ.*, Spring 1989, 21(1), pp. 57–76.

Osano, Hiroshi. Implicit Contracts and Reputa-

tions. *Econ. Stud. Quart.*, June 1989, 40(2), pp. 109–21.

Osband, Kent. Optimal Forecasting Incentives. *J. Polit. Econ.*, October 1989, 97(5), pp. 1091–1112.

———. Reforming the Soviet Cartel. *Contemp. Policy Issues*, January 1989, 7(1), pp. 53–69.

Osborn, Denise R. and Smith, Jeremy P. The Performance of Periodic Autoregressive Models in Forecasting Seasonal U. K. Consumption. *J. Bus. Econ. Statist.*, January 1989, 7(1), pp. 117–27.

Osborne, Clark; McGrann, James M. and Karkosh, Kedrick. Agricultural Financial Analysis Expert Systems: Software Description. *Can. J. Agr. Econ.*, Part 1, December 1989, 37(4), pp. 695–708.

Osers, Jan. Die antitechnokratische gesellschaft von Joseph Huber. (With English summary.) *Jahr. Wirtsch. Osteuropas*, 1989, 13(1), pp. 153–75.

———. Die tschechoslowakische "Wirtschaftsdemokratie" als wegbereiter des prager frühlings. (With English summary.) *Jahr. Wirtsch. Osteuropas*, 1989, 13(2), pp. 115–40.

Oshikoya, W. T. Foreign Borrowing, Agricultural Productivity, and the Nigerian Economy: A Macro-sectoral Analysis. *J. Policy Modeling*, Winter 1989, 11(4), pp. 531–46.

Oshima, Harry T. Human Resources in the Agro-industrial Transition. **In** *Chakravarty, S.*, ed., 1989, pp. 7–23.

———. Japan's Role in the Future of the Asian-Pacific Economies. **In** *Shinohara, M. and Lo, F.*, eds., 1989, pp. 54–67.

Osipenko, O. V. and Kozlov, Iu. G. What Is It That Casts a Shadow? *Prob. Econ.*, November 1989, 32(7), pp. 29–42.

Oskam, Arie. Principles of the EC Dairy Model. *Europ. Rev. Agr. Econ.*, 1989, 16(4), pp. 463–97.

———; **Reinhard, A. and Thijssen, G.** Wasmodel-2: A Disaggregated Agricultural Sector Model Partly Based on Prior Information. **In** *Bauer, S. and Henrichsmeyer, W.*, eds., 1989, pp. 53–69.

Osmani, S. R. Limits to the Alleviation of Poverty through Non-farm Credit. *Bangladesh Devel. Stud.*, December 1989, 17(4), pp. 1–19.

Ospina Sardi, Jorge. Trade Policy in Latin America. **In** *Naya, S., et al.*, eds., 1989, pp. 77–91.

Ostanello, Anna and Norese, Maria Franca. Identification and Development of Alternatives: Introduction to the Recognition of Process Typologies. **In** *Lockett, A. G. and Islei, G.*, eds., 1989, pp. 112–23.

Östblom, Göran. Productivity Changes and Changes in the Requirements of Imports in the Swedish Economy, 1957–1980: An Input–Output Study. *Econ. Systems Res.*, 1989, 1(1), pp. 97–110.

Oster, Clinton V., Jr. and Zorn, C. Kurt. Is It Still Safe to Fly? **In** *Moses, L. N. and Savage, I.*, eds., 1989, pp. 129–52.

Osterberg, William P. Tobin's q, Investment, and

the Endogenous Adjustment of Financial Structure. *J. Public Econ.*, December 1989, *40*(3), pp. 293–318.

Osterfeld, David. Radical Federalism: Responsiveness, Conflict, and Efficiency. In *Brennan, G. and Lomasky, L. E.*, eds., 1989, pp. 149–73.

Østergaard, Tom. Aiming beyond Conventional Development Assistance: An Analysis of Nordic Aid to the SADCC Region. In *Odén, B. and Othman, H.*, eds., 1989, pp. 127–79.

Osterhammel, Jürgen. British Business in China, 1860s–1950s. In *Davenport-Hines, R. P. T. and Jones, G.*, eds., 1989, pp. 189–216.

Osterman, Paul and Lynch, Lisa M. Technological Innovation and Employment in Telecommunications. *Ind. Relat.*, Spring 1989, *28*(2), pp. 188–206.

Östermark, Ralf. Kapitalmarknadsmodeller och portföljeffektivitet. (Capital Market Models and Portfolio Efficiency. With English summary.) *Ekon. Samfundets Tidskr.*, 1989, *42*(2), pp. 101–12.

_____; **Zeleny, Milan and Kasanen, Eero.** Gestalt System of Holistic Graphics: New Management Support View of MCDM. In *Lockett, A. G. and Islei, G.*, eds., 1989, pp. 143–56.

Osterwoldt, Ralph. Implementation and Enforcement Issues in the Protection of Migratory Species: Two Case Studies: Waterfowl in North America, Seals in Europe. *Natural Res. J.*, Fall 1989, *29*(4), pp. 1017–49.

Ostroy, Joseph M. The Informational Efficiency of Monetary Exchange. In *Starr, R. M.*, ed., 1989, *1973*, pp. 115–28.

_____ **and Starr, Ross M.** Money and the Decentralization of Exchange. In *Starr, R. M.*, ed., 1989, *1974*, pp. 149–69.

Ostry, Sylvia. The Role of International Institutions in Surveillance and Policy Coordination: Comment. In *Bryant, R. C., et al.*, eds., 1989, pp. 365–68.

Oswald, Andrew J. Wages and Employment in Unionized Economies: Theory and Evidence: Comment. In *Holmlund, B.; Löfgren, K.-G. and Engström, L.*, 1989, pp. 105–13.

_____ **and Blanchflower, David G.** Housing, Wages and UK Labour Markets: Comments. *Oxford Bull. Econ. Statist.*, March 1989, *51*(2), pp. 137–43.

_____ **and Blanchflower, David G.** Housing, Wages and UK Labour Markets: Reply. *Oxford Bull. Econ. Statist.*, March 1989, *51*(2), pp. 159–62.

Otani, Ichiro and Villanueva, Delano. Major Determinants of Long-term Growth in LDCs. *Finance Devel.*, September 1989, *26*(3), pp. 41–43.

_____ **and Villanueva, Delano.** Theoretical Aspects of Growth in Developing Countries: External Debt Dynamics and the Role of Human Capital. *Int. Monet. Fund Staff Pap.*, June 1989, *36*(2), pp. 307–42.

Otani, Kiyoshi. A Collapse of a Fixed Rate Regime with a Discrete Realignment of the Exchange

Rate. *J. Japanese Int. Economies*, September 1989, *3*(3), pp. 250–69.

Otayek, René. Burkina Faso: Between Feeble State and Total State, the Swing Continues. In *Cruise O'Brien, D. B.; Dunn, J. and Rathbone, R.*, eds., 1989, pp. 13–30.

Otero, Manuel and Cirio, Felix M. Agricultural Trade in Argentina: Impacts on the Global Economy and Strategies for the GATT Negotiations. In *Whalley, J.*, ed., *Vol. 2*, 1989, pp. 161–78.

Othman, Shehu. Nigeria: Power for Profit—Class, Corporatism, and Factionalism in the Military. In *Cruise O'Brien, D. B.; Dunn, J. and Rathbone, R.*, eds., 1989, pp. 113–44.

Otsuka, Allen S. and Lin, Steven A. Y. Determinants of U.S. Direct Manufacturing Investments in East Asia. In *Missouri Valley Economic Association*, 1989, pp. 123–28.

Otsuka, Keijiro and Murakami, Naoki. Incentives and Enforcement under Contract: The Taxicab in Kyoto. *J. Japanese Int. Economies*, September 1989, *3*(3), pp. 231–49.

Otsuki, Mikiro. Mechanisms and Institutions: Comment. In *Shiraishi, T. and Tsuru, S.*, eds., 1989, pp. 105–06.

Ott, Mack. Is America Being Sold Out? *Fed. Res. Bank St. Louis Rev.*, March–April 1989, *71*(2), pp. 47–64.

_____ **and Belongia, Michael T.** The U.S. Monetary Policy Regime, Interest Differentials, and Dollar Exchange Rate Risk Premia. *J. Int. Money Finance*, March 1989, *8*(1), pp. 137–45.

Otto, Daniel M.; Edelman, Mark A. and Orazem, Peter F. An Analysis of Farmers' Agricultural Policy Preferences. *Amer. J. Agr. Econ.*, November 1989, *71*(4), pp. 837–46.

Ottoz, Elisabetta. Discriminazione intertemporale in un modello di diffusione tecnologica. (Intertemporal Discrimination in a Model of Technological Diffusion. With English summary.) *Rivista Int. Sci. Econ. Com.*, April–May 1989, *36*(4–5), pp. 371–87.

Ou, Jane A. and Penman, Stephen H. Accounting Measurement, Price–Earnings Ratio, and the Information Content of Security Prices. *J. Acc. Res.*, Supplement, 1989, *27*, pp. 111–44.

_____ **and Penman, Stephen H.** Financial Statement Analysis and the Prediction of Stock Returns. *J. Acc. Econ.*, November 1989, *11*(4), pp. 295–329.

Ouliaris, Sam and Corbae, Dean. A Random Walk through the Gibson Paradox. *J. Appl. Econometrics*, July–Sept. 1989, *4*(3), pp. 295–303.

Oulton, Nicholas. Productivity Growth in Manufacturing, 1963–85: The Roles of New Investment and Scrapping. *Nat. Inst. Econ. Rev.*, February 1989, (127), pp. 64–75.

Oum, Tae Hoon. Alternative Demand Models and Their Elasticity Estimates. *J. Transp. Econ. Policy*, May 1989, *23*(2), pp. 163–87.

_____ **and Tretheway, Michael W.** Hedonic vs. General Specifications of the Translog Cost

Function. *Logist. Transp. Rev.*, March 1989, 25(1), pp. 3–21.

_____; Tretheway, Michael W. and Gillen, David W. Privatization of Air Canada: Why It Is Necessary in a Deregulated Environment. *Can. Public Policy*, September 1989, 15(3), pp. 285–99.

van Ours, Jan C. Durations of Dutch Job Vacancies. *De Economist*, 1989, 137(3), pp. 309–27.

Ouwersloot, H. and Rietveld, Piet. Intraregional Income Distribution and Poverty: Some Investigations for the Netherlands, 1960–81. *Environ. Planning A*, July 1989, 21(7), pp. 881–904.

Overlaet, B. and Shokkaert, E. Moral Intuitions and Economic Models of Distributive Justice. *Soc. Choice Welfare*, January 1989, 6(1), pp. 19–31.

Ovsienko, V. V. and Gerasimovich, V. N. A Reform of the Mechanism of International Economic Relations: Basic Concepts and Problems. *Matekon*, Winter 1989–90, 26(2), pp. 27–37.

Owen, A. D. Economic Growth and Energy Efficiency: Towards a More Rational Use of Energy. In *Owen, A. D., ed.*, 1989, pp. 25–37.

Owen, Bruce M. and Noll, Roger G. The Anticompetitive Uses of Regulation: *United States v. AT&T*. In *Kwoka, J. E., Jr. and White, L. J., eds.*, 1989, pp. 290–337.

Owen, D. W. and Green, A. E. The Changing Geography of Occupations in Engineering in Britain, 1978–1987. *Reg. Stud.*, February 1989, 23(1), pp. 27–42.

_____ and Green, A. E. Labour Market Accounts for Travel-to-Work Areas, 1981–1984. *Reg. Stud.*, February 1989, 23(1), pp. 69–72.

Owen, Guillermo; Grofman, Bernard and Feld, Scott L. Proving a Distribution-Free Generalization of the Condorcet Jury Theorem. *Math. Soc. Sci.*, February 1989, 17(1), pp. 1–16.

_____ and Maschler, M. The Consistent Shapley Value for Hyperplane Games. *Int. J. Game Theory*, 1989, 18(4), pp. 389–407.

_____ and Shapley, L. S. Optimal Location of Candidates in Ideological Space. *Int. J. Game Theory*, 1989, 18(3), pp. 339–56.

Owen, John D. Labor Supply over the Life Cycle: The Long-term Forecasting Problem. *Int. J. Forecasting*, 1989, 5(2), pp. 249–57.

Owen, Nicholas and Müller, Jürgen. The Effect of Trade on Plant Size. In *Jacquemin, A. and Sapir, A., eds.*, 1989, 1985, pp. 173–84.

Owen, Norman G. Subsistence in the Slump: Agricultural Adjustment in the Provincial Philippines. In *Brown, I., ed.*, 1989, pp. 95–114.

Owen, P. Dorian and Solis-Fallas, Otton. Unorganized Money Markets and 'Unproductive' Assets in the New Structuralist Critique of Financial Liberalization. *J. Devel. Econ.*, October 1989, 31(2), pp. 341–55.

Owen, Roger. Egypt in the World Depression: Agricultural Recession and Industrial Expansion. In *Brown, I., ed.*, 1989, pp. 137–51.

_____. The Movement of Labor in and out of the Middle East over the Last Two Centuries:

Peasants, Patterns, and Policies. In *Sabagh, G., ed.*, 1989, pp. 29–43.

Owen, Thomas C. A Standard Ruble of Account for Russian Business History, 1769–1914: A Note. *J. Econ. Hist.*, September 1989, 49(3), pp. 699–706.

Owen, Virginia Lee. The Economic Legacy of Gothic Cathedral Building: France and England Compared. *J. Cult. Econ.*, June 1989, 13(1), pp. 89–100.

Owens, Emiel W. Economic and Health Consequences of Undernutrition. *Int. J. Soc. Econ.*, 1989, 16(12), pp. 5–13.

Owens, Jeffrey P. and Messere, Ken C. Long-Term Revenue Trends and Current Tax Reform Issues in OECD Countries. In *Chiancone, A. and Messere, K., eds.*, 1989, pp. 21–35.

Oxley, James; Fox, Glenn C. and Moschini, Giancarlo. An Analysis of the Structural and Welfare Effects of Bovine Somatotropin on the Ontario Dairy Industry. *Can. J. Agr. Econ.*, November 1989, 37(3), pp. 393–406.

Oyejide, T. Ademola. Primary Commodities in the International Trading System. In *Whalley, J., ed., Vol. 1*, 1989, pp. 91–111.

_____. Resource Exports, Adjustment Problems and Liberalization Prospects in Nigeria. In *Whalley, J., ed., Vol. 2*, 1989, pp. 40–57.

_____. Sector Proportions and Growth in the Development of the Nigerian Economy. In *Williamson, J. G. and Panchamukhi, V. R., eds.*, 1989, pp. 190–218.

_____ and Tran, Lien H. Food and Agricultural Imports of Sub-Saharan Africa. In *Islam, N., ed.*, 1989, pp. 147–64.

Ozaki, Tohru and Ozaki, Valerie H. Statistical Identification of Nonlinear Dynamics in Macroeconomics Using Nonlinear Time Series Models. In *Hackl, P., ed.*, 1989, pp. 345–65.

Ozaki, Valerie H. and Ozaki, Tohru. Statistical Identification of Nonlinear Dynamics in Macroeconomics Using Nonlinear Time Series Models. In *Hackl, P., ed.*, 1989, pp. 345–65.

Ozawa, Terutomo and Sato, Mitsuaki. JETRO, Japan's Adaptive Innovation in the Organization of Trade. *J. World Trade*, August 1989, 23(4), pp. 15–24.

Ozernoy, Vladimir M. and Jelassi, M. Tawfik. A Framework for Building an Expert System for MCDM Models Selection. In *Lockett, A. G. and Islei, G., eds.*, 1989, pp. 553–62.

Özler, Şule. Commercial Bank Lending to Developing Countries: The Expansion of the Market. *Contemp. Policy Issues*, July 1989, 7(3), pp. 1–10.

_____. On the Relation between Reschedulings and Bank Value. *Amer. Econ. Rev.*, December 1989, 79(5), pp. 1117–31.

Paarlberg, Don. The (Negative) Role of Food Aid and Technical Assistance: A Comment. In *Horwich, G. and Lynch, G. J., eds.*, 1989, pp. 130–31.

_____. Why Is Agricultural Policy So Difficult to Reform? Commentary. In *Krämer, C. S., ed.*, 1989, pp. 34–35.

Paarlberg, Philip L. and Seitzinger, Ann Hillberg. A Simulation Model of the U.S. Export Enhancement Program for Wheat in the Presence of an EC Response. *Europ. Rev. Agr. Econ.*, 1989, *16*(4), pp. 445–62.

Paarlberg, Robert L. International Agricultural Policy Coordination: An Aid to Liberal Reform? In *von Witzke, H.; Runge, C. F. and Job, B.*, eds., 1989, pp. 177–211.

_____. Is There Anything "American" about American Agricultural Policy? In *Krämer, C. S.*, ed., 1989, pp. 37–55.

Paavonen, Tapani. Neutrality, Protectionism and the International Community: Finnish Foreign Economic Policy in the Period of Reconstruction of the International Economy, 1945–1950. *Scand. Econ. Hist. Rev.*, 1989, *37*(1), pp. 23–40.

de Pablo, Juan Carlos. Economic Policy without Political Context: Guido, 1962–63. In *di Tella, G. and Dornbusch, R.*, eds., 1989, pp. 129–41.

_____. Economic Policy without Political Context: Guido, 1962–63: Response. In *di Tella, G. and Dornbusch, R.*, eds., 1989, pp. 146.

_____. External Shocks and Policy Reforms in the Southern Cone: A Reassessment: Comment. In *[Díaz-Alejandro, C.]*, 1989, pp. 263–64.

Pachauri, R. K. Energy and Growth: Beyond the Myths and Myopia. *Energy J.*, January 1989, *10*(1), pp. 1–19.

Paché, Gilles. Conflits et pouvoirs dans la commercialisation des produits agro-alimentaires: Industriels, distributeurs, prestataires logistiques. (Conflicts and Powers in the Commercialization of Food Produce: Manufacturers, Distributors, and Logistical Intermediaries. With English summary.) *Écon. Societes*, July 1989, *23*(7), pp. 217–29.

Paci, Massimo. Public and Private in the Italian Welfare System. In *Lange, P. and Regini, M.*, eds., 1989, pp. 217–34.

Paci, Pierella; Wagstaff, Adam and van Doorslaer, Eddy. Equity in the Finance and Delivery of Health Care: Some Tentative Cross-country Comparisons. *Oxford Rev. Econ. Policy*, Spring 1989, *5*(1), pp. 89–112.

Pack, Janet Rothenberg. Privatization and Cost Reduction. *Policy Sciences*, March 1989, *22*(1), pp. 1–25.

Pack, Ludwig. Gewinnmaximale oder rentabilitätsmaximale Losgrösse bzw. Bestellmenge? (With English summary.) *Z. Betriebswirtshaft*, January 1989, *59*(1), pp. 5–26.

Packard, Michael D. and Reno, Virginia P. A Look at Very Early Retirees. *Soc. Sec. Bull.*, March 1989, *52*(3), pp. 16–29.

Paczynski, Jerzy. Nonlinear Computer Models—Issues of Generation and Differentiation. In *Lewandowski, A. and Wierzbicki, A. P.*, eds., 1989, pp. 172–79.

Padberg, Daniel I. Break-Out Session I—Issues for Hunger, Malnutrition, Agriculture, and Food Policy: Recommendations: Private Sector Agribusiness. In *Helmuth, J. W. and Johnson, S. R.*, eds., Vol. 1, 1989, pp. 125–26.

Padoa Schioppa, Fiorella. Factor Flexibility, Uncertainty and Exchange Rate Regimes: Discussion. In *De Cecco, M. and Giovannini, A.*, eds., 1989, pp. 121–26.

_____; Rossi, Nicola and Modigliani, Franco. Aggregate Unemployment in Italy, 1960–1983. In *Modigliani, F.*, *Vol. 4*, 1989, *1986*, pp. 253–87.

Paech, Niko. Umweltbewusstsein, Qualitätsunsicherheit und die Wirkung einer Emissionspublizität. (Environmental Consciousness, Quality Uncertainty and the Impact of an Emission Publicity. With English summary.) *Z. Wirtschaft. Sozialwissen.*, 1989, *109*(3), pp. 385–98.

Paga, Leslaw A. and Lulek, Andrzej F. The Spheres of Inequality in a Centrally Planned Economy: The Case of Poland. *Int. J. Soc. Econ.*, 1989, *16*(1), pp. 27–39.

Pagan, Adrian R. On the Role of Simulation in the Statistical Evaluation of Econometric Models. *J. Econometrics*, January 1989, *40*(1), pp. 125–39.

_____. Twenty Years After: Econometrics, 1966–1986. In *Cornet, B. and Tulkens, H.*, eds., 1989, pp. 319–83.

_____ and Hoffman, Dennis L. Post-Sample Prediction Tests for Generalized Method of Moments Estimators. *Oxford Bull. Econ. Statist.*, August 1989, *51*(3), pp. 333–43.

_____ and Hong, Y. Some Simulation Studies of Nonparametric Estimators. In *Ullah, A.*, ed., 1989, *1988*, pp. 129–44.

_____ and Vella, Frank. Diagnostic Tests for Models Based on Individual Data: A Survey. *J. Appl. Econometrics*, Supplement, December 1989, *4*, pp. S29–59.

_____ and Wickens, Michael R. A Survey of Some Recent Econometric Methods. *Econ. J.*, December 1989, *99*(398), pp. 962–1025.

Pagano, Marco. Endogenous Market Thinness and Stock Price Volatility. *Rev. Econ. Stud.*, April 1989, *56*(2), pp. 269–87.

_____. Monetary Policy, Capital Controls and Seigniorage in an Open Economy: Discussion. In *De Cecco, M. and Giovannini, A.*, eds., 1989, pp. 37–52.

_____. Trading Volume and Asset Liquidity. *Quart. J. Econ.*, May 1989, *104*(2), pp. 255–74.

_____ and Jappelli, Tullio. Consumption and Capital Market Imperfections: An International Comparison. *Amer. Econ. Rev.*, December 1989, *79*(5), pp. 1088–1105.

_____; Modigliani, Franco and Jappelli, Tullio. The Impact of Fiscal Policy and Inflation on National Saving: A Reply. *Banca Naz. Lavoro Quart. Rev.*, June 1989, (169), pp. 239–44.

Page, F. H., Jr. Incentive Compatible Strategies for General Stackelberg Games with Incomplete Information. *Int. J. Game Theory*, 1989, *18*(4), pp. 409–21.

Page, John M., Jr. and Nishimizu, Mieko. Productivity Change and Growth in Industry and Agriculture: An International Comparison. In *Williamson, J. G. and Panchamukhi, V. R.*, eds., 1989, pp. 390–413.

Paggi, Mechel S. and Mjelde, James W. An Empirical Analysis of Interregional Price Linkages. *J. Reg. Sci.*, May 1989, *29*(2), pp. 171–89.

Paglin, Morton. On the Measurement and Trend of Inequality: Reply. *Amer. Econ. Rev.*, March 1989, *79*(1), pp. 265–66.

Pagoulatos, Angelos; Debertin, David L. and Sjarkowi, Fachurrozi. Soil Erosion, Intertemporal Profit, and the Soil Conservation Decision. *Southern J. Agr. Econ.*, December 1989, *21*(2), pp. 55–62.

Painter, Joe and Massey, Doreen. The Changing Geography of Trade Unions. In *Mohan, J., ed.*, 1989, pp. 130–50.

Pajestka, Józef. Institutional Change for the Future: Socialist Experience and New Horizons. In *Shiraishi, T. and Tsuru, S., eds.*, 1989, pp. 111–25.

_____. Revaluation of the Past Experience and the Future of Economic Reform in Poland. In *Gomulka, S.; Ha, Y.-C. and Kim, C.-O., eds.*, 1989, pp. 170–80.

Pakes, Ariel. Employee Retirement and a Firm's Pension Plan: Comment. In *Wise, D. A., ed.*, 1989, pp. 330–33.

_____ **and Pollard, David.** Simulation and the Asymptotics of Optimization Estimators. *Econometrica*, September 1989, *57*(5), pp. 1027–57.

_____ **and Simpson, Margaret.** Patent Renewal Data. *Brookings Pap. Econ. Act.*, Microeconomics, 1989, pp. 331–401.

Pal, S. P. On the Feasibility of Reducing Budgetary Food Subsidies in India. *Margin*, July–Sept. 1989, *21*(4), pp. 30–42.

Paladini, Ruggero. Kalecki and Fiscal Policy. In *Sebastiani, M., ed.*, 1989, pp. 220–30.

Palasek, Karen. The Case for a Laissez-Faire Monetary System. *Cato J.*, Fall 1989, *9*(2), pp. 399–403.

Palazzi, Paolo and Buccellato, Claudio. Deindustrializzazione e sviluppo: Alcuni confronti internazionali. (Deindustrialization and Development: Some International Comparison. With English summary.) *Econ. Lavoro*, Jan.–March 1989, *23*(1), pp. 53–75.

Paldam, Martin. Theoretical Developments in the Light of Macroeconomic Policy and Empirical Research: Comment. *Scand. J. Econ.*, 1989, *91*(2), pp. 339–45.

_____. A Wage Structure Theory of Inflation, Industrial Conflicts and Trade Unions. *Scand. J. Econ.*, 1989, *91*(1), pp. 63–81.

Palepu, Krishna G.; Asquith, Paul and Healy, Paul. Earnings and Stock Splits. *Accounting Rev.*, July 1989, *64*(3), pp. 387–403.

Palfrey, Thomas R. A Mathematical Proof of Duverger's Law. In *Ordeshook, P. C., ed.*, 1989, pp. 69–91.

_____; **Forsythe, Robert and Isaac, R. Mark.** Theories and Tests of "Blind Bidding" in Sealed-Bid Auctions. *Rand J. Econ.*, Summer 1989, *20*(2), pp. 214–38.

_____ **and Jagannathan, Ravi.** Effects of Insider Trading Disclosures on Speculative Activity

and Future Prices. *Econ. Inquiry*, July 1989, *27*(3), pp. 411–30.

_____ **and Srivastava, Sanjay.** Implementation with Incomplete Information in Exchange Economies. *Econometrica*, January 1989, *57*(1), pp. 115–34.

_____ **and Srivastava, Sanjay.** Mechanism Design with Incomplete Information: A Solution to the Implementation Problem. *J. Polit. Econ.*, June 1989, *97*(3), pp. 668–91.

Palia, Aspy P. and Williams, Harold R. Impact of TPM on U.S. Steel Imports from Japan. *Rivista Int. Sci. Econ. Com.*, December 1989, *36*(12), pp. 1109–21.

Pallini, Andrea and Giorgi, Giovanni Maria. Upper Bounds on Gini Index: A Measure for Geometric Comparison. *Econ. Notes*, 1989, (2), pp. 282–86.

Palloni, Alberto and Kephart, George. The Effects of Breastfeeding and Contraception on the Natural Rate of Increase: Are There Compensating Effects? *Population Stud.*, November 1989, *43*(3), pp. 455–78.

Pallottino, Stefano and Nguyen, Sang. Hyperpaths and Shortest Hyperpaths. In *Simeone, B., ed.*, 1989, pp. 258–71.

Palm, Franz C. and Winder, C. C. A. Intertemporal Consumer Behaviour under Structural Changes in Income: Reply. *Econometric Rev.*, 1989, *8*(1), pp. 143–48.

_____ **and Winder, C. C. A.** Intertemporal Consumer Behaviour under Structural Changes in Income. *Econometric Rev.*, 1989, *8*(1), pp. 1–87.

de Palma, André and Leruth, Luc. Congestion and Game in Capacity: A Duopoly Analysis in the Presence of Network Externalities. *Ann. Écon. Statist.*, July–Dec. 1989, (15–16), pp. 389–407.

_____ **and Thisse, Jacques-François.** Les modèles de choix discrets. (Discrete Choice Models. With English summary.) *Ann. Écon. Statist.*, April–June 1989, (14), pp. 151–90.

_____; **Thisse, Jacques-François and Anderson, Simon P.** Demand for Differentiated Products, Discrete Choice Models, and the Characteristics Approach. *Rev. Econ. Stud.*, January 1989, *56*(1), pp. 21–35.

_____; **Thisse, Jacques-François and Anderson, Simon P.** Spatial Price Policies Reconsidered. *J. Ind. Econ.*, September 1989, *38*(1), pp. 1–18.

_____; **Thisse, Jacques-François and Ben-Akiva, Moshe.** Spatial Competition with Differentiated Products. *Reg. Sci. Urban Econ.*, February 1989, *19*(1), pp. 5–19.

Palma, J. Gabriel and Marcel, Mario. Kaldor on the 'Discreet Charm' of the Chilean Bourgeoisie. *Cambridge J. Econ.*, March 1989, *13*(1), pp. 245–72.

_____ **and Marcel, Mario.** Kaldor on the 'Discreet Charm' of the Chilean Bourgeoisie. In *Lawson, T.; Palma, J. G. and Sender, J., eds.*, 1989, pp. 245–72.

_____; **Sender, John and Lawson, Tony.** Kaldor's Contribution to Economics: An Introduction. *Cambridge J. Econ.*, March 1989, *13*(1), pp. 1–8.

Palma, Pedro A. Commodity Price Contractions, Debt and Economic Growth in Developing Economies: The Venezuelan Case. In *[Adams, F. G.]*, 1989, pp. 101–27.

Palme, Mårten and Palmer, Edward E. A Macroeconomic Analysis of Employer-Contribution Financed Social Security. In *Gustafsson, B. A. and Klevmarken, N. A.*, eds., 1989, pp. 113–42.

Palmer, Bruce A. Tax Reform and Retirement Income Replacement Ratios. *J. Risk Ins.*, December 1989, *56*(4), pp. 702–25.

Palmer, Derek. Improving Britain's Transport Links with Europe. *Nat. Westminster Bank Quart. Rev.*, August 1989, pp. 29–38.

Palmer, Edward E.; Gottfries, Nils and Persson, Torsten. Regulation, Financial Buffer Stocks, and Short-run Adjustment: An Econometric Case-Study of Sweden, 1970–82. *Europ. Econ. Rev.*, October 1989, *33*(8), pp. 1545–65.

_____ **and Palme, Mårten.** A Macroeconomic Analysis of Employer-Contribution Financed Social Security. In *Gustafsson, B. A. and Klevmarken, N. A.*, eds., 1989, pp. 113–42.

Palmer, George R. The Economics of Australian Hospitals: Forum: The Funding of Hospitals Using Diagnosis Related Groups: Problems and Solutions. In *Smith, C. S.*, ed., 1989, pp. 308–17.

_____. Hospital Output and the Use of Diagnosis Related Groups for Purposes of Economic and Financial Analysis. In *Butler, J. R. G. and Doessel, D. P.*, eds., 1989, *1986*, pp. 322–43.

Palmer, Michael and Gordon, Kenneth R. A Comparison of the Financial Institutions' View and the Market's View of Country Creditworthiness. *J. Finan. Services Res.*, June 1989, *2*(2), pp. 73–87.

Palmer, Paul R.; Harmon, Bruce R. and Ward, Lisa M. Schedule Estimating Relationships for Tactical Aircraft. In *Gulledge, T. R., Jr. and Litteral, L. A.*, eds., 1989, pp. 259–80.

Palmeter, N. David. Agriculture and Trade Regulation: Selected Issues in the Application of U.S. Antidumping and Countervailing Duty Laws. *J. World Trade*, February 1989, *23*(1), pp. 47–68.

_____. Agriculture and Trade Regulation: Selected Issues in the Application of U.S. Antidumping and Countervailing Duty Laws. *J. World Trade*, February 1989, *23*(1), pp. 47–68.

_____. The Impact of the U.S. Antidumping Law on China–U.S. Trade. *J. World Trade*, August 1989, *23*(4), pp. 5–14.

Palmquist, Raymond B. Land as a Differentiated Factor of Production: A Hedonic Model and Its Implications for Welfare Measurement. *Land Econ.*, February 1989, *65*(1), pp. 23–28.

_____ **and Danielson, Leon E.** A Hedonic Study of the Effects of Erosion Control and Drainage on Farmland Values. *Amer. J. Agr. Econ.*, February 1989, *71*(1), pp. 55–62.

Palmrose, Zoe-Vonna. The Relation of Audit Con-

tract Type to Audit Fees and Hours. *Accounting Rev.*, July 1989, *64*(3), pp. 488–99.

Palokangas, Tapio. Union Power in the Long Run Reconsidered. *Scand. J. Econ.*, 1989, *91*(3), pp. 625–35.

Palterovich, D. Competition and Democratization. *Prob. Econ.*, February 1989, *31*(10), pp. 60–77.

_____. Competition and Democratization. In *Jones, A. and Moskoff, W.*, eds., 1989, *1989*, pp. 60–77.

Paltiel, Khayyam Zev. Canadian Election Expense Legislation, 1963–85: A Critical Appraisal or Was the Effort Worth It? In *Alexander, H. E.*, ed., 1989, pp. 51–75.

Palumbo, Giovanni. The Disregard of a Legal Entity for Tax Purposes: Italy. In *International Fiscal Association*, ed. *(II)*, 1989, pp. 335–54.

Palyi, Melchior. The Introduction of Adam Smith on the Continent. In *Clark, J. M., et al.*, 1989, pp. 180–233.

Pan, Pu-Sen and Kim, Yoon Hyung. Patterns and Important Issues in Supply. In *Kim, Y. H. and Smith, K. R.*, eds., 1989, pp. 107–43.

Panagariya, Arvind and Narayana, A. V. L. Excise Tax Evasion: Reply. *Public Finance*, 1989, *44*(3), pp. 510–12.

Panas, Epaminondas E. and Kintis, Andreas A. The Capital–Energy Controversy: Further Results. *Energy Econ.*, July 1989, *11*(3), pp. 201–12.

Panayotou, Theodore. Thailand: The Experience of a Food Exporter. In *Sicular, T.*, ed., 1989, pp. 65–108.

Panchamukhi, Vadiraj R.; Nambiar, R. G. and Mehta, Rajesh. Structural Change and Economic Growth in Developing Countries. In *Williamson, J. G. and Panchamukhi, V. R.*, eds., 1989, pp. 54–84.

_____ **and Williamson, Jeffrey G.** The Balance between Industry and Agriculture in Economic Development: Introduction. In *Williamson, J. G. and Panchamukhi, V. R.*, eds., 1989, pp. xxi–xxxii.

Pandey, R. K. and Sarup, Shanti. Study of Rice Production Function in India. *Margin*, Jan.–March 1989, *21*(2), pp. 52–61.

Pandey, Sushil. The Econometrics of Damage Control: Comment. *Amer. J. Agr. Econ.*, May 1989, *71*(2), pp. 443–44.

_____. Irrigation and Crop Yield Variability: A Review. In *Anderson, J. R. and Hazell, P. B. R.*, eds., 1989, pp. 234–41.

Pandit, V. N.; Sastry, D. U. and Krishnamurty, K. India: Medium Term Economic Outlook, 1988–90. In *Reddy, J. M., et al.*, eds. *(II)*, 1989, pp. 1–22.

_____; **Sharma, P. D. and Krishnamurty, K.** Parameters of Growth in a Developing Mixed Economy: The Indian Experience. *J. Quant. Econ.*, July 1989, *5*(2), pp. 295–325.

Pang, Eul-Soo. Debt, Adjustment, and Democratic Cacophony in Brazil. In *Stallings, B. and Kaufman, R.*, eds., 1989, pp. 127–42.

Pangestu, Mari. East Kalimantan: Beyond the

Timber and Oil Boom. In *Hill, H., ed.*, 1989, pp. 151–75.

Panić, M. and Schioppa, C. Europe's Long-Term Capital Flows Since 1971. In *Gordon, I. and Thirlwall, A. P., eds.*, 1989, pp. 166–94.

Panik, Michael J.; Sullivan, Jack J. and Kolluri, Bharat R. Wagner's Law of Public Expenditure Revisited. In *Missouri Valley Economic Association*, 1989, pp. 98–104.

Pankratz, John and Schmisseur, Ed. XLAYER: An Expert System Providing Management Advice to Commercial Layer Managers. *Southern J. Agr. Econ.*, December 1989, 21(2), pp. 183–93.

Pannell, David J. REFLIST: A Program to Assist in Preparation of Reference Lists in Theses and Journal Articles. *Rev. Marketing Agr. Econ.*, April, Aug., Dec. 1989, 57(1–2–3), pp. 129–33.

Panov, O. and Djarova, J. Strategic Planning and Economic Growth in Bulgaria. In *Krelle, W., ed.*, 1989, pp. 407–17.

Pant, Manoj. A Financial Model of the Multinational Corporation. *Indian Econ. Rev.*, July–Dec. 1989, 24(2), pp. 207–23.

_____ **and Das, Sandwip Kumar.** On Export Diversification and Earning Instability—Theory and Evidence. *Indian Econ. J.*, Jan.–March 1989, 36(3), pp. 65–71.

Panton, Don B. The Relevance of the Distributional Form of Common Stock Returns to the Construction of Optimal Portfolios: Comment. *J. Finan. Quant. Anal.*, March 1989, 24(1), pp. 129–30.

Panuccio, Theresa. Rural Women in Ghana: Their Workloads, Access and Organizations. In *Lineberry, W. P., ed.*, 1989, pp. 85–129.

Panunzi, Fausto. Barriere multiple all'entrata e ottimalitá della strategia di entry-deterrence. (Multiple Barriers to Entry and the Optimality of the Entry-Deterrence Strategy. (With English summary.) *Rivista Int. Sci. Econ. Com.*, September 1989, 36(9), pp. 857–72.

Pany, Kurt; Pourciau, Susan and Margheim, Loren. Controlling Audit Staff Underreporting of Time and Premature Signoffs: Some Preliminary Findings. In *Gangolly, J., ed.*, 1989, pp. 181–94.

_____; **Wheeler, Stephen and Chewning, Gene.** Auditor Reporting Decisions Involving Accounting Principle Changes: Some Evidence on Materiality Thresholds. *J. Acc. Res.*, Spring 1989, 27(1), pp. 78–96.

Panzar, John C. Technological Determinants of Firm and Industry Structure. In *Schmalensee, R. and Willig, R. D., eds.*, Vol. 1, 1989, pp. 3–59.

_____ **and Braeutigam, Ronald R.** Diversification Incentives under "Price-Based" and "Cost-Based" Regulation. *Rand J. Econ.*, Autumn 1989, 20(3), pp. 373–91.

_____ **and Savage, Ian.** Regulation, Deregulation, and Safety: An Economic Analysis. In *Moses, L. N. and Savage, I., eds.*, 1989, pp. 31–49.

_____ **and Sibley, David S.** Optimal Two-Part

Tariffs for Inputs: The Case of Imperfect Competition. *J. Public Econ.*, November 1989, 40(2), pp. 237–49.

Papademos, Lucas and Modigliani, Franco. Inflation, Financial and Fiscal Structure, and the Monetary Mechanism. In *Modigliani, F., Vol. 4*, 1989, *1983*, pp. 48–95.

_____ **and Modigliani, Franco.** Money, Credit and the Monetary Mechanism. In *Modigliani, F., Vol. 4*, 1989, *1987*, pp. 96–135.

_____ **and Modigliani, Franco.** Optimal Demand Policies against Stagflation. In *Modigliani, F., Vol. 4*, 1989, *1978*, pp. 155–201.

_____ **and Modigliani, Franco.** The Structure of Financial Markets and the Monetary Mechanism. In *Modigliani, F., Vol. 4*, 1989, *1980*, pp. 3–47.

Papageorgiou, Demetris; Michaely, Michael and Choksi, Armeane. The Design of Trade Liberalization. *Finance Devel.*, March 1989, 26(1), pp. 2–5.

Papageorgiou, Yorgos Y. and Beckmann, Martin J. Heterogeneous Tastes and Residential Location. *J. Reg. Sci.*, August 1989, 29(3), pp. 317–23.

_____ **and Pines, David.** The Exponential Density Function: First Principles, Comparative Statics, and Empirical Evidence. *J. Urban Econ.*, September 1989, 26(2), pp. 264–68.

Papava, V. G. A Unified Approach to the Analysis of Dynamic Interindustry Balance Models. *Matekon*, Spring 1989, 25(3), pp. 3–18.

Papell, David H. Monetary Policy in the United States under Flexible Exchange Rates. *Amer. Econ. Rev.*, December 1989, 79(5), pp. 1106–16.

Papi, Luca and Muscatelli, Anton. Un modello con aspettative razionali per la domanda di moneta: Un giudizio critico. (With English summary.) *Econ. Int.*, Feb.–March 1989, 42(1–2), pp. 90–108.

Papić, Augustin. The Interconnection between International Trade, Finance and Debt—The Implications for North–South Economic Relations. In *Mrak, M., ed.*, 1989, pp. 63–93.

Papola, T. S. Restructuring in Indian Industry: Implications for Employment and Industrial Relations. In *Edgren, G., ed.*, 1989, pp. 29–75.

Pappas, Milton. A Perfect Foresight Model of Economic Growth, Inflation and the Balance of International Indebtedness. In *Singer, H. W. and Sharma, S., eds. (I)*, 1989, pp. 277–95.

Paquet, Gilles. Multiculturalism as National Policy. *J. Cult. Econ.*, June 1989, 13(1), pp. 17–34.

Parai, Amar K. and Beck, John H. The Incidence of Classified Property Taxes in a Three-Sector Model with an Imperfectly Mobile Population. *J. Urban Econ.*, January 1989, 25(1), pp. 77–92.

_____ **and Yu, Eden S. H.** Factor Immobility and Gains from Trade. *Southern Econ. J.*, January 1989, 55(3), pp. 601–09.

_____ **and Yu, Eden S. H.** Factor Mobility and

Customs Unions Theory. *Southern Econ. J.*, April 1989, *55*(4), pp. 842–52.

Paraskevopoulos, Christos C.; Andrikopoulos, Andreas A. and Brox, James A. Interfuel and Interfactor Substitution in Ontario Manufacturing, 1962–82. *Appl. Econ.*, December 1989, *21*(12), pp. 1667–81.

Parcel, Toby L. Comparable Worth, Occupational Labor Markets, and Occupational Earnings: Results from the 1980 Census. In *Michael, R. T.; Hartmann, H. I. and O'Farrell, B., eds.*, 1989, pp. 134–52.

Pardal, Francisco Rodrigues. El no reconocimiento fiscal de entidades legales: Portugal. (The Disregard of a Legal Entity for Tax Purposes: Portugal. With English summary.) In *International Fiscal Association, ed. (II)*, 1989, pp. 447–62.

Parden, Shannon A. The Milagro Beanfield War Revisited in Ensenada Land and Water Association v. Sleeper: Public Welfare Defies Transfer of Water Rights. *Natural Res. J.*, Summer 1989, *29*(3), pp. 861–76.

Pardey, Philip G. The Agricultural Knowledge Production Function: An Empirical Look. *Rev. Econ. Statist.*, August 1989, *71*(3), pp. 453–61.

_____ **and Craig, Barbara.** Causal Relationships between Public Sector Agricultural Research Expenditures and Output. *Amer. J. Agr. Econ.*, February 1989, *71*(1), pp. 9–19.

Paredes, Gonzalo L. and Brodie, J. Douglas. Land Value and the Linkage between Stand and Forest Level Analyses. *Land Econ.*, May 1989, *65*(2), pp. 158–66.

Paredes M., Ricardo and Riveros C., Luis. Sesgo de selección y el efecto de los salarios mínimos. (With English summary.) *Cuadernos Econ.*, December 1989, *26*(79), pp. 367–83.

Parenta, Tajuddin; Sturgess, Neil H. and Kristanto, Kustiah. South Sulawesi: New Directions in Agriculture? In *Hill, H., ed.*, 1989, pp. 386–407.

Parguez, Alain. Cet âge de l'austérité. (This Age of Austerity. With English summary.) *Écon. Appl.*, 1989, *42*(1), pp. 71–89.

_____. Money and Financial Money Capital within a Keynesian Framework. In *Barrère, A., ed.*, 1989, pp. 3–15.

Parhizgari, Ali M.; Prakash, Arun J. and LaCava, Gerald. A General Proof of Merton's Analytic Derivation of the Efficient Portfolio Frontier. *Quart. J. Bus. Econ.*, Summer 1989, *28*(3), pp. 67–77.

Pari, Robert A.; Rosenthal, Leonard and Johnson, James M. The Impact of In-substance Defeasance on Bondholder and Shareholder Wealth. *J. Finance*, September 1989, *44*(4), pp. 1049–57.

Parikh, Kirit S.; Frohberg, Klaus K. and Fischer, Günther. International Effects of CAP Trade Liberalization. In *Tarditi, S., et al., eds.*, 1989, pp. 27–46.

_____ **and Tims, Wouter.** Food and Agricultural Policies and Programs of Major Countries and Regions: Reaction. In *Helmuth, J. W. and*

Johnson, S. R., eds., Vol. 1, 1989, pp. 37–39.

_____ **and Tims, Wouter.** Food Consumption, Dietary Status, and Chronic Hunger: An Assessment of Its Extent and Policy Options. In *Helmuth, J. W. and Johnson, S. R., eds., Vol. 2*, 1989, pp. 3–44.

Paris, Quirino. Broken Symmetry, Symmetry, and Price Uncertainty: Or, Short and Long-run Comparative Statics of the Competitive Firm. *Europ. Econ. Rev.*, July 1989, *33*(6), pp. 1227–39.

_____. Revenue and Cost Uncertainty, Generalized Mean–Variance and the Linear Complementarity Problem: Reply. *Amer. J. Agr. Econ.*, August 1989, *71*(3), pp. 810–12.

_____. Stochastic Technology and Prices: Reply. *Amer. J. Agr. Econ.*, August 1989, *71*(3), pp. 817–19.

_____. A Sure Bet on Symmetry. *Amer. J. Agr. Econ.*, May 1989, *71*(2), pp. 344–51.

_____ **and Knapp, Keith C.** Estimation of von Liebig Response Functions. *Amer. J. Agr. Econ.*, February 1989, *71*(1), pp. 178–86.

Pariser, David B. and Khilji, Nasir M. Monopsony and Federal Coal Leasing—A Bargaining Approach. *Energy Econ.*, July 1989, *11*(3), pp. 169–74.

Park, C. Whan; Iyer, Easwar S. and Smith, Daniel C. The Effects of Situational Factors on In-Store Grocery Shopping Behavior: The Role of Store Environment and Time Available for Shopping. *J. Cons. Res.*, March 1989, *15*(4), pp. 422–33.

_____ **and Smith, Daniel C.** Product-Level Choice: A Top-Down or Bottom-Up Process? *J. Cons. Res.*, December 1989, *16*(3), pp. 289–99.

Park, Daekeun and Han, Aaron K. Testing for Structural Change in Panel Data: Application to a Study of U. S. Foreign Trade in Manufacturing Goods. *Rev. Econ. Statist.*, February 1989, *71*(1), pp. 135–42.

Park, Kang H. Determinants of Intra-industry Trade. In *Missouri Valley Economic Association*, 1989, pp. 110–15.

Park, Se-Hark. Linkages between Industry and Services and Their Implications for Urban Employment Generation in Developing Countries. *J. Devel. Econ.*, April 1989, *30*(2), pp. 359–79.

_____ **and Chan, Kenneth S.** A Cross-Country Input–Output Analysis of Intersectoral Relationships between Manufacturing and Services and Their Employment Implications. *World Devel.*, February 1989, *17*(2), pp. 199–212.

_____ **and Chan, Kenneth S.** A Cross-Country Study on the Role of the Service Sector. *J. Econ. Devel.*, December 1989, *14*(2), pp. 35–54.

Park, Thae S. Federal Personal Income Tax Liabilities and Payments: Revised and Updated Estimates, 1986–87. *Surv. Curr. Bus.*, September 1989, *69*(9), pp. 19–20.

_____. Relationship between Personal Income and Adjusted Gross Income: Revised Estimates, 1985–87. *Surv. Curr. Bus.*, August 1989, *69*(8), pp. 30–32.

Park, Wankyu. General Grants System in Korea: Toward Horizontal Equity and Tax Effort. *J. Econ. Devel.*, December 1989, *14*(2), pp. 153–65.

Park, Won-Am. U.S. International Macroeconomic Policy: Discussion. In *Bayard, T. O. and Young, S.-G., eds.*, 1989, pp. 37–42.

_____ **and Collins, Susan M.** External Debt and Macroeconomic Performance in South Korea. In *Sachs, J. D., ed. (II)*, 1989, pp. 121–40.

_____ **and Collins, Susan M.** External Debt and Macroeconomic Performance in South Korea. In *Sachs, J. D. and Collins, S. M., eds.*, 1989, pp. 151–369.

Park, Won J. and Larsen, James E. Non-uniform Percentage Brokerage Commissions and Real Estate Market Performance. *Amer. Real Estate Urban Econ. Assoc. J.*, Winter 1989, *17*(4), pp. 422–38.

Park, Young-il and Anderson, Kym. China and the International Relocation of World Textile and Clothing Activity. *Weltwirtsch. Arch.*, 1989, *125*(1), pp. 129–48.

Park, Yung Chul. The Little Dragons and Structural Change in Pacific Asia. *World Econ.*, June 1989, *12*(2), pp. 125–61.

_____ **and Yoo, Jung-Ho.** More Free Trade Areas: A Korean Perspective. In *Schott, J. J., ed.*, 1989, pp. 141–58.

Parke, William R.; Chib, Siddhartha and Cooley, Thomas F. Predictive Efficiency for Simple Non-linear Models. *J. Econometrics,* January 1989, *40*(1), pp. 33–44.

Parker, Darrell F. Production Dynamics, Inventories, and the Transmission Mechanism. In *Missouri Valley Economic Association*, 1989, pp. 183–89.

Parker, Glenn R. Looking Beyond Reelection: Revising Assumptions about the Factors Motivating Congressional Behavior. *Public Choice*, December 1989, *63*(3), pp. 237–52.

Parker, John. Who Has a Drug Lag? *Managerial Dec. Econ.*, December 1989, *10*(4), pp. 299–309.

Parker, Larry M. and Tucker, Michael J. CPAs as Financial Planners: Responsibilities under the Investment Advisers Act of 1940. In *Gangolly, J., ed.*, 1989, pp. 89–101.

Parker, Randall E. Some Evidence on the Persistence of Price and Output Shocks in the Pre–World War I and Post–World War II Eras. *Econ. Notes*, 1989, (3), pp. 413–22.

Parker, Robert P. Dispute Settlement in the GATT and the Canada–U.S. Free Trade Agreement. *J. World Trade*, June 1989, *23*(3), pp. 83–93.

Parker, William N. The Study of European Economic History in Europe: Impressions and Conjectures. *Econ. Rec.*, September 1989, *65*(190), pp. 282–86.

Parkin, David. Comparing Health Service Efficiency Across Countries. *Oxford Rev. Econ. Policy*, Spring 1989, *5*(1), pp. 75–88.

Parkinson, Martin and Bernanke, Ben S. Unemployment, Inflation, and Wages in the American Depression: Are There Lessons for Europe? *Amer. Econ. Rev.*, May 1989, *79*(2), pp. 210–14.

Parks, William, II and Howe, Wayne J. Labor Market Completes Sixth Year of Expansion in 1988. *Mon. Lab. Rev.*, February 1989, *112*(2), pp. 3–14.

_____ **and Markey, James P.** Occupational Change: Pursuing a Different Kind of Work. *Mon. Lab. Rev.*, September 1989, *112*(9), pp. 3–12.

Parle, William M. and Lawler, James J. Expansion of the Public Trust Doctrine in Environmental Law: An Examination of Judicial Policy Making by State Courts. *Soc. Sci. Quart.*, March 1989, *70*(1), pp. 134–48.

Parliament, Claudia; Tsur, Yacov and Zilberman, David. Cooperative Labor Allocation under Uncertainty. *J. Compar. Econ.*, December 1989, *13*(4), pp. 539–52.

Parmenter, B. R. and Adams, Philip D. Economic Prospects: 1988–89 to 1994–95. *Australian Econ. Rev.*, Spring 1989, (87), pp. 5–15.

_____ **and Meagher, G. A.** Forecasting the Demand for Engineers in Australia, 1986–87 to 1991–92. *Australian Bull. Lab.*, June 1989, *15*(3), pp. 185–99.

Parnell, Allan M. and Rindfuss, Ronald R. The Varying Connection between Marital Status and Childbearing in the United States. *Population Devel. Rev.*, September 1989, *15*(3), pp. 447–70.

Parodi, Giuliana. A Structural Model of Trade Union Behaviour under Uncertainty, with Sticky Wage. *Labour*, Winter 1989, *3*(3), pp. 93–108.

Paroush, Jacob and Karotkin, D. Robustness of Optimal Majority Rules over Teams with Changing Size. *Soc. Choice Welfare*, April 1989, *6*(2), pp. 127–38.

_____ **and Wolf, Avner.** Production and Hedging Decisions in the Presence of Basis Risk. *J. Futures Markets*, December 1989, *9*(6), pp. 547–63.

Parr, J. B. and O'Neill, G. J. Aspects of the Lognormal Function in the Analysis of Regional Population Distribution. *Environ. Planning A,* July 1989, *21*(7), pp. 961–73.

Parra, Alirio A. The Oil Market and Production Control. In *[Evans, J. K.]*, 1989, pp. 139–46.

de la Parra, Gonzalo Afcha and Melvin, Michael. Dollar Currency in Latin America: A Bolivian Application. *Econ. Letters*, December 1989, *31*(4), pp. 393–97.

Parrinello, Sergio. Individualismo metodologico contro altri "ismi" in economia: Un commento. (Methodological Individualism and Economic Equilibrium: A Comment. With English summary.) *Econ. Politica*, April 1989, *6*(1), pp. 123–32.

_____. Individualismo metodologico ed equilibrio: Una replica. (Methodological Individualism and Economic Equilibrium: A Rejoinder. With English summary.) *Econ. Politica*, April 1989, *6*(1), pp. 147–49.

_____. The Marshallian Core of the General Theory. In *Barrère, A., ed.*, 1989, pp. 170–81.

_____. Norme sociali, fluttuazioni e moneta nel modello $(1 + r)$ **Ap** + w**l** = **Bp**. (Social Norms, Fluctuations and Money in the Model $(1 + r)$ **Ap** + w**l** = **Bp**. With English summary.) *Econ. Politica*, August 1989, *6*(2), pp. 235–54.

_____. Uncertainty and the Residual Hypothesis. In *[Weintraub, S.]*, 1989, pp. 123–32.

Parry, Jonathan. On the Moral Perils of Exchange. In *Parry, J. and Bloch, M., eds.*, 1989, pp. 64–93.

_____ **and Bloch, Maurice.** Money and the Morality of Exchange: Introduction. In *Parry, J. and Bloch, M., eds.*, 1989, pp. 1–32.

Parry, Martin L. and Carter, T. R. The Effect of Climatic Variations of Food Production. In *Oram, P. A., et al.*, 1989, pp. 429–49.

_____; **Crosson, Pierre R. and Easterling, William E., III.** Adapting Future Agriculture to Changes in Climate. In *Rosenberg, N. J., et al., eds.*, 1989, pp. 91–104.

Parsons, David; Kirby, Michael G. and Gunasekera, H. Don B. H. Liberalizing Agricultural Trade: Some Perspectives for Developing Countries. In *Whalley, J., ed., Vol. 1*, 1989, pp. 238–57.

Parsons, Donald O. and Goldin, Claudia. Parental Altruism and Self-Interest: Child Labor among Late Nineteenth-Century American Families. *Econ. Inquiry*, October 1989, *27*(4), pp. 637–59.

Parsons, George R. On the Value of the Condition of a Forest Stock: Comment. *Land Econ.*, February 1989, *65*(1), pp. 68–72.

Parsons, John E. Estimating the Strategic Value of Long-term Forward Purchase Contracts Using Auction Models. *J. Finance*, September 1989, *44*(4), pp. 981–1010.

Partch, M. Megan and Mikkelson, Wayne H. Managers' Voting Rights and Corporate Control. *J. Finan. Econ.*, December 1989, *25*(2), pp. 263–90.

Parthasarathy, T. and Sinha, S. Existence of Stationary Equilibrium Strategies in Non-zero Sum Discounted Stochastic Games with Uncountable State Space and State-Independent Transitions. *Int. J. Game Theory*, 1989, *18*(2), pp. 189–94.

Pártos, Gy. Questions Posed by Hungarian Telecommunications in the Age of Microelectronics. *Acta Oecon.*, 1989, *40*(3–4), pp. 339–51.

Partow, Zeinab and Warford, Jeremy J. Evolution of the World Bank's Environmental Policy. *Finance Devel.*, December 1989, *26*(4), pp. 5–8.

Partridge, Mark; Mutti, John and Morgan, William E. The Incidence of Regional Taxes in a General Equilibrium Framework. *J. Public Econ.*, June 1989, *39*(1), pp. 83–107.

Partridge, William R. and Vlahakis, John G. Assessment of Security at Facilities that Produce Nuclear Weapons. In *Golden, B. L.; Wasil, E. A. and Harker, P. T., eds.*, 1989, pp. 182–91.

Parvin, Manoucher. Islamic Rule, Economics,

Woman, and Man: An Overview of Ideology and Reality. *Comp. Econ. Stud.*, Fall 1989, *31*(3), pp. 85–102.

Pascha, Werner. The Internationalization of Japan's and West Germany's Textile and Clothing Industries, 1970–1985. In *Dams, T. and Matsugi, T., eds.*, 1989, pp. 215–46.

Paschos, P. Einkommenswirkungen der EG-Agrarpolitik in Griechenland. (Income Effects of the EEC Agricultural Policy (CAP) in Greece. With English summary.) *Jahr. Nationalökon. Statist.*, March 1989, *206*(2), pp. 117–27.

Pasha, Hafiz A.; Ghaus, Aisha and Malik, Salman. The Economic Cost of Power Outages in the Industrial Sector of Pakistan. *Energy Econ.*, October 1989, *11*(4), pp. 301–18.

_____ **and Wasti, S. Ashraf.** Unemployment and Rates of Return to Education. *Singapore Econ. Rev.*, October 1989, *34*(2), pp. 64–77.

Pashardes, Panos and Fry, Vanessa. Constructing the True Cost of Living Index from the Engel Curves of the Piglog Model. *J. Appl. Econometrics*, Jan.–March 1989, *4*(1), pp. 41–56.

Pasinetti, Luigi L. Government Deficit Spending Is Not Incompatible with the Cambridge Theorem of the Rate of Profit: A Reply. *J. Post Keynesian Econ.*, Summer 1989, *11*(4), pp. 641–47.

_____. Growing Subsystems and Vertically Hyper-Integrated Sectors: A Note of Clarification. *Cambridge J. Econ.*, September 1989, *13*(3), pp. 479–80.

_____. A Note on the Evaluation of Public Deficits: Net or Gross of Interest? *Banca Naz. Lavoro Quart. Rev.*, September 1989, (170), pp. 303–11.

_____. Ricardian Debt/Taxation Equivalence in the Kaldor Theory of Profits and Income Distribution. *Cambridge J. Econ.*, March 1989, *13*(1), pp. 25–36.

_____. Ricardian Debt/Taxation Equivalence in the Kaldor Theory of Profits and Income Distribution. In *Lawson, T.; Palma, J. G. and Sender, J., eds.*, 1989, pp. 25–36.

Pasour, E. C., Jr. The Efficient-Markets Hypothesis and Entrepreneurship. In *Rothbard, M. N. and Block, W., eds.*, 1989, pp. 95–107.

_____. Nonconventional Costs of Rent-Seeking: X-inefficiency in the Political Process. *Public Choice*, October 1989, *63*(1), pp. 87–91.

Pasquino, Gianfranco. Unregulated Regulators: Parties and Party Government. In *Lange, P. and Regini, M., eds.*, 1989, pp. 29–50.

Passamani, Giuliana. Empirical Analyses of Causal Relationships among Estimated Aggregate Unemployment Duration and Some Properly Chosen Economic Variables. *Labour*, Spring 1989, *3*(1), pp. 149–69.

Passy, Ury and Hackman, Steven T. A Consistent, Reflexive Duality Framework of Production: An Application of Quasi-Concave Conjugacy Theory. *J. Econ. (Z. Nationalökon.)*, 1989, *49*(2), pp. 183–198.

Pastor, Manuel, Jr. Annual Review of Nations:

Year 1988: Mexico. In *Haberman, L. and Sacks, P. M., eds.*, 1989, pp. 213–31.

──────. Current Account Deficits and Debt Accumulation in Latin America: Debate and Evidence. *J. Devel. Econ.*, July 1989, *31*(1), pp. 77–97.

Pastore, José Maria Dagnino. The Role of the Economist in Government: An International Perspective: Argentina. In *Pechman, J. A., ed.*, 1989, pp. 195–212.

Pasurka, Carl; Färe, Rolf and Grosskopf, Shawna. The Effect of Environmental Regulations on the Efficiency of Electric Utilities: 1969 versus 1975. *Appl. Econ.*, February 1989, *21*(2), pp. 225–35.

────── and Grabowski, Richard. The Relative Efficiency of Slave Agriculture: An Application of a Stochastic Production Frontier. *Appl. Econ.*, May 1989, *21*(5), pp. 587–95.

────── and Grabowski, Richard. The Relative Technical Efficiency of Slave and Non-slave Farms in Southern Agriculture. *Eastern Econ. J.*, July–Sept. 1989, *15*(3), pp. 245–58.

Patel, I. G. Images of Joan. In *Feiwel, G. R., ed. (II)*, 1989, pp. 863–65.

Patel, Pari and Pavitt, Keith. A Comparison of Technological Activities in West Germany and the United Kingdom. *Nat. Westminster Bank Quart. Rev.*, May 1989, pp. 27–42.

Patell, James M. On the Usefulness of Earnings and Earnings Research: Lessons and Directions from Two Decades of Empirical Research: Discussion. *J. Acc. Res.*, Supplement, 1989, *27*, pp. 193–201.

Paterson, Donald G. and Shearer, Ronald A. Terminating Building Societies in Quebec City, 1850–1864. *Bus. Hist. Rev.*, Summer 1989, *63*(2), pp. 384–415.

Paterson, William and Bulmer, Simon. West Germany's Role in Europe: 'Man-Mountain' or 'Semi-Gulliver'? *J. Common Market Stud.*, December 1989, *28*(2), pp. 95–117.

Patinkin, Don. Keynes and the Keynesian Cross: A Further Note. *Hist. Polit. Econ.*, Fall 1989, *21*(3), pp. 537–44.

──────. Keynesian Economics Rehabilitated: A Rejoinder to Professor Hicks. In *Wood, J. C. and Woods, R. N., eds., Vol. 2*, 1989, *1959*, pp. 29–35.

──────. Michal Kalecki and the General Theory. In *Sebastiani, M., ed.*, 1989, pp. 25–44.

────── and Steiger, Otto. In Search of the "Veil of Money" and the "Neutrality of Money": A Note on the Origin of Terms. *Scand. J. Econ.*, 1989, *91*(1), pp. 131–46.

Patnaik, Prabhat. Marx's Transformation Problem and Ricardo's Invariant Measure. *Cambridge J. Econ.*, December 1989, *13*(4), pp. 555–62.

──────; Sanyal, Amal and Mukherji, Anjan. Stocks, Credit and the Commodity Market: A Preliminary Exercise. In *Rakshit, M., ed.*, 1989, pp. 111–28.

Patnaik, Utsa. Some Paradoxes of Capitalist Development in Indian Agriculture. *Rev. Radical Polit. Econ.*, Fall 1989, *21*(3), pp. 118–22.

Patrick, Melanie K. and Carlson, George N. Ad-

dressing the Regressivity of a Value-Added Tax. *Nat. Tax J.*, September 1989, *42*(3), pp. 339–51.

Patridge, Mark; Morgan, William E. and Mutti, John. A Regional Equilibrium Model of the United States: Tax Effects on Factor Movements and Regional Production. *Rev. Econ. Statist.*, November 1989, *71*(4), pp. 626–35.

Patrulescu, M.; Dumitrescu, Vl. and Somnea, D. Software Simulation of Bigger Fonts Printing on Dot Matrix Graphical Printers. *Econ. Computat. Econ. Cybern. Stud. Res.*, 1989, *24*(2–3), pp. 103–09.

Patry, Michel; Raynauld, Jacques and Beaulieu, Anne. L'analyse de la productivité des transporteurs aériens canadiens dans le années soixante-dix: Pour un autre plan de vol. (With English summary.) *L'Actual. Econ.*, June 1989, *65*(2), pp. 183–207.

Patsouratis, Vassilis. Corporate Taxation and Dividend Behavior: An Empirical Analysis. *Greek Econ. Rev.*, 1989, *11*(2), pp. 323–38.

Pattanaik, Prasanta K. and Barrett, C. Richard. Fuzzy Sets, Preference and Choice: Some Conceptual Issues. *Bull. Econ. Res.*, October 1989, *41*(4), pp. 229–53.

Patterson, Douglas M. and Ashley, Richard A. Linear versus Nonlinear Macroeconomies: A Statistical Test. *Int. Econ. Rev.*, August 1989, *30*(3), pp. 685–704.

────── and Hinich, Melvin J. Evidence of Nonlinearity in the Trade-by-Trade Stock Market Return Generating Process. In *Barnett, W. A.; Geweke, J. and Shell, K., eds.*, 1989, pp. 383–409.

Patterson, Eliza. Food Safety and International Trade: The U.S.–EC Meat and Hormone Controversies: Commentary. In *Krämer, C. S., ed.*, 1989, pp. 234–36.

Patterson, Gardner. Implications for the GATT and the World Trading System. In *Schott, J. J., ed.*, 1989, pp. 353–65.

Patterson, Kerry D. Erratum Notification [The Stability of Some Annual Consumption Functions]. *Oxford Econ. Pap.*, April 1989, *41*(2), pp. 458.

──────. Modelling Price Expectations. *Appl. Econ.*, March 1989, *21*(3), pp. 413–26.

────── and Harnett, Ian. An Analysis of Changes in the Structural and Simulation Properties of the Bank of England Quarterly Model of the UK Economy. *Econ. Modelling*, January 1989, *6*(1), pp. 20–55.

Patterson, Perry L. Domestic Economic Reform in the Soviet Union and Eastern Europe: Causes and Interdependence. *Jahr. Wirtsch. Osteuropas*, 1989, *13*(2), pp. 7–40.

Pattie, C. J. and Johnston, R. J. The Changing Electoral Geography of Great Britain. In *Mohan, J., ed.*, 1989, pp. 51–68.

Paul, Allen B. Research on Futures Markets: Discussion. *Western J. Agr. Econ.*, July 1989, *14*(1), pp. 140–42.

Paul, Chris and Mbaku, John M. Political Instability in Africa: A Rent-Seeking Approach. *Public Choice*, October 1989, *63*(1), pp. 63–72.

_____ and **Wilhite, Al.** Corporate Campaign Contributions and Legislative Voting. *Quart. Rev. Econ. Bus.*, Autumn 1989, *29*(3), pp. 73–85.

Paul, Mohinder. Composition and Distribution of Income among Rural Households in Haryana. *Margin*, Jan.–March 1989, *21*(2), pp. 62–76.

Paul, P. B.; Sar, N. L. and Bui-Lan, A. Forecasting Sawntimber Consumption: The Application of an End-Use Model. *Australian J. Agr. Econ.*, December 1989, *33*(3), pp. 219–32.

Paul, Satya. A Model of Constructing the Poverty Line. *J. Devel. Econ.*, January 1989, *30*(1), pp. 129–44.

_____. A Note on Social Statistics in India. *Indian Econ. J.*, April–June 1989, *36*(4), pp. 71–74.

_____ and **Dasgupta, Ajit K.** Inheritance and Wealth Inequality: The Case of the Punjab. *J. Devel. Econ.*, April 1989, *30*(2), pp. 301–24.

Paulsen, George E. The Federal Trade Commission versus the National Recovery Administration: Fair Trade Practices and Voluntary Codes, 1935. *Soc. Sci. Quart.*, March 1989, *70*(1), pp. 149–63.

Paulson, David M. Nationalist Guerrillas in the Sino-Japanese War: The "Die-Hards" of Shandong Province. In *Hartford, K. and Goldstein, S. M., eds.*, 1989, pp. 128–50.

Pauly, Daniel; Silvestre, Geronimo and Smith, Ian R. On Development, Fisheries and Dynamite: A Brief Review of Tropical Fisheries Management. *Natural Res. Modeling*, Summer 1989, *3*(3), pp. 307–29.

Pauly, Louis. Changing International Financial Markets. *Finance Devel.*, December 1989, *26*(4), pp. 34–37.

Pauly, Peter. Foreign Debt and the Structure of World Trade. In *Krelle, W., ed.*, 1989, pp. 515–25.

_____. Sectoral Output, Employment, and Real Wages: Long-Run Trends for the U.S. Economy. In *Krelle, W., ed.*, 1989, pp. 301–10.

_____ and **Diebold, Francis X.** Forecasting in Situations of Structural Change: A General Approach. In *Hackl, P., ed.*, 1989, pp. 297–318.

Pauly, Ralf; Hauke, Wolfgang and Opitz, Otto. Explorative Data Analysis and Macroeconomics. In *Opitz, O., ed.*, 1989, pp. 416–31.

_____ and **Schell, A.** Calendar Effects in Structural Time Series Models with Trend and Season. *Empirical Econ.*, 1989, *14*(3), pp. 241–56.

Paunio, J. and Pekkarinen, Jukka. The Hicksian Revision of the Multiplier Analysis of Expansion. In *Wood, J. C. and Woods, R. N., eds.*, Vol. 3, 1989, *1976*, pp. 114–26.

Paus, Eva. The Political Economy of Manufactured Export Growth: Argentina and Brazil in the 1970s. *J. Developing Areas*, January 1989, *23*(2), pp. 173–99.

Pavitt, Keith. Strategic Management in the Innovating Firm. In *Mansfield, R., ed.*, 1989, pp. 79–95.

_____ and **Patel, Pari.** A Comparison of Techno-

logical Activities in West Germany and the United Kingdom. *Nat. Westminster Bank Quart. Rev.*, May 1989, pp. 27–42.

Pavlenko, S. Iu. and Ryvkina, Rozalina V. Managerial Behavior of Executives of Agricultural Enterprises. In *Yanowitch, M., ed.*, 1989, *1987*, pp. 23–35.

Pavlopoulos, P. G. and Kouzelis, A. K. Cost Behaviour in the Banking Industry: Evidence from a Greek Commercial Bank. *Appl. Econ.*, March 1989, *21*(3), pp. 285–93.

Paxton, Kenneth W.; Lavergne, David R. and Vandeveer, Lonnie R. Irrigation and Potential Diversification Benefits in Humid Climates. *Southern J. Agr. Econ.*, December 1989, *21*(2), pp. 167–74.

Paye, Jean-Claude. Growth among the Advanced Nations. In *Cerami, C. A., ed.*, 1989, pp. 53–61.

Payne, Bill. Lights Dim for Domestic Uranium Producers: Note. *Natural Res. J.*, Fall 1989, *29*(4), pp. 1079–91.

Payne, Bruce L. Spiro Agnew and Maryland Customs. In *Heidenheimer, A. J.; Johnston, M. and LeVine, V. T., eds.*, 1989, *1981*, pp. 601–25.

Payne, James E. A Small-Scale Macroeconometric Model of Yugoslavia: 1952–1985. *Econ. Anal. Workers' Manage.*, 1989, *23*(4), pp. 335–54.

_____ and **Zuehlke, Thomas W.** Tests of the Rational Expectations–Permanent Income Hypothesis for Developing Economies. *J. Macroecon.*, Summer 1989, *11*(3), pp. 423–33.

Payne, Joan. Trade Union Membership and Activism among Young People in Great Britain. *Brit. J. Ind. Relat.*, March 1989, *27*(1), pp. 111–32.

Payne, Philip. Public Health and Functional Consequences of Seasonal Hunger and Malnutrition. In *Sahn, D. E., ed.*, 1989, pp. 19–46.

Payner, Brook S.; Butler, Richard J. and Heckman, James J. The Impact of the Economy and the State on the Economic Status of Blacks: A Study of South Carolina. In *Galenson, D. W., ed.*, 1989, pp. 231–346.

_____ and **Heckman, James J.** Determining the Impact of Federal Antidiscrimination Policy on the Economic Status of Blacks: A Study of South Carolina. *Amer. Econ. Rev.*, March 1989, *79*(1), pp. 138–77.

Paz Espinosa, Maria and Rhee, Changyong. Efficient Wage Bargaining as a Repeated Game. *Quart. J. Econ.*, August 1989, *104*(3), pp. 565–88.

Peacock, Alan. Deregulation and the Future of Commercial Television: Introduction. In *Hughes, G. and Vines, D., eds.*, 1989, pp. 1–8.

_____. Economic Freedom and Modern Libertarian Thinking. In *Johnson, C., ed.*, 1989, pp. 37–50.

_____. The Future of Public Service Broadcasting. In *Veljanovski, C., ed. (I)*, 1989, pp. 51–62.

_____. Pioneers of Modern Economics in Britain:

Volume 2: Introduction. **In** *Greenaway, D. and Presley, J. R., eds.*, 1989, pp. 1–10.

_____ **and Willgerodt, Hans.** German Liberalism and Economic Revival. **In** *Peacock, A. and Willgerodt, H., eds. (II)*, 1989, pp. 1–14.

_____ **and Willgerodt, Hans.** Overall View of the German Liberal Movement. **In** *Peacock, A. and Willgerodt, H., eds. (I)*, 1989, pp. 1–15.

Pearce, David and Pearce, Maria Rosaria Di Nucci. Economics and Technological Change: Some Conceptual and Methodological Issues. **In** *Balzer, W. and Hamminga, B., eds.*, 1989, pp. 101–27.

Pearce, David G.; Stacchetti, Ennio and Geanakoplos, John. Psychological Games and Sequential Rationality. *Games Econ. Behav.*, March 1989, *1*(1), pp. 60–79.

Pearce, David W. and Button, Kenneth J. Infrastructure Restoration as a Tool for Stimulating Urban Renewal—The Glasgow Canal. *Urban Stud.*, December 1989, *26*(6), pp. 559–71.

_____ **and Markandya, Anil.** Marginal Opportunity Cost as a Planning Concept in Natural Resource Management. **In** *Schramm, G. and Warford, J. J., eds.*, 1989, pp. 39–55.

Pearce, Jone L. and Rosener, Judy. Advisory Board Performance: Managing Ambiguity and Limited Commitment in Public Television. **In** *Herman, R. D. and Van Til, J., eds.*, 1989, pp. 36–47.

Pearce, Maria Rosaria Di Nucci and Pearce, David. Economics and Technological Change: Some Conceptual and Methodological Issues. **In** *Balzer, W. and Hamminga, B., eds.*, 1989, pp. 101–27.

Pearman, A. D., et al. The Use of Multicriteria Techniques to Rank Highway Investment Proposals. **In** *Lockett, A. G. and Islei, G., eds.*, 1989, pp. 157–65.

Pearson, Mark; Smith, Stephen R. and Micklewright, John. Has Britain an Early School-Leaving Problem? *Fisc. Stud.*, February 1989, *10*(1), pp. 1–16.

_____; **Smith, Stephen R. and White, Stuart.** Demographic Influences on Public Spending. *Fisc. Stud.*, May 1989, *10*(2), pp. 48–65.

Pearson, P. J. G. Proactive Energy–Environment Policy Strategies: A Role for Input–Output Analysis? *Environ. Planning A*, October 1989, *21*(10), pp. 1329–48.

Pearson, Ruth. Women's Employment and Multinationals in the UK: Restructuring and Flexibility. **In** *Elson, D. and Pearson, R., eds.*, 1989, pp. 12–37.

_____ **and Elson, Diane.** Nimble Fingers and Foreign Investments: Introduction. **In** *Elson, D. and Pearson, R., eds.*, 1989, pp. 1–11.

Pebley, Anne R. and Hill, Kenneth. Child Mortality in the Developing World. *Population Devel. Rev.*, December 1989, *15*(4), pp. 657–87.

Pécaut, Daniel. The State, Industrial Relations and the Labour Movement in Latin America: Volume 1: Colombia. **In** *Carrière, J.; Haworth, N. and Roddick, J., eds.*, 1989, pp. 263–303.

Pechman, Joseph A. The Role of the Economist

in Government: An International Perspective: The United States. **In** *Pechman, J. A., ed.*, 1989, pp. 109–24.

Peck, Anne E. and Nahmias, Antoinette M. Hedging Your Advice: Do Portfolio Models Explain Hedging? *Food Res. Inst. Stud.*, 1989, *21*(2), pp. 193–204.

Peck, James and Shell, Karl. On the Nonequivalence of the Arrow-Securities Game and the Contingent-Commodities Game. **In** *Barnett, W. A.; Geweke, J. and Shell, K., eds.*, 1989, pp. 61–85.

Peck, Jamie A. and Haughton, Graham. Local Labour Market Analysis, Skill Shortages and the Skills Audit Approach. *Reg. Stud.*, June 1989, *23*(3), pp. 271–76.

_____ **and Lloyd, Peter E.** Conceptualising Processes of Skill Change: A Local Labour Market Approach. **In** *Linge, G. J. R. and van der Knaap, G. A., eds.*, 1989, pp. 107–27.

Peck, Linda Levy. Corruption and Political Development in Early Modern Britain. **In** *Heidenheimer, A. J.; Johnston, M. and LeVine, V. T., eds.*, 1989, *1978*, pp. 219–31.

Peck, Merton J. Industrial Organization and the Gains from Europe 1992. *Brookings Pap. Econ. Act.*, 1989, (2), pp. 277–99.

Peck, N. T. and Khan, M. Ali. On the Interiors of Production Sets in Infinite Dimensional Spaces. *J. Math. Econ.*, 1989, *18*(1), pp. 29–39.

Peck, Richard M. Taxation, Risk, and Returns to Scale. *J. Public Econ.*, December 1989, *40*(3), pp. 319–30.

Peck, Stephen C.; Uhler, Robert G. and Nelson, Charles R. The NERC Fan in Retrospect and Lessons for the Future. *Energy J.*, April 1989, *10*(2), pp. 91–107.

Peden, Edgar A. and Bradley, Michael D. Government Size, Productivity, and Economic Growth: The Post-war Experience. *Public Choice*, June 1989, *61*(3), pp. 229–45.

Peden, G. C. Britain in the 1930s: A Managed Economy? A Comment. *Econ. Hist. Rev., 2nd Ser.*, November 1989, *42*(4), pp. 538–43.

Pedersen, Jørgen Lindgaard. Technology Policy in Denmark: Introduction. **In** *Pedersen, J. L., ed.*, 1989, pp. 13–27.

_____; **Arnfred, Niels and Hansen, Annegrethe.** Bio-technology and Politics, Danish Experiences. **In** *Pedersen, J. L., ed.*, 1989, pp. 159–84.

Pedersen, Lars Haagen. Overskudsdeling i en lille åben økonomi. (Profit Sharing in a Small Open Economy. With English summary.) *Nationaløkon. Tidsskr.*, 1989, *127*(1), pp. 59–73.

Pedersen, Peder J. Arbejdsmarkedspension og fremtidens pensionsstruktur. (A Review of a Recent Report on Labour Market Pensions Issued by the Danish Ministry of Labour. With English summary.) *Nationaløkon. Tidsskr.*, 1989, *127*(2), pp. 200–212.

_____ **and Søndergaard, Jørgen.** Det inflationaere danske arbejdsmarked. (The Inflationary Bias in the Danish Economy. With English summary.) *Nationaløkon. Tidsskr.*, 1989, *127*(1), pp. 1–20.

Pederson, Kendra and Schoney, Richard A. An Economic Evaluation of Alternative Crop Leases. *Can. J. Agr. Econ.*, November 1989, *37*(3), pp. 525–37.

Pedone, Antonio. International Coordination of Fiscal Policies: Current and Future Issues: Comment. In *Monti, M., ed.*, 1989, pp. 50–53.

_____. Taxation of Income from Capital and the Creation of a European Financial Area. *Rev. Econ. Cond. Italy*, Sept.–Dec. 1989, (3), pp. 285–300.

Peebles, Gavin. The "Second Law of Demand": A Search for It in Textbooks. *Hong Kong Econ. Pap.*, 1989, (19), pp. 49–65.

Peek, Joe and Hendershott, Patric H. Aggregate U.S. Private Saving: Conceptual Measures and Empirical Tests. In *Lipsey, R. E. and Tice, H. S., eds.*, 1989, pp. 185–223.

_____ **and Hendershott, Patric H.** Household Saving in the United States: Measurement and Behavior. *J. Bus. Econ. Statist.*, January 1989, *7*(1), pp. 11–19.

Peel, David A. New Classical Macroeconomics. In *Greenaway, D., ed.*, 1989, pp. 45–67.

_____. On Testing the Properties of Directly Obtained Expectations Data. *Econ. Letters*, August 1989, *30*(2), pp. 137–39.

_____ **and Pope, Peter F.** Empirical Evidence on the Properties of Exchange Rate Forecasts and the Risk Premium. *Econ. Letters*, December 1989, *31*(4), pp. 387–91.

_____ **and Pope, Peter F.** Information, Prices and Efficiency in a Fixed-Odds Betting Market. *Economica*, August 1989, *56*(223), pp. 323–41.

Peel, M. J. and Wilson, Nicholas. The Liquidation/Merger Alternative: Some Results for the UK Corporate Sector. *Managerial Dec. Econ.*, September 1989, *10*(3), pp. 209–20.

Peele, Gillian. Contemporary Conservatism and the Borders of the State. In *Helm, D., ed.*, 1989, pp. 153–79.

Peelle, Elizabeth. Innovative Process and Inventive Solutions: Nuclear Waste Packaging Facility Case Study. In *Dysart, B. C., III and Clawson, M., eds.*, 1989, pp. 143–67.

Pehkonen, Jaakko. The Causes of Unemployment in Finland 1970–82: Some Further Empirical Evidence. *Appl. Econ.*, June 1989, *21*(6), pp. 723–39.

Pehlivanov, Vassil. Reconstruction of Pricing of the Means of Production. In *Bulgarian Academy of Sciences, Institute of Economics*, 1989, pp. 75–83.

Peil, J. A New Look at Adam Smith. *Int. J. Soc. Econ.*, 1989, *16*(1), pp. 52–72.

Peiser, Richard B. Density and Urban Sprawl. *Land Econ.*, August 1989, *65*(3), pp. 193–204.

Pejovich, Steve. Liberty, Property Rights, and Innovation in Eastern Europe. *Cato J.*, Spring–Summer 1989, *9*(1), pp. 57–71.

Pekkarinen, Jukka. Early Hicks and Keynesian Monetary Theory: Different Views on Liquid-

ity Preference. In *Wood, J. C. and Woods, R. N., eds., Vol. 4*, 1989, *1986*, pp. 286–99.

_____. Keynesianism and the Scandinavian Models of Economic Policy. In *Hall, P. A., ed.*, 1989, pp. 311–45.

_____ **and Paunio, J.** The Hicksian Revision of the Multiplier Analysis of Expansion. In *Wood, J. C. and Woods, R. N., eds., Vol. 3*, 1989, *1976*, pp. 114–26.

Pelaez, Rolando F. Interest Rates as Predictors of Inflation Revisited. *Southern Econ. J.*, April 1989, *55*(4), pp. 1025–28.

Peles, Yoram C. and Schneller, Meir I. The Duration of the Adjustment Process of Financial Ratios. *Rev. Econ. Statist.*, August 1989, *71*(3), pp. 527–32.

Pelikan, Pavel. Evolution, Economic Competence, and the Market for Corporate Control. *J. Econ. Behav. Organ.*, December 1989, *12*(3), pp. 279–303.

Pelkmans, Jacques. Industrial Integration: The Core of the EC Rediscovered. In *Tarditi, S., et al., eds.*, 1989, pp. 207–26.

Pellegrini, Claudio. Managers as Employees: Italy. In *Roomkin, M. J., ed.*, 1989, pp. 228–51.

van Pelt, Michiel and Nijkamp, Peter. Spatial Impact Analysis in Developing Countries: Method and Application. *Int. Reg. Sci. Rev.*, 1989, *12*(2), pp. 211–28.

Pelton, Joseph N. INTELSAT and Separate Satellite Systems Issues. In *Jussawalla, M.; Okuma, T. and Araki, T., eds.*, 1989, pp. 264–71.

Peltzman, Sam. The Control and Performance of State-Owned Enterprises: Comment. In *MacAvoy, P. W., et al.*, 1989, pp. 69–75.

_____. The Economic Theory of Regulation after a Decade of Deregulation. *Brookings Pap. Econ. Act.*, Microeconomics, 1989, pp. 1–41.

Pemberton, James. The Macroeconomics of Inflation Non-neutrality. *Econ. J.*, March 1989, *99*(394), pp. 62–82.

_____. Marshall's Rules for Derived Demand: A Critique and a Generalisation. *Scot. J. Polit. Econ.*, November 1989, *36*(4), pp. 396–405.

_____. Union Responses to Changes in Non-labour Input Prices. *Econ. Letters*, August 1989, *30*(2), pp. 181–83.

_____. Wage and Employment Determination When Employment Adjustment Is Costly. *Bull. Econ. Res.*, January 1989, *41*(1), pp. 77–80.

Peña, Devon G. Development Policy in the 1980s: The Twin Plants, a Lesson for the Enterprise Zone Proposal? In *Martin, M. T. and Kandal, T. R., eds.*, 1989, pp. 316–45.

Peña Sánchez de Rivera, Daniel. Sobre la robustez a la muestra de un modelo econométrico dinámico. (With English summary.) *Revista Española Econ.*, 1989, *6*(1–2), pp. 193–214.

Penati, Alessandro; Gultekin, Mustafa N. and Gultekin, N. Bulent. Capital Controls and International Capital Market Segmentation: The Evidence from the Japanese and American Stock Markets. *J. Finance*, September 1989, *44*(4), pp. 849–69.

_____ **and Pennacchi, George G.** Optimal Portfolio Choice and the Collapse of a Fixed-Exchange Rate Regime. *J. Int. Econ.*, August 1989, *27*(1–2), pp. 1–24.

_____; **Porta, Angelo and Bruni, Franco.** Financial Regulation, Implicit Taxes, and Fiscal Adjustment in Italy. In *Monti, M., ed.*, 1989, pp. 197–230.

Pencak, William. New York and the Rise of American Capitalism: Introduction. In *Pencak, W. and Wright, C. E., eds.*, 1989, pp. xi–xx.

Pendleton, John W. and Lawson, T. L. Climatic Variability and Sustainability of Crop Yields in the Humid Tropics. In *Oram, P. A., et al.*, 1989, pp. 57–68.

Peng, Jianfeng and Shao, Daosheng. Changing Patterns in Workers' View of Life. *Chinese Econ. Stud.*, Summer 1989, *22*(4), pp. 39–43.

Penkov, Peter. The Insurance Fund of Socialist Society. In *Bulgarian Academy of Sciences, Institute of Economics*, 1989, pp. 184–91.

Penkrot, Joseph L. Can AFDC Parents Pay Child Support? *J. Policy Anal. Manage.*, Winter 1989, *8*(1), pp. 104–10.

Penman, Stephen H. and Ou, Jane A. Accounting Measurement, Price–Earnings Ratio, and the Information Content of Security Prices. *J. Acc. Res.*, Supplement, 1989, *27*, pp. 111–44.

_____ **and Ou, Jane A.** Financial Statement Analysis and the Prediction of Stock Returns. *J. Acc. Econ.*, November 1989, *11*(4), pp. 295–329.

Penn, J. B. The SAEA: After Twenty Years. *Southern J. Agr. Econ.*, July 1989, *21*(1), pp. 55–60.

_____. Selective Perceptions and the Politics of Agricultural Policy: Commentary. In *Krämer, C. S., ed.*, 1989, pp. 78–79.

Pennacchi, George G. and Penati, Alessandro. Optimal Portfolio Choice and the Collapse of a Fixed-Exchange Rate Regime. *J. Int. Econ.*, August 1989, *27*(1–2), pp. 1–24.

Pennella, Giuseppe. Productivity in the Italian Administration. Methods, Comparisons and Results. *Labour*, Winter 1989, *3*(3), pp. 169–87.

Penner, Rudolph G. Credit Rationing and Government Loan Programs: A Welfare Analysis: Comments. *Amer. Real Estate Urban Econ. Assoc. J.*, Summer 1989, *17*(2), pp. 194–96.

Penning de Vries, F. W. T., et al. Simulated Yields of Wheat and Rice in Current Weather and When Ambient CO_2 Has Doubled. In *Oram, P. A., et al.*, 1989, pp. 347–57.

Pennisi, Giuseppe. Economic Appraisal of Environment-Related Projects. Many Certainties and a Few Uncertainties. *Econ. Scelte Pubbliche/J. Public Finance Public Choice*, Jan.–Aug. 1989, *7*(1–2), pp. 29–43.

Pennock, J. Roland. The Justification of Democracy. In *Brennan, G. and Lomasky, L. E., eds.*, 1989, pp. 11–41.

_____. Markets and Justice: NOMOS XXXI: Epilogue. In *Chapman, J. W. and Pennock, J. R., eds.*, 1989, pp. 328–30.

_____ **and Chapman, John W.** Markets and Jus-

tice: NOMOS XXXI: Introduction. In *Chapman, J. W. and Pennock, J. R., eds.*, 1989, pp. 1–10.

Penrose, Edith. History, the Social Sciences and Economic 'Theory,' with Special Reference to Multinational Enterprise. In *Teichova, A.; Lévy-Leboyer, M. and Nussbaum, H., eds.*, 1989, pp. 7–13.

_____. Oil and the International Economy: Multinational Aspects 1900–73. In *Ferrier, R. W. and Fursenko, A., eds.*, 1989, pp. 3–16.

Peoples, James H., Jr. Merger Activity and Wage Levels in U.S. Manufacturing. *J. Lab. Res.*, Spring 1989, *10*(2), pp. 183–96.

Pepall, Lynne M. The Informational Role of Spanning in Competitive Product Selection. *Can. J. Econ.*, February 1989, *22*(1), pp. 37–49.

_____ **and Shapiro, Daniel M.** The Military–Industrial Complex in Canada. *Can. Public Policy*, September 1989, *15*(3), pp. 265–84.

Pera, Alberto. Deregulation and Privatisation in an Economy-Wide Context. *OECD Econ. Stud.*, Spring 1989, (12), pp. 159–204.

Perali, Federico; Berni, Pietro and Begalli, Diego. Importance of Risk in the Acreage Supply Decision of Italian Rice Producers. In *Bauer, S. and Henrichsmeyer, W., eds.*, 1989, pp. 43–52.

Perasso, Giancarlo. The Pricing of LDC Debt in the Secondary Market: An Empirical Analysis. *Kyklos*, 1989, *42*(4), pp. 533–55.

_____ **and Lall, Sanjaya.** Determinants of the Debt Problem in Eastern and Southern Africa: A Statistical Analysis. *Rivista Int. Sci. Econ. Com.*, Oct.–Nov. 1989, *36*(10–11), pp. 985–92.

Perée, Eric and Steinherr, Alfred. Exchange Rate Uncertainty and Foreign Trade. *Europ. Econ. Rev.*, July 1989, *33*(6), pp. 1241–64.

Pereira, Pedro L. Valls; Markwald, Ricardo A. and Moreira, Ajax R. Bello. Previsão da produção industrial: Indicadores antecedentes e modelos de série temporal. (With English summary.) *Pesquisa Planejamento Econ.*, August 1989, *19*(2), pp. 233–54.

Perelman, Michael A. Adam Smith and Dependent Social Relations. *Hist. Polit. Econ.*, Fall 1989, *21*(3), pp. 503–20.

Perelman, Sergio and Barla, Philippe. Technical Efficiency in Airlines under Regulated and Deregulated Environments. *Ann. Pub. Coop. Econ.*, 1989, *60*(1), pp. 103–24.

_____ **and Fecher, Fabienne.** Productivité, progrès technique et efficacité: Une étude comparative de 14 secteurs industriels belges. (Total Factor Productivity, Technical Progress and Efficiency: A Comparative Study of 14 Belgian Industrial Sectors. With English summary.) *Ann. Écon. Statist.*, Jan.–March 1989, (13), pp. 93–118.

_____ **and Thiry, Bernard.** Measuring the Performance of Public Transport Companies. *Ann. Pub. Coop. Econ.*, 1989, *60*(1), pp. 3–7.

Perepelkin, L.; Shkaratan, O. and Koroteeva, V. From Bureaucratic Centralism to Economic Integration of Sovereign Republics. *Prob. Econ.*, July 1989, *32*(3), pp. 36–56.

Peretiatkowicz, Anatol. Democracy in Selected Polish State Enterprises. *Econ. Anal. Workers' Manage.*, 1989, *23*(1), pp. 31–41.

Pérez García, Francisco. Financiación y déficit con dos niveles de Gobierno. Comportamientos estratégicos. (With English summary.) *Invest. Ecón.*, January 1989, *13*(1), pp. 85–114.

Pérez-López, Jorge F. Case for a GATT Code on Temporary Measures. *World Econ.*, March 1989, *12*(1), pp. 53–67.

_____. Sugar and Structural Change in the Cuban Economy. *World Devel.*, October 1989, *17*(10), pp. 1627–46.

_____. Wages, Earnings, Hours of Work, and Retail Prices in Cuba. In *Mesa-Lago, C., ed.*, 1989, pp. 199–224.

Pérez Motta, Eduardo and Bucay, Nisso. Trade Negotiation Strategy for Mexico. In *Whalley, J., ed., Vol. 2*, 1989, pp. 230–43.

Pérez Porrúa, Juan Manuel. The Equilibrium Exchange Rate of the Mexican Peso: A Monetary Approach. In *Brock, P. L.; Connolly, M. B. and González-Vega, C., eds.*, 1989, pp. 187–94.

Perez, Roland. Contraintes stratégiques et logiques d'action des groupes alimentaires. (Strategic Constraints and the Logic of the Food Industry Groups' Activity. With English summary.) *Écon. Societes*, July 1989, *23*(7), pp. 9–26.

Peristiani, Stavros and Hardouvelis, Gikas A. Do Margin Requirements Matter? Evidence from U.S. and Japanese Stock Markets. *Fed. Res. Bank New York Quart. Rev.*, Winter 1989–90, *14*(4), pp. 16–35.

_____; **Saunders, Anthony and Allen, Linda.** Bank Size, Collateral, and Net Purchase Behavior in the Federal Funds Market: Empirical Evidence. *J. Bus.*, October 1989, *62*(4), pp. 501–15.

Perkins, Edwin J. The Entrepreneurial Spirit in Colonial America: The Foundations of Modern Business History. *Bus. Hist. Rev.*, Spring 1989, *63*(1), pp. 160–86.

Perkins, James O. N. Austerity and Australia. *Écon. Appl.*, 1989, *42*(1), pp. 239–67.

Perkins, John. German Shipping and Australia before the First World War. *Australian Econ. Hist. Rev.*, March 1989, *29*(1), pp. 42–59.

Perlman, Mark. Institutions and Agriculture in Old-Régime France: Comment. *J. Inst. Theoretical Econ.*, March 1989, *145*(1), pp. 182–84.

Perlman, Morris. Adam Smith and the Paternity of the Real Bills Doctrine. *Hist. Polit. Econ.*, Spring 1989, *21*(1), pp. 77–90.

Perlman, Richard and Drago, Robert. Microeconomic Issues in Labour Economics: New Approaches: Introduction. In *Drago, R. and Perlman, R., eds.*, 1989, pp. 1–15.

_____ **and Drago, Robert.** Supervision and High Wages as Competing Incentives: A Basis for Labour Segmentation Theory. In *Drago, R. and Perlman, R., eds.*, 1989, pp. 41–61.

Perloff, Jeffrey M. and Fargeix, André. The Effect of Tariffs in Markets with Vertical Restraints. *J. Int. Econ.*, February 1989, *26*(1/2), pp. 99–117.

_____ **and Karp, Larry S.** Dynamic Oligopoly in the Rice Export Market. *Rev. Econ. Statist.*, August 1989, *71*(3), pp. 462–70.

_____ **and Karp, Larry S.** Estimating Market Structure and Tax Incidence: The Japanese Television Market. *J. Ind. Econ.*, March 1989, *37*(3), pp. 225–39.

Pern, A. L. The Family Budget in the Mirror of Statistics. *Prob. Econ.*, July 1989, *32*(3), pp. 81–88.

Perold, André F. and Gammill, James F., Jr. The Changing Character of Stock Market Liquidity. *J. Portfol. Manage.*, Spring 1989, *15*(3), pp. 13–18.

Perras, James and Wilman, Elizabeth A. The Substitute Price Variable in the Travel Cost Equation. *Can. J. Agr. Econ.*, July 1989, *37*(2), pp. 249–61.

Perreault, J. and George, M. V. Methodological Issues in the Projection of Households and Families in Canada. *Statist. J.*, 1989, *6*(4), pp. 325–36.

Perri, Stefano and Gallegati, Mauro. Un modello ricardiano di crescita e distribuzione: Un approccio integrato. (A Ricardian Model of Distribution and Growth: An Integrated Approach. With English summary.) *Econ. Politica*, December 1989, *6*(3), pp. 381–402.

Perri, Timothy. Imprecise Testing and Endogenous Limits to Bonds. *Econ. Letters*, 1989, *29*(2), pp. 195–97.

Perrings, Charles. The Adjustment Programme and the Perverse Effects of Poverty in Sub-Saharan Africa. In *Singer, H. W. and Sharma, S., eds. (I)*, 1989, pp. 321–34.

_____. An Optimal Path to Extinction? Poverty and Resource Degradation in the Open Agrarian Economy. *J. Devel. Econ.*, January 1989, *30*(1), pp. 1–24.

Perron, Pierre. The Great Crash, the Oil Price Shock, and the Unit Root Hypothesis. *Econometrica*, November 1989, *57*(6), pp. 1361–1401.

Perrot, Anne and Zylberberg, André. Salaire d'efficience et dualisme du marché du travail. (Efficiency Wage and Dual Labour Market. With English summary.) *Revue Écon.*, January 1989, *40*(1), pp. 5–20.

Perrucci, Robert and Potter, Harry R. The Collective Actor in Organizational Analysis. In *Perrucci, R. and Potter, H. R., eds.*, 1989, pp. 1–15.

Perry, George L. The Debt Overhang of Developing Countries: Comment. In *[Díaz-Alejandro, C.]*, 1989, pp. 103–05.

Perry, Gregory M. and Pope, C. Arden, III. Individual versus Social Discount Rates in Allocating Depletable Natural Resources over Time. *Econ. Letters*, 1989, *29*(3), pp. 257–64.

_____, **et al.** Incorporating Government Program Provisions into a Mean–Variance Framework. *Southern J. Agr. Econ.*, December 1989, *21*(2), pp. 95–105.

_____. Modeling Government Program Participation Decisions at the Farm Level. *Amer. J. Agr. Econ.*, November 1989, *71*(4), pp. 1011–20.

Perry, Martin K. Vertical Integration: Determinants and Effects. In *Schmalensee, R. and Willig, R. D., eds., Vol. 1*, 1989, pp. 183–255.

Perry, Philip R.; Hartigan, James C. and Kamma, Sreenivas. The Injury Determination Category and the Value of Relief from Dumping. *Rev. Econ. Statist.*, February 1989, *71*(1), pp. 183–86.

Perry Robinson, Julian P. Adequacy versus Feasibility in the Scope of the Projected Chemical Weapons Convention. In *Rotblat, J. and Goldanskii, V. I., eds.*, 1989, pp. 105–11.

_____. Verification Procedures for a Chemical Weapons Treaty. In *Altmann, J. and Rotblat, J., eds.*, 1989, pp. 201–09.

Perry, Stephen David. The Promise: "Uncaptured" Peasantry, the State and Development in Bhutan. *Can. J. Devel. Stud.*, 1989, *10*(2), pp. 257–72.

Perry, William J. Defense Investment Strategy. *Foreign Aff.*, Spring 1989, *68*(2), pp. 72–92.

Persaud, B. Population, Resources, and Limits to Growth: Commentary. In *DeGregori, T. R., ed.*, 1989, pp. 129–35.

_____. Theory and Practice in World Agriculture: Commentary. In *DeGregori, T. R., ed.*, 1989, pp. 79–86.

Persaud, Vishnu. Alister McIntyre and North–South Economic Relations. *Soc. Econ. Stud.*, June 1989, *38*(2), pp. 5–23.

Persky, Allan. An Uncertain Fine for Pollution as a Fixed Cost that Affects Output. *Amer. Economist*, Spring 1989, *33*(1), pp. 24–27.

Persky, Joseph. Adam Smith's Invisible Hands. *J. Econ. Perspectives*, Fall 1989, *3*(4), pp. 195–201.

_____. Black Economic Thought and the Southern Economy. *Rev. Black Polit. Econ.*, Spring 1989, *17*(4), pp. 27–44.

Personick, Martin E. and Biddle, Elyce A. Job Hazards Underscored in Woodworking Study. *Mon. Lab. Rev.*, September 1989, *112*(9), pp. 18–23.

_____ and Daley, Judy R. Profiles in Safety and Health: Work Hazards of Mobile Homes. *Mon. Lab. Rev.*, July 1989, *112*(7), pp. 15–20.

_____ and Taylor-Shirley, Katherine. Profiles in Safety and Health: Occupational Hazards of Meatpacking. *Mon. Lab. Rev.*, January 1989, *112*(1), pp. 3–9.

Personick, Valerie A. Industry Output and Employment: A Slower Trend for the Nineties. *Mon. Lab. Rev.*, November 1989, *112*(11), pp. 25–41.

_____. The Outlook for U.S. Industries: Projections to the Year 2000. In *Libecap, G. D., ed.*, 1989, pp. 219–28.

Persson, Torsten. Management of a Common Currency: Discussion. In *De Cecco, M. and Giovannini, A., eds.*, 1989, pp. 156–58.

_____; Palmer, Edward E. and Gottfries, Nils. Regulation, Financial Buffer Stocks, and Short-run Adjustment: An Econometric Case-Study

of Sweden, 1970–82. *Europ. Econ. Rev.*, October 1989, *33*(8), pp. 1545–65.

_____ and Svensson, Lars E. O. Exchange Rate Variability and Asset Trade. *J. Monet. Econ.*, May 1989, *23*(3), pp. 485–509.

_____ and Svensson, Lars E. O. Why a Stubborn Conservative Would Run a Deficit: Policy with Time-Inconsistent Preferences. *Quart. J. Econ.*, May 1989, *104*(2), pp. 325–45.

Perttunen, Jukka and Martikainen, Teppo. On the Proportionality Assumption of Financial Ratios. *Liiketaloudellinen Aikak.*, 1989, *38*(4), pp. 343–59.

Perumal, M. Economic Growth and Income Inequality in Malaysia, 1957–1984. *Singapore Econ. Rev.*, October 1989, *34*(2), pp. 33–46.

Pesaran, Bahram and Magnus, Jan R. The Exact Multi-period Mean-Square Forecast Error for the First-Order Autoregressive Model with an Intercept. *J. Econometrics*, October 1989, *42*(2), pp. 157–79.

Pesaran, M. Hashem. Consistency of Short-term and Long-term Expectations. *J. Int. Money Finance*, December 1989, *8*(4), pp. 511–16.

_____ and Pierse, Richard G. A Proof of the Asymptotic Validity of a Test for Perfect Aggregation. *Econ. Letters*, 1989, *30*(1), pp. 41–47.

_____; Pierse, Richard G. and Kumar, Mohan S. Econometric Analysis of Aggregation in the Context of Linear Prediction Models. *Econometrica*, July 1989, *57*(4), pp. 861–88.

Pesciarelli, Enzo. Smith, Bentham, and the Development of Contrasting Ideas on Entrepreneurship. *Hist. Polit. Econ.*, Fall 1989, *21*(3), pp. 521–36.

Pessanha, José Miguel. Specification and Estimation of a Conditional Normal Linear Hierarchical Model. *Economia (Portugal)*, October 1989, *13*(3), pp. 359–88.

Pestieau, Pierre. Measuring the Performance of Public Enterprises: A Must in Times of Privatization. *Ann. Pub. Coop. Econ.*, 1989, *60*(3), pp. 293–305.

_____; Wibaut, Serge and Marchand, Maurice. Optimal Commodity Taxation and Tax Reform under Unemployment. *Scand. J. Econ.*, 1989, *91*(3), pp. 547–63.

_____; Wildasin, David E. and Boadway, Robin W. Non-cooperative Behavior and Efficient Provision of Public Goods. *Public Finance*, 1989, *44*(1), pp. 1–17.

_____; Wildasin, David E. and Boadway, Robin W. Tax-Transfer Policies and the Voluntary Provision of Public Goods. *J. Public Econ.*, July 1989, *39*(2), pp. 157–76.

Peters, Donald L. Receipts and Expenditures of State Governments and of Local Governments: Revised and Updated Estimates, 1985–88. *Surv. Curr. Bus.*, October 1989, *69*(10), pp. 24–27.

Peters, Hans and Hendrikse, George. A Note on Partial Vertical Integration. *Econ. Letters*, September 1989, *30*(3), pp. 249–52.

Peters, John G. and Welch, Susan. Gradients of Corruption in Perceptions of American Public

Life. In *Heidenheimer, A. J.; Johnston, M. and LeVine, V. T., eds.*, 1989, *1978*, pp. 723–41.

Peters, Lon L. Managing Competition in German Coal, 1893–1913. *J. Econ. Hist.*, June 1989, *49*(2), pp. 419–33.

Peters, Michael and Hosios, Arthur J. Repeated Insurance Contracts with Adverse Selection and Limited Commitment. *Quart. J. Econ.*, May 1989, *104*(2), pp. 229–53.

Peters, Michael H. Process Control with Lot Sizing. In *Gulledge, T. R., Jr. and Litteral, L. A., eds.*, 1989, pp. 311–23.

Peters, Richard T. The Changing Nature of Debt and Equity: A Legal Perspective: Discussion. In *Kopcke, R. W. and Rosengren, E. S., eds.*, 1989, pp. 67–72.

Peters, Roy H. Population, Pensions and Public Sector Surpluses. *Nat. Westminster Bank Quart. Rev.*, November 1989, pp. 22–30.

Peters, Thomas A. The Exact Moments of OLS in Dynamic Regression Models with Non-normal Errors. *J. Econometrics*, February 1989, *40*(2), pp. 279–305.

Petersen, Jørn Henrik. Pensionsproblemer i europæisk perspektiv. (Main Characteristics and Problems of European Pension Systems. With English summary.) *Nationaløkon. Tidsskr.*, 1989, *127*(3), pp. 289–307.

_____. The Process of Retirement in Denmark: Trends, Public Discussion and Institutional Framework. In *Schmähl, W., ed.*, 1989, pp. 63–81.

Petersen, Niels Helveg. Dansk økonomi og det indre marked. (The Danish Economy and the Internal Market in the EEC. With English summary.) *Nationaløkon. Tidsskr.*, 1989, *127*(1), pp. 21–34.

_____. Den økonomiske politik i Danmark. (Structural Problems in Danish Economic Policy. With English summary.) *Nationaløkon. Tidsskr.*, 1989, *127*(3), pp. 275–88.

_____. Det indre marked—En udfordring fur dansk økonomisk politik og det nordiske samarbejde. (The Internal Market—A Challenge for Danish Economic Policy and Nordic Cooperation. With English summary.) *Ekon. Samfundets Tidskr.*, 1989, *42*(4), pp. 215–27.

Peterson, C. James, et al. Genetic Improvement and the Variability in Wheat Yields in the Great Plains. In *Anderson, J. R. and Hazell, P. B. R., eds.*, 1989, pp. 175–84.

Peterson, Christine E.; Antel, John and Hosek, James R. Military Enlistment and Attrition: An Analysis of Decision Reversal. In *Ehrenberg, R. G., ed.*, 1989, pp. 207–63.

Peterson, David R. and Dickinson, Amy. Seasonality in the Option Market. *Financial Rev.*, November 1989, *24*(4), pp. 529–40.

_____ and Klein, Linda S. Earnings Forecast Revisions Associated with Stock Split Announcements. *J. Finan. Res.*, Winter 1989, *12*(4), pp. 319–28.

Peterson, Dean F. Irrigation as a Factor in Food Security. In *Oram, P. A., et al.*, 1989, pp. 515–32.

Peterson, E. Wesley F.; Grant, Warren R. and

Ito, Shoichi. Rice in Asia: Is It Becoming an Inferior Good? *Amer. J. Agr. Econ.*, February 1989, *71*(1), pp. 32–42.

Peterson, Esther. The Colston Warne Legacy. *J. Cons. Aff.*, Winter 1989, *23*(2), pp. 213–25.

Peterson, G. Paul; Nantz, Kathryn A. and Buss, James A. A Comparison of Distributive Justice in OECD Countries. *Rev. Soc. Econ.*, Spring 1989, *47*(1), pp. 1–14.

Peterson, George and Mendelsohn, Robert. Welfare Measurement with Expenditure-Constrained Demand Models. *Rev. Econ. Statist.*, February 1989, *71*(1), pp. 164–67.

Peterson, George E. and Godwin, Stephen R. Developing a Comprehensive Condition Assessment System. In *Matzer, J., Jr., ed.*, 1989, *1984*, pp. 65–73.

Peterson, Janice. The Feminization of Poverty: A Reply. *J. Econ. Issues*, March 1989, *23*(1), pp. 238–45.

Peterson, John. International Trade in Services: The Uruguay Round and Cultural and Information Services. *Nat. Westminster Bank Quart. Rev.*, August 1989, pp. 56–67.

Peterson, Mark F.; Smith, Peter B. and Tayeb, Monir. The Cultural Context of Leadership Actions: A Cross-Cultural Analysis. In *Davies, J., et al., eds.*, 1989, pp. 85–92.

Peterson, Pamela P. Event Studies: A Review of Issues and Methodology. *Quart. J. Bus. Econ.*, Summer 1989, *28*(3), pp. 36–66.

Peterson, Paul E. and Chubb, John E. American Political Institutions and the Problem of Governance. In *Chubb, J. E. and Peterson, P. E., eds.*, 1989, pp. 1–43.

_____ and Rom, Mark. Macroeconomic Policymaking: Who Is In Control? In *Chubb, J. E. and Peterson, P. E., eds.*, 1989, pp. 139–82.

Peterson, Richard B. and Sullivan, Jerry. Japanese Management Theories: A Research Agenda. In *Prasad, S. B., ed.*, 1989, pp. 255–75.

Peterson, Richard L.; Ma, Christopher K. and Rao, Ramesh P. The Resiliency of the High-Yield Bond Market: The LTV Default. *J. Finance*, September 1989, *44*(4), pp. 1085–97.

Peterson, Wallace C. Market Power: The Missing Element in Keynesian Economics. *J. Econ. Issues*, June 1989, *23*(2), pp. 379–91.

_____. Power and Economic Performance. In *Tool, M. R. and Samuels, W. J., eds. (I)*, 1989, *1980*, pp. 89–131.

_____. The U.S. "Welfare State" and the Conservative Counterrevolution. In *Tool, M. R. and Samuels, W. J., eds. (II)*, 1989, *1985*, pp. 455–95.

Peterson, William. Supply Functions in an Input–Output Framework. In *Miller, R. E.; Polenske, K. R. and Rose, A. Z., eds.*, 1989, pp. 22–34.

Peterson, Willis L. International Food Stamps. In *Helmuth, J. W. and Johnson, S. R., eds.*, Vol. 2, 1989, pp. 191–200.

_____. Rates of Return on Capital: An International Comparison. *Kyklos*, 1989, *42*(2), pp. 203–17.

_____. World Hunger, Malnutrition, and Food

Production and Distribution Systems: Reaction. In *Helmuth, J. W. and Johnson, S. R.*, eds., *Vol. 1*, 1989, pp. 188–91.

Pethig, Rüdiger. Efficiency versus Self-financing in Water Quality Management. *J. Public Econ.*, February 1989, *38*(1), pp. 75–93.

_____ **and Fiedler, Klaus.** Effluent Charges on Municipal Wastewater Treatment Facilities: In Search of Their Theoretical Rationale. *J. Econ. (Z. Nationalökon.)*, 1989, *49*(1), pp. 71–94.

Petit, Maria Luisa. Fiscal and Monetary Policy Co-ordination: A Differential Game Approach. *J. Appl. Econometrics*, April–June 1989, *4*(2), pp. 161–79.

Petit, Michel. Is There Anything "American" about American Agricultural Policy? Commentary. In *Krämer, C. S., ed.*, 1989, pp. 56–60.

_____. The Role of the World Bank in the Debate on Aid, Trade, and Agricultural Policies. In *Swegle, W. E. and Ligon, P. C., eds.*, 1989, pp. 29–39.

Petit, Pascal and Tahar, Gabriel. Dynamics of Technological Change and Schemes of Diffusion. *Manchester Sch. Econ. Soc. Stud.*, December 1989, *57*(4), pp. 370–86.

_____ **and Tahar, Gabriel.** Effets productivité et qualité de l'automatisation: Une approche macro-économique. (Productivity and Quality Effects of Automation: A Macroeconomic Approach. With English summary.) *Revue Écon.*, January 1989, *40*(1), pp. 35–54.

_____; **Tahar, Gabriel and Antonelli, Cristiano.** Technological Diffusion and Investment Behaviour: The Case of the Textile Industry. *Weltwirtsch. Arch.*, 1989, *125*(4), pp. 782–803.

Petitbó i Juan, Amadeu. El control de los mercados de productos industriales en la economía española. (The Control of Industrial Products Markets in the Spanish Economy. With English summary.) *Écon. Societes*, February 1989, *23*(2), pp. 189–238.

Petith, Howard C. A Shorter Version of Ståhl's Theorem T_{10}. *Scand. J. Econ.*, 1989, *91*(1), pp. 169–70.

Petöcz, Gy. Reflections about an All-Round Inquiry. *Acta Oecon.*, 1989, *40*(3–4), pp. 279–83.

Petrakos, George. Urbanization and International Trade in Developing Countries. *World Devel.*, August 1989, *17*(8), pp. 1269–77.

_____ **and Brada, Josef C.** Metropolitan Concentration in Developing Countries. *Kyklos*, 1989, *42*(4), pp. 557–78.

Petrakov, N. I. The Development of Mathematical Economic Methods: Results, Problems, Prospects (Continued). *Matekon*, Spring 1989, *25*(3), pp. 57–59.

_____. Distributing Responsibility and Democratizing the Management of the Economy. *Prob. Econ.*, January 1989, *31*(9), pp. 82–97.

_____. On Differences in the Interpretation of the Role of the Commodity–Money Mechanism in a Transition Economy. *Matekon*, Fall 1989, *26*(1), pp. 50–72.

Petras, James F. Class and Political-Economic

Development in the Mediterranean: An Overview. In *Martin, M. T. and Kandal, T. R.*, eds., 1989, pp. 299–315.

_____ **and Morley, Morris H.** The Imperial State in the Rise and Fall of U.S. Imperialism. In *MacEwan, A. and Tabb, W. K., eds.*, 1989, pp. 44–63.

Petrecolla, Alberto. Unbalanced Development, 1958–62. In *di Tella, G. and Dornbusch, R.*, eds., 1989, pp. 108–25.

Petrera Pavone, Margarita. Effectiveness and Efficiency of Social Security in the Economic Cycle: The Peruvian Case. In *WHO, Pan American Health Organization*, 1989, pp. 73–85.

Petri, Peter A. and Carter, Anne P. Leontief's Contribution to Economics. *J. Policy Modeling*, Spring 1989, *11*(1), pp. 7–30.

_____ **and Leipziger, Danny M.** Korean Incentive Policies towards Industry and Agriculture. In *Williamson, J. G. and Panchamukhi, V. R.*, eds., 1989, pp. 167–89.

Petříček, Václav. New Trends in Foreign-Trade Planning. *Czech. Econ. Digest.*, February 1989, (1), pp. 21–33.

Petrovich, Giuliano. Politiche fiscali e frazionamento del lavoro. (Fiscal Policies and Work Splitting. With English summary.) *Rivista Int. Sci. Econ. Com.*, January 1989, *36*(1), pp. 39–54.

Petruzzi, Christopher R. and Lee, Chi-Wen Jevons. Inventory Accounting Switch and Uncertainty. *J. Acc. Res.*, Autumn 1989, *27*(2), pp. 277–96.

Pettengill, Glenn N. Daily Return Correlations: A Reexamination. *Quart. J. Bus. Econ.*, Summer 1989, *28*(3), pp. 122–41.

_____. Holiday Closings and Security Returns. *J. Finan. Res.*, Spring 1989, *12*(1), pp. 57–67.

Pettigrew, Andrew M. Longitudinal Methods to Study Change: Theory and Practice. In *Mansfield, R., ed.*, 1989, pp. 21–49.

_____; **Sparrow, Paul and Hendry, Chris.** Linking Strategic Change, Competitive Performance and Human Resource Management: Results of a UK Empirical Study. In *Mansfield, R., ed.*, 1989, pp. 195–220.

_____; **Whipp, Richard and Rosenfeld, Robert.** Competitiveness and the Management of Strategic Change Process. In *Francis, A. and Tharakan, P. K. M., eds.*, 1989, pp. 110–36.

Pettway, Richard H.; Scanlon, Kevin P. and Trifts, Jack W. Impacts of Relative Size and Industrial Relatedness on Returns to Shareholders of Acquiring Firms. *J. Finan. Res.*, Summer 1989, *12*(2), pp. 103–12.

Petzel, Todd E. Financial Risk Management Needs of Developing Countries: Discussion. *Amer. J. Agr. Econ.*, May 1989, *71*(2), pp. 531–33.

Pezzini, Mario. The Small-Firm Economy's Odd Man Out: The Case of Ravenna. In *Goodman, E. and Bamford, J., eds.*, 1989, pp. 223–38.

Pfaff, Anita B. and Pfaff, Martin. Distributive Effects of Alternative Health-Care Financing Mechanisms: Cost-Sharing and Risk-Equivalent Contributions. In *Chiancone, A. and Messere, K., eds.*, 1989, pp. 375–401.

Pfaff, Martin and Pfaff, Anita B. Distributive Effects of Alternative Health-Care Financing Mechanisms: Cost-Sharing and Risk-Equivalent Contributions. In *Chiancone, A. and Messere, K., eds.*, 1989, pp. 375–401.

Pfaffenberger, Roger C. and Dielman, Terry E. Efficiency of Ordinary Least Squares for Linear Models with Autocorrelation. *J. Amer. Statist. Assoc.*, March 1989, *84*(405), pp. 248.

Pfann, Gerard A.; Ridder, Geert and Hartog, Joop. (Non-)graduation and the Earnings Function: An Inquiry on Self-Selection. *Europ. Econ. Rev.*, September 1989, *33*(7), pp. 1373–95.

——— **and Verspagen, Bart.** The Structure of Adjustment Costs for Labour in the Dutch Manufacturing Sector. *Econ. Letters*, 1989, *29*(4), pp. 365–71.

Pfeffer, Max J. Part-time Farming and the Stability of Family Farms in the Federal Republic of Germany. *Europ. Rev. Agr. Econ.*, 1989, *16*(4), pp. 425–44.

———. Structural Dimensions of Farm Crisis in the Federal Republic of Germany. In *Goodman, D. and Redclift, M., eds.*, 1989, pp. 183–204.

Pfeffermann, D. and Allon, J. Multivariate Exponential Smoothing: Method and Practice. *Int. J. Forecasting*, 1989, *5*(1), pp. 83–98.

Pfeffermann, Guy and Bond, Gary. IFC and Development. *Finance Devel.*, December 1989, *26*(4), pp. 41–43.

Pfeiffer, Glenn M. and Bowen, Robert M. The Year-End LIFO Purchase Decision: The Case of Farmer Brothers Company. *Accounting Rev.*, January 1989, *64*(1), pp. 152–71.

Pfeiffer, W. H. and Braun, H. J. Yield Stability in Bread Wheat. In *Anderson, J. R. and Hazell, P. B. R., eds.*, 1989, pp. 157–74.

Pfeiffer, Wayne C. Necessary Prior Considerations for the Construction of Agricultural Expert Systems: The Case of the Ontario Beef Sire Selection Expert System. *Can. J. Agr. Econ.*, Part 1, December 1989, *37*(4), pp. 709–22.

Pfingsten, Andreas. Der Einsatz von monetären Anreizsystemen in der Planung. (With English summary.) *Z. Betriebswirtshaft*, December 1989, *59*(12), pp. 1285–96.

———. Incentives to Forecast Honestly. In *Bamberg, G. and Spremann, K., eds.*, 1989, pp. 117–33.

Pfister, Ulrich. Proto-industrialization and Demographic Change: The Canton of Zürich Revisited. *J. Europ. Econ. Hist.*, Winter 1989, *18*(3), pp. 629–62.

——— **and Suter, Christian.** Global Debt Cycles and the Role of Political Regimes. In *Avery, W. P. and Rapkin, D. P., eds.*, 1989, pp. 17–55.

Pfleiderer, Paul and Admati, Anat R. Divide and Conquer: A Theory of Intraday and Day-of-the-Week Mean Effects. *Rev. Financial Stud.*, 1989, *2*(2), pp. 189–223.

Pham, H. N.; Waddington, S. R. and Crossa, J. Yield Stability of CIMMYT Maize Germplasm in International and On-Farm Trials. In *Anderson, J. R. and Hazell, P. B. R., eds.*, 1989, pp. 185–205.

Phaneuf, Louis and Ambler, Steve. Accommodation, Price Flexibility and Fluctuations. *Econ. Letters*, September 1989, *30*(3), pp. 185–90.

——— **and Ambler, Steve.** The Stablizing Effects of Price Flexibility in Contract-Based Models. *J. Macroecon.*, Spring 1989, *11*(2), pp. 233–46.

Phang, Sock Yong. Welfare Implications of HDB Policy on the Public Housing Price Gradient. *Singapore Econ. Rev.*, October 1989, *34*(2), pp. 16–32.

Phelan, John J., Jr. Ethical Leadership and the Investment Industry. In *Williams, O. F.; Reilly, F. K. and Houck, J. W., eds.*, 1989, pp. 23–33.

Phelps, Edmund S. New Channels in the Transmission of Foreign Shocks. In *[Díaz-Alejandro, C.]*, 1989, pp. 315–23.

———. Overview [Monetary Policy, Capital Controls and Seigniorage in an Open Economy] [Seigniorage in Europe]. In *De Cecco, M. and Giovannini, A., eds.*, 1989, pp. 90–94.

Phelps, John J.; Sheets, Robert G. and Nord, Stephen. Service Industries and Structural Underemployment in Urban Areas in the United States. *Rivista Int. Sci. Econ. Com.*, September 1989, *36*(9), pp. 785–800.

Philip, George. Britain and Latin America: Oil and Minerals. In *Bulmer-Thomas, V., ed.*, 1989, pp. 136–47.

Philippatos, George C. and Guth, Michael A. S. A Reexamination of Arbitrage Pricing Theory (APT) under Common Knowledge Beliefs. *Rivista Int. Sci. Econ. Com.*, August 1989, *36*(8), pp. 729–46.

——— **and Puri, Tribhuvan N.** On the Pricing of Foreign Exchange Contracts. *Rivista Int. Sci. Econ. Com.*, April–May 1989, *36*(4–5), pp. 389–406.

Phillips, Almarin. New Technologies and Diversified Telecommunications Services: Policy Problems in an ISDN Environment. In *Crew, M. A., ed.*, 1989, pp. 107–25.

Phillips, David R. and Yeh, Anthony G. O. Special Economic Zones. In *Goodman, D. S. G., ed.*, 1989, pp. 112–34.

Phillips, G. Michael and Jennings, William P. Risk as a Discount Rate Determinant in Wrongful Death and Injury Cases. *J. Risk Ins.*, March 1989, *56*(1), pp. 122–27.

Phillips, Garry D. A. and Harvey, Andrew C. Testing for Structural Change in Simultaneous Equation Models. In *Hackl, P., ed.*, 1989, pp. 25–36.

——— **and McCabe, Brendan P. M.** A Sequential Approach to Testing for Structural Change in Econometric Models. In *Kramer, W., ed.*, 1989, pp. 87–101.

——— **and McCabe, Brendan P. M.** A Sequential Approach to Testing for Structural Change in

Econometric Models. *Empirical Econ.*, 1989, *14*(2), pp. 151–65.

Phillips, Gordon. The British Labour Movement before 1914. **In** *Geary, D., ed.*, 1989, pp. 11–47.

Phillips, Keith R. and Brown, Stephen P. A. Oil Demand and Prices in the 1990s. *Fed. Res. Bank Dallas Econ. Rev.*, January 1989, pp. 1–8.

_____ **and Gruben, William C.** Diversifying Texas: Recent History and Prospects. *Fed. Res. Bank Dallas Econ. Rev.*, July 1989, pp. 1–12.

Phillips-Patrick, Frederick J. The Effect of Asset and Ownership Structure on Political Risk: Some Evidence from Mitterrand's Election in France. *J. Banking Finance*, September 1989, *13*(4–5), pp. 651–71.

Phillips, Ronnie J. Is There a "Texas School" of Economics. *J. Econ. Issues*, September 1989, *23*(3), pp. 863–72.

_____ . The Minsky–Simons–*Veblen* Connection: Comment. *J. Econ. Issues*, September 1989, *23*(3), pp. 889–91.

_____ . Radical Institutionalism and the Texas School of Economics. **In** *Dugger, W. M., ed.*, 1989, pp. 21–37.

Phillips, William E. and Armstrong, Glen W. The Optimal Timing of Land Use Changes from Forestry to Agriculture. *Can. J. Agr. Econ.*, March 1989, *37*(1), pp. 125–34.

Phillips, William H. The Economic Performance of Late Victorian Britain: Traditional Historians and Growth. *J. Europ. Econ. Hist.*, Fall 1989, *18*(2), pp. 393–414.

Philpott, J. C. Public Policy and Local Development: The Case of Stevenage New Town. **In** *Gibbs, D., ed.*, 1989, pp. 266–85.

Phipps, Tim T. Externalities and the Returns to Agricultural Research: Discussion. *Amer. J. Agr. Econ.*, May 1989, *71*(2), pp. 466–67.

Phlips, Louis. Time Series and Cross Sectional Studies of Industrial Structure. *Europ. Econ. Rev.*, March 1989, *33*(2/3), pp. 321–24.

_____ **and Richard, Jean-François.** A Dynamic Oligopoly Model with Demand Inertia and Inventories. *Math. Soc. Sci.*, August 1989, *18*(1), pp. 1–32.

Pi Anguita, Joaquín. La eficiencia del tipo de cambio peseta-dólar en un contexto multimercado. (With English summary.) *Invest. Ecón.*, January 1989, *13*(1), pp. 167–80.

Piatier, André. 1980–1990: dix ans de surf. (10 Years "Surfing": 1980–1990. With English summary.) *Écon. Societes*, March 1989, *23*(3), pp. 5–41.

Picard, Pierre. Prix fictifs et déséquilibres macroéconomiques. (With English summary.) *Revue Écon. Politique*, March–April 1989, *99*(2), pp. 252–75.

_____ ; **Rey, Patrick and Guesnerie, Roger.** Adverse Selection and Moral Hazard with Risk Neutral Agents. *Europ. Econ. Rev.*, April 1989, *33*(4), pp. 807–23.

Picci, Giorgio. Aggregation of Linear Systems in a Completely Deterministic Framework. **In** *[Willems, J. C.]*, 1989, pp. 358–81.

_____ . Parametrization of Factor Analysis Models. *J. Econometrics*, May 1989, *41*(1), pp. 17–38.

Piccioni, Marco. Distribuzione e quantita' prodotte nell'impostazione classica. (With English summary.) *Studi. Econ.*, 1989, *44*(37), pp. 179–218.

Picciotto, Sol. Slicing a Shadow: Business Taxation in an International Framework. **In** *Hancher, L. and Moran, M., eds.*, 1989, pp. 11–47.

Pichelmann, Karl and Neudorfer, Peter. Measuring Shock Persistence in Austrian Unemployment: A Note. *Empirica*, 1989, *16*(2), pp. 193–208.

Pichler, Eva. Eine Anmerkung zu Incentive-Effekten eines Entlohnungsschemas mit fixen Anteilen am Gesamtprodukt. (A Note on the Inventive Effects of Compensation Schemas with Fixed Shares on Output. With English summary.) *Z. Wirtschaft. Sozialwissen.*, 1989, *109*(3), pp. 421–30.

Picht, Hartmut and Nunnenkamp, Peter. Willful Default by Developing Countries in the 1980s: A Cross-Country Analysis of Major Determinants. *Weltwirtsch. Arch.*, 1989, *125*(4), pp. 681–702.

Pick, Daniel H. and Carter, Colin A. The J-Curve Effect and the U.S. Agricultural Trade Balance. *Amer. J. Agr. Econ.*, August 1989, *71*(3), pp. 712–20.

Pickett, John C. and Kluender, Richard A. Public Policy Implications for the Supply of Pine Sawlogs. *Natural Res. J.*, Summer 1989, *29*(3), pp. 723–35.

Pickles, A. R. and O'Farrell, P. N. Entrepreneurial Behaviour within Male Work Histories: A Sector-Specific Analysis. *Environ. Planning A*, March 1989, *21*(3), pp. 311–31.

Picory, Christian. Orthodoxie libérale et hétérodoxie marginaliste: Clément Colson. (Liberal Orthodoxy and Marginalist Heterodoxy: Clement Colson. With English summary.) *Revue Écon.*, July 1989, *40*(4), pp. 679–707.

Picot, Arnold and Kaulmann, Thomas. Comparative Performance of Government-Owned and Privately-Owned Industrial Corporations—Empirical Results from Six Countries. *J. Inst. Theoretical Econ.*, June 1989, *145*(2), pp. 298–316.

Piddington, Kenneth. The Bank and the Environment: Questions and Answers. *Finance Devel.*, September 1989, *26*(3), pp. 44–45.

Pieper, Paul J. Construction Price Statistics Revisited. **In** *Jorgenson, D. W. and Landau, R., eds.*, 1989, pp. 293–330.

_____ . Why Construction Industry Productivity Is Declining: Comment. *Rev. Econ. Statist.*, August 1989, *71*(3), pp. 543–46.

_____ **and Eisner, Robert.** Inflation-Adjusted Government Budget Deficits and Real Economic Activity: Rejoinder. *Ann. Écon. Statist.*, Jan.–March 1989, (13), pp. 139–47.

Pieptea, Dan R. Decision Support Systems for Bond Portfolio Management: A Review of Underlying Theory and Empirical Work. **In** *Lee, C. F., ed.*, 1989, pp. 95–120.

———. A Shortcut to Itô's Lemma for Financial Applications: The Case of Hedging with Interest Rate Futures. *Finance*, December 1989, *10*(2), pp. 51–58.

——— and Merville, Larry J. Stock-Price Volatility, Mean-Reverting Diffusion, and Noise. *J. Finan. Econ.*, September 1989, *24*(1), pp. 193–214.

Pierani, Pierpaolo and Frohberg, Klaus K. Impact of CAP Trade Liberalization on Agricultural Supply. In *Tarditi, S., et al., eds.*, 1989, pp. 123–41.

Pierce, David A. Sensitivity Analysis of Seasonal Adjustments: Empirical Case Studies: Comment. *J. Amer. Statist. Assoc.*, March 1989, *84*(405), pp. 21–22.

Pierse, Richard G.; Kumar, Mohan S. and Pesaran, M. Hashem. Econometric Analysis of Aggregation in the Context of Linear Prediction Models. *Econometrica*, July 1989, *57*(4), pp. 861–88.

——— and Pesaran, M. Hashem. A Proof of the Asymptotic Validity of a Test for Perfect Aggregation. *Econ. Letters*, 1989, *30*(1), pp. 41–47.

Pieters, Rik G. M. A Note on Cost in Economic Psychology. *J. Econ. Psych.*, 1989, *10*(4), pp. 441–55.

Piganiol, Claude. Industrial Relations and Enterprise Restructuring in France. *Int. Lab. Rev.*, 1989, *128*(5), pp. 621–38.

Piggott, John. Wealth Taxation for Australia. *Australian Tax Forum*, 1989, *6*(3), pp. 327–46.

Piggott, Roley R. and Fleming, Euan M. Assessment of Policy Options for Agricultural Export Stabilization in the South Pacific. *J. Developing Areas*, January 1989, *23*(2), pp. 271–89.

Pigott, Charles. Economic Consequences of Continued U.S. External Deficits. *Fed. Res. Bank New York Quart. Rev.*, Winter–Spring 1989, *13-14*(4–1), pp. 4–15.

———; Rodrigues, Anthony P. and Hung, Juann. Financial Implications of the U.S. External Deficit. *Fed. Res. Bank New York Quart. Rev.*, Winter–Spring 1989, *13-14*(4–1), pp. 33–51.

Piha, Kalevi. Organization Structure and Changing Marketing. *Liiketaloudellinen Aikak.*, 1989, *38*(2), pp. 71–81.

Pihlanto, Pekka. Holistinen ihmiskäsitys ja johdon laskentatoimen tutkimuksen aktorinäkemys. (The Holistic Concept of Man and the Notion of an Actor in Management Accounting Research. With English summary.) *Liiketaloudellinen Aikak.*, 1989, *38*(2), pp. 117–41.

van der Pijl, Kees. The Capitalist Class: The International Level. In *Bottomore, T. and Brym, R. J., eds.*, 1989, pp. 237–66.

Pike, John. Recent Developments in Space Weapons. In *Altmann, J. and Rotblat, J., eds.*, 1989, pp. 114–20.

———. Threshold Limits on Anti-missile Systems. In *Rotblat, J. and Goldanskii, V. I., eds.*, 1989, pp. 25–33.

Pike, Richard and Sharp, John. Trends in the Use of Management Science Techniques in Capital Budgeting. *Managerial Dec. Econ.*, June 1989, *10*(2), pp. 135–40.

Pikkarainen, Pentti and Virén, Matti. Granger Causality between Money, Output, Prices and Interest Rates: Some Cross-country Evidence from the Period 1875–1984. *Weltwirtsch. Arch.*, 1989, *125*(1), pp. 74–82.

Pikoulakis, Emmanuel. Efficient and Credible Exchange Rate and Monetary Policies for Stabilising the Economy. *Greek Econ. Rev.*, 1989, *11*(2), pp. 305–22.

———. The Exchange Rate and the Current Account When Prices Evolve Sluggishly: A Simplification of the Dynamics and a Reconciliation with the Absorption Approach. In *MacDonald, R. and Taylor, M. P., eds.*, 1989, pp. 178–94.

Pillarisetti, Janaki Ram and Chang, Yang-Ming. Debt and the Developing Countries: A Note on Optimal International Borrowing. *J. Devel. Stud.*, July 1989, *25*(4), pp. 576–79.

Pinch, S. P. The Restructuring Thesis and the Study of Public Services. *Environ. Planning A*, July 1989, *21*(7), pp. 905–26.

Pinckney, Thomas C. The Multiple Effects of Procurement Price on Production and Procurement of Wheat in Pakistan. *Pakistan Devel. Rev.*, Summer 1989, *28*(2), pp. 95–119.

——— and Valdés, Alberto. Trade and Macroeconomic Policies' Impact on Agricultural Growth: Evidence To-date. *Eastern Afr. Econ. Rev.*, June 1989, *5*(1), pp. 42–61.

Pinder, John. The Single Market: A Step towards European Union. In *Lodge, J., ed.*, 1989, pp. 94–110.

Pindyck, Robert S. and Majd, Saman. The Learning Curve and Optimal Production under Uncertainty. *Rand J. Econ.*, Autumn 1989, *20*(3), pp. 331–43.

Pinegar, J. Michael and Chang, Eric C. Seasonal Fluctuations in Industrial Production and Stock Market Seasonals. *J. Finan. Quant. Anal.*, March 1989, *24*(1), pp. 59–74.

Pines, David and Papageorgiou, Yorgos Y. The Exponential Density Function: First Principles, Comparative Statics, and Empirical Evidence. *J. Urban Econ.*, September 1989, *26*(2), pp. 264–68.

———; Schwartz, Abba and Eldor, Rafael. Determinants of an Individual's Demand for Hedging Instruments. *J. Futures Markets*, April 1989, *9*(2), pp. 135–41.

Pinheiro, Armando Castelar and Matesco, Virene. Relação capital/produto incremental: Estimativas para o período 1948/87. (With English summary.) *Pesquisa Planejamento Econ.*, December 1989, *19*(3), pp. 597–612.

de Piniés, Jaime. Debt Sustainability and Overadjustment. *World Devel.*, January 1989, *17*(1), pp. 29–43.

Pink, George H. Government Restriction on Foreign Investment by Pension Funds: An Empirical Evaluation. *Can. Public Policy*, September 1989, *15*(3), pp. 300–312.

Pinkerton, Evelyn. Attaining Better Fisheries Management through Co-management—Prospects, Problems, and Propositions. In *Pinkerton, E., ed.*, 1989, pp. 3–33.

_____; Rettig, R. Bruce and Berkes, Fikret. The Future of Fisheries Co-management: A Multidisciplinary Assessment. In *Pinkerton, E., ed.,* 1989, pp. 273–89.

Pinstrup-Andersen, Per. Prevalence of Malnutrition and Dietary Deficiencies as They Relate to Health and Performance Problems. In *Helmuth, J. W. and Johnson, S. R., eds., Vol. 2,* 1989, pp. 201–18.

_____. World Hunger, Malnutrition, and Food Production and Distribution Systems: Reaction. In *Helmuth, J. W. and Johnson, S. R., eds., Vol. 1,* 1989, pp. 191–93.

_____ and Jaramillo, Mauricio. The Impact of Drought and Technological Change in Rice Production on Intrayear Fluctuations in Food Consumption: The Case of North Arcot, India. In *Sahn, D. E., ed.,* 1989, pp. 264–84.

Pinto Barbosa, António S. and Buchanan, James M. Convexity Constraints in Public Goods Theory. In *Buchanan, J. M. (II),* 1989, pp. 218–27.

Pinto, Brian. Black Market Premia, Exchange Rate Unification, and Inflation in Sub-Saharan Africa. *World Bank Econ. Rev.,* September 1989, 3(3), pp. 321–38.

_____ and Kharas, Homi. Exchange Rate Rules, Black Market Premia and Fiscal Deficits: The Bolivian Hyperinflation. *Rev. Econ. Stud.,* July 1989, 56(3), pp. 435–47.

Pinto-Duschinsky, Michael. Trends in British Political Funding, 1979–84. In *Alexander, H. E., ed.,* 1989, pp. 24–50.

Pinto, James V. and Hildred, William M. Estimates of Passive Tax Expenditures, 1984. *J. Econ. Issues,* March 1989, 23(1), pp. 93–106.

Piontek, E. Polish Foreign Investment Law 1988. *J. World Trade,* October 1989, 23(5), pp. 5–26.

Piore, Michael J. Fissure and Discontinuity in U.S. Labor Management Relations. In *Rosenberg, S., ed.,* 1989, pp. 47–61.

Piotrowski, Wiktor and Sysło, Maciej M. A Characterization of Centroidal Graphs. In *Simeone, B., ed.,* 1989, pp. 272–81.

Pipe, G. Russell. International Views on the Tradeability of Telecommunications. In *Robinson, P.; Sauvant, K. P. and Govitrikar, V. P., eds.,* 1989, pp. 121–27.

Pippenger, John and Davutyan, Nurhan. Excess Returns and Official Intervention: Canada 1952–1960. *Econ. Inquiry,* July 1989, 27(3), pp. 489–500.

_____ and Maasoumi, Esfandiar. Transaction Costs and the Interest Parity Theorem: Comment. *J. Polit. Econ.,* February 1989, 97(1), pp. 236–43.

Pirchi, Anat and Fershtman, Chaim. Perceived Wealth and Government Bonds: A Diagrammatic Exposition. *Amer. Economist,* Spring 1989, 33(1), pp. 83–86.

Piron, Robert. Good Asset Management: A Real Laffer. *Challenge,* Nov.–Dec. 1989, 32(6), pp. 56–57.

_____. A Note on Non-Archimedean Utility with Moral Dimensions. *Indian Econ. J.,* April–June 1989, 36(4), pp. 75–79.

_____. Rationing Medical Care: Tragic Choices and Fundamental Values. *Challenge,* May–June 1989, 32(3), pp. 50–51.

Pisano, Gary P. Using Equity Participation to Support Exchange: Evidence from the Biotechnology Industry. *J. Law, Econ., Organ.,* Spring 1989, 5(1), pp. 109–26.

_____ and Teece, David J. Collaborative Arrangements and Global Technology Strategy: Some Evidence from the Telecommunications Equipment Industry. In *Rosenbloom, R. S. and Burgelman, R. A., eds.,* 1989, pp. 227–56.

Pissarides, Christopher A. Unemployment and Macroeconomics. *Economica,* February 1989, 56(221), pp. 1–14.

_____. Unemployment Consequences of an Aging Population: An Application of Insider–Outsider Theory. *Europ. Econ. Rev.,* March 1989, 33(2/3), pp. 355–66.

_____; Jackman, R. and Layard, Richard. On Vacancies. *Oxford Bull. Econ. Statist.,* November 1989, 51(4), pp. 377–94.

_____; Meghir, Costas and Ioannides, Yannis M. Female Participation and Male Unemployment Duration in Greece: Evidence from the Labour Force Survey. *Europ. Econ. Rev.,* March 1989, 33(2/3), pp. 395–406.

_____ and Wadsworth, Jonathan. Unemployment and the Inter-regional Mobility of Labour. *Econ. J.,* September 1989, 99(397), pp. 739–55.

_____ and Weber, Guglielmo. An Expenditure-Based Estimate of Britain's Black Economy. *J. Public Econ.,* June 1989, 39(1), pp. 17–32.

Pitcher, Hugh M. IQ and Lead Exposure: Analytic Issues Arising in the Water Lead and Gasoline Lead Standards. *Amer. J. Agr. Econ.,* May 1989, 71(2), pp. 475–79.

Pitchford, John D. Optimum Borrowing and the Current Account When There Are Fluctuations in Income. *J. Int. Econ.,* May 1989, 26(3/4), pp. 345–58.

_____. A Sceptical View of Australia's Current Account and Debt Problem. *Australian Econ. Rev.,* Winter 1989, (86), pp. 5–14.

Pitelis, Christos N. The Transnational Corporation: A Synthesis. *Rev. Radical Polit. Econ.,* Winter 1989, 21(4), pp. 1–11.

Pitkänen, K. J.; Mielke, J. H. and Jorde, L. B. Smallpox and Its Eradication in Finland: Implications for Disease Control. *Population Stud.,* March 1989, 43(1), pp. 95–111.

Pitt, Mark M. and Slemrod, Joel. The Compliance Cost of Itemizing Deductions: Evidence from Individual Tax Returns. *Amer. Econ. Rev.,* December 1989, 79(5), pp. 1224–32.

Pitt, Martyn. Corporate Birth, Crisis and Rebirth: The Emergence of Four Small UK Service Firms. In *Mansfield, R., ed.,* 1989, pp. 262–77.

Pittman, Russell. On Predation and Victimless Crime: A Comment. *Antitrust Bull.,* Spring 1989, 34(1), pp. 231–34.

Plambeck, Donald L. The Implication of Board Member Composition for Fund-Raising Success. In *Herman, R. D. and Van Til, J., eds.,* 1989, pp. 60–66.

Plambeck, T. and Gangolli, A. A Note on Periodicity in Some Octal Games. *Int. J. Game Theory,* 1989, *18*(3), pp. 311–20.

Plane, David A. The Interregional Impacts of U.S. Core–Periphery Net Migration. In *Gibson, L. J. and Stimson, R. J., eds.,* 1989, pp. 33–46.

———. Population Migration and Economic Restructuring in the United States. *Int. Reg. Sci. Rev.,* 1989, *12*(3), pp. 263–80.

Planting, Mark A. The History and Development of the U.S. Annual Input–Output Accounts. In *Franz, A. and Rainer, N., eds.,* 1989, pp. 215–31.

Plasman, Robert. Les politiques d'emploi en Belgique: Analyse et estimation de leur impact macroéconomique. (With English summary.) *Cah. Écon. Bruxelles,* 2nd Trimester 1989, (122), pp. 133–74.

———; **Guillaume, Y. and Meulders, Danièle.** Simulation des impacts de l'achèvement du marché intérieur. Le cas de la Belgique. (With English summary.) *Cah. Écon. Bruxelles,* 4th Trimester 1989, (124), pp. 449–73.

Plassard, Jean-Michel. Discrimination statistique et marché du travail. (With English summary.) *Rech. Écon. Louvain,* 1989, *55*(2), pp. 177–202.

——— **and Vincens, Jean.** Âge, emploi, salaire. (With English summary.) *Revue Écon. Politique,* May–June 1989, *99*(3), pp. 393–45.

Plasschaert, Sylvain R. The Relative Merits of Schedular, Global and Dualistic Patterns of Income Taxation. In *Chiancone, A. and Messere, K., eds.,* 1989, pp. 53–71.

Plath, D. Anthony and Nunnally, Bennie H., Jr. Leasing versus Borrowing: Evaluating Alternative Forms of Consumer Credit. *J. Cons. Aff.,* Winter 1989, *23*(2), pp. 383–92.

Platt, D. C. M. Social Welfare, 1850–1950: Australia, Argentina and Canada Compared: Introduction. In *Platt, D. C. M., ed.,* 1989, pp. 1–21.

Platt, Harlan D. The Determinants of Interindustry Failure. *J. Econ. Bus.,* May 1989, *41*(2), pp. 107–26.

——— **and Platt, Marjorie A.** Failure in the Oil Patch: An Examination of the Production and Oil Field Services Industries. *Energy J.,* July 1989, *10*(3), pp. 35–49.

——— **and Welch, Jonathan B.** Factors that Influence Public Utility Performance. *Energy Econ.,* July 1989, *11*(3), pp. 219–27.

Platt, Harold L. The Cost of Energy: Technological Change, Rate Structures, and Public Policy in Chicago, 1880–1920. *Urban Stud.,* February 1989, *26*(1), pp. 32–44.

Platt, Marjorie A. and Platt, Harlan D. Failure in the Oil Patch: An Examination of the Production and Oil Field Services Industries. *Energy J.,* July 1989, *10*(3), pp. 35–49.

Please, Stanley; Landell-Mills, Pierre and Agarwala, Ramgopal. From Crisis to Sustainable Growth in Sub-Saharan Africa. *Finance Devel.,* December 1989, *26*(4), pp. 26–29.

Plein, L. Christopher and Webber, David J. Biotechnology and Agriculture in the Congressional Policy Arena. In *Krämer, C. S., ed.,* 1989, pp. 179–200.

Pleskovic, Boris. Interindustry Flows in a General Equilibrium Model of Fiscal Incidence: An Application to Egypt. *J. Policy Modeling,* Spring 1989, *11*(1), pp. 157–77.

Plessis, Alain. La Révolution et les banques en France: De la Caisse d'escompte à la Banque de France. (The Revolution and the Banks in France: From the *Caisse d'escompte* to the Bank of France. With English summary.) *Revue Écon.,* November 1989, *40*(6), pp. 1001–14.

Pletcher, James. Rice and Padi Market Management in West Malaysia, 1957–1986. *J. Developing Areas,* April 1989, *23*(3), pp. 363–83.

Plewes, Thomas J. The Statistics Corner. *Bus. Econ.,* October 1989, *24*(4), pp. 49–51.

Plewis, I. F. School Roll Forecasts: Their Uses, Their Accuracy and Educational Reform: Comments. *J. Roy. Statist. Society,* 1989, *152*(3), pp. 301–02.

Pliskin, Jeffrey and Jones, Derek C. British Evidence on the Employment Effects of Profit Sharing. *Ind. Relat.,* Spring 1989, *28*(2), pp. 276–98.

Ploberger, Werner. The Local Power of the CUSUM-SQ Test against Heteroscedasticity. In *Hackl, P., ed.,* 1989, pp. 127–33.

———; **Krämer, Walter and Alt, Raimund.** A Modification of the CUSUM Test in the Linear Regression Model with Lagged Dependent Variables. In *Kramer, W., ed.,* 1989, pp. 1–11.

———; **Krämer, Walter and Alt, Raimund.** A Modification of the CUSUM Test in the Linear Regression Model with Lagged Dependent Variables. *Empirical Econ.,* 1989, *14*(2), pp. 65–75.

———; **Krämer, Walter and Kontrus, Karl.** A New Test for Structural Stability in the Linear Regression Model. *J. Econometrics,* February 1989, *40*(2), pp. 307–18.

van der Ploeg, Frederick. Disposable Income, Unemployment, Inflation and State Spending in a Dynamic Political–Economic Model. *Public Choice,* March 1989, *60*(3), pp. 211–39.

———. The Political Economy of Overvaluation. *Econ. J.,* September 1989, *99*(397), pp. 850–55.

———. The Use of Simple Rules for International Policy Agreements: Discussion. In *Miller, M.; Eichengreen, B. and Portes, R., eds.,* 1989, pp. 321–24.

——— **and van de Klundert, Theo.** Fiscal Policy and Finite Lives in Interdependent Economies with Real and Nominal Wage Rigidity. *Oxford Econ. Pap.,* July 1989, *41*(3), pp. 459–89.

——— **and van de Klundert, Theo.** Wage Rigidity and Capital Mobility in an Optimizing Model of a Small Open Economy. *De Economist,* 1989, *137*(1), pp. 47–75.

_____ and ten Raa, Thijs. A Statistical Approach to the Problem of Negatives in Input–Output Analysis. *Econ. Modelling*, January 1989, *6*(1), pp. 2–19.

_____ and de Zeeuw, Aart J. Conflict over Arms Accumulation in Market and Command Economies. In *[Verheyen, P.]*, 1989, pp. 91–119.

_____ and de Zeeuw, Aart J. Dynamic Policy Games in Economics: Introduction. In *[Verheyen, P.]*, 1989, pp. 1–8.

Ploix, Hélène. The World Economic and Financial System: Progress in International Coordination and Debt Financing. In *Kaushik, S. K., ed.*, 1989, pp. 67–80.

Plosser, Charles I. Risk, Exchange Market Intervention, and Private Speculative Behavior in a Small Open Economy: Commentary. In *Stone, C. C., ed.*, 1989, pp. 73–75.

_____. Understanding Real Business Cycles. *J. Econ. Perspectives*, Summer 1989, *3*(3), pp. 51–77.

Plotnick, Robert D. How Much Poverty Is Reduced by State Income Transfers? *Mon. Lab. Rev.*, July 1989, *112*(7), pp. 21–26.

_____. Poverty and Income Transfer Policy at the State Level. *Growth Change*, Fall 1989, *20*(4), pp. 41–50.

Plott, Charles R. An Updated Review of Industrial Organization: Applications of Experimental Methods. In *Schmalensee, R. and Willig, R. D., eds., Vol. 2*, 1989, pp. 1109–76.

_____ and Johnson, Michael D. The Effect of Two Trading Institutions on Price Expectations and the Stability of Supply-Response Lag Markets. *J. Econ. Psych.*, June 1989, *10*(2), pp. 189–216.

Plourde, André and Waverman, Leonard. Canadian Energy Trade: The Past and the Future. In *Watkins, G. C., ed.*, 1989, pp. 141–80.

Plourde, Charles and Smith, J. Barry. Crop Sharing in the Fishery and Industry Equilibrium. *Marine Resource Econ.*, 1989, *6*(3), pp. 179–93.

_____ and Yeung, David. Harvesting of a Transboundary Replenishable Fish Stock: A Noncooperative Game Solution. *Marine Resource Econ.*, 1989, *6*(1), pp. 57–70.

_____ and Yeung, David. A Model of Industrial Pollution in a Stochastic Environment. *J. Environ. Econ. Manage.*, March 1989, *16*(2), pp. 97–105.

Plumb of Coleshill [Lord]. Food and Agricultural Policy Issues of the European Community. In *Helmuth, J. W. and Johnson, S. R., eds., Vol. 1*, 1989, pp. 17–24.

Plumlee, R. David; Chow, Chee W. and McNamee, Alan H. Focusing Audit Aids for Enhanced Audit Efficiency and Effectiveness. In *Gangolly, J., ed.*, 1989, pp. 195–204.

_____ and Moeckel, Cindy L. Auditors' Confidence in Recognition of Audit Evidence. *Accounting Rev.*, October 1989, *64*(4), pp. 653–66.

Plummer, Mark and Mathios, Alan D. The Regulation of Advertising by the Federal Trade Commission: Capital Market Effects. In *Zerbe, R. O., ed.*, 1989, pp. 77–93.

Png, Ivan P. L. Reservations: Customer Insurance in the Marketing of Capacity. *Marketing Sci.*, Summer 1989, *8*(3), pp. 248–64.

_____ and Mookherjee, Dilip. Optimal Auditing, Insurance, and Redistribution. *Quart. J. Econ.*, May 1989, *104*(2), pp. 399–415.

_____ and Zolt, Eric M. Efficient Deterrence and the Tax Treatment of Monetary Sanctions. *Int. Rev. Law Econ.*, December 1989, *9*(2), pp. 209–17.

Poddar, Satya N. Integration of Tax Expenditures into the Expenditure Management System: The Canadian Experience. In *Bruce, N., ed.*, 1989, pp. 259–68.

_____ and Harley, Nancy. Problems in Moving from a Flawed to a Neutral and Broad-Based Consumption Tax: The Canadian Experience. *Australian Tax Forum*, 1989, *6*(3), pp. 303–26.

_____ and Watson, Vinita. Problems of Transition and of Implementation of Different Revenue Structures. In *Chiancone, A. and Messere, K., eds.*, 1989, pp. 265–84.

Podgursky, Michael and Swaim, Paul. Do More-Educated Workers Fare Better Following Job Displacement? *Mon. Lab. Rev.*, August 1989, *112*(8), pp. 43–46.

Podkaminer, Leon. Corrigendum [Disequilibrium in Poland's Consumer Markets: Further Evidence on Intermarket Spillovers]. *J. Compar. Econ.*, December 1989, *13*(4), pp. 583.

_____. Macroeconomic Disequilibrium in Centrally Planned Economies: Identifiability of Econometric Models Based on the Theory of Household Behavior under Quantity Constraints. *J. Compar. Econ.*, March 1989, *13*(1), pp. 47–60.

_____. Macroeconomic Disequilibrium in Centrally Planned Economies: Reply. *J. Compar. Econ.*, December 1989, *13*(4), pp. 580–82.

Podrecca, Elena and Neri, Fabio. Dalla curva di beveridge ad una matrice per qualifiche. (From the Beveridge Curve to a Job Category Matrix. With English summary.) *Econ. Lavoro*, July–Sept. 1989, *23*(3), pp. 87–98.

Podsakoff, Philip M. and Williams, Larry J. Longitudinal Field Methods for Studying Reciprocal Relationships in Organizational Behavior Research: Toward Improved Casual Analysis. In *Cummings, L. L. and Staw, B. M., eds.*, 1989, pp. 247–92.

Pogány, Ágnes. From the Cradle to the Grave? Banking and Industry in Budapest in the 1910s and 1920s. *J. Europ. Econ. Hist.*, Winter 1989, *18*(3), pp. 529–49.

Pogorel, Gérard. Information Technology from Social Impact to Social Input: A European Perspective. In *Jussawalla, M.; Okuma, T. and Araki, T., eds.*, 1989, pp. 205–11.

Pogue, Thomas F. and Sgontz, Larry G. Taxing to Control Social Costs: The Case of Alcohol. *Amer. Econ. Rev.*, March 1989, *79*(1), pp. 235–43.

Pohl, Gerhard. Trade Policymaking in China. In *Nau, H. R., ed.*, 1989, pp. 51–68.

Pöhl, Karl Otto. Preconditions for the Creation of a European Currency. In *Franz, O., ed.*, 1989, pp. 109–17.

Pohlmeier, Winfried and König, Heinz. Worksharing and Factor Prices: A Comparison of Three Flexible Functional Forms for Nonlinear Cost Schemes. *J. Inst. Theoretical Econ.*, June 1989, *145*(2), pp. 343–57.

Poiesz, Theo B. C. The Image Concept: Its Place in Consumer Psychology. *J. Econ. Psych.*, 1989, *10*(4), pp. 457–72.

Poirier, Dale J. A Report from the Battlefront. *J. Bus. Econ. Statist.*, January 1989, 7(1), pp. 137–39.

Poitevin, Michel. Collusion and the Banking Structure of a Duopoly. *Can. J. Econ.*, May 1989, *22*(2), pp. 263–77.

_____. Financial Signalling and the "Deep-Pocket" Argument. *Rand J. Econ.*, Spring 1989, *20*(1), pp. 26–40.

Poitras, Geoffrey. Do Changes in Debt Maturity Composition Affect the Term Structure? Some Canadian Evidence. *Appl. Econ.*, April 1989, *21*(4), pp. 553–66.

_____. The Market Value of Government of Canada Debt: A Comment on the Importance of Correct Valuation of Non-marketable Debt. *Can. J. Econ.*, May 1989, *22*(2), pp. 395–405.

_____. Optimal Futures Spread Positions. *J. Futures Markets*, April 1989, *9*(2), pp. 123–33.

Pola, Giancarlo and Brosio, Giorgio. A Survey of Various Attempts to Explain the Distribution of Tax Revenues among Levels of Government. In *Chiancone, A. and Messere, K., eds.*, 1989, pp. 403–20.

Polachek, Dora E. and Polachek, Solomon W. An Indirect Test of Children's Influence on Efficiencies in Parental Consumer Behavior. *J. Cons. Aff.*, Summer 1989, *23*(1), pp. 91–110.

Polachek, Solomon W. and Polachek, Dora E. An Indirect Test of Children's Influence on Efficiencies in Parental Consumer Behavior. *J. Cons. Aff.*, Summer 1989, *23*(1), pp. 91–110.

Polak, Jacques J. The Role of International Institutions in Surveillance and Policy Coordination: Comment. In *Bryant, R. C., et al., eds.*, 1989, pp. 368–80.

_____. Strengthening the Role of the IMF in the International Monetary System. In *Gwin, C. and Feinberg, R. E., eds.*, 1989, pp. 45–68.

Polanski, Boris and Tellier, Luc-Normand. The Weber Problem: Frequency of Different Solution Types and Extension to Repulsive Forces and Dynamic Processes. *J. Reg. Sci.*, August 1989, *29*(3), pp. 387–405.

Polasek, Wolfgang. Local Autoregression Models for Detection of Changes in Causality. In *Hackl, P., ed.*, 1989, pp. 407–40.

_____ and Pötzelberger, Klaus. Robust Bayesian Analysis of a Parameter Change in Linear Regression. In *Kramer, W., ed.*, 1989, pp. 59–73.

_____ and Pötzelberger, Klaus. Robust Bayesian Analysis of a Parameter Change in Linear Re-

gression. *Empirical Econ.*, 1989, *14*(2), pp. 123–37.

Polemarchakis, H. M. and Donsimoni, Marie-Paule. Intertemporal Equilibrium and Disadvantageous Growth. *Europ. Econ. Rev.*, January 1989, *33*(1), pp. 59–65.

_____ and Dutta, J. Credit Constraints and Investment Finance: Some Evidence from Greece. In *Monti, M., ed.*, 1989, pp. 158–82.

Polenske, Karen R. Historical and New International Perspectives on Input–Output Accounts. In *Miller, R. E.; Polenske, K. R. and Rose, A. Z., eds.*, 1989, pp. 37–50.

_____. System of Input–Output Accounts for Corporate Planning. In *Franz, A. and Rainer, N., eds.*, 1989, pp. 375–88.

Polese, Mario and Verreault, Roger. Trade in Information-Intensive Services: How and Why Regions Develop Export Advantages. *Can. Public Policy*, December 1989, *15*(4), pp. 376–86.

Poli, Giorgio; Basevi, Giorgio and Kind, Paolo. International Co-operation of Monetary Policies and Confrontation of Commercial and Financial Policies: An Application to U.S.–EC Relations and to Problems of the European Monetary System. In *Hodgman, D. R. and Wood, G. E., eds.*, 1989, pp. 217–49.

Polich, C. L. and Iversen, L. H. The Provision of Long-Term Care in Risk-Based HMOs. In *Scheffler, R. M. and Rossiter, L. F., eds.*, 1989, pp. 351–60.

Polinsky, A. Mitchell and Rubinfeld, Daniel L. A Note on Optimal Public Enforcement with Settlements and Litigation Costs. In *Zerbe, R. O., ed.*, 1989, pp. 1–8.

_____ and Shavell, Steven. Legal Error, Litigation, and the Incentive to Obey the Law. *J. Law, Econ., Organ.*, Spring 1989, *5*(1), pp. 99–108.

Polivka, Anne E. and Nardone, Thomas. On the Definition of "Contingent Work." *Mon. Lab. Rev.*, December 1989, *112*(12), pp. 9–16.

Pollack, Gerald A. and Nicolich, Lillian. The Business Economist at Work: Overseas Shipholding Group. *Bus. Econ.*, July 1989, *24*(3), pp. 48–51.

Pollack, Molly. Poverty and the Labour Market in Costa Rica. In *Rodgers, G., ed.*, 1989, pp. 65–80.

_____ and López M., Cecilia. The Incorporation of Women in Development Policies. *CEPAL Rev.*, December 1989, (39), pp. 37–46.

_____ and Uthoff, Andras. Poverty and the Labour Market: Greater Santiago, 1969–85. In *Rodgers, G., ed.*, 1989, pp. 117–43.

Pollack, Robert A. Consumer Durables in a Cost-of-Living Index. In *Pollak, R. A.*, 1989, pp. 186–89.

_____. Group Cost-of-Living Indexes. In *Pollak, R. A.*, 1989, *1980*, pp. 119–27.

_____. The Intertemporal Cost-of-Living Index. In *Pollak, R. A.*, 1989, *1975*, pp. 70–89.

_____. Mortgage Interest Rates in the CPI. In *Pollak, R. A.*, 1989, pp. 190–92.

_____. The Social Cost-of-Living Index. In *Pollak, R. A.*, 1989, *1981*, pp. 128–52.

_____. Subindexes in the Cost-of-Living Index. In *Pollak, R. A.*, 1989, *1975*, pp. 53–69.

_____. The Theory of the Cost-of-Living Index. In *Pollak, R. A.*, 1989, *1983*, pp. 3–52.

_____. The Treatment of "Quality" in the Cost-of-Living Index. In *Pollak, R. A.*, 1989, *1983*, pp. 153–80.

_____. The Treatment of Taxes in the Consumer Price Index. In *Pollak, R. A.*, 1989, pp. 193–99.

_____. The Treatment of the Environment in the Cost-of-Living Index. In *Pollak, R. A.*, 1989, pp. 181–85.

_____. Welfare Comparisons and Equivalence Scales. In *Pollak, R. A.*, 1989, *1979*, pp. 111–18.

_____. Welfare Evaluation and the Cost-of-Living Index in the Household Production Model. In *Pollak, R. A.*, 1989, *1978*, pp. 90–110.

_____; **Taubman, Paul and Behrman, Jere R.** Family Resources, Family Size, and Access to Financing for College Education. *J. Polit. Econ.*, April 1989, *97*(2), pp. 398–419.

Pollakowski, Henry O. Housing Patterns and Mobility of the Aged: The United States and West Germany: Comment. In *Wise, D. A., ed.*, 1989, pp. 115–18.

Pollard, David and Pakes, Ariel. Simulation and the Asymptotics of Optimization Estimators. *Econometrica*, September 1989, *57*(5), pp. 1027–57.

Pollard, Stephen K. Pacific Atoll Economies. *Asian-Pacific Econ. Lit.*, March 1989, *3*(1), pp. 65–83.

_____ **and Canarella, Giorgio.** Unanticipated Monetary Growth, Output, and the Price Level in Latin America: An Empirical Investigation. *J. Devel. Econ.*, April 1989, *30*(2), pp. 345–58.

Pollard, W. A.; Alpert, W. T. and Greenberg, E. Statistical Properties of Data Stretching. *J. Appl. Econometrics*, Oct.–Dec. 1989, *4*(4), pp. 383–91.

Pollin, Robert. Debt-Dependent Growth and Financial Innovation: Instability in the United States and Latin America. In *MacEwan, A. and Tabb, W. K., eds.*, 1989, pp. 121–44.

_____. Growing Federal Deficits and Declining U.S. Growth: What Is the Connection? *Rev. Radical Polit. Econ.*, Fall 1989, *21*(3), pp. 51–57.

Pollio, Howard R.; Thompson, Craig J. and Locander, William B. Putting Consumer Experience Back into Consumer Research: The Philosophy and Method of Existential-Phenomenology. *J. Cons. Res.*, September 1989, *16*(2), pp. 133–46.

Pollock, Andrew C. A Model of UK Real Effective Exchange Rate Behaviour. *Appl. Econ.*, December 1989, *21*(12), pp. 1563–87.

Pollock, Richard L. and Moncur, James E. T. Scarcity Rents for Water: A Valuation and Pricing Model: Reply. *Land Econ.*, November 1989, *65*(4), pp. 425–28.

Polonchek, John; Slovin, Myron B. and Sushka, Marie E. Valuation Effects of Commercial Bank Securities Offerings: A Test of the Information Hypothesis. *J. Banking Finance*, July 1989, *13*(3), pp. 443–61.

Polterovich, V. M. and Khenkin, G. M. An Evolutionary Model with Interaction between Development and Adoption of New Technologies. *Matekon*, Fall 1989, *26*(1), pp. 3–19.

Pomfret, Richard. The Economics of Voluntary Export Restraint Agreements. *J. Econ. Surveys*, 1989, *3*(3), pp. 199–211.

_____. The Theory of Preferential Trading Arrangements. In *Jacquemin, A. and Sapir, A., eds.*, 1989, *1986*, pp. 44–70.

_____. Voluntary Export Restraints in the Presence of Monopoly Power. *Kyklos*, 1989, *42*(1), pp. 61–72.

Pommer, Evert and de Groot, Hans. The Stability of Stated Preferences for Public Goods: Evidence from Recent Budget Games. *Public Choice*, February 1989, *60*(2), pp. 123–32.

Pommerehne, Werner W. and Frey, Bruno S. Art Investment: An Empirical Inquiry. *Southern Econ. J.*, October 1989, *56*(2), pp. 396–409.

_____ **and Weck-Hannemann, Hannelore.** Einkommensteuerhinterziehung in der Schweiz: Eine empirische Analyse. (Income Tax Evasion in Switzerland: An Empirical Analysis. With English summary.) *Schweiz. Z. Volkswirtsch. Statist.*, December 1989, *125*(4), pp. 515–56.

Pomp, Richard D. The Experience of the Philippines in Taxing Its Nonresident Citizens. In *Bhagwati, J. N. and Wilson, J. D., eds.*, 1989, pp. 43–81.

Pompelli, Greg and Heien, Dale M. The Demand for Alcoholic Beverages: Economic and Demographic Effects. *Southern Econ. J.*, January 1989, *55*(3), pp. 759–70.

Ponssard, Jean-Pierre. Concurrence imparfaite et rendements croissants: Une approche en termes de fair-play. (Imperfect Competition and Increasing Returns: An Approach Using Fairness Considerations. With English summary.) *Ann. Écon. Statist.*, July–Dec. 1989, (15–16), pp. 151–72.

_____ **and Tanguy, Hervé.** Un cadre conceptuel commun à la planification et à la concurrence formalisation théorique et implications pratiques. (With English summary.) *L'Actual. Econ.*, March 1989, *65*(1), pp. 86–104.

du Pont, Pete. Education in America: The Opportunity to Choose. In *Crane, E. H. and Boaz, D.*, 1989, pp. 239–49.

Pontecorvo, Giulio. The State of Worldwide Fishery Statistics: A Modest Proposal: Reply. *Marine Resource Econ.*, 1989, *6*(1), pp. 87–88.

Poole, William. Stability under the Gold Standard in Practice: Comment. In *[Schwartz, A. J.]*, 1989, pp. 195–200.

_____ **and Feinman, Joshua.** Federal Reserve Policymaking: An Overview and Analysis of the Policy Process: Comment. *Carnegie–Rochester Conf. Ser. Public Policy*, Spring 1989, *30*, pp. 63–74.

_____, **et al.** Challenges of Macro Policy in the

Open U.S. Economy. *Contemp. Policy Issues*, January 1989, 7(1), pp. 1–34.

Poos, Jaques F. Strengthening the United States–Europe Partnership. In *Cerami, C. A., ed.*, 1989, pp. 93–102.

Poot, Jacques; Siegers, Jacques J. and van Mourik, Aad. Trends in Occupational Segregation of Women and Men in New Zealand: Some New Evidence. *New Zealand Econ. Pap.*, 1989, 23, pp. 29–50.

Pope, C. Arden, III and Perry, Gregory M. Individual versus Social Discount Rates in Allocating Depletable Natural Resources over Time. *Econ. Letters*, 1989, 29(3), pp. 257–64.

Pope, Clayne L. Households on the American Frontier: The Distribution of Income and Wealth in Utah, 1850–1900. In *Galenson, D. W., ed.*, 1989, pp. 148–89.

_____ **and Galenson, David W.** Economic and Geographic Mobility on the Farming Frontier: Evidence from Appanoose County, Iowa, 1850–1870. *J. Econ. Hist.*, September 1989, 49(3), pp. 635–55.

Pope, Gregory C. Hospital Nonprice Competition and Medicare Reimbursement Policy. *J. Health Econ.*, June 1989, 8(2), pp. 147–72.

_____ **and Hurdle, Sylvia.** Physician Productivity: Trends and Determinants. *Inquiry*, Spring 1989, 26(1), pp. 100–115.

Pope, Jeff. The Compliance Costs of Personal Income Taxation—A Review of the Issues. *Australian Tax Forum*, 1989, 6(2), pp. 125–42.

Pope, Peter F. and Peel, David A. Empirical Evidence on the Properties of Exchange Rate Forecasts and the Risk Premium. *Econ. Letters*, December 1989, 31(4), pp. 387–91.

_____ **and Peel, David A.** Information, Prices and Efficiency in a Fixed-Odds Betting Market. *Economica*, August 1989, 56(223), pp. 323–41.

Pope, Rulon D. and Chambers, Robert G. Price Aggregation When Price-Taking Firms' Prices Vary. *Rev. Econ. Stud.*, April 1989, 56(2), pp. 297–309.

Popescu, Ileana and Rizzoli, Irina. Computation of the Eigenvalues for a Tridiagonal, Symmetric, Real Matrix. *Econ. Computat. Econ. Cybern. Stud. Res.*, 1989, 24(2–3), pp. 85–89.

Popescu, Oreste. Económica Indiana. (The "Indian" Economics in Latin America. With English summary.) *Económica (La Plata)*, 1989, 35(1–2), pp. 37–69.

Popkin, Barry M.; Guilkey, David K. and Haines, Pamela S. Food Consumption Changes of Adult Women between 1977 and 1985. *Amer. J. Agr. Econ.*, November 1989, 71(4), pp. 949–59.

Popkov, Yu S. A New Class of Dynamic Macrosystem Models with Self-reproduction. *Environ. Planning A*, June 1989, 21(6), pp. 739–51.

Popkova, L. Where are the *Pirogi* Meatier? In *Jones, A. and Moskoff, W., eds.*, 1989, 1988, pp. 99–103.

Popov, Gavriil. A Discussion on Problems of Bureaucratism. *Prob. Econ.*, September 1989, 32(5), pp. 6–12.

_____. The Goals and the Mechanism. *Prob. Econ.*, March 1989, 31(11), pp. 33–47.

_____. The Journal and Restructuring. *Prob. Econ.*, February 1989, 31(10), pp. 6–25.

Porell, F.; Gruenberg, L. and Tompkins, C. The Health Status and Utilization Patterns of the Elderly: Implications for Setting Medicare Payments to HMOs. In *Scheffler, R. M. and Rossiter, L. F., eds.*, 1989, pp. 41–73.

Poret, Pierre and Barbone, Luca. Structural Conditions and Macroeconomic Responses to Shocks: A Sensitivity Analysis for Four European Countries. *OECD Econ. Stud.*, Spring 1989, (12), pp. 131–58.

Porket, J. L. Full Employment in Soviet Theory and Practice. *Brit. J. Ind. Relat.*, July 1989, 27(2), pp. 264–79.

Porras, J. International Comparability of Statistics of Education. *Statist. J.*, 1989, 6(3), pp. 223–54.

Porta, Angelo; Bruni, Franco and Penati, Alessandro. Financial Regulation, Implicit Taxes, and Fiscal Adjustment in Italy. In *Monti, M., ed.*, 1989, pp. 197–230.

Porta, Fernando and Chudnovsky, Daniel. On Argentine–Brazilian Economic Integration. *CEPAL Rev.*, December 1989, (39), pp. 115–34.

Porta, Pier Luigi. Adam Smith's Subjective Stance. A Comment on Professor Hutchison's "Before Adam Smith." *Econ. Scelte Pubbliche/ J. Public Finance Public Choice*, Sept.–Dec. 1989, 7(3), pp. 191–201.

Portait, Roland and Allemane, Rémy. L'évaluation et la gestion d'un portefeuille comprenant des contrats MATIF, BTAN et des options sur BTAN et sur contrats MATIF. (Valuation and Management of a Portfolio Including Interest Rate Futures, Bonds and Options on Bonds and Futures. With English summary.) *Finance*, June 1989, 10(1), pp. 41–67.

Portantiero, Juan Carlos. Political and Economic Crises in Argentina. In *di Tella, G. and Dornbusch, R., eds.*, 1989, pp. 16–24.

Porteous, Mike; Barber, John and Metcalfe, Stanley. Barriers to Growth: The ACARD Study. In *Barber, J.; Metcalfe, J. S. and Porteous, M., eds.*, 1989, pp. 1–19.

Porteous, Samuel D. and Verbeke, Alain. The Implementation of Strategic Export Controls in Canada. *Can. Public Policy*, March 1989, 15(1), pp. 12–24.

Porter, David P.; Banks, Jeffrey S. and Ledyard, John O. Allocating Uncertain and Unresponsive Resources: An Experimental Approach. *Rand J. Econ.*, Spring 1989, 20(1), pp. 1–25.

Porter, Douglas R. Financing Infrastructure with Special Districts. In *Matzer, J., Jr., ed.*, 1989, 1987, pp. 162–69.

Porter, Philip K. and Davis, Michael L. A Test for Pure or Apparent Ideology in Congressional Voting. *Public Choice*, February 1989, 60(2), pp. 101–11.

Porter, Richard C. Recent Trends in LDC Military Expenditures. *World Devel.*, October 1989, 17(10), pp. 1573–84.

and Grobar, Lisa M. Benoit Revisited: Defense Spending and Economic Growth in LDCs. *J. Conflict Resolution*, June 1989, *33*(2), pp. 318–45.

Porter, Richard D. and Bayer, Amanda S. Monetary Perspective on Underground Economic Activity in the United States. In *Feige, E. L., ed.*, 1989, pp. 129–57.

and Small, David H. Understanding the Behavior of M2 and V2. *Fed. Res. Bull.*, April 1989, *75*(4), pp. 244–54.

; Small, David H. and Hallman, Jeffrey J. M2 per Unit of Potential GNP as an Anchor for the Price Level. *Fed. Res. Bull.*, April 1989, *75*(4), pp. 263–64.

Porter, Robert H. and Hendricks, Kenneth. Collusion in Auctions. *Ann. Écon. Statist.*, July–Dec. 1989, (15–16), pp. 217–30.

; Spady, Richard H. and Hendricks, Kenneth. Random Reservation Prices and Bidding Behavior in OCS Drainage Auctions. *J. Law Econ.*, Part 2, October 1989, *32*(2), pp. S83–106.

Portes, Alejandro and Castells, Manuel. World Underneath: The Origins, Dynamics, and Effects of the Informal Economy. In *Portes, A.; Castells, M. and Benton, L. A., eds.*, 1989, pp. 11–37.

; Castells, Manuel and Benton, Lauren A. The Policy Implications of Informality: Conclusion. In *Portes, A.; Castells, M. and Benton, L. A., eds.*, 1989, pp. 298–311.

and Johns, Michael. The Polarization of Class and Space in the Contemporary Latin American City. In *Canak, W. L., ed.*, 1989, pp. 111–37.

Portes, Richard. Economic Reforms, International Capital Flows and the Development of the Domestic Capital Market in CPEs. *Europ. Econ. Rev.*, March 1989, *33*(2/3), pp. 466–71.

. Fiscal Adjustment, Debt Management, and Conditionality: Comment. In *Monti, M., ed.*, 1989, pp. 148–50.

. The Monetary Unification Process in 19th-Century Germany: Relevance and Lessons for Europe Today: Discussion. In *De Cecco, M. and Giovannini, A., eds.*, 1989, pp. 241–43.

and Eichengreen, Barry. After the Deluge: Default, Negotiation, and Readjustment during the Interwar Years. In *Eichengreen, B. and Lindert, P. H., eds.*, 1989, pp. 12–47.

and Eichengreen, Barry. Dealing with Debt: The 1930s and the 1980s. In *Husain, I. and Diwan, I., eds.*, 1989, pp. 69–86.

; Miller, Marcus H. and Eichengreen, Barry. Blueprints for Exchange-Rate Management: Introduction. In *Miller, M.; Eichengreen, B. and Portes, R., eds.*, 1989, pp. 1–10.

and Quandt, Richard E. Macroeconomic Disequilibrium in Centrally Planned Economies: Comment. *J. Compar. Econ.*, December 1989, *13*(4), pp. 576–79.

Portillo, Michael. The Reform of Social Security: A Government View. In *Dilnot, A. and Walker, I., eds.*, 1989, pp. 192–99.

Portney, Paul R. Assessing and Managing the Risks of Climate Change. In *Rosenberg, N. J., et al., eds.*, 1989, pp. 83–88.

; McGartland, Albert M. and Oates, Wallace E. The *Net* Benefits of Incentive-Based Regulation: A Case Study of Environmental Standard Setting. *Amer. Econ. Rev.*, December 1989, *79*(5), pp. 1233–42.

Porto, Alberto. Economía del bienestar: Teoría y política económica. (Theory and Policy in Welfare Economics. With English summary.) *Económica (La Plata)*, 1989, *35*(1–2), pp. 71–100.

Portugal, Pedro and Addison, John T. The Endogeneity of Union Status and the Application of the Hausman Test. *J. Lab. Res.*, Fall 1989, *10*(4), pp. 437–41.

and Addison, John T. Job Displacement, Relative Wage Changes, and Duration of Unemployment. *J. Lab. Econ.*, July 1989, *7*(3), pp. 281–302.

and Addison, John T. On the Costs of Worker Displacement: The Case of Dissipated Firm-Specific Training Investments. *Southern Econ. J.*, July 1989, *56*(1), pp. 166–82.

Portwood, Derek. Strategic Responses of Local Authorities in the United Kingdom to Long-Term Unemployment. In *Dyson, K., ed.*, 1989, pp. 180–93.

Posner, M. V. and Kay, John A. Routes to Economic Integration: 1992 in the European Community. *Nat. Inst. Econ. Rev.*, August 1989, (129), pp. 55–68.

Posner, Richard A. and Landes, William M. An Economic Analysis of Copyright Law. *J. Legal Stud.*, June 1989, *18*(2), pp. 325–63.

Posnett, John and Sandler, Todd. Demand for Charity Donations in Private Non-profit Markets: The Case of the U.K. *J. Public Econ.*, November 1989, *40*(2), pp. 187–200.

Post, James E. Corporate Social Performance and Policy from the 1980s to 1990s. In *Post, J. E., ed.*, 1989, pp. ix–xvii.

and Waddock, Sandra A. Social Cause Partnerships and the "Mega-event": Hunger, Homelessness and Hands across America. In *Post, J. E., ed.*, 1989, pp. 181–205.

Postel-Vinay, Gilles. Debt and Agricultural Performance in the Languedocian Vineyard, 1870–1914. In *Grantham, G. and Leonard, C. S., eds., Pt. A*, 1989, pp. 161–86.

. A la recherche de la révolution économique dans les campagnes (1789–1815). (In Search of the Economic Impact of Revolution and Wars on French Agriculture, 1789–1815. With English summary.) *Revue Écon.*, November 1989, *40*(6), pp. 1015–46.

Postlewaite, Andrew and Matthews, Steven A. Pre-play Communication in Two-Person Sealed-Bid Double Auctions. *J. Econ. Theory*, June 1989, *48*(1), pp. 238–63.

and McLean, Richard P. Excess Functions and Nucleolus Allocations of Pure Exchange Economies. *Games Econ. Behav.*, June 1989, *1*(2), pp. 131–43.

and Wettstein, David. Feasible and Continuous Implementation. *Rev. Econ. Stud.*, October 1989, *56*(4), pp. 603–11.

Potepan, Michael J. Interest Rates, Income, and Home Improvement Decisions. *J. Urban Econ.*, May 1989, *25*(3), pp. 282–94.

Poterba, James M. Aging, Moving, and Housing Wealth: Comment. In *Wise, D. A., ed.*, 1989, pp. 48–54.

_____. Capital Gains Tax Policy toward Entrepreneurship. *Nat. Tax J.*, September 1989, *42*(3), pp. 375–89.

_____. Lifetime Incidence and the Distributional Burden of Excise Taxes. *Amer. Econ. Rev.*, May 1989, *79*(2), pp. 325–30.

_____. Tax Reform and the Market for Tax-Exempt Debt. *Reg. Sci. Urban Econ.*, August 1989, *19*(3), pp. 537–62.

_____. Venture Capital and Capital Gains Taxation. In *Summers, L. H., ed.*, 1989, pp. 47–67.

_____ **and Manchester, Joyce M.** Second Mortgages and Household Saving. *Reg. Sci. Urban Econ.*, May 1989, *19*(2), pp. 325–46.

_____; **Summers, Lawrence H. and Cutler, David M.** What Moves Stock Prices? *J. Portfol. Manage.*, Spring 1989, *15*(3), pp. 4–12.

Potestio, Paola. Alternative Aspects of Monetary Theory in the "General Theory": Significance and Implications. *Rech. Écon. Louvain*, 1989, *55*(3), pp. 257–72.

_____. Real Wages and Employment: Some Macroeconomic Models Compared. *Econ. Notes*, 1989, (3), pp. 299–313.

Pötscher, Benedikt M. and Prucha, Ingmar R. A Uniform Law of Large Numbers for Dependent and Heterogeneous Data Processes. *Econometrica*, May 1989, *57*(3), pp. 675–83.

Potter, Clive. Approaching Limits: Farming Contraction and Environmental Conservation in the UK. In *Goodman, D. and Redclift, M., eds.*, 1989, pp. 135–55.

Potter, Harry R. and Perrucci, Robert. The Collective Actor in Organizational Analysis. In *Perrucci, R. and Potter, H. R., eds.*, 1989, pp. 1–15.

Potter, Lesley and Hasymi, Ali. South Kalimantan: The Banjarese Heartland. In *Hill, H., ed.*, 1989, pp. 473–99.

Potter, Robert B. Rural–Urban Interaction in Barbados and the Southern Caribbean: Patterns and Processes of Dependent Development in Small Countries. In *[Mountjoy, A. B.]*, 1989, pp. 257–93.

_____. Urban–Rural Interaction, Spatial Polarisation and Development Planning. In *[Mountjoy, A. B.]*, 1989, pp. 323–33.

Potters, Jos; Tijs, Stef and Muto, Shigeo. Information Market Games. *Int. J. Game Theory*, 1989, *18*(2), pp. 209–26.

_____, **et al.** Clan Games. *Games Econ. Behav.*, September 1989, *1*(3), pp. 275–93.

Pötzelberger, Klaus and Polasek, Wolfgang. Robust Bayesian Analysis of a Parameter Change in Linear Regression. *Empirical Econ.*, 1989, *14*(2), pp. 123–37.

_____ **and Polasek, Wolfgang.** Robust Bayesian Analysis of a Parameter Change in Linear Regression. In *Kramer, W., ed.*, 1989, pp. 59–73.

Pouliquen, Alain. The Structural Modernization of Polish Private Agriculture: The Turning Point in the 1980's. *Comp. Econ. Stud.*, Summer 1989, *31*(2), pp. 66–91.

Poulon, Frédéric. La France, nation salariée. (France, Salaried Nation. With English summary.) *Écon. Societes*, August 1989, *23*(8), pp. 77–89.

_____. Libéralisme et sortie de crise. (Liberalism and the Way Out of the Crisis. With English summary.) *Écon. Appl.*, 1989, *42*(1), pp. 7–21.

Poulsen, Annette B. and Jarrell, Gregg A. Stock Trading before the Announcement of Tender Offers: Insider Trading or Market Anticipation? *J. Law, Econ., Organ.*, Fall 1989, *5*(2), pp. 225–48.

_____ **and Lehn, Kenneth.** Free Cash Flow and Stockholder Gains in Going Private Transactions. *J. Finance*, July 1989, *44*(3), pp. 771–87.

Pound, John. Shareholder Activism and Share Values: The Causes and Consequences of Countersolicitations against Management Antitakeover Proposals. *J. Law Econ.*, Part 1, October 1989, *32*(2), pp. 357–79.

_____ **and Shiller, Robert J.** Survey Evidence on Diffusion of Interest and Information among Investors. *J. Econ. Behav. Organ.*, August 1989, *12*(1), pp. 47–66.

Pourciau, Susan; Margheim, Loren and Pany, Kurt. Controlling Audit Staff Underreporting of Time and Premature Signoffs: Some Preliminary Findings. In *Gangolly, J., ed.*, 1989, pp. 181–94.

Pourgerami, Abbas and Djeto, Assane. Inflation–Growth Trade-Off in an Export-Oriented Rural Economy: The Case of Ghana. *Eastern Afr. Econ. Rev.*, June 1989, *5*(1), pp. 32–41.

_____ **and von Hirschhausen, Christian R.** Aggregate Demand for Energy and Dynamics of Energy Demand Elasticities in Non-Oil-Developing Countries. *J. Energy Devel.*, Spring 1989, *14*(2), pp. 237–52.

Poussou, Jean-Pierre. Le dynamisme de l'économie française sous Louis XVI. (The Dynamism of French Economy under the Reign of Louis XVI. With English summary.) *Revue Écon.*, November 1989, *40*(6), pp. 965–84.

_____. Les activités urbaines en France pendant la Révolution. (The Economic Activities of French Cities during the Revolution. With English summary.) *Revue Écon.*, November 1989, *40*(6), pp. 1061–77.

Powell, Andrew. The Management of Risk in Developing Country Finance. *Oxford Rev. Econ. Policy*, Winter 1989, *5*(4), pp. 69–87.

_____; **Anderson, Ronald W. and Gilbert, Christopher L.** Securitization and Commodity Contingency in International Lending. *Amer. J. Agr. Econ.*, May 1989, *71*(2), pp. 523–30.

Powell, James L.; Stock, James H. and Stoker, Thomas M. Semiparametric Estimation of Index Coefficients. *Econometrica*, November 1989, *57*(6), pp. 1403–30.

Powell, Martha C.; Williams, Carol J. and Fazio, Russell H. The Role of Attitude Accessibility in the Attitude-to-Behavior Process. *J. Cons. Res.*, December 1989, *16*(3), pp. 280–89.

Powell, Melanie. Tax Harmonisation in the European Community. In *Robinson, D.; Maynard, A. and Chester, R., eds.*, 1989, pp. 131–47.

Powell, R. A. Windows on a New World: Microelectronics. In *Finkelstein, J., ed.*, 1989, pp. 1–40.

Powell, Robert. The Dynamics of Longer Brinkmanship Crises. In *Ordeshook, P. C., ed.*, 1989, pp. 151–75.

Powell, Roy A. and Jensen, Rodney C. Regional Economic Structure: An Input–Output Approach. In *Higgins, B. and Zagorski, K., eds.*, 1989, pp. 173–95.

Powell, Stephen J. and Slater, Valerie A. Ramifications of U.S. Trade and National Security Laws for Petroleum Imports. *J. Energy Devel.*, Spring 1989, *14*(2), pp. 293–317.

Powelz, Herbert J. H. Ein System zur Ist-Soll-Abweichungs- Ursachenanalyse von Erlösen. (With English summary.) *Z. Betriebswirtshaft*, November 1989, *59*(11), pp. 1229–34.

Power, A. P. and Russell, N. P. UK Government Expenditure—Implications of Changes in Agricultural Output under the Common Agricultural Policy. *J. Agr. Econ.*, January 1989, *40*(1), pp. 32–39.

Power, Anthony; Kruger, Michael W. and Dennerlein, John. Deciphering Distribution Effects: Commentary. *Marketing Sci.*, Spring 1989, *8*(2), pp. 129–30.

Power, Marilyn. The Reagan Administration and the Regulation of Labor: The Curious Case of Affirmative Action. In *Rosenberg, S., ed.*, 1989, pp. 197–206.

Powers, Marian and Revsine, Lawrence. Lessors' Accounting and Residual Values: Comdisco, *Barron's* and GAAP. *Accounting Rev.*, April 1989, *64*(2), pp. 346–68.

Pownall, Grace and Waymire, Gregory. Voluntary Disclosure Choice and Earnings Information Transfer. *J. Acc. Res.*, Supplement, 1989, *27*, pp. 85–105.

_____ **and Waymire, Gregory.** Voluntary Disclosure Credibility and Securities Prices: Evidence from Management Earnings Forecasts, 1969–73. *J. Acc. Res.*, Autumn 1989, *27*(2), pp. 227–45.

Pozdniakov, E. Is It Possible to Be "A Little Pregnant"? A Dilettante's Opinion [Where Are the *Pirogi* Meatier?]. In *Jones, A. and Moskoff, W., eds.*, 1989, *1988*, pp. 104–10.

Pozsgay, Imre. In Search of Legitimacy: Interview. *Challenge*, Nov.–Dec. 1989, *32*(6), pp. 11–14.

van Praag, Bernard M. S. and Oostendorp, Remco H. On the Stability of the Social Security System. In *Gustafsson, B. A. and Klevmarken, N. A., eds.*, 1989, pp. 97–111.

_____ **and Wesselman, Bertram M.** Elliptical

Multivariate Analysis. *J. Econometrics*, June 1989, *41*(2), pp. 189–203.

Praagman, Jaap. Bahadur Efficiency of Tests for a Shift in Location of Normal Populations. In *Hackl, P., ed.*, 1989, pp. 135–65.

Prabalolane, B. Regional Structure of Agricultural Economy in Pondicherry. *Margin*, July–Sept. 1989, *21*(4), pp. 65–75.

Pradhan, Mahmood; Wood, Geoffrey E. and Capie, Forrest H. Prices and Price Controls: Are Price Controls a Policy Instrument? In *Hodgman, D. R. and Wood, G. E., eds.*, 1989, pp. 109–38.

Pradhan, Rajesh K. On Helping Small Enterprises in Developing Countries. *World Devel.*, January 1989, *17*(1), pp. 157–59.

Prados de la Escosura, Leandro and Molinas, César. Was Spain Different? Spanish Historical Backwardness Revisited. *Exploration Econ. Hist.*, October 1989, *26*(4), pp. 385–402.

Praet, Peter and Vuchelen, Jef. The Contribution of Consumer Confidence Indexes in Forecasting the Effects of Oil Prices on Private Consumption. *Int. J. Forecasting*, 1989, *5*(3), pp. 393–97.

Prager, Robin A. The Effects of Regulatory Policies on the Cost of Debt for Electric Utilities: An Empirical Investigation. *J. Bus.*, January 1989, *62*(1), pp. 33–53.

_____. Using Stock Price Data to Measure the Effects of Regulation: The Interstate Commerce Act and the Railroad Industry. *Rand J. Econ.*, Summer 1989, *20*(2), pp. 280–90.

Prahalad, C. K.; Doz, Yves and Angelmar, R. Assessing the Scope of Innovations: A Dilemma for Top Management. In *Rosenbloom, R. S. and Burgelman, R. A., eds.*, 1989, pp. 257–81.

Prais, S. J. How Europe Would See the New British Initiative for Standardising Vocational Qualifications. *Nat. Inst. Econ. Rev.*, August 1989, (129), pp. 52–54.

_____. Qualified Manpower in Engineering: Britain and Other Industrially Advanced Countries. *Nat. Inst. Econ. Rev.*, February 1989, (127), pp. 76–83.

_____ **and Jarvis, Valerie.** Two Nations of Shopkeepers: Training for Retailing in France and Britain. *Nat. Inst. Econ. Rev.*, May 1989, (128), pp. 58–74.

_____; **Jarvis, Valerie and Wagner, Karin.** Productivity and Vocational Skills in Services in Britain and Germany: Hotels. *Nat. Inst. Econ. Rev.*, November 1989, (130), pp. 52–74.

Prakash, Arun J.; LaCava, Gerald and Parhizgari, Ali M. A General Proof of Merton's Analytic Derivation of the Efficient Portfolio Frontier. *Quart. J. Bus. Econ.*, Summer 1989, *28*(3), pp. 67–77.

Prasad, Bhagwan. Small Scale Sector and the Seventh Five-Year Plan—Performance and Prospects. In *Reddy, J. M., et al., eds. (II)*, 1989, pp. 93–100.

Prasad, Pradhan H. Agrarian Violence in Bihar. In *Prasad, P. H.*, 1989, *1987*, pp. 75–94.

_____. Employment and Income in Rural India. In *Prasad, P. H.*, 1989, *1972*, pp. 20–26.

_____. Growth in the Macro-economic Perspective. In *Prasad, P. H.*, 1989, *1967*, pp. 5–13.

_____. Planning and Growth in India. In *Prasad, P. H.*, 1989, *1967*, pp. 14–19.

_____. Poverty and Agricultural Development. In *Prasad, P. H.*, 1989, *1985*, pp. 63–74.

_____. Poverty and Bondage. In *Prasad, P. H.*, 1989, *1976*, pp. 44–54.

_____. Production Relations: Achilles' Heel of Indian Planning. In *Prasad, P. H.*, 1989, *1973*, pp. 27–36.

_____. Reactionary Role of Usurer's Capital in Rural India. In *Prasad, P. H.*, 1989, *1974*, pp. 37–43.

_____. Rising Middle Peasantry in North India. In *Prasad, P. H.*, 1989, *1980*, pp. 55–62.

_____. Roots of Uneven Regional Growth in India. In *Prasad, P. H.*, 1989, *1988*, pp. 107–19.

_____. Towards a Theory of Transformation of Semi-feudal Agriculture. In *Prasad, P. H.*, 1989, *1987*, pp. 95–106.

Prasad, S. Benjamin. Advances in International Comparative Management: Epilogue. In *Prasad, S. B.*, ed., 1989, pp. 277–81.

Prat, G. and Durand, J.-J. Analyse de la relation entre la masse monétaire et la base monétaire en France, 1950–1987. (Analysis of the Relationship between the Money Stock and the Monetary Base in France, 1950–1987. With English summary.) *Écon. Societes*, April–May 1989, *23*(4–5), pp. 185–230.

Prates, Suzana and Fortuna, Juan Carlos. Informal Sector versus Informalized Labor Relations in Uruguay. In *Portes, A.; Castells, M. and Benton, L. A.*, eds., 1989, pp. 78–94.

Pratt, James B. and Baker, Samuel H. Experience as a Barrier to Contestability in Airline Markets. *Rev. Econ. Statist.*, May 1989, *71*(2), pp. 352–56.

Pratt, John W. Risk Aversion in the Small and in the Large. In *Diamond, P. and Rothschild, M.*, eds., 1989, *1964*, pp. 61–79.

_____. Utility Functions, Interest Rates, and the Demand for Bonds. In *[Hadar, J.]*, 1989, pp. 225–31.

_____ and Zeckhauser, Richard J. The Impact of Risk Sharing on Efficient Decision. *J. Risk Uncertainty*, September 1989, *2*(3), pp. 219–34.

Pratt, Joseph and Castaneda, Chris. New Markets, Outmoded Manufacturing: The Transition from Manufactured Gas to Natural Gas by Northeastern Utilities after World War II. In *Hausman, W. J.*, ed., 1989, pp. 238–47.

Pratt, Michael D. and Millner, Edward L. An Experimental Investigation of Efficient Rent-Seeking. *Public Choice*, August 1989, *62*(2), pp. 139–51.

Prawoto, Hendro. The Energy Outlook in Indonesia. In *James, W. E.*, ed., 1989, pp. 167–73.

Prazniak, Roxann. Feminist Humanism: Socialism and Neofeminism in the Writings of Zhang

Jie. In *Dirlik, A. and Meisner, M.*, eds., 1989, pp. 269–93.

Prebble, John. New Zealand's 1988 International Tax Regime for Trusts. *Australian Tax Forum*, 1989, *6*(1), pp. 65–87.

Preckel, Paul V.; Huang, Wen-Yuan and Hertel, Thomas W. The CARD Linear Programming Model of U.S. Agriculture. *J. Agr. Econ. Res.*, Spring 1989, *41*(2), pp. 20–23.

_____ and Nelson, Carl H. The Conditional Beta Distribution as a Stochastic Production Function. *Amer. J. Agr. Econ.*, May 1989, *71*(2), pp. 370–78.

_____ and Nelson, Carl H. Erratum [The Conditional Beta Distribution as a Stochastic Production Function]. *Amer. J. Agr. Econ.*, November 1989, *71*(4), pp. 1045.

Prell, Mark A. The Measurement of Housing Output: U.S. and Soviet Case Studies. *Rev. Income Wealth*, September 1989, *35*(3), pp. 297–315.

_____. The Role of the Service Sector in Soviet GNP and Productivity Estimates: Reply. *J. Compar. Econ.*, December 1989, *13*(4), pp. 574–75.

_____. The Role of the Service Sector in Soviet GNP and Productivity Estimates. *J. Compar. Econ.*, September 1989, *13*(3), pp. 383–405.

Premus, Robert and Swaney, James A. Modern Empiricism and Quantum Leap Theorizing in Economics. In *Tool, M. R. and Samuels, W. J.*, eds. *(II)*, 1989, *1982*, pp. 189–206.

Prentice, Barry and Storey, Gary. Flaxseed: Victim of Crowding Out? *Can. J. Agr. Econ.*, Part 2, December 1989, *37*(4), pp. 1165–79.

Prentice, N. J. Secs. 765–767 and Controlled Foreign Companies Legislation: United Kingdom. *Bull. Int. Fiscal Doc.*, February 1989, *43*(2), pp. 84–93.

Prescod, Ronald and Holder, Carlos. The Distribution of Personal Income in Barbados. *Soc. Econ. Stud.*, March 1989, *38*(1), pp. 87–113.

Prescott, David M.; Stengos, Thanasis and Moschini, Giancarlo. Nonparametric Kernel Estimation Applied to Forecasting: An Evaluation Based on the Bootstrap. In *Ullah, A.*, ed., 1989, *1988*, pp. 19–32.

Prescott, Edward C. Building Blocks of Market Clearing Business Cycle Models: Comment. In *Blanchard, O. J. and Fischer, S.*, eds., 1989, pp. 287–91.

_____; Chari, Varadarajan V. and Kehoe, Patrick J. Time Consistency and Policy. In *Barro, R. J.*, ed., 1989, pp. 265–305.

_____ and Lucas, Robert E., Jr. Equilibrium Search and Unemployment. In *Diamond, P. and Rothschild, M.*, eds., 1989, *1974*, pp. 517–38.

Prescott, Kate and Buckley, Peter J. The Structure of British Industry's Sales in Foreign Markets. *Managerial Dec. Econ.*, September 1989, *10*(3), pp. 189–208.

Prescott, Victor. Maritime Boundaries in the Southwest Pacific Region. In *Couper, A. D.*, ed., 1989, pp. 4–21.

Presley, John R. J. M. Keynes and D. H. Robertson: Three Phases of Collaboration. **In** *Samu-els, W. J., ed. (II)*, 1989, pp. 31–46.

_____. Sir John R. Hicks, 1904– **In** *Greenaway, D. and Presley, J. R., eds.*, 1989, pp. 96–119.

Press, Jon and Harvey, Charles. Overseas Investment and the Professional Advance of British Metal Mining Engineers, 1851–1914. *Econ. Hist. Rev., 2nd Ser.*, February 1989, *42*(1), pp. 64–86.

Press, S. James and Arnold, Barry C. Bayesian Estimation and Prediction for Pareto Data. *J. Amer. Statist. Assoc.*, December 1989, *84*(408), pp. 1079–84.

Presser, Harriet B. Can We Make Time for Children? The Economy, Work Schedules, and Child Care. *Demography*, November 1989, *26*(4), pp. 523–43.

Presser, Stanley. Collection and Design Issues: Discussion. **In** *Kasprzyk, D., et al., eds.*, 1989, pp. 75–79.

_____. Is Inaccuracy on Factual Survey Items Item-Specific or Respondent-Specific? **In** *Singer, E. and Presser, S., eds.*, 1989, *1984*, pp. 344–55.

_____ **and Schuman, Howard.** The Measurement of a Middle Position in Attitude Surveys. **In** *Singer, E. and Presser, S., eds.*, 1989, *1980*, pp. 108–23.

Pressman, Steven. Comment of Peterson's "The Feminization of Poverty." *J. Econ. Issues*, March 1989, *23*(1), pp. 231–38.

Preston, Anne E. The Nonprofit Worker in a For-Profit World. *J. Lab. Econ.*, October 1989, *7*(4), pp. 438–63.

_____ **and Ichniowski, Casey.** The Persistence of Organized Crime in New York City Construction: An Economic Perspective. *Ind. Lab. Relat. Rev.*, July 1989, *42*(4), pp. 549–65.

Preston, David A. Too Busy to Farm: Under-utilisation of Farm Land in Central Java. *J. Devel. Stud.*, October 1989, *26*(1), pp. 43–57.

Preston, Lee E. Territorial Restraints: GTE *Sylvania*. **In** *Kwoka, J. E., Jr. and White, L. J., eds.*, 1989, pp. 273–89.

Preston, Samuel H.; Himes, Christine and Eggers, Mitchell. Demographic Conditions Responsible for Population Aging. *Demography*, November 1989, *26*(4), pp. 691–704.

Prestowitz, Clyde. Strengthening Japan–U.S. Co-operation and the Concept of Japan–U.S. Free Trade Arrangements: Comments. **In** *Schott, J. J., ed.*, 1989, pp. 136–40.

Price, Barry and Simowitz, Roslyn. In Defense of Government Regulation. **In** *Tool, M. R. and Samuels, W. J., eds. (III)*, 1989, *1986*, pp. 263–75.

Price, Brian. Frank and Lillian Gilbreth and the Manufacture and Marketing of Motion Study, 1908–1924. **In** *Hausman, W. J., ed.*, 1989, pp. 88–98.

Price, Catherine. Gas Privatization: Effects on Pricing Policy. **In** *Helm, D.; Kay, J. and Thompson, D., eds.*, 1989, pp. 263–78.

Price, J. Michael; McDowell, Howard and Kramer, Randall A. An Analysis of U.S. Farm Income Policies: Historical, Market-Deter-

mined, and Sector-Wide Stabilization. *Southern J. Agr. Econ.*, December 1989, *21*(2), pp. 1–11.

Price, Jacob M. What Did Merchants Do? Reflections on British Overseas Trade, 1660–1790. *J. Econ. Hist.*, June 1989, *49*(2), pp. 267–84.

Price, L. D. D. External Impacts of the United States' Financial Policies: Comment. **In** *Hamouda, O. F.; Rowley, R. and Wolf, B. M., eds.*, 1989, pp. 127–28.

Price, Victoria Curzon. Three Models of European Integration. **In** *Dahrendorf, R., et al.*, 1989, pp. 23–38.

Priddat, Birger P. Schmoller on Ethics and Economics. *Int. J. Soc. Econ.*, 1989, *16*(9–10–11), pp. 47–68.

Prilutskii, Oleg F.; Rodionov, Stanislav N. and Fetter, Steve. Passive Detection of Nuclear Warheads. **In** *Altmann, J. and Rotblat, J., eds.*, 1989, pp. 48–59.

Prime, Penelope B. Socialism and Economic Development: The Politics of Accumulation in China. **In** *Dirlik, A. and Meisner, M., eds.*, 1989, pp. 136–51.

Primeaux, Walter J., Jr. Electricity Supply: An End to Natural Monopoly. **In** *Veljanovski, C., ed. (II)*, 1989, pp. 129–34.

_____ **and Fiegenbaum, Avi.** An Empirical Examination of Strategic Groups in Three Manufacturing Industries. **In** *Lee, C. F., ed.*, 1989, pp. 281–310.

Primrose, Neil. Issues in the Development of the International Information Economy: A View from the Southwest. **In** *Jussawalla, M.; Okuma, T. and Araki, T., eds.*, 1989, pp. 74–82.

Primus, Wendell E. Children in Poverty: A Committee Prepares for an Informed Debate. *J. Policy Anal. Manage.*, Winter 1989, *8*(1), pp. 23–34.

Prince, Gé. Dutch Economic Policy in Indonesia, 1870–1942. **In** *Maddison, A. and Prince, G., eds.*, 1989, pp. 203–26.

_____. Economic Growth in Indonesia, 1820–1940: Introduction. **In** *Maddison, A. and Prince, G., eds.*, 1989, pp. 1–13.

Prince, Michael J. and Doern, G. Bruce. The Political Administration of School Closures: Administrators, Trustees and Community Groups. *Can. Public Policy*, December 1989, *15*(4), pp. 450–69.

Prince, Raymond and Milliman, Scott R. Firm Incentives to Promote Technological Change in Pollution Control. *J. Environ. Econ. Manage.*, November 1989, *17*(3), pp. 247–65.

Pringle, W. A. and Döckel, J. A. The South African Angora Goat and Mohair Industry. *S. Afr. J. Econ.*, September 1989, *57*(3), pp. 215–30.

Prinz, Aloys. Wie beeinflussen Grundeinkommenssysteme das Arbeitsangebot? (Income Transfer Systems and Labor Supply. With English summary.) *Konjunkturpolitik*, 1989, *35*(1–2), pp. 110–28.

Prinzinger, Joseph and Newman, Jeffry. Is Hospice a Cost Effective Alternative to Medicaid

Conventional Care? *Atlantic Econ. J.*, March 1989, *17*(1), pp. 95.

Prisching, M. Evolution and Design of Social Institutions in Austrian Theory. *J. Econ. Stud.*, 1989, *16*(2), pp. 47–62.

Pritchett, Jonathan B. The Burden of Negro Schooling: Tax Incidence and Racial Redistribution in Postbellum North Carolina. *J. Econ. Hist.*, December 1989, *49*(4), pp. 966–73.

Profit, Alain J. Minitel: A French Entry into Information Services. In *National Economic Research Associates*, 1989, pp. 163–80.

Propper, Carol. An Econometric Analysis of the Demand for Private Health Insurance in England and Wales. *Appl. Econ.*, June 1989, *21*(6), pp. 777–92.

Prosi, Gerhard. The Economic Significance of Ethics. In *Rueschhoff, N. and Schaum, K.*, eds., 1989, pp. 77–87.

Prosser, Tony. Regulation of Privatized Enterprises: Institutions and Procedures. In *Hancher, L. and Moran, M.*, eds., 1989, pp. 135–65.

Provenzano, George. Alternative National Policies and the Location Patterns of Energy-Related Facilities. In *Labys, W. C.; Takayama, T. and Uri, N. D.*, eds., 1989, pp. 189–223.

Provopoulos, George A. Some Evidence on Unbalanced Productivity Growth: The Case of the Greek Public Sector. *Ann. Pub. Coop. Econ.*, 1989, *60*(3), pp. 359–67.

Prucha, Ingmar R. and Madan, Dilip B. A Note on the Estimation of Nonsymmetric Dynamic Factor Demand Models. *J. Econometrics*, October 1989, *42*(2), pp. 275–83.

_____ **and Pötscher, Benedikt M.** A Uniform Law of Large Numbers for Dependent and Heterogeneous Data Processes. *Econometrica*, May 1989, *57*(3), pp. 675–83.

Prud'homme, Remy. Internal Mobilization of Resources. In *World Bank and Istituto Italo-Africano*, 1989, pp. 99–105.

_____. Main Issues in Decentralization. In *World Bank and Istituto Italo-Africano*, 1989, pp. 71–75.

Pruitt, Stephen W. and Wei, K. C. John. Institutional Ownership and Changes in the S&P 500. *J. Finance*, June 1989, *44*(2), pp. 509–13.

_____; **Wei, K. C. John and Bansal, Vipul K.** An Empirical Reexamination of the Impact of CBOE Option Initiation on the Volatility and Trading Volume of the Underlying Equaties: 1973–1986. *Financial Rev.*, February 1989, *24*(1), pp. 19–29.

_____ **and White, Richard E.** Exchange-Traded Options and CRISMA Trading. *J. Portfol. Manage.*, Summer 1989, *15*(4), pp. 55–56.

Pryke, Richard. Performance of the Public Sector Energy Utilities between 1968 and 1978. In *Helm, D.; Kay, J. and Thompson, D.*, eds., 1989, pp. 115–32.

Pryor, Frederic L. Marxist Regime Series: IV: Review Article. *J. Compar. Econ.*, June 1989, *13*(2), pp. 340–49.

_____. What Is Comparative Economic Systems

All About? *Comp. Econ. Stud.*, Fall 1989, *31*(3), pp. 1–6.

Psacharopoulos, George. Time Trends of the Returns to Education: Cross-National Evidence. *Econ. Educ. Rev.*, 1989, *8*(3), pp. 225–31.

_____ **and Arriagada, Ana Maria.** The Determinants of Early Age Human Capital Formation: Evidence from Brazil. *Econ. Devel. Cult. Change*, July 1989, *37*(4), pp. 683–708.

_____ **and Kugler, Bernardo.** Earnings and Education in Argentina: An Analysis of the 1985 Buenos Aires Household Survey. *Econ. Educ. Rev.*, 1989, *8*(4), pp. 353–65.

_____ **and Tzannatos, Zafiris.** Female Labor Force Participation: An International Perspective. *World Bank Res. Observer*, July 1989, *4*(2), pp. 187–201.

Pu, Shan. Planning and the Market. *Cato J.*, Winter 1989, *8*(3), pp. 581–84.

_____. Trade and Economic Cooperation in the Asian-Pacific Region: Comment. In *Shinohara, M. and Lo, F.*, eds., 1989, pp. 514–515.

Pucik, Vladimir. Managerial Career Progression in Large Japanese Manufacturing Firms. In *Nedd, A.*, ed., 1989, pp. 257–76.

_____ **and Roomkin, Myron J.** Managers as Employees: Japan. In *Roomkin, M. J.*, ed., 1989, pp. 255–78.

Pugel, Thomas A. The Implementation of Industrial Policy in the United States and Japan: Tax Reform and Corporate Taxation. In *Hayashi, K.*, ed., 1989, pp. 265–312.

Pugliaresi, Lucian and Berliner, Diane T. Policy Analysis at the Department of State: The Policy Planning Staff. *J. Policy Anal. Manage.*, Summer 1989, *8*(3), pp. 379–94.

Puglisi, Donald J. and D'Souza, Rudolph E. A Note on Fiscal Agent Pricing of Federal Agency Debt. *J. Banking Finance*, May 1989, *13*(2), pp. 311–20.

Pugna, Irina and Burlacu, Veronica. Optimizing the Reliability of Coherent Binary Systems in the Designing Stage. *Econ. Computat. Econ. Cybern. Stud. Res.*, 1989, *24*(2–3), pp. 51–60.

Pugno, Maurizio. Labour's Share, Growth and Structural Change: The Case of U.S. Industrialisation. In *Di Matteo, M.; Goodwin, R. M. and Vercelli, A.*, eds., 1989, pp. 242–66.

Pulitini, Francesco. Le "New Properties" e il decentramento delle scelte pubbliche. (The "New Properties" and the Decentralization of Public Choices. With English summary.) *Econ. Scelte Pubbliche/J. Public Finance Public Choice*, Jan.–Aug. 1989, *7*(1–2), pp. 55–66.

Pullen, J. M. In Defence of Senior's Last Hour-and-Twenty-Five Minutes. *Hist. Polit. Econ.*, Summer 1989, *21*(2), pp. 299–309.

_____. Senior's Last Hour: Rejoinder. *Hist. Polit. Econ.*, Summer 1989, *21*(2), pp. 311–12.

Pulleyblank, William R.; Ball, Michael O. and Liu, Wei-Guo. Two-Terminal Steiner Tree Polyhedra. In *Cornet, B. and Tulkens, H.*, eds., 1989, pp. 251–84.

Pullum, Thomas W.; Tedrow, Lucky M. and Herting, Jerald R. Measuring Change and

Continuity in Parity Distributions. *Demography*, August 1989, *26*(3), pp. 485–98.

Pulsinelli, Robert W. and Borland, Melvin V. Household Commodity Production and Social Harassment Costs. *Southern Econ. J.*, October 1989, *56*(2), pp. 291–301.

Pulsipher, Allan G. and Gilmer, Robert William. Structural Change in Southern Manufacturing: Expansion in the Tennessee Valley. *Growth Change*, Spring 1989, *20*(2), pp. 62–70.

Punnett, Betty Jane. International Human Resource Management. In *Rugman, A. M., ed.*, 1989, pp. 330–46.

_____ **and Jain, Hem C.** Management Styles: Some Similarities and Differences between Japanese and Canadian Managers in Canada. In *Prasad, S. B., ed.*, 1989, pp. 183–97.

Punzo, Lionello F. Von Neumann and Karl Menger's Mathematical Colloquium. In *Dore, M.; Chakravarty, S. and Goodwin, R., eds.*, 1989, pp. 29–65.

Purcell, John and Ahlstrand, Bruce. Corporate Strategy and the Management of Employee Relations in the Multi-divisional Company. *Brit. J. Ind. Relat.*, November 1989, *27*(3), pp. 396–417.

Puri, Tribhuvan N. and Philippatos, George C. On the Pricing of Foreign Exchange Contracts. *Rivista Int. Sci. Econ. Com.*, April–May 1989, *36*(4–5), pp. 389–406.

Purohit, Devavrat and Levinthal, Daniel A. Durable Goods and Product Obsolescence. *Marketing Sci.*, Winter 1989, *8*(1), pp. 35–56.

Purver, Ronald G. Aspects of Sovereignty and Security in the Artic. In *McRae, D. and Munro, G., eds.*, 1989, pp. 165–88.

Puskin, Dena and Cromwell, Jerry. Hospital Productivity and Intensity Trends: 1980–87. *Inquiry*, Fall 1989, *26*(3), pp. 366–80.

Pustay, Michael W. Deregulation and the U.S. Trucking Industry. In *Button, K. and Swann, D., eds.*, 1989, pp. 236–56.

_____. Liberalization of U.S. International Aviation Policy: A Preliminary Assessment. *Quart. Rev. Econ. Bus.*, Summer 1989, *29*(2), pp. 15–26.

_____ **and Zardkoohi, Asghar.** Does Transferability Affect the Social Costs of Licensing? *Public Choice*, August 1989, *62*(2), pp. 187–90.

Putman, S. H. and Chung, S.-H. Effects of Spatial System Design on Spatial Interaction Models: 1. The Spatial System Definition Problem. *Environ. Planning A*, January 1989, *21*(1), pp. 27–46.

Putnam, Robert D. and Henning, C. Randall. The Bonn Summit of 1978: A Case Study in Coordination. In *Cooper, R. N., et al.*, 1989, pp. 12–140.

Putsis, William P., Jr. Product Diffusion, Product Differentiation and the Timing of New Product Introduction: The Television and VCR Market 1964–85. *Managerial Dec. Econ.*, March 1989, *10*(1), pp. 37–50.

Putterman, Louis. Agricultural Producer Cooperatives. In *Bardhan, P., ed. (II)*, 1989,

pp. 319–39.

_____. Commodification of Labor Follows Commodification of the Firm on a Theorem of the New Institutional Economics. *Ann. Pub. Coop. Econ.*, 1989, *60*(2), pp. 161–79.

_____ **and Hsiung, Bingyuang.** Pre- and Postreform Income Distribution in a Chinese Commune: The Case of Dahe Township in Hebei Province. *J. Compar. Econ.*, September 1989, *13*(3), pp. 406–45.

Puu, Tönu. On Growth and Dispersal of Populations. *Ann. Reg. Sci.*, 1989, *23*(3), pp. 171–86.

_____. On the Spatiotemporal Dynamics of Capital and Labour. In *Andersson, Å. E., et al., eds.*, 1989, pp. 121–31.

Puumanen, Kari. Exchange Rate Management and Macroeconomic Policy: A National Perspective: Comment. *Scand. J. Econ.*, 1989, *91*(2), pp. 471–72.

_____. Real Exchange Rates and Macroeconomics: A Selective Survey. *Scand. J. Econ.*, 1989, *91*(2), pp. 433–34.

Pyatt, Everett. Procurement Competition at Work: The Navy's Experience. *Yale J. Regul.*, Summer 1989, *6*(2), pp. 319–31.

Pyatt, Graham. The Method of Apportionment and Accounting Multipliers. *J. Policy Modeling*, Spring 1989, *11*(1), pp. 111–30.

Pyle, Kenneth B. The Burden of Japanese History and the Politics of Burden Sharing. In *Makin, J. H. and Hellmann, D. C., eds.*, 1989, pp. 41–77.

Pyles, David. Demand Theory and Elasticity Matrix Construction. In *Tweeten, L., ed.*, 1989, pp. 56–72.

_____; **Henneberry, Shida and Tweeten, Luther.** Supply and Elasticity Estimation. In *Tweeten, L., ed.*, 1989, pp. 73–95.

Pylkkönen, Pertti and Lahti, Ari. News and Stock Prices. *Liiketaloudellinen Aikak.*, 1989, *38*(3), pp. 184–93.

Pylypchuk, M. H. The Role of Private Consultants in Farm Business Management. *Can. J. Agr. Econ.*, Part 1, December 1989, *37*(4), pp. 587–89.

Pyun, Chong Soo and Chung, Kee Ho. The Effects of Risk, Inflation and Dividend Yield on Common Stock Returns: The Case of Korea. *Int. Econ. J.*, Winter 1989, *3*(4), pp. 69–78.

Pywell, C. and Amin, Ash. Is Technology Policy Enough for Local Economic Revitalization? The Case of Tyne and Wear in the North East of England. *Reg. Stud.*, October 1989, *23*(5), pp. 463–77.

Qi, Qingfu. The "Asiatic Mode of Production" Is Not a Marxist Scientific Concept. In *Brook, T., ed.*, 1989, pp. 136–48.

Qin, Duo. Formalization of Identification Theory. *Oxford Econ. Pap.*, January 1989, *41*(1), pp. 73–93.

_____. Formalization of Identification Theory. In *de Marchi, N. and Gilbert, C., eds.*, 1989, pp. 73–93.

Qin, Yuzheng. In the Construction of New Coalpits, We Should Pay Attention to Co-ordination of Production and Demand in the Locality. In

Howe, C. and Walker, K. R., eds., 1989, *1958*, pp. 181–85.

Qiu, Xu-Yao; Yu, Ke-Chun and Xu, Chan-Min. An Evolutionary Account of Management and the Role of Management Development in China. In *Davies, J., et al., eds.*, 1989, pp. 112–24.

Quack, Sigrid and Büchtemann, Christoph F. "Bridges" or "Traps"? Non-standard Employment in the Federal Republic of Germany. In *Rodgers, G. and Rodgers, J., eds.*, 1989, pp. 109–48.

Quah, Danny and Blanchard, Olivier Jean. The Dynamic Effects of Aggregate Demand and Supply Disturbances. *Amer. Econ. Rev.*, September 1989, *79*(4), pp. 655–73.

_____ **and Ito, Takatoshi.** Hypothesis Testing with Restricted Spectral Density Matrices, with an Application to Uncovered Interest Parity. *Int. Econ. Rev.*, February 1989, *30*(1), pp. 203–15.

Quah, Euston. Country Studies and the Value of Household Production. *Appl. Econ.*, December 1989, *21*(12), pp. 1631–46.

_____ **and Kho, Timothy.** Economic Aspects of Legal Issues Involving Women in Singapore: Matrimonial Property Division and Rape. *Singapore Econ. Rev.*, April 1989, *34*(1), pp. 30–42.

_____ **and Rieber, William.** Value of Children in Compensation for Wrongful Death. *Int. Rev. Law Econ.*, December 1989, *9*(2), pp. 165–79.

Quah, Jon S. T. Singapore's Experience in Curbing Corruption. In *Heidenheimer, A. J.; Johnston, M. and LeVine, V. T., eds.*, 1989, pp. 841–53.

Qualls, John H. The PC Corner. *Bus. Econ.*, April 1989, *24*(2), pp. 53–54.

_____. The PC Corner. *Bus. Econ.*, October 1989, *24*(4), pp. 52–54.

Quam, Lois. Post-war American Health Care: The Many Costs of Market Failure. *Oxford Rev. Econ. Policy*, Spring 1989, *5*(1), pp. 113–23.

Quan, Daniel C. and Quigley, John M. Inferring an Investment Return Series for Real Estate from Observations on Sales. *Amer. Real Estate Urban Econ. Assoc. J.*, Summer 1989, *17*(2), pp. 218–30.

Quan, Nguyen T. Concentration of Income and Land Holdings: Prediction by Latent Variables Model and Partial Least Squares. *J. Devel. Econ.*, July 1989, *31*(1), pp. 55–76.

Quandt, Richard E. and Portes, Richard. Macroeconomic Disequilibrium in Centrally Planned Economies: Comment. *J. Compar. Econ.*, December 1989, *13*(4), pp. 576–79.

_____ **and Rosen, Harvey S.** Endogenous Output in an Aggregate Model of the Labor Market. *Rev. Econ. Statist.*, August 1989, *71*(3), pp. 394–400.

Quandt, William B. Middle East Challenges. In *Bosworth, B. P., et al.*, 1989, pp. 160–65.

Quarmby, D. A. Developments in the Retail Market and Their Effect on Freight Distribution. *J. Transp. Econ. Policy*, January 1989, *23*(1), pp. 75–87.

Quddus, Munir; Liu, Jin-Tan and Butler, John S. Money, Prices, and Causality: The Chinese Hyperinflation, 1946–49, Reexamined. *J. Macroecon.*, Summer 1989, *11*(3), pp. 447–53.

Quenneville, B.; Rao, J. N. K. and Srinath, K. P. Estimation of Level and Change Using Current Preliminary Data. In *Kasprzyk, D., et al., eds.*, 1989, pp. 457–79.

Quibria, M. G. International Migration and Real Wages: Is There Any Neo-classical Ambiguity? *J. Devel. Econ.*, July 1989, *31*(1), pp. 177–83.

_____. Neoclassical Political Economy: An Application to Trade Policies. *J. Econ. Surveys*, 1989, *3*(2), pp. 107–36.

_____ **and Rivera-Batiz, Francisco L.** International Migration and Real Wages: A Resolution Note. *J. Devel. Econ.*, July 1989, *31*(1), pp. 193–94.

Quick, R. and Bronckers, M. What Is a Countervailable Subsidy under EEC Trade Law? *J. World Trade*, December 1989, *23*(6), pp. 5–31.

Quiggin, John. The Role and Consequences of Special Interest Groups and Political Factors. In *[Gruen, F. H.]*, 1989, pp. 60–80.

Quiggin, Pat; Caldwell, John C. and Caldwell, Pat. The Social Context of AIDS in Sub-Saharan Africa. *Population Devel. Rev.*, June 1989, *15*(2), pp. 185–234.

Quigley, John M. Household Dissolution and the Choice of Alternative Living Arrangements among Elderly Americans: Comment. In *Wise, D. A., ed.*, 1989, pp. 147–49.

_____ **and Quan, Daniel C.** Inferring an Investment Return Series for Real Estate from Observations on Sales. *Amer. Real Estate Urban Econ. Assoc. J.*, Summer 1989, *17*(2), pp. 218–30.

_____ **and Rubinfeld, Daniel L.** Unobservables in Consumer Choice: Residential Energy and the Demand for Comfort. *Rev. Econ. Statist.*, August 1989, *71*(3), pp. 416–25.

_____ **and Varaiya, Pravin.** On the Dynamics of Regulated Markets, Construction Standards, Energy Standards and Durable Goods: A Cautionary Tale. In *Andersson, Å. E., et al., eds.*, 1989, pp. 263–71.

Quigley, Neil C. The Bank of Nova Scotia in the Caribbean, 1889–1940. *Bus. Hist. Rev.*, Winter 1989, *63*(4), pp. 797–838.

_____. The Mortgage Market in New Zealand, and the Origins of the Government Advances to Settlers Act, 1894. *New Zealand Econ. Pap.*, 1989, *23*, pp. 51–79.

Quijano, Alicia M. Capital Expenditures by Majority-Owned Foreign Affiliates of U.S. Companies, 1989. *Surv. Curr. Bus.*, March 1989, *69*(3), pp. 20–25.

Quince, Annabelle and Lansbury, Russell D. Managers as Employees: Australia. In *Roomkin, M. J., ed.*, 1989, pp. 97–130.

Quinn, Joseph F. and Burkhauser, Richard V. American Patterns of Work and Retirement. In *Schmähl, W., ed.*, 1989, pp. 91–113.

Quintanilla, S. Antonio Ruiz and England, George W. Major Work Meaning Patterns in the National Labor Forces of Germany, Japan and the United States. In *Prasad, S. B., ed.*, 1989, pp. 77–94.

Quintas, L. G. A Note on Polymatrix Games. *Int. J. Game Theory*, 1989, *18*(3), pp. 261–72.

Quirk, James and Habibagahi, Hamid. Hicksian Stability and Walras' Law. In *Wood, J. C. and Woods, R. N., eds., Vol. 2*, 1989, *1973*, pp. 249–61.

———; **Womer, Keith and Terasawa, Katsuaki L.** Turbulence, Cost Escalation and Capital Intensity Bias in Defense Contracting. In *Gulledge, T. R., Jr. and Litteral, L. A., eds.*, 1989, pp. 97–116.

Quirk, Peter J. The Case for Open Foreign Exchange Systems. *Finance Devel.*, June 1989, *26*(2), pp. 30–33.

Quisumbing, M. Agnes R. and Taylor, Lance. Resource Transfers from Agriculture. In *Chakravarty, S., ed.*, 1989, pp. 116–45.

Quizon, Jaime B. and Binswanger, Hans P. What Can Agriculture Do for the Poorest Rural Groups? In *Adelman, I. and Lane, S., eds.*, 1989, pp. 110–35.

Qureshi, Muzaffar and Diwan, Romesh. Interfirm Diffusion of Innovations: Shuttleless Looms in Pakistan. *Indian J. Quant. Econ.*, 1989, *5*(1), pp. 47–62.

ten Raa, Thijs; Chakraborty, Debesh and Das, Tuhin. Working Capital in an Input–Output Model. *Econ. Systems Res.*, 1989, *1*(1), pp. 53–68.

——— **and van der Ploeg, Frederick.** A Statistical Approach to the Problem of Negatives in Input–Output Analysis. *Econ. Modelling*, January 1989, *6*(1), pp. 2–19.

Raabe, William A. and Reichenstein, William R. Investment Returns and Inflation Neutrality under Alternative Tax Structures: Investment and Public Policy Implications. In *Jones, S. M., ed.*, 1989, pp. 149–63.

van Raaij, W. Fred. Economic News, Expectations and Macro-economic Behaviour. *J. Econ. Psych.*, 1989, *10*(4), pp. 473–93.

——— **and van Houwelingen, Jeannet H.** The Effect of Goal-Setting and Daily Electronic Feedback on In-home Energy Use. *J. Cons. Res.*, June 1989, *16*(1), pp. 98–105.

Rabár, Ferenc and Csáki, Csaba. Current and Prospective Problems of Hunger and Malnutrition: Beyond the Reach of the Invisible Hand. In *Helmuth, J. W. and Johnson, S. R., eds., Vol. 2*, 1989, pp. 141–55.

Rabeau, Yves and Duguay, Pierre. Les effets macro-économiques de la politique budgétaire: De Keynes à la synthèse néo-classique. (The Macroeconomic Effects of Fiscal Policy: From Keynes to the Neo-classical Synthesis. With English summary.) *Revue Écon.*, July 1989, *40*(4), pp. 597–620.

Rabianski, Joseph S. and Stone, Jack H. A Pedagogical Note on Monopoly Supply. *Amer. Economist*, Spring 1989, *33*(1), pp. 80–82.

Rabin, Alan and Birch, Dan. Aggregate Demand Curves: A Reply. *J. Macroecon.*, Winter 1989, *11*(1), pp. 145–47.

Rabinovitch, Ramon. Pricing Stock and Bond Options When the Default-Free Rate Is Stochastic. *J. Finan. Quant. Anal.*, December 1989, *24*(4), pp. 447–57.

Rabkina, N. and Rimashevskaia, N. M. Should We Fear Inflation? *Prob. Econ.*, May 1989, *32*(1), pp. 6–14.

——— **and Vladova, N.** Property and the Market. *Prob. Econ.*, July 1989, *32*(3), pp. 6–24.

Rabushka, Alvin. A Free-Market Constitution for Hong Kong: A Blueprint for China. *Cato J.*, Winter 1989, *8*(3), pp. 641–52.

Raday, Frances. Costs of Dismissal: An Analysis in Community Justice and Efficiency. *Int. Rev. Law Econ.*, December 1989, *9*(2), pp. 181–207.

Radhakrishna, Meena. The Criminal Tribes Act in Madras Presidency: Implications for Itinerant Trading Communities. *Indian Econ. Soc. Hist. Rev.*, July–Sept. 1989, *26*(3), pp. 269–95.

Radice, Hugo. British Capitalism in a Changing Global Economy. In *MacEwan, A. and Tabb, W. K., eds.*, 1989, pp. 64–81.

Radin, Margaret Jane. Justice and the Market Domain. In *Chapman, J. W. and Pennock, J. R., eds.*, 1989, pp. 165–97.

Radner, Barbara. Inner-City Economics: The Back of the Book. In *Missouri Valley Economic Association*, 1989, pp. 41–47.

Radner, Daniel B. Net Worth and Financial Assets of Age Groups in 1984. *Soc. Sec. Bull.*, March 1989, *52*(3), pp. 2–15.

———. The Wealth of the Aged and Nonaged, 1984. In *Lipsey, R. E. and Tice, H. S., eds.*, 1989, pp. 645–84.

Radner, Roy. Competitive Equilibrium under Uncertainty. In *Diamond, P. and Rothschild, M., eds.*, 1989, *1968*, pp. 177–204.

———; **Leininger, Wolfgang and Linhart, Peter B.** Equilibria of the Sealed-Bid Mechanism for Bargaining with Incomplete Information. *J. Econ. Theory*, June 1989, *48*(1), pp. 63–106.

——— **and Linhart, Peter B.** Minimax-Regret Strategies for Bargaining over Several Variables. *J. Econ. Theory*, June 1989, *48*(1), pp. 152–78.

———; **Satterthwaite, Mark A. and Linhart, Peter B.** Symposium on Noncooperative Bargaining: Introduction. *J. Econ. Theory*, June 1989, *48*(1), pp. 1–17.

——— **and Schotter, Andrew.** The Sealed-Bid Mechanism: An Experimental Study. *J. Econ. Theory*, June 1989, *48*(1), pp. 179–220.

Radoulov, Lalyu. The Commodity Character of the Socialist Economy and Its Planned Development. In *Bulgarian Academy of Sciences, Institute of Economics*, 1989, pp. 58–65.

Radu, Michael S. and Somerville, Keith. People's Republic of Congo: Politics, Economics and Society. In *Allen, C., et al.*, 1989, pp. 145–236.

Radzicki, Michael J. Incorporating Christian Values into Business Simulations: An Institutional Dynamics Approach. In *Rueschhoff, N. and Schaum, K., eds.*, 1989, pp. 157–72.

Rae, Douglas A. and Lareau, Thomas J. Valuing

WTP for Diesel Odor Reductions: An Application of Contingent Ranking Technique. *Southern Econ. J.*, January 1989, *55*(3), pp. 728–42.

Rae, Patti L. and Rothschild, Leonard W., Jr. Highlights of the Sec. 482 White Paper: United States. *Bull. Int. Fiscal Doc.*, April 1989, *43*(4), pp. 177–80.

Rafaeli, Anat and Sutton, Robert I. The Expression of Emotion in Organizational Life. In *Cummings, L. L. and Staw, B. M., eds.*, 1989, pp. 1–42.

Rafalko, Robert J. Henry George's Labor Theory of Value: He Saw the Entrepreneurs and Workers as Employers of Capital and Land, and Not the Reverse. *Amer. J. Econ. Sociology*, July 1989, *48*(3), pp. 311–20.

Raffer, Kunibert. A Critique of the Socialist Countries' Theory and Practice of the New International Economic Order. In *Schulz, B. H. and Hansen, W. W., eds.*, 1989, pp. 91–109.

_____. Global Structural Adjustment, Dependence and Unequal Exchange: Bleak Prospects for the Periphery. In *Wohlmuth, K., ed.*, 1989, pp. 283–317.

_____. International Debts: A Crisis for Whom? In *Singer, H. W. and Sharma, S., eds. (I)*, 1989, pp. 51–62.

Raffiee, Kambiz; Adrangi, Bahram and Doroodian, Khosrow. Exchange Rates, Import Costs, and Domestic Wage and Price Levels. *Atlantic Econ. J.*, March 1989, *17*(1), pp. 91.

Ragan, James F., Jr. and Slottje, Daniel J. Alternatives to Unemployment-Based Funding Formulas in the Allocation of Federal Grants. *Growth Change*, Winter 1989, *20*(1), pp. 17–33.

Raghuram, C. Some Aspects of Industrialisation in the Large Scale Sector. In *Reddy, J. M., et al., eds. (II)*, 1989, pp. 62–79.

Ragin, Charles and Walton, John. Austerity and Dissent: Social Bases of Popular Struggle in Latin America. In *Canak, W. L., ed.*, 1989, pp. 216–32.

Rahim, Eric and Aftab, Khalid. 'Barriers' to the Growth of Informal Sector Firms: A Case Study. *J. Devel. Stud.*, July 1989, *25*(4), pp. 490–507.

Rahman, Sultan Hafeez. Forecasting of Yarn and Cloth Availability and Prices in Bangladesh: An Econometric Approach. *Bangladesh Devel. Stud.*, December 1989, *17*(4), pp. 21–52.

Rahmeyer, Fritz. The Evolutionary Approach to Innovation Activity. *J. Inst. Theoretical Econ.*, June 1989, *145*(2), pp. 275–97.

Rahn, Richard W. Private Money: An Idea Whose Time Has Come. *Cato J.*, Fall 1989, *9*(2), pp. 353–62.

Raichur, Satish and Van Ness, Peter. Dilemmas of Socialist Development: An Analysis of Strategic Lines in China, 1949–1981. In *Van Ness, P., ed.*, 1989, pp. 143–69.

Raiiman, Hussain Zillur. Mode of Production Debate Revisited: Conceptual Issues in Bengal's Agrarian Transition. *Bangladesh Devel. Stud.*, December 1989, *17*(4), pp. 53–70.

Raiklin, Ernest. On People's Welfare in Aganbe-

gyan's *The Economic Challenge of Perestroika*. *Int. J. Soc. Econ.*, 1989, *16*(7), pp. 16–33.

_____. On Three Non-ideological Consequences of Specialisation among Economists. *Int. J. Soc. Econ.*, 1989, *16*(5), pp. 32–45.

_____. Reflections on Economic Aspects of Gorbachev's Book *Perestroika:* Wishful Thinking for a Make-Believe World? *Int. J. Soc. Econ.*, 1989, *16*(3), pp. 9–33.

_____ and McCormick, Ken. The Conditional View of the Neoclassical and Marxist Approaches to the Concept of Productive Labour. *Int. J. Soc. Econ.*, 1989, *16*(1), pp. 13–26.

Raimondo, Henry J. Leviathan and Federalism in the United States. *Public Finance Quart.*, April 1989, *17*(2), pp. 204–15.

Rainbow, Roger. Oil Industry and the Environment. In *Owen, A. D., ed.*, 1989, pp. 57–61.

Rainer, Norbert. Descriptive versus Analytical Make-Use Systems: Some Austrian Experiences. In *Miller, R. E.; Polenske, K. R. and Rose, A. Z., eds.*, 1989, pp. 51–64.

_____ and Franz, Alfred. Compilation of Input–Output Data: Introduction and Summary. In *Franz, A. and Rainer, N., eds.*, 1989, pp. 7–20.

_____ and Richter, Josef. The SNA Make-Use Framework as a Descriptive Basis for IQ Analysis. In *Franz, A. and Rainer, N., eds.*, 1989, pp. 233–55.

Raines, J. Patrick. Frank H. Knight's Contributions to Social Economics. *Rev. Soc. Econ.*, Fall 1989, *47*(3), pp. 280–92.

Rainwater, Lee; Simpson, Rick and Smeeding, Timothy M. Comparative Cross-National Research on Income and Economic Well-Being: The Luxembourg Income Study. *Surv. Curr. Bus.*, March 1989, *69*(3), pp. 62–67.

_____; Smeeding, Timothy M. and Coder, John. Inequality among Children and Elderly in Ten Modern Nations: The United States in an International Context. *Amer. Econ. Rev.*, May 1989, *79*(2), pp. 320–24.

Raisian, John and Hashimoto, Masanori. Investments in Employer–Employee Attachments by Japanese and U.S. Workers in Firms of Varying Size. *J. Japanese Int. Economies*, March 1989, *3*(1), pp. 31–48.

Raj, Baldev and Siklos, Pierre L. The Role of Fiscal Policy in the St. Louis Model: Nonparametric Estimates for a Small Open Economy. In *Ullah, A., ed.*, 1989, *1988*, pp. 47–64.

_____ and Taylor, Timothy G. Do 'Bootstrap Tests' Provide Significance Levels Equivalent to the Exact Test? Empirical Evidence from Testing Linear Within-Equation Restrictions in Large Demand Systems. *J. Quant. Econ.*, January 1989, *5*(1), pp. 73–89.

Raj, S. P.; Krishnamurthi, Lakshman and Narayan, Jack. Intervention Analysis Using Control Series and Exogenous Variables in a Transfer Function Model: A Case Study. *Int. J. Forecasting*, 1989, *5*(1), pp. 21–27.

Rajagopalan, V. and Ajjan, N. An Analysis of Supply Response of the Tea Industry in South India. *Singapore Econ. Rev.*, April 1989, *34*(1), pp. 68–74.

———— and Ajjan, N. An Analysis of Supply Response of the Tea Industry in South India. *Singapore Econ. Rev.*, October 1989, *34*(2), pp. 89–96.

Rajan, Roby. Endogenous Coalition Formation in Cooperative Oligopolies. *Int. Econ. Rev.*, November 1989, *30*(4), pp. 863–76.

Rajasenan, D. and Sankaranarayanan, K. C. Cost–Benefit Analysis of Mechanised Fishing: A Case Study. *Margin*, Oct. 1989–March 1990, *22*(1–2), pp. 80–91.

Rakitskaia, G. The Development of a Socialist Attitude toward Work. *Prob. Econ.*, February 1989, *31*(10), pp. 78–94.

Rakitskii, B. The Reform of Management and the Dialectics of Interests. In *Yanowitch, M., ed., 1989, 1987*, pp. 47–52.

Rakshit, Mihir. Effective Demand in a Developing Country: Approaches and Issues. In *Rakshit, M., ed.*, 1989, pp. 1–25.

————. Underdevelopment of Commodity, Credit and Land Markets: Some Macroeconomic Implications. In *Rakshit, M., ed.*, 1989, pp. 148–82.

Rall, Wilhelm. Organisation für den Weltmarkt. (With English summary.) *Z. Betriebswirtshaft*, October 1989, *59*(10), pp. 1074–89.

Ram, Kewal and Sarma, Atul. Income, Output and Employment Linkages and Import Intensities of Manufacturing Industries in India. *J. Devel. Stud.*, January 1989, *25*(2), pp. 192–209.

Ram, Rati. Can Educational Expansion Reduce Income Inequality in Less-Developed Countries? *Econ. Educ. Rev.*, 1989, *8*(2), pp. 185–95.

————. Government Size and Economic Growth: A New Framework and Some Evidence from Cross-Section and Time-Series Data: Reply. *Amer. Econ. Rev.*, March 1989, *79*(1), pp. 281–84.

————. Level of Development and Income Inequality: An Extension of Kuznets-Hypothesis to the World Economy. *Kyklos*, 1989, *42*(1), pp. 73–88.

————. Wagner's Hypothesis and Tests of Granger-Causality: Reply. *Public Finance*, 1989, *44*(1), pp. 139–49.

———— and Ramsey, David D. Government Capital and Private Output in the United States: Additional Evidence. *Econ. Letters*, September 1989, *30*(3), pp. 223–26.

Raman, K. K.; Wilson, Earl R. and Ingram, Robert W. The Information in Governmental Annual Reports: A Contemporaneous Price Reaction Approach. *Accounting Rev.*, April 1989, *64*(2), pp. 250–68.

Ramanadham, V. V. Privatisation in Developing Countries: Concluding Review. In *Ramanadham, V. V., ed.*, 1989, pp. 405–32.

————. Privatisation: The UK Experience and Developing Countries. In *Ramanadham, V. V., ed.*, 1989, pp. 3–93.

Ramanan, Ramachandran and Rubin, Marc A. State Policy Regarding Local Government Au-

ditors. In *Chan, J. L. and Patton, J. M., eds.*, 1989, pp. 57–69.

Ramanjeneyulu, S. and Rao, G. Chandrasekar. Role of Domestic Debt in Plan Finances. In *Reddy, J. M., et al., eds. (I)*, 1989, pp. 51–57.

Ramaswamy, Vijaya. Aspects of Women and Work in Early South India. *Indian Econ. Soc. Hist. Rev.*, Jan.–March 1989, *26*(1), pp. 81–99.

Ramesh, K.; Han, Jerry C. Y. and Wild, John J. Managers' Earnings Forecasts and Intra-industry Information Transfers. *J. Acc. Econ.*, February 1989, *11*(1), pp. 3–33.

Ramesh, R.; Karwan, Mark H. and Zionts, Stanley. Performance Characteristics of Three Interactive Solution Strategies for Bicriteria Integer Programming. In *Lockett, A. G. and Islei, G., eds.*, 1989, pp. 472–85.

Ramey, Valerie A. Inventories as Factors of Production and Economic Fluctuations. *Amer. Econ. Rev.*, June 1989, *79*(3), pp. 338–54.

Ramírez, Miguel D. The Social and Economic Consequences of the National Austerity Program in Mexico. In *Handelman, H. and Baer, W., eds.*, 1989, pp. 143–70.

Ramos-Elorduy, Julieta and Rocha-Hernandez, Alma E. 1988 World Food Conference: Proceedings: Appendix: The Use of Insects in Human and Animal Nutrition. In *Helmuth, J. W. and Johnson, S. R., eds., Vol. 1*, 1989, pp. 263–65.

Ramos, Joseph. El cuestionamiento de la estrategia del desarrollo y del papel del Estado a la luz de la crisis. (With English summary.) *Cuadernos Econ.*, December 1989, *26*(79), pp. 299–310.

————. Neo-Keynesian Macroeconomics as Seen from the South. *CEPAL Rev.*, August 1989, (38), pp. 7–29.

Ramos, Roberto Luis Olinto and Braz de Oliveira e Silva, Antonio. A Commodity Flow Balancing Procedure for the Base Year of the New Brazilian System of National Accounts. In *Franz, A. and Rainer, N., eds.*, 1989, pp. 301–24.

Rampa, Giorgio. Conjectures, Learning, and Equilibria in Monopolistic Competition. *J. Econ. (Z. Nationalökon.)*, 1989, *49*(2), pp. 139–63.

————; Vaggi, Gianni and Lunghini, Giorgio. The Age of Waste: Some Ideas on Full Employment. *Écon. Appl.*, 1989, *42*(1), pp. 115–33.

Rampilla, Narayana Rao. A Developing Judicial Perspective to India's Monopolies and Restrictive Trade Practices Act of 1969. *Antitrust Bull.*, Fall 1989, *34*(3), pp. 655–82.

Ramsaran, Ramesh. Capital Movements—The Experience of Commonwealth Caribbean Countries, 1970–1984. In *Worrell, D. and Bourne, C., eds.*, 1989, pp. 48–64.

Ramsay, J. O. and Abrahamowicz, M. Binomial Regression with Monotone Splines: A Psychometric Application. *J. Amer. Statist. Assoc.*, December 1989, *84*(408), pp. 906–15.

Ramsey, David D. and Ram, Rati. Government Capital and Private Output in the United

States: Additional Evidence. *Econ. Letters,* September 1989, *30*(3), pp. 223–26.

Ramseyer, J. Mark. Water Law in Imperial Japan: Public Goods, Private Claims, and Legal Convergence. *J. Legal Stud.,* January 1989, *18*(1), pp. 51–77.

———— **and Nakazato, Minoru.** The Rational Litigant: Settlement Amounts and Verdict Rates in Japan. *J. Legal Stud.,* June 1989, *18*(2), pp. 263–90.

Ramstad, Yngve. A Pragmatist's Quest for Holistic Knowledge: The Scientific Methodology of John R. Commons. In *Tool, M. R. and Samuels, W. J., eds. (II),* 1989, *1986,* pp. 207–45.

————. "Reasonable Value" versus "Instrumental Value:" Competing Paradigms in Institutional Economics. *J. Econ. Issues,* September 1989, *23*(3), pp. 761–77.

Ramstetter, Eric D. and Lee, Chung H. Trade in Services and Returns on Foreign Direct Investment. *Weltwirtsch. Arch.,* 1989, *125*(2), pp. 375–85.

Rana, Ratna. Technological Innovation in the Asian-Pacific Region: Facts and Economic Interpretations: Comment. In *Shinohara, M. and Lo, F., eds.,* 1989, pp. 348–50.

Ranade, C. G. Hicks Coefficient to Depict Direction of Movements in Relative Factor Shares in Agricultural Production. In *Wood, J. C. and Woods, R. N., eds., Vol. 3,* 1989, *1977,* pp. 163–72.

Randall, Adrian J. Work, Culture and Resistance to Machinery in the West of England Woollen Industry. In *Hudson, P., ed.,* 1989, pp. 175–98.

Randall, Alan; Bergstrom, John C. and Stoll, John R. Information Effects in Contingent Markets. *Amer. J. Agr. Econ.,* August 1989, *71*(3), pp. 685–91.

———— **and Hoehn, John P.** Benefit Estimation for Complex Policies. In *Folmer, H. and van Ierland, E., eds.,* 1989, pp. 219–29.

———— **and Hoehn, John P.** Too Many Proposals Pass the Benefit Cost Test. *Amer. Econ. Rev.,* June 1989, *79*(3), pp. 544–51.

Randall, Richard E. Can the Market Evaluate Asset Quality Exposure in Banks? *New Eng. Econ. Rev.,* July–Aug. 1989, pp. 3–24.

Randall, Stephen J. The State and Private Enterprise in United States–Latin American Oil Policy. In *Teichova, A.; Lévy-Leboyer, M. and Nussbaum, H., eds.,* 1989, pp. 191–200.

Randolph, Susan. Intertemporal Aspects of Male Earnings Inequality in Malaysia, 1968 to 1976. *Singapore Econ. Rev.,* April 1989, *34*(1), pp. 13–29.

———— **and Trzcinski, Eileen.** Relative Earnings Mobility in a Third World Country. *World Devel.,* April 1989, *17*(4), pp. 513–24.

Randolph, William C.; Auten, Gerald E. and Burman, Leonard E. Estimation and Interpretation of Capital Gains Realization Behavior: Evidence from Panel Data. *Nat. Tax J.,* September 1989, *42*(3), pp. 353–74.

———— **and Moulton, Brent R.** Alternative Tests

of the Error Components Model. *Econometrica,* May 1989, *57*(3), pp. 685–93.

von Randow, Philipp and Wehrt, Klaus. New Technologies, Liability Rules and Adaptive Behavior: Comment. In *Faure, M. and Van den Bergh, R., eds.,* 1989, pp. 107–16.

Rangan, Nanda K.; Eyssell, Thomas H. and Fraser, Donald R. Debt–Equity Swaps, Regulation K, and Bank Stock Returns. *J. Banking Finance,* December 1989, *13*(6), pp. 853–68.

————; **Stanley, Thomas and Ogden, William, Jr.** Risk Reduction in S&L Mortgage Loan Portfolios through Geographic Diversification. *J. Finan. Services Res.,* February 1989, *2*(1), pp. 39–48.

————, **et al.** Production Costs for Consolidated Multibank Holding Companies Compared to One-Bank Organizational Forms. *J. Econ. Bus.,* November 1989, *41*(4), pp. 317–25.

Rangarajan, Anuradha and Moffitt, Robert. The Effect of Transfer Programmes on Work Effort and Human Capital Formation: Evidence from the U.S. In *Dilnot, A. and Walker, I., eds.,* 1989, pp. 116–36.

Rangarajan, C. The Exchange Rate System: Some Key Issues. *Indian Econ. J.,* Jan.–March 1989, *36*(3), pp. 14–27.

————. Issues in Monetary Management. *Indian Econ. J.,* Jan.–March 1989, *36*(3), pp. 1–13.

———— **and Ahluwalia, Isher Judge.** A Study of Linkages between Agriculture and Industry: The Indian Experience. In *Williamson, J. G. and Panchamukhi, V. R., eds.,* 1989, pp. 219–50.

Rangazas, Peter. Redistributive Taxation in a Simple Life-Cycle Model. *Economica,* November 1989, *56*(224), pp. 487–503.

———— **and Abdullah, Dewan A.** Inflation, Tax Rates, and Investment with Endogenous Financial Behavior. *Southern Econ. J.,* April 1989, *55*(4), pp. 870–79.

Ranis, Gustav. Debt, Adjustment and Development. In *Singer, H. W. and Sharma, S., eds. (I),* 1989, pp. 227–38.

————. Economic Liberalization and the Equilibrium Real Exchange Rate in Developing Countries: Comment. In *[Díaz-Alejandro, C.],* 1989, pp. 188–90.

————. Macro Policies, the Terms of Trade and the Spatial Dimension of Balanced Growth. In *Islam, N., ed.,* 1989, pp. 39–60.

————. The Role of Institutions in Transition Growth: The East Asian Newly Industrializing Countries. *World Devel.,* Special Issue, September 1989, *17*(9), pp. 1443–53.

Ranis, Peter. Redemocratization and the Argentine Working Class. *Can. J. Devel. Stud.,* 1989, *10*(2), pp. 293–302.

Ránki, György. The Introduction and Evolution of Planning in Hungary. In *Van Ness, P., ed.,* 1989, pp. 31–51.

Rankin, Neil. Monetary, Fiscal and Exchange Intervention Policy in a Two-Country Intertemporal Disequilibrium Model. *Europ. Econ. Rev.,* September 1989, *33*(7), pp. 1463–80.

————. Stabilization Policy, Fixed Exchange

Rates and Target Zones: Discussion. **In** *Miller, M.; Eichengreen, B. and Portes, R., eds.*, 1989, pp. 95–97.

Ransom, Roger L. and Sutch, Richard. The Trend in the Rate of Labor Force Participation of Older Men, 1870–1930: A Reply. *J. Econ. Hist.*, March 1989, *49*(1), pp. 170–83.

Ranson, Baldwin. The Increasing Importance of Financial Capital in the U.S. Economy: A Note. *J. Econ. Issues*, March 1989, *23*(1), pp. 245–47.

Rantala, Olavi. HELIBOR-korkojen aikasarjaprosessi ja aikarakenne. (The Time Series Process and the Term Structure of Interest Rates in Finland. With English summary.) *Liiketaloudellinen Aikak.*, 1989, *38*(2), pp. 142–55.

Rao, Ambar G. and Eastlack, Joseph O., Jr. Advertising Experiments at the Campbell Soup Company: Reply. *Marketing Sci.*, Winter 1989, *8*(1), pp. 76–77.

———— **and Eastlack, Joseph O., Jr.** Advertising Experiments at the Campbell Soup Company. *Marketing Sci.*, Winter 1989, *8*(1), pp. 57–71.

Rao, B. Bhaskara and Srivastava, Virendra K. The Specification and Estimation of the Output Equation in the Rational Expectations Model with Gradual Price Adjustment. *Australian Econ. Pap.*, December 1989, *28*(53), pp. 201–08.

Rao, C. P. and Rosenberg, L. Joseph. William T. Dillard: A Pioneer Merchant in Suburban Shopping Centers. **In** *Perkins, E. J., ed.*, 1989, pp. 230–36.

Rao, D. S. Prasada and Shepherd, William F. Trends in Average Earnings of Production Workers in Australia and in OECD Member Countries. *Australian Bull. Lab.*, December 1989, *15*(5), pp. 400–425.

Rao, G. Chandrasekar and Ramanjeneyulu, S. Role of Domestic Debt in Plan Finances. **In** *Reddy, J. M., et al., eds. (I)*, 1989, pp. 51–57.

Rao, G. R. K.; Acharya, H. S. and Rao, N. Ganga Prasada. Yield Stability of Sorghum and Millet across Climates. **In** *Oram, P. A., et al.*, 1989, pp. 165–86.

Rao, J. Mohan. Taxing Agriculture: Instruments and Incidence. *World Devel.*, June 1989, *17*(6), pp. 809–23.

Rao, J. N. K.; Srinath, K. P. and Quenneville, B. Estimation of Level and Change Using Current Preliminary Data. **In** *Kasprzyk, D., et al., eds.*, 1989, pp. 457–79.

Rao, J. S. Narayan. Returns to Investments in Indian Planning. **In** *Reddy, J. M., et al., eds. (I)*, 1989, pp. 58–66.

Rao, M. J. Manohar and Datta, Ramesh C. Rates of Return in the Indian Private Sector. *Econ. Letters*, October 1989, *30*(4), pp. 373–78.

———— **and Datta, Ramesh C.** The Screening Hypothesis and the Marginal Productivity Theory. *Econ. Letters*, October 1989, *30*(4), pp. 379–84.

Rao, N. Ganga Prasada; Rao, G. R. K. and Acharya, H. S. Yield Stability of Sorghum and Millet across Climates. **In** *Oram, P. A., et al.*, 1989, pp. 165–86.

Rao, N. H.; Swaminathan, M. S. and Sinha, S. K. Food Security in the Changing Global Climate. **In** *Oram, P. A., et al.*, 1989, pp. 579–97.

Rao, P. Purnachandra and Kumar, R. Nanda. Savings in Household Sector as a Source of Finance. **In** *Reddy, J. M., et al., eds. (I)*, 1989, pp. 138–45.

Rao, P. V. Krishna and Sastry, K. P. Restrictive Trade Practices Policy in India. *J. Ind. Econ.*, June 1989, *37*(4), pp. 427–35.

Rao, Ramesh K. S. and Harlow, W. V. Asset Pricing in a Generalized Mean-Lower Partial Moment Framework: Theory and Evidence. *J. Finan. Quant. Anal.*, September 1989, *24*(3), pp. 285–311.

Rao, Ramesh P.; Hiraki, Takato and Aggarwal, Raj. Skewness and Kurtosis in Japanese Equity Returns: Empirical Evidence. *J. Finan. Res.*, Fall 1989, *12*(3), pp. 253–60.

————**; Peterson, Richard L. and Ma, Christopher K.** The Resiliency of the High-Yield Bond Market: The LTV Default. *J. Finance*, September 1989, *44*(4), pp. 1085–97.

————**; Sears, R. Stephen and Ma, Christopher K.** Limit Moves and Price Resolution: The Case of the Treasury Bond Futures Market. *J. Futures Markets*, August 1989, *9*(4), pp. 321–35.

————**; Sears, R. Stephen and Ma, Christopher K.** Volatility, Price Resolution, and the Effectiveness of Price Limits. *J. Finan. Services Res.*, December 1989, *3*(2–3), pp. 165–99.

————**; Sears, R. Stephen and Ma, Christopher K.** Volatility, Price Resolution, and the Effectiveness of Price Limits. **In** *Edwards, F. R., ed.*, 1989, pp. 67–101.

Rao, S. Kishan. The Strategy of Development: The Twin Goals of Reduction in Poverty and Unemployment—A Critique. **In** *Reddy, J. M., et al., eds. (II)*, 1989, pp. 149–62.

Rao, T. Divakara. Resources for the Seventh Plan of Andhra Pradesh State—A Search for Alternatives. **In** *Reddy, J. M., et al., eds. (I)*, 1989, pp. 112–24.

Rao, V. M. The Impact of Rural Development Programmes on the Economic Structure of Rural Communities. **In** *Adelman, I. and Lane, S., eds.*, 1989, pp. 97–109.

Rao, V. V. Bhanoji. Government Size and Economic Growth: A New Framework and Some Evidence from Cross-Section and Time-Series Data: Comment. *Amer. Econ. Rev.*, March 1989, *79*(1), pp. 272–80.

————. Income Inequality and Poverty in East Asia: Trends and Implications. *Indian Econ. J.*, Oct.–Dec. 1989, *37*(2), pp. 57–64.

Rapaczynski, Andrzej. The Vagaries of Consent: A Response to John Gray. **In** *Chapman, J. W. and Pennock, J. R., eds.*, 1989, pp. 59–71.

Raphael, David E. The Information Industry: A New Portrait. *Bus. Econ.*, July 1989, *24*(3), pp. 28–33.

Rapkin, David P. and Avery, William P. Markets,

Politics, and Change in the Global Political Economy. In *Avery, W. P. and Rapkin, D. P., eds.*, 1989, pp. 1–16.

Rapoport, Amnon and Bornstein, Gary. Solving Public Good Problems in Competition between Equal and Unequal Size Groups. *J. Conflict Resolution*, September 1989, *33*(3), pp. 460–79.

Rapp, David. Agriculture and the Failure of the Budget Process: Commentary. In *Krämer, C. S., ed.*, 1989, pp. 103–04.

Rappoport, Peter and Reichlin, Lucrezia. On Broken Trends, Random Walks and Non-Stationary Cycles. In *Di Matteo, M.; Goodwin, R. M. and Vercelli, A., eds.*, 1989, pp. 305–31.

_____ **and Reichlin, Lucrezia.** Segmented Trends and Non-stationary Time Series. *Econ. J.*, Supplement, 1989, *99*(395), pp. 168–77.

Rasche, Robert H. Money-Income Causality—A Critical Review of the Literature since *A Monetary History:* Comment. In *[Schwartz, A. J.]*, 1989, pp. 151–56.

Rasey, Keith P. and Dommel, Paul R. Coping with the Loss of General Revenue Sharing in Ohio. *Public Budg. Finance*, Autumn 1989, *9*(3), pp. 43–51.

Rashid, Muhammad; Riener, Kenneth D. and Gandhi, Devinder K. Intertemporal Resolution of Uncertainty and Portfolio Behavior. *Financial Rev.*, August 1989, *24*(3), pp. 491–97.

Rashid, Salim. Adam Smith as a Historian of Economic Thought: Reply. *Quart. Rev. Econ. Bus.*, Winter 1989, *29*(4), pp. 96–99.

_____. Backhouse's *A History of Modern Economic Analysis* and Dasgupta's *Epochs in Economic Theory:* Review Essay. In *Samuels, W. J., ed. (II)*, 1989, pp. 239–45.

_____. English Financial Pamphleteers of the Mid-Eighteenth Century: The Last Phase of Pragmatic Political Economy. In *Walker, D. A., ed.*, 1989, pp. 3–18.

_____ **and Oran, Ahmad.** Fiscal Policy in Early Islam. *Public Finance*, 1989, *44*(1), pp. 75–101.

Rashid, Zakariah Abdul. Price Structure, Technological Obsolescence and Labour Productivity—A Vintage Hypothesis Approach. *Singapore Econ. Rev.*, April 1989, *34*(1), pp. 50–67.

Raskin, A. H. Cyrus S. Ching: Pioneer in Industrial Peacemaking. *Mon. Lab. Rev.*, August 1989, *112*(8), pp. 22–35.

Rasmusen, Eric. A Simple Model of Product Quality with Elastic Demand. *Econ. Letters*, 1989, *29*(4), pp. 281–83.

_____ **and Hirshleifer, David.** Cooperation in a Repeated Prisoners' Dilemma with Ostracism. *J. Econ. Behav. Organ.*, August 1989, *12*(1), pp. 87–106.

Rasmussen, David W.; Fournier, Gary M. and Charity, Douglas A. The Impact of Cost of Living Differentials on Migration of Elderly People to Florida. *Rev. Reg. Stud.*, Spring 1989, *19*(2), pp. 48–54.

Rasmussen, Svend and Nielsen, A. Hjortshøj. The Impact of Quotas on the Optimal Adjust-

ment of Milk Production at the Farm Level: Reply. *Europ. Rev. Agr. Econ.*, 1989, *16*(4), pp. 523–24.

Rasmusson, Eugene M. Global Climate Variability: Interannual and Intraseasonal Time Scales. In *Oram, P. A., et al.*, 1989, pp. 237–48.

Rassekh, Farhad and Mokhtari, Manouchehr. The Tendency towards Factor Price Equalization among OECD Countries. *Rev. Econ. Statist.*, November 1989, *71*(4), pp. 636–42.

Rastoin, Jean-Louis. Stratégies des industries de l'agro-fourniture: La nouvelle donne. (Agribusiness Firm Strategies: The New Challenge. With English summary.) *Écon. Societes*, July 1989, *23*(7), pp. 69–90.

Ratcliffe, Barrie M. Bureaucracy and Early French Railroads: The Myth and the Reality. *J. Europ. Econ. Hist.*, Fall 1989, *18*(2), pp. 331–70.

Rathbone, Richard and Cruise O'Brien, Donal B. Contemporary West African States: Introduction. In *Cruise O'Brien, D. B.; Dunn, J. and Rathbone, R., eds.*, 1989, pp. 1–11.

Rattsø, Jørn. Macrodynamic Adjustment Mechanisms in a Dual Semi-industrialized Economy. *J. Devel. Econ.*, January 1989, *30*(1), pp. 47–69.

Rauch, James E. Increasing Returns to Scale and the Pattern of Trade. *J. Int. Econ.*, May 1989, *26*(3/4), pp. 359–69.

Rauscher, Michael. Foreign Debt and Renewable Resources. *Metroecon.*, February 1989, *40*(1), pp. 57–66.

Rausser, Gordon C. The Macroeconomic Dimension of Agricultural and Food Policy Reform. In *Helmuth, J. W. and Johnson, S. R., eds.*, Vol. 2, 1989, pp. 90–110.

_____ **and Foster, William E.** A Coherent Policy for U.S. Agriculture. In *Horwich, G. and Lynch, G. J., eds.*, 1989, pp. 191–237.

_____ **and Foster, William E.** Impacts of Economic Reform for Agricultural and Food Policy: Reaction. In *Helmuth, J. W. and Johnson, S. R., eds., Vol. 1*, 1989, pp. 95–99.

_____ **and Innes, Robert D.** Incomplete Markets and Government Agricultural Policy. *Amer. J. Agr. Econ.*, November 1989, *71*(4), pp. 915–31.

_____ **and Kitchen, John.** Interest Rates and Commodity Prices. *J. Agr. Econ. Res.*, Spring 1989, *41*(2), pp. 5–11.

_____ **and Wright, Brian D.** Alternative Strategies for Trade Policy Reform. In *von Witzke, H.; Runge, C. F. and Job, B., eds.*, 1989, pp. 117–59.

Raut, Lakshmi and Virmani, Arvind. Determinants of Consumption and Savings Behavior in Developing Countries. *World Bank Econ. Rev.*, September 1989, *3*(3), pp. 379–93.

Ravallion, Martin. Land-Contingent Poverty Alleviation Schemes. *World Devel.*, August 1989, *17*(8), pp. 1223–33.

_____. The Welfare Cost of Housing Standards: Theory with Application to Jakarta. *J. Urban Econ.*, September 1989, *26*(2), pp. 197–211.

_____ **and Chao, Kalvin.** Targeted Policies for

Poverty Alleviation under Imperfect Information: Algorithms and Applications. *J. Policy Modeling*, Summer 1989, *11*(2), pp. 213–24.

Raveh, Adi. A Nonmetric Approach to Linear Discriminant Analysis. *J. Amer. Statist. Assoc.*, March 1989, *84*(405), pp. 176–83.

Ravenal, Earl C. The Price of Defense. In *Crane, E. H. and Boaz, D.*, 1989, pp. 131–45.

Ravenscraft, David J. and Scherer, F. M. The Profitability of Mergers. *Int. J. Ind. Organ.*, Special Issue, March 1989, *7*(1), pp. 101–16.

Raviv, Artur and Harris, Milton. The Design of Securities. *J. Finan. Econ.*, October 1989, *24*(2), pp. 255–87.

Rawabdeh, M. A. and Civelek, M. A. An Empirical Investigation of the Portfolio Behaviour of the Jordanian Commercial Banks. *Middle East Bus. Econ. Rev.*, July 1989, *1*(2), pp. 27–35.

Rawson, Don and Hancock, Keith. Industrial Relations: Stability and Turmoil. In *Hancock, K.*, ed., 1989, pp. 166–91.

Ray, Aswini K. The International Political System and the Developing World: A View from the Periphery. In *Thomas, C. and Saravanamuttu, P.*, eds., 1989, pp. 13–28.

Ray, Brian; Rosenberg, Mark W. and Moore, Eric G. Redistribution of Immigrant Groups in Canada. In *Beach, C. M. and Green, A. G.*, 1989, pp. 62–79.

Ray, D. and Nachane, D. M. The Money-Multiplier: A Re-examination of the Indian Evidence. *Indian Econ. J.*, July–Sept. 1989, *37*(1), pp. 56–73.

Ray, Daryll E. Regression and Statistical Methods. In *Tweeten, L.*, ed., 1989, pp. 11–45.

Ray, Debraj. Credible Coalitions and the Core. *Int. J. Game Theory*, 1989, *18*(2), pp. 185–87.

_____ **and Bernheim, B. Douglas.** Collective Dynamic Consistency in Repeated Games. *Games Econ. Behav.*, December 1989, *1*(4), pp. 295–326.

_____ **and Bernheim, B. Douglas.** Markov Perfect Equilibria in Altruistic Growth Economies with Production Uncertainty. *J. Econ. Theory*, February 1989, *47*(1), pp. 195–202.

_____ **and Dutta, Bhaskar.** A Concept of Egalitarianism under Participation Constraints. *Econometrica*, May 1989, *57*(3), pp. 615–35.

_____ **and Sengupta, Kunal.** Interlinkages and the Pattern of Competition. In *Bardhan, P.*, ed. (*II*), 1989, pp. 243–63.

_____; **Sengupta, Kunal and Dutta, Bhaskar.** Contracts with Eviction in Infinitely Repeated Principal–Agent Relationships. In *Bardhan, P.*, ed. (*II*), 1989, pp. 93–121.

Ray, Edward John. The Determinants of Foreign Direct Investment in the United States, 1979–85. In *Feenstra, R. C.*, ed., 1989, pp. 53–77.

_____. The Impact of Rent Seeking Activity on U.S. Preferential Trade and World Debt. *Weltwirtsch. Arch.*, 1989, *125*(3), pp. 619–38.

Ray, George F. British Coal. *Nat. Inst. Econ. Rev.*, November 1989, (130), pp. 75–84.

Ray, Himanshu Prabha. Early Historical Trade: An Overview. *Indian Econ. Soc. Hist. Rev.*, Oct.–Dec. 1989, *26*(4), pp. 437–57.

Ray, Ranjan. Impact of Demographic Variables on Optimal Commodity Taxes: Evidence from U.K. Family Expenditure Surveys, 1967–85. *Public Finance*, 1989, *44*(3), pp. 437–52.

_____. A New Class of Decomposable Poverty Measures. *Indian Econ. J.*, April–June 1989, *36*(4), pp. 30–38.

_____ **and Murty, M. N.** A Computational Procedure for Calculating Optimal Commodity Taxes with Illustrative Evidence from Indian Budget Data. *Scand. J. Econ.*, 1989, *91*(4), pp. 655–70.

Ray, S.; Ghosh, S. and Lall, Sanjaya. The Determinants and Promotion of South–South Trade in Manufactured Products. In *Ventura-Dias, V.*, ed., 1989, pp. 131–64.

Ray, Subhash C. Consumer Demand in a System of Partial Rationing and Dual Pricing. *Indian Econ. Rev.*, Jan.–June 1989, *24*(1), pp. 25–43.

_____. Legal Control of Drunken Driving: A Time Series Study of California Data. *Int. J. Forecasting*, 1989, *5*(4), pp. 515–22.

_____ **and Segerson, Kathleen.** On the Equivalence of Alternative Measures of the Elasticity of Substitution. *Bull. Econ. Res.*, July 1989, *41*(3), pp. 207–12.

Ray, Sunil Baran. Planning for Rural Industrialisation: Some Basic Issues. In *Reddy, J. M.*, et al., eds. (*II*), 1989, pp. 112–21.

Ray, Tim, et al. Competition and the Momentum of Technical Change. In *Francis, A. and Tharakan, P. K. M.*, eds., 1989, pp. 165–99.

Ray, W. D. Rates of Convergence to Steady State for the Linear Growth Version of a Dynamic Linear Model (DLM). *Int. J. Forecasting*, 1989, *5*(4), pp. 537–45.

Rayment, Paul and Kol, Jacob. Allyn Young Specialisation and Intermediate Goods in Intra-industry Trade. In *Tharakan, P. K. M. and Kol, J.*, eds., 1989, pp. 51–68.

Raymond, José Luis; Argimón, Isabel and Valdés, Teófilo. Evolución de la recaudación en el IRPF: Determinación de las causas y estimación de efectos. (With English summary.) *Invest. Econ.*, January 1989, *13*(1), pp. 15–43.

Raynauld, Jacques; Beaulieu, Anne and Patry, Michel. L'analyse de la productivité des transporteurs aériens canadiens dans le années soixante-dix: Pour un autre plan de vol. (With English summary.) *L'Actual. Econ.*, June 1989, *65*(2), pp. 183–207.

Rayner, A. J.; Bates, J. M. and McDonald, J. R. S. Market Power in the Food Industry: A Note. *J. Agr. Econ.*, January 1989, *40*(1), pp. 101–08.

_____; **Hine, Robert C. and Ingersent, K. A.** Agriculture in the Uruguay Round: From the Punta del Este Declaration to the Geneva Accord. *J. Agr. Econ.*, September 1989, *40*(3), pp. 385–97.

Raz, Baruch. A Proposal for a Cooperative Water Project: The Aqaba-Eilat Canal/Port. In *Fishelson, G.*, ed., 1989, pp. 327–45.

Raza, Bilquees and Khan, Ashfaque H. The Demand for Money in Pakistan: Quarterly Results

1972–1987. *Pakistan Econ. Soc. Rev.*, Summer 1989, *27*(1), pp. 33–48.

Razin, Assaf and Frenkel, Jacob A. Exchange-Rate Management Viewed as Tax Policies. *Europ. Econ. Rev.*, April 1989, *33*(4), pp. 761–81.

_____ **and Frenkel, Jacob A.** International Effects of Tax Reforms. *Econ. J.*, Supplement, 1989, *99*(395), pp. 38–58.

Rea, Edward. Budget Accounting: Another View. *Public Budg. Finance*, Autumn 1989, *9*(3), pp. 102–03.

Rea, Samuel A., Jr. An Economic Analysis of Buyer's Breach: A Comment. *Can. J. Econ.*, November 1989, *22*(4), pp. 904–09.

Read, Christopher. Labour and Socialism in Tsarist Russia. In *Geary, D., ed.*, 1989, pp. 137–81.

Read, James A., Jr.; Carpenter, Paul R. and Graves, Frank C. Estimating the Cost of Switching Rights on Natural Gas Pipelines. *Energy J.*, October 1989, *10*(4), pp. 59–81.

Read, Martin and Gear, Tony. On-Line Group Decision Support. In *Lockett, A. G. and Islei, G., eds.*, 1989, pp. 124–33.

Read, Peter and Ulph, Alistair. Monopoly Extraction under Performance Constraints. *Bull. Econ. Res.*, April 1989, *41*(2), pp. 107–22.

Read, William A. and O'Brien, James L. The Involved Hospital. In *Eisdorfer, C.; Kessler, D. A. and Spector, A. N., eds.*, 1989, pp. 157–83.

Reading, Brian. Monetarism and Stagflation. In *Llewellyn, D. T., ed.*, 1989, pp. 83–107.

Reagan, Patricia B. and Stulz, René M. Contracts, Delivery Lags, and Currency Risks. *J. Int. Money Finance*, March 1989, *8*(1), pp. 89–103.

Realfonzo, Riccardo. Una "bibliografia ragionata" per lo studio dell'influenza di Schumpeter sul pensiero economico italiano (1907–1939). (With English summary.) *Studi. Econ.*, 1989, *44*(37), pp. 85–124.

Reardon, Thomas and Matlon, Peter. Seasonal Food Insecurity and Vulnerability in Drought-Affected Regions of Burkina Faso. In *Sahn, D. E., ed.*, 1989, pp. 118–36.

Reati, Angelo. A Note on the Alleged Redundancy of Labor Value. *Rev. Radical Polit. Econ.*, 1989, *21*(1–2), pp. 169–74.

Rebick, Marcus E. and Freeman, Richard B. Crumbling Pillar? Declining Union Density in Japan. *J. Japanese Int. Economies*, December 1989, *3*(4), pp. 578–605.

Rebitzer, James B. Efficiency Wages and Implicit Contracts: An Institutional Evaluation. In *Drago, R. and Perlman, R., eds.*, 1989, pp. 16–40.

_____. Unemployment, Long-term Employment Relations and the Determination of Unit Labour Cost Growth in U.S. Manufacturing Industries. *Int. Rev. Applied Econ.*, June 1989, *3*(2), pp. 125–47.

Rebstock, Wolfgang and Hoffman Friedrich. Unternehmungsethik. Eine Herausforderung an die Unternehmung. (With English summary.) *Z. Betriebswirtshaft*, June 1989, *59*(6), pp. 667–87.

Reckers, Philip M. J.; Duncan, William A. and LaRue, David. An Empirical Examination of the Influence of Selected Economic and Noneconomic Variables on Decision Making by Tax Professionals. In *Jones, S. M., ed.*, 1989, pp. 91–106.

_____ **and LaRue, David.** An Empirical Examination of the Influence of Selected Factors on Professional Tax Preparers' Decision Processes. In *Schwartz, B. N., ed.*, 1989, pp. 37–50.

Redclift, Michael. The Environmental Consequences of Latin America's Agricultural Development: Some Thoughts on the Brundtland Commission Report. *World Devel.*, March 1989, *17*(3), pp. 365–77.

_____ **and Goodman, David.** The International Farm Crisis: Introduction. In *Goodman, D. and Redclift, M., eds.*, 1989, pp. 1–22.

Reddaway, Brian. Tax Reform in the United Kingdom. In *Lawson, T.; Palma, J. G. and Sender, J., eds.*, 1989, pp. 141–54.

_____. Tax Reform in the United Kingdom. *Cambridge J. Econ.*, March 1989, *13*(1), pp. 141–54.

_____ **and Oppenheimer, Peter M.** The U.S. Economy: Performance and Prospects. *Nat. Inst. Econ. Rev.*, February 1989, (127), pp. 52–63.

Reddy, C. Subbarami and Reddy, P. Raja Sekhara. Inverse Labour Demand Equations in Selected Indian Industries. *Margin*, Jan.–March 1989, *21*(2), pp. 30–33.

Reddy, G. Pakki and Misra, R. K. Surplus Generation by Public Enterprises for the Financing of Seventh Plan: A Case of State Level Public Enterprises of Andhra Pradesh. In *Reddy, J. M., et al., eds. (I)*, 1989, pp. 125–37.

Reddy, G. Raghava. External Finance: India's Sixth and Seventh Plans. In *Reddy, J. M., et al., eds. (I)*, 1989, pp. 72–78.

Reddy, G. Raji. Financial Resources for the Seventh Five-Year Plan: Review and Prospects. In *Reddy, J. M., et al., eds. (II)*, 1989, pp. 219–39.

_____. Pattern of Financing Five-Year Plans: Changes and Implications. In *Reddy, J. M., et al., eds. (I)*, 1989, pp. 22–50.

_____. Performance and Prospects of Financing the Seventh Five-Year Plan. In *Reddy, J. M., et al., eds. (II)*, 1989, pp. 206–18.

Reddy, J. Mahender. Exports in the Seventh Five-Year Plan: Performance and Prospects. In *Reddy, J. M., et al., eds. (II)*, 1989, pp. 163–83.

_____. Foreign Aid to India: Some Aspects. In *Reddy, J. M., et al., eds. (I)*, 1989, pp. 79–99.

Reddy, K. C. A Note on the Growth and Structure of Indian Imports. In *Reddy, J. M., et al., eds. (II)*, 1989, pp. 184–88.

Reddy, K. N. Financing of the Seventh Five-Year Plan (1985–90): Retrospect and Prospect. In *Reddy, J. M., et al., eds. (II)*, 1989, pp. 189–205.

Reddy, P. Raja Sekhara and Reddy, C. Subba-rami. Inverse Labour Demand Equations in Selected Indian Industries. *Margin,* Jan.–March 1989, *21*(2), pp. 30–33.

Reddy, Tippa. Priorities and Allocations in Seventh Plan: Their Implications for Growth and Social Justice. In *Reddy, J. M., et al., eds. (II),* 1989, pp. 23–34.

Reddy, Y. Venugopal. Privatisation in India. In *Ramanadham, V. V., ed.,* 1989, pp. 178–98.

Redfern, Philip. Population Registers: Some Administrative and Statistical Pros and Cons. *J. Roy. Statist. Society,* 1989, *152*(1), pp. 1–28.

Redmond, J. Was Sterling Overvalued in 1925? A Comment. *Econ. Hist. Rev., 2nd Ser.,* February 1989, *42*(1), pp. 87–89.

Redstone, John and Switzer, Lorne N. The Impact of a Canada–U.S. Bilateral Free Trade Accord on the Canadian Minerals Industry. *Appl. Econ.,* February 1989, *21*(2), pp. 273–84.

Reece, B. F. and Van Hoa, Tran. An Empirical Study of Optimal Taxation on Australian Financial Institutions. *Econ. Letters,* 1989, *29*(2), pp. 163–66.

Reece, William S. and Zeischang, Kimberly D. Evidence on Taxation and Charitable Giving from the 1983 U.S. Treasury Tax Model File. *Econ. Letters,* November 1989, *31*(1), pp. 49–53.

Reed, Gary E.; Kram, Kathy E. and Yeager, Peter C. Decisions and Dilemmas: The Ethical Dimension in the Corporate Context. In *Post, J. E., ed.,* 1989, pp. 21–54.

Reed, J. David and Lesage, James P. The Dynamic Relationship between Export, Local, and Total Area Employment. *Reg. Sci. Urban Econ.,* December 1989, *19*(4), pp. 615–36.

——— **and Lesage, James P.** Interregional Wage Transmission in an Urban Hierarchy: Tests Using Vector Autoregressive Models. *Int. Reg. Sci. Rev.,* 1989, *12*(3), pp. 305–18.

Reed, Lowell C. A World Energy Outlook. In *Hawdon, D., ed.,* 1989, pp. 20–38.

Reed, Michael R.; Skees, Jerry R. and Vantreese, Valerie L. Mandatory Production Controls and Asset Values: A Case Study of Burley Tobacco Quotas. *Amer. J. Agr. Econ.,* May 1989, *71*(2), pp. 319–25.

Reed, Robert G., III. The Future of Independent Oil Refiners in the United States. In *[Evans, J. K.],* 1989, pp. 147–61.

Reed, Sarah A. and Koch, Bruce S. Resource Allocation Decisions by Charitable Organizations: An Experiment. In *Chan, J. L. and Patton, J. M., eds.,* 1989, pp. 99–122.

Reed, Thomas F. Do Union Organizers Matter? Individual Differences, Campaign Practices, and Representation Election Outcomes. *Ind. Lab. Relat. Rev.,* October 1989, *43*(1), pp. 103–19.

Reed, W. Robert. Information in Political Markets: A Little Knowledge Can Be a Dangerous Thing. *J. Law, Econ., Organ.,* Fall 1989, *5*(2), pp. 355–74.

——— **and Lott, John R., Jr.** Shirking and Sorting in a Political Market with Finite-Lived Politicians. *Public Choice,* April 1989, *61*(1), pp. 75–96.

Reed, William J. Optimal Investment in the Protection of a Vulnerable Biological Resource. *Natural Res. Modeling,* Fall 1989, *3*(4), pp. 463–80.

——— **and Clarke, Harry R.** The Tree-Cutting Problem in a Stochastic Environment: The Case of Age-Dependent Growth. *J. Econ. Dynam. Control,* October 1989, *13*(4), pp. 569–95.

——— **and Errico, Darrell.** A New Look at Whole-Forest Modeling. *Natural Res. Modeling,* Summer 1989, *3*(3), pp. 399–427.

Rees, P. H. Research Policy and Review 30. How to Add Value to Migration Data from the 1991 Census. *Environ. Planning A,* October 1989, *21*(10), pp. 1363–79.

Rees, Ray. Modelling Public Enterprise Performance. In *Helm, D.; Kay, J. and Thompson, D., eds.,* 1989, pp. 92–114.

———. Uncertainty, Information and Insurance. In *Hey, J. D., ed.,* 1989, pp. 47–78.

Reese, Joachim and Fandel, Günter. "Just-in-Time"-Logistik am Beispiel eines Zulieferbetriebs in der Automobilindustrie. (With English summary.) *Z. Betriebswirtschaft,* January 1989, *59*(1), pp. 55–69.

Reetz, Norbert. Wachstumsgleichgewicht und Verteilungsspielraum in einer kleinen offenen Volkswirtschaft. (Growth Equilibrium and Distribution in a Small Open Economy. With English summary.) *Schweiz. Z. Volkswirtsch. Statist.,* March 1989, *125*(1), pp. 19–42.

Reeves, Gary R.; Gonzales, Juan J. and Franz, Lori S. The Effect of Decision Maker Characteristics on Group Decision Making. In *Lockett, A. G. and Islei, G., eds.,* 1989, pp. 134–42.

Regan, Edward J. The Strategic Importance of Telecommunications to Banking. In *Jussawalla, M.; Okuma, T. and Araki, T., eds.,* 1989, pp. 118–23.

Regel, Roy W. and Murray, Dennis. Staff Performance Evaluation by Auditors: The Effect of Training on Accuracy and Consensus. In *Schwartz, B. N., ed.,* 1989, pp. 223–39.

Regens, James L. Congressional Cosponsorship of Acid Rain Controls. *Soc. Sci. Quart.,* June 1989, *70*(2), pp. 505–12.

Reggiani, Aura and Nijkamp, Peter. Spatial Interaction and Input–Output Models: A Dynamic Stochastic Multiobjective Framework. In *Miller, R. E.; Polenske, K. R. and Rose, A. Z., eds.,* 1989, pp. 193–205.

Regibeau, Pierre and Matutes, Carmen. Standardization across Markets and Entry. *J. Ind. Econ.,* June 1989, *37*(4), pp. 359–71.

Regini, Marino and Lange, Peter. Interests and Institutions—Forms of Social Regulation and Public Policy-Making. In *Lange, P. and Regini, M., eds.,* 1989, pp. 1–25.

——— **and Lange, Peter.** The Italian Case between Continuity and Change. In *Lange, P. and Regini, M., eds.*, 1989, pp. 249–72.

Register, Charles A. Racial Employment and Earnings Differentials: The Impact of the Reagan Administration—Reply. *Rev. Black Polit. Econ.*, Spring 1989, *17*(4), pp. 85–87.

———— **and Bruning, Edward R.** Technical Efficiency within Hospitals: Do Profit Incentives Matter? *Appl. Econ.*, September 1989, *21*(9), pp. 1217–33.

———— **and Sharp, Ansel M.** For-Profit Hospital Performance: The Impact of Time. *J. Behav. Econ.*, Winter 1989, *18*(4), pp. 307–16.

Regonini, Gloria and Dente, Bruno. Politics and Policies in Italy. In *Lange, P. and Regini, M., eds.*, 1989, pp. 51–79.

Reheis, Fritz. The Just State: Observations on Gustav von Schmoller's Political Theory. *Int. J. Soc. Econ.*, 1989, *16*(9–10–11), pp. 93–100.

Reher, David Sven and Iriso-Napal, Pedro Luis. Marital Fertility and Its Determinants in Rural and in Urban Spain, 1887–1930. *Population Stud.*, November 1989, *43*(3), pp. 405–27.

Reich, Michael R. and Marui, Eiji. International Cooperation for Health: Problems, Prospects, and Priorities: Overview and Introduction. In *Reich, M. R. and Marui, E., eds.*, 1989, pp. 1–20.

Reich, Simon. Roads to Follow: Regulating Direct Foreign Investment. *Int. Organ.*, Autumn 1989, *43*(4), pp. 543–84.

Reich, Utz-Peter. Essence and Appearance: Reflections on Input–Output Methodology in Terms of a Classical Paradigm. *Econ. Systems Res.*, 1989, *1*(4), pp. 417–28.

————; **Stäglin, Reiner and Stahmer, Carsten.** The Implementation of a Consistent System of Input–Output Tables for the Federal Republic of Germany. In *Franz, A. and Rainer, N., eds.*, 1989, pp. 111–30.

Reichelderfer, Katherine H. Externalities and the Returns to Agricultural Research: Discussion. *Amer. J. Agr. Econ.*, May 1989, *71*(2), pp. 464–65.

———— **and Hinkle, Maureen Kuwano.** The Evolution of Pesticide Policy: Environmental Interests and Agriculture. In *Krämer, C. S., ed.*, 1989, pp. 147–73.

Reichelstein, Stefan and Melumad, Nahum D. Value of Communication in Agencies. *J. Econ. Theory*, April 1989, *47*(2), pp. 334–68.

Reichenstein, William R. Martingales and Efficient Forecasts of Effective Mortgage Rates. *J. Real Estate Finance Econ.*, December 1989, *2*(4), pp. 317–30.

———— **and Raabe, William A.** Investment Returns and Inflation Neutrality under Alternative Tax Structures: Investment and Public Policy Implications. In *Jones, S. M., ed.*, 1989, pp. 149–63.

Reichert, Alan K.; Brewer, Elijah, III and Garcia, Gillian G. A Statistical Analysis of S&L Accounting Profits. In *Lee, C. F., ed.*, 1989, pp. 163–93.

Reichlin, Lucrezia. Intertemporal Consumer Behaviour under Structural Changes in Income:

Comment. *Econometric Rev.*, 1989, *8*(1), pp. 123–31.

————. Structural Change and Unit Root Econometrics. *Econ. Letters*, December 1989, *31*(3), pp. 231–33.

———— **and Rappoport, Peter.** On Broken Trends, Random Walks and Non-Stationary Cycles. In *Di Matteo, M.; Goodwin, R. M. and Vercelli, A., eds.*, 1989, pp. 305–31.

———— **and Rappoport, Peter.** Segmented Trends and Non-stationary Time Series. *Econ. J.*, Supplement, 1989, *99*(395), pp. 168–77.

Reid, Bradford G. Government Budgets and Aggregate Consumption: Cross-sectional Evidence from Canadian Provincial Data. *J. Macroecon.*, Winter 1989, *11*(1), pp. 121–32.

———— **and Boothe, Paul M.** Asset Returns and Government Budgets in a Small Open Economy: Empirical Evidence for Canada. *J. Monet. Econ.*, January 1989, *23*(1), pp. 65–77.

Reid, Donald W. and Tew, Bernard V. Land Allocation under Uncertainty for Alternative Specifications of Return Distributions: Comment. *Amer. J. Agr. Econ.*, May 1989, *71*(2), pp. 439–40.

Reid, Frank; Gunderson, Morley and Kervin, John. The Effect of Labour Relations Legislation on Strike Incidence. *Can. J. Econ.*, November 1989, *22*(4), pp. 779–94.

Reid, Gary J. Measuring Government Performance: The Case of Government Waste. *Nat. Tax J.*, March 1989, *42*(1), pp. 29–44.

Reid, Gavin C. Adam Smith's Stadial Analysis as a Sequence of Societal Growth Trajectories. *Scot. J. Polit. Econ.*, February 1989, *36*(1), pp. 59–70.

———— **and Wolfe, J. N.** Hicks, John R. In *Wood, J. C. and Woods, R. N., eds.*, Vol. 3, 1989, *1979*, pp. 217–21.

Reid, Joseph D., Jr. and Kurth, Michael M. Public Employees in Political Firms: Part B. Civil Service and Militancy. *Public Choice*, January 1989, *60*(1), pp. 41–54.

Reid, Robert J. and Vaillancourt, François. Administrative and Compliance Costs of Taxation: Canada. In *International Fiscal Association, ed. (I)*, 1989, pp. 267–90.

Reiffen, David and Levy, David T. Vertical Integration in a Spatial Setting: Implications of the Successive Monopoly Distortion. *Econ. Letters*, 1989, *29*(1), pp. 77–81.

Reig Martínez, Ernest; Sanchis i Marco, Manuel and Castillo Gimenez, Juana. Spain's Trade and Development Strategies. In *Yannopoulos, G. N., ed.*, 1989, pp. 40–65.

Reilly, Susan. An Analysis of the Factors Influencing the Second Tier and Its Evolution. *Australian Bull. Lab.*, June 1989, *15*(3), pp. 200–222.

Reilly, William K. The Future of Environmental Law. *Yale J. Regul.*, Summer 1989, *6*(2), pp. 351–55.

Reimers, Cordelia W. Pension Wealth, Age-Wealth Profiles, and the Distribution of Net Worth: Comment. In *Lipsey, R. E. and Tice, H. S., eds.*, 1989, pp. 731–36.

———— **and Honig, Marjorie.** Is It Worth Eliminating the Retirement Test? *Amer. Econ. Rev.*, May 1989, 79(2), pp. 103–07.

———— **and Honig, Marjorie.** The Retirement Process in the United States: Mobility among Full-Time Work, Partial Retirement, and Full Retirement. In *Schmähl, W., ed.*, 1989, pp. 115–31.

Reimers, Hans-Eggert and Siebeck, Karin. Ein einfaches Modell kontinuierlicher Anpassung für den Arbeits- und Gütermarkt—Einige empirische Befunde. (A Simple Continuous Time Adjustment Model for the Labour and the Goods Market—Some Empirical Evidence. With English summary.) *Ifo-Studien*, 1989, 35(1), pp. 27–52.

Reimers, Roland. The Verification of Conventional Disarmament Treaties by Remote Sensing. In *Altmann, J. and Rotblat, J., eds.*, 1989, pp. 172–83.

Reinert, Kenneth A. Nontradable Goods and the Timmer–Falcon Effect. *Developing Econ.*, June 1989, 27(2), pp. 206–13.

Reinganum, Jennifer F. The Timing of Innovation: Research, Development, and Diffusion. In *Schmalensee, R. and Willig, R. D., eds.*, Vol. 1, 1989, pp. 849–908.

Reingen, Peter H.; Kelley, Craig A. and Gaidis, William C. The Use of Vivid Stimuli to Enhance Comprehension of the Content of Product Warning Messages. *J. Cons. Aff.*, Winter 1989, 23(2), pp. 243–66.

Reinhard, A.; Thijssen, G. and Oskam, Arie. Wasmodel-2: A Disaggregated Agricultural Sector Model Partly Based on Prior Information. In *Bauer, S. and Henrichsmeyer, W., eds.*, 1989, pp. 53–69.

Reinhardt, Forest and McCraw, Thomas K. Losing to Win: U.S. Steel's Pricing, Investment Decisions, and Market Share, 1901–1938. *J. Econ. Hist.*, September 1989, 49(3), pp. 593–619.

Reinhardt, Uwe E. Economists in Health Care: Saviors, or Elephants in a Porcelain Shop? *Amer. Econ. Rev.*, May 1989, 79(2), pp. 337–42.

Reining, Robert. Two Methods for Estimating Real Structural Change in Agriculture. *J. Agr. Econ. Res.*, Winter 1989, 41(1), pp. 39–43.

Reinsel, Gregory C. and Chi, Eric M. Models for Longitudinal Data with Random Effects and AR(1) Errors. *J. Amer. Statist. Assoc.*, June 1989, 84(406), pp. 452–59.

Reisen, Helmut. Public Debt, North and South. In *Husain, I. and Diwan, I., eds.*, 1989, pp. 116–27.

Reishus, David. Financing Child Care: Who Will Pay for the Kids? *Nat. Tax J.*, September 1989, 42(3), pp. 249–59.

Reisman, David A. In Memoriam: John Richard Hicks. *Singapore Econ. Rev.*, October 1989, 34(2), pp. 9–15.

Reiss, Peter C. and Spiller, Pablo T. Competition and Entry in Small Airline Markets. *J. Law Econ.*, Part 2, October 1989, 32(2), pp. S179–202.

Reiss, Winfried; Landes, Thomas and Loistl,

Otto. The Determinants of the Fundamental Value Part of a Share Price. In *Loistl, O. and Landes, T., ed.*, 1989, pp. 129–63.

————; **Landes, Thomas and Loistl, Otto.** The Market Microstructure and the Dynamic Pricing of Financial Assets. In *Loistl, O. and Landes, T., ed.*, 1989, pp. 53–108.

———— **and Loistl, Otto.** Pricebuilding Mechanisms and Their Modelling in the Literature. In *Loistl, O. and Landes, T., ed.*, 1989, pp. 13–51.

Reitzes, Donald C. and Mutran, Elizabeth. Labor Force Participation and Health: A Cohort Comparison of Older Male Workers. *Soc. Sci. Quart.*, June 1989, 70(2), pp. 449–67.

Rejda, George E. and Lee, Kyung W. State Unemployment Compensation Programs: Immediate Reforms Needed. *J. Risk Ins.*, December 1989, 56(4), pp. 649–69.

Rele, J. R. and Retherford, Robert D. A Decomposition of Recent Fertility Changes in South Asia. *Population Devel. Rev.*, December 1989, 15(4), pp. 739–47.

Remington, Robin Alison. Romania: Boundary Disintegration between East and South. In *Schulz, B. H. and Hansen, W. W., eds.*, 1989, pp. 197–211.

Renard, Mary-Françoise. Les régions françaises et la qualification régionale. (With English summary.) *Revue Écon. Politique*, Sept.–Oct. 1989, 99(5), pp. 744–61.

Renault, Eric; Gourieroux, Christian and Monfort, Alan. Testing for Common Roots. *Econometrica*, January 1989, 57(1), pp. 171–85.

Renes, Gusta and Hagenaars, Aldi. The Perceived Distribution of Job Characteristics. *Europ. Econ. Rev.*, April 1989, 33(4), pp. 845–62.

Reno, Virginia P. and Packard, Michael D. A Look at Very Early Retirees. *Soc. Sec. Bull.*, March 1989, 52(3), pp. 16–29.

Renshaw, Edward F. An Alternative Plan for Cutting the Cost of Social Security. *Challenge*, July–Aug. 1989, 32(4), pp. 54–56.

————. An Oil Import Fee and Drilling Activity in the USA. *Energy Econ.*, April 1989, 11(2), pp. 158–60.

Renshaw, Geoff T. Market Liberalisation, Equity and Development: Summary and Conclusions. In *Renshaw, G. T., ed.*, 1989, pp. 141–67.

Rentzler, Joel; Elton, Edwin J. and Gruber, Martin J. New Public Offerings, Information, and Investor Rationality: The Case of Publicly Offered Commodity Funds. *J. Bus.*, January 1989, 62(1), pp. 1–15.

Reny, Philip J.; McAfee, R. Preston and McMillan, John. Extracting the Surplus in the Common-Value Auction. *Econometrica*, November 1989, 57(6), pp. 1451–59.

Repetto, Robert. Economic Incentives for Sustainable Production. In *Schramm, G. and Warford, J. J., eds.*, 1989, pp. 69–86.

————. Nature's Resources as Productive Assets. *Challenge*, Sept.–Oct. 1989, 32(5), pp. 16–20.

Reponen, Tapio. Aligning Information Systems Strategy to Business Strategy: Case Finnpap.

Liiketaloudellinen Aikak., 1989, *38*(4), pp. 360–73.

Reppy, Judith. Conversion from Military Research and Development: Economic Aspects. In *Rotblat, J. and Goldanskii, V. I., eds.*, 1989, pp. 171–77.

Repullo, Rafael. Los efectos económicos de los coeficientes bancarios: Un análisis teórico. (With English summary.) *Invest. Econ.*, May 1989, *13*(2), pp. 227–44.

_____. On the Efficiency of Equilibrium with Transaction Costs. *Economica*, February 1989, *56*(221), pp. 49–59.

Reschovsky, Andrew and Chernick, Howard. Federal Tax Reform and the Taxation of Urban Residents. *Public Finance Quart.*, April 1989, *17*(2), pp. 123–57.

Resek, Robert W. and Hodgman, Donald R. Italian Monetary and Foreign Exchange Policy. In *Hodgman, D. R. and Wood, G. E., eds.*, 1989, pp. 62–86.

Resnick, Bruce G. and Klemkosky, Robert C. An Analysis of Variance Test for Linearity of the Two-Parameter Asset Pricing Model. *J. Econ. Bus.*, November 1989, *41*(4), pp. 265–82.

Resnick, Stephen and Wolff, Richard. The New Marxian Economics: Building on Althusser's Legacy. *Écon. Societes*, June 1989, *23*(6), pp. 185–200.

Resnik, Harvey L. P. and Tamerin, John S. Risk Taking by Individual Option—Case Study: Cigarette Smoking. In *Diamond, P. and Rothschild, M., eds.*, 1989, *1972*, pp. 5–16.

Restoy, Fernando. Posibilidades de sustitución entre inputs energéticos en la industria manufacturera española. (With English summary.) *Invest. Econ.*, September 1989, *13*(3), pp. 407–37.

Reszke, Irena. Actual and Potential Effects of Patterns of Working Time on the Status of Women in Poland. In *Agassi, J. B. and Heycock, S., eds.*, 1989, pp. 229–37.

Retherford, Robert D. and Rele, J. R. A Decomposition of Recent Fertility Changes in South Asia. *Population Devel. Rev.*, December 1989, *15*(4), pp. 739–47.

Rettig, R. Bruce; Berkes, Fikret and Pinkerton, Evelyn. The Future of Fisheries Co-management: A Multi-disciplinary Assessment. In *Pinkerton, E., ed.*, 1989, pp. 273–89.

Reubens, Beatrice G. Unemployment Insurance in the United States and Europe, 1973–83. *Mon. Lab. Rev.*, April 1989, *112*(4), pp. 22–31.

Reus, Estiva and Dupont, Frédéric. Le profit macroéconomique monétaire. (Monetary Macroeconomic Profit. With English summary.) *Écon. Appl.*, 1989, *42*(2), pp. 87–114.

ReVelle, Charles; Cohon, Jared and Klimberg, Ronald K. NMIS: A National Model for Inspection Selection with Limited Resources. In *Lockett, A. G. and Islei, G., eds.*, 1989, pp. 244–53.

Revelle, Roger R. Food, Population and Conflict in Africa. In *Rotblat, J. and Goldanskii, V. I., eds.*, 1989, pp. 240–47.

_____. Thoughts on Abatement and Adaptation. In *Rosenberg, N. J., et al., eds.*, 1989, pp. 167–74.

Revenga, Ana L. and Katz, Lawrence F. Changes in the Structure of Wages: The United States vs Japan. *J. Japanese Int. Economies*, December 1989, *3*(4), pp. 522–53.

Révész, Gábor. How the Economic Reforms Were Distorted. *Eastern Europ. Econ.*, Spring 1989, *27*(3), pp. 61–84.

Revesz, John T. The Optimal Taxation of Labour Income. *Public Finance*, 1989, *44*(3), pp. 453–75.

Revesz, Richard L. and Kornhauser, Lewis A. Sharing Damages among Multiple Tortfeasors. *Yale Law J.*, March 1989, *98*(5), pp. 831–84.

Revsine, Lawrence and Powers, Marian. Lessors' Accounting and Residual Values: Comdisco, Barron's and GAAP. *Accounting Rev.*, April 1989, *64*(2), pp. 346–68.

Rexroat, Cynthia. Economic Transformation, Family Structure, and Poverty Rates of Black Children in Metropolitan Areas. *Amer. Econ. Rev.*, May 1989, *79*(2), pp. 67–70.

Rey, Guido. Small Firms: Profile and Analysis, 1981–85. In *Goodman, E. and Bamford, J., eds.*, 1989, pp. 69–110.

Rey, Patrick; Guesnerie, Roger and Picard, Pierre. Adverse Selection and Moral Hazard with Risk Neutral Agents. *Europ. Econ. Rev.*, April 1989, *33*(4), pp. 807–23.

Reyneri, Emilio. The Italian Labor Market: Between State Control and Social Regulation. In *Lange, P. and Regini, M., eds.*, 1989, pp. 129–45.

Reynolds, Clark W. and Camard, Wayne. Flow-of-Funds and National Income and Product Account Savings Estimates in Latin America. In *Lipsey, R. E. and Tice, H. S., eds.*, 1989, pp. 153–80.

Reynolds, John E.; Moss, Charles B. and Shonkwiler, J. S. Government Payments to Farmers and Real Agricultural Asset Values in the 1980s. *Southern J. Agr. Econ.*, December 1989, *21*(2), pp. 139–53.

Reynolds, Morgan O. and Lott, John R., Jr. Production Costs and Deregulation. *Public Choice*, May 1989, *61*(2), pp. 183–86.

Reynolds, R. Larry. The Delivery of Medical Care and Institutional Change. *J. Econ. Issues*, March 1989, *23*(1), pp. 215–29.

_____. Institutionally Determined Property Claims. In *Tool, M. R. and Samuels, W. J., eds. (III)*, 1989, *1985*, pp. 237–45.

_____. Reply [Medical Care and Institutional Change]. *J. Econ. Issues*, December 1989, *23*(4), pp. 1179–80.

_____ and Barney, L. Dwayne, Jr. An Economic Analysis of Transplant Organs. *Atlantic Econ. J.*, September 1989, *17*(3), pp. 12–20.

Reynolds, Robert J.; Logan, John W. and Masson, Robert T. Efficient Regulation with Little Information: Reality in the Limit? *Int. Econ. Rev.*, November 1989, *30*(4), pp. 851–61.

Reynoso, Alejandro and Dornbusch, Rudiger. Financial Factors in Economic Development. *Amer. Econ. Rev.*, May 1989, 79(2), pp. 204–09.

de Rezende, Condorcet Pereira. The Disregard of a Legal Entity for Tax Purposes: General Report. In *International Fiscal Association, ed. (II)*, 1989, pp. 19–40.

de Rezende, Gervásio Castro. Agricultura e ajuste externo no Brasil: Novas considerações. (With English summary.) *Pesquisa Planejamento Econ.*, December 1989, 19(3), pp. 553–78.

Rhee, Changyong and Paz Espinosa, Maria. Efficient Wage Bargaining as a Repeated Game. *Quart. J. Econ.*, August 1989, 104(3), pp. 565–88.

Rhind, D. W. and Mounsey, H. M. The Chorley Committee and "Handling Geographic Information." *Environ. Planning A*, May 1989, 21(5), pp. 571–85.

Rhine, Sherrie L. W. The Effect of State Mandates on Student Performance. *Amer. Econ. Rev.*, May 1989, 79(2), pp. 231–35.

————; **Santos, Maria C. and Cohn, Elchanan.** Institutions of Higher Education as Multiproduct Firms: Economies of Scale and Scope. *Rev. Econ. Statist.*, May 1989, 71(2), pp. 284–90.

Rho, Jeong Hyun and Kim, Tschangcho John. Solving a Three-Dimensional Urban Activity Model of Land Use Intensity and Transport Congestion. *J. Reg. Sci.*, November 1989, 29(4), pp. 595–613.

Rhoades, Stephen A. and Amel, Dean F. Empirical Evidence on the Motives for Bank Mergers. *Eastern Econ. J.*, Jan.–March 1989, 15(1), pp. 17–27.

Rhode, Paul and Olmstead, Alan L. The U.S. Energy Crisis of 1920 and the Search for New Oil Supplies. In *Ferrier, R. W. and Fursenko, A., eds.*, 1989, pp. 83–93.

Rhodes, Carolyn. Reciprocity in Trade: The Utility of a Bargaining Strategy. *Int. Organ.*, Spring 1989, 43(2), pp. 273–99.

Rhodes, George F., Jr. and Sampath, R. K. A Note on Optimal Pricing of Publicly Produced Intermediate Inputs: Response. *Atlantic Econ. J.*, September 1989, 17(3), pp. 47–48.

Rhodes, Larry E. and Valenta, Lee. Industry-Based Supported Employment: An Enclave Approach. In *Wehman, P. and Kregel, J., eds.*, 1989, pp. 53–68.

Rhodes, Martin. Whither Regulation? 'Disorganized Capitalism' and the West European Labour Market. In *Hancher, L. and Moran, M., eds.*, 1989, pp. 227–67.

Rhodes, V. James. A Markov Chain Analysis of Pork Farm Size Distributions in the South: Comment. *Southern J. Agr. Econ.*, December 1989, 21(2), pp. 217–18.

Rhodus, W. Timothy; Baldwin, E. Dean and Henderson, Dennis R. Pricing Accuracy and Efficiency in a Pilot Electronic Hog Market. *Amer. J. Agr. Econ.*, November 1989, 71(4), pp. 874–82.

Rhys, John and Allsopp, Christopher. The Macroeconomic Impact of North Sea Oil. In *Helm, D.; Kay, J. and Thompson, D., eds.*, 1989, pp. 377–410.

Ribaudo, Marc O. Targeting the Conservation Reserve Program to Maximize Water Quality Benefits. *Land Econ.*, November 1989, 65(4), pp. 320–32.

Ribhegge, Hermann. Widersprüche in der Geldmengenpolitik der Deutschen Bundesbank. (Contradictions in the Money Supply Policy of the Deutsche Bundesbank. With English summary.) *Kredit Kapital*, 1989, 22(2), pp. 197–220.

Ricart i Costa, Joan E. On Managerial Contracting with Asymmetric Information. *Europ. Econ. Rev.*, December 1989, 33(9), pp. 1805–29.

Ricca, Sergio. The Behaviour of the State and Precarious Work. In *Rodgers, G. and Rodgers, J., eds.*, 1989, pp. 287–93.

Rice, Charles Owen. Confessions of an Anti-communist. *Labor Hist.*, Summer 1989, 30(3), pp. 449–62.

Rice, Dorothy P. The Characteristics and Health of the Elderly. In *Eisdorfer, C.; Kessler, D. A. and Spector, A. N., eds.*, 1989, pp. 3–26.

————. Health and Long-term Care for the Aged. *Amer. Econ. Rev.*, May 1989, 79(2), pp. 343–48.

———— **and Kelman, Sander.** Measuring Comorbidity and Overlap in the Hospitalization Cost for Alcohol and Drug Abuse and Mental Illness. *Inquiry*, Summer 1989, 26(2), pp. 249–60.

Rice, Edward M. and Karpoff, Jonathan M. Organizational Form, Share Transferability, and Firm Performance: Evidence from the ANCSA Corporations. *J. Finan. Econ.*, September 1989, 24(1), pp. 69–105.

Rice, G. Randolph. The After-Tax Income Distribution in the U.S. during an Inflationary Decade: A Look Backwards at the 1970s. *Rev. Soc. Econ.*, Fall 1989, 47(3), pp. 322–32.

————. Capital–Skill Complementarity and the Interregional Distribution of Human Capital in U.S. Manufacturing. *Appl. Econ.*, August 1989, 21(8), pp. 1087–98.

Rice, Martha Larus; Metzler, Helen M. D. and Shafer, Michael S. Integration in the Workplace: Perceptions and Experiences of Employees without Disabilities. In *Wehman, P. and Kregel, J., eds.*, 1989, pp. 137–59.

Rice, Phillip and Frater, Philip. The Demand for Petrol with Explicit New Car Fuel Efficiency Effects: A UK Study 1977–86. *Energy Econ.*, April 1989, 11(2), pp. 95–104.

Rice, Robert C. Riau and Jambi: Rapid Growth in Dualistic Natural Resource-Intensive Economies. In *Hill, H., ed.*, 1989, pp. 124–50.

Rich, Daniel P. and Goel, Rajeev K. On the Economic Incentives for Taking Bribes. *Public Choice*, June 1989, 61(3), pp. 269–75.

Rich, Georg. Canadian Banks, Gold, and the Crisis of 1907. *Exploration Econ. Hist.*, April 1989, 26(2), pp. 135–60.

Rich, Robert W. Testing the Rationality of Inflation Forecasts from Survey Data: Another Look at the SRC Expected Price Change Data. *Rev. Econ. Statist.*, November 1989, *71*(4), pp. 682–86.

Richard, Jean-François and Hendry, David F. Recent Developments in the Theory of Encompassing. In *Cornet, B. and Tulkens, H., eds.*, 1989, pp. 393–440.

_____ and Phlips, Louis. A Dynamic Oligopoly Model with Demand Inertia and Inventories. *Math. Soc. Sci.*, August 1989, *18*(1), pp. 1–32.

Richard, Patricia Bayer. Alternative Abortion Policies: What Are the Health Consequences? *Soc. Sci. Quart.*, December 1989, *70*(4), pp. 941–55.

Richard, Scott F. A New Approach to Production Equilibria in Vector Lattices. *J. Math. Econ.*, 1989, *18*(1), pp. 41–56.

_____ and Roll, Richard. Prepayments on Fixed-Rate Mortgage-Backed Securities. *J. Portfol. Manage.*, Spring 1989, *15*(3), pp. 73–82.

Richards, Daniel J. and Garman, David M. Policy Rules, Inflationary Bias, and Cyclical Stability. *J. Money, Credit, Banking*, November 1989, *21*(4), pp. 409–21.

Richards, P. J. Market Liberalisation, Equity and Development: Preface. In *Renshaw, G. T., ed.*, 1989, pp. v–xii.

Richards, Steven and Livingston, Lori A. U.S. Import and Export Prices Continued to Register Sizable Gains in 1988. *Mon. Lab. Rev.*, May 1989, *112*(5), pp. 11–33.

Richardson, B. J. The Economics of Australian Hospitals: Forum: The NSW Public Accounts Committee Inquiry into Payments to Visiting Medical Officers. In *Smith, C. S., ed.*, 1989, pp. 291–300.

Richardson, David. Accounting for Profits in the British Trade in Slaves: Reply. *Exploration Econ. Hist.*, October 1989, *26*(4), pp. 492–99.

_____. The Eighteenth-Century British Slave Trade: Estimates of Its Volume and Coastal Distribution in Africa. In *Ransom, R. L., ed.*, 1989, pp. 151–95.

Richardson, Greg D.; Michener, H. Andrew and Salzer, Mark S. Extensions of Value Solutions in Constant-Sum Non-sidepayment Games. *J. Conflict Resolution*, September 1989, *33*(3), pp. 530–53.

Richardson, Harry W. and Brennan, Ellen M. Asian Megacity Characteristics, Problems, and Policies. *Int. Reg. Sci. Rev.*, 1989, *12*(2), pp. 117–29.

_____; Gordon, Peter and Kumar, Ajay. Congestion, Changing Metropolitan Structure, and City Size in the United States. *Int. Reg. Sci. Rev.*, 1989, *12*(1), pp. 45–56.

_____; Gordon, Peter and Kumar, Ajay. Gender Differences in Metropolitan Travel Behavior. *Reg. Stud.*, December 1989, *23*(6), pp. 499–510.

_____; Gordon, Peter and Kumar, Ajay. The Influence of Metropolitan Spatial Structure on Commuting Time. *J. Urban Econ.*, September 1989, *26*(2), pp. 138–51.

_____; Gordon, Peter and Kumar, Ajay. The Spatial Mismatch Hypothesis: Some New Evidence. *Urban Stud.*, June 1989, *26*(3), pp. 315–26.

Richardson, J. Health Care Economics in Singapore: Trends and Issues: Commentary. In *Smith, C. S., ed.*, 1989, pp. 169–71.

_____; Hall, Jane and Salkeld, G. Cost Utility Analysis: The Compatibility of Measurement Techniques and the Measurement of Utility through Time. In *Smith, C. S., ed.*, 1989, pp. 31–60.

Richardson, J. David. Empirical Research on Trade Liberalisation with Imperfect Competition: A Survey. *OECD Econ. Stud.*, Spring 1989, (12), pp. 7–50.

Richardson, James W. and Bowker, J. M. Impacts of Alternative Farm Policies on Rural Communities. *Southern J. Agr. Econ.*, December 1989, *21*(2), pp. 35–46.

Richardson, Jeff R. The Inducement Hypothesis: That Doctors Generate Demand for Their Own Services. In *Butler, J. R. G. and Doessel, D. P., eds.*, 1989, *1981*, pp. 215–37.

_____. Ownership and Regulation in the Health Care Sector. In *Butler, J. R. G. and Doessel, D. P., eds.*, 1989, *1987*, pp. 87–108.

Richardson, Matthew and Stock, James H. Drawing Inferences from Statistics Based on Multiyear Asset Returns. *J. Finan. Econ.*, December 1989, *25*(2), pp. 323–48.

Richardson, Miles and Green, Bill. The Fisheries Co-management Initiative in Haida Gwaii. In *Pinkerton, E., ed.*, 1989, pp. 249–61.

Richardson, Philip. The Structure of Capital during the Industrial Revolution Revisited: Two Case Studies form the Cotton Textile Industry. *Econ. Hist. Rev., 2nd Ser.*, November 1989, *42*(4), pp. 484–503.

Richardson, Ray and Kelly, John. Annual Review Article 1988. *Brit. J. Ind. Relat.*, March 1989, *27*(1), pp. 133–54.

_____ and Wood, Stephen. Productivity Change in the Coal Industry and the New Industrial Relations. *Brit. J. Ind. Relat.*, March 1989, *27*(1), pp. 33–55.

Richardson, Stephen R. Corporate Tax Reform and Its Economic Impact: An Evaluation of the Phase 1 Proposals: Comment: Corporate Tax Incentives and Tax Losses. In *Mintz, J. and Whalley, J., eds.*, 1989, pp. 130–36.

Richardson, Sue and McNabb, Robert. Earnings, Education and Experience: Is Australia Different? *Australian Econ. Pap.*, June 1989, *28*(52), pp. 57–75.

Richardson, Thomas and Clayton, Elizabeth. Soviet Control of City Size. *Econ. Devel. Cult. Change*, October 1989, *38*(1), pp. 155–65.

Richardson, William. Architecture, Urban Planning and Housing during the First Five Year Plans: Hannes Meyer in the USSR, 1930–1936. *Urban Stud.*, February 1989, *26*(1), pp. 155–63.

Richelle, Yves; Allard, Marie and Bronsard, Camille. Temporary Pareto Optimum Theory. *J. Public Econ.*, April 1989, *38*(3), pp. 343–68.

Richter, Josef and Rainer, Norbert. The SNA Make-Use Framework as a Descriptive Basis for IQ Analysis. In *Franz, A. and Rainer, N., eds.*, 1989, pp. 233–55.

Richter, Lothar. Improving Employment and Manpower Information in Developing Countries: Results and Lessons of an ILO Technical Co-operation Programme. *Int. Lab. Rev.*, 1989, *128*(5), pp. 661–73.

Richter, Rudolf. The Louvre Accord from the Viewpoint of the New Institutional Economics. *J. Inst. Theoretical Econ.*, December 1989, *145*(4), pp. 704–19.

_____. Views and Comments on Transaction Costs and the Governance Structure of Political Institutions. *J. Inst. Theoretical Econ.*, December 1989, *145*(4), pp. 659–60.

_____ **and Furubotn, Eirik G.** The New Institutional Approach to Economic History. *J. Inst. Theoretical Econ.*, March 1989, *145*(1), pp. 1–15.

Richter, Sándor. Trade with the Soviet Union. A Comparison of the Experiences of Austria, Finland, Yugoslavia and Hungary. *Acta Oecon.*, 1989, *41*(1–2), pp. 27–52.

Richter, Walther. Impact of Information Technology on Education, Training, and Employment in European OECD Countries. In *Jussawalla, M.; Okuma, T. and Araki, T., eds.*, 1989, pp. 199–204.

Richtering, Jürgen. The Debt Situation of the Developing Countries: A Medium-Term Scenario Analysis. In *Krelle, W., ed.*, 1989, pp. 527–39.

Riddell-Dixon, Elizabeth. Canada at the Preparatory Commission: Policies and Challenges. In *McRae, D. and Munro, G., eds.*, 1989, pp. 69–91.

Ridder, Geert; Hartog, Joop and Pfann, Gerard A. (Non-)graduation and the Earnings Function: An Inquiry on Self-Selection. *Europ. Econ. Rev.*, September 1989, *33*(7), pp. 1373–95.

Rideout, Douglas B. and Hof, John G. Limitations of the With and Without Principle in Benefit–Cost Analysis. *Public Finance Quart.*, April 1989, *17*(2), pp. 216–26.

Ridings, Eugene W. Business Associationalism, the Legitimation of Enterprise, and the Emergence of a Business Elite in Nineteenth-Century Brazil. *Bus. Hist. Rev.*, Winter 1989, *63*(4), pp. 757–96.

Rie, Michael A. Professional Ethics and Political Power. In *Strosberg, M. A.; Fein, I. A. and Carroll, J. D., eds.*, 1989, pp. 82–86.

Riebel, Paul. Wirtschaftsdynamik, Unternehmensführung und Unternehmensrechnung. (With English summary.) Z. *Betriebswirtshaft*, March 1989, *59*(3), pp. 247–59.

Rieber, William and Quah, Euston. Value of Children in Compensation for Wrongful Death. *Int. Rev. Law Econ.*, December 1989, *9*(2), pp. 165–79.

Riebsame, William E. Assessing the Social Impli-

cations of Climate Fluctuation through Climate Impact Studies. In *Oram, P. A., et al.*, 1989, pp. 451–67.

Riedel, James. The Demand for LDC Exports of Manufactures: Estimates from Hong Kong: A Rejoinder. *Econ. J.*, June 1989, *99*(396), pp. 467–70.

Riefler, Roger F. Chinese Urban Location Patterns. *Reg. Sci. Persp.*, 1989, *19*(1), pp. 25–39.

Rieger, Hans Christoph. Regional Economic Co-operation in the Asia-Pacific Region. *Asian-Pacific Econ. Lit.*, September 1989, *3*(2), pp. 5–33.

Rieke, Wolfgang. The Prospects for a European Central Bank: Panel Discussion. In *De Cecco, M. and Giovannini, A., eds.*, 1989, pp. 343–47.

Riemenschneider, Charles H. and Young, Robert E., II. Agriculture and the Failure of the Budget Process. In *Krämer, C. S., ed.*, 1989, pp. 87–102.

Riemer, Jeremiah M. and Allen, Christopher S. The Industrial Policy Controversy in West Germany: Organized Adjustment and the Emergence of Meso-corporatism. In *Foglesong, R. E. and Wolfe, J. D., eds.*, 1989, pp. 45–64.

Riener, Kenneth D.; Gandhi, Devinder K. and Rashid, Muhammad. Intertemporal Resolution of Uncertainty and Portfolio Behavior. *Financial Rev.*, August 1989, *24*(3), pp. 491–97.

Rieper, Bernd. Zahlungs- oder erfolgsorientierte Entscheidungsrechnungen? Eine Erörterung am Beispiel der Bestellmengenrechnung unter Beachtung von Zahlungskonditionen. (With English summary.) Z. *Betriebswirtshaft*, August 1989, *59*(8), pp. 875–87.

Rieser, Vittorio and Cerruti, Giancarlo. Professionalità in transizione. (Professionalism in Transition. With English summary.) *Econ. Lavoro*, July–Sept. 1989, *23*(3), pp. 99–117.

Riesman, Janet A. Republican Revisions: Political Economy in New York after the Panic of 1819. In *Pencak, W. and Wright, C. E., eds.*, 1989, pp. 1–44.

Rietveld, Piet. Infrastructure and Regional Development: A Survey of Multiregional Economic Models. *Ann. Reg. Sci.*, 1989, *23*(4), pp. 255–74.

_____. Regional Income Inequality and Economic Development: A Comment. *Reg. Sci. Urban Econ.*, December 1989, *19*(4), pp. 637–44.

_____ **and Nijkamp, Peter.** Multiple-Objective Optimization in a Macroeconomic Context. In *Muller, F. and Zwezerijnen, W. J., eds.*, 1989, pp. 133–49.

_____ **and Ouwersloot, H.** Intraregional Income Distribution and Poverty: Some Investigations for the Netherlands, 1960–81. *Environ. Planning A*, July 1989, *21*(7), pp. 881–904.

Riezman, Raymond and Cooper, Russell. Uncertainty and the Choice of Trade Policy in Oligopolistic Industries. *Rev. Econ. Stud.*, January 1989, *56*(1), pp. 129–40.

Rigaud, Jacques. French Culture. In *Frankel, A. V. and Heck, C. B.*, eds., 1989, pp. 18–23.

Rigby, David L. and Anderson, William P. Estimating Capital Stocks and Capital Ages in Canada's Regions: 1961–1981. *Reg. Stud.*, April 1989, *23*(2), pp. 117–26.

Riggenbach, Jeff. The Drug Prohibition Problem. In *Crane, E. H. and Boaz, D.*, 1989, pp. 267–81.

Riis, Christian. Strategic Wage Contracts. *J. Econ. (Z. Nationalökon.)*, 1989, *50*(2), pp. 129–37.

_____ and Thonstad, Tore. A Counterfactual Study of Economic Impacts of Norwegian Emigration and Capital Imports. In *Gordon, I. and Thirlwall, A. P.*, eds., 1989, pp. 116–32.

Riker, William H. and Wright, Stephen G. Plurality and Ronoff Systems and Numbers of Candidates. *Public Choice*, February 1989, *60*(2), pp. 155–75.

Riley, Gerald F. and Bye, Barry V. Eliminating the Medicare Waiting Period for Social Security Disabled-Worker Beneficiaries. *Soc. Sec. Bull.*, May 1989, *52*(5), pp. 2–15.

Riley, James C. and Alter, George. Fraility, Sickness, and Death: Models of Morbidity and Mortality in Historical Populations. *Population Stud.*, March 1989, *43*(1), pp. 25–45.

Riley, John G. Expected Revenue from Open and Sealed Bid Auctions. *J. Econ. Perspectives*, Summer 1989, *3*(3), pp. 41–50.

_____ and Hirshleifer, Jack. The Analytics of Uncertainty and Information: An Expository Survey. In *Hirshleifer, J.*, 1989, *1979*, pp. 152–206.

_____ and Maskin, Eric. Optimal Multi-unit Auctions. In *Hahn, F.*, ed., 1989, pp. 312–35.

Riley, Jonathan. Justice under Capitalism. In *Chapman, J. W. and Pennock, J. R.*, eds., 1989, pp. 122–62.

_____. Rights to Liberty in Purely Private Matters. *Econ. Philos.*, October 1989, *5*(2), pp. 121–66.

Riley, N. T. Aid for Maritime Developments in the Pacific. In *Couper, A. D.*, ed., 1989, pp. 160–67.

Rima, Ingrid H. The "Black Box" of Technical Change and Innovation. *Eastern Econ. J.*, Oct.–Dec. 1989, *15*(4), pp. 377–79.

Rimashevskaia, N. M. Public Well-Being: Myth and Reality. *Prob. Econ.*, April 1989, *31*(12), pp. 34–49.

_____ and Rabkina, N. Should We Fear Inflation? *Prob. Econ.*, May 1989, *32*(1), pp. 6–14.

Rimlinger, G. V. Labour and the State on the Continent, 1800–1939. In *Mathias, P. and Pollard, S.*, eds., 1989, pp. 549–606.

Rimmer, Peter J. Urban Change and the International Economy: Japanese Construction Contractors and Developers under Three Administrations. In *Smith, M. P.*, ed., 1989, pp. 156–99.

Rimmer, Russell J. Boulding's Theory of Distribution in a Neo-Pasinetti Framework. *Cambridge J. Econ.*, September 1989, *13*(3), pp. 453–58.

_____. Employment Implications of Improved Labour Productivity in the Australian Iron and Steel Industry. *Econ. Rec.*, June 1989, *65*(189), pp. 114–25.

Rindell, Krister. Arbitrage med indexoptioner och-terminer. (Arbitrage with Stock Index Options and Futures. With English summary.) *Ekon. Samfundets Tidskr.*, 1989, *42*(2), pp. 113–22.

Rindfuss, Ronald R. and Parnell, Allan M. The Varying Connection between Marital Status and Childbearing in the United States. *Population Devel. Rev.*, September 1989, *15*(3), pp. 447–70.

Ring, Raymond J., Jr. The Proportion of Consumers' and Producers' Goods in the General Sales Tax. *Nat. Tax J.*, June 1989, *42*(2), pp. 167–79.

Rinholm, R. A. and Schoney, Richard A. Capital Cost Allowance and Tax Neutrality: A Case Study of Saskatchewan Farmers' Claims versus Actual Depreciation. *Can. J. Agr. Econ.*, March 1989, *37*(1), pp. 47–62.

Rinnooy Kan, Alexander H. G. Twenty Years of Mathematical Programming: Comments. In *Cornet, B. and Tulkens, H.*, eds., 1989, pp. 232–36.

Riordan, Michael H. and McLean, Richard P. Industry Structure with Sequential Technology Choice. *J. Econ. Theory*, February 1989, *47*(1), pp. 1–21.

_____ and Sappington, David E. M. Second Sourcing. *Rand J. Econ.*, Spring 1989, *20*(1), pp. 41–58.

Riordan, Timothy H.; Oria, Maria E. and Tuss, Joseph P. Dayton's Capital Allocation Process. In *Matzer, J., Jr.*, ed., 1989, *1987*, pp. 21–37.

Ritchart, Dean L. Microcomputers as Tools for Infrastructure Management. In *Matzer, J., Jr.*, ed., 1989, *1986*, pp. 110–14.

Ritchie, J. B. Economic Implications of the New Environmentalism for the Australian Coal Industry. In *Owen, A. D.*, ed., 1989, pp. 51–56.

Rittenberg, Libby. Nobel Laureates in Economic Sciences: A Biographical Dictionary: James McGill Buchanan: 1986. In *Katz, B. S.*, ed., 1989, pp. 30–39.

Ritter, Jay R. and Chopra, Navin. Portfolio Rebalancing and the Turn-of-the-Year Effect. *J. Finance*, March 1989, *44*(1), pp. 149–66.

Ritzen, Jozef M. M. Revenue and Demographic Change. In *Chiancone, A. and Messere, K.*, eds., 1989, pp. 305–22.

_____ and van Imhoff, Evert. Comparing Employment Opportunities of Graduates and Dropouts of Full-Time Education and an In-Service Training Program. *Econ. Educ. Rev.*, 1989, *8*(2), pp. 159–67.

Rivera-Batiz, Francisco L. The Impact of International Migration on Real Wages: Another Look. *J. Devel. Econ.*, July 1989, *31*(1), pp. 185–92.

_____ and Quibria, M. G. International Migration and Real Wages: A Resolution Note. *J. Devel. Econ.*, July 1989, *31*(1), pp. 193–94.

Rivera Vilas, Luis Miguel and Garcia Alvarez-Coque, José Maréa. El modelo multiatributo de utilidad esperada con relaciones de sustitución constantes. (With English summary.) *Invest. Econ.*, September 1989, *13*(3), pp. 453–63.

Riveros C., Luis and Paredes M., Ricardo. Sesgo de selección y el efecto de los salarios mínimos. (With English summary.) *Cuadernos Econ.*, December 1989, *26*(79), pp. 367–83.

Riviére, Pascal and Lantieri, Charles. Peut-on estimer la demande d'actifs á partir d'un modèle de portefeuille? (An Estimation of the Demand for Money Derived from a Portfolio Model. With English summary.) *Revue Écon.*, January 1989, *40*(1), pp. 55–79.

Rivlin, Alice M. The Continuing Search for a Popular Tax. *Amer. Econ. Rev.*, May 1989, *79*(2), pp. 113–17.

Rivoli, Pietra and Aggarwal, Reena. Seasonal and Day-of-the-Week Effects in Four Emerging Stock Markets. *Financial Rev.*, November 1989, *24*(4), pp. 541–50.

Rizzi, Dino. Poverty in Italy: 1984. *Ricerche Econ.*, July–Sept. 1989, *43*(3), pp. 357–81.

Rizzo, John A. The Impact of Medical Malpractice Insurance Rate Regulation. *J. Risk Ins.*, September 1989, *56*(3), pp. 482–500.

Rizzoli, Irina and Popescu, Ileana. Computation of the Eigenvalues for a Tridiagonal, Symmetric, Real Matrix. *Econ. Computat. Econ. Cybern. Stud. Res.*, 1989, *24*(2–3), pp. 85–89.

Ro, Sung-Tae and Kim, Mahn-Je. Korean International Macroeconomic Policy. In *Bayard, T. O. and Young, S.-G., eds.*, 1989, pp. 43–65.

Rob, Rafael. Pollution Claim Settlements under Private Information. *J. Econ. Theory*, April 1989, *47*(2), pp. 307–33.

_____ **and Jovanovic, Boyan.** The Growth and Diffusion of Knowledge. *Rev. Econ. Stud.*, October 1989, *56*(4), pp. 569–82.

Roback, Jennifer. Racism as Rent Seeking. *Econ. Inquiry*, October 1989, *27*(4), pp. 661–81.

Robb, A. L. and Burbidge, J. B. Consumption, Income, and Retirement. *Can. J. Econ.*, August 1989, *22*(3), pp. 522–42.

Robb, Richard and Heckman, James J. The Value of Longitudinal Data for Solving the Problem of Selection Bias in Evaluating the Impact of Treatments on Outcomes. In *Kasprzyk, D., et al., eds.*, 1989, pp. 512–38.

Robben, Henry S. J., et al. A Cross-National Comparison of Attitudes, Personality, Behaviour, and Social Comparison in Tax Evasion Experiments. In *Grunert, K. G. and Ölander, F., eds.*, 1989, pp. 121–34.

Robbie, K.; Wright, Mike and Thompson, R. S. Privatisation via Management and Employee Buyouts: Analysis and U.K. Experience. *Ann. Pub. Coop. Econ.*, 1989, *60*(4), pp. 399–429.

Robbins, Walter; Apostolou, Nicholas and Kee, Robert. Capital Budgeting Practices of U.S. Cities: A Survey. In *Matzer, J., Jr., ed.*, 1989, *1987*, pp. 100–109.

Roberds, William. Money and the Economy: Puzzles from the 1980s' Experience. *Fed. Res.* Bank Atlanta Econ. Rev., Sept.–Oct. 1989, *74*(5), pp. 20–35.

Roberg, Arlene G. and Werbel, James D. A Role Theory Perspective on Career Decision Making. In *Ferris, G. R. and Rowland, K. M., eds.*, 1989, pp. 227–58.

Robert, Jacques and Kuhn, Peter. Seniority and Distribution in a Two-Worker Trade Union. *Quart. J. Econ.*, August 1989, *104*(3), pp. 485–505.

Roberti, Paolo. Some Critical Reflections on the Principles and Instruments of the Welfare State. *Labour*, Spring 1989, *3*(1), pp. 95–125.

Roberts, Ben. The Social Dimension of European Labour Markets. In *Dahrendorf, R., et al.*, 1989, pp. 39–49.

Roberts, Brian E. Voters, Investors, and the Consumption of Political Information. In *Ordeshook, P. C., ed.*, 1989, pp. 31–47.

Roberts, Bryan R. Employment Structure, Life Cycle, and Life Chances: Formal and Informal Sectors in Guadalajara. In *Portes, A.; Castells, M. and Benton, L. A., eds.*, 1989, pp. 41–59.

Roberts, David C. and Gill, Harley Leroy. New Car Warranty Repair: Theory and Evidence. *Southern Econ. J.*, January 1989, *55*(3), pp. 662–78.

Roberts, David L. and Anderson, Gary A. Stability in the Present Value Assessment of Lost Earnings. *J. Risk Ins.*, March 1989, *56*(1), pp. 50–66.

Roberts, Fred S. and Aczél, János. On the Possible Merging Functions. *Math. Soc. Sci.*, June 1989, *17*(3), pp. 205–43.

Roberts, James. A Micro-economic Analysis of Tea Production Using a Separable Restricted Profit Function. *J. Agr. Econ.*, May 1989, *40*(2), pp. 185–97.

_____. Tea Production Economics in Sri Lanka. *Can. J. Devel. Stud.*, 1989, *10*(2), pp. 241–56.

Roberts, John M. Equilibrium without Market Clearing. In *Cornet, B. and Tulkens, H., eds.*, 1989, pp. 145–58.

_____. Involuntary Unemployment and Imperfect Competition: A Game-Theoretic Macromodel. In *Feiwel, G. R., ed. (I)*, 1989, pp. 146–65.

_____; **Boskin, Michael J. and Robinson, Marc S.** New Estimates of Federal Government Tangible Capital and Net Investment. In *Jorgenson, D. W. and Landau, R., eds.*, 1989, pp. 451–83.

_____ **and Bulow, Jeremy.** The Simple Economics of Optimal Auctions. *J. Polit. Econ.*, October 1989, *97*(5), pp. 1060–90.

Roberts, Judith and Grossman, Jean Baldwin. Welfare Savings from Employment and Training Programs for Welfare Recipients. *Rev. Econ. Statist.*, August 1989, *71*(3), pp. 532–37.

Roberts, Mark J. and Nelson, Jon P. Ramsey Numbers and the Role of Competing Interest Groups in Electric Utility Regulation. *Quart. Rev. Econ. Bus.*, Autumn 1989, *29*(3), pp. 21–42.

_____; **Samuelson, Larry and Dunne, Timothy.** Firm Entry and Postentry Performance in the

U.S. Chemical Industries. *J. Law Econ.*, Part 2, October 1989, *32*(2), pp. S233–71.

_____; Samuelson, Larry and Dunne, Timothy. The Growth and Failure of U.S. Manufacturing Plants. *Quart. J. Econ.*, November 1989, *104*(4), pp. 671–98.

_____; Samuelson, Larry and Dunne, Timothy. Plant Turnover and Gross Employment Flows in the U.S. Manufacturing Sector. *J. Lab. Econ.*, January 1989, *7*(1), pp. 48–71.

Roberts, P. W. Coal and the Environment: Planning and Management Issues for the Future of the Coalfields. *Environ. Planning A*, October 1989, *21*(10), pp. 1285–96.

Roberts, Paul Craig. America in the World Economy: A Strategy for the 1990s: Commentary. In *Hamilton, E. K., ed.*, 1989, pp. 113–21.

_____. Comment: How Economists Wrought a Nonsystem. In *Dorn, J. A. and Niskanen, W. A., eds.*, 1989, *1988*, pp. 143–45.

_____. Supply-Side Economics: An Assessment of the American Experience in the 1980s. *Nat. Westminster Bank Quart. Rev.*, February 1989, pp. 60–75.

Roberts, Russell D. and Lott, John R., Jr. Why Comply: One-Sided Enforcement of Price Controls and Victimless Crime Laws. *J. Legal Stud.*, June 1989, *18*(2), pp. 403–14.

Roberts, Tanya. Human Illness Costs of Foodborne Bacteria. *Amer. J. Agr. Econ.*, May 1989, *71*(2), pp. 468–74.

Robertson, D. H. The Interrelations of Shifts in Demand. In *Wood, J. C. and Woods, R. N., eds., Vol. 1*, 1989, *1944*, pp. 95–96.

Robertson, James W.; Wykoff, Frank C. and Hulten, Charles R. Energy, Obsolescence, and the Productivity Slowdown. In *Jorgenson, D. W. and Landau, R., eds.*, 1989, pp. 225–58.

Robertson, Matthew. Temporary Layoffs and Unemployment in Canada. *Ind. Relat.*, Winter 1989, *28*(1), pp. 82–90.

Robertson, Paul L. and Langlois, Richard N. Explaining Vertical Integration: Lessons from the American Automobile Industry. *J. Econ. Hist.*, June 1989, *49*(2), pp. 361–75.

Robertson, Peter. Some Explanations for the Growth of Part-Time Unemployment in Australia. *Australian Bull. Lab.*, December 1989, *15*(5), pp. 384–99.

Robertson, Thomas S.; Gatignon, Hubert and Eliashberg, Jehoshua. Modeling Multinational Diffusion Patterns: An Efficient Methodology. *Marketing Sci.*, Summer 1989, *8*(3), pp. 231–47.

Robins, Philip K. and Blau, David M. Fertility, Employment, and Child-Care Costs. *Demography*, May 1989, *26*(2), pp. 287–99.

Robinson, Ann. Taxation and the Family. In *[Sandford, C.]*, 1989, pp. 55–66.

Robinson, Bill. The Economics of Coal. In *Helm, D.; Kay, J. and Thompson, D., eds.*, 1989, pp. 313–46.

_____. Reforming the Taxation of Capital Gains, Gifts and Inheritances. *Fisc. Stud.*, February 1989, *10*(1), pp. 32–40.

_____ and Lee, Catherine. Can Household Surveys Help Explain the Fall in the Savings Ratio? *Fisc. Stud.*, August 1989, *10*(3), pp. 60–71.

Robinson, Chris. The Joint Determination of Union Status and Union Wage Effects: Some Tests of Alternative Models. *J. Polit. Econ.*, June 1989, *97*(3), pp. 639–67.

_____. Union Endogeneity and Self-selection. *J. Lab. Econ.*, January 1989, *7*(1), pp. 106–12.

Robinson, Colin. Privatising the Energy Industries. In *Veljanovski, C., ed. (II)*, 1989, pp. 113–28.

_____ and Marshall, Eileen. Liberalizing the British Coal Industry. In *Helm, D.; Kay, J. and Thompson, D., eds.*, 1989, *1986*, pp. 289–312.

Robinson, David. Controlling Legal Addictions: 'Taking Advantage of What's There'. In *Robinson, D.; Maynard, A. and Chester, R., eds.*, 1989, pp. 1–23.

Robinson, David J. and Mansur, Ahsan H. Transmission of Effects of the Fiscal Deficit in Industrial Countries to the Fiscal Deficit of Developing Countries. In *Blejer, M. I. and Chu, K., eds.*, 1989, pp. 132–68.

Robinson, James D., III. Third World Debt: The Next Phase: Concluding Impressions. In *Fried, E. R. and Trezise, P. H., eds.*, 1989, pp. 101–03.

Robinson, John B. Comments in Response to "Beyond Accuracy." *Int. J. Forecasting*, 1989, *5*(4), pp. 485–89.

Robinson, Kenneth J. and Ely, David P. The Stock Market and Inflation: A Synthesis of the Theory and Evidence. *Fed. Res. Bank Dallas Econ. Rev.*, March 1989, pp. 17–29.

_____ and Hill, John K. Money, Wages, and Factor Scarcity as Predictors of Inflation. *Fed. Res. Bank Dallas Econ. Rev.*, May 1989, pp. 21–29.

Robinson, Lindsay. A Third-Party Perspective on Reimbursement Policy. In *Strosberg, M. A.; Fein, I. A. and Carroll, J. D., eds.*, 1989, pp. 64–69.

Robinson, M. Silvan. Oil Trading: Yesterday, Today, and Tomorrow. In *[Evans, J. K.]*, 1989, pp. 162–71.

Robinson, Marc S.; Huber, Alan M. and Boskin, Michael J. Government Saving, Capital Formation, and Wealth in the United States, 1947–85. In *Lipsey, R. E. and Tice, H. S., eds.*, 1989, pp. 287–353.

_____; Roberts, John M. and Boskin, Michael J. New Estimates of Federal Government Tangible Capital and Net Investment. In *Jorgenson, D. W. and Landau, R., eds.*, 1989, pp. 451–83.

Robinson, Michael A. and Christy, Francis T., Jr. The State of Worldwide Fishery Statistics: A Modest Proposal: Comment. *Marine Resource Econ.*, 1989, *6*(1), pp. 83–84.

Robinson, Michael D.; Bramley, Donald G. and Wunnava, Phanindra V. A Note on Union–Non-union Benefit Differentials and Size of Establishment. *Econ. Letters*, 1989, *30*(1), pp. 85–88.

_____ and King, Robin A. Assessing Structural Adjustment Programs: A Summary of Country Experience. In *Weeks, J. F., ed.*, 1989, pp. 103–23.

_____ and Wunnava, Phanindra V. Measuring Direct Discrimination in Labor Markets Using a Frontier Approach: Evidence from CPS Female Earnings Data. *Southern Econ. J.*, July 1989, *56*(1), pp. 212–18.

Robinson, Michele. A Review of Monetary Policies in the Jamaican Economy, 1980–1985. In *Worrell, D. and Bourne, C., eds.*, 1989, pp. 125–31.

Robinson, Peter. Information Technology and the Relationship among OECD Countries. In *Jussawalla, M.; Okuma, T. and Araki, T., eds.*, 1989, pp. 40–46.

Robinson, Peter M. Hypothesis Testing in Semiparametric and Nonparametric Models for Econometric Time Series. *Rev. Econ. Stud.*, October 1989, *56*(4), pp. 511–34.

_____. Nonparametric Estimation of Time-Varying Parameters. In *Hackl, P., ed.*, 1989, pp. 253–64.

_____ and Bera, Anil K. Tests for Serial Dependence and Other Specification Analysis in Models of Markets in Disequilibrium. *J. Bus. Econ. Statist.*, July 1989, *7*(3), pp. 343–52.

Robinson, Roger J. and Schmitz, Lelde. Jamaica: Navigating through a Troubled Decade. *Finance Devel.*, December 1989, *26*(4), pp. 30–33.

Robinson, Saranna and Meltzer, Allan H. Stability under the Gold Standard in Practice. In *[Schwartz, A. J.]*, 1989, pp. 163–95.

Robinson, Sherman; Kilkenny, Maureen and Adelman, Irma. The Effect of Agricultural Trade Liberalization on the U.S. Economy: Projections to 1991. In *Stoeckel, A. B.; Vincent, D. and Cuthbertson, S., eds.*, 1989, pp. 222–59.

_____ and de Melo, Jaime. Product Differentiation and the Treatment of Foreign Trade in Computable General Equilibrium Models of Small Economies. *J. Int. Econ.*, August 1989, *27*(1–2), pp. 47–67.

_____; Schluter, Gerald and Fohlin, Caroline. Terms of Trade and Factor Commitments in Agriculture. *J. Agr. Econ. Res.*, Fall 1989, *41*(4), pp. 6–11.

Robles, Barbara and Betancourt, Roger. Credit, Money and Production: Empirical Evidence. *Rev. Econ. Statist.*, November 1989, *71*(4), pp. 712–17.

Robson, Arthur J. On the Uniqueness of Endogenous Strategic Timing. *Can. J. Econ.*, November 1989, *22*(4), pp. 917–21.

Robson, Mark H. Measuring the Cost of Capital When Taxes Are Changing with Foresight. *J. Public Econ.*, December 1989, *40*(3), pp. 261–92.

Robson, Martin. Unemployment and Real Wages in Britain, 1967–1983. *Oxford Econ. Pap.*, October 1989, *41*(4), pp. 789–801.

Rocco, Fedor. The Place and Role of Marketing in Yugoslav Economic Theory and Practice. In *Macesich, G., ed.*, 1989, pp. 71–81.

Rocha-Hernandez, Alma E. and Ramos-Elorduy, Julieta. 1988 World Food Conference: Proceedings: Appendix: The Use of Insects in Human and Animal Nutrition. In *Helmuth, J. W. and Johnson, S. R., eds., Vol. 1*, 1989, pp. 263–65.

Rochaix, Lise. Information Asymmetry and Search in the Market for Physicians' Services. *J. Health Econ.*, March 1989, *8*(1), pp. 53–84.

Rochet, Jean-Charles and Bajeux, Isabelle. Opérations d'initiés: une analyse de surplus. (Insider Trading: A Surplus Analysis. With English summary.) *Finance*, June 1989, *10*(1), pp. 7–19.

_____ and Champsaur, Paul. Multiproduct Duopolists. *Econometrica*, May 1989, *57*(3), pp. 533–57.

Rock, James M. Book IV: The Inducement to Invest. *Amer. Economist*, Spring 1989, *33*(1), pp. 45–51.

Rock, L. L.; Craigwell, R. C. and Sealy, R. C. Public Deficits and Private Consumption: Empirical Evidence from Small Open Economies. *Appl. Econ.*, May 1989, *21*(5), pp. 697–710.

Rocke, David M. Bootstrap Bartlett Adjustment in Seemingly Unrelated Regression. *J. Amer. Statist. Assoc.*, June 1989, *84*(406), pp. 598–601.

Rockoff, Hugh. A Note on Anna J. Schwartz's Contribution to Pre-1867 Monetary History. In *[Schwartz, A. J.]*, 1989, pp. 70–75.

Roddick, Jacqueline. The State, Industrial Relations and the Labour Movement in Latin America: Volume 1: Chile. In *Carrière, J.; Haworth, N. and Roddick, J., eds.*, 1989, pp. 178–262.

_____; Carrière, Jean and Haworth, Nigel. Proletarianisation, Industrialisation and Patterns of Action. In *Carrière, J.; Haworth, N. and Roddick, J., eds.*, 1989, pp. 1–20.

_____ and van Niekerk, Nico. The State, Industrial Relations and the Labour Movement in Latin America: Volume 1: Bolivia. In *Carrière, J.; Haworth, N. and Roddick, J., eds.*, 1989, pp. 128–77.

Rodgers, Gerry. Precarious Work in Western Europe: The State of the Debate. In *Rodgers, G. and Rodgers, J., eds.*, 1989, pp. 1–16.

_____. Trends in Urban Poverty and Labour Market Access. In *Rodgers, G., ed.*, 1989, pp. 1–33.

Rodgers, Willard L. Comparisons of Alternative Approaches to the Estimation of Simple Causal Models from Panel Data. In *Kasprzyk, D., et al., eds.*, 1989, pp. 432–56.

Rodionov, Stanislav N. Verification of a Ban on Space Weapons. In *Altmann, J. and Rotblat, J., eds.*, 1989, pp. 121–24.

_____; Fetter, Steve and Prilutskii, Oleg F. Passive Detection of Nuclear Warheads. In *Altmann, J. and Rotblat, J., eds.*, 1989, pp. 48–59.

Rodman, Kenneth A. Markets, Sovereignty, and

International Regime Change: Constraints on Nationalization Strategies in Peru and Jamaica. In *Avery, W. P. and Rapkin, D. P.*, eds., 1989, pp. 127–49.

Rodrigo, Chandra and Jayatissa, R. A. Maximising Benefits from Labour Migration: Sri Lanka. In *Amjad, R.*, ed., 1989, pp. 255–302.

Rodrigues, Anthony P. and Engel, Charles. Tests of International CAPM with Time-Varying Covariances. *J. Appl. Econometrics*, April–June 1989, *4*(2), pp. 119–38.

_____; **Hung, Juann and Pigott, Charles.** Financial Implications of the U.S. External Deficit. *Fed. Res. Bank New York Quart. Rev.*, Winter–Spring 1989, *13-14*(4–1), pp. 33–51.

Rodrigues, Denise A.; Dias, Antonio José R. and Façanha, Luis Otávio. Financiamentos públicos para projetos de pesquisa e desenvolvimento: Uma experiência de avaliação na Finep. (With English summary.) *Pesquisa Planejamento Econ.*, April 1989, *19*(1), pp. 133–60.

Rodriguez, Alvaro. The Existence of an Optimal Inflation Rate in a Cash-in-Advance Economy. *J. Macroecon.*, Spring 1989, *11*(2), pp. 309–14.

Rodriguez, Carlos Alfredo. Argentina's Foreign Debt: Origins and Alternatives. In *Edwards, S. and Larrain, F.*, eds., 1989, pp. 181–204.

_____. The Strategy of Debt Buy-Backs: A Theoretical Analysis of the Competitive Case. In *Frenkel, J. A.; Dooley, M. P. and Wickham, P.*, eds., 1989, pp. 346–58.

_____ **and Folkerts-Landau, David.** Mexican Debt Exchange: Lessons and Issues. In *Frenkel, J. A.; Dooley, M. P. and Wickham, P.*, eds., 1989, pp. 359–71.

Rodriguez D., Cristina; Blum V., Roberto and Rubio F., Luis. The Making of Mexico's Trade Policy and the Uruguay Round. In *Nau, H. R.*, ed., 1989, pp. 167–90.

Rodríguez, Flavia. Recession and Adjustment in the Dominican Republic: 1983–1985. In *Brock, P. L.; Connolly, M. B. and González-Vega, C.*, eds., 1989, pp. 210–24.

_____. Savings, Investment and Uncertainty in Latin America. *Soc. Econ. Stud.*, December 1989, *38*(4), pp. 1–52.

Rodriguez, J. and Namkoong, G. Optimum Growth and Reproduction Schedules for Forest Trees. *Natural Res. Modeling*, Fall 1989, *3*(4), pp. 539–51.

Rodríguez, José Miguel. The Crisis in Spanish Private Banks: A Logit Analysis. *Finance*, June 1989, *10*(1), pp. 69–88.

_____. The Crisis in Spanish Private Banks: An Empirical Analysis. *Rivista Int. Sci. Econ. Com.*, Oct.–Nov. 1989, *36*(10–11), pp. 1033–55.

Rodríguez Mendoza, Miguel. Multilateral Trade Negotiations. In *Naya, S., et al.*, eds., 1989, pp. 231–48.

Rodriguez, Ricardo J. and Kolb, Robert W. The Regression Tendencies of Betas: A Reappraisal. *Financial Rev.*, May 1989, *24*(2), pp. 319–34.

Rodrik, Dani. Credibility of Trade Reform—A Policy Maker's Guide. *World Econ.*, March 1989, *12*(1), pp. 1–16.

_____. Fiscal Adjustment and Deficit Financing during the Debt Crisis: Comment. In *Husain, I. and Diwan, I.*, eds., 1989, pp. 113–15.

_____. Optimal Trade Taxes for a Large Country with Non-atomistic Firms. *J. Int. Econ.*, February 1989, *26*(1/2), pp. 157–67.

_____. Promises, Promises: Credible Policy Reform via Signalling. *Econ. J.*, September 1989, *99*(397), pp. 756–72.

_____ **and Celâsun, Merih.** Debt, Adjustment, and Growth: Turkey. In *Sachs, J. D. and Collins, S. M.*, eds., 1989, pp. 615–808.

_____ **and Celâsun, Merih.** Turkish Experience with Debt: Macroeconomic Policy and Performance. In *Sachs, J. D.*, ed. *(II)*, 1989, pp. 193–211.

_____ **and Devarajan, Shantayanan.** Trade Liberalization in Developing Countries: Do Imperfect Competition and Scale Economies Matter? *Amer. Econ. Rev.*, May 1989, *79*(2), pp. 283–87.

Rodway, John. Tax Reform Proposals: Trinidad and Tobago. *Bull. Int. Fiscal Doc.*, June 1989, *43*(6), pp. 292–93.

Roe, Alan R. Interest Rate Policy, Employment and Income Distribution. In *Renshaw, G. T.*, ed., 1989, pp. 71–103.

Roe, Emery M. Narrative Analysis for the Policy Analyst: A Case Study of the 1980–1982 Medfly Controversy in California. *J. Policy Anal. Manage.*, Spring 1989, *8*(2), pp. 251–73.

_____ **and Omolehinwa, Eddy.** Boom and Bust Budgeting: Repetitive Budgetary Processes in Nigeria, Kenya and Ghana. *Public Budg. Finance*, Summer 1989, *9*(2), pp. 43–65.

Roe, Terry L. Agricultural Policies in Developing Countries: The Transfer of Resources from Agriculture. In *Horwich, G. and Lynch, G. J.*, eds., 1989, pp. 91–119.

_____ **and Yen, Steven T.** Estimation of a Two-Level Demand System with Limited Dependent Variables. *Amer. J. Agr. Econ.*, February 1989, *71*(1), pp. 85–98.

Roebroek, Joop M. Social Welfare in Developed Market Countries: Netherlands. In *Dixon, J. and Scheurell, R. P.*, eds., 1989, pp. 147–89.

Roehl, Thomas. A Comparison of U.S.–Japanese Firms' Parts-Supply Systems: What besides Nationality Matters? In *Hayashi, K.*, ed., 1989, pp. 127–54.

Roehner, B. An Empirical Study of Price Correlations: 1. How Should Spatial Interactions between Interdependent Markets Be Measured? *Environ. Planning A*, February 1989, *21*(2), pp. 161–73.

_____. An Empirical Study of Price Correlations: 2. The Decrease in Price Correlation with Distance and the Concept of Correlation Length. *Environ. Planning A*, March 1989, *21*(3), pp. 289–98.

Roemer, John E. An Axiomatic Approach to Marxian Political Philosophy. In *Feiwel, G. R.*, ed. *(II)*, 1989, pp. 833–50.

_____. Marxism and Contemporary Social Science. *Rev. Soc. Econ.*, Winter 1989, *47*(4), pp. 377–91.

_____ **and Moulin, Hervé.** Public Ownership of the External World and Private Ownership of Self. *J. Polit. Econ.*, April 1989, *97*(2), pp. 347–67.

Roemer, Michael. The Macroeconomics of Counterpart Funds Revisited. *World Devel.*, June 1989, *17*(6), pp. 795–807.

_____; **Devarajan, Shantayanan and Jones, Christine.** Markets under Price Controls in Partial and General Equilibrium. *World Devel.*, December 1989, *17*(12), pp. 1881–93.

_____ **and Jones, Christine.** Modeling and Measuring Parallel Markets in Developing Countries: Editors' Introduction. *World Devel.*, December 1989, *17*(12), pp. 1861–70.

Roenfeldt, Rodney L.; Moore, William T. and Christensen, Donald G. Equity Valuation Effects of Forming Master Limited Partnerships. *J. Finan. Econ.*, September 1989, *24*(1), pp. 107–24.

Roett, Riordan. How the 'Haves' Manage the 'Have-Nots': Latin America and the Debt Crisis. In *Stallings, B. and Kaufman, R., eds.*, 1989, pp. 59–73.

_____. Paraguay after Stroessner. *Foreign Aff.*, Spring 1989, *68*(2), pp. 124–42.

Rofel, Lisa. Hegemony and Productivity: Workers in Post-Mao China. In *Dirlik, A. and Meisner, M., eds.*, 1989, pp. 235–52.

Rofman, Alejandro. Austerity and Regional Development Strategy in Argentina and Latin America. In *Canak, W. L., ed.*, 1989, pp. 98–110.

Rogalski, Richard J. and Gultekin, N. Bulent. Duration as a Measure of Basis Risk: The Wrong Answer at Low Cost—Answer to Rejoinder. *J. Portfol. Manage.*, Summer 1989, *15*(4), pp. 86–87.

_____ **and Gultekin, N. Bulent.** Duration: Response to Critics: Comment. *J. Portfol. Manage.*, Spring 1989, *15*(3), pp. 83–87.

_____ **and Maloney, Kevin J.** Call-Option Pricing and the Turn of the Year. *J. Bus.*, October 1989, *62*(4), pp. 539–52.

Roger, Patrick. Agrégation de l'information par les prix et dépendance des sources d'information. (Aggregation of Information by Prices and Dependency on Data Origins. With English summary.) *Écon. Societes*, January 1989, *23*(1), pp. 85–109.

_____ **and Rousseau, Patrick.** Sur l'évaluation des taux de change: Une approche par le modèle d'arbitrage. (Exchange Rate Pricing: An Arbitrage Approach. With English summary.) *Écon. Societes*, December 1989, *23*(12), pp. 159–82.

Rogers, Andrei and McNown, Robert F. Forecasting Mortality: A Parameterized Time Series Approach. *Demography*, November 1989, *26*(4), pp. 645–60.

Rogers, Carol Ann. Debt Restructuring with a Public Good. *Scand. J. Econ.*, 1989, *91*(1), pp. 117–30.

Rogers, David F. Optimal Strategies for Invest-

ment in Setup Cost Reductions in a Just-in-Time Environment. In *Gulledge, T. R., Jr. and Litteral, L. A., eds.*, 1989, pp. 298–310.

Rogers, J. Scott and Rowse, John G. Canadian Interregional Electricity Trade: Analysing the Gains from System Integration during 1990–2020. *Energy Econ.*, April 1989, *11*(2), pp. 105–18.

Rogers, John D. Cultural Nationalism and Social Reform: The 1904 Temperance Movement in Sri Lanka. *Indian Econ. Soc. Hist. Rev.*, July–Sept. 1989, *26*(3), pp. 319–41.

_____. Theories of Crime and Development: An Historical Perspective. *J. Devel. Stud.*, April 1989, *25*(3), pp. 314–28.

Rogers, P. Health Insurance Choice: An Econometric Analysis of A.B.S. Health and Health Insurance Surveys: Commentary. In *Smith, C. S., ed.*, 1989, pp. 195.

Rogers, R. Mark. Tracking the Economy: Fundamentals for Understanding Data. *Fed. Res. Bank Atlanta Econ. Rev.*, March–April 1989, *74*(2), pp. 30–48.

Rogers, Richard G. Ethnic and Birth Weight Differences in Cause-Specific Infant Mortality. *Demography*, May 1989, *26*(2), pp. 335–43.

_____. Ethnic Differences in Infant Mortality: Fact or Artifact? *Soc. Sci. Quart.*, September 1989, *70*(3), pp. 642–49.

Rogers, Robert P. and Mathios, Alan D. The Impact of Alternative Forms of State Regulation of AT&T on Direct-Dial, Long-Distance Telephone Rates. *Rand J. Econ.*, Autumn 1989, *20*(3), pp. 437–53.

Rogers, Ronald C.; Mais, Eric L. and Moore, William T. A Re-examination of Shareholder Wealth Effects of Calls of Convertible Preferred Stock. *J. Finance*, December 1989, *44*(5), pp. 1401–10.

Rogers, Theresa F. Interviews by Telephone and in Person: Quality of Responses and Field Performance. In *Singer, E. and Presser, S., eds.*, 1989, *1976*, pp. 193–207.

Rogers, William D. Third World Debt: The Next Phase: The Situation in Latin America. In *Fried, E. R. and Trezise, P. H., eds.*, 1989, pp. 39–43.

Rogerson, R. J., et al. Indicators of Quality of Life: Some Methodological Issues. *Environ. Planning A*, December 1989, *21*(12), pp. 1655–66.

Rogerson, Richard and Loungani, Prakash. Cyclical Fluctuations and Sectoral Reallocation: Evidence from the PSID. *J. Monet. Econ.*, March 1989, *23*(2), pp. 259–73.

Rogerson, William P. Profit Regulation of Defense Contractors and Prizes for Innovation. *J. Polit. Econ.*, December 1989, *97*(6), pp. 1284–1305.

Rogner, Hans-Holger. Dynamic Energy Complex Analysis for Metropolitan Regions. In *Andersson, Å. E., et al., eds.*, 1989, pp. 273–89.

Rogoff, Kenneth. Market-Based Debt Reduction: Comment. In *Husain, I. and Diwan, I., eds.*, 1989, pp. 273–75.

_____. Reputation, Coordination, and Monetary

Policy. **In** *Barro, R. J., ed.*, 1989, pp. 236–64.

———— **and Bulow, Jeremy.** A Constant Recontracting Model of Sovereign Debt. *J. Polit. Econ.*, February 1989, *97*(1), pp. 155–78.

———— **and Bulow, Jeremy.** Multilateral Negotiations for Rescheduling Developing Country Debt. **In** *Frenkel, J. A.; Dooley, M. P. and Wickham, P., eds.*, 1989, pp. 194–207.

———— **and Bulow, Jeremy.** Sovereign Debt: Is to Forgive to Forget? *Amer. Econ. Rev.*, March 1989, *79*(1), pp. 43–50.

Rogovin, V. Z. Social Justice and the Socialist Distribution of Vital Goods. **In** *Yanowitch, M., ed.*, 1989, *1986*, pp. 133–54.

———— **and Naumova, N. F.** The Task of Justice. **In** *Yanowitch, M., ed.*, 1989, *1987*, pp. 155–69.

Rogowski, Tadeusz. Dynamic Aspects of Multiobjective Trajectory Optimization in Decision Support Systems. **In** *Lewandowski, A. and Wierzbicki, A. P., eds.*, 1989, pp. 92–105.

————; **Sobczyk, Jerzy and Wierzbicki, Andrzej P.** IAC–DIDAS–L: A Dynamic Interactive Decision Analysis and Support System for Multicriteria Analysis of Linear and Dynamic Linear Models on Professional Microcomputers. **In** *Lewandowski, A. and Wierzbicki, A. P., eds.*, 1989, pp. 373–75.

Rogowsky, Robert A. Sub Rosa Regulation: The Iceberg beneath the Surface. **In** *Meiners, R. E. and Yandle, B., eds.*, 1989, pp. 209–22.

———— **and MacLeod, William C.** Consumer Protection at the FTC during the Reagan Administration. **In** *Meiners, R. E. and Yandle, B., eds.*, 1989, pp. 71–88.

Roh, Jae-Sun; Nelson, Carl H. and Braden, John B. Asset Fixity and Investment Asymmetry in Agriculture. *Amer. J. Agr. Econ.*, November 1989, *71*(4), pp. 970–79.

Rohatyn, Felix G. America's Economic Dependence. *Foreign Aff.*, 1988–89, *68*(1), pp. 53–65.

————. Needed: Restraints on the Takeover Mania. **In** *Guttmann, R., ed.*, 1989, *1986*, pp. 170–74.

Rohlfs, Jeffrey H. "Miles to Go": The Need for Additional Reforms in Capital Recovery Methods. **In** *National Economic Research Associates*, 1989, pp. 63–93.

Rohr-Zänker, R. and Müller, W. The Fiscal Crisis and the Local State: Examination of the Structuralist Concept. *Environ. Planning A*, December 1989, *21*(12), pp. 1619–38.

Rohrbach, Kermit and Chandra, Ramesh. The Power of Beaver's U against a Variance Increase in Market Model Residuals. *J. Acc. Res.*, Spring 1989, *27*(1), pp. 145–55.

Rohrlich, George F. On the Quest for Knowledge and the Duty to Kow. *Int. J. Soc. Econ.*, 1989, *16*(5), pp. 56–59.

Rohwer, Bernd. Möglichkeiten und Grenzen der Wachstumspolitik. (Growth Policy Opportunities and Limits. With English summary.) *Kredit Kapital*, 1989, *22*(4), pp. 487–507.

van Roij, G. The International Interbank-Market

and the Stability of the Banking System. **In** *Sijben, J. J., ed.*, 1989, pp. 107–53.

Rojas R., Patricio and Matte E., Ricardo. Evolución reciente del mercado monetario y una estimación de la demanda por dinero en Chile. (With English summary.) *Cuadernos Econ.*, August 1989, *26*(78), pp. 195–216.

Rojot, Jacques. Managers as Employees: France. **In** *Roomkin, M. J., ed.*, 1989, pp. 202–27.

————. The Myth of French Exceptionalism. **In** *Barbash, J. and Barbash, K., eds.*, 1989, pp. 76–88.

————. National Experiences in Labour Market Flexibility. **In** *OECD*, 1989, pp. 37–60.

Roland-Holst, David W. Bias and Stability of Multiplier Estimates. *Rev. Econ. Statist.*, November 1989, *71*(4), pp. 718–21.

————. Savings Promotion, Investment Promotion, and International Competitiveness: Comment. **In** *Feenstra, R. C., ed.*, 1989, pp. 45–46.

Roland-Lévy, Christine and Lassarre, Dominique. Understanding Children's Economic Socialization. **In** *Grunert, K. G. and Ölander, F., eds.*, 1989, pp. 347–68.

Rolfe, Robert J. and Doupnik, Timothy S. The Relevance of Level of Aggregation of Geographic Area Data in the Assessment of Foreign Investment Risk. **In** *Schwartz, B. N., ed.*, 1989, pp. 51–65.

Roll, Richard. Price Volatility, International Market Links, and Their Implications for Regulatory Policies. **In** *Edwards, F. R., ed.*, 1989, pp. 113–48.

————. Price Volatility, International Market Links, and Their Implications for Regulatory Policies. *J. Finan. Services Res.*, December 1989, *3*(2–3), pp. 211–46.

———— **and Richard, Scott F.** Prepayments on Fixed-Rate Mortgage-Backed Securities. *J. Portfol. Manage.*, Spring 1989, *15*(3), pp. 73–82.

Röller, Lars-Hendrik and Deolalikar, Anil B. Patenting by Manufacturing Firms in India: Its Production and Impact. *J. Ind. Econ.*, March 1989, *37*(3), pp. 303–14.

Rom, Mark and Peterson, Paul E. Macroeconomic Policymaking: Who Is In Control? **In** *Chubb, J. E. and Peterson, P. E., eds.*, 1989, pp. 139–82.

Roman, Emmanuel; Hakanoğlu, Erol and Kopprasch, Robert. Constant Proportion Portfolio Insurance for Fixed-Income Investment. *J. Portfol. Manage.*, Summer 1989, *15*(4), pp. 58–66.

Roman, Paul M. and Blum, Terry C. Employee Assistance Programs and Human Resources Management. **In** *Ferris, G. R. and Rowland, K. M., eds.*, 1989, pp. 259–312.

Romanelli, Elaine. Organization Birth and Population Variety: A Community Perspective on Origins. **In** *Cummings, L. L. and Staw, B. M., eds.*, 1989, pp. 211–46.

Romani, Franco. Taxation of Financial Activities: Round Table. *Rev. Econ. Cond. Italy*, Sept.–Dec. 1989, (3), pp. 373–79.

Romanin-Jacur, G. F.M.S. Queueing Network Models Theory and Applications. **In** *Archetti, F.; Lucertini, M. and Serafini, P., eds.*, 1989, pp. 213–36.

Romano, Richard E. Aspects of R&D Subsidization. *Quart. J. Econ.*, November 1989, *104*(4), pp. 863–73.

_____; **Blair, Roger D. and Kaserman, David L.** A Pedagogical Treatment of Bilateral Monopoly. *Southern Econ. J.*, April 1989, *55*(4), pp. 831–41.

Romer, Christina D. The Prewar Business Cycle Reconsidered: New Estimates of Gross National Product, 1869–1908. *J. Polit. Econ.*, February 1989, *97*(1), pp. 1–37.

_____ **and Romer, David H.** Does Monetary Policy Matter? A New Test in the Spirit of Friedman and Schwartz. **In** *Blanchard, O. J. and Fischer, S., eds.*, 1989, pp. 121–70.

Romer, Daniel; McQueen, Josh and Deighton, John. Using Drama to Persuade. *J. Cons. Res.*, December 1989, *16*(3), pp. 335–43.

Romer, David H. Institutional Change and the Efficacy of Monetary Policy: Comments. *Brookings Pap. Econ. Act.*, 1989, (1), pp. 114–19.

_____. Output Persistence, Economic Structure, and the Choice of Stabilization Policy: Comments. *Brookings Pap. Econ. Act.*, 1989, (2), pp. 117–25.

_____ **and Ball, Laurence.** Are Prices Too Sticky? *Quart. J. Econ.*, August 1989, *104*(3), pp. 507–24.

_____ **and Ball, Laurence.** The Equilibrium and Optimal Timing of Price Changes. *Rev. Econ. Stud.*, April 1989, *56*(2), pp. 179–98.

_____ **and Romer, Christina D.** Does Monetary Policy Matter? A New Test in the Spirit of Friedman and Schwartz. **In** *Blanchard, O. J. and Fischer, S., eds.*, 1989, pp. 121–70.

Romer, Paul M. Capital Accumulation in the Theory of Long-Run Growth. **In** *Barro, R. J., ed.*, 1989, pp. 51–127.

_____; **Kehoe, Timothy J. and Levine, David K.** Steady States and Determinacy of Equilibria in Economies with Infinitely Lived Agents. **In** *Feiwel, G. R., ed. (II)*, 1989, pp. 521–44.

Romer, Thomas; Cassidy, Glenn and Epple, Dennis. Redistribution by Local Governments in a Monocentric Urban Area. *Reg. Sci. Urban Econ.*, August 1989, *19*(3), pp. 421–54.

_____ **and Epple, Dennis.** On the Flexibility of Municipal Boundaries. *J. Urban Econ.*, November 1989, *26*(3), pp. 307–19.

Roncaglia, Alessandro. Research in Fusion as Investment. *Giorn. Econ.*, July–Aug. 1989, *48*(7–8), pp. 293–307.

Roncesvalles, Orlando. IMF Quotas: A Briefing. *Finance Devel.*, December 1989, *26*(4), pp. 10.

Rond, Philip C., III and Imershein, Allen W. Elite Fragmentation in Health Care: Proprietary and Nonproprietary Hospitals in Florida. *Soc. Sci. Quart.*, March 1989, *70*(1), pp. 53–71.

Ronen, Joshua. The Rise and Decay of Entrepreneurship: A Different Perspective. *J. Behav. Econ.*, Fall 1989, *18*(3), pp. 167–84.

_____ **and Aharoni, A.** The Choice among Accounting Alternatives and Management Compensation: Effects of Corporate Tax. *Accounting Rev.*, January 1989, *64*(1), pp. 69–86.

_____; **Gilad, B. and Kaish, S.** Information, Search, and Entrepreneurship: A Pilot Study. *J. Behav. Econ.*, Fall 1989, *18*(3), pp. 217–35.

Rones, Philip L. and Herz, Diane E. Institutional Barriers to Employment of Older Workers. *Mon. Lab. Rev.*, April 1989, *112*(4), pp. 14–21.

_____ **and Klein, Bruce W.** A Profile of the Working Poor. *Mon. Lab. Rev.*, October 1989, *112*(10), pp. 3–13.

Roningen, Vernon O. and Dixit, Praveen M. Quantitative Impacts of Creating an Agricultural Free Trade Area between the United States and Canada. *Can. J. Agr. Econ.*, Part 2, December 1989, *37*(4), pp. 1023–33.

Ronn, Aimee Gerbarg and Ronn, Ehud I. The Box Spread Arbitrage Conditions: Theory, Tests, and Investment Strategies. *Rev. Financial Stud.*, 1989, *2*(1), pp. 91–108.

Ronn, Ehud I. and Bliss, Robert R., Jr. Arbitrage-Based Estimation of Nonstationary Shifts in the Term Structure of Interest Rates. *J. Finance*, July 1989, *44*(3), pp. 591–610.

_____ **and Ronn, Aimee Gerbarg.** The Box Spread Arbitrage Conditions: Theory, Tests, and Investment Strategies. *Rev. Financial Stud.*, 1989, *2*(1), pp. 91–108.

_____ **and Verma, Avinash K.** Risk-Based Capital Adequacy Standards for a Sample of 43 Major Banks. *J. Banking Finance*, March 1989, *13*(1), pp. 21–29.

Ronning, Gerd. A Microeconometric Study of Travelling Behaviour. **In** *Opitz, O., ed.*, 1989, pp. 432–40.

Roomkin, Myron J. Managers as Employees: An Overview. **In** *Roomkin, M. J., ed.*, 1989, pp. 3–13.

_____. Managers as Employees: United States. **In** *Roomkin, M. J., ed.*, 1989, pp. 57–96.

_____ **and Pucik, Vladimir.** Managers as Employees: Japan. **In** *Roomkin, M. J., ed.*, 1989, pp. 255–78.

Roos, C. An $0(n^3L)$ Approximate Center Method for Linear Programming. **In** *Dolecki, S., ed.*, 1989, pp. 147–58.

Roosa, Robert V. The Gap between Trade Theory and Capital Flows. **In** *Guttmann, R., ed.*, 1989, *1983*, pp. 257–60.

Roper, Stephen. The Economics of Job Vacancies. *Brit. Rev. Econ. Issues*, Spring 1989, *11*(24), pp. 49–73.

Röpke, Wilhelm. Interdependence of Domestic and International Economic Systems. **In** *Peacock, A. and Willgerodt, H., eds. (II)*, 1989, *1951*, pp. 68–81.

Rorke, C. Harvey; Jog, Vijay M. and Fowler, David J. A Bias-Correcting Procedure for Beta Estimation in the Presence of Thin Trading. *J. Finan. Res.*, Spring 1989, *12*(1), pp. 23–32.

Rosa, Jean-Jacques; Grubel, Herbert G. and

Hammes, David L. The National Accounts, Household Service Consumption and Its Monetization. *Kyklos*, 1989, *42*(1), pp. 3–15.

Rosaasen, Ken A.; Furtan, W. Hartley and Fulton, Murray E. Agricultural Subsidies in Canada: Explicit and Implicit. In *Schmitz, A., ed.*, 1989, pp. 329–62.

Rosanvallon, Pierre. The Development of Keynesianism in France. In *Hall, P. A., ed.*, 1989, pp. 171–93.

Rosati, Furio Camillo. L'offerta di lavoro in Italia: Un test dell'ipotesi di sostituibilità intertemporale. (The Intertemporal Substitution Hypothesis: A Test for the Italian Economy. With English summary.) *Ricerche Econ.*, July–Sept. 1989, *43*(3), pp. 283–303.

Rose-Ackerman, Susan. Corruption and the Private Sector. In *Heidenheimer, A. J.; Johnston, M. and LeVine, V. T., eds.*, 1989, pp. 661–83.

_____. Dikes, Dams, and Vicious Hogs: Entitlement and Efficiency in Tort Law. *J. Legal Stud.*, January 1989, *18*(1), pp. 25–50.

_____. Which Bureaucracies Are Less Corruptible? In *Heidenheimer, A. J.; Johnston, M. and LeVine, V. T., eds.*, 1989, pp. 803–25.

Rose, Adam Z. and Allison, Timothy. On the Plausibility of the Supply-Driven Input–Output Model: Empirical Evidence on Joint Stability. *J. Reg. Sci.*, August 1989, *29*(3), pp. 451–58.

_____ **and Beaumont, Paul M.** Interrelational Income Distribution Multipliers for the U.S. Economy. In *Miller, R. E.; Polenske, K. R. and Rose, A. Z., eds.*, 1989, pp. 134–47.

_____ **and Miernyk, William.** Input–Output Analysis: The First Fifty Years. *Econ. Systems Res.*, 1989, *1*(2), pp. 229–71.

Rose, Andrew K. and Yellen, Janet L. Is There a J-Curve? *J. Monet. Econ.*, July 1989, *24*(1), pp. 53–68.

Rose, Carol M. Environmental Faust Succumbs to Temptations of Economic Mephistopheles, or, Value by Any Other Name Is Preference. *Mich. Law Rev.*, May 1989, *87*(6), pp. 1631–46.

Rose, David C. The Effect of Changes in Firm Diversification on Union Wage Settlements for 15 Major U.S. Industrial Firms. *Southern Econ. J.*, April 1989, *55*(4), pp. 896–907.

Rose, David J. and Smith, Kirk R. Nuclear Power. In *Kim, Y. II. and Smith, K. R., eds.*, 1989, pp. 145–85.

Rose, Jerome C. Biological Consequences of Segregation and Economic Deprivation: A Post-Slavery Population from Southwest Arkansas. *J. Econ. Hist.*, June 1989, *49*(2), pp. 351–60.

Rose, Leslie S. and Kingma, Hildy L. Seasonal Migration of Retired Persons: Estimating Its Extent and Its Implications for the State of Florida. *J. Econ. Soc. Meas.*, 1989, *15*(1), pp. 91–104.

Rose, Louis A. Topographical Constraints and Urban Land Supply Indexes. *J. Urban Econ.*, November 1989, *26*(3), pp. 335–47.

_____. Urban Land Supply: Natural and Contrived Restrictions. *J. Urban Econ.*, May 1989, *25*(3), pp. 325–45.

_____ **and La Croix, Sumner J.** A Simulation Study of the Interactive Effects of Taxes and Inflation on the Relative Price of Land. *Land Econ.*, May 1989, *65*(2), pp. 100–117.

_____ **and La Croix, Sumner J.** Urban Land Price: The Extraordinary Case of Honolulu Hawaii. *Urban Stud.*, June 1989, *26*(3), pp. 301–14.

Rose, Marshall and Rosenthal, Donald. The Timing of Oil and Gas Leasing on the Outer Continental Shelf: Theory and Policies. *Energy J.*, April 1989, *10*(2), pp. 109–31.

Rose, Nancy L. Financial Influences on Airline Safety. In *Moses, L. N. and Savage, I., eds.*, 1989, pp. 93–114.

_____ **and Joskow, Paul L.** The Effects of Economic Regulation. In *Schmalensee, R. and Willig, R. D., eds., Vol. 2*, 1989, pp. 1449–1506.

Rose, Peter S. Diversification of the Banking Firm. *Financial Rev.*, May 1989, *24*(2), pp. 251–80.

Rose, Richard. Political Economy and Public Policy: The Problem of Joint Appraisal. In *Samuels, W. J., ed. (I)*, 1989, pp. 147–56.

_____. Privatization: A Question of Quantities and Qualities. In *Fels, G. and von Furstenberg, G. M., eds.*, 1989, pp. 247–76.

Rosefielde, Steven. The Distorted World of Soviet-Type Economies. *Atlantic Econ. J.*, December 1989, *17*(4), pp. 83–86.

Rosegrant, Mark W. and Mongkolsmai, Dow. The Effect of Irrigation on Seasonal Rice Prices, Farm Income, and Labor Demand in Thailand. In *Sahn, D. E., ed.*, 1989, pp. 246–63.

Roseingrave, Tomas. The Role of Local Employment Initiatives in Combating Long-Term Unemployment in the European Community. In *Dyson, K., ed.*, 1989, pp. 132–51.

Rosen, Christine Meisner. Business, Democracy, and Progressive Reform in the Redevelopment of Baltimore after the Great Fire of 1904. *Bus. Hist. Rev.*, Summer 1989, *63*(2), pp. 283–328.

Rosen, Harvey S. and Holtz-Eakin, Douglas. The 'Rationality' of Municipal Capital Spending: Evidence from New Jersey. *Reg. Sci. Urban Econ.*, August 1989, *19*(3), pp. 517–36.

_____; **Holtz-Eakin, Douglas and Newey, Whitney K.** The Revenues–Expenditures Nexus: Evidence from Local Government Data. *Int. Econ. Rev.*, May 1989, *30*(2), pp. 415–29.

_____ **and Quandt, Richard E.** Endogenous Output in an Aggregate Model of the Labor Market. *Rev. Econ. Statist.*, August 1989, *71*(3), pp. 394–400.

Rosen, Howard F. The U.S.–Israel Free Trade Area Agreement: How Well Is It Working and What Have We Learned? In *Schott, J. J., ed.*, 1989, pp. 97–119.

Rosen, Richard J., et al. New Banking Powers: A Portfolio Analysis of Bank Investment in Real Estate. *J. Banking Finance*, July 1989, *13*(3), pp. 355–66.

Rosen, Sherwin. The Accumulation of Human and Nonhuman Capital, 1948–84: Comment. In

Lipsey, R. E. and Tice, H. S., eds., 1989, pp. 282–85.

Rosen, Stacey and Shapouri, Shahla. Export Growth, Instability and Shortfall: The Impact on Economic Performance in Africa. *Can. J. Agr. Econ.*, Part 2, December 1989, *37*(4), pp. 1241–50.

Rosenbach, Margo L. and Mitchell, Janet B. Feasibility of Case-Based Payment for Inpatient Radiology, Anesthesia, and Pathology Services. *Inquiry*, Winter 1989, *26*(4), pp. 457–67.

Rosenbaum, David I. An Empirical Test of the Effect of Excess Capacity in Price Setting, Capacity-Constrained Supergames. *Int. J. Ind. Organ.*, June 1989, *7*(2), pp. 231–41.

_____. The Impact of Market Structure on Technological Adoption in the Portland Cement Industry. *Quart. Rev. Econ. Bus.*, Autumn 1989, *29*(3), pp. 102–10.

_____ **and MacPhee, Craig R.** The Asymmetric Effects of Reversible Tariff Changes under the United States GSP. *Southern Econ. J.*, July 1989, *56*(1), pp. 105–25.

_____ **and MacPhee, Craig R.** Has the European Community GSP Increased LDC Exports? *Appl. Econ.*, June 1989, *21*(6), pp. 823–41.

_____ **and Ye, Meng-Hua.** (*s*,*S*) Pricing Policy When Adjustment Costs Affect Demand. *Econ. Letters*, November 1989, *31*(1), pp. 77–80.

Rosenberg, Alexander. Are Generic Predictions Enough? In *Balzer, W. and Hamminga, B., eds.*, 1989, pp. 43–68.

Rosenberg, Jacob and Katz, Eliakim. Rent-Seeking for Budgetary Allocation: Preliminary Results for 20 Countries. *Public Choice*, February 1989, *60*(2), pp. 133–44.

Rosenberg, L. Joseph and Rao, C. P. William T. Dillard: A Pioneer Merchant in Suburban Shopping Centers. In *Perkins, E. J., ed.*, 1989, pp. 230–36.

Rosenberg, Mark W.; Moore, Eric G. and Ray, Brian. Redistribution of Immigrant Groups in Canada. In *Beach, C. M. and Green, A. G.*, 1989, pp. 62–79.

Rosenberg, Nathan and Aoki, Masahiko. The Japanese Firm as an Innovating Institution. In *Shiraishi, T. and Tsuru, S., eds.*, 1989, pp. 137–54.

Rosenberg, Norman J. Potential Effects on Crop Production of Carbon Dioxide Enrichment in the Atmosphere and Greenhouse-Induced Climate Change. In *Oram, P. A., et al.*, 1989, pp. 359–73.

_____ **and Schneider, Stephen H.** The Greenhouse Effect: Its Causes, Possible Impacts, and Associated Uncertainties. In *Rosenberg, N. J., et al., eds.*, 1989, pp. 7–34.

_____, **et al.** Greenhouse Warming: Abatement and Adaptation: Introduction. In *Rosenberg, N. J., et al., eds.*, 1989, pp. 1–4.

Rosenberg, Robert Allen; Hendon, Willliam S. and Costa, Frank. The General Public and the Art Museum: Case Studies of Visitors to Several Institutions Identify Characteristics of Their Publics. *Amer. J. Econ. Sociology*, April 1989, *48*(2), pp. 231–43.

Rosenberg, Samuel. Labor Market Restructuring in Europe and the United States: The Search for Flexibility. In *Rosenberg, S., ed.*, 1989, pp. 3–16.

_____. The Restructuring of the Labor Market, the Labor Force, and the Nature of Employment Relations in the United States in the 1980s. In *Rosenberg, S., ed.*, 1989, pp. 63–85.

_____. The State and the Labor Market: An Evaluation. In *Rosenberg, S., ed.*, 1989, pp. 235–49.

Rosenblatt, David. Letter to the Editors [Co-integration, Error Correction, and Aggregation in Dynamic Models: A Comment]. *Oxford Bull. Econ. Statist.*, August 1989, *51*(3), pp. 351.

Rosenbloom, Joshua L. Is Wage Rate Dispersion a Good Index of Labor Market Integration: A Comment. *J. Econ. Hist.*, March 1989, *49*(1), pp. 166–69.

Rosenbloom, Richard S. and Burgelman, Robert A. Technology Strategy: An Evolutionary Process Perspective. In *Rosenbloom, R. S. and Burgelman, R. A., eds.*, 1989, pp. 1–23.

Rosenblum, Harvey and Cox, William Michael. Money and Inflation in a Deregulated Financial Environment: An Overview. *Fed. Res. Bank Dallas Econ. Rev.*, May 1989, pp. 1–19.

Rosende, Francisco. Mexico's Debt Burden: Comment. In *Edwards, S. and Larrain, F., eds.*, 1989, pp. 292–93.

Rosener, Judy and Pearce, Jone L. Advisory Board Performance: Managing Ambiguity and Limited Commitment in Public Television. In *Herman, R. D. and Van Til, J., eds.*, 1989, pp. 36–47.

Rosenfeld, Ahron; Lewellen, Wilbur and Loderer, Claudio F. Mergers, Executive Risk Reduction, and Stockholder Wealth. *J. Finan. Quant. Anal.*, December 1989, *24*(4), pp. 459–72.

Rosenfeld, Raymond A. Federal Grants and Local Capital Improvements: The Impact of Reagan Budgets. *Public Budg. Finance*, Spring 1989, *9*(1), pp. 74–84.

Rosenfeld, Robert. Evidence of Functional and Hierarchical Cultures in a Multinational Company. In *Prasad, S. B., ed.*, 1989, pp. 61–73.

_____; **Pettigrew, Andrew M. and Whipp, Richard.** Competitiveness and the Management of Strategic Change Process. In *Francis, A. and Tharakan, P. K. M., eds.*, 1989, pp. 110–36.

Rosengren, Eric S. and Kopcke, Richard W. Are the Distinctions between Debt and Equity Disappearing? An Overview. In *Kopcke, R. W. and Rosengren, E. S., eds.*, 1989, pp. 1–11.

_____ **and Kopcke, Richard W.** Regulation of Debt and Equity. In *Kopcke, R. W. and Rosengren, E. S., eds.*, 1989, pp. 173–206.

Rosenheim, James M. County Governance and Elite Withdrawal in Norfolk, 1660–1720. In *[Stone, L.]*, 1989, pp. 95–125.

Rosenmüller, Joachim. Homogeneous Games with Countably Many Players. *Math. Soc. Sci.*, April 1989, *17*(2), pp. 131–59.

Rosenstock, Adolf. Zinsertragsteuern und internationale Zinsdifferenzen. (Interest Yield Taxation and International Interest Rate Differentials. With English summary.) *Kredit Kapital*, 1989, *22*(1), pp. 92–116.

Rosenthal, Donald and Rose, Marshall. The Timing of Oil and Gas Leasing on the Outer Continental Shelf: Theory and Policies. *Energy J.*, April 1989, *10*(2), pp. 109–31.

Rosenthal, Gert. Latin American and Caribbean Development in the 1980s and the Outlook for the Future. *CEPAL Rev.*, December 1989, (39), pp. 7–17.

Rosenthal, Leonard; Johnson, James M. and Pari, Robert A. The Impact of In-substance Defeasance on Bondholder and Shareholder Wealth. *J. Finance*, September 1989, *44*(4), pp. 1049–57.

Rosenthal, Leslie. Income and Price Elasticities of Demand for Owner-Occupied Housing in the UK: Evidence from Pooled Cross-Sectional and Time-Series Data. *Appl. Econ.*, June 1989, *21*(6), pp. 761–75.

Rosenthal, Michael. An American Attempt to Control International Corruption. In *Heidenheimer, A. J.; Johnston, M. and LeVine, V. T., eds.*, 1989, pp. 701–15.

Rosenthal, Neal H. More Than Wages at Issue in Job Quality Debate. *Mon. Lab. Rev.*, December 1989, *112*(12), pp. 4–8.

Rosenthal, Robert W. A Bounded-Rationality Approach to the Study of Noncooperative Games. *Int. J. Game Theory*, 1989, *18*(3), pp. 273–91.

_____ **and Masso, Jordi.** More on the 'Anti-Folk Theorem.' *J. Math. Econ.*, 1989, *18*(3), pp. 281–90.

_____ **and Spady, Richard H.** Duopoly with Both Ruin and Entry. *Can. J. Econ.*, November 1989, *22*(4), pp. 834–51.

Rosenthal, Stephen R. Producing Results in Government: Moving beyond Project Management and Its Limited View of Success. *J. Policy Anal. Manage.*, Winter 1989, *8*(1), pp. 110–16.

Rosenthal, Stuart S. and Gabriel, Stuart A. Household Location and Race: Estimates of a Multinomial Logit Model. *Rev. Econ. Statist.*, May 1989, *71*(2), pp. 240–49.

Rosenwaike, Ira and Bradshaw, Benjamin S. Mortality of the Spanish Surname Population of the Southwest: 1980. *Soc. Sci. Quart.*, September 1989, *70*(3), pp. 631–41.

Rosenzweig, Mark R. and Jasso, Guillermina. Language Skill Acquisition, Labor Markets and Locational Choice: The Foreign-Born in the United States, 1900 and 1980. In *van Dijk, J., et al., eds.*, 1989, pp. 217–39.

_____ **and Schultz, T. Paul.** Schooling, Information and Nonmarket Productivity: Contraceptive Use and Its Effectiveness. *Int. Econ. Rev.*, May 1989, *30*(2), pp. 457–77.

_____ **and Stark, Oded.** Consumption Smoothing, Migration, and Marriage: Evidence from Rural India. *J. Polit. Econ.*, August 1989, *97*(4), pp. 905–26.

Rosier, Bernard and Dockès, Pierre. Un schéma explicatif des rythmes longs: Application à la "crise" contemporaine. (A Schema for Explaining Long Waves: An Application to the Present Crisis. With English summary.) *Écon. Societes*, March 1989, *23*(3), pp. 43–55.

Rosine, John and Walraven, Nicholas. Drought, Agriculture, and the Economy. *Fed. Res. Bull.*, January 1989, *75*(1), pp. 1–12.

Roskamp, Karl W. Optimal Lifetime Consumption, Asset Constraints and Tax Structure Changes: Toward a Computable Model. In *Chiancone, A. and Messere, K., eds.*, 1989, pp. 183–96.

Rosko, Michael D. A Comparison of Hospital Performance under the Partial-Payer Medicare PPS and State All-Payer Rate-Setting Systems. *Inquiry*, Spring 1989, *26*(1), pp. 48–61.

Rosner, Peter and Winckler, Georg. Aspects of Austrian Economics in the 1920s and 1930s. In *Samuels, W. J., ed. (II)*, 1989, pp. 19–30.

Ross, A. D. The Disregard of a Legal Entity for Tax Purposes: United Kingdom. In *International Fiscal Association, ed. (II)*, 1989, pp. 473–87.

Ross, Andrew L. Full Circle: Conventional Proliferation, the International Arms Trade, and Third World Arms Exports. In *Baek, K.-I.; McLaurin, R. D. and Moon, C., eds.*, 1989, pp. 1–31.

Ross, Bruce W. The Leisure Factor in Entrepreneurial Success: A Lesson from the "Robber Baron" Era. *Econ. Soc. Rev.*, April 1989, *20*(3), pp. 243–55.

Ross, David R. and Bradburd, Ralph M. Can Small Firms Find and Defend Strategic Niches? A Test of the Porter Hypothesis. *Rev. Econ. Statist.*, May 1989, *71*(2), pp. 258–62.

Ross, Hermann. Economic Growth and Structural Change of OECD Countries. In *Krelle, W., ed.*, 1989, pp. 83–118.

Ross, Jean. Pay the Man: Effects of Demographic Composition on Prescribed Wage Rates in the California Civil Service: Commentary. In *Michael, R. T.; Hartmann, H. I. and O'Farrell, B., eds.*, 1989, pp. 131–33.

Ross, Myron H. and Zondervan, Scott. Capital Gains and the Rate of Return on a Stradivarius. *Econ. Inquiry*, July 1989, *27*(3), pp. 529–40.

Ross, Stephen A. Information and Volatility: The No-Arbitrage Martingale Approach to Timing and Resolution Irrelevancy. *J. Finance*, March 1989, *44*(1), pp. 1–17.

_____ . Institutional Markets, Financial Marketing, and Financial Innovation. *J. Finance*, July 1989, *44*(3), pp. 541–56.

_____ . Using Tax Policy to Curb Speculative Short-term Trading: Commentary. *J. Finan. Services Res.*, December 1989, *3*(2–3), pp. 117–20.

_____ . Using Tax Policy to Curb Speculative Short-Term Trading: Commentary. In *Edwards, F. R., ed.*, 1989, pp. 19–22.

_____ ; **Shanken, Jay and Gibbons, Michael R.** A Test of the Efficiency of a Given Portfolio. *Econometrica*, September 1989, *57*(5), pp. 1121–52.

Rossana, Robert J. and Tomiyama, Ken. Two-Stage Optimal Control Problems with an Explicit Switch Point Dependence: Optimality Criteria and and Example of Delivery Lags and Investment. *J. Econ. Dynam. Control,* July 1989, *13*(3), pp. 319–37.

Rosser, J. Barkley, Jr.; Sheehan, Richard G. and Ahmed, Ehsan. A Comparison of National and International Aggregate Supply and Demand VAR Models: The United States, Japan and the European Economic Community. *Weltwirtsch. Arch.,* 1989, *125*(2), pp. 252–72.

Rossi, José W. The Demand for Money in Brazil: What Happened in the 1980s? *J. Devel. Econ.,* October 1989, *31*(2), pp. 357–67.

———— **and Braga, Helson C.** A produtividade total dos fatores de produção na indústria brasileira: 1970/83. (With English summary.) *Pesquisa Planejamento Econ.,* August 1989, *19*(2), pp. 255–76.

Rossi, Nicola. Dependency Rates and Private Savings Behavior in Developing Countries. *Int. Monet. Fund Staff Pap.,* March 1989, *36*(1), pp. 166–81.

————. Government Spending, the Real Interest Rate, and Liquidity-Constrained Consumers' Behavior in Developing Countries. In *Blejer, M. I. and Chu, K., eds.,* 1989, *1988,* pp. 238–75.

————. The Impact of Fiscal Policy and Inflation on National Saving: A Comment. *Banca Naz. Lavoro Quart. Rev.,* June 1989, (169), pp. 229–37.

———— **and Bollini, Andrea C.** Demographic Variables in Demand Systems and Related Measures of the Cost of Changing Family Size. *Giorn. Econ.,* Sept.–Oct. 1989, *48*(9–10), pp. 449–65.

———— **and Faini, Riccardo.** La macroeconometria ed il comportamento degli agenti privati: Il caso del modello econometrico della Banca d'Italia. (With English summary.) *Politica. Econ.,* April 1989, *5*(1), pp. 69–89.

————; **Modigliani, Franco and Padoa Schioppa, Fiorella.** Aggregate Unemployment in Italy, 1960–1983. In *Modigliani, F., Vol. 4,* 1989, *1986,* pp. 253–87.

Rossi, S. and Micossi, S. Restrictions on International Capital Flows: The Case of Italy. In *Gordon, I. and Thirlwall, A. P., eds.,* 1989, pp. 195–214.

Rossiter, John R. and Winter, Franz L. Pattern-Matching Purchase Behavior and Stochastic Brand Choice: A Low Involvement Model. *J. Econ. Psych.,* 1989, *10*(4), pp. 559–85.

Rossiter, L. F., et al. Medicare's Expanded Choices Program: Issues and Evidence from the HMO Experience. In *Scheffler, R. M. and Rossiter, L. F., eds.,* 1989, pp. 3–40.

Rossmiller, George E. and Elliott, Barbara J. Agriculture in the GATT: A Perspective from the United States. *Can. J. Agr. Econ.,* Part 2, December 1989, *37*(4), pp. 853–61.

———— **and Tutwiler, M. Ann.** The Potential for Agricultural Trade Reform. In *Helmuth, J. W. and Johnson, S. R., eds., Vol. 2,* 1989, pp. 303–12.

Rosson, Philip J. Exporting in the Smaller Cana-

dian Firm. In *Rugman, A. M., ed.,* 1989, pp. 86–105.

Roszkowski, Wojciech. The Growth of the State Sector in the Polish Economy in the Years 1918–1926. *J. Europ. Econ. Hist.,* Spring 1989, *18*(1), pp. 105–26.

Rota, Paola. Salari di efficienza, contrattazione salariale e Insiders–Outsiders: Una rassegna dei più recenti modelli di determinazione del salario. (Efficiency Wages, Union Bargaining, and Insiders–Outsiders: A Survey of the Most Recent Models of Wage Determination. With English summary.) *Politica. Econ.,* August 1989, *5*(2), pp. 301–39.

———— **and Del Boca, Alessandra.** Wage Compensation and Employment: Some Empirical Evidence from Microdata. *Giorn. Econ.,* March–April 1989, *48*(3–4), pp. 147–57.

Rotberg, Eugene H. Institutional Approaches to Debt Relief. In *Dornbusch, R.; Makin, J. H. and Zlowe, D., eds.,* 1989, pp. 65–68.

Rotemberg, Julio J. Comparative Estimates of a Macroeconomic Disequilibrium Model: France, Germany, the U.K. and the U.S.A.: Comment. *Europ. Econ. Rev.,* May 1989, *33*(5), pp. 989–93.

———— **and Giovannini, Alberto.** Exchange-Rate Dynamics with Sticky Prices: The Deutsche Mark, 1974–1982. *J. Bus. Econ. Statist.,* April 1989, *7*(2), pp. 169–78.

———— **and Saloner, Garth.** The Cyclical Behavior of Strategic Inventories. *Quart. J. Econ.,* February 1989, *104*(1), pp. 73–97.

———— **and Saloner, Garth.** Tariffs vs Quotas with Implicit Collusion. *Can. J. Econ.,* May 1989, *22*(2), pp. 237–44.

Rotenberg, W. and Krinsky, I. Signalling and the Valuation of Unseasoned New Issues Revisited. *J. Finan. Quant. Anal.,* June 1989, *24*(2), pp. 257–66.

———— **and Krinsky, I.** The Transition to Competitive Pricing on the Toronto Stock Exchange. *Can. Public Policy,* June 1989, *15*(2), pp. 135–44.

Rotfeld, Adam. Confidence- and Security-Building Measures in Europe. In *Rotblat, J. and Goldanskii, V. I., eds.,* 1989, pp. 136–42.

Roth, Alvin E. Risk Aversion and the Relationship between Nash's Solution and Subgame Perfect Equilibrium of Sequential Bargaining. *J. Risk Uncertainty,* December 1989, *2*(4), pp. 353–65.

————. Two-Sided Matching with Incomplete Information about Others' Preferences. *Games Econ. Behav.,* June 1989, *1*(2), pp. 191–209.

———— **and Ochs, Jack.** An Experimental Study of Sequential Bargaining. *Amer. Econ. Rev.,* June 1989, *79*(3), pp. 355–84.

———— **and Sotomayor, Marilda.** The College Admissions Problem Revisited. *Econometrica,* May 1989, *57*(3), pp. 559–70.

Roth, Michael, et al. Land Ownership Security and Farm Investment: Comment. *Amer. J. Agr. Econ.,* February 1989, *71*(1), pp. 211–14.

Roth, Timothy P. Two-Stage Optimization, Tax Rates, and Saving: Some Time Series Evidence. *Public Finance Quart.*, October 1989, *17*(4), pp. 375–90.

Roth, William V. Trade Policy: The View from Congress. In *Cerami, C. A., ed.*, 1989, pp. 63–71.

Rothbard, Murray N. The Hermeneutical Invasion of Philosophy and Economics. In *Rothbard, M. N. and Block, W., eds.*, 1989, pp. 45–59.

Rothbart, George S.; Fine, Michelle and Sudman, Seymour. On Finding and Interviewing the Needles in the Haystack: The Use of Multiplicity Sampling. In *Singer, E. and Presser, S., eds.*, 1989, *1982*, pp. 18–31.

Rothberg, James P.; Nothaft, Frank E. and Gabriel, Stuart A. On the Determinants of Yield Spreads between Mortgage Pass-Through and Treasury Securities. *J. Real Estate Finance Econ.*, December 1989, *2*(4), pp. 301–15.

Rothenberg, Lawrence S. Putting the Puzzle Together: Why People Join Public Interest Groups. *Public Choice*, March 1989, *60*(3), pp. 241–57.

Rothgeb, John M., Jr. Direct Foreign Investment, Repression, Reform, and Political Conflict in Third World States. In *Avery, W. P. and Rapkin, D. P., eds.*, 1989, pp. 105–25.

Rothschild, Kurt W. The Economist as Preacher: A Note [Economic Efficiency versus Egalitarian Rights]. *Kyklos*, 1989, *42*(2), pp. 257–59.

_____. Some Reflections on the Growth of Female Labour Supply and the Tertiary Sector. *Int. Rev. Applied Econ.*, June 1989, *3*(2), pp. 233–42.

Rothschild, Leonard W., Jr. and Rae, Patti L. Highlights of the Sec. 482 White Paper: United States. *Bull. Int. Fiscal Doc.*, April 1989, *43*(4), pp. 177–80.

Rothschild, Michael. Models of Market Organization with Imperfect Information: A Survey. In *Diamond, P. and Rothschild, M., eds.*, 1989, *1973*, pp. 461–86.

_____. Searching for the Lowest Price When the Distribution of Prices Is Unknown. In *Diamond, P. and Rothschild, M., eds.*, 1989, *1974*, pp. 427–49.

_____ **and Stiglitz, Joseph E.** Equilibrium in Competitive Insurance Markets: An Essay on the Economics of Imperfect Information. In *Diamond, P. and Rothschild, M., eds.*, 1989, *1976*, pp. 259–79.

_____ **and Stiglitz, Joseph E.** Increasing Risk: I. A Definition. In *Diamond, P. and Rothschild, M., eds.*, 1989, *1970*, pp. 101–19.

_____; **Stiglitz, Joseph E. and Brock, William A.** Stochastic Capital Theory. In *Feiwel, G. R., ed. (II)*, 1989, pp. 591–622.

Rothwell, Geoffrey S. Stock Market Reaction to Nuclear Reactor Failures. *Contemp. Policy Issues*, July 1989, *7*(3), pp. 96–106.

_____ **and Dubin, Jeffrey A.** Risk and Reactor Safety Systems Adoption. *J. Econometrics*, October 1989, *42*(2), pp. 201–18.

Rothwell, Roy and Beesley, Mark. The Importance of Technology Transfer. In *Barber, J.;*

Metcalfe, J. S. and Porteous, M., eds., 1989, pp. 87–104.

Rotwein, Eugene. Empiricism and Economic Method: Several Views Considered. In *Tool, M. R. and Samuels, W. J., eds. (II)*, 1989, *1973*, pp. 118–39.

Roubini, Nouriel. High Public Debt: The Italian Experience: A Review Essay. *J. Monet. Econ.*, November 1989, *24*(3), pp. 471–78.

_____ **and Sachs, Jeffrey D.** Fiscal Policy: Government Spending and Budget Deficits in the Industrial Countries. *Econ. Policy: A Europ. Forum*, April 1989, (8), pp. 99–132.

_____ **and Sachs, Jeffrey D.** Political and Economic Determinants of Budget Deficits in the Industrial Democracies. *Europ. Econ. Rev.*, May 1989, *33*(5), pp. 903–33.

_____; **Sachs, Jeffrey D. and McKibbin, Warwick J.** Correcting Global Imbalances: A Simulation Approach. In *Stern, R. M., ed.*, 1989, pp. 379–424.

Roukens de Lange, A. The Impact of Macro-economic Policies on the South African Economy: Analysis Based on a Social Accounting Matrix. *J. Stud. Econ. Econometrics*, November 1989, *13*(3), pp. 21–44.

Roulston, Carmel. Women on the Margin: The Women's Movement in Northern Ireland, 1973–1988. *Sci. Society*, Summer 1989, *53*(2), pp. 219–36.

Roumasset, James A. Decentralization and Local Public Goods: Getting the Incentives Right. *Philippine Rev. Econ. Bus.*, June 1989, *26*(1), pp. 1–13.

_____, **et al.** Fertilizer and Crop Yield Variability: A Review. In *Anderson, J. R. and Hazell, P. B. R., eds.*, 1989, pp. 223–33.

Roumi, Ebrahim and Schnabel, Jacques A. Corporate Insurance and the Underinvestment Problem: An Extension. *J. Risk Ins.*, March 1989, *56*(1), pp. 155–59.

Round, Jeffery I. Decomposition of Input–Output and Economy-Wide Multipliers in a Regional Setting. In *Miller, R. E.; Polenske, K. R. and Rose, A. Z., eds.*, 1989, pp. 103–18.

Roura-Agusti, J. Bernat and Vargas, Luis G. Business Strategy Formulation for a Financial Institution in a Developing Country. In *Golden, B. L.; Wasil, E. A. and Harker, P. T., eds.*, 1989, pp. 251–65.

Rouse, William and Hurd, Richard W. Progressive Union Organizing: The SEIU Justice for Janitors Campaign. *Rev. Radical Polit. Econ.*, Fall 1989, *21*(3), pp. 70–75.

Roush, Fred W. and Kim, K. H. Kelly's Conjecture. *Math. Soc. Sci.*, April 1989, *17*(2), pp. 189–94.

Rousseas, Stephen. Anti Systems. *J. Post Keynesian Econ.*, Spring 1989, *11*(3), pp. 385–98.

_____. Can the U.S. Financial System Survive the Revolution? *Challenge*, March–April 1989, *32*(2), pp. 39–43.

_____. The Financial Counterrevolution in the American Economy. *Écon. Appl.*, 1989, *42*(1), pp. 161–70.

_____. On the Endogeneity of Money Once

More: Comment. *J. Post Keynesian Econ.*, Spring 1989, *11*(3), pp. 474–78.

Rousseau, J. M. and Kauffmann, P. La théorie des choix de portefeuille: reformulation par une approche en termes de caractéristiques aléatoires. (Portfolio Theory Revisited: The Analysis of Random Characteristics. With English summary.) *Écon. Societes*, April–May 1989, *23*(4–5), pp. 249–64.

Rousseau, Patrick and Roger, Patrick. Sur l'évaluation des taux de change: Une approche par le modèle d'arbitrage. (Exchange Rate Pricing: An Arbitrage Approach. With English summary.) *Écon. Societes*, December 1989, *23*(12), pp. 159–82.

Rousslang, Donald J. Estimates of the Elasticities of Substitution between Imports and Home Goods for the United States: Comment. *Weltwirtsch. Arch.*, 1989, *125*(2), pp. 366–70.

_____ **and Méndez, José A.** Does the Central American Common Market Benefit Its Members? *Econ. Inquiry*, July 1989, *27*(3), pp. 473–87.

_____ **and Méndez, José A.** Liberalizing U.S. Trade with the Eastern Bloc: What Are the Consequences? *J. Compar. Econ.*, December 1989, *13*(4), pp. 491–507.

_____ **and Murray, Tracy.** A Method for Estimating Injury Caused by Unfair Trade Practices. *Int. Rev. Law Econ.*, December 1989, *9*(2), pp. 149–64.

Routh, Guy. Economics and Chaos. *Challenge*, July–Aug. 1989, *32*(4), pp. 47–52.

Rouwendal, Jan and Nijkamp, Peter. Endogenous Production of R and D and Stable Economic Development. *De Economist*, 1989, *137*(2), pp. 202–16.

le Roux, W. C. Die Voorkoms van Verbruikerskrediet in Suid-Afrika 1965–1987 met Spesiale Verwysing na Meubels en Motors. (With English summary.) *J. Stud. Econ. Econometrics*, November 1989, *13*(3), pp. 45–59.

Rovetta, A. and Filippini, L. Economic Aspects in Factory Automation in Relation to System Flexibility. In *Archetti, F.; Lucertini, M. and Serafini, P., eds.*, 1989, pp. 135–51.

Rowcroft, J. E.; Brander, J. R. G. and Cook, B. A. Deregulated Airline Markets as Open Access Commons. *De Economist*, 1989, *137*(4), pp. 466–75.

Rowe, Nicholas. Do Small Menu Costs Cause Bigger and Badder Business Cycles in Monopolistic Macroeconomies? *J. Macroecon.*, Winter 1989, *11*(1), pp. 25–48.

Rowland, Diane; Lyons, Barbara and Davis, Karen. Catastrophic Coverage under the Medicare Program. In *Eisdorfer, C.; Kessler, D. A. and Spector, A. N., eds.*, 1989, pp. 106–24.

Rowlands, Marie B. Continuity and Change in an Industrialising Society: The Case of the West Midlands Industries. In *Hudson, P., ed.*, 1989, pp. 103–31.

Rowley, Charles K. and Crew, Michael A. Feasibility of Deregulation: A Public Choice Analysis. In *Crew, M. A., ed.*, 1989, pp. 5–20.

Rowley, J. C. R. and Antoniou, A. Canadian Corporate Structure: The Importance of Shadow Groups. *S. Afr. J. Econ.*, December 1989, *57*(4), pp. 380–92.

Rowley, Keith A. and McKinney, Joseph. Voluntary Restraint Arrangements on Steel Imports: Policy Development and Sectoral Effects. *J. World Trade*, June 1989, *23*(3), pp. 69–81.

Rowley, Robin and Hamouda, Omar F. Disturbance in the World Economy. In *Hamouda, O. F.; Rowley, R. and Wolf, B. M., eds.*, 1989, pp. 1–3.

Rowse, John G. and Rogers, J. Scott. Canadian Interregional Electricity Trade: Analysing the Gains from System Integration during 1990–2020. *Energy Econ.*, April 1989, *11*(2), pp. 105–18.

Roxborough, Ian. Organized Labor: A Major Victim of the Debt Crisis. In *Stallings, B. and Kaufman, R., eds.*, 1989, pp. 91–108.

Roy, Durgadas. A Theory of Cooperation: Some Conflicting Ideas. *Indian Econ. J.*, April–June 1989, *36*(4), pp. 81–89.

Roy, R. and Dufour, Jean-Marie. Some Robust Exact Results on Sample Autocorrelations and Tests of Randomness: Corrigendum. *J. Econometrics*, June 1989, *41*(2), pp. 279–81.

Roy, Suby; Imada, Pearl and Naya, Seiji. Lessons in Development: A Comparative Study of Asia and Latin America: Introduction. In *Naya, S., et al., eds.*, 1989, pp. 3–12.

Royer, Jacques. South–South Trade in Steel Goods. In *Ventura-Dias, V., ed.*, 1989, pp. 197–215.

Rozek, Richard P. Competitive Bidding in Electricity Markets: A Survey. *Energy J.*, October 1989, *10*(4), pp. 117–38.

Rozo, Carlos A. Failures of the Renegotiation Process. In *Singer, H. W. and Sharma, S., eds. (II)*, 1989, pp. 134–45.

Ruane, Frances. Payroll Taxes, Capital Grants and Irish Unemployment: A Comment. *Econ. Soc. Rev.*, October 1989, *21*(1), pp. 122–25.

Rübel, Gerhard. Einige Zweifel an der langfristig vollbeschäftigungssichernden Wirkung eines Beteiligungslohnsystems. (Some Doubts Concerning the Ability of a Share Economy to Ensure Long Run Full Employment. With English summary.) *Jahr. Nationalökon. Statist.*, December 1989, *206*(6), pp. 583–90.

Rubel, Maximilien. Marx penseur de la Révolution française. (Marx on the French Revolution. With English summary.) *Écon. Societes*, September 1989, *23*(9), pp. 7–59.

_____ . A quand la "Glasnost" dans le Karl-Marx-Haus à Trèves? ("Glastnost" at the Karl-Marx-Haus in Triers. With English summary.) *Écon. Societes*, September 1989, *23*(9), pp. 121–59.

Ruben, George. Collective Bargaining and Labor–Management Relations, 1988. *Mon. Lab. Rev.*, January 1989, *112*(1), pp. 25–39.

Rubery, Jill. Precarious Forms of Work in the United Kingdom. In *Rodgers, G. and Rodgers, J., eds.*, 1989, pp. 49–73.

_____ ; **Wilkinson, Frank and Tarling, Roger.** Government Policy and the Labor Market: The

Case of the United Kingdom. **In** *Rosenberg, S., ed.,* 1989, pp. 23–45.

Rubin, Beth A. Unionism and Income Inequality: Reply. *Ind. Lab. Relat. Rev.,* October 1989, *43*(1), pp. 137–39.

Rubin, Bruce and Seifert, Bruce. Spin-Offs and the Listing Phenomena. *J. Econ. Bus.,* February 1989, *41*(1), pp. 1–19.

Rubin, Marc A. and Ramanan, Ramachandran. State Policy Regarding Local Government Auditors. **In** *Chan, J. L. and Patton, J. M., eds.,* 1989, pp. 57–69.

Rubinfeld, Daniel L. and Cooter, Robert D. Economic Analysis of Legal Disputes and Their Resolution. *J. Econ. Lit.,* September 1989, *27*(3), pp. 1067–97.

_____ **and Polinsky, A. Mitchell.** A Note on Optimal Public Enforcement with Settlements and Litigation Costs. **In** *Zerbe, R. O., ed.,* 1989, pp. 1–8.

_____ **and Quigley, John M.** Unobservables in Consumer Choice: Residential Energy and the Demand for Comfort. *Rev. Econ. Statist.,* August 1989, *71*(3), pp. 416–25.

_____ **and Shapiro, Perry.** Micro-estimation of the Demand for Schooling: Evidence from Michigan and Massachusetts. *Reg. Sci. Urban Econ.,* August 1989, *19*(3), pp. 381–98.

Rubinstein, Ariel. Competitive Equilibrium in a Market with Decentralized Trade and Strategic Behavior: An Introduction. **In** *Feiwel, G. R., ed. (I),* 1989, pp. 243–59.

_____. The Electronic Mail Game: Strategic Behavior under "Almost Common Knowledge." *Amer. Econ. Rev.,* June 1989, *79*(3), pp. 385–91.

_____; **Wilson, Charles and Kornhauser, Lewis A.** Reputation and Patience in the 'War of Attrition.' *Economica,* February 1989, *56*(221), pp. 15–24.

Rubinstein, David. Victorian Feminists: Henry and Millicent Garrett Fawcett. **In** *Goldman, L., ed.,* 1989, pp. 71–90.

Rubio F., Luis; Rodriguez D., Cristina and Blum V., Roberto. The Making of Mexico's Trade Policy and the Uruguay Round. **In** *Nau, H. R., ed.,* 1989, pp. 167–90.

Rubio, Mariano. European Currency—A Spanish View. **In** *Franz, O., ed.,* 1989, pp. 103–06.

Rubli-Kaiser, Federico. The Economic Adjustment Process in Latin America: A Conceptual Evaluation. **In** *Singer, H. W. and Sharma, S., eds. (I),* 1989, pp. 261–76.

Ruccio, David F. The Costs of Austerity in Nicaragua: The Worker–Peasant Alliance (1979–1987). **In** *Handelman, H. and Baer, W., eds.,* 1989, pp. 224–50.

_____. Fordism on a World Scale: International Dimensions of Regulation. *Rev. Radical Polit. Econ.,* Winter 1989, *21*(4), pp. 33–53.

Rudd, Andrew; Stefek, Dan and Grinold, Richard C. Gobal Factors: Fact or Fiction? *J. Portfol. Manage.,* Fall 1989, *16*(1), pp. 79–88.

Rudebusch, Glenn D. An Empirical Disequilibrium Model of Labor, Consumption, and

Investment. *Int. Econ. Rev.,* August 1989, *30*(3), pp. 633–54.

_____ **and Diebold, Francis X.** Long Memory and Persistence in Aggregate Output. *J. Monet. Econ.,* September 1989, *24*(2), pp. 189–209.

_____ **and Diebold, Francis X.** Scoring the Leading Indicators. *J. Bus.,* July 1989, *62*(3), pp. 369–91.

Rudloff, Darren and Horrigan, John. Telecommunications Policy and Economic Development: The New State Role: Illinois. **In** *Schmandt, J.; Williams, F. and Wilson, R. H., eds.,* 1989, pp. 63–82.

Rudney, Gabriel and Young, Paula. The Nonprofit Sector of the U.S. Economy: A Methodological Statement. *Rev. Income Wealth,* March 1989, *35*(1), pp. 56–80.

Rudolph, Patricia M. The Insolvent Thrifts of 1982: Where Are They Now? *Amer. Real Estate Urban Econ. Assoc. J.,* Winter 1989, *17*(4), pp. 450–62.

_____; **Selby, Edward B., Jr. and Lindley, James T.** Credit Card Possession and Use: Changes over Time. *J. Econ. Bus.,* May 1989, *41*(2), pp. 127–42.

Rudra, Ashok. Emergence of the Intelligentsia as a Ruling Class in India. *Indian Econ. Rev.,* July–Dec. 1989, *24*(2), pp. 155–83.

_____. Field Survey Methods. **In** *Bardhan, P., ed. (I),* 1989, pp. 218–37.

Rueschemeyer, Marilyn. New Towns in the German Democratic Republic: The *Neubaugebiete* of Rostock. **In** *Rueschemeyer, M. and Lemke, C., eds.,* 1989, pp. 117–43.

_____ **and Lemke, Christiane.** The Quality of Life in the German Democratic Republic: Conclusion. **In** *Rueschemeyer, M. and Lemke, C., eds.,* 1989, pp. 228–35.

Rueschhoff, Norlin G. Intercultural Business Values: A European–American Dialogue. **In** *Rueschhoff, N. and Schaum, K., eds.,* 1989, pp. 4–8.

_____ **and Mussner, Werner.** Institutional Infrastructures as an Element of Intercultural Value Analysis. **In** *Rueschhoff, N. and Schaum, K., eds.,* 1989, pp. 106–22.

_____ **and Schaum, Konrad.** Christian Business Values in an Intercultural Environment: Perspectives for Further Research. **In** *Rueschhoff, N. and Schaum, K., eds.,* 1989, pp. 182–88.

Ruff, Charles F. C. Federal Prosecution of Local Corruption. **In** *Heidenheimer, A. J.; Johnston, M. and LeVine, V. T., eds.,* 1989, *1977,* pp. 627–37.

Ruffing, Kenneth G. Impacts of Economic Reform for Agricultural and Food Policy: Reaction. **In** *Helmuth, J. W. and Johnson, S. R., eds., Vol. 1,* 1989, pp. 93–95.

_____. Macroeconomic and Monetary Policies and Economic Growth. **In** *Helmuth, J. W. and Johnson, S. R., eds., Vol. 2,* 1989, pp. 111–20.

Rugege, Sam and Santho, Sehoai. Contract Farming and Outgrower Schemes: Asparagus Production in Lesotho. *Eastern Afr. Econ. Rev.*, Special Issue, August 1989, pp. 20–41.

Ruggles, Patricia and Williams, Roberton. Longitudinal Measures of Poverty: Accounting for Income and Assets over Time. *Rev. Income Wealth*, September 1989, *35*(3), pp. 225–43.

Rugina, Anghel N. Principia Methodologica 1: A Bridge from Economics to All Other Natural Sciences: Towards a Methodological Unification of All Sciences. *Int. J. Soc. Econ.*, 1989, *16*(4), pp. 1–76.

_____. The Quest for Independence of *Principia Logica:* Toward a Third Revolution in Logic. *Rivista Int. Sci. Econ. Com.*, March 1989, *36*(3), pp. 193–220.

Rugman, Alan M. U.S. Administered Protection and Canadian Trade Policy. In *Rugman, A. M., ed.*, 1989, pp. 106–22.

_____ **and Anderson, Andrew.** Subsidies in the U.S. Steel Industry: A New Conceptual Framework and Literature Review. *J. World Trade*, December 1989, *23*(6), pp. 59–83.

_____ **and Verbeke, Alain.** Strategic Management and Trade Policy. In *Rugman, A. M., ed.*, 1989, pp. 144–59.

_____ **and Warner, Mark.** Strategies for the Canadian Multinationals. In *Rugman, A. M., ed.*, 1989, pp. 200–229.

_____ **and Yeung, Bernard.** Trade in Services and Returns on Multinational Activity. *Weltwirtsch. Arch.*, 1989, *125*(2), pp. 686–91.

Rugumamu, Severine. The Textile Industry in Tanzania. *Rev. Radical Polit. Econ.*, Winter 1989, *21*(4), pp. 54–72.

Ruhfus, Jürgen. How East–West Trade Fits the Picture. In *Cerami, C. A., ed.*, 1989, pp. 213–22.

Rühmann, Peter and Lohmann, Karl. Marktverzinsung und Erhaltungskonzeptionen bei abnutzbaren Anlagegegenständen. (With English summary.) *Z. Betriebswirtshaft*, December 1989, *59*(12), pp. 1324–37.

Ruin, Olof. Features and Phases of the "Swedish Model." *CEPAL Rev.*, December 1989, (39), pp. 19–26.

Ruina, Jack. Controlling Military Research and Development. In *Rotblat, J. and Goldanskii, V. I., eds.*, 1989, pp. 165–70.

Ruiz-Castillo, Javier; Thomas, Duncan and Deaton, Angus S. The Influence of Household Composition on Household Expenditure Patterns: Theory and Spanish Evidence. *J. Polit. Econ.*, February 1989, *97*(1), pp. 179–200.

Rumbiak, Michael and Manning, Chris. Irian Jaya: Economic Change, Migrants, and Indigenous Welfare. In *Hill, H., ed.*, 1989, pp. 76–106.

Rumelt, Richard P. and Liebeskind, Julia. Markets for Experience Goods with Performance Uncertainty. *Rand J. Econ.*, Winter 1989, *20*(4), pp. 601–21.

Runge, C. Ford; Job, Brian and von Witzke, Harald. Policy Coordination in World Agriculture: Introduction. In *von Witzke, H.; Runge, C. F. and Job, B., eds.*, 1989, pp. 1–5.

_____ **and von Witzke, Harald.** Agricultural Integration: Problems and Perspectives. In *Tarditi, S., et al., eds.*, 1989, pp. 227–43.

_____; **von Witzke, Harald and Thompson, Shelley J.** International Agricultural and Trade Policy: A Political Economic Coordination Game. In *von Witzke, H.; Runge, C. F. and Job, B., eds.*, 1989, pp. 89–116.

Runkle, David E. The U.S. Economy in 1990 and 1991: Continued Expansion Likely. *Fed. Res. Bank Minn. Rev.*, Fall 1989, *13*(4), pp. 19–26.

_____ **and Keane, Michael P.** Are Economic Forecasts Rational? *Fed. Res. Bank Minn. Rev.*, Spring 1989, *13*(2), pp. 26–33.

_____ **and Miller, Preston J.** The U.S. Economy in 1989 and 1990: Walking a Fine Line. *Fed. Res. Bank Minn. Rev.*, Winter 1989, *13*(1), pp. 3–10.

Runner, Diana. Changes in Unemployment Insurance Legislation during 1988. *Mon. Lab. Rev.*, January 1989, *112*(1), pp. 59–65.

Rupp, Agnes and Taube, Carl A. Analysis of the Effect of Disproportionately Large Share of Low-Income Patients on Psychiatric Costs in General Hospitals. *Inquiry*, Summer 1989, *26*(2), pp. 216–21.

Ruppert, David and Aldershof, Brian. Transformations to Symmetry and Homoscedasticity. *J. Amer. Statist. Assoc.*, June 1989, *84*(406), pp. 437–46.

de Rus, Ginés. El transporte público urbano en España: Comportamiento de los costes y regulación de la industria. (With English summary.) *Invest. Econ.*, May 1989, *13*(2), pp. 207–25.

Rusek, Antonin. Industrial Growth in Czechoslovakia 1971–1985: Total Factor Productivity and Capital–Labor Substitution. *J. Compar. Econ.*, June 1989, *13*(2), pp. 301–13.

Rush, Mark and Denslow, Dave. Supply Shocks and the Interest Rate. *Econ. Inquiry*, July 1989, *27*(3), pp. 501–10.

_____ **and Hakkio, Craig S.** Market Efficiency and Cointegration: An Application to the Sterling and Deutschemark Exchange Markets. *J. Int. Money Finance*, March 1989, *8*(1), pp. 75–88.

Rushton, G. and Thill, J.-C. The Effect of Distance Metric on the Degree of Spatial Competition between Firms. *Environ. Planning A*, April 1989, *21*(4), pp. 499–507.

Rusmich, Ladislav. The Restructuring of Prices: From Theory to Practice. *Czech. Econ. Digest.*, April 1989, (2), pp. 37–43.

_____ **and Hrnčířová, M.** Disputes around Economic Prognoses. *Czech. Econ. Digest.*, August 1989, (5), pp. 3–19.

Russek, Frank S. and Miller, Stephen M. Are the Twin Deficits Really Related? *Contemp. Policy Issues*, October 1989, *7*(4), pp. 91–115.

Russell, Graeme; Goodnow, Jacqueline and Burns, Ailsa. Australian Families: Pictures and Interpretations. In *Hancock, K., ed.*, 1989, pp. 23–43.

Russell, N. P. and Power, A. P. UK Government Expenditure—Implications of Changes in Agricultural Output under the Common Agricultural Policy. *J. Agr. Econ.*, January 1989, *40*(1), pp. 32–39.

Russell, R. Robert and Blackorby, Charles. The Morishima Elasticity of Substitution; Symmetry, Constancy, Separability, and Its Relationship to the Hicks and Allen Elasticities. **In** *Wood, J. C. and Woods, R. N., eds., Vol. 3,* 1989, *1981,* pp. 258–73.

_____ **and Blackorby, Charles.** Will the Real Elasticity of Substitution Please Stand Up? (A Comparison of the Allen/Uzawa and Morishima Elasticities). *Amer. Econ. Rev.*, September 1989, *79*(4), pp. 882–88.

Russell, Thomas. On 'Maxwell's Laws' of Individual Behaviour. *Econ. Letters*, October 1989, *30*(4), pp. 307–11.

Russell, W. R. and Seo, T. K. Representative Sets for Stochastic Dominance Rules. **In** *[Hadar, J.],* 1989, pp. 59–76.

Russo, Benjamin; Gandar, John M. and Zuber, Richard A. Market Rationality Tests Based on Cross-Equation Restrictions. *J. Monet. Econ.*, November 1989, *24*(3), pp. 455–70.

Russo, Margherita. Technical Change and the Industrial District: The Role of Inter-firm Relations in the Growth and Transformation of Ceramic Tile Production in Italy. **In** *Goodman, E. and Bamford, J., eds.,* 1989, pp. 198–222.

Russo, Massimo. The European Monetary Union: An Agnostic Evaluation: Comment. **In** *Bryant, R. C., et al., eds.,* 1989, pp. 338–40.

_____. The Prospects for a European Central Bank: Panel Discussion. **In** *De Cecco, M. and Giovannini, A., eds.,* 1989, pp. 347–54.

Russon, Manuel G. and Hollingshead, Craig A. Aircraft Size as a Quality of Service Variable in a Short-Haul Market. *Int. J. Transport Econ.*, October 1989, *16*(3), pp. 297–311.

_____ **and Hollingshead, Craig A.** Convenience and Circuity in a Short-Haul Model of Air Passenger Demand. *Rev. Reg. Stud.*, Winter 1989, *19*(1), pp. 50–56.

Rust, John. A Dynamic Programming Model of Retirement Behavior. **In** *Wise, D. A., ed.,* 1989, pp. 359–98.

Rust, Roland T. and Donthu, Naveen. Estimating Geographic Customer Densities Using Kernel Density Estimation. *Marketing Sci.*, Spring 1989, *8*(2), pp. 191–203.

Ruszczynski, Andrzej. Modern Techniques for Linear Dynamic and Stochastic Programs. **In** *Lewandowski, A. and Wierzbicki, A. P., eds.,* 1989, pp. 48–67.

_____. Regularized Decomposition and Augmented Lagrangian Decomposition for Angular Linear Programming Problems. **In** *Lewandowski, A. and Wierzbicki, A. P., eds.,* 1989, pp. 80–91.

_____ **and Gondzio, Jacek.** A Sensitivity Method for Solving Multistage Stochastic Linear Programming Problems. **In** *Lewandowski, A. and Wierzbicki, A. P., eds.,* 1989, pp. 68–79.

Rutgaizer, V. and Nikiforov, L. V. Leasing Relations in the Economic System of Socialism. *Prob. Econ.*, November 1989, *32*(7), pp. 49–62.

Rutherford, Malcolm. Some Issues in the Comparison of Austrian and Institutional Economics. **In** *Samuels, W. J., ed. (II),* 1989, pp. 159–72.

Rutherford, Thomas F.; Wooton, Ian and Harrison, Glenn W. The Economic Impact of the European Community. *Amer. Econ. Rev.*, May 1989, *79*(2), pp. 288–94.

Rutledge, Gary L. and Farber, Kit D. Pollution Abatement and Control Expenditures, 1984–87. *Surv. Curr. Bus.*, June 1989, *69*(6), pp. 19–26.

Rutman, Gilbert L. and Ault, David E. Land Scarcity, Economic Efficiency, and African Common Law. **In** *Zerbe, R. O., ed.,* 1989, pp. 33–54.

Rutström, E. E.; Wigle, Randall M. and Harrison, Glenn W. Costs of Agricultural Trade Wars. **In** *Stoeckel, A. B.; Vincent, D. and Cuthbertson, S., eds.,* 1989, pp. 330–67.

Ruttan, Vernon W. Assistance for Economic Development. **In** *Samuels, W. J., ed. (I),* 1989, pp. 157–65.

_____. Assistance to Expand Agricultural Production. **In** *Krueger, A. O.; Michalopoulos, C. and Ruttan, V. W.,* 1989, pp. 140–69.

_____. Improving the Quality of Life in Rural Areas. **In** *Krueger, A. O.; Michalopoulos, C. and Ruttan, V. W.,* 1989, pp. 170–84.

_____. Institutional Innovation and Agricultural Development. *World Devel.*, Special Issue, September 1989, *17*(9), pp. 1375–87.

_____. Market Integration in Agriculture: An Historical Overview. **In** *von Witzke, H.; Runge, C. F. and Job, B., eds.,* 1989, pp. 6–55.

_____. Why Foreign Economic Assistance? *Econ. Devel. Cult. Change*, January 1989, *37*(2), pp. 411–24.

_____ **and Krueger, Anne O.** Assistance to Korea. **In** *Krueger, A. O.; Michalopoulos, C. and Ruttan, V. W.,* 1989, pp. 226–49.

_____ **and Krueger, Anne O.** Assistance to Turkey. **In** *Krueger, A. O.; Michalopoulos, C. and Ruttan, V. W.,* 1989, pp. 250–68.

_____ **and Krueger, Anne O.** Development Thought and Development Assistance. **In** *Krueger, A. O.; Michalopoulos, C. and Ruttan, V. W.,* 1989, pp. 13–31.

_____ **and Krueger, Anne O.** Toward a Theory of Development Assistance. **In** *Krueger, A. O.; Michalopoulos, C. and Ruttan, V. W.,* 1989, pp. 32–52.

_____; **Krueger, Anne O. and Michalopoulos, Constantine.** Aid and Development: Introduction. **In** *Krueger, A. O.; Michalopoulos, C. and Ruttan, V. W.,* 1989, pp. 1–10.

_____; **Krueger, Anne O. and Michalopoulos, Constantine.** Some Lessons from Development Assistance. **In** *Krueger, A. O.; Michalopoulos, C. and Ruttan, V. W.,* 1989 , pp. 305–23.

_____ **and Sartorius, Rolf H.** The Sources of the Basic Human Needs Mandate. *J. Developing Areas*, April 1989, *23*(3), pp. 331–361.

Ruusunen, Jukka and Hamalainen, Raimo P. Project Selection by an Integrated Decision

Aid. **In** *Golden, B. L.; Wasil, E. A. and Harker, P. T., eds.*, 1989, pp. 101–21.

Ryan, Alan. Value-Judgements and Welfare. **In** *Helm, D., ed.*, 1989, pp. 46–65.

Ryan, David L. and Livernois, John R. Testing for Non-jointness in Oil and Gas Exploration: A Variable Profit Function Approach. *Int. Econ. Rev.*, May 1989, *30*(2), pp. 479–504.

Ryan, Paul. Youth Interventions, Job Substitution, and Trade Union Policy in Great Britain, 1976–1986. **In** *Rosenberg, S., ed.*, 1989, pp. 175–96.

_____ **and Marsden, David.** Statistical Tests for the Universality of Youth Employment Mechanisms in Segmented Labour Markets. *Int. Rev. Applied Econ.*, June 1989, *3*(2), pp. 148–69.

_____ **and McNabb, Robert.** Segmented Labour Markets. **In** *Sapsford, D. and Tzannatos, Z., eds.*, 1989, pp. 151–76.

Rybczynski, Tad M. Corporate Restructuring. *Nat. Westminster Bank Quart. Rev.*, August 1989, pp. 18–28.

_____. The European Community and the World Economy. *Bus. Econ.*, October 1989, *24*(4), pp. 24–29.

Ryder, Harl E. and Galor, Oded. Existence, Uniqueness, and Stability of Equilibrium in an Overlapping-Generations Model with Productive Capital. *J. Econ. Theory*, December 1989, *49*(2), pp. 360–75.

Rymes, Thomas K. Technical Progress, Research and Development. **In** *Feiwel, G. R., ed. (II)*, 1989, pp. 660–76.

_____. The Theory and Measurement of the Nominal Output of Banks, Sectoral Rates of Savings, and Wealth in the National Accounts: Reply. **In** *Lipsey, R. E. and Tice, H. S., eds.*, 1989, pp. 393–400.

_____. The Theory and Measurement of the Nominal Output of Banks, Sectoral Rates of Savings, and Wealth in the National Accounts. **In** *Lipsey, R. E. and Tice, H. S., eds.*, 1989, pp. 357–90.

Rys, Tomasz and Dobrowolski, Grzegorz. Architecture and Functionality of MIDA. **In** *Lewandowski, A. and Wierzbicki, A. P., eds.*, 1989, pp. 339–70.

Ryscavage, Paul. Understanding Real Income Trends: An Analysis of Conflicting Signals. *Bus. Econ.*, January 1989, *24*(1), pp. 36–42.

Ryvkina, Rozalina V. Economic Culture as Society's Memory. *Prob. Econ.*, October 1989, *32*(6), pp. 70–87.

_____ **and Pavlenko, S. Iu.** Managerial Behavior of Executives of Agricultural Enterprises. **In** *Yanowitch, M., ed.*, 1989, *1987*, pp. 23–35.

_____ **and Zaslavskaia, Tat'iana I.** The Subject Matter of Economic Sociology. **In** *Yanowitch, M., ed.*, 1989, *1984*, pp. 103–17.

_____ **and Zaslavskaia, Tat'iana I.** The Subject of Economic Sociology. **In** *Zaslavskaia, T. I.*, 1989, *1987*, pp. 20–37.

Sa-Aadu, J. and Sirmans, C. F. The Pricing of Adjustable Rate Mortgage Contracts. *J. Real Estate Finance Econ.*, December 1989, *2*(4), pp. 253–66.

_____; **Sirmans, C. F. and Benjamin, John D.** Financing and House Prices. *J. Finan. Res.*, Spring 1989, *12*(1), pp. 83–91.

Saari, Donald G. A Dictionary for Voting Paradoxes. *J. Econ. Theory*, August 1989, *48*(2), pp. 443–75.

Saaty, Thomas L. Group Decision Making and the AHP. **In** *Golden, B. L.; Wasil, E. A. and Harker, P. T., eds.*, 1989, pp. 59–67.

Saavedra-Rivano, Neantro. Taxa de juros e inflação de custos. (With English summary.) *Pesquisa Planejamento Econ.*, August 1989, *19*(2), pp. 397–408.

Saba, Richard P.; Caudill, Steven B. and Ault, Richard W. Efficient Estimation of the Costs of Rent Controls. *Rev. Econ. Statist.*, February 1989, *71*(1), pp. 154–59.

Sabani, Laura. Simultaneous and Sequential Modelling in International Trade Analysis: The Italian Empirical Evidence (1960/84). *Econ. Notes*, 1989, (2), pp. 243–73.

Sabel, Charles F. Flexible Specialisation and the Re-emergence of Regional Economies. **In** *Hirst, P. and Zeitlin, J., eds.*, 1989, pp. 17–70.

Sabot, Richard H. Human Capital Accumulation in Post-green Revolution Pakistan: Some Preliminary Results. *Pakistan Devel. Rev.*, Winter 1989, *28*(4), pp. 413–31.

_____. In Praise of Development Economics: Comments. *Pakistan Devel. Rev.*, Winter 1989, *28*(4), pp. 379–81.

Sabourian, Hamid. Repeated Games: A Survey. **In** *Hahn, F., ed.*, 1989, pp. 62–105.

_____. Repeated Games: Some Applications to Under-Cutting and Harassment in the Labour Market. *Europ. Econ. Rev.*, March 1989, *33*(2/3), pp. 625–34.

Sacco, Pier Luigi. Sui fondamenti di equilibrio generale dell'economia dinamica: Una rassegna critica. (On the General Equilibrium Foundations of the Dynamic Economics: A Critical Survey. With English summary.) *Giorn. Econ.*, July–Aug. 1989, *48*(7–8), pp. 347–400.

Sachs, Jeffrey D. Conditionality, Debt Relief, and the Developing Country Debt Crisis. **In** *Sachs, J. D., ed. (II)*, 1989, pp. 275–84.

_____. Conditionality, Debt Relief, and the Developing Country Debt Crisis. **In** *Sachs, J. D., ed. (I)*, 1989, pp. 255–95.

_____. The Debt Overhang of Developing Countries. **In** *[Díaz-Alejandro, C.]*, 1989, pp. 80–102.

_____. Developing Country Debt and Economic Performance: The International Financial System: Introduction. **In** *Sachs, J. D., ed. (I)*, 1989, pp. 1–35.

_____. Developing Country Debt and the World Economy: Introduction. **In** *Sachs, J. D., ed. (II)*, 1989, pp. 1–33.

_____. Efficient Debt Reduction. **In** *Husain, I. and Diwan, I., eds.*, 1989, pp. 239–57.

_____. Making the Brady Plan Work. *Foreign Aff.*, Summer 1989, *68*(3), pp. 87–104.

_____. Strengthening IMF Programs in Highly Indebted Countries. **In** *Gwin, C. and Feinberg, R. E., eds.*, 1989, pp. 101–22.

_____ and Jorgensen, Erika. Default and Renegotiation of Latin American Foreign Bonds in the Interwar Period. In *Eichengreen, B. and Lindert, P. H., eds.*, 1989, pp. 48–85.

_____ and McKibbin, Warwick J. Implications of Policy Rules for the World Economy. In *Bryant, R. C., et al., eds.*, 1989, pp. 151–94.

_____; McKibbin, Warwick J. and Roubini, Nouriel. Correcting Global Imbalances: A Simulation Approach. In *Stern, R. M., ed.*, 1989, pp. 379–424.

_____ and Morales, Juan Antonio. Bolivia's Economic Crisis. In *Sachs, J. D., ed. (II)*, 1989, pp. 57–79.

_____ and Roubini, Nouriel. Fiscal Policy: Government Spending and Budget Deficits in the Industrial Countries. *Econ. Policy: A Europ. Forum*, April 1989, (8), pp. 99–132.

_____ and Roubini, Nouriel. Political and Economic Determinants of Budget Deficits in the Industrial Democracies. *Europ. Econ. Rev.*, May 1989, 33(5), pp. 903–33.

Sacks, Paul M. and Canavan, T. Christopher. Safe Passage through Dire Straits: Managing an Orderly Exit from the Debt Crisis. In *Weeks, J. F., ed.*, 1989, pp. 75–87.

Sadanand, Asha. Protection of Seller's Interests under Buyer's Breach. *Can. J. Econ.*, November 1989, 22(4), pp. 910–16.

_____; Sadanand, Venkatraman and Marks, Denton. Probationary Contracts in Agencies with Bilateral Asymmetric Information. *Can. J. Econ.*, August 1989, 22(3), pp. 643–61.

Sadanand, Venkatraman. Endogenous Diffusion of Technology. *Int. J. Ind. Organ.*, December 1989, 7(4), pp. 471–87.

_____; Marks, Denton and Sadanand, Asha. Probationary Contracts in Agencies with Bilateral Asymmetric Information. *Can. J. Econ.*, August 1989, 22(3), pp. 643–61.

Sadao, Fujiwara. Foreign Trade, Investment, and Industrial Imperialism in Postwar Japan. In *Morris-Suzuki, T. and Seiyama, T., eds.*, 1989, pp. 166–206.

Sadler, Barry. National Parks, Wilderness Preservation, and Native Peoples in Northern Canada. *Natural Res. J.*, Winter 1989, 29(1), pp. 185–204.

Sadli, Mohammad. The Oil Problem—With Special Relevance to Indonesia. In *Shinohara, M. and Lo, F., eds.*, 1989, pp. 249–57.

_____. Trade and Economic Cooperation in the Asian-Pacific Region: Comment. In *Shinohara, M. and Lo, F., eds.*, 1989, pp. 515–17.

Sadoulet, Elisabeth; Fafchamps, Marcel and de Janvry, Alain. Agrarian Structure, Technological Innovations, and the State. In *Bardhan, P., ed. (II)*, 1989, pp. 356–82.

_____ and de Janvry, Alain. Growth and Equity in Agriculture-Led Growth. In *Adelman, I. and Lane, S., eds.*, 1989, pp. 81–96.

_____ and de Janvry, Alain. Investment Strategies to Combat Rural Poverty: A Proposal for Latin America. *World Devel.*, August 1989, 17(8), pp. 1203–21.

_____ and de Janvry, Alain. A Study in Resistance to Institutional Change: The Lost Game of Latin American Land Reform. *World Devel.*, Special Issue, September 1989, 17(9), pp. 1397–1407.

_____; Wilcox, Linda and de Janvry, Alain. Rural Labour in Latin America. *Int. Lab. Rev.*, Special Issue, 1989, 128(6), pp. 701–29.

Sadovski, Aleander N. Experience with Environment Statistics in the Bulgarian Environmental Monitoring System. *Statist. J.*, 1989, 6(1), pp. 69–73.

Saenko, O. P. and Mal'ginova, E. G. Property and Family Well-Being. *Prob. Econ.*, July 1989, 32(3), pp. 72–80.

Saenz, Rogelio; Hwang, Sean-Shong and Aguirre, B. E. Discrimination and the Assimilation and Ethnic Competition Perspectives. *Soc. Sci. Quart.*, September 1989, 70(3), pp. 594–606.

Saerbeck, Rainer. Semi–Input-Output Analysis to Estimate National Economic Parameters: An Application to Botswana. *Industry Devel.*, June 1989, (27), pp. 45–66.

Safaříková, Vlasta. CMEA Common Market—Utopia or Prospect? *Czech. Econ. Digest.*, August 1989, (5), pp. 57–75.

Saffer, Henry and Chaloupka, Frank. Breath Testing and Highway Fatality Rates. *Appl. Econ.*, July 1989, 21(7), pp. 901–12.

Saffran, Bernard. Markets and Justice: An Economist's Perspective. In *Chapman, J. W. and Pennock, J. R., eds.*, 1989, pp. 303–27.

_____. Recommendations for Further Reading. *J. Econ. Perspectives*, Spring 1989, 3(2), pp. 175–79.

_____. Recommendations for Further Reading. *J. Econ. Perspectives*, Fall 1989, 3(4), pp. 203–06.

_____. Recommendations for Further Reading. *J. Econ. Perspectives*, Winter 1989, 3(1), pp. 183–88.

_____. Recommendations for Further Reading. *J. Econ. Perspectives*, Summer 1989, 3(3), pp. 175–78.

Safra, Zvi and Karni, Edi. Dynamic Consistency, Revelations in Auctions and the Structure of Preferences. *Rev. Econ. Stud.*, July 1989, 56(3), pp. 421–33.

Safranski, Scott R. and Kwon, Ik-Whan. Religio-cultural Values in Management: Isolating Specific Relationships. In *Rueschhoff, N. and Schaum, K., eds.*, 1989, pp. 143–56.

_____ and Kwon, Ik-Whan. Religion and Management: Exploring Specific Relationships. In *Prasad, S. B., ed.*, 1989, pp. 171–82.

Sagar, Sushma. Poverty Measurement: Some Issues. *Indian Econ. J.*, April–June 1989, 36(4), pp. 48–56.

Sage, Colin. Drugs and Economic Development in Latin America: A Study in the Political Economy of Cocaine in Bolivia. In *Ward, P. M., ed.*, 1989, pp. 38–57.

Saggar, Mridul and Keshari, Pradeep Kumar. A Firm Level Study of the Determinants of Export Performance in Machinery and Transport Equipment Industry of India. *Indian Econ. J.*, Jan.–March 1989, *36*(3), pp. 36–48.

Sah, Raaj Kumar. Comparative Properties of Sums of Independent Binomials with Different Parameters. *Econ. Letters*, November 1989, *31*(1), pp. 27–30.

_____ **and Stiglitz, Joseph E.** Sources of Technological Divergence between Developed and Less Developed Economies. In *[Díaz-Alejandro, C.]*, 1989, pp. 423–46.

_____ **and Stiglitz, Joseph E.** Technological Learning, Social Learning and Technological Change. In *Chakravarty, S., ed.*, 1989, pp. 285–98.

Saha, Govind P. The Energy Sector and Economic Issues in New Zealand. In *James, W. E., ed.*, 1989, pp. 77–96.

Sahai, Hardeo. Subpopulation Comparisons of Aptitude Scores of the 1980 High School Seniors: An Analysis of the High School and Beyond Survey. *J. Econ. Soc. Meas.*, 1989, *15*(1), pp. 71–89.

Sahi, Siddhartha and Yao, Shuntian. The Noncooperative Equilibria of a Trading Economy with Complete Markets and Consistent Prices. *J. Math. Econ.*, 1989, *18*(4), pp. 325–46.

Sahn, David E. A Conceptual Framework for Examining the Seasonal Aspects of Household Food Security. In *Sahn, D. E., ed.*, 1989, pp. 3–16.

_____. Policy Recommendations for Improving Food Security. In *Sahn, D. E., ed.*, 1989, pp. 301–16.

_____ **and Alderman, Harold.** Understanding the Seasonality of Employment, Wages, and Income. In *Sahn, D. E., ed.*, 1989, pp. 81–106.

_____ **and von Braun, Joachim.** The Implications of Variability in Food Production for National and Household Food Security. In *Anderson, J. R. and Hazell, P. B. R., eds.*, 1989, pp. 320–38.

_____ **and Delgado, Christopher.** The Nature and Implications for Market Interventions of Seasonal Food Price Variability. In *Sahn, D. E., ed.*, 1989, pp. 179–95.

Sahni, Balbir S.; Ahsan, Syed M. and Kwan, Andy C. C. Causality between Government Consumption Expenditure and National Income: OECD Countries. *Public Finance*, 1989, *44*(2), pp. 204–24.

Sahota, Gian S. Theory of the Core and Decentralization in Federal Systems: A Cross-Country Analysis with Special Reference to India. *Indian J. Quant. Econ.*, 1989, *5*(2), pp. 1–47.

Saint-Germain, Michelle A. Does Their Difference Make a Difference? The Impact of Women on Public Policy in the Arizona Legislature. *Soc. Sci. Quart.*, December 1989, *70*(4), pp. 956–68.

Saint-Marc, Michèle. Monetary History in the Long Run: How Are Monetarization and Monetarism Implicated in France, in the U.K. and in U.S.A.? *J. Europ. Econ. Hist.*, Winter 1989, *18*(3), pp. 551–82.

Sainz O., Manuel; Chevez, Pablo and Kiehnle,

Herman. The Disregard of a Legal Entity for Tax Purposes: Mexico. In *International Fiscal Association, ed. (II)*, 1989, pp. 381–89.

Saith, Ashwani. Macro-economic Issues in International Labour Migration: A Review. In *Amjad, R., ed.*, 1989, pp. 28–54.

Saito, Kunio. The Future Role of Japan as a Financial Centre in the Asian-Pacific Area: Comment. In *Shinohara, M. and Lo, F., eds.*, 1989, pp. 398–99.

Saito, Osamu. Bringing the Covert Structure of the Past to Light: Review Article. *J. Econ. Hist.*, December 1989, *49*(4), pp. 992–99.

Saito, Takao. The Influence of German Business Administration on Japanese Business Administration—Especially in Reference to Accounting. In *Dams, T. and Matsugi, T., eds.*, 1989, pp. 107–17.

Saito, Yasuhiko; Ingegneri, Dominique and Crimmins, Eileen M. Changes in Life Expectancy and Disability-Free Life Expectancy in the United States. *Population Devel. Rev.*, June 1989, *15*(2), pp. 235–67.

Sakai, Ken-ichi. The Simple Analytics of Implicit Labour Contracts: A Comment. *Bull. Econ. Res.*, January 1989, *41*(1), pp. 81–83.

Sakai, Yasuhiro and Yamato, Takehiko. Oligopoly, Information and Welfare. *J. Econ. (Z. Nationalökon.)*, 1989, *49*(1), pp. 3–24.

Sakamoto, Masahiro. Japan's Role in the International System. In *Makin, J. H. and Hellmann, D. C., eds.*, 1989, pp. 175–202.

Sakashita, Noboru. Market Equilibrium and Optimum Social Welfare in a Two-Region Economy. In *Sato, R. and Negishi, T., eds.*, 1989, pp. 43–58.

Sakawa, Masatoshi and Yano, Hitoshi. Personal Computer-Aided Interactive Decision Making for Multiobjective Linear Programming Problems with Fuzzy Coefficients and Its Applications. In *Lockett, A. G. and Islei, G., eds.*, 1989, pp. 462–71.

SaKong, Il. The International Economic Position of Korea. In *Bayard, T. O. and Young, S.-G., eds.*, 1989, pp. 7–17.

Sakurai, Masao. Formulators and Legislators of International Trade and Industrial Policy in Japan and the United States. In *Hayashi, K., ed.*, 1989, pp. 160–93.

Salais, Robert. L'analyse économique des conventions du travail. (The Economic Analysis of Labour Conventions. With English summary.) *Revue Écon.*, March 1989, *40*(2), pp. 199–240.

Salama, Abdin Ahmed. Direct Taxation in the Sudan. *Bull. Int. Fiscal Doc.*, January 1989, *43*(1), pp. 17–21.

Salamon, Gerald L. Accounting Rates of Return: Reply. *Amer. Econ. Rev.*, March 1989, *79*(1), pp. 290–93.

Salamon, Lester M. Beyond Privatization: The Tools of Government Action: Conclusion. In *Salamon, L. M., ed.*, 1989, pp. 255–64.

_____. The Changing Tools of Government Action: An Overview. In *Salamon, L. M., ed.*, 1989, pp. 3–22.

_____ **and Lund, Michael S.** The Tools Approach: Basic Analytics. In *Salamon, L. M.,* *ed.*, 1989, pp. 23–49.

Salanie, Bernard and Laroque, Guy. Estimation of Multi-market Fix-Price Models: An Application of Pseudo Maximum Likelihood Methods. *Econometrica*, July 1989, 57(4), pp. 831–60.

Salant, David and McTaggart, Douglas. Time Consistency and Subgame Perfect Equilibria in a Monetary Policy Game. *J. Macroecon.,* Fall 1989, 11(4), pp. 575–88.

Salant, Stephen W. When Is Inducing Self-selection Suboptimal for a Monopolist? *Quart. J. Econ.*, May 1989, 104(2), pp. 391–97.

_____; **Swierzbinski, Joseph E. and Bagnoli, Mark.** Durable-Goods Monopoly with Discrete Demand. *J. Polit. Econ.,* December 1989, 97(6), pp. 1459–78.

Salant, Walter S. The Spread of Keynesian Doctrines and Practices in the United States. In *Hall, P. A., ed.*, 1989, pp. 27–51.

Salanti, Andrea. Distinguishing "Internal" from "External" Criticism in Economic Methodology. *Hist. Polit. Econ.*, Winter 1989, 21(4), pp. 635–39.

_____. "Internal" Criticisms in Economic Theory: Are They Really Conclusive? *Econ. Notes,* 1989, (1), pp. 1–15.

_____. Recent Work in Economic Methodology: Much Ado about What? *Ricerche Econ.*, Jan.– June 1989, 43(1–2), pp. 21–39.

Salati, Eneas. Deforestation and Climatic Changes in the Amazon Basin. In *Oram, P. A., et al.*, 1989, pp. 469–75.

Salatka, William K. The Impact of SFAS No. 8 on Equity Prices of Early and Late Adopting Firms: An Events Study and Cross-Sectional Analysis. *J. Acc. Econ.*, February 1989, 11(1), pp. 35–69.

Salazar, Debra J. Regulatory Politics and Environment: State Regulation of Logging Practices. In *Zerbe, R. O., ed.*, 1989, pp. 95–117.

Salchenberger, Linda M. Sole Owner Harvesting Policies under the Threat of Entry: A Two-Stage Linear Game. *J. Environ. Econ. Manage.*, March 1989, 16(2), pp. 121–33.

Saldanha, Fernando B. Fixprice Analysis of Labor-Managed Economies. *J. Compar. Econ.*, June 1989, 13(2), pp. 227–53.

Saleh, A. K. Md. Ehsanes; Sen, Pranab K. and Gupta, Arjun K. Improved Estimation in a Contingency Table: Independence Structure. *J. Amer. Statist. Assoc.*, June 1989, 84(406), pp. 525–32.

Saleh, Abdul Karim; Kristanto, Kustiah and Makaliwe, Willem H. South-east Sulawesi: Isolation and Dispersed Settlement. In *Hill, H., ed.*, 1989, pp. 566–83.

Saleh, M. Zainuddin and Adnan, M. Anuar. Resource Endowment and Allocation in Islamic Countries for Economic Co-operation: Appendix. In *Choudhury, M. A.*, 1989, pp. 155–58.

Salehi-Isfahani, Djavad. Oil Exports, Real Exchange Rate Appreciation, and Demand for Imports in Nigeria. *Econ. Devel. Cult. Change*, April 1989, 37(3), pp. 495–512.

_____ and **Crémer, Jacques.** The Rise and Fall of Oil Prices: A Competitive View. *Ann. Écon. Statist.*, July–Dec. 1989, (15–16), pp. 427–54.

_____ and **Esfahani, Hadi S.** Effort Observability and Worker Productivity: Towards an Explanation of Economic Dualism. *Econ. J.*, September 1989, 99(397), pp. 818–36.

Salengros, Pierre; van de Leemput, Cécile and Mubikangiey, Luc. Psychological and Sociological Perspectives on Precarious Employment in Belgium. In *Rodgers, G. and Rodgers, J., eds.*, 1989, pp. 197–223.

Salerno, Joseph T. Why Austrians Are Wrong about Depressions: Comment. In *Rothbard, M. N. and Block, W., eds.*, 1989, pp. 141–45.

Salinelli, Ernesto and Cigola, Margherita. Sui contratti di "Interest Rate Swap" a capitale variabile. (On Roller-Coaster Swaps. With English summary.) *Giorn. Econ.*, Nov.–Dec. 1989, 48(11–12), pp. 593–606.

Salinger, Michael A. The Meaning of "Upstream" and "Downstream" and the Implications for Modeling Vertical Mergers. *J. Ind. Econ.*, June 1989, 37(4), pp. 373–87.

_____. Stock Market Margin Requirements and Volatility: Implications for Regulation of Stock Index Futures. *J. Finan. Services Res.*, December 1989, 3(2–3), pp. 121–38.

_____. Stock Market Margin Requirements and Volatility: Implications for Regulation of Stock Index Futures. In *Edwards, F. R., ed.*, 1989, pp. 23–40.

Salkeld, G.; Richardson, J. and Hall, Jane. Cost Utility Analysis: The Compatibility of Measurement Techniques and the Measurement of Utility through Time. In *Smith, C. S., ed.*, 1989, pp. 31–60.

Salles, M. The Best Voting Method: A Review. *Soc. Choice Welfare*, October 1989, 6(4), pp. 337–46.

Sallnäs, Ola and Eriksson, Ljusk Ola. Management Variation and Price Expectations in an Intertemporal Forest Sector Model. *Natural Res. Modeling*, Summer 1989, 3(3), pp. 385–98.

Sallnow, Mike J. Precious Metals in the Andean Moral Economy. In *Parry, J. and Bloch, M., eds.*, 1989, pp. 209–31.

Salm, Cláudio and Eichenberg, Luiz C. Integration Trends in the Brazilian Labour Market. *CEPAL Rev.*, December 1989, (39), pp. 63–72.

Saloner, Garth and Besen, Stanley M. The Economics of Telecommunications Standards. In *Crandall, R. W. and Flamm, K., eds.*, 1989, pp. 177–220.

_____ and **Ordover, Janusz A.** Predation, Monopolization, and Antitrust. In *Schmalensee, R. and Willig, R. D., eds., Vol. 1*, 1989, pp. 537–96.

_____ and **Rotemberg, Julio J.** The Cyclical Behavior of Strategic Inventories. *Quart. J. Econ.*, February 1989, 104(1), pp. 73–97.

_____ and **Rotemberg, Julio J.** Tariffs vs Quotas with Implicit Collusion. *Can. J. Econ.*, May 1989, 22(2), pp. 237–44.

Salsbäck, Johan. The Disregard of a Legal Entity for Tax Purposes: Sweden. In *International Fiscal Association, ed. (II)*, 1989, pp. 489–99.

Salter, V. A. Caribbean Perspectives of Alister McIntyre. *Soc. Econ. Stud.*, June 1989, 38(2), pp. 1–4.

Saltik, Haşim. High Speed Trans-Turkey Railway Lines Will Open Up the Asian Gateway. In *Candemir, Y., ed.*, 1989, pp. 300–313.

Salvanes, Kjell Gunnar. The Structure of the Norwegian Fish Farming Industry: An Empirical Analysis of Economies of Scale and Substitution Possibilities. *Marine Resource Econ.*, 1989, 6(4), pp. 349–73.

Salvati, Michele. A Long Cycle in Industrial Relations, or: Regulation Theory and Political Economy. *Labour*, Spring 1989, 3(1), pp. 41–72.

Salvatore, Dominick. A Model of Dumping and Protectionism in the United States. *Weltwirtsch. Arch.*, 1989, 125(4), pp. 763–81.

Salyer, Kevin D. Exchange Rate Volatility: The Role of Real Shocks and the Velocity of Money. *Econ. Inquiry*, July 1989, 27(3), pp. 387–409.

Salzer, Mark S.; Richardson, Greg D. and Michener, H. Andrew. Extensions of Value Solutions in Constant-Sum Non-sidepayment Games. *J. Conflict Resolution*, September 1989, 33(3), pp. 530–53.

Samanta, Subarna K. Average of Forecasts: Some Further Results. *Atlantic Econ. J.*, September 1989, 17(3), pp. 82.

——— **and Beladi, Hamid.** Price Advertising Decision under Uncertainty. *Indian Econ. J.*, Oct.–Dec. 1989, 37(2), pp. 28–39.

Samarasinghe, S. W. R. de A. Japanese and U.S. Health Assistance to Sri Lanka. In *Reich, M. R. and Marui, E., eds.*, 1989, pp. 91–118.

Sambharya, Rakesh B.; Bobko, Philip and Johnson, Nancy Brown. Deregulation, Business Strategy, and Wages in the Airline Industry. *Ind. Relat.*, Fall 1989, 28(3), pp. 419–30.

Samet, Dov and Gilboa, Itzhak. Bounded versus Unbounded Rationality: The Tyranny of the Weak. *Games Econ. Behav.*, September 1989, 1(3), pp. 213–21.

——— **; Kamien, Morton I. and Li, Lode.** Bertrand Competition with Subcontracting. *Rand J. Econ.*, Winter 1989, 20(4), pp. 553–67.

——— **and Monderer, Dov.** Approximating Common Knowledge with Common Beliefs. *Games Econ. Behav.*, June 1989, 1(2), pp. 170–90.

Sami, Heibatollah and Hartman, Bart P. The Impact of the Accounting Treatment of Leasing Contracts on Use Decision Making: A Field Experiment. In *Schwartz, B. N., ed.*, 1989, pp. 23–35.

Samiei, S. H. Purchasing Power Parity and Administered Exchange Rates. *Econ. Letters*, November 1989, 31(1), pp. 61–64.

Sammartino, Frank; Gramlich, Edward M. and Kasten, Richard. Deficit Reduction and Income Redistribution. *Amer. Econ. Rev.*, May 1989, 79(2), pp. 315–19.

Samoff, Joel. Popular Initiatives and Local Government in Tanzania. *J. Developing Areas*, October 1989, 24(1), pp. 1–18.

Samorodov, Aleksandr. Coping with the Employment Effects of Restructuring in Eastern Europe. *Int. Lab. Rev.*, 1989, 128(3), pp. 357–71.

Sampaio e Mello, António. Insider Trading and Dealer Pricing. *Economia (Portugal)*, May 1989, 13(2), pp. 163–77.

Sampath, R. K. and Rhodes, George F., Jr. A Note on Optimal Pricing of Publicly Produced Intermediate Inputs: Response. *Atlantic Econ. J.*, September 1989, 17(3), pp. 47–48.

Sampson, Gary P. Developing Countries and the Liberalization of Trade in Services. In *Whalley, J., ed., Vol. 1*, 1989, pp. 132–48.

———. Developing Countries and the Uruguay Round of Trade Negotiations: Comment. In *Fischer, S. and de Tray, D., eds.*, 1989, pp. 49–53.

———. Non-tariff Barriers Facing Developing Country Exports. In *Whalley, J., ed., Vol. 1*, 1989, pp. 171–88.

———. Protection in Agriculture and Manufacturing: Meeting the Objectives of the Uruguay Round. In *Islam, N., ed.*, 1989, pp. 219–42.

Sampson, Michael J. and Gregory, Allan W. Markov Chain Tests of the Unbiasedness Hypothesis in the Forward Foreign Exchange Market. *J. Quant. Econ.*, January 1989, 5(1), pp. 143–54.

Sampson, R. Neil. Maintaining Agricultural Land as the Petroleum Era Passes. In *Dysart, B. C., III and Clawson, M., eds.*, 1989, pp. 61–81.

Samuel, John. Immigration Issues: A National Perspective. In *Beach, C. M. and Green, A. G.*, 1989, pp. 12–15.

Samuels, Richard J. Consuming for Production: Japanese National Security, Nuclear Fuel Procurement, and the Domestic Economy. *Int. Organ.*, Autumn 1989, 43(4), pp. 625–46.

Samuels, Warren J. Austrian and Institutional Economics: Some Common Elements. In *Samuels, W. J., ed. (II)*, 1989, pp. 53–71.

———. Determinate Solutions and Valuational Processes: Overcoming the Foreclosure of Process. *J. Post Keynesian Econ.*, Summer 1989, 11(4), pp. 531–46.

———. Diverse Approaches to the Economic Role of Government: An Interpretive Essay. In *Samuels, W. J., ed. (I)*, 1989, pp. 213–49.

———. Economics as a Science and Its Relation to Policy: The Example of Free Trade. In *Tool, M. R. and Samuels, W. J., eds. (II)*, 1989, 1980, pp. 406–28.

———. The Methodology of Economics and the Case for Policy Diffidence and Restraint. *Rev. Soc. Econ.*, Summer 1989, 47(2), pp. 113–33.

———. On the Nature and Existence of Economic Coercion: The Correspondence of Robert Lee Hale and Thomas Nixon Carver. In *Tool, M. R. and Samuels, W. J., eds. (III)*, 1989, 1984, pp. 177–98.

———. Response: Comparing Austrian and Institutional Economics. In *Samuels, W. J., ed. (II)*, 1989, pp. 203–25.

_____. Some Fundamentals of the Economic Role of Government. In *Samuels, W. J., ed. (I)*, 1989, pp. 167–72.

_____. Some Fundamentals of the Economic Role of Government. *J. Econ. Issues*, June 1989, *23*(2), pp. 427–33.

Samuelson, Larry. Brem's *Pioneering Economic Theory, 1630–1980: A Mathematical Restatement:* Review Essay. In *Samuels, W. J., ed. (II)*, 1989, pp. 229–37.

_____ **and Bond, Eric W.** Bargaining with Commitment, Choice of Techniques, and Direct Foreign Investment. *J. Int. Econ.*, February 1989, *26*(1/2), pp. 77–97.

_____ **and Bond, Eric W.** Strategic Behaviour and the Rules for International Taxation of Capital. *Econ. J.*, December 1989, *99*(398), pp. 1099–1111.

_____; **Dunne, Timothy and Roberts, Mark J.** Firm Entry and Postentry Performance in the U.S. Chemical Industries. *J. Law Econ.*, Part 2, October 1989, *32*(2), pp. S233–71.

_____; **Dunne, Timothy and Roberts, Mark J.** The Growth and Failure of U.S. Manufacturing Plants. *Quart. J. Econ.*, November 1989, *104*(4), pp. 671–98.

_____; **Dunne, Timothy and Roberts, Mark J.** Plant Turnover and Gross Employment Flows in the U.S. Manufacturing Sector. *J. Lab. Econ.*, January 1989, *7*(1), pp. 48–71.

_____ **and Mirman, Leonard J.** Information and Equilibrium with Inside Traders. *Econ. J.*, Supplement, 1989, *99*(395), pp. 152–67.

Samuelson, Pamela. Innovation and Competition: Conflicts over Intellectual Property Rights in New Technologies. In *Weil, V. and Snapper, J. W., eds.*, 1989, pp. 169–92.

Samuelson, Paul A. Complementarity—An Essay on the 40th Anniversary of the Hicks–Allen Revolution in Demand Theory. In *Wood, J. C. and Woods, R. N., eds., Vol. 3*, 1989, *1974*, pp. 63–106.

_____. The Judgment of Economic Science on Rational Portfolio Management: Indexing, Timing and Long-Horizon Effects. *J. Portfol. Manage.*, Fall 1989, *16*(1), pp. 4–12.

_____. The Relation between Hicksian Stability and True Dynamic Stability. In *Wood, J. C. and Woods, R. N., eds., Vol. 1*, 1989, *1944*, pp. 106–07.

_____. Remembering Joan. In *Feiwel, G. R., ed. (II)*, 1989, pp. 121–43.

_____. A Revisionist View of von Neumann's Growth Model. In *Dore, M.; Chakravarty, S. and Goodwin, R., eds.*, 1989, pp. 100–122.

_____. Ricardo Was Right! *Scand. J. Econ.*, 1989, *91*(1), pp. 47–62.

_____. Robert Solow: An Affectionate Portrait. *J. Econ. Perspectives*, Summer 1989, *3*(3), pp. 91–97.

_____. The Stability of Equilibrium: Comparative Statics and Dynamics. In *Wood, J. C. and Woods, R. N., eds., Vol. 1*, 1989, *1941*, pp. 45–68.

Sanchez, Aurora. Economic Growth and Stock Market Development. *Philippine Rev. Econ.*

Bus., June 1989, *26*(1), pp. 109–40.

Sánchez Choliz, Julio. La razon patron de Sraffa y el cambio técnico. (With English summary.) *Invest. Ecón.*, January 1989, *13*(1), pp. 137–54.

Sanchez de la Cal, Manuel and Barbosa, Fernando de Holanda. Brazilian Experience with External Debt and Prospects for Growth. In *Singer, H. W. and Sharma, S., eds. (I)*, 1989, pp. 397–412.

Sanchez, José; Dominguez, José M. and Molina, Agustín. El impuesto sobre el gasto personal: Algunas cuestiones básicas para el caso español. (With English summary.) *Invest. Ecón.*, May 1989, *13*(2), pp. 269–81.

Sanchez, Juana and Felix, David. Pooling Foreign Assets and Liabilities of Latin American Debtors to Solve Their Debt Crisis: Estimates of Capital Flight and Alternative Pooling Mechanisms. In *Gray, H. P., ed.*, 1989, pp. 43–61.

Sanchez, Nicolas and Nugent, Jeffrey B. The Efficiency of the Mesta: A Parable. *Exploration Econ. Hist.*, July 1989, *26*(3), pp. 261–84.

Sanchis i Marco, Manuel; Castillo Gimenez, Juana and Reig Martínez, Ernest. Spain's Trade and Development Strategies. In *Yannopoulos, G. N., ed.*, 1989, pp. 40–65.

Sandee, Henry and Weijland, Hermine. Rural Cottage Industry in Transition: The Roof Tile Industry in *Kabupaten* Boyolali, Central Java. *Bull. Indonesian Econ. Stud.*, August 1989, *25*(2), pp. 79–98.

Sandelands, Lloyd E. and Buckner, Georgette C. Of Art and Work: Aesthetic Experience and the Psychology of Work Feelings. In *Cummings, L. L. and Staw, B. M., eds.*, 1989, pp. 105–131.

Sandelin, Bo. Knight's Crusonia Plant—A Short Cut to the Wicksell Effect. *Hist. Polit. Econ.*, Spring 1989, *21*(1), pp. 15–26.

_____. Wicksells felslut om genomsnittlig investeringstid. (Average Investment Time—Wicksell's Conclusion Wrong. With English summary.) *Ekon. Samfundets Tidskr.*, 1989, *42*(1), pp. 19–24.

Sander, William and Ferber, Marianne A. Of Women, Men, and Divorce: Not by Economics Alone. *Rev. Soc. Econ.*, Spring 1989, *47*(1), pp. 15–26.

Sanders, Debra L. and Wyndelts, Robert W. An Examination of Tax Practioners' Decisions under Uncertainty. In *Jones, S. M., ed.*, 1989, pp. 41–72.

Sanders, Hy. Problems with Conventional Expenditure Tax Wisdom or State Policy Analysis with Sales and Excise Taxes and Problems with the Data. *Nat. Tax J.*, September 1989, *42*(3), pp. 315–22.

Sanderson, Fred H. Effects of a Reduction in U.S. Agricultural Protection. In *Tarditi, S., et al., eds.*, 1989, pp. 70–77.

Sanderson, Stephen E. Mexican Agricultural Policy in the Shadow of the U.S. Farm Crisis. In *Goodman, D. and Redclift, M., eds.*, 1989, pp. 205–33.

Sanderson, Warren; Gertler, Paul and Locay,

Luis. Are User Fees Regressive? The Welfare Implications of Charging for Medical Care in Peru. In *WHO, Pan American Health Organization*, 1989, pp. 86–106.

Sandford, Cedric. Administrative and Compliance Costs of Taxation: General Report. In *International Fiscal Association, ed. (I)*, 1989, pp. 19–40.

Sandler, Todd and Cornes, Richard. Public Goods, Growth, and Welfare. *Soc. Choice Welfare*, July 1989, *6*(3), pp. 243–51.

―――― **and Lee, Dwight R.** On the Optimal Retaliation against Terrorists: The Paid-Rider Option. *Public Choice*, May 1989, *61*(2), pp. 141–52.

―――― **and Posnett, John.** Demand for Charity Donations in Private Non-profit Markets: The Case of the U.K. *J. Public Econ.*, November 1989, *40*(2), pp. 187–200.

Sandmo, Agnar. Differential Taxation and the Encouragement of Risk-Taking. *Econ. Letters*, November 1989, *31*(1), pp. 55–59.

Sándor, Lászlóó. Labor Needs a Clear Policy: Interview. *Challenge*, Nov.–Dec. 1989, *32*(6), pp. 14–17.

Sandrock, Otto. International Arbitration as a Means to Solve Disputes between Multinational Corporations. In *Negandhi, A. R., ed.*, 1989, pp. 153–69.

Sands, Barbara N. Agricultural Decision-Making under Uncertainty: The Case of the Shanxi Farmers, 1931–1936. *Exploration Econ. Hist.*, July 1989, *26*(3), pp. 339–59.

――――. Market-Clearing by Corruption: The Political Economy of China's Recent Economic Reforms. *J. Inst. Theoretical Econ.*, March 1989, *145*(1), pp. 116–26.

Sandström, Arne and Nygård, Fredrik. Income Inequality Measures Based on Sample Surveys. *J. Econometrics*, September 1989, *42*(1), pp. 81–95.

Sandver, Marcus H. and Heneman, Herbert G., III. Union Characteristics and Organizing Success. *J. Lab. Res.*, Fall 1989, *10*(4), pp. 377–89.

Sanford, Jonathan E. The World Bank and Poverty: A Review of the Evidence on Whether the Agency Has Diminished Emphasis on Aid to the Poor. *Amer. J. Econ. Sociology*, April 1989, *48*(2), pp. 151–64.

Sanger, Gary C. and Lamoureux, Christopher G. Firm Size and Turn-of-the-Year Effects in the OTC/NASDAQ Market. *J. Finance*, December 1989, *44*(5), pp. 1219–45.

Sanglier, M. and Allen, P. M. Evolutionary Models of Urban Systems: An Application to the Belgian Provinces. *Environ. Planning A*, April 1989, *21*(4), pp. 477–98.

Saniga, Erwin M.; Kolari, James and McInish, Thomas H. A Note on the Distribution Types of Financial Ratios in the Commercial Banking Industry. *J. Banking Finance*, July 1989, *13*(3), pp. 463–71.

Sankaranarayanan, K. C. and Rajasenan, D. Cost–Benefit Analysis of Mechanised Fishing: A Case Study. *Margin*, Oct. 1989–March 1990, *22*(1–2), pp. 80–91.

Sankey, John. Domestically Prohibited Goods and Hazardous Substances—A New GATT Working Group Is Established. *J. World Trade*, December 1989, *23*(6), pp. 99–108.

Sannucci, Valeria. The Establishment of a Central Bank: Italy in the 19th Century. In *De Cecco, M. and Giovannini, A., eds.*, 1989, pp. 244–80.

―――― **and Cotula, Franco.** Nota sulla ricerca storica della Banca d'Italia. (Note on the Historical Research Undertaken by the Bank of Italy. With English summary.) *Rivista Storia Econ.*, S.S., October 1989, *6*(3), pp. 369–75.

Sanso, Marcos; Cuairán, Rogelio and Sanz, Fernando. Flujos bilaterales de comercio internacional, ecuación de gravedad y teoria Heckscher–Ohlin. (With English summary.) *Invest. Ecón.*, January 1989, *13*(1), pp. 155–66.

Santarelli, Enrico. Financial and Technological Innovations during the Phases of Capitalist Development. In *Di Matteo, M.; Goodwin, R. M. and Vercelli, A., eds.*, 1989, pp. 384–402.

―――― **and Archibugi, Daniele.** Tecnologia e struttura del commercio internazionale: La posizione dell'Italia. (Technology and Trade Structure: The Case of Italy. With English summary.) *Ricerche Econ.*, Oct.–Dec. 1989, *43*(4), pp. 427–55.

Santerre, Rexford E. Representative versus Direct Democracy: Are There Any Expenditure Differences? *Public Choice*, February 1989, *60*(2), pp. 145–54.

―――― **and Neun, Stephen P.** Managerial Control and Executive Compensation in the 1930s: A Reexamination. *Quart. J. Bus. Econ.*, Autumn 1989, *28*(4), pp. 100–118.

Santho, Sehoai and Rugege, Sam. Contract Farming and Outgrower Schemes: Asparagus Production in Lesotho. *Eastern Afr. Econ. Rev.*, Special Issue, August 1989, pp. 20–41.

Santiago, Carlos E. The Dynamics of Minimum Wage Policy in Economic Development: A Multiple Time-Series Approach. *Econ. Devel. Cult. Change*, October 1989, *38*(1), pp. 1–30.

Santini, Carlo. The Impact of Fiscal Policy on the Balance of Payments: Recent Experience in the United States: Comment. In *Monti, M., ed.*, 1989, pp. 77–80.

Santini, Jean-Jacques and Encaoua, David. Les privatisations en France: Éléments d'analyse et bilan. (With English summary.) *L'Actual. Econ.*, March 1989, *65*(1), pp. 21–52.

Santomero, Anthony M. The Changing Structure of Financial Institutions: A Review Essay. *J. Monet. Econ.*, September 1989, *24*(2), pp. 321–28.

Santoni, G. J. and Hermann, Werner. The Cost of Restricting Corporate Takeovers: A Lesson from Switzerland. *Fed. Res. Bank San Francisco Rev.*, Nov.–Dec. 1989, *71*(6), pp. 3–11.

Santos, Anibal. Models of Privatization and Market Structure. *Economia (Portugal)*, January 1989, *13*(1), pp. 56–81.

Santos, Eduardo. Poverty in Ecuador. *CEPAL Rev.*, August 1989, (38), pp. 121–32.

dos Santos, João Nunes. Causalidade entre moeda e rendimento na economia portuguesa: 1958–1984. (With English summary.) *Economia (Portugal)*, October 1989, *13*(3), pp. 335–57.

Santos, Manuel S. and Bona, Jerry L. On the Structure of the Equilibrium Price Set of Overlapping-Generations Economies. *J. Math. Econ.*, 1989, *18*(3), pp. 209–30.

Santos, Maria C.; Cohn, Elchanan and Rhine, Sherrie L. W. Institutions of Higher Education as Multi-product Firms: Economies of Scale and Scope. *Rev. Econ. Statist.*, May 1989, *71*(2), pp. 284–90.

Sanyal, Amal; Mukherji, Anjan and Patnaik, Prabhat. Stocks, Credit and the Commodity Market: A Preliminary Exercise. In *Rakshit, M., ed.*, 1989, pp. 111–28.

Sanz, Fernando; de la Cruz Navarro, María and Martinez Mongay, Carlos. Selección y explotación de los sistemas de alarma y prevención de quiebra. (With English summary.) *Invest. Ecón.*, September 1989, *13*(3), pp. 465–84.

_____; **Sanso, Marcos and Cuairán, Rogelio.** Flujos bilaterales de comercio internacional, ecuación de gravedad y teoria Heckscher–Ohlin. (With English summary.) *Invest. Ecón.*, January 1989, *13*(1), pp. 155–66.

Sapir, André. Europe 1992 and Its Possible Implications for Nonmember Countries: Comments. In *Schott, J. J., ed.*, 1989, pp. 313–15.

_____. Les aspects extérieurs du grand marché européen. (With English summary.) *Revue Écon. Politique*, Sept.–Oct. 1989, *99*(5), pp. 692–719.

_____. Trade among Developing Countries in Investment-Related Technological Services. In *Ventura-Dias, V., ed.*, 1989, pp. 165–96.

_____ **and Jacquemin, Alexis.** The European Internal Market: Introduction: 1992: A Single but Imperfect Market. In *Jacquemin, A. and Sapir, A., eds.*, 1989, pp. 1–9.

_____ **and Jacquemin, Alexis.** International Trade and Integration of the European Community: An Econometric Analysis. In *Jacquemin, A. and Sapir, A., eds.*, 1989, *1988*, pp. 202–12.

Sappington, David E. M. and Demski, Joel S. Hierarchical Structure and Responsibility Accounting. *J. Acc. Res.*, Spring 1989, *27*(1), pp. 40–58.

_____ **and Lewis, Tracy R.** Countervailing Incentives in Agency Problems. *J. Econ. Theory*, December 1989, *49*(2), pp. 294–313.

_____ **and Lewis, Tracy R.** Inflexible Rules in Incentive Problems. *Amer. Econ. Rev.*, March 1989, *79*(1), pp. 69–84.

_____ **and Lewis, Tracy R.** Regulatory Options and Price-Cap Regulation. *Rand J. Econ.*, Autumn 1989, *20*(3), pp. 405–16.

_____ **and Riordan, Michael H.** Second Sourcing. *Rand J. Econ.*, Spring 1989, *20*(1), pp. 41–58.

Sapra, Sunil K. Instrumental Variable Estimation in Nonlinear Simultaneous Equation Models with Limited Dependent Variables. *Bull. Econ. Res.*, October 1989, *41*(4), pp. 275–85.

Sapsford, David. Strikes: Models and Evidence. In *Sapsford, D. and Tzannatos, Z., eds.*, 1989, pp. 126–50.

_____ **and Tzannatos, Zafiris.** Labour Economics: An Overview of Some Recent Theoretical and Empirical Developments. In *Sapsford, D. and Tzannatos, Z., eds.*, 1989, pp. 1–6.

Sar, N. L.; Bui-Lan, A. and Paul, P. B. Forecasting Sawntimber Consumption: The Application of an End-Use Model. *Australian J. Agr. Econ.*, December 1989, *33*(3), pp. 219–32.

Sarafopoulos, N. and Valavanidis, A. Occupational Health and Safety in Greece: Current Problems and Perspectives. *Int. Lab. Rev.*, 1989, *128*(2), pp. 249–58.

Sarantis, Nicholas. Macroeconomic Policy and Activity in an Open Economy with Oligopoly and Collective Bargaining. *J. Econ. (Z. Nationalökon.)*, 1989, *49*(1), pp. 25–46.

Saravanamuttu, Paikiasothy. Alliances, Bases and Security: A Southern Perspective. In *Thomas, C. and Saravanamuttu, P., eds.*, 1989, pp. 77–88.

_____. Conflict and Consensus in South/North Security: Conclusion. In *Thomas, C. and Saravanamuttu, P., eds.*, 1989, pp. 195–99.

Saraydar, Edward. The Conflation of Productivity and Efficiency in Economics and Economic History. *Econ. Philos.*, April 1989, *5*(1), pp. 55–67.

Sarbanes, Paul S. Third World Debt: The Next Phase: Perspectives of Politicians. In *Fried, E. R. and Trezise, P. H., eds.*, 1989, pp. 80–84.

Sarcinelli, Mario. The Mezzogiorno and the Single European Market: Complementary or Conflicting Aims? *Banca Naz. Lavoro Quart. Rev.*, June 1989, (169), pp. 129–64.

Sardoni, Claudio. Some Aspects of Kalecki's Theory of Profits: Its Relationship to Marx's Schemes of Reproduction. In *Sebastiani, M., ed.*, 1989, pp. 206–19.

_____ **and Bruno, Sergio.** Productivity Competitiveness among Non Cooperating Integrated Economies: A Negative-Sum Game. *Labour*, Spring 1989, *3*(1), pp. 73–94.

Sargent, John. Tax Expenditures and Government Policy: Introductory Remarks. In *Bruce, N., ed.*, 1989, pp. 15–20.

Sargent, Thomas J. Two Models of Measurements and the Investment Accelerator. *J. Polit. Econ.*, April 1989, *97*(2), pp. 251–87.

_____ **and Brandt, Loren.** Interpreting New Evidence about China and U.S. Silver Purchases. *J. Monet. Econ.*, January 1989, *23*(1), pp. 31–51.

_____ **and Marcet, Albert.** Convergence of Least-Squares Learning in Environments with Hidden State Variables and Private Information. *J. Polit. Econ.*, December 1989, *97*(6), pp. 1306–22.

_____ **and Marcet, Albert.** Convergence of Least Squares Learning Mechanisms in Self-referential Linear Stochastic Models. *J. Econ. Theory*, August 1989, *48*(2), pp. 337–68.

_____ **and Marcet, Albert.** Least-Squares Learning and the Dynamics of Hyperflation. In *Barnett, W. A.; Geweke, J. and Shell, K., eds.,* 1989, pp. 119–37.

Sarig, Oded and Warga, Arthur. Bond Price Data and Bond Market Liquidity. *J. Finan. Quant. Anal.,* September 1989, *24*(3), pp. 367–78.

_____ **and Warga, Arthur.** Some Empirical Estimates of the Risk Structure of Interest Rates. *J. Finance,* December 1989, *44*(5), pp. 1351–60.

Sarin, Rakesh K. and Becker, Joao L. Decision Analysis Using Lottery-Dependent Utility. *J. Risk Uncertainty,* April 1989, *2*(1), pp. 105–17.

Sarkar, Abhirup. Effective Demand, Trade and Employment. *J. Quant. Econ.,* January 1989, *5*(1), pp. 29–35.

_____. A Keynesian Model of North–South Trade. *J. Devel. Econ.,* January 1989, *30*(1), pp. 179–88.

Sarma, Atul and Ram, Kewal. Income, Output and Employment Linkages and Import Intensities of Manufacturing Industries in India. *J. Devel. Stud.,* January 1989, *25*(2), pp. 192–209.

Sarma, J. S. Famine and National and International Food Prices. In *Oram, P. A., et al.,* 1989, pp. 375–87.

Sarmad, Khwaja. The Determinants of Import Demand in Pakistan. *World Devel.,* October 1989, *17*(10), pp. 1619–25.

_____. Planning Priorities in South Asia's Development: Comments. *Pakistan Devel. Rev.,* Winter 1989, *28*(4), pp. 544–45.

Sarna, A. C. and Bhatia, N. L. Transport Systems for Metropolitan Cities of India—A Review. In *Candemir, Y., ed.,* 1989, pp. 539–51.

Sarnat, Marshall. The Emergence of Israel's Security Market: A Note. *J. Econ. Hist.,* September 1989, *49*(3), pp. 693–98.

Sarno, Domenico. Approcci teorici, metodologici ed empirici all'analisi della produttività nella pubblica amministrazione. (Theoretical, Methodological and Empirical Approaches to the Analysis of Productivity in Public Administration. With English summary.) *Econ. Lavoro,* Jan.–March 1989, *23*(1), pp. 77–93.

Sarrazin, Hermann and Krelle, Wilhelm. Growth of the West German Economy: Forecast by the Bonn Model 11. In *Krelle, W., ed.,* 1989, pp. 399–405.

Sarris, Alexander H. Price Policies and International Distortions in the Wheat Market. In *Tarditi, S., et al., eds.,* 1989, pp. 171–89.

_____. Prospects for EC Agricultural Trade with Developing Countries. *Europ. Rev. Agr. Econ.,* 1989, *16*(2), pp. 169–86.

Sartor, Nicola. Flessibilità automatica e variazioni discrezionali: Le ritenute Irpef sui redditi da lavoro dipendente. (Built-in Flexibility and Discretionary Changes: The Case of the Italian Progressive Tax on Labour Income. With English summary.) *Ricerche Econ.,* Oct.–Dec. 1989, *43*(4), pp. 479–93.

Sartorius, Rolf H. and Ruttan, Vernon W. The Sources of the Basic Human Needs Mandate.

J. Developing Areas, April 1989, *23*(3), pp. 331–361.

Sarup, Shanti and Pandey, R. K. Study of Rice Production Function in India. *Margin,* Jan.– March 1989, *21*(2), pp. 52–61.

Sarwar, Ghulam and Anderson, Dale G. Railroad Rate Deregulation and Uncertainty of Farm-Level Prices for Corn. *Amer. J. Agr. Econ.,* November 1989, *71*(4), pp. 883–91.

_____; **Dhaliwal, Naginder S. and Yanagida, John F.** Uncertainty and the Stability of Money Demand Functions for the U.S. Agricultural Sector. *Can. J. Agr. Econ.,* July 1989, *37*(2), pp. 279–89.

Sarwar, Sehba and Korzick, Amy M. Telecommunications Policy and Economic Development: The New State Role: Virginia. In *Schmandt, J.; Williams, F. and Wilson, R. H., eds.,* 1989, pp. 213–39.

Sasaki, Komei. On a Possible Bias in Estimates of Hedonic Price Functions. *J. Urban Econ.,* January 1989, *25*(1), pp. 138–42.

_____. Transportation System Change and Urban Structure in Two-Transport Mode Setting. *J. Urban Econ.,* May 1989, *25*(3), pp. 346–67.

Sasieni, Maurice W. Optimal Advertising Strategies. *Marketing Sci.,* Fall 1989, *8*(4), pp. 358–70.

Sass, Steven A. Professionalization in Pensions and the U.S. Economy: A Chandlerian Framework for the Post-Chandlerian Age. In *Hausman, W. J., ed.,* 1989, pp. 197–206.

Sass, Tim R. and Gisser, Micha. Agency Cost, Firm Size, and Exclusive Dealing. *J. Law Econ.,* Part 1, October 1989, *32*(2), pp. 381–400.

Sassen-Koob, Saskia. New York City's Informal Economy. In *Portes, A.; Castells, M. and Benton, L. A., eds.,* 1989, pp. 60–77.

Sastry, D. U.; Krishnamurty, K. and Pandit, V. N. India: Medium Term Economic Outlook, 1988–90. In *Reddy, J. M., et al., eds. (II),* 1989, pp. 1–22.

Sastry, D. V. S. and Kelkar, Ujwala R. On Decomposition of Total Inequality by Factor Components. *Margin,* Oct. 1989–March 1990, *22*(1–2), pp. 98–102.

Sastry, K. P. and Rao, P. V. Krishna. Restrictive Trade Practices Policy in India. *J. Ind. Econ.,* June 1989, *37*(4), pp. 427–35.

Sathar, Zeba A. Seeking Explanations for High Levels of Infant Mortality in Pakistan: Response. *Pakistan Devel. Rev.,* Autumn 1989, *28*(3), pp. 258–59.

_____ **and Kazi, Shahnaz.** Female Employment and Fertility: Further Investigation of an Ambivalent Association. *Pakistan Devel. Rev.,* Autumn 1989, *28*(3), pp. 175–93.

Sathiendrakumar, R. and Tisdell, Clem A. Comments on a Note on Optimal Effort in the Maldivian Tuna Industry. *Marine Resource Econ.,* 1989, *6*(2), pp. 177–78.

Satish, A. Economics of Irrigation Management: A Study of Public Tubewells in U.P. *Margin,* July–Sept. 1989, *21*(4), pp. 53–64.

Sato, Kazuo and Leff, Nathaniel H. Modelling

the Demand for Foreign Savings in Developing Countries: Testing a Hypothesis with Latin American Data. *J. Devel. Stud.*, July 1989, 25(4), pp. 537–49.

Sato, Mitsuaki and Ozawa, Terutomo. JETRO, Japan's Adaptive Innovation in the Organization of Trade. *J. World Trade*, August 1989, 23(4), pp. 15–24.

Sato, Ryuzo and Matsushita, Masahiro. Estimations of Self-Dual Demand Functions: An International Comparison. In *Sato, R. and Negishi, T., eds.*, 1989, pp. 253–73.

_____ **and Mitchell, Thomas M.** The Economics of Technical Progress. *Eastern Econ. J.*, Oct.–Dec. 1989, 15(4), pp. 309–36.

Sato, Seizaburo and Suzuki, Yuji. A New Stage of the United States–Japan Alliance. In *Makin, J. H. and Hellmann, D. C., eds.*, 1989, pp. 153–74.

Sato, Toshio. Satellite Communications: Technologies and Services. In *Jussawalla, M.; Okuma, T. and Araki, T., eds.*, 1989, pp. 272–77.

Sato, Yoshio. A Comparison of U.S.–Japanese Firms' Parts-Supply Systems: What Besides Nationality Matters? Commentary. In *Hayashi, K., ed.*, 1989, pp. 158–59.

Sattar, Zaidi. Interest-Free Economics and the Islamic Macroeconomic System. *Pakistan Econ. Soc. Rev.*, Winter 1989, 27(2), pp. 109–38.

_____. Privatizing Public Enterprises in Bangladesh: A Simulation Analysis of Macroeconomic Impacts. *Appl. Econ.*, September 1989, 21(9), pp. 1159–76.

Satterthwaite, Mark A. and Gresik, Thomas A. The Rate at Which a Simple Market Converges to Efficiency as the Number of Traders Increases: An Asymptotic Result for Optimal Trading Mechanisms. *J. Econ. Theory*, June 1989, 48(1), pp. 304–32.

_____; **Linhart, Peter B. and Radner, Roy.** Symposium on Noncooperative Bargaining: Introduction. *J. Econ. Theory*, June 1989, 48(1), pp. 1–17.

_____ **and Williams, Steven R.** Bilateral Trade with the Sealed Bid k-Double Auction: Existence and Efficiency. *J. Econ. Theory*, June 1989, 48(1), pp. 107–33.

_____ **and Williams, Steven R.** The Rate of Convergence to Efficiency in the Buyer's Bid Double Auction as the Market Becomes Large. *Rev. Econ. Stud.*, October 1989, 56(4), pp. 477–98.

Satyanarayan, B. External Resources in Economic Development. In *Reddy, J. M., et al., eds. (I)*, 1989, pp. 100–111.

Sauerhaft, Daniel and Wang, George H. K. Examination Ratings and the Identification of Problem/Non-problem Thrift Institutions. *J. Finan. Services Res.*, October 1989, 2(4), pp. 319–42.

Saulnier, Raymond J. The President's Economic Report: A Critique. *J. Portfol. Manage.*, Summer 1989, 15(4), pp. 78–79.

Saunders, Anthony. The Commercial Bank Claims on Developing Countries: How Have

Banks Been Affected? Comment. In *Husain, I. and Diwan, I., eds.*, 1989, pp. 143–45.

_____. Forward Foreign Exchange Markets: Organization and Micro-structure for a Kenyan-Type Economy. In *[Marjolin, R.]*, 1989, pp. 135–49.

_____; **Allen, Linda and Peristiani, Stavros.** Bank Size, Collateral, and Net Purchase Behavior in the Federal Funds Market: Empirical Evidence. *J. Bus.*, October 1989, 62(4), pp. 501–15.

_____ **and Walter, Ingo.** Competitive Performance, Regulation and Trade in Banking Services. In *Vosgerau, H.-J., ed.*, 1989, pp. 238–50.

Saunders, Christopher. Investment, Debt and Growth: A Diversity of Experience. In *Singer, H. W. and Sharma, S., eds. (I)*, 1989, pp. 63–78.

Saunders, Edward M. and Lusht, Kenneth M. Direct Tests of the Divergence of Opinion Hypothesis in the Market for Racetrack Betting. *J. Finan. Res.*, Winter 1989, 12(4), pp. 285–91.

Saunders, Harold H. The Arab–Israeli Conflict in a Global Perspective. In *Steinbruner, J. D., ed.*, 1989, pp. 221–51.

Saunders, Harry D. "Macroeconomic Impacts of Energy Shocks," the Energy Modeling Forum Comparison of Models: Comment. *Energy J.*, October 1989, 10(4), pp. 175–88.

Saunders, Norman C. The Aggregate Structure of the Economy. *Mon. Lab. Rev.*, November 1989, 112(11), pp. 13–24.

Saunders, Peter. Space, Urbanism and the Created Environment. In *Held, D. and Thompson, J. B., eds.*, 1989, pp. 215–34.

Saunders, Peter; Bradbury, Bruce and Whiteford, Peter. Unemployment Benefit Replacement Rates. *Australian Bull. Lab.*, June 1989, 15(3), pp. 223–44.

Saunders, Peter J. Federal Budget Deficits, Interest Rates, and Inflation: Their Implication for Growth. *Eastern Econ. J.*, July–Sept. 1989, 15(3), pp. 213–19.

Saupe, William E. and Gould, Brian W. Off-Farm Labor Market Entry and Exit. *Amer. J. Agr. Econ.*, November 1989, 71(4), pp. 960–69.

_____; **Klemme, Richard M. and Gould, Brian W.** Conservation Tillage: The Role of Farm and Operator Characteristics and the Perception of Soil Erosion. *Land Econ.*, May 1989, 65(2), pp. 167–82.

Sauvant, Karl P. Electronic Highways for World Trade: Services and Data Services. In *Robinson, P.; Sauvant, K. P. and Govitrikar, V. P., eds.*, 1989, pp. 3–12.

Savage, Elizabeth and Apps, Patricia. Labour Supply, Welfare Rankings and the Measurement of Inequality. *J. Public Econ.*, August 1989, 39(3), pp. 335–64.

Savage, Ian and Moses, Leon N. The Effect of Airline Pilot Characteristics on Perceptions of Job Safety Risks. *J. Risk Uncertainty*, December 1989, 2(4), pp. 335–51.

_____ **and Moses, Leon N.** Summary of Other

Aviation Issues. In *Moses, L. N. and Savage, I., eds.*, 1989, pp. 206–15.

_____ and Moses, Leon N. Transportation Safety in an Age of Deregulation: Introduction. In *Moses, L. N. and Savage, I., eds.*, 1989, pp. 3–7.

_____ and Moses, Leon N. Transportation Safety in an Age of Deregulation: Summary and Policy Implications. In *Moses, L. N. and Savage, I., eds.*, 1989, pp. 308–31.

_____ and Panzar, John C. Regulation, Deregulation, and Safety: An Economic Analysis. In *Moses, L. N. and Savage, I., eds.*, 1989, pp. 31–49.

Savas, E. S. Improving the Performance of Public Enterprises through Competition. In *UNDTCD*, 1989, pp. 76–93.

Savastano, Miguel and Edwards, Sebastian. Latin America's Intra-regional Trade: Evolution and Future Prospects. In *Greenaway, D.; Hyclak, T. and Thornton, R. J., eds.*, 1989, pp. 189–233.

Savit, Robert. Nonlinearities and Chaotic Effects in Options Prices. *J. Futures Markets*, December 1989, *9*(6), pp. 507–18.

Săvulescu, B. and Vasiliu, D. P. Total Maximal Flow in a Network Having Random Capacities. *Econ. Computat. Econ. Cybern. Stud. Res.*, 1989, *24*(2–3), pp. 91–101.

Sawa, Takamitsu and Mori, Shunsuke. Revaluation of Durable Capital Stock in Japanese Manufacturing and Its Application for the Measurement of Potential Growth Rate during the OPEC Decade. In *Sato, R. and Negishi, T., eds.*, 1989, pp. 125–44.

Sawchuk, Gary D.; Webster, Gloria and Jenkins, Glenn P. Trade, Protectionism and Industrial Adjustment: Three North American Case Studies: Case Study 3: The Consumer Electronics Industry in North America. In *North–South Institute*, 1989, pp. 105–46.

Sawers, David. Financing for Broadcasting. In *Veljanovski, C., ed. (I)*, 1989, pp. 79–98.

Sawers, Larry. Urban Primacy in Tanzania. *Econ. Devel. Cult. Change*, July 1989, *37*(4), pp. 841–59.

Sawhill, Isabel V. Concentrated Deviance and the "Underclass" Hypothesis: Comment. *J. Policy Anal. Manage.*, Spring 1989, *8*(2), pp. 282–83.

_____. Reaganomics in Retrospect: Lessons for a New Administration. *Challenge*, May–June 1989, *32*(3), pp. 57–59.

Sawhney, Harmeet S. and Jennings, Larkin. Telecommunications Policy and Economic Development: The New State Role: New York. In *Schmandt, J.; Williams, F. and Wilson, R. H., eds.*, 1989, pp. 111–50.

Sawyer, Malcolm C. Kalecki's Economics and Explanations of the Economic Crisis. In *Sebastiani, M., ed.*, 1989, pp. 275–308.

Sawyer, W. Charles and Niroomand, Farhang. The Extent of Scale Economies in U.S. Foreign Trade. *J. World Trade*, December 1989, *23*(6), pp. 137–46.

_____ and Sprinkle, Richard L. Alternative Empirical Estimates of Trade Creation and Trade

Diversion: A Comparison of the Baldwin–Murray and Verdoorn Models. *Weltwirtsch. Arch.*, 1989, *125*(1), pp. 61–73.

_____; Sprinkle, Richard L. and Clark, Don P. Determinants of Industry Participation under Offshore Assembly Provisions in the United States Tariff Code. *J. World Trade*, October 1989, *23*(5), pp. 123–30.

_____; Sprinkle, Richard L. and Deyak, Timothy A. An Empirical Examination of the Structural Stability of Disaggregated U.S. Import Demand. *Rev. Econ. Statist.*, May 1989, *71*(2), pp. 337–41.

Saxena, K. K. Key Sectors of the Indian Economy (Based on I–0 Exercise). *Indian J. Quant. Econ.*, 1989, *5*(2), pp. 69–76.

Saxena, Pradeep Kumar. Rural Female Work Participation Rate in Gujarat: An Inter-District Analysis. *Margin*, Oct. 1989–March 1990, *22*(1–2), pp. 124–32.

Saxonhouse, Gary R. Differentiated Products, Economies of Scale, and Access to the Japanese Market. In *Feenstra, R. C., ed.*, 1989, pp. 145–74.

_____ and Stern, Robert M. An Analytical Survey of Formal and Informal Barriers to International Trade and Investment in the United States, Canada, and Japan. In *Stern, R. M., ed.*, 1989, pp. 293–353.

Sayer, Stuart. Macroeconomic Theory and Policy. *J. Econ. Surveys*, 1989, *3*(4), pp. 353–74.

Sayre, Gregory G. and Calzonetti, Frank J. The Politics of Acid Rain and Canadian Power Imports. In *Calzonetti, F. J., et al.*, 1989, pp. 129–43.

al-Sayyid-Marsot, Afaf Lutfi. Women and Social Change. In *Sabagh, G., ed.*, 1989, pp. 112–29.

Sazanami, Yoko. Trade and Investment Patterns and Barriers in the United States, Canada, and Japan. In *Stern, R. M., ed.*, 1989, pp. 90–126.

Scalmani, Teodoro and Vivarelli, Marco. La disoccupazione come categoria economica: Il contributo di Emil Lederer. (Unemployment as an Economic Concept: The Contribution of Emil Lederer. With English summary.) *Giorn. Econ.*, Nov.–Dec. 1989, *48*(11–12), pp. 569–92.

Scandizzo, Pasquale Lucio. Il valore del tempo: Consumo, salario e tempo libero. (Time Value: Consumption Wages and Free Time. With English summary.) *Econ. Lavoro*, Jan.–March 1989, *23*(1), pp. 95–113.

_____. Measures of Industrial Protectionism: Relevance for Trade and Labour Policies. *Labour*, Winter 1989, *3*(3), pp. 129–67.

_____. Misure indirette dell'occupazione con i modelli di equilibrio economico generale. (Indirect Employment Measures with General Economic Models. With English summary.) *Econ. Lavoro*, Oct.–Dec. 1989, *23*(4), pp. 61–71.

Scanlon, Kevin P.; Trifts, Jack W. and Pettway, Richard H. Impacts of Relative Size and Industrial Relatedness on Returns to Shareholders of Acquiring Firms. *J. Finan. Res.*, Summer 1989, *12*(2), pp. 103–12.

Scanlon, William J. and Feder, Judith. Paying for Long-Term Care. In *Eisdorfer, C.; Kessler, D. A. and Spector, A. N., eds.*, 1989, pp. 125–36.

_____ **and Feder, Judith.** Problems and Prospects in Financing Long-Term Care. In *McLennan, K. and Meyer, J. A., eds.*, 1989, pp. 67–85.

Scarborough, Cathy. Conceptualizing Black Women's Employment Experiences. *Yale Law J.*, May 1989, *98*(7), pp. 1457–78.

Scarfe, Brian L. Energy Investment and Security of Supply. In *Watkins, G. C., ed.*, 1989, pp. 181–92.

Scarpa, Carlo. La liberalizzazione del commercio internazionale di servizi: Schemi teorici per l'intervento pubblico. (The Liberalization of the International Trade of Services: A Theoretical Framework for Public Intervention. With English summary.) *Rivista Int. Sci. Econ. Com.*, April–May 1989, *36*(4–5), pp. 437–58.

_____ . On the Effectiveness of Average Cost Pricing Regulation in the Presence of Learning-by-Doing. *Giorn. Econ.*, Jan.–Feb. 1989, *48*(1–2), pp. 73–90.

_____ . Politiche commerciali in un contesto strategico: La rilevanza della struttura di mercato. (With English summary.) *Studi. Econ.*, 1989, *44*(39), pp. 113–36.

Scarsini, Marco and Muliere, Pietro. Multivariate Decisions with Unknown Price Vector. *Econ. Letters*, 1989, *29*(1), pp. 13–19.

_____ **and Muliere, Pietro.** A Note on Stochastic Dominance and Inequality Measures. *J. Econ. Theory*, December 1989, *49*(2), pp. 314–23.

Scazzieri, Roberto. Economic Theory as Rational Reconstruction. *Ricerche Econ.*, Jan.–June 1989, *43*(1–2), pp. 40–56.

Schachter, Joseph and Althaus, Paul G. An Equilibrium Model of Gross Migration. *J. Reg. Sci.*, May 1989, *29*(2), pp. 143–59.

Schackmann-Fallis, Karl-Peter. External Control and Regional Development within the Federal Republic of Germany. *Int. Reg. Sci. Rev.*, 1989, *12*(3), pp. 245–61.

Schadé, Rosemarie Sanderson. Tax Treaty Overrides in the Technical and Miscellaneous Revenue Act of 1988: United States. *Bull. Int. Fiscal Doc.*, May 1989, *43*(5), pp. 214–17.

Schaede, Ulrike. Forwards and Futures in Tokugawa-Period Japan: A New Perspective on the Dojima Rice Market. *J. Banking Finance*, September 1989, *13*(4–5), pp. 487–513.

Schaefer, Donald F. Locational Choice in the Antebellum South. *J. Econ. Hist.*, March 1989, *49*(1), pp. 145–65.

Schaefer, Jeffrey M. and Strongin, David G. Foreign Portfolio Investment in the United States. In *Kaushik, S. K., ed.*, 1989, pp. 155–80.

_____ **and Strongin, David G.** Why All the Fuss about Foreign Investment. *Challenge*, May–June 1989, *32*(3), pp. 31–35.

Schaefer, Thomas and Hopwood, William. Firm-Specific Responsiveness to Input Price Changes and the Incremental Information in Current Cost Income. *Accounting Rev.*, April 1989, *64*(2), pp. 313–28.

Schaeffer, Nora Cate and Bradburn, Norman M. Respondent Behavior in Magnitude Estimation. *J. Amer. Statist. Assoc.*, June 1989, *84*(406), pp. 402–13.

Schaeffer, Robert. Devolution, Partition, and War in the Interstate System. In *Schaeffer, R. K., ed.*, 1989, pp. 99–108.

_____ . War in the World-System: Introduction. In *Schaeffer, R. K., ed.*, 1989, pp. 1–8.

Schäfer, Dieter and Stahmer, Carsten. Input–Output Model for the Analysis of Environmental Protection Activities. *Econ. Systems Res.*, 1989, *1*(2), pp. 203–28.

Schaffer, Mark E. Are Profit-Maximisers the Best Survivors? A Darwinian Model of Economic Natural Selection. *J. Econ. Behav. Organ.*, August 1989, *12*(1), pp. 29–45.

_____ . The Credible-Commitment Problem in the Center–Enterprise Relationship. *J. Compar. Econ.*, September 1989, *13*(3), pp. 359–82.

Schankerman, Mark and Lach, Saul. Dynamics of R&D and Investment in the Scientific Sector. *J. Polit. Econ.*, August 1989, *97*(4), pp. 880–904.

Schanze, Erich. Contract, Agency, and the Delegation of Decision Making. In *Bamberg, G. and Spremann, K., eds.*, 1989, pp. 461–71.

_____ . Distributional Issues in Contracting for Property Rights: Comment. *J. Inst. Theoretical Econ.*, March 1989, *145*(1), pp. 32–37.

Schapiro, Morton Owen; Winston, Gordon C. and McPherson, Michael S. Recent Trends in U.S. Higher Education Costs and Prices: The Role of Government Funding. *Amer. Econ. Rev.*, May 1989, *79*(2), pp. 253–57.

Scharer, Linda K. and Brickner, Philip W. Alcoholism among the Elderly. In *Eisdorfer, C.; Kessler, D. A. and Spector, A. N., eds.*, 1989, pp. 341–57.

Scharf, C. Bradley. Social Policy and Social Conditions in the GDR. In *Rueschemeyer, M. and Lemke, C., eds.*, 1989, pp. 3–24.

Scharfstein, David S.; Stein, Jeremy C. and Froot, Kenneth A. LDC Debt: Forgiveness, Indexation, and Investment Incentives. *J. Finance*, December 1989, *44*(5), pp. 1335–50.

Schatz, Klaus-Werner. Differences in Income Elasticities and Trends in Real Exchange Rates: Comment. *Europ. Econ. Rev.*, May 1989, *33*(5), pp. 1050–54.

_____ **and Donges, Juergen B.** The Iberian Countries in the EEC—Risks and Chances for Their Manufacturing Industries. In *Yannopoulos, G. N., ed.*, 1989, pp. 254–306.

Schatzer, Raymond Joe; Tilley, Daniel S. and Moesel, Douglas. Consumer Expenditures at Direct Produce Markets. *Southern J. Agr. Econ.*, July 1989, *21*(1), pp. 131–38.

Schaum, Konrad and Rueschhoff, Norlin G. Christian Business Values in an Intercultural Environment: Perspectives for Further Research. In *Rueschhoff, N. and Schaum, K.*, *eds.*, 1989, pp. 182–88.

Schaum, Wolfgang and Dirrigl, Hans. Ausschüttungsplanung nach der Steurerreform 1990. (With English summary.) *Z. Betriebswirtshaft*, March 1989, *59*(3), pp. 291–309.

Schedvin, C. B. Australian Economic History. *Econ. Rec.*, September 1989, *65*(190), pp. 287–90.

Scheffler, Richard M.; Haas-Wilson, Deborah and Cheadle, Allen. Demand for Mental Health Services: An Episode of Treatment Approach. *Southern Econ. J.*, July 1989, *56*(1), pp. 219–32.

_____ **and Miller, Angela Browne.** Demand Analysis of Mental Health Service Use among Ethnic Subpopulations. *Inquiry*, Summer 1989, *26*(2), pp. 202–15.

Scheffman, David T. and Holt, Charles A. Strategic Business Behavior and Antitrust. In *Larner, R. J. and Meehan, J. W., Jr., eds.*, 1989, pp. 39–82.

_____ **and Langenfeld, James.** Innovation and U.S. Competition Policy. *Antitrust Bull.*, Spring 1989, *34*(1), pp. 1–63.

_____ **and Spiller, Pablo T.** Empirical Approaches to Market Power: Introduction. *J. Law Econ.*, Part 2, October 1989, *32*(2), pp. S3–10.

Scheide, Joachim. A K-Percent Rule for Monetary Policy in West Germany. *Weltwirtsch. Arch.*, 1989, *125*(2), pp. 326–36.

_____. On Real and Monetary Causes for Business Cycles in West Germany. *Schweiz. Z. Volkswirtsch. Statist.*, December 1989, *125*(4), pp. 583–95.

_____ **and Sinn, Stefan.** How Strong Is the Case for International Coordination? In *Dorn, J. A. and Niskanen, W. A., eds.*, 1989, pp. 397–422.

Scheinkman, José A. and LeBaron, Blake. Nonlinear Dynamics and GNP Data. In *Barnett, W. A.; Geweke, J. and Shell, K., eds.*, 1989, pp. 213–27.

_____ **and LeBaron, Blake.** Nonlinear Dynamics and Stock Returns. *J. Bus.*, July 1989, *62*(3), pp. 311–37.

Schell, A. and Pauly, Ralf. Calendar Effects in Structural Time Series Models with Trend and Season. *Empirical Econ.*, 1989, *14*(3), pp. 241–56.

Schellenkens, Jona. Mortality and Socio-economic Status in Two Eighteenth-Century Dutch Villages. *Population Stud.*, November 1989, *43*(3), pp. 391–404.

Schellhaass, Horst-Manfred and Neumann, Uwe. Missbrauchsaufsicht im Lebensmitteleinzelhandel. (With English summary.) *Z. Betriebswirtshaft*, May 1989, *59*(5), pp. 566–78.

Schembri, Lawrence. Export Prices and Exchange Rates: An Industry Approach. In *Feenstra, R. C., ed.*, 1989, pp. 185–206.

Schenk, Hans. Corruption . . . What Corruption? Notes on Bribery and Dependency in Urban India. In *Ward, P. M., ed.*, 1989, pp. 110–22.

Schenone, Osvaldo H. El "Cuentapropismo," la legislación laboral y la acumulación de capital. (With English summary.) *Cuadernos Econ.*, December 1989, *26*(79), pp. 321–34.

Scherer, F. M. Does Antitrust Compromise Technological Efficiency? *Eastern Econ. J.*, Jan.–March 1989, *15*(1), pp. 1–5.

_____. Merger in the Petroleum Industry: The *Mobil–Marathon* Case. In *Kwoka, J. E., Jr. and White, L. J., eds.*, 1989, pp. 19–45.

_____. Merger Policy in the 1970s and 1980s. In *Larner, R. J. and Meehan, J. W., Jr., eds.*, 1989, pp. 83–101.

_____. Patents: Recent Trends and Puzzles: Comments. *Brookings Pap. Econ. Act.*, Microeconomics, 1989, pp. 325–28.

_____ **and Ravenscraft, David J.** The Profitability of Mergers. *Int. J. Ind. Organ.*, Special Issue, March 1989, *7*(1), pp. 101–16.

Scherf, Wolfgang. Zur Abgrenzung und finanzpolitischen Bedeutung verschiedener Arten der Staatsverschuldung. (Public Debt: Different Types and Their Policy Implications. With English summary.) *Jahr. Nationalökon. Statist.*, March 1989, *206*(2), pp. 136–51.

_____ **and Oberhauser, Alois.** Interactions between the External Economy and the Fiscal and Monetary Policy of the Federal Republic of Germany, in View of Stabilization Policy. In *Dams, T. and Matsugi, T., eds.*, 1989, pp. 275–97.

Scherr, Fredrick C. and Sugrue, Timothy F. An Empirical Test of Ross's Cash Flow Beta Theory of Capital Structure. *Financial Rev.*, August 1989, *24*(3), pp. 355–70.

Scherr, Sara J. Agriculture in an Export Boom Economy: A Comparative Analysis of Policy and Performance in Indonesia, Mexico and Nigeria. *World Devel.*, April 1989, *17*(4), pp. 543–60.

Scherzer, Kenneth A. The Politics of Default: Financial Restructure and Reform in Depression Era Fall River, Massachusetts. *Urban Stud.*, February 1989, *26*(1), pp. 164–76.

Schettkat, Ronald. The Impact of Taxes on Female Labour Supply. *Int. Rev. Applied Econ.*, January 1989, *3*(1), pp. 1–24.

Scheu, Tim and Colwell, Peter F. Optimal Lot Size and Configuration. *J. Urban Econ.*, July 1989, *26*(1), pp. 90–109.

Scheurell, Robert P. and Dixon, John. Social Welfare in Developed Market Countries: Preface. In *Dixon, J. and Scheurell, R. P., eds.*, 1989, pp. vii–xii.

Scheuren, Fritz. Panel Surveys: Nonresponse Adjustments: Discussion. In *Kasprzyk, D., et al., eds.*, 1989, pp. 426–31.

_____. The Social Policy Simulation Database and Model: An Example of Survey and Administrative Data Integration: A Comment. *Surv. Curr. Bus.*, May 1989, *69*(5), pp. 40–41.

Schiantarelli, Fabio; Low, William and McIntosh, James. A Qualitative Response Analysis of UK Firms' Employment and Output Decisions. *J. Appl. Econometrics*, July–Sept. 1989, *4*(3), pp. 251–64.

Schick, Allen. Health Policy: Spending More and

Protecting Less. In *Lewin, M. E. and Sullivan, S., eds.*, 1989, pp. 29–52.

Schiek, William A. and Babb, Emerson M. Impact of Reverse Osmosis on Southeast Milk Markets. *Southern J. Agr. Econ.*, December 1989, *21*(2), pp. 63–75.

van Schijndel, Geert-Jan C. Th.; Jørgensen, Steffen and Kort, Peter M. Optimal Investment, Financing, and Dividends: A Stackelberg Differential Game. *J. Econ. Dynam. Control*, July 1989, *13*(3), pp. 339–77.

Schildbach, Thomas. Zur Diskussion über das Bernoulli-Prinzip in Deutschland und im Ausland. (With English summary.) *Z. Betriebswirtshaft*, July 1989, *59*(7), pp. 766–78.

Schiller, Christian and Heller, Peter S. The Fiscal Impact of Privatization, with Some Examples from Arab Countries. *World Devel.*, May 1989, *17*(5), pp. 757–67.

_____ **and Heller, Peter S.** The Fiscal Impact of Privatization, with Some Examples from Arab Countries. In *El-Naggar, S., ed.*, 1989, pp. 85–112.

Schilling, Don. Estimating the Present Value of Future Income Losses 1900–1982; an Historical Simulation: Reply. *J. Risk Ins.*, September 1989, *56*(3), pp. 560–63.

Schinasi, Garry J. and Swamy, P. A. V. B. The Out-of-Sample Forecasting Performance of Exchange Rate Models When Coefficients Are Allowed to Change. *J. Int. Money Finance*, September 1989, *8*(3), pp. 375–90.

Schindler, Klaus and Welcker, Johannes. Währungsoptionsscheine und der Rückerstattung-Währungsoptionsschein (RWOS—Money-Back Currency Warrant) der Nordiska Investeringsbanken (NIB). (Money-Back Currency Warrants of the Nordiska Investeringsbanken. With English summary.) *Kredit Kapital*, 1989, *22*(2), pp. 239–66.

Schindler, Robert M. and Holbrook, Morris B. Some Exploratory Findings on the Development of Musical Tastes. *J. Cons. Res.*, June 1989, *16*(1), pp. 119–24.

Schioppa, C. and Panić, M. Europe's Long-Term Capital Flows Since 1971. In *Gordon, I. and Thirlwall, A. P., eds.*, 1989, pp. 166–94.

Schipper, Katherine; Smith, Abbie and Marais, M. Laurentius. Wealth Effects of Going Private for Senior Securities. *J. Finan. Econ.*, June 1989, *23*(1), pp. 155–91.

Schips, Bernd. Geldmengenpolitik und Wechselkursentwicklung. (Monetary Policy and the Development of Exchange Rates. With English summary.) *Aussenwirtschaft*, June 1989, *44*(2), pp. 237–51.

_____ **and Abrahamsen, Yngve.** Specification and Stability Tests versus Jackknifing: Some Illustrative Examples. In *Hackl, P., ed.*, 1989, pp. 37–43.

Schirm, David C.; Ferri, Michael G. and Moore, Scott B. The Listing, Size, and Value of Equity Warrants. *Financial Rev.*, February 1989, *24*(1), pp. 135–46.

_____ **; Sheehan, Richard G. and Ferri, Michael G.** Financial Market Responses to Treasury

Debt Announcements: A Note. *J. Money, Credit, Banking*, August 1989, *21*(3), pp. 394–400.

Schlack, Robert F. Economic Change in the People's Republic of China: An Institutionalist Approach. *J. Econ. Issues*, March 1989, *23*(1), pp. 155–88.

Schlagenhauf, Don; Talu, Ayhan and Melvin, Michael. The U.S. Budget Deficit and the Foreign Exchange Value of the Dollar. *Rev. Econ. Statist.*, August 1989, *71*(3), pp. 500–505.

Schleef, Harold J. Whole Life Cost Comparisons Based upon the Year of Required Protection. *J. Risk Ins.*, March 1989, *56*(1), pp. 83–103.

Schlegelmilch, B. B. and Tynan, A. C. The Scope for Market Segmentation within the Charity Market: An Empirical Analysis. *Managerial Dec. Econ.*, June 1989, *10*(2), pp. 127–34.

Schleicher, Stefan. Structural Adjustment, Productivity and Capital Accumulation in Austria. In *Krelle, W., ed.*, 1989, pp. 487–95.

Schlenker, Robert E. and Shaughnessy, Peter W. Swing-Bed Hospital Cost and Reimbursement. *Inquiry*, Winter 1989, *26*(4), pp. 508–21.

Schlesinger, Harris. On the Analytics of Pure Public Good Provision. *Public Finance*, 1989, *44*(1), pp. 102–09.

Schloss, Zvi H. Variable Exchange Rates and the Quality of Credit. In *[Marjolin, R.]*, 1989, pp. 215–24.

Schlottmann, Alan M.; Fox, William F. and Herzog, Henry W., Jr. Metropolitan Fiscal Structure and Migration. *J. Reg. Sci.*, November 1989, *29*(4), pp. 523–36.

_____ **and Herzog, Henry W., Jr.** Environmental Regulation and the Valuation of Life: Interindustry Mobility and the Market Price of Safety. In *Folmer, H. and van Ierland, E., eds.*, 1989, pp. 139–57.

_____ **and Herzog, Henry W., Jr.** High-Technology Location and Worker Mobility in the U.S. In *Andersson, Å. E.; Batten, D. F. and Karlsson, C., eds.*, 1989, pp. 219–32.

_____ **and Watson, Robin A.** Air Quality Standards, Coal Conversion and the Steam-Electric Coal Market. In *Labys, W. C.; Takayama, T. and Uri, N. D., eds.*, 1989, pp. 105–27.

Schluter, Gerald; Fohlin, Caroline and Robinson, Sherman. Terms of Trade and Factor Commitments in Agriculture. *J. Agr. Econ. Res.*, Fall 1989, *41*(4), pp. 6–11.

Schmähl, Winfried. Retirement at the Cross-Roads: Tasks and Problems under Changing Economic and Demographic Conditions: Some Introductory Remarks. In *Schmähl, W., ed.*, 1989, pp. 1–12.

_____ **and Jacobs, Klaus.** The Process of Retirement in Germany: Trends, Public Discussion and Options for Its Redefinition. In *Schmähl, W., ed.*, 1989, pp. 13–38.

Schmalensee, Richard. Good Regulatory Regimes. *Rand J. Econ.*, Autumn 1989, *20*(3), pp. 417–36.

_____ . Inter-industry Studies of Structure and

Performance. In *Schmalensee, R. and Willig, R. D., eds., Vol. 2*, 1989, pp. 951–1009.

————. Intra-industry Profitability Differences in U.S. Manufacturing, 1953–1983. *J. Ind. Econ.*, June 1989, 37(4), pp. 337–57.

————. The Potential of Incentive Regulation. In *Helm, D.; Kay, J. and Thompson, D., eds.*, 1989, pp. 178–87.

Schmandt, Jurgen; Weintraub, Sidney and Bean, Frank D. Mexican and Central American Population and U.S. Immigration Policy: Introduction. In *Bean, F. D.; Schmandt, J. and Weintraub, S., eds.*, 1989, pp. 1–4.

Schmaus, Guenther; Stephenson, Geoffrey and O'Higgins, Michael. Income Distribution and Redistribution: A Microdata Analysis for Seven Countries. *Rev. Income Wealth*, June 1989, 35(2), pp. 107–31.

Schmeidler, David. Subjective Probability and Expected Utility without Additivity. *Econometrica*, May 1989, 57(3), pp. 571–87.

———— **and Gilboa, Itzhak.** Maxmin Expected Utility with Non-unique Prior. *J. Math. Econ.*, 1989, 18(2), pp. 141–53.

Schmid, A. Allan. Economy and State: An Institutionalist Theory of Process and Learning. In *Samuels, W. J., ed. (I)*, 1989, pp. 173–78.

Schmid, Hans. Soll die Schweiz mit der EG Freizügigkeit für Arbeitnehmer vereinbaren? (Should Switzerland Set Up a Contract with the EC for Free Migration of Workers? With English summary.) *Aussenwirtschaft*, June 1989, 44(2), pp. 159–77.

Schmidt, Christian. Quels fondements pour le calcul économique public? (With English summary.) *Revue Écon. Politique*, March–April 1989, 99(2), pp. 204–16.

Schmidt, Herbert G. The Social Impact of Small Business. In *Gemper, B. B., ed.*, 1989, pp. 34–46.

Schmidt, Karsten and Stahlecker, Peter. Zur Ausnutzung von a priori Informationen bei der Schätzung einer gesamtwirtschaftlichen Cobb–Douglas-Produktionsfunktion. (On the Estimation of a Macroeconomic Cobb–Douglas Production Function Using Prior Information. With English summary.) *Jahr. Nationalökon. Statist.*, December 1989, 206(6), pp. 599–605.

Schmidt, Klaus-Dieter; Donges, Juergen B. and Klodt, Henning. Prospective Structural Changes in the West German Economy. In *Krelle, W., ed.*, 1989, pp. 385–98.

Schmidt, Kurt. The Public Sector in a Market Economy. In *Peacock, A. and Willgerodt, H., eds. (II)*, 1989, 1956, pp. 195–207.

Schmidt, Paul-Günther. Debt Equity Swaps: Konzeption, Anwendung und Probleme. (Debt Equity Swaps: Concepts, Application and Problems. With English summary.) *Kredit Kapital*, 1989, 22(2), pp. 296–322.

Schmidt, Peter; Breusch, Trevor S. and Mizon, Grayham E. Efficient Estimation Using Panel Data. *Econometrica*, May 1989, 57(3), pp. 695–700.

———— **and Guilkey, David K.** Extended Tabulations for Dickey–Fuller Tests. *Econ. Letters*, December 1989, 31(4), pp. 355–57.

———— **and Witte, Ann Dryden.** Predicting Criminal Recidivism Using 'Split Population' Survival Time Models. *J. Econometrics*, January 1989, 40(1), pp. 141–59.

Schmidt, Ralf-Bodo. "Unternehmungsphilosophie" and Human Concept—Questions to the Research of Real Theory. In *Dams, T. and Matsugi, T., eds.*, 1989, pp. 1–20.

Schmidt, Reinhard H. Agency Costs Are Not a "Flop"! In *Bamberg, G. and Spremann, K., eds.*, 1989, pp. 495–509.

Schmidt, Ronald H. Natural Resources and Regional Growth. *Fed. Res. Bank San Francisco Econ. Rev.*, Fall 1989, (4), pp. 3–19.

Schmidt, Rudi and Trinczek, Rainer. Standardised and Differentiated Working Hours in the Context of an Increasing Deregulation of Working Conditions—The West German Experience. In *Agassi, J. B. and Heycock, S., eds.*, 1989, pp. 129–36.

Schmidt-Trenz, Hans-Jörg. The State of Nature in the Shadow of Contract Formation: Adding a Missing Link to J. M. Buchanan's Social Contract Theory. *Public Choice*, September 1989, 62(3), pp. 237–51.

Schmidtz, David; Walker, James M. and Isaac, R. Mark. The Assurance Problem in a Laboratory Market. *Public Choice*, September 1989, 62(3), pp. 217–36.

Schmisseur, Ed and Pankratz, John. XLAYER: An Expert System Providing Management Advice to Commercial Layer Managers. *Southern J. Agr. Econ.*, December 1989, 21(2), pp. 183–93.

Schmit, Joan T. and Moore, William T. The Risk Retention Act of 1986: Effects on Insurance Firm Shareholders' Wealth. *J. Risk Ins.*, March 1989, 56(1), pp. 137–45.

Schmitt, Bernard. La France appauvrie par le service de sa dette extérieure. (The Double Burden of France's External Debt. With English summary.) *Écon. Societes*, August 1989, 23(8), pp. 91–100.

Schmitt, George F. The Information Revolution and the Regulatory Old Regime. In *National Economic Research Associates*, 1989, pp. 213–21.

Schmitt, Günther. Farms, Farm Households, and Productivity of Resource Use in Agriculture. *Europ. Rev. Agr. Econ.*, 1989, 16(2), pp. 257–84.

————. Simon Kuznets' "Sectoral Shares in Labor Force": A Different Explanation of His $(I + S)/A$ Ratio. *Amer. Econ. Rev.*, December 1989, 79(5), pp. 1262–76.

Schmitt, Harrison H. Energy Realities for the Third Millennium. *Energy J.*, October 1989, 10(4), pp. i–iii.

Schmitz, Andrew. Agricultural Diversification Strategies: Canada and the United States. In *Schmitz, A., ed.*, 1989, pp. 8–36.

————. Discussion: Livestock: Constraints and Opportunities. In *Buse, R. C., ed.*, 1989, pp. 359–66.

_____. Free Trade and Agricultural Diversification: Canada and the United States: Introduction. In *Schmitz, A., ed.*, 1989, pp. 1–7.

_____. Trade in Primary Products: Canada, the United States, and Japan. In *Stern, R. M., ed.*, 1989, pp. 141–67.

_____. United States Agricultural Trade: Where Are the Gains? Reply. *Western J. Agr. Econ.*, December 1989, 14(2), pp. 313–15.

_____ and Just, Richard E. The Effect of U.S. Farm Programs on Diversification. In *Schmitz, A., ed.*, 1989, pp. 303–28.

Schmitz, Edward J.; Dale, Charles and Drisko, Alan F. The Use of the Army College Fund: Implications for Program Cost Effectiveness. In *Gulledge, T. R., Jr. and Litteral, L. A., eds.*, 1989, pp. 407–22.

Schmitz, Heinz-Peter and Scott, David W. Calibrating Histograms with Application to Economic Data. In *Ullah, A., ed.*, 1989, 1988, pp. 33–46.

Schmitz, Hubert and Carvalho, Ruy de Quadros. Automation and Labour in the Brazilian Car Industry. *J. Devel. Stud.*, October 1989, 26(1), pp. 81–119.

Schmitz, James A., Jr. Imitation, Entrepreneurship, and Long-run Growth. *J. Polit. Econ.*, June 1989, 97(3), pp. 721–39.

Schmitz, Lelde and Robinson, Roger J. Jamaica: Navigating through a Troubled Decade. *Finance Devel.*, December 1989, 26(4), pp. 30–33.

Schmitz, Susanne and Gabriel, Paul E. The Effect of Occupational Segregation on the Relative Earnings of Black Males. *Econ. Letters*, 1989, 30(1), pp. 77–83.

Schnabel, Claus; Addison, John T. and Genosko, Joachim. Gewerkschaften, Produktivität und Rent Seeking. (Union, Productivity, and Rent Seeking. With English summary.) *Jahr. Nationalökon. Statist.*, March 1989, 206(2), pp. 102–16.

Schnabel, Jacques A. Exposure to Foreign Exchange Risk: A Multi-currency Extension. *Managerial Dec. Econ.*, December 1989, 10(4), pp. 331–33.

_____ and Roumi, Ebrahim. Corporate Insurance and the Underinvestment Problem: An Extension. *J. Risk Ins.*, March 1989, 56(1), pp. 155–59.

Schnare, Ann B. and McKinney, Scott. Trends in Residential Segregation by Race: 1960–1980. *J. Urban Econ.*, November 1989, 26(3), pp. 269–80.

Schneider, Ben Ross. Annual Review of Nations: Year 1988: Brazil. In *Haberman, L. and Sacks, P. M., eds.*, 1989, pp. 37–53.

Schneider, Dieter. Agency Costs and Transaction Costs: Flops in the Principal-Agent-Theory of Financial Markets. In *Bamberg, G. and Spremann, K., eds.*, 1989, pp. 481–94.

Schneider, Hans-Peter. The New German System of Party Funding: The Presidential Committee Report of 1983 and Its Realization. In *Alexander, H. E., ed.*, 1989, pp. 220–35.

Schneider, Hilmar and Hujer, Reinhard. The Analysis of Labor Market Mobility Using Panel Data. *Europ. Econ. Rev.*, March 1989, 33(2/3), pp. 530–36.

Schneider, John C. Homeless Men and Housing Policy in Urban America, 1850–1920. *Urban Stud.*, February 1989, 26(1), pp. 90–99.

Schneider, Mark. Intercity Competition and the Size of the Local Public Work Force. *Public Choice*, December 1989, 63(3), pp. 253–65.

Schneider, Stephen H. and Rosenberg, Norman J. The Greenhouse Effect: Its Causes, Possible Impacts, and Associated Uncertainties. In *Rosenberg, N. J., et al., eds.*, 1989, pp. 7–34.

Schneidewind, Dieter. Management of a German Subsidiary in Japan—Experiences, Challenges, Solutions. In *Dams, T. and Matsugi, T., eds.*, 1989, pp. 43–63.

Schnell, Daniel; Hanson, Steven D. and Baumel, C. Phillip. Impact of Railroad Contracts on Grain Bids to Farmers. *Amer. J. Agr. Econ.*, August 1989, 71(3), pp. 638–46.

Schneller, Meir I. and Peles, Yoram C. The Duration of the Adjustment Process of Financial Ratios. *Rev. Econ. Statist.*, August 1989, 71(3), pp. 527–32.

Schnitkey, Gary D.; Taylor, C. Robert and Barry, Peter J. Evaluating Farmland Investments Considering Dynamic Stochastic Returns and Farmland Prices. *Western J. Agr. Econ.*, July 1989, 14(1), pp. 143–56.

Schnytzer, Adi and Guttman, Joel M. Strategic Work Interactions and the Kibbutz–Kolkhoz Paradox. *Econ. J.*, September 1989, 99(397), pp. 686–99.

Schodt, David W. Austerity Policies in Ecuador: Christian Democratic and Social Christian Versions of the Gospel. In *Handelman, H. and Baer, W., eds.*, 1989, pp. 171–94.

Schoemaker, Paul J. H. Preferences for Information on Probabilities versus Prizes: The Role of Risk-Taking Attitudes. *J. Risk Uncertainty*, April 1989, 2(1), pp. 37–60.

Schoeman, N. J. The Development of Economic Thought in the Economic Culture of South Africa. In *Gemper, B. B., ed.*, 1989, pp. 98–103.

Schoen, Richard M. Variational Theory for the Total Scalar Curvature Functional for Riemannian Metrics and Related Topics. In *Giaquinta, M., ed.*, 1989, pp. 120–54.

Schoen, Robert; Woolredge, John and Thomas, Barbara. Ethnic and Educational Effects on Marriage Choice. *Soc. Sci. Quart.*, September 1989, 70(3), pp. 617–30.

Schoenberger, Erica. Some Dilemmas of Automation: Strategic and Operational Aspects of Technological Change in Production. *Econ. Geogr.*, July 1989, 65(3), pp. 232–47.

Schoenbrod, David. Environmental Law and Growing Up. *Yale J. Regul.*, Summer 1989, 6(2), pp. 357–68.

Schoenfeldt, Lyle F. and Steger, Joseph A. Identification and Development of Management Talent. In *Ferris, G. R. and Rowland, K. M., eds.*, 1989, pp. 121–81.

Schoening, Niles C. and Sweeney, Larry E. Applying an Industrial Diversification Decision

Model to Small Regions. *Rev. Reg. Stud.*, Fall 1989, *19*(3), pp. 14–17.

Schokkaert, Erik and Decoster, André. Equity and Efficiency of a Reform of Belgian Indirect Taxes. *Rech. Écon. Louvain*, 1989, 55(2), pp. 155–76.

Schöler, Bärbel and Gensior, Sabine. Women's Employment and Multinationals in the Federal Republic of Germany: The Job-Export Question. In *Elson, D. and Pearson, R., eds.*, 1989, pp. 60–79.

Schöler, Klaus. Competitive Retailing and Monopolistic Wholesaling in a Spatial Market. *Ann. Reg. Sci.*, 1989, *23*(1), pp. 19–28.

_____. Risk and Illegal Trade. *Metroecon.*, February 1989, *40*(1), pp. 87–97.

_____. Some Properties of Vertically Related Markets in a Spatial Context. *J. Inst. Theoretical Econ.*, September 1989, *145*(3), pp. 525–32.

_____. Zu den Kausalitätsbeziehungen zwischen Geldmenge, Sozialprodukt und Preisniveau. (With English summary.) *Z. Wirtschaft. Sozialwissen.*, 1989, *109*(2), pp. 287–301.

Scholes, Myron S. and Wolfson, Mark A. Decentralized Investment Banking: The Case of Discount Dividend-Reinvestment and Stock-Purchase Plans. *J. Finan. Econ.*, September 1989, *24*(1), pp. 7–35.

Scholl, Russell B. The International Investment Position of the United States in 1988. *Surv. Curr. Bus.*, June 1989, *69*(6), pp. 41–49.

Schollaert, Paul T. and Teachman, Jay D. Gender of Children and Birth Timing. *Demography*, August 1989, *26*(3), pp. 411–23.

Scholliers, Peter. Introductory Remarks: Comparing Real Wages in the 19th and 20th Centuries. In *Scholliers, P., ed.*, 1989, pp. 1–19.

_____. Select Bibliography of Wages, Prices and Real Wages in Europe in the 19th and 20th Centuries, with Special Emphasis on Statistics and Methodological Problems. In *Scholliers, P., ed.*, 1989, pp. 236–44.

_____ and Hannes, Jules. Some Conclusions and Suggestions for Further Research. In *Scholliers, P., ed.*, 1989, pp. 229–35.

Scholtz, Edwin and Naude, Peter. A Hybrid Model of Strategic Planning. In *Lockett, A. G. and Islei, G., eds.*, 1989, pp. 305–13.

Schoner, Bertram and Wedley, William C. Alternative Scales in AHP. In *Lockett, A. G. and Islei, G., eds.*, 1989, pp. 345–54.

Schoney, Richard A. and Pederson, Kendra. An Economic Evaluation of Alternative Crop Leases. *Can. J. Agr. Econ.*, November 1989, *37*(3), pp. 525–37.

_____ and Rinholm, R. A. Capital Cost Allowance and Tax Neutrality: A Case Study of Saskatchewan Farmers' Claims versus Actual Depreciation. *Can. J. Agr. Econ.*, March 1989, *37*(1), pp. 47–62.

_____ and Weisensel, Ward P. An Analysis of the Yield–Price Risk Associated with Specialty Crops. *Western J. Agr. Econ.*, December 1989, *14*(2), pp. 293–99.

Schoonbeek, Lambert. Stability and Structural Forms of Economic Models. *Econ. Modelling*, April 1989, *6*(2), pp. 182–88.

Schoop, P. and Hanus, H. Influence of Nitrogen Fertilizer and Fungicide on Yield and Yield Variability in Wheat and Barley. In *Anderson, J. R. and Hazell, P. B. R., eds.*, 1989, pp. 265–84.

Schor, Juliet B. and Epstein, Gerald A. The Divorce of the Banca d'Italia and the Italian Treasury: A Case Study of Central Bank Independence. In *Lange, P. and Regini, M., eds.*, 1989, pp. 147–64.

Schotman, Peter and Koedijk, Kees. Dominant Real Exchange Rate Movements. *J. Int. Money Finance*, December 1989, *8*(4), pp. 517–31.

Schott, Jeffrey J. Economic Sanctions and the Middle East. In *Fishelson, G., ed.*, 1989, pp. 123–40.

_____. More Free Trade Areas? In *Schott, J. J., ed.*, 1989, pp. 1–58.

_____. U.S. Trade Policy: Implications for U.S.–Korean Relations. In *Bayard, T. O. and Young, S.-G., eds.*, 1989, pp. 83–105.

Schotter, Andrew. Market and Institutions: Comment. In *Shiraishi, T. and Tsuru, S., eds.*, 1989, pp. 50–55.

_____ and Radner, Roy. The Sealed-Bid Mechanism: An Experimental Study. *J. Econ. Theory*, June 1989, *48*(1), pp. 179–220.

Schrader, H. Consumption of Farm Households and Agricultural Sector Modelling: Experiences for the FRG. In *Bauer, S. and Henrichsmeyer, W., eds.*, 1989, pp. 113–23.

Schram, Arthur and van Winden, Frans. Revealed Preferences for Public Goods: Applying a Model of Voter Behavior. *Public Choice*, March 1989, *60*(3), pp. 259–82.

Schram, Sanford F. and Wilken, Paul H. It's No 'Laffer' Matter: Claim that Increasing Welfare Aid Breeds Poverty and Dependence Fails Statistical Test. *Amer. J. Econ. Sociology*, April 1989, *48*(2), pp. 203–17.

Schramm, Gunter. Optimal Timing of Transmission Line Investments. *Energy Econ.*, July 1989, *11*(3), pp. 181–88.

_____ and Armitage, Jane. Managing the Supply of and Demand for Fuelwood in Africa. In *Schramm, G. and Warford, J. J., eds.*, 1989, pp. 139–71.

Schramm, Ronald. International Default and Rescheduling under Interest Rate Uncertainty. In *Singer, H. W. and Sharma, S., eds. (II)*, 1989, pp. 160–71.

Schran, Peter. On the Organization of Production under Socialism. In *Dirlik, A. and Meisner, M., eds.*, 1989, pp. 59–78.

Schreiber, Richard K. and Grady, Gerald J. Expert System Applications in the IRS. *J. Policy Anal. Manage.*, Spring 1989, *8*(2), pp. 193–99.

Schreiner, Dean F. Agricultural Project Investment Analysis. In *Tweeten, L., ed.*, 1989, pp. 238–77.

_____ and Kang, Suki. Analysis of Public Subsidy to Rural Community Water Systems. *Reg. Sci. Persp.*, 1989, *19*(1), pp. 40–64.

_____, et al. Policy Applications in Natural Resource Projects. In *Tweeten, L., ed.*, 1989, pp. 278–321.

Schremmer, D. E. Taxation and Public Finance: Britain, France, and Germany. In *Mathias, P. and Pollard, S., eds.*, 1989, pp. 315–494.

Schreüder, Willem A. and van Dyk, Esbeth. A Multidimensional Scaling Model for Qualitative Pair Wise Comparisons. In *Lockett, A. G. and Islei, G., eds.*, 1989, pp. 68–77.

Schreuel, Evert-J.; Makaliwe-Watupongoh, J. A. A. and Makaliwe, Willem H. Central Sulawesi: Facing Communication and Erosion Problems. In *Hill, H., ed.*, 1989, pp. 511–27.

Schrimper, Ronald A. Cross-Sectional Data for Demand Analysis. In *Buse, R. C., ed.*, 1989, pp. 74–92.

Schroath, Frederick W. and Korth, Christopher M. Managerial Barriers to the Internationalization of U.S. Property and Liability Insurers: Theory and Perspectives. *J. Risk Ins.*, December 1989, *56*(4), pp. 630–48.

Schroder, Mark Douglas. Computing the Constant Elasticity of Variance Option Pricing Formula. *J. Finance*, March 1989, *44*(1), pp. 211–19.

Schroder, W. R.; Taylor, N. W. and Johnson, R. W. M. Deregulation and the New Zealand Agricultural Sector: A Review. *Rev. Marketing Agr. Econ.*, April, Aug., Dec. 1989, *57*(1–2–3), pp. 47–74.

Schröder, Wolfgang. Anmerkungen zur normativen Interpretation von Leistungsbilanzsalden. (Observations on the Normative Approach to Interpreting Net Balance on Current Account. With English summary.) *Kredit Kapital*, 1989, *22*(4), pp. 508–19.

Schroeder, Gertrude E. The Implementation and Integration of Innovations in Soviet-Type Economies. *Cato J.*, Spring–Summer 1989, *9*(1), pp. 35–55.

Schroeder, John and Haus, Joseph W. Lasers: Now the Age of Light. In *Finkelstein, J., ed.*, 1989, pp. 67–107.

Schroeder, Larry. Business Taxes and Fees. In *Schroeder, L., ed.*, 1989, pp. 161–73.

_____. Governmental Decentralization in Bangladesh. In *Schroeder, L., ed.*, 1989, pp. 1–22.

_____. Strengthening Local Governments in Bangladesh. In *Schroeder, L., ed.*, 1989, pp. 191–208.

_____ and Maniruzzaman. Local Government Structure. In *Schroeder, L., ed.*, 1989, pp. 23–50.

_____ and Wasylenko, Michael. Public Sector Forecasting in the Third World. *Int. J. Forecasting*, 1989, *5*(3), pp. 333–45.

Schroeven, Chris and Solar, P. The Construction of Historical Price Indices, with an Illustration from Interwar Belgium. In *Scholliers, P., ed.*, 1989, pp. 149–75.

Schubert, Eric S. Arbitrage in the Foreign Exchange Markets of London and Amsterdam during the 18th Century. *Exploration Econ. Hist.*, January 1989, *26*(1), pp. 1–20.

Schubert, Walt. Unemployment Insurance Costs:

Issues and Dilemmas. *Int. J. Soc. Econ.*, 1989, *16*(8), pp. 60–67.

Schudlich, Edwin. Between Consensus and Conflict: On the Development of Industrial Working Times in the Federal Republic of Germany. In *Agassi, J. B. and Heycock, S., eds.*, 1989, pp. 29–40.

Schuessler, Rudolf. Exit Threats and Cooperation under Anonymity. *J. Conflict Resolution*, December 1989, *33*(4), pp. 728–49.

Schuh, G. Edward. Exchange Rates and Pricing: Impacts on National Economies, Food Consumption, and Agriculture. In *Helmuth, J. W. and Johnson, S. R., eds., Vol. 2*, 1989, pp. 77–89.

_____. Impact of the International Macro Environment on the World Food Situation. In *Horwich, G. and Lynch, G. J., eds.*, 1989, pp. 11–20.

_____. Impacts of Economic Reform for Agricultural and Food Policy: Reaction. In *Helmuth, J. W. and Johnson, S. R., eds., Vol. 1*, 1989, pp. 91–93.

_____. Redesigning International Institutions and Agricultural Sectors. In *von Witzke, H.; Runge, C. F. and Job, B., eds.*, 1989, pp. 160–76.

von der Schulenburg, J.-Matthias Graf and Finsinger, Jörg. Der Sonntagsverkauf. (The Effects of Sunday Trading. With English summary.) *Z. Wirtschaft. Sozialwissen.*, 1989, *109*(1), pp. 119–28.

Schulhofer, Stephen J. Just Punishment in an Imperfect World. *Mich. Law Rev.*, May 1989, *87*(6), pp. 1263–93.

Schulmann, Horst. Third World Debt: The Next Phase: Concluding Impressions. In *Fried, E. R. and Trezise, P. H., eds.*, 1989, pp. 106–09.

Schultz, Richard. Privatization in Canada: Ideology, Symbolism or Substance? Comment. In *MacAvoy, P. W., et al.*, 1989, pp. 337–40.

Schultz, Siegfried. Trends and Issues of German Aid Policy. *Konjunkturpolitik*, 1989, *35*(6), pp. 361–82.

Schultz, T. Paul and Rosenzweig, Mark R. Schooling, Information and Nonmarket Productivity: Contraceptive Use and Its Effectiveness. *Int. Econ. Rev.*, May 1989, *30*(2), pp. 457–77.

Schultz, Theodore W. The Economics of Historical Economics. In *Galenson, D. W., ed.*, 1989, pp. 1–4.

_____. Investing in People: Schooling in Low Income Countries. *Econ. Educ. Rev.*, 1989, *8*(3), pp. 219–23.

Schultze, Charles L. Alternative Approaches to the Political Business Cycle: Comments. *Brookings Pap. Econ. Act.*, 1989, (2), pp. 56–63.

_____. Industry Rents: Evidence and Implications: Comments. *Brookings Pap. Econ. Act.*, Microeconomics, 1989, pp. 280–83.

_____ and Lawrence, Robert Z. Barriers to European Growth: Overview. In *Jacquemin, A. and Sapir, A., eds.*, 1989, pp. 251–97.

_____; Litan, Robert E. and Lawrence, Robert Z. Improving American Living Standards. In *Bosworth, B. P., et al.*, 1989, pp. 29–48.

_____ and Mann, Thomas E. Getting Rid of the Budget Deficit: Why We Should and How We Can. In *Bosworth, B. P., et al.*, 1989, pp. 1–28.

Schulz, Brigitte H. The German Democratic Republic and Sub-Saharan Africa: The Limits of East–South Economic Relations. In *Schulz, B. H. and Hansen, W. W., eds.*, 1989, pp. 213–35.

Schulz, Norbert and Stahl, Konrad. Good and Bad Competition in Spatial Markets for Search Goods: The Case of Linear Utility Functions. *Ann. Écon. Statist.*, July–Dec. 1989, (15–16), pp. 113–36.

_____ and Weimann, Joachim. Competition of Newspapers and the Location of Political Parties. *Public Choice*, November 1989, 63(2), pp. 125–47.

Schulze-Böing, Matthias; Wohlrab-Sahr, Monika and Brose, Hanns-Georg. Discontinuity and Flexibility in Working Time and Work Careers: The Example of Temporary Work. In *Agassi, J. B. and Heycock, S., eds.*, 1989, pp. 99–113.

Schulze, Peter W. Socialist Transformation and Soviet Foreign Policy in the Gorbachev Era. In *Schulz, B. H. and Hansen, W. W., eds.*, 1989, pp. 53–76.

Schumacher, Dieter. North–South Trade and Structural Changes in Developed Countries. *Konjunkturpolitik*, 1989, 35(3), pp. 129–59.

Schumacher, Johannes M. Linear System Representations. In *[Willems, J. C.]*, 1989, pp. 382–408.

Schuman, Howard and Converse, Jean M. The Effects of Black and White Interviewers on Black Responses. In *Singer, E. and Presser, S., eds.*, 1989, 1971, pp. 247–71.

_____; Kalton, Graham and Ludwig, Jacob. Context and Contiguity in Survey Questionnaires. In *Singer, E. and Presser, S., eds.*, 1989, 1983, pp. 151–54.

_____ and Presser, Stanley. The Measurement of a Middle Position in Attitude Surveys. In *Singer, E. and Presser, S., eds.*, 1989, 1980, pp. 108–23.

Schumann, Michael and Kern, Horst. New Concepts of Production in West German Plants. In *Katzenstein, P. J., ed.*, 1989, pp. 87–110.

Schumpeter, Elizabeth Boody. Bibliography of the Writings of Joseph A. Schumpeter. In *Schumpeter, J. A.*, 1989, pp. 330–41.

Schumpeter, Joseph A. The Analysis of Economic Change. In *Schumpeter, J. A.*, 1989, 1935, pp. 134–49.

_____. Capitalism. In *Schumpeter, J. A.*, 1989, 1946, pp. 189–210.

_____. Capitalism in the Postwar World. In *Schumpeter, J. A.*, 1989, 1943, pp. 175–88.

_____. The Common Sense of Econometrics. In *Schumpeter, J. A.*, 1989, 1933, pp. 100–107.

_____. The Creative Response in Economic History. In *Schumpeter, J. A.*, 1989, 1947, pp. 221–31.

_____. The Decade of the Twenties. In *Schumpeter, J. A.*, 1989, 1946, pp. 211–20.

_____. Economic Theory and Entrepreneurial History. In *Schumpeter, J. A.*, 1989, 1949, pp. 253–71.

_____. English Economists and the State-Managed Economy. In *Schumpeter, J. A.*, 1989, 1949, pp. 306–21.

_____. The Explanation of the Business Cycle. In *Schumpeter, J. A.*, 1989, 1927, pp. 21–46.

_____. The Historical Approach to the Analysis of Business Cycles. In *Schumpeter, J. A.*, 1989, 1949, pp. 322–29.

_____. The Influence of Protective Tariffs on the Industrial Development of the United States. In *Schumpeter, J. A.*, 1989, 1940, pp. 169–74.

_____. The Instability of Capitalism. In *Schumpeter, J. A.*, 1989, 1928, pp. 47–72.

_____. Mitchell's Business Cycles. In *Schumpeter, J. A.*, 1989, 1930, pp. 73–95.

_____. The Nature and Necessity of a Price System. In *Schumpeter, J. A.*, 1989, 1934, pp. 118–24.

_____. On the Concept of Social Value. In *Schumpeter, J. A.*, 1989, 1909, pp. 1–20.

_____. Preface to Japanese Edition of "Theorie Der Wirtschaftlichen Entwicklung." In *Schumpeter, J. A.*, 1989, 1937, pp. 165–68.

_____. The Present World Depression: A Tentative Diagnosis. In *Schumpeter, J. A.*, 1989, 1931, pp. 96–99.

_____. Professor Taussig on Wages and Capital. In *Schumpeter, J. A.*, 1989, 1936, pp. 150–59.

_____. Review of Keynes's *General Theory*. In *Schumpeter, J. A.*, 1989, 1936, pp. 160–64.

_____. Review of Robinson's Economics of Imperfect Competition. In *Schumpeter, J. A.*, 1989, 1934, pp. 125–33.

_____. Science and Ideology. In *Schumpeter, J. A.*, 1989, 1949, pp. 272–86.

_____. Theoretical Problems of Economic Growth. In *Schumpeter, J. A.*, 1989, 1947, pp. 232–40.

_____. There Is Still Time to Stop Inflation. In *Schumpeter, J. A.*, 1989, 1948, pp. 241–52.

_____. The *Communist Manifesto* in Sociology and Economics. In *Schumpeter, J. A.*, 1989, 1949, pp. 287–305.

van Schuppen, J. H. Stochastic Realization Problems. In *[Willems, J. C.]*, 1989, pp. 480–523.

Schuster, J. Mark Davidson. The British Deed of Covenant as a Tax Incentive for Charitable Donations: Vestige or Viable Alternative? In *James, E., ed.*, 1989, pp. 267–85.

Schwab, Barry H.; Sen, Pranab K. and Chinchilli, Vernon M. Inference Based on Ranks for the Multiple-Design Multivariate Linear Model. *J. Amer. Statist. Assoc.*, June 1989, 84(406), pp. 517–24.

Schwab, Robert; Zampelli, Ernest M. and Dynarski, Mark. Local Characteristics and Public Production: The Case of Education. *J. Urban Econ.*, September 1989, 26(2), pp. 250–63.

Schwab, Stewart. Coase Defends Coase: Why

Lawyers Listen and Economists Do Not. *Mich. Law Rev.*, May 1989, *87*(6), pp. 1171–98.

Schwalbach, Joachim; Grasshoff, Ulrike and Mahmood, Talat. The Dynamics of Corporate Profits. *Europ. Econ. Rev.*, October 1989, *33*(8), pp. 1625–39.

Schwallie, Daniel P. Measuring the Effects of Federal Grants-in-Aid on Total Public Sector Size. *Public Finance Quart.*, April 1989, *17*(2), pp. 185–203.

Schwann, Gregory M. and Capozza, Dennis R. The Asset Approach to Pricing Urban Land: Empirical Evidence. *Amer. Real Estate Urban Econ. Assoc. J.*, Summer 1989, *17*(2), pp. 161–74.

Schwartz, Abba; Eldor, Rafael and Pines, David. Determinants of an Individual's Demand for Hedging Instruments. *J. Futures Markets*, April 1989, *9*(2), pp. 135–41.

Schwartz, Alan. Defensive Tactics and Optimal Search. *J. Law, Econ., Organ.*, Fall 1989, *5*(2), pp. 413–24.

_____. A Theory of Loan Priorities. *J. Legal Stud.*, June 1989, *18*(2), pp. 209–61.

Schwartz, Alex; Fainstein, Norman I. and Fainstein, Susan S. Economic Shifts and Land Use in the Global City: New York, 1940–1987. In *Beauregard, R. A., ed.*, 1989, pp. 45–85.

Schwartz, Anna J. Does Monetary Policy Matter? A New Test in the Spirit of Friedman and Schwartz: Comment. In *Blanchard, O. J. and Fischer, S., eds.*, 1989, pp. 170–76.

_____. International Debts: What's Fact and What's Fiction. *Econ. Inquiry*, January 1989, *27*(1), pp. 1–19.

_____. Long-term Trends in Bank Regulation: Comments. *J. Finan. Services Res.*, September 1989, *2*(3), pp. 185–88.

_____. The Theory and Measurement of the Nominal Output of Banks, Sectoral Rates of Savings, and Wealth in the National Accounts: Comment. In *Lipsey, R. E. and Tice, H. S., eds.*, 1989, pp. 390–93.

_____ **and Bordo, Michael D.** Transmission of Real and Monetary Disturbances under Fixed and Floating Exchange Rates. In *Dorn, J. A. and Niskanen, W. A., eds.*, 1989, *1988*, pp. 237–58.

Schwartz, David S. Idealism and Realism: An Institutionalist View of Corporate Power in the Regulated Utilities. In *Tool, M. R. and Samuels, W. J., eds. (I)*, 1989, *1985*, pp. 361–81.

Schwartz, Eduardo S. and Brennan, Michael J. Portfolio Insurance and Financial Market Equilibrium. *J. Bus.*, October 1989, *62*(4), pp. 455–72.

_____; **Stangeland, David and Morck, Randall.** The Valuation of Forestry Resources under Stochastic Prices and Inventories. *J. Finan. Quant. Anal.*, December 1989, *24*(4), pp. 473–87.

_____ **and Torous, Walter N.** Prepayment and the Valuation of Mortgage-Backed Securities. *J. Finance*, June 1989, *44*(2), pp. 375–92.

_____; **Zechner, Josef and Giammarino, Ronald.** Market Valuation of Bank Assets and Deposit Insurance in Canada. *Can. J. Econ.*, February 1989, *22*(1), pp. 109–27.

Schwartz, Eli. The Problem of the Savings and Loans. In *Schwartz, E. and Vasconcellos, G. M., eds.*, 1989, pp. 5–38.

_____. Summary: Looking to the Future. In *Schwartz, E. and Vasconcellos, G. M., eds.*, 1989, pp. 39–42.

Schwartz, Gail Garfield. Regulatory Scrutiny of Company Decisions. In *National Economic Research Associates*, 1989, pp. 95–102.

Schwartz, Marius. Investments in Oligopoly: Welfare Effects and Tests for Predation. *Oxford Econ. Pap.*, October 1989, *41*(4), pp. 698–719.

Schwartz, Saul and Baum, Sandra R. What Strategy for the "Education President"? *Challenge*, Jan.–Feb. 1989, *32*(1), pp. 44–50.

_____; **Hutchens, Robert M. and Jakubson, George H.** AFDC and the Formation of Subfamilies. *J. Human Res.*, Fall 1989, *24*(4), pp. 599–628.

Schwartz, Steven; Erekson, O. Homer and Moser, James W. Evenhandedness in Arbitration: The Case of Major League Baseball. *Eastern Econ. J.*, April–June 1989, *15*(2), pp. 117–27.

Schwartzman, Kathleen C. The Economic Origins of Political Instability: Why the Portuguese Bourgeoisie Abandoned Its First Republic. In *Avery, W. P. and Rapkin, D. P., eds.*, 1989, pp. 151–72.

Schwarz, Anne Naylor and Louscher, David J. Patterns of Third World Military Technology Acquisition. In *Baek, K.-I.; McLaurin, R. D. and Moon, C., eds.*, 1989, pp. 33–56.

Schwarz, Jonathan S. International Tax Aspects of Charities: General Report. *Bull. Int. Fiscal Doc.*, December 1989, *43*(12), pp. 539–43.

_____. Recent Developments from a United Kingdom Perspective on the Canada–United Kingdom Tax Convention. *Bull. Int. Fiscal Doc.*, February 1989, *43*(2), pp. 69–72.

Schwarz, L. D. The Formation of the Wage: Some Problems. In *Scholliers, P., ed.*, 1989, pp. 21–39.

Schwarz, Norbert, et al. Response Scales: Effects of Category Range on Reported Behavior and Comparative Judgments. In *Singer, E. and Presser, S., eds.*, 1989, *1985*, pp. 165–72.

Schwefel, Detlef. The Product-Path-Analysis: A Method of Socio-economic Project Appraisal. *Can. J. Devel. Stud.*, 1989, *10*(2), pp. 211–23.

Schweikart, Larry. Financing the Urban Frontier: Entrepreneurial Creativity and Western Cities, 1945–1975. *Urban Stud.*, February 1989, *26*(1), pp. 177–86.

Schweinberger, A. G. Foreign Capital Flows, Tariffs, and Welfare: A Global Analysis. *Can. J. Econ.*, May 1989, *22*(2), pp. 310–27.

de Schweinitz, Karl, Jr. What Is Economic Imperialism? In *Tool, M. R. and Samuels, W. J., eds. (III)*, 1989, *1981*, pp. 397–423.

Schweitzer, Mary M. State-Issued Currency and the Ratification of the U.S. Constitution. *J. Econ. Hist.*, June 1989, *49*(2), pp. 311–22.

Schweitzer, Robert and Bundt, Thomas P. Deregulation, Deposit Markets, and Banks' Costs of Funds. *Financial Rev.*, August 1989, *24*(3), pp. 417–30.

_____ **and Lee, Insup.** Shareholder Wealth Effects of Interstate Banking: The Case of Delaware's Financial Center Development Act. *J. Finan. Services Res.*, June 1989, *2*(2), pp. 65–72.

Schweizer, B. and Janowitz, M. F. Ordinal and Percentile Clustering. *Math. Soc. Sci.*, October 1989, *18*(2), pp. 135–86.

Schweizer, Urs. Litigation and Settlement under Two-Sided Incomplete Information. *Rev. Econ. Stud.*, April 1989, *56*(2), pp. 163–77.

Schweninger, Loren. Black-Owned Businesses in the South, 1790–1880. *Bus. Hist. Rev.*, Spring 1989, *63*(1), pp. 22–60.

Schwert, G. William. Business Cycles, Financial Crises, and Stock Volatility. *Carnegie–Rochester Conf. Ser. Public Policy*, Autumn 1989, *31*, pp. 83–125.

_____. Business Cycles, Financial Crises, and Stock Volatility: Reply. *Carnegie–Rochester Conf. Ser. Public Policy*, Autumn 1989, *31*, pp. 133–37.

_____. Margin Requirement and Stock Volatility. In *Edwards, F. R., ed.*, 1989, pp. 55–66.

_____. Margin Requirements and Stock Volatility. *J. Finan. Services Res.*, December 1989, *3*(2–3), pp. 153–64.

_____. Tests for Unit Roots: A Monte Carlo Investigation. *J. Bus. Econ. Statist.*, April 1989, *7*(2), pp. 147–59.

_____. Why Does Stock Market Volatility Change over Time? *J. Finance*, December 1989, *44*(5), pp. 1115–53.

Schwier, Ann S. and Schwier, Jerome F. Pareto's Practical View of Socialist Systems. In *Missouri Valley Economic Association*, 1989, pp. 1–9.

Schwier, Jerome F. and Schwier, Ann S. Pareto's Practical View of Socialist Systems. In *Missouri Valley Economic Association*, 1989, pp. 1–9.

Schydlowsky, Daniel M. Argentina: Macroeconomic Policy, 1966–73: Comment: Argentine Commercial Policy, 1969: Structure and Consequences. In *di Tella, G. and Dornbusch, R., eds.*, 1989, pp. 175–88.

Sciberras, E. Technical Change and Competitiveness. In *Punset, E. and Sweeney, G., eds.*, 1989, pp. 67–77.

Sciomachen, A. and Archetti, F. Development, Analysis and Simulation of Petri Net Models: An Application to AGV Systems. In *Archetti, F.; Lucertini, M. and Serafini, P., eds.*, 1989, pp. 91–113.

Scitovsky, Tibor. Culture is a Good Thing: A Welfare–Economic Judgment. *J. Cult. Econ.*, June 1989, *13*(1), pp. 1–16.

_____. Growth in the Affluent Society. In *Johnson, C., ed.*, 1989, pp. 151–62.

_____. My First Encounter with Joan Robinson. In *Feiwel, G. R., ed. (II)*, 1989, pp. 866–67.

Scorgie, Michael E. The Role of Negative Numbers in the Development of Double Entry Bookkeeping: A Comment. *J. Acc. Res.*, Autumn 1989, *27*(2), pp. 316–18.

Scotchmer, Suzanne. Equivalent Variation with Uncertain Prices. *Econ. Letters*, 1989, *29*(2), pp. 127–28.

_____. Equivalent Variation with Uncertain Prices. *Econ. Letters*, August 1989, *30*(2), pp. 117–18.

_____. Who Profits from Taxpayer Confusion? *Econ. Letters*, 1989, *29*(1), pp. 49–55.

_____ **and Slemrod, Joel.** Randomness in Tax Enforcement. *J. Public Econ.*, February 1989, *38*(1), pp. 17–32.

Scott, A. and Sheldrick, B. Energy and Environment: Deriving a Research Agenda. *Environ. Planning A*, October 1989, *21*(10), pp. 1349–62.

Scott, Allen J. and Kwok, E. C. Inter-firm Subcontracting and Locational Agglomeration: A Case Study of the Printed Circuits Industry in Southern California. *Reg. Stud.*, October 1989, *23*(5), pp. 405–16.

_____ **and Mattingly, Doreen J.** The Aircraft and Parts Industry in Southern California: Continuity and Change from the Inter-war years to the 1990s. *Econ. Geogr.*, January 1989, *65*(1), pp. 48–71.

Scott, Carole E. Competition and State Government in Antebellum Georgia and South Carolina. In *Perkins, E. J., ed.*, 1989, pp. 140–58.

Scott, Charles G. Resources of Supplemental Security Income Recipients. *Soc. Sec. Bull.*, August 1989, *52*(8), pp. 2–9.

_____. A Study of Supplemental Security Income Awardees. *Soc. Sec. Bull.*, February 1989, *52*(2), pp. 2–13.

Scott, Clyde and Odewahn, Charles. An Analysis of Multi-union Elections Involving Incumbent Unions. *J. Lab. Res.*, Spring 1989, *10*(2), pp. 197–205.

_____ **and Shadoan, Elizabeth.** The Effect of Gender on Arbitration Decisions. *J. Lab. Res.*, Fall 1989, *10*(4), pp. 429–36.

Scott, David W. and Schmitz, Heinz-Peter. Calibrating Histograms with Application to Economic Data. In *Ullah, A., ed.*, 1989, *1988*, pp. 33–46.

Scott, Elton and Tucker, Alan L. Predicting Currency Return Volatility. *J. Banking Finance*, December 1989, *13*(6), pp. 839–51.

Scott, Frank A., Jr.; Berger, Mark C. and Black, Dan A. Effects of the Tax Treatment of Fringe Benefits on Labor Market Segmentation. *Ind. Lab. Relat. Rev.*, January 1989, *42*(2), pp. 216–29.

_____ **and Gulley, O. David.** Lottery Effects on Pari-mutual Tax Revenues. *Nat. Tax J.*, March 1989, *42*(1), pp. 89–93.

Scott, James C. Corruption, Machine Politics and Political Change. In *Heidenheimer, A. J.; Johnston, M. and LeVine, V. T., eds.*, 1989, *1969*, pp. 275–86.

_____. Handling Historical Comparisons Cross-Nationally. In *Heidenheimer, A. J.; Johnston, M. and LeVine, V. T., eds.*, 1989, pp. 129–43.

Scott, James H., Jr. and Chatterjee, Sris. Explaining Differences in Corporate Capital Structure: Theory and New Evidence. *J. Banking Finance*, May 1989, *13*(2), pp. 283–309.

Scott, John T. Purposive Diversification as a Motive for Merger. *Int. J. Ind. Organ.*, Special Issue, March 1989, *7*(1), pp. 35–47.

Scott, Jonathan A. and Leeth, John D. The Incidence of Secured Debt: Evidence from the Small Business Community. *J. Finan. Quant. Anal.*, September 1989, *24*(3), pp. 379–94.

Scott, Kenneth E. Domestic Bank Regulation in a World of International Banking. In *Vosgerau, H.-J., ed.*, 1989, pp. 125–49.

Scott, Loren C.; Moore, William J. and Newman, Robert J. Welfare Expenditures and the Decline of Unions. *Rev. Econ. Statist.*, August 1989, *71*(3), pp. 538–42.

Scott, Louis O. Estimating the Marginal Rate of Substitution in the Intertemporal Capital Asset Pricing Model. *Rev. Econ. Statist.*, August 1989, *71*(3), pp. 365–75.

_____. Stock Price Changes with Random Volatility and Jumps: Some Empirical Evidence. *Quart. Rev. Econ. Bus.*, Spring 1989, *29*(1), pp. 21–32.

_____ and Chesney, Marc. Pricing European Currency Options: A Comparison of the Modified Black–Scholes Model and a Random Variance Model. *J. Finan. Quant. Anal.*, September 1989, *24*(3), pp. 267–84.

Scott, M. Maintaining Capital Intact. In *Wood, J. C. and Woods, R. N., eds., Vol. 4, 1989, 1984,* pp. 91–104.

Scott, Robert E. The Changing Nature of Debt and Equity: A Legal Perspective: Discussion. In *Kopcke, R. W. and Rosengren, E. S., eds.*, 1989, pp. 73–79.

Scotton, R. B. Integrating Medicare with Private Health Insurance: The Best of Both Worlds? In *Smith, C. S., ed.*, 1989, pp. 219–38.

_____. Membership of Voluntary Health Insurance. In *Butler, J. R. G. and Doessel, D. P., eds.*, 1989, *1969*, pp. 113–27.

_____ and Deeble, J. S. Compulsory Health Insurance for Australia. In *Butler, J. R. G. and Doessel, D. P., eds.*, 1989, *1968*, pp. 128–44.

Scrawell, Helga and Joignaux, Guy. Enjeux et stratégies autour de la filière bio-éthanol. (Aims and Strategies in the Production of Bio-ethanol. With English summary.) *Écon. Societes*, July 1989, *23*(7), pp. 159–78.

Screpanti, Ernesto. Monetary Dynamics, Speculation, and the Term Structure of Interest Rates. *Econ. Notes*, 1989, (2), pp. 167–91.

_____. Some Demographic and Social Processes and the Problem of Kondratieff Cycle Periodicity. In *Di Matteo, M.; Goodwin, R. M. and Vercelli, A., eds.*, 1989, pp. 114–29.

Scrime, Alan J. The Grand System: Telecommunications in the United States. In *Finkelstein, J., ed.*, 1989, pp. 153–72.

Scully, Gerald W. The Size of the State, Economic Growth and the Efficient Utilization of National Resources. *Public Choice*, November 1989, *63*(2), pp. 149–64.

_____ and Slottje, Daniel J. The Paradox of Politics and Policy in Redistributing Income. *Public Choice*, January 1989, *60*(1), pp. 55–70.

Sdogati, Fabio and Hester, Donald D. European Financial Integration: Some Lessons from Italy. *Banca Naz. Lavoro Quart. Rev.*, September 1989, (170), pp. 313–44.

Seabright, Paul and Gatsios, Konstantine. Regulation in the European Community. *Oxford Rev. Econ. Policy*, Summer 1989, *5*(2), pp. 37–60.

_____ and McGowan, Francis. Deregulating European Airlines. *Econ. Policy: A Europ. Forum*, October 1989, (9), pp. 283–344.

Seaks, Terry G.; Smith, W. James and Formby, John P. On the Measurement and Trend of Inequality: A Reconsideration. *Amer. Econ. Rev.*, March 1989, *79*(1), pp. 256–64.

Sealy, L. S. British and European Company Law. In *Dahrendorf, R., et al.*, 1989, pp. 89–101.

Sealy, R. C.; Rock, L. L. and Craigwell, R. C. Public Deficits and Private Consumption: Empirical Evidence from Small Open Economies. *Appl. Econ.*, May 1989, *21*(5), pp. 697–710.

Sears, R. Stephen; Ma, Christopher K. and Rao, Ramesh P. Limit Moves and Price Resolution: The Case of the Treasury Bond Futures Market. *J. Futures Markets*, August 1989, *9*(4), pp. 321–35.

_____; Ma, Christopher K. and Rao, Ramesh P. Volatility, Price Resolution, and the Effectiveness of Price Limits. *J. Finan. Services Res.*, December 1989, *3*(2–3), pp. 165–99.

_____; Ma, Christopher K. and Rao, Ramesh P. Volatility, Price Resolution, and the Effectiveness of Price Limits. In *Edwards, F. R., ed.*, 1989, pp. 67–101.

Seaver, Bill L. and Triantis, Konstantinos P. The Implications of Using Messy Data to Estimate Production-Frontier–Based Technical Efficiency Measures. *J. Bus. Econ. Statist.*, January 1989, *7*(1), pp. 49–59.

Sebastian, Bernard J. The Role of the Securities Market in Mobilizing Resources for the Region. *Soc. Econ. Stud.*, December 1989, *38*(4), pp. 115–32.

Sebastiani, Mario. Kalecki and Marx on Effective Demand. *Atlantic Econ. J.*, December 1989, *17*(4), pp. 22–28.

_____. Long-Period Perspectives on Unemployment in Kalecki and in Keynes. In *Sebastiani, M., ed.*, 1989, pp. 81–97.

Sebastiao, Manuel and de Macedo, Jorge Braga. Public Debt and Implicit Taxes: The Portuguese Experience. *Europ. Econ. Rev.*, March 1989, *33*(2/3), pp. 573–79.

Sebstad, Jennefer and Grown, Caren A. Introduction: Toward a Wider Perspective on Women's Employment. *World Devel.*, July 1989, *17*(7), pp. 937–52.

Seccareccia, Mario and Lavoie, Marc. Les idées révolutionnaires de Keynes en politique économique et le déclin du capitalisme rentier. (The Keynesian Revolution in the Theory of Economic Policy and the Twilight of Rentiers

Capitalism. With English summary.) *Écon. Appl.*, 1989, *42*(1), pp. 47–70.

Sechzer, Selig L. Factor Intensity Conditions for Welfare-Improving Foreign Investment in Tariff-Distorted Economies: A Comment. *Int. Econ. Rev.*, November 1989, *30*(4), pp. 999–1003.

Seddon, David. The Politics of 'Adjustment' in Morocco. In *Campbell, B. K. and Loxley, J., eds.*, 1989, pp. 234–65.

Sedjo, Roger A. and Solomon, Allen M. Climate and Forests. In *Rosenberg, N. J., et al., eds.*, 1989, pp. 105–19.

Sedov, L. From Bureaucracy to Logocracy: Based on Materials Relating to Soviet Society from the 1930s to the 1970s. *Prob. Econ.*, September 1989, *32*(5), pp. 89–94.

Seeborg, Michael C. and DeBoer, Larry. The Unemployment Rates of Men and Women: A Transition Probability Analysis. *Ind. Lab. Relat. Rev.*, April 1989, *42*(3), pp. 404–14.

Seeler, Hans-Joachim. The Ecu as a Force for Integration in the European Community. In *Franz, O., ed.*, 1989, pp. 32–37.

Sefer, Berislav. Social Policy in a Socialist Self-Managing Society. In *Macesich, G., ed.*, 1989, pp. 189–206.

Seff, Eric J. and Choie, Kenneth S. TIPP: Insurance without Complexity: Comment. *J. Portfol. Manage.*, Fall 1989, *16*(1), pp. 107–08.

Segal, Uzi and Spivak, Avia. Firm Size and Optimal Growth Rates. *Europ. Econ. Rev.*, January 1989, *33*(1), pp. 159–67.

Segar, James; Hatch, Upton and Atwood, Joseph A. An Application of Safety-First Probability Limits in a Discrete Stochastic Farm Management Programming Model. *Southern J. Agr. Econ.*, July 1989, *21*(1), pp. 65–72.

Segarra, Eduardo and Ervin, R. Terry. Agricultural Economists and Multidisciplinary Research: Comment. *Amer. J. Agr. Econ.*, May 1989, *71*(2), pp. 437–38.

————, et al. Nitrogen Carry-over Impacts in Irrigated Cotton Production, Southern High Plains of Texas. *Western J. Agr. Econ.*, December 1989, *14*(2), pp. 300–309.

Seger, Martha R. Statement to the U.S. House Subcommittee on Consumer Affairs and Coinage of the Committee on Banking, Finance and Urban Affairs, May 16, 1989. *Fed. Res. Bull.*, July 1989, *75*(7), pp. 493–95.

————. Statement to the U.S. House Subcommittee on Consumer Affairs and Coinage of the Committee on Banking, Finance and Urban Affairs, October 17, 1989. *Fed. Res. Bull.*, December 1989, *75*(12), pp. 786–90.

————. Statement to the U.S. Senate Subcommittee on Consumer and Regulatory Affairs of the Committee on Banking, Housing, and Urban Affairs, June 7, 1989. *Fed. Res. Bull.*, August 1989, *75*(8), pp. 550–57.

Segerson, Kathleen. Risk and Incentives in the Financing of Hazardous Waste Cleanup. *J. Environ. Econ. Manage.*, January 1989, *16*(1), pp. 1–8.

———— and Ray, Subhash C. On the Equivalence

of Alternative Measures of the Elasticity of Substitution. *Bull. Econ. Res.*, July 1989, *41*(3), pp. 207–12.

Seguino, Stephanie and Grafton, Quentin. The Haitian Coffee Market: A Case Study of Different Approaches to Social Science Research. *Can. J. Devel. Stud.*, 1989, *10*(1), pp. 91–102.

Segura, Julio. Descomposiciones alternativas de las variaciones de los requerimientos de empleo: Una nota. (With English summary.) *Invest. Ecón.*, September 1989, *13*(3), pp. 517–21.

Seibel, Wolfgang. The Function of Mellow Weakness: Nonprofit Organizations as Problem Nonsolvers in Germany. In *James, E., ed.*, 1989, pp. 177–92.

Seidel, Hans. The Role of the Economist in Government: An International Perspective: Austria. In *Pechman, J. A., ed.*, 1989, pp. 89–106.

Seidman, Harold. Government Sponsored Enterprises: Viewpoints. *Public Budg. Finance*, Autumn 1989, *9*(3), pp. 76–80.

Seidman, L. William. How to Solve the S&L Mess. *Challenge*, Jan.–Feb. 1989, *32*(1), pp. 56–58.

————. Third World Debt: The Next Phase: Perspectives of Commercial Bank Creditors. In *Fried, E. R. and Trezise, P. H., eds.*, 1989, pp. 55–56.

Seidman, Laurence S. Boost Saving with a Personal Consumption Tax. *Challenge*, Nov.–Dec. 1989, *32*(6), pp. 44–50.

————. Complements and Substitutes: The Importance of Minding p's and q's. *Southern Econ. J.*, July 1989, *56*(1), pp. 183–90.

————. The Welfare Cost of a Relativistic Economy. *J. Post Keynesian Econ.*, Winter 1988–89, *11*(2), pp. 295–304.

Seidman, Robert B. Contract Law, the Free Market, and State Intervention: A Jurisprudential Perspective. In *Tool, M. R. and Samuels, W. J., eds. (III)*, 1989, *1973*, pp. 17–39.

———— and Makgetla, Neva Seidman. The Applicability of Law and Economics to Policymaking in the Third World. *J. Econ. Issues*, March 1989, *23*(1), pp. 35–78.

———— and Makgetla, Neva Seidman. On the Appropriate Arenas for Government Intervention in the Third World. In *Samuels, W. J., ed. (I)*, 1989, pp. 131–46.

Seifert, Bruce and Rubin, Bruce. Spin-Offs and the Listing Phenomena. *J. Econ. Bus.*, February 1989, *41*(1), pp. 1–19.

Seifert, Eberhard K. The Just State—Observations on Schmoller's Political Theory: Comment. *Int. J. Soc. Econ.*, 1989, *16*(9–10–11), pp. 101–05.

————. Schmoller on Justice—Today. *Int. J. Soc. Econ.*, 1989, *16*(9–10–11), pp. 69–92.

Seitz, Helmut. Die Quantifizierung von Tendenzbefragungsdaten: Ein Überblick. (The Quantification of Tendency Data: A Survey. With English summary.) *Ifo-Studien*, 1989, *35*(1), pp. 1–26.

_____ and **König, Heinz.** Zur Transmission von Nachfrage- und Kostenschocks auf Lagerhaltung, Preise und Produktion. (The Transmission of Demand and Cost Shocks on Inventories, Prices and Production. With English summary.) *Jahr. Nationalökon. Statist.*, October 1989, *206*(4–5), pp. 421–33.

Seitzinger, Ann Hillberg and Paarlberg, Philip L. A Simulation Model of the U.S. Export Enhancement Program for Wheat in the Presence of an EC Response. *Europ. Rev. Agr. Econ.*, 1989, *16*(4), pp. 445–62.

Seják, Josef; Klusoň, Václav and Hrnčíř, Miroslav. The Directions of Development of Intensive Type Economic Mechanism. *Czech. Econ. Pap.*, 1989, (26), pp. 31–49.

Sekkat, Khalid. L'analyse de causalité comme méthode de détermination des filières industrielles. (Causality as a Method for Detecting Key Industrial Linkages. With English summary.) *Ann. Écon. Statist.*, April–June 1989, (14), pp. 191–223.

Sekulović, Slobodan. The Complete or Total Coefficient of Aggregate Demand Elasticity. *Econ. Anal. Workers' Manage.*, 1989, *23*(2), pp. 167–83.

Selby, Edward B., Jr.; Lindley, James T. and Rudolph, Patricia M. Credit Card Possession and Use: Changes over Time. *J. Econ. Bus.*, May 1989, *41*(2), pp. 127–42.

Selden, Mark. Mao Zedong and the Political Economy of Chinese Development. In *Dirlik, A. and Meisner, M., eds.*, 1989, pp. 43–58.

Seldon, Arthur. Economic Scholarship and Political Interest: IEA Thinking and Government Policies. In *Gamble, A., et al.*, 1989, pp. 75–98.

Seldon, Barry J. and Doroodian, Khosrow. A Simultaneous Model of Cigarette Advertising: Effects on Demand and Industry Response to Public Policy. *Rev. Econ. Statist.*, November 1989, *71*(4), pp. 673–77.

Seldon, Zena A. Seasonality in Movement Patterns on the Upper Mississippi. *Logist. Transp. Rev.*, March 1989, *25*(1), pp. 23–38.

Selgin, George A. The Analytical Framework of the Real-Bills Doctrine. *J. Inst. Theoretical Econ.*, September 1989, *145*(3), pp. 489–507.

_____. Commercial Banks as Pure Intermediaries: Between "Old" and "New" Views. *Southern Econ. J.*, July 1989, *56*(1), pp. 80–86.

_____. Legal Restrictions, Financial Weakening, and the Lender of Late Resort. *Cato J.*, Fall 1989, *9*(2), pp. 429–59.

_____ and **White, Lawrence H.** The Evolution of a Free Banking System. In *White, L. H.*, 1989, *1987*, pp. 218–42.

Seligman, Ben B. Philosophic Perspectives in Economic Thought. In *Tool, M. R. and Samuels, W. J., eds.* (II), 1989, *1971*, pp. 253–76.

Seliunin, Vasilii. A Profound Reform or the Revenge of the Bureaucracy? *Prob. Econ.*, March 1989, *31*(11), pp. 6–32.

Sell, Friedrich L. Die Rolle ökonomischer Verhaltensweisen für "Timing" und "Sequenc-ing" handelspolitischer Liberalisierungsprogramme. (The Political Economy of Trade Liberalization: Consequences for "Timing" and "Sequencing." With English summary.) *Z. Wirtschaft. Sozialwissen.*, 1989, *109*(3), pp. 449–66.

Sellar, Christine; Chavas, Jean-Paul and Stoll, John R. On the Commodity Value of Travel Time in Recreational Activities. *Appl. Econ.*, June 1989, *21*(6), pp. 711–22.

Sellgren, J. Assisting Local Economies: An Assessment of Emerging Patterns of Local Authority Economic Development Activities. In *Gibbs, D., ed.*, 1989, pp. 232–65.

Sellström, Tor. Some Factors behind Nordic Relations with Southern Africa. In *Odén, B. and Othman, H., eds.*, 1989, pp. 13–46.

Sellwood, D. J. Reduction of Errors in a Consumer Price Index. In *Turvey, R.*, 1989, pp. 147–54.

Selnes, Fred and Troye, Sigurd Villads. Buying Expertise, Information Search, and Problem Solving. *J. Econ. Psych.*, November 1989, *10*(3), pp. 411–28.

Selnow, Gary; Blosser, Lois and Marlowe, Julia. A Content Analysis of Problem-Resolution Appeals in Television Commercials. *J. Cons. Aff.*, Summer 1989, *23*(1), pp. 175–94.

Selowsky, Marcelo. Efficient Debt Reduction: Comment. In *Husain, I. and Diwan, I., eds.*, 1989, pp. 257.

Selvanathan, E. Antony. Advertising and Consumer Demand: A Differential Approach. *Econ. Letters*, December 1989, *31*(3), pp. 215–19.

_____. A Note on the Stochastic Approach to Index Numbers. *J. Bus. Econ. Statist.*, October 1989, 7(4), pp. 471–74.

Semmler, Willi. Financial Dynamics and Business Cycles: New Perspectives: Introduction. In *Semmler, W., ed.*, 1989, pp. xi–xxi.

_____ and **Franke, Reiner.** Debt-Financing of Firms, Stability, and Cycles in a Dynamical Macroeconomic Growth Model. In *Semmler, W., ed.*, 1989, pp. 38–64.

Sen, Amartya. Food and Freedom. *World Devel.*, June 1989, *17*(6), pp. 769–81.

_____. The Living Standard. In *Wood, J. C. and Woods, R. N., eds., Vol. 4*, 1989, *1984*, pp. 105–21.

_____. The Moral Standing of the Market. In *Helm, D., ed.*, 1989, pp. 92–109.

_____. The Profit Motive. In *Johnson, C., ed.*, 1989, pp. 106–24.

Sen, Binayak and Sobhan, Rehman. Trends in the Repayment Performance to the DFIs: Implications for the Development of Entrepreneurship in Bangladesh. *Bangladesh Devel. Stud.*, September 1989, *17*(3), pp. 21–66.

Sen, Partha and Turnovsky, Stephen J. Deterioration of the Terms of Trade and Capital Accumulation: A Re-examination of the Laursen-Metzler Effect. *J. Int. Econ.*, May 1989, *26*(3/4), pp. 227–50.

_____ and **Turnovsky, Stephen J.** Tariffs, Capital Accumulation, and the Current Account in a

Small Open Economy. *Int. Econ. Rev.*, November 1989, *30*(4), pp. 811–31.

Sen, Pranab K. Change Point Problem Relating to the Poverty Structure. In *Hackl, P., ed.*, 1989, pp. 329–44.

_____; **Chinchilli, Vernon M. and Schwab, Barry H.** Inference Based on Ranks for the Multiple-Design Multivariate Linear Model. *J. Amer. Statist. Assoc.*, June 1989, *84*(406), pp. 517–24.

_____ **and Ghosh, Malay.** Median Unbiasedness and Pitman Closeness. *J. Amer. Statist. Assoc.*, December 1989, *84*(408), pp. 1089–91.

_____; **Gupta, Arjun K. and Saleh, A. K. Md. Ehsanes.** Improved Estimation in a Contingency Table: Independence Structure. *J. Amer. Statist. Assoc.*, June 1989, *84*(406), pp. 525–32.

_____ **and Hušková, Marie.** Nonparametric Tests for Shift and Change in Regression at an Unknown Time Point. In *Hackl, P., ed.*, 1989, pp. 71–85.

Sen, Somnath and Murshed, S. Mansoob. Inflation and Macroeconomic Adjustments in a North–South Model. *Greek Econ. Rev.*, 1989, *11*(1), pp. 95–118.

Sen, Subrata K. and Coughlan, Anne T. Salesforce Compensation: Theory and Managerial Implications. *Marketing Sci.*, Fall 1989, *8*(4), pp. 324–42.

Sen, Sunanda. Lender Paradoxes and the Recent Turnarounds in International Capital Markets. In *Singer, H. W. and Sharma, S., eds. (II)*, 1989, pp. 172–91.

Senauer, Ben. Discussion: Effects of Demographic Factors. In *Buse, R. C., ed.*, 1989, pp. 297–304.

Sender, John; Lawson, Tony and Palma, J. Gabriel. Kaldor's Contribution to Economics: An Introduction. *Cambridge J. Econ.*, March 1989, *13*(1), pp. 1–8.

Şenesen, M. U. and Günlük-Şenesen, G. An Analysis of the Turkish Transportation Sector in the Context of a Two-Group Industry Model. In *Candemir, Y., ed.*, 1989, pp. 145–60.

Senf, David R. Measures of Shifts in Regional Retail Trade. *Rev. Reg. Stud.*, Fall 1989, *19*(3), pp. 18–23.

Sengenberger, Werner and Bosch, Gerhard. Employment Policy, the State, and the Unions in the Federal Republic of Germany. In *Rosenberg, S., ed.*, 1989, pp. 87–106.

Sengupta, Jati K. Nonparametric Tests of Efficiency of Portfolio Investment. *J. Econ. (Z. Nationalökon.)*, 1989, *50*(1), pp. 1–15.

Sengupta, Kunal; Dutta, Bhaskar and Ray, Debraj. Contracts with Eviction in Infinitely Repeated Principal–Agent Relationships. In *Bardhan, P., ed. (II)*, 1989, pp. 93–121.

_____ **and Ray, Debraj.** Interlinkages and the Pattern of Competition. In *Bardhan, P., ed. (II)*, 1989, pp. 243–63.

Senser, Robert A. How Poland's Solidarity Won Freedom of Association. *Mon. Lab. Rev.*, September 1989, *112*(9), pp. 34–38.

Şenses, Fikret. The Nature and Main Characteristics of Recent Turkish Growth in Export of Manufactures. *Developing Econ.*, March 1989, *27*(1), pp. 19–33.

Seo, Bong Chul. The Multinationalization of Korean Business and the New Direction of FDI from Korea. In *Negandhi, A. R., ed.*, 1989, pp. 323–36.

Seo, Fumiko. Construction of a Multiattribute Risk Function and Its Properties for Assessing Hazardous Events. In *Lockett, A. G. and Islei, G., eds.*, 1989, pp. 400–409.

Seo, T. K. and Russell, W. R. Representative Sets for Stochastic Dominance Rules. In *[Hadar, J.]*, 1989, pp. 59–76.

Sepassi, Gholam Reza. Single-Generation Environmental Clubs under the Assumption of Threshold Value. *METU*, 1989, *16*(3–4), pp. 147–78.

Sephton, Peter S. Anticipated Monetary Policy in Canada: Some New Evidence. *Econ. Letters*, 1989, *30*(1), pp. 11–17.

_____. Causality between Export Growth and Industrial Development: Empirical Evidence from the NICs—A Comment. *J. Devel. Econ.*, October 1989, *31*(2), pp. 413–15.

_____. A Note on Exchange Rate Trend-Stationarity. *Int. Econ. J.*, Summer 1989, *3*(2), pp. 73–77.

_____. On Exchange Intervention, Sterilization, and Bank Reserve Accounting. *J. Int. Money Finance*, September 1989, *8*(3), pp. 445–50.

_____. On the Exchange-Rate Elasticity of the Demand for International Reserves: Some Evidence from Industrial Countries: A Comment. *Weltwirtsch. Arch.*, 1989, *125*(2), pp. 392–93.

_____. Relative Prices and Money: Some Canadian Evidence. *Can. J. Agr. Econ.*, July 1989, *37*(2), pp. 269–77.

Serafini, P., et al. Job Shop Scheduling: A Case Study. In *Archetti, F.; Lucertini, M. and Serafini, P., eds.*, 1989, pp. 237–46.

Serapio, Manuel G., Jr.; Shin, Mansoo and Negandhi, Anant R. Multinationals and Newly Industrialized Countries: Strategies, Environmental Imperatives, and Practices: Introduction: Multinationals in the Twenty-first Century. In *Negandhi, A. R., ed.*, 1989, pp. 1–8.

Serletis, Apostolos and Afxentiou, Panayiotis C. Long Term Trends in Canadian Economic Development. *Econ. Notes*, 1989, (3), pp. 362–75.

_____ **and Fisher, Douglas.** Velocity and the Growth of Money in the United States, 1970–1985. *J. Macroecon.*, Summer 1989, *11*(3), pp. 323–32.

Seror, Ann C. An Empirical Analysis of Strategies for Managerial Control: The United States and Japan. In *Prasad, S. B., ed.*, 1989, pp. 19–44.

Serrano Perez, Felipe. Las desregulaciones en la crisis: El caso de la Seguridad Social española. (The "Deregulations" in the Crisis: The Case of the Spanish Social Security System. With English summary.) *Écon. Societes*, February 1989, *23*(2), pp. 101–28.

Sertel, Murat. On the Continuity of Closed Convex Hull. *Math. Soc. Sci.*, December 1989, *18*(3), pp. 297–99.

Séruzier, Michel. Compilation of National Accounts in High Inflation Countries. *Rev. Income Wealth*, March 1989, *35*(1), pp. 81–100.

Servais, J.-M. The Social Clause in Trade Agreements: Wishful Thinking or an Instrument of Social Progress? *Int. Lab. Rev.*, 1989, *128*(4), pp. 423–32.

Servais, Marita; Duncan, Greg J. and Solenberger, Peter. Data Base Management Approaches to Household Panel Studies. In *Kasprzyk, D., et al., eds.*, 1989, pp. 190–225.

Seshu, D. V., et al. Effect of Weather and Climate on Production and Vulnerability of Rice. In *Oram, P. A., et al.*, 1989, pp. 93–113.

Šestáková, Monika. Financial Operations of U.S. Transnational Corporations: Development after the Second World War and Recent Tendencies. In *Teichova, A.; Lévy-Leboyer, M. and Nussbaum, H., eds.*, 1989, pp. 69–75.

Sestito, Paolo. Alcune note sull'occupazione indipendente in Italia. (Some Short Notes on Self-Employment in Italy. With English summary.) *Econ. Lavoro*, July–Sept. 1989, *23*(3), pp. 71–85.

Seth, Rama. Distributional Issues in Privatization. *Fed. Res. Bank New York Quart. Rev.*, Summer 1989, *14*(2), pp. 29–43.

Seton, Francis. Eigenprices Revisited—Recapitulation and Apologia. *Econ. Systems Res.*, 1989, *1*(2), pp. 273–83.

Settle, Suzanne R. Telecommunications Policy in the United States. In *Jussawalla, M.; Okuma, T. and Araki, T., eds.*, 1989, pp. 69–73.

Sevón, Guje and Weckström, Sonja. The Development of Reasoning about Economic Events: A Study of Finnish Children. *J. Econ. Psych.*, 1989, *10*(4), pp. 495–514.

Seward, Shirley B. The Role of Immigration: Policy Context of Immigration to Canada. In *Beach, C. M. and Green, A. G.*, 1989, pp. 3–8.

Sewell, W. R. Derrick; Dearden, Philip and Dumbrell, John. Wilderness Decisionmaking and the Role of Environmental Interest Groups: A Comparison of the Franklin Dam, Tasmania and South Moresby, British Columbia Cases. *Natural Res. J.*, Winter 1989, *29*(1), pp. 147–69.

Sexton, Jean. Controlling Corruption in the Construction Industry: The Quebec Approach. *Ind. Lab. Relat. Rev.*, July 1989, *42*(4), pp. 524–35.

Sexton, Jerry. Long-Term Unemployment: The International Perspective (1). In *Dyson, K., ed.*, 1989, pp. 28–50.

Sexton, Richard J.; Wilson, Brooks M. and Wann, Joyce J. Some Tests of the Economic Theory of Cooperatives: Methodology and Application to Cotton Ginning. *Western J. Agr. Econ.*, July 1989, *14*(1), pp. 56–66.

_____, **et al.** The Conservation and Welfare Effects of Information in a Time-of-Day Pricing Experiment. *Land Econ.*, August 1989, *65*(3), pp. 272–79.

Sexton, Robert L.; Graves, Philip E. and Lee, Dwight R. Statutes versus Enforcement: The Case of the Optimal Speed Limit. *Amer. Econ. Rev.*, September 1989, *79*(4), pp. 932–36.

Seyedian, Mojtaba. Nobel Laureates in Economic Sciences: A Biographical Dictionary: Franco Modigliani: 1985. In *Katz, B. S., ed.*, 1989, pp. 203–17.

Sforzi, Fabio. The Geography of Industrial Districts in Italy. In *Goodman, E. and Bamford, J., eds.*, 1989, pp. 153–73.

Sgontz, Larry G. and Pogue, Thomas F. Taxing to Control Social Costs: The Case of Alcohol. *Amer. Econ. Rev.*, March 1989, *79*(1), pp. 235–43.

Sgro, Pasquale M.; Hazari, Bharat R. and Muir, S. Rationing Black Markets and Welfare of the Poor. *Indian Econ. J.*, April–June 1989, *36*(4), pp. 39–47.

Shaaf, Mohammad and Smith, Paula A. The Role of the Regional Economy in Oklahoma Bank Failures. In *Missouri Valley Economic Association*, 1989, pp. 86–91.

Shabad, Theodore. Siberian Development under Gorbachev. *Int. Reg. Sci. Rev.*, 1989, *12*(3), pp. 281–89.

Shabman, Leonard A. and Bosch, Darrell J. The Decline of Private Sector Oyster Culture in Virginia: Causes and Remedial Policies. *Marine Resource Econ.*, 1989, *6*(3), pp. 227–43.

Shackle, G. L. S. Sir John Hicks' 'IS–LM': An Explanation': A Comment. In *Wood, J. C. and Woods, R. N., eds., Vol. 3*, 1989, *1982*, pp. 298–301.

_____. What Did the *General Theory* Do? In *Pheby, J., ed.*, 1989, pp. 48–58.

Shackleton, Michael. The Budget of the European Community. In *Lodge, J., ed.*, 1989, pp. 129–47.

Shadoan, Elizabeth and Scott, Clyde. The Effect of Gender on Arbitration Decisions. *J. Lab. Res.*, Fall 1989, *10*(4), pp. 429–36.

Shafer, Carl E. Price and Value Effects of Pecan Crop Forecasts, 1971–1987. *Southern J. Agr. Econ.*, July 1989, *21*(1), pp. 97–103.

_____; **Anderson, Carl G. and Wood, Wendell C.** Frequency and Duration of Profitable Hedging Margins for Texas Cotton Producers, 1980–1986. *J. Futures Markets*, December 1989, *9*(6), pp. 519–28.

Shafer, Jeffrey R. Simulating the Effects of Some Simple Coordinated versus Uncoordinated Policy Rules: Comment. In *Bryant, R. C., et al., eds.*, 1989, pp. 240–44.

_____. Summit Agendas: A Symposium: Present and Future Agendas. *Can. Public Policy*, Supplement, February 1989, *15*, pp. S78–82.

Shafer, Michael S. An Introduction to Supported Employment. In *Wehman, P. and Kregel, J., eds.*, 1989, pp. 3–18.

_____; **Rice, Martha Larus and Metzler, Helen M. D.** Integration in the Workplace: Perceptions and Experiences of Employees without Disabilities. In *Wehman, P. and Kregel, J., eds.*, 1989, pp. 137–59.

Shaffer, James Duncan. On the Fundamentals of the Economic Role of Government—The Rules Governing Economic Activity. In *Samuels, W. J., ed. (I)*, 1989, pp. 179–85.

_____. Selective Perceptions and the Politics of Agricultural Policy. In *Krämer, C. S., ed.*, 1989, pp. 61–77.

Shaffer, John W. Agrarian Change and Landlord–Tenant Relations in the French Nivernais. In *Grantham, G. and Leonard, C. S., eds., Pt. A*, 1989, pp. 125–36.

Shaffer, Sherrill. Annuities and Infraction. *Atlantic Econ. J.*, March 1989, *17*(1), pp. 96.

_____. Competition in the U.S. Banking Industry. *Econ. Letters*, 1989, *29*(4), pp. 321–23.

_____. Optimal Regulation of a Consistent Conjectures Duopoly. *Econ. Letters*, November 1989, *31*(1), pp. 87–89.

_____. Predatory Entrapment. *Econ. Letters*, 1989, *29*(1), pp. 83–86.

_____. Structuring an Option to Facilitate Replication with Transaction Costs. *Econ. Letters*, December 1989, *31*(2), pp. 183–87.

_____. Volatility-Invariant Hedging. *Econ. Letters*, 1989, *29*(3), pp. 249–51.

Shahabuddin, Quazi. Pattern of Food Consumption in Bangladesh: An Analysis of Household Expenditure Survey Data. *Bangladesh Devel. Stud.*, September 1989, *17*(3), pp. 101–17.

Shahi, Manoj and Adelman, M. A. Oil Development–Operating Cost Estimates, 1955–85. *Energy Econ.*, January 1989, *11*(1), pp. 2–10.

Shahin, Wassim N. Money Supply Implications of Financing Deficits through Captive Buyers in a Dual Loan System. *Quart. Rev. Econ. Bus.*, Summer 1989, *29*(2), pp. 87–95.

_____ **and Islam, Muhammad Q.** Economic Methodology Applied to Political Hostage-Taking in Light of the Iran-Contra Affair. *Southern Econ. J.*, April 1989, *55*(4), pp. 1019–24.

Shaikh, Anwar. Accumulation, Finance, and Effective Demand in Marx, Keynes, and Kalecki. In *Semmler, W., ed.*, 1989, pp. 65–86.

Shaked, Avner; Sutton, John and Binmore, Ken. An Outside Option Experiment. *Quart. J. Econ.*, November 1989, *104*(4), pp. 753–70.

Shalen, C. T. The Optimal Maturity of Hedges and Participation of Hedgers in Futures and Forward Markets. *J. Futures Markets*, June 1989, *9*(3), pp. 215–24.

Shaller, Douglas R. and Shiba, Tsunemasa. Price Smoothing and Demand Noise: On Business Behavior and Macromodels. *Weltwirtsch. Arch.*, 1989, *125*(1), pp. 83–96.

Shams, M. The Dynamism of World Oil Industry: An Economic Analysis. *Middle East Bus. Econ. Rev.*, July 1989, *1*(2), pp. 1–9.

_____. The Impact of Oil Revenues on OPEC Economy. *Rivista Int. Sci. Econ. Com.*, Oct.–Nov. 1989, *36*(10–11), pp. 977–84.

_____. The Impact of Oil Revenues on the OPEC Economy. *Energy Econ.*, October 1989, *11*(4), pp. 242–46.

_____. Money-Velocity Causality Detection: Evidence from Some Developing Countries. *Econ. Letters*, September 1989, *30*(3), pp. 227–30.

Shanahan, James L. Private Support for the Arts in U.S. Metropolitan Areas with United Arts Funds. *J. Cult. Econ.*, December 1989, *13*(2), pp. 35–51.

Shand, R. T. and Kalirajan, K. P. A Generalized Measure of Technical Efficiency. *Appl. Econ.*, January 1989, *21*(1), pp. 25–34.

Shane, Mathew. Government Intervention, Financial Constraint, and the World Food Situation. In *Horwich, G. and Lynch, G. J., eds.*, 1989, pp. 65–90.

Shani, Y.; Bresler, Eshel and Feinerman, Eli. Economic Optimisation of Sprinkler Irrigation Considering Uncertainty of Spatial Water Distribution. *Australian J. Agr. Econ.*, August 1989, *33*(2), pp. 88–107.

Shanken, Jay; Gibbons, Michael R. and Ross, Stephen A. A Test of the Efficiency of a Given Portfolio. *Econometrica*, September 1989, *57*(5), pp. 1121–52.

Shannon, John and Kee, James Edwin. The Rise of Competitive Federalism. *Public Budg. Finance*, Winter 1989, *9*(4), pp. 5–20.

Shao, Daosheng and Hong, Fenglin. Workers' Assessment of Party Spirit and Interpersonal Relations. *Chinese Econ. Stud.*, Summer 1989, *22*(4), pp. 44–54.

_____ **and Peng, Jianfeng.** Changing Patterns in Workers' View of Life. *Chinese Econ. Stud.*, Summer 1989, *22*(4), pp. 39–43.

Shao, Jun. Monte Carlo Approximations in Bayesian Decision Theory. *J. Amer. Statist. Assoc.*, September 1989, *84*(407), pp. 727–32.

Shapiro, Carl. Market Power and Mergers in Durable-Good Industries: Comment. *J. Law Econ.*, Part 2, October 1989, *32*(2), pp. S227–32.

_____. Theories of Oligopoly Behavior. In *Schmalensee, R. and Willig, R. D., eds., Vol. 1*, 1989, pp. 329–414.

_____. The Theory of Business Strategy. *Rand J. Econ.*, Spring 1989, *20*(1), pp. 125–37.

_____ **and Farrell, Joseph.** Optimal Contracts with Lock-In. *Amer. Econ. Rev.*, March 1989, *79*(1), pp. 51–68.

Shapiro, Daniel M. and Pepall, Lynne M. The Military–Industrial Complex in Canada. *Can. Public Policy*, September 1989, *15*(3), pp. 265–84.

_____ **and Stelcner, Morton.** Canadian Public–Private Sector Earnings Differentials, 1970–1980. *Ind. Relat.*, Winter 1989, *28*(1), pp. 72–81.

Shapiro, David. A Descriptive Overview of Traditional Farms and Farm Households in Zaire. *Rev. Black Polit. Econ.*, Fall 1989, *18*(2), pp. 87–96.

Shapiro, Helen. State Intervention and Industrialization: The Origins of the Brazilian Automotive Industry. In *Hausman, W. J., ed.*, 1989, pp. 26–30.

Shapiro, Kenneth and Ellsworth, Lynn. Seasonality in Burkina Faso Grain Marketing: Farmer

Strategies and Government Policy. In *Sahn, D. E., ed.*, 1989, pp. 196–205.

Shapiro, Matthew D. Assessing the Federal Reserve's Measures of Capacity and Utilization. *Brookings Pap. Econ. Act.*, 1989, (1), pp. 181–225.

_____. Inventories, Orders, Temporary and Permanent Layoffs: An Econometric Analysis: Comment. *Carnegie–Rochester Conf. Ser. Public Policy*, Spring 1989, *30*, pp. 367–73.

Shapiro, Nina. Dow's Methodology and Macroeconomics: Review Essay. In *Samuels, W. J., ed. (II)*, 1989, pp. 269–76.

Shapiro, Perry and Fischel, William A. A Constitutional Choice Model of Compensation for Takings. *Int. Rev. Law Econ.*, December 1989, *9*(2), pp. 115–28.

_____ **and Rubinfeld, Daniel L.** Micro-estimation of the Demand for Schooling: Evidence from Michigan and Massachusetts. *Reg. Sci. Urban Econ.*, August 1989, *19*(3), pp. 381–98.

Shapiro, Sidney A. and McGarity, Thomas O. Reorienting OSHA: Regulatory Alternatives and Legislative Reform. *Yale J. Regul.*, Winter 1989, *6*(1), pp. 1–63.

Shapiro, Stephen L.; Borg, Mary O'Malley and Mason, Paul M. The Case of Effort Variables in Student Performance. *J. Econ. Educ.*, Summer 1989, *20*(3), pp. 308–13.

_____; **Borg, Mary O'Malley and Mason, Paul M.** Gaming Tax Incidence for Three Groups of Las Vegas Gamblers. *Appl. Econ.*, September 1989, *21*(9), pp. 1267–77.

Shapiro, Thomas M. and Oliver, Melvin L. Race and Wealth. *Rev. Black Polit. Econ.*, Spring 1989, *17*(4), pp. 5–25.

Shapley, L. S. and Owen, Guillermo. Optimal Location of Candidates in Ideological Space. *Int. J. Game Theory*, 1989, *18*(3), pp. 339–56.

Shaposhnikov, A. N. and Lisov, V. A. Methods and Results of Constructing a Typology of Families Based on Level of Material Well-Being: Example of the Rural Population. *Prob. Econ.*, May 1989, *32*(1), pp. 33–51.

_____; **Zaslavskaia, Tat'iana I. and Smirnov, V.** Restructuring the Management of Soviet Society's Agrarian Sector. *Prob. Econ.*, January 1989, *31*(9), pp. 39–54.

Shapouri, Shahla and Rosen, Stacey. Export Growth, Instability and Shortfall: The Impact on Economic Performance in Africa. *Can. J. Agr. Econ.*, Part 2, December 1989, *37*(4), pp. 1241–50.

Sharif, M. A Technique for Estimating a Direct Utility Function. *J. Stud. Econ. Econometrics*, August 1989, *13*(2), pp. 1–23.

Sharkey, William W. Game Theoretic Modeling of Increasing Returns to Scale. *Games Econ. Behav.*, December 1989, *1*(4), pp. 370–431.

Sharma, Basu. The Effect of Strikes on Economic Growth. *Atlantic Econ. J.*, March 1989, *17*(1), pp. 87.

_____. Korean Trade Union Growth during the Period 1962–1984. *Econ. Letters*, November 1989, *31*(1), pp. 105–08.

_____. Union Growth in Malaysia and Singapore. *Ind. Relat.*, Fall 1989, *28*(3), pp. 446–58.

Sharma, D. Deo. Technical Consultancy as a Network of Relationships. In *Hallén, L. and Johanson, J., eds.*, 1989, pp. 57–74.

Sharma, H. R. and Diwakar, Ashok. Transfer of Technology and Response of Small Farmers. *Margin*, Jan.–March 1989, *21*(2), pp. 45–51.

Sharma, P. D.; Krishnamurty, K. and Pandit, V. N. Parameters of Growth in a Developing Mixed Economy: The Indian Experience. *J. Quant. Econ.*, July 1989, *5*(2), pp. 295–325.

Sharma, Soumitra. External Debt Management and Economic Growth: An Introduction. In *Singer, H. W. and Sharma, S., eds. (II)*, 1989, pp. 3–11.

Sharp, Ansel M. and Register, Charles A. For-Profit Hospital Performance: The Impact of Time. *J. Behav. Econ.*, Winter 1989, *18*(4), pp. 307–16.

Sharp, John and Pike, Richard. Trends in the Use of Management Science Techniques in Capital Budgeting. *Managerial Dec. Econ.*, June 1989, *10*(2), pp. 135–40.

Sharp, Keith P. Mortgage Rate Insurance Pricing under an Interest Rate Diffusion with Drift. *J. Risk Ins.*, March 1989, *56*(1), pp. 34–49.

Sharp, Margaret. Biotechnology in Britain and France: The Evolution of Policy. In *Sharp, M. and Holmes, P., eds.*, 1989, pp. 119–59.

_____. The Community and New Technologies. In *Lodge, J., ed.*, 1989, pp. 202–20.

_____ **and Holmes, Peter.** Conclusions: Farewell to the National Champion. In *Sharp, M. and Holmes, P., eds.*, 1989, pp. 212–39.

_____ **and Holmes, Peter.** The State: Captor or Captive? In *Sharp, M. and Holmes, P., eds.*, 1989, pp. 1–18.

Sharples, Jerry A. and Holland, Forrest D. World Wheat Trade: Implications for U.S. Exports. In *Labys, W. C.; Takayama, T. and Uri, N. D., eds.*, 1989, pp. 299–329.

Shastri, Kuldeep and Choi, J. Y. Bid–Ask Spreads and Volatility Estimates: The Implications for Option Pricing. *J. Banking Finance*, May 1989, *13*(2), pp. 207–19.

Shatalin, S. Social Development and Economic Growth. In *Jones, A. and Moskoff, W., eds.*, 1989, *1987*, pp. 195–214.

Shatalov, Sergei. African Debt: Options for Cooperative Approach. In *Mrak, M., ed.*, 1989, pp. 189–202.

Shaughnessy, Peter W. and Schlenker, Robert E. Swing-Bed Hospital Cost and Reimbursement. *Inquiry*, Winter 1989, *26*(4), pp. 508–21.

Shavell, Steven. Optimal Sanctions and the Incentive to Provide Evidence to Legal Tribunals. *Int. Rev. Law Econ.*, June 1989, *9*(1), pp. 3–11.

_____. Sharing of Information Prior to Settlement or Litigation. *Rand J. Econ.*, Summer 1989, *20*(2), pp. 183–95.

_____ **and Polinsky, A. Mitchell.** Legal Error, Litigation, and the Incentive to Obey the Law.

J. Law, Econ., Organ., Spring 1989, *5*(1), pp. 99–108.

Shaw, Douglas V. The Great Northern Railroad and the Promotion of Tourism. *J. Cult. Econ.*, June 1989, *13*(1), pp. 65–76.

Shaw, G. K. Expectations in Macroeconomics. In *Greenaway, D., ed.*, 1989, pp. 22–44.

_____. Joan Robinson, 1903–83. In *Greenaway, D. and Presley, J. R., eds.*, 1989, pp. 144–69.

Shaw, Gareth; Greenwood, Justin and Williams, Alan M. From Tourist to Tourism Entrepreneur, From Consumption to Production: Evidence from Cornwall, England. *Environ. Planning A*, December 1989, *21*(12), pp. 1639–53.

Shaw, James B.; Ismail, Abdul Jalil Bin and Fisher, Cynthia D. A Cognitive Categorization Approach to Managerial Performance Appraisal: Analysis of the Singapore Manager. In *Nedd, A., ed.*, 1989, pp. 339–57.

Shaw, Kathryn L. Intertemporal Labor Supply and the Distribution of Family Income. *Rev. Econ. Statist.*, May 1989, *71*(2), pp. 196–205.

_____. Life-Cycle Labor Supply with Human Capital Accumulation. *Int. Econ. Rev.*, May 1989, *30*(2), pp. 431–56.

_____. Wage Variability in the 1970s: Sectoral Shifts or Cyclical Sensitivity. *Rev. Econ. Statist.*, February 1989, *71*(1), pp. 26–36.

Shaw, L. M. E. The Inquisition and the Portuguese Economy. *J. Europ. Econ. Hist.*, Fall 1989, *18*(2), pp. 415–31.

Shaw, Marguerite and Frenkel, Stephen J. No Tears for the Second Tier: Productivity Bargaining in the Australian Metal Industry. *Australian Bull. Lab.*, March 1989, *15*(2), pp. 90–114.

Shaw, Martin. War and the Nation-State in Social Theory. In *Held, D. and Thompson, J. B., eds.*, 1989, pp. 129–46.

Shaw, Timothy M. The UN Economic Commission for Africa: Continental Development and Self-Reliance. In *[Gordenker, L.]*, 1989, pp. 98–111.

Shaw, W. Douglass. Valuing the Effect of Acidification Damages on the Adirondack Fishery: Comment. *Amer. J. Agr. Econ.*, February 1989, *71*(1), pp. 217–20.

Shea, Gary S. *Ex-Post* Rational Price Approximations and the Empirical Reliability of the Present-Value Relation. *J. Appl. Econometrics*, April–June 1989, *4*(2), pp. 139–59.

Shea, Koon-Lam and Lau, Man-Lui. A Choice Theoretic Model of the Kaldorian Growth: The Most Rapid Approach Path Analysis. *Hong Kong Econ. Pap.*, 1989, (19), pp. 43–47.

_____ and Manning, Richard. Perfect Discrimination and the Long-run National Advantage. *J. Econ. (Z. Nationalökon.)*, 1989, *49*(3), pp. 299–313.

_____ and Manning, Richard. Perfectly Discriminatory Policy towards International Capital Movements in a Dynamic World. *Int. Econ. Rev.*, May 1989, *30*(2), pp. 329–48.

Sheard, Paul. The Japanese General Trading Company as an Aspect of Interfirm Risk-Sharing. *J. Japanese Int. Economies*, September 1989, *3*(3), pp. 308–22.

_____. The Main Bank System and Corporate Monitoring and Control in Japan. *J. Econ. Behav. Organ.*, May 1989, *11*(3), pp. 399–422.

Shearer, Ronald A. and Paterson, Donald G. Terminating Building Societies in Quebec City, 1850–1864. *Bus. Hist. Rev.*, Summer 1989, *63*(2), pp. 384–415.

Sheate, W. R. and Macrory, R. B. Agriculture and the EC Environmental Assessment Directive: Lessons for Community Policy-Making. *J. Common Market Stud.*, September 1989, *28*(1), pp. 68–81.

Shechter, Mordechai; Kim, Moshe and Golan, Lorette. Valuing a Public Good: Direct and Indirect Valuation Approaches to the Measurement of the Benefits from Pollution Abatement. In *Folmer, H. and van Ierland, E., eds.*, 1989, pp. 123–37.

Sheehan, Dennis P. and Loderer, Claudio F. Corporate Bankruptcy and Managers' Self-Serving Behavior. *J. Finance*, September 1989, *44*(4), pp. 1059–75.

Sheehan, Richard G.; Ahmed, Ehsan and Rosser, J. Barkley, Jr. A Comparison of National and International Aggregate Supply and Demand VAR Models: The United States, Japan and the European Economic Community. *Weltwirtsch. Arch.*, 1989, *125*(2), pp. 252–72.

_____; Ferri, Michael G. and Schirm, David C. Financial Market Responses to Treasury Debt Announcements: A Note. *J. Money, Credit, Banking*, August 1989, *21*(3), pp. 394–400.

_____ and Hafer, R. W. The Sensitivity of VAR Forecasts to Alternative Lag Structures. *Int. J. Forecasting*, 1989, *5*(3), pp. 399–408.

Sheen, Jeffrey Ralph. Modelling the Floating Australian Dollar: Can the Random Walk Be Encompassed by a Model Using a Permanent Decomposition of Money and Output? *J. Int. Money Finance*, June 1989, *8*(2), pp. 253–76.

Sheets, Robert G.; Nord, Stephen and Phelps, John J. Service Industries and Structural Underemployment in Urban Areas in the United States. *Rivista Int. Sci. Econ. Com.*, September 1989, *36*(9), pp. 785–800.

Sheffer, Eliezer. The Economic Burden of the Arms Race in the Middle East. In *Fishelson, G., ed.*, 1989, pp. 15–29.

Sheffrin, Steven M. Joan Robinson and the New Classical Economists as Critics of Keynesian Economics. In *Feiwel, G. R., ed. (I)*, 1989, pp. 631–45.

_____ and Joerding, Wayne. Consumption Spending and Output Fluctuations: A Multicountry Study. *Appl. Econ.*, July 1989, *21*(7), pp. 891–99.

Shefrin, Hersh; Madan, Dilip B. and Milne, Frank. The Multinomial Option Pricing Model and Its Brownian and Poisson Limits. *Rev. Financial Stud.*, 1989, *2*(2), pp. 251–65.

Sheikh, Aamir M. Stock Splits, Volatility Increases, and Implied Volatilities. *J. Finance*, December 1989, *44*(5), pp. 1361–72.

Sheikh, Munir A. A Theory of Risk, Smuggling and Welfare. *World Devel.*, December 1989, *17*(12), pp. 1931–44.

Sheinis, L. Z. Steady Joint Work by Clients and Developers Is Needed. *Matekon*, Spring 1989, *25*(3), pp. 63–65.

Shejhetov, Boris M. and Egorova, Elena N. Simulated Analysis of the Integration of Science and Industry. *Econ. Systems Res.*, 1989, *1*(4), pp. 481–89.

Sheldon, George and Blattner, Niklaus. Foreign Labour, Growth and Productivity: The Case of Switzerland. In *Gordon, I. and Thirlwall, A. P., eds.*, 1989, pp. 148–65.

_____; Kugler, Peter and Müller, Urs. Non-neutral Technical Change, Capital, White-Collar and Blue-Collar Labor: Some Empirical Results. *Econ. Letters*, November 1989, *31*(1), pp. 91–94.

Sheldon, Ian M. and McCorriston, Steve. Measuring Patterns of Intra-industry Specialisation within the EC. *Scot. J. Polit. Econ.*, February 1989, *36*(1), pp. 96–102.

_____ and McCorriston, Steve. Trade and Welfare Effects of EC Accession on the UK Agricultural Supply Industries. *J. Agr. Econ.*, September 1989, *40*(3), pp. 302–13.

_____ and McCorriston, Steve. The Welfare Implications of Nitrogen Limitation Policies. *J. Agr. Econ.*, May 1989, *40*(2), pp. 143–51.

Sheldrick, B. and Scott, A. Energy and Environment: Deriving a Research Agenda. *Environ. Planning A*, October 1989, *21*(10), pp. 1349–62.

Shell, Karl and Cass, David. Sunspot Equilibrium in an Overlapping-Generations Economy with an Idealized Contingent-Commodities Market. In *Barnett, W. A.; Geweke, J. and Shell, K., eds.*, 1989, pp. 3–20.

_____ and Peck, James. On the Nonequivalence of the Arrow-Securities Game and the Contingent-Commodities Game. In *Barnett, W. A.; Geweke, J. and Shell, K., eds.*, 1989, pp. 61–85.

Shen, Patrick; Lu, Wen-he and Gale, James R. Cross Section Evidence on the Demand for Money by the Household Sector. In *Missouri Valley Economic Association*, 1989, pp. 63–69.

Shepherd, Geoffrey; Webber, Douglas and Cawson, Alan. Governments, Markets, and Regulation in the West European Consumer Electronics Industry. In *Hancher, L. and Moran, M., eds.*, 1989, pp. 109–33.

Shepherd, Phil. Transnational Corporations and the Denationalisation of the Latin American Cigarette Industry. In *Teichova, A.; Lévy-Leboyer, M. and Nussbaum, H., eds.*, 1989, pp. 201–28.

Shepherd, William F. and Rao, D. S. Prasada. Trends in Average Earnings of Production Workers in Australia and in OECD Member Countries. *Australian Bull. Lab.*, December 1989, *15*(5), pp. 400–425.

Shepherd, William G. Capital Gains as Economic Rent. *Rev. Soc. Econ.*, Summer 1989, *47*(2), pp. 155–72.

_____. Efficient Profits vs. Unlimited Capture, as a Reward for Superior Performance: Analysis and Cases. *Antitrust Bull.*, Spring 1989, *34*(1), pp. 121–52.

Shepherdson, Ian C. The Secondary Market in Less Developed Countries' Debt: A Survey. *Nat. Westminster Bank Quart. Rev.*, November 1989, pp. 31–41.

Sheppard, Stephen and Cheshire, Paul. British Planning Policy and Access to Housing: Some Empirical Estimates. *Urban Stud.*, October 1989, *26*(5), pp. 469–85.

Shepsle, Kenneth A. The Changing Textbook Congress. In *Chubb, J. E. and Peterson, P. E., eds.*, 1989, pp. 238–66.

Sherer, Peter D. and Cappelli, Peter. Spanning the Union/Nonunion Boundary. *Ind. Relat.*, Spring 1989, *28*(2), pp. 206–26.

_____ and Morishima, Motohiro. Roads and Roadblocks to Dual Commitment: Similar and Dissimilar Antecedents of Union and Company Commitment. *J. Lab. Res.*, Summer 1989, *10*(3), pp. 311–30.

Shergill, G. S. and Hamilton, R. T. Diversification Patterns in New Zealand Listed Companies. *New Zealand Econ. Pap.*, 1989, *23*, pp. 3–11.

Sherk, George William. Equitable Apportionment after *Vermejo:* The Demise of a Doctrine. *Natural Res. J.*, Spring 1989, *29*(2), pp. 565–83.

Sherman, Howard J. Real and Financial Factors in the Business Cycle. *Rev. Radical Polit. Econ.*, Fall 1989, *21*(3), pp. 45–50.

_____. Theories of Economic Crisis: Demand-Side, Supply-Side, and Profit Squeeze. *Sci. Society*, Spring 1989, *53*(1), pp. 62–71.

Sherman, Lawrence W. The Mobilization of Scandal. In *Heidenheimer, A. J.; Johnston, M. and LeVine, V. T., eds.*, 1989, pp. 887–911.

Sherman, Philip D. Out from Competence: Commercial and Investment Banks in the 1990s. In *Kaushik, S. K., ed.*, 1989, pp. 145–54.

Sherman, Roger. Efficiency Aspects of Diversification by Public Utilities. In *Crew, M. A., ed.*, 1989, pp. 43–63.

Sherman, Sally R. Public Attitudes toward Social Security. *Soc. Sec. Bull.*, December 1989, *52*(12), pp. 2–16.

Sherr, Avrom and Domberger, Simon. The Impact of Competition on Pricing and Quality of Legal Services. *Int. Rev. Law Econ.*, June 1989, *9*(1), pp. 41–56.

Sherry, John F., Jr.; Belk, Russell W. and Wallendorf, Melanie. The Sacred and the Profane in Consumer Behavior: Theodicy on the Odyssey. *J. Cons. Res.*, June 1989, *16*(1), pp. 1–38.

Sherry, Robert L. Teaching Economics to Trade Unionists. *J. Econ. Educ.*, Spring 1989, *20*(2), pp. 173–79.

Sherwood-Call, Carolyn. Undocumented Workers and Regional Differences in Apparel Labor Markets. *Fed. Res. Bank San Francisco Econ. Rev.*, Winter 1989, (1), pp. 53–63.

Sheshinski, Eytan. Note on the Shape of the Optimum Income Tax Schedule. *J. Public Econ.*, November 1989, *40*(2), pp. 201–15.

_____. A Simple Model of Optimum Life-Cycle Consumption with Earnings Uncertainty. *J. Econ. Theory*, October 1989, *49*(1), pp. 169–78.

_____; Slutsky, Steven M. and Hamilton, Jonathan H. Production Externalities and Long-run Equilibria: Bargaining and Pigovian Taxation. *Econ. Inquiry*, July 1989, *27*(3), pp. 453–71.

Shevlin, Terry; Bowen, Robert M. and Johnson, Marilyn F. Informational Efficiency and the Information Content of Earnings during the Market Crash of October 1987. *J. Acc. Econ.*, July 1989, *11*(2–3), pp. 225–54.

Shew, William B. Telephone Profits from Cable Television? In *National Economic Research Associates*, 1989, pp. 155–61.

Shi, Tian. Research into the Problem of the Scale of Urban Development. In *Howe, C. and Walker, K. R., eds.*, 1989, *1958*, pp. 358–65.

Shiba, Tsunemasa and Shaller, Douglas R. Price Smoothing and Demand Noise: On Business Behavior and Macromodels. *Weltwirtsch. Arch.*, 1989, *125*(1), pp. 83–96.

Shibata, Ritei. Statistical Aspects of Model Selection. In *Willems, J. C., ed.*, 1989, pp. 215–40.

Shideed, Kamil H. and McIntosh, Christopher S. The Effect of Government Programs on Acreage Response over Time: The Case of Corn Production in Iowa. *Western J. Agr. Econ.*, July 1989, *14*(1), pp. 38–44.

_____ and White, Fred C. Alternative Forms of Price Expectations in Supply Analysis for U.S. Corn and Soybean Acreages. *Western J. Agr. Econ.*, December 1989, *14*(2), pp. 281–92.

Shieh, Yeung-Nan. The Beckmann–Zipf Effect and Plant Location under Uniform Pricing. *Econ. Letters*, 1989, *30*(1), pp. 89–92.

_____. Demand, Location, and the Theory of Production. *Ann. Reg. Sci.*, 1989, *23*(2), pp. 93–103.

_____. Treasury Bill Financing, Perpetuity Financing, and the Government Budget Constraint. *Public Finance*, 1989, *44*(1), pp. 150–52.

_____ and Ekelund, Robert B., Jr. Jevons on Utility, Exchange, and Demand Theory: A Reassessment. *Manchester Sch. Econ. Soc. Stud.*, March 1989, *57*(1), pp. 17–33.

_____ and Logan, Bob. Location and Corporate Decisions in a Truly Profit Maximizing Model. *Reg. Sci. Urban Econ.*, February 1989, *19*(1), pp. 125–31.

_____ and O'Brien, J. Patrick. Transportation Rates, Production and Location in the Moses–Weber Triangle: A Note. *Reg. Sci. Urban Econ.*, February 1989, *19*(1), pp. 133–42.

_____ and Olson, Dennis O. Estimating Functional Forms in Cost-Prices. *Europ. Econ. Rev.*, September 1989, *33*(7), pp. 1445–61.

Shields, David and Eichenseher, John W. Corporate Capital Structure and Auditor 'Fit.' In *Gangolly, J., ed.*, 1989, pp. 39–56.

_____ and Kluger, Brian D. Auditor Changes, Information Quality and Bankruptcy Prediction. *Managerial Dec. Econ.*, December 1989, *10*(4), pp. 275–82.

Shields, Gail M. and Shields, Michael P. The Emergence of Migration Theory and a Suggested New Direction. *J. Econ. Surveys*, 1989, *3*(4), pp. 277–304.

_____ and Shields, Michael P. Family Migration and Nonmarket Activities in Costa Rica. *Econ. Devel. Cult. Change*, October 1989, *38*(1), pp. 73–88.

Shields, Michael D.; Whittenburg, Gerald E. and Chow, Chee W. The Quality of Practioners' Judgments Regarding Substantial Authority: An Exploratory Empirical Investigation. In *Jones, S. M., ed.*, 1989, pp. 165–80.

Shields, Michael P. The Machinery Question: Can Technological Improvements Reduce Real Output? *Economica*, May 1989, *56*(222), pp. 215–24.

_____ and Grabowski, Richard. Lewis and Ricardo: A Reinterpretation. *World Devel.*, February 1989, *17*(2), pp. 193–97.

_____ and Shields, Gail M. The Emergence of Migration Theory and a Suggested New Direction. *J. Econ. Surveys*, 1989, *3*(4), pp. 277–304.

_____ and Shields, Gail M. Family Migration and Nonmarket Activities in Costa Rica. *Econ. Devel. Cult. Change*, October 1989, *38*(1), pp. 73–88.

Shiells, Clinton R. Competition and Complementarity between U.S. Imports from Developed and Newly Industrializing Countries. *Weltwirtsch. Arch.*, 1989, *125*(1), pp. 114–28.

_____ and Bednarzik, Robert W. Labor Market Changes and Adjustments: How Do the U.S. and Japan Compare? *Mon. Lab. Rev.*, February 1989, *112*(2), pp. 31–42.

_____; Stern, Robert M. and Deardorff, Alan V. Estimates of the Elasticities of Substitution between Imports and Home Goods for the United States: Reply. *Weltwirtsch. Arch.*, 1989, *125*(2), pp. 371–74.

Shih, Jun-ji. Edgeworth's Contribution to the Theory of "Ramsey Pricing." *Hist. Polit. Econ.*, Summer 1989, *21*(2), pp. 345–49.

Shiller, Robert J. The Behavior of Home Buyers in Boom and Post-boom Markets. In *Shiller, R. J., 1989, 1988*, pp. 403–30.

_____. Bond Market Volatility: An Introductory Survey. In *Shiller, R. J.*, 1989, pp. 219–36.

_____. Business Cycles, Financial Crises, and Stock Volatility: A Comment. *Carnegie–Rochester Conf. Ser. Public Policy*, Autumn 1989, *31*, pp. 127–32.

_____. Cointegration and Tests of Present Value Models. In *Shiller, R. J., 1989, 1987*, pp. 288–316.

_____. Comovements in Stock Prices and Comovements in Dividends. In *Shiller, R. J.*, 1989, pp. 183–96.

_____. Comovements in Stock Prices and Comovements in Dividends. *J. Finance*, July 1989, *44*(3), pp. 719–29.

———. The Determinants of the Variability of Stock Market Prices. In *Shiller, R. J.*, 1989, *1981*, pp. 359–67.

———. The Dividend Ratio Model and Small Sample Bias: A Monte Carlo Study. In *Shiller, R. J.*, 1989, pp. 174–82.

———. Do Stock Prices Move Too Much to Be Justified by Subsequent Changes in Dividends? In *Shiller, R. J.*, 1989, *1981*, pp. 105–30.

———. Econometric Tests of Rationality and Market Efficiency: A Comment. *Econometric Rev.*, 1989, *8*(2), pp. 201–05.

———. The Efficiency of the Market for Single Family Homes. In *Shiller, R. J.*, 1989, pp. 322–41.

———. Factors and Fundamentals. In *Shiller, R. J.*, 1989, pp. 197–214.

———. Fashions, Fads, and Bubbles in Financial Markets. In *Shiller, R. J.*, 1989, *1988*, pp. 49–68.

———. The Gibson Paradox and Historical Movements in Real Interest Rates. In *Shiller, R. J.*, 1989, *1977*, pp. 237–55.

———. International Stock Price Movements: Links and Messages: Comments. *Brookings Pap. Econ. Act.*, 1989, (1), pp. 171–75.

———. Investor Behavior in the October 1987 Stock Market Crash: Survey Evidence. In *Shiller, R. J.*, 1989, pp. 379–402.

———. Market Volatility: Concluding Notes. In *Shiller, R. J.*, 1989, pp. 431–38.

———. Market Volatility: Data Series. In *Shiller, R. J.*, 1989, pp. 439–51.

———. Market Volatility: Introduction. In *Shiller, R. J.*, 1989, pp. 1–4.

———. The Probability of Gross Violations of a Present Value Variance Inequality. In *Shiller, R. J.*, 1989, *1988*, pp. 149–52.

———. Stock Price Volatility: An Introductory Survey. In *Shiller, R. J.*, 1989, pp. 77–104.

———. Stock Prices and Social Dynamics. In *Shiller, R. J.*, 1989, *1984*, pp. 7–48.

———. Stock Prices, Earnings, and Expected Dividends. In *Shiller, R. J.*, 1989, *1988*, pp. 153–73.

———. Ultimate Sources of Aggregate Variability. In *Shiller, R. J.*, 1989, *1987*, pp. 350–58.

———. The Use of Volatility Measures in Assessing Market Efficiency. In *Shiller, R. J.*, 1989, *1981*, pp. 131–48.

———. The Volatility of Long-Term Interest Rates and Expectations Models of the Term Structure. In *Shiller, R. J.*, 1989, *1979*, pp. 256–87.

——— and Campbell, John Y. The Dividend Ratio Model and Small Sample Bias: A Monte Carlo Study. *Econ. Letters*, 1989, *29*(4), pp. 325–31.

——— and Case, Karl E. The Efficiency of the Market for Single-Family Homes. *Amer. Econ. Rev.*, March 1989, *79*(1), pp. 125–37.

——— and Fair, Ray C. The Informational Context of Ex Ante Forecasts. *Rev. Econ. Statist.*, May 1989, *71*(2), pp. 325–31.

——— and Modigliani, Franco. Coupon and Tax Effects on New and Seasoned Bond Yields and the Measurement of the Cost of Debt Capital. In *Modigliani, F., Vol. 5*, 1989, *1979*, pp. 371–92.

——— and Pound, John. Survey Evidence on Diffusion of Interest and Information among Investors. *J. Econ. Behav. Organ.*, August 1989, *12*(1), pp. 47–66.

Shilling, James D. and Hendershott, Patric H. The Impact of the Agencies on Conventional Fixed-Rate Mortgage Yields. *J. Real Estate Finance Econ.*, June 1989, *2*(2), pp. 101–15.

——— and Hendershott, Patric H. Reforming Conforming Loan Limits: The Impact on Thrift Earnings and Taxpayer Outlays. *J. Finan. Services Res.*, December 1989, *3*(4), pp. 311–31.

———; Sirmans, C. F. and Benjamin, John D. Flood Insurance, Wealth Redistribution, and Urban Property Values. *J. Urban Econ.*, July 1989, *26*(1), pp. 43–53.

Shilling, Jon. The Baker Plan and Brady Reformulation: An Evaluation: Comment. In *Husain, I. and Diwan, I., eds.*, 1989, pp. 193–96.

Shim, Sangdal and Eun, Cheol S. International Transmission of Stock Market Movements. *J. Finan. Quant. Anal.*, June 1989, *24*(2), pp. 241–56.

Shim, Seung-Jin; Akiyama, Yutaka and Torii, Yasuhiko. Effects of Tariff Reductions on Trade in the Asia-Pacific Region. In *Miller, R. E.; Polenske, K. R. and Rose, A. Z., eds.*, 1989, pp. 165–79.

Shimao, Tadao. Institutional Capacity for Disease Research and Control: Tuberculosis. In *Reich, M. R. and Marui, E., eds.*, 1989, pp. 58–75.

Shimko, David C. The Equilibrium Valuation of Risky Discrete Cash Flows in Continuous Time. *J. Finance*, December 1989, *44*(5), pp. 1357–83.

Shimomura, Koji and Kemp, Murray C. A Neglected Corner: Labor Unions and the Pattern of International Trade. In *Feiwel, G. R., ed. (II)*, 1989, pp. 774–90.

Shimono, Keiko and Amemiya, Takeshi. An Application of Nested Logit Models to the Labor Supply of the Elderly. *Econ. Stud. Quart.*, March 1989, *40*(1), pp. 14–22.

Shin, Eui-Hang and Chang, Kyung-Sup. Intra- and Intersectoral Processes of Wage Growth: An Examination of Wage Growth Dynamics and Contexts. *Soc. Sci. Quart.*, June 1989, *70*(2), pp. 323–40.

Shin, Jeong-Shik. Effects of Oil Price Changes on the Korean Economy. In *James, W. E., ed.*, 1989, pp. 113–21.

Shin, Kwang-Shik. Information, Transaction Costs, and the Organization of Distribution: The Case of Japan's General Trading Companies. *J. Japanese Int. Economies*, September 1989, *3*(3), pp. 292–307.

Shin, M. J. and Tabucanon, M. T. A Multicriterion Optimization Model for Industrial Promotion: The Case of Korea. In *Lockett, A. G. and Islei, G., eds.*, 1989, pp. 275–86.

Shin, Mansoo; Negandhi, Anant R. and Serapio, Manuel G., Jr. Multinationals and Newly Industrialized Countries: Strategies, Environmental Imperatives, and Practices: Introduction: Multinationals in the Twenty-first Century. In *Negandhi, A. R.*, *ed.*, 1989, pp. 1–8.

Shinjo, Koji and Doi, Noriyuki. Welfare Loss Calculation for Japanese Industries. *Int. J. Ind. Organ.*, June 1989, 7(2), pp. 243–56.

Shinkai, Yoichi. On the International Coordination of Macro Policies. *Econ. Stud. Quart.*, March 1989, 40(1), pp. 1–13.

Shinn, Christine H. Universities, Education and the National Economy: Setting the Scene: Whose University? In *Stephens, M. D.*, *ed.*, 1989, pp. 3–25.

Shinnear, Reuel, et al. Estimation of the Economic Rate of Return for Industrial Companies. *J. Bus.*, July 1989, 62(3), pp. 417–45.

Shinohara, Miyohei. Global Adjustment and the Future of Asian-Pacific Economies. In *Shinohara, M. and Lo, F.*, *eds.*, 1989, pp. 1–14.

_____ **and Lo, Fu-chen.** Global Adjustment and the Future of Asian-Pacific Economy: Introduction: An Overview of Issues. In *Shinohara, M. and Lo, F.*, *eds.*, 1989, pp. ix–xxi.

Shionoya, Yuichi. The Schumpeter Family in Třešť. *Hitotsubashi J. Econ.*, December 1989, 30(2), pp. 157–66.

Shipp, Stephanie; Brown, Gregory and Jacobs, Eva. Families of Working Wives Spending More on Services and Nondurables. *Mon. Lab. Rev.*, February 1989, 112(2), pp. 15–23.

Shirakawa, Hiromichi. Bond Futures Market in Japan—Its Structure and Some Empirical Tests. *Bank Japan Monet. Econ. Stud.*, April 1989, 7(1), pp. 131–58.

Shirk, Susan. The Political Economy of Chinese Industrial Reform. In *Nee, V. and Stark, D.*, *eds.*, 1989, pp. 328–62.

Shirom, Arie. Toward a Diagnostic Framework of Power in Union-Management Relationships. In *Barbash, J. and Barbash, K.*, *eds.*, 1989, pp. 226–40.

Shironin, V. M. and Aven, Petr O. The Reform of the Economic Mechanism: The Realism of the Projected Transformations. In *Jones, A. and Moskoff, W.*, *eds.*, 1989, 1988, pp. 251–66.

Shishkin, V. A. Soviet Oil Exports between the Two World Wars. In *Ferrier, R. W. and Fursenko, A.*, *eds.*, 1989, pp. 74–82.

Shishkov, Iu. V. *Perestroika* and the Phantom of Convergence. *Prob. Econ.*, November 1989, 32(7), pp. 6–28.

Shitovitz, Benyamin. The Bargaining Set and the Core in Mixed Markets with Atoms and an Atomless Sector. *J. Math. Econ.*, 1989, 18(4), pp. 377–83.

_____; **Spiegel, M. and Weber, Shlomo.** 'Top of the Line' Quality as an Optimal Solution for a Multi-quality Monopolist. *Europ. Econ. Rev.*, October 1989, 33(8), pp. 1641–52.

Shkaratan, O.; Koroteeva, V. and Perepelkin, L. From Bureaucratic Centralism to Economic Integration of Sovereign Republics. *Prob. Econ.*, July 1989, 32(3), pp. 36–56.

Shkredov, Vladimir P. Socialism and Property. *Prob. Econ.*, April 1989, 31(12), pp. 6–19.

Shkurti, William J. and Winefordner, Darrell. The Politics of State Revenue Forecasting in Ohio, 1984–1987: A Case Study and Research Implications. *Int. J. Forecasting*, 1989, 5(3), pp. 361–71.

Shleifer, Andrei and Vishny, Robert W. Management Entrenchment: The Case of Manager-Specific Investments. *J. Finan. Econ.*, November 1989, 25(1), pp. 123–39.

_____; **Vishny, Robert W. and Morck, Randall.** Alternative Mechanisms for Corporate Control. *Amer. Econ. Rev.*, September 1989, 79(4), pp. 842–52.

_____; **Vishny, Robert W. and Murphy, Kevin M.** Building Blocks of Market Clearing Business Cycle Models. In *Blanchard, O. J. and Fischer, S.*, *eds.*, 1989, pp. 247–87.

_____; **Vishny, Robert W. and Murphy, Kevin M.** Income Distribution, Market Size, and Industrialization. *Quart. J. Econ.*, August 1989, 104(3), pp. 537–64.

_____; **Vishny, Robert W. and Murphy, Kevin M.** Industrialization and the Big Push. *J. Polit. Econ.*, October 1989, 97(5), pp. 1003–26.

Shmelev, Nikolai. Economics and Common Sense. *Prob. Econ.*, March 1989, 31(11), pp. 58–67.

_____. Economics and Common Sense. In *Jones, A. and Moskoff, W.*, *eds.*, 1989, 1989, pp. 267–76.

_____. New Anxieties. *Prob. Econ.*, January 1989, 31(9), pp. 6–38.

Shoemaker, Robbin. Agricultural Land Values and Rents under the Conservation Reserve Program. *Land Econ.*, May 1989, 65(2), pp. 131–37.

Shogren, Jason F. Fairness in Bargaining Requires a Context: An Experimental Examination of Loyalty. *Econ. Letters*, December 1989, 31(4), pp. 319–23.

_____ **and d'Arge, Ralph C.** Non-market Asset Prices: A Comparison of Three Valuation Approaches. In *Folmer, H. and van Ierland, E.*, *eds.*, 1989, pp. 15–36.

Shojai, Siamack. Nobel Laureates in Economic Sciences: A Biographical Dictionary: Gerard Debreu: 1983. In *Katz, B. S.*, *ed.*, 1989, pp. 40–52.

_____. Optimal Oil Production in OPEC Members under Macroeconomic Constraints. *J. Econ. Devel.*, June 1989, 14(1), pp. 135–48.

Shokhin, A.; Guzanova, A. and Liberman, L. Prices through the Eyes of the Population. *Prob. Econ.*, June 1989, 32(2), pp. 6–13.

Shokkaert, E. and Overlaet, B. Moral Intuitions and Economic Models of Distributive Justice. *Soc. Choice Welfare*, January 1989, 6(1), pp. 19–31.

Shone, Ronald. Software for Solving Equations: EUREKA: THE SOLVER, TK SOLVER PLUS and MathCAD. *J. Econ. Surveys*, 1989, 3(1), pp. 83–95.

Shonkwiler, J. S.; Reynolds, John E. and Moss, Charles B. Government Payments to Farmers and Real Agricultural Asset Values in the 1980s. *Southern J. Agr. Econ.*, December 1989, *21*(2), pp. 139–53.

Shooshan, Harry M., III. Reforming Regulation of Local Exchange Carriers or It *Is* Broke, So Let's Fix It! In *National Economic Research Associates*, 1989, pp. 181–89.

Shopov, Dimiter. On the Relationship of Wages with Labour Productivity and Intensity. In *Bulgarian Academy of Sciences, Institute of Economics*, 1989, pp. 172–83.

Shorey, John. The Consequences of Job Search Requirements on Unemployment Benefits. *Scot. J. Polit. Econ.*, February 1989, *36*(1), pp. 36–58.

Shorrocks, A. F. and Davies, James B. Optimal Grouping of Income and Wealth Data. *J. Econometrics*, September 1989, *42*(1), pp. 97–108.

Short, Brian. The De-industrialisation Process: A Case Study of the Weald, 1600–1850. In *Hudson, P., ed.*, 1989, pp. 156–74.

Short, Pamela Farley and Taylor, Amy K. Premiums, Benefits, and Employee Choice of Health Insurance Options. *J. Health Econ.*, December 1989, *8*(3), pp. 293–311.

Shortle, James S. and McSweeny, William T. Stochastic Technology and Prices: Comment. *Amer. J. Agr. Econ.*, August 1989, *71*(3), pp. 813–16.

Shoup, Carl S. Rules for Distributing a Free Government Service among Areas of a City. *Nat. Tax J.*, June 1989, *42*(2), pp. 103–21.

Shove, G. F. A Review of *The Theory of Wages* by J. R. Hicks. In *Wood, J. C. and Woods, R. N., eds., Vol. 1*, 1989, *1933*, pp. 1–11.

Shoven, John B. The Japanese Tax Reform and the Effective Rate of Tax on Japanese Corporate Investments. In *Summers, L. H., ed.*, 1989, pp. 97–115.

_____. The Wealth and Poverty of Widows: Assets before and after the Husband's Death: Comment. In *Wise, D. A., ed.*, 1989, pp. 199–200.

_____ **and Bagwell, Laurie Simon.** Cash Distributions to Shareholders. *J. Econ. Perspectives*, Summer 1989, *3*(3), pp. 129–40.

_____; **Spivak, Avia and Kotlikoff, Laurence J.** Annuity Insurance, Savings, and Inequality. In *Kotlikoff, L. J.*, 1989, pp. 109–40.

_____; **Sundberg, Jeffrey O. and Bunker, John P.** The Social Security Cost of Smoking. In *Wise, D. A., ed.*, 1989, pp. 231–50.

Shrestha, Keshab. Empirical Measurement of an Inflation Index: A Multiple-Indicators Distributed-Lag Approach. *J. Bus. Econ. Statist.*, April 1989, *7*(2), pp. 219–25.

Shrestha, Rajendra B.; Gopalakrishnan, Chennat and Khaleghi, Gholam H. Energy–Non-energy Input Substitution in U.S. Agriculture: Some Findings. *Appl. Econ.*, May 1989, *21*(5), pp. 673–79.

Shrestha, Ram M. and Clarke, Harry R. Traditional Energy Programs and the Theory of Open Access Forest Resources. *Energy J.*, July 1989, *10*(3), pp. 139–55.

_____ **and Clarke, Harry R.** Traditional Energy

Programs with an Open Access Forest Resource: Policy Implications. *Energy J.*, October 1989, *10*(4), pp. 45–57.

Shridharan, L. Warehousing Requirements for Fertiliser: 2000 AD. *Margin*, Oct. 1989–March 1990, *22*(1–2), pp. 57–79.

Shrieves, Ronald E. and Dahl, Drew. Evidence on the Role of Holding Company Acquisitions in the Management of Bank Capital. *J. Finan. Services Res.*, February 1989, *2*(1), pp. 21–37.

Shriver, Donald W., Jr. Ethical Discipline and Religious Hope in the Investment Industry. In *Williams, O. F.; Reilly, F. K. and Houck, J. W., eds.*, 1989, pp. 233–50.

Shriver, Keith A. and Dugan, Michael T. The Effects of Estimation Period, Industry, and Proxy on the Calculation of the Degree of Operating Leverage. *Financial Rev.*, February 1989, *24*(1), pp. 109–22.

_____ **and Dugan, Michael T.** FASB Statement 33 Data Base: Compositional Characteristics, Potential Uses, and Sources of Measurement Error. *J. Econ. Soc. Meas.*, 1989, *15*(1), pp. 27–36.

Shropshire, William O. Who Is My Neighbour? *Int. J. Soc. Econ.*, 1989, *16*(5), pp. 18–31.

Shubik, Martin and Verkerke, J. Hoult. Open Questions in Defense Economics and Economic Warfare. *J. Conflict Resolution*, September 1989, *33*(3), pp. 480–99.

_____ **and Yao, Shuntian.** Gold, Liquidity and Secured Loans in a Multistage Economy: Part I: Gold as Money. *J. Econ. (Z. Nationalökon.)*, 1989, *49*(3), pp. 245–77.

Shuchman, Carol. Family Transfers and Household Living Arrangements among the Elderly. In *Goldscheider, F. K. and Goldscheider, C., eds.*, 1989, pp. 127–46.

Shucksmith, D. M., et al. Pluriactivity, Farm Structures and Rural Change. *J. Agr. Econ.*, September 1989, *40*(3), pp. 345–60.

Shugart, Herman H. and Batie, Sandra S. The Biological Consequences of Climate Changes: An Ecological and Economic Assessment. In *Rosenberg, N. J., et al., eds.*, 1989, pp. 121–31.

Shughart, William F., II. Antitrust Policy in the Reagan Administration: Pyrrhic Victories? In *Meiners, R. E. and Yandle, B., eds.*, 1989, pp. 89–103.

_____ **and Boudreaux, Donald J.** The Effects of Monetary Instability on the Extent of Vertical Integration. *Atlantic Econ. J.*, June 1989, *17*(2), pp. 1–10.

_____ **and Kimenyi, Mwangi S.** Political Successions and the Growth of Government. *Public Choice*, August 1989, *62*(2), pp. 173–79.

_____; **Tollison, Robert D. and Anderson, Gary M.** On the Incentives of Judges to Enforce Legislative Wealth Transfers. *J. Law Econ.*, April 1989, *32*(1), pp. 215–28.

_____; **Tollison, Robert D. and Anderson, Gary M.** Political Entry Barriers and Tax Incidence: The Political Economy of Sales and Excise Taxes. *Public Finance*, 1989, *44*(1), pp. 8–18.

_____; **Tollison, Robert D. and Fleisher, Arthur**

A., III. Ownership Structure in Professional Sports. In *Zerbe, R. O., ed.*, 1989, pp. 71–75.

_____; **Tollison, Robert D. and Higgins, Richard S.** Price Leadership with Incomplete Information. *J. Econ. Behav. Organ.*, May 1989, *11*(3), pp. 423–29.

Shukla, Jagadish. Predictability of Weather and Climate: Long-Range Forecasting of Indian Monsoons. In *Oram, P. A., et al.*, 1989, pp. 305–10.

Shula, Emmanuel W. C. and Nyirongo, Griffin K. Contract Farming and Smallholder Outgrower Schemes in Zambia. *Eastern Afr. Econ. Rev.*, Special Issue, August 1989, pp. 83–96.

Shull, Bernard. Provisional Markets, Relevant Markets and Banking Markets: The Justice Department's Merger Guidelines in Wise County, Virginia. *Antitrust Bull.*, Summer 1989, *34*(2), pp. 411–28.

Shulman, Steven. Controversies in the Marxian Analysis of Racial Discrimination. *Rev. Radical Polit. Econ.*, Winter 1989, *21*(4), pp. 73–80.

_____. A Critique of the Declining Discrimination Hypothesis. In *Shulman, S. and Darity, W., Jr., eds.*, 1989, pp. 126–50.

_____. The Natural Rate of Unemployment: Concept and Critique. *J. Post Keynesian Econ.*, Summer 1989, *11*(4), pp. 509–21.

_____ and **Darity, William A., Jr.** The Question of Discrimination: Racial Inequality in the U.S. Labor Market: Introduction. In *Shulman, S. and Darity, W., Jr., eds.*, 1989, pp. 1–6.

Shumway, C. Richard. Testing Structure and Behavior with First- and Second-Order Taylor Series Expansions. *Can. J. Agr. Econ.*, March 1989, *37*(1), pp. 95–109.

_____ and **Howard, Wayne H.** Technical Change and Applications of Dynamic Duality to Agriculture: Reply. *Amer. J. Agr. Econ.*, August 1989, *71*(3), pp. 805.

Shupe, Steven J.; Weatherford, Gary D. and Checchio, Elizabeth. Western Water Rights: The Era of Reallocation. *Natural Res. J.*, Spring 1989, *29*(2), pp. 413–34.

Shuttleworth, Graham. Policies in Transition: Lessons from Madagascar. *World Devel.*, March 1989, *17*(3), pp. 397–408.

Shuzō, Teruoka. Land Reform and Postwar Japanese Capitalism. In *Morris-Suzuki, T. and Seiyama, T., eds.*, 1989, pp. 74–104.

Shy, Oz. External Effects and Pareto Inferior Trade. *Southern Econ. J.*, July 1989, *56*(1), pp. 56–63.

Shyy, Gang. Bullish or Bearish: A Bayesian Dichotomous Model to Forecast Turning Points in the Foreign Exchange Market. *J. Econ. Bus.*, February 1989, *41*(1), pp. 49–60.

_____. Gambler's Ruin and Optimal Stop Loss Strategy. *J. Futures Markets*, December 1989, *9*(6), pp. 565–71.

Siahaan, Pulo and Daroesman, Ruth. West Kalimantan: Uneven Development? In *Hill, H., ed.*, 1989, pp. 528–47.

Sibert, Anne. The Risk Premium in the Foreign Exchange Market. *J. Money, Credit, Banking*, February 1989, *21*(1), pp. 49–65.

Sibley, David S. Asymmetric Information, Incentives and Price-Cap Regulation. *Rand J. Econ.*, Autumn 1989, *20*(3), pp. 392–404.

_____ and **Panzar, John C.** Optimal Two-Part Tariffs for Inputs: The Case of Imperfect Competition. *J. Public Econ.*, November 1989, *40*(2), pp. 237–49.

Sichel, Daniel E. Are Business Cycles Asymmetric? A Correction. *J. Polit. Econ.*, October 1989, *97*(5), pp. 1255–60.

Sichel, Werner. The State of Economic Science: Views of Six Nobel Laureates: Introduction. In *Sichel, W., ed.*, 1989, pp. 1–8.

Sicilia, David B. and Dyer, Davis. From Commodity to Specialty Chemicals: Cellulose Products and Naval Stores at the Hercules Powder Company, 1919–1939. In *Hausman, W. J., ed.*, 1989, pp. 59–71.

Sick, Gordon A. Multiperiod Risky Project Valuation: A Mean–Covariance Certainty-Equivalent Approach. In *Lee, C. F., ed.*, 1989, pp. 1–36.

_____; **Zechner, Josef and Maksimovic, Vojislav.** Forward Markets, Stock Markets, and the Theory of the Firm: Comment. *J. Finance*, June 1989, *44*(2), pp. 525–28.

Sickles, Robin C. An Analysis of Simultaneous Limited Dependent Variable Models and Some Nonstandard Cases. In *Mariano, R. S.; Lim, K. S. and Ling, K. D., eds.*, 1989, pp. 85–122.

Sicsic, Pierre. Estimation du stock de monnaie métallique en France à la fin du XIXᵉ siècle. (Estimation of Metal Money in France at the End of the XIXth Century. With English summary.) *Revue Écon.*, July 1989, *40*(4), pp. 709–36.

Sicular, Terry. China: Food Pricing under Socialism. In *Sicular, T., ed.*, 1989, pp. 243–88.

_____. Food Price Policy in Asia: Introduction. In *Sicular, T., ed.*, 1989, pp. 1–21.

_____. Structure and Motifs in the Food Price Policy Story: Conclusion. In *Sicular, T., ed.*, 1989, pp. 289–95.

Siddharthan, N. S. Impact of Import Liberalisation on Export Intensities: A Study of the Indian Private Corporate Sector. *Indian Econ. J.*, Oct.–Dec. 1989, *37*(2), pp. 103–11.

Siddiq, E. A. and Momtaz, A. Extending Rice Cultivation to New Areas in Egypt. In *International Rice Research Institute*, 1989, pp. 275–90.

Siddiqi, Muhammad Yasin Mazhar. Role of Booty in the Economy during the Prophet's Time. *J. King Abdulaziz Univ.: Islamic Econ.*, 1989, *1*, pp. 83–116.

Siddiqui, Anjum. The Causal Relation between Money and Inflation in a Developing Economy. *Int. Econ. J.*, Summer 1989, *3*(2), pp. 79–96.

Siddiqui, Shamim Ahmad and Zaman, Asad. Investment and Income Distribution Pattern under Musharka Finance: The Certainty Case.

Pakistan J. Appl. Econ., Summer 1989, *8*(1), pp. 1–30.

———— **and Zaman, Asad.** Investment and Income Distribution Patterns under Musharka Finance: The Uncertainty Case. *Pakistan J. Appl. Econ.*, Summer 1989, *8*(1), pp. 31–71.

Sidhu, J. S. and Sidhu, Rajinder S. Demand for and Productivity of Major Plant Nutrients and Policy Implications for Their Balanced Use in India. *Indian J. Quant. Econ.*, 1989, *5*(1), pp. 1–11.

Sidhu, Rajinder S. and Sidhu, J. S. Demand for and Productivity of Major Plant Nutrients and Policy Implications for Their Balanced Use in India. *Indian J. Quant. Econ.*, 1989, *5*(1), pp. 1–11.

Siebeck, Karin and Reimers, Hans-Eggert. Ein einfaches Modell kontinuierlicher Anpassung für den Arbeits- und Gütermarkt—Einige empirische Befunde. (A Simple Continuous Time Adjustment Model for the Labour and the Goods Market—Some Empirical Evidence. With English summary.) *Ifo-Studien*, 1989, *35*(1), pp. 27–52.

Siebert, Horst. The Half and the Full Debt Cycle. *Weltwirtsch. Arch.*, 1989, *125*(2), pp. 217–29.

————. Institutional Arrangements for Natural Resources. In *Vosgerau, H.-J., ed.*, 1989, pp. 333–65.

————. Perspektiven zur Vollendung des europäischen Binnenmarktes. (With English summary.) *Kyklos*, 1989, *42*(2), pp. 181–201.

———— **and Long, Ngo Van.** Optimal Foreign Borrowing: The Impact of the Planning Horizon on the Half and Full Debt Cycle. *J. Econ. (Z. Nationalökon.)*, 1989, *49*(3), pp. 279–97.

Siebert, W. Stanley. Inequality of Opportunity: An Analysis Based on the Microeconomics of the Family. In *Drago, R. and Perlman, R., eds.*, 1989, pp. 177–97.

Siedentopf, Heinrich and König, Klaus. Privatisation: Singapore's Experience in Perspective: An International Perspective II: Privatisation and Institutional Modernisation in Asia and Europe. In *Thynne, I. and Ariff, M., eds.*, 1989, pp. 167–86.

Siedmann, Daniel J. The Real Effects of Nominal Price Rigidity. *Europ. Econ. Rev.*, December 1989, *33*(9), pp. 1831–38.

Siegan, Bernard H. Economic Liberties and the Constitution. *Bus. Econ.*, January 1989, *24*(1), pp. 23–28.

Siegel, Daniel R.; Israel, Ronen and Ofer, Aharon R. The Information Content of Equity-for-Debt Swaps: An Investigation of Analyst Forecasts of Firm Cash Flows. *J. Finan. Econ.*, December 1989, *25*(2), pp. 349–70.

Siegenthaler, Hansjörg. Organization, Ideology and the Free Rider Problem. *J. Inst. Theoretical Econ.*, March 1989, *145*(1), pp. 215–31.

Siegers, Jacques J.; van Mourik, Aad and Poot, Jacques. Trends in Occupational Segregation of Women and Men in New Zealand: Some New Evidence. *New Zealand Econ. Pap.*, 1989, *23*, pp. 29–50.

Siegmann, Heinrich. Enhancing Conventional

Stability in Europe. In *Altmann, J. and Rotblat, J., eds.*, 1989, pp. 131–38.

Sienknecht, Hans-Peter and Hansen, Gerd. A Comparison of Demand Systems—A Case Study for West Germany. *Empirical Econ.*, 1989, *14*(1), pp. 43–61.

Sigel, Louis T. Economic Reform and the Open Policy in China: Commentary. In *Zerby, J., ed.*, 1989, pp. 59–71.

Sigelman, Lee. Question-Order Effects on Presidential Popularity. In *Singer, E. and Presser, S., eds.*, 1989, *1981*, pp. 142–50.

———— **and Welch, Susan.** A Black Gender Gap? *Soc. Sci. Quart.*, March 1989, *70*(1), pp. 120–33.

Signorino, Guido. Trasformazione dei dati e verifica della stabilità strutturale in modelli con errori AR(1). (Transforming Data and Testing for Structural Change in Models with AR(1) Errors. With English summary.) *Rivista Int. Sci. Econ. Com.*, March 1989, *36*(3), pp. 233–47.

Sihag, Balbir S. and McDonough, Carol C. Shift-Share Analysis: The International Dimension. *Growth Change*, Summer 1989, *20*(3), pp. 80–88.

Sijben, Jac J. External Disequilibria and the Burden of Economic Adjustment in the World Economy. In *Sijben, J. J., ed.*, 1989, pp. 1–13.

Sikdar, Soumyen. Deficit Financing, Administered Prices and Indirect Taxation: A Macroeconomic Exercise. In *Rakshit, M., ed.*, 1989, pp. 94–110.

Siklos, Pierre L. The End of the Hungarian Hyperinflation of 1945–1946. *J. Money, Credit, Banking*, May 1989, *21*(2), pp. 135–47.

————. Unit Root Behavior in Velocity: Cross-Country Tests Using Recursive Estimation. *Econ. Letters*, September 1989, *30*(3), pp. 231–36.

———— **and Raj, Baldev.** The Role of Fiscal Policy in the St. Louis Model: Nonparametric Estimates for a Small Open Economy. In *Ullah, A., ed.*, 1989, *1988*, pp. 47–64.

Šilac, Mirta. Otplata zajma varijabilnim anuitetima. (Periodical Payments by Variable Amounts. With English summary.) *Econ. Anal. Workers' Manage.*, 1989, *23*(2), pp. 185–98.

Silagi, Michael. Henry George and Europe: As Dissident Economist and Path-Breaking Philosopher, He Was a Catalyst for British Social Reform. *Amer. J. Econ. Sociology*, January 1989, *48*(1), pp. 113–22.

Silber, Jacques G. Factor Components, Population Subgroups and the Computation of the Gini Index of Inequality. *Rev. Econ. Statist.*, February 1989, *71*(1), pp. 107–15.

————. On the Measurement of Employment Segregation. *Econ. Letters*, September 1989, *30*(3), pp. 237–43.

———— **and Berrebi, Z. M.** Deprivation, the Gini Index of Inequality and the Flatness of an Income Distribution. *Math. Soc. Sci.*, December 1989, *18*(3), pp. 229–37.

Silberman, Jonathan and Klock, Mark. The Behavior of Respondents in Contingent Valuation: Evidence on Starting Bids. *J. Behav. Econ.*, Spring 1989, *18*(1), pp. 51–60.

Silberstein, Adriana R. and Jacobs, Curtis A. Symptoms of Repeated Interview Effects in the Consumer Expenditure Interview Survey. In *Kasprzyk, D., et al., eds.*, 1989, pp. 289–303.

Silk, Leonard. Issues in International Banking and Finance. In *Kaushik, S. K., ed.*, 1989, pp. xi–xviii.

_____. Yes, Virginia, Institutionalists Do Exist. *J. Post Keynesian Econ.*, Fall 1989, *12*(1), pp. 3–9.

da Silva, Armindo. The Portuguese Experience of European Integration—A Quantitative Assessment of the Effects of EFTA and EEC Tariff Preferences. In *Yannopoulos, G. N., ed.*, 1989, pp. 87–143.

de Silva, Charles and Crichton, Noel. Financial Development and Economic Growth: Trinidad and Tobago, 1973–1987. *Soc. Econ. Stud.*, December 1989, *38*(4), pp. 133–64.

Silva-Echenique, Julio. Quasi-vertical Integration and Rate-of-Return Regulation. *Can. J. Econ.*, November 1989, *22*(4), pp. 852–66.

da Silva, Eivany Antonio. The New Income Tax and the Treaties to Prevent Double Taxation: Brazil. *Bull. Int. Fiscal Doc.*, Aug.–Sept. 1989, *43*(8–9), pp. 399–402.

Silva-Herzog, Jesús. Third World Debt: The Next Phase: Concluding Impressions. In *Fried, E. R. and Trezise, P. H., eds.*, 1989, pp. 97–99.

da Silva Martins, Ives Gandra. Inflation and Taxation: Brazil. *Bull. Int. Fiscal Doc.*, Aug.–Sept. 1989, *43*(8–9), pp. 403–07.

Silver, Brian D. and Anderson, Barbara A. The Changing Shape of Soviet Mortality, 1958–1985: An Evaluation of Old and New Evidence. *Population Stud.*, July 1989, *43*(2), pp. 243–65.

_____ **and Anderson, Barbara A.** Demographic Sources of the Changing Ethnic Composition of the Soviet Union. *Population Devel. Rev.*, December 1989, *15*(4), pp. 609–56.

_____ **and Anderson, Barbara A.** Patterns of Cohort Mortality in the Soviet Population. *Population Devel. Rev.*, September 1989, *15*(3), pp. 471–501.

Silver, J. Lew and Ali, Mukhtar M. Testing Slutsky Symmetry in Systems of Linear Demand Equations. *J. Econometrics*, June 1989, *41*(2), pp. 251–66.

Silver, Jessica Dunsay and Besharov, Douglas J. Rationing Access to Advanced Medical Techniques. In *McLennan, K. and Meyer, J. A., eds.*, 1989, pp. 41–66.

Silver, Mick S. and Lowe, J. F. An Appraisal of the Performance of Manufacturing Industry in Wales. *J. Econ. Stud.*, 1989, *16*(1), pp. 31–46.

_____ **and Mahdavy, Khashayar.** The Measurement of a Nation's Terms of Trade Effect and Real National Disposable Income within a National Accounting Framework. *J. Roy. Statist. Society*, 1989, *152*(1), pp. 87–107.

Silver, Stephen and Sumner, Scott. Real Wages, Employment, and the Phillips Curve. *J. Polit. Econ.*, June 1989, *97*(3), pp. 706–20.

Silverstone, Brian. MacroSolve. *J. Econ. Surveys*, 1989, *3*(2), pp. 171–78.

Silvestre, Geronimo; Smith, Ian R. and Pauly, Daniel. On Development, Fisheries and Dynamite: A Brief Review of Tropical Fisheries Management. *Natural Res. Modeling*, Summer 1989, *3*(3), pp. 307–29.

Silvestre, Joaquim. Who Benefits from Unemployment? In *Feiwel, G. R., ed. (I)*, 1989, pp. 462–81.

_____ **and Mas-Colell, Andreu.** Cost Share Equilibria: A Lindahlian Approach. *J. Econ. Theory*, April 1989, *47*(2), pp. 239–56.

Silvestri, George and Lukasiewicz, John. Projections of Occupational Employment, 1988–2000. *Mon. Lab. Rev.*, November 1989, *112*(11), pp. 42–65.

Silvia, John E. America in Debt: A President's Dilemma. *Challenge*, Jan.–Feb. 1989, *32*(1), pp. 27–34.

_____ **and Whall, Barry.** Home Equity Loans and the Business Cycle. *Bus. Econ.*, January 1989, *24*(1), pp. 43–45.

Simandjuntak, Djisman S. Survey of Recent Developments. *Bull. Indonesian Econ. Stud.*, April 1989, *25*(1), pp. 3–30.

Simar, Léopold and Deprins, Dominique. Estimating Technical Inefficiencies with Correction for Environmental Conditions: With an Application to Railway Companies. *Ann. Pub. Coop. Econ.*, 1989, *60*(1), pp. 81–102.

_____ **and Deprins, Dominique.** Estimation de frontières déterministes avec facteurs exogènes d'inefficacité. (Estimating Deterministic Frontier Functions with Exogeneous Factors for the Inefficiency. With English summary.) *Ann. Écon. Statist.*, April–June 1989, (14), pp. 117–50.

Simeone, Bruno and Hammer, Peter L. Quadratic Functions of Binary Variables. In *Simeone, B., ed.*, 1989, pp. 1–56.

Simmons, Peter. Bad Luck and Fixed Costs in Personal Bankruptcies. *Econ. J.*, March 1989, *99*(394), pp. 92–107.

Simmons, Richard P. Ingredients for Success in a Globally Competitive Environment. In *Ahlbrandt, R. S., Jr., ed.*, 1989, pp. 12–16.

Simms, Richard A. Equitable Apportionment—Priorities and New Uses. *Natural Res. J.*, Spring 1989, *29*(2), pp. 549–63.

Simnett, Richard E. Contestable Markets and Telecommunications. In *Crew, M. A., ed.*, 1989, pp. 127–42.

Simnett, Roger and Trotman, Ken. Auditor versus Model: Information Choice and Information Processing. *Accounting Rev.*, July 1989, *64*(3), pp. 514–28.

Simon, András. Analysis and Forecasts of Growth of the Hungarian Economy. In *Krelle, W., ed.*, 1989, pp. 477–86.

_____. A Search Model of Shortages. *Acta Oecon.*, 1989, *41*(1–2), pp. 137–56.

Simon, Carl P. Some Fine-Tuning for Dominant

Diagonal Matrices. *Econ. Letters*, September 1989, *30*(3), pp. 217–21.

Simon, Carol J. The Effect of the 1933 Securities Act on Investor Information and the Performance of New Issues. *Amer. Econ. Rev.*, June 1989, *79*(3), pp. 295–318.

Simon, Curtis J.; Warner, John T. and Diamond, Charles A. Evidence on the Fit of the Log-Linear Income Model versus a General Statistical Specification. *Econ. Letters*, December 1989, *31*(3), pp. 293–98.

Simon, David. Rural–Urban Interaction and Development in Southern Africa: The Implications of Reduced Labour Migration. In *[Mountjoy, A. B.]*, 1989, pp. 141–68.

Simon, David P. Expectations and Risk in the Treasury Bill Market: An Instrumental Variables Approach. *J. Finan. Quant. Anal.*, September 1989, *24*(3), pp. 357–65.

———. The Rationality of Federal Funds Rate Expectations: Evidence from a Survey: A Note. *J. Money, Credit, Banking*, August 1989, *21*(3), pp. 388–93.

Simon, Herbert A. The State of Economic Science: Views of Six Nobel Laureates: Dr. Herbert A. Simon. In *Sichel, W., ed.*, 1989, pp. 97–110.

Simon, Hermann. Die Zeit als strategischer Erfolgsfaktor. (With English summary.) *Z. Betriebswirtschaft*, January 1989, *59*(1), pp. 70–93.

Simon, Julian L. Lebensraum: Paradoxically, Population Growth May Eventually End Wars. *J. Conflict Resolution*, March 1989, *33*(1), pp. 164–80.

———. On Aggregate Empirical Studies Relating Population Variables to Economic Development. *Population Devel. Rev.*, June 1989, *15*(2), pp. 323–32.

———. The Positive Worth of Waste: A Reply. *Soc. Sci. Quart.*, December 1989, *70*(4), pp. 898–91.

———. Robinson Crusoe Was Not Mainly a Resource Allocator. *Soc. Sci. Quart.*, June 1989, *70*(2), pp. 471–78.

——— **and Levy, Haim.** A Generalization That Makes Useful the Dorfman–Steiner Theorem with Respect to Advertising. *Managerial Dec. Econ.*, March 1989, *10*(1), pp. 85–87.

——— **and Sullivan, Richard J.** Population Size, Knowledge Stock, and Other Determinants of Agricultural Publication and Patenting: England, 1541–1850. *Exploration Econ. Hist.*, January 1989, *26*(1), pp. 21–44.

Simon, Jürgen and Finsinger, Jörg. An Economic Assessment of the EC Product Liability Directive and the Product Liability Law of the Federal Republic of Germany. In *Faure, M. and Van den Bergh, R., eds.*, 1989, pp. 185–214.

Simon, Leo K. and Stinchcombe, Maxwell B. Extensive Form Games in Continuous Time: Pure Strategies. *Econometrica*, September 1989, *57*(5), pp. 1171–1214.

Simon, Leonard S. Alternative Strategies for Success: Panel Presentation. In *Federal Home Loan Bank of San Francisco*, 1989, pp. 115–18.

Simon, Roy D., Jr. Fee Sharing between Lawyers and Public Interest Groups. *Yale Law J.*, April 1989, *98*(6), pp. 1069–1133.

Simonis, Udo Ernst. Development and Environment: A Plea for Harmonization. In *Wohlmuth, K., ed.*, 1989, pp. 209–27.

——— **and Leipert, Christian.** Environmental Protection Expenditures: The German Example. *Rivista Int. Sci. Econ. Com.*, March 1989, *36*(3), pp. 255–70.

Simonovits, András. Hidden Investment Cycles in Socialist Economies. *Scand. J. Econ.*, 1989, *91*(3), pp. 583–97.

———. Keynesian Issues and Economic Theory: Comment. *Scand. J. Econ.*, 1989, *91*(2), pp. 301–06.

Simons, Fisher. An Agenda for Tax Policy. In *Crane, E. H. and Boaz, D.*, 1989, pp. 31–53.

Simons, Joseph J. and Harris, Barry C. Focusing Market Definition: How Much Substitution Is Necessary? In *Zerbe, R. O., ed.*, 1989, pp. 207–26.

Simons, Katerina. Measuring Credit Risk in Interest Rate Swaps. *New Eng. Econ. Rev.*, Nov.–Dec. 1989, pp. 29–38.

Simonson, Itamar. Choice Based on Reasons: The Case of Attraction and Compromise Effects. *J. Cons. Res.*, September 1989, *16*(2), pp. 158–74.

Simowitz, Roslyn and Price, Barry. In Defense of Government Regulation. In *Tool, M. R. and Samuels, W. J., eds. (III)*, 1989, *1986*, pp. 263–75.

Simpson, Douglas G. Hellinger Deviance Tests: Efficiency, Breakdown Points, and Examples. *J. Amer. Statist. Assoc.*, March 1989, *84*(405), pp. 107–13.

Simpson, John. The International Political System and the Developing World: A View from the North. In *Thomas, C. and Saravanamuttu, P., eds.*, 1989, pp. 29–42.

Simpson, Liv Hobbelstad. Computerised Input–Output Tables Integrated with National Accounts for Developing Countries. In *Franz, A. and Rainer, N., eds.*, 1989, pp. 257–79.

Simpson, Margaret and Pakes, Ariel. Patent Renewal Data. *Brookings Pap. Econ. Act.*, Microeconomics, 1989, pp. 331–401.

Simpson, Rick; Smeeding, Timothy M. and Rainwater, Lee. Comparative Cross-National Research on Income and Economic Well-Being: The Luxembourg Income Study. *Surv. Curr. Bus.*, March 1989, *69*(3), pp. 62–67.

Simpson, Stephen. School Roll Forecasts: Their Uses, Their Accuracy and Educational Reform: Reply. *J. Roy. Statist. Society*, 1989, *152*(3), pp. 303–04.

———. School Roll Forecasts: Their Uses, Their Accuracy and Educational Reform. *J. Roy. Statist. Society*, 1989, *152*(3), pp. 287–301.

Sims, Christopher A. Models and Their Uses. *Amer. J. Agr. Econ.*, May 1989, *71*(2), pp. 489–94.

———. New Indexes of Coincident and Leading Economic Indicators: Comment. In *Blanch-*

ard, O. J. and Fischer, S., eds., 1989, pp. 394–97.

_____. Output Persistence, Economic Structure, and the Choice of Stabilization Policy: Comments. *Brookings Pap. Econ. Act.*, 1989, (2), pp. 125–29.

_____. What Kind of a Science is Economics? A Review Article on *Causality in Economics* by John R. Hicks. In *Wood, J. C. and Woods, R. N., eds., Vol. 3*, 1989, *1981*, pp. 286–90.

Sims, Geoffrey D. Universities, Education and the National Economy: Setting the Scene: The Universities. In *Stephens, M. D., ed.*, 1989, pp. 26–40.

_____. Universities, Education and the National Economy: Case Studies: Engineering. In *Stephens, M. D., ed.*, 1989, pp. 72–86.

Sinai, Allen and Stokes, Houston H. Money Balances in the Production Function: A Retrospective Look. *Eastern Econ. J.*, Oct.–Dec. 1989, *15*(4), pp. 349–63.

Sinclair, M. Thea and Sutcliffe, Charles. Truncated Income Multipliers and Local Income Generation over Time. *Appl. Econ.*, December 1989, *21*(12), pp. 1621–30.

Sinclair, Peter. Some Reasons Why International Economic Policy Coordination Only Sometimes Pays. *Greek Econ. Rev.*, 1989, *11*(2), pp. 235–56.

Sindelar, Jody and Mullahy, John. Life-Cycle Effects of Alcoholism on Education, Earnings, and Occupation. *Inquiry*, Summer 1989, *26*(2), pp. 272–82.

Singell, Larry D. and Lillydahl, Jane H. Some Alternative Definitions of Youth Unemployment: A Means for Improved Understanding and Policy Formulation. *Amer. J. Econ. Sociology*, October 1989, *48*(4), pp. 457–71.

Singer, Burton. The World Fertility Survey: An Appraisal of Methodology: Comment. *J. Amer. Statist. Assoc.*, September 1989, *84*(407), pp. 771–72.

_____; Manton, Kenneth G. and Berkman, Lisa F. Black/White Differences in Health Status and Mortality among the Elderly. *Demography*, November 1989, *26*(4), pp. 661–78.

Singer, Eleanor; Frankel, Martin R. and Glassman, Marc B. The Effect of Interviewer Characteristics and Expectations on Response. In *Singer, E. and Presser, S., eds.*, 1989, *1983*, pp. 272–87.

Singer, H. W. Food Aid and Structural Adjustment Lending. In *Singer, H. W. and Sharma, S., eds. (I)*, 1989, pp. 239–44.

_____. The World Bank: Human Face or Facelift? Some Comments in the Light of the World Bank's Annual Report. *World Devel.*, August 1989, *17*(8), pp. 1313–16.

_____. The 1980s: A Lost Decade—Development in Reverse? In *Singer, H. W. and Sharma, S., eds. (II)*, 1989, pp. 46–56.

Singer, Paul. Democracy and Inflation, in the Light of the Brazilian Experience. In *Canak, W. L., ed.*, 1989, pp. 31–46.

_____. Inflation and Market as Alternative Sys-

tems of Regulation. In *Davidson, P. and Kregel, J., eds.*, 1989, pp. 230–40.

Singer, S. Fred. How to Trim Oil Imports, Dampen Price Swings. *J. Policy Anal. Manage.*, Winter 1989, *8*(1), pp. 116–19.

_____. VIF Vivit: Reply. *Energy J.*, October 1989, *10*(4), pp. 171–72.

Singh, Ajit. Third World Competition and De-industrialisation in Advanced Countries. *Cambridge J. Econ.*, March 1989, *13*(1), pp. 103–20.

_____. Third World Competition and De-industrialisation in Advanced Countries. In *Lawson, T.; Palma, J. G. and Sender, J., eds.*, 1989, pp. 103–20.

Singh, Harbhajan and Dhesi, Autar Singh. Education, Labour Market Distortions and Relative Earnings of Different Religion-Caste Categories in India (A Case Study of Delhi.) *Can. J. Devel. Stud.*, 1989, *10*(1), pp. 75–89.

Singh, Harinder. Modeling Endogenous Monetary Stock Behavior. A Simultaneous Transfer Function Approach. *Empirical Econ.*, 1989, *14*(4), pp. 291–305.

_____ and Gerber, Jim. On-the-Job Leisure–Income Tradeoffs: A Test of Rational Behavior. *Econ. Letters*, 1989, *29*(1), pp. 91–94.

Singh, J. P. Terms of Trade in Punjab Agriculture. *Indian Econ. Rev.*, July–Dec. 1989, *24*(2), pp. 263–76.

Singh, Jagdip. Determinants of Consumers' Decisions to Seek Third Party Redress: An Empirical Study of Dissatisfied Patients. *J. Cons. Aff.*, Winter 1989, *23*(2), pp. 329–63.

Singh, Manmohan. Development Policy Research: The Task Ahead. In *Fischer, S. and de Tray, D., eds.*, 1989, pp. 11–20.

Singh, Neelam. Trade Behaviour of Firms: An Empirical Study of the Size and Foreign Collaboration Effects. *Indian Econ. Rev.*, Jan.–June 1989, *24*(1), pp. 45–66.

Singh, Nirvikar. Theories of Sharecropping. In *Bardhan, P., ed. (II)*, 1989, pp. 31–72.

_____ and Data-Chaudhuri, Mrinal. Tariffs vs. Quotas with Uncertain Substitutability between Inputs. *J. Quant. Econ.*, July 1989, *5*(2), pp. 251–65.

_____ and Kohli, Inderjit. Exports and Growth: Critical Minimum Effort and Diminishing Returns. *J. Devel. Econ.*, April 1989, *30*(2), pp. 391–400.

_____ and Thomas, Ravi. Matching Grants versus Block Grants with Imperfect Information. *Nat. Tax J.*, June 1989, *42*(2), pp. 191–203.

Singh, Sudama and Joshi, Yamini. Structural Changes in the Economy of Uttar Pradesh during Seventies: An Input–Output Study. *Indian Econ. J.*, Oct.–Dec. 1989, *37*(2), pp. 19–27.

Singh, Tarlok. Monetary–Fiscal Dynamics in the Mechanics of Aggregate Economic Activity—An Indian Experience. *Indian J. Quant. Econ.*, 1989, *5*(2), pp. 77–98.

_____. Planning Priorities in South Asia's Development. *Pakistan Devel. Rev.*, Winter 1989, *28*(4), pp. 529–43.

Singhal, K. C. and Kumar, Narinder. India's Export Instability. *Indian Econ. J.*, Jan.–March 1989, *36*(3), pp. 72–79.

Singleton, John. Japanese Folkcraft Pottery Apprenticeship: Cultural Patterns of an Educational Institution. In *Coy, M. W., ed.*, 1989, pp. 13–30.

Singleton, W. Ron. A Comparative Analysis of Tax Expenditure Budget Trends. In *Jones, S. M., ed.*, 1989, pp. 73–89.

Singpurwalla, Nozer D. and Meinhold, Richard J. Robustification of Kalman Filter Models. *J. Amer. Statist. Assoc.*, June 1989, *84*(406), pp. 479–86.

Sinha, Anup K. and Dasgupta, Sudipto. Erratic Dynamics of Dual Economies. In *Rakshit, M., ed.*, 1989, pp. 129–47.

Sinha, Prabhakant and Manrai, Ajay K. Elimination-by-Cutoffs. *Marketing Sci.*, Spring 1989, *8*(2), pp. 133–52.

Sinha, S. and Parthasarathy, T. Existence of Stationary Equilibrium Strategies in Non-zero Sum Discounted Stochastic Games with Uncountable State Space and State-Independent Transitions. *Int. J. Game Theory*, 1989, *18*(2), pp. 189–94.

Sinha, S. K. and Khanna-Chopra, Renu. Impact of Climate Variation on Production of Pulses. In *Oram, P. A., et al.*, 1989, pp. 219–36.

_____; **Rao, N. H. and Swaminathan, M. S.** Food Security in the Changing Global Climate. In *Oram, P. A., et al.*, 1989, pp. 579–97.

Siniscalco, Domenico. Defining and Measuring Output and Productivity in the Service Sector. In *Giersch, H., ed.*, 1989, pp. 38–58.

_____ **and Carraro, Carlo.** L'OPEC e il mercato del greggio: Uno schema di oligopolio. (OPEC and the Oil Market: An Oligopoly Model. With English summary.) *Econ. Politica*, April 1989, *6*(1), pp. 31–65.

Sinn, Hans-Werner. Expected Utility and the Siegel Paradox. *J. Econ. (Z. Nationalökon.)*, 1989, *50*(3), pp. 257–68.

_____. Two-Moment Decision Models and Expected Utility Maximization: Comment. *Amer. Econ. Rev.*, June 1989, *79*(3), pp. 601–02.

_____ **and Howitt, Peter.** Gradual Reforms of Capital Income Taxation. *Amer. Econ. Rev.*, March 1989, *79*(1), pp. 106–24.

Sinn, Stefan and Scheide, Joachim. How Strong Is the Case for International Coordination? In *Dorn, J. A. and Niskanen, W. A., eds.*, 1989, pp. 397–422.

Sioshansi, F. P.; Sorooshian, Soroosh and Kher, Lov. Noisy Data and Uncertain Coefficients: A Reply. *Energy J.*, January 1989, *10*(1), pp. 171–74.

Siow, Aloysius. Fixed Cost of Work and the Demand for Lotteries. *Econ. Letters*, 1989, *29*(4), pp. 299–302.

Sipos, Aladár. Socialist Technically Oriented Production Systems: The Case of Hungarian Agriculture. In *Adelman, I. and Lane, S., eds.*, 1989, pp. 197–210.

_____ **and Tardos, Márton.** Economic Control and the Structural Interdependence of Organizations in Hungary at the End of the Second

Reform Decade. *Eastern Europ. Econ.*, Fall 1989, *28*(1), pp. 17–33.

Sira, F. N. and Craig, J. G. Dilemmas in Cooperative Development in Third World Countries. *Ann. Pub. Coop. Econ.*, 1989, *60*(2), pp. 229–49.

Sirmans, C. F.; Benjamin, John D. and Sa-Aadu, J. Financing and House Prices. *J. Finan. Res.*, Spring 1989, *12*(1), pp. 83–91.

_____; **Benjamin, John D. and Shilling, James D.** Flood Insurance, Wealth Redistribution, and Urban Property Values. *J. Urban Econ.*, July 1989, *26*(1), pp. 43–53.

_____ **and Sa-Aadu, J.** The Pricing of Adjustable Rate Mortgage Contracts. *J. Real Estate Finance Econ.*, December 1989, *2*(4), pp. 253–66.

Sirmans, G. Stacy and Ferreira, Eurico J. Selling Price, Financing Premiums, and Days on the Market. *J. Real Estate Finance Econ.*, September 1989, *2*(3), pp. 209–22.

Sirotković, Jakov. The UN Development Decade and the World Debt Problem. In *Singer, H. W. and Sharma, S., eds. (I)*, 1989, pp. 129–34.

Sisler, Daniel G.; Habicht, Jean-Pierre and Berman, Peter. Equity in Public-Sector Primary Health Care: The Role of Service Organization in Indonesia. *Econ. Devel. Cult. Change*, July 1989, *37*(4), pp. 778–803.

Sisneros, Phillip M.; Chatfield, Robert E. and Moyer, R. Charles. The Accuracy of Long-term Earnings Forecasts for Industrial Firms. *Quart. J. Bus. Econ.*, Summer 1989, *28*(3), pp. 91–104.

_____; **Moyer, R. Charles and Chatfield, Robert E.** Security Analysts Monitoring Activity: Agency Costs and Information Demands. *J. Finan. Quant. Anal.*, December 1989, *24*(4), pp. 503–12.

Sithole, Vincent Majozi and Boeren, Clasina C. M. Contract Farming Schemes in Swaziland: Vuvulane Irrigated Farms and Mphetseni Settlement Scheme. *Eastern Afr. Econ. Rev.*, Special Issue, August 1989, pp. 59–69.

Sivakumar, M. V. K. Climate Vulnerability of Sorghum and Millet. In *Oram, P. A., et al.*, 1989, pp. 187–92.

_____. Some Strategies to Cope with Drought in the Sahelian Zone. In *Oram, P. A., et al.*, 1989, pp. 541–55.

Siven, Claes-Henric. La Scuola di Stoccolma in prospettiva. (With English summary.) *Studi. Econ.*, 1989, *44*(37), pp. 17–40.

_____ **and Blomquist, Soren.** Nobel Laureates in Economic Sciences: A Biographical Dictionary: Bertil Ohlin: 1977. In *Katz, B. S., ed.*, 1989, pp. 229–40.

Siwaraksa, Subhak; Adams, F. Gerard and Faulhaber, Gerald R. Measuring Services Output—The Wharton Index of Services Production. *J. Econ. Soc. Meas.*, 1989, *15*(2), pp. 155–66.

Sjaastad, Larry A. Argentine Economic Policy, 1976–81. In *di Tella, G. and Dornbusch, R., eds.*, 1989, pp. 254–75.

———. Debt, Depression, and Real Rates of Interest in Latin America. In *Brock, P. L.; Connolly, M. B. and González-Vega, C., eds.*, 1989, pp. 21–39.

Sjafrizaland Dawood, Dayan. Aceh: The LNG Boom and Enclave Development. In *Hill, H., ed.*, 1989, pp. 107–23.

Sjahrirand Mackie, J. A. C. Survey of Recent Developments. *Bull. Indonesian Econ. Stud.*, December 1989, 25(3), pp. 3–34.

Sjarkowi, Fachurrozi; Pagoulatos, Angelos and Debertin, David L. Soil Erosion, Intertemporal Profit, and the Soil Conservation Decision. *Southern J. Agr. Econ.*, December 1989, 21(2), pp. 55–62.

Sjoquist, David L. and Ihlanfeldt, Keith R. The Impact of Job Decentralization on the Economic Welfare of Central City Blacks. *J. Urban Econ.*, July 1989, 26(1), pp. 110–30.

Sjostrom, William. Collusion in Ocean Shipping: A Test of Monopoly and Empty Core Models. *J. Polit. Econ.*, October 1989, 97(5), pp. 1160–79.

———. On the Origin of Shipping Conferences: Excess Capacity and the Opening of the Suez Canal. *Int. J. Transport Econ.*, October 1989, 16(3), pp. 329–35.

Sjovold, Arve R. and Morrison, Damon C. Rocket Propulsion Cost Modeling. In *Gulledge, T. R., Jr. and Litteral, L. A., eds.*, 1989, pp. 226–58.

Skaburskis, Andrejs. Impact Attenuation in Nonconflict Situations: The Price Effects of a Nuisance Land-Use. *Environ. Planning A*, March 1989, 21(3), pp. 375–83.

———. Inversions in Urban Density Gradients: A Brief Look at the Vancouver Metropolitan Area's Density Profile. *Urban Stud.*, August 1989, 26(4), pp. 397–401.

Skaggs, Neil T. A Reappraisal of John Fullarton's "Banking School" System in Light of Modern Theory. In *Missouri Valley Economic Association*, 1989, pp. 80–85.

Skalmierski, Slawomir and Kulpinska, Jolanta. The Taming of New Technology. A Polish Case Study on the Introduction of a Flexible Manufacturing System. In *Francis, A. and Grootings, P., eds.*, 1989, pp. 140–64.

Skånland, Hermod. European Currency—A Norwegian View. In *Franz, O., ed.*, 1989, pp. 94–97.

Skees, Jerry R.; Vantreese, Valerie L. and Reed, Michael R. Mandatory Production Controls and Asset Values: A Case Study of Burley Tobacco Quotas. *Amer. J. Agr. Econ.*, May 1989, 71(2), pp. 319–25.

Škegro, Borislav and Burkett, John P. Capitalism, Socialism, and Productivity: An Econometric Analysis of CES and Translog Functions. *Europ. Econ. Rev.*, July 1989, 33(6), pp. 1115–33.

———; Gapinski, James H. and Anušić, Zoran. Policy Initiatives for Improving Yugoslav Economic Performance. *Int. Econ. J.*, Winter 1989, 3(4), pp. 95–107.

———; Zuehlke, Thomas W. and Gapinski, James H. A Model of Yugoslav Economic Performance. *J. Compar. Econ.*, March 1989, 13(1), pp. 15–46.

Skidelsky, Robert. Keynes and the State. In *Helm, D., ed.*, 1989, pp. 144–52.

Skiles, Marilyn. Dealing with Debt: The 1930s and the 1980s: Comment. In *Husain, I. and Diwan, I., eds.*, 1989, pp. 86–88.

Skinner, Douglas J. Options Markets and Stock Return Volatility. *J. Finan. Econ.*, June 1989, 23(1), pp. 61–78.

Skinner, Jonathan. Housing Wealth and Aggregate Saving. *Reg. Sci. Urban Econ.*, May 1989, 19(2), pp. 305–24.

——— and Feenberg, Daniel R. Sources of IRA Saving. In *Summers, L. H., ed.*, 1989, pp. 25–46.

Skocz, Maciej; Zebrowski, Maciej and Ziembla, Wieslaw. Spatial Allocation and Investment Scheduling in the Development Programming. In *Lewandowski, A. and Wierzbicki, A. P., eds.*, 1989, pp. 322–38.

Skogh, Göran. The Combination of Private and Public Regulation of Safety. In *Faure, M. and Van den Bergh, R., eds.*, 1989, pp. 87–101.

———. The Transactions Cost Theory of Insurance: Contracting Impediments and Costs. *J. Risk Ins.*, December 1989, 56(4), pp. 726–32.

——— and Bowles, Roger. Reputation, Monitoring and the Organisation of the Law Firm. In *Faure, M. and Van den Bergh, R., eds.*, 1989, pp. 33–47.

Skold, Karl D. and Holt, Matthew T. Dynamic Elasticities and Flexibilities in a Quarterly Model of the U.S. Pork Sector. *Appl. Econ.*, December 1989, 21(12), pp. 1683–1700.

Skolka, Jiří. Input–Output Structural Decomposition Analysis for Austria. *J. Policy Modeling*, Spring 1989, 11(1), pp. 45–66.

———. Tax Content of Final Demand in Austria. *Econ. Systems Res.*, 1989, 1(3), pp. 393–401.

Skott, Peter. Effective Demand, Class Struggle and Cyclical Growth. *Int. Econ. Rev.*, February 1989, 30(1), pp. 231–47.

Skousen, Mark. Why the U.S. Economy Is Not Depression-Proof. In *Rothbard, M. N. and Block, W., eds.*, 1989, pp. 75–94.

Skulimowski, Andrzej M. J. and Gorecki, Henryk. Safety Principle in Multiobjective Decision Support in the Decision Space Defined by Availability of Resources. In *Lewandowski, A. and Wierzbicki, A. P., eds.*, 1989, pp. 145–57.

Skurski, Roger and Andreae, Clemens-August. Global Values, Institutions and Policies: A Conceptual Framework. In *Rueschhoff, N. and Schaum, K., eds.*, 1989, pp. 1–3.

Skuse, Frank and Arestis, Philip. Austerity Policies and the New Right: Recent UK Experience. *Écon. Appl.*, 1989, 42(1), pp. 171–202.

Slade, Margaret E. The Fictitious Payoff-Function: Two Applications to Dynamic Games. *Ann. Écon. Statist.*, July–Dec. 1989, (15–16), pp. 193–216.

———. Modeling Stochastic and Cyclical Components of Technical Change: An Application of the Kalman Filter. *J. Econometrics*, July 1989, *41*(3), pp. 363–83.

_____. Price Wars in Price-Setting Supergames. *Economica*, August 1989, *56*(223), pp. 295–310.

_____. The Two Pricing Systems for Nonferrous Metals. In *Jackson, L. M. and Richardson, P. R., eds.*, 1989, pp. 26–45.

_____ and Jacquemin, Alexis. Cartels, Collusion, and Horizontal Merger. In *Schmalensee, R. and Willig, R. D., eds., Vol. 1*, 1989, pp. 415–73.

Slater, Martin. The Rationale for Marginal Cost Pricing. In *Helm, D.; Kay, J. and Thompson, D., eds.*, 1989, pp. 133–54.

Slater, Miriam. 'Il Magnifico.' In *[Stone, L.]*, 1989, pp. 15–20.

Slater, P. B. A Field Theory of Spatial Interaction. *Environ. Planning A*, January 1989, *21*(1), pp. 121–26.

_____. Response [Point-to-Point Migration Functions and Gravity Model Renormalization: Approaches to Aggregation in Spatial Interaction Modeling]. *Environ. Planning A*, September 1989, *21*(9), pp. 1265–66.

Slater, Susanne V. Curriculum Development for Public Sector Financial Management. *Public Budg. Finance*, Spring 1989, *9*(1), pp. 85–91.

Slater, Valerie A. and Powell, Stephen J. Ramifications of U.S. Trade and National Security Laws for Petroleum Imports. *J. Energy Devel.*, Spring 1989, *14*(2), pp. 293–317.

Sleemi, Fehmida and Davis, William M. Collective Bargaining in 1989: Negotiators Will Face Diverse Issues. *Mon. Lab. Rev.*, January 1989, *112*(1), pp. 10–24.

Slemrod, Joel. Are Estimated Tax Elasticities Really Just Tax Evasion Elasticities? The Case of Charitable Contributions. *Rev. Econ. Statist.*, August 1989, *71*(3), pp. 517–22.

_____. Rank Reversals and the Tax Elasticity of Capital Gains Realizations. *Nat. Tax J.*, December 1989, *42*(4), pp. 503–07.

_____. The Return to Tax Simplification: An Econometric Analysis. *Public Finance Quart.*, January 1989, *17*(1), pp. 3–27.

_____ and Pitt, Mark M. The Compliance Cost of Itemizing Deductions: Evidence from Individual Tax Returns. *Amer. Econ. Rev.*, December 1989, *79*(5), pp. 1224–32.

_____ and Scotchmer, Suzanne. Randomness in Tax Enforcement. *J. Public Econ.*, February 1989, *38*(1), pp. 17–32.

Slesnick, Daniel T. The Measurement of Horizontal Inequality. *Rev. Econ. Statist.*, August 1989, *71*(3), pp. 481–90.

_____. Specific Egalitarianism and Total Welfare Inequality: A Decompositional Analysis. *Rev. Econ. Statist.*, February 1989, *71*(1), pp. 116–27.

Sleuwaegen, Leo E.; DeBondt, Raymond R. and Dehandschutter, Wim V. The Herfindahl Index and Concentration Ratios Revisited. *Antitrust Bull.*, Fall 1989, *34*(3), pp. 625–40.

_____; Weiss, Leonard W. and Yamawaki, Hideki. Industry Competition and the Formation of the European Common Market. In *Weiss, L. W., ed.*, 1989, pp. 112–43.

_____; Yamawaki, Hideki and Audretsch, David B. The Convergence of International and Domestic Markets: Foreword. In *Audretsch, D. B.; Sleuwaegen, L. and Yamawaki, H., eds.*, 1989, pp. vii–x.

_____; Yamawaki, Hideki and Audretsch, David B. The Dynamics of Export Competition. In *Audretsch, D. B.; Sleuwaegen, L. and Yamawaki, H., eds.*, 1989, pp. 211–45.

Sloan, Frank A.; Wedig, Gerard J. and Hassan, Mahmud. Hospital Investment Decisions and the Cost of Capital. *J. Bus.*, October 1989, *62*(4), pp. 517–37.

Sloan, Judith. The Australian Labour Market, March 1989. *Australian Bull. Lab.*, March 1989, *15*(2), pp. 71–89.

_____ and Wooden, Mark. The Australian Labour Market: September 1989. *Australian Bull. Lab.*, September 1989, *15*(4), pp. 259–86.

_____; Wooden, Mark and Blandy, Richard. Reforming the Trade Union Structure in Australia. *Australian Bull. Lab.*, December 1989, *15*(5), pp. 370–83.

Sloane, Peter and Dex, Shirley. The Economics of Discrimination: How Far Have We Come? In *Drago, R. and Perlman, R., eds.*, 1989, pp. 83–104.

Slottje, Daniel J.; Basmann, R. L. and Nieswiadomy, Michael L. On the Empirical Relationship between Several Well-Known Inequality Measures. *J. Econometrics*, September 1989, *42*(1), pp. 49–66.

_____; Black, Dan A. and Hayes, Kathy J. Demographic Change and Inequality in the Size Distributions of Labor and Nonlabor Income. *Rev. Income Wealth*, September 1989, *35*(3), pp. 283–96.

_____ and Hayes, Kathy J. The Efficacy of State and Local Governments' Redistributional Policies. *Public Finance Quart.*, July 1989, *17*(3), pp. 304–22.

_____ and Hirschberg, Joseph G. Remembrance of Things Past the Distribution of Earnings across Occupations and the Kappa Criterion. *J. Econometrics*, September 1989, *42*(1), pp. 121–30.

_____; Hirschberg, Joseph G. and Molina, David J. Errata [A Selection Criterion for Choosing between Functional Forms of Income Distribution]. *Econometric Rev.*, 1989, *8*(2), pp. 227.

_____ and Ragan, James F., Jr. Alternatives to Unemployment-Based Funding Formulas in the Allocation of Federal Grants. *Growth Change*, Winter 1989, *20*(1), pp. 17–33.

_____ and Scully, Gerald W. The Paradox of Politics and Policy in Redistributing Income. *Public Choice*, January 1989, *60*(1), pp. 55–70.

Slovin, Myron B.; Sushka, Marie E. and Polonchek, John. Valuation Effects of Commercial Bank Securities Offerings: A Test of the Information Hypothesis. *J. Banking Finance*, July 1989, *13*(3), pp. 443–61.

Slutsky, Steven M.; Hamilton, Jonathan H. and

Sheshinski, Eytan. Production Externalities and Long-run Equilibria: Bargaining and Pigovian Taxation. *Econ. Inquiry,* July 1989, 27(3), pp. 453–71.

Smaldone, Joseph P. and McLaurin, Ronald D. Supplier Controls in U.S. Arms Transfer Policy. In *Baek, K.-I.; McLaurin, R. D. and Moon, C., eds.,* 1989, pp. 101–12.

Small, David H.; Hallman, Jeffrey J. and Porter, Richard D. M2 per Unit of Potential GNP as an Anchor for the Price Level. *Fed. Res. Bull.,* April 1989, 75(4), pp. 263–64.

_____ **and Porter, Richard D.** Understanding the Behavior of M2 and V2. *Fed. Res. Bull.,* April 1989, 75(4), pp. 244–54.

Small, J. L. and Morss, Mark F. Deriving Electricity Demand Elasticities from a Simulation Model. *Energy J.,* July 1989, 10(3), pp. 51–76.

_____ **and Morss, Mark F.** The Effect of Wood and Coal Stoves on Household Use of Electricity. *Land Econ.,* February 1989, 65(1), pp. 29–37.

Small, Kenneth A. and Brownstone, David. Efficient Estimation of Nested Logit Models. *J. Bus. Econ. Statist.,* January 1989, 7(1), pp. 67–74.

Smallwood, David M.; Haidacher, Richard C. and Blaylock, James R. A Review of the Research Literature on Meat Demand. In *Buse, R. C., ed.,* 1989, pp. 93–124.

Smart, Denise T. and Martin, Charles L. Consumer Correspondence: An Exploratory Investigation of Consistency between Business Policy and Practice. *J. Cons. Aff.,* Winter 1989, 23(2), pp. 364–82.

Smeeding, Timothy M. Poverty, Affluence, and the Income Costs of Children: Cross-national Evidence from the Luxembourg Income Study (LIS). *J. Post Keynesian Econ.,* Winter 1988–89, 11(2), pp. 222–40.

_____. Poverty, Affluence and the Income Costs of Children: Cross-National Evidence from the Luxembourg Income Study (LIS). In *Davidson, P. and Kregel, J., eds.,* 1989, pp. 98–114.

_____; **Coder, John and Rainwater, Lee.** Inequality among Children and Elderly in Ten Modern Nations: The United States in an International Context. *Amer. Econ. Rev.,* May 1989, 79(2), pp. 320–24.

_____ **and Moon, Marilyn.** Can the Elderly Afford Long-Term Care? In *Lewin, M. E. and Sullivan, S., eds.,* 1989, pp. 137–60.

_____; **Rainwater, Lee and Simpson, Rick.** Comparative Cross-National Research on Income and Economic Well-Being: The Luxembourg Income Study. *Surv. Curr. Bus.,* March 1989, 69(3), pp. 62–67.

Smeets, Heinz-Dieter. The 'True Protection' Concept—A Comment. *J. Devel. Stud.,* April 1989, 25(3), pp. 401–07.

Smidovich, Nikita P. Challenge Inspections in a Chemical Weapons Convention. In *Altmann, J. and Rotblat, J., eds.,* 1989, pp. 196–200.

Smidt, Seymour and Lakonishok, Josef. Past Price Changes and Current Trading Volume. *J. Portfol. Manage.,* Summer 1989, 15(4), pp. 18–24.

Smil, Vaclav. Coronary Heart Disease, Diet, and Western Mortality. *Population Devel. Rev.,* September 1989, 15(3), pp. 399–424.

Smirnov, V.; Shaposhnikov, A. N. and Zaslavskaia, Tat'iana I. Restructuring the Management of Soviet Society's Agrarian Sector. *Prob. Econ.,* January 1989, 31(9), pp. 39–54.

Smit, B.; McIlravey, G. P. and Joseph, A. E. Consumer Preferences for Rural Residences: A Conjoint Analysis in Ontario, Canada. *Environ. Planning A,* January 1989, 21(1), pp. 47–63.

Smit, E. van der M.; de Coning, T. J. and Tromp, D. Die Soeke na Suksesfaktore in Klein Ondernemings—'n Pragmatiese Benadering. (With English summary.) *J. Stud. Econ. Econometrics,* March 1989, 13(1), pp. 1–17.

Smit, Hidde P. and Burger, Kees. Long-term and Short-term Analysis of the Natural Rubber Market. *Weltwirtsch. Arch.,* 1989, 125(4), pp. 718–47.

Smit, M. R. and Fourie, F. C. v. N. Trends in Economic Concentration in South Africa. *S. Afr. J. Econ.,* September 1989, 57(3), pp. 241–56.

Smith, A. D. New Measures of British Service Outputs. *Nat. Inst. Econ. Rev.,* May 1989, (128), pp. 75–88.

Smith, Abbie; Marais, M. Laurentius and Schipper, Katherine. Wealth Effects of Going Private for Senior Securities. *J. Finan. Econ.,* June 1989, 23(1), pp. 155–91.

Smith, Alasdair; Venables, Anthony J. and Gasiorek, Michael. Tariffs, Subsidies and Retaliation. *Europ. Econ. Rev.,* March 1989, 33(2/3), pp. 480–89.

Smith, Amy L.; Wunnava, Phanindra V. and Olsen, Katherine. An Empirical Study of the Life-Cycle Hypothesis with Respect to Alumni Donations. *Amer. Economist,* Fall 1989, 33(2), pp. 60–63.

Smith, Ben. The Impact and Management of Minerals Development. In *[Gruen, F. H.],* 1989, pp. 210–39.

Smith, Brian H. More than Altruism: The Politics of European International Charities. In *James, E., ed.,* 1989, pp. 319–38.

Smith, Bruce D. A Business Cycle Model with Private Information. *J. Lab. Econ.,* April 1989, 7(2), pp. 210–37.

_____. Legal Restrictions, "Sunspots," and Cycles. *J. Econ. Theory,* April 1989, 47(2), pp. 369–92.

_____. A Model of Nominal Contracts. *J. Lab. Econ.,* October 1989, 7(4), pp. 392–414.

_____. Unemployment, the Variability of Hours, and the Persistence of "Disturbances": A Private Information Approach. *Int. Econ. Rev.,* November 1989, 30(4), pp. 921–38.

_____ **and Cooley, Thomas F.** Dynamic Coalition Formation and Equilibrium Policy Selection. *J. Monet. Econ.,* September 1989, 24(2), pp. 211–33.

_____ **and Stutzer, Michael J.** Credit Rationing

and Government Loan Programs: A Welfare Analysis. *Amer. Real Estate Urban Econ. Assoc. J.*, Summer 1989, *17*(2), pp. 177–93.

Smith, Bruce H. A Comment on Work Disincentive Effects of Government Income Maintenance Programs. *Amer. Economist*, Fall 1989, *33*(2), pp. 68–69.

Smith, C. Selby. Effects of Payment and Ownership on Hospital Efficiency: Commentary. In *Smith, C. S., ed.*, 1989, pp. 283–90.

Smith, Carol A. Survival Strategies among Petty Commodity Producers in Guatemala. *Int. Lab. Rev.*, Special Issue, 1989, *128*(6), pp. 791–813.

Smith, Charles David. Peasant Resistance to the "Grow More Coffee" Campaign in Kagera Region, Tanzania. *Can. J. Devel. Stud.*, 1989, *10*(2), pp. 273–87.

Smith, Creston M. The Social Security Administration's Continuous Work History Sample. *Soc. Sec. Bull.*, October 1989, *52*(10), pp. 20–28.

Smith, Daniel C. and Park, C. Whan. Product-Level Choice: A Top-Down or Bottom-Up Process? *J. Cons. Res.*, December 1989, *16*(3), pp. 289–99.

_____; **Park, C. Whan and Iyer, Easwar S.** The Effects of Situational Factors on In-Store Grocery Shopping Behavior: The Role of Store Environment and Time Available for Shopping. *J. Cons. Res.*, March 1989, *15*(4), pp. 422–33.

Smith, Darlene Brannigan and Bloom, Paul N. Using Content Analysis to Understand the Consumer Movement. *J. Cons. Aff.*, Winter 1989, *23*(2), pp. 301–28.

Smith, David F. Managers as Employees: New Zealand. In *Roomkin, M. J., ed.*, 1989, pp. 131–48.

Smith, Douglas A. and Vodden, Keith. Global Environmental Policy: The Case of Ozone Depletion. *Can. Public Policy*, December 1989, *15*(4), pp. 413–23.

Smith, Eldon D. Reflections on Human Resources in the Strategy of Rural Economic Development. *Rev. Reg. Stud.*, Winter 1989, *19*(1), pp. 13–22.

Smith, Fred L., Jr. Getting Deregulation Back on Track. In *Crane, E. H. and Boaz, D.*, 1989, pp. 73–90.

Smith, Gregor W. Transactions Demand for Money with a Stochastic, Time-Varying Interest Rate. *Rev. Econ. Stud.*, October 1989, *56*(4), pp. 623–33.

_____ **and Milbourne, Ross D.** How Informative Are Preliminary Announcements of the Money Stock in Canada? *Can. J. Econ.*, August 1989, *22*(3), pp. 595–606.

Smith, Helen Lawton; Smith, Stephen R. and Dickson, Keith. Interfirm Collaboration and Innovation: Strategic Alliances or Reluctant Partnerships? In *Mansfield, R., ed.*, 1989, pp. 140–60.

Smith, Herbert L. Integrating Theory and Research on the Institutional Determinants of Fertility. *Demography*, May 1989, *26*(2), pp. 171–84.

Smith, Ian R.; Pauly, Daniel and Silvestre, Ger-

onimo. On Development, Fisheries and Dynamite: A Brief Review of Tropical Fisheries Management. *Natural Res. Modeling*, Summer 1989, *3*(3), pp. 307–29.

Smith, J. Barry and Plourde, Charles. Crop Sharing in the Fishery and Industry Equilibrium. *Marine Resource Econ.*, 1989, *6*(3), pp. 179–93.

_____ **and Weber, Shlomo.** Contemporaneous Externalities, Rational Expectations, and Equilibrium Production Functions in Natural Resource Models. *J. Environ. Econ. Manage.*, September 1989, *17*(2), pp. 155–70.

_____ **and Weber, Shlomo.** Rent-Seeking Behaviour of Retaliating Agents. *Public Choice*, May 1989, *61*(2), pp. 153–66.

Smith, James A. Think Tanks and the Politics of Ideas. In *Colander, D. C. and Coats, A. W., eds.*, 1989, pp. 175–94.

Smith, James P. Career Wage Mobility. In *Shulman, S. and Darity, W., Jr., eds.*, 1989, pp. 109–25.

_____. Children among the Poor. *Demography*, May 1989, *26*(2), pp. 235–48.

_____. Occupational Segregation, Compensating Differentials, and Comparable Worth: Commentary. In *Michael, R. T.; Hartmann, H. I. and O'Farrell, B., eds.*, 1989, pp. 171–75.

_____ **and Ward, Michael.** Women in the Labor Market and in the Family. *J. Econ. Perspectives*, Winter 1989, *3*(1), pp. 9–23.

_____ **and Welch, Finis R.** Black Economic Progress after Myrdal. *J. Econ. Lit.*, June 1989, *27*(2), pp. 519–64.

Smith, Jeffrey W. A Theoretical Analysis of the Supply of Housing. *J. Urban Econ.*, September 1989, *26*(2), pp. 174–88.

Smith, Jeremy P. and Osborn, Denise R. The Performance of Periodic Autoregressive Models in Forecasting Seasonal U. K. Consumption. *J. Bus. Econ. Statist.*, January 1989, *7*(1), pp. 117–27.

Smith, Jillian and Judge, Ken. Purchase of Service in England. In *James, E., ed.*, 1989, pp. 139–61.

Smith, Kay A. Intra-industry Trade Patterns: A Test of the Variety Hypothesis. In *Gray, H. P., ed.*, 1989, pp. 81–127.

Smith, Kenneth L. and Brocato, Joe. Velocity and the Variability of Money Growth: Evidence from Granger-Causality Tests: Comment. *J. Money, Credit, Banking*, May 1989, *21*(2), pp. 258–61.

_____; **Brocato, Joe and Kumar, Akhil.** Individual versus Group Spot Price Forecasting in the International Petroleum Market: A Case Study. *Managerial Dec. Econ.*, March 1989, *10*(1), pp. 13–24.

Smith, Kirk R. and Kim, Yoon Hyung. Electric Power in Development: Lessons from Northeast Asia. In *Kim, Y. H. and Smith, K. R., eds.*, 1989, pp. 225–49.

_____ **and Kim, Yoon Hyung.** Electricity in Northeast Asia: The Principal Historical Trends. In *Kim, Y. H. and Smith, K. R., eds.*, 1989, pp. 1–19.

——— **and Rose, David J.** Nuclear Power. In *Kim, Y. H. and Smith, K. R., eds.*, 1989, pp. 145–85.

Smith, L. C., Jr. and Smith, L. Murphy. Microcomputer Applications for Teaching Microeconomic Concepts: Some Old and New Approaches. *J. Econ. Educ.*, Winter 1989, *20*(1), pp. 73–92.

Smith, L. D. Structural Adjustment, Price Reform and Agricultural Performance in Sub-Saharan Africa. *J. Agr. Econ.*, January 1989, *40*(1), pp. 21–31.

Smith, L. Murphy and Smith, L. C., Jr. Microcomputer Applications for Teaching Microeconomic Concepts: Some Old and New Approaches. *J. Econ. Educ.*, Winter 1989, *20*(1), pp. 73–92.

Smith, Lawrence B. and Fallis, George. Tax Reform and Residential Real Estate. In *Mintz, J. and Whalley, J., eds.*, 1989, pp. 336–65.

Smith, Lois M. Progress, Science and Myth: The Health Education of Cuban Women. In *Mesa-Lago, C., ed.*, 1989, pp. 167–96.

Smith, Marc T. and Delaney, Charles J. Impact Fees and the Price of New Housing: An Empirical Study. *Amer. Real Estate Urban Econ. Assoc. J.*, Spring 1989, *17*(1), pp. 41–54.

——— **and Delaney, Charles J.** Pricing Implications of Development Exactions on Existing Housing Stock. *Growth Change*, Fall 1989, *20*(4), pp. 1–12.

——— **and Hendershott, Patric H.** Transfer Programs and Aggregate Household Formations. *Population Res. Policy Rev.*, September 1989, *8*(3), pp. 227–45.

Smith, Marcia Datlow and Juhrs, Patricia D. Community-Based Employment for Persons with Autism. In *Wehman, P. and Kregel, J., eds.*, 1989, pp. 163–75.

Smith, Mark E. Food Aid Policy and Food Demand Patterns: Changes in Farm, Trade, and Aid Legislation and U.S. Food Aid. In *Helmuth, J. W. and Johnson, S. R., eds., Vol. 1*, 1989, pp. 132–36.

Smith, Maxwell and Kraus, Alan. Market Created Risk. *J. Finance*, July 1989, *44*(3), pp. 557–69.

Smith, Michael B. Korea as a U.S. Trading Partner. In *Bayard, T. O. and Young, S.-G., eds.*, 1989, pp. 77–82.

Smith, Michael L. Investment Returns and Yields to Holders of Insurance. *J. Bus.*, January 1989, *62*(1), pp. 81–98.

Smith, Michael Peter. Pacific Rim Cities in the World Economy: Introduction. In *Smith, M. P., ed.*, 1989, pp. 3–8.

Smith, Michael R. Marchak on Free Trade: A Response. *Can. Public Policy*, September 1989, *15*(3), pp. 339–44.

———. A Sociological Appraisal of the Free Trade Agreement. *Can. Public Policy*, March 1989, *15*(1), pp. 57–71.

Smith, Murray G. and Lipsey, Richard G. The Canada–U.S. Free Trade Agreement: Special Case or Wave of the Future? In *Schott, J. J., ed.*, 1989, pp. 317–35.

Smith, N. Craig. The Case Study: A Vital Yet Misunderstood Research Method for Management. In *Mansfield, R., ed.*, 1989, pp. 50–64.

Smith, Nina. Kan økonomiske teorier forklare kvinders placering på arbejdsmarkedet? (Can Economic Theories Explain Female Labour Market Behaviour? With English summary.) *Nationaløkon. Tidsskr.*, 1989, *127*(3), pp. 321–38.

Smith, P. J. The Rehousing/Relocation Issue in an Early Slum Clearance Scheme: Edinburgh 1865–1885. *Urban Stud.*, February 1989, *26*(1), pp. 100–114.

Smith, P. N. and Wickens, Michael R. Assessing the Effects of Monetary Shocks on Exchange Rate Variability with a Stylised Econometric Model of the UK. *Greek Econ. Rev.*, 1989, *11*(1), pp. 76–94.

Smith, Paula A. and Shaaf, Mohammad. The Role of the Regional Economy in Oklahoma Bank Failures. In *Missouri Valley Economic Association*, 1989, pp. 86–91.

Smith, Peter and Holly, Sean. Interrelated Factor Demands for Manufacturing: A Dynamic Translog Cost Function Approach. *Europ. Econ. Rev.*, January 1989, *33*(1), pp. 111–26.

Smith, Peter B.; Tayeb, Monir and Peterson, Mark F. The Cultural Context of Leadership Actions: A Cross-Cultural Analysis. In *Davies, J., et al., eds.*, 1989, pp. 85–92.

Smith, Philip J. Is Two-Phase Sampling Really Better for Estimating Age Composition? *J. Amer. Statist. Assoc.*, December 1989, *84*(408), pp. 916–21.

Smith, R. I.; Fowler, D. and Cape, J. N. The Statistics of Phytotoxic Air Pollutants. *J. Roy. Statist. Society*, 1989, *152*(2), pp. 183–98.

Smith, R. P. Models of Military Expenditure. *J. Appl. Econometrics*, Oct.–Dec. 1989, *4*(4), pp. 345–59.

Smith, Richard A. The Effects of Local Fair Housing Ordinances on Housing Segregation: Their Impact Is Small, but It's an Important Positive Change toward Integration. *Amer. J. Econ. Sociology*, April 1989, *48*(2), pp. 219–30.

——— **and Larkey, Patrick D.** Bias in the Formulation of Local Government Budget Problems. *Policy Sciences*, May 1989, *22*(2), pp. 123–66.

Smith, Richard J. On the Use of Distributional Mis-specification Checks in Limited Dependent Variable Models. *Econ. J.*, Supplement, 1989, *99*(395), pp. 178–92.

——— **and Blundell, Richard W.** Estimation in a Class of Simultaneous Equation Limited Dependent Variable Models. *Rev. Econ. Stud.*, January 1989, *56*(1), pp. 37–57.

Smith, Robert F. and Watts, Michael. Economics in Literature and Drama. *J. Econ. Educ.*, Summer 1989, *20*(3), pp. 291–307.

Smith, Rodney T. Water Transfers, Irrigation Districts, and the Compensation Problem. *J. Policy Anal. Manage.*, Summer 1989, *8*(3), pp. 446–65.

Smith, Roger S. Identifying Tax Expenditures: Comment. In *Bruce, N., ed.*, 1989, pp. 226–30.

_____ and Mirus, Rolf. Canada's Underground Economy. In *Feige, E. L., ed.*, 1989, pp. 267–80.

Smith, Roy C. International Stock Market Transactions. In *Noyelle, T., ed.*, 1989, pp. 7–29.

Smith, Sharon P. Bargaining Realities: Responding to a Changing World. In *Huang, W.-C., ed.*, 1989, pp. 13–26.

Smith, Stanley D.; Syed, Azmat A. and Liu, Pu. The Exploitation of Inside Information at the *Wall Street Journal:* A Test of Strong Form Efficiency. *Financial Rev.*, November 1989, *24*(4), pp. 567–79.

Smith, Stanley K. Toward a Methodology for Estimating Temporary Residents. *J. Amer. Statist. Assoc.*, June 1989, *84*(406), pp. 430–36.

Smith, Stephen C. and Ye, Meng-Hua. Dynamic Allocation in a Labor-Manged Firm: Reply. *J. Compar. Econ.*, June 1989, *13*(2), pp. 338–39.

Smith, Stephen D. and Morgan, George Emir. Some Notes on Risk Management via Forward Contracting. *Southern Econ. J.*, July 1989, *56*(1), pp. 240–52.

Smith, Stephen R. European Perspectives on the Shadow Economy. *Europ. Econ. Rev.*, March 1989, *33*(2/3), pp. 589–96.

_____; Dickson, Keith and Smith, Helen Lawton. Interfirm Collaboration and Innovation: Strategic Alliances or Reluctant Partnerships? In *Mansfield, R., ed.*, 1989, pp. 140–60.

_____ and Helm, Dieter. The Assessment: Economic Integration and the Role of the European Community. *Oxford Rev. Econ. Policy*, Summer 1989, *5*(2), pp. 1–19.

_____ and Helm, Dieter. The Decentralized State: The Economic Borders of Local Government. In *Helm, D., ed.*, 1989, pp. 275–96.

_____; Micklewright, John and Pearson, Mark. Has Britain an Early School-Leaving Problem? *Fisc. Stud.*, February 1989, *10*(1), pp. 1–16.

_____; White, Stuart and Pearson, Mark. Demographic Influences on Public Spending. *Fisc. Stud.*, May 1989, *10*(2), pp. 48–65.

Smith, Steve. The Fall and Rise of the State in International Politics. In *Duncan, G., ed.*, 1989, pp. 33–55.

Smith, Susan J. The Politics of 'Race' and a New Segregationalism. In *Mohan, J., ed.*, 1989, pp. 151–71.

Smith, Theodore M. Corruption, Tradition, and Change in Indonesia. In *Heidenheimer, A. J.; Johnston, M. and LeVine, V. T., eds.*, 1989, *1971*, pp. 423–40.

Smith, Tom W. The Hidden 25 Percent: An Analysis of Nonresponse on the 1980 General Social Survey. In *Singer, E. and Presser, S., eds.*, 1989, *1983*, pp. 50–68.

_____. In Search of House Effects: A Comparison of Responses to Various Questions by Different Survey Organizations. In *Singer, E. and Presser, S., eds.*, 1989, *1978*, pp. 224–44.

_____. That Which We Call Welfare by Any Other Name Would Smell Sweeter: An Analysis of the Impact of Question Wording on Response Patterns. In *Singer, E. and Presser, S., eds.*, 1989, *1987*, pp. 99–107.

Smith, Tony. Roemer on Marx's Theory of Exploitation: Shortcomings of a Non-dialectical Approach. *Sci. Society*, Fall 1989, *53*(3), pp. 327–40.

Smith, Tony E. Finite Spectral Analysis of Multiregional Time Series. In *Andersson, Å. E., et al., eds.*, 1989, pp. 133–63.

Smith, V. Kerry. Taking Stock of Progress with Travel Cost Recreation Demand Methods: Theory and Implementation. *Marine Resource Econ.*, 1989, *6*(4), pp. 279–310.

_____ and Desvousges, William H. Subjective versus Technical Risk Estimates: Do Risk Communication Policies Increase Consistency? *Econ. Letters*, December 1989, *31*(3), pp. 287–91.

_____ and Kopp, Raymond J. Benefit Estimation Goes to Court: The Case of Natural Resource Damage Assessments. *J. Policy Anal. Manage.*, Fall 1989, *8*(4), pp. 593–612.

_____ and Mork, Knut Anton. Testing the Life-Cycle Hypothesis with a Norwegian Household Panel. *J. Bus. Econ. Statist.*, July 1989, *7*(3), pp. 287–96.

Smith, Verity A. Recent Trends in Cuban Criticism and Literature. In *Mesa-Lago, C., ed.*, 1989, pp. 81–99.

Smith, Vernon L. Theory, Experiment and Economics. *J. Econ. Perspectives*, Winter 1989, *3*(1), pp. 151–69.

Smith, W. James; Formby, John P. and Seaks, Terry G. On the Measurement and Trend of Inequality: A Reconsideration. *Amer. Econ. Rev.*, March 1989, *79*(1), pp. 256–64.

Smith, William B. A View from Wall Street. In *Williams, O. F.; Reilly, F. K. and Houck, J. W., eds.*, 1989, pp. 47–51.

Smith, William C. Heterodox Shocks and the Political Economy of Democratic Transition in Argentina and Brazil. In *Canak, W. L., ed.*, 1989, pp. 138–66.

Smithin, John N. The Composition of Government Expenditures and the Effectiveness of Fiscal Policy. In *Pheby, J., ed.*, 1989, pp. 209–27.

_____. A Neglected Monetary Standard Alternative: Gold/Commodity Bimetallism: Comment. In *Hamouda, O. F.; Rowley, R. and Wolf, B. M., eds.*, 1989, pp. 210–11.

Smits, Helen L.; Berkman, Lisa F. and Kapp, Mary C. The Value of Medical Care: Four Case Studies. In *Eisdorfer, C.; Kessler, D. A. and Spector, A. N., eds.*, 1989, pp. 322–40.

Smolensky, Eugene. Survey Estimates of Wealth: An Assessment of Quality: Comment. In *Lipsey, R. E. and Tice, H. S., eds.*, 1989, pp. 548–551.

_____; Danziger, Sheldon and Gottschalk, Peter. How the Rich Have Fared, 1973–87. *Amer. Econ. Rev.*, May 1989, *79*(2), pp. 310–14.

_____ and Hoyt, William H. The Distributed Effects of Revenue Structures. In *Chiancone, A. and Messere, K., eds.*, 1989, pp. 215–30.

Smuts, R. Malcolm. Public Ceremony and Royal

Charisma: The English Royal Entry in London, 1485–1642. In *[Stone, L.]*, 1989, pp. 65–93.

Smyth, David J. Aggregate Demand Curves: Static and Dynamic. *J. Macroecon.*, Winter 1989, *11*(1), pp. 133–40.

_____. The Specification of Mortgage Availability in Models of Housing Demand: Theory and Evidence. In *Missouri Valley Economic Association*, 1989, pp. 162–68.

_____ **and Arora, Harjit.** A Temporary Equilibrium Model of the Mortgage Market. *J. Macroecon.*, Spring 1989, *11*(2), pp. 261–68.

_____ **and Dua, Pami.** The Public's Indifference Map between Inflation and Unemployment: Empirical Evidence for the Nixon, Ford, Carter and Reagan Presidencies. *Public Choice*, January 1989, *60*(1), pp. 71–85.

_____; **Washburn, Susan K. and Dua, Pami.** Social Preferences, Inflation, Unemployment, and Political Business Cycles: Econometric Evidence for the Reagan Presidency. *Southern Econ. J.*, October 1989, *56*(2), pp. 336–48.

Snape, Ed and Bamber, Greg. Managerial and Professional Employees: Conceptualising Union Strategies and Structures. *Brit. J. Ind. Relat.*, March 1989, *27*(1), pp. 93–110.

_____ **and Bamber, Greg.** Managers as Employees: Britain. In *Roomkin, M. J.*, *ed.*, 1989, pp. 17–56.

Snape, Richard H. A Free Trade Agreement with Australia? In *Schott, J. J.*, *ed.*, 1989, pp. 167–96.

Snapper, John W. and Weil, Vivian. Owning Scientific and Technical Information: Value and Ethical Issues: Introduction. In *Weil, V. and Snapper, J. W.*, *eds.*, 1989, pp. 1–12.

Sneed, Joseph D. Micro-economic Models of Problem Choice in Basic Science. In *Balzer, W. and Hamminga, B.*, *eds.*, 1989, pp. 207–24.

Sneessens, Henri; Calcoen, Francis and Eeckhoudt, Louis. L'épargne de précaution: Une analyse géométrique. (Precautionary Saving: A Geometric Analysis. With English summary.) *Revue Écon.*, January 1989, *40*(1), pp. 21–34.

Snehota, Ivan and Fiocca, Renato. High Technology and Management of the Market Differential. In *Hallén, L. and Johanson, J.*, *eds.*, 1989, pp. 199–209.

Snell, Andrew. Information, Rational Expectations and Macroeconomic Modelling. *J. Econ. Surveys*, 1989, *3*(2), pp. 179–98.

_____ **and Landesmann, Michael.** The Consequences of Mrs. Thatcher for U.K. Manufacturing Exports. *Econ. J.*, March 1989, *99*(394), pp. 1–27.

_____ **and Landesmann, Michael.** Implications of a Modernization Strategy for the United Kingdom. In *Krelle, W.*, *ed.*, 1989, pp. 353–84.

Snickars, Folke. Infrastructure: A Treat for Regional Science Research. *Ann. Reg. Sci.*, 1989, *23*(4), pp. 251–53.

Snider, Lewis W. Supplier Control and Recipient Autonomy: Problems and Prospects. In *Baek,*

K.-I.; McLaurin, R. D. and Moon, C., *eds.*, 1989, pp. 231–70.

Sniezek, Janet A. An Examination of Group Process in Judgmental Forecasting. *Int. J. Forecasting*, 1989, *5*(2), pp. 171–78.

Snijders, D. Global Company and World Financial Markets. In *Sijben, J. J.*, *ed.*, 1989, pp. 59–74.

_____. Investment Policy Viewed from the Perspective of a Multinational Company—"Some Unconnected Thoughts." In *Muller, F. and Zwezerijnen, W. J.*, *eds.*, 1989, pp. 100–106.

Snoek, Harry. Problems of Bank Supervision in LDCs. *Finance Devel.*, December 1989, *26*(4), pp. 14–16.

Snow, Arthur and Warren, Ronald S., Jr. Tax Rates and Labor Supply in Fiscal Equilibrium. *Econ. Inquiry*, July 1989, *27*(3), pp. 511–20.

Snow, Marcellus and Jussawalla, Meheroo. Deregulatory Trends in OECD Countries. In *Jussawalla, M.; Okuma, T. and Araki, T.*, *eds.*, 1989, pp. 21–39.

Snowball, Doug; Tubbs, Richard M. and Bamber, E. Michael. Audit Structure and Its Relation to Role Conflict and Role Ambiguity: An Empirical Investigation. *Accounting Rev.*, April 1989, *64*(2), pp. 285–99.

Snowden, P. N. The Interpretation of Market Discounts in Assessing Buy-Back Benefits. *Int. Monet. Fund Staff Pap.*, September 1989, *36*(3), pp. 733–35.

Snower, Dennis J. and Lindbeck, Assar. Macroeconomic Policy and Insider Power. *Amer. Econ. Rev.*, May 1989, *79*(2), pp. 370–76.

Snyder, Donald. Speeding, Coordination, and the 55-MPH Limit: Comment. *Amer. Econ. Rev.*, September 1989, *79*(4), pp. 922–25.

Snyder, Donald C. A Data Base with Income and Assets of New Retirees by Race and Hispanic Origin. *Rev. Black Polit. Econ.*, Spring 1989, *17*(4), pp. 73–81.

Snyder, Donald L.; Biswas, Basudeb and Bhattacharyya, Rabindra N. The Optimal Forest Rotation: Some Economic Dimensions. *Indian Econ. J.*, Oct.–Dec. 1989, *37*(2), pp. 69–82.

Snyder, Edward A. New Insights into the Decline of Antitrust Enforcement. *Contemp. Policy Issues*, October 1989, *7*(4), pp. 1–18.

_____ **and Hughes, James W.** Evaluating Medical Malpractice Reforms. *Contemp. Policy Issues*, April 1989, *7*(2), pp. 83–98.

_____ **and Hughes, James W.** Policy Analysis of Medical Malpractice Reforms: What Can We Learn from Claims Data? *J. Bus. Econ. Statist.*, October 1989, *7*(4), pp. 423–31.

_____; **Masten, Scott E. and Meehan, James W., Jr.** Vertical Integration in the U.S. Auto Industry: A Note on the Influence of Transaction Specific Assets. *J. Econ. Behav. Organ.*, October 1989, *12*(2), pp. 265–73.

Snyder, James M. Election Goals and the Allocation of Campaign Resources. *Econometrica*, May 1989, *57*(3), pp. 637–60.

_____. Political Geography and Interest-Group Power. *Soc. Choice Welfare*, April 1989, *6*(2), pp. 103–25.

Snyder, Ralph D. A Review of the Forecasting Package Stamp. *J. Econ. Surveys*, 1989, *3*(4), pp. 345–51.

Snyder, Ralph W., Jr. Stabilizing World Oil Prices (SWOP): A Security Strategy. In *[Evans, J. K.]*, 1989, pp. 172–81.

Snyder, Susan D. and Broadway, Michael J. The Persistence of Urban Deprivation: The Example of Wichita, Kansas, in the 1970s. *Growth Change*, Spring 1989, *20*(2), pp. 50–61.

Soares, F. B. A Differential Approach to Modelling the Agricultural Sector. In *Bauer, S. and Henrichsmeyer, W., eds.*, 1989, pp. 253–59.

Sobczyk, Jerzy; Wierzbicki, Andrzej P. and Rogowski, Tadeusz. IAC–DIDAS–L: A Dynamic Interactive Decision Analysis and Support System for Multicriteria Analysis of Linear and Dynamic Linear Models on Professional Microcomputers. In *Lewandowski, A. and Wierzbicki, A. P., eds.*, 1989, pp. 373–75.

Soberman, R. M.; Cubukgil, A. and Harltos, Z. J. Transportation Research Needs of Developing Countries: The Case for a New Centre. In *Candemir, Y., ed.*, 1989, pp. 196–209.

Sobhan, Rehman. Employment and Social Issues in the Formulation of Policy for the Handloom Industry. *Bangladesh Devel. Stud.*, March–June 1989, *17*(1–2), pp. 157–74.

_____ **and Sen, Binayak.** Trends in the Repayment Performance to the DFIs: Implications for the Development of Entrepreneurship in Bangladesh. *Bangladesh Devel. Stud.*, September 1989, *17*(3), pp. 21–66.

Sockell, Donna and Delaney, John Thomas. The Mandatory-Permissive Distinction and Collective Bargaining Outcomes. *Ind. Lab. Relat. Rev.*, July 1989, *42*(4), pp. 566–83.

Söderberg, Johan. Hard Times in 19th-Century Sweden: Comment. *Exploration Econ. Hist.*, October 1989, *26*(4), pp. 477–91.

Södersten, Jan. The Investment Funds System Reconsidered. *Scand. J. Econ.*, 1989, *91*(4), pp. 671–87.

Söderström, Lars. Almost Genuine Insurance Schemes as an Alternative to Tax-Financed Pensions and Other Social Security Benefits. In *Chiancone, A. and Messere, K., eds.*, 1989, pp. 339–50.

_____ **and Kruse, Agneta.** Early Retirement in Sweden. In *Schmähl, W., ed.*, 1989, pp. 39–61.

Soenen, Luc A. and Aggarwal, Raj. The ECU Currency Cocktail: Its Performance as a Risk-Reducing Investment. *Rivista Int. Sci. Econ. Com.*, Oct.–Nov. 1989, *36*(10–11), pp. 1019–32.

Soesastro, M. Hadi. East Timor: Questions of Economic Viability. In *Hill, H., ed.*, 1989, pp. 207–29.

van Soest, Arthur. Minimum Wage Rates and Unemployment in the Netherlands. *De Economist*, 1989, *137*(3), pp. 279–308.

Šohinger, Jasminka. On the Notion of Equilibrium in Marx's Economics. *Econ. Anal. Workers' Manage.*, 1989, *23*(2), pp. 129–37.

Sohrabian, Ahmad. An Empirical Analysis of the Intertemporal Substitution Hypothesis. *Appl. Econ.*, August 1989, *21*(8), pp. 1109–28.

Soja, Edward; Morales, Rebecca and Wolff, Goetz. Urban Restructuring: An Analysis of Social and Spatial Change in Los Angeles. In *Beauregard, R. A., ed.*, 1989, pp. 87–122.

Sojo, Ana. Social Policies in Costa Rica. *CEPAL Rev.*, August 1989, (38), pp. 105–19.

Sojo, E. and Klein, Lawrence R. Combinations of High and Low Frequency Data in Macroeconometric Models. In *[Adams, F. G.]*, 1989, pp. 3–16.

Sokil, Catherine M. Hungarian Financial and Labor Market Reforms: Developing Conditions for the Market Mechanism? *Eastern Europ. Econ.*, Fall 1989, *28*(1), pp. 53–63.

Sokołowska, Joanna. Application of the Valence-Instrumentality-Expectancy and Multiattribute Utility Models in the Prediction of Worker Effort. In *Grunert, K. G. and Ölander, F., eds.*, 1989, pp. 231–45.

Sokolsky, Joel J. Striking a New Balance: Seapower, Security, Sovereignty, and Canada. In *McRae, D. and Munro, G., eds.*, 1989, pp. 189–213.

Solar, P. and Schroeven, Chris. The Construction of Historical Price Indices, with an Illustration from Interwar Belgium. In *Scholliers, P., ed.*, 1989, pp. 149–75.

Solberg, Donald P. and McCabe, George M. Hedging in the Treasury Bill Futures Market When the Hedged Instrument and the Deliverable Instrument Are Not Matched. *J. Futures Markets*, December 1989, *9*(6), pp. 529–37.

Solberg, Ronald L. Developing Country Creditworthiness and Financial Market Innovation. In *Singer, H. W. and Sharma, S., eds. (I)*, 1989, pp. 167–80.

Solé, Jose Manuel. Adjusting to Freer Trade: Spain's First Economic Steps in the EEC. In *Nieuwenhuysen, J., ed.*, 1989, pp. 85–99.

Solenberger, Peter; Servais, Marita and Duncan, Greg J. Data Base Management Approaches to Household Panel Studies. In *Kasprzyk, D., et al., eds.*, 1989, pp. 190–225.

Solimano, Andrés. Argentina's Foreign Debt: Origins and Alternatives: Comment. In *Edwards, S. and Larrain, F., eds.*, 1989, pp. 205–07.

Solis-Fallas, Otton and Owen, P. Dorian. Unorganized Money Markets and 'Unproductive' Assets in the New Structuralist Critique of Financial Liberalization. *J. Devel. Econ.*, October 1989, *31*(2), pp. 341–55.

Solnik, B. and Brennan, Michael J. International Risk Sharing and Capital Mobility. *J. Int. Money Finance*, September 1989, *8*(3), pp. 359–73.

Solo, Robert A. Institutional Economics. In *Hey, J. D., ed.*, 1989, pp. 263–76.

_____. Organizational Structure, Technological Advance, and the New Tasks of Government. In *Tool, M. R. and Samuels, W. J., eds. (I)*, 1989, *1972*, pp. 193–210.

Solocha, Andrew; Soskin, Mark D. and Kasoff, Mark J. Canadian Investment in Northern

New York: Impact of Exchange Rates on Foreign Direct Investment. *Growth Change*, Winter 1989, *20*(1), pp. 1–16.

Solodkov, M. and Mikheev, I. A Stage-by-Stage Transition to Wholesale Trade in the Means of Production. *Prob. Econ.*, January 1989, *31*(9), pp. 98–112.

Solomatin, D. P. Problem Structuring Tools for Pre-MCDM Stage. In *Lockett, A. G. and Islei, G., eds.*, 1989, pp. 522–33.

Solomon, Allen M. and Sedjo, Roger A. Climate and Forests. In *Rosenberg, N. J., et al., eds.*, 1989, pp. 105–19.

Solomon, Anthony M. New Strategies for the Federal Reserve? In *Guttmann, R., ed.*, 1989, *1982*, pp. 139–45.

_____. Unresolved Issues in Monetary Policy. *Fed. Res. Bank New York Quart. Rev.*, Special Issue, 1989, pp. 42–47.

Solomon, D. A Revision of the Theory of Local Government Borrowing. *S. Afr. J. Econ.*, September 1989, *57*(3), pp. 231–40.

Solomon, Robert. International Dimensions of Monetary Policy: Coordination versus Autonomy: Commentary. In *Federal Reserve Bank of Kansas City*, 1989, pp. 233–36.

_____. International Monetary Reform: The Future Is Not What It Used to Be! In *Hamouda, O. F.; Rowley, R. and Wolf, B. M., eds.*, 1989, pp. 10–16.

Solomou, Solomos and Kitson, Michael. The Macroeconomics of Protectionism: The Case of Britain in the 1930s. In *Lawson, T.; Palma, J. G. and Sender, J., eds.*, 1989, pp. 155–69.

_____ and Kitson, Michael. The Macroeconomics of Protectionism: The Case of Britain in the 1930s. *Cambridge J. Econ.*, March 1989, *13*(1), pp. 155–69.

Solon, Gary. Biases in the Estimation of Intergenerational Earnings Correlations. *Rev. Econ. Statist.*, February 1989, *71*(1), pp. 172–74.

_____. The Value of Panel Data in Economic Research. In *Kasprzyk, D., et al., eds.*, 1989, pp. 486–96.

Soloveitchik, David I. Inconsistent Linear Constraints and Objectives in MOLP Problems. In *Lockett, A. G. and Islei, G., eds.*, 1989, pp. 370–79.

Solow, Andrew R. and Broadus, James M. Loss Functions in Estimating Offshore Oil Resources. *Resources & Energy*, March 1989, *11*(1), pp. 81–92.

Solow, John L. and Malueg, David A. A Note on Welfare in the Durable-Goods Monopoly. *Economica*, November 1989, *56*(224), pp. 523–27.

Solow, Robert M. How Economic Ideas Turn to Mush. In *Colander, D. C. and Coats, A. W., eds.*, 1989, pp. 75–83.

_____. Mr Hicks and the Classics. In *Wood, J. C. and Woods, R. N., eds., Vol. 4*, 1989, *1984*, pp. 57–69.

_____. The State of Economic Science: Views of Six Nobel Laureates: Dr. Robert M. Solow. In *Sichel, W., ed.*, 1989, pp. 25–39.

_____ and Blinder, Alan S. Does Fiscal Policy

Matter? In *Blinder, A. S.*, 1989, *1973*, pp. 1–16.

Solt, Michael E. and Statman, Meir. Good Companies, Bad Stocks. *J. Portfol. Manage.*, Summer 1989, *15*(4), pp. 39–44.

Soltow, Lee. The Life Cycle of Ownership in Norway, 1664–1930. *J. Europ. Econ. Hist.*, Fall 1989, *18*(2), pp. 433–46.

_____. The Rich and the Destitute in Sweden, 1805–1855: A Test of Tocqueville's Inequality Hypotheses. *Econ. Hist. Rev., 2nd Ser.*, February 1989, *42*(1), pp. 43–63.

Soltwedel, Rüdiger. Supply-Side Policies since 1982? The Lessons Are Still to Be Learned. In *Fels, G. and von Furstenberg, G. M., eds.*, 1989, pp. 73–99.

Somayajulu, V. V. N. Indian Plan Priorities, Strategies and Research Gaps in Development Plan Modelling and Policy Analysis. In *Reddy, J. M., et al., eds. (II)*, 1989, pp. 35–61.

_____. Integration of Financial and Physical Planning. In *Reddy, J. M., et al., eds. (I)*, 1989, pp. 1–21.

Somers, Anne R. Is Comprehensive Care for the Elderly Fiscally Viable? In *Eisdorfer, C.; Kessler, D. A. and Spector, A. N., eds.*, 1989, pp. 467–81.

Somers, Stephen A. and Merrill, Jeffrey C. Long-Term Care: The Great Debate on the Wrong Issue. *Inquiry*, Fall 1989, *26*(3), pp. 317–20.

Somerville, Keith and Baxter, Joan. Burkina Faso: Politics, Economics and Society. In *Allen, C., et al.*, 1989, pp. 237–86.

_____ and Radu, Michael S. People's Republic of Congo: Politics, Economics and Society. In *Allen, C., et al.*, 1989, pp. 145–236.

Sommariva, Andrea and Tullio, Giuseppe. The German Depression and the Stock Market Crash of the Thirties: The Role of Macropolicies and of the International Business Cycle. *J. Banking Finance*, September 1989, *13*(4–5), pp. 515–36.

Somnea, D.; Patrulescu, M. and Dumitrescu, Vl. Software Simulation of Bigger Fonts Printing on Dot Matrix Graphical Printers. *Econ. Computat. Econ. Cybern. Stud. Res.*, 1989, *24*(2–3), pp. 103–09.

Somwaru, A.; Vasavada, Utpal and Ball, V. E. Modeling Dynamic Adjustment Subject to Integrability Conditions. In *Bauer, S. and Henrichsmeyer, W., eds.*, 1989, pp. 279–86.

Sondakh, Lucky and Jones, Gavin W. North Sulawesi: Unexploited Potential. In *Hill, H., ed.*, 1989, pp. 364–85.

Søndergaard, Jørgen and Pedersen, Peder J. Det inflationaere danske arbejdsmarked. (The Inflationary Bias in the Danish Economy. With English summary.) *Nationaløkon. Tidsskr.*, 1989, *127*(1), pp. 1–20.

Song, Byung-Nak; Furukawa, Shunichi and Lo, Fu-chen. Patterns of Development and Interdependence among the East and Southeast Asian Economies. In *Shinohara, M. and Lo, F., eds.*, 1989, pp. 108–27.

Song, In-Man and Lobo, Gerald J. The Incremental Information in SFAS No. 33 Income Disclosures over Historical Cost Income and Its Cash and Accrual Components. *Accounting Rev.*, April 1989, *64*(2), pp. 329–43.

Song, Min. The Scientific Validity of the Concept of the Asiatic Mode of Production. In *Brook, T., ed.*, 1989, pp. 149–56.

Song, Ping. Why We Must Implement a Rational, Low Wage System. In *Howe, C. and Walker, K. R., eds.*, 1989, *1957*, pp. 335–44.

Sonis, Michael and Hewings, Geoffrey J. D. Error and Sensitivity Input–Output Analysis: A New Approach. In *Miller, R. E.; Polenske, K. R. and Rose, A. Z., eds.*, 1989, pp. 232–44.

_____; **Jackson, Randall W. and Hewings, Geoffrey J. D.** Decomposition Approaches to the Identification of Change in Regional Economies. *Econ. Geogr.*, July 1989, *65*(3), pp. 216–31.

Sonka, Steven T. and Easterling, William E., III. Economic Adjustments to Climatic Variability. In *Oram, P. A., et al.*, 1989, pp. 389–404.

_____; **Hornbaker, Robert H. and Dixon, Bruce L.** Estimating Production Activity Costs for Multioutput Firms with a Random Coefficient Regression Model. *Amer. J. Agr. Econ.*, February 1989, *71*(1), pp. 167–77.

_____; **Mjelde, James W. and Dixon, Bruce L.** Estimating the Value of Sequential Updating Solutions for Intrayear Crop Management. *Western J. Agr. Econ.*, July 1989, *14*(1), pp. 1–8.

Sonnenschein, Hugo and Duffie, Darrell. Arrow and General Equilibrium Theory. *J. Econ. Lit.*, June 1989, *27*(2), pp. 565–98.

Sonstegaard, Miles H. Efficient Pricing and Budgetary Balance. *J. Polit. Econ.*, February 1989, *97*(1), pp. 244–49.

Sonstelie, Jon and Deacon, Robert T. Price Controls and Rent-Seeking Behavior in Developing Countries. *World Devel.*, December 1989, *17*(12), pp. 1945–54.

_____ **and Deacon, Robert T.** The Welfare Costs of Rationing by Waiting. *Econ. Inquiry*, April 1989, *27*(2), pp. 179–96.

Soo, Chung Hwa and Kihwan, Kim. Korea's Domestic Trade Politics and the Uruguay Round. In *Nau, H. R., ed.*, 1989, pp. 135–65.

Soper, John C. and Walstad, William B. What Is High School Economics? Factors Contributing to Student Achievement and Attitudes. *J. Econ. Educ.*, Winter 1989, *20*(1), pp. 23–38.

Sordi, Serena. Some Notes on the Second Version of Kalecki's Business-Cycle Theory. In *Sebastiani, M., ed.*, 1989, pp. 252–74.

Sorensen, A. D. and Weinand, H. Australian Nonmetropolitan Settlements: Some Aspects of Population Growth. In *Gibson, L. J. and Stimson, R. J., eds.*, 1989, pp. 125–34.

Sørensen, Christen. Økonomisk politik i Danmark—En kritik. (Danish Economic Policy—A Critical Evaluation. With English summary.) *Nationaløkon. Tidsskr.*, 1989, *127*(2), pp. 165–83.

Sorensen, Elaine. Measuring the Effect of Occupational Sex and Race Composition on Earn-

ings. In *Michael, R. T.; Hartmann, H. I. and O'Farrell, B., eds.*, 1989, pp. 49–69.

_____. Measuring the Pay Disparity between Typically Female Occupations and Other Jobs: A Bivariate Selectivity Approach. *Ind. Lab. Relat. Rev.*, July 1989, *42*(4), pp. 624–39.

_____. The Wage Effects of Occupational Sex Composition: A Review and New Findings. In *Hill, M. A. and Killingsworth, M. R., eds.*, 1989, pp. 57–79.

Sorenson, Ann Marie. Husbands' and Wives' Characteristics and Fertility Decisions: A Diagonal Mobility Model. *Demography*, February 1989, *26*(1), pp. 125–35.

van Sorge, Wim and van Bochove, Cornelis A. Constant Wealth National Income: Accounting for War Damage with an Application to the Netherlands, 1940–45. *Rev. Income Wealth*, June 1989, *35*(2), pp. 187–208.

Sorger, Gerhard. Competitive Dynamic Advertising: A Modification of the Case Game. *J. Econ. Dynam. Control*, January 1989, *13*(1), pp. 55–80.

_____. On the Optimality and Stability of Competitive Paths in Continuous Time Growth Models. *J. Econ. Theory*, August 1989, *48*(2), pp. 526–47.

_____ **and Feichtinger, Gustav.** Intertemporal Sharecropping: A Differential Game Approach. In *Bamberg, G. and Spremann, K., eds.*, 1989, pp. 415–38.

Sorin, Sylvain. On Repeated Games without a Recursive Structure: Existence of Lim V_n. *Int. J. Game Theory*, 1989, *18*(1), pp. 45–55.

_____ **and Aumann, Robert J.** Cooperation and Bounded Recall. *Games Econ. Behav.*, March 1989, *1*(1), pp. 5–39.

Soro, Bruno. Il moltiplicatore input–output del commercio estero nell'economia italiana, 1970–1985. (The Italian Input–Output Foreign Trade Multiplier, 1970–1985. With English summary.) *Ricerche Econ.*, Oct.–Dec. 1989, *43*(4), pp. 494–509.

Sorokin, D. The Restructuring of Property Relations: A Socialist Choice. *Prob. Econ.*, August 1989, *32*(4), pp. 17–23.

Sorooshian, Soroosh; Kher, Lov and Sioshansi, F. P. Noisy Data and Uncertain Coefficients: A Reply. *Energy J.*, January 1989, *10*(1), pp. 171–74.

Sorrentino, Constance E. Adjusted Japanese Unemployment Rate Remains below 3 Percent in 1987–88. *Mon. Lab. Rev.*, June 1989, *112*(6), pp. 36–38.

_____ **and Kutscher, Ronald E.** Employment and Unemployment Patterns in the U.S. and Europe, 1973–1987. *J. Lab. Res.*, Winter 1989, *10*(1), pp. 5–22.

Soskice, David and Carlin, Wendy. Medium-Run Keynesianism: Hysteresis and Capital Scrapping. In *Davidson, P. and Kregel, J., eds.*, 1989, pp. 241–55.

Soskin, Mark D.; Kasoff, Mark J. and Solocha, Andrew. Canadian Investment in Northern New York: Impact of Exchange Rates on Foreign Direct Investment. *Growth Change*, Winter 1989, *20*(1), pp. 1–16.

Sosnowski, Janusz S. and Makowski, Marek. HYBRID: A Mathematical Programming Package. In *Lewandowski, A. and Wierzbicki, A. P.*, eds., 1989, pp. 376–77.

_____ **and Makowski, Marek.** Mathematical Programming Package HYBRID. In *Lewandowski, A. and Wierzbicki, A. P.*, eds., 1989, pp. 106–44.

Sota, Martha Salgado. Relaxing Distributional Assumptions in the Estimation of Female Labour Supply Models. *Oxford Bull. Econ. Statist.*, November 1989, *51*(4), pp. 429–50.

Sotomayor, Marilda and Roth, Alvin E. The College Admissions Problem Revisited. *Econometrica*, May 1989, *57*(3), pp. 559–70.

Soubeyran, Antoine. When Decentralized Trade Unions Are Better for Their Members than Centralized Ones. *Labour*, Spring 1989, *3*(1), pp. 21–39.

Soubie, Raymond. French Society. In *Frankel, A. V. and Heck, C. B.*, eds., 1989, pp. 29–33.

Soubra, Yehia. The Construction and Engineering Design Services Sector: Some Trade and Development Aspects. *J. World Trade*, February 1989, *23*(1), pp. 97–124.

_____. The Construction and Engineering Design Services Sector: Some Trade and Development Aspects. *J. World Trade*, February 1989, *23*(1), pp. 97–124.

Soufflet, J. F. Les stratégies industrielles dans la filière viande bovine française. (Industrial Strategies in the French Beef Meat Sector. With English summary.) *Écon. Societes*, July 1989, *23*(7), pp. 179–96.

Southall, Aidan. The African Port City: Docks and Suburbs: Review Article. *Econ. Devel. Cult. Change*, October 1989, *38*(1), pp. 167–89.

Southgate, Douglas and Macke, Robert. The Downstream Benefits of Soil Conservation in Third World Hydroelectric Watersheds. *Land Econ.*, February 1989, *65*(1), pp. 38–48.

Southwick, Lawrence, Jr. and Hamlen, William A., Jr. Quality in the MBA Program: Inputs, Outputs or Value Added? *J. Econ. Soc. Meas.*, 1989, *15*(1), pp. 1–26.

Souton, Marc; Dumontier, Pascal and Brunet, Jean-Michel. Les caractéristiques financières des sociétés françaises acquises par offre publique. (Financial Ratios as Predictors of French Takeovers. With English summary.) *Écon. Societes*, December 1989, *23*(12), pp. 107–28.

de Souza, Nali de Jesus. O método dos dígrafos: Uma aplicação para a matriz de relações interindustriais do Brasil de 1975. (With English summary.) *Pesquisa Planejamento Econ.*, December 1989, *19*(3), pp. 613–41.

Spady, Richard H.; Hendricks, Kenneth and Porter, Robert H. Random Reservation Prices and Bidding Behavior in OCS Drainage Auctions. *J. Law Econ.*, Part 2, October 1989, *32*(2), pp. S83–106.

_____ **and Rosenthal, Robert W.** Duopoly with Both Ruin and Entry. *Can. J. Econ.*, November 1989, *22*(4), pp. 834–51.

Spahn, Heinz-Peter. Competition between the D-Mark and the Dollar: The Policies of the Bundesbank in the 1970s and 1980s. *Écon. Appl.*, 1989, *42*(2), pp. 5–33.

Spahn, P. Bernd and Kaiser, Helmut. On the Efficiency and Distributive Justice of Consumption Taxes: A Study on VAT in West Germany. *J. Econ. (Z. Nationalökon.)*, 1989, *49*(2), pp. 199–218.

Spahr, Ronald W.; Herbst, Anthony F. and Maberly, Edwin D. An Analysis of Daily Patterns in Stock Returns across Indices: Spot versus Futures. *Quart. J. Bus. Econ.*, Winter 1989, *28*(1), pp. 55–67.

Spanos, Aris. Early Empirical Findings on the Consumption Function, Stylized Facts or Fiction: A Retrospective View. *Oxford Econ. Pap.*, January 1989, *41*(1), pp. 150–69.

_____. Early Empirical Findings on the Consumption Function, Stylized Facts or Fiction: A Retrospective View. In *de Marchi, N. and Gilbert, C.*, eds., 1989, pp. 150–69.

Sparrow, Paul; Hendry, Chris and Pettigrew, Andrew M. Linking Strategic Change, Competitive Performance and Human Resource Management: Results of a UK Empirical Study. In *Mansfield, R.*, ed., 1989, pp. 195–220.

Spaventa, Luigi. Seigniorage in Europe: Discussion. In *De Cecco, M. and Giovannini, A.*, eds., 1989, pp. 84–88.

_____. Seigniorage: Old and New Policy Issues: Introduction. *Europ. Econ. Rev.*, March 1989, *33*(2/3), pp. 557–63.

_____ **and Giavazzi, Francesco.** Italy: The Real Effects of Inflation and Disinflation. *Econ. Policy: A Europ. Forum*, April 1989, (8), pp. 133–71.

_____, **et al.** Towards a Public Debt Policy in Italy. *Banca Naz. Lavoro Quart. Rev.*, September 1989, (170), pp. 253–302.

Speaker, Paul J.; Mitchell, Douglas W. and Gelles, Gregory M. Geometric Combination Lags as Flexible Infinite Distributed Lag Estimators. *J. Econ. Dynam. Control*, April 1989, *13*(2), pp. 171–85.

Spear, Stephen E. Are Sunspots Necessary? *J. Polit. Econ.*, August 1989, *97*(4), pp. 965–73.

_____. Learning Rational Expectations under Computability Constraints. *Econometrica*, July 1989, *57*(4), pp. 889–910.

_____. When Are Small Frictions Negligible? In *Barnett, W. A.; Geweke, J. and Shell, K.*, eds., 1989, pp. 291–308.

Spears, Annie and Nagarajan, P. Comment on Causality Testing of the Wagner's Law. *Atlantic Econ. J.*, March 1989, *17*(1), pp. 90.

_____ **and Nagarajan, P.** "No Causality" between Government Expenditure and Economic Growth: A Comment. *Public Finance*, 1989, *44*(1), pp. 134–38.

Specker, Konrad. Madras Handlooms in the Nineteenth Century. *Indian Econ. Soc. Hist. Rev.*, April–June 1989, *26*(2), pp. 131–66.

Spector, Abby N.; Eisdorfer, Carl and Kessler,

David A. Caring for the Elderly: Introduction. In *Eisdorfer, C.; Kessler, D. A. and Spector, A. N., eds.*, 1989, pp. xix–xxi.

Spector, Lee C. and Gohmann, Stephan F. Test Scrambling and Student Performance. *J. Econ. Educ.*, Summer 1989, *20*(3), pp. 235–38.

Speight, Alan E. H. and MacDonald, Ronald. Consumption, Saving and Rational Expectations: Some Further Evidence for the U.K. *Econ. J.*, March 1989, *99*(394), pp. 83–91.

_____ **and MacDonald, Ronald.** Does the Public Sector Obey the Rational Expectations–Permanent Income Hypothesis? A Multi-country Study of the Time Series Properties of Government Expenditures. *Appl. Econ.*, September 1989, *21*(9), pp. 1257–66.

_____ **and MacDonald, Ronald.** Government Expenditure under Rational Expectations: Some Estimates for the U.K., Canada, Germany, and the U.S. *Public Finance*, 1989, *44*(3), pp. 419–36.

Spellman, Lewis J. Reducing Default Premia on Insured Deposits: The Policy Alternatives. In *Federal Home Loan Bank of San Francisco*, 1989, pp. 169–85.

Spence, Michael. Job Market Signaling. In *Diamond, P. and Rothschild, M., eds.*, 1989, *1973*, pp. 283–304.

Spencer, Barbara J. and Brander, James A. Moral Hazard and Limited Liability: Implications for the Theory of the Firm. *Int. Econ. Rev.*, November 1989, *30*(4), pp. 833–49.

_____ **and Jones, Ronald W.** Raw Materials, Processing Activities, and Protectionism. *Can. J. Econ.*, August 1989, *22*(3), pp. 469–86.

Spencer, David E. Does Money Matter? The Robustness of Evidence from Vector Autoregressions. *J. Money, Credit, Banking*, November 1989, *21*(4), pp. 442–54.

Spencer, Michael and Hartwick, John M. An Oil-Exporting Region versus an Industrialized Region. In *Andersson, Å. E., et al., eds.*, 1989, pp. 67–79.

Spencer, Peter D. Housing, Wages and UK Labour Markets: Comments. *Oxford Bull. Econ. Statist.*, March 1989, *51*(2), pp. 153–57.

_____. How to Make the Central Bank Look Good: A Reply. *J. Polit. Econ.*, February 1989, *97*(1), pp. 233–35.

_____. Speculative and Precautionary Balances as Complements in the Portfolio: The Case of the U.K. Banking Sector: 1972–1980. *J. Banking Finance*, December 1989, *13*(6), pp. 811–30.

Spencer, Roger W. and Walz, Daniel T. The Informational Content of Forward Rates: Further Evidence. *J. Finan. Res.*, Spring 1989, *12*(1), pp. 69–81.

Spero, Joan E. The Information Revolution and Financial Services: A New North–South Issue? In *Jussawalla, M.; Okuma, T. and Araki, T., eds.*, 1989, pp. 109–17.

Speyrer, Janet Furman. The Effect of Land-Use Restrictions on Market Values of Single-Family Homes in Houston. *J. Real Estate Finance Econ.*, June 1989, *2*(2), pp. 117–30.

Spiegel, M.; Weber, Shlomo and Shitovitz, Benyamin. 'Top of the Line' Quality as an Optimal Solution for a Multi-quality Monopolist. *Europ. Econ. Rev.*, October 1989, *33*(8), pp. 1641–52.

Spiegel, Uriel; Friedman, Joseph and Hakim, Simon. The Difference between Short and Long Run Effects of Police Outlays on Crime: Policing Deters Criminals Initially, but Later They May 'Learn by Doing.' *Amer. J. Econ. Sociology*, April 1989, *48*(2), pp. 177–91.

Spiess, Lorraine. Canada–China Mineral Trade. In *Jackson, L. M. and Richardson, P. R., eds.*, 1989, pp. 7–14.

Spiller, Pablo T. A Note on Pricing of Hub-and-Spoke Networks. *Econ. Letters*, August 1989, *30*(2), pp. 165–69.

_____ **and Reiss, Peter C.** Competition and Entry in Small Airline Markets. *J. Law Econ.*, Part 2, October 1989, *32*(2), pp. S179–202.

_____ **and Scheffman, David T.** Empirical Approaches to Market Power: Introduction. *J. Law Econ.*, Part 2, October 1989, *32*(2), pp. S3–10.

Spindt, Paul A. and Benveniste, Lawrence M. How Investment Bankers Determine the Offer Price and Allocation of New Issues. *J. Finan. Econ.*, October 1989, *24*(2), pp. 343–61.

_____ **and Stolz, Richard W.** The Expected Stop-Out Price in a Discriminating Auction. *Econ. Letters*, December 1989, *31*(2), pp. 133–37.

_____ **and Tarhan, Vefa.** Bank Reserve Adjustment Process and the Use of Reserve Carry-over as a Reserve Management Tool: Reply. *J. Banking Finance*, March 1989, *13*(1), pp. 37–40.

Spinelli, Franco and Dooley, Michael P. The Early Stages of Financial Innovation and Money Demand in France and Italy. *Manchester Sch. Econ. Soc. Stud.*, June 1989, *57*(2), pp. 107–24.

Spiro, Erwin. The 1989 Budget Policy: South Africa. *Bull. Int. Fiscal Doc.*, June 1989, *43*(6), pp. 286–88.

Spiro, Michael H. and Makhija, Anil K. Determinants of Earned Rates of Return on Equity of U.S. Electric Utilities, 1976–1984. *Econ. Letters*, October 1989, *30*(4), pp. 367–71.

Spiro, Peter S. Improving a Group Forecast by Removing the Conservative Bias in Its Components. *Int. J. Forecasting*, 1989, *5*(1), pp. 127–31.

Spithoven, A. H. G. M. Distribution of Income and Unemployment in the Netherlands 1965–85. In *Davidson, P. and Kregel, J., eds.*, 1989, pp. 280–87.

Spivak, Avia and Kotlikoff, Laurence J. The Family as an Incomplete Annuities Market. In *Kotlikoff, L. J.*, 1989, *1981*, pp. 88–108.

_____; **Kotlikoff, Laurence J. and Shoven, John B.** Annuity Insurance, Savings, and Inequality. In *Kotlikoff, L. J.*, 1989, pp. 109–40.

_____ **and Segal, Uzi.** Firm Size and Optimal Growth Rates. *Europ. Econ. Rev.*, January 1989, *33*(1), pp. 159–67.

_____; **Summers, Lawrence H. and Kotlikoff,**

Laurence J. The Adequacy of Savings. In *Kotlikoff, L. J.*, 1989, *1982*, pp. 429–54.

Spivey, Michael F. The Cost of Including a Call Provision in Municipal Debt Contracts. *J. Finan. Res.*, Fall 1989, *12*(3), pp. 203–16.

Spofford, Walter O., Jr.; Harrington, Winston and Krupnick, Alan J. The Economic Losses of a Waterborne Disease Outbreak. *J. Urban Econ.*, January 1989, *25*(1), pp. 116–37.

Spohn, Willfried and Bodemann, Y. Michal. The Capitalist Class: Federal Republic of Germany. In *Bottomore, T. and Brym, R. J.*, eds., 1989, pp. 73–108.

Sporleder, Thomas L. Pricing Efficiency in Agricultural Markets: Discussion. *Western J. Agr. Econ.*, July 1989, *14*(1), pp. 122–25.

Spotton, Brenda and Kompas, Tom. A Note on Rational Speculative Bubbles. *Econ. Letters*, October 1989, *30*(4), pp. 327–31.

Spraos, John. Kaldor on Commodities. *Cambridge J. Econ.*, March 1989, *13*(1), pp. 201–22.

_____. Kaldor on Commodities. In *Lawson, T.; Palma, J. G. and Sender, J.*, eds., 1989, pp. 201–22.

Spremann, Klaus. Agent and Principal. In *Bamberg, G. and Spremann, K.*, eds., 1989, pp. 3–37.

_____. Stakeholder-Ansatz versus Agency-Theorie. (With English summary.) *Z. Betriebswirtshaft*, July 1989, *59*(7), pp. 742–46.

_____ and Jung, Michael. Transaktionsrisiken. (With English summary.) *Z. Betriebswirtshaft*, January 1989, *59*(1), pp. 94–112.

Spriggs, John and Taylor, J. S. Effects of the Monetary Macro-economy on Canadian Agricultural Prices. *Can. J. Econ.*, May 1989, *22*(2), pp. 278–89.

Sprinkel, Beryl W. Supply-Side Economics: Lessons from the U.S. Experience. In *Fels, G. and von Furstenberg, G. M.*, eds., 1989, pp. 135–51.

Sprinkle, Richard L.; Clark, Don P. and Sawyer, W. Charles. Determinants of Industry Participation under Offshore Assembly Provisions in the United States Tariff Code. *J. World Trade*, October 1989, *23*(5), pp. 123–30.

_____; Deyak, Timothy A. and Sawyer, W. Charles. An Empirical Examination of the Structural Stability of Disaggregated U.S. Import Demand. *Rev. Econ. Statist.*, May 1989, *71*(2), pp. 337–41.

_____ and Sawyer, W. Charles. Alternative Empirical Estimates of Trade Creation and Trade Diversion: A Comparison of the Baldwin–Murray and Verdoorn Models. *Weltwirtsch. Arch.*, 1989, *125*(1), pp. 61–73.

Spronk, Jaap. Multi Factorial Financial Planning. In *Lockett, A. G. and Islei, G.*, eds., 1989, pp. 380–89.

Sproul, Allan. Reflections of a Central Banker. *Fed. Res. Bank New York Quart. Rev.*, Special Issue, 1989, pp. 21–28.

Spuches, Charles M. and Evensky, Jerry M. The Syracuse University Experience: Lessons in Multiteacher Course Design. *J. Econ. Educ.*, Spring 1989, *20*(2), pp. 181–98.

Spudeck, Raymond E. and Moyer, R. Charles. A Note on the Stock Market's Reaction to the Accident at Three Mile Island. *J. Econ. Bus.*, August 1989, *41*(3), pp. 235–40.

Spulber, Daniel F. Product Variety and Competitive Discounts. *J. Econ. Theory*, August 1989, *48*(2), pp. 510–25.

_____. The Second Best Core. *Int. Econ. Rev.*, August 1989, *30*(3), pp. 623–31.

_____ and Besanko, David. Antitrust Enforcement under Asymmetric Information. *Econ. J.*, June 1989, *99*(396), pp. 408–25.

_____ and Besanko, David. Delegated Law Enforcement and Noncooperative Behavior. *J. Law, Econ., Organ.*, Spring 1989, *5*(1), pp. 25–52.

_____; Stangle, Bruce E. and MacAvoy, Paul W. Is Competitive Entry Free? Bypass and Partial Deregulation in Natural Gas Markets. *Yale J. Regul.*, Summer 1989, *6*(2), pp. 209–47.

Srinagesh, Padmanabhan and Bradburd, Ralph M. Quality Distortion by a Discriminating Monopolist. *Amer. Econ. Rev.*, March 1989, *79*(1), pp. 96–105.

Srinath, K. P.; Quenneville, B. and Rao, J. N. K. Estimation of Level and Change Using Current Preliminary Data. In *Kasprzyk, D., et al.*, eds., 1989, pp. 457–79.

Srinidhi, Bin N. and Vasarhelyi, M. A. Adaptation and Use of Reliability Concepts in Internal Control Evaluation. In *Gangolly, J.*, ed., 1989, pp. 141–57.

Srinivasan, Aruna. Measuring State and Local Fiscal Capacities in the Southeast. *Fed. Res. Bank Atlanta Econ. Rev.*, Sept.–Oct. 1989, *74*(5), pp. 36–46.

_____. Public Finance and Economic Growth in the Southeast. *Fed. Res. Bank Atlanta Econ. Rev.*, Jan.–Feb. 1989, *74*(1), pp. 48–62.

Srinivasan, P. V. Redistributive Impact of 'Optimal' Commodity Taxes: Evidence from Indian Data. *Econ. Letters*, October 1989, *30*(4), pp. 385–88.

Srinivasan, T. N. Food Aid: A Cause of Development Failure or an Instrument for Success? *World Bank Econ. Rev.*, January 1989, *3*(1), pp. 39–65.

_____. The Noncompetitive Theory of International Trade and Trade Policy: Comment. In *Fischer, S. and de Tray, D.*, eds., 1989, pp. 217–21.

_____. North–South Models and the Evolution of Global Interdependence: Comment. In *[Díaz-Alejandro, C.]*, 1989, pp. 421–22.

_____. On Choice among Creditors and Bonded Labour Contracts. In *Bardhan, P.*, ed. *(II)*, 1989, pp. 203–20.

_____. On Studying Socio-Economic Change in Rural India. In *Bardhan, P.*, ed. *(I)*, 1989, pp. 238–49.

_____. Recent Theories of Imperfect Competition and International Trade: Any Implications for Development Strategy? *Indian Econ. Rev.*, Jan.–June 1989, *24*(1), pp. 1–23.

_____. The Theory of International Trade, Steady-State Analysis and Economics of Development. In *Feiwel, G. R., ed. (II)*, 1989, pp. 687–701.

_____ and Bell, Clive. Interlinked Transactions in Rural Markets: An Empirical Study of Andhra Pradesh, Bihar and Punjab. *Oxford Bull. Econ. Statist.*, February 1989, *51*(1), pp. 73–83.

_____ and Bell, Clive. Some Aspects of Linked Product and Credit Market Contracts among Risk-Neutral Agents. In *Bardhan, P., ed. (II)*, 1989, pp. 221–36.

_____; Buiter, Willem H. and Kletzer, Kenneth M. Some Thoughts on the Brady Plan: Putting a Fourth Leg on the Donkey? *World Devel.*, October 1989, *17*(10), pp. 1661–64.

Srinivasan, V.; Abeele, P. Vanden and Butaye, I. The Factor Structure of Multidimensional Response to Marketing Stimuli: A Comparison of Two Approaches. *Marketing Sci.*, Winter 1989, *8*(1), pp. 78–88.

_____ and Basu, Amiya K. The Metric Quality of Ordered Categorical Data. *Marketing Sci.*, Summer 1989, *8*(3), pp. 205–30.

Srinivasan, Venkat and Bolster, Paul J. An Expert System for Assigning Investment Quality Ratings Using the AHP. In *Lockett, A. G. and Islei, G., eds.*, 1989, pp. 563–74.

_____; Kim, Yong H. and Bolster, Paul J. A Framework for Integrating the Leasing Alternative with the Capital Budgeting Decision. In *Lee, C. F., ed.*, 1989, pp. 75–93.

Srivastava, A. K. and Tracy, D. S. On Approximating the Minimum Risk Estimator in Linear Regression Models. *Econ. Letters*, 1989, *29*(2), pp. 153–56.

Srivastava, J. P. Development of Crop Germplasm with Improved Tolerance for Environmental and Biotic Stresses. In *Oram, P. A., et al.*, 1989, pp. 489–501.

Srivastava, Rajendra P. Measurement of the Reliability Parameters of Internal Accounting Control Components: A Field Study. In *Gangolly, J., ed.*, 1989, pp. 159–78.

Srivastava, Sanjay and Palfrey, Thomas R. Implementation with Incomplete Information in Exchange Economies. *Econometrica*, January 1989, *57*(1), pp. 115–34.

_____ and Palfrey, Thomas R. Mechanism Design with Incomplete Information: A Solution to the Implementation Problem. *J. Polit. Econ.*, June 1989, *97*(3), pp. 668–91.

Srivastava, Vinita. Urban Industrial Workers in India: Differentiated Labour and Differentiated Hours of Work. In *Agassi, J. B. and Heycock, S., eds.*, 1989, pp. 145–60.

Srivastava, Virendra K. and Rao, B. Bhaskara. The Specification and Estimation of the Output Equation in the Rational Expectations Model with Gradual Price Adjustment. *Australian Econ. Pap.*, December 1989, *28*(53), pp. 201–08.

_____; Ullah, Aman and Carter, R. A. L. Corrigendum [The Sampling Distribution of Shrinkage Estimators and Their *F*-Ratios in the Re-gression Model]. *J. Econometrics*, February 1989, *40*(2), pp. 339.

St. Louis, Larry V. Empirical Tests of Some Semisurvey Update Procedures Applied to Rectangular Input–Output Tables. *J. Reg. Sci.*, August 1989, *29*(3), pp. 373–85.

Sta. Romana, Elpidio R. The Philippine State's Hegemony and Fiscal Base, 1950–1985. *Developing Econ.*, June 1989, *27*(2), pp. 185–205.

Staaf, Robert J. and De Alessi, Louis. Subjective Value in Contract Law. *J. Inst. Theoretical Econ.*, December 1989, *145*(4), pp. 561–77.

Staatz, John M.; Dioné, Josué and Dembélé, N. Nango. Cereals Market Liberalization in Mali. *World Devel.*, May 1989, *17*(5), pp. 703–18.

Stabler, Jack C. Dualism and Development in the Northwest Territories. *Econ. Devel. Cult. Change*, July 1989, *37*(4), pp. 805–39.

_____ and Howe, Eric C. Canada Divided: The Optimal Division of an Economy into Regions. *J. Reg. Sci.*, May 1989, *29*(2), pp. 191–211.

Stacchetti, Ennio; Geanakoplos, John and Pearce, David G. Psychological Games and Sequential Rationality. *Games Econ. Behav.*, March 1989, *1*(1), pp. 60–79.

Stacey, J. A. and Strain, W. J. Investment in Canada. *Bull. Int. Fiscal Doc.*, February 1989, *43*(2), pp. 55–62.

Stach, Patricia Burgess. Real Estate Development and Urban Form: Roadblocks in the Path to Residential Exclusivity. *Bus. Hist. Rev.*, Summer 1989, *63*(2), pp. 356–83.

Stachurski, Andrzej and Kiwiel, Krzysztof C. Issues of Effectiveness Arising in the Design of a System of Nondifferentiable Optimization Algorithms. In *Lewandowski, A. and Wierzbicki, A. P., eds.*, 1989, pp. 180–92.

Stackhouse, Lee Ann and Christiansen, Robert E. The Privatization of Agricultural Trading in Malawi. *World Devel.*, May 1989, *17*(5), pp. 729–40.

Staehle, Wolfgang H. Employment of Older Persons from a Management Point of View. In *Schmähl, W., ed.*, 1989, pp. 163–73.

Staelin, Richard and Keller, Kevin Lane. Assessing Biases in Measuring Decision Effectiveness and Information Overload. *J. Cons. Res.*, March 1989, *15*(4), pp. 504–08.

Stafford, Bernard. De-industrialization in Advanced Economies: Review Article. *Cambridge J. Econ.*, December 1989, *13*(4), pp. 541–54.

Stafford, H. A. Geographic Implications of Plant Closure Legislation in the USA. In *Gibbs, D., ed.*, 1989, pp. 95–116.

Stager, David A. A. and Foot, David K. Intertemporal Market Effect on Gender Earnings Differentials: Lawyers in Canada, 1970–80. *Appl. Econ.*, August 1989, *21*(8), pp. 1011–28.

_____ and Foot, David K. Lawyers' Earnings under Market Growth and Differentiation, 1970–80. *Can. J. Econ.*, February 1989, *22*(1), pp. 150–63.

Stäglin, Reiner. Toward an Input–Output Subsystem for the Information Sector. In *Miller, R. E.; Polenske, K. R. and Rose, A. Z., eds.*, 1989, pp. 65–78.

_____; **Stahmer, Carsten and Reich, Utz-Peter.**
The Implementation of a Consistent System
of Input–Output Tables for the Federal Republic of Germany. In *Franz, A. and Rainer, N.,
eds.*, 1989, pp. 111–30.

Stagni, Anna; Bosi, Paolo and Golinelli, Roberto.
Le origini del debito pubblico e il costo della
stabilizzazione. (With English summary.) *Politica. Econ.*, December 1989, 5(3), pp. 389–
425.

Stahl, Charles W. and Habib, Ahsanul. The Impact of Overseas Workers' Remittances on Indigenous Industries: Evidence from Bangladesh. *Developing Econ.*, September 1989,
27(3), pp. 269–85.

Stahl, Dale O., II. Oligopolistic Pricing with Sequential Consumer Search. *Amer. Econ. Rev.*,
September 1989, 79(4), pp. 700–712.

Ståhl, I. The Slope of the Union's Resistance
Curve in Collective Bargaining—A Solution to
the Hicks–Shackle Controversy: Comment. In
Wood, J. C. and Woods, R. N., eds., Vol. 3,
1989, *1980*, pp. 226–29.

**Stahl, Joseph W.; Levine, Daniel B. and Horow-
itz, Stanley A.** The Effect of Technology on
the Supportability and Cost of Avionics Equipment. In *Gulledge, T. R., Jr. and Litteral, L.
A., eds.*, 1989, pp. 214–25.

Stahl, Konrad. Housing Patterns and Mobility of
the Aged: The United States and West Germany. In *Wise, D. A., ed.*, 1989, pp. 93–115.

_____ **and Schulz, Norbert.** Good and Bad Competition in Spatial Markets for Search Goods:
The Case of Linear Utility Functions. *Ann.
Écon. Statist.*, July–Dec. 1989, (15–16), pp.
113–36.

Ståhlberg, Ann-Charlotte. Redistribution Effects
of Social Policy in a Lifetime Analytical Framework. In *Gustafsson, B. A. and Klevmarken,
N. A., eds.*, 1989, pp. 51–65.

Stahlecker, Peter and Schmidt, Karsten. Zur
Ausnutzung von a priori Informationen bei der
Schätzung einer gesamtwirtschaftlichen Cobb–
Douglas-Produktionsfunktion. (On the Estima-
tion of a Macroeconomic Cobb–Douglas Pro-
duction Function Using Prior Information.
With English summary.) *Jahr. Nationalökon.
Statist.*, December 1989, 206(6), pp. 599–605.

**Stahmer, Carsten; Reich, Utz-Peter and Stäglin,
Reiner.** The Implementation of a Consistent
System of Input–Output Tables for the Federal
Republic of Germany. In *Franz, A. and
Rainer, N., eds.*, 1989, pp. 111–30.

_____ **and Schäfer, Dieter.** Inpu–Output Model
for the Analysis of Environmental Protection
Activities. *Econ. Systems Res.*, 1989, *1*(2), pp.
203–28.

Staiger, Robert W. U.S.–Canada Bilateral Tariff
Elimination: The Role of Product Differentia-
tion and Market Structure: Comment. In
Feenstra, R. C., ed., 1989, pp. 246–50.

_____ **and Bagwell, Kyle.** The Role of Export
Subsidies When Product Quality is Unknown.
J. Int. Econ., August 1989, 27(1–2), pp. 69–
89.

_____ **and Tabellini, Guido.** Rules and Discretion in Trade Policy. *Europ. Econ. Rev.*, July
1989, 33(6), pp. 1265–77.

Stajner, Rikard. The System of International Economic Relations. In *Macesich, G., ed.*, 1989,
pp. 180–88.

Stalder, Peter. A Disequilibrium Model with
Smooth Regime Transitions and a Keynesian
Spillover for Switzerland's Labor Market. *Eu-
rop. Econ. Rev.*, April 1989, 33(4), pp. 863–93.

_____. Excess Demand and Capacity Utiliza-
tion—An Empirical Analysis with Swiss Business Survey Data. *Appl. Econ.*, October 1989,
21(10), pp. 1383–95.

Staley, Tom. Nobel Laureates in Economic Sciences: A Biographical Dictionary: Paul Anthony Samuelson: 1970. In *Katz, B. S., ed.*,
1989, pp. 240–52.

Stallings, Barbara. Political Economy of Democratic Transition: Chile in the 1980s. In *Stallings, B. and Kaufman, R., eds.*, 1989, pp. 181–
99.

_____ **and Kaufman, Robert R.** Debt and Democracy in the 1980s: The Latin American Experience. In *Stallings, B. and Kaufman, R.,
eds.*, 1989, pp. 201–23.

Stallman, Judith I. Relevancy of the Social Sciences in the Policy Arena: Implications for Agricultural Economics: Discussion. *Southern J.
Agr. Econ.*, July 1989, 21(1), pp. 53–54.

**Stam, Antonie; Joachimsthaler, Erich A. and
Gardiner, Lorraine R.** Multicriteria Issues in
Marketing: A Sales Resource Allocation Exam-
ple and Potential Areas of Future Research.
In *Lockett, A. G. and Islei, G., eds.*, 1989,
pp. 224–33.

Stambaugh, Robert F. and Kandel, Shmuel. A
Mean–Variance Framework for Tests of Asset
Pricing Models. *Rev. Financial Stud.*, 1989,
2(2), pp. 125–56.

Stanbury, William T. Privatization in Canada:
Ideology, Symbolism or Substance? In *Mac-
Avoy, P. W., et al.*, 1989, pp. 273–329.

_____. Reforming Direct Regulation in Canada.
In *Button, K. and Swann, D., eds.*, 1989, pp.
49–78.

Standaert, Stan. Did Algeria Experience Re-
pressed Inflation in the 1970s? *Econ. Modelling*, January 1989, 6(1), pp. 94–104.

Standing, Guy. The "British Experiment": Structural Adjustment or Accelerated Decline? In
*Portes, A.; Castells, M. and Benton, L. A.,
eds.*, 1989, pp. 279–97.

_____. Global Feminization through Flexible La-
bor. *World Devel.*, July 1989, 17(7), pp. 1077–
95.

Stanev, Stefan. Rate of Plant Utilization and Its
Effect on the Balance of Economic Growth.
In *Bulgarian Academy of Sciences, Institute
of Economics*, 1989, pp. 100–106.

Stanfield, James Ronald. Karl Polanyi and Contemporary Economic Thought. *Rev. Soc.
Econ.*, Fall 1989, 47(3), pp. 266–79.

_____. Of Paradigms and Discipline. In *Samuels,
W. J., ed. (II)*, 1989, pp. 173–79.

_____. U.S. Marxist Economics in Veblenian

Perspective. In *Dugger, W. M., ed.*, 1989, pp. 83–104.

———. Veblenian and Neo-Marxian Perspectives on the Cultural Crisis of Late Capitalism. *J. Econ. Issues*, September 1989, 23(3), pp. 717–34.

Stanford, William. Symmetric Paths and Evolution to Equilibrium in the Discounted Prisoners' Dilemma. *Econ. Letters*, December 1989, 31(2), pp. 139–43.

Stangeland, David; Morck, Randall and Schwartz, Eduardo S. The Valuation of Forestry Resources under Stochastic Prices and Inventories. *J. Finan. Quant. Anal.*, December 1989, 24(4), pp. 473–87.

Stangle, Bruce E.; MacAvoy, Paul W. and Spulber, Daniel F. Is Competitive Entry Free? Bypass and Partial Deregulation in Natural Gas Markets. *Yale J. Regul.*, Summer 1989, 6(2), pp. 209–47.

Staniswalis, Joan G. The Kernel Estimate of a Regression Function in Likelihood-Based Models. *J. Amer. Statist. Assoc.*, March 1989, 84(405), pp. 276–83.

———. Local Bandwidth Selection for Kernel Estimates. *J. Amer. Statist. Assoc.*, March 1989, 84(405), pp. 284–88.

Stankovsky, Jan and Gabrisch, Hubert. Special Forms of East–West Trade. *Soviet E. Europ. Foreign Trade*, Spring 1989, 25(1), pp. 1–132.

——— and Gabrisch, Hubert. Special Forms of East–West Trade. *Soviet E. Europ. Foreign Trade*, Summer 1989, 25(2), pp. 1–117.

Stanley, Guy. Annual Review of Nations: Year 1988: Canada. In *Haberman, L. and Sacks, P. M., eds.*, 1989, pp. 55–73.

Stanley, Michael A.; Balachandran, Chandra S. and Fisher, Peter F. An Expert System Approach to Rural Development: A Prototype (TIHSO). *J. Developing Areas*, January 1989, 23(2), pp. 259–70.

Stanley, T. D. and Jarrell, Stephen B. Meta-Regression Analysis: A Quantitative Method of Literature Surveys. *J. Econ. Surveys*, 1989, 3(2), pp. 161–70.

Stanley, Thomas; Ogden, William, Jr. and Rangan, Nanda K. Risk Reduction in S&L Mortgage Loan Portfolios through Geographic Diversification. *J. Finan. Services Res.*, February 1989, 2(1), pp. 39–48.

Stano, Miron and Folland, Sherman. Sources of Small Area Variations in the Use of Medical Care. *J. Health Econ.*, March 1989, 8(1), pp. 85–107.

Stanovnik, Tine. The Direct Measurement of Welfare Levels in Slovene Households. *Econ. Anal. Workers' Manage.*, 1989, 23(1), pp. 43–54.

Stanton, Julie; Tarr, David and de Melo, Jaime. Revenue-Raising Taxes: General Equilibrium Evaluation of Alternative Taxation in U.S. Petroleum Industries. *J. Policy Modeling*, Fall 1989, 11(3), pp. 425–49.

Stanton, Thomas H. Government Sponsored Enterprises: Another View. *Public Budg. Finance*, Autumn 1989, 9(3), pp. 81–86.

Stanton, Timothy J. Regional Conflict and the Clean Air Act. *Rev. Reg. Stud.*, Fall 1989, 19(3), pp. 24–30.

Staples, A. C. Memoirs of William Prinsep: Calcutta Years, 1817–1842. *Indian Econ. Soc. Hist. Rev.*, Jan.–March 1989, 26(1), pp. 61–79.

Staples, Katharine and Nawrocki, David. A Customized LPM Risk Measure for Portfolio Analysis. *Appl. Econ.*, February 1989, 21(2), pp. 205–18.

Stapleton, David C. Cohort Size and the Academic Labor Market. *J. Human Res.*, Spring 1989, 24(2), pp. 221–52.

Starck, Christian C. Consumption and Income in Finland, 1960–1983: A Multiple Time Series Analysis. *Liiketaloudellinen Aikak.*, 1989, 38(3), pp. 225–39.

Stark, David. Coexisting Organizational Forms in Hungary's Emerging Mixed Economy. In *Nee, V. and Stark, D., eds.*, 1989, pp. 137–68.

——— and Nee, Victor. Toward an Institutional Analysis of State Socialism. In *Nee, V. and Stark, D., eds.*, 1989, pp. 1–31.

Stark, Graham and Dilnot, Andrew. The Poverty Trap, Tax Cuts, and the Reform of Social Security. In *Dilnot, A. and Walker, I., eds.*, 1989, pp. 169–78.

——— and Fry, Vanessa. The Take-Up of Supplementary Benefit: Gaps in the 'Safety Net'? In *Dilnot, A. and Walker, I., eds.*, 1989, pp. 179–91.

——— and Johnson, Paul. Ten Years of Mrs Thatcher: The Distributional Consequences. *Fisc. Stud.*, May 1989, 10(2), pp. 29–37.

Stark, Oded. Altruism and the Quality of Life. *Amer. Econ. Rev.*, May 1989, 79(2), pp. 86–90.

——— and Katz, Eliakim. International Labour Migration under Alternative Informational Regimes: A Diagrammatic Analysis. *Europ. Econ. Rev.*, January 1989, 33(1), pp. 127–42.

——— and Rosenzweig, Mark R. Consumption Smoothing, Migration, and Marriage: Evidence from Rural India. *J. Polit. Econ.*, August 1989, 97(4), pp. 905–26.

——— and Taylor, J. Edward. Relative Deprivation and International Migration. *Demography*, February 1989, 26(1), pp. 1–14.

Starkey, Betty J. Annual Review of Nations: Year 1988: Australia. In *Haberman, L. and Sacks, P. M., eds.*, 1989, pp. 19–35.

———. Annual Review of Nations: Year 1988: Philippines. In *Haberman, L. and Sacks, P. M., eds.*, 1989, pp. 267–84.

———. Annual Review of Nations: Year 1988: Thailand. In *Haberman, L. and Sacks, P. M., eds.*, 1989, pp. 335–52.

Starkey, Ken. Time and Professionalism: Disputes Concerning the Nature of Contract. *Brit. J. Ind. Relat.*, November 1989, 27(3), pp. 375–95.

———. Time and Work: A Psychological Perspective. In *Blyton, P., et al.*, 1989, pp. 35–56.

Starkie, David. British Rail: Competition on the

Network. In *Veljanovski, C., ed. (II)*, 1989, *1984*, pp. 178–88.

———. Deregulation: The Australian Experience. In *Button, K. and Swann, D., eds.*, 1989, pp. 104–23.

Starleaf, Dennis. Break-Out Session I—Issues for Hunger, Malnutrition, Agriculture, and Food Policy: Recommendations: Financial and Trading Firms and Organizations. In *Helmuth, J. W. and Johnson, S. R., eds., Vol. 1*, 1989, pp. 128–30.

Starmer, Chris and Sugden, Robert. Probability and Juxtaposition Effects: An Experimental Investigation of the Common Ratio Effect. *J. Risk Uncertainty*, June 1989, *2*(2), pp. 159–78.

———; **Sugden, Robert and Loomes, Graham.** Preference Reversal: Information-Processing Effect or Rational Non-transitive Choice? *Econ. J.*, Supplement, 1989, *99*(395), pp. 140–51.

Starodubrovskaia, I.; Tolstikov, S. and Gromkovskii, V. Bureaucratism in the Socialist Economy: Its Essence and Forms, and Means of Overcoming It. *Prob. Econ.*, September 1989, *32*(5), pp. 13–34.

Starr, Joyce R. A Marshall Plan for the Middle East: The U.S. Response. In *Fishelson, G., ed.*, 1989, pp. 163–66.

Starr, Ross M. Decentralized Non-monetary Trade. In *Starr, R. M., ed.*, 1989, *1976*, pp. 172–74.

———. General Equilibrium Models of Monetary Economies: Studies in the Static Foundations of Monetary Theory: Open Questions: A Research Agenda. In *Starr, R. M., ed.*, 1989, pp. 339–42.

———. Money in a Sequence Economy: A Correction. In *Starr, R. M., ed.*, 1989, *1978*, pp. 241.

———. The Price of Money in a Pure Exchange Monetary Economy with Taxation. In *Starr, R. M., ed.*, 1989, *1974*, pp. 326–35.

———. The Structure of Exchange in Barter and Monetary Economies. In *Starr, R. M., ed.*, 1989, *1972*, pp. 131–43.

——— **and Goldman, Steven M.** Pairwise, *t*-Wise, and Pareto Optimalities. In *Starr, R. M., ed.*, 1989, *1982*, pp. 99–112.

——— **and Heller, Walter P.** Equilibrium with Non-convex Transactions Costs: Monetary and Non-monetary Economies. In *Starr, R. M., ed.*, 1989, *1976*, pp. 267–87.

——— **and Ostroy, Joseph M.** Money and the Decentralization of Exchange. In *Starr, R. M., ed.*, 1989, *1974*, pp. 149–69.

Starrett, David A. Inefficiency and the Demand for "Money" in a Sequence Economy. In *Starr, R. M., ed.*, 1989, *1973*, pp. 229–40.

Startz, Richard. Monopolistic Competition as a Foundation for Keynesian Macroeconomic Models. *Quart. J. Econ.*, November 1989, *104*(4), pp. 737–52.

———. The Stochastic Behavior of Durable and Nondurable Consumption. *Rev. Econ. Statist.*, May 1989, *71*(2), pp. 356–63.

———; **Nelson, Charles R. and Turner, Christo-** pher M. A Markov Model of Heteroskedasticity, Risk, and Learning in the Stock Market. *J. Finan. Econ.*, November 1989, *25*(1), pp. 3–22.

Staten, Michael and Umbeck, John. Economic Inefficiency: A Failure of Economists. *J. Econ. Educ.*, Winter 1989, *20*(1), pp. 57–72.

——— **and Umbeck, John.** Shipping the Good Students Out: The Effect of a Fixed Charge on Student Enrollments. *J. Econ. Educ.*, Spring 1989, *20*(2), pp. 165–71.

Statman, Meir and Solt, Michael E. Good Companies, Bad Stocks. *J. Portfol. Manage.*, Summer 1989, *15*(4), pp. 39–44.

Staudhammer, Rainer; Steinert, Heinz and Blankenburg, Erhard. Political Scandals and Corruption Issues in West Germany. In *Heidenheimer, A. J.; Johnston, M. and LeVine, V. T., eds.*, 1989, pp. 913–32.

Stavenhagen, Lutz G. Der europäische Binnenmarkt—Chancen und Risiken für die deutsche Wirtschaft. (The European Single Market—Opportunities and Risks for the German Economy. With English summary.) *Jahr. Nationalökon. Statist.*, October 1989, *206*(4–5), pp. 476–86.

Stayman, Douglas M. and Deshpande, Rohit. Situational Ethnicity and Consumer Behavior. *J. Cons. Res.*, December 1989, *16*(3), pp. 361–71.

Steckel, Joel H.; Winer, Russell S. and Glazer, Rashi. The Formation of Key Marketing Variable Expectations and Their Impact on Firm Performance: Some Experimental Evidence. *Marketing Sci.*, Winter 1989, *8*(1), pp. 18–34.

Steckel, Richard H. Household Migration and Rural Settlement in the United States, 1850–1860. *Exploration Econ. Hist.*, April 1989, *26*(2), pp. 190–218.

Stedman, Louellen and Hakim, Peter. Political Change and Economic Policy in Latin America and the Caribbean in 1988. In *Weeks, J. F., ed.*, 1989, pp. 165–74.

Steedman, Hilary and Wagner, Karin. Productivity, Machinery and Skills: Clothing Manufacture in Britain and Germany. *Nat. Inst. Econ. Rev.*, May 1989, (128), pp. 40–57.

Steedman, Ian. Economic Theory and Intrinsically Non-autonomous Preferences and Beliefs. In *Steedman, I.*, 1989, *1980*, pp. 205–21.

———. Heterogeneous Labour and 'Classical' Theory. In *Steedman, I.*, 1989, *1980*, pp. 1–13.

———. Heterogeneous Labour, Money Wages and Marx's Theory. In *Steedman, I.*, 1989, *1985*, pp. 14–39.

———. Jevons's Theory of Capital and Interest. In *Steedman, I.*, 1989, *1972*, pp. 145–67.

———. Marx on Ricardo. In *Steedman, I.*, 1989, *1975*, pp. 51–84.

———. Natural Prices, Differential Profit Rates and the Classical Competitive Process. In *Steedman, I.*, 1989, *1984*, pp. 98–116.

———. On Pasinetti's 'G' Matrix. *Metroecon.*, February 1989, *40*(1), pp. 3–15.

———. On the 'Impossibility' of Hicks-Neutral

Technical Change. In *Wood, J. C. and Woods, R. N., eds., Vol. 4*, 1989, *1985*, pp. 231–45.

———. P. H. Wicksteed's Jevonian Critique of Marx. In *Steedman, I.*, 1989, pp. 117–44.

———. Positive Profits with Negative Surplus Value. In *Steedman, I.*, 1989, *1975*, pp. 85–97.

———. Rationality, Economic Man and Altruism in P. H. Wicksteed's *Common Sense of Political Economy*. In *Steedman, I.*, 1989, *1986*, pp. 185–204.

———. Time Preference, the Rate of Interest and Abstinence from Accumulation. In *Steedman, I.*, 1989, *1981*, pp. 222–45.

———. Trade Interest versus Class Interest. In *Steedman, I.*, 1989, *1986*, pp. 168–84.

——— and Metcalfe, J. S. 'On Foreign Trade.' In *Steedman, I.*, 1989, *1973*, pp. 40–50.

Steeh, Charlotte G. Trends in Nonresponse Rates, 1952–1979. In *Singer, E. and Presser, S., eds.*, 1989, *1981*, pp. 32–49.

Steel, Brent S.; Lovrich, Nicholas P. and Warner, Rebecca L. Conditions Associated with the Advent of Representative Bureaucracy: The Case of Women in Policing. *Soc. Sci. Quart.*, September 1989, *70*(3), pp. 562–78.

Steele, H. Keith C. The Australian Antidumping System. In *Jackson, J. H. and Vermulst, E. A., eds.*, 1989, pp. 223–86.

Steenbergen, Jacques. Some Comments on EEC Antidumping Enforcement. In *Jackson, J. H. and Vermulst, E. A., eds.*, 1989, pp. 396–99.

Steenge, Albert E. Second Thoughts on the Commodity Technology and the Industry Technology Approaches. In *Franz, A. and Rainer, N., eds.*, 1989, pp. 411–39.

Steers, Richard M. The Cultural Imperative in HRM Research. In *Nedd, A., ed.*, 1989, pp. 23–32.

Ştefănescu, Maria Viorica. General Algorithms for a Hierarchical Classification. *Econ. Computat. Econ. Cybern. Stud. Res.*, 1989, *24*(2–3), pp. 61–74.

Ştefănescu, Poliana and Ştefănescu, St. A Simple Monte Carlo Simulation Technique with Applications in Large Systems. *Econ. Computat. Econ. Cybern. Stud. Res.*, 1989, *24*(2–3), pp. 117–25.

Ştefănescu, St. and Ştefănescu, Poliana. A Simple Monte Carlo Simulation Technique with Applications in Large Systems. *Econ. Computat. Econ. Cybern. Stud. Res.*, 1989, *24*(2–3), pp. 117–25.

Stefanizzi, Sonia and Tarrow, Sidney. Protest and Regulation: The Interaction of State and Society in the Cycle of 1965–74. In *Lange, P. and Regini, M., eds.*, 1989, pp. 81–107.

Stefanou, Spiro E. Learning, Experience, and Firm Size. *J. Econ. Bus.*, November 1989, *41*(4), pp. 283–96.

———. Returns to Scale in the Long Run: The Dynamic Theory of Cost. *Southern Econ. J.*, January 1989, *55*(3), pp. 570–79.

Stefanski, Leonard A.; Carroll, Raymond J. and Künsch, Hans R. Conditionally Unbiased Bounded-Influence Estimation in General Regression Models, with Applications to General-ized Linear Models. *J. Amer. Statist. Assoc.*, June 1989, *84*(406), pp. 460–66.

Stefek, Dan; Grinold, Richard C. and Rudd, Andrew. Gobal Factors: Fact or Fiction? *J. Portfol. Manage.*, Fall 1989, *16*(1), pp. 79–88.

Stegemann, Klaus. Policy Rivalry among Industrial States: What Can We Learn from Models of Strategic Trade Policy? *Int. Organ.*, Winter 1989, *43*(1), pp. 73–100.

Steger, Joseph A. and Schoenfeldt, Lyle F. Identification and Development of Management Talent. In *Ferris, G. R. and Rowland, K. M., eds.*, 1989, pp. 121–81.

Stehle, John F. A Proof That God Would Be a Capitalist. *Atlantic Econ. J.*, September 1989, *17*(3), pp. 81.

Steiger, Otto and Heinsohn, Gunnar. The Veil of Barter: The Solution to 'The Task of Obtaining Representations of an Economy in Which Money Is Essential.' In *[Weintraub, S.]*, 1989, pp. 175–201.

——— and Patinkin, Don. In Search of the "Veil of Money" and the "Neutrality of Money": A Note on the Origin of Terms. *Scand. J. Econ.*, 1989, *91*(1), pp. 131–46.

Stein, Herbert. America's Second Fiscal Revolution. *Challenge*, July–Aug. 1989, *32*(4), pp. 4–10.

Stein, Jeremy C. Cheap Talk and the Fed: A Theory of Imprecise Policy Announcements. *Amer. Econ. Rev.*, March 1989, *79*(1), pp. 32–42.

———. Efficient Capital Markets, Inefficient Firms: A Model of Myopic Corporate Behavior. *Quart. J. Econ.*, November 1989, *104*(4), pp. 655–69.

———. Overreactions in the Options Market. *J. Finance*, September 1989, *44*(4), pp. 1011–23.

———; Froot, Kenneth A. and Scharfstein, David S. LDC Debt: Forgiveness, Indexation, and Investment Incentives. *J. Finance*, December 1989, *44*(5), pp. 1335–50.

Stein, Leslie. Third World Poverty, Economic Growth and Income Distribution. *Can. J. Devel. Stud.*, 1989, *10*(2), pp. 225–40.

Stein, Michael H. Treatment for Injury Purposes of Transactions Not at LTFV. In *Jackson, J. H. and Vermulst, E. A., eds.*, 1989, pp. 400–404.

Steinberg, Dan. Induced Work Participation and the Returns to Experience for Welfare Women: Evidence from a Social Experiment. *J. Econometrics*, July 1989, *41*(3), pp. 321–40.

Steinberg, Earl P. and Heyssel, Robert M. Medical Research and Teaching in a Market-Driven Health Care System. In *McLennan, K. and Meyer, J. A., eds.*, 1989, pp. 133–45.

Steinberg, Gerald and Mintz, Alex. Coping with Supplier Control: The Israeli Experience. In *Baek, K.-I.; McLaurin, R. D. and Moon, C., eds.*, 1989, pp. 137–51.

Steinbruner, John D. The Prospect of Cooperative Security. In *Bosworth, B. P., et al.*, 1989, pp. 71–94.

———. The Prospect of Cooperative Security. In *Steinbruner, J. D., ed.*, 1989, pp. 94–118.

_____. Restructuring American Foreign Policy: Introduction. In *Steinbruner, J. D., ed.*, 1989, pp. 1–11.

Steindel, Charles and Englander, A. Steven. Evaluating Recent Trends in Capital Formation. *Fed. Res. Bank New York Quart. Rev.*, Autumn 1989, *14*(3), pp. 7–19.

Steindl, Josef. Reflections on Kalecki's Dynamics. In *Sebastiani, M., ed.*, 1989, pp. 309–13.

_____. Saving and Debt. In *Barrère, A., ed.*, 1989, pp. 71–78.

Steiner, Viktor. Berufswechsel und Erwerbsstatus von Lehrabsolventen. Ein bivariates Probit-Modell. (Apprenticeship Training, Occupational Change and Employment Status of Youth—A Bivariate Probit Model. With English summary.) *Z. Wirtschaft. Sozialwissen.*, 1989, *109*(4), pp. 603–23.

_____. Causes of Recurrent Unemployment—An Empirical Analysis. *Empirica*, 1989, *16*(1), pp. 53–65.

_____ and Flaig, Gebhard. Stability and Dynamic Properties of Labour Demand in West German Manufacturing. *Oxford Bull. Econ. Statist.*, November 1989, *51*(4), pp. 395–412.

Steinert, Heinz; Blankenburg, Erhard and Staudhammer, Rainer. Political Scandals and Corruption Issues in West Germany. In *Heidenheimer, A. J.; Johnston, M. and LeVine, V. T., eds.*, 1989, pp. 913–32.

Steinherr, Alfred and Perée, Eric. Exchange Rate Uncertainty and Foreign Trade. *Europ. Econ. Rev.*, July 1989, *33*(6), pp. 1241–64.

Steinhorst, R. Kirk and Byers, C. Randall. An Alternative Interpretation of Freedman's Nonresponse Case Study: Reply. *J. Bus. Econ. Statist.*, January 1989, *7*(1), pp. 33.

_____ and Byers, C. Randall. An Alternative Interpretation of Freedman's Nonresponse Case Study. *J. Bus. Econ. Statist.*, January 1989, *7*(1), pp. 27–28.

Steinitz, Klaus and Heinrichs, Wolfgang. Problems of an Industrial Economy with Intensive Agricultural Production: The German Democratic Republic. In *Williamson, J. G. and Panchamukhi, V. R., eds.*, 1989, pp. 288–301.

Steinmann, Gunter. Population, Resources, and Limits to Growth. In *DeGregori, T. R., ed.*, 1989, pp. 87–128.

Steinmann, Horst and Kumar, B. Nino. Small and Medium-Sized Multinationals and Development: Suitability of International Strategy of German Small and Medium-Sized Firms in Newly Industrializing Countries. In *Negandhi, A. R., ed.*, 1989, pp. 105–24.

Steinmeier, Thomas L. and Gustman, Alan L. An Analysis of Pension Benefit Formulas, Pension Wealth, and Incentives from Pensions. In *Ehrenberg, R. G., ed.*, 1989, pp. 53–106.

Stelcner, Morton; van der Gaag, Jacques and Vijverberg, Wim. A Switching Regression Model of Public–Private Sector Wage Differentials in Peru: 1985–86. *J. Human Res.*, Summer 1989, *24*(3), pp. 545–59.

_____ and Shapiro, Daniel M. Canadian Public–Private Sector Earnings Differentials, 1970–1980. *Ind. Relat.*, Winter 1989, *28*(1), pp. 72–81.

_____; Vijverberg, Wim and van der Gaag, Jacques. Wage Differentials and Moonlighting by Civil Servants: Evidence from Côte d'Ivoire and Peru. *World Bank Econ. Rev.*, January 1989, *3*(1), pp. 67–95.

Stella, Peter. Do Tax Amnesties Work? *Finance Devel.*, December 1989, *26*(4), pp. 38–40.

Stelzer, Irwin M. Privatisation and Regulation: Oft-Necessary Complements. In *Veljanovski, C., ed. (II)*, 1989, pp. 70–77.

Stemp, Peter and Wohar, Mark E. The Indeterminacy of the Optimal Monetary Aggregate for Stabilization Policy under Rational Expectations. *Econ. Int.*, Aug.–Nov. 1989, *42*(3–4), pp. 258–78.

Stengos, Thanasis and Frank, Murray. Measuring the Strangeness of Gold and Silver Rates of Return. *Rev. Econ. Stud.*, October 1989, *56*(4), pp. 553–67.

_____; Moschini, Giancarlo and Prescott, David M. Nonparametric Kernel Estimation Applied to Forecasting: An Evaluation Based on the Bootstrap. In *Ullah, A., ed.*, 1989, *1988*, pp. 19–32.

Stenios, Marianne. Klarar vi av boomen inom postgradual utbildning? (Can We Cope with the Boom in Postgraduate Education? With English summary.) *Ekon. Samfundets Tidskr.*, 1989, *42*(4), pp. 213–14.

Stensland, Gunnar; Bjørstad, Heidi and Hefting, Tom. A Model for Exploration Decisions. *Energy Econ.*, July 1989, *11*(3), pp. 189–200.

_____ and Olsen, Trond E. Optimal Sequencing of Resource Pools under Uncertainty. *J. Environ. Econ. Manage.*, July 1989, *17*(1), pp. 83–92.

_____ and Tjøstheim, Dag. Optimal Investments Using Empirical Dynamic Programming with Application to Natural Resources. *J. Bus.*, January 1989, *62*(1), pp. 99–120.

Stephens, Mark A. and Hsieh, Chang-tseh. A Simultaneous-Equations Model for Examining Taiwan–U.S. Trade Relations. In *Lee, C. F. and Hu, S.-C., eds.*, 1989, pp. 139–55.

Stephens, Michael D. Universities, Education and the National Economy: Conclusion. In *Stephens, M. D., ed.*, 1989, pp. 129–35.

Stephenson, Geoffrey; O'Higgins, Michael and Schmaus, Guenther. Income Distribution and Redistribution: A Microdata Analysis for Seven Countries. *Rev. Income Wealth*, June 1989, *35*(2), pp. 107–31.

Stepick, Alex. Miami's Two Informal Sectors. In *Portes, A.; Castells, M. and Benton, L. A., eds.*, 1989, pp. 111–31.

Sterlacchini, Alessandro. R&D, Innovations, and Total Factor Productivity Growth in British Manufacturing. *Appl. Econ.*, November 1989, *21*(11), pp. 1549–62.

Sterling, Arlie and Modigliani, Franco. Determinants of Private Saving with Special Reference to the Role of Social Security—Cross-Country Tests. In *Modigliani, F., Vol. 5*, 1989, *1983*, pp. 3–34.

bined Training: Evidence of Economic Impact. *Econ. Educ. Rev.*, 1989, *8*(1), pp. 31–35.

Stevens, Deloris V. Funding Status of Private Pension Plans, 1985: Termination Funding Ratios. In *Turner, J. A. and Beller, D. J., eds.*, 1989, pp. 119–36.

Stevens, Guy V. G. Developments and Prospects in Macroeconometric Modeling: A Comment. *Eastern Econ. J.*, Oct.–Dec. 1989, *15*(4), pp. 305–08.

Stevens, Jerry L. and Vandell, Robert F. Evidence of Superior Performance from Timing. *J. Portfol. Manage.*, Spring 1989, *15*(3), pp. 38–42.

Stevens, Kevin T. Multistate Apportionment of Income: An Empirical Analysis. In *Jones, S. M., ed.*, 1989, pp. 181–200.

Stevens, Paul. Middle East Oil Supplies in the 1990s. In *Hawdon, D., ed.*, 1989, pp. 61–79.

Stevens, Thomas J. and VanSickle, John J. Market Information Systems: An Online Agricultural Market News Retrieval System. *Southern J. Agr. Econ.*, December 1989, *21*(2), pp. 195–201.

Stevenson, A. The Canadian Decentralization Experience. In *World Bank and Istituto Italo-Africano*, 1989, pp. 136–39.

Stevenson, Adlai E. and Frye, Alton. Trading with the Communists. *Foreign Aff.*, Spring 1989, *68*(2), pp. 53–71.

Stevenson, Andrew; Vines, David and Muscatelli, Vito Antonio. Uncovered Interest Parity, Exchange Rate Risk and Exchange Rate Dynamics. In *MacDonald, R. and Taylor, M. P., eds.*, 1989, pp. 159–77.

Stevenson, Glenn G. The Production, Distribution, and Consumption of Fuelwood in Haiti. *J. Developing Areas*, October 1989, *24*(1), pp. 59–76.

Stevenson, Richard. Nobel Laureates in Economic Sciences: A Biographical Dictionary: John Richard Hicks: 1972. In *Katz, B. S., ed.*, 1989, pp. 94–109.

Stevers, Ester and Wilkinson, Christopher. "Appropriate Regulation" for Communication and Information Services. In *Robinson, P.; Sauvant, K. P. and Govitrikar, V. P., eds.*, 1989, pp. 155–80.

Stewart, Frances. Sources of Technological Divergence between Developed and Less Developed Economies: Comment. In *[Díaz-Alejandro, C.]*, 1989, pp. 447–50.

Stewart, Geoff. Profit-Sharing in Cournot Oligopoly. *Econ. Letters*, December 1989, *31*(3), pp. 221–24.

Stewart, Ian. The Role of the Economist in Government: An International Perspective: Canada. In *Pechman, J. A., ed.*, 1989, pp. 125–45.

Stewart, J. C. Transfer Pricing: Some Empirical Evidence from Ireland. *J. Econ. Stud.*, 1989, *16*(3), pp. 40–56.

Stewart, James B. and Benjamin, Lois. The Self-Concept of Black and White Women: The Influences upon Its Formation of Welfare Dependency, Work Effort, Family Networks, and Ill-

nesses. *Amer. J. Econ. Sociology*, April 1989, *48*(2), pp. 165–75.

———— **and Benjamin, Lois.** Values, Beliefs, and Welfare Recipiency: Is There a Connection? *Rev. Black Polit. Econ.*, Winter 1989, *17*(3), pp. 43–67.

———— **and MacPherson, David A.** The Labor Force Participation and Earnings Profiles of Married Female Immigrants. *Quart. Rev. Econ. Bus.*, Autumn 1989, *29*(3), pp. 57–72.

———— **and Macpherson, David A.** The Labor Supply and School Attendance of Black Women in Extended and Nonextended Households. *Amer. Econ. Rev.*, May 1989, *79*(2), pp. 71–74.

Stewart, Jenice P. The Prediction Accuracy of Alternative Income Reporting Measures: An Empirical Investigation. In *Schwartz, B. N., ed.*, 1989, pp. 85–112.

Stewart, Mark and Harrison, Alan. Cyclical Fluctuations in Strike Durations. *Amer. Econ. Rev.*, September 1989, *79*(4), pp. 827–41.

Stickel, Scott E. The Timing of and Incentives for Annual Earnings Forecasts Near Interim Earnings Announcements. *J. Acc. Econ.*, July 1989, *11*(2–3), pp. 275–92.

Stigile, Arthur W. National Economic Commission: Another View. *Public Budg. Finance*, Autumn 1989, *9*(3), pp. 64–73.

Stigler, George J. The Butcher, the Baker, and the Policy-Maker: Adam Smith on Public Choice: Reply. *Hist. Polit. Econ.*, Winter 1989, *21*(4), pp. 659–60.

————. Two Notes on the Coase Theorem. *Yale Law J.*, December 1989, *99*(3), pp. 631–33.

Stiglitz, Joseph E. Financial Markets and Development. *Oxford Rev. Econ. Policy*, Winter 1989, *5*(4), pp. 55–68.

————. Imperfect Information in the Product Market. In *Schmalensee, R. and Willig, R. D., eds., Vol. 1*, 1989, pp. 769–847.

————. Incentives, Information, and Organizational Design. *Empirica*, 1989, *16*(1), pp. 3–29.

————. Markets, Market Failures, and Development. *Amer. Econ. Rev.*, May 1989, *79*(2), pp. 197–203.

————. Monopolistic Competition and the Capital Market. In *Feiwel, G. R., ed. (I)*, 1989, pp. 485–507.

————. Rational Peasants, Efficient Institutions, and a Theory of Rural Organization: Methodological Remarks for Development Economics. In *Bardhan, P., ed. (II)*, 1989, pp. 18–29.

————. Reflections on the State of Economics: 1988. *Econ. Rec.*, March 1989, *65*(188), pp. 66–72.

————. Using Tax Policy to Curb Speculative Short-Term Trading. In *Edwards, F. R., ed.*, 1989, pp. 3–17.

————. Using Tax Policy to Curb Speculative Short-term Trading. *J. Finan. Services Res.*, December 1989, *3*(2–3), pp. 101–15.

———— **and Arnott, Richard J.** Congestion Pricing to Improve Air Travel Safety. In *Moses, L. N. and Savage, I., eds.*, 1989, pp. 167–85.

_____ and Blinder, Alan S. Money, Credit Constraints, and Economic Activity. In *Blinder, A. S.*, 1989, *1983*, pp. 17–24.

_____ and Braverman, Avishay. Credit Rationing, Tenancy, Productivity, and the Dynamics of Inequality. In *Bardhan, P., ed. (II)*, 1989, pp. 185–202.

_____; Brock, William A. and Rothschild, Michael. Stochastic Capital Theory. In *Feiwel, G. R., ed. (II)*, 1989, pp. 591–622.

_____ and Gale, Ian L. The Informational Content of Initial Public Offerings. *J. Finance*, June 1989, *44*(2), pp. 469–77.

_____ and Greenwald, Bruce C. Toward a Theory of Rigidities. *Amer. Econ. Rev.*, May 1989, *79*(2), pp. 364–69.

_____ and Rothschild, Michael. Equilibrium in Competitive Insurance Markets: An Essay on the Economics of Imperfect Information. In *Diamond, P. and Rothschild, M., eds.*, 1989, *1976*, pp. 259–79.

_____ and Rothschild, Michael. Increasing Risk: I. A Definition. In *Diamond, P. and Rothschild, M., eds.*, 1989, *1970*, pp. 101–19.

_____ and Sah, Raaj Kumar. Sources of Technological Divergence between Developed and Less Developed Economies. In *[Díaz-Alejandro, C.]*, 1989, pp. 423–46.

_____ and Sah, Raaj Kumar. Technological Learning, Social Learning and Technological Change. In *Chakravarty, S., ed.*, 1989, pp. 285–98.

Stimson, R. J. and Gibson, L. J. The United States and Australia: Observations and Speculations about Two Mature Economies. In *Gibson, L. J. and Stimson, R. J., eds.*, 1989, pp. 1–6.

Stinchcombe, Arthur L. An Outsider's View of Network Analyses of Power. In *Perrucci, R. and Potter, H. R., eds.*, 1989, pp. 119–33.

Stinchcombe, Maxwell B. and Simon, Leo K. Extensive Form Games in Continuous Time: Pure Strategies. *Econometrica*, September 1989, *57*(5), pp. 1171–1214.

Stipdonk, Bill P.; Warren, Cathy J. and Mountain, Dean C. Technological Innovation and a Changing Energy Mix—A Parametric and Flexible Approach to Modeling Ontario Manufacturing. *Energy J.*, October 1989, *10*(4), pp. 139–58.

Stipetić, Vladimir. Agriculture and Managing the Debt Crisis. In *Singer, H. W. and Sharma, S., eds. (II)*, 1989, pp. 127–33.

Stirling, Kate J. Women Who Remain Divorced: The Long-term Economic Consequences. *Soc. Sci. Quart.*, September 1989, *70*(3), pp. 549–61.

Stirrat, R. L. Money, Men and Women. In *Parry, J. and Bloch, M., eds.*, 1989, pp. 94–116.

Stober, Thomas L. and Bernard, Victor L. The Nature and Amount of Information in Cash Flows and Accruals. *Accounting Rev.*, October 1989, *64*(4), pp. 624–52.

Stock, James H. Hysteresis and the Evolution of Postwar U.S. and U.K. Unemployment. In

Barnett, W. A.; Geweke, J. and Shell, K., eds., 1989, pp. 361–82.

_____. Nonparametric Policy Analysis. *J. Amer. Statist. Assoc.*, June 1989, *84*(406), pp. 567–75.

_____ and Richardson, Matthew. Drawing Inferences from Statistics Based on Multiyear Asset Returns. *J. Finan. Econ.*, December 1989, *25*(2), pp. 323–48.

_____; Stoker, Thomas M. and Powell, James L. Semiparametric Estimation of Index Coefficients. *Econometrica*, November 1989, *57*(6), pp. 1403–30.

_____ and Watson, Mark W. Interpreting the Evidence on Money–Income Causality. *J. Econometrics*, January 1989, *40*(1), pp. 161–81.

_____ and Watson, Mark W. New Indexes of Coincident and Leading Economic Indicators. In *Blanchard, O. J. and Fischer, S., eds.*, 1989, pp. 351–94.

Stockman, Alan C. The Cash-in-Advance Constraint in International Economics. In *Tsiang, S. C.*, 1989, pp. 377–93.

_____. Factor Flexibility, Uncertainty and Exchange Rate Regimes: Discussion. In *De Cecco, M. and Giovannini, A., eds.*, 1989, pp. 126–30.

_____. The International Transmission of Inflation Afloat: Comment. In *[Schwartz, A. J.]*, 1989, pp. 236–40.

_____ and Baxter, Marianne. Business Cycles and the Exchange-Rate Regime: Some International Evidence. *J. Monet. Econ.*, May 1989, *23*(3), pp. 377–400.

_____ and Dellas, Harris. International Portfolio Nondiversification and Exchange Rate Variability. *J. Int. Econ.*, May 1989, *26*(3/4), pp. 271–89.

Stockton, David J. and Struckmeyer, Charles S. Tests of the Specification and Predictive Accuracy of Nonnested Models of Inflation. *Rev. Econ. Statist.*, May 1989, *71*(2), pp. 275–83.

_____ and Wallich, Henry C. A Macroeconomic Perspective on Tax-Based Incomes Policies. In *[Weintraub, S.]*, 1989, pp. 47–67.

Stoddart, Greg L. and Muldoon, Jacqueline M. Publicly Financed Competition in Health Care Delivery: A Canadian Simulation Model. *J. Health Econ.*, December 1989, *8*(3), pp. 313–38.

Stoeckel, Andrew B. and Breckling, Jens. Some Economywide Effects of Agricultural Policies in the European Community: A General Equilibrium Study. In *Stoeckel, A. B.; Vincent, D. and Cuthbertson, S., eds.*, 1989, pp. 94–124.

_____; Vincent, David and Cuthbertson, Sandy. Macroeconomic Consequences of Farm Support Policies: Overview. In *Stoeckel, A. B.; Vincent, D. and Cuthbertson, S., eds.*, 1989, pp. 1–63.

Stoecker, Arthur L. and Epplin, Francis M. Mathematical Programming. In *Tweeten, L., ed.*, 1989, pp. 212–37.

_____ and Li, Elton. Using Microcomputers for Policy Analysis. In *Tweeten, L., ed.*, 1989, pp. 46–55.

Stoever, William A. Foreign Collaborations Policy in India: A Review. *J. Developing Areas*, July 1989, *23*(4), pp. 485–504.

Stoffelsma, Ronald J. and Oosterhaven, Jan. Social Security Benefits and Interregional Income Inequalities: The Case of the Netherlands. *Ann. Reg. Sci.*, 1989, *23*(3), pp. 223–40.

Stoker, G. Urban Development Corporations: A Review. *Reg. Stud.*, April 1989, *23*(2), pp. 159–67.

Stoker, Thomas M. Tests of Additive Derivative Constraints. *Rev. Econ. Stud.*, October 1989, *56*(4), pp. 535–52.

_____ **and Härdle, Wolfgang.** Investigating Smooth Multiple Regression by the Method of Average Derivatives. *J. Amer. Statist. Assoc.*, December 1989, *84*(408), pp. 986–95.

_____; **Powell, James L. and Stock, James H.** Semiparametric Estimation of Index Coefficients. *Econometrica*, November 1989, *57*(6), pp. 1403–30.

Stokes, Ernie. Macroeconomic Impact of the Canada–U.S. Free Trade Agreement. *J. Policy Modeling*, Summer 1989, *11*(2), pp. 225–45.

Stokes, Gale. The Social Origins of East European Politics. In *Chirot, D., ed.*, 1989, pp. 210–51.

Stokes, Houston H. and Sinai, Allen. Money Balances in the Production Function: A Retrospective Look. *Eastern Econ. J.*, Oct.–Dec. 1989, *15*(4), pp. 349–63.

Stokes, Robert L. and Munro, Gordon R. The Canada–United States Pacific Salmon Treaty. In *McRae, D. and Munro, G., eds.*, 1989, pp. 17–35.

Stokey, Nancy L. Reputation and Time Consistency. *Amer. Econ. Rev.*, May 1989, *79*(2), pp. 134–39.

Stoll, Hans R. Inferring the Components of the Bid–Ask Spread: Theory and Empirical Tests. *J. Finance*, March 1989, *44*(1), pp. 115–34.

_____ **and Haller, Andreas.** Market Structure and Transaction Costs: Implied Spreads in the German Stock Market. *J. Banking Finance*, September 1989, *13*(4–5), pp. 697–708.

Stoll, John R. and Bergstrom, John C. Application of Experimental Economics Concepts and Precepts to CVM Field Survey Procedures. *Western J. Agr. Econ.*, July 1989, *14*(1), pp. 98–109.

_____; **Randall, Alan and Bergstrom, John C.** Information Effects in Contingent Markets. *Amer. J. Agr. Econ.*, August 1989, *71*(3), pp. 685–91.

_____; **Sellar, Christine and Chavas, Jean-Paul.** On the Commodity Value of Travel Time in Recreational Activities. *Appl. Econ.*, June 1989, *21*(6), pp. 711–22.

Stollar, Andrew J.; Thompson, G. Rodney and Grubaugh, Stephen G. Socialist Structural Gaps: A Simultaneous Inference Analysis. *Rev. Econ. Statist.*, November 1989, *71*(4), pp. 693–98.

Stollberg, Rudhard; Assmann, Georg and Nagel, Detlev. The Introduction of New Technology in Industrial Enterprises of the German Demo-cratic Republic: Two Case Studies. In *Francis, A. and Grootings, P., eds.*, 1989, pp. 61–87.

Stollery, K. R. and Androkovich, Robert A. Regulation of Stochastic Fisheries: A Comparison of Alternative Methods in the Pacific Halibut Fishery. *Marine Resource Econ.*, 1989, *6*(2), pp. 109–22.

Stolp, Chandler; Warner, David C. and Juretic, Mark. Patterns of Inpatient Mental Health, Mental Retardation, and Substance Abuse Service Utilization in California. *Soc. Sci. Quart.*, September 1989, *70*(3), pp. 687–707.

Stolper, Wolfgang W. The German Slump and Hitler's Economic Policies. *J. Inst. Theoretical Econ.*, December 1989, *145*(4), pp. 720–29.

_____. Spiethoff, Schumpeter und *Das Wesen des Geldes:* Comments and Additions. *Kyklos*, 1989, *42*(3), pp. 435–38.

Stolz, Richard W. and Spindt, Paul A. The Expected Stop-Out Price in a Discriminating Auction. *Econ. Letters*, December 1989, *31*(2), pp. 133–37.

Stone, Bruce and Tong, Zhong. Changing Patterns of Variability in Chinese Cereal Production. In *Anderson, J. R. and Hazell, P. B. R., eds.*, 1989, pp. 35–59.

Stone, Charles Austin and Zissu, Anne-Marie. A Causality-Effect between Bid Premium and Outcome of Tender Offer. *Econ. Letters*, 1989, *29*(4), pp. 349–51.

Stone, Gary and Englander, A. Steven. Inflation Expectations Surveys as Predictors of Inflation and Behavior in Financial and Labor Markets. *Fed. Res. Bank New York Quart. Rev.*, Autumn 1989, *14*(3), pp. 20–32.

Stone, Jack H. and Allen, Ralph C. The Locational Criteria of Footloose Firms: A Formal Model. *Rev. Reg. Stud.*, Spring 1989, *19*(2), pp. 13–17.

_____ **and Rabianski, Joseph S.** A Pedagogical Note on Monopoly Supply. *Amer. Economist*, Spring 1989, *33*(1), pp. 80–82.

Stone, Joe A. and Haynes, Stephen E. An Integrated Test for Electoral Cycles in the U.S. Economy. *Rev. Econ. Statist.*, August 1989, *71*(3), pp. 426–34.

Stone, John C.; Dantzig, George B. and McAllister, Patrick H. Deriving a Utility Function for the U.S. Economy. *J. Policy Modeling*, Fall 1989, *11*(3), pp. 391–424.

_____; **Dantzig, George B. and McAllister, Patrick H.** Integrability of the Multiple-Period Equilibrium Model: Part II. *J. Policy Modeling*, Winter 1989, *11*(4), pp. 569–92.

Stone, Lawrence. Epilogue: Lawrence Stone—As Seen by Himself. In *[Stone, L.]*, 1989, pp. 575–95.

Stone, Susan; Koziara, Edward C. and Yan, Chiou-Shuang. Employer Strike Insurance. In *Perkins, E. J., ed.*, 1989, pp. 220–29.

Stonehouse, D. P. and Trelawny, P. M. The Effects of Introducing Supplemental Bovine Somatotropin to the Canadian Dairy Industry. *Can. J. Agr. Econ.*, July 1989, *37*(2), pp. 191–209.

Stoneman, Colin. The World Bank and the IMF

in Zimbabwe. **In** *Campbell, B. K. and Loxley, J., eds.*, 1989, pp. 37–66.

Stoneman, P. Technological Diffusion, Vertical Product Differentiation and Quality Improvement. *Econ. Letters*, December 1989, *31*(3), pp. 277–80.

Stonich, Susan C. The Dynamics of Social Processes and Environmental Destruction: A Central American Case Study. *Population Devel. Rev.*, June 1989, *15*(2), pp. 269–96.

Storaci, Marina. Il gold exchange standard in Italia: 1927–31. (The Gold Exchange Standard in Italy: 1927–31. With English summary.) *Rivista Storia Econ.*, S.S., October 1989, *6*(3), pp. 283–319.

Storey, Gary and Prentice, Barry. Flaxseed: Victim of Crowding Out? *Can. J. Agr. Econ.*, Part 2, December 1989, *37*(4), pp. 1165–79.

Storper, Michael. The Transition to Flexible Specialisation in the U.S. Film Industry: External Economies, the Division of Labour, and the Crossing of Industrial Divides. *Cambridge J. Econ.*, June 1989, *13*(2), pp. 273–305.

_____ **and Christopherson, Susan.** The Effects of Flexible Specialization on Industrial Politics and the Labor Market: The Motion Picture Industry. *Ind. Lab. Relat. Rev.*, April 1989, *42*(3), pp. 331–47.

Stott, Richard. Hinterland Development and Differences in Work Setting: The New York City Region, 1820–1870. **In** *Pencak, W. and Wright, C. E., eds.*, 1989, pp. 45–71.

Stoughton, Neal M. and Darrough, Masako N. A Bargaining Approach to Profit Sharing in Joint Ventures. *J. Bus.*, April 1989, *62*(2), pp. 237–70.

_____ **and Jorion, Philippe.** An Empirical Investigation of the Early Exercise Premium of Foreign Currency Options. *J. Futures Markets*, October 1989, *9*(5), pp. 365–75.

Stover, John. The Latest Figures on World Population Growth. *Challenge*, July–Aug. 1989, *32*(4), pp. 56–57.

Stoykov, Tsanko. Some Theoretical and Methodological Problems Pertaining to a Differentiated Approach to the Analysis and Planning of the Living Standards. **In** *Bulgarian Academy of Sciences, Institute of Economics*, 1989, pp. 164–71.

Strain, W. J. and Stacey, J. A. Investment in Canada. *Bull. Int. Fiscal Doc.*, February 1989, *43*(2), pp. 55–62.

Strand, Ivar E. and McConnell, Kenneth E. Benefits from Commercial Fisheries When Demand and Supply Depend on Water Quality. *J. Environ. Econ. Manage.*, November 1989, *17*(3), pp. 284–92.

_____, **Jr.; Bockstael, Nancy E. and McConnell, Kenneth E.** Measuring the Benefits of Improvements in Water Quality: The Chesapeake Bay. *Marine Resource Econ.*, 1989, *6*(1), pp. 1–18.

_____; **Bockstael, Nancy E. and McConnell, Kenneth E.** A Random Utility Model for Sportfishing: Some Preliminary Results for Florida. *Marine Resource Econ.*, 1989, *6*(3), pp. 245–60.

_____ **and Lipton, Douglas W.** The Effect of Common Property on the Optimal Structure of the Fishing Industry. *J. Environ. Econ. Manage.*, January 1989, *16*(1), pp. 45–51.

Stránský, František. Greater Integration Is the Solution. *Czech. Econ. Digest.*, May 1989, (3), pp. 16–20.

Strassmann, W. Paul. The Rise, Fall, and Transformation of Overseas Construction Contracting. *World Devel.*, June 1989, *17*(6), pp. 783–94.

Stratford, Mike; Islei, Gerd and Cox, Barry. Ranking, Monitoring and Control of Research Projects in the Pharmaceutical Industry. **In** *Lockett, A. G. and Islei, G., eds.*, 1989, pp. 191–202.

Stratton, Kay. Union Democracy in the International Typographical Union: Thirty Years Later. *J. Lab. Res.*, Winter 1989, *10*(1), pp. 119–34.

Straubhaar, Thomas. Ökologische Grenzen des Bevölkerungswachstums? (Are There Ecological Limits of Population Growth? With English summary.) *Schweiz. Z. Volkswirtsch. Statist.*, September 1989, *125*(3), pp. 473–85.

Strauss, George. Industrial Relations as an Academic Field: What's Wrong with It. **In** *Barbash, J. and Barbash, K., eds.*, 1989, pp. 241–60.

Strauss, John; Thomas, Duncan and Henriques, Maria Helena. Mortalidade infantil, estado nutricional e características do domicílio: A evidência brasileira. (With English summary.) *Pesquisa Planejamento Econ.*, December 1989, *19*(3), pp. 427–82.

Strauss-Kahn, Marc-Olivier; Bordes, Christian and Driscoll, Michael J. Price Inertia and Nominal Aggregate Demand in Major European Countries. *Rech. Écon. Louvain*, 1989, *55*(2), pp. 105–28.

_____; **Chouraqui, J. C. and Driscoll, Michael J.** The Effects of Monetary Policy on the Real Sector: What Do We Know? *Banca Naz. Lavoro Quart. Rev.*, March 1989, (168), pp. 3–46.

Strauss, Robert P. Federal Tax Policy and the Market for Corporate Control: Relationships and Consequences. **In** *McKee, D. L., ed.*, 1989, pp. 116–39.

_____; **Banker, Rajiv D. and Bunch, Beverly S.** Factors Influencing School District Financial Reporting Practices. **In** *Chan, J. L. and Patton, J. M., eds.*, 1989, pp. 27–56.

Straussman, Jeffrey D. and Thurmaier, Kurt. Budgeting Rights: The Case of Jail Litigation. *Public Budg. Finance*, Summer 1989, *9*(2), pp. 30–42.

Strawser, Jerry R.; Cassidy, Judith H. and Friedberg, Alan H. Factors Affecting Materiality Judgments: A Comparison of "Big Eight" Accounting Firms' Materiality Views with the Results of Empirical Research. **In** *Schwartz, B. N., ed.*, 1989, pp. 187–201.

Strayer, Kerry and Twenhafel, David. Telecommunications Policy and Economic Development: The New State Role: Washington. In *Schmandt, J.; Williams, F. and Wilson, R. H., eds.*, 1989, pp. 241–65.

Strecker, Heinrich and Wiegert, Rolf. Wirtschaftsstatistiche Daten und ökonomische Realität. (Economic Statistical Data and Economic Reality. With English summary.) *Jahr. Nationalökon. Statist.*, October 1989, *206*(4–5), pp. 487–509.

Streeck, Wolfgang. Successful Adjustment to Turbulent Markets: The Automobile Industry. In *Katzenstein, P. J., ed.*, 1989, pp. 113–56.

Street, John. Controlling Interests: Technology, State Control and Democracy. In *Duncan, G., ed.*, 1989, pp. 215–31.

Streeten, Paul. Disguised Unemployment and Underemployment. In *Feiwel, G. R., ed. (II)*, 1989, pp. 723–26.

_____. Global Institutions for an Interdependent World. *World Devel.*, Special Issue, September 1989, *17*(9), pp. 1349–59.

_____. Interests, Ideology and Institutions: A Review of Bhagwati on Protectionism. *World Devel.*, February 1989, *17*(2), pp. 293–98.

_____. International Co-operation and Global Justice. In *Adelman, I. and Lane, S., eds.*, 1989, pp. 3–17.

_____. The Politics of Food Prices. In *Islam, N., ed.*, 1989, pp. 61–71.

_____. Surpluses for a Capital-Hungry World. In *Singer, H. W. and Sharma, S., eds. (I)*, 1989, pp. 23–26.

Stren, Richard E. Accountability in Africa. In *World Bank and Istituto Italo-Africano*, 1989, pp. 123–29.

_____. Institutional Arrangements. In *World Bank and Istituto Italo-Africano*, 1989, pp. 92–98.

Streng, M.; Twilt, F. and Jonker, P. Gradient Newton Flows for Complex Polynomials. In *Dolecki, S., ed.*, 1989, pp. 177–90.

Strom, Sharon Hartman. "Light Manufacturing": The Feminization of American Office Work, Work, 1900–1930. *Ind. Lab. Relat. Rev.*, October 1989, *43*(1), pp. 53–71.

Strøm, Steinar. Why Does Unemployment Persist? Comment. *Scand. J. Econ.*, 1989, *91*(2), pp. 397–400.

_____ and Isachsen, Arne Jon. The Hidden Economy in Norway with Special Emphasis on the Hidden Labor Market. In *Feige, E. L., ed.*, 1989, pp. 251–65.

Stromsdorfer, Ernest W.; Farkas, George and Hotchkiss, Lawrence. Vocational Training, Supply Constraints, and Individual Economic Outcomes. *Econ. Educ. Rev.*, 1989, *8*(1), pp. 17–30.

Strømsheim, Gunvor. Working Time Reforms in a Welfare Society: Preferences, Interests and Conflicts. In *Agassi, J. B. and Heycock, S., eds.*, 1989, pp. 48–63.

Strong, Benjamin. Federal Reserve Control of Credit. *Fed. Res. Bank New York Quart. Rev.*, Special Issue, 1989, pp. 6–14.

_____. The Formation of the Federal Reserve

System. *Fed. Res. Bank New York Quart. Rev.*, Special Issue, 1989, pp. 4–5.

Strong, John S. The Market Valuation of Credit Market Debt. In *Jorgenson, D. W. and Landau, R., eds.*, 1989, pp. 373–408.

_____. The Market Valuation of Credit Market Debt. *J. Money, Credit, Banking*, August 1989, *21*(3), pp. 307–20.

Strong, Maurice. International Cooperation for Survival. In *Rotblat, J. and Goldanskii, V. I., eds.*, 1989, pp. 218–23.

Strongin, David G. and Schaefer, Jeffrey M. Foreign Portfolio Investment in the United States. In *Kaushik, S. K., ed.*, 1989, pp. 155–80.

_____ and Schaefer, Jeffrey M. Why All the Fuss about Foreign Investment. *Challenge*, May–June 1989, *32*(3), pp. 31–35.

Strosberg, Martin A. Rationing of Medical Care for the Critically Ill: Introduction. In *Strosberg, M. A.; Fein, I. A. and Carroll, J. D., eds.*, 1989, pp. 1–10.

Stroup, Richard L. The Unpredictable Politics behind Regulation: The Institutional Basis. In *Meiners, R. E. and Yandle, B., eds.*, 1989, pp. 242–52.

Struckmeyer, Charles S. and Stockton, David J. Tests of the Specification and Predictive Accuracy of Nonnested Models of Inflation. *Rev. Econ. Statist.*, May 1989, *71*(2), pp. 275–83.

Strumwasser, Ira, et al. The Triple Option Choice: Self-selection Bias in Traditional Coverage, HMOs, and PPOs. *Inquiry*, Winter 1989, *26*(4), pp. 432–41.

Struthers, John and Young, Alistair. Economics of Voting: Theories and Evidence. *J. Econ. Stud.*, 1989, *16*(5), pp. 1–43.

Strydom, P. D. F. International Economics: Review Note. *S. Afr. J. Econ.*, June 1989, *57*(2), pp. 175–80.

Stryjakiewicz, Tadeusz and Matykowski, Roman. The Changing Organisation of Labour and Its Impacts on Daily Activities. In *Linge, G. J. R. and van der Knaap, G. A., eds.*, 1989, pp. 128–43.

Stryker, J. Dirck. Technology, Human Pressure, and Ecology in the Arid and Semi-arid Tropics. In *Leonard, H. J., ed.*, 1989, pp. 87–109.

_____ and Tuluy, Hasan A. Assistance to Ghana and the Ivory Coast. In *Krueger, A. O.; Michalopoulos, C. and Ruttan, V. W.*, 1989, pp. 269–302.

Stuart, Charles and Hansson, Ingemar. The Marginal Cost of Public Funds: Methods and Prospects. In *Chiancone, A. and Messere, K., eds.*, 1989, pp. 231–41.

_____ and Hansson, Ingemar. Social Security as Trade among Living Generations. *Amer. Econ. Rev.*, December 1989, *79*(5), pp. 1182–95.

_____ and Hansson, Ingemar. Why Is Investment Subsidized? *Int. Econ. Rev.*, August 1989, *30*(3), pp. 549–59.

Stuart, O. D. J. The Leading Characteristics of Consumer Sentiment Data. *J. Stud. Econ. Econometrics*, August 1989, *13*(2), pp. 79–95.

Stübler, Walter. A Social Account for International Comparisons. *Statist. J.*, 1989, 6(4), pp. 359–68.

Studzinski, Krzysztof; Zorychta, Krystian and Ogryczak, Wlodzimierz. DINAS: Dynamic Interactive Network Analysis System. In *Lewandowski, A. and Wierzbicki, A. P., eds.*, 1989, pp. 385–87.

_____**; Zorychta, Krystian and Ogryczak, Wlodzimierz.** Dynamic Interactive Network Analysis System. In *Lockett, A. G. and Islei, G., eds.*, 1989, pp. 444–53.

_____**; Zorychta, Krystian and Ogryczak, Wlodzimierz.** A Generalized Reference Point Approach to Multiobjective Transshipment Problem with Facility Location. In *Lewandowski, A. and Wierzbicki, A. P., eds.*, 1989, pp. 213–29.

_____**; Zorychta, Krystian and Ogryczak, Wlodzimierz.** Solving Multiobjective Distribution–Location Problems with the DINAS System. In *Lewandowski, A. and Wierzbicki, A. P., eds.*, 1989, pp. 230–50.

Stuetzle, Werner and Hastie, Trevor. Principal Curves. *J. Amer. Statist. Assoc.*, June 1989, 84(406), pp. 502–16.

Stull, William J. and Kushnirsky, Fyodor I. Productive and Unproductive Labour: Smith, Marx, and the Soviets. In *Walker, D. A., ed.*, 1989, pp. 82–103.

Stulz, René M. and Bailey, Warren. The Pricing of Stock Index Options in a General Equilibrium Model. *J. Finan. Quant. Anal.*, March 1989, 24(1), pp. 1–12.

_____ **and Chan, K. C.** Risk and the Economy: A Finance Perspective. In *Stone, C. C., ed.*, 1989, pp. 79–117.

_____ **and Reagan, Patricia B.** Contracts, Delivery Lags, and Currency Risks. *J. Int. Money Finance*, March 1989, 8(1), pp. 89–103.

_____**; Walkling, Ralph A. and Lang, Larry H. P.** Managerial Performance, Tobin's Q, and the Gains from Successful Tender Offers. *J. Finan. Econ.*, September 1989, 24(1), pp. 137–54.

Sturgeon, James I. and Munkirs, John R. Oligopolistic Cooperation: Conceptual and Empirical Evidence of Market Structure Evolution. In *Tool, M. R. and Samuels, W. J., eds. (I)*, 1989, 1985, pp. 337–59.

_____ **and Williams, W. D.** Linkages: A Personal Computer-Based Implementation of John Munkirs's Tableau. *J. Econ. Issues*, September 1989, 23(3), pp. 895–96.

Sturgess, Brian. Advertising Revenue and Broadcasting. In *Veljanovski, C., ed. (I)*, 1989, pp. 114–25.

Sturgess, Neil H. and Esparon, N. M. The Measurement of Technical Efficiency Using Frontier Production Functions of Rice Farms in West Java. *Bull. Indonesian Econ. Stud.*, December 1989, 25(3), pp. 99–119.

_____**; Kristanto, Kustiah and Parenta, Tajuddin.** South Sulawesi: New Directions in Agriculture? In *Hill, H., ed.*, 1989, pp. 386–407.

Sturzenegger, Federico. Explicando las fluctuaciones del producto en la Argentina. (Explaining Output Fluctuations in Argentina. With

English summary.) *Económica (La Plata)*, 1989, 35(1–2), pp. 101–52.

Stutzer, Michael J. and Smith, Bruce D. Credit Rationing and Government Loan Programs: A Welfare Analysis. *Amer. Real Estate Urban Econ. Assoc. J.*, Summer 1989, 17(2), pp. 177–93.

Su, Hong-Lin and Little, Roderick J. A. Item Nonresponse in Panel Surveys. In *Kasprzyk, D., et al., eds.*, 1989, pp. 400–425.

Su, Kaihua. The Meaning of the "Asiatic Mode of Production" and the Origin of the Term. In *Brook, T., ed.*, 1989, pp. 157–63.

Su, Shao-zhi. A Chinese View on the Reform of the Economic Mechanism in Hungary: A Comment. In *Van Ness, P., ed.*, 1989, pp. 194–211.

_____. Telecommunications and Development: The Case of China. In *Jussawalla, M.; Okuma, T. and Araki, T., eds.*, 1989, pp. 289–92.

Suárez Burguet, Celestino; Fernández Guerrero, Ismael and Gonzalez, Agustin. Spanish External Trade and EEC Preferences. In *Yannopoulos, G. N., ed.*, 1989, pp. 144–68.

Suarez Pandiello, Javier. Una propuesta para la integración multijurisdiccional del IRPF. (With English summary.) *Invest. Econ.*, May 1989, 13(2), pp. 245–67.

Suarez-Villa, Luiz. Reestruturação industrial, mudança tecnológica e planejamento do desenvolvimento metropolitano. (With English summary.) *Pesquisa Planejamento Econ.*, April 1989, 19(1), pp. 161–82.

Subich, Linda Mezydlo, et al. The Effects of Sex-Role-Related Factors on Occupational Choice and Salary. In *Michael, R. T.; Hartmann, H. I. and O'Farrell, B., eds.*, 1989, pp. 91–104.

Subrahmanya, M. H. Bala. Rural Industries in Karnataka: Structure and Growth. *Margin*, Jan.–March 1989, 21(2), pp. 34–44.

Subrahmanyam, Krishnaswami. Revision of the Non-proliferation Treaty. In *Rotblat, J. and Goldanskii, V. I., eds.*, 1989, pp. 52–60.

Subrahmanyam, Marti G.; Brenner, Menachem and Courtadon, Georges. Options on Stock Indices and Options on Futures. *J. Banking Finance*, September 1989, 13(4–5), pp. 773–82.

_____**; Uno, Jun and Brenner, Menachem.** The Behavior of Prices in the Nikkei Spot and Futures Market. *J. Finan. Econ.*, August 1989, 23(2), pp. 363–83.

Subrahmanyam, Sanjay. The Coromandel Trade of the Danish East India Company, 1618–1649. *Scand. Econ. Hist. Rev.*, 1989, 37(1), pp. 41–56.

_____. Warfare and State Finance in Wodeyar Mysore, 1724–25: A Missionary Perspective. *Indian Econ. Soc. Hist. Rev.*, April–June 1989, 26(2), pp. 203–33.

Subramaniam, Kamla. The Relevance of Multipe Switching in the Theory of Capital. *Indian Econ. Rev.*, July–Dec. 1989, 24(2), pp. 225–45.

Subramanian, A. and Islam, Nurul. Agricultural Exports of Developing Countries: Estimates of Income and Price Elasticities of Demand and Supply. *J. Agr. Econ.*, May 1989, *40*(2), pp. 221–31.

Subramanian, S. Poverty Minimization in the Light of 'Life-Boat Ethics.' *J. Quant. Econ.*, July 1989, *5*(2), pp. 239–49.

Sudhölter, P. Homogeneous Games as Anti Step Functions. *Int. J. Game Theory*, 1989, *18*(4), pp. 433–69.

Sudman, Seymour; Rothbart, George S. and Fine, Michelle. On Finding and Interviewing the Needles in the Haystack: The Use of Multiplicity Sampling. In *Singer, E. and Presser, S., eds.*, 1989, *1982*, pp. 18–31.

Suen, Wing. Rationing and Rent Dissipation in the Presence of Heterogeneous Individuals. *J. Polit. Econ.*, December 1989, *97*(6), pp. 1384–94.

Sufrin, Sidney C. The Pivots of Economic Development. *Rivista Int. Sci. Econ. Com.*, August 1989, *36*(8), pp. 689–702.

Sugden, Robert. Spontaneous Order. *J. Econ. Perspectives*, Fall 1989, *3*(4), pp. 85–97.

_____; **Loomes, Graham and Starmer, Chris.** Preference Reversal: Information-Processing Effect or Rational Non-transitive Choice? *Econ. J.*, Supplement, 1989, *99*(395), pp. 140–51.

_____ **and Starmer, Chris.** Probability and Juxtaposition Effects: An Experimental Investigation of the Common Ratio Effect. *J. Risk Uncertainty*, June 1989, *2*(2), pp. 159–78.

Sugden, Roger and Cowling, Keith. Exchange Rate Adjustment and Oligopoly Pricing Behaviour. *Cambridge J. Econ.*, September 1989, *13*(3), pp. 373–93.

Sugihara, Kaoru. Japan's Industrial Recovery, 1931–6. In *Brown, I., ed.*, 1989, pp. 152–69.

Sugrue, Timothy F. and Scherr, Fredrick C. An Empirical Test of Ross's Cash Flow Beta Theory of Capital Structure. *Financial Rev.*, August 1989, *24*(3), pp. 355–70.

Sujan, Ivan. Economic Development of the CSSR: Analysis and Conditional Forecasts. In *Krelle, W., ed.*, 1989, pp. 461–476.

Sukhatme, Vasant A. Assistance to India. In *Krueger, A. O.; Michalopoulos, C. and Ruttan, V. W.*, 1989, pp. 203–25.

_____ **and Michalopoulos, Constantine.** The Impact of Development Assistance: A Review of the Quantitative Evidence. In *Krueger, A. O.; Michalopoulos, C. and Ruttan, V. W.*, 1989, pp. 111–24.

Sukhotin, Iu. V. Political Economy—In Breadth or in Depth? *Prob. Econ.*, October 1989, *32*(6), pp. 88–103.

_____. Property: The Restructuring of Relations. *Prob. Econ.*, August 1989, *32*(4), pp. 75–81.

Sulak, Donna B. and Montgomery, Mark R. Female First Marriage in East and Southeast Asia: A Kiefer–Neumann Model. *J. Devel. Econ.*, April 1989, *30*(2), pp. 225–40.

Sulcoski, Carol J. Looking a Gift of Stock in the Mouth: Donative Transfers and Rule 10b-5. *Mich. Law Rev.*, December 1989, *88*(3), pp. 604–34.

Suliman, Ali Ahmed. Liberalization and Privatization: An Overview: Comment. In *El-Naggar, S., ed.*, 1989, pp. 45–49.

Suliman, M. Osman. Inflation and Labor Unions: Empirical Evidence from the U.S. *Econ. Int.*, Aug.–Nov. 1989, *42*(3–4), pp. 198–206.

_____ **and El-Gaghdadi, Mahdi.** Global Approaches to Commodity Price Stabilization. *J. World Trade*, August 1989, *23*(4), pp. 25–34.

Sullivan, A. Charlene and Worden, Debra Drecnik. Deregulation, Tax Reform, and the Use of Consumer Credit. *J. Finan. Services Res.*, October 1989, *3*(1), pp. 77–91.

Sullivan, Daniel. Monopsony Power in the Market for Nurses. *J. Law Econ.*, Part 2, October 1989, *32*(2), pp. S135–78.

Sullivan, David F. State and Local Government Fiscal Position in 1988. *Surv. Curr. Bus.*, February 1989, *69*(2), pp. 18–20.

Sullivan, Edward J. and McCain, Roger A. RATS: An Econometric Package for Microcomputers. *J. Econ. Surveys*, 1989, *3*(3), pp. 253–60.

Sullivan, Gene D. and Avery, David. Southeastern Manufacturing: Recent Changes and Prospects. *Fed. Res. Bank Atlanta Econ. Rev.*, Jan.–Feb. 1989, *74*(1), pp. 2–15.

Sullivan, Jack J.; Kolluri, Bharat R. and Panik, Michael J. Wagner's Law of Public Expenditure Revisited. In *Missouri Valley Economic Association*, 1989, pp. 98–104.

Sullivan, Jerry and Peterson, Richard B. Japanese Management Theories: A Research Agenda. In *Prasad, S. B., ed.*, 1989, pp. 255–75.

Sullivan, John; Wainio, John and Krissoff, Barry. Opening Agricultural Markets: Implications for Developing Countries. *Can. J. Agr. Econ.*, Part 2, December 1989, *37*(4), pp. 1265–75.

Sullivan, Martin A. and Cordes, Joseph J. Resolving the Thrift Industry Crisis: A Public Finance Perspective. *Nat. Tax J.*, September 1989, *42*(3), pp. 233–47.

Sullivan, Richard J. England's "Age of Invention": The Acceleration of Patents and Patentable Invention during the Industrial Revolution. *Exploration Econ. Hist.*, October 1989, *26*(4), pp. 424–52.

_____ **and Simon, Julian L.** Population Size, Knowledge Stock, and Other Determinants of Agricultural Publication and Patenting: England, 1541–1850. *Exploration Econ. Hist.*, January 1989, *26*(1), pp. 21–44.

Sullivan, Roger C. Privatisation in Ethiopia, Malawi and Uganda. In *Ramanadham, V. V., ed.*, 1989, pp. 352–57.

Sullivan, Sean and Lewin, Marion Ein. The Care of Tomorrow's Elderly: Introduction. In *Lewin, M. E. and Sullivan, S., eds.*, 1989, pp. 1–10.

Sümer, M. Y. M. The Concept of Tolerance in Railway Transportation Systems. In *Candemir, Y., ed.*, 1989, pp. 552–65.

Summa, Timo and Kumbhakar, Subal C. Technical Efficiency of Finnish Brewing Plants: A Production Frontier Approach. *Scand. J. Econ.*, 1989, *91*(1), pp. 147–60.

Summary, Rebecca M. A Political–Economic Model of U.S. Bilateral Trade. *Rev. Econ. Statist.*, February 1989, *71*(1), pp. 179–82.

_____; **Vasegh-Daneshvary, Nasser and France, Judith.** The Impact of Economic Education Courses on the Knowledge and Retention of Knowledge of Secondary and Primary School Teachers. *J. Econ. Educ.*, Fall 1989, *20*(4), pp. 346–54.

Summerfield, Gale and Aslanbeigui, Nahid. Impact of the Responsibility System on Women in Rural China: An Application of Sen's Theory of Entitlements. *World Devel.*, March 1989, *17*(3), pp. 343–50.

Summers, Lawrence H. Assessing the Federal Reserve's Measures of Capacity and Utilization: Comments. *Brookings Pap. Econ. Act.*, 1989, (1), pp. 235–38.

_____. Recent Trends in U.S. Earnings and Family Incomes: Comment. In *Blanchard, O. J. and Fischer, S., eds.*, 1989, pp. 114–19.

_____. Some Simple Economics of Mandated Benefits. *Amer. Econ. Rev.*, May 1989, *79*(2), pp. 177–83.

_____. Tax Reform after the Tax Reform Act of 1986. In *Mintz, J. and Whalley, J., eds.*, 1989, pp. 137–41.

_____; **Cutler, David M. and Poterba, James M.** What Moves Stock Prices? *J. Portfol. Manage.*, Spring 1989, *15*(3), pp. 4–12.

_____ **and Fischer, Stanley.** Should Governments Learn to Live with Inflation? *Amer. Econ. Rev.*, May 1989, *79*(2), pp. 382–87.

_____ **and Goulder, Lawrence H.** Tax Policy, Asset Prices, and Growth: A General Equilibrium Analysis. *J. Public Econ.*, April 1989, *38*(3), pp. 265–96.

_____ **and Katz, Lawrence F.** Can Interindustry Wage Differentials Justify Strategic Trade Policy? In *Feenstra, R. C., ed.*, 1989, pp. 85–116.

_____ **and Katz, Lawrence F.** Industry Rents: Evidence and Implications. *Brookings Pap. Econ. Act.*, Microeconomics, 1989, pp. 209–75.

_____ **and Kotlikoff, Laurence J.** The Role of Intergenerational Transfers in Aggregate Capital Accumulation. In *Kotlikoff, L. J.*, 1989, *1981*, pp. 43–67.

_____; **Kotlikoff, Laurence J. and Spivak, Avia.** The Adequacy of Savings. In *Kotlikoff, L. J.*, 1989, *1982*, pp. 429–54.

_____ **and Summers, Victoria P.** When Financial Markets Work Too Well: A Cautious Case for a Securities Transactions Tax. In *Edwards, F. R., ed.*, 1989, pp. 163–88.

_____ **and Summers, Victoria P.** When Financial Markets Work Too Well: A Cautious Case for Securities Transactions Tax. *J. Finan. Services Res.*, December 1989, *3*(2–3), pp. 261–86.

Summers, Robert A. Experience with INF Treaty Verification and Prospects for Effective Verification of Strategic Arms Reductions. In *Altmann, J. and Rotblat, J., eds.*, 1989, pp. 16–26.

Summers, Victoria P. and Summers, Lawrence H. When Financial Markets Work Too Well: A Cautious Case for Securities Transactions Tax. *J. Finan. Services Res.*, December 1989, *3*(2–3), pp. 261–86.

_____ **and Summers, Lawrence H.** When Financial Markets Work too Well: A Cautious Case for a Securities Transactions Tax. In *Edwards, F. R., ed.*, 1989, pp. 163–88.

Sumner, Daniel A. and Frazao, Elizabeth. Wage Rates in a Poor Rural Area with Emphasis on the Impact of Farm and Nonfarm Experience. *Econ. Devel. Cult. Change*, July 1989, *37*(4), pp. 709–18.

_____ **and Mueller, Rolf A. E.** Are Harvest Forecasts News? USDA Announcements and Futures Market Reactions. *Amer. J. Agr. Econ.*, February 1989, *71*(1), pp. 1–8.

Sumner, Michael. Investment, Q, and Taxes. *Public Finance*, 1989, *44*(2), pp. 285–94.

Sumner, Scott. Using Futures Instrument Prices to Target Nominal Income. *Bull. Econ. Res.*, April 1989, *41*(2), pp. 157–62.

_____ **and Grubaugh, Stephen G.** Commodity Prices, Money Surprises, and Fed Credibility: A Comment. *J. Money, Credit, Banking*, August 1989, *21*(3), pp. 407–08.

_____ **and Silver, Stephen.** Real Wages, Employment, and the Phillips Curve. *J. Polit. Econ.*, June 1989, *97*(3), pp. 706–20.

Sun, Li-Teh; Zhang, Shi-Ying and Ge, Minghao. Prospects of Chinese Wage Reform: A Synergy of Market and Planning Systems. *Int. J. Soc. Econ.*, 1989, *16*(8), pp. 26–34.

Sundaram, Anant K. Syndications in Sovereign Lending. *J. Int. Money Finance*, September 1989, *8*(3), pp. 451–64.

_____ **and Deolalikar, Anil B.** Technology Choice, Adaptation and Diffusion in Private- and State-Owned Enterprises in India. In *James, J., ed.*, 1989, pp. 73–138.

Sundaram, K. Agriculture–Industry Interrelations in India: Issues of Migration. In *Chakravarty, S., ed.*, 1989, pp. 177–206.

_____; **Tendulkar, Suresh D. and Jain, L. R.** Level of Living and Incidence of Poverty in Rural India—A Cross-Sectional Analysis. *J. Quant. Econ.*, January 1989, *5*(1), pp. 187–209.

Sundaram, Rangarajan K. Corrigendum [Perfect Equilibrium in Non-randomized Strategies in a Class of Symmetric Dynamic Games]. *J. Econ. Theory*, December 1989, *49*(2), pp. 385–87.

_____. Perfect Equilibrium in Non-randomized Strategies in a Class of Symmetric Dynamic Games. *J. Econ. Theory*, February 1989, *47*(1), pp. 153–77.

Sundararajan, S. and Bhole, L. M. Functional Form of the Import Demand Function. *Margin*, April–June 1989, *21*(3), pp. 52–65.

Sundaresan, Suresh M. Intertemporally Dependent Preferences and the Volatility of Consumption and Wealth. *Rev. Financial Stud.*, 1989, *2*(1), pp. 73–89.

Sundberg, Heimer. The Flexible Pensionable Age in Finland. In *Schmähl, W., ed.*, 1989, pp. 83–89.

Sundberg, Jeffrey O.; Bunker, John P. and Shoven, John B. The Social Security Cost of Smoking. In *Wise, D. A., ed.*, 1989, pp. 231–50.

Sundberg, Lennart and Carlén, Göran. Allocation Mechanisms in Public Provision of Transport and Communication Infrastructure. *Ann. Reg. Sci.*, 1989, *23*(4), pp. 311–27.

Sunding, David and Adelman, Irma. Joan Robinson as a Development Economist. In *Feiwel, G. R., ed. (II)*, 1989, pp. 702–22.

Sundquist, W. Burt and Cooke, Stephen C. Cost Efficiency in U.S. Corn Production. *Amer. J. Agr. Econ.*, November 1989, *71*(4), pp. 1003–10.

Sundstrom, Eric and Altman, Irwin. Physical Environments and Work-Group Effectiveness. In *Cummings, L. L. and Staw, B. M., eds.*, 1989, pp. 175–209.

Sung, Bom Yong; Becker, Robert A. and Boyd, John H., III. Recursive Utility and Optimal Capital Accumulation. I. Existence. *J. Econ. Theory*, February 1989, *47*(1), pp. 76–100.

Sunkel, Osvaldo. From Adjustment and Restructuring to Development. In *Weeks, J. F., ed.*, 1989, pp. 223–32.

_____. Institutionalism and Structuralism. *CEPAL Rev.*, August 1989, (38), pp. 146–55.

_____. Structuralism, Dependency and Institutionalism: An Exploration of Common Ground and Disparities. *J. Econ. Issues*, June 1989, *23*(2), pp. 519–33.

Sunley, Emil M. Tax Policy and Corporate Borrowing: Discussion. In *Kopcke, R. W. and Rosengren, E. S., eds.*, 1989, pp. 169–72.

_____. The Tax Reform Act of 1986 and Economic Growth: Comment. In *Black, S. W., ed.*, 1989, pp. 151–53.

_____ **and Clark, Richard A.** Corporate Debt: What Are the Issues and What Are the Choices. *Nat. Tax J.*, September 1989, *42*(3), pp. 273–82.

Sunstein, Cass R. Disrupting Voluntary Transactions. In *Chapman, J. W. and Pennock, J. R., eds.*, 1989, pp. 279–302.

Suominen, Ilkka. Privatiseringsprocessen i Europa och hos oss. (The Privatization Process in Europe and Finland. With English summary.) *Ekon. Samfundets Tidskr.*, 1989, *42*(3), pp. 169–78.

Suominen, Kari. Administrative and Compliance Costs of Taxation: Finland. In *International Fiscal Association, ed. (I)*, 1989, pp. 349–60.

Suplicy, Eduardo Matarazzo. Income and Citizens' Rights Distribution. In *Davidson, P. and Kregel, J., eds.*, 1989, pp. 216–29.

Supple, Barry. Historical Studies in International Corporate Business: Introduction: Multinational Enterprise. In *Teichova, A.; Lévy-Leboyer, M. and Nussbaum, H., eds.*, 1989, pp. 1–6.

_____. Storia quantitativa e storia economica: Interventi degli esperti. (In English.) In *Cavaciocchi, S., ed.*, 1989, pp. 325–30.

Suranyi, György and Gadó, Ottó. Desirable Changes in the Hungarian Tax Structure. In *Chiancone, A. and Messere, K., eds.*, 1989, pp. 167–81.

Surekha, K. and Griffiths, W. E. Additive and Multiplicative Heteroscedasticity: A Bayesian Analysis with an Application to an Expenditure Model. *J. Quant. Econ.*, January 1989, *5*(1), pp. 43–58.

Suret, Jean-Marc and Gagnon, Jean-Marie. The Canadian Tax Reform and Dividends: A Reexamination. *Finance*, December 1989, *10*(2), pp. 27–49.

Surrey, M. J. C. Aggregate Consumption and Saving. In *Greenaway, D., ed.*, 1989, pp. 132–62.

_____. Money, Commodity Prices and Inflation: Some Simple Tests. *Oxford Bull. Econ. Statist.*, August 1989, *51*(3), pp. 219–38.

Surry, Yves. An Econometric Model of the French Compound Feed Sector. In *Bauer, S. and Henrichsmeyer, W., eds.*, 1989, pp. 31–42.

_____; **McClatchy, Don and Cahill, Sean.** Exchange Rates and Multilateral Free Trade in Agriculture. *Can. J. Agr. Econ.*, Part 2, December 1989, *37*(4), pp. 993–1007.

Sury, M. M. 1989/90 Budget: A Tightrope Walking: India. *Bull. Int. Fiscal Doc.*, June 1989, *43*(6), pp. 280–82.

Sushka, Marie E.; Polonchek, John and Slovin, Myron B. Valuation Effects of Commercial Bank Securities Offerings: A Test of the Information Hypothesis. *J. Banking Finance*, July 1989, *13*(3), pp. 443–61.

Suslow, Valerie Y. and Bresnahan, Timothy F. Oligopoly Pricing with Capacity Constraints. *Ann. Écon. Statist.*, July–Dec. 1989, (15–16), pp. 267–89.

_____ **and Bresnahan, Timothy F.** Short-run Supply with Capacity Constraints. *J. Law Econ.*, Part 2, October 1989, *32*(2), pp. S11–42.

Susman, Paul. Exporting the Crisis: U.S. Agriculture and the Third World. *Econ. Geogr.*, October 1989, *65*(4), pp. 293–313.

Sussmann, H. J. Optimal Control. In *[Willems, J. C.]*, 1989, pp. 409–25.

Sussna, Edward. Managing in a Global Competitive Environment: Comments. In *Ahlbrandt, R. S., Jr., ed.*, 1989, pp. 65–66.

Sutch, Richard and Ransom, Roger L. The Trend in the Rate of Labor Force Participation of Older Men, 1870–1930: A Reply. *J. Econ. Hist.*, March 1989, *49*(1), pp. 170–83.

Sutcliffe, Charles and Sinclair, M. Thea. Truncated Income Multipliers and Local Income Generation over Time. *Appl. Econ.*, December 1989, *21*(12), pp. 1621–30.

Sutela, Pekka. Ideology as a Means of Economic Debate or the Strange Case of Objective Economic Laws of Socialism. *Jahr. Wirtsch. Osteuropas*, 1989, *13*(1), pp. 198–220.

Suter, Christian and Pfister, Ulrich. Global Debt Cycles and the Role of Political Regimes. In *Avery, W. P. and Rapkin, D. P., eds.*, 1989, pp. 17–55.

Sutherland, Ronald G. International Machinery

for Monitoring a Chemical Weapons Convention. In *Rotblat, J. and Goldanskii, V. I., eds.*, 1989, pp. 98–104.

Sutherland, Ronald J. An Analysis of the U.S. Department of Energy's Civilian R&D Budget. *Energy J.*, January 1989, *10*(1), pp. 35–54.

Sutherland, William M. Policy, Law and Management in Pacific Island Fisheries. In *Couper, A. D., ed.*, 1989, pp. 33–46.

Sutomo, Slamet. Income, Food Consumption and Estimation of Energy and Protein Intake of Households: A Study Based on the 1975 and 1980 Indonesian Social Accounting Matrices. *Bull. Indonesian Econ. Stud.*, December 1989, *25*(3), pp. 57–72.

Suttle, Philip. The Problem of Forecasting Debt Servicing Difficulties. In *Bird, G., ed.*, 1989, pp. 20–40.

Sutton, John. Endogenous Sunk Costs and the Structure of Advertising Intensive Industries. *Europ. Econ. Rev.*, March 1989, *33*(2/3), pp. 335–44.

_____. Is Imperfect Competition Empirically Empty? In *Feiwel, G. R., ed. (I)*, 1989, pp. 225–40.

_____; **Binmore, Ken and Shaked, Avner.** An Outside Option Experiment. *Quart. J. Econ.*, November 1989, *104*(4), pp. 753–70.

Sutton, Keith. The Role of Urban Bias in Perpetuating Rural–Urban and Regional Disparities in the Maghreb. In *[Mountjoy, A. B.]*, 1989, pp. 68–108.

Sutton, Robert I. and Rafaeli, Anat. The Expression of Emotion in Organizational Life. In *Cummings, L. L. and Staw, B. M., eds.*, 1989, pp. 1–42.

Suwanmala, Charas. Crisis and Response: Treasury Cash Balance Crisis in Thailand 1980–1982. *Public Budg. Finance*, Autumn 1989, *9*(3), pp. 27–36.

Suzuki, Katsuhiko. Choice between International Capital and Labor Mobility for Diversified Economies. *J. Int. Econ.*, November 1989, *27*(3–4), pp. 347–61.

Suzuki, Kazuyuki and Goto, Akira. R&D Capital, Rate of Return on R&D Investment and Spillover of R&D in Japanese Manufacturing Industries. *Rev. Econ. Statist.*, November 1989, *71*(4), pp. 555–64.

_____; **Honda, Tetsushi and Nambu, Tsuruhiko.** Deregulation in Japan. In *Crandall, R. W. and Flamm, K., eds.*, 1989, pp. 147–73.

Suzuki, Norihiko. International Product Development Scanning across the Pacific: A Conceptual Approach. In *Negandhi, A. R., ed.*, 1989, pp. 283–304.

_____. The Trading House and the Challenge from the Far East. In *Hallén, L. and Johanson, J., eds.*, 1989, pp. 249–58.

_____ **and Irie, Itaro.** The Cooperative Development of Research Projects on MNCs between Taiwan and Japan: Past, Present, and Future. In *Negandhi, A. R., ed.*, 1989, pp. 231–37.

Suzuki, Yoshio. The Future Role of Japan as a Financial Centre in the Asian-Pacific Area. In

Shinohara, M. and Lo, F., eds., 1989, pp. 384–97.

_____. Policy Targets and Operating Procedures in the 1990s: The Case of Japan. In *Federal Reserve Bank of Kansas City*, 1989, pp. 161–73.

Suzuki, Yuji and Sato, Seizaburo. A New Stage of the United States–Japan Alliance. In *Makin, J. H. and Hellmann, D. C., eds.*, 1989, pp. 153–74.

Svanidze, Adelaida. Processi di urbanizzazione: Interventi degli esperti. (In English.) In *Cavaciocchi, S., ed.*, 1989, pp. 235–37.

Svejnar, Jan. Models of Modern-Sector Labor Market Institutions in Developing Countries. *World Devel.*, Special Issue, September 1989, *17*(9), pp. 1409–15.

Svensson, L.-G. Fairness, the Veil of Ignorance and Social Choice. *Soc. Choice Welfare*, January 1989, *6*(1), pp. 1–17.

Svensson, Lars E. O. Exchange Rate Management and Macroeconomic Policy: A National Perspective: Comment. *Scand. J. Econ.*, 1989, *91*(2), pp. 473–76.

_____. Portfolio Choice with Non-expected Utility in Continuous Time. *Econ. Letters*, October 1989, *30*(4), pp. 313–17.

_____. Real Exchange Rates and Macroeconomics: A Selective Survey: Comment. *Scand. J. Econ.*, 1989, *91*(2), pp. 435–38.

_____. Trade in Nominal Assets: Monetary Policy, and Price Level and Exchange Rate Risk. *J. Int. Econ.*, February 1989, *26*(1/2), pp. 1–28.

_____ **and Persson, Torsten.** Exchange Rate Variability and Asset Trade. *J. Monet. Econ.*, May 1989, *23*(3), pp. 485–509.

_____ **and Persson, Torsten.** Why a Stubborn Conservative Would Run a Deficit: Policy with Time-Inconsistent Preferences. *Quart. J. Econ.*, May 1989, *104*(2), pp. 325–45.

_____ **and van Wijnbergen, Sweder.** Excess Capacity, Monopolistic Competition, and International Transmission of Monetary Disturbances. *Econ. J.*, September 1989, *99*(397), pp. 785–805.

Swaan, Wim. Price Regulation in Hungary: Indirect but Comprehensive Bureaucratic Control. *Comp. Econ. Stud.*, Winter 1989, *31*(4), pp. 10–52.

Swagler, Roger M. and Wheeler, Paula. Rental-Purchase Agreements: A Preliminary Investigation of Consumer Attitudes and Behaviors. *J. Cons. Aff.*, Summer 1989, *23*(1), pp. 145–60.

Swaim, Paul and Podgursky, Michael. Do More-Educated Workers Fare Better Following Job Displacement? *Mon. Lab. Rev.*, August 1989, *112*(8), pp. 43–46.

Swales, J. K. Are Discretionary Regional Subsidies Cost-Effective? *Reg. Stud.*, August 1989, *23*(4), pp. 361–68.

_____; **Holden, Darryl R. and Nairn, Alasdair G. M.** Shift-Share Analysis of Regional Growth and Policy: A Critique. *Oxford Bull. Econ. Statist.*, February 1989, *51*(1), pp. 15–34.

Swaminathan, M. S. No Time to Relax. In *Inter-*

national Rice Research Institute, 1989, pp. 11–24.

_____; Sinha, S. K. and Rao, N. H. Food Security in the Changing Global Climate. In *Oram, P. A., et al.*, 1989, pp. 579–97.

Swamy, P. A. V. B.; Conway, Roger K. and LeBlanc, Michael R. The Stochastic Coefficients Approach to Econometric Modeling, Part III: Estimation, Stability Testing, and Prediction. *J. Agr. Econ. Res.*, Winter 1989, *41*(1), pp. 4–20.

_____ and Schinasi, Garry J. The Out-of-Sample Forecasting Performance of Exchange Rate Models When Coefficients Are Allowed to Change. *J. Int. Money Finance*, September 1989, *8*(3), pp. 375–90.

_____ and Tavlas, George S. Financial Deregulation, the Demand for Money, and Monetary Policy in Australia. *Int. Monet. Fund Staff Pap.*, March 1989, *36*(1), pp. 63–101.

_____ and Tavlas, George S. Modeling Buffer Stock Money: An Appraisal. *J. Policy Modeling*, Winter 1989, *11*(4), pp. 593–612.

Swan, John E. and Oliver, Richard L. Equity and Disconfirmation Perceptions as Influences on Merchant and Product Satisfaction. *J. Cons. Res.*, December 1989, *16*(3), pp. 372–83.

Swan, Peter L. and Bateson, Jeff. Economies of Scale and Utilization: An Analysis of the Multiplant Generation Costs of the Electricity Commission of New South Wales, 1970/71–1984/85. *Econ. Rec.*, December 1989, *65*(191), pp. 329–44.

Swan, T. W. The Principle of Effective Demand—A 'Real Life' Model. *Econ. Rec.*, December 1989, *65*(191), pp. 378–98.

Swanepoel, J. J. and van der Walt, I. N. A. Indicative Labour and Capital Programming: An Exercise on the Frontiers of Empirical Economics. In *Gemper, B. B., ed.*, 1989, pp. 65–86.

Swaney, James A. Our Obsolete Technology Mentality. *J. Econ. Issues*, June 1989, *23*(2), pp. 569–78.

_____ and Evers, Martin A. The Social Cost Concepts of K. William Kapp and Karl Polanyi. *J. Econ. Issues*, March 1989, *23*(1), pp. 7–33.

_____ and Premus, Robert. Modern Empiricism and Quantum Leap Theorizing in Economics. In *Tool, M. R. and Samuels, W. J., eds. (II)*, 1989, *1982*, pp. 189–206.

Swann, Dennis. The Regulatory Scene: An Overview. In *Button, K. and Swann, D., eds.*, 1989, pp. 1–23.

_____ and Button, Kenneth J. European Community Airlines—Deregulation and Its Problems. *J. Common Market Stud.*, June 1989, *27*(4), pp. 259–82.

_____ and Button, Kenneth J. Regulatory Reform: The Way Forward. In *Button, K. and Swann, D., eds.*, 1989, pp. 321–32.

Swann, G. M. Peter. Nobel Laureates in Economic Sciences: A Biographical Dictionary: Ragnar Anton Kittil Frisch: 1969. In *Katz, B. S., ed.*, 1989, pp. 66–80.

Swanson, David A. A State-Based Regression Model for Estimating Substate Life Expectancy. *Demography*, February 1989, *26*(1), pp. 161–70.

Swanson, David H. Recommendations for Economic, Agricultural, and Trade Policies to Improve the Functioning of the World Food Production and Distribution Systems. In *Helmuth, J. W. and Johnson, S. R., eds., Vol. 1*, 1989, pp. 220–30.

Swanson, Eric V. and Hartley, Michael J. Maximum Likelihood Estimation of the Truncated and Censored Normal Regression Models. In *Mariano, R. S.; Lim, K. S. and Ling, K. D., eds.*, 1989, pp. 159–204.

_____ and Hartley, Michael J. Retention of Basic Skills among Dropouts from Egyptian Primary Schools. In *Mariano, R. S.; Lim, K. S. and Ling, K. D., eds.*, 1989, pp. 205–45.

Swanson, James A. A Test for Selectivity Bias in the Estimation of the Wage Equations of Older Male Workers. In *Missouri Valley Economic Association*, 1989, pp. 150–55.

Swanson, Louis. Selective Perceptions and the Politics of Agricultural Policy: Commentary. In *Krämer, C. S., ed.*, 1989, pp. 80–83.

Swanson, Paul A. Market Value and the Choice of Technique. *Rev. Radical Polit. Econ.*, 1989, *21*(1–2), pp. 57–74.

Swanstrom, Thomas E. The Savings Solution. *Bus. Econ.*, July 1989, *24*(3), pp. 10–16.

Swanstrom, Todd and Kerstein, Robert. Job and Housing Displacement: A Review of Competing Policy Perspectives. In *Smith, M. P., ed.*, 1989, pp. 254–96.

Swaroop, Vinaya. Uniform Labor-Income Taxation and Economic Efficiency. *J. Public Econ.*, February 1989, *38*(1), pp. 117–36.

Swart, Koenraad W. The Sale of Public Offices. In *Heidenheimer, A. J.; Johnston, M. and LeVine, V. T., eds.*, 1989, pp. 87–99.

Swartz, Katherine. How the Overlap between the Poverty and Medicaid Populations Changed between 1979 and 1983, or Lessons for the Next Recession. *J. Human Res.*, Spring 1989, *24*(2), pp. 319–30.

_____ and Hadley, Jack. The Impacts on Hospital Costs between 1980 and 1984 of Hospital Rate Regulation, Competition, and Changes in Health Insurance Coverage. *Inquiry*, Spring 1989, *26*(1), pp. 35–47.

Sweat, Mike; Brueggemann, John and Boswell, Terry E. War in the Core of the World-System: Testing the Goldstein Thesis. In *Schaeffer, R. K., ed.*, 1989, pp. 9–26.

Swedberg, Richard. Essays on Entrepreneurs, Innovations, Business Cycles, and the Evolution of Capitalism: Introduction to the Transaction Edition. In *Schumpeter, J. A.*, 1989, pp. vii–xxxix.

_____. Joseph A. Schumpeter and the Tradition of Economic Sociology. *J. Inst. Theoretical Econ.*, September 1989, *145*(3), pp. 508–24.

Sweeney, Gerry. Information Resources and Corporate Growth: Introduction: Information and Corporate Growth. In *Punset, E. and Sweeney, G., eds.*, 1989, pp. 1–15.

Sweeney, James L.; Hickman, Bert G. and Huntington, Hillard G. On Economic Policy Responses to Disruptions: Reply. *Energy J.*, October 1989, *10*(4), pp. 189–98.

Sweeney, Larry E. and Schoening, Niles C. Applying an Industrial Diversification Decision Model to Small Regions. *Rev. Reg. Stud.*, Fall 1989, *19*(3), pp. 14–17.

Sweet, Arnold L. and Bartolomei, Sonia M. A Note on a Comparison of Exponential Smoothing Methods for Forecasting Seasonal Series. *Int. J. Forecasting*, 1989, *5*(1), pp. 111–116.

Sweet, Richard. The Institutional Context of Industry Training, with Particular Reference to the French Experience. *Australian Bull. Lab.*, September 1989, *15*(4), pp. 326–42.

Sweezy, Paul and Magdoff, Harry. The Financial Explosion. In *Guttmann, R., ed.*, 1989, *1985*, pp. 129–33.

Swegle, Wayne E. and Ligon, Polly C. Aid, Trade, and Farm Policies: A Sourcebook on Issues and Interrelationships: Introduction. In *Swegle, W. E. and Ligon, P. C., eds.*, 1989, pp. xi–xv.

Swetnam, John. What Else Did Indians Have to Do with Their Time? Alternatives to Labor Migration in Prerevolutionary Guatemala. *Econ. Devel. Cult. Change*, October 1989, *38*(1), pp. 89–112.

Swierzbinski, Joseph E.; Bagnoli, Mark and Salant, Stephen W. Durable-Goods Monopoly with Discrete Demand. *J. Polit. Econ.*, December 1989, *97*(6), pp. 1459–78.

—— **and Mendelsohn, Robert.** Exploration and Exhaustible Resources: The Microfoundations of Aggregate Models. *Int. Econ. Rev.*, February 1989, *30*(1), pp. 175–86.

—— **and Mendelsohn, Robert.** Information and Exhaustible Resources: A Bayesian Analysis. *J. Environ. Econ. Manage.*, May 1989, *16*(3), pp. 193–208.

Swift, John. Merger Policy: Certainty or Lottery? In *Fairburn, J. and Kay, J., eds.*, 1989, pp. 264–80.

Swinbank, Alan. The Common Agricultural Policy and the Politics of European Decision Making. *J. Common Market Stud.*, June 1989, *27*(4), pp. 303–22.

Swings, André A. L. Dollar Dominance or YE$-Troika? Europe's ECU: A New Geopolitic Instrument. In *Kaushik, S. K., ed.*, 1989, pp. 49–65.

Swirsky, Benjamin. Tax Reform and Residential Real Estate: Comment. In *Mintz, J. and Whalley, J., eds.*, 1989, pp. 366–72.

Switalski, Marion and Kistner, Klaus-Peter. Hierarchische Produktionsplanung. (With English summary.) *Z. Betriebswirtshaft*, May 1989, *59*(5), pp. 477–503.

Switzer, Lorne N. and Redstone, John. The Impact of a Canada–U.S. Bilateral Free Trade Accord on the Canadian Minerals Industry. *Appl. Econ.*, February 1989, *21*(2), pp. 273–84.

Swoboda, Alexander K. The Dollar in the 1990s: Competitiveness and the Challenges of New Economic Blocs: Commentary. In *Federal Reserve Bank of Kansas City*, 1989, pp. 283–90.

—— **and Genberg, Hans.** Policy and Current Account Determination under Floating Exchange Rates. *Int. Monet. Fund Staff Pap.*, March 1989, *36*(1), pp. 1–30.

Swoboda, Peter. The Liquidation Decision as a Principal–Agent Problem. In *Bamberg, G. and Spremann, K., eds.*, 1989, pp. 167–77.

Syed, Azmat A.; Liu, Pu and Smith, Stanley D. The Exploitation of Inside Information at the *Wall Street Journal:* A Test of Strong Form Efficiency. *Financial Rev.*, November 1989, *24*(4), pp. 567–79.

Syeduzzaman, M. Impacts of Global Adjustment on the Asian-Pacific Economy: Comment. In *Shinohara, M. and Lo, F., eds.*, 1989, pp. 323–27.

Sylos Labini, Paolo. Recollections of Joan. In *Feiwel, G. R., ed. (II)*, 1989, pp. 870–73.

Symansky, Steven A. and Dooley, Michael P. Comparing Menu Items: Methodological Considerations and Policy Issues. In *Frenkel, J. A.; Dooley, M. P. and Wickham, P., eds.*, 1989, pp. 398–411.

Symons, Elizabeth and Walker, Ian. The Revenue and Welfare Effects of Fiscal Harmonization for the UK. *Oxford Rev. Econ. Policy*, Summer 1989, *5*(2), pp. 61–75.

Symons, James S. V. and Bean, Charles R. Ten Years of Mrs. T. In *Blanchard, O. J. and Fischer, S., eds.*, 1989, pp. 13–61.

—— **and Newell, Andrew.** Stylised Facts and the Labour Demand Curve. *Labour*, Winter 1989, *3*(3), pp. 3–21.

Syron, Richard F. A Framework for the Future: A Panel Presentation. In *Federal Home Loan Bank of San Francisco*, 1989, pp. 215–18.

Syrquin, Moshe. Sector Proportions and Economic Development: The Evidence since 1950. In *Williamson, J. G. and Panchamukhi, V. R., eds.*, 1989, pp. 32–53.

—— **and Deutsch, Joseph.** Economic Development and the Structure of Production. *Econ. Systems Res.*, 1989, *1*(4), pp. 447–64.

Sysło, Maciej M. and Piotrowski, Wiktor. A Characterization of Centroidal Graphs. In *Simeone, B., ed.*, 1989, pp. 272–81.

Szafarz, A.; Broze, L. and Gourieroux, Christian. Speculative Bubbles and Exchange of Information on the Market of a Storable Good. In *Barnett, W. A.; Geweke, J. and Shell, K., eds.*, 1989, pp. 101–18.

Szalai, Erzsébet. See-Saw: The Economic Mechanism and Large-Company Interests. *Acta Oecon.*, 1989, *41*(1–2), pp. 101–36.

Szamuely, László. An Iron Hoop Made of Wood. *Acta Oecon.*, 1989, *40*(3–4), pp. 267–71.

——. Ideological Features Yet to Be Overcome in Soviet-Type Economies. In *Gomulka, S.; Ha, Y.-C. and Kim, C.-O., eds.*, 1989, pp. 156–69.

——. Intentions and Constraints: Reflections on Reading Iván T. Berend's Study. *Acta Oecon.*, 1989, *40*(1–2), pp. 150–59.

Szapiro, T. and Michalowski, W. A Safe Choice

Procedure in Interactive Programming. In *Lockett, A. G. and Islei, G., eds.*, 1989, pp. 454–61.

Szegö, Andrea. Taxation and Income Distribution: A Kaleckian Approach. In *Davidson, P. and Kregel, J., eds.*, 1989, pp. 179–94.

Székely, Alberto. Yellow-Fin Tuna: A Transboundary Resource of the Eastern Pacific. *Natural Res. J.*, Fall 1989, *29*(4), pp. 1051–65.

Székely, Gabriel. Dilemmas of Export Diversification in a Developing Economy: Mexican Oil in the 1980s. *World Devel.*, November 1989, *17*(11), pp. 1777–97.

Székely, István. Economic Growth and Structural Change in Developing Countries. In *Krelle, W., ed.*, 1989, pp. 173–98.

_____ and Dobrinsky, Rumen Nikolov. Growth in and Interdependent World Economy: Linking the National Models through International Trade. In *Krelle, W., ed.*, 1989, pp. 199–232.

Szelenyi, Ivan. Eastern Europe in an Epoch of Transition: Toward a Socialist Mixed Economy? In *Nee, V. and Stark, D., eds.*, 1989, pp. 208–32.

Szénási, Magdolna. A Dispute on the Changes in Property Rights. *Acta Oecon.*, 1989, *40*(1–2), pp. 165–72.

Szidarovszky, Ferenc. On Non-negative Solvability of Nonlinear Input–Output Systems. *Econ. Letters*, October 1989, *30*(4), pp. 319–21.

_____ and Okuguchi, Koji. An Adaptive Model of Oligopoly with Multi-product Firms. *Econ. Stud. Quart.*, March 1989, *40*(1), pp. 48–52.

_____ and Okuguchi, Koji. A Non-differentiable Input–Output Model. *Math. Soc. Sci.*, October 1989, *18*(2), pp. 187–90.

Szilágyi, György. International Demand Analysis. *Statist. J.*, 1989, *6*(4), pp. 305–14.

Sziráczki, György and Galasi, Péter. State Regulation, Enterprise Behavior, and the Labor Market in Hungary, 1968–1983. In *Rosenberg, S., ed.*, 1989, pp. 151–70.

Szostak, Rick. The Organization of Work: The Emergence of the Factory Revisited. *J. Econ. Behav. Organ.*, May 1989, *11*(3), pp. 343–58.

Szulc, Bohdan J. Price Indices below the Basic Aggregation Level. In *Turvey, R.*, 1989, pp. 167–78.

Szumski, J. S. The Transformation Problem Solved? *Cambridge J. Econ.*, September 1989, *13*(3), pp. 431–52.

Szusterman, Celia. The 'Revolución Libertadora', 1955–58. In *di Tella, G. and Dornbusch, R., eds.*, 1989, pp. 89–102.

Szymanowski, W. and Ogryczak, Wlodzimierz. The Analysis of Liquid Milk Supply to Urban Agglomeration by Bicriterion Linear Transportation Model with the MPSX/370 Package. In *Lockett, A. G. and Islei, G., eds.*, 1989, pp. 203–11.

Szymanski, Stefan; Kay, John A. and Manning, Alan. The Economic Benefits of the Channel Tunnel. *Econ. Policy: A Europ. Forum*, April 1989, (8), pp. 211–34.

Szyrmer, Janusz. Trade-Off between Error and Information in the RAS Procedure. In *Miller,*

R. E.; Polenske, K. R. and Rose, A. Z., eds., 1989, pp. 258–78.

Tabb, William K. Capital Mobility, the Restructuring of Production, and the Politics of Labor. In *MacEwan, A. and Tabb, W. K., eds.*, 1989, pp. 259–78.

_____ and MacEwan, Arthur. Instability and Change in the World Economy. In *MacEwan, A. and Tabb, W. K., eds.*, 1989, pp. 23–43.

_____ and MacEwan, Arthur. Instability and Change in the World Economy: Introduction. In *MacEwan, A. and Tabb, W. K., eds.*, 1989, pp. 7–20.

Tabellini, Guido. Management of a Common Currency: Discussion. In *De Cecco, M. and Giovannini, A., eds.*, 1989, pp. 158–61.

_____ and Alesina, Alberto. External Debt, Capital Flight and Political Risk. *J. Int. Econ.*, November 1989, *27*(3–4), pp. 199–220.

_____ and La Via, Vincenzo. Money, Deficit and Public Debt in the United States. *Rev. Econ. Statist.*, February 1989, *71*(1), pp. 15–25.

_____ and Staiger, Robert W. Rules and Discretion in Trade Policy. *Europ. Econ. Rev.*, July 1989, *33*(6), pp. 1265–77.

Tabor, Steven R.; Altemeier, Klaus and Adinugroho, Bambang. Foodcrop Demand in Indonesia: A Systems Approach. *Bull. Indonesian Econ. Stud.*, August 1989, *25*(2), pp. 31–51.

Tabors, Richard and Castillo Bonet, Manuel. Load Management. In *Kim, Y. H. and Smith, K. R., eds.*, 1989, pp. 65–105.

Tabucanon, M. T. and Shin, M. J. A Multicriterion Optimization Model for Industrial Promotion: The Case of Korea. In *Lockett, A. G. and Islei, G., eds.*, 1989, pp. 275–86.

Tachibanaki, Toshiaki and Ichioka, Osamu. General Equilibrium Evaluations of Tariffs, Nontariff Barriers and Subsidies for Agriculture in Japan. *Econ. Stud. Quart.*, December 1989, *40*(4), pp. 317–35.

Taga, Leonore Shever. The Soviet Firm in the 'Large-Scale Experiment.' *Comp. Econ. Stud.*, Summer 1989, *31*(2), pp. 92–134.

Taggart, Robert A., Jr. Still Searching for Optimal Capital Structure: Discussion. In *Kopcke, R. W. and Rosengren, E. S., eds.*, 1989, pp. 100–105.

Tahar, Gabriel; Antonelli, Cristiano and Petit, Pascal. Technological Diffusion and Investment Behaviour: The Case of the Textile Industry. *Weltwirtsch. Arch.*, 1989, *125*(4), pp. 782–803.

_____ and Petit, Pascal. Dynamics of Technological Change and Schemes of Diffusion. *Manchester Sch. Econ. Soc. Stud.*, December 1989, *57*(4), pp. 370–86.

_____ and Petit, Pascal. Effets productivité et qualité de l'automatisation: Une approche macro-économique. (Productivity and Quality Effects of Automation: A Macroeconomic Approach. With English summary.) *Revue Écon.*, January 1989, *40*(1), pp. 35–54.

Taira, Koji. Development, Growth, and the Long Run: Review Article. *Econ. Devel. Cult.*

Change, January 1989, *37*(2), pp. 425–33.

———. Labor Market Segmentation, Human Resource Utilization, and Economic Development: The Case of Japan in Historical Perspective. In *Sato, R. and Negishi, T., eds.*, 1989, pp. 181–96.

Tait, Alan A. Misconceptions about the Value-Added Tax. *Finance Devel.*, March 1989, *26*(1), pp. 25–27.

———. Not So General Equilibrium and Not So Optimal Taxation. *Public Finance*, 1989, *44*(2), pp. 169–82.

Taiwo, I. O. Determinants of Federal Government Expenditure in Nigeria. *Soc. Econ. Stud.*, September 1989, *38*(3), pp. 205–22.

———. Potential Effects of Privatization on Economic Growth: The Nigerian Case. *Eastern Afr. Econ. Rev.*, June 1989, *5*(1), pp. 62–73.

Taixeira, John A. and Bina, Cyrus. Leveraged Buyouts: Robber Barons of the Eighties. *Challenge*, Sept.–Oct. 1989, *32*(5), pp. 53–57.

Takagi, Keizo. The Rise of Land Prices in Japan: The Determination Mechanism and the Effect of Taxation System. *Bank Japan Monet. Econ. Stud.*, August 1989, *7*(2), pp. 93–139.

Takagi, Shinji. An Alternative Approach to the Divergence Indicator in the European Monetary System. *De Economist*, 1989, *137*(3), pp. 360–66.

———. The Japanese Equity Market: Past and Present. *J. Banking Finance*, September 1989, *13*(4–5), pp. 537–70.

Takagi, Yasuoki. Growth with External Debt and Inflation. In *Singer, H. W. and Sharma, S., eds. (II)*, 1989, pp. 80–96.

Takahara, Iwane. The Role of Industrial Nations in Building Communications Infrastructure for Developing Countries. In *Jussawalla, M.; Okuma, T. and Araki, T., eds.*, 1989, pp. 296–98.

Takahashi, H. and Byron, R. P. An Analysis of the Effect of Schooling, Experience and Sex on Earnings in the Government and Private Sectors of Urban Java. *Bull. Indonesian Econ. Stud.*, April 1989, *25*(1), pp. 105–17.

Takayama, Akira. Economic Expansion, Industrialization, and Dutch Disease Economics in the Context of International Monetary Economics. In *Sato, R. and Negishi, T., eds.*, 1989, pp. 59–82.

——— and Ide, Toyonari. On Homothetic Functions. *Scand. J. Econ.*, 1989, *91*(3), pp. 621–23.

——— and Ide, Toyonari. Returns to Scale under Non-homotheticity and Homotheticity and the Shape of Average Cost. *J. Inst. Theoretical Econ.*, June 1989, *145*(2), pp. 367–88.

Takayama, Shigeo. Keys to Accessing Japanese Markets. In *Matsuo, H., ed.*, 1989, pp. 25–31.

Takayama, Takashi and Hashimoto, Hideo. A Comparative Study of Linear Complementarity Programming Models and Linear Programming Models in Multi-region Investment Analysis: Aluminium and Bauxite. In *Labys, W. C.; Takayama, T. and Uri, N. D., eds.*, 1989, pp. 129–63.

———, et al. Application of the Spatial and Temporal Price and Allocation Model to the World Food Economy. In *Labys, W. C.; Takayama, T. and Uri, N. D., eds.*, 1989, pp. 227–78.

Takeda, Masahiko. Bank Failures and Optimal Bank Audit Policy. *Bank Japan Monet. Econ. Stud.*, April 1989, *7*(1), pp. 99–130.

Takeda, Shigeo. Joint Production and the Non-substitution Theorem. *Econ. Stud. Quart.*, March 1989, *40*(1), pp. 53–65.

Takemori, Shumpei and Jones, Ronald W. Foreign Monopoly and Optimal Tariffs for the Small Open Economy. *Europ. Econ. Rev.*, December 1989, *33*(9), pp. 1691–1707.

Takeuchi, Yoshiyuki and Yoshikawa, Hiroshi. Real Wages and the Japanese Economy. *Bank Japan Monet. Econ. Stud.*, April 1989, *7*(1), pp. 1–40.

Takurō, Seiyama. A Radical Interpretation of Postwar Economic Policies. In *Morris-Suzuki, T. and Seiyama, T., eds.*, 1989, pp. 28–73.

Ta-lang, Shih. The Role of the People's Republic of China's Hong Kong–Based Conglomerates as Agents of Development. In *Negandhi, A. R., ed.*, 1989, pp. 215–30.

Talley, Wayne K. Joint Cost and Competitive Value-of-Service Pricing. *Int. J. Transport Econ.*, June 1989, *16*(2), pp. 119–30.

———. Optimization of Bus Frequency and Speed of Service: A System Approach. *Logist. Transp. Rev.*, June 1989, *25*(2), pp. 139–56.

———. Regulatory Reform of the U.S. and U.K. Inter-city Bus Industries. In *Button, K. and Swann, D., eds.*, 1989, pp. 257–78.

——— and Chaffin, Wilkie W. Diffusion Indexes and a Statistical Test for Predicting Turning Points in Business Cycles. *Int. J. Forecasting*, 1989, *5*(1), pp. 29–36.

Tallman, Ellis W. Financial Asset Pricing Theory: A Review of Recent Developments. *Fed. Res. Bank Atlanta Econ. Rev.*, Nov.–Dec. 1989, *74*(6), pp. 26–41.

Talmor, Eli. Tax Arbitrage Restrictions and Financial Leverage Clienteles. *J. Banking Finance*, December 1989, *13*(6), pp. 831–38.

Talu, Ayhan; Melvin, Michael and Schlagenhauf, Don. The U.S. Budget Deficit and the Foreign Exchange Value of the Dollar. *Rev. Econ. Statist.*, August 1989, *71*(3), pp. 500–505.

Tam, Joseph N. K. Corporate Social Awareness and Responsibility: Implications for Management Education in Hong Kong. In *Davies, J., et al., eds.*, 1989, pp. 152–59.

Tam, On-kit. Economic Policy in China: Commentary. In *Zerby, J., ed.*, 1989, pp. 118–20.

Tamerin, John S. and Resnik, Harvey L. P. Risk Taking by Individual Option—Case Study: Cigarette Smoking. In *Diamond, P. and Rothschild, M., eds.*, 1989, *1972*, pp. 5–16.

Tan, Augustine. Payments Imbalances, Sudden Surges and Safeguards. *World Econ.*, September 1989, *12*(3), pp. 325–38.

Tan, Chwee Huat. Confucianism and Nation Building in Singapore. *Int. J. Soc. Econ.*, 1989, *16*(8), pp. 5–16.

————. Human Resource Management Reforms in the People's Republic of China. In *Nedd, A., ed.*, 1989, pp. 45–58.

Tan, Edita A. and Canlas, Dante B. Migrant's Saving Remittance and Labour Supply Behaviour: The Philippines Case. In *Amjad, R., ed.*, 1989, pp. 223–54.

Tanaka, Kazuyoshi and Ohkawa, Masayuki. A Note on Tariffs and Employment under Flexible Exchange Rates. *Scand. J. Econ.*, 1989, *91*(4), pp. 741–46.

Tanaka, Kunikazu. On a Theory Concerning International Fiscal Policies. *Kobe Univ. Econ.*, 1989, (35), pp. 81–101.

Tanchoco, J. M. A. and Noble, James S. Cost Modeling for Design Justification. In *Gulledge, T. R., Jr. and Litteral, L. A., eds.*, 1989, pp. 197–213.

Tandon, Pankaj. A Note on Optimal Pricing of Publicly Produced Intermediate Inputs. *Atlantic Econ. J.*, September 1989, *17*(3), pp. 43–46.

Tang, Xiaobing. Textiles and the Uruguay Round of Multilateral Trade Negotiations. *J. World Trade*, June 1989, *23*(3), pp. 51–68.

Tangermann, Stefan. Evaluation of the Current CAP Reform Package. *World Econ.*, June 1989, *12*(2), pp. 175–88.

————. Progress and Issues in the GATT Negotiations: An EC Perspective. *Can. J. Agr. Econ.*, Part 2, December 1989, *37*(4), pp. 863–74.

Tangri, Shanti S. Annual Review of Nations: Year 1988: India. In *Haberman, L. and Sacks, P. M., eds.*, 1989, pp. 117–33.

Tanguy, Hervé and Ponssard, Jean-Pierre. Un cadre conceptuel commun à la planification et à la concurrence formalisation théorique et implications pratiques. (With English summary.) *L'Actual. Econ.*, March 1989, *65*(1), pp. 86–104.

Tanizaki, Hisashi. The Kalman Filter Model under the Assumption of the First-Order Autoregressive Process in the Disturbance Terms. *Econ. Letters*, December 1989, *31*(2), pp. 145–49.

Tank, Frederick E. and Abdullah, Dewan A. The Determinants of Fixed Investment over the Business Cycle: Some Time Series Evidence. *J. Macroecon.*, Winter 1989, *11*(1), pp. 49–65.

Tannenwald, Robert. The Changing Level and Mix of Federal Aid to State and Local Governments. *New Eng. Econ. Rev.*, May–June 1989, pp. 41–55.

Tansel, Aysit. Factors Affecting Traffic Accidents in Turkey. In *Candemir, Y., ed.*, 1989, pp. 126–36.

Tanton, Morgan and Easterby-Smith, Mark. Is the Western View Inevitable? A Model of the Development of Management Education. In *Davies, J., et al., eds.*, 1989, pp. 11–22.

Tanzer, Michael. Growing Instability in the International Oil Industry. In *MacEwan, A. and Tabb, W. K., eds.*, 1989, pp. 225–40.

Tanzi, Vito. Fiscal Policy, Growth, and the Design of Stabilization Programs. In *Blejer, M. I. and Chu, K., eds.*, 1989, pp. 13–32.

————. Fiscal Policy Responses to Exogenous Shocks in Developing Countries. In *Blejer, M. I. and Chu, K., eds.*, 1989, *1986*, pp. 101–08.

————. The Impact of Macroeconomic Policies on the Level of Taxation and the Fiscal Balance in Developing Countries. *Int. Monet. Fund Staff Pap.*, September 1989, *36*(3), pp. 633–56.

————. International Coordination of Fiscal Policies: Current and Future Issues. In *Monti, M., ed.*, 1989, pp. 7–37.

————. Lags in Tax Collection and the Case for Inflationary Finance: Theory with Simulations. In *Blejer, M. I. and Chu, K., eds.*, 1989, pp. 208–37.

————. Public Debt, North and South: Comment. In *Husain, I. and Diwan, I., eds.*, 1989, pp. 127–28.

————. The Theory and Practice of International Policy Coordination: Does Coordination Pay? Comment. In *Bryant, R. C., et al., eds.*, 1989, pp. 47–50.

———— **and Bovenberg, A. Lans.** Economic Interdependence and the International Implications of Supply-Side Policies. In *Fels, G. and von Furstenberg, G. M., eds.*, 1989, pp. 153–79.

———— **and Casanegra de Jantscher, Milka.** The Use of Presumptive Income in Modern Tax Systems. In *Chiancone, A. and Messere, K., eds.*, 1989, pp. 37–51.

Tapiero, Charles S. The Utility of Manufacturing Cooperatives. *J. Econ. Dynam. Control*, July 1989, *13*(3), pp. 471–83.

Taplin, Ian M. Acknowledging Labor's Record of Success: Reply. *Challenge*, March–April 1989, *32*(2), pp. 53–54.

————. Segmentation and the Organisation of Work in the Italian Apparel Industry. *Soc. Sci. Quart.*, June 1989, *70*(2), pp. 408–24.

Tapon, Francis. A Transaction Costs Analysis of Innovations in the Organization of Pharmaceutical R and D. *J. Econ. Behav. Organ.*, October 1989, *12*(2), pp. 197–213.

Tappeiner, Gottfried and Holub, Hans Werner. An Extension of Input–Output Employment Models. *Econ. Systems Res.*, 1989, *1*(3), pp. 297–309.

———— **and Holub, Hans Werner.** Structural Consequences of Different Models of Transformation in the SNA. In *Franz, A. and Rainer, N., eds.*, 1989, pp. 389–410.

Tarascio, Vincent J. Economic and War Cycles. *Hist. Polit. Econ.*, Spring 1989, *21*(1), pp. 91–101.

————. Marxian Perspectives and Modern Political Economy. *Atlantic Econ. J.*, December 1989, *17*(4), pp. 1–5.

Tardiff, Timothy J. Measuring Competitiveness in Telecommunications Markets. In *National Economic Research Associates*, 1989, pp. 21–34.

———— **and Hausman, Jerry A.** Competition in Telecommunications for Large Users in New York. In *National Economic Research Associates*, 1989, pp. 1–19.

Tarditi, Secondo, et al. Agricultural Trade Liberalization and the European Community: Introduction. In *Tarditi, S., et al., eds.*, 1989, pp. 1–23.

Tardos, Márton. Can Hungary's Monetary Policy Succeed? *Eastern Europ. Econ.*, Fall 1989, *28*(1), pp. 64–78.

_____. Economic Organizations and Ownership. *Acta Oecon.*, 1989, *40*(1–2), pp. 17–37.

_____. We Must Return to Democracy. *Acta Oecon.*, 1989, *40*(3–4), pp. 271–74.

_____ **and Sipos, Aladár.** Economic Control and the Structural Interdependence of Organizations in Hungary at the End of the Second Reform Decade. *Eastern Europ. Econ.*, Fall 1989, *28*(1), pp. 17–33.

Targetti, F. and Thirlwall, A. P. The Essential Kaldor: Introduction. In *Kaldor, N.*, 1989, pp. 1–23.

Targetti Lenti, Renata. I modelli di equilibrio economico generale calcolabili (CGE) e la metodologia SAM. (CGE Models and the Social Accounting Matrix [SAM] Methodology. With English summary.) *Giorn. Econ.*, July–Aug. 1989, *48*(7–8), pp. 309–45.

Tarhan, Vefa and Spindt, Paul A. Bank Reserve Adjustment Process and the Use of Reserve Carryover as a Reserve Management Tool: Reply. *J. Banking Finance*, March 1989, *13*(1), pp. 37–40.

Tarling, Roger; Rubery, Jill and Wilkinson, Frank. Government Policy and the Labor Market: The Case of the United Kingdom. In *Rosenberg, S., ed.*, 1989, pp. 23–45.

Tarlock, A. Dan and DuMars, Charles T. New Challenges to State Water Allocation Sovereignty: Symposium Introduction. *Natural Res. J.*, Spring 1989, *29*(2), pp. 331–46.

Tarr, David; de Melo, Jaime and Stanton, Julie. Revenue-Raising Taxes: General Equilibrium Evaluation of Alternative Taxation in U.S. Petroleum Industries. *J. Policy Modeling*, Fall 1989, *11*(3), pp. 425–49.

Tarrant, John R. An Analysis of Variability in Soviet Grain Production. In *Anderson, J. R. and Hazell, P. B. R., eds.*, 1989, pp. 60–77.

Tarrius, Alain. Looking for a Transport Supply Adapted to Larger Metropolitan Areas Peripheries. In *Candemir, Y., ed.*, 1989, pp. 401–06.

Tarrow, Sidney and Stefanizzi, Sonia. Protest and Regulation: The Interaction of State and Society in the Cycle of 1965–74. In *Lange, P. and Regini, M., eds.*, 1989, pp. 81–107.

Tarshis, Lorie. Debts, Deficits and Interest Rates. In *Feiwel, G. R., ed. (I)*, 1989, pp. 694–708.

_____. Disarming the Debt Bomb. In *Guttmann, R., ed.*, 1989, *1987*, pp. 213–18.

_____. Keynes's Co-operative Economy and the Aggregate Supply Function. In *Pheby, J., ed.*, 1989, pp. 35–47.

_____. Remembering Joan Robinson. In *Feiwel, G. R., ed. (II)*, 1989, pp. 918–20.

_____. A Return Visit to the International Debt Problem of the LDCs. In *Hamouda, O. F.;*

Rowley, R. and Wolf, B. M., eds., 1989, pp. 160–69.

Taslim, M. A. Allocative Efficiency of Cropshare Cultivation: Interpreting the Empirical Evidence. *Pakistan Devel. Rev.*, Autumn 1989, *28*(3), pp. 233–50.

_____. Short-term Leasing, Resource Allocation, and Crop-Share Tenancy. *Amer. J. Agr. Econ.*, August 1989, *71*(3), pp. 785–90.

_____. Supervision Problems and the Size–Productivity Relation in Bangladesh Agriculture. *Oxford Bull. Econ. Statist.*, February 1989, *51*(1), pp. 55–71.

Tatarevic, Ljiljana. Razvoj regionalnih i meduregionalnih modela. (Review of the Development of Regional and Intra-regional Models. With English summary.) *Econ. Anal. Workers' Manage.*, 1989, *23*(3), pp. 273–96.

Tatom, John A. U.S. Investment in the 1980s: The Real Story. *Fed. Res. Bank St. Louis Rev.*, March–April 1989, *71*(2), pp. 3–15.

Taub, Bart M. Aggregate Fluctuations as an Information Transmission Mechanism. *J. Econ. Dynam. Control*, January 1989, *13*(1), pp. 113–50.

_____. Dynamic Consistency of Insurance Contracts under Enforcement by Exclusion. *J. Econ. Dynam. Control*, January 1989, *13*(1), pp. 93–112.

_____. Insurance and Economic Growth. *J. Public Econ.*, March 1989, *38*(2), pp. 249–64.

_____. The Optimum Quantity of Money in a Stochastic Economy. *Int. Econ. Rev.*, May 1989, *30*(2), pp. 255–73.

Taube, Carl A. and Goldman, Howard H. State Strategies to Restructure Psychiatric Hospitals: A Selective Review. *Inquiry*, Summer 1989, *26*(2), pp. 146–56.

_____ **and Rupp, Agnes.** Analysis of the Effect of Disproportionately Large Share of Low-Income Patients on Psychiatric Costs in General Hospitals. *Inquiry*, Summer 1989, *26*(2), pp. 216–21.

Taube, Paul M. An Analysis of the Influence of Self-assesed Health on Expenditure in a Complete Demand System. *J. Econ. Psych.*, March 1989, *10*(1), pp. 101–16.

Taubman, Paul. Role of Parental Income in Educational Attainment. *Amer. Econ. Rev.*, May 1989, *79*(2), pp. 57–61.

_____. The Social Security Cost of Smoking: Comment. In *Wise, D. A., ed.*, 1989, pp. 250–53.

_____ **and Behrman, Jere R.** Is Schooling "Mostly in the Genes"? Nature–Nurture Decomposition Using Data on Relatives. *J. Polit. Econ.*, December 1989, *97*(6), pp. 1425–46.

_____ **and Behrman, Jere R.** A Test of the Easterlin Fertility Model Using Income for Two Generations and a Comparison with the Becker Model. *Demography*, February 1989, *26*(1), pp. 117–23.

_____; **Behrman, Jere R. and Pollack, Robert A.** Family Resources, Family Size, and Access to Financing for College Education. *J. Polit. Econ.*, April 1989, *97*(2), pp. 398–419.

Tauchen, George and Gallant, Ronald. Seminonparametric Estimation of Conditionally Constrained Heterogeneous Processes: Asset Pricing Applications. *Econometrica*, September 1989, 57(5), pp. 1091–1120.

Tauer, Loren W. and Weersink, Alfons J. Comparative Analysis of Investment Models for New York Dairy Farms. *Amer. J. Agr. Econ.*, February 1989, 71(1), pp. 136–45.

Tavares Mareira, José Alberto. European Currency—A Portuguese View. In *Franz, O., ed.*, 1989, pp. 98–102.

Taveira, Elisa M. Ferreira. Portugal's Accession to the EEC and Its Impact on Foreign Direct Investment. In *Yannopoulos, G. N., ed.*, 1989, pp. 169–226.

Tavlas, George S. The Demand for Money in South Africa: A Test of the Buffer Stock Model. *S. Afr. J. Econ.*, March 1989, 57(1), pp. 1–13.

_____. Economic Policy Effectiveness in Hicksian Analysis: A Reply. In *Wood, J. C. and Woods, R. N., eds., Vol. 3*, 1989, 1982, pp. 294–97.

_____. Economic Policy Effectiveness in Hicksian Analysis: An Extension. In *Wood, J. C. and Woods, R. N., eds., Vol. 3*, 1989, 1980, pp. 230–39.

_____. Interpreting Keynes: Reflections on the Leijonhufvud–Yeager Discussion. *Cato J.*, Spring–Summer 1989, 9(1), pp. 237–52.

_____ and Bailey, Martin J. Trade and Investment under Floating Rates: The U.S. Experience. In *Dorn, J. A. and Niskanen, W. A., eds.*, 1989, 1988, pp. 207–28.

_____ and Swamy, P. A. V. B. Financial Deregulation, the Demand for Money, and Monetary Policy in Australia. *Int. Monet. Fund Staff Pap.*, March 1989, 36(1), pp. 63–101.

_____ and Swamy, P. A. V. B. Modeling Buffer Stock Money: An Appraisal. *J. Policy Modeling*, Winter 1989, 11(4), pp. 593–612.

Tavolaro, Agostinho Toffoli. Taxation Agreements under the New Constitution: Brazil. *Bull. Int. Fiscal Doc.*, Aug.–Sept. 1989, 43(8–9), pp. 371–75.

Tayeb, Monir; Peterson, Mark F. and Smith, Peter B. The Cultural Context of Leadership Actions: A Cross-Cultural Analysis. In *Davies, J., et al., eds.*, 1989, pp. 85–92.

Taylor, Amy K. and Short, Pamela Farley. Premiums, Benefits, and Employee Choice of Health Insurance Options. *J. Health Econ.*, December 1989, 8(3), pp. 293–311.

Taylor, C. Robert. Duality, Optimization, and Microeconomic Theory: Pitfalls for the Applied Researcher. *Western J. Agr. Econ.*, December 1989, 14(2), pp. 200–212.

_____; Barry, Peter J. and Schnitkey, Gary D. Evaluating Farmland Investments Considering Dynamic Stochastic Returns and Farmland Prices. *Western J. Agr. Econ.*, July 1989, 14(1), pp. 143–56.

_____ and Burt, Oscar R. Reduction of State Variable Dimension in Stochastic Dynamic Optimization Models Which Use Time-Series Data. *Western J. Agr. Econ.*, December 1989, 14(2), pp. 213–22.

Taylor, D. Wayne. The Economic Effects of the Direct Regulation of the Taxicab Industry in Metropolitan Toronto. *Logist. Transp. Rev.*, June 1989, 25(2), pp. 169–82.

Taylor, Daniel B. and Kazmierczak, Tamra Kirkpatrick. VEGMARC II(c): A Computerized Record Keeping System for Vegetable Marketing Cooperatives. *Southern J. Agr. Econ.*, July 1989, 21(1), pp. 149–55.

Taylor, David T. and Jacobs, James J. The Increasing Role of States in Water Management: The Wyoming Experience. *Western J. Agr. Econ.*, December 1989, 14(2), pp. 261–67.

Taylor, Dean. How to Make the Central Bank Look Good. *J. Polit. Econ.*, February 1989, 97(1), pp. 226–32.

_____. Stopping Inflation in the Dornbusch Model: Optimal Monetary Policies with Alternative Price-Adjustment Equations. *J. Macroecon.*, Spring 1989, 11(2), pp. 199–216.

_____ and Connolly, Michael B. Adjustment to Interest Rate Shocks in Latin America and the Caribbean. In *Brock, P. L.; Connolly, M. B. and González-Vega, C., eds.*, 1989, pp. 80–95.

Taylor, Donald C. Designing Electricity Rate Structures for Irrigation. *Land Econ.*, November 1989, 65(4), pp. 394–409.

Taylor, Elizabeth Newlin. Pushing State Regulatory Commissions behind the Bright Line: FERC Jurisdiction Prevails in *Mississippi Power & Light Co. v. Mississippi ex rel. Moore*, 487 U.S. __, 108 S. Ct. 2428 (1988). Note. *Natural Res. J.*, Spring 1989, 29(2), pp. 607–20.

Taylor, J. Edward and Stark, Oded. Relative Deprivation and International Migration. *Demography*, February 1989, 26(1), pp. 1–14.

Taylor, J. S. and Spriggs, John. Effects of the Monetary Macro-economy on Canadian Agricultural Prices. *Can. J. Econ.*, May 1989, 22(2), pp. 278–89.

Taylor, Jack and Gravelle, Jane G. Financing Long-term Care for the Elderly. *Nat. Tax J.*, September 1989, 42(3), pp. 219–32.

Taylor, Jeremy M. G.; Lange, Kenneth L. and Little, Roderick J. A. Robust Statistical Modeling Using the t Distribution. *J. Amer. Statist. Assoc.*, December 1989, 84(408), pp. 881–96.

Taylor, Jim and Johnes, Jill. The First Destination of New Graduates: Comparisons between Universities. *Appl. Econ.*, March 1989, 21(3), pp. 357–73.

Taylor, John B. Differences in Economic Fluctuations in Japan and the United States: The Role of Nominal Rigidities. *J. Japanese Int. Economies*, June 1989, 3(2), pp. 127–44.

_____. The Evolution of Ideas in Macroeconomics. *Econ. Rec.*, June 1989, 65(189), pp. 185–89.

_____. Monetary Policy and the Stability of Macroeconomic Relationships. *J. Appl. Econometrics*, Supplement, December 1989, 4, pp. S161–78.

———. Policy Analysis with a Multicountry Model. In *Bryant, R. C., et al., eds.*, 1989, pp. 122–41.

Taylor, Keith F. and Van Kooten, G. C. Measuring the Marginal Welfare Impacts of Government Regulation: The Case of Supply Management. *Can. J. Econ.*, November 1989, 22(4), pp. 892–903.

Taylor, Lance. Demand Composition, Income Distribution, and Growth. In *Feiwel, G. R., ed. (II)*, 1989, pp. 623–37.

———. Theories of Sectoral Balance. In *Williamson, J. G. and Panchamukhi, V. R., eds.*, 1989, pp. 3–31.

——— and O'Connell, Stephen A. A Minsky Crisis. In *Semmler, W., ed.*, 1989, pp. 3–17.

——— and Quisumbing, M. Agnes R. Resource Transfers from Agriculture. In *Chakravarty, S., ed.*, 1989, pp. 116–45.

Taylor, Larry W. An Application of Extended Rational Approximants to White's Information Matrix Test. *Econ. Letters*, 1989, 30(1), pp. 49–53.

———. Deriving Covariance Matrices for Specification Tests. *J. Quant. Econ.*, July 1989, 5(2), pp. 267–73.

Taylor, Mark P. Covered Interest Arbitrage and Market Turbulence. *Econ. J.*, June 1989, 99(396), pp. 376–91.

———. Expectations, Risk and Uncertainty in the Foreign Exchange Market: Some Results Based on Survey Data. *Manchester Sch. Econ. Soc. Stud.*, June 1989, 57(2), pp. 142–53.

———. Vector Autogressive Tests of Uncovered Interest Rate Parity with Allowance for Conditional Heteroscedasticity. *Scot. J. Polit. Econ.*, August 1989, 36(3), pp. 238–52.

——— and Artis, Michael J. Abolishing Exchange Control: The UK Experience. *Greek Econ. Rev.*, 1989, 11(1), pp. 19–48.

——— and Artis, Michael J. The Achievements of the European Monetary System. *Econ. Soc. Rev.*, January 1989, 20(2), pp. 121–45.

——— and Artis, Michael J. Some Issues Concerning the Long-Run Credibility of the European Monetary System. In *MacDonald, R. and Taylor, M. P., eds.*, 1989, pp. 295–306.

——— and Cuthbertson, Keith. Anticipated and Unanticipated Variables in the Demand for M1 in the U.K. *Manchester Sch. Econ. Soc. Stud.*, December 1989, 57(4), pp. 319–39.

———; Hall, Stephen G. and Miles, David K. Modelling Asset Prices with Time-Varying Betas. *Manchester Sch. Econ. Soc. Stud.*, December 1989, 57(4), pp. 340–56.

——— and MacDonald, Ronald. Economic Analysis of Foreign Exchange Markets: An Expository Survey. In *MacDonald, R. and Taylor, M. P., eds.*, 1989, pp. 3–107.

——— and MacDonald, Ronald. Foreign Exchange Market Efficiency and Cointegration: Some Evidence from the Recent Float. *Econ. Letters*, 1989, 29(1), pp. 63–68.

——— and MacDonald, Ronald. Interest Rate Parity: Some New Evidence. *Bull. Econ. Res.*, October 1989, 41(4), pp. 255–74.

——— and MacDonald, Ronald. International Parity Conditions. *Greek Econ. Rev.*, 1989, 11(2), pp. 257–90.

——— and MacDonald, Ronald. Rational Expectations, Risk and Efficiency in the London Metal Exchange: An Empirical Analysis. *Appl. Econ.*, February 1989, 21(2), pp. 143–53.

——— and Mills, Terence C. Random Walk Components in Output and Exchange Rates: Some Robust Tests on UK Data. *Bull. Econ. Res.*, April 1989, 41(2), pp. 123–35.

——— and Tonks, Ian. The Internationalisation of Stock Markets and the Abolition of U.K. Exchange Control. *Rev. Econ. Statist.*, May 1989, 71(2), pp. 332–36.

Taylor, Michael and Garlick, Steve. Commonwealth Government Involvement in Regional Development in the 1980s: A Local Approach. In *Higgins, B. and Zagorski, K., eds.*, 1989, pp. 79–103.

Taylor, N. W.; Johnson, R. W. M. and Schroder, W. R. Deregulation and the New Zealand Agricultural Sector: A Review. *Rev. Marketing Agr. Econ.*, April, Aug., Dec. 1989, 57(1–2–3), pp. 47–74.

Taylor, Paul. The New Dynamics of EC Integration in the 1980s. In *Lodge, J., ed.*, 1989, pp. 3–25.

Taylor, Peter J. Britain's Changing Role in the World-Economy. In *Mohan, J., ed.*, 1989, pp. 18–34.

Taylor, R. H. Advanced Robotics in FMS. In *Archetti, F.; Lucertini, M. and Serafini, P., eds.*, 1989, pp. 247–59.

Taylor-Shirley, Katherine and Personick, Martin E. Profiles in Safety and Health: Occupational Hazards of Meatpacking. *Mon. Lab. Rev.*, January 1989, 112(1), pp. 3–9.

Taylor, Stanley A. A Comparison of Classical Tests of Criterion when Determining Granger Causality with a Bivariate ARMA Model. *Empirical Econ.*, 1989, 14(3), pp. 257–71.

Taylor, Stephen. World Payments Imbalances and U.S. Statistics. In *Lipsey, R. E. and Tice, H. S., eds.*, 1989, pp. 401–29.

Taylor, Theodore B. Can Nuclear Weapons Be Developed without Full Testing? In *Altmann, J. and Rotblat, J., eds.*, 1989, pp. 82–85.

———. Roles of Technological Innovation in the Arms Race. In *Rotblat, J. and Goldanskii, V. I., eds.*, 1989, pp. 158–64.

Taylor, Timothy G. and Raj, Baldev. Do 'Bootstrap Tests' Provide Significance Levels Equivalent to the Exact Test? Empirical Evidence from Testing Linear Within-Equation Restrictions in Large Demand Systems. *J. Quant. Econ.*, January 1989, 5(1), pp. 73–89.

Taylor, William. Statement to the U.S. House Subcommittee on International Development, Finance, Trade and Monetary Policy of the Committee on Banking, Finance and Urban Affairs, June 27, 1989. *Fed. Res. Bull.*, August 1989, 75(8), pp. 563–65.

Taylor, William. Universities, Education and the National Economy: Case Studies: Education and the Economy. In *Stephens, M. D., ed.*,

1989, pp. 51–71.

Taylor, William E. Regulating Competition for IntraLATA Services. In *National Economic Research Associates*, 1989, pp. 35–50.

Tayman, Jeff and Fonseca, Lois. Postcensal Estimates of Household Income Distributions. *Demography*, February 1989, *26*(1), pp. 149–59.

Tayyab, Ahsan and Kumar, Ramesh C. Money, Working Capital and Production in a Developing Economy: A Disequilibrium Econometric Model of Production for India, 1950–1980. *Empirical Econ.*, 1989, *14*(3), pp. 229–39.

Tchijov, Iouri. Economic Structural Changes: The Problems of Forecasting. In *Krelle, W., ed.*, 1989, pp. 571–79.

Teachman, Jay D. and Schollaert, Paul T. Gender of Children and Birth Timing. *Demography*, August 1989, *26*(3), pp. 411–23.

Teague, Paul. Constitution or Regime? The Social Dimension to the 1992 Project. *Brit. J. Ind. Relat.*, November 1989, *27*(3), pp. 310–29.

――――. Economic Development in Northern Ireland: Has Pathfinder Lost Its Way? *Reg. Stud.*, February 1989, *23*(1), pp. 63–69.

――――. Pathfinder: A Reply [Economic Development in Northern Ireland: Has Pathfinder Lost Its Way?]. *Reg. Stud.*, October 1989, *23*(5), pp. 483–85.

Teal, Francis and Dinwiddy, Caroline. Project Appraisal and Foreign Exchange Constraints: A Response. *Econ. J.*, June 1989, *99*(396), pp. 483.

――――― **and Dinwiddy, Caroline.** Relative Shadow Prices and the Shadow Exchange Rate. *J. Public Econ.*, December 1989, *40*(3), pp. 349–58.

Teboulle, M. and Ben-Tal, A. A Smoothing Technique for Nondifferentiable Optimization Problems. In *Dolecki, S., ed.*, 1989, pp. 1–11.

Tecson, Gwendolyn R. Structural Change and Barriers to Philippine Manufactured Exports. *Developing Econ.*, March 1989, *27*(1), pp. 34–59.

Tedeschi, Jardena. The Expected Employment Impact of a Change in the Pattern of Foreign Trade of Goods and Services: Some Methodological Notes. *Giorn. Econ.*, Jan.–Feb. 1989, *48*(1–2), pp. 35–54.

Tedeschi, Piero and Bull, Clive. Optimal Probation for New Hires. *J. Inst. Theoretical Econ.*, December 1989, *145*(4), pp. 627–42.

Tedrow, Lucky M.; Herting, Jerald R. and Pullum, Thomas W. Measuring Change and Continuity in Parity Distributions. *Demography*, August 1989, *26*(3), pp. 485–98.

Teece, David J. Inter-organizational Requirements of the Innovation Process. *Managerial Dec. Econ.*, Special Issue, Spring 1989, pp. 35–42.

――――― **and Pisano, Gary P.** Collaborative Arrangements and Global Technology Strategy: Some Evidence from the Telecommunications Equipment Industry. In *Rosenbloom, R. S. and Burgelman, R. A., eds.*, 1989, pp. 227–56.

Teel, Jesse E.; Bearden, William O. and Netemeyer, Richard G. Measurement of Consumer Susceptibility to Interpersonal Influence. *J. Cons. Res.*, March 1989, *15*(4), pp. 473–81.

Tegene, Abebayehu. The Monetarist Explanation of Inflation: The Experience of Six African Countries. *J. Econ. Stud.*, 1989, *16*(1), pp. 5–18.

――――. On the Effects of Relative Prices and Effective Exchange Rates on Trade Flows of LDCs. *Appl. Econ.*, November 1989, *21*(11), pp. 1447–63.

Tehranian, Hassan and Millon-Cornett, Marcia H. Stock Market Reactions to the Depository Institutions Deregulation and Monetary Control Act of 1980. *J. Banking Finance*, March 1989, *13*(1), pp. 81–100.

Tehranian, Majid. Information Society and Democratic Prospects. In *Jussawalla, M.; Okuma, T. and Araki, T., eds.*, 1989, pp. 212–21.

Teich, Mikuláš. Electrical Research, Standardisation and the Beginnings of the Corporate Economy. In *Teichova, A.; Lévy-Leboyer, M. and Nussbaum, H., eds.*, 1989, pp. 29–42.

Teichman, Judith. The Politics of the Mexican Debt Crisis. In *Campbell, B. K., ed.*, 1989, pp. 163–86.

Teichova, Alice. East-Central and South-East Europe, 1919–39. In *Mathias, P. and Pollard, S., eds.*, 1989, pp. 887–983.

Teillet, Pierre; Vanoli, André and Milot, Jean-Paul. How to Treat Non-produced Assets and Exceptional Events in the National Accounts? Considerations on the Variations in Wealth Accounting. *Rev. Income Wealth*, June 1989, *35*(2), pp. 163–86.

Teitel, Simón. The Baker Plan and Brady Reformulation: An Evaluation: Comment. In *Husain, I. and Diwan, I., eds.*, 1989, pp. 196–98.

――――. Industrialisation, Primary Commodities and Exports of Manufactures. In *Islam, N., ed.*, 1989, pp. 315–41.

Teixeira Pinto, Luiz Fernando. Brazilian Tax Treatment of Foreign Investments. *Bull. Int. Fiscal Doc.*, Aug.–Sept. 1989, *43*(8–9), pp. 376–78.

――――. The Tax System Pursuant to the New Federal Constitution of 1988: Brazil. *Bull. Int. Fiscal Doc.*, April 1989, *43*(4), pp. 183–86.

Tejada de Rivero, David. The Financing of Health: Conditions for Effectiveness and Equity: Commentary. In *WHO, Pan American Health Organization*, 1989, pp. 174–81.

di Tella, Guido. Argentina's Economy under a Labour-Based Government, 1973–76. In *di Tella, G. and Dornbusch, R., eds.*, 1989, pp. 213–46.

――――. The Political Economy of Argentina, 1946–83: Postscript. In *di Tella, G. and Dornbusch, R., eds.*, 1989, pp. 320–24.

――――― **and Dornbusch, Rudiger.** The Political Economy of Argentina, 1946–83: Introduction. In *di Tella, G. and Dornbusch, R., eds.*, 1989, pp. 1–15.

Tellér, Gyula. Structural Questions of Cooperative Ownership and Income Redistribution in

Hungarian Agriculture. *Acta Oecon.*, 1989, *41*(3–4), pp. 435–53.

Tellier, Luc-Normand and Polanski, Boris. The Weber Problem: Frequency of Different Solution Types and Extension to Repulsive Forces and Dynamic Processes. *J. Reg. Sci.*, August 1989, *29*(3), pp. 387–405.

Temin, Peter. Capital Exports, 1870–1914: A Reply. *Econ. Hist. Rev.*, *2nd Ser.*, May 1989, *42*(2), pp. 265–66.

Tempro, Elizabeth M. and Liburd, Eustace E. An Assessment of Monetary and Credit Policies in the OECS Region, 1975–1985. In *Worrell, D. and Bourne, C.*, eds., 1989, pp. 132–46.

Tena-Junguito, Antonio. On the Accuracy of Foreign Trade Statistics: Italy, 1890–1938. *Rivista Storia Econ.*, *S.S.*, February 1989, *6*(1), pp. 87–112.

Tendler, Judith. What Ever Happened to Poverty Alleviation? *World Devel.*, July 1989, *17*(7), pp. 1033–44.

Tendulkar, Suresh D. An Approach towards Integrating Large- and Small-Scale Surveys. In *Bardhan, P.*, ed. *(I)*, 1989, pp. 200–217.

_____ **and Jain, L. R.** On a Relationship between the Real and the Nominal Relative Disparities in the Consumption of Cereals in Rural India. *J. Devel. Econ.*, October 1989, *31*(2), pp. 271–95.

_____; **Jain, L. R. and Sundaram, K.** Level of Living and Incidence of Poverty in Rural India—A Cross-Sectional Analysis. *J. Quant. Econ.*, January 1989, *5*(1), pp. 187–209.

Tenenbaum, Susan. Social Discounting: Retrieving the Civic Dimension. *Econ. Philos.*, April 1989, *5*(1), pp. 33–46.

Teodorovic, Ivan and Nusinovic, Mustafa. Investment Decisionmaking. In *Macesich, G.*, ed., 1989, pp. 101–32.

Teranishi, Juro. The Sectoral Flow of Funds in Pre-war Japan: A Reconsideration. In *Chakravarty, S.*, ed., 1989, pp. 146–68.

_____ **and Khosla, Anil.** Exchange Rate Pass-through in Export Prices—An International Comparison. *Hitotsubashi J. Econ.*, June 1989, *30*(1), pp. 31–48.

Terasawa, Katsuaki L. and Besen, Stanley M. The Prototype Model of Defense Procurement. In *Gulledge, T. R., Jr. and Litteral, L. A.*, eds., 1989, pp. 1–33.

_____; **Quirk, James and Womer, Keith.** Turbulence, Cost Escalation and Capital Intensity Bias in Defense Contracting. In *Gulledge, T. R., Jr. and Litteral, L. A.*, eds., 1989, pp. 97–116.

Teres, Daniel. Triage: An Everyday Occurrence in the Intensive Care Unit. In *Strosberg, M. A.; Fein, I. A. and Carroll, J. D.*, eds., 1989, pp. 70–75.

Terker, Bruce; Blume, Marshall E. and MacKinlay, A. Craig. Order Imbalances and Stock Price Movements on October 19 and 20, 1987. *J. Finance*, September 1989, *44*(4), pp. 827–48.

Terleckyj, Nestor E. Growth of the Telecommunications and Computer Industries. In *Cran-*

dall, R. W. and Flamm, K., eds., 1989, pp. 328–70.

_____ **and Levy, David M.** Problems Identifying Returns to R&D in an Industry. *Managerial Dec. Econ.*, Special Issue, Spring 1989, pp. 43–49.

Terlizzese, Daniele; Visco, Ignazio and Galli, Giampaolo. Un modello trimestrale per la previsione e la politica economica: Le proprietà di breve e di lungo periodo del modello della Banca d'Italia. (With English summary.) *Politica. Econ.*, April 1989, *5*(1), pp. 3–51.

Termini, Valeria. Arbitraggisti, speculatori e hedgers nei futures finanziari. Un'ipotesi di ruttura dell'equilibrio. (Speculators, Arbitragents and Hedgers in Financial Futures. A Definition of Risk. With English summary.) *Econ. Politica*, December 1989, *6*(3), pp. 403–25.

_____. A Note on Hicks's 'Contemporaneous Causality.' In *Wood, J. C. and Woods, R. N.*, eds., Vol. 4, 1989, *1984*, pp. 38–44.

Terrell, Katherine. An Analysis of the Wage Structure in Guatemala City. *J. Developing Areas*, April 1989, *23*(3), pp. 405–23.

Tersine, Richard J.; Larson, Paul D. and Barman, Samir. An Economic Inventory/Transport Model with Freight Rate Discounts. *Logist. Transp. Rev.*, December 1989, *25*(4), pp. 291–306.

Tervo, Hannu. A Micro-Level Approach to the Analysis of the Displacement Effects of Regional Incentive Policy: The Case of Finland. *Reg. Stud.*, December 1989, *23*(6), pp. 511–21.

Terza, Joseph V. and Fishback, Price V. Are Estimates of Sex Discrimination by Employers Robust? The Use of Never-Marrieds. *Econ. Inquiry*, April 1989, *27*(2), pp. 271–85.

_____; **Khalifah, Noor Aini and Coughlin, Cletus C.** The Determinants of Escape Clause Petitions. *Rev. Econ. Statist.*, May 1989, *71*(2), pp. 341–47.

Terzi, Andrea. Three Questions on Finance: Preliminary Remarks. *Écon. Appl.*, 1989, *42*(2), pp. 115–24.

Tether, Philip. Legal Controls and Voluntary Agreements. In *Robinson, D.; Maynard, A. and Chester, R.*, eds., 1989, pp. 203–20.

Teulings, Coen and Koopmanschap, Marc. An Econometric Model of Crowding Out of Lower Education Levels. *Europ. Econ. Rev.*, October 1989, *33*(8), pp. 1653–64.

Tew, Bernard V. and Reid, Donald W. Land Allocation under Uncertainty for Alternative Specifications of Return Distributions: Comment. *Amer. J. Agr. Econ.*, May 1989, *71*(2), pp. 439–40.

Tew, Brian. Financial Deregulation and Monetary Policy. In *[Marjolin, R.]*, 1989, pp. 227–42.

_____. A Review of *Critical Essays in Monetary Theory* by Sir John Hicks. In *Wood, J. C. and Woods, R. N.*, eds., Vol. 2, 1989, *1968*, pp. 72–74.

Tewari, Devi D. and Kulshreshtha, Surendra N.

Impacts of Rising Energy Prices on Saskatchewan Agriculture: A Reply. *Can. J. Agr. Econ.*, July 1989, *37*(2), pp. 323–25.

Texter, Pamela A. and Ord, J. Keith. Forecasting Using Automatic Identification Procedures: A Comparative Analysis. *Int. J. Forecasting,* 1989, *5*(2), pp. 209–15.

Thacher, Thomas D., II and Jacobs, James B. Attacking Corruption in Union–Management Relations: A Symposium. *Ind. Lab. Relat. Rev.*, July 1989, *42*(4), pp. 501–07.

Thage, Bent. Input–Output Tables and the Value Concepts of the SNA. In *Franz, A. and Rainer, N., eds.*, 1989, pp. 281–99.

_____ **and Berner, Ole.** Kvartalsvise nationalregnskaber fra Danmarks Statistik—Og nogle udenlandske erfaringer. (The Sources and Methods of the New Official Quarterly National Accounts for Denmark. With English summary.) *Nationaløkon. Tidsskr.*, 1989, *127*(1), pp. 95–109.

Thakor, Anjan V. Competitive Equilibrium with Type Convergence in an Asymmetrically Informed Market. *Rev. Financial Stud.*, 1989, *2*(1), pp. 49–71.

_____ **and Greenbaum, Stuart I.** Bank Reserve Requirements as an Impediment to Signaling. *Econ. Inquiry,* January 1989, *27*(1), pp. 75–91.

Thalassinos, Lefteris I. East–West Trade Prospectives. *Indian Econ. J.*, Jan.–March 1989, *36*(3), pp. 28–35.

Thaler, Richard H. Interindustry Wage Differentials. *J. Econ. Perspectives*, Spring 1989, *3*(2), pp. 181–93.

_____ **and De Bondt, Werner F. M.** A Mean-Reverting Walk Down Wall Street. *J. Econ. Perspectives*, Winter 1989, *3*(1), pp. 189–202.

_____ **and Loewenstein, George.** Intertemporal Choice. *J. Econ. Perspectives*, Fall 1989, *3*(4), pp. 181–93.

Thampapillai, Dodo J. The Elimination of Absolute Poverty: Approaches to Monetary Valuation. *Indian Econ. J.*, April–June 1989, *36*(4), pp. 19–29.

Thanawala, Kishor. Social Economic Aspects of India's Development. *Int. J. Soc. Econ.*, 1989, *16*(7), pp. 34–47.

Thane, Pat. Old Age: Burden or Benefit? In *Joshi, H., ed.*, 1989, pp. 56–71.

Tharakan, P. K. M. Bilateral Intra-industry Trade between Countries with Different Factor Endowment Patterns. In *Tharakan, P. K. M. and Kol, J., eds.*, 1989, pp. 69–91.

_____ **and Kol, Jacob.** Intra-industry Trade, Traditional Trade Theory and Its Extensions. In *Tharakan, P. K. M. and Kol, J., eds.*, 1989, pp. 1–14.

_____, **et al.** Comparative Advantage and Competitiveness in a Small, 'Open' Economy. In *Francis, A. and Tharakan, P. K. M., eds.*, 1989, pp. 41–63.

Thatcher, John G. and Kon, Stanley J. The Effect of Bankruptcy Laws on the Valuation of Risky Consumer Debt. *Financial Rev.*, August 1989, *24*(3), pp. 371–95.

Thee, Kian Wie. The Development of Sumatra, 1820–1940. In *Maddison, A. and Prince, G., eds.*, 1989, pp. 133–58.

_____ **and Barlow, Colin.** North Sumatra: Growth with Unbalanced Development. In *Hill, H., ed.*, 1989, pp. 408–36.

Theeuwes, Jules J. M. On Reducing Unemployment. In *Muller, F. and Zwezerijnen, W. J., eds.*, 1989, pp. 47–61.

_____; **Koopmans, Carl C. and van Opstal, Rocus.** Human Capital and Job Levels: Explaining the Age–Income Funnel. *Europ. Econ. Rev.*, December 1989, *33*(9), pp. 1839–49.

Theil, Henri. The Development of International Inequality: 1960–1985. *J. Econometrics*, September 1989, *42*(1), pp. 145–55.

_____ **and Narduzzi, Susan A.** The Statistical Structure of Real-Income Changes. *Econ. Letters*, 1989, *29*(3), pp. 271–73.

Theilmann, John and Wilhite, Al. Campaign Contributions by Political Parties Ideology *vs.* Winning. *Atlantic Econ. J.*, June 1989, *17*(2), pp. 11–20.

Thelen, Kathleen. Neoliberalism and the Battle over Working-Time Reduction in West Germany. In *Foglesong, R. E. and Wolfe, J. D., eds.*, 1989, pp. 65–85.

Theodore, Karl. Government Influence in an Enclave Economy: An Exercise in Modelling. *Soc. Econ. Stud.*, March 1989, *38*(1), pp. 37–59.

Théoret, Raymond. Du comportement différent des dépôts des particuliers au Québec et en Ontario. (With English summary.) *L'Actual. Econ.*, June 1989, *65*(2), pp. 231–47.

Therrien, G. A. The Future Role of the Farm Management Expert. *Can. J. Agr. Econ.*, Part 1, December 1989, *37*(4), pp. 801–03.

Theuerkauf, Ingo. Kundennutzenmessung mit Conjoint. (With English summary.) *Z. Betriebswirtshaft*, November 1989, *59*(11), pp. 1179–1218.

Theunissen, A. J. and Whittaker, John. Does Money Supply Endogeneity Matter? A Comment. *S. Afr. J. Econ.*, June 1989, *57*(2), pp. 201–02.

Thévenot, Laurent. Équilibre et rationalité dans un univers complexe. (Equilibrium and Rationality in a Complex Universe. With English summary.) *Revue Écon.*, March 1989, *40*(2), pp. 147–97.

Thibodeau, Thomas G. Housing Price Indexes from the 1974–1983 SIMSA Annual Housing Surveys. *Amer. Real Estate Urban Econ. Assoc. J.*, Spring 1989, *17*(1), pp. 100–117.

_____ **and Giliberto, S. Michael.** Modeling Conventional Residential Mortgage Refinancings. *J. Real Estate Finance Econ.*, December 1989, *2*(4), pp. 285–99.

Thierstein, Alain and Fischer, Georges. Internationale Wettbewerbsfähigkeit und regionale Entwicklung. (International Competitiveness and Regional Development. With English summary.) *Aussenwirtschaft*, June 1989, *44*(2), pp. 197–222.

Thies, Clifford F. and Baum, Christopher F. The Term Structure of Interest Rates and the Demand for Money during the Great Depression. *Southern Econ. J.*, October 1989, *56*(2), pp. 490–98.

_____ **and Gerlowski, Daniel A.** Deposit Insurance: A History of Failure. *Cato J.*, Winter 1989, *8*(3), pp. 677–93.

Thiessen, Gordon G. Foreign Exchange Markets Viewed from a Macro-policy Perspective. *Can. Public Policy*, Supplement, February 1989, *15*, pp. S67–70.

Thieu, Tran Vu. Improvement and Implementation of Some Algorithms for Nonconvex Optimization Problems. In *Dolecki, S., ed.*, 1989, pp. 159–70.

Thijssen, G.; Oskam, Arie and Reinhard, A. Wasmodel-2: A Disaggregated Agricultural Sector Model Partly Based on Prior Information. In *Bauer, S. and Henrichsmeyer, W., eds.*, 1989, pp. 53–69.

Thill, J.-C. and Rushton, G. The Effect of Distance Metric on the Degree of Spatial Competition between Firms. *Environ. Planning A*, April 1989, *21*(4), pp. 499–507.

Thirlwall, A. P. Kaldor As a Policy Adviser. *Cambridge J. Econ.*, March 1989, *13*(1), pp. 121–39.

_____. Kaldor as a Policy Adviser. In *Lawson, T.; Palma, J. G. and Sender, J., eds.*, 1989, pp. 121–39.

_____ **and Gibson, Heather D.** An International Comparison of the Causes of Changes in the Debt Service Ratio 1980–1985. *Banca Naz. Lavoro Quart. Rev.*, March 1989, (168), pp. 73–95.

_____ **and Gibson, Heather D.** Errata Corrige [An International Comparison of the Causes of Changes in the Debt Service Ratio 1980–1985]. *Banca Naz. Lavoro Quart. Rev.*, June 1989, (169), pp. 245.

_____ **and Gordon, Ian.** European Factor Mobility: Introduction. In *Gordon, I. and Thirlwall, A. P., eds.*, 1989, pp. 1–12.

_____ **and Kennedy, C.** Extended Hicks Neutral Technical Change—A Comment. In *Wood, J. C. and Woods, R. N., eds., Vol. 3*, 1989, *1977*, pp. 178–79.

_____ **and Mendes, A. J. Marques.** The Balance of Payments Constraint and Growth in Portugal: 1951–1984. In *Yannopoulos, G. N., ed.*, 1989, pp. 21–39.

_____ **and Targetti, F.** The Essential Kaldor: Introduction. In *Kaldor, N.*, 1989, pp. 1–23.

Thirsk, Joan. Specializzazione e diversificazione dell'economia rurale: Relazione introduttiva. (In English.) In *Cavaciocchi, S., ed.*, 1989, pp. 127–44.

Thirtle, C. and Bottomley, P. The Rate of Return to Public Sector Agricultural R&D in the UK, 1965–80. *Appl. Econ.*, August 1989, *21*(8), pp. 1063–86.

Thiry, Bernard; Frank, M. and Jeanfils, Ph. La réforme de 1988 relative à l'impôt sur le revenu et aux droits d'accises. (With English summary.) *Cah. Écon. Bruxelles*, 1st Trimester 1989, (121), pp. 69–115.

_____ **and Perelman, Sergio.** Measuring the Per-formance of Public Transport Companies. *Ann. Pub. Coop. Econ.*, 1989, *60*(1), pp. 3–7.

_____ **and Tulkens, Henry.** Productivity, Efficiency and Technical Progress: Concepts and Measurement. *Ann. Pub. Coop. Econ.*, 1989, *60*(1), pp. 9–42.

Thisen, Jean K. The Private versus the Social Man. *Int. J. Soc. Econ.*, 1989, *16*(8), pp. 35–48.

Thisse, Jacques-François; Anderson, Simon P. and de Palma, André. Demand for Differentiated Products, Discrete Choice Models, and the Characteristics Approach. *Rev. Econ. Stud.*, January 1989, *56*(1), pp. 21–35.

_____; **Anderson, Simon P. and de Palma, André.** Spatial Price Policies Reconsidered. *J. Ind. Econ.*, September 1989, *38*(1), pp. 1–18.

_____; **Ben-Akiva, Moshe and de Palma, André.** Spatial Competition with Differentiated Products. *Reg. Sci. Urban Econ.*, February 1989, *19*(1), pp. 5–19.

_____; **Cremer, Helmuth and Marchand, Maurice.** The Public Firm as an Instrument for Regulating an Oligopolistic Market. *Oxford Econ. Pap.*, April 1989, *41*(2), pp. 283–301.

_____ **and Gabszewicz, Jean Jaskold.** Competitive Discriminatory Pricing. In *Feiwel, G. R., ed. (I)*, 1989, pp. 387–406.

_____ **and Neven, Damien J.** Choix des produits: Concurrence en qualité et en variété. (Products Selection: Competition in Quality and Variety. With English summary.) *Ann. Écon. Statist.*, July–Dec. 1989, (15–16), pp. 85–112.

_____ **and de Palma, André.** Les modèles de choix discrets. (Discrete Choice Models. With English summary.) *Ann. Écon. Statist.*, April–June 1989, (14), pp. 151–90.

_____; **Weskamp, Anita and Hamilton, Jonathan H.** Spatial Discrimination: Bertrand vs. Cournot in a Model of Location Choice. *Reg. Sci. Urban Econ.*, February 1989, *19*(1), pp. 87–102.

Thistle, Paul D. Duality between Generalized Lorenz Curves and Distribution Functions. *Econ. Stud. Quart.*, June 1989, *40*(2), pp. 183–87.

_____. Ranking Distributions with Generalized Lorenz Curves. *Southern Econ. J.*, July 1989, *56*(1), pp. 1–12.

_____; **Bishop, John A. and Chakraborti, S.** Asymptotically Distribution-Free Statistical Inference for Generalized Lorenz Curves. *Rev. Econ. Statist.*, November 1989, *71*(4), pp. 725–27.

_____; **McLeod, Robert W. and Conrad, B. Lynne.** Interest Rates and Bank Portfolio Adjustments. *J. Banking Finance*, March 1989, *13*(1), pp. 151–61.

Thom, Rodney. In Search of a Causal Relationship between Industrial Output and Employment in Ireland: A Comment. *Econ. Soc. Rev.*, October 1989, *21*(1), pp. 68–70.

_____. Real Exchange Rates, Co-integration and Purchasing Power Parity: Irish Experience in the EMS. *Econ. Soc. Rev.*, January 1989, *20*(2), pp. 147–63.

Thoma, Mark A. Do Prices Lead Money? A Reexamination of the Neutrality Hypothesis. *Econ. Inquiry*, April 1989, 27(2), pp. 197–217.

Thomas, Alan and Cornforth, Chris. A Model for Democratic Decision-Making: The Case of Worker Co-operatives. *Econ. Anal. Workers' Manage.*, 1989, 23(1), pp. 1–15.

Thomas, Barbara; Schoen, Robert and Woolredge, John. Ethnic and Educational Effects on Marriage Choice. *Soc. Sci. Quart.*, September 1989, 70(3), pp. 617–30.

Thomas, Caroline. Conflict and Consensus in South/North Security: Introduction. In *Thomas, C. and Saravanamuttu, P., eds.*, 1989, pp. 1–10.

Thomas, Christina and Lalli, Marco. Public Opinion and Decision Making in the Community. Evaluation of Residents' Attitudes towards Town Planning Measures. *Urban Stud.*, August 1989, 26(4), pp. 435–47.

Thomas, Christopher R.; Maurice, S. Charles and Crumbley, D. Larry. Vertical Integration, Price Squeezing, and the Percentage Depletion Allowance. *Quart. Rev. Econ. Bus.*, Winter 1989, 29(4), pp. 26–36.

Thomas, Clive Y. Foreign Currency Black Markets: Lessons from Guyana. *Soc. Econ. Stud.*, June 1989, 38(2), pp. 137–84.

_____. Restructuring of the World Economy and Its Political Implications for the Third World. In *MacEwan, A. and Tabb, W. K., eds.*, 1989, pp. 331–48.

Thomas, David. The United States Factor in British Relations with Latin America. In *Bulmer-Thomas, V., ed.*, 1989, pp. 68–82.

Thomas, Desmond. The Small-Country Assumption and the Theoretical Analysis of Devaluation. *Soc. Econ. Stud.*, December 1989, 38(4), pp. 53–69.

Thomas, Duncan; Deaton, Angus S. and Ruiz-Castillo, Javier. The Influence of Household Composition on Household Expenditure Patterns: Theory and Spanish Evidence. *J. Polit. Econ.*, February 1989, 97(1), pp. 179–200.

_____; Henriques, Maria Helena and Strauss, John. Mortalidade infantil, estado nutricional e características do domicílio: A evidência brasileira. (With English summary.) *Pesquisa Planejamento Econ.*, December 1989, 19(3), pp. 427–82.

Thomas, Howard and Lewis, Pam. The Linkage between Strategy, Strategic Groups and Performance in the UK Retail Grocery Industry. In *Mansfield, R., ed.*, 1989, pp. 163–79.

Thomas, J. J. The Early Econometric History of the Consumption Function. *Oxford Econ. Pap.*, January 1989, 41(1), pp. 131–49.

_____. The Early Econometric History of the Consumption Function. In *de Marchi, N. and Gilbert, C., eds.*, 1989, pp. 131–49.

Thomas, J. William and Ashcraft, Marie L. F. Measuring Severity of Illness: A Comparison of Interrater Reliability among Severity Methodologies. *Inquiry*, Winter 1989, 26(4), pp. 483–92.

Thomas, Jacob K. Unusual Patterns in Reported Earnings. *Accounting Rev.*, October 1989, 64(4), pp. 773–87.

_____. Why Do Firms Terminate Their Overfunded Pension Plans? *J. Acc. Econ.*, November 1989, 11(4), pp. 361–98.

_____ and Bernard, Victor L. Post-Earnings-Announcement Drift: Delayed Price Response or Risk Premium? *J. Acc. Res.*, Supplement, 1989, 27, pp. 1–36.

Thomas, Janet M. An Empirical Investigation of Product Differentiation and Pricing Strategy: An Application to the Household Goods Motor Carrier Industry. *Southern Econ. J.*, July 1989, 56(1), pp. 64–79.

_____ and Callan, Scott J. Constant Returns to Scale in the Post-Deregulatory Period; the Case of Specialized Motor Carriers. *Logist. Transp. Rev.*, September 1989, 25(3), pp. 271–88.

Thomas, John W. and Grindle, Merilee S. Policy Makers, Policy Choices, and Policy Outcomes: The Political Economy of Reform in Developing Countries. *Policy Sciences*, November 1989, 22(3–4), pp. 213–48.

Thomas, Jonathan P. Institutional Arrangements for Natural Resources: Summary of the Discussion. In *Vosgerau, H.-J., ed.*, 1989, pp. 366–67.

_____. Some Micro and Macro Implications of Inventories. In *Hahn, F., ed.*, 1989, pp. 437–51.

_____ and Lockwood, Ben. Asymptotic Efficiency in Principal–Agent Models with Hidden Information. *Econ. Letters*, October 1989, 30(4), pp. 297–301.

Thomas, Lacy Glenn. Advertising in Consumer Goods Industries: Durability, Economies of Scale, and Heterogeneity. *J. Law Econ.*, April 1989, 32(1), pp. 163–93.

Thomas, Paul A. and Hammond, Thomas H. The Impossibility of a Neutral Hierarchy. *J. Law, Econ., Organ.*, Spring 1989, 5(1), pp. 155–84.

Thomas, Raju G. C. Strategies of Recipient Autonomy: The Case of India. In *Baek, K.-I.; McLaurin, R. D. and Moon, C., eds.*, 1989, pp. 185–200.

Thomas, Ravi and Singh, Nirvikar. Matching Grants versus Block Grants with Imperfect Information. *Nat. Tax J.*, June 1989, 42(2), pp. 191–203.

Thomas, Stephen C. Market Reforms and Human Rights in China. In *Van Ness, P., ed.*, 1989, pp. 170–93.

Thomas, Stephen H. Whose Crisis Is the Debt Crisis? A View from the North. In *Thomas, C. and Saravanamuttu, P., eds.*, 1989, pp. 123–32.

_____; Lloyd-Ellis, H. and McKenzie, G. W. Using Country Balance Sheet Data to Predict Debt Rescheduling. *Econ. Letters*, December 1989, 31(2), pp. 173–77.

Thomas, Valerie. Verification of Sea-Launched Cruise Missiles. In *Altmann, J. and Rotblat, J., eds.*, 1989, pp. 38–47.

Thomas, Vinod and Chhibber, Ajay. Experience

with Policy Reforms under Adjustment. *Finance Devel.*, March 1989, *26*(1), pp. 28–31.

Thomas, Wade L.; Musgrave, Frank W. and Vaughan, Michael B. The Evolving Health Care System: Economic Integration through Reciprocity. *J. Econ. Issues*, June 1989, *23*(2), pp. 493–502.

Thomassin, Paul J. and Baker, Laurie. Institutional Change and Its Impact on Farm Management. *Can. J. Agr. Econ.*, Part 1, December 1989, *37*(4), pp. 775–94.

Thommesen, Sven and Ekelund, Robert B., Jr. Disequilibrium Theory and Thornton's Assault on the Laws of Supply and Demand. *Hist. Polit. Econ.*, Winter 1989, *21*(4), pp. 567–92.

Thompson, Alicia and Foster, Jerry R. Motor Carrier Salespeople: Can They Adapt? *Logist. Transp. Rev.*, December 1989, *25*(4), pp. 307–24.

Thompson, Craig J.; Locander, William B. and Pollio, Howard R. Putting Consumer Experience Back into Consumer Research: The Philosophy and Method of Existential-Phenomenology. *J. Cons. Res.*, September 1989, *16*(2), pp. 133–46.

Thompson, Cynthia. Compensation for Death and Dismemberment. *Mon. Lab. Rev.*, September 1989, *112*(9), pp. 13–17.

Thompson, David. Introducing Competition and Regulatory Requirements. In *Ramanadham, V. V., ed.*, 1989, pp. 125–32.

_____; **Hammond, Elizabeth and Helm, Dieter.** Competition in Electricity Supply: Has the Energy Act Failed? In *Helm, D.; Kay, J. and Thompson, D., eds.*, 1989, *1986*, pp. 157–77.

_____; **Helm, Dieter and Kay, John A.** The Market for Energy: Introduction: Energy Policy and the Role of the State in the Market for Energy. In *Helm, D.; Kay, J. and Thompson, D., eds.*, 1989, pp. 1–20.

_____; **Toker, Saadet and Geroski, Paul A.** Vertical Separation and Price Discrimination: Cellular Phones in the UK. *Fisc. Stud.*, November 1989, *10*(4), pp. 83–103.

Thompson, Donald J., II and Zivney, Terry L. The Effect of Market Proxy Rebalancing Policies on Detecting Abnormal Performance. *J. Finan. Res.*, Winter 1989, *12*(4), pp. 293–99.

_____ **and Zivney, Terry L.** The Specification and Power of the Sign Test in Measuring Security Price Performance: Comments and Analysis. *Financial Rev.*, November 1989, *24*(4), pp. 581–88.

Thompson, F. M. L. Rural Society and Agricultural Change in Nineteenth-Century Britain. In *Grantham, G. and Leonard, C. S., eds.*, Pt. A, 1989, pp. 187–202.

Thompson, Fred. Privatization at the State and Local Level: Comment. In *MacAvoy, P. W., et al.*, 1989, pp. 203–07.

Thompson, G. Rodney; Billingsley, Randall S. and Fraser, Donald R. Shareholder Wealth and Stock Repurchases by Bank Holding Companies. *Quart. J. Bus. Econ.*, Winter 1989, *28*(1), pp. 3–25.

_____; **Grubaugh, Stephen G. and Stollar, Andrew J.** Socialist Structural Gaps: A Simultaneous Inference Analysis. *Rev. Econ. Statist.*, November 1989, *71*(4), pp. 693–98.

Thompson, Gary D. and Langworthy, Mark. Profit Function Approximations and Duality Applications to Agriculture. *Amer. J. Agr. Econ.*, August 1989, *71*(3), pp. 791–98.

_____ **and Lyon, Charles C.** Marketing Order Impacts on Farm–Retail Price Spreads: The Suspension of Prorates on California–Arizona Navel Oranges. *Amer. J. Agr. Econ.*, August 1989, *71*(3), pp. 647–60.

Thompson, Gerald L. John von Neumann's Contributions to Mathematical Programming Economics. In *Dore, M.; Chakravarty, S. and Goodwin, R., eds.*, 1989, pp. 221–37.

Thompson, Gregory L. Misused Product Costing in the American Railroad Industry: Southern Pacific Passenger Service between the Wars. *Bus. Hist. Rev.*, Autumn 1989, *63*(3), pp. 511–54.

Thompson, Henry. Do Tariffs Protect Specific Factors? *Can. J. Econ.*, May 1989, *22*(2), pp. 406–12.

_____. Variable Employment and Income in General Equilibrium. *Southern Econ. J.*, January 1989, *55*(3), pp. 679–83.

_____ **and Wickham, Elizabeth.** An Empirical Analysis of Intra-industry Trade and Multinational Firms. In *Tharakan, P. K. M. and Kol, J., eds.*, 1989, pp. 121–44.

Thompson, James F. and Edwards, W. F. The Retail Price Effect of the Kentucky and Tennessee Milk Marketing Laws. *Southern J. Agr. Econ.*, December 1989, *21*(2), pp. 211–15.

Thompson, John B. The Theory of Structuration. In *Held, D. and Thompson, J. B., eds.*, 1989, pp. 56–76.

_____ **and Held, David.** Social Theory of Modern Societies: Anthony Giddens and His Critics: Introduction. In *Held, D. and Thompson, J. B., eds.*, 1989, pp. 1–18.

Thompson, Judith Kenner. Pressure to Change: A Case Analysis of Union Use of Corporate Campaigns. In *Post, J. E., ed.*, 1989, pp. 119–50.

Thompson, Patrick A., et al. Multivariate Time Series Projections of Parameterized Age-Specific Fertility Rates. *J. Amer. Statist. Assoc.*, September 1989, *84*(407), pp. 689–99.

Thompson, Peter J. Providing a Qualified Society to Meet the Challenge. *Nat. Westminster Bank Quart. Rev.*, February 1989, pp. 22–29.

Thompson, R. S. Circulation versus Advertiser Appeal in the Newspaper Industry: An Empirical Investigation. *J. Ind. Econ.*, March 1989, *37*(3), pp. 259–71.

_____; **Robbie, K. and Wright, Mike.** Privatisation via Management and Employee Buyouts: Analysis and U.K. Experience. *Ann. Pub. Coop. Econ.*, 1989, *60*(4), pp. 399–429.

_____ **and Wright, Mike.** Bonding, Agency Costs and Management Buyouts: A Note. *Bull. Econ. Res.*, January 1989, *41*(1), pp. 69–75.

Thompson, Randal Joy. Importation and Local Generation of Technology by the Third World:

An Institutionalist Perspective: Commentary. In *DeGregori, T. R., ed.*, 1989, pp. 371–84.

Thompson, Robert L. Farm, Trade, and Development Policies: What They Mean for Future U.S. Export Markets. In *Swegle, W. E. and Ligon, P. C., eds.*, 1989, pp. 1–9.

_____. Spatial and Temporal Price Equilibrium Agricultural Models. In *Labys, W. C.; Takayama, T. and Uri, N. D., eds.*, 1989, pp. 49–65.

_____; **Tsigas, Marinos E. and Hertel, Thomas W.** Economywide Effects of Unilateral Trade and Policy Liberalization in U.S. Agriculture. In *Stoeckel, A. B.; Vincent, D. and Cuthbertson, S., eds.*, 1989, pp. 260–92.

Thompson, Shelley J.; Runge, C. Ford and von Witzke, Harald. International Agricultural and Trade Policy: A Political Economic Coordination Game. In *von Witzke, H.; Runge, C. F. and Job, B., eds.*, 1989, pp. 89–116.

Thompson, Stanley R. and Myers, Robert J. Generalized Optimal Hedge Ratio Estimation. *Amer. J. Agr. Econ.*, November 1989, *71*(4), pp. 858–68.

_____ **and Myers, Robert J.** Optimal Portfolios of External Debt in Developing Countries: The Potential Role of Commodity-Linked Bonds. *Amer. J. Agr. Econ.*, May 1989, *71*(2), pp. 517–22.

Thompson, T. Scott and Manski, Charles F. Estimation of Best Predictors of Binary Response. *J. Econometrics*, January 1989, *40*(1), pp. 97–123.

Thompson, Velma Montoya. AIDS Testing: An Economic Assessment of Evolving Public Policy. *Econ. Inquiry*, April 1989, *27*(2), pp. 259–69.

Thoms, David and Donnelly, Tom. Trade Unions, Management and the Search for Production in the Coventry Motor Car Industry, 1939–75. In *Harvey, C. and Turner, J., eds.*, 1989, pp. 98–113.

Thomson, Graeme. A Single Market for Goods and Services in the Antipodes. *World Econ.*, June 1989, *12*(2), pp. 206–18.

Thomson, J. M. The Journal's First 21 Years: Preface. *J. Transp. Econ. Policy*, January 1989, *23*(1), pp. 11–16.

Thomson, James B. Errors in Recorded Security Prices and the Turn-of-the-Year Effect. *J. Finan. Quant. Anal.*, December 1989, *24*(4), pp. 513–26.

Thomson, Kenneth J. Budgetary and Economic Effects of CAP Trade Liberalization. In *Tarditi, S., et al., eds.*, 1989, pp. 110–19.

Thomson, Randall J. and Newman, Barbara A. Economic Growth and Social Development: A Longitudinal Analysis of Causal Priority. *World Devel.*, April 1989, *17*(4), pp. 461–71.

Thomson, Ross. Invention, Markets, and the Scope of the Firm: The Nineteenth Century U.S. Shoe Machinery Industry. In *Hausman, W. J., ed.*, 1989, pp. 140–49.

Thomson, William and Chun, Youngsub. Bargaining Solutions and Relative Guarantees. *Math. Soc. Sci.*, June 1989, *17*(3), pp. 285–95.

_____ **and Diamantaras, Dimitrios.** A Refinement and Extension of the No-Envy Concept. *Econ. Letters*, August 1989, *30*(2), pp. 103–07.

Thonstad, Tore and Riis, Christian. A Counterfactual Study of Economic Impacts of Norwegian Emigration and Capital Imports. In *Gordon, I. and Thirlwall, A. P., eds.*, 1989, pp. 116–32.

Thorbecke, Erik. Planning Techniques for Social Justice. In *Adelman, I. and Lane, S., eds.*, 1989, pp. 45–71.

_____ **and Khan, Haider A.** Macroeconomic Effects of Technology Choice: Multiplier and Structural Path Analysis within a SAM Framework. *J. Policy Modeling*, Spring 1989, *11*(1), pp. 131–56.

_____ **and Morrisson, Christian.** Institutions, Policies and Agricultural Performance: A Comparative Analysis. *World Devel.*, Special Issue, September 1989, *17*(9), pp. 1485–98.

Thornborrow, Nancy M. Nobel Laureates in Economic Sciences: A Biographical Dictionary: Milton Friedman: 1976. In *Katz, B. S., ed.*, 1989, pp. 53–65.

Thorner, John A. Acid Rain: The Cross-Media Aspects. In *Dysart, B. C., III and Clawson, M., eds.*, 1989, pp. 115–23.

Thornicroft, Kenneth W. Airline Deregulation and the Airline Labor Market. *J. Lab. Res.*, Spring 1989, *10*(2), pp. 163–81.

Thorns, David C. The New International Division of Labor and Urban Change: A New Zealand Case Study. In *Smith, M. P., ed.*, 1989, pp. 68–101.

Thornton, Daniel L. The Effect of Unanticipated Money on the Money and Foreign Exchange Markets. *J. Int. Money Finance*, December 1989, *8*(4), pp. 573–87.

_____. Tests of Covered Interest Rate Parity. *Fed. Res. Bank St. Louis Rev.*, July–Aug. 1989, *71*(4), pp. 55–66.

_____ **and Garfinkel, Michelle R.** The Link between M1 and the Monetary Base in the 1980s. *Fed. Res. Bank St. Louis Rev.*, Sept.–Oct. 1989, *71*(5), pp. 35–52.

Thornton, John. The Demand for Money in India: A Test of McKinnon's Complementarity Hypothesis. *Indian Econ. J.*, July–Sept. 1989, *37*(1), pp. 82–86.

Thornton, John H.; Cross, Mark L. and Davidson, Wallace N., III. The Impact of Directors and Officers' Liability Suits on Firm Value. *J. Risk Ins.*, March 1989, *56*(1), pp. 128–36.

Thornton, Judith and Leary, Neil A. Are Socialist Industries Inoculated against Innovation? A Case Study of Technological Change in Steelmaking. *Comp. Econ. Stud.*, Summer 1989, *31*(2), pp. 42–65.

Thornton, Michael C. and White-Means, Shelley I. Factors Influencing the Use of the Hospital Emergency Room among Black Americans. *Rev. Black Polit. Econ.*, Spring 1989, *17*(4), pp. 59–71.

Thornton, P. K. Risk Decisions for Beef Production Systems in the Colombian Savannas. *J. Agr. Econ.*, May 1989, *40*(2), pp. 198–208.

Thornton, Robert J. and Innes, Jon T. Interpreting Semilogarithmic Regression Coefficients in Labor Research. *J. Lab. Res.*, Fall 1989, *10*(4), pp. 443–47.

Thorpe, Andy. The Religious Opium of Liberation: Redemption Politicised? *Int. J. Soc. Econ.*, 1989, *16*(12), pp. 14–25.

Thorpe, Kenneth E. Costs and Distributional Impacts of Employer Health Insurance Mandates and Medicaid Expansion. *Inquiry*, Fall 1989, *26*(3), pp. 335–44.

Thorson, John E. Water Marketing in Big Sky Country: An Interim Assessment. *Natural Res. J.*, Spring 1989, *29*(2), pp. 479–88.

Thoumi, Francisco E. Bilateral Trade Flows and Economic Integration in Latin America and the Caribbean. *World Devel.*, March 1989, *17*(3), pp. 421–29.

_____. Smuggler's Blues at the Central Bank: Lessons from Sudan: Comment. In *[Díaz-Alejandro, C.]*, 1989, pp. 211–13.

_____. Trade Flows and Economic Integration among the LDCs of the Caribbean Basin. *Soc. Econ. Stud.*, June 1989, *38*(2), pp. 215–33.

Thrall, Robert M. Classification Transitions under Expansion of Inputs and Outputs in Data Envelopment Analysis. *Managerial Dec. Econ.*, June 1989, *10*(2), pp. 159–62.

Thrift, Nigel J.; Leyshon, A. and Daniels, Peter W. Internationalisation of Professional Producer Services: Accountancy Conglomerates. In *Enderwick, P.*, 1989, pp. 79–106.

Throop, Adrian W. Fiscal Policy, the Dollar, and International Trade: A Synthesis of Two Views. *Fed. Res. Bank San Francisco Econ. Rev.*, Summer 1989, (3), pp. 27–44.

_____. Reagan Fiscal Policy and the Dollar. *Fed. Res. Bank San Francisco Econ. Rev.*, Summer 1989, (3), pp. 18–26.

Throup, David and Anderson, David. The Agrarian Economy of Central Province, Kenya, 1918 to 1939. In *Brown, I., ed.*, 1989, pp. 8–28.

Thuijsman, F. and Vrieze, O. J. On Equilibria in Repeated Games with Absorbing States. *Int. J. Game Theory*, 1989, *18*(3), pp. 293–310.

Thurik, A. R. and van der Hoeven, W. H. M. Manufacturing Margins: Differences between Small and Large Firms. *Econ. Letters*, 1989, *29*(4), pp. 353–59.

_____ and van der Hoeven, W. H. M. Profit Margins and Concentration. *Atlantic Econ. J.*, June 1989, *17*(2), pp. 79.

Thurmaier, Kurt and Straussman, Jeffrey D. Budgeting Rights: The Case of Jail Litigation. *Public Budg. Finance*, Summer 1989, *9*(2), pp. 30–42.

Thurman, Walter N. Have Meat Price and Income Elasticities Changed? Their Connection with Changes in Marketing Channels. In *Buse, R. C., ed.*, 1989, pp. 157–69.

_____ and Fisher, Douglas. Sweden's Financial Sophistication in the Nineteenth Century: An Appraisal. *J. Econ. Hist.*, September 1989, *49*(3), pp. 621–34.

_____ and Wohlgenant, Michael K. Consistent Estimation of General Equilibrium Welfare Effects. *Amer. J. Agr. Econ.*, November 1989, *71*(4), pp. 1041–45.

Thuronyi, Victor. Direct Expenditures versus Tax Expenditures for Economic and Social Policy: Comment. In *Bruce, N., ed.*, 1989, pp. 330–32.

Thurow, Lester C. An Establishment or an Oligarchy? *Nat. Tax J.*, December 1989, *42*(4), pp. 405–11.

Thursby, Jerry G. A Comparison of Several Specification Error Tests for a General Alternative. *Int. Econ. Rev.*, February 1989, *30*(1), pp. 217–30.

_____. Expected MSE of Errors-in-Variables and Omitted Variables Models. *Econ. Letters*, September 1989, *30*(3), pp. 211–16.

Thursby, M. C.; Blackorby, Charles and Lovell, C. A. Knox. Extended Hicks Neutral Technical Change. In *Wood, J. C. and Woods, R. N., eds., Vol. 3*, 1989, *1976*, pp. 153–62.

Thury, Gerhard. Dynamic Specification of Consumer Expenditure on Non-durable and Services in Austria. *Empirica*, 1989, *16*(1), pp. 67–83.

Thwaites, A. T.; Williams, H. and Gillespie, A. E. Industrial Dynamics and Policy Debate in the Information Technology Production Industries. In *Gibbs, D., ed.*, 1989, pp. 55–69.

Thygesen, Lars. Prospects for Socio-demographic Risk Research in Denmark. *Statist. J.*, 1989, *6*(1), pp. 1–15.

Thygesen, Niels. Er den økonomiske og monetære union kommet nærmere? (The Content of and the Attitudes to the Delors Committee's Report on an Economic and Monetary Union in Europe. With English summary.) *Nationaløkon. Tidsskr.*, 1989, *127*(2), pp. 143–59.

_____. The Prospects for a European Central Bank: Panel Discussion. In *De Cecco, M. and Giovannini, A., eds.*, 1989, pp. 354–64.

Thynne, Ian. Privatisation: Singapore's Experience in Perspective: The Administrative State in Transition. In *Thynne, I. and Ariff, M., eds.*, 1989, pp. 19–58.

_____. Privatisation: Singapore's Experience in Perspective: A Framework for Analysis. In *Thynne, I. and Ariff, M., eds.*, 1989, pp. 1–17.

Thys-Clément, F.; Jeanfils, Ph. and Kestens, P. 1992 en perspective 2000: Les performances de la Belgique suite à l'ouverture européenne des frontières. (With English summary.) *Cah. Écon. Bruxelles*, 4th Trimester 1989, (124), pp. 475–91.

Tian, Guoqiang. Implementation of the Lindahl Correspondence by a Single-Valued, Feasible, and Continuous Mechanism. *Rev. Econ. Stud.*, October 1989, *56*(4), pp. 613–21.

Tian, Yuan. Price Reform and the Transfer of the Property Rights System. *Chinese Econ. Stud.*, Spring 1989, *22*(3), pp. 89–102.

Tice, Helen Stone and Lipsey, Robert E. The Measurement of Saving, Investment, and

Wealth: Introduction. In *Lipsey, R. E. and Tice, H. S., eds.*, 1989, pp. 1–19.

Ticovschi, V. and Costake, N. On Some Aspects of Scientific Research, Technological Development and the Application of Technical Advances. *Econ. Computat. Econ. Cybern. Stud. Res.*, 1989, *24*(1), pp. 25–36.

_____ **and Costake, N.** On Some Aspects of Scientific Research, Technological Development and the Application of Technical Advance (II). *Econ. Computat. Econ. Cybern. Stud. Res.*, 1989, *24*(2–3), pp. 17–27.

_____ **and Costake, N.** On Some Aspects of Scientific Research, Technological Development and the Application of Technical Advance (III). *Econ. Computat. Econ. Cybern. Stud. Res.*, 1989, *24*(4), pp. 5–19.

Tideman, T. N. and Zavist, T. M. Complete Independence of Clones in the Ranked Pairs Rule. *Soc. Choice Welfare*, April 1989, *6*(2), pp. 167–73.

Tierney, Luke; Kass, Robert E. and Kadane, Joseph B. Fully Exponential Laplace Approximations to Expectations and Variances of Nonpositive Functions. *J. Amer. Statist. Assoc.*, September 1989, *84*(407), pp. 710–16.

Tierney, Paul E., Jr. Ethics and Takeovers: A Debate (1) The Ethos of Wall Street. In *Williams, O. F.; Reilly, F. K. and Houck, J. W., eds.*, 1989, pp. 65–76.

Tietenberg, Thomas H. Acid Rain Reduction Credits. *Challenge*, March–April 1989, *32*(2), pp. 25–29.

_____. Indivisible Toxic Torts: The Economics of Joint and Several Liability. *Land Econ.*, November 1989, *65*(4), pp. 305–19.

Tietzel, Manfred. Prognoselogik oder: Warum prognostiker irren dürfen. (On the Logic of Economic Forecasting. With English summary.) *Jahr. Nationalökon. Statist.*, December 1989, *206*(6), pp. 546–62.

Tigre, Paulo Bastos and Evans, Peter B. Going Beyond Clones in Brazil and Korea: A Comparative Analysis of NIC Strategies in the Computer Industry. *World Devel.*, November 1989, *17*(11), pp. 1751–68.

Tijs, Stef; Muto, Shigeo and Potters, Jos. Information Market Games. *Int. J. Game Theory*, 1989, *18*(2), pp. 209–26.

Tikka, Kari S. The Disregard of a Legal Entity for Tax Purposes: Finland. In *International Fiscal Association, ed. (II)*, 1989, pp. 259–68.

Tilak, Jandhyala B. G. Rates of Return to Education and Income Distribution. *De Economist*, 1989, *137*(4), pp. 454–65.

_____ **and Bhatt, G. K.** Educational Development in Haryana: An Inter-district Analysis. *Margin*, Oct. 1989–March 1990, *22*(1–2), pp. 108–23.

Tilley, Daniel S. Value-Added Activities as a Rural Development Strategy: Discussion. *Southern J. Agr. Econ.*, July 1989, *21*(1), pp. 37–40.

_____; **Moesel, Douglas and Schatzer, Raymond Joe.** Consumer Expenditures at Direct Produce Markets. *Southern J. Agr. Econ.*, July 1989, *21*(1), pp. 131–38.

Tillotson, John. International Commodity Agreements and the European Community: Questions of Competence and Will. *J. World Trade*, December 1989, *23*(6), pp. 109–25.

Tilly, Richard H. Banking Institutions in Historical and Comparative Perspective: Germany, Great Britain and the United States in the Nineteenth and Early Twentieth Century. *J. Inst. Theoretical Econ.*, March 1989, *145*(1), pp. 189–209.

_____. German Industrialization and Gerschenkronian Backwardness. *Rivista Storia Econ.*, S.S., June 1989, *6*(2), pp. 139–64.

Tilman, Rick. Social Value Theory, Corporate Power, and Political Elites: Appraisals of Lindblom's *Politics and Markets*. In *Tool, M. R. and Samuels, W. J., eds. (I)*, 1989, *1983*, pp. 245–61.

_____ **and Edgell, Stephen.** The Intellectual Antecedents of Thorstein Veblen: A Reappraisal. *J. Econ. Issues*, December 1989, *23*(4), pp. 1003–26.

Tilton, John E. Changing Patterns of Mineral Trade. In *Jackson, L. M. and Richardson, P. R., eds.*, 1989, pp. 15–25.

_____. The New View of Minerals and Economic Growth. *Econ. Rec.*, September 1989, *65*(190), pp. 265–78.

Timár, János. The Defense of Worktime in Hungary: Worktime and the Economic Reform. *Eastern Europ. Econ.*, Winter 1989–90, *28*(2), pp. 172–87.

Timberlake, Richard H., Jr. The Government's License to Create Money. *Cato J.*, Fall 1989, *9*(2), pp. 301–21.

_____. Marginal Utility Equilibrium between Money and Goods: A Reply to Professor Barnett's Criticism. In *Rothbard, M. N. and Block, W., eds.*, 1989, pp. 159–61.

Timbrell, Martin. Contracts and Market-Clearing in the Labour Market. In *Greenaway, D., ed.*, 1989, pp. 68–90.

Timko, M. and Loyns, R. M. A. Market Information Needs for Prairie Farmers. *Can. J. Agr. Econ.*, Part 1, December 1989, *37*(4), pp. 609–27.

Timme, Stephen G. and Hunter, William Curt. Does Multiproduct Production in Large Banks Reduce Costs? *Fed. Res. Bank Atlanta Econ. Rev.*, May–June 1989, *74*(3), pp. 2–11.

Timmer, C. Peter. Indonesia: Transition from Food Importer to Exporter. In *Sicular, T., ed.*, 1989, pp. 22–64.

Timmermann, Allan. Børskrakket i oktober 1987. (The Stock Exchange Crash in October 1987. With English summary.) *Nationaløkon. Tidsskr.*, 1989, *127*(1), pp. 74–94.

Timmermans, Daniëlle; Vlek, Charles and Hendrickx, Laurie. An Experimental Study of the Effectiveness of Computer-Programmed Decision Support. In *Lockett, A. G. and Islei, G., eds.*, 1989, pp. 13–23.

Timmermans, H. J. P.; Borgers, A. W. J. and van der Heijden, R. E. C. M. A Variety Seeking Model of Spatial Choice-Behaviour. *Envi-*

ron. Planning A, August 1989, *21*(8), pp. 1037–48.

Timmins, S. A. and Kassem, M. S. A Descriptive of the Need in Family Businesses to Juggle Family Values and Business Decision Making: The Saudi Arabian Case. *Middle East Bus. Econ. Rev.*, July 1989, *1*(2), pp. 37–42.

Tims, Wouter and Parikh, Kirit S. Food and Agricultural Policies and Programs of Major Countries and Regions: Reaction. In *Helmuth, J. W. and Johnson, S. R., eds., Vol. 1*, 1989, pp. 37–39.

_____ **and Parikh, Kirit S.** Food Consumption, Dietary Status, and Chronic Hunger: An Assessment of Its Extent and Policy Options. In *Helmuth, J. W. and Johnson, S. R., eds., Vol. 2*, 1989, pp. 3–44.

Tinbergen, Jan. The Economics of Warfare: Joan Robinson's Challenge. In *Feiwel, G. R., ed. (I)*, 1989, pp. 749–68.

_____. The Impact of the Forecasting Capacity of One Science on That of Other Sciences. *Int. J. Forecasting*, 1989, *5*(1), pp. 3–5.

Tindemans, Leo. What the Developing Nations Must Contribute. In *Cerami, C. A., ed.*, 1989, pp. 169–81.

Tingley, Daniel H. and Fortin, Guy. The Disregard of a Legal Entity for Tax Purposes: Canada. In *International Fiscal Association, ed. (II)*, 1989, pp. 223–37.

Tingsabadh, Charit. Maximising Development Benefits from Labour Migration: Thailand. In *Amjad, R., ed.*, 1989, pp. 303–42.

Tinsley, LaVerne C. State Workers' Compensation: Enactments in 1988. *Mon. Lab. Rev.*, January 1989, *112*(1), pp. 66–71.

Tirard, Jean-Marc and Courtois, Pierre. La non-reconnaissance des personnes juridiques en matière fiscale: France. (The Disregard of a Legal Entity for Tax Purposes: France. With English summary.) In *International Fiscal Association, ed. (II)*, 1989, pp. 269–87.

Tirelli, Patrizio. Politiche monetarie e fiscali in un regime di cambi flessibili: Il ruolo delle partite correnti. (With English summary.) *Politica. Econ.*, April 1989, *5*(1), pp. 189–212.

_____ **and Boggio, Luciano.** Economic Growth, Exports and International Competitiveness. *Econ. Int.*, Feb.–March 1989, *42*(1–2), pp. 22–46.

Tirole, Jean and Fudenberg, Drew. Noncooperative Game Theory for Industrial Organization: An Introduction and Overview. In *Schmalensee, R. and Willig, R. D., eds., Vol. 1*, 1989, pp. 259–327.

_____ **and Holmstrom, Bengt R.** The Theory of the Firm. In *Schmalensee, R. and Willig, R. D., eds., Vol. 1*, 1989, pp. 61–133.

Tisdell, Clem A. Giant Clams in the Pacific—The Socio-economic Potential of a Developing Technology for Their Mariculture. In *Couper, A. D., ed.*, 1989, pp. 74–88.

_____. Transfer Pricing: Technical and Productivity Change within the Firm. *Managerial Dec. Econ.*, September 1989, *10*(3), pp. 253–56.

_____ **and Alauddin, Mohammad.** Biochemical

Technology and Bangladeshi Land Productivity: Diwan and Kallianpur's Analysis Reapplied and Critically Examined. *Appl. Econ.*, June 1989, *21*(6), pp. 741–60.

_____ **and Alauddin, Mohammad.** New Crop Varieties: Impact on Diversification and Stability of Yields. *Australian Econ. Pap.*, June 1989, *28*(52), pp. 123–40.

_____ **and Alauddin, Mohammad.** Poverty, Resource Distribution and Security: The Impact of New Agricultural Technology in Rural Bangladesh. *J. Devel. Stud.*, July 1989, *25*(4), pp. 550–70.

_____ **and McKee, David L.** Urbanization and the Development Problem in Small Island Nations. *METU*, 1989, *16*(1–2), pp. 85–98.

_____ **and Sathiendrakumar, R.** Comments on a Note on Optimal Effort in the Maldivian Tuna Industry. *Marine Resource Econ.*, 1989, *6*(2), pp. 177–78.

Tishler, Asher. The Response of Large Firms to Different Schemes of Time-of-Use Pricing When the Production Function is Quadratic. *Energy J.*, April 1989, *10*(2), pp. 69–90.

Titman, Sheridan D. and Grinblatt, Mark. Mutual Fund Performance: An Analysis of Quarterly Portfolio Holdings. *J. Bus.*, July 1989, *62*(3), pp. 393–416.

_____ **and Torous, Walter N.** Valuing Commercial Mortgages: An Empirical Investigation of the Contingent-Claims Approach to Pricing Risky Debt. *J. Finance*, June 1989, *44*(2), pp. 345–73.

_____ **and Warga, Arthur.** Stock Returns as Predictors of Interest Rates and Inflation. *J. Finan. Quant. Anal.*, March 1989, *24*(1), pp. 47–58.

Tittel, Manfred and Degens, Paul O. Isotonic Regression—For a Monotone Index on a Hierarchy. In *Opitz, O., ed.*, 1989, pp. 212–21.

Tiwari, R. C.; Jammalamadaka, S. R. and Chib, Siddhartha. Bayes Prediction Density and Regression Estimation—A Semiparametric Approach. In *Ullah, A., ed.*, 1989, *1988*, pp. 87–100.

Tiwari, R. S. and Kashyap, S. P. Size Distribution of Firms in Diamond Processing Industry in India: An Exploratory Analysis. *Indian J. Quant. Econ.*, 1989, *5*(1), pp. 63–83.

Tjønneland, Elling Njål. South Africa's Regional Policies in the Late and Post-Apartheid Periods. In *Odén, B. and Othman, H., eds.*, 1989, pp. 47–61.

Tjøstheim, Dag and Stensland, Gunnar. Optimal Investments Using Empirical Dynamic Programming with Application to Natural Resources. *J. Bus.*, January 1989, *62*(1), pp. 99–120.

To, Minh-Chau and Marcil, Benoît. La transaction programmée et la volatilité. (With English summary.) *L'Actual. Econ.*, June 1989, *65*(2), pp. 248–62.

Tobin, James. Growth and Distribution: A Neoclassical Kaldor–Robinson Exercise. *Cambridge J. Econ.*, March 1989, *13*(1), pp. 37–45.

_____. Growth and Distribution: A Neoclassical

Kaldor–Robinson Exercise. In *Lawson, T.; Palma, J. G. and Sender, J., eds.*, 1989, pp. 37–45.

———. Money, Capital, and Other Stores of Value. In *Starr, R. M., ed.*, 1989, *1961*, pp. 26–37.

———. On the Efficiency of the Financial System. In *Johnson, C., ed.*, 1989, pp. 125–38.

———. The State of Economic Science: Views of Six Nobel Laureates: Dr. James Tobin. In *Sichel, W., ed.*, 1989, pp. 61–76.

——— and Baumol, William J. The Optimal Cash Balance Proposition: Maurice Allais' Priority. *J. Econ. Lit.*, September 1989, *27*(3), pp. 1160–62.

Todd, Michael J. and Mitchell, John E. On the Relationship between the Search Directions in the Affine and Projective Variants of Karmarkar's Linear Programming Algorithm. In *Cornet, B. and Tulkens, H., eds.*, 1989, pp. 237–50.

Todd, Richard M. Policy Analysis with Time-Series Econometric Models: Discussion. *Amer. J. Agr. Econ.*, May 1989, *71*(2), pp. 509–10.

Todd, Walker F. Variations on a Theme: Long-term Growth of Government: Comments. *J. Finan. Services Res.*, September 1989, *2*(3), pp. 167–70.

Togan, Subidey. Lessons to Be Learned from the European Unemployment of the 80s: Comments. *Pakistan Devel. Rev.*, Winter 1989, *28*(4), pp. 329–30.

Toharia, Luis; Fina, Lluis and Meixide, Alberto. Reregulating the Labor Market amid an Economic and Political Crisis: Spain, 1975–1986. In *Rosenberg, S., ed.*, 1989, pp. 107–25.

Toker, Saadet; Geroski, Paul A. and Thompson, David. Vertical Separation and Price Discrimination: Cellular Phones in the UK. *Fisc. Stud.*, November 1989, *10*(4), pp. 83–103.

Tokman, Víctor E. Policies for a Heterogeneous Informal Sector in Latin America. *World Devel.*, July 1989, *17*(7), pp. 1067–76.

———; García, Álvero and Infante, Ricardo. Paying Off the Social Debt in Latin America. *Int. Lab. Rev.*, 1989, *128*(4), pp. 467–83.

Tolley, George and Miller, Tracy. Technology Adoption and Agricultural Price Policy. *Amer. J. Agr. Econ.*, November 1989, *71*(4), pp. 847–57.

Tolley, H. Dennis; Bahr, Michael D. and Dotson, Peter K. A Statistical Method for Monitoring Social Insurance Claims. *J. Risk Ins.*, December 1989, *56*(4), pp. 670–85.

Tollison, Robert D. Chicago Political Economy. *Public Choice*, December 1989, *63*(3), pp. 293–97.

———. The Exercise of Market Power in Laboratory Experiments: Comment. *J. Law Econ.*, Part 2, October 1989, *32*(2), pp. S131–33.

———. Superdissipation. *Public Choice*, April 1989, *61*(1), pp. 97–98.

———; Anderson, Gary M. and Ekelund, Robert B., Jr. Nassau Senior as Economic Consultant: The Factory Acts Reconsidered. *Economica*, February 1989, *56*(221), pp. 71–81.

———; Anderson, Gary M. and Levy, David M. The Half-Life of Dead Economists. *Can. J. Econ.*, February 1989, *22*(1), pp. 174–83.

———; Anderson, Gary M. and Shughart, William F., II. On the Incentives of Judges to Enforce Legislative Wealth Transfers. *J. Law Econ.*, April 1989, *32*(1), pp. 215–28.

———; Anderson, Gary M. and Shughart, William F., II. Political Entry Barriers and Tax Incidence: The Political Economy of Sales and Excise Taxes. *Public Finance*, 1989, *44*(1), pp. 8–18.

———; Ekelund, Robert B., Jr. and Hébert, Robert F. An Economic Model of the Medieval Church: Usury as a Form of Rent Seeking. *J. Law, Econ., Organ.*, Fall 1989, *5*(2), pp. 307–31.

———; Fleisher, Arthur A., III and Shughart, William F., II. Ownership Structure in Professional Sports. In *Zerbe, R. O., ed.*, 1989, pp. 71–75.

——— and Goff, Brian L. The Allocation of Death in the Vietnam War: Reply. *Southern Econ. J.*, April 1989, *55*(4), pp. 1034–35.

———; Higgins, Richard S. and Shughart, William F., II. Price Leadership with Incomplete Information. *J. Econ. Behav. Organ.*, May 1989, *11*(3), pp. 423–29.

Tolnay, Stewart E. A New Look at the Effect of Venereal Disease on Black Fertility: The Deep South in 1940. *Demography*, November 1989, *26*(4), pp. 679–90.

Tolstikov, S.; Gromkovskii, V. and Starodubrovskaia, I. Bureaucratism in the Socialist Economy: Its Essence and Forms, and Means of Overcoming It. *Prob. Econ.*, September 1989, *32*(5), pp. 13–34.

Toma, Eugenia Froedge and Hoyt, William H. State Mandates and Interest Group Lobbying. *J. Public Econ.*, March 1989, *38*(2), pp. 199–213.

Toma, Mark. The Policy Effectiveness of Open Market Operations in the 1920s. *Exploration Econ. Hist.*, January 1989, *26*(1), pp. 99–116.

———. Will Bounty-Hunting Revenue Agents Increase Enforcement? *Public Choice*, June 1989, *61*(3), pp. 247–60.

Toman, Michael A. and Macauley, Molly K. No Free Launch: Efficient Space Transportation Pricing. *Land Econ.*, May 1989, *65*(2), pp. 91–99.

Tomiyama, Ken and Rossana, Robert J. Two-Stage Optimal Control Problems with an Explicit Switch Point Dependence: Optimality Criteria and and Example of Delivery Lags and Investment. *J. Econ. Dynam. Control*, July 1989, *13*(3), pp. 319–37.

Tomlins, Christopher L. The Ties That Bind: Master and Servant in Massachusetts, 1800–1850. *Labor Hist.*, Spring 1989, *30*(2), pp. 193–227.

Tomlinson, B. R. British Business in India, 1860–1970. In *Davenport-Hines, R. P. T. and Jones, G., eds.*, 1989, pp. 92–116.

Tomlinson, Jim. Macro-economic Management

and Industrial Policy. In *Hirst, P. and Zeitlin, J., eds.*, 1989, pp. 248–68.

Tompkins, C.; Porell, F. and Gruenberg, L. The Health Status and Utilization Patterns of the Elderly: Implications for Setting Medicare Payments to HMOs. In *Scheffler, R. M. and Rossiter, L. F., eds.*, 1989, pp. 41–73.

Tompson, William and Klehr, Harvey. Self-determination in the Black Belt: Origins of a Communist Policy. *Labor Hist.*, Summer 1989, *30*(3), pp. 354–66.

Toms, Miroslav. On the Conception and Measurement of Final Economic Results. *Czech. Econ. Pap.*, 1989, (27), pp. 65–83.

_____ **and Hájek, Mojmír.** Theoretical Questions of Forecasting the Intensification Process and Its Growth Rate Alternatives. *Czech. Econ. Pap.*, 1989, (26), pp. 51–71.

Tone, Kaoru and Yanagisawa, Shigeru. Site Selection for a Large Scale Integrated Circuits Factory. In *Golden, B. L.; Wasil, E. A. and Harker, P. T., eds.*, 1989, pp. 242–50.

Tonelson, Alan. A New Central America and Caribbean Policy. In *Crane, E. H. and Boaz, D.*, 1989, pp. 183–201.

Toner, Phillip. A Note on New Labour Market Data for the Building and Construction Industry. *Australian Bull. Lab.*, March 1989, *15*(2), pp. 139–42.

Tong, Howell. Thresholds, Stability, Nonlinear Forecasting and Irregularly Sampled Data. In *Hackl, P., ed.*, 1989, pp. 279–96.

_____ **and Chan, K. S.** A Survey on the Statistical Analysis of a Univariate Threshold Autoregressive Model. In *Mariano, R. S.; Lim, K. S. and Ling, K. D., eds.*, 1989, pp. 1–42.

Tong, Zhong and Stone, Bruce. Changing Patterns of Variability in Chinese Cereal Production. In *Anderson, J. R. and Hazell, P. B. R., eds.*, 1989, pp. 35–59.

Toniolo, Gianni. The Establishment of a Central Bank: Italy in the 19th Century: Discussion. In *De Cecco, M. and Giovannini, A., eds.*, 1989, pp. 285–89.

_____. Storia quantitativa e storia economica: Interventi degli esperti. (In English.) In *Cavaciocchi, S., ed.*, 1989, pp. 330–38.

Tonks, Ian and Bulkley, I. George. Are U.K. Stock Prices Excessively Volatile? Trading Rules and Variance Bounds Tests. *Econ. J.*, December 1989, *99*(398), pp. 1083–98.

_____ **and Taylor, Mark P.** The Internationalisation of Stock Markets and the Abolition of U.K. Exchange Control. *Rev. Econ. Statist.*, May 1989, *71*(2), pp. 332–36.

Tool, Marc R. An Institutionalist Legacy. *J. Econ. Issues*, June 1989, *23*(2), pp. 327–36.

_____. The Social Value Theory of Orthodoxy: A Review and Critique. In *Tool, M. R. and Samuels, W. J., eds. (II)*, 1989, *1980*, pp. 92–109.

Toolson, Richard B. The Charitable Contribution Deduction: New Evidence of a Tax Incentive Effect. In *Jones, S. M., ed.*, 1989, pp. 107–29.

Topel, Robert H. Industry Rents: Evidence and Implications: Comments. *Brookings Pap.*

Econ. Act., Microeconomics, 1989, pp. 283–88.

Topol, R.; Avouyi-Dovi, S. and Boutillier, M. Du peu de pertinence des anticipations sur le taux d'intérêt à court terme: Retour à la théorie de l'habitat préféré. (Weak Relevance of Short Term Interest Rate Expectations and Return to the Preferred Habitat Theory. With English summary.) *Écon. Societes*, April–May 1989, *23*(4–5), pp. 43–70.

Torelli, Nicola and Trivellato, Ugo. Youth Unemployment Duration from the Italian Labour Force Survey: Accuracy Issues and Modelling Attempts. *Europ. Econ. Rev.*, March 1989, *33*(2/3), pp. 407–15.

Toren, Christina. Drinking Cash: The Purification of Money through Ceremonial Exchange in Fiji. In *Parry, J. and Bloch, M., eds.*, 1989, pp. 142–64.

Torigian, Michael. National Unity on the Waterfront: Communist Politics and the ILWU during the Second World War. *Labor Hist.*, Summer 1989, *30*(3), pp. 409–32.

Torii, Yasuhiko; Shim, Seung-Jin and Akiyama, Yutaka. Effects of Tariff Reductions on Trade in the Asia-Pacific Region. In *Miller, R. E.; Polenske, K. R. and Rose, A. Z., eds.*, 1989, pp. 165–79.

Torkanovskii, Evgenii P. The Participation of Working People in the Management of Production as a Factor in Heightening Labor Activism. In *Jones, A. and Moskoff, W., eds.*, 1989, *1987*, pp. 78–88.

_____. Property and Self-management. *Prob. Econ.*, August 1989, *32*(4), pp. 56–74.

_____. Socialist Self-Management of Production. In *Yanowitch, M., ed.*, 1989, *1987*, pp. 36–46.

_____. What Lies Ahead for Self-management in Production? *Prob. Econ.*, April 1989, *31*(12), pp. 20–33.

Törmä, Hannu and Ilmakunnas, Pekka. Structural Change in Factor Substitution in Finnish Manufacturing. *Scand. J. Econ.*, 1989, *91*(4), pp. 705–21.

Tornell, Aaron. Inconsistencia dinámica de los programas proteccionistas. (The Inconsistency of Protectionist Programs. With English summary.) *Estud. Econ.*, Jan.–June 1989, *4*(1), pp. 61–82.

Törnkvist, Birgitta and Westlund, Anders H. On the Identification of Time for Structural Changes by MOSUM-SQ and CUSUM-SQ Procedures. In *Hackl, P., ed.*, 1989, pp. 97–126.

Torous, Walter N. and Franks, Julian R. An Empirical Investigation of U.S. Firms in Reorganization. *J. Finance*, July 1989, *44*(3), pp. 747–69.

_____ **and Schwartz, Eduardo S.** Prepayment and the Valuation of Mortgage-Backed Securities. *J. Finance*, June 1989, *44*(2), pp. 375–92.

_____ **and Titman, Sheridan D.** Valuing Commercial Mortgages: An Empirical Investigation of the Contingent-Claims Approach to Pricing

Risky Debt. *J. Finance,* June 1989, *44*(2), pp. 345–73.

Torrance, Thomas S.; Addison, John T. and Burton, John. Causation, Social Science and Sir John Hicks. In *Wood, J. C. and Woods, R. N., eds., Vol. 4,* 1989, *1984,* pp. 27–37.

_____ **and MacDonald, Ronald.** Some Survey-Based Tests of Uncovered Interest Parity. In *MacDonald, R. and Taylor, M. P., eds.,* 1989, pp. 239–48.

Torre, André. Allocation du crédit et changement structurel. L'exemple français (Une Analyse Verticalement Intégrée de la période 1978–1986). (Credit Allocation and Structural Change: The French Experience. With English summary.) *Écon. Appl.,* 1989, *42*(2), pp. 35–54.

de la Torre, Lidia and Korn, Francis. Housing in Buenos Aires 1887–1914. In *Platt, D. C. M., ed.,* 1989, pp. 87–104.

Torrence, William D. and Love, Douglas O. The Value of Advance Notice of Worker Displacement. *Southern Econ. J.,* January 1989, *55*(3), pp. 626–43.

Torres, Francisco S. Portugal's Monetary Integration into a Changing Europe: A Proposal. *Economia (Portugal),* October 1989, *13*(3), pp. 395–405.

_____ . Sobre a adesão a uma união monetária com liderança e mobilidade perfeita de capitais. (With English summary.) *Economia (Portugal),* May 1989, *13*(2), pp. 233–54.

Torricelli, Costanza. A Survey in the Theory of Futures Markets. *Ricerche Econ.,* Oct.–Dec. 1989, *43*(4), pp. 516–42.

Torto, Raymond G. and Wheaton, William C. Income and Appraised Values: A Reexamination of the FRC Returns Data. *Amer. Real Estate Urban Econ. Assoc. J.,* Winter 1989, *17*(4), pp. 439–49.

Toshio, Kurokawa. Problems of the Japanese Working Class in Historical Perspective. In *Morris-Suzuki, T. and Seiyama, T., eds.,* 1989, pp. 131–65.

Toshio, Sumiya. The Structure and Operation of Monopoly Capital in Japan. In *Morris-Suzuki, T. and Seiyama, T., eds.,* 1989, pp. 105–30.

Toshkova, Svetla. Eminent Theoretician in Economics in Bulgaria (On the 90th Anniversary of the Birth of Professor Todor Vladigerov). In *Bulgarian Academy of Sciences, Institute of Economics,* 1989, pp. 207–15.

Totterdill, Peter and Zeitlin, Jonathan. Markets, Technology and Local Intervention: The Case of Clothing. In *Hirst, P. and Zeitlin, J., eds.,* 1989, pp. 155–90.

Tovey, C. A.; Trick, Michael A. and Bartholdi, J. J., III. The Computational Difficulty of Manipulating an Election. *Soc. Choice Welfare,* July 1989, *6*(3), pp. 227–41.

_____ ; **Trick, Michael A. and Bartholdi, J. J., III.** Voting Schemes for Which It Can Be Difficult to Tell Who Won the Election. *Soc. Choice Welfare,* April 1989, *6*(2), pp. 157–65.

Tovias, Alfred. Iberian Countries, Iberoamerica and the European Community. *World Econ.,* March 1989, *12*(1), pp. 105–15.

_____ . The Impact of the Entry of Spain into the EEC on the Prices of Factors of Production. *Econ. Int.,* Aug.–Nov. 1989, *42*(3–4), pp. 207–18.

Towe, Christopher M. Balanced Budget Constraints and the Time Consistency of Optimal Policy in a Non-Ricardian Economy. *Southern Econ. J.,* January 1989, *55*(3), pp. 547–58.

_____ . Exchange Rate "Fundamentals" versus Speculation in a Developing Economy: An Illustrative Example Using Lebanese Data. *Int. Monet. Fund Staff Pap.,* September 1989, *36*(3), pp. 678–707.

Tower, Edward. Excise Tax Evasion: Comment. *Public Finance,* 1989, *44*(3), pp. 506–09.

_____ . On the Dispersion of Optimum Tariffs on Goods with Fixed World Prices. *Rivista Int. Sci. Econ. Com.,* April–May 1989, *36*(4–5), pp. 407–12.

_____ **and Loo, Thomas.** Agricultural Protectionism and the Less Developed Countries: The Relationship between Agricultural Prices, Debt Servicing Capacities, and the Need for Development Aid. In *Stoeckel, A. B.; Vincent, D. and Cuthbertson, S., eds.,* 1989, pp. 64–93.

_____ ; **Webb, Michael A. and Copeland, Brian R.** On Negotiated Quotas, Tariffs, and Transfers. *Oxford Econ. Pap.,* October 1989, *41*(4), pp. 774–88.

Towers, Brian. Running the Gauntlet: British Trade Unions under Thatcher, 1979–1988. *Ind. Lab. Relat. Rev.,* January 1989, *42*(2), pp. 163–88.

Towey, Richard E. Economics Instruction with Lotus 1–2–3. *Econ. Inquiry,* April 1989, *27*(2), pp. 363–66.

Town, Robert and Milliman, Scott R. Competition in Deregulated Air Fares. In *Weiss, L. W., ed.,* 1989, pp. 163–67.

Townroe, Peter M. The Case for Experimental, Adaptive Restraint Policies in Developing Nation Metropolitan Areas. *Int. Reg. Sci. Rev.,* 1989, *12*(2), pp. 131–46.

Townsend, Gary and Constantino, Luis. Modeling Operating Rate Decisions in the Canadian Forest Industries. *Western J. Agr. Econ.,* December 1989, *14*(2), pp. 268–80.

Townsend, Robert M. Currency and Credit in a Private Information Economy. *J. Polit. Econ.,* December 1989, *97*(6), pp. 1323–44.

Toy, William W. and Zurack, Mark A. Tracking the Euro-Pac Index. *J. Portfol. Manage.,* Winter 1989, *15*(2), pp. 55–58.

Toyama, Nate and Train, Kenneth E. Pareto Dominance through Self-selecting Tariffs: The Case of TOU Electricity Rates for Agricultural Customers. *Energy J.,* January 1989, *10*(1), pp. 91–109.

Toye, John. Nicholas Kaldor and Tax Reform in Developing Countries. *Cambridge J. Econ.,* March 1989, *13*(1), pp. 183–200.

_____ . Nicholas Kaldor and Tax Reform in Developing Countries. In *Lawson, T.; Palma, J. G. and Sender, J.*, eds., 1989, pp. 183–200.

Toyoda, Toshihisa and Ohtani, Kazuhiro. A Switching Regression Model with Different Change-Points for Individual Coefficients and Its Application to the Energy Demand Equations for Japan. In *Kramer, W.*, ed., 1989, pp. 29–39.

_____ **and Ohtani, Kazuhiro.** A Switching Regression Model with Different Change-Points for Individual Coefficients and Its Application to the Energy Demand Equations for Japan. *Empirical Econ.*, 1989, 14(2), pp. 93–103.

_____ **and Ohtani, Kazuhiro.** Testing Equality between Sets of Coefficients in Two Linear Regressions When Error Terms Are Autocorrelated. *Econ. Stud. Quart.*, March 1989, 40(1), pp. 35–47.

Trabelsi, Abdelwahed and Hillmer, Steven C. A Benchmarking Approach to Forecast Combination. *J. Bus. Econ. Statist.*, July 1989, 7(3), pp. 353–62.

Tracy, D. S. and Srivastava, A. K. On Approximating the Minimum Risk Estimator in Linear Regression Models. *Econ. Letters*, 1989, 29(2), pp. 153–56.

Tracy, Joseph S. and Abowd, John M. Market Structure, Strike Activity, and Union Wage Settlements. *Ind. Relat.*, Spring 1989, 28(2), pp. 227–50.

_____ **and Gyourko, Joseph.** The Importance of Local Fiscal Conditions in Analyzing Local Labor Markets. *J. Polit. Econ.*, October 1989, 97(5), pp. 1208–31.

_____ **and Gyourko, Joseph.** Local Public Sector Rent-Seeking and Its Impact on Local Land Values. *Reg. Sci. Urban Econ.*, August 1989, 19(3), pp. 493–516.

_____ **and Gyourko, Joseph.** On the Political Economy of Land Value Capitalization and Local Public Sector Rent Seeking in a Tiebout Model. *J. Urban Econ.*, September 1989, 26(2), pp. 152–73.

Train, Kenneth E.; Ben-Akiva, Moshe and Atherton, Terry. Consumption Patterns and Self-selecting Tariffs. *Rev. Econ. Statist.*, February 1989, 71(1), pp. 62–73.

_____ **and Toyama, Nate.** Pareto Dominance through Self-selecting Tariffs: The Case of TOU Electricity Rates for Agricultural Customers. *Energy J.*, January 1989, 10(1), pp. 91–109.

Trainor, Richard. The Gentrification of Victorian and Edwardian Industrialists. In *[Stone, L.]*, 1989, pp. 167–97.

Trajtenberg, Manuel. The Welfare Analysis of Product Innovations, with an Application to Computed Tomography Scanners. *J. Polit. Econ.*, April 1989, 97(2), pp. 444–79.

_____ **and Yitzhaki, Shlomo.** The Diffusion of Innovations: A Methodological Reappraisal. *J. Bus. Econ. Statist.*, January 1989, 7(1), pp. 35–47.

Tramontozzi, Paul N. and Besharov, Douglas J. Federal Child Care Assistance: A Growing Middle-Class Entitlement. *J. Policy Anal. Manage.*, Spring 1989, 8(2), pp. 313–18.

Tran, Lien H. and Oyejide, T. Ademola. Food and Agricultural Imports of Sub-Saharan Africa. In *Islam, N.*, ed., 1989, pp. 147–64.

Tran-Nguyen, Anh-Nga. Can Debt Conversions Be a Solution to the Debt Problem? In *Mrak, M.*, ed., 1989, pp. 145–72.

_____. The Monetary and Financial Aspects of South–South Trade. In *Ventura-Dias, V.*, ed., 1989, pp. 82–109.

Trant, Gerald I. Agriculture's Contribution to Development. *Can. J. Agr. Econ.*, Part 2, December 1989, 37(4), pp. 805–12.

_____. Population Growth, Food Consumption Requirements, and the Problem of Hunger. In *Helmuth, J. W. and Johnson, S. R.*, eds., Vol. 1, 1989, pp. 149–55.

Traore, Kalilou and Konate, M. Operational Agroclimatic Assistance to Agriculture in Sub-Saharan Africa: A Case Study. In *Oram, P. A., et al.*, 1989, pp. 193–202.

Trapp, James N. A Commodity Market Simulation Game for Teaching Market Risk Management. *Southern J. Agr. Econ.*, July 1989, 21(1), pp. 139–47.

_____. The Dawning of the Age of Dynamic Theory: Its Implication for Agricultural Economics Research and Teaching. *Southern J. Agr. Econ.*, July 1989, 21(1), pp. 1–11.

_____. Simulation and Systems Modeling. In *Tweeten, L.*, ed., 1989, pp. 128–88.

Traugott, Michael W.; Groves, Robert M. and Lepkowski, James M. Using Dual Frame Designs to Reduce Nonresponse in Telephone Surveys. In *Singer, E. and Presser, S.*, eds., 1989, 1987, pp. 79–96.

_____ **and Katosh, John P.** The Consequences of Validated and Self-Reported Voting Measures. In *Singer, E. and Presser, S.*, eds., 1989, 1981, pp. 327–43.

Travaglini, Guido. Keynesian versus Walrasian Price and Quantity Determination. A Technical Note. *Rivista Int. Sci. Econ. Com.*, April–May 1989, 36(4–5), pp. 359–69.

Travers, T. C.; Clements, L. C. and Allen, D. N. Pricing of New Vehicles in the Australian Consumer Price Index: Adjusting for Quality Change. In *Turvey, R.*, 1989, pp. 163–65.

Travlos, Nickolaos G. and Millon-Cornett, Marcia H. Information Effects Associated with Debt-for-Equity and Equity-for-Debt Exchange Offers. *J. Finance*, June 1989, 44(2), pp. 451–68.

de Tray, Dennis. The Interface between Population and Development Models, Plans and Policies: Comments. *Pakistan Devel. Rev.*, Winter 1989, 28(4), pp. 408–11.

_____. Reducing Poverty in Developing Countries—Some Basic Principles for Policy Design. *Pakistan Devel. Rev.*, Winter 1989, 28(4), pp. 437–60.

_____ **and Fischer, Stanley.** Proceedings of the World Bank Annual Conference on Development Economics 1989: Introduction. In *Fischer, S. and de Tray, D.*, eds., 1989, pp. 1–9.

Treadgold, Malcolm L. and Hall, Peter H. Aggregate Demand Curves: A Response. *J. Macroecon.*, Winter 1989, *11*(1), pp. 141–43.

Treat, Barbara Laflin and Treat, John Elting. The Future of "Futures." In *[Evans, J. K.]*, 1989, pp. 182–95.

Treat, John Elting and Treat, Barbara Laflin. The Future of "Futures." In *[Evans, J. K.]*, 1989, pp. 182–95.

Trebilcock, Anne M. AIDS and the Workplace: Some Policy Pointers from International Labour Standards. *Int. Lab. Rev.*, 1989, *128*(1), pp. 29–45.

Trebilcock, Michael J. A Depressed View of Policies for Depressed Industries: Comment. In *Stern, R. M., ed.*, 1989, pp. 213–18.

Trebing, Harry M. Apologetics of Deregulation in Energy and Telecommunications: An Institutionalist Assessment. In *Tool, M. R. and Samuels, W. J., eds. (III)*, 1989, *1986*, pp. 333–52.

_____. Public Control of Enterprise: Neoclassical Assault and Neoinstitutional Reform. In *Tool, M. R. and Samuels, W. J., eds. (II)*, 1989, *1984*, pp. 496–511.

_____. Realism and Relevance in Public Utility Regulation. In *Tool, M. R. and Samuels, W. J., eds. (III)*, 1989, *1974*, pp. 307–31.

_____. Restoring Purposeful Government: The Galbraithian Contribution. *J. Econ. Issues*, June 1989, *23*(2), pp. 393–411.

Treble, John G. The 'Chilling Effect' of Conventional Arbitration: A Counterexample. *Bull. Econ. Res.*, January 1989, *41*(1), pp. 59–67.

_____ and Barmby, Tim. A Note on Absenteeism. *Brit. J. Ind. Relat.*, March 1989, *27*(1), pp. 155–58.

Treglia, Michael. Manipulation of the Pareto Semi-optimal Rule. *Econ. Letters*, 1989, *29*(2), pp. 121–25.

Trehan, Bharat. Forecasting Growth in Current Quarter Real GNP. *Fed. Res. Bank San Francisco Econ. Rev.*, Winter 1989, (1), pp. 39–52.

_____ and Judd, John P. Unemployment-Rate Dynamics: Aggregate-Demand and -Supply Interactions. *Fed. Res. Bank San Francisco Econ. Rev.*, Fall 1989, (4), pp. 20–37.

Trelawny, P. M. and Stonehouse, D. P. The Effects of Introducing Supplemental Bovine Somatotropin to the Canadian Dairy Industry. *Can. J. Agr. Econ.*, July 1989, *37*(2), pp. 191–209.

Tremblay, Diane G. From Work-Sharing to the Flexibilisation of Working Hours: A Comparative Analysis of the Cases of Canada and France. In *Agassi, J. B. and Heycock, S., eds.*, 1989, pp. 67–83.

Treml, Vladimir G. Dr. Vanous's "Dark Side of Glasnost" Revisited. *Comp. Econ. Stud.*, Winter 1989, *31*(4), pp. 95–109.

_____. The Most Recent Input–Output Table: A Milestone in Soviet Statistics. *Soviet Econ.*, Oct.–Dec. 1989, *5*(4), pp. 341–59.

Trengove, C. D. and Logan, J. Extract from "Forum on Health Insurance in Australia: Financing Health Care—Which Way from Here?" In *Butler, J. R. G. and Doessel, D. P., eds.*, 1989, *1988*, pp. 185–88.

Trenkler, G. and Wijekoon, P. Mean Square Error Matrix Superiority of Estimators under Linear Restrictions and Misspecification. *Econ. Letters*, August 1989, *30*(2), pp. 141–49.

de Trenqualye, Pierre. Stable Implementation of Lindahl Allocations. *Econ. Letters*, 1989, *29*(4), pp. 291–94.

Tresch, Richard W. Fundamentals Relating to the Economic Functions of Government. In *Samuels, W. J., ed. (I)*, 1989, pp. 187–96.

Trescott, Paul B. Scottish Political Economy Comes to the Far East: The Burton–Chambers *Political Economy* and the Introduction of Western Economic Ideas into Japan and China. *Hist. Polit. Econ.*, Fall 1989, *21*(3), pp. 481–502.

Tresnowski, Bernard R. Have We Reached a New Threshold of Major Change? *Inquiry*, Winter 1989, *26*(4), pp. 415–17.

_____. Hospitals' Responses to Fiscal Pressures May Hold Lessons for Us. *Inquiry*, Fall 1989, *26*(3), pp. 315–16.

Tretheway, Michael W.; Gillen, David W. and Oum, Tae Hoon. Privatization of Air Canada: Why It Is Necessary in a Deregulated Environment. *Can. Public Policy*, September 1989, *15*(3), pp. 285–99.

_____ and Oum, Tae Hoon. Hedonic vs. General Specifications of the Translog Cost Function. *Logist. Transp. Rev.*, March 1989, *25*(1), pp. 3–21.

Treuer, Philip and Briesemeister, Janee. Telecommunications Policy and Economic Development: The New State Role: Vermont. In *Schmandt, J.; Williams, F. and Wilson, R. H., eds.*, 1989, pp. 185–212.

Trevor, Leigh B. Hostile Takeovers: A U.S. Falkland Islands Where the Argentines Always Win. In *McKee, D. L., ed.*, 1989, pp. 16–32.

Treyz, George I.; Lahr, Michael L. and Stevens, Benjamin H. On the Comparative Accuracy of RPC Estimating Techniques. In *Miller, R. E.; Polenske, K. R. and Rose, A. Z., eds.*, 1989, pp. 245–57.

Trezise, Philip H. What's Next with Export Controls? In *Bosworth, B. P., et al.*, 1989, pp. 170–75.

_____ and Fried, Edward R. Third World Debt: The Next Phase: Overview. In *Fried, E. R. and Trezise, P. H., eds.*, 1989, pp. 3–16.

_____ and Fried, Edward R. Third World Debt: The Next Phase: Preface. In *Fried, E. R. and Trezise, P. H., eds.*, 1989, pp. vii–viii.

Triantis, Konstantinos P. and Seaver, Bill L. The Implications of Using Messy Data to Estimate Production-Frontier–Based Technical Efficiency Measures. *J. Bus. Econ. Statist.*, January 1989, *7*(1), pp. 49–59.

Tribedy, Gopal; Beladi, Hamid and Biswas, Basudeb. General Equilibrium Analysis of Negative Value-Added. *J. Econ. Stud.*, 1989, *16*(1), pp. 47–53.

Trick, Michael A. Recognizing Single-Peaked Preferences on a Tree. *Math. Soc. Sci.*, June 1989, *17*(3), pp. 329–34.

———; **Bartholdi, J. J., III and Tovey, C. A.** The Computational Difficulty of Manipulating an Election. *Soc. Choice Welfare*, July 1989, *6*(3), pp. 227–41.

———; **Bartholdi, J. J., III and Tovey, C. A.** Voting Schemes for Which It Can Be Difficult to Tell Who Won the Election. *Soc. Choice Welfare*, April 1989, *6*(2), pp. 157–65.

Triffin, Robert. Alternative or Complementary Anchors for the Paper-Exchange Standard: The Dollar and Its Major Rivals, or a Reformed SDR and the ECU? In *Kaushik, S. K., ed.*, 1989, pp. 17–33.

———. Correcting the World Monetary Scandal. In *Guttmann, R., ed.*, 1989, *1986*, pp. 271–81.

———. A European Monetary Bank with Central Bank Functions. In *Franz, O., ed.*, 1989, pp. 131–41.

———. The Intermixture of Politics and Economics in the World Monetary Scandal: Diagnosis and Prescription. *Amer. Economist*, Spring 1989, *33*(1), pp. 5–15.

———. The International Monetary System and the Paper-Exchange Standard. In *Hamouda, O. F.; Rowley, R. and Wolf, B. M., eds.*, 1989, pp. 35–41.

Trifts, Jack W.; Pettway, Richard H. and Scanlon, Kevin P. Impacts of Relative Size and Industrial Relatedness on Returns to Shareholders of Acquiring Firms. *J. Finan. Res.*, Summer 1989, *12*(2), pp. 103–12.

Trigilia, Carlo. Small-Firm Development and Political Subcultures in Italy. In *Goodman, E. and Bamford, J., eds.*, 1989, pp. 174–97.

Trigueros, Ignacio. A Free Trade Agreement between Mexico and the United States? In *Schott, J. J., ed.*, 1989, pp. 255–67.

Trimble, John L.; Johnson, Ruth C. and Kaserman, David L. Equilibration in a Negotiated Market: Evidence from Housing. *J. Urban Econ.*, July 1989, *26*(1), pp. 30–42.

Trimble, Robert F. and Augustine, Norman R. Procurement Competition at Work: The Manufacturer's Experience. *Yale J. Regul.*, Summer 1989, *6*(2), pp. 333–47.

Trinczek, Rainer and Schmidt, Rudi. Standardised and Differentiated Working Hours in the Context of an Increasing Deregulation of Working Conditions—The West German Experience. In *Agassi, J. B. and Heycock, S., eds.*, 1989, pp. 129–36.

Triplett, Jack E. Price and Technological Change in a Capital Good: A Survey of Research on Computers. In *Jorgenson, D. W. and Landau, R., eds.*, 1989, pp. 127–213.

———; **Cole, Rosanne and Dulberger, Ellen R.** The Postwar Evolution of Computer Prices: Comment. In *Jorgenson, D. W. and Landau, R., eds.*, 1989, pp. 215–19.

Tripp, James T. B. and Dudek, Daniel J. Institutional Guidelines for Designing Successful Transferable Rights Programs. *Yale J. Regul.*, Summer 1989, *6*(2), pp. 369–91.

Trippi, Robert R. A Discount Rate Adjustment for Calculation of Expected Net Present Values and Internal Rates of Return of Investments Whose Lives Are Uncertain. *J. Econ. Bus.*, May 1989, *41*(2), pp. 143–51.

Tříska, Dušan and Klaus, Václav. The Economic Centre: The Restructuring and Equilibrium. *Czech. Econ. Digest.*, February 1989, (1), pp. 34–56.

Tristani, M. Gloria. Interior Turns Off Tap for Wilderness Areas. *Natural Res. J.*, Summer 1989, *29*(3), pp. 877–94.

Trivedi, P. K. and Alexander, J. N. Reemployment Probability and Multiple Unemployment Spells: A Partial-Likelihood Approach. *J. Bus. Econ. Statist.*, July 1989, *7*(3), pp. 395–401.

——— **and Yeo, Stephen J.** On Using Ridge-Type Estimators for a Distributed Lag Model. *Oxford Bull. Econ. Statist.*, February 1989, *51*(1), pp. 85–90.

Trivedi, Prajapati. The Demand for Working Capital: A Rejoinder. *Appl. Econ.*, January 1989, *21*(1), pp. 141–42.

Trivellato, Ugo and Bordignon, Silvano. The Optimal Use of Provisional Data in Forecasting with Dynamic Models. *J. Bus. Econ. Statist.*, April 1989, *7*(2), pp. 275–86.

——— **and Torelli, Nicola.** Youth Unemployment Duration from the Italian Labour Force Survey: Accuracy Issues and Modelling Attempts. *Europ. Econ. Rev.*, March 1989, *33*(2/3), pp. 407–15.

Trockel, Walter. Classification of Budget-Invariant Monotonic Preferences. *Econ. Letters*, 1989, *30*(1), pp. 7–10.

Troesken, Werner. A Note on the Efficacy of the German Steel and Coal Syndicates. *J. Europ. Econ. Hist.*, Winter 1989, *18*(3), pp. 595–603.

Trombley, Mark A. Accounting Method Choice in the Software Industry: Characteristics of Firms Electing Early Adoption of SFAS No. 86. *Accounting Rev.*, July 1989, *64*(3), pp. 529–38.

Tromp, D.; Smit, E. van der M. and de Coning, T. J. Die Soeke na Suksesfaktore in Klein Ondernemings—'n Pragmatiese Benadering. (With English summary.) *J. Stud. Econ. Econometrics*, March 1989, *13*(1), pp. 1–17.

Tronstad, Russell and McNeill, Thomas J. Asymmetric Price Risk: An Econometric Analysis of Aggregate Sow Farrowings, 1973–86. *Amer. J. Agr. Econ.*, August 1989, *71*(3), pp. 630–37.

Tropeano, Domenico. Exchange Rate Determination Theory During World War I: Cassel versus Wicksell. *Econ. Notes*, 1989, (2), pp. 210–28.

Trotman, Ken and Simnett, Roger. Auditor versus Model: Information Choice and Information Processing. *Accounting Rev.*, July 1989, *64*(3), pp. 514–28.

Troutt, Marvin D. and Clinton, Roy J. Interactive Optimization: An Optimal Scaling and Step Sizing Approach for the Method of Abstract

Forces. In *Lockett, A. G. and Islei, G., eds.*, 1989, pp. 58–67.

Troye, Sigurd Villads and Selnes, Fred. Buying Expertise, Information Search, and Problem Solving. *J. Econ. Psych.*, November 1989, *10*(3), pp. 411–28.

Trueblood, Michael Alan. Agricultural Production Function Estimates from Aggregate Intercountry Observations: A Selected Survey. *Can. J. Agr. Econ.*, Part 2, December 1989, *37*(4), pp. 1045–60.

Truett, Dale B. and Truett, Lila J. An Intertemporal Cross-Section Analysis of Economies of Scale in Mexican Manufacturing. *Growth Change*, Fall 1989, *20*(4), pp. 66–80.

_____ **and Truett, Lila J.** Level of Development and the U.S. Generalised System of Preferences: Malaysia and Mexico. *J. Devel. Stud.*, January 1989, *25*(2), pp. 226–39.

Truett, Lila J. and Truett, Dale B. An Intertemporal Cross-Section Analysis of Economies of Scale in Mexican Manufacturing. *Growth Change*, Fall 1989, *20*(4), pp. 66–80.

_____ **and Truett, Dale B.** Level of Development and the U.S. Generalised System of Preferences: Malaysia and Mexico. *J. Devel. Stud.*, January 1989, *25*(2), pp. 226–39.

Truman, Edwin M. Correcting Global Imbalances: A Simulation Approach: Comment. In *Stern, R. M., ed.*, 1989, pp. 424–27.

_____. U.S. Policy on the Problems of International Debt. *Fed. Res. Bull.*, November 1989, *75*(11), pp. 727–35.

Trumble, David and Hirst, Eric. Effects of the Hood River Conservation Project on Electricity Use and Savings in Single-Family Homes. *Appl. Econ.*, August 1989, *21*(8), pp. 1029–42.

Trumbull, William N. Estimations of the Economic Model of Crime Using Aggregate and Individual Level Data. *Southern Econ. J.*, October 1989, *56*(2), pp. 423–39.

Truong, T. P.; Nguyen, V. A. and Hall, V. B. Responses to World Oil and Coal Shocks, in a Short-run Fuel Substitution Tax Model. *Australian Econ. Rev.*, Spring 1989, (87), pp. 25–38.

Trussell, James; van de Walle, Etienne and van de Walle, Francine. Norms and Behaviour in Burkinabe Fertility. *Population Stud.*, November 1989, *43*(3), pp. 429–54.

Truu, M. L. Economics of Perestroika: Review Article. *S. Afr. J. Econ.*, June 1989, *57*(2), pp. 161–74.

_____. Sir John Hicks on *Monetary Theory* (Review Article). In *Wood, J. C. and Woods, R. N., eds., Vol. 2*, 1989, *1970*, pp. 131–46.

_____. Where Was Economics When the Renaissance Happened? *S. Afr. J. Econ.*, December 1989, *57*(4), pp. 362–79.

Tryon, Ralph. Policy Analysis with a Multicountry Model: Comment. In *Bryant, R. C., et al., eds.*, 1989, pp. 146–50.

Trzcinski, Eileen and Randolph, Susan. Relative Earnings Mobility in a Third World Country. *World Devel.*, April 1989, *17*(4), pp. 513–24.

Trzeciakowski, Witold. Reform, Restructuring,

Indebtedness. *Eastern Europ. Econ.*, Spring 1989, *27*(3), pp. 5–23.

Tsai, Pan-Long. Foreign Investment, Technology Transfer and Foreign Capital Impact Function. *Int. Econ. J.*, Summer 1989, *3*(2), pp. 43–56.

_____. A Note on the Symmetry between Lerner's Case and Metzler's Paradox. *J. Int. Econ.*, November 1989, *27*(3–4), pp. 373–79.

Tsakaloyannis, Panos. The EC: From Civilian Power to Military Integration. In *Lodge, J., ed.*, 1989, pp. 241–55.

Tsanacas, Demetri P. Market Share Effects of the Lomé Convention and the GSP. In *Gray, H. P., ed.*, 1989, pp. 129–207.

Tsang, Mun C. and Levin, Henry M. The Economics of Overeducation: Reply. *Econ. Educ. Rev.*, 1989, *8*(2), pp. 209.

Tsaur, Tien-wang; Liu, Shun-chieh and Chen, Chau-nan. Currency Substitution, Foreign Inflation, and Terms-of-Trade Dynamics. *J. Polit. Econ.*, August 1989, *97*(4), pp. 955–64.

Tsay, Ruey S. Parsimonious Parameterization of Vector Autoregressive Moving Average Models. *J. Bus. Econ. Statist.*, July 1989, *7*(3), pp. 327–41.

_____. Testing and Modeling Threshold Autoregressive Processes. *J. Amer. Statist. Assoc.*, March 1989, *84*(405), pp. 231–40.

Tschinkel, Sheila L.; Whitehead, David D. and King, B. Frank. Interstate Banking Developments in the 1980s. *Fed. Res. Bank Atlanta Econ. Rev.*, May–June 1989, *74*(3), pp. 32–51.

Tschirhart, John. Partial Regulation of Natural Monopoly. In *Shogren, J. F., ed.*, 1989, pp. 55–81.

_____. Ranking Economics Departments in Areas of Expertise. *J. Econ. Educ.*, Spring 1989, *20*(2), pp. 199–222.

Tse, David K.; Belk, Russell W. and Zhou, Nan. Becoming a Consumer Society: A Longitudinal and Cross-cultural Content Analysis of Print Ads from Hong Kong, the People's Republic of China, and Taiwan. *J. Cons. Res.*, March 1989, *15*(4), pp. 457–72.

Tse, Edison T. S. and Khilnani, Arvind. A Note on the Radius of Convergence of the U.S.A. Algorithm. *J. Econ. Dynam. Control*, April 1989, *13*(2), pp. 313–16.

_____ **and Viswanathan, Nagarathnam.** Monopolistic Provision of Congested Service with Incentive-Based Allocation of Priorities. *Int. Econ. Rev.*, February 1989, *30*(1), pp. 153–74.

Tse, Senyo and Freeman, Robert N. The Multiperiod Information Content of Accounting Earnings: Confirmations and Contradictions of Previous Earnings Reports. *J. Acc. Res.*, Supplement, 1989, *27*, pp. 49–79.

Tse, Y. K. A Proportional Random Utility Approach to Qualitative Response Models. *J. Bus. Econ. Statist.*, January 1989, *7*(1), pp. 61–65.

_____ **and Kalirajan, K. P.** Technical Efficiency Measures for the Malaysian Food Manufacturing Industry. *Developing Econ.*, June 1989, *27*(2), pp. 174–84.

_____ **and Tse, Y. M.** Exact Maximum Likelihood Estimation of Vector ARMA Processes.

In *Mariano, R. S.; Lim, K. S. and Ling, K. D., eds.*, 1989, pp. 71–84.

Tse, Y. M. and Tse, Y. K. Exact Maximum Likelihood Estimation of Vector ARMA Processes. In *Mariano, R. S.; Lim, K. S. and Ling, K. D., eds.*, 1989, pp. 71–84.

Tseng, Tseng-Tsai. Energy Sector Performance and Economic Development in Taiwan. In *James, W. E., ed.*, 1989, pp. 123–32.

Tsenova, Victoria. Long-Term Programmes in Forming the Strategy of Scientific and Technological Development. In *Bulgarian Academy of Sciences, Institute of Economics*, 1989, pp. 84–88.

Tsiang, S. C. A Critical Note on the Optimum Supply of Money. In *Tsiang, S. C.*, 1989, *1969*, pp. 331–48.

_____. The Diffusion of Reserves and the Money Supply Multiplier. In *Tsiang, S. C.*, 1989, *1978*, pp. 249–69.

_____. Fashions and Misconceptions in Monetary Theory and Their Influences on Financial and Banking Policies. In *Tsiang, S. C.*, 1989, *1979*, pp. 107–30.

_____. Feasibility and Desirability of a U.S.–Taiwan Free Trade Agreement. In *Schott, J. J., ed.*, 1989, pp. 159–66.

_____. Finance Constraints and the Theory of Money: Selected Papers: Introduction. In *Tsiang, S. C.*, 1989, pp. 1–24.

_____. The Flow Formulation of the Money Market Equilibrium for an Open Economy and the Determination of the Exchange Rate. In *Tsiang, S. C.*, 1989, *1988*, pp. 191–217.

_____. Keynes' "Finance" Demand for Liquidity, Robertson's Loanable Funds Theory, and Friedman's Monetarism. In *Tsiang, S. C.*, 1989, *1980*, pp. 303–30.

_____. Liquidity Preference and Loanable Funds Theories, Multiplier and Velocity Analyses: A Synthesis. In *Tsiang, S. C.*, 1989, *1956*, pp. 49–76.

_____. The Monetary Theoretic Foundation of the Modern Monetary Approach to the Balance of Payments. In *Tsiang, S. C.*, 1989, *1977*, pp. 153–75.

_____. A Note on Speculation and Income Stability. In *Tsiang, S. C.*, 1989, *1943*, pp. 27–47.

_____. The Rationale of the Mean-Standard Deviation Analysis, Skewness Preference, and the Demand for Money. In *Tsiang, S. C.*, 1989, *1972*, pp. 221–48.

_____. The Role of Money in Trade-Balance Stability: Synthesis of the Elasticity and Absorption Approaches. In *Tsiang, S. C.*, 1989, *1961*, pp. 77–106.

_____. Stock or Portfolio Approach to Monetary Theory and the Neo-Keynesian School of James Tobin. In *Tsiang, S. C.*, 1989, *1982*, pp. 271–99.

_____. The Total Inadequacy of "Keynesian" Balance of Payments Theory, or Rather That of "Walras' Law"? In *Tsiang, S. C.*, 1989, *1985*, pp. 177–89.

_____. Walras' Law, Say's Law, and Liquidity Preference in General Equilibrium Analysis.

In *Tsiang, S. C.*, 1989, *1966*, pp. 133–51.

Tsigas, Marinos E. and Hertel, Thomas W. Testing Dynamic Models of the Farm Firm. *Western J. Agr. Econ.*, July 1989, *14*(1), pp. 20–29.

_____; **Hertel, Thomas W. and Thompson, Robert L.** Economywide Effects of Unilateral Trade and Policy Liberalization in U.S. Agriculture. In *Stoeckel, A. B.; Vincent, D. and Cuthbertson, S., eds.*, 1989, pp. 260–92.

Tsoukias, Alexis and Balestra, Gabriella. Preparing an Intelligent Interface for the Use of Multicriteria Outranking Methods. In *Lockett, A. G. and Islei, G., eds.*, 1989, pp. 575–84.

Tsoulfidis, Lefteris. The Physiocratic Theory of Tax Incidence. *Scot. J. Polit. Econ.*, August 1989, *36*(3), pp. 301–10.

Tsuang, Grace W. Assuring Equal Access of Asian Americans to Highly Selective Universities. *Yale Law J.*, January 1989, *98*(3), pp. 659–78.

Tsuchiya, Moriaki. The Changing Pacific Rim Economy, with Special Reference to Japanese Transnational Corporations: A View from Australia: Comment. In *Shiraishi, T. and Tsuru, S., eds.*, 1989, pp. 79–81.

Tsui, Kam-Wah; Leonard, Tom and Hsu, John S. J. Bayesian Marginal Inference. *J. Amer. Statist. Assoc.*, December 1989, *84*(408), pp. 1051–58.

Tsukuda, Yoshihiko. Comparison of Single Equation Methods of Prediction in a Simultaneous Equation System. *Econ. Stud. Quart.*, March 1989, *40*(1), pp. 23–34.

Tsukui, Jinkichi and Hori, Hajime. Rolling Plans and the Turnpike in a Dynamic Input–Output System: A Simulation Study. *J. Policy Modeling*, Spring 1989, *11*(1), pp. 91–109.

Tsuneki, Atsushi. The Measurement of the Benefits of Public Inputs with Distortionary Taxation. *Can. J. Econ.*, November 1989, *22*(4), pp. 885–91.

_____. The Measurement of Waste with Increasing Returns to Scale. *Econ. Stud. Quart.*, September 1989, *40*(3), pp. 276–88.

Tsur, Yacov. On Testing for Revealed Preference Conditions. *Econ. Letters*, December 1989, *31*(4), pp. 359–62.

_____; **Zilberman, David and Parliament, Claudia.** Cooperative Labor Allocation under Uncertainty. *J. Compar. Econ.*, December 1989, *13*(4), pp. 539–52.

Tsuru, Shigeto. Keynote Address: Economics of Institutions or Institutional Economics. In *Shiraishi, T. and Tsuru, S., eds.*, 1989, pp. 1–23.

Tsurumi, Hiroki. Detection of Join Point in Regression Models. In *Hackl, P., ed.*, 1989, pp. 87–95.

Tsutsui, Yoshiro and Mori, Nobuhiro. Bank Market Structure and Performance: Evidence from Japan. *Econ. Stud. Quart.*, December 1989, *40*(4), pp. 296–316.

Tubbs, Richard M.; Bamber, E. Michael and Snowball, Doug. Audit Structure and Its Relation to Role Conflict and Role Ambiguity: An Empirical Investigation. *Accounting Rev.*, April 1989, *64*(2), pp. 285–99.

Tubiana, Laurence. World Trade in Agricultural Products: From Global Regulation to Market Fragmentation. In *Goodman, D. and Redclift, M., eds.*, 1989, pp. 23–45.

Tuccillo, John A. The Thrift Crisis and the Financing of Real Estate. In *Schwartz, E. and Vasconcellos, G. M., eds.*, 1989, pp. 43–47.

Tuchtfeldt, Egon. Will Communism and Capitalism Become Similar Economic Systems? In *Peacock, A. and Willgerodt, H., eds. (II)*, 1989, *1969*, pp. 87–105.

Tucker, Alan L. and Scott, Elton. Predicting Currency Return Volatility. *J. Banking Finance*, December 1989, *13*(6), pp. 839–51.

Tucker, Michael J. and Parker, Larry M. CPAs as Financial Planners: Responsibilities under the Investment Advisers Act of 1940. In *Gangolly, J., ed.*, 1989, pp. 89–101.

Tucker, Paula K. and Clair, Robert T. Interstate Banking and the Federal Reserve: A Historical Perspective. *Fed. Res. Bank Dallas Econ. Rev.*, November 1989, pp. 1–20.

Tuckman, Howard P. and Chang, Cyril F. Teacher Training and Teacher Optimism about the American Economic System. *J. Econ. Educ.*, Fall 1989, *20*(4), pp. 335–45.

Tufano, Peter. Financial Innovation and First-Mover Advantages. *J. Finan. Econ.*, December 1989, *25*(2), pp. 213–40.

Tukey, John W.; Ericksen, Eugene P. and Kadane, Joseph B. Adjusting the 1980 Census of Population and Housing. *J. Amer. Statist. Assoc.*, December 1989, *84*(408), pp. 927–44.

Tulipana, F. Peter and Herman, Robert Dean. Board–Staff Relations and Perceived Effectiveness in Nonprofit Organizations. In *Herman, R. D. and Van Til, J., eds.*, 1989, pp. 48–59.

Tulkens, Henry and Thiry, Bernard. Productivity, Efficiency and Technical Progress: Concepts and Measurement. *Ann. Pub. Coop. Econ.*, 1989, *60*(1), pp. 9–42.

Tull, Donald S. and Albaum, Gerald S. Bias in Random Digit Dialed Surveys. In *Singer, E. and Presser, S., eds.*, 1989, *1977*, pp. 11–17.

Tullberg, Rita. External Debt: The Moral Dimension. In *Hamouda, O. F.; Rowley, R. and Wolf, B. M., eds.*, 1989, pp. 195–96.

Tullio, Giuseppe. Inflation Adjusted Government Budget Deficits and Their Impact on the Business Cycle: Empirical Evidence for Eight Industrial Countries. *Ann. Écon. Statist.*, Jan.–March 1989, (13), pp. 119–37.

————. Smith and Ricardo on the Long-run Effects of the Growth of Government Expenditure, Taxation, and Debt: Is Their Theory Relevant Today? *Hist. Polit. Econ.*, Winter 1989, *21*(4), pp. 723–36.

———— **and Bekx, P.** A Note on the European Monetary System, and the Determination of the DM–Dollar Exchange Rate. *Cah. Écon. Bruxelles*, 3rd Trimester 1989, (123), pp. 329–43.

———— **and Sommariva, Andrea.** The German Depression and the Stock Market Crash of the Thirties: The Role of Macropolicies and of the

International Business Cycle. *J. Banking Finance*, September 1989, *13*(4–5), pp. 515–36.

Tullock, Gordon. Changing Incentives to Make Economics More Relevant. In *Colander, D. C. and Coats, A. W., eds.*, 1989, pp. 235–47.

————. Why Austrians Are Wrong about Depressions: Reply. In *Rothbard, M. N. and Block, W., eds.*, 1989, pp. 147–49.

———— **and Grier, Kevin B.** An Empirical Analysis of Cross-National Economic Growth, 1951–80. *J. Monet. Econ.*, September 1989, *24*(2), pp. 259–76.

Tuluy, Hasan A. and Stryker, J. Dirck. Assistance to Ghana and the Ivory Coast. In *Krueger, A. O.; Michalopoulos, C. and Ruttan, V. W.*, 1989, pp. 269–302.

Tuma, Elias H. The Economic Impact of the Capitulations: The Middle East and Europe: A Reinterpretation. *J. Europ. Econ. Hist.*, Winter 1989, *18*(3), pp. 663–82.

————. The Economics of Occupation in Palestine since 1948 and the Costs of Noncooperation. In *Fishelson, G., ed.*, 1989, pp. 79–104.

Tumlir, Jan. Economic Policy for a Stable World Order. In *Dorn, J. A. and Niskanen, W. A., eds.*, 1989, *1984*, pp. 423–31.

————. Franz Böhm and the Development of Economic-Constitutional Analysis. In *Peacock, A. and Willgerodt, H., eds. (I)*, 1989, pp. 125–41.

Turan, Osman. A Passenger/Vehicle Ferry Design for the Mediterranean. In *Candemir, Y., ed.*, 1989, pp. 266–80.

Turay, Abdul M. and Hamdar, Bassam. The New International Debt Strategy for Indebted Nations: A Problem of Liquidity. *Econ. Int.*, Aug.–Nov. 1989, *42*(3–4), pp. 219–33.

Turchiano, B.; Maione, B. and Fanti, M. P. Large Scale Markov Chain Modelling of Transfer Lines. In *Archetti, F.; Lucertini, M. and Serafini, P., eds.*, 1989, pp. 193–211.

deTurck, Mark A. and Goldhaber, Gerald M. Effectiveness of Product Warning Labels: Effects of Consumers' Information Processing Objectives. *J. Cons. Aff.*, Summer 1989, *23*(1), pp. 111–26.

Ture, Norman B. What Can We Learn from the United States' Experience? In *Fels, G. and von Furstenberg, G. M., eds.*, 1989, pp. 107–32.

Turek, Otakar and Ježek, Tomáš. Structural Changes and the Economic Mechanism. *Czech. Econ. Digest.*, November 1989, (7), pp. 53–79.

Turke, Paul W. Evolution and the Demand for Children. *Population Devel. Rev.*, March 1989, *15*(1), pp. 61–90.

Turnbull, Geoffrey K. Household Behavior in a Monocentric Urban Area with a Public Sector. *J. Urban Econ.*, January 1989, *25*(1), pp. 103–15.

————. Land Markets and Tax Reform: The Effects of Passive Loss Limitations. *Land Econ.*, May 1989, *65*(2), pp. 118–30.

———— **and Boyd, Roy.** Dynamic Adjustment to Land Taxation Policy: Neutrality and Welfare

Implications. *J. Environ. Econ. Manage.*, May 1989, *16*(3), pp. 242–52.

_____ **and Boyd, Roy.** The Effects of Greenspace Tax Laws on Urban Development. *Rev. Reg. Stud.*, Spring 1989, *19*(2), pp. 30–39.

Turnbull, Peter and Mayhew, Ken. Models of Union Behaviour: A Critique of Recent Literature. In *Drago, R. and Perlman, R., eds.*, 1989, pp. 105–29.

Turnbull, Stuart M. and Boyle, Phelim P. Pricing and Hedging Capped Options. *J. Futures Markets*, February 1989, *9*(1), pp. 41–54.

Turner, Anthony G. The World Fertility Survey: An Appraisal of Methodology: Comment. *J. Amer. Statist. Assoc.*, September 1989, *84*(407), pp. 768–69.

Turner, Brian. U.S. Trade Policy: Implications for U.S.–Korean Relations: Discussion. In *Bayard, T. O. and Young, S.-G., eds.*, 1989, pp. 110–17.

Turner, Charlie G. Japanese Import Restrictions. *Quart. Rev. Econ. Bus.*, Spring 1989, *29*(1), pp. 82–91.

Turner, Christopher M.; Startz, Richard and Nelson, Charles R. A Markov Model of Heteroskedasticity, Risk, and Learning in the Stock Market. *J. Finan. Econ.*, November 1989, *25*(1), pp. 3–22.

Turner, David S. and Macdonald, Garry. A Ready Reckoner Package for Macroeconomics Teaching. *Oxford Bull. Econ. Statist.*, March 1989, *51*(2), pp. 193–211.

_____; **Wallis, Kenneth F. and Whitley, John D.** Differences in the Properties of Large-Scale Macroeconometric Models: The Role of Labour Market Specifications. *J. Appl. Econometrics*, Oct.–Dec. 1989, *4*(4), pp. 317–44.

Turner, Janet L. Who Cares Who Owns America? *Bus. Econ.*, April 1989, *24*(2), pp. 35–40.

Turner, John. Labour and Business in Modern Britain. In *Harvey, C. and Turner, J., eds.*, 1989, pp. 1–7.

Turner, John A. and Beller, Daniel J. Trends in Pensions: Introduction and Summary of Major Findings. In *Turner, J. A. and Beller, D. J., eds.*, 1989, pp. 1–14.

_____ **and Dailey, Lorna M.** U.S. Pensions in World Perspective. In *Turner, J. A. and Beller, D. J., eds.*, 1989, pp. 15–27.

_____ **and McCarthy, David D.** Pension Rates of Return in Large and Small Plans. In *Turner, J. A. and Beller, D. J., eds.*, 1989, pp. 235–86.

Turner, Louis. Oil Companies as Multinationals: The New Environment. In *[Evans, J. K.]*, 1989, pp. 196–204.

Turner, Martha J. and Hilton, Ronald W. Use of Accounting Product-Costing Systems in Making Production Decisions. *J. Acc. Res.*, Autumn 1989, *27*(2), pp. 297–312.

Turner, Michael. Benefits but at Cost: The Debates about Parliamentary Enclosure. In *Grantham, G. and Leonard, C. S., eds.*, Pt. A, 1989, pp. 49–67.

Turner, Paul. Monetary Interdependence and Deflation in Britain and the United States be-

tween the Wars: Discussion. In *Miller, M.; Eichengreen, B. and Portes, R., eds.*, 1989, pp. 71–72.

Turner, Robert W. Fringe Benefits: Should We Milk This Sacred Cow? *Nat. Tax J.*, September 1989, *42*(3), pp. 293–300.

Turnovsky, Stephen J. Risk, Exchange Market Intervention, and Private Speculative Behavior in a Small Open Economy. In *Stone, C. C., ed.*, 1989, pp. 41–72.

_____. The Term Structure of Interest Rates and the Effects of Macroeconomic Policy. *J. Money, Credit, Banking*, August 1989, *21*(3), pp. 321–47.

_____ **and Bianconi, Marcelo.** Strategic Wages Policy and the Gains from Cooperation. In *[Verheyen, P.]*, 1989, pp. 191–222.

_____ **and d'Orey, Vasco.** The Choice of Monetary Instrument in Two Interdependent Economies under Uncertainty. *J. Monet. Econ.*, January 1989, *23*(1), pp. 121–33.

_____ **and Sen, Partha.** Deterioration of the Terms of Trade and Capital Accumulation: A Re-examination of the Laursen–Metzler Effect. *J. Int. Econ.*, May 1989, *26*(3/4), pp. 227–50.

_____ **and Sen, Partha.** Tariffs, Capital Accumulation, and the Current Account in a Small Open Economy. *Int. Econ. Rev.*, November 1989, *30*(4), pp. 811–31.

Turok, Ivan. Evaluation and Understanding in Local Economic Policy. *Urban Stud.*, December 1989, *26*(6), pp. 587–606.

Turunen-Red, A. H.; Woodland, A. D. and Diewert, W. E. Productivity- and Pareto-Improving Changes in Taxes and Tariffs. *Rev. Econ. Stud.*, April 1989, *56*(2), pp. 199–215.

Turvey, Calum G. The Relationship between Hedging with Futures and the Financing Function of Farm Management. *Can. J. Agr. Econ.*, Part 1, December 1989, *37*(4), pp. 629–38.

_____ **and Amanor-Boadu, Vincent.** Evaluating Premiums for a Farm Income Insurance Policy. *Can. J. Agr. Econ.*, July 1989, *37*(2), pp. 233–47.

_____ **and Baker, Timothy G.** Optimal Hedging under Alternative Capital Structures and Risk Aversion. *Can. J. Agr. Econ.*, March 1989, *37*(1), pp. 135–43.

Tusell, Fernando; Zubiri, Ignacio and Gallastegui, Immaculada. Cálculo del efecto de alteraciones fiscales en una economía abierta: El caso del I.V.A. en el País Vasco. (With English summary.) *Invest. Econ.*, May 1989, *13*(2), pp. 283–300.

Tüshaus, Ulrich. On the Interpretation of Median Relations. In *Opitz, O., ed.*, 1989, pp. 222–29.

Tushman, Michael L. and Nadler, David A. Leadership for Organizational Change. In *Mohrman, A. M., Jr., et al.*, 1989, pp. 100–119.

Tuss, Joseph P.; Riordan, Timothy H. and Oria, Maria E. Dayton's Capital Allocation Process. In *Matzer, J., Jr., ed.*, 1989, *1987*, pp. 21–37.

Tutwiler, M. Ann and Rossmiller, George E. The Potential for Agricultural Trade Reform. In *Helmuth, J. W. and Johnson, S. R., eds., Vol. 2*, 1989, pp. 303–12.

Tversky, Amos and Kahneman, Daniel. Judgment under Uncertainty: Heuristics and Biases. In *Diamond, P. and Rothschild, M., eds.*, 1989, *1974*, pp. 19–34.

Tweeten, Luther. Classical Welfare Analysis. In *Tweeten, L., ed.*, 1989, pp. 96–127.

———. Index Numbers and Aggregation. In *Tweeten, L., ed.*, 1989, pp. 373–91.

———. Macroeconomic Linkages to Agriculture. In *Tweeten, L., ed.*, 1989, pp. 355–72.

———; **Pyles, David and Henneberry, Shida.** Supply and Elasticity Estimation. In *Tweeten, L., ed.*, 1989, pp. 73–95.

Twenhafel, David and Strayer, Kerry. Telecommunications Policy and Economic Development: The New State Role: Washington. In *Schmandt, J.; Williams, F. and Wilson, R. H., eds.*, 1989, pp. 241–65.

———, **et al.** Telecommunications Policy and Economic Development: The New State Role: Introduction. In *Schmandt, J.; Williams, F. and Wilson, R. H., eds.*, 1989, pp. 1–16.

Twight, Charlotte. Institutional Underpinnings of Parochialism: The Case of Military Base Closures. *Cato J.*, Spring–Summer 1989, *9*(1), pp. 73–105.

Twilt, F.; Jonker, P. and Streng, M. Gradient Newton Flows for Complex Polynomials. In *Dolecki, S., ed.*, 1989, pp. 177–90.

Twomey, Michael J. The Debt Crisis and Latin American Agriculture. *J. Developing Areas*, July 1989, *23*(4), pp. 545–66.

Tybout, Alice M. and Meyers-Levy, Joan. Schema Congruity as a Basis for Product Evaluation. *J. Cons. Res.*, June 1989, *16*(1), pp. 39–54.

Tye, William B. Incentive Compatibility of the Revenue/Variable Cost Test for Rail Competitive Access. *Antitrust Bull.*, Spring 1989, *34*(1), pp. 153–84.

Tyers, Rodney and Anderson, Kym. Price Elasticities in International Food Trade: Synthetic Estimates from a Global Model. *J. Policy Modeling*, Fall 1989, *11*(3), pp. 315–44.

——— **and Falvey, Rodney E.** Border Price Changes and Domestic Welfare in the Presence of Subsidised Exports. *Oxford Econ. Pap.*, April 1989, *41*(2), pp. 434–51.

——— **and Yang, Yongzheng.** The Economic Costs of Food Self-Sufficiency in China. *World Devel.*, February 1989, *17*(2), pp. 237–53.

Tylecote, Andrew. The South in the Long Wave: Technological Dependence and the Dynamics of World Economic Growth. In *Di Matteo, M.; Goodwin, R. M. and Vercelli, A., eds.*, 1989, pp. 206–24.

Tynan, A. C. and Schlegelmilch, B. B. The Scope for Market Segmentation within the Charity Market: An Empirical Analysis. *Managerial Dec. Econ.*, June 1989, *10*(2), pp. 127–34.

Tyrchniewicz, Edward W. and Farrell, Carlyle A. J. Trade Preferences for Developing Countries: An Analysis of Canada's Trade with the Caribbean Basin. *Can. J. Agr. Econ.*, Part 2, December 1989, *37*(4), pp. 1231–40.

Tyson, Karen W., et al. The Value of Weapon System Reliability in a Combat Environment: Costs and Performance. In *Gulledge, T. R., Jr. and Litteral, L. A., eds.*, 1989, pp. 387–406.

Tyson, Laura D'Andrea. Differentiated Products, Economies of Scale, and Access to the Japanese Market: Comment. In *Feenstra, R. C., ed.*, 1989, pp. 175–80.

Tytgat, Bernard and Meulders, Danièle. The Emergence of Atypical Employment in the European Community. In *Rodgers, G. and Rodgers, J., eds.*, 1989, pp. 179–96.

Tzannatos, Zafiris. The Economics of Discrimination: Theory and British Evidence. In *Sapsford, D. and Tzannatos, Z., eds.*, 1989, pp. 177–207.

——— **and Psacharopoulos, George.** Female Labor Force Participation: An International Perspective. *World Bank Res. Observer*, July 1989, *4*(2), pp. 187–201.

——— **and Sapsford, David.** Labour Economics: An Overview of Some Recent Theoretical and Empirical Developments. In *Sapsford, D. and Tzannatos, Z., eds.*, 1989, pp. 1–6.

Tzeng, Gwo-Hshiung. Modeling Energy Demand and Socioeconomic Development of Taiwan. *Energy J.*, April 1989, *10*(2), pp. 133–52.

U.K. Department of Energy. The Demand for Energy. In *Helm, D.; Kay, J. and Thompson, D., eds.*, 1989, pp. 77–91.

Uchitelle, Elliot. The Effectiveness of Tax Amnesty Programs in Selected Countries. *Fed. Res. Bank New York Quart. Rev.*, Autumn 1989, *14*(3), pp. 48–53.

Uckmar, Victor. The Fiscal Treatment of Savings in Italy. *Rev. Econ. Cond. Italy*, Sept.–Dec. 1989, (3), pp. 331–35.

Uctum, Merih and Wickens, Michael R. Exchange Rate Determination, the Stock Market and Investment Finance. In *MacDonald, R. and Taylor, M. P., eds.*, 1989, pp. 142–58.

Udell, Gregory F. Loan Quality, Commercial Loan Review and Loan Officer Contracting. *J. Banking Finance*, July 1989, *13*(3), pp. 367–82.

Udgaonkar, Bhalchandra. Contributions of Science and Technology to the Alleviation of Underdevelopment. In *Rotblat, J. and Goldanskii, V. I., eds.*, 1989, pp. 235–39.

Udry, Chris; Binswanger, Hans P. and McIntire, John. Production Relations in Semi-arid African Agriculture. In *Bardhan, P., ed. (II)*, 1989, pp. 122–44.

Uekusa, Masu. The Effects of Innovations in Information Technology on Corporate and Industrial Organisation in Japan. In *Shiraishi, T. and Tsuru, S., eds.*, 1989, pp. 162–83.

Ugolini, G. Marco. Alcune considerazioni sull'importanza del turismo estero per la bilancia dei pagamenti italiana. (Some Considerations on the Importance of Foreign Tourism for the Italian Balance of Payments. With English summary.) *Econ. Int.*, Aug.–Nov. 1989, *42*(3–4), pp. 234–43.

Uhlaner, Carole Jean. "Relational Goods" and Participation: Incorporating Sociability into a Theory of Rational Action. *Public Choice*, September 1989, *62*(3), pp. 253–85.

Uhler, Robert G.; Nelson, Charles R. and Peck, Stephen C. The NERC Fan in Retrospect and Lessons for the Future. *Energy J.*, April 1989, *10*(2), pp. 91–107.

Uhlmann, Bernd and Kaas, Klaus Peter. Pharma-Marketing. Möglichkeiten und Grenzen nach der Strukturreform des Gesundheitswesens. (With English summary.) *Z. Betriebswirtshaft*, June 1989, *59*(6), pp. 620–36.

Ujihara, A. and Lichtenberg, A. J. Application of Nonlinear Mapping Theory to Commodity Price Fluctuations. *J. Econ. Dynam. Control*, April 1989, *13*(2), pp. 225–46.

Ulan, Michael and Dewald, William G. The U.S. Net International Investment Position: Misstated and Misunderstood. In *Dorn, J. A. and Niskanen, W. A., eds.*, 1989, pp. 363–94.

Ulbrich, Holley H. and Wallace, Myles S. Determinants of Club Membership: An Economic Approach. *Atlantic Econ. J.*, March 1989, *17*(1), pp. 8–15.

_____; **Wallace, Myles S. and Bowles, David.** Default Risk, Interest Differentials and Fiscal Policy: A New Look at Crowding Out. *Eastern Econ. J.*, July–Sept. 1989, *15*(3), pp. 203–12.

de Ulhoa Canto, Gilberto. The Constitutional Tax Reform 1988: An Overview: Brazil. *Bull. Int. Fiscal Doc.*, Aug.–Sept. 1989, *43*(8–9), pp. 379–82.

Ullah, Aman. Nonparametric Estimation and Hypothesis Testing in Econometric Models. In *Ullah, A., ed.*, 1989, pp. 101–27.

_____; **Carter, R. A. L. and Srivastava, Virendra K.** Corrigendum [The Sampling Distribution of Shrinkage Estimators and Their F-Ratios in the Regression Model]. *J. Econometrics*, February 1989, *40*(2), pp. 339.

_____; **Cribbett, P. F. and Lye, J. N.** Evaluation of the Two-Stage Least Squares Distribution Function by Imhof's Procedure. *J. Quant. Econ.*, January 1989, *5*(1), pp. 91–96.

Ullmo, Bernard. Le taux de change et l'emploi une critique des modèles macroéconomiques. (With English summary.) *Revue Écon. Politique*, Jan.–Feb. 1989, *99*(1), pp. 55–77.

Ulmer, Melville J. Human Values and Economic Science. In *Tool, M. R. and Samuels, W. J., eds. (II)*, 1989, *1974*, pp. 140–51.

Ulph, Alistair. The Incentives to Make Commitments in Wage Bargains. *Rev. Econ. Stud.*, July 1989, *56*(3), pp. 449–65.

_____. A Review of Books on Resource and Environmental Economics. *Bull. Econ. Res.*, July 1989, *41*(3), pp. 219–28.

_____ **and Read, Peter.** Monopoly Extraction under Performance Constraints. *Bull. Econ. Res.*, April 1989, *41*(2), pp. 107–22.

_____ **and Ulph, David.** Gains and Losses from Cartelisation in Markets for Exhaustible Re-

sources in the Absence of Binding Future Contracts. In *[Verheyen, P.]*, 1989, pp. 157–89.

_____ **and Ulph, David.** Labor Markets and Innovation. *J. Japanese Int. Economies*, December 1989, *3*(4), pp. 403–23.

_____ **and Ulph, David.** Union Bargaining: A Survey of Recent Work. In *Sapsford, D. and Tzannatos, Z., eds.*, 1989, pp. 86–125.

Ulph, David; Beath, John and Katsoulacos, Yannis. The Game-Theoretic Analysis of Innovation: A Survey. *Bull. Econ. Res.*, July 1989, *41*(3), pp. 163–84.

_____; **Beath, John and Katsoulacos, Yannis.** Strategic R&D Policy. *Econ. J.*, Supplement, 1989, *99*(395), pp. 74–83.

_____ **and Ulph, Alistair.** Gains and Losses from Cartelisation in Markets for Exhaustible Resources in the Absence of Binding Future Contracts. In *[Verheyen, P.]*, 1989, pp. 157–89.

_____ **and Ulph, Alistair.** Labor Markets and Innovation. *J. Japanese Int. Economies*, December 1989, *3*(4), pp. 403–23.

_____ **and Ulph, Alistair.** Union Bargaining: A Survey of Recent Work. In *Sapsford, D. and Tzannatos, Z., eds.*, 1989, pp. 86–125.

Ulybin, K. On Criteria of the Socialist Nature of Property Relations. *Prob. Econ.*, August 1989, *32*(4), pp. 24–39.

Umbeck, John and Staten, Michael. Economic Inefficiency: A Failure of Economists. *J. Econ. Educ.*, Winter 1989, *20*(1), pp. 57–72.

_____ **and Staten, Michael.** Shipping the Good Students Out: The Effect of a Fixed Charge on Student Enrollments. *J. Econ. Educ.*, Spring 1989, *20*(2), pp. 165–71.

Unakul, Snoh. Impacts of Global Adjustment on the Asian-Pacific Economy: Comment. In *Shinohara, M. and Lo, F., eds.*, 1989, pp. 322–23.

Unal, Haluk. Impact of Deposit-Rate Ceiling Changes on Bank Stock Returns. *J. Money, Credit, Banking*, May 1989, *21*(2), pp. 206–20.

Underwood, Daniel A. Estimation, Verification, and Prognostication: For What? *J. Econ. Issues*, June 1989, *23*(2), pp. 587–95.

Underwood, John. The World Bank's Response to the Developing Country Debt Crisis. *Contemp. Policy Issues*, April 1989, *7*(2), pp. 50–65.

_____ **and Humphreys, Charles.** The External Debt Difficulties of Low-Income Africa. In *Husain, I. and Diwan, I., eds.*, 1989, pp. 45–65.

Ungerer, Horst. The European Monetary System and the International Monetary System. *J. Common Market Stud.*, March 1989, *27*(3), pp. 231–48.

Unninayar, S. Basic Data Requirements of an Agroclimatic System. In *Oram, P. A., et al.*, 1989, pp. 341–46.

Uno, Jun; Brenner, Menachem and Subrahmanyam, Marti G. The Behavior of Prices in the Nikkei Spot and Futures Market. *J. Finan. Econ.*, August 1989, *23*(2), pp. 363–83.

Uno, Kimio. Service Economy in an Input–Output Framework—The Case of R&D. In *Franz, A. and Rainer, N., eds.*, 1989, pp. 131–51.

Unterwurzacher, Erich and Wirl, Franz. Transaction Costs and Their Impact on Energy Demand Behaviour. In *Gulledge, T. R., Jr. and Litteral, L. A., eds.*, 1989, pp. 130–41.

Unwin, Tim. The Urban–Rural Context of Agrarian Change in the Arabian Peninsula. In *[Mountjoy, A. B.]*, 1989, pp. 169–203.

_____. Urban–Rural Interaction in Developing Countries: A Theoretical Perspective. In *[Mountjoy, A. B.]*, 1989, pp. 11–32.

Upadhyay, K. S. The Implications of Changes in the Economic Policy during the Seventh Plan. In *Reddy, J. M., et al., eds. (II)*, 1989, pp. 80–92.

UpCher, M. R. and McLaren, K. R. Specification, Identification and Estimation of a Continuous-Time Portfolio Model of Asset Demands. *J. Quant. Econ.*, July 1989, *5*(2), pp. 275–94.

Urata, Masutaro. Formulators and Legislators of International Trade and Industrial Policy in Japan and the United States: Commentary. In *Hayashi, K., ed.*, 1989, pp. 194–95.

Urata, Shujiro. Sources of Economic Growth and Structural Change: An International Comparison. In *Williamson, J. G. and Panchamukhi, V. R., eds.*, 1989, pp. 144–66.

Urbain, J. P. Model Selection Criteria and Granger Causality Tests: An Empirical Note. *Econ. Letters*, 1989, *29*(4), pp. 317–20.

Urban, Jan. Strategy for a Rising Standard of Living. *Czech. Econ. Digest.*, November 1989, (7), pp. 80–107.

Urban, Peter and FitzGerald, Vince. Causes and Consequences of Changes in the Terms of Trade and the Balance of Payments. In *[Gruen, F. H.]*, 1989, pp. 240–61.

Urbany, Joel E.; Dickson, Peter R. and Wilkie, William L. Buyer Uncertainty and Information Search. *J. Cons. Res.*, September 1989, *16*(2), pp. 208–15.

Uri, Noel D. Delineating the Nature and Extent of the Market for Agricultural Commodities. *J. Econ. Devel.*, June 1989, *14*(1), pp. 47–64.

_____. Linear Complementarity Programming: Electrical Energy as a Case Study. In *Labys, W. C.; Takayama, T. and Uri, N. D., eds.*, 1989, pp. 165–88.

_____. Natural Gas Demand by Agriculture in the USA. *Energy Econ.*, April 1989, *11*(2), pp. 137–46.

_____. Quantitative Methods for Market-Oriented Economic Analysis over Space and Time: Introduction. In *Labys, W. C.; Takayama, T. and Uri, N. D., eds.*, 1989, pp. 3–15.

_____. A Reconsideration of the Impact of Recalls on the Market Valuation of a Product. *Econ. Modelling*, October 1989, *6*(4), pp. 457–66.

_____. The Structure of Agricultural Unemployment in the United States. *Growth Change*, Summer 1989, *20*(3), pp. 1–13.

_____ and Boyd, Roy. The Effects on Agriculture in the United States of an Oil Import Fee. *Appl. Econ.*, December 1989, *21*(12), pp. 1647–66.

_____ and Boyd, Roy. The Impacts of an Oil Import Fee on U.S. Agriculture. *J. Econ. Devel.*, December 1989, *14*(2), pp. 55–75.

_____; Mixon, J. Wilson, Jr. and Kyer, Ben L. An Analysis of the Automatic Stabilizers Associated with Taxes and Transfer Payments. *Int. Rev. Applied Econ.*, January 1989, *3*(1), pp. 46–56.

_____; Mixon, J. Wilson, Jr. and Kyer, Ben L. Automatic Stabilizers Reconsidered. *Public Finance*, 1989, *44*(3), pp. 476–91.

Urrutia, Miguel. Asia and Latin America: Main Issues for Further Research. In *Naya, S., et al., eds.*, 1989, pp. 251–57.

_____ and Krueger, Anne O. Remarks on Country Studies. In *Sachs, J. D., ed. (II)*, 1989, pp. 212–22.

Ursprung, Heinrich W. and Karacaoglu, Girol. Exchange-Rate Dynamics under Gradual Portfolio and Commodity-Price Adjustment. *Europ. Econ. Rev.*, July 1989, *33*(6), pp. 1205–26.

Urzúa, Carlos M. and Cuddington, John T. Trends and Cycles in Colombia's Real GDP and Fiscal Deficit. *J. Devel. Econ.*, April 1989, *30*(2), pp. 325–43.

_____ and Cuddington, John T. Trends and Cycles in the Net Barter Terms of Trade: A New Approach. *Econ. J.*, June 1989, *99*(396), pp. 426–42.

Usher, Dan. The Concept of Neutrality as a Basis for Identifying and Classifying Tax Expenditures. In *Bruce, N., ed.*, 1989, pp. 407–14.

_____. The Dynastic Cycle and the Stationary State. *Amer. Econ. Rev.*, December 1989, *79*(5), pp. 1031–44.

Usher, Lisa and Duke, John. Multifactor Productivity Slips in the Nonrubber Footwear Industry. *Mon. Lab. Rev.*, April 1989, *112*(4), pp. 32–38.

Ushio, Yoshiaki. Efficiency Properties of Large Dynamic Markets. *Int. Econ. Rev.*, August 1989, *30*(3), pp. 537–47.

Uslaner, Eric M. Is American Energy Politics Ideological? *Energy J.*, January 1989, *10*(1), pp. 55–75.

Usunier, Jean-Claude. Marketing International et rémunérations occultes. (Bribing in International Contracts: Tentative Economic Explanations. With English summary.) *Écon. Societes*, December 1989, *23*(12), pp. 221–42.

Uthoff, Andras and Pollack, Molly. Poverty and the Labour Market: Greater Santiago, 1969–85. In *Rodgers, G., ed.*, 1989, pp. 117–43.

Uttley, Stephen. Social Welfare in Developed Market Countries: New Zealand. In *Dixon, J. and Scheurell, R. P., eds.*, 1989, pp. 190–227.

Utton, Albert E. and Hayton, Robert D. Transboundary Groundwaters: The Bellagio Draft Treaty. *Natural Res. J.*, Summer 1989, *29*(3), pp. 663–722.

Uusitalo, Liisa. Economic Man or Social Man—Exploring Free Riding in the Production of Collective Goods. In *Grunert, K. G. and Ölander, F., eds.*, 1989, pp. 267–83.

Vach, Werner. Least Squares Approximation of

Additive Trees. In *Opitz, O., ed.*, 1989, pp. 230–38.

Vaciago, Giacomo. The New Market in Government Securities: Efficiency and Liquidity. *Rev. Econ. Cond. Italy*, Jan.–April 1989, (1), pp. 43–60.

Văduva, I. On the Probability Distribution of the Values of a Distribution Density. *Econ. Computat. Econ. Cybern. Stud. Res.*, 1989, 24(2–3), pp. 111–15.

Vaez-Zadeh, Reza. Oil Wealth and Economic Behavior: The Case of Venezuela, 1965–81. *Int. Monet. Fund Staff Pap.*, June 1989, 36(2), pp. 343–84.

Vaggi, Gianni. A Two-Sector, Four-Class Model. In *Chakravarty, S., ed.*, 1989, pp. 94–115.

———; **Lunghini, Giorgio and Rampa, Giorgio.** The Age of Waste: Some Ideas on Full Employment. *Écon. Appl.*, 1989, 42(1), pp. 115–33.

Vahcic, Ales. Capital Markets, Management Takeovers and Creation of New Firms in a Reformed Self-Managed Economy: Some Lessons from the Nova Gorica (Yugoslavia) Experiment. *Europ. Econ. Rev.*, March 1989, 33(2/3), pp. 456–65.

Vaidyanathan, A. Macro and Micro Approaches to Studying Rural Economic Change: Some Pointers from Indian Experience. In *Bardhan, P., ed. (I)*, 1989, pp. 13–31.

Vaillancourt, François. Incidence of Tax Expenditures in a Lifetime Framework: Theory and an Application to RRSPs: Comment. In *Bruce, N., ed.*, 1989, pp. 372–74.

———. The View of Immigration from Quebec—Quebec's Immigration Policy: An Economic Assessment of Its Rationale and Impact. In *Beach, C. M. and Green, A. G.*, 1989, pp. 16–26.

——— **and Fortin, Pierre.** Panel Discussion on Canadian Immigration Objectives: Levels, Composition, and Directions. In *Beach, C. M. and Green, A. G.*, 1989, pp. 92–93.

——— **and Reid, Robert J.** Administrative and Compliance Costs of Taxation: Canada. In *International Fiscal Association, ed. (I)*, 1989, pp. 267–90.

Vainshtein, B. Fictitious Problems in a Specific Economy. *Prob. Econ.*, September 1989, 32(5), pp. 60–68.

Vakneen, Yitzhak and Yitzhaki, Shlomo. On the Shadow Price of a Tax Inspector. *Public Finance*, 1989, 44(3), pp. 492–505.

Valach, Vladimír. The Establishment of State Enterprises—Only the First Step. *Czech. Econ. Digest.*, May 1989, (3), pp. 37–45.

Valavanidis, A. and Sarafopoulos, N. Occupational Health and Safety in Greece: Current Problems and Perspectives. *Int. Lab. Rev.*, 1989, 128(2), pp. 249–58.

Valdés, Alberto. The Policy Response of Agriculture: Comment. In *Fischer, S. and de Tray, D., eds.*, 1989, pp. 263–68.

——— **and Pinckney, Thomas C.** Trade and Macroeconomic Policies' Impact on Agricultural Growth: Evidence To-date. *Eastern Afr. Econ. Rev.*, June 1989, 5(1), pp. 42–61.

——— **and Zietz, Joachim.** Lowering Agricultural Protection: A Developing Country Perspective towards the Uruguay Round. In *Islam, N., ed.*, 1989, pp. 243–57.

Valdés, Dennis Nodín. Betabeleros: The Formation of an Agricultural Proletariat in the Midwest, 1897–1930. *Labor Hist.*, Fall 1989, 30(4), pp. 536–62.

Valdés, Teófilo; Raymond, José Luis and Argimón, Isabel. Evolución de la recaudación en el IRPF: Determinación de las causas y estimación de efectos. (With English summary.) *Invest. Econ.*, January 1989, 13(1), pp. 15–43.

Valdmanis, Vivian and Byrnes, Patricia. Variable Cost Frontiers and Efficiency: An Investigation of Labor Costs in Hospitals. In *Gulledge, T. R., Jr. and Litteral, L. A., eds.*, 1989, pp. 160–75.

Valenta, František. The Essence of the Restructuring. *Czech. Econ. Digest.*, June 1989, (4), pp. 52–61.

———. Industrial Production in Agricultural Co-operatives: A Factor Accelerating Technical Progress in Czechoslovak Agriculture. In *Chakravarty, S., ed.*, 1989, pp. 323–37.

Valenta, Lee and Rhodes, Larry E. Industry-Based Supported Employment: An Enclave Approach. In *Wehman, P. and Kregel, J., eds.*, 1989, pp. 53–68.

Valério, Nuno; Nunes, Ana Bela and Mata, Eugénia. Portuguese Economic Growth, 1833–1985. *J. Europ. Econ. Hist.*, Fall 1989, 18(2), pp. 291–330.

Valette-Florence, Pierre. Valeurs et marketing: Origine historique, spécificités et champs d'application. (Values and Marketing. Historical Origin, Specificities and Fields of Application. With English summary.) *Écon. Societes*, December 1989, 23(12), pp. 7–56.

Valletta, Robert G. The Impact of Unionism on Municipal Expenditures and Revenues. *Ind. Lab. Relat. Rev.*, April 1989, 42(3), pp. 430–42.

Valli, Vittorio and Checchi, Daniele. Investimenti ed occupazione: Un approccio strutturale. (Investment and Employment: A Structural Approach. With English summary.) *Giorn. Econ.*, Jan.–Feb. 1989, 48(1–2), pp. 3–34.

Valliant, Richard and Miller, Stephen M. A Class of Multiplicative Estimators of Laspeyres Price Indexes. *J. Bus. Econ. Statist.*, July 1989, 7(3), pp. 382–94.

Valovaia, T. The Difficult Road of Cognition: Restrictions on a Timely Book and a Sensational Article. In *Jones, A. and Moskoff, W., eds.*, 1989, 1988, pp. 116–23.

Van Arkadie, Brian. The Role of Institutions in Development. In *Fischer, S. and de Tray, D., eds.*, 1989, pp. 153–75.

Van Atta, Don. Theorists of Agrarian *Perestroika*. *Soviet Econ.*, Jan.–March 1989, 5(1), pp. 70–99.

Van Bael, Ivo. Lessons for the EEC: More Transparency, Less Discretion, and, at Last, a Debate? In *Jackson, J. H. and Vermulst, E. A., eds.*, 1989, pp. 405–08.

Van de Stadt, Huib; Zeelenberg, Kees and Huigen, René. Socio-Economic Accounts for the Netherlands. *Rev. Income Wealth*, September 1989, 35(3), pp. 317–34.

Van de Ven, Andrew H. and Garud, Raghu. A Framework for Understanding the Emergence of New Industries. In *Rosenbloom, R. S. and Burgelman, R. A., eds.*, 1989, pp. 195–225.

Van den Bergh, Roger and Faure, Michael. Essays in Law and Economics: Corporations, Accident Prevention and Compensation for Losses: Introduction. In *Faure, M. and Van den Bergh, R., eds.*, 1989, pp. 15–20.

Van den Bosch, K.; Deleeck, H. and De Lathouwer, L. Regional Differences in the Distribution of Social Security Benefits in Belgium: Facts and Causes. *Cah. Écon. Bruxelles*, 3rd Trimester 1989, (123), pp. 265–310.

Van den Bossche, Anne-Marie. GATT: The Indispensable Link between the EEC and Hungary? *J. World Trade*, June 1989, 23(3), pp. 141–55.

Van der Borg, Jan and Martellato, Dino. Dinamica occupazionale nei sistemi urbani italiani. (Employment Dynamics in Italian Urban Systems. With English summary.) *Econ. Lavoro*, Oct.–Dec. 1989, 23(4), pp. 31–47.

Van Der Klaauw, W.; Dolton, P. J. and Makepeace, G. H. Occupational Choice and Earnings Determination: The Role of Sample Selection and Non-pecuniary Factors. *Oxford Econ. Pap.*, July 1989, 41(3), pp. 573–94.

Van der Wee, Herman and Buyst, Erik. Europe and the World Economy during the Inter-war Period. In *[Fischer, W.],* 1989, pp. 239–59.

Van der Woude, Ad. Specializzazione e diversificazione dell'economia rurale: Interventi degli esperti. (In English.) In *Cavaciocchi, S., ed.,* 1989, pp. 174–80.

Van Hoa, Tran. System Estimation of Generalized Working Models: A Semiparametric Approach. *Econ. Letters*, December 1989, 31(4), pp. 363–66.

_____ **and Ironmonger, D. S.** Equivalence Scales: A Household Production Approach. *Econ. Letters*, December 1989, 31(4), pp. 407–10.

_____ **and Reece, B. F.** An Empirical Study of Optimal Taxation on Australian Financial Institutions. *Econ. Letters*, 1989, 29(2), pp. 163–66.

Van Huyck, John B. and Cosimano, Thomas F. Dynamic Monetary Control and Interest Rate Stabilization. *J. Monet. Econ.*, January 1989, 23(1), pp. 53–63.

Van Kooten, G. C. Stochastic Dynamic Modeling: Discussion. *Western J. Agr. Econ.*, July 1989, 14(1), pp. 166–67.

_____ **and Taylor, Keith F.** Measuring the Marginal Welfare Impacts of Government Regulation: The Case of Supply Management. *Can. J. Econ.*, November 1989, 22(4), pp. 892–903.

_____**; Weisensel, Ward P. and de Jong, E.** Estimating the Costs of Soil Erosion: A Reply. *Can.*

J. Agr. Econ., November 1989, 37(3), pp. 555–62.

_____**; Weisensel, Ward P. and de Jong, E.** Estimating the Costs of Soil Erosion in Saskatchewan. *Can. J. Agr. Econ.*, March 1989, 37(1), pp. 63–75.

Van Lear, William M. The Restructuring of the Oil Industry. *J. Econ. Issues*, March 1989, 23(1), pp. 147–54.

Van Loon, Richard. Converting Exemptions and Deductions into Credits: An Economic Assessment: Comment. In *Mintz, J. and Whalley, J., eds.*, 1989, pp. 78–82.

Van Maanen, John and Kunda, Gideon. "Real Feelings": Emotional Expression and Organizational Culture. In *Cummings, L. L. and Staw, B. M., eds.*, 1989, pp. 43–103.

Van Ness, Peter. Market Reforms in Socialist Societies: Comparing China and Hungary: Introduction. In *Van Ness, P., ed.*, 1989, pp. 1–26.

_____ **and Loehr, William.** The Cost of Self-Reliance: The Case of China. In *Van Ness, P., ed.*, 1989, pp. 262–80.

_____ **and Raichur, Satish.** Dilemmas of Socialist Development: An Analysis of Strategic Lines in China, 1949–1981. In *Van Ness, P., ed.*, 1989, pp. 143–69.

Van Order, Robert and Capozza, Dennis R. Spatial Competition with Consistent Conjectures. *J. Reg. Sci.*, February 1989, 29(1), pp. 1–13.

_____ **and Hendershott, Patric H.** Integration of Mortgage and Capital Markets and the Accumulation of Residential Capital. *Reg. Sci. Urban Econ.*, May 1989, 19(2), pp. 189–210.

Van Scyoc, Lee J. Effects of Airline Deregulation on Profitability. *Logist. Transp. Rev.*, March 1989, 25(1), pp. 39–51.

Van Wicklin, Warren A., III and Finsterbusch, Kurt. Beneficiary Participation in Development Projects: Empirical Tests of Popular Theories. *Econ. Devel. Cult. Change*, April 1989, 37(3), pp. 573–93.

Vanags, A. and Hale, C. Spot and Period Rates in the Dry Bulk Market: Some Tests for the Period 1980–1986. *J. Transp. Econ. Policy*, September 1989, 23(3), pp. 281–91.

Vanagunas, Stanley. Max Weber's Authority Models and the Theory of X-Inefficiency: The Economic Sociologist's Analysis Adds More Structure to Leibenstein's Critique of Rationality. *Amer. J. Econ. Sociology*, October 1989, 48(4), pp. 393–400.

Vanberg, Viktor and Buchanan, James M. Organization Theory and Fiscal Economics: Society, State, and Public Debt. In *Buchanan, J. M. (II),* 1989, pp. 329–43.

_____ **and Buchanan, James M.** A Theory of Leadership and Deference in Constitutional Construction. *Public Choice*, April 1989, 61(1), pp. 15–27.

Vandell, Kerry D. and Lane, Jonathan S. The Economics of Architecture and Urban Design: Some Preliminary Findings. *Amer. Real Estate Urban Econ. Assoc. J.*, Summer 1989, 17(2), pp. 235–60.

Vandell, Robert F. and Stevens, Jerry L. Evidence of Superior Performance from Timing. *J. Portfol. Manage.*, Spring 1989, *15*(3), pp. 38–42.

VanDerhei, Jack L. and Harrington, Scott E. Pension Asset Reversions. In *Turner, J. A. and Beller, D. J., eds.*, 1989, pp. 187–210.

Vanderkamp, John. The Role of Migration in Regional Adjustment. In *van Dijk, J., et al., eds.*, 1989, pp. 147–75.

Vanderpooten, Daniel. The Use of Preference Information in Multiple Criteria Interactive Procedures. In *Lockett, A. G. and Islei, G., eds.*, 1989, pp. 390–99.

VanderZwaag, David. Canada and Marine Environmental Protection: The Changing Tides of Law and Policy. In *McRae, D. and Munro, G., eds.*, 1989, pp. 95–132.

Vandeveer, Lonnie R.; Paxton, Kenneth W. and Lavergne, David R. Irrigation and Potential Diversification Benefits in Humid Climates. *Southern J. Agr. Econ.*, December 1989, *21*(2), pp. 167–74.

Vaner, Josef. The Main Linkage of the Economic Mechanism. *Czech. Econ. Digest.*, June 1989, (4), pp. 62–77.

Vanhamme, Geneviève and Ginsburgh, Victor. Price Differences in the EC Car Market: Some Further Results. *Ann. Écon. Statist.*, July–Dec. 1989, (15–16), pp. 137–49.

VanHoose, David D. Monetary Targeting and Price Level Non-Trend-Stationarity: A Note. *J. Money, Credit, Banking*, May 1989, *21*(2), pp. 232–39.

_____. Reverse-Lag Reserve Accounting, Bank Behavior, and Monetary Control: A Formal Analysis. *Atlantic Econ. J.*, September 1989, *17*(3), pp. 34–38.

_____ and Waller, Christopher J. Endogenous Wage Indexation and Optimal Monetary Policy with and without a Balanced Budget. *J. Econ. Bus.*, February 1989, *41*(1), pp. 21–31.

_____ and Waller, Christopher J. Islands, Indexation and Monetary Policy. *Econ. Inquiry*, October 1989, *27*(4), pp. 705–17.

_____ and Waller, Christopher J. Optimal Monetary Policy and Alternative Wage Indexation Schemes in a Model with Interest-Sensitive Labor Supply. *J. Macroecon.*, Spring 1989, *11*(2), pp. 163–80.

Vanoli, André; Milot, Jean-Paul and Teillet, Pierre. How to Treat Non-produced Assets and Exceptional Events in the National Accounts? Considerations on the Variations in Wealth Accounting. *Rev. Income Wealth*, June 1989, *35*(2), pp. 163–86.

Vansant, Jerry. Opportunities and Risks for Private Voluntary Organizations as Agents of LDC Policy Change. *World Devel.*, November 1989, *17*(11), pp. 1723–31.

VanSickle, John J. and Stevens, Thomas J. Market Information Systems: An Online Agricultural Market News Retrieval System. *Southern J. Agr. Econ.*, December 1989, *21*(2), pp. 195–201.

VanTassell, Larry W. and Nixon, Clair J. A Further Look at the Effect of Federal Tax Laws on Optimal Machinery Replacement. *Southern J. Agr. Econ.*, December 1989, *21*(2), pp. 77–84.

Vantreese, Valerie L.; Reed, Michael R. and Skees, Jerry R. Mandatory Production Controls and Asset Values: A Case Study of Burley Tobacco Quotas. *Amer. J. Agr. Econ.*, May 1989, *71*(2), pp. 319–25.

Vanzetti, David and Kennedy, John. Optimal Retaliation in International Commodity Markets. *Rev. Marketing Agr. Econ.*, April, Aug., Dec. 1989, *57*(1–2–3), pp. 93–117.

Varady, David P. The Impact of City/Suburban Location on Moving Plans: A Cincinnati Study. *Growth Change*, Spring 1989, *20*(2), pp. 35–49.

Varaiya, Nikhil P. and Alberts, William W. Assessing the Profitability of Growth by Acquisition: A 'Premium Recapture' Approach. *Int. J. Ind. Organ.*, Special Issue, March 1989, *7*(1), pp. 133–49.

_____ and Giliberto, S. Michael. The Winner's Curse and Bidder Competition in Acquisitions: Evidence from Failed Bank Auctions. *J. Finance*, March 1989, *44*(1), pp. 59–75.

Varaiya, Pravin. Productivity in Manufacturing and the Division of Mental Labor. In *Andersson, Å. E.; Batten, D. F. and Karlsson, C., eds.*, 1989, pp. 17–23.

_____ and Quigley, John M. On the Dynamics of Regulated Markets, Construction Standards, Energy Standards and Durable Goods: A Cautionary Tale. In *Andersson, Å. E., et al., eds.*, 1989, pp. 263–71.

Vårdal, E. and Brunstad, R. J. Goal Conflicts in the Norwegian Farming Industry: Allocational Loss through the Pursuit of Non-efficiency Goals. In *Bauer, S. and Henrichsmeyer, W., eds.*, 1989, pp. 97–101.

Vargas, Luis G. and Roura-Agusti, J. Bernat. Business Strategy Formulation for a Financial Institution in a Developing Country. In *Golden, B. L.; Wasil, E. A. and Harker, P. T., eds.*, 1989, pp. 251–65.

Várhegyi, Éva. Results and Failures of Monetary Restriction (Some Lessons of Hungarian Financial Policy in 1988). *Acta Oecon.*, 1989, *41*(3–4), pp. 403–20.

Varian, Hal R. Differences of Opinion in Financial Markets. In *Stone, C. C., ed.*, 1989, pp. 3–37.

_____. Price Discrimination. In *Schmalensee, R. and Willig, R. D., eds., Vol. 1*, 1989, pp. 597–654.

_____ and Gordon, Roger H. Taxation of Asset Income in the Presence of a World Securities Market. *J. Int. Econ.*, May 1989, *26*(3/4), pp. 205–26.

Varley, Ann. Settlement, Illegality, and Legalization: The Need for Reassessment. In *Ward, P. M., ed.*, 1989, pp. 156–87.

Varman, Benu. Some Remarks on the Definition and Magnitude of Recent Capital Flight from Developing Countries. *Kredit Kapital*, 1989, *22*(4), pp. 565–97.

Varoufakis, Yanis. Worker Solidarity and Strikes. *Australian Econ. Pap.*, June 1989, *28*(52), pp. 76–92.

_____ **and Lyons, Bruce.** Game Theory, Oligopoly and Bargaining. In *Hey, J. D., ed.*, 1989, pp. 79–126.

Varshney, Ashutosh. Ideas, Interest and Institutions in Policy Change: Transformation of India's Agricultural Strategy in the Mid-1960's. *Policy Sciences*, November 1989, *22*(3–4), pp. 289–323.

Vasarhelyi, M. A. and Srinidhi, Bin N. Adaptation and Use of Reliability Concepts in Internal Control Evaluation. In *Gangolly, J., ed.*, 1989, pp. 141–57.

Vasavada, Utpal and Baffes, John. On the Choice of Functional Forms in Agricultural Production Analysis. *Appl. Econ.*, August 1989, *21*(8), pp. 1053–61.

_____; **Ball, V. E. and Somwaru, A.** Modeling Dynamic Adjustment Subject to Integrability Conditions. In *Bauer, S. and Henrichsmeyer, W., eds.*, 1989, pp. 279–86.

_____ **and Chambers, Robert G.** Technical Change and Applications of Dynamic Duality to Agriculture: Reply. *Amer. J. Agr. Econ.*, August 1989, *71*(3), pp. 803–04.

Vascik, George. The Brussels Convention of 1902: Reevaluating the Roles of State and Industry in Wilhelmine Germany. In *Perkins, E. J., ed.*, 1989, pp. 91–100.

Vasegh-Daneshvary, Nasser; France, Judith and Summary, Rebecca M. The Impact of Economic Education Courses on the Knowledge and Retention of Knowledge of Secondary and Primary School Teachers. *J. Econ. Educ.*, Fall 1989, *20*(4), pp. 346–54.

Vashist, B. K. Macro-economic Policy: A Meade–Mundell Synthesis and Extension. *Indian Econ. J.*, Jan.–March 1989, *36*(3), pp. 80–87.

Vasil'eva, N. A. First Steps of the New Economic Mechanism. *Matekon*, Winter 1989–90, *26*(2), pp. 38–49.

Vasiliu, D. P. and Săvulescu, B. Total Maximal Flow in a Network Having Random Capacities. *Econ. Computat. Econ. Cybern. Stud. Res.*, 1989, *24*(2–3), pp. 91–101.

Vasko, Tibor. Technology, Structural Change and Long-Term Fluctuations. In *Di Matteo, M.; Goodwin, R. M. and Vercelli, A., eds.*, 1989, pp. 167–76.

Vassilakis, Spyros. Increasing Returns and Strategic Behavior: The Worker–Firm Ratio. *Rand J. Econ.*, Winter 1989, *20*(4), pp. 622–36.

Vastrup, Claus. Economic Policy and Adjustment in Denmark. In *Monti, M., ed.*, 1989, pp. 87–105.

Vatnick, Silvina. The Market-Based Menu Approach in Action: The 1988 Brazilian Financing Package: Comment. In *Husain, I. and Diwan, I., eds.*, 1989, pp. 174–75.

Vatter, Harold G. and Walker, John F. Why Has the United States Operated Below Potential since World War II? *J. Post Keynesian Econ.*, Spring 1989, *11*(3), pp. 327–46.

Vaubel, Roland. The European Monetary System: A Regional Bretton Woods or an Institutional Innovation? Comments. In *Vosgerau, H.-J., ed.*, 1989, pp. 119–22.

Vaughan, D. R. and Booth, P. The Economic Importance of Tourism and the Arts in Merseyside. *J. Cult. Econ.*, December 1989, *13*(2), pp. 21–34.

Vaughan, Denton R. Development and Evaluation of a Survey-Based Type of Benefit Classification for the Social Security Program. *Soc. Sec. Bull.*, January 1989, *52*(1), pp. 12–26.

Vaughan, Michael B.; Thomas, Wade L. and Musgrave, Frank W. The Evolving Health Care System: Economic Integration through Reciprocity. *J. Econ. Issues*, June 1989, *23*(2), pp. 493–502.

Vaupel, James W. and Zeng, Yi. The Impact of Urbanization and Delayed Childbearing on Population Growth and Aging in China. *Population Devel. Rev.*, September 1989, *15*(3), pp. 425–45.

Väyrynen, Raimo. Economic Fluctuations, Military Expenditures, and Warfare in International Relations. In *Schaeffer, R. K., ed.*, 1989, pp. 109–26.

Vazquez, Andres. A Note on the Application of the Derivation of Price Elasticity of Demand from Total Revenue Response to Price Changes: Some Clarifications. *Econ. Notes*, 1989, (3), pp. 423–31.

Veall, Michael R. and Giordano, Rosanna. A Note on Log–Log Regressions with Dummy Variables: Why Units Matter. *Oxford Bull. Econ. Statist.*, February 1989, *51*(1), pp. 95–96.

_____ **and McAleer, Michael.** How Fragile Are Fragile Inferences? A Re-evaluation of the Deterrent Effect of Capital Punishment. *Rev. Econ. Statist.*, February 1989, *71*(1), pp. 99–106.

Vedder, Richard and Gallaway, Lowell. The Tullock–Bastiat Hypothesis and Rawlsian Distribution Strategies. *Public Choice*, May 1989, *61*(2), pp. 177–81.

Vedder, Richard K. Three Cheers for the Corporate Raider. In *McKee, D. L., ed.*, 1989, pp. 3–15.

Vedlitz, Arnold; Worchel, Stephen and Dyer, James. Social Distance among Racial and Ethnic Groups in Texas: Some Demographic Correlates. *Soc. Sci. Quart.*, September 1989, *70*(3), pp. 607–16.

Vedovato, Claudio and Lundahl, Mats. The State and Economic Development in Haiti and the Dominican Republic. *Scand. Econ. Hist. Rev.*, 1989, *37*(3), pp. 39–59.

Veeman, Michele and Chen, Peter. Estimating Market Demand Functions for Meat: An Update of Elasticity Estimates. *Can. J. Agr. Econ.*, Part 2, December 1989, *37*(4), pp. 1061–69.

Veeman, Terrence S. Sustainable Development: Its Economic Meaning and Policy Implications. *Can. J. Agr. Econ.*, Part 2, December 1989, *37*(4), pp. 875–86.

van der Veen, Dirk J. The Sophistication of Real-Wage Series. In *Scholliers, P., ed.*, 1989, pp. 176–78.

_____ **and van Zanden, Jan Luiten.** Real-Wage Trends and Consumption Patterns in the Netherlands, c. 1870–1940. In *Scholliers, P., ed.*, 1989, pp. 205–28.

van der Veen, Jaap. Changing Agricultural Policies in the North and the South. In *Helmuth, J. W. and Johnson, S. R., eds., Vol. 1*, 1989, pp. 56–65.

Veendorp, E. C. H. Instability, the Hicks Conditions, and the Choice of the Numéraire. In *Wood, J. C. and Woods, R. N., eds., Vol. 2, 1989, 1970*, pp. 121–30.

Veeneklaas, F. R. Analysis by Optimization. In *Muller, F. and Zwezerijnen, W. J., eds.*, 1989, pp. 150–62.

Veenhoven, Ruut. National Wealth and Individual Happiness. In *Grunert, K. G. and Ölander, F., eds.*, 1989, pp. 9–32.

de Veer, Jan. National Effects of CAP Trade Liberalization. In *Tarditi, S., et al., eds.*, 1989, pp. 99–109.

Vega-Redondo, Fernando. Extrapolative Expectations and Market Stability. *Int. Econ. Rev.*, August 1989, *30*(3), pp. 513–17.

_____. Implementation of Lindahl Equilibrium: An Integration of the Static and Dynamic Approaches. *Math. Soc. Sci.*, December 1989, *18*(3), pp. 211–28.

Végh, Carlos A. Government Spending and Inflationary Finance: A Public Finance Approach. *Int. Monet. Fund Staff Pap.*, September 1989, *36*(3), pp. 657–77.

_____. The Optimal Inflation Tax in the Presence of Currency Substitution. *J. Monet. Econ.*, July 1989, *24*(1), pp. 139–46.

Vehmanen, Petri. Alternative Views of Financial Accounting. *Liiketaloudellinen Aikak.*, 1989, *38*(3), pp. 240–54.

Vekov, Angel. Krustyu Rakovski—Socio-political and Economic Activity. In *Bulgarian Academy of Sciences, Institute of Economics*, 1989, pp. 198–206.

Velasco, Andres and Nayfeld, Alejandro. Annual Review of Nations: Year 1988: Argentina. In *Haberman, L. and Sacks, P. M., eds.*, 1989, pp. 1–18.

Veldheer, Linda C.; Getzel, Elizabeth Evans and Kregel, John. Projecting the Service Needs of Transition-Aged Young Adults Exiting Public School Programs: A Statewide Analysis. In *Wehman, P. and Kregel, J., eds.*, 1989, pp. 243–56.

Veljanovski, Cento. Competition in Broadcasting. In *Veljanovski, C., ed. (I)*, 1989, pp. 3–24.

_____. Privatisation: Monopoly Money or Competition? In *Veljanovski, C., ed. (II)*, 1989, pp. 26–51.

_____. The Role of Advertising in Broadcasting Policy. In *Veljanovski, C., ed. (I)*, 1989, pp. 99–113.

_____. Whose Europe? Competing Visions for 1992: Foreword. In *Dahrendorf, R., et al.*, 1989, pp. ix–xi.

Vella, Frank and Pagan, Adrian R. Diagnostic Tests for Models Based on Individual Data: A Survey. *J. Appl. Econometrics*, Supplement, December 1989, *4*, pp. S29–59.

Velupillai, Kumaraswamy. What Have We Learned in the Path from Gödel and Turing to Artificial Intelligence? In *Andersson, Å. E.; Batten, D. F. and Karlsson, C., eds.*, 1989, pp. 25–30.

_____ **and Jespersen, Jesper.** Et farvel til o "klassiske" økonomer. (The Contributions to Economic Theory of John Hicks [1904–89] and Richard Kahn [1905–89]. With English summary.) *Nationaløkon. Tidsskr.*, 1989, *127*(2), pp. 264–68.

Venables, Anthony J.; Gasiorek, Michael and Smith, Alasdair. Tariffs, Subsidies and Retaliation. *Europ. Econ. Rev.*, March 1989, *33*(2/3), pp. 480–89.

Vencill, C. Daniel. Nobel Laureates in Economic Sciences: A Biographical Dictionary: Kenneth J. Arrow: 1972. In *Katz, B. S., ed.*, 1989, pp. 9–30.

Vencovský, František. Economic Prerequisites of Freely Convertible Currency. *Czech. Econ. Digest.*, February 1989, (1), pp. 57–84.

_____. Monetary Policy in the New Concept of Central Plans. *Czech. Econ. Digest.*, April 1989, (2), pp. 19–36.

Venezia, Itzhak; Greenbaum, Stuart I. and Kanatas, George. Equilibrium Loan Pricing under the Bank–Client Relationship. *J. Banking Finance*, May 1989, *13*(2), pp. 221–35.

Venezian, Emilio C.; Nye, Blaine F. and Hofflander, Alfred E. The Distribution of Claims for Professional Malpractice: Some Statistical and Public Policy Aspects. *J. Risk Ins.*, December 1989, *56*(4), pp. 686–701.

Venieris, George J. Agricultural Cooperatives vs. Public Companies in the Greek Wine Industry. *Europ. Rev. Agr. Econ.*, 1989, *16*(1), pp. 129–35.

Venkataram, J. V. and Nagaraja, G. N. Institutional Short-Term Loan Facilities for Farmers: A Taluk-Level Study in Karnataka. *Margin*, Oct. 1989–March 1990, *22*(1–2), pp. 92–97.

Venkataraman, Krishnaswamy. Management of Technological Change. *Industry Devel.*, April 1989, (26), pp. 57–82.

Venkatesh, P. C. The Impact of Dividend Initiation on the Earnings Announcements and Returns Volatility. *J. Bus.*, April 1989, *62*(2), pp. 175–97.

Venkateswarlu, B. Vulnerability of Rice to Climate. In *Oram, P. A., et al.*, 1989, pp. 115–21.

Venkateswarlu, Tadiboyina. History of Economic Thought: Survey of Course Outlines in Universities in Canada and the United States of America. *Amer. Economist*, Fall 1989, *33*(2), pp. 71–90.

Venti, Steven F. and Wise, David A. Aging, Moving, and Housing Wealth. In *Wise, D. A., ed.*, 1989, pp. 9–48.

Ventura-Días, Vivianne. The Old Logics of the New International Economic Order. *CEPAL Rev.*, April 1989, (37), pp. 105–21.

_____. South–South Trade: Trends, Issues, and Obstacles to Its Growth: Introduction. In *Ventura-Dias, V., ed.*, 1989, pp. xvii–xxvii.

_____. The Structure of South–South Trade. In *Ventura-Dias, V., ed.*, 1989, pp. 25–81.

_____. The Theoretical Background for Analysis of South–South Trade. In *Ventura-Dias, V., ed.*, 1989, pp. 1–24.

Verbeke, Alain. A Note on Neglected Behavioural Aspects in the *X*-Efficiency Theory. *Rivista Int. Sci. Econ. Com.*, July 1989, *36*(7), pp. 643–60.

_____ and de Lombaerde, P. Assessing International Seaport Competition: A Tool for Strategic Decision Making. *Int. J. Transport Econ.*, June 1989, *16*(2), pp. 175–92.

_____ and Porteous, Samuel D. The Implementation of Strategic Export Controls in Canada. *Can. Public Policy*, March 1989, *15*(1), pp. 12–24.

_____ and Rugman, Alan M. Strategic Management and Trade Policy. In *Rugman, A. M., ed.*, 1989, pp. 144–59.

Verbon, H. A. A. Conversion Policies for Public Pension Plans in a Small Open Economy. In *Gustafsson, B. A. and Klevmarken, N. A., eds.*, 1989, pp. 83–95.

Vercelli, Alessandro. "Keynes dopo Lucas." Una replica. ("Keynes dopo Lucas." A Reply. With English summary.) *Econ. Politica*, August 1989, *6*(2), pp. 265–73.

_____. La formazione dei giovani economisti alla luce di alcune recenti tendenze evolutive negli studi economici. (The Training of Young Economists in the Light of Recent Tendencies in Economic Studies. With English summary.) *Econ. Politica*, August 1989, *6*(2), pp. 203–13.

_____. Uncertainty, Technological Flexibility and Long Term Fluctuations. In *Di Matteo, M.; Goodwin, R. M. and Vercelli, A., eds.*, 1989, pp. 130–44.

_____; Di Matteo, Massimo and Goodwin, Richard M. Technological and Social Factors in Long Term Fluctuations: Proceedings of an International Workshop Held in Siena, Italy, December 16–18, 1986: Introduction. In *Di Matteo, M.; Goodwin, R. M. and Vercelli, A., eds.*, 1989, pp. v–ix.

Verdugo, Naomi Turner and Verdugo, Richard R. The Impact of Surplus Schooling on Earnings: Some Additional Findings. *J. Human Res.*, Fall 1989, *24*(4), pp. 629–43.

Verdugo, Richard R. and Verdugo, Naomi Turner. The Impact of Surplus Schooling on Earnings: Some Additional Findings. *J. Human Res.*, Fall 1989, *24*(4), pp. 629–43.

Vergani, G. and Bogahawatte, C. An Interregional Equilibrium Model to Evaluate the Impact of Agricultural Policy Measures or Development Projects on the Agricultural Sector of Developing Countries. Case Study: Sri Lanka. In *Bauer, S. and Henrichsmeyer, W., eds.*, 1989, pp. 85–95.

Verges, Joaquín. Medición de la diferencia en cuanto a costes sociales por congestión entre el transporte individual y transporte público urbano. Con una aplicación para el area urbana de Barcelona. (With English summary.) *Invest. Econ.*, May 1989, *13*(2), pp. 183–205.

Vergottis, Andreas and Beenstock, Michael. An Econometric Model of the World Market for Dry Cargo Freight and Shipping. *Appl. Econ.*, March 1989, *21*(3), pp. 339–56.

_____ and Beenstock, Michael. An Econometric Model of the World Tanker Market. *J. Transp. Econ. Policy*, September 1989, *23*(3), pp. 263–80.

Verhage, Bronislaw J. and Goodwin, Cathy. Role Perceptions of Services: A Cross-cultural Comparison with Behavioral Implications. *J. Econ. Psych.*, 1989, *10*(4), pp. 543–58.

Verhoeff, René. The Spatial Diffusion of the Performing Arts in the Netherlands. *J. Cult. Econ.*, December 1989, *13*(2), pp. 53–68.

Verkerke, J. Hoult. Compensating Victims of Preferential Employment Discrimination Remedies. *Yale Law J.*, May 1989, *98*(7), pp. 479–99.

_____ and Shubik, Martin. Open Questions in Defense Economics and Economic Warfare. *J. Conflict Resolution*, September 1989, *33*(3), pp. 480–99.

Verma, Anil. Joint Participation Programs: Self-help or Suicide for Labor? *Ind. Relat.*, Fall 1989, *28*(3), pp. 401–10.

Verma, Avinash K. and Ronn, Ehud I. Risk-Based Capital Adequacy Standards for a Sample of 43 Major Banks. *J. Banking Finance*, March 1989, *13*(1), pp. 21–29.

Verma, V. and Cleland, J. The World Fertility Survey: An Appraisal of Methodology. *J. Amer. Statist. Assoc.*, September 1989, *84*(407), pp. 756–67.

Vermaelen, Theo and Eckel, Catherine C. The Financial Fallout from Chernobyl: Risk Perceptions and Regulatory Response. In *Crew, M. A., ed.*, 1989, pp. 183–201.

Vermersch, D. and Guyomard, H. Economy and Technology of the French Cereal Sector: A Dual Approach. In *Bauer, S. and Henrichsmeyer, W., eds.*, 1989, pp. 260–77.

Vermulst, Edwin A. The Antidumping Systems of Australia, Canada, the EEC and the USA: Have Antidumping Laws Become a Problem in International Trade? In *Jackson, J. H. and Vermulst, E. A., eds.*, 1989, pp. 425–66.

_____; Waer, Paul and Bellis, Jean-François. Further Changes in the EEC Anti-dumping Regulation: A Codification of Controversial Methodologies. *J. World Trade*, April 1989, *23*(2), pp. 21–34.

Vernon, Raymond. Conceptual Aspects of Privatization. *CEPAL Rev.*, April 1989, (37), pp. 143–49.

Vernon-Wortzel, Heidi and Wortzel, Lawrence H. Privatization: Not the Only Answer. *World Devel.*, May 1989, *17*(5), pp. 633–41.

Verreault, Roger and Polese, Mario. Trade in

Information-Intensive Services: How and Why Regions Develop Export Advantages. *Can. Public Policy*, December 1989, *15*(4), pp. 376–86.

Verspagen, Bart and Pfann, Gerard A. The Structure of Adjustment Costs for Labour in the Dutch Manufacturing Sector. *Econ. Letters*, 1989, *29*(4), pp. 365–71.

Vesenka, Mary H. Economic Interests and Ideological Conviction: A Note on PACs and Agricultural Acts. *J. Econ. Behav. Organ.*, October 1989, *12*(2), pp. 259–63.

Vessillier, Elisabeth and Euzéby, Alain. Analyse d'un prélèvement sur les salaires: Les cotisations sociales. (With English summary.) In *Chiancone, A. and Messere, K., eds.*, 1989, pp. 323–37.

Vestal, James E. Evidence on the Determinants and Factor Content Characteristics of Japanese Technology Trade 1977–1981. *Rev. Econ. Statist.*, November 1989, *71*(4), pp. 565–71.

Vestøl, Jon Åge and Høie, Henning. Sustainable Agriculture: Assessments of Agricultural Pollution in the SIMJAR Model. *Statist. J.*, 1989, *6*(3), pp. 255–67.

Vetsuypens, Michael R. and Hite, Gailen L. Management Buyouts of Divisions and Shareholder Wealth. *J. Finance*, September 1989, *44*(4), pp. 953–70.

_____ **and Millon-Cornett, Marcia H.** Voting Rights and Shareholder Wealth: The Issuance of Limited Voting Common Stock. *Managerial Dec. Econ.*, September 1989, *10*(3), pp. 175–88.

_____ **and Muscarella, Chris J.** A Simple Test of Baron's Model of IPO Underpricing. *J. Finan. Econ.*, September 1989, *24*(1), pp. 125–35.

_____ **and Muscarella, Chris J.** The Underpricing of "Second" Initial Public Offerings. *J. Finan. Res.*, Fall 1989, *12*(3), pp. 183–92.

Vetter, Ernst Günter. Role of Trade Unions in a Market Economy. In *Peacock, A. and Willgerodt, H., eds. (II)*, 1989, *1972*, pp. 140–51.

Veugelers, Reinhilde. Wage Premia, Price–Cost Margins and Bargaining Power in Belgian Manufacturing. *Europ. Econ. Rev.*, January 1989, *33*(1), pp. 169–80.

Vial, Jean-Philippe. A Unified Approach to Projective Algorithms for Linear Programming. In *Dolecki, S., ed.*, 1989, pp. 191–220.

_____ **and Fraley, C.** Numerical Study of Projective Methods for Linear Programming. In *Dolecki, S., ed.*, 1989, pp. 25–38.

Vial, Joaquín. El mercado mundial del Cobre. Antecedentes para un análisis sistemático. (The World Market for Copper: Background for a Systematic Analysis. With English summary.) *Colección Estud. CIEPLAN*, June 1989, (26), pp. 91–125.

Vianello, Ferdinando. Effective Demand and the Rate of Profits: Some Thoughts on Marx, Kalecki and Sraffa. In *Sebastiani, M., ed.*, 1989, pp. 164–90.

Vicarelli, Fausto. On the Extension of Sraffa's Theory to a Growing Economy. In *[Weintraub, S.]*, 1989, pp. 203–12.

Vickerman, R. W. Measuring Changes in Regional Competitiveness: The Effects of International Infrastructure Investments. *Ann. Reg. Sci.*, 1989, *23*(4), pp. 275–86.

Vickers, Douglas. The Illusion of the Economic Margin. *J. Post Keynesian Econ.*, Fall 1989, *12*(1), pp. 88–97.

_____. The Money Capital Constraint and Decisions in the Firm. In *[Weintraub, S.]*, 1989, pp. 155–73.

Vickers, John. The Nature of Costs and the Number of Firms at Cournot Equilibrium. *Int. J. Ind. Organ.*, December 1989, *7*(4), pp. 503–09.

_____ **and Yarrow, George.** Privatization in Britain. In *MacAvoy, P. W., et al.*, 1989, pp. 209–45.

Vickers, Stephen P. and Belton, Valerie. V·I·S·A—VIM for MCDA. In *Lockett, A. G. and Islei, G., eds.*, 1989, pp. 287–304.

Vicuñna, Francisco Orrego. Latin American Trade with the Asia-Pacific Region. In *Naya, S., et al., eds.*, 1989, pp. 213–29.

Vieille, Jean-Noël. Liens entre stratégie et performance de quelques groupes agro-alimentaires mondiaux. (Interaction between Strategy and Financial Performance of Some World Food Industry Groups. With English summary.) *Écon. Societes*, July 1989, *23*(7), pp. 53–67.

Vigderhous, Gideon. Scheduling Telephone Interviews: A Study of Seasonal Patterns. In *Singer, E. and Presser, S., eds.*, 1989, *1981*, pp. 69–78.

Vijverberg, Wim and van der Gaag, Jacques. Wage Determinants in Côte d'Ivoire: Experience, Credentials, and Human Capital. *Econ. Devel. Cult. Change*, January 1989, *37*(2), pp. 371–81.

_____; **van der Gaag, Jacques and Stelcner, Morton.** Wage Differentials and Moonlighting by Civil Servants: Evidence from Côte d'Ivoire and Peru. *World Bank Econ. Rev.*, January 1989, *3*(1), pp. 67–95.

_____; **Stelcner, Morton and van der Gaag, Jacques.** A Switching Regression Model of Public–Private Sector Wage Differentials in Peru: 1985–86. *J. Human Res.*, Summer 1989, *24*(3), pp. 545–59.

Vikhanskii, Oleg S. The Reorganization of Management in the Soviet Union. *Econ. Rev. (Keizai Kenkyu)*, January 1989, *40*(1), pp. 69–72.

_____. There Is No Nation More Open . . . *Prob. Econ.*, December 1989, *32*(8), pp. 59–77.

Vila, Jean-Luc. Simple Games of Market Manipulation. *Econ. Letters*, 1989, *29*(1), pp. 21–26.

_____ **and Grossman, Sanford J.** Portfolio Insurance in Complete Markets: A Note. *J. Bus.*, October 1989, *62*(4), pp. 473–76.

Vila, Xavier. Decisión bajo riesgo y relaciones de similitud: Observaciones sobre la conjetura de Rubinstein. (With English summary.) *Invest. Ecón.*, September 1989, *13*(3), pp. 439–51.

Viladomiu, Lourdes and Etxezarreta, Miren. The Restructuring of Spanish Agriculture, and Spain's Accession to the EEC. In *Goodman, D. and Redclift, M., eds.*, 1989, pp. 156–82.

Vilas, Carlos M. International Constraints on Progressive Change in Peripheral Societies: The Case of Nicaragua. In *MacEwan, A. and Tabb, W. K., eds.*, 1989, pp. 316–30.

Vilcassim, Naufel J. Extending the Rotterdam Model to Test Hierarchical Market Structures. *Marketing Sci.*, Spring 1989, *8*(2), pp. 181–90.

Villa, A. Hierarchical Architectures for Production Planning and Control. In *Archetti, F.; Lucertini, M. and Serafini, P., eds.*, 1989, pp. 261–88.

Villa, Paola and Bettio, Francesca. Non-wage Work and Disguised Wage Employment in Italy. In *Rodgers, G. and Rodgers, J., eds.*, 1989, pp. 149–78.

_____ **and Brusco, Sebastiano.** The State, the Unions, and the Labor Market: The Italian Case, 1969–1985. In *Rosenberg, S., ed.*, 1989, pp. 127–50.

Villanueva, Delano and Otani, Ichiro. Major Determinants of Long-term Growth in LDCs. *Finance Devel.*, September 1989, *26*(3), pp. 41–43.

_____ **and Otani, Ichiro.** Theoretical Aspects of Growth in Developing Countries: External Debt Dynamics and the Role of Human Capital. *Int. Monet. Fund Staff Pap.*, June 1989, *36*(2), pp. 307–42.

Villanueva, Javier. Economic Policy during Illia's Period in Office, 1963–66: Comment. In *di Tella, G. and Dornbusch, R., eds.*, 1989, pp. 162–65.

Villaseñor, José A. and Arnold, Barry C. Elliptical Lorenz Curves. *J. Econometrics*, February 1989, *40*(2), pp. 327–38.

Villegas, Daniel J. The Impact of Usury Ceilings on Consumer Credit. *Southern Econ. J.*, July 1989, *56*(1), pp. 126–41.

Villeneuve, Paul. Gender, Employment and Territory in Metropolitan Environments. In *Linge, G. J. R. and van der Knaap, G. A., eds.*, 1989, pp. 67–86.

Vincens, Jean and Plassard, Jean-Michel. Âge, emploi, salaire. (With English summary.) *Revue Écon. Politique*, May–June 1989, *99*(3), pp. 393–45.

Vincent, Daniel R. Bargaining with Common Values. *J. Econ. Theory*, June 1989, *48*(1), pp. 47–62.

Vincent, David. Domestic Effects of Agricultural Protection in Asian Countries with Special Reference to Korea. In *Stoeckel, A. B.; Vincent, D. and Cuthbertson, S., eds.*, 1989, pp. 150–72.

_____. Effects of Agricultural Protection in Japan: An Economywide Analysis. In *Stoeckel, A. B.; Vincent, D. and Cuthbertson, S., eds.*, 1989, pp. 173–99.

_____; **Cuthbertson, Sandy and Stoeckel, Andrew B.** Macroeconomic Consequences of Farm Support Policies: Overview. In *Stoeckel,*

A. B.; Vincent, D. and Cuthbertson, S., eds., 1989, pp. 1–63.

Vincent, James W. and Hagen, Daniel A. On the Pricing of Independently-Generated Electricity. *Southern Econ. J.*, April 1989, *55*(4), pp. 935–53.

Vinci, Salvatore. Disoccupazione e Mezzogiorno. (Unemployment and the "Mezzogiorno." With English summary.) *Econ. Lavoro*, Oct.–Dec. 1989, *23*(4), pp. 23–29.

Vinciguerra, Marlisa. The Aftermath of *Meritor:* A Search for Standards in the Law of Sexual Harassment. *Yale Law J.*, June 1989, *98*(8), pp. 1717–38.

Vincke, Philippe. La modélisation des préférences. (With English summary.) *Revue Écon. Politique*, March–April 1989, *99*(2), pp. 217–34.

Viner, Jacob. Adam Smith and Laissez Faire. In *Clark, J. M., et al.*, 1989, pp. 116–55.

Vines, David. Policy Assignment Strategies with Somewhat Flexible Exchange Rates: Discussion. In *Miller, M.; Eichengreen, B. and Portes, R., eds.*, 1989, pp. 155–59.

_____ **and Hughes, Gordon.** Regulation and Strategic Behaviour in Commercial Television. In *Hughes, G. and Vines, D., eds.*, 1989, pp. 38–90.

_____ **and Molana, Hassan H.** North–South Growth and the Terms of Trade: A Model on Kaldorian Lines. *Econ. J.*, June 1989, *99*(396), pp. 443–53.

_____ **and Moutos, Thomas.** The Simple Macroeconomics of North–South Interaction. *Amer. Econ. Rev.*, May 1989, *79*(2), pp. 270–76.

_____ **and Muscatelli, Anton.** Macroeconomic Interactions between the North and South. In *Bryant, R. C., et al., eds.*, 1989, pp. 381–412.

_____; **Muscatelli, Vito Antonio and Stevenson, Andrew.** Uncovered Interest Parity, Exchange Rate Risk and Exchange Rate Dynamics. In *MacDonald, R. and Taylor, M. P., eds.*, 1989, pp. 159–77.

Viney, Rosalie. Cost Benefit Analysis of Non-drug Treatment of Hypertension. In *Smith, C. S., ed.*, 1989, pp. 123–43.

Vining, Aidan R. and Boardman, Anthony E. Ownership and Performance in Competitive Environments: A Comparison of the Performance of Private, Mixed, and State-Owned Enterprises. *J. Law Econ.*, April 1989, *32*(1), pp. 1–33.

Vink, N. and Nieuwoudt, W. L. The Effects of Increased Earnings from Traditional Agriculture in Southern Africa. *S. Afr. J. Econ.*, September 1989, *57*(3), pp. 257–69.

Vintrová, Ruženka. Continuity or Restructuring? Some Problems of Long-term Socio-economic Forecasts. *Czech. Econ. Pap.*, 1989, (27), pp. 7–23.

Violette, Daniel M.; Fisher, Ann and Chestnut, Lauraine G. The Value of Reducing Risks of Death: A Note on New Evidence. *J. Policy Anal. Manage.*, Winter 1989, *8*(1), pp. 88–100.

Viotti, Staffan; Englund, Peter and Hörngren, Lars. Discount Window Borrowing and Money

Market Interest Rates. *Scand. J. Econ.*, 1989, *91*(3), pp. 517–33.

Vipond, Joan. Australian Experiments with Regional Policies. In *Higgins, B. and Zagorski, K., eds.*, 1989, pp. 65–78.

Virén, Matti. The Long-run Relationship between Interest Rates and Inflation: Some Cross-Country Evidence. *J. Banking Finance*, September 1989, *13*(4–5), pp. 571–85.

——. Saving, Investment and the Current Account: A Review of Recent Evidence. *Econ. Notes*, 1989, (1), pp. 69–75.

—— **and Koskela, Erkki.** International Differences in Saving Rates and the Life Cycle Hypothesis: A Comment. *Europ. Econ. Rev.*, September 1989, *33*(7), pp. 1489–98.

—— **and Pikkarainen, Pentti.** Granger Causality between Money, Output, Prices and Interest Rates: Some Cross-country Evidence from the Period 1875–1984. *Weltwirtsch. Arch.*, 1989, *125*(1), pp. 74–82.

Virmani, Arvind. Credit Markets and Credit Policy in Developing Countries: Myths and Reality. *Greek Econ. Rev.*, 1989, *11*(1), pp. 49–75.

——. Indirect Tax Evasion and Production Efficiency. *J. Public Econ.*, July 1989, *39*(2), pp. 223–37.

——. Technical Possibilities, Usable Blue Prints and Physical Plant Capacity: A Simple Model of Endogenous Technical Change. *Indian Econ. Rev.*, July–Dec. 1989, *24*(2), pp. 185–96.

—— **and Raut, Lakshmi.** Determinants of Consumption and Savings Behavior in Developing Countries. *World Bank Econ. Rev.*, September 1989, *3*(3), pp. 379–93.

Virmani, S. M. Cropping Systems Strategies for Coping with Climatic Fluctuations. In *Oram, P. A., et al.*, 1989, pp. 533–40.

Virtanen, Ilkka and Yli-Olli, Paavo. Kassavirtaperusteisten tunnuslukujen jakaumaominaisuudet ja jakaumien ajallinen pysyvyys. (On Cross-Sectional Properties and Time-Series Persistence of Finnish Cash-Flow Based Financial Ratio Distributions. With English summary.) *Liiketaloudellinen Aikak.*, 1989, *38*(4), pp. 373–404.

Virts, Nancy and Ng, Kenneth. The Value of Freedom. *J. Econ. Hist.*, December 1989, *49*(4), pp. 958–65.

Visaggio, Mauro. On Ricardo's Public Debt Theory. *Econ. Notes*, 1989, (2), pp. 149–66.

Visco, Ignazio; Galli, Giampaolo and Terlizzese, Daniele. Un modello trimestrale per la previsione e la politica economica: Le proprietà di breve e di lungo periodo del modello della Banca d'Italia. (With English summary.) *Politica. Econ.*, April 1989, *5*(1), pp. 3–51.

Visco, Vincenzo. Taxation of Financial Activities: Round Table. *Rev. Econ. Cond. Italy*, Sept.–Dec. 1989, (3), pp. 380–89.

Viscusi, W. Kip. The Effect of Transportation Deregulation on Worker Safety. In *Moses, L. N. and Savage, I., eds.*, 1989, pp. 70–89.

——. The Interaction between Product Liability and Workers' Compensation as Ex Post Remedies for Workplace Injuries. *J. Law, Econ., Organ.*, Spring 1989, *5*(1), pp. 185–210.

——. The Political Economy of Risk Communication Policies for Food and Alcoholic Beverages. In *Shogren, J. F., ed.*, 1989, pp. 83–129.

——. Prospective Reference Theory: Toward an Explanation of the Paradoxes. *J. Risk Uncertainty*, September 1989, *2*(3), pp. 235–63.

——. Toward a Diminished Role for Tort Liability: Social Insurance, Government Regulation, and Contemporary Risks to Health and Safety. *Yale J. Regul.*, Winter 1989, *6*(1), pp. 65–107.

—— **and Moore, Michael J.** Promoting Safety through Workers' Compensation: The Efficacy and Net Wage Costs of Injury Insurance. *Rand J. Econ.*, Winter 1989, *20*(4), pp. 499–515.

—— **and Moore, Michael J.** Rates of Time Preference and Valuations of the Duration of Life. *J. Public Econ.*, April 1989, *38*(3), pp. 297–317.

Vishny, Robert W.; Morck, Randall and Shleifer, Andrei. Alternative Mechanisms for Corporate Control. *Amer. Econ. Rev.*, September 1989, *79*(4), pp. 842–52.

——; **Murphy, Kevin M. and Shleifer, Andrei.** Building Blocks of Market Clearing Business Cycle Models. In *Blanchard, O. J. and Fischer, S., eds.*, 1989, pp. 247–87.

——; **Murphy, Kevin M. and Shleifer, Andrei.** Income Distribution, Market Size, and Industrialization. *Quart. J. Econ.*, August 1989, *104*(3), pp. 537–64.

——; **Murphy, Kevin M. and Shleifer, Andrei.** Industrialization and the Big Push. *J. Polit. Econ.*, October 1989, *97*(5), pp. 1003–26.

—— **and Shleifer, Andrei.** Management Entrenchment: The Case of Manager-Specific Investments. *J. Finan. Econ.*, November 1989, *25*(1), pp. 123–39.

Vishwanath, Tara. Job Search, Stigma Effect, and Escape Rate from Unemployment. *J. Lab. Econ.*, October 1989, *7*(4), pp. 487–502.

Visser, H. Exchange Rate Theories. *De Economist*, 1989, *137*(1), pp. 16–46.

Viswanath, P. V. Taxes and the Futures-Forward Price Difference in the 91-Day T-Bill Market. *J. Money, Credit, Banking*, May 1989, *21*(2), pp. 190–205.

Viswanathan, Nagarathnam and Tse, Edison T. S. Monopolistic Provision of Congested Service with Incentive-Based Allocation of Priorities. *Int. Econ. Rev.*, February 1989, *30*(1), pp. 153–74.

Vitaliano, Donald F. and Mazeya, Y. E. Public Debt and the Size Distribution of Income. In *Davidson, P. and Kregel, J., eds.*, 1989, pp. 56–77.

Viterito, Arthur and Lowe, John C. Differential Spatial Attraction of Private Colleges and Universities in the United States. *Econ. Geogr.*, July 1989, *65*(3), pp. 208–15.

Viton, Philip A. The Desirability of Private-Sector Urban Transportation. *Int. J. Transport Econ.*, June 1989, *16*(2), pp. 131–63.

Vivarelli, Marco and Scalmani, Teodoro. La disoccupazione come categoria economica: Il contributo di Emil Lederer. (Unemployment as an Economic Concept: The Contribution of Emil Lederer. With English summary.) *Giorn. Econ.*, Nov.–Dec. 1989, *48*(11–12), pp. 569–92.

Vives, Xavier. Cournot and the Oligopoly Problem. *Europ. Econ. Rev.*, March 1989, *33*(2/3), pp. 503–14.

———. Technological Competition, Uncertainty, and Oligopoly. *J. Econ. Theory*, August 1989, *48*(2), pp. 386–415.

Vizayakumar, K. and Mohapatra, P. K. J. An Approach to Environmental Impact Assessment by Using Cross Impact Simulation. *Environ. Planning A*, June 1989, *21*(6), pp. 831–37.

Vlachos, Evan C. Comprehensive Planning and Environmental Ethos. In *Dysart, B. C., III and Clawson, M., eds.*, 1989, pp. 126–34.

Vlachou, Andriana S. and Efthymoglou, Prodromos G. Productivity in the Vertically Integrated System of the Greek Electricity Utility, 1970–85. *Energy Econ.*, April 1989, *11*(2), pp. 119–26.

Vladeck, Bruce C. and Freeman, Iris C. The Nursing Home Conundrum. In *Eisdorfer, C.; Kessler, D. A. and Spector, A. N., eds.*, 1989, pp. 224–34.

Vladov, Hristo. Justice, Economic Equality and Welfare in the Conditions of Optimal Functioning of the Economy. In *Bulgarian Academy of Sciences, Institute of Economics*, 1989, pp. 36–46.

Vladova, N. and Rabkina, N. Property and the Market. *Prob. Econ.*, July 1989, *32*(3), pp. 6–24.

Vlahakis, John G. and Partridge, William R. Assessment of Security at Facilities that Produce Nuclear Weapons. In *Golden, B. L.; Wasil, E. A. and Harker, P. T., eds.*, 1989, pp. 182–91.

Vlahos, Kiriakos and Bunn, Derek. Evaluation of the Long-term Effects on UK Electricity Prices following Privatisation. *Fisc. Stud.*, November 1989, *10*(4), pp. 104–16.

——— **and Bunn, Derek.** Evaluation of the Nuclear Constraint in a Privatised Electricity Supply Industry. *Fisc. Stud.*, February 1989, *10*(1), pp. 41–52.

Vlasselaer, M.; Lemaitre, N. and Khrouz, F. Secteur de l'Audit: Analyse structurelle et identification des avantages concurrentiels. (With English summary.) *Cah. Écon. Bruxelles*, 3rd Trimester 1989, (123), pp. 311–27.

Vlek, Charles; Hendrickx, Laurie and Timmermans, Daniëlle. An Experimental Study of the Effectiveness of Computer-Programmed Decision Support. In *Lockett, A. G. and Islei, G., eds.*, 1989, pp. 13–23.

Vleminckx, A. The Impact of the Quality of Debts for the Vulnerability of the International Banking System: Commentary. In *Sijben, J. J., ed.*, 1989, pp. 97–106.

de Vletter, Fion. Footloose Foreign Investment

in Swaziland. In *Whiteside, A. W., ed.*, 1989, pp. 142–66.

Vodă, V. G. and Isaic-Maniu, Al. Estimation of the Average Life of Products by the Aid of Minimum Length Confidence Intervals. *Econ. Computat. Econ. Cybern. Stud. Res.*, 1989, *24*(1), pp. 53–59.

Vodden, Keith and Smith, Douglas A. Global Environmental Policy: The Case of Ozone Depletion. *Can. Public Policy*, December 1989, *15*(4), pp. 413–23.

Voeller, Joachim. A Note on Fair Equality of Rules. In *Bamberg, G. and Spremann, K., eds.*, 1989, pp. 473–80.

Vogel, Joseph H. Entrepreneurship, Evolution, and the Entropy Law. *J. Behav. Econ.*, Fall 1989, *18*(3), pp. 185–204.

Vogelsang, Ingo. Price Cap Regulation of Telecommunications Services: A Long-Run Approach. In *Crew, M. A., ed.*, 1989, pp. 21–42.

———. Two-Part Tariffs as Regulatory Constraints. *J. Public Econ.*, June 1989, *39*(1), pp. 45–66.

——— **and Acton, Jan Paul.** Price-Cap Regulation: Introduction. *Rand J. Econ.*, Autumn 1989, *20*(3), pp. 369–72.

Vogt, Michael G. Bank Reserve Adjustment Process and the Use of Reserve Carryover as a Reserve Management Tool: Comment. *J. Banking Finance*, March 1989, *13*(1), pp. 31–36.

Vojnic, Dragomir; Lang, Rikard and Marendic, Bozo. The Socioeconomic Model of Socialist Self-Management. In *Macesich, G., ed.*, 1989, pp. 12–55.

Volcker, Paul A. The Contributions and Limitations of "Monetary" Analysis. *Fed. Res. Bank New York Quart. Rev.*, Special Issue, 1989, pp. 35–41.

———. Facing Up to the Twin Deficits. In *Guttmann, R., ed.*, 1989, *1984*, pp. 223–28.

———. How Serious Is U.S. Bank Exposure? In *Guttmann, R., ed.*, 1989, *1983*, pp. 180–88.

———. The Political Economy of the Dollar. In *Johnson, C., ed.*, 1989, pp. 53–73.

———. Third World Debt: The Next Phase: Status, Issues, and Prospects. In *Fried, E. R. and Trezise, P. H., eds.*, 1989, pp. 19–21.

Volkonskii, A., et al. The Activation of Labor and Personal Income. *Matekon*, Fall 1989, *26*(1), pp. 39–49.

Von Glinow, Mary Ann and Chung, Byung Jae. Comparative Human Resource Management Practices in the United States, Japan, Korea, and the People's Republic of China. In *Nedd, A., ed.*, 1989, pp. 153–71.

——— **and Chung, Byung Jae.** Korean Chaebols and the Changing Business Environment. In *Chung, K. H. and Lee, H. C., eds.*, 1989, pp. 27–38.

Vona, Stefano and Bini-Smaghi, Lorenzo. The Effects of Economic Convergence and Competitiveness on Trade among the EMS Countries. In *Hodgman, D. R. and Wood, G. E., eds.*, 1989, pp. 272–326.

Voos, Paula B. The Influence of Cooperative Programs on Union–Management Relations, Flexibility, and Other Labor Relations Outcomes. *J. Lab. Res.*, Winter 1989, *10*(1), pp. 103–17.

_____ and Eaton, Adrienne E. The Ability of Unions to Adapt to Innovative Workplace Arrangements. *Amer. Econ. Rev.*, May 1989, *79*(2), pp. 172–76.

Vorasopontaviporn, P. and Kim, Kwan S. International Trade, Employment, and Income: The Case of Thailand. *Developing Econ.*, March 1989, *27*(1), pp. 60–74.

Vorhies, Frank and Glahe, Fred. Liberty and Development in Africa. *S. Afr. J. Econ.*, September 1989, *57*(3), pp. 279–91.

_____ and Glahe, Fred. Religion, Liberty and Economic Development: An Empirical Investigation. *Public Choice*, September 1989, *62*(3), pp. 201–15.

Vos, Rob. Accounting for the World Economy. *Rev. Income Wealth*, December 1989, *35*(4), pp. 389–408.

_____. Ecuador: Windfall Gains, Unbalanced Growth and Stabilization. In *Fitzgerald, E. V. K. and Vos, R.*, 1989, pp. 187–232.

_____. International Finance, Global Adjustment and North–South Relations. In *Fitzgerald, E. V. K. and Vos, R.*, 1989, pp. 115–53.

_____ and FitzGerald, E. V. K. Financing Economic Development: A Structural Approach to Monetary Policy: Introduction. In *Fitzgerald, E. V. K. and Vos, R.*, 1989, pp. 1–15.

_____ and FitzGerald, E. V. K. The Foundations of Development Finance: Economic Structure, Accumulation Balances and Income Distribution. In *Fitzgerald, E. V. K. and Vos, R.*, 1989, pp. 17–54.

Vosburgh, Richard E.; Frisbee, William R. and Fast, Janet. The Effects of Consumer Education on Consumer Search. *J. Cons. Aff.*, Summer 1989, *23*(1), pp. 65–90.

Vosgerau, Hans-Jürgen. International Capital Movements and Trade in an Intertemporal Setting. In *Gordon, I. and Thirlwall, A. P., eds.*, 1989, pp. 215–32.

_____. New Institutional Arrangements for the World Economy: Introduction. In *Vosgerau, H.-J., ed.*, 1989, pp. 1–6.

Vošický, Emilián. Development of Czechoslovakia's Relations with the European Communities. *Czech. Econ. Digest.*, May 1989, (3), pp. 46–50.

Vostatek, Jaroslav. Prognostic Scenarios. *Czech. Econ. Digest.*, May 1989, (3), pp. 21–30.

_____. System of Children's Allowances and Their Relation to Wage Income Taxation. *Czech. Econ. Pap.*, 1989, (27), pp. 85–94.

Voucheva, Hristina. On the Interaction between Prices and Finances. In *Bulgarian Academy of Sciences, Institute of Economics*, 1989, pp. 135–44.

Vougias, S. and Naniopoulos, A. Evaluation of the Port of Volos for the Transport of Goods between Europe and Middle East. In *Candemir, Y., ed.*, 1989, pp. 355–69.

Voute, Caesar. Prospects of Satellite Verification in Europe. In *Rotblat, J. and Goldanskii, V. I., eds.*, 1989, pp. 147–54.

Vredin, Anders and Hörngren, Lars. Exchange Risk Premia in a Currency Basket System. *Weltwirtsch. Arch.*, 1989, *125*(2), pp. 310–25.

Vriend, Nick and Hartog, Joop. Post-war International Labour Mobility: The Netherlands. In *Gordon, I. and Thirlwall, A. P., eds.*, 1989, pp. 74–94.

de Vries, Jan. Processi di urbanizzazione: Interventi degli esperti. (In English.) In *Cavaciocchi, S., ed.*, 1989, pp. 240–44.

Vrieze, O. J. and Thuijsman, F. On Equilibria in Repeated Games with Absorbing States. *Int. J. Game Theory*, 1989, *18*(3), pp. 293–310.

Vroman, Susan B. Inflation Uncertainty and Contract Duration. *Rev. Econ. Statist.*, November 1989, *71*(4), pp. 677–81.

_____. A Longitudinal Analysis of Strike Activity in U.S. Manufacturing: 1957–1984. *Amer. Econ. Rev.*, September 1989, *79*(4), pp. 816–26.

_____ and Vroman, Wayne. The Increase in Early Retirement since 1969. In *Lewin, M. E. and Sullivan, S., eds.*, 1989, pp. 81–101.

Vroman, Wayne and Vroman, Susan B. The Increase in Early Retirement since 1969. In *Lewin, M. E. and Sullivan, S., eds.*, 1989, pp. 81–101.

Vrooman, David M. The Cooperative Traffic Program: Employee Participation on the Baltimore & Ohio Railroad, Phase 2. In *Perkins, E. J., ed.*, 1989, pp. 159–75.

Vuchelen, Jef. Labour Unions, International Competition and the Social Reproduction Cost of Labour. In *Scholliers, P., ed.*, 1989, pp. 201–04.

_____ and Heyndels, B. De efficiëntie van de belastinginning. (With English summary.) *Cah. Écon. Bruxelles*, 2nd Trimester 1989, (122), pp. 221–34.

_____ and Praet, Peter. The Contribution of Consumer Confidence Indexes in Forecasting the Effects of Oil Prices on Private Consumption. *Int. J. Forecasting*, 1989, *5*(3), pp. 393–97.

Vuong, Quang H. Likelihood Ratio Tests for Model Selection and Non-nested Hypotheses. *Econometrica*, March 1989, *57*(2), pp. 307–33.

Vuthipongse, Prakrom. Institutional Capacity to Address Health Problems. In *Reich, M. R. and Marui, E., eds.*, 1989, pp. 37–57.

van Vuuren, Willem and Fox, Glenn C. Estimating the Costs of Soil Erosion: A Comment. *Can. J. Agr. Econ.*, November 1989, *37*(3), pp. 549–53.

_____; Fox, Glenn C. and McKenney, D. W. An Economic Comparison of Alternative Tree Improvement Strategies: A Simulation Approach. *Can. J. Agr. Econ.*, July 1989, *37*(2), pp. 211–32.

Vyslozil, Wilfried and Mühlbacher, Hans. Making Corporate Strategies Work: The Role of Values, Norms, and Attitudes. In *Rueschhoff, N. and Schaum, K., eds.*, 1989, pp. 123–42.

Waagstein, Thorbjørn. Begrebet "strukturforandringer" i økonomisk teori. (The Concept of "Structure" in Economic Theory. With English summary.) *Nationaløkon. Tidsskr.*, 1989, *127*(1), pp. 35–44.

de Waal, Alex. Famine Mortality: A Case Study of Darfur, Sudan 1984–5. *Population Stud.*, March 1989, *43*(1), pp. 5–24.

de Waal, D. P. and Lynas, M. G. Use of External Support Sources in the Planning Processes of Small Firms in Natal, South Africa. *J. Stud. Econ. Econometrics*, March 1989, *13*(1), pp. 77–88.

Wachtel, Howard M. The Global Funny Money Game. In *Guttmann, R., ed.*, 1989, *1988*, pp. 261–65.

Wachtel, Jeffrey M.; Ebrahimi, Bahman and Miner, John B. The Managerial Motivation of Potential Managers in the United States and Other Countries of the World: Implications for National Competitiveness and the Productivity Problem. In *Prasad, S. B., ed.*, 1989, pp. 147–70.

Wachtel, Paul. Present NIPA Saving Measures: Their Characteristics and Limitations: Comment. In *Lipsey, R. E. and Tice, H. S., eds.*, 1989, pp. 93–100.

Wachter, Kenneth W. and Lee, Ronald D. U.S. Births and Limit Cycle Models. *Demography*, February 1989, *26*(1), pp. 99–115.

Wachter, Michael L. and Carter, William H. Norm Shifts in Union Wages: Will 1989 Be a Replay of 1969? *Brookings Pap. Econ. Act.*, 1989, (2), pp. 233–64.

Wachter, Susan and Linneman, Peter D. The Impacts of Borrowing Constraints on Homeownership. *Amer. Real Estate Urban Econ. Assoc. J.*, Winter 1989, *17*(4), pp. 389–402.

Waddington, S. R.; Crossa, J. and Pham, H. N. Yield Stability of CIMMYT Maize Germplasm in International and On-Farm Trials. In *Anderson, J. R. and Hazell, P. B. R., eds.*, 1989, pp. 185–205.

Waddock, Sandra A. and Post, James E. Social Cause Partnerships and the "Mega-event": Hunger, Homelessness and Hands across America. In *Post, J. E., ed.*, 1989, pp. 181–205.

Wade, Larry L. On the Economic Role of Government. In *Samuels, W. J., ed. (I)*, 1989, pp. 197–204.

Wade, Robert. Politics and Graft: Recruitment, Appointment, and Promotions to Public Office in India. In *Ward, P. M., ed.*, 1989, pp. 73–109.

Wadensjö, Eskil and Edebalk, Per Gunnar. Contractually Determined Insurance Schemes for Manual Workers. In *Gustafsson, B. A. and Klevmarken, N. A., eds.*, 1989, pp. 195–210.

Wadewitz, Sabine; Willenbockel, Dirk and Funke, Michael. Tobin's Q and Sectoral Investment in West Germany and Great Britain: A Pooled Cross-Section and Time-Series Study. *Z. Wirtschaft. Sozialwissen.*, 1989, *109*(3), pp. 399–420.

Wadhwani, Sushil. Price Volatility, International Market Links, and Their Implications for Regu-

latory Policies: Commentary. In *Edwards, F. R., ed.*, 1989, pp. 157–61.

_____. Price Volatility, International Market Links, and Their Implications for Regulatory Policies: Commentary. *J. Finan. Services Res.*, December 1989, *3*(2–3), pp. 255–59.

_____ **and Estrin, Saul.** Profit-Sharing. In *Sapsford, D. and Tzannatos, Z., eds.*, 1989, pp. 227–58.

_____ **and Mullins, Mark.** The Effect of the Stock Market on Investment: A Comparative Study. *Europ. Econ. Rev.*, May 1989, *33*(5), pp. 939–56.

Wadley, Susan S. and Derr, Bruce W. Karimpur 1925–1984: Understanding Rural India through Restudies. In *Bardhan, P., ed. (I)*, 1989, pp. 76–126.

Wadsworth, Jonathan and Pissarides, Christopher A. Unemployment and the Inter-regional Mobility of Labour. *Econ. J.*, September 1989, *99*(397), pp. 739–55.

Waelbroeck, Jean. Comparative Estimates of a Macroeconomic Disequilibrium Model: France, Germany, the U.K. and the U.S.A.: Comment. *Europ. Econ. Rev.*, May 1989, *33*(5), pp. 993–95.

_____. Twenty Years After: Econometrics, 1966–1986: Comments. In *Cornet, B. and Tulkens, H., eds.*, 1989, pp. 388–92.

_____; **Adelman, Irma and Bourniaux, Jean-Marc.** Agricultural Development-Led Industrialisation in a Global Perspective. In *Williamson, J. G. and Panchamukhi, V. R., eds.*, 1989, pp. 320–39.

Waer, Paul; Bellis, Jean-François and Vermulst, Edwin A. Further Changes in the EEC Antidumping Regulation: A Codification of Controversial Methodologies. *J. World Trade*, April 1989, *23*(2), pp. 21–34.

Wagatsuma, Takashi. Japan's Development Assistance in Health. In *Reich, M. R. and Marui, E., eds.*, 1989, pp. 372–81.

Wagener, H.-J. A Sketchy View on the Socialist Market Economy. *Acta Oecon.*, 1989, *40*(3–4), pp. 274–79.

_____ **and Hoen, H. W.** Hungary's Exports to the OECD: A Constant Market Shares Analysis. *Acta Oecon.*, 1989, *40*(1–2), pp. 65–77.

Wagenhofer, Alfred. Investigation Strategies with Costly Perfect Information. In *Bamberg, G. and Spremann, K., eds.*, 1989, pp. 347–77.

Wagner, Adolf. Makroökonomisches Kreislauf-und/oder Marktgleichgewicht. (Macroeconomic Flow and/or Market Equilibrium. With English summary.) *Jahr. Nationalökon. Statist.*, October 1989, *206*(4–5), pp. 510–16.

Wagner, Helmut M. Alternatives of Disinflation and Stability Policy—Costs, Efficiency and Implementability: A Comparison between Japan and West Germany. *Bank Japan Monet. Econ. Stud.*, April 1989, *7*(1), pp. 41–97.

_____. Durch Gewinnbeteiligung zur Vollbeschäftigung? (Full Employment through Gain Sharing? With English summary.) *Konjunkturpolitik*, 1989, *35*(6), pp. 329–45.

Wagner, Joachim. Structural Change and Em-

ployment in an Open Economy with Segmented Labour Markets: The Case of the Federal Republic of Germany. In *Wohlmuth, K.,
ed.*, 1989, pp. 359–77.

_____ and Bellmann, Lutz. Adjustment Strategies and Employment in Import-Sensitive
Manufacturing Industries: An Econometric
Study for the Federal Republic of Germany,
1976–1983. In *Wohlmuth, K., ed.*, 1989, pp.
379–401.

_____ and Bellmann, Lutz. The Employment
of Female and Foreign Workers in West Germany Manufacturing Industries, 1977–1983.
Econ. Lavoro, Jan.–March 1989, *23*(1), pp.
131–38.

_____; Bellmann, Lutz and Breitung, Jörg. Bias
Correction and Bootstrapping of Error Component Models for Panel Data: Theory and Applications. *Empirical Econ.*, 1989, *14*(4), pp. 329–
42.

_____ and Lorenz, Wilhelm. Einkommensfunktionsschätzungen mit Längsschnittdaten
für vollzeiterwerbstätige deutsche Männer.
(Estimates of Earnings Functions for Full-
Time Working German Men Using Longitudinal Data. With English summary.) *Konjunkturpolitik*, 1989, *35*(1–2), pp. 99–109.

Wagner, Karin; Prais, S. J. and Jarvis, Valerie.
Productivity and Vocational Skills in Services
in Britain and Germany: Hotels. *Nat. Inst.
Econ. Rev.*, November 1989, (130), pp. 52–
74.

_____ and Steedman, Hilary. Productivity, Ma-
chinery and Skills: Clothing Manufacture in
Britain and Germany. *Nat. Inst. Econ. Rev.*,
May 1989, (128), pp. 40–57.

Wagner, Michael. Spatial Determinants of Social
Mobility: An Analysis with Life History Data
for Three West German Cohorts. In *van Dijk,
J., et al., eds.*, 1989, pp. 241–64.

Wagner, R. Harrison. Uncertainty, Rational
Learning, and Bargaining in the Cuban Missile
Crisis. In *Ordeshook, P. C., ed.*, 1989, pp.
177–205.

Wagner, Richard E. Constitutional Order in a
Federal Republic. *Public Choice*, May 1989,
61(2), pp. 187–92.

_____ and Buchanan, James M. Dialogues Concerning Fiscal Religion. In *Buchanan, J. M.
(II)*, 1989, pp. 283–93.

Wagstaff, Adam. Econometric Studies in Health
Economics: A Survey of the British Literature.
J. Health Econ., March 1989, *8*(1), pp. 1–
51.

_____. Estimating Efficiency in the Hospital Sec-
tor: A Comparison of Three Statistical Cost
Frontier Models. *Appl. Econ.*, May 1989,
21(5), pp. 659–72.

_____ and Barrow, Michael. Efficiency Measurement in the Public Sector: An Appraisal.
Fisc. Stud., February 1989, *10*(1), pp. 72–97.

_____; van Doorslaer, Eddy and Paci, Pierella.
Equity in the Finance and Delivery of Health
Care: Some Tentative Cross-country Comparisons. *Oxford Rev. Econ. Policy*, Spring 1989,
5(1), pp. 89–112.

Wahl, Jenny Bourne. Tax Treatment of Foreign
Exchange Gains and Losses and the Tax Reform Act of 1986. *Nat. Tax J.*, March 1989,
42(1), pp. 59–68.

Wahlroos, Björn. De finansiella marknadernas
roll och framtid. (The Role and Future of Financial Markets. With English summary.)
Ekon. Samfundets Tidskr., 1989, *42*(2), pp. 95–
100.

Wahlund, Richard. Perception and Judgment of
Marginal Tax Rates after a Tax Reduction. In
Grunert, K. G. and Ölander, F., eds., 1989,
pp. 135–79.

Waincymer, Jeffrey. Antidumping Regulations in
the Australian Context: A Commentary. In
Jackson, J. H. and Vermulst, E. A., eds., 1989,
pp. 409–17.

Wainio, John; Krissoff, Barry and Sullivan, John.
Opening Agricultural Markets: Implications for
Developing Countries. *Can. J. Agr. Econ.*,
Part 2, December 1989, *37*(4), pp. 1265–75.

_____ and Liu, Karen. Sources of Instability in
the World Soybean Market. *Can. J. Agr.
Econ.*, Part 2, December 1989, *37*(4), pp.
1315–23.

Wakabayashi, Mitsuru and Graen, George. Human Resource Development of Japanese Managers: Leadership and Career Investment. In
Nedd, A., ed., 1989, pp. 235–56.

Wakasugi, Ryuhei. Japan's Import Structure and
Trade Policy: Realities and Economic Considerations. In *Nieuwenhuysen, J., ed.*, 1989, pp.
70–84.

_____. Technological Innovation in the Asian-Pa-
cific Region: Facts and Economic Interpretations. In *Shinohara, M. and Lo, F., eds.*, 1989,
pp. 328–45.

Wakefield, Joseph C. Federal Fiscal Programs.
Surv. Curr. Bus., January 1989, *69*(1), pp. 29–
35.

Wakefield, W. B. School Roll Forecasts: Their
Uses, Their Accuracy and Educational Reform.
J. Roy. Statist. Society, 1989, *152*(3), pp. 302–
03.

Wakita, Shigeru. Are Survey Forecasts Trusted?:
American Trade Account Deficit and Yen/Dol-
lar Rate. *Econ. Letters*, 1989, *29*(4), pp. 339–
44.

Wakker, Peter. Continuous Subjective Expected
Utility with Non-additive Probabilities. *J.
Math. Econ.*, 1989, *18*(1), pp. 1–27.

Walbert, Mark S. Grading Software Programs Ac-
companying Selected Principles Texts. *Econ.
Inquiry*, January 1989, *27*(1), pp. 169–79.

_____. Writing Better Software for Economics
Principles Textbooks. *J. Econ. Educ.*, Summer
1989, *20*(3), pp. 281–89.

Waldie, Bruce. Accounting Software: The Answer
to Better Farm Records? *Can. J. Agr. Econ.*,
Part 1, December 1989, *37*(4), pp. 727–32.

Waldman, Donald M. and Becker, William E.
A Graphical Interpretation of Probit Coefficients. *J. Econ. Educ.*, Fall 1989, *20*(4), pp.
371–78.

Waldman, Michael and Haltiwanger, John C.
Limited Rationality and Strategic Comple-

ments: The Implications for Macroeconomics. *Quart. J. Econ.*, August 1989, *104*(3), pp. 463–83.

_____ **and Haltiwanger, John C.** Rational Expectations in the Aggregate. *Econ. Inquiry*, October 1989, *27*(4), pp. 619–36.

Walker, David A. Effects of Economic Reforms on the Banking System in China. *Econ. Int.*, Aug.–Nov. 1989, *42*(3–4), pp. 244–57.

_____ **and Koot, Ronald S.** Economic Stability and the Federal Deficit. *Rivista Int. Sci. Econ. Com.*, Oct.–Nov. 1989, *36*(10–11), pp. 905–16.

Walker, Donald A. Keynes's Anticipation of Monetarism. *Australian Econ. Pap.*, June 1989, *28*(52), pp. 1–15.

Walker, Ian. Microeconometric Modelling and Microeconomic Policy Analysis. In *Hey, J. D., ed.*, 1989, pp. 209–35.

_____ **and Dilnot, Andrew.** Economic Issues in Social Security: Introduction. In *Dilnot, A. and Walker, I., eds.*, 1989, pp. 1–15.

_____ **and Symons, Elizabeth.** The Revenue and Welfare Effects of Fiscal Harmonization for the UK. *Oxford Rev. Econ. Policy*, Summer 1989, *5*(2), pp. 61–75.

Walker, James M.; Isaac, R. Mark and Schmidtz, David. The Assurance Problem in a Laboratory Market. *Public Choice*, September 1989, *62*(3), pp. 217–36.

Walker, James R. and Heckman, James J. Forecasting Aggregate Period-Specific Birth Rates: The Time Series Properties of a Microdynamic Neoclassical Model of Fertility. *J. Amer. Statist. Assoc.*, December 1989, *84*(408), pp. 958–65.

Walker, John F. and Vatter, Harold G. Why Has the United States Operated Below Potential since World War II? *J. Post Keynesian Econ.*, Spring 1989, *11*(3), pp. 327–46.

Walker, Lilly J. Schubert. Fitting Farm Management Strategies to Family Style. *Can. J. Agr. Econ.*, Part 1, December 1989, *37*(4), pp. 747–54.

Walker, Mark. Conflicting Interests, Decomposability, and Comparative Statics. *Math. Soc. Sci.*, August 1989, *18*(1), pp. 57–79.

Walker, Mary Beth and Brown, Bryan W. The Random Utility Hypothesis and Inference in Demand Systems. *Econometrica*, July 1989, *57*(4), pp. 815–29.

Walker, Michael A. and Grubel, Herbert G. Services and the Changing Economic Structure. In *Giersch, H., ed.*, 1989, pp. 1–34.

Walker, P. and Dunn, R. District-Level Variations in the Configuration of Service Provision in England: A Graphical Approach to Classification. *Environ. Planning A*, October 1989, *21*(10), pp. 1397–1411.

Walker, Thomas S. High-Yielding Varieties and Variability in Sorghum and Pearl Millet Production in India. In *Anderson, J. R. and Hazell, P. B. R., eds.*, 1989, pp. 91–99.

_____. Yield and Household Income Variability in India's Semi-Arid Tropics. In *Anderson, J. R. and Hazell, P. B. R., eds.*, 1989, pp. 309–19.

Walkling, Ralph A.; Lang, Larry H. P. and Stulz, René M. Managerial Performance, Tobin's Q, and the Gains from Successful Tender Offers. *J. Finan. Econ.*, September 1989, *24*(1), pp. 137–54.

Wall, Geoffrey and Mitchell, Claire J. A. The Arts and Employment: A Case Study of the Stratford Festival. *Growth Change*, Fall 1989, *20*(4), pp. 31–40.

Wall, Jerry L. and MacDonald, Don N. An Experimental Study of the Allais Paradox over Losses: Some Preliminary Evidence. *Quart. J. Bus. Econ.*, Autumn 1989, *28*(4), pp. 43–60.

Wall, Larry D. Capital Requirements for Banks: A Look at the 1981 and 1988 Standards. *Fed. Res. Bank Atlanta Econ. Rev.*, March–April 1989, *74*(2), pp. 14–29.

_____. Interest Rate Swaps in an Agency Theoretic Model with Uncertain Interest Rates. *J. Banking Finance*, May 1989, *13*(2), pp. 261–70.

_____. A Plan for Reducing Future Deposit Insurance Losses: Puttable Subordinated Debt. *Fed. Res. Bank Atlanta Econ. Rev.*, July–Aug. 1989, *74*(4), pp. 2–17.

_____; **Cheng, David C. and Gup, Benton E.** Financial Determinants of Bank Takeovers: A Note. *J. Money, Credit, Banking*, November 1989, *21*(4), pp. 524–36.

_____ **and Hunter, William Curt.** Bank Merger Motivations: A Review of the Evidence and an Examination of Key Target Bank Characteristics. *Fed. Res. Bank Atlanta Econ. Rev.*, Sept.–Oct. 1989, *74*(5), pp. 2–19.

Wall, M. Danny. The Tasks Ahead. In *Federal Home Loan Bank of San Francisco*, 1989, pp. 231–37.

Wall, Richard. Leaving Home and Living Alone: An Historical Perspective. *Population Stud.*, November 1989, *43*(3), pp. 369–89.

_____. The Place of the Unskilled Male Worker in the Economy of a Nation: A Comment. In *Scholliers, P., ed.*, 1989, pp. 66–73.

Wallace, Fred. The Neutrality of Optimal Government Financial Policy: Supplying the Intergenerational Free Lunch: A Comment. *Eastern Econ. J.*, April–June 1989, *15*(2), pp. 147–50.

Wallace, Helen. The Best Is the Enemy of the 'Could': Bargaining in the European Community. In *Tarditi, S., et al., eds.*, 1989, pp. 193–206.

Wallace, John. The Promotion of Effective Management Development. In *Davies, J., et al., eds.*, 1989, pp. 167–84.

_____, **et al.** Management and Organizational Development in Bulgaria. In *Davies, J., et al., eds.*, 1989, pp. 238–46.

Wallace, Michael B. Nepal: Food Pricing with an Open Border. In *Sicular, T., ed.*, 1989, pp. 183–242.

Wallace, Myles S.; Bowles, David and Ulbrich, Holley H. Default Risk, Interest Differentials and Fiscal Policy: A New Look at Crowding

Out. *Eastern Econ. J.*, July–Sept. 1989, *15*(3), pp. 203–12.

_____ **and McNown, Robert F.** Co-integration Tests for Long Run Equilibrium in the Monetary Exchange Rate Model. *Econ. Letters*, December 1989, *31*(3), pp. 263–67.

_____ **and McNown, Robert F.** National Price Levels, Purchasing Power Parity, and Cointegration: A Test of Four High Inflation Economies. *J. Int. Money Finance*, December 1989, *8*(4), pp. 533–45.

_____ **and Ulbrich, Holley H.** Determinants of Club Membership: An Economic Approach. *Atlantic Econ. J.*, March 1989, *17*(1), pp. 8–15.

Wallace, Nancy E. and Inaba, Fred S. Spatial Price Competition and the Demand for Freight Transportation. *Rev. Econ. Statist.*, November 1989, *71*(4), pp. 614–25.

Wallace, Neil. Some Alternative Monetary Models and Their Implications for the Role of Open-Market Policy. **In** *Barro, R. J., ed.*, 1989, pp. 306–28.

Wallace, R. 'Homelessness,' Contagious Destruction of Housing, and Municipal Service Cuts in New York City: 1. Demographics of a Housing Deficit. *Environ. Planning A*, December 1989, *21*(12), pp. 1585–1602.

Wallace, Robert. The Industries Assistance Commission's Report on Pharmaceutical Products. **In** *Butler, J. R. G. and Doessel, D. P., eds.*, 1989, *1987*, pp. 348–62.

_____. Medifinance: A Proposal for an Alternative Health Insurance System. **In** *Butler, J. R. G. and Doessel, D. P., eds.*, 1989, *1977*, pp. 167–84.

Wallace, Wanda A. An "Early Warning" Signal from the Market: Its Potential as an Audit Tool. **In** *Gangolly, J., ed.*, 1989, pp. 205–31.

_____. Are Audit Fees Sufficiently Risk Adjusted? **In** *Gangolly, J., ed.*, 1989, pp. 3–37.

Wallack, Stanley and Lewin, Marion Ein. Strategies for Financing Long-Term Care. **In** *Lewin, M. E. and Sullivan, S., eds.*, 1989, pp. 161–76.

van de Walle, Etienne and Garenne, Michel. Polygyny and Fertility among the Sereer of Senegal. *Population Stud.*, July 1989, *43*(2), pp. 267–83.

_____; **van de Walle, Francine and Trussell, James.** Norms and Behaviour in Burkinabe Fertility. *Population Stud.*, November 1989, *43*(3), pp. 429–54.

van de Walle, Francine; Trussell, James and van de Walle, Etienne. Norms and Behaviour in Burkinabe Fertility. *Population Stud.*, November 1989, *43*(3), pp. 429–54.

van de Walle, Nicolas. Privatization in Developing Countries: A Review of the Issues. *World Devel.*, May 1989, *17*(5), pp. 601–15.

Wallendorf, Melanie; Sherry, John F., Jr. and Belk, Russell W. The Sacred and the Profane in Consumer Behavior: Theodicy on the Odyssey. *J. Cons. Res.*, June 1989, *16*(1), pp. 1–38.

Wallenius, Jyrki and Korhonen, Pekka. A Careful Look at Efficiency in Multiple Objective Linear Programming. **In** *Lockett, A. G. and Islei, G., eds.*, 1989, pp. 334–44.

Waller, Christopher J. Efficiency Wages, Wage Indexation and Macroeconomic Stabilization. *Econ. Letters*, August 1989, *30*(2), pp. 125–28.

_____. Monetary Policy Games and Central Bank Politics. *J. Money, Credit, Banking*, November 1989, *21*(4), pp. 422–31.

_____ **and VanHoose, David D.** Endogenous Wage Indexation and Optimal Monetary Policy with and without a Balanced Budget. *J. Econ. Bus.*, February 1989, *41*(1), pp. 21–31.

_____ **and VanHoose, David D.** Islands, Indexation and Monetary Policy. *Econ. Inquiry*, October 1989, *27*(4), pp. 705–17.

_____ **and VanHoose, David D.** Optimal Monetary Policy and Alternative Wage Indexation Schemes in a Model with Interest-Sensitive Labor Supply. *J. Macroecon.*, Spring 1989, *11*(2), pp. 163–80.

Waller, Mary Ellen. The Business Side of Media Development: Popular Women's Magazines in the Late Nineteenth Century. **In** *Perkins, E. J., ed.*, 1989, pp. 40–59.

Waller, William T., Jr. Criticism of Institutionalism, Methodology, and Value Theory: Comment. *J. Econ. Issues*, September 1989, *23*(3), pp. 873–79.

_____. The Impossibility of Fiscal Policy. *J. Econ. Issues*, December 1989, *23*(4), pp. 1047–58.

_____. Methodological Aspects of Radical Institutionalism. **In** *Dugger, W. M., ed.*, 1989, pp. 39–49.

Waller-Zuckerman, Mary Ellen. Marketing the Women's Journals, 1873–1900. **In** *Hausman, W. J., ed.*, 1989, pp. 99–108.

_____. "Old Homes, in a City of Perpetual Change": Women's Magazines, 1890–1916. *Bus. Hist. Rev.*, Winter 1989, *63*(4), pp. 715–56.

Wallerstein, Immanuel; Arrighi, Giovanni and Keyder, Çağlar. Southern Europe in the World Economy in the Twentieth Century: Implications for Political and Social Transformations. **In** *Martin, M. T. and Kandal, T. R., eds.*, 1989, pp. 409–17.

Wallich, Henry C. Whither American Banking Reform? **In** *Guttmann, R., ed.*, 1989, *1985*, pp. 152–55.

_____ **and Stockton, David J.** A Macroeconomic Perspective on Tax-Based Incomes Policies. **In** *[Weintraub, S.]*, 1989, pp. 47–67.

Wallin, Jan. Profitability, Capital Structure and Debt Servicing Behaviour: Empirical Analysis of Patterns in Small and Middle-Size Companies. *Liiketaloudellinen Aikak.*, 1989, *38*(1), pp. 31–46.

Wallis, John Joseph. Employment in the Great Depression: New Data and Hypotheses. *Exploration Econ. Hist.*, January 1989, *26*(1), pp. 45–72.

_____. Towards a Positive Economic Theory of Institutional Change. *J. Inst. Theoretical Econ.*, March 1989, *145*(1), pp. 98–112.

Wallis, Kenneth F. Macroeconomic Forecasting: A Survey. *Econ. J.*, March 1989, *99*(394), pp. 28–61.

_____; **Whitley, John D. and Turner, David S.** Differences in the Properties of Large-Scale Macroeconometric Models: The Role of Labour Market Specifications. *J. Appl. Econometrics*, Oct.–Dec. 1989, *4*(4), pp. 317–44.

Wallis, W. Allen. On European Economic Integration. *Amer. J. Econ. Sociology*, April 1989, *48*(2), pp. 142.

Walliser, Bernard. Articulation entre microéconomie et macaroéconomie dans l'évaluation des projets. (With English summary.) *Revue Écon. Politique*, March–April 1989, *99*(2), pp. 235–51.

_____. Théorie des jeux et genèse des institutions. (With English summary.) *Rech. Écon. Louvain*, 1989, *55*(4), pp. 339–64.

Wallschutzsky, Ian. Achieving Compliance in Developing Countries: International. *Bull. Int. Fiscal Doc.*, May 1989, *43*(5), pp. 234–44.

Walraven, Nicholas and Rosine, John. Drought, Agriculture, and the Economy. *Fed. Res. Bull.*, January 1989, *75*(1), pp. 1–12.

Walsh, Brendan M. Tests for Macroeconomic Feedback from Large-Scale Migration Based on the Irish Experience, 1948–87: A Note. *Econ. Soc. Rev.*, April 1989, *20*(3), pp. 257–66.

_____. Tests for the Macroeconomic Effects of Large-Scale Migration Based on the Irish Experience, 1948–87: A Rejoinder. *Econ. Soc. Rev.*, April 1989, *20*(3), pp. 278–79.

Walsh, Frank A.; Woelger, Ernestine and Walsh, Patrick P. The Real Wage Gap and Its Development over Time: The Irish Experience 1960–1987. *Econ. Soc. Rev.*, October 1989, *21*(1), pp. 87–102.

Walsh, Lorena S. Plantation Management in the Chesapeake, 1620–1820. *J. Econ. Hist.*, June 1989, *49*(2), pp. 393–406.

Walsh, Michael J. Energy Tax Credits and Housing Improvement. *Energy Econ.*, October 1989, *11*(4), pp. 275–84.

Walsh, Patrick P.; Walsh, Frank A. and Woelger, Ernestine. The Real Wage Gap and Its Development over Time: The Irish Experience 1960–1987. *Econ. Soc. Rev.*, October 1989, *21*(1), pp. 87–102.

Walsh, Richard G.; Johnson, Donn M. and McKean, John R. Issues in Nonmarket Valuation and Policy Application: A Retrospective Glance. *Western J. Agr. Econ.*, July 1989, *14*(1), pp. 178–88.

Walsh, Tim. Part-Time Employment and Labour Market Policies. *Nat. Westminster Bank Quart. Rev.*, May 1989, pp. 43–55.

Walsh, Vivian. Joan Robinson and 'Getting into Equilibrium,' in Short and Long Periods. **In** *Feiwel, G. R., ed. (II)*, 1989, pp. 303–10.

_____. A View of Joan Robinson's Last Decade. **In** *Feiwel, G. R., ed. (II)*, 1989, pp. 881–91.

Walstad, William B. and Soper, John C. What Is High School Economics? Factors Contribut-ing to Student Achievement and Attitudes. *J. Econ. Educ.*, Winter 1989, *20*(1), pp. 23–38.

Walston, Roderick E. The Public Trust Doctrine in the Water Rights Context. *Natural Res. J.*, Spring 1989, *29*(2), pp. 585–92.

van der Walt, I. N. A. and Swanepoel, J. J. Indicative Labour and Capital Programming: An Exercise on the Frontiers of Empirical Economics. **In** *Gemper, B. B., ed.*, 1989, pp. 65–86.

Walter, Ingo and Levich, Richard M. The Regulation of Global Financial Markets. **In** *Noyelle, T., ed.*, 1989, pp. 51–89.

_____ **and Saunders, Anthony.** Competitive Performance, Regulation and Trade in Banking Services. **In** *Vosgerau, H.-J., ed.*, 1989, pp. 238–50.

Walter, Jean-Luc and Day, Richard H. Economic Growth in the Very Long Run: On the Multiple-Phase Interaction of Population, Technology, and Social Infrastructure. **In** *Barnett, W. A.; Geweke, J. and Shell, K., eds.*, 1989, pp. 253–89.

Walter, John R. Monetary Aggregates: A User's Guide. *Fed. Res. Bank Richmond Econ. Rev.*, Jan.–Feb. 1989, *75*(1), pp. 20–28.

_____ **and Gup, Benton E.** Top Performing Small Banks: Making Money the Old-Fashioned Way. *Fed. Res. Bank Richmond Econ. Rev.*, Nov.–Dec. 1989, *75*(6), pp. 23–35.

_____ **and Welker, Donald L.** Fifth District Banks' Return on Assets: Highest in Decade. *Fed. Res. Bank Richmond Econ. Rev.*, May–June 1989, *75*(3), pp. 16–22.

Walter, Norbert. Implications of EC Financial Integration. *Bus. Econ.*, October 1989, *24*(4), pp. 18–23.

_____. Protection and the Structure of the Banking Industry in an International Context: Comment. **In** *Giersch, H., ed.*, 1989, pp. 219–21.

_____. Supply-Side Economics: Struggling for Rebirth. **In** *Fels, G. and von Furstenberg, G. M., eds.*, 1989, pp. 405–16.

Walter, Terry and Koh, Francis. A Direct Test of Rock's Model of the Pricing of Unseasoned Issues. *J. Finan. Econ.*, August 1989, *23*(2), pp. 251–72.

Walters, Alan. Comment: A Critical View of the EMS. **In** *Dorn, J. A. and Niskanen, W. A., eds.*, 1989, *1988*, pp. 289–92.

_____. Liberalization and Privatization: An Overview. **In** *El-Naggar, S., ed.*, 1989, pp. 18–41.

_____. A Life Philosophy. *Amer. Economist*, Fall 1989, *33*(2), pp. 18–24.

_____. Privatization in Britain: Comment. **In** *MacAvoy, P. W., et al.*, 1989, pp. 247–57.

_____. Supply-Side Policies: The Lessons from the U.K. **In** *Fels, G. and von Furstenberg, G. M., eds.*, 1989, pp. 185–214.

_____ **and Minford, Patrick.** Modelling the Role of Government Deficits in Developing Countries. *Econ. Modelling*, April 1989, *6*(2), pp. 106–73.

Walters, Jon. Renegotiating Dependency: The Case of the Southern African Customs Union. *J. Common Market Stud.*, September 1989, *28*(1), pp. 29–52.

Walters, Stephen J. K.; Jordan, John M. and Meador, Mark. Academic Research Productivity, Department Size and Organization: Further Results. *Econ. Educ. Rev.*, 1989, 8(4), pp. 345–52.

Walton, Clarence C. Investment Bankers from Ethical Perspectives . . . with Special Emphasis on the Theory of Agency. In *Williams, O. F.; Reilly, F. K. and Houck, J. W., eds.*, 1989, pp. 217–32.

Walton, David and Hook, Alison. Commodity Price Indicators: A Case for Discretion Rather Than Rules. In *Miller, M.; Eichengreen, B. and Portes, R., eds.*, 1989, pp. 99–119.

Walton, John and Ragin, Charles. Austerity and Dissent: Social Bases of Popular Struggle in Latin America. In *Canak, W. L., ed.*, 1989, pp. 216–32.

Walton, John K. Proto-industrialisation and the First Industrial Revolution: The Case of Lancashire. In *Hudson, P., ed.*, 1989, pp. 41–68.

Walton, Thomas F. and Langenfeld, James. Regulatory Reform under Reagan—The Right Way and the Wrong Way. In *Meiners, R. E. and Yandle, B., eds.*, 1989, pp. 41–70.

Walz, Daniel T. and Spencer, Roger W. The Informational Content of Forward Rates: Further Evidence. *J. Finan. Res.*, Spring 1989, 12(1), pp. 69–81.

Walz, Uwe and Bletzinger, Matthias. Zum Schattenpreis- und Einkommensbegriff in der ökonomischen Theorie der Fertilität. (Shadow Price and Income Concepts in the Economic Theory of Fertility. With English summary.) *Jahr. Nationalökon. Statist.*, December 1989, 206(6), pp. 591–98.

Walzer, N.; Deller, Steven C. and Chicoine, David L. Representative vs. Direct Democracy and Government Spending in a Median Voter Model. *Public Finance*, 1989, 44(2), pp. 225–36.

Wan, G. H.; Anderson, Jock R. and Findlay, Carly J. Are Modern Cultivars More Risky? A Question of Stochastic Efficiency. In *Anderson, J. R. and Hazell, P. B. R., eds.*, 1989, pp. 301–08.

Wan, Henry, Jr. and Clemhout, Simone. On Games of Cake-Eating. In *[Verheyen, P.]*, 1989, pp. 121–55.

_____ **and Fields, Gary S.** Wage-Setting Institutions and Economic Growth. *World Devel.*, Special Issue, September 1989, 17(9), pp. 1471–83.

Wand, Yair and Weber, Ron. A Model of Control and Audit Procedure Change in Evolving Data Processing Systems. *Accounting Rev.*, January 1989, 64(1), pp. 87–107.

Wang, Chun-Yuan. Optimal Monetary–Fiscal Stabilizers under an Indexed versus Nonindexed Tax Structure—A Correction. *J. Econ. Bus.*, February 1989, 41(1), pp. 89–92.

Wang, Dunshu and Yu, Ke. Further Comments on the "Asiatic Mode of Production." In *Brook, T., ed.*, 1989, pp. 118–35.

Wang, George H. K. and Sauerhaft, Daniel. Examination Ratings and the Identification of Problem/Non-problem Thrift Institutions. *J. Finan. Services Res.*, October 1989, 2(4), pp. 319–42.

Wang, Guangwei. The Basic Tasks of China's First Five-Year Plan. In *Howe, C. and Walker, K. R., eds.*, 1989, 1955, pp. 10–19.

Wang, Heshou. Developing the National Iron and Steel Industry at Top Speed. In *Howe, C. and Walker, K. R., eds.*, 1989, 1957, pp. 165–71.

Wang, Hui-Ling; Matsuda, Yoshiro and Mizoguchi, Toshiyuki. A Comparison of Real Consumption Level between Japan and People's Republic of China—The First Approach of Application of ICP Method to Chinese Data. *Hitotsubashi J. Econ.*, June 1989, 30(1), pp. 15–29.

Wang, Jane-Ling; Gastwirth, Joseph L. and Nayak, Tapan K. Statistical Properties of Measures of Between-Group Income Differentials. *J. Econometrics*, September 1989, 42(1), pp. 5–19.

Wang, Leonard F. S. Resource Policy, Investment, and Employment under Variable Returns to Scale. *J. Devel. Econ.*, April 1989, 30(2), pp. 381–89.

_____. Urban Unemployment, Economies of Scale and Customs Unions. In *Missouri Valley Economic Association*, 1989, pp. 175–82.

Wang, Qiwen and Golden, Bruce L. An Alternate Measure of Consistency. In *Golden, B. L.; Wasil, E. A. and Harker, P. T., eds.*, 1989, pp. 68–81.

Wang, Rongjiu and Liu, Yunhui. Appraising the Adjustment of Autumn Grain Prices. In *Howe, C. and Walker, K. R., eds.*, 1989, 1959, pp. 265–67.

Wang, Susheng. Trade Balance and Exchange Rate with the PPP Theory. *Econ. Letters*, October 1989, 30(4), pp. 363–66.

Wang, Tzu-ying. What Lessons Have Been Gained through the Experience of Preparing and Implementing the 1956 State Budget? In *Howe, C. and Walker, K. R., eds.*, 1989, 1957, pp. 41–51.

Wang, Xiangming. The Population Policy, and Balanced Growth of Industry and Agriculture in China. In *Chakravarty, S., ed.*, 1989, pp. 43–56.

Wang, Xiaoqiang. Transcending the Logic of Private Ownership: The Separation between Contracted Production and Corporate Property. *Chinese Econ. Stud.*, Fall 1989, 23(1), pp. 43–56.

_____; **Gao, Shangquan and Chen, Yizi.** Investigation of Reforms in Hungary and Yugoslavia. *Chinese Econ. Stud.*, Spring 1989, 22(3), pp. 80–88.

_____ **and Ji, Xiaoming.** Thoughts on Not Establishing a Stockholding System for Enterprises. *Chinese Econ. Stud.*, Fall 1989, 23(1), pp. 33–42.

_____ **and Ji, Xiaoming.** Thoughts on the Model of Nonstock Enterprises. *Chinese Econ. Stud.*, Winter 1988–89, 22(2), pp. 38–46.

Wang, Zhigang and Zou, Gang. Interests of the Entrepreneur and Behavior of the Enterprise.

Chinese Econ. Stud., Winter 1988–89, 22(2), pp. 82–94.

Wann, Joyce J.; Sexton, Richard J. and Wilson, Brooks M. Some Tests of the Economic Theory of Cooperatives: Methodology and Application to Cotton Ginning. *Western J. Agr. Econ.*, July 1989, *14*(1), pp. 56–66.

Wanous, John P. and Colella, Adrienne. Organizational Entry Research: Current Status and Future Directions. In *Ferris, G. R. and Rowland, K. M., eds.*, 1989, pp. 59–120.

Wansbeek, Tom and Kapteyn, Arie. Estimation of the Error-Components Model with Incomplete Panels. *J. Econometrics*, July 1989, *41*(3), pp. 341–61.

Wansley, James W. and Dhillon, Upinder S. Determinants of Valuation Effects for Security Offerings of Commercial Bank Holding Companies. *J. Finan. Res.*, Fall 1989, *12*(3), pp. 217–33.

_____ **and Lamoureux, Christopher G.** The Pricing of When-Issued Securities. *Financial Rev.*, May 1989, *24*(2), pp. 183–98.

_____; **Lane, William R. and Looney, Stephen W.** An Examination of Misclassifications with Bank Failure Prediction Models. *J. Econ. Bus.*, November 1989, *41*(4), pp. 327–36.

Waqif, Arif A. The Structure of Unemployment and Employment Generating Strategies. In *Reddy, J. M., et al., eds. (II)*, 1989, pp. 130–48.

Waragai, Tomoki and Akiba, Hiroya. An Analysis of Structural Changes in the Seven Major Exchange Rates. In *Singer, H. W. and Sharma, S., eds. (II)*, 1989, pp. 146–59.

_____ **and Akiba, Hiroya.** An Arbitrariness-Free Method of Detecting Structural Changes. *Econ. Letters*, 1989, *29*(1), pp. 27–30.

Ward, Charles W. R. and Choi, Daniel F. S. The Reconciliation of the Smith's and Jarrow and Rudd's Option Sensitivity Formulae: A Teaching Note. *Financial Rev.*, August 1989, *24*(3), pp. 507–10.

Ward, Clement E.; Kahl, Kandice H. and Hudson, Michael A. Cash Settlement Issues for Live Cattle Futures Contracts. *J. Futures Markets*, June 1989, *9*(3), pp. 237–48.

Ward, David A. The Canadian Approach to Anti-avoidance Provisions: Background to the New Anti-avoidance Rule. *Bull. Int. Fiscal Doc.*, February 1989, *43*(2), pp. 73–76.

Ward, Frank A. Efficiently Managing Spatially Competing Water Uses: New Evidence from a Regional Recreation Demand Model. *J. Reg. Sci.*, May 1989, *29*(2), pp. 229–46.

Ward, Hugh. Testing the Waters: Taking Risks to Gain Reassurance in Public Goods Games. *J. Conflict Resolution*, June 1989, *33*(2), pp. 274–308.

Ward, Karen. From Executive to Feminist: The Business Women's Legislative Council of Los Angeles, 1927–1932. In *Perkins, E. J., ed.*, 1989, pp. 60–75.

Ward, Lisa M.; Palmer, Paul R. and Harmon, Bruce R. Schedule Estimating Relationships for Tactical Aircraft. In *Gulledge, T. R., Jr. and Litteral, L. A., eds.*, 1989, pp. 259–80.

Ward, Michael and Smith, James P. Women in the Labor Market and in the Family. *J. Econ. Perspectives*, Winter 1989, *3*(1), pp. 9–23.

Ward, Oliver O. Job Creation and European Employment Issues: A Business Owner's Perspective. *J. Lab. Res.*, Winter 1989, *10*(1), pp. 57–60.

Ward, Peter. Corruption, Development and Inequality: Introduction. In *Ward, P. M., ed.*, 1989, pp. 1–12.

_____. Local Leadership and the Distributional Benefits Wrought by Illegality in Third World Community Development. In *Ward, P. M., ed.*, 1989, pp. 143–55.

Ward, Ronald W. and Dixon, Bruce L. Effectiveness of Fluid Milk Advertising since the Dairy and Tobacco Adjustment Act of 1983. *Amer. J. Agr. Econ.*, August 1989, *71*(3), pp. 730–40.

Wardlow, Penelope S. and Friar, Shirley A. Local Government Procurement of CPA Audit Services: The Role of the States. *Public Budg. Finance*, Spring 1989, *9*(1), pp. 92–106.

_____ **and Godfrey, James T.** Pers Reports and Users' Information Needs. In *Chan, J. L. and Patton, J. M., eds.*, 1989, pp. 71–97.

Ware, Harold and Bidwell, Miles O. Regulatory Scrutiny of Marketing Expenses: Competitive Necessity vs. Regulatory Hang-Ups. In *National Economic Research Associates*, 1989, pp. 117–31.

Ware, Roger; Lewis, Tracy R. and Feenstra, Robert C. Eliminating Price Supports: A Political Economy Perspective. *J. Public Econ.*, November 1989, *40*(2), pp. 159–85.

Warf, Barney and Cox, Joseph C. Military Prime Contracts and Taxes in the New York Metropolitan Region: A Short-run Analysis. *Reg. Stud.*, June 1989, *23*(3), pp. 241–51.

Warford, Jeremy J. Environmental Management and Economic Policy in Developing Countries. In *Schramm, G. and Warford, J. J., eds.*, 1989, pp. 7–22.

_____ **and Partow, Zeinab.** Evolution of the World Bank's Environmental Policy. *Finance Devel.*, December 1989, *26*(4), pp. 5–8.

Warga, Arthur. Experimental Design in Tests of Linear Factor Models. *J. Bus. Econ. Statist.*, April 1989, *7*(2), pp. 191–98.

_____ **and Sarig, Oded.** Bond Price Data and Bond Market Liquidity. *J. Finan. Quant. Anal.*, September 1989, *24*(3), pp. 367–78.

_____ **and Sarig, Oded.** Some Empirical Estimates of the Risk Structure of Interest Rates. *J. Finance*, December 1989, *44*(5), pp. 1351–60.

_____ **and Titman, Sheridan D.** Stock Returns as Predictors of Interest Rates and Inflation. *J. Finan. Quant. Anal.*, March 1989, *24*(1), pp. 47–58.

Warley, T. K. and Meilke, Karl D. Agriculture in the Uruguay Round: A Canadian Perspective. *Can. J. Agr. Econ.*, Part 2, December 1989, *37*(4), pp. 825–52.

Warner, David C.; Juretic, Mark and Stolp, Chandler. Patterns of Inpatient Mental Health, Mental Retardation, and Substance Abuse Service Utilization in California. *Soc. Sci. Quart.*, September 1989, 70(3), pp. 687–707.

Warner, John T.; Diamond, Charles A. and Simon, Curtis J. Evidence on the Fit of the Log-Linear Income Model versus a General Statistical Specification. *Econ. Letters*, December 1989, 31(3), pp. 293–98.

Warner, Malcolm; Campbell, Adrian and Currie, Wendy. Innovation, Skills and Training: Micro-electronics and Manpower in the United Kingdom and West Germany. **In** *Hirst, P. and Zeitlin, J., eds.*, 1989, pp. 133–54.

Warner, Mark and Rugman, Alan M. Strategies for the Canadian Multinationals. **In** *Rugman, A. M., ed.*, 1989, pp. 200–229.

Warner, Rebecca L.; Steel, Brent S. and Lovrich, Nicholas P. Conditions Associated with the Advent of Representative Bureaucracy: The Case of Women in Policing. *Soc. Sci. Quart.*, September 1989, 70(3), pp. 562–78.

Warner, Sam Bass, Jr. The Evolution of High Technology in the Boston Region 1920–1980. **In** *Andersson, Å. E.; Batten, D. F. and Karlsson, C., eds.*, 1989, pp. 133–41.

Wärneryd, Karl. Legal Restrictions and the Evolution of Media of Exchange. *J. Inst. Theoretical Econ.*, December 1989, 145(4), pp. 613–26.

Wärneryd, Karl-Erik. On the Psychology of Saving: An Essay on Economic Behavior. *J. Econ. Psych.*, 1989, 10(4), pp. 515–41.

Warr, Peter G. Export Processing Zones and Trade Policy. *Finance Devel.*, June 1989, 26(2), pp. 34–36.

_____. Export Processing Zones: The Economics of Enclave Manufacturing. *World Bank Res. Observer*, January 1989, 4(1), pp. 65–88.

Warren-Boulton, Frederick R. Resale Price Maintenance Reexamined: *Monsanto v. Spray-Rite*. **In** *Kwoka, J. E., Jr. and White, L. J., eds.*, 1989, pp. 371–404.

Warren, Cathy J.; Mountain, Dean C. and Stipdonk, Bill P. Technological Innovation and a Changing Energy Mix—A Parametric and Flexible Approach to Modeling Ontario Manufacturing. *Energy J.*, October 1989, 10(4), pp. 139–58.

Warren, Ronald S., Jr. and Snow, Arthur. Tax Rates and Labor Supply in Fiscal Equilibrium. *Econ. Inquiry*, July 1989, 27(3), pp. 511–20.

Warsh, David. The Development of the Ideas: Strategic Trade Policy and Competitiveness. **In** *Colander, D. C. and Coats, A. W., eds.*, 1989, pp. 85–93.

Warshawsky, Mark J. The Adequacy and Consistency of Margin Requirements in the Markets for Stocks and Derivative Products. *Fed. Res. Bull.*, September 1989, 75(9), pp. 610–11.

_____. The Adequacy of Funding of Private Defined Benefit Pension Plans. **In** *Turner, J. A. and Beller, D. J., eds.*, 1989, pp. 153–86.

_____. The Institutional and Regulatory Environ-

ment of Defined Benefit Pension Plans. **In** *Turner, J. A. and Beller, D. J., eds.*, 1989, pp. 29–38.

_____. Tax Reform and Corporate Capital Structure. *Public Finance*, 1989, 44(2), pp. 295–307.

Wascher, William L. and Gay, Robert S. Persistence Effects in Labor Force Participation. *Eastern Econ. J.*, July–Sept. 1989, 15(3), pp. 177–87.

Washburn, Susan K.; Dua, Pami and Smyth, David J. Social Preferences, Inflation, Unemployment, and Political Business Cycles: Econometric Evidence for the Reagan Presidency. *Southern Econ. J.*, October 1989, 56(2), pp. 336–48.

Washington, Mary T. and Mock, Theodore J. Risk Concepts and Risk Assessment in Auditing. **In** *Gangolly, J., ed.*, 1989, pp. 105–17.

Wasil, Edward A.; Harker, Patrick T. and Golden, Bruce L. The Analytic Hierarchy Process: Applications and Studies: Introduction. **In** *Golden, B. L.; Wasil, E. A. and Harker, P. T., eds.*, 1989, pp. 1–2.

_____; Levy, Doug E. and Golden, Bruce L. Applications of the Analytic Hierarchy Process: A Categorized, Annotated Bibliography. **In** *Golden, B. L.; Wasil, E. A. and Harker, P. T., eds.*, 1989, pp. 37–58.

_____ and Mitchell, Kenneth H. AHP in Practice: Applications and Observations from a Management Consulting Perspective. **In** *Golden, B. L.; Wasil, E. A. and Harker, P. T., eds.*, 1989, pp. 192–212.

Wasilewski, Zbigniew. The Use of Graphical Displays in the Analysis of Structural Change. **In** *Hackl, P., ed.*, 1989, pp. 167–88.

Wasley, Charles E.; Handa, Puneet and Kothari, S. P. The Relation between the Return Interval and Betas: Implications for the Size Effect. *J. Finan. Econ.*, June 1989, 23(1), pp. 79–100.

_____ and Kothari, S. P. Measuring Security Price Performance in Size-Clustered Samples. *Accounting Rev.*, April 1989, 64(2), pp. 228–49.

Wass von Czege, Andreas. Ungarns Integration in die Weltwirtschaft: Vision oder Alptraum? (Hungary's Integration into the World Economy: A Vision or a Nightmare? With English summary.) *Aussenwirtschaft*, December 1989, 44(3–4), pp. 425–52.

Wasserfallen, Walter. Flexible Exchange Rates: A Closer Look. *J. Monet. Econ.*, May 1989, 23(3), pp. 511–21.

_____. Macroeconomics News and the Stock Market: Evidence from Europe. *J. Banking Finance*, September 1989, 13(4–5), pp. 613–26.

Wassermann, Wolfram. Worker Participation in Technological Change. **In** *OECD*, 1989, pp. 61–74.

Wassink, Darwin and Carbaugh, Robert. Dollar–Yen Exchange Rate Effects on Trade. *Rivista Int. Sci. Econ. Com.*, December 1989, 36(12), pp. 1075–88.

_____ and Carbaugh, Robert. Evaluation of U.S.–Canada Free Trade Agreement. **In** *Mis-*

souri Valley Economic Association, 1989, pp. 135–42.

Wasti, S. Ashraf and Pasha, Hafiz A. Unemployment and Rates of Return to Education. *Singapore Econ. Rev.*, October 1989, *34*(2), pp. 64–77.

Waswo, Ann. Japan's Rural Economy in Crisis. In *Brown, I., ed.*, 1989, pp. 115–36.

Wasylenko, Michael and Schroeder, Larry. Public Sector Forecasting in the Third World. *Int. J. Forecasting*, 1989, *5*(3), pp. 333–45.

Watad, Mahmoud and Garcia, Danny B., III. Telecommunications Policy and Economic Development: The New State Role: California. In *Schmandt, J.; Williams, F. and Wilson, R. H., eds.*, 1989, pp. 17–39.

Watanabe, Shinichi and Mitsui, Toshihide. Monetary Growth in a Turnpike Environment. *J. Monet. Econ.*, July 1989, *24*(1), pp. 123–37.

Waterbury, John. Endemic and Planned Corruption in a Monarchical Regime. In *Heidenheimer, A. J.; Johnston, M. and LeVine, V. T., eds.*, 1989, *1973*, pp. 339–61.

_____. The Political Management of Economic Adjustment and Reform. In *Roe, A.; Roy, J. and Sengupta, J.*, 1989, pp. 55–65.

_____. The Political Management of Economic Adjustment and Reform. In *Nelson, J. M., ed.*, 1989, pp. 39–56.

_____ **and Bienen, Henry.** The Political Economy of Privatization in Developing Countries. *World Devel.*, May 1989, *17*(5), pp. 617–32.

Waters, Alan Rufus. The Anxious Course: Achieving Change in Washington, D.C. In *Meiners, R. E. and Yandle, B., eds.*, 1989, pp. 275–93.

_____. The Debate over Monetarism: Monetary Policy and Economic Development. In *DeGregori, T. R., ed.*, 1989, pp. 191–221.

Waters, D. M. Improved Education and Training for New Marine Technology and Social Change in the Pacific Island Nations—A Preliminary Appraisal of the Task. In *Couper, A. D., ed.*, 1989, pp. 179–87.

Waters, Timothy J. Antitrust Law and Policy: Rule of Law or Economic Assumptions? In *Larner, R. J. and Meehan, J. W., Jr., eds.*, 1989, pp. 151–77.

Waterson, Michael. Models of Product Differentiation. *Bull. Econ. Res.*, January 1989, *41*(1), pp. 1–27.

_____ **and Molho, Ian.** Modelling Supermarket Store Locations. *Scot. J. Polit. Econ.*, November 1989, *36*(4), pp. 375–84.

Waterton, Jennifer and Lievesley, Denise. Evidence of Conditioning Effects in the British Social Attitudes Panel. In *Kasprzyk, D., et al., eds.*, 1989, pp. 319–39.

Watkins, Alfred J. Latin America's Prospects in the Financial Markets. *CEPAL Rev.*, April 1989, (37), pp. 45–63.

Watkins, G. Campbell. Eccentric Orbits: Canadian Oil and Gas Pricing, 1947 to 1987. In *Watkins, G. C., ed.*, 1989, pp. 105–40.

Watkins, Paul R.; Karlinsky, Stewart S. and Milliron, Valerie C. Policy Judgments of Taxpay-

ers: An Analysis of Criteria Employed. In *Jones, S. M., ed.*, 1989, pp. 201–21.

Watrin, Christian. Towards a More Humane Society? In *Peacock, A. and Willgerodt, H., eds. (II)*, 1989, *1975*, pp. 106–23.

Watson, C. Maxwell and Dooley, Michael P. Reinvigorating the Debt Strategy. *Finance Devel.*, September 1989, *26*(3), pp. 8–11.

Watson, Harry. An Analysis of the Formation and Behavior of Partnerships. *Public Finance Quart.*, July 1989, *17*(3), pp. 281–303.

Watson, Hilbourne A. Surplus Labor, Unequal Exchange, and Merchant Capital: Rethinking Caribbean Migration Theory. In *Martin, M. T. and Kandal, T. R., eds.*, 1989, pp. 242–66.

Watson, Mark W. MTS: A Review. *J. Appl. Econometrics*, April–June 1989, *4*(2), pp. 205–06.

_____. Recursive Solution Methods for Dynamic Linear Rational Expectations Models. *J. Econometrics*, May 1989, *41*(1), pp. 65–89.

_____. Sensitivity Analysis of Seasonal Adjustments: Empirical Case Studies: Comment. *J. Amer. Statist. Assoc.*, March 1989, *84*(405), pp. 27–28.

_____ **and Stock, James H.** Interpreting the Evidence on Money–Income Causality. *J. Econometrics*, January 1989, *40*(1), pp. 161–81.

_____ **and Stock, James H.** New Indexes of Coincident and Leading Economic Indicators. In *Blanchard, O. J. and Fischer, S., eds.*, 1989, pp. 351–94.

Watson, Robin A. and Schlottmann, Alan M. Air Quality Standards, Coal Conversion and the Steam-Electric Coal Market. In *Labys, W. C.; Takayama, T. and Uri, N. D., eds.*, 1989, pp. 105–27.

Watson, Vinita and Poddar, Satya N. Problems of Transition and of Implementation of Different Revenue Structures. In *Chiancone, A. and Messere, K., eds.*, 1989, pp. 265–84.

Watterson, P. A.; Woodward, J. H. and Woods, R. I. The Causes of Rapid Infant Mortality Decline in England and Wales, 1861–1921. Part II. *Population Stud.*, March 1989, *43*(1), pp. 113–32.

Wattleworth, Michael and Larsen, Flemming. Structural Policies in Industrial Countries. *Finance Devel.*, September 1989, *26*(3), pp. 20–23.

Watts, Michael and Lynch, Gerald J. The Principles Courses Revisited. *Amer. Econ. Rev.*, May 1989, *79*(2), pp. 236–41.

_____ **and Smith, Robert F.** Economics in Literature and Drama. *J. Econ. Educ.*, Summer 1989, *20*(3), pp. 291–307.

Watts, Myles J. and Johnson, Ronald N. Contractual Stipulations, Resource Use, and Interest Groups: Implications from Federal Grazing Contracts. *J. Environ. Econ. Manage.*, January 1989, *16*(1), pp. 87–96.

Waverman, Leonard. U.S. Interexchange Competition. In *Crandall, R. W. and Flamm, K., eds.*, 1989, pp. 63–113.

_____ **and Plourde, André.** Canadian Energy

Trade: The Past and the Future. In *Watkins, G. C., ed.*, 1989, pp. 141–80.

—— and Wilson, Thomas A. Is the Process the Message? *Can. Public Policy*, Supplement, February 1989, *15*, pp. S1–9.

Way, Peter. Shovel and Shamrock: Irish Workers and Labor Violence in the Digging of the Chesapeake and Ohio Canal. *Labor Hist.*, Fall 1989, *30*(4), pp. 489–517.

Waymire, Gregory and Pownall, Grace. Voluntary Disclosure Choice and Earnings Information Transfer. *J. Acc. Res.*, Supplement, 1989, *27*, pp. 85–105.

—— and Pownall, Grace. Voluntary Disclosure Credibility and Securities Prices: Evidence from Management Earnings Forecasts, 1969–73. *J. Acc. Res.*, Autumn 1989, *27*(2), pp. 227–45.

Weatherford, Gary D.; Checchio, Elizabeth and Shupe, Steven J. Western Water Rights: The Era of Reallocation. *Natural Res. J.*, Spring 1989, *29*(2), pp. 413–34.

Weatherford, M. Stephen and Fukui, Haruhiro. Domestic Adjustment to International Shocks in Japan and the United States. *Int. Organ.*, Autumn 1989, *43*(4), pp. 585–623.

Weatherstone, Dennis. A U.S. Perspective on Europe 1992. In *Noyelle, T., ed.*, 1989, pp. 115–18.

Weaver, James H.; Wilber, Charles K. and Jameson, Kenneth P. Strategies of Development: A Survey. In *DeGregori, T. R., ed.*, 1989, pp. 137–77.

Weaver, John. The Denial of Social Experiment in Canadian Housing Policy before the Second World War. In *Platt, D. C. M., ed.*, 1989, pp. 71–86.

Weaver, R. Kent. Coming to Grips with Indexing. In *Bosworth, B. P., et al.*, 1989, pp. 146–51.

Weaver, Robert D. and Lass, Daniel A. Corner Solutions in Duality Models: A Cross-Section Analysis of Dairy Production Decisions. *Amer. J. Agr. Econ.*, November 1989, *71*(4), pp. 1025–40.

Webb, Alan J, et al. Impact of the Soviet Grain Embargo; A Comparison of Methods. *J. Policy Modeling*, Fall 1989, *11*(3), pp. 361–89.

Webb-Carter, David. The Illicit Drug Trade. In *Bulmer-Thomas, V., ed.*, 1989, pp. 186–202.

Webb, David C. and de Meza, David. The Role of Interest Rate Taxes in Credit Markets with Divisible Projects and Asymmetric Information. *J. Public Econ.*, June 1989, *39*(1), pp. 33–44.

Webb, Michael A.; Copeland, Brian R. and Tower, Edward. On Negotiated Quotas, Tariffs, and Transfers. *Oxford Econ. Pap.*, October 1989, *41*(4), pp. 774–88.

Webb, Nick C. and Moore, M. Roger. Residence in the United Kingdom and the Scope of U.K. Taxation for Individuals—A Consultative Document. *Bull. Int. Fiscal Doc.*, March 1989, *43*(3), pp. 119–21.

Webb, Patrick J. R. and von Braun, Joachim. The Impact of New Crop Technology on the Agricultural Division of Labor in a West Afri-

can Setting. *Econ. Devel. Cult. Change*, April 1989, *37*(3), pp. 513–34.

Webb, Roy H. and Whelpley, William. Labor Market Data. *Fed. Res. Bank Richmond Econ. Rev.*, Nov.–Dec. 1989, *75*(6), pp. 15–22.

—— and Willemse, Rob. Macroeconomic Price Indexes. *Fed. Res. Bank Richmond Econ. Rev.*, July–Aug. 1989, *75*(4), pp. 22–32.

Webb, Steven and Dilnot, Andrew. Reforming National Insurance Contributions: A Progress Report. *Fisc. Stud.*, May 1989, *10*(2), pp. 38–47.

—— and Dilnot, Andrew. The 1988 Social Security Reforms. In *Dilnot, A. and Walker, I., eds.*, 1989, pp. 239–67.

—— and Disney, Richard. Is There a Market Failure in Occupational Sick Pay? In *Dilnot, A. and Walker, I., eds.*, 1989, pp. 52–68.

—— and Johnson, Paul. Counting People with Low Incomes: The Impact of Recent Changes in Official Statistics. *Fisc. Stud.*, November 1989, *10*(4), pp. 66–82.

Webb, Steven B. Saving in Developing Countries: Theory and Review: Comment. In *Fischer, S. and de Tray, D., eds.*, 1989, pp. 101–03.

Webber, David J. and Plein, L. Christopher. Biotechnology and Agriculture in the Congressional Policy Arena. In *Krämer, C. S., ed.*, 1989, pp. 179–200.

Webber, Douglas; Cawson, Alan and Shepherd, Geoffrey. Governments, Markets, and Regulation in the West European Consumer Electronics Industry. In *Hancher, L. and Moran, M., eds.*, 1989, pp. 109–33.

Webber, Michael. Capital Flows and Rates of Profit. *Rev. Radical Polit. Econ.*, 1989, *21*(1–2), pp. 113–35.

Weber, Guglielmo and Attanasio, Orazio P. Intertemporal Substitution, Risk Aversion and the Euler Equation for Consumption. *Econ. J.*, Supplement, 1989, *99*(395), pp. 59–73.

—— and Pissarides, Christopher A. An Expenditure-Based Estimate of Britain's Black Economy. *J. Public Econ.*, June 1989, *39*(1), pp. 17–32.

Weber, Luc. Les besoins en information statistique des années 1990. (The Needs for Statistical Information in the Year 1990. With English summary.) *Schweiz. Z. Volkswirtsch. Statist.*, September 1989, *125*(3), pp. 355–66.

Weber, Martin; Camerer, Colin F. and Loewenstein, George. The Curse of Knowledge in Economic Settings: An Experimental Analysis. *J. Polit. Econ.*, October 1989, *97*(5), pp. 1232–54.

Weber, Ron and Wand, Yair. A Model of Control and Audit Procedure Change in Evolving Data Processing Systems. *Accounting Rev.*, January 1989, *64*(1), pp. 87–107.

Weber, Shlomo; Shitovitz, Benyamin and Spiegel, M. 'Top of the Line' Quality as an Optimal Solution for a Multi-quality Monopolist. *Europ. Econ. Rev.*, October 1989, *33*(8), pp. 1641–52.

—— and Smith, J. Barry. Contemporaneous Externalities, Rational Expectations, and Equilibrium Production Functions in Natural Resource Models. *J. Environ. Econ. Manage.*, September 1989, *17*(2), pp. 155–70.

_____ and Smith, J. Barry. Rent-Seeking Behaviour of Retaliating Agents. *Public Choice*, May 1989, *61*(2), pp. 153–66.

Weber, William L.; Färe, Rolf and Grosskopf, Shawna. Measuring School District Performance. *Public Finance Quart.*, October 1989, *17*(4), pp. 409–28.

Webster, Gloria; Jenkins, Glenn P. and Sawchuk, Gary D. Trade, Protectionism and Industrial Adjustment: Three North American Case Studies: Case Study 3: The Consumer Electronics Industry in North America. In *North–South Institute*, 1989, pp. 105–46.

Webster, Paul and Williams, Nigel T. Variability in Wheat and Barley Production in Southeast England. In *Anderson, J. R. and Hazell, P. B. R., eds.*, 1989, pp. 107–17.

Weck-Hannemann, Hannelore and Pommerehne, Werner W. Einkommensteuerhinterziehung in der Schweiz: Eine empirische Analyse. (Income Tax Evasion in Switzerland: An Empirical Analysis. With English summary.) *Schweiz. Z. Volkswirtsch. Statist.*, December 1989, *125*(4), pp. 515–56.

Wecker, William E. Assessing the Accuracy of Time Series Model Forecasts of Count Observations: Comment. *J. Bus. Econ. Statist.*, October 1989, *7*(4), pp. 418–19.

Weckström, Sonja and Sevón, Guje. The Development of Reasoning about Economic Events: A Study of Finnish Children. *J. Econ. Psych.*, 1989, *10*(4), pp. 495–514.

Wedeman, Andrew H. Annual Review of Nations: Year 1988: People's Republic of China. In *Haberman, L. and Sacks, P. M., eds.*, 1989, pp. 247–65.

_____. Annual Review of Nations: Year 1988: Republic of China (Taiwan). In *Haberman, L. and Sacks, P. M., eds.*, 1989, pp. 285–99.

Wedemeyer, Dan J. and Barber, Richard J. Emerging Technological Possibilities: ISDN and Its Impact on Interdependence, 1986–2016. In *Jussawalla, M.; Okuma, T. and Araki, T., eds.*, 1989, pp. 247–63.

Wedig, Gerard J.; Hassan, Mahmud and Sloan, Frank A. Hospital Investment Decisions and the Cost of Capital. *J. Bus.*, October 1989, *62*(4), pp. 517–37.

Wedley, William C.; Lam, K. F. and Choo, E. U. Linear Goal Programming in Estimation of Classification Probability. In *Lockett, A. G. and Islei, G., eds.*, 1989, pp. 166–78.

_____ and Schoner, Bertram. Alternative Scales in AHP. In *Lockett, A. G. and Islei, G., eds.*, 1989, pp. 345–54.

Weeks, John F. Debt Disaster? Banks, Governments, and Multilaterals Confront the Crisis: Introduction. In *Weeks, J. F., ed.*, 1989, pp. xix–xxii.

_____. Losers Pay Reparations, or How the Third World Lost the Lending War. In *Weeks, J. F., ed.*, 1989, pp. 41–63.

_____. A Macroeconomic Overview of the Cen-

tral American Economies. In *Irvin, G. and Holland, S., eds.*, 1989, pp. 23–43.

Weeks, Melvyn J. and Batey, Peter W. J. The Effects of Household Disaggregation in Extended Input–Output Models. In *Miller, R. E.; Polenske, K. R. and Rose, A. Z., eds.*, 1989, pp. 119–33.

Weems, Kerry and McCoy, John L. Disabled-Worker Beneficiaries and Disabled SSI Recipients: A Profile of Demographic and Program Characteristics. *Soc. Sec. Bull.*, May 1989, *52*(5), pp. 16–28.

Weersink, Alfons J. and Tauer, Loren W. Comparative Analysis of Investment Models for New York Dairy Farms. *Amer. J. Agr. Econ.*, February 1989, *71*(1), pp. 136–45.

Weffort, Francisco C. Features and Phases of the "Swedish Model": Comments. *CEPAL Rev.*, December 1989, (39), pp. 31–35.

Wegner, Manfred. The European Monetary System: A Regional Bretton Woods or an Institutional Innovation? In *Vosgerau, H.-J., ed.*, 1989, pp. 89–118.

_____. The Role of the Economist in Government: An International Perspective: The European Economic Community. In *Pechman, J. A., ed.*, 1989, pp. 279–99.

Wegner, Trevor and Brice, Helene. A Quantitative Approach to Corporate Social Responsibility Programme Formulation. *Managerial Dec. Econ.*, June 1989, *10*(2), pp. 163–71.

_____; Money, Arthur and Naude, Peter. A Comparison of Multi-attribute Utility Generation Methods. In *Lockett, A. G. and Islei, G., eds.*, 1989, pp. 46–57.

Wehman, Paul and Kregel, John. An Analysis of the Employment Outcomes of Young Adults with Mental Retardation. In *Wehman, P. and Kregel, J., eds.*, 1989, pp. 257–67.

_____; Kregel, John and Banks, P. David. Competitive Employment for Persons with Mental Retardation: A Decade Later. In *Wehman, P. and Kregel, J., eds.*, 1989, pp. 97–113.

_____, et al. The Supported Work Model of Competitive Employment: Illustrations of Competence in Workers with Severe and Profound Handicaps. In *Wehman, P. and Kregel, J., eds.*, 1989, pp. 19–52.

Wehrt, Klaus and von Randow, Philipp. New Technologies, Liability Rules and Adaptive Behavior: Comment. In *Faure, M. and Van den Bergh, R., eds.*, 1989, pp. 107–16.

Wehrung, Donald A., et al. Adjusting Risky Situations: A Theoretical Framework and Empirical Test. *J. Risk Uncertainty*, June 1989, *2*(2), pp. 189–212.

Wei, I. On the Question of Agricultural Investment in China's First Five-Year Plan. In *Howe, C. and Walker, K. R., eds.*, 1989, 1955, pp. 20–28.

Wei, K. C. John; Bansal, Vipul K. and Pruitt, Stephen W. An Empirical Reexamination of the Impact of CBOE Option Initiation on the Volatility and Trading Volume of the Underlying Equaties: 1973–1986. *Financial Rev.*, February 1989, *24*(1), pp. 19–29.

_____; **Bubnys, Edward L. and Lee, Cheng Few.** The APT versus the Multi-factor CAPM: Empirical Evidence. *Quart. Rev. Econ. Bus.*, Winter 1989, *29*(4), pp. 6–25.

_____ **and Pruitt, Stephen W.** Institutional Ownership and Changes in the S&P 500. *J. Finance,* June 1989, *44*(2), pp. 509–13.

Wei, L. J. and Lin, D. Y. The Robust Inference for the Cox Proportional Hazards Model. *J. Amer. Statist. Assoc.*, December 1989, *84*(408), pp. 1074–78.

Wei, Ning and Bing, Zhao. Developments in Foreign Trade Reform. In *Zerby, J., ed.*, 1989, pp. 33–45.

_____ **and Bing, Zhao.** Direct Foreign Investment in China. In *Zerby, J., ed.*, 1989, pp. 46–58.

Wei, William. Law and Order: The Role of Guomindang Security Forces in the Suppression of the Communist Bases during the Soviet Period. In *Hartford, K. and Goldstein, S. M., eds.*, 1989, pp. 34–61.

Weibull, Jörgen W. A Note on the Continuity of Incentive Schedules. *J. Public Econ.*, July 1989, *39*(2), pp. 239–43.

Weicher, John C. Wealth and Poverty among the Elderly. In *Lewin, M. E. and Sullivan, S., eds.*, 1989, pp. 11–27.

_____ **and Woodward, Susan E.** Goring the Wrong Ox: A Defense of the Mortgage Interest Deduction. *Nat. Tax J.*, September 1989, *42*(3), pp. 301–13.

Weidemann, Anna and Hill, Hal. Regional Development in Indonesia: Patterns and Issues. In *Hill, H., ed.*, 1989, pp. 3–54.

Weidenbaum, Murray L. Is the American Economy Reaching a Turning Point? *Challenge*, Sept.–Oct. 1989, *32*(5), pp. 57–59.

_____. Lifting the Heavy Hand of Government: Lessons for West Germany from the American Experience. In *Fels, G. and von Furstenberg, G. M., eds.*, 1989, pp. 279–96.

Weiermair, Klaus and Leibenstein, Harvey. X-Efficiency, Managerial Discretion, and the Nature of Employment-Relations: A Game-Theoretical Approach. In *Leibenstein, H., Vol. 2,* 1989, *1988*, pp. 212–27.

Weiher, Kenneth. Macroeconomic Causes and Consequences of Major Stock Market Reversals: An Historical Study. In *Perkins, E. J., ed.*, 1989, pp. 124–39.

van der Weijden, C. J. Competition Policy in the Netherlands: Law, Theory and Policy. In *Muller, F. and Zwezerijnen, W. J., eds.*, 1989, pp. 72–81.

Weijland, Hermine and Sandee, Henry. Rural Cottage Industry in Transition: The Roof Tile Industry in *Kabupaten* Boyolali, Central Java. *Bull. Indonesian Econ. Stud.*, August 1989, *25*(2), pp. 79–98.

Weil, David N. and Mankiw, N. Gregory. The Baby Boom, the Baby Bust, and the Housing Market. *Reg. Sci. Urban Econ.*, May 1989, *19*(2), pp. 235–58.

Weil, Max Harry. Rationing of Medical Care for the Critically Ill: Alternatives to Rationing. In

Strosberg, M. A.; Fein, I. A. and Carroll, J. D., eds., 1989, pp. 17–23.

Weil, Philippe. The Equity Premium Puzzle and the Risk-Free Rate Puzzle. *J. Monet. Econ.*, November 1989, *24*(3), pp. 401–21.

_____. Increasing Returns and Animal Spirits. *Amer. Econ. Rev.*, September 1989, *79*(4), pp. 889–94.

_____. Money, Time Preference and External Balance. *Europ. Econ. Rev.*, March 1989, *33*(2/3), pp. 564–72.

_____. Overlapping Families of Infinitely-Lived Agents. *J. Public Econ.*, March 1989, *38*(2), pp. 183–98.

Weil, Vivian and Snapper, John W. Owning Scientific and Technical Information: Value and Ethical Issues: Introduction. In *Weil, V. and Snapper, J. W., eds.*, 1989, pp. 1–12.

Weilenmann, Paul. Dezentrale Führung: Leistungsbeurteilung und Verrechnungspreise. (With English summary.) *Z. Betriebswirtshaft*, September 1989, *59*(9), pp. 932–56.

Weiler, William C. A Flexible Approach to Modelling Enrollment Choice Behavior. *Econ. Educ. Rev.*, 1989, *8*(3), pp. 277–83.

Weiman, David F. Families, Farms and Rural Society in Preindustrial America. In *Grantham, G. and Leonard, C. S., eds., Pt. B*, 1989, pp. 255–77.

Weimann, Joachim. Überlegungen zum Theoriebegriff der Wirtschaftswissenschaften. (With English summary.) *Z. Wirtschaft. Sozialwissen.*, 1989, *109*(2), pp. 233–64.

_____ **and Schulz, Norbert.** Competition of Newspapers and the Location of Political Parties. *Public Choice*, November 1989, *63*(2), pp. 125–47.

Weinand, H. and Sorensen, A. D. Australian Nonmetropolitan Settlements: Some Aspects of Population Growth. In *Gibson, L. J. and Stimson, R. J., eds.*, 1989, pp. 125–34.

Weinberg, John A. and Lacker, Jeffrey M. Optimal Contracts under Costly State Falsification. *J. Polit. Econ.*, December 1989, *97*(6), pp. 1345–63.

Weinblatt, J.; Friedman, Joseph and Hakim, Simon. Casino Gambling as a "Growth Pole" Strategy and Its Effect on Crime. *J. Reg. Sci.*, November 1989, *29*(4), pp. 615–23.

Weindlmaier, Hannes. Effects of Decreasing Agricultural Prices on the Cereal Markets. In *Tarditi, S., et al., eds.*, 1989, pp. 157–70.

Weinel, Ivan and Crossland, Philip D. The Scientific Foundations of Technological Progress. *J. Econ. Issues*, September 1989, *23*(3), pp. 795–808.

Weiner, Charles. Patenting and Academic Research: Historical Case Studies. In *Weil, V. and Snapper, J. W., eds.*, 1989, pp. 87–109.

Weiner, Robert J.; Benjamin, Nancy C. and Devarajan, Shantayanan. The 'Dutch' Disease in a Developing Country: Oil Reserves in Cameroon. *J. Devel. Econ.*, January 1989, *30*(1), pp. 71–92.

_____ **and Devarajan, Shantayanan.** Dynamic Policy Coordination: Stockpiling for Energy

Security. *J. Environ. Econ. Manage.*, January 1989, *16*(1), pp. 9–22.

_____ **and Hubbard, R. Glenn.** Contracting and Price Adjustment in Commodity Markets: Evidence from Copper and Oil. *Rev. Econ. Statist.*, February 1989, *71*(1), pp. 80–89.

Weingast, Barry R. The Political Institutions of Representative Government: Legislatures. *J. Inst. Theoretical Econ.*, December 1989, *145*(4), pp. 693–703.

_____; **Gilligan, Thomas W. and Marshall, William J.** Regulation and the Theory of Legislative Choice: The Interstate Commerce Act of 1887. *J. Law Econ.*, April 1989, *32*(1), pp. 35–61.

_____ **and North, Douglass C.** Constitutions and Commitment: The Evolution of Institutions Governing Public Choice in Seventeenth-Century England. *J. Econ. Hist.*, December 1989, *49*(4), pp. 803–32.

Weintraub, Cathy and Cross, Sam Y. Treasury and Federal Reserve Foreign Exchange Operations: May–June 1989. *Fed. Res. Bank New York Quart. Rev.*, Autumn 1989, *14*(3), pp. 61–66.

Weintraub, E. Roy. Methodology Doesn't Matter, but the History of Thought Might. *Scand. J. Econ.*, 1989, *91*(2), pp. 477–93.

Weintraub, Sidney. Hicks on *IS–LM:* More Explanation? In *Wood, J. C. and Woods, R. N., eds., Vol. 3*, 1989, *1982*, pp. 307–13.

_____. Implications of Mexican Demographic Developments for the United States. In *Bean, F. D.; Schmandt, J. and Weintraub, S., eds.*, 1989, pp. 179–99.

_____. Revision and Recantation in Hicksian Economics: A Review Article. In *Wood, J. C. and Woods, R. N., eds., Vol. 3*, 1989, *1976*, pp. 138–46.

_____; **Bean, Frank D. and Schmandt, Jurgen.** Mexican and Central American Population and U.S. Immigration Policy: Introduction. In *Bean, F. D.; Schmandt, J. and Weintraub, S., eds.*, 1989, pp. 1–4.

Weintrop, Joseph; Choi, Dosoung and Kamma, Sreenivas. The Delaware Courts, Poison Pills, and Shareholder Wealth. *J. Law, Econ., Organ.*, Fall 1989, *5*(2), pp. 375–93.

Weir, David R. Tontines, Public Finance, and Revolution in France and England, 1688–1789. *J. Econ. Hist.*, March 1989, *49*(1), pp. 95–124.

Weir, Margaret. Ideas and Politics: The Acceptance of Keynesianism in Britain and the United States. In *Hall, P. A., ed.*, 1989, pp. 53–86.

Weir, Ron. Rationalization and Diversification in the Scotch Whiskey Industry, 1900–1939: Another Look at 'Old' and 'New' Industries. *Econ. Hist. Rev., 2nd Ser.*, August 1989, *42*(3), pp. 375–95.

Weisensel, Ward P.; de Jong, E. and Van Kooten, G. C. Estimating the Costs of Soil Erosion: A Reply. *Can. J. Agr. Econ.*, November 1989, *37*(3), pp. 555–62.

_____; **de Jong, E. and Van Kooten, G. C.** Estimating the Costs of Soil Erosion in Saskatche-

wan. *Can. J. Agr. Econ.*, March 1989, *37*(1), pp. 63–75.

_____ **and Schoney, Richard A.** An Analysis of the Yield–Price Risk Associated with Specialty Crops. *Western J. Agr. Econ.*, December 1989, *14*(2), pp. 293–99.

Weisman, Dennis L.,. Optimal Re-contracting, Market Risk and the Regulated Firm in Competitive Transition. In *Zerbe, R. O., ed.*, 1989, pp. 153–72.

Weiss, Frank D. Defining and Measuring Output and Productivity in the Service Sector: Comment. In *Giersch, H., ed.*, 1989, pp. 59–62.

_____. Domestic Dimensions of the Uruguay Round: The Case of West Germany in the European Communities. In *Nau, H. R., ed.*, 1989, pp. 69–89.

Weiss, John. Industrial Reform in Jamaica in the 1980s: An Export Promotion Strategy. *Int. Rev. Applied Econ.*, June 1989, *3*(2), pp. 191–213.

Weiss, Karl-Heinz and Hanusch, Horst. Tax Reform in a Recovering Economy: From Income Taxes to Indirect Taxation. In *Chiancone, A. and Messere, K., eds.*, 1989, pp. 197–213.

Weiss, Leonard W. Concentration and Price: Conclusions. In *Weiss, L. W., ed.*, 1989, pp. 266–84.

_____. A Review of Concentration–Price Studies in Banking. In *Weiss, L. W., ed.*, 1989, pp. 219–54.

_____. Why Study Concentration and Price? In *Weiss, L. W., ed.*, 1989, pp. 1–14.

_____ **and Belman, Dale L.** Concentration and Wages: Direct and Indirect Effects. In *Weiss, L. W., ed.*, 1989, pp. 85–111.

_____; **Brannman, Lance and Klein, J. Douglass.** The Price Effects of Increased Competition in Auction Markets. In *Weiss, L. W., ed.*, 1989, pp. 67–84.

_____ **and Kelton, Christina M. L.** Change in Concentration, Change in Cost, Change in Demand, and Change in Price. In *Weiss, L. W., ed.*, 1989, pp. 41–66.

_____ **and Koller, Roland H., II.** Price Levels and Seller Concentration: The Case of Portland Cement. In *Weiss, L. W., ed.*, 1989, pp. 17–40.

_____ **and Nakazawa, Toshiaki.** The Legal Cartels of Japan. *Antitrust Bull.*, Fall 1989, *34*(3), pp. 641–53.

_____; **Yamawaki, Hideki and Sleuwaegen, Leo E.** Industry Competition and the Formation of the European Common Market. In *Weiss, L. W., ed.*, 1989, pp. 112–43.

Weiss, Marc A. Marketing and Financing Home Ownership: Mortgage Lending and Public Policy in the United States, 1918–1989. In *Hausman, W. J., ed.*, 1989, pp. 109–18.

_____. Real Estate History: An Overview and Research Agenda. *Bus. Hist. Rev.*, Summer 1989, *63*(2), pp. 241–82.

_____. Richard T. Ely and the Contribution of Economic Research to National Housing Policy, 1920–1940. In *Perkins, E. J., ed.*, 1989, pp. 1–24.

_____. Richard T. Ely and the Contribution of

Economic Research to National Housing Policy, 1920–1940. *Urban Stud.*, February 1989, *26*(1), pp. 115–26.

_____ **and Metzger, John T.** Planning for Chicago: The Changing Politics of Metropolitan Growth and Neighborhood Development. In *Beauregard, R. A., ed.*, 1989, pp. 123–51.

Weiss, Peter; Maier, Gunther and Gerking, Shelby. The Economics of Traffic Accidents on Austrian Roads: Risk Lovers or Policy Deficit? *Empirica*, 1989, *16*(2), pp. 177–92.

Weiss, Thomas G. The UN Code of Conduct for Transnational Corporations. In *[Gordenker, L.]*, 1989, pp. 86–97.

Weissert, William G. and Cready, Cynthia Matthews. A Prospective Budgeting Model for Home- and Community-Based Long-Term Care. *Inquiry*, Spring 1989, *26*(1), pp. 116–29.

_____ **and Wilson, Catharine E.** Private Long-term Care Insurance: After Coverage Restrictions Is There Anything Left? *Inquiry*, Winter 1989, *26*(4), pp. 493–507.

Weisskopf, Thomas E.; Bowles, Samuel and Gordon, David M. Business Ascendancy and Economic Impasse: A Structural Retrospective on Conservative Economics, 1979–87. *J. Econ. Perspectives*, Winter 1989, *3*(1), pp. 107–34.

Weistroffer, H. Roland and Narula, Subhash C. Algorithms for Multi-objective Nonlinear Programming Problems: An Overview. In *Lockett, A. G. and Islei, G., eds.*, 1989, pp. 434–43.

Weithers, John G. Ethics within the Securities Industry. In *Williams, O. F.; Reilly, F. K. and Houck, J. W., eds.*, 1989, pp. 35–39.

Weitz, Barton and Anderson, Erin. Determinants of Continuity in Conventional Industrial Channel Dyads. *Marketing Sci.*, Fall 1989, *8*(4), pp. 310–23.

Weitzman, Martin L. The Promise of Profit Sharing. In *Huang, W.-C., ed.*, 1989, pp. 91–109.

_____. A Theory of Wage Dispersion and Job Market Segmentation. *Quart. J. Econ.*, February 1989, *104*(1), pp. 121–37.

_____ **and Freeman, Richard B.** Bonuses and Employment in Japan. In *Freeman, R. B.*, 1989, *1987*, pp. 249–69.

von Weizsäcker, C. C. Learning Industries with Special Reference to Telecommunications. *Tijdschrift Econ. Manage.*, June 1989, *34*(3), pp. 249–78.

von Weizsäcker, Robert K. Demographic Change and Income Distribution. *Europ. Econ. Rev.*, March 1989, *33*(2/3), pp. 377–88.

_____. Demographischer Wandel und staatliche Einkommenssicherung: Eine Inzidenzanalyse. (Demographic Change and State Income Support: An Incidence Analysis. With English summary.) *Jahr. Nationalökon. Statist.*, July 1989, *206*(3), pp. 181–207.

_____ **and Bös, Dieter.** Economic Consequences of an Aging Population. *Europ. Econ. Rev.*, March 1989, *33*(2/3), pp. 345–54.

Welch, David A. Crisis Decision Making Reconsidered. *J. Conflict Resolution,* September 1989, *33*(3), pp. 430–45.

Welch, Finis R. Affirmative Action and Discrimination. In *Shulman, S. and Darity, W., Jr., eds.*, 1989, pp. 153–89.

_____ **and Smith, James P.** Black Economic Progress after Myrdal. *J. Econ. Lit.*, June 1989, *27*(2), pp. 519–64.

Welch, Ivo. Seasoned Offerings, Imitation Costs, and the Underpricing of Initial Public Offerings. *J. Finance*, June 1989, *44*(2), pp. 421–49.

Welch, John H. The Variability of Inflation in Brazil: 1974–1982. *J. Econ. Devel.*, June 1989, *14*(1), pp. 149–62.

Welch, Jonathan B. and Platt, Harlan D. Factors that Influence Public Utility Performance. *Energy Econ.*, July 1989, *11*(3), pp. 219–27.

Welch, Susan and Peters, John G. Gradients of Corruption in Perceptions of American Public Life. In *Heidenheimer, A. J.; Johnston, M. and LeVine, V. T., eds.*, 1989, *1978*, pp. 723–41.

_____ **and Sigelman, Lee.** A Black Gender Gap? *Soc. Sci. Quart.*, March 1989, *70*(1), pp. 120–33.

Welch, W. Pete. Improving Medicare Payments to HMOs: Urban Core versus Suburban Ring. *Inquiry*, Spring 1989, *26*(1), pp. 62–71.

_____. Restructuring the Federal Employees Health Benefits Program: The Private Sector Option. *Inquiry*, Fall 1989, *26*(3), pp. 321–34.

Welcker, Johannes and Schindler, Klaus. Währungsoptionsscheine und der Rückerstattung-Währungsoptionsschein (RWOS—Money-Back Currency Warrant) der Nordiska Investeringsbanken (NIB). (Money-Back Currency Warrants of the Nordiska Investeringsbanken. With English summary.) *Kredit Kapital*, 1989, *22*(2), pp. 239–66.

Welfe, Wladyslaw and Czyzewski, Adam B. The Growth of the Polish Economy and Prospects for Structural Change. In *Krelle, W., ed.*, 1989, pp. 419–43.

Welfens, Paul J. J. Innovation, Trade, External Debt and Growth in the World Economy. In *Singer, H. W. and Sharma, S., eds. (I)*, 1989, pp. 87–106.

Welford, Richard. Growth Aspirations and the Participation–Performance Nexus: The Case of U.K. Producer Cooperatives. *Econ. Anal. Workers' Manage.*, 1989, *23*(1), pp. 17–29.

Welker, Donald L. and Walter, John R. Fifth District Banks' Return on Assets: Highest in Decade. *Fed. Res. Bank Richmond Econ. Rev.*, May–June 1989, *75*(3), pp. 16–22.

Weller, Barry R. National Indicator Series as Quantitative Predictors of Small Region Monthly Employment Levels. *Int. J. Forecasting*, 1989, *5*(2), pp. 241–47.

_____ **and Kurre, James A.** Forecasting the Local Economy, Using Time-Series and Shift-Share Techniques. *Environ. Planning A*, June 1989, *21*(6), pp. 753–70.

_____ **and Kurre, James A.** Regional Cyclical Instability: An Empirical Examination of Wage, Hours and Employment Adjustments, and an Application of the Portfolio Variance

Technique. *Reg. Stud.*, August 1989, *23*(4), pp. 315–29.

Weller, Paul and Miller, Marcus H. Exchange Rate Bands and Realignments in a Stationary Stochastic Setting. In *Miller, M.; Eichengreen, B. and Portes, R.*, eds., 1989, pp. 161–73.

_____; **Williamson, John and Miller, Marcus H.** The Stabilizing Properties of Target Zones. In *Bryant, R. C., et al.*, eds., 1989, pp. 248–71.

Wellhofer, E. Spencer. Core and Periphery: Territorial Dimensions in Politics. *Urban Stud.*, June 1989, *26*(3), pp. 340–55.

Welling, Linda A. Satisfaction Guaranteed or Money (Partially) Refunded: Efficient Refunds under Asymmetric Information. *Can. J. Econ.*, February 1989, *22*(1), pp. 62–78.

Wells, Graeme and Evans, Lewis. Time Series Estimates of Tariff Incidence. *Appl. Econ.*, September 1989, *21*(9), pp. 1191–1202.

Wells, Jerome C. On the Agricultural Performance of Developing Nations, 1950–85. *Food Res. Inst. Stud.*, 1989, *21*(2), pp. 165–91.

Wells, Rosalind. Consumers to Play a Supportive, Not Leading Role. *Bus. Econ.*, July 1989, *24*(3), pp. 23–27.

Welsch, Heinz. An Application of Statistical Specification Error Tests. *Energy Econ.*, October 1989, *11*(4), pp. 285–92.

_____. Habit Persistence and the Structure of International Commodity Trade: A Demand System Analysis for Nine Industrialized Countries. *Empirical Econ.*, 1989, *14*(1), pp. 21–42.

_____. Modeling Exchange Rates and Foreign Trade of Developed Market Economies. In *Krelle, W.*, ed., 1989, pp. 233–258.

_____ **and Krelle, Wilhelm.** Determination of Exchange Rates and Capital Flows for OECD Countries. In *Gordon, I. and Thirlwall, A. P.*, eds., 1989, pp. 233–50.

Welsh, Richard; Beilock, Richard and Burkhart, Jeffrey. Risk Permits: An Alterntive Approach to Transportation Safety Regulations. *Logist. Transp. Rev.*, September 1989, *25*(3), pp. 195–207.

Welzel, Peter. Strategische Effekte ertragsorientierter Entlohnung in Oligopolen. (Strategic Effects of Profit Sharing in Oligopoly. With English summary.) *Jahr. Nationalökon. Statist.*, January 1989, *206*(1), pp. 61–74.

Wen, Guifang. Energetically Promote the Circulation of the Means of Production and Price Reform. *Chinese Econ. Stud.*, Spring 1989, *22*(3), pp. 67–79.

Wenders, John T. Deregulating Telecommunications. In *Meiners, R. E. and Yandle, B.*, eds., 1989, pp. 104–31.

Wenzel, Georg; Dejon, Bruno and Güldner, Bernhard. Direct Equilibria of Economies and Their Perfect Homogeneity Limits. In *Andersson, Å. E., et al.*, eds., 1989, pp. 81–105.

Werbel, James D. and Roberg, Arlene G. A Role Theory Perspective on Career Decision Making. In *Ferris, G. R. and Rowland, K. M.*, eds., 1989, pp. 227–58.

Werden, Gregory J. Price-Fixing and Civil Dam-

ages: Setting the Record Straight. *Antitrust Bull.*, Summer 1989, *34*(2), pp. 307–35.

_____ **and Williams, Michael A.** Can the Concentration-Collusion Hypothesis Be Refuted Empirically? *Econ. Letters*, September 1989, *30*(3), pp. 253–57.

_____ **and Williams, Michael A.** The Role of Stock Market Studies in Formulating Antitrust Policy toward Horizontal Mergers: Reply. *Quart. J. Bus. Econ.*, Autumn 1989, *28*(4), pp. 39–42.

_____ **and Williams, Michael A.** The Role of Stock Market Studies in Formulating Antitrust Policy toward Horizontal Mergers. *Quart. J. Bus. Econ.*, Autumn 1989, *28*(4), pp. 3–21.

Were, Miriam K. Public Health Aspects of Hunger and Malnutrition for Populations in Developing Countries. In *Helmuth, J. W. and Johnson, S. R.*, eds., Vol. 2, 1989, pp. 219–39.

Werge, Thomas. Corporate Kingdoms and the Kingdom of God in America. In *Rueschhoff, N. and Schaum, K.*, eds., 1989, pp. 57–76.

Werlang, Sérgio Ribeiro da Costa and Marques, Maria Silvia Bastos. Moratória interna, dívida pública e juros reais. (With English summary.) *Pesquisa Planejamento Econ.*, April 1989, *19*(1), pp. 19–43.

Werneck, Rogério L. F. Aspectos macroeconômicos da privatização no Brasil. (With English summary.) *Pesquisa Planejamento Econ.*, August 1989, *19*(2), pp. 277–307.

Werner, Jan. Equilibrium with Incomplete Markets without Ordered Preferences. *J. Econ. Theory*, December 1989, *49*(2), pp. 379–82.

Werner, Josua and Mauch, Gerhard. Friedrich List und die Lehre von den produktiven Kräften. (Friedrich List and the Theory of Productive Forces. With English summary.) *Jahr. Nationalökon. Statist.*, December 1989, *206*(6), pp. 533–45.

Werner, Pierre. A Common European Currency—No Longer Utopian! In *Franz, O.*, ed., 1989, pp. 142–43.

Werner, Simcha B. The Development of Political Corruption in Israel. In *Heidenheimer, A. J.; Johnston, M. and LeVine, V. T.*, eds., 1989, 1983, pp. 251–74.

Wernerfelt, Birger. Tacit Collusion in Differentiated Cournot Games. *Econ. Letters*, 1989, *29*(4), pp. 303–06.

Wescott, Robert F. and Yates, Mary V. The PC Corner: Desktop Publishing is for Economists. *Bus. Econ.*, January 1989, *24*(1), pp. 51–53.

Weskamp, Anita; Hamilton, Jonathan H. and Thisse, Jacques-François. Spatial Discrimination: Bertrand vs. Cournot in a Model of Location Choice. *Reg. Sci. Urban Econ.*, February 1989, *19*(1), pp. 87–102.

Wesselman, Bertram M. and van Praag, Bernard M. S. Elliptical Multivariate Analysis. *J. Econometrics*, June 1989, *41*(2), pp. 189–203.

Wessels, Hans. Beschäftigungswirkungen computergestützter Technologien—Dargestellt am Beispiel der Montageroboter. (With English summary.) *Z. Betriebswirtshaft*, November 1989, *59*(11), pp. 1159–78.

_____ **and Meyer-Krahmer, Frieder.** Intersektorale Verflechtung von Technologiegebern und Technologienehmern—Eine empirische Analyse für die Bundesrepublik Deutschland. (Intersectoral Technology Flow: Network between Producer and User—An Empirical Analysis for the Federal Republic of Germany. With English summary.) *Jahr. Nationalökon. Statist.*, December 1989, *206*(6), pp. 563–82.

West, Donald A. Adjustment of Fruit and Vegetable Processing to the Canada–United States Trade Agreement. *Can. J. Agr. Econ.*, Part 2, December 1989, *37*(4), pp. 1287–1300.

West, Douglas S. Evaluating a Supermarket Relocation Strategy Using Spatial Competition Analysis. *Ann. Reg. Sci.*, 1989, *23*(2), pp. 137–54.

West, Edwin G. Nonprofit Organizations: Revised Theory and New Evidence. *Public Choice*, November 1989, *63*(2), pp. 165–74.

_____. Open Enrollment: A Vehicle for Market Competition in Schooling? *Cato J.*, Spring–Summer 1989, *9*(1), pp. 253–62.

West, Guy R. and Jackson, Randall W. Perspectives on Probabilistic Input–Output Analysis. In *Miller, R. E.; Polenske, K. R. and Rose, A. Z., eds.*, 1989, pp. 209–21.

_____ **and Jensen, Rodney C.** On Objectivity in Economic Research: A Response. *Environ. Planning A*, March 1989, *21*(3), pp. 405–07.

West, Heidimarie and Hyman, Leonard S. Diversification, Deregulation, and Competition: Cost of Capital Implications for Electric Utilities. In *Crew, M. A., ed.*, 1989, pp. 165–81.

West, Kenneth D. Estimation of Linear Rational Expectations Models, in the Presence of Deterministic Terms. *J. Monet. Econ.*, November 1989, *24*(3), pp. 437–42.

_____. Order Backlogs and Production Smoothing. In *Kollintzas, T., ed.*, 1989, pp. 246–69.

Westerfield, Randolph and Jaffe, Jeffrey F. Is There a Monthly Effect in Stock Market Returns? Evidence from Foreign Countries. *J. Banking Finance*, May 1989, *13*(2), pp. 237–44.

_____; **Jaffe, Jeffrey F. and Keim, Donald B.** Earnings Yields, Market Values, and Stock Returns. *J. Finance*, March 1989, *44*(1), pp. 135–48.

_____; **Ma, Christopher K. and Jaffe, Jeffrey F.** A Twist on the Monday Effect in Stock Prices: Evidence from the U.S. and Foreign Stock Markets. *J. Banking Finance*, September 1989, *13*(4–5), pp. 641–50.

Westergård-Nielsen, Niels. Empirical Studies of the European Labour Market Using Microeconomic Data Sets: Introduction. *Europ. Econ. Rev.*, March 1989, *33*(2/3), pp. 389–94.

_____. The Use of Register Data in Economic Analysis. *Schweiz. Z. Volkswirtsch. Statist.*, September 1989, *125*(3), pp. 391–403.

Westley, Glenn D. Commercial Electricity Demand in a Central American Economy. *Appl. Econ.*, January 1989, *21*(1), pp. 1–17.

_____. Nontraditional Partial Adjustment Models and Their Use in Estimating the Residential Demand for Electricity in Costa Rica. *Land Econ.*, August 1989, *65*(3), pp. 254–71.

Westlund, Anders H. and Hackl, Peter. Statistical Analysis of "Structural Change": An Annotated Bibliography. *Empirical Econ.*, 1989, *14*(2), pp. 167–92.

_____ **and Hackl, Peter.** Statistical Analysis of "Structural Change": An Annotated Bibliography. In *Kramer, W., ed.*, 1989, pp. 103–28.

_____ **and Törnkvist, Birgitta.** On the Identification of Time for Structural Changes by MOSUM-SQ and CUSUM-SQ Procedures. In *Hackl, P., ed.*, 1989, pp. 97–126.

Westoff, Charles F.; Moreno, Lorenzo and Goldman, Noreen. The Demographic Impact of Changes in Contraceptive Practice in Third World Populations. *Population Devel. Rev.*, March 1989, *15*(1), pp. 91–106.

Weston, Ann and Mark, Janette. The Havana Charter Experience: Lessons for Developing Countries. In *Whalley, J., ed., Vol. 1*, 1989, pp. 45–65.

Weston, J. Fred. Strategy and Business Economics. *Bus. Econ.*, April 1989, *24*(2), pp. 5–12.

de Wet, Geert L. The Effect of Labour-Intensive Production on Progress. In *Gemper, B. B., ed.*, 1989, pp. 87–97.

Wetle, Terrie. Ethical Issues and Value Conflicts in Geriatric Care. In *Eisdorfer, C.; Kessler, D. A. and Spector, A. N., eds.*, 1989, pp. 403–12.

Wets, Roger J.-B. and Artstein, Zvi. Decentralized Allocation of Resources among Many Producers. *J. Math. Econ.*, 1989, *18*(4), pp. 303–24.

Wettstein, David and Postlewaite, Andrew. Feasible and Continuous Implementation. *Rev. Econ. Stud.*, October 1989, *56*(4), pp. 603–11.

Wetzel, James N. Economic Issues Involving Property Rights to School Attendance. *Econ. Educ. Rev.*, 1989, *8*(3), pp. 255–62.

Wetzstein, Michael E.; Noles, Richard K. and McClelland, John W. Optimal Replacement Policies for Rejuvenated Assets. *Amer. J. Agr. Econ.*, February 1989, *71*(1), pp. 147–57.

Wever, Kirsten R. Toward a Structural Account of Union Participation in Management: The Case of Western Airlines. *Ind. Lab. Relat. Rev.*, July 1989, *42*(4), pp. 600–609.

Weyman-Jones, Thomas. U.S. and U.K. Energy Policy. In *Button, K. and Swann, D., eds.*, 1989, pp. 279–99.

Whalen, Charles J. John R. Commons's *Institutional Economics*: A Re-examination. *J. Econ. Issues*, June 1989, *23*(2), pp. 443–54.

_____. The Minsky–Simons–*Veblen* Connection: Reply. *J. Econ. Issues*, September 1989, *23*(3), pp. 891–95.

Whall, Barry and Silvia, John E. Home Equity Loans and the Business Cycle. *Bus. Econ.*, January 1989, *24*(1), pp. 43–45.

Whalley, John. Developing Countries and the Global Trading System: Introduction. In *Whalley, J., ed., Vol. 2*, 1989, pp. 1–16.

_____. Implications for the GATT and the World

Trading System: Comments. In *Schott, J. J., ed.*, 1989, pp. 366–73.

_____. Tax Expenditures and Public Management and Accounting: Comment. In *Bruce, N., ed.*, 1989, pp. 127–29.

_____. Taxes in Canada, Japan, and the United States: Influences on Trade and Investment Flows, and the Role of Tax-Based Trade Irritants. In *Stern, R. M., ed.*, 1989, pp. 219–40.

_____. U.S.–Canada Bilateral Tariff Elimination: The Role of Product Differentiation and Market Structure: Comment. In *Feenstra, R. C., ed.*, 1989, pp. 250–53.

_____ and Clarete, Ramon L. Trade-Restricting Effects of Exchange Rate Regimes: Implications for Developed–Developing Country Trade Negotiations. In *Whalley, J., ed., Vol. 1*, 1989, pp. 66–88.

_____ and Hamilton, Bob. Efficiency and Distributional Effects of the Tax Reform Package. In *Mintz, J. and Whalley, J., eds.*, 1989, pp. 373–98.

_____ and Hamilton, Bob. Geographically Discriminatory Trade Arrangements. In *Jacquemin, A. and Sapir, A., eds.*, 1989, *1985*, pp. 213–26.

_____ and Hamilton, Bob. Reforming Indirect Taxes in Canada: Some General Equilibrium Estimates. *Can. J. Econ.*, August 1989, *22*(3), pp. 561–75.

_____; Hamilton, Bob and Davies, James B. Capital Income Taxation in a Two-Commodity Life Cycle Model: The Role of Factor Intensity and Asset Capitalization Effects. *J. Public Econ.*, June 1989, *39*(1), pp. 109–26.

_____ and Hamilton, Colleen. Coalitions in the Uruguay Round. *Weltwirtsch. Arch.*, 1989, *125*(3), pp. 547–62.

_____ and Hamilton, Colleen. Developing Countries and the Global Trading System: Introduction. In *Whalley, J., ed., Vol. 1*, 1989, pp. 3–25.

_____ and Jones, Rich. A Canadian Regional General Equilibrium Model and Some Applications. *J. Urban Econ.*, May 1989, *25*(3), pp. 368–404.

_____ and Nguyen, Trien T. General Equilibrium Analysis of Black and White Markets: A Computational Approach. *J. Public Econ.*, December 1989, *40*(3), pp. 331–47.

_____; Zhu, Lijing and McMillan, John. The Impact of China's Economic Reforms on Agricultural Productivity Growth. *J. Polit. Econ.*, August 1989, *97*(4), pp. 781–807.

Wharton, Amy S. Gender Segregation in Private-Sector, Public-Sector, and Self-employed Occupations, 1950–1981. *Soc. Sci. Quart.*, December 1989, *70*(4), pp. 923–40.

Wharton, J. D. and Harmatz, H. R. An Exploratory Investigation of How Cultural Attitudes Relate to Life Insurance Holdings: A Cross-Cultural Comparison. *J. Econ. Psych.*, June 1989, *10*(2), pp. 217–27.

Whatmore, S. J.; Marsden, T. K. and Munton, R. J. Part-Time Farming and Its Implications

for the Rural Landscape: A Preliminary Analysis. *Environ. Planning A*, April 1989, *21*(4), pp. 523–36.

Wheatley, Simon M. A Critique of Latent Variable Tests of Asset Pricing Models. *J. Finan. Econ.*, August 1989, *23*(2), pp. 325–38.

Wheaton, William C. On the Use of the Financial Option Price Model to Value and Explain Vacant Urban Land: Comments. *Amer. Real Estate Urban Econ. Assoc. J.*, Summer 1989, *17*(2), pp. 159–60.

_____ and Torto, Raymond G. Income and Appraised Values: A Reexamination of the FRC Returns Data. *Amer. Real Estate Urban Econ. Assoc. J.*, Winter 1989, *17*(4), pp. 439–49.

Wheeler, Hoyt N. Social Dominance and Industrial Relations. In *Barbash, J. and Barbash, K., eds.*, 1989, pp. 184–93.

Wheeler, James O. and Bagchi-Sen, Sharmistha. A Spatial and Temporal Model of Foreign Direct Investment in the United States. *Econ. Geogr.*, April 1989, *65*(2), pp. 113–29.

Wheeler, Joseph C. The Critical Role for Official Development Assistance in the 1990s. *Finance Devel.*, September 1989, *26*(3), pp. 38–40.

Wheeler, Paula and Swagler, Roger M. Rental-Purchase Agreements: A Preliminary Investigation of Consumer Attitudes and Behaviors. *J. Cons. Aff.*, Summer 1989, *23*(1), pp. 145–60.

Wheeler, Stephen; Chewning, Gene and Pany, Kurt. Auditor Reporting Decisions Involving Accounting Principle Changes: Some Evidence on Materiality Thresholds. *J. Acc. Res.*, Spring 1989, *27*(1), pp. 78–96.

Wheelock, David C. The Strategy, Effectiveness, and Consistency of Federal Reserve Monetary Policy 1924–1933. *Exploration Econ. Hist.*, October 1989, *26*(4), pp. 453–76.

Wheelwright, Edward L. and Crough, Greg J. The Changing Pacific Rim Economy, with Special Reference to Japanese Transnational Corporations: A View from Australia. In *Shiraishi, T. and Tsuru, S., eds.*, 1989, pp. 61–78.

Whelpley, William and Webb, Roy H. Labor Market Data. *Fed. Res. Bank Richmond Econ. Rev.*, Nov.–Dec. 1989, *75*(6), pp. 15–22.

Whichard, Obie G. U.S. Multinational Companies: Operations in 1987. *Surv. Curr. Bus.*, June 1989, *69*(6), pp. 27–39.

Whiddon, Beverly and Martin, Patricia Yancey. Organizational Democracy and Work Quality in a State Welfare Agency. *Soc. Sci. Quart.*, September 1989, *70*(3), pp. 667–86.

Whinston, Michael D.; McAfee, R. Preston and McMillan, John. Multiproduct Monopoly, Commodity Bundling, and Correlation of Values. *Quart. J. Econ.*, May 1989, *104*(2), pp. 371–83.

Whipp, Richard; Rosenfeld, Robert and Pettigrew, Andrew M. Competitiveness and the Management of Strategic Change Process. In *Francis, A. and Tharakan, P. K. M., eds.*, 1989, pp. 110–36.

Whipple, Glen D. and Menkhaus, Dale J. Supply Response in the U.S. Sheep Industry. *Amer.*

J. Agr. Econ., February 1989, *71*(1), pp. 126–35.

Whitaker, John K. The Cambridge Background to Imperfect Competition. **In** *Feiwel, G. R., ed. (I),* 1989, pp. 169–96.

_____. Palgrave Resurrected: A Review Article. *J. Polit. Econ.*, April 1989, *97*(2), pp. 480–96.

Whitby, Kenny J. and Gilliam, Franklin D., Jr. Race, Class, and Attitudes toward Social Welfare Spending: An Ethclass Interpretation. *Soc. Sci. Quart.*, March 1989, *70*(1), pp. 88–100.

White, B. and Ennew, C. T. The Implications of Quotas and Supply Control Policy in the British Potato Market. *Europ. Rev. Agr. Econ.*, 1989, *16*(2), pp. 243–56.

White, Christine. British Business in Russian Asia since the 1860s: An Opportunity Lost? **In** *Davenport-Hines, R. P. T. and Jones, G., eds.,* 1989, pp. 68–91.

White, Eugene Nelson. Was There a Solution to the Ancien Régime's Financial Dilemma? *J. Econ. Hist.*, September 1989, *49*(3), pp. 545–68.

White, Fred C. and Centner, Terence J. Protecting Inventors' Intellectual Property Rights in Biotechnology. *Western J. Agr. Econ.*, December 1989, *14*(2), pp. 189–99.

_____ **and Maligaya, Arlyn R.** Agricultural Output Supply and Input Demand Relationships with Endogenous Land Rents. *Southern J. Agr. Econ.*, December 1989, *21*(2), pp. 13–20.

_____ **and Shideed, Kamil H.** Alternative Forms of Price Expectations in Supply Analysis for U.S. Corn and Soybean Acreages. *Western J. Agr. Econ.*, December 1989, *14*(2), pp. 281–92.

White, Gordon. Restructuring the Working Class: Labor Reform in Post-Mao China. **In** *Dirlik, A. and Meisner, M., eds.,* 1989, pp. 152–68.

_____ **and Bowles, Paul.** Contradictions in China's Financial Reforms: The Relationship between Banks and Enterprises. *Cambridge J. Econ.*, December 1989, *13*(4), pp. 481–95.

White, Graham S. and Elshabani, Abdelgader. Regional Transportation Planning Issues in the Context of Comprehensive Development Plans. **In** *Candemir, Y., ed.,* 1989, pp. 161–83.

White, Halbert. Some Asymptotic Results for Learning in Single Hidden-Layer Feedforward Network Models. *J. Amer. Statist. Assoc.*, December 1989, *84*(408), pp. 1003–13.

_____**; Kamstra, Mark and Granger, C. W. J.** Interval Forecasting: An Analysis Based upon ARCH-Quantile Estimators. *J. Econometrics*, January 1989, *40*(1), pp. 87–96.

White, Harry L. and Maris, Brian A. Valuing and Hedging Fixed Rate Mortgage Commitments. *J. Real Estate Finance Econ.*, September 1989, *2*(3), pp. 223–32.

White, James R. and Grieson, Ronald E. The Existence and Capitalization of Neighborhood Externalities: A Reassessment. *J. Urban Econ.*, January 1989, *25*(1), pp. 68–76.

White, James W. Economic Development and Sociopolitical Unrest in Nineteenth-Century Japan. *Econ. Devel. Cult. Change*, January 1989, *37*(2), pp. 231–60.

White-Jones, Marcia and Due, Jean M. Differences in Earning, Labour Inputs, Decision-Making and Perception of Development between Farm and Market: A Case Study in Zambia. *Eastern Afr. Econ. Rev.*, December 1989, *5*(2), pp. 91–103.

White, Kenneth J. NAG Fortran Workstation Library: A Review. *J. Appl. Econometrics*, Jan.–March 1989, *4*(1), pp. 93–96.

White, Lawrence H. Accounting for Non-interest-bearing Currency: A Critique of the Legal Restrictions Theory of Money. **In** *White, L. H.,* 1989, *1987*, pp. 243–54.

_____. Alternative Perspectives on the Cashless Competitive Payments System. *J. Post Keynesian Econ.*, Spring 1989, *11*(3), pp. 378–84.

_____. Comment: Toward an International Fiat Standard? **In** *Dorn, J. A. and Niskanen, W. A., eds.,* 1989, *1988*, pp. 135–42.

_____. Competitive Money, Inside and Out. **In** *White, L. H.,* 1989, *1983*, pp. 48–69.

_____. Competitive Payments Systems and the Unit of Account. **In** *White, L. H.,* 1989, *1984*, pp. 169–94.

_____. Competitive Payments Systems: Reply. **In** *White, L. H.,* 1989, *1986*, pp. 195–202.

_____. Depoliticizing the Supply of Money. **In** *White, L. H.,* 1989, *1988*, pp. 91–110.

_____. Fix or Float? The International Monetary Dilemma. **In** *White, L. H.,* 1989, *1983*, pp. 137–47.

_____. Free Banking and the Gold Standard. **In** *White, L. H.,* 1989, *1985*, pp. 148–66.

_____. Free Banking as an Alternative Monetary System. **In** *White, L. H.,* 1989, *1984*, pp. 13–47.

_____. Gold, Dollars, and Private Currencies. **In** *White, L. H.,* 1989, *1981*, pp. 127–36.

_____. Privatization of Financial Institutions in Developing Countries. **In** *White, L. H.,* 1989, *1987*, pp. 111–23.

_____. Problems Inherent in Political Money Supply Regimes: Some Historical and Theoretical Lessons. **In** *White, L. H.,* 1989, *1988*, pp. 70–90.

_____. A Subjectivist Perspective on the Definition and Identification of Money. **In** *White, L. H.,* 1989, *1986*, pp. 203–17.

_____. What Kinds of Monetary Institutions Would a Free Market Deliver? *Cato J.*, Fall 1989, *9*(2), pp. 367–91.

_____ **and Selgin, George A.** The Evolution of a Free Banking System. **In** *White, L. H.,* 1989, *1987*, pp. 218–42.

White, Lawrence J. Application of the Merger Guidelines: The Proposed Merger of Coca-Cola and Dr Pepper. **In** *Kwoka, J. E., Jr. and White, L. J., eds.,* 1989, pp. 80–98.

_____. A Framework for the Future: Panel Presentation. **In** *Federal Home Loan Bank of San Francisco,* 1989, pp. 221–24.

_____. The Reform of Federal Deposit Insurance. *J. Econ. Perspectives*, Fall 1989, *3*(4), pp. 11–29.

_____. Restrictions on Financial Intermediaries and Implications for Aggregate Fluctuations: Canada and the United States 1870–1913: Comment. In *Blanchard, O. J. and Fischer, S., eds.*, 1989, pp. 345–49.

_____. The Revolution in Antitrust Analysis of Vertical Relationships: How Did We Get from There to Here? In *Larner, R. J. and Meehan, J. W., Jr., eds.*, 1989, pp. 103–21.

_____ and Kwoka, John E., Jr. The Antitrust Revolution: Introduction. In *Kwoka, J. E., Jr. and White, L. J., eds.*, 1989, pp. 1–5.

_____ and Kwoka, John E., Jr. The Economic and Legal Context of Horizontal Practices. In *Kwoka, J. E., Jr. and White, L. J., eds.*, 1989, pp. 122–33.

_____ and Kwoka, John E., Jr. The Economic and Legal Context of Horizontal Structure. In *Kwoka, J. E., Jr. and White, L. J., eds.*, 1989, pp. 8–18.

_____ and Kwoka, John E., Jr. The Economic and Legal Context of Vertical Arrangements. In *Kwoka, J. E., Jr. and White, L. J., eds.*, 1989, pp. 264–72.

White, Leonard A. A Proper Interpretation of the Market Definition within an Antitrust Context. In *Missouri Valley Economic Association*, 1989, pp. 10–15.

White-Means, Shelley I. Consumer Information, Insurance, and Doctor Shopping: The Elderly Consumer's Perspective. *J. Cons. Aff.*, Summer 1989, *23*(1), pp. 45–64.

_____ and Thornton, Michael C. Factors Influencing the Use of the Hospital Emergency Room among Black Americans. *Rev. Black Polit. Econ.*, Spring 1989, *17*(4), pp. 59–71.

White, Michael D. Conscription and the Size of Armed Forces. *Soc. Sci. Quart.*, September 1989, *70*(3), pp. 772–81.

White, Michael V. Jevons's "Antipodean Interlude": The Question of Early Influences: Rejoinder. *Hist. Polit. Econ.*, Winter 1989, *21*(4), pp. 623–31.

_____. Why Are There No Supply and Demand Curves in Jevons? *Hist. Polit. Econ.*, Fall 1989, *21*(3), pp. 425–56.

White, Michelle J. An Empirical Test of the Comparative and Contributory Negligence Rules in Accident Law. *Rand J. Econ.*, Autumn 1989, *20*(3), pp. 308–30.

_____. The Corporate Bankruptcy Decision. *J. Econ. Perspectives*, Spring 1989, *3*(2), pp. 129–51.

White, Nancy; Bresnock, Anne E. and Graves, Philip E. Multiple-Choice Testing: Question and Response Position. *J. Econ. Educ.*, Summer 1989, *20*(3), pp. 239–45.

White, Richard E. and Pruitt, Stephen W. Exchange-Traded Options and CRISMA Trading. *J. Portfol. Manage.*, Summer 1989, *15*(4), pp. 55–56.

White, Stuart; Pearson, Mark and Smith, Stephen R. Demographic Influences on Public

Spending. *Fisc. Stud.*, May 1989, *10*(2), pp. 48–65.

White, T. Kelley. Trade and Agriculture. In *Horwich, G. and Lynch, G. J., eds.*, 1989, pp. 21–49.

Whiteford, Peter. Taxation and Social Security: An Overview. *Australian Tax Forum*, 1989, *6*(1), pp. 1–39.

_____; Saunders, Peter and Bradbury, Bruce. Unemployment Benefit Replacement Rates. *Australian Bull. Lab.*, June 1989, *15*(3), pp. 223–44.

Whitehead, David D. and Goudreau, Robert E. Commercial Bank Profitability: Improved in 1988. *Fed. Res. Bank Atlanta Econ. Rev.*, July–Aug. 1989, *74*(4), pp. 34–47.

_____; King, B. Frank and Tschinkel, Sheila L. Interstate Banking Developments in the 1980s. *Fed. Res. Bank Atlanta Econ. Rev.*, May–June 1989, *74*(3), pp. 32–51.

Whitehead, Laurence. Britain, Latin America and the European Community. In *Bulmer-Thomas, V., ed.*, 1989, pp. 83–100.

_____. Democratization and Disinflation: A Comparative Approach. In *Nelson, J. M., ed.*, 1989, pp. 79–93.

_____. On Presidential Graft: The Latin American Evidence. In *Heidenheimer, A. J.; Johnston, M. and LeVine, V. T., eds.*, 1989, *1983*, pp. 781–800.

Whitehouse, Michael A. and Dykes, Sayre Ellen. The Establishment and Evolution of the Federal Reserve Board: 1913–23. *Fed. Res. Bull.*, April 1989, *75*(4), pp. 227–43.

Whitelegg, John. Transport Policy: Off the Rails? In *Mohan, J., ed.*, 1989, pp. 187–207.

Whitesell, Robert S. Estimates of the Output Loss from Allocative Inefficiency: A Comparison of Hungary and West Germany. *Eastern Europ. Econ.*, Winter 1989–90, *28*(2), pp. 95–125.

Whitesell, William C. The Demand for Currency versus Debitable Accounts: A Note. *J. Money, Credit, Banking*, May 1989, *21*(2), pp. 246–57.

Whiteside, Alan. Industrialization and Investment in Malawi. In *Whiteside, A. W., ed.*, 1989, pp. 84–102.

_____. Industrialization and Investment Incentives in Southern Africa: Introduction. In *Whiteside, A. W., ed.*, 1989, pp. 1–10.

_____. A Summary of Incentives Available in the Southern Africa States. In *Whiteside, A. W., ed.*, 1989, pp. 218–39.

_____ and Gallagher, Sally. Mozambique: Incentives and Industrialization in a Centrally Planned State. In *Whiteside, A. W., ed.*, 1989, pp. 103–20.

_____ and McGrath, John. Industry, Investment Incentives and the Foreign Exchange Crisis: Zambia—A Case Study. In *Whiteside, A. W., ed.*, 1989, pp. 167–83.

Whiteside, M. M. and Narayanan, A. Reverse Regression, Collinearity, and Employment Discrimination. *J. Bus. Econ. Statist.*, July 1989, *7*(3), pp. 403–06.

Whitford, David T. and Davis, Wayne J. Tests

of Composition Models for Resource Allocation: Good News and Bad News. In *Lee, C. F., ed.*, 1989, pp. 375–93.

Whitley, John D.; Turner, David S. and Wallis, Kenneth F. Differences in the Properties of Large-Scale Macroeconometric Models: The Role of Labour Market Specifications. *J. Appl. Econometrics*, Oct.–Dec. 1989, *4*(4), pp. 317–44.

Whitman, Ray D. and Bezdek, Roger H. Federal Reimbursement for Mandates on State and Local Governments. *Public Budg. Finance*, Spring 1989, *9*(1), pp. 47–62.

Whitmore, G. A. Stochastic Dominance for the Class of Completely Monotonic Utility Functions. In *[Hadar, J.]*, 1989, pp. 77–88.

Whitmore, R. W., et al. Using Health Indicators in Calculating the AAPCC. In *Scheffler, R. M. and Rossiter, L. F., eds.*, 1989, pp. 75–109.

Whitson, David and Macintosh, Donald. Rational Planning vs. Regional Interests: The Professionalization of Canadian Amateur Sport. *Can. Public Policy*, December 1989, *15*(4), pp. 436–49.

Whitt, J. Allen. Organizational Ties and Urban Growth. In *Perrucci, R. and Potter, H. R., eds.*, 1989, pp. 97–109.

Whitt, Joseph A., Jr. Purchasing-Power Parity and Exchange Rates in the Long Run. *Fed. Res. Bank Atlanta Econ. Rev.*, July–Aug. 1989, *74*(4), pp. 18–32.

Whittaker, John and Abraham, Haim. Is Dynamic Stability of Walrasian Equilibrium Achieved through Falling Target Utilities? *Int. Econ. Rev.*, August 1989, *30*(3), pp. 507–11.

_____ **and Barr, G. D. I.** The Price Elasticity of Electricity Demand in South Africa. *Appl. Econ.*, September 1989, *21*(9), pp. 1153–57.

_____ **and Theunissen, A. J.** Does Money Supply Endogeneity Matter? A Comment. *S. Afr. J. Econ.*, June 1989, *57*(2), pp. 201–02.

Whitten, David O. Weighing the Output of Academic Economists: Survey Results Reveal the Fringes of an Elusive Measuring Device. In *Perkins, E. J., ed.*, 1989, pp. 247–54.

Whittenburg, Gerald E.; Chow, Chee W. and Shields, Michael D. The Quality of Practioners' Judgments Regarding Substantial Authority: An Exploratory Empirical Investigation. In *Jones, S. M., ed.*, 1989, pp. 165–80.

Whittingham, Wilfred. The United States Government's Caribbean Basin Initiative. *CEPAL Rev.*, December 1989, (39), pp. 73–92.

Whittington, Geoffrey. Reporting the Incidence of Corporation Tax. In *[Sandford, C.]*, 1989, pp. 67–85.

Whittlesey, Norman K.; Halverson, Philip and Hamilton, Joel R. Interruptible Water Markets in the Pacific Northwest. *Amer. J. Agr. Econ.*, February 1989, *71*(1), pp. 63–75.

Whyatt, Anna. National/Local Relationships in Policies towards Long-Term Unemployment. In *Dyson, K., ed.*, 1989, pp. 227–36.

Whynes, David K. The Economic Role of Government as a Constitutional Problem. In *Samuels, W. J., ed. (I)*, 1989, pp. 205–11.

_____. The Political Business Cycle. In *Greenaway, D., ed.*, 1989, pp. 111–31.

Whyte, Ian D. Proto-industrialisation in Scotland. In *Hudson, P., ed.*, 1989, pp. 228–51.

Whyte, Martin King. Who Hates Bureaucracy? A Chinese Puzzle. In *Nee, V. and Stark, D., eds.*, 1989, pp. 233–54.

Wiatr, Jerzy J. Economic and Political Reforms in Socialist Countries of Eastern Europe: A Comparative Analysis. In *Gomulka, S.; Ha, Y.-C. and Kim, C.-O., eds.*, 1989, pp. 123–38.

Wiatrowski, William J. and Houff, James N. Analyzing Short-term Disability Benefits. *Mon. Lab. Rev.*, June 1989, *112*(6), pp. 3–9.

_____ **and Meisenheimer, Joseph R., II.** Flexible Benefits Plans: Employees Who Have a Choice. *Mon. Lab. Rev.*, December 1989, *112*(12), pp. 17–23.

Wibaut, Serge; Marchand, Maurice and Pestieau, Pierre. Optimal Commodity Taxation and Tax Reform under Unemployment. *Scand. J. Econ.*, 1989, *91*(3), pp. 547–63.

Wibisono, Makarim. The Politics of Indonesian Textile Policy: The Interests of Government Agencies and the Private Sector. *Bull. Indonesian Econ. Stud.*, April 1989, *25*(1), pp. 31–52.

Wichers, C. Robert and Maeshiro, Asatoshi. Estimating Money Demand in Log-First-Difference Form: Comment. *Southern Econ. J.*, April 1989, *55*(4), pp. 1036–39.

_____ **and Maeshiro, Asatoshi.** On the Relationship between the Estimates of Level Models and Difference Models. *Amer. J. Agr. Econ.*, May 1989, *71*(2), pp. 432–36.

Wickens, M. R. Econometric Tests of Rationality and Market Efficiency: Comment. *Econometric Rev.*, 1989, *8*(2), pp. 207–12.

Wickens, Michael R. Intertemporal Consumer Behaviour under Structural Changes in Income: Comment. *Econometric Rev.*, 1989, *8*(1), pp. 133–41.

_____ **and Pagan, Adrian R.** A Survey of Some Recent Econometric Methods. *Econ. J.*, December 1989, *99*(398), pp. 962–1025.

_____ **and Smith, P. N.** Assessing the Effects of Monetary Shocks on Exchange Rate Variability with a Stylised Econometric Model of the UK. *Greek Econ. Rev.*, 1989, *11*(1), pp. 76–94.

_____ **and Uctum, Merih.** Exchange Rate Determination, the Stock Market and Investment Finance. In *MacDonald, R. and Taylor, M. P., eds.*, 1989, pp. 142–58.

Wickham, Elizabeth and Thompson, Henry. An Empirical Analysis of Intra-industry Trade and Multinational Firms. In *Tharakan, P. K. M. and Kol, J., eds.*, 1989, pp. 121–44.

Wickham-Jones, Mark. New Directions in Radical Political Economy. *J. Econ. Surveys*, 1989, *3*(3), pp. 261–76.

Wickham, Peter; Frenkel, Jacob A. and Dooley, Michael P. An Introduction to Analytical Issues in Debt. In *Frenkel, J. A.; Dooley, M. P. and Wickham, P., eds.*, 1989, pp. 1–9.

Wicklund, Robert A. and Braun, Ottmar L. Psychological Antecedents of Conspicuous Consumption. *J. Econ. Psych.*, June 1989, *10*(2), pp. 161–87.

Wickström, Bengt-Arne. The Norwegian Social-Security System: Present State and Future Prospects. In *Faure, M. and Van den Bergh, R., eds.*, 1989, pp. 163–84.

———. The Speed Limit as Life Saver: Comment. In *Faure, M. and Van den Bergh, R., eds.*, 1989, pp. 157–61.

Widdows, Kealoha and Kovenock, Dan. The Sequencing of Union Contract Negotiations. *Managerial Dec. Econ.*, December 1989, *10*(4), pp. 283–89.

Widmer, Candace. Minority Participation on Boards of Directors of Human Service Agencies: Some Evidence and Suggestions. In *Herman, R. D. and Van Til, J., eds.*, 1989, pp. 139–51.

———. Why Board Members Participate. In *Herman, R. D. and Van Til, J., eds.*, 1989, pp. 8–23.

Widmer, Lorne; Brinkman, George L. and Fox, Glenn C. Benefit Analysis of Agricultural Research: A Reply. *Can. J. Agr. Econ.*, March 1989, *37*(1), pp. 149–52.

Wieand, Kenneth F. Security Prices in a Production Economy with Durable Capital. *J. Real Estate Finance Econ.*, June 1989, *2*(2), pp. 81–100.

Wiedemann, Raimund and Opitz, Otto. An Agglomerative Algorithm of Overlapping Clustering. In *Opitz, O., ed.*, 1989, pp. 201–11.

Wiegert, Rolf and Strecker, Heinrich. Wirtschaftsstatistiche Daten und ökonomische Realität. (Economic Statistical Data and Economic Reality. With English summary.) *Jahr. Nationalökon. Statist.*, October 1989, *206*(4–5), pp. 487–509.

Wiener, Joshua M. Taking Care of the Uninsured. In *Bosworth, B. P., et al.*, 1989, pp. 127–31.

Wierzbicki, Andrzej P. Multiobjective Decision Support for Simulated Gaming. In *Lockett, A. G. and Islei, G., eds.*, 1989, pp. 498–509.

———; **Bronisz, Piotr and Krus, Lech.** Towards Interactive Solutions in a Bargaining Problem. In *Lewandowski, A. and Wierzbicki, A. P., eds.*, 1989, pp. 251–68.

——— **and Lewandowski, Andrzej.** Decision Support Systems Using Reference Point Optimization. In *Lewandowski, A. and Wierzbicki, A. P., eds.*, 1989, pp. 3–20.

———; **Rogowski, Tadeusz and Sobczyk, Jerzy.** IAC–DIDAS–L: A Dynamic Interactive Decision Analysis and Support System for Multicriteria Analysis of Linear and Dynamic Linear Models on Professional Microcomputers. In *Lewandowski, A. and Wierzbicki, A. P., eds.*, 1989, pp. 373–75.

Wiggins, James B. and Jarrow, Robert A. Option Pricing and Implicit Volatilities. *J. Econ. Surveys*, 1989, *3*(1), pp. 59–81.

Wiggins, Steven N. Social Control and Labor Relations in the American South before the Mechanization of the Cotton Harvest in the 1950s:

Comment. *J. Inst. Theoretical Econ.*, March 1989, *145*(1), pp. 158–61.

Wigington, Ian and Hazledine, Tim. Canadian Auto Policy Revisited: Reply. *Can. Public Policy*, March 1989, *15*(1), pp. 107–08.

Wigle, Randall M.; Harrison, Glenn W. and Rutström, E. E. Costs of Agricultural Trade Wars. In *Stoeckel, A. B.; Vincent, D. and Cuthbertson, S., eds.*, 1989, pp. 330–67.

——— **and Markusen, James R.** Nash Equilibrium Tariffs for the United States and Canada: The Roles of Country Size, Scale Economies, and Capital Mobility. *J. Polit. Econ.*, April 1989, *97*(2), pp. 368–86.

Wijekoon, P. and Trenkler, G. Mean Square Error Matrix Superiority of Estimators under Linear Restrictions and Misspecification. *Econ. Letters*, August 1989, *30*(2), pp. 141–49.

Wijkman, Per Magnus. The Effect of New Free Trade Areas on EFTA. In *Schott, J. J., ed.*, 1989, pp. 281–92.

——— **and Lindström, Eva Sundkvist.** Pacific Basin Integration: A Step towards Freer Trade. In *Nieuwenhuysen, J., ed.*, 1989, pp. 144–62.

Wijnberg, Nachoem M. Industry and Innovation. *De Economist*, 1989, *137*(4), pp. 499–505.

van Wijnbergen, Sweder. External Debt, Inflation, and the Public Sector: Towards Fiscal Policy for Sustainable Growth. In *Roe, A.; Roy, J. and Sengupta, J.*, 1989, pp. 34–54.

———. External Debt, Inflation, and the Public Sector: Toward Fiscal Policy for Sustainable Growth. *World Bank Econ. Rev.*, September 1989, *3*(3), pp. 297–320.

——— **and Anand, Ritu.** Inflation and the Financing of Government Expenditure: An Introductory Analysis with an Application to Turkey. *World Bank Econ. Rev.*, January 1989, *3*(1), pp. 17–38.

——— **and Cumby, Robert E.** Financial Policy and Speculative Runs with a Crawling Peg: Argentina 1979–1981. *J. Int. Econ.*, August 1989, *27*(1–2), pp. 111–27.

——— **and Svensson, Lars E. O.** Excess Capacity, Monopolistic Competition, and International Transmission of Monetary Disturbances. *Econ. J.*, September 1989, *99*(397), pp. 785–805.

Wikström, Solveig R.; Elg, Ulf and Johansson, Ulf. From the Consumption of Necessities to Experience-Seeking Consumption. In *Grunert, K. G. and Ölander, F., eds.*, 1989, pp. 287–308.

Wiktorin, Marianne. Stayers and Returners in Swedish Rental Housing Improvement. *Urban Stud.*, August 1989, *26*(4), pp. 403–18.

Wilber, Charles K.; Jameson, Kenneth P. and Weaver, James H. Strategies of Development: A Survey. In *DeGregori, T. R., ed.*, 1989, pp. 137–77.

Wilcox, Christopher J. Social Costs of Regulation of Primary Industry: An Application to Animal Welfare Regulation of the Victorian Pig Industry. *Australian J. Agr. Econ.*, December 1989, *33*(3), pp. 187–202.

Wilcox, David W. Social Security Benefits, Consumption Expenditure, and the Life Cycle Hypothesis. *J. Polit. Econ.*, April 1989, *97*(2), pp. 288–304.

———. The Sustainability of Government Deficits: Implications of the Present-Value Borrowing Constraint. *J. Money, Credit, Banking*, August 1989, *21*(3), pp. 291–306.

———; English, William B. and Miron, Jeffrey A. Seasonal Fluctuations and the Life Cycle–Permanent Income Model of Consumption: A Correction. *J. Polit. Econ.*, August 1989, *97*(4), pp. 988–91.

Wilcox, James A. Liquidity Constraints on Consumption: The Real Effects of "Real" Lending Policies. *Fed. Res. Bank San Francisco Econ. Rev.*, Fall 1989, (4), pp. 39–52.

Wilcox, Linda; de Janvry, Alain and Sadoulet, Elisabeth. Rural Labour in Latin America. *Int. Lab. Rev.*, Special Issue, 1989, *128*(6), pp. 701–29.

Wild, John J.; Ramesh, K. and Han, Jerry C. Y. Managers' Earnings Forecasts and Intra-industry Information Transfers. *J. Acc. Econ.*, February 1989, *11*(1), pp. 3–33.

Wildasin, David E. Demand Estimation for Public Goods: Distortionary Taxation and Other Sources of Bias. *Reg. Sci. Urban Econ.*, August 1989, *19*(3), pp. 353–79.

———. Interjurisdictional Capital Mobility: Fiscal Externality and a Corrective Subsidy. *J. Urban Econ.*, March 1989, *25*(2), pp. 193–212.

———. Tax Expenditures: The Personal Standard. In *Bruce, N., ed.*, 1989, pp. 135–79.

——— and Boadway, Robin W. A Median Voter Model of Social Security. *Int. Econ. Rev.*, May 1989, *30*(2), pp. 307–28.

——— and Boadway, Robin W. Voting Models of Social Security Determination. In *Gustafsson, B. A. and Klevmarken, N. A., eds.*, 1989, pp. 29–50.

———; Boadway, Robin W. and Pestieau, Pierre. Non-cooperative Behavior and Efficient Provision of Public Goods. *Public Finance*, 1989, *44*(1), pp. 1–17.

———; Boadway, Robin W. and Pestieau, Pierre. Tax-Transfer Policies and the Voluntary Provision of Public Goods. *J. Public Econ.*, July 1989, *39*(2), pp. 157–76.

Wilde, Louis L.; Graetz, Michael J. and Dubin, Jeffrey A. Administrative and Compliance Costs of Taxation: United States. In *International Fiscal Association, ed. (I)*, 1989, pp. 311–47.

Wildemann, Horst. Fabrikorganisation: Kundennahe Produktion durch Fertigungssegmentierung. (With English summary.) *Z. Betriebswirtshaft*, January 1989, *59*(1), pp. 27–54.

Wilder, Patricia S. Productivity in the Retail Auto and Home Supply Store Industry. *Mon. Lab. Rev.*, August 1989, *112*(8), pp. 36–40.

Wilen, James E.; Gardner, B. Delworth and Huffaker, Ray G. Multiple Use Benefits on Public Rangelands: An Incentive-Based Fee System. *Amer. J. Agr. Econ.*, August 1989, *71*(3), pp. 670–78.

——— and Huffaker, Ray G. Dynamics of Opti-

mal Stocking in Plant/Herbivore Systems. *Natural Res. Modeling*, Fall 1989, *3*(4), pp. 553–75.

Wilhelm, Jochen E. M. On Stakeholders' Unanimity. In *Bamberg, G. and Spremann, K., eds.*, 1989, pp. 179–204.

Wilhite, Al and Bryant, Richard. Additional Interpretations of Dummy Variables in Semilogarithmic Equations. *Atlantic Econ. J.*, December 1989, *17*(4), pp. 88.

——— and Paul, Chris. Corporate Campaign Contributions and Legislative Voting. *Quart. Rev. Econ. Bus.*, Autumn 1989, *29*(3), pp. 73–85.

——— and Theilmann, John. Campaign Contributions by Political Parties Ideology *vs.* Winning. *Atlantic Econ. J.*, June 1989, *17*(2), pp. 11–20.

Wilhite, D. A. and Easterling, William E., III. Improving Response to Drought. In *Oram, P. A., et al.*, 1989, pp. 321–31.

Wilimovsky, Norman J. Policy Statements on Canadian Research in Aquatic Science. In *McRae, D. and Munro, G., eds.*, 1989, pp. 133–41.

Wilk, G. Mitchell. Telecommunications in a Competitive Environment: Informal Remarks. In *National Economic Research Associates*, 1989, pp. 223–26.

Wilken, Paul H. and Schram, Sanford F. It's No 'Laffer' Matter: Claim that Increasing Welfare Aid Breeds Poverty and Dependence Fails Statistical Test. *Amer. J. Econ. Sociology*, April 1989, *48*(2), pp. 203–17.

Wilkie, J. Scott. The Canada–United Kingdom Income Tax Convention. *Bull. Int. Fiscal Doc.*, February 1989, *43*(2), pp. 63–68.

Wilkie, William L.; Urbany, Joel E. and Dickson, Peter R. Buyer Uncertainty and Information Search. *J. Cons. Res.*, September 1989, *16*(2), pp. 208–15.

Wilkinson, Barry and Oliver, Nick. Japanese Manufacturing Techniques and Personnel and Industrial Relations Practice in Britain: Evidence and Implications. *Brit. J. Ind. Relat.*, March 1989, *27*(1), pp. 73–91.

Wilkinson, Bruce W. The Saskatchewan Potash Industry and the 1987 U.S. Antidumping Action. *Can. Public Policy*, June 1989, *15*(2), pp. 145–61.

Wilkinson, Christopher and Stevers, Ester. "Appropriate Regulation" for Communication and Information Services. In *Robinson, P.; Sauvant, K. P. and Govitrikar, V. P., eds.*, 1989, pp. 155–80.

Wilkinson, Frank; Tarling, Roger and Rubery, Jill. Government Policy and the Labor Market: The Case of the United Kingdom. In *Rosenberg, S., ed.*, 1989, pp. 23–45.

Wilkinson, Maurice. Aggregate Inventory Behavior in Large European Economies. *Europ. Econ. Rev.*, January 1989, *33*(1), pp. 181–94.

Wilkinson, Paul. Political Violence and the International System: A View from the North. In *Thomas, C. and Saravanamuttu, P., eds.*, 1989, pp. 175–94.

Wilkinson, Philip [Sir] and Lomax, David F. Lessons for Banking from the 1980s and the Recent Past. *Nat. Westminster Bank Quart. Rev.*, May 1989, pp. 2–16.

Wilks, Stephen. Corporate Strategy and State Support in the European Motor Industry. In *Hancher, L. and Moran, M., eds.*, 1989, pp. 167–98.

Willemain, Thomas R. Graphical Adjustment of Statistical Forecasts. *Int. J. Forecasting*, 1989, *5*(2), pp. 179–85.

Willems, J. C. and Heij, C. A Deterministic Approach to Approximate Modelling. In *Willems, J. C., ed.*, 1989, pp. 49–134.

Willems, J. L. Robust Stabilization of Uncertain Dynamic Systems. In *[Willems, J. C.]*, 1989, pp. 524–41.

Willemse, Rob and Webb, Roy H. Macroeconomic Price Indexes. *Fed. Res. Bank Richmond Econ. Rev.*, July–Aug. 1989, *75*(4), pp. 22–32.

Willenbockel, Dirk; Funke, Michael and Wadewitz, Sabine. Tobin's Q and Sectoral Investment in West Germany and Great Britain: A Pooled Cross-Section and Time-Series Study. *Z. Wirtschaft. Sozialwissen.*, 1989, *109*(3), pp. 399–420.

Willett, Keith. Optimality and the Government's Risk Management Programs. *Managerial Dec. Econ.*, June 1989, *10*(2), pp. 107–13.

Willett, Thomas D. Country Risk and the Structure of International Financial Intermediation: Commentary. In *Stone, C. C., ed.*, 1989, pp. 228–33.

_____. Key Exchange Rate Regimes: A Constitutional Perspective. In *Dorn, J. A. and Niskanen, W. A., eds.*, 1989, *1988*, pp. 191–206.

_____. Policy Motives and International Trade Restrictions: Comments. In *Vosgerau, H.-J., ed.*, 1989, pp. 303–09.

_____. A Public Choice Analysis of Strategies for Restoring International Economic Stability. In *Vosgerau, H.-J., ed.*, 1989, pp. 9–30.

_____ **and Kaempfer, William H.** Combining Rent-Seeking and Public Choice Theory in the Analysis of Tariffs versus Quotas. *Public Choice*, October 1989, *63*(1), pp. 79–86.

_____; **Kaempfer, William H. and McClure, J. Harold, Jr.** Incremental Protection and Efficient Political Choice between Tariffs and Quotas. *Can. J. Econ.*, May 1989, *22*(2), pp. 228–36.

Willey, Phillip C. T. and Ghiat, Boufeldja. The Impact of Local Culture and Attitudes on Organizational Effectiveness in Algeria. In *Davies, J., et al., eds.*, 1989, pp. 66–74.

Willgerodt, Hans and Peacock, Alan. German Liberalism and Economic Revival. In *Peacock, A. and Willgerodt, H., eds. (II)*, 1989, pp. 1–14.

_____ **and Peacock, Alan.** Overall View of the German Liberal Movement. In *Peacock, A. and Willgerodt, H., eds. (I)*, 1989, pp. 1–15.

Willheim, Ernst. Australia–Indonesia Sea-Bed Boundary Negotiations: Proposals for a Joint Development Zone in the "Timor Gap." *Natural Res. J.*, Summer 1989, *29*(3), pp. 821–42.

Williams, Alan M.; Shaw, Gareth and Greenwood, Justin. From Tourist to Tourism Entrepreneur, From Consumption to Production: Evidence from Cornwall, England. *Environ. Planning A*, December 1989, *21*(12), pp. 1639–53.

Williams, Byron K. Review of Dynamic Optimization Methods in Renewable Natural Resource Management. *Natural Res. Modeling*, Spring 1989, *3*(2), pp. 137–216.

Williams, C. G. and Hornsby, H. H. Vocationalism in U.S. and U.K. High Schools. *Econ. Educ. Rev.*, 1989, *8*(1), pp. 37–47.

Williams, Carol J.; Fazio, Russell H. and Powell, Martha C. The Role of Attitude Accessibility in the Attitude-to-Behavior Process. *J. Cons. Res.*, December 1989, *16*(3), pp. 280–89.

Williams, Donald R. Job Characteristics and the Labor Force Participation Behavior of Black and White Male Youth. *Rev. Black Polit. Econ.*, Fall 1989, *18*(2), pp. 5–24.

Williams, Gethin. Experimentation in Reflective Practice: A Conceptual Framework for Managers in Highly Professionalized Organizations. In *Mansfield, R., ed.*, 1989, pp. 65–75.

Williams, H.; Gillespie, A. E. and Thwaites, A. T. Industrial Dynamics and Policy Debate in the Information Technology Production Industries. In *Gibbs, D., ed.*, 1989, pp. 55–69.

Williams, Harold R. and Palia, Aspy P. Impact of TPM on U.S. Steel Imports from Japan. *Rivista Int. Sci. Econ. Com.*, December 1989, *36*(12), pp. 1109–21.

Williams, Harry B. What Temporary Workers Earn: Findings from New BLS Survey. *Mon. Lab. Rev.*, March 1989, *112*(3), pp. 3–6.

Williams, Jeffrey C. and Wright, Brian D. A Theory of Negative Prices for Storage. *J. Futures Markets*, February 1989, *9*(1), pp. 1–13.

Williams, Joan C. Deconstructing Gender. *Mich. Law Rev.*, February 1989, *87*(4), pp. 797–845.

Williams, Karel, et al. Facing Up to Manufacturing Failure. In *Hirst, P. and Zeitlin, J., eds.*, 1989, pp. 71–94.

Williams, Kenneth; Collier, Kenneth and Ordeshook, Peter C. The Rationally Uninformed Electorate: Some Experimental Evidence. *Public Choice*, January 1989, *60*(1), pp. 3–29.

Williams, Larry J. and Podsakoff, Philip M. Longitudinal Field Methods for Studying Reciprocal Relationships in Organizational Behavior Research: Toward Improved Casual Analysis. In *Cummings, L. L. and Staw, B. M., eds.*, 1989, pp. 247–92.

Williams, Lynn R. Collective Bargaining: An Essential Element for Successful Labor–Management Participation. In *Ahlbrandt, R. S., Jr., ed.*, 1989, pp. 53–57.

Williams, Marc A. The Developing Countries and the International Economic Order: A View from the South. In *Thomas, C. and Saravanamuttu, P., eds.*, 1989, pp. 45–58.

Williams, Marion. Regulation of Financial Institutions in the Caribbean: Implications for Growth and Development. *Soc. Econ. Stud.*, December 1989, *38*(4), pp. 181–99.

Williams, Martin and Laumas, Prem S. The Demand for Working Capital: A Reply. *Appl. Econ.*, January 1989, *21*(1), pp. 139–40.

_____ and Moomaw, Ronald L. Capital and Labour Efficiencies: A Regional Analysis. *Urban Stud.*, December 1989, *26*(6), pp. 573–85.

Williams, Michael A. and Werden, Gregory J. Can the Concentration-Collusion Hypothesis Be Refuted Empirically? *Econ. Letters*, September 1989, *30*(3), pp. 253–57.

_____ and Werden, Gregory J. The Role of Stock Market Studies in Formulating Antitrust Policy toward Horizontal Mergers: Reply. *Quart. J. Bus. Econ.*, Autumn 1989, *28*(4), pp. 39–42.

_____ and Werden, Gregory J. The Role of Stock Market Studies in Formulating Antitrust Policy toward Horizontal Mergers. *Quart. J. Bus. Econ.*, Autumn 1989, *28*(4), pp. 3–21.

Williams, Nigel T. and Webster, Paul. Variability in Wheat and Barley Production in Southeast England. In *Anderson, J. R. and Hazell, P. B. R., eds.*, 1989, pp. 107–17.

Williams, Patricia. The Obliging Shell: An Informal Essay on Formal Equal Opportunity. *Mich. Law Rev.*, August 1989, *87*(8), pp. 2128–51.

Williams, Phil. Intervention in the Developing World: A Northern Perspective. In *Thomas, C. and Saravanamuttu, P., eds.*, 1989, pp. 144–56.

Williams, Rick L.; Folsom, Ralph and LaVange, Lisa. A Probability Sampling Perspective on Panel Data Analysis. In *Kasprzyk, D., et al., eds.*, 1989, pp. 108–38.

Williams, Roberton and Ruggles, Patricia. Longitudinal Measures of Poverty: Accounting for Income and Assets over Time. *Rev. Income Wealth*, September 1989, *35*(3), pp. 225–43.

Williams, Steven R. and Satterthwaite, Mark A. Bilateral Trade with the Sealed Bid *k*-Double Auction: Existence and Efficiency. *J. Econ. Theory*, June 1989, *48*(1), pp. 107–33.

_____ and Satterthwaite, Mark A. The Rate of Convergence to Efficiency in the Buyer's Bid Double Auction as the Market Becomes Large. *Rev. Econ. Stud.*, October 1989, *56*(4), pp. 477–98.

Williams, T. Franklin. Approaches to Health. In *Eisdorfer, C.; Kessler, D. A. and Spector, A. N., eds.*, 1989, pp. 482–89.

Williams, W. D. and Sturgeon, James I. Linkages: A Personal Computer-Based Implementation of John Munkirs's Tableau. *J. Econ. Issues*, September 1989, *23*(3), pp. 895–96.

Williamson, James. The Need for a Geriatrics Specialty: Lessons from the United Kingdom. In *Eisdorfer, C.; Kessler, D. A. and Spector, A. N., eds.*, 1989, pp. 291–306.

Williamson, Jeffrey G. The Constraints on Industrialisation: Some Lessons from the First Industrial Revolution. In *Williamson, J. G. and Panchamukhi, V. R., eds.*, 1989, pp. 85–105.

_____. Factor Market Distortions, Applied General Equilibrium, and History. *Australian Econ. Hist. Rev.*, March 1989, *29*(1), pp. 3–20.

_____. The Future of Economic History: A View from North America. *Econ. Rec.*, September 1989, *65*(190), pp. 291–95.

_____ and Boyer, George R. A Quantitative Assessment of the Fertility Transition in England, 1851–1911. In *Ransom, R. L., ed.*, 1989, pp. 93–117.

_____ and Panchamukhi, Vadiraj R. The Balance between Industry and Agriculture in Economic Development: Introduction. In *Williamson, J. G. and Panchamukhi, V. R., eds.*, 1989, pp. xxi–xxxii.

Williamson, John. The Brady Initiative: Alternatives and Evaluation. In *Mrak, M., ed.*, 1989, pp. 49–62.

_____. The Case for Roughly Stabilizing the Real Value of the Dollar. *Amer. Econ. Rev.*, May 1989, *79*(2), pp. 41–45.

_____. Comment: Conflicting Views of the Twin Deficits. In *Dorn, J. A. and Niskanen, W. A., eds.*, 1989, *1988*, pp. 325–28.

_____. A Comparison of Alternative Regimes for International Macropolicy Coordination: Discussion. In *Miller, M.; Eichengreen, B. and Portes, R., eds.*, 1989, pp. 203–06.

_____. The Global Economic Environment and Prospects for Recovery in Latin America. In *Edwards, S. and Larrain, F., eds.*, 1989, pp. 126–52.

_____. Indian Macroeconomic Policies: Comment. In *[Díaz-Alejandro, C.]*, 1989, pp. 309–12.

_____. International Dimensions of Monetary Policy: Coordination versus Autonomy: Commentary. In *Federal Reserve Bank of Kansas City*, 1989, pp. 237–43.

_____. Korean International Macroeconomic Policy: Discussion. In *Bayard, T. O. and Young, S.-G., eds.*, 1989, pp. 71–76.

_____ and Miller, Marcus H. The International Monetary System: An Analysis of Alternative Regimes. In *Hamouda, O. F.; Rowley, R. and Wolf, B. M., eds.*, 1989, pp. 68–84.

_____; Miller, Marcus H. and Weller, Paul. The Stabilizing Properties of Target Zones. In *Bryant, R. C., et al., eds.*, 1989, pp. 248–71.

Williamson, Oliver E. Transaction Cost Economics. In *Schmalensee, R. and Willig, R. D., eds.*, Vol. 1, 1989, pp. 135–82.

Williamson, Stephen D. Bank Failures, Financial Restrictions, and Aggregate Fluctuations: Canada and the United States, 1870–1913. *Fed. Res. Bank Minn. Rev.*, Summer 1989, *13*(3), pp. 20–40.

_____. Restrictions on Financial Intermediaries and Implications for Aggregate Fluctuations: Canada and the United States 1870–1913. In *Blanchard, O. J. and Fischer, S., eds.*, 1989, pp. 303–40.

_____ and Greenwood, Jeremy. International Financial Intermediation and Aggregate Fluctuations under Alternative Exchange Rate Regimes. *J. Monet. Econ.*, May 1989, *23*(3), pp. 401–31.

Willinger, G. Lee; Bathke, Allen W., Jr. and Lorek, Kenneth S. Firm-Size and the Predictive Ability of Quarterly Earnings Data. *Accounting Rev.*, January 1989, *64*(1), pp. 49–68.

Willinger, Marc. Risk Aversion and the Value of Information. *J. Risk Ins.*, March 1989, *56*(1), pp. 104–12.

Willis, K. G. On Objectivity in Economic Research and Input–Output Tables: A Reply. *Environ. Planning A*, March 1989, *21*(3), pp. 408–10.

Willis, Norman. A Worker's Right to Train. *Nat. Westminster Bank Quart. Rev.*, February 1989, pp. 13–21.

Willke, Richard J. and Cotter, Patrick S. Young Physicians and Changes in Medical Practice Characteristics between 1975 and 1987. *Inquiry*, Spring 1989, *26*(1), pp. 84–99.

Willman, Alpo. Devaluation Expectations and Speculative Attacks on the Currency. *Scand. J. Econ.*, 1989, *91*(1), pp. 97–116.

Willmore, Larry. Determinants of Industrial Structure: A Brazilian Case Study. *World Devel.*, October 1989, *17*(10), pp. 1601–17.

———. Export Promotion and Import Substitution in Central American Industry. *CEPAL Rev.*, August 1989, (38), pp. 48–67.

Willms, Manfred. Fiscal Deficits, Interest Rates and Monetary Policy in West Germany. In *Hodgman, D. R. and Wood, G. E., eds.*, 1989, pp. 87–108.

Willner, Johan. Price Leadership and Welfare Losses in U.S. Manufacturing: Comment. *Amer. Econ. Rev.*, June 1989, *79*(3), pp. 604–09.

Wills, Robert L. and Mueller, Willard F. Brand Pricing and Advertising. *Southern Econ. J.*, October 1989, *56*(2), pp. 383–95.

Wilman, Elizabeth A. and Perras, James. The Substitute Price Variable in the Travel Cost Equation. *Can. J. Agr. Econ.*, July 1989, *37*(2), pp. 249–61.

Wilmouth, Robert K. Futures Market and Self-Regulation. In *Williams, O. F.; Reilly, F. K. and Houck, J. W., eds.*, 1989, pp. 53–58.

Wilson, Arlette C. and Glezen, G. William. The Effect of the Length of Prediction Interval on Prediction Error of Regression Models Used in Analytical Review. In *Schwartz, B. N., ed.*, 1989, pp. 173–86.

Wilson, Brooks M.; Wann, Joyce J. and Sexton, Richard J. Some Tests of the Economic Theory of Cooperatives: Methodology and Application to Cotton Ginning. *Western J. Agr. Econ.*, July 1989, *14*(1), pp. 56–66.

Wilson, Catharine E. and Weissert, William G. Private Long-term Care Insurance: After Coverage Restrictions Is There Anything Left? *Inquiry*, Winter 1989, *26*(4), pp. 493–507.

Wilson, Charles; Kornhauser, Lewis A. and Rubinstein, Ariel. Reputation and Patience in the 'War of Attrition.' *Economica*, February 1989, *56*(221), pp. 15–24.

Wilson, Earl R.; Ingram, Robert W. and Raman, K. K. The Information in Governmental Annual Reports: A Contemporaneous Price Reaction Approach. *Accounting Rev.*, April 1989, *64*(2), pp. 250–68.

Wilson, J. S. G. The Money Market in France. *Banca Naz. Lavoro Quart. Rev.*, June 1989, (169), pp. 191–206.

Wilson, Jack W. and Jones, Charles P. The Analysis of the January Effect in Stocks and Interest Rates under Varying Monetary Regimes. *J. Finan. Res.*, Winter 1989, *12*(4), pp. 341–54.

Wilson, James Q. Corruption: The Shame of the States. In *Heidenheimer, A. J.; Johnston, M. and LeVine, V. T., eds.*, 1989, *1966*, pp. 589–600.

Wilson, John Douglas. The Effect of Potential Emigration on the Optimal Linear Income Tax. In *Bhagwati, J. N. and Wilson, J. D., eds.*, 1989, *1980*, pp. 97–112.

———. On the Optimal Tax Base for Commodity Taxation. *Amer. Econ. Rev.*, December 1989, *79*(5), pp. 1196–1206.

———. Optimal Income Taxation and Migration: A World Welfare Point of View. In *Bhagwati, J. N. and Wilson, J. D., eds.*, 1989, *1982*, pp. 201–19.

———. Optimal Linear Income Taxation in the Presence of Emigration. In *Bhagwati, J. N. and Wilson, J. D., eds.*, 1989, *1982*, pp. 141–58.

——— and Bhagwati, Jagdish N. Income Taxation in the Presence of International Personal Mobility: An Overview. In *Bhagwati, J. N. and Wilson, J. D., eds.*, 1989, pp. 3–39.

——— and Gordon, Roger H. Measuring the Efficiency Cost of Taxing Risky Capital Income. *Amer. Econ. Rev.*, June 1989, *79*(3), pp. 427–39.

Wilson, John F., et al. Measuring Household Saving: Recent Experience from the Flow-of-Funds Perspective. In *Lipsey, R. E. and Tice, H. S., eds.*, 1989, pp. 101–45.

Wilson, Lee. Addition of a Climate Variable to the Howe and Linaweaver Western Sprinkling Equation. *Water Resources Res.*, June 1989, *25*(6), pp. 1067–69.

Wilson, Lynn O. and Norton, John A. Optimal Entry Timing for a Product Line Extension. *Marketing Sci.*, Winter 1989, *8*(1), pp. 1–17.

Wilson, Nicholas and Cable, John. Profit-Sharing and Productivity: An Analysis of UK Engineering Firms. *Econ. J.*, June 1989, *99*(396), pp. 366–75.

——— and Peel, M. J. The Liquidation/Merger Alternative: Some Results for the UK Corporate Sector. *Managerial Dec. Econ.*, September 1989, *10*(3), pp. 209–20.

Wilson, Paul W. Scheduling Costs and the Value of Travel Time. *Urban Stud.*, June 1989, *26*(3), pp. 356–66.

Wilson, R. A. and Bosworth, Derek L. Infrastructure for Technological Change: Intellectual Property Rights. In *Andersson, Å. E.; Batten, D. F. and Karlsson, C., eds.*, 1989, pp. 197–215.

Wilson, Robert B. Efficient and Competitive Rationing. *Econometrica*, January 1989, *57*(1), pp. 1–40.

_____. Entry and Exit. In *Feiwel, G. R., ed. (I)*, 1989, pp. 260–304.

_____ and **Kennan, John.** Strategic Bargaining Models and Interpretation of Strike Data. *J. Appl. Econometrics*, Supplement, December 1989, *4*, pp. S87–130.

Wilson, Robert H. and Grubb, W. Norton. Sources of Increasing Inequality in Wages and Salaries, 1960–80. *Mon. Lab. Rev.*, April 1989, *112*(4), pp. 3–13.

_____; **Monts, Ken and Blissett, Marlan.** Weather Normalization of Electricity Sales to the School Sector: Potential Model Misspecification. *Energy Econ.*, April 1989, *11*(2), pp. 127–32.

Wilson, Robert K. Background to Early Regional Development. In *Higgins, B. and Zagorski, K., eds.*, 1989, pp. 17–41.

Wilson, Thomas A. and Devereux, Michael. International Co-ordination of Macroeconomic Policies: A Review. *Can. Public Policy*, Supplement, February 1989, *15*, pp. S20–34.

_____ and **Waverman, Leonard.** Is the Process the Message? *Can. Public Policy*, Supplement, February 1989, *15*, pp. S1–9.

Wilson, William W. Differentiation and Implicit Prices in Export Wheat Markets. *Western J. Agr. Econ.*, July 1989, *14*(1), pp. 67–77.

_____. Price Discovery and Hedging in the Sunflower Market. *J. Futures Markets*, October 1989, *9*(5), pp. 377–91.

_____; **Carter, Colin A. and Karrenbrock, Jeffrey D.** Freer Trade in the North American Beer and Flour Markets. In *Schmitz, A., ed.*, 1989, pp. 139–86.

Wiltgen, Richard. The Evolution of Marx's Perspective of Mercantilism. *Int. J. Soc. Econ.*, 1989, *16*(7), pp. 48–56.

Winai Ström, Gabriele. Labour and Migrant Labour in Destabilized and Future Southern Africa. In *Odén, B. and Othman, H., eds.*, 1989, pp. 63–76.

Winch, Donald. Keynes, Keynesianism, and State Intervention. In *Hall, P. A., ed.*, 1989, pp. 107–27.

_____. The Plain Man's Political Economist: A Discussion. In *Goldman, L., ed.*, 1989, pp. 111–19.

Winckler, Georg and Rosner, Peter. Aspects of Austrian Economics in the 1920s and 1930s. In *Samuels, W. J., ed. (II)*, 1989, pp. 19–30.

van Winden, Frans and Schram, Arthur. Revealed Preferences for Public Goods: Applying a Model of Voter Behavior. *Public Choice*, March 1989, *60*(3), pp. 259–82.

Winder, C. C. A. and Palm, Franz C. Intertemporal Consumer Behaviour under Structural Changes in Income. *Econometric Rev.*, 1989, *8*(1), pp. 1–87.

_____ and **Palm, Franz C.** Intertemporal Consumer Behaviour under Structural Changes in Income: Reply. *Econometric Rev.*, 1989, *8*(1), pp. 143–48.

Winder, Robert C. Nobel Laureates in Economic Sciences: A Biographical Dictionary: Lawrence

R. Klein: 1980. In *Katz, B. S., ed.*, 1989, pp. 122–35.

Windle, Robert and McShan, Scott. The Implications of Hub-and-Spoke Routing for Airline Costs and Competitiveness. *Logist. Transp. Rev.*, September 1989, *25*(3), pp. 209–30.

Windolf, Paul. Productivity Coalitions and the Future of European Corporatism. *Ind. Relat.*, Winter 1989, *28*(1), pp. 1–20.

Winefordner, Darrell and Shkurti, William J. The Politics of State Revenue Forecasting in Ohio, 1984–1987: A Case Study and Research Implications. *Int. J. Forecasting*, 1989, *5*(3), pp. 361–71.

Winer, Russell S.; Glazer, Rashi and Steckel, Joel H. The Formation of Key Marketing Variable Expectations and Their Impact on Firm Performance: Some Experimental Evidence. *Marketing Sci.*, Winter 1989, *8*(1), pp. 18–34.

Winer, Stanley L. and Hettich, Walter. Tax Expenditures and the Democratic Process. In *Bruce, N., ed.*, 1989, pp. 379–405.

Wingender, John R. and Groff, James E. On Stochastic Dominance Analysis of Day-of-the-Week Return Patterns. *J. Finan. Res.*, Spring 1989, *12*(1), pp. 51–55.

_____ and **Lau, Hon-Shiang.** The Analytics of the Intervaling Effect on Skewness and Kurtosis of Stock Returns. *Financial Rev.*, May 1989, *24*(2), pp. 215–33.

Winglee, Peter. Agricultural Trade Policies of Industrial Countries. *Finance Devel.*, March 1989, *26*(1), pp. 9–11.

Winiecki, Jan. Buying Out Property Rights to the Economy from the Ruling Stratum: The Case of Soviet-Type States. *Int. Rev. Law Econ.*, June 1989, *9*(1), pp. 79–85.

_____. Eastern Europe: Challenge of 1992 Dwarfed by Pressures of System's Decline. *Aussenwirtschaft*, December 1989, *44*(3–4), pp. 345–65.

Winkel, Harald. Zur Interdependenz von Agrarökonomie und Wirtschaftstheorie. (The Interdependence of Economic Theory and Agricultural Economics. With English summary.) *Jahr. Nationalökon. Statist.*, October 1989, *206*(4–5), pp. 517–26.

Winkler, G. Michael. Intermediation under Trade Restrictions. *Quart. J. Econ.*, May 1989, *104*(2), pp. 299–324.

Winkler, Robert L. Combining Forecasts: A Philosophical Basis and Some Current Issues. *Int. J. Forecasting*, 1989, *5*(4), pp. 605–09.

_____. Uncertainty about Processes That Shift over Time: Modeling and Analysis: Comment. *J. Bus. Econ. Statist.*, October 1989, *7*(4), pp. 419–22.

_____ and **McCardle, Kevin F.** All Roads Lead to Risk Preference: A Turnpike Theorem for Conditionally Independent Returns. *J. Finan. Quant. Anal.*, March 1989, *24*(1), pp. 13–28.

Winpenny, Thomas R. From Peripatetic Boilermaker to Successful Industrialist: A World-Class Apprenticeship Pays Off for John Best. In *Perkins, E. J., ed.*, 1989, pp. 190–205.

Winrich, J. Steven. Self-Reference and the Incomplete Structure of Neoclassical Economics. In *Tool, M. R. and Samuels, W. J., eds. (II)*, 1989, *1984*, pp. 170–88.

Winsberg, Morton D. Income Polarization between the Central Cities and Suburbs of U.S. Metropolises, 1950–1980. *Amer. J. Econ. Sociology*, January 1989, *48*(1), pp. 3–10.

_____. Life Cycle Neighborhood Changes in Chicago Suburbs 1960–80. *Growth Change*, Spring 1989, *20*(2), pp. 71–80.

Winsborough, Halliman H. Data Base Management: Discussion. In *Kasprzyk, D., et al., eds.*, 1989, pp. 242–48.

Winsby, Roger and Brinner, Roger E. The Evolution of the Business of Business Economics. *Bus. Econ.*, April 1989, *24*(2), pp. 32–34.

Winship, Christopher. Salaries, Salary Growth, and Promotions of Men and Women in a Large, Private Firm: Commentary. In *Michael, R. T.; Hartmann, H. I. and O'Farrell, B., eds.*, 1989, pp. 44–48.

Winslow, E. G. 'Human Logic' and Keynes's Economics: A Reply. *Eastern Econ. J.*, Jan.–March 1989, *15*(1), pp. 67–70.

_____. Organic Interdependence, Uncertainty and Economic Analysis. *Econ. J.*, December 1989, *99*(398), pp. 1173–82.

Winston, Clifford and Morrison, Steven A. Enhancing the Performance of the Deregulated Air Transportation System. *Brookings Pap. Econ. Act.*, Microeconomics, 1989, pp. 61–112.

Winston, Gordon C. Imperfectly Rational Choice: Rationality as the Result of a Costly Activity. *J. Econ. Behav. Organ.*, August 1989, *12*(1), pp. 67–86.

_____; McPherson, Michael S. and Schapiro, Morton Owen. Recent Trends in U.S. Higher Education Costs and Prices: The Role of Government Funding. *Amer. Econ. Rev.*, May 1989, *79*(2), pp. 253–57.

Winter, Eyal. A Value for Cooperative Games with Levels Structure of Cooperation. *Int. J. Game Theory*, 1989, *18*(2), pp. 227–40.

Winter, Franz L. and Rossiter, John R. Pattern-Matching Purchase Behavior and Stochastic Brand Choice: A Low Involvement Model. *J. Econ. Psych.*, 1989, *10*(4), pp. 559–85.

Winter, Michael; Cox, Graham and Lowe, Philip. The Farm Crisis in Britain. In *Goodman, D. and Redclift, M., eds.*, 1989, pp. 113–34.

Winter, Pawel. Topological Network Synthesis. In *Simeone, B., ed.*, 1989, pp. 282–303.

Winter, Ralph and Mathewson, Frank. The Economic Effects of Automobile Dealer Regulation. *Ann. Écon. Statist.*, July–Dec. 1989, (15–16), pp. 409–26.

Winter, Sidney G. Patents in Complex Contexts: Incentives and Effectiveness. In *Weil, V. and Snapper, J. W., eds.*, 1989, pp. 41–60.

Winterrowd, James. Saving a Plant through Labor–Management Cooperation. In *Ahlbrandt, R. S., Jr., ed.*, 1989, pp. 61–63.

Winters, L. Alan. Britain in Europe: A Survey of Quantitative Trade Studies. In *Jacquemin, A. and Sapir, A., eds.*, 1989, *1987*, pp. 122–42.

_____. The So-Called "Non-economic" Objectives of Agricultural Support. *OECD Econ. Stud.*, Winter 1989–1990, (13), pp. 237–66.

Wirl, Franz. Impact of Environmental Regulation on Economic Activity—Austria. *Empirica*, 1989, *16*(2), pp. 209–33.

_____. Optimal Capacity Expansion of Hydro Power Plants. *Energy Econ.*, April 1989, *11*(2), pp. 133–36.

_____ and Unterwurzacher, Erich. Transaction Costs and Their Impact on Energy Demand Behaviour. In *Gulledge, T. R., Jr. and Litteral, L. A., eds.*, 1989, pp. 130–41.

Wirt, John G., et al. National Assessment of Vocational Education: Testimony before the House Education and Labour Committee, March 7, 1989. *Econ. Educ. Rev.*, 1989, *8*(4), pp. 383–92.

Wirth, Michael O. and Bloch, Harry. Concentration and the Price of Local Television Advertising Time. In *Weiss, L. W., ed.*, 1989, pp. 155–58.

Wise, Carol. Democratization, Crisis, and the APRA's Modernization Project in Peru. In *Stallings, B. and Kaufman, R., eds.*, 1989, pp. 163–80.

Wise, David A. The Economics of Aging: Overview. In *Wise, D. A., ed.*, 1989, pp. 1–7.

_____ and Hurd, Michael D. The Wealth and Poverty of Widows: Assets before and after the Husband's Death. In *Wise, D. A., ed.*, 1989, pp. 177–99.

_____ and Kotlikoff, Laurence J. Employee Retirement and a Firm's Pension Plan. In *Wise, D. A., ed.*, 1989, pp. 279–330.

_____ and Venti, Steven F. Aging, Moving, and Housing Wealth. In *Wise, D. A., ed.*, 1989, pp. 9–48.

Wise, Lois Recascino and Jonzon, Björn. Getting Young People to Work: An Evaluation of Swedish Youth Employment Policy. *Int. Lab. Rev.*, 1989, *128*(3), pp. 337–56.

Wiseman, A. Clark. Projected Long-term Demographic Trends and Aggregate Personal Saving in the United States. *J. Post Keynesian Econ.*, Summer 1989, *11*(4), pp. 497–508.

Wiseman, Frederick. Methodological Bias in Public Opinion Surveys. In *Singer, E. and Presser, S., eds.*, 1989, *1972*, pp. 189–92.

Wiseman, Jack. Beyond Positive Economics—Dream and Reality. In *Wiseman, J.*, 1989, *1983*, pp. 156–70.

_____. Cost, Choice and Political Economy: 'Talks Too Much . . . ' In *Wiseman, J.*, 1989, pp. 1–35.

_____. Costs and Decisions. In *Wiseman, J.*, 1989, *1980*, pp. 140–55.

_____. Economic Efficiency and Efficient Public Policy. In *Wiseman, J.*, 1989, *1985*, pp. 171–85.

_____. General Equilibrium or Market Process: An Evaluation. In *Wiseman, J.*, 1989, pp. 213–33.

_____. Growing without Nationalisation. In *Veljanovski, C., ed. (II)*, 1989, *1964*, pp. 3–14.

_____. The Political Economy of Federalism: A

Critical Appraisal. In *Wiseman, J.*, 1989, *1987*, pp. 71–111.

_____. The Political Economy of Government Revenues. In *Wiseman, J.*, 1989, pp. 199–212.

_____. The Political Economy of Government Revenues. In *Chiancone, A. and Messere, K.*, eds., 1989, pp. 9–20.

_____. The Political Economy of Nationalized Industry. In *Wiseman, J.*, 1989, *1978*, pp. 125–39.

_____. Social Policy and the Social Market Economy. In *Peacock, A. and Willgerodt, H.*, eds. (I), 1989, pp. 160–78.

_____. Some Reflections on the Economics of Group Behaviour. In *Wiseman, J.*, 1989, *1978*, pp. 112–24.

_____. The Theory of Public Utility Price: An Empty Box. In *Wiseman, J.*, 1989, *1957*, pp. 49–70.

_____. Uncertainty, Costs and Collectivist Economic Planning. In *Wiseman, J.*, 1989, *1953*, pp. 36–48.

_____. The Way Ahead: A New Political Economy. In *Wiseman, J.*, 1989, pp. 265–85.

_____ and Littlechild, Stephen C. Crusoe's Kingdom: Cost, Choice and Political Economy. In *Wiseman, J.*, 1989, pp. 234–64.

_____ and Littlechild, Stephen C. The Political Economy of Restriction of Choice. In *Wiseman, J.*, 1989, *1986*, pp. 186–98.

Wiseman, Michael. Economic Expansion and Establishment Growth on the Periphery. In *Andersson, Å. E.; Batten, D. F. and Karlsson, C.*, eds., 1989, pp. 233–49.

_____. Proposition 13 and Effective Property Tax Rates. *Public Finance Quart.*, October 1989, 17(4), pp. 391–408.

Wisman, Jon D. Economic Knowledge, Evolutionary Epistemology, and Human Interests. *J. Econ. Issues*, June 1989, 23(2), pp. 647–56.

Wisniewski, Kenneth J. and Blattberg, Robert C. Price-Induced Patterns of Competition. *Marketing Sci.*, Fall 1989, 8(4), pp. 291–309.

Witcombe, John R. Variability in the Yield of Pearl Millet Varieties and Hybrids in India and Pakistan. In *Anderson, J. R. and Hazell, P. B. R.*, eds., 1989, pp. 206–20.

Withers, Glenn. Artists' Subsidy of the Arts: Reply. *Australian Econ. Pap.*, December 1989, 28(53), pp. 288–89.

_____. Living and Working in Australia. In *Hancock, K.*, ed., 1989, pp. 1–22.

Withers, Ramsey M. Transportation Safety and Economic Regulatory Reform—The Canadian Perspective. In *Moses, L. N. and Savage, I.*, eds., 1989, pp. 300–307.

Withycombe, Richard. Forecasting with Combined Seasonal Indices. *Int. J. Forecasting*, 1989, 5(4), pp. 547–52.

Witkowski, Terrence H. Colonial Consumers in Revolt: Buyer Values and Behavior during the Nonimportation Movement, 1764–1776. *J. Cons. Res.*, September 1989, 16(2), pp. 216–26.

Witt, Stephen F. and Martin, Christine A. Fore-casting Tourism Demand: A Comparison of the Accuracy of Several Quantitative Methods. *Int. J. Forecasting*, 1989, 5(1), pp. 7–19.

Witt, Tom S.; Allison, Timothy and Calzonetti, Frank J. Electricity Supply and Demand. In *Calzonetti, F. J., et al.*, 1989, pp. 19–51.

Witt, Ulrich. The Evolution of Economic Institutions as a Propagation Process. *Public Choice*, August 1989, 62(2), pp. 155–72.

_____. Subjectivism in Economics—A Suggested Reorientation. In *Grunert, K. G. and Ölander, F.*, eds., 1989, pp. 409–31.

Witte, Ann Dryden and Schmidt, Peter. Predicting Criminal Recidivism Using 'Split Population' Survival Time Models. *J. Econometrics*, January 1989, 40(1), pp. 141–59.

Witte, Eberhard. Managers as Employee: Germany. In *Roomkin, M. J.*, ed., 1989, pp. 151–75.

Witte, Willard E. and Marquis, Milton H. Cash Management and the Demand for Money by Firms. *J. Macroecon.*, Summer 1989, 11(3), pp. 333–50.

Witteveen, H. Financing the World Economy in the Nineties: Opening Address. In *Sijben, J. J.*, ed., 1989, pp. 15–17.

Wittink, Dick R., et al. Conjoint Reliability Measures. *Marketing Sci.*, Fall 1989, 8(4), pp. 371–74.

Wittman, Donald. Pressure Group Size and the Politics of Income Redistribution. *Soc. Choice Welfare*, October 1989, 6(4), pp. 275–86.

_____. Why Democracies Produce Efficient Results. *J. Polit. Econ.*, December 1989, 97(6), pp. 1395–1424.

Witzke, H. P. and Erkes, H. T. Base Model (Version B): Feed Component. In *Bauer, S. and Henrichsmeyer, W.*, eds., 1989, pp. 399–405.

von Witzke, Harald and Runge, C. Ford. Agricultural Integration: Problems and Perspectives. In *Tarditi, S., et al.*, eds., 1989, pp. 227–43.

_____; Runge, C. Ford and Job, Brian. Policy Coordination in World Agriculture: Introduction. In *von Witzke, H.; Runge, C. F. and Job, B.*, eds., 1989, pp. 1–5.

_____; Thompson, Shelley J. and Runge, C. Ford. International Agricultural and Trade Policy: A Political Economic Coordination Game. In *von Witzke, H.; Runge, C. F. and Job, B.*, eds., 1989, pp. 89–116.

Wizarat, Shahida. Sources of Growth in Pakistan's Large-Scale Manufacturing Sector: 1955–56 to 1980–81. *Pakistan Econ. Soc. Rev.*, Winter 1989, 27(2), pp. 139–58.

Woelger, Ernestine; Walsh, Patrick P. and Walsh, Frank A. The Real Wage Gap and Its Development over Time: The Irish Experience 1960–1987. *Econ. Soc. Rev.*, October 1989, 21(1), pp. 87–102.

Woellner, Robin and Burns, Lee. International Information Flows—The Tax Implications. *Australian Tax Forum*, 1989, 6(2), pp. 143–200.

Wohar, Mark E. and Burkett, Paul G. External Shocks and Fiscal Deficits in a Monetary Model of International Reserve Determination: Honduras, 1960–83. *Appl. Econ.*, July 1989, *21*(7), pp. 921–29.

_____ and Stemp, Peter. The Indeterminacy of the Optimal Monetary Aggregate for Stabilization Policy under Rational Expectations. *Econ. Int.*, Aug.–Nov. 1989, *42*(3–4), pp. 258–78.

Wohlert, Klaus. Multinational Enterprise—Financing, Trade, Diplomacy: The Swedish Case. In *Teichova, A.; Lévy-Leboyer, M. and Nussbaum, H., eds.*, 1989, pp. 77–86.

Wohlgemuth, Arno. The Laws on Foreign Investment and Import/Export Taxes: Viet-Nam. *Bull. Int. Fiscal Doc.*, January 1989, *43*(1), pp. 22–24.

Wohlgenant, Michael K. Demand for Farm Output in a Complete System of Demand Functions. *Amer. J. Agr. Econ.*, May 1989, *71*(2), pp. 241–52.

_____. Effects on the Changing Composition of Beef Consumption on the Elasticities for Beef and Poultry. In *Buse, R. C., ed.*, 1989, pp. 170–86.

_____ and Lemieux, Catharine M. *Ex Ante* Evaluation of the Economic Impact of Agricultural Biotechnology: The Case of Porcine Somatotropin. *Amer. J. Agr. Econ.*, November 1989, *71*(4), pp. 903–14.

_____; Mullen, J. D. and Alston, Julian M. The Impact of Farm and Processing Research on the Australian Wool Industry. *Australian J. Agr. Econ.*, April 1989, *33*(1), pp. 32–47.

_____ and Thurman, Walter N. Consistent Estimation of General Equilibrium Welfare Effects. *Amer. J. Agr. Econ.*, November 1989, *71*(4), pp. 1041–45.

Wohlmuth, Karl. Structural Adjustment and East–West–South Economic Cooperation: Key Issues. In *Wohlmuth, K., ed.*, 1989, pp. 11–61.

_____. Sudan's Industrialisation after Independence: A Case of Africa's Crisis of Industrialisation. In *Islam, N., ed.*, 1989, pp. 357–79.

_____ and Hansohm, Dirk. Sudan's East–South and South–South Economic Cooperation. In *Wohlmuth, K., ed.*, 1989, pp. 481–513.

Wohlrab-Sahr, Monika; Brose, Hanns-Georg and Schulze-Böing, Matthias. Discontinuity and Flexibility in Working Time and Work Careers: The Example of Temporary Work. In *Agassi, J. B. and Heycock, S., eds.*, 1989, pp. 99–113.

Wohltmann, Hans-Werner. Theorie des Angebotsmonopols bei stochastischer Nachfrage. Eine Übersicht. (Theory of the Monopoly Facing Stochastic Demand: A Survey. With English summary.) *Jahr. Nationalökon. Statist.*, January 1989, *206*(1), pp. 1–17.

_____ and Krömer, Wolfgang. On the Notion of Time-Consistency: Comment. *Europ. Econ. Rev.*, July 1989, *33*(6), pp. 1283–88.

Woittiez, Isolde; ten Hacken, Peter and Kapteyn, Arie. Unemployment Benefits and the Labor Market, A Micro/Macro Approach. In *Gustafsson, B. A. and Klevmarken, N. A., eds.*, 1989, pp. 143–64.

Wojnilower, Albert M. Regulation of Debt and Equity: Discussion. In *Kopcke, R. W. and Rosengren, E. S., eds.*, 1989, pp. 212–20.

Wolak, Frank A. Testing Inequality Constraints in Linear Econometric Models. *J. Econometrics*, June 1989, *41*(2), pp. 205–35.

Wolcher, Louis E. Price Discrimination and Inefficient Risk Allocation under the Rule of *Hadley v. Baxendale*. In *Zerbe, R. O., ed.*, 1989, pp. 9–31.

Woldseth, Kjell. The Disregard of a Legal Entity for Tax Purposes: Norway. In *International Fiscal Association, ed. (II)*, 1989, pp. 391–405.

Wolf, Avner and Paroush, Jacob. Production and Hedging Decisions in the Presence of Basis Risk. *J. Futures Markets*, December 1989, *9*(6), pp. 547–63.

Wolf, Bernard M. American Subsidiaries in Canada and the Free Trade Agreement. In *Rugman, A. M., ed.*, 1989, pp. 178–88.

_____. The International Monetary System: A Look Ahead. In *Hamouda, O. F.; Rowley, R. and Wolf, B. M., eds.*, 1989, pp. 214–19.

Wolf, Karin and Degens, Paul O. On Properties of Additive Tree Algorithms. In *Opitz, O., ed.*, 1989, pp. 256–65.

Wolf, Martin. Is There a Case for Free Trade Areas? Comments. In *Schott, J. J., ed.*, 1989, pp. 89–95.

_____. Why Voluntary Export Restraints? An Historical Analysis. *World Econ.*, September 1989, *12*(3), pp. 273–91.

Wolf, W. Base-Model (BM). In *Bauer, S. and Henrichsmeyer, W., eds.*, 1989, pp. 365–74.

_____. Short-Term Forecast and Simulation System (SFSS). In *Bauer, S. and Henrichsmeyer, W., eds.*, 1989, pp. 375–78.

Wolfe, Barbara L. and Behrman, Jere R. Does More Schooling Make Women Better Nourished and Healthier? Adult Sibling Random and Fixed Effects Estimates for Nicaragua. *J. Human Res.*, Fall 1989, *24*(4), pp. 644–63.

_____; Haveman, Robert H. and Gottschalk, Peter. Health Care Financing in the U.S., U.K. and Netherlands: Distributional Consequences. In *Chiancone, A. and Messere, K., eds.*, 1989, pp. 351–73.

Wolfe, David A. and Muszynski, Leon. New Technology and Training: Lessons from Abroad. *Can. Public Policy*, September 1989, *15*(3), pp. 245–64.

Wolfe, J. N. and Reid, Gavin C. Hicks, John R. In *Wood, J. C. and Woods, R. N., eds., Vol. 3*, 1989, *1979*, pp. 217–21.

Wolfe, Joel D. Democracy and Economic Adjustment: A Comparative Analysis of Political Change. In *Foglesong, R. E. and Wolfe, J. D., eds.*, 1989, pp. 153–76.

_____. Reorganizing Interest Representation: A Political Analysis of Privatization in Britain. In *Foglesong, R. E. and Wolfe, J. D., eds.*, 1989, pp. 9–25.

_____ and Foglesong, Richard E. The Politics of Economic Adjustment: Pluralism, Corporatism, and Privatization: Introduction. In *Foglesong, R. E. and Wolfe, J. D., eds.*, 1989, pp. 1–8.

Wolff, Christian C. P. Exchange Rate Models and Parameter Variation: The Case of the Dollar–Mark Exchange Rate. *J. Econ. (Z. National-ökon.)*, 1989, *50*(1), pp. 55–62.

_____. Share Ownership and Efficiency: Comment. In *Faure, M. and Van den Bergh, R.*, eds., 1989, pp. 81–83.

Wolff, Edward N. Trends in Aggregate Household Wealth in the U.S., 1900–83. *Rev. Income Wealth*, March 1989, *35*(1), pp. 1–29.

_____ **and Baumol, William J.** Three Fundamental Productivity Concepts: Principles and Measurement. In *Feiwel, G. R., ed. (II)*, 1989, pp. 638–59.

_____ **and Howell, David R.** Labor Quality and Productivity Growth in the United States: An Input–Output Growth-Accounting Framework. In *Miller, R. E.; Polenske, K. R. and Rose, A. Z.*, eds., 1989, pp. 148–62.

_____ **and Marley, Marcia.** Long-Term Trends in U.S. Wealth Inequality: Methodological Issues and Results. In *Lipsey, R. E. and Tice, H. S.*, eds., 1989, pp. 765–839.

Wolff, Eric D.; Asquith, Paul and Mullins, David W., Jr. Original Issue High Yield Bonds: Aging Analyses of Defaults, Exchanges, and Calls. *J. Finance*, September 1989, *44*(4), pp. 923–52.

Wolff, Goetz; Soja, Edward and Morales, Rebecca. Urban Restructuring: An Analysis of Social and Spatial Change in Los Angeles. In *Beauregard, R. A.*, ed., 1989, pp. 87–122.

Wolff, Richard and Resnick, Stephen. The New Marxian Economics: Building on Althusser's Legacy. *Écon. Societes*, June 1989, *23*(6), pp. 185–200.

Wolff, Ulrich. Die Nichtanerkennung von juristischen Personen im Steuerrecht: Deutschland. (The Disregard of a Legal Entity for Tax Purposes: Germany. With English summary.) In *International Fiscal Association, ed. (II)*, 1989, pp. 139–56.

Wolfgarten, H. Supply Component. In *Bauer, S. and Henrichsmeyer, W.*, eds., 1989, pp. 385–89.

_____ **and Ferber, P.** Market Component. In *Bauer, S. and Henrichsmeyer, W.*, eds., 1989, pp. 395–98.

Wolfson, Mark A. and Scholes, Myron S. Decentralized Investment Banking: The Case of Discount Dividend-Reinvestment and Stock-Purchase Plans. *J. Finan. Econ.*, September 1989, *24*(1), pp. 7–35.

Wolfson, Martin H. Comparison of Theories of Financial Crises. In *Guttmann, R.*, ed., *1986*, pp. 69–73.

_____. The Stock Market and Recession. *Rev. Radical Polit. Econ.*, Fall 1989, *21*(3), pp. 40–44.

_____. Theories of Financial Crises. In *Semmler, W.*, ed., 1989, pp. 221–27.

_____ **and McLaughlin, Mary M.** Recent Developments in the Profitability and Lending Practices of Commercial Banks. *Fed. Res. Bull.*, July 1989, *75*(7), pp. 461–84.

Wolfson, Michael C. Divorce, Homemaker Pensions and Lifecycle Analysis. *Population Res. Policy Rev.*, January 1989, *8*(1), pp. 25–54.

_____, **et al.** The Social Policy Simulation Database and Model: An Example of Survey and Administrative Data Integration. *Surv. Curr. Bus.*, May 1989, *69*(5), pp. 36–40.

Wolfstetter, Elmar and Brown, Murray. Tripartite Income–Employment Contracts and Coalition Incentive Compatibility. *Rand J. Econ.*, Autumn 1989, *20*(3), pp. 291–307.

Wolken, John D. and Daskin, Alan J. An Empirical Investigation of the Critical Herfindahl Index in Banking. *J. Econ. Bus.*, May 1989, *41*(2), pp. 95–105.

_____ **and Hannan, Timothy H.** Returns to Bidders and Targets in the Acquisition Process: Evidence from the Banking Industry. *J. Finan. Services Res.*, October 1989, *3*(1), pp. 5–16.

Wolpin, Kenneth I. and Eckstein, Zvi. Dynamic Labour Force Participation of Married Women and Endogenous Work Experience. *Rev. Econ. Stud.*, July 1989, *56*(3), pp. 375–90.

_____ **and Eckstein, Zvi.** The Specification and Estimation of Dynamic Stochastic Discrete Choice Models: A Survey. *J. Human Res.*, Fall 1989, *24*(4), pp. 562–98.

Wolrath, Björn. Nordisk försäkring inför 1992. (Nordic Insurance in the Year 1992. With English summary.) *Ekon. Samfundets Tidskr.*, 1989, *42*(3), pp. 153–63.

Womack, Abner W. World Grain and Oilseed Outlook. *Can. J. Agr. Econ.*, Part 2, December 1989, *37*(4), pp. 1193–97.

_____; **Meyers, William H. and Frohberg, Klaus K.** Food and Agricultural Policies and Programs of Major Countries and Regions: Reaction. In *Helmuth, J. W. and Johnson, S. R.*, eds., *Vol. 1*, 1989, pp. 39–41.

Womer, Keith; Terasawa, Katsuaki L. and Quirk, James. Turbulence, Cost Escalation and Capital Intensity Bias in Defense Contracting. In *Gulledge, T. R., Jr. and Litteral, L. A.*, eds., 1989, pp. 97–116.

Wong, Christine P. W. Between Plan and Market: The Role of the Local Sector in Post-Mao Reforms in China. In *Gomulka, S.; Ha, Y.-C. and Kim, C.-O.*, eds., 1989, pp. 36–55.

Wong, Chung Ming. Welfare Implications of Price Stabilization with Monopolistic Trade. *Amer. J. Agr. Econ.*, February 1989, *71*(1), pp. 43–54.

Wong, David Y. Inflation, Taxation, and the International Allocation of Capital. *Int. Econ. J.*, Spring 1989, *3*(1), pp. 17–34.

Wong, G. Wenchi; Maberly, Edwin D. and Ma, Christopher K. The Daily Effect in the Gold Market: A Reply. *J. Futures Markets*, April 1989, *9*(2), pp. 175–77.

Wong, John. The ASEAN Model of Regional Cooperation. In *Naya, S., et al.*, eds., 1989, pp. 121–41.

Wong, Kar-yiu. National Defense and Foreign Trade: The Sweet and Sour Relationship between the United States and Japan. In *Makin, J. H. and Hellmann, D. C.*, eds., 1989, pp. 81–126.

Wong, Kie Ann. The Firm Size Effect on Stock Returns in a Developing Stock Market. *Econ. Letters*, 1989, *30*(1), pp. 61–65.

Wong, Lung-Fai. Agricultural Productivity in China and India: A Comparative Analysis. *Can. J. Agr. Econ.*, March 1989, *37*(1), pp. 77–93.

Wong, Richard Y. C. Freedom and Reform in Asian–Pacific Economies. *Cato J.*, Winter 1989, *8*(3), pp. 653–56.

Wong, Shee Q. Monetary Regimes, Inflation Expectations, and Real Activity. *Quart. J. Bus. Econ.*, Spring 1989, *28*(2), pp. 50–60.

Wong, William and O'Conor, Karen. Measuring the Precision of the Employment Cost Index. *Mon. Lab. Rev.*, March 1989, *112*(3), pp. 29–36.

Wonham W. M.. On the Control of Discrete-Event Systems. In *[Willems, J. C.]*, 1989, pp. 542–62.

Wonnacott, Paul and Lutz., Mark. Is There a Case for Free Trade Areas? In *Schott, J. J., ed.*, 1989, pp. 59–84.

Wonnacott, Ronald J. Trade and Investment Patterns and Barriers in the United States, Canada, and Japan: Comment. In *Stern, R. M., ed.*, 1989, pp. 133–38.

Woo, Wing Thye. Savings Promotion, Investment Promotion, and International Competitiveness: Comment. In *Feenstra, R. C., ed.*, 1989, pp. 47–51.

_____ **and Nasution, Anwar.** The Conduct of Economic Policies in Indonesia and Its Impact on External Debt. In *Sachs, J. D., ed. (II)*, 1989, pp. 101–20.

_____ **and Nasution, Anwar.** Indonesian Economic Policies and Their Relation to External Debt Management. In *Sachs, J. D. and Collins, S. M., eds.*, 1989, pp. 17–149.

Wood, Adrian. Deceleration of Inflation with Acceleration of Price Reform: Vietnam's Remarkable Recent Experience. *Cambridge J. Econ.*, December 1989, *13*(4), pp. 563–71.

Wood, C. and Hooper, P. The Effects of the Relaxation of Planning Controls in Enterprise Zones on Industrial Pollution. *Environ. Planning A*, September 1989, *21*(9), pp. 1157–67.

Wood, D. Robley, Jr. and Harrison, William B. The Development of a Bank Classification Scheme through Discriminant Analysis. *Atlantic Econ. J.*, March 1989, *17*(1), pp. 35–42.

Wood, David O.; Harper, Michael J. and Berndt, Ernst R. Rates of Return and Capital Aggregation Using Alternative Rental Prices. In *Jorgenson, D. W. and Landau, R., eds.*, 1989, pp. 331–72.

Wood, Gavin; Avenell, Simon and Leeson, Robert. Measuring Exchange Rate Uncertainty: The Case of the Australian Dollar 1969 to 1987. *Australian Econ. Rev.*, Winter 1989, (86), pp. 34–42.

Wood, Geoffrey E. Banking and Monetary Control after 1992—A Central Bank for Europe? In *Dahrendorf, R., et al.*, 1989, pp. 51–67.

_____. The Origins of Cheaper Money: Comments. *Econ. Hist. Rev., 2nd Ser.*, August 1989, *42*(3), pp. 396–400.

_____ **and Capie, Forrest H.** Anna Schwartz's Perspective on British Economic History. In *[Schwartz, A. J.]*, 1989, pp. 79–104.

_____; **Capie, Forrest H. and Pradhan, Mahmood.** Prices and Price Controls: Are Price Controls a Policy Instrument? In *Hodgman, D. R. and Wood, G. E., eds.*, 1989, pp. 109–38.

_____ **and Coughlin, Cletus C.** An Introduction to Non-tariff Barriers to Trade. *Fed. Res. Bank St. Louis Rev.*, Jan.–Feb. 1989, *71*(1), pp. 32–46.

_____ **and Hodgman, Donald R.** Macroeconomic Policy and Economic Interdependence: Introduction. In *Hodgman, D. R. and Wood, G. E., eds.*, 1989, pp. vii–xvi.

Wood, John Cunningham and Woods, Ronald N. Sir John R. Hicks: Critical Assessments: General Commentary. In *Wood, J. C. and Woods, R. N., eds., Vol. 1*, 1989, pp. xxi–lv.

Wood, Robert E. The International Monetary Fund and the World Bank in a Changing World Economy. In *MacEwan, A. and Tabb, W. K., eds.*, 1989, pp. 298–315.

Wood, Stephen and Richardson, Ray. Productivity Change in the Coal Industry and the New Industrial Relations. *Brit. J. Ind. Relat.*, March 1989, *27*(1), pp. 33–55.

Wood, Wendell C.; Shafer, Carl E. and Anderson, Carl G. Frequency and Duration of Profitable Hedging Margins for Texas Cotton Producers, 1980–1986. *J. Futures Markets*, December 1989, *9*(6), pp. 519–28.

Wooden, Mark. Workers' Compensation, Unemployment and Industrial Accidents: An Intertemporal Analysis. *Australian Econ. Pap.*, December 1989, *28*(53), pp. 219–35.

_____; **Blandy, Richard and Sloan, Judith.** Reforming the Trade Union Structure in Australia. *Australian Bull. Lab.*, December 1989, *15*(5), pp. 370–83.

_____; **Kriegler, Roy and Dawkins, Peter.** Towards Organizational Effectiveness: An Overview with an Australian Perspective. *Australian Bull. Lab.*, March 1989, *15*(2), pp. 115–38.

_____ **and Sloan, Judith.** The Australian Labour Market: September 1989. *Australian Bull. Lab.*, September 1989, *15*(4), pp. 259–86.

Wooders, Myrna Holtz. A Tiebout Theorem. *Math. Soc. Sci.*, August 1989, *18*(1), pp. 33–55.

_____; **Hammond, Peter J. and Kaneko, Mamoru.** Continuum Economies with Finite Coalitions: Core, Equilibria, and Widespread Externalities. *J. Econ. Theory*, October 1989, *49*(1), pp. 113–34.

_____ **and Kaneko, Mamoru.** The Core of a Continuum Economy with Widespread Externalities and Finite Coalitions: From Finite to Continuum Economies. *J. Econ. Theory*, October 1989, *49*(1), pp. 135–68.

Woodford, Michael. Finance, Instability, and Cycles. In *Semmler, W., ed.*, 1989, pp. 18–37.

_____. Imperfect Financial Intermediation and Complex Dynamics. In *Barnett, W. A.; Geweke, J. and Shell, K., eds.*, 1989, pp. 309–34.

Woodhouse, Thomas J. and Hanson, Kathleen M. The Treatment of Finance-Related Commodities in a Consumers' Price Index. In *Turvey, R.*, 1989, pp. 155–61.

Woodland, A. D.; Diewert, W. E. and Turunen-Red, A. H. Productivity- and Pareto-Improving Changes in Taxes and Tariffs. *Rev. Econ. Stud.*, April 1989, *56*(2), pp. 199–215.

Woodrow, R. Brian. Trade in Telecommunication and Data Services: A "Constitutional" Analysis. In *Robinson, P.; Sauvant, K. P. and Govitrikar, V. P., eds.*, 1989, pp. 15–41.

Woods, Alan. USAID and U.S. Farmers: Common Goals and Concerns. In *Swegle, W. E. and Ligon, P. C., eds.*, 1989, pp. 23–27.

Woods, John E. A Note on Hicks' Composite Commodity Theorem. In *Wood, J. C. and Woods, R. N., eds., Vol. 3*, 1989, *1979*, pp. 180–82.

_____ **and Bidard, Christian.** Taxes, Lands and Non-basics in Joint Production. *Oxford Econ. Pap.*, October 1989, *41*(4), pp. 802–12.

Woods, John R. Pension Coverage among Private Wage and Salary Workers: Preliminary Findings from the 1988 Survey of Employee Benefits. *Soc. Sec. Bull.*, October 1989, *52*(10), pp. 2–19.

Woods, R. I.; Watterson, P. A. and Woodward, J. H. The Causes of Rapid Infant Mortality Decline in England and Wales, 1861–1921. Part II. *Population Stud.*, March 1989, *43*(1), pp. 113–32.

Woods, Ronald N. and Wood, John Cunningham. Sir John R. Hicks: Critical Assessments: General Commentary. In *Wood, J. C. and Woods, R. N., eds., Vol. 1*, 1989, pp. xxi–lv.

Woodward, G. Thomas. Government Sponsored Enterprises: Another View. *Public Budg. Finance*, Autumn 1989, *9*(3), pp. 87–93.

_____ **and Makinen, Gail E.** A Monetary Interpretation of the Poincaré Stabilization of 1926. *Southern Econ. J.*, July 1989, *56*(1), pp. 191–211.

_____ **and Makinen, Gail E.** The Taiwanese Hyperinflation and Stabilization of 1945–1952. *J. Money, Credit, Banking*, February 1989, *21*(1), pp. 90–105.

Woodward, J. H.; Woods, R. I. and Watterson, P. A. The Causes of Rapid Infant Mortality Decline in England and Wales, 1861–1921. Part II. *Population Stud.*, March 1989, *43*(1), pp. 113–32.

Woodward, Nick. Some Organisational Implications of Privatisation. In *Ramanadham, V. V., ed.*, 1989, pp. 133–41.

Woodward, Susan E. and Weicher, John C. Goring the Wrong Ox: A Defense of the Mortgage Interest Deduction. *Nat. Tax J.*, September 1989, *42*(3), pp. 301–13.

Wooldridge, Jeffrey M. A Computationally Simple Heteroskedasticity and Serial Correlation Robust Standard Error for the Linear Regression Model. *Econ. Letters*, December 1989, *31*(3), pp. 239–43.

Woolf, Stuart. L'impact de l'occupation française sur l'économie italienne (1796–1815). (The Impact of the French Revolution on the Italian Economy, 1796–1815. With English summary.) *Revue Écon.*, November 1989, *40*(6), pp. 1097–1118.

Woolley, J. Michael. The Competitive Effects of Horizontal Mergers in the Hospital Industry. *J. Health Econ.*, December 1989, *8*(3), pp. 271–91.

Woolredge, John; Thomas, Barbara and Schoen, Robert. Ethnic and Educational Effects on Marriage Choice. *Soc. Sci. Quart.*, September 1989, *70*(3), pp. 617–30.

Woolridge, J. R. and Ghosh, C. Stock-Market Reaction to Growth-Induced Dividend Cuts: Are Investors Myopic? *Managerial Dec. Econ.*, March 1989, *10*(1), pp. 25–35.

Wooton, Ian; Harrison, Glenn W. and Rutherford, Thomas F. The Economic Impact of the European Community. *Amer. Econ. Rev.*, May 1989, *79*(2), pp. 288–94.

Worchel, Stephen; Dyer, James and Vedlitz, Arnold. Social Distance among Racial and Ethnic Groups in Texas: Some Demographic Correlates. *Soc. Sci. Quart.*, September 1989, *70*(3), pp. 607–16.

Worden, Debra Drecnik and Sullivan, A. Charlene. Deregulation, Tax Reform, and the Use of Consumer Credit. *J. Finan. Services Res.*, October 1989, *3*(1), pp. 77–91.

Wörner, Manfred. The Atlantic Alliance and Changing East–West Relations. In *Frankel, A. V. and Heck, C. B., eds.*, 1989, pp. 87–91.

Woronoff, Denis. L'industrialisation de la France de 1789 à 1815. Un essai de bilan. (French of the Industrialization of 1789 to 1815. With English summary.) *Revue Écon.*, November 1989, *40*(6), pp. 1047–60.

Worrall, Tim. Labour Contract Theory. In *Hahn, F., ed.*, 1989, pp. 336–59.

Worrell, DeLisle. Recent Economic Experience and the Search for New Guidelines. In *Worrell, D. and Bourne, C., eds.*, 1989, pp. 1–11.

_____ . The Tax System of Barbados. *Bull. Int. Fiscal Doc.*, October 1989, *43*(10), pp. 457–62.

_____ **and Codrington, Harold.** Trade and Economic Growth in Small Developing Economies: Research on the Caribbean. In *Worrell, D. and Bourne, C., eds.*, 1989, pp. 28–47.

Worrell, Keith. Rational Expectations, Causality and Integrative Fiscal–Monetary Policy in the Caribbean: Comment. *Soc. Econ. Stud.*, March 1989, *38*(1), pp. 157–60.

Worsick, Janice and Naini, Abbas. The Impact of Energy Prices on Alberta's Economic Outlook. *Energy Econ.*, January 1989, *11*(1), pp. 46–52.

Worthington, Paula R. On the Distinction between Structure and Conduct: Adjustment Costs, Concentration, and Price Behavior. *J. Ind. Econ.*, December 1989, *38*(2), pp. 235–38.

Wortzel, Lawrence H. and Vernon-Wortzel, Heidi. Privatization: Not the Only Answer. *World Devel.*, May 1989, *17*(5), pp. 633–41.

Woś, Augustyn. The Allocation of Resources of Labour in the Process of the Economic Development of Poland. **In** *Chakravarty, S., ed.,* 1989, pp. 266–76.

Wosinski, Marek. A Model of Consumer Behaviour in the Situation of Shortages. **In** *Grunert, K. G. and Ölander, F., eds.,* 1989, pp. 369–89.

Wozny, James; Alm, James and Miller, Barbara Diane. The Land Development Tax. **In** *Schroeder, L., ed.,* 1989, pp. 115–43.

Wray, L. Randall. A Keynesian Presentation of the Relations among Government Deficits, Investment, Saving, and Growth. *J. Econ. Issues,* December 1989, *23*(4), pp. 977–1002.

_____. A Keynesian Theory of Banking: A Comment. *J. Post Keynesian Econ.,* Fall 1989, *12*(1), pp. 152–56.

Wrege, Charles and Greenwood, Ronald G. Origins of Midvale Steel (1866–1880): Birthplace of Scientific Management. **In** *Perkins, E. J., ed.,* 1989, pp. 206–19.

Wren, Colin. Factors Underlying the Employment Effects of Financial Assistance Policies. *Appl. Econ.,* April 1989, *21*(4), pp. 497–513.

_____. The Revised Regional Development Grant Scheme: A Case Study in Cleveland County of a Marginal Employment Subsidy. *Reg. Stud.,* April 1989, *23*(2), pp. 127–37.

Wren-Lewis, Simon. Exchange-Rate Regimes and Policy Coordination: Discussion. **In** *Miller, M.; Eichengreen, B. and Portes, R., eds.,* 1989, pp. 237–38.

_____. Recent Developments in the Institute's Domestic Macromodel. *Nat. Inst. Econ. Rev.,* November 1989, (130), pp. 47–51.

_____ **and Currie, David A.** An Appraisal of Alternative Blueprints for International Policy Coordination. *Europ. Econ. Rev.,* December 1989, *33*(9), pp. 1769–85.

_____ **and Currie, David A.** A Comparison of Alternative Regimes for International Macropolicy Coordination. **In** *Miller, M.; Eichengreen, B. and Portes, R., eds.,* 1989, pp. 181–201.

_____ **and Currie, David A.** Evaluating Blueprints for the Conduct of International Macro Policy. *Amer. Econ. Rev.,* May 1989, *79*(2), pp. 264–69.

_____ **and Ireland, Jonathan.** Terminal Dates and the Dynamic Properties of National Institute Model 11. *Nat. Inst. Econ. Rev.,* May 1989, (128), pp. 91–93.

Wright, Arnold and Ashton, Robert H. Identifying Audit Adjustments with Attention-Directing Procedures. *Accounting Rev.,* October 1989, *64*(4), pp. 710–28.

Wright, Arthur W. History as Prologue: Lessons from Canadian and United States Energy Policy, 1970–1988. **In** *Watkins, G. C., ed.,* 1989, pp. 17–39.

Wright, Brian D. and Newbery, David M. Financial Instruments for Consumption Smoothing by Commodity-Dependent Exporters. *Amer. J. Agr. Econ.,* May 1989, *71*(2), pp. 511–16.

_____ **and Rausser, Gordon C.** Alternative Stra-

tegies for Trade Policy Reform. **In** *von Witzke, H.; Runge, C. F. and Job, B., eds.,* 1989, pp. 117–59.

_____ **and Williams, Jeffrey C.** A Theory of Negative Prices for Storage. *J. Futures Markets,* February 1989, *9*(1), pp. 1–13.

Wright, Charlotte J. and Groff, James E. The Market for Corporate Control and Its Implications for Accounting Policy Choice. **In** *Schwartz, B. N., ed.,* 1989, pp. 3–21.

Wright, Erik Olin. Models of Historical Trajectory: An Assessment of Giddens's Critique of Marxism. **In** *Held, D. and Thompson, J. B., eds.,* 1989, pp. 77–102.

Wright, George and Ayton, Peter. Judgemental Probability Forecasts for Personal and Impersonal Events. *Int. J. Forecasting,* 1989, *5*(1), pp. 117–25.

Wright, John Winthrop. A Proposal for a New and Stable International Currency. **In** *Kaushik, S. K., ed.,* 1989, pp. 35–48.

Wright, Mike; Chiplin, Brian and Coyne, John. The Market for Corporate Control: The Divestment Option. **In** *Fairburn, J. and Kay, J., eds.,* 1989, pp. 116–32.

_____ **and Thompson, R. S.** Bonding, Agency Costs and Management Buyouts: A Note. *Bull. Econ. Res.,* January 1989, *41*(1), pp. 69–75.

_____; **Thompson, R. S. and Robbie, K.** Privatisation via Management and Employee Buyouts: Analysis and U.K. Experience. *Ann. Pub. Coop. Econ.,* 1989, *60*(4), pp. 399–429.

Wright, Peter and Kirmani, Amna. Money Talks: Perceived Advertising Expense and Expected Product Quality. *J. Cons. Res.,* December 1989, *16*(3), pp. 344–53.

Wright, Randall and Burdett, Kenneth. Optimal Firm Size, Taxes, and Unemployment. *J. Public Econ.,* August 1989, *39*(3), pp. 275–87.

_____ **and Burdett, Kenneth.** Unemployment Insurance and Short-Time Compensation: The Effects on Layoffs, Hours per Worker, and Wages. *J. Polit. Econ.,* December 1989, *97*(6), pp. 1479–96.

_____ **and Kiyotaki, Nobuhiro.** On Money as a Medium of Exchange. *J. Polit. Econ.,* August 1989, *97*(4), pp. 927–54.

Wright, Richard. Robbins as a Political Economist: A Response. *Econ. J.,* June 1989, *99*(396), pp. 471–78.

_____. Validity of Antidumping Remedies—Some Thoughts. **In** *Jackson, J. H. and Vermulst, E. A., eds.,* 1989, pp. 418–24.

Wright, Richard W. Japanese Investment in Canada. **In** *Rugman, A. M., ed.,* 1989, pp. 55–66.

Wright, Robert E. The Easterlin Hypothesis and European Fertility Rates. *Population Devel. Rev.,* March 1989, *15*(1), pp. 107–22.

_____ **and Ermisch, John F.** Welfare Benefits and the Duration of Single Parenthood. *Nat. Inst. Econ. Rev.,* November 1989, (130), pp. 85–90.

Wright, Stephen G. and Riker, William H. Plurality and Ronoff Systems and Numbers of Candidates. *Public Choice*, February 1989, *60*(2), pp. 155–75.

Wrigley, Edward Anthony. Popolazione e famiglie: Interventi degli esperti. (In English.) **In** *Cavaciocchi, S., ed.*, 1989, pp. 108–12.

Wrigley, N. The Lure of the USA: Further Reflections on the Internationalisation of British Grocery Retailing Capital. *Environ. Planning A*, March 1989, *21*(3), pp. 283–88.

Wruck, Karen Hopper. Equity Ownership Concentration and Firm Value: Evidence from Private Equity Financings. *J. Finan. Econ.*, June 1989, *23*(1), pp. 3–28.

_____ **and Baker, George P.** Organizational Changes and Value Creation in Leveraged Buyouts: The Case of the O.M. Scott and Sons Company. *J. Finan. Econ.*, December 1989, *25*(2), pp. 163–90.

Wu, Chunchi and Kim, Moon K. Performance of Mutual Funds in the Pre- versus Post-Mayday Periods. *Quart. J. Bus. Econ.*, Spring 1989, *28*(2), pp. 61–84.

_____ **and Lee, Cheng Few.** Using Zellner's Errors-in-Variables Model to Reexamine MM's Valuation Model for the Electric Utility Industry. **In** *Lee, C. F., ed.*, 1989, pp. 63–73.

Wu, Dakun. Some Questions Concerning Research on the Asiatic Mode of Production. **In** *Brook, T., ed.*, 1989, pp. 35–46.

Wu, De-Min. An Empirical Analysis of Japanese Direct Investment in Taiwan: A Neoclassical Approach. **In** *Lee, C. F. and Hu, S.-C., eds.*, 1989, pp. 9–64.

Wu, Jiaxiang and Jin, Lizuo. Establishing a Stockholding System for Enterprises: One Line of Thought for Further Promotion of the Reform. *Chinese Econ. Stud.*, Fall 1989, *23*(1), pp. 24–32.

_____ **and Jin, Lizuo.** Sharing Enterprises: An Approach to Further Reform. *Chinese Econ. Stud.*, Winter 1988–89, *22*(2), pp. 24–37.

Wu, Mingyu and Bao, Ke. Policy Studies in China. **In** *Zerby, J., ed.*, 1989, pp. 110–17.

Wu, Pei-Ing; Braden, John B. and Johnson, Gary V. Efficient Control of Cropland Sediment: Storm Event versus Annual Average Loads. *Water Resources Res.*, February 1989, *25*(2), pp. 161–68.

Wu, Rong-I. Economic Development Strategies and the Role of Direct Foreign Investment in Taiwan. **In** *Lee, C. F. and Hu, S.-C., eds.*, 1989, pp. 65–89.

_____. Industrialization in a Resources-Poor and Labor-Rich Developing Country: The Experience in Taiwan. **In** *Gemper, B. B., ed.*, 1989, pp. 171–88.

Wu, S. Y. and Horen, J. Vertical Transactions under Uncertainty. **In** *[Hadar, J.]*, 1989, pp. 157–86.

Wu, Shouhui and Guo, Jinhua. Workers' Evaluation of and Hopes for Trade Unions. *Chinese Econ. Stud.*, Summer 1989, *22*(4), pp. 55–68.

Wu, Terry Y. S. Economic Reforms in China: The Case of the Agricultural Sector. *J. Econ. Devel.*, December 1989, *14*(2), pp. 167–75.

Wu, Yu and Li, Xu. Prerequisite Conditions to

Enforcement of the Bankruptcy Law. *Chinese Econ. Stud.*, Winter 1988–89, *22*(2), pp. 16–23.

Wu, Zhipu. From Agricultural Producers' Co-operative to People's Commune. **In** *Howe, C. and Walker, K. R., eds.*, 1989, *1958*, pp. 251–64.

Wulff, Jochen C. Global Product Development. **In** *Ahlbrandt, R. S., Jr., ed.*, 1989, pp. 49–51.

Wulwick, Nancy J. Phillips' Approximate Regression. **In** *de Marchi, N. and Gilbert, C., eds.*, 1989, pp. 170–88.

_____. Phillips' Approximate Regression. *Oxford Econ. Pap.*, January 1989, *41*(1), pp. 170–88.

Wunnava, Phanindra V.; Olsen, Katherine and Smith, Amy L. An Empirical Study of the Life-Cycle Hypothesis with Respect to Alumni Donations. *Amer. Economist*, Fall 1989, *33*(2), pp. 60–63.

_____ **and Robinson, Michael D.** Measuring Direct Discrimination in Labor Markets Using a Frontier Approach: Evidence from CPS Female Earnings Data. *Southern Econ. J.*, July 1989, *56*(1), pp. 212–18.

_____; **Robinson, Michael D. and Bramley, Donald G.** A Note on Union–Non-union Benefit Differentials and Size of Establishment. *Econ. Letters*, 1989, *30*(1), pp. 85–88.

Wurm, Clemens A. International Industrial Cartels, the State and Politics: Great Britain between the Wars. **In** *Teichova, A.; Lévy-Leboyer, M. and Nussbaum, H., eds.*, 1989, pp. 111–22.

Wurst, John; Neter, John and Godfrey, James T. Efficiency of Sieve Sampling in Auditing. *J. Bus. Econ. Statist.*, April 1989, *7*(2), pp. 199–205.

Wuyts, Marc. Money and the Agrarian Question: The Mozambican Experience. **In** *Fitzgerald, E. V. K. and Vos, R.*, 1989, pp. 233–61.

Wyatt, Steve B. and Adams, Paul D. On the Pricing of European and American Foreign Currency Options: A Clarification. *J. Int. Money Finance*, June 1989, *8*(2), pp. 305–11.

Wyckoff, Andrew W. and Blair, Peter D. The Changing Structure of the U.S. Economy: An Input–Output Analysis. **In** *Miller, R. E.; Polenske, K. R. and Rose, A. Z., eds.*, 1989, pp. 293–307.

Wyckoff, J. and Eubanks, L. Voluntary Contributions to State Nongame Wildlife Programs. *J. Environ. Econ. Manage.*, January 1989, *16*(1), pp. 38–44.

Wyckoff, Paul Gary. Bureaucracy and the 'Publicness' of Local Public Goods: A Reply. *Public Choice*, July 1989, *62*(1), pp. 79–82.

Wydler, Daniel. Swiss Stocks, Bonds, and Inflation, 1926–1987. *J. Portfol. Manage.*, Winter 1989, *15*(2), pp. 27–32.

Wyer, Robert S., Jr. and Hong, Sung-Tai. Effects of Country-of-Origin and Product-Attribute Information on Product Evaluation: An Information Processing Perspective. *J. Cons. Res.*, September 1989, *16*(2), pp. 175–87.

Wykoff, Frank C. Economic Depreciation and the

User Cost of Business-Leased Automobiles. In *Jorgenson, D. W. and Landau, R., eds.*, 1989, pp. 259–92.

_____. Economics: On-line and Interactive. *Econ. Inquiry*, July 1989, *27*(3), pp. 547–54.

_____; Hulten, Charles R. and Robertson, James W. Energy, Obsolescence, and the Productivity Slowdown. In *Jorgenson, D. W. and Landau, R., eds.*, 1989, pp. 225–58.

Wylie, Peter J. Technological Adaptation in Canadian Manufacturing, 1900–1929. *J. Econ. Hist.*, September 1989, *49*(3), pp. 569–91.

Wyman, Donald and Gereffi, Gary. Determinants of Development Strategies in Latin America and East Asia. In *Haggard, S. and Moon, C., eds.*, 1989, pp. 23–52.

Wyndelts, Robert W. and Sanders, Debra L. An Examination of Tax Practioners' Decisions under Uncertainty. In *Jones, S. M., ed.*, 1989, pp. 41–72.

van Wyngen, Gerry. Impact of International Tax Changes on Australian Investments. *Australian Tax Forum*, 1989, *6*(1), pp. 89–97.

Wynn, R. F. K. Sovereign-Risk Quantification Methodologies: A Critique. In *Singer, H. W. and Sharma, S., eds. (II)*, 1989, pp. 192–210.

Wynne-Edwards, Hugh. Marketing of Nonferrous Metals: Product Development. In *Jackson, L. M. and Richardson, P. R., eds.*, 1989, pp. 87–97.

Wynne, Kevin J. and Harris, Malcolm C., Sr. Explaining the Decline of Nuclear Power in the United States: Evidence from Plant Cancellation Decisions. *J. Energy Devel.*, Spring 1989, *14*(2), pp. 251–67.

Wyplosz, Charles. Asymmetry in the EMS: Intentional or Systemic? *Europ. Econ. Rev.*, March 1989, *33*(2/3), pp. 310–20.

_____. The Costs and Benefits of a European Currency: Discussion. In *De Cecco, M. and Giovannini, A., eds.*, 1989, pp. 212–15.

_____. The Impact of Fiscal Policy on the Balance of Payments: Recent Experience in the United States: Comment. In *Monti, M., ed.*, 1989, pp. 81–86.

_____ and Cohen, Daniel. The European Monetary Union: An Agnostic Evaluation. In *Bryant, R. C., et al., eds.*, 1989, pp. 311–37.

Wyrick, Thomas L. and Arnold, Roger A. Earmarking as a Deterrent to Rent-Seeking. *Public Choice*, March 1989, *60*(3), pp. 283–91.

Wyzan, Michael L. and Nelson, Michael A. Public Policy, Local Labor Demand, and Migration in Sweden, 1979–84. *J. Reg. Sci.*, May 1989, *29*(2), pp. 247–64.

Xian, Zhang Wen. On the Socialist Market System and Its Model. *Int. J. Soc. Econ.*, 1989, *16*(2), pp. 54–58.

Xie, Yu. An Alternative Purging Method: Controlling the Composition-Dependent Interaction in an Analysis of Rates. *Demography*, November 1989, *26*(4), pp. 711–16.

Xin, Naiquan and Cheng, Yannian. The Relationship between Fluctuations in Food Crop Yields and Meteorological Conditions in China. In *Oram, P. A., et al.*, 1989, pp. 85–92.

Xing, Hua. A Few Problems that Need to Be Addressed Immediately in Workers' Daily Lives. *Chinese Econ. Stud.*, Summer 1989, *22*(4), pp. 92–110.

Xu, Chan-Min; Qiu, Xu-Yao and Yu, Ke-Chun. An Evolutionary Account of Management and the Role of Management Development in China. In *Davies, J., et al., eds.*, 1989, pp. 112–24.

Xu, Pengfei. Establishing a New Order of the Socialist Commodity Economy. *Cato J.*, Winter 1989, *8*(3), pp. 607–11.

Xue, Muqiao. Several Problems Concerning Prices. *Chinese Econ. Stud.*, Spring 1989, *22*(3), pp. 24–33.

Yaari, Menahem E. Some Remarks on Measures of Risk Aversion and on Their Uses. In *Diamond, P. and Rothschild, M., eds.*, 1989, *1969*, pp. 83–97.

Yaari, Uzi; Choi, Jongmoo Jay and Fabozzi, Frank J. Optimum Corporate Leverage with Risky Debt: A Demand Approach. *J. Finan. Res.*, Summer 1989, *12*(2), pp. 129–42.

_____; Coyne, Christopher and Fabozzi, Frank J. Taxation of Capital Gains with Deferred Realization. *Nat. Tax J.*, December 1989, *42*(4), pp. 475–85.

Yadav, Manjit S. and Klein, Noreen M. Context Effects on Effort and Accuracy in Choice: An Enquiry into Adaptive Decision Making. *J. Cons. Res.*, March 1989, *15*(4), pp. 411–21.

Yaghmaian, Behzad. Economic Development and the Determinants of Third World Debt. *Rev. Radical Polit. Econ.*, Fall 1989, *21*(3), pp. 99–104.

Yagil, Joseph. Mergers and Bankruptcy Costs. *J. Econ. Bus.*, November 1989, *41*(4), pp. 307–15.

Yakita, Akira. The Optimal Rate of Inflation and Taxation. *J. Public Econ.*, April 1989, *38*(3), pp. 369–85.

Yamada, Motonari. Process Innovation and Small Firms in Japan. In *Dams, T. and Matsugi, T., eds.*, 1989, pp. 77–90.

Yamada, Tadashi; Chaloupka, Frank and Yamada, Tetsuji. Nutrition and Infant Health in Japan. *J. Human Res.*, Fall 1989, *24*(4), pp. 725–36.

Yamada, Tetsuji; Yamada, Tadashi and Chaloupka, Frank. Nutrition and Infant Health in Japan. *J. Human Res.*, Fall 1989, *24*(4), pp. 725–36.

Yamaguchi, Hiroichi. The South Asian Economy and Asian-Pacific Region: Comment. In *Shinohara, M. and Lo, F., eds.*, 1989, pp. 246–48.

Yamaguchi, Kaoru. On the Theory of "Value." *Rev. Radical Polit. Econ.*, 1989, *21*(1–2), pp. 27–56.

Yamaguchi, Kazuo. A Formal Theory for Male-Preferring Stopping Rules of Childbearing: Sex Differences in Birth Order and in the Number of Siblings. *Demography*, August 1989, *26*(3), pp. 451–65.

Yamamura, Kozo. Shedding History's Inertia: The U.S.–Japanese Alliance in a Changed

World. In *Makin, J. H. and Hellmann, D. C.*, eds., 1989, pp. 203–36.

Yamasaki, Shigeru. Compilation of Asian International Input–Output Table for 1985. In *Franz, A. and Rainer, N.*, eds., 1989, pp. 153–67.

Yamato, Takehiko and Sakai, Yasuhiro. Oligopoly, Information and Welfare. *J. Econ. (Z. Nationalökon.)*, 1989, *49*(1), pp. 3–24.

Yamawaki, Hideki. A Comparative Analysis of Intertemporal Behavior of Profits: Japan and the United States. *J. Ind. Econ.*, June 1989, *37*(4), pp. 389–409.

_____; **Audretsch, David B. and Sleuwaegen, Leo E.** The Convergence of International and Domestic Markets: Foreword. In *Audretsch, D. B.; Sleuwaegen, L. and Yamawaki, H.*, eds., 1989, pp. vii–x.

_____; **Audretsch, David B. and Sleuwaegen, Leo E.** The Dynamics of Export Competition. In *Audretsch, D. B.; Sleuwaegen, L. and Yamawaki, H.*, eds., 1989, pp. 211–45.

_____; **Sleuwaegen, Leo E. and Weiss, Leonard W.** Industry Competition and the Formation of the European Common Market. In *Weiss, L. W.*, ed., 1989, pp. 112–43.

Yamazaki, Hiroaki. Mitsui Bussan during the 1920s. In *Teichova, A.; Lévy-Leboyer, M. and Nussbaum, H.*, eds., 1989, pp. 163–76.

Yamazawa, Ippei. The Changing Role of the Asian NICs in the Asian-Pacific Region towards the Year 2000: Comment. In *Shinohara, M. and Lo, F.*, eds., 1989, pp. 232–33.

_____. Industrialisation through Full Utilisation of Foreign Trade: The Case of Some East Asian Economies. In *Islam, N.*, ed., 1989, pp. 343–55.

Yan, Chiou-Shuang; Stone, Susan and Koziara, Edward C. Employer Strike Insurance. In *Perkins, E. J.*, ed., 1989, pp. 220–29.

Yan, Jianyu. A Discussion of the Momentous Significance of New China's First Population Census Viewed from Several Questions Concerning Population. In *Howe, C. and Walker, K. R.*, eds., 1989, *1953*, pp. 294–99.

Yan, Ruxian. Marriage, Family and Social Progress of China's Minority Nationalities. In *Chiao, C. and Tapp, N.*, eds., 1989, pp. 79–87.

Yanagida, John F.; Sarwar, Ghulam and Dhaliwal, Naginder S. Uncertainty and the Stability of Money Demand Functions for the U.S. Agricultural Sector. *Can. J. Agr. Econ.*, July 1989, *37*(2), pp. 279–89.

Yanagida, Tatsuo. An Open Macro Model with a Goods Inventory. (In Japanese. With English summary.) *Econ. Stud. Quart.*, June 1989, *40*(2), pp. 166–77.

Yanagihara, Tōru. The Debt Problem and Structural Adjustment. In *Shinohara, M. and Lo, F.*, eds., 1989, pp. 295–321.

_____. The Dual-Industrial Growth in Prewar Japan. *Developing Econ.*, December 1989, *27*(4), pp. 359–80.

Yanagisawa, Haruka. Mixed Trends in Landholding in Lalgudi Taluk: 1895–1925. *Indian Econ.*

Soc. Hist. Rev., Oct.–Dec. 1989, *26*(4), pp. 405–35.

Yanagisawa, Shigeru and Tone, Kaoru. Site Selection for a Large Scale Integrated Circuits Factory. In *Golden, B. L.; Wasil, E. A. and Harker, P. T.*, eds., 1989, pp. 242–50.

Yancey, T. A.; Judge, G. G. and Bohrer, Robert. Sampling Performance of Some Joint One-Sided Preliminary Test Estimators under Squared Error Loss. *Econometrica*, September 1989, *57*(5), pp. 1221–28.

Yandle, Bruce. Bootleggers and Baptists in the Market for Regulation. In *Shogren, J. F.*, ed., 1989, pp. 29–53.

_____. Taxation, Political Action, and Superfund. *Cato J.*, Winter 1989, *8*(3), pp. 751–64.

_____ **and Meiners, Roger E.** Regulatory Lessons from the Reagan Era: Introduction. In *Meiners, R. E. and Yandle, B.*, eds., 1989, pp. 3–15.

Yanelle, Marie-Odile. The Strategic Analysis of Intermediation. *Europ. Econ. Rev.*, March 1989, *33*(2/3), pp. 294–301.

Yang, Chin-Wei. A Note on the Musgravian Transformation. *Eastern Econ. J.*, July–Sept. 1989, *15*(3), pp. 229–34.

_____ **and Labys, Walter C.** A Sensitivity Analysis of the Linear Complementarity Programming Model: Appalachian Steam Coal and Natural Gas. In *Labys, W. C.; Takayama, T. and Uri, N. D.*, eds., 1989, pp. 69–86.

_____ **and McNamara, James Bray.** Two Quadratic Programming Acquisition Models with Reciprocal Services. In *Gulledge, T. R., Jr. and Litteral, L. A.*, eds., 1989, pp. 338–49.

Yang, Chingwen. Two Problems of Industrial Location. In *Howe, C. and Walker, K. R.*, eds., 1989, *1957*, pp. 172–80.

Yang, Haitian and Chang, Hiuze. Contracting, Leasing, and Selling All Unprofitable Enterprises. *Chinese Econ. Stud.*, Winter 1988–89, *22*(2), pp. 95–104.

Yang, Xiaokai and Huang, Youguang. Why Should China Implement the Policy of Converting Enterprises to Management by the People in One Single Leap "Across the River"? A Discussion of the Reform of the Ownership System. *Chinese Econ. Stud.*, Fall 1989, *23*(1), pp. 64–81.

Yang, Yongzheng and Tyers, Rodney. The Economic Costs of Food Self-Sufficiency in China. *World Devel.*, February 1989, *17*(2), pp. 237–53.

Yannacopoulos, Nicos A. A Graph-Theoretic Interpretation of a Proposition on the Theory of Monetary Exchange. *Rivista Int. Sci. Econ. Com.*, March 1989, *36*(3), pp. 249–54.

Yannopoulos, George N. The Effects of Tariff Preferences on Export Expansion, Export Diversification and Investment Diversion: A Comparative Analysis of the Iberian and Other Mediterranean Economies. In *Yannopoulos, G. N.*, ed., 1989, pp. 66–86.

_____. European Integration and the Iberian Economies: Introduction. In *Yannopoulos, G. N.*, ed., 1989, pp. 1–20.

———. The Management of Trade-Induced Structural Adjustment: An Evaluation of the EC's Integrated Mediterranean Programmes. *J. Common Market Stud.*, June 1989, 27(4), pp. 283–301.

———. Trade Policy Options in the Design of Development Strategies. In *Gray, H. P., ed.*, 1989, pp. 209–23.

Yano, Adrian S. Configurations for Arbitrage Using Financial Futures Contracts. *J. Futures Markets*, October 1989, 9(5), pp. 439–48.

Yano, Hitoshi and Sakawa, Masatoshi. Personal Computer-Aided Interactive Decision Making for Multiobjective Linear Programming Problems with Fuzzy Coefficients and Its Applications. In *Lockett, A. G. and Islei, G., eds.*, 1989, pp. 462–71.

Yano, Makoto. Comparative Statics in Dynamic Stochastic Models: Differential Analysis of a Stochastic Modified Golden Rule State in a Banach Space. *J. Math. Econ.*, 1989, 18(2), pp. 169–85.

———. Voluntary Export Restraints and Expectations: An Analysis of Export Quotas in Oligopolistic Markets. *Int. Econ. Rev.*, November 1989, 30(4), pp. 707–23.

Yanowitch, Murray. The Influence of Tat'iana I. Zaslavskaia on Soviet Social Thought. In *Zaslavskaia, T. I.*, 1989, pp. vii–xix.

———. The Widening Scope of Soviet Reformist Thought. In *Yanowitch, M., ed.*, 1989, pp. vii–xxvi.

Yao, Dennis A. and Anton, James J. Split Awards, Procurement, and Innovation. *Rand J. Econ.*, Winter 1989, 20(4), pp. 538–52.

——— and Faulhaber, Gerald R. "Fly-By-Night" Firms and the Market for Product Reviews. *J. Ind. Econ.*, September 1989, 38(1), pp. 65–77.

Yao, Shujie. Policy Modelling for the Chinese Grain Sector within a Framework of Quadratic Spatial Equilibrium. *Indian J. Quant. Econ.*, 1989, 5(2), pp. 49–68.

Yao, Shuntian and Sahi, Siddhartha. The Noncooperative Equilibria of a Trading Economy with Complete Markets and Consistent Prices. *J. Math. Econ.*, 1989, 18(4), pp. 325–46.

——— and Shubik, Martin. Gold, Liquidity and Secured Loans in a Multistage Economy: Part I: Gold as Money. *J. Econ. (Z. Nationalökon.)*, 1989, 49(3), pp. 245–77.

Yapp, Graham A. Wilderness in Kakadu National Park: Aboriginal and Other Interests. *Natural Res. J.*, Winter 1989, 29(1), pp. 171–84.

Yardley, James A.; Callaghan, Joseph H. and Mittelstaedt, H. Fred. Auditors' Incompatible Economic Incentives. In *Gangolly, J., ed.*, 1989, pp. 57–64.

Yarrow, George. Does Ownership Matter? In *Veljanovski, C., ed. (II)*, 1989, pp. 52–69.

———. Privatization and Economic Performance in Britain. *Carnegie–Rochester Conf. Ser. Public Policy*, Autumn 1989, 31, pp. 303–44.

———. Regulatory Issues in the Electricity Supply Industry. In *Helm, D.; Kay, J. and Thompson, D., eds.*, 1989, pp. 188–205.

——— and Vickers, John. Privatization in Britain. In *MacAvoy, P. W., et al.*, 1989, pp. 209–45.

Yashiro, Masamoto. Economy and Culture: The Case of U.S.–Japan Economic Relations: Commentary. In *Hayashi, K., ed.*, 1989, pp. 19–21.

Yashiv, Eran. Optimal Inflation and the Government Revenue Mix. *Econ. Letters*, December 1989, 31(2), pp. 151–54.

Yasin, Mesghena. Testing the Monetary Approach to the Balance of Payments in the Presence of Nontraded Goods. In *Missouri Valley Economic Association*, 1989, pp. 48–54.

Yassin, Ibrahim Hassan. The Estimation of the Grant Element of Loans Reconsidered. *Pakistan Devel. Rev.*, Summer 1989, 28(2), pp. 121–32.

Yates, JoAnne. Information Systems for Handling Manufacturing and Marketing Data in American Firms, 1880–1920. In *Hausman, W. J., ed.*, 1989, pp. 207–17.

Yates, Judith. Housing Policy Reform: A Constructive Critique. *Urban Stud.*, August 1989, 26(4), pp. 419–33.

Yates, Mary V. and Wescott, Robert F. The PC Corner: Desktop Publishing is for Economists. *Bus. Econ.*, January 1989, 24(1), pp. 51–53.

Yayla, Nadir. The Transportation Problems of Istanbul—Suggestions. In *Candemir, Y., ed.*, 1989, pp. 418–30.

Ybarra, Josep-Antoni. Informalization in the Valencian Economy: A Model for Underdevelopment. In *Portes, A.; Castells, M. and Benton, L. A., eds.*, 1989, pp. 216–27.

Ye, Meng-Hua and Rosenbaum, David I. (s,S) Pricing Policy When Adjustment Costs Affect Demand. *Econ. Letters*, November 1989, 31(1), pp. 77–80.

——— and Smith, Stephen C. Dynamic Allocation in a Labor-Manged Firm: Reply. *J. Compar. Econ.*, June 1989, 13(2), pp. 338–39.

Yeager, Leland B. A Competitive Payments System: Some Objections Considered. *J. Post Keynesian Econ.*, Spring 1989, 11(3), pp. 370–77.

———. Domestic Stability versus Exchange Rate Stability. In *Dorn, J. A. and Niskanen, W. A., eds.*, 1989, 1988, pp. 39–55.

———. Why Subjectivism? Reply. In *Rothbard, M. N. and Block, W., eds.*, 1989, pp. 139–40.

——— and Greenfield, Robert L. Can Monetary Disequilibrium Be Eliminated? *Cato J.*, Fall 1989, 9(2), pp. 405–21.

Yeager, Peter C.; Reed, Gary E. and Kram, Kathy E. Decisions and Dilemmas: The Ethical Dimension in the Corporate Context. In *Post, J. E., ed.*, 1989, pp. 21–54.

Yeager, Rodger. Democratic Pluralism and Ecological Crisis in Botswana. *J. Developing Areas*, April 1989, 23(3), pp. 385–404.

Yeats, Alexander J. Developing Countries' Exports of Manufactures: Past and Future Implications of Shifting Patterns of Comparative Advantage. *Developing Econ.*, June 1989, 27(2), pp. 109–45.

_____ and Laird, Samuel. Nontariff Barriers of Developed Countries, 1966–86. *Finance Devel.*, March 1989, *26*(1), pp. 12–13.

Yeh, Anthony G. O. and Phillips, David R. Special Economic Zones. In *Goodman, D. S. G., ed.*, 1989, pp. 112–34.

Yeh, Yeong-Her. Tariffs *vs.* Export Quotas. *Atlantic Econ. J.*, June 1989, *17*(2), pp. 65–67.

Yeldan, A. Erinc. Structural Adjustment and Trade in Turkey: Investigating the Alternatives "Beyond Export-led Growth." *J. Policy Modeling*, Summer 1989, *11*(2), pp. 273–96.

Yellen, Janet L. The Beveridge Curve: Comments. *Brookings Pap. Econ. Act.*, 1989, (1), pp. 65–71.

_____. Symposium on the Budget Deficit. *J. Econ. Perspectives*, Spring 1989, *3*(2), pp. 17–21.

_____ and Rose, Andrew K. Is There a J-Curve? *J. Monet. Econ.*, July 1989, *24*(1), pp. 53–68.

Yellowitz, Irwin. Samuel Gompers: A Half Century in Labor's Front Rank. *Mon. Lab. Rev.*, July 1989, *112*(7), pp. 27–33.

Yen, Eva C. and Yen, Gili. On Phone Reservations: Public versus Private Teaching Hospitals. *Atlantic Econ. J.*, March 1989, *17*(1), pp. 92.

_____; Yen, Gili and Chang, T. L. On the Management of State-Owned Manufacturing Enterprises in Taiwan: An Application of Financial Ratio Analysis. In *Lee, C. F. and Hu, S.-C., eds.*, 1989, pp. 243–62.

_____; Yen, Gili and Liu, Ben-C. Cultural and Family Effects on Fertility Decisions in Taiwan, R.O.C.: Traditional Values and Family Structure Are as Relevant as Income Measures. *Amer. J. Econ. Sociology*, October 1989, *48*(4), pp. 415–26.

Yen, Gili. Is Managerial Resistance "Strategic" or "Self-Serving"? A Case Study of Merger Proposals. In *Lee, C. F., ed.*, 1989, pp. 351–73.

_____; Chang, T. L. and Yen, Eva C. On the Management of State-Owned Manufacturing Enterprises in Taiwan: An Application of Financial Ratio Analysis. In *Lee, C. F. and Hu, S.-C., eds.*, 1989, pp. 243–62.

_____; Liu, Ben-C. and Yen, Eva C. Cultural and Family Effects on Fertility Decisions in Taiwan, R.O.C.: Traditional Values and Family Structure Are as Relevant as Income Measures. *Amer. J. Econ. Sociology*, October 1989, *48*(4), pp. 415–26.

_____ and Yen, Eva C. On Phone Reservations: Public versus Private Teaching Hospitals. *Atlantic Econ. J.*, March 1989, *17*(1), pp. 92.

Yen, Steven T. and Roe, Terry L. Estimation of a Two-Level Demand System with Limited Dependent Variables. *Amer. J. Agr. Econ.*, February 1989, *71*(1), pp. 85–98.

Yeo, Stephen J. and Trivedi, P. K. On Using Ridge-Type Estimators for a Distributed Lag Model. *Oxford Bull. Econ. Statist.*, February 1989, *51*(1), pp. 85–90.

Yeon, Ha Cheong. An Approach to Developing Primary Health Care in Korea. In *Reich, M. R. and Marui, E., eds.*, 1989, pp. 119–44.

Yetley, Mervin and Marks, Suzanne. Food Aid Policy and Food Demand Patterns: Changing Food Demand Patterns Reveal Potential for Trade. In *Helmuth, J. W. and Johnson, S. R., eds., Vol. 1*, 1989, pp. 136–45.

Yeung, Bernard and Mirus, Rolf. Exchange Rate Behaviour: Theory and Managerial Implications. In *Rugman, A. M., ed.*, 1989, pp. 270–90.

_____ and Rugman, Alan M. Trade in Services and Returns on Multinational Activity. *Weltwirtsch. Arch.*, 1989, *125*(2), pp. 686–91.

Yeung, David. The Choice of Numeraire in Price Uncertainty Models. *Atlantic Econ. J.*, June 1989, *17*(2), pp. 77.

_____ and Hartwick, John M. Production Cost Uncertainty and Industry Equilibrium for Nonrenewable Resource Extraction. *Natural Res. Modeling*, Fall 1989, *3*(4), pp. 577–88.

_____ and Plourde, Charles. Harvesting of a Transboundary Replenishable Fish Stock: A Noncooperative Game Solution. *Marine Resource Econ.*, 1989, *6*(1), pp. 57–70.

_____ and Plourde, Charles. A Model of Industrial Pollution in a Stochastic Environment. *J. Environ. Econ. Manage.*, March 1989, *16*(2), pp. 97–105.

Yeutter, Clayton. Multilateral Trade Negotiations and Food and Agricultural Policy Change. In *Helmuth, J. W. and Johnson, S. R., eds., Vol. 1*, 1989, pp. 30–36.

Yi, Gyoseob. Classical Welfare Theorems in Economies with the Overtaking Criterion. *J. Math. Econ.*, 1989, *18*(1), pp. 57–75.

Yi, Youjae; Bagozzi, Richard P. and Baumgartner, Johann. An Investigation into the Role of Intentions as Mediators of the Attitude–Behavior Relationship. *J. Econ. Psych.*, March 1989, *10*(1), pp. 35–62.

Yildirim, Erhan. Total Factor Productivity Growth in Turkish Manufacturing Industry between 1963–1983: An Analysis. *METU*, 1989, *16*(3–4), pp. 65–96.

Yildirim, Fetih. Estimation of the Weibull Parameters by Examining the Behaviour of the Likelihood Function. *METU*, 1989, *16*(1–2), pp. 67–84.

Yinger, John and Ladd, Helen F. The Determinants of State Assistance to Central Cities. *Nat. Tax J.*, December 1989, *42*(4), pp. 413–28.

Yip, Chong K. Tariffs, Employment and Wage Bargaining. *Econ. Letters*, December 1989, *31*(2), pp. 169–71.

_____ and Fender, John. Tariffs and Employment: An Intertemporal Approach. *Econ. J.*, September 1989, *99*(397), pp. 806–17.

Yip, George S. An Integrated Approach to Global Competitive Strategy. In *Mansfield, R., ed.*, 1989, pp. 180–94.

Yitzhaki, Shlomo and Lerman, Robert I. Improving the Accuracy of Estimates of Gini Coefficients. *J. Econometrics*, September 1989, *42*(1), pp. 43–47.

_____ and Trajtenberg, Manuel. The Diffusion of Innovations: A Methodological Reappraisal.

J. Bus. Econ. Statist., January 1989, 7(1), pp. 35–47.

_____ and Vakneen, Yitzhak. On the Shadow Price of a Tax Inspector. *Public Finance*, 1989, 44(3), pp. 492–505.

Yli-Olli, Paavo and Virtanen, Ilkka. Kassavirta-perusteisten tunnuslukujen jakaumaomina-isuudet ja jakaumien ajallinen pysyvyys. (On Cross-Sectional Properties and Time-Series Persistence of Finnish Cash-Flow Based Financial Ratio Distributions. With English summary.) *Liiketaloudellinen Aikak.*, 1989, 38(4), pp. 373–404.

Yngvesson, Barbara. Inventing Law in Local Settings: Rethinking Popular Legal Culture. *Yale Law J.*, June 1989, 98(8), pp. 1689–1709.

Yoder, James A. and Levy, Haim. Applying the Black–Scholes Model after Large Market Shocks. *J. Portfol. Manage.*, Fall 1989, 16(1), pp. 103–06.

Yoder, Lois J. The Corporate Takeover Regulatory Arena. In *McKee, D. L., ed.*, 1989, pp. 85–99.

Yoffie, David B. American Trade Policy: An Obsolete Bargain? In *Chubb, J. E. and Peterson, P. E., eds.*, 1989, pp. 100–138.

_____. The Newly Industrializing Countries and the Political Economy of Protectionism. In *Haggard, S. and Moon, C., eds.*, 1989, pp. 331–57.

_____ and Milner, Helen V. Between Free Trade and Protectionism: Strategic Trade Policy and a Theory of Corporate Trade Demands. *Int. Organ.*, Spring 1989, 43(2), pp. 239–72.

Yohe, Gary W. More on the Properties of a Tax cum Subsidy Pollution Control Strategy. *Econ. Letters*, December 1989, 31(2), pp. 193–98.

Yoho, DeVon L. Fairmodel: Microcomputer Software to Teach Macroeconomic Concepts. *J. Econ. Educ.*, Winter 1989, 20(1), pp. 107–13.

Yokoyama, Hisashi. Export-Led Industrialization and the Dutch Disease. *Developing Econ.*, December 1989, 27(4), pp. 427–45.

_____ and Itoga, Shigeru. A Test of the Dual-Industrial Growth Hypothesis: The Case of the Philippines and Thailand. *Developing Econ.*, December 1989, 27(4), pp. 381–88.

_____, et al. Factor Abundance in East and Southeast Asian Countries: An Empirical Study with Leontief's and Leamer's Formulas. *Developing Econ.*, December 1989, 27(4), pp. 389–406.

Yonezawa, Masakatsu. International Communications Policy of Japan. In *Jussawalla, M.; Okuma, T. and Araki, T., eds.*, 1989, pp. 54–59.

Yoo, Byung-Kook and Kim, Jae-Cheol. Partial Compliance with the Minimum Wage Law. *Bull. Econ. Res.*, July 1989, 41(3), pp. 197–206.

Yoo, Jang H. and Harrison, William B. Altruism in the "Market" for Giving and Receiving: A Case of Higher Education. *Econ. Educ. Rev.*, 1989, 8(4), pp. 367–76.

Yoo, Jung-Ho. U.S. Trade Policy: Implications for U.S.–Korean Relations: Discussion. In *Bayard, T. O. and Young, S.-G., eds.*, 1989, pp. 106–10.

_____ and Park, Yung Chul. More Free Trade Areas: A Korean Perspective. In *Schott, J. J., ed.*, 1989, pp. 141–58.

Yoo, Kil-Sang. Does Human Capital Investment Increase Inequality of Earnings in Korea? *J. Econ. Devel.*, June 1989, 14(1), pp. 163–74.

Yoon, Haejin. A Korean Agricultural General Equilibrium Model of Trade. *Philippine Rev. Econ. Bus.*, December 1989, 26(2), pp. 236–61.

Yoon, Y. J. Technological Change and Embodiment Hypothesis. *Econ. Letters*, August 1989, 30(2), pp. 119–23.

York, Robert and Lipsey, Richard G. The Canada–U.S. Free Trade Agreement. In *Rugman, A. M., ed.*, 1989, pp. 123–43.

Yoshii, Masahiko. On Interbranch Scientific–Technical Complexes: A New Soviet Scientific–Technical Organization. *Kobe Univ. Econ.*, 1989, (35), pp. 69–80.

Yoshikawa, Hiroshi and Ohtake, Fumio. An Analysis of Female Labor Supply, Housing Demand and the Saving Rate in Japan. *Europ. Econ. Rev.*, May 1989, 33(5), pp. 997–1023.

_____ and Takeuchi, Yoshiyuki. Real Wages and the Japanese Economy. *Bank Japan Monet. Econ. Stud.*, April 1989, 7(1), pp. 1–40.

Yoshikawa, Kazuhiro; Kobayashi, Kiyoshi and Zhang, Wei-Bin. Taste Change and Conservation Laws in the Housing Market. In *Andersson, Å. E., et al., eds.*, 1989, pp. 291–307.

Yoshino, Bunroku. Japan and the Uruguay Round. In *Nau, H. R., ed.*, 1989, pp. 111–34.

Yoshitomi, Masaru. Changing U.S.–Japan Economic Relationships and International Payments Imbalances. *Bus. Econ.*, January 1989, 24(1), pp. 29–35.

_____. Present International Imbalances and Exchange Rate Effects. In *Shinohara, M. and Lo, F., eds.*, 1989, pp. 279–94.

Yotopoulos, Pan A. Distributions of Real Income: Within Countries and by World Income Classes. *Rev. Income Wealth*, December 1989, 35(4), pp. 357–76.

_____. The (Rip)Tide of Privatization: Lessons from Chile. *World Devel.*, May 1989, 17(5), pp. 683–702.

_____. Trade and Foreign-Owned Production in Services: Some Conceptual and Theoretical Issues: Comment. In *Giersch, H., ed.*, 1989, pp. 151–55.

_____ and Lau, Lawrence J. The Meta-production Function Approach to Technological Change in World Agriculture. *J. Devel. Econ.*, October 1989, 31(2), pp. 241–69.

Youker, Robert. Lessons from Evaluation in Africa for External Funding Bodies. In *Davies, J., et al., eds.*, 1989, pp. 75–84.

Young, Alistair and Struthers, John. Economics of Voting: Theories and Evidence. *J. Econ. Stud.*, 1989, 16(5), pp. 1–43.

Young, Allan H. Alternative Measures of Real GNP. *Surv. Curr. Bus.*, April 1989, 69(4), pp. 27–34.

_____. BEA's Measurement of Computer Output. *Surv. Curr. Bus.*, July 1989, *69*(7), pp. 108–15.

Young, Allan Richard. An Economic Rationale for Door Prizes. *Marketing Sci.*, Fall 1989, *8*(4), pp. 375–80.

Young, Claire F. L. Identifying Tax Expenditures: Comment. In *Bruce, N., ed.*, 1989, pp. 231–34.

Young, Douglas J. A 'Fair Share' Model of Public Good Provision. *J. Econ. Behav. Organ.*, January 1989, *11*(1), pp. 137–47.

Young, George; Mims, Anne M. and Duffy, Patricia A. Effects of Alternative Acreage Restriction Provisions on Alabama Cotton Farms. *Southern J. Agr. Econ.*, December 1989, *21*(2), pp. 85–94.

Young, James C.; Fisher, Ronald C. and Goddeeris, John H. Participation in Tax Amnesties: The Individual Income Tax. *Nat. Tax J.*, March 1989, *42*(1), pp. 15–27.

Young, Kan H. The Effects of Taxes and Rates of Return on Foreign Direct Investment in the United States: Reply. *Nat. Tax J.*, June 1989, *42*(2), pp. 209.

Young, Leslie and Boyle, Glenn W. Forward and Futures Prices in a General Equilibrium Monetary Model. *J. Finan. Econ.*, October 1989, *24*(2), pp. 319–41.

Young, Marilyn. Chicken Little in China: Some Reflections on Women. In *Dirlik, A. and Meisner, M., eds.*, 1989, pp. 253–68.

Young, Oran R. The Politics of International Regime Formation: Managing Natural Resources and the Environment. *Int. Organ.*, Summer 1989, *43*(3), pp. 349–75.

Young, Paula and Rudney, Gabriel. The Nonprofit Sector of the U.S. Economy: A Methodological Statement. *Rev. Income Wealth*, March 1989, *35*(1), pp. 56–80.

Young, Peg and Ord, J. Keith. Model Selection and Estimation for Technological Growth Curves. *Int. J. Forecasting*, 1989, *5*(4), pp. 501–13.

Young, Peter. Privatization: Better Services at Less Cost. In *Crane, E. H. and Boaz, D.*, 1989, pp. 251–65.

Young, Peter C. Local Government Risk Financing and Risk Control Pools: Understanding Their Forms, Functions, and Purposes. *Public Budg. Finance*, Winter 1989, *9*(4), pp. 40–54.

Young, R. A. Political Scientists, Economists, and the Canada–U.S. Free Trade Agreement. *Can. Public Policy*, March 1989, *15*(1), pp. 49–56.

Young, Richard A. and Fellingham, John C. Special Allocations, Investment Decisions, and Transactions Costs in Partnerships. *J. Acc. Res.*, Autumn 1989, *27*(2), pp. 179–200.

Young, Robert E., II and Riemenschneider, Charles H. Agriculture and the Failure of the Budget Process. In *Krämer, C. S., ed.*, 1989, pp. 87–102.

Young, Ronald. Lessons from Strathclyde's Experience: Boosting People's Self-Confidence. In *Dyson, K., ed.*, 1989, pp. 194–217.

Young, S. David. "Black Monday" and Reforming the Capital Markets. In *Crane, E. H. and Boaz, D.*, 1989, pp. 91–103.

Young, Soo-Gil. Korean Trade Policy: Implications for Korea–U.S. Cooperation. In *Bayard, T. O. and Young, S.-G., eds.*, 1989, pp. 119–58.

Younger, Benet and Harper, Joellen M. Telecommunications Policy and Economic Development: The New State Role: Nebraska. In *Schmandt, J.; Williams, F. and Wilson, R. H., eds.*, 1989, pp. 83–110.

Yu, Ben T. The Delineation of Rights on Technology Transfer. In *Zerbe, R. O., ed.*, 1989, pp. 267–78.

Yu, Eden S. H. and Chen, Guo-quan. On Fuzzy Quantity and Fuzzy Isoquant. *Math. Soc. Sci.*, February 1989, *17*(1), pp. 17–31.

_____ and Ingene, Charles A. Optimal Intervention Policies for a Region Facing Pollution-Induced Uncertainty. *Ann. Reg. Sci.*, 1989, *23*(1), pp. 3–18.

_____ and Parai, Amar K. Factor Immobility and Gains from Trade. *Southern Econ. J.*, January 1989, *55*(3), pp. 601–09.

_____ and Parai, Amar K. Factor Mobility and Customs Unions Theory. *Southern Econ. J.*, April 1989, *55*(4), pp. 842–52.

Yu, Ke and Wang, Dunshu. Further Comments on the "Asiatic Mode of Production." In *Brook, T., ed.*, 1989, pp. 118–35.

Yu, Ke-Chun; Xu, Chan-Min and Qiu, Xu-Yao. An Evolutionary Account of Management and the Role of Management Development in China. In *Davies, J., et al., eds.*, 1989, pp. 112–24.

Yu, Ming-Fang and Ames, Glenn C. W. An Analysis of Removal of Agricultural Trade Barriers between the United States and Canada with Emphasis on the Southeast. *Can. J. Agr. Econ.*, Part 2, December 1989, *37*(4), pp. 1035–43.

Yu, Oliver S.; Nakamura, Mitsugu and Kim, Yoon Hyung. Structure, Parameters, and Prediction of Demand. In *Kim, Y. H. and Smith, K. R., eds.*, 1989, pp. 21–64.

Yu, Po-Lung and Datta, Deepak K. Acquisitions, Mergers and Habitual Domains Analysis. In *Lockett, A. G. and Islei, G., eds.*, 1989, pp. 1–12.

_____; Huang, Shu-De and Zhang, Dazhi. Decision Rationality and Habitual Domain Analysis. In *Lockett, A. G. and Islei, G., eds.*, 1989, pp. 24–33.

Yu, Shirley S. and McNiel, Douglas W. Blue Laws: Impact on Regional Retail Activity. *Population Res. Policy Rev.*, September 1989, *8*(3), pp. 267–78.

Yu, Weiqiu and Dickson, V. A. Welfare Losses in Canadian Manufacturing under Alternative Oligopoly Regimes. *Int. J. Ind. Organ.*, June 1989, *7*(2), pp. 257–67.

Yu, Yong-ding. China's Economic Policy towards Asian-Pacific Economies. In *Shinohara, M. and Lo, F., eds.*, 1989, pp. 176–204.

Yuan, Yufei and Gafni, Amiram. Students Performance vs. Hospital Performance in the Labor

Market for Medical Interns and Residents: Do Hospitals Perform Better Due to Asymmetry in Information Available to Them Relative to Students? *J. Health Econ.*, December 1989, 8(3), pp. 353–60.

Yuanzheng, Luo. China's Economic Structural Reform and Agricultural Development. In *Adelman, I. and Lane, S., eds.*, 1989, pp. 211–15.

Yüce, Rüştü. The Behavior of Flexible Pavements under Increased Axle Loads and Tire Pressured with Emphasis on Turkish Transit Highways (TETEK) Project. In *Candemir, Y., ed.*, 1989, pp. 314–33.

Yücel, Mine Kuban. Scarcity Rent Reconsidered: The Effects of Exploration. *Resources & Energy*, March 1989, 11(1), pp. 93–101.

_____. Severance Taxes and Market Structure in an Exhaustible Resource Industry. *J. Environ. Econ. Manage.*, March 1989, 16(2), pp. 134–48.

Yudelman, Montague. Sustainable and Equitable Development in Irrigated Environments. In *Leonard, H. J., ed.*, 1989, pp. 61–85.

Yung, Kenneth; Gay, Gerald D. and Kolb, Robert W. Trader Rationality in the Exercise of Futures Options. *J. Finan. Econ.*, August 1989, 23(2), pp. 339–61.

Yunker, James A. Some Empirical Evidence on the Social Welfare Maximization Hypothesis. *Public Finance*, 1989, 44(1), pp. 110–33.

Yurdusev, A. Nuri. Camp David Meetings: An Analysis within the Framework of Bargaining Game Models. *METU*, 1989, 16(3–4), pp. 97–126.

Yushi, Mao and Hare, Paul G. Chinese Experience in the Introduction of a Market Mechanism into a Planned Economy: The Role of Pricing. *J. Econ. Surveys*, 1989, 3(2), pp. 137–58.

Zabalza Martí, Antonio. Uso de modelos para el análisis y la predicción económica. (With English summary.) *Revista Española Econ.*, 1989, 6(1–2), pp. 215–29.

Zachariah, O. E. R.; Fox, Glenn C. and Brinkman, George L. Product Market Distortions and the Returns to Broiler Chicken Research in Canada. *J. Agr. Econ.*, January 1989, 40(1), pp. 40–51.

Zacharias, Thomas P.; Ojemakinde, Abiodun and Lange, Mark D. Modelling the Firm-Level Multiproduct Cost Structure of Agricultural Production. In *Gulledge, T. R., Jr. and Litteral, L. A., eds.*, 1989, pp. 117–29.

Zadoks, Jan C. Coping with Climatic Variation in Plant Disease Control. In *Oram, P. A., et al.*, 1989, pp. 269–76.

Zafiriou, Margaret. The Canadian Experience with Lean Beef. In *Buse, R. C., ed.*, 1989, pp. 346–58.

Zagari, Eugenio. Verso la teoria economica di Marx: J. C. Sismondi. (With English summary.) *Studi. Econ.*, 1989, 44(37), pp. 145–77.

Zagaris, Bruce. The Carribean Basin Tax Information Exchange Agreements Program of the United States: Eat Softly and Carry a Big Stick. *Bull. Int. Fiscal Doc.*, March 1989, 43(3), pp. 115–18.

_____. Developments in the Offshore Financial Sector: Barbados. *Bull. Int. Fiscal Doc.*, October 1989, 43(10), pp. 463–64.

Zagorski, Krzysztof. Main Dimensions of Regional Differentiation. In *Higgins, B. and Zagorski, K., eds.*, 1989, pp. 151–72.

Zagouras, N. G.; Caouris, Y. G. and Kantsos, E. T. Production and Cost Functions of Water Low-Temperature Solar Desalination. *Appl. Econ.*, September 1989, 21(9), pp. 1177–89.

Zahid, Shahid N. and Mujahid-Mukhtar, Eshya. Impact of Agricultural Research and Extension on Crop Productivity in Pakistan: A Comment. *World Devel.*, April 1989, 17(4), pp. 589–90.

Záhlava, Frantisek. The Nature and Role of Agricultural Cooperative Societies in Czechoslovakia. *Int. Rev. Applied Econ.*, June 1989, 3(2), pp. 214–32.

Zahler, Roberto. After the Debt Crisis: Modes of Development for the Longer Run in Latin America: Comment. In *Edwards, S. and Larrain, F., eds.*, 1989, pp. 121–25.

Zaidi, Akbar. Explanations for High Levels of Infant Mortality in Pakistan—A Dissenting View: Comment. *Pakistan Devel. Rev.*, Autumn 1989, 28(3), pp. 251–57.

Zaidi, Mahmood A.; Atmiyanandana, Vinita and Lawler, John J. Human Resource Strategies in Southeast Asia: The Case of Thailand. In *Nedd, A., ed.*, 1989, pp. 201–21.

_____ and Bemmels, Brian G. Industrial Relations: The Minnesota Model. In *Barbash, J. and Barbash, K., eds.*, 1989, pp. 203–10.

Zaidi, S. Akbar. Poverty and Disease: Need for Structural Change. *Indian Econ. J.*, April–June 1989, 36(4), pp. 1–18.

Zaidi, Sunita. The Mughal State and Tribes in Seventeenth Century Sind. *Indian Econ. Soc. Hist. Rev.*, July–Sept. 1989, 26(3), pp. 343–62.

Zaima, Janis K. and Hirschey, Mark. Insider Trading, Ownership Structure, and the Market Assessment of Corporate Sell-Offs. *J. Finance*, September 1989, 44(4), pp. 971–80.

Zain, Djumilah and Mackie, J. A. C. East Java: Balanced Growth and Diversification. In *Hill, H., ed.*, 1989, pp. 306–29.

Zalai, Ernö. Eigenvalues and Labour Values: Contributions to the Quantitative Analysis of Value. *Econ. Systems Res.*, 1989, 1(3), pp. 403–09.

Zalesskii, A. B. Efficiency of Enterprises and Their Associations under Conditions of Full Financial Accountability. *Matekon*, Fall 1989, 26(1), pp. 20–38.

Zalokar, Nadja. Careers of Young Women during the Transitional Decade of the 1970s. *Contemp. Policy Issues*, January 1989, 7(1), pp. 95–109.

Zamagni, Stefano and Donzelli, Franco. Epistemology and Economic Theory: Introduction. *Ricerche Econ.*, Jan.–June 1989, 43(1–2), pp. 3–7.

Zamagni, Vera. An International Comparison of

Real Industrial Wages, 1890–1913: Methodological Issues and Results. In *Scholliers, P.*, *ed.*, 1989, pp. 107–39.

Zaman, Asad and Siddiqui, Shamim Ahmad. Investment and Income Distribution Pattern under Musharka Finance: The Certainty Case. *Pakistan J. Appl. Econ.*, Summer 1989, 8(1), pp. 1–30.

———— **and Siddiqui, Shamim Ahmad.** Investment and Income Distribution Patterns under Musharka Finance: The Uncertainty Case. *Pakistan J. Appl. Econ.*, Summer 1989, 8(1), pp. 31–71.

Zame, William and Duffie, Darrell. The Consumption-Based Capital Asset Pricing Model. *Econometrica*, November 1989, 57(6), pp. 1279–97.

von Zameck, Walburga. Tax Evasion and Tax Revenue Loss: Another Elaboration of the Peacock–Shaw Approach. *Public Finance*, 1989, 44(2), pp. 308–15.

Zammit, E. L. and Baldacchino, G. Fifth International Conference on the Economics of Self-management (Vienna, Austria, July 1988): Workers on the Board—A Sociological Comment on Recent Developments in Workers' Participation in Malta. *Econ. Anal. Workers' Manage.*, 1989, 23(1), pp. 79–94.

Zampelli, Ernest M.; Dynarski, Mark and Schwab, Robert. Local Characteristics and Public Production: The Case of Education. *J. Urban Econ.*, September 1989, 26(2), pp. 250–63.

———— **and Forbes, Kevin F.** Is Leviathan a Mythical Beast? *Amer. Econ. Rev.*, June 1989, 79(3), pp. 568–77.

Zandamela, Rogério L. Wage Indexation, Openness and Inflation Uncertainty. The Case of Italy. *Appl. Econ.*, May 1989, 21(5), pp. 651–57.

van Zanden, Jan Luiten. One Cost of Living Index? In *Scholliers, P., ed.*, 1989, pp. 179–81.

———— **and van der Veen, Dirk J.** Real-Wage Trends and Consumption Patterns in the Netherlands, c. 1870–1940. In *Scholliers, P., ed.*, 1989, pp. 205–28.

Zanders, Eva and Baches-Gellner, Uschi. Lehre und Forschung als Verbundproduktion. Data-Envelopment-Analysen und organisationsökonomische Interpretationen der Realität in wirtschaftswissenschaftlichen Fachbereichen. (With English summary.) *Z. Betriebswirtschaft*, March 1989, 59(3), pp. 271–90.

Zandi, Farrokh R. and Anam, Mahmudul. Immiserising Factor Growth and the Non-equivalence of Quotas and VERs. *Int. Econ. J.*, Autumn 1989, 3(3), pp. 23–30.

Zangeneh, Hamid. Islamic Banking: Theory and Practice in Iran. *Comp. Econ. Stud.*, Fall 1989, 31(3), pp. 67–84.

———— **and Falls, Gregory A.** The Interest Rate Volatility and the Demand for Money: The Empirical Evidence. *Quart. J. Bus. Econ.*, Winter 1989, 28(1), pp. 26–42.

Zanier, Claudio. Japan as a Newcomer in the World Silk Market: The European Assessment

(1848–1898). *Rivista Int. Sci. Econ. Com.*, February 1989, 36(2), pp. 135–42.

Zäpfel, Günther. Wirtschaftliche Rechtfertigung einer computerintegrierten Produktion (CIM): Probleme und Anforderung an die investitionsrechnung. (With English summary.) *Z. Betriebswirtshaft*, October 1989, 59(10), pp. 1058–73.

Zardkoohi, Asghar; Backhaus, Jürgen G. and Holcombe, Randall G. Public Investment and the Burden of the Public Debt: Reply. *Southern Econ. J.*, October 1989, 56(2), pp. 532–34.

———— **and Pustay, Michael W.** Does Transferability Affect the Social Costs of Licensing? *Public Choice*, August 1989, 62(2), pp. 187–90.

Zarinnejadan, Milad. L'évaluation financière et l'investissement physique privé en Suisse 1949–1986. (Financial Valuation and Fixed Private Investment in Switzerland, 1949–86. With English summary.) *Schweiz. Z. Volkswirtsch. Statist.*, December 1989, 125(4), pp. 557–81.

Zarkin, Gary A. and Biddle, Jeff E. Choice among Wage-Hours Packages: An Empirical Investigation of Male Labor Supply. *J. Lab. Econ.*, October 1989, 7(4), pp. 415–37.

Zarkovich, S. S. The Overcount in Censuses of Population. *Jahr. Nationalökon. Statist.*, December 1989, 206(6), pp. 606–09.

Zarnowitz, Victor and Braun, Phillip. New Indexes of Coincident and Leading Economic Indicators: Comment. In *Blanchard, O. J. and Fischer, S., eds.*, 1989, pp. 397–408.

Zarowin, Paul. Does the Stock Market Overreact to Corporate Earnings Information? *J. Finance*, December 1989, 44(5), pp. 1385–99.

————. Short-run Market Overreaction: Size and Seasonality Effects. *J. Portfol. Manage.*, Spring 1989, 15(3), pp. 26–29.

————; **Amit, Raphael and Livnat, Joshua.** The Mode of Corporate Diversification: Internal Ventures versus Acquisitions. *Managerial Dec. Econ.*, June 1989, 10(2), pp. 89–100.

Zarruk, Emilio R. Bank Spread with Uncertain Deposit Level and Risk Aversion. *J. Banking Finance*, December 1989, 13(6), pp. 797–810.

Zaslavskaia, Tat'iana I. Creative Activity of the Masses: Social Reserves of Growth. In *Zaslavskaia, T. I.*, 1989, 1987, pp. 66–84.

————. Economic Behavior and Economic Development. In *Zaslavskaia, T. I.*, 1989, 1980, pp. 3–19.

————. Economics through the Prism of Sociology. In *Zaslavskaia, T. I.*, 1989, 1986, pp. 38–53.

————. The Role of Sociology in Accelerating the Development of Soviet Society. In *Zaslavskaia, T. I.*, 1989, 1987, pp. 104–22.

————. Social Justice and the Human Factor in Economic Development. In *Yanowitch, M., ed.*, 1989, 1986, pp. 118–32.

————. Social Justice and the Human Factor in Economic Development. In *Zaslavskaia, T. I.*, 1989, 1987, pp. 85–103.

————. The Social Mechanism of the Economy. In *Zaslavskaia, T. I.*, 1989, 1987, pp. 54–65.

_____. Urgent Problems in the Theory of Economic Sociology. In *Zaslavskaia, T. I.*, 1989, *1988*, pp. 123–39.

_____ and Ryvkina, Rozalina V. The Subject Matter of Economic Sociology. In *Yanowitch, M., ed.*, 1989, *1984*, pp. 103–17.

_____ and Ryvkina, Rozalina V. The Subject of Economic Sociology. In *Zaslavskaia, T. I.*, 1989, *1987*, pp. 20–37.

_____; Smirnov, V. and Shaposhnikov, A. N. Restructuring the Management of Soviet Society's Agrarian Sector. *Prob. Econ.*, January 1989, *31*(9), pp. 39–54.

Zaslavskii, I. Ia. Turnpike Theorems in Models with Changing Technology. *Matekon*, Winter 1989–90, *26*(2), pp. 17–26.

Zavel'ski, M. G. To Be Closer to Economic Reality. *Matekon*, Spring 1989, *25*(3), pp. 68–71.

Zavist, T. M. and Tideman, T. N. Complete Independence of Clones in the Ranked Pairs Rule. *Soc. Choice Welfare*, April 1989, *6*(2), pp. 167–73.

Zax, Jeffrey S. Employment and Local Public Sector Unions. *Ind. Relat.*, Winter 1989, *28*(1), pp. 21–31.

_____. Initiatives and Government Expenditures. *Public Choice*, December 1989, *63*(3), pp. 267–77.

_____. Is There a Leviathan in Your Neighborhood? *Amer. Econ. Rev.*, June 1989, *79*(3), pp. 560–67.

_____. Quits and Race. *J. Human Res.*, Summer 1989, *24*(3), pp. 469–93.

Zbesko, John. Determinants of Performance in the Bull Market. *J. Portfol. Manage.*, Winter 1989, *15*(2), pp. 38–44.

Zdep, S. M., et al. The Validity of the Randomized Response Technique. In *Singer, E. and Presser, S., eds.*, 1989, *1979*, pp. 385–90.

Zdravomyslov, A. G. The New Sociopolitical Thinking and the Problem of the "Technological Challenge." In *Yanowitch, M., ed.*, 1989, *1987*, pp. 61–77.

Zdunic, Stjepan. Macroeconomic Models in the Planning Process of the Yugoslav Economy. In *Macesich, G., ed.*, 1989, pp. 168–79.

Zeager, Lester A. and Flacco, Paul R. The Competitive Firm with Uncertainty in the Rate of Labor Turnover. *Southern Econ. J.*, October 1989, *56*(2), pp. 457–66.

Zebrowski, Maciej. Multiobjective Evaluation of Industrial Structures. In *Lewandowski, A. and Wierzbicki, A. P., eds.*, 1989, pp. 294–309.

_____ and Dobrowolski, Grzegorz. Basic Model of an Industrial Structure. In *Lewandowski, A. and Wierzbicki, A. P., eds.*, 1989, pp. 287–93.

_____ and Dobrowolski, Grzegorz. Hierarchical Multiobjective Approach to a Programming Problem. In *Lewandowski, A. and Wierzbicki, A. P., eds.*, 1989, pp. 310–21.

_____ and Kopytowski, Jerzy. MIDA: Experience in Theory, Software and Application of DSS in the Chemical Industry. In *Lewandowski, A. and Wierzbicki, A. P., eds.*, 1989, pp. 271–86.

_____; Ziembla, Wieslaw and Skocz, Maciej. Spatial Allocation and Investment Scheduling in the Development Programming. In *Lewandowski, A. and Wierzbicki, A. P., eds.*, 1989, pp. 322–38.

Zecchini, Salvatore. Fiscal Adjustment, Debt Management, and Conditionality: Comment. In *Monti, M., ed.*, 1989, pp. 151–57.

Zech, Charles E. and Mathis, Edward J. The Median Voter Model Fails an Empirical Test: The Procedure, Useful in the Absence of a Better One, Is Not Valid for Multidimensional Issues. *Amer. J. Econ. Sociology*, January 1989, *48*(1), pp. 79–87.

Zechner, Josef; Fischer, Edwin O. and Heinkel, Robert. Dynamic Capital Structure Choice: Theory and Tests. *J. Finance*, March 1989, *44*(1), pp. 19–40.

_____; Fischer, Edwin O. and Heinkel, Robert. Dynamic Recapitalization Policies and the Role of Call Premia and Issue Discounts. *J. Finan. Quant. Anal.*, December 1989, *24*(4), pp. 427–46.

_____; Giammarino, Ronald and Schwartz, Eduardo S. Market Valuation of Bank Assets and Deposit Insurance in Canada. *Can. J. Econ.*, February 1989, *22*(1), pp. 109–27.

_____; Maksimovic, Vojislav and Sick, Gordon A. Forward Markets, Stock Markets, and the Theory of the Firm: Comment. *J. Finance*, June 1989, *44*(2), pp. 525–28.

Zeckhauser, Richard J. Reflections of Thomas Schelling. *J. Econ. Perspectives*, Spring 1989, *3*(2), pp. 153–64.

_____ and Horn, Murray. The Control and Performance of State-Owned Enterprises. In *MacAvoy, P. W., et al.*, 1989, pp. 7–57.

_____ and Pratt, John W. The Impact of Risk Sharing on Efficient Decision. *J. Risk Uncertainty*, September 1989, *2*(3), pp. 219–34.

Zeelenberg, Kees; Huigen, René and Van de Stadt, Huib. Socio-Economic Accounts for the Netherlands. *Rev. Income Wealth*, September 1989, *35*(3), pp. 317–34.

de Zeeuw, Aart J. and van der Ploeg, Frederick. Conflict over Arms Accumulation in Market and Command Economies. In *[Verheyen, P.]*, 1989, pp. 91–119.

_____ and van der Ploeg, Frederick. Dynamic Policy Games in Economics: Introduction. In *[Verheyen, P.]*, 1989, pp. 1–8.

Zeger, Scott L. and Diggle, Peter J. A Non-Gaussian Model for Time Series with Pulses. *J. Amer. Statist. Assoc.*, June 1989, *84*(406), pp. 354–59.

_____ and Liang, Kung-Yee. A Class of Logistic Regression Models for Multivariate Binary Time Series. *J. Amer. Statist. Assoc.*, June 1989, *84*(406), pp. 447–51.

Zegveld, Walter. New Issues in Science and Technology Policy: Discontinuities in the Process of Knowledge Generation, Knowledge Transfer and Knowledge Transformation. In *Andersson, Å. E.; Batten, D. F. and Karlsson, C., eds.*, 1989, pp. 279–89.

_____. Promotion of a Regional Information

Economy: The Role of Government and Public Sector Institutions in Partnership with Industry. In *Punset, E. and Sweeney, G., eds.*, 1989, pp. 119–30.

Zeigler, Donald J. and Johnson, James H., Jr. Nuclear Protective Action Advisories: A Policy Analysis and Evaluation. *Growth Change*, Fall 1989, *20*(4), pp. 51–65.

Zeira, Joseph. Inflationary Inertia in a Wage-Price Spiral Model. *Europ. Econ. Rev.*, October 1989, *33*(8), pp. 1665–83.

Zeischang, Kimberly D. and Reece, William S. Evidence on Taxation and Charitable Giving from the 1983 U.S. Treasury Tax Model File. *Econ. Letters*, November 1989, *31*(1), pp. 49–53.

Zeitlin, Jonathan and McKinlay, Alan. The Meanings of Managerial Prerogative: Industrial Relations and the Organisation of Work in British Engineering, 1880–1939. In *Harvey, C. and Turner, J., eds.*, 1989, pp. 32–47.

———— **and Totterdill, Peter.** Markets, Technology and Local Intervention: The Case of Clothing. In *Hirst, P. and Zeitlin, J., eds.*, 1989, pp. 155–90.

Zejan, Mario C. Intra-firm Trade and Swedish Multinationals. *Weltwirtsch. Arch.*, 1989, *125*(4), pp. 814–33.

———— **and Aguilar, Renato.** Debt Repayment Capacity in Argentina and Uruguay. In *Singer, H. W. and Sharma, S., eds. (I)*, 1989, pp. 383–95.

Zeldes, Stephen P. Consumption and Liquidity Constraints: An Empirical Investigation. *J. Polit. Econ.*, April 1989, *97*(2), pp. 305–46.

————. Optimal Consumption with Stochastic Income: Deviations from Certainty Equivalence. *Quart. J. Econ.*, May 1989, *104*(2), pp. 275–98.

———— **and Miron, Jeffrey A.** Production, Sales, and the Change in Inventories: An Identity That Doesn't Add Up. *J. Monet. Econ.*, July 1989, *24*(1), pp. 31–51.

———— **and Miron, Jeffrey A.** Seasonality, Cost Shocks, and the Production Smoothing Model of Inventories. In *Kollintzas, T., ed.*, 1989, pp. 199–244.

Zeleny, Milan; Kasanen, Eero and Östermark, Ralf. Gestalt System of Holistic Graphics: New Management Support View of MCDM. In *Lockett, A. G. and Islei, G., eds.*, 1989, pp. 143–56.

Zelhorst, Dick and de Haan, Jakob. Stabilization of the Economy: Some More International Evidence. *Banca Naz. Lavoro Quart. Rev.*, December 1989, (171), pp. 431–40.

Zellers, Wendy K.; Brown, Lawrence D. and McLaughlin, Catherine G. Health Care Coalitions: Characteristics, Activities, and Prospects. *Inquiry*, Spring 1989, *26*(1), pp. 72–83.

Zellner, Arnold. Risk and the Economy: A Finance Perspective: Commentary. In *Stone, C. C., ed.*, 1989, pp. 118–24.

———— **and Hong, Chansik.** Forecasting International Growth Rates Using Bayesian Shrinkage

and Other Procedures. *J. Econometrics*, January 1989, *40*(1), pp. 183–202.

Zellner, James A. A Simultaneous Analysis of Food Industry Conduct. *Amer. J. Agr. Econ.*, February 1989, *71*(1), pp. 105–15.

Zeman, Karl. Structural Change in the Czechoslovak Economy to the Year 2000. In *Krelle, W., ed.*, 1989, pp. 445–60.

Zemel, Eitan. Small Talk and Cooperation: A Note on Bounded Rationality. *J. Econ. Theory*, October 1989, *49*(1), pp. 1–9.

———— **and Gilboa, Itzhak.** Nash and Correlated Equilibria: Some Complexity Considerations. *Games Econ. Behav.*, March 1989, *1*(1), pp. 80–93.

Zeng, Yi. Is the Chinese Family Planning Program "Tightening Up"? *Population Devel. Rev.*, June 1989, *15*(2), pp. 333–37.

———— **and Vaupel, James W.** The Impact of Urbanization and Delayed Childbearing on Population Growth and Aging in China. *Population Devel. Rev.*, September 1989, *15*(3), pp. 425–45.

Zerbato, Michel. Bouclage monétaire du circuit et austérité. (The Closing of the Currency Circulation and Austerity. With English summary.) *Écon. Appl.*, 1989, *42*(1), pp. 91–113.

Zerby, John. Contemporary Economic Issues in China: Introduction. In *Zerby, J., ed.*, 1989, pp. 1–5.

————. Introduction to the South Pacific Economies. In *Lodewijks, J. and Zerby, J., eds.*, 1989, pp. 1–21.

————. Recent Developments in the South Pacific Island Economies: Summary and Concluding Remarks. In *Lodewijks, J. and Zerby, J., eds.*, 1989, pp. 88–91.

————. Recent Trade Patterns in the South Pacific Economies. In *Lodewijks, J. and Zerby, J., eds.*, 1989, pp. 67–87.

————. A Survey of Economic Reform in China. In *Zerby, J., ed.*, 1989, pp. 7–32.

Zesch, Scott K. Forms of Business Organization and Rural Enterprise Development: Some Examples from Anglophone Africa. *World Devel.*, November 1989, *17*(11), pp. 1841–52.

Zezza, Gennaro and Godley, Wynne. Foreign Debt, Foreign Trade and Living Conditions, with Special Reference to Denmark. *Nationaløkon. Tidsskr.*, 1989, *127*(2), pp. 229–35.

Zhang, Dazhi; Yu, Po-Lung and Huang, Shu-De. Decision Rationality and Habitual Domain Analysis. In *Lockett, A. G. and Islei, G., eds.*, 1989, pp. 24–33.

Zhang, Qingwu. Why Must We Reduce Urban Population? In *Howe, C. and Walker, K. R., eds.*, 1989, *1958*, pp. 345–50.

Zhang, Shi-Ying; Ge, Minghao and Sun, Li-Teh. Prospects of Chinese Wage Reform: A Synergy of Market and Planning Systems. *Int. J. Soc. Econ.*, 1989, *16*(8), pp. 26–34.

Zhang, Shihong. Give Enterprises Appropriate Powers of Autonomy. In *Howe, C. and Walker, K. R., eds.*, 1989, *1956*, pp. 153–57.

Zhang, Wei-Bin. Oscillations in the Rodriguez Model of Entry and Price Dynamics. *J. Econ.*

Dynam. Control, July 1989, *13*(3), pp. 485–97.

_____; Yoshikawa, Kazuhiro and Kobayashi, Kiyoshi. Taste Change and Conservation Laws in the Housing Market. In *Andersson, Å. E., et al., eds.,* 1989, pp. 291–307.

Zhang, Weiying. On the Line of Thought in Price Reform Guided Chiefly by the Notion of "Letting Go." *Chinese Econ. Stud.,* Spring 1989, *22*(3), pp. 50–66.

Zhang, Wenxian and Jiang, Xiaorong. The Economic Law of Population Distribution and Migration. *Int. J. Soc. Econ.,* 1989, *16*(1), pp. 5–12.

_____ and Jiang, Xiaorong. The Transformation of the Agricultural Population and the Urbanisation Process in China. *Int. J. Soc. Econ.,* 1989, *16*(1), pp. 40–51.

Zhao, Lisheng. The Well-Field System in Relation to the Asiatic Mode of Production. In *Brook, T., ed.,* 1989, pp. 65–84.

Zheng, Yingping. Incentive Control of Humanistic Systems. *Math. Soc. Sci.,* December 1989, *18*(3), pp. 263–74.

Zhou, Nan; Tse, David K. and Belk, Russell W. Becoming a Consumer Society: A Longitudinal and Cross-cultural Content Analysis of Print Ads from Hong Kong, the People's Republic of China, and Taiwan. *J. Cons. Res.,* March 1989, *15*(4), pp. 457–72.

Zhou, Su and Melvin, Michael. Do Centrally Planned Exchange Rates Behave Differently from Capitalist Rates? *J. Compar. Econ.,* June 1989, *13*(2), pp. 325–34.

Zhou, Xiaochuan and Lou, Jiwei. On the Direction of Reform in the Price System. *Chinese Econ. Stud.,* Spring 1989, *22*(3), pp. 14–23.

Zhu, Jiazhen. Some Questions Concerning Research on the Theory of the Asiatic Mode of Production. In *Brook, T., ed.,* 1989, pp. 104–17.

Zhu, Lijing; McMillan, John and Whalley, John. The Impact of China's Economic Reforms on Agricultural Productivity Growth. *J. Polit. Econ.,* August 1989, *97*(4), pp. 781–807.

Zick, Cathleen D.; Burton, John R. and Mayer, Robert N. Consumer Representation and Local Telephone Rates. *J. Cons. Aff.,* Winter 1989, *23*(2), pp. 267–84.

Ziebart, David A. The Information Content of Annual Accounting Data: An Empirical Modeling Approach Using Structural Equation Techniques. In *Lee, C. F., ed.,* 1989, pp. 121–41.

Ziegler, Peter A. Transfer Pricing: A Problem Seeking a Solution. *Australian Tax Forum,* 1989, *6*(4), pp. 455–94.

Ziegler, Richard E. and Fess, Philip E. Perceptions of Bankers and Analysts of the CPA's Responsibilities for Audited Financial Statements. In *Gangolly, J., ed.,* 1989, pp. 65–88.

Ziembla, Wieslaw; Skocz, Maciej and Zebrowski, Maciej. Spatial Allocation and Investment Scheduling in the Development Programming. In *Lewandowski, A. and Wierzbicki, A. P., eds.,* 1989, pp. 322–38.

Zieschang, Kimberley D.; Miller, Richard D. and

Garner, Thesia I. Using the Consumer Expenditure Survey Data: Past, Present, and Future Research. *J. Econ. Soc. Meas.,* 1989, *15*(3–4), pp. 237–79.

Zietz, Joachim. Negotiations on GATT Reform and Political Incentives. *World Econ.,* March 1989, *12*(1), pp. 39–52.

_____ and Valdés, Alberto. Lowering Agricultural Protection: A Developing Country Perspective towards the Uruguay Round. In *Islam, N., ed.,* 1989, pp. 243–57.

Zilberfarb, Ben-Zion. The Effect of Automated Teller Machines on Demand Deposits: An Empirical Analysis. *J. Finan. Services Res.,* February 1989, *2*(1), pp. 49–57.

_____. Exchange Rates and the Geographic Distribution of Exports: Some Evidence from a Developing Open Economy. *Weltwirtsch. Arch.,* 1989, *125*(1), pp. 149–57.

_____. Interest Rate Determination in a High Inflation Economy. *J. Macroecon.,* Fall 1989, *11*(4), pp. 533–49.

_____. Overdraft Banking: An Empirical Analysis. *J. Banking Finance,* December 1989, *13*(6), pp. 869–81.

Zilberman, David; Bogen, Kenneth T. and Lichtenberg, Erik. Regulating Environmental Health Risks under Uncertainty: Groundwater Contamination in California. *J. Environ. Econ. Manage.,* July 1989, *17*(1), pp. 22–34.

_____; Casterline, Gary and Dinar, Ariel. The Adoption of Modern Irrigation Technologies in the United States. In *Schmitz, A., ed.,* 1989, pp. 222–48.

_____ and Collender, Robert N. Land Allocation under Uncertainty for Alternative Specifications of Return Distributions: Reply. *Amer. J. Agr. Econ.,* May 1989, *71*(2), pp. 441–42.

_____ and Harper, Carolyn R. Pest Externalities from Agricultural Inputs. *Amer. J. Agr. Econ.,* August 1989, *71*(3), pp. 692–702.

_____ and Lichtenberg, Erik. The Econometrics of Damage Contol: Reply. *Amer. J. Agr. Econ.,* May 1989, *71*(2), pp. 445–46.

_____; Parliament, Claudia and Tsur, Yacov. Cooperative Labor Allocation under Uncertainty. *J. Compar. Econ.,* December 1989, *13*(4), pp. 539–52.

Zilcha, Itzhak and Karni, Edi. Aggregate and Distributional Effects of Fair Social Security. *J. Public Econ.,* October 1989, *40*(1), pp. 37–56.

Ziliotti, Marco. Controllo dell'impresa e struttura finanziaria ottimale. (Firm Control and Optimal Financial Structure. With English summary.) *Rivista Int. Sci. Econ. Com.,* January 1989, *36*(1), pp. 55–74.

_____. Decisioni di liquidazione e di fallimento nella teoria dell'impresa. (Liquidation and Bankruptcy Decisions in the Theory of the Firm. With English summary.) *Giorn. Econ.,* March–April 1989, *48*(3–4), pp. 159–73.

Zimbalist, Andrew. The State of the Art of Comparative Economics. *Comp. Econ. Stud.,* Fall 1989, *31*(3), pp. 6–15.

_____ and Joglekar, Gitanjali. Dollar GDP per Capita in Cuba: Estimates and Observations on the Use of the Physical Indicators Method. *J. Compar. Econ.*, March 1989, *13*(1), pp. 85–114.

Zimmer, Michael A. and Nakosteen, Robert A. Minimum Wages and Labor Market Prospects of Women. *Southern Econ. J.*, October 1989, *56*(2), pp. 302–14.

Zimmer, Steven A. and McCauley, Robert N. Explaining International Differences in the Cost of Capital. *Fed. Res. Bank New York Quart. Rev.*, Summer 1989, *14*(2), pp. 7–28.

Zimmerman, Dennis. Tax-Exempt Bonds: A Sacred Cow That Gave (Some) Milk. *Nat. Tax J.*, September 1989, *42*(3), pp. 283–92.

Zimmerman, Gary C. The Growing Presence of Japanese Banks in California. *Fed. Res. Bank San Francisco Econ. Rev.*, Summer 1989, (3), pp. 3–17.

Zimmerman, Martin B. and Borenstein, Severin. Losses in Airline Demand and Value Following Accidents. In *Moses, L. N. and Savage, I.,* eds., 1989, pp. 50–55.

Zimmermann, Heinz and Dubacher, René. A Simple Measure of Bond Convexity with Applications. *Jahr. Nationalökon. Statist.*, January 1989, *206*(1), pp. 48–60.

Zimmermann, Klaus F. Die Konkurrenz der Genüsse: Ein Brentano-Modell des Geburtenrückgangs. (The Competition of Pleasures: A Brentano Model of Fertility Decisions. With English summary.) *Z. Wirtschaft. Sozialwissen.*, 1989, *109*(3), pp. 467–83.

_____. Innovative Activity and Industrial Structure. *Empirica*, 1989, *16*(1), pp. 85–110.

Zin, Stanley E.; Backus, David K. and Gregory, Allan W. Risk Premiums in the Term Structure: Evidence from Artificial Economies. *J. Monet. Econ.*, November 1989, *24*(3), pp. 371–99.

_____ **and Epstein, Larry G.** Substitution, Risk Aversion, and the Temporal Behavior of Consumption and Asset Returns: A Theoretical Framework. *Econometrica*, July 1989, *57*(4), pp. 937–69.

Zinam, Oleg. On the Demise of Capitalism: Theories of Doom in Historical Perspective. *Rivista Int. Sci. Econ. Com.*, July 1989, *36*(7), pp. 593–607.

_____. Quality of Life, Quality of the Individual, Technology and Economic Development. *Amer. J. Econ. Sociology*, January 1989, *48*(1), pp. 55–68.

Zini, Alvaro, Jr. Brazil at the Crossroads: Foreign Debt and Fiscal Exhaustion. In *[Marjolin, R.],* 1989, pp. 67–83.

Zionts, Stanley; Ramesh, R. and Karwan, Mark H. Performance Characteristics of Three Interactive Solution Strategies for Bicriteria Integer Programming. In *Lockett, A. G. and Islei, G.,* eds., 1989, pp. 472–85.

Zis, George. Is There Still a Case for Flexible Exchange Rates? *Brit. Rev. Econ. Issues,* Spring 1989, *11*(24), pp. 1–20.

_____ **and McDonald, Frank.** The European Monetary System: Towards 1992 and Beyond.

J. Common Market Stud., March 1989, *27*(3), pp. 183–202.

Zissu, Anne-Marie. The Information Content of Post Tender Offer Movement in the Price of Target Shares. *Econ. Letters,* 1989, *29*(3), pp. 253–55.

_____ **and Stone, Charles Austin.** A Causality-Effect between Bid Premium and Outcome of Tender Offer. *Econ. Letters,* 1989, *29*(4), pp. 349–51.

Zivney, Terry L. Aggregation Bias in Applying the Pure-Play Technique. *J. Econ. Bus.*, February 1989, *41*(1), pp. 33–47.

_____ **and Alderson, Michael J.** Optimal Cross-Hedge Portfolios for Hedging Stock Index Options. *J. Futures Markets*, February 1989, *9*(1), pp. 67–75.

_____ **and Marcus, Richard D.** The Day the United States Defaulted on Treasury Bills. *Financial Rev.*, August 1989, *24*(3), pp. 475–89.

_____ **and Thompson, Donald J., II.** The Effect of Market Proxy Rebalancing Policies on Detecting Abnormal Performance. *J. Finan. Res.*, Winter 1989, *12*(4), pp. 293–99.

_____ **and Thompson, Donald J., II.** The Specification and Power of the Sign Test in Measuring Security Price Performance: Comments and Analysis. *Financial Rev.*, November 1989, *24*(4), pp. 581–88.

Zmijewski, Mark E. and Easton, Peter D. Cross-sectional Variation in the Stock Market Response to Accounting Earnings Announcements. *J. Acc. Econ.*, July 1989, *11*(2–3), pp. 117–41.

Zobrist, Frederick A. and Gould, Michael S. An Overview of Water Resources Planning in West Africa. *World Devel.*, November 1989, *17*(11), pp. 1717–22.

Zodrow, George R. and Mieszkowski, Peter. Taxation and the Tiebout Model: The Differential Effects of Head Taxes, Taxes on Land Rents, and Property Taxes. *J. Econ. Lit.*, September 1989, *27*(3), pp. 1098–1146.

Zografos, Kostas G., et al. A Multiobjective Model for Locating Public Facilities on an Uncongested Transportation Network. In *Lockett, A. G. and Islei, G.,* eds., 1989, pp. 264–74.

Zohir, Sajjad. Wage and Labour Market in Agriculture: Some Comments. *Bangladesh Devel. Stud.*, December 1989, *17*(4), pp. 83–91.

Zolt, Eric M. and Png, I. P. L. Efficient Deterrence and the Tax Treatment of Monetary Sanctions. *Int. Rev. Law Econ.*, December 1989, *9*(2), pp. 209–17.

Zondervan, Scott and Ross, Myron H. Capital Gains and the Rate of Return on a Stradivarius. *Econ. Inquiry*, July 1989, *27*(3), pp. 529–40.

Zorn, C. Kurt and Oster, Clinton V., Jr. Is It Still Safe to Fly? In *Moses, L. N. and Savage, I.,* eds., 1989, pp. 129–52.

Zorn, Peter M. Mobility–Tenure Decisions and Financial Credit: Do Mortgage Qualification Requirements Constrain Homeownership? *Amer. Real Estate Urban Econ. Assoc. J.*, Spring 1989, *17*(1), pp. 1–16.

_____ **and Lea, Michael J.** Mortgage Borrower

Repayment Behavior: A Microeconomic Analysis with Canadian Adjustable Rate Mortgage Data. *Amer. Real Estate Urban Econ. Assoc. J.*, Spring 1989, *17*(1), pp. 118–36.

Zorychta, Krystian; Ogryczak, Wlodzimierz and Studzinski, Krzysztof. DINAS: Dynamic Interactive Network Analysis System. In *Lewandowski, A. and Wierzbicki, A. P., eds.*, 1989, pp. 385–87.

_____; **Ogryczak, Wlodzimierz and Studzinski, Krzysztof.** Dynamic Interactive Network Analysis System. In *Lockett, A. G. and Islei, G., eds.*, 1989, pp. 444–53.

_____; **Ogryczak, Wlodzimierz and Studzinski, Krzysztof.** A Generalized Reference Point Approach to Multiobjective Transshipment Problem with Facility Location. In *Lewandowski, A. and Wierzbicki, A. P., eds.*, 1989, pp. 213–29.

_____; **Ogryczak, Wlodzimierz and Studzinski, Krzysztof.** Solving Multiobjective Distribution–Location Problems with the DINAS System. In *Lewandowski, A. and Wierzbicki, A. P., eds.*, 1989, pp. 230–50.

Zou, Gang and Wang, Zhigang. Interests of the Entrepreneur and Behavior of the Enterprise. *Chinese Econ. Stud.*, Winter 1988–89, *22*(2), pp. 82–94.

Zouari, Abderrazak. Collective Action and Governance Structure in Tunisia's Labor Organization. In *Nabli, M. K. and Nugent, J. B., eds.*, 1989, pp. 323–51.

Zouboulakis, Michel. La construction de l'objet économique dans la tradition ricardienne. (The Construction of Economy as an Object in the Ricardian Tradition. With English summary.) *Écon. Societes*, June 1989, *23*(6), pp. 41–63.

Zoványi, G. The Evolution of a National Urban Development Strategy in Hungary. *Environ. Planning A*, March 1989, *21*(3), pp. 333–47.

Zuber, Richard A.; Johnson, R. Stafford and Fiore, Lyle C. The Investment Performance of Common Stocks in Relation to Their Price–Earnings Ratios: An Update of the Basu Study. *Financial Rev.*, August 1989, *24*(3), pp. 499–505.

_____; **Russo, Benjamin and Gandar, John M.** Market Rationality Tests Based on Cross-Equation Restrictions. *J. Monet. Econ.*, November 1989, *24*(3), pp. 455–70.

Zuberi, Habib A. Production Function, Institutional Credit and Agricultural Development in Pakistan. *Pakistan Devel. Rev.*, Spring 1989, *28*(1), pp. 43–55.

Zuberi, Matin. Intervention in the Developing World: A Southern Perspective. In *Thomas, C. and Saravanamuttu, P., eds.*, 1989, pp. 135–43.

Zubiri, Ignacio; Gallastegui, Immaculada and Tusell, Fernando. Cálculo del efecto de alteraciones fiscales en una economía abierta: El caso del I.V.A. en el País Vasco. (With English summary.) *Invest. Econ.*, May 1989, *13*(2), pp. 283–300.

Zuehlke, Thomas W. Transformations to Normality and Selectivity Bias in Hedonic Price Func-

tions. *J. Real Estate Finance Econ.*, September 1989, *2*(3), pp. 173–80.

_____ **and Fournier, Gary M.** Litigation and Settlement: An Empirical Approach. *Rev. Econ. Statist.*, May 1989, *71*(2), pp. 189–95.

_____; **Gapinski, James H. and Škegro, Borislav.** A Model of Yugoslav Economic Performance. *J. Compar. Econ.*, March 1989, *13*(1), pp. 15–46.

_____ **and Payne, James E.** Tests of the Rational Expectations–Permanent Income Hypothesis for Developing Economies. *J. Macroecon.*, Summer 1989, *11*(3), pp. 423–33.

Zukerman, Stephen; Feder, Judith and Hadley, Jack. Profits and Fiscal Pressure in the Prospective Payment System: Their Impacts on Hospitals. *Inquiry*, Fall 1989, *26*(3), pp. 354–65.

Zupan, Mark A. Cable Franchise Renewals: Do Incumbent Firms Behave Opportunistically? *Rand J. Econ.*, Winter 1989, *20*(4), pp. 473–82.

_____. A Cross-institutional Comparison of the Extent to which Political Representatives' Voting Behavior Reflects Constituents' Preferences. *Econ. Letters*, October 1989, *30*(4), pp. 291–95.

_____. The Efficacy of Franchise Bidding Schemes in the Case of Cable Television: Some Systematic Evidence. *J. Law Econ.*, Part 1, October 1989, *32*(2), pp. 401–56.

_____. Non-price Concessions and the Effect of Franchise Bidding Schemes on Cable Company Costs. *Appl. Econ.*, March 1989, *21*(3), pp. 305–23.

Zurack, Mark A. and Toy, William W. Tracking the Euro-Pac Index. *J. Portfol. Manage.*, Winter 1989, *15*(2), pp. 55–58.

Zurzolo, Antonio. Taxation of Financial Activities: Introductory Address. *Rev. Econ. Cond. Italy*, Sept.–Dec. 1989, (3), pp. 281–84.

Zusman, Pinhas. Peasants' Risk Aversion and the Choice of Marketing Intermediaries and Contracts: A Bargaining Theory of Equilibrium Marketing Contracts. In *Bardhan, P., ed. (II)*, 1989, pp. 297–315.

_____ **and Bell, Clive.** The Equilibrium Vector of Pairwise-Bargained Agency Contracts with Diverse Actors and Principals Owning a Fixed Resource. *J. Econ. Behav. Organ.*, January 1989, *11*(1), pp. 91–114.

Zwart, Anthony C. and Blandford, David. Market Intervention and International Price Stability. *Amer. J. Agr. Econ.*, May 1989, *71*(2), pp. 379–88.

Zweifel, P. and Ferrari, M. Multiple Versorgungsrisiken und optimale Reservekapazitäten in der schweizerischen Energieversorgung. (Multiple Risks in Energy Supply and Optimal Reserve Capacities—The Case of Switzerland. With English summary.) *Schweiz. Z. Volkswirtsch. Statist.*, March 1989, *125*(1), pp. 1–17.

Zwezerijnen, W. J. Economic Policy: A Survey. In *Muller, F. and Zwezerijnen, W. J., eds.*, 1989, pp. 1–16.

Zwick, Martin and Attaran, Mohsen. An Information Theory Approach to Measuring Industrial Diversification. *J. Econ. Stud.*, 1989, *16*(1), pp. 19–30.

Zwiener, Rudolf. Die Einkommensverteilungseffekte öffentlicher Defizite in einer unterbeschäftigten Wirtschaft. Analyse anhand eines ökonometrischen Konjunkturmodells für die Bundesrepublik Deutschland. (Effects of Public Deficits on Income Distribution during a Situation of Unemployment—Results of an Econometric Business Cycle Model for the Federal Republic of Germany. With English summary.) *Konjunkturpolitik*, 1989, *35*(1–2), pp. 53–76.

Zwingli, Michael E.; Hardy, William E., Jr. and Adrian, John L., Jr. Reduced Risk Rotations for Fresh Vegetable Crops: An Analysis for the Sand Mountain and Tennessee Valley Regions of Alabama. *Southern J. Agr. Econ.*, December 1989, *21*(2), pp. 155–65.

Zylberberg, André and Perrot, Anne. Salaire d'efficience et dualisme du marché du travail. (Efficiency Wage and Dual Labour Market. With English summary.) *Revue Écon.*, January 1989, *40*(1), pp. 5–20.